Pokémon X™ Pokémon Y™

The Official Kalos Region Pokédex & Postgame Adventure Guide

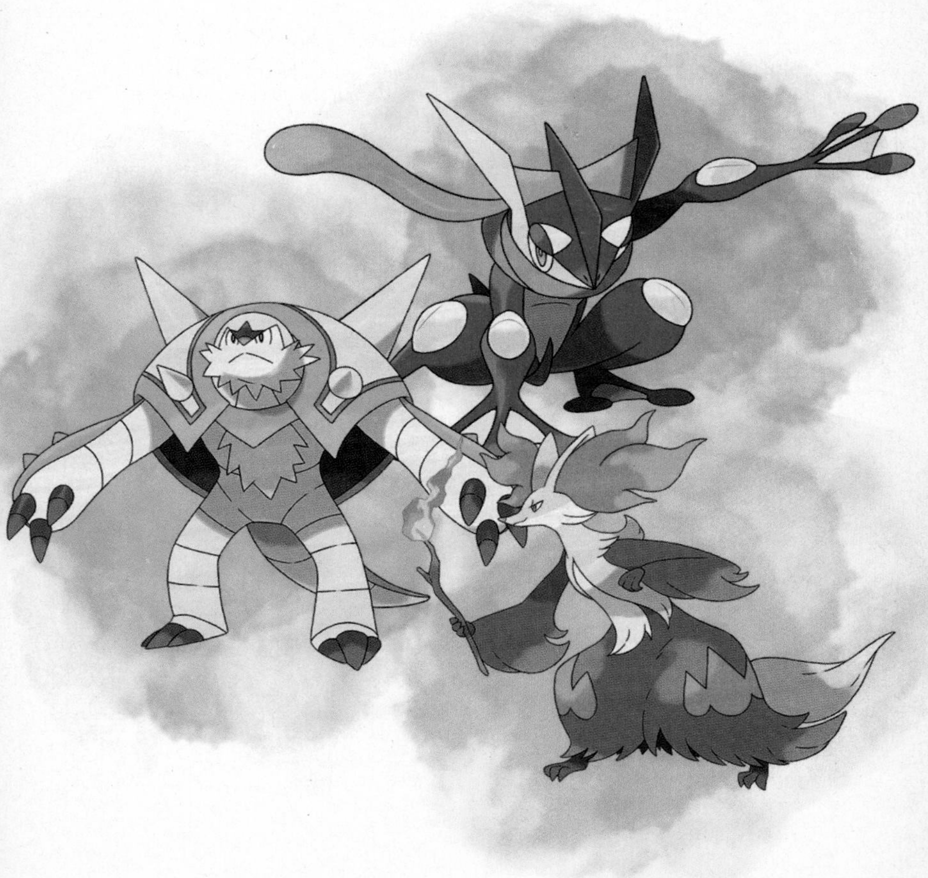

Table of Contents

Kalos Region Map 8

After the Hall of Fame
Recommended Route 10

Your Adventure after the Hall of Fame

Post-game Walkthrough 12
Vaniville Town 12
Lumiose City 13
Kiloude City 18
Battle Maison.. 22
Friend Safari 24
Anlstar City... 27
Geosenge Town.. 28
Reflection Cave 28
Ambrette Town 28
Terminus Cave... 29
Azure Bay 33
Chamber of Emptiness................................ 37
Unknown Dungeon 38
Post-game Activities 40
Battle Institute 40
Looker Events 42
Completing Your Pokédex 59
Eggs & Pokémon 61
Hunting for Fossils in Glittering Cave 81
Fishing Guide.. 82
Mega Stones 83
Poké Radar 85
Getting Rewards for
Pokédex Completion.................................... 87
Daily Events 88

Kalos Region Pokédex

*Reference the Pokémon Alphabetical Index on the next page
for a full list of the Pokémon in the Kalos region Pokédex*

Kalos Pokédex Guide................................... 94

Central Kalos Pokédex 98
Coastal Kalos Pokédex......................... 269
Mountain Kalos Pokédex 431

How and Where to Meet
Special Pokémon 598

Adventure Data

Pokémon Moves... 600
Where to Find TMs and HMs
and Learn Other Moves 616
Pokémon Abilities....................................... 618
Pokémon's Natures and
Characteristics.. 624
Base Stats Raised through Defeating
Wild Pokémon in the Kalos Region 625
Items 631
Key Items 640
Poké Balls 641
Items Held by Wild Pokémon
in Kalos.. 642
Berries 644
Where to Obtain Items 648
Pokémon Moves Reverse Lookup.............. 650
Pokémon Abilities Reverse Lookup 713
Pokémon Weakness Chart—
Kalos Regional Pokédex............................ 718
Type Matchup Chart................................... 734
Inverse Type Matchup Chart..................... 735

NEW Index of Mega Evolutions

Abomasnow...529
Absol 278
Aerodactyl...340
Aggron 542
Alakazam...219
Ampharos 404
Banette..566
Blastoise 201
Charizard 196, 197
Garchomp..439
Gardevoir...172
Gengar 464
Gyarados 154
Heracross...408
Houndoom 350
Kangaskhan 332
Lucario...168
Manectric...347
Mawile 334
Medicham 262
Mewtwo 596, 597
Pinsir 406
Scizor...581
Tyranitar..546
Venusaur..192

Alphabetical Index

A

Abomasnow.................. 528
Mega Abomasnow....... 529
Abra 216
Absol 277
Mega Absol 278
Accelgor....................... 456
Aegislash
(Blade Forme)............... 236
Aegislash
(Shield Forme) 235
Aerodactyl 339
Mega Aerodactyl.......... 340
Aggron 541
Mega Aggron.............. 542
Alakazam...................... 218
Mega Alakazam.......... 219
Alomomola 426
Altaria.......................... 584
Amaura......................... 337
Amoonguss................... 486
Ampharos 403
Mega Ampharos 404
Arbok 470
Ariados 550
Aromatisse.................... 247
Aron 539
Articuno....................... 428
Audino......................... 240
Aurorus......................... 338
Avalugg 519
Axew 266
Azumarill 144
Azurill 142

B

Bagon........................... 283
Banette......................... 565
Mega Banette.............. 566

Barbaracle.................... 291
Barboach 472
Basculin 492
Beartic 521
Beedrill 129
Bellossom 223
Bellsprout 457
Bergmite 518
Bibarel 140
Bidoof.......................... 139
Binacle......................... 290
Bisharp 481
Blastoise 200
Mega Blastoise 201
Boldore......................... 395
Bonsly.......................... 572
Braixen 102
Budew 180
Buizel........................... 490
Bulbasaur..................... 189
Bunnelby...................... 107
Burmy 145
Butterfree..................... 126

C

Carbink......................... 398
Carnivine 460
Carvanha 159
Caterpie....................... 124
Chandelure 501
Charizard 195
Mega Charizard X....... 196
Mega Charizard Y 197
Charmander.................. 193
Charmeleon 194
Chatot 415
Chesnaught 100
Chespin 98
Chimecho 386

Chinchou 424
Chingling 385
Clamperl 418
Clauncher 301
Clawitzer 302
Cloyster 306
Combee 185
Conkeldurr 535
Corphish 155
Corsola 423
Crawdaunt.................... 156
Croagunk 242
Crobat 265
Crustle.......................... 293
Cryogonal 553
Cubchoo 520
Cubone.......................... 329

D

Dedenne 384
Deino............................ 586
Delcatty 188
Delibird........................ 530
Delphox 103
Diggersby...................... 108
Diglett.......................... 431
Ditto 582
Dodrio 209
Doduo........................... 208
Doublade 234
Dragalge 300
Dragonair..................... 590
Dragonite..................... 591
Drapion......................... 447
Dratini.......................... 589
Drifblim........................ 270
Drifloon........................ 269
Druddigon..................... 585
Ducklett........................ 244

Alphabetical Index

Dugtrio 432
Dunsparce..................... 141
Duosion 390
Durant 548
Dwebble 292

E

Eevee............................. 351
Ekans............................. 469
Electrike........................ 345
Electrode....................... 512
Emolga 360
Escavalier...................... 454
Espeon.......................... 355
Espurr 229
Exeggcute 413
Exeggutor 414
Exploud......................... 259

F

Farfetch'd 165
Fearow.......................... 552
Fennekin 101
Ferroseed 341
Ferrothorn 342
Flaaffy.......................... 402
Flabébé......................... 174
Flabébé (Blue Flower)..... 175
Flabébé (Orange Flower).. 175
Flabébé (Red Flower)...... 175
Flabébé (White Flower).... 175
Flabébé (Yellow Flower)... 175
Flareon 354
Fletchinder 112
Fletchling 111
Floatzel......................... 491
Floette 176
Floette (Blue Flower) 177
Floette (Orange Flower).. 177
Floette (Red Flower) 177
Floette (White Flower).... 177
Floette (Yellow Flower) ... 177
Florges.......................... 178
Florges (Blue Flower)...... 179

Florges (Orange Flower) ... 179
Florges (Red Flower)....... 179
Florges (White Flower).... 179
Florges (Yellow Flower) ... 179
Flygon........................... 435
Foongus 485
Fraxure.......................... 267
Froakie.......................... 104
Frogadier 105
Furfrou 206
Furfrou (Dandy Trim)....... 207
Furfrou (Debutante Trim)...207
Furfrou (Diamond Trim)... 207
Furfrou (Heart Trim) 207
Furfrou (Kabuki Trim) 207
Furfrou (La Reine Trim).... 207
Furfrou (Matron Trim) 207
Furfrou (Pharaoh Trim).... 207
Furfrou (Star Trim) 207
Furret............................ 225

G

Gabite........................... 437
Gallade 173
Garbodor 514
Garchomp 438
  Mega Garchomp.......... 439
Gardevoir...................... 171
  Mega Gardevoir........... 172
Gastly 461
Gengar 463
  Mega Gengar 464
Geodude........................ 440
Gible............................. 436
Gigalith......................... 396
Glaceon 358
Gligar 557
Gliscor 558
Gloom........................... 221
Gogoat 203
Golbat 264
Goldeen 157
Golduck 164
Golem........................... 442

Golett 365
Golurk 366
Goodra 452
Goomy........................... 450
Gorebyss 420
Gothita 569
Gothitelle 571
Gothorita 570
Gourgeist....................... 497
Gourgeist
(Large Size) 498
Gourgeist
(Small Size) 498
Gourgeist
(Super Size)................... 498
Granbull......................... 344
Graveler 441
Greninja......................... 106
Grumpig 276
Gulpin........................... 212
Gurdurr......................... 534
Gyarados........................ 153
  Mega Gyarados............ 154

H

Hariyama 370
Haunter 462
Hawlucha....................... 363
Haxorus 268
Heatmor......................... 547
Heliolisk........................ 316
Helioptile 315
Heracross 407
  Mega Heracross 408
Hippopotas 317
Hippowdon 318
Honchkrow 484
Honedge........................ 233
Hoothoot 559
Hoppip.......................... 252
Horsea 308
Houndoom..................... 349
  Mega Houndoom.......... 350
Houndour 348

Huntail.......................... 419
Hydreigon 588

I

Igglybuff 561
Illumise 251
Inkay............................. 279
Ivysaur 190

J

Jigglypuff 562
Jolteon......................... 353
Jumpluff....................... 254
Jynx 523

K

Kadabra 217
Kakuna 128
Kangaskhan................... 331
  Mega Kangaskhan 332
Karrablast 453
Kecleon......................... 232
Kingdra 310
Kirlia 170
Klefki 482
Krokorok 313
Krookodile 314

L

Lairon 540
Lampent 500
Lanturn 425
Lapras........................... 427
Larvitar 543
Leafeon......................... 357
Ledian........................... 184
Ledyba.......................... 183
Lickilicky 578
Lickitung 577
Liepard 475
Linoone......................... 110
Litleo 161
Litwick 499

Lombre 488
Lotad 487
Loudred 258
Lucario.......................... 167
  Mega Lucario.............. 168
Ludicolo 489
Lunatone 281
Luvdisc......................... 298

M

Machamp....................... 328
Machoke 327
Machop 326
Magcargo 444
Magikarp 152
Magnemite 508
Magneton 509
Magnezone................... 510
Makuhita 369
Malamar 280
Mamoswine 517
Manectric...................... 346
  Mega Manectric.......... 347
Mantine........................ 417
Mantyke........................ 416
Mareep......................... 401
Marill 143
Marowak 330
Masquerain................... 151
Mawile 333
  Mega Mawile 334
Medicham...................... 261
  Mega Medicham.......... 262
Meditite 260
Meowstic (Female) 231
Meowstic (Male) 230
Metapod 125
Mewtwo 595, 598
  Mega Mewtwo X 596
  Mega Mewtwo Y 597
Mienfoo 271
Mienshao...................... 272
Mightyena...................... 477
Miltank 400

Mime Jr. 387
Minun............................ 211
Moltres 430
Mothim.......................... 149
Mr. Mime 388
Munchlax....................... 255
Murkrow........................ 483

N

Nidoking........................ 383
Nidoqueen 380
Nidoran ♀ 378
Nidoran ♂ 381
Nidorina......................... 379
Nidorino 382
Nincada 226
Ninjask 227
Noctowl 560
Noibat 555
Noivern 556
Nosepass 367

O

Octillery 422
Oddish 220
Onix.............................. 322

P

Pachirisu 409
Pancham....................... 204
Pangoro 205
Panpour 134
Pansage 130
Pansear........................ 132
Patrat............................ 478
Pawniard....................... 480
Pelipper......................... 287
Phantump 493
Pichu 136
Pidgeot 116
Pidgeotto 115
Pidgey........................... 114
Pikachu......................... 137

Piloswine 516
Pinsir 405
  Mega Pinsir 406
Plusle 210
Politoed 468
Poliwag 465
Poliwhirl 466
Poliwrath 467
Poochyena 476
Probopass 368
Psyduck 163
Pumpkaboo 495
Pumpkaboo
(Large Size) 496
Pumpkaboo
(Small Size) 496
Pumpkaboo
(Super Size) 496
Pupitar 544
Purrloin 474
Pyroar 162

Q

Quagsire 449
Quilladin 99
Qwilfish 307

R

Raichu 138
Ralts 169
Relicanth 311
Remoraid 421
Reuniclus 391
Rhydon 320
Rhyhorn 319
Rhyperior 321
Riolu 166
Roggenrola 394
Roselia 181
Roserade 182
Rotom 502
Rotom (Fan Rotom) 506
Rotom (Frost Rotom) 505

Rotom (Heat Rotom) 503
Rotom (Mow Rotom) 507
Rotom (Wash Rotom) 504

S

Sableye 397
Salamence 285
Sandile 312
Sandshrew 537
Sandslash 538
Sawk 372
Scatterbug 117
Scizor 580
  Mega Scizor 581
Scolipede 239
Scrafty 215
Scraggy 214
Scyther 579
Seadra 309
Seaking 158
Sentret 224
Seviper 274
Sharpedo 160
Shedinja 228
Shelgon 284
Shellder 305
Shelmet 455
Shuckle 445
Shuppet 564
Sigilyph 364
Simipour 135
Simisage 131
Simisear 133
Skarmory 554
Skiddo 202
Skiploom 253
Skitty 187
Skorupi 446
Skrelp 299
Skuntank 377
Sliggoo 451
Slowbro 411
Slowking 412

Slowpoke 410
Slugma 443
Slurpuff 249
Smeargle 241
Smoochum 522
Sneasel 531
Snorlax 256
Snover 527
Snubbull 343
Solosis 389
Solrock 282
Spearow 551
Spewpa 118
Spinarak 549
Spinda 574
Spoink 275
Spritzee 246
Squirtle 198
Staraptor 375
Staravia 374
Starly 373
Starmie 304
Staryu 303
Steelix 323
Stunfisk 471
Stunky 376
Sudowoodo 573
Surskit 150
Swablu 583
Swalot 213
Swanna 245
Swellow 289
Swinub 515
Swirlix 248
Swoobat 325
Sylveon 359

T

Taillow 288
Talonflame 113
Tauros 399
Teddiursa 575
Tentacool 294

Tentacruel 295
Throh 371
Timburr 533
Torkoal........................... 536
Toxicroak 243
Trapinch 433
Trevenant 494
Trubbish 513
Tyrantrum 336
Tyranitar........................ 545
  Mega Tyranitar............ 546
Tyrunt 335

U

Umbreon........................ 356
Ursaring......................... 576

V

Vanillish 525
Vanillite 524
Vanilluxe 526
Vaporeon 352
Venipede........................ 237
Venusaur....................... 191
  Mega Venusaur............ 192
Vespiquen 186
Vibrava 434
Victreebel....................... 459
Vileplume....................... 222
Vivillon........................... 119
Vivillon
(Archipelago Pattern)...... 122
Vivillon
(Continental Pattern) 120
Vivillon
(Elegant Pattern) 121
Vivillon
(Garden Pattern) 121

Vivillon
(High Plains Pattern)....... 122
Vivillon
(Icy Snow Pattern) 120
Vivillon
(Jungle Pattern) 123
Vivillon
(Marine Pattern) 121
Vivillon
(Meadow Pattern) 121
Vivillon
(Modern Pattern)............ 121
Vivillon
(Monsoon Pattern) 122
Vivillon
(Ocean Pattern) 123
Vivillon
(Polar Pattern) 120
Vivillon
(River Pattern) 122
Vivillon
(Sandstorm Pattern)........ 122
Vivillon
(Savanna Pattern) 123
Vivillon
(Sun Pattern) 123
Vivillon
(Tundra Pattern) 120
Volbeat 250
Voltorb........................... 511

W

Wailmer 296
Wailord 297
Wartortle 199
Watchog 479
Weavile........................... 531
Weedle 127
Weepinbell..................... 458

Whirlipede 238
Whiscash 473
Whismur 257
Wigglytuff...................... 563
Wingull 286
Wobbuffet...................... 393
Woobat.......................... 324
Wooper.......................... 448
Wormadam
(Plant Cloak) 146
Wormadam
(Sandy Cloak)................. 147
Wormadam
(Trash Cloak) 148
Wynaut.......................... 392

X

Xerneas 592

Y

Yanma 361
Yanmega......................... 362
Yveltal 593

Z

Zangoose....................... 273
Zapdos........................... 429
Zigzagoon...................... 109
Zoroark 568
Zorua 567
Zubat............................. 263
Zweilous 587
Zygarde.......................... 594

Kalos Region Map

(after entering the Hall of Fame)

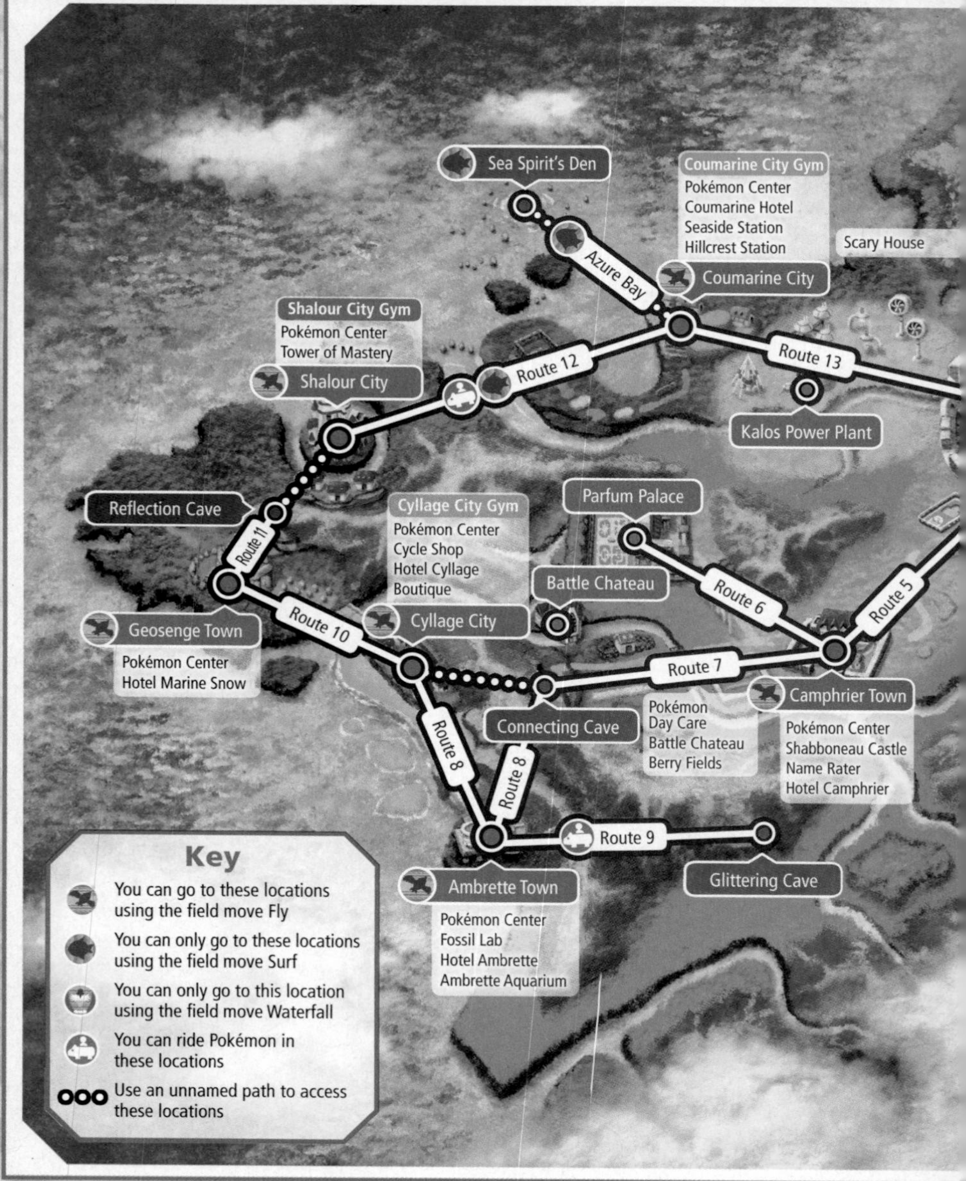

Sea Spirit's Den

Coumarine City Gym
Pokémon Center
Coumarine Hotel
Seaside Station
Hillcrest Station

Scary House

Azure Bay

Coumarine City

Shalour City Gym
Pokémon Center
Tower of Mastery

Route 13

Route 12

Shalour City

Kalos Power Plant

Reflection Cave

Route 11

Parfum Palace

Cyllage City Gym
Pokémon Center
Cycle Shop
Hotel Cyllage
Boutique

Battle Chateau

Route 6

Route 5

Route 10

Cyllage City

Route 7

Camphrier Town

Geosenge Town
Pokémon Center
Hotel Marine Snow

Pokémon
Day Care
Battle Chateau
Berry Fields

Camphrier Town
Pokémon Center
Shabboneau Castle
Name Rater
Hotel Camphrier

Route 8

Connecting Cave

Route 8

Route 9

Glittering Cave

Ambrette Town

Pokémon Center
Fossil Lab
Hotel Ambrette
Ambrette Aquarium

Key

- You can go to these locations using the field move Fly
- You can only go to these locations using the field move Surf
- You can only go to this location using the field move Waterfall
- You can ride Pokémon in these locations
- **ooo** Use an unnamed path to access these locations

This is the map of the Kalos region, where your adventure awaits. All of the cities, towns, routes, caves, and other important places are shown. Routes are labeled in white, towns and cities in red, caves or naturally occurring locations in gray, and buildings in blue.

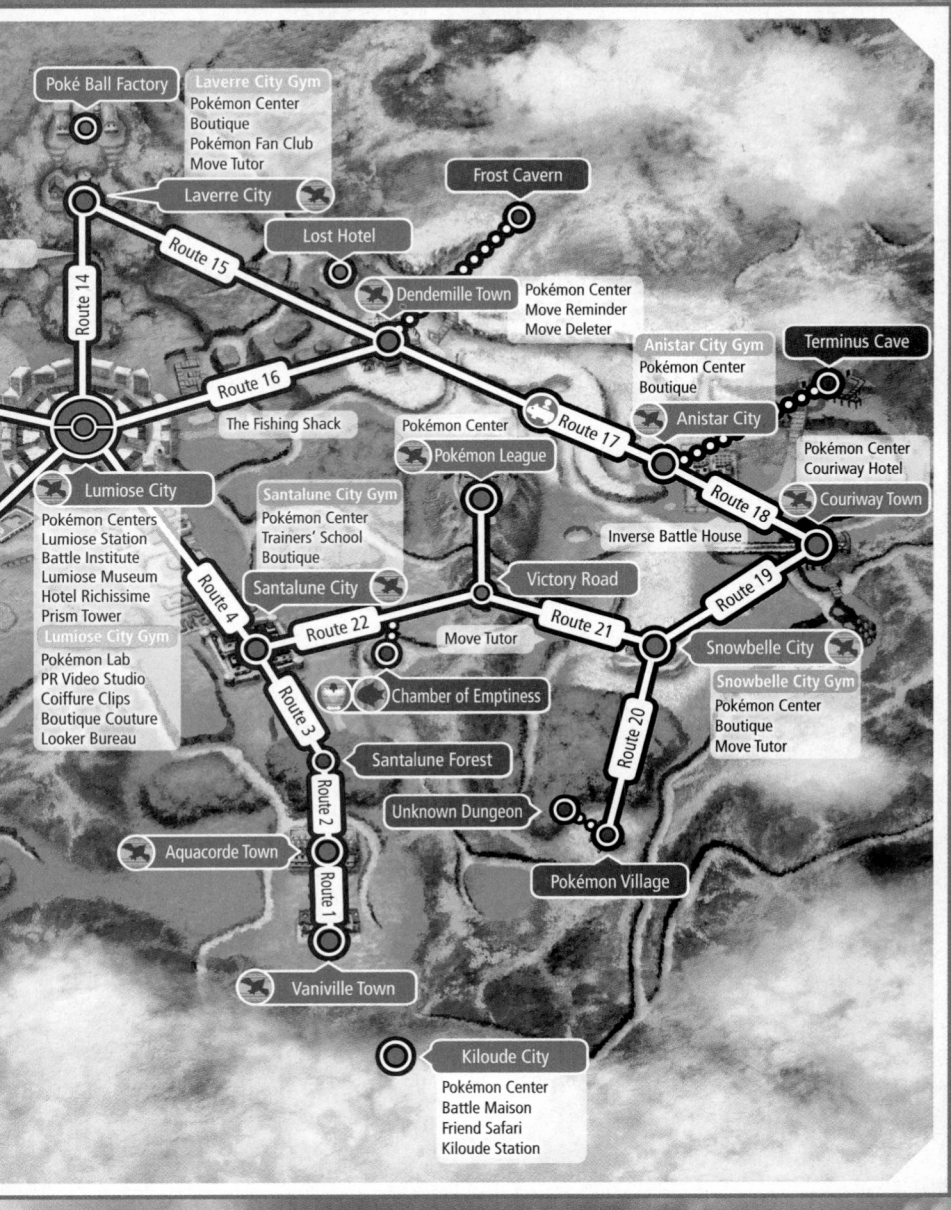

Poké Ball Factory

Laverre City Gym
Pokémon Center
Boutique
Pokémon Fan Club
Move Tutor

Frost Cavern

Laverre City

Route 15

Lost Hotel

Route 14

Dendemille Town

Pokémon Center
Move Reminder
Move Deleter

Anistar City Gym
Pokémon Center
Boutique

Terminus Cave

Route 16

The Fishing Shack

Pokémon Center
Pokémon League

Route 17

Anistar City

Route 18

Pokémon Center
Couriway Hotel

Couriway Town

Lumiose City

Santalune City Gym
Pokémon Center
Trainers' School
Boutique

Inverse Battle House

Route 19

Pokémon Centers
Lumiose Station
Battle Institute
Lumiose Museum
Hotel Richissime
Prism Tower

Santalune City

Victory Road

Route 4

Route 22

Route 21

Route 20

Snowbelle City

Lumiose City Gym

Move Tutor

Snowbelle City Gym
Pokémon Center
Boutique
Move Tutor

Pokémon Lab
PR Video Studio
Coiffure Clips
Boutique Couture
Looker Bureau

Route 3

Chamber of Emptiness

Santalune Forest

Route 2

Unknown Dungeon

Aquacorde Town

Route 1

Pokémon Village

Vaniville Town

Kiloude City

Pokémon Center
Battle Maison
Friend Safari
Kiloude Station

9

Recommended Route

Below is the recommended route for the adventures that await you after becoming the Champion of the Kalos region. Check this guide to ensure that you experience all of the major events that await you after facing the Pokémon League!

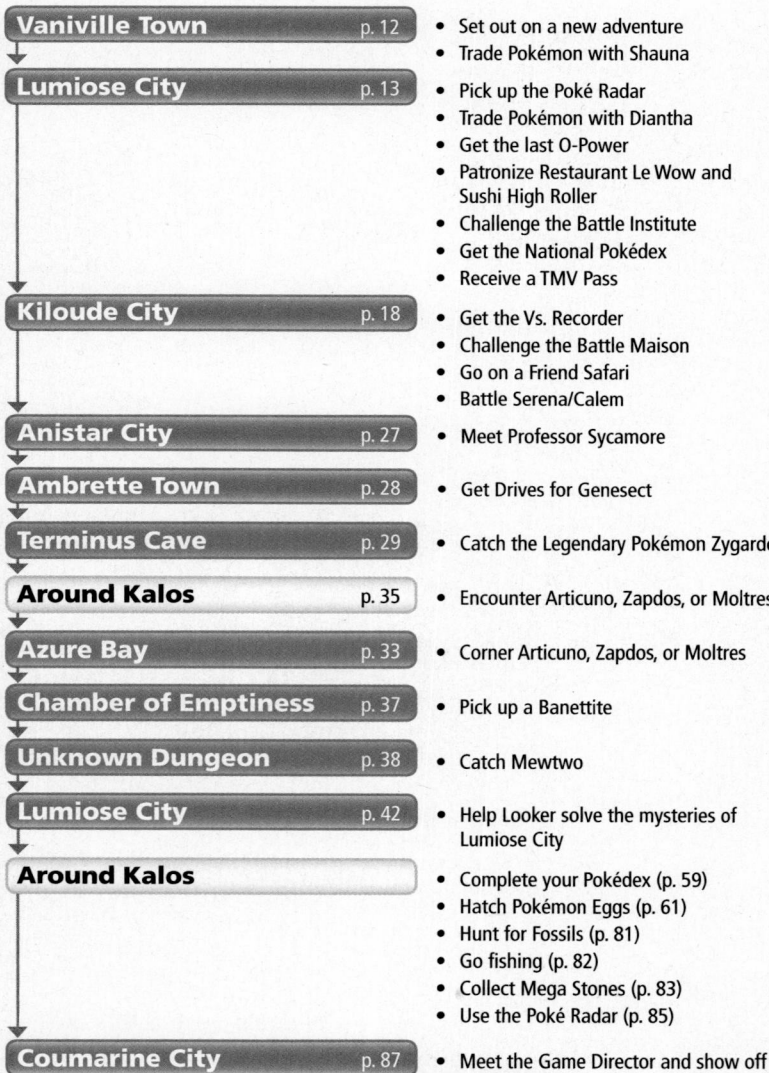

Vaniville Town — p. 12
- Set out on a new adventure
- Trade Pokémon with Shauna

Lumiose City — p. 13
- Pick up the Poké Radar
- Trade Pokémon with Diantha
- Get the last O-Power
- Patronize Restaurant Le Wow and Sushi High Roller
- Challenge the Battle Institute
- Get the National Pokédex
- Receive a TMV Pass

Kiloude City — p. 18
- Get the Vs. Recorder
- Challenge the Battle Maison
- Go on a Friend Safari
- Battle Serena/Calem

Anistar City — p. 27
- Meet Professor Sycamore

Ambrette Town — p. 28
- Get Drives for Genesect

Terminus Cave — p. 29
- Catch the Legendary Pokémon Zygarde

Around Kalos — p. 35
- Encounter Articuno, Zapdos, or Moltres

Azure Bay — p. 33
- Corner Articuno, Zapdos, or Moltres

Chamber of Emptiness — p. 37
- Pick up a Banettite

Unknown Dungeon — p. 38
- Catch Mewtwo

Lumiose City — p. 42
- Help Looker solve the mysteries of Lumiose City

Around Kalos
- Complete your Pokédex (p. 59)
- Hatch Pokémon Eggs (p. 61)
- Hunt for Fossils (p. 81)
- Go fishing (p. 82)
- Collect Mega Stones (p. 83)
- Use the Poké Radar (p. 85)

Coumarine City — p. 87
- Meet the Game Director and show off your Pokédex

Your Adventure after the Hall of Fame

AFTER THE HALL OF FAME

CENTRAL KALOS

COASTAL KALOS

MOUNTAIN KALOS

ADVENTURE DATA

Post-game Walkthrough

Continue your adventures in the Kalos region! After being returned to your home in Vaniville Town, you can reach areas that were not accessible before you entered the Hall of Fame. Get ready to catch Legendary Pokémon and encounter Pokémon from other regions!

VANIVILLE TOWN Receive a message from Professor Sycamore

I received a message from Professor Sycamore. He says he wants to meet you at Lumiose Station.

Following your induction into the Hall of Fame and a well-deserved night's rest, you awaken back in your bed in Vaniville Town. Go downstairs to find your mom making breakfast. She tells you that she received a message from Professor Sycamore, inviting you to meet him at Lumiose Station. It seems that the dashing professor still has a few surprises in store!

VANIVILLE TOWN Trade Pokémon with Shauna

Your good friend Shauna awaits you just outside your home. She's still reeling from the excitement of yesterday's parade and wishes to trade Pokémon with you. Shauna will accept any Pokémon in trade for her Chespin (if you chose Fennekin as your first Pokémon partner at the beginning of the game), Fennekin (if you chose Froakie), or Froakie (if you chose Chespin), so give her any Pokémon you like.

Trade

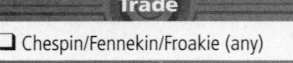

☐ Chespin/Fennekin/Froakie (any)

Lumiose City

Lumiose City remains a spacious hub of excitement and activity. All of its familiar shops and destinations are available, and now that you've entered the Hall of Fame, even more activities can be enjoyed.

Field Moves Needed

Items

- ☐ Destiny Knot
- ☐ Elixir
- ☐ Gardevoirite
- ☐ Nugget
- ☐ Poké Radar
- ☐ TMV Pass

North Boulevard Poké Mart

Heal Ball	300
Nest Ball	1,000
Net Ball	1,000

South Boulevard Poké Mart

TM11 Sunny Day	50,000
TM18 Rain Dance	50,000
TM75 Swords Dance	10,000
TM76 Struggle Bug	10,000
TM78 Bulldoze	10,000

Herboriste (Vernal Avenue)

Energy Powder	500
Energy Root	800
Heal Powder	450
Revival Herb	2,800

Juice Shoppe (Autumnal Avenue)

Fresh Berry Juices	Free (with Berries)
Premium Berry Juices	Varies*

*The more expensive the juice, the greater its effects will be.

Lumiose Galette Stand (North Boulevard)

Galette	100

Trade

- ☐ Ralts (any)

Poké Ball Boutique (Autumnal Avenue)

Dive Ball	1,000
Dusk Ball	1,000
Heal Ball	300
Luxury Ball	1,000
Nest Ball	1,000
Net Ball	1,000
Premier Ball	200
Quick Ball	1,000
Repeat Ball	1,000
Timer Ball	1,000

Stone Emporium (Vernal Avenue)

Venusaurite or Charizardite X (**X**) or Charizardite Y (**Y**) or Blastoisinite	1,000,000
Fire Stone	2,100
Leaf Stone	2,100
Water Stone	2,100

NOTE *Item prices and availability in Lumiose City shops may vary based on how stylish the clerk deems you to be. Learn more about enhancing your style in Pokémon X & Pokémon Y: The Official Kalos Region Guidebook, p. 119.*

STEP
1 ▸ Receive the Poké Radar at the Sycamore Pokémon Lab

It's the Pokémon Radar, or Poké Radar for short.

Fly or travel to Lumiose City next. Before rushing off to meet Professor Sycamore at Lumiose Station, pay a visit to Sycamore Labs on South Boulevard. Speak to a lab assistant on the second floor to receive a new item: the Poké Radar! Now you can easily search the tall grass for wild Pokémon of the same species.

AFTER THE HALL OF FAME

CENTRAL KALOS

COASTAL KALOS

MOUNTAIN KALOS

ADVENTURE DATA

 TIP *Use the Poké Radar to catch many Pokémon of the same species. They will be more likely to find Eggs at the Pokémon Day Care on Route 7 when left together (p. 61). For more on how to use the Poké Radar, turn to page 85.*

STEP 2 > Trade Pokémon with Diantha in Café Soleil

how would you feel about trading one of your Pokémon for my Ralts here?

Pop by Café Soleil, which is located along South Boulevard, and you'll find none other than the Kalos region's former Champion, Diantha, enjoying some refreshment. Speak to Diantha, and she'll offer to trade Pokémon with you. Diantha will accept any Pokémon in exchange for her Ralts, so think it over and give her any Pokémon you like. To further sweeten the deal, the traded Ralts will be holding a Gardevoirite.

STEP 3 > Receive final O-Power from Mr. Bonding

Finally, the time has come! The time for me to give you the last power!

If you've learned every O-Power from Mr. Bonding up to this point, and if you're stylish enough, then the final O-Power is within your grasp. Find Mr. Bonding in Café Introversion on South Boulevard and speak to him to obtain Hatching Power.

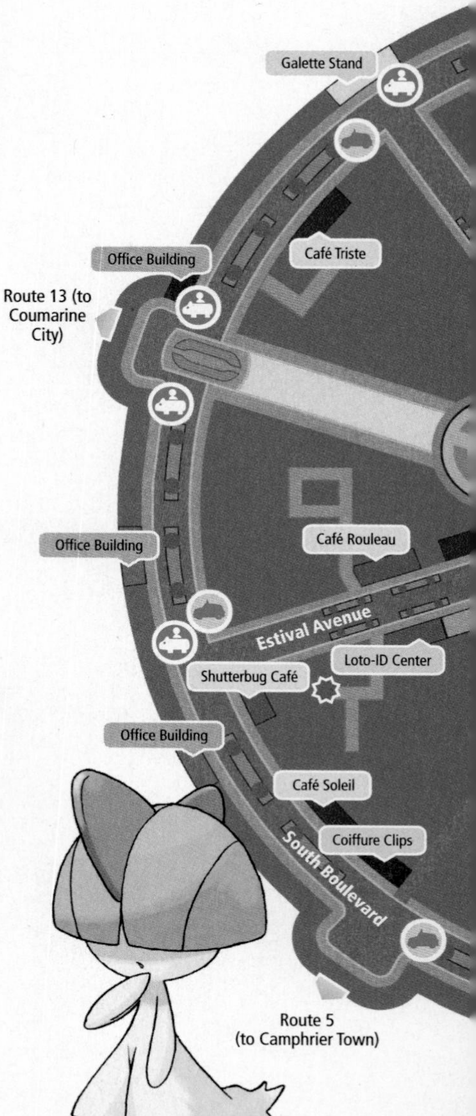

Galette Stand

Office Building

Café Triste

Route 13 (to Coumarine City)

Office Building

Café Rouleau

Estival Avenue

Loto-ID Center

Shutterbug Café

Office Building

Café Soleil

Coiffure Clips

South Boulevard

Route 5 (to Camphrier Town)

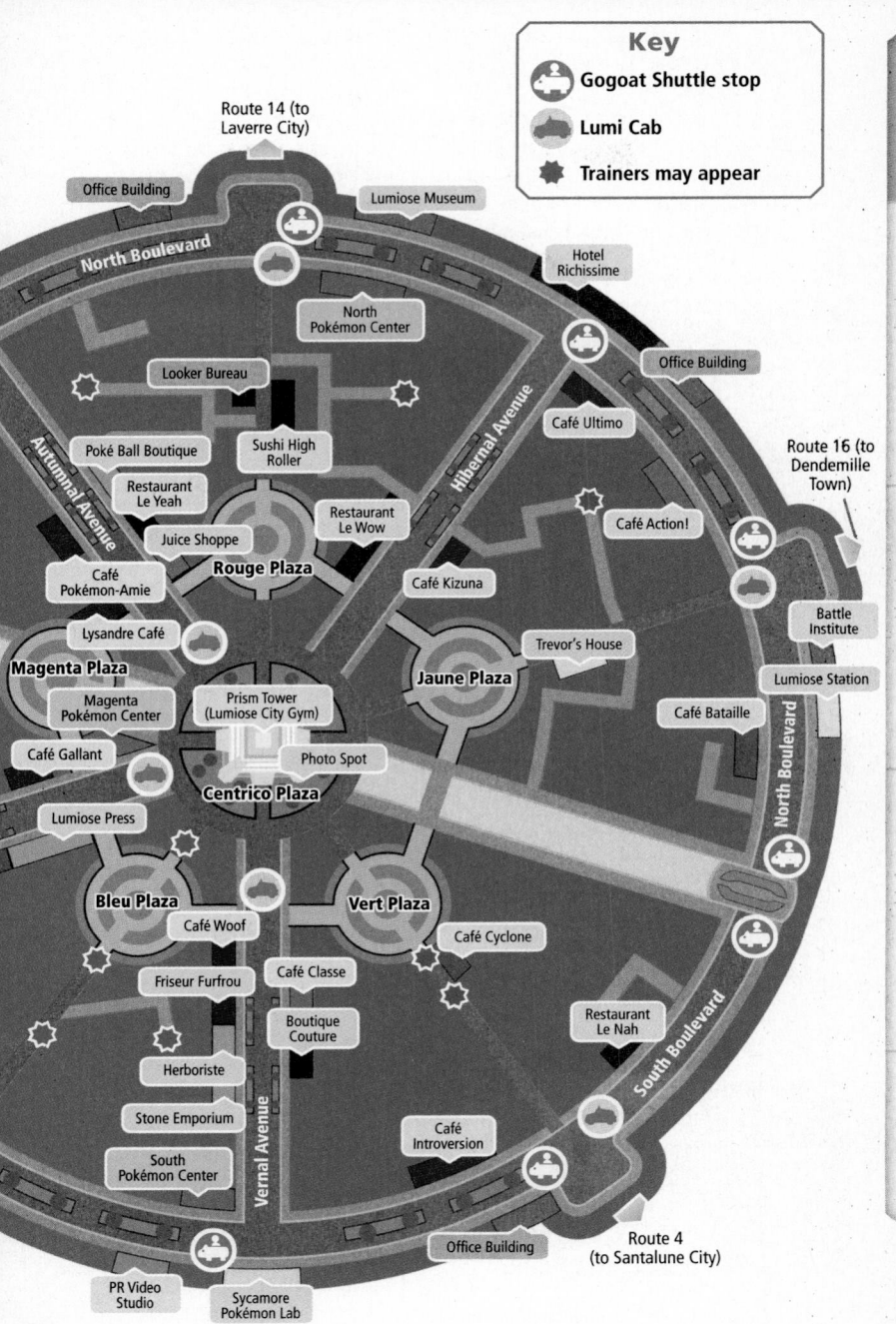

Key

- Gogoat Shuttle stop
- Lumi Cab
- Trainers may appear

Route 14 (to Laverre City)

Office Building

Lumiose Museum

North Boulevard

Hotel Richissime

North Pokémon Center

Office Building

Looker Bureau

Café Ultimo

Hibernal Avenue

Poké Ball Boutique

Sushi High Roller

Café Action!

Autumnal Avenue

Restaurant Le Yeah

Restaurant Le Wow

Route 16 (to Dendemille Town)

Juice Shoppe

Rouge Plaza

Café Kizuna

Battle Institute

Café Pokémon-Amie

Trevor's House

Lumiose Station

Lysandre Café

Jaune Plaza

Magenta Plaza

Café Bataille

Magenta Pokémon Center

Prism Tower (Lumiose City Gym)

North Boulevard

Café Gallant

Photo Spot

Centrico Plaza

Lumiose Press

Bleu Plaza

Vert Plaza

Café Woof

Café Cyclone

Friseur Furfrou

Café Classe

Boutique Couture

Restaurant Le Nah

South Boulevard

Herboriste

Stone Emporium

Vernal Avenue

Café Introversion

South Pokémon Center

PR Video Studio

Sycamore Pokémon Lab

Office Building

Route 4 (to Santalune City)

AFTER THE HALL OF FAME

CENTRAL KALOS

COASTAL KALOS

MOUNTAIN KALOS

ADVENTURE DATA

NOTE *Learn more about enhancing your style in* Pokémon X & Pokémon Y: The Official Kalos Region Guidebook, *p. 119.*

If Mr. Bonding does not appear at Café Introversion, then you may have missed him at one of his previous locations, or you may not have developed your style enough. Revisit the following locations to ensure that you've met Mr. Bonding everywhere, and perform lots of actions around Lumiose City to increase your style rating.

Mr. Bonding's locations

City/Town	Location	O-Power(s) Learned
Lumiose City	Route 5 Gate	Attack Power and Defense Power
Camphrier Town	Hotel Camphrier	Sp. Atk Power
Ambrette Town	Hotel Ambrette	Sp. Def Power
Cyllage City	Hotel Cyllage	Prize Money Power
Geosenge Town	Hotel Marine Snow	Speed Power
Shalour City	Pokémon Center	Critical Power
Coumarine City	Hillcrest Station	Befriending Power
Lumiose City	Hotel Richissime	Bargain Power
Laverre City	Pokémon Center	Encounter Power
Dendemille Town	Pokémon Center	Accuracy Power
Anistar City	Pokémon Center	Exp. Point Power
Couriway Town	Couriway Hotel	Stealth Power
Snowbelle City	Pokémon Center	PP Restoring Power
Lumiose City	Café Introversion	Hatching Power

 NOTES *If Mr. Bonding doesn't appear at one of these locations, then you've already met him there.*

You start off with the Capture Power and HP Restoring Power. These are the only two O-Powers you don't have to meet Mr. Bonding to access.

STEP
④ Satisfy your hunger for battle

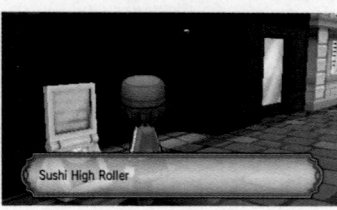

Sushi High Roller

Now that you have proven yourself to be as strong as a Champion, you can get into Restaurant Le Wow on Hibernal Avenue. If you're stylish enough, you will also find the staff at Sushi High Roller welcoming you in at last. Visit this classy sushi restaurant north of Rouge Plaza, right across from that vacant storefront that finally seems to have been rented out.

STEP 5 » See how you measure up with a Battle Test

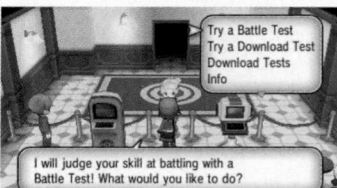

You can finally access all of the Battle Tests at the Battle Institute on North Boulevard. See what rank you can achieve and earn great prizes and BP for your efforts. To learn more about Battle Tests, see page 40.

STEP 6 » Obtain the National Pokédex at Lumiose Station

Now it's time to head at last to Lumiose Station, which is located along North Boulevard. Sina and Dexio call out to you as you enter the station. They promptly update your Pokédex again. Now you can register many more Pokémon in the National Pokédex!

STEP 7 » Meet up with Professor Sycamore at Lumiose Station

Professor Sycamore has been waiting patiently inside Lumiose Station, so take a moment to speak with him. The professor gives you something special: a TMV Pass to Kiloude City! Now you can use the super-fast TMV trains in Lumiose Station to travel to Kiloude City, where more excitement and adventure awaits.

STEP 8 » Board a TMV train and travel to Kiloude City

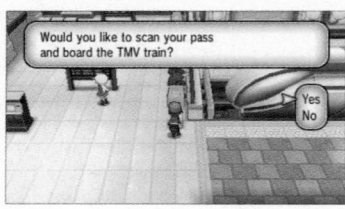

There's lots more to see and do in Kiloude City, so what are you waiting for? Approach the nearby orange scanning machine and press Ⓐ to scan your new TMV Pass. You'll automatically board the train afterward and speed off to Kiloude City. What a way to travel!

AFTER THE HALL OF FAME

CENTRAL KALOS

COASTAL KALOS

MOUNTAIN KALOS

ADVENTURE DATA

Kiloude City

After you enter the Hall of Fame, Professor Sycamore will give you a special pass to Kiloude City. This pass lets you use the high-speed trains at Lumiose Station to travel to Kiloude City anytime you like. Kiloude City offers exciting places to visit, including the Battle Maison and Friend Safari.

Field Moves Needed

Pokémon Trainer Serena/Calem

Friend Safari

Battle Maison

Kiloude Station (to Lumiose Station)

Pokémon Center

Items
☐ Absolite
☐ Bamboo Sprig Hat or Sundae Dress
☐ DNA Splicers
☐ Lansat Berry
☐ Max Revive
☐ Nugget
☐ Revive
☐ Starf Berry
☐ TM58 Sky Drop
☐ TM91 Flash Cannon
☐ Vs. Recorder

Hidden Items
☐ Max Revive
☐ PP Up

Poké Mart	
TM16 Light Screen	30,000
TM33 Reflect	30,000
TM50 Overheat	80,000
TM68 Giga Impact	90,000
TM93 Wild Charge	50,000

STEP 1 >> Answer a quiz and receive a Max Revive

You have a Pokédex, right?
I'll give you a Pokémon quiz!

Speak to a youth inside Kiloude Station, and you'll be quizzed about Pokémon. Even if you can't answer the quiz correctly the first time, you can keep guessing until you get it right and receive a valuable Max Revive.

STEP 2 >> Receive the Vs. Recorder

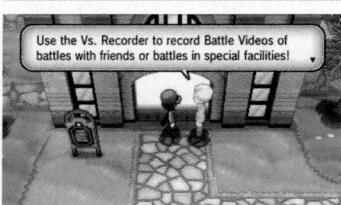

Use the Vs. Recorder to record Battle Videos of battles with friends or battles in special facilities!

A man greets you as you exit Kiloude Station. He recognizes you from the parade in Lumiose City and gives you a special tool called a Vs. Recorder. With this device, you can record Battle Videos whenever you battle against other players or inside special facilities! You may then choose to make your Battle Videos public by posting them online for other players to watch, and you can view a Battle Video that has been recorded by another player when you connect to the Internet and search for it using a code from a friend. How cool is that?

NOTE *The Vs. Recorder also lets you retry most types of battle that you've recorded. Simply open the Vs. Recorder in your Bag, highlight a battle that you've recorded, and then tap the top-right button to begin a mock battle. You can choose to battle with the Pokémon in your party or the ones in your Battle Box. See if you can perform even better this time around!*

STEP 3 >> Show off a Pokémon that knows Petal Blizzard to receive a Revive

Yes! That's it! Petal Blizzard!
Take this as a thank-you gift, OK?

The Pokémon Center isn't far, but make a quick stop in the house that you pass along the way. If you have a Pokémon that knows the Petal Blizzard move, show it to the woman who lives here. She'll reward you with a Revive.

AFTER THE HALL OF FAME

CENTRAL KALOS

COASTAL KALOS

MOUNTAIN KALOS

ADVENTURE DATA

STEP
④ Meet the Judge at the Pokémon Center

Enter the Pokémon Center next and speak to the Judge. This man has the unique ability to discern the potential of any Pokémon in your party. Just show the Judge a Pokémon, and he'll tell you which of its stats are the most powerful and which are weak (if any). The Poké Mart here offers some special goods, too, so be sure to check them out.

 If you've caught multiple Pokémon of the same species, the Judge can help you determine which ones have the greatest potential.

STEP
⑤ Listen to the bard's final ballad

Speak to the traveling bard in the Pokémon Center. If you have listened to all the earlier parts, you can hear the conclusion of his epic ballad. The bard appears in the following places. You can revisit them and listen to each part of his ballad if you missed one earlier.

1. Parfum Palace
2. Cyllage City Pokémon Center
3. Laverre City Pokémon Center
4. Snowbelle City Pokémon Center

STEP
⑥ Snap up TM91 Flash Cannon

Enter Kiloude City's southeast house and speak to the kid upstairs to obtain TM91 Flash Cannon. This TM unleashes a powerful Steel-type move, which are hard to come by. This is the only TM that will teach Pokémon a forceful Steel-type special move.

STEP 7 Obtain TM58 Sky Drop

Sky Drop carries the target into the sky on the first turn and drops it to the

Take a moment to chat with a young girl in one of Kiloude City's northwest houses next, and she'll give you TM58 Sky Drop. This two-stage move lifts the opposing Pokémon up into the air—preventing it from taking any action until after it's dropped to the ground on the next turn. Ouch!

STEP 8 Show off Kyurem and receive DNA Splicers

The Pokémon Kyurem...

Enter the other northwest house and show a woman the Pokémon named Kyurem, and she'll give you DNA Splicers. This useful item lets you absofuse (merge) Kyurem with Reshiram or Zekrom to make White Kyurem or Black Kyurem. You can also use the DNA Splicers again to undo this process. Reshiram, Zekrom, and Kyurem are Legendary Pokémon from the Unova region, as seen in *Pokémon Black*, *Pokémon White*, *Pokémon Black 2*, and *Pokémon White 2*.

STEP 9 Inspire an artist and snag some groovy threads

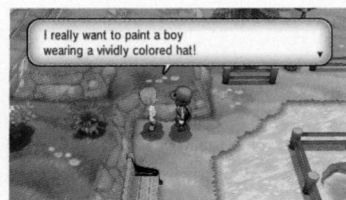

I really want to paint a boy wearing a vividly colored hat!

Head up to the north pond to find an artist that's in need of inspiration. If you're playing as the male character, put on a vividly colored hat and shoes, and you'll help this artist snap out of her creative slump. Female characters must dress in lots of ruffles and frills to inspire her. You'll be rewarded with either a Bamboo Sprig Hat (if your character is male) or a Sundae Dress (if your character is female).

STEP
10 Check out the Battle Maison

By now you've surely noticed the large building in the center of Kiloude City. This is the Battle Maison! Enter to participate in competitive Single Battles, Double Battles, Triple Battles, and Rotation Battles. Join with friends and you can undertake special Multi Battles with them!

Participate in Battle Maison Battles!

Battle Maison battles are unique for several reasons. For starters, your goal is to win as many battles as possible in a row without losing. You can take a break and save your progress between battles without fear, since your winning streak will be preserved. Your winning streak is broken only when you lose a battle.

Battle Maison options

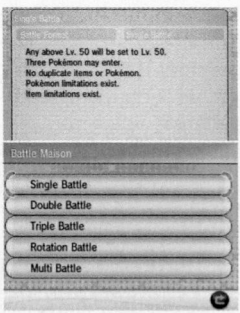

When setting up a Battle Maison battle, you have a number of options. When playing solo, you can choose to participate in Single, Double, Triple, or Rotation Battles. You can even do Multi Battles when you're alone, by calling for help from one of your friends in the game, like Tierno or Trevor. You can also get a little help from any Friends you have registered on your Nintendo 3DS system, even if they're not actively playing with you. You maintain a different winning streak in each battle type (Single, Double, Triple, Rotation, and Multi).

After setting up your battle options, you'll need to choose your Pokémon. You can use the Pokémon in your party, or you can use the ones in your Battle Box. Use the PC in the Battle Maison to fill your party and Battle Box with your favorite Pokémon.

 You can even change the music that you'll battle to, if you'd like!

Battle Maison rewards

Every time you win at the Battle Maison, you'll earn some BP (Battle Points). You earn 1–2 BP for each battle in the regular battle formats, and 20 BP for beating the Battle Chatelaines. You earn 2–7 BP for each battle in the Super battle formats, and 50 BP for the Battle Chatelaines there. The more wins you rack up, the more BP you'll earn. Spend these precious points at the two Exchange Service Corners in the Battle Maison's front lobby to purchase all sorts of neat prizes. The selection is impressive, so enjoy yourself at the Battle Maison and stock up on lots of cool stuff!

Kiloude City

AFTER THE
HALL OF FAME

CENTRAL
KALOS

COASTAL
KALOS

MOUNTAIN
KALOS

ADVENTURE
DATA

Nita / Single Battles

Evelyn / Double Battles

Morgan / Rotation Battles

Dana / Triple Battles

You'll also receive special prizes when you reach winning-streak milestones at the Battle Maison.

- Win 19 battles in a row, and you'll meet one of the Battle Maison's four owners: the Battle Chatelaines. The Battle Chatelaine you meet in your 20th battle depends on the battle format you're attempting (Single, Double, Triple, Rotation, or Multi). After you defeat each Battle Chatelaine, you will unlock the corresponding Super battle format.
- Win 50 Super battles in a row, and a monument will appear in the entrance to the Battle Maison. Aim to get the monuments for all five battle formats: Single, Double, Triple, Rotation, and Multi.

- Win 100 battles in a row to receive a Lansat Berry from the girl at the entrance to the Battle Maison.
- Win 200 battles in a row to earn a Starf Berry from the girl at the entrance to the Battle Maison.
- Be sure to plant the Battle Maison's rare Berries at the Berry fields on Route 7 so you can grow lots more of them.

Battle Maison notes

A few more important notes about the Battle Maison.

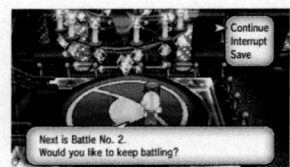

- You can save your progress by choosing "Interrupt" to leave the battle and autosave your game. Interrupting your advancement between battles will not break your winning streak.
- Losing a battle will break your winning streak, as will closing or resetting the game during battle. Be sure you have your battery sufficiently charged when challenging the Battle Maison and don't press that HOME Button!
- You can't use items from your Bag while battling in the Battle House.
- You can use the Pokémon in your Battle Box or the Pokémon in your party.
- You use three Pokémon for Single Battles, four Pokémon for Double Battles, six Pokémon for Triple Battles, and four Pokémon for Rotation Battles. Each Trainer in a Multi Battle will use two Pokémon.
- Pokémon over Lv. 50 will be temporarily reduced to Lv. 50 for the duration of each battle.
- All Pokémon and their held items must be different—no Pokémon or held items may have the same name (except when battling

with friends in Multi Battles). Additionally, no Pokémon may hold a Soul Dew.
- Some Pokémon are not allowed in the Battle Maison battles. These include: Mewtwo, Mew, Ho-Oh, Lugia, Celebi, Kyogre, Groudon, Rayquaza, Jirachi, Deoxys, Palkia, Dialga, Giratina, Phione, Manaphy, Darkrai, Shaymin, Arceus, Zekrom, Reshiram, Kyurem, Victini, Keldeo, Meloetta, Genesect, Xerneas, Yveltal, and Zygarde.
- In Multi Battles, you can play with friends using your infrared connection. If you don't have someone to play with at the moment, you can have an AI Trainer come help you. You get your choice of your friends in the game, like Tierno and Shauna. If you call on friends you have registered on your Nintendo 3DS system, they will be able to send someone to aid you in battle. This helper will have a different appearance and team based on the friend code you use.

STEP
11 ▶ Check out the Friend Safari

Welcome to the Friend Safari!

Kiloude City is also famous for another Trainer attraction: the Friend Safari! Here, you can go on the Safari of a Friend who's registered in your friend list. Going on a Friend Safari is lots of fun and totally free, and it's also the only way to catch certain Pokémon. For example, you can catch beginning Pokémon partners from previous games in Friend Safaris, rather than having to trade for them or transfer them from a previous game. Why not give it a try?

 If one of your friends is also playing Pokémon X *or* Pokémon Y, *more Pokémon will pop up while you participate in his or her Safari. This is the ideal time to try a Friend Safari!*

Go on a Friend Safari!

You'll unlock a different Friend Safari for each friend code that's registered to your Nintendo 3DS system. Register lots of friend codes to unlock more Safaris. The more Safaris that are available to you, the more Pokémon you can discover!

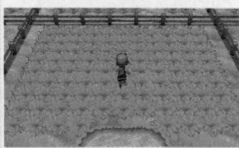

Simply choose which Friend Safari you'd like to take, and then go outside and run through the tall grass. It won't be long before you encounter wild Pokémon.

A wild Wartortle appeared!

The Pokémon you encounter will all be of the type indicated when you chose the Safari. This makes Friend Safaris a great way to easily round out your Pokédex with Pokémon of specific types. Register lots of friend codes and participate in plenty of Friend Safaris and see how many Pokémon you can catch!

Special Notes

A few special notes regarding Friend Safaris.

- Usually you can only meet two kinds of Pokémon in a Friend Safari. But if you play a Safari of a Friend who has entered the Hall of Fame, you can meet three kinds of Pokémon instead of just two. Also, Pokémon that you catch may have a Hidden Ability.

- Pokémon you catch during a Friend Safari may have great potential. Speak to the Judge in Kiloude City's Pokémon Center to discover the potential of your Pokémon (see p. 20 for more information about the Judge).

Pokémon that can appear during Friend Safaris (by Safari type)

Normal	Aipom	Audino	Chansey	Ditto	Dunsparce	Eevee
	Kecleon	Lillipup	Loudred	Minccino	Smeargle	Teddiursa
Fire	Braixen*	Charmeleon*	Fletchinder	Growlithe	Larvesta	Magmar
	Ninetales	Pansear	Ponyta	Pyroar	Slugma	
Water	Azumarill	Bibarel	Floatzel	Frogadier*	Gyarados	Krabby
	Octillery	Panpour	Poliwhirl	Quagsire	Wartortle*	
Grass	Gogoat	Ivysaur*	Maractus	Oddish	Pansage	Petilil
	Quilladin*	Sawsbuck	Sunkern	Swadloon	Tangela	
Electric	Dedenne	Electabuzz	Electrode	Emolga	Galvantula	Helioptile
	Luxio	Manectric	Pachirisu	Pikachu	Stunfisk	Zebstrika
Ice	Beartic	Bergmite	Cloyster	Delibird	Dewgong	Lapras
	Piloswine	Sneasel	Snorunt	Snover	Spheal	
Fighting	Breloom	Hariyama	Machoke	Mankey	Meditite	Mienfoo
	Pancham	Riolu	Sawk	Throh	Tyrogue	
Poison	Ariados	Cascoon	Drapion	Garbodor	Gloom	Kakuna
	Muk	Seviper	Swalot	Toxicroak	Venomoth	Whirlipede
Ground	Camerupt	Diggersby	Dugtrio	Gastrodon	Marowak	Nincada
	Palpitoad	Phanpy	Sandshrew	Trapinch	Wooper	
Flying	Doduo	Farfetch'd	Fletchinder	Hawlucha	Hoothoot	Pidgey
	Rufflet	Spearow	Swanna	Tranquill	Tropius	Woobat
Psychic	Abra	Drowzee	Duosion	Espurr	Girafarig	Gothorita
	Grumpig	Munna	Sigilyph	Wobbuffet	Xatu	
Bug	Beautifly	Butterfree	Combee	Heracross	Illumise	Ledyba
	Masquerain	Paras	Pinsir	Venomoth	Vivillon	Volbeat
Rock	Barbaracle	Boldore	Corsola	Dwebble	Magcargo	Nosepass
	Onix	Pupitar	Rhydon	Shuckle		
Ghost	Drifblim	Dusclops	Golurk	Lampent	Phantump	Pumpkaboo
	Shuppet	Spiritomb				
Dragon	Dragonair	Druddigon	Fraxure	Gabite	Noibat	Shelgon
	Sliggoo					
Dark	Absol	Cacturne	Crawdaunt	Inkay	Liepard	Mightyena
	Nuzleaf	Pawniard	Sableye	Sandile	Sneasel	Vullaby
Steel	Bronzong	Excadrill	Ferroseed	Forretress	Klang	Klefki
	Magneton	Mawile	Metang	Skarmory		
Fairy	Clefairy	Dedenne	Floette	Jigglypuff	Kirlia	Mawile
	Snubbull	Spritzee	Swirlix	Togepi		

Pokémon that can usually only be obtained from a Pokémon Professor or through trades

STEP 12 Have a friendly battle against Serena/Calem and receive Absolite

Will you have a battle with me?
I think you're in for a surprise!

Yes
No

After you've completed at least one battle in the Battle Maison, you'll find Serena/Calem near Kiloude City's north pond. Serena/Calem will offer to battle you here once each day. This is a great way to gain experience and prize money. As a bonus, Serena/Calem will give you a Mega Stone (Absolite) after your first victory!

Vs. Serena/Calem's Pokémon

Serena/Calem's Default Pokémon

The following Pokémon are always used by Serena/Calem, regardless of the Pokémon you chose at the start of the game.

Meowstic ♀/♂ Lv. 66 Psychic
Weak to: Bug Ghost Dark

Clefable ♀ Lv. 68 Fairy
Weak to: Poison Steel

Altaria ♀ Lv. 67 Dragon Flying
Weak to: 4x! Ice Rock Dragon / Fairy

Absol ♂ Lv. 68 Dark
Weak to: Fighting Bug Fairy

If you chose Chespin:

Jolteon ♂ Lv. 66 Electric
Weak to: Ground

Delphox ♂ Lv. 70 Fire Psychic
Weak to: Water Ground Rock / Ghost Dark

If you chose Fennekin:

Flareon ♂ Lv. 66 Fire
Weak to: Water Ground Rock

Greninja ♂ Lv. 70 Water Dark
Weak to: Grass Electric Fighting / Bug Fairy

If you chose Froakie:

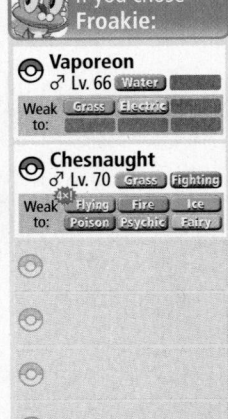

Vaporeon ♂ Lv. 66 Water
Weak to: Grass Electric

Chesnaught ♂ Lv. 70 Grass Fighting
Weak to: 4x! Flying Fire Ice / Poison Psychic Fairy

NOTES

The gender of Serena/Calem's Pokémon varies depending on whether or not you're battling Serena or Calem. Serena will have more female Pokémon, while Calem will have more male Pokémon.

One of Serena/Calem's Pokémon will be a fully evolved Pokémon that she or he has been using ever since you first met. Serena/Calem's final Pokémon will be powered up by Mega Evolution. Be prepared!

STEP
13 Head to Anistar City after defeating Serena/Calem

I have a message from Professor Sycamore.

Speak to Serena/Calem after you defeat her/him, and she/he will give you a message from Professor Sycamore. The professor is waiting for you at Anistar City, near the giant sundial, with news of a Mega Evolution breakthrough. You'd better hurry over there!

ANISTAR CITY
Learn the secret of the sundial from Professor Sycamore

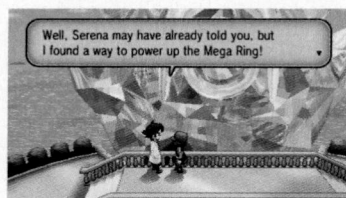

Well, Serena may have already told you, but I found a way to power up the Mega Ring!

Make a beeline for the sundial and speak to Professor Sycamore. The professor informs you of his latest theory: Mega Stones are actually leftover debris from the use of the ultimate weapon 3,000 years ago. He asks you to touch the sundial. It powers up your Mega Ring! Now you can use the Mega Ring to locate Mega Stones for one hour every evening, between 8 P.M. and 9 P.M.

NOTE

Pokémon X and Pokémon Y use your Nintendo 3DS system's internal clock. Just wait until 8 P.M. to get started searching for precious Mega Stones.

ANISTAR CITY
Check up on the lonely old man

It's a Poké Ball with Caterpie inside. There's a letter next to it, too.

Before you race off to hunt for Mega Stones, pay a quick visit to the house of the lonely old man whom you met during your first visit to Anistar City. The old man is gone, and a single Poké Ball remains on the floor. Inspect it to reclaim the Pokémon you lent him. You'll also discover a thank-you letter from the old man, along with a valuable Comet Shard.

AFTER THE HALL OF FAME

CENTRAL KALOS

COASTAL KALOS

MOUNTAIN KALOS

ADVENTURE DATA

GEOSENGE TOWN > ## Receive daily Mega Evolution tips from Trevor

According to Professor Sycamore's research, Scizor has a potential Mega Evolution!

What better place to begin your search for Mega Stones than Geosenge Town? Well, unfortunately, you won't find any new Mega Stones here. But you will find your buddy Trevor standing around outside! Speak to Trevor to learn the name of a Pokémon that has the potential for Mega Evolution. Trevor will tell you about another Pokémon with Mega Evolution potential each day, so have a word with him daily to learn what you can about these amazing Pokémon.

TIP *See page 83 to learn more about Mega Stones, including a chart that reveals where every Mega Stone can be found.*

Get a Reveal Glass for Thundurus, Landorus,
REFLECTION CAVE > and Tornadus

Xavier obtained the Reveal Glass!

Go back to Reflection Cave and talk to the Scientist on 1F when you have Thundurus, Landorus, or Tornadus in your party. She will give you a Reveal Glass which allows these special Pokémon from *Pokémon Black*, *Pokémon White*, *Pokémon Black 2*, and *Pokémon White 2* to change forms.

AMBRETTE TOWN > ## Get Drives for Genesect in Ambrette Town

Is that Pokémon with you... Genesect?!

If you have managed to obtain the rare Pokémon Genesect, go back to Ambrette Town and visit the Fossil Lab. A Hiker there will give you Drives that will allow your Genesect to change the type of its Techno Blast move. While you're in the area, why not also swing by Glittering Cave for some Fossil hunting (p. 81)? When you're done with all that, get ready to return to Terminus Cave!

A coal mine that was closed a few years ago due to rumors of a monster living deep within it.

Terminus Cave

A chill wind flows through this foreboding cave, which lies along Route 18. Many wild Pokémon reside here, and there's plenty of treasure for bold adventurers to discover. Rumor even has it that a powerful Pokémon may reside in the cave's deepest reaches...

Field Moves Needed

Rock Smash

Entrance 1

A

Entrance

2F

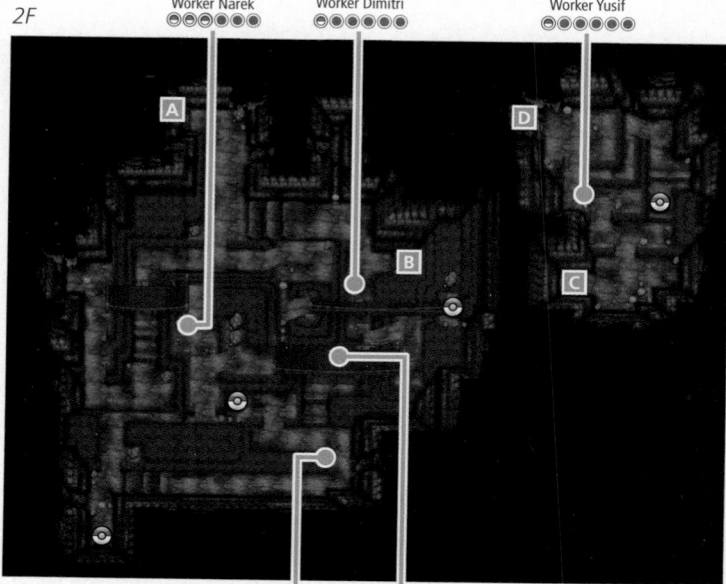

Worker Narek

Worker Dimitri

Worker Yusif

A

D

B

C

Hiker Bergin   Hiker Aaron

AFTER THE HALL OF FAME

CENTRAL KALOS

COASTAL KALOS

MOUNTAIN KALOS

ADVENTURE DATA

AFTER THE
HALL OF FAME

CENTRAL
KALOS

COASTAL
KALOS

MOUNTAIN
KALOS

ADVENTURE
DATA

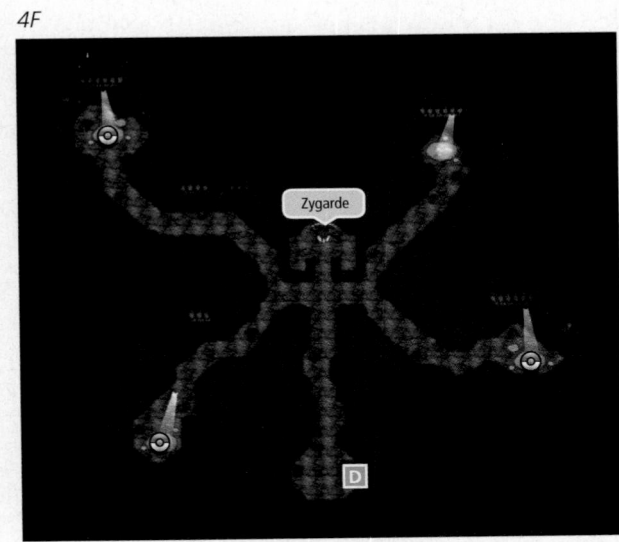

3F

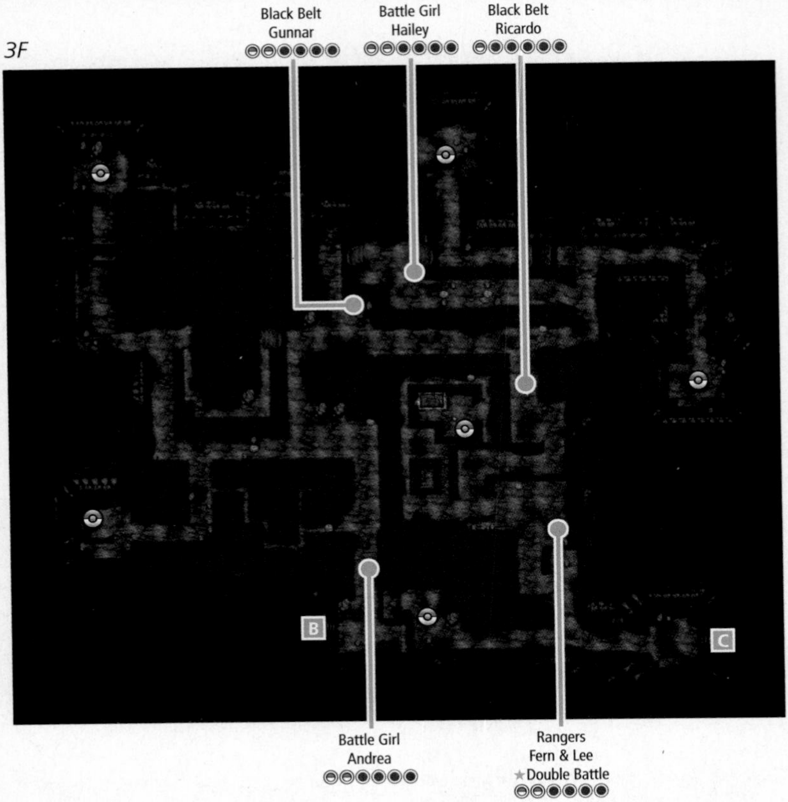

Black Belt
Gunnar
◉◎◉◉◉◉

Battle Girl
Hailey
◉◎◉◉◉◉

Black Belt
Ricardo
◉◎◉◉◉◉

B

C

Battle Girl
Andrea
◉◎◉◉◉◉

Rangers
Fern & Lee
★Double Battle
◉◎◉◉◉◉

4F

Zygarde

D

Entrance 2

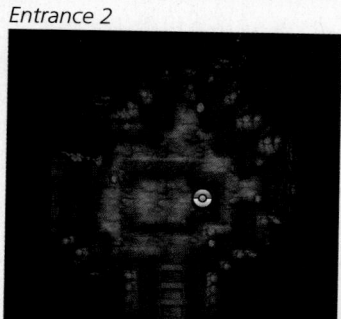

Entrance 3

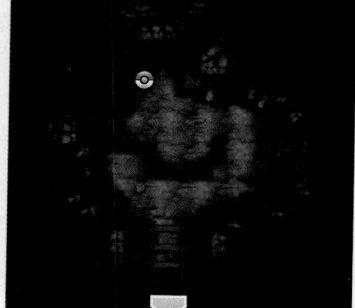

Entrance

Entrance

AFTER THE
HALL OF FAME

CENTRAL
KALOS

COASTAL
KALOS

MOUNTAIN
KALOS

ADVENTURE
DATA

Items
Second floor
☐ Escape Rope
☐ Heat Rock
☐ Reaper Cloth
☐ Star Piece
Third Floor
☐ Dusk Stone
☐ Elixir
☐ Full Heal
☐ Iron Plate
☐ TM30 Shadow Ball
☐ X Attack
Fourth Floor
☐ Adamant Orb
☐ Griseous Orb
☐ Lustrous Orb
Entrance 2
☐ Dragon Scale
Entrance 3
☐ TM31 Brick Break

Hidden Items
Second floor
☐ Dusk Ball
☐ Hyper Potion
☐ Max Repel
☐ Moon Stone
Third floor
☐ Dire Hit
☐ Iron
☐ Max Potion
Fourth floor
☐ Big Nugget
Entrance 2
☐ Normal Gem

Cave		
☐ Durant	◎	
☐ Graveler	○	
☐ Lairon	○	✗
☐ Pupitar	○	Y
☐ Sandslash	○	

Horde Encounter		
☐ Aron ×5	△	✗
☐ Durant ×5	◎	
☐ Geodude ×5	○	
☐ Larvitar ×5	△	Y

Cracked Rock		
☐ Graveler	◎	
☐ Shuckle	▲	

Ambush (cave)		
☐ Ariados	◎	
☐ Noibat	△	

◎ frequent ○ average △ rare ▲ almost never

1 ⟩ Find the right entrance

If you haven't already visited Terminus Cave, you'll find that it features three entrances, but only one of them leads to its main floors. Use the entrance near the Inverse Battle house to begin a complete exploration of Terminus Cave.

 Be sure to check the cave's two other entrances as well. Each leads to a small chamber that houses additional items.

STEP
2 Battle and catch Zygarde

Zzzz-dddd-aaaaaa!

Make your way to Terminus Cave's final floor, and you'll have a chance to battle a mighty Pokémon named Zygarde. This is a tough battle due to Zygarde's high Sp. Atk and even higher Attack stat combining with dangerous moves such as Earthquake and Dragon Pulse. But if you wear Zygarde down without defeating it, you'll have a chance to catch this unique Pokémon!

TIP *Try using a Dusk Ball to catch Zygarde—it has a good chance of success when used against cave-dwelling Pokémon.*

NOTE *If you fail to catch Zygarde, it will retreat into hiding. Don't worry; it will come back the next day. You'll just have to return to Terminus Cave and try again!*

Catch Zygarde!

Lv. 70 [Dragon] [Ground]

Weak to: [4×] Ice [Dragon] [Fairy]

STEP
3 Search Zygarde's den for precious items

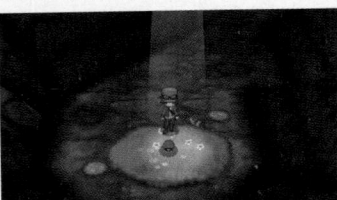

Terminus Cave's final floor also houses several priceless items. Explore each side path to its end to discover these top-notch treats in beams of light.

Adamant Orb: A brightly gleaming orb to be held by Dialga. It boosts the power of Dragon- and Steel-type moves when it is held.

Griseous Orb: A glowing orb to be held by Giratina. It boosts the power of Dragon- and Ghost-type moves when it is held.

Lustrous Orb: A beautifully glowing orb to be held by Palkia. It boosts the power of Dragon- and Water-type moves when it is held.

Azure Bay

This spacious bay is a favorite vacationing spot for surfers around the Kalos region. Even if you've already plundered the many treasures found around the bay's isles, the Sea Spirit's Den to the north comes into play during your pursuit of Legendary Pokémon.

Field Moves
Needed

Surf

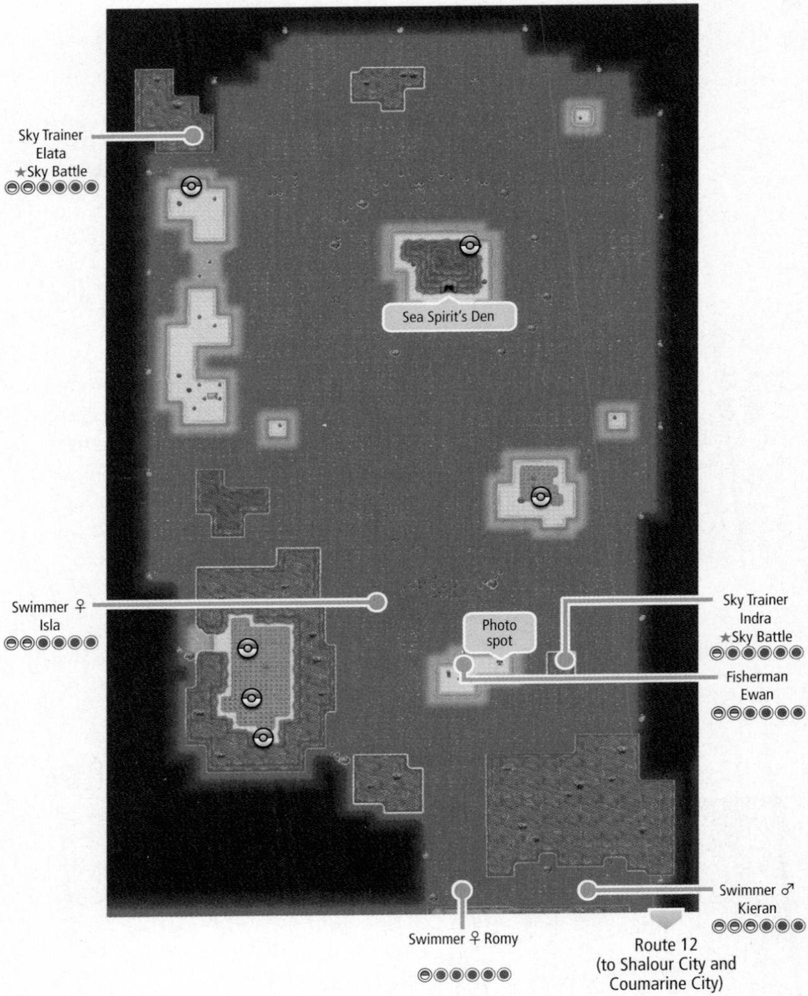

Sky Trainer
Elata
★Sky Battle
◉◉◉◉◉◉

Sea Spirit's Den

Swimmer ♀
Isla
◉◉◉◉◉◉

Photo
spot

Sky Trainer
Indra
★Sky Battle
◉◉◉◉◉◉

Fisherman
Ewan
◉◉◉◉◉◉

Swimmer ♂
Kieran
◉◉◉◉◉◉

Swimmer ♀ Romy
◉◉◉◉◉◉

Route 12
(to Shalour City and
Coumarine City)

Items

- ☐ Ampharosite
- ☐ Big Pearl
- ☐ Deep Sea Scale
- ☐ Deep Sea Tooth
- ☐ Dive Ball
- ☐ Splash Plate
- ☐ TM81 X-Scissor

Hidden Items

- ☐ Heart Scale
- ☐ Hyper Potion
- ☐ Star Piece

Tall Grass

☐ Chatot	○
☐ Exeggcute	△
☐ Inkay	△
☐ Slowpoke	◎

Cracked Rock

☐ Binacle	○
☐ Dwebble	◎

Horde Encounter

☐ Exeggcute ×5	△
☐ Slowpoke ×5	○
☐ Wingull ×5	◎

◎ frequent ○ average
△ rare ▲ almost never

Fishing

Old Rod

☐ Luvdisc	◎

Good Rod

☐ Chinchou	○
☐ Remoraid	◎

Super Rod

☐ Alomomola	◎
☐ Lanturn	▲
☐ Octillery	○

Water Surface

☐ Lapras	▲
☐ Mantyke	△
☐ Tentacool	◎

STEP 1 Explore the great bay

If you haven't already explored Azure Bay, you'll find this tranquil place to be quite large and filled with many small isles to explore. Spend some time surfing the sea, but remember to use your Dowsing Machine to detect hidden goodies whenever you reach dry land while also keeping an eye out for two Sky Trainers.

> **TIP** Surf Azure Bay in peace by using Max Repels to prevent random encounters.

STEP 2 Catch Legendary Pokémon at the Sea Spirit's Den

Zapdos appeared!

The Sea Spirit's Den is a small cave that lies at Azure Bay's north end. This cave is small and empty, but it will become an important backdrop during your pursuit of Articuno, Zapdos, or Moltres. After chasing the Legendary Pokémon all over Kalos, you'll eventually be able to battle and capture it here at the Sea Spirit's Den. See the following pages to learn all about these Legendary Pokémon.

Catch Articuno!

◉ Lv. 70 | Ice | Flying |
Weak⁴ˣ¹ to: | Rock | Fire | Electric |
| Steel | | |

Catch Moltres!

◉ Lv. 70 | Fire | Flying |
Weak⁴ˣ¹ to: | Rock | Water | Electric |

Catch Zapdos!

◉ Lv. 70 | Electric | Flying |
Weak to: | Ice | Rock |

Catching Legendary Pokémon

Catching these Legendary Pokémon is no easy feat, but it's possible now that you've entered the Hall of Fame. Simply run around the tall grass or flowers located along one of the following Routes to catch your first glimpse of one of these three Legendary Pokémon.

- Route 4
- Route 5
- Route 7
- Route 10
- Route 11
- Route 12
- Route 14
- Route 15
- Route 16
- Route 18
- Route 19
- Route 21
- Route 22

Catching Legendary Pokémon (continued)

After you enter the Hall of Fame, a Legendary Pokémon will appear during your very first wild Pokémon encounter in these areas. The exact Legendary Pokémon you encounter varies depending on the first Pokémon partner you chose at the beginning of the adventure.

Articuno appears if you chose Chespin as your first partner.
Moltres appears if you chose Froakie as your first partner.
Zapdos appears if you chose Fennekin as your first partner.

Unfortunately, the Legendary Pokémon flees soon after you encounter it. Don't worry—you haven't missed your chance to catch it! Bring up your Coastal Kalos Pokédex and find the Legendary Pokémon's entry (it will be near the bottom of the list). Press Ⓐ to select the Legendary Pokémon and call up its Habitat information.

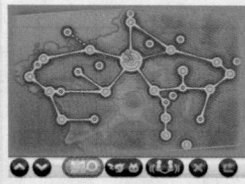

The Habitat screen shows the most likely place where the Legendary Pokémon may go to take shelter. Look for a flashing red area on the map. That's where you need to go!

You may not want to use Fly to get around, because the Legendary Pokémon tends to relocate when you use Fly. Pursue the Legendary Pokémon on foot unless you want to chance seeing if it will move to another nearby location. If traveling over land, use your Roller Skates and Bicycle to hasten your travels.

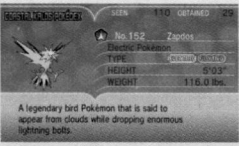

Pursue the Legendary Pokémon around the Kalos region until you've encountered it 10 more times. At that point, the Legendary Pokémon will seek refuge within the Sea Spirit's Den. That's where you'll have your final battle with it. Save your game before the battle and do your best to catch it. If you accidentally defeat the Legendary Pokémon, you'll just need to try catching it again another day.

A mysterious void. It is said that nothing can exist within it.

Chamber of Emptiness

You've tracked down a couple of powerful Pokémon by this point, but now it's time to get some more Mega Stones. Return to Route 22, and along it you will find the Chamber of Emptiness. Despite popular rumor, you'll definitely find something worth discovering here!

Field Moves Needed

Strength   Surf

Waterfall

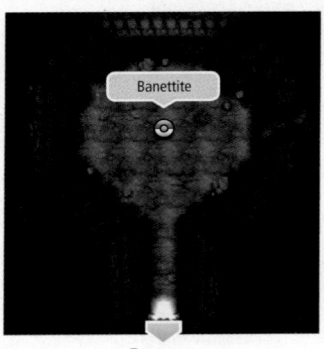

Banettite

Entrance

Items
- ☐ Banettite
- ☐ Spooky Plate

STEP
1 ▸ Use Surf and Waterfall to find the entrance

Though you don't need any field moves once you're inside the Chamber of Emptiness, you do need the Surf and Waterfall field moves to reach it. First, use Surf to reach Route 22's southern waterfall, and then use Waterfall to ride down to a lower area. Continue using Surf as you navigate the river, heading for the cave's entrance.

STEP
2 ▸ Enter between 8 P.M. and 9 P.M. for a Mega Stone

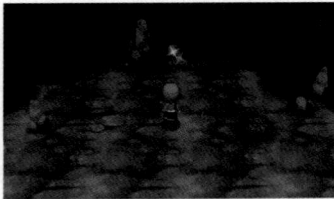

The Chamber of Emptiness *almost* lives up to its name. Just one item rests on the ground. After Professor Sycamore has powered up your Mega Ring at Anistar City (p. 27), visit the Chamber of Emptiness between 8 P.M. and 9 P.M., and you'll notice a sparkling area. Inspect this area to discover a Mega Stone: Banettite!

NOTE *Even if you know where to look, you cannot obtain the Banettite Mega Stone unless you see the area sparkling.*

AFTER THE HALL OF FAME

CENTRAL KALOS

COASTAL KALOS

MOUNTAIN KALOS

ADVENTURE DATA

37

Unknown Dungeon

Return to the Pokémon Village and you'll have access at last to the Unknown Dungeon. Within it you will find a very rare and very powerful Pokémon: Mewtwo, a species of Pokémon that was artificially created through cloning.

AFTER THE
HALL OF FAME

CENTRAL
KALOS

COASTAL
KALOS

MOUNTAIN
KALOS

ADVENTURE
DATA

Field Moves
Needed

Surf

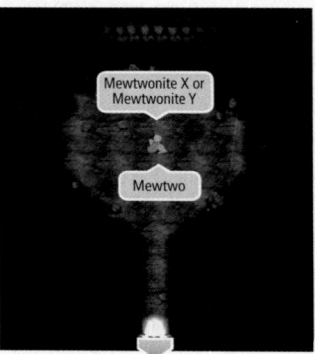

Mewtwonite X or
Mewtwonite Y

Mewtwo

Entrance

Catching Mewtwo

This Legendary Pokémon resides in the Pokémon Village in a cave called the Unknown Dungeon. Use the Surf field move to cross the Pokémon Village's west river and reach the cave.

A man may have blocked your way if you tried to enter the Unknown Dungeon before taking on the Pokémon League, but return to the Pokémon Village after entering the Hall of Fame and the man will be gone, allowing you access to the cave.

A towering Pokémon stands in the Unknown Dungeon. It's Mewtwo! Prepare your party and save your game before approaching this Legendary Pokémon.

AFTER THE
HALL OF FAME

CENTRAL
KALOS

COASTAL
KALOS

MOUNTAIN
KALOS

ADVENTURE
DATA

Catching Mewtwo (continued)

Mewtwo is challenging to catch due to its strong defensive moves. It will use Barrier to increase its Defense, and Recover to restore its lost HP. Settle in for a long battle, make use of status conditions, and try using a Timer Ball to catch Mewtwo after several turns have passed. You can buy Timer Balls at the Poké Marts in Coumarine City and Snowbelle City. If you catch Mewtwo, you'll get a Mewtwonite X or Mewtwonite Y, depending on which game you're playing.

Catch Mewtwo!

◉ Lv. 70 | Psychic

Weak to: | Bug | Ghost | Dark

Mega Mewtwo X (✗)

Mega Mewtwo Y (Ⓨ)

Post-game Activities

Now that you've completed the post-game walkthrough, take a moment to participate in fun and interesting activities around Lumiose City! After entering the Hall of Fame, a few new places become available to you—two of them are the Battle Institute and the Looker Bureau.

Battle Institute

The Battle Institute on Lumiose City's North Boulevard allows you to take a Battle Test after you enter the Hall of Fame. Step up with your well-trained Pokémon, and your skill in raising them will be evaluated. Aim for Master Rank!

How the Battle Test Works

1 Choose your Pokémon

Choose Pokémon from your party or Battle Box: three for Single Battles; four for Double Battles. You can't use more than one Pokémon with the same Pokédex number. No two Pokémon can hold the same item.

2 Battle five Trainers

After each battle, your Pokémon will be healed. Even if you lose a battle, the Battle Test will continue until you've battled all five Trainers.

3 See the results

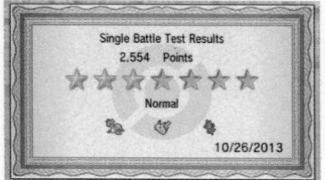

How you battled against these five Trainers will be evaluated and the result determined. You'll earn points, prizes, and a rank. You can always check your past records using the PC that is to the right of the receptionist.

Battle Institute Rewards

Fight hard to reach higher and higher ranks at the Battle Institute, and you'll be entitled to special rewards.

Beginner Rank (0–999): 3 BP and either Health Wing, Muscle Wing, Resist Wing, Genius Wing, Clever Wing, or Swift Wing

Novice Rank (1,000–1,999): 5 BP and either Health Wing, Muscle Wing, Resist Wing, Genius Wing, Clever Wing, or Swift Wing

Normal Rank (2,000–2,999): 7 BP and either Health Wing, Muscle Wing, Resist Wing, Genius Wing, Clever Wing, or Swift Wing

Super Rank (3,000–3,999): 9 BP and either Protein, Iron, Calcium, Zinc, Carbos, or HP Up

Hyper Rank (4,000–4,999): 11 BP and either Protein, Iron, Calcium, Zinc, Carbos, or HP Up

Elite Rank (5,000–5,999): 13 BP and either Protein, Iron, Calcium, Zinc, Carbos, or HP Up

Master Rank (6,000 points or more): 15 BP and PP Up

Tips for Getting a High Score

There are tricks to getting a high score in a Battle Test. If you take the test while keeping these six points in mind, you should be able to earn a high score and a better rank.

1. **Don't let your Pokémon faint.**
2. **Defeat your opponent in as few turns as possible.**
3. **Win with a lot of HP remaining.**
4. **Use a variety of moves.**
5. **Hit opposing Pokémon with supereffective moves.**
6. **Switch your Pokémon.**

Battle Institute Notes

Keep the following in mind when testing your skills at the Battle Institute:

- You can't use items from the Bag during the battles.
- All Pokémon will be set to Level 50 for the test.
- You can't quit the test once it has begun, but you can give up on each battle by choosing to run. If you run from a battle, it will be treated as a loss.
- Some Pokémon can't take part, including: Mewtwo, Mew, Ho-Oh, Lugia, Celebi, Kyogre, Groudon, Rayquaza, Jirachi, Deoxys, Palkia, Dialga, Giratina, Phione, Manaphy, Darkrai, Shaymin, Arceus, Zekrom, Reshiram, Kyurem, Victini, Meloetta, Keldeo, Genesect, Xerneas, Yveltal, and Zygarde.

Looker Events

Chapter 1: That Man's a Real...Looker

After you've entered the Hall of Fame and traveled to Kiloude City, you'll receive an enigmatic Holo Clip from an unknown person the next time you visit Lumiose City. The message invites you to visit the Looker Bureau, which has recently opened. Sounds intriguing!

Locating the Looker Bureau can be tricky. Look for it in an unassuming alley between North Boulevard and Rouge Plaza. To find it fast, just use a Lumi Cab. The Looker Bureau is listed under Facilities.

Enter the Looker Bureau and speak with a hard-boiled detective named Looker. The man needs help cleaning up Lumiose City and asks that you team up with him. Agree to help Looker, and he'll waste no time in giving you your first assignment.

Your first task involves seeking out five sparkling Looker Tickets that Looker has hidden around Lumiose City. This would be a daunting task in such a sprawling metropolis, but Looker has scribbled down a few notes about the location of each Looker Ticket. His notes are as follows:

1. In the Pokémon Center next to Magenta Plaza
2. In Centrico Plaza, in the tower illuminating the city
3. On Vernal Avenue, at a shop selling medicines
4. On North Boulevard, 1F, in a place where people rest
5. On North Boulevard, 1F, in a place filled with art

 TIP *Looker also includes his notes in a Holo Clip message after you leave the Bureau. Refer to this Holo Clip message if you've forgotten his notes.*

Looker's notes are pretty clear, but here's a visual guide to help you discover each Looker Ticket.

Looker Ticket locations

1. Magenta Pokémon Center

2. Prism Tower

3. Herboriste

4. Hotel Richissime

5. Lumiose Museum

I'll send you a message on your Holo Caster whenever we have a job to do!

After discovering all five sparkling Looker Tickets, return to the Looker Bureau to receive your promotion. Congratulations! You're now a full-fledged detective, ready to take on Lumiose City's toughest cases!

Chapter 2: In the Back Alleys

I want to talk to you about something important! Could you come to the Looker Bureau, please?

Shortly after you leave the Looker Bureau, Looker contacts you via the Holo Caster. When you're ready, return to the Looker Bureau to begin your first official case!

★ Details: "Kids in Lumiose City seem to be spending a lot of time in back alleys recently."

Read Looker's notebook to learn all about the case at hand. It seems that a representative from a local mothers' group has voiced concerns about kids spending too much time in Lumiose City's back alleys. What might those kids be up to in these shadowy, suspicious places? Inquiring mothers want to know!

My gut tells me there's something fishy about the alley leading off South Boulevard.

Looker asks you to explore the alleys around Lumiose City and get to the bottom of this issue. His gut tells him that there's something fishy in the back alley along South Boulevard, so that's where you should begin your investigation. Looker also adds more notes to his notebook, indicating where each of Lumiose City's four alleys is found.

Lumiose City alley locations

South Boulevard alley: Beside Restaurant Le Nah

North Boulevard alley 1: Across from the Galette Stand

North Boulevard alley 2: Across from Lumiose Station

North Boulevard alley 3: Beside Café Triste

Mimi and the homeless girl

you're gonna hafta beat me in battle!

Yes
No

Make your way to South Boulevard and enter the dark alley to the right of Restaurant Le Nah. Looker's instincts were spot on, and in the alley you'll find a group of kids! Unfortunately, these tykes don't take kindly to grown-ups invading their secret hideout. You must battle all four kids to make your way through the alley.

Vs. Preschooler Natalie's Pokémon

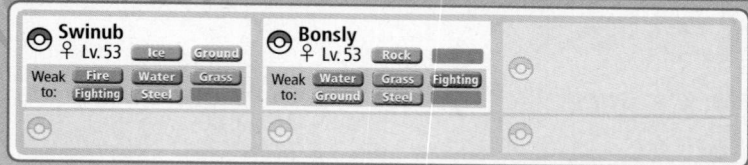

Swinub ♀ Lv. 53 — Ice / Ground
Weak to: Fire / Water / Grass / Fighting / Steel

Bonsly ♀ Lv. 53 — Rock
Weak to: Water / Grass / Fighting / Ground / Steel

Vs. Preschooler Lily's Pokémon

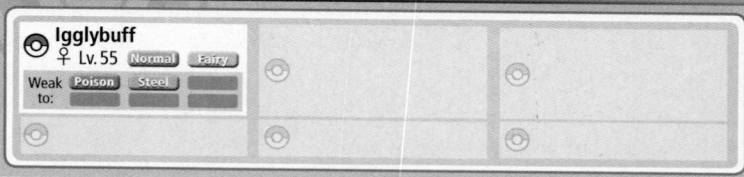

Igglybuff ♀ Lv. 55 — Normal / Fairy
Weak to: Poison / Steel

Vs. Schoolgirl Callie's Pokémon

Rapidash
♀ Lv. 53 [Fire]
Weak to: [Water] [Ground] [Rock]

Kingler
♀ Lv. 53 [Water]
Weak to: [Grass] [Electric]

Leavanny
♀ Lv. 53 [Bug] [Grass]
Weak to: [4x][Fire] [4x][Flying] [Ice] [Poison] [Bug] [Rock]

Vs. Schoolboy Macon's Pokémon

Spiritomb
♂ Lv. 56 [Ghost] [Dark]
Weak to: [Fairy]

Looker arrives on the scene when you reach the alley's end. It turns out that a homeless girl and her Pokémon friend, Mimi, are the leaders of this little group. There's nothing sinister going on here, however, for she and the kids are simply playing together in the alley.

Looker suddenly has an idea. To encourage the homeless girl to get off the streets, he invites her to become his assistant and live at the Looker Bureau. Mimi doesn't like the idea, though, and quickly runs off. Still, Looker maintains a positive outlook and believes he can win Mimi over in time. What's more, he asks you to try to befriend Mimi and win the Pokémon's trust!

Befriending Mimi

Mimi has fled to the alleys along North Boulevard, and it's up to you to track it down. Leave the alley and turn left to run into North Boulevard. As you leave the alley, you'll receive a Holo Clip from Looker with vital information: Mimi does not like being petted by strangers!

AFTER THE
HALL OF FAME

CENTRAL
KALOS

COASTAL
KALOS

MOUNTAIN
KALOS

ADVENTURE
DATA

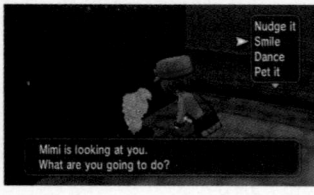

Begin searching the three alleys along North Boulevard for Mimi. One alley is across the street from Lumiose Station, another lies across the street from the Galette Stand, and the third is right next to Café Triste. You'll find Mimi in one of these alleys. When you find Mimi, approach the little Pokémon and choose to either smile, sing, or dance. Just don't pet or nudge it!

Mimi may flee to another of North Boulevard's three alleys depending on how much it has warmed up to you. Keep checking the North Boulevard's alleys for Mimi and choose how to interact with the little Pokémon each time you track it down. Try to mix up your overtures to win Mimi's trust!

Mimi always flees through the alleys in the same pattern. It starts with the one near Café Triste and ends at the one across from Lumiose Station.

It won't be long before Mimi takes a liking to you. The little Pokémon then agrees to move into the Looker Bureau along with the homeless girl, who reveals that her name is Emma. Now that Emma and Mimi are off the streets, those kids are sure to stop hanging out in Lumiose City's back alleys. Case closed!

Chapter 3: Detective, Tourist, Gang

Shortly after you leave the Looker Bureau, Looker calls you back in, eager to talk about Emma. It seems that Emma has been a bit stressed since she moved into Looker's office. Before you can inquire much further about Emma's issues, a tourist suddenly barges in.

Unfortunately, the tourist isn't fluent in your language, and although she seems agitated, she can't be understood. Using his powers of deduction, Looker assumes that the tourist is upset because she hasn't been offered a cup of tea. The great detective leaves straight away to buy some.

And the real reason she is so troubled is that her precious Pokémon were stolen!

Emma and Mimi soon arrive, and as luck would have it, the girl understands the tourist's words. Mimi also unleashes a mystical power that lets you understand the tourist's thoughts. It soon becomes clear that the woman is not interested in tea. She's upset because her precious Pokémon have been stolen!

Pardon? Whom? The Lumiose Gang?

Looker returns, tea in hand, and more details emerge. The tourist's Pokémon were stolen from her at Lumiose Station. Emma believes that the dangerous Lumiose Gang is involved, and she urges Looker to drop the case. Looker will have none of that, though, and heads out to investigate Lumiose Station.

Return that tourist's stolen Pokémon!

Emma implores you to follow Looker, warning that the Lumiose Gang is not to be trifled with. Before leaving the Bureau, read Looker's notebook to get his early impressions of Emma and Mimi. Leave the Bureau and turn left to reach North Boulevard. Turn right when you get there and hurry to Lumiose Station, where you'll find Looker in a tight spot, surrounded by Lumiose Gang members.

We need Emma here with us, got it?!

The gang members seem to know Emma, but that doesn't stop them from picking a fight with you. Teach each member of the Lumiose Gang a lesson by beating them all in battle.

Vs. Lumiose Gang Member Sedna's Pokémon

Mandibuzz
♀ Lv. 58 Dark Flying
Weak to: Electric Ice Rock Fairy

Vs. Lumiose Gang Member Eris's Pokémon

Pangoro
♂ Lv. 56 [Fighting] [Dark]
Weak to: [x4] [Fairy] [Fighting] [Flying]

Bouffalant
♀ Lv. 56 [Normal]
Weak to: [Fighting]

Vs. Lumiose Gang Member Nix's Pokémon

Druddigon
♂ Lv. 56 [Dragon]
Weak to: [Ice] [Dragon] [Fairy]

Krookodile
♂ Lv. 56 [Ground] [Dark]
Weak to: [Water] [Grass] [Ice] [Fighting] [Bug] [Fairy]

Emma arrives after you defeat all three gang members, and you soon learn that not only was she involved with the Lumiose Gang, she was considered their leader! Emma insists that she never wanted to be part of the gang, but they declared her their leader after she took them down in a fight. She convinces the gang to return the Pokémon they stole from the tourist. Case closed!

We're all done wi' chorin' an' cheatin'. We're lookin' for honest work.

Back at the Looker Bureau, Emma receives a surprise visit from one of the Lumiose Gang members. The punk insists that his crew are going to stop stealing and start looking for honest work. And it seems that all this talk about work makes Emma begin to wonder if she should be contributing somehow as well.

Chapter 4: An Unforgivable Crime

Late last night, an intruder broke into the Lumiose Museum and damaged a painting.

This case appears while you're having a chat with Looker about Emma. You receive a Holo Caster news bulletin that reveals that a piece of art in the Lumiose Museum has been defaced. You'd better hurry over and find out what happened!

Turn left after leaving the Looker Bureau and sprint into North Boulevard. The Lumiose Museum is located along the street's north side. An Artist inside the museum tells you that a piece on the third floor was damaged.

But who could be responsible for this shocking work?

Head up to the third floor to find the museum director staring at a defaced mural in disbelief. The damage is quite extensive. The piece has been covered in graffiti! Who could have done such a thing?

Newscaster: We have another special bulletin. Poké Ball thefts are rampant in Lumiose City.

There's nothing more for you to accomplish at the museum, so head back outside. You'll soon receive another Holo Caster news bulletin: Poké Ball thefts are rampant in Lumiose City! It seems that the culprit strikes directly after Pokémon battles, when Trainers let their guard down. The crimes are most common in the city's back alleys, where there are few witnesses.

Looker's plan

I have devised an absolutely amazing plan that will bring an immediate solution.

After the news bulletin, Looker contacts you via the Holo Caster. Hurry back to the Looker Bureau to learn the details of Looker's latest plan: a sting! You'll play the role of the victim, luring the Poké Ball thief into a battle in a back alley. Looker will remain hidden until the moment is right to make the bust!

If you have a moment, how about a little battle with me?

Yes
No

The nearest alley isn't far. Turn left as you exit the Looker Bureau and run back up to North Boulevard. Turn left again and run a short distance to reach the alley across from the Galette Stand. Inside, you discover a Suspicious Woman who invites you to battle.

Vs. Suspicious Woman ???'s Pokémon

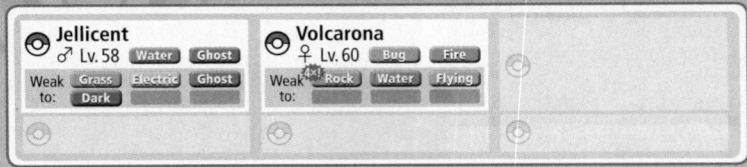

Jellicent
♂ Lv. 58 `Water` `Ghost`
Weak to: `Grass` `Electric` `Ghost` `Dark`

Volcarona
♀ Lv. 60 `Bug` `Fire`
Weak to: `Rock`(4x!) `Water` `Flying`

OBSTRUCTION DETECTED.
PROCESS JEOPARDIZED.

After the battle, the woman reveals her true form. She appears to be clad in some sort of robotic suit. Luckily, Looker springs his trap before your Pokémon can be stolen, and the mysterious thief flees. A master of deduction, Looker's keen insight helps him determine the alley to which the suspect has fled.

Pursuing the Poké Ball thief

Hiya! You're a Trainer, right?
How about a Pokémon battle?

Yes
No

Exit the alley, turn left, and race to the alley near Café Triste. Here, you'll discover a Suspicious Child who's eager to battle. Defeat the child, and it turns out to be the same culprit again! Looker springs his trap and prevents your Pokémon from being plundered, but the thief manages to escape again.

Vs. Suspicious Child ???'s Pokémon

Whimsicott
♀ Lv. 57 `Grass` `Fairy`
Weak to: `Poison`(4x!) `Fire` `Ice` `Flying` `Steel`

Mawile
♀ Lv. 57 `Steel` `Fairy`
Weak to: `Fire` `Ground`

Granbull
♂ Lv. 57 `Fairy`
Weak to: `Poison` `Steel`

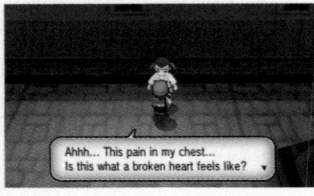

Ahhh... This pain in my chest...
Is this what a broken heart feels like?

This crook must be caught! Looker believes the suspect has fled to the alley across from Lumiose Station this time. Leave the current alley, turn right, and go all the way down North Boulevard to find the alley. Unfortunately, the suspect is not here—only her latest victim!

The victim is still reeling from the battle, but Looker manages to extract some information from him. The Poké Ball thief has probably fled to the lone alley on South Boulevard. Exit the current alley, turn right, and then run a short distance to reach South Boulevard.

The South Boulevard alley is right nearby, next to Restaurant Le Nah. Battle a Suspicious Lady here to expose the thief and spring Looker's trap as you've done before.

Vs. Suspicious Lady ???'s Pokémon

Persian
♀ Lv. 60 Normal
Weak to: Fighting

The plot thickens

Looker arrives right on cue, but this time, the suspect isn't so quick to flee. Before things can turn ugly, Mimi appears. The little Pokémon seems to know the suspect and begins jumping around for joy. It seems impossible, but Looker's keen sense of deduction tells him that the suspect can only be Emma!

The masked thief denies that she is Emma and instead insists that her name is Essentia. After a tussle with Looker, the enigmatic Essentia flees, and Looker asks for your help in returning to the Bureau. Case closed...or is it?

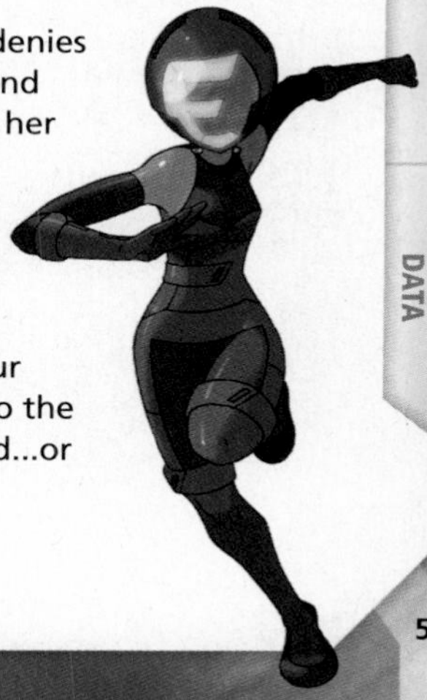

Chapter 5: A Fiery Woman and the Truth Revealed

Emma contacts you next via the Holo Caster. She's shocked to learn that Looker is recovering at the hospital, and she quickly leaves the Bureau to visit him.

Please allow me to begin the battle at once!

You receive a surprise visitor at the Bureau shortly after Emma leaves. Before introducing himself, the mysterious man asks if he may test your battle skill. Defeat the man in battle to prove your worthiness.

Vs. Butler Chalmers's Pokémon

Braviary
♂ Lv. 62 Normal Flying
Weak to: Electric Ice Rock

You must hurry to Hotel Richissime's Royal Suite at once!

Impressed with your skill, the man finally begins to talk. His name is Butler Chalmers, and he formerly served as an admin of Team Flare. Chalmers goes on to say that he's merely here to pass along a message from his mistress. He asks you to hurry to Hotel Richissime's Royal Suite at once to meet her.

A meeting with Malva

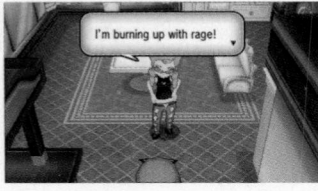

I'm burning up with rage!

Race to Hotel Richissime on North Boulevard. Once you arrive, take the elevator up to the fifth floor, where the royal suites are found. Sprint to the southwest suite to find none other than ex–Team Flare member Malva awaiting you!

If you want to help the girl, you need to put a stop to Xerosic.

Malva is steamed about having to wait for you. Douse the flames of her rage with a quick battle, and Malva will reveal all sorts of secrets. It seems that Emma is using a piece of technology called the Expansion Suit to become Essentia. This suit was created by the villainous Team Flare Scientist, Dr. Xerosic, whom Malva sees as the source of all the trouble.

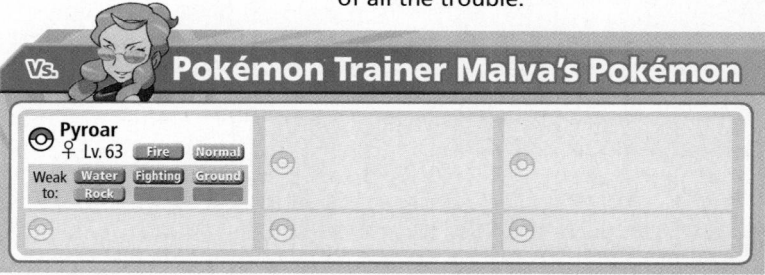

Pokémon Trainer Malva's Pokémon

Pyroar
♀ Lv. 63   Fire   Normal
Weak to: Water   Fighting   Ground
Rock

Race to the café

There's no time to lose! Malva has revealed that Dr. Xerosic can be found at Lysandre Café, so head there on the double. The café is located near the central Pokémon Center near Magenta Plaza. If you're having trouble finding it, just hop into a Lumi Cab.

 **TIP** *Rest your Pokémon in the nearby Pokémon Center before visiting the Lysandre Café. Challenging battles are in store!*

Now you have access to the secret floor of Lysandre Labs.

Malva waits for you inside the Lysandre Café. How'd she get here so fast? No matter—follow Malva into Lysandre Labs, where she enters a secret code at the elevator, enabling you to reach a hidden floor.

Back in the labs

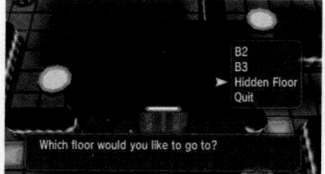

B2
B3
► Hidden Floor
Quit

Which floor would you like to go to?

Enter the elevator after Malva departs and select Hidden Floor as your destination. You'll be challenged to battle by a Scientist the moment you step off the elevator, so be prepared!

AFTER THE HALL OF FAME

CENTRAL KALOS

COASTAL KALOS

MOUNTAIN KALOS

ADVENTURE DATA

The Hidden Floor has the same layout as the Lysandre Labs' main floor, but there are no items to find and all of the side rooms are sealed. Navigate the various spin panels and warp panels to reach the floor's northeast corner. You'll battle a few Scientists and former Lumiose Gang members along the way.

Well, I got onto a part-time job as a security guard. See?

Use the northeast warp panel to zip over to the north warp panel. Nix, a former member of the Lumiose Gang, guards a side room here. Defeat Nix and he'll let you check out the room he's guarding.

Essential research

EXPANSION SUIT SPECS
1. Physical Enhancement

The small room that Nix was guarding is filled with books and stolen Poké Balls. You can't take the Poké Balls, so begin reading the many books on the shelves. Inspect every bookshelf and read every book, and then speak to Nix again.

After you've read every book in the room, a clock will sound, indicating that Nix's shift is over. After Nix leaves, none other than the ex–Team Flare scientist, Dr. Xerosic, barges into the room.

Rescuing Emma

Now, battle! Battle, my Essentia!

Lost in thought, Dr. Xerosic takes little notice of you at first. But it's not long before he summons Essentia to battle you. You must defeat Essentia three times, in three separate battles. Fortunately, you have the opportunity to save the game and use items to heal your Pokémon between each battle.

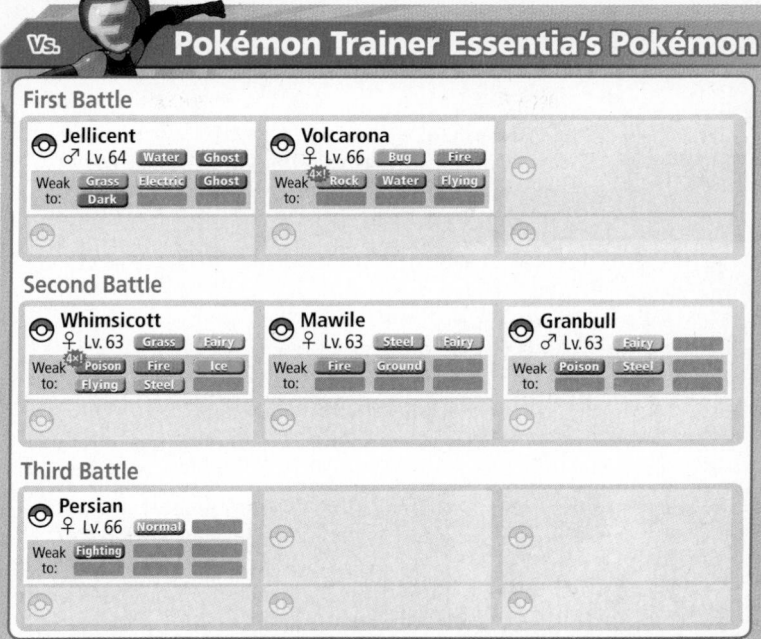

Vs. Pokémon Trainer Essentia's Pokémon

First Battle

Jellicent
♂ Lv. 64 — Water, Ghost
Weak to: Grass, Electric, Ghost, Dark

Volcarona
♀ Lv. 66 — Bug, Fire
Weak to: Rock (4x!), Water, Flying

Second Battle

Whimsicott
♀ Lv. 63 — Grass, Fairy
Weak to: Poison (4x!), Fire, Ice, Flying, Steel

Mawile
♀ Lv. 63 — Steel, Fairy
Weak to: Fire, Ground

Granbull
♂ Lv. 63 — Fairy
Weak to: Poison, Steel

Third Battle

Persian
♀ Lv. 66 — Normal
Weak to: Fighting

The one in control of Essentia is not Emma, but me!

Keep fighting and defeating Essentia, and Looker will eventually arrive on the scene. The hard-boiled detective tries his best to get through to Emma, but it's no use. As long as she wears the Expansion Suit, Dr. Xerosic is in complete control!

This is all I am able to do! Please aid me!.

To save Emma, you must defeat Essentia a fourth time. Speak to Looker before approaching Essentia, and he'll quickly restore your Pokémon's health. Approach Essentia afterward to begin the final battle.

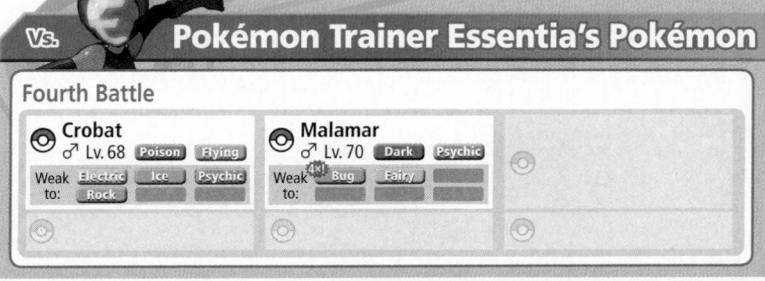

Vs. Pokémon Trainer Essentia's Pokémon

Fourth Battle

Crobat
♂ Lv. 68 — Poison, Flying
Weak to: Electric, Ice, Psychic, Rock

Malamar
♂ Lv. 70 — Dark, Psychic
Weak to: Bug (4x!), Fairy

Remote control...
Power down. Deactivate.

After you defeat Essentia for the final time, she begins to malfunction. There is no way to help her! As you witness the malfunction, Dr. Xerosic suddenly has a change of heart. The mad scientist decides to relinquish his control over Essentia, and Emma soon awakens from her deep sleep.

Dr. Xerosic was telling the truth. Emma was placed in a coma-like state while wearing the Expansion Suit, and she had no knowledge of her recent criminal acts. She merely answered Dr. Xerosic's ad and agreed to help him in his research, hoping to make a little money to help pay back Looker.

Once I have everything in order, I will ask you to accompany me to the station.

Emma is out of danger and the case is finally closed. Back at the Bureau, Looker accepts Dr. Xerosic's surprisingly heartfelt confession, which clears Emma of wrongdoing. Looker has a job to do, though, and will see that Dr. Xerosic pays for his crimes.

Final Chapter: Here's Lookin' at You, Kid

I think it's holding something...

Emma is safe and sound, and it's not long before she contacts you on the Holo Caster, asking you to meet her at the Bureau. She's planning on throwing a surprise party for Looker, who has been released from the hospital. Mimi shows up before Looker, however, and Emma notices that the little Pokémon is holding a letter.

I must say good-bye to this lovely region. And, more painfully, to you, my friends.

The letter is from Looker, and Emma reads it aloud. In his letter, Looker confesses that he's not merely a detective, but also an officer of the International Police! The good news is that Looker is perfectly healthy, while the bad news is that Looker has concluded his work in Kalos. With heartfelt thanks for all of your help, Looker bids you, Emma, and Mimi farewell.

Emma is shocked that Looker would just up and leave so quickly, and runs out of the office to track him down. Read Looker's notebook for a more personal good-bye message, then hurry after Emma.

Before you can leave the Bureau, former Lumiose Gang member Nix walks through the door. He was hoping to visit Emma, but she's already gone after Looker. As you try to leave again, Nix mentions that Looker was on his way to the Lumiose Museum. Maybe you can still catch him!

Looking for Looker

Leave the Looker Bureau, and turn left to reach North Boulevard. Enter the Lumiose Museum and zip up to the third floor. Speak to the museum director to find that the painting has been fully restored—and that Looker just left.

Drat, you're too late! Dash back downstairs and leave the museum. The Artist you met before recognizes you on your way out and confirms that Looker just left. Where could he have gone?

Fortunately, it doesn't take long before you have an answer. Emma calls you on the Holo Caster and says that Looker and Dr. Xerosic are at Lysandre Café. Hightail it over there—this could be your last chance to see them!

The big good-bye

Sure enough, you find Looker and Dr. Xerosic at Lysandre Café. Looker is leaning on Dr. Xerosic to ensure he hasn't kept any stolen Poké Balls, and he's surprised to see you, Emma, and Mimi.

The meeting is emotional, but everything turns out for the best. Looker places Emma in charge of the Looker Bureau, and Dr. Xerosic gives her the Expansion Suit and all of his Pokémon to help her keep Lumiose City free of crime.

Time is short, for Looker and Dr. Xerosic have a train to catch. With a final fond farewell, Detective/Officer Looker of the International Police takes his leave of Lumiose City. Well done!

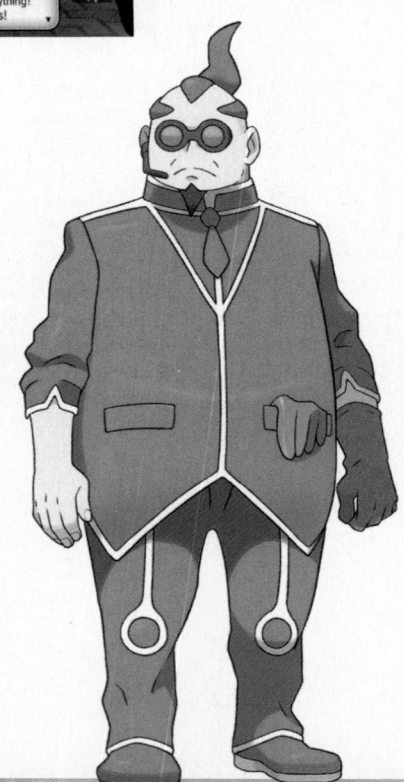

Completing Your Pokédex

After experiencing practically everything there is to see and do around the Kalos region, the time has now come to focus on completing your Pokédex! Catching every Pokémon around the Kalos region is far from easy, but the following sections will steer you in the right direction. You should also consult the Pokédex pages for specifics on how to obtain each individual Pokémon.

In the Field

Many Pokémon can be encountered simply by running around through the tall grass, flowers, swamps, deserts, and caves that fill the Kalos region. You will also obtain fishing rods during the game that will allow you to fish for certain Pokémon. For more on fishing, turn to page 82.

Horde Encounters

Some Pokémon, like Scraggy, Hoppip, Wingull, and others, are only available in Horde Encounters. Horde Encounters are a new type of battle introduced in *Pokémon X* and *Pokémon Y* where you take on five wild Pokémon at once. Using Honey in the field will make it more likely that you will experience a Horde Encounter.

Shaking Trash Cans

In the Lost Hotel and Pokémon Village, you will see the large green trash cans shake from time to time. Several Pokémon can only be found in these trash cans. These include Rotom, Trubbish, and even Banette—which can Mega Evolve into Mega Banette!

Pokémon Ambushes

Sometimes shadows may appear on the ground outside or in caves. These indicate that there is a Pokémon above, just waiting to swoop down upon you! These ambushes are the only way to encounter some Pokémon in the wild, such as Woobat, Ariados, Fearow, Skarmory, and Noibat. You may also find bushes shaking on the side of a route. Walk by and a wild Pokémon will leap out to ambush you! This is the only way to encounter Venipede and Audino in the wild.

AFTER THE HALL OF FAME

CENTRAL KALOS

COASTAL KALOS

MOUNTAIN KALOS

ADVENTURE DATA

AFTER THE
HALL OF FAME

CENTRAL
KALOS

COASTAL
KALOS

MOUNTAIN
KALOS

ADVENTURE
DATA

Smashing Rocks

Once you learn the Rock Smash move, you'll be able to smash cracked rocks that you find in the field. These may yield items, but at other times contain wild Pokémon. Some Pokémon, such as Dwebble, Slugma, Shuckle, and the newly-discovered Binacle, can only be found by smashing these rocks to smithereens.

Restoring Fossils

Numerous Pokémon can only be restored by collecting their Fossils and having them restored by the researchers at the Fossil Lab. For more information, turn to page 81 for a guide on Fossil hunting.

Pokémon Eggs

Many Pokémon can only be obtained by finding an Egg and catching it. This includes Pokémon like Pichu, Munchlax, and Makuhita, which will not appear in the wild in the Kalos region. If you want one for your Pokédex, turn to the section on Pokémon Eggs that begins on page 61.

Riding Pokémon

In certain areas in the Kalos region, you can ride on some Pokémon to get over the rough terrain and find other Pokémon. Riding atop Rhyhorn, for example, is the only way that you will encounter Helioptile, Sandile, and Hippopotas. You will also only encounter Snover, Delibird, and Sneasel from the back of Mamoswine.

Friend Safari

Along with getting Pokémon you won't get anywhere else, this feature will allow you to get many Pokémon with great stats. You can also catch Braixen, Frogadier, and Quilladin in Friend Safaris, allowing you to secure all three of the partner Pokémon which you were offered at the beginning of the game. Go to page 24 if you don't know how to use the Friend Safari.

Link Trades

Doing a Link Trade with other players is the only ways to evolve some Pokémon. It is also the only way to get Pokémon that are only available in *Pokémon X* or only in *Pokémon Y*. You can also collect special Pokémon, such as the many differently patterned Vivillon that players around the world will be able to offer up on the GTS or through Wonder Trade.

Legendary Pokémon

Xerneas and Yveltal are not the only Legendary Pokémon that you may come across in your adventures in Kalos. Be sure you also catch Articuno, Zapdos, or Moltres, and Mewtwo and Zygarde. Legendary Pokémon can only be encountered in special locations, and you will only be able to obtain them once in your game.

Eggs & Pokémon

I'm the Day-Care Lady.

Leave two Pokémon at the Pokémon Day Care on Route 7, and sometimes an Egg will be discovered. Many Pokémon species in the Kalos Pokédex can be obtained by hatching them from Eggs. Use these steps to discover Eggs and get the Pokémon you're after.

Steps Leading to Egg Discovery

1 Deposit Pokémon	2 Take the Egg	3 Hatch the Egg
Try leaving two Pokémon of opposite gender.	If the male and female Pokémon left at the Day Care get along well, an Egg will be discovered.	Put the Egg in your party and carry it around on your adventure. Eventually, a Pokémon will hatch from the Egg.

Clues concerning Egg discovery

The two don't really seem to like each other very much.

When you leave two Pokémon at the Pokémon Day Care, the man outside tells you how well they get along. His words also reveal how likely it is that an Egg will be discovered. The Egg that is found will be of the same species as the female Pokémon, or an earlier species in its evolutionary line (unless you use a Ditto).

The Day-Care Man's messages

The two seem to get along very well!	Eggs are likely to be found.
The two seem to get along.	Eggs may be found.
The two don't really seem to like each other very much.	Eggs are unlikely to be found.
The two prefer to play with other Pokémon more than with each other.	Eggs will not be found.

Egg Groups

To find Eggs, the simplest method is to leave two Pokémon of the same species but opposite genders at the Pokémon Day Care. Another method is to pair Pokémon by Egg Group. If you leave two different species of Pokémon of opposite gender but the same Egg Group, you may find an Egg. In this case, the Egg found will hatch a Pokémon of the same species as the female Pokémon. Use the following charts to help you match Pokémon by Egg Group.

 TIPS

With a Ditto, you can find almost any kind of Egg! Ditto are commonly found in the Pokémon Village, so be sure to catch one. It will allow you to find Eggs even for Pokémon of unknown gender, where normally no Eggs can be found.

Eggs don't just inherit their species from the Pokémon that are left at the Pokémon Day Care. A Pokémon that hatches from an Egg can also inherit moves that it would normally only learn at a higher level, if both of the Pokémon left at the Day Care know it. It can also inherit moves that would normally be impossible to learn, or only available from a TM, from the male Pokémon left at the Pokémon Day Care. Even Abilities and Hidden Abilities are inheritable from the female Pokémon left at the Pokémon Day Care.

Key to the Tables

- Pokémon listed as ♂ are only male, while those listed as ♀ are only female
- Pokémon listed as ♂/♀ have both male and female
- Pokémon listed as "Unknown" do not have a known gender

Grass Group

● Grass Egg Group only

	Amoonguss	♂/♀
	Bellossom	♂/♀
	Bellsprout	♂/♀
	Carnivine	♂/♀
	Exeggcute	♂/♀
	Exeggutor	♂/♀
	Foongus	♂/♀
	Gloom	♂/♀
	Lilligant	♀
	Maractus	♂/♀
	Oddish	♂/♀
	Petilil	♀
	Sunflora	♂/♀
	Sunkern	♂/♀
	Tangela	♂/♀
	Tangrowth	♂/♀
	Victreebel	♂/♀
	Vileplume	♂/♀
	Weepinbell	♂/♀

● Grass and Bug Egg Groups

	Paras	♂/♀
	Parasect	♂/♀

● Grass and Human-Like Egg Groups

	Cacnea	♂/♀
	Cacturne	♂/♀

● Grass and Monster Egg Groups

	Abomasnow	♂/♀
	Bayleef	♂/♀
	Bulbasaur	♂/♀
	Chikorita	♂/♀
	Grotle	♂/♀
	Ivysaur	♂/♀
	Meganium	♂/♀
	Snover	♂/♀
	Torterra	♂/♀
	Tropius	♂/♀
	Turtwig	♂/♀
	Venusaur	♂/♀

● Grass and Fairy Egg Groups

	Breloom	♂/♀
	Cherrim	♂/♀
	Cherubi	♂/♀
	Cottonee	♂/♀
	Hoppip	♂/♀
	Jumpluff	♂/♀
	Roselia	♂/♀
	Roserade	♂/♀
	Shroomish	♂/♀
	Skiploom	♂/♀
	Whimsicott	♂/♀

● Grass and Mineral Egg Groups

	Ferroseed	♂/♀
	Ferrothorn	♂/♀

● Grass and Field Egg Groups

	Nuzleaf	♂/♀
	Seedot	♂/♀
	Serperior	♂/♀
	Servine	♂/♀
	Shiftry	♂/♀
	Snivy	♂/♀

● Grass and Water 1 Egg Groups

	Lombre	♂/♀
	Lotad	♂/♀
	Ludicolo	♂/♀

● Grass and Amorphous Egg Groups

	Phantump	♂/♀
	Trevenant	♂/♀

There is no crossover between the Grass Egg Group and the following Egg Groups:

- Flying
- Dragon
- Water 2
- Water 3
- Ditto
- No Eggs Discovered

AFTER THE HALL OF FAME

CENTRAL KALOS

COASTAL KALOS

MOUNTAIN KALOS

ADVENTURE DATA

Bug Group

● Bug Egg Group only

Accelgor	♂/♀	Nincada	♂/♀
Ariados	♂/♀	Ninjask	♂/♀
Beautifly	♂/♀	Pineco	♂/♀
Beedrill	♂/♀	Pinsir	♂/♀
Burmy	♂/♀	Scatterbug	♂/♀
Butterfree	♂/♀	Scizor	♂/♀
Cascoon	♂/♀	Scolipede	♂/♀
Caterpie	♂/♀	Scyther	♂/♀
Combee	♂/♀	Sewaddle	♂/♀
Durant	♂/♀	Shelmet	♂/♀
Dustox	♂/♀	Shuckle	♂/♀
Escavalier	♂/♀	Silcoon	♂/♀
Flygon	♂/♀	Spewpa	♂/♀
Forretress	♂/♀	Spinarak	♂/♀
Galvantula	♂/♀	Swadloon	♂/♀
Gligar	♂/♀	Trapinch	♂/♀
Gliscor	♂/♀	Venipede	♂/♀
Heracross	♂/♀	Venomoth	♂/♀
Joltik	♂/♀	Venonat	♂/♀
Kakuna	♂/♀	Vespiquen	♀
Karrablast	♂/♀	Vibrava	♂/♀
Kricketot	♂/♀	Vivillon	♂/♀
Kricketune	♂/♀	Volcarona	♂/♀
Larvesta	♂/♀	Weedle	♂/♀
Leavanny	♂/♀	Whirlipede	♂/♀
Ledian	♂/♀	Wormadam	♀
Ledyba	♂/♀	Wurmple	♂/♀
Metapod	♂/♀	Yanma	♂/♀
Mothim	♂	Yanmega	♂/♀

● Bug and Grass Egg Groups

Paras	♂/♀
Parasect	♂/♀

● Bug and Human-Like Egg Groups

Illumise	♀
Volbeat	♂

● Bug and Mineral Egg Groups

Crustle	♂/♀
Dwebble	♂/♀

● Bug and Water 1 Egg Groups

Masquerain	♂/♀
Surskit	♂/♀

● Bug and Water 3 Egg Groups

Drapion	♂/♀
Skorupi	♂/♀

There is no crossover between the Bug Egg Group and the following Egg Groups:

● Flying
● Fairy
● Dragon
● Amorphous
● Water 2
● Ditto
● Monster
● No Eggs Discovered

Have Pokémon inherit level-up moves

The two Pokémon you leave at the Pokémon Day Care can pass on a move they have learned to a Pokémon hatched from an Egg. Usually, newly hatched Pokémon only know the moves that the Pokémon would know at Lv. 1. However, if both of the two Pokémon you left at the Pokémon Day Care have learned a move that the hatched Pokémon can learn by leveling up, the hatched Pokémon will know that move. This is a great way to give Pokémon powerful moves from the start.

Remember: If both Pokémon at the Day Care know the same level-up move, the hatched Pokémon may know that level-up move.

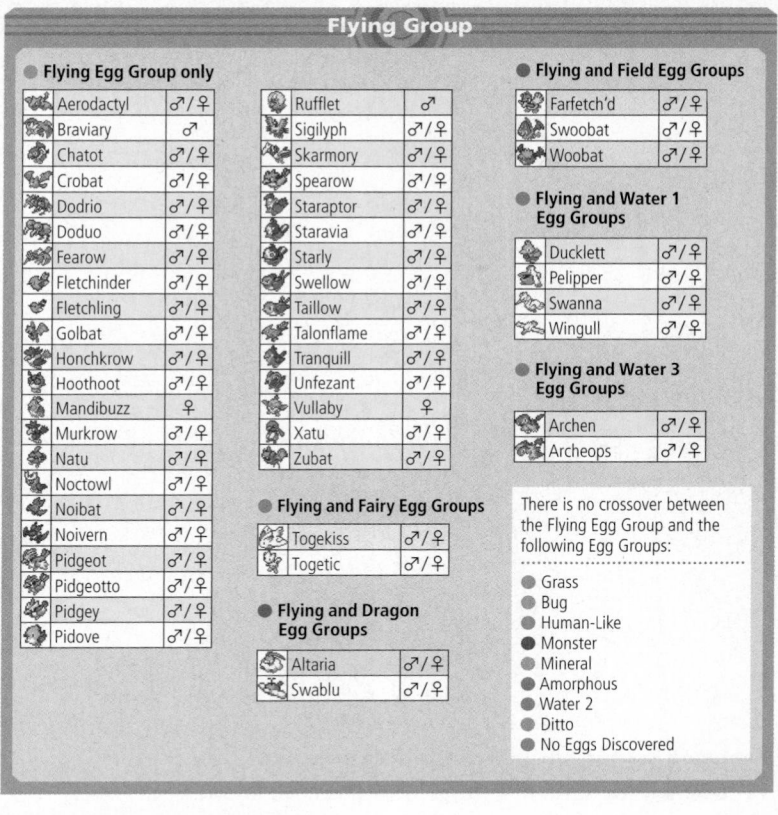

Flying Group

● Flying Egg Group only

Aerodactyl	♂/♀
Braviary	♂
Chatot	♂/♀
Crobat	♂/♀
Dodrio	♂/♀
Doduo	♂/♀
Fearow	♂/♀
Fletchinder	♂/♀
Fletchling	♂/♀
Golbat	♂/♀
Honchkrow	♂/♀
Hoothoot	♂/♀
Mandibuzz	♀
Murkrow	♂/♀
Natu	♂/♀
Noctowl	♂/♀
Noibat	♂/♀
Noivern	♂/♀
Pidgeot	♂/♀
Pidgeotto	♂/♀
Pidgey	♂/♀
Pidove	♂/♀

Rufflet	♂
Sigilyph	♂/♀
Skarmory	♂/♀
Spearow	♂/♀
Staraptor	♂/♀
Staravia	♂/♀
Starly	♂/♀
Swellow	♂/♀
Taillow	♂/♀
Talonflame	♂/♀
Tranquill	♂/♀
Unfezant	♂/♀
Vullaby	♀
Xatu	♂/♀
Zubat	♂/♀

● Flying and Fairy Egg Groups

Togekiss	♂/♀
Togetic	♂/♀

● Flying and Dragon Egg Groups

Altaria	♂/♀
Swablu	♂/♀

● Flying and Field Egg Groups

Farfetch'd	♂/♀
Swoobat	♂/♀
Woobat	♂/♀

● Flying and Water 1 Egg Groups

Ducklett	♂/♀
Pelipper	♂/♀
Swanna	♂/♀
Wingull	♂/♀

● Flying and Water 3 Egg Groups

Archen	♂/♀
Archeops	♂/♀

There is no crossover between the Flying Egg Group and the following Egg Groups:
....
- ● Grass
- ● Bug
- ● Human-Like
- ● Monster
- ● Mineral
- ● Amorphous
- ● Water 2
- ● Ditto
- ● No Eggs Discovered

Have Pokémon inherit TM moves

The male Pokémon you leave at the Pokémon Day Care can pass on a move that it has learned to the Pokémon that hatches from a found Egg if the hatched Pokémon is able to learn that move regularly from a TM.

Remember: A move that the male Pokémon knows and that the hatched Pokémon could learn from a TM can be passed on.

Teach your Pokémon Egg Moves

Pokémon from Eggs may hatch already knowing moves that they usually can't learn, called Egg Moves. For example, Riolu can't learn the move Bullet Punch by leveling up. But if a male Pokémon left at the Pokémon Day Care knows Bullet Punch, the Riolu that hatches from the Egg found there might know the move Bullet Punch. Many Egg Moves are unexpected, letting you take opponents by surprise.

Remember: A move that the male Pokémon knows and that the hatched Pokémon can learn as an Egg Move can be passed on.

Eggs & Pokémon

AFTER THE HALL OF FAME

CENTRAL KALOS

COASTAL KALOS

MOUNTAIN KALOS

ADVENTURE DATA

Human-Like Group

Human-Like Egg Group only

Abra	♂/♀
Alakazam	♂/♀
Beheeyem	♂/♀
Bisharp	♂/♀
Conkeldurr	♂/♀
Croagunk	♂/♀
Drowzee	♂/♀
Electabuzz	♂/♀
Electivire	♂/♀
Elgyem	♂/♀
Gothita	♂/♀
Gothitelle	♂/♀
Gothorita	♂/♀
Gurdurr	♂/♀
Hariyama	♂/♀
Hawlucha	♂/♀
Hitmonchan	♂
Hitmonlee	♂
Hitmontop	♂
Hypno	♂/♀
Jynx	♀
Kadabra	♂/♀
Machamp	♂/♀
Machoke	♂/♀

Machop	♂/♀
Magmar	♂/♀
Magmortar	♂/♀
Makuhita	♂/♀
Medicham	♂/♀
Meditite	♂/♀
Mr. Mime	♂/♀
Pawniard	♂/♀
Sableye	♂/♀
Sawk	♂
Throh	♂
Timburr	♂/♀
Toxicroak	♂/♀

Human-Like and Grass Egg Groups

Cacnea	♂/♀
Cacturne	♂/♀

Human-Like and Bug Egg Groups

Illumise	♀
Volbeat	♂

Human-Like and Field Egg Groups

Buneary	♂/♀
Chimchar	♂/♀
Infernape	♂/♀
Lopunny	♂/♀
Lucario	♂/♀
Mienfoo	♂/♀
Mienshao	♂/♀
Monferno	♂/♀
Pancham	♂/♀
Pangoro	♂/♀
Spinda	♂/♀

There is no crossover between the Human-Like Egg Group and the following Egg Groups:

- Flying
- Monster
- Fairy
- Dragon
- Mineral
- Amorphous
- Water 1
- Water 2
- Water 3
- Ditto
- No Eggs Discovered

Pokémon Eggs found with the help of incense

In general, the Pokémon hatched from Eggs you find at a Pokémon Day Care will be the first in their Evolutionary line. However, there are exceptions. For example, dropping off a female Wobbuffet and a male Pokémon from the Amorphous Group will not result in finding a Wynaut Egg, although Wynaut is the pre-Evolution of Wobbuffet. It will be a Wobbuffet Egg. To get a Wynaut Egg, you'll need to give one of the Pokémon a Lax Incense before you drop it off, which you can get at the stand in Coumarine City.

Eggs that require incense

Egg Discovered	Female Pokémon	Male Pokémon Egg Group	Necessary Item
Azurill	Marill or Azumarill	Fairy Group or Water Group 1	Sea Incense
Wynaut	Wobbuffet	Amorphous Group	Lax Incense
Budew	Roselia or Roserade	Fairy Group or Grass Group	Rose Incense
Chingling	Chimecho	Amorphous Group	Pure Incense
Bonsly	Sudowoodo	Mineral Group	Rock Incense
Mime Jr.	Mr. Mime	Human-Like Group	Odd Incense
Happiny	Chansey or Blissey	Fairy Group	Luck Incense
Munchlax	Snorlax	Monster Group	Full Incense
Mantyke	Mantine	Water Group 1	Wave Incense

Monster Group

Monster Egg Group only

Aggron	♂ / ♀
Amaura	♂ / ♀
Aron	♂ / ♀
Aurorus	♂ / ♀
Avalugg	♂ / ♀
Bastiodon	♂ / ♀
Bergmite	♂ / ♀
Cranidos	♂ / ♀
Cubone	♂ / ♀
Kangaskhan	♀
Lairon	♂ / ♀
Larvitar	♂ / ♀
Lickilicky	♂ / ♀
Lickitung	♂ / ♀
Marowak	♂ / ♀
Pupitar	♂ / ♀
Rampardos	♂ / ♀
Shieldon	♂ / ♀
Snorlax	♂ / ♀
Tyranitar	♂ / ♀

Monster and Grass Egg Groups

Abomasnow	♂ / ♀
Bayleef	♂ / ♀
Bulbasaur	♂ / ♀
Chikorita	♂ / ♀
Grotle	♂ / ♀
Ivysaur	♂ / ♀
Meganium	♂ / ♀
Snover	♂ / ♀
Torterra	♂ / ♀
Tropius	♂ / ♀
Turtwig	♂ / ♀
Venusaur	♂ / ♀

Monster and Dragon Egg Groups

Axew	♂ / ♀
Charizard	♂ / ♀
Charmander	♂ / ♀
Charmeleon	♂ / ♀
Druddigon	♂ / ♀
Fraxure	♂ / ♀
Gabite	♂ / ♀
Garchomp	♂ / ♀
Gible	♂ / ♀
Grovyle	♂ / ♀
Haxorus	♂ / ♀
Heliolisk	♂ / ♀
Helioptile	♂ / ♀
Sceptile	♂ / ♀
Treecko	♂ / ♀
Tyrantrum	♂ / ♀
Tyrunt	♂ / ♀

Monster and Field Egg Groups

Ampharos	♂ / ♀
Exploud	♂ / ♀
Flaaffy	♂ / ♀
Loudred	♂ / ♀
Mareep	♂ / ♀
Nidoking	♂
Nidoran ♀	♀
Nidoran ♂	♂
Nidorino	♂
Rhydon	♂ / ♀
Rhyhorn	♂ / ♀
Rhyperior	♂ / ♀
Whismur	♂ / ♀

Monster and Water 1 Egg Groups

Blastoise	♂ / ♀
Croconaw	♂ / ♀
Feraligatr	♂ / ♀
Lapras	♂ / ♀
Marshtomp	♂ / ♀
Mudkip	♂ / ♀
Slowbro	♂ / ♀
Slowking	♂ / ♀
Slowpoke	♂ / ♀
Squirtle	♂ / ♀
Swampert	♂ / ♀
Totodile	♂ / ♀
Wartortle	♂ / ♀

There is no crossover between the Monster Egg Group and the following Egg Groups:

- Bug
- Flying
- Human-Like
- Fairy
- Mineral
- Amorphous
- Water 2
- Water 3
- Ditto
- No Eggs Discovered

Either one of the two Abilities can be inherited

You don't know which Ability a Pokémon hatched from an Egg will have until it hatches. For example, Axew can have either the Rivalry or Mold Breaker Ability. Sometimes when you leave a female Haxorus with the Mold Breaker Ability at the Pokémon Day Care, the Egg that hatches will be an Axew with the Rivalry Ability. This is the basic rule about the Abilities of Pokémon hatched from Eggs.

Remember: The Ability of a Pokémon hatched from an Egg is more likely to be the Ability of the female Pokémon left at the Pokémon Day Care.

Eggs & Pokémon

AFTER THE HALL OF FAME

CENTRAL KALOS

COASTAL KALOS

MOUNTAIN KALOS

ADVENTURE DATA

Fairy Group

● Fairy Egg Group only

	Aromatisse	♂/♀
	Audino	♂/♀
	Blissey	♀
	Chansey	♀
	Clefable	♂/♀
	Clefairy	♂/♀
	Flabébé	♀
	Floette	♀
	Florges	♀
	Jigglypuff	♂/♀
	Minun	♂/♀
	Plusle	♂/♀
	Slurpuff	♂/♀
	Spritzee	♂/♀
	Swirlix	♂/♀
	Wigglytuff	♂/♀

● Fairy and Grass Egg Groups

	Breloom	♂/♀
	Cherrim	♂/♀
	Cherubi	♂/♀
	Cottonee	♂/♀
	Hoppip	♂/♀
	Jumpluff	♂/♀
	Roselia	♂/♀
	Roserade	♂/♀
	Shroomish	♂/♀
	Skiploom	♂/♀
	Whimsicott	♂/♀

● Fairy and Flying Egg Groups

	Togekiss	♂/♀
	Togetic	♂/♀

● Fairy and Mineral Egg Groups

	Carbink	Unknown
	Froslass	♀
	Glalie	♂/♀
	Snorunt	♂/♀

● Fairy and Field Egg Groups

	Dedenne	♂/♀
	Delcatty	♂/♀
	Granbull	♂/♀
	Mawile	♂/♀
	Pachirisu	♂/♀
	Pikachu	♂/♀
	Raichu	♂/♀
	Skitty	♂/♀
	Snubbull	♂/♀

● Fairy and Amorphous Egg Groups

	Castform	♂/♀

● Fairy and Water 1 Egg Groups

	Azumarill	♂/♀
	Manaphy	Unknown
	Marill	♂/♀
	Phione	Unknown

There is no crossover between the Fairy Egg Group and the following Egg Groups:

● Bug
● Human-Like
● Monster
● Dragon
● Water 2
● Water 3
● Ditto
● No Eggs Discovered

Hidden Abilities can be inherited

Certain Pokémon have rare Abilities called "Hidden Abilities." If you are lucky enough to get one, you can pass on these Hidden Abilities. If you leave a female Pokémon with a Hidden Ability at the Pokémon Day Care, you may find an Egg that hatches into a Pokémon with the same Ability. For example, Watchog can have the Hidden Ability Analytic. If you discover an Egg when you leave a female Watchog with the Analytic Ability at the Pokémon Day Care, you may find an Egg of a Patrat with Run Away, Keen Eye, or the same Hidden Ability, Analytic.

Remember: You can sometimes hatch a Pokémon with a Hidden Ability if and only if the female Pokémon left at the Pokémon Day Care had that Hidden Ability.

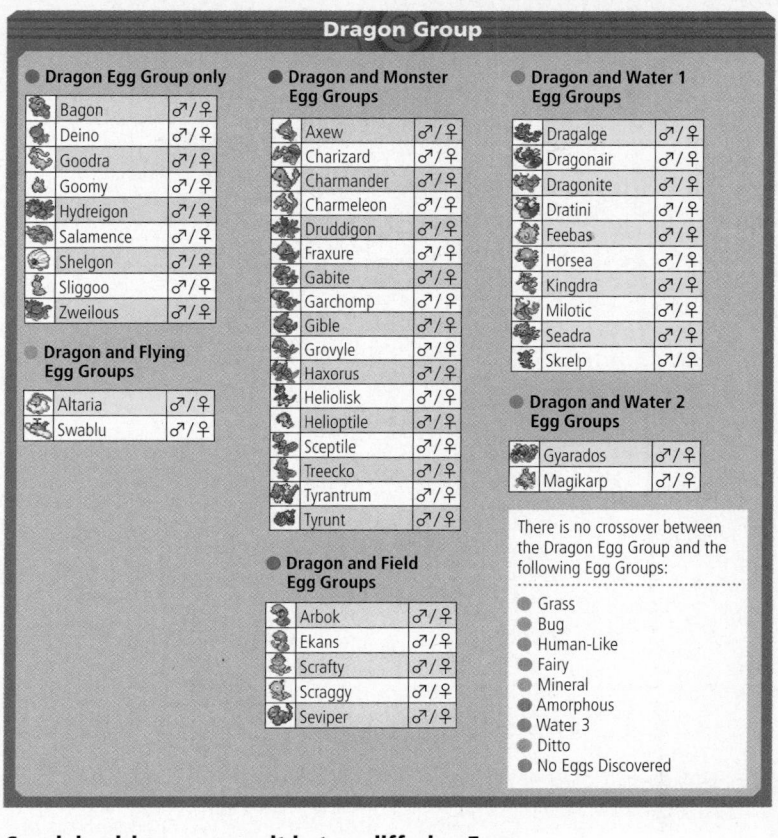

Dragon Group

Dragon Egg Group only

	Bagon	♂/♀
	Deino	♂/♀
	Goodra	♂/♀
	Goomy	♂/♀
	Hydreigon	♂/♀
	Salamence	♂/♀
	Shelgon	♂/♀
	Sliggoo	♂/♀
	Zweilous	♂/♀

Dragon and Flying Egg Groups

	Altaria	♂/♀
	Swablu	♂/♀

Dragon and Monster Egg Groups

	Axew	♂/♀
	Charizard	♂/♀
	Charmander	♂/♀
	Charmeleon	♂/♀
	Druddigon	♂/♀
	Fraxure	♂/♀
	Gabite	♂/♀
	Garchomp	♂/♀
	Gible	♂/♀
	Grovyle	♂/♀
	Haxorus	♂/♀
	Heliolisk	♂/♀
	Helioptile	♂/♀
	Sceptile	♂/♀
	Treecko	♂/♀
	Tyrantrum	♂/♀
	Tyrunt	♂/♀

Dragon and Field Egg Groups

	Arbok	♂/♀
	Ekans	♂/♀
	Scrafty	♂/♀
	Scraggy	♂/♀
	Seviper	♂/♀

Dragon and Water 1 Egg Groups

	Dragalge	♂/♀
	Dragonair	♂/♀
	Dragonite	♂/♀
	Dratini	♂/♀
	Feebas	♂/♀
	Horsea	♂/♀
	Kingdra	♂/♀
	Milotic	♂/♀
	Seadra	♂/♀
	Skrelp	♂/♀

Dragon and Water 2 Egg Groups

	Gyarados	♂/♀
	Magikarp	♂/♀

There is no crossover between the Dragon Egg Group and the following Egg Groups:

- Grass
- Bug
- Human-Like
- Fairy
- Mineral
- Amorphous
- Water 3
- Ditto
- No Eggs Discovered

AFTER THE HALL OF FAME

CENTRAL KALOS

COASTAL KALOS

MOUNTAIN KALOS

ADVENTURE DATA

Special pairings can result in two differing Eggs

It is usually a given that only one kind of Pokémon can be hatched from a particular Pokémon pairing, but that doesn't mean that there aren't certain special conditions which defy this common sense. If you drop off a Nidoran ♀ with a male Pokémon from either the Monster Group or the Field Group, the Egg that you find could be either a Nidoran ♀ or a Nidoran ♂. This also works if you leave the male Pokémon at the Day Care with a Ditto.

Remember: Certain Pokémon have the chance of hatching different Pokémon from the Eggs that you find.

AFTER THE HALL OF FAME

CENTRAL KALOS

COASTAL KALOS

MOUNTAIN KALOS

ADVENTURE DATA

Mineral Group

Mineral Egg Group only

Aegislash	♂ / ♀
Baltoy	Unknown
Beldum	Unknown
Boldore	♂ / ♀
Bronzong	Unknown
Bronzor	Unknown
Claydol	Unknown
Cryogonal	Unknown
Doublade	♂ / ♀
Electrode	Unknown
Garbodor	♂ / ♀
Geodude	♂ / ♀
Gigalith	♂ / ♀
Golem	♂ / ♀
Golett	Unknown
Golurk	Unknown
Graveler	♂ / ♀
Honedge	♂ / ♀
Klang	Unknown
Klefki	♂ / ♀
Klink	Unknown
Klinklang	Unknown

Lunatone	Unknown
Magnemite	Unknown
Magneton	Unknown
Magnezone	Unknown
Metagross	Unknown
Metang	Unknown
Nosepass	♂ / ♀
Onix	♂ / ♀
Porygon	Unknown
Porygon2	Unknown
Porygon-Z	Unknown
Probopass	♂ / ♀
Roggenrola	♂ / ♀
Shedinja	Unknown
Solrock	Unknown
Steelix	♂ / ♀
Sudowoodo	♂ / ♀
Trubbish	♂ / ♀
Vanillish	♂ / ♀
Vanillite	♂ / ♀
Vanilluxe	♂ / ♀
Voltorb	Unknown

Mineral and Grass Egg Groups

Ferroseed	♂ / ♀
Ferrothorn	♂ / ♀

Mineral and Bug Egg Groups

Crustle	♂ / ♀
Dwebble	♂ / ♀

Mineral and Fairy Egg Groups

Carbink	Unknown
Froslass	♀
Glalie	♂ / ♀
Snorunt	♂ / ♀

Mineral and Amorphous Egg Groups

Cofagrigus	♂ / ♀
Yamask	♂ / ♀

There is no crossover between the Mineral Egg Group and the following Egg Groups:

- Flying
- Human-Like
- Monster
- Dragon
- Field
- Water 1
- Water 2
- Water 3
- Ditto
- No Eggs Discovered

Field Group

● **Field Egg Group only**

Absol	♂/♀		Hippopotas	♂/♀		Samurott	♂/♀
Aipom	♂/♀		Hippowdon	♂/♀		Sandile	♂/♀
Ambipom	♂/♀		Houndoom	♂/♀		Sandshrew	♂/♀
Arcanine	♂/♀		Houndour	♂/♀		Sandslash	♂/♀
Beartic	♂/♀		Jolteon	♂/♀		Sawsbuck	♂/♀
Blaziken	♂/♀		Kecleon	♂/♀		Sentret	♂/♀
Blitzle	♂/♀		Krokorok	♂/♀		Shinx	♂/♀
Bouffalant	♂/♀		Krookodile	♂/♀		Simipour	♂/♀
Braixen	♂/♀		Leafeon	♂/♀		Simisage	♂/♀
Bunnelby	♂/♀		Liepard	♂/♀		Simisear	♂/♀
Camerupt	♂/♀		Lillipup	♂/♀		Skiddo	♂/♀
Chesnaught	♂/♀		Linoone	♂/♀		Skuntank	♂/♀
Chespin	♂/♀		Litleo	♂/♀		Slaking	♂/♀
Cinccino	♂/♀		Luxio	♂/♀		Slakoth	♂/♀
Combusken	♂/♀		Luxray	♂/♀		Smeargle	♂/♀
Cubchoo	♂/♀		Mamoswine	♂/♀		Sneasel	♂/♀
Cyndaquil	♂/♀		Manectric	♂/♀		Spoink	♂/♀
Darmanitan	♂/♀		Mankey	♂/♀		Stantler	♂/♀
Darumaka	♂/♀		Meowstic	♂/♀		Stoutland	♂/♀
Deerling	♂/♀		Meowth	♂/♀		Stunky	♂/♀
Delphox	♂/♀		Mightyena	♂/♀		Swinub	♂/♀
Dewott	♂/♀		Miltank	♀		Sylveon	♂/♀
Diggersby	♂/♀		Minccino	♂/♀		Tauros	♂
Diglett	♂/♀		Munna	♂/♀		Teddiursa	♂/♀
Donphan	♂/♀		Musharna	♂/♀		Tepig	♂/♀
Drilbur	♂/♀		Ninetales	♂/♀		Torchic	♂/♀
Dugtrio	♂/♀		Numel	♂/♀		Torkoal	♂/♀
Dunsparce	♂/♀		Oshawott	♂/♀		Typhlosion	♂/♀
Eevee	♂/♀		Panpour	♂/♀		Umbreon	♂/♀
Electrike	♂/♀		Pansage	♂/♀		Ursaring	♂/♀
Emboar	♂/♀		Pansear	♂/♀		Vaporeon	♂/♀
Emolga	♂/♀		Patrat	♂/♀		Vigoroth	♂/♀
Espeon	♂/♀		Persian	♂/♀		Vulpix	♂/♀
Espurr	♂/♀		Phanpy	♂/♀		Watchog	♂/♀
Excadrill	♂/♀		Pignite	♂/♀		Weavile	♂/♀
Fennekin	♂/♀		Piloswine	♂/♀		Zangoose	♂/♀
Flareon	♂/♀		Ponyta	♂/♀		Zebstrika	♂/♀
Furfrou	♂/♀		Poochyena	♂/♀		Zigzagoon	♂/♀
Furret	♂/♀		Primeape	♂/♀		Zoroark	♂/♀
Girafarig	♂/♀		Purrloin	♂/♀		Zorua	♂/♀
Glaceon	♂/♀		Purugly	♂/♀			
Glameow	♂/♀		Pyroar	♂/♀			
Gogoat	♂/♀		Quilava	♂/♀			
Growlithe	♂/♀		Quilladin	♂/♀			
Grumpig	♂/♀		Rapidash	♂/♀			
Heatmor	♂/♀		Raticate	♂/♀			
Herdier	♂/♀		Rattata	♂/♀			

AFTER THE HALL OF FAME

CENTRAL KALOS

COASTAL KALOS

MOUNTAIN KALOS

ADVENTURE DATA

Field Group (continued)

● Field and Grass Egg Groups

Nuzleaf	♂/♀
Seedot	♂/♀
Serperior	♂/♀
Servine	♂/♀
Shiftry	♂/♀
Snivy	♂/♀

● Field and Flying Egg Groups

Farfetch'd	♂/♀
Swoobat	♂/♀
Woobat	♂/♀

● Field and Human-Like Egg Groups

Buneary	♂/♀
Chimchar	♂/♀
Infernape	♂/♀
Lopunny	♂/♀
Lucario	♂/♀
Mienfoo	♂/♀
Mienshao	♂/♀
Monferno	♂/♀
Pancham	♂/♀
Pangoro	♂/♀
Spinda	♂/♀

● Field and Monster Egg Groups

Ampharos	♂/♀
Exploud	♂/♀
Flaaffy	♂/♀
Loudred	♂/♀
Mareep	♂/♀
Nidoking	♂
Nidoran ♀	♀
Nidoran ♂	♂
Nidorino	♂
Rhydon	♂/♀
Rhyhorn	♂/♀
Rhyperior	♂/♀
Whismur	♂/♀

● Field and Fairy Egg Groups

Dedenne	♂/♀
Delcatty	♂/♀
Granbull	♂/♀
Mawile	♂/♀
Pachirisu	♂/♀
Pikachu	♂/♀
Raichu	♂/♀
Skitty	♂/♀
Snubbull	♂/♀

● Field and Dragon Egg Groups

Arbok	♂/♀
Ekans	♂/♀
Scrafty	♂/♀
Scraggy	♂/♀
Seviper	♂/♀

● Field and Water 1 Egg Groups

Bibarel	♂/♀
Bidoof	♂/♀
Buizel	♂/♀
Delibird	♂/♀
Dewgong	♂/♀
Empoleon	♂/♀
Floatzel	♂/♀
Golduck	♂/♀
Piplup	♂/♀
Prinplup	♂/♀
Psyduck	♂/♀
Quagsire	♂/♀
Sealeo	♂/♀
Seel	♂/♀
Spheal	♂/♀
Walrein	♂/♀
Wooper	♂/♀

● Field and Water 2 Egg Groups

Wailmer	♂/♀
Wailord	♂/♀

There is no crossover between the Field Egg Group and the following Egg Groups:

- ● Bug
- ● Mineral
- ● Amorphous
- ● Water 3
- ● Ditto
- ● No Eggs Discovered

Pokémon may inherit Natures

The Pokémon hatched from an Egg may inherit the Nature of the female Pokémon that was left at the Pokémon Day Care. You will be able to pass along a Pokémon's Nature with certainty if it is holding an item called an Everstone. Natures affect how a Pokémon's stats grow upon leveling up.

Remember: Pokémon hatched from Eggs can inherit Natures from the Pokémon left at the Pokémon Day Care.

Amorphous Group

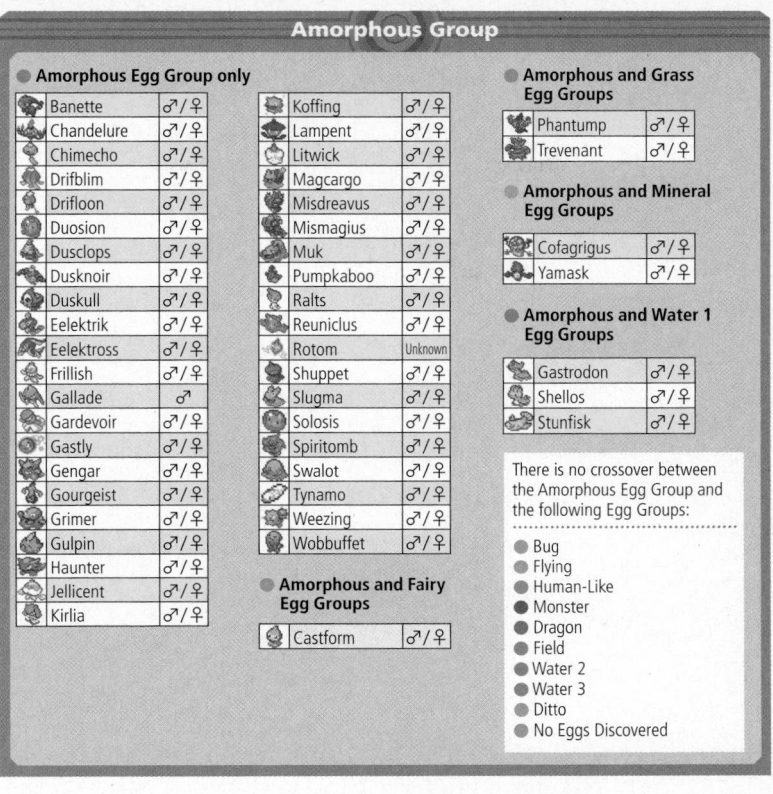

Amorphous Egg Group only

Banette	♂/♀		Koffing	♂/♀
Chandelure	♂/♀		Lampent	♂/♀
Chimecho	♂/♀		Litwick	♂/♀
Drifblim	♂/♀		Magcargo	♂/♀
Drifloon	♂/♀		Misdreavus	♂/♀
Duosion	♂/♀		Mismagius	♂/♀
Dusclops	♂/♀		Muk	♂/♀
Dusknoir	♂/♀		Pumpkaboo	♂/♀
Duskull	♂/♀		Ralts	♂/♀
Eelektrik	♂/♀		Reuniclus	♂/♀
Eelektross	♂/♀		Rotom	Unknown
Frillish	♂/♀		Shuppet	♂/♀
Gallade	♂		Slugma	♂/♀
Gardevoir	♂/♀		Solosis	♂/♀
Gastly	♂/♀		Spiritomb	♂/♀
Gengar	♂/♀		Swalot	♂/♀
Gourgeist	♂/♀		Tynamo	♂/♀
Grimer	♂/♀		Weezing	♂/♀
Gulpin	♂/♀		Wobbuffet	♂/♀
Haunter	♂/♀			
Jellicent	♂/♀			
Kirlia	♂/♀			

Amorphous and Fairy Egg Groups

Castform	♂/♀

Amorphous and Grass Egg Groups

Phantump	♂/♀
Trevenant	♂/♀

Amorphous and Mineral Egg Groups

Cofagrigus	♂/♀
Yamask	♂/♀

Amorphous and Water 1 Egg Groups

Gastrodon	♂/♀
Shellos	♂/♀
Stunfisk	♂/♀

There is no crossover between the Amorphous Egg Group and the following Egg Groups:

- Bug
- Flying
- Human-Like
- Monster
- Dragon
- Field
- Water 2
- Water 3
- Ditto
- No Eggs Discovered

Use your special Abilities and O-Powers to help hatch Eggs

There is an O-Power called Hatching Power that will aid you by making Pokémon Eggs hatch faster than usual. For Egg enthusiasts, this O-Power will be a great boon. And like all other O-Powers, the more you use it, the stronger it will become. It is not an easy O-Power to obtain, though. You will have to obtain every other O-Power first and fulfill certain other conditions. If you are up to this challenge, Mr. Bonding will bestow this power upon you. Don't forget that you can also use the O-Powers of those around you. Having a Pokémon in your party with certain Abilities will also help you hatch an Egg that you are carrying around. Abilities like Flame Body or Magma Armor will keep the Egg warm, and make it hatch faster.

Remember: You can obtain a special O-Power that will help you to hatch Eggs more quickly. You can also use Abilities to help an Egg hatch faster.

AFTER THE HALL OF FAME

CENTRAL KALOS

COASTAL KALOS

MOUNTAIN KALOS

ADVENTURE DATA

Water Group 1

Water Egg Group 1 only

	Clamperl	♂/♀
	Froakie	♂/♀
	Frogadier	♂/♀
	Gorebyss	♂/♀
	Greninja	♂/♀
	Huntail	♂/♀
	Mantine	♂/♀
	Palpitoad	♂/♀
	Politoed	♂/♀
	Poliwag	♂/♀
	Poliwhirl	♂/♀
	Poliwrath	♂/♀
	Seismitoad	♂/♀
	Tympole	♂/♀

Water 1 and Grass Egg Groups

	Lombre	♂/♀
	Lotad	♂/♀
	Ludicolo	♂/♀

Water 1 and Bug Egg Groups

	Masquerain	♂/♀
	Surskit	♂/♀

Water 1 and Flying Egg Groups

	Ducklett	♂/♀
	Pelipper	♂/♀
	Swanna	♂/♀
	Wingull	♂/♀

Water 1 and Monster Egg Groups

	Blastoise	♂/♀
	Croconaw	♂/♀
	Feraligatr	♂/♀
	Lapras	♂/♀
	Marshtomp	♂/♀
	Mudkip	♂/♀
	Slowbro	♂/♀
	Slowking	♂/♀
	Slowpoke	♂/♀
	Squirtle	♂/♀
	Swampert	♂/♀
	Totodile	♂/♀
	Wartortle	♂/♀

Water 1 and Fairy Egg Groups

	Azumarill	♂/♀
	Manaphy	Unknown
	Marill	♂/♀
	Phione	Unknown

Water 1 and Dragon Egg Groups

	Dragalge	♂/♀
	Dragonair	♂/♀
	Dragonite	♂/♀
	Dratini	♂/♀
	Feebas	♂/♀
	Horsea	♂/♀
	Kingdra	♂/♀
	Milotic	♂/♀
	Seadra	♂/♀
	Skrelp	♂/♀

Water 1 and Field Egg Groups

	Bibarel	♂/♀
	Bidoof	♂/♀
	Buizel	♂/♀
	Delibird	♂/♀
	Dewgong	♂/♀
	Empoleon	♂/♀
	Floatzel	♂/♀
	Golduck	♂/♀
	Piplup	♂/♀
	Prinplup	♂/♀
	Psyduck	♂/♀
	Quagsire	♂/♀
	Sealeo	♂/♀
	Seel	♂/♀
	Spheal	♂/♀
	Walrein	♂/♀
	Wooper	♂/♀

Water 1 and Amorphous Egg Groups

	Gastrodon	♂/♀
	Shellos	♂/♀
	Stunfisk	♂/♀

Water 1 and Water 2 Egg Groups

	Alomomola	♂/♀
	Inkay	♂/♀
	Malamar	♂/♀
	Octillery	♂/♀
	Relicanth	♂/♀
	Remoraid	♂/♀

Water 1 and Water 3 Egg Groups

	Carracosta	♂/♀
	Clauncher	♂/♀
	Clawitzer	♂/♀
	Corphish	♂/♀
	Corsola	♂/♀
	Crawdaunt	♂/♀
	Kabuto	♂/♀
	Kabutops	♂/♀
	Omanyte	♂/♀
	Omastar	♂/♀
	Tirtouga	♂/♀

There is no crossover between the Water Egg Group 1 and the following Egg Groups:

- Human-Like
- Mineral
- Ditto
- No Eggs Discovered

Water Group 2

● Water Egg Group 2 only

	Barboach	♂/♀
	Basculin	♂/♀
	Carvanha	♂/♀
	Chinchou	♂/♀
	Finneon	♂/♀
	Goldeen	♂/♀
	Lanturn	♂/♀
	Lumineon	♂/♀
	Luvdisc	♂/♀
	Qwilfish	♂/♀
	Seaking	♂/♀
	Sharpedo	♂/♀
	Whiscash	♂/♀

● Water 2 and Dragon Egg Groups

	Gyarados	♂/♀
	Magikarp	♂/♀

● Water 2 and Field Egg Groups

	Wailmer	♂/♀
	Wailord	♂/♀

● Water 2 and Water 1 Egg Groups

	Alomomola	♂/♀
	Inkay	♂/♀
	Malamar	♂/♀
	Octillery	♂/♀
	Relicanth	♂/♀
	Remoraid	♂/♀

There is no crossover between the Water Egg Group 2 and the following Egg Groups:

- Grass
- Bug
- Flying
- Human-Like
- Monster
- Fairy
- Mineral
- Amorphous
- Water 3
- Ditto
- No Eggs Discovered

Water Group 3

● Water Egg Group 3 only

	Anorith	♂/♀
	Armaldo	♂/♀
	Barbaracle	♂/♀
	Binacle	♂/♀
	Cloyster	♂/♀
	Cradily	♂/♀
	Kingler	♂/♀
	Krabby	♂/♀
	Lileep	♂/♀
	Shellder	♂/♀
	Starmie	Unknown
	Staryu	Unknown
	Tentacool	♂/♀
	Tentacruel	♂/♀

● Water 3 and Bug Egg Groups

	Drapion	♂/♀
	Skorupi	♂/♀

● Water 3 and Flying Egg Groups

	Archen	♂/♀
	Archeops	♂/♀

● Water 3 and Water 1 Egg Groups

	Carracosta	♂/♀
	Clauncher	♂/♀
	Clawitzer	♂/♀
	Corphish	♂/♀
	Corsola	♂/♀
	Crawdaunt	♂/♀
	Kabuto	♂/♀
	Kabutops	♂/♀
	Omanyte	♂/♀
	Omastar	♂/♀
	Tirtouga	♂/♀

There is no crossover between the Water Egg Group 3 and the following Egg Groups:

- Grass
- Human-Like
- Monster
- Fairy
- Dragon
- Mineral
- Field
- Amorphous
- Water 2
- Ditto
- No Eggs Discovered

AFTER THE HALL OF FAME

CENTRAL KALOS

COASTAL KALOS

MOUNTAIN KALOS

ADVENTURE DATA

AFTER THE HALL OF FAME

CENTRAL KALOS

COASTAL KALOS

MOUNTAIN KALOS

ADVENTURE DATA

Ditto Group

● **Ditto Group**

Ditto	Unknown

The Ditto Group is a special Group. Ditto is not a part of any other Egg Group, yet if you drop it off at a Pokémon Day Care with almost any other Pokémon, you will find an Egg for that Pokémon. You cannot find a Ditto Egg.

No Eggs Discovered Group

● **No Eggs Discovered**

None of the Pokémon in the No Eggs Discovered Group belong to any other Egg Group

Arceus	Unknown	Mew	Unknown
Articuno	Unknown	Mewtwo	Unknown
Azelf	Unknown	Mime Jr.	♂/♀
Azurill	♂/♀	Moltres	Unknown
Bonsly	♂/♀	Munchlax	♂/♀
Budew	♂/♀	Nidoqueen	♀
Celebi	Unknown	Nidorina	♀
Chingling	♂/♀	Palkia	Unknown
Cleffa	♂/♀	Pichu	♂/♀
Cobalion	Unknown	Raikou	Unknown
Cresselia	♀	Rayquaza	Unknown
Darkrai	Unknown	Regice	Unknown
Deoxys	Unknown	Regigigas	Unknown
Dialga	Unknown	Regirock	Unknown
Elekid	♂/♀	Registeel	Unknown
Entei	Unknown	Reshiram	Unknown
Genesect	Unknown	Riolu	♂/♀
Giratina	Unknown	Shaymin	Unknown
Groudon	Unknown	Smoochum	♀
Happiny	♀	Suicune	Unknown
Heatran	♂/♀	Terrakion	Unknown
Ho-Oh	Unknown	Thundurus	♂
Igglybuff	♂/♀	Togepi	♂/♀
Jirachi	Unknown	Tornadus	♂
Keldeo	Unknown	Tyrogue	♂
Kyogre	Unknown	Unown	Unknown
Kyurem	Unknown	Uxie	Unknown
Landorus	♂	Victini	Unknown
Latias	♀	Virizion	Unknown
Latios	♂	Wynaut	♂/♀
Lugia	Unknown	Xerneas	Unknown
Magby	♂/♀	Yveltal	Unknown
Mantyke	♂/♀	Zapdos	Unknown
Meloetta	Unknown	Zekrom	Unknown
Mesprit	Unknown	Zygarde	Unknown

Inheriting Moves

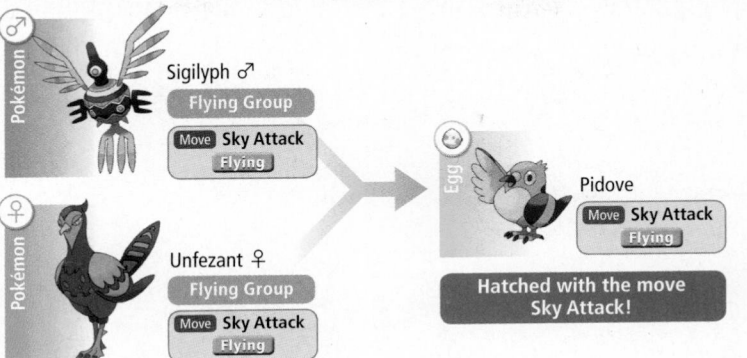

The two Pokémon you leave at the Pokémon Day Care can pass on a move they have learned to a Pokémon that hatches from an Egg. Usually, a newly hatched Pokémon only knows Lv. 1 moves. However, if both the Pokémon you left at the Day Care have learned a move that the hatched Pokémon can learn by leveling up, the hatched Pokémon will know that move. Check the following rules for details.

Info about inheriting moves

1. If both Pokémon at the Pokémon Day Care know the same level-up move, the hatched Pokémon may know that level-up move.

2. A move that the male Pokémon knows and that the hatched Pokémon could learn from a TM can be passed on.

Egg Moves

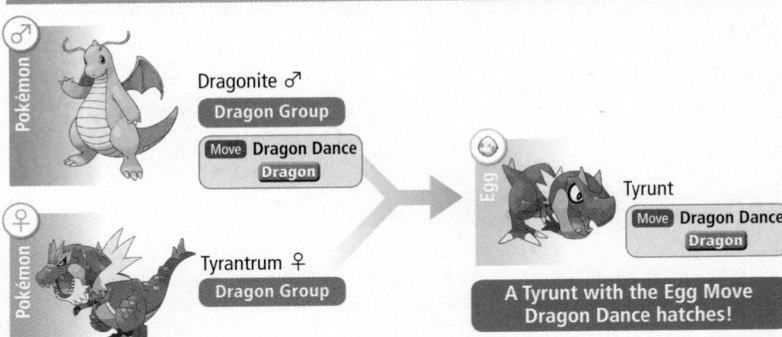

Pokémon may hatch from Eggs already knowing moves that they usually can't learn. For example, Tyrantrum can't learn the move Dragon Dance by leveling up. But if the male Pokémon left at the Pokémon Day Care

AFTER THE HALL OF FAME

CENTRAL KALOS

COASTAL KALOS

MOUNTAIN KALOS

ADVENTURE DATA

AFTER THE HALL OF FAME

CENTRAL KALOS

COASTAL KALOS

MOUNTAIN KALOS

ADVENTURE DATA

is a Dragonite that knows Dragon Dance, the Tyrunt that hatches from the Egg might know the move Dragon Dance. Because many Egg Moves are so unexpected, you can surprise an opposing Trainer in battle.

Inheriting Egg Moves

A move that the male Pokémon knows and that the hatched Pokémon can learn as an Egg Move can be passed on.

Inheriting Abilities

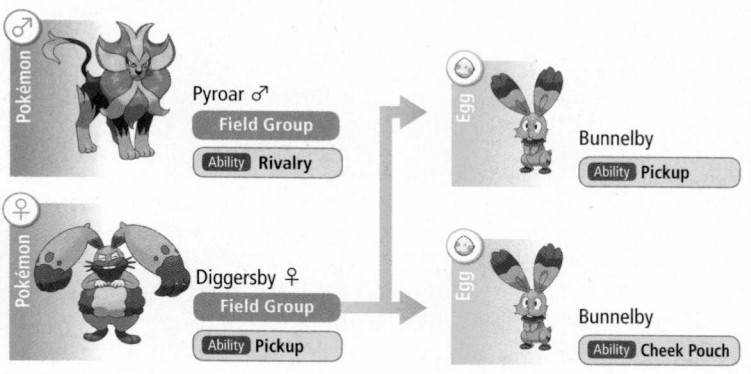

Pyroar ♂
Field Group
Ability **Rivalry**

Diggersby ♀
Field Group
Ability **Pickup**

Bunnelby
Ability **Pickup**

Bunnelby
Ability **Cheek Pouch**

You don't know which Ability a Pokémon will have until it hatches. For example, Diggersby can have either the Pickup or Cheek Pouch Ability. Sometimes when you leave a female Diggersby with the Pickup Ability at the Pokémon Day Care, the Egg that hatches will be a Bunnelby with the Cheek Pouch Ability.

Abilities of hatched Pokémon

1 When the female Pokémon has two possible Abilities, the hatched Pokémon could have either one.

2 The Ability of a Pokémon hatched from an Egg is more likely to be the Ability of the female Pokémon left at the Pokémon Day Care.

Item that affects Pokémon's Abilities

Ability Capsule

This new item in *Pokémon X* and *Pokémon Y* allows you to change the Ability of a Pokémon whose species can have more than one Ability. For example, Audino can normally have the Healer or Regenerator Abilities. If you caught an Audino with the Healer Ability, but you are hoping to pass along the Regenerator Ability, you can use an Ability Capsule to switch your Audino's Ability from Healer to Regenerator. Unfortunately, you can't swap to a Hidden Ability. You can get an Ability Capsule for 200 BP in Kiloude City's Battle Maison.

Inheriting Hidden Abilities

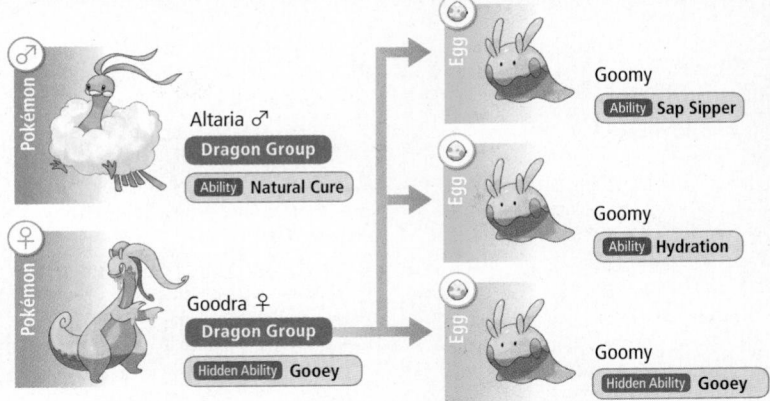

If you leave a female Pokémon with a Hidden Ability at the Pokémon Day Care, you may find an Egg that hatches into a Pokémon with the same Ability. For example, Goodra can have the Hidden Ability Gooey. If you discover an Egg when you leave a female Goodra with the Gooey Ability at the Pokémon Day Care, you may find an Egg containing a Goomy with Sap Sipper, Hydration, or the same Hidden Ability, Gooey. When the female Pokémon at the Pokémon Day Care has a Hidden Ability, you can sometimes hatch a Pokémon with a Hidden Ability. The Hidden Ability will not be passed down if the female was paired with a Ditto.

Inheriting Stats

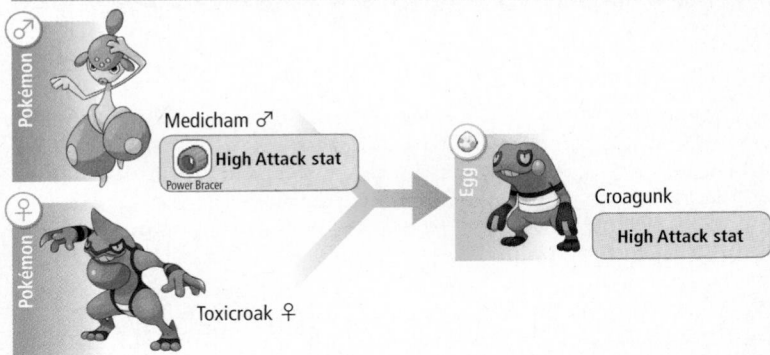

There are ways to pass inherent strength on to a Pokémon that hatches from an Egg. For example, when you leave a Pokémon that has a high inherent strength in Attack at the Pokémon Day Care, have it hold a Power Bracer. It passes the holder's inherent strength in Attack on to the Pokémon that will hatch from the Egg. When you are raising Pokémon for battles, try to find many Eggs using this method, then hatch them and pick a newly hatched Pokémon with overall high stats.

Items that pass on inherent strengths

 **Power Weight**

Passes the holder's inherent strength in HP on to the Pokémon that hatches from the Egg.

Power Bracer

Passes the holder's inherent strength in Attack on to the Pokémon that hatches from the Egg.

Power Belt

Passes the holder's inherent strength in Defense on to the Pokémon that hatches from the Egg.

Power Lens

Passes the holder's inherent strength in Sp. Atk on to the Pokémon that hatches from the Egg.

Power Band

Passes the holder's inherent strength in Sp. Def on to the Pokémon that hatches from the Egg.

Power Anklet

Passes the holder's inherent strength in Speed on to the Pokémon that hatches from the Egg.

Inheriting Natures

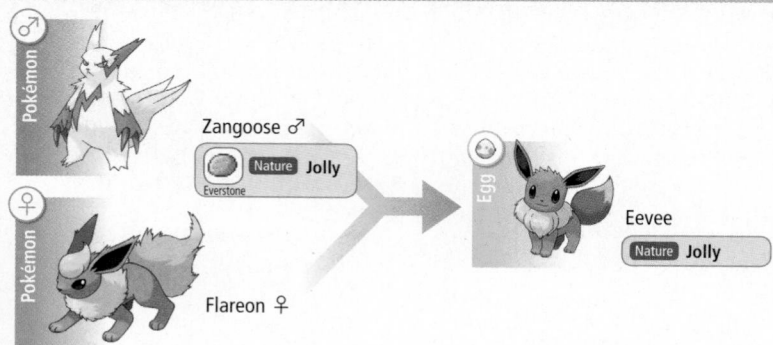

Pokémon ♂

Zangoose ♂

Everstone | Nature **Jolly**

Pokémon ♀

Flareon ♀

Egg

Eevee

Nature **Jolly**

Nature is essential in raising a Pokémon with high stats. Which stat increases quickly when the Pokémon levels up is determined by its Nature. So, for example, if you want to pass on the Jolly Nature of the Pokémon you left at the Pokémon Day Care to a hatched Pokémon, have the Pokémon hold an Everstone. The hatched Pokémon will always have the same Jolly Nature.

Increasing Shiny Pokémon

Leave two Pokémon from *Pokémon X* or *Pokémon Y* games registered in different parts of the world to increase the odds of finding a Shiny Pokémon. For example, matching a Japanese Flareon with an American Zangoose will give you a better chance of finding an Egg for a Shiny Pokémon than leaving two Pokémon from the same country.

Hunting for Fossils in Glittering Cave

If you want to obtain more Pokémon, you'll need to get your hands dirty back at Glittering Cave. Teach a Pokémon the Rock Smash move so you can use it in the field. Return to Glittering Cave after you've entered the Hall of Fame.

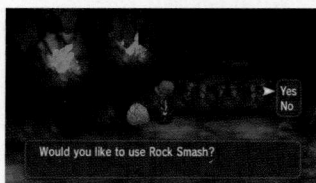

Sprint straight through the cave's first tunnel system to reach the second. As you explore the second tunnel system, keep a lookout for small, cracked rocks. Use the Rock Smash field move on these special rocks to shatter them.

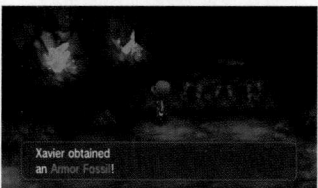

Be careful. After shattering a cracked rock with Rock Smash, you might be forced to battle a wild Pokémon. If you're really lucky, however, you may instead discover a long-lost Pokémon Fossil!

 Pokémon Fossils can only be found by smashing rocks inside Glittering Cave. No other area's cracked rocks contain Pokémon Fossils.

 Exit and re-enter Glittering Cave as many times as you like to refresh the deposits of cracked rocks and try for more Fossils.

When you've finished raiding Glittering Cave, make your way back through Route 9 and visit Ambrette Town. (Or use Fly to get there.) Visit the Fossil Lab in Ambrette Town and speak to the researcher at the front desk. He'll happily accept any Fossils you found in Glittering Cave and restore them into ancient and powerful Pokémon. Restore lots of Fossils to fill out your Pokédex!

 Fossils of the same name will always be restored to the same Pokémon. For example, the Old Amber will always be restored into Aerodactyl.

AFTER THE
HALL OF FAME

CENTRAL
KALOS

COASTAL
KALOS

MOUNTAIN
KALOS

ADVENTURE
DATA

Fossil finder's guide

The following Fossils can all be found by smashing small, cracked rocks inside Glittering Cave.

- Old Amber (restores to Aerodactyl)
- Cover Fossil (restores to Tirtouga)
- Plume Fossil (restores to Archen)
- Armor Fossil (restores to Shieldon)
- Skull Fossil (restores to Cranidos)

- Root Fossil* (restores to Lileep)
- Claw Fossil* (restores to Anorith)
- Helix Fossil** (restores to Omanyte)
- Dome Fossil** (restores to Kabuto)

*Only appears in *Pokémon X*
**Only appears in *Pokémon Y*

Fishing Guide

Many Pokémon make their home in rivers or under the sea, and fishing with a rod is the only way to encounter these aquatic catches. Note that the Pokémon you encounter while traveling across the sea with Surf are different than the ones you can catch by fishing.

Yeah!
Not now.

I just so happen to have a spare rod right here.
Whaddya say?

The Pokémon you will catch by fishing will depend on your rod. There are three different rods to discover, each one better than the last. Seek out three generous fishermen around Kalos. They will part with their spare rods if you speak to them at the following locations.

Fishing rods

Rod	Quality	Where to get it
Old Rod	Poor	Ambrette Town (Ambrette Aquarium)
Good Rod	Good	Coumarine City (pier)
Super Rod	Excellent	Route 16 (fishing shack)

Once you've secured a fishing rod, you're ready to start fishing. Approach any body of water and equip your fishing rod to cast your line. Press Ⓐ to reel in your catch the moment you get a bite. You'll know you've gotten a nibble when a pair of exclamation points appears over your head.

 NOTE   *"Consecutive fishing" occurs when you hook several Pokémon in a row without missing. Use the Super Rod to help you achieve this. Hook eight Pokémon in a row without missing, and you'll be entitled to a special reward from the Fisherman in the fishing shack on Route 16!*

A wild Clawitzer appeared!

After you've hooked a Pokémon, you just need to battle and catch it. Wear it down with moves and status conditions, and then throw a Poké Ball. Dive Balls and Net Balls are ideal for catching Water-type Pokémon. You can buy Dive Balls and Net Balls at the Poké Ball Boutique in Lumiose City (Autumnal Avenue).

Mega Stones

Mega Stones grant certain Pokémon the power to use Mega Evolution during battle. These items must be held by the proper Pokémon to enable Mega Evolution.

The following Mega Stones are obtained over the course of the adventure.

Mega Stones obtained during the main story

Mega Stone	Pokémon	Location	Note
Venusaurite	Mega Venusaur	Lumiose City	When you chose Bulbasaur at the Sycamore Pokémon Lab. The other two Pokémon's Mega Stones can be obtained at the Stone Emporium on Vernal Avenue.
Charizardite X*	Mega Charizard X	Lumiose City	When you chose Charmander at the Sycamore Pokémon Lab. The other two Pokémon's Mega Stones can be obtained at the Stone Emporium on Vernal Avenue.
Charizardite Y**	Mega Charizard Y	Lumiose City	When you chose Charmander at the Sycamore Pokémon Lab. The other two Pokémon's Mega Stones can be obtained at the Stone Emporium on Vernal Avenue.
Blastoisinite	Mega Blastoise	Lumiose City	When you chose Squirtle at the Sycamore Pokémon Lab. The other two Pokémon's Mega Stones can be obtained at the Stone Emporium on Vernal Avenue.
Aerodactylite	Mega Aerodactyl	Ambrette Town	Get it from a Scientist at the Fossil Lab after you return from Glittering Cave.
Ampharosite	Mega Ampharos	Azure Bay	Get it from the man near the photo spot in Azure Bay.
Lucarionite	Mega Lucario	Shalour City	When you receive Lucario from Korrina at the top of the Tower of Mastery.
Gengarite	Mega Gengar	Laverre City	Get it from a Hex Maniac in Laverre City after seeing Gastly, Haunter, or Gengar.
Abomasite	Mega Abomasnow	Frost Cavern	Talk to Abomasnow after rescuing it from Team Flare.

*Only appears in *Pokémon X*   **Only appears in *Pokémon Y*

Many more Mega Stones can be obtained by exploring Kalos after you've entered the Hall of Fame. Your Mega Ring must be powered up by the sundial at Anistar City in order to discover some of these long-lost Mega Stones. Here's a quick course on how to get your Mega Ring powered up.

1 Defeat the Champion and enter the Hall of Fame.

2 Obtain TMV Pass from Professor Sycamore at Lumiose Station.

3 Try at least one battle in Kiloude City's Battle Maison.

4 Defeat Serena/Calem near Kiloude City's north pond.

5 Talk to Serena/Calem to hear the professor's message.

6 Meet Professor Sycamore near the great sundial at Anistar City.

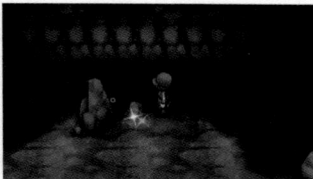

Once your Mega Ring has been super-charged by the sundial, you'll be able to detect hidden Mega Stones in certain areas just by visiting them between 8 P.M. and 9 P.M. Check your Nintendo 3DS System Settings to verify the time of day.

Mega Stones obtained after entering the Hall of Fame

Mega Stone	Pokémon	Location	Note
Absolite	Mega Absol	Kiloude City	Receive from Serena/Calem after battling.
Aggronite**	Mega Aggron	Cyllage City	Look in the Pokémon Gym.
Alakazite	Mega Alakazam	Reflection Cave	Find in the deepest part of the cave.
Banettite	Mega Banette	Chamber of Emptiness	—
Garchompite	Mega Garchomp	Victory Road	Investigate near where you once battled Serena/Calem.
Gardevoirite	Mega Gardevoir	Lumiose City	Receive by trading Pokémon with Diantha at Café Soleil.
Gyaradosite	Mega Gyarados	Couriway Town	Search near the waterfalls.
Heracronite**	Mega Heracross	Santalune Forest	Investigate the tall grass.
Houndoominite**	Mega Houndoom	Route 16	Find near the Roller Skaters.
Kangaskhanite	Mega Kangaskhan	Glittering Cave	Look in the first part of the cave.
Manectite*	Mega Manectric	Route 16	Search near the Roller Skaters.

*Only appears in *Pokémon X*   **Only appears in *Pokémon Y*

Mega Stones obtained after entering the Hall of Fame (continued)

Mega Stone	Pokémon	Location	Note
Mawilite	Mega Mawile	Camphrier Town	Find within Shabboneau Castle.
Medichamite	Mega Medicham	Laverre City	Look near the well.
Mewtwonite X*	Mega Mewtwo X	Pokémon Village	Find when you catch Mewtwo.
Mewtwonite Y**	Mega Mewtwo Y	Pokémon Village	Find when you catch Mewtwo.
Pinsirite*	Mega Pinsir	Santalune Forest	Discover in the tall grass.
Scizorite	Mega Scizor	Frost Cavern	Search where Abomasnow was once attacked.
Tyranitarite*	Mega Tyranitar	Cyllage City	Investigate the Pokémon Gym.

*Only appears in *Pokémon X*   **Only appears in *Pokémon Y*

Poké Radar

When used in tall grass (including flower patches), the Poké Radar causes nearby areas to shake, revealing where wild Pokémon are hiding. This Key Item can help you complete your Pokédex with greater ease.

After you enter the Hall of Fame, the Poké Radar can be obtained from a Scientist on the second floor of the Sycamore Pokémon Lab in Lumiose City (South Boulevard).

 Every use of the Poké Radar depletes its battery. Walk or run 50 paces to recharge it.

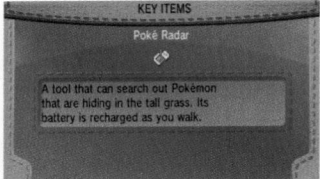

The Poké Radar makes it easier to meet Pokémon of the same species. When you use the Poké Radar, look for patches of shaking grass (up to four paces away). If you catch or defeat the Pokémon that appears in the shaking grass, the Poké Radar will tune to that species of Pokémon, and will help you discover more Pokémon of that same species.

AFTER THE
HALL OF FAME

CENTRAL
KALOS

COASTAL
KALOS

MOUNTAIN
KALOS

ADVENTURE
DATA

 TIP If you aren't interested in tuning your Poké Radar to the current wild Pokémon that has appeared, simply flee from the battle and then use the Poké Radar again.

Kinds of Shaking Grass

Shaking Grass

- You will definitely encounter a Pokémon.

Violently Shaking Grass

- You will definitely encounter a Pokémon.
- You are more likely to meet the same kind of Pokémon as you just battled.

Weakly Shaking Grass

- You will not encounter a Pokémon.
- Enter this kind of grass and the effects of the Poké Radar will end.

Sparkling Grass

- You will definitely encounter a Shiny Pokémon.

 NOTE The more of the same Pokémon you meet in shaking grass, the easier it becomes to meet Shiny Pokémon.

Actions That End the Poké Radar Effect

Any of these actions will cancel the Poké Radar's effect, causing the background music to return to normal.

- If no grass shakes after the battle
- If you run from battle
- If you are drawn into battle with a Pokémon outside of a shaking grass patch (avoid this by using Repels)
- If you encounter a different Pokémon in the shaking grass than the last species you battled (you break the chain)
- If you enter weakly shaking grass
- If you are drawn into a Trainer battle
- If you leave the current area
- If you use the Bicycle or Roller Skates
- If you use a hidden move or other field move
- If you use an item or move that makes you meet wild Pokémon (Honey, Sweet Scent, and the like)
- If you use your Dowsing Machine
- If you use a fishing rod
- If you trigger a story event
- If you save your game and then load it again

Records and Rewards

A record of how many of the same species of Pokémon you've encountered in a row is kept on the machine on the second floor of the Sycamore Pokémon Lab in Lumiose City (South Boulevard). Here's what the machine shows.

- The 1st, 2nd, and 3rd best records in the past
- The most recent record
- The record for the current target Pokémon

The target Pokémon changes daily. Talk to the Scientist near the record machine to find out the target Pokémon for the day. He will want you to encounter as many of that Pokémon in a row as you can. When you talk to the Scientist after reaching a new record, you can receive the following rewards.

1–10 Pokémon: Ultra Ball	**21–30 Pokémon:** PP Max
11–20 Pokémon: PP Up	**31 or more Pokémon:** Rare Candy

 You get all the rewards for your record and below. For example, if you record 20, you'll receive the PP Up and the Ultra Ball. If your record is 31, you'll get all four items at once.

Getting Rewards for Pokédex Completion

Completing your Pokédex is not only fun, but also earns you respect from those around you. You get an award for completing each of the three Pokédexes in the Kalos region, and another for completing the National Pokédex. When you obtain an award, you'll find it proudly hanging on your bedroom wall at home. Swing by the Coumarine Hotel in Coumarine City and speak to the Game Director on the second floor to claim these fabulous awards!

AFTER THE
HALL OF FAME

CENTRAL
KALOS

COASTAL
KALOS

MOUNTAIN
KALOS

ADVENTURE
DATA

Hoo ha! You've found 70 or more!
Now we're talking! This is for you!

Don't forget that there were some other prizes to be claimed around Kalos for completing your Pokédex! A Scientist in Shalour City will give you an Eviolite if you've seen 40 or more Pokémon from the Coastal Kalos Pokédex. In Dendemille Town, a Monsieur will give you a Shell Bell if you've seen 70 or more Pokémon from the Mountain Kalos Pokédex!

Some Pokémon don't need to be registered in your Pokédex for it to be considered complete. These include Mewtwo, Articuno, Zapdos, and Moltres, among others. There are 150 Pokémon needed in each of the Central, Coastal, and Mountain Kalos Pokédexes for them to be considered complete. There are 705 Pokémon that will have to be registered in your National Pokédex for it to be considered complete. You don't need to have all Mythical Pokémon registered for the National Pokédex to be considered complete.

Daily Events

Here are some of the many things you can accomplish every day around the Kalos region. Get in the habit of checking them out daily! Events colored ● become accessible only after you enter the Hall of Fame.

Check boutiques for new goods

How to buy items
Try on!
Nothing

Hello!
What would you like to do?

Where: Santalune, Lumiose, Cyllage, Laverre, Anistar, Snowbelle

The boutiques around the Kalos region change their stock each day, so check in on them daily to see what new shipments might have come in. If you hope to complete your wardrobe or find your perfect look, you'll want to be diligent on this one!

Examine shaking garbage cans

Xavier found an HP Up!

Where: The Lost Hotel (Route 15), The Pokémon Village (Route 20)

Some of the large green garbage cans in the Lost Hotel and the Pokémon Village shake, rattle, and roll. You might find items or wild Pokémon inside, so crack 'em open. Different Pokémon may appear on different days.

Buy some fresh-baked galettes

Xavier obtained
a Lumiose Galette!

Where: North Lumiose City (North Boulevard)

Lumiose Galettes are a favorite souvenir from the famed City of Light. They are available for a few hours after each new batch is baked—but they do sell out so be sure to get them before they're gone! They'll heal all of a Pokémon's status conditions.

Try your luck at Loto-ID

Where: South Lumiose City (Estival Avenue)

On Estival Avenue is the Loto-ID Center, where you can draw a different number each day. Win prizes based on how closely the number drawn matches the ID of your Pokémon—best of all, it's absolutely free to play!

Enjoy juice at the Juice Shoppe

Where: South Lumiose City (Vernal Avenue)

You can get fresh-squeezed juice and premium juice made for you each day at the Juice Shoppe. Depending on what Berries you put into your blends, you may improve your Pokémon's base stats or help them level up.

Battle Trainers in the twisting alleys

Where: All around Lumiose City

There are 10 Trainers who can appear in the alleys that twist through the heart of Lumiose City. Each time you beat one, another will appear in a different location. Some may even give you prizes for winning!

Get a Luxury Ball or some Heal Balls

Where: South Lumiose City (Vernal Avenue)

Talk to the young girl in the Poké Ball Boutique and she will ask if you like round things. Agree that you do and she will give you either a Luxury Ball or three Heal Balls. Visit her every day for more!

Spruce up your Trainer PR Videos

Where: North Lumiose City (North Boulevard)

If you're confident in your style, talk to the Rich Boy in Café Action on North Boulevard. He is a copywriter, and each day he'll come up with new blurbs that you can include in your Trainer PR Videos.

Earn some cash for part-time work

Where: North Lumiose City (North Boulevard)

You can do each of the three part-time tasks at Hotel Richissime once a day. Become a master at changing beds, taking room-service orders, and finding lost items, and you'll be making bank before long!

AFTER THE HALL OF FAME

CENTRAL KALOS

COASTAL KALOS

MOUNTAIN KALOS

ADVENTURE DATA

Get an Aspear, Cheri, Chesto, Pecha, or Rawst Berry

Where: Camphrier Town

If you can show a man in Camphrier Town a Pokémon of the type that he's interested in, he'll let you choose from an Aspear Berry, Cheri Berry, Chesto Berry, Pecha Berry, or Rawst Berry for your reward.

Get a Sweet Heart from a sweetheart

Where: Camphrier Town

In the same house as the man who gave you Berries is a Maid who will give you a Sweet Heart every day, simply for being you. Be sure to visit this house each day for both of these nice finds.

Take care of your Berry fields

Where: Route 7

Try to check in on your Berry fields each day to check that they are well-watered and free from Bug-type Pokémon. Harvest any Berries that are mature and plant new trees to get started on your next crop!

Get a Dive Ball for a Poké Ball

Where: Ambrette Town

Talk to the Punk Guy who is standing in the middle of Ambrette Town, and he'll offer you a great deal. He'll trade you a valuable Dive Ball, great for catching Water-type Pokémon, for a regular old Poké Ball!

Get a Health Wing

Where: Ambrette Town

Bring your swiftest Pokémon with you to Ambrette Town, because if you show this Ace Trainer a Pokémon with a Speed at or above the level she asks for, she'll give you a Health Wing in return.

Get your Pokémon a massage

Where: Cyllage City

If you wish, this woman will provide one of the Pokémon in your party with a massage once a day. This special treat will help make that Pokémon feel more friendly toward you, so show a little love!

Snag some unattended Berries

A nice Rawst Berry is on the table with a sign saying, "Help yourself."

Where: Coumarine City

An unattended stand in Coumarine City is stocked each day with either an Aspear Berry, a Cheri Berry, a Chesto Berry, a Pecha Berry, or a Rawst Berry. It's not stealing—the sign tells you they are free to take.

Trot out your very large Pokémon

Xavier obtained a Poké Doll.

Where: Laverre City

A Lass in Laverre City wants to see very large Pokémon. Only a Pokémon that stands 9'10" or above will satisfy her interest. Every day that you show her that you have one on your team, she'll give you a Poké Doll.

Parade around your very small Pokémon

Xavier obtained a Poké Doll.

Where: Laverre City

A Rich Boy near the gate in Laverre City wants to see teeny-tiny Pokémon. If you have a Pokémon on your team that is less than a foot in height, he will give you a Poké Doll each day.

Show off your TMs for profit

Xavier obtained a Leppa Berry!

Where: Dendemille Town

There is an Ace Trainer in Dendemille Town who is quite a TM enthusiast. Each day, she'll name a TM. If you can show her that you have it, she'll give you a Leppa Berry.

Take part in an Inverse Battle

Would you care to try an Inverse Battle?   Yes / No

Where: Route 18

A very peculiar kind of Psychic lives on Route 18. You can challenge him to an Inverse Battle once a day. Using his mystic powers, he'll reverse all the Pokémon's strengths and weaknesses!

Freshen up with Fresh Water

Xavier obtained a Fresh Water!

Where: Couriway Town

A man to the east of the hotel in Couriway Town sells one bottle of Fresh Water per day. Each bottle will restore 50 HP to a Pokémon. He may even give you a Berry as a bonus!

Work up an appetite in Lumiose

Where: All around Lumiose City

Once you enter the Hall of Fame and show some real style, there will be two more restaurants in Lumiose City available to you. Stop by all four restaurants to enjoy the fine dining, rigorous battles, and some great prizes!

Get Ultra Balls for helping out

Where: South Lumiose City (South Boulevard)

A Scientist in the Sycamore Pokémon Lab will give you the Poké Radar after you enter the Hall of Fame. Use it to help him with his research. If you are successful, you can earn an Ultra Ball each day, and more!

Learn more about Mega Evolution from Trevor

Where: Geosenge Town

Trevor can be found hanging around Geosenge Town after you enter the Hall of Fame. Talk to him there, and each day he'll tell you about one Pokémon that is capable of Mega Evolution.

Show off your moves for Tierno

Where: Coumarine City

Out on the bluff to the east of the Coumarine City Pokémon Gym, you'll find Tierno admiring the view. Each day he'll ask about a different move. If you can show it to him, you'll get a Heart Scale.

Take on Serena/Calem

Where: Kiloude City

After you beat Serena/Calem once and go to meet Professor Sycamore in Anistar City, you'll find your rival back in Kiloude City again. She or he will be happy to battle you once a day, high on the hill in Kiloude City.

Battle Essentia in her devastating mobile suit

Where: Lumiose City

After you clear all six chapters of Looker's detective story, you'll be able to meet Essentia in the Looker Bureau on Tuesdays, Thursdays, and Saturdays. Challenge her if you're ready for one tough battle!

Kalos Pokédex Guide

Pokémon

6 Abilities

The Pokémon's Ability. If two Abilities are listed, each individual Pokémon will have one of the two. If an Ability for a Pokémon that appeared in *Pokémon Black 2* and *Pokémon White 2* has changed in *Pokémon X* and *Pokémon Y*, the Ability is shown in blue.

7 Hidden Ability

Some Pokémon have Hidden Abilities. You can obtain Pokémon with Hidden Abilities in special conditions. For example, a Pokémon in a Horde Encounter may have a Hidden Ability, as could a wild Pokémon in a Friend Safari. If a Hidden Ability for a Pokémon that appeared in *Pokémon Black 2* and *Pokémon White 2* has changed in *Pokémon X* and *Pokémon Y*, the Hidden Ability is shown in blue.

8 Stat growth rates

The growth rates of the Pokémon's stats are listed here. They are calculated by comparing the stat to the stats of other Pokémon in the National Pokédex. There are 10 stat growth rates. The first 5 are shown in green, and 6–10 are shown in red.

9 Egg Groups

The Egg Group the Pokémon belongs to. When two Egg Groups are listed, the Pokémon belongs to both (p. 62).

10 Items sometimes held by wild Pokémon

Some wild Pokémon will have a held item. The type of item that the Pokémon may be holding is shown. If you use a Poké Ball to catch that Pokémon when it has a held item, you will also receive the item.

11 Evolution

If the Pokémon evolves, this shows the course of Evolution for the Pokémon as well as any conditions governing its Evolution.

12 Can be used in

The battle formats and facilities that the Pokémon can join are listed here. There are six types: Inverse Battle, Sky Battle, Battle Chateau, Battle Institute, Battle Maison, and Random Matchup.

1 Pokédex area and Pokédex number

The area of the Kalos region that the Pokédex features and the Kalos Pokédex number of the Pokémon.

2 Pokémon category and species

A Pokémon's category, such as Spiny Nut, may provide a pointer to its traits or attributes. Pokémon of different species, such as Fennekin and Vulpix, may belong to the same category (in this case, Fox Pokémon).

3 Height, weight, and gender

The height and weight of the Pokémon, as well as which genders, if any, the Pokémon has.

4 Pokédex entry

This is the summary of the Pokémon's characteristics given in the Kalos Pokédex. The summary in *Pokémon X* usually differs from that in *Pokémon Y*.

5 Type

The Pokémon's type. Some Pokémon have two types. If a type for a Pokémon that appeared in *Pokémon Black 2* and *Pokémon White 2* has changed in *Pokémon X* and *Pokémon Y*, the type is shown in blue.

13 Damage taken in normal battles

Damage taken when the Pokémon is attacked by a move in a normal battle. It increases or decreases depending on the move type. If the effect of an Ability changes damage, ❶ is shown. If damage for a Pokémon that appeared in *Pokémon Black 2* and *Pokémon White 2* has changed in *Pokémon X* and *Pokémon Y*, the damage is shown in blue.

14 Damage taken in Inverse Battles

Damage taken when the Pokémon is attacked by a move in an Inverse Battle. You can try the battle with Psychic Inver in a house on Route 18. If the effect of an Ability changes damage, ❶ is shown.

15 How to obtain for your Kalos Pokédex

The methods for adding Pokémon to the Kalos Pokédex are shown. These are not the only ways to obtain the Pokémon. There are three Kalos Pokédexes: Central, Coastal, and Mountain Kalos Pokédex. If you need to trade Pokémon by PSS, it's indicated here.

16 Appearance

Here you can see how the Pokémon looks from the front, the side, and the back. If the male and female have different appearances, they will be shown here. If the Pokémon can change Formes, each Forme will be shown here, too.

17 Level-up moves

A list of the moves that the Pokémon can learn by leveling up. If a move has been added for a Pokémon that appeared in *Pokémon Black 2* and *Pokémon White 2*, the move is shown in red, and if the level to learn a move has changed, the move name is shown in blue.

18 TM & HM moves

A list of the moves the Pokémon can learn by using a TM or an HM. TMs and HMs do not go away once used, so they can be used to teach Pokémon moves as many times as you like. Added moves for Pokémon that appeared in *Pokémon Black 2* and *Pokémon White 2* are shown in red.

19 Moves taught by people

A list of moves that people can teach Pokémon. There are ultimate moves, battle-combo moves, and the strongest Dragon-type moves.

20 Egg Moves

These moves are occasionally learned by the Pokémon upon hatching from an Egg as long as they are known by the male Pokémon you left at the Pokémon Day Care (p. 61). Added moves for Pokémon that appeared in *Pokémon Black 2* and *Pokémon White 2* are shown in red.

Range Guide

■ **Normal**
The move affects the selected target. If the move is used by a Pokémon in the middle position during a Triple Battle, the move can target any of the other five Pokémon (including allies). If the move is used by a Pokémon during a Double Battle or Multi Battle, or in the left or right position during a Triple Battle, the move can target any of the three surrounding Pokémon (including its ally).

■ **Many Others**
The move affects multiple Pokémon at the same time. If the move is used by a Pokémon in the middle position during a Triple Battle, the move will affect all three opposing Pokémon. If the move is used by a Pokémon during a Double Battle or Multi Battle, or in the left or right position during a Triple Battle, the move will affect two opposing Pokémon.

■ **1 Random**
The move affects one of the opposing Pokémon at random.

■ **Adjacent**
The move affects the surrounding Pokémon at the same time. If the move is used by a Pokémon in the middle position during a Triple Battle, the move will affect the other five Pokémon (including allies) simultaneously. If the move is used by a Pokémon during a Double Battle or Multi Battle, or in the left or right position during a Triple Battle, the move will affect the three surrounding Pokémon (including its ally) simultaneously.

■ **1 Ally**
This move affects an adjacent ally during a Double Battle, Triple Battle, or Multi Battle. It has no effect in a Single Battle.

■ **Self/Ally**
The move affects the user or one of its allies. In a Single Battle, it affects only the user. In a Double Battle, Triple Battle, or Multi Battle, it affects one of the allies (including the user).

■ **Self**
The move affects only the user.

■ **Your Party**
The move affects your entire party, including Pokémon that are in their Poké Balls.

■ **Other Side**
The move affects all Pokémon on the opponent's side of the field. Since the move affects the field, the move's effects continue even if the Pokémon are swapped out (except for moves that only work for one turn).

■ **Your Side**
The move affects all Pokémon on your side of the field. Since the move affects the field, the move's effects continue even if the Pokémon are swapped out (except for moves that only work for one turn).

■ **Both Sides**
The move affects all Pokémon on the field, regardless of which side they are on. Since the move affects the field, the move's effects continue even if the Pokémon are swapped out.

■ **Varies**
The move is influenced by factors such as the opposing Pokémon's move or the user's type, so the range is not fixed.

Move List Guide

Lv.	The level at which the move can be learned	Pow.	The move's attack power
No.	The TM or HM's number	Acc.	The move's accuracy
Type	The move's type	PP	How many times the move can be used
Kind	Whether the move is a physical, special, or status move	Range	The number and range of targets the move can affect

Physical Move: Does more damage the higher the Attack stat is.
Special Move: Does more damage the higher the Sp. Atk stat is.
Status Move: Damages stats or inflicts status condition on the target(s), or various other effects.

Mega Evolution

1) Mega Evolution symbol

The symbol indicates that the Pokémon Mega Evolves.

2) Height, weight, and gender

The height and weight of the Pokémon, as well as which genders, if any, the Pokémon has. If the data changes after Mega Evolution, it's shown in blue.

3) Type

The Pokémon's type. If the type changes after Mega Evolution, it's shown in blue.

4) Abilities

The Pokémon's Ability. If the Ability changes after Mega Evolution, it's shown in blue.

5) Stat growth rates

The growth rates of the Pokémon's stats are listed here. They are calculated by comparing the stat to the stats of other Pokémon in the National Pokédex. There are 10 stat growth rates. The first 5 are shown in green, and 6–10 are shown in red. If the stats change after Mega Evolution, they are shown in blue.

6) Mega Stone required

It shows the Mega Stone necessary for the Pokémon to Mega Evolve, and how to obtain it.

7) Damage taken in normal battles

Damage taken when the Pokémon is attacked by a move in a normal battle. It increases or decreases depending on the move type. If the effect of an Ability changes damage, ❶ is shown. If the damage changes due to the type change caused by Mega Evolution, it's shown in blue.

8) Damage taken in Inverse Battles

Damage taken when the Pokémon is attacked by a move in an Inverse Battle. You can try the battle with Psychic Inver in a house on Route 18. If the effect of an Ability changes damage, ❶ is shown. If the damage changes due to the type change caused by Mega Evolution, it's shown in blue.

9) Can be used in

The battle formats and facilities that the Pokémon can join are listed here. There are six types: Inverse Battle, Sky Battle, Battle Chateau, Battle Institute, Battle Maison, and Random Matchup.

10) Appearance

See how the Mega-Evolved Pokémon looks from the front, the side, and the back.

What Is Mega Evolution?

A New Form of Evolution That Releases a Pokémon's Hidden Energy

Mega Evolution is a temporarily evolved state of Pokémon that were thought to be unable to evolve any further. It releases the Pokémon's hidden power. Mega Evolution can change the Pokémon's type, Ability, stats, height, and weight. Damage done by the opponent's move also changes if the Pokémon's type changes.

Mega Evolution happens only during battle. When a battle ends, the Pokémon returns to normal. If you have a Pokémon Mega Evolve, it will be registered in "APPEARANCE/CRY" in a Kalos Pokédex. However, you can complete a Kalos Pokédex without this.

To have a Pokémon Mega Evolve, you need a Mega Ring in which a mysterious stone is embedded, and an appropriate Mega Stone. A Mega Ring is a band for a Pokémon Trainer to wear on his/her wrist. A Mega Stone is an item that you can give a Pokémon to hold. When a Pokémon Trainer equipped with a Mega Ring uses a Pokémon that holds the required Mega Stone in a battle, the Pokémon can Mega Evolve.

You can receive a Mega Ring from the Mega Evolution successor, Korrina, in the Tower of Mastery in Shalour City, and you can obtain Mega Stones in various places during your adventure in the Kalos region. You can find many Mega Stones after you enter the Hall of Fame.

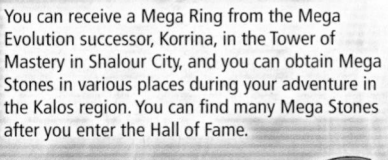

The number of Pokémon that can Mega Evolve is unknown. Mega Evolution, the Mega Ring, and Mega Stones are still veiled in mystery.

AFTER THE HALL OF FAME

CENTRAL KALOS

001

Chespin

COASTAL KALOS

MOUNTAIN KALOS

ADVENTURE DATA

Central Kalos 001
Spiny Nut Pokémon
☑ **Chespin**

HEIGHT: 1'04" WEIGHT: 19.8 lbs.
GENDER: ♂/♀

The quills on its head are usually soft. When it flexes them, the points become so hard and sharp that they can pierce rock.

Such a thick shell of wood covers its head and back that even a direct hit from a truck wouldn't faze it.

TYPE Grass

ABILITY
Overgrow

HIDDEN ABILITY
Bulletproof

STAT GROWTH RATES
HP	■■
Attack	■■■
Defense	■■■
Sp. Atk	■■
Sp. Def	■■
Speed	■■

EGG GROUP
Field

EVOLUTION

Chespin — Lv. 16 → Quilladin — Lv. 36 → Chesnaught

ITEMS SOMETIMES HELD BY WILD POKÉMON
None

Can be used in
Inverse Battle
—
Battle Chateau
Battle Institute
Battle Maison
Random Matchup

Damage taken in normal battles	
Normal	×1
Fire	×2
Water	×0.5
Grass	×0.5
Electric	×0.5
Ice	×2
Fighting	×1
Poison	×2
Ground	×0.5
Flying	×2
Psychic	×1
Bug	×2
Rock	×1
Ghost	×1
Dragon	×1
Dark	×1
Steel	×1
Fairy	×1

Damage taken in Inverse Battles	
Normal	×1
Fire	×0.5
Water	×2
Grass	×2
Electric	×2
Ice	×0.5
Fighting	×1
Poison	×0.5
Ground	×2
Flying	×0.5
Psychic	×1
Bug	×0.5
Rock	×1
Ghost	×1
Dragon	×1
Dark	×1
Steel	×1
Fairy	×1

How to obtain for your Central Kalos Pokédex

❶ Receive from Tierno in Aquacorde Town.

❷ Trade with Shauna after entering the Hall of Fame (if you chose Fennekin at the beginning of the game).

❶ Receive from Tierno in Aquacorde Town.

❷ Trade with Shauna after entering the Hall of Fame (if you chose Fennekin at the beginning of the game).

Same form for ♂/♀

● LEVEL-UP MOVES

Lv.	Name	Type	Kind	Pow.	Acc.	PP	Range
1	Tackle	Normal	Physical	50	100	35	Normal
1	Growl	Normal	Status	—	100	40	Many Others
5	Vine Whip	Grass	Physical	45	100	25	Normal
8	Rollout	Rock	Physical	30	90	20	Normal
11	Bite	Dark	Physical	60	100	25	Normal
15	Leech Seed	Grass	Status	—	90	10	Normal
18	Pin Missile	Bug	Physical	25	95	20	Normal
27	Take Down	Normal	Physical	90	85	20	Normal
32	Seed Bomb	Grass	Physical	80	100	15	Normal
35	Mud Shot	Ground	Special	55	95	15	Normal
39	Bulk Up	Fighting	Status	—	—	20	Self
42	Body Slam	Normal	Physical	85	100	15	Normal
45	Pain Split	Normal	Status	—	—	20	Normal
48	Wood Hammer	Grass	Physical	120	100	15	Normal

● TM & HM MOVES

No.	Name	Type	Kind	Pow.	Acc.	PP	Range
TM05	Roar	Normal	Status	—	—	20	Normal
TM06	Toxic	Poison	Status	—	90	10	Normal
TM08	Bulk Up	Fighting	Status	—	—	20	Self
TM10	Hidden Power	Normal	Special	60	100	15	Normal
TM11	Sunny Day	Fire	Status	—	—	5	Both Sides
TM12	Taunt	Dark	Status	—	100	20	Normal
TM17	Protect	Normal	Status	—	—	10	Self
TM21	Frustration	Normal	Physical	—	100	20	Normal
TM22	Solar Beam	Grass	Special	120	100	10	Normal
TM23	Smack Down	Rock	Physical	50	100	15	Normal
TM27	Return	Normal	Physical	—	100	20	Normal
TM28	Dig	Ground	Physical	80	100	10	Normal
TM31	Brick Break	Fighting	Physical	75	100	15	Normal
TM32	Double Team	Normal	Status	—	—	15	Self
TM33	Reflect	Psychic	Status	—	—	20	Your Side
TM36	Sludge Bomb	Poison	Special	90	100	10	Normal
TM39	Rock Tomb	Rock	Physical	60	95	15	Normal
TM40	Aerial Ace	Flying	Physical	60	—	20	Normal
TM42	Facade	Normal	Physical	70	100	20	Normal
TM44	Rest	Psychic	Status	—	—	10	Self
TM45	Attract	Normal	Status	—	100	15	Normal
TM47	Low Sweep	Fighting	Physical	65	100	20	Normal
TM48	Round	Normal	Special	60	100	15	Normal
TM53	Energy Ball	Grass	Special	90	100	10	Normal
TM56	Fling	Dark	Physical	—	100	10	Normal
TM65	Shadow Claw	Ghost	Physical	70	100	15	Normal
TM66	Payback	Dark	Physical	50	100	10	Normal
TM67	Retaliate	Normal	Physical	70	100	5	Normal
TM70	Flash	Normal	Status	—	100	20	Normal
TM71	Stone Edge	Rock	Physical	100	80	5	Normal
TM74	Gyro Ball	Steel	Physical	—	100	5	Normal
TM75	Swords Dance	Normal	Status	—	—	20	Self
TM78	Bulldoze	Ground	Physical	60	100	20	Adjacent

No.	Name	Type	Kind	Pow.	Acc.	PP	Range
TM80	Rock Slide	Rock	Physical	75	90	10	Many Others
TM84	Poison Jab	Poison	Physical	80	100	20	Normal
TM86	Grass Knot	Grass	Special	—	100	20	Normal
TM87	Swagger	Normal	Status	—	90	15	Normal
TM88	Sleep Talk	Normal	Status	—	—	10	Self
TM90	Substitute	Normal	Status	—	—	10	Self
TM94	Rock Smash	Fighting	Physical	40	100	15	Normal
TM96	Nature Power	Normal	Status	—	—	20	Normal
TM98	Power-Up Punch	Fighting	Physical	40	100	20	Normal
TM100	Confide	Normal	Status	—	—	20	Normal
HM01	Cut	Normal	Physical	50	95	30	Normal
HM04	Strength	Normal	Physical	80	100	15	Normal

● MOVES TAUGHT BY PEOPLE

Name	Type	Kind	Pow.	Acc.	PP	Range
Grass Pledge	Grass	Special	80	100	10	Normal

● EGG MOVES

Name	Type	Kind	Pow.	Acc.	PP	Range
Synthesis	Grass	Status	—	—	5	Self
Belly Drum	Normal	Status	—	—	10	Self
Curse	Ghost	Status	—	—	10	Varies
Quick Guard	Fighting	Status	—	—	15	Your Side
Spikes	Ground	Status	—	—	20	Other Side
Defense Curl	Normal	Status	—	—	40	Self
Rollout	Rock	Physical	30	90	20	Normal

Central Kalos
Spiny Armor Pokémon
☑ **Quilladin**

002

HEIGHT: 2'04" WEIGHT: 63.9 lbs.
GENDER: ♂ / ♀

TYPE Grass

ABILITY
Overgrow

HIDDEN ABILITY
Bulletproof

STAT GROWTH RATES
HP	■■■
Attack	■■■■
Defense	■■■■
Sp. Atk	■■■
Sp. Def	■■
Speed	■■■

EGG GROUP
Field

❌ It relies on its sturdy shell to deflect predators' attacks. It counterattacks with its sharp quills.

🅨 They strengthen their lower bodies by running into one another. They are very kind and won't start fights.

⬛ EVOLUTION

Chespin → Lv. 16 → Quilladin → Lv. 36 → Chesnaught

ITEMS SOMETIMES HELD BY WILD POKÉMON
None

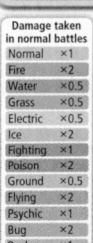

Damage taken in normal battles	
Normal	×1
Fire	×2
Water	×0.5
Grass	×0.5
Electric	×0.5
Ice	×2
Fighting	×1
Poison	×2
Ground	×0.5
Flying	×2
Psychic	×1
Bug	×2
Rock	×1
Ghost	×1
Dragon	×1
Dark	×1
Steel	×1
Fairy	×1

Damage taken in Inverse Battles	
Normal	×1
Fire	×0.5
Water	×2
Grass	×2
Electric	×2
Ice	×0.5
Fighting	×1
Poison	×0.5
Ground	×2
Flying	×0.5
Psychic	×1
Bug	×0.5
Rock	×1
Ghost	×1
Dragon	×1
Dark	×1
Steel	×1
Fairy	×1

Can be used in	
Inverse Battle	Battle Institute
—	Battle Maison
Battle Chateau	Random Matchup

Same form for ♂ / ♀

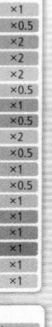 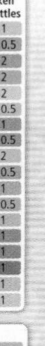

How to obtain for your Central Kalos Pokédex

❶ Level up Chespin to Lv. 16.
❷ Link Trade or transfer from another game.

❶ Level up Chespin to Lv. 16.
❷ Link Trade or transfer from another game.

● **LEVEL-UP MOVES**

Lv.	Name	Type	Kind	Pow.	Acc.	PP	Range
1	Tackle	Normal	Physical	50	100	35	Normal
1	Growl	Normal	Status	—	100	40	Many Others
5	Vine Whip	Grass	Physical	45	100	25	Normal
8	Rollout	Rock	Physical	30	90	20	Normal
11	Bite	Dark	Physical	60	100	25	Normal
15	Leech Seed	Grass	Status	—	90	10	Normal
20	Pin Missile	Bug	Physical	25	95	20	Normal
26	Needle Arm	Grass	Physical	60	100	15	Normal
30	Take Down	Normal	Physical	90	85	20	Normal
35	Seed Bomb	Grass	Physical	80	100	15	Normal
39	Mud Shot	Ground	Special	55	95	15	Normal
44	Bulk Up	Fighting	Status	—	—	20	Self
48	Body Slam	Normal	Physical	85	100	15	Normal
52	Pain Split	Normal	Status	—	—	20	Normal
55	Wood Hammer	Grass	Physical	120	100	15	Normal

● **TM & HM MOVES**

No.	Name	Type	Kind	Pow.	Acc.	PP	Range
TM01	Hone Claws	Dark	Status	—	—	15	Self
TM05	Roar	Normal	Status	—	—	20	Normal
TM06	Toxic	Poison	Status	—	90	10	Normal
TM08	Bulk Up	Fighting	Status	—	—	20	Self
TM10	Hidden Power	Normal	Special	60	100	15	Normal
TM11	Sunny Day	Fire	Status	—	—	5	Both Sides
TM12	Taunt	Dark	Status	—	100	20	Normal
TM17	Protect	Normal	Status	—	—	10	Self
TM21	Frustration	Normal	Physical	—	100	20	Normal
TM22	Solar Beam	Grass	Special	120	100	10	Normal
TM23	Smack Down	Rock	Physical	50	100	15	Normal
TM27	Return	Normal	Physical	—	100	20	Normal
TM28	Dig	Ground	Physical	80	100	10	Normal
TM33	Reflect	Psychic	Status	—	—	20	Your Side
TM36	Sludge Bomb	Poison	Special	90	100	10	Normal
TM39	Rock Tomb	Rock	Physical	60	95	15	Normal
TM40	Aerial Ace	Flying	Physical	60	—	20	Normal
TM42	Facade	Normal	Physical	70	100	20	Normal
TM44	Rest	Psychic	Status	—	—	10	Self
TM45	Attract	Normal	Status	—	100	15	Normal
TM47	Low Sweep	Fighting	Physical	65	100	20	Normal
TM48	Round	Normal	Special	60	100	15	Normal
TM53	Energy Ball	Grass	Special	90	100	10	Normal
TM56	Fling	Dark	Physical	—	100	10	Normal
TM65	Shadow Claw	Ghost	Physical	70	100	15	Normal
TM66	Payback	Dark	Physical	50	100	10	Normal
TM67	Retaliate	Normal	Physical	70	100	5	Normal
TM70	Flash	Normal	Status	—	100	20	Normal
TM71	Stone Edge	Rock	Physical	100	80	5	Normal
TM74	Gyro Ball	Steel	Physical	—	100	5	Normal
TM75	Swords Dance	Normal	Status	—	—	20	Self

No.	Name	Type	Kind	Pow.	Acc.	PP	Range
TM78	Bulldoze	Ground	Physical	60	100	20	Adjacent
TM80	Rock Slide	Rock	Physical	75	90	10	Many Others
TM84	Poison Jab	Poison	Physical	80	100	20	Normal
TM86	Grass Knot	Grass	Special	—	100	20	Normal
TM87	Swagger	Normal	Status	—	90	15	Normal
TM88	Sleep Talk	Normal	Status	—	—	10	Self
TM90	Substitute	Normal	Status	—	—	10	Self
TM94	Rock Smash	Fighting	Physical	40	100	15	Normal
TM96	Nature Power	Normal	Status	—	—	20	Normal
TM98	Power-Up Punch	Fighting	Physical	40	100	20	Normal
TM100	Confide	Normal	Status	—	—	20	Normal
HM01	Cut	Normal	Physical	50	95	30	Normal
HM04	Strength	Normal	Physical	80	100	15	Normal

● **MOVES TAUGHT BY PEOPLE**

Name	Type	Kind	Pow.	Acc.	PP	Range
Grass Pledge	Grass	Special	80	100	10	Normal

AFTER THE HALL OF FAME

CENTRAL KALOS

002 | Quilladin

COASTAL KALOS

MOUNTAIN KALOS

ADVENTURE DATA

AFTER THE HALL OF FAME

CENTRAL KALOS

003

Chesnaught

COASTAL KALOS

MOUNTAIN KALOS

ADVENTURE DATA

🏠 Central Kalos — 003
Spiny Armor Pokémon
☑ Chesnaught

HEIGHT: 5'03" WEIGHT: 198.4 lbs.
GENDER: ♂/♀

TYPE Grass Fighting

ABILITY
Overgrow

HIDDEN ABILITY
Bulletproof

STAT GROWTH RATES
HP	■■■■
Attack	■■■■■
Defense	■■■■■
Sp. Atk	■■■■
Sp. Def	■■■
Speed	■■■■

EGG GROUP
Field

❌ Its Tackle is forceful enough to flip a 50-ton tank. It shields its allies from danger with its own body.

❓ When it takes a defensive posture with its fists guarding its face, it could withstand a bomb blast.

🔺 EVOLUTION

Lv. 16 — Lv. 36

Chespin — Quilladin — Chesnaught

ITEMS SOMETIMES HELD BY WILD POKÉMON
None

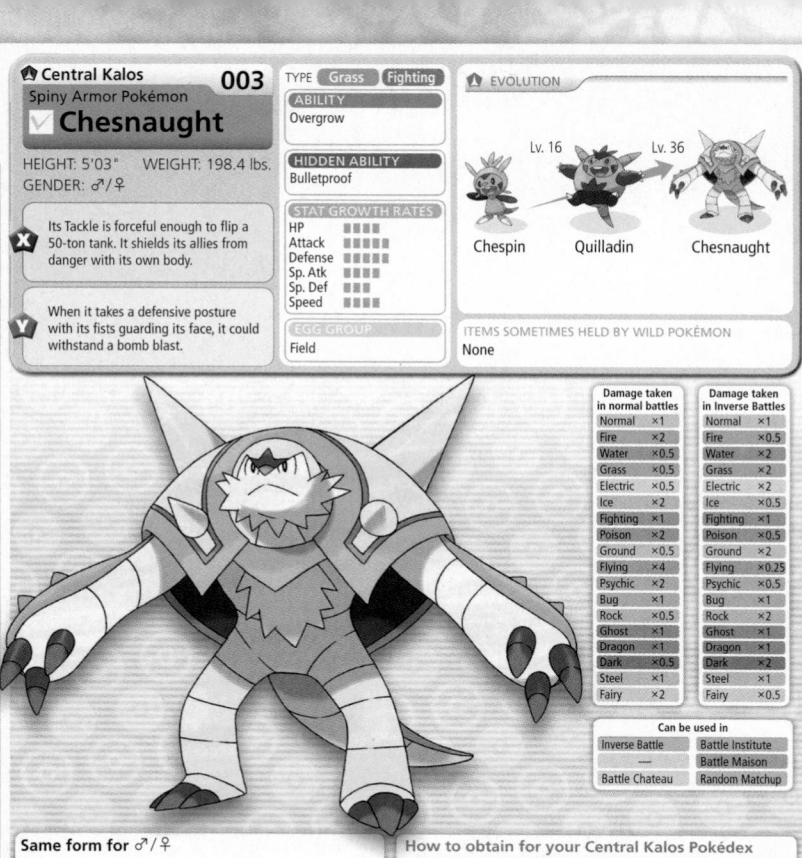

Damage taken in normal battles		Damage taken in Inverse Battles	
Normal	×1	Normal	×1
Fire	×2	Fire	×0.5
Water	×0.5	Water	×2
Grass	×0.5	Grass	×2
Electric	×0.5	Electric	×2
Ice	×2	Ice	×0.5
Fighting	×1	Fighting	×1
Poison	×2	Poison	×0.5
Ground	×0.5	Ground	×2
Flying	×4	Flying	×0.25
Psychic	×2	Psychic	×0.5
Bug	×1	Bug	×1
Rock	×0.5	Rock	×2
Ghost	×1	Ghost	×1
Dragon	×1	Dragon	×1
Dark	×0.5	Dark	×2
Steel	×1	Steel	×1
Fairy	×2	Fairy	×0.5

Can be used in	
Inverse Battle	Battle Institute
—	Battle Maison
Battle Chateau	Random Matchup

Same form for ♂/♀

How to obtain for your Central Kalos Pokédex

❶ Level up Quilladin to Lv. 36.
❷ Link Trade or transfer from another game.

❶ Level up Quilladin to Lv. 36.
❷ Link Trade or transfer from another game.

● LEVEL-UP MOVES

Lv.	Name	Type	Kind	Pow.	Acc.	PP	Range
1	Feint	Normal	Physical	30	100	10	Normal
1	Hammer Arm	Fighting	Physical	100	90	10	Normal
1	Belly Drum	Normal	Status	—	—	10	Self
1	Tackle	Normal	Physical	50	100	35	Normal
1	Growl	Normal	Status	—	100	40	Many Others
5	Vine Whip	Grass	Physical	45	100	25	Normal
8	Rollout	Rock	Physical	30	90	20	Normal
11	Bite	Dark	Physical	60	100	25	Normal
15	Leech Seed	Grass	Status	—	90	10	Normal
22	Pin Missile	Bug	Physical	25	95	20	Normal
26	Needle Arm	Grass	Physical	60	100	15	Normal
30	Take Down	Normal	Physical	90	85	20	Normal
35	Seed Bomb	Grass	Physical	80	100	15	Normal
36	Spiky Shield	Grass	Status	—	—	10	Self
41	Mud Shot	Ground	Special	55	95	15	Normal
44	Bulk Up	Fighting	Status	—	—	20	Self
48	Body Slam	Normal	Physical	85	100	15	Normal
52	Pain Split	Normal	Status	—	—	20	Normal
55	Wood Hammer	Grass	Physical	120	100	15	Normal
60	Hammer Arm	Fighting	Physical	100	90	10	Normal
70	Giga Impact	Normal	Physical	150	90	5	Normal
75	Spiky Shield	Grass	Status	—	—	10	Self

● TM & HM MOVES

No.	Name	Type	Kind	Pow.	Acc.	PP	Range
TM01	Hone Claws	Dark	Status	—	—	15	Self
TM02	Dragon Claw	Dragon	Physical	80	100	15	Normal
TM05	Roar	Normal	Status	—	—	20	Normal
TM06	Toxic	Poison	Status	—	90	10	Normal
TM08	Bulk Up	Fighting	Status	—	—	20	Self
TM10	Hidden Power	Normal	Special	60	100	15	Normal
TM11	Sunny Day	Fire	Status	—	—	5	Both Sides
TM12	Taunt	Dark	Status	—	100	20	Normal
TM15	Hyper Beam	Normal	Special	150	90	5	Normal
TM17	Protect	Normal	Status	—	—	10	Self
TM21	Frustration	Normal	Physical	—	100	20	Normal
TM22	Solar Beam	Grass	Special	120	100	10	Normal
TM23	Smack Down	Rock	Physical	50	100	15	Normal
TM26	Earthquake	Ground	Physical	100	100	10	Adjacent
TM27	Return	Normal	Physical	—	100	20	Normal
TM28	Dig	Ground	Physical	80	100	10	Normal
TM31	Brick Break	Fighting	Physical	75	100	15	Normal
TM32	Double Team	Normal	Status	—	—	15	Self
TM33	Reflect	Psychic	Status	—	—	20	Your Side
TM36	Sludge Bomb	Poison	Special	90	100	10	Normal
TM39	Rock Tomb	Rock	Physical	60	95	15	Normal
TM40	Aerial Ace	Flying	Physical	60	—	20	Normal
TM42	Facade	Normal	Physical	70	100	20	Normal
TM44	Rest	Psychic	Status	—	—	10	Self
TM45	Attract	Normal	Status	—	100	15	Normal
TM47	Low Sweep	Fighting	Physical	65	100	20	Normal
TM48	Round	Normal	Special	60	100	15	Normal
TM52	Focus Blast	Fighting	Special	120	70	5	Normal
TM53	Energy Ball	Grass	Special	90	100	10	Normal
TM56	Fling	Dark	Physical	—	100	10	Normal
TM65	Shadow Claw	Ghost	Physical	70	100	15	Normal
TM66	Payback	Dark	Physical	50	100	10	Normal
TM67	Retaliate	Normal	Physical	70	100	5	Normal

No.	Name	Type	Kind	Pow.	Acc.	PP	Range
TM68	Giga Impact	Normal	Physical	150	90	5	Normal
TM70	Flash	Normal	Status	—	100	20	Normal
TM71	Stone Edge	Rock	Physical	100	80	5	Normal
TM74	Gyro Ball	Steel	Physical	—	100	5	Normal
TM75	Swords Dance	Normal	Status	—	—	20	Self
TM78	Bulldoze	Ground	Physical	60	100	20	Adjacent
TM80	Rock Slide	Rock	Physical	75	90	10	Many Others
TM84	Poison Jab	Poison	Physical	80	100	20	Normal
TM86	Grass Knot	Grass	Special	—	100	20	Normal
TM87	Swagger	Normal	Status	—	90	15	Normal
TM88	Sleep Talk	Normal	Status	—	—	10	Self
TM90	Substitute	Normal	Status	—	—	10	Self
TM94	Rock Smash	Fighting	Physical	40	100	15	Normal
TM96	Nature Power	Normal	Status	—	—	20	Normal
TM98	Power-Up Punch	Fighting	Physical	40	100	20	Normal
TM100	Confide	Normal	Status	—	—	20	Normal
HM01	Cut	Normal	Physical	50	95	30	Normal
HM04	Strength	Normal	Physical	80	100	15	Normal

● MOVES TAUGHT BY PEOPLE

Name	Type	Kind	Pow.	Acc.	PP	Range
Grass Pledge	Grass	Special	80	100	10	Normal
Frenzy Plant	Grass	Special	150	90	5	Normal

Central Kalos

Fox Pokémon

Fennekin

004

HEIGHT: 1'04" WEIGHT: 20.7 lbs.
GENDER: ♂/♀

X Eating a twig fills it with energy, and its roomy ears give vent to air hotter than 390 degrees Fahrenheit.

Y As it walks, it munches on a twig in place of a snack. It intimidates opponents by puffing hot air out of its ears.

TYPE Fire

ABILITY
Blaze

HIDDEN ABILITY
Magician

STAT GROWTH RATES
HP	■
Attack	■■
Defense	■■
Sp. Atk	■■■
Sp. Def	■■■
Speed	■■■

EGG GROUP
Field

EVOLUTION

	Lv. 16		Lv. 36	
Fennekin		Braixen		Delphox

ITEMS SOMETIMES HELD BY WILD POKÉMON
None

Damage taken in normal battles		Damage taken in Inverse Battles		Can be used in
Normal	×1	Normal	×1	Inverse Battle
Fire	×0.5	Fire	×2	—
Water	×2	Water	×0.5	Battle Chateau
Grass	×0.5	Grass	×2	Battle Institute
Electric	×1	Electric	×1	Battle Maison
Ice	×0.5	Ice	×2	Random Matchup
Fighting	×1	Fighting	×1	
Poison	×1	Poison	×1	
Ground	×2	Ground	×0.5	
Flying	×1	Flying	×1	
Psychic	×1	Psychic	×1	
Bug	×0.5	Bug	×2	
Rock	×2	Rock	×0.5	
Ghost	×1	Ghost	×1	
Dragon	×1	Dragon	×1	
Dark	×1	Dark	×1	
Steel	×0.5	Steel	×2	
Fairy	×0.5	Fairy	×2	

How to obtain for your Central Kalos Pokédex

❶ Receive from Tierno in Aquacorde Town.
❷ Trade with Shauna after entering the Hall of Fame (if you chose Froakie at the beginning of the game).

❶ Receive from Tierno in Aquacorde Town.
❷ Trade with Shauna after entering the Hall of Fame (if you chose Froakie at the beginning of the game).

Same form for ♂/♀

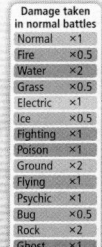
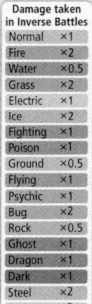

● LEVEL-UP MOVES

Lv.	Name	Type	Kind	Pow.	Acc.	PP	Range
1	Scratch	Normal	Physical	40	100	35	Normal
1	Tail Whip	Normal	Status	—	100	30	Many Others
5	Ember	Fire	Special	40	100	25	Normal
11	Howl	Normal	Status	—	—	40	Self
14	Flame Charge	Fire	Physical	50	100	20	Normal
17	Psybeam	Psychic	Special	65	100	20	Normal
20	Fire Spin	Fire	Special	35	85	15	Normal
25	Lucky Chant	Normal	Status	—	—	30	Your Side
27	Light Screen	Psychic	Status	—	—	30	Your Side
31	Psyshock	Psychic	Special	80	100	10	Normal
35	Flamethrower	Fire	Special	90	100	15	Normal
38	Will-O-Wisp	Fire	Status	—	85	15	Normal
41	Psychic	Psychic	Special	90	100	10	Normal
43	Sunny Day	Fire	Status	—	—	5	Both Sides
46	Magic Room	Psychic	Status	—	—	10	Both Sides
48	Fire Blast	Fire	Special	110	85	5	Normal

● TM & HM MOVES

No.	Name	Type	Kind	Pow.	Acc.	PP	Range
TM03	Psyshock	Psychic	Special	80	100	10	Normal
TM06	Toxic	Poison	Status	—	90	10	Normal
TM10	Hidden Power	Normal	Special	60	100	15	Normal
TM11	Sunny Day	Fire	Status	—	—	5	Both Sides
TM16	Light Screen	Psychic	Status	—	—	30	Your Side
TM17	Protect	Normal	Status	—	—	10	Self
TM18	Rain Dance	Water	Status	—	—	5	Both Sides
TM20	Safeguard	Normal	Status	—	—	25	Your Side
TM21	Frustration	Normal	Physical	—	100	20	Normal
TM22	Solar Beam	Grass	Special	120	100	10	Normal
TM27	Return	Normal	Physical	—	100	20	Normal
TM29	Psychic	Psychic	Special	90	100	10	Normal
TM32	Double Team	Normal	Status	—	—	15	Self
TM35	Flamethrower	Fire	Special	90	100	15	Normal
TM38	Fire Blast	Fire	Special	110	85	5	Normal
TM42	Facade	Normal	Physical	70	100	20	Normal
TM43	Flame Charge	Fire	Physical	50	100	20	Normal
TM44	Rest	Psychic	Status	—	—	10	Self
TM45	Attract	Normal	Status	—	100	15	Normal
TM46	Thief	Dark	Physical	60	100	25	Normal
TM48	Round	Normal	Special	60	100	15	Normal
TM49	Echoed Voice	Normal	Special	40	100	15	Normal
TM50	Overheat	Fire	Special	130	90	5	Normal
TM59	Incinerate	Fire	Special	60	100	15	Many Others
TM61	Will-O-Wisp	Fire	Status	—	85	15	Normal
TM63	Embargo	Dark	Status	—	100	15	Normal
TM77	Psych Up	Normal	Status	—	—	10	Normal
TM85	Dream Eater	Psychic	Special	100	100	15	Normal
TM86	Grass Knot	Grass	Special	—	100	20	Normal
TM87	Swagger	Normal	Status	—	90	15	Normal
TM88	Sleep Talk	Normal	Status	—	—	10	Self
TM90	Substitute	Normal	Status	—	—	10	Self
TM98	Power-Up Punch	Fighting	Physical	40	100	20	Normal

No.	Name	Type	Kind	Pow.	Acc.	PP	Range
TM100	Confide	Normal	Status	—	—	20	Normal
HM01	Cut	Normal	Physical	50	95	30	Normal

● MOVES TAUGHT BY PEOPLE

Name	Type	Kind	Pow.	Acc.	PP	Range
Fire Pledge	Fire	Special	80	100	10	Normal

● EGG MOVES

Name	Type	Kind	Pow.	Acc.	PP	Range
Wish	Normal	Status	—	—	10	Self
Hypnosis	Psychic	Status	—	60	20	Normal
Heat Wave	Fire	Special	95	90	10	Many Others
Magic Coat	Psychic	Status	—	—	15	Self

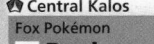

AFTER THE HALL OF FAME

CENTRAL KALOS

005

Braixen

COASTAL KALOS

MOUNTAIN KALOS

ADVENTURE DATA

Central Kalos — 005

Fox Pokémon

Braixen

HEIGHT: 3'03" WEIGHT: 32.0 lbs.
GENDER: ♂/♀

X It has a twig stuck in its tail. With friction from its tail fur, it sets the twig on fire and launches into battle.

Y When the twig is plucked from its tail, friction sets the twig alight. The flame is used to send signals to its allies.

TYPE Fire

ABILITY
Blaze

HIDDEN ABILITY
Magician

STAT GROWTH RATES
HP	■ ■ ■
Attack	■ ■ ■
Defense	■ ■ ■
Sp. Atk	■ ■ ■ ■
Sp. Def	■ ■ ■
Speed	■ ■ ■ ■

EGG GROUP
Field

EVOLUTION

Lv. 16	Lv. 36
Fennekin	Braixen	Delphox

ITEMS SOMETIMES HELD BY WILD POKÉMON
None

Can be used in
Inverse Battle
—
Battle Chateau
Battle Institute
Battle Maison
Random Matchup

Damage taken in normal battles	
Normal	×1
Fire	×0.5
Water	×2
Grass	×0.5
Electric	×1
Ice	×0.5
Fighting	×1
Poison	×1
Ground	×2
Flying	×1
Psychic	×1
Bug	×0.5
Rock	×2
Ghost	×1
Dragon	×1
Dark	×1
Steel	×0.5
Fairy	×0.5

Damage taken in Inverse Battles	
Normal	×1
Fire	×2
Water	×0.5
Grass	×2
Electric	×1
Ice	×2
Fighting	×1
Poison	×1
Ground	×0.5
Flying	×1
Psychic	×1
Bug	×2
Rock	×0.5
Ghost	×1
Dragon	×1
Dark	×1
Steel	×2
Fairy	×2

How to obtain for your Central Kalos Pokédex

❶ Level up Fennekin to Lv. 16.
❷ Link Trade or transfer from another game.

❶ Level up Fennekin to Lv. 16.
❷ Link Trade or transfer from another game.

Same form for ♂/♀

● LEVEL-UP MOVES

Lv.	Name	Type	Kind	Pow.	Acc.	PP	Range
1	Scratch	Normal	Physical	40	100	35	Normal
1	Tail Whip	Normal	Status	—	100	30	Many Others
5	Ember	Fire	Special	40	100	25	Normal
11	Howl	Normal	Status	—	—	40	Self
14	Flame Charge	Fire	Physical	50	100	20	Normal
18	Psybeam	Psychic	Special	65	100	20	Normal
22	Fire Spin	Fire	Special	35	85	15	Normal
27	Lucky Chant	Normal	Status	—	—	30	Your Side
30	Light Screen	Psychic	Status	—	—	30	Your Side
34	Psyshock	Psychic	Special	80	100	10	Normal
41	Flamethrower	Fire	Special	90	100	15	Normal
45	Will-O-Wisp	Fire	Status	—	85	15	Normal
48	Psychic	Psychic	Special	90	100	10	Normal
51	Sunny Day	Fire	Status	—	—	5	Both Sides
53	Magic Room	Psychic	Status	—	—	10	Both Sides
55	Fire Blast	Fire	Special	110	85	5	Normal

● TM & HM MOVES

No.	Name	Type	Kind	Pow.	Acc.	PP	Range
TM03	Psyshock	Psychic	Special	80	100	10	Normal
TM06	Toxic	Poison	Status	—	90	10	Normal
TM10	Hidden Power	Normal	Special	60	100	15	Normal
TM11	Sunny Day	Fire	Status	—	—	5	Both Sides
TM16	Light Screen	Psychic	Status	—	—	30	Your Side
TM17	Protect	Normal	Status	—	—	10	Self
TM18	Rain Dance	Water	Status	—	—	5	Both Sides
TM20	Safeguard	Normal	Status	—	—	25	Your Side
TM21	Frustration	Normal	Physical	—	100	20	Normal
TM22	Solar Beam	Grass	Special	120	100	10	Normal
TM27	Return	Normal	Physical	—	100	20	Normal
TM29	Psychic	Psychic	Special	90	100	10	Normal
TM32	Double Team	Normal	Status	—	—	15	Self
TM35	Flamethrower	Fire	Special	90	100	15	Normal
TM38	Fire Blast	Fire	Special	110	85	5	Normal
TM42	Facade	Normal	Physical	70	100	20	Normal
TM43	Flame Charge	Fire	Physical	50	100	20	Normal
TM44	Rest	Psychic	Status	—	—	10	Self
TM45	Attract	Normal	Status	—	100	15	Normal
TM46	Thief	Dark	Physical	60	100	25	Normal
TM48	Round	Normal	Special	60	100	15	Normal
TM49	Echoed Voice	Normal	Special	40	100	15	Normal
TM50	Overheat	Fire	Special	130	90	5	Normal
TM59	Incinerate	Fire	Special	60	100	15	Many Others
TM61	Will-O-Wisp	Fire	Status	—	85	15	Normal
TM63	Embargo	Dark	Status	—	100	15	Normal
TM77	Psych Up	Normal	Status	—	—	10	Normal
TM85	Dream Eater	Psychic	Special	100	100	15	Normal
TM86	Grass Knot	Grass	Special	—	100	20	Normal
TM87	Swagger	Normal	Status	—	90	15	Normal
TM88	Sleep Talk	Normal	Status	—	—	10	Self
TM90	Substitute	Normal	Status	—	—	10	Self
TM98	Power-Up Punch	Fighting	Physical	40	100	20	Normal

No.	Name	Type	Kind	Pow.	Acc.	PP	Range
TM100	Confide	Normal	Status	—	—	20	Normal
HM01	Cut	Normal	Physical	50	95	30	Normal

● MOVES TAUGHT BY PEOPLE

Name	Type	Kind	Pow.	Acc.	PP	Range
Fire Pledge	Fire	Special	80	100	10	Normal

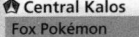 Central Kalos — 006

AFTER THE HALL OF FAME

CENTRAL KALOS | 006 | Delphox

COASTAL KALOS

MOUNTAIN KALOS

ADVENTURE DATA

Fox Pokémon
☑ Delphox

HEIGHT: 4'11" WEIGHT: 86.0 lbs.
GENDER: ♂ / ♀

X It gazes into the flame at the tip of its branch to achieve a focused state, which allows it to see into the future.

Y Using psychic power, it generates a fiery vortex of 5,400 degrees Fahrenheit, incinerating foes swept into this whirl of flame.

ABILITY
Blaze

HIDDEN ABILITY
Magician

STAT GROWTH RATES

HP	■■■
Attack	■■■■
Defense	■■■
Sp. Atk	■■■■■■
Sp. Def	■■■■
Speed	■■■■■

EGG GROUP
Field

EVOLUTION

Lv. 16   Lv. 36

Fennekin   Braixen   Delphox

ITEMS SOMETIMES HELD BY WILD POKÉMON
None

Damage taken in normal battles			Damage taken in Inverse Battles	
Normal	×1		Normal	×1
Fire	×0.5		Fire	×2
Water	×2		Water	×0.5
Grass	×0.5		Grass	×2
Electric	×1		Electric	×1
Ice	×0.5		Ice	×2
Fighting	×0.5		Fighting	×2
Poison	×1		Poison	×1
Ground	×2		Ground	×0.5
Flying	×1		Flying	×1
Psychic	×0.5		Psychic	×2
Bug	×1		Bug	×1
Rock	×2		Rock	×0.5
Ghost	×2		Ghost	×0.5
Dragon	×1		Dragon	×1
Dark	×2		Dark	×0.5
Steel	×0.5		Steel	×2
Fairy	×2		Fairy	×2

Can be used in	
Inverse Battle	Battle Institute
—	Battle Maison
Battle Chateau	Random Matchup

Same form for ♂ / ♀

How to obtain for your Central Kalos Pokédex

❶ Level up Braixen to Lv. 36.
❷ Link Trade or transfer from another game.

❶ Level up Braixen to Lv. 36.
❷ Link Trade or transfer from another game.

● LEVEL-UP MOVES

Lv.	Name	Type	Kind	Pow.	Acc.	PP	Range
1	Future Sight	Psychic	Special	120	100	10	Normal
1	Role Play	Psychic	Status	—	—	10	Normal
1	Switcheroo	Dark	Status	—	100	10	Normal
1	Shadow Ball	Ghost	Special	80	100	15	Normal
1	Scratch	Normal	Physical	40	100	35	Many Others
1	Tail Whip	Normal	Status	—	100	30	Many Others
5	Ember	Fire	Special	40	100	25	Normal
11	Howl	Normal	Status	—	—	40	Self
14	Flame Charge	Fire	Physical	50	100	20	Normal
18	Psybeam	Psychic	Special	65	100	20	Normal
22	Fire Spin	Fire	Special	35	85	15	Normal
27	Lucky Chant	Normal	Status	—	—	30	Your Side
30	Light Screen	Psychic	Status	—	—	30	Your Side
34	Psyshock	Psychic	Special	80	100	10	Normal
36	Mystical Fire	Fire	Special	65	100	10	Normal
42	Flamethrower	Fire	Special	90	100	15	Normal
47	Will-O-Wisp	Fire	Status	—	85	15	Normal
51	Psychic	Psychic	Special	90	100	10	Normal
55	Sunny Day	Fire	Status	—	—	5	Both Sides
58	Magic Room	Psychic	Status	—	—	10	Both Sides
61	Fire Blast	Fire	Special	110	85	5	Normal
69	Future Sight	Psychic	Special	120	100	10	Normal
75	Mystical Fire	Fire	Special	65	100	10	Normal

● TM & HM MOVES

No.	Name	Type	Kind	Pow.	Acc.	PP	Range
TM03	Psyshock	Psychic	Special	80	100	10	Normal
TM04	Calm Mind	Psychic	Status	—	—	20	Self
TM06	Toxic	Poison	Status	—	90	10	Normal
TM10	Hidden Power	Normal	Special	60	100	15	Normal
TM11	Sunny Day	Fire	Status	—	—	5	Both Sides
TM15	Hyper Beam	Normal	Special	150	90	5	Normal
TM16	Light Screen	Psychic	Status	—	—	30	Your Side
TM17	Protect	Normal	Status	—	—	10	Self
TM18	Rain Dance	Water	Status	—	—	5	Both Sides
TM20	Safeguard	Normal	Status	—	—	25	Your Side
TM21	Frustration	Normal	Physical	—	100	20	Normal
TM22	Solar Beam	Grass	Special	120	100	10	Normal
TM27	Return	Normal	Physical	—	100	20	Normal
TM29	Psychic	Psychic	Special	90	100	10	Normal
TM30	Shadow Ball	Ghost	Special	80	100	15	Normal
TM32	Double Team	Normal	Status	—	—	15	Self
TM35	Flamethrower	Fire	Special	90	100	15	Normal
TM38	Fire Blast	Fire	Special	110	85	5	Normal
TM42	Facade	Normal	Physical	70	100	20	Normal
TM43	Flame Charge	Fire	Physical	50	100	20	Normal
TM44	Rest	Psychic	Status	—	—	10	Self
TM45	Attract	Normal	Status	—	100	15	Normal
TM46	Thief	Dark	Physical	60	100	25	Normal
TM48	Round	Normal	Special	60	100	15	Normal
TM49	Echoed Voice	Normal	Special	40	100	15	Normal
TM50	Overheat	Fire	Special	130	90	5	Normal
TM59	Incinerate	Fire	Special	60	100	15	Many Others
TM61	Will-O-Wisp	Fire	Status	—	85	15	Normal
TM63	Embargo	Dark	Status	—	100	15	Normal
TM68	Giga Impact	Normal	Physical	150	90	5	Normal
TM77	Psych Up	Normal	Status	—	—	10	Normal
TM85	Dream Eater	Psychic	Special	100	100	15	Normal
TM86	Grass Knot	Grass	Special	—	100	20	Normal
TM87	Swagger	Normal	Status	—	90	15	Normal
TM88	Sleep Talk	Normal	Status	—	—	10	Self
TM90	Substitute	Normal	Status	—	—	10	Self
TM92	Trick Room	Psychic	Status	—	—	5	Both Sides
TM98	Power-Up Punch	Fighting	Physical	40	100	20	Normal
TM100	Confide	Normal	Status	—	—	20	Normal
HM01	Cut	Normal	Physical	50	95	30	Normal

● MOVES TAUGHT BY PEOPLE

Name	Type	Kind	Pow.	Acc.	PP	Range
Fire Pledge	Fire	Special	80	100	10	Normal
Blast Burn	Fire	Special	150	90	5	Normal

AFTER THE HALL OF FAME

CENTRAL KALOS

007

Froakie

COASTAL KALOS

MOUNTAIN KALOS

ADVENTURE DATA

🏠 Central Kalos 007
Bubble Frog Pokémon
☑ Froakie

HEIGHT: 1'00" WEIGHT: 15.4 lbs.
GENDER: ♂ / ♀

X It secretes flexible bubbles from its chest and back. The bubbles reduce the damage it would otherwise take when attacked.

Y It protects its skin by covering its body in delicate bubbles. Beneath its happy-go-lucky air, it keeps a watchful eye on its surroundings.

TYPE Water

ABILITY
Torrent

HIDDEN ABILITY
Protean

STAT GROWTH RATES
HP	■ ■
Attack	■ ■ ■
Defense	■ ■
Sp. Atk	■ ■ ■
Sp. Def	■ ■
Speed	■ ■ ■ ■

EGG GROUP
Water 1

🏠 EVOLUTION

Froakie — Lv. 16 → Frogadier — Lv. 36 → Greninja

ITEMS SOMETIMES HELD BY WILD POKÉMON
None

Damage taken in normal battles		Damage taken in Inverse Battles	
Normal	×1	Normal	×1
Fire	×0.5	Fire	×2
Water	×0.5	Water	×2
Grass	×2	Grass	×0.5
Electric	×2	Electric	×0.5
Ice	×0.5	Ice	×2
Fighting	×1	Fighting	×1
Poison	×1	Poison	×1
Ground	×1	Ground	×1
Flying	×1	Flying	×1
Psychic	×1	Psychic	×1
Bug	×1	Bug	×1
Rock	×1	Rock	×1
Ghost	×1	Ghost	×1
Dragon	×1	Dragon	×1
Dark	×1	Dark	×1
Steel	×0.5	Steel	×2
Fairy	×1	Fairy	×1

Can be used in	
Inverse Battle	Battle Institute
—	Battle Maison
Battle Chateau	Random Matchup

Same form for ♂ / ♀

How to obtain for your Central Kalos Pokédex

❶ Receive from Tierno in Aquacorde Town.
❷ Trade with Shauna after entering the Hall of Fame.

❶ Receive from Tierno in Aquacorde Town.
❷ Trade with Shauna after entering the Hall of Fame.

● LEVEL-UP MOVES

Lv.	Name	Type	Kind	Pow.	Acc.	PP	Range
1	Pound	Normal	Physical	40	100	35	Normal
1	Growl	Normal	Status	—	100	40	Many Others
5	Bubble	Water	Special	40	100	30	Many Others
8	Quick Attack	Normal	Physical	40	100	30	Normal
10	Lick	Ghost	Physical	30	100	30	Normal
14	Water Pulse	Water	Special	60	100	20	Normal
18	Smokescreen	Normal	Status	—	100	20	Normal
21	Round	Normal	Special	60	100	15	Normal
25	Fling	Dark	Physical	—	100	10	Normal
29	Smack Down	Rock	Physical	50	100	15	Normal
35	Substitute	Normal	Status	—	—	10	Self
39	Bounce	Flying	Physical	85	85	5	Normal
43	Double Team	Normal	Status	—	—	15	Self
48	Hydro Pump	Water	Special	110	80	5	Normal

● TM & HM MOVES

No.	Name	Type	Kind	Pow.	Acc.	PP	Range
TM06	Toxic	Poison	Status	—	90	10	Normal
TM10	Hidden Power	Normal	Special	60	100	15	Normal
TM12	Taunt	Dark	Status	—	100	20	Normal
TM13	Ice Beam	Ice	Special	90	100	10	Normal
TM14	Blizzard	Ice	Special	110	70	5	Many Others
TM17	Protect	Normal	Status	—	—	10	Self
TM18	Rain Dance	Water	Status	—	—	5	Both Sides
TM21	Frustration	Normal	Physical	—	100	20	Normal
TM23	Smack Down	Rock	Physical	50	100	15	Normal
TM27	Return	Normal	Physical	—	100	20	Normal
TM28	Dig	Ground	Physical	80	100	10	Normal
TM32	Double Team	Normal	Status	—	—	15	Self
TM39	Rock Tomb	Rock	Physical	60	95	15	Normal
TM40	Aerial Ace	Flying	Physical	60	—	20	Normal
TM42	Facade	Normal	Physical	70	100	20	Normal
TM44	Rest	Psychic	Status	—	—	10	Self
TM45	Attract	Normal	Status	—	100	15	Normal
TM46	Thief	Dark	Physical	60	100	25	Normal
TM48	Round	Normal	Special	60	100	15	Normal
TM49	Echoed Voice	Normal	Special	40	100	15	Normal
TM55	Scald	Water	Special	80	100	15	Normal
TM56	Fling	Dark	Physical	—	100	10	Normal
TM62	Acrobatics	Flying	Physical	55	100	15	Normal
TM80	Rock Slide	Rock	Physical	75	90	10	Many Others
TM86	Grass Knot	Grass	Special	—	100	20	Normal
TM87	Swagger	Normal	Status	—	90	15	Normal
TM88	Sleep Talk	Normal	Status	—	—	10	Self
TM89	U-turn	Bug	Physical	70	100	20	Normal
TM90	Substitute	Normal	Status	—	—	10	Self
TM94	Rock Smash	Fighting	Physical	40	100	15	Normal
TM98	Power-Up Punch	Fighting	Physical	40	100	20	Normal
TM100	Confide	Normal	Status	—	—	20	Normal
HM01	Cut	Normal	Physical	50	95	30	Normal

No.	Name	Type	Kind	Pow.	Acc.	PP	Range
HM03	Surf	Water	Special	90	100	15	Adjacent
HM04	Strength	Normal	Physical	80	100	15	Normal
HM05	Waterfall	Water	Physical	80	100	15	Normal

● MOVES TAUGHT BY PEOPLE

Name	Type	Kind	Pow.	Acc.	PP	Range
Water Pledge	Water	Special	80	100	10	Normal

● EGG MOVES

Name	Type	Kind	Pow.	Acc.	PP	Range
Bestow	Normal	Status	—	—	15	Normal
Mind Reader	Normal	Status	—	—	5	Normal
Toxic Spikes	Poison	Status	—	—	20	Other Side
Mud Sport	Ground	Status	—	—	15	Both Sides
Camouflage	Normal	Status	—	—	20	Self
Water Sport	Water	Status	—	—	15	Both Sides

Central Kalos

008

Bubble Frog Pokémon

☑ **Frogadier**

HEIGHT: 2'00" WEIGHT: 24.0 lbs.
GENDER: ♂/♀

X It can throw bubble-covered pebbles with precise control, hitting empty cans up to a hundred feet away.

Y Its swiftness is unparalleled. It can scale a tower of more than 2,000 feet in a minute's time.

TYPE Water

ABILITY
Torrent

HIDDEN ABILITY
Protean

STAT GROWTH RATES
HP	■■
Attack	■■■
Defense	■■
Sp. Atk	■■■■
Sp. Def	■■■
Speed	■■■■■

EGG GROUP
Water 1

EVOLUTION

Lv. 16 → Lv. 36

Froakie   Frogadier   Greninja

ITEMS SOMETIMES HELD BY WILD POKÉMON
None

Damage taken in normal battles		Damage taken in Inverse Battles	
Normal	×1	Normal	×1
Fire	×0.5	Fire	×2
Water	×0.5	Water	×2
Grass	×2	Grass	×0.5
Electric	×2	Electric	×0.5
Ice	×0.5	Ice	×2
Fighting	×1	Fighting	×1
Poison	×1	Poison	×1
Ground	×1	Ground	×1
Flying	×1	Flying	×1
Psychic	×1	Psychic	×1
Bug	×1	Bug	×1
Rock	×1	Rock	×1
Ghost	×1	Ghost	×1
Dragon	×1	Dragon	×1
Dark	×1	Dark	×1
Steel	×0.5	Steel	×2
Fairy	×1	Fairy	×1

Can be used in	
Inverse Battle	Battle Institute
—	Battle Maison
Battle Chateau	Random Matchup

Same form for ♂/♀

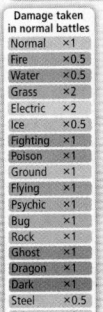

How to obtain for your Central Kalos Pokédex

❶ Level up Froakie to Lv. 16.
❷ Link Trade or transfer from another game.

❶ Level up Froakie to Lv. 16.
❷ Link Trade or transfer from another game.

LEVEL-UP MOVES

Lv.	Name	Type	Kind	Pow.	Acc.	PP	Range
1	Pound	Normal	Physical	40	100	35	Normal
1	Growl	Normal	Status	—	100	40	Many Others
5	Bubble	Water	Special	40	100	30	Many Others
8	Quick Attack	Normal	Physical	40	100	30	Normal
10	Lick	Ghost	Physical	30	100	30	Normal
14	Water Pulse	Water	Special	60	100	20	Normal
20	Smokescreen	Normal	Status	—	100	20	Normal
23	Round	Normal	Special	60	100	15	Normal
28	Fling	Dark	Physical	—	100	10	Normal
33	Smack Down	Rock	Physical	50	100	15	Normal
38	Substitute	Normal	Status	—	—	10	Self
44	Bounce	Flying	Physical	85	85	5	Normal
48	Double Team	Normal	Status	—	—	15	Self
55	Hydro Pump	Water	Special	110	80	5	Normal

TM & HM MOVES

No.	Name	Type	Kind	Pow.	Acc.	PP	Range
TM06	Toxic	Poison	Status	—	90	10	Normal
TM10	Hidden Power	Normal	Special	60	100	15	Normal
TM12	Taunt	Dark	Status	—	100	20	Normal
TM13	Ice Beam	Ice	Special	90	100	10	Normal
TM14	Blizzard	Ice	Special	110	70	5	Many Others
TM17	Protect	Normal	Status	—	—	10	Self
TM18	Rain Dance	Water	Status	—	—	5	Both Sides
TM21	Frustration	Normal	Physical	—	100	20	Normal
TM23	Smack Down	Rock	Physical	50	100	15	Normal
TM27	Return	Normal	Physical	—	100	20	Normal
TM28	Dig	Ground	Physical	80	100	10	Normal
TM32	Double Team	Normal	Status	—	—	15	Self
TM39	Rock Tomb	Rock	Physical	60	95	15	Normal
TM40	Aerial Ace	Flying	Physical	60	—	20	Normal
TM42	Facade	Normal	Physical	70	100	20	Normal
TM44	Rest	Psychic	Status	—	—	10	Self
TM45	Attract	Normal	Status	—	100	15	Normal
TM46	Thief	Dark	Physical	60	100	25	Normal
TM48	Round	Normal	Special	60	100	15	Normal
TM49	Echoed Voice	Normal	Special	40	100	15	Normal
TM55	Scald	Water	Special	80	100	15	Normal
TM56	Fling	Dark	Physical	—	100	10	Normal
TM62	Acrobatics	Flying	Physical	55	100	15	Normal
TM80	Rock Slide	Rock	Physical	75	90	10	Many Others
TM86	Grass Knot	Grass	Special	—	100	20	Normal
TM87	Swagger	Normal	Status	—	90	15	Normal
TM88	Sleep Talk	Normal	Status	—	—	10	Self
TM89	U-turn	Bug	Physical	70	100	20	Normal
TM90	Substitute	Normal	Status	—	—	10	Self
TM94	Rock Smash	Fighting	Physical	40	100	15	Normal
TM97	Dark Pulse	Dark	Special	80	100	15	Normal
TM98	Power-Up Punch	Fighting	Physical	40	100	20	Normal
TM100	Confide	Normal	Status	—	—	20	Normal

No.	Name	Type	Kind	Pow.	Acc.	PP	Range
HM01	Cut	Normal	Physical	50	95	30	Normal
HM03	Surf	Water	Special	90	100	15	Adjacent
HM04	Strength	Normal	Physical	80	100	15	Normal
HM05	Waterfall	Water	Physical	80	100	15	Normal

MOVES TAUGHT BY PEOPLE

Name	Type	Kind	Pow.	Acc.	PP	Range
Water Pledge	Water	Special	80	100	10	Normal

AFTER THE HALL OF FAME

CENTRAL KALOS

008

Frogadier

COASTAL KALOS

MOUNTAIN KALOS

ADVENTURE DATA

AFTER THE HALL OF FAME

CENTRAL KALOS
009
Greninja

COASTAL KALOS

MOUNTAIN KALOS

ADVENTURE DATA

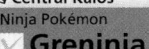

Central Kalos 009

Ninja Pokémon

☑ Greninja

HEIGHT: 4'11"   WEIGHT: 88.2 lbs.
GENDER: ♂ / ♀

X It creates throwing stars out of compressed water. When it spins them and throws them at high speed, these stars can split metal in two.

Y It appears and vanishes with a ninja's grace. It toys with its enemies using swift movements, while slicing them with throwing stars of sharpest water.

TYPE Water Dark

ABILITY
Torrent

HIDDEN ABILITY
Protean

STAT GROWTH RATES

HP	▪▪▪
Attack	▪▪▪▪▪
Defense	▪▪▪
Sp. Atk	▪▪▪▪▪
Sp. Def	▪▪▪
Speed	▪▪▪▪▪▪▪

EGG GROUP
Water 1

⬆ EVOLUTION

Froakie   Lv. 16 Frogadier   Lv. 36 Greninja

ITEMS SOMETIMES HELD BY WILD POKÉMON
None

Damage taken in normal battles		Damage taken in Inverse Battles	
Normal	×1	Normal	×1
Fire	×0.5	Fire	×2
Water	×0.5	Water	×2
Grass	×2	Grass	×0.5
Electric	×2	Electric	×0.5
Ice	×0.5	Ice	×2
Fighting	×2	Fighting	×0.5
Poison	×1	Poison	×1
Ground	×1	Ground	×1
Flying	×1	Flying	×1
Psychic	×0	Psychic	×2
Bug	×2	Bug	×0.5
Rock	×1	Rock	×1
Ghost	×2	Ghost	×0.5
Dragon	×1	Dragon	×1
Dark	×0.5	Dark	×2
Steel	×0.5	Steel	×2
Fairy	×2	Fairy	×0.5

Can be used in	
Inverse Battle	Battle Institute
—	Battle Maison
Battle Chateau	Random Matchup

Same form for ♂ / ♀

How to obtain for your Central Kalos Pokédex

❶ Level up Frogadier to Lv. 36.
❷ Link Trade or transfer from another game.

❶ Level up Frogadier to Lv. 36.
❷ Link Trade or transfer from another game.

● LEVEL-UP MOVES

Lv.	Name	Type	Kind	Pow.	Acc.	PP	Range
1	Night Slash	Dark	Physical	70	100	15	Normal
1	Role Play	Psychic	Status	—	—	10	Normal
1	Mat Block	Fighting	Status	—	—	10	Your Side
1	Pound	Normal	Physical	40	100	35	Normal
1	Growl	Normal	Status	—	100	40	Many Others
5	Bubble	Water	Special	40	100	30	Many Others
8	Quick Attack	Normal	Physical	40	100	30	Normal
10	Lick	Ghost	Physical	30	100	30	Normal
14	Water Pulse	Water	Special	60	100	20	Normal
20	Smokescreen	Normal	Status	—	100	20	Normal
23	Shadow Sneak	Ghost	Physical	40	100	30	Normal
28	Spikes	Ground	Status	—	—	20	Other Side
33	Feint Attack	Dark	Physical	60	—	20	Normal
36	Water Shuriken	Water	Physical	15	100	20	Normal
43	Substitute	Normal	Status	—	—	10	Self
49	Extrasensory	Psychic	Special	80	100	20	Normal
52	Double Team	Normal	Status	—	—	15	Self
56	Haze	Ice	Status	—	—	30	Both Sides
60	Hydro Pump	Water	Special	110	80	5	Normal
70	Night Slash	Dark	Physical	70	100	15	Normal
75	Water Shuriken	Water	Physical	15	100	20	Normal

● TM & HM MOVES

No.	Name	Type	Kind	Pow.	Acc.	PP	Range
TM06	Toxic	Poison	Status	—	90	10	Normal
TM10	Hidden Power	Normal	Special	60	100	15	Normal
TM12	Taunt	Dark	Status	—	100	20	Normal
TM13	Ice Beam	Ice	Special	90	100	10	Normal
TM14	Blizzard	Ice	Special	110	70	5	Many Others
TM15	Hyper Beam	Normal	Special	150	90	5	Normal
TM17	Protect	Normal	Status	—	—	10	Self
TM18	Rain Dance	Water	Status	—	—	5	Both Sides
TM21	Frustration	Normal	Physical	—	100	20	Normal
TM23	Smack Down	Rock	Physical	50	100	15	Normal
TM27	Return	Normal	Physical	—	100	20	Normal
TM28	Dig	Ground	Physical	80	100	10	Normal
TM32	Double Team	Normal	Status	—	—	15	Self
TM39	Rock Tomb	Rock	Physical	60	95	15	Normal
TM40	Aerial Ace	Flying	Physical	60	—	20	Normal
TM42	Facade	Normal	Physical	70	100	20	Normal
TM44	Rest	Psychic	Status	—	—	10	Self
TM45	Attract	Normal	Status	—	100	15	Normal
TM46	Thief	Dark	Physical	60	100	25	Normal
TM48	Round	Normal	Special	60	100	15	Normal
TM49	Echoed Voice	Normal	Special	40	100	15	Normal
TM55	Scald	Water	Special	80	100	15	Normal
TM56	Fling	Dark	Physical	—	100	10	Normal
TM62	Acrobatics	Flying	Physical	55	100	15	Normal
TM68	Giga Impact	Normal	Physical	150	90	5	Normal
TM80	Rock Slide	Rock	Physical	75	90	10	Many Others
TM86	Grass Knot	Grass	Special	—	100	20	Normal
TM87	Swagger	Normal	Status	—	90	15	Normal
TM88	Sleep Talk	Normal	Status	—	—	10	Self
TM89	U-turn	Bug	Physical	70	100	20	Normal
TM90	Substitute	Normal	Status	—	—	10	Self
TM94	Rock Smash	Fighting	Physical	40	100	15	Normal
TM97	Dark Pulse	Dark	Special	80	100	15	Normal

No.	Name	Type	Kind	Pow.	Acc.	PP	Range
TM98	Power-Up Punch	Fighting	Physical	40	100	20	Normal
TM100	Confide	Normal	Status	—	—	20	Normal
HM01	Cut	Normal	Physical	50	95	30	Normal
HM03	Surf	Water	Special	90	100	15	Adjacent
HM04	Strength	Normal	Physical	80	100	15	Normal
HM05	Waterfall	Water	Physical	80	100	15	Normal

● MOVES TAUGHT BY PEOPLE

Name	Type	Kind	Pow.	Acc.	PP	Range
Water Pledge	Water	Special	80	100	10	Normal
Hydro Cannon	Water	Special	150	90	5	Normal

⬛ Central Kalos

Digging Pokémon

☑ Bunnelby

010

HEIGHT: 1'04" WEIGHT: 11.0 lbs.
GENDER: ♂/♀

TYPE Normal

ABILITIES
Pickup
Cheek Pouch

HIDDEN ABILITY
Huge Power

STAT GROWTH RATES
HP	▪▪
Attack	▪▪
Defense	▪▪
Sp. Atk	▪▪
Sp. Def	▪▪
Speed	▪▪▪

EGG GROUP
Field

X They use their large ears to dig burrows. They will dig the whole night through.

Y It has ears like shovels. Digging holes strengthens its ears so much that they can sever thick roots effortlessly.

⬛ EVOLUTION

Lv. 20

Bunnelby → Diggersby

ITEMS SOMETIMES HELD BY WILD POKÉMON
None

Damage taken in normal battles		Damage taken in Inverse Battles	
Normal	×1	Normal	×1
Fire	×1	Fire	×1
Water	×1	Water	×1
Grass	×1	Grass	×1
Electric	×1	Electric	×1
Ice	×1	Ice	×1
Fighting	×2	Fighting	×0.5
Poison	×1	Poison	×1
Ground	×1	Ground	×1
Flying	×1	Flying	×1
Psychic	×1	Psychic	×1
Bug	×1	Bug	×1
Rock	×1	Rock	×1
Ghost	×0	Ghost	×2
Dragon	×1	Dragon	×1
Dark	×1	Dark	×1
Steel	×1	Steel	×1
Fairy	×1	Fairy	×1

Can be used in
Inverse Battle
—
Battle Chateau
Battle Institute
Battle Maison
Random Matchup

How to obtain for your Central Kalos Pokédex

❶ Catch in the tall grass on Route 2.

❷ Catch in the tall grass on Route 3.

❶ Catch in the tall grass on Route 2.

❷ Catch in the tall grass on Route 3.

Same form for ♂/♀

● LEVEL-UP MOVES

Lv.	Name	Type	Kind	Pow.	Acc.	PP	Range
1	Tackle	Normal	Physical	50	100	35	Normal
1	Agility	Psychic	Status	—	—	30	Self
1	Leer	Normal	Status	—	100	30	Many Others
7	Quick Attack	Normal	Physical	40	100	30	Normal
10	Double Slap	Normal	Physical	15	85	10	Normal
13	Mud-Slap	Ground	Special	20	100	10	Normal
15	Take Down	Normal	Physical	90	85	20	Normal
18	Mud Shot	Ground	Special	55	95	15	Normal
20	Double Kick	Fighting	Physical	30	100	30	Normal
25	Odor Sleuth	Normal	Status	—	—	40	Normal
29	Flail	Normal	Physical	—	100	15	Normal
33	Dig	Ground	Physical	80	100	10	Normal
38	Bounce	Flying	Physical	85	85	5	Normal
42	Super Fang	Normal	Physical	—	90	10	Normal
47	Facade	Normal	Physical	70	100	20	Normal
49	Earthquake	Ground	Physical	100	100	10	Adjacent

● TM & HM MOVES

No.	Name	Type	Kind	Pow.	Acc.	PP	Range
TM06	Toxic	Poison	Status	—	90	10	Normal
TM08	Bulk Up	Fighting	Status	—	—	20	Self
TM10	Hidden Power	Normal	Special	60	100	15	Normal
TM17	Protect	Normal	Status	—	—	10	Self
TM21	Frustration	Normal	Physical	—	100	20	Normal
TM23	Smack Down	Rock	Physical	50	100	15	Normal
TM26	Earthquake	Ground	Physical	100	100	10	Adjacent
TM27	Return	Normal	Physical	—	100	20	Normal
TM28	Dig	Ground	Physical	80	100	10	Normal
TM31	Brick Break	Fighting	Physical	75	100	15	Normal
TM32	Double Team	Normal	Status	—	—	15	Self
TM36	Sludge Bomb	Poison	Special	90	100	10	Normal
TM37	Sandstorm	Rock	Status	—	—	10	Both Sides
TM39	Rock Tomb	Rock	Physical	60	95	15	Normal
TM41	Torment	Dark	Status	—	100	15	Normal
TM42	Facade	Normal	Physical	70	100	20	Normal
TM44	Rest	Psychic	Status	—	—	10	Self
TM45	Attract	Normal	Status	—	100	15	Normal
TM46	Thief	Dark	Physical	60	100	25	Normal
TM48	Round	Normal	Special	60	100	15	Normal
TM56	Fling	Dark	Physical	—	100	10	Normal
TM66	Payback	Dark	Physical	50	100	10	Normal
TM71	Stone Edge	Rock	Physical	100	80	5	Normal
TM78	Bulldoze	Ground	Physical	60	100	20	Adjacent
TM80	Rock Slide	Rock	Physical	75	90	10	Many Others
TM86	Grass Knot	Grass	Special	—	100	20	Normal
TM87	Swagger	Normal	Status	—	90	15	Normal
TM88	Sleep Talk	Normal	Status	—	—	10	Self
TM89	U-turn	Bug	Physical	70	100	20	Normal
TM90	Substitute	Normal	Status	—	—	10	Self
TM93	Wild Charge	Electric	Physical	90	100	15	Normal
TM94	Rock Smash	Fighting	Physical	40	100	15	Normal
TM96	Nature Power	Normal	Status	—	—	20	Normal

No.	Name	Type	Kind	Pow.	Acc.	PP	Range
TM98	Power-Up Punch	Fighting	Physical	40	100	20	Normal
TM100	Confide	Normal	Status	—	—	20	Normal
HM01	Cut	Normal	Physical	50	95	30	Normal
HM03	Surf	Water	Special	90	100	15	Adjacent
HM04	Strength	Normal	Physical	80	100	15	Normal

● MOVES TAUGHT BY PEOPLE

Name	Type	Kind	Pow.	Acc.	PP	Range

● EGG MOVES

Name	Type	Kind	Pow.	Acc.	PP	Range
Spikes	Ground	Status	—	—	20	Other Side
Defense Curl	Normal	Status	—	—	40	Self
Rollout	Rock	Physical	30	90	20	Normal

AFTER THE HALL OF FAME

CENTRAL KALOS

011

Diggersby

COASTAL KALOS

MOUNTAIN KALOS

ADVENTURE DATA

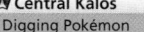

Central Kalos

Digging Pokémon

✓ Diggersby

011

HEIGHT: 3'03" WEIGHT: 93.5 lbs.
GENDER: ♂/♀

| TYPE | Normal | Ground |

ABILITIES
Pickup
Cheek Pouch

HIDDEN ABILITY
Huge Power

STAT GROWTH RATES
HP ▪▪▪
Attack ▪▪▪
Defense ▪▪▪
Sp. Atk ▪▪
Sp. Def ▪▪▪
Speed ▪▪▪▪

EGG GROUP
Field

X — With their powerful ears, they can heft boulders of a ton or more with ease. They can be a big help at construction sites.

Y — As powerful as an excavator, its ears can reduce dense bedrock to rubble. When it's finished digging, it lounges lazily.

EVOLUTION

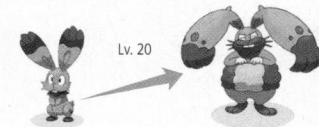

Lv. 20

Bunnelby → Diggersby

ITEMS SOMETIMES HELD BY WILD POKÉMON
None

Damage taken in normal battles	
Normal	×1
Fire	×1
Water	×2
Grass	×2
Electric	×0
Ice	×2
Fighting	×2
Poison	×0.5
Ground	×1
Flying	×1
Psychic	×1
Bug	×1
Rock	×0.5
Ghost	×0
Dragon	×1
Dark	×1
Steel	×1
Fairy	×1

Damage taken in Inverse Battles	
Normal	×1
Fire	×1
Water	×0.5
Grass	×0.5
Electric	×2
Ice	×0.5
Fighting	×0.5
Poison	×2
Ground	×1
Flying	×1
Psychic	×1
Bug	×1
Rock	×2
Ghost	×2
Dragon	×1
Dark	×1
Steel	×1
Fairy	×1

Can be used in	
Inverse Battle	Battle Institute
—	Battle Maison
Battle Chateau	Random Matchup

Same form for ♂/♀

How to obtain for your Central Kalos Pokédex

❶ Catch in the yellow flowers on Route 22.
❷ Level up Bunnelby to Lv. 20.

❶ Catch in the yellow flowers on Route 22.
❷ Level up Bunnelby to Lv. 20.

● LEVEL-UP MOVES

Lv.	Name	Type	Kind	Pow.	Acc.	PP	Range
1	Hammer Arm	Fighting	Physical	100	90	10	Normal
1	Rototiller	Ground	Status	—	—	10	Adjacent
1	Bulldoze	Ground	Physical	60	100	20	Adjacent
1	Swords Dance	Normal	Status	—	—	20	Self
1	Tackle	Normal	Physical	50	100	35	Normal
1	Agility	Psychic	Status	—	—	30	Self
1	Leer	Normal	Status	—	100	30	Many Others
7	Quick Attack	Normal	Physical	40	100	30	Normal
13	Mud-Slap	Ground	Special	20	100	10	Normal
15	Take Down	Normal	Physical	90	85	20	Normal
18	Mud Shot	Ground	Special	55	95	15	Normal
20	Double Kick	Fighting	Physical	30	100	30	Normal
26	Odor Sleuth	Normal	Status	—	—	40	Normal
31	Flail	Normal	Physical	—	100	15	Normal
37	Dig	Ground	Physical	80	100	10	Normal
42	Bounce	Flying	Physical	85	85	5	Normal
48	Super Fang	Normal	Physical	—	90	10	Normal
53	Facade	Normal	Physical	70	100	20	Normal
57	Earthquake	Ground	Physical	100	100	10	Adjacent
60	Hammer Arm	Fighting	Physical	100	90	10	Normal

● TM & HM MOVES

No.	Name	Type	Kind	Pow.	Acc.	PP	Range
TM06	Toxic	Poison	Status	—	90	10	Normal
TM08	Bulk Up	Fighting	Status	—	—	20	Self
TM10	Hidden Power	Normal	Special	60	100	15	Normal
TM15	Hyper Beam	Normal	Special	150	90	5	Normal
TM17	Protect	Normal	Status	—	—	10	Self
TM21	Frustration	Normal	Physical	—	100	20	Normal
TM23	Smack Down	Rock	Physical	50	100	15	Normal
TM26	Earthquake	Ground	Physical	100	100	10	Adjacent
TM27	Return	Normal	Physical	—	100	20	Normal
TM28	Dig	Ground	Physical	80	100	10	Normal
TM31	Brick Break	Fighting	Physical	75	100	15	Normal
TM32	Double Team	Normal	Status	—	—	15	Self
TM36	Sludge Bomb	Poison	Special	90	100	10	Normal
TM37	Sandstorm	Rock	Status	—	—	10	Both Sides
TM39	Rock Tomb	Rock	Physical	60	95	15	Normal
TM41	Torment	Dark	Status	—	100	15	Normal
TM42	Facade	Normal	Physical	70	100	20	Normal
TM44	Rest	Psychic	Status	—	—	10	Self
TM45	Attract	Normal	Status	—	100	15	Normal
TM46	Thief	Dark	Physical	60	100	25	Normal
TM48	Round	Normal	Special	60	100	15	Normal
TM56	Fling	Dark	Physical	—	100	10	Normal
TM66	Payback	Dark	Physical	50	100	10	Normal
TM68	Giga Impact	Normal	Physical	150	90	5	Normal
TM71	Stone Edge	Rock	Physical	100	80	5	Normal
TM75	Swords Dance	Normal	Status	—	—	20	Self
TM78	Bulldoze	Ground	Physical	60	100	20	Adjacent
TM80	Rock Slide	Rock	Physical	75	90	10	Many Others
TM86	Grass Knot	Grass	Special	—	100	20	Normal
TM87	Swagger	Normal	Status	—	90	15	Normal
TM88	Sleep Talk	Normal	Status	—	—	10	Self
TM89	U-turn	Bug	Physical	70	100	20	Normal
TM90	Substitute	Normal	Status	—	—	10	Self

No.	Name	Type	Kind	Pow.	Acc.	PP	Range
TM93	Wild Charge	Electric	Physical	90	100	15	Normal
TM94	Rock Smash	Fighting	Physical	40	100	15	Normal
TM96	Nature Power	Normal	Status	—	—	20	Normal
TM98	Power-Up Punch	Fighting	Physical	40	100	20	Normal
TM100	Confide	Normal	Status	—	—	20	Normal
HM01	Cut	Normal	Physical	50	95	30	Normal
HM03	Surf	Water	Special	90	100	15	Adjacent
HM04	Strength	Normal	Physical	80	100	15	Normal

● MOVES TAUGHT BY PEOPLE

Name	Type	Kind	Pow.	Acc.	PP	Range

🏠 **Central Kalos**

Tiny Raccoon Pokémon

012

✓ **Zigzagoon**

HEIGHT: 1'04" WEIGHT: 38.6 lbs.
GENDER: ♂ / ♀

X It walks in zigzag fashion. It's good at finding items in the grass and even in the ground.

Y A Pokémon with abundant curiosity. It shows an interest in everything, so it always zigzags.

TYPE **Normal**

ABILITIES
Pickup
Gluttony

HIDDEN ABILITY
Quick Feet

STAT GROWTH RATES
HP	▪▪
Attack	▪▪
Defense	▪▪
Sp. Atk	▪
Sp. Def	▪▪
Speed	▪▪▪

EGG GROUP
Field

EVOLUTION

Lv. 20

Zigzagoon → Linoone

ITEMS SOMETIMES HELD BY WILD POKÉMON
None

Damage taken in normal battles		Damage taken in Inverse Battles	
Normal	×1	Normal	×1
Fire	×1	Fire	×1
Water	×1	Water	×1
Grass	×1	Grass	×1
Electric	×1	Electric	×1
Ice	×1	Ice	×1
Fighting	×2	Fighting	×0.5
Poison	×1	Poison	×1
Ground	×1	Ground	×1
Flying	×1	Flying	×1
Psychic	×1	Psychic	×1
Bug	×1	Bug	×1
Rock	×1	Rock	×1
Ghost	×0	Ghost	×2
Dragon	×1	Dragon	×1
Dark	×1	Dark	×1
Steel	×1	Steel	×1
Fairy	×1	Fairy	×1

Can be used in	
Inverse Battle	Battle Institute
—	Battle Maison
Battle Chateau	Random Matchup

Same form for ♂ / ♀

How to obtain for your Central Kalos Pokédex

Catch in the tall grass on Route 2.

Catch in the tall grass on Route 2.

● **LEVEL-UP MOVES**

Lv.	Name	Type	Kind	Pow.	Acc.	PP	Range
1	Growl	Normal	Status	—	100	40	Many Others
1	Tackle	Normal	Physical	50	100	35	Normal
5	Tail Whip	Normal	Status	—	100	30	Many Others
9	Headbutt	Normal	Physical	70	100	15	Normal
11	Baby-Doll Eyes	Fairy	Status	—	100	30	Normal
13	Sand Attack	Ground	Status	—	100	15	Normal
17	Odor Sleuth	Normal	Status	—	—	40	Normal
21	Mud Sport	Ground	Status	—	—	15	Both Sides
25	Pin Missile	Bug	Physical	25	95	20	Normal
29	Covet	Normal	Physical	60	100	25	Normal
33	Bestow	Normal	Status	—	—	15	Normal
37	Flail	Normal	Physical	—	100	15	Normal
41	Rest	Psychic	Status	—	—	10	Self
45	Belly Drum	Normal	Status	—	—	10	Self
49	Fling	Dark	Physical	—	100	10	Normal

● **TM & HM MOVES**

No.	Name	Type	Kind	Pow.	Acc.	PP	Range
TM01	Hone Claws	Dark	Status	—	—	15	Self
TM06	Toxic	Poison	Status	—	90	10	Normal
TM10	Hidden Power	Normal	Special	60	100	15	Normal
TM11	Sunny Day	Fire	Status	—	—	5	Both Sides
TM13	Ice Beam	Ice	Special	90	100	10	Normal
TM14	Blizzard	Ice	Special	110	70	5	Many Others
TM17	Protect	Normal	Status	—	—	10	Self
TM18	Rain Dance	Water	Status	—	—	5	Both Sides
TM21	Frustration	Normal	Physical	—	100	20	Normal
TM24	Thunderbolt	Electric	Special	90	100	15	Normal
TM25	Thunder	Electric	Special	110	70	10	Normal
TM27	Return	Normal	Physical	—	100	20	Normal
TM28	Dig	Ground	Physical	80	100	10	Normal
TM30	Shadow Ball	Ghost	Special	80	100	15	Normal
TM32	Double Team	Normal	Status	—	—	15	Self
TM42	Facade	Normal	Physical	70	100	20	Normal
TM44	Rest	Psychic	Status	—	—	10	Self
TM45	Attract	Normal	Status	—	100	15	Normal
TM46	Thief	Dark	Physical	60	100	25	Normal
TM48	Round	Normal	Special	60	100	15	Normal
TM49	Echoed Voice	Normal	Special	40	100	15	Normal
TM56	Fling	Dark	Physical	—	100	10	Normal
TM57	Charge Beam	Electric	Special	50	90	10	Normal
TM67	Retaliate	Normal	Physical	70	100	5	Normal
TM73	Thunder Wave	Electric	Status	—	100	20	Normal
TM86	Grass Knot	Grass	Special	—	100	20	Normal
TM87	Swagger	Normal	Status	—	90	15	Normal
TM88	Sleep Talk	Normal	Status	—	—	10	Self
TM90	Substitute	Normal	Status	—	—	10	Self
TM94	Rock Smash	Fighting	Physical	40	100	15	Normal
TM100	Confide	Normal	Status	—	—	20	Normal
HM01	Cut	Normal	Physical	50	95	30	Normal
HM03	Surf	Water	Special	90	100	15	Adjacent

● **MOVES TAUGHT BY PEOPLE**

Name	Type	Kind	Pow.	Acc.	PP	Range

● **EGG MOVES**

Name	Type	Kind	Pow.	Acc.	PP	Range
Charm	Fairy	Status	—	100	20	Normal
Pursuit	Dark	Physical	40	100	20	Normal
Tickle	Normal	Status	—	100	20	Normal
Trick	Psychic	Status	—	100	10	Normal
Helping Hand	Normal	Status	—	—	20	1 Ally
Mud-Slap	Ground	Special	20	100	10	Normal
Sleep Talk	Normal	Status	—	—	10	Self
Rock Climb	Normal	Physical	90	85	20	Normal
Simple Beam	Normal	Status	—	100	15	Normal

AFTER THE HALL OF FAME

CENTRAL KALOS

013

Linoone

COASTAL KALOS

MOUNTAIN KALOS

ADVENTURE DATA

Central Kalos — 013

Rushing Pokémon

☑ Linoone

HEIGHT: 1'08" WEIGHT: 71.6 lbs.
GENDER: ♂/♀

X When running in a straight line, it can easily top 60 miles an hour. It has a tough time with curved roads.

Y It charges prey at speeds over 60 miles an hour. However, because it can only run straight, it often fails.

TYPE: Normal

ABILITIES
Pickup
Gluttony

HIDDEN ABILITY
Quick Feet

STAT GROWTH RATES
HP	■■■
Attack	■■■■
Defense	■■■
Sp. Atk	■■
Sp. Def	■■■
Speed	■■■■■

EGG GROUP
Field

EVOLUTION

Lv. 20

Zigzagoon → Linoone

ITEMS SOMETIMES HELD BY WILD POKÉMON
None

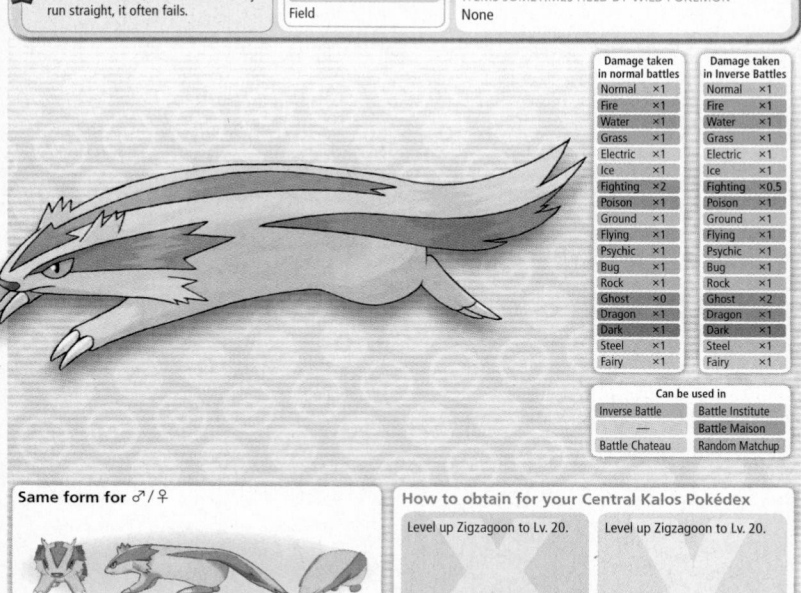

Damage taken in normal battles	
Normal	×1
Fire	×1
Water	×1
Grass	×1
Electric	×1
Ice	×1
Fighting	×2
Poison	×1
Ground	×1
Flying	×1
Psychic	×1
Bug	×1
Rock	×1
Ghost	×0
Dragon	×1
Dark	×1
Steel	×1
Fairy	×1

Damage taken in Inverse Battles	
Normal	×1
Fire	×1
Water	×1
Grass	×1
Electric	×1
Ice	×1
Fighting	×0.5
Poison	×1
Ground	×1
Flying	×1
Psychic	×1
Bug	×1
Rock	×1
Ghost	×2
Dragon	×1
Dark	×1
Steel	×1
Fairy	×1

Can be used in	
Inverse Battle	Battle Institute
—	Battle Maison
Battle Chateau	Random Matchup

Same form for ♂/♀

How to obtain for your Central Kalos Pokédex

Level up Zigzagoon to Lv. 20. (X)

Level up Zigzagoon to Lv. 20. (Y)

● LEVEL-UP MOVES

Lv.	Name	Type	Kind	Pow.	Acc.	PP	Range
1	Play Rough	Fairy	Physical	90	90	10	Normal
1	Rototiller	Ground	Status	—	—	10	Adjacent
1	Switcheroo	Dark	Status	—	100	10	Normal
1	Tackle	Normal	Physical	50	100	35	Normal
1	Growl	Normal	Status	—	100	40	Many Others
1	Tail Whip	Normal	Status	—	100	30	Many Others
1	Headbutt	Normal	Physical	70	100	15	Normal
5	Tail Whip	Normal	Status	—	100	30	Many Others
9	Headbutt	Normal	Physical	70	100	15	Normal
13	Sand Attack	Ground	Status	—	100	15	Normal
17	Odor Sleuth	Normal	Status	—	—	40	Normal
23	Mud Sport	Ground	Status	—	—	15	Both Sides
29	Fury Swipes	Normal	Physical	18	80	15	Normal
35	Covet	Normal	Physical	60	100	25	Normal
41	Bestow	Normal	Status	—	—	15	Normal
47	Slash	Normal	Physical	70	100	20	Normal
53	Rest	Psychic	Status	—	—	10	Self
59	Belly Drum	Normal	Status	—	—	10	Self
65	Fling	Dark	Physical	—	100	10	Normal

● TM & HM MOVES

No.	Name	Type	Kind	Pow.	Acc.	PP	Range
TM01	Hone Claws	Dark	Status	—	—	15	Self
TM05	Roar	Normal	Status	—	—	20	Normal
TM06	Toxic	Poison	Status	—	90	10	Normal
TM10	Hidden Power	Normal	Special	60	100	15	Normal
TM11	Sunny Day	Fire	Status	—	—	5	Both Sides
TM13	Ice Beam	Ice	Special	90	100	10	Normal
TM14	Blizzard	Ice	Special	110	70	5	Many Others
TM15	Hyper Beam	Normal	Special	150	90	5	Normal
TM17	Protect	Normal	Status	—	—	10	Self
TM18	Rain Dance	Water	Status	—	—	5	Both Sides
TM21	Frustration	Normal	Physical	—	100	20	Normal
TM24	Thunderbolt	Electric	Special	90	100	15	Normal
TM25	Thunder	Electric	Special	110	70	10	Normal
TM27	Return	Normal	Physical	—	100	20	Normal
TM28	Dig	Ground	Physical	80	100	10	Normal
TM30	Shadow Ball	Ghost	Special	80	100	15	Normal
TM32	Double Team	Normal	Status	—	—	15	Self
TM42	Facade	Normal	Physical	70	100	20	Normal
TM44	Rest	Psychic	Status	—	—	10	Self
TM45	Attract	Normal	Status	—	100	15	Normal
TM46	Thief	Dark	Physical	60	100	25	Normal
TM48	Round	Normal	Special	60	100	15	Normal
TM49	Echoed Voice	Normal	Special	40	100	15	Normal
TM56	Fling	Dark	Physical	—	100	10	Normal
TM57	Charge Beam	Electric	Special	50	90	10	Normal
TM65	Shadow Claw	Ghost	Physical	70	100	15	Normal
TM67	Retaliate	Normal	Physical	70	100	5	Normal
TM68	Giga Impact	Normal	Physical	150	90	5	Normal
TM73	Thunder Wave	Electric	Status	—	100	20	Normal
TM86	Grass Knot	Grass	Special	—	100	20	Normal
TM87	Swagger	Normal	Status	—	90	15	Normal
TM88	Sleep Talk	Normal	Status	—	—	10	Self
TM90	Substitute	Normal	Status	—	—	10	Self

No.	Name	Type	Kind	Pow.	Acc.	PP	Range
TM94	Rock Smash	Fighting	Physical	40	100	15	Normal
TM100	Confide	Normal	Status	—	—	20	Normal
HM01	Cut	Normal	Physical	50	95	30	Normal
HM03	Surf	Water	Special	90	100	15	Adjacent
HM04	Strength	Normal	Physical	80	100	15	Normal

● MOVES TAUGHT BY PEOPLE

Name	Type	Kind	Pow.	Acc.	PP	Range

Central Kalos

Tiny Robin Pokémon

☑ Fletchling

014

HEIGHT: 1'00"   WEIGHT: 3.7 lbs.
GENDER: ♂/♀

X These friendly Pokémon send signals to one another with beautiful chirps and tail-feather movements.

Y Despite the beauty of its lilting voice, it's merciless to intruders that enter its territory.

TYPE 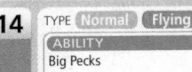 Normal Flying

ABILITY
Big Pecks

HIDDEN ABILITY
Gale Wings

STAT GROWTH RATES

HP	■■
Attack	■■■
Defense	■■
Sp. Atk	■■
Sp. Def	■■
Speed	■■■

EGG GROUP
Flying

▲ EVOLUTION

Fletchling   Lv. 17 → Fletchinder   Lv. 35 → Talonflame

ITEMS SOMETIMES HELD BY WILD POKÉMON
None

AFTER THE HALL OF FAME

CENTRAL KALOS

014 Fletchling

COASTAL KALOS

MOUNTAIN KALOS

ADVENTURE DATA

Damage taken in normal battles		Damage taken in Inverse Battles	
Normal	×1	Normal	×1
Fire	×1	Fire	×1
Water	×1	Water	×1
Grass	×0.5	Grass	×2
Electric	×2	Electric	×0.5
Ice	×2	Ice	×0.5
Fighting	×1	Fighting	×1
Poison	×1	Poison	×1
Ground	×0	Ground	×2
Flying	×1	Flying	×1
Psychic	×1	Psychic	×1
Bug	×0.5	Bug	×2
Rock	×2	Rock	×0.5
Ghost	×0	Ghost	×2
Dragon	×1	Dragon	×1
Dark	×1	Dark	×1
Steel	×1	Steel	×1
Fairy	×1	Fairy	×1

Can be used in	
Inverse Battle	Battle Institute
—	Battle Maison
Battle Chateau	Random Matchup

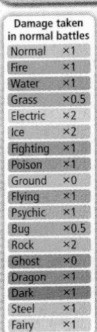

Same form for ♂/♀

How to obtain for your Central Kalos Pokédex

❶ Catch in the tall grass on Route 2.
❷ Catch in the tall grass on Route 3.

❶ Catch in the tall grass on Route 2.
❷ Catch in the tall grass on Route 3.

● LEVEL-UP MOVES

Lv.	Name	Type	Kind	Pow.	Acc.	PP	Range
1	Tackle	Normal	Physical	50	100	35	Normal
1	Growl	Normal	Status	—	100	40	Many Others
6	Quick Attack	Normal	Physical	40	100	30	Normal
10	Peck	Flying	Physical	35	100	35	Normal
13	Agility	Psychic	Status	—	—	30	Self
16	Flail	Normal	Physical	—	100	15	Normal
21	Roost	Flying	Status	—	—	10	Self
25	Razor Wind	Normal	Special	80	100	10	Many Others
29	Natural Gift	Normal	Physical	—	100	15	Normal
34	Flame Charge	Fire	Physical	50	100	20	Normal
39	Acrobatics	Flying	Physical	55	100	15	Normal
41	Me First	Normal	Status	—	—	20	Varies
45	Tailwind	Flying	Status	—	—	15	Your Side
48	Steel Wing	Steel	Physical	70	90	25	Normal

● TM & HM MOVES

No.	Name	Type	Kind	Pow.	Acc.	PP	Range
TM06	Toxic	Poison	Status	—	90	10	Normal
TM10	Hidden Power	Normal	Special	60	100	15	Normal
TM11	Sunny Day	Fire	Status	—	—	5	Both Sides
TM12	Taunt	Dark	Status	—	100	20	Normal
TM17	Protect	Normal	Status	—	—	10	Self
TM21	Frustration	Normal	Physical	—	100	20	Normal
TM27	Return	Normal	Physical	—	100	20	Normal
TM32	Double Team	Normal	Status	—	—	15	Self
TM40	Aerial Ace	Flying	Physical	60	—	20	Normal
TM42	Facade	Normal	Physical	70	100	20	Normal
TM43	Flame Charge	Fire	Physical	50	100	20	Normal
TM44	Rest	Psychic	Status	—	—	10	Self
TM45	Attract	Normal	Status	—	100	15	Normal
TM46	Thief	Dark	Physical	60	100	25	Normal
TM48	Round	Normal	Special	60	100	15	Normal
TM50	Overheat	Fire	Special	130	90	5	Normal
TM51	Steel Wing	Steel	Physical	70	90	25	Normal
TM62	Acrobatics	Flying	Physical	55	100	15	Normal
TM75	Swords Dance	Normal	Status	—	—	20	Self
TM87	Swagger	Normal	Status	—	90	15	Normal
TM88	Sleep Talk	Normal	Status	—	—	10	Self
TM89	U-turn	Bug	Physical	70	100	20	Normal
TM90	Substitute	Normal	Status	—	—	10	Self
TM100	Confide	Normal	Status	—	—	20	Normal
HM02	Fly	Flying	Physical	90	95	15	Normal

No.	Name	Type	Kind	Pow.	Acc.	PP	Range

● MOVES TAUGHT BY PEOPLE

Name	Type	Kind	Pow.	Acc.	PP	Range

● EGG MOVES

Name	Type	Kind	Pow.	Acc.	PP	Range
Tailwind	Flying	Status	—	—	15	Your Side
Snatch	Dark	Status	—	—	10	Self
Quick Guard	Fighting	Status	—	—	15	Your Side

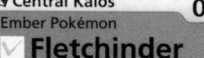

Central Kalos 015

Ember Pokémon

✓ **Fletchinder**

HEIGHT: 2'04" WEIGHT: 35.3 lbs.
GENDER: ♂ / ♀

X From its beak, it expels embers that set the tall grass on fire. Then it pounces on the bewildered prey that pop out of the grass.

Y The hotter the flame sac on its belly, the faster it can fly, but it takes some time to get the fire going.

TYPE	Fire	Flying

ABILITY
Flame Body

HIDDEN ABILITY
Gale Wings

STAT GROWTH RATES
HP	■■■
Attack	■■■■
Defense	■■■
Sp. Atk	■■■
Sp. Def	■■
Speed	■■■■■

EGG GROUP
Flying

EVOLUTION

Lv. 17   Lv. 35

Fletchling   Fletchinder   Talonflame

ITEMS SOMETIMES HELD BY WILD POKÉMON
None

Damage taken in normal battles	
Normal	×1
Fire	×0.5
Water	×2
Grass	×0.25
Electric	×2
Ice	×1
Fighting	×0.5
Poison	×1
Ground	×0
Flying	×1
Psychic	×1
Bug	×0.25
Rock	×4
Ghost	×1
Dragon	×1
Dark	×1
Steel	×0.5
Fairy	×0.5

Damage taken in Inverse Battles	
Normal	×1
Fire	×2
Water	×0.5
Grass	×4
Electric	×0.5
Ice	×1
Fighting	×2
Poison	×1
Ground	×1
Flying	×1
Psychic	×1
Bug	×4
Rock	×0.25
Ghost	×1
Dragon	×1
Dark	×1
Steel	×2
Fairy	×2

Can be used in	
Inverse Battle	Battle Institute
Sky Battle	Battle Maison
Battle Chateau	Random Matchup

Same form for ♂ / ♀

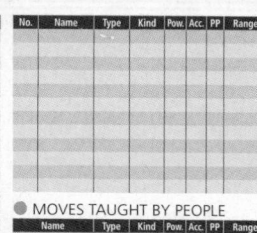

How to obtain for your Central Kalos Pokédex

Level up Fletchling to Lv. 17.

Level up Fletchling to Lv. 17.

X   Y

● LEVEL-UP MOVES

Lv.	Name	Type	Kind	Pow.	Acc.	PP	Range
1	Tackle	Normal	Physical	50	100	35	Normal
1	Growl	Normal	Status	—	100	40	Many Others
6	Quick Attack	Normal	Physical	40	100	30	Normal
10	Peck	Flying	Physical	35	100	35	Normal
13	Agility	Psychic	Status	—	—	30	Self
16	Flail	Normal	Physical	—	100	15	Normal
17	Ember	Fire	Special	40	100	25	Normal
25	Roost	Flying	Status	—	—	10	Self
27	Razor Wind	Normal	Special	80	100	10	Many Others
31	Natural Gift	Normal	Physical	—	100	15	Normal
38	Flame Charge	Fire	Physical	50	100	20	Normal
42	Acrobatics	Flying	Physical	55	100	15	Normal
46	Me First	Normal	Status	—	—	20	Varies
51	Tailwind	Flying	Status	—	—	15	Your Side
55	Steel Wing	Steel	Physical	70	90	25	Normal

● TM & HM MOVES

No.	Name	Type	Kind	Pow.	Acc.	PP	Range
TM06	Toxic	Poison	Status	—	90	10	Normal
TM10	Hidden Power	Normal	Special	60	100	15	Normal
TM11	Sunny Day	Fire	Status	—	—	5	Both Sides
TM12	Taunt	Dark	Status	—	100	20	Normal
TM17	Protect	Normal	Status	—	—	10	Self
TM19	Roost	Flying	Status	—	—	10	Self
TM21	Frustration	Normal	Physical	—	100	20	Normal
TM27	Return	Normal	Physical	—	100	20	Normal
TM32	Double Team	Normal	Status	—	—	15	Self
TM35	Flamethrower	Fire	Special	90	100	15	Normal
TM38	Fire Blast	Fire	Special	110	85	5	Normal
TM40	Aerial Ace	Flying	Physical	60	—	20	Normal
TM42	Facade	Normal	Physical	70	100	20	Normal
TM43	Flame Charge	Fire	Physical	50	100	20	Normal
TM44	Rest	Psychic	Status	—	—	10	Self
TM45	Attract	Normal	Status	—	100	15	Normal
TM46	Thief	Dark	Physical	60	100	25	Normal
TM48	Round	Normal	Special	60	100	15	Normal
TM50	Overheat	Fire	Special	130	90	5	Normal
TM51	Steel Wing	Steel	Physical	70	90	25	Normal
TM59	Incinerate	Fire	Special	60	100	15	Many Others
TM61	Will-O-Wisp	Fire	Status	—	85	15	Normal
TM62	Acrobatics	Flying	Physical	55	100	15	Normal
TM75	Swords Dance	Normal	Status	—	—	20	Self
TM87	Swagger	Normal	Status	—	90	15	Normal
TM88	Sleep Talk	Normal	Status	—	—	10	Self
TM89	U-turn	Bug	Physical	70	100	20	Normal
TM90	Substitute	Normal	Status	—	—	10	Self
TM100	Confide	Normal	Status	—	—	20	Normal
HM02	Fly	Flying	Physical	90	95	15	Normal

No.	Name	Type	Kind	Pow.	Acc.	PP	Range

● MOVES TAUGHT BY PEOPLE

Name	Type	Kind	Pow.	Acc.	PP	Range

AFTER THE HALL OF FAME

CENTRAL KALOS

015

Fletchinder

COASTAL KALOS

MOUNTAIN KALOS

ADVENTURE DATA

Central Kalos **016**
Scorching Pokémon
 Talonflame

HEIGHT: 3'11" WEIGHT: 54.0 lbs.
GENDER: ♂/♀

> **X** In the fever of an exciting battle, it showers embers from the gaps between its feathers and takes to the air.

> **Y** When attacking prey, it can reach speeds of up to 310 mph. It finishes its prey off with a colossal kick.

TYPE Fire Flying

ABILITY
Flame Body

HIDDEN ABILITY
Gale Wings

STAT GROWTH RATES
HP
Attack
Defense
Sp. Atk
Sp. Def
Speed

EGG GROUP
Flying

EVOLUTION

Lv. 17 Lv. 35

Fletchling Fletchinder Talonflame

ITEMS SOMETIMES HELD BY WILD POKÉMON
None

Damage taken in normal battles		Damage taken in Inverse Battles	
Normal	×1	Normal	×1
Fire	×0.5	Fire	×2
Water	×2	Water	×0.5
Grass	×0.25	Grass	×4
Electric	×2	Electric	×0.5
Ice	×1	Ice	×1
Fighting	×0.5	Fighting	×2
Poison	×1	Poison	×1
Ground	×0	Ground	×1
Flying	×1	Flying	×1
Psychic	×1	Psychic	×1
Bug	×0.25	Bug	×4
Rock	×4	Rock	×0.25
Ghost	×1	Ghost	×1
Dragon	×1	Dragon	×1
Dark	×1	Dark	×1
Steel	×0.5	Steel	×2
Fairy	×0.5	Fairy	×2

Can be used in	
Inverse Battle	Battle Institute
Sky Battle	Battle Maison
Battle Chateau	Random Matchup

Same form for ♂/♀

How to obtain for your Central Kalos Pokédex

Level up Fletchinder to Lv. 35. Level up Fletchinder to Lv. 35.

● **LEVEL-UP MOVES**

Lv.	Name	Type	Kind	Pow.	Acc.	PP	Range
1	Brave Bird	Flying	Physical	120	100	15	Normal
1	Flare Blitz	Fire	Physical	120	100	15	Normal
1	Tackle	Normal	Physical	50	100	35	Normal
1	Growl	Normal	Status	—	100	40	Many Others
6	Quick Attack	Normal	Physical	40	100	30	Normal
10	Peck	Flying	Physical	35	100	35	Normal
13	Agility	Psychic	Status	—	—	30	Self
16	Flail	Normal	Physical	—	100	15	Normal
17	Ember	Fire	Special	40	100	25	Normal
25	Roost	Flying	Status	—	—	10	Self
27	Razor Wind	Normal	Special	80	100	10	Many Others
31	Natural Gift	Normal	Physical	—	100	15	Normal
39	Flame Charge	Fire	Physical	50	100	20	Normal
44	Acrobatics	Flying	Physical	55	100	15	Normal
49	Me First	Normal	Status	—	—	20	Varies
55	Tailwind	Flying	Status	—	—	15	Your Side
60	Steel Wing	Steel	Physical	70	90	25	Normal
64	Brave Bird	Flying	Physical	120	100	15	Normal

● **TM & HM MOVES**

No.	Name	Type	Kind	Pow.	Acc.	PP	Range
TM01	Hone Claws	Dark	Status	—	—	15	Self
TM06	Toxic	Poison	Status	—	90	10	Normal
TM08	Bulk Up	Fighting	Status	—	—	20	Self
TM10	Hidden Power	Normal	Special	60	100	15	Normal
TM11	Sunny Day	Fire	Status	—	—	5	Both Sides
TM12	Taunt	Dark	Status	—	100	20	Normal
TM15	Hyper Beam	Normal	Special	150	90	5	Normal
TM17	Protect	Normal	Status	—	—	10	Self
TM19	Roost	Flying	Status	—	—	10	Self
TM21	Frustration	Normal	Physical	—	100	20	Normal
TM22	Solar Beam	Grass	Special	120	100	10	Normal
TM27	Return	Normal	Physical	—	100	20	Normal
TM32	Double Team	Normal	Status	—	—	15	Self
TM35	Flamethrower	Fire	Special	90	100	15	Normal
TM38	Fire Blast	Fire	Special	110	85	5	Normal
TM40	Aerial Ace	Flying	Physical	60	—	20	Normal
TM42	Facade	Normal	Physical	70	100	20	Normal
TM43	Flame Charge	Fire	Physical	50	100	20	Normal
TM44	Rest	Psychic	Status	—	—	10	Self
TM45	Attract	Normal	Status	—	100	15	Normal
TM46	Thief	Dark	Physical	60	100	25	Normal
TM48	Round	Normal	Special	60	100	15	Normal
TM50	Overheat	Fire	Special	130	90	5	Normal
TM51	Steel Wing	Steel	Physical	70	90	25	Normal
TM59	Incinerate	Fire	Special	60	100	15	Many Others
TM61	Will-O-Wisp	Fire	Status	—	85	15	Normal
TM62	Acrobatics	Flying	Physical	55	100	15	Normal
TM68	Giga Impact	Normal	Physical	150	90	5	Normal
TM75	Swords Dance	Normal	Status	—	—	20	Self
TM87	Swagger	Normal	Status	—	90	15	Normal
TM88	Sleep Talk	Normal	Status	—	—	10	Self
TM89	U-turn	Bug	Physical	70	100	20	Normal
TM90	Substitute	Normal	Status	—	—	10	Self

No.	Name	Type	Kind	Pow.	Acc.	PP	Range
TM100	Confide	Normal	Status	—	—	20	Normal
HM02	Fly	Flying	Physical	90	95	15	Normal

● **MOVES TAUGHT BY PEOPLE**

Name	Type	Kind	Pow.	Acc.	PP	Range

AFTER THE HALL OF FAME

CENTRAL KALOS

016 Talonflame

COASTAL KALOS

MOUNTAIN KALOS

ADVENTURE DATA

AFTER THE HALL OF FAME

CENTRAL KALOS
017
Pidgey

COASTAL KALOS

MOUNTAIN KALOS

ADVENTURE DATA

🔼 Central Kalos — 017
Tiny Bird Pokémon
∨ Pidgey

HEIGHT: 1'00" WEIGHT: 4.0 lbs.
GENDER: ♂/♀

TYPE Normal Flying

ABILITIES
Keen Eye
Tangled Feet

HIDDEN ABILITY
Big Pecks

STAT GROWTH RATES
HP	▪▪
Attack	▪▪
Defense	▪▪
Sp. Atk	▪▪
Sp. Def	▪▪
Speed	▪▪▪

EGG GROUP
Flying

X A common sight in forests and woods. It flaps its wings at ground level to kick up blinding sand.

Y It is docile and prefers to avoid conflict. If disturbed, however, it can ferociously strike back.

🔼 EVOLUTION

Lv. 18 → Lv. 36 →

Pidgey   Pidgeotto   Pidgeot

ITEMS SOMETIMES HELD BY WILD POKÉMON
None

Can be used in
Inverse Battle
—
Battle Chateau
Battle Institute
Battle Maison
Random Matchup

Damage taken in normal battles		Damage taken in Inverse Battles	
Normal	×1	Normal	×1
Fire	×1	Fire	×1
Water	×1	Water	×1
Grass	×0.5	Grass	×2
Electric	×2	Electric	×0.5
Ice	×2	Ice	×0.5
Fighting	×1	Fighting	×1
Poison	×1	Poison	×1
Ground	×0	Ground	×2
Flying	×1	Flying	×1
Psychic	×1	Psychic	×1
Bug	×0.5	Bug	×2
Rock	×2	Rock	×0.5
Ghost	×0	Ghost	×2
Dragon	×1	Dragon	×1
Dark	×1	Dark	×1
Steel	×1	Steel	×1
Fairy	×1	Fairy	×1

How to obtain for your Central Kalos Pokédex

❶ Catch in the tall grass on Route 2.
❷ Catch in the tall grass on Route 3.

❶ Catch in the tall grass on Route 2.
❷ Catch in the tall grass on Route 3.

Same form for ♂/♀

● LEVEL-UP MOVES

Lv.	Name	Type	Kind	Pow.	Acc.	PP	Range
1	Tackle	Normal	Physical	50	100	35	Normal
5	Sand Attack	Ground	Status	—	100	15	Normal
9	Gust	Flying	Special	40	100	35	Normal
13	Quick Attack	Normal	Physical	40	100	30	Normal
17	Whirlwind	Normal	Status	—	—	20	Normal
21	Twister	Dragon	Special	40	100	20	Many Others
25	Feather Dance	Flying	Status	—	100	15	Normal
29	Agility	Psychic	Status	—	—	30	Self
33	Wing Attack	Flying	Physical	60	100	35	Normal
37	Roost	Flying	Status	—	—	10	Self
41	Tailwind	Flying	Status	—	—	15	Your Side
45	Mirror Move	Flying	Status	—	—	20	Normal
49	Air Slash	Flying	Special	75	95	15	Normal
53	Hurricane	Flying	Special	110	70	10	Normal

● TM & HM MOVES

No.	Name	Type	Kind	Pow.	Acc.	PP	Range
TM06	Toxic	Poison	Status	—	90	10	Normal
TM10	Hidden Power	Normal	Special	60	100	15	Normal
TM11	Sunny Day	Fire	Status	—	—	5	Both Sides
TM17	Protect	Normal	Status	—	—	10	Self
TM18	Rain Dance	Water	Status	—	—	5	Both Sides
TM19	Roost	Flying	Status	—	—	10	Self
TM21	Frustration	Normal	Physical	—	100	20	Normal
TM27	Return	Normal	Physical	—	100	20	Normal
TM32	Double Team	Normal	Status	—	—	15	Self
TM40	Aerial Ace	Flying	Physical	60	—	20	Normal
TM42	Facade	Normal	Physical	70	100	20	Normal
TM44	Rest	Psychic	Status	—	—	10	Self
TM45	Attract	Normal	Status	—	100	15	Normal
TM46	Thief	Dark	Physical	60	100	25	Normal
TM48	Round	Normal	Special	60	100	15	Normal
TM51	Steel Wing	Steel	Physical	70	90	25	Normal
TM87	Swagger	Normal	Status	—	90	15	Normal
TM88	Sleep Talk	Normal	Status	—	—	10	Self
TM89	U-turn	Bug	Physical	70	100	20	Normal
TM90	Substitute	Normal	Status	—	—	10	Self
TM100	Confide	Normal	Status	—	—	20	Normal
HM02	Fly	Flying	Physical	90	95	15	Normal

● MOVES TAUGHT BY PEOPLE

Name	Type	Kind	Pow.	Acc.	PP	Range

● EGG MOVES

Name	Type	Kind	Pow.	Acc.	PP	Range
Pursuit	Dark	Physical	40	100	20	Normal
Feint Attack	Dark	Physical	60	—	20	Normal
Foresight	Normal	Status	—	—	40	Normal
Steel Wing	Steel	Physical	70	90	25	Normal
Air Cutter	Flying	Special	60	95	25	Many Others
Air Slash	Flying	Special	75	95	15	Normal
Brave Bird	Flying	Physical	120	100	15	Normal
Uproar	Normal	Special	90	100	10	1 Random
Defog	Flying	Status	—	—	15	Normal

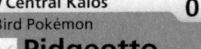
Pidgeotto

018

Bird Pokémon

TYPE: Normal / Flying

HEIGHT: 3'07" WEIGHT: 66.1 lbs.
GENDER: ♂/♀

ABILITIES
Keen Eye
Tangled Feet

HIDDEN ABILITY
Big Pecks

X — The claws on its feet are well developed. It can carry prey such as an Exeggcute to its nest over 60 miles away.

Y — Very protective of its sprawling territorial area, this Pokémon will fiercely peck at any intruder.

STAT GROWTH RATES
HP	■■■
Attack	■■■
Defense	■■■
Sp. Atk	■■
Sp. Def	■■
Speed	■■■■

EGG GROUP
Flying

EVOLUTION

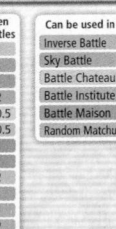

Pidgey —Lv. 18→ Pidgeotto —Lv. 36→ Pidgeot

ITEMS SOMETIMES HELD BY WILD POKÉMON
None

Damage taken in normal battles		Damage taken in Inverse Battles		Can be used in
Normal	×1	Normal	×1	Inverse Battle
Fire	×1	Fire	×1	Sky Battle
Water	×1	Water	×1	Battle Chateau
Grass	×0.5	Grass	×2	Battle Institute
Electric	×2	Electric	×0.5	Battle Maison
Ice	×2	Ice	×0.5	Random Matchup
Fighting	×1	Fighting	×1	
Poison	×1	Poison	×1	
Ground	×0	Ground	×2	
Flying	×1	Flying	×1	
Psychic	×1	Psychic	×1	
Bug	×0.5	Bug	×2	
Rock	×2	Rock	×0.5	
Ghost	×0	Ghost	×2	
Dragon	×1	Dragon	×1	
Dark	×1	Dark	×1	
Steel	×1	Steel	×1	
Fairy	×1	Fairy	×1	

How to obtain for your Central Kalos Pokédex

X	Y
Level up Pidgey to Lv. 18.	Level up Pidgey to Lv. 18.

Same form for ♂/♀

AFTER THE HALL OF FAME

CENTRAL KALOS

018 Pidgeotto

COASTAL KALOS

MOUNTAIN KALOS

ADVENTURE DATA

● LEVEL-UP MOVES

Lv.	Name	Type	Kind	Pow.	Acc.	PP	Range
1	Tackle	Normal	Physical	50	100	35	Normal
1	Sand Attack	Ground	Status	—	100	15	Normal
1	Gust	Flying	Special	40	100	35	Normal
5	Sand Attack	Ground	Status	—	100	15	Normal
9	Gust	Flying	Special	40	100	35	Normal
13	Quick Attack	Normal	Physical	40	100	30	Normal
17	Whirlwind	Normal	Status	—	—	20	Normal
22	Twister	Dragon	Special	40	100	20	Many Others
27	Feather Dance	Flying	Status	—	100	15	Normal
32	Agility	Psychic	Status	—	—	30	Self
37	Wing Attack	Flying	Physical	60	100	35	Normal
42	Roost	Flying	Status	—	—	10	Self
47	Tailwind	Flying	Status	—	—	15	Your Side
52	Mirror Move	Flying	Status	—	—	20	Normal
57	Air Slash	Flying	Special	75	95	15	Normal
62	Hurricane	Flying	Special	110	70	10	Normal

● TM & HM MOVES

No.	Name	Type	Kind	Pow.	Acc.	PP	Range
TM06	Toxic	Poison	Status	—	90	10	Normal
TM10	Hidden Power	Normal	Special	60	100	15	Normal
TM11	Sunny Day	Fire	Status	—	—	5	Both Sides
TM17	Protect	Normal	Status	—	—	10	Self
TM18	Rain Dance	Water	Status	—	—	5	Both Sides
TM19	Roost	Flying	Status	—	—	10	Self
TM21	Frustration	Normal	Physical	—	100	20	Normal
TM27	Return	Normal	Physical	—	100	20	Normal
TM32	Double Team	Normal	Status	—	—	15	Self
TM40	Aerial Ace	Flying	Physical	60	—	20	Normal
TM42	Facade	Normal	Physical	70	100	20	Normal
TM44	Rest	Psychic	Status	—	—	10	Self
TM45	Attract	Normal	Status	—	100	15	Normal
TM46	Thief	Dark	Physical	60	100	25	Normal
TM48	Round	Normal	Special	60	100	15	Normal
TM51	Steel Wing	Steel	Physical	70	90	25	Normal
TM87	Swagger	Normal	Status	—	90	15	Normal
TM88	Sleep Talk	Normal	Status	—	—	10	Self
TM89	U-turn	Bug	Physical	70	100	20	Normal
TM90	Substitute	Normal	Status	—	—	10	Self
TM100	Confide	Normal	Status	—	—	20	Normal
HM02	Fly	Flying	Physical	90	95	15	Normal

● MOVES TAUGHT BY PEOPLE

Name	Type	Kind	Pow.	Acc.	PP	Range

Central Kalos — 019

Bird Pokémon

✓ Pidgeot

HEIGHT: 4'11" WEIGHT: 87.1 lbs.
GENDER: ♂/♀

TYPE Normal Flying

ABILITIES
Keen Eye
Tangled Feet

HIDDEN ABILITY
Big Pecks

X When hunting, it skims the surface of water at high speed to pick off unwary prey such as Magikarp.

Y It spreads its gorgeous wings widely to intimidate enemies. It races through the skies at Mach-2 speed.

STAT GROWTH RATES
HP ■■■
Attack ■■■■
Defense ■■■■
Sp. Atk ■■■
Sp. Def ■■■
Speed ■■■■■

EGG GROUP
Flying

EVOLUTION

Lv. 18 → Lv. 36

Pidgey Pidgeotto Pidgeot

ITEMS SOMETIMES HELD BY WILD POKÉMON
None

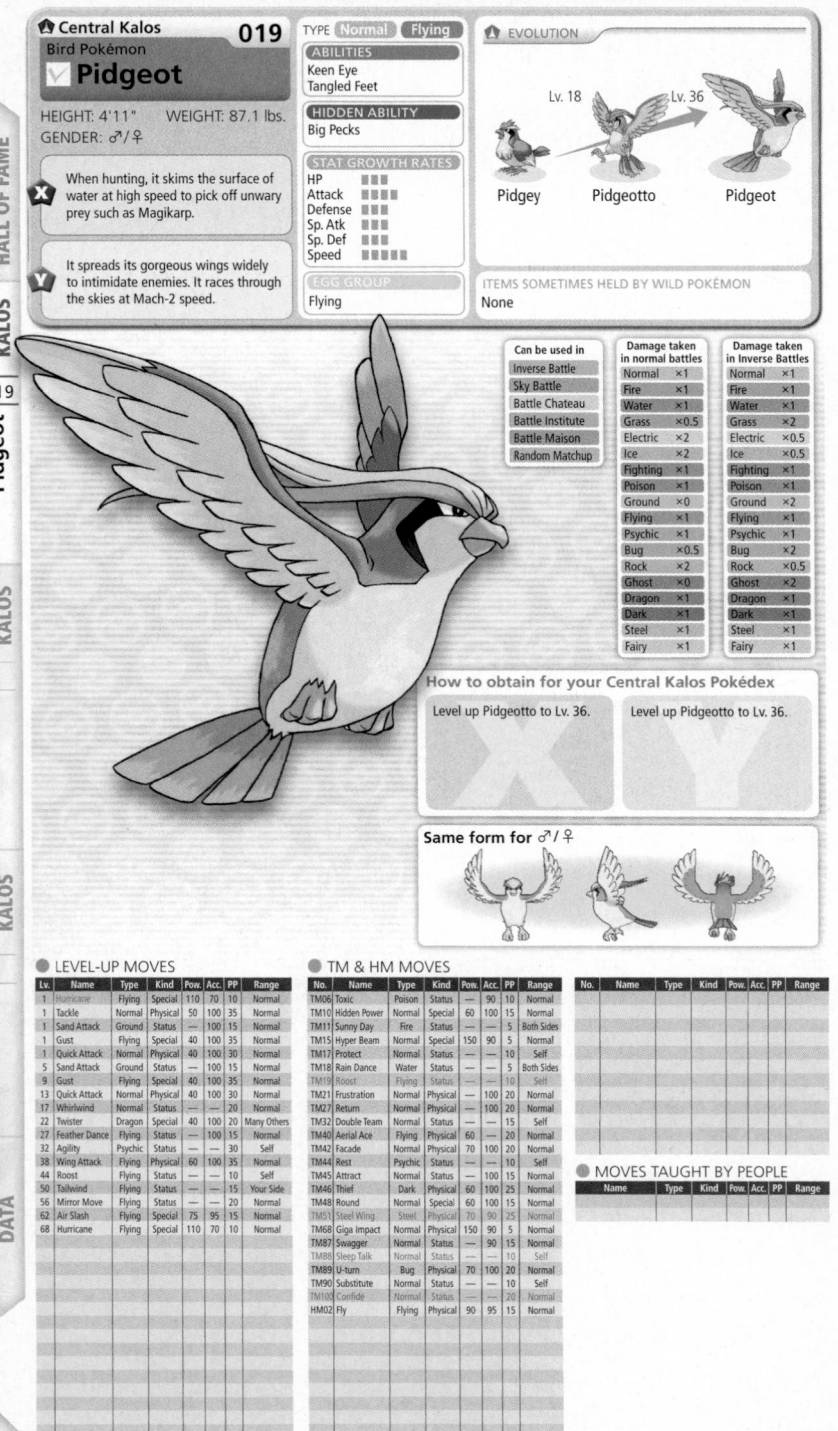

Can be used in
Inverse Battle
Sky Battle
Battle Chateau
Battle Institute
Battle Maison
Random Matchup

Damage taken in normal battles
Normal	×1
Fire	×1
Water	×1
Grass	×0.5
Electric	×2
Ice	×2
Fighting	×1
Poison	×1
Ground	×0
Flying	×1
Psychic	×1
Bug	×0.5
Rock	×2
Ghost	×0
Dragon	×1
Dark	×1
Steel	×1
Fairy	×1

Damage taken in Inverse Battles
Normal	×1
Fire	×1
Water	×1
Grass	×2
Electric	×0.5
Ice	×0.5
Fighting	×1
Poison	×1
Ground	×2
Flying	×1
Psychic	×1
Bug	×2
Rock	×0.5
Ghost	×2
Dragon	×1
Dark	×1
Steel	×1
Fairy	×1

How to obtain for your Central Kalos Pokédex

X: Level up Pidgeotto to Lv. 36.
Y: Level up Pidgeotto to Lv. 36.

Same form for ♂/♀

● LEVEL-UP MOVES

Lv.	Name	Type	Kind	Pow.	Acc.	PP	Range
1	Hurricane	Flying	Special	110	70	10	Normal
1	Tackle	Normal	Physical	50	100	35	Normal
1	Sand Attack	Ground	Status	—	100	15	Normal
1	Gust	Flying	Special	40	100	35	Normal
5	Quick Attack	Normal	Physical	40	100	30	Normal
5	Sand Attack	Ground	Status	—	100	15	Normal
9	Gust	Flying	Special	40	100	35	Normal
13	Quick Attack	Normal	Physical	40	100	30	Normal
17	Whirlwind	Normal	Status	—	—	20	Normal
22	Twister	Dragon	Special	40	100	20	Many Others
27	Feather Dance	Flying	Status	—	100	15	Normal
32	Agility	Psychic	Status	—	—	30	Self
38	Wing Attack	Flying	Physical	60	100	35	Normal
44	Roost	Flying	Status	—	—	10	Self
50	Tailwind	Flying	Status	—	—	15	Your Side
56	Mirror Move	Flying	Status	—	—	20	Normal
62	Air Slash	Flying	Special	75	95	15	Normal
68	Hurricane	Flying	Special	110	70	10	Normal

● TM & HM MOVES

No.	Name	Type	Kind	Pow.	Acc.	PP	Range
TM06	Toxic	Poison	Status	—	90	10	Normal
TM10	Hidden Power	Normal	Special	60	100	15	Normal
TM11	Sunny Day	Fire	Status	—	—	5	Both Sides
TM15	Hyper Beam	Normal	Special	150	90	5	Normal
TM17	Protect	Normal	Status	—	—	10	Self
TM18	Rain Dance	Water	Status	—	—	5	Both Sides
TM19	Roost	Flying	Status	—	—	10	Self
TM21	Frustration	Normal	Physical	—	100	20	Normal
TM27	Return	Normal	Physical	—	100	20	Normal
TM32	Double Team	Normal	Status	—	—	15	Self
TM40	Aerial Ace	Flying	Physical	60	—	20	Normal
TM42	Facade	Normal	Physical	70	100	20	Normal
TM44	Rest	Psychic	Status	—	—	10	Self
TM45	Attract	Normal	Status	—	100	15	Normal
TM46	Thief	Dark	Physical	60	100	25	Normal
TM48	Round	Normal	Special	60	100	15	Normal
TM51	Steel Wing	Steel	Physical	70	90	25	Normal
TM68	Giga Impact	Normal	Physical	150	90	5	Normal
TM87	Swagger	Normal	Status	—	90	15	Normal
TM88	Sleep Talk	Normal	Status	—	—	10	Self
TM89	U-turn	Bug	Physical	70	100	20	Normal
TM90	Substitute	Normal	Status	—	—	10	Self
TM100	Confide	Normal	Status	—	—	20	Normal
HM02	Fly	Flying	Physical	90	95	15	Normal

● MOVES TAUGHT BY PEOPLE

Name	Type	Kind	Pow.	Acc.	PP	Range

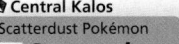
Scatterdust Pokémon
☑ Scatterbug

020

HEIGHT: 1'00" WEIGHT: 5.5 lbs.
GENDER: ♂/♀

X When under attack from bird Pokémon, it spews a poisonous black powder that causes paralysis on contact.

Y The powder that covers its body regulates its temperature, so it can live in any region or climate.

TYPE Bug

ABILITIES
Shield Dust
Compound Eyes

HIDDEN ABILITY
Friend Guard

STAT GROWTH RATES
HP	■■
Attack	■■
Defense	■■
Sp. Atk	■
Sp. Def	■
Speed	■■

EGG GROUP
Bug

EVOLUTION

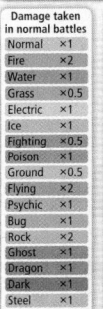 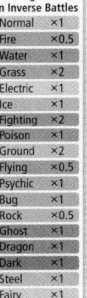 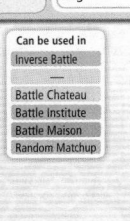

Scatterbug Lv. 9 Spewpa Lv. 12 Vivillon

ITEMS SOMETIMES HELD BY WILD POKÉMON
None

Damage taken in normal battles		Damage taken in Inverse Battles		Can be used in
Normal	×1	Normal	×1	Inverse Battle
Fire	×2	Fire	×0.5	—
Water	×1	Water	×1	Battle Chateau
Grass	×0.5	Grass	×2	Battle Institute
Electric	×1	Electric	×1	Battle Maison
Ice	×1	Ice	×1	Random Matchup
Fighting	×0.5	Fighting	×2	
Poison	×1	Poison	×1	
Ground	×0.5	Ground	×2	
Flying	×2	Flying	×0.5	
Psychic	×1	Psychic	×1	
Bug	×1	Bug	×1	
Rock	×2	Rock	×0.5	
Ghost	×1	Ghost	×1	
Dragon	×1	Dragon	×1	
Dark	×1	Dark	×1	
Steel	×1	Steel	×1	
Fairy	×1	Fairy	×1	

How to obtain for your Central Kalos Pokédex

❶ Catch in the tall grass on Route 2.
❷ Catch in the tall grass in Santalune Forest.

❶ Catch in the tall grass on Route 2.
❷ Catch in the tall grass in Santalune Forest.

Same form for ♂/♀

  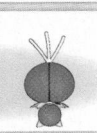

● LEVEL-UP MOVES
Lv.	Name	Type	Kind	Pow.	Acc.	PP	Range
1	Tackle	Normal	Physical	50	100	35	Normal
1	String Shot	Bug	Status	—	95	40	Many Others
6	Stun Spore	Grass	Status	—	75	30	Normal
15	Bug Bite	Bug	Physical	60	100	20	Normal

● TM & HM MOVES
No.	Name	Type	Kind	Pow.	Acc.	PP	Range

No.	Name	Type	Kind	Pow.	Acc.	PP	Range

● MOVES TAUGHT BY PEOPLE
Name	Type	Kind	Pow.	Acc.	PP	Range

● EGG MOVES
Name	Type	Kind	Pow.	Acc.	PP	Range
Stun Spore	Grass	Status	—	75	30	Normal
Poison Powder	Poison	Status	—	75	35	Normal
Rage Powder	Bug	Status	—	—	20	Self

AFTER THE HALL OF FAME

CENTRAL KALOS

020 Scatterbug

COASTAL KALOS

MOUNTAIN KALOS

ADVENTURE DATA

AFTER THE HALL OF FAME

CENTRAL KALOS

021

Spewpa

COASTAL KALOS

MOUNTAIN KALOS

ADVENTURE DATA

🏠 **Central Kalos** **021**

Scatterdust Pokémon

☑ Spewpa

HEIGHT: 1'00" WEIGHT: 18.5 lbs.
GENDER: ♂/♀

X It lives hidden within thicket shadows. When predators attack, it quickly bristles the fur covering its body in an effort to threaten them.

Y The beaks of bird Pokémon can't begin to scratch its stalwart body. To defend itself, it spews powder.

TYPE **Bug**

ABILITY
Shed Skin

HIDDEN ABILITY
Friend Guard

STAT GROWTH RATES
HP	■■
Attack	■
Defense	■■■
Sp. Atk	■
Sp. Def	■
Speed	■■

EGG GROUP
Bug

🦋 EVOLUTION

Lv. 9 Lv. 12

Scatterbug Spewpa Vivillon

ITEMS SOMETIMES HELD BY WILD POKÉMON
None

Damage taken in normal battles	
Normal	×1
Fire	×2
Water	×1
Grass	×0.5
Electric	×1
Ice	×1
Fighting	×0.5
Poison	×1
Ground	×0.5
Flying	×2
Psychic	×1
Bug	×1
Rock	×2
Ghost	×1
Dragon	×1
Dark	×1
Steel	×1
Fairy	×1

Damage taken in Inverse Battles	
Normal	×1
Fire	×0.5
Water	×1
Grass	×2
Electric	×1
Ice	×1
Fighting	×2
Poison	×1
Ground	×2
Flying	×0.5
Psychic	×1
Bug	×1
Rock	×0.5
Ghost	×1
Dragon	×1
Dark	×1
Steel	×1
Fairy	×1

Can be used in	
Inverse Battle	Battle Institute
—	Battle Maison
Battle Chateau	Random Matchup

Same form for ♂/♀

How to obtain for your Central Kalos Pokédex

Level up Scatterbug to Lv. 9.

Level up Scatterbug to Lv. 9.

● LEVEL-UP MOVES

Lv.	Name	Type	Kind	Pow.	Acc.	PP	Range
1	Harden	Normal	Status	—	—	30	Self
9	Protect	Normal	Status	—	—	10	Self

● TM & HM MOVES

No.	Name	Type	Kind	Pow.	Acc.	PP	Range
TM17	Protect	Normal	Status	—	—	10	Self

No.	Name	Type	Kind	Pow.	Acc.	PP	Range

● MOVES TAUGHT BY PEOPLE

Name	Type	Kind	Pow.	Acc.	PP	Range

AFTER THE HALL OF FAME

CENTRAL KALOS

022 Vivillon

COASTAL KALOS

MOUNTAIN KALOS

ADVENTURE DATA

Central Kalos 022

Scale Pokémon

Vivillon

HEIGHT: 3'11"　　WEIGHT: 37.5 lbs.
GENDER: ♂ / ♀

X Vivillon with many different patterns are found all over the world. These patterns are affected by the climate of their habitat.

Y The patterns on this Pokémon's wings depend on the climate and topography of its habitat. It scatters colorful scales.

TYPE Bug　Flying

ABILITIES
Shield Dust
Compound Eyes

HIDDEN ABILITY
Friend Guard

STAT GROWTH RATES
HP	■■■
Attack	■■■
Defense	■■
Sp. Atk	■■■■
Sp. Def	■■
Speed	■■■■■

EGG GROUP
Bug

EVOLUTION

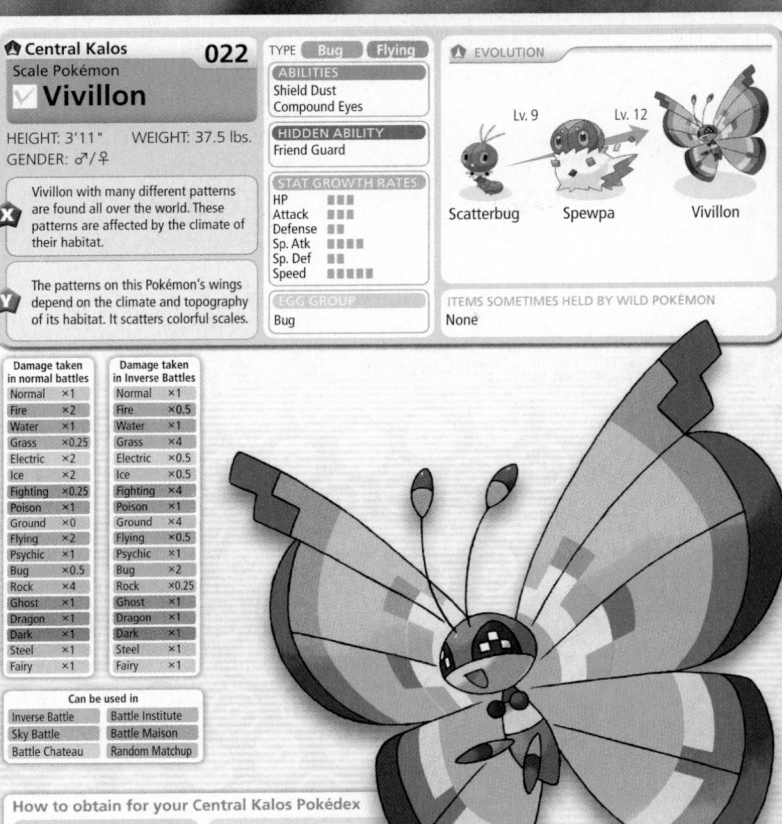

Scatterbug　Lv. 9　Spewpa　Lv. 12　Vivillon

ITEMS SOMETIMES HELD BY WILD POKÉMON
None

Damage taken in normal battles		Damage taken in Inverse Battles	
Normal	×1	Normal	×1
Fire	×2	Fire	×0.5
Water	×1	Water	×1
Grass	×0.25	Grass	×4
Electric	×2	Electric	×0.5
Ice	×2	Ice	×0.5
Fighting	×0.25	Fighting	×4
Poison	×1	Poison	×1
Ground	×0	Ground	×4
Flying	×2	Flying	×0.5
Psychic	×1	Psychic	×1
Bug	×0.5	Bug	×2
Rock	×4	Rock	×0.25
Ghost	×1	Ghost	×1
Dragon	×1	Dragon	×1
Dark	×1	Dark	×1
Steel	×1	Steel	×1
Fairy	×1	Fairy	×1

Can be used in	
Inverse Battle	Battle Institute
Sky Battle	Battle Maison
Battle Chateau	Random Matchup

How to obtain for your Central Kalos Pokédex

Level up Spewpa to Lv. 12.	Level up Spewpa to Lv. 12.

● LEVEL-UP MOVES

Lv.	Name	Type	Kind	Pow.	Acc.	PP	Range
1	Powder	Bug	Status	—	100	20	Normal
1	Sleep Powder	Grass	Status	—	75	15	Normal
1	Poison Powder	Poison	Status	—	75	35	Normal
1	Stun Spore	Grass	Status	—	75	30	Normal
1	Gust	Flying	Special	40	100	35	Normal
1	Light Screen	Psychic	Status	—	—	30	Your Side
12	Struggle Bug	Bug	Special	50	100	20	Many Others
17	Psybeam	Psychic	Special	65	100	20	Normal
21	Supersonic	Normal	Status	—	55	20	Normal
25	Draining Kiss	Fairy	Special	50	100	10	Normal
31	Aromatherapy	Grass	Status	—	—	5	Your Party
35	Bug Buzz	Bug	Special	90	100	10	Normal
41	Safeguard	Normal	Status	—	—	25	Your Side
45	Quiver Dance	Bug	Status	—	—	20	Self
50	Hurricane	Flying	Special	110	70	10	Normal
55	Powder	Bug	Status	—	100	20	Normal

● TM & HM MOVES

No.	Name	Type	Kind	Pow.	Acc.	PP	Range
TM04	Calm Mind	Psychic	Status	—	—	20	Self
TM06	Toxic	Poison	Status	—	90	10	Normal
TM10	Hidden Power	Normal	Special	60	100	15	Normal
TM11	Sunny Day	Fire	Status	—	—	5	Both Sides
TM15	Hyper Beam	Normal	Special	150	90	5	Normal
TM16	Light Screen	Psychic	Status	—	—	30	Your Side
TM17	Protect	Normal	Status	—	—	10	Self
TM18	Rain Dance	Water	Status	—	—	5	Both Sides
TM19	Roost	Flying	Status	—	—	10	Self
TM20	Safeguard	Normal	Status	—	—	25	Your Side
TM21	Frustration	Normal	Physical	—	100	20	Normal
TM22	Solar Beam	Grass	Special	120	100	10	Normal
TM27	Return	Normal	Physical	—	100	20	Normal
TM29	Psychic	Psychic	Special	90	100	10	Normal
TM32	Double Team	Normal	Status	—	—	15	Self
TM40	Aerial Ace	Flying	Physical	60	—	20	Normal
TM42	Facade	Normal	Physical	70	100	20	Normal
TM44	Rest	Psychic	Status	—	—	10	Self
TM45	Attract	Normal	Status	—	100	15	Normal
TM46	Thief	Dark	Physical	60	100	25	Normal
TM48	Round	Normal	Special	60	100	15	Normal
TM53	Energy Ball	Grass	Special	90	100	10	Normal
TM62	Acrobatics	Flying	Physical	55	100	15	Normal
TM68	Giga Impact	Normal	Physical	150	90	5	Normal
TM70	Flash	Normal	Status	—	100	20	Normal
TM76	Struggle Bug	Bug	Special	50	100	20	Many Others
TM77	Psych Up	Normal	Status	—	—	10	Normal
TM83	Infestation	Bug	Special	20	100	20	Normal
TM85	Dream Eater	Psychic	Special	100	100	15	Normal
TM87	Swagger	Normal	Status	—	90	15	Normal
TM88	Sleep Talk	Normal	Status	—	—	10	Self
TM89	U-turn	Bug	Physical	70	100	20	Normal
TM90	Substitute	Normal	Status	—	—	10	Self

No.	Name	Type	Kind	Pow.	Acc.	PP	Range
TM100	Confide	Normal	Status	—	—	20	Normal

● MOVES TAUGHT BY PEOPLE

Name	Type	Kind	Pow.	Acc.	PP	Range

AFTER THE HALL OF FAME

CENTRAL KALOS

022

Vivillon

COASTAL KALOS

MOUNTAIN KALOS

ADVENTURE DATA

⊙ Vivillon has different wing colors and patterns

The colors and patterns of Vivillon's wings are different depending on the areas where the players are playing *Pokémon X* and *Pokémon Y*. Enjoy various beautiful patterns of Vivillon's wings.

The areas where Vivillon with the Icy Snow Pattern appear

Icy Snow Pattern: Same form for ♂ / ♀

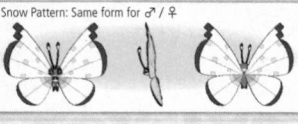

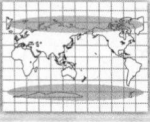

The areas where Vivillon with the Polar Pattern appear

Polar Pattern: Same form for ♂ / ♀

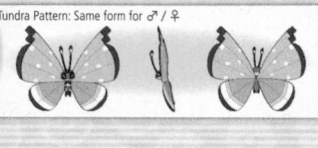

The areas where Vivillon with the Tundra Pattern appear

Tundra Pattern: Same form for ♂ / ♀

The areas where Vivillon with the Continental Pattern appear

Continental Pattern: Same form for ♂ / ♀

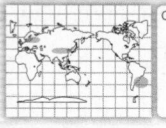

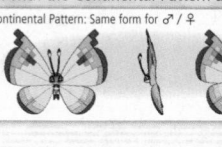

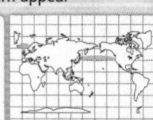

The areas where Vivillon with the Garden Pattern appear

Garden Pattern: Same form for ♂ / ♀

The area where Vivillon with the Elegant Pattern appear

 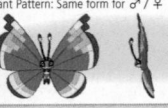 

Elegant Pattern: Same form for ♂ / ♀

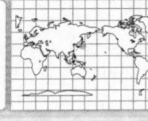

The area where Vivillon with the Meadow Pattern appear

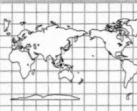  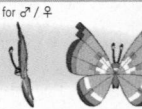

Meadow Pattern: Same form for ♂ / ♀

The area where Vivillon with the Modern Pattern appear

Modern Pattern: Same form for ♂ / ♀

The areas where Vivillon with the Marine Pattern appear

Marine Pattern: Same form for ♂ / ♀

AFTER THE HALL OF FAME

CENTRAL KALOS

022

Vivillon

COASTAL KALOS

MOUNTAIN KALOS

ADVENTURE DATA

The areas where Vivillon with the Archipelago Pattern appear

Archipelago Pattern: Same form for ♂ / ♀

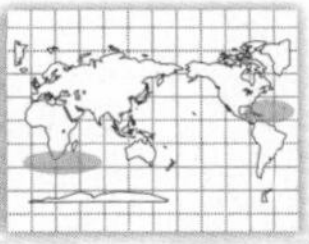

The areas where Vivillon with the High Plains Pattern appear

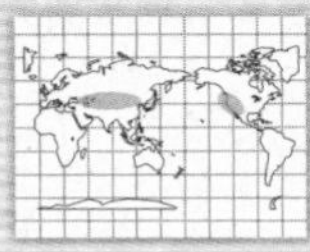

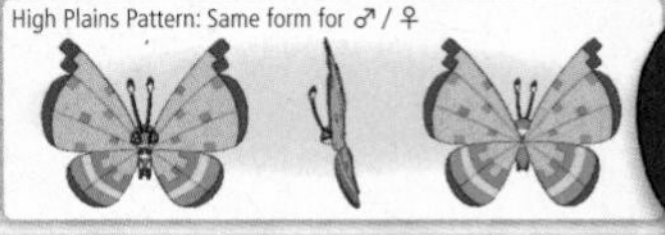

High Plains Pattern: Same form for ♂ / ♀

The area where Vivillon with the Sandstorm Pattern appear

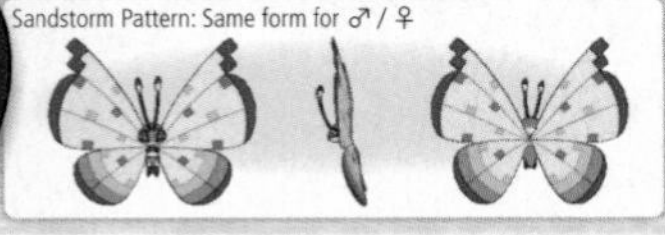

Sandstorm Pattern: Same form for ♂ / ♀

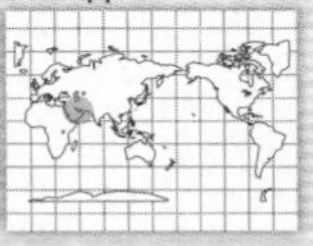

The areas where Vivillon with the River Pattern appear

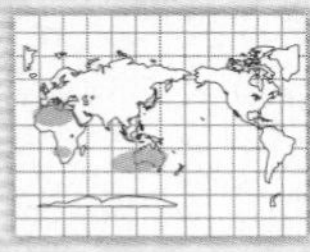

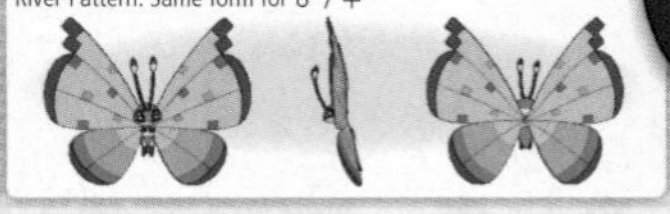

River Pattern: Same form for ♂ / ♀

The area where Vivillon with the Monsoon Pattern appear

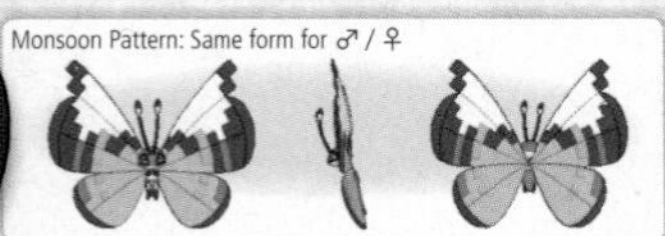

Monsoon Pattern: Same form for ♂ / ♀

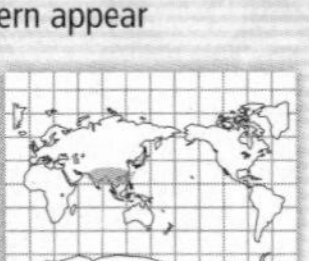

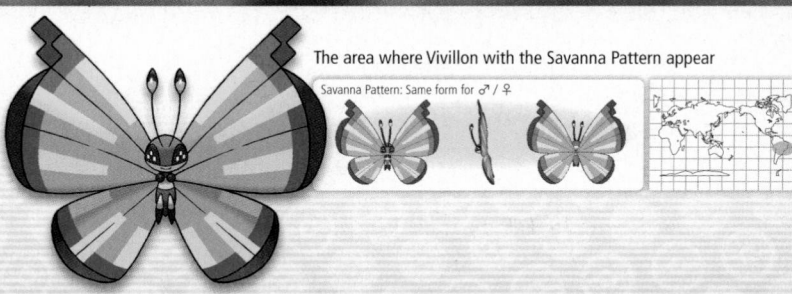

The area where Vivillon with the Savanna Pattern appear

Savanna Pattern: Same form for ♂ / ♀

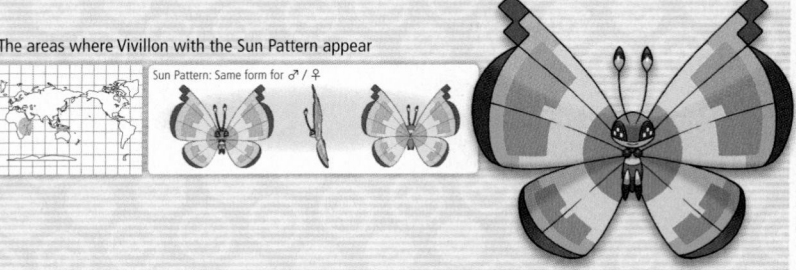

The areas where Vivillon with the Sun Pattern appear

Sun Pattern: Same form for ♂ / ♀

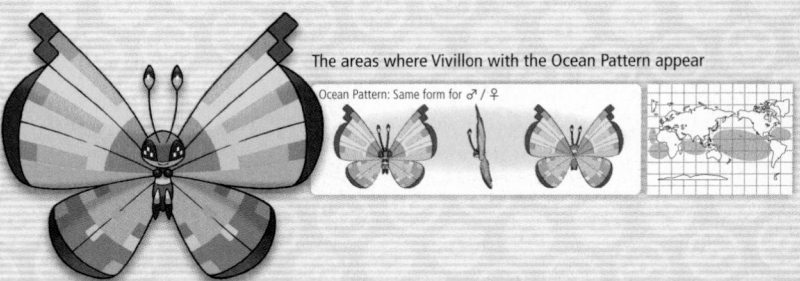

The areas where Vivillon with the Ocean Pattern appear

Ocean Pattern: Same form for ♂ / ♀

The areas where Vivillon with the Jungle Pattern appear

Jungle Pattern: Same form for ♂ / ♀

As of now, 18 different wing patterns of Vivillon have been confirmed. Trade Pokémon via PSS and collect all kinds of Vivillon.

AFTER THE HALL OF FAME

CENTRAL KALOS

023

Caterpie

COASTAL KALOS

MOUNTAIN KALOS

ADVENTURE DATA

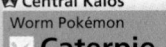

🏠 **Central Kalos** **023**

Worm Pokémon

✔ **Caterpie**

HEIGHT: 1'00" WEIGHT: 6.4 lbs.
GENDER: ♂/♀

X For protection, it releases a horrible stench from the antennae on its head to drive away enemies.

Y Its feet have suction cups designed to stick to any surface. It tenaciously climbs trees to forage.

TYPE **Bug**

ABILITY
Shield Dust

HIDDEN ABILITY
Run Away

STAT GROWTH RATES

HP	■■
Attack	■■
Defense	■■
Sp. Atk	■
Sp. Def	■
Speed	■■■

EGG GROUP
Bug

🔺 **EVOLUTION**

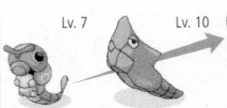

Lv. 7   Lv. 10

Caterpie   Metapod   Butterfree

ITEMS SOMETIMES HELD BY WILD POKÉMON
None

Damage taken in normal battles	
Normal	×1
Fire	×2
Water	×1
Grass	×0.5
Electric	×1
Ice	×1
Fighting	×0.5
Poison	×1
Ground	×0.5
Flying	×2
Psychic	×1
Bug	×1
Rock	×2
Ghost	×1
Dragon	×1
Dark	×1
Steel	×1
Fairy	×1

Damage taken in Inverse Battles	
Normal	×1
Fire	×0.5
Water	×1
Grass	×2
Electric	×1
Ice	×1
Fighting	×2
Poison	×1
Ground	×2
Flying	×0.5
Psychic	×1
Bug	×1
Rock	×0.5
Ghost	×1
Dragon	×1
Dark	×1
Steel	×1
Fairy	×1

Can be used in	
Inverse Battle	Battle Institute
—	Battle Maison
Battle Chateau	Random Matchup

Same form for ♂/♀

How to obtain for your Central Kalos Pokédex

Catch in the tall grass in Santalune Forest.

❶ Catch in the tall grass on Route 2.
❷ Catch in the tall grass in Santalune Forest.

● **LEVEL-UP MOVES**

Lv.	Name	Type	Kind	Pow.	Acc.	PP	Range
1	Tackle	Normal	Physical	50	100	35	Normal
1	String Shot	Bug	Status	—	95	40	Many Others
15	Bug Bite	Bug	Physical	60	100	20	Normal

● **TM & HM MOVES**

No.	Name	Type	Kind	Pow.	Acc.	PP	Range

No.	Name	Type	Kind	Pow.	Acc.	PP	Range

● **MOVES TAUGHT BY PEOPLE**

Name	Type	Kind	Pow.	Acc.	PP	Range

● **EGG MOVES**

Name	Type	Kind	Pow.	Acc.	PP	Range

AFTER THE HALL OF FAME

CENTRAL KALOS

024 Metapod

COASTAL KALOS

MOUNTAIN KALOS

ADVENTURE DATA

Central Kalos 024

Cocoon Pokémon

Metapod

HEIGHT: 2'04"   WEIGHT: 21.8 lbs.
GENDER: ♂/♀

X A steel-hard shell protects its tender body. It quietly endures hardships while awaiting evolution.

Y This Pokémon is vulnerable to attack while its shell is soft, exposing its weak and tender body.

TYPE **Bug**

ABILITY
Shed Skin

HIDDEN ABILITY
None

STAT GROWTH RATES
HP	■ ■
Attack	■
Defense	■ ■ ■
Sp. Atk	■
Sp. Def	■
Speed	■ ■

EGG GROUP
Bug

EVOLUTION

	Lv. 7		Lv. 10	
Caterpie		Metapod		Butterfree

ITEMS SOMETIMES HELD BY WILD POKÉMON
None

Damage taken in normal battles		Damage taken in Inverse Battles	
Normal	×1	Normal	×1
Fire	×2	Fire	×0.5
Water	×1	Water	×1
Grass	×0.5	Grass	×2
Electric	×1	Electric	×1
Ice	×1	Ice	×1
Fighting	×0.5	Fighting	×2
Poison	×1	Poison	×1
Ground	×0.5	Ground	×2
Flying	×2	Flying	×0.5
Psychic	×1	Psychic	×1
Bug	×1	Bug	×1
Rock	×2	Rock	×0.5
Ghost	×1	Ghost	×1
Dragon	×1	Dragon	×1
Dark	×1	Dark	×1
Steel	×1	Steel	×1
Fairy	×1	Fairy	×1

Can be used in	
Inverse Battle	Battle Institute
—	Battle Maison
Battle Chateau	Random Matchup

Same form for ♂/♀

How to obtain for your Central Kalos Pokédex

Level up Caterpie to Lv. 7.

❶ Catch in the tall grass in Santalune Forest.
❷ Level up Caterpie to Lv. 7.

● LEVEL-UP MOVES

Lv.	Name	Type	Kind	Pow.	Acc.	PP	Range
1	Harden	Normal	Status	—	—	30	Self
7	Harden	Normal	Status	—	—	30	Self

● TM & HM MOVES

No.	Name	Type	Kind	Pow.	Acc.	PP	Range		No.	Name	Type	Kind	Pow.	Acc.	PP	Range

● MOVES TAUGHT BY PEOPLE

Name	Type	Kind	Pow.	Acc.	PP	Range

Central Kalos — 025

Butterfly Pokémon

☑ Butterfree

HEIGHT: 3'07" WEIGHT: 70.5 lbs.
GENDER: ♂/♀

X It loves the honey of flowers and can locate flower patches that have even tiny amounts of pollen.

Y The wings are protected by rain-repellent dust. As a result, this Pokémon can fly about even in rain.

TYPE: Bug / Flying

ABILITY
Compound Eyes

HIDDEN ABILITY
Tinted Lens

STAT GROWTH RATES
HP	■ ■ ■
Attack	■ ■
Defense	■ ■
Sp. Atk	■ ■ ■ ■
Sp. Def	■ ■ ■
Speed	■ ■ ■ ■

EGG GROUP
Bug

EVOLUTION

Caterpie — Lv. 7 — Metapod — Lv. 10 — Butterfree

ITEMS SOMETIMES HELD BY WILD POKÉMON
None

Damage taken in normal battles		Damage taken in Inverse Battles	
Normal	×1	Normal	×1
Fire	×2	Fire	×0.5
Water	×1	Water	×1
Grass	×0.25	Grass	×4
Electric	×2	Electric	×0.5
Ice	×2	Ice	×0.5
Fighting	×0.25	Fighting	×4
Poison	×1	Poison	×1
Ground	×0	Ground	×4
Flying	×2	Flying	×0.5
Psychic	×1	Psychic	×1
Bug	×0.5	Bug	×2
Rock	×4	Rock	×0.25
Ghost	×1	Ghost	×1
Dragon	×1	Dragon	×1
Dark	×1	Dark	×1
Steel	×1	Steel	×1
Fairy	×1	Fairy	×1

Can be used in
Inverse Battle
Sky Battle
Battle Chateau
Battle Institute
Battle Maison
Random Matchup

How to obtain for your Central Kalos Pokédex

Level up Metapod to Lv. 10. | Level up Metapod to Lv. 10.

♂    ♀

The base of a male's lower wings is white, while a female's is black.

● LEVEL-UP MOVES

Lv.	Name	Type	Kind	Pow.	Acc.	PP	Range
1	Confusion	Psychic	Special	50	100	25	Normal
10	Confusion	Psychic	Special	50	100	25	Normal
12	Poison Powder	Poison	Status	—	75	35	Normal
12	Stun Spore	Grass	Status	—	75	30	Normal
12	Sleep Powder	Grass	Status	—	75	15	Normal
16	Gust	Flying	Special	40	100	35	Normal
18	Supersonic	Normal	Status	—	55	20	Normal
22	Whirlwind	Normal	Status	—	—	20	Normal
24	Psybeam	Psychic	Special	65	100	20	Normal
28	Silver Wind	Bug	Special	60	100	5	Normal
30	Tailwind	Flying	Status	—	—	15	Your Side
34	Rage Powder	Bug	Status	—	—	20	Self
36	Safeguard	Normal	Status	—	—	25	Your Side
40	Captivate	Normal	Status	—	100	20	Many Others
42	Bug Buzz	Bug	Special	90	100	10	Normal
46	Quiver Dance	Bug	Status	—	—	20	Self

● TM & HM MOVES

No.	Name	Type	Kind	Pow.	Acc.	PP	Range
TM06	Toxic	Poison	Status	—	90	10	Normal
TM09	Venoshock	Poison	Special	65	100	10	Normal
TM10	Hidden Power	Normal	Special	60	100	15	Normal
TM11	Sunny Day	Fire	Status	—	—	5	Both Sides
TM15	Hyper Beam	Normal	Special	150	90	5	Normal
TM17	Protect	Normal	Status	—	—	10	Self
TM18	Rain Dance	Water	Status	—	—	5	Both Sides
TM19	Roost	Flying	Status	—	—	10	Self
TM20	Safeguard	Normal	Status	—	—	25	Your Side
TM21	Frustration	Normal	Physical	—	100	20	Normal
TM22	Solar Beam	Grass	Special	120	100	10	Normal
TM27	Return	Normal	Physical	—	100	20	Normal
TM29	Psychic	Psychic	Special	90	100	10	Normal
TM30	Shadow Ball	Ghost	Special	80	100	15	Normal
TM32	Double Team	Normal	Status	—	—	15	Self
TM40	Aerial Ace	Flying	Physical	60	—	20	Normal
TM42	Facade	Normal	Physical	70	100	20	Normal
TM44	Rest	Psychic	Status	—	—	10	Self
TM45	Attract	Normal	Status	—	100	15	Normal
TM46	Thief	Dark	Physical	60	100	25	Normal
TM48	Round	Normal	Special	60	100	15	Normal
TM53	Energy Ball	Grass	Special	90	100	10	Normal
TM62	Acrobatics	Flying	Physical	55	100	15	Normal
TM68	Giga Impact	Normal	Physical	150	90	5	Normal
TM70	Flash	Normal	Status	—	100	20	Normal
TM76	Struggle Bug	Bug	Special	50	100	20	Many Others
TM77	Psych Up	Normal	Status	—	—	10	Normal
TM83	Infestation	Bug	Special	20	100	20	Normal
TM85	Dream Eater	Psychic	Special	100	100	15	Normal
TM87	Swagger	Normal	Status	—	90	15	Normal
TM88	Sleep Talk	Normal	Status	—	—	10	Self
TM89	U-turn	Bug	Physical	70	100	20	Normal
TM90	Substitute	Normal	Status	—	—	10	Self

No.	Name	Type	Kind	Pow.	Acc.	PP	Range
TM100	Confide	Normal	Status	—	—	20	Normal

● MOVES TAUGHT BY PEOPLE

Name	Type	Kind	Pow.	Acc.	PP	Range

Side tabs: AFTER THE HALL OF FAME · CENTRAL KALOS · COASTAL KALOS · MOUNTAIN KALOS · ADVENTURE DATA · 025 Butterfree

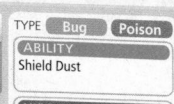

Central Kalos

Hairy Bug Pokémon

☑ Weedle

026

HEIGHT: 1'00"   WEIGHT: 7.1 lbs.
GENDER: ♂ / ♀

TYPE Bug Poison

ABILITY
Shield Dust

HIDDEN ABILITY
Run Away

STAT GROWTH RATES
HP
Attack
Defense
Sp. Atk
Sp. Def
Speed

EGG GROUP
Bug

X — Often found in forests and grasslands. It has a sharp, toxic barb of around two inches on top of its head.

Y — Its poison stinger is very powerful. Its bright-colored body is intended to warn off its enemies.

⚅ EVOLUTION

Weedle → Lv. 7 → Kakuna → Lv. 10 → Beedrill

ITEMS SOMETIMES HELD BY WILD POKÉMON
None

Damage taken in normal battles	
Normal	×1
Fire	×2
Water	×1
Grass	×0.25
Electric	×1
Ice	×1
Fighting	×0.25
Poison	×0.5
Ground	×1
Flying	×2
Psychic	×2
Bug	×0.5
Rock	×2
Ghost	×1
Dragon	×1
Dark	×1
Steel	×1
Fairy	×0.5

Damage taken in Inverse Battles	
Normal	×1
Fire	×0.5
Water	×1
Grass	×4
Electric	×1
Ice	×1
Fighting	×4
Poison	×2
Ground	×1
Flying	×0.5
Psychic	×0.5
Bug	×2
Rock	×0.5
Ghost	×1
Dragon	×1
Dark	×1
Steel	×1
Fairy	×2

Can be used in	
Inverse Battle	Battle Institute
—	Battle Maison
Battle Chateau	Random Matchup

Same form for ♂ / ♀

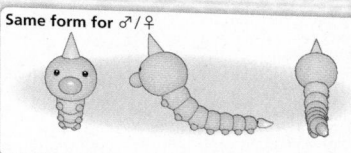

How to obtain for your Central Kalos Pokédex

❶ Catch in the tall grass on Route 2.
❷ Catch in the tall grass in Santalune Forest.

Catch in the tall grass in Santalune Forest.

● LEVEL-UP MOVES

Lv.	Name	Type	Kind	Pow.	Acc.	PP	Range
1	Poison Sting	Poison	Physical	15	100	35	Normal
1	String Shot	Bug	Status	—	95	40	Many Others
15	Bug Bite	Bug	Physical	60	100	20	Normal

● TM & HM MOVES

No.	Name	Type	Kind	Pow.	Acc.	PP	Range

No.	Name	Type	Kind	Pow.	Acc.	PP	Range

● MOVES TAUGHT BY PEOPLE

Name	Type	Kind	Pow.	Acc.	PP	Range

● EGG MOVES

Name	Type	Kind	Pow.	Acc.	PP	Range

AFTER THE HALL OF FAME

CENTRAL KALOS

026 Weedle

COASTAL KALOS

MOUNTAIN KALOS

ADVENTURE DATA

AFTER THE HALL OF FAME

CENTRAL KALOS

027

Kakuna

COASTAL KALOS

MOUNTAIN KALOS

ADVENTURE DATA

Central Kalos 027

Cocoon Pokémon

Kakuna

HEIGHT: 2'00" WEIGHT: 22.0 lbs.
GENDER: ♂/♀

TYPE: Bug Poison

ABILITY
Shed Skin

HIDDEN ABILITY
None

STAT GROWTH RATES
HP ■■
Attack ■
Defense ■■
Sp. Atk ■
Sp. Def ■
Speed ■■

EGG GROUP
Bug

X Almost incapable of moving, this Pokémon can only harden its shell to protect itself when it is in danger.

Y While awaiting evolution, it hides from predators under leaves and in nooks of branches.

EVOLUTION

Weedle — Lv. 7 → Kakuna — Lv. 10 → Beedrill

ITEMS SOMETIMES HELD BY WILD POKÉMON
None

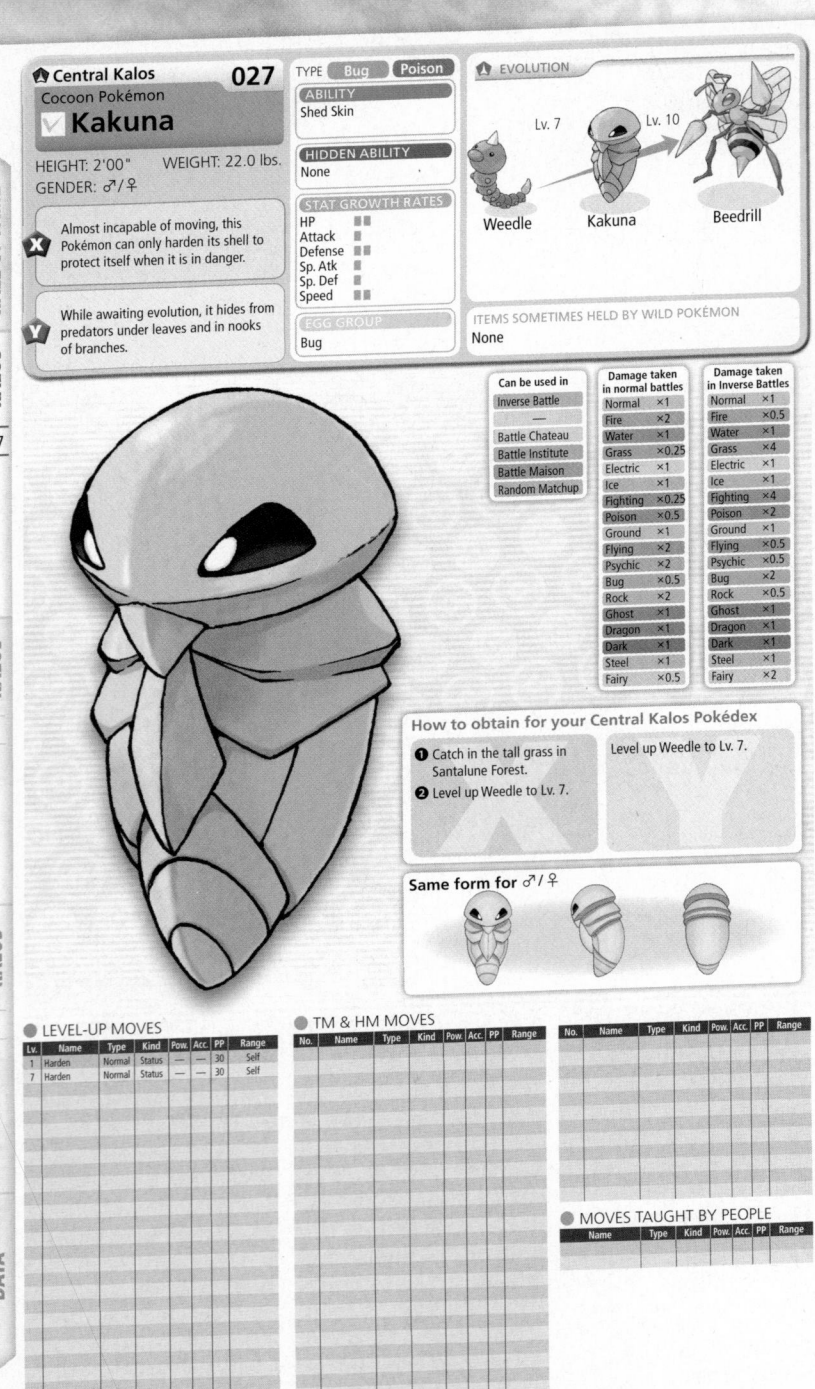

Can be used in
Inverse Battle
—
Battle Chateau
Battle Institute
Battle Maison
Random Matchup

Damage taken in normal battles		Damage taken in Inverse Battles	
Normal	×1	Normal	×1
Fire	×2	Fire	×0.5
Water	×1	Water	×1
Grass	×0.25	Grass	×4
Electric	×1	Electric	×1
Ice	×1	Ice	×1
Fighting	×0.25	Fighting	×4
Poison	×0.5	Poison	×2
Ground	×1	Ground	×1
Flying	×2	Flying	×0.5
Psychic	×2	Psychic	×0.5
Bug	×0.5	Bug	×2
Rock	×2	Rock	×0.5
Ghost	×1	Ghost	×1
Dragon	×1	Dragon	×1
Dark	×1	Dark	×1
Steel	×1	Steel	×1
Fairy	×0.5	Fairy	×2

How to obtain for your Central Kalos Pokédex
1 Catch in the tall grass in Santalune Forest.
2 Level up Weedle to Lv. 7.

Level up Weedle to Lv. 7.

Same form for ♂/♀

● LEVEL-UP MOVES

Lv.	Name	Type	Kind	Pow.	Acc.	PP	Range
1	Harden	Normal	Status	—	—	30	Self
7	Harden	Normal	Status	—	—	30	Self

● TM & HM MOVES

No.	Name	Type	Kind	Pow.	Acc.	PP	Range

No.	Name	Type	Kind	Pow.	Acc.	PP	Range

● MOVES TAUGHT BY PEOPLE

Name	Type	Kind	Pow.	Acc.	PP	Range

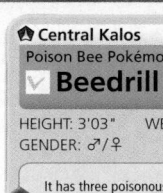

Central Kalos

Poison Bee Pokémon

☑ Beedrill

028

HEIGHT: 3'03" WEIGHT: 65.0 lbs.
GENDER: ♂/♀

Ⓧ It has three poisonous stingers on its forelegs and its tail. They are used to jab its enemy repeatedly.

Ⓨ May appear in a swarm. Flies at violent speeds, all the while stabbing with the toxic stinger on its rear.

TYPE **Bug** **Poison**

ABILITY
Swarm

HIDDEN ABILITY
Sniper

STAT GROWTH RATES

HP	▪▪▪
Attack	▪▪▪▪▪
Defense	▪▪
Sp. Atk	▪▪
Sp. Def	▪▪▪
Speed	▪▪▪▪

EGG GROUP
Bug

⟁ EVOLUTION

Lv. 7   Lv. 10

Weedle   Kakuna   Beedrill

ITEMS SOMETIMES HELD BY WILD POKÉMON
None

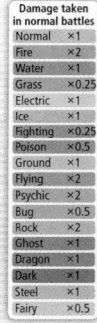

Damage taken in normal battles	
Normal	×1
Fire	×2
Water	×1
Grass	×0.25
Electric	×1
Ice	×1
Fighting	×0.25
Poison	×0.5
Ground	×1
Flying	×2
Psychic	×2
Bug	×0.5
Rock	×2
Ghost	×1
Dragon	×1
Dark	×1
Steel	×1
Fairy	×0.5

Damage taken in Inverse Battles	
Normal	×1
Fire	×0.5
Water	×1
Grass	×4
Electric	×1
Ice	×1
Fighting	×4
Poison	×2
Ground	×1
Flying	×0.5
Psychic	×0.5
Bug	×1
Rock	×0.5
Ghost	×1
Dragon	×1
Dark	×1
Steel	×1
Fairy	×2

Can be used in	
Inverse Battle	Battle Institute
—	Battle Maison
Battle Chateau	Random Matchup

Same form for ♂/♀

How to obtain for your Central Kalos Pokédex

Level up Kakuna to Lv. 10.   Level up Kakuna to Lv. 10.

● LEVEL-UP MOVES

Lv.	Name	Type	Kind	Pow.	Acc.	PP	Range
1	Fury Attack	Normal	Physical	15	85	20	Normal
10	Fury Attack	Normal	Physical	15	85	20	Normal
13	Focus Energy	Normal	Status	—	—	30	Self
16	Twineedle	Bug	Physical	25	100	20	Normal
19	Rage	Normal	Physical	20	100	20	Normal
22	Pursuit	Dark	Physical	40	100	20	Normal
25	Toxic Spikes	Poison	Status	—	—	20	Other Side
28	Pin Missile	Bug	Physical	25	95	20	Normal
31	Agility	Psychic	Status	—	—	30	Self
34	Assurance	Dark	Physical	60	100	10	Normal
37	Poison Jab	Poison	Physical	80	100	20	Normal
40	Endeavor	Normal	Physical	—	100	5	Normal
45	Fell Stinger	Bug	Physical	30	100	25	Normal

● TM & HM MOVES

No.	Name	Type	Kind	Pow.	Acc.	PP	Range
TM06	Toxic	Poison	Status	—	90	10	Normal
TM09	Venoshock	Poison	Special	65	100	10	Normal
TM10	Hidden Power	Normal	Special	60	100	15	Normal
TM11	Sunny Day	Fire	Status	—	—	5	Both Sides
TM15	Hyper Beam	Normal	Special	150	90	5	Normal
TM17	Protect	Normal	Status	—	—	10	Self
TM19	Roost	Flying	Status	—	—	10	Self
TM21	Frustration	Normal	Physical	—	100	20	Normal
TM22	Solar Beam	Grass	Special	120	100	10	Normal
TM27	Return	Normal	Physical	—	100	20	Normal
TM31	Brick Break	Fighting	Physical	75	100	15	Normal
TM32	Double Team	Normal	Status	—	—	15	Self
TM36	Sludge Bomb	Poison	Special	90	100	10	Normal
TM40	Aerial Ace	Flying	Physical	60	—	20	Normal
TM42	Facade	Normal	Physical	70	100	20	Normal
TM44	Rest	Psychic	Status	—	—	10	Self
TM45	Attract	Normal	Status	—	100	15	Normal
TM46	Thief	Dark	Physical	60	100	25	Normal
TM48	Round	Normal	Special	60	100	15	Normal
TM54	False Swipe	Normal	Physical	40	100	40	Normal
TM62	Acrobatics	Flying	Physical	55	100	15	Normal
TM66	Payback	Dark	Physical	50	100	10	Normal
TM68	Giga Impact	Normal	Physical	150	90	5	Normal
TM70	Flash	Normal	Status	—	100	20	Normal
TM75	Swords Dance	Normal	Status	—	—	20	Self
TM76	Struggle Bug	Bug	Special	50	100	20	Many Others
TM81	X-Scissor	Bug	Physical	80	100	15	Normal
TM83	Infestation	Bug	Special	20	100	20	Normal
TM84	Poison Jab	Poison	Physical	80	100	20	Normal
TM87	Swagger	Normal	Status	—	90	15	Normal
TM88	Sleep Talk	Normal	Status	—	—	10	Self
TM89	U-turn	Bug	Physical	70	100	20	Normal
TM90	Substitute	Normal	Status	—	—	10	Self
TM94	Rock Smash	Fighting	Physical	40	100	15	Normal
TM100	Confide	Normal	Status	—	—	20	Normal
HM01	Cut	Normal	Physical	50	95	30	Normal

● MOVES TAUGHT BY PEOPLE

Name	Type	Kind	Pow.	Acc.	PP	Range

AFTER THE HALL OF FAME

CENTRAL KALOS

028 | Beedrill

COASTAL KALOS

MOUNTAIN KALOS

ADVENTURE DATA

AFTER THE HALL OF FAME

CENTRAL KALOS

029

Pansage

COASTAL KALOS

MOUNTAIN KALOS

ADVENTURE DATA

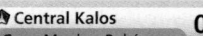 **Central Kalos** **029**
Grass Monkey Pokémon
Pansage

HEIGHT: 2'00" WEIGHT: 23.1 lbs.
GENDER: ♂/♀

X It shares the leaf on its head with weary-looking Pokémon. These leaves are known to relieve stress.

Y It's good at finding berries and gathers them from all over. It's kind enough to share them with friends.

 TYPE Grass

ABILITY
Gluttony

HIDDEN ABILITY
Overgrow

STAT GROWTH RATES
HP	■■
Attack	■■■
Defense	■■
Sp. Atk	■■■
Sp. Def	■■
Speed	■■■■

EGG GROUP
Field

EVOLUTION

Leaf Stone

Pansage → Simisage

ITEMS SOMETIMES HELD BY WILD POKÉMON
None

Can be used in
Inverse Battle
—
Battle Chateau
Battle Institute
Battle Maison
Random Matchup

Damage taken in normal battles
Normal	×1
Fire	×2
Water	×0.5
Grass	×0.5
Electric	×0.5
Ice	×2
Fighting	×1
Poison	×2
Ground	×0.5
Flying	×2
Psychic	×1
Bug	×2
Rock	×1
Ghost	×1
Dragon	×1
Dark	×1
Steel	×1
Fairy	×1

Damage taken in Inverse Battles
Normal	×1
Fire	×0.5
Water	×2
Grass	×2
Electric	×2
Ice	×0.5
Fighting	×1
Poison	×0.5
Ground	×2
Flying	×0.5
Psychic	×1
Bug	×0.5
Rock	×1
Ghost	×1
Dragon	×1
Dark	×1
Steel	×1
Fairy	×1

Same form for ♂/♀

How to obtain for your Central Kalos Pokédex

Catch in the tall grass in Santalune Forest.

Catch in the tall grass in Santalune Forest.

● LEVEL-UP MOVES
Lv.	Name	Type	Kind	Pow.	Acc.	PP	Range
1	Scratch	Normal	Physical	40	100	35	Normal
1	Play Nice	Normal	Status	—	—	20	Normal
4	Leer	Normal	Status	—	100	30	Many Others
7	Lick	Ghost	Physical	30	100	30	Normal
10	Vine Whip	Grass	Physical	45	100	25	Normal
13	Fury Swipes	Normal	Physical	18	80	15	Normal
16	Leech Seed	Grass	Status	—	90	10	Normal
19	Bite	Dark	Physical	60	100	25	Normal
22	Seed Bomb	Grass	Physical	80	100	15	Normal
25	Torment	Dark	Status	—	100	15	Normal
28	Fling	Dark	Physical	—	100	10	Normal
31	Acrobatics	Flying	Physical	55	100	15	Normal
34	Grass Knot	Grass	Special	—	100	20	Normal
37	Recycle	Normal	Status	—	—	10	Self
40	Natural Gift	Normal	Physical	—	100	15	Normal
43	Crunch	Dark	Physical	80	100	15	Normal

● TM & HM MOVES
No.	Name	Type	Kind	Pow.	Acc.	PP	Range
TM01	Hone Claws	Dark	Status	—	—	15	Self
TM06	Toxic	Poison	Status	—	90	10	Normal
TM10	Hidden Power	Normal	Special	60	100	15	Normal
TM11	Sunny Day	Fire	Status	—	—	5	Both Sides
TM12	Taunt	Dark	Status	—	100	20	Normal
TM17	Protect	Normal	Status	—	—	10	Self
TM21	Frustration	Normal	Physical	—	100	20	Normal
TM22	Solar Beam	Grass	Special	120	100	10	Normal
TM27	Return	Normal	Physical	—	100	20	Normal
TM28	Dig	Ground	Physical	80	100	10	Normal
TM32	Double Team	Normal	Status	—	—	15	Self
TM39	Rock Tomb	Rock	Physical	60	95	15	Normal
TM41	Torment	Dark	Status	—	100	15	Normal
TM42	Facade	Normal	Physical	70	100	20	Normal
TM44	Rest	Psychic	Status	—	—	10	Self
TM45	Attract	Normal	Status	—	100	15	Normal
TM46	Thief	Dark	Physical	60	100	25	Normal
TM48	Round	Normal	Special	60	100	15	Normal
TM53	Energy Ball	Grass	Special	90	100	10	Normal
TM56	Fling	Dark	Physical	—	100	10	Normal
TM62	Acrobatics	Flying	Physical	55	100	15	Normal
TM65	Shadow Claw	Ghost	Physical	70	100	15	Normal
TM66	Payback	Dark	Physical	50	100	10	Normal
TM70	Flash	Normal	Status	—	100	20	Normal
TM86	Grass Knot	Grass	Special	—	100	20	Normal
TM87	Swagger	Normal	Status	—	90	15	Normal
TM88	Sleep Talk	Normal	Status	—	—	10	Self
TM90	Substitute	Normal	Status	—	—	10	Self
TM94	Rock Smash	Fighting	Physical	40	100	15	Normal
TM96	Nature Power	Normal	Status	—	—	20	Normal
TM100	Confide	Normal	Status	—	—	20	Normal
HM01	Cut	Normal	Physical	50	95	30	Normal

No.	Name	Type	Kind	Pow.	Acc.	PP	Range

● MOVES TAUGHT BY PEOPLE
Name	Type	Kind	Pow.	Acc.	PP	Range

● EGG MOVES
Name	Type	Kind	Pow.	Acc.	PP	Range
Covet	Normal	Physical	60	100	25	Normal
Low Kick	Fighting	Physical	—	100	20	Normal
Tickle	Normal	Status	—	100	20	Normal
Nasty Plot	Dark	Status	—	—	20	Self
Role Play	Psychic	Status	—	—	10	Normal
Astonish	Ghost	Physical	30	100	15	Normal
Grass Whistle	Grass	Status	—	55	15	Normal
Magical Leaf	Grass	Special	60	—	20	Normal
Bullet Seed	Grass	Physical	25	100	30	Normal
Leaf Storm	Grass	Special	130	90	5	Normal
Disarming Voice	Fairy	Special	40	—	15	Many Others

Central Kalos **030**
Thorn Monkey Pokémon
 Simisage

HEIGHT: 3'07"   WEIGHT: 67.2 lbs.
GENDER: ♂/♀

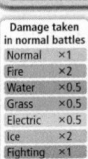
X It attacks enemies with strikes of its thorn-covered tail. This Pokémon is wild tempered.

Y Ill tempered, it fights by swinging its barbed tail around wildly. The leaf growing on its head is very bitter.

TYPE Grass

ABILITY
Gluttony

HIDDEN ABILITY
Overgrow

STAT GROWTH RATES
HP	■■■
Attack	■■■■■
Defense	■■■
Sp. Atk	■■■■■
Sp. Def	■■■
Speed	■■■■■

EGG GROUP
Field

EVOLUTION

Leaf Stone

Pansage   Simisage

ITEMS SOMETIMES HELD BY WILD POKÉMON
None

AFTER THE HALL OF FAME

CENTRAL KALOS

030

Simisage

COASTAL KALOS

MOUNTAIN KALOS

ADVENTURE DATA

Damage taken in normal battles		Damage taken in Inverse Battles		Can be used in
Normal	×1	Normal	×1	Inverse Battle
Fire	×2	Fire	×0.5	—
Water	×0.5	Water	×2	Battle Chateau
Grass	×0.5	Grass	×2	Battle Institute
Electric	×0.5	Electric	×2	Battle Maison
Ice	×2	Ice	×0.5	Random Matchup
Fighting	×1	Fighting	×1	
Poison	×2	Poison	×0.5	
Ground	×0.5	Ground	×2	
Flying	×2	Flying	×0.5	
Psychic	×1	Psychic	×1	
Bug	×2	Bug	×0.5	
Rock	×1	Rock	×1	
Ghost	×1	Ghost	×1	
Dragon	×1	Dragon	×1	
Dark	×1	Dark	×1	
Steel	×1	Steel	×1	
Fairy	×1	Fairy	×1	

How to obtain for your Central Kalos Pokédex

Use a Leaf Stone on Pansage.   Use a Leaf Stone on Pansage.

X   **Y**

Same form for ♂/♀

● LEVEL-UP MOVES

Lv.	Name	Type	Kind	Pow.	Acc.	PP	Range
1	Leer	Normal	Status	—	100	30	Many Others
1	Lick	Ghost	Physical	30	100	30	Normal
1	Fury Swipes	Normal	Physical	18	80	15	Normal
1	Seed Bomb	Grass	Physical	80	100	15	Normal

■ TM & HM MOVES

No.	Name	Type	Kind	Pow.	Acc.	PP	Range
TM01	Hone Claws	Dark	Status	—	—	15	Self
TM06	Toxic	Poison	Status	—	90	10	Normal
TM10	Hidden Power	Normal	Special	60	100	15	Normal
TM11	Sunny Day	Fire	Status	—	—	5	Both Sides
TM12	Taunt	Dark	Status	—	100	20	Normal
TM15	Hyper Beam	Normal	Special	150	90	5	Normal
TM17	Protect	Normal	Status	—	—	10	Self
TM21	Frustration	Normal	Physical	—	100	20	Normal
TM22	Solar Beam	Grass	Special	120	100	10	Normal
TM27	Return	Normal	Physical	—	100	20	Normal
TM28	Dig	Ground	Physical	80	100	10	Normal
TM31	Brick Break	Fighting	Physical	75	100	15	Normal
TM32	Double Team	Normal	Status	—	—	15	Self
TM39	Rock Tomb	Rock	Physical	60	95	15	Normal
TM41	Torment	Dark	Status	—	100	15	Normal
TM42	Facade	Normal	Physical	70	100	20	Normal
TM44	Rest	Psychic	Status	—	—	10	Self
TM45	Attract	Normal	Status	—	100	15	Normal
TM46	Thief	Dark	Physical	60	100	25	Normal
TM47	Low Sweep	Fighting	Physical	65	100	20	Normal
TM48	Round	Normal	Special	60	100	15	Normal
TM52	Focus Blast	Fighting	Special	120	70	5	Normal
TM53	Energy Ball	Grass	Special	90	100	10	Normal
TM56	Fling	Dark	Physical	—	100	10	Normal
TM62	Acrobatics	Flying	Physical	55	100	15	Normal
TM65	Shadow Claw	Ghost	Physical	70	100	15	Normal
TM66	Payback	Dark	Physical	50	100	10	Normal
TM68	Giga Impact	Normal	Physical	150	90	5	Normal
TM70	Flash	Normal	Status	—	100	20	Normal
TM80	Rock Slide	Rock	Physical	75	90	10	Many Others
TM86	Grass Knot	Grass	Special	—	100	20	Normal
TM87	Swagger	Normal	Status	—	90	15	Normal
TM88	Sleep Talk	Normal	Status	—	—	10	Self

No.	Name	Type	Kind	Pow.	Acc.	PP	Range
TM90	Substitute	Normal	Status	—	—	10	Self
TM94	Rock Smash	Fighting	Physical	40	100	15	Normal
TM96	Nature Power	Normal	Status	—	—	20	Normal
TM98	Power-Up Punch	Fighting	Physical	40	100	20	Normal
TM100	Confide	Normal	Status	—	—	20	Normal
HM01	Cut	Normal	Physical	50	95	30	Normal

● MOVES TAUGHT BY PEOPLE

Name	Type	Kind	Pow.	Acc.	PP	Range

AFTER THE HALL OF FAME

CENTRAL KALOS

031

Pansear

COASTAL KALOS

MOUNTAIN KALOS

ADVENTURE DATA

🔺 Central Kalos — 031

High Temp Pokémon
☑ Pansear

HEIGHT: 2'00"　WEIGHT: 24.3 lbs.
GENDER: ♂/♀

TYPE Fire

ABILITY
Gluttony

HIDDEN ABILITY
Blaze

STAT GROWTH RATES
HP	■■
Attack	■■■
Defense	■■
Sp. Atk	■■■
Sp. Def	■■
Speed	■■■■

EGG GROUP
Field

❌ Very intelligent, it roasts berries before eating them. It likes to help people.

🔵 This Pokémon lives in caves in volcanoes. The fire within the tuft on its head can reach 600 degrees Fahrenheit.

🔺 EVOLUTION

Pansear → Fire Stone → Simisear

ITEMS SOMETIMES HELD BY WILD POKÉMON
None

Damage taken in normal battles	
Normal	×1
Fire	×0.5
Water	×2
Grass	×0.5
Electric	×1
Ice	×0.5
Fighting	×1
Poison	×1
Ground	×2
Flying	×1
Psychic	×1
Bug	×0.5
Rock	×2
Ghost	×1
Dragon	×1
Dark	×1
Steel	×0.5
Fairy	×0.5

Damage taken in Inverse Battles	
Normal	×1
Fire	×2
Water	×0.5
Grass	×2
Electric	×1
Ice	×2
Fighting	×1
Poison	×1
Ground	×0.5
Flying	×1
Psychic	×1
Bug	×2
Rock	×0.5
Ghost	×1
Dragon	×1
Dark	×1
Steel	×2
Fairy	×2

Can be used in	
Inverse Battle	Battle Institute
—	Battle Maison
Battle Chateau	Random Matchup

Same form for ♂/♀

How to obtain for your Central Kalos Pokédex

Catch in the tall grass in Santalune Forest.	Catch in the tall grass in Santalune Forest.
X	Y

● LEVEL-UP MOVES

Lv.	Name	Type	Kind	Pow.	Acc.	PP	Range
1	Scratch	Normal	Physical	40	100	35	Normal
1	Play Nice	Normal	Status	—	—	20	Normal
4	Leer	Normal	Status	—	100	30	Many Others
7	Lick	Ghost	Physical	30	100	30	Normal
10	Incinerate	Fire	Special	60	100	15	Many Others
16	Fury Swipes	Normal	Physical	18	80	15	Normal
19	Yawn	Normal	Status	—	—	10	Normal
19	Bite	Dark	Physical	60	100	25	Normal
22	Flame Burst	Fire	Special	70	100	15	Normal
25	Amnesia	Psychic	Status	—	—	20	Self
28	Fling	Dark	Physical	—	100	10	Normal
31	Acrobatics	Flying	Physical	55	100	15	Normal
34	Fire Blast	Fire	Special	110	85	5	Normal
37	Recycle	Normal	Status	—	—	10	Self
40	Natural Gift	Normal	Physical	—	100	15	Normal
43	Crunch	Dark	Physical	80	100	15	Normal

● TM & HM MOVES

No.	Name	Type	Kind	Pow.	Acc.	PP	Range
TM01	Hone Claws	Dark	Status	—	—	15	Self
TM06	Toxic	Poison	Status	—	90	10	Normal
TM10	Hidden Power	Normal	Special	60	100	15	Normal
TM11	Sunny Day	Fire	Status	—	—	5	Both Sides
TM12	Taunt	Dark	Status	—	100	20	Normal
TM17	Protect	Normal	Status	—	—	10	Self
TM21	Frustration	Normal	Physical	—	100	20	Normal
TM22	Solar Beam	Grass	Special	120	100	10	Normal
TM27	Return	Normal	Physical	—	100	20	Normal
TM28	Dig	Ground	Physical	80	100	10	Normal
TM32	Double Team	Normal	Status	—	—	15	Self
TM35	Flamethrower	Fire	Special	90	100	15	Normal
TM38	Fire Blast	Fire	Special	110	85	5	Normal
TM39	Rock Tomb	Rock	Physical	60	95	15	Normal
TM41	Torment	Dark	Status	—	100	15	Normal
TM42	Facade	Normal	Physical	70	100	20	Normal
TM43	Flame Charge	Fire	Physical	50	100	20	Normal
TM44	Rest	Psychic	Status	—	—	10	Self
TM45	Attract	Normal	Status	—	100	15	Normal
TM46	Thief	Dark	Physical	60	100	25	Normal
TM47	Low Sweep	Fighting	Physical	65	100	20	Normal
TM48	Round	Normal	Special	60	100	15	Normal
TM50	Overheat	Fire	Special	130	90	5	Normal
TM56	Fling	Dark	Physical	—	100	10	Normal
TM59	Incinerate	Fire	Special	60	100	15	Many Others
TM61	Will-O-Wisp	Fire	Status	—	85	15	Normal
TM62	Acrobatics	Flying	Physical	55	100	15	Normal
TM65	Shadow Claw	Ghost	Physical	70	100	15	Normal
TM66	Payback	Dark	Physical	50	100	10	Normal
TM86	Grass Knot	Grass	Special	—	100	20	Normal
TM87	Swagger	Normal	Status	—	90	15	Normal
TM88	Sleep Talk	Normal	Status	—	—	10	Self
TM90	Substitute	Normal	Status	—	—	10	Self

No.	Name	Type	Kind	Pow.	Acc.	PP	Range
TM94	Rock Smash	Fighting	Physical	40	100	15	Normal
TM100	Confide	Normal	Status	—	—	20	Normal
HM01	Cut	Normal	Physical	50	95	30	Normal

● MOVES TAUGHT BY PEOPLE

Name	Type	Kind	Pow.	Acc.	PP	Range

● EGG MOVES

Name	Type	Kind	Pow.	Acc.	PP	Range
Covet	Normal	Physical	60	100	25	Normal
Low Kick	Fighting	Physical	—	100	20	Normal
Tickle	Normal	Status	—	100	20	Normal
Nasty Plot	Dark	Status	—	—	20	Self
Role Play	Psychic	Status	—	—	10	Normal
Astonish	Ghost	Physical	30	100	15	Normal
Sleep Talk	Normal	Status	—	—	10	Self
Fire Spin	Fire	Special	35	85	15	Normal
Fire Punch	Fire	Physical	75	100	15	Normal
Heat Wave	Fire	Special	95	90	10	Many Others
Disarming Voice	Fairy	Special	40	—	15	Many Others

AFTER THE HALL OF FAME

CENTRAL KALOS

032 | Simisear

COASTAL KALOS

MOUNTAIN KALOS

ADVENTURE DATA

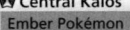

Central Kalos — 032

Ember Pokémon

☑ Simisear

HEIGHT: 3'03" WEIGHT: 61.7 lbs.
GENDER: ♂/♀

 A flame burns inside its body. It scatters embers from its head and tail to sear its opponents.

 When it gets excited, embers rise from its head and tail and it gets hot. For some reason, it loves sweets.

TYPE Fire

ABILITY
Gluttony

HIDDEN ABILITY
Blaze

STAT GROWTH RATES

HP	■■■
Attack	■■■■■
Defense	■■■
Sp. Atk	■■■■■
Sp. Def	■■■
Speed	■■■■■

EGG GROUP
Field

ITEMS SOMETIMES HELD BY WILD POKÉMON
None

⬆ EVOLUTION

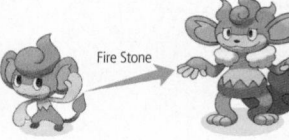

Pansear → (Fire Stone) → Simisear

Damage taken in normal battles		Damage taken in Inverse Battles	
Normal	×1	Normal	×1
Fire	×0.5	Fire	×2
Water	×2	Water	×0.5
Grass	×0.5	Grass	×2
Electric	×1	Electric	×1
Ice	×0.5	Ice	×2
Fighting	×1	Fighting	×1
Poison	×1	Poison	×1
Ground	×2	Ground	×0.5
Flying	×1	Flying	×1
Psychic	×1	Psychic	×1
Bug	×0.5	Bug	×2
Rock	×2	Rock	×0.5
Ghost	×1	Ghost	×1
Dragon	×1	Dragon	×1
Dark	×1	Dark	×1
Steel	×0.5	Steel	×2
Fairy	×0.5	Fairy	×2

Can be used in	
Inverse Battle	Battle Institute
—	Battle Maison
Battle Chateau	Random Matchup

Same form for ♂/♀

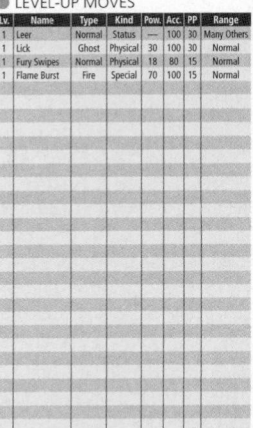

How to obtain for your Central Kalos Pokédex

Use a Fire Stone on Pansear.   Use a Fire Stone on Pansear.

● LEVEL-UP MOVES

Lv.	Name	Type	Kind	Pow.	Acc.	PP	Range
1	Leer	Normal	Status	—	100	30	Many Others
1	Lick	Ghost	Physical	30	100	30	Normal
1	Fury Swipes	Normal	Physical	18	80	15	Normal
1	Flame Burst	Fire	Special	70	100	15	Normal

● TM & HM MOVES

No.	Name	Type	Kind	Pow.	Acc.	PP	Range
TM01	Hone Claws	Dark	Status	—	—	15	Self
TM06	Toxic	Poison	Status	—	90	10	Normal
TM10	Hidden Power	Normal	Special	60	100	15	Normal
TM11	Sunny Day	Fire	Status	—	—	5	Both Sides
TM12	Taunt	Dark	Status	—	100	20	Normal
TM15	Hyper Beam	Normal	Special	150	90	5	Normal
TM17	Protect	Normal	Status	—	—	10	Self
TM21	Frustration	Normal	Physical	—	100	20	Normal
TM22	Solar Beam	Grass	Special	120	100	10	Normal
TM27	Return	Normal	Physical	—	100	20	Normal
TM28	Dig	Ground	Physical	80	100	10	Normal
TM31	Brick Break	Fighting	Physical	75	100	15	Normal
TM32	Double Team	Normal	Status	—	—	15	Self
TM35	Flamethrower	Fire	Special	90	100	15	Normal
TM38	Fire Blast	Fire	Special	110	85	5	Normal
TM39	Rock Tomb	Rock	Physical	60	95	15	Normal
TM41	Torment	Dark	Status	—	100	15	Normal
TM42	Facade	Normal	Physical	70	100	20	Normal
TM43	Flame Charge	Fire	Physical	50	100	20	Normal
TM44	Rest	Psychic	Status	—	—	10	Self
TM45	Attract	Normal	Status	—	100	15	Normal
TM46	Thief	Dark	Physical	60	100	25	Normal
TM47	Low Sweep	Fighting	Physical	65	100	20	Normal
TM48	Round	Normal	Special	60	100	15	Normal
TM50	Overheat	Fire	Special	130	90	5	Normal
TM52	Focus Blast	Fighting	Special	120	70	5	Normal
TM56	Fling	Dark	Physical	—	100	10	Normal
TM59	Incinerate	Fire	Special	60	100	15	Many Others
TM61	Will-O-Wisp	Fire	Status	—	85	15	Normal
TM62	Acrobatics	Flying	Physical	55	100	15	Normal
TM65	Shadow Claw	Ghost	Physical	70	100	15	Normal
TM66	Payback	Dark	Physical	50	100	10	Normal
TM68	Giga Impact	Normal	Physical	150	90	5	Normal

No.	Name	Type	Kind	Pow.	Acc.	PP	Range
TM80	Rock Slide	Rock	Physical	75	90	10	Many Others
TM86	Grass Knot	Grass	Special	—	100	20	Normal
TM87	Swagger	Normal	Status	—	90	15	Normal
TM88	Sleep Talk	Normal	Status	—	—	10	Self
TM90	Substitute	Normal	Status	—	—	10	Self
TM94	Rock Smash	Fighting	Physical	40	100	15	Normal
TM98	Power-Up Punch	Fighting	Physical	40	100	20	Normal
TM100	Confide	Normal	Status	—	—	20	Normal
HM01	Cut	Normal	Physical	50	95	30	Normal

● MOVES TAUGHT BY PEOPLE

Name	Type	Kind	Pow.	Acc.	PP	Range

AFTER THE HALL OF FAME

CENTRAL KALOS
033
Panpour

COASTAL KALOS

MOUNTAIN KALOS

ADVENTURE DATA

Central Kalos 033

Spray Pokémon

☑ **Panpour**

HEIGHT: 2'00" WEIGHT: 29.8 lbs.
GENDER: ♂/♀

X The water stored inside the tuft on its head is full of nutrients. It waters plants with it using its tail.

Y The water stored inside the tuft on its head is full of nutrients. Plants that receive its water grow large.

TYPE Water

ABILITY
Gluttony

HIDDEN ABILITY
Torrent

STAT GROWTH RATES
HP	■■
Attack	■■■
Defense	■■
Sp. Atk	■■■
Sp. Def	■■
Speed	■■■■

EGG GROUP
Field

EVOLUTION

Panpour → Water Stone → Simipour

ITEMS SOMETIMES HELD BY WILD POKÉMON
None

	Damage taken in normal battles		Damage taken in Inverse Battles
Normal	×1	Normal	×1
Fire	×0.5	Fire	×2
Water	×0.5	Water	×2
Grass	×2	Grass	×0.5
Electric	×2	Electric	×0.5
Ice	×0.5	Ice	×2
Fighting	×1	Fighting	×1
Poison	×1	Poison	×1
Ground	×1	Ground	×1
Flying	×1	Flying	×1
Psychic	×1	Psychic	×1
Bug	×1	Bug	×1
Rock	×1	Rock	×1
Ghost	×1	Ghost	×1
Dragon	×1	Dragon	×1
Dark	×1	Dark	×1
Steel	×0.5	Steel	×2
Fairy	×1	Fairy	×1

Can be used in	
Inverse Battle	Battle Institute
—	Battle Maison
Battle Chateau	Random Matchup

Same form for ♂/♀

How to obtain for your Central Kalos Pokédex

Catch in the tall grass in Santalune Forest.

Catch in the tall grass in Santalune Forest.

● LEVEL-UP MOVES

Lv.	Name	Type	Kind	Pow.	Acc.	PP	Range
1	Scratch	Normal	Physical	40	100	35	Normal
1	Play Nice	Normal	Status	—	—	20	Normal
4	Leer	Normal	Status	—	100	30	Many Others
7	Lick	Ghost	Physical	30	100	30	Normal
10	Water Gun	Water	Special	40	100	25	Normal
13	Fury Swipes	Normal	Physical	18	80	15	Normal
16	Water Sport	Water	Status	—	—	15	Both Sides
19	Bite	Dark	Physical	60	100	25	Normal
22	Scald	Water	Special	80	100	15	Normal
25	Taunt	Dark	Status	—	100	20	Normal
28	Fling	Dark	Physical	—	100	10	Normal
31	Acrobatics	Flying	Physical	55	100	15	Normal
34	Brine	Water	Special	65	100	10	Normal
37	Recycle	Normal	Status	—	—	10	Self
40	Natural Gift	Normal	Physical	—	100	15	Normal
43	Crunch	Dark	Physical	80	100	15	Normal

● TM & HM MOVES

No.	Name	Type	Kind	Pow.	Acc.	PP	Range
TM01	Hone Claws	Dark	Status	—	—	15	Self
TM06	Toxic	Poison	Status	—	90	10	Normal
TM07	Hail	Ice	Status	—	—	10	Both Sides
TM10	Hidden Power	Normal	Special	60	100	15	Normal
TM12	Taunt	Dark	Status	—	100	20	Normal
TM13	Ice Beam	Ice	Special	90	100	10	Normal
TM14	Blizzard	Ice	Special	110	70	5	Many Others
TM17	Protect	Normal	Status	—	—	10	Self
TM18	Rain Dance	Water	Status	—	—	5	Both Sides
TM21	Frustration	Normal	Physical	—	100	20	Normal
TM27	Return	Normal	Physical	—	100	20	Normal
TM28	Dig	Ground	Physical	80	100	10	Normal
TM32	Double Team	Normal	Status	—	—	15	Self
TM39	Rock Tomb	Rock	Physical	60	95	15	Normal
TM41	Torment	Dark	Status	—	100	15	Normal
TM42	Facade	Normal	Physical	70	100	20	Normal
TM44	Rest	Psychic	Status	—	—	10	Self
TM45	Attract	Normal	Status	—	100	15	Normal
TM46	Thief	Dark	Physical	60	100	25	Normal
TM47	Low Sweep	Fighting	Physical	65	100	20	Normal
TM48	Round	Normal	Special	60	100	15	Normal
TM55	Scald	Water	Special	80	100	15	Normal
TM56	Fling	Dark	Physical	—	100	10	Normal
TM62	Acrobatics	Flying	Physical	55	100	15	Normal
TM66	Payback	Dark	Physical	50	100	10	Normal
TM86	Grass Knot	Grass	Special	—	100	20	Normal
TM87	Swagger	Normal	Status	—	90	15	Normal
TM88	Sleep Talk	Normal	Status	—	—	10	Self
TM90	Substitute	Normal	Status	—	—	10	Self
TM94	Rock Smash	Fighting	Physical	40	100	15	Normal
TM100	Confide	Normal	Status	—	—	20	Normal
HM01	Cut	Normal	Physical	50	95	30	Normal

No.	Name	Type	Kind	Pow.	Acc.	PP	Range
HM03	Surf	Water	Special	90	100	15	Adjacent
HM05	Waterfall	Water	Physical	80	100	15	Normal

● MOVES TAUGHT BY PEOPLE

Name	Type	Kind	Pow.	Acc.	PP	Range

● EGG MOVES

Name	Type	Kind	Pow.	Acc.	PP	Range
Covet	Normal	Physical	60	100	25	Normal
Low Kick	Fighting	Physical	—	100	20	Normal
Tickle	Normal	Status	—	100	20	Normal
Nasty Plot	Dark	Status	—	—	20	Self
Role Play	Psychic	Status	—	—	10	Normal
Astonish	Ghost	Physical	30	100	15	Normal
Aqua Ring	Water	Status	—	—	20	Self
Aqua Tail	Water	Physical	90	90	10	Normal
Mud Sport	Ground	Status	—	—	15	Both Sides
Hydro Pump	Water	Special	110	80	5	Normal
Disarming Voice	Fairy	Special	40	—	15	Many Others

Central Kalos

Geyser Pokémon

☑ **Simipour** **034**

HEIGHT: 3'03" WEIGHT: 63.9 lbs.
GENDER: ♂/♀

X The high-pressure water expelled from its tail is so powerful, it can destroy a concrete wall.

Y It prefers places with clean water. When its tuft runs low, it replenishes it by siphoning up water with its tail.

TYPE Water

ABILITY
Gluttony

HIDDEN ABILITY
Torrent

STAT GROWTH RATES

HP	■■■
Attack	■■■■■
Defense	■■■
Sp. Atk	■■■■■
Sp. Def	■■■
Speed	■■■■■

EGG GROUP
Field

EVOLUTION

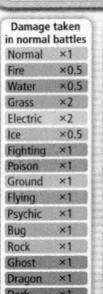

Panpour → Water Stone → Simipour

ITEMS SOMETIMES HELD BY WILD POKÉMON
None

Damage taken in normal battles			Damage taken in Inverse Battles			Can be used in
Normal	×1		Normal	×1		Inverse Battle
Fire	×0.5		Fire	×2		
Water	×0.5		Water	×2		Battle Chateau
Grass	×2		Grass	×0.5		Battle Institute
Electric	×2		Electric	×0.5		Battle Maison
Ice	×0.5		Ice	×2		Random Matchup
Fighting	×1		Fighting	×1		
Poison	×1		Poison	×1		
Ground	×1		Ground	×1		
Flying	×1		Flying	×1		
Psychic	×1		Psychic	×1		
Bug	×1		Bug	×1		
Rock	×1		Rock	×1		
Ghost	×1		Ghost	×1		
Dragon	×1		Dragon	×1		
Dark	×1		Dark	×1		
Steel	×0.5		Steel	×2		
Fairy	×1		Fairy	×1		

How to obtain for your Central Kalos Pokédex

Use a Water Stone on Panpour.	Use a Water Stone on Panpour.

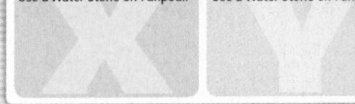

Same form for ♂/♀

● LEVEL-UP MOVES

Lv.	Name	Type	Kind	Pow.	Acc.	PP	Range
1	Leer	Normal	Status	—	100	30	Many Others
1	Lick	Ghost	Physical	30	100	30	Normal
1	Fury Swipes	Normal	Physical	18	80	15	Normal
1	Scald	Water	Special	80	100	15	Normal

● TM & HM MOVES

No.	Name	Type	Kind	Pow.	Acc.	PP	Range
TM01	Hone Claws	Dark	Status	—	—	15	Self
TM06	Toxic	Poison	Status	—	90	10	Normal
TM07	Hail	Ice	Status	—	—	10	Both Sides
TM10	Hidden Power	Normal	Special	60	100	15	Normal
TM12	Taunt	Dark	Status	—	100	20	Normal
TM13	Ice Beam	Ice	Special	90	100	10	Normal
TM14	Blizzard	Ice	Special	110	70	5	Many Others
TM15	Hyper Beam	Normal	Special	150	90	5	Normal
TM17	Protect	Normal	Status	—	—	10	Self
TM18	Rain Dance	Water	Status	—	—	5	Both Sides
TM21	Frustration	Normal	Physical	—	100	20	Normal
TM27	Return	Normal	Physical	—	100	20	Normal
TM28	Dig	Ground	Physical	80	100	10	Normal
TM31	Brick Break	Fighting	Physical	75	100	15	Normal
TM32	Double Team	Normal	Status	—	—	15	Self
TM39	Rock Tomb	Rock	Physical	60	95	15	Normal
TM41	Torment	Dark	Status	—	100	15	Normal
TM42	Facade	Normal	Physical	70	100	20	Normal
TM44	Rest	Psychic	Status	—	—	10	Self
TM45	Attract	Normal	Status	—	100	15	Normal
TM46	Thief	Dark	Physical	60	100	25	Normal
TM47	Low Sweep	Fighting	Physical	65	100	20	Normal
TM48	Round	Normal	Special	60	100	15	Normal
TM52	Focus Blast	Fighting	Special	120	70	5	Normal
TM55	Scald	Water	Special	80	100	15	Normal
TM56	Fling	Dark	Physical	—	100	10	Normal
TM62	Acrobatics	Flying	Physical	55	100	15	Normal
TM65	Shadow Claw	Ghost	Physical	70	100	15	Normal
TM66	Payback	Dark	Physical	50	100	10	Normal
TM68	Giga Impact	Normal	Physical	150	90	5	Normal
TM80	Rock Slide	Rock	Physical	75	90	10	Many Others
TM86	Grass Knot	Grass	Special	—	100	20	Normal
TM87	Swagger	Normal	Status	—	90	15	Normal

No.	Name	Type	Kind	Pow.	Acc.	PP	Range
TM88	Sleep Talk	Normal	Status	—	—	10	Self
TM90	Substitute	Normal	Status	—	—	10	Self
TM94	Rock Smash	Fighting	Physical	40	100	15	Normal
TM98	Power-Up Punch	Fighting	Physical	40	100	20	Normal
TM100	Confide	Normal	Status	—	—	20	Normal
HM01	Cut	Normal	Physical	50	95	30	Normal
HM03	Surf	Water	Special	90	100	15	Adjacent
HM05	Waterfall	Water	Physical	80	100	15	Normal

● MOVES TAUGHT BY PEOPLE

Name	Type	Kind	Pow.	Acc.	PP	Range

AFTER THE HALL OF FAME

CENTRAL KALOS | 034 | Simipour

COASTAL KALOS

MOUNTAIN KALOS

ADVENTURE DATA

AFTER THE HALL OF FAME

CENTRAL KALOS

035
Pichu

COASTAL KALOS

MOUNTAIN KALOS

ADVENTURE DATA

Central Kalos — 035

Tiny Mouse Pokémon

☑ Pichu

HEIGHT: 1'00" WEIGHT: 4.4 lbs.
GENDER: ♂/♀

TYPE Electric

ABILITY
Static

HIDDEN ABILITY
Lightning Rod

STAT GROWTH RATES
HP	■
Attack	■■
Defense	■
Sp. Atk	■■
Sp. Def	■■
Speed	■■■

EGG GROUP
No Eggs Discovered

X It plays with others by touching tails and setting off sparks. This appears to be a test of courage.

Y It is not yet skilled at storing electricity. It may send out a jolt if amused or startled.

EVOLUTION

Level up with high friendship → Thunder Stone

Pichu → Pikachu → Raichu

ITEMS SOMETIMES HELD BY WILD POKÉMON
None

Damage taken in normal battles		Damage taken in Inverse Battles	
Normal	×1	Normal	×1
Fire	×1	Fire	×1
Water	×1	Water	×1
Grass	×1	Grass	×1
Electric	×0.5	Electric	×2
Ice	×1	Ice	×1
Fighting	×1	Fighting	×1
Poison	×1	Poison	×1
Ground	×2	Ground	×0.5
Flying	×0.5	Flying	×2
Psychic	×1	Psychic	×1
Bug	×1	Bug	×1
Rock	×1	Rock	×1
Ghost	×1	Ghost	×1
Dragon	×1	Dragon	×1
Dark	×1	Dark	×1
Steel	×0.5	Steel	×2
Fairy	×1	Fairy	×1

Can be used in	
Inverse Battle	Battle Institute
—	Battle Maison
Battle Chateau	Random Matchup

Same form for ♂/♀

How to obtain for your Central Kalos Pokédex

Leave Pikachu or Raichu at the Pokémon Day Care, and hatch the Egg that is found.

Leave Pikachu or Raichu at the Pokémon Day Care, and hatch the Egg that is found.

● LEVEL-UP MOVES

Lv.	Name	Type	Kind	Pow.	Acc.	PP	Range
1	Thunder Shock	Electric	Special	40	100	30	Normal
1	Charm	Fairy	Status	—	100	20	Normal
5	Tail Whip	Normal	Status	—	100	30	Many Others
10	Sweet Kiss	Fairy	Status	—	75	10	Normal
13	Thunder Wave	Electric	Status	—	100	20	Normal
18	Nasty Plot	Dark	Status	—	—	20	Self

● TM & HM MOVES

No.	Name	Type	Kind	Pow.	Acc.	PP	Range
TM06	Toxic	Poison	Status	—	90	10	Normal
TM10	Hidden Power	Normal	Special	60	100	15	Normal
TM16	Light Screen	Psychic	Status	—	—	30	Your Side
TM17	Protect	Normal	Status	—	—	10	Self
TM18	Rain Dance	Water	Status	—	—	5	Both Sides
TM21	Frustration	Normal	Physical	—	100	20	Normal
TM24	Thunderbolt	Electric	Special	90	100	15	Normal
TM25	Thunder	Electric	Special	110	70	10	Normal
TM27	Return	Normal	Physical	—	100	20	Normal
TM32	Double Team	Normal	Status	—	—	15	Self
TM42	Facade	Normal	Physical	70	100	20	Normal
TM44	Rest	Psychic	Status	—	—	10	Self
TM45	Attract	Normal	Status	—	100	15	Normal
TM48	Round	Normal	Special	60	100	15	Normal
TM49	Echoed Voice	Normal	Special	40	100	15	Normal
TM56	Fling	Dark	Physical	—	100	10	Normal
TM57	Charge Beam	Electric	Special	50	90	10	Normal
TM70	Flash	Normal	Status	—	100	20	Normal
TM72	Volt Switch	Electric	Special	70	100	20	Normal
TM73	Thunder Wave	Electric	Status	—	100	20	Normal
TM86	Grass Knot	Grass	Special	—	100	20	Normal
TM87	Swagger	Normal	Status	—	90	15	Normal
TM88	Sleep Talk	Normal	Status	—	—	10	Self
TM90	Substitute	Normal	Status	—	—	10	Self
TM93	Wild Charge	Electric	Physical	90	100	15	Normal
TM100	Confide	Normal	Status	—	—	20	Normal

No.	Name	Type	Kind	Pow.	Acc.	PP	Range

● MOVES TAUGHT BY PEOPLE

Name	Type	Kind	Pow.	Acc.	PP	Range

● EGG MOVES

Name	Type	Kind	Pow.	Acc.	PP	Range
Reversal	Fighting	Physical	—	100	15	Normal
Bide	Normal	Physical	—	—	10	Self
Present	Normal	Physical	—	90	15	Normal
Encore	Normal	Status	—	100	5	Normal
Double Slap	Normal	Physical	15	85	10	Normal
Wish	Normal	Status	—	—	10	Self
Charge	Electric	Status	—	—	20	Self
Fake Out	Normal	Physical	40	100	10	Normal
Thunder Punch	Electric	Physical	75	100	15	Normal
Tickle	Normal	Status	—	100	20	Normal
Flail	Normal	Physical	—	100	15	Normal
Endure	Normal	Status	—	—	10	Self
Lucky Chant	Normal	Status	—	—	30	Your Side
Bestow	Normal	Status	—	—	15	Normal
Disarming Voice	Fairy	Special	40	—	15	Many Others
Volt Tackle*	Electric	Physical	120	100	15	Normal

*To have a Pichu learn the egg move Volt Tackle, you have to have one of the Pokémon hold a Light Ball when you leave it at the Pokémon Day Care. Wild Pikachu sometimes have a Light Ball.

Central Kalos 036
Mouse Pokémon
☑ **Pikachu**

HEIGHT: 1'04"   WEIGHT: 13.2 lbs.
GENDER: ♂/♀

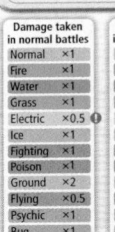

X It raises its tail to check its surroundings. The tail is sometimes struck by lightning in this pose.

Y It has small electric sacs on both its cheeks. If threatened, it looses electric charges from the sacs.

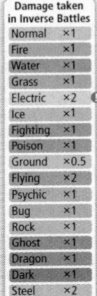

TYPE Electric

ABILITY
Static

HIDDEN ABILITY
Lightning Rod

STAT GROWTH RATES
HP	■■
Attack	■■■
Defense	■■
Sp. Atk	■■
Sp. Def	■■
Speed	■■■■■

EGG GROUPS
Field, Fairy

EVOLUTION

Level up with high friendship → Thunder Stone

Pichu   Pikachu   Raichu

ITEMS SOMETIMES HELD BY WILD POKÉMON
Light Ball

Damage taken in normal battles		Damage taken in inverse Battles	
Normal	×1	Normal	×1
Fire	×1	Fire	×1
Water	×1	Water	×1
Grass	×1	Grass	×1
Electric	×0.5 ❶	Electric	×2 ❶
Ice	×1	Ice	×1
Fighting	×1	Fighting	×1
Poison	×1	Poison	×1
Ground	×2	Ground	×0.5
Flying	×0.5	Flying	×2
Psychic	×1	Psychic	×1
Bug	×1	Bug	×1
Rock	×1	Rock	×1
Ghost	×1	Ghost	×1
Dragon	×1	Dragon	×1
Dark	×1	Dark	×1
Steel	×0.5	Steel	×2
Fairy	×1	Fairy	×1

Can be used in
Inverse Battle
—
Battle Chateau
Battle Institute
Battle Maison
Random Matchup

How to obtain for your Central Kalos Pokédex

❶ Catch in the tall grass in Santalune Forest.
❷ Catch in the tall grass on Route 3.

❶ Catch in the tall grass in Santalune Forest.
❷ Catch in the tall grass on Route 3.

The tip of a male's tail is straight. A female has a notch at the end of its tail.

● LEVEL-UP MOVES

Lv.	Name	Type	Kind	Pow.	Acc.	PP	Range
1	Tail Whip	Normal	Status	—	100	30	Many Others
1	Thunder Shock	Electric	Special	40	100	30	Normal
5	Growl	Normal	Status	—	100	40	Many Others
7	Play Nice	Normal	Status	—	—	20	Normal
10	Quick Attack	Normal	Physical	40	100	30	Normal
13	Thunder Wave	Electric	Status	—	100	20	Normal
18	Electro Ball	Electric	Special	—	100	10	Normal
21	Double Team	Normal	Status	—	—	15	Self
23	Nuzzle	Electric	Physical	20	100	20	Normal
26	Slam	Normal	Physical	80	75	20	Normal
29	Thunderbolt	Electric	Special	90	100	15	Normal
34	Feint	Normal	Physical	30	100	10	Normal
37	Agility	Psychic	Status	—	—	30	Self
42	Discharge	Electric	Special	80	100	15	Adjacent
45	Light Screen	Psychic	Status	—	—	30	Your Side
50	Thunder	Electric	Special	110	70	10	Normal

● TM & HM MOVES

No.	Name	Type	Kind	Pow.	Acc.	PP	Range
TM06	Toxic	Poison	Status	—	90	10	Normal
TM10	Hidden Power	Normal	Special	60	100	15	Normal
TM16	Light Screen	Psychic	Status	—	—	30	Your Side
TM17	Protect	Normal	Status	—	—	10	Self
TM18	Rain Dance	Water	Status	—	—	5	Both Sides
TM21	Frustration	Normal	Physical	—	100	20	Normal
TM24	Thunderbolt	Electric	Special	90	100	15	Normal
TM25	Thunder	Electric	Special	110	70	10	Normal
TM27	Return	Normal	Physical	—	100	20	Normal
TM28	Dig	Ground	Physical	80	100	10	Normal
TM31	Brick Break	Fighting	Physical	75	100	15	Normal
TM32	Double Team	Normal	Status	—	—	15	Self
TM42	Facade	Normal	Physical	70	100	20	Normal
TM44	Rest	Psychic	Status	—	—	10	Self
TM45	Attract	Normal	Status	—	100	15	Normal
TM48	Round	Normal	Special	60	100	15	Normal
TM49	Echoed Voice	Normal	Special	40	100	15	Normal
TM56	Fling	Dark	Physical	—	100	10	Normal
TM57	Charge Beam	Electric	Special	50	90	10	Normal
TM70	Flash	Normal	Status	—	100	20	Normal
TM72	Volt Switch	Electric	Special	70	100	20	Normal
TM73	Thunder Wave	Electric	Status	—	100	20	Normal
TM86	Grass Knot	Grass	Special	—	100	20	Normal
TM87	Swagger	Normal	Status	—	90	15	Normal
TM88	Sleep Talk	Normal	Status	—	—	10	Self
TM90	Substitute	Normal	Status	—	—	10	Self
TM93	Wild Charge	Electric	Physical	90	100	15	Normal
TM94	Rock Smash	Fighting	Physical	40	100	15	Normal
TM100	Confide	Normal	Status	—	—	20	Normal
HM04	Strength	Normal	Physical	80	100	15	Normal

No.	Name	Type	Kind	Pow.	Acc.	PP	Range

● MOVES TAUGHT BY PEOPLE

Name	Type	Kind	Pow.	Acc.	PP	Range

AFTER THE HALL OF FAME

CENTRAL KALOS

037

Raichu

COASTAL KALOS

MOUNTAIN KALOS

ADVENTURE DATA

Central Kalos

037 — Raichu

Mouse Pokémon

TYPE: Electric

HEIGHT: 2'07" **WEIGHT:** 66.1 lbs.
GENDER: ♂/♀

ABILITY
Static

HIDDEN ABILITY
Lightning Rod

X When its electricity builds, its muscles are stimulated, and it becomes more aggressive than usual.

Y It can loose 100,000-volt bursts of electricity, instantly downing foes several times its size.

STAT GROWTH RATES
HP	■■■
Attack	■■■■■
Defense	■■■■
Sp. Atk	■■■■
Sp. Def	■■■■
Speed	■■■■■■

EGG GROUPS
Field, Fairy

EVOLUTION

Level up with high friendship → Thunder Stone

Pichu → Pikachu → Raichu

ITEMS SOMETIMES HELD BY WILD POKÉMON
None

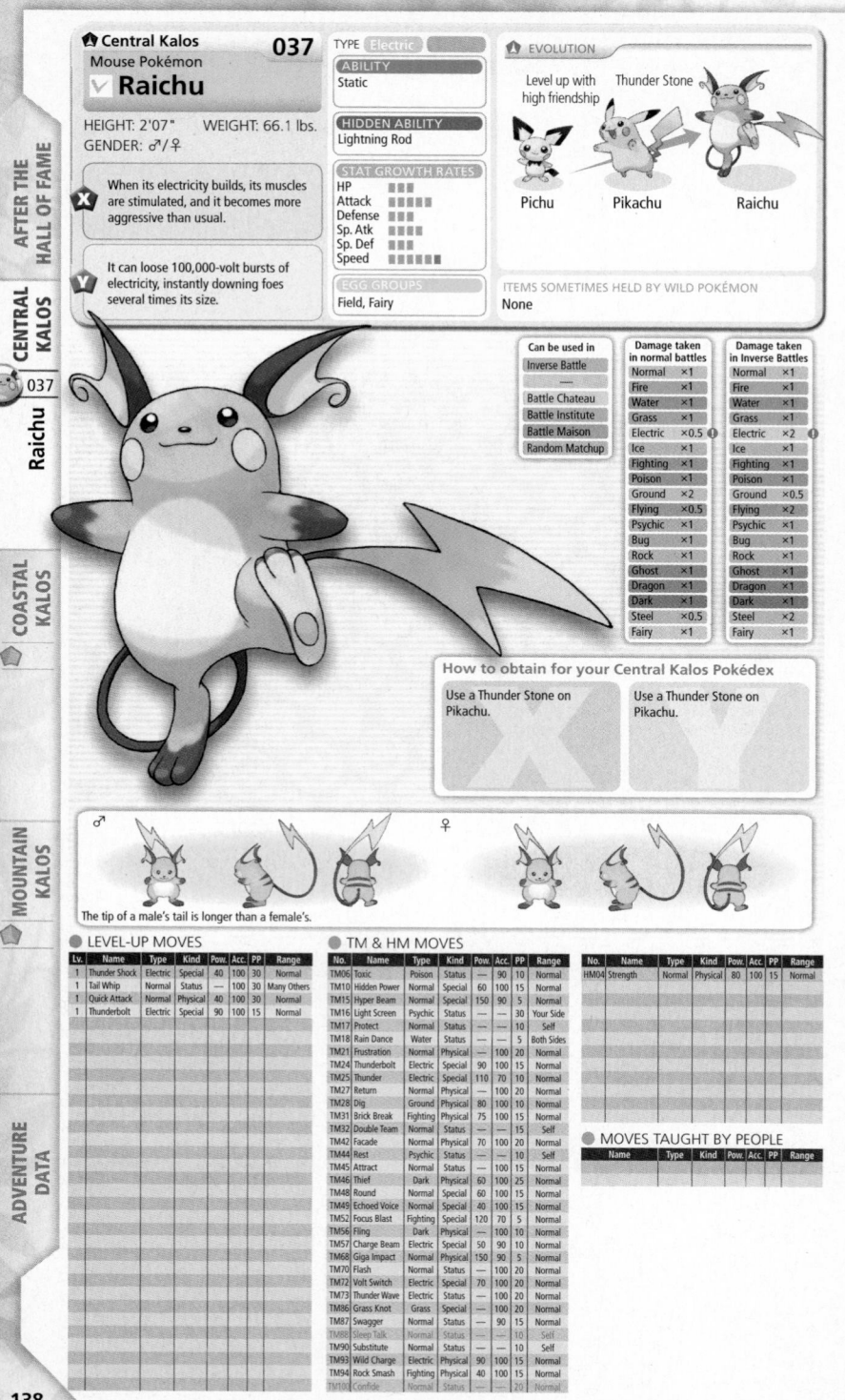

Can be used in
Inverse Battle
—
Battle Chateau
Battle Institute
Battle Maison
Random Matchup

Damage taken in normal battles
Normal	×1
Fire	×1
Water	×1
Grass	×1
Electric	×0.5
Ice	×1
Fighting	×1
Poison	×1
Ground	×2
Flying	×0.5
Psychic	×1
Bug	×1
Rock	×1
Ghost	×1
Dragon	×1
Dark	×1
Steel	×0.5
Fairy	×1

Damage taken in Inverse Battles
Normal	×1
Fire	×1
Water	×1
Grass	×1
Electric	×2
Ice	×1
Fighting	×1
Poison	×1
Ground	×0.5
Flying	×2
Psychic	×1
Bug	×1
Rock	×1
Ghost	×1
Dragon	×1
Dark	×1
Steel	×2
Fairy	×1

How to obtain for your Central Kalos Pokédex

X: Use a Thunder Stone on Pikachu.

Y: Use a Thunder Stone on Pikachu.

♂ / ♀

The tip of a male's tail is longer than a female's.

● LEVEL-UP MOVES

Lv.	Name	Type	Kind	Pow.	Acc.	PP	Range
1	Thunder Shock	Electric	Special	40	100	30	Normal
1	Tail Whip	Normal	Status	—	100	30	Many Others
1	Quick Attack	Normal	Physical	40	100	30	Normal
1	Thunderbolt	Electric	Special	90	100	15	Normal

● TM & HM MOVES

No.	Name	Type	Kind	Pow.	Acc.	PP	Range
TM06	Toxic	Poison	Status	—	90	10	Normal
TM10	Hidden Power	Normal	Special	60	100	15	Normal
TM15	Hyper Beam	Normal	Special	150	90	5	Normal
TM16	Light Screen	Psychic	Status	—	—	30	Your Side
TM17	Protect	Normal	Status	—	—	10	Self
TM18	Rain Dance	Water	Status	—	—	5	Both Sides
TM21	Frustration	Normal	Physical	—	100	20	Normal
TM24	Thunderbolt	Electric	Special	90	100	15	Normal
TM25	Thunder	Electric	Special	110	70	10	Normal
TM27	Return	Normal	Physical	—	100	20	Normal
TM28	Dig	Ground	Physical	80	100	10	Normal
TM31	Brick Break	Fighting	Physical	75	100	15	Normal
TM32	Double Team	Normal	Status	—	—	15	Self
TM42	Facade	Normal	Physical	70	100	20	Normal
TM44	Rest	Psychic	Status	—	—	10	Self
TM45	Attract	Normal	Status	—	100	15	Normal
TM46	Thief	Dark	Physical	60	100	25	Normal
TM48	Round	Normal	Special	60	100	15	Normal
TM49	Echoed Voice	Normal	Special	40	100	15	Normal
TM52	Focus Blast	Fighting	Special	120	70	5	Normal
TM56	Fling	Dark	Physical	—	100	10	Normal
TM57	Charge Beam	Electric	Special	50	90	10	Normal
TM68	Giga Impact	Normal	Physical	150	90	5	Normal
TM70	Flash	Normal	Status	—	100	20	Normal
TM72	Volt Switch	Electric	Special	70	100	20	Normal
TM73	Thunder Wave	Electric	Status	—	100	20	Normal
TM86	Grass Knot	Grass	Special	—	100	20	Normal
TM87	Swagger	Normal	Status	—	90	15	Normal
TM88	Sleep Talk	Normal	Status	—	—	10	Self
TM90	Substitute	Normal	Status	—	—	10	Self
TM93	Wild Charge	Electric	Physical	90	100	15	Normal
TM94	Rock Smash	Fighting	Physical	40	100	15	Normal
TM100	Confide	Normal	Status	—	—	20	Normal

No.	Name	Type	Kind	Pow.	Acc.	PP	Range
HM04	Strength	Normal	Physical	80	100	15	Normal

● MOVES TAUGHT BY PEOPLE

Name	Type	Kind	Pow.	Acc.	PP	Range

Central Kalos
Plump Mouse Pokémon
038

 Bidoof

HEIGHT: 1'08" WEIGHT: 44.1 lbs.
GENDER: ♂/♀

TYPE Normal

ABILITIES
Simple
Unaware

HIDDEN ABILITY
Moody

EVOLUTION

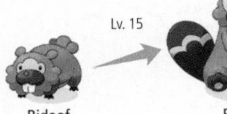

Bidoof → Lv. 15 → Bibarel

X	With nerves of steel, nothing can perturb it. It is more agile and active than it appears.

Y	It constantly gnaws on logs and rocks to whittle down its front teeth. It nests alongside water.

STAT GROWTH RATES

HP	■ ■ ■
Attack	■ ■
Defense	■ ■
Sp. Atk	■ ■
Sp. Def	■ ■
Speed	■ ■

EGG GROUPS
Water 1, Field

ITEMS SOMETIMES HELD BY WILD POKÉMON
None

Damage taken in normal battles		Damage taken in Inverse Battles		Can be used in
Normal	×1	Normal	×1	Inverse Battle
Fire	×1	Fire	×1	—
Water	×1	Water	×1	Battle Chateau
Grass	×1	Grass	×1	Battle Institute
Electric	×1	Electric	×1	Battle Maison
Ice	×1	Ice	×1	Random Matchup
Fighting	×2	Fighting	×0.5	
Poison	×1	Poison	×1	
Ground	×1	Ground	×1	
Flying	×1	Flying	×1	
Psychic	×1	Psychic	×1	
Bug	×1	Bug	×1	
Rock	×1	Rock	×1	
Ghost	×0	Ghost	×2	
Dragon	×1	Dragon	×1	
Dark	×1	Dark	×1	
Steel	×1	Steel	×1	
Fairy	×1	Fairy	×1	

How to obtain for your Central Kalos Pokédex

❶ Catch in the tall grass on Route 3.
❷ Catch in the tall grass on Route 22.

❶ Catch in the tall grass on Route 3.
❷ Catch in the tall grass on Route 22.

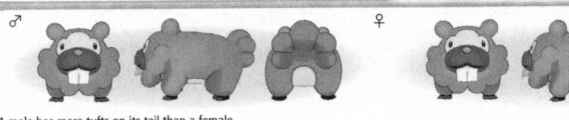

♂   ♀

A male has more tufts on its tail than a female.

● LEVEL-UP MOVES

Lv.	Name	Type	Kind	Pow.	Acc.	PP	Range
1	Tackle	Normal	Physical	50	100	35	Normal
5	Growl	Normal	Status	—	100	40	Many Others
9	Defense Curl	Normal	Status	—	—	40	Self
13	Rollout	Rock	Physical	30	90	20	Normal
17	Headbutt	Normal	Physical	70	100	15	Normal
21	Hyper Fang	Normal	Physical	80	90	15	Normal
25	Yawn	Normal	Status	—	—	10	Normal
29	Amnesia	Psychic	Status	—	—	20	Self
33	Take Down	Normal	Physical	90	85	20	Normal
37	Super Fang	Normal	Physical	—	90	10	Normal
41	Superpower	Fighting	Physical	120	100	5	Normal
45	Curse	Ghost	Status	—	—	10	Varies

● TM & HM MOVES

No.	Name	Type	Kind	Pow.	Acc.	PP	Range
TM06	Toxic	Poison	Status	—	90	10	Normal
TM10	Hidden Power	Normal	Special	60	100	15	Normal
TM11	Sunny Day	Fire	Status	—	—	5	Both Sides
TM12	Taunt	Dark	Status	—	100	20	Normal
TM13	Ice Beam	Ice	Special	90	100	10	Normal
TM14	Blizzard	Ice	Special	110	70	5	Many Others
TM17	Protect	Normal	Status	—	—	10	Self
TM18	Rain Dance	Water	Status	—	—	5	Both Sides
TM21	Frustration	Normal	Physical	—	100	20	Normal
TM24	Thunderbolt	Electric	Special	90	100	15	Normal
TM25	Thunder	Electric	Special	110	70	10	Normal
TM27	Return	Normal	Physical	—	100	20	Normal
TM28	Dig	Ground	Physical	80	100	10	Normal
TM30	Shadow Ball	Ghost	Special	80	100	15	Normal
TM32	Double Team	Normal	Status	—	—	15	Self
TM42	Facade	Normal	Physical	70	100	20	Normal
TM44	Rest	Psychic	Status	—	—	10	Self
TM45	Attract	Normal	Status	—	100	15	Normal
TM46	Thief	Dark	Physical	60	100	25	Normal
TM48	Round	Normal	Special	60	100	15	Normal
TM49	Echoed Voice	Normal	Special	40	100	15	Normal
TM57	Charge Beam	Electric	Special	50	90	10	Normal
TM67	Retaliate	Normal	Physical	70	100	5	Normal
TM73	Thunder Wave	Electric	Status	—	100	20	Normal
TM86	Grass Knot	Grass	Special	—	100	20	Normal
TM87	Swagger	Normal	Status	—	90	15	Normal
TM88	Sleep Talk	Normal	Status	—	—	10	Self
TM90	Substitute	Normal	Status	—	—	10	Self
TM94	Rock Smash	Fighting	Physical	40	100	15	Normal
TM100	Confide	Normal	Status	—	—	20	Normal
HM01	Cut	Normal	Physical	50	95	30	Normal

● MOVES TAUGHT BY PEOPLE

Name	Type	Kind	Pow.	Acc.	PP	Range

● EGG MOVES

Name	Type	Kind	Pow.	Acc.	PP	Range
Quick Attack	Normal	Physical	40	100	30	Normal
Water Sport	Water	Status	—	—	15	Both Sides
Double-Edge	Normal	Physical	120	100	15	Normal
Fury Swipes	Normal	Physical	18	80	15	Normal
Defense Curl	Normal	Status	—	—	40	Self
Rollout	Rock	Physical	30	90	20	Normal
Odor Sleuth	Normal	Status	—	—	40	Normal
Aqua Tail	Water	Physical	90	90	10	Normal
Rock Climb	Normal	Physical	90	85	20	Normal
Sleep Talk	Normal	Status	—	—	10	Self
Endure	Normal	Status	—	—	10	Self
Skull Bash	Normal	Physical	130	100	10	Normal

AFTER THE HALL OF FAME

CENTRAL KALOS

039

Bibarel

COASTAL

MOUNTAIN KALOS

ADVENTURE DATA

Central Kalos — 039

Beaver Pokémon

Bibarel

HEIGHT: 3'03" WEIGHT: 69.4 lbs.
GENDER: ♂ / ♀

X It busily makes its nest with stacks of branches and roots it has cut up with its sharp incisors.

Y It makes its nest by damming streams with bark and mud. It is known as an industrious worker.

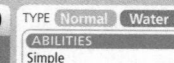

TYPE Normal Water

ABILITIES
Simple
Unaware

HIDDEN ABILITY
Moody

STAT GROWTH RATES
HP	■■■
Attack	■■■
Defense	■■■
Sp. Atk	■■■
Sp. Def	■■■
Speed	■■■■

EGG GROUPS
Water, Field

EVOLUTION

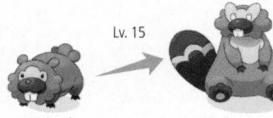

Lv. 15

Bidoof → Bibarel

ITEMS SOMETIMES HELD BY WILD POKÉMON
None

Can be used in
Inverse Battle
—
Battle Chateau
Battle Institute
Battle Maison
Random Matchup

Damage taken in normal battles	
Normal	×1
Fire	×0.5
Water	×0.5
Grass	×2
Electric	×2
Ice	×0.5
Fighting	×2
Poison	×1
Ground	×1
Flying	×1
Psychic	×1
Bug	×1
Rock	×1
Ghost	×0
Dragon	×1
Dark	×1
Steel	×0.5
Fairy	×1

Damage taken in Inverse Battles	
Normal	×1
Fire	×2
Water	×2
Grass	×0.5
Electric	×0.5
Ice	×2
Fighting	×0.5
Poison	×1
Ground	×1
Flying	×1
Psychic	×1
Bug	×1
Ghost	×2
Dragon	×1
Dark	×1
Steel	×2
Fairy	×1

How to obtain for your Central Kalos Pokédex

❶ Catch in the yellow flowers on Route 22.
❷ Level up Bidoof to Lv. 15.

❶ Catch in the yellow flowers on Route 22.
❷ Level up Bidoof to Lv. 15.

♂ ♀

The patch of white fur on the male's face is larger. The patch of white fur on the female's face is smaller.

● LEVEL-UP MOVES

Lv.	Name	Type	Kind	Pow.	Acc.	PP	Range
1	Rototiller	Ground	Status	—	—	10	Adjacent
1	Tackle	Normal	Physical	50	100	35	Normal
1	Growl	Normal	Status	—	100	40	Many Others
5	Growl	Normal	Status	—	100	40	Many Others
9	Defense Curl	Normal	Status	—	—	40	Self
13	Rollout	Rock	Physical	30	90	20	Normal
15	Water Gun	Water	Special	40	100	25	Normal
18	Headbutt	Normal	Physical	70	100	15	Normal
23	Hyper Fang	Normal	Physical	80	90	15	Normal
28	Yawn	Normal	Status	—	—	10	Normal
33	Amnesia	Psychic	Status	—	—	20	Self
38	Take Down	Normal	Physical	90	85	20	Normal
43	Super Fang	Normal	Physical	—	90	10	Normal
48	Superpower	Fighting	Physical	120	100	5	Normal
53	Curse	Ghost	Status	—	—	10	Varies

● TM & HM MOVES

No.	Name	Type	Kind	Pow.	Acc.	PP	Range
TM06	Toxic	Poison	Status	—	90	10	Normal
TM10	Hidden Power	Normal	Special	60	100	15	Normal
TM11	Sunny Day	Fire	Status	—	—	5	Both Sides
TM12	Taunt	Dark	Status	—	100	20	Normal
TM13	Ice Beam	Ice	Special	90	100	10	Normal
TM14	Blizzard	Ice	Special	110	70	5	Many Others
TM15	Hyper Beam	Normal	Special	150	90	5	Normal
TM17	Protect	Normal	Status	—	—	10	Self
TM18	Rain Dance	Water	Status	—	—	5	Both Sides
TM21	Frustration	Normal	Physical	—	100	20	Normal
TM24	Thunderbolt	Electric	Special	90	100	15	Normal
TM25	Thunder	Electric	Special	110	70	10	Normal
TM27	Return	Normal	Physical	—	100	20	Normal
TM28	Dig	Ground	Physical	80	100	10	Normal
TM30	Shadow Ball	Ghost	Special	80	100	15	Normal
TM32	Double Team	Normal	Status	—	—	15	Self
TM42	Facade	Normal	Physical	70	100	20	Normal
TM44	Rest	Psychic	Status	—	—	10	Self
TM45	Attract	Normal	Status	—	100	15	Normal
TM46	Thief	Dark	Physical	60	100	25	Normal
TM48	Round	Normal	Special	60	100	15	Normal
TM49	Echoed Voice	Normal	Special	40	100	15	Normal
TM55	Scald	Water	Special	80	100	15	Normal
TM56	Fling	Dark	Physical	—	100	10	Normal
TM57	Charge Beam	Electric	Special	50	90	10	Normal
TM67	Retaliate	Normal	Physical	70	100	5	Normal
TM68	Giga Impact	Normal	Physical	150	90	5	Normal
TM73	Thunder Wave	Electric	Status	—	100	20	Normal
TM78	Bulldoze	Ground	Physical	60	100	20	Adjacent
TM86	Grass Knot	Grass	Special	—	100	20	Normal
TM87	Swagger	Normal	Status	—	90	15	Normal
TM88	Sleep Talk	Normal	Status	—	—	10	Self
TM90	Substitute	Normal	Status	—	—	10	Self

No.	Name	Type	Kind	Pow.	Acc.	PP	Range
TM94	Rock Smash	Fighting	Physical	40	100	15	Normal
TM100	Confide	Normal	Status	—	—	20	Normal
HM01	Cut	Normal	Physical	50	95	30	Normal
HM03	Surf	Water	Special	90	100	15	Adjacent
HM04	Strength	Normal	Physical	80	100	15	Normal
HM05	Waterfall	Water	Physical	80	100	15	Normal

● MOVES TAUGHT BY PEOPLE

Name	Type	Kind	Pow.	Acc.	PP	Range

Central Kalos 040
Land Snake Pokémon

☑ **Dunsparce**

HEIGHT: 4'11" WEIGHT: 30.9 lbs.
GENDER: ♂/♀

X When spotted, this Pokémon escapes backward by furiously boring into the ground with its tail.

Y It digs into the ground with its tail and makes a mazelike nest. It can fly just a little.

TYPE **Normal**

ABILITIES
Serene Grace
Run Away

HIDDEN ABILITY
Rattled

STAT GROWTH RATES
HP	■■■■
Attack	■■■■
Defense	■■■
Sp. Atk	■■■
Sp. Def	■■■
Speed	■■■

EGG GROUP
Field

EVOLUTION

Does not evolve

ITEMS SOMETIMES HELD BY WILD POKÉMON
None

Damage taken in normal battles			Damage taken in Inverse Battles	
Normal	×1		Normal	×1
Fire	×1		Fire	×1
Water	×1		Water	×1
Grass	×1		Grass	×1
Electric	×1		Electric	×1
Ice	×1		Ice	×1
Fighting	×2		Fighting	×0.5
Poison	×1		Poison	×1
Ground	×1		Ground	×1
Flying	×1		Flying	×1
Psychic	×1		Psychic	×1
Bug	×1		Bug	×1
Rock	×1		Rock	×1
Ghost	×0		Ghost	×2
Dragon	×1		Dragon	×1
Dark	×1		Dark	×1
Steel	×1		Steel	×1
Fairy	×1		Fairy	×1

Can be used in	
Inverse Battle	Battle Institute
—	Battle Maison
Battle Chateau	Random Matchup

Same form for ♂/♀

How to obtain for your Central Kalos Pokédex

❶ Catch in the tall grass on Route 3.
❷ Catch in the tall grass on Route 22.

❶ Catch in the tall grass on Route 3.
❷ Catch in the tall grass on Route 22.

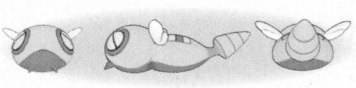

● LEVEL-UP MOVES

Lv.	Name	Type	Kind	Pow.	Acc.	PP	Range
1	Rage	Normal	Physical	20	100	20	Normal
1	Defense Curl	Normal	Status	—	—	40	Self
4	Rollout	Rock	Physical	30	90	20	Normal
7	Spite	Ghost	Status	—	100	10	Normal
10	Pursuit	Dark	Physical	40	100	20	Normal
13	Screech	Normal	Status	—	85	40	Normal
16	Yawn	Normal	Status	—	—	10	Normal
19	Ancient Power	Rock	Special	60	100	5	Normal
22	Take Down	Normal	Physical	90	85	20	Normal
25	Roost	Flying	Status	—	—	10	Self
28	Glare	Normal	Status	—	100	30	Normal
31	Dig	Ground	Physical	80	100	10	Normal
34	Double-Edge	Normal	Physical	120	100	15	Normal
37	Coil	Poison	Status	—	—	20	Self
40	Endure	Normal	Status	—	—	10	Self
43	Drill Run	Ground	Physical	80	95	10	Normal
46	Endeavor	Normal	Physical	—	100	5	Normal
49	Flail	Normal	Physical	—	100	15	Normal

● TM & HM MOVES

No.	Name	Type	Kind	Pow.	Acc.	PP	Range
TM04	Calm Mind	Psychic	Status	—	—	20	Self
TM06	Toxic	Poison	Status	—	90	10	Normal
TM10	Hidden Power	Normal	Special	60	100	15	Normal
TM11	Sunny Day	Fire	Status	—	—	5	Both Sides
TM13	Ice Beam	Ice	Special	90	100	10	Normal
TM14	Blizzard	Ice	Special	110	70	5	Many Others
TM17	Protect	Normal	Status	—	—	10	Self
TM18	Rain Dance	Water	Status	—	—	5	Both Sides
TM19	Roost	Flying	Status	—	—	10	Self
TM21	Frustration	Normal	Physical	—	100	20	Normal
TM22	Solar Beam	Grass	Special	120	100	10	Normal
TM24	Thunderbolt	Electric	Special	90	100	15	Normal
TM25	Thunder	Electric	Special	110	70	10	Normal
TM26	Earthquake	Ground	Physical	100	100	10	Adjacent
TM27	Return	Normal	Physical	—	100	20	Normal
TM28	Dig	Ground	Physical	80	100	10	Normal
TM30	Shadow Ball	Ghost	Special	80	100	15	Normal
TM32	Double Team	Normal	Status	—	—	15	Self
TM35	Flamethrower	Fire	Special	90	100	15	Normal
TM38	Fire Blast	Fire	Special	110	85	5	Normal
TM39	Rock Tomb	Rock	Physical	60	95	15	Normal
TM42	Facade	Normal	Physical	70	100	20	Normal
TM44	Rest	Psychic	Status	—	—	10	Self
TM45	Attract	Normal	Status	—	100	15	Normal
TM46	Thief	Dark	Physical	60	100	25	Normal
TM48	Round	Normal	Special	60	100	15	Normal
TM57	Charge Beam	Electric	Special	50	90	10	Normal
TM59	Incinerate	Fire	Special	60	100	15	Many Others
TM67	Retaliate	Normal	Physical	70	100	5	Normal
TM73	Thunder Wave	Electric	Status	—	100	20	Normal
TM74	Gyro Ball	Steel	Physical	—	100	5	Normal
TM77	Psych Up	Normal	Status	—	—	10	Normal
TM78	Bulldoze	Ground	Physical	60	100	20	Adjacent

No.	Name	Type	Kind	Pow.	Acc.	PP	Range
TM80	Rock Slide	Rock	Physical	75	90	10	Many Others
TM84	Poison Jab	Poison	Physical	80	100	20	Normal
TM85	Dream Eater	Psychic	Special	100	100	15	Normal
TM87	Swagger	Normal	Status	—	90	15	Normal
TM88	Sleep Talk	Normal	Status	—	—	10	Self
TM90	Substitute	Normal	Status	—	—	10	Self
TM93	Wild Charge	Electric	Physical	90	100	15	Normal
TM94	Rock Smash	Fighting	Physical	40	100	15	Normal
TM100	Confide	Normal	Status	—	—	20	Normal
HM04	Strength	Normal	Physical	80	100	15	Normal

● MOVES TAUGHT BY PEOPLE

Name	Type	Kind	Pow.	Acc.	PP	Range

● EGG MOVES

Name	Type	Kind	Pow.	Acc.	PP	Range
Bide	Normal	Physical	—	—	10	Self
Ancient Power	Rock	Special	60	100	5	Normal
Bite	Dark	Physical	60	100	25	Normal
Headbutt	Normal	Physical	70	100	15	Normal
Astonish	Ghost	Physical	30	100	15	Normal
Curse	Ghost	Status	—	—	10	Varies
Trump Card	Normal	Special	—	—	5	Normal
Magic Coat	Psychic	Status	—	—	15	Self
Snore	Normal	Special	50	100	15	Normal
Agility	Psychic	Status	—	—	30	Self
Secret Power	Normal	Physical	70	100	20	Normal
Sleep Talk	Normal	Status	—	—	10	Self
Hex	Ghost	Special	65	100	10	Normal

AFTER THE HALL OF FAME

CENTRAL KALOS

041

Azurill

COASTAL KALOS

MOUNTAIN KALOS

ADVENTURE DATA

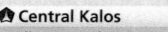

Central Kalos 041
Polka Dot Pokémon
☑ **Azurill**

HEIGHT: 0'08" WEIGHT: 4.4 lbs.
GENDER: ♂/♀

X A Pokémon that lives by water. It moves quickly on land by bouncing on its big tail.

Y It swings its large, nutrient-filled tail around to fight opponents bigger than itself.

TYPE | Normal | Fairy

ABILITIES
Thick Fat
Huge Power

HIDDEN ABILITY
Sap Sipper

STAT GROWTH RATES
HP	■■
Attack	■■
Defense	■■
Sp. Atk	■
Sp. Def	■
Speed	■

EGG GROUP
No Eggs Discovered

EVOLUTION

Level up with high friendship
Lv. 18

Azurill → Marill → Azumarill

ITEMS SOMETIMES HELD BY WILD POKÉMON
None

Damage taken in normal battles		Damage taken in Inverse Battles	
Normal	×1	Normal	×1
Fire	×1	Fire	×1
Water	×1	Water	×1
Grass	×1	Grass	×1
Electric	×1	Electric	×1
Ice	×1	Ice	×1
Fighting	×1	Fighting	×1
Poison	×2	Poison	×0.5
Ground	×1	Ground	×1
Flying	×1	Flying	×1
Psychic	×1	Psychic	×1
Bug	×0.5	Bug	×2
Rock	×1	Rock	×1
Ghost	×0	Ghost	×1
Dragon	×0	Dragon	×2
Dark	×0.5	Dark	×2
Steel	×2	Steel	×0.5
Fairy	×1	Fairy	×1

Can be used in	
Inverse Battle	Battle Institute
—	Battle Maison
Battle Chateau	Random Matchup

Same form for ♂/♀

How to obtain for your Central Kalos Pokédex

❶ Catch in the tall grass on Route 3.
❷ Catch in the tall grass on Route 22.

❶ Catch in the tall grass on Route 3.
❷ Catch in the tall grass on Route 22.

● **LEVEL-UP MOVES**

Lv.	Name	Type	Kind	Pow.	Acc.	PP	Range
1	Splash	Normal	Status	—	—	40	Self
1	Water Gun	Water	Special	40	100	25	Normal
2	Tail Whip	Normal	Status	—	100	30	Many Others
5	Water Sport	Water	Status	—	—	15	Both Sides
7	Bubble	Water	Special	40	100	30	Many Others
10	Charm	Fairy	Status	—	100	20	Normal
13	Bubble Beam	Water	Special	65	100	20	Normal
16	Helping Hand	Normal	Status	—	—	20	1 Ally
20	Slam	Normal	Physical	80	75	20	Normal
23	Bounce	Flying	Physical	85	85	5	Normal

● **TM & HM MOVES**

No.	Name	Type	Kind	Pow.	Acc.	PP	Range
TM06	Toxic	Poison	Status	—	90	10	Normal
TM07	Hail	Ice	Status	—	—	10	Both Sides
TM10	Hidden Power	Normal	Special	60	100	15	Normal
TM13	Ice Beam	Ice	Special	90	100	10	Normal
TM14	Blizzard	Ice	Special	110	70	5	Many Others
TM16	Light Screen	Psychic	Status	—	—	30	Your Side
TM17	Protect	Normal	Status	—	—	10	Self
TM18	Rain Dance	Water	Status	—	—	5	Both Sides
TM21	Frustration	Normal	Physical	—	100	20	Normal
TM27	Return	Normal	Physical	—	100	20	Normal
TM32	Double Team	Normal	Status	—	—	15	Self
TM42	Facade	Normal	Physical	70	100	20	Normal
TM44	Rest	Psychic	Status	—	—	10	Self
TM45	Attract	Normal	Status	—	100	15	Normal
TM48	Round	Normal	Special	60	100	15	Normal
TM55	Scald	Water	Special	80	100	15	Normal
TM87	Swagger	Normal	Status	—	90	15	Normal
TM88	Sleep Talk	Normal	Status	—	—	10	Self
TM90	Substitute	Normal	Status	—	—	10	Self
TM100	Confide	Normal	Status	—	—	20	Normal
HM03	Surf	Water	Special	90	100	15	Adjacent
HM05	Waterfall	Water	Physical	80	100	15	Normal

No.	Name	Type	Kind	Pow.	Acc.	PP	Range

● **MOVES TAUGHT BY PEOPLE**

Name	Type	Kind	Pow.	Acc.	PP	Range

● **EGG MOVES**

Name	Type	Kind	Pow.	Acc.	PP	Range
Encore	Normal	Status	—	100	5	Normal
Sing	Normal	Status	—	55	15	Normal
Refresh	Normal	Status	—	—	20	Self
Slam	Normal	Physical	80	75	20	Normal
Tickle	Normal	Status	—	100	20	Normal
Fake Tears	Dark	Status	—	100	20	Normal
Body Slam	Normal	Physical	85	100	15	Normal
Water Sport	Water	Status	—	—	15	Both Sides
Soak	Water	Status	—	100	20	Normal
Muddy Water	Water	Special	90	85	10	Many Others
Copycat	Normal	Status	—	—	20	Self
Camouflage	Normal	Status	—	—	20	Self

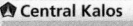

Central Kalos

042

Aqua Mouse Pokémon

☑ **Marill**

HEIGHT: 1'04" WEIGHT: 18.7 lbs.
GENDER: ♂/♀

X The fur on its body naturally repels water. It can stay dry, even when it plays in the water.

Y The tip of its tail is filled with oil that is lighter than water, so it acts as a float.

TYPE | Water | Fairy

ABILITIES
Thick Fat
Huge Power

HIDDEN ABILITY
Sap Sipper

STAT GROWTH RATES
HP ■■■
Attack ■
Defense ■■
Sp. Atk ■
Sp. Def ■■
Speed ■■

EGG GROUPS
Water 1, Fairy

EVOLUTION
Level up with high friendship → Azurill → Marill → Lv. 18 → Azumarill

ITEMS SOMETIMES HELD BY WILD POKÉMON
None

AFTER THE HALL OF FAME

CENTRAL KALOS

042 Marill

COASTAL KALOS

MOUNTAIN KALOS

ADVENTURE DATA

Damage taken in normal battles		Damage taken in Inverse Battles	
Normal	×1	Normal	×1
Fire	×0.5	Fire	×2
Water	×0.5	Water	×2
Grass	×2	Grass	×0.5
Electric	×2	Electric	×0.5
Ice	×0.5	Ice	×2
Fighting	×0.5	Fighting	×2
Poison	×2	Poison	×0.5
Ground	×1	Ground	×1
Flying	×1	Flying	×1
Psychic	×1	Psychic	×1
Bug	×0.5	Bug	×2
Rock	×1	Rock	×1
Ghost	×1	Ghost	×1
Dragon	×0	Dragon	×2
Dark	×0.5	Dark	×2
Steel	×1	Steel	×1
Fairy	×1	Fairy	×1

Can be used in

Inverse Battle	Battle Institute
—	Battle Maison
Battle Chateau	Random Matchup

Same form for ♂/♀

How to obtain for your Central Kalos Pokédex
❶ Catch on the surface of the water on Route 3.
❷ Level up Azurill with high friendship.

❶ Catch on the surface of the water on Route 3.
❷ Level up Azurill with high friendship.

LEVEL-UP MOVES

Lv.	Name	Type	Kind	Pow.	Acc.	PP	Range
1	Tackle	Normal	Physical	50	100	35	Normal
1	Water Gun	Water	Special	40	100	25	Normal
1	Tail Whip	Normal	Status	—	100	30	Many Others
5	Water Sport	Water	Status	—	—	15	Both Sides
7	Bubble	Water	Special	40	100	30	Many Others
10	Defense Curl	Normal	Status	—	—	40	Self
10	Rollout	Rock	Physical	30	90	20	Normal
13	Bubble Beam	Water	Special	65	100	20	Normal
16	Helping Hand	Normal	Status	—	—	20	1 Ally
20	Aqua Tail	Water	Physical	90	90	10	Normal
23	Double-Edge	Normal	Physical	120	100	15	Normal
28	Aqua Ring	Water	Status	—	—	20	Self
31	Rain Dance	Water	Status	—	—	5	Both Sides
37	Superpower	Fighting	Physical	120	100	5	Normal
40	Hydro Pump	Water	Special	110	80	5	Normal
45	Play Rough	Fairy	Physical	90	90	10	Normal

TM & HM MOVES

No.	Name	Type	Kind	Pow.	Acc.	PP	Range
TM06	Toxic	Poison	Status	—	90	10	Normal
TM07	Hail	Ice	Status	—	—	10	Both Sides
TM10	Hidden Power	Normal	Special	60	100	15	Normal
TM13	Ice Beam	Ice	Special	90	100	10	Normal
TM14	Blizzard	Ice	Special	110	70	5	Many Others
TM16	Light Screen	Psychic	Status	—	—	30	Your Side
TM17	Protect	Normal	Status	—	—	10	Self
TM18	Rain Dance	Water	Status	—	—	5	Both Sides
TM21	Frustration	Normal	Physical	—	100	20	Normal
TM27	Return	Normal	Physical	—	100	20	Normal
TM28	Dig	Ground	Physical	80	100	10	Normal
TM31	Brick Break	Fighting	Physical	75	100	15	Normal
TM32	Double Team	Normal	Status	—	—	15	Self
TM42	Facade	Normal	Physical	70	100	20	Normal
TM44	Rest	Psychic	Status	—	—	10	Self
TM45	Attract	Normal	Status	—	100	15	Normal
TM48	Round	Normal	Special	60	100	15	Normal
TM55	Scald	Water	Special	80	100	15	Normal
TM56	Fling	Dark	Physical	—	100	10	Normal
TM86	Grass Knot	Grass	Special	—	100	20	Normal
TM87	Swagger	Normal	Status	—	90	15	Normal
TM88	Sleep Talk	Normal	Status	—	—	10	Self
TM90	Substitute	Normal	Status	—	—	10	Self
TM94	Rock Smash	Fighting	Physical	40	100	15	Normal
TM98	Power-Up Punch	Fighting	Physical	40	100	20	Normal
TM100	Confide	Normal	Status	—	—	20	Normal
HM03	Surf	Water	Special	90	100	15	Adjacent
HM04	Strength	Normal	Physical	80	100	15	Normal
HM05	Waterfall	Water	Physical	80	100	15	Normal

MOVES TAUGHT BY PEOPLE

Name	Type	Kind	Pow.	Acc.	PP	Range

EGG MOVES

Name	Type	Kind	Pow.	Acc.	PP	Range
Present	Normal	Physical	—	90	15	Normal
Amnesia	Psychic	Status	—	—	20	Self
Future Sight	Psychic	Special	120	100	10	Normal
Belly Drum	Normal	Status	—	—	10	Self
Perish Song	Normal	Status	—	—	5	Adjacent
Supersonic	Normal	Status	—	55	20	Normal
Aqua Jet	Water	Physical	40	100	20	Normal
Superpower	Fighting	Physical	120	100	5	Normal
Refresh	Normal	Status	—	—	20	Self
Body Slam	Normal	Physical	85	100	15	Normal
Water Sport	Water	Status	—	—	15	Both Sides
Muddy Water	Water	Special	90	85	10	Many Others
Camouflage	Normal	Status	—	—	20	Self

AFTER THE HALL OF FAME

CENTRAL KALOS

043

Azumarill

COASTAL KALOS

MOUNTAIN KALOS

ADVENTURE DATA

Central Kalos 043
Aqua Rabbit Pokémon
☑ Azumarill

HEIGHT: 2'07" WEIGHT: 62.8 lbs.
GENDER: ♂/♀

TYPE **Water** **Fairy**

ABILITIES
Thick Fat
Huge Power

HIDDEN ABILITY
Sap Sgiver — Sap Sipper

X Its long ears are superb sensors. It can distinguish the movements of living things on riverbeds.

Y The bubble-like pattern on its stomach helps it camouflage itself when it's in the water.

STAT GROWTH RATES
HP
Attack
Defense
Sp. Atk
Sp. Def
Speed

EGG GROUPS
Water 1, Fairy

EVOLUTION
Level up with high friendship — Lv. 18
Azurill Marill Azumarill

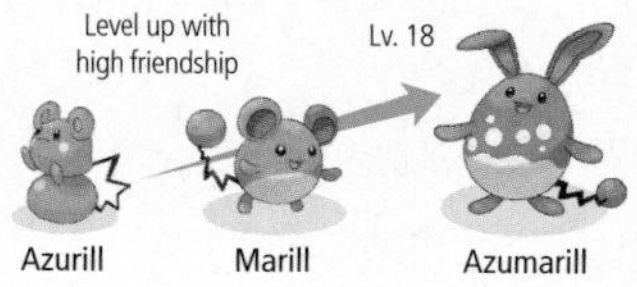

ITEMS SOMETIMES HELD BY WILD POKÉMON
None

Damage taken in normal battles		Damage taken in Inverse Battles	
Normal	×1	Normal	×1
Fire	×0.5	Fire	×2
Water	×0.5	Water	×2
Grass	×2	Grass	×0.5
Electric	×2	Electric	×0.5
Ice	×0.5	Ice	×2
Fighting	×0.5	Fighting	×2
Poison	×2	Poison	×0.5
Ground	×1	Ground	×1
Flying	×1	Flying	×1
Psychic	×1	Psychic	×1
Bug	×0.5	Bug	×2
Rock	×1	Rock	×1
Ghost	×1	Ghost	×1
Dragon	×0	Dragon	×2
Dark	×0.5	Dark	×2
Steel	×1	Steel	×1
Fairy	×1	Fairy	×1

Can be used in	
Inverse Battle	Battle Institute
—	Battle Maison
Battle Chateau	Random Matchup

Same form for ♂/♀

How to obtain for your Central Kalos Pokédex
❶ Catch in the yellow flowers or on the surface of the water on Route 22.
❷ Level up Marill to Lv. 18.

❶ Catch in the yellow flowers or on the surface of the water on Route 22.
❷ Level up Marill to Lv. 18.

● LEVEL-UP MOVES

Lv.	Name	Type	Kind	Pow.	Acc.	PP	Range
1	Tackle	Normal	Physical	50	100	35	Normal
1	Water Gun	Water	Special	40	100	25	Normal
1	Tail Whip	Normal	Status	—	100	30	Many Others
1	Water Sport	Water	Status	—	—	15	Both Sides
2	Tail Whip	Normal	Status	—	100	30	Many Others
5	Water Sport	Water	Status	—	—	15	Both Sides
5	Bubble	Water	Special	40	100	30	Many Others
10	Defense Curl	Normal	Status	—	—	40	Self
10	Rollout	Rock	Physical	30	90	20	Normal
13	Bubble Beam	Water	Special	65	100	20	Normal
16	Helping Hand	Normal	Status	—	—	20	1 Ally
21	Aqua Tail	Water	Physical	90	90	10	Normal
25	Double-Edge	Normal	Physical	120	100	15	Normal
31	Aqua Ring	Water	Status	—	—	20	Self
35	Rain Dance	Water	Status	—	—	5	Both Sides
42	Superpower	Fighting	Physical	120	100	5	Normal
46	Hydro Pump	Water	Special	110	80	5	Normal
50	Play Rough	Fairy	Physical	90	90	10	Normal

● TM & HM MOVES

No.	Name	Type	Kind	Pow.	Acc.	PP	Range
TM06	Toxic	Poison	Status	—	90	10	Normal
TM07	Hail	Ice	Status	—	—	10	Both Sides
TM10	Hidden Power	Normal	Special	60	100	15	Normal
TM13	Ice Beam	Ice	Special	90	100	10	Normal
TM14	Blizzard	Ice	Special	110	70	5	Many Others
TM15	Hyper Beam	Normal	Special	150	90	5	Normal
TM16	Light Screen	Psychic	Status	—	—	30	Your Side
TM17	Protect	Normal	Status	—	—	10	Self
TM18	Rain Dance	Water	Status	—	—	5	Both Sides
TM21	Frustration	Normal	Physical	—	100	20	Normal
TM27	Return	Normal	Physical	—	100	20	Normal
TM28	Dig	Ground	Physical	80	100	10	Normal
TM31	Brick Break	Fighting	Physical	75	100	15	Normal
TM32	Double Team	Normal	Status	—	—	15	Self
TM42	Facade	Normal	Physical	70	100	20	Normal
TM44	Rest	Psychic	Status	—	—	10	Self
TM45	Attract	Normal	Status	—	100	15	Normal
TM48	Round	Normal	Special	60	100	15	Normal
TM52	Focus Blast	Fighting	Special	120	70	5	Normal
TM55	Scald	Water	Special	80	100	15	Normal
TM56	Fling	Dark	Physical	—	100	10	Normal
TM68	Giga Impact	Normal	Physical	150	90	5	Normal
TM78	Bulldoze	Ground	Physical	60	100	20	Adjacent
TM86	Grass Knot	Grass	Special	—	100	20	Normal
TM87	Swagger	Normal	Status	—	90	15	Normal
TM88	Sleep Talk	Normal	Status	—	—	10	Self
TM90	Substitute	Normal	Status	—	—	10	Self
TM94	Rock Smash	Fighting	Physical	40	100	15	Normal
TM98	Power-Up Punch	Fighting	Physical	40	100	20	Normal
TM100	Confide	Normal	Status	—	—	20	Normal
HM03	Surf	Water	Special	90	100	15	Adjacent
HM04	Strength	Normal	Physical	80	100	15	Normal
HM05	Waterfall	Water	Physical	80	100	15	Normal

● MOVES TAUGHT BY PEOPLE

Name	Type	Kind	Pow.	Acc.	PP	Range

🏠 Central Kalos

044

Bagworm Pokémon

✓ # Burmy

HEIGHT: 0'08" WEIGHT: 7.5 lbs.
GENDER: ♂ / ♀

X To shelter itself from cold, wintry winds, it covers itself with a cloak made of twigs and leaves.

Y If its cloak is broken in battle, it quickly remakes the cloak with materials nearby.

TYPE | Bug

ABILITIES
Shed Skin

HIDDEN ABILITY
None

STAT GROWTH RATES
HP	■■
Attack	■■
Defense	■■
Sp. Atk	■
Sp. Def	■■
Speed	■■

EGG GROUP
Bug

🏠 EVOLUTION

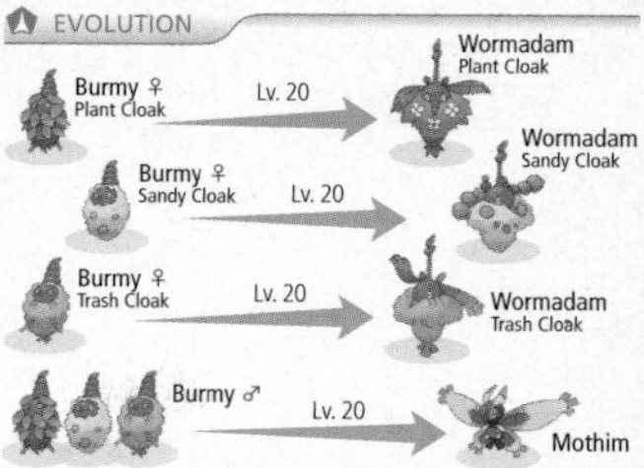

Burmy ♀ Plant Cloak → Lv. 20 → Wormadam Plant Cloak

Burmy ♀ Sandy Cloak → Lv. 20 → Wormadam Sandy Cloak

Burmy ♀ Trash Cloak → Lv. 20 → Wormadam Trash Cloak

Burmy ♂ → Lv. 20 → Mothim

ITEMS SOMETIMES HELD BY WILD POKÉMON
None

Plant Cloak

Sandy Cloak

Trash Cloak

Damage taken in normal battles	
Normal	×1
Fire	×2
Water	×1
Grass	×0.5
Electric	×1
Ice	×1
Fighting	×0.5
Poison	×1
Ground	×0.5
Flying	×2
Psychic	×1
Bug	×1
Rock	×2
Ghost	×1
Dragon	×1
Dark	×1
Steel	×1
Fairy	×1

Damage taken in Inverse Battles	
Normal	×1
Fire	×0.5
Water	×1
Grass	×2
Electric	×1
Ice	×1
Fighting	×2
Poison	×1
Ground	×2
Flying	×0.5
Psychic	×1
Bug	×1
Rock	×0.5
Ghost	×1
Dragon	×1
Dark	×1
Steel	×1
Fairy	×1

Can be used in
Inverse Battle
—
Battle Chateau
Battle Institute
Battle Maison
Random Matchup

Same form for ♂ / ♀

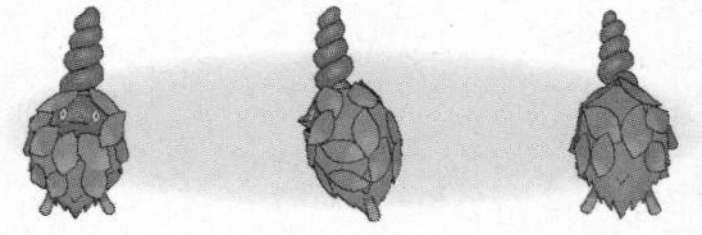

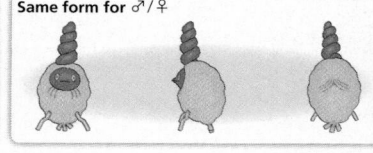

Same form for ♂ / ♀

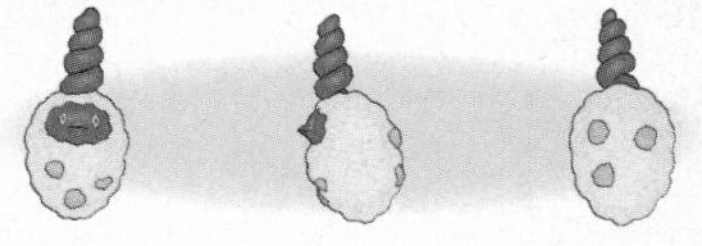

Same form for ♂ / ♀

How to obtain for your Central Kalos Pokédex

X Catch in the tall grass on Route 3.

Y Catch in the tall grass on Route 3.

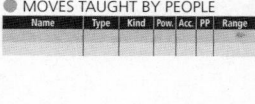

● LEVEL-UP MOVES
Lv.	Name	Type	Kind	Pow.	Acc.	PP	Range
1	Protect	Normal	Status	—	—	10	Self
10	Tackle	Normal	Physical	50	100	35	Normal
15	Bug Bite	Bug	Physical	60	100	20	Normal
20	Hidden Power	Normal	Special	60	100	15	Normal

● TM & HM MOVES
No.	Name	Type	Kind	Pow.	Acc.	PP	Range
TM10	Hidden Power	Normal	Special	60	100	15	Normal
TM17	Protect	Normal	Status	—	—	10	Self

● MOVES TAUGHT BY PEOPLE
Name	Type	Kind	Pow.	Acc.	PP	Range

Burmy's form changes based on the environment in which it last battled (Plant Cloak in tall grass / out of doors, Sandy Cloak in caves / on beaches, Trash Cloak inside buildings).

AFTER THE HALL OF FAME

CENTRAL KALOS

045

Wormadam
Plant Cloak

COASTAL KALOS

MOUNTAIN KALOS

ADVENTURE DATA

🏠 **Central Kalos** 045

Bagworm Pokémon

Wormadam
Plant Cloak

HEIGHT: 1'08" WEIGHT: 14.3 lbs.
GENDER: ♀

X Its appearance changes depending on where it evolved. The materials on hand become a part of its body.

Y When Burmy evolved, its cloak became a part of this Pokémon's body. The cloak is never shed.

TYPE Bug Grass

ABILITY
Anticipation

HIDDEN ABILITY
None

STAT GROWTH RATES
HP	■■■
Attack	■■■
Defense	■■■
Sp. Atk	■■■■
Sp. Def	■■■■
Speed	■■

EGG GROUP
Bug

🏠 EVOLUTION

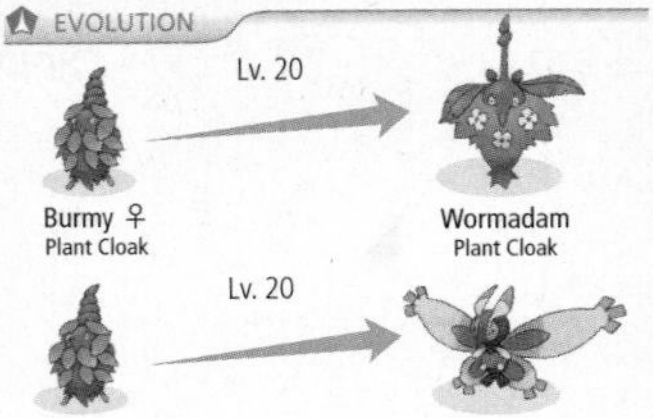

Lv. 20

Burmy ♀
Plant Cloak → Wormadam
Plant Cloak

Lv. 20

Burmy ♂
Plant Cloak → Mothim

ITEMS SOMETIMES HELD BY WILD POKÉMON
None

Can be used in
Inverse Battle
—
Battle Chateau
Battle Institute
Battle Maison
Random Matchup

Damage taken in normal battles	
Normal	×1
Fire	×4
Water	×0.5
Grass	×0.25
Electric	×0.5
Ice	×2
Fighting	×0.5
Poison	×2
Ground	×0.25
Flying	×4
Psychic	×1
Bug	×2
Rock	×2
Ghost	×1
Dragon	×1
Dark	×1
Steel	×1
Fairy	×1

Damage taken in Inverse Battles	
Normal	×1
Fire	×0.25
Water	×2
Grass	×4
Electric	×2
Ice	×0.5
Fighting	×2
Poison	×0.5
Ground	×4
Flying	×0.25
Psychic	×1
Bug	×0.5
Rock	×0.5
Ghost	×1
Dragon	×1
Dark	×1
Steel	×1
Fairy	×1

How to obtain for your Central Kalos Pokédex

Level up Burmy ♀ (Plant Cloak) to Lv. 20.

Level up Burmy ♀ (Plant Cloak) to Lv. 20.

♀

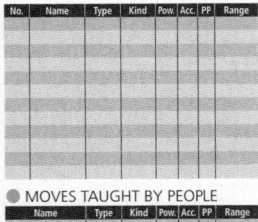

● LEVEL-UP MOVES

Lv.	Name	Type	Kind	Pow.	Acc.	PP	Range
1	Tackle	Normal	Physical	50	100	35	Normal
10	Protect	Normal	Status	—	—	10	Self
15	Bug Bite	Bug	Physical	60	100	20	Normal
20	Hidden Power	Normal	Special	60	100	15	Normal
23	Confusion	Psychic	Special	50	100	25	Normal
26	Razor Leaf	Grass	Physical	55	95	25	Many Others
29	Growth	Normal	Status	—	—	20	Self
32	Psybeam	Psychic	Special	65	100	20	Normal
35	Captivate	Normal	Status	—	100	20	Many Others
38	Flail	Normal	Physical	—	100	15	Normal
41	Attract	Normal	Status	—	100	15	Normal
44	Psychic	Psychic	Special	90	100	10	Normal
47	Leaf Storm	Grass	Special	130	90	5	Normal

● TM & HM MOVES

No.	Name	Type	Kind	Pow.	Acc.	PP	Range
TM06	Toxic	Poison	Status	—	90	10	Normal
TM09	Venoshock	Poison	Special	65	100	10	Normal
TM10	Hidden Power	Normal	Special	60	100	15	Normal
TM11	Sunny Day	Fire	Status	—	—	5	Both Sides
TM15	Hyper Beam	Normal	Special	150	90	5	Normal
TM17	Protect	Normal	Status	—	—	10	Self
TM18	Rain Dance	Water	Status	—	—	5	Both Sides
TM20	Safeguard	Normal	Status	—	—	25	Your Side
TM21	Frustration	Normal	Physical	—	100	20	Normal
TM22	Solar Beam	Grass	Special	120	100	10	Normal
TM27	Return	Normal	Physical	—	100	20	Normal
TM29	Psychic	Psychic	Special	90	100	10	Normal
TM30	Shadow Ball	Ghost	Special	80	100	15	Normal
TM32	Double Team	Normal	Status	—	—	15	Self
TM42	Facade	Normal	Physical	70	100	20	Normal
TM44	Rest	Psychic	Status	—	—	10	Self
TM45	Attract	Normal	Status	—	100	15	Normal
TM46	Thief	Dark	Physical	60	100	25	Normal
TM48	Round	Normal	Special	60	100	15	Normal
TM53	Energy Ball	Grass	Special	90	100	10	Normal
TM68	Giga Impact	Normal	Physical	150	90	5	Normal
TM70	Flash	Normal	Status	—	100	20	Normal
TM76	Struggle Bug	Bug	Special	50	100	20	Many Others
TM77	Psych Up	Normal	Status	—	—	10	Normal
TM83	Infestation	Bug	Special	20	100	20	Normal
TM85	Dream Eater	Psychic	Special	100	100	15	Normal
TM86	Grass Knot	Grass	Special	—	100	20	Normal
TM87	Swagger	Normal	Status	—	90	15	Normal
TM88	Sleep Talk	Normal	Status	—	—	10	Self
TM90	Substitute	Normal	Status	—	—	10	Self
TM100	Confide	Normal	Status	—	—	20	Normal

No.	Name	Type	Kind	Pow.	Acc.	PP	Range

● MOVES TAUGHT BY PEOPLE

Name	Type	Kind	Pow.	Acc.	PP	Range

Central Kalos
Bagworm Pokémon
Wormadam
Sandy Cloak

045

HEIGHT: 1'08" **WEIGHT:** 14.3 lbs.
GENDER: ♀

X — Its appearance changes depending on where it evolved. The materials on hand become a part of its body.

Y — When Burmy evolved, its cloak became a part of this Pokémon's body. The cloak is never shed.

TYPE Bug Ground

ABILITY
Anticipation

HIDDEN ABILITY
None

STAT GROWTH RATES
HP	■■■
Attack	■■■■
Defense	■■■■■
Sp. Atk	■■■
Sp. Def	■■■■■
Speed	■■

EGG GROUP
Bug

EVOLUTION

Burmy ♀
Sandy Cloak → Lv. 20 → Wormadam
Sandy Cloak

Burmy ♂
Sandy Cloak → Lv. 20 → Mothim

ITEMS SOMETIMES HELD BY WILD POKÉMON
None

Damage taken in normal battles		Damage taken in Inverse Battles		Can be used in
Normal	×1	Normal	×1	Inverse Battle
Fire	×2	Fire	×0.5	—
Water	×2	Water	×0.5	Battle Chateau
Grass	×1	Grass	×1	Battle Institute
Electric	×0	Electric	×2	Battle Maison
Ice	×2	Ice	×0.5	Random Matchup
Fighting	×0.5	Fighting	×2	
Poison	×0.5	Poison	×2	
Ground	×0.5	Ground	×2	
Flying	×2	Flying	×0.5	
Psychic	×1	Psychic	×1	
Bug	×1	Bug	×1	
Rock	×1	Rock	×1	
Ghost	×1	Ghost	×1	
Dragon	×1	Dragon	×1	
Dark	×1	Dark	×1	
Steel	×1	Steel	×1	
Fairy	×1	Fairy	×1	

How to obtain for your Central Kalos Pokédex

Level up Burmy ♀ (Sandy Cloak) to Lv. 20.

Level up Burmy ♀ (Sandy Cloak) to Lv. 20.

♀

● LEVEL-UP MOVES
Lv.	Name	Type	Kind	Pow.	Acc.	PP	Range
1	Tackle	Normal	Physical	50	100	35	Normal
10	Protect	Normal	Status	—	—	10	Self
15	Bug Bite	Bug	Physical	60	100	20	Normal
20	Hidden Power	Normal	Special	60	100	15	Normal
23	Confusion	Psychic	Special	50	100	25	Normal
26	Rock Blast	Rock	Physical	25	90	10	Normal
29	Harden	Normal	Status	—	—	30	Self
32	Psybeam	Psychic	Special	65	100	20	Normal
35	Captivate	Normal	Status	—	100	20	Many Others
38	Flail	Normal	Physical	—	100	15	Normal
41	Attract	Normal	Status	—	100	15	Normal
44	Psychic	Psychic	Special	90	100	10	Normal
47	Fissure	Ground	Physical	—	30	5	Normal

● TM & HM MOVES
No.	Name	Type	Kind	Pow.	Acc.	PP	Range
TM06	Toxic	Poison	Status	—	90	10	Normal
TM09	Venoshock	Poison	Special	65	100	10	Normal
TM10	Hidden Power	Normal	Special	60	100	15	Normal
TM11	Sunny Day	Fire	Status	—	—	5	Both Sides
TM15	Hyper Beam	Normal	Special	150	90	5	Normal
TM17	Protect	Normal	Status	—	—	10	Self
TM18	Rain Dance	Water	Status	—	—	5	Both Sides
TM20	Safeguard	Normal	Status	—	—	25	Your Side
TM21	Frustration	Normal	Physical	—	100	20	Normal
TM26	Earthquake	Ground	Physical	100	100	10	Adjacent
TM27	Return	Normal	Physical	—	100	20	Normal
TM28	Dig	Ground	Physical	80	100	10	Normal
TM29	Psychic	Psychic	Special	90	100	10	Normal
TM30	Shadow Ball	Ghost	Special	80	100	15	Normal
TM32	Double Team	Normal	Status	—	—	15	Self
TM37	Sandstorm	Rock	Status	—	—	10	Both Sides
TM39	Rock Tomb	Rock	Physical	60	95	15	Normal
TM42	Facade	Normal	Physical	70	100	20	Normal
TM44	Rest	Psychic	Status	—	—	10	Self
TM45	Attract	Normal	Status	—	100	15	Normal
TM46	Thief	Dark	Physical	60	100	25	Normal
TM48	Round	Normal	Special	60	100	15	Normal
TM68	Giga Impact	Normal	Physical	150	90	5	Normal
TM70	Flash	Normal	Status	—	100	20	Normal
TM76	Struggle Bug	Bug	Special	50	100	20	Many Others
TM77	Psych Up	Normal	Status	—	—	10	Self
TM78	Bulldoze	Ground	Physical	60	100	20	Adjacent
TM83	Infestation	Bug	Special	20	100	20	Normal
TM85	Dream Eater	Psychic	Special	100	100	15	Normal
TM87	Swagger	Normal	Status	—	90	15	Normal
TM88	Sleep Talk	Normal	Status	—	—	10	Self
TM90	Substitute	Normal	Status	—	—	10	Self
TM100	Confide	Normal	Status	—	—	20	Normal

● MOVES TAUGHT BY PEOPLE
Name	Type	Kind	Pow.	Acc.	PP	Range

AFTER THE HALL OF FAME

CENTRAL KALOS

045 Wormadam Sandy Cloak

COASTAL KALOS

MOUNTAIN KALOS

ADVENTURE DATA

045

Bagworm Pokémon

☑ Wormadam
Trash Cloak

HEIGHT: 1'08" WEIGHT: 14.3 lbs.
GENDER: ♀

| TYPE | Bug | Steel |

ABILITY
Anticipation

HIDDEN ABILITY
None

STAT GROWTH RATES
HP	■■■
Attack	■■■■
Defense	■■■■
Sp. Atk	■■■
Sp. Def	■■■■
Speed	■■

EGG GROUP
Bug

X Its appearance changes depending on where it evolved. The materials on hand become a part of its body.

Y When Burmy evolved, its cloak became a part of this Pokémon's body. The cloak is never shed.

⬆ EVOLUTION

Burmy ♀
Trash Cloak
— Lv. 20 → Wormadam
Trash Cloak

Burmy ♂
Trash Cloak
— Lv. 20 → Mothim

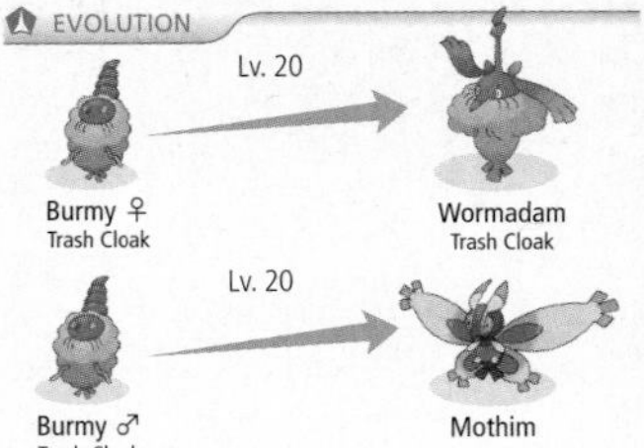

ITEMS SOMETIMES HELD BY WILD POKÉMON
None

Can be used in
| Inverse Battle |
| — |
| Battle Chateau |
| Battle Institute |
| Battle Maison |
| Random Matchup |

Damage taken in normal battles		Damage taken in Inverse Battles	
Normal	×0.5	Normal	×2
Fire	×4	Fire	×0.25
Water	×1	Water	×1
Grass	×0.25	Grass	×4
Electric	×1	Electric	×1
Ice	×0.5	Ice	×2
Fighting	×1	Fighting	×1
Poison	×0	Poison	×1
Ground	×1	Ground	×1
Flying	×1	Flying	×1
Psychic	×0.5	Psychic	×2
Bug	×0.5	Bug	×2
Rock	×1	Rock	×1
Ghost	∞	Ghost	×1
Dragon	×0.5	Dragon	×2
Dark	∞	Dark	×1
Steel	×0.5	Steel	×2
Fairy	×0.5	Fairy	×2

How to obtain for your Central Kalos Pokédex

Level up Burmy ♀ (Trash Cloak) to Lv. 20.

Level up Burmy ♀ (Trash Cloak) to Lv. 20.

♀

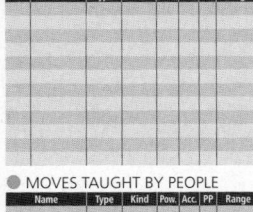

● LEVEL-UP MOVES

Lv.	Name	Type	Kind	Pow.	Acc.	PP	Range
1	Tackle	Normal	Physical	50	100	35	Normal
10	Protect	Normal	Status	—	—	10	Self
15	Bug Bite	Bug	Physical	60	100	20	Normal
20	Hidden Power	Normal	Special	60	100	15	Normal
23	Confusion	Psychic	Special	50	100	25	Normal
26	Mirror Shot	Steel	Special	65	85	10	Normal
29	Metal Sound	Steel	Status	—	85	40	Normal
32	Psybeam	Psychic	Special	65	100	20	Normal
35	Captivate	Normal	Status	—	100	20	Many Others
38	Flail	Normal	Physical	—	100	15	Normal
41	Attract	Normal	Status	—	100	15	Normal
44	Psychic	Psychic	Special	90	100	10	Normal
47	Iron Head	Steel	Physical	80	100	15	Normal

● TM & HM MOVES

No.	Name	Type	Kind	Pow.	Acc.	PP	Range
TM06	Toxic	Poison	Status	—	90	10	Normal
TM09	Venoshock	Poison	Special	65	100	10	Normal
TM10	Hidden Power	Normal	Special	60	100	15	Normal
TM11	Sunny Day	Fire	Status	—	—	5	Both Sides
TM15	Hyper Beam	Normal	Special	150	90	5	Normal
TM17	Protect	Normal	Status	—	—	10	Self
TM18	Rain Dance	Water	Status	—	—	5	Both Sides
TM20	Safeguard	Normal	Status	—	—	25	Your Side
TM21	Frustration	Normal	Physical	—	100	20	Normal
TM27	Return	Normal	Physical	—	100	20	Normal
TM29	Psychic	Psychic	Special	90	100	10	Normal
TM30	Shadow Ball	Ghost	Special	80	100	15	Normal
TM32	Double Team	Normal	Status	—	—	15	Self
TM42	Facade	Normal	Physical	70	100	20	Normal
TM44	Rest	Psychic	Status	—	—	10	Self
TM45	Attract	Normal	Status	—	100	15	Normal
TM46	Thief	Dark	Physical	60	100	25	Normal
TM48	Round	Normal	Special	60	100	15	Normal
TM68	Giga Impact	Normal	Physical	150	90	5	Normal
TM70	Flash	Normal	Status	—	100	20	Normal
TM74	Gyro Ball	Steel	Physical	—	100	5	Normal
TM76	Struggle Bug	Bug	Special	50	100	20	Many Others
TM77	Psych Up	Normal	Status	—	—	10	Normal
TM83	Infestation	Bug	Special	20	100	20	Normal
TM85	Dream Eater	Psychic	Special	100	100	15	Normal
TM87	Swagger	Normal	Status	—	90	15	Normal
TM88	Sleep Talk	Normal	Status	—	—	10	Self
TM90	Substitute	Normal	Status	—	—	10	Self
TM91	Flash Cannon	Steel	Special	80	100	10	Normal
TM100	Confide	Normal	Status	—	—	20	Normal

No.	Name	Type	Kind	Pow.	Acc.	PP	Range

● MOVES TAUGHT BY PEOPLE

Name	Type	Kind	Pow.	Acc.	PP	Range

AFTER THE HALL OF FAME

CENTRAL KALOS
045
Wormadam
Trash Cloak

COASTAL KALOS

MOUNTAIN KALOS

ADVENTURE DATA

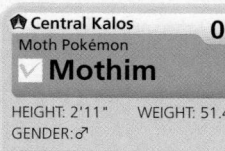

Central Kalos 046
Moth Pokémon
☑ Mothim

HEIGHT: 2'11"   WEIGHT: 51.4 lbs.
GENDER: ♂

X It loves the honey of flowers and steals honey collected by Combee.

Y It flutters around at night and steals honey from the Combee hive.

TYPE: Bug | Flying

ABILITY
Swarm

HIDDEN ABILITY
Tinted Lens

STAT GROWTH RATES
HP	■■■
Attack	■■■■■
Defense	■■
Sp. Atk	■■■■■
Sp. Def	■■
Speed	■■■■

EGG GROUP
Bug

EVOLUTION

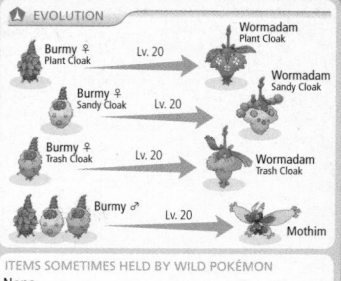

Burmy ♀ Plant Cloak — Lv. 20 → Wormadam Plant Cloak

Burmy ♀ Sandy Cloak — Lv. 20 → Wormadam Sandy Cloak

Burmy ♀ Trash Cloak — Lv. 20 → Wormadam Trash Cloak

Burmy ♂ — Lv. 20 → Mothim

ITEMS SOMETIMES HELD BY WILD POKÉMON
None

Damage taken in normal battles		Damage taken in Inverse Battles	
Normal	×1	Normal	×1
Fire	×2	Fire	×0.5
Water	×1	Water	×1
Grass	×0.25	Grass	×4
Electric	×2	Electric	×0.5
Ice	×2	Ice	×0.5
Fighting	×0.25	Fighting	×4
Poison	×1	Poison	×1
Ground	×0	Ground	×4
Flying	×2	Flying	×0.5
Psychic	×1	Psychic	×1
Bug	×0.5	Bug	×2
Rock	×4	Rock	×0.25
Ghost	×1	Ghost	×1
Dragon	×1	Dragon	×1
Dark	×1	Dark	×1
Steel	×1	Steel	×1
Fairy	×1	Fairy	×1

Can be used in	
Inverse Battle	Battle Institute
Sky Battle	Battle Maison
Battle Chateau	Random Matchup

♂

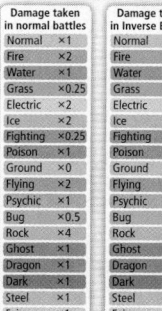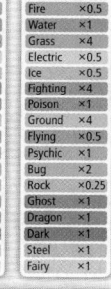

How to obtain for your Central Kalos Pokédex

Level up Burmy ♂ to Lv. 20.   Level up Burmy ♂ to Lv. 20.

● LEVEL-UP MOVES

Lv.	Name	Type	Kind	Pow.	Acc.	PP	Range
1	Tackle	Normal	Physical	50	100	35	Normal
10	Protect	Normal	Status	—	—	10	Self
15	Bug Bite	Bug	Physical	60	100	20	Normal
20	Hidden Power	Normal	Special	60	100	15	Normal
23	Confusion	Psychic	Special	50	100	25	Normal
26	Gust	Flying	Special	40	100	35	Normal
29	Poison Powder	Poison	Status	—	75	35	Normal
32	Psybeam	Psychic	Special	65	100	20	Normal
35	Camouflage	Normal	Status	—	—	20	Self
38	Silver Wind	Bug	Special	60	100	5	Normal
41	Air Slash	Flying	Special	75	95	15	Normal
44	Psychic	Psychic	Special	90	100	10	Normal
47	Bug Buzz	Bug	Special	90	100	10	Normal
50	Quiver Dance	Bug	Status	—	—	20	Self

● TM & HM MOVES

No.	Name	Type	Kind	Pow.	Acc.	PP	Range
TM06	Toxic	Poison	Status	—	90	10	Normal
TM09	Venoshock	Poison	Special	65	100	10	Normal
TM10	Hidden Power	Normal	Special	60	100	15	Normal
TM11	Sunny Day	Fire	Status	—	—	5	Both Sides
TM15	Hyper Beam	Normal	Special	150	90	5	Normal
TM17	Protect	Normal	Status	—	—	10	Self
TM18	Rain Dance	Water	Status	—	—	5	Both Sides
TM19	Roost	Flying	Status	—	—	10	Self
TM20	Safeguard	Normal	Status	—	—	25	Your Side
TM21	Frustration	Normal	Physical	—	100	20	Normal
TM22	Solar Beam	Grass	Special	120	100	10	Normal
TM27	Return	Normal	Physical	—	100	20	Normal
TM29	Psychic	Psychic	Special	90	100	10	Normal
TM30	Shadow Ball	Ghost	Special	80	100	15	Normal
TM32	Double Team	Normal	Status	—	—	15	Self
TM40	Aerial Ace	Flying	Physical	60	—	20	Normal
TM42	Facade	Normal	Physical	70	100	20	Normal
TM44	Rest	Psychic	Status	—	—	10	Self
TM45	Attract	Normal	Status	—	100	15	Normal
TM46	Thief	Dark	Physical	60	100	25	Normal
TM48	Round	Normal	Special	60	100	15	Normal
TM53	Energy Ball	Grass	Special	90	100	10	Normal
TM62	Acrobatics	Flying	Physical	55	100	15	Normal
TM68	Giga Impact	Normal	Physical	150	90	5	Normal
TM70	Flash	Normal	Status	—	100	20	Normal
TM76	Struggle Bug	Bug	Special	50	100	20	Many Others
TM77	Psych Up	Normal	Status	—	—	10	Normal
TM83	Infestation	Bug	Special	20	100	20	Normal
TM85	Dream Eater	Psychic	Special	100	100	15	Normal
TM87	Swagger	Normal	Status	—	90	15	Normal
TM88	Sleep Talk	Normal	Status	—	—	10	Self
TM89	U-turn	Bug	Physical	70	100	20	Normal
TM90	Substitute	Normal	Status	—	—	10	Self

No.	Name	Type	Kind	Pow.	Acc.	PP	Range
TM100	Confide	Normal	Status	—	—	20	Normal

● MOVES TAUGHT BY PEOPLE

Name	Type	Kind	Pow.	Acc.	PP	Range

AFTER THE HALL OF FAME

CENTRAL KALOS

047

Surskit

COASTAL KALOS

MOUNTAIN KALOS

ADVENTURE DATA

🏠 Central Kalos — 047
Pond Skater Pokémon
✓ Surskit

HEIGHT: 1'08" WEIGHT: 3.7 lbs.
GENDER: ♂/♀

TYPE Bug | Water

ABILITY
Swift Swim

HIDDEN ABILITY
Rain Dish

STAT GROWTH RATES
HP	▪▪
Attack	▪▪
Defense	▪▪
Sp. Atk	▪▪
Sp. Def	▪▪
Speed	▪▪▪▪

EGG GROUPS
Water 1, Bug

X They usually live on ponds, but after an evening shower, they may appear on puddles in towns.

Y It appears as if it is skating on water. It draws prey with a sweet scent from the tip of its head.

🔺 EVOLUTION

Lv. 22

Surskit → Masquerain

ITEMS SOMETIMES HELD BY WILD POKÉMON
None

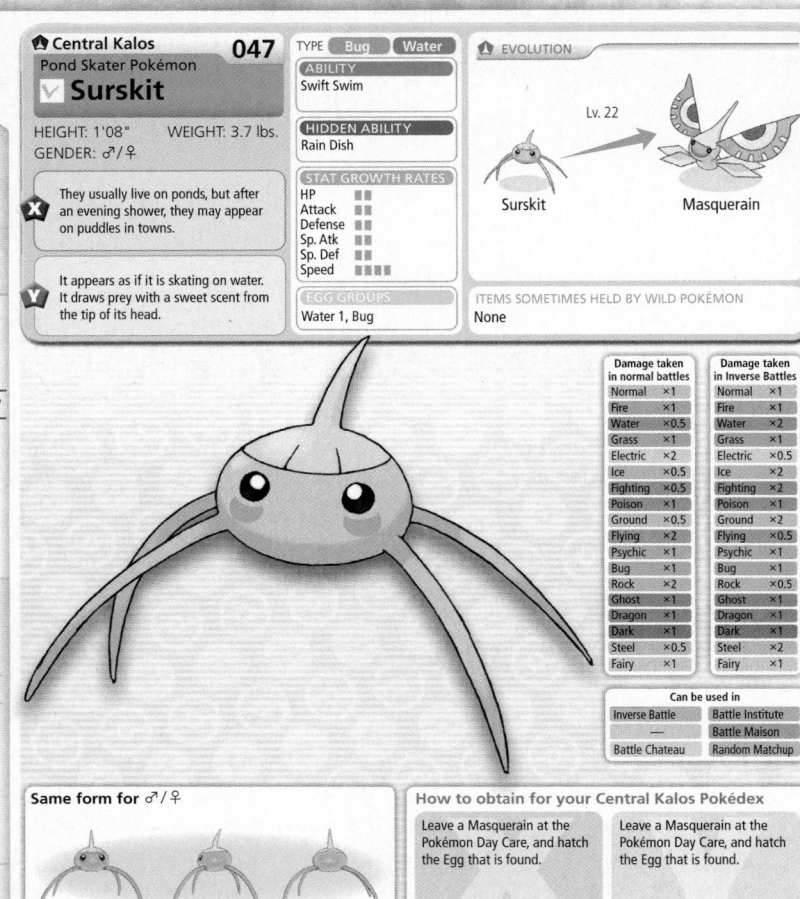

Damage taken in normal battles	
Normal	×1
Fire	×1
Water	×0.5
Grass	×1
Electric	×2
Ice	×0.5
Fighting	×0.5
Poison	×1
Ground	×0.5
Flying	×2
Psychic	×1
Bug	×1
Rock	×2
Ghost	×1
Dragon	×1
Dark	×1
Steel	×0.5
Fairy	×1

Damage taken in Inverse Battles	
Normal	×1
Fire	×1
Water	×2
Grass	×1
Electric	×0.5
Ice	×2
Fighting	×2
Poison	×1
Ground	×2
Flying	×0.5
Psychic	×1
Bug	×1
Rock	×0.5
Ghost	×1
Dragon	×1
Dark	×1
Steel	×2
Fairy	×1

Can be used in	
Inverse Battle	Battle Institute
—	Battle Maison
Battle Chateau	Random Matchup

Same form for ♂/♀

How to obtain for your Central Kalos Pokédex
Leave a Masquerain at the Pokémon Day Care, and hatch the Egg that is found.

Leave a Masquerain at the Pokémon Day Care, and hatch the Egg that is found.

● LEVEL-UP MOVES
Lv.	Name	Type	Kind	Pow.	Acc.	PP	Range
1	Bubble	Water	Special	40	100	30	Many Others
7	Quick Attack	Normal	Physical	40	100	30	Normal
13	Sweet Scent	Normal	Status	—	100	20	Many Others
19	Water Sport	Water	Status	—	—	15	Both Sides
25	Bubble Beam	Water	Special	65	100	20	Normal
31	Agility	Psychic	Status	—	—	30	Self
37	Mist	Ice	Status	—	—	30	Your Side
37	Haze	Ice	Status	—	—	30	Both Sides
43	Baton Pass	Normal	Status	—	—	40	Self
46	Sticky Web	Bug	Status	—	—	20	Other Side

● TM & HM MOVES
No.	Name	Type	Kind	Pow.	Acc.	PP	Range
TM06	Toxic	Poison	Status	—	90	10	Normal
TM10	Hidden Power	Normal	Special	60	100	15	Normal
TM11	Sunny Day	Fire	Status	—	—	5	Both Sides
TM13	Ice Beam	Ice	Special	90	100	10	Normal
TM14	Blizzard	Ice	Special	110	70	5	Many Others
TM17	Protect	Normal	Status	—	—	10	Self
TM18	Rain Dance	Water	Status	—	—	5	Both Sides
TM21	Frustration	Normal	Physical	—	100	20	Normal
TM22	Solar Beam	Grass	Special	120	100	10	Normal
TM27	Return	Normal	Physical	—	100	20	Normal
TM30	Shadow Ball	Ghost	Special	80	100	15	Normal
TM32	Double Team	Normal	Status	—	—	15	Self
TM42	Facade	Normal	Physical	70	100	20	Normal
TM44	Rest	Psychic	Status	—	—	10	Self
TM45	Attract	Normal	Status	—	100	15	Normal
TM46	Thief	Dark	Physical	60	100	25	Normal
TM48	Round	Normal	Special	60	100	15	Normal
TM55	Scald	Water	Special	80	100	15	Normal
TM70	Flash	Normal	Status	—	100	20	Normal
TM76	Struggle Bug	Bug	Special	50	100	20	Many Others
TM77	Psych Up	Normal	Status	—	—	10	Normal
TM83	Infestation	Bug	Special	20	100	20	Normal
TM87	Swagger	Normal	Status	—	90	15	Normal
TM88	Sleep Talk	Normal	Status	—	—	10	Self
TM90	Substitute	Normal	Status	—	—	10	Self
TM100	Confide	Normal	Status	—	—	20	Normal

No.	Name	Type	Kind	Pow.	Acc.	PP	Range

● MOVES TAUGHT BY PEOPLE
Name	Type	Kind	Pow.	Acc.	PP	Range

● EGG MOVES
Name	Type	Kind	Pow.	Acc.	PP	Range
Foresight	Normal	Status	—	—	40	Normal
Mud Shot	Ground	Special	55	95	15	Normal
Psybeam	Psychic	Special	65	100	20	Normal
Hydro Pump	Water	Special	110	80	5	Normal
Mind Reader	Normal	Status	—	—	5	Normal
Signal Beam	Bug	Special	75	100	15	Normal
Bug Bite	Bug	Physical	60	100	20	Normal
Aqua Jet	Water	Physical	40	100	20	Normal
Endure	Normal	Status	—	—	10	Self
Fell Stinger	Bug	Physical	30	100	25	Normal
Power Split	Psychic	Status	—	—	10	Normal

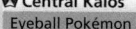
Eyeball Pokémon

Masquerain

048

HEIGHT: 2'07" WEIGHT: 7.9 lbs.
GENDER: ♂/♀

 Its antennae have eye patterns on them. Its four wings enable it to hover and fly in any direction.

Y It flaps its four wings to hover and fly freely in any direction—to and fro and sideways.

AFTER THE HALL OF FAME

CENTRAL KALOS

048 | Masquerain

COASTAL KALOS

MOUNTAIN KALOS

ADVENTURE DATA

| TYPE | Bug | Flying |

ABILITY
Intimidate

HIDDEN ABILITY
Unnerve

STAT GROWTH RATES

HP	■ ■
Attack	■ ■
Defense	■ ■
Sp. Atk	■ ■ ■
Sp. Def	■ ■
Speed	■ ■

EGG GROUPS
Water 1, Bug

EVOLUTION

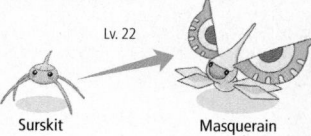

Surskit — Lv. 22 → Masquerain

ITEMS SOMETIMES HELD BY WILD POKÉMON
Silver Powder

Damage taken in normal battles		Damage taken in Inverse Battles	
Normal	×1	Normal	×1
Fire	×2	Fire	×0.5
Water	×1	Water	×1
Grass	×0.25	Grass	×4
Electric	×2	Electric	×0.5
Ice	×2	Ice	×0.5
Fighting	×0.25	Fighting	×4
Poison	×1	Poison	×1
Ground	×0	Ground	×4
Flying	×2	Flying	×0.5
Psychic	×1	Psychic	×1
Bug	×0.5	Bug	×2
Rock	×4	Rock	×0.25
Ghost	×1	Ghost	×1
Dragon	×1	Dragon	×1
Dark	×1	Dark	×1
Steel	×1	Steel	×1
Fairy	×1	Fairy	×1

Can be used in	
Inverse Battle	Battle Institute
Sky Battle	Battle Maison
Battle Chateau	Random Matchup

Same form for ♂/♀

How to obtain for your Central Kalos Pokédex

Catch on the surface of the water on Route 3.

Catch on the surface of the water on Route 3.

● LEVEL-UP MOVES

Lv.	Name	Type	Kind	Pow.	Acc.	PP	Range
1	Quiver Dance	Bug	Status	—	—	20	Self
1	Bug Buzz	Bug	Special	90	100	10	Normal
1	Whirlwind	Normal	Status	—	—	20	Normal
1	Ominous Wind	Ghost	Special	60	100	5	Normal
1	Bubble	Water	Special	40	100	30	Many Others
1	Quick Attack	Normal	Physical	40	100	30	Normal
1	Sweet Scent	Normal	Status	—	100	20	Many Others
1	Water Sport	Water	Status	—	—	15	Both Sides
7	Quick Attack	Normal	Physical	40	100	30	Normal
13	Sweet Scent	Normal	Status	—	100	20	Many Others
19	Water Sport	Water	Status	—	—	15	Both Sides
22	Gust	Flying	Special	40	100	35	Normal
26	Scary Face	Normal	Status	—	100	10	Normal
33	Stun Spore	Grass	Status	—	75	30	Normal
40	Silver Wind	Bug	Special	60	100	5	Normal
47	Air Slash	Flying	Special	75	95	15	Normal
54	Whirlwind	Normal	Status	—	—	20	Normal
61	Bug Buzz	Bug	Special	90	100	10	Normal
68	Quiver Dance	Bug	Status	—	—	20	Self

● TM & HM MOVES

No.	Name	Type	Kind	Pow.	Acc.	PP	Range
TM06	Toxic	Poison	Status	—	90	10	Normal
TM10	Hidden Power	Normal	Special	60	100	15	Normal
TM11	Sunny Day	Fire	Status	—	—	5	Both Sides
TM13	Ice Beam	Ice	Special	90	100	10	Normal
TM14	Blizzard	Ice	Special	110	70	5	Many Others
TM15	Hyper Beam	Normal	Special	150	90	5	Normal
TM17	Protect	Normal	Status	—	—	10	Self
TM18	Rain Dance	Water	Status	—	—	5	Both Sides
TM19	Roost	Flying	Status	—	—	10	Self
TM21	Frustration	Normal	Physical	—	100	20	Normal
TM22	Solar Beam	Grass	Special	120	100	10	Normal
TM27	Return	Normal	Physical	—	100	20	Normal
TM30	Shadow Ball	Ghost	Special	80	100	15	Normal
TM32	Double Team	Normal	Status	—	—	15	Self
TM40	Aerial Ace	Flying	Physical	60	—	20	Normal
TM42	Facade	Normal	Physical	70	100	20	Normal
TM44	Rest	Psychic	Status	—	—	10	Self
TM45	Attract	Normal	Status	—	100	15	Normal
TM46	Thief	Dark	Physical	60	100	25	Normal
TM48	Round	Normal	Special	60	100	15	Normal
TM53	Energy Ball	Grass	Special	90	100	10	Normal
TM55	Scald	Water	Special	80	100	15	Normal
TM68	Giga Impact	Normal	Physical	150	90	5	Normal
TM70	Flash	Normal	Status	—	100	20	Normal
TM76	Struggle Bug	Bug	Special	50	100	20	Many Others
TM77	Psych Up	Normal	Status	—	—	10	Normal
TM83	Infestation	Bug	Special	20	100	20	Normal
TM87	Swagger	Normal	Status	—	90	15	Normal
TM88	Sleep Talk	Normal	Status	—	—	10	Self
TM89	U-turn	Bug	Physical	70	100	20	Normal
TM90	Substitute	Normal	Status	—	—	10	Self
TM100	Confide	Normal	Status	—	—	20	Normal

No.	Name	Type	Kind	Pow.	Acc.	PP	Range

● MOVES TAUGHT BY PEOPLE

Name	Type	Kind	Pow.	Acc.	PP	Range

AFTER THE HALL OF FAME

CENTRAL KALOS

049

Magikarp

COASTAL KALOS

MOUNTAIN KALOS

ADVENTURE DATA

🏠 Central Kalos **049**

Fish Pokémon

Magikarp

HEIGHT: 2'11"　　WEIGHT: 22.0 lbs.
GENDER: ♂/♀

X It is virtually worthless in terms of both power and speed. It is the most weak and pathetic Pokémon in the world.

Y In the distant past, it was somewhat stronger than the horribly weak descendants that exist today.

TYPE　Water

ABILITY
Swift Swim

HIDDEN ABILITY
Rattled

STAT GROWTH RATES
HP	■
Attack	■
Defense	■ ■ ■
Sp. Atk	■
Sp. Def	■
Speed	■ ■ ■ ■

EGG GROUPS
Water 2, Dragon

EVOLUTION

Magikarp　→ Lv. 20 →　Gyarados

ITEMS SOMETIMES HELD BY WILD POKÉMON
None

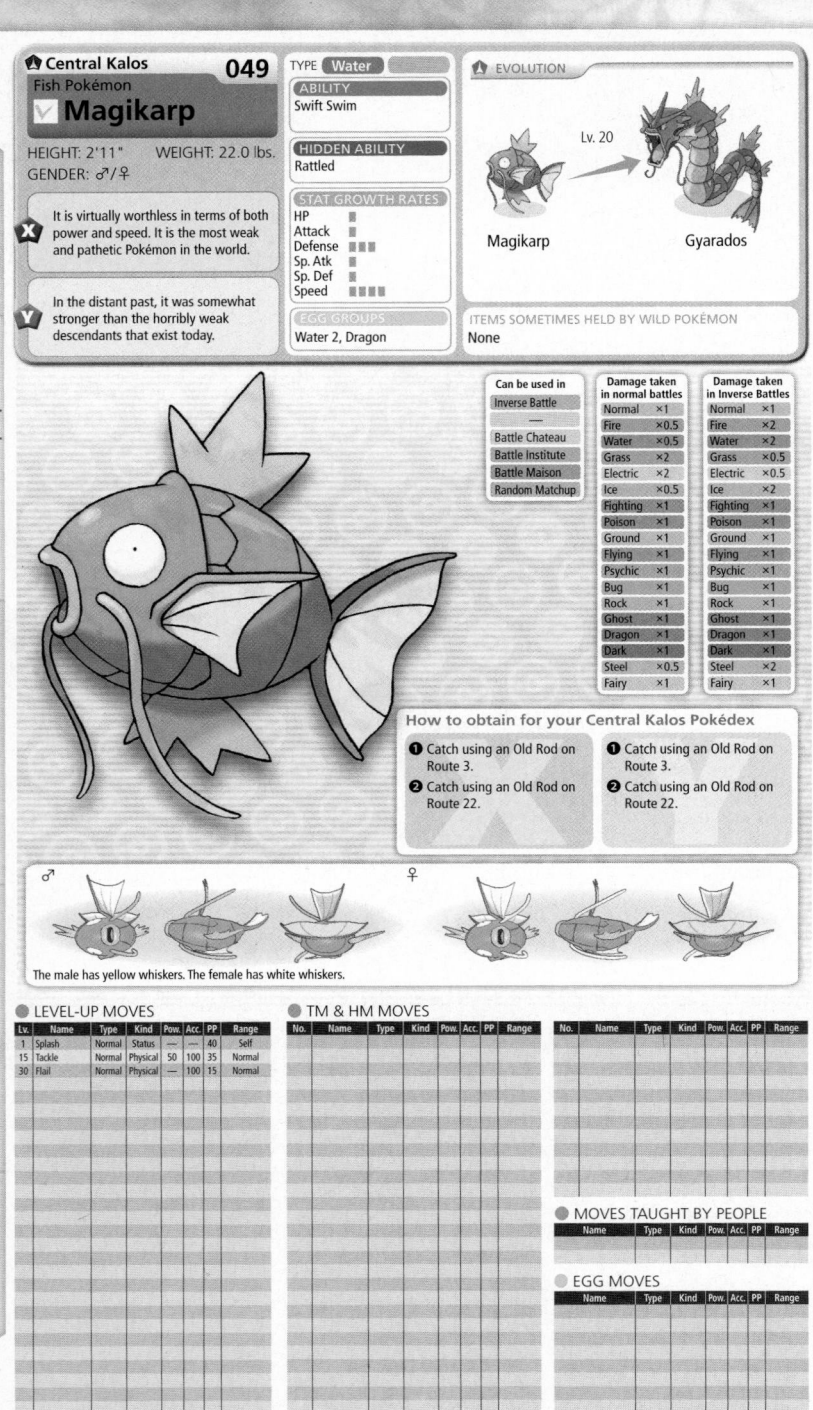

Can be used in
Inverse Battle
—
Battle Chateau
Battle Institute
Battle Maison
Random Matchup

Damage taken in normal battles
Normal	×1
Fire	×0.5
Water	×0.5
Grass	×2
Electric	×2
Ice	×0.5
Fighting	×1
Poison	×1
Ground	×1
Flying	×1
Psychic	×1
Bug	×1
Rock	×1
Ghost	×1
Dragon	×1
Dark	×1
Steel	×0.5
Fairy	×1

Damage taken in Inverse Battles
Normal	×1
Fire	×2
Water	×2
Grass	×0.5
Electric	×0.5
Ice	×2
Fighting	×1
Poison	×1
Ground	×1
Flying	×1
Psychic	×1
Bug	×1
Rock	×1
Ghost	×1
Dragon	×1
Dark	×1
Steel	×2
Fairy	×1

How to obtain for your Central Kalos Pokédex

❶ Catch using an Old Rod on Route 3.
❷ Catch using an Old Rod on Route 22.

❶ Catch using an Old Rod on Route 3.
❷ Catch using an Old Rod on Route 22.

♂　　　　　　　♀

The male has yellow whiskers. The female has white whiskers.

● LEVEL-UP MOVES

Lv.	Name	Type	Kind	Pow.	Acc.	PP	Range
1	Splash	Normal	Status	—	—	40	Self
15	Tackle	Normal	Physical	50	100	35	Normal
30	Flail	Normal	Physical	—	100	15	Normal

● TM & HM MOVES

No.	Name	Type	Kind	Pow.	Acc.	PP	Range

No.	Name	Type	Kind	Pow.	Acc.	PP	Range

● MOVES TAUGHT BY PEOPLE

Name	Type	Kind	Pow.	Acc.	PP	Range

● EGG MOVES

Name	Type	Kind	Pow.	Acc.	PP	Range

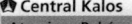

Central Kalos
Atrocious Pokémon
Gyarados
050

HEIGHT: 21'04" WEIGHT: 518.1 lbs.
GENDER: ♂/♀

X In ancient literature, there is a record of a Gyarados that razed a village when violence flared.

Y Rarely seen in the wild. Huge and vicious, it is capable of destroying entire cities in a rage.

TYPE Water Flying

ABILITY
Intimidate

HIDDEN ABILITY
Moxie

STAT GROWTH RATES
HP	■■■■
Attack	■■■■■■
Defense	■■■
Sp. Atk	■■■
Sp. Def	■■■■
Speed	■■■■

EGG GROUPS
Water 2, Dragon

EVOLUTION

Magikarp → Lv. 20 → Gyarados

ITEMS SOMETIMES HELD BY WILD POKÉMON
None

Damage taken in normal battles	
Normal	×1
Fire	×0.5
Water	×0.5
Grass	×1
Electric	×4
Ice	×1
Fighting	×0.5
Poison	×1
Ground	×0
Flying	×1
Psychic	×1
Bug	×0.5
Rock	×2
Ghost	×1
Dragon	×1
Dark	×1
Steel	×0.5
Fairy	×1

Damage taken in Inverse Battles	
Normal	×1
Fire	×2
Water	×2
Grass	×1
Electric	×0.25
Ice	×1
Fighting	×2
Poison	×1
Ground	×2
Flying	×1
Psychic	×1
Bug	×2
Rock	×0.5
Ghost	×1
Dragon	×1
Dark	×1
Steel	×2
Fairy	×1

Can be used in
Inverse Battle
Sky Battle
Battle Chateau
Battle Institute
Battle Maison
Random Matchup

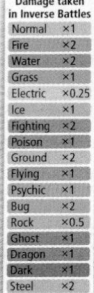

♂

♀

The male has blue whiskers. The female has white whiskers.

How to obtain for your Central Kalos Pokédex

❶ Catch using a Super Rod on Route 3 or Route 22.
❷ Level up Magikarp to Lv. 20.

❶ Catch using a Super Rod on Route 3 or Route 22.
❷ Level up Magikarp to Lv. 20.

● LEVEL-UP MOVES

Lv.	Name	Type	Kind	Pow.	Acc.	PP	Range
1	Thrash	Normal	Physical	120	100	10	1 Random
20	Bite	Dark	Physical	60	100	25	Normal
23	Dragon Rage	Dragon	Special	—	100	10	Normal
26	Leer	Normal	Status	—	100	30	Many Others
29	Twister	Dragon	Special	40	100	20	Many Others
32	Ice Fang	Ice	Physical	65	95	15	Normal
35	Aqua Tail	Water	Physical	90	90	10	Normal
38	Rain Dance	Water	Status	—	—	5	Both Sides
41	Hydro Pump	Water	Special	110	80	5	Normal
44	Dragon Dance	Dragon	Status	—	—	20	Self
47	Hyper Beam	Normal	Special	150	90	5	Normal

● TM & HM MOVES

No.	Name	Type	Kind	Pow.	Acc.	PP	Range
TM05	Roar	Normal	Status	—	—	20	Normal
TM06	Toxic	Poison	Status	—	90	10	Normal
TM07	Hail	Ice	Status	—	—	10	Both Sides
TM10	Hidden Power	Normal	Special	60	100	15	Normal
TM12	Taunt	Dark	Status	—	100	20	Normal
TM13	Ice Beam	Ice	Special	90	100	10	Normal
TM14	Blizzard	Ice	Special	110	70	5	Many Others
TM15	Hyper Beam	Normal	Special	150	90	5	Normal
TM17	Protect	Normal	Status	—	—	10	Self
TM18	Rain Dance	Water	Status	—	—	5	Both Sides
TM21	Frustration	Normal	Physical	—	100	20	Normal
TM24	Thunderbolt	Electric	Special	90	100	15	Normal
TM25	Thunder	Electric	Special	110	70	10	Normal
TM26	Earthquake	Ground	Physical	100	100	10	Adjacent
TM27	Return	Normal	Physical	—	100	20	Normal
TM32	Double Team	Normal	Status	—	—	15	Self
TM35	Flamethrower	Fire	Special	90	100	15	Normal
TM37	Sandstorm	Rock	Status	—	—	10	Both Sides
TM38	Fire Blast	Fire	Special	110	85	5	Normal
TM41	Torment	Dark	Status	—	100	15	Normal
TM42	Facade	Normal	Physical	70	100	20	Normal
TM44	Rest	Psychic	Status	—	—	10	Self
TM45	Attract	Normal	Status	—	100	15	Normal
TM48	Round	Normal	Special	60	100	15	Normal
TM55	Scald	Water	Special	80	100	15	Normal
TM59	Incinerate	Fire	Special	60	100	15	Many Others
TM66	Payback	Dark	Physical	50	100	10	Normal
TM68	Giga Impact	Normal	Physical	150	90	5	Normal
TM71	Stone Edge	Rock	Physical	100	80	5	Normal
TM73	Thunder Wave	Electric	Status	—	100	20	Normal
TM78	Bulldoze	Ground	Physical	60	100	20	Adjacent
TM82	Dragon Tail	Dragon	Physical	60	90	10	Normal
TM87	Swagger	Normal	Status	—	90	15	Normal
TM88	Sleep Talk	Normal	Status	—	—	10	Self
TM90	Substitute	Normal	Status	—	—	10	Self
TM94	Rock Smash	Fighting	Physical	40	100	15	Normal
TM97	Dark Pulse	Dark	Special	80	100	15	Normal
TM100	Confide	Normal	Status	—	—	20	Normal
HM03	Surf	Water	Special	90	100	15	Adjacent
HM04	Strength	Normal	Physical	80	100	15	Normal
HM05	Waterfall	Water	Physical	80	100	15	Normal

● MOVES TAUGHT BY PEOPLE

Name	Type	Kind	Pow.	Acc.	PP	Range

AFTER THE
HALL OF FAME

CENTRAL
KALOS

Mega Gyarados

COASTAL
KALOS

MOUNTAIN
KALOS

ADVENTURE
DATA

Mega Evolution

Atrocious Pokémon

☑ **Mega Gyarados**

HEIGHT: 21'04"   WEIGHT: 672.4 lbs.   GENDER: ♂/♀

TYPE **Water** **Dark**

ABILITY
Mold Breaker

STAT GROWTH RATES

HP	
Attack	
Defense	
Sp. Atk	
Sp. Def	
Speed	

MEGA STONE REQUIRED

Gyaradosite
Obtain in Couriway Town between
8 P.M. and 8:59 P.M., after entering
the Hall of Fame and speaking with
Professor Sycamore in Anistar City.

Damage taken in normal battles		Damage taken in Inverse Battles	
Normal	×1	Normal	×1
Fire	×0.5	Fire	×2
Water	×0.5	Water	×2
Grass	×2	Grass	×0.5
Electric	×2	Electric	×0.5
Ice	×0.5	Ice	×2
Fighting	×2	Fighting	×0.5
Poison	×1	Poison	×1
Ground	×1	Ground	×1
Flying	×1	Flying	×1
Psychic	×0	Psychic	×2
Bug	×2	Bug	×0.5
Rock	×1	Rock	×1
Ghost	×0.5	Ghost	×2
Dragon	×1	Dragon	×1
Dark	×0.5	Dark	×2
Steel	×0.5	Steel	×2
Fairy	×2	Fairy	×0.5

Can be used in	
Inverse Battle	Battle Institute
Sky Battle	Battle Maison
Battle Chateau	Random Matchup

Same form for ♂/♀

154

⬦ Central Kalos
Ruffian Pokémon
☑ Corphish

051

HEIGHT: 2'00"   WEIGHT: 25.4 lbs.
GENDER: ♂ / ♀

X No matter how dirty the water in the river, it will adapt and thrive. It has a strong will to survive.

Y Its hardy vitality enables it to adapt to any environment. Its pincers will never release prey.

TYPE Water

ABILITIES
Hyper Cutter
Shell Armor

HIDDEN ABILITY
Adaptability

STAT GROWTH RATES
HP	■■
Attack	■■■■
Defense	■■■
Sp. Atk	■■
Sp. Def	■■
Speed	■■

EGG GROUPS
Water 1, Water 3

⬦ EVOLUTION

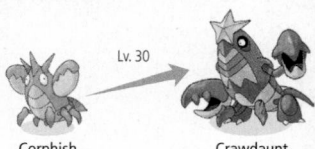

Corphish → Lv. 30 → Crawdaunt

ITEMS SOMETIMES HELD BY WILD POKÉMON
None

Damage taken in normal battles		Damage taken in Inverse Battles	
Normal	×1	Normal	×1
Fire	×0.5	Fire	×2
Water	×0.5	Water	×2
Grass	×2	Grass	×0.5
Electric	×2	Electric	×0.5
Ice	×0.5	Ice	×2
Fighting	×1	Fighting	×1
Poison	×1	Poison	×1
Ground	×1	Ground	×1
Flying	×1	Flying	×1
Psychic	×1	Psychic	×1
Bug	×1	Bug	×1
Rock	×1	Rock	×1
Ghost	×1	Ghost	×1
Dragon	×1	Dragon	×1
Dark	×1	Dark	×1
Steel	×0.5	Steel	×2
Fairy	×1	Fairy	×1

Can be used in	
Inverse Battle	Battle Institute
—	Battle Maison
Battle Chateau	Random Matchup

Same form for ♂ / ♀

How to obtain for your Central Kalos Pokédex

❶ Catch using a Good Rod on Route 3.

❷ Catch using a Good Rod at Parfum Palace.

❶ Catch using a Good Rod on Route 3.

❷ Catch using a Good Rod at Parfum Palace.

● LEVEL-UP MOVES

Lv.	Name	Type	Kind	Pow.	Acc.	PP	Range
1	Bubble	Water	Special	40	100	30	Many Others
7	Harden	Normal	Status	—	—	30	Self
10	Vice Grip	Normal	Physical	55	100	30	Normal
13	Leer	Normal	Status	—	100	30	Many Others
20	Bubble Beam	Water	Special	65	100	20	Normal
23	Protect	Normal	Status	—	—	10	Self
26	Knock Off	Dark	Physical	65	100	20	Normal
32	Taunt	Dark	Status	—	100	20	Normal
35	Night Slash	Dark	Physical	70	100	15	Normal
38	Crabhammer	Water	Physical	100	90	10	Normal
44	Swords Dance	Normal	Status	—	—	20	Self
47	Crunch	Dark	Physical	80	100	15	Normal
53	Guillotine	Normal	Physical	—	30	5	Normal

● TM & HM MOVES

No.	Name	Type	Kind	Pow.	Acc.	PP	Range
TM01	Hone Claws	Dark	Status	—	—	15	Self
TM06	Toxic	Poison	Status	—	90	10	Normal
TM07	Hail	Ice	Status	—	—	10	Both Sides
TM10	Hidden Power	Normal	Special	60	100	15	Normal
TM12	Taunt	Dark	Status	—	100	20	Normal
TM13	Ice Beam	Ice	Special	90	100	10	Normal
TM14	Blizzard	Ice	Special	110	70	5	Many Others
TM17	Protect	Normal	Status	—	—	10	Self
TM18	Rain Dance	Water	Status	—	—	5	Both Sides
TM21	Frustration	Normal	Physical	—	100	20	Normal
TM27	Return	Normal	Physical	—	100	20	Normal
TM28	Dig	Ground	Physical	80	100	10	Normal
TM31	Brick Break	Fighting	Physical	75	100	15	Normal
TM32	Double Team	Normal	Status	—	—	15	Self
TM36	Sludge Bomb	Poison	Special	90	100	10	Normal
TM39	Rock Tomb	Rock	Physical	60	95	15	Normal
TM40	Aerial Ace	Flying	Physical	60	—	20	Normal
TM42	Facade	Normal	Physical	70	100	20	Normal
TM44	Rest	Psychic	Status	—	—	10	Self
TM45	Attract	Normal	Status	—	100	15	Normal
TM48	Round	Normal	Special	60	100	15	Normal
TM54	False Swipe	Normal	Physical	40	100	40	Normal
TM55	Scald	Water	Special	80	100	15	Normal
TM56	Fling	Dark	Physical	—	100	10	Normal
TM66	Payback	Dark	Physical	50	100	10	Normal
TM75	Swords Dance	Normal	Status	—	—	20	Self
TM80	Rock Slide	Rock	Physical	75	90	10	Many Others
TM81	X-Scissor	Bug	Physical	80	100	15	Normal
TM87	Swagger	Normal	Status	—	90	15	Normal
TM88	Sleep Talk	Normal	Status	—	—	10	Self
TM90	Substitute	Normal	Status	—	—	10	Self
TM94	Rock Smash	Fighting	Physical	40	100	15	Normal
TM100	Confide	Normal	Status	—	—	20	Normal

No.	Name	Type	Kind	Pow.	Acc.	PP	Range
HM01	Cut	Normal	Physical	50	95	30	Normal
HM03	Surf	Water	Special	90	100	15	Adjacent
HM04	Strength	Normal	Physical	80	100	15	Normal
HM05	Waterfall	Water	Physical	80	100	15	Normal

● MOVES TAUGHT BY PEOPLE

Name	Type	Kind	Pow.	Acc.	PP	Range

● EGG MOVES

Name	Type	Kind	Pow.	Acc.	PP	Range
Mud Sport	Ground	Status	—	—	15	Both Sides
Endeavor	Normal	Physical	—	100	5	Normal
Body Slam	Normal	Physical	85	100	15	Normal
Ancient Power	Rock	Special	60	100	5	Normal
Knock Off	Dark	Physical	65	100	20	Normal
Superpower	Fighting	Physical	120	100	5	Normal
Metal Claw	Steel	Physical	50	95	35	Normal
Dragon Dance	Dragon	Status	—	—	20	Self
Trump Card	Normal	Special	—	—	5	Normal
Chip Away	Normal	Physical	70	100	20	Normal
Double-Edge	Normal	Physical	120	100	15	Normal
Aqua Jet	Water	Physical	40	100	20	Normal
Switcheroo	Dark	Status	—	100	10	Normal

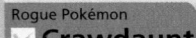

AFTER THE HALL OF FAME

CENTRAL KALOS

052

Crawdaunt

COASTAL KALOS

MOUNTAIN KALOS

ADVENTURE DATA

Central Kalos 052

Rogue Pokémon

Crawdaunt

HEIGHT: 3'07" WEIGHT: 72.3 lbs.
GENDER: ♂/♀

TYPE Water / Dark

ABILITIES
Hyper Cutter
Shell Armor

HIDDEN ABILITY
Adaptability

STAT GROWTH RATES
HP ■■■
Attack ■■■■■■
Defense ■■■■
Sp. Atk ■■■■
Sp. Def ■■■■
Speed ■■■

EGG GROUPS
Water 1, Water 3

X It is a ruffian that uses its pincers to pick up and toss out other Pokémon from its pond.

Y Loving to battle, this Pokémon pinches all Pokémon that enter its territory with its pincers and throws them out.

EVOLUTION

Lv. 30

Corphish → Crawdaunt

ITEMS SOMETIMES HELD BY WILD POKÉMON
None

Damage taken in normal battles	
Normal	×1
Fire	×0.5
Water	×0.5
Grass	×2
Electric	×2
Ice	×0.5
Fighting	×2
Poison	×1
Ground	×1
Flying	×1
Psychic	×0
Bug	×2
Rock	×1
Ghost	×0.5
Dragon	×1
Dark	×0.5
Steel	×0.5
Fairy	×2

Damage taken in Inverse Battles	
Normal	×1
Fire	×2
Water	×2
Grass	×0.5
Electric	×0.5
Ice	×2
Fighting	×0.5
Poison	×1
Ground	×1
Flying	×1
Psychic	×2
Bug	×0.5
Rock	×1
Ghost	×2
Dragon	×1
Dark	×2
Steel	×2
Fairy	×0.5

Can be used in	
Inverse Battle	Battle Institute
—	Battle Maison
Battle Chateau	Random Matchup

Same form for ♂/♀

How to obtain for your Central Kalos Pokédex

❶ Catch using a Super Rod on Route 3 or at Parfum Palace.
❷ Level up Corphish to Lv. 30.

❶ Catch using a Super Rod on Route 3 or at Parfum Palace.
❷ Level up Corphish to Lv. 30.

● LEVEL-UP MOVES

Lv.	Name	Type	Kind	Pow.	Acc.	PP	Range
1	Guillotine	Normal	Physical	—	30	5	Normal
1	Bubble	Water	Special	40	100	30	Many Others
1	Harden	Normal	Status	—	—	30	Self
1	Vice Grip	Normal	Physical	55	100	30	Normal
1	Leer	Normal	Status	—	100	30	Many Others
7	Harden	Normal	Status	—	—	30	Self
10	Vice Grip	Normal	Physical	55	100	30	Normal
13	Leer	Normal	Status	—	100	30	Many Others
20	Bubble Beam	Water	Special	65	100	20	Normal
23	Protect	Normal	Status	—	—	10	Self
26	Knock Off	Dark	Physical	65	100	20	Normal
30	Swift	Normal	Special	60	—	20	Many Others
34	Taunt	Dark	Status	—	100	20	Normal
39	Night Slash	Dark	Physical	70	100	15	Normal
44	Crabhammer	Water	Physical	100	90	10	Normal
52	Swords Dance	Normal	Status	—	—	20	Self
57	Crunch	Dark	Physical	80	100	15	Normal
65	Guillotine	Normal	Physical	—	30	5	Normal

● TM & HM MOVES

No.	Name	Type	Kind	Pow.	Acc.	PP	Range
TM01	Hone Claws	Dark	Status	—	—	15	Self
TM06	Toxic	Poison	Status	—	90	10	Normal
TM07	Hail	Ice	Status	—	—	10	Both Sides
TM10	Hidden Power	Normal	Special	60	100	15	Normal
TM12	Taunt	Dark	Status	—	100	20	Normal
TM13	Ice Beam	Ice	Special	90	100	10	Normal
TM14	Blizzard	Ice	Special	110	70	5	Many Others
TM15	Hyper Beam	Normal	Special	150	90	5	Normal
TM17	Protect	Normal	Status	—	—	10	Self
TM18	Rain Dance	Water	Status	—	—	5	Both Sides
TM21	Frustration	Normal	Physical	—	100	20	Normal
TM27	Return	Normal	Physical	—	100	20	Normal
TM28	Dig	Ground	Physical	80	100	10	Normal
TM31	Brick Break	Fighting	Physical	75	100	15	Normal
TM32	Double Team	Normal	Status	—	—	15	Self
TM34	Sludge Wave	Poison	Special	95	100	10	Adjacent
TM36	Sludge Bomb	Poison	Special	90	100	10	Normal
TM39	Rock Tomb	Rock	Physical	60	95	15	Normal
TM40	Aerial Ace	Flying	Physical	60	—	20	Normal
TM42	Facade	Normal	Physical	70	100	20	Normal
TM44	Rest	Psychic	Status	—	—	10	Self
TM45	Attract	Normal	Status	—	100	15	Normal
TM48	Round	Normal	Special	60	100	15	Normal
TM54	False Swipe	Normal	Physical	40	100	40	Normal
TM55	Scald	Water	Special	80	100	15	Normal
TM56	Fling	Dark	Physical	—	100	10	Normal
TM66	Payback	Dark	Physical	50	100	10	Normal
TM67	Retaliate	Normal	Physical	70	100	5	Normal
TM68	Giga Impact	Normal	Physical	150	90	5	Normal
TM75	Swords Dance	Normal	Status	—	—	20	Self
TM80	Rock Slide	Rock	Physical	75	90	10	Many Others
TM81	X-Scissor	Bug	Physical	80	100	15	Normal
TM87	Swagger	Normal	Status	—	90	15	Normal

No.	Name	Type	Kind	Pow.	Acc.	PP	Range
TM88	Sleep Talk	Normal	Status	—	—	10	Self
TM90	Substitute	Normal	Status	—	—	10	Self
TM94	Rock Smash	Fighting	Physical	40	100	15	Normal
TM95	Snarl	Dark	Special	55	95	15	Many Others
TM96	Nature Power	Normal	Status	—	—	20	Normal
TM97	Dark Pulse	Dark	Special	80	100	15	Normal
TM100	Confide	Normal	Status	—	—	20	Normal
HM01	Cut	Normal	Physical	50	95	30	Normal
HM03	Surf	Water	Special	90	100	15	Adjacent
HM04	Strength	Normal	Physical	80	100	15	Normal
HM05	Waterfall	Water	Physical	80	100	15	Normal

● MOVES TAUGHT BY PEOPLE

Name	Type	Kind	Pow.	Acc.	PP	Range

Central Kalos
Goldfish Pokémon
053
☑ Goldeen

HEIGHT: 2'00"   WEIGHT: 33.1 lbs.
GENDER: ♂/♀

> It swims at a steady 5 knots. If it senses danger, it will strike back with its sharp horn.

> Its dorsal, pectoral, and tail fins wave elegantly in water. That is why it is known as the water dancer.

TYPE Water

ABILITIES
Swift Swim
Water Veil

HIDDEN ABILITY
None

STAT GROWTH RATES
HP	■ ■
Attack	■ ■ ■ ■
Defense	■ ■ ■
Sp. Atk	■ ■
Sp. Def	■ ■
Speed	■ ■ ■

EGG GROUP
Water 2

⚡ EVOLUTION

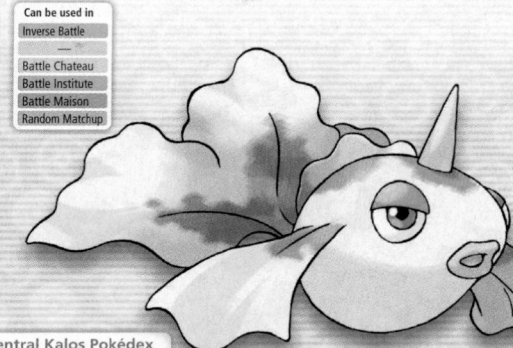

Lv. 33

Goldeen   Seaking

ITEMS SOMETIMES HELD BY WILD POKÉMON
None

Damage taken in normal battles		Damage taken in Inverse Battles	
Normal	×1	Normal	×1
Fire	×0.5	Fire	×2
Water	×0.5	Water	×2
Grass	×2	Grass	×0.5
Electric	×2	Electric	×0.5
Ice	×0.5	Ice	×2
Fighting	×1	Fighting	×1
Poison	×1	Poison	×1
Ground	×1	Ground	×1
Flying	×1	Flying	×1
Psychic	×1	Psychic	×1
Bug	×1	Bug	×1
Rock	×1	Rock	×1
Ghost	×1	Ghost	×1
Dragon	×1	Dragon	×1
Dark	×1	Dark	×1
Steel	×0.5	Steel	×2
Fairy	×1	Fairy	×1

Can be used in
Inverse Battle
- —
Battle Chateau
Battle Institute
Battle Maison
Random Matchup

How to obtain for your Central Kalos Pokédex

❶ Catch using a Good Rod on Route 3.

❷ Catch using a Good Rod on Route 22.

❶ Catch using a Good Rod on Route 3.

❷ Catch using a Good Rod on Route 22.

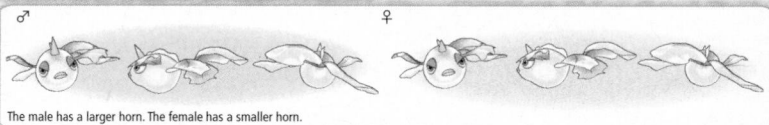

♂   ♀

The male has a larger horn. The female has a smaller horn.

● LEVEL-UP MOVES

Lv.	Name	Type	Kind	Pow.	Acc.	PP	Range
1	Peck	Flying	Physical	35	100	35	Normal
1	Tail Whip	Normal	Status	—	100	30	Many Others
1	Water Sport	Water	Status	—	—	15	Both Sides
7	Supersonic	Normal	Status	—	55	20	Normal
11	Horn Attack	Normal	Physical	65	100	25	Normal
17	Water Pulse	Water	Special	60	100	20	Normal
21	Flail	Normal	Physical	—	100	15	Normal
27	Aqua Ring	Water	Status	—	—	20	Self
31	Fury Attack	Normal	Physical	15	85	20	Normal
37	Waterfall	Water	Physical	80	100	15	Normal
41	Horn Drill	Normal	Physical	—	30	5	Normal
47	Agility	Psychic	Status	—	—	30	Self
50	Scald	Water	Status	—	100	20	Normal
57	Megahorn	Bug	Physical	120	85	10	Normal

● TM & HM MOVES

No.	Name	Type	Kind	Pow.	Acc.	PP	Range
TM06	Toxic	Poison	Status	—	90	10	Normal
TM07	Hail	Ice	Status	—	—	10	Both Sides
TM10	Hidden Power	Normal	Special	60	100	15	Normal
TM13	Ice Beam	Ice	Special	90	100	10	Normal
TM14	Blizzard	Ice	Special	110	70	5	Many Others
TM17	Protect	Normal	Status	—	—	10	Self
TM18	Rain Dance	Water	Status	—	—	5	Both Sides
TM21	Frustration	Normal	Physical	—	100	20	Normal
TM27	Return	Normal	Physical	—	100	20	Normal
TM32	Double Team	Normal	Status	—	—	15	Self
TM42	Facade	Normal	Physical	70	100	20	Normal
TM44	Rest	Psychic	Status	—	—	10	Self
TM45	Attract	Normal	Status	—	100	15	Normal
TM48	Round	Normal	Special	60	100	15	Normal
TM55	Scald	Water	Special	80	100	15	Normal
TM84	Poison Jab	Poison	Physical	80	100	20	Normal
TM87	Swagger	Normal	Status	—	90	15	Normal
TM88	Sleep Talk	Normal	Status	—	—	10	Self
TM90	Substitute	Normal	Status	—	—	10	Self
TM100	Confide	Normal	Status	—	—	20	Normal
HM03	Surf	Water	Special	90	100	15	Adjacent
HM05	Waterfall	Water	Physical	80	100	15	Normal

● MOVES TAUGHT BY PEOPLE

Name	Type	Kind	Pow.	Acc.	PP	Range

● EGG MOVES

Name	Type	Kind	Pow.	Acc.	PP	Range
Psybeam	Psychic	Special	65	100	20	Normal
Haze	Ice	Status	—	—	30	Both Sides
Hydro Pump	Water	Special	110	80	5	Normal
Sleep Talk	Normal	Status	—	—	10	Self
Mud Sport	Ground	Status	—	—	15	Both Sides
Mud-Slap	Ground	Special	20	100	10	Normal
Aqua Tail	Water	Physical	90	90	10	Normal
Body Slam	Normal	Physical	85	100	15	Normal
Mud Shot	Ground	Special	55	95	15	Normal
Skull Bash	Normal	Physical	130	100	10	Normal
Signal Beam	Bug	Special	75	100	15	Normal

AFTER THE HALL OF FAME

CENTRAL KALOS
053
Goldeen

COASTAL KALOS

MOUNTAIN KALOS

ADVENTURE DATA

AFTER THE HALL OF FAME

CENTRAL KALOS

054

Seaking

COASTAL KALOS

MOUNTAIN KALOS

ADVENTURE DATA

🏠 Central Kalos — 054

Goldfish Pokémon

☑ Seaking

HEIGHT: 4'03" WEIGHT: 86.0 lbs.
GENDER: ♂/♀

TYPE	Water

ABILITIES
Swift Swim
Water Veil

HIDDEN ABILITY
None

STAT GROWTH RATES
HP ▪▪▪
Attack ▪▪▪▪▪
Defense ▪▪▪
Sp. Atk ▪▪▪
Sp. Def ▪▪▪
Speed ▪▪▪▪

EGG GROUP
Water 2

❌ In the autumn spawning season, they can be seen swimming powerfully up rivers and creeks.

🔵 It makes its nest by hollowing out boulders in streams with its horn. It defends its eggs with its life.

🔼 EVOLUTION

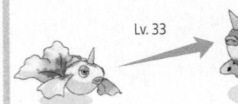

Lv. 33

Goldeen → Seaking

ITEMS SOMETIMES HELD BY WILD POKÉMON
None

Can be used in
Inverse Battle
—
Battle Chateau
Battle Institute
Battle Maison
Random Matchup

Damage taken in normal battles		Damage taken in Inverse Battles	
Normal	×1	Normal	×1
Fire	×0.5	Fire	×2
Water	×0.5	Water	×2
Grass	×2	Grass	×0.5
Electric	×2	Electric	×0.5
Ice	×0.5	Ice	×2
Fighting	×1	Fighting	×1
Poison	×1	Poison	×1
Ground	×1	Ground	×1
Flying	×1	Flying	×1
Psychic	×1	Psychic	×1
Bug	×1	Bug	×1
Rock	×1	Rock	×1
Ghost	×1	Ghost	×1
Dragon	×1	Dragon	×1
Dark	×1	Dark	×1
Steel	×0.5	Steel	×2
Fairy	×1	Fairy	×1

How to obtain for your Central Kalos Pokédex

❶ Catch using a Super Rod on Route 3 or Route 22.
❷ Level up Goldeen to Lv. 33.

❶ Catch using a Super Rod on Route 3 or Route 22.
❷ Level up Goldeen to Lv. 33.

♂

♀

The male has a larger horn. The female has a smaller horn.

● LEVEL-UP MOVES

Lv.	Name	Type	Kind	Pow.	Acc.	PP	Range
1	Megahorn	Bug	Physical	120	85	10	Normal
1	Poison Jab	Poison	Physical	80	100	20	Normal
1	Peck	Flying	Physical	35	100	35	Normal
1	Tail Whip	Normal	Status	—	100	30	Many Others
1	Water Sport	Water	Status	—	—	15	Both Sides
1	Supersonic	Normal	Status	—	55	20	Normal
7	Supersonic	Normal	Status	—	55	20	Normal
11	Horn Attack	Normal	Physical	65	100	25	Normal
17	Water Pulse	Water	Special	60	100	20	Normal
21	Flail	Normal	Physical	—	100	15	Normal
27	Aqua Ring	Water	Status	—	—	20	Self
31	Fury Attack	Normal	Physical	15	85	20	Normal
40	Waterfall	Water	Physical	80	100	15	Normal
47	Horn Drill	Normal	Physical	—	30	5	Normal
56	Agility	Psychic	Status	—	—	30	Self
63	Soak	Water	Status	—	100	20	Normal
72	Megahorn	Bug	Physical	120	85	10	Normal

■ TM & HM MOVES

No.	Name	Type	Kind	Pow.	Acc.	PP	Range
TM06	Toxic	Poison	Status	—	90	10	Normal
TM07	Hail	Ice	Status	—	—	10	Both Sides
TM10	Hidden Power	Normal	Special	60	100	15	Normal
TM13	Ice Beam	Ice	Special	90	100	10	Normal
TM14	Blizzard	Ice	Special	110	70	5	Many Others
TM15	Hyper Beam	Normal	Special	150	90	5	Normal
TM17	Protect	Normal	Status	—	—	10	Self
TM18	Rain Dance	Water	Status	—	—	5	Both Sides
TM21	Frustration	Normal	Physical	—	100	20	Normal
TM27	Return	Normal	Physical	—	100	20	Normal
TM32	Double Team	Normal	Status	—	—	15	Self
TM42	Facade	Normal	Physical	70	100	20	Normal
TM44	Rest	Psychic	Status	—	—	10	Self
TM45	Attract	Normal	Status	—	100	15	Normal
TM48	Round	Normal	Special	60	100	15	Normal
TM55	Scald	Water	Special	80	100	15	Normal
TM68	Giga Impact	Normal	Physical	150	90	5	Normal
TM84	Poison Jab	Poison	Physical	80	100	20	Normal
TM87	Swagger	Normal	Status	—	90	15	Normal
TM88	Sleep Talk	Normal	Status	—	—	10	Self
TM90	Substitute	Normal	Status	—	—	10	Self
TM100	Confide	Normal	Status	—	—	20	Normal
HM03	Surf	Water	Special	90	100	15	Adjacent
HM05	Waterfall	Water	Physical	80	100	15	Normal

● MOVES TAUGHT BY PEOPLE

Name	Type	Kind	Pow.	Acc.	PP	Range

Central Kalos
Savage Pokémon
 Carvanha **055**

HEIGHT: 2'07" WEIGHT: 45.9 lbs.
GENDER: ♂/♀

X They form packs to attack boats and rip out their hulls to sink them. They live in rivers in the jungle.

Y It lives in massive rivers that course through jungles. It swarms prey that enter its territory.

 TYPE Water | Dark

ABILITY
Rough Skin

HIDDEN ABILITY
None

STAT GROWTH RATES
HP	■■
Attack	■■■■■
Defense	■
Sp. Atk	■■■
Sp. Def	■
Speed	■■■■

EGG GROUP
Water 2

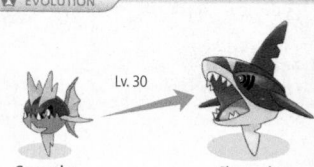

⬆ EVOLUTION
Lv. 30

Carvanha → Sharpedo

ITEMS SOMETIMES HELD BY WILD POKÉMON
Deep Sea Tooth

Damage taken in normal battles		Damage taken in Inverse Battles	
Normal	×1	Normal	×1
Fire	×0.5	Fire	×2
Water	×0.5	Water	×2
Grass	×2	Grass	×0.5
Electric	×2	Electric	×0.5
Ice	×0.5	Ice	×2
Fighting	×2	Fighting	×0.5
Poison	×1	Poison	×1
Ground	×1	Ground	×1
Flying	×1	Flying	×1
Psychic	×0	Psychic	×2
Bug	×2	Bug	×0.5
Rock	×1	Rock	×1
Ghost	×0.5	Ghost	×2
Dragon	×1	Dragon	×1
Dark	×0.5	Dark	×2
Steel	×0.5	Steel	×2
Fairy	×2	Fairy	×0.5

Can be used in	
Inverse Battle	Battle Institute
—	Battle Maison
Battle Chateau	Random Matchup

Same form for ♂/♀

How to obtain for your Central Kalos Pokédex

Catch using a Good Rod on Route 22.

Catch using a Good Rod on Route 22.

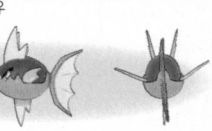

● **LEVEL-UP MOVES**

Lv.	Name	Type	Kind	Pow.	Acc.	PP	Range
1	Leer	Normal	Status	—	100	30	Many Others
1	Bite	Dark	Physical	60	100	25	Normal
6	Rage	Normal	Physical	20	100	20	Normal
8	Focus Energy	Normal	Status	—	—	30	Self
11	Scary Face	Normal	Status	—	100	10	Normal
16	Ice Fang	Ice	Physical	65	95	15	Normal
18	Screech	Normal	Status	—	85	40	Normal
21	Swagger	Normal	Status	—	90	15	Normal
26	Assurance	Dark	Physical	60	100	10	Normal
28	Crunch	Dark	Physical	80	100	15	Normal
31	Aqua Jet	Water	Physical	40	100	20	Normal
36	Agility	Psychic	Status	—	—	30	Self
38	Take Down	Normal	Physical	90	85	20	Normal

● **TM & HM MOVES**

No.	Name	Type	Kind	Pow.	Acc.	PP	Range
TM06	Toxic	Poison	Status	—	90	10	Normal
TM07	Hail	Ice	Status	—	—	10	Both Sides
TM10	Hidden Power	Normal	Special	60	100	15	Normal
TM12	Taunt	Dark	Status	—	100	20	Normal
TM13	Ice Beam	Ice	Special	90	100	10	Normal
TM14	Blizzard	Ice	Special	110	70	5	Many Others
TM17	Protect	Normal	Status	—	—	10	Self
TM18	Rain Dance	Water	Status	—	—	5	Both Sides
TM21	Frustration	Normal	Physical	—	100	20	Normal
TM27	Return	Normal	Physical	—	100	20	Normal
TM32	Double Team	Normal	Status	—	—	15	Self
TM41	Torment	Dark	Status	—	100	15	Normal
TM42	Facade	Normal	Physical	70	100	20	Normal
TM44	Rest	Psychic	Status	—	—	10	Self
TM45	Attract	Normal	Status	—	100	15	Normal
TM46	Thief	Dark	Physical	60	100	25	Normal
TM48	Round	Normal	Special	60	100	15	Normal
TM55	Scald	Water	Special	80	100	15	Normal
TM66	Payback	Dark	Physical	50	100	10	Normal
TM67	Retaliate	Normal	Physical	70	100	5	Normal
TM87	Swagger	Normal	Status	—	90	15	Normal
TM88	Sleep Talk	Normal	Status	—	—	10	Self
TM90	Substitute	Normal	Status	—	—	10	Self
TM95	Snarl	Dark	Special	55	95	15	Many Others
TM97	Dark Pulse	Dark	Special	80	100	15	Normal
TM100	Confide	Normal	Status	—	—	20	Normal
HM03	Surf	Water	Special	90	100	15	Adjacent
HM05	Waterfall	Water	Physical	80	100	15	Normal

● **MOVES TAUGHT BY PEOPLE**

Name	Type	Kind	Pow.	Acc.	PP	Range

● **EGG MOVES**

Name	Type	Kind	Pow.	Acc.	PP	Range
Hydro Pump	Water	Special	110	80	5	Normal
Double-Edge	Normal	Physical	120	100	15	Normal
Thrash	Normal	Physical	120	100	10	1 Random
Ancient Power	Rock	Special	60	100	5	Normal
Swift	Normal	Special	60	—	20	Many Others
Brine	Water	Special	65	100	10	Normal
Destiny Bond	Ghost	Status	—	—	5	Self

AFTER THE HALL OF FAME

CENTRAL KALOS

055

Carvanha

COASTAL KALOS

MOUNTAIN KALOS

ADVENTURE DATA

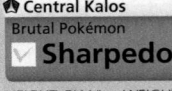

Central Kalos 056

Brutal Pokémon

Sharpedo

HEIGHT: 5'11" WEIGHT: 195.8 lbs.
GENDER: ♂/♀

TYPE Water Dark

ABILITIES
Rough Skin

HIDDEN ABILITY
None

STAT GROWTH RATES
HP	■■■
Attack	■■■■■
Defense	■■
Sp. Atk	■■■
Sp. Def	■■
Speed	■■■■■

EGG GROUP
Water 2

X Its fangs rip through sheet iron. It swims at 75 mph and is known as "The Bully of the Sea."

Y It can swim at speeds of 75 mph by jetting seawater through its body. It is the bandit of the sea.

EVOLUTION

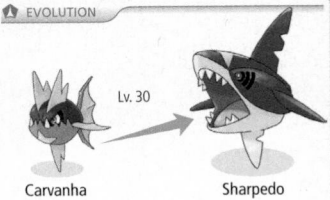

Carvanha → Lv. 30 → Sharpedo

ITEMS SOMETIMES HELD BY WILD POKÉMON
Deep Sea Tooth

Can be used in
Inverse Battle
—
Battle Chateau
Battle Institute
Battle Maison
Random Matchup

Damage taken in normal battles		Damage taken in Inverse Battles	
Normal	×1	Normal	×1
Fire	×0.5	Fire	×2
Water	×0.5	Water	×2
Grass	×2	Grass	×0.5
Electric	×2	Electric	×0.5
Ice	×0.5	Ice	×2
Fighting	×2	Fighting	×0.5
Poison	×1	Poison	×1
Ground	×1	Ground	×1
Flying	×1	Flying	×1
Psychic	×0	Psychic	×2
Bug	×2	Bug	×0.5
Rock	×1	Rock	×1
Ghost	×0.5	Ghost	×2
Dragon	×1	Dragon	×1
Dark	×0.5	Dark	×2
Steel	×0.5	Steel	×2
Fairy	×2	Fairy	×0.5

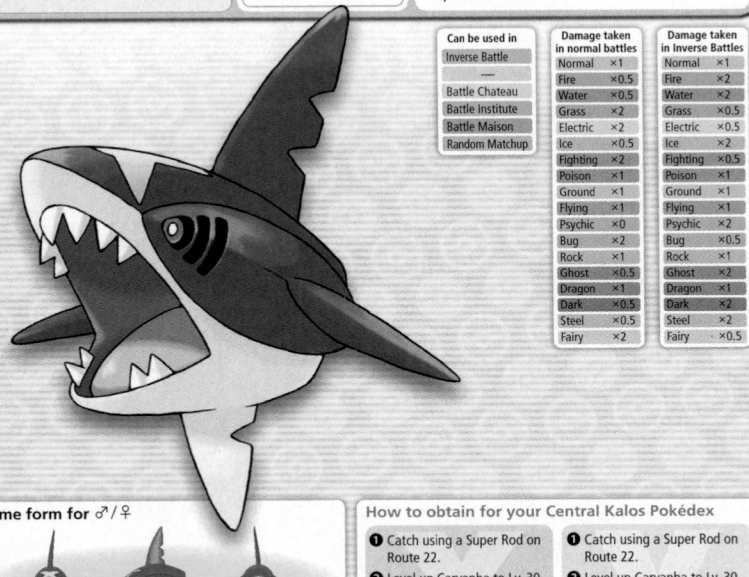

Same form for ♂/♀

How to obtain for your Central Kalos Pokédex
1. Catch using a Super Rod on Route 22.
2. Level up Carvanha to Lv. 30.

1. Catch using a Super Rod on Route 22.
2. Level up Carvanha to Lv. 30.

● LEVEL-UP MOVES

Lv.	Name	Type	Kind	Pow.	Acc.	PP	Range
1	Night Slash	Dark	Physical	70	100	15	Normal
1	Feint	Normal	Physical	30	100	10	Normal
1	Leer	Normal	Status	—	100	30	Many Others
1	Bite	Dark	Physical	60	100	25	Normal
1	Rage	Normal	Physical	20	100	20	Normal
1	Focus Energy	Normal	Status	—	—	30	Self
6	Rage	Normal	Physical	20	100	20	Normal
8	Focus Energy	Normal	Status	—	—	30	Self
11	Scary Face	Normal	Status	—	100	10	Normal
16	Ice Fang	Ice	Physical	65	95	15	Normal
18	Screech	Normal	Status	—	85	40	Normal
21	Swagger	Normal	Status	—	90	15	Normal
26	Assurance	Dark	Physical	60	100	10	Normal
28	Crunch	Dark	Physical	80	100	15	Normal
30	Slash	Normal	Physical	70	100	20	Normal
34	Aqua Jet	Water	Physical	40	100	20	Normal
40	Taunt	Dark	Status	—	100	20	Normal
45	Agility	Psychic	Status	—	—	30	Self
50	Skull Bash	Normal	Physical	130	100	10	Normal
56	Night Slash	Dark	Physical	70	100	15	Normal

● TM & HM MOVES

No.	Name	Type	Kind	Pow.	Acc.	PP	Range
TM05	Roar	Normal	Status	—	—	20	Normal
TM06	Toxic	Poison	Status	—	90	10	Normal
TM07	Hail	Ice	Status	—	—	10	Both Sides
TM10	Hidden Power	Normal	Special	60	100	15	Normal
TM12	Taunt	Dark	Status	—	100	20	Normal
TM13	Ice Beam	Ice	Special	90	100	10	Normal
TM14	Blizzard	Ice	Special	110	70	5	Many Others
TM15	Hyper Beam	Normal	Special	150	90	5	Normal
TM17	Protect	Normal	Status	—	—	10	Self
TM18	Rain Dance	Water	Status	—	—	5	Both Sides
TM21	Frustration	Normal	Physical	—	100	20	Normal
TM26	Earthquake	Ground	Physical	100	100	10	Adjacent
TM27	Return	Normal	Physical	—	100	20	Normal
TM32	Double Team	Normal	Status	—	—	15	Self
TM39	Rock Tomb	Rock	Physical	60	95	15	Normal
TM41	Torment	Dark	Status	—	100	15	Normal
TM42	Facade	Normal	Physical	70	100	20	Normal
TM44	Rest	Psychic	Status	—	—	10	Self
TM45	Attract	Normal	Status	—	100	15	Normal
TM46	Thief	Dark	Physical	60	100	25	Normal
TM48	Round	Normal	Special	60	100	15	Normal
TM55	Scald	Water	Special	80	100	15	Normal
TM66	Payback	Dark	Physical	50	100	10	Normal
TM67	Retaliate	Normal	Physical	70	100	5	Normal
TM68	Giga Impact	Normal	Physical	150	90	5	Normal
TM78	Bulldoze	Ground	Physical	60	100	20	Adjacent
TM84	Poison Jab	Poison	Physical	80	100	20	Normal
TM87	Swagger	Normal	Status	—	90	15	Normal
TM88	Sleep Talk	Normal	Status	—	—	10	Self
TM90	Substitute	Normal	Status	—	—	10	Self
TM94	Rock Smash	Fighting	Physical	40	100	15	Normal
TM95	Snarl	Dark	Special	55	95	15	Many Others
TM97	Dark Pulse	Dark	Special	80	100	15	Normal

No.	Name	Type	Kind	Pow.	Acc.	PP	Range
TM100	Confide	Normal	Status	—	—	20	Normal
HM03	Surf	Water	Special	90	100	15	Adjacent
HM04	Strength	Normal	Physical	80	100	15	Normal
HM05	Waterfall	Water	Physical	80	100	15	Normal

● MOVES TAUGHT BY PEOPLE

Name	Type	Kind	Pow.	Acc.	PP	Range

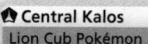 **Central Kalos**

Lion Cub Pokémon

✔ Litleo 057

HEIGHT: 2'00" WEIGHT: 29.8 lbs.
GENDER: ♂ / ♀

❌ The stronger the opponent it faces, the more heat surges from its mane and the more power flows through its body.

❓ They set off on their own from their pride and live by themselves to become stronger. These hot-blooded Pokémon are quick to fight.

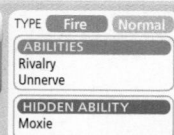

TYPE Fire Normal

ABILITIES
Rivalry
Unnerve

HIDDEN ABILITY
Moxie

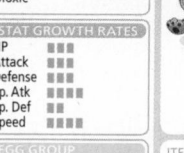

STAT GROWTH RATES

HP	■■■
Attack	■■■
Defense	■■
Sp. Atk	■■■
Sp. Def	■■
Speed	■■■

EGG GROUP
Field

🔆 **EVOLUTION**

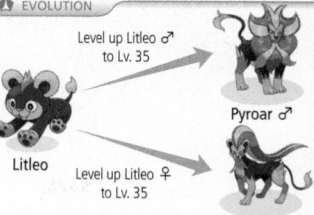

Level up Litleo ♂ to Lv. 35 → Pyroar ♂

Litleo

Level up Litleo ♀ to Lv. 35 → Pyroar ♀

ITEMS SOMETIMES HELD BY WILD POKÉMON
None

Damage taken in normal battles		Damage taken in Inverse Battles	
Normal	×1	Normal	×1
Fire	×0.5	Fire	×2
Water	×2	Water	×0.5
Grass	×0.5	Grass	×2
Electric	×1	Electric	×1
Ice	×0.5	Ice	×2
Fighting	×2	Fighting	×0.5
Poison	×1	Poison	×1
Ground	×2	Ground	×0.5
Flying	×1	Flying	×1
Psychic	×1	Psychic	×1
Bug	×0.5	Bug	×2
Rock	×1	Rock	×0.5
Ghost	×0	Ghost	×2
Dragon	×1	Dragon	×1
Dark	×1	Dark	×1
Steel	×0.5	Steel	×2
Fairy	×0.5	Fairy	×2

Can be used in	
Inverse Battle	Battle Institute
—	Battle Maison
Battle Chateau	Random Matchup

Same form for ♂ / ♀

How to obtain for your Central Kalos Pokédex

❶ Catch in the tall grass on Route 22.
❷ Catch in the yellow flowers on Route 22.

❶ Catch in the tall grass on Route 22.
❷ Catch in the yellow flowers on Route 22.

● **LEVEL-UP MOVES**

Lv.	Name	Type	Kind	Pow.	Acc.	PP	Range
1	Tackle	Normal	Physical	50	100	35	Normal
1	Leer	Normal	Status	—	100	30	Many Others
5	Ember	Fire	Special	40	100	25	Normal
8	Work Up	Normal	Status	—	—	30	Self
11	Headbutt	Normal	Physical	70	100	15	Normal
15	Noble Roar	Normal	Status	—	100	30	Normal
20	Take Down	Normal	Physical	90	85	20	Normal
23	Fire Fang	Fire	Physical	65	95	15	Normal
28	Endeavor	Normal	Physical	—	100	5	Normal
33	Echoed Voice	Normal	Special	40	100	15	Normal
36	Flamethrower	Fire	Special	90	100	15	Normal
39	Crunch	Dark	Physical	80	100	15	Normal
43	Hyper Voice	Normal	Special	90	100	10	Many Others
46	Incinerate	Fire	Special	60	100	15	Many Others
50	Overheat	Fire	Special	130	90	5	Normal

● **TM & HM MOVES**

No.	Name	Type	Kind	Pow.	Acc.	PP	Range
TM05	Roar	Normal	Status	—	—	20	Normal
TM06	Toxic	Poison	Status	—	90	10	Normal
TM10	Hidden Power	Normal	Special	60	100	15	Normal
TM11	Sunny Day	Fire	Status	—	—	5	Both Sides
TM12	Taunt	Dark	Status	—	100	20	Normal
TM17	Protect	Normal	Status	—	—	10	Self
TM18	Rain Dance	Water	Status	—	—	5	Both Sides
TM21	Frustration	Normal	Physical	—	100	20	Normal
TM22	Solar Beam	Grass	Special	120	100	10	Normal
TM27	Return	Normal	Physical	—	100	20	Normal
TM28	Dig	Ground	Physical	80	100	10	Normal
TM32	Double Team	Normal	Status	—	—	15	Self
TM35	Flamethrower	Fire	Special	90	100	15	Normal
TM38	Fire Blast	Fire	Special	110	85	5	Normal
TM42	Facade	Normal	Physical	70	100	20	Normal
TM43	Flame Charge	Fire	Physical	50	100	20	Normal
TM44	Rest	Psychic	Status	—	—	10	Self
TM45	Attract	Normal	Status	—	100	15	Normal
TM46	Thief	Dark	Physical	60	100	25	Normal
TM48	Round	Normal	Special	60	100	15	Normal
TM49	Echoed Voice	Normal	Special	40	100	15	Normal
TM50	Overheat	Fire	Special	130	90	5	Normal
TM59	Incinerate	Fire	Special	60	100	15	Many Others
TM61	Will-O-Wisp	Fire	Status	—	85	15	Normal
TM66	Payback	Dark	Physical	50	100	10	Normal
TM67	Retaliate	Normal	Physical	70	100	5	Normal
TM78	Bulldoze	Ground	Physical	60	100	20	Adjacent
TM87	Swagger	Normal	Status	—	90	15	Normal
TM88	Sleep Talk	Normal	Status	—	—	10	Self
TM90	Substitute	Normal	Status	—	—	10	Self
TM93	Wild Charge	Electric	Physical	90	100	15	Normal
TM94	Rock Smash	Fighting	Physical	40	100	15	Normal
TM95	Snarl	Dark	Special	55	95	15	Many Others

No.	Name	Type	Kind	Pow.	Acc.	PP	Range
TM97	Dark Pulse	Dark	Special	80	100	15	Normal
TM100	Confide	Normal	Status	—	—	20	Normal
HM04	Strength	Normal	Physical	80	100	15	Normal

● **MOVES TAUGHT BY PEOPLE**

Name	Type	Kind	Pow.	Acc.	PP	Range

● **EGG MOVES**

Name	Type	Kind	Pow.	Acc.	PP	Range
Entrainment	Normal	Status	—	100	15	Normal
Yawn	Normal	Status	—	—	10	Normal
Snatch	Dark	Status	—	—	10	Self
Fire Spin	Fire	Special	35	85	15	Normal

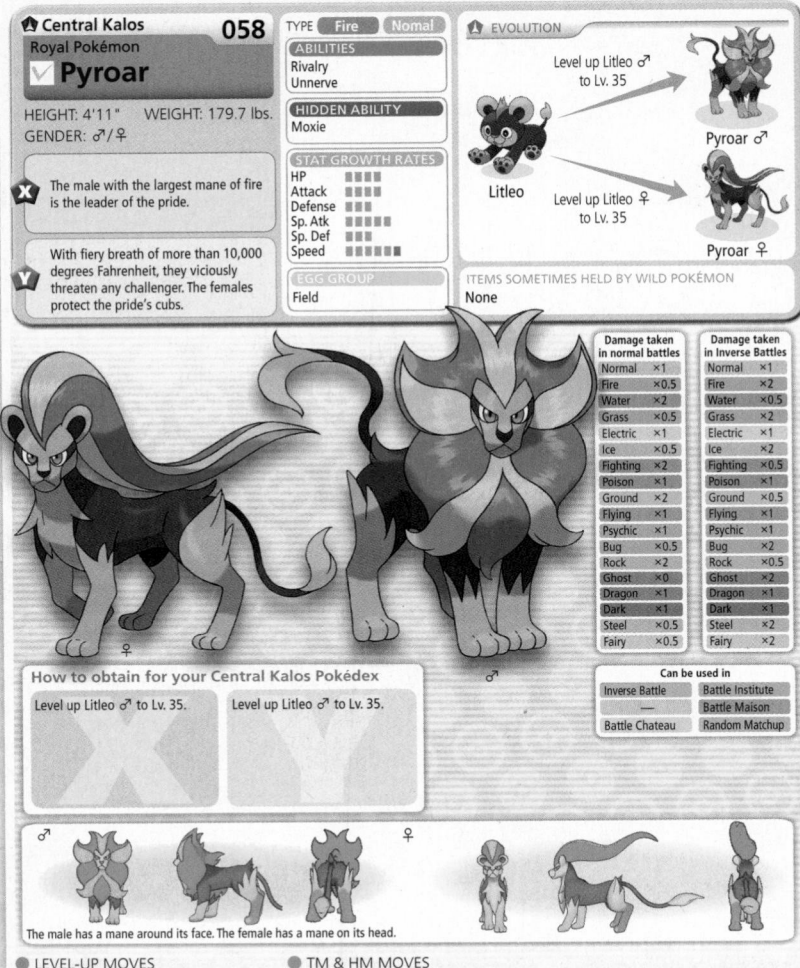

Central Kalos — 058

Royal Pokémon

☑ Pyroar

HEIGHT: 4'11" WEIGHT: 179.7 lbs.
GENDER: ♂/♀

TYPE: Fire / Normal

ABILITIES: Rivalry, Unnerve
HIDDEN ABILITY: Moxie

❌ The male with the largest mane of fire is the leader of the pride.

◆ With fiery breath of more than 10,000 degrees Fahrenheit, they viciously threaten any challenger. The females protect the pride's cubs.

STAT GROWTH RATES
HP ▪▪▪▪
Attack ▪▪▪▪
Defense ▪▪▪
Sp. Atk ▪▪▪▪▪
Sp. Def ▪▪▪
Speed ▪▪▪▪▪▪

EGG GROUP: Field

EVOLUTION

Litleo — Level up Litleo ♂ to Lv. 35 → Pyroar ♂
Litleo — Level up Litleo ♀ to Lv. 35 → Pyroar ♀

ITEMS SOMETIMES HELD BY WILD POKÉMON: None

Damage taken in normal battles		Damage taken in Inverse Battles	
Normal	×1	Normal	×1
Fire	×0.5	Fire	×2
Water	×2	Water	×0.5
Grass	×0.5	Grass	×2
Electric	×1	Electric	×1
Ice	×0.5	Ice	×2
Fighting	×2	Fighting	×0.5
Poison	×1	Poison	×1
Ground	×2	Ground	×0.5
Flying	×1	Flying	×1
Psychic	×1	Psychic	×1
Bug	×0.5	Bug	×2
Rock	×2	Rock	×0.5
Ghost	×0	Ghost	×2
Dragon	×1	Dragon	×1
Dark	×1	Dark	×1
Steel	×0.5	Steel	×2
Fairy	×0.5	Fairy	×2

Can be used in: Inverse Battle, Battle Institute, —, Battle Maison, Battle Chateau, Random Matchup

How to obtain for your Central Kalos Pokédex

Level up Litleo ♂ to Lv. 35. (X) Level up Litleo ♀ to Lv. 35. (Y)

The male has a mane around its face. The female has a mane on its head.

● LEVEL-UP MOVES

Lv.	Name	Type	Kind	Pow.	Acc.	PP	Range
1	Hyper Beam	Normal	Special	150	90	5	Normal
1	Tackle	Normal	Physical	50	100	35	Normal
1	Leer	Normal	Status	—	100	30	Many Others
5	Ember	Fire	Special	40	100	25	Normal
8	Work Up	Normal	Status	—	—	30	Self
11	Headbutt	Normal	Physical	70	100	15	Normal
15	Noble Roar	Normal	Status	—	100	30	Normal
20	Take Down	Normal	Physical	90	85	20	Normal
23	Fire Fang	Fire	Physical	65	95	15	Normal
28	Endeavor	Normal	Physical	—	100	5	Normal
33	Echoed Voice	Normal	Special	40	100	15	Normal
38	Flamethrower	Fire	Special	90	100	15	Normal
42	Crunch	Dark	Physical	80	100	15	Normal
47	Hyper Voice	Normal	Special	90	100	10	Many Others
51	Incinerate	Fire	Special	60	100	15	Many Others
57	Overheat	Fire	Special	130	90	5	Normal

■ TM & HM MOVES

No.	Name	Type	Kind	Pow.	Acc.	PP	Range
TM05	Roar	Normal	Status	—	—	20	Normal
TM06	Toxic	Poison	Status	—	90	10	Normal
TM10	Hidden Power	Normal	Special	60	100	15	Normal
TM11	Sunny Day	Fire	Status	—	—	5	Both Sides
TM12	Taunt	Dark	Status	—	100	20	Normal
TM15	Hyper Beam	Normal	Special	150	90	5	Normal
TM17	Protect	Normal	Status	—	—	10	Self
TM18	Rain Dance	Water	Status	—	—	5	Both Sides
TM21	Frustration	Normal	Physical	—	100	20	Normal
TM22	Solar Beam	Grass	Special	120	100	10	Normal
TM27	Return	Normal	Physical	—	100	20	Normal
TM28	Dig	Ground	Physical	80	100	10	Normal
TM32	Double Team	Normal	Status	—	—	15	Self
TM35	Flamethrower	Fire	Special	90	100	15	Normal
TM38	Fire Blast	Fire	Special	110	85	5	Normal
TM42	Facade	Normal	Physical	70	100	20	Normal
TM43	Flame Charge	Fire	Physical	50	100	20	Normal
TM44	Rest	Psychic	Status	—	—	10	Self
TM45	Attract	Normal	Status	—	100	15	Normal
TM46	Thief	Dark	Physical	60	100	25	Normal
TM48	Round	Normal	Special	60	100	15	Normal
TM49	Echoed Voice	Normal	Special	40	100	15	Normal
TM50	Overheat	Fire	Special	130	90	5	Normal
TM59	Incinerate	Fire	Special	60	100	15	Many Others
TM61	Will-O-Wisp	Fire	Status	—	85	15	Normal
TM66	Payback	Dark	Physical	50	100	10	Normal
TM67	Retaliate	Normal	Physical	70	100	5	Normal
TM68	Giga Impact	Normal	Physical	150	90	5	Normal
TM78	Bulldoze	Ground	Physical	60	100	20	Adjacent
TM87	Swagger	Normal	Status	—	90	15	Normal
TM88	Sleep Talk	Normal	Status	—	—	10	Self
TM90	Substitute	Normal	Status	—	—	10	Self
TM93	Wild Charge	Electric	Physical	90	100	15	Normal

No.	Name	Type	Kind	Pow.	Acc.	PP	Range
TM94	Rock Smash	Fighting	Physical	40	100	15	Normal
TM95	Snarl	Dark	Special	55	95	15	Many Others
TM97	Dark Pulse	Dark	Special	80	100	15	Normal
TM100	Confide	Normal	Status	—	—	20	Normal
HM04	Strength	Normal	Physical	80	100	15	Normal

● MOVES TAUGHT BY PEOPLE

Name	Type	Kind	Pow.	Acc.	PP	Range

Central Kalos
Duck Pokémon

059

Psyduck

TYPE **Water**

HEIGHT: 2'07" WEIGHT: 43.2 lbs.
GENDER: ♂/♀

ABILITIES
Damp
Cloud Nine

HIDDEN ABILITY
Swift Swim

STAT GROWTH RATES
HP	▪▪
Attack	▪▪▪
Defense	▪▪
Sp. Atk	▪▪▪
Sp. Def	▪▪
Speed	▪▪▪

EGG GROUPS
Water 1, Field

X It is constantly wracked by a headache. When the headache turns intense, it begins using mysterious powers.

Y It has mystical powers but doesn't recall that it has used them. That is why it always looks puzzled.

EVOLUTION

Psyduck — Lv. 33 → Golduck

ITEMS SOMETIMES HELD BY WILD POKÉMON
None

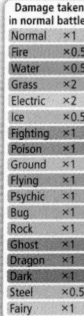

Damage taken in normal battles		Damage taken in Inverse Battles	
Normal	×1	Normal	×1
Fire	×0.5	Fire	×2
Water	×0.5	Water	×2
Grass	×2	Grass	×0.5
Electric	×2	Electric	×0.5
Ice	×0.5	Ice	×2
Fighting	×1	Fighting	×1
Poison	×1	Poison	×1
Ground	×1	Ground	×1
Flying	×1	Flying	×1
Psychic	×1	Psychic	×1
Bug	×1	Bug	×1
Rock	×1	Rock	×1
Ghost	×1	Ghost	×1
Dragon	×1	Dragon	×1
Dark	×1	Dark	×1
Steel	×0.5	Steel	×2
Fairy	×1	Fairy	×1

Can be used in	
Inverse Battle	Battle Institute
—	Battle Maison
Battle Chateau	Random Matchup

Same form for ♂/♀

How to obtain for your Central Kalos Pokédex

❶ Catch in the yellow flowers on Route 22.
❷ Catch on the surface of the water on Route 22.

❶ Catch in the yellow flowers on Route 22.
❷ Catch on the surface of the water on Route 22.

● LEVEL-UP MOVES

Lv.	Name	Type	Kind	Pow.	Acc.	PP	Range
1	Water Sport	Water	Status	—	—	15	Both Sides
1	Scratch	Normal	Physical	40	100	35	Normal
4	Tail Whip	Normal	Status	—	100	30	Many Others
8	Water Gun	Water	Special	40	100	25	Normal
11	Disable	Normal	Status	—	100	20	Normal
15	Confusion	Psychic	Special	50	100	25	Normal
18	Water Pulse	Water	Special	60	100	20	Normal
22	Fury Swipes	Normal	Physical	18	80	15	Normal
25	Screech	Normal	Status	—	85	40	Normal
29	Zen Headbutt	Psychic	Physical	80	90	15	Normal
32	Aqua Tail	Water	Physical	90	90	10	Normal
36	Soak	Water	Status	—	100	20	Normal
39	Psych Up	Normal	Status	—	—	10	Normal
43	Amnesia	Psychic	Status	—	—	20	Self
46	Hydro Pump	Water	Special	110	80	5	Normal
50	Wonder Room	Psychic	Status	—	—	10	Both Sides

● TM & HM MOVES

No.	Name	Type	Kind	Pow.	Acc.	PP	Range
TM01	Hone Claws	Dark	Status	—	—	15	Self
TM03	Psyshock	Psychic	Special	80	100	10	Normal
TM04	Calm Mind	Psychic	Status	—	—	20	Self
TM06	Toxic	Poison	Status	—	90	10	Normal
TM07	Hail	Ice	Status	—	—	10	Both Sides
TM10	Hidden Power	Normal	Special	60	100	15	Normal
TM13	Ice Beam	Ice	Special	90	100	10	Normal
TM14	Blizzard	Ice	Special	110	70	5	Many Others
TM16	Light Screen	Psychic	Status	—	—	30	Your Side
TM17	Protect	Normal	Status	—	—	10	Self
TM18	Rain Dance	Water	Status	—	—	5	Both Sides
TM21	Frustration	Normal	Physical	—	100	20	Normal
TM27	Return	Normal	Physical	—	100	20	Normal
TM28	Dig	Ground	Physical	80	100	10	Normal
TM29	Psychic	Psychic	Special	90	100	10	Normal
TM31	Brick Break	Fighting	Physical	75	100	15	Normal
TM32	Double Team	Normal	Status	—	—	15	Self
TM40	Aerial Ace	Flying	Physical	60	—	20	Normal
TM42	Facade	Normal	Physical	70	100	20	Normal
TM44	Rest	Psychic	Status	—	—	10	Self
TM45	Attract	Normal	Status	—	100	15	Normal
TM48	Round	Normal	Special	60	100	15	Normal
TM55	Scald	Water	Special	80	100	15	Normal
TM56	Fling	Dark	Physical	—	100	10	Normal
TM65	Shadow Claw	Ghost	Physical	70	100	15	Normal
TM70	Flash	Normal	Status	—	100	20	Normal
TM77	Psych Up	Normal	Status	—	—	10	Normal
TM87	Swagger	Normal	Status	—	90	15	Normal
TM88	Sleep Talk	Normal	Status	—	—	10	Self
TM90	Substitute	Normal	Status	—	—	10	Self
TM94	Rock Smash	Fighting	Physical	40	100	15	Normal
TM98	Power-Up Punch	Fighting	Physical	40	100	20	Normal
TM100	Confide	Normal	Status	—	—	20	Normal

No.	Name	Type	Kind	Pow.	Acc.	PP	Range
HM03	Surf	Water	Special	90	100	15	Adjacent
HM04	Strength	Normal	Physical	80	100	15	Normal
HM05	Waterfall	Water	Physical	80	100	15	Normal

● MOVES TAUGHT BY PEOPLE

Name	Type	Kind	Pow.	Acc.	PP	Range

● EGG MOVES

Name	Type	Kind	Pow.	Acc.	PP	Range
Hypnosis	Psychic	Status	—	60	20	Normal
Psybeam	Psychic	Special	65	100	20	Normal
Foresight	Normal	Status	—	—	40	Normal
Future Sight	Psychic	Special	120	100	10	Normal
Cross Chop	Fighting	Physical	100	80	5	Normal
Refresh	Normal	Status	—	—	20	Self
Confuse Ray	Ghost	Status	—	100	10	Normal
Yawn	Normal	Status	—	—	10	Normal
Mud Bomb	Ground	Special	65	85	10	Normal
Encore	Normal	Status	—	100	5	Normal
Secret Power	Normal	Physical	70	100	20	Normal
Sleep Talk	Normal	Status	—	—	10	Self
Synchronoise	Psychic	Special	120	100	10	Adjacent
Simple Beam	Normal	Status	—	100	15	Normal
Clear Smog	Poison	Special	50	—	15	Normal

AFTER THE HALL OF FAME

CENTRAL KALOS
059
Psyduck

COASTAL KALOS

MOUNTAIN KALOS

ADVENTURE DATA

AFTER THE HALL OF FAME

CENTRAL KALOS

060

Golduck

COASTAL KALOS

MOUNTAIN KALOS

ADVENTURE DATA

Central Kalos 060
Duck Pokémon
Golduck

HEIGHT: 5'07" WEIGHT: 168.9 lbs.
GENDER: ♂/♀

X It appears by waterways at dusk. It may use telekinetic powers if its forehead glows mysteriously.

Y The forelegs are webbed, helping to make it an adept swimmer. It can be seen swimming elegantly in lakes, etc.

TYPE Water

ABILITIES
Damp
Cloud Nine

HIDDEN ABILITY
Swift Swim

STAT GROWTH RATES
HP	■■■
Attack	■■■
Defense	■■■
Sp. Atk	■■■■■
Sp. Def	■■■
Speed	■■■■

EGG GROUPS
Water 1, Field

EVOLUTION

Psyduck → Lv. 33 → Golduck

ITEMS SOMETIMES HELD BY WILD POKÉMON
None

Damage taken in normal battles		Damage taken in Inverse Battles	
Normal	×1	Normal	×1
Fire	×0.5	Fire	×2
Water	×0.5	Water	×2
Grass	×2	Grass	×0.5
Electric	×2	Electric	×0.5
Ice	×0.5	Ice	×2
Fighting	×1	Fighting	×1
Poison	×1	Poison	×1
Ground	×1	Ground	×1
Flying	×1	Flying	×1
Psychic	×1	Psychic	×1
Bug	×1	Bug	×1
Rock	×1	Rock	×1
Ghost	×1	Ghost	×1
Dragon	×1	Dragon	×1
Dark	×1	Dark	×1
Steel	×0.5	Steel	×2
Fairy	×1	Fairy	×1

Can be used in	
Inverse Battle	Battle Institute
—	Battle Maison
Battle Chateau	Random Matchup

Same form for ♂/♀

How to obtain for your Central Kalos Pokédex

X Level up Psyduck to Lv. 33.

Y Level up Psyduck to Lv. 33.

● LEVEL-UP MOVES

Lv.	Name	Type	Kind	Pow.	Acc.	PP	Range
1	Aqua Jet	Water	Physical	40	100	20	Normal
1	Water Sport	Water	Status	—	—	15	Both Sides
1	Scratch	Normal	Physical	40	100	35	Normal
1	Tail Whip	Normal	Status	—	100	30	Many Others
1	Water Gun	Water	Special	40	100	25	Normal
4	Tail Whip	Normal	Status	—	100	30	Many Others
8	Water Gun	Water	Special	40	100	25	Normal
11	Disable	Normal	Status	—	100	20	Normal
15	Confusion	Psychic	Special	50	100	25	Normal
18	Water Pulse	Water	Special	60	100	20	Normal
22	Fury Swipes	Normal	Physical	18	80	15	Normal
25	Screech	Normal	Status	—	85	40	Normal
29	Zen Headbutt	Psychic	Physical	80	90	15	Normal
32	Aqua Tail	Water	Physical	90	90	10	Normal
38	Soak	Water	Status	—	100	20	Normal
43	Psych Up	Normal	Status	—	—	10	Normal
49	Amnesia	Psychic	Status	—	—	20	Self
54	Hydro Pump	Water	Special	110	80	5	Normal
60	Wonder Room	Psychic	Status	—	—	10	Both Sides

● TM & HM MOVES

No.	Name	Type	Kind	Pow.	Acc.	PP	Range
TM01	Hone Claws	Dark	Status	—	—	15	Self
TM03	Psyshock	Psychic	Special	80	100	10	Normal
TM04	Calm Mind	Psychic	Status	—	—	20	Self
TM06	Toxic	Poison	Status	—	90	10	Normal
TM07	Hail	Ice	Status	—	—	10	Both Sides
TM10	Hidden Power	Normal	Special	60	100	15	Normal
TM13	Ice Beam	Ice	Special	90	100	10	Normal
TM14	Blizzard	Ice	Special	110	70	5	Many Others
TM15	Hyper Beam	Normal	Special	150	90	5	Normal
TM16	Light Screen	Psychic	Status	—	—	30	Your Side
TM17	Protect	Normal	Status	—	—	10	Self
TM18	Rain Dance	Water	Status	—	—	5	Both Sides
TM21	Frustration	Normal	Physical	—	100	20	Normal
TM27	Return	Normal	Physical	—	100	20	Normal
TM28	Dig	Ground	Physical	80	100	10	Normal
TM29	Psychic	Psychic	Special	90	100	10	Normal
TM31	Brick Break	Fighting	Physical	75	100	15	Normal
TM32	Double Team	Normal	Status	—	—	15	Self
TM40	Aerial Ace	Flying	Physical	60	—	20	Normal
TM42	Facade	Normal	Physical	70	100	20	Normal
TM44	Rest	Psychic	Status	—	—	10	Self
TM45	Attract	Normal	Status	—	100	15	Normal
TM47	Low Sweep	Fighting	Physical	65	100	20	Normal
TM48	Round	Normal	Special	60	100	15	Normal
TM52	Focus Blast	Fighting	Special	120	70	5	Normal
TM55	Scald	Water	Special	80	100	15	Normal
TM56	Fling	Dark	Physical	—	100	10	Normal
TM65	Shadow Claw	Ghost	Physical	70	100	15	Normal
TM68	Giga Impact	Normal	Physical	150	90	5	Normal
TM70	Flash	Normal	Status	—	100	20	Normal
TM77	Psych Up	Normal	Status	—	—	10	Normal
TM87	Swagger	Normal	Status	—	90	15	Normal
TM88	Sleep Talk	Normal	Status	—	—	10	Self

No.	Name	Type	Kind				Range
TM90	Substitute	Normal	Status	—	—	10	Self
TM94	Rock Smash	Fighting	Physical	40	100	15	Normal
TM98	Power-Up Punch	Fighting	Physical	40	100	20	Normal
TM100	Confide	Normal	Status	—	—	20	Normal
HM03	Surf	Water	Special	90	100	15	Adjacent
HM04	Strength	Normal	Physical	80	100	15	Normal
HM05	Waterfall	Water	Physical	80	100	15	Normal

● MOVES TAUGHT BY PEOPLE

Name	Type	Kind	Pow.	Acc.	PP	Range

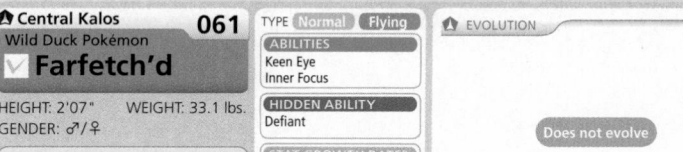

Central Kalos 061
Wild Duck Pokémon
☑ Farfetch'd

HEIGHT: 2'07" WEIGHT: 33.1 lbs.
GENDER: ♂/♀

X The plant stalk it holds is its weapon. The stalk is used like a sword to cut all sorts of things.

Y It always walks about with a plant stalk clamped in its beak. The stalk is used for building its nest.

TYPE **Normal** **Flying**

ABILITIES
Keen Eye
Inner Focus

HIDDEN ABILITY
Defiant

STAT GROWTH RATES
HP	■■
Attack	■■■
Defense	■■■
Sp. Atk	■■■
Sp. Def	■■■
Speed	■■■

EGG GROUPS
Flying, Field

EVOLUTION
Does not evolve

ITEMS SOMETIMES HELD BY WILD POKÉMON
Stick

Damage taken in normal battles		Damage taken in Inverse Battles	
Normal	×1	Normal	×1
Fire	×1	Fire	×1
Water	×1	Water	×1
Grass	×0.5	Grass	×2
Electric	×2	Electric	×0.5
Ice	×2	Ice	×0.5
Fighting	×1	Fighting	×1
Poison	×1	Poison	×1
Ground	×0	Ground	×2
Flying	×1	Flying	×1
Psychic	×1	Psychic	×1
Bug	×0.5	Bug	×2
Rock	×2	Rock	×0.5
Ghost	×0	Ghost	×2
Dragon	×1	Dragon	×1
Dark	×1	Dark	×1
Steel	×1	Steel	×1
Fairy	×1	Fairy	×1

Can be used in	
Inverse Battle	Battle Institute
—	Battle Maison
Battle Chateau	Random Matchup

Same form for ♂/♀

How to obtain for your Central Kalos Pokédex

❶ Catch in the tall grass on Route 22.
❷ Catch in the yellow flowers on Route 22.

❶ Catch in the tall grass on Route 22.
❷ Catch in the yellow flowers on Route 22.

● LEVEL-UP MOVES

Lv.	Name	Type	Kind	Pow.	Acc.	PP	Range
1	Brave Bird	Flying	Physical	120	100	15	Normal
1	Poison Jab	Poison	Physical	80	100	20	Normal
1	Peck	Flying	Physical	35	100	35	Normal
1	Sand Attack	Ground	Status	—	100	15	Normal
1	Leer	Normal	Status	—	100	30	Many Others
1	Fury Cutter	Bug	Physical	40	95	20	Normal
7	Fury Attack	Normal	Physical	15	85	20	Normal
9	Aerial Ace	Flying	Physical	60	—	20	Normal
13	Knock Off	Dark	Physical	65	100	20	Normal
19	Slash	Normal	Physical	70	100	20	Normal
21	Air Cutter	Flying	Special	60	95	25	Many Others
25	Swords Dance	Normal	Status	—	—	20	Self
31	Agility	Psychic	Status	—	—	30	Self
33	Night Slash	Dark	Physical	70	100	15	Normal
37	Acrobatics	Flying	Physical	55	100	15	Normal
43	Feint	Normal	Physical	30	100	10	Normal
45	False Swipe	Normal	Physical	40	100	40	Normal
49	Air Slash	Flying	Special	75	95	15	Normal
55	Brave Bird	Flying	Physical	120	100	15	Normal

● TM & HM MOVES

No.	Name	Type	Kind	Pow.	Acc.	PP	Range
TM06	Toxic	Poison	Status	—	90	10	Normal
TM10	Hidden Power	Normal	Special	60	100	15	Normal
TM11	Sunny Day	Fire	Status	—	—	5	Both Sides
TM17	Protect	Normal	Status	—	—	10	Self
TM19	Roost	Flying	Status	—	—	10	Self
TM21	Frustration	Normal	Physical	—	100	20	Normal
TM27	Return	Normal	Physical	—	100	20	Normal
TM32	Double Team	Normal	Status	—	—	15	Self
TM40	Aerial Ace	Flying	Physical	60	—	20	Normal
TM42	Facade	Normal	Physical	70	100	20	Normal
TM44	Rest	Psychic	Status	—	—	10	Self
TM45	Attract	Normal	Status	—	100	15	Normal
TM46	Thief	Dark	Physical	60	100	25	Normal
TM48	Round	Normal	Special	60	100	15	Normal
TM51	Steel Wing	Steel	Physical	70	90	25	Normal
TM54	False Swipe	Normal	Physical	40	100	40	Normal
TM62	Acrobatics	Flying	Physical	55	100	15	Normal
TM67	Retaliate	Normal	Physical	70	100	5	Normal
TM75	Swords Dance	Normal	Status	—	—	20	Self
TM77	Psych Up	Normal	Status	—	—	10	Normal
TM84	Poison Jab	Poison	Physical	80	100	20	Normal
TM87	Swagger	Normal	Status	—	90	15	Normal
TM88	Sleep Talk	Normal	Status	—	—	10	Self
TM89	U-turn	Bug	Physical	70	100	20	Normal
TM90	Substitute	Normal	Status	—	—	10	Self
TM100	Confide	Normal	Status	—	—	20	Normal
HM01	Cut	Normal	Physical	50	95	30	Normal
HM02	Fly	Flying	Physical	90	95	15	Normal

● MOVES TAUGHT BY PEOPLE

Name	Type	Kind	Pow.	Acc.	PP	Range

● EGG MOVES

Name	Type	Kind	Pow.	Acc.	PP	Range
Steel Wing	Steel	Physical	70	90	25	Normal
Foresight	Normal	Status	—	—	40	Normal
Mirror Move	Flying	Status	—	—	20	Normal
Gust	Flying	Special	40	100	35	Normal
Quick Attack	Normal	Physical	40	100	30	Normal
Flail	Normal	Physical	—	100	15	Normal
Feather Dance	Flying	Status	—	100	15	Normal
Curse	Ghost	Status	—	—	10	Varies
Covet	Normal	Physical	60	100	25	Normal
Mud-Slap	Ground	Special	20	100	10	Normal
Night Slash	Dark	Physical	70	100	15	Normal
Leaf Blade	Grass	Physical	90	100	15	Normal
Revenge	Fighting	Physical	60	100	10	Normal
Roost	Flying	Status	—	—	10	Self
Trump Card	Normal	Special	—	—	5	Normal
Simple Beam	Normal	Status	—	100	15	Normal

AFTER THE HALL OF FAME

CENTRAL KALOS

062

Riolu

COASTAL KALOS

MOUNTAIN KALOS

ADVENTURE DATA

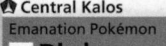

Central Kalos 062

Emanation Pokémon

☑ **Riolu**

HEIGHT: 2'04"   WEIGHT: 44.5 lbs.
GENDER: ♂/♀

TYPE Fighting

ABILITIES
Steadfast
Inner Focus

HIDDEN ABILITY
Prankster

STAT GROWTH RATES
HP	▪▪
Attack	▪▪▪▪
Defense	▪▪
Sp. Atk	▪▪
Sp. Def	▪▪
Speed	▪▪▪

EGG GROUP
No Eggs Discovered

X It uses the shapes of auras, which change according to emotion, to communicate with others.

Y The aura that emanates from its body intensifies to alert others if it is afraid or sad.

EVOLUTION

Level up with high friendship between 4 A.M. and 7:59 P.M.

Riolu → Lucario

ITEMS SOMETIMES HELD BY WILD POKÉMON
None

Can be used in
Inverse Battle
—
Battle Chateau
Battle Institute
Battle Maison
Random Matchup

Damage taken in normal battles	
Normal	×1
Fire	×1
Water	×1
Grass	×1
Electric	×1
Ice	×1
Fighting	×1
Poison	×1
Ground	×1
Flying	×2
Psychic	×2
Bug	×0.5
Rock	×0.5
Ghost	×1
Dragon	×1
Dark	×0.5
Steel	×1
Fairy	×2

Damage taken in Inverse Battles	
Normal	×1
Fire	×1
Water	×1
Grass	×1
Electric	×1
Ice	×1
Fighting	×1
Poison	×1
Ground	×1
Flying	×0.5
Psychic	×0.5
Bug	×2
Rock	×2
Ghost	×1
Dragon	×1
Dark	×2
Steel	×1
Fairy	×0.5

How to obtain for your Central Kalos Pokédex

❶ Catch in the tall grass on Route 22.

❷ Catch in the yellow flowers on Route 22.

❶ Catch in the tall grass on Route 22.

❷ Catch in the yellow flowers on Route 22.

Same form for ♂/♀

● **LEVEL-UP MOVES**

Lv.	Name	Type	Kind	Pow.	Acc.	PP	Range
1	Foresight	Normal	Status	—	—	40	Normal
1	Quick Attack	Normal	Physical	40	100	30	Normal
1	Endure	Normal	Status	—	—	10	Self
6	Counter	Fighting	Physical	—	100	20	Varies
11	Feint	Normal	Physical	30	100	10	Normal
15	Force Palm	Fighting	Physical	60	100	10	Normal
19	Copycat	Normal	Status	—	—	20	Self
24	Screech	Normal	Status	—	85	40	Normal
29	Reversal	Fighting	Physical	—	100	15	Normal
47	Nasty Plot	Dark	Status	—	—	20	Self
50	Final Gambit	Fighting	Special	—	100	5	Normal

● **TM & HM MOVES**

No.	Name	Type	Kind	Pow.	Acc.	PP	Range
TM05	Roar	Normal	Status	—	—	20	Normal
TM06	Toxic	Poison	Status	—	90	10	Normal
TM08	Bulk Up	Fighting	Status	—	—	20	Self
TM10	Hidden Power	Normal	Special	60	100	15	Normal
TM11	Sunny Day	Fire	Status	—	—	5	Both Sides
TM17	Protect	Normal	Status	—	—	10	Self
TM18	Rain Dance	Water	Status	—	—	5	Both Sides
TM21	Frustration	Normal	Physical	—	100	20	Normal
TM26	Earthquake	Ground	Physical	100	100	10	Adjacent
TM27	Return	Normal	Physical	—	100	20	Normal
TM28	Dig	Ground	Physical	80	100	10	Normal
TM31	Brick Break	Fighting	Physical	75	100	15	Normal
TM32	Double Team	Normal	Status	—	—	15	Self
TM39	Rock Tomb	Rock	Physical	60	95	15	Normal
TM42	Facade	Normal	Physical	70	100	20	Normal
TM44	Rest	Psychic	Status	—	—	10	Self
TM45	Attract	Normal	Status	—	100	15	Normal
TM47	Low Sweep	Fighting	Physical	65	100	20	Normal
TM48	Round	Normal	Special	60	100	15	Normal
TM52	Focus Blast	Fighting	Special	120	70	5	Normal
TM56	Fling	Dark	Physical	—	100	10	Normal
TM65	Shadow Claw	Ghost	Physical	70	100	15	Normal
TM66	Payback	Dark	Physical	50	100	10	Normal
TM67	Retaliate	Normal	Physical	70	100	5	Normal
TM75	Swords Dance	Normal	Status	—	—	20	Self
TM78	Bulldoze	Ground	Physical	60	100	20	Adjacent
TM80	Rock Slide	Rock	Physical	75	90	10	Many Others
TM84	Poison Jab	Poison	Physical	80	100	20	Normal
TM87	Swagger	Normal	Status	—	90	15	Normal
TM88	Sleep Talk	Normal	Status	—	—	10	Self
TM90	Substitute	Normal	Status	—	—	10	Self
TM94	Rock Smash	Fighting	Physical	40	100	15	Normal
TM98	Power-Up Punch	Fighting	Physical	40	100	20	Normal
TM100	Confide	Normal	Status	—	—	20	Normal
HM04	Strength	Normal	Physical	80	100	15	Normal

● **MOVES TAUGHT BY PEOPLE**

Name	Type	Kind	Pow.	Acc.	PP	Range

● **EGG MOVES**

Name	Type	Kind	Pow.	Acc.	PP	Range
Cross Chop	Fighting	Physical	100	80	5	Normal
Detect	Fighting	Status	—	—	5	Self
Bite	Dark	Physical	60	100	25	Normal
Mind Reader	Normal	Status	—	—	5	Normal
Sky Uppercut	Fighting	Physical	85	90	15	Normal
High Jump Kick	Fighting	Physical	130	90	10	Normal
Agility	Psychic	Status	—	—	30	Self
Vacuum Wave	Fighting	Special	40	100	30	Normal
Crunch	Dark	Physical	80	100	15	Normal
Low Kick	Fighting	Physical	—	100	20	Normal
Iron Defense	Steel	Status	—	—	15	Self
Blaze Kick	Fire	Physical	85	90	10	Normal
Bullet Punch	Steel	Physical	40	100	30	Normal
Follow Me	Normal	Status	—	—	20	Self
Circle Throw	Fighting	Physical	60	90	10	Normal

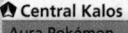

Central Kalos

063

Aura Pokémon

✓ Lucario

HEIGHT: 3'11" WEIGHT: 119.0 lbs.
GENDER: ♂/♀

X By catching the aura emanating from others, it can read their thoughts and movements.

Y By reading the auras of all things, it can tell how others are feeling from over half a mile away.

TYPE [Fighting] [Steel]

ABILITIES
Steadfast
Inner Focus

HIDDEN ABILITY
Justified

STAT GROWTH RATES
HP	■■■
Attack	■■■■■
Defense	■■■
Sp. Atk	■■■■■■
Sp. Def	■■■
Speed	■■■■■

EGG GROUPS
Field, Human-Like

EVOLUTION

Level up with high friendship between 4 A.M. and 7:59 P.M.

Riolu → Lucario

ITEMS SOMETIMES HELD BY WILD POKÉMON
None

Damage taken in normal battles		Damage taken in Inverse Battles	
Normal	×0.5	Normal	×2
Fire	×2	Fire	×0.5
Water	×1	Water	×1
Grass	×0.5	Grass	×2
Electric	×1	Electric	×1
Ice	×0.5	Ice	×2
Fighting	×2	Fighting	×0.5
Poison	×0	Poison	×2
Ground	×2	Ground	×0.5
Flying	×1	Flying	×1
Psychic	×1	Psychic	×1
Bug	×0.25	Bug	×4
Rock	×0.25	Rock	×4
Ghost	×1	Ghost	×1
Dragon	×1	Dragon	×2
Dark	×0.5	Dark	×2
Steel	×0.5	Steel	×2
Fairy	×1	Fairy	×1

Can be used in
Inverse Battle
—
Battle Chateau
Battle Institute
Battle Maison
Random Matchup

How to obtain for your Central Kalos Pokédex

❶ Receive from Korrina after defeating her in the Tower of Mastery in Shalour City.
❷ Level up Riolu with high friendship between 4 A.M. and 7:59 P.M.

❶ Receive from Korrina after defeating her in the Tower of Mastery in Shalour City.
❷ Level up Riolu with high friendship between 4 A.M. and 7:59 P.M.

Same form for ♂/♀

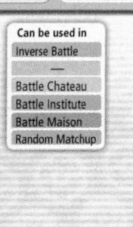

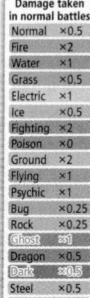 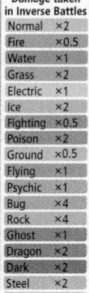

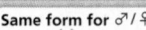

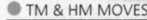

● LEVEL-UP MOVES

Lv.	Name	Type	Kind	Pow.	Acc.	PP	Range
1	Extreme Speed	Normal	Physical	80	100	5	Normal
1	Dragon Pulse	Dragon	Special	85	100	10	Normal
1	Close Combat	Fighting	Physical	120	100	5	Normal
1	Aura Sphere	Fighting	Special	80	—	20	Normal
1	Foresight	Normal	Status	—	—	40	Normal
1	Quick Attack	Normal	Physical	40	100	30	Normal
1	Detect	Fighting	Status	—	—	5	Self
1	Metal Claw	Steel	Physical	50	95	35	Normal
6	Counter	Fighting	Physical	—	100	20	Varies
11	Feint	Normal	Physical	30	100	10	Normal
15	Power-Up Punch	Fighting	Physical	40	100	20	Normal
19	Swords Dance	Normal	Status	—	—	20	Self
24	Metal Sound	Steel	Status	—	85	40	Normal
29	Bone Rush	Ground	Physical	25	90	10	Normal
33	Quick Guard	Fighting	Status	—	—	15	Your Side
37	Me First	Normal	Status	—	—	20	Varies
42	Aura Sphere	Fighting	Special	80	—	20	Normal
47	Calm Mind	Psychic	Status	—	—	20	Self
51	Heal Pulse	Psychic	Status	—	—	10	Normal
55	Close Combat	Fighting	Physical	120	100	5	Normal
60	Dragon Pulse	Dragon	Special	85	100	10	Normal
65	Extreme Speed	Normal	Physical	80	100	5	Normal

● TM & HM MOVES

No.	Name	Type	Kind	Pow.	Acc.	PP	Range
TM01	Hone Claws	Dark	Status	—	—	15	Self
TM04	Calm Mind	Psychic	Status	—	—	20	Self
TM05	Roar	Normal	Status	—	—	20	Normal
TM06	Toxic	Poison	Status	—	90	10	Normal
TM08	Bulk Up	Fighting	Status	—	—	20	Self
TM10	Hidden Power	Normal	Special	60	100	15	Normal
TM11	Sunny Day	Fire	Status	—	—	5	Both Sides
TM15	Hyper Beam	Normal	Special	150	90	5	Normal
TM17	Protect	Normal	Status	—	—	10	Self
TM18	Rain Dance	Water	Status	—	—	5	Both Sides
TM21	Frustration	Normal	Physical	—	100	20	Normal
TM26	Earthquake	Ground	Physical	100	100	10	Adjacent
TM27	Return	Normal	Physical	—	100	20	Normal
TM28	Dig	Ground	Physical	80	100	10	Normal
TM29	Psychic	Psychic	Special	90	100	10	Normal
TM30	Shadow Ball	Ghost	Special	80	100	15	Normal
TM31	Brick Break	Fighting	Physical	75	100	15	Normal
TM32	Double Team	Normal	Status	—	—	15	Self
TM39	Rock Tomb	Rock	Physical	60	95	15	Normal
TM42	Facade	Normal	Physical	70	100	20	Normal
TM44	Rest	Psychic	Status	—	—	10	Self
TM45	Attract	Normal	Status	—	100	15	Normal
TM47	Low Sweep	Fighting	Physical	65	100	20	Normal
TM48	Round	Normal	Special	60	100	15	Normal
TM52	Focus Blast	Fighting	Special	120	70	5	Normal
TM56	Fling	Dark	Physical	—	100	10	Normal
TM65	Shadow Claw	Ghost	Physical	70	100	15	Normal
TM66	Payback	Dark	Physical	50	100	10	Normal
TM67	Retaliate	Normal	Physical	70	100	5	Normal
TM68	Giga Impact	Normal	Physical	150	90	5	Normal
TM71	Stone Edge	Rock	Physical	100	80	5	Normal
TM75	Swords Dance	Normal	Status	—	—	20	Self
TM78	Bulldoze	Ground	Physical	60	100	20	Adjacent

No.	Name	Type	Kind	Pow.	Acc.	PP	Range
TM80	Rock Slide	Rock	Physical	75	90	10	Many Others
TM84	Poison Jab	Poison	Physical	80	100	20	Normal
TM87	Swagger	Normal	Status	—	90	15	Normal
TM88	Sleep Talk	Normal	Status	—	—	10	Self
TM90	Substitute	Normal	Status	—	—	10	Self
TM91	Flash Cannon	Steel	Special	80	100	10	Normal
TM94	Rock Smash	Fighting	Physical	40	100	15	Normal
TM97	Dark Pulse	Dark	Special	80	100	15	Normal
TM98	Power-Up Punch	Fighting	Physical	40	100	20	Normal
TM100	Confide	Normal	Status	—	—	20	Normal
HM04	Strength	Normal	Physical	80	100	15	Normal

● MOVES TAUGHT BY PEOPLE

Name	Type	Kind	Pow.	Acc.	PP	Range

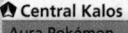

AFTER THE HALL OF FAME

CENTRAL KALOS

063

Lucario

COASTAL KALOS

MOUNTAIN KALOS

ADVENTURE DATA

Mega Evolution

Aura Pokémon

☑ **Mega Lucario**

HEIGHT: 4'03" WEIGHT: 126.8 lbs. GENDER: ♂ / ♀

TYPE Fighting Steel

ABILITY
Adaptability

STAT GROWTH RATES

HP	▦▦▦
Attack	▦▦▦▦▦▦▦
Defense	▦▦▦▦
Sp. Atk	▦▦▦▦▦▦▦
Sp. Def	▦▦▦
Speed	▦▦▦▦▦▦

MEGA STONE REQUIRED

Lucarionite
The Lucario you receive after defeating Korrina in the Tower of Mastery in Shalour City is holding it.

Damage taken in normal battles		Damage taken in Inverse Battles	
Normal	×0.5	Normal	×2
Fire	×2	Fire	×0.5
Water	×1	Water	×1
Grass	×0.5	Grass	×2
Electric	×1	Electric	×1
Ice	×0.5	Ice	×2
Fighting	×2	Fighting	×0.5
Poison	×0	Poison	×2
Ground	×2	Ground	×0.5
Flying	×1	Flying	×1
Psychic	×1	Psychic	×1
Bug	×0.25	Bug	×4
Rock	×0.25	Rock	×4
Ghost	×1	Ghost	×1
Dragon	×0.5	Dragon	×2
Dark	×0.5	Dark	×2
Steel	×0.5	Steel	×2
Fairy	×1	Fairy	×1

Can be used in	
Inverse Battle	Battle Institute
—	Battle Maison
Battle Chateau	Random Matchup

Same form for ♂ / ♀

AFTER THE HALL OF FAME

CENTRAL KALOS

Mega Lucario

COASTAL KALOS

MOUNTAIN KALOS

ADVENTURE DATA

🏠 Central Kalos — 064
Feeling Pokémon
☑ Ralts

HEIGHT: 1'04"   WEIGHT: 14.6 lbs.
GENDER: ♂ / ♀

TYPE Psychic Fairy

ABILITIES
Synchronize
Trace

HIDDEN ABILITY
Telepathy

STAT GROWTH RATES
HP	▪
Attack	▪
Defense	▪
Sp. Atk	▪▪
Sp. Def	▪▪
Speed	▪▪

EGG GROUP
Amorphous

X If its horns capture the warm feelings of people or Pokémon, its body warms up slightly.

Y It is highly attuned to the emotions of people and Pokémon. It hides if it senses hostility.

EVOLUTION
Ralts — Lv. 20 → Kirlia — Lv. 30 → Gardevoir
Kirlia — Use a Dawn Stone on Kirlia ♂ → Gallade

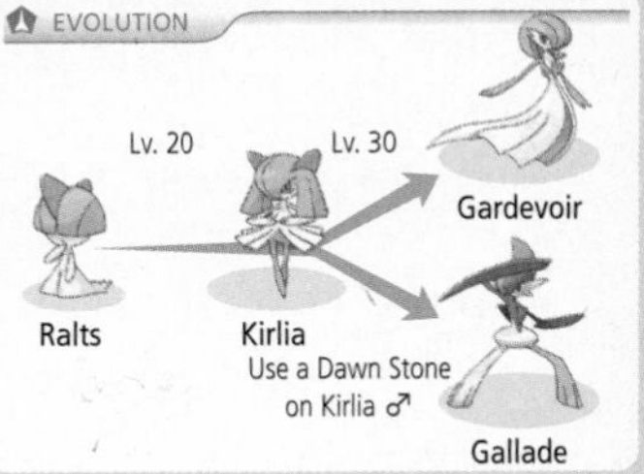

ITEMS SOMETIMES HELD BY WILD POKÉMON
None

Damage taken in normal battles		Damage taken in Inverse Battles	
Normal	×1	Normal	×1
Fire	×1	Fire	×1
Water	×1	Water	×1
Grass	×1	Grass	×1
Electric	×1	Electric	×1
Ice	×1	Ice	×1
Fighting	×0.25	Fighting	×4
Poison	×2	Poison	×0.5
Ground	×1	Ground	×1
Flying	×1	Flying	×1
Psychic	×0.5	Psychic	×2
Bug	×1	Bug	×1
Rock	×1	Rock	×1
Ghost	×2	Ghost	×0.5
Dragon	×0	Dragon	×2
Dark	×1	Dark	×1
Steel	×2	Steel	×0.5
Fairy	×1	Fairy	×1

Can be used in
Inverse Battle
—
Battle Chateau
Battle Institute
Battle Maison
Random Matchup

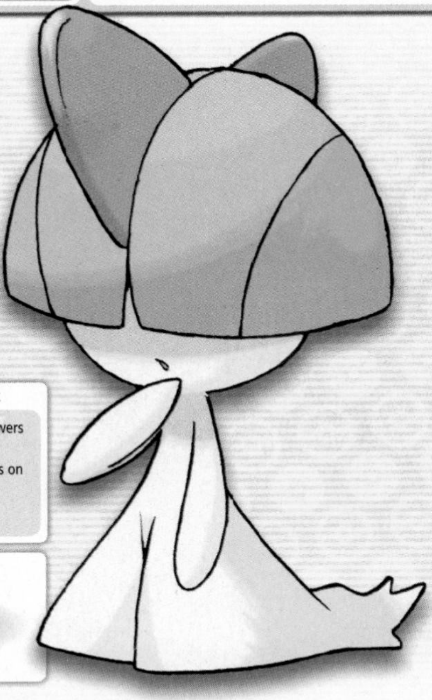

How to obtain for your Central Kalos Pokédex
❶ Catch in the yellow flowers on Route 4.
❷ Catch in the red flowers on Route 4.

❶ Catch in the yellow flowers on Route 4.
❷ Catch in the red flowers on Route 4.

Same form for ♂ / ♀

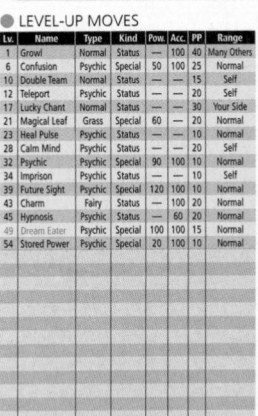

● LEVEL-UP MOVES
Lv.	Name	Type	Kind	Pow.	Acc.	PP	Range
1	Growl	Normal	Status	—	100	40	Many Others
6	Confusion	Psychic	Special	50	100	25	Normal
10	Double Team	Normal	Status	—	—	15	Self
12	Teleport	Psychic	Status	—	—	20	Self
17	Lucky Chant	Normal	Status	—	—	30	Your Side
21	Magical Leaf	Grass	Special	60	—	20	Normal
24	Heal Pulse	Psychic	Status	—	—	10	Normal
28	Calm Mind	Psychic	Status	—	—	20	Self
32	Psychic	Psychic	Special	90	100	10	Normal
34	Imprison	Psychic	Status	—	—	10	Self
39	Future Sight	Psychic	Special	120	100	10	Normal
43	Charm	Fairy	Status	—	100	20	Normal
46	Hypnosis	Psychic	Status	—	60	20	Normal
49	Dream Eater	Psychic	Special	100	100	15	Normal
54	Stored Power	Psychic	Special	20	100	10	Normal

● TM & HM MOVES
No.	Name	Type	Kind	Pow.	Acc.	PP	Range
TM03	Psyshock	Psychic	Special	80	100	10	Normal
TM04	Calm Mind	Psychic	Status	—	—	20	Self
TM06	Toxic	Poison	Status	—	90	10	Normal
TM10	Hidden Power	Normal	Special	60	100	15	Normal
TM11	Sunny Day	Fire	Status	—	—	5	Both Sides
TM12	Taunt	Dark	Status	—	100	20	Normal
TM16	Light Screen	Psychic	Status	—	—	30	Your Side
TM17	Protect	Normal	Status	—	—	10	Self
TM18	Rain Dance	Water	Status	—	—	5	Both Sides
TM20	Safeguard	Normal	Status	—	—	25	Your Side
TM21	Frustration	Normal	Physical	—	100	20	Normal
TM24	Thunderbolt	Electric	Special	90	100	15	Normal
TM27	Return	Normal	Physical	—	100	20	Normal
TM29	Psychic	Psychic	Special	90	100	10	Normal
TM30	Shadow Ball	Ghost	Special	80	100	15	Normal
TM32	Double Team	Normal	Status	—	—	15	Self
TM33	Reflect	Psychic	Status	—	—	20	Your Side
TM41	Torment	Dark	Status	—	100	15	Normal
TM42	Facade	Normal	Physical	70	100	20	Normal
TM44	Rest	Psychic	Status	—	—	10	Self
TM45	Attract	Normal	Status	—	100	15	Normal
TM46	Thief	Dark	Physical	60	100	25	Normal
TM48	Round	Normal	Special	60	100	15	Normal
TM49	Echoed Voice	Normal	Special	40	100	15	Normal
TM56	Fling	Dark	Physical	—	100	10	Normal
TM57	Charge Beam	Electric	Special	50	90	10	Normal
TM61	Will-O-Wisp	Fire	Status	—	85	15	Normal
TM70	Flash	Normal	Status	—	100	20	Normal
TM73	Thunder Wave	Electric	Status	—	100	20	Normal
TM77	Psych Up	Normal	Status	—	—	10	Normal
TM85	Dream Eater	Psychic	Special	100	100	15	Normal
TM86	Grass Knot	Grass	Special	—	100	20	Normal
TM87	Swagger	Normal	Status	—	90	15	Normal
TM88	Sleep Talk	Normal	Status	—	—	10	Self
TM90	Substitute	Normal	Status	—	—	10	Self
TM92	Trick Room	Psychic	Status	—	—	5	Both Sides
TM99	Dazzling Gleam	Fairy	Special	80	100	10	Many Others
TM100	Confide	Normal	Status	—	—	20	Normal

● MOVES TAUGHT BY PEOPLE
Name	Type	Kind	Pow.	Acc.	PP	Range

● EGG MOVES
Name	Type	Kind	Pow.	Acc.	PP	Range
Disable	Normal	Status	—	100	20	Normal
Mean Look	Normal	Status	—	—	5	Normal
Memento	Dark	Status	—	100	10	Normal
Destiny Bond	Ghost	Status	—	—	5	Self
Grudge	Ghost	Status	—	—	5	Self
Shadow Sneak	Ghost	Physical	40	100	30	Normal
Confuse Ray	Ghost	Status	—	100	10	Normal
Encore	Normal	Status	—	100	5	Normal
Synchronoise	Psychic	Special	120	100	10	Adjacent
Skill Swap	Psychic	Status	—	—	10	Normal
Misty Terrain	Fairy	Status	—	—	10	Both Sides
Ally Switch	Psychic	Status	—	—	15	Self

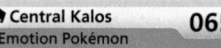

Central Kalos — 065
Emotion Pokémon
☑ Kirlia

HEIGHT: 2'07" WEIGHT: 44.5 lbs.
GENDER: ♂/♀

TYPE Psychic / Fairy

ABILITIES
Synchronize
Trace

HIDDEN ABILITY
Telepathy

STAT GROWTH RATES
HP	▪▪
Attack	▪▪
Defense	▪▪
Sp. Atk	▪▪▪
Sp. Def	▪▪▪
Speed	▪▪▪

EGG GROUP
Amorphous

X The cheerful spirit of its Trainer gives it energy for its psychokinetic power. It spins and dances when happy.

Y It has a psychic power that enables it to distort the space around it and see into the future.

EVOLUTION

Ralts — Lv. 20 → Kirlia — Lv. 30 → Gardevoir

Kirlia — Use a Dawn Stone on Kirlia ♂ → Gallade

ITEMS SOMETIMES HELD BY WILD POKÉMON
None

Can be used in
Inverse Battle
—
Battle Chateau
Battle Institute
Battle Maison
Random Matchup

Damage taken in normal battles
Normal	×1
Fire	×1
Water	×1
Grass	×1
Electric	×1
Ice	×1
Fighting	×0.25
Poison	×2
Ground	×1
Flying	×1
Psychic	×0.5
Bug	×2
Rock	×1
Ghost	×2
Dragon	×0
Dark	×2
Steel	×2
Fairy	×1

Damage taken in Inverse Battles
Normal	×1
Fire	×1
Water	×1
Grass	×1
Electric	×1
Ice	×1
Fighting	×4
Poison	×0.5
Ground	×1
Flying	×1
Psychic	×2
Bug	×1
Rock	×1
Ghost	×0.5
Dragon	×2
Dark	×1
Steel	×0.5
Fairy	×1

How to obtain for your Central Kalos Pokédex

 Level up Ralts to Lv. 20.

 Level up Ralts to Lv. 20.

Same form for ♂ / ♀

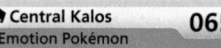

● LEVEL-UP MOVES
Lv.	Name	Type	Kind	Pow.	Acc.	PP	Range
1	Growl	Normal	Status	—	100	40	Many Others
1	Confusion	Psychic	Special	50	100	25	Normal
1	Double Team	Normal	Status	—	—	15	Self
1	Teleport	Psychic	Status	—	—	20	Self
6	Confusion	Psychic	Special	50	100	25	Normal
10	Double Team	Normal	Status	—	—	15	Self
12	Teleport	Psychic	Status	—	—	20	Self
17	Lucky Chant	Normal	Status	—	—	30	Your Side
22	Magical Leaf	Grass	Special	60	—	20	Normal
25	Heal Pulse	Psychic	Status	—	—	10	Normal
31	Calm Mind	Psychic	Status	—	—	20	Self
36	Psychic	Psychic	Special	90	100	10	Normal
39	Imprison	Psychic	Status	—	—	10	Self
45	Future Sight	Psychic	Special	120	100	10	Normal
48	Charm	Fairy	Status	—	100	20	Normal
53	Hypnosis	Psychic	Status	—	60	20	Normal
59	Dream Eater	Psychic	Special	100	100	15	Normal
64	Stored Power	Psychic	Special	20	100	10	Normal

● TM & HM MOVES
No.	Name	Type	Kind	Pow.	Acc.	PP	Range
TM03	Psyshock	Psychic	Special	80	100	10	Normal
TM04	Calm Mind	Psychic	Status	—	—	20	Self
TM06	Toxic	Poison	Status	—	90	10	Normal
TM10	Hidden Power	Normal	Special	60	100	15	Normal
TM11	Sunny Day	Fire	Status	—	—	5	Both Sides
TM12	Taunt	Dark	Status	—	100	20	Normal
TM16	Light Screen	Psychic	Status	—	—	30	Your Side
TM17	Protect	Normal	Status	—	—	10	Self
TM18	Rain Dance	Water	Status	—	—	5	Both Sides
TM20	Safeguard	Normal	Status	—	—	25	Your Side
TM21	Frustration	Normal	Physical	—	100	20	Normal
TM24	Thunderbolt	Electric	Special	90	100	15	Normal
TM27	Return	Normal	Physical	—	100	20	Normal
TM29	Psychic	Psychic	Special	90	100	10	Normal
TM30	Shadow Ball	Ghost	Special	80	100	15	Normal
TM32	Double Team	Normal	Status	—	—	15	Self
TM33	Reflect	Psychic	Status	—	—	20	Your Side
TM41	Torment	Dark	Status	—	100	15	Normal
TM42	Facade	Normal	Physical	70	100	20	Normal
TM44	Rest	Psychic	Status	—	—	10	Self
TM45	Attract	Normal	Status	—	100	15	Normal
TM48	Round	Normal	Special	60	100	15	Normal
TM46	Thief	Dark	Physical	60	100	25	Normal
TM49	Echoed Voice	Normal	Special	40	100	15	Normal
TM56	Fling	Dark	Physical	—	100	10	Normal
TM57	Charge Beam	Electric	Special	50	90	10	Normal
TM61	Will-O-Wisp	Fire	Status	—	85	15	Normal
TM70	Flash	Normal	Status	—	100	20	Normal
TM73	Thunder Wave	Electric	Status	—	100	20	Normal
TM77	Psych Up	Normal	Status	—	—	10	Normal
TM85	Dream Eater	Psychic	Special	100	100	15	Normal
TM86	Grass Knot	Grass	Special	—	100	20	Normal
TM87	Swagger	Normal	Status	—	90	15	Normal
TM88	Sleep Talk	Normal	Status	—	—	10	Self
TM90	Substitute	Normal	Status	—	—	10	Self
TM92	Trick Room	Psychic	Status	—	—	5	Both Sides
TM99	Dazzling Gleam	Fairy	Special	80	100	10	Many Others
TM100	Confide	Normal	Status	—	—	20	Normal

● MOVES TAUGHT BY PEOPLE
Name	Type	Kind	Pow.	Acc.	PP	Range

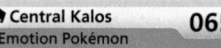

AFTER THE HALL OF FAME
CENTRAL KALOS
065 Kirlia
COASTAL KALOS
MOUNTAIN KALOS
ADVENTURE DATA

AFTER THE HALL OF FAME

CENTRAL KALOS

066

Gardevoir

COASTAL KALOS

MOUNTAIN KALOS

ADVENTURE DATA

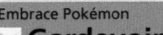 **Central Kalos** **066**

Embrace Pokémon

 Gardevoir

HEIGHT: 5'03" WEIGHT: 106.7 lbs.
GENDER: ♂/♀

X To protect its Trainer, it will expend all its psychic power to create a small black hole.

Y It has the power to predict the future. Its power peaks when it is protecting its Trainer.

TYPE **Psychic** Fairy

ABILITIES
Synchronize
Trace

HIDDEN ABILITY
Telepathy

STAT GROWTH RATES
HP	■■■
Attack	■■■
Defense	■■■
Sp. Atk	■■■■■■
Sp. Def	■■■■■
Speed	■■■■

EGG GROUP
Amorphous

EVOLUTION

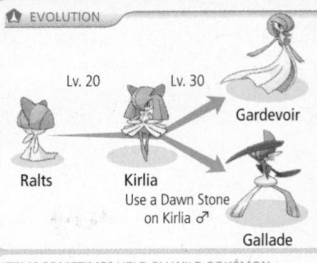

Lv. 20   Lv. 30

                            Gardevoir

Ralts   Kirlia
             Use a Dawn Stone
             on Kirlia ♂

                            Gallade

ITEMS SOMETIMES HELD BY WILD POKÉMON
None

Damage taken in normal battles		Damage taken in Inverse Battles		Can be used in
Normal	×1	Normal	×1	Inverse Battle
Fire	×1	Fire	×1	—
Water	×1	Water	×1	Battle Chateau
Grass	×1	Grass	×1	Battle Institute
Electric	×1	Electric	×1	Battle Maison
Ice	×1	Ice	×1	Random Matchup
Fighting	×0.25	Fighting	×4	
Poison	×2	Poison	×0.5	
Ground	×1	Ground	×1	
Flying	×1	Flying	×1	
Psychic	×0.5	Psychic	×2	
Bug	×1	Bug	×1	
Rock	×1	Rock	×1	
Ghost	×2	Ghost	×0.5	
Dragon	×0	Dragon	×2	
Dark	×1	Dark	×1	
Steel	×2	Steel	×0.5	
Fairy	×1	Fairy	×1	

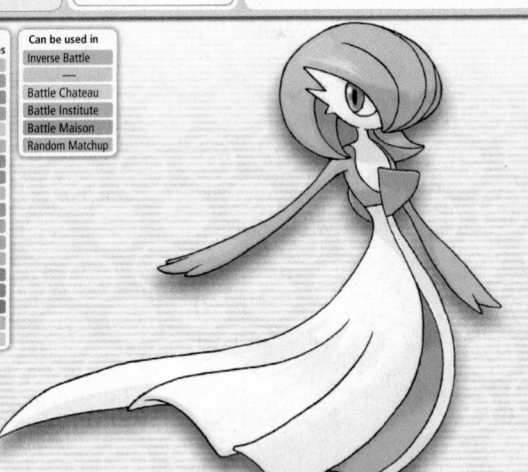

Same form for ♂/♀

 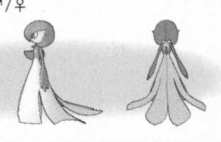

How to obtain for your Central Kalos Pokédex

Level up Kirlia to Lv. 30.   Level up Kirlia to Lv. 30.

● LEVEL-UP MOVES

Lv.	Name	Type	Kind	Pow.	Acc.	PP	Range
1	Moonblast	Fairy	Special	95	100	15	Normal
1	Stored Power	Psychic	Special	20	100	10	Normal
1	Misty Terrain	Fairy	Status	—	—	10	Both Sides
1	Healing Wish	Psychic	Status	—	—	10	Self
1	Growl	Normal	Status	—	100	40	Many Others
1	Confusion	Psychic	Special	50	100	25	Normal
1	Double Team	Normal	Status	—	—	15	Self
1	Teleport	Psychic	Status	—	—	20	Self
6	Confusion	Psychic	Special	50	100	25	Normal
10	Double Team	Normal	Status	—	—	15	Self
12	Teleport	Psychic	Status	—	—	20	Self
17	Wish	Normal	Status	—	—	10	Self
22	Magical Leaf	Grass	Special	60	—	20	Normal
25	Heal Pulse	Psychic	Status	—	—	10	Normal
33	Calm Mind	Psychic	Status	—	—	20	Self
40	Psychic	Psychic	Special	90	100	10	Normal
45	Imprison	Psychic	Status	—	—	10	Self
53	Future Sight	Psychic	Special	120	100	10	Normal
60	Captivate	Normal	Status	—	100	20	Many Others
65	Hypnosis	Psychic	Status	—	60	20	Normal
73	Dream Eater	Psychic	Special	100	100	15	Normal
80	Stored Power	Psychic	Special	20	100	10	Normal
85	Moonblast	Fairy	Special	95	100	15	Normal

● TM & HM MOVES

No.	Name	Type	Kind	Pow.	Acc.	PP	Range
TM03	Psyshock	Psychic	Special	80	100	10	Normal
TM04	Calm Mind	Psychic	Status	—	—	20	Self
TM06	Toxic	Poison	Status	—	90	10	Normal
TM10	Hidden Power	Normal	Special	60	100	15	Normal
TM11	Sunny Day	Fire	Status	—	—	5	Both Sides
TM12	Taunt	Dark	Status	—	100	20	Normal
TM15	Hyper Beam	Normal	Special	150	90	5	Normal
TM16	Light Screen	Psychic	Status	—	—	30	Your Side
TM17	Protect	Normal	Status	—	—	10	Self
TM18	Rain Dance	Water	Status	—	—	5	Both Sides
TM20	Safeguard	Normal	Status	—	—	25	Your Side
TM21	Frustration	Normal	Physical	—	100	20	Normal
TM24	Thunderbolt	Electric	Special	90	100	15	Normal
TM27	Return	Normal	Physical	—	100	20	Normal
TM29	Psychic	Psychic	Special	90	100	10	Normal
TM30	Shadow Ball	Ghost	Special	80	100	15	Normal
TM32	Double Team	Normal	Status	—	—	15	Self
TM33	Reflect	Psychic	Status	—	—	20	Your Side
TM41	Torment	Dark	Status	—	100	15	Normal
TM42	Facade	Normal	Physical	70	100	20	Normal
TM44	Rest	Psychic	Status	—	—	10	Self
TM45	Attract	Normal	Status	—	100	15	Normal
TM46	Thief	Dark	Physical	60	100	25	Normal
TM48	Round	Normal	Special	60	100	15	Normal
TM49	Echoed Voice	Normal	Special	40	100	15	Normal
TM52	Focus Blast	Fighting	Special	120	70	5	Normal
TM53	Energy Ball	Grass	Special	90	100	10	Normal
TM56	Fling	Dark	Physical	—	100	10	Normal
TM57	Charge Beam	Electric	Special	50	90	10	Normal
TM61	Will-O-Wisp	Fire	Status	—	85	15	Normal
TM68	Giga Impact	Normal	Physical	150	90	5	Normal
TM70	Flash	Normal	Status	—	100	20	Normal
TM73	Thunder Wave	Electric	Status	—	100	20	Normal
TM77	Psych Up	Normal	Status	—	—	10	Normal
TM85	Dream Eater	Psychic	Special	100	100	15	Normal
TM86	Grass Knot	Grass	Special	—	100	20	Normal
TM87	Swagger	Normal	Status	—	90	15	Normal
TM88	Sleep Talk	Normal	Status	—	—	10	Self
TM90	Substitute	Normal	Status	—	—	10	Self
TM92	Trick Room	Psychic	Status	—	—	5	Both Sides
TM99	Dazzling Gleam	Fairy	Special	80	100	10	Many Others
TM100	Confide	Normal	Status	—	—	20	Normal

● MOVES TAUGHT BY PEOPLE

Name	Type	Kind	Pow.	Acc.	PP	Range

AFTER THE HALL OF FAME

CENTRAL KALOS

Mega Gardevoir

COASTAL KALOS

MOUNTAIN KALOS

ADVENTURE DATA

Mega Evolution

Embrace Pokémon

☑ **Mega Gardevoir**

TYPE **Psychic** **Fairy**

ABILITY
Pixilate

STAT GROWTH RATES
HP	■■■
Attack	■■■■
Defense	■■■
Sp. Atk	■■■■■■■■
Sp. Def	■■■■■■
Speed	■■■■■

MEGA STONE REQUIRED

Gardevoirite
The Ralts you trade with Diantha at Café Soleil on South Boulevard in Lumiose City after entering the Hall of Fame is holding it.

HEIGHT: 5'03"   WEIGHT: 106.7 lbs.   GENDER: ♂ / ♀

Can be used in
Inverse Battle	Battle Institute
—	Battle Maison
Battle Chateau	Random Matchup

Damage taken in normal battles
Normal	×1
Fire	×1
Water	×1
Grass	×1
Electric	×1
Ice	×1
Fighting	×0.25
Poison	×2
Ground	×1
Flying	×1
Psychic	×0.5
Bug	×1
Rock	×1
Ghost	×2
Dragon	×0
Dark	×1
Steel	×2
Fairy	×1

Damage taken in Inverse Battles
Normal	×1
Fire	×1
Water	×1
Grass	×1
Electric	×1
Ice	×1
Fighting	×4
Poison	×0.5
Ground	×1
Flying	×1
Psychic	×2
Bug	×1
Rock	×1
Ghost	×0.5
Dragon	×2
Dark	×1
Steel	×0.5
Fairy	×1

Same form for ♂ / ♀

AFTER THE HALL OF FAME

CENTRAL KALOS

067 Gallade

COASTAL KALOS

MOUNTAIN KALOS

ADVENTURE DATA

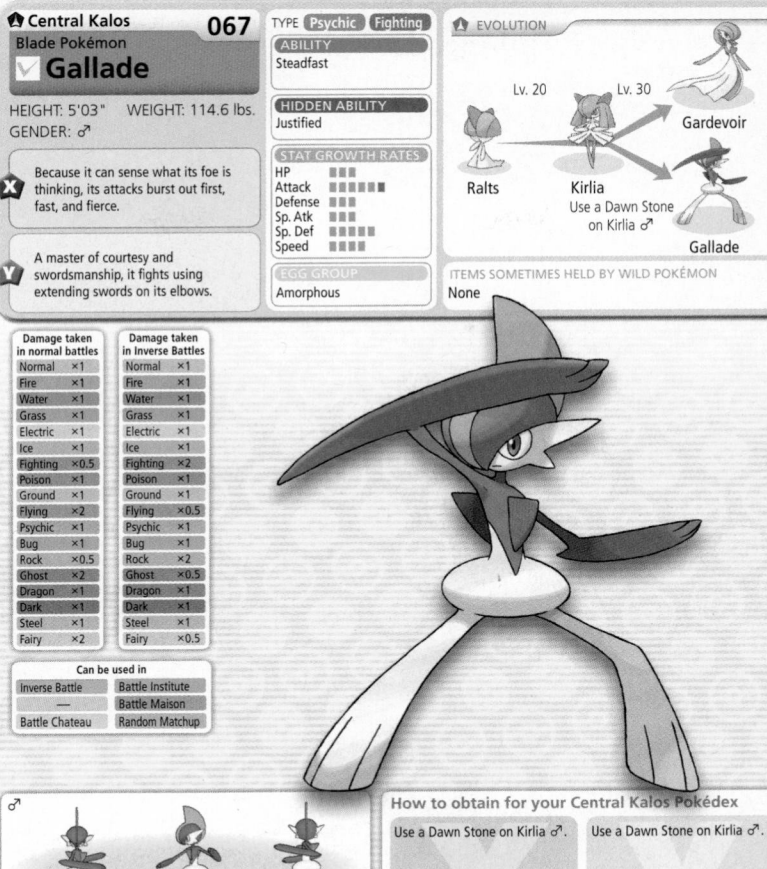

⬆ Central Kalos — 067
Blade Pokémon
☑ Gallade

HEIGHT: 5'03" WEIGHT: 114.6 lbs.
GENDER: ♂

X Because it can sense what its foe is thinking, its attacks burst out first, fast, and fierce.

Y A master of courtesy and swordsmanship, it fights using extending swords on its elbows.

TYPE Psychic Fighting

ABILITY
Steadfast

HIDDEN ABILITY
Justified

STAT GROWTH RATES
HP	■■■
Attack	■■■■■■
Defense	■■■
Sp. Atk	■■■
Sp. Def	■■■
Speed	■■■■

EGG GROUP
Amorphous

EVOLUTION

Ralts — Lv. 20 → Kirlia — Lv. 30 → Gardevoir
Use a Dawn Stone on Kirlia ♂ → Gallade

ITEMS SOMETIMES HELD BY WILD POKÉMON
None

Damage taken in normal battles		Damage taken in Inverse Battles	
Normal	×1	Normal	×1
Fire	×1	Fire	×1
Water	×1	Water	×1
Grass	×1	Grass	×1
Electric	×1	Electric	×1
Ice	×1	Ice	×1
Fighting	×0.5	Fighting	×2
Poison	×1	Poison	×1
Ground	×1	Ground	×1
Flying	×2	Flying	×0.5
Psychic	×1	Psychic	×1
Bug	×1	Bug	×1
Rock	×0.5	Rock	×2
Ghost	×2	Ghost	×0.5
Dragon	×1	Dragon	×1
Dark	×1	Dark	×1
Steel	×1	Steel	×1
Fairy	×2	Fairy	×0.5

Can be used in	
Inverse Battle	Battle Institute
—	Battle Maison
Battle Chateau	Random Matchup

♂

How to obtain for your Central Kalos Pokédex

X	Y
Use a Dawn Stone on Kirlia ♂.	Use a Dawn Stone on Kirlia ♂.

● LEVEL-UP MOVES

Lv.	Name	Type	Kind	Pow.	Acc.	PP	Range
1	Stored Power	Psychic	Special	20	100	10	Normal
1	Close Combat	Fighting	Physical	120	100	5	Normal
1	Leaf Blade	Grass	Physical	90	100	15	Normal
1	Night Slash	Dark	Physical	70	100	15	Normal
1	Leer	Normal	Status	—	100	30	Many Others
1	Confusion	Psychic	Special	50	100	25	Normal
1	Double Team	Normal	Status	—	—	15	Self
1	Teleport	Psychic	Status	—	—	20	Self
6	Confusion	Psychic	Special	50	100	25	Normal
10	Double Team	Normal	Status	—	—	15	Self
12	Teleport	Psychic	Status	—	—	20	Self
17	Fury Cutter	Bug	Physical	40	95	20	Normal
22	Slash	Normal	Physical	70	100	20	Normal
25	Heal Pulse	Psychic	Status	—	—	10	Normal
31	Swords Dance	Normal	Status	—	—	20	Self
36	Psycho Cut	Psychic	Physical	70	100	20	Normal
39	Helping Hand	Normal	Status	—	—	20	1 Ally
45	Feint	Normal	Physical	30	100	10	Normal
50	False Swipe	Normal	Physical	40	100	40	Normal
53	Protect	Normal	Status	—	—	10	Self
59	Close Combat	Fighting	Physical	120	100	5	Normal
64	Stored Power	Psychic	Special	20	100	10	Normal

● TM & HM MOVES

No.	Name	Type	Kind	Pow.	Acc.	PP	Range
TM03	Psyshock	Psychic	Special	80	100	10	Normal
TM04	Calm Mind	Psychic	Status	—	—	20	Self
TM06	Toxic	Poison	Status	—	90	10	Normal
TM08	Bulk Up	Fighting	Status	—	—	20	Self
TM10	Hidden Power	Normal	Special	60	100	15	Normal
TM11	Sunny Day	Fire	Status	—	—	5	Both Sides
TM12	Taunt	Dark	Status	—	100	20	Normal
TM15	Hyper Beam	Normal	Special	150	90	5	Normal
TM16	Light Screen	Psychic	Status	—	—	30	Your Side
TM17	Protect	Normal	Status	—	—	10	Self
TM18	Rain Dance	Water	Status	—	—	5	Both Sides
TM20	Safeguard	Normal	Status	—	—	25	Your Side
TM21	Frustration	Normal	Physical	—	100	20	Normal
TM24	Thunderbolt	Electric	Special	90	100	15	Normal
TM26	Earthquake	Ground	Physical	100	100	10	Adjacent
TM27	Return	Normal	Physical	—	100	20	Normal
TM29	Psychic	Psychic	Special	90	100	10	Normal
TM30	Shadow Ball	Ghost	Special	80	100	15	Normal
TM31	Brick Break	Fighting	Physical	75	100	15	Normal
TM32	Double Team	Normal	Status	—	—	15	Self
TM33	Reflect	Psychic	Status	—	—	20	Your Side
TM39	Rock Tomb	Rock	Physical	60	95	15	Normal
TM40	Aerial Ace	Flying	Physical	60	—	20	Normal
TM41	Torment	Dark	Status	—	100	15	Normal
TM42	Facade	Normal	Physical	70	100	20	Normal
TM44	Rest	Psychic	Status	—	—	10	Self
TM45	Attract	Normal	Status	—	100	15	Normal
TM46	Thief	Dark	Physical	60	100	25	Normal
TM47	Low Sweep	Fighting	Physical	65	100	20	Normal
TM48	Round	Normal	Special	60	100	15	Normal
TM49	Echoed Voice	Normal	Special	40	100	15	Normal
TM52	Focus Blast	Fighting	Special	120	70	5	Normal
TM54	False Swipe	Normal	Physical	40	100	40	Normal

No.	Name	Type	Kind	Pow.	Acc.	PP	Range
TM56	Fling	Dark	Physical	—	100	10	Normal
TM57	Charge Beam	Electric	Special	50	90	10	Normal
TM61	Will-O-Wisp	Fire	Status	—	85	15	Normal
TM67	Retaliate	Normal	Physical	70	100	5	Normal
TM68	Giga Impact	Normal	Physical	150	90	5	Normal
TM70	Flash	Normal	Status	—	100	20	Normal
TM71	Stone Edge	Rock	Physical	100	80	5	Normal
TM73	Thunder Wave	Electric	Status	—	100	20	Normal
TM75	Swords Dance	Normal	Status	—	—	20	Self
TM77	Psych Up	Normal	Status	—	—	10	Normal
TM78	Bulldoze	Ground	Physical	60	100	20	Adjacent
TM80	Rock Slide	Rock	Physical	75	90	10	Many Others
TM81	X-Scissor	Bug	Physical	80	100	15	Normal
TM84	Poison Jab	Poison	Physical	80	100	20	Normal
TM85	Dream Eater	Psychic	Special	100	100	15	Normal
TM86	Grass Knot	Grass	Special	—	100	20	Normal
TM87	Swagger	Normal	Status	—	90	15	Normal
TM88	Sleep Talk	Normal	Status	—	—	10	Self
TM90	Substitute	Normal	Status	—	—	10	Self
TM92	Trick Room	Psychic	Status	—	—	5	Both Sides
TM94	Rock Smash	Fighting	Physical	40	100	15	Normal
TM98	Power-Up Punch	Fighting	Physical	40	100	20	Normal
TM99	Dazzling Gleam	Fairy	Special	80	100	10	Many Others
TM100	Confide	Normal	Status	—	—	20	Normal
HM01	Cut	Normal	Physical	50	95	30	Normal
HM04	Strength	Normal	Physical	80	100	15	Normal

● MOVES TAUGHT BY PEOPLE

Name	Type	Kind	Pow.	Acc.	PP	Range

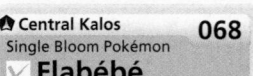

Central Kalos
Single Bloom Pokémon
✓ Flabébé

068

HEIGHT: 0'04" WEIGHT: 0.2 lbs.
GENDER: ♀

It draws out and controls the hidden power of flowers. The flower Flabébé holds is most likely part of its body.

When it finds a flower it likes, it dwells on that flower its whole life long. It floats in the wind's embrace with an untroubled heart.

TYPE Fairy

ABILITY
Flower Veil

HIDDEN ABILITY
Symbiosis

STAT GROWTH RATES
HP	■■
Attack	■■
Defense	■■
Sp. Atk	■■■
Sp. Def	■■■
Speed	■■

EGG GROUP
Fairy

EVOLUTION

Lv. 19 — Shiny Stone

Flabébé → Floette → Florges

ITEMS SOMETIMES HELD BY WILD POKÉMON
None

Damage taken in normal battles		Damage taken in Inverse Battles	
Normal	×1	Normal	×1
Fire	×1	Fire	×1
Water	×1	Water	×1
Grass	×1	Grass	×1
Electric	×1	Electric	×1
Ice	×1	Ice	×1
Fighting	×0.5	Fighting	×2
Poison	×2	Poison	×0.5
Ground	×1	Ground	×1
Flying	×1	Flying	×1
Psychic	×1	Psychic	×1
Bug	×0.5	Bug	×2
Rock	×1	Rock	×1
Ghost	×1	Ghost	×1
Dragon	×0	Dragon	×2
Dark	×0.5	Dark	×2
Steel	×2	Steel	×0.5
Fairy	×1	Fairy	×1

Can be used in	
Inverse Battle	Battle Institute
—	Battle Maison
Battle Chateau	Random Matchup

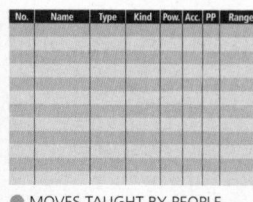

● LEVEL-UP MOVES

Lv.	Name	Type	Kind	Pow.	Acc.	PP	Range
1	Tackle	Normal	Physical	50	100	35	Normal
1	Vine Whip	Grass	Physical	45	100	25	Normal
6	Fairy Wind	Fairy	Special	40	100	30	Normal
10	Lucky Chant	Normal	Status	—	—	30	Your Side
15	Razor Leaf	Grass	Physical	55	95	25	Many Others
20	Wish	Normal	Status	—	—	10	Self
22	Magical Leaf	Grass	Special	60	—	20	Normal
24	Grassy Terrain	Grass	Status	—	—	10	Both Sides
28	Petal Blizzard	Grass	Physical	90	100	15	Adjacent
33	Aromatherapy	Grass	Status	—	—	5	Your Party
41	Misty Terrain	Fairy	Status	—	—	10	Both Sides
41	Moonblast	Fairy	Special	95	100	15	Normal
45	Petal Dance	Grass	Special	120	100	10	1 Random
48	Solar Beam	Grass	Special	120	100	10	Normal

● TM & HM MOVES

No.	Name	Type	Kind	Pow.	Acc.	PP	Range
TM04	Calm Mind	Psychic	Status	—	—	20	Self
TM06	Toxic	Poison	Status	—	90	10	Normal
TM10	Hidden Power	Normal	Special	60	100	15	Normal
TM11	Sunny Day	Fire	Status	—	—	5	Both Sides
TM17	Protect	Normal	Status	—	—	10	Self
TM18	Rain Dance	Water	Status	—	—	5	Both Sides
TM20	Safeguard	Normal	Status	—	—	25	Your Side
TM21	Frustration	Normal	Physical	—	100	20	Normal
TM22	Solar Beam	Grass	Special	120	100	10	Normal
TM27	Return	Normal	Physical	—	100	20	Normal
TM29	Psychic	Psychic	Special	90	100	10	Normal
TM32	Double Team	Normal	Status	—	—	15	Self
TM42	Facade	Normal	Physical	70	100	20	Normal
TM44	Rest	Psychic	Status	—	—	10	Self
TM45	Attract	Normal	Status	—	100	15	Normal
TM48	Round	Normal	Special	60	100	15	Normal
TM49	Echoed Voice	Normal	Special	40	100	15	Normal
TM53	Energy Ball	Grass	Special	90	100	10	Normal
TM70	Flash	Normal	Status	—	100	20	Normal
TM86	Grass Knot	Grass	Special	—	100	20	Normal
TM87	Swagger	Normal	Status	—	90	15	Normal
TM88	Sleep Talk	Normal	Status	—	—	10	Self
TM90	Substitute	Normal	Status	—	—	10	Self
TM96	Nature Power	Normal	Status	—	—	20	Normal
TM99	Dazzling Gleam	Fairy	Special	80	100	10	Many Others
TM100	Confide	Normal	Status	—	—	20	Normal

No.	Name	Type	Kind	Pow.	Acc.	PP	Range

● MOVES TAUGHT BY PEOPLE

Name	Type	Kind	Pow.	Acc.	PP	Range

● EGG MOVES

Name	Type	Kind	Pow.	Acc.	PP	Range
Copycat	Normal	Status	—	—	20	Self
Captivate	Normal	Status	—	100	20	Many Others
Camouflage	Normal	Status	—	—	20	Self

AFTER THE HALL OF FAME

CENTRAL KALOS

068

Flabébé

COASTAL KALOS

MOUNTAIN KALOS

ADVENTURE DATA

Flabébé with different colors of flowers

There are five different colors of flowers that Flabébé hold.

The places where wild Flabébé appear depend on their flower colors.

Red Flower: ♀

How to obtain for your
Central Kalos Pokédex

Catch in the red flowers
on Route 4.

Catch in the red flowers
on Route 4.

Yellow Flower: ♀

How to obtain for your
Central Kalos Pokédex

❶ Catch in the yellow
flowers on Route 4.
❷ Catch in the yellow
flowers on Route 7.

❶ Catch in the yellow
flowers on Route 4.
❷ Catch in the yellow
flowers on Route 7.

Orange Flower: ♀

How to obtain for your
Central Kalos Pokédex

❶ Catch in the yellow
flowers on Route 4.
❷ Catch in the red
flowers on Route 4.

❶ Catch in the yellow
flowers on Route 4.
❷ Catch in the red
flowers on Route 4.

Blue Flower: ♀

How to obtain for your
Central Kalos Pokédex

Catch in the purple
flowers on Route 7.

Catch in the purple
flowers on Route 7.

White Flower: ♀

How to obtain for your
Central Kalos Pokédex

❶ Catch in the yellow
flowers on Route 4.
❷ Catch in the red
flowers on Route 4.

❶ Catch in the yellow
flowers on Route 4.
❷ Catch in the red
flowers on Route 4.

AFTER THE HALL OF FAME

CENTRAL KALOS

069

Floette

COASTAL KALOS

MOUNTAIN KALOS

ADVENTURE DATA

🏠 Central Kalos

Single Bloom Pokémon

069

☑ **Floette**

HEIGHT: 0'08"   WEIGHT: 2.0 lbs.

GENDER: ♀

TYPE Fairy

ABILITY
Flower Veil

HIDDEN ABILITY
Symbiosis

STAT GROWTH RATES
HP	■■
Attack	■■
Defense	■■
Sp. Atk	■■
Sp. Def	■■■■
Speed	■■■

EGG GROUP
Fairy

ITEMS SOMETIMES HELD BY WILD POKÉMON
None

⬆ EVOLUTION

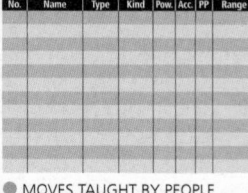

Flabébé — Lv. 19 → Floette — Shiny Stone → Florges

X It flutters around fields of flowers and cares for flowers that are starting to wilt. It draws out the hidden power of flowers to battle.

Y When the flowers of a well-tended flower bed bloom, it appears and celebrates with an elegant dance.

Damage taken in normal battles	
Normal	×1
Fire	×1
Water	×1
Grass	×1
Electric	×1
Ice	×1
Fighting	×0.5
Poison	×2
Ground	×1
Flying	×1
Psychic	×1
Bug	×0.5
Rock	×1
Ghost	×1
Dragon	×0
Dark	×0.5
Steel	×2
Fairy	×1

Damage taken in Inverse Battles	
Normal	×1
Fire	×1
Water	×1
Grass	×1
Electric	×1
Ice	×1
Fighting	×2
Poison	×0.5
Ground	×1
Flying	×1
Psychic	×1
Bug	×2
Rock	×2
Ghost	×1
Dragon	×2
Dark	×2
Steel	×0.5
Fairy	×1

Can be used in	
Inverse Battle	Battle Institute
—	Battle Maison
Battle Chateau	Random Matchup

● LEVEL-UP MOVES

Lv.	Name	Type	Kind	Pow.	Acc.	PP	Range
1	Tackle	Normal	Physical	50	100	35	Normal
1	Vine Whip	Grass	Physical	45	100	25	Normal
6	Fairy Wind	Fairy	Special	40	100	30	Normal
10	Lucky Chant	Normal	Status	—	—	30	Your Side
15	Razor Leaf	Grass	Physical	55	95	25	Many Others
20	Wish	Normal	Status	—	—	10	Self
25	Magical Leaf	Grass	Special	60	—	20	Normal
27	Grassy Terrain	Grass	Status	—	—	10	Both Sides
33	Petal Blizzard	Grass	Physical	90	100	15	Adjacent
38	Aromatherapy	Grass	Status	—	—	5	Your Party
43	Misty Terrain	Fairy	Status	—	—	10	Both Sides
46	Moonblast	Fairy	Special	95	100	15	Normal
51	Petal Dance	Grass	Special	120	100	10	1 Random
58	Solar Beam	Grass	Special	120	100	10	Normal

● TM & HM MOVES

No.	Name	Type	Kind	Pow.	Acc.	PP	Range
TM04	Calm Mind	Psychic	Status	—	—	20	Self
TM06	Toxic	Poison	Status	—	90	10	Normal
TM10	Hidden Power	Normal	Special	60	100	15	Normal
TM11	Sunny Day	Fire	Status	—	—	5	Both Sides
TM17	Protect	Normal	Status	—	—	10	Self
TM18	Rain Dance	Water	Status	—	—	5	Both Sides
TM20	Safeguard	Normal	Status	—	—	25	Your Side
TM21	Frustration	Normal	Physical	—	100	20	Normal
TM22	Solar Beam	Grass	Special	120	100	10	Normal
TM27	Return	Normal	Physical	—	100	20	Normal
TM29	Psychic	Psychic	Special	90	100	10	Normal
TM32	Double Team	Normal	Status	—	—	15	Self
TM42	Facade	Normal	Physical	70	100	20	Normal
TM44	Rest	Psychic	Status	—	—	10	Self
TM45	Attract	Normal	Status	—	100	15	Normal
TM48	Round	Normal	Special	60	100	15	Normal
TM49	Echoed Voice	Normal	Special	40	100	15	Normal
TM53	Energy Ball	Grass	Special	90	100	10	Normal
TM70	Flash	Normal	Status	—	100	20	Normal
TM86	Grass Knot	Grass	Special	—	100	20	Normal
TM87	Swagger	Normal	Status	—	90	15	Normal
TM88	Sleep Talk	Normal	Status	—	—	10	Self
TM90	Substitute	Normal	Status	—	—	10	Self
TM96	Nature Power	Normal	Status	—	—	20	Normal
TM99	Dazzling Gleam	Fairy	Special	80	100	10	Many Others
TM100	Confide	Normal	Status	—	—	20	Normal

● MOVES TAUGHT BY PEOPLE

Name	Type	Kind	Pow.	Acc.	PP	Range

◎ Floette with different colors of flowers

There are five different colors of flowers that Floette hold.

Floette won't appear in the wild. They evolve inheriting the flower colors of Flabébé.

Red Flower: ♀

How to obtain for your Central Kalos Pokédex

Level up Red Flower Flabébé to Lv. 19.

Level up Red Flower Flabébé to Lv. 19.

Yellow Flower: ♀

How to obtain for your Central Kalos Pokédex

Level up Yellow Flower Flabébé to Lv. 19.

Level up Yellow Flower Flabébé to Lv. 19.

Orange Flower: ♀

How to obtain for your Central Kalos Pokédex

Level up Orange Flower Flabébé to Lv. 19.

Level up Orange Flower Flabébé to Lv. 19.

Blue Flower: ♀

How to obtain for your Central Kalos Pokédex

Level up Blue Flower Flabébé to Lv. 19.

Level up Blue Flower Flabébé to Lv. 19.

White Flower: ♀

How to obtain for your Central Kalos Pokédex

Level up White Flower Flabébé to Lv. 19.

Level up White Flower Flabébé to Lv. 19.

AFTER THE HALL OF FAME

CENTRAL KALOS

069 | Floette

COASTAL KALOS

MOUNTAIN KALOS

ADVENTURE DATA

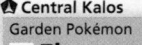
Garden Pokémon

☑ Florges

HEIGHT: 3'07"   WEIGHT: 22.0 lbs.
GENDER: ♀

X It claims exquisite flower gardens as its territory, and it obtains power from basking in the energy emitted by flowering plants.

Y In times long past, governors of castles would invite Florges to create flower gardens to embellish the castle domains.

TYPE Fairy

ABILITY
Flower Veil

HIDDEN ABILITY
Symbiosis

STAT GROWTH RATES
HP	■■■
Attack	■■■
Defense	■■■
Sp. Atk	■■■■■
Sp. Def	■■■■■■
Speed	■■■■

EGG GROUP
Fairy

● EVOLUTION

Lv. 19   Shiny Stone

Flabébé   Floette   Florges

ITEMS SOMETIMES HELD BY WILD POKÉMON
None

Damage taken in normal battles	
Normal	×1
Fire	×1
Water	×1
Grass	×1
Electric	×1
Ice	×1
Fighting	×0.5
Poison	×2
Ground	×1
Flying	×1
Psychic	×1
Bug	×0.5
Rock	×1
Ghost	×1
Dragon	×0
Dark	×0.5
Steel	×2
Fairy	×1

Damage taken in Inverse Battles	
Normal	×1
Fire	×1
Water	×1
Grass	×1
Electric	×1
Ice	×1
Fighting	×2
Poison	×0.5
Ground	×1
Flying	×1
Psychic	×1
Bug	×2
Rock	×1
Ghost	×1
Dragon	×2
Dark	×2
Steel	×0.5
Fairy	×1

Can be used in	
Inverse Battle	Battle Institute
—	Battle Maison
Battle Chateau	Random Matchup

AFTER THE HALL OF FAME

CENTRAL KALOS

070

Florges

COASTAL KALOS

MOUNTAIN KALOS

ADVENTURE DATA

● LEVEL-UP MOVES

Lv.	Name	Type	Kind	Pow.	Acc.	PP	Range
1	Disarming Voice	Fairy	Special	40	—	15	Many Others
1	Lucky Chant	Normal	Status	—	—	30	Your Side
1	Wish	Normal	Status	—	—	10	Self
1	Magical Leaf	Grass	Special	60	—	20	Normal
1	Flower Shield	Fairy	Status	—	—	10	Adjacent
1	Grass Knot	Grass	Special	—	100	20	Normal
1	Grassy Terrain	Grass	Status	—	—	10	Both Sides
1	Petal Blizzard	Grass	Physical	90	100	15	Adjacent
1	Misty Terrain	Fairy	Status	—	—	10	Both Sides
1	Moonblast	Fairy	Special	95	100	15	Normal
1	Petal Dance	Grass	Special	120	100	10	1 Random
1	Aromatherapy	Grass	Status	—	—	5	Your Party

● TM & HM MOVES

No.	Name	Type	Kind	Pow.	Acc.	PP	Range
TM04	Calm Mind	Psychic	Status	—	—	20	Self
TM06	Toxic	Poison	Status	—	90	10	Normal
TM10	Hidden Power	Normal	Special	60	100	15	Normal
TM11	Sunny Day	Fire	Status	—	—	5	Both Sides
TM15	Hyper Beam	Normal	Special	150	90	5	Normal
TM16	Light Screen	Psychic	Status	—	—	30	Your Side
TM17	Protect	Normal	Status	—	—	10	Self
TM18	Rain Dance	Water	Status	—	—	5	Both Sides
TM20	Safeguard	Normal	Status	—	—	25	Your Side
TM21	Frustration	Normal	Physical	—	100	20	Normal
TM22	Solar Beam	Grass	Special	120	100	10	Normal
TM27	Return	Normal	Physical	—	100	20	Normal
TM29	Psychic	Psychic	Special	90	100	10	Normal
TM32	Double Team	Normal	Status	—	—	15	Self
TM42	Facade	Normal	Physical	70	100	20	Normal
TM44	Rest	Psychic	Status	—	—	10	Self
TM45	Attract	Normal	Status	—	100	15	Normal
TM48	Round	Normal	Special	60	100	15	Normal
TM49	Echoed Voice	Normal	Special	40	100	15	Normal
TM53	Energy Ball	Grass	Special	90	100	10	Normal
TM68	Giga Impact	Normal	Physical	150	90	5	Normal
TM70	Flash	Normal	Status	—	100	20	Normal
TM86	Grass Knot	Grass	Special	—	100	20	Normal
TM87	Swagger	Normal	Status	—	90	15	Normal
TM88	Sleep Talk	Normal	Status	—	—	10	Self
TM90	Substitute	Normal	Status	—	—	10	Self
TM96	Nature Power	Normal	Status	—	—	20	Normal
TM99	Dazzling Gleam	Fairy	Special	80	100	10	Many Others
TM100	Confide	Normal	Status	—	—	20	Normal

No.	Name	Type	Kind	Pow.	Acc.	PP	Range

● MOVES TAUGHT BY PEOPLE

Name	Type	Kind	Pow.	Acc.	PP	Range

◯ Florges with different colors of flowers

There are five different colors of flowers that Florges hold.

Florges won't appear in the wild. They evolve inheriting the flower colors of Floette.

AFTER THE HALL OF FAME

CENTRAL KALOS

070 Florges

COASTAL KALOS

MOUNTAIN KALOS

ADVENTURE DATA

Red Flower: ♀

How to obtain for your Central Kalos Pokédex

Use a Shiny Stone on Red Flower Floette.

Use a Shiny Stone on Red Flower Floette.

Yellow Flower: ♀

How to obtain for your Central Kalos Pokédex

Use a Shiny Stone on Yellow Flower Floette.

Use a Shiny Stone on Yellow Flower Floette.

Orange Flower: ♀

How to obtain for your Central Kalos Pokédex

Use a Shiny Stone on Orange Flower Floette.

Use a Shiny Stone on Orange Flower Floette.

Blue Flower: ♀

How to obtain for your Central Kalos Pokédex

Use a Shiny Stone on Blue Flower Floette.

Use a Shiny Stone on Blue Flower Floette.

White Flower: ♀

How to obtain for your Central Kalos Pokédex

Use a Shiny Stone on White Flower Floette.

Use a Shiny Stone on White Flower Floette.

AFTER THE HALL OF FAME

CENTRAL KALOS

071

Budew

COASTAL KALOS

MOUNTAIN KALOS

ADVENTURE DATA

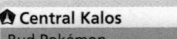

🏠 Central Kalos — 071
Bud Pokémon
∨ **Budew**

HEIGHT: 0'08" WEIGHT: 2.6 lbs.
GENDER: ♂/♀

TYPE Grass | Poison

ABILITIES
Natural Cure
Poison Point

HIDDEN ABILITY
Leaf Guard

STAT GROWTH RATES
HP
Attack
Defense
Sp. Atk
Sp. Def
Speed

EGG GROUP
No Eggs Discovered

X When it feels the sun's warm touch, it opens its bud to release pollen. It lives alongside clear pools.

Y Over the winter, it closes its bud and endures the cold. In spring, the bud opens and releases pollen.

⬆ EVOLUTION

Level up with high friendship between 4 A.M. and 7:59 P.M.   Shiny Stone

Budew   Roselia   Roserade

ITEMS SOMETIMES HELD BY WILD POKÉMON
Poison Barb

Damage taken in normal battles		Damage taken in Inverse Battles	
Normal	×1	Normal	×1
Fire	×2	Fire	×0.5
Water	×0.5	Water	×2
Grass	×0.25	Grass	×4
Electric	×0.5	Electric	×2
Ice	×2	Ice	×0.5
Fighting	×0.5	Fighting	×2
Poison	×1	Poison	×1
Ground	×1	Ground	×1
Flying	×2	Flying	×0.5
Psychic	×2	Psychic	×0.5
Bug	×1	Bug	×1
Rock	×1	Rock	×1
Ghost	×1	Ghost	×1
Dragon	×1	Dragon	×1
Dark	×1	Dark	×1
Steel	×1	Steel	×1
Fairy	×0.5	Fairy	×2

Can be used in	
Inverse Battle	Battle Institute
—	Battle Maison
Battle Chateau	Random Matchup

Same form for ♂/♀

How to obtain for your Central Kalos Pokédex

❶ Catch in the yellow flowers on Route 4.
❷ Catch in the red flowers on Route 4.

❶ Catch in the yellow flowers on Route 4.
❷ Catch in the red flowers on Route 4.

● LEVEL-UP MOVES

Lv.	Name	Type	Kind	Pow.	Acc.	PP	Range
1	Absorb	Grass	Special	20	100	25	Normal
4	Growth	Normal	Status	—	—	20	Self
7	Water Sport	Water	Status	—	—	15	Both Sides
10	Stun Spore	Grass	Status	—	75	30	Normal
13	Mega Drain	Grass	Special	40	100	15	Normal
16	Worry Seed	Grass	Status	—	100	10	Normal

■ TM & HM MOVES

No.	Name	Type	Kind	Pow.	Acc.	PP	Range
TM06	Toxic	Poison	Status	—	90	10	Normal
TM09	Venoshock	Poison	Special	65	100	10	Normal
TM10	Hidden Power	Normal	Special	60	100	15	Normal
TM11	Sunny Day	Fire	Status	—	—	5	Both Sides
TM17	Protect	Normal	Status	—	—	10	Self
TM18	Rain Dance	Water	Status	—	—	5	Both Sides
TM21	Frustration	Normal	Physical	—	100	20	Normal
TM22	Solar Beam	Grass	Special	120	100	10	Normal
TM27	Return	Normal	Physical	—	100	20	Normal
TM30	Shadow Ball	Ghost	Special	80	100	15	Normal
TM32	Double Team	Normal	Status	—	—	15	Self
TM36	Sludge Bomb	Poison	Special	90	100	10	Normal
TM42	Facade	Normal	Physical	70	100	20	Normal
TM44	Rest	Psychic	Status	—	—	10	Self
TM45	Attract	Normal	Status	—	100	15	Normal
TM48	Round	Normal	Special	60	100	15	Normal
TM53	Energy Ball	Grass	Special	90	100	10	Normal
TM70	Flash	Normal	Status	—	100	20	Normal
TM75	Swords Dance	Normal	Status	—	—	20	Self
TM77	Psych Up	Normal	Status	—	—	10	Self
TM86	Grass Knot	Grass	Special	—	100	20	Normal
TM87	Swagger	Normal	Status	—	90	15	Normal
TM88	Sleep Talk	Normal	Status	—	—	10	Self
TM90	Substitute	Normal	Status	—	—	10	Self
TM96	Nature Power	Normal	Status	—	—	20	Normal
TM99	Dazzling Gleam	Fairy	Special	80	100	10	Many Others
TM100	Confide	Normal	Status	—	—	20	Normal
HM01	Cut	Normal	Physical	50	95	30	Normal

No.	Name	Type	Kind	Pow.	Acc.	PP	Range

● MOVES TAUGHT BY PEOPLE

Name	Type	Kind	Pow.	Acc.	PP	Range

● EGG MOVES

Name	Type	Kind	Pow.	Acc.	PP	Range
Spikes	Ground	Status	—	—	20	Other Side
Synthesis	Grass	Status	—	—	5	Self
Pin Missile	Bug	Physical	25	95	20	Normal
Cotton Spore	Grass	Status	—	100	40	Many Others
Sleep Powder	Grass	Status	—	75	15	Normal
Razor Leaf	Grass	Physical	55	95	25	Many Others
Mind Reader	Normal	Status	—	—	5	Normal
Leaf Storm	Grass	Special	130	90	5	Normal
Extrasensory	Psychic	Special	80	100	20	Normal
Seed Bomb	Grass	Physical	80	100	15	Normal
Giga Drain	Grass	Special	75	100	10	Normal
Natural Gift	Normal	Physical	—	100	15	Normal
Grass Whistle	Grass	Status	—	55	15	Normal

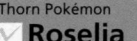

Central Kalos — 072

Thorn Pokémon

☑ Roselia

HEIGHT: 1'00"   WEIGHT: 4.4 lbs.
GENDER: ♂/♀

TYPE Grass / Poison

ABILITIES
Natural Cure
Poison Point

HIDDEN ABILITY
Leaf Guard

STAT GROWTH RATES
HP	■■
Attack	■■
Defense	■■
Sp. Atk	■■■■■
Sp. Def	■■■
Speed	■■■

EGG GROUPS
Fairy, Grass

X It uses the different poisons in each hand separately when it attacks. The stronger its aroma, the healthier it is.

Y Roselia that drink nutritionally rich springwater are said to reveal rare coloration when they bloom.

EVOLUTION

Level up with high friendship between 4 A.M. and 7:59 P.M.   Shiny Stone

Budew   Roselia   Roserade

ITEMS SOMETIMES HELD BY WILD POKÉMON
Poison Barb

Damage taken in normal battles	
Normal	×1
Fire	×2
Water	×0.5
Grass	×0.25
Electric	×0.5
Ice	×2
Fighting	×0.5
Poison	×1
Ground	×1
Flying	×2
Psychic	×2
Bug	×1
Rock	×1
Ghost	×1
Dragon	×1
Dark	×1
Steel	×1
Fairy	×0.5

Damage taken in Inverse Battles	
Normal	×1
Fire	×0.5
Water	×2
Grass	×4
Electric	×2
Ice	×0.5
Fighting	×2
Poison	×1
Ground	×1
Flying	×0.5
Psychic	×0.5
Bug	×1
Rock	×1
Ghost	×1
Dragon	×1
Dark	×1
Steel	×1
Fairy	×2

Can be used in
Inverse Battle
——
Battle Chateau
Battle Institute
Battle Maison
Random Matchup

How to obtain for your Central Kalos Pokédex

❶ Catch in the yellow or the purple flowers on Route 7.
❷ Level up Budew with high friendship between 4 A.M. and 7:59 P.M.

❶ Catch in the yellow or the purple flowers on Route 7.
❷ Level up Budew with high friendship between 4 A.M. and 7:59 P.M.

 ♂

   ♀

The male has a smaller leaf on its front. The female has a larger leaf on its front.

● LEVEL-UP MOVES

Lv.	Name	Type	Kind	Pow.	Acc.	PP	Range
1	Absorb	Grass	Special	20	100	25	Normal
4	Growth	Normal	Status	—	—	20	Self
7	Poison Sting	Poison	Physical	15	100	35	Normal
10	Stun Spore	Grass	Status	—	75	30	Normal
13	Mega Drain	Grass	Special	40	100	15	Normal
16	Leech Seed	Grass	Status	—	90	10	Normal
19	Magical Leaf	Grass	Special	60	—	20	Normal
22	Grass Whistle	Grass	Status	—	55	15	Normal
25	Giga Drain	Grass	Special	75	100	10	Normal
28	Toxic Spikes	Poison	Status	—	—	20	Other Side
31	Sweet Scent	Normal	Status	—	100	20	Many Others
34	Ingrain	Grass	Status	—	—	20	Self
37	Petal Dance	Grass	Special	120	100	10	1 Random
40	Toxic	Poison	Status	—	90	10	Normal
43	Aromatherapy	Grass	Status	—	—	5	Your Party
46	Synthesis	Grass	Status	—	—	5	Self
50	Petal Blizzard	Grass	Physical	90	100	15	Adjacent

● TM & HM MOVES

No.	Name	Type	Kind	Pow.	Acc.	PP	Range
TM06	Toxic	Poison	Status	—	90	10	Normal
TM09	Venoshock	Poison	Special	65	100	10	Normal
TM10	Hidden Power	Normal	Special	60	100	15	Normal
TM11	Sunny Day	Fire	Status	—	—	5	Both Sides
TM17	Protect	Normal	Status	—	—	10	Self
TM18	Rain Dance	Water	Status	—	—	5	Both Sides
TM21	Frustration	Normal	Physical	—	100	20	Normal
TM22	Solar Beam	Grass	Special	120	100	10	Normal
TM27	Return	Normal	Physical	—	100	20	Normal
TM30	Shadow Ball	Ghost	Special	80	100	15	Normal
TM32	Double Team	Normal	Status	—	—	15	Self
TM36	Sludge Bomb	Poison	Special	90	100	10	Normal
TM42	Facade	Normal	Physical	70	100	20	Normal
TM44	Rest	Psychic	Status	—	—	10	Self
TM45	Attract	Normal	Status	—	100	15	Normal
TM48	Round	Normal	Special	60	100	15	Normal
TM53	Energy Ball	Grass	Special	90	100	10	Normal
TM70	Flash	Normal	Status	—	100	20	Normal
TM75	Swords Dance	Normal	Status	—	—	20	Self
TM77	Psych Up	Normal	Status	—	—	10	Normal
TM84	Poison Jab	Poison	Physical	80	100	20	Normal
TM86	Grass Knot	Grass	Special	—	100	20	Normal
TM87	Swagger	Normal	Status	—	90	15	Normal
TM88	Sleep Talk	Normal	Status	—	—	10	Self
TM90	Substitute	Normal	Status	—	—	10	Self
TM96	Nature Power	Normal	Status	—	—	20	Normal
TM99	Dazzling Gleam	Fairy	Special	80	100	10	Many Others
TM100	Confide	Normal	Status	—	—	20	Normal
HM01	Cut	Normal	Physical	50	95	30	Normal

● MOVES TAUGHT BY PEOPLE

Name	Type	Kind	Pow.	Acc.	PP	Range

● EGG MOVES

Name	Type	Kind	Pow.	Acc.	PP	Range
Spikes	Ground	Status	—	—	20	Other Side
Synthesis	Grass	Status	—	—	5	Self
Pin Missile	Bug	Physical	25	95	20	Normal
Cotton Spore	Grass	Status	—	100	40	Many Others
Sleep Powder	Grass	Status	—	75	15	Normal
Razor Leaf	Grass	Physical	55	95	25	Many Others
Mind Reader	Normal	Status	—	—	5	Normal
Leaf Storm	Grass	Special	130	90	5	Normal
Seed Bomb	Grass	Physical	80	100	15	Normal
Giga Drain	Grass	Special	75	100	10	Normal
Natural Gift	Normal	Physical	—	100	15	Normal
Grass Whistle	Grass	Status	—	55	15	Normal
Bullet Seed	Grass	Physical	25	100	30	Normal

AFTER THE HALL OF FAME

CENTRAL KALOS

072 | Roselia

COASTAL KALOS

MOUNTAIN KALOS

ADVENTURE DATA

Bouquet Pokémon

☑️ **Roserade**

HEIGHT: 2'11"   WEIGHT: 32.0 lbs.
GENDER: ♂/♀

TYPE	Grass	Poison

ABILITIES
Natural Cure
Poison Point

HIDDEN ABILITY
Technician

STAT GROWTH RATES

HP	▪▪▪
Attack	▪▪▪
Defense	▪▪▪
Sp. Atk	▪▪▪▪▪▪
Sp. Def	▪▪▪▪
Speed	▪▪▪▪

EGG GROUPS
Fairy, Grass

🅧 Luring prey with a sweet scent, it uses poison whips on its arms to poison, bind, and finish off the prey.

🅨 With the movements of a dancer, it strikes with whips that are densely lined with poison thorns.

⬆ EVOLUTION

Level up with high friendship between 4 A.M. and 7:59 P.M.

Shiny Stone

Budew   Roselia   Roserade

ITEMS SOMETIMES HELD BY WILD POKÉMON
None

Can be used in
Inverse Battle
—
Battle Chateau
Battle Institute
Battle Maison
Random Matchup

Damage taken in normal battles	
Normal	×1
Fire	×2
Water	×0.5
Grass	×0.25
Electric	×0.5
Ice	×2
Fighting	×0.5
Poison	×1
Ground	×1
Flying	×2
Psychic	×2
Bug	×1
Rock	×1
Ghost	×1
Dragon	×1
Dark	×1
Steel	×1
Fairy	×0.5

Damage taken in Inverse Battles	
Normal	×1
Fire	×0.5
Water	×2
Grass	×4
Electric	×2
Ice	×0.5
Fighting	×2
Poison	×1
Ground	×1
Flying	×0.5
Psychic	×0.5
Bug	×1
Rock	×1
Ghost	×1
Dragon	×1
Dark	×1
Steel	×1
Fairy	×2

How to obtain for your Central Kalos Pokédex

Use a Shiny Stone on Roselia.   Use a Shiny Stone on Roselia.

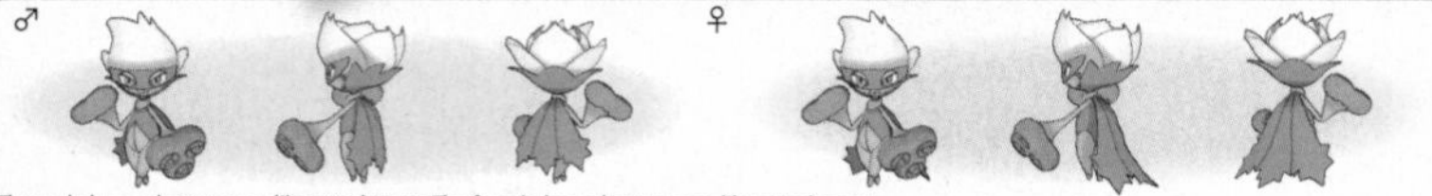

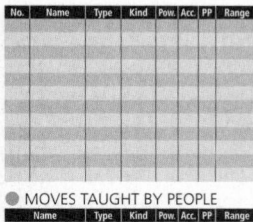

The male has a shorter cape-like attachment. The female has a longer cape-like attachment.

● LEVEL-UP MOVES

Lv.	Name	Type	Kind	Pow.	Acc.	PP	Range
1	Venom Drench	Poison	Status	—	100	20	Many Others
1	Grassy Terrain	Grass	Status	—	—	10	Both Sides
1	Weather Ball	Normal	Special	50	100	10	Normal
1	Poison Sting	Poison	Physical	15	100	35	Normal
1	Mega Drain	Grass	Special	40	100	15	Normal
1	Magical Leaf	Grass	Special	60	—	20	Normal
1	Sweet Scent	Normal	Status	—	100	20	Many Others

● TM & HM MOVES

No.	Name	Type	Kind	Pow.	Acc.	PP	Range
TM06	Toxic	Poison	Status	—	90	10	Normal
TM09	Venoshock	Poison	Special	65	100	10	Normal
TM10	Hidden Power	Normal	Special	60	100	15	Normal
TM11	Sunny Day	Fire	Status	—	—	5	Both Sides
TM15	Hyper Beam	Normal	Special	150	90	5	Normal
TM17	Protect	Normal	Status	—	—	10	Self
TM18	Rain Dance	Water	Status	—	—	5	Both Sides
TM21	Frustration	Normal	Physical	—	100	20	Normal
TM22	Solar Beam	Grass	Special	120	100	10	Normal
TM27	Return	Normal	Physical	—	100	20	Normal
TM30	Shadow Ball	Ghost	Special	80	100	15	Normal
TM32	Double Team	Normal	Status	—	—	15	Self
TM36	Sludge Bomb	Poison	Special	90	100	10	Normal
TM42	Facade	Normal	Physical	70	100	20	Normal
TM44	Rest	Psychic	Status	—	—	10	Self
TM45	Attract	Normal	Status	—	100	15	Normal
TM48	Round	Normal	Special	60	100	15	Normal
TM53	Energy Ball	Grass	Special	90	100	10	Normal
TM68	Giga Impact	Normal	Physical	150	90	5	Normal
TM70	Flash	Normal	Status	—	100	20	Normal
TM75	Swords Dance	Normal	Status	—	—	20	Self
TM77	Psych Up	Normal	Status	—	—	10	Normal
TM84	Poison Jab	Poison	Physical	80	100	20	Normal
TM86	Grass Knot	Grass	Special	—	100	20	Normal
TM87	Swagger	Normal	Status	—	90	15	Normal
TM88	Sleep Talk	Normal	Status	—	—	10	Self
TM90	Substitute	Normal	Status	—	—	10	Self
TM96	Nature Power	Normal	Status	—	—	20	Normal
TM99	Dazzling Gleam	Fairy	Special	80	100	10	Many Others
TM100	Confide	Normal	Status	—	—	20	Normal
HM01	Cut	Normal	Physical	50	95	30	Normal

No.	Name	Type	Kind	Pow.	Acc.	PP	Range

● MOVES TAUGHT BY PEOPLE

Name	Type	Kind	Pow.	Acc.	PP	Range

AFTER THE HALL OF FAME

CENTRAL KALOS

073

Roserade

COASTAL KALOS

MOUNTAIN KALOS

ADVENTURE DATA

AFTER THE HALL OF FAME

CENTRAL KALOS

074 | Ledyba

COASTAL KALOS

MOUNTAIN KALOS

ADVENTURE DATA

🔺 Central Kalos — 074
Five Star Pokémon
✓ Ledyba

HEIGHT: 3'03" WEIGHT: 23.8 lbs.
GENDER: ♂ / ♀

TYPE	Bug	Flying

ABILITIES
Swarm
Early Bird

HIDDEN ABILITY
Rattled

STAT GROWTH RATES

HP	▪▪
Attack	▪
Defense	▪▪
Sp. Atk	▪▪
Sp. Def	▪▪
Speed	▪▪▪

EGG GROUP
Bug

X When the weather turns cold, lots of Ledyba gather from everywhere to cluster and keep each other warm.

Y It is timid and clusters together with others. The fluid secreted by its feet indicates its location.

EVOLUTION

Ledyba → Ledian (Lv. 18)

ITEMS SOMETIMES HELD BY WILD POKÉMON
None

Damage taken in normal battles		Damage taken in Inverse Battles		Can be used in
Normal	×1	Normal	×1	Inverse Battle
Fire	×2	Fire	×0.5	Sky Battle
Water	×1	Water	×1	Battle Chateau
Grass	×0.25	Grass	×4	Battle Institute
Electric	×2	Electric	×0.5	Battle Maison
Ice	×2	Ice	×0.5	Random Matchup
Fighting	×0.25	Fighting	×4	
Poison	×1	Poison	×1	
Ground	×0	Ground	×4	
Flying	×1	Flying	×0.5	
Psychic	×1	Psychic	×1	
Bug	×0.5	Bug	×2	
Rock	×4	Rock	×0.25	
Ghost	×1	Ghost	×1	
Dragon	×1	Dragon	×1	
Dark	×1	Dark	×1	
Steel	×1	Steel	×1	
Fairy	×1	Fairy	×1	

How to obtain for your Central Kalos Pokédex

❶ Catch in the yellow flowers on Route 4.
❷ Catch in the red flowers on Route 4.

❶ Catch in the yellow flowers on Route 4.
❷ Catch in the red flowers on Route 4.

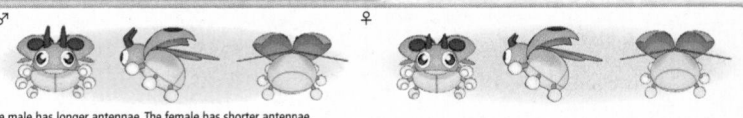

The male has longer antennae. The female has shorter antennae.

● LEVEL-UP MOVES

Lv.	Name	Type	Kind	Pow.	Acc.	PP	Range
1	Tackle	Normal	Physical	50	100	35	Normal
6	Supersonic	Normal	Status	—	55	20	Normal
9	Comet Punch	Normal	Physical	18	85	15	Normal
14	Light Screen	Psychic	Status	—	—	30	Your Side
14	Reflect	Psychic	Status	—	—	20	Your Side
14	Safeguard	Normal	Status	—	—	25	Your Side
17	Mach Punch	Fighting	Physical	40	100	30	Normal
22	Baton Pass	Normal	Status	—	—	40	Self
25	Silver Wind	Bug	Special	60	100	5	Normal
30	Agility	Psychic	Status	—	—	30	Self
33	Swift	Normal	Special	60	—	20	Many Others
38	Double-Edge	Normal	Physical	120	100	15	Normal
41	Bug Buzz	Bug	Special	90	100	10	Normal

● TM & HM MOVES

No.	Name	Type	Kind	Pow.	Acc.	PP	Range
TM06	Toxic	Poison	Status	—	90	10	Normal
TM10	Hidden Power	Normal	Special	60	100	15	Normal
TM11	Sunny Day	Fire	Status	—	—	5	Both Sides
TM16	Light Screen	Psychic	Status	—	—	30	Your Side
TM17	Protect	Normal	Status	—	—	10	Self
TM19	Roost	Flying	Status	—	—	10	Self
TM20	Safeguard	Normal	Status	—	—	25	Your Side
TM21	Frustration	Normal	Physical	—	100	20	Normal
TM22	Solar Beam	Grass	Special	120	100	10	Normal
TM27	Return	Normal	Physical	—	100	20	Normal
TM28	Dig	Ground	Physical	80	100	10	Normal
TM31	Brick Break	Fighting	Physical	75	100	15	Normal
TM32	Double Team	Normal	Status	—	—	15	Self
TM33	Reflect	Psychic	Status	—	—	20	Your Side
TM40	Aerial Ace	Flying	Physical	60	—	20	Normal
TM42	Facade	Normal	Physical	70	100	20	Normal
TM44	Rest	Psychic	Status	—	—	10	Self
TM45	Attract	Normal	Status	—	100	15	Normal
TM46	Thief	Dark	Physical	60	100	25	Normal
TM48	Round	Normal	Special	60	100	15	Normal
TM56	Fling	Dark	Physical	—	100	10	Normal
TM62	Acrobatics	Flying	Physical	55	100	15	Normal
TM70	Flash	Normal	Status	—	100	20	Normal
TM75	Swords Dance	Normal	Status	—	—	20	Self
TM76	Struggle Bug	Bug	Special	50	100	20	Many Others
TM83	Infestation	Bug	Special	20	100	20	Normal
TM87	Swagger	Normal	Status	—	90	15	Normal
TM88	Sleep Talk	Normal	Status	—	—	10	Self
TM89	U-turn	Bug	Physical	70	100	20	Normal
TM90	Substitute	Normal	Status	—	—	10	Self
TM98	Power-Up Punch	Fighting	Physical	40	100	20	Normal
TM100	Confide	Normal	Status	—	—	20	Normal

No.	Name	Type	Kind	Pow.	Acc.	PP	Range

● MOVES TAUGHT BY PEOPLE

Name	Type	Kind	Pow.	Acc.	PP	Range

● EGG MOVES

Name	Type	Kind	Pow.	Acc.	PP	Range
Psybeam	Psychic	Special	65	100	20	Normal
Bide	Normal	Physical	—	—	10	Self
Silver Wind	Bug	Special	60	100	5	Normal
Bug Buzz	Bug	Special	90	100	10	Normal
Screech	Normal	Status	—	85	40	Normal
Encore	Normal	Status	—	100	5	Normal
Knock Off	Dark	Physical	65	100	20	Normal
Bug Bite	Bug	Physical	60	100	20	Normal
Focus Punch	Fighting	Physical	150	100	20	Normal
Drain Punch	Fighting	Physical	75	100	10	Normal
Dizzy Punch	Normal	Physical	70	100	10	Normal
Tailwind	Flying	Status	—	—	15	Your Side

AFTER THE HALL OF FAME

CENTRAL KALOS
075

Ledian

COASTAL KALOS

MOUNTAIN KALOS

ADVENTURE DATA

🔺 Central Kalos 075
Five Star Pokémon
☑ Ledian

HEIGHT: 4'07"   WEIGHT: 78.5 lbs.
GENDER: ♂/♀

X When the stars flicker in the night sky, it flutters about, scattering a glowing powder.

Y The spot patterns on its back grow larger or smaller depending on the number of stars in the night sky.

TYPE: Bug / Flying

ABILITIES
Swarm
Early Bird

HIDDEN ABILITY
Rattled

STAT GROWTH RATES
HP	▪▪
Attack	▪▪
Defense	▪▪
Sp. Atk	▪▪▪
Sp. Def	▪▪▪▪▪
Speed	▪▪▪▪▪

EGG GROUP
Bug

● EVOLUTION

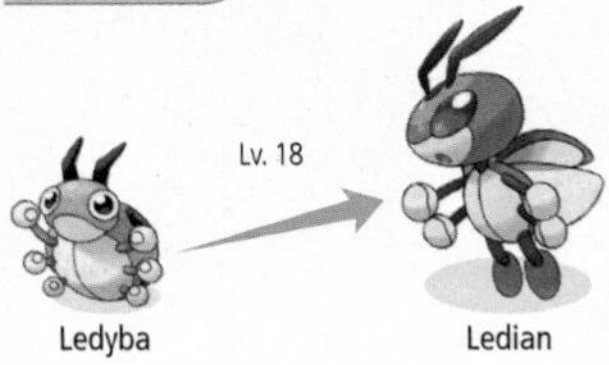

Ledyba → (Lv. 18) → Ledian

ITEMS SOMETIMES HELD BY WILD POKÉMON
None

Can be used in
Inverse Battle
Sky Battle
Battle Chateau
Battle Institute
Battle Maison
Random Matchup

Damage taken in normal battles		Damage taken in Inverse Battles	
Normal	×1	Normal	×1
Fire	×2	Fire	×0.5
Water	×1	Water	×1
Grass	×0.25	Grass	×4
Electric	×2	Electric	×0.5
Ice	×2	Ice	×0.5
Fighting	×0.25	Fighting	×4
Poison	×1	Poison	×1
Ground	×0	Ground	×4
Flying	×2	Flying	×0.5
Psychic	×1	Psychic	×1
Bug	×0.5	Bug	×2
Rock	×4	Rock	×0.25
Ghost	×1	Ghost	×1
Dragon	×1	Dragon	×1
Dark	×1	Dark	×1
Steel	×1	Steel	×1
Fairy	×1	Fairy	×1

How to obtain for your Central Kalos Pokédex

Level up Ledyba to Lv. 18.	Level up Ledyba to Lv. 18.
X	Y

♂   ♀

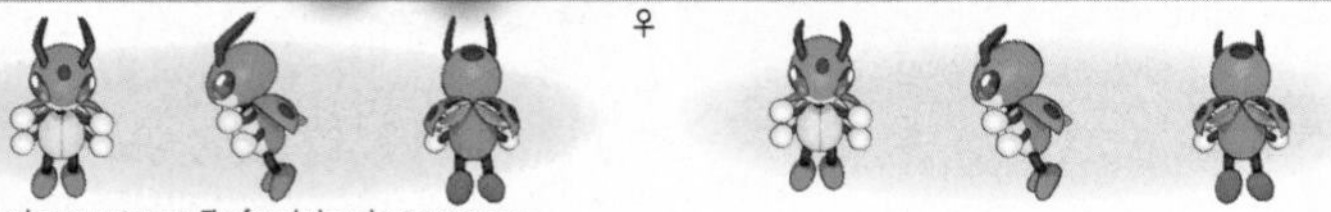

The male has longer antennae. The female has shorter antennae.

● LEVEL-UP MOVES

Lv.	Name	Type	Kind	Pow.	Acc.	PP	Range
1	Tackle	Normal	Physical	50	100	35	Normal
1	Supersonic	Normal	Status	—	55	20	Normal
1	Comet Punch	Normal	Physical	18	85	15	Normal
6	Supersonic	Normal	Status	—	55	20	Normal
9	Comet Punch	Normal	Physical	18	85	15	Normal
14	Light Screen	Psychic	Status	—	—	30	Your Side
14	Reflect	Psychic	Status	—	—	20	Your Side
14	Safeguard	Normal	Status	—	—	25	Your Side
17	Mach Punch	Fighting	Physical	40	100	30	Normal
24	Baton Pass	Normal	Status	—	—	40	Self
29	Silver Wind	Bug	Special	60	100	5	Normal
36	Agility	Psychic	Status	—	—	30	Self
41	Swift	Normal	Special	60	—	20	Many Others
48	Double-Edge	Normal	Physical	120	100	15	Normal
53	Bug Buzz	Bug	Special	90	100	10	Normal

● TM & HM MOVES

No.	Name	Type	Kind	Pow.	Acc.	PP	Range
TM06	Toxic	Poison	Status	—	90	10	Normal
TM10	Hidden Power	Normal	Special	60	100	15	Normal
TM11	Sunny Day	Fire	Status	—	—	5	Both Sides
TM15	Hyper Beam	Normal	Special	150	90	5	Normal
TM16	Light Screen	Psychic	Status	—	—	30	Your Side
TM17	Protect	Normal	Status	—	—	10	Self
TM19	Roost	Flying	Status	—	—	10	Self
TM20	Safeguard	Normal	Status	—	—	25	Your Side
TM21	Frustration	Normal	Physical	—	100	20	Normal
TM22	Solar Beam	Grass	Special	120	100	10	Normal
TM27	Return	Normal	Physical	—	100	20	Normal
TM28	Dig	Ground	Physical	80	100	10	Normal
TM31	Brick Break	Fighting	Physical	75	100	15	Normal
TM32	Double Team	Normal	Status	—	—	15	Self
TM33	Reflect	Psychic	Status	—	—	20	Your Side
TM40	Aerial Ace	Flying	Physical	60	—	20	Normal
TM42	Facade	Normal	Physical	70	100	20	Normal
TM44	Rest	Psychic	Status	—	—	10	Self
TM45	Attract	Normal	Status	—	100	15	Normal
TM46	Thief	Dark	Physical	60	100	25	Normal
TM48	Round	Normal	Special	60	100	15	Normal
TM52	Focus Blast	Fighting	Special	120	70	5	Normal
TM56	Fling	Dark	Physical	—	100	10	Normal
TM62	Acrobatics	Flying	Physical	55	100	15	Normal
TM68	Giga Impact	Normal	Physical	150	90	5	Normal
TM70	Flash	Normal	Status	—	100	20	Normal
TM75	Swords Dance	Normal	Status	—	—	20	Self
TM76	Struggle Bug	Bug	Special	50	100	20	Many Others
TM83	Infestation	Bug	Special	20	100	20	Normal
TM87	Swagger	Normal	Status	—	90	15	Normal
TM88	Sleep Talk	Normal	Status	—	—	10	Self
TM89	U-turn	Bug	Physical	70	100	20	Normal
TM90	Substitute	Normal	Status	—	—	10	Self

No.	Name	Type	Kind	Pow.	Acc.	PP	Range
TM94	Rock Smash	Fighting	Physical	40	100	15	Normal
TM98	Power-Up Punch	Fighting	Physical	40	100	20	Normal
TM100	Confide	Normal	Status	—	—	20	Normal
HM04	Strength	Normal	Physical	80	100	15	Normal

● MOVES TAUGHT BY PEOPLE

Name	Type	Kind	Pow.	Acc.	PP	Range

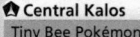 **Central Kalos**

Tiny Bee Pokémon

▽ Combee

076

HEIGHT: 1'00" WEIGHT: 12.1 lbs.
GENDER: ♂/♀

X The trio is together from birth. It constantly gathers honey from flowers to please Vespiquen.

V It collects and delivers honey to its colony. At night, they cluster to form a beehive and sleep.

TYPE **Bug** **Flying**

ABILITY
Honey Gather

HIDDEN ABILITY
Hustle

STAT GROWTH RATES
HP	■ ■
Attack	■ ■
Defense	■ ■
Sp. Atk	■
Sp. Def	■ ■
Speed	■ ■ ■ ■

EGG GROUP
Bug

EVOLUTION

Level up Combee ♀ to Lv. 21

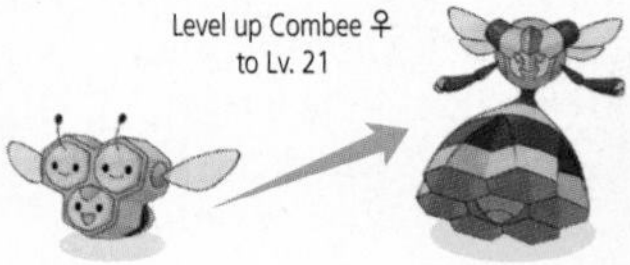

Combee → Vespiquen

ITEMS SOMETIMES HELD BY WILD POKÉMON
Honey

Damage taken in normal battles		Damage taken in Inverse Battles		Can be used in
Normal	×1	Normal	×1	Inverse Battle
Fire	×2	Fire	×0.5	Sky Battle
Water	×1	Water	×1	Battle Chateau
Grass	×0.25	Grass	×4	Battle Institute
Electric	×2	Electric	×0.5	Battle Maison
Ice	×2	Ice	×0.5	Random Matchup
Fighting	×0.25	Fighting	×4	
Poison	×1	Poison	×1	
Ground	×0	Ground	×4	
Flying	×2	Flying	×0.5	
Psychic	×1	Psychic	×1	
Bug	×0.5	Bug	×2	
Rock	×4	Rock	×0.25	
Ghost	×1	Ghost	×1	
Dragon	×1	Dragon	×1	
Dark	×1	Dark	×1	
Steel	×1	Steel	×1	
Fairy	×1	Fairy	×1	

How to obtain for your Central Kalos Pokédex

❶ Catch in the yellow flowers on Route 4.
❷ Catch in the red flowers on Route 4.

❶ Catch in the yellow flowers on Route 4.
❷ Catch in the red flowers on Route 4.

♂　　　　　　♀

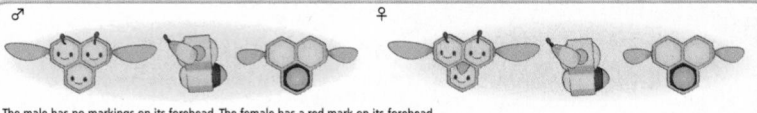

The male has no markings on its forehead. The female has a red mark on its forehead.

● **LEVEL-UP MOVES**

Lv.	Name	Type	Kind	Pow.	Acc.	PP	Range
1	Sweet Scent	Normal	Status	—	100	20	Many Others
1	Gust	Flying	Special	40	100	35	Normal
13	Bug Bite	Bug	Physical	60	100	20	Normal
29	Bug Buzz	Bug	Special	90	100	10	Normal

● **TM & HM MOVES**

No.	Name	Type	Kind	Pow.	Acc.	PP	Range

No.	Name	Type	Kind	Pow.	Acc.	PP	Range

● **MOVES TAUGHT BY PEOPLE**

Name	Type	Kind	Pow.	Acc.	PP	Range

● **EGG MOVES**

Name	Type	Kind	Pow.	Acc.	PP	Range

AFTER THE HALL OF FAME

CENTRAL KALOS

077

Vespiquen

COASTAL KALOS

MOUNTAIN KALOS

ADVENTURE DATA

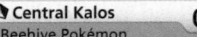

Central Kalos — 077

Beehive Pokémon

☑ Vespiquen

HEIGHT: 3'11" WEIGHT: 84.9 lbs.
GENDER: ♀

TYPE Bug | Flying

ABILITY
Pressure

HIDDEN ABILITY
Unnerve

STAT GROWTH RATES

HP	▪▪▪
Attack	▪▪▪▪
Defense	▪▪▪▪
Sp. Atk	▪▪▪▪
Sp. Def	▪▪▪▪
Speed	▪▪

EGG GROUP
Bug

X — It houses its colony in cells in its body and releases various pheromones to make those grubs do its bidding.

Y — Its abdomen is a honeycomb for grubs. It raises its grubs on honey collected by Combee.

⬆ EVOLUTION

Level up Combee ♀ to Lv. 21

Combee → Vespiquen

ITEMS SOMETIMES HELD BY WILD POKÉMON
None

Can be used in
- Inverse Battle
- Sky Battle
- Battle Chateau
- Battle Institute
- Battle Maison
- Random Matchup

Damage taken in normal battles	
Normal	×1
Fire	×2
Water	×1
Grass	×0.25
Electric	×2
Ice	×2
Fighting	×0.25
Poison	×1
Ground	×0
Flying	×2
Psychic	×1
Bug	×0.5
Rock	×4
Ghost	×1
Dragon	×1
Dark	×1
Steel	×1
Fairy	×1

Damage taken in Inverse Battles	
Normal	×1
Fire	×0.5
Water	×1
Grass	×4
Electric	×0.5
Ice	×0.5
Fighting	×4
Poison	×1
Ground	×4
Flying	×0.5
Psychic	×1
Bug	×2
Rock	×0.25
Ghost	×1
Dragon	×1
Dark	×1
Steel	×1
Fairy	×1

How to obtain for your Central Kalos Pokédex

Level up Combee ♀ to Lv. 21.
X

Level up Combee ♀ to Lv. 21.
Y

♀

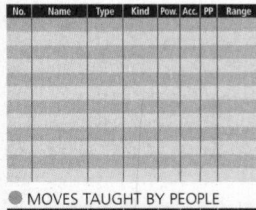

● LEVEL-UP MOVES

Lv.	Name	Type	Kind	Pow.	Acc.	PP	Range
1	Fell Stinger	Bug	Physical	30	100	25	Normal
1	Destiny Bond	Ghost	Status	—	—	5	Self
1	Sweet Scent	Normal	Status	—	100	20	Many Others
1	Gust	Flying	Special	40	100	35	Normal
1	Poison Sting	Poison	Physical	15	100	35	Normal
1	Confuse Ray	Ghost	Status	—	100	10	Normal
9	Pursuit	Dark	Physical	40	100	20	Normal
13	Fury Swipes	Normal	Physical	18	80	15	Normal
17	Defend Order	Bug	Status	—	—	10	Self
21	Slash	Normal	Physical	70	100	20	Normal
25	Power Gem	Rock	Special	80	100	20	Normal
29	Heal Order	Bug	Status	—	—	10	Self
33	Toxic	Poison	Status	—	90	10	Normal
37	Air Slash	Flying	Special	75	95	15	Normal
41	Captivate	Normal	Status	—	100	20	Many Others
45	Attack Order	Bug	Physical	90	100	15	Normal
49	Swagger	Normal	Status	—	90	15	Normal
53	Destiny Bond	Ghost	Status	—	—	5	Self
57	Fell Stinger	Bug	Physical	30	100	25	Normal

● TM & HM MOVES

No.	Name	Type	Kind	Pow.	Acc.	PP	Range
TM01	Hone Claws	Dark	Status	—	—	15	Self
TM06	Toxic	Poison	Status	—	90	10	Normal
TM09	Venoshock	Poison	Special	65	100	10	Normal
TM10	Hidden Power	Normal	Special	60	100	15	Normal
TM11	Sunny Day	Fire	Status	—	—	5	Both Sides
TM15	Hyper Beam	Normal	Special	150	90	5	Normal
TM17	Protect	Normal	Status	—	—	10	Self
TM18	Rain Dance	Water	Status	—	—	5	Both Sides
TM19	Roost	Flying	Status	—	—	10	Self
TM21	Frustration	Normal	Physical	—	100	20	Normal
TM27	Return	Normal	Physical	—	100	20	Normal
TM32	Double Team	Normal	Status	—	—	15	Self
TM36	Sludge Bomb	Poison	Special	90	100	10	Normal
TM40	Aerial Ace	Flying	Physical	60	—	20	Normal
TM42	Facade	Normal	Physical	70	100	20	Normal
TM44	Rest	Psychic	Status	—	—	10	Self
TM45	Attract	Normal	Status	—	100	15	Normal
TM46	Thief	Dark	Physical	60	100	25	Normal
TM48	Round	Normal	Special	60	100	15	Normal
TM56	Fling	Dark	Physical	—	100	10	Normal
TM60	Quash	Dark	Status	—	100	15	Normal
TM62	Acrobatics	Flying	Physical	55	100	15	Normal
TM68	Giga Impact	Normal	Physical	150	90	5	Normal
TM70	Flash	Normal	Status	—	100	20	Normal
TM76	Struggle Bug	Bug	Special	50	100	20	Many Others
TM81	X-Scissor	Bug	Physical	80	100	15	Normal
TM83	Infestation	Bug	Special	20	100	20	Normal
TM87	Swagger	Normal	Status	—	90	15	Normal
TM88	Sleep Talk	Normal	Status	—	—	10	Self
TM89	U-turn	Bug	Physical	70	100	20	Normal
TM90	Substitute	Normal	Status	—	—	10	Self
TM100	Confide	Normal	Status	—	—	20	Normal
HM01	Cut	Normal	Physical	50	95	30	Normal

No.	Name	Type	Kind	Pow.	Acc.	PP	Range

● MOVES TAUGHT BY PEOPLE

Name	Type	Kind	Pow.	Acc.	PP	Range

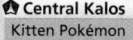 **Central Kalos**
Kitten Pokémon
078

☑ **Skitty**

HEIGHT: 2'00" WEIGHT: 24.3 lbs.
GENDER: ♂/♀

X It can't stop itself from chasing moving things, and it runs in a circle, chasing its own tail.

Y It shows its cute side by chasing its own tail until it gets dizzy.

TYPE Normal

ABILITIES
Cute Charm
Normalize

HIDDEN ABILITY
Wonder Skin

STAT GROWTH RATES
HP
Attack
Defense
Sp. Atk
Sp. Def
Speed

EGG GROUPS
Field, Fairy

EVOLUTION

Moon Stone

Skitty → Delcatty

ITEMS SOMETIMES HELD BY WILD POKÉMON
None

Damage taken in normal battles		Damage taken in Inverse Battles	
Normal	×1	Normal	×1
Fire	×1	Fire	×1
Water	×1	Water	×1
Grass	×1	Grass	×1
Electric	×1	Electric	×1
Ice	×1	Ice	×1
Fighting	×2	Fighting	×0.5
Poison	×1	Poison	×1
Ground	×1	Ground	×1
Flying	×1	Flying	×1
Psychic	×1	Psychic	×1
Bug	×1	Bug	×1
Rock	×1	Rock	×1
Ghost	×0	Ghost	×2
Dragon	×1	Dragon	×1
Dark	×1	Dark	×1
Steel	×1	Steel	×1
Fairy	×1	Fairy	×1

Can be used in	
Inverse Battle	Battle Institute
—	Battle Maison
Battle Chateau	Random Matchup

Same form for ♂ / ♀

How to obtain for your Central Kalos Pokédex

❶ Catch in the yellow flowers on Route 4.

❷ Catch in the red flowers on Route 4.

❶ Catch in the yellow flowers on Route 4.

❷ Catch in the red flowers on Route 4.

● **LEVEL-UP MOVES**

Lv.	Name	Type	Kind	Pow.	Acc.	PP	Range
1	Fake Out	Normal	Physical	40	100	10	Normal
1	Growl	Normal	Status	—	100	40	Many Others
1	Tail Whip	Normal	Status	—	100	30	Many Others
1	Tackle	Normal	Physical	50	100	35	Normal
4	Foresight	Normal	Status	—	—	40	Normal
8	Attract	Normal	Status	—	100	15	Normal
11	Sing	Normal	Status	—	55	15	Normal
15	Double Slap	Normal	Physical	15	85	10	Normal
18	Copycat	Normal	Status	—	—	20	Self
22	Assist	Normal	Status	—	—	20	Self
25	Charm	Fairy	Status	—	100	20	Normal
29	Feint Attack	Dark	Physical	60	—	20	Normal
32	Wake-Up Slap	Fighting	Physical	70	100	10	Normal
36	Covet	Normal	Physical	60	100	25	Normal
39	Heal Bell	Normal	Status	—	—	5	Your Party
42	Double-Edge	Normal	Physical	120	100	15	Normal
46	Captivate	Normal	Status	—	100	20	Many Others
49	Play Rough	Fairy	Physical	90	90	10	Normal

● **TM & HM MOVES**

No.	Name	Type	Kind	Pow.	Acc.	PP	Range
TM04	Calm Mind	Psychic	Status	—	—	20	Self
TM06	Toxic	Poison	Status	—	90	10	Normal
TM10	Hidden Power	Normal	Special	60	100	15	Normal
TM11	Sunny Day	Fire	Status	—	—	5	Both Sides
TM13	Ice Beam	Ice	Special	90	100	10	Normal
TM14	Blizzard	Ice	Special	110	70	5	Many Others
TM17	Protect	Normal	Status	—	—	10	Self
TM18	Rain Dance	Water	Status	—	—	5	Both Sides
TM20	Safeguard	Normal	Status	—	—	25	Your Side
TM21	Frustration	Normal	Physical	—	100	20	Normal
TM22	Solar Beam	Grass	Special	120	100	10	Normal
TM24	Thunderbolt	Electric	Special	90	100	15	Normal
TM25	Thunder	Electric	Special	110	70	10	Normal
TM27	Return	Normal	Physical	—	100	20	Normal
TM28	Dig	Ground	Physical	80	100	10	Normal
TM30	Shadow Ball	Ghost	Special	80	100	15	Normal
TM32	Double Team	Normal	Status	—	—	15	Self
TM42	Facade	Normal	Physical	70	100	20	Normal
TM44	Rest	Psychic	Status	—	—	10	Self
TM45	Attract	Normal	Status	—	100	15	Normal
TM48	Round	Normal	Special	60	100	15	Normal
TM49	Echoed Voice	Normal	Special	40	100	15	Normal
TM57	Charge Beam	Electric	Special	50	90	10	Normal
TM66	Payback	Dark	Physical	50	100	10	Normal
TM67	Retaliate	Normal	Physical	70	100	5	Normal
TM70	Flash	Normal	Status	—	100	20	Normal
TM73	Thunder Wave	Electric	Status	—	100	20	Normal
TM77	Psych Up	Normal	Status	—	—	10	Normal
TM85	Dream Eater	Psychic	Special	100	100	15	Normal
TM86	Grass Knot	Grass	Special	—	100	20	Normal
TM87	Swagger	Normal	Status	—	90	15	Normal
TM88	Sleep Talk	Normal	Status	—	—	10	Self
TM90	Substitute	Normal	Status	—	—	10	Self

No.	Name	Type	Kind	Pow.	Acc.	PP	Range
TM93	Wild Charge	Electric	Physical	90	100	15	Normal
TM100	Confide	Normal	Status	—	—	20	Normal

● **MOVES TAUGHT BY PEOPLE**

Name	Type	Kind	Pow.	Acc.	PP	Range

● **EGG MOVES**

Name	Type	Kind	Pow.	Acc.	PP	Range
Helping Hand	Normal	Status	—	—	20	1 Ally
Uproar	Normal	Special	90	100	10	1 Random
Fake Tears	Dark	Status	—	100	20	Normal
Wish	Normal	Status	—	—	10	Self
Baton Pass	Normal	Status	—	—	40	Self
Tickle	Normal	Status	—	100	20	Normal
Last Resort	Normal	Physical	140	100	5	Normal
Fake Out	Normal	Physical	40	100	10	Normal
Zen Headbutt	Psychic	Physical	80	90	15	Normal
Sucker Punch	Dark	Physical	80	100	5	Normal
Mud Bomb	Ground	Special	65	85	10	Normal
Simple Beam	Normal	Status	—	100	15	Normal
Captivate	Normal	Status	—	100	20	Many Others
Cosmic Power	Psychic	Status	—	—	20	Self

AFTER THE HALL OF FAME

CENTRAL KALOS
079

Delcatty

COASTAL KALOS

MOUNTAIN KALOS

ADVENTURE DATA

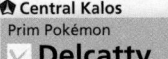 Central Kalos **079**
Prim Pokémon
Delcatty

HEIGHT: 3'07" WEIGHT: 71.9 lbs.
GENDER: ♂/♀

X It dislikes dirty places. It often searches for a comfortable place in which to groom itself.

Y It is highly popular among female Trainers for its sublime fur. It does not keep a nest.

TYPE Normal

ABILITIES
Cute Charm
Normalize

HIDDEN ABILITY
Wonder Skin

STAT GROWTH RATES
HP	■■■
Attack	■■■
Defense	■■■
Sp. Atk	■■■
Sp. Def	■■
Speed	■■■■

EGG GROUPS
Field, Fairy

EVOLUTION

Moon Stone

Skitty   Delcatty

ITEMS SOMETIMES HELD BY WILD POKÉMON
None

Can be used in
Inverse Battle
—
Battle Chateau
Battle Institute
Battle Maison
Random Matchup

Damage taken in normal battles		Damage taken in Inverse Battles	
Normal	×1	Normal	×1
Fire	×1	Fire	×1
Water	×1	Water	×1
Grass	×1	Grass	×1
Electric	×1	Electric	×1
Ice	×1	Ice	×1
Fighting	×2	Fighting	×0.5
Poison	×1	Poison	×1
Ground	×1	Ground	×1
Flying	×1	Flying	×1
Psychic	×1	Psychic	×1
Bug	×1	Bug	×1
Rock	×1	Rock	×1
Ghost	×0	Ghost	×2
Dragon	×1	Dragon	×1
Dark	×1	Dark	×1
Steel	×1	Steel	×1
Fairy	×1	Fairy	×1

How to obtain for your Central Kalos Pokédex

Use a Moon Stone on Skitty.	Use a Moon Stone on Skitty.

Same form for ♂/♀

● LEVEL-UP MOVES

Lv.	Name	Type	Kind	Pow.	Acc.	PP	Range
1	Fake Out	Normal	Physical	40	100	10	Normal
1	Attract	Normal	Status	—	100	15	Normal
1	Sing	Normal	Status	—	55	15	Normal
1	Double Slap	Normal	Physical	15	85	10	Normal

● TM & HM MOVES

No.	Name	Type	Kind	Pow.	Acc.	PP	Range
TM04	Calm Mind	Psychic	Status	—	—	20	Self
TM06	Toxic	Poison	Status	—	90	10	Normal
TM10	Hidden Power	Normal	Special	60	100	15	Normal
TM11	Sunny Day	Fire	Status	—	—	5	Both Sides
TM13	Ice Beam	Ice	Special	90	100	10	Normal
TM14	Blizzard	Ice	Special	110	70	5	Many Others
TM15	Hyper Beam	Normal	Special	150	90	5	Normal
TM17	Protect	Normal	Status	—	—	10	Self
TM18	Rain Dance	Water	Status	—	—	5	Both Sides
TM20	Safeguard	Normal	Status	—	—	25	Your Side
TM21	Frustration	Normal	Physical	—	100	20	Normal
TM22	Solar Beam	Grass	Special	120	100	10	Normal
TM24	Thunderbolt	Electric	Special	90	100	15	Normal
TM25	Thunder	Electric	Special	110	70	10	Normal
TM27	Return	Normal	Physical	—	100	20	Normal
TM28	Dig	Ground	Physical	80	100	10	Normal
TM30	Shadow Ball	Ghost	Special	80	100	15	Normal
TM32	Double Team	Normal	Status	—	—	15	Self
TM42	Facade	Normal	Physical	70	100	20	Normal
TM44	Rest	Psychic	Status	—	—	10	Self
TM45	Attract	Normal	Status	—	100	15	Normal
TM48	Round	Normal	Special	60	100	15	Normal
TM49	Echoed Voice	Normal	Special	40	100	15	Normal
TM57	Charge Beam	Electric	Special	50	90	10	Normal
TM66	Payback	Dark	Physical	50	100	10	Normal
TM67	Retaliate	Normal	Physical	70	100	5	Normal
TM68	Giga Impact	Normal	Physical	150	90	5	Normal
TM70	Flash	Normal	Status	—	100	20	Normal
TM73	Thunder Wave	Electric	Status	—	100	20	Normal
TM77	Psych Up	Normal	Status	—	—	10	Normal
TM85	Dream Eater	Psychic	Special	100	100	15	Normal
TM86	Grass Knot	Grass	Special	—	100	20	Normal
TM87	Swagger	Normal	Status	—	90	15	Normal
TM88	Sleep Talk	Normal	Status	—	—	10	Self
TM90	Substitute	Normal	Status	—	—	10	Self
TM93	Wild Charge	Electric	Physical	90	100	15	Normal
TM94	Rock Smash	Fighting	Physical	40	100	15	Normal
TM100	Confide	Normal	Status	—	—	20	Normal
HM04	Strength	Normal	Physical	80	100	15	Normal

● MOVES TAUGHT BY PEOPLE

Name	Type	Kind	Pow.	Acc.	PP	Range

AFTER THE HALL OF FAME

CENTRAL KALOS

080 | Bulbasaur

COASTAL KALOS

MOUNTAIN KALOS

ADVENTURE DATA

Central Kalos
Seed Pokémon

080

☑ Bulbasaur

HEIGHT: 2'04" WEIGHT: 15.2 lbs.
GENDER: ♂/♀

TYPE Grass Poison

ABILITY
Overgrow

HIDDEN ABILITY
Chlorophyll

STAT GROWTH RATES
HP	■■
Attack	■■■
Defense	■■
Sp. Atk	■■■
Sp. Def	■■■
Speed	■■■

EGG GROUPS
Monster, Grass

X A strange seed was planted on its back at birth. The plant sprouts and grows with this Pokémon.

Y For some time after its birth, it grows by gaining nourishment from the seed on its back.

EVOLUTION

Lv. 16   Lv. 32

Bulbasaur   Ivysaur   Venusaur

ITEMS SOMETIMES HELD BY WILD POKÉMON
None

Damage taken in normal battles		Damage taken in Inverse Battles	
Normal	×1	Normal	×1
Fire	×2	Fire	×0.5
Water	×0.5	Water	×2
Grass	×0.25	Grass	×4
Electric	×1	Electric	×2
Ice	×2	Ice	×0.5
Fighting	×0.5	Fighting	×2
Poison	×1	Poison	×1
Ground	×1	Ground	×1
Flying	×2	Flying	×0.5
Psychic	×2	Psychic	×0.5
Bug	×1	Bug	×1
Rock	×1	Rock	×1
Ghost	×1	Ghost	×1
Dragon	×1	Dragon	×1
Dark	×1	Dark	×1
Steel	×1	Steel	×1
Fairy	×0.5	Fairy	×2

Can be used in	
Inverse Battle	Battle Institute
—	Battle Maison
Battle Chateau	Random Matchup

Same form for ♂/♀

How to obtain for your Central Kalos Pokédex

❶ Receive from Professor Sycamore in Lumiose City.
❷ Link Trade or transfer from another game.

❶ Receive from Professor Sycamore in Lumiose City.
❷ Link Trade or transfer from another game.

● LEVEL-UP MOVES

Lv.	Name	Type	Kind	Pow.	Acc.	PP	Range
1	Tackle	Normal	Physical	50	100	35	Normal
3	Growl	Normal	Status	—	100	40	Many Others
7	Leech Seed	Grass	Status	—	90	10	Normal
9	Vine Whip	Grass	Physical	45	100	25	Normal
13	Poison Powder	Poison	Status	—	75	35	Normal
13	Sleep Powder	Grass	Status	—	75	15	Normal
15	Take Down	Normal	Physical	90	85	20	Normal
19	Razor Leaf	Grass	Physical	55	95	25	Many Others
21	Sweet Scent	Normal	Status	—	100	20	Many Others
25	Growth	Normal	Status	—	—	20	Self
27	Double-Edge	Normal	Physical	120	100	15	Normal
31	Worry Seed	Grass	Status	—	100	10	Normal
33	Synthesis	Grass	Status	—	—	5	Self
37	Seed Bomb	Grass	Physical	80	100	15	Normal

● TM & HM MOVES

No.	Name	Type	Kind	Pow.	Acc.	PP	Range
TM06	Toxic	Poison	Status	—	90	10	Normal
TM09	Venoshock	Poison	Special	65	100	10	Normal
TM10	Hidden Power	Normal	Special	60	100	15	Normal
TM11	Sunny Day	Fire	Status	—	—	5	Both Sides
TM16	Light Screen	Psychic	Status	—	—	30	Your Side
TM17	Protect	Normal	Status	—	—	10	Self
TM20	Safeguard	Normal	Status	—	—	25	Your Side
TM21	Frustration	Normal	Physical	—	100	20	Normal
TM22	Solar Beam	Grass	Special	120	100	10	Normal
TM27	Return	Normal	Physical	—	100	20	Normal
TM32	Double Team	Normal	Status	—	—	15	Self
TM36	Sludge Bomb	Poison	Special	90	100	10	Normal
TM42	Facade	Normal	Physical	70	100	20	Normal
TM44	Rest	Psychic	Status	—	—	10	Self
TM45	Attract	Normal	Status	—	100	15	Normal
TM48	Round	Normal	Special	60	100	15	Normal
TM49	Echoed Voice	Normal	Special	40	100	15	Normal
TM53	Energy Ball	Grass	Special	90	100	10	Normal
TM70	Flash	Normal	Status	—	100	20	Normal
TM75	Swords Dance	Normal	Status	—	—	20	Self
TM86	Grass Knot	Grass	Special	—	100	20	Normal
TM87	Swagger	Normal	Status	—	90	15	Normal
TM88	Sleep Talk	Normal	Status	—	—	10	Self
TM90	Substitute	Normal	Status	—	—	10	Self
TM94	Rock Smash	Fighting	Physical	40	100	15	Normal
TM96	Nature Power	Normal	Status	—	—	20	Normal
TM100	Confide	Normal	Status	—	—	20	Normal
HM01	Cut	Normal	Physical	50	95	30	Normal
HM04	Strength	Normal	Physical	80	100	15	Normal

No.	Name	Type	Kind	Pow.	Acc.	PP	Range

● MOVES TAUGHT BY PEOPLE

Name	Type	Kind	Pow.	Acc.	PP	Range
Grass Pledge	Grass	Special	80	100	10	Normal

● EGG MOVES

Name	Type	Kind	Pow.	Acc.	PP	Range
Skull Bash	Normal	Physical	130	100	10	Normal
Charm	Fairy	Status	—	100	20	Normal
Petal Dance	Grass	Special	120	100	10	1 Random
Magical Leaf	Grass	Special	60	—	20	Normal
Grass Whistle	Grass	Status	—	55	15	Normal
Curse	Ghost	Status	—	—	10	Varies
Ingrain	Grass	Status	—	—	20	Self
Nature Power	Normal	Status	—	—	20	Normal
Amnesia	Psychic	Status	—	—	20	Self
Leaf Storm	Grass	Special	130	90	5	Normal
Power Whip	Grass	Physical	120	85	10	Normal
Sludge	Poison	Special	65	100	20	Normal
Endure	Normal	Status	—	—	10	Self
Giga Drain	Grass	Special	75	100	10	Normal
Grassy Terrain	Grass	Status	—	—	10	Both Sides

Central Kalos 081
Ivysaur
Seed Pokémon

HEIGHT: 3'03" WEIGHT: 28.7 lbs.
GENDER: ♂/♀

TYPE Grass Poison

ABILITY
Overgrow

HIDDEN ABILITY
Chlorophyll

STAT GROWTH RATES
HP
Attack
Defense
Sp. Atk
Sp. Def
Speed

EGG GROUPS
Monster, Grass

X: There is a plant bulb on its back. When it absorbs nutrients, the bulb is said to blossom into a large flower.

Y: When the bud on its back starts swelling, a sweet aroma wafts to indicate the flower's coming bloom.

EVOLUTION

Lv. 16 → Lv. 32
Bulbasaur — Ivysaur — Venusaur

ITEMS SOMETIMES HELD BY WILD POKÉMON
None

	Damage taken in normal battles		Damage taken in Inverse Battles
Normal	×1	Normal	×1
Fire	×2	Fire	×0.5
Water	×0.5	Water	×2
Grass	×0.25	Grass	×4
Electric	×0.5	Electric	×2
Ice	×2	Ice	×0.5
Fighting	×0.5	Fighting	×2
Poison	×1	Poison	×1
Ground	×1	Ground	×1
Flying	×2	Flying	×0.5
Psychic	×2	Psychic	×0.5
Bug	×1	Bug	×1
Rock	×1	Rock	×1
Ghost	×1	Ghost	×1
Dragon	×1	Dragon	×1
Dark	×1	Dark	×1
Steel	×1	Steel	×1
Fairy	×0.5	Fairy	×2

Can be used in
Inverse Battle | Battle Institute
— | Battle Maison
Battle Chateau | Random Matchup

Same form for ♂/♀

How to obtain for your Central Kalos Pokédex
❶ Level up Bulbasaur to Lv. 16.
❷ Link Trade or transfer from another game.

❶ Level up Bulbasaur to Lv. 16.
❷ Link Trade or transfer from another game.

● LEVEL-UP MOVES
Lv.	Name	Type	Kind	Pow.	Acc.	PP	Range
1	Tackle	Normal	Physical	50	100	35	Normal
1	Growl	Normal	Status	—	100	40	Many Others
1	Leech Seed	Grass	Status	—	90	10	Normal
3	Growl	Normal	Status	—	100	40	Many Others
7	Leech Seed	Grass	Status	—	90	10	Normal
9	Vine Whip	Grass	Physical	45	100	25	Normal
13	Poison Powder	Poison	Status	—	75	35	Normal
13	Sleep Powder	Grass	Status	—	75	15	Normal
15	Take Down	Normal	Physical	90	85	20	Normal
20	Razor Leaf	Grass	Physical	55	95	25	Many Others
23	Sweet Scent	Normal	Status	—	100	20	Many Others
28	Growth	Normal	Status	—	—	20	Self
31	Double-Edge	Normal	Physical	120	100	15	Normal
36	Worry Seed	Grass	Status	—	100	10	Normal
39	Synthesis	Grass	Status	—	—	5	Self
44	Solar Beam	Grass	Special	120	100	10	Normal

● TM & HM MOVES
No.	Name	Type	Kind	Pow.	Acc.	PP	Range
TM06	Toxic	Poison	Status	—	90	10	Normal
TM09	Venoshock	Poison	Special	65	100	10	Normal
TM10	Hidden Power	Normal	Special	60	100	15	Normal
TM11	Sunny Day	Fire	Status	—	—	5	Both Sides
TM16	Light Screen	Psychic	Status	—	—	30	Your Side
TM17	Protect	Normal	Status	—	—	10	Self
TM20	Safeguard	Normal	Status	—	—	25	Your Side
TM21	Frustration	Normal	Physical	—	100	20	Normal
TM22	Solar Beam	Grass	Special	120	100	10	Normal
TM27	Return	Normal	Physical	—	100	20	Normal
TM32	Double Team	Normal	Status	—	—	15	Self
TM36	Sludge Bomb	Poison	Special	90	100	10	Normal
TM42	Facade	Normal	Physical	70	100	20	Normal
TM44	Rest	Psychic	Status	—	—	10	Self
TM45	Attract	Normal	Status	—	100	15	Normal
TM48	Round	Normal	Special	60	100	15	Normal
TM49	Echoed Voice	Normal	Special	40	100	15	Normal
TM53	Energy Ball	Grass	Special	90	100	10	Normal
TM70	Flash	Normal	Status	—	100	20	Normal
TM75	Swords Dance	Normal	Status	—	—	20	Self
TM86	Grass Knot	Grass	Special	—	100	20	Normal
TM87	Swagger	Normal	Status	—	90	15	Normal
TM88	Sleep Talk	Normal	Status	—	—	10	Self
TM90	Substitute	Normal	Status	—	—	10	Self
TM94	Rock Smash	Fighting	Physical	40	100	15	Normal
TM96	Nature Power	Normal	Status	—	—	20	Normal
TM100	Confide	Normal	Status	—	—	20	Normal
HM01	Cut	Normal	Physical	50	95	30	Normal
HM04	Strength	Normal	Physical	80	100	15	Normal

● MOVES TAUGHT BY PEOPLE
Name	Type	Kind	Pow.	Acc.	PP	Range
Grass Pledge	Grass	Special	80	100	10	Normal

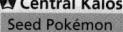

Central Kalos
Seed Pokémon
Venusaur

082

HEIGHT: 6'07" WEIGHT: 220.5 lbs.
GENDER: ♂/♀

TYPE `Grass` `Poison`

ABILITY
Overgrow

HIDDEN ABILITY
Chlorophyll

STAT GROWTH RATES

HP	▪▪▪
Attack	▪▪▪▪
Defense	▪▪▪▪
Sp. Atk	▪▪▪▪▪
Sp. Def	▪▪▪▪▪
Speed	▪▪▪▪

EGG GROUPS
Monster, Grass

X By spreading the broad petals of its flower and catching the sun's rays, it fills its body with power.

Y After a rainy day, the flower on its back smells stronger. The scent attracts other Pokémon.

EVOLUTION

Bulbasaur — Lv. 16 → Ivysaur — Lv. 32 → Venusaur

ITEMS SOMETIMES HELD BY WILD POKÉMON
None

Damage taken in normal battles		Damage taken in Inverse Battles		Can be used in
Normal	×1	Normal	×1	Inverse Battle
Fire	×2	Fire	×0.5	—
Water	×0.5	Water	×2	Battle Chateau
Grass	×0.25	Grass	×4	Battle Institute
Electric	×0.5	Electric	×2	Battle Maison
Ice	×2	Ice	×0.5	Random Matchup
Fighting	×0.5	Fighting	×2	
Poison	×1	Poison	×1	
Ground	×1	Ground	×1	
Flying	×2	Flying	×0.5	
Psychic	×2	Psychic	×0.5	
Bug	×1	Bug	×1	
Rock	×1	Rock	×1	
Ghost	×1	Ghost	×1	
Dragon	×1	Dragon	×1	
Dark	×1	Dark	×1	
Steel	×1	Steel	×1	
Fairy	×0.5	Fairy	×2	

How to obtain for your Central Kalos Pokédex

❶ Level up Ivysaur to Lv. 32.
❷ Link Trade or transfer from another game.

❶ Level up Ivysaur to Lv. 32.
❷ Link Trade or transfer from another game.

♂   ♀

The male has no pistil in its bloom. The female has a pistil in its bloom.

● LEVEL-UP MOVES

Lv.	Name	Type	Kind	Pow.	Acc.	PP	Range
1	Tackle	Normal	Physical	50	100	35	Normal
1	Growl	Normal	Status	—	100	40	Many Others
1	Leech Seed	Grass	Status	—	90	10	Normal
1	Vine Whip	Grass	Physical	45	100	25	Normal
3	Growl	Normal	Status	—	100	40	Many Others
7	Leech Seed	Grass	Status	—	90	10	Normal
9	Vine Whip	Grass	Physical	45	100	25	Normal
13	Poison Powder	Poison	Status	—	75	35	Normal
13	Sleep Powder	Grass	Status	—	75	15	Normal
15	Take Down	Normal	Physical	90	85	20	Normal
20	Razor Leaf	Grass	Physical	55	95	25	Many Others
23	Sweet Scent	Normal	Status	—	100	20	Many Others
28	Growth	Normal	Status	—	—	20	Self
31	Double-Edge	Normal	Physical	120	100	15	Normal
32	Petal Dance	Grass	Special	120	100	10	1 Random
39	Worry Seed	Grass	Status	—	100	10	Normal
45	Synthesis	Grass	Status	—	—	5	Self
50	Petal Blizzard	Grass	Physical	90	100	15	Adjacent
53	Solar Beam	Grass	Special	120	100	10	Normal

● TM & HM MOVES

No.	Name	Type	Kind	Pow.	Acc.	PP	Range
TM05	Roar	Normal	Status	—	—	20	Normal
TM06	Toxic	Poison	Status	—	90	10	Normal
TM09	Venoshock	Poison	Special	65	100	10	Normal
TM10	Hidden Power	Normal	Special	60	100	15	Normal
TM11	Sunny Day	Fire	Status	—	—	5	Both Sides
TM15	Hyper Beam	Normal	Special	150	90	5	Normal
TM16	Light Screen	Psychic	Status	—	—	30	Your Side
TM17	Protect	Normal	Status	—	—	10	Self
TM20	Safeguard	Normal	Status	—	—	25	Your Side
TM21	Frustration	Normal	Physical	—	100	20	Normal
TM22	Solar Beam	Grass	Special	120	100	10	Normal
TM26	Earthquake	Ground	Physical	100	100	10	Adjacent
TM27	Return	Normal	Physical	—	100	20	Normal
TM32	Double Team	Normal	Status	—	—	15	Self
TM36	Sludge Bomb	Poison	Special	90	100	10	Normal
TM42	Facade	Normal	Physical	70	100	20	Normal
TM44	Rest	Psychic	Status	—	—	10	Self
TM45	Attract	Normal	Status	—	100	15	Normal
TM48	Round	Normal	Special	60	100	15	Normal
TM49	Echoed Voice	Normal	Special	40	100	15	Normal
TM53	Energy Ball	Grass	Special	90	100	10	Normal
TM68	Giga Impact	Normal	Physical	150	90	5	Normal
TM70	Flash	Normal	Status	—	100	20	Normal
TM75	Swords Dance	Normal	Status	—	—	20	Self
TM78	Bulldoze	Ground	Physical	60	100	20	Adjacent
TM86	Grass Knot	Grass	Special	—	100	20	Normal
TM87	Swagger	Normal	Status	—	90	15	Normal
TM88	Sleep Talk	Normal	Status	—	—	10	Self
TM90	Substitute	Normal	Status	—	—	10	Self
TM94	Rock Smash	Fighting	Physical	40	100	15	Normal
TM96	Nature Power	Normal	Status	—	—	20	Normal
TM100	Confide	Normal	Status	—	—	20	Normal
HM01	Cut	Normal	Physical	50	95	30	Normal

No.	Name	Type	Kind	Pow.	Acc.	PP	Range
HM04	Strength	Normal	Physical	80	100	15	Normal

● MOVES TAUGHT BY PEOPLE

Name	Type	Kind	Pow.	Acc.	PP	Range
Grass Pledge	Grass	Special	80	100	10	Normal
Frenzy Plant	Grass	Special	150	90	5	Normal

AFTER THE HALL OF FAME

CENTRAL KALOS

082 | Venusaur

COASTAL KALOS

MOUNTAIN KALOS

ADVENTURE DATA

AFTER THE HALL OF FAME

CENTRAL KALOS

Mega Venusaur

COASTAL KALOS

MOUNTAIN KALOS

ADVENTURE DATA

Mega Evolution

Seed Pokémon

☑ Mega Venusaur

TYPE	Grass	Poison

ABILITY
Thick Fat

STAT GROWTH RATES

HP	▪▪▪
Attack	▪▪▪▪
Defense	▪▪▪▪▪
Sp. Atk	▪▪▪▪▪
Sp. Def	▪▪▪▪▪
Speed	▪▪▪▪

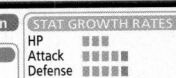 **MEGA STONE REQUIRED**

Venusaurite
Professor Sycamore gives it to you if you receive Bulbasaur in his Pokémon Lab in Lumiose City. You can also buy one at Lumiose City's Stone Emporium.

HEIGHT: 7'10"   WEIGHT: 342.8 lbs.   GENDER: ♂ / ♀

Damage taken in normal battles	
Normal	×1
Fire	×2
Water	×0.5
Grass	×0.25
Electric	×0.5
Ice	×2
Fighting	×0.5
Poison	×1
Ground	×1
Flying	×2
Psychic	×2
Bug	×1
Rock	×1
Ghost	×1
Dragon	×1
Dark	×1
Steel	×1
Fairy	×0.5

Damage taken in Inverse Battles	
Normal	×1
Fire	×0.5
Water	×2
Grass	×4
Electric	×2
Ice	×0.5
Fighting	×2
Poison	×1
Ground	×1
Flying	×0.5
Psychic	×0.5
Bug	×1
Rock	×1
Ghost	×1
Dragon	×1
Dark	×1
Steel	×1
Fairy	×2

Can be used in	
Inverse Battle	Battle Institute
—	Battle Maison
Battle Chateau	Random Matchup

Same form for ♂ / ♀

192

Central Kalos
Lizard Pokémon
☑ Charmander **083**

HEIGHT: 2'00" WEIGHT: 18.7 lbs.
GENDER: ♂/♀

X The flame on its tail indicates Charmander's life force. If it is healthy, the flame burns brightly.

Y From the time it is born, a flame burns at the tip of its tail. Its life would end if the flame were to go out.

TYPE Fire

ABILITY
Blaze

HIDDEN ABILITY
Solar Power

STAT GROWTH RATES
HP	■■
Attack	■■■
Defense	■■
Sp. Atk	■■■
Sp. Def	■■
Speed	■■■■

EGG GROUPS
Monster, Dragon

⬆ EVOLUTION

Lv. 16   Lv. 36

Charmander   Charmeleon   Charizard

ITEMS SOMETIMES HELD BY WILD POKÉMON
None

Damage taken in normal battles		Damage taken in Inverse Battles	
Normal	×1	Normal	×1
Fire	×0.5	Fire	×2
Water	×2	Water	×0.5
Grass	×0.5	Grass	×2
Electric	×1	Electric	×1
Ice	×0.5	Ice	×2
Fighting	×1	Fighting	×1
Poison	×1	Poison	×1
Ground	×2	Ground	×0.5
Flying	×1	Flying	×1
Psychic	×1	Psychic	×1
Bug	×0.5	Bug	×2
Rock	×2	Rock	×0.5
Ghost	×1	Ghost	×1
Dragon	×1	Dragon	×1
Dark	×1	Dark	×1
Steel	×0.5	Steel	×2
Fairy	×0.5	Fairy	×2

Can be used in	
Inverse Battle	Battle Institute
—	Battle Maison
Battle Chateau	Random Matchup

Same form for ♂/♀

How to obtain for your Central Kalos Pokédex
❶ Receive from Professor Sycamore in Lumiose City.
❷ Link Trade or transfer from another game.

❶ Receive from Professor Sycamore in Lumiose City.
❷ Link Trade or transfer from another game.

● LEVEL-UP MOVES

Lv.	Name	Type	Kind	Pow.	Acc.	PP	Range
1	Scratch	Normal	Physical	40	100	35	Normal
1	Growl	Normal	Status	—	100	40	Many Others
7	Ember	Fire	Special	40	100	25	Normal
10	Smokescreen	Normal	Status	—	100	20	Normal
16	Dragon Rage	Dragon	Special	—	100	10	Normal
19	Scary Face	Normal	Status	—	100	10	Normal
25	Fire Fang	Fire	Physical	65	95	15	Normal
28	Flame Burst	Fire	Special	70	100	15	Normal
34	Slash	Normal	Physical	70	100	20	Normal
37	Flamethrower	Fire	Special	90	100	15	Normal
43	Fire Spin	Fire	Special	35	85	15	Normal
46	Inferno	Fire	Special	100	50	5	Normal

● TM & HM MOVES

No.	Name	Type	Kind	Pow.	Acc.	PP	Range
TM01	Hone Claws	Dark	Status	—	—	15	Self
TM02	Dragon Claw	Dragon	Physical	80	100	15	Normal
TM06	Toxic	Poison	Status	—	90	10	Normal
TM10	Hidden Power	Normal	Special	60	100	15	Normal
TM11	Sunny Day	Fire	Status	—	—	5	Both Sides
TM17	Protect	Normal	Status	—	—	10	Self
TM21	Frustration	Normal	Physical	—	100	20	Normal
TM27	Return	Normal	Physical	—	100	20	Normal
TM28	Dig	Ground	Physical	80	100	10	Normal
TM31	Brick Break	Fighting	Physical	75	100	15	Normal
TM32	Double Team	Normal	Status	—	—	15	Self
TM35	Flamethrower	Fire	Special	90	100	15	Normal
TM38	Fire Blast	Fire	Special	110	85	5	Normal
TM39	Rock Tomb	Rock	Physical	60	95	15	Normal
TM40	Aerial Ace	Flying	Physical	60	—	20	Normal
TM42	Facade	Normal	Physical	70	100	20	Normal
TM43	Flame Charge	Fire	Physical	50	100	20	Normal
TM44	Rest	Psychic	Status	—	—	10	Self
TM45	Attract	Normal	Status	—	100	15	Normal
TM48	Round	Normal	Special	60	100	15	Normal
TM49	Echoed Voice	Normal	Special	40	100	15	Normal
TM50	Overheat	Fire	Special	130	90	5	Normal
TM56	Fling	Dark	Physical	—	100	10	Normal
TM59	Incinerate	Fire	Special	60	100	15	Many Others
TM61	Will-O-Wisp	Fire	Status	—	85	15	Normal
TM65	Shadow Claw	Ghost	Physical	70	100	15	Normal
TM75	Swords Dance	Normal	Status	—	—	20	Self
TM80	Rock Slide	Rock	Physical	75	90	10	Many Others
TM87	Swagger	Normal	Status	—	90	15	Normal
TM88	Sleep Talk	Normal	Status	—	—	10	Self
TM90	Substitute	Normal	Status	—	—	10	Self
TM94	Rock Smash	Fighting	Physical	40	100	15	Normal
TM98	Power-Up Punch	Fighting	Physical	40	100	20	Normal

No.	Name	Type	Kind	Pow.	Acc.	PP	Range
TM100	Confide	Normal	Status	—	—	20	Normal
HM01	Cut	Normal	Physical	50	95	30	Normal
HM04	Strength	Normal	Physical	80	100	15	Normal

● MOVES TAUGHT BY PEOPLE

Name	Type	Kind	Pow.	Acc.	PP	Range
Fire Pledge	Fire	Special	80	100	10	Normal

● EGG MOVES

Name	Type	Kind	Pow.	Acc.	PP	Range
Belly Drum	Normal	Status	—	—	10	Self
Ancient Power	Rock	Special	60	100	5	Normal
Bite	Dark	Physical	60	100	25	Normal
Outrage	Dragon	Physical	120	100	10	1 Random
Beat Up	Dark	Physical	—	100	10	Normal
Dragon Dance	Dragon	Status	—	—	20	Self
Crunch	Dark	Physical	80	100	15	Normal
Dragon Rush	Dragon	Physical	100	75	10	Normal
Metal Claw	Steel	Physical	50	95	35	Normal
Flare Blitz	Fire	Physical	120	100	15	Normal
Counter	Fighting	Physical	—	100	20	Varies
Dragon Pulse	Dragon	Special	85	100	10	Normal
Focus Punch	Fighting	Physical	150	100	20	Normal
Air Cutter	Flying	Special	60	95	25	Many Others

AFTER THE HALL OF FAME

CENTRAL KALOS

084

Charmeleon

COASTAL KALOS

MOUNTAIN KALOS

ADVENTURE DATA

Central Kalos   084
Flame Pokémon
☑ Charmeleon

HEIGHT: 3'07"   WEIGHT: 41.9 lbs.
GENDER: ♂/♀

X It lashes about with its tail to knock down its foe. It then tears up the fallen opponent with sharp claws.

Y When it swings its burning tail, it elevates the air temperature to unbearably high levels.

TYPE Fire

ABILITY
Blaze

HIDDEN ABILITY
Solar Power

STAT GROWTH RATES
HP	■■■
Attack	■■■
Defense	■■■
Sp. Atk	■■■■
Sp. Def	■■■
Speed	■■■■

EGG GROUPS
Monster, Dragon

EVOLUTION

Lv. 16   Lv. 36

Charmander   Charmeleon   Charizard

ITEMS SOMETIMES HELD BY WILD POKÉMON
None

Damage taken in normal battles	
Normal	×1
Fire	×0.5
Water	×2
Grass	×0.5
Electric	×1
Ice	×0.5
Fighting	×1
Poison	×1
Ground	×2
Flying	×1
Psychic	×1
Bug	×0.5
Rock	×2
Ghost	×1
Dragon	×1
Dark	×1
Steel	×0.5
Fairy	×0.5

Damage taken in Inverse Battles	
Normal	×1
Fire	×2
Water	×0.5
Grass	×2
Electric	×1
Ice	×2
Fighting	×1
Poison	×1
Ground	×0.5
Flying	×1
Psychic	×1
Bug	×2
Rock	×0.5
Ghost	×1
Dragon	×1
Dark	×1
Steel	×2
Fairy	×2

Can be used in	
Inverse Battle	Battle Institute
—	Battle Maison
Battle Chateau	Random Matchup

Same form for ♂/♀

How to obtain for your Central Kalos Pokédex

❶ Level up Charmander to Lv. 16.
❷ Link Trade or transfer from another game.

❶ Level up Charmander to Lv. 16.
❷ Link Trade or transfer from another game.

● LEVEL-UP MOVES

Lv.	Name	Type	Kind	Pow.	Acc.	PP	Range
1	Scratch	Normal	Physical	40	100	35	Normal
1	Growl	Normal	Status	—	100	40	Many Others
1	Ember	Fire	Special	40	100	25	Normal
7	Ember	Fire	Special	40	100	25	Normal
13	Smokescreen	Normal	Status	—	100	20	Normal
17	Dragon Rage	Dragon	Special	—	100	10	Normal
21	Scary Face	Normal	Status	—	100	10	Normal
28	Fire Fang	Fire	Physical	65	95	15	Normal
32	Flame Burst	Fire	Special	70	100	15	Normal
39	Slash	Normal	Physical	70	100	20	Normal
43	Flamethrower	Fire	Special	90	100	15	Normal
50	Fire Spin	Fire	Special	35	85	15	Normal
54	Inferno	Fire	Special	100	50	5	Normal

● TM & HM MOVES

No.	Name	Type	Kind	Pow.	Acc.	PP	Range
TM01	Hone Claws	Dark	Status	—	—	15	Self
TM02	Dragon Claw	Dragon	Physical	80	100	15	Normal
TM06	Toxic	Poison	Status	—	90	10	Normal
TM10	Hidden Power	Normal	Special	60	100	15	Normal
TM11	Sunny Day	Fire	Status	—	—	5	Both Sides
TM17	Protect	Normal	Status	—	—	10	Self
TM21	Frustration	Normal	Physical	—	100	20	Normal
TM27	Return	Normal	Physical	—	100	20	Normal
TM28	Dig	Ground	Physical	80	100	10	Normal
TM31	Brick Break	Fighting	Physical	75	100	15	Normal
TM32	Double Team	Normal	Status	—	—	15	Self
TM35	Flamethrower	Fire	Special	90	100	15	Normal
TM38	Fire Blast	Fire	Special	110	85	5	Normal
TM39	Rock Tomb	Rock	Physical	60	95	15	Normal
TM40	Aerial Ace	Flying	Physical	60	—	20	Normal
TM42	Facade	Normal	Physical	70	100	20	Normal
TM43	Flame Charge	Fire	Physical	50	100	20	Normal
TM44	Rest	Psychic	Status	—	—	10	Self
TM45	Attract	Normal	Status	—	100	15	Normal
TM48	Round	Normal	Special	60	100	15	Normal
TM49	Echoed Voice	Normal	Special	40	100	15	Normal
TM50	Overheat	Fire	Special	130	90	5	Normal
TM56	Fling	Dark	Physical	—	100	10	Normal
TM59	Incinerate	Fire	Special	60	100	15	Many Others
TM61	Will-O-Wisp	Fire	Status	—	85	15	Normal
TM65	Shadow Claw	Ghost	Physical	70	100	15	Normal
TM75	Swords Dance	Normal	Status	—	—	20	Self
TM80	Rock Slide	Rock	Physical	75	90	10	Many Others
TM87	Swagger	Normal	Status	—	90	15	Normal
TM88	Sleep Talk	Normal	Status	—	—	10	Self
TM90	Substitute	Normal	Status	—	—	10	Self
TM94	Rock Smash	Fighting	Physical	40	100	15	Normal
TM98	Power-Up Punch	Fighting	Physical	40	100	20	Normal

No.	Name	Type	Kind	Pow.	Acc.	PP	Range
TM100	Confide	Normal	Status	—	—	20	Normal
HM01	Cut	Normal	Physical	50	95	30	Normal
HM04	Strength	Normal	Physical	80	100	15	Normal

● MOVES TAUGHT BY PEOPLE

Name	Type	Kind	Pow.	Acc.	PP	Range
Fire Pledge	Fire	Special	80	100	10	Normal

AFTER THE HALL OF FAME

CENTRAL KALOS

085 Charizard

COASTAL KALOS

MOUNTAIN KALOS

ADVENTURE DATA

Central Kalos
Flame Pokémon
☑ Charizard

085

HEIGHT: 5'07" WEIGHT: 199.5 lbs.
GENDER: ♂/♀

TYPE Fire | Flying

ABILITY
Blaze

HIDDEN ABILITY
Solar Power

STAT GROWTH RATES
HP	▪▪▪
Attack	▪▪▪
Defense	▪▪▪
Sp. Atk	▪▪▪▪▪
Sp. Def	▪▪▪
Speed	▪▪▪▪

EGG GROUPS
Monster, Dragon

X When expelling a blast of superhot fire, the red flame at the tip of its tail burns more intensely.

Y Its wings can carry this Pokémon close to an altitude of 4,600 feet. It blows out fire at very high temperatures.

EVOLUTION

Lv. 16 Lv. 36

Charmander Charmeleon Charizard

ITEMS SOMETIMES HELD BY WILD POKÉMON
None

Damage taken in normal battles		Damage taken in Inverse Battles	
Normal	×1	Normal	×1
Fire	×0.5	Fire	×2
Water	×2	Water	×0.5
Grass	×0.25	Grass	×4
Electric	×2	Electric	×0.5
Ice	×1	Ice	×1
Fighting	×0.5	Fighting	×2
Poison	×1	Poison	×1
Ground	×0	Ground	×1
Flying	×1	Flying	×1
Psychic	×1	Psychic	×1
Bug	×0.25	Bug	×4
Rock	×4	Rock	×0.25
Ghost	×1	Ghost	×1
Dragon	×1	Dragon	×1
Dark	×1	Dark	×1
Steel	×0.5	Steel	×2
Fairy	×0.5	Fairy	×2

Can be used in	
Inverse Battle	Battle Institute
Sky Battle	Battle Maison
Battle Chateau	Random Matchup

Same form for ♂/♀

How to obtain for your Central Kalos Pokédex

❶ Level up Charmeleon to Lv. 36.
❷ Link Trade or transfer from another game.

❶ Level up Charmeleon to Lv. 36.
❷ Link Trade or transfer from another game.

● LEVEL-UP MOVES

Lv.	Name	Type	Kind	Pow.	Acc.	PP	Range
1	Flare Blitz	Fire	Physical	120	100	15	Normal
1	Heat Wave	Fire	Special	95	90	10	Many Others
1	Dragon Claw	Dragon	Physical	80	100	15	Normal
1	Shadow Claw	Ghost	Physical	70	100	15	Normal
1	Air Slash	Flying	Special	75	95	15	Normal
1	Scratch	Normal	Physical	40	100	35	Normal
1	Growl	Normal	Status	—	100	40	Many Others
1	Ember	Fire	Special	40	100	25	Normal
1	Smokescreen	Normal	Status	—	100	20	Normal
7	Ember	Fire	Special	40	100	25	Normal
10	Smokescreen	Normal	Status	—	100	20	Normal
17	Dragon Rage	Dragon	Special	—	100	10	Normal
21	Scary Face	Normal	Status	—	100	10	Normal
28	Fire Fang	Fire	Physical	65	95	15	Normal
32	Flame Burst	Fire	Special	70	100	15	Normal
36	Wing Attack	Flying	Physical	60	100	35	Normal
41	Slash	Normal	Physical	70	100	20	Normal
47	Flamethrower	Fire	Special	90	100	15	Normal
56	Fire Spin	Fire	Special	35	85	15	Normal
62	Inferno	Fire	Special	100	50	5	Normal
71	Heat Wave	Fire	Special	95	90	10	Many Others
77	Flare Blitz	Fire	Physical	120	100	15	Normal

● TM & HM MOVES

No.	Name	Type	Kind	Pow.	Acc.	PP	Range
TM01	Hone Claws	Dark	Status	—	—	15	Self
TM02	Dragon Claw	Dragon	Physical	80	100	15	Normal
TM05	Roar	Normal	Status	—	—	20	Normal
TM06	Toxic	Poison	Status	—	90	10	Normal
TM10	Hidden Power	Normal	Special	60	100	15	Normal
TM11	Sunny Day	Fire	Status	—	—	5	Both Sides
TM15	Hyper Beam	Normal	Special	150	90	5	Normal
TM17	Protect	Normal	Status	—	—	10	Self
TM19	Roost	Flying	Status	—	—	10	Self
TM21	Frustration	Normal	Physical	—	100	20	Normal
TM22	Solar Beam	Grass	Special	120	100	10	Normal
TM26	Earthquake	Ground	Physical	100	100	10	Adjacent
TM27	Return	Normal	Physical	—	100	20	Normal
TM28	Dig	Ground	Physical	80	100	10	Normal
TM31	Brick Break	Fighting	Physical	75	100	15	Normal
TM32	Double Team	Normal	Status	—	—	15	Self
TM35	Flamethrower	Fire	Special	90	100	15	Normal
TM38	Fire Blast	Fire	Special	110	85	5	Normal
TM39	Rock Tomb	Rock	Physical	60	95	15	Normal
TM40	Aerial Ace	Flying	Physical	60	—	20	Normal
TM42	Facade	Normal	Physical	70	100	20	Normal
TM43	Flame Charge	Fire	Physical	50	100	20	Normal
TM44	Rest	Psychic	Status	—	—	10	Self
TM45	Attract	Normal	Status	—	100	15	Normal
TM48	Round	Normal	Special	60	100	15	Normal
TM49	Echoed Voice	Normal	Special	40	100	15	Normal
TM50	Overheat	Fire	Special	130	90	5	Normal
TM51	Steel Wing	Steel	Physical	70	90	25	Normal
TM52	Focus Blast	Fighting	Special	120	70	5	Normal
TM56	Fling	Dark	Physical	—	100	10	Normal
TM58	Sky Drop	Flying	Physical	60	100	10	Normal
TM59	Incinerate	Fire	Special	60	100	15	Many Others
TM61	Will-O-Wisp	Fire	Status	—	85	15	Normal
TM65	Shadow Claw	Ghost	Physical	70	100	15	Normal
TM68	Giga Impact	Normal	Physical	150	90	5	Normal
TM75	Swords Dance	Normal	Status	—	—	20	Self
TM78	Bulldoze	Ground	Physical	60	100	20	Adjacent
TM80	Rock Slide	Rock	Physical	75	90	10	Many Others
TM82	Dragon Tail	Dragon	Physical	60	90	10	Normal
TM87	Swagger	Normal	Status	—	90	15	Normal
TM88	Sleep Talk	Normal	Status	—	—	10	Self
TM90	Substitute	Normal	Status	—	—	10	Self
TM94	Rock Smash	Fighting	Physical	40	100	15	Normal
TM98	Power-Up Punch	Fighting	Physical	40	100	20	Normal
TM100	Confide	Normal	Status	—	—	20	Normal
HM01	Cut	Normal	Physical	50	95	30	Normal
HM02	Fly	Flying	Physical	90	95	15	Normal
HM04	Strength	Normal	Physical	80	100	15	Normal

● MOVES TAUGHT BY PEOPLE

Name	Type	Kind	Pow.	Acc.	PP	Range
Fire Pledge	Fire	Special	80	100	10	Normal
Blast Burn	Fire	Special	150	90	5	Normal

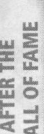

AFTER THE HALL OF FAME

CENTRAL KALOS

Mega Charizard X

COASTAL KALOS

MOUNTAIN KALOS

ADVENTURE DATA

Mega Evolution
Flame Pokémon
✓ Mega Charizard X

TYPE	Fire	Dragon

ABILITY
Tough Claws

STAT GROWTH RATES	
HP	■■■
Attack	■■■■■■■
Defense	■■■■■
Sp. Atk	■■■■
Sp. Def	■■■■
Speed	■■■■■■

MEGA STONE REQUIRED

Charizardite X
Professor Sycamore gives it to you if you receive Charizard in his Pokémon Lab in Lumiose City (in *Pokémon X*). You can also buy one at Lumiose City's Stone Emporium (in *Pokémon X*).

HEIGHT: 5'07"   WEIGHT: 243.6 lbs.   GENDER: ♂ / ♀

Damage taken in normal battles	
Normal	×1
Fire	×0.25
Water	×1
Grass	×0.25
Electric	×0.5
Ice	×1
Fighting	×1
Poison	×1
Ground	×2
Flying	×1
Psychic	×1
Bug	×0.5
Rock	×2
Ghost	×1
Dragon	×2
Dark	×1
Steel	×0.5
Fairy	×1

Damage taken in Inverse Battles	
Normal	×1
Fire	×4
Water	×1
Grass	×4
Electric	×2
Ice	×1
Fighting	×1
Poison	×1
Ground	×0.5
Flying	×1
Psychic	×1
Bug	×2
Rock	×0.5
Ghost	×1
Dragon	×0.5
Dark	×1
Steel	×2
Fairy	×1

Can be used in	
Inverse Battle	Battle Institute
Sky Battle	Battle Maison
Battle Chateau	Random Matchup

Same form for ♂ / ♀

Mega Evolution

Flame Pokémon

✔ Mega Charizard Y

TYPE	Fire / Flying
ABILITY	Drought

HEIGHT: 5'07"   WEIGHT: 221.6 lbs.   GENDER: ♂/♀

STAT GROWTH RATES

HP	■■■
Attack	■■■■
Defense	■■■
Sp. Atk	■■■■■
Sp. Def	■■■■
Speed	■■■■■

🌀 MEGA STONE REQUIRED

Charizardite Y
Professor Sycamore gives it to you if you receive Charizard in his Pokémon Lab in Lumiose City (in *Pokémon Y*). You can also buy one at Lumiose City's Stone Emporium (in *Pokémon Y*).

Same form for ♂/♀

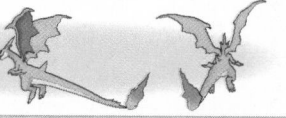

Damage taken in normal battles		Damage taken in Inverse Battles	
Normal	×1	Normal	×1
Fire	×0.5	Fire	×2
Water	×2	Water	×0.5
Grass	×0.25	Grass	×4
Electric	×2	Electric	×0.5
Ice	×1	Ice	×1
Fighting	×0.5	Fighting	×2
Poison	×1	Poison	×1
Ground	×0	Ground	×1
Flying	×1	Flying	×1
Psychic	×1	Psychic	×1
Bug	×0.25	Bug	×4
Rock	×4	Rock	×0.25
Ghost	×1	Ghost	×1
Dragon	×1	Dragon	×1
Dark	×1	Dark	×1
Steel	×0.5	Steel	×2
Fairy	×0.5	Fairy	×2

Can be used in	
Inverse Battle	Battle Institute
Sky Battle	Battle Maison
Battle Chateau	Random Matchup

AFTER THE HALL OF FAME

CENTRAL KALOS

086

Squirtle

COASTAL KALOS

MOUNTAIN KALOS

ADVENTURE DATA

Central Kalos — 086

Tiny Turtle Pokémon

Squirtle

HEIGHT: 1'08" WEIGHT: 19.8 lbs.
GENDER: ♂/♀

TYPE Water

ABILITY
Torrent

HIDDEN ABILITY
Rain Dish

STAT GROWTH RATES

HP	■■
Attack	■■■
Defense	■■■
Sp. Atk	■■
Sp. Def	■■
Speed	■■

EGG GROUPS
Monster, Water 1

X It shelters itself in its shell, then strikes back with spouts of water at every opportunity.

Y Shoots water at prey while in the water. Withdraws into its shell when in danger.

EVOLUTION

Squirtle — Lv. 16 → Wartortle — Lv. 36 → Blastoise

ITEMS SOMETIMES HELD BY WILD POKÉMON
None

Damage taken in normal battles		Damage taken in Inverse Battles	
Normal	×1	Normal	×1
Fire	×0.5	Fire	×2
Water	×0.5	Water	×2
Grass	×2	Grass	×0.5
Electric	×2	Electric	×0.5
Ice	×0.5	Ice	×2
Fighting	×1	Fighting	×1
Poison	×1	Poison	×1
Ground	×1	Ground	×1
Flying	×1	Flying	×1
Psychic	×1	Psychic	×1
Bug	×1	Bug	×1
Rock	×1	Rock	×1
Ghost	×1	Ghost	×1
Dragon	×1	Dragon	×1
Dark	×1	Dark	×1
Steel	×0.5	Steel	×2
Fairy	×1	Fairy	×1

Can be used in	
Inverse Battle	Battle Institute
—	Battle Maison
Battle Chateau	Random Matchup

Same form for ♂/♀

How to obtain for your Central Kalos Pokédex

1. Receive from Professor Sycamore in Lumiose City.
2. Link Trade or transfer from another game.

1. Receive from Professor Sycamore in Lumiose City.
2. Link Trade or transfer from another game.

LEVEL-UP MOVES

Lv.	Name	Type	Kind	Pow.	Acc.	PP	Range
1	Tackle	Normal	Physical	50	100	35	Normal
4	Tail Whip	Normal	Status	—	100	30	Many Others
7	Water Gun	Water	Special	40	100	25	Normal
10	Withdraw	Water	Status	—	—	40	Self
13	Bubble	Water	Special	40	100	30	Many Others
16	Bite	Dark	Physical	60	100	25	Normal
19	Rapid Spin	Normal	Physical	20	100	40	Normal
22	Protect	Normal	Status	—	—	10	Self
25	Water Pulse	Water	Special	60	100	20	Normal
28	Aqua Tail	Water	Physical	90	90	10	Normal
31	Skull Bash	Normal	Physical	130	100	10	Normal
34	Iron Defense	Steel	Status	—	—	15	Self
37	Rain Dance	Water	Status	—	—	5	Both Sides
40	Hydro Pump	Water	Special	110	80	5	Normal

TM & HM MOVES

No.	Name	Type	Kind	Pow.	Acc.	PP	Range
TM06	Toxic	Poison	Status	—	90	10	Normal
TM07	Hail	Ice	Status	—	—	10	Both Sides
TM10	Hidden Power	Normal	Special	60	100	15	Normal
TM13	Ice Beam	Ice	Special	90	100	10	Normal
TM14	Blizzard	Ice	Special	110	70	5	Many Others
TM17	Protect	Normal	Status	—	—	10	Self
TM18	Rain Dance	Water	Status	—	—	5	Both Sides
TM21	Frustration	Normal	Physical	—	100	20	Normal
TM27	Return	Normal	Physical	—	100	20	Normal
TM28	Dig	Ground	Physical	80	100	10	Normal
TM31	Brick Break	Fighting	Physical	75	100	15	Normal
TM32	Double Team	Normal	Status	—	—	15	Self
TM39	Rock Tomb	Rock	Physical	60	95	15	Normal
TM42	Facade	Normal	Physical	70	100	20	Normal
TM44	Rest	Psychic	Status	—	—	10	Self
TM45	Attract	Normal	Status	—	100	15	Normal
TM48	Round	Normal	Special	60	100	15	Normal
TM55	Scald	Water	Special	80	100	15	Normal
TM56	Fling	Dark	Physical	—	100	10	Normal
TM74	Gyro Ball	Steel	Physical	—	100	5	Normal
TM87	Swagger	Normal	Status	—	90	15	Normal
TM88	Sleep Talk	Normal	Status	—	—	10	Self
TM90	Substitute	Normal	Status	—	—	10	Self
TM94	Rock Smash	Fighting	Physical	40	100	15	Normal
TM98	Power-Up Punch	Fighting	Physical	40	100	20	Normal
TM100	Confide	Normal	Status	—	—	20	Normal
HM03	Surf	Water	Special	90	100	15	Adjacent
HM04	Strength	Normal	Physical	80	100	15	Normal
HM05	Waterfall	Water	Physical	80	100	15	Normal

MOVES TAUGHT BY PEOPLE

Name	Type	Kind	Pow.	Acc.	PP	Range
Water Pledge	Water	Special	80	100	10	Normal

EGG MOVES

Name	Type	Kind	Pow.	Acc.	PP	Range
Mirror Coat	Psychic	Special	—	100	20	Varies
Haze	Ice	Status	—	—	30	Both Sides
Mist	Ice	Status	—	—	30	Your Side
Foresight	Normal	Status	—	—	40	Normal
Flail	Normal	Physical	—	100	15	Normal
Refresh	Normal	Status	—	—	20	Self
Mud Sport	Ground	Status	—	—	15	Both Sides
Yawn	Normal	Status	—	—	10	Normal
Muddy Water	Water	Special	90	85	10	Many Others
Fake Out	Normal	Physical	40	100	10	Normal
Aqua Ring	Water	Status	—	—	20	Self
Aqua Jet	Water	Physical	40	100	20	Normal
Water Spout	Water	Special	150	100	5	Many Others
Brine	Water	Special	65	100	10	Normal
Dragon Pulse	Dragon	Special	85	100	10	Normal
Aura Sphere	Fighting	Special	80	—	20	Normal

AFTER THE HALL OF FAME

CENTRAL KALOS

087 | Wartortle

COASTAL KALOS

MOUNTAIN KALOS

ADVENTURE DATA

🔺 Central Kalos — 087
Turtle Pokémon
☑ Wartortle

HEIGHT: 3'03" WEIGHT: 49.6 lbs.
GENDER: ♂/♀

TYPE Water

ABILITY
Torrent

HIDDEN ABILITY
Rain Dish

X When tapped, this Pokémon will pull in its head, but its tail will still stick out a little bit.

Y It is said to live 10,000 years. Its furry tail is popular as a symbol of longevity.

STAT GROWTH RATES
HP	■■■
Attack	■■■
Defense	■■■■
Sp. Atk	■■■
Sp. Def	■■■
Speed	■■■

EGG GROUPS
Monster, Water 1

EVOLUTION

Squirtle — Lv. 16 → Wartortle — Lv. 36 → Blastoise

ITEMS SOMETIMES HELD BY WILD POKÉMON
None

Damage taken in normal battles	
Normal	×1
Fire	×0.5
Water	×0.5
Grass	×2
Electric	×2
Ice	×0.5
Fighting	×1
Poison	×1
Ground	×1
Flying	×1
Psychic	×1
Bug	×1
Rock	×1
Ghost	×1
Dragon	×1
Dark	×1
Steel	×0.5
Fairy	×1

Damage taken in Inverse Battles	
Normal	×1
Fire	×2
Water	×2
Grass	×0.5
Electric	×0.5
Ice	×2
Fighting	×1
Poison	×1
Ground	×1
Flying	×1
Psychic	×1
Bug	×1
Rock	×1
Ghost	×1
Dragon	×1
Dark	×1
Steel	×2
Fairy	×1

Can be used in
Inverse Battle	Battle Institute
—	Battle Maison
Battle Chateau	Random Matchup

Same form for ♂/♀

How to obtain for your Central Kalos Pokédex
1. Level up Squirtle to Lv. 16.
2. Link Trade or transfer from another game.

1. Level up Squirtle to Lv. 16.
2. Link Trade or transfer from another game.

● LEVEL-UP MOVES
Lv.	Name	Type	Kind	Pow.	Acc.	PP	Range
1	Tackle	Normal	Physical	50	100	35	Normal
1	Tail Whip	Normal	Status	—	100	30	Many Others
1	Water Gun	Water	Special	40	100	25	Normal
4	Tail Whip	Normal	Status	—	100	30	Many Others
7	Water Gun	Water	Special	40	100	25	Normal
10	Withdraw	Water	Status	—	—	40	Self
13	Bubble	Water	Special	40	100	30	Many Others
16	Bite	Dark	Physical	60	100	25	Normal
20	Rapid Spin	Normal	Physical	20	100	40	Normal
24	Protect	Normal	Status	—	—	10	Self
28	Water Pulse	Water	Special	60	100	20	Normal
32	Aqua Tail	Water	Physical	90	90	10	Normal
36	Skull Bash	Normal	Physical	130	100	10	Normal
40	Iron Defense	Steel	Status	—	—	15	Self
44	Rain Dance	Water	Status	—	—	5	Both Sides
48	Hydro Pump	Water	Special	110	80	5	Normal

● TM & HM MOVES
No.	Name	Type	Kind	Pow.	Acc.	PP	Range
TM06	Toxic	Poison	Status	—	90	10	Normal
TM07	Hail	Ice	Status	—	—	10	Both Sides
TM10	Hidden Power	Normal	Special	60	100	15	Normal
TM13	Ice Beam	Ice	Special	90	100	10	Normal
TM14	Blizzard	Ice	Special	110	70	5	Many Others
TM17	Protect	Normal	Status	—	—	10	Self
TM18	Rain Dance	Water	Status	—	—	5	Both Sides
TM21	Frustration	Normal	Physical	—	100	20	Normal
TM27	Return	Normal	Physical	—	100	20	Normal
TM28	Dig	Ground	Physical	80	100	10	Normal
TM31	Brick Break	Fighting	Physical	75	100	15	Normal
TM32	Double Team	Normal	Status	—	—	15	Self
TM39	Rock Tomb	Rock	Physical	60	95	15	Normal
TM42	Facade	Normal	Physical	70	100	20	Normal
TM44	Rest	Psychic	Status	—	—	10	Self
TM45	Attract	Normal	Status	—	100	15	Normal
TM48	Round	Normal	Special	60	100	15	Normal
TM55	Scald	Water	Special	80	100	15	Normal
TM56	Fling	Dark	Physical	—	100	10	Normal
TM74	Gyro Ball	Steel	Physical	—	100	5	Normal
TM87	Swagger	Normal	Status	—	90	15	Normal
TM88	Sleep Talk	Normal	Status	—	—	10	Self
TM90	Substitute	Normal	Status	—	—	10	Self
TM94	Rock Smash	Fighting	Physical	40	100	15	Normal
TM98	Power-Up Punch	Fighting	Physical	40	100	20	Normal
TM100	Confide	Normal	Status	—	—	20	Normal
HM03	Surf	Water	Special	90	100	15	Adjacent
HM04	Strength	Normal	Physical	80	100	15	Normal
HM05	Waterfall	Water	Physical	80	100	15	Normal

No.	Name	Type	Kind	Pow.	Acc.	PP	Range

● MOVES TAUGHT BY PEOPLE
Name	Type	Kind	Pow.	Acc.	PP	Range
Water Pledge	Water	Special	80	100	10	Normal

AFTER THE HALL OF FAME

CENTRAL KALOS

088

Blastoise

COASTAL KALOS

MOUNTAIN KALOS

ADVENTURE DATA

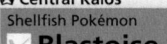

⬆ Central Kalos

Shellfish Pokémon

☑ Blastoise

088

HEIGHT: 5'03" WEIGHT: 188.5 lbs.
GENDER: ♂/♀

X It crushes its foe under its heavy body to cause fainting. In a pinch, it will withdraw inside its shell.

Y The pressurized water jets on this brutal Pokémon's shell are used for high-speed tackles.

TYPE Water

ABILITY
Torrent

HIDDEN ABILITY
Rain Dish

STAT GROWTH RATES
HP	■■■
Attack	■■■■
Defense	■■■■
Sp. Atk	■■■
Sp. Def	■■■
Speed	■■■■

EGG GROUPS
Monster, Water 1

⬆ EVOLUTION

Lv. 16   Lv. 36

Squirtle   Wartortle   Blastoise

ITEMS SOMETIMES HELD BY WILD POKÉMON
None

Can be used in
Inverse Battle
—
Battle Chateau
Battle Institute
Battle Maison
Random Matchup

Damage taken in normal battles
Normal	×1
Fire	×0.5
Water	×0.5
Grass	×2
Electric	×2
Ice	×0.5
Fighting	×1
Poison	×1
Ground	×1
Flying	×1
Psychic	×1
Bug	×1
Rock	×1
Ghost	×1
Dragon	×1
Dark	×1
Steel	×0.5
Fairy	×1

Damage taken in Inverse Battles
Normal	×1
Fire	×2
Water	×2
Grass	×0.5
Electric	×0.5
Ice	×2
Fighting	×1
Poison	×1
Ground	×1
Flying	×1
Psychic	×1
Bug	×1
Rock	×1
Ghost	×1
Dragon	×1
Dark	×1
Steel	×2
Fairy	×1

How to obtain for your Central Kalos Pokédex

❶ Level up Wartortle to Lv. 36.
❷ Link Trade or transfer from another game.

❶ Level up Wartortle to Lv. 36.
❷ Link Trade or transfer from another game.

Same form for ♂/♀

● LEVEL-UP MOVES

Lv.	Name	Type	Kind	Pow.	Acc.	PP	Range
1	Flash Cannon	Steel	Special	80	100	10	Normal
1	Tackle	Normal	Physical	50	100	35	Normal
1	Tail Whip	Normal	Status	—	100	30	Many Others
1	Water Gun	Water	Special	40	100	25	Normal
1	Withdraw	Water	Status	—	—	40	Self
4	Tail Whip	Normal	Status	—	100	30	Many Others
7	Water Gun	Water	Special	40	100	25	Normal
10	Withdraw	Water	Status	—	—	40	Self
13	Bubble	Water	Special	40	100	30	Many Others
16	Bite	Dark	Physical	60	100	25	Normal
20	Rapid Spin	Normal	Physical	20	100	40	Normal
24	Protect	Normal	Status	—	—	10	Self
28	Water Pulse	Water	Special	60	100	20	Normal
32	Aqua Tail	Water	Physical	90	90	10	Normal
39	Rain Dance	Normal	Status	—	—	15	Both Sides
42	Skull Bash	Normal	Physical	130	100	10	Normal
46	Iron Defense	Steel	Status	—	—	15	Self
53	Rain Dance	Water	Status	—	—	5	Both Sides
60	Hydro Pump	Water	Special	110	80	5	Normal

■ TM & HM MOVES

No.	Name	Type	Kind	Pow.	Acc.	PP	Range
TM05	Roar	Normal	Status	—	—	20	Normal
TM06	Toxic	Poison	Status	—	90	10	Normal
TM07	Hail	Ice	Status	—	—	10	Both Sides
TM10	Hidden Power	Normal	Special	60	100	15	Normal
TM13	Ice Beam	Ice	Special	90	100	10	Normal
TM14	Blizzard	Ice	Special	110	70	5	Many Others
TM15	Hyper Beam	Normal	Special	150	90	5	Normal
TM17	Protect	Normal	Status	—	—	10	Self
TM18	Rain Dance	Water	Status	—	—	5	Both Sides
TM21	Frustration	Normal	Physical	—	100	20	Normal
TM23	Smack Down	Rock	Physical	50	100	15	Normal
TM26	Earthquake	Ground	Physical	100	100	10	Adjacent
TM27	Return	Normal	Physical	—	100	20	Normal
TM28	Dig	Ground	Physical	80	100	10	Normal
TM31	Brick Break	Fighting	Physical	75	100	15	Normal
TM32	Double Team	Normal	Status	—	—	15	Self
TM39	Rock Tomb	Rock	Physical	60	95	15	Normal
TM42	Facade	Normal	Physical	70	100	20	Normal
TM44	Rest	Psychic	Status	—	—	10	Self
TM45	Attract	Normal	Status	—	100	15	Normal
TM48	Round	Normal	Special	60	100	15	Normal
TM52	Focus Blast	Fighting	Special	120	70	5	Normal
TM55	Scald	Water	Special	80	100	15	Normal
TM56	Fling	Dark	Physical	—	100	10	Normal
TM68	Giga Impact	Normal	Physical	150	90	5	Normal
TM74	Gyro Ball	Steel	Physical	—	100	5	Normal
TM78	Bulldoze	Ground	Physical	60	100	20	Adjacent
TM80	Rock Slide	Rock	Physical	75	90	10	Many Others
TM82	Dragon Tail	Dragon	Physical	60	90	10	Normal
TM87	Swagger	Normal	Status	—	90	15	Normal
TM88	Sleep Talk	Normal	Status	—	—	10	Self
TM90	Substitute	Normal	Status	—	—	10	Self
TM91	Flash Cannon	Steel	Special	80	100	10	Normal

No.	Name	Type	Kind	Pow.	Acc.	PP	Range
TM94	Rock Smash	Fighting	Physical	40	100	15	Normal
TM97	Dark Pulse	Dark	Special	80	100	15	Normal
TM98	Power-Up Punch	Fighting	Physical	40	100	20	Normal
TM100	Confide	Normal	Status	—	—	20	Normal
HM03	Surf	Water	Special	90	100	15	Adjacent
HM04	Strength	Normal	Physical	80	100	15	Normal
HM05	Waterfall	Water	Physical	80	100	15	Normal

● MOVES TAUGHT BY PEOPLE

Name	Type	Kind	Pow.	Acc.	PP	Range
Water Pledge	Water	Special	80	100	10	Normal
Hydro Cannon	Water	Special	150	90	5	Normal

Mega Evolution

Shellfish Pokémon

☑ **Mega Blastoise**

HEIGHT: 5'03" WEIGHT: 222.9 lbs. GENDER: ♂/♀

TYPE **Water**

ABILITY
Mega Launcher

STAT GROWTH RATES

HP	▪▪▪
Attack	▪▪▪▪
Defense	▪▪▪▪▪
Sp. Atk	▪▪▪▪▪▪▪
Sp. Def	▪▪▪▪▪
Speed	▪▪▪▪

MEGA STONE REQUIRED

Blastoisinite
Professor Sycamore gives it to you if you receive Squirtle in the Sycamore Pokémon Lab in Lumiose City. You can also buy one at Lumiose City's Stone Emporium.

Can be used in

Inverse Battle	Battle Institute
—	Battle Maison
Battle Chateau	Random Matchup

Damage taken in normal battles

Normal	×1
Fire	×0.5
Water	×0.5
Grass	×2
Electric	×2
Ice	×0.5
Fighting	×1
Poison	×1
Ground	×1
Flying	×1
Psychic	×1
Bug	×1
Rock	×1
Ghost	×1
Dragon	×1
Dark	×1
Steel	×0.5
Fairy	×1

Damage taken in Inverse Battles

Normal	×1
Fire	×2
Water	×2
Grass	×0.5
Electric	×0.5
Ice	×2
Fighting	×1
Poison	×1
Ground	×1
Flying	×1
Psychic	×1
Bug	×1
Rock	×1
Ghost	×1
Dragon	×1
Dark	×1
Steel	×2
Fairy	×1

Same form for ♂/♀

AFTER THE HALL OF FAME

CENTRAL KALOS

089

Skiddo

COASTAL KALOS

MOUNTAIN KALOS

ADVENTURE DATA

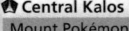

Central Kalos 089

Mount Pokémon

Skiddo

HEIGHT: 2'11"   WEIGHT: 68.3 lbs.
GENDER: ♂/♀

X Thought to be one of the first Pokémon to live in harmony with humans, it has a placid disposition.

Y If it has sunshine and water, it doesn't need to eat, because it can generate energy from the leaves on its back.

TYPE | Grass

ABILITY
Sap Sipper

HIDDEN ABILITY
Grass Pelt

STAT GROWTH RATES
HP	▓▓▓
Attack	▓▓▓
Defense	▓▓
Sp. Atk	▓▓▓
Sp. Def	▓▓
Speed	▓▓▓

EGG GROUP
Field

EVOLUTION

Skiddo   Lv. 32 →   Gogoat

ITEMS SOMETIMES HELD BY WILD POKÉMON
None

Can be used in
Inverse Battle
—
Battle Chateau
Battle Institute
Battle Maison
Random Matchup

Damage taken in normal battles	
Normal	×1
Fire	×2
Water	×0.5
Grass	×0.5
Electric	×0.5
Ice	×2
Fighting	×1
Poison	×2
Ground	×0.5
Flying	×2
Psychic	×1
Bug	×2
Rock	×1
Ghost	×1
Dragon	×1
Dark	×1
Steel	×1
Fairy	×1

Damage taken in Inverse Battles	
Normal	×1
Fire	×0.5
Water	×2
Grass	×2
Electric	×2
Ice	×0.5
Fighting	×1
Poison	×0.5
Ground	×2
Flying	×0.5
Psychic	×1
Bug	×0.5
Rock	×1
Ghost	×1
Dragon	×1
Dark	×1
Steel	×1
Fairy	×1

How to obtain for your Central Kalos Pokédex

❶ Catch in the tall grass on Route 5.
❷ Catch in the purple flowers on Route 5.

❶ Catch in the tall grass on Route 5.
❷ Catch in the purple flowers on Route 5.

Same form for ♂ / ♀

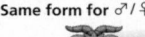 

● LEVEL-UP MOVES

Lv.	Name	Type	Kind	Pow.	Acc.	PP	Range
1	Tackle	Normal	Physical	50	100	35	Normal
1	Growth	Normal	Status	—	—	20	Self
7	Vine Whip	Grass	Physical	45	100	25	Normal
9	Tail Whip	Normal	Status	—	100	30	Many Others
12	Leech Seed	Grass	Status	—	90	10	Normal
13	Razor Leaf	Grass	Physical	55	95	25	Many Others
16	Worry Seed	Grass	Status	—	100	10	Normal
20	Synthesis	Grass	Status	—	—	5	Self
22	Take Down	Normal	Physical	90	85	20	Normal
26	Bulldoze	Ground	Physical	60	100	20	Adjacent
30	Seed Bomb	Grass	Physical	80	100	15	Normal
34	Bulk Up	Fighting	Status	—	—	20	Self
38	Double-Edge	Normal	Physical	120	100	15	Normal
42	Horn Leech	Grass	Physical	75	100	10	Normal
45	Leaf Blade	Grass	Physical	90	100	15	Normal
50	Milk Drink	Normal	Status	—	—	10	Self

● TM & HM MOVES

No.	Name	Type	Kind	Pow.	Acc.	PP	Range
TM05	Roar	Normal	Status	—	—	20	Normal
TM06	Toxic	Poison	Status	—	90	10	Normal
TM08	Bulk Up	Fighting	Status	—	—	20	Self
TM10	Hidden Power	Normal	Special	60	100	15	Normal
TM11	Sunny Day	Fire	Status	—	—	5	Both Sides
TM17	Protect	Normal	Status	—	—	10	Self
TM18	Rain Dance	Water	Status	—	—	5	Both Sides
TM21	Frustration	Normal	Physical	—	100	20	Normal
TM22	Solar Beam	Grass	Special	120	100	10	Normal
TM27	Return	Normal	Physical	—	100	20	Normal
TM28	Dig	Ground	Physical	80	100	10	Normal
TM31	Brick Break	Fighting	Physical	75	100	15	Normal
TM32	Double Team	Normal	Status	—	—	15	Self
TM42	Facade	Normal	Physical	70	100	20	Normal
TM44	Rest	Psychic	Status	—	—	10	Self
TM45	Attract	Normal	Status	—	100	15	Normal
TM48	Round	Normal	Special	60	100	15	Normal
TM53	Energy Ball	Grass	Special	90	100	10	Normal
TM66	Payback	Dark	Physical	50	100	10	Normal
TM67	Retaliate	Normal	Physical	70	100	5	Normal
TM78	Bulldoze	Ground	Physical	60	100	20	Adjacent
TM80	Rock Slide	Rock	Physical	75	90	10	Many Others
TM86	Grass Knot	Grass	Special	—	100	20	Normal
TM87	Swagger	Normal	Status	—	90	15	Normal
TM88	Sleep Talk	Normal	Status	—	—	10	Self
TM90	Substitute	Normal	Status	—	—	10	Self
TM93	Wild Charge	Electric	Physical	90	100	15	Normal
TM94	Rock Smash	Fighting	Physical	40	100	15	Normal
TM96	Nature Power	Normal	Status	—	—	20	Normal
TM100	Confide	Normal	Status	—	—	20	Normal
HM03	Surf	Water	Special	90	100	15	Adjacent
HM04	Strength	Normal	Physical	80	100	15	Normal

● MOVES TAUGHT BY PEOPLE

Name	Type	Kind	Pow.	Acc.	PP	Range

● EGG MOVES

Name	Type	Kind	Pow.	Acc.	PP	Range
Defense Curl	Normal	Status	—	—	40	Self
Rollout	Rock	Physical	30	90	20	Normal
Milk Drink	Normal	Status	—	—	10	Self

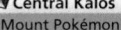
Central Kalos
Mount Pokémon
☑ Gogoat

090

HEIGHT: 5'07" WEIGHT: 200.6 lbs.
GENDER: ♂ / ♀

❌ It can tell how its Trainer is feeling by subtle shifts in the grip on its horns. This empathic sense lets them run as if one being.

✓ They inhabit mountainous regions. The leader of the herd is decided by a battle of clashing horns.

TYPE | Grass

ABILITY
Sap Sipper

HIDDEN ABILITY
Grass Pelt

STAT GROWTH RATES
HP	■■■■
Attack	■■■■■
Defense	■■■
Sp. Atk	■■■■■
Sp. Def	■■■
Speed	■■■■

EGG GROUP
Field

EVOLUTION

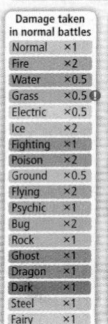
Skiddo

Lv. 32

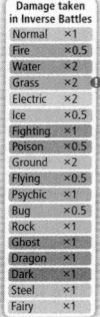
Gogoat

ITEMS SOMETIMES HELD BY WILD POKÉMON
None

Damage taken in normal battles	
Normal	×1
Fire	×2
Water	×0.5
Grass	×0.5
Electric	×0.5
Ice	×2
Fighting	×1
Poison	×2
Ground	×0.5
Flying	×2
Psychic	×1
Bug	×2
Rock	×1
Ghost	×1
Dragon	×1
Dark	×1
Steel	×1
Fairy	×1

Damage taken in Inverse Battles	
Normal	×1
Fire	×0.5
Water	×2
Grass	×2
Electric	×2
Ice	×0.5
Fighting	—
Poison	×0.5
Ground	×2
Flying	×0.5
Psychic	×1
Bug	×0.5
Rock	×1
Ghost	×1
Dragon	×1
Dark	×1
Steel	×1
Fairy	×1

Can be used in
Inverse Battle
—
Battle Chateau
Battle Institute
Battle Maison
Random Matchup

How to obtain for your Central Kalos Pokédex

Level up Skiddo to Lv. 32.

Level up Skiddo to Lv. 32.

Same form for ♂ / ♀

● LEVEL-UP MOVES

Lv.	Name	Type	Kind	Pow.	Acc.	PP	Range
1	Aerial Ace	Flying	Physical	60	—	20	Normal
1	Tackle	Normal	Physical	50	100	35	Normal
1	Growth	Normal	Status	—	—	20	Self
7	Vine Whip	Grass	Physical	45	100	25	Normal
9	Tail Whip	Normal	Status	—	100	30	Many Others
12	Leech Seed	Grass	Status	—	90	10	Normal
13	Razor Leaf	Grass	Physical	55	95	25	Many Others
16	Worry Seed	Grass	Status	—	100	10	Normal
20	Synthesis	Grass	Status	—	—	5	Self
22	Take Down	Normal	Physical	90	85	20	Normal
26	Bulldoze	Ground	Physical	60	100	20	Adjacent
30	Seed Bomb	Grass	Physical	80	100	15	Normal
34	Bulk Up	Fighting	Status	—	—	20	Self
40	Double-Edge	Normal	Physical	120	100	15	Normal
47	Horn Leech	Grass	Physical	75	100	10	Normal
55	Leaf Blade	Grass	Physical	90	100	15	Normal
58	Milk Drink	Normal	Status	—	—	10	Self
60	Earthquake	Ground	Physical	100	100	10	Adjacent
65	Aerial Ace	Flying	Physical	60	—	20	Normal

● TM & HM MOVES

No.	Name	Type	Kind	Pow.	Acc.	PP	Range
TM05	Roar	Normal	Status	—	—	20	Normal
TM06	Toxic	Poison	Status	—	90	10	Normal
TM08	Bulk Up	Fighting	Status	—	—	20	Self
TM10	Hidden Power	Normal	Special	60	100	15	Normal
TM11	Sunny Day	Fire	Status	—	—	5	Both Sides
TM15	Hyper Beam	Normal	Special	150	90	5	Normal
TM17	Protect	Normal	Status	—	—	10	Self
TM18	Rain Dance	Water	Status	—	—	5	Both Sides
TM21	Frustration	Normal	Physical	—	100	20	Normal
TM22	Solar Beam	Grass	Special	120	100	10	Normal
TM26	Earthquake	Ground	Physical	100	100	10	Adjacent
TM27	Return	Normal	Physical	—	100	20	Normal
TM28	Dig	Ground	Physical	80	100	10	Normal
TM31	Brick Break	Fighting	Physical	75	100	15	Normal
TM32	Double Team	Normal	Status	—	—	15	Self
TM40	Aerial Ace	Flying	Physical	60	—	20	Normal
TM42	Facade	Normal	Physical	70	100	20	Normal
TM44	Rest	Psychic	Status	—	—	10	Self
TM45	Attract	Normal	Status	—	100	15	Normal
TM48	Round	Normal	Special	60	100	15	Normal
TM53	Energy Ball	Grass	Special	90	100	10	Normal
TM66	Payback	Dark	Physical	50	100	10	Normal
TM67	Retaliate	Normal	Physical	70	100	5	Normal
TM68	Giga Impact	Normal	Physical	150	90	5	Normal
TM78	Bulldoze	Ground	Physical	60	100	20	Adjacent
TM80	Rock Slide	Rock	Physical	75	90	10	Many Others
TM86	Grass Knot	Grass	Special	—	100	20	Normal
TM87	Swagger	Normal	Status	—	90	15	Normal
TM88	Sleep Talk	Normal	Status	—	—	10	Self
TM90	Substitute	Normal	Status	—	—	10	Self
TM93	Wild Charge	Electric	Physical	90	100	15	Normal
TM94	Rock Smash	Fighting	Physical	40	100	15	Normal
TM96	Nature Power	Normal	Status	—	—	20	Normal

No.	Name	Type	Kind	Pow.	Acc.	PP	Range
TM100	Confide	Normal	Status	—	—	20	Normal
HM03	Surf	Water	Special	90	100	15	Adjacent
HM04	Strength	Normal	Physical	80	100	15	Normal

● MOVES TAUGHT BY PEOPLE

Name	Type	Kind	Pow.	Acc.	PP	Range

AFTER THE HALL OF FAME

CENTRAL KALOS

090 | Gogoat

COASTAL KALOS

MOUNTAIN KALOS

ADVENTURE DATA

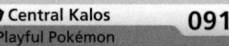

Central Kalos
Playful Pokémon
☑ Pancham
091

HEIGHT: 2'00" WEIGHT: 17.6 lbs.
GENDER: ♂/♀

TYPE Fighting

ABILITIES
Iron Fist
Mold Breaker

HIDDEN ABILITY
Scrappy

> ✕ It does its best to be taken seriously by its enemies, but its glare is not sufficiently intimidating. Chewing on a leaf is its trademark.

> Y It does its level best to glare and pull a scary face, but it can't help grinning if anyone pats its head.

STAT GROWTH RATES
HP	■■■
Attack	■■■■
Defense	■■■
Sp. Atk	■■
Sp. Def	■■
Speed	■■

EGG GROUPS
Field, Human-Like

⬆ EVOLUTION
Lv. 32 with a Dark-type Pokémon in your party

Pancham → Pangoro

ITEMS SOMETIMES HELD BY WILD POKÉMON
Mental Herb

Can be used in
Inverse Battle
—
Battle Chateau
Battle Institute
Battle Maison
Random Matchup

Damage taken in normal battles	
Normal	×1
Fire	×1
Water	×1
Grass	×1
Electric	×1
Ice	×1
Fighting	×1
Poison	×1
Ground	×1
Flying	×2
Psychic	×2
Bug	×0.5
Rock	×0.5
Ghost	×1
Dragon	×1
Dark	×0.5
Steel	×1
Fairy	×2

Damage taken in Inverse Battles	
Normal	×1
Fire	×1
Water	×1
Grass	×1
Electric	×1
Ice	×1
Fighting	×1
Poison	×1
Ground	×1
Flying	×0.5
Psychic	×0.5
Bug	×2
Rock	×2
Ghost	×1
Dragon	×1
Dark	×2
Steel	×1
Fairy	×0.5

How to obtain for your Central Kalos Pokédex
❶ Catch in the tall grass on Route 5.
❷ Catch in the purple flowers on Route 5.

❶ Catch in the tall grass on Route 5.
❷ Catch in the purple flowers on Route 5.

Same form for ♂/♀

● LEVEL-UP MOVES
Lv.	Name	Type	Kind	Pow.	Acc.	PP	Range
1	Tackle	Normal	Physical	50	100	35	Normal
1	Leer	Normal	Status	—	100	30	Many Others
7	Arm Thrust	Fighting	Physical	15	100	20	Normal
10	Work Up	Normal	Status	—	—	30	Self
12	Karate Chop	Fighting	Physical	50	100	25	Normal
15	Comet Punch	Normal	Physical	18	85	15	Normal
20	Slash	Normal	Physical	70	100	20	Normal
25	Circle Throw	Fighting	Physical	60	90	10	Normal
27	Vital Throw	Fighting	Physical	70	—	10	Normal
33	Body Slam	Normal	Physical	85	100	15	Normal
39	Crunch	Dark	Physical	80	100	15	Normal
42	Entrainment	Normal	Status	—	100	15	Normal
45	Parting Shot	Dark	Status	—	100	20	Normal
48	Sky Uppercut	Fighting	Physical	85	90	15	Normal

● TM & HM MOVES
No.	Name	Type	Kind	Pow.	Acc.	PP	Range
TM05	Roar	Normal	Status	—	—	20	Normal
TM06	Toxic	Poison	Status	—	90	10	Normal
TM08	Bulk Up	Fighting	Status	—	—	20	Self
TM10	Hidden Power	Normal	Special	60	100	15	Normal
TM11	Sunny Day	Fire	Status	—	—	5	Both Sides
TM17	Protect	Normal	Status	—	—	10	Self
TM18	Rain Dance	Water	Status	—	—	5	Both Sides
TM21	Frustration	Normal	Physical	—	100	20	Normal
TM27	Return	Normal	Physical	—	100	20	Normal
TM28	Dig	Ground	Physical	80	100	10	Normal
TM31	Brick Break	Fighting	Physical	75	100	15	Normal
TM32	Double Team	Normal	Status	—	—	15	Self
TM36	Sludge Bomb	Poison	Special	90	100	10	Normal
TM39	Rock Tomb	Rock	Physical	60	95	15	Normal
TM40	Aerial Ace	Flying	Physical	60	—	20	Normal
TM41	Torment	Dark	Status	—	100	15	Normal
TM42	Facade	Normal	Physical	70	100	20	Normal
TM44	Rest	Psychic	Status	—	—	10	Self
TM45	Attract	Normal	Status	—	100	15	Normal
TM47	Low Sweep	Fighting	Physical	65	100	20	Normal
TM48	Round	Normal	Special	60	100	15	Normal
TM49	Echoed Voice	Normal	Special	40	100	15	Normal
TM54	False Swipe	Normal	Physical	40	100	40	Normal
TM56	Fling	Dark	Physical	—	100	10	Normal
TM65	Shadow Claw	Ghost	Physical	70	100	15	Normal
TM66	Payback	Dark	Physical	50	100	10	Normal
TM67	Retaliate	Normal	Physical	70	100	5	Normal
TM68	Giga Impact	Normal	Physical	150	90	5	Normal
TM71	Stone Edge	Rock	Physical	100	80	5	Normal
TM75	Swords Dance	Normal	Status	—	—	20	Self
TM78	Bulldoze	Ground	Physical	60	100	20	Adjacent
TM80	Rock Slide	Rock	Physical	75	90	10	Many Others
TM86	Grass Knot	Grass	Special	—	100	20	Normal
TM87	Swagger	Normal	Status	—	90	15	Normal

No.	Name	Type	Kind	Pow.	Acc.	PP	Range
TM88	Sleep Talk	Normal	Status	—	—	10	Self
TM90	Substitute	Normal	Status	—	—	10	Self
TM94	Rock Smash	Fighting	Physical	40	100	15	Normal
TM97	Dark Pulse	Dark	Special	80	100	15	Normal
TM98	Power-Up Punch	Fighting	Physical	40	100	20	Normal
TM100	Confide	Normal	Status	—	—	20	Normal
HM01	Cut	Normal	Physical	50	95	30	Normal
HM03	Surf	Water	Special	90	100	15	Normal
HM04	Strength	Normal	Physical	80	100	15	Normal

● MOVES TAUGHT BY PEOPLE
Name	Type	Kind	Pow.	Acc.	PP	Range

● EGG MOVES
Name	Type	Kind	Pow.	Acc.	PP	Range
Quash	Dark	Status	—	100	15	Normal
Me First	Normal	Status	—	—	20	Varies
Quick Guard	Fighting	Status	—	—	15	Your Side
Foul Play	Dark	Physical	95	100	15	Normal
Storm Throw	Fighting	Physical	60	100	10	Normal

AFTER THE HALL OF FAME
CENTRAL KALOS
091
Pancham
COASTAL KALOS
MOUNTAIN KALOS
ADVENTURE DATA

Central Kalos — 092

Daunting Pokémon

Pangoro

HEIGHT: 6'11" WEIGHT: 299.8 lbs.
GENDER: ♂/♀

TYPE Fighting Dark

ABILITIES
Iron Fist
Mold Breaker

HIDDEN ABILITY
Scrappy

STAT GROWTH RATES
HP
Attack
Defense
Sp. Atk
Sp. Def
Speed

EGG GROUPS
Field, Human-Like

X Although it possesses a violent temperament, it won't put up with bullying. It uses the leaf in its mouth to sense the movements of its enemies.

Y It charges ahead and bashes its opponents like a berserker, uncaring about any hits it might take. Its arms are mighty enough to snap a telephone pole.

EVOLUTION

Lv. 32 with a Dark-type Pokémon in your party

Pancham → Pangoro

ITEMS SOMETIMES HELD BY WILD POKÉMON
None

Damage taken in normal battles		Damage taken in Inverse Battles	
Normal	×1	Normal	×1
Fire	×1	Fire	×1
Water	×1	Water	×1
Grass	×1	Grass	×1
Electric	×1	Electric	×1
Ice	×1	Ice	×1
Fighting	×2	Fighting	×0.5
Poison	×1	Poison	×1
Ground	×1	Ground	×1
Flying	×2	Flying	×0.5
Psychic	×0	Psychic	×1
Bug	×1	Bug	×1
Rock	×0.5	Rock	×2
Ghost	×0.5	Ghost	×2
Dragon	×1	Dragon	×1
Dark	×0.25	Dark	×4
Steel	×1	Steel	×1
Fairy	×4	Fairy	×0.25

Can be used in	
Inverse Battle	Battle Institute
—	Battle Maison
Battle Chateau	Random Matchup

Same form for ♂/♀

How to obtain for your Central Kalos Pokédex

Level up Pancham to Lv. 32 while having a Dark-type Pokémon in your party.

Level up Pancham to Lv. 32 while having a Dark-type Pokémon in your party.

● LEVEL-UP MOVES

Lv.	Name	Type	Kind	Pow.	Acc.	PP	Range
1	Entrainment	Normal	Status	—	100	15	Normal
1	Hammer Arm	Fighting	Physical	100	90	10	Normal
1	Tackle	Normal	Physical	50	100	35	Normal
1	Leer	Normal	Status	—	100	30	Many Others
7	Arm Thrust	Fighting	Physical	15	100	20	Normal
9	Work Up	Normal	Status	—	—	30	Self
12	Karate Chop	Fighting	Physical	50	100	25	Normal
15	Comet Punch	Normal	Physical	18	85	15	Normal
20	Slash	Normal	Physical	70	100	20	Normal
23	Circle Throw	Fighting	Physical	60	90	10	Normal
27	Vital Throw	Fighting	Physical	70	—	10	Normal
33	Body Slam	Normal	Physical	85	100	15	Normal
42	Crunch	Dark	Physical	80	100	15	Normal
45	Entrainment	Normal	Status	—	100	15	Normal
48	Parting Shot	Dark	Status	—	100	20	Normal
52	Sky Uppercut	Fighting	Physical	85	90	15	Normal
57	Hammer Arm	Fighting	Physical	100	90	10	Normal
65	Taunt	Dark	Status	—	100	20	Normal
70	Low Sweep	Fighting	Physical	65	100	20	Normal

● TM & HM MOVES

No.	Name	Type	Kind	Pow.	Acc.	PP	Range
TM01	Hone Claws	Dark	Status	—	—	15	Self
TM02	Dragon Claw	Dragon	Physical	80	100	15	Normal
TM05	Roar	Normal	Status	—	—	20	Normal
TM06	Toxic	Poison	Status	—	90	10	Normal
TM08	Bulk Up	Fighting	Status	—	—	20	Self
TM10	Hidden Power	Normal	Special	60	100	15	Normal
TM11	Sunny Day	Fire	Status	—	—	5	Both Sides
TM12	Taunt	Dark	Status	—	100	20	Normal
TM15	Hyper Beam	Normal	Special	150	90	5	Normal
TM17	Protect	Normal	Status	—	—	10	Self
TM18	Rain Dance	Water	Status	—	—	5	Both Sides
TM21	Frustration	Normal	Physical	—	100	20	Normal
TM26	Earthquake	Ground	Physical	100	100	10	Adjacent
TM27	Return	Normal	Physical	—	100	20	Normal
TM28	Dig	Ground	Physical	80	100	10	Normal
TM31	Brick Break	Fighting	Physical	75	100	15	Normal
TM32	Double Team	Normal	Status	—	—	15	Self
TM36	Sludge Bomb	Poison	Special	90	100	10	Normal
TM39	Rock Tomb	Rock	Physical	60	95	15	Normal
TM40	Aerial Ace	Flying	Physical	60	—	20	Normal
TM41	Torment	Dark	Status	—	100	15	Normal
TM42	Facade	Normal	Physical	70	100	20	Normal
TM44	Rest	Psychic	Status	—	—	10	Self
TM45	Attract	Normal	Status	—	100	15	Normal
TM46	Thief	Dark	Physical	60	100	25	Normal
TM47	Low Sweep	Fighting	Physical	65	100	20	Normal
TM48	Round	Normal	Special	60	100	15	Normal
TM49	Echoed Voice	Normal	Special	40	100	15	Normal
TM52	Focus Blast	Fighting	Special	120	70	5	Normal
TM54	False Swipe	Normal	Physical	40	100	40	Normal
TM56	Fling	Dark	Physical	—	100	10	Normal
TM60	Quash	Dark	Status	—	100	15	Normal
TM63	Embargo	Dark	Status	—	100	15	Normal

No.	Name	Type	Kind	Pow.	Acc.	PP	Range
TM65	Shadow Claw	Ghost	Physical	70	100	15	Normal
TM66	Payback	Dark	Physical	50	100	10	Normal
TM67	Retaliate	Normal	Physical	70	100	5	Normal
TM68	Giga Impact	Normal	Physical	150	90	5	Normal
TM75	Swords Dance	Normal	Status	—	—	20	Self
TM78	Bulldoze	Ground	Physical	60	100	20	Adjacent
TM80	Rock Slide	Rock	Physical	75	90	10	Many Others
TM81	X-Scissor	Bug	Physical	80	100	15	Normal
TM83	Infestation	Bug	Special	20	100	20	Normal
TM84	Poison Jab	Poison	Physical	80	100	20	Normal
TM86	Grass Knot	Grass	Special	—	100	20	Normal
TM87	Swagger	Normal	Status	—	90	15	Normal
TM88	Sleep Talk	Normal	Status	—	—	10	Self
TM90	Substitute	Normal	Status	—	—	10	Self
TM94	Rock Smash	Fighting	Physical	40	100	15	Normal
TM95	Snarl	Dark	Special	55	95	15	Many Others
TM97	Dark Pulse	Dark	Special	80	100	15	Normal
TM98	Power-Up Punch	Fighting	Physical	40	100	20	Normal
TM100	Confide	Normal	Status	—	—	20	Normal
HM01	Cut	Normal	Physical	50	95	30	Normal
HM03	Surf	Water	Special	90	100	15	Adjacent
HM04	Strength	Normal	Physical	80	100	15	Normal

● MOVES TAUGHT BY PEOPLE

Name	Type	Kind	Pow.	Acc.	PP	Range

AFTER THE HALL OF FAME

CENTRAL KALOS

093

Furfrou

COASTAL KALOS

MOUNTAIN KALOS

ADVENTURE DATA

🏠 **Central Kalos**

Poodle Pokémon

✔ Furfrou

093

HEIGHT: 3'11" WEIGHT: 61.7 lbs.
GENDER: ♂/♀

TYPE Normal

ABILITY
Fur Coat

HIDDEN ABILITY
None

STAT GROWTH RATES
HP	■■■
Attack	■■■■
Defense	■■■
Sp. Atk	■■■
Sp. Def	■■■
Speed	■■■■■

EGG GROUP
Field

❌ Trimming its fluffy fur not only makes it more elegant but also increases the swiftness of its movements.

✔ Historically, in the Kalos region, these Pokémon were the designated guardians of the king.

🏠 **EVOLUTION**

Does not evolve

ITEMS SOMETIMES HELD BY WILD POKÉMON
None

Can be used in
Inverse Battle
——
Battle Chateau
Battle Institute
Battle Maison
Random Matchup

Damage taken in normal battles
Normal	×1
Fire	×1
Water	×1
Grass	×1
Electric	×1
Ice	×1
Fighting	×2
Poison	×1
Ground	×1
Flying	×1
Psychic	×1
Bug	×1
Rock	×1
Ghost	×0
Dragon	×1
Dark	×1
Steel	×1
Fairy	×1

Damage taken in Inverse Battles
Normal	×1
Fire	×1
Water	×1
Grass	×1
Electric	×1
Ice	×1
Fighting	×0.5
Poison	×1
Ground	×1
Flying	×1
Psychic	×1
Bug	×1
Rock	×1
Ghost	×2
Dragon	×1
Dark	×1
Steel	×1
Fairy	×1

Furfrou
Natural Form

Furfrou
Diamond Trim

Furfrou
Star Trim

Furfrou
Heart Trim

How to obtain for your Central Kalos Pokédex

❶ Catch in the tall grass on Route 5.

❷ Catch in the purple flowers on Route 5.

❶ Catch in the tall grass on Route 5.

❷ Catch in the purple flowers on Route 5.

● LEVEL-UP MOVES

Lv.	Name	Type	Kind	Pow.	Acc.	PP	Range
1	Tackle	Normal	Physical	50	100	35	Normal
1	Growl	Normal	Status	—	100	40	Many Others
5	Sand Attack	Ground	Status	—	100	15	Normal
9	Baby-Doll Eyes	Fairy	Status	—	100	30	Normal
12	Headbutt	Normal	Physical	70	100	15	Normal
15	Tail Whip	Normal	Status	—	100	30	Many Others
22	Bite	Dark	Physical	60	100	25	Normal
27	Odor Sleuth	Normal	Status	—	—	40	Normal
33	Retaliate	Normal	Physical	70	100	5	Normal
35	Take Down	Normal	Physical	90	85	20	Normal
38	Charm	Fairy	Status	—	100	20	Normal
42	Sucker Punch	Dark	Physical	80	100	5	Normal
48	Cotton Guard	Grass	Status	—	—	10	Self

● TM & HM MOVES

No.	Name	Type	Kind	Pow.	Acc.	PP	Range
TM05	Roar	Normal	Status	—	—	20	Normal
TM06	Toxic	Poison	Status	—	90	10	Normal
TM10	Hidden Power	Normal	Special	60	100	15	Normal
TM11	Sunny Day	Fire	Status	—	—	5	Both Sides
TM17	Protect	Normal	Status	—	—	10	Self
TM18	Rain Dance	Water	Status	—	—	5	Both Sides
TM21	Frustration	Normal	Physical	—	100	20	Normal
TM27	Return	Normal	Physical	—	100	20	Normal
TM28	Dig	Ground	Physical	80	100	10	Normal
TM32	Double Team	Normal	Status	—	—	15	Self
TM42	Facade	Normal	Physical	70	100	20	Normal
TM44	Rest	Psychic	Status	—	—	10	Self
TM45	Attract	Normal	Status	—	100	15	Normal
TM48	Round	Normal	Special	60	100	15	Normal
TM49	Echoed Voice	Normal	Special	40	100	15	Normal
TM57	Charge Beam	Electric	Special	50	90	10	Normal
TM67	Retaliate	Normal	Physical	70	100	5	Normal
TM68	Giga Impact	Normal	Physical	150	90	5	Normal
TM70	Flash	Normal	Status	—	100	20	Normal
TM73	Thunder Wave	Electric	Status	—	100	20	Normal
TM86	Grass Knot	Grass	Special	—	100	20	Normal
TM87	Swagger	Normal	Status	—	90	15	Normal
TM88	Sleep Talk	Normal	Status	—	—	10	Self

No.	Name	Type	Kind	Pow.	Acc.	PP	Range
TM89	U-turn	Bug	Physical	70	100	20	Normal
TM90	Substitute	Normal	Status	—	—	10	Self
TM93	Wild Charge	Electric	Physical	90	100	15	Normal
TM94	Rock Smash	Fighting	Physical	40	100	15	Normal
TM95	Snarl	Dark	Special	55	95	15	Many Others
TM97	Dark Pulse	Dark	Special	80	100	15	Normal
TM100	Confide	Normal	Status	—	—	20	Normal
HM03	Surf	Water	Special	90	100	15	Adjacent

● MOVES TAUGHT BY PEOPLE

Name	Type	Kind	Pow.	Acc.	PP	Range

● EGG MOVES

Name	Type	Kind	Pow.	Acc.	PP	Range
Role Play	Psychic	Status	—	—	10	Normal
Work Up	Normal	Status	—	—	30	Self
Mimic	Normal	Status	—	—	10	Normal
Captivate	Normal	Status	—	100	20	Many Others
Refresh	Normal	Status	—	—	20	Self

Furfrou change their forms when trimmed

Furfrou change their forms when they are trimmed at the Friseur Furfrou on South Boulevard in Lumiose City. La Reine Trim, Kabuki Trim, and Pharaoh Trim forms will be available when you become stylish, and Debutante Trim, Matron Trim, and Dandy Trim will be available when you become even more stylish.

Natural Form: Same form for ♂ / ♀

Heart Trim: Same form for ♂ / ♀

Star Trim: Same form for ♂ / ♀

Diamond Trim: Same form for ♂ / ♀

La Reine Trim: Same form for ♂ / ♀

Kabuki Trim: Same form for ♂ / ♀

Pharaoh Trim: Same form for ♂ / ♀

Debutante Trim: Same form for ♂ / ♀

Matron Trim: Same form for ♂ / ♀

Dandy Trim: Same form for ♂ / ♀

AFTER THE HALL OF FAME

CENTRAL KALOS

093 Furfrou

COASTAL KALOS

MOUNTAIN KALOS

ADVENTURE DATA

AFTER THE HALL OF FAME

CENTRAL KALOS

094

Doduo

COASTAL KALOS

MOUNTAIN KALOS

ADVENTURE DATA

🏠 Central Kalos — 094
Twin Bird Pokémon
✅ Doduo

HEIGHT: 4'07" WEIGHT: 86.4 lbs.
GENDER: ♂/♀

TYPE Normal / Flying

ABILITIES
Run Away
Early Bird

HIDDEN ABILITY
Tangled Feet

STAT GROWTH RATES	
HP	▪▪
Attack	▪▪▪▪
Defense	▪▪
Sp. Atk	▪▪
Sp. Def	▪▪
Speed	▪▪▪▪

EGG GROUP
Flying

X A two-headed Pokémon that was discovered as a sudden mutation. It runs at a pace of over 60 miles per hour.

Y The brains in its two heads appear to communicate emotions to each other with a telepathic power.

⬆ EVOLUTION

Doduo → Lv. 31 → Dodrio

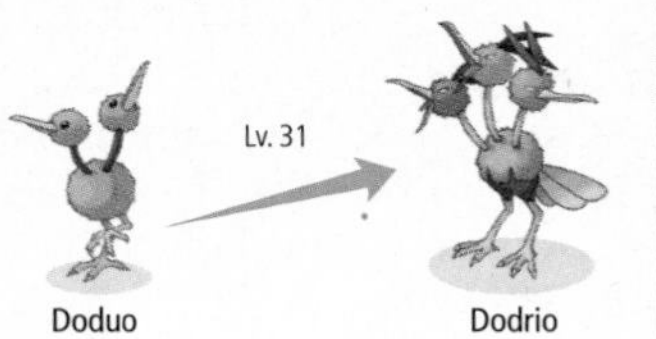

ITEMS SOMETIMES HELD BY WILD POKÉMON
Sharp Beak

Can be used in
Inverse Battle
—
Battle Chateau
Battle Institute
Battle Maison
Random Matchup

Damage taken in normal battles	
Normal	×1
Fire	×1
Water	×1
Grass	×0.5
Electric	×2
Ice	×2
Fighting	×1
Poison	×1
Ground	×0
Flying	×1
Psychic	×1
Bug	×0.5
Rock	×2
Ghost	×0
Dragon	×1
Dark	×1
Steel	×1
Fairy	×1

Damage taken in Inverse Battles	
Normal	×1
Fire	×1
Water	×1
Grass	×2
Electric	×0.5
Ice	×0.5
Fighting	×1
Poison	×1
Ground	×2
Flying	×1
Psychic	×1
Bug	×2
Rock	×0.5
Ghost	×2
Dragon	×1
Dark	×1
Steel	×1
Fairy	×1

How to obtain for your Central Kalos Pokédex

❶ Catch in the tall grass on Route 5.
❷ Catch in the purple flowers on Route 5.

❶ Catch in the tall grass on Route 5.
❷ Catch in the purple flowers on Route 5.

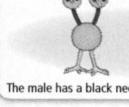
♂

♀

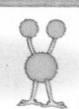

The male has a black neck. The female has a beige neck.

● LEVEL-UP MOVES

Lv.	Name	Type	Kind	Pow.	Acc.	PP	Range
1	Peck	Flying	Physical	35	100	35	Normal
1	Growl	Normal	Status	—	100	40	Many Others
5	Quick Attack	Normal	Physical	40	100	30	Normal
10	Rage	Normal	Physical	20	100	20	Normal
14	Fury Attack	Normal	Physical	15	85	20	Normal
19	Pursuit	Dark	Physical	40	100	20	Normal
23	Uproar	Normal	Special	90	100	10	1 Random
28	Acupressure	Normal	Status	—	—	30	Self/Ally
32	Double Hit	Normal	Physical	35	90	10	Normal
37	Agility	Psychic	Status	—	—	30	Self
41	Drill Peck	Flying	Physical	80	100	20	Normal
46	Endeavor	Normal	Physical	—	100	5	Normal
50	Thrash	Normal	Physical	120	100	10	1 Random

● TM & HM MOVES

No.	Name	Type	Kind	Pow.	Acc.	PP	Range
TM06	Toxic	Poison	Status	—	90	10	Normal
TM10	Hidden Power	Normal	Special	60	100	15	Normal
TM11	Sunny Day	Fire	Status	—	—	5	Both Sides
TM17	Protect	Normal	Status	—	—	10	Self
TM19	Roost	Flying	Status	—	—	10	Self
TM21	Frustration	Normal	Physical	—	100	20	Normal
TM27	Return	Normal	Physical	—	100	20	Normal
TM32	Double Team	Normal	Status	—	—	15	Self
TM40	Aerial Ace	Flying	Physical	60	—	20	Normal
TM42	Facade	Normal	Physical	70	100	20	Normal
TM44	Rest	Psychic	Status	—	—	10	Self
TM45	Attract	Normal	Status	—	100	15	Normal
TM46	Thief	Dark	Physical	60	100	25	Normal
TM48	Round	Normal	Special	60	100	15	Normal
TM49	Echoed Voice	Normal	Special	40	100	15	Normal
TM51	Steel Wing	Steel	Physical	70	90	25	Normal
TM87	Swagger	Normal	Status	—	90	15	Normal
TM88	Sleep Talk	Normal	Status	—	—	10	Self
TM90	Substitute	Normal	Status	—	—	10	Self
TM100	Confide	Normal	Status	—	—	20	Normal
HM02	Fly	Flying	Physical	90	95	15	Normal

● MOVES TAUGHT BY PEOPLE

Name	Type	Kind	Pow.	Acc.	PP	Range

● EGG MOVES

Name	Type	Kind	Pow.	Acc.	PP	Range
Quick Attack	Normal	Physical	40	100	30	Normal
Supersonic	Normal	Status	—	55	20	Normal
Haze	Ice	Status	—	—	30	Both Sides
Feint Attack	Dark	Physical	60	—	20	Normal
Flail	Normal	Physical	—	100	15	Normal
Endeavor	Normal	Physical	—	100	5	Normal
Mirror Move	Flying	Status	—	—	20	Normal
Brave Bird	Flying	Physical	120	100	15	Normal
Natural Gift	Normal	Physical	—	100	15	Normal
Assurance	Dark	Physical	60	100	10	Normal

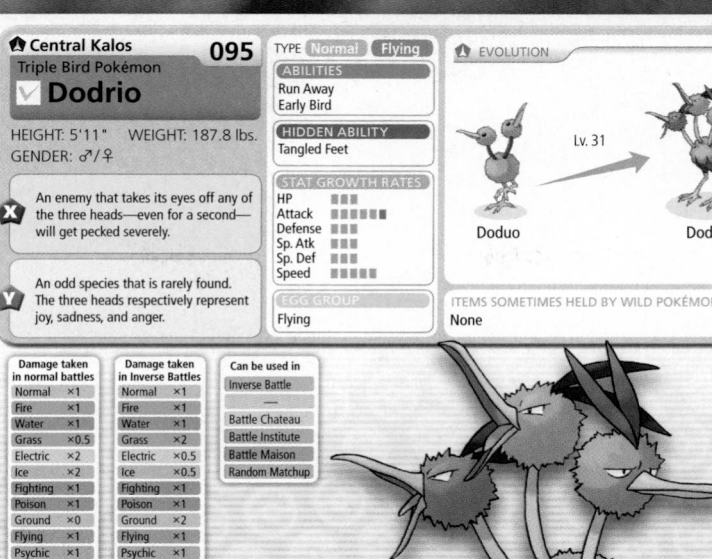

⌂ Central Kalos — 095

Triple Bird Pokémon

☑ Dodrio

HEIGHT: 5'11" WEIGHT: 187.8 lbs.
GENDER: ♂/♀

X An enemy that takes its eyes off any of the three heads—even for a second—will get pecked severely.

Y An odd species that is rarely found. The three heads respectively represent joy, sadness, and anger.

TYPE Normal / Flying

ABILITIES
Run Away
Early Bird

HIDDEN ABILITY
Tangled Feet

STAT GROWTH RATES
HP ▪▪▪
Attack ▪▪▪▪▪
Defense ▪▪▪
Sp. Atk ▪▪▪
Sp. Def ▪▪▪
Speed ▪▪▪▪▪

EGG GROUP
Flying

↑ EVOLUTION

Doduo → (Lv. 31) → Dodrio

ITEMS SOMETIMES HELD BY WILD POKÉMON
None

Damage taken in normal battles		Damage taken in Inverse Battles	
Normal	×1	Normal	×1
Fire	×1	Fire	×1
Water	×1	Water	×1
Grass	×0.5	Grass	×2
Electric	×2	Electric	×0.5
Ice	×2	Ice	×0.5
Fighting	×1	Fighting	×1
Poison	×1	Poison	×1
Ground	×0	Ground	×2
Flying	×1	Flying	×1
Psychic	×1	Psychic	×1
Bug	×0.5	Bug	×2
Rock	×2	Rock	×0.5
Ghost	×0	Ghost	×2
Dragon	×1	Dragon	×1
Dark	×1	Dark	×1
Steel	×1	Steel	×1
Fairy	×1	Fairy	×1

Can be used in
Inverse Battle
———
Battle Chateau
Battle Institute
Battle Maison
Random Matchup

How to obtain for your Central Kalos Pokédex

X	Y
Level up Doduo to Lv. 31.	Level up Doduo to Lv. 31.

♂   ♀

The male has a black neck. The female has a beige neck.

● LEVEL-UP MOVES

Lv.	Name	Type	Kind	Pow.	Acc.	PP	Range
1	Pluck	Flying	Physical	60	100	20	Normal
1	Peck	Flying	Physical	35	100	35	Normal
1	Growl	Normal	Status	—	100	40	Many Others
1	Quick Attack	Normal	Physical	40	100	30	Normal
1	Rage	Normal	Physical	20	100	20	Normal
5	Quick Attack	Normal	Physical	40	100	30	Normal
10	Rage	Normal	Physical	20	100	20	Normal
14	Fury Attack	Normal	Physical	15	85	20	Normal
19	Pursuit	Dark	Physical	40	100	20	Normal
23	Uproar	Normal	Special	90	100	10	1 Random
28	Acupressure	Normal	Status	—	—	30	Self/Ally
34	Tri Attack	Normal	Special	80	100	10	Normal
41	Agility	Psychic	Status	—	—	30	Self
47	Drill Peck	Flying	Physical	80	100	20	Normal
54	Endeavor	Normal	Physical	—	100	5	Normal
60	Thrash	Normal	Physical	120	100	10	1 Random

● TM & HM MOVES

No.	Name	Type	Kind	Pow.	Acc.	PP	Range
TM06	Toxic	Poison	Status	—	90	10	Normal
TM10	Hidden Power	Normal	Special	60	100	15	Normal
TM11	Sunny Day	Fire	Status	—	—	5	Both Sides
TM12	Taunt	Dark	Status	—	100	20	Normal
TM15	Hyper Beam	Normal	Special	150	90	5	Normal
TM17	Protect	Normal	Status	—	—	10	Self
TM19	Roost	Flying	Status	—	—	10	Self
TM21	Frustration	Normal	Physical	—	100	20	Normal
TM27	Return	Normal	Physical	—	100	20	Normal
TM32	Double Team	Normal	Status	—	—	15	Self
TM40	Aerial Ace	Flying	Physical	60	—	20	Normal
TM41	Torment	Dark	Status	—	100	15	Normal
TM42	Facade	Normal	Physical	70	100	20	Normal
TM44	Rest	Psychic	Status	—	—	10	Self
TM45	Attract	Normal	Status	—	100	15	Normal
TM46	Thief	Dark	Physical	60	100	25	Normal
TM48	Round	Normal	Special	60	100	15	Normal
TM49	Echoed Voice	Normal	Special	40	100	15	Normal
TM51	Steel Wing	Steel	Physical	70	90	25	Normal
TM66	Payback	Dark	Physical	50	100	10	Normal
TM68	Giga Impact	Normal	Physical	150	90	5	Normal
TM87	Swagger	Normal	Status	—	90	15	Normal
TM88	Sleep Talk	Normal	Status	—	—	10	Self
TM90	Substitute	Normal	Status	—	—	10	Self
TM100	Confide	Normal	Status	—	—	20	Normal
HM02	Fly	Flying	Physical	90	95	15	Normal

No.	Name	Type	Kind	Pow.	Acc.	PP	Range

● MOVES TAUGHT BY PEOPLE

Name	Type	Kind	Pow.	Acc.	PP	Range

AFTER THE HALL OF FAME

CENTRAL KALOS

095

Dodrio

COASTAL KALOS

MOUNTAIN KALOS

ADVENTURE DATA

AFTER THE HALL OF FAME

CENTRAL KALOS

096

Plusle

COASTAL KALOS

MOUNTAIN KALOS

ADVENTURE DATA

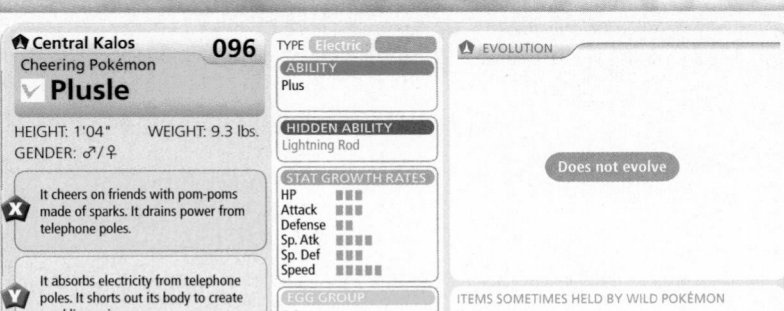

Central Kalos 096
Cheering Pokémon
☑ Plusle

HEIGHT: 1'04"　　WEIGHT: 9.3 lbs.
GENDER: ♂/♀

TYPE Electric

ABILITY
Plus

HIDDEN ABILITY
Lightning Rod

STAT GROWTH RATES
HP	■■■
Attack	■■■
Defense	■■
Sp. Atk	■■■
Sp. Def	■■■
Speed	■■■■■

EGG GROUP
Fairy

X It cheers on friends with pom-poms made of sparks. It drains power from telephone poles.

Y It absorbs electricity from telephone poles. It shorts out its body to create crackling noises.

EVOLUTION

Does not evolve

ITEMS SOMETIMES HELD BY WILD POKÉMON
None

Can be used in
Inverse Battle
—
Battle Chateau
Battle Institute
Battle Maison
Random Matchup

Damage taken in normal battles		Damage taken in Inverse Battles	
Normal	×1	Normal	×1
Fire	×1	Fire	×1
Water	×1	Water	×1
Grass	×1	Grass	×1
Electric	×0.5	Electric	×2
Ice	×1	Ice	×1
Fighting	×1	Fighting	×1
Poison	×1	Poison	×1
Ground	×2	Ground	×0.5
Flying	×0.5	Flying	×2
Psychic	×1	Psychic	×1
Bug	×1	Bug	×1
Rock	×1	Rock	×1
Ghost	×1	Ghost	×1
Dragon	×1	Dragon	×1
Dark	×1	Dark	×1
Steel	×0.5	Steel	×2
Fairy	×1	Fairy	×1

How to obtain for your Central Kalos Pokédex

❶ Catch in the tall grass on Route 5.

❷ Catch in the purple flowers on Route 5.

Catch in a Horde Encounter on Route 5.

Same form for ♂/♀

● LEVEL-UP MOVES

Lv.	Name	Type	Kind	Pow.	Acc.	PP	Range
1	Nasty Plot	Dark	Status	—	—	20	Self
1	Nuzzle	Electric	Physical	20	100	20	Normal
1	Entrainment	Normal	Status	—	100	15	Normal
1	Play Nice	Normal	Status	—	—	20	Normal
1	Growl	Normal	Status	—	100	40	Many Others
3	Thunder Wave	Electric	Status	—	100	20	Normal
7	Quick Attack	Normal	Physical	40	100	30	Normal
10	Helping Hand	Normal	Status	—	—	20	1 Ally
15	Spark	Electric	Physical	65	100	20	Normal
17	Encore	Normal	Status	—	100	5	Normal
21	Play Nice	Normal	Status	—	—	20	Normal
24	Copycat	Normal	Status	—	—	20	Self
29	Electro Ball	Electric	Special	—	100	10	Normal
31	Swift	Normal	Special	60	—	20	Many Others
35	Fake Tears	Dark	Status	—	100	20	Normal
38	Charge	Electric	Status	—	—	20	Self
42	Thunder	Electric	Special	110	70	10	Normal
44	Baton Pass	Normal	Status	—	—	40	Self
48	Agility	Psychic	Status	—	—	30	Self
50	Last Resort	Normal	Physical	140	100	5	Normal
56	Nasty Plot	Dark	Status	—	—	20	Self
63	Entrainment	Normal	Status	—	100	15	Normal

● TM & HM MOVES

No.	Name	Type	Kind	Pow.	Acc.	PP	Range
TM06	Toxic	Poison	Status	—	90	10	Normal
TM10	Hidden Power	Normal	Special	60	100	15	Normal
TM16	Light Screen	Psychic	Status	—	—	30	Your Side
TM17	Protect	Normal	Status	—	—	10	Self
TM18	Rain Dance	Water	Status	—	—	5	Both Sides
TM21	Frustration	Normal	Physical	—	100	20	Normal
TM24	Thunderbolt	Electric	Special	90	100	15	Normal
TM25	Thunder	Electric	Special	110	70	10	Normal
TM27	Return	Normal	Physical	—	100	20	Normal
TM32	Double Team	Normal	Status	—	—	15	Self
TM42	Facade	Normal	Physical	70	100	20	Normal
TM44	Rest	Psychic	Status	—	—	10	Self
TM45	Attract	Normal	Status	—	100	15	Normal
TM48	Round	Normal	Special	60	100	15	Normal
TM49	Echoed Voice	Normal	Special	40	100	15	Normal
TM56	Fling	Dark	Physical	—	100	10	Normal
TM57	Charge Beam	Electric	Special	50	90	10	Normal
TM70	Flash	Normal	Status	—	100	20	Normal
TM72	Volt Switch	Electric	Special	70	100	20	Normal
TM73	Thunder Wave	Electric	Status	—	100	20	Normal
TM86	Grass Knot	Grass	Special	—	100	20	Normal
TM87	Swagger	Normal	Status	—	90	15	Normal
TM88	Sleep Talk	Normal	Status	—	—	10	Self
TM90	Substitute	Normal	Status	—	—	10	Self
TM93	Wild Charge	Electric	Physical	90	100	15	Normal
TM100	Confide	Normal	Status	—	—	20	Normal

● MOVES TAUGHT BY PEOPLE

Name	Type	Kind	Pow.	Acc.	PP	Range

● EGG MOVES

Name	Type	Kind	Pow.	Acc.	PP	Range
Wish	Normal	Status	—	—	10	Self
Sing	Normal	Status	—	55	15	Normal
Sweet Kiss	Fairy	Status	—	75	10	Normal
Discharge	Electric	Special	80	100	15	Adjacent
Lucky Chant	Normal	Status	—	—	30	Your Side

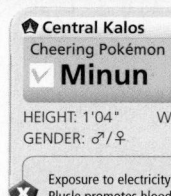

Central Kalos

Cheering Pokémon

∨ Minun   097

HEIGHT: 1'04"   WEIGHT: 9.3 lbs.
GENDER: ♂/♀

TYPE `Electric`

ABILITY
Minus

HIDDEN ABILITY
Volt Absorb

STAT GROWTH RATES
HP	■■■
Attack	■■
Defense	■■
Sp. Atk	■■■■
Sp. Def	■■■■
Speed	■■■■■

EGG GROUP
Fairy

✖ Exposure to electricity from Minun and Plusle promotes blood circulation and relaxes muscles.

∨ It cheers on friends. If its friends are losing, its body lets off more and more sparks.

⚡ EVOLUTION

Does not evolve

ITEMS SOMETIMES HELD BY WILD POKÉMON
None

Damage taken in normal battles		Damage taken in Inverse Battles		Can be used in
Normal	×1	Normal	×1	Inverse Battle
Fire	×1	Fire	×1	----
Water	×1	Water	×1	Battle Chateau
Grass	×1	Grass	×1	Battle Institute
Electric	×0.5 ❶	Electric	×2 ❶	Battle Maison
Ice	×1	Ice	×1	Random Matchup
Fighting	×1	Fighting	×1	
Poison	×1	Poison	×1	
Ground	×2	Ground	×0.5	
Flying	×0.5	Flying	×2	
Psychic	×1	Psychic	×1	
Bug	×1	Bug	×1	
Rock	×1	Rock	×1	
Ghost	×1	Ghost	×1	
Dragon	×1	Dragon	×1	
Dark	×1	Dark	×1	
Steel	×0.5	Steel	×2	
Fairy	×1	Fairy	×1	

How to obtain for your Central Kalos Pokédex

Catch in a Horde Encounter on Route 5.

❶ Catch in the tall grass on Route 5.
❷ Catch in the purple flowers on Route 5.

Same form for ♂/♀

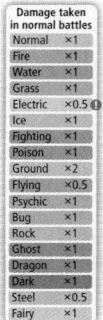 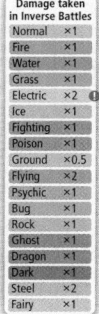

● LEVEL-UP MOVES

Lv.	Name	Type	Kind	Pow.	Acc.	PP	Range
1	Nasty Plot	Dark	Status	—	—	20	Self
1	Nuzzle	Electric	Physical	20	100	20	Normal
1	Entrainment	Normal	Status	—	100	15	Normal
1	Play Nice	Normal	Status	—	—	20	Normal
3	Growl	Normal	Status	—	100	40	Many Others
3	Thunder Wave	Electric	Status	—	100	20	Normal
7	Quick Attack	Normal	Physical	40	100	30	Normal
10	Helping Hand	Normal	Status	—	—	20	1 Ally
15	Spark	Electric	Physical	65	100	20	Normal
17	Encore	Normal	Status	—	100	5	Normal
21	Charm	Fairy	Status	—	100	20	Normal
24	Copycat	Normal	Status	—	—	20	Self
29	Electro Ball	Electric	Special	—	100	10	Normal
31	Swift	Normal	Special	60	—	20	Many Others
35	Fake Tears	Dark	Status	—	100	20	Normal
38	Charge	Electric	Status	—	—	20	Self
42	Thunder	Electric	Special	110	70	10	Normal
44	Baton Pass	Normal	Status	—	—	40	Self
48	Agility	Psychic	Status	—	—	30	Self
51	Trump Card	Normal	Special	—	—	5	Normal
56	Nasty Plot	Dark	Status	—	—	20	Self
63	Entrainment	Normal	Status	—	100	15	Normal

● TM & HM MOVES

No.	Name	Type	Kind	Pow.	Acc.	PP	Range
TM06	Toxic	Poison	Status	—	90	10	Normal
TM10	Hidden Power	Normal	Special	60	100	15	Normal
TM16	Light Screen	Psychic	Status	—	—	30	Your Side
TM17	Protect	Normal	Status	—	—	10	Self
TM18	Rain Dance	Water	Status	—	—	5	Both Sides
TM21	Frustration	Normal	Physical	—	100	20	Normal
TM24	Thunderbolt	Electric	Special	90	100	15	Normal
TM25	Thunder	Electric	Special	110	70	10	Normal
TM27	Return	Normal	Physical	—	100	20	Normal
TM32	Double Team	Normal	Status	—	—	15	Self
TM42	Facade	Normal	Physical	70	100	20	Normal
TM44	Rest	Psychic	Status	—	—	10	Self
TM45	Attract	Normal	Status	—	100	15	Normal
TM48	Round	Normal	Special	60	100	15	Normal
TM49	Echoed Voice	Normal	Special	40	100	15	Normal
TM56	Fling	Dark	Physical	—	100	10	Normal
TM57	Charge Beam	Electric	Special	50	90	10	Normal
TM70	Flash	Normal	Status	—	100	20	Normal
TM72	Volt Switch	Electric	Special	70	100	20	Normal
TM73	Thunder Wave	Electric	Status	—	100	20	Normal
TM86	Grass Knot	Grass	Special	—	100	20	Normal
TM87	Swagger	Normal	Status	—	90	15	Normal
TM88	Sleep Talk	Normal	Status	—	—	10	Self
TM90	Substitute	Normal	Status	—	—	10	Self
TM93	Wild Charge	Electric	Physical	90	100	15	Normal
TM100	Confide	Normal	Status	—	—	20	Normal

● MOVES TAUGHT BY PEOPLE

Name	Type	Kind	Pow.	Acc.	PP	Range

● EGG MOVES

Name	Type	Kind	Pow.	Acc.	PP	Range
Wish	Normal	Status	—	—	10	Self
Sing	Normal	Status	—	55	15	Normal
Sweet Kiss	Fairy	Status	—	75	10	Normal
Discharge	Electric	Special	80	100	15	Adjacent
Lucky Chant	Normal	Status	—	—	30	Your Side

AFTER THE HALL OF FAME

CENTRAL KALOS

098

Gulpin

COASTAL KALOS

MOUNTAIN KALOS

ADVENTURE DATA

🏠 Central Kalos — 098

Stomach Pokémon

☑ Gulpin

HEIGHT: 1'04"   WEIGHT: 22.7 lbs.
GENDER: ♂/♀

TYPE (Poison)

ABILITIES
Liquid Ooze
Sticky Hold

HIDDEN ABILITY
Gluttony

STAT GROWTH RATES
HP	■ ■ ■
Attack	■ ■
Defense	■ ■
Sp. Atk	■ ■
Sp. Def	■ ■
Speed	■ ■

EGG GROUP
Amorphous

🔺 EVOLUTION

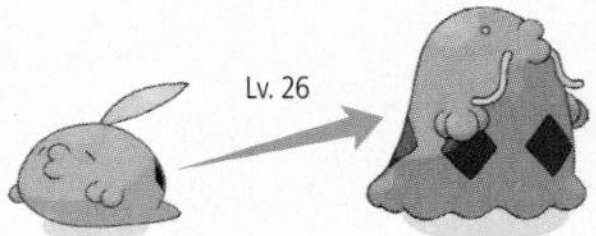

Gulpin → Lv. 26 → Swalot

ITEMS SOMETIMES HELD BY WILD POKÉMON
Oran Berry

✖ It has a small heart and brain. Its stomach comprises most of its body, with enzymes to dissolve anything.

Y There is nothing its stomach can't digest. While it is digesting, vile, overpowering gases are expelled.

Can be used in
Inverse Battle
—
Battle Chateau
Battle Institute
Battle Maison
Random Matchup

Damage taken in normal battles		Damage taken in Inverse Battles	
Normal	×1	Normal	×1
Fire	×1	Fire	×1
Water	×1	Water	×1
Grass	×0.5	Grass	×2
Electric	×1	Electric	×1
Ice	×1	Ice	×1
Fighting	×0.5	Fighting	×2
Poison	×0.5	Poison	×2
Ground	×2	Ground	×0.5
Flying	×1	Flying	×1
Psychic	×2	Psychic	×0.5
Bug	×0.5	Bug	×2
Rock	×1	Rock	×1
Ghost	×1	Ghost	×1
Dragon	×1	Dragon	×1
Dark	×1	Dark	×1
Steel	×1	Steel	×1
Fairy	×0.5	Fairy	×2

How to obtain for your Central Kalos Pokédex

❶ Catch in the tall grass on Route 5.
❷ Catch in the purple flowers on Route 5.

❶ Catch in the tall grass on Route 5.
❷ Catch in the purple flowers on Route 5.

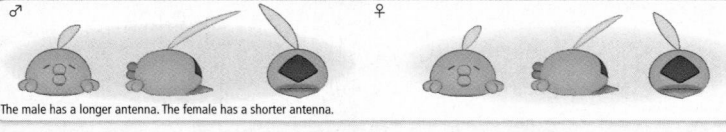

♂   ♀

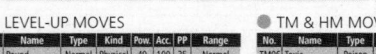

The male has a longer antenna. The female has a shorter antenna.

● LEVEL-UP MOVES

Lv.	Name	Type	Kind	Pow.	Acc.	PP	Range
1	Pound	Normal	Physical	40	100	35	Normal
6	Yawn	Normal	Status	—	—	10	Normal
9	Poison Gas	Poison	Status	—	90	40	Many Others
14	Sludge	Poison	Special	65	100	20	Normal
17	Amnesia	Psychic	Status	—	—	20	Self
23	Encore	Normal	Status	—	100	5	Normal
28	Toxic	Poison	Status	—	90	10	Normal
34	Acid Spray	Poison	Special	40	100	20	Normal
39	Stockpile	Normal	Status	—	—	20	Self
39	Spit Up	Normal	Special	—	100	10	Normal
39	Swallow	Normal	Status	—	—	10	Self
40	Belch	Poison	Special	120	90	10	Normal
44	Sludge Bomb	Poison	Special	90	100	10	Normal
49	Gastro Acid	Poison	Status	—	100	10	Normal
54	Wring Out	Normal	Special	—	100	5	Normal
59	Gunk Shot	Poison	Physical	120	80	5	Normal

● TM & HM MOVES

No.	Name	Type	Kind	Pow.	Acc.	PP	Range
TM06	Toxic	Poison	Status	—	90	10	Normal
TM09	Venoshock	Poison	Special	65	100	10	Normal
TM10	Hidden Power	Normal	Special	60	100	15	Normal
TM11	Sunny Day	Fire	Status	—	—	5	Both Sides
TM13	Ice Beam	Ice	Special	90	100	10	Normal
TM17	Protect	Normal	Status	—	—	10	Self
TM18	Rain Dance	Water	Status	—	—	5	Both Sides
TM21	Frustration	Normal	Physical	—	100	20	Normal
TM22	Solar Beam	Grass	Special	120	100	10	Normal
TM27	Return	Normal	Physical	—	100	20	Normal
TM30	Shadow Ball	Ghost	Special	80	100	15	Normal
TM32	Double Team	Normal	Status	—	—	15	Self
TM34	Sludge Wave	Poison	Special	95	100	10	Adjacent
TM36	Sludge Bomb	Poison	Special	90	100	10	Normal
TM42	Facade	Normal	Physical	70	100	20	Normal
TM44	Rest	Psychic	Status	—	—	10	Self
TM45	Attract	Normal	Status	—	100	15	Normal
TM48	Round	Normal	Special	60	100	15	Normal
TM64	Explosion	Normal	Physical	250	100	5	Adjacent
TM83	Infestation	Bug	Special	20	100	20	Normal
TM85	Dream Eater	Psychic	Special	100	100	15	Normal
TM87	Swagger	Normal	Status	—	90	15	Normal
TM88	Sleep Talk	Normal	Status	—	—	10	Self
TM90	Substitute	Normal	Status	—	—	10	Self
TM94	Rock Smash	Fighting	Physical	40	100	15	Normal
TM98	Power-Up Punch	Fighting	Physical	40	100	20	Normal
TM100	Confide	Normal	Status	—	—	20	Normal
HM04	Strength	Normal	Physical	80	100	15	Normal

● MOVES TAUGHT BY PEOPLE

Name	Type	Kind	Pow.	Acc.	PP	Range

● EGG MOVES

Name	Type	Kind	Pow.	Acc.	PP	Range
Acid Armor	Poison	Status	—	—	20	Self
Smog	Poison	Special	30	70	20	Normal
Pain Split	Normal	Status	—	—	20	Normal
Curse	Ghost	Status	—	—	10	Varies
Destiny Bond	Ghost	Status	—	—	5	Self
Mud-Slap	Ground	Special	20	100	10	Normal
Gunk Shot	Poison	Physical	120	80	5	Normal
Venom Drench	Poison	Status	—	100	20	Many Others

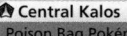 Central Kalos **099**

Poison Bag Pokémon

 Swalot

HEIGHT: 5'07" WEIGHT: 176.4 lbs.
GENDER: ♂ / ♀

TYPE **Poison**

ABILITIES
Liquid Ooze
Sticky Hold

HIDDEN ABILITY
Gluttony

STAT GROWTH RATES

HP	▪▪▪▪
Attack	▪▪▪▪
Defense	▪▪▪▪
Sp. Atk	▪▪▪▪
Sp. Def	▪▪▪▪
Speed	▪▪▪

EGG GROUP
Amorphous

 It swallows anything whole. It sweats toxic fluids from its follicles to douse foes.

It gulps anything that fits in its mouth. Its special enzymes can dissolve anything.

EVOLUTION

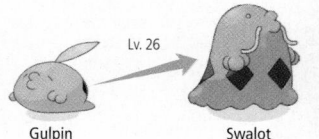

Gulpin → Lv. 26 → Swalot

ITEMS SOMETIMES HELD BY WILD POKÉMON
None

Damage taken in normal battles		Damage taken in Inverse Battles		Can be used in
Normal	×1	Normal	×1	Inverse Battle
Fire	×1	Fire	×1	—
Water	×1	Water	×1	Battle Chateau
Grass	×0.5	Grass	×2	Battle Institute
Electric	×1	Electric	×1	Battle Maison
Ice	×1	Ice	×1	Random Matchup
Fighting	×0.5	Fighting	×2	
Poison	×0.5	Poison	×2	
Ground	×2	Ground	×0.5	
Flying	×1	Flying	×1	
Psychic	×2	Psychic	×0.5	
Bug	×0.5	Bug	×2	
Rock	×1	Rock	×1	
Ghost	×1	Ghost	×1	
Dragon	×1	Dragon	×1	
Dark	×1	Dark	×1	
Steel	×1	Steel	×1	
Fairy	×0.5	Fairy	×2	

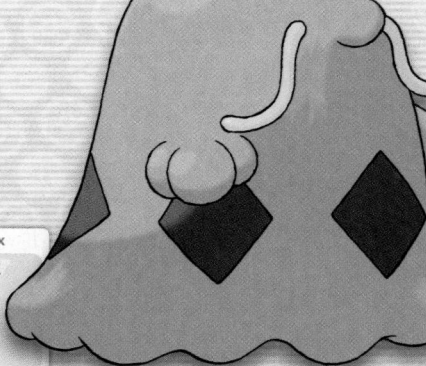

How to obtain for your Central Kalos Pokédex

Level up Gulpin to Lv. 26.	Level up Gulpin to Lv. 26.
X	Y

 ♂  ♀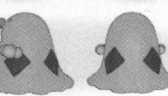

The male has longer whiskers than the female.

● **LEVEL-UP MOVES**

Lv.	Name	Type	Kind	Pow.	Acc.	PP	Range
1	Gunk Shot	Poison	Physical	120	80	5	Normal
1	Wring Out	Normal	Special	—	100	5	Normal
1	Pound	Normal	Physical	40	100	35	Normal
1	Yawn	Normal	Status	—	—	10	Normal
1	Poison Gas	Poison	Status	—	90	40	Many Others
1	Sludge	Poison	Special	65	100	20	Normal
6	Yawn	Normal	Status	—	—	10	Normal
9	Poison Gas	Poison	Status	—	90	40	Many Others
14	Sludge	Poison	Special	65	100	20	Normal
17	Amnesia	Psychic	Status	—	—	20	Self
23	Encore	Normal	Status	—	100	5	Normal
26	Body Slam	Normal	Physical	85	100	15	Normal
30	Toxic	Poison	Status	—	90	10	Normal
38	Acid Spray	Poison	Special	40	100	20	Normal
45	Stockpile	Normal	Status	—	—	20	Self
45	Spit Up	Normal	Special	—	100	10	Normal
45	Swallow	Normal	Status	—	—	10	Self
46	Belch	Poison	Special	120	90	10	Normal
52	Sludge Bomb	Poison	Special	90	100	10	Normal
59	Gastro Acid	Poison	Status	—	100	10	Normal
66	Wring Out	Normal	Special	—	100	5	Normal
73	Gunk Shot	Poison	Physical	120	80	5	Normal

● **TM & HM MOVES**

No.	Name	Type	Kind	Pow.	Acc.	PP	Range
TM06	Toxic	Poison	Status	—	90	10	Normal
TM09	Venoshock	Poison	Special	65	100	10	Normal
TM10	Hidden Power	Normal	Special	60	100	15	Normal
TM11	Sunny Day	Fire	Status	—	—	5	Both Sides
TM13	Ice Beam	Ice	Special	90	100	10	Normal
TM15	Hyper Beam	Normal	Special	150	90	5	Normal
TM17	Protect	Normal	Status	—	—	10	Self
TM18	Rain Dance	Water	Status	—	—	5	Both Sides
TM21	Frustration	Normal	Physical	—	100	20	Normal
TM22	Solar Beam	Grass	Special	120	100	10	Normal
TM26	Earthquake	Ground	Physical	100	100	10	Adjacent
TM27	Return	Normal	Physical	—	100	20	Normal
TM30	Shadow Ball	Ghost	Special	80	100	15	Normal
TM32	Double Team	Normal	Status	—	—	15	Self
TM34	Sludge Wave	Poison	Special	95	100	10	Adjacent
TM36	Sludge Bomb	Poison	Special	90	100	10	Normal
TM42	Facade	Normal	Physical	70	100	20	Normal
TM44	Rest	Psychic	Status	—	—	10	Self
TM45	Attract	Normal	Status	—	100	15	Normal
TM48	Round	Normal	Special	60	100	15	Normal
TM64	Explosion	Normal	Physical	250	100	5	Adjacent
TM68	Giga Impact	Normal	Physical	150	90	5	Normal
TM78	Bulldoze	Ground	Physical	60	100	20	Adjacent
TM83	Infestation	Bug	Special	20	100	20	Normal
TM85	Dream Eater	Psychic	Special	100	100	15	Normal
TM87	Swagger	Normal	Status	—	90	15	Normal
TM88	Sleep Talk	Normal	Status	—	—	10	Self
TM90	Substitute	Normal	Status	—	—	10	Self
TM94	Rock Smash	Fighting	Physical	40	100	15	Normal
TM98	Power-Up Punch	Fighting	Physical	40	100	20	Normal
TM100	Confide	Normal	Status	—	—	20	Normal
HM04	Strength	Normal	Physical	80	100	15	Normal

No.	Name	Type	Kind	Pow.	Acc.	PP	Range

● **MOVES TAUGHT BY PEOPLE**

Name	Type	Kind	Pow.	Acc.	PP	Range

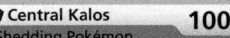

AFTER THE HALL OF FAME

CENTRAL KALOS

100

Scraggy

COASTAL KALOS

MOUNTAIN KALOS

ADVENTURE DATA

Central Kalos — 100

Shedding Pokémon

☑ **Scraggy**

HEIGHT: 2'00" WEIGHT: 26.0 lbs.
GENDER: ♂ / ♀

TYPE Dark / Fighting

ABILITIES
Shed Skin
Moxie

HIDDEN ABILITY
Intimidate

STAT GROWTH RATES
HP	■■
Attack	■■■
Defense	■■
Sp. Atk	■■
Sp. Def	■■
Speed	■■■

EGG GROUPS
Field, Dragon

X Its skin has a rubbery elasticity, so it can reduce damage by defensively pulling its skin up to its neck.

Y Proud of its sturdy skull, it suddenly headbutts everything, but its weight makes it unstable, too.

EVOLUTION

Scraggy → (Lv. 39) → Scrafty

ITEMS SOMETIMES HELD BY WILD POKÉMON
Shed Shell

Can be used in
Inverse Battle
—
Battle Chateau
Battle Institute
Battle Maison
Random Matchup

Damage taken in normal battles		Damage taken in Inverse Battles	
Normal	×1	Normal	×1
Fire	×1	Fire	×1
Water	×1	Water	×1
Grass	×1	Grass	×1
Electric	×1	Electric	×1
Ice	×1	Ice	×1
Fighting	×2	Fighting	×0.5
Poison	×1	Poison	×1
Ground	×1	Ground	×1
Flying	×2	Flying	×0.5
Psychic	×0	Psychic	×1
Bug	×1	Bug	×1
Rock	×0.5	Rock	×2
Ghost	×0.5	Ghost	×2
Dragon	×1	Dragon	×1
Dark	×0.25	Dark	×4
Steel	×1	Steel	×1
Fairy	×4	Fairy	×0.25

How to obtain for your Central Kalos Pokédex

Catch in a Horde Encounter on Route 5. (X)

Catch in a Horde Encounter on Route 5. (Y)

Same form for ♂ / ♀

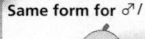

● LEVEL-UP MOVES

Lv.	Name	Type	Kind	Pow.	Acc.	PP	Range
1	Leer	Normal	Status	—	100	30	Many Others
1	Low Kick	Fighting	Physical	—	100	20	Normal
5	Sand Attack	Ground	Status	—	100	15	Normal
9	Feint Attack	Dark	Physical	60	—	20	Normal
12	Headbutt	Normal	Physical	70	100	15	Normal
16	Swagger	Normal	Status	—	90	15	Normal
20	Brick Break	Fighting	Physical	75	100	15	Normal
23	Payback	Dark	Physical	50	100	10	Normal
27	Chip Away	Normal	Physical	70	100	20	Normal
31	High Jump Kick	Fighting	Physical	130	90	10	Normal
34	Scary Face	Normal	Status	—	100	10	Normal
38	Crunch	Dark	Physical	80	100	15	Normal
42	Facade	Normal	Physical	70	100	20	Normal
45	Rock Climb	Normal	Physical	90	85	20	Normal
48	Focus Punch	Fighting	Physical	150	100	20	Normal
50	Head Smash	Rock	Physical	150	80	5	Normal

■ TM & HM MOVES

No.	Name	Type	Kind	Pow.	Acc.	PP	Range
TM02	Dragon Claw	Dragon	Physical	80	100	15	Normal
TM05	Roar	Normal	Status	—	—	20	Normal
TM06	Toxic	Poison	Status	—	90	10	Normal
TM08	Bulk Up	Fighting	Status	—	—	20	Self
TM10	Hidden Power	Normal	Special	60	100	15	Normal
TM11	Sunny Day	Fire	Status	—	—	5	Both Sides
TM17	Taunt	Dark	Status	—	100	20	Normal
TM17	Protect	Normal	Status	—	—	10	Self
TM18	Rain Dance	Water	Status	—	—	5	Both Sides
TM21	Frustration	Normal	Physical	—	100	20	Normal
TM23	Smack Down	Rock	Physical	50	100	15	Normal
TM27	Return	Normal	Physical	—	100	20	Normal
TM28	Dig	Ground	Physical	80	100	10	Normal
TM31	Brick Break	Fighting	Physical	75	100	15	Normal
TM32	Double Team	Normal	Status	—	—	15	Self
TM36	Sludge Bomb	Poison	Special	90	100	10	Normal
TM39	Rock Tomb	Rock	Physical	60	95	15	Normal
TM41	Torment	Dark	Status	—	100	15	Normal
TM42	Facade	Normal	Physical	70	100	20	Normal
TM44	Rest	Psychic	Status	—	—	10	Self
TM45	Attract	Normal	Status	—	100	15	Normal
TM47	Low Sweep	Fighting	Physical	65	100	20	Normal
TM48	Round	Normal	Special	60	100	15	Normal
TM52	Focus Blast	Fighting	Special	120	70	5	Normal
TM56	Fling	Dark	Physical	—	100	10	Normal
TM59	Incinerate	Fire	Special	60	100	15	Many Others
TM66	Payback	Dark	Physical	50	100	10	Normal
TM67	Retaliate	Normal	Physical	70	100	5	Normal
TM71	Stone Edge	Rock	Physical	100	80	5	Normal
TM80	Rock Slide	Rock	Physical	75	90	10	Many Others
TM82	Dragon Tail	Dragon	Physical	60	90	10	Normal
TM84	Poison Jab	Poison	Physical	80	100	20	Normal
TM86	Grass Knot	Grass	Special	—	100	20	Normal

No.	Name	Type	Kind	Pow.	Acc.	PP	Range
TM87	Swagger	Normal	Status	—	90	15	Normal
TM88	Sleep Talk	Normal	Status	—	—	10	Self
TM90	Substitute	Normal	Status	—	—	10	Self
TM94	Rock Smash	Fighting	Physical	40	100	15	Normal
TM95	Snarl	Dark	Special	55	95	15	Many Others
TM97	Dark Pulse	Dark	Special	80	100	15	Normal
TM98	Power-Up Punch	Fighting	Physical	40	100	20	Normal
TM100	Confide	Normal	Status	—	—	20	Normal
HM04	Strength	Normal	Physical	80	100	15	Normal

● MOVES TAUGHT BY PEOPLE

Name	Type	Kind	Pow.	Acc.	PP	Range

● EGG MOVES

Name	Type	Kind	Pow.	Acc.	PP	Range
Drain Punch	Fighting	Physical	75	100	10	Normal
Counter	Fighting	Physical	—	100	20	Varies
Dragon Dance	Dragon	Status	—	—	20	Self
Detect	Fighting	Status	—	—	5	Self
Fake Out	Normal	Physical	40	100	10	Normal
Fire Punch	Fire	Physical	75	100	15	Normal
Ice Punch	Ice	Physical	75	100	15	Normal
Thunder Punch	Electric	Physical	75	100	15	Normal
Amnesia	Psychic	Status	—	—	20	Self
Feint Attack	Dark	Physical	60	—	20	Normal
Zen Headbutt	Psychic	Physical	80	90	15	Normal
Quick Guard	Fighting	Status	—	—	15	Your Side

Hoodlum Pokémon

☑ Scrafty

HEIGHT: 3'07" WEIGHT: 66.1 lbs.
GENDER: ♂/♀

TYPE Dark Fighting

ABILITIES
Shed Skin
Moxie

HIDDEN ABILITY
Intimidate

STAT GROWTH RATES
HP ▪▪▪
Attack ▪▪▪▪▪
Defense ▪▪▪▪▪
Sp. Atk ▪▪
Sp. Def ▪▪▪▪▪
Speed ▪▪▪

EGG GROUPS
Field, Dragon

⚜ EVOLUTION

Lv. 39

Scraggy   Scrafty

ITEMS SOMETIMES HELD BY WILD POKÉMON
None

X It pulls up its shed skin to protect itself while it kicks. The bigger the crest, the more respected it is.

Y It can smash concrete blocks with its kicking attacks. The one with the biggest crest is the group leader.

AFTER THE HALL OF FAME

CENTRAL KALOS

101 Scrafty

COASTAL KALOS

MOUNTAIN KALOS

ADVENTURE DATA

Damage taken in normal battles		Damage taken in Inverse Battles	
Normal	×1	Normal	×1
Fire	×1	Fire	×1
Water	×1	Water	×1
Grass	×1	Grass	×1
Electric	×1	Electric	×1
Ice	×1	Ice	×1
Fighting	×2	Fighting	×0.5
Poison	×1	Poison	×1
Ground	×1	Ground	×1
Flying	×2	Flying	×0.5
Psychic	×0	Psychic	×1
Bug	×1	Bug	×1
Rock	×0.5	Rock	×2
Ghost	×0.5	Ghost	×2
Dragon	×1	Dragon	×1
Dark	×0.25	Dark	×4
Steel	×1	Steel	×1
Fairy	×4	Fairy	×0.25

Can be used in
Inverse Battle
—
Battle Chateau
Battle Institute
Battle Maison
Random Matchup

How to obtain for your Central Kalos Pokédex

Level up Scraggy to Lv. 39. Level up Scraggy to Lv. 39.

Same form for ♂/♀

● LEVEL-UP MOVES

Lv.	Name	Type	Kind	Pow.	Acc.	PP	Range
1	Leer	Normal	Status	—	100	30	Many Others
1	Low Kick	Fighting	Physical	—	100	20	Normal
1	Sand Attack	Ground	Status	—	100	15	Normal
1	Feint Attack	Dark	Physical	60	—	20	Normal
5	Sand Attack	Ground	Status	—	100	15	Normal
9	Feint Attack	Dark	Physical	60	—	20	Normal
12	Headbutt	Normal	Physical	70	100	15	Normal
16	Swagger	Normal	Status	—	90	15	Normal
20	Brick Break	Fighting	Physical	75	100	15	Normal
23	Payback	Dark	Physical	50	100	10	Normal
27	Chip Away	Normal	Physical	70	100	20	Normal
31	High Jump Kick	Fighting	Physical	130	90	10	Normal
34	Scary Face	Normal	Status	—	100	10	Normal
38	Crunch	Dark	Physical	80	100	15	Normal
45	Facade	Normal	Physical	70	100	20	Normal
51	Rock Climb	Normal	Physical	90	85	20	Normal
58	Focus Punch	Fighting	Physical	150	100	20	Normal
65	Head Smash	Rock	Physical	150	80	5	Normal

● TM & HM MOVES

No.	Name	Type	Kind	Pow.	Acc.	PP	Range
TM02	Dragon Claw	Dragon	Physical	80	100	15	Normal
TM05	Roar	Normal	Status	—	—	20	Normal
TM06	Toxic	Poison	Status	—	90	10	Normal
TM08	Bulk Up	Fighting	Status	—	—	20	Self
TM10	Hidden Power	Normal	Special	60	100	15	Normal
TM11	Sunny Day	Fire	Status	—	—	5	Both Sides
TM12	Taunt	Dark	Status	—	100	20	Normal
TM15	Hyper Beam	Normal	Special	150	90	5	Normal
TM17	Protect	Normal	Status	—	—	10	Self
TM18	Rain Dance	Water	Status	—	—	5	Both Sides
TM21	Frustration	Normal	Physical	—	100	20	Normal
TM23	Smack Down	Rock	Physical	50	100	15	Normal
TM27	Return	Normal	Physical	—	100	20	Normal
TM28	Dig	Ground	Physical	80	100	10	Normal
TM31	Brick Break	Fighting	Physical	75	100	15	Normal
TM32	Double Team	Normal	Status	—	—	15	Self
TM36	Sludge Bomb	Poison	Special	90	100	10	Normal
TM39	Rock Tomb	Rock	Physical	60	95	15	Normal
TM41	Torment	Dark	Status	—	100	15	Normal
TM42	Facade	Normal	Physical	70	100	20	Normal
TM44	Rest	Psychic	Status	—	—	10	Self
TM45	Attract	Normal	Status	—	100	15	Normal
TM46	Thief	Dark	Physical	60	100	25	Normal
TM47	Low Sweep	Fighting	Physical	65	100	20	Normal
TM48	Round	Normal	Special	60	100	15	Normal
TM52	Focus Blast	Fighting	Special	120	70	5	Normal
TM56	Fling	Dark	Physical	—	100	10	Normal
TM59	Incinerate	Fire	Special	60	100	15	Many Others
TM66	Payback	Dark	Physical	50	100	10	Normal
TM67	Retaliate	Normal	Physical	70	100	5	Normal
TM68	Giga Impact	Normal	Physical	150	90	5	Normal
TM71	Stone Edge	Rock	Physical	100	80	5	Normal
TM80	Rock Slide	Rock	Physical	75	90	10	Many Others
TM82	Dragon Tail	Dragon	Physical	60	90	10	Normal
TM84	Poison Jab	Poison	Physical	80	100	20	Normal
TM86	Grass Knot	Grass	Special	—	100	20	Normal
TM87	Swagger	Normal	Status	—	90	15	Normal
TM88	Sleep Talk	Normal	Status	—	—	10	Self
TM90	Substitute	Normal	Status	—	—	10	Self
TM94	Rock Smash	Fighting	Physical	40	100	15	Normal
TM95	Snarl	Dark	Special	55	95	15	Many Others
TM97	Dark Pulse	Dark	Special	80	100	15	Normal
TM98	Power-Up Punch	Fighting	Physical	40	100	20	Normal
TM100	Confide	Normal	Status	—	—	20	Normal
HM04	Strength	Normal	Physical	80	100	15	Normal

● MOVES TAUGHT BY PEOPLE

Name	Type	Kind	Pow.	Acc.	PP	Range

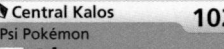

Central Kalos — 102

Psi Pokémon

✓ Abra

HEIGHT: 2'11" WEIGHT: 43.0 lbs.
GENDER: ♂/♀

TYPE Psychic

ABILITIES
Synchronize
Inner Focus

HIDDEN ABILITY
Magic Guard

STAT GROWTH RATES
HP	▌
Attack	▌
Defense	▌
Sp. Atk	▌▌▌▌▌
Sp. Def	▌▌
Speed	▌▌▌▌▌

EGG GROUP
Human-Like

X It sleeps for 18 hours a day. It uses a variety of extrasensory powers even while asleep.

Y It senses impending attacks and teleports away to safety before the actual attacks can strike.

EVOLUTION

Abra → Kadabra → Alakazam
Lv. 16 → Link Trade

ITEMS SOMETIMES HELD BY WILD POKÉMON
Twisted Spoon

Damage taken in normal battles		Damage taken in Inverse Battles	
Normal	×1	Normal	×1
Fire	×1	Fire	×1
Water	×1	Water	×1
Grass	×1	Grass	×1
Electric	×1	Electric	×1
Ice	×1	Ice	×1
Fighting	×0.5	Fighting	×2
Poison	×1	Poison	×1
Ground	×1	Ground	×1
Flying	×1	Flying	×1
Psychic	×0.5	Psychic	×1
Bug	×2	Bug	×0.5
Rock	×1	Rock	×1
Ghost	×2	Ghost	×0.5
Dragon	×1	Dragon	×1
Dark	×2	Dark	×0.5
Steel	×1	Steel	×1
Fairy	×1	Fairy	×1

Can be used in	
Inverse Battle	Battle Institute
—	Battle Maison
Battle Chateau	Random Matchup

Same form for ♂/♀

How to obtain for your Central Kalos Pokédex

❶ Catch in the tall grass on Route 5.
❷ Catch in the purple flowers on Route 5.

❶ Catch in the tall grass on Route 5.
❷ Catch in the purple flowers on Route 5.

● LEVEL-UP MOVES

Lv.	Name	Type	Kind	Pow.	Acc.	PP	Range
1	Teleport	Psychic	Status	—	—	20	Self

● TM & HM MOVES

No.	Name	Type	Kind	Pow.	Acc.	PP	Range
TM03	Psyshock	Psychic	Special	80	100	10	Normal
TM04	Calm Mind	Psychic	Status	—	—	20	Self
TM06	Toxic	Poison	Status	—	90	10	Normal
TM10	Hidden Power	Normal	Special	60	100	15	Normal
TM11	Sunny Day	Fire	Status	—	—	5	Both Sides
TM12	Taunt	Dark	Status	—	100	20	Normal
TM16	Light Screen	Psychic	Status	—	—	30	Your Side
TM17	Protect	Normal	Status	—	—	10	Self
TM18	Rain Dance	Water	Status	—	—	5	Both Sides
TM20	Safeguard	Normal	Status	—	—	25	Your Side
TM21	Frustration	Normal	Physical	—	100	20	Normal
TM27	Return	Normal	Physical	—	100	20	Normal
TM29	Psychic	Psychic	Special	90	100	10	Normal
TM30	Shadow Ball	Ghost	Special	80	100	15	Normal
TM32	Double Team	Normal	Status	—	—	15	Self
TM33	Reflect	Psychic	Status	—	—	20	Your Side
TM41	Torment	Dark	Status	—	100	15	Normal
TM42	Facade	Normal	Physical	70	100	20	Normal
TM44	Rest	Psychic	Status	—	—	10	Self
TM45	Attract	Normal	Status	—	100	15	Normal
TM46	Thief	Dark	Physical	60	100	25	Normal
TM48	Round	Normal	Special	60	100	15	Normal
TM53	Energy Ball	Grass	Special	90	100	10	Normal
TM56	Fling	Dark	Physical	—	100	10	Normal
TM57	Charge Beam	Electric	Special	50	90	10	Normal
TM63	Embargo	Dark	Status	—	100	15	Normal
TM70	Flash	Normal	Status	—	100	20	Normal
TM73	Thunder Wave	Electric	Status	—	100	20	Normal
TM77	Psych Up	Normal	Status	—	—	10	Normal
TM85	Dream Eater	Psychic	Special	100	100	15	Normal
TM86	Grass Knot	Grass	Special	—	100	20	Normal
TM87	Swagger	Normal	Status	—	90	15	Normal
TM88	Sleep Talk	Normal	Status	—	—	10	Self

No.	Name	Type	Kind	Pow.	Acc.	PP	Range
TM90	Substitute	Normal	Status	—	—	10	Self
TM92	Trick Room	Psychic	Status	—	—	5	Both Sides
TM99	Dazzling Gleam	Fairy	Special	80	100	10	Many Others
TM100	Confide	Normal	Status	—	—	20	Normal

● MOVES TAUGHT BY PEOPLE

Name	Type	Kind	Pow.	Acc.	PP	Range

● EGG MOVES

Name	Type	Kind	Pow.	Acc.	PP	Range
Encore	Normal	Status	—	100	5	Normal
Barrier	Psychic	Status	—	—	20	Self
Knock Off	Dark	Physical	65	100	20	Normal
Fire Punch	Fire	Physical	75	100	15	Normal
Thunder Punch	Electric	Physical	75	100	15	Normal
Ice Punch	Ice	Physical	75	100	15	Normal
Power Trick	Psychic	Status	—	—	10	Self
Guard Swap	Psychic	Status	—	—	10	Normal
Skill Swap	Psychic	Status	—	—	10	Normal
Guard Split	Psychic	Status	—	—	10	Normal
Psycho Shift	Psychic	Status	—	100	10	Normal
Ally Switch	Psychic	Status	—	—	15	Normal

AFTER THE HALL OF FAME

CENTRAL KALOS

102

Abra

COASTAL KALOS

MOUNTAIN KALOS

ADVENTURE DATA

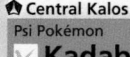

Central Kalos
Psi Pokémon
☑ **Kadabra**

103

HEIGHT: 4'03" WEIGHT: 124.6 lbs.
GENDER: ♂/♀

 When it uses its psychic power, it emits strong alpha waves that can ruin precision devices.

 If it uses its abilities, it emits special alpha waves that cause machines to malfunction.

TYPE **Psychic**

ABILITIES
Synchronize
Inner Focus

HIDDEN ABILITY
Magic Guard

STAT GROWTH RATES
HP	▪▪
Attack	▪▪
Defense	▪▪
Sp. Atk	▪▪▪▪▪▪
Sp. Def	▪▪▪
Speed	▪▪▪▪▪▪

EGG GROUP
Human-Like

EVOLUTION

Lv. 16 → Link Trade →

Abra — Kadabra — Alakazam

ITEMS SOMETIMES HELD BY WILD POKÉMON
None

Damage taken in normal battles		Damage taken in Inverse Battles		Can be used in
Normal	×1	Normal	×1	Inverse Battle
Fire	×1	Fire	×1	
Water	×1	Water	×1	Battle Chateau
Grass	×1	Grass	×1	Battle Institute
Electric	×1	Electric	×1	Battle Maison
Ice	×1	Ice	×1	Random Matchup
Fighting	×0.5	Fighting	×2	
Poison	×1	Poison	×1	
Ground	×1	Ground	×1	
Flying	×1	Flying	×1	
Psychic	×0.5	Psychic	×2	
Bug	×2	Bug	×0.5	
Rock	×1	Rock	×1	
Ghost	×2	Ghost	×0.5	
Dragon	×1	Dragon	×1	
Dark	×2	Dark	×0.5	
Steel	×1	Steel	×1	
Fairy	×1	Fairy	×1	

How to obtain for your Central Kalos Pokédex

Level up Abra to Lv. 16. | Level up Abra to Lv. 16.

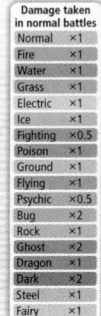 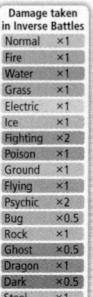 ♂ 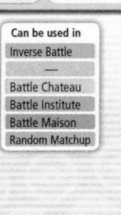 ♀

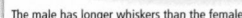

The male has longer whiskers than the female.

● LEVEL-UP MOVES

Lv.	Name	Type	Kind	Pow.	Acc.	PP	Range
1	Teleport	Psychic	Status	—	—	20	Self
1	Kinesis	Psychic	Status	—	80	15	Normal
1	Confusion	Psychic	Special	50	100	25	Normal
16	Confusion	Psychic	Special	50	100	25	Normal
18	Disable	Normal	Status	—	100	20	Normal
22	Miracle Eye	Psychic	Status	—	—	40	Normal
24	Ally Switch	Psychic	Status	—	—	15	Self
28	Psybeam	Psychic	Special	65	100	20	Normal
30	Reflect	Psychic	Status	—	—	20	Your Side
34	Telekinesis	Psychic	Status	—	—	15	Normal
36	Recover	Normal	Status	—	—	10	Self
40	Psycho Cut	Psychic	Physical	70	100	20	Normal
42	Role Play	Psychic	Status	—	—	10	Normal
46	Psychic	Psychic	Special	90	100	10	Normal
48	Future Sight	Psychic	Special	120	100	10	Normal
50	Trick	Psychic	Status	—	100	10	Normal

● TM & HM MOVES

No.	Name	Type	Kind	Pow.	Acc.	PP	Range
TM03	Psyshock	Psychic	Special	80	100	10	Normal
TM04	Calm Mind	Psychic	Status	—	—	20	Self
TM06	Toxic	Poison	Status	—	90	10	Normal
TM10	Hidden Power	Normal	Special	60	100	15	Normal
TM11	Sunny Day	Fire	Status	—	—	5	Both Sides
TM12	Taunt	Dark	Status	—	100	20	Normal
TM16	Light Screen	Psychic	Status	—	—	30	Your Side
TM17	Protect	Normal	Status	—	—	10	Self
TM18	Rain Dance	Water	Status	—	—	5	Both Sides
TM20	Safeguard	Normal	Status	—	—	25	Your Side
TM21	Frustration	Normal	Physical	—	100	20	Normal
TM27	Return	Normal	Physical	—	100	20	Normal
TM29	Psychic	Psychic	Special	90	100	10	Normal
TM30	Shadow Ball	Ghost	Special	80	100	15	Normal
TM32	Double Team	Normal	Status	—	—	15	Self
TM33	Reflect	Psychic	Status	—	—	20	Your Side
TM41	Torment	Dark	Status	—	100	15	Normal
TM42	Facade	Normal	Physical	70	100	20	Normal
TM44	Rest	Psychic	Status	—	—	10	Self
TM45	Attract	Normal	Status	—	100	15	Normal
TM46	Thief	Dark	Physical	60	100	25	Normal
TM48	Round	Normal	Special	60	100	15	Normal
TM53	Energy Ball	Grass	Special	90	100	10	Normal
TM56	Fling	Dark	Physical	—	100	10	Normal
TM57	Charge Beam	Electric	Special	50	90	10	Normal
TM63	Embargo	Dark	Status	—	100	15	Normal
TM70	Flash	Normal	Status	—	100	20	Normal
TM73	Thunder Wave	Electric	Status	—	100	20	Normal
TM77	Psych Up	Normal	Status	—	—	10	Normal
TM85	Dream Eater	Psychic	Special	100	100	15	Normal
TM86	Grass Knot	Grass	Special	—	100	20	Normal
TM87	Swagger	Normal	Status	—	90	15	Normal
TM88	Sleep Talk	Normal	Status	—	—	10	Self

No.	Name	Type	Kind	Pow.	Acc.	PP	Range
TM90	Substitute	Normal	Status	—	—	10	Self
TM92	Trick Room	Psychic	Status	—	—	5	Both Sides
TM99	Dazzling Gleam	Fairy	Special	80	100	10	Many Others
TM100	Confide	Normal	Status	—	—	20	Normal

● MOVES TAUGHT BY PEOPLE

Name	Type	Kind	Pow.	Acc.	PP	Range

AFTER THE HALL OF FAME

CENTRAL KALOS

103

Kadabra

COASTAL KALOS

MOUNTAIN KALOS

ADVENTURE DATA

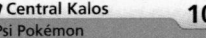

AFTER THE HALL OF FAME

CENTRAL KALOS

104

Alakazam

COASTAL KALOS

MOUNTAIN KALOS

ADVENTURE DATA

Central Kalos 104

Psi Pokémon

Alakazam

HEIGHT: 4'11" WEIGHT: 105.8 lbs.
GENDER: ♂/♀

TYPE Psychic

ABILITIES
Synchronize
Inner Focus

HIDDEN ABILITY
Magic Guard

STAT GROWTH RATES
HP	■■■
Attack	■■■
Defense	■■
Sp. Atk	■■■■■■■■
Sp. Def	■■■■
Speed	■■■■■■■

EGG GROUP
Human-Like

X Its brain cells multiply continually until it dies. As a result, it remembers everything.

Y Its brain can outperform a supercomputer. Its IQ (intelligence quotient) is said to be around 5,000.

EVOLUTION

Lv. 16   Link Trade

Abra   Kadabra   Alakazam

ITEMS SOMETIMES HELD BY WILD POKÉMON
None

Can be used in
Inverse Battle
—
Battle Chateau
Battle Institute
Battle Maison
Random Matchup

Damage taken in normal battles	
Normal	×1
Fire	×1
Water	×1
Grass	×1
Electric	×1
Ice	×1
Fighting	×0.5
Poison	×1
Ground	×1
Flying	×1
Psychic	×0.5
Bug	×2
Rock	×1
Ghost	×2
Dragon	×1
Dark	×2
Steel	×1
Fairy	×1

Damage taken in Inverse Battles	
Normal	×1
Fire	×1
Water	×1
Grass	×1
Electric	×1
Ice	×1
Fighting	×2
Poison	×1
Ground	×1
Flying	×1
Psychic	×2
Bug	×0.5
Rock	×1
Ghost	×0.5
Dragon	×1
Dark	×0.5
Steel	×1
Fairy	×1

How to obtain for your Central Kalos Pokédex

Receive Kadabra by Link Trade, and have it evolve.

Receive Kadabra by Link Trade, and have it evolve.

The male has longer whiskers than the female.

● LEVEL-UP MOVES

Lv.	Name	Type	Kind	Pow.	Acc.	PP	Range
1	Teleport	Psychic	Status	—	—	20	Self
1	Kinesis	Psychic	Status	—	80	15	Normal
1	Confusion	Psychic	Special	50	100	25	Normal
16	Confusion	Psychic	Special	50	100	25	Normal
18	Disable	Normal	Status	—	100	20	Normal
22	Miracle Eye	Psychic	Status	—	—	40	Normal
24	Ally Switch	Psychic	Status	—	—	15	Self
28	Psybeam	Psychic	Special	65	100	20	Normal
30	Reflect	Psychic	Status	—	—	20	Your Side
34	Telekinesis	Psychic	Status	—	—	15	Normal
36	Recover	Normal	Status	—	—	10	Self
40	Psycho Cut	Psychic	Physical	70	100	20	Normal
42	Calm Mind	Psychic	Status	—	—	20	Self
46	Psychic	Psychic	Special	90	100	10	Normal
48	Future Sight	Psychic	Special	120	100	10	Normal
50	Trick	Psychic	Status	—	100	10	Normal

● TM & HM MOVES

No.	Name	Type	Kind	Pow.	Acc.	PP	Range
TM03	Psyshock	Psychic	Special	80	100	10	Normal
TM04	Calm Mind	Psychic	Status	—	—	20	Self
TM06	Toxic	Poison	Status	—	90	10	Normal
TM10	Hidden Power	Normal	Special	60	100	15	Normal
TM11	Sunny Day	Fire	Status	—	—	5	Both Sides
TM12	Taunt	Dark	Status	—	100	20	Normal
TM15	Hyper Beam	Normal	Special	150	90	5	Normal
TM16	Light Screen	Psychic	Status	—	—	30	Your Side
TM17	Protect	Normal	Status	—	—	10	Self
TM18	Rain Dance	Water	Status	—	—	5	Both Sides
TM20	Safeguard	Normal	Status	—	—	25	Your Side
TM21	Frustration	Normal	Physical	—	100	20	Normal
TM27	Return	Normal	Physical	—	100	20	Normal
TM29	Psychic	Psychic	Special	90	100	10	Normal
TM30	Shadow Ball	Ghost	Special	80	100	15	Normal
TM32	Double Team	Normal	Status	—	—	15	Self
TM33	Reflect	Psychic	Status	—	—	20	Your Side
TM41	Torment	Dark	Status	—	100	15	Normal
TM42	Facade	Normal	Physical	70	100	20	Normal
TM44	Rest	Psychic	Status	—	—	10	Self
TM45	Attract	Normal	Status	—	100	15	Normal
TM46	Thief	Dark	Physical	60	100	25	Normal
TM48	Round	Normal	Special	60	100	15	Normal
TM52	Focus Blast	Fighting	Special	120	70	5	Normal
TM53	Energy Ball	Grass	Special	90	100	10	Normal
TM56	Fling	Dark	Physical	—	100	10	Normal
TM57	Charge Beam	Electric	Special	50	90	10	Normal
TM63	Embargo	Dark	Status	—	100	15	Normal
TM68	Giga Impact	Normal	Physical	150	90	5	Normal
TM70	Flash	Normal	Status	—	100	20	Normal
TM73	Thunder Wave	Electric	Status	—	100	20	Normal
TM77	Psych Up	Normal	Status	—	—	10	Normal
TM85	Dream Eater	Psychic	Special	100	100	15	Normal

No.	Name	Type	Kind	Pow.	Acc.	PP	Range
TM86	Grass Knot	Grass	Special	—	100	20	Normal
TM87	Swagger	Normal	Status	—	90	15	Normal
TM88	Sleep Talk	Normal	Status	—	—	10	Self
TM90	Substitute	Normal	Status	—	—	10	Self
TM92	Trick Room	Psychic	Status	—	—	5	Both Sides
TM99	Dazzling Gleam	Fairy	Special	80	100	10	Many Others
TM100	Confide	Normal	Status	—	—	20	Normal

● MOVES TAUGHT BY PEOPLE

Name	Type	Kind	Pow.	Acc.	PP	Range

Mega Evolution

Psi Pokémon

☑ Mega Alakazam

HEIGHT: 3'11"   WEIGHT: 105.8 lbs.   GENDER: ♂/♀

TYPE **Psychic**

ABILITY
Trace

STAT GROWTH RATES

HP	██
Attack	██
Defense	███
Sp. Atk	█████████
Sp. Def	████
Speed	████████

MEGA STONE REQUIRED

Alakazite
Obtain in Reflection Cave between 8 P.M. and 8:59 P.M., after entering the Hall of Fame and speaking with Professor Sycamore in Anistar City.

AFTER THE HALL OF FAME

CENTRAL KALOS   Mega Alakazam

COASTAL KALOS

MOUNTAIN KALOS

ADVENTURE DATA

Damage taken in normal battles	
Normal	×1
Fire	×1
Water	×1
Grass	×1
Electric	×1
Ice	×1
Fighting	×0.5
Poison	×1
Ground	×1
Flying	×1
Psychic	×0.5
Bug	×2
Rock	×1
Ghost	×2
Dragon	×1
Dark	×2
Steel	×1
Fairy	×1

Damage taken in Inverse Battles	
Normal	×1
Fire	×1
Water	×1
Grass	×1
Electric	×1
Ice	×1
Fighting	×2
Poison	×1
Ground	×1
Flying	×1
Psychic	×2
Bug	×0.5
Rock	×1
Ghost	×0.5
Dragon	×1
Dark	×0.5
Steel	×1
Fairy	×1

Can be used in	
Inverse Battle	Battle Institute
—	Battle Maison
Battle Chateau	Random Matchup

Same form for ♂/♀

AFTER THE HALL OF FAME

CENTRAL KALOS

105

Oddish

COASTAL KALOS

MOUNTAIN KALOS

ADVENTURE DATA

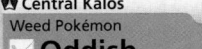

Central Kalos 105

Weed Pokémon

✅ Oddish

HEIGHT: 1'08" WEIGHT: 11.9 lbs.
GENDER: ♂/♀

X — During the day, it stays in the cold underground to avoid the sun. It grows by bathing in moonlight.

Y — Its scientific name is "Oddium Wanderus." At night, it is said to walk nearly 1,000 feet on its two roots.

TYPE | Grass | Poison

ABILITY
Chlorophyll

HIDDEN ABILITY
Run Away

STAT GROWTH RATES
HP	■■
Attack	■■
Defense	■■■
Sp. Atk	■■■■
Sp. Def	■■■
Speed	■■

EGG GROUP
Grass

EVOLUTION

Oddish → Gloom

Leaf Stone → Vileplume
Sun Stone → Bellossom

Lv. 21

ITEMS SOMETIMES HELD BY WILD POKÉMON
None

Damage taken in normal battles	
Normal	×1
Fire	×2
Water	×0.5
Grass	×0.25
Electric	×0.5
Ice	×2
Fighting	×0.5
Poison	×1
Ground	×1
Flying	×2
Psychic	×2
Bug	×1
Rock	×1
Ghost	×1
Dragon	×1
Dark	×1
Steel	×1
Fairy	×0.5

Damage taken in Inverse Battles	
Normal	×1
Fire	×0.5
Water	×2
Grass	×4
Electric	×2
Ice	×0.5
Fighting	×2
Poison	×1
Ground	×1
Flying	×0.5
Psychic	×0.5
Bug	×1
Rock	×1
Ghost	×1
Dragon	×1
Dark	×1
Steel	×1
Fairy	×2

Can be used in	
Inverse Battle	Battle Institute
—	Battle Maison
Battle Chateau	Random Matchup

Same form for ♂/♀

How to obtain for your Central Kalos Pokédex

Catch in the very tall grass on Route 6. (X)

Catch in the very tall grass on Route 6. (Y)

● LEVEL-UP MOVES

Lv.	Name	Type	Kind	Pow.	Acc.	PP	Range
1	Absorb	Grass	Special	20	100	25	Normal
5	Sweet Scent	Normal	Status	—	100	20	Many Others
9	Acid	Poison	Special	40	100	30	Many Others
13	Poison Powder	Poison	Status	—	75	35	Normal
15	Stun Spore	Grass	Status	—	75	30	Normal
17	Sleep Powder	Grass	Status	—	75	15	Normal
21	Mega Drain	Grass	Special	40	100	15	Normal
25	Lucky Chant	Normal	Status	—	—	30	Your Side
29	Natural Gift	Normal	Physical	—	100	15	Normal
33	Moonlight	Fairy	Status	—	—	5	Self
37	Giga Drain	Grass	Special	75	100	10	Normal
41	Petal Dance	Grass	Special	120	100	10	1 Random
45	Grassy Terrain	Grass	Status	—	—	10	Both Sides

● TM & HM MOVES

No.	Name	Type	Kind	Pow.	Acc.	PP	Range
TM06	Toxic	Poison	Status	—	90	10	Normal
TM09	Venoshock	Poison	Special	65	100	10	Normal
TM10	Hidden Power	Normal	Special	60	100	15	Normal
TM11	Sunny Day	Fire	Status	—	—	5	Both Sides
TM17	Protect	Normal	Status	—	—	10	Self
TM21	Frustration	Normal	Physical	—	100	20	Normal
TM22	Solar Beam	Grass	Special	120	100	10	Normal
TM27	Return	Normal	Physical	—	100	20	Normal
TM32	Double Team	Normal	Status	—	—	15	Self
TM36	Sludge Bomb	Poison	Special	90	100	10	Normal
TM42	Facade	Normal	Physical	70	100	20	Normal
TM44	Rest	Psychic	Status	—	—	10	Self
TM45	Attract	Normal	Status	—	100	15	Normal
TM48	Round	Normal	Special	60	100	15	Normal
TM53	Energy Ball	Grass	Special	90	100	10	Normal
TM70	Flash	Normal	Status	—	100	20	Normal
TM75	Swords Dance	Normal	Status	—	—	20	Self
TM83	Infestation	Bug	Special	20	100	20	Normal
TM86	Grass Knot	Grass	Special	—	100	20	Normal
TM87	Swagger	Normal	Status	—	90	15	Normal
TM88	Sleep Talk	Normal	Status	—	—	10	Self
TM90	Substitute	Normal	Status	—	—	10	Self
TM96	Nature Power	Normal	Status	—	—	20	Normal
TM99	Dazzling Gleam	Fairy	Special	80	100	10	Many Others
TM100	Confide	Normal	Status	—	—	20	Normal
HM01	Cut	Normal	Physical	50	95	30	Normal

● MOVES TAUGHT BY PEOPLE

Name	Type	Kind	Pow.	Acc.	PP	Range

● EGG MOVES

Name	Type	Kind	Pow.	Acc.	PP	Range
Razor Leaf	Grass	Physical	55	95	25	Many Others
Flail	Normal	Physical	—	100	15	Normal
Synthesis	Grass	Status	—	—	5	Self
Charm	Fairy	Status	—	100	20	Normal
Ingrain	Grass	Status	—	—	20	Self
Tickle	Normal	Status	—	100	20	Normal
Teeter Dance	Normal	Status	—	100	20	Adjacent
Secret Power	Normal	Physical	70	100	20	Normal
Nature Power	Normal	Status	—	—	20	Normal
After You	Normal	Status	—	—	15	Normal

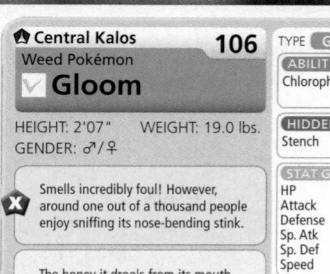

♠ Central Kalos

106

Weed Pokémon

☑ **Gloom**

HEIGHT: 2'07" WEIGHT: 19.0 lbs.
GENDER: ♂/♀

X Smells incredibly foul! However, around one out of a thousand people enjoy sniffing its nose-bending stink.

Y The honey it drools from its mouth smells so atrocious, it can curl noses more than a mile away.

TYPE **Grass** **Poison**

ABILITY
Chlorophyll

HIDDEN ABILITY
Stench

STAT GROWTH RATES
HP	▪▪▪
Attack	▪▪▪
Defense	▪▪▪
Sp. Atk	▪▪▪▪
Sp. Def	▪▪▪
Speed	▪▪

EGG GROUP
Grass

⬆ EVOLUTION

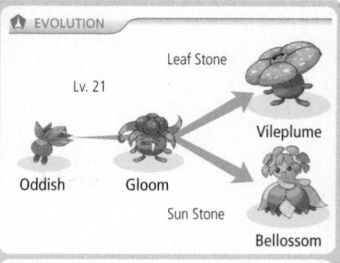

Leaf Stone

Lv. 21

Vileplume

Oddish   Gloom

Sun Stone

Bellossom

ITEMS SOMETIMES HELD BY WILD POKÉMON
None

Damage taken in normal battles		Damage taken in Inverse Battles	
Normal	×1	Normal	×1
Fire	×2	Fire	×0.5
Water	×0.5	Water	×2
Grass	×0.25	Grass	×4
Electric	×1	Electric	×1
Ice	×2	Ice	×0.5
Fighting	×0.5	Fighting	×2
Poison	×1	Poison	×1
Ground	×1	Ground	×1
Flying	×2	Flying	×0.5
Psychic	×2	Psychic	×0.5
Bug	×1	Bug	×1
Rock	×1	Rock	×1
Ghost	×1	Ghost	×1
Dragon	×1	Dragon	×1
Dark	×1	Dark	×1
Steel	×1	Steel	×1
Fairy	×0.5	Fairy	×2

Can be used in
Inverse Battle
—
Battle Chateau
Battle Institute
Battle Maison
Random Matchup

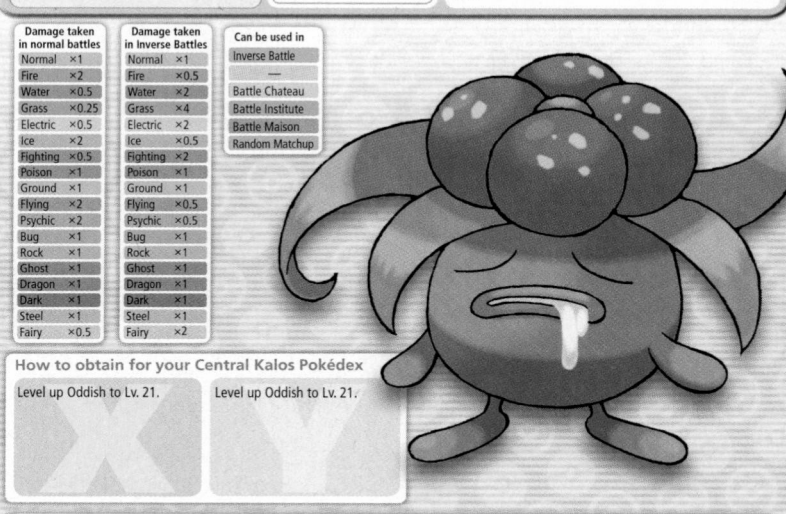

How to obtain for your Central Kalos Pokédex

Level up Oddish to Lv. 21.   Level up Oddish to Lv. 21.

X   Y

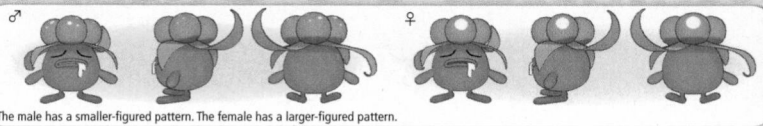

♂   ♀

The male has a smaller-figured pattern. The female has a larger-figured pattern.

● LEVEL-UP MOVES

Lv.	Name	Type	Kind	Pow.	Acc.	PP	Range
1	Absorb	Grass	Special	20	100	25	Normal
1	Sweet Scent	Normal	Status	—	100	20	Many Others
1	Acid	Poison	Special	40	100	30	Many Others
5	Sweet Scent	Normal	Status	—	100	20	Many Others
9	Acid	Poison	Special	40	100	30	Many Others
13	Poison Powder	Poison	Status	—	75	35	Normal
15	Stun Spore	Grass	Status	—	75	30	Normal
17	Sleep Powder	Grass	Status	—	75	15	Normal
23	Mega Drain	Grass	Special	40	100	15	Normal
29	Lucky Chant	Normal	Status	—	—	30	Your Side
35	Natural Gift	Normal	Physical	—	100	15	Normal
41	Moonlight	Fairy	Status	—	—	5	Self
47	Giga Drain	Grass	Special	75	100	10	Normal
50	Petal Blizzard	Grass	Physical	90	100	15	Adjacent
53	Petal Dance	Grass	Special	120	100	10	1 Random
56	Grassy Terrain	Grass	Status	—	—	10	Both Sides

● TM & HM MOVES

No.	Name	Type	Kind	Pow.	Acc.	PP	Range
TM06	Toxic	Poison	Status	—	90	10	Normal
TM09	Venoshock	Poison	Special	65	100	10	Normal
TM10	Hidden Power	Normal	Special	60	100	15	Normal
TM11	Sunny Day	Fire	Status	—	—	5	Both Sides
TM17	Protect	Normal	Status	—	—	10	Self
TM21	Frustration	Normal	Physical	—	100	20	Normal
TM22	Solar Beam	Grass	Special	120	100	10	Normal
TM27	Return	Normal	Physical	—	100	20	Normal
TM32	Double Team	Normal	Status	—	—	15	Self
TM36	Sludge Bomb	Poison	Special	90	100	10	Normal
TM42	Facade	Normal	Physical	70	100	20	Normal
TM44	Rest	Psychic	Status	—	—	10	Self
TM45	Attract	Normal	Status	—	100	15	Normal
TM48	Round	Normal	Special	60	100	15	Normal
TM53	Energy Ball	Grass	Special	90	100	10	Normal
TM56	Fling	Dark	Physical	—	100	10	Normal
TM70	Flash	Normal	Status	—	100	20	Normal
TM75	Swords Dance	Normal	Status	—	—	20	Self
TM83	Infestation	Bug	Special	20	100	20	Normal
TM86	Grass Knot	Grass	Special	—	100	20	Normal
TM87	Swagger	Normal	Status	—	90	15	Normal
TM88	Sleep Talk	Normal	Status	—	—	10	Self
TM90	Substitute	Normal	Status	—	—	10	Self
TM96	Nature Power	Normal	Status	—	—	20	Normal
TM99	Dazzling Gleam	Fairy	Special	80	100	10	Many Others
TM100	Confide	Normal	Status	—	—	20	Normal
HM01	Cut	Normal	Physical	50	95	30	Normal

● MOVES TAUGHT BY PEOPLE

Name	Type	Kind	Pow.	Acc.	PP	Range

AFTER THE HALL OF FAME

CENTRAL KALOS

107

Vileplume

COASTAL

MOUNTAIN KALOS

ADVENTURE DATA

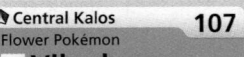

Central Kalos — 107
Flower Pokémon
✓ Vileplume

HEIGHT: 3'11" WEIGHT: 41.0 lbs.
GENDER: ♂/♀

TYPE Grass Poison

ABILITY
Chlorophyll

HIDDEN ABILITY
Effect Spore

STAT GROWTH RATES
HP	■■■
Attack	■■■
Defense	■■■
Sp. Atk	■■■■■
Sp. Def	■■■■
Speed	■■■

EGG GROUP
Grass

X The larger its petals, the more toxic pollen it contains. Its big head is heavy and hard to hold up.

Y It has the world's largest petals. With every step, the petals shake out heavy clouds of toxic pollen.

EVOLUTION

Oddish — Gloom — Lv. 21 → Vileplume (Leaf Stone)
Gloom — Sun Stone → Bellossom

ITEMS SOMETIMES HELD BY WILD POKÉMON
None

Can be used in
Inverse Battle
—
Battle Chateau
Battle Institute
Battle Maison
Random Matchup

Damage taken in normal battles	
Normal	×1
Fire	×2
Water	×0.5
Grass	×0.25
Electric	×0.5
Ice	×2
Fighting	×0.5
Poison	×1
Ground	×1
Flying	×2
Psychic	×2
Bug	×1
Rock	×1
Ghost	×1
Dragon	×1
Dark	×1
Steel	×1
Fairy	×0.5

Damage taken in Inverse Battles	
Normal	×1
Fire	×0.5
Water	×2
Grass	×4
Electric	×2
Ice	×0.5
Fighting	×2
Poison	×1
Ground	×1
Flying	×0.5
Psychic	×0.5
Bug	×1
Rock	×1
Ghost	×1
Dragon	×1
Dark	×1
Steel	×1
Fairy	×2

How to obtain for your Central Kalos Pokédex

X: Use a Leaf Stone on Gloom.

Y: Use a Leaf Stone on Gloom.

♂ (left three) ♀ (right three)

The male has a smaller-figured pattern. The females has a larger-figured pattern.

● LEVEL-UP MOVES

Lv.	Name	Type	Kind	Pow.	Acc.	PP	Range
1	Mega Drain	Grass	Special	40	100	15	Normal
1	Aromatherapy	Grass	Status	—	—	5	Your Party
1	Stun Spore	Grass	Status	—	75	30	Normal
1	Poison Powder	Poison	Status	—	75	35	Normal
50	Petal Blizzard	Grass	Physical	90	100	15	Adjacent
53	Petal Dance	Grass	Special	120	100	10	1 Random
65	Solar Beam	Grass	Special	120	100	10	Normal

■ TM & HM MOVES

No.	Name	Type	Kind	Pow.	Acc.	PP	Range
TM06	Toxic	Poison	Status	—	90	10	Normal
TM09	Venoshock	Poison	Special	65	100	10	Normal
TM10	Hidden Power	Normal	Special	60	100	15	Normal
TM11	Sunny Day	Fire	Status	—	—	5	Both Sides
TM15	Hyper Beam	Normal	Special	150	90	5	Normal
TM17	Protect	Normal	Status	—	—	10	Self
TM20	Safeguard	Normal	Status	—	—	25	Your Side
TM21	Frustration	Normal	Physical	—	100	20	Normal
TM22	Solar Beam	Grass	Special	120	100	10	Normal
TM27	Return	Normal	Physical	—	100	20	Normal
TM32	Double Team	Normal	Status	—	—	15	Self
TM36	Sludge Bomb	Poison	Special	90	100	10	Normal
TM42	Facade	Normal	Physical	70	100	20	Normal
TM44	Rest	Psychic	Status	—	—	10	Self
TM45	Attract	Normal	Status	—	100	15	Normal
TM48	Round	Normal	Special	60	100	15	Normal
TM53	Energy Ball	Grass	Special	90	100	10	Normal
TM56	Fling	Dark	Physical	—	100	10	Normal
TM68	Giga Impact	Normal	Physical	150	90	5	Normal
TM70	Flash	Normal	Status	—	100	20	Normal
TM75	Swords Dance	Normal	Status	—	—	20	Self
TM83	Infestation	Bug	Special	20	100	20	Normal
TM86	Grass Knot	Grass	Special	—	100	20	Normal
TM87	Swagger	Normal	Status	—	90	15	Normal
TM88	Sleep Talk	Normal	Status	—	—	10	Self
TM90	Substitute	Normal	Status	—	—	10	Self
TM96	Nature Power	Normal	Status	—	—	20	Normal
TM99	Dazzling Gleam	Fairy	Special	80	100	10	Many Others
TM100	Confide	Normal	Status	—	—	20	Normal
HM01	Cut	Normal	Physical	50	95	30	Normal

No.	Name	Type	Kind	Pow.	Acc.	PP	Range

● MOVES TAUGHT BY PEOPLE

Name	Type	Kind	Pow.	Acc.	PP	Range

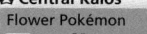
Flower Pokémon

☑ **Bellossom**

108

TYPE Grass

ABILITY
Chlorophyll

HIDDEN ABILITY
Healer

STAT GROWTH RATES

HP	▪▪▪
Attack	▪▪▪▪
Defense	▪▪▪▪
Sp. Atk	▪▪▪▪
Sp. Def	▪▪▪
Speed	▪▪▪

EGG GROUP
Grass

HEIGHT: 1'04"   WEIGHT: 12.8 lbs.
GENDER: ♂ / ♀

X Bellossom gather at times and seem to dance. They say that the dance is a ritual to summon the sun.

Y When the heavy rainfall season ends, it is drawn out by warm sunlight to dance in the open.

EVOLUTION

Oddish — Lv. 21 → Gloom

Gloom — Leaf Stone → Vileplume

Gloom — Sun Stone → Bellossom

ITEMS SOMETIMES HELD BY WILD POKÉMON
None

Damage taken in normal battles		Damage taken in Inverse Battles		Can be used in
Normal	×1	Normal	×1	Inverse Battle
Fire	×2	Fire	×0.5	—
Water	×0.5	Water	×2	Battle Chateau
Grass	×0.5	Grass	×2	Battle Institute
Electric	×0.5	Electric	×2	Battle Maison
Ice	×2	Ice	×0.5	Random Matchup
Fighting	×1	Fighting	×1	
Poison	×2	Poison	×0.5	
Ground	×0.5	Ground	×2	
Flying	×2	Flying	×0.5	
Psychic	×1	Psychic	×1	
Bug	×2	Bug	×0.5	
Rock	×1	Rock	×1	
Ghost	×1	Ghost	×1	
Dragon	×1	Dragon	×1	
Dark	×1	Dark	×1	
Steel	×1	Steel	×1	
Fairy	×1	Fairy	×1	

Same form for ♂ / ♀

How to obtain for your Central Kalos Pokédex

Use a Sun Stone on Gloom.   Use a Sun Stone on Gloom.

● LEVEL-UP MOVES

Lv.	Name	Type	Kind	Pow.	Acc.	PP	Range
1	Leaf Storm	Grass	Special	130	90	5	Normal
1	Leaf Blade	Grass	Physical	90	100	15	Normal
1	Mega Drain	Grass	Special	40	100	15	Normal
1	Sweet Scent	Normal	Status	—	100	20	Many Others
1	Stun Spore	Grass	Status	—	75	30	Normal
1	Sunny Day	Fire	Status	—	—	5	Both Sides
23	Magical Leaf	Grass	Special	60	—	20	Normal
50	Petal Blizzard	Grass	Physical	90	100	15	Adjacent
53	Leaf Storm	Grass	Special	130	90	5	Normal

● TM & HM MOVES

No.	Name	Type	Kind	Pow.	Acc.	PP	Range
TM06	Toxic	Poison	Status	—	90	10	Normal
TM09	Venoshock	Poison	Special	65	100	10	Normal
TM10	Hidden Power	Normal	Special	60	100	15	Normal
TM11	Sunny Day	Fire	Status	—	—	5	Both Sides
TM15	Hyper Beam	Normal	Special	150	90	5	Normal
TM17	Protect	Normal	Status	—	—	10	Self
TM20	Safeguard	Normal	Status	—	—	25	Your Side
TM21	Frustration	Normal	Physical	—	100	20	Normal
TM22	Solar Beam	Grass	Special	120	100	10	Normal
TM27	Return	Normal	Physical	—	100	20	Normal
TM32	Double Team	Normal	Status	—	—	15	Self
TM36	Sludge Bomb	Poison	Special	90	100	10	Normal
TM42	Facade	Normal	Physical	70	100	20	Normal
TM44	Rest	Psychic	Status	—	—	10	Self
TM45	Attract	Normal	Status	—	100	15	Normal
TM48	Round	Normal	Special	60	100	15	Normal
TM53	Energy Ball	Grass	Special	90	100	10	Normal
TM56	Fling	Dark	Physical	—	100	10	Normal
TM68	Giga Impact	Normal	Physical	150	90	5	Normal
TM70	Flash	Normal	Status	—	100	20	Normal
TM75	Swords Dance	Normal	Status	—	—	20	Self
TM83	Infestation	Bug	Special	20	100	20	Normal
TM86	Grass Knot	Grass	Special	—	100	20	Normal
TM87	Swagger	Normal	Status	—	90	15	Normal
TM88	Sleep Talk	Normal	Status	—	—	10	Self
TM90	Substitute	Normal	Status	—	—	10	Self
TM96	Nature Power	Normal	Status	—	—	20	Normal
TM99	Dazzling Gleam	Fairy	Special	80	100	10	Many Others
TM100	Confide	Normal	Status	—	—	20	Normal
HM01	Cut	Normal	Physical	50	95	30	Normal

● MOVES TAUGHT BY PEOPLE

Name	Type	Kind	Pow.	Acc.	PP	Range

AFTER THE HALL OF FAME

CENTRAL KALOS

108 Bellossom

COASTAL KALOS

MOUNTAIN KALOS

ADVENTURE DATA

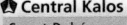

AFTER THE HALL OF FAME

CENTRAL KALOS

109

Sentret

COASTAL KALOS

MOUNTAIN KALOS

ADVENTURE DATA

Central Kalos — **109**

Scout Pokémon

☑ **Sentret**

HEIGHT: 2'07" WEIGHT: 13.2 lbs.
GENDER: ♂/♀

TYPE: Normal

ABILITIES
Run Away
Keen Eye

HIDDEN ABILITY
Frisk

STAT GROWTH RATES
HP
Attack
Defense
Sp. Atk
Sp. Def
Speed

EGG GROUP
Field

X — When acting as a lookout, it warns others of danger by screeching and hitting the ground with its tail.

Y — It stands on its tail so it can see a long way. If it spots an enemy, it cries loudly to warn its kind.

EVOLUTION

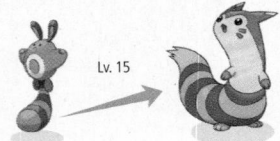

Sentret → Lv. 15 → Furret

ITEMS SOMETIMES HELD BY WILD POKÉMON
None

Can be used in
Inverse Battle
—
Battle Chateau
Battle Institute
Battle Maison
Random Matchup

Damage taken in normal battles	
Normal	×1
Fire	×1
Water	×1
Grass	×1
Electric	×1
Ice	×1
Fighting	×2
Poison	×1
Ground	×1
Flying	×1
Psychic	×1
Bug	×1
Rock	×1
Ghost	×0
Dragon	×1
Dark	×1
Steel	×1
Fairy	×1

Damage taken in Inverse Battles	
Normal	×1
Fire	×1
Water	×1
Grass	×1
Electric	×1
Ice	×1
Fighting	×0.5
Poison	×1
Ground	×1
Flying	×1
Psychic	×1
Bug	×1
Rock	×1
Ghost	×2
Dragon	×1
Dark	×1
Steel	×1
Fairy	×1

How to obtain for your Central Kalos Pokédex

Catch in the very tall grass on Route 6.

Catch in the very tall grass on Route 6.

Same form for ♂/♀

● **LEVEL-UP MOVES**

Lv.	Name	Type	Kind	Pow.	Acc.	PP	Range
1	Scratch	Normal	Physical	40	100	35	Normal
1	Foresight	Normal	Status	—	—	40	Normal
4	Defense Curl	Normal	Status	—	—	40	Self
7	Quick Attack	Normal	Physical	40	100	30	Normal
13	Fury Swipes	Normal	Physical	18	80	15	Normal
16	Helping Hand	Normal	Status	—	—	20	1 Ally
19	Follow Me	Normal	Status	—	—	20	Self
25	Slam	Normal	Physical	80	75	20	Normal
28	Rest	Psychic	Status	—	—	10	Self
31	Sucker Punch	Dark	Physical	80	100	5	Normal
36	Amnesia	Psychic	Status	—	—	20	Self
39	Baton Pass	Normal	Status	—	—	40	Self
42	Me First	Normal	Status	—	—	20	Varies
47	Hyper Voice	Normal	Special	90	100	10	Many Others

● **TM & HM MOVES**

No.	Name	Type	Kind	Pow.	Acc.	PP	Range
TM01	Hone Claws	Dark	Status	—	—	15	Self
TM06	Toxic	Poison	Status	—	90	10	Normal
TM10	Hidden Power	Normal	Special	60	100	15	Normal
TM11	Sunny Day	Fire	Status	—	—	5	Both Sides
TM13	Ice Beam	Ice	Special	90	100	10	Normal
TM17	Protect	Normal	Status	—	—	10	Self
TM18	Rain Dance	Water	Status	—	—	5	Both Sides
TM21	Frustration	Normal	Physical	—	100	20	Normal
TM22	Solar Beam	Grass	Special	120	100	10	Normal
TM24	Thunderbolt	Electric	Special	90	100	15	Normal
TM27	Return	Normal	Physical	—	100	20	Normal
TM28	Dig	Ground	Physical	80	100	10	Normal
TM30	Shadow Ball	Ghost	Special	80	100	15	Normal
TM31	Brick Break	Fighting	Physical	75	100	15	Normal
TM32	Double Team	Normal	Status	—	—	15	Self
TM35	Flamethrower	Fire	Special	90	100	15	Normal
TM42	Facade	Normal	Physical	70	100	20	Normal
TM44	Rest	Psychic	Status	—	—	10	Self
TM45	Attract	Normal	Status	—	100	15	Normal
TM46	Thief	Dark	Physical	60	100	25	Normal
TM48	Round	Normal	Special	60	100	15	Normal
TM49	Echoed Voice	Normal	Special	40	100	15	Normal
TM56	Fling	Dark	Physical	—	100	10	Normal
TM57	Charge Beam	Electric	Special	50	90	10	Normal
TM65	Shadow Claw	Ghost	Physical	70	100	15	Normal
TM67	Retaliate	Normal	Physical	70	100	5	Normal
TM86	Grass Knot	Grass	Special	—	100	20	Normal
TM87	Swagger	Normal	Status	—	90	15	Normal
TM88	Sleep Talk	Normal	Status	—	—	10	Self
TM89	U-turn	Bug	Physical	70	100	20	Normal
TM90	Substitute	Normal	Status	—	—	10	Self
TM98	Power-Up Punch	Fighting	Physical	40	100	20	Normal
TM100	Confide	Normal	Status	—	—	20	Normal

No.	Name	Type	Kind	Pow.	Acc.	PP	Range
HM01	Cut	Normal	Physical	50	95	30	Normal
HM03	Surf	Water	Special	90	100	15	Adjacent

● **MOVES TAUGHT BY PEOPLE**

Name	Type	Kind	Pow.	Acc.	PP	Range

● **EGG MOVES**

Name	Type	Kind	Pow.	Acc.	PP	Range
Double-Edge	Normal	Physical	120	100	15	Normal
Pursuit	Dark	Physical	40	100	20	Normal
Slash	Normal	Physical	70	100	20	Normal
Focus Energy	Normal	Status	—	—	30	Self
Reversal	Fighting	Physical	—	100	15	Normal
Trick	Psychic	Status	—	100	10	Normal
Assist	Normal	Status	—	—	20	Self
Last Resort	Normal	Physical	140	100	5	Normal
Charm	Fairy	Status	—	100	20	Normal
Covet	Normal	Physical	60	100	25	Normal
Natural Gift	Normal	Physical	—	100	15	Normal
Iron Tail	Steel	Physical	100	75	15	Normal
Captivate	Normal	Status	—	100	20	Many Others

Central Kalos

110

Long Body Pokémon

Furret ✓

HEIGHT: 5'11" WEIGHT: 71.6 lbs.
GENDER: ♂/♀

X The mother puts its offspring to sleep by curling up around them. It corners foes with speed.

Y It makes a nest to suit its long and skinny body. The nest is impossible for other Pokémon to enter.

TYPE **Normal**

ABILITIES
Run Away
Keen Eye

HIDDEN ABILITY
Frisk

STAT GROWTH RATES
HP	▪▪▪
Attack	▪▪▪▪
Defense	▪▪▪
Sp. Atk	▪▪
Sp. Def	▪▪
Speed	▪▪▪▪▪

EGG GROUP
Field

EVOLUTION

Sentret Lv. 15 Furret

ITEMS SOMETIMES HELD BY WILD POKÉMON
None

Damage taken in normal battles	
Normal	×1
Fire	×1
Water	×1
Grass	×1
Electric	×1
Ice	×1
Fighting	×2
Poison	×1
Ground	×1
Flying	×1
Psychic	×1
Bug	×1
Rock	×1
Ghost	×0
Dragon	×1
Dark	×1
Steel	×1
Fairy	×1

Damage taken in Inverse Battles	
Normal	×1
Fire	×1
Water	×1
Grass	×1
Electric	×1
Ice	×1
Fighting	×0.5
Poison	×1
Ground	×1
Flying	×1
Psychic	×1
Bug	×1
Rock	×1
Ghost	×2
Dragon	×1
Dark	×1
Steel	×1
Fairy	×1

Can be used in
Inverse Battle
——
Battle Chateau
Battle Institute
Battle Maison
Random Matchup

Same form for ♂/♀

How to obtain for your Central Kalos Pokédex

Level up Sentret to Lv. 15.

Level up Sentret to Lv. 15.

X Y

● LEVEL-UP MOVES

Lv.	Name	Type	Kind	Pow.	Acc.	PP	Range
1	Scratch	Normal	Physical	40	100	35	Normal
1	Foresight	Normal	Status	—	—	40	Normal
1	Defense Curl	Normal	Status	—	—	40	Self
4	Quick Attack	Normal	Physical	40	100	30	Normal
4	Defense Curl	Normal	Status	—	—	40	Self
7	Quick Attack	Normal	Physical	40	100	30	Normal
13	Fury Swipes	Normal	Physical	18	80	15	Normal
17	Helping Hand	Normal	Status	—	—	20	1 Ally
21	Follow Me	Normal	Status	—	—	20	Self
28	Slam	Normal	Physical	80	75	20	Normal
32	Rest	Psychic	Status	—	—	10	Self
36	Sucker Punch	Dark	Physical	80	100	5	Normal
42	Amnesia	Psychic	Status	—	—	20	Self
46	Baton Pass	Normal	Status	—	—	40	Self
50	Me First	Normal	Status	—	—	20	Varies
56	Hyper Voice	Normal	Special	90	100	10	Many Others

● TM & HM MOVES

No.	Name	Type	Kind	Pow.	Acc.	PP	Range
TM01	Hone Claws	Dark	Status	—	—	15	Self
TM06	Toxic	Poison	Status	—	90	10	Normal
TM10	Hidden Power	Normal	Special	60	100	15	Normal
TM11	Sunny Day	Fire	Status	—	—	5	Both Sides
TM13	Ice Beam	Ice	Special	90	100	10	Normal
TM14	Blizzard	Ice	Special	110	70	5	Many Others
TM15	Hyper Beam	Normal	Special	150	90	5	Normal
TM17	Protect	Normal	Status	—	—	10	Self
TM18	Rain Dance	Water	Status	—	—	5	Both Sides
TM21	Frustration	Normal	Physical	—	100	20	Normal
TM22	Solar Beam	Grass	Special	120	100	10	Normal
TM24	Thunderbolt	Electric	Special	90	100	15	Normal
TM25	Thunder	Electric	Special	110	70	10	Normal
TM27	Return	Normal	Physical	—	100	20	Normal
TM28	Dig	Ground	Physical	80	100	10	Normal
TM30	Shadow Ball	Ghost	Special	80	100	15	Normal
TM31	Brick Break	Fighting	Physical	75	100	15	Normal
TM32	Double Team	Normal	Status	—	—	15	Self
TM35	Flamethrower	Fire	Special	90	100	15	Normal
TM42	Facade	Normal	Physical	70	100	20	Normal
TM44	Rest	Psychic	Status	—	—	10	Self
TM45	Attract	Normal	Status	—	100	15	Normal
TM46	Thief	Dark	Physical	60	100	25	Normal
TM48	Round	Normal	Special	60	100	15	Normal
TM49	Echoed Voice	Normal	Special	40	100	15	Normal
TM52	Focus Blast	Fighting	Special	120	70	5	Normal
TM56	Fling	Dark	Physical	—	100	10	Normal
TM57	Charge Beam	Electric	Special	50	90	10	Normal
TM65	Shadow Claw	Ghost	Physical	70	100	15	Normal
TM67	Retaliate	Normal	Physical	70	100	5	Normal
TM68	Giga Impact	Normal	Physical	150	90	5	Normal
TM86	Grass Knot	Grass	Special	—	100	20	Normal
TM87	Swagger	Normal	Status	—	90	15	Normal

No.	Name	Type	Kind	Pow.	Acc.	PP	Range
TM88	Sleep Talk	Normal	Status	—	—	10	Self
TM89	U-turn	Bug	Physical	70	100	20	Normal
TM90	Substitute	Normal	Status	—	—	10	Self
TM94	Rock Smash	Fighting	Physical	40	100	15	Normal
TM98	Power-Up Punch	Fighting	Physical	40	100	20	Normal
TM100	Confide	Normal	Status	—	—	20	Normal
HM01	Cut	Normal	Physical	50	95	30	Normal
HM03	Surf	Water	Special	90	100	15	Adjacent
HM04	Strength	Normal	Physical	80	100	15	Normal

● MOVES TAUGHT BY PEOPLE

Name	Type	Kind	Pow.	Acc.	PP	Range

AFTER THE HALL OF FAME

CENTRAL KALOS
111
Nincada

COASTAL KALOS

MOUNTAIN KALOS

ADVENTURE DATA

Central Kalos 111
Trainee Pokémon
✓ Nincada

HEIGHT: 1'08" WEIGHT: 12.1 lbs.
GENDER: ♂/♀

X Because it lived almost entirely underground, it is nearly blind. It uses its antennae instead.

Y It can sometimes live underground for more than 10 years. It absorbs nutrients from the roots of trees.

TYPE: Bug / Ground

ABILITY: Compound Eyes

HIDDEN ABILITY: Run Away

STAT GROWTH RATES
HP ▪▪
Attack ▪▪
Defense ▪▪▪▪
Sp. Atk ▪
Sp. Def ▪
Speed ▪▪

EGG GROUP: Bug

EVOLUTION

Nincada — Lv. 20 → Ninjask

Lv. 20 with an open space in your party and a Poké Ball → Shedinja

ITEMS SOMETIMES HELD BY WILD POKÉMON: None

Can be used in
Inverse Battle
—
Battle Chateau
Battle Institute
Battle Maison
Random Matchup

Damage taken in normal battles	
Normal	×1
Fire	×2
Water	×2
Grass	×1
Electric	×0
Ice	×2
Fighting	×0.5
Poison	×0.5
Ground	×0.5
Flying	×1
Psychic	×1
Bug	×1
Rock	×1
Ghost	×1
Dragon	×1
Dark	×1
Steel	×1
Fairy	×1

Damage taken in Inverse Battles	
Normal	×1
Fire	×0.5
Water	×0.5
Grass	×1
Electric	×2
Ice	×0.5
Fighting	×2
Poison	×2
Ground	×2
Flying	×0.5
Psychic	×1
Bug	×1
Rock	×1
Ghost	×1
Dragon	×1
Dark	×1
Steel	×1
Fairy	×1

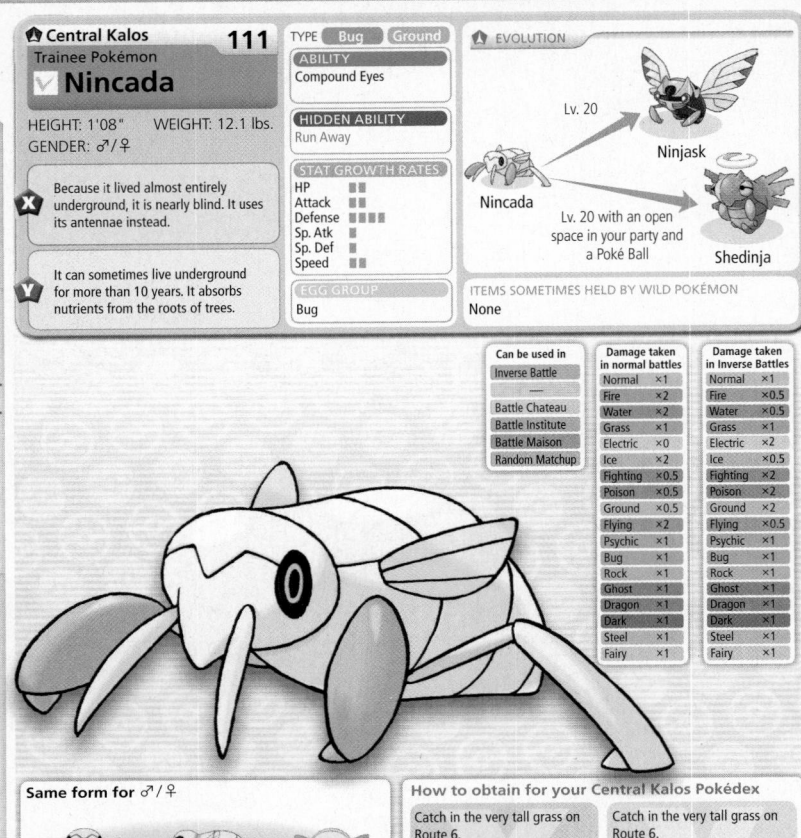

Same form for ♂/♀

How to obtain for your Central Kalos Pokédex
Catch in the very tall grass on Route 6.
Catch in the very tall grass on Route 6.

LEVEL-UP MOVES
Lv.	Name	Type	Kind	Pow.	Acc.	PP	Range
1	Scratch	Normal	Physical	40	100	35	Normal
1	Harden	Normal	Status	—	—	30	Self
5	Leech Life	Bug	Physical	20	100	15	Normal
9	Sand Attack	Ground	Status	—	100	15	Normal
14	Fury Swipes	Normal	Physical	18	80	15	Normal
19	Mind Reader	Normal	Status	—	—	5	Normal
25	False Swipe	Normal	Physical	40	100	40	Normal
31	Mud-Slap	Ground	Special	20	100	10	Normal
38	Metal Claw	Steel	Physical	50	95	35	Normal
45	Dig	Ground	Physical	80	100	10	Normal

TM & HM MOVES
No.	Name	Type	Kind	Pow.	Acc.	PP	Range
TM01	Hone Claws	Dark	Status	—	—	15	Self
TM06	Toxic	Poison	Status	—	90	10	Normal
TM10	Hidden Power	Normal	Special	60	100	15	Normal
TM11	Sunny Day	Fire	Status	—	—	5	Both Sides
TM17	Protect	Normal	Status	—	—	10	Self
TM21	Frustration	Normal	Physical	—	100	20	Normal
TM22	Solar Beam	Grass	Special	120	100	10	Normal
TM27	Return	Normal	Physical	—	100	20	Normal
TM28	Dig	Ground	Physical	80	100	10	Normal
TM30	Shadow Ball	Ghost	Special	80	100	15	Normal
TM32	Double Team	Normal	Status	—	—	15	Self
TM37	Sandstorm	Rock	Status	—	—	10	Both Sides
TM40	Aerial Ace	Flying	Physical	60	—	20	Normal
TM42	Facade	Normal	Physical	70	100	20	Normal
TM44	Rest	Psychic	Status	—	—	10	Self
TM48	Round	Normal	Special	60	100	15	Normal
TM54	False Swipe	Normal	Physical	40	100	40	Normal
TM70	Flash	Normal	Status	—	100	20	Normal
TM76	Struggle Bug	Bug	Special	50	100	20	Many Others
TM81	X-Scissor	Bug	Physical	80	100	15	Normal
TM87	Swagger	Normal	Status	—	90	15	Normal
TM88	Sleep Talk	Normal	Status	—	—	10	Self
TM90	Substitute	Normal	Status	—	—	10	Self
TM100	Confide	Normal	Status	—	—	20	Normal
HM01	Cut	Normal	Physical	50	95	30	Normal

MOVES TAUGHT BY PEOPLE
Name	Type	Kind	Pow.	Acc.	PP	Range

EGG MOVES
Name	Type	Kind	Pow.	Acc.	PP	Range
Endure	Normal	Status	—	—	10	Self
Feint Attack	Dark	Physical	60	—	20	Normal
Gust	Flying	Special	40	100	35	Normal
Silver Wind	Bug	Special	60	100	5	Normal
Bug Buzz	Bug	Special	90	100	10	Normal
Night Slash	Dark	Physical	70	100	15	Normal
Bug Bite	Bug	Physical	60	100	20	Normal
Final Gambit	Fighting	Special	—	100	5	Normal

Ninja Pokémon
Ninjask

HEIGHT: 2'07" WEIGHT: 26.5 lbs.
GENDER: ♂/♀

X Its cry leaves a lasting headache if heard for too long. It moves so quickly that it is almost invisible.

Y Because it moves so quickly, it sometimes becomes unseeable. It congregates around tree sap.

TYPE Bug Flying

ABILITY
Speed Boost

HIDDEN ABILITY
Infiltrator

STAT GROWTH RATES

HP	■■■
Attack	■■■■■
Defense	■■
Sp. Atk	■■
Sp. Def	■■
Speed	■■■■■■■■

EGG GROUP
Bug

EVOLUTION

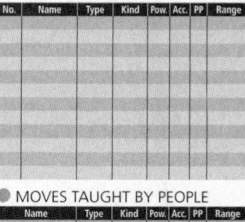

Lv. 20 → Ninjask

Nincada

Lv. 20 with an open space in your party and a Poké Ball → Shedinja

ITEMS SOMETIMES HELD BY WILD POKÉMON
None

Damage taken in normal battles		Damage taken in Inverse Battles	
Normal	×1	Normal	×1
Fire	×2	Fire	×0.5
Water	×1	Water	×1
Grass	×0.25	Grass	×4
Electric	×2	Electric	×0.5
Ice	×2	Ice	×0.5
Fighting	×0.25	Fighting	×4
Poison	×1	Poison	×1
Ground	×0	Ground	×4
Flying	×2	Flying	×0.5
Psychic	×1	Psychic	×1
Bug	×0.5	Bug	×2
Rock	×4	Rock	×0.25
Ghost	×1	Ghost	×1
Dragon	×1	Dragon	×1
Dark	×1	Dark	×1
Steel	×1	Steel	×1
Fairy	×1	Fairy	×1

Can be used in	
Inverse Battle	Battle Institute
Sky Battle	Battle Maison
Battle Chateau	Random Matchup

Same form for ♂/♀

How to obtain for your Central Kalos Pokédex

Level up Nincada to Lv. 20. Level up Nincada to Lv. 20.

AFTER THE HALL OF FAME

CENTRAL KALOS

112 Ninjask

COASTAL KALOS

MOUNTAIN KALOS

ADVENTURE DATA

● LEVEL-UP MOVES

Lv.	Name	Type	Kind	Pow.	Acc.	PP	Range
1	Bug Bite	Bug	Physical	60	100	20	Normal
1	Scratch	Normal	Physical	40	100	35	Normal
1	Harden	Normal	Status	—	—	30	Self
1	Leech Life	Bug	Physical	20	100	15	Normal
1	Sand Attack	Ground	Status	—	100	15	Normal
5	Leech Life	Bug	Physical	20	100	15	Normal
9	Sand Attack	Ground	Status	—	100	15	Normal
14	Fury Swipes	Normal	Physical	18	80	15	Normal
19	Mind Reader	Normal	Status	—	—	5	Normal
20	Double Team	Normal	Status	—	—	15	Self
20	Fury Cutter	Bug	Physical	40	95	20	Normal
20	Screech	Normal	Status	—	85	40	Normal
25	Swords Dance	Normal	Status	—	—	20	Self
31	Slash	Normal	Physical	70	100	20	Normal
38	Agility	Psychic	Status	—	—	30	Self
45	Baton Pass	Normal	Status	—	—	40	Self
52	X-Scissor	Bug	Physical	80	100	15	Normal

● TM & HM MOVES

No.	Name	Type	Kind	Pow.	Acc.	PP	Range
TM01	Hone Claws	Dark	Status	—	—	15	Self
TM06	Toxic	Poison	Status	—	90	10	Normal
TM10	Hidden Power	Normal	Special	60	100	15	Normal
TM11	Sunny Day	Fire	Status	—	—	5	Both Sides
TM15	Hyper Beam	Normal	Special	150	90	5	Normal
TM17	Protect	Normal	Status	—	—	10	Self
TM19	Roost	Flying	Status	—	—	10	Self
TM21	Frustration	Normal	Physical	—	100	20	Normal
TM22	Solar Beam	Grass	Special	120	100	10	Normal
TM27	Return	Normal	Physical	—	100	20	Normal
TM28	Dig	Ground	Physical	80	100	10	Normal
TM30	Shadow Ball	Ghost	Special	80	100	15	Normal
TM32	Double Team	Normal	Status	—	—	15	Self
TM37	Sandstorm	Rock	Status	—	—	10	Both Sides
TM40	Aerial Ace	Flying	Physical	60	—	20	Normal
TM42	Facade	Normal	Physical	70	100	20	Normal
TM44	Rest	Psychic	Status	—	—	10	Self
TM45	Attract	Normal	Status	—	100	15	Normal
TM46	Thief	Dark	Physical	60	100	25	Normal
TM48	Round	Normal	Special	60	100	15	Normal
TM54	False Swipe	Normal	Physical	40	100	40	Normal
TM68	Giga Impact	Normal	Physical	150	90	5	Normal
TM70	Flash	Normal	Status	—	100	20	Normal
TM75	Swords Dance	Normal	Status	—	—	20	Self
TM76	Struggle Bug	Bug	Special	50	100	20	Many Others
TM81	X-Scissor	Bug	Physical	80	100	15	Normal
TM87	Swagger	Normal	Status	—	90	15	Normal
TM88	Sleep Talk	Normal	Status	—	—	10	Self
TM89	U-turn	Bug	Physical	70	100	20	Normal
TM90	Substitute	Normal	Status	—	—	10	Self
TM100	Confide	Normal	Status	—	—	20	Normal
HM01	Cut	Normal	Physical	50	95	30	Normal

● MOVES TAUGHT BY PEOPLE

Name	Type	Kind	Pow.	Acc.	PP	Range

AFTER THE HALL OF FAME

CENTRAL KALOS

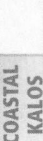
113
Shedinja

COASTAL KALOS

MOUNTAIN KALOS

ADVENTURE DATA

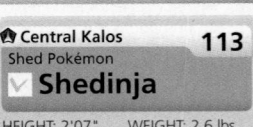

Central Kalos 113

Shed Pokémon

☑ **Shedinja**

HEIGHT: 2'07" WEIGHT: 2.6 lbs.
GENDER: unknown

X A discarded bug shell that came to life. Peering into the crack on its back is said to steal one's spirit.

Y A most peculiar Pokémon that somehow appears in a Poké Ball when a Nincada evolves.

TYPE: Bug Ghost

ABILITY
Wonder Guard

HIDDEN ABILITY
None

STAT GROWTH RATES
HP	▪
Attack	▪▪▪▪▪
Defense	▪▪
Sp. Atk	▪
Sp. Def	▪
Speed	▪▪

EGG GROUP
Mineral

EVOLUTION

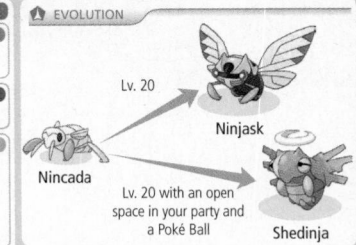

Nincada

Lv. 20 → Ninjask

Lv. 20 with an open space in your party and a Poké Ball → Shedinja

ITEMS SOMETIMES HELD BY WILD POKÉMON
None

Damage taken in normal battles	
Normal	×0
Fire	×2
Water	×1
Grass	×0.5
Electric	×1
Ice	×1
Fighting	×0
Poison	×0.5
Ground	×0.5
Flying	×2
Psychic	×1
Bug	×0.5
Rock	×2
Ghost	×2
Dragon	×1
Dark	×2
Steel	×1
Fairy	×1

Damage taken in Inverse Battles	
Normal	×2
Fire	×0.5
Water	×1
Grass	×2
Electric	×1
Ice	×1
Fighting	×4
Poison	×2
Ground	×2
Flying	×0.5
Psychic	×1
Bug	×2
Rock	×0.5
Ghost	×0.5
Dragon	×1
Dark	×0.5
Steel	×1
Fairy	×1

Can be used in	
Inverse Battle	Battle Institute
—	Battle Maison
Battle Chateau	Random Matchup

Gender unknown

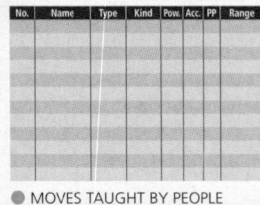

How to obtain for your Central Kalos Pokédex

Level up Nincada to Lv. 20 with an open space in your party and a Poké Ball.

Level up Nincada to Lv. 20 with an open space in your party and a Poké Ball.

● **LEVEL-UP MOVES**

Lv.	Name	Type	Kind	Pow.	Acc.	PP	Range
1	Scratch	Normal	Physical	40	100	35	Normal
1	Harden	Normal	Status	—	—	30	Self
5	Leech Life	Bug	Physical	20	100	15	Normal
9	Sand Attack	Ground	Status	—	100	15	Normal
14	Fury Swipes	Normal	Physical	18	80	15	Normal
19	Mind Reader	Normal	Status	—	—	5	Normal
25	Spite	Ghost	Status	—	100	10	Normal
31	Confuse Ray	Ghost	Status	—	100	10	Normal
38	Shadow Sneak	Ghost	Physical	40	100	30	Normal
43	Grudge	Ghost	Status	—	—	5	Self
47	Phantom Force	Ghost	Physical	90	100	10	Normal
50	Heal Block	Psychic	Status	—	100	15	Many Others
59	Shadow Ball	Ghost	Special	80	100	15	Normal

● **TM & HM MOVES**

No.	Name	Type	Kind	Pow.	Acc.	PP	Range
TM01	Hone Claws	Dark	Status	—	—	15	Self
TM06	Toxic	Poison	Status	—	90	10	Normal
TM10	Hidden Power	Normal	Special	60	100	15	Normal
TM11	Sunny Day	Fire	Status	—	—	5	Both Sides
TM15	Hyper Beam	Normal	Special	150	90	5	Normal
TM17	Protect	Normal	Status	—	—	10	Self
TM21	Frustration	Normal	Physical	—	100	20	Normal
TM22	Solar Beam	Grass	Special	120	100	10	Normal
TM27	Return	Normal	Physical	—	100	20	Normal
TM28	Dig	Ground	Physical	80	100	10	Normal
TM30	Shadow Ball	Ghost	Special	80	100	15	Normal
TM32	Double Team	Normal	Status	—	—	15	Self
TM37	Sandstorm	Rock	Status	—	—	10	Both Sides
TM40	Aerial Ace	Flying	Physical	60	—	20	Normal
TM42	Facade	Normal	Physical	70	100	20	Normal
TM44	Rest	Psychic	Status	—	—	10	Self
TM46	Thief	Dark	Physical	60	100	25	Normal
TM48	Round	Normal	Special	60	100	15	Normal
TM54	False Swipe	Normal	Physical	40	100	40	Normal
TM61	Will-O-Wisp	Fire	Status	—	85	15	Normal
TM65	Shadow Claw	Ghost	Physical	70	100	15	Normal
TM68	Giga Impact	Normal	Physical	150	90	5	Normal
TM70	Flash	Normal	Status	—	100	20	Normal
TM76	Struggle Bug	Bug	Special	50	100	20	Many Others
TM81	X-Scissor	Bug	Physical	80	100	15	Normal
TM85	Dream Eater	Psychic	Special	100	100	15	Normal
TM87	Swagger	Normal	Status	—	90	15	Normal
TM88	Sleep Talk	Normal	Status	—	—	10	Self
TM90	Substitute	Normal	Status	—	—	10	Self
TM100	Confide	Normal	Status	—	—	20	Normal
HM01	Cut	Normal	Physical	50	95	30	Normal

No.	Name	Type	Kind	Pow.	Acc.	PP	Range

● **MOVES TAUGHT BY PEOPLE**

Name	Type	Kind	Pow.	Acc.	PP	Range

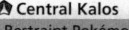 **Central Kalos**
Restraint Pokémon

☑ Espurr

114

TYPE: **Psychic**

HEIGHT: 1'00" WEIGHT: 7.7 lbs.
GENDER: ♂ / ♀

ABILITIES
Keen Eye
Infiltrator

HIDDEN ABILITY
Own Tempo

X The organ that emits its intense psychic power is sheltered by its ears to keep power from leaking out.

Y It has enough psychic energy to blast everything within 300 feet of itself, but it has no control over its power.

STAT GROWTH RATES
HP	■■■
Attack	■■■
Defense	■■
Sp. Atk	■■■
Sp. Def	■■■
Speed	■■■■

EGG GROUP
Field

⬤ EVOLUTION

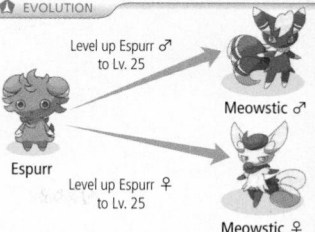

Level up Espurr ♂ to Lv. 25 → Meowstic ♂

Espurr

Level up Espurr ♀ to Lv. 25 → Meowstic ♀

ITEMS SOMETIMES HELD BY WILD POKÉMON
None

Damage taken in normal battles		Damage taken in Inverse Battles		Can be used in
Normal	×1	Normal	×1	Inverse Battle
Fire	×1	Fire	×1	—
Water	×1	Water	×1	Battle Chateau
Grass	×1	Grass	×1	Battle Institute
Electric	×1	Electric	×1	Battle Maison
Ice	×1	Ice	×1	Random Matchup
Fighting	×0.5	Fighting	×2	
Poison	×1	Poison	×1	
Ground	×1	Ground	×1	
Flying	×1	Flying	×1	
Psychic	×0.5	Psychic	×2	
Bug	×2	Bug	×0.5	
Rock	×1	Rock	×1	
Ghost	×2	Ghost	×0.5	
Dragon	×1	Dragon	×1	
Dark	×2	Dark	×0.5	
Steel	×1	Steel	×1	
Fairy	×1	Fairy	×1	

How to obtain for your Central Kalos Pokédex

X Catch in the very tall grass on Route 6.

Y Catch in the very tall grass on Route 6.

Same form for ♂ / ♀

⬤ LEVEL-UP MOVES
Lv.	Name	Type	Kind	Pow.	Acc.	PP	Range
1	Scratch	Normal	Physical	40	100	35	Normal
1	Leer	Normal	Status	—	100	30	Many Others
5	Covet	Normal	Physical	60	100	25	Normal
9	Confusion	Psychic	Special	50	100	25	Normal
13	Light Screen	Psychic	Status	—	—	30	Your Side
17	Psybeam	Psychic	Special	65	100	20	Normal
19	Fake Out	Normal	Physical	40	100	10	Normal
22	Disarming Voice	Fairy	Special	40	—	15	Many Others
25	Psyshock	Psychic	Special	80	100	10	Normal

⬤ TM & HM MOVES
No.	Name	Type	Kind	Pow.	Acc.	PP	Range
TM03	Psyshock	Psychic	Special	80	100	10	Normal
TM04	Calm Mind	Psychic	Status	—	—	20	Self
TM06	Toxic	Poison	Status	—	90	10	Normal
TM10	Hidden Power	Normal	Special	60	100	15	Normal
TM11	Sunny Day	Fire	Status	—	—	5	Both Sides
TM16	Light Screen	Psychic	Status	—	—	30	Your Side
TM17	Protect	Normal	Status	—	—	10	Self
TM18	Rain Dance	Water	Status	—	—	5	Both Sides
TM20	Safeguard	Normal	Status	—	—	25	Your Side
TM21	Frustration	Normal	Physical	—	100	20	Normal
TM24	Thunderbolt	Electric	Special	90	100	15	Normal
TM27	Return	Normal	Physical	—	100	20	Normal
TM29	Psychic	Psychic	Special	90	100	10	Normal
TM32	Double Team	Normal	Status	—	—	15	Self
TM33	Reflect	Psychic	Status	—	—	20	Your Side
TM41	Torment	Dark	Status	—	100	15	Normal
TM42	Facade	Normal	Physical	70	100	20	Normal
TM44	Rest	Psychic	Status	—	—	10	Self
TM45	Attract	Normal	Status	—	100	15	Normal
TM48	Round	Normal	Special	60	100	15	Normal
TM49	Echoed Voice	Normal	Special	40	100	15	Normal
TM53	Energy Ball	Grass	Special	90	100	10	Normal
TM57	Charge Beam	Electric	Special	50	90	10	Normal
TM66	Payback	Dark	Physical	50	100	10	Normal
TM70	Flash	Normal	Status	—	100	20	Normal
TM73	Thunder Wave	Electric	Status	—	100	20	Normal
TM77	Psych Up	Normal	Status	—	—	10	Normal
TM85	Dream Eater	Psychic	Special	100	100	15	Normal
TM87	Swagger	Normal	Status	—	90	15	Normal
TM88	Sleep Talk	Normal	Status	—	—	10	Self
TM90	Substitute	Normal	Status	—	—	10	Self
TM92	Trick Room	Psychic	Status	—	—	5	Both Sides
TM97	Dark Pulse	Dark	Special	80	100	15	Normal

No.	Name	Type	Kind	Pow.	Acc.	PP	Range
TM100	Confide	Normal	Status	—	—	20	Normal
HM01	Cut	Normal	Physical	50	95	30	Normal

⬤ MOVES TAUGHT BY PEOPLE
Name	Type	Kind	Pow.	Acc.	PP	Range

⬤ EGG MOVES
Name	Type	Kind	Pow.	Acc.	PP	Range
Trick	Psychic	Status	—	100	10	Normal
Yawn	Normal	Status	—	—	10	Normal
Assist	Normal	Status	—	—	20	Self
Barrier	Psychic	Status	—	—	20	Self

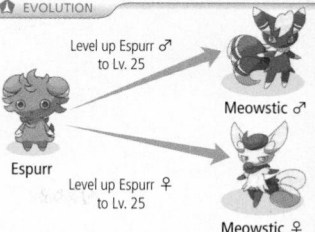

AFTER THE HALL OF FAME

CENTRAL KALOS

114

Espurr

COASTAL KALOS

MOUNTAIN KALOS

ADVENTURE DATA

AFTER THE HALL OF FAME

CENTRAL KALOS

115

Meowstic
Male Form

COASTAL KALOS

MOUNTAIN KALOS

ADVENTURE DATA

Central Kalos — 115

Constraint Pokémon

Meowstic

HEIGHT: 2'00" WEIGHT: 18.7 lbs.
GENDER: ♂

TYPE Psychic

ABILITIES
Keen Eye
Infiltrator

HIDDEN ABILITY
Prankster

STAT GROWTH RATES
HP ■■■
Attack ■■■
Defense ■■■
Sp. Atk ■■■■
Sp. Def ■■■
Speed ■■■■■■

EGG GROUP
Field

X When in danger, it raises its ears and releases enough psychic power to grind a 10-ton truck into dust.

Y The eyeball patterns on the interior of its ears emit psychic energy. It keeps the patterns tightly covered because that power is too immense.

EVOLUTION

Espurr

Level up Espurr ♂ to Lv. 25 → Meowstic ♂

Level up Espurr ♀ to Lv. 25 → Meowstic ♀

ITEMS SOMETIMES HELD BY WILD POKÉMON
None

Damage taken in normal battles		Damage taken in Inverse Battles	
Normal	×1	Normal	×1
Fire	×1	Fire	×1
Water	×1	Water	×1
Grass	×1	Grass	×1
Electric	×1	Electric	×1
Ice	×1	Ice	×1
Fighting	×0.5	Fighting	×2
Poison	×1	Poison	×1
Ground	×1	Ground	×1
Flying	×1	Flying	×1
Psychic	×0.5	Psychic	×2
Bug	×2	Bug	×0.5
Rock	×1	Rock	×1
Ghost	×2	Ghost	×0.5
Dragon	×1	Dragon	×1
Dark	×2	Dark	×0.5
Steel	×1	Steel	×1
Fairy	×1	Fairy	×1

Can be used in	
Inverse Battle	Battle Institute
—	Battle Maison
Battle Chateau	Random Matchup

♂

How to obtain for your Central Kalos Pokédex

X Level up Espurr ♂ to Lv. 25.

Y Level up Espurr ♂ to Lv. 25.

● LEVEL-UP MOVES

Lv.	Name	Type	Kind	Pow.	Acc.	PP	Range
1	Quick Guard	Fighting	Status	—	—	15	Your Side
1	Mean Look	Normal	Status	—	—	5	Normal
1	Helping Hand	Normal	Status	—	—	20	1 Ally
1	Scratch	Normal	Physical	40	100	35	Normal
1	Leer	Normal	Status	—	100	30	Many Others
5	Covet	Normal	Physical	60	100	25	Normal
9	Confusion	Psychic	Special	50	100	25	Normal
13	Light Screen	Psychic	Status	—	—	30	Your Side
17	Psybeam	Psychic	Special	65	100	20	Normal
19	Fake Out	Normal	Physical	40	100	10	Normal
22	Disarming Voice	Fairy	Special	40	—	15	Many Others
25	Psyshock	Psychic	Special	80	100	10	Normal
28	Charm	Fairy	Status	—	100	20	Normal
31	Miracle Eye	Psychic	Status	—	—	40	Normal
35	Reflect	Psychic	Status	—	—	20	Your Side
40	Psychic	Psychic	Special	90	100	10	Normal
43	Role Play	Psychic	Status	—	—	10	Normal
45	Imprison	Psychic	Status	—	—	10	Self
48	Sucker Punch	Dark	Physical	80	100	5	Normal
50	Misty Terrain	Fairy	Status	—	—	10	Both Sides
53	Quick Guard	Fighting	Status	—	—	15	Your Side

● TM & HM MOVES

No.	Name	Type	Kind	Pow.	Acc.	PP	Range
TM03	Psyshock	Psychic	Special	80	100	10	Normal
TM04	Calm Mind	Psychic	Status	—	—	20	Self
TM06	Toxic	Poison	Status	—	90	10	Normal
TM10	Hidden Power	Normal	Special	60	100	15	Normal
TM11	Sunny Day	Fire	Status	—	—	5	Both Sides
TM15	Hyper Beam	Normal	Special	150	90	5	Normal
TM16	Light Screen	Psychic	Status	—	—	30	Your Side
TM17	Protect	Normal	Status	—	—	10	Self
TM18	Rain Dance	Water	Status	—	—	5	Both Sides
TM20	Safeguard	Normal	Status	—	—	25	Your Side
TM21	Frustration	Normal	Physical	—	100	20	Normal
TM24	Thunderbolt	Electric	Special	90	100	15	Normal
TM27	Return	Normal	Physical	—	100	20	Normal
TM28	Dig	Ground	Physical	80	100	10	Normal
TM29	Psychic	Psychic	Special	90	100	10	Normal
TM30	Shadow Ball	Ghost	Special	80	100	15	Normal
TM32	Double Team	Normal	Status	—	—	15	Self
TM33	Reflect	Psychic	Status	—	—	20	Your Side
TM41	Torment	Dark	Status	—	100	15	Normal
TM42	Facade	Normal	Physical	70	100	20	Normal
TM44	Rest	Psychic	Status	—	—	10	Self
TM45	Attract	Normal	Status	—	100	15	Normal
TM48	Round	Normal	Special	60	100	15	Normal
TM49	Echoed Voice	Normal	Special	40	100	15	Normal
TM53	Energy Ball	Grass	Special	90	100	10	Normal
TM57	Charge Beam	Electric	Special	50	90	10	Normal
TM66	Payback	Dark	Physical	50	100	10	Normal
TM68	Giga Impact	Normal	Physical	150	90	5	Normal
TM70	Flash	Normal	Status	—	100	20	Normal
TM73	Thunder Wave	Electric	Status	—	100	20	Normal
TM77	Psych Up	Normal	Status	—	—	10	Normal
TM85	Dream Eater	Psychic	Special	100	100	15	Normal
TM87	Swagger	Normal	Status	—	90	15	Normal

No.	Name	Type	Kind	Pow.	Acc.	PP	Range
TM88	Sleep Talk	Normal	Status	—	—	10	Self
TM90	Substitute	Normal	Status	—	—	10	Self
TM92	Trick Room	Psychic	Status	—	—	5	Both Sides
TM97	Dark Pulse	Dark	Special	80	100	15	Normal
TM98	Power-Up Punch	Fighting	Physical	40	100	20	Normal
TM100	Confide	Normal	Status	—	—	20	Normal
HM01	Cut	Normal	Physical	50	95	30	Normal

● MOVES TAUGHT BY PEOPLE

Name	Type	Kind	Pow.	Acc.	PP	Range

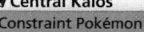 **Central Kalos**
Constraint Pokémon **115**
 Meowstic

HEIGHT: 2'00"   WEIGHT: 18.7 lbs.
GENDER: ♀

 When in danger, it raises its ears and releases enough psychic power to grind a 10-ton truck into dust.

When in danger, it raises its ears and releases enough psychic power to grind a 10-ton truck into dust.

The eyeball patterns on the interior of its ears emit psychic energy. It keeps the patterns tightly covered because that power is too immense.

TYPE **Psychic**

ABILITIES
Keen Eye
Infiltrator

HIDDEN ABILITY
Competitive

STAT GROWTH RATES
HP	■■■
Attack	■■■
Defense	■■■
Sp. Atk	■■■■
Sp. Def	■■■
Speed	■■■■■

EGG GROUP
Field

EVOLUTION

Espurr → Level up Espurr ♂ to Lv. 25 → Meowstic ♂
Espurr → Level up Espurr ♀ to Lv. 25 → Meowstic ♀

ITEMS SOMETIMES HELD BY WILD POKÉMON
None

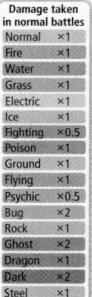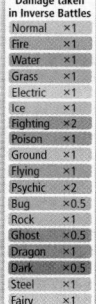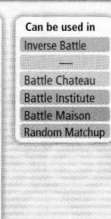

AFTER THE HALL OF FAME

CENTRAL KALOS

115

Meowstic Female Form

COASTAL KALOS

MOUNTAIN KALOS

ADVENTURE DATA

Damage taken in normal battles	
Normal	×1
Fire	×1
Water	×1
Grass	×1
Electric	×1
Ice	×1
Fighting	×0.5
Poison	×1
Ground	×1
Flying	×1
Psychic	×0.5
Bug	×2
Rock	×1
Ghost	×2
Dragon	×1
Dark	×2
Steel	×1
Fairy	×1

Damage taken in Inverse Battles	
Normal	×1
Fire	×1
Water	×1
Grass	×1
Electric	×1
Ice	×1
Fighting	×2
Poison	×1
Ground	×1
Flying	×1
Psychic	×2
Bug	×0.5
Rock	×1
Ghost	×0.5
Dragon	×1
Dark	×0.5
Steel	×1
Fairy	×1

Can be used in
Inverse Battle
—
Battle Chateau
Battle Institute
Battle Maison
Random Matchup

How to obtain for your Central Kalos Pokédex

Level up Espurr ♀ to Lv. 25.   Level up Espurr ♀ to Lv. 25.

♀

● LEVEL-UP MOVES

Lv.	Name	Type	Kind	Pow.	Acc.	PP	Range
1	Stored Power	Psychic	Special	20	100	10	Normal
1	Me First	Normal	Status	—	—	20	Varies
1	Magical Leaf	Grass	Special	60	—	20	Normal
1	Scratch	Normal	Physical	40	100	35	Normal
1	Leer	Normal	Status	—	100	30	Many Others
5	Covet	Normal	Physical	60	100	25	Normal
9	Confusion	Psychic	Special	50	100	25	Normal
13	Light Screen	Psychic	Status	—	—	30	Your Side
17	Psybeam	Psychic	Special	65	100	20	Normal
19	Fake Out	Normal	Physical	40	100	10	Normal
22	Disarming Voice	Fairy	Special	40	—	15	Many Others
25	Psyshock	Psychic	Special	80	100	10	Normal
28	Charge Beam	Electric	Special	50	90	10	Normal
31	Shadow Ball	Ghost	Special	80	100	15	Normal
35	Extrasensory	Psychic	Special	80	100	20	Normal
40	Psychic	Psychic	Special	90	100	10	Normal
43	Role Play	Psychic	Status	—	—	10	Normal
45	Signal Beam	Bug	Special	75	100	15	Normal
48	Sucker Punch	Dark	Physical	80	100	5	Normal
50	Future Sight	Psychic	Special	120	100	10	Normal
53	Stored Power	Psychic	Special	20	100	10	Normal

● TM & HM MOVES

No.	Name	Type	Kind	Pow.	Acc.	PP	Range
TM03	Psyshock	Psychic	Special	80	100	10	Normal
TM04	Calm Mind	Psychic	Status	—	—	20	Self
TM06	Toxic	Poison	Status	—	90	10	Normal
TM10	Hidden Power	Normal	Special	60	100	15	Normal
TM11	Sunny Day	Fire	Status	—	—	5	Both Sides
TM15	Hyper Beam	Normal	Special	150	90	5	Normal
TM16	Light Screen	Psychic	Status	—	—	30	Your Side
TM17	Protect	Normal	Status	—	—	10	Self
TM18	Rain Dance	Water	Status	—	—	5	Both Sides
TM20	Safeguard	Normal	Status	—	—	25	Your Side
TM21	Frustration	Normal	Physical	—	100	20	Normal
TM24	Thunderbolt	Electric	Special	90	100	15	Normal
TM27	Return	Normal	Physical	—	100	20	Normal
TM28	Dig	Ground	Physical	80	100	10	Normal
TM29	Psychic	Psychic	Special	90	100	10	Normal
TM30	Shadow Ball	Ghost	Special	80	100	15	Normal
TM32	Double Team	Normal	Status	—	—	15	Self
TM33	Reflect	Psychic	Status	—	—	20	Your Side
TM41	Torment	Dark	Status	—	100	15	Normal
TM42	Facade	Normal	Physical	70	100	20	Normal
TM44	Rest	Psychic	Status	—	—	10	Self
TM45	Attract	Normal	Status	—	100	15	Normal
TM48	Round	Normal	Special	60	100	15	Normal
TM49	Echoed Voice	Normal	Special	40	100	15	Normal
TM53	Energy Ball	Grass	Special	90	100	10	Normal
TM57	Charge Beam	Electric	Special	50	90	10	Normal
TM66	Payback	Dark	Physical	50	100	10	Normal
TM68	Giga Impact	Normal	Physical	150	90	5	Normal
TM70	Flash	Normal	Status	—	100	20	Normal
TM73	Thunder Wave	Electric	Status	—	100	20	Normal
TM77	Psych Up	Normal	Status	—	—	10	Normal
TM85	Dream Eater	Psychic	Special	100	100	15	Normal
TM87	Swagger	Normal	Status	—	90	15	Normal
TM88	Sleep Talk	Normal	Status	—	—	10	Self
TM90	Substitute	Normal	Status	—	—	10	Self
TM92	Trick Room	Psychic	Status	—	—	5	Both Sides
TM97	Dark Pulse	Dark	Special	80	100	15	Normal
TM98	Power-Up Punch	Fighting	Physical	40	100	20	Normal
TM100	Confide	Normal	Status	—	—	20	Normal
HM01	Cut	Normal	Physical	50	95	30	Normal

● MOVES TAUGHT BY PEOPLE

Name	Type	Kind	Pow.	Acc.	PP	Range

AFTER THE HALL OF FAME

CENTRAL KALOS
116
Kecleon

COASTAL KALOS

MOUNTAIN KALOS

ADVENTURE DATA

Central Kalos — 116

Color Swap Pokémon

✅ Kecleon

HEIGHT: 3'03" WEIGHT: 48.5 lbs.
GENDER: ♂/♀

TYPE Normal

ABILITY
Color Change

HIDDEN ABILITY
Protean

STAT GROWTH RATES
HP	■■■
Attack	■■■■
Defense	■■■
Sp. Atk	■■■
Sp. Def	■■■■■
Speed	■■

EGG GROUP
Field

X It can freely change its body's color. The zigzag pattern on its belly doesn't change, however.

Y It changes its shading to match its surroundings so it can sneak up on prey. Only its belly patterns stay fixed.

EVOLUTION
Does not evolve

ITEMS SOMETIMES HELD BY WILD POKÉMON
None

Damage taken in normal battles		Damage taken in Inverse Battles	
Normal	×1	Normal	×1
Fire	×1	Fire	×1
Water	×1	Water	×1
Grass	×1	Grass	×1
Electric	×1	Electric	×1
Ice	×1	Ice	×1
Fighting	×2	Fighting	×0.5
Poison	×1	Poison	×1
Ground	×1	Ground	×1
Flying	×1	Flying	×1
Psychic	×1	Psychic	×1
Bug	×1	Bug	×1
Rock	×1	Rock	×1
Ghost	×0	Ghost	×2
Dragon	×1	Dragon	×1
Dark	×1	Dark	×1
Steel	×1	Steel	×1
Fairy	×1	Fairy	×1

Can be used in	
Inverse Battle	Battle Institute
—	Battle Maison
Battle Chateau	Random Matchup

Same form for ♂/♀

How to obtain for your Central Kalos Pokédex

Catch in the very tall grass on Route 6.

Catch in the very tall grass on Route 6.

● LEVEL-UP MOVES

Lv.	Name	Type	Kind	Pow.	Acc.	PP	Range
1	Synchronoise	Psychic	Special	120	100	10	Adjacent
1	Ancient Power	Rock	Special	60	100	5	Normal
1	Thief	Dark	Physical	60	100	25	Normal
1	Tail Whip	Normal	Status	—	100	30	Many Others
1	Astonish	Ghost	Physical	30	100	15	Normal
1	Lick	Ghost	Physical	30	100	30	Normal
1	Scratch	Normal	Physical	40	100	35	Normal
4	Bind	Normal	Physical	15	85	20	Normal
7	Feint Attack	Dark	Physical	60	—	20	Normal
10	Fury Swipes	Normal	Physical	18	80	15	Normal
14	Feint	Normal	Physical	30	100	10	Normal
18	Psybeam	Psychic	Special	65	100	20	Normal
22	Shadow Sneak	Ghost	Physical	40	100	30	Normal
27	Slash	Normal	Physical	70	100	20	Normal
32	Screech	Normal	Status	—	85	40	Normal
37	Substitute	Normal	Status	—	—	10	Self
43	Sucker Punch	Dark	Physical	80	100	5	Normal
49	Shadow Claw	Ghost	Physical	70	100	15	Normal
55	Ancient Power	Rock	Special	60	100	5	Normal
58	Synchronoise	Psychic	Special	120	100	10	Adjacent

● TM & HM MOVES

No.	Name	Type	Kind	Pow.	Acc.	PP	Range
TM01	Hone Claws	Dark	Status	—	—	15	Self
TM06	Toxic	Poison	Status	—	90	10	Normal
TM10	Hidden Power	Normal	Special	60	100	15	Normal
TM11	Sunny Day	Fire	Status	—	—	5	Both Sides
TM13	Ice Beam	Ice	Special	90	100	10	Normal
TM14	Blizzard	Ice	Special	110	70	5	Many Others
TM17	Protect	Normal	Status	—	—	10	Self
TM18	Rain Dance	Water	Status	—	—	5	Both Sides
TM21	Frustration	Normal	Physical	—	100	20	Normal
TM22	Solar Beam	Grass	Special	120	100	10	Normal
TM24	Thunderbolt	Electric	Special	90	100	15	Normal
TM25	Thunder	Electric	Special	110	70	10	Normal
TM27	Return	Normal	Physical	—	100	20	Normal
TM28	Dig	Ground	Physical	80	100	10	Normal
TM30	Shadow Ball	Ghost	Special	80	100	15	Normal
TM31	Brick Break	Fighting	Physical	75	100	15	Normal
TM32	Double Team	Normal	Status	—	—	15	Self
TM35	Flamethrower	Fire	Special	90	100	15	Normal
TM38	Fire Blast	Fire	Special	110	85	5	Normal
TM39	Rock Tomb	Rock	Physical	60	95	15	Normal
TM40	Aerial Ace	Flying	Physical	60	—	20	Normal
TM42	Facade	Normal	Physical	70	100	20	Normal
TM44	Rest	Psychic	Status	—	—	10	Self
TM45	Attract	Normal	Status	—	100	15	Normal
TM46	Thief	Dark	Physical	60	100	25	Normal
TM48	Round	Normal	Special	60	100	15	Normal
TM56	Fling	Dark	Physical	—	100	10	Normal
TM57	Charge Beam	Electric	Special	50	90	10	Normal
TM59	Incinerate	Fire	Special	60	100	15	Many Others
TM65	Shadow Claw	Ghost	Physical	70	100	15	Normal
TM67	Retaliate	Normal	Physical	70	100	5	Normal
TM70	Flash	Normal	Status	—	100	20	Normal
TM73	Thunder Wave	Electric	Status	—	100	20	Normal
TM77	Psych Up	Normal	Status	—	—	10	Normal
TM80	Rock Slide	Rock	Physical	75	90	10	Many Others
TM86	Grass Knot	Grass	Special	—	100	20	Normal
TM87	Swagger	Normal	Status	—	90	15	Normal
TM88	Sleep Talk	Normal	Status	—	—	10	Self
TM90	Substitute	Normal	Status	—	—	10	Self
TM92	Trick Room	Psychic	Status	—	—	5	Both Sides
TM94	Rock Smash	Fighting	Physical	40	100	15	Normal
TM98	Power-Up Punch	Fighting	Physical	40	100	20	Normal
TM100	Confide	Normal	Status	—	—	20	Normal
HM01	Cut	Normal	Physical	50	95	30	Normal
HM04	Strength	Normal	Physical	80	100	15	Normal

● MOVES TAUGHT BY PEOPLE

Name	Type	Kind	Pow.	Acc.	PP	Range

● EGG MOVES

Name	Type	Kind	Pow.	Acc.	PP	Range
Disable	Normal	Status	—	100	20	Normal
Magic Coat	Psychic	Status	—	—	15	Self
Trick	Psychic	Status	—	100	10	Normal
Fake Out	Normal	Physical	40	100	10	Normal
Nasty Plot	Dark	Status	—	—	20	Self
Dizzy Punch	Normal	Physical	70	100	10	Normal
Recover	Normal	Status	—	—	10	Self
Skill Swap	Psychic	Status	—	—	10	Normal
Snatch	Dark	Status	—	—	10	Self
Foul Play	Dark	Physical	95	100	15	Normal
Camouflage	Normal	Status	—	—	20	Self

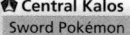 **Central Kalos**

Sword Pokémon

117

Honedge

HEIGHT: 2'07" WEIGHT: 4.4 lbs.
GENDER: ♂/♀

X	Apparently this Pokémon is born when a departed spirit inhabits a sword. It attaches itself to people and drinks their life force.
Y	If anyone dares to grab its hilt, it wraps a blue cloth around that person's arm and drains that person's life energy completely.

TYPE Steel / Ghost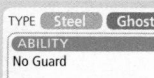

ABILITY
No Guard

HIDDEN ABILITY
None

STAT GROWTH RATES
HP ▪▪
Attack ▪▪▪▪
Defense ▪▪▪▪
Sp. Atk ▪▪
Sp. Def ▪▪
Speed ▪▪

EGG GROUP
Mineral

EVOLUTION

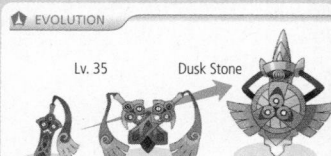

Honedge — Lv. 35 → Doublade — Dusk Stone → Aegislash Shield Forme

ITEMS SOMETIMES HELD BY WILD POKÉMON
None

Damage taken in normal battles

Normal	×0
Fire	×2
Water	×1
Grass	×0.5
Electric	×1
Ice	×0.5
Fighting	×0
Poison	×0
Ground	×2
Flying	×0.5
Psychic	×0.5
Bug	×0.25
Rock	×0.5
Ghost	×2
Dragon	×0.5
Dark	×2
Steel	×0.5
Fairy	×0.5

Damage taken in Inverse Battles

Normal	×4
Fire	×0.5
Water	×1
Grass	×2
Electric	×1
Ice	×2
Fighting	×1
Poison	×4
Ground	×0.5
Flying	×2
Psychic	×2
Bug	×4
Rock	×2
Ghost	×2
Dragon	×2
Dark	×0.5
Steel	×2
Fairy	×2

Can be used in

Inverse Battle
——
Battle Chateau
Battle Institute
Battle Maison
Random Matchup

How to obtain for your Central Kalos Pokédex

Catch in the very tall grass on Route 6.	Catch in the very tall grass on Route 6.
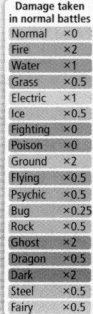	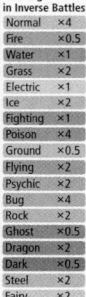

Same form for ♂/♀

● LEVEL-UP MOVES

Lv.	Name	Type	Kind	Pow.	Acc.	PP	Range
1	Tackle	Normal	Physical	50	100	35	Normal
1	Swords Dance	Normal	Status	—	—	20	Self
5	Fury Cutter	Bug	Physical	40	95	20	Normal
8	Metal Sound	Steel	Status	—	85	40	Normal
13	Pursuit	Dark	Physical	40	100	20	Normal
18	Autotomize	Steel	Status	—	—	15	Self
20	Shadow Sneak	Ghost	Physical	40	100	30	Normal
22	Aerial Ace	Flying	Physical	60	—	20	Normal
26	Retaliate	Normal	Physical	70	100	5	Normal
29	Slash	Normal	Physical	70	100	20	Normal
32	Iron Defense	Steel	Status	—	—	15	Self
35	Night Slash	Dark	Physical	70	100	15	Normal
39	Power Trick	Psychic	Status	—	—	10	Self
42	Iron Head	Steel	Physical	80	100	15	Normal
47	Sacred Sword	Fighting	Physical	90	100	15	Normal

● TM & HM MOVES

No.	Name	Type	Kind	Pow.	Acc.	PP	Range
TM06	Toxic	Poison	Status	—	90	10	Normal
TM10	Hidden Power	Normal	Special	60	100	15	Normal
TM17	Protect	Normal	Status	—	—	10	Self
TM18	Rain Dance	Water	Status	—	—	5	Both Sides
TM21	Frustration	Normal	Physical	—	100	20	Normal
TM27	Return	Normal	Physical	—	100	20	Normal
TM31	Brick Break	Fighting	Physical	75	100	15	Normal
TM32	Double Team	Normal	Status	—	—	15	Self
TM33	Reflect	Psychic	Status	—	—	20	Your Side
TM40	Aerial Ace	Flying	Physical	60	—	20	Normal
TM42	Facade	Normal	Physical	70	100	20	Normal
TM44	Rest	Psychic	Status	—	—	10	Self
TM45	Attract	Normal	Status	—	100	15	Normal
TM54	False Swipe	Normal	Physical	40	100	40	Normal
TM65	Shadow Claw	Ghost	Physical	70	100	15	Normal
TM67	Retaliate	Normal	Physical	70	100	5	Normal
TM74	Gyro Ball	Steel	Physical	—	100	5	Normal
TM75	Swords Dance	Normal	Status	—	—	20	Self
TM80	Rock Slide	Rock	Physical	75	90	10	Many Others
TM87	Swagger	Normal	Status	—	90	15	Normal
TM88	Sleep Talk	Normal	Status	—	—	10	Self
TM90	Substitute	Normal	Status	—	—	10	Self
TM91	Flash Cannon	Steel	Special	80	100	10	Normal
TM94	Rock Smash	Fighting	Physical	40	100	15	Normal
TM100	Confide	Normal	Status	—	—	20	Normal
HM01	Cut	Normal	Physical	50	95	30	Normal

● MOVES TAUGHT BY PEOPLE

Name	Type	Kind	Pow.	Acc.	PP	Range

● EGG MOVES

Name	Type	Kind	Pow.	Acc.	PP	Range
Metal Sound	Steel	Status	—	85	40	Normal
Shadow Sneak	Ghost	Physical	40	100	30	Normal
Destiny Bond	Ghost	Status	—	—	5	Self
Wide Guard	Rock	Status	—	—	10	Your Side

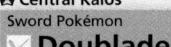

AFTER THE HALL OF FAME

CENTRAL KALOS

118

Doublade

COASTAL KALOS

MOUNTAIN KALOS

ADVENTURE DATA

⬆ Central Kalos **118**

Sword Pokémon

☑ Doublade

HEIGHT: 2'07" WEIGHT: 9.9 lbs.
GENDER: ♂ / ♀

ⓧ When Honedge evolves, it divides into two swords, which cooperate via telepathy to coordinate attacks and slash their enemies to ribbons.

ⓨ The complex attack patterns of its two swords are unstoppable, even for an opponent greatly accomplished at swordplay.

TYPE Steel Ghost

ABILITY
No Guard

HIDDEN ABILITY
None

STAT GROWTH RATES
HP ■■■
Attack ■■■
Defense ■■■■■■
Sp. Atk ■■
Sp. Def ■■
Speed ■■

EGG GROUP
Mineral

⬆ EVOLUTION

Honedge → (Lv. 35) Doublade → (Dusk Stone) Aegislash Shield Forme

ITEMS SOMETIMES HELD BY WILD POKÉMON
None

	Damage taken in normal battles		Damage taken in Inverse Battles
Normal	×0	Normal	×4
Fire	×2	Fire	×0.5
Water	×1	Water	×1
Grass	×0.5	Grass	×2
Electric	×1	Electric	×1
Ice	×0.5	Ice	×2
Fighting	×0	Fighting	×1
Poison	×0	Poison	×4
Ground	×2	Ground	×0.5
Flying	×0.5	Flying	×2
Psychic	×0.5	Psychic	×2
Bug	×0.25	Bug	×4
Rock	×2	Rock	×0.5
Ghost	×2	Ghost	×0.5
Dragon	×0.5	Dragon	×2
Dark	×2	Dark	×0.5
Steel	×0.5	Steel	×2
Fairy	×0.5	Fairy	×2

Can be used in

Inverse Battle	Battle Institute
—	Battle Maison
Battle Chateau	Random Matchup

Same form for ♂ / ♀

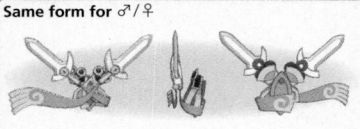

How to obtain for your Central Kalos Pokédex

Level up Honedge to Lv. 35. | Level up Honedge to Lv. 35.

● LEVEL-UP MOVES

Lv.	Name	Type	Kind	Pow.	Acc.	PP	Range
1	Tackle	Normal	Physical	50	100	35	Normal
1	Swords Dance	Normal	Status	—	—	20	Self
5	Fury Cutter	Bug	Physical	40	95	20	Normal
8	Metal Sound	Steel	Status	—	85	40	Normal
13	Pursuit	Dark	Physical	40	100	20	Normal
18	Autotomize	Steel	Status	—	—	15	Self
20	Shadow Sneak	Ghost	Physical	40	100	30	Normal
22	Aerial Ace	Flying	Physical	60	—	20	Normal
26	Retaliate	Normal	Physical	70	100	5	Normal
29	Slash	Normal	Physical	70	100	20	Normal
32	Iron Defense	Steel	Status	—	—	15	Self
36	Night Slash	Dark	Physical	70	100	15	Normal
41	Power Trick	Psychic	Status	—	—	10	Self
45	Iron Head	Steel	Physical	80	100	15	Normal
51	Sacred Sword	Fighting	Physical	90	100	15	Normal

● TM & HM MOVES

No.	Name	Type	Kind	Pow.	Acc.	PP	Range
TM06	Toxic	Poison	Status	—	90	10	Normal
TM10	Hidden Power	Normal	Special	60	100	15	Normal
TM17	Protect	Normal	Status	—	—	10	Self
TM18	Rain Dance	Water	Status	—	—	5	Both Sides
TM21	Frustration	Normal	Physical	—	100	20	Normal
TM27	Return	Normal	Physical	—	100	20	Normal
TM31	Brick Break	Fighting	Physical	75	100	15	Normal
TM32	Double Team	Normal	Status	—	—	15	Self
TM33	Reflect	Psychic	Status	—	—	20	Your Side
TM40	Aerial Ace	Flying	Physical	60	—	20	Normal
TM42	Facade	Normal	Physical	70	100	20	Normal
TM44	Rest	Psychic	Status	—	—	10	Self
TM45	Attract	Normal	Status	—	100	15	Normal
TM54	False Swipe	Normal	Physical	40	100	40	Normal
TM65	Shadow Claw	Ghost	Physical	70	100	15	Normal
TM67	Retaliate	Normal	Physical	70	100	5	Normal
TM74	Gyro Ball	Steel	Physical	—	100	5	Normal
TM75	Swords Dance	Normal	Status	—	—	20	Self
TM80	Rock Slide	Rock	Physical	75	90	10	Many Others
TM87	Swagger	Normal	Status	—	90	15	Normal
TM88	Sleep Talk	Normal	Status	—	—	10	Self
TM90	Substitute	Normal	Status	—	—	10	Self
TM91	Flash Cannon	Steel	Special	80	100	10	Normal
TM94	Rock Smash	Fighting	Physical	40	100	15	Normal
TM100	Confide	Normal	Status	—	—	20	Normal
HM01	Cut	Normal	Physical	50	95	30	Normal

● MOVES TAUGHT BY PEOPLE

Name	Type	Kind	Pow.	Acc.	PP	Range

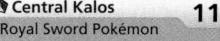

Central Kalos — 119

Royal Sword Pokémon

☑ # Aegislash
Shield Forme

HEIGHT: 5'07" WEIGHT: 116.8 lbs.
GENDER: ♂/♀

| TYPE | Steel | Ghost |

ABILITY
Stance Change

HIDDEN ABILITY
None

STAT GROWTH RATES
HP ■■■
Attack ■■■
Defense ■■■■■■
Sp. Atk ■■■■■■
Sp. Def ■■■
Speed ■■■

EGG GROUP
Mineral

X Generations of kings were attended by these Pokémon, which used their spectral power to manipulate and control people and Pokémon.

Y Apparently, it can detect the innate qualities of leadership. According to legend, whoever it recognizes is destined to become king.

⬆ EVOLUTION

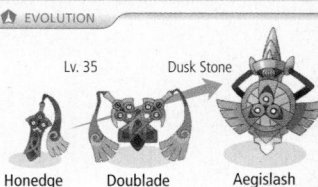

| | Lv. 35 | | Dusk Stone | |
| Honedge | | Doublade | | Aegislash Shield Forme |

ITEMS SOMETIMES HELD BY WILD POKÉMON
None

Damage taken in normal battles		Damage taken in Inverse Battles	
Normal	×0	Normal	×4
Fire	×2	Fire	×0.5
Water	×1	Water	×1
Grass	×0.5	Grass	×2
Electric	×1	Electric	×1
Ice	×0.5	Ice	×2
Fighting	×0	Fighting	×1
Poison	×0	Poison	×4
Ground	×2	Ground	×0.5
Flying	×0.5	Flying	×2
Psychic	×0.5	Psychic	×2
Bug	×0.25	Bug	×4
Rock	×0.5	Rock	×2
Ghost	×2	Ghost	×0.5
Dragon	×2	Dragon	×2
Dark	×2	Dark	×0.5
Steel	×0.5	Steel	×2
Fairy	×0.5	Fairy	×2

Can be used in	
Inverse Battle	Battle Institute
—	Battle Maison
Battle Chateau	Random Matchup

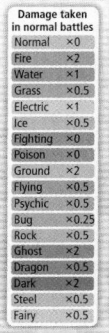

Same form for ♂/♀

How to obtain for your Central Kalos Pokédex

Use a Dusk Stone on Doublade.*	Use a Dusk Stone on Doublade.*

● LEVEL-UP MOVES

Lv.	Name	Type	Kind	Pow.	Acc.	PP	Range
1	Fury Cutter	Bug	Physical	40	95	20	Normal
1	Pursuit	Dark	Physical	40	100	20	Normal
1	Autotomize	Steel	Status	—	—	15	Self
1	Shadow Sneak	Ghost	Physical	40	100	30	Normal
1	Slash	Normal	Physical	70	100	20	Normal
1	Iron Defense	Steel	Status	—	—	15	Self
1	Night Slash	Dark	Physical	70	100	15	Normal
1	Power Trick	Psychic	Status	—	—	10	Self
1	Iron Head	Steel	Physical	80	100	15	Normal
1	Head Smash	Rock	Physical	150	80	5	Normal
1	Swords Dance	Normal	Status	—	—	20	Self
1	Aerial Ace	Flying	Physical	60	—	20	Normal
1	King's Shield	Steel	Status	—	—	10	Self
1	Sacred Sword	Fighting	Physical	90	100	15	Normal

■ TM & HM MOVES

No.	Name	Type	Kind	Pow.	Acc.	PP	Range
TM06	Toxic	Poison	Status	—	90	10	Normal
TM10	Hidden Power	Normal	Special	60	100	15	Normal
TM11	Sunny Day	Fire	Status	—	—	5	Both Sides
TM15	Hyper Beam	Normal	Special	150	90	5	Normal
TM17	Protect	Normal	Status	—	—	10	Self
TM18	Rain Dance	Water	Status	—	—	5	Both Sides
TM21	Frustration	Normal	Physical	—	100	20	Normal
TM27	Return	Normal	Physical	—	100	20	Normal
TM30	Shadow Ball	Ghost	Special	80	100	15	Normal
TM31	Brick Break	Fighting	Physical	75	100	15	Normal
TM32	Double Team	Normal	Status	—	—	15	Self
TM33	Reflect	Psychic	Status	—	—	20	Your Side
TM40	Aerial Ace	Flying	Physical	60	—	20	Normal
TM42	Facade	Normal	Physical	70	100	20	Normal
TM44	Rest	Psychic	Status	—	—	10	Self
TM45	Attract	Normal	Status	—	100	15	Normal
TM48	Round	Normal	Special	60	100	15	Normal
TM54	False Swipe	Normal	Physical	40	100	40	Normal
TM65	Shadow Claw	Ghost	Physical	70	100	15	Normal
TM67	Retaliate	Normal	Physical	70	100	5	Normal
TM68	Giga Impact	Normal	Physical	150	90	5	Normal
TM74	Gyro Ball	Steel	Physical	—	100	5	Normal
TM75	Swords Dance	Normal	Status	—	—	20	Self
TM80	Rock Slide	Rock	Physical	75	90	10	Many Others
TM87	Swagger	Normal	Status	—	90	15	Normal
TM88	Sleep Talk	Normal	Status	—	—	10	Self
TM90	Substitute	Normal	Status	—	—	10	Self
TM91	Flash Cannon	Steel	Special	80	100	10	Normal
TM94	Rock Smash	Fighting	Physical	40	100	15	Normal
TM100	Confide	Normal	Status	—	—	20	Normal
HM01	Cut	Normal	Physical	50	95	30	Normal

No.	Name	Type	Kind	Pow.	Acc.	PP	Range

● MOVES TAUGHT BY PEOPLE

Name	Type	Kind	Pow.	Acc.	PP	Range

*Aegislash's Forme changes based on the moves it uses in battle. It begins each battle in Shield Forme. Using a physical or special move will make it change into its Blade Forme. Using the move King's Shield will return it to its Shield Forme.

AFTER THE HALL OF FAME

CENTRAL KALOS

119

Aegislash
Shield Forme

COASTAL KALOS

MOUNTAIN KALOS

ADVENTURE DATA

119

COASTAL KALOS

MOUNTAIN KALOS

ADVENTURE DATA

🏠 Central Kalos — 119
Royal Sword Pokémon
☑ Aegislash
Blade Forme

HEIGHT: 5'07" WEIGHT: 116.8 lbs.
GENDER: ♂/♀

| TYPE | Steel | Ghost |

ABILITY
Stance Change

HIDDEN ABILITY
None

STAT GROWTH RATES
HP	▪▪▪
Attack	▪▪▪▪▪▪▪▪
Defense	▪▪
Sp. Atk	▪▪▪▪▪▪▪
Sp. Def	▪▪
Speed	▪▪▪

EGG GROUP
Mineral

X Generations of kings were attended by these Pokémon, which used their spectral power to manipulate and control people and Pokémon.

Y Apparently, it can detect the innate qualities of leadership. According to legend, whoever it recognizes is destined to become king.

⚔ EVOLUTION

Lv. 35   Dusk Stone

Honedge   Doublade   Aegislash (Shield Forme)   Aegislash (Blade Forme)

ITEMS SOMETIMES HELD BY WILD POKÉMON
None

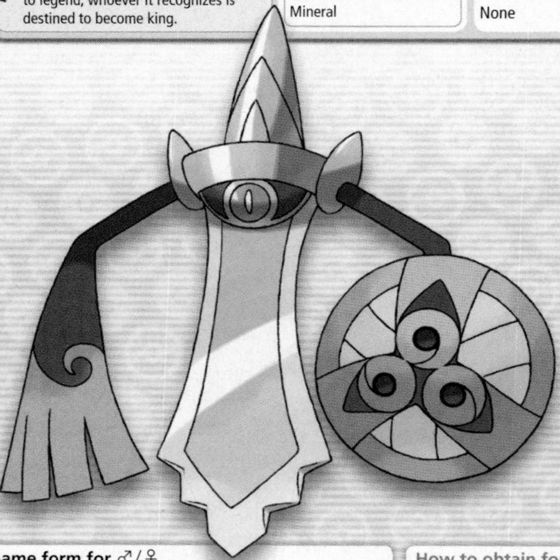

Damage taken in normal battles	
Normal	×0
Fire	×2
Water	×1
Grass	×0.5
Electric	×1
Ice	×0.5
Fighting	×0
Poison	×0
Ground	×2
Flying	×0.5
Psychic	×0.5
Bug	×0.25
Rock	×0.5
Ghost	×2
Dragon	×0.5
Dark	×2
Steel	×0.5
Fairy	×0.5

Damage taken in Inverse Battles	
Normal	×4
Fire	×0.5
Water	×1
Grass	×2
Electric	×1
Ice	×2
Fighting	×1
Poison	×1
Ground	×0.5
Flying	×2
Psychic	×2
Bug	×4
Rock	×2
Ghost	×0.5
Dragon	×2
Dark	×0.5
Steel	×2
Fairy	×2

Can be used in	
Inverse Battle	Battle Institute
—	Battle Maison
Battle Chateau	Random Matchup

Same form for ♂/♀

How to obtain for your Central Kalos Pokédex

X Use a Dusk Stone on Doublade.*

Y Use a Dusk Stone on Doublade.*

● LEVEL-UP MOVES

Lv.	Name	Type	Kind	Pow.	Acc.	PP	Range
1	Fury Cutter	Bug	Physical	40	95	20	Normal
1	Pursuit	Dark	Physical	40	100	20	Normal
1	Autotomize	Steel	Status	—	—	15	Self
1	Shadow Sneak	Ghost	Physical	40	100	30	Normal
1	Slash	Normal	Physical	70	100	20	Normal
1	Iron Defense	Steel	Status	—	—	15	Self
1	Night Slash	Dark	Physical	70	100	15	Normal
1	Power Trick	Psychic	Status	—	—	10	Self
1	Iron Head	Steel	Physical	80	100	15	Normal
1	Head Smash	Rock	Physical	150	80	5	Normal
1	Swords Dance	Normal	Status	—	—	20	Self
1	Aerial Ace	Flying	Physical	60	—	20	Normal
1	King's Shield	Steel	Status	—	—	10	Self
1	Sacred Sword	Fighting	Physical	90	100	15	Normal

● TM & HM MOVES

No.	Name	Type	Kind	Pow.	Acc.	PP	Range
TM06	Toxic	Poison	Status	—	90	10	Normal
TM10	Hidden Power	Normal	Special	60	100	15	Normal
TM11	Sunny Day	Fire	Status	—	—	5	Both Sides
TM15	Hyper Beam	Normal	Special	150	90	5	Normal
TM17	Protect	Normal	Status	—	—	10	Self
TM18	Rain Dance	Water	Status	—	—	5	Both Sides
TM21	Frustration	Normal	Physical	—	100	20	Normal
TM27	Return	Normal	Physical	—	100	20	Normal
TM30	Shadow Ball	Ghost	Special	80	100	15	Normal
TM31	Brick Break	Fighting	Physical	75	100	15	Normal
TM32	Double Team	Normal	Status	—	—	15	Self
TM33	Reflect	Psychic	Status	—	—	20	Your Side
TM40	Aerial Ace	Flying	Physical	60	—	20	Normal
TM42	Facade	Normal	Physical	70	100	20	Normal
TM44	Rest	Psychic	Status	—	—	10	Self
TM45	Attract	Normal	Status	—	100	15	Normal
TM48	Round	Normal	Special	60	100	15	Normal
TM54	False Swipe	Normal	Physical	40	100	40	Normal
TM65	Shadow Claw	Ghost	Physical	70	100	15	Normal
TM67	Retaliate	Normal	Physical	70	100	5	Normal
TM68	Giga Impact	Normal	Physical	150	90	5	Normal
TM74	Gyro Ball	Steel	Physical	—	100	5	Normal
TM75	Swords Dance	Normal	Status	—	—	20	Self
TM80	Rock Slide	Rock	Physical	75	90	10	Many Others
TM87	Swagger	Normal	Status	—	90	15	Normal
TM88	Sleep Talk	Normal	Status	—	—	10	Self
TM90	Substitute	Normal	Status	—	—	10	Self
TM91	Flash Cannon	Steel	Special	80	100	10	Normal
TM94	Rock Smash	Fighting	Physical	40	100	15	Normal
TM100	Confide	Normal	Status	—	—	20	Normal
HM01	Cut	Normal	Physical	50	95	30	Normal

● MOVES TAUGHT BY PEOPLE

Name	Type	Kind	Pow.	Acc.	PP	Range

*Aegislash's Forme changes based on the moves it uses in battle. It begins each battle in Shield Forme. Using a physical or special move will make it change into its Blade Forme. Using the move King's Shield will return it to its Shield Forme.

AFTER THE HALL OF FAME

CENTRAL KALOS

120

Venipede

COASTAL KALOS

MOUNTAIN KALOS

ADVENTURE DATA

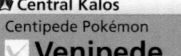 Central Kalos

Centipede Pokémon

Venipede

120

HEIGHT: 1'04"　WEIGHT: 11.7 lbs.
GENDER: ♂ / ♀

X It discovers what is going on around it by using the feelers on its head and tail. It is brutally aggressive.

Y Its bite injects a potent poison, enough to paralyze large bird Pokémon that try to prey on it.

TYPE	Bug	Poison

ABILITIES
Poison Point
Swarm

HIDDEN ABILITY
Speed Boost

STAT GROWTH RATES
HP	▪▪
Attack	▪▪
Defense	▪▪▪
Sp. Atk	▪
Sp. Def	▪▪
Speed	▪▪▪

EGG GROUP
Bug

EVOLUTION

Lv. 22 　　 Lv. 30

Venipede　　Whirlipede　　Scolipede

ITEMS SOMETIMES HELD BY WILD POKÉMON
Poison Barb

Damage taken in normal battles		Damage taken in Inverse Battles	
Normal	×1	Normal	×1
Fire	×2	Fire	×0.5
Water	×1	Water	×1
Grass	×0.25	Grass	×4
Electric	×1	Electric	×1
Ice	×1	Ice	×1
Fighting	×0.25	Fighting	×4
Poison	×0.5	Poison	×2
Ground	×1	Ground	×1
Flying	×2	Flying	×0.5
Psychic	×2	Psychic	×0.5
Bug	×0.5	Bug	×2
Rock	×2	Rock	×0.5
Ghost	×1	Ghost	×1
Dragon	×1	Dragon	×1
Dark	×1	Dark	×1
Steel	×1	Steel	×1
Fairy	×0.5	Fairy	×2

Can be used in	
Inverse Battle	Battle Institute
—	Battle Maison
Battle Chateau	Random Matchup

Same form for ♂ / ♀

How to obtain for your Central Kalos Pokédex

Catch when it jumps out of the shaking bush on Route 6.

Catch when it jumps out of the shaking bush on Route 6.

● LEVEL-UP MOVES

Lv.	Name	Type	Kind	Pow.	Acc.	PP	Range
1	Defense Curl	Normal	Status	—	—	40	Self
1	Rollout	Rock	Physical	30	90	20	Normal
5	Poison Sting	Poison	Physical	15	100	35	Normal
8	Screech	Normal	Status	—	85	40	Normal
12	Pursuit	Dark	Physical	40	100	20	Normal
15	Protect	Normal	Status	—	—	10	Self
19	Poison Tail	Poison	Physical	50	100	25	Normal
22	Bug Bite	Bug	Physical	60	100	20	Normal
26	Venoshock	Poison	Special	65	100	10	Normal
29	Agility	Psychic	Status	—	—	30	Self
33	Steamroller	Bug	Physical	65	100	20	Normal
36	Toxic	Poison	Status	—	90	10	Normal
38	Venoshock	Poison	Special	65	100	10	Normal
40	Rock Climb	Normal	Physical	90	85	20	Normal
43	Double-Edge	Normal	Physical	120	100	15	Normal

● TM & HM MOVES

No.	Name	Type	Kind	Pow.	Acc.	PP	Range
TM06	Toxic	Poison	Status	—	90	10	Normal
TM09	Venoshock	Poison	Special	65	100	10	Normal
TM10	Hidden Power	Normal	Special	60	100	15	Normal
TM11	Sunny Day	Fire	Status	—	—	5	Both Sides
TM17	Protect	Normal	Status	—	—	10	Self
TM21	Frustration	Normal	Physical	—	100	20	Normal
TM22	Solar Beam	Grass	Special	120	100	10	Normal
TM27	Return	Normal	Physical	—	100	20	Normal
TM32	Double Team	Normal	Status	—	—	15	Self
TM36	Sludge Bomb	Poison	Special	90	100	10	Normal
TM42	Facade	Normal	Physical	70	100	20	Normal
TM44	Rest	Psychic	Status	—	—	10	Self
TM45	Attract	Normal	Status	—	100	15	Normal
TM48	Round	Normal	Special	60	100	15	Normal
TM66	Payback	Dark	Physical	50	100	10	Normal
TM74	Gyro Ball	Steel	Physical	—	100	5	Normal
TM76	Struggle Bug	Bug	Special	30	100	20	Many Others
TM83	Infestation	Bug	Special	20	100	20	Normal
TM84	Poison Jab	Poison	Physical	80	100	20	Normal
TM87	Swagger	Normal	Status	—	90	15	Normal
TM88	Sleep Talk	Normal	Status	—	—	10	Self
TM90	Substitute	Normal	Status	—	—	10	Self
TM94	Rock Smash	Fighting	Physical	40	100	15	Normal
TM100	Confide	Normal	Status	—	—	20	Normal

No.	Name	Type	Kind	Pow.	Acc.	PP	Range

● MOVES TAUGHT BY PEOPLE

Name	Type	Kind	Pow.	Acc.	PP	Range

● EGG MOVES

Name	Type	Kind	Pow.	Acc.	PP	Range
Twineedle	Bug	Physical	25	100	20	Normal
Pin Missile	Bug	Physical	25	95	20	Normal
Toxic Spikes	Poison	Status	—	—	20	Other Side
Spikes	Ground	Status	—	—	20	Other Side
Take Down	Normal	Physical	90	85	20	Normal
Rock Climb	Normal	Physical	90	85	20	Normal

AFTER THE HALL OF FAME

CENTRAL KALOS

121

Whirlipede

COASTAL KALOS

MOUNTAIN KALOS

ADVENTURE DATA

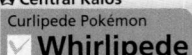

🏠 Central Kalos 121

Curlipede Pokémon

✓ Whirlipede

HEIGHT: 3'11" WEIGHT: 129.0 lbs.
GENDER: ♂/♀

X Protected by a hard shell, it spins its body like a wheel and crashes furiously into its enemies.

Y It is usually motionless, but when attacked, it rotates at high speed and then crashes into its opponent.

TYPE Bug | Poison

ABILITIES
Poison Point
Swarm

HIDDEN ABILITY
Speed Boost

STAT GROWTH RATES
HP	■■
Attack	■■
Defense	■■■■
Sp. Atk	■■
Sp. Def	■■■
Speed	■■■

EGG GROUP
Bug

⬆ EVOLUTION

Lv. 22 → Lv. 30

Venipede → Whirlipede → Scolipede

ITEMS SOMETIMES HELD BY WILD POKÉMON
None

Damage taken in normal battles		Damage taken in Inverse Battles	
Normal	×1	Normal	×1
Fire	×2	Fire	×0.5
Water	×1	Water	×1
Grass	×0.25	Grass	×4
Electric	×1	Electric	×1
Ice	×1	Ice	×1
Fighting	×0.25	Fighting	×4
Poison	×0.5	Poison	×2
Ground	×1	Ground	×1
Flying	×2	Flying	×0.5
Psychic	×2	Psychic	×0.5
Bug	×0.5	Bug	×2
Rock	×2	Rock	×0.5
Ghost	×1	Ghost	×1
Dragon	×1	Dragon	×1
Dark	×1	Dark	×1
Steel	×1	Steel	×1
Fairy	×0.5	Fairy	×2

Can be used in	
Inverse Battle	Battle Institute
—	Battle Maison
Battle Chateau	Random Matchup

Same form for ♂/♀

How to obtain for your Central Kalos Pokédex

Level up Venipede to Lv. 22. Level up Venipede to Lv. 22.

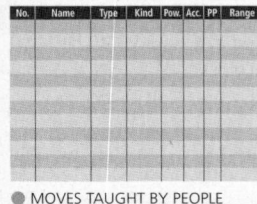

● LEVEL-UP MOVES

Lv.	Name	Type	Kind	Pow.	Acc.	PP	Range
1	Defense Curl	Normal	Status	—	—	40	Self
1	Rollout	Rock	Physical	30	90	20	Normal
1	Poison Sting	Poison	Physical	15	100	35	Normal
1	Screech	Normal	Status	—	85	40	Normal
5	Poison Sting	Poison	Physical	15	100	35	Normal
8	Screech	Normal	Status	—	85	40	Normal
12	Pursuit	Dark	Physical	40	100	20	Normal
15	Protect	Normal	Status	—	—	10	Self
19	Poison Tail	Poison	Physical	50	100	25	Normal
22	Iron Defense	Steel	Status	—	—	15	Self
23	Bug Bite	Bug	Physical	60	100	20	Normal
28	Venoshock	Poison	Special	65	100	10	Normal
32	Agility	Psychic	Status	—	—	30	Self
37	Steamroller	Bug	Physical	65	100	20	Normal
41	Toxic	Poison	Status	—	90	10	Normal
43	Venom Drench	Poison	Status	—	100	10	Many Others
46	Rock Climb	Normal	Physical	90	85	20	Normal
50	Double-Edge	Normal	Physical	120	100	15	Normal

● TM & HM MOVES

No.	Name	Type	Kind	Pow.	Acc.	PP	Range
TM06	Toxic	Poison	Status	—	90	10	Normal
TM09	Venoshock	Poison	Special	65	100	10	Normal
TM10	Hidden Power	Normal	Special	60	100	15	Normal
TM11	Sunny Day	Fire	Status	—	—	5	Both Sides
TM17	Protect	Normal	Status	—	—	10	Self
TM21	Frustration	Normal	Physical	—	100	20	Normal
TM22	Solar Beam	Grass	Special	120	100	10	Normal
TM27	Return	Normal	Physical	—	100	20	Normal
TM32	Double Team	Normal	Status	—	—	15	Self
TM36	Sludge Bomb	Poison	Special	90	100	10	Normal
TM42	Facade	Normal	Physical	70	100	20	Normal
TM44	Rest	Psychic	Status	—	—	10	Self
TM45	Attract	Normal	Status	—	100	15	Normal
TM48	Round	Normal	Special	60	100	15	Normal
TM66	Payback	Dark	Physical	50	100	10	Normal
TM74	Gyro Ball	Steel	Physical	—	100	5	Normal
TM76	Struggle Bug	Bug	Special	50	100	20	Many Others
TM83	Infestation	Bug	Special	20	100	20	Normal
TM84	Poison Jab	Poison	Physical	80	100	20	Normal
TM87	Swagger	Normal	Status	—	90	15	Normal
TM88	Sleep Talk	Normal	Status	—	—	10	Self
TM90	Substitute	Normal	Status	—	—	10	Self
TM94	Rock Smash	Fighting	Physical	40	100	15	Normal
TM100	Confide	Normal	Status	—	—	20	Normal

No.	Name	Type	Kind	Pow.	Acc.	PP	Range

● MOVES TAUGHT BY PEOPLE

Name	Type	Kind	Pow.	Acc.	PP	Range

AFTER THE HALL OF FAME

CENTRAL KALOS

122 | Scolipede

COASTAL KALOS

MOUNTAIN KALOS

ADVENTURE DATA

🔺 Central Kalos

Megapede Pokémon

☑ Scolipede

122

TYPE Bug | Poison

ABILITIES
Poison Point
Swarm

HIDDEN ABILITY
Speed Boost

STAT GROWTH RATES
HP	■■■
Attack	■■■■■
Defense	■■■■
Sp. Atk	■■■
Sp. Def	■■■
Speed	■■■■■■

EGG GROUP
Bug

HEIGHT: 8'02" WEIGHT: 442.0 lbs.
GENDER: ♂ / ♀

❌ It clasps its prey with the claws on its neck until it stops moving. Then it finishes it off with deadly poison.

🅨 With quick movements, it chases down its foes, attacking relentlessly with its horns until it prevails.

EVOLUTION

Venipede → Lv. 22 → Whirlipede → Lv. 30 → Scolipede

ITEMS SOMETIMES HELD BY WILD POKÉMON
None

Damage taken in normal battles		Damage taken in Inverse Battles	
Normal	×1	Normal	×1
Fire	×2	Fire	×0.5
Water	×1	Water	×1
Grass	×0.25	Grass	×4
Electric	×1	Electric	×1
Ice	×1	Ice	×1
Fighting	×0.25	Fighting	×4
Poison	×0.5	Poison	×2
Ground	×1	Ground	×1
Flying	×2	Flying	×0.5
Psychic	×2	Psychic	×0.5
Bug	×0.5	Bug	×2
Rock	×2	Rock	×0.5
Ghost	×1	Ghost	×1
Dragon	×1	Dragon	×1
Dark	×1	Dark	×1
Steel	×1	Steel	×1
Fairy	×0.5	Fairy	×2

Can be used in	
Inverse Battle	Battle Institute
—	Battle Maison
Battle Chateau	Random Matchup

Same form for ♂ / ♀

How to obtain for your Central Kalos Pokédex

X	Y
Level up Whirlipede to Lv. 30.	Level up Whirlipede to Lv. 30.

● LEVEL-UP MOVES

Lv.	Name	Type	Kind	Pow.	Acc.	PP	Range
1	Megahorn	Bug	Physical	120	85	10	Normal
1	Defense Curl	Normal	Status	—	—	40	Self
1	Rollout	Rock	Physical	30	90	20	Normal
1	Poison Sting	Poison	Physical	15	100	35	Normal
1	Screech	Normal	Status	—	85	40	Normal
5	Poison Sting	Poison	Physical	15	100	35	Normal
8	Screech	Normal	Status	—	85	40	Normal
12	Pursuit	Dark	Physical	40	100	20	Normal
15	Protect	Normal	Status	—	—	10	Self
19	Poison Tail	Poison	Physical	50	100	25	Normal
23	Bug Bite	Bug	Physical	60	100	20	Normal
28	Venoshock	Poison	Special	65	100	10	Normal
30	Baton Pass	Normal	Status	—	—	40	Self
33	Agility	Psychic	Status	—	—	30	Self
39	Steamroller	Bug	Physical	65	100	20	Normal
44	Toxic	Poison	Status	—	90	10	Normal
47	Venom Drench	Poison	Status	—	100	20	Many Others
50	Rock Climb	Normal	Physical	90	85	20	Normal
55	Double-Edge	Normal	Physical	120	100	15	Normal
65	Megahorn	Bug	Physical	120	85	10	Normal

● TM & HM MOVES

No.	Name	Type	Kind	Pow.	Acc.	PP	Range
TM06	Toxic	Poison	Status	—	90	10	Normal
TM09	Venoshock	Poison	Special	65	100	10	Normal
TM10	Hidden Power	Normal	Special	60	100	15	Normal
TM11	Sunny Day	Fire	Status	—	—	5	Both Sides
TM15	Hyper Beam	Normal	Special	150	90	5	Normal
TM17	Protect	Normal	Status	—	—	10	Self
TM21	Frustration	Normal	Physical	—	100	20	Normal
TM22	Solar Beam	Grass	Special	120	100	10	Normal
TM26	Earthquake	Ground	Physical	100	100	10	Adjacent
TM27	Return	Normal	Physical	—	100	20	Normal
TM28	Dig	Ground	Physical	80	100	10	Normal
TM32	Double Team	Normal	Status	—	—	15	Self
TM36	Sludge Bomb	Poison	Special	90	100	10	Normal
TM39	Rock Tomb	Rock	Physical	60	95	15	Normal
TM42	Facade	Normal	Physical	70	100	20	Normal
TM44	Rest	Psychic	Status	—	—	10	Self
TM45	Attract	Normal	Status	—	100	15	Normal
TM48	Round	Normal	Special	60	100	15	Normal
TM66	Payback	Dark	Physical	50	100	10	Normal
TM68	Giga Impact	Normal	Physical	150	90	5	Normal
TM74	Gyro Ball	Steel	Physical	—	100	5	Normal
TM75	Swords Dance	Normal	Status	—	—	20	Self
TM76	Struggle Bug	Bug	Special	50	100	20	Many Others
TM78	Bulldoze	Ground	Physical	60	100	20	Adjacent
TM80	Rock Slide	Rock	Physical	75	90	10	Many Others
TM81	X-Scissor	Bug	Physical	80	100	15	Normal
TM83	Infestation	Bug	Special	20	100	20	Normal
TM84	Poison Jab	Poison	Physical	80	100	20	Normal
TM87	Swagger	Normal	Status	—	90	15	Normal
TM88	Sleep Talk	Normal	Status	—	—	10	Self
TM90	Substitute	Normal	Status	—	—	10	Self
TM94	Rock Smash	Fighting	Physical	40	100	15	Normal
TM100	Confide	Normal	Status	—	—	20	Normal

No.	Name	Type	Kind	Pow.	Acc.	PP	Range
HM01	Cut	Normal	Physical	50	95	30	Normal
HM04	Strength	Normal	Physical	80	100	15	Normal

● MOVES TAUGHT BY PEOPLE

Name	Type	Kind	Pow.	Acc.	PP	Range

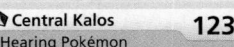

Central Kalos 123

Hearing Pokémon

☑ Audino

HEIGHT: 3'07" WEIGHT: 68.3 lbs.
GENDER: ♂ / ♀

| TYPE | Normal |

ABILITIES
Healer
Regenerator

HIDDEN ABILITY
Klutz

STAT GROWTH RATES
HP	▪▪▪▪
Attack	▪▪▪
Defense	—
Sp. Atk	▪▪▪
Sp. Def	▪▪▪
Speed	▪▪▪

EGG GROUP
Fairy

X Using the feelers on its ears, it can tell how someone is feeling or when an egg might hatch.

Y It touches others with the feelers on its ears, using the sound of their heartbeats to tell how they are feeling.

EVOLUTION

Does not evolve

ITEMS SOMETIMES HELD BY WILD POKÉMON
Oran Berry, Sitrus Berry

Can be used in
Inverse Battle
—
Battle Chateau
Battle Institute
Battle Maison
Random Matchup

Damage taken in normal battles	
Normal	×1
Fire	×1
Water	×1
Grass	×1
Electric	×1
Ice	×1
Fighting	×2
Poison	×1
Ground	×1
Flying	×1
Psychic	×1
Bug	×1
Rock	×1
Ghost	×0
Dragon	×1
Dark	×1
Steel	×1
Fairy	×1

Damage taken in Inverse Battles	
Normal	×1
Fire	×1
Water	×1
Grass	×1
Electric	×1
Ice	×1
Fighting	×0.5
Poison	×1
Ground	×1
Flying	×1
Psychic	×1
Bug	×1
Rock	×1
Ghost	×2
Dragon	×1
Dark	×1
Steel	×1
Fairy	×1

How to obtain for your Central Kalos Pokédex

Catch when it jumps out of the shaking bush on Route 6.

Catch when it jumps out of the shaking bush on Route 6.

Same form for ♂ / ♀

● LEVEL-UP MOVES

Lv.	Name	Type	Kind	Pow.	Acc.	PP	Range
1	Last Resort	Normal	Physical	140	100	5	Normal
1	Play Nice	Normal	Status	—	—	20	Normal
1	Pound	Normal	Physical	40	100	35	Normal
1	Growl	Normal	Status	—	100	40	Many Others
1	Helping Hand	Normal	Status	—	—	20	1 Ally
5	Refresh	Normal	Status	—	—	20	Self
10	Double Slap	Normal	Physical	15	85	10	Normal
15	Attract	Normal	Status	—	100	15	Normal
20	Secret Power	Normal	Physical	70	100	20	Normal
25	Entrainment	Normal	Status	—	100	15	Normal
30	Take Down	Normal	Physical	90	85	20	Normal
35	Heal Pulse	Psychic	Status	—	—	10	Normal
40	After You	Normal	Status	—	—	15	Normal
45	Simple Beam	Normal	Status	—	100	15	Normal
50	Double-Edge	Normal	Physical	120	100	15	Normal
55	Last Resort	Normal	Physical	140	100	5	Normal

● TM & HM MOVES

No.	Name	Type	Kind	Pow.	Acc.	PP	Range
TM03	Psyshock	Psychic	Special	80	100	10	Normal
TM04	Calm Mind	Psychic	Status	—	—	20	Self
TM06	Toxic	Poison	Status	—	90	10	Normal
TM10	Hidden Power	Normal	Special	60	100	15	Normal
TM11	Sunny Day	Fire	Status	—	—	5	Both Sides
TM13	Ice Beam	Ice	Special	90	100	10	Normal
TM14	Blizzard	Ice	Special	110	70	5	Many Others
TM15	Hyper Beam	Normal	Special	150	90	5	Normal
TM16	Light Screen	Psychic	Status	—	—	30	Your Side
TM17	Protect	Normal	Status	—	—	10	Self
TM18	Rain Dance	Water	Status	—	—	5	Both Sides
TM20	Safeguard	Normal	Status	—	—	25	Your Side
TM21	Frustration	Normal	Physical	—	100	20	Normal
TM22	Solar Beam	Grass	Special	120	100	10	Normal
TM24	Thunderbolt	Electric	Special	90	100	15	Normal
TM25	Thunder	Electric	Special	110	70	10	Normal
TM27	Return	Normal	Physical	—	100	20	Normal
TM28	Dig	Ground	Physical	80	100	10	Normal
TM29	Psychic	Psychic	Special	90	100	10	Normal
TM30	Shadow Ball	Ghost	Special	80	100	15	Normal
TM32	Double Team	Normal	Status	—	—	15	Self
TM33	Reflect	Psychic	Status	—	—	20	Your Side
TM35	Flamethrower	Fire	Special	90	100	15	Normal
TM38	Fire Blast	Fire	Special	110	85	5	Normal
TM42	Facade	Normal	Physical	70	100	20	Normal
TM44	Rest	Psychic	Status	—	—	10	Self
TM45	Attract	Normal	Status	—	100	15	Normal
TM48	Round	Normal	Special	60	100	15	Normal
TM49	Echoed Voice	Normal	Special	40	100	15	Normal
TM56	Fling	Dark	Physical	—	100	10	Normal
TM57	Charge Beam	Electric	Special	50	90	10	Normal
TM59	Incinerate	Fire	Special	60	100	15	Many Others
TM67	Retaliate	Normal	Physical	70	100	5	Normal

No.	Name	Type	Kind	Pow.	Acc.	PP	Range
TM70	Flash	Normal	Status	—	100	20	Normal
TM73	Thunder Wave	Electric	Status	—	100	20	Normal
TM77	Psych Up	Normal	Status	—	—	10	Normal
TM85	Dream Eater	Psychic	Special	100	100	15	Normal
TM86	Grass Knot	Grass	Special	—	100	20	Normal
TM87	Swagger	Normal	Status	—	90	15	Normal
TM88	Sleep Talk	Normal	Status	—	—	10	Self
TM90	Substitute	Normal	Status	—	—	10	Self
TM92	Trick Room	Psychic	Status	—	—	5	Both Sides
TM93	Wild Charge	Electric	Physical	90	100	15	Normal
TM98	Power-Up Punch	Fighting	Physical	40	100	20	Normal
TM99	Dazzling Gleam	Fairy	Special	80	100	10	Many Others
TM100	Confide	Normal	Status	—	—	20	Normal
HM03	Surf	Water	Special	90	100	15	Adjacent

● MOVES TAUGHT BY PEOPLE

Name	Type	Kind	Pow.	Acc.	PP	Range

● EGG MOVES

Name	Type	Kind	Pow.	Acc.	PP	Range
Wish	Normal	Status	—	—	10	Self
Heal Bell	Normal	Status	—	—	5	Your Party
Lucky Chant	Normal	Status	—	—	30	Your Side
Encore	Normal	Status	—	100	5	Normal
Bestow	Normal	Status	—	—	15	Normal
Sweet Kiss	Fairy	Status	—	75	10	Normal
Yawn	Normal	Status	—	—	10	Normal
Sleep Talk	Normal	Status	—	—	10	Self
Healing Wish	Psychic	Status	—	—	10	Self
Amnesia	Psychic	Status	—	—	20	Self
Draining Kiss	Fairy	Special	50	100	10	Normal

AFTER THE HALL OF FAME

CENTRAL KALOS

124

Smeargle

COASTAL KALOS

MOUNTAIN KALOS

ADVENTURE DATA

⬆ Central Kalos
Painter Pokémon
☑ Smeargle
124

HEIGHT: 3'11"   WEIGHT: 127.9 lbs.
GENDER: ♂/♀

TYPE Normal

ABILITIES
Own Tempo
Technician

HIDDEN ABILITY
Moody

X It marks its territory by using its tail like a paintbrush. There are more than 5,000 different marks.

Y Once it becomes an adult, it has a tendency to let its comrades plant footprints on its back.

STAT GROWTH RATES
HP	▪▪
Attack	▪
Defense	▪▪
Sp. Atk	▪
Sp. Def	▪▪
Speed	▪▪▪▪

EGG GROUP
Field

⬆ EVOLUTION

Does not evolve

ITEMS SOMETIMES HELD BY WILD POKÉMON
None

Damage taken in normal battles		Damage taken in Inverse Battles	
Normal	×1	Normal	×1
Fire	×1	Fire	×1
Water	×1	Water	×1
Grass	×1	Grass	×1
Electric	×1	Electric	×1
Ice	×1	Ice	×1
Fighting	×2	Fighting	×0.5
Poison	×1	Poison	×1
Ground	×1	Ground	×1
Flying	×1	Flying	×1
Psychic	×1	Psychic	×1
Bug	×1	Bug	×1
Rock	×1	Rock	×1
Ghost	×0	Ghost	×2
Dragon	×1	Dragon	×1
Dark	×1	Dark	×1
Steel	×1	Steel	×1
Fairy	×1	Fairy	×1

Can be used in
Inverse Battle
—
Battle Chateau
Battle Institute
Battle Maison
Random Matchup

How to obtain for your Central Kalos Pokédex

❶ Catch in the yellow flowers on Route 7.

❷ Catch in the tall grass on Route 7.

❶ Catch in the yellow flowers on Route 7.

❷ Catch in the tall grass on Route 7.

Same form for ♂/♀

● LEVEL-UP MOVES

Lv.	Name	Type	Kind	Pow.	Acc.	PP	Range
1	Sketch	Normal	Status	—	—	1	Normal
11	Sketch	Normal	Status	—	—	1	Normal
21	Sketch	Normal	Status	—	—	1	Normal
31	Sketch	Normal	Status	—	—	1	Normal
41	Sketch	Normal	Status	—	—	1	Normal
51	Sketch	Normal	Status	—	—	1	Normal
61	Sketch	Normal	Status	—	—	1	Normal
71	Sketch	Normal	Status	—	—	1	Normal
81	Sketch	Normal	Status	—	—	1	Normal
91	Sketch	Normal	Status	—	—	1	Normal

● TM & HM MOVES

No.	Name	Type	Kind	Pow.	Acc.	PP	Range

No.	Name	Type	Kind	Pow.	Acc.	PP	Range

● MOVES TAUGHT BY PEOPLE

Name	Type	Kind	Pow.	Acc.	PP	Range

● EGG MOVES

Name	Type	Kind	Pow.	Acc.	PP	Range

AFTER THE HALL OF FAME

CENTRAL KALOS

125

Croagunk

COASTAL KALOS

MOUNTAIN KALOS

ADVENTURE DATA

🏠 Central Kalos 125
Toxic Mouth Pokémon
☑ Croagunk

HEIGHT: 2'04" WEIGHT: 50.7 lbs.
GENDER: ♂/♀

TYPE Poison Fighting

ABILITIES
Anticipation
Dry Skin

HIDDEN ABILITY
Poison Touch

STAT GROWTH RATES
HP	■■
Attack	■■■
Defense	■■
Sp. Atk	■■■
Sp. Def	■■
Speed	■■■

EGG GROUP
Human-Like

Ⓧ Its cheeks hold poison sacs. It tries to catch foes off guard and jab them with toxic fingers.

Ⓨ Inflating its poison sacs, it fills the area with an odd sound and hits flinching opponents with a poison jab.

⬆ EVOLUTION

Croagunk — Lv. 37 → Toxicroak

ITEMS SOMETIMES HELD BY WILD POKÉMON
Black Sludge

Can be used in
Inverse Battle
—
Battle Chateau
Battle Institute
Battle Maison
Random Matchup

Damage taken in normal battles	
Normal	×1
Fire	×1
Water	×1
Grass	×0.5
Electric	×1
Ice	×1
Fighting	×0.5
Poison	×0.5
Ground	×2
Flying	×2
Psychic	×4
Bug	×0.25
Rock	×0.5
Ghost	×1
Dragon	×1
Dark	×0.5
Steel	×1
Fairy	×1

Damage taken in Inverse Battles	
Normal	×1
Fire	×1
Water	×1
Grass	×2
Electric	×1
Ice	×1
Fighting	×2
Poison	×2
Ground	×0.5
Flying	×0.5
Psychic	×0.25
Bug	×4
Rock	×2
Ghost	×1
Dragon	×1
Dark	×2
Steel	×1
Fairy	×1

How to obtain for your Central Kalos Pokédex

❶ Catch in the tall grass on Route 7.
❷ Catch in the yellow flowers on Route 7.

❶ Catch in the tall grass on Route 7.
❷ Catch in the yellow flowers on Route 7.

♂ ♀

The male's stripes on its abdomen are located lower than the female's stripes.

● LEVEL-UP MOVES

Lv.	Name	Type	Kind	Pow.	Acc.	PP	Range
1	Astonish	Ghost	Physical	30	100	15	Normal
3	Mud-Slap	Ground	Special	20	100	10	Normal
8	Poison Sting	Poison	Physical	15	100	35	Normal
10	Taunt	Dark	Status	—	100	20	Normal
15	Pursuit	Dark	Physical	40	100	20	Normal
17	Feint Attack	Dark	Physical	60	—	20	Normal
22	Revenge	Fighting	Physical	60	100	10	Normal
24	Swagger	Normal	Status	—	90	15	Normal
29	Mud Bomb	Ground	Special	65	85	10	Normal
31	Sucker Punch	Dark	Physical	80	100	5	Normal
36	Venoshock	Poison	Special	65	100	10	Normal
38	Nasty Plot	Dark	Status	—	—	20	Self
43	Poison Jab	Poison	Physical	80	100	20	Normal
45	Sludge Bomb	Poison	Special	90	100	10	Normal
47	Belch	Poison	Special	120	90	10	Normal
50	Flatter	Dark	Status	—	100	15	Normal

● TM & HM MOVES

No.	Name	Type	Kind	Pow.	Acc.	PP	Range
TM06	Toxic	Poison	Status	—	90	10	Normal
TM08	Bulk Up	Fighting	Status	—	20	20	Self
TM09	Venoshock	Poison	Special	65	100	10	Normal
TM10	Hidden Power	Normal	Special	60	100	15	Normal
TM11	Sunny Day	Fire	Status	—	—	5	Both Sides
TM12	Taunt	Dark	Status	—	100	20	Normal
TM17	Protect	Normal	Status	—	—	10	Self
TM18	Rain Dance	Water	Status	—	—	5	Both Sides
TM21	Frustration	Normal	Physical	—	100	20	Normal
TM26	Earthquake	Ground	Physical	100	100	10	Adjacent
TM27	Return	Normal	Physical	—	100	20	Normal
TM28	Dig	Ground	Physical	80	100	10	Normal
TM30	Shadow Ball	Ghost	Special	80	100	15	Normal
TM31	Brick Break	Fighting	Physical	75	100	15	Normal
TM32	Double Team	Normal	Status	—	—	15	Self
TM34	Sludge Wave	Poison	Special	95	100	10	Adjacent
TM36	Sludge Bomb	Poison	Special	90	100	10	Normal
TM39	Rock Tomb	Rock	Physical	60	95	15	Normal
TM41	Torment	Dark	Status	—	100	15	Normal
TM42	Facade	Normal	Physical	70	100	20	Normal
TM44	Rest	Psychic	Status	—	—	10	Self
TM45	Attract	Normal	Status	—	100	15	Normal
TM46	Thief	Dark	Physical	60	100	25	Normal
TM47	Low Sweep	Fighting	Physical	65	100	20	Normal
TM48	Round	Normal	Special	60	100	15	Normal
TM52	Focus Blast	Fighting	Special	120	70	5	Normal
TM56	Fling	Dark	Physical	—	100	10	Normal
TM63	Embargo	Dark	Status	—	100	15	Normal
TM66	Payback	Dark	Physical	50	100	10	Normal
TM67	Retaliate	Normal	Physical	70	100	5	Normal
TM78	Bulldoze	Ground	Physical	60	100	20	Adjacent
TM80	Rock Slide	Rock	Physical	75	90	10	Many Others
TM81	X-Scissor	Bug	Physical	80	100	15	Normal

No.	Name	Type	Kind	Pow.	Acc.	PP	Range
TM84	Poison Jab	Poison	Physical	80	100	20	Normal
TM87	Swagger	Normal	Status	—	90	15	Normal
TM88	Sleep Talk	Normal	Status	—	—	10	Self
TM90	Substitute	Normal	Status	—	—	10	Self
TM94	Rock Smash	Fighting	Physical	40	100	15	Normal
TM97	Dark Pulse	Dark	Special	80	100	15	Normal
TM98	Power-Up Punch	Fighting	Physical	40	100	20	Normal
TM100	Confide	Normal	Status	—	—	20	Normal
HM04	Strength	Normal	Physical	80	100	15	Normal

● MOVES TAUGHT BY PEOPLE

Name	Type	Kind	Pow.	Acc.	PP	Range

● EGG MOVES

Name	Type	Kind	Pow.	Acc.	PP	Range
Me First	Normal	Status	—	—	20	Varies
Feint	Normal	Physical	30	100	10	Normal
Dynamic Punch	Fighting	Physical	100	50	5	Normal
Headbutt	Normal	Physical	70	100	15	Normal
Vacuum Wave	Fighting	Special	40	100	30	Normal
Meditate	Psychic	Status	—	—	40	Self
Fake Out	Normal	Physical	40	100	10	Normal
Wake-Up Slap	Fighting	Physical	70	100	10	Normal
Smelling Salts	Normal	Physical	70	100	10	Normal
Cross Chop	Fighting	Physical	100	80	5	Normal
Bullet Punch	Steel	Physical	40	100	30	Normal
Counter	Fighting	Physical	—	100	20	Varies
Drain Punch	Fighting	Physical	75	100	10	Normal
Acupressure	Normal	Status	—	—	30	Self/Ally
Quick Guard	Fighting	Status	—	—	15	Your Side

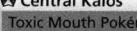

Central Kalos
Toxic Mouth Pokémon

126

 Toxicroak

HEIGHT: 4'03" WEIGHT: 97.9 lbs.
GENDER: ♂/♀

X	It has a poison sac at its throat. When it croaks, the stored poison is churned for greater potency.
Y	Its knuckle claws secrete a toxin so vile that even a scratch could prove fatal.

TYPE Poison Fighting

ABILITIES
Anticipation
Dry Skin

HIDDEN ABILITY
Poison Touch

STAT GROWTH RATES
HP ■■■
Attack ■■■■
Defense ■■■
Sp. Atk ■■■■
Sp. Def ■■■
Speed ■■■■

EGG GROUP
Human-Like

EVOLUTION

Croagunk → Lv. 37 → Toxicroak

ITEMS SOMETIMES HELD BY WILD POKÉMON
None

Damage taken in normal battles		Damage taken in Inverse Battles	
Normal	×1	Normal	×1
Fire	×1	Fire	×1
Water	×1	Water	×1
Grass	×0.5	Grass	×2
Electric	×1	Electric	×1
Ice	×1	Ice	×1
Fighting	×0.5	Fighting	×2
Poison	×0.5	Poison	×2
Ground	×2	Ground	×0.5
Flying	×2	Flying	×0.5
Psychic	×4	Psychic	×0.25
Bug	×0.25	Bug	×4
Rock	×0.5	Rock	×2
Ghost	×1	Ghost	×1
Dragon	×1	Dragon	×1
Dark	×0.5	Dark	×2
Steel	×1	Steel	×1
Fairy	×1	Fairy	×1

Can be used in
Inverse Battle
—
Battle Chateau
Battle Institute
Battle Maison
Random Matchup

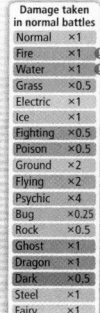
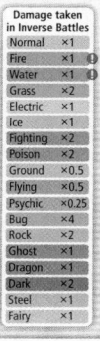
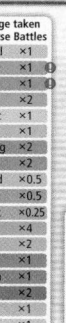

How to obtain for your Central Kalos Pokédex

Level up Croagunk to Lv. 37.	Level up Croagunk to Lv. 37.

 ♂   ♀

The male has a bigger throat sac. The female has a smaller throat sac.

● LEVEL-UP MOVES

Lv.	Name	Type	Kind	Pow.	Acc.	PP	Range
1	Astonish	Ghost	Physical	30	100	15	Normal
1	Mud-Slap	Ground	Special	20	100	10	Normal
1	Poison Sting	Poison	Physical	15	100	35	Normal
3	Mud-Slap	Ground	Special	20	100	10	Normal
8	Poison Sting	Poison	Physical	15	100	35	Normal
10	Taunt	Dark	Status	—	100	20	Normal
15	Pursuit	Dark	Physical	40	100	20	Normal
17	Feint Attack	Dark	Physical	60	—	20	Normal
22	Revenge	Fighting	Physical	60	100	10	Normal
24	Swagger	Normal	Status	—	90	15	Normal
29	Mud Bomb	Ground	Special	65	85	10	Normal
31	Sucker Punch	Dark	Physical	80	100	5	Normal
36	Venoshock	Poison	Special	65	100	10	Normal
41	Nasty Plot	Dark	Status	—	—	20	Self
49	Poison Jab	Poison	Physical	80	100	20	Normal
54	Sludge Bomb	Poison	Special	90	100	10	Normal
58	Belch	Poison	Special	120	90	10	Normal
62	Flatter	Dark	Status	—	100	15	Normal

● TM & HM MOVES

No.	Name	Type	Kind	Pow.	Acc.	PP	Range
TM06	Toxic	Poison	Status	—	90	10	Normal
TM08	Bulk Up	Fighting	Status	—	—	20	Self
TM09	Venoshock	Poison	Special	65	100	10	Normal
TM10	Hidden Power	Normal	Special	60	100	15	Normal
TM11	Sunny Day	Fire	Status	—	—	5	Both Sides
TM12	Taunt	Dark	Status	—	100	20	Normal
TM15	Hyper Beam	Normal	Special	150	90	5	Normal
TM17	Protect	Normal	Status	—	—	10	Self
TM18	Rain Dance	Water	Status	—	—	5	Both Sides
TM21	Frustration	Normal	Physical	—	100	20	Normal
TM26	Earthquake	Ground	Physical	100	100	10	Adjacent
TM27	Return	Normal	Physical	—	100	20	Normal
TM28	Dig	Ground	Physical	80	100	10	Normal
TM30	Shadow Ball	Ghost	Special	80	100	15	Normal
TM31	Brick Break	Fighting	Physical	75	100	15	Normal
TM32	Double Team	Normal	Status	—	—	15	Self
TM34	Sludge Wave	Poison	Special	95	100	10	Adjacent
TM36	Sludge Bomb	Poison	Special	90	100	10	Normal
TM39	Rock Tomb	Rock	Physical	60	95	15	Normal
TM41	Torment	Dark	Status	—	100	15	Normal
TM42	Facade	Normal	Physical	70	100	20	Normal
TM44	Rest	Psychic	Status	—	—	10	Self
TM45	Attract	Normal	Status	—	100	15	Normal
TM46	Thief	Dark	Physical	60	100	25	Normal
TM47	Low Sweep	Fighting	Physical	65	100	20	Normal
TM48	Round	Normal	Special	60	100	15	Normal
TM52	Focus Blast	Fighting	Special	120	70	5	Normal
TM56	Fling	Dark	Physical	—	100	10	Normal
TM63	Embargo	Dark	Status	—	100	15	Normal
TM66	Payback	Dark	Physical	50	100	10	Normal
TM67	Retaliate	Normal	Physical	70	100	5	Normal
TM68	Giga Impact	Normal	Physical	150	90	5	Normal
TM71	Stone Edge	Rock	Physical	100	80	5	Normal

No.	Name	Type	Kind	Pow.	Acc.	PP	Range
TM75	Swords Dance	Normal	Status	—	—	20	Self
TM78	Bulldoze	Ground	Physical	60	100	20	Adjacent
TM80	Rock Slide	Rock	Physical	75	90	10	Many Others
TM81	X-Scissor	Bug	Physical	80	100	15	Normal
TM84	Poison Jab	Poison	Physical	80	100	20	Normal
TM87	Swagger	Normal	Status	—	90	15	Normal
TM88	Sleep Talk	Normal	Status	—	—	10	Self
TM90	Substitute	Normal	Status	—	—	10	Self
TM94	Rock Smash	Fighting	Physical	40	100	15	Normal
TM97	Dark Pulse	Dark	Special	80	100	15	Normal
TM98	Power-Up Punch	Fighting	Physical	40	100	20	Normal
TM100	Confide	Normal	Status	—	—	20	Normal
HM01	Cut	Normal	Physical	50	95	30	Normal
HM04	Strength	Normal	Physical	80	100	15	Normal

● MOVES TAUGHT BY PEOPLE

Name	Type	Kind	Pow.	Acc.	PP	Range

AFTER THE HALL OF FAME

CENTRAL KALOS

127

Ducklett

COASTAL KALOS

MOUNTAIN KALOS

ADVENTURE DATA

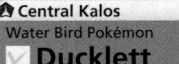 **Central Kalos** **127**

Water Bird Pokémon

✓ **Ducklett**

HEIGHT: 1'08" WEIGHT: 12.1 lbs.
GENDER: ♂/♀

ⓧ When attacked, it uses its feathers to splash water, escaping under cover of the spray.

Ⓥ They are better at swimming than flying, and they happily eat their favorite food, peat moss, as they dive underwater.

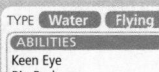 TYPE **Water** **Flying**

ABILITIES
Keen Eye
Big Pecks

HIDDEN ABILITY
Hydration

STAT GROWTH RATES
HP	▪▪▪
Attack	▪▪
Defense	▪▪
Sp. Atk	▪▪
Sp. Def	▪▪
Speed	▪▪

EGG GROUPS
Water 1, Flying

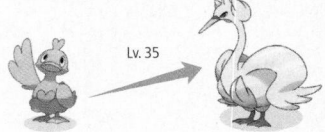 🔄 **EVOLUTION**

Ducklett — Lv. 35 → Swanna

ITEMS SOMETIMES HELD BY WILD POKÉMON
None

Damage taken in normal battles		Damage taken in Inverse Battles	
Normal	×1	Normal	×1
Fire	×0.5	Fire	×2
Water	×0.5	Water	×2
Grass	×1	Grass	×1
Electric	×4	Electric	×0.25
Ice	×1	Ice	×1
Fighting	×0.5	Fighting	×2
Poison	×1	Poison	×1
Ground	×0	Ground	×2
Flying	×1	Flying	×1
Psychic	×1	Psychic	×1
Bug	×0.5	Bug	×2
Rock	×2	Rock	×0.5
Ghost	×1	Ghost	×1
Dragon	×1	Dragon	×1
Dark	×1	Dark	×1
Steel	×0.5	Steel	×2
Fairy	×1	Fairy	×1

Can be used in	
Inverse Battle	Battle Institute
—	Battle Maison
Battle Chateau	Random Matchup

Same form for ♂/♀

How to obtain for your Central Kalos Pokédex

❶ Catch in the yellow flowers on Route 7.
❷ Catch in the purple flowers on Route 7.

❶ Catch in the yellow flowers on Route 7.
❷ Catch in the purple flowers on Route 7.

● **LEVEL-UP MOVES**

Lv.	Name	Type	Kind	Pow.	Acc.	PP	Range
1	Water Gun	Water	Special	40	100	25	Normal
3	Water Sport	Water	Status	—	—	15	Both Sides
6	Defog	Flying	Status	—	—	15	Normal
9	Wing Attack	Flying	Physical	60	100	35	Normal
13	Water Pulse	Water	Special	60	100	20	Normal
15	Aerial Ace	Flying	Physical	60	—	20	Normal
19	Bubble Beam	Water	Special	65	100	20	Normal
21	Feather Dance	Flying	Status	—	100	15	Normal
24	Aqua Ring	Water	Status	—	—	20	Self
27	Air Slash	Flying	Special	75	95	15	Normal
30	Roost	Flying	Status	—	—	10	Self
34	Rain Dance	Water	Status	—	—	5	Both Sides
37	Tailwind	Flying	Status	—	—	15	Your Side
41	Brave Bird	Flying	Physical	120	100	15	Normal
46	Hurricane	Flying	Special	110	70	10	Normal

● **TM & HM MOVES**

No.	Name	Type	Kind	Pow.	Acc.	PP	Range
TM06	Toxic	Poison	Status	—	90	10	Normal
TM07	Hail	Ice	Status	—	—	10	Both Sides
TM10	Hidden Power	Normal	Special	60	100	15	Normal
TM13	Ice Beam	Ice	Special	90	100	10	Normal
TM17	Protect	Normal	Status	—	—	10	Self
TM18	Rain Dance	Water	Status	—	—	5	Both Sides
TM19	Roost	Flying	Status	—	—	10	Self
TM21	Frustration	Normal	Physical	—	100	20	Normal
TM27	Return	Normal	Physical	—	100	20	Normal
TM32	Double Team	Normal	Status	—	—	15	Self
TM40	Aerial Ace	Flying	Physical	60	—	20	Normal
TM44	Facade	Normal	Physical	70	100	20	Normal
TM45	Rest	Psychic	Status	—	—	10	Self
TM45	Attract	Normal	Status	—	100	15	Normal
TM48	Round	Normal	Special	60	100	15	Normal
TM51	Steel Wing	Steel	Physical	70	90	25	Normal
TM55	Scald	Water	Special	80	100	15	Normal
TM87	Swagger	Normal	Status	—	90	15	Normal
TM88	Sleep Talk	Normal	Status	—	—	10	Self
TM90	Substitute	Normal	Status	—	—	10	Self
TM100	Confide	Normal	Status	—	—	20	Normal
HM02	Fly	Flying	Physical	90	95	15	Normal
HM03	Surf	Water	Special	90	100	15	Adjacent

● **MOVES TAUGHT BY PEOPLE**

Name	Type	Kind	Pow.	Acc.	PP	Range

● **EGG MOVES**

Name	Type	Kind	Pow.	Acc.	PP	Range
Steel Wing	Steel	Physical	70	90	25	Normal
Brine	Water	Special	65	100	10	Normal
Gust	Flying	Special	40	100	35	Normal
Air Cutter	Flying	Special	60	95	25	Many Others
Mirror Move	Flying	Status	—	—	20	Normal
Me First	Normal	Status	—	—	20	Varies
Lucky Chant	Normal	Status	—	—	30	Your Side
Mud Sport	Ground	Status	—	—	15	Both Sides

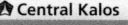

Central Kalos

128

White Bird Pokémon

 Swanna

HEIGHT: 4'03" WEIGHT: 53.4 lbs.
GENDER: ♂/♀

TYPE Water Flying

ABILITIES
Keen Eye
Big Pecks

HIDDEN ABILITY
Hydration

STAT GROWTH RATES
HP ▪▪▪
Attack ▪▪▪▪
Defense ▪▪▪
Sp. Atk ▪▪▪▪
Sp. Def ▪▪▪
Speed ▪▪▪▪▪

EGG GROUPS
Water 1, Flying

EVOLUTION

Ducklett → Lv. 35 → Swanna

X Despite their elegant appearance, they can flap their wings strongly and fly for thousands of miles.

Y Swanna start to dance at dusk. The one dancing in the middle is the leader of the flock.

ITEMS SOMETIMES HELD BY WILD POKÉMON
None

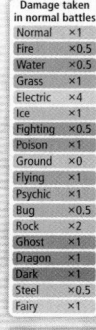

Damage taken in normal battles	
Normal	×1
Fire	×0.5
Water	×0.5
Grass	×1
Electric	×4
Ice	×1
Fighting	×0.5
Poison	×1
Ground	×0
Flying	×1
Psychic	×1
Bug	×0.5
Rock	×2
Ghost	×1
Dragon	×1
Dark	×1
Steel	×0.5
Fairy	×1

Damage taken in Inverse Battles	
Normal	×1
Fire	×2
Water	×2
Grass	×1
Electric	×0.25
Ice	×1
Fighting	×2
Poison	×1
Ground	×2
Flying	×1
Psychic	×1
Bug	×2
Rock	×0.5
Ghost	×1
Dragon	×1
Dark	×1
Steel	×2
Fairy	×1

Can be used in
Inverse Battle
Sky Battle
Battle Chateau
Battle Institute
Battle Maison
Random Matchup

How to obtain for your Central Kalos Pokédex

Level up Ducklett to Lv. 35.	Level up Ducklett to Lv. 35.

X Y

Same form for ♂/♀

● LEVEL-UP MOVES

Lv.	Name	Type	Kind	Pow.	Acc.	PP	Range
1	Water Gun	Water	Special	40	100	25	Normal
1	Water Sport	Water	Status	—	—	15	Both Sides
1	Defog	Flying	Status	—	—	15	Normal
1	Wing Attack	Flying	Physical	60	100	35	Normal
3	Water Sport	Water	Status	—	—	15	Both Sides
6	Defog	Flying	Status	—	—	15	Normal
9	Wing Attack	Flying	Physical	60	100	35	Normal
13	Water Pulse	Water	Special	60	100	20	Normal
15	Aerial Ace	Flying	Physical	60	—	20	Normal
19	Bubble Beam	Water	Special	65	100	20	Normal
21	Feather Dance	Flying	Status	—	100	15	Normal
24	Aqua Ring	Water	Status	—	—	20	Self
27	Air Slash	Flying	Special	75	95	15	Normal
30	Roost	Flying	Status	—	—	10	Self
34	Rain Dance	Water	Status	—	—	5	Both Sides
40	Tailwind	Flying	Status	—	—	15	Your Side
47	Brave Bird	Flying	Physical	120	100	15	Normal
55	Hurricane	Flying	Special	110	70	10	Normal

● TM & HM MOVES

No.	Name	Type	Kind	Pow.	Acc.	PP	Range
TM06	Toxic	Poison	Status	—	90	10	Normal
TM07	Hail	Ice	Status	—	—	10	Both Sides
TM10	Hidden Power	Normal	Special	60	100	15	Normal
TM13	Ice Beam	Ice	Special	90	100	10	Normal
TM15	Hyper Beam	Normal	Special	150	90	5	Normal
TM17	Protect	Normal	Status	—	—	10	Self
TM18	Rain Dance	Water	Status	—	—	5	Both Sides
TM21	Frustration	Normal	Physical	—	100	20	Normal
TM27	Return	Normal	Physical	—	100	20	Normal
TM32	Double Team	Normal	Status	—	—	15	Self
TM40	Aerial Ace	Flying	Physical	60	—	20	Normal
TM42	Facade	Normal	Physical	70	100	20	Normal
TM44	Rest	Psychic	Status	—	—	10	Self
TM45	Attract	Normal	Status	—	100	15	Normal
TM48	Round	Normal	Special	60	100	15	Normal
TM51	Steel Wing	Steel	Physical	70	90	25	Normal
TM55	Scald	Water	Special	80	100	15	Normal
TM68	Giga Impact	Normal	Physical	150	90	5	Normal
TM87	Swagger	Normal	Status	—	90	15	Normal
TM88	Sleep Talk	Normal	Status	—	—	10	Self
TM90	Substitute	Normal	Status	—	—	10	Self
TM100	Confide	Normal	Status	—	—	20	Normal
HM02	Fly	Flying	Physical	90	95	15	Normal
HM03	Surf	Water	Special	90	100	15	Adjacent

● MOVES TAUGHT BY PEOPLE

Name	Type	Kind	Pow.	Acc.	PP	Range

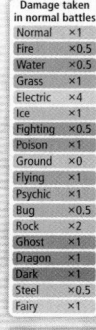

Swanna

128

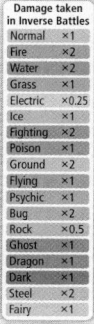

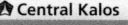

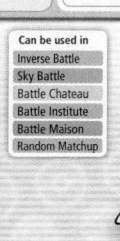

AFTER THE HALL OF FAME

CENTRAL KALOS

128 | Swanna

COASTAL KALOS

MOUNTAIN KALOS

ADVENTURE DATA

AFTER THE HALL OF FAME

CENTRAL KALOS

129

Spritzee

COASTAL KALOS

MOUNTAIN KALOS

ADVENTURE DATA

🏠 Central Kalos

129

Perfume Pokémon

✔ Spritzee

HEIGHT: 0'08" WEIGHT: 1.1 lbs.
GENDER: ♂/♀

X It emits a scent that enraptures those who smell it. This fragrance changes depending on what it has eaten.

Y In the past, rather than using perfume, royal ladies carried a Spritzee that would waft a fragrance they liked.

TYPE Fairy

ABILITY
Healer

HIDDEN ABILITY
Aroma Veil

STAT GROWTH RATES

HP	▪▪▪
Attack	▪▪▪
Defense	▪▪▪
Sp. Atk	▪▪▪
Sp. Def	▪▪▪
Speed	▪

EGG GROUP
Fairy

ITEMS SOMETIMES HELD BY WILD POKÉMON
None

EVOLUTION

Link Trade with Sachet

Spritzee → Aromatisse

Damage taken in normal battles		Damage taken in Inverse Battles	
Normal	×1	Normal	×1
Fire	×1	Fire	×1
Water	×1	Water	×1
Grass	×1	Grass	×1
Electric	×1	Electric	×1
Ice	×1	Ice	×1
Fighting	×0.5	Fighting	×2
Poison	×2	Poison	×0.5
Ground	×1	Ground	×1
Flying	×1	Flying	×1
Psychic	×1	Psychic	×1
Bug	×0.5	Bug	×2
Rock	×1	Rock	×1
Ghost	×1	Ghost	×1
Dragon	×0	Dragon	×2
Dark	×0.5	Dark	×2
Steel	×2	Steel	×0.5
Fairy	×1	Fairy	×1

Can be used in	
Inverse Battle	Battle Institute
—	Battle Maison
Battle Chateau	Random Matchup

Same form for ♂/♀

How to obtain for your Central Kalos Pokédex

Link Trade or transfer from another game.

❶ Catch in the yellow flowers on Route 7.
❷ Catch in the purple flowers on Route 7.

● LEVEL-UP MOVES

Lv.	Name	Type	Kind	Pow.	Acc.	PP	Range
1	Sweet Scent	Normal	Status	—	100	20	Many Others
1	Fairy Wind	Fairy	Special	40	100	30	Normal
6	Sweet Kiss	Fairy	Status	—	75	10	Normal
8	Odor Sleuth	Normal	Status	—	—	40	Normal
13	Echoed Voice	Normal	Special	40	100	15	Normal
17	Calm Mind	Psychic	Status	—	—	20	Self
21	Draining Kiss	Fairy	Special	50	100	10	Normal
25	Aromatherapy	Grass	Status	—	—	5	Your Party
29	Attract	Normal	Status	—	100	15	Normal
33	Moonblast	Fairy	Special	95	100	15	Normal
35	Charm	Fairy	Status	—	100	20	Normal
38	Flail	Normal	Physical	—	100	15	Normal
42	Misty Terrain	Fairy	Status	—	—	10	Both Sides
44	Skill Swap	Psychic	Status	—	—	10	Normal
48	Psychic	Psychic	Special	90	100	10	Normal
50	Disarming Voice	Fairy	Special	40	—	15	Many Others

● TM & HM MOVES

No.	Name	Type	Kind	Pow.	Acc.	PP	Range
TM04	Calm Mind	Psychic	Status	—	—	20	Self
TM06	Toxic	Poison	Status	—	90	10	Normal
TM10	Hidden Power	Normal	Special	60	100	15	Normal
TM11	Sunny Day	Fire	Status	—	—	5	Both Sides
TM16	Light Screen	Psychic	Status	—	—	30	Your Side
TM17	Protect	Normal	Status	—	—	10	Self
TM18	Rain Dance	Water	Status	—	—	5	Both Sides
TM21	Frustration	Normal	Physical	—	100	20	Normal
TM24	Thunderbolt	Electric	Special	90	100	15	Normal
TM27	Return	Normal	Physical	—	100	20	Normal
TM29	Psychic	Psychic	Special	90	100	10	Normal
TM32	Double Team	Normal	Status	—	—	15	Self
TM33	Reflect	Psychic	Status	—	—	20	Your Side
TM41	Torment	Dark	Status	—	100	15	Normal
TM42	Facade	Normal	Physical	70	100	20	Normal
TM44	Rest	Psychic	Status	—	—	10	Self
TM45	Attract	Normal	Status	—	100	15	Normal
TM48	Round	Normal	Special	60	100	15	Normal
TM49	Echoed Voice	Normal	Special	40	100	15	Normal
TM53	Energy Ball	Grass	Special	90	100	10	Normal
TM57	Charge Beam	Electric	Special	50	90	10	Normal
TM70	Flash	Normal	Status	—	100	20	Normal
TM74	Gyro Ball	Steel	Physical	—	100	5	Normal
TM77	Psych Up	Normal	Status	—	—	10	Normal
TM85	Dream Eater	Psychic	Special	100	100	15	Normal
TM87	Swagger	Normal	Status	—	90	15	Normal
TM88	Sleep Talk	Normal	Status	—	—	10	Self
TM90	Substitute	Normal	Status	—	—	10	Self
TM91	Flash Cannon	Steel	Special	80	100	10	Normal
TM92	Trick Room	Psychic	Status	—	—	5	Both Sides
TM99	Dazzling Gleam	Fairy	Special	80	100	10	Many Others
TM100	Confide	Normal	Status	—	—	20	Normal

No.	Name	Type	Kind	Pow.	Acc.	PP	Range

● MOVES TAUGHT BY PEOPLE

Name	Type	Kind	Pow.	Acc.	PP	Range

● EGG MOVES

Name	Type	Kind	Pow.	Acc.	PP	Range
Disable	Normal	Status	—	100	20	Normal
Wish	Normal	Status	—	—	10	Self
Captivate	Normal	Status	—	100	20	Many Others
Refresh	Normal	Status	—	—	20	Self

AFTER THE HALL OF FAME

CENTRAL KALOS

130

Aromatisse

COASTAL KALOS

MOUNTAIN KALOS

ADVENTURE DATA

Central Kalos
Fragrance Pokémon

Aromatisse

130

HEIGHT: 2'07" WEIGHT: 34.2 lbs.
GENDER: ♂/♀

X It devises various scents, pleasant and unpleasant, and emits scents that its enemies dislike in order to gain an edge in battle.

Y Its scent is so overpowering that, unless a Trainer happens to really enjoy the smell, he or she will have a hard time walking alongside it.

TYPE Fairy

ABILITY
Healer

HIDDEN ABILITY
Aroma Veil

STAT GROWTH RATES
HP
Attack
Defense
Sp. Atk
Sp. Def
Speed

EGG GROUP
Fairy

EVOLUTION

Link Trade with Sachet

Spritzee → Aromatisse

ITEMS SOMETIMES HELD BY WILD POKÉMON
None

Damage taken in normal battles		Damage taken in Inverse Battles	
Normal	×1	Normal	×1
Fire	×1	Fire	×1
Water	×1	Water	×1
Grass	×1	Grass	×1
Electric	×1	Electric	×1
Ice	×1	Ice	×1
Fighting	×0.5	Fighting	×2
Poison	×2	Poison	×0.5
Ground	×1	Ground	×1
Flying	×1	Flying	×1
Psychic	×1	Psychic	×1
Bug	×0.5	Bug	×2
Rock	×1	Rock	×1
Ghost	×1	Ghost	×1
Dragon	×0	Dragon	×2
Dark	×0.5	Dark	×2
Steel	×2	Steel	×0.5
Fairy	×1	Fairy	×1

Can be used in	
Inverse Battle	Battle Institute
—	Battle Maison
Battle Chateau	Random Matchup

Same form for ♂/♀

How to obtain for your Central Kalos Pokédex

❶ Link Trade or transfer from another game.

❷ Receive Spritzee with Sachet by Link Trade, and have it evolve.

Receive Spritzee with Sachet by Link Trade, and have it evolve.

● LEVEL-UP MOVES

Lv.	Name	Type	Kind	Pow.	Acc.	PP	Range
1	Aromatic Mist	Fairy	Status	—	—	20	1 Ally
1	Heal Pulse	Psychic	Status	—	—	10	Normal
1	Sweet Scent	Normal	Status	—	100	20	Many Others
1	Fairy Wind	Fairy	Special	40	100	30	Normal
6	Sweet Kiss	Fairy	Status	—	75	10	Normal
8	Odor Sleuth	Normal	Status	—	—	40	Normal
13	Echoed Voice	Normal	Special	40	100	15	Normal
17	Calm Mind	Psychic	Status	—	—	20	Self
21	Draining Kiss	Fairy	Special	50	100	10	Normal
25	Aromatherapy	Grass	Status	—	—	5	Your Party
28	Attract	Normal	Status	—	100	15	Normal
31	Moonblast	Fairy	Special	95	100	15	Normal
35	Charm	Fairy	Status	—	100	20	Normal
38	Flail	Normal	Physical	—	100	15	Normal
42	Misty Terrain	Fairy	Status	—	—	10	Both Sides
44	Skill Swap	Psychic	Status	—	—	10	Normal
48	Psychic	Psychic	Special	90	100	10	Normal
53	Disarming Voice	Fairy	Special	40	—	15	Many Others
57	Reflect	Psychic	Status	—	—	20	Your Side
64	Psych Up	Normal	Status	—	—	10	Normal

● TM & HM MOVES

No.	Name	Type	Kind	Pow.	Acc.	PP	Range
TM03	Psyshock	Psychic	Special	80	100	10	Normal
TM04	Calm Mind	Psychic	Status	—	—	20	Self
TM06	Toxic	Poison	Status	—	90	10	Normal
TM10	Hidden Power	Normal	Special	60	100	15	Normal
TM11	Sunny Day	Fire	Status	—	—	5	Both Sides
TM15	Hyper Beam	Normal	Special	150	90	5	Normal
TM16	Light Screen	Psychic	Status	—	—	30	Your Side
TM17	Protect	Normal	Status	—	—	10	Self
TM18	Rain Dance	Water	Status	—	—	5	Both Sides
TM21	Frustration	Normal	Physical	—	100	20	Normal
TM24	Thunderbolt	Electric	Special	90	100	15	Normal
TM25	Thunder	Electric	Special	110	70	10	Normal
TM27	Return	Normal	Physical	—	100	20	Normal
TM29	Psychic	Psychic	Special	90	100	10	Normal
TM32	Double Team	Normal	Status	—	—	15	Self
TM33	Reflect	Psychic	Status	—	—	20	Your Side
TM41	Torment	Dark	Status	—	100	15	Normal
TM42	Facade	Normal	Physical	70	100	20	Normal
TM44	Rest	Psychic	Status	—	—	10	Self
TM45	Attract	Normal	Status	—	100	15	Normal
TM48	Round	Normal	Special	60	100	15	Normal
TM49	Echoed Voice	Normal	Special	40	100	15	Normal
TM53	Energy Ball	Grass	Special	90	100	10	Normal
TM57	Charge Beam	Electric	Special	50	90	10	Normal
TM68	Giga Impact	Normal	Physical	150	90	5	Normal
TM70	Flash	Normal	Status	—	100	20	Normal
TM74	Gyro Ball	Steel	Physical	—	100	5	Normal
TM77	Psych Up	Normal	Status	—	—	10	Normal
TM85	Dream Eater	Psychic	Special	100	100	15	Normal
TM87	Swagger	Normal	Status	—	90	15	Normal
TM88	Sleep Talk	Normal	Status	—	—	10	Self
TM90	Substitute	Normal	Status	—	—	10	Self
TM91	Flash Cannon	Steel	Special	80	100	10	Normal

No.	Name	Type	Kind	Pow.	Acc.	PP	Range
TM92	Trick Room	Psychic	Status	—	—	5	Both Sides
TM99	Dazzling Gleam	Fairy	Special	80	100	10	Many Others
TM100	Confide	Normal	Status	—	—	20	Normal

● MOVES TAUGHT BY PEOPLE

Name	Type	Kind	Pow.	Acc.	PP	Range

AFTER THE HALL OF FAME

CENTRAL KALOS

131

Swirlix

COASTAL KALOS

MOUNTAIN KALOS

ADVENTURE DATA

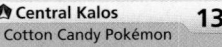

Central Kalos   131
Cotton Candy Pokémon

Swirlix

HEIGHT: 1'04"   WEIGHT: 7.7 lbs.
GENDER: ♂/♀

TYPE Fairy

ABILITY
Sweet Veil

HIDDEN ABILITY
Unbearden

STAT GROWTH RATES
HP	■■■
Attack	■■■
Defense	■■■
Sp. Atk	■■■
Sp. Def	■■
Speed	■■

EGG GROUP
Fairy

(X) To entangle its opponents in battle, it extrudes white threads as sweet and sticky as cotton candy.

(Y) Because it eats nothing but sweets, its fur is as sticky sweet as cotton candy.

EVOLUTION

Link Trade with Whipped Dream

Swirlix → Slurpuff

ITEMS SOMETIMES HELD BY WILD POKÉMON
None

Can be used in
Inverse Battle
—
Battle Chateau
Battle Institute
Battle Maison
Random Matchup

Damage taken in normal battles
Normal	×1
Fire	×1
Water	×1
Grass	×1
Electric	×1
Ice	×1
Fighting	×0.5
Poison	×2
Ground	×1
Flying	×1
Psychic	×1
Bug	×0.5
Rock	×1
Ghost	×1
Dragon	×0
Dark	×0.5
Steel	×2
Fairy	×1

Damage taken in Inverse Battles
Normal	×1
Fire	×1
Water	×1
Grass	×1
Electric	×1
Ice	×1
Fighting	×2
Poison	×0.5
Ground	×1
Flying	×1
Psychic	×1
Bug	×2
Rock	×1
Ghost	×1
Dragon	×2
Dark	×2
Steel	×0.5
Fairy	×1

How to obtain for your Central Kalos Pokédex

❶ Catch in the yellow flowers on Route 7.

❷ Catch in the purple flowers on Route 7.

Link Trade or transfer from another game.

Same form for ♂ / ♀

● LEVEL-UP MOVES

Lv.	Name	Type	Kind	Pow.	Acc.	PP	Range
1	Sweet Scent	Normal	Status	—	100	20	Many Others
1	Tackle	Normal	Physical	50	100	35	Normal
5	Fairy Wind	Fairy	Special	40	100	30	Normal
8	Play Nice	Normal	Status	—	—	20	Normal
13	Fake Tears	Dark	Status	—	100	20	Normal
13	Round	Normal	Special	60	100	15	Normal
17	Cotton Spore	Grass	Status	—	100	40	Many Others
21	Endeavor	Normal	Physical	—	100	5	Normal
26	Aromatherapy	Grass	Status	—	—	5	Your Party
31	Draining Kiss	Fairy	Special	50	100	10	Normal
36	Energy Ball	Grass	Special	90	100	10	Normal
41	Cotton Guard	Grass	Status	—	—	10	Self
45	Wish	Normal	Status	—	—	10	Self
49	Play Rough	Fairy	Physical	90	90	10	Normal
58	Light Screen	Psychic	Status	—	—	30	Your Side
67	Safeguard	Normal	Status	—	—	25	Your Side

● TM & HM MOVES

No.	Name	Type	Kind	Pow.	Acc.	PP	Range
TM04	Calm Mind	Psychic	Status	—	—	20	Self
TM06	Toxic	Poison	Status	—	90	10	Normal
TM10	Hidden Power	Normal	Special	60	100	15	Normal
TM11	Sunny Day	Fire	Status	—	—	5	Both Sides
TM16	Light Screen	Psychic	Status	—	—	30	Your Side
TM17	Protect	Normal	Status	—	—	10	Self
TM18	Rain Dance	Water	Status	—	—	5	Both Sides
TM20	Safeguard	Normal	Status	—	—	25	Your Side
TM21	Frustration	Normal	Physical	—	100	20	Normal
TM24	Thunderbolt	Electric	Special	90	100	15	Normal
TM27	Return	Normal	Physical	—	100	20	Normal
TM29	Psychic	Psychic	Special	90	100	10	Normal
TM32	Double Team	Normal	Status	—	—	15	Self
TM35	Flamethrower	Fire	Special	90	100	15	Normal
TM42	Facade	Normal	Physical	70	100	20	Normal
TM44	Rest	Psychic	Status	—	—	10	Self
TM45	Attract	Normal	Status	—	100	15	Normal
TM46	Thief	Dark	Physical	60	100	25	Normal
TM48	Round	Normal	Special	60	100	15	Normal
TM53	Energy Ball	Grass	Special	90	100	10	Normal
TM70	Flash	Normal	Status	—	100	20	Normal
TM77	Psych Up	Normal	Status	—	—	10	Normal
TM85	Dream Eater	Psychic	Special	100	100	15	Normal
TM87	Swagger	Normal	Status	—	90	15	Normal
TM88	Sleep Talk	Normal	Status	—	—	10	Self
TM90	Substitute	Normal	Status	—	—	10	Self
TM99	Dazzling Gleam	Fairy	Special	80	100	10	Many Others
TM100	Confide	Normal	Status	—	—	20	Normal
HM03	Surf	Water	Special	90	100	15	Adjacent

● MOVES TAUGHT BY PEOPLE

Name	Type	Kind	Pow.	Acc.	PP	Range

● EGG MOVES

Name	Type	Kind	Pow.	Acc.	PP	Range
After You	Normal	Status	—	—	15	Normal
Yawn	Normal	Status	—	—	10	Normal
Belly Drum	Normal	Status	—	—	10	Self
Copycat	Normal	Status	—	—	20	Self

AFTER THE HALL OF FAME

CENTRAL KALOS

132 | Slurpuff

COASTAL KALOS

MOUNTAIN KALOS

ADVENTURE DATA

🏠 Central Kalos   **132**

Meringue Pokémon

☑ Slurpuff

HEIGHT: 2'07" WEIGHT: 11.0 lbs.
GENDER: ♂ / ♀

X	It can distinguish the faintest of scents. It puts its sensitive sense of smell to use by helping pastry chefs in their work.
Y	Its sense of smell is 100 million times better than a human's, so even the faintest scent tells it about everything in the area. It's like it can see with its nose!

TYPE   Fairy

ABILITY
Sweet Veil

HIDDEN ABILITY
Unburden

STAT GROWTH RATES
HP ▪▪▪
Attack ▪▪▪
Defense ▪▪▪▪
Sp. Atk ▪▪▪▪
Sp. Def ▪▪▪
Speed ▪▪▪▪

EGG GROUP
Fairy

🔺 EVOLUTION

Link Trade with
Whipped Dream

Swirlix   Slurpuff

ITEMS SOMETIMES HELD BY WILD POKÉMON
None

Damage taken in normal battles		Damage taken in Inverse Battles	
Normal	×1	Normal	×1
Fire	×1	Fire	×1
Water	×1	Water	×1
Grass	×1	Grass	×1
Electric	×1	Electric	×1
Ice	×1	Ice	×1
Fighting	×0.5	Fighting	×2
Poison	×2	Poison	×0.5
Ground	×1	Ground	×1
Flying	×1	Flying	×1
Psychic	×1	Psychic	×1
Bug	×0.5	Bug	×2
Rock	×1	Rock	×1
Ghost	×1	Ghost	×1
Dragon	×0	Dragon	×2
Dark	×0.5	Dark	×2
Steel	×2	Steel	×0.5
Fairy	×1	Fairy	×1

Can be used in	
Inverse Battle	Battle Institute
—	Battle Maison
Battle Chateau	Random Matchup

Same form for ♂ / ♀

How to obtain for your Central Kalos Pokédex

Receive Swirlix with Whipped Dream by Link Trade, and have it evolve.

❶ Link Trade or transfer from another game.
❷ Receive Swirlix with Whipped Dream by Link Trade, and have it evolve.

● LEVEL-UP MOVES

Lv.	Name	Type	Kind	Pow.	Acc.	PP	Range
1	Sweet Scent	Normal	Status	—	100	20	Many Others
1	Tackle	Normal	Physical	50	100	35	Normal
5	Fairy Wind	Fairy	Special	40	100	30	Normal
8	Play Nice	Normal	Status	—	—	20	Normal
10	Fake Tears	Dark	Status	—	100	20	Normal
13	Round	Normal	Special	60	100	15	Normal
17	Cotton Spore	Grass	Status	—	100	40	Many Others
21	Endeavor	Normal	Physical	—	100	5	Normal
26	Aromatherapy	Grass	Status	—	—	5	Your Party
31	Draining Kiss	Fairy	Special	50	100	10	Normal
36	Energy Ball	Grass	Special	90	100	10	Normal
41	Cotton Guard	Grass	Status	—	—	10	Self
45	Wish	Normal	Status	—	—	10	Self
49	Play Rough	Fairy	Physical	90	90	10	Normal
58	Light Screen	Psychic	Status	—	—	30	Your Side
67	Safeguard	Normal	Status	—	—	25	Your Side

● TM & HM MOVES

No.	Name	Type	Kind	Pow.	Acc.	PP	Range
TM04	Calm Mind	Psychic	Status	—	—	20	Self
TM06	Toxic	Poison	Status	—	90	10	Normal
TM10	Hidden Power	Normal	Special	60	100	15	Normal
TM11	Sunny Day	Fire	Status	—	—	5	Both Sides
TM15	Hyper Beam	Normal	Special	150	90	5	Normal
TM16	Light Screen	Psychic	Status	—	—	30	Your Side
TM17	Protect	Normal	Status	—	—	10	Self
TM18	Rain Dance	Water	Status	—	—	5	Both Sides
TM20	Safeguard	Normal	Status	—	—	25	Your Side
TM21	Frustration	Normal	Physical	—	100	20	Normal
TM24	Thunderbolt	Electric	Special	90	100	15	Normal
TM27	Return	Normal	Physical	—	100	20	Normal
TM29	Psychic	Psychic	Special	90	100	10	Normal
TM32	Double Team	Normal	Status	—	—	15	Self
TM35	Flamethrower	Fire	Special	90	100	15	Normal
TM42	Facade	Normal	Physical	70	100	20	Normal
TM44	Rest	Psychic	Status	—	—	10	Self
TM45	Attract	Normal	Status	—	100	15	Normal
TM46	Thief	Dark	Physical	60	100	25	Normal
TM48	Round	Normal	Special	60	100	15	Normal
TM53	Energy Ball	Grass	Special	90	100	10	Normal
TM68	Giga Impact	Normal	Physical	150	90	5	Normal
TM70	Flash	Normal	Status	—	100	20	Normal
TM77	Psych Up	Normal	Status	—	—	10	Self
TM85	Dream Eater	Psychic	Special	100	100	15	Normal
TM87	Swagger	Normal	Status	—	90	15	Normal
TM88	Sleep Talk	Normal	Status	—	—	10	Self
TM90	Substitute	Normal	Status	—	—	10	Self
TM99	Dazzling Gleam	Fairy	Special	80	100	10	Many Others
TM100	Confide	Normal	Status	—	—	20	Normal
HM03	Surf	Water	Special	90	100	15	Adjacent

No.	Name	Type	Kind	Pow.	Acc.	PP	Range

● MOVES TAUGHT BY PEOPLE

Name	Type	Kind	Pow.	Acc.	PP	Range

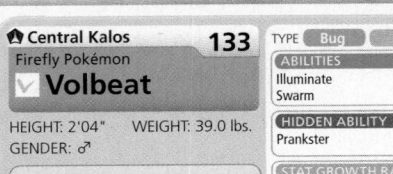

Central Kalos 133

Firefly Pokémon

Volbeat

HEIGHT: 2'04" WEIGHT: 39.0 lbs.
GENDER: ♂

TYPE Bug

ABILITIES
Illuminate
Swarm

HIDDEN ABILITY
Prankster

STAT GROWTH RATES
HP	■■■
Attack	■■■■
Defense	■■■
Sp. Atk	■■
Sp. Def	■■
Speed	■■■■■

EGG GROUPS
Bug, Human-Like

EVOLUTION

Does not evolve

ITEMS SOMETIMES HELD BY WILD POKÉMON
None

X It communicates with others by lighting up its rear at night. It loves Illumise's sweet aroma.

Y It lives around clean ponds. At night, its rear lights up. It converses with others by flashing its light.

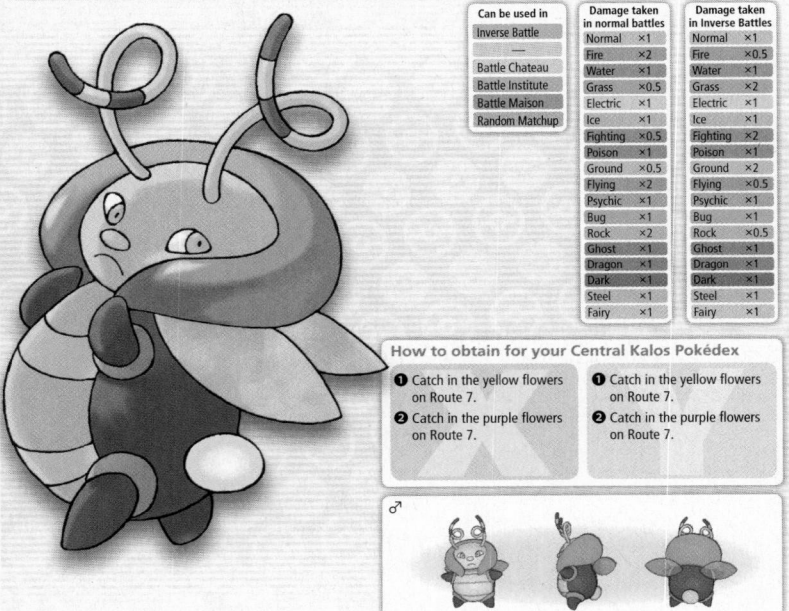

Can be used in
Inverse Battle
—
Battle Chateau
Battle Institute
Battle Maison
Random Matchup

Damage taken in normal battles	
Normal	×1
Fire	×2
Water	×1
Grass	×0.5
Electric	×1
Ice	×1
Fighting	×0.5
Poison	×1
Ground	×0.5
Flying	×2
Psychic	×1
Bug	×1
Rock	×2
Ghost	×1
Dragon	×1
Dark	×1
Steel	×1
Fairy	×1

Damage taken in Inverse Battles	
Normal	×1
Fire	×0.5
Water	×1
Grass	×2
Electric	×1
Ice	×1
Fighting	×2
Poison	×1
Ground	×1
Flying	×0.5
Psychic	×1
Bug	×1
Rock	×0.5
Ghost	×1
Dragon	×1
Dark	×1
Steel	×1
Fairy	×1

How to obtain for your Central Kalos Pokédex

❶ Catch in the yellow flowers on Route 7.
❷ Catch in the purple flowers on Route 7.

❶ Catch in the yellow flowers on Route 7.
❷ Catch in the purple flowers on Route 7.

♂

AFTER THE HALL OF FAME

CENTRAL KALOS

133

Volbeat

COASTAL KALOS

MOUNTAIN KALOS

ADVENTURE DATA

● LEVEL-UP MOVES

Lv.	Name	Type	Kind	Pow.	Acc.	PP	Range
1	Flash	Normal	Status	—	100	20	Normal
1	Tackle	Normal	Physical	50	100	35	Normal
5	Double Team	Normal	Status	—	—	15	Self
9	Confuse Ray	Ghost	Status	—	100	10	Normal
13	Moonlight	Fairy	Status	—	—	5	Self
17	Quick Attack	Normal	Physical	40	100	30	Normal
21	Tail Glow	Bug	Status	—	—	20	Self
25	Signal Beam	Bug	Special	75	100	15	Normal
29	Protect	Normal	Status	—	—	10	Self
33	Helping Hand	Normal	Status	—	—	20	1 Ally
37	Zen Headbutt	Psychic	Physical	80	90	15	Normal
41	Bug Buzz	Bug	Special	90	100	10	Normal
45	Double-Edge	Normal	Physical	120	100	15	Normal

● TM & HM MOVES

No.	Name	Type	Kind	Pow.	Acc.	PP	Range
TM06	Toxic	Poison	Status	—	90	10	Normal
TM10	Hidden Power	Normal	Special	60	100	15	Normal
TM11	Sunny Day	Fire	Status	—	—	5	Both Sides
TM16	Light Screen	Psychic	Status	—	—	30	Your Side
TM17	Protect	Normal	Status	—	—	10	Self
TM18	Rain Dance	Water	Status	—	—	5	Both Sides
TM19	Roost	Flying	Status	—	—	10	Self
TM21	Frustration	Normal	Physical	—	100	20	Normal
TM22	Solar Beam	Grass	Special	120	100	10	Normal
TM24	Thunderbolt	Electric	Special	90	100	15	Normal
TM25	Thunder	Electric	Special	110	70	10	Normal
TM27	Return	Normal	Physical	—	100	20	Normal
TM30	Shadow Ball	Ghost	Special	80	100	15	Normal
TM31	Brick Break	Fighting	Physical	75	100	15	Normal
TM32	Double Team	Normal	Status	—	—	15	Self
TM40	Aerial Ace	Flying	Physical	60	—	20	Normal
TM42	Facade	Normal	Physical	70	100	20	Normal
TM44	Rest	Psychic	Status	—	—	10	Self
TM45	Attract	Normal	Status	—	100	15	Normal
TM46	Thief	Dark	Physical	60	100	25	Normal
TM48	Round	Normal	Special	60	100	15	Normal
TM56	Fling	Dark	Physical	—	100	10	Normal
TM57	Charge Beam	Electric	Special	50	90	10	Normal
TM62	Acrobatics	Flying	Physical	55	100	15	Normal
TM70	Flash	Normal	Status	—	100	20	Normal
TM73	Thunder Wave	Electric	Status	—	100	20	Normal
TM76	Struggle Bug	Bug	Special	50	100	20	Many Others
TM77	Psych Up	Normal	Status	—	—	10	Normal
TM87	Swagger	Normal	Status	—	90	15	Normal
TM88	Sleep Talk	Normal	Status	—	—	10	Self
TM89	U-turn	Bug	Physical	70	100	20	Normal
TM90	Substitute	Normal	Status	—	—	10	Self
TM98	Power-Up Punch	Fighting	Physical	40	100	20	Normal

No.	Name	Type	Kind	Pow.	Acc.	PP	Range
TM99	Dazzling Gleam	Fairy	Special	80	100	10	Many Others
TM100	Confide	Normal	Status	—	—	20	Normal

● MOVES TAUGHT BY PEOPLE

Name	Type	Kind	Pow.	Acc.	PP	Range

● EGG MOVES

Name	Type	Kind	Pow.	Acc.	PP	Range
Baton Pass	Normal	Status	—	—	40	Self
Silver Wind	Bug	Special	60	100	5	Normal
Trick	Psychic	Status	—	100	10	Normal
Encore	Normal	Status	—	100	5	Normal
Bug Buzz	Bug	Special	90	100	10	Normal
Dizzy Punch	Normal	Physical	70	100	10	Normal
Seismic Toss	Fighting	Physical	—	100	20	Normal

AFTER THE HALL OF FAME

CENTRAL KALOS

134

Illumise

COASTAL KALOS

MOUNTAIN KALOS

ADVENTURE DATA

Central Kalos

134

Firefly Pokémon

Illumise

HEIGHT: 2'00" WEIGHT: 39.0 lbs.
GENDER: ♀

TYPE Bug

ABILITIES
Oblivious
Tinted Lens

HIDDEN ABILITY
Prankster

STAT GROWTH RATES
HP	■■■
Attack	■■■
Defense	■■■
Sp. Atk	■■■■
Sp. Def	■■■
Speed	■■■■■

EGG GROUPS
Bug, Human-Like

EVOLUTION

Does not evolve

X Its fragrance attracts a swarm of Volbeat, so they draw over 200 patterns in the night sky.

Y With its sweet aroma, it guides Volbeat to draw signs with light in the night sky.

ITEMS SOMETIMES HELD BY WILD POKÉMON
None

Damage taken in normal battles		Damage taken in Inverse Battles	
Normal	×1	Normal	×1
Fire	×2	Fire	×0.5
Water	×1	Water	×1
Grass	×0.5	Grass	×2
Electric	×1	Electric	×1
Ice	×1	Ice	×1
Fighting	×0.5	Fighting	×2
Poison	×1	Poison	×1
Ground	×0.5	Ground	×2
Flying	×2	Flying	×0.5
Psychic	×1	Psychic	×1
Bug	×1	Bug	×1
Rock	×2	Rock	×0.5
Ghost	×1	Ghost	×1
Dragon	×1	Dragon	×1
Dark	×1	Dark	×1
Steel	×1	Steel	×1
Fairy	×1	Fairy	×1

Can be used in
Inverse Battle
—
Battle Chateau
Battle Institute
Battle Maison
Random Matchup

How to obtain for your Central Kalos Pokédex

❶ Catch in the yellow flowers on Route 7.
❷ Catch in the purple flowers on Route 7.

❶ Catch in the yellow flowers on Route 7.
❷ Catch in the purple flowers on Route 7.

♀

● LEVEL-UP MOVES

Lv.	Name	Type	Kind	Pow.	Acc.	PP	Range
1	Tackle	Normal	Physical	50	100	35	Normal
1	Play Nice	Normal	Status	—	—	20	Normal
5	Sweet Scent	Normal	Status	—	100	20	Many Others
9	Charm	Fairy	Status	—	100	20	Normal
13	Moonlight	Fairy	Status	—	—	5	Self
17	Quick Attack	Normal	Physical	40	100	30	Normal
21	Wish	Normal	Status	—	—	10	Self
25	Encore	Normal	Status	—	100	5	Normal
29	Flatter	Dark	Status	—	100	15	Normal
33	Helping Hand	Normal	Status	—	—	20	1 Ally
37	Zen Headbutt	Psychic	Physical	80	90	15	Normal
41	Bug Buzz	Bug	Special	90	100	10	Normal
45	Covet	Normal	Physical	60	100	25	Normal

● TM & HM MOVES

No.	Name	Type	Kind	Pow.	Acc.	PP	Range
TM06	Toxic	Poison	Status	—	90	10	Normal
TM10	Hidden Power	Normal	Special	60	100	15	Normal
TM11	Sunny Day	Fire	Status	—	—	5	Both Sides
TM16	Light Screen	Psychic	Status	—	—	30	Your Side
TM17	Protect	Normal	Status	—	—	10	Self
TM18	Rain Dance	Water	Status	—	—	5	Both Sides
TM19	Roost	Flying	Status	—	—	10	Self
TM21	Frustration	Normal	Physical	—	100	20	Normal
TM22	Solar Beam	Grass	Special	120	100	10	Normal
TM24	Thunderbolt	Electric	Special	90	100	15	Normal
TM25	Thunder	Electric	Special	110	70	10	Normal
TM27	Return	Normal	Physical	—	100	20	Normal
TM30	Shadow Ball	Ghost	Special	80	100	15	Normal
TM31	Brick Break	Fighting	Physical	75	100	15	Normal
TM32	Double Team	Normal	Status	—	—	15	Self
TM40	Aerial Ace	Flying	Physical	60	—	20	Normal
TM42	Facade	Normal	Physical	70	100	20	Normal
TM44	Rest	Psychic	Status	—	—	10	Self
TM45	Attract	Normal	Status	—	100	15	Normal
TM46	Thief	Dark	Physical	60	100	25	Normal
TM48	Round	Normal	Special	60	100	15	Normal
TM56	Fling	Dark	Physical	—	100	10	Normal
TM57	Charge Beam	Electric	Special	50	90	10	Normal
TM62	Acrobatics	Flying	Physical	55	100	15	Normal
TM70	Flash	Normal	Status	—	100	20	Normal
TM73	Thunder Wave	Electric	Status	—	100	20	Normal
TM76	Struggle Bug	Bug	Special	50	100	20	Many Others
TM77	Psych Up	Normal	Status	—	—	10	Normal
TM87	Swagger	Normal	Status	—	90	15	Normal
TM88	Sleep Talk	Normal	Status	—	—	10	Self
TM89	U-turn	Bug	Physical	70	100	20	Normal
TM90	Substitute	Normal	Status	—	—	10	Self
TM98	Power-Up Punch	Fighting	Physical	40	100	20	Normal

No.	Name	Type	Kind	Pow.	Acc.	PP	Range
TM99	Dazzling Gleam	Fairy	Special	80	100	10	Many Others
TM100	Confide	Normal	Status	—	—	20	Normal

● MOVES TAUGHT BY PEOPLE

Name	Type	Kind	Pow.	Acc.	PP	Range

● EGG MOVES

Name	Type	Kind	Pow.	Acc.	PP	Range
Baton Pass	Normal	Status	—	—	40	Self
Silver Wind	Bug	Special	60	100	5	Normal
Growth	Normal	Status	—	—	20	Self
Encore	Normal	Status	—	100	5	Normal
Bug Buzz	Bug	Special	90	100	10	Normal
Captivate	Normal	Status	—	100	20	Many Others
Fake Tears	Dark	Status	—	100	20	Normal
Confuse Ray	Ghost	Status	—	100	10	Normal

AFTER THE HALL OF FAME

CENTRAL KALOS

135

Hoppip

COASTAL KALOS

MOUNTAIN KALOS

ADVENTURE DATA

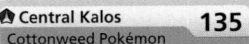

🔺 Central Kalos — 135

Cottonweed Pokémon

✓ Hoppip

HEIGHT: 1'04"　WEIGHT: 1.1 lbs.
GENDER: ♂ / ♀

TYPE Grass　Flying

ABILITIES
Chlorophyll
Leaf Guard

HIDDEN ABILITY
Infiltrator

STAT GROWTH RATES

HP	▪▪
Attack	▪▪
Defense	▪▪
Sp. Atk	▪▪
Sp. Def	▪▪
Speed	▪▪▪

EGG GROUPS
Fairy, Grass

X Its body is so light, it must grip the ground firmly with its feet to keep from being blown away.

Y It drifts on winds. It is said that when Hoppip gather in fields and mountains, spring is on the way.

🔺 EVOLUTION

Lv. 18　　Lv. 27

Hoppip　　Skiploom　　Jumpluff

ITEMS SOMETIMES HELD BY WILD POKÉMON
None

Damage taken in normal battles		Damage taken in Inverse Battles	
Normal	×1	Normal	×1
Fire	×2	Fire	×0.5
Water	×0.5	Water	×2
Grass	×0.25	Grass	×4
Electric	×1	Electric	×1
Ice	×2	Ice	×0.25
Fighting	×0.5	Fighting	×2
Poison	×2	Poison	×0.5
Ground	×0	Ground	×4
Flying	×2	Flying	×0.5
Psychic	×1	Psychic	×1
Bug	×1	Bug	×1
Rock	×2	Rock	×0.5
Ghost	×1	Ghost	×1
Dragon	×1	Dragon	×1
Dark	×1	Dark	×1
Steel	×1	Steel	×1
Fairy	×1	Fairy	×1

Can be used in	
Inverse Battle	Battle Institute
Sky Battle	Battle Maison
Battle Chateau	Random Matchup

Same form for ♂ / ♀

How to obtain for your Central Kalos Pokédex

Catch in a Horde Encounter on Route 7.	Catch in a Horde Encounter on Route 7.
X	**Y**

● LEVEL-UP MOVES

Lv.	Name	Type	Kind	Pow.	Acc.	PP	Range
1	Splash	Normal	Status	—	—	40	Self
4	Synthesis	Grass	Status	—	—	5	Self
6	Tail Whip	Normal	Status	—	100	30	Many Others
8	Tackle	Normal	Physical	50	100	35	Normal
10	Fairy Wind	Fairy	Special	40	100	30	Normal
12	Poison Powder	Poison	Status	—	75	35	Normal
14	Stun Spore	Grass	Status	—	75	30	Normal
16	Sleep Powder	Grass	Status	—	75	15	Normal
19	Bullet Seed	Grass	Physical	25	100	30	Normal
22	Leech Seed	Grass	Status	—	90	10	Normal
25	Mega Drain	Grass	Special	40	100	15	Normal
28	Acrobatics	Flying	Physical	55	100	15	Normal
31	Rage Powder	Bug	Status	—	—	20	Self
34	Cotton Spore	Grass	Status	—	100	40	Many Others
37	U-turn	Bug	Physical	70	100	20	Normal
40	Worry Seed	Grass	Status	—	100	10	Normal
43	Giga Drain	Grass	Special	75	100	10	Normal
46	Bounce	Flying	Physical	85	85	5	Normal
49	Memento	Dark	Status	—	100	10	Normal

● TM & HM MOVES

No.	Name	Type	Kind	Pow.	Acc.	PP	Range
TM06	Toxic	Poison	Status	—	90	10	Normal
TM10	Hidden Power	Normal	Special	60	100	15	Normal
TM11	Sunny Day	Fire	Status	—	—	5	Both Sides
TM17	Protect	Normal	Status	—	—	10	Self
TM21	Frustration	Normal	Physical	—	100	20	Normal
TM22	Solar Beam	Grass	Special	120	100	10	Normal
TM27	Return	Normal	Physical	—	100	20	Normal
TM32	Double Team	Normal	Status	—	—	15	Self
TM33	Reflect	Psychic	Status	—	—	20	Your Side
TM40	Aerial Ace	Flying	Physical	60	—	20	Normal
TM42	Facade	Normal	Physical	70	100	20	Normal
TM44	Rest	Psychic	Status	—	—	10	Self
TM45	Attract	Normal	Status	—	100	15	Normal
TM48	Round	Normal	Special	60	100	15	Normal
TM53	Energy Ball	Grass	Special	90	100	10	Normal
TM62	Acrobatics	Flying	Physical	55	100	15	Normal
TM70	Flash	Normal	Status	—	100	20	Normal
TM75	Swords Dance	Normal	Status	—	—	20	Self
TM77	Psych Up	Normal	Status	—	—	10	Normal
TM83	Infestation	Bug	Special	20	100	20	Normal
TM86	Grass Knot	Grass	Special	—	100	20	Normal
TM87	Swagger	Normal	Status	—	90	15	Normal
TM88	Sleep Talk	Normal	Status	—	—	10	Self
TM89	U-turn	Bug	Physical	70	100	20	Normal
TM90	Substitute	Normal	Status	—	—	10	Self
TM99	Dazzling Gleam	Fairy	Special	80	100	10	Many Others
TM100	Confide	Normal	Status	—	—	20	Normal

● MOVES TAUGHT BY PEOPLE

Name	Type	Kind	Pow.	Acc.	PP	Range

● EGG MOVES

Name	Type	Kind	Pow.	Acc.	PP	Range
Confusion	Psychic	Special	50	100	25	Normal
Encore	Normal	Status	—	100	5	Normal
Double-Edge	Normal	Physical	120	100	15	Normal
Amnesia	Psychic	Status	—	—	20	Self
Helping Hand	Normal	Status	—	—	20	1 Ally
Aromatherapy	Grass	Status	—	—	5	Your Party
Worry Seed	Grass	Status	—	100	10	Normal
Cotton Guard	Grass	Status	—	—	10	Self
Seed Bomb	Grass	Physical	80	100	15	Normal
Endure	Normal	Status	—	—	10	Self
Grassy Terrain	Grass	Status	—	—	10	Both Sides

Central Kalos

Cottonweed Pokémon

Skiploom ☑

136

HEIGHT: 2'00" WEIGHT: 2.2 lbs.
GENDER: ♂/♀

| TYPE | Grass | Flying |

ABILITIES
Chlorophyll
Leaf Guard

HIDDEN ABILITY
Infiltrator

STAT GROWTH RATES
HP ▪▪
Attack ▪▪
Defense ▪▪
Sp. Atk ▪▪
Sp. Def ▪▪▪
Speed ▪▪▪▪

EGG GROUPS
Fairy, Grass

X The bloom on top of its head opens and closes as the temperature fluctuates up and down.

Y It spreads its petals to absorb sunlight. It also floats in the air to get closer to the sun.

EVOLUTION

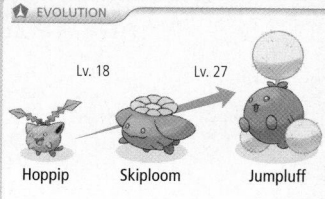

Hoppip → Lv. 18 → Skiploom → Lv. 27 → Jumpluff

ITEMS SOMETIMES HELD BY WILD POKÉMON
None

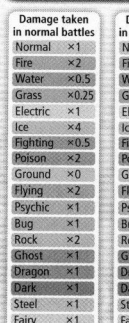

Damage taken in normal battles	
Normal	×1
Fire	×2
Water	×0.5
Grass	×0.25
Electric	×1
Ice	×4
Fighting	×0.5
Poison	×2
Ground	×0
Flying	×2
Psychic	×1
Bug	×1
Rock	×2
Ghost	×1
Dragon	×1
Dark	×1
Steel	×1
Fairy	×1

Damage taken in Inverse Battles	
Normal	×1
Fire	×0.5
Water	×2
Grass	×4
Electric	×1
Ice	×0.25
Fighting	×2
Poison	×0.5
Ground	×4
Flying	×0.5
Psychic	×1
Bug	×1
Rock	×0.5
Ghost	×1
Dragon	×1
Dark	×1
Steel	×1
Fairy	×1

Can be used in	
Inverse Battle	Battle Institute
Sky Battle	Battle Maison
Battle Chateau	Random Matchup

Same form for ♂/♀

How to obtain for your Central Kalos Pokédex

Level up Hoppip to Lv. 18.

Level up Hoppip to Lv. 18.

● LEVEL-UP MOVES

Lv.	Name	Type	Kind	Pow.	Acc.	PP	Range
1	Splash	Normal	Status	—	—	40	Self
1	Synthesis	Grass	Status	—	—	5	Self
1	Tail Whip	Normal	Status	—	100	30	Many Others
1	Tackle	Normal	Physical	50	100	35	Normal
4	Synthesis	Grass	Status	—	—	5	Self
6	Tail Whip	Normal	Status	—	100	30	Many Others
8	Tackle	Normal	Physical	50	100	35	Normal
10	Fairy Wind	Fairy	Special	40	100	30	Normal
12	Poison Powder	Poison	Status	—	75	35	Normal
14	Stun Spore	Grass	Status	—	75	30	Normal
16	Sleep Powder	Grass	Status	—	75	15	Normal
20	Bullet Seed	Grass	Physical	25	100	30	Normal
24	Leech Seed	Grass	Status	—	90	10	Normal
28	Mega Drain	Grass	Special	40	100	15	Normal
32	Acrobatics	Flying	Physical	55	100	15	Normal
36	Rage Powder	Bug	Status	—	—	20	Self
40	Cotton Spore	Grass	Status	—	100	40	Many Others
44	U-turn	Bug	Physical	70	100	20	Normal
48	Worry Seed	Grass	Status	—	100	10	Normal
52	Giga Drain	Grass	Special	75	100	10	Normal
56	Bounce	Flying	Physical	85	85	5	Normal
60	Memento	Dark	Status	—	100	10	Normal

● TM & HM MOVES

No.	Name	Type	Kind	Pow.	Acc.	PP	Range
TM06	Toxic	Poison	Status	—	90	10	Normal
TM10	Hidden Power	Normal	Special	60	100	15	Normal
TM11	Sunny Day	Fire	Status	—	—	5	Both Sides
TM17	Protect	Normal	Status	—	—	10	Self
TM21	Frustration	Normal	Physical	—	100	20	Normal
TM22	Solar Beam	Grass	Special	120	100	10	Normal
TM27	Return	Normal	Physical	—	100	20	Normal
TM32	Double Team	Normal	Status	—	—	15	Self
TM33	Reflect	Psychic	Status	—	—	20	Your Side
TM40	Aerial Ace	Flying	Physical	60	—	20	Normal
TM42	Facade	Normal	Physical	70	100	20	Normal
TM44	Rest	Psychic	Status	—	—	10	Self
TM45	Attract	Normal	Status	—	100	15	Normal
TM48	Round	Normal	Special	60	100	15	Normal
TM53	Energy Ball	Grass	Special	90	100	10	Normal
TM62	Acrobatics	Flying	Physical	55	100	15	Normal
TM70	Flash	Normal	Status	—	100	20	Normal
TM75	Swords Dance	Normal	Status	—	—	20	Self
TM77	Psych Up	Normal	Status	—	—	10	Normal
TM83	Infestation	Bug	Special	20	100	20	Normal
TM86	Grass Knot	Grass	Special	—	100	20	Normal
TM87	Swagger	Normal	Status	—	90	15	Normal
TM88	Sleep Talk	Normal	Status	—	—	10	Self
TM89	U-turn	Bug	Physical	70	100	20	Normal
TM90	Substitute	Normal	Status	—	—	10	Self
TM99	Dazzling Gleam	Fairy	Special	80	100	10	Many Others
TM100	Confide	Normal	Status	—	—	20	Normal

● MOVES TAUGHT BY PEOPLE

Name	Type	Kind	Pow.	Acc.	PP	Range

AFTER THE HALL OF FAME

CENTRAL KALOS

136 | Skiploom

COASTAL KALOS

MOUNTAIN KALOS

ADVENTURE DATA

AFTER THE HALL OF FAME

CENTRAL KALOS

137

Jumpluff

COASTAL KALOS

MOUNTAIN KALOS

ADVENTURE DATA

🏠 **Central Kalos** **137**

Cottonweed Pokémon

☑ **Jumpluff**

TYPE Grass Flying

ABILITIES
Chlorophyll
Leaf Guard

HIDDEN ABILITY
Infiltrator

HEIGHT: 2'07"   WEIGHT: 6.6 lbs.
GENDER: ♂/♀

STAT GROWTH RATES
HP	■■■
Attack	■■■
Defense	■■■
Sp. Atk	■■■
Sp. Def	■■■■
Speed	■■■■■■

🕹 **EVOLUTION**

Lv. 18   Lv. 27

Hoppip   Skiploom   Jumpluff

X — Blown by seasonal winds, it circles the globe, scattering cotton spores as it goes.

Y — Even in the fiercest wind, it can control its fluff to make its way to any place in the world it wants.

EGG GROUPS
Fairy, Grass

ITEMS SOMETIMES HELD BY WILD POKÉMON
None

Can be used in
Inverse Battle
Sky Battle
Battle Chateau
Battle Institute
Battle Maison
Random Matchup

Damage taken in normal battles	
Normal	×1
Fire	×2
Water	×0.5
Grass	×0.25
Electric	×1
Ice	×4
Fighting	×0.5
Poison	×2
Ground	×0
Flying	×2
Psychic	×1
Bug	×1
Rock	×2
Ghost	×1
Dragon	×1
Dark	×1
Steel	×1
Fairy	×1

Damage taken in Inverse Battles	
Normal	×1
Fire	×0.5
Water	×2
Grass	×4
Electric	×1
Ice	×0.25
Fighting	×2
Poison	×0.5
Ground	×4
Flying	×0.5
Psychic	×1
Bug	×1
Rock	×0.5
Ghost	×1
Dragon	×1
Dark	×1
Steel	×1
Fairy	×1

How to obtain for your Central Kalos Pokédex

Level up Skiploom to Lv. 27.

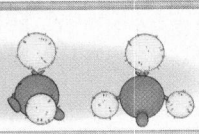
Level up Skiploom to Lv. 27.

Same form for ♂/♀

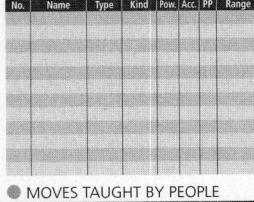

● **LEVEL-UP MOVES**

Lv.	Name	Type	Kind	Pow.	Acc.	PP	Range
1	Splash	Normal	Status	—	—	40	Self
1	Synthesis	Grass	Status	—	—	5	Self
1	Tail Whip	Normal	Status	—	100	30	Many Others
1	Tackle	Normal	Physical	50	100	35	Normal
4	Synthesis	Grass	Status	—	—	5	Self
6	Tail Whip	Normal	Status	—	100	30	Many Others
8	Tackle	Normal	Physical	50	100	35	Normal
10	Fairy Wind	Fairy	Special	40	100	30	Normal
12	Poison Powder	Poison	Status	—	75	35	Normal
14	Stun Spore	Grass	Status	—	75	30	Normal
16	Sleep Powder	Grass	Status	—	75	15	Normal
20	Bullet Seed	Grass	Physical	25	100	30	Normal
24	Leech Seed	Grass	Status	—	90	10	Normal
29	Mega Drain	Grass	Special	40	100	15	Normal
34	Acrobatics	Flying	Physical	55	100	15	Normal
39	Rage Powder	Bug	Status	—	—	20	Self
44	Cotton Spore	Grass	Status	—	100	40	Many Others
49	U-turn	Bug	Physical	70	100	20	Normal
54	Worry Seed	Grass	Status	—	100	10	Normal
59	Giga Drain	Grass	Special	75	100	10	Normal
64	Bounce	Flying	Physical	85	85	5	Normal
69	Memento	Dark	Status	—	100	10	Normal

● **TM & HM MOVES**

No.	Name	Type	Kind	Pow.	Acc.	PP	Range
TM06	Toxic	Poison	Status	—	90	10	Normal
TM10	Hidden Power	Normal	Special	60	100	15	Normal
TM11	Sunny Day	Fire	Status	—	—	5	Both Sides
TM15	Hyper Beam	Normal	Special	150	90	5	Normal
TM17	Protect	Normal	Status	—	—	10	Self
TM21	Frustration	Normal	Physical	—	100	20	Normal
TM22	Solar Beam	Grass	Special	120	100	10	Normal
TM27	Return	Normal	Physical	—	100	20	Normal
TM32	Double Team	Normal	Status	—	—	15	Self
TM33	Reflect	Psychic	Status	—	—	20	Your Side
TM40	Aerial Ace	Flying	Physical	60	—	20	Normal
TM42	Facade	Normal	Physical	70	100	20	Normal
TM44	Rest	Psychic	Status	—	—	10	Self
TM45	Attract	Normal	Status	—	100	15	Normal
TM48	Round	Normal	Special	60	100	15	Normal
TM53	Energy Ball	Grass	Special	90	100	10	Normal
TM62	Acrobatics	Flying	Physical	55	100	15	Normal
TM68	Giga Impact	Normal	Physical	150	90	5	Normal
TM70	Flash	Normal	Status	—	100	20	Normal
TM75	Swords Dance	Normal	Status	—	—	20	Self
TM77	Psych Up	Normal	Status	—	—	10	Normal
TM83	Infestation	Bug	Special	20	100	20	Normal
TM86	Grass Knot	Grass	Special	—	100	20	Normal
TM87	Swagger	Normal	Status	—	90	15	Normal
TM88	Sleep Talk	Normal	Status	—	—	10	Self
TM89	U-turn	Bug	Physical	70	100	20	Normal
TM90	Substitute	Normal	Status	—	—	10	Self
TM99	Dazzling Gleam	Fairy	Special	80	100	10	Many Others
TM100	Confide	Normal	Status	—	—	20	Normal

No.	Name	Type	Kind	Pow.	Acc.	PP	Range

● **MOVES TAUGHT BY PEOPLE**

Name	Type	Kind	Pow.	Acc.	PP	Range

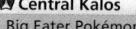

⛰ Central Kalos

138

Big Eater Pokémon

∨ **Munchlax**

HEIGHT: 2'00" WEIGHT: 231.5 lbs.
GENDER: ♂/♀

X It hides food under its long body hair. However, it forgets it has hidden the food.

Y It conceals food under the long fur on its body. It carts around this food stash and swallows it without chewing.

TYPE Normal

ABILITIES
Pickup
Thick Fat

HIDDEN ABILITY
None

STAT GROWTH RATES

HP	▪▪▪▪▪
Attack	▪▪▪▪
Defense	▪▪
Sp. Atk	▪▪
Sp. Def	▪▪
Speed	▪▪▪

EGG GROUP
No Eggs Discovered

⛰ EVOLUTION

Level up with high friendship

Munchlax → Snorlax

ITEMS SOMETIMES HELD BY WILD POKÉMON
None

Damage taken in normal battles		Damage taken in Inverse Battles	
Normal	×1	Normal	×1
Fire	×1	Fire	×1
Water	×1	Water	×1
Grass	×1	Grass	×1
Electric	×1	Electric	×1
Ice	×1	Ice	×1
Fighting	×2	Fighting	×0.5
Poison	×1	Poison	×1
Ground	×1	Ground	×1
Flying	×1	Flying	×1
Psychic	×1	Psychic	×1
Bug	×1	Bug	×1
Rock	×1	Rock	×1
Ghost	×0	Ghost	×2
Dragon	×1	Dragon	×1
Dark	×1	Dark	×1
Steel	×1	Steel	×1
Fairy	×1	Fairy	×1

Can be used in

Inverse Battle	Battle Institute
—	Battle Maison
Battle Chateau	Random Matchup

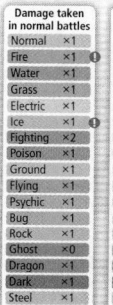

Same form for ♂/♀

How to obtain for your Central Kalos Pokédex

Have Snorlax hold Full Incense and leave it at the Pokémon Day Care, and hatch the Egg that is found.

Have Snorlax hold Full Incense and leave it at the Pokémon Day Care, and hatch the Egg that is found.

● LEVEL-UP MOVES

Lv.	Name	Type	Kind	Pow.	Acc.	PP	Range
1	Last Resort	Normal	Physical	140	100	5	Normal
1	Snatch	Dark	Status	—	—	10	Self
1	Lick	Ghost	Physical	30	100	30	Normal
1	Metronome	Normal	Status	—	—	10	Self
1	Odor Sleuth	Normal	Status	—	—	40	Normal
1	Tackle	Normal	Physical	50	100	35	Normal
4	Defense Curl	Normal	Status	—	—	40	Self
9	Amnesia	Psychic	Status	—	—	20	Self
12	Lick	Ghost	Physical	30	100	30	Normal
17	Chip Away	Normal	Physical	70	100	20	Normal
20	Screech	Normal	Status	—	85	40	Normal
25	Body Slam	Normal	Physical	85	100	15	Normal
28	Stockpile	Normal	Status	—	—	20	Self
33	Swallow	Normal	Status	—	—	10	Self
36	Rollout	Rock	Physical	30	90	20	Normal
41	Fling	Dark	Physical	—	100	10	Normal
44	Belly Drum	Normal	Status	—	—	10	Self
49	Natural Gift	Normal	Physical	—	100	15	Normal
52	Snatch	Dark	Status	—	—	10	Self
57	Last Resort	Normal	Physical	140	100	5	Normal

● TM & HM MOVES

No.	Name	Type	Kind	Pow.	Acc.	PP	Range
TM06	Toxic	Poison	Status	—	90	10	Normal
TM10	Hidden Power	Normal	Special	60	100	15	Normal
TM11	Sunny Day	Fire	Status	—	—	5	Both Sides
TM13	Ice Beam	Ice	Special	90	100	10	Normal
TM14	Blizzard	Ice	Special	110	70	5	Many Others
TM17	Protect	Normal	Status	—	—	10	Self
TM18	Rain Dance	Water	Status	—	—	5	Both Sides
TM21	Frustration	Normal	Physical	—	100	20	Normal
TM22	Solar Beam	Grass	Special	120	100	10	Normal
TM24	Thunderbolt	Electric	Special	90	100	15	Normal
TM25	Thunder	Electric	Special	110	70	10	Normal
TM26	Earthquake	Ground	Physical	100	100	10	Adjacent
TM27	Return	Normal	Physical	—	100	20	Normal
TM29	Psychic	Psychic	Special	90	100	10	Normal
TM30	Shadow Ball	Ghost	Special	80	100	15	Normal
TM31	Brick Break	Fighting	Physical	75	100	15	Normal
TM32	Double Team	Normal	Status	—	—	15	Self
TM35	Flamethrower	Fire	Special	90	100	15	Normal
TM37	Sandstorm	Rock	Status	—	—	10	Both Sides
TM38	Fire Blast	Fire	Special	110	85	5	Normal
TM39	Rock Tomb	Rock	Physical	60	95	15	Normal
TM42	Facade	Normal	Physical	70	100	20	Normal
TM44	Rest	Psychic	Status	—	—	10	Self
TM45	Attract	Normal	Status	—	100	15	Normal
TM48	Round	Normal	Special	60	100	15	Normal
TM56	Fling	Dark	Physical	—	100	10	Normal
TM59	Incinerate	Fire	Special	60	100	15	Many Others
TM67	Retaliate	Normal	Physical	70	100	5	Normal
TM78	Bulldoze	Ground	Physical	60	100	20	Adjacent
TM80	Rock Slide	Rock	Physical	75	90	10	Many Others
TM87	Swagger	Normal	Status	—	90	15	Normal
TM88	Sleep Talk	Normal	Status	—	—	10	Self
TM90	Substitute	Normal	Status	—	—	10	Self

No.	Name	Type	Kind	Pow.	Acc.	PP	Range
TM94	Rock Smash	Fighting	Physical	40	100	15	Normal
TM98	Power-Up Punch	Fighting	Physical	40	100	20	Normal
TM100	Confide	Normal	Status	—	—	20	Normal
HM03	Surf	Water	Special	90	100	15	Adjacent
HM04	Strength	Normal	Physical	80	100	15	Normal

● MOVES TAUGHT BY PEOPLE

Name	Type	Kind	Pow.	Acc.	PP	Range

● EGG MOVES

Name	Type	Kind	Pow.	Acc.	PP	Range
Lick	Ghost	Physical	30	100	30	Normal
Charm	Fairy	Status	—	100	20	Normal
Double-Edge	Normal	Physical	120	100	15	Normal
Curse	Ghost	Status	—	—	10	Varies
Whirlwind	Normal	Status	—	—	20	Normal
Pursuit	Dark	Physical	40	100	20	Normal
Zen Headbutt	Psychic	Physical	80	90	15	Normal
Counter	Fighting	Physical	—	100	20	Varies
Natural Gift	Normal	Physical	—	100	15	Normal
After You	Normal	Status	—	—	15	Normal
Self-Destruct	Normal	Physical	200	100	5	Adjacent
Belch	Poison	Special	120	90	10	Normal

AFTER THE HALL OF FAME

CENTRAL KALOS

138 Munchlax

COASTAL KALOS

MOUNTAIN KALOS

ADVENTURE DATA

AFTER THE HALL OF FAME

CENTRAL KALOS

139

Snorlax

COASTAL KALOS

MOUNTAIN KALOS

ADVENTURE DATA

🏠 Central Kalos — 139

Sleeping Pokémon

☑ Snorlax

HEIGHT: 6'11" WEIGHT: 1014.1 lbs.
GENDER: ♂ / ♀

TYPE Normal

ABILITIES
Immunity
Thick Fat

HIDDEN ABILITY
None

STAT GROWTH RATES

HP	■■■■■■
Attack	■■■■
Defense	■■■
Sp. Atk	■■
Sp. Def	■■■■■
Speed	■■

EGG GROUP
Monster

X It is not satisfied unless it eats over 880 pounds of food every day. When it is done eating, it goes promptly to sleep.

Y Its stomach can digest any kind of food, even if it happens to be moldy or rotten.

⚡ EVOLUTION

Level up with high friendship

Munchlax → Snorlax

ITEMS SOMETIMES HELD BY WILD POKÉMON
None

Damage taken in normal battles			Damage taken in Inverse Battles	
Normal	×1		Normal	×1
Fire	×1		Fire	×1
Water	×1		Water	×1
Grass	×1		Grass	×1
Electric	×1		Electric	×1
Ice	×1		Ice	×1
Fighting	×2		Fighting	×0.5
Poison	×1		Poison	×1
Ground	×1		Ground	×1
Flying	×1		Flying	×1
Psychic	×1		Psychic	×1
Bug	×1		Bug	×1
Rock	×1		Rock	×1
Ghost	×0		Ghost	×2
Dragon	×1		Dragon	×1
Dark	×1		Dark	×1
Steel	×1		Steel	×1
Fairy	×1		Fairy	×1

Can be used in	
Inverse Battle	Battle Institute
—	Battle Maison
Battle Chateau	Random Matchup

Same form for ♂ / ♀

How to obtain for your Central Kalos Pokédex

Use the Poké Flute to wake the Snorlax sleeping on Route 7, and catch it.

Use the Poké Flute to wake the Snorlax sleeping on Route 7, and catch it.

● LEVEL-UP MOVES

Lv.	Name	Type	Kind	Pow.	Acc.	PP	Range
1	Tackle	Normal	Physical	50	100	35	Normal
4	Defense Curl	Normal	Status	—	—	40	Self
9	Amnesia	Psychic	Status	—	—	20	Self
12	Lick	Ghost	Physical	30	100	30	Normal
17	Chip Away	Normal	Physical	70	100	20	Normal
20	Yawn	Normal	Status	—	—	10	Normal
25	Body Slam	Normal	Physical	85	100	15	Normal
28	Rest	Psychic	Status	—	—	10	Self
28	Snore	Normal	Special	50	100	15	Normal
33	Sleep Talk	Normal	Status	—	—	10	Self
36	Rollout	Rock	Physical	30	90	20	Normal
41	Block	Normal	Status	—	—	5	Normal
44	Belly Drum	Normal	Status	—	—	10	Self
49	Crunch	Dark	Physical	80	100	15	Normal
50	Heavy Slam	Steel	Physical	—	100	10	Normal
57	Giga Impact	Normal	Physical	150	90	5	Normal

● TM & HM MOVES

No.	Name	Type	Kind	Pow.	Acc.	PP	Range
TM06	Toxic	Poison	Status	—	90	10	Normal
TM10	Hidden Power	Normal	Special	60	100	15	Normal
TM11	Sunny Day	Fire	Status	—	—	5	Both Sides
TM13	Ice Beam	Ice	Special	90	100	10	Normal
TM14	Blizzard	Ice	Special	110	70	5	Many Others
TM15	Hyper Beam	Normal	Special	150	90	5	Normal
TM17	Protect	Normal	Status	—	—	10	Self
TM18	Rain Dance	Water	Status	—	—	5	Both Sides
TM21	Frustration	Normal	Physical	—	100	20	Normal
TM22	Solar Beam	Grass	Special	120	100	10	Normal
TM23	Smack Down	Rock	Physical	50	100	15	Normal
TM24	Thunderbolt	Electric	Special	90	100	15	Normal
TM25	Thunder	Electric	Special	110	70	10	Normal
TM26	Earthquake	Ground	Physical	100	100	10	Adjacent
TM27	Return	Normal	Physical	—	100	20	Normal
TM29	Psychic	Psychic	Special	90	100	10	Normal
TM30	Shadow Ball	Ghost	Special	80	100	15	Normal
TM31	Brick Break	Fighting	Physical	75	100	15	Normal
TM32	Double Team	Normal	Status	—	—	15	Self
TM35	Flamethrower	Fire	Special	90	100	15	Normal
TM37	Sandstorm	Rock	Status	—	—	10	Both Sides
TM38	Fire Blast	Fire	Special	110	85	5	Normal
TM39	Rock Tomb	Rock	Physical	60	95	15	Normal
TM42	Facade	Normal	Physical	70	100	20	Normal
TM44	Rest	Psychic	Status	—	—	10	Self
TM45	Attract	Normal	Status	—	100	15	Normal
TM48	Round	Normal	Special	60	100	15	Normal
TM52	Focus Blast	Fighting	Special	120	70	5	Normal
TM56	Fling	Dark	Physical	—	100	10	Normal
TM59	Incinerate	Fire	Special	60	100	15	Many Others
TM67	Retaliate	Normal	Physical	70	100	5	Normal
TM68	Giga Impact	Normal	Physical	150	90	5	Normal
TM78	Bulldoze	Ground	Physical	60	100	20	Adjacent
TM80	Rock Slide	Rock	Physical	75	90	10	Many Others
TM87	Swagger	Normal	Status	—	90	15	Normal
TM88	Sleep Talk	Normal	Status	—	—	10	Self
TM90	Substitute	Normal	Status	—	—	10	Self
TM93	Wild Charge	Electric	Physical	90	100	15	Normal
TM94	Rock Smash	Fighting	Physical	40	100	15	Normal
TM98	Power-Up Punch	Fighting	Physical	40	100	20	Normal
TM100	Confide	Normal	Status	—	—	20	Normal
HM03	Surf	Water	Special	90	100	15	Adjacent
HM04	Strength	Normal	Physical	80	100	15	Normal

● MOVES TAUGHT BY PEOPLE

Name	Type	Kind	Pow.	Acc.	PP	Range

● EGG MOVES

Name	Type	Kind	Pow.	Acc.	PP	Range
Lick	Ghost	Physical	30	100	30	Normal
Charm	Fairy	Status	—	100	20	Normal
Double-Edge	Normal	Physical	120	100	15	Normal
Curse	Ghost	Status	—	—	10	Varies
Fissure	Ground	Physical	—	30	5	Normal
Whirlwind	Normal	Status	—	—	20	Normal
Pursuit	Dark	Physical	40	100	20	Normal
Counter	Fighting	Physical	—	100	20	Varies
Natural Gift	Normal	Physical	—	100	15	Normal
After You	Normal	Status	—	—	15	Normal
Belch	Poison	Special	120	90	10	Normal

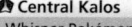 Central Kalos

140

Whisper Pokémon

Whismur

HEIGHT: 2'00" WEIGHT: 35.9 lbs.
GENDER: ♂/♀

 It usually murmurs but starts crying loudly if it senses danger. It stops when its ear covers are shut.

 If it senses danger, it scares the foe by crying out with the volume of a jet-plane engine.

TYPE **Normal**

ABILITY
Soundproof

HIDDEN ABILITY
Rattled

STAT GROWTH RATES

HP	■■■
Attack	■■■
Defense	■■
Sp. Atk	■■■
Sp. Def	■
Speed	■■

EGG GROUPS
Monster, Field

EVOLUTION

Whismur	Loudred	Exploud
	Lv. 20	Lv. 40

ITEMS SOMETIMES HELD BY WILD POKÉMON
None

Damage taken in normal battles		Damage taken in Inverse Battles	
Normal	×1	Normal	×1
Fire	×1	Fire	×1
Water	×1	Water	×1
Grass	×1	Grass	×1
Electric	×1	Electric	×1
Ice	×1	Ice	×1
Fighting	×2	Fighting	×0.5
Poison	×1	Poison	×1
Ground	×1	Ground	×1
Flying	×1	Flying	×1
Psychic	×1	Psychic	×1
Bug	×1	Bug	×1
Rock	×1	Rock	×1
Ghost	×0	Ghost	×2
Dragon	×1	Dragon	×1
Dark	×1	Dark	×1
Steel	×1	Steel	×1
Fairy	×1	Fairy	×1

Can be used in	
Inverse Battle	Battle Institute
—	Battle Maison
Battle Chateau	Random Matchup

Same form for ♂/♀

How to obtain for your Central Kalos Pokédex

❶ Catch in the Connecting Cave.
❷ Catch in a Horde Encounter in the Connecting Cave.

❶ Catch in the Connecting Cave.
❷ Catch in a Horde Encounter in the Connecting Cave.

● LEVEL-UP MOVES

Lv.	Name	Type	Kind	Pow.	Acc.	PP	Range
1	Pound	Normal	Physical	40	100	35	Normal
5	Uproar	Normal	Special	90	100	10	1 Random
11	Astonish	Ghost	Physical	30	100	15	Normal
15	Howl	Normal	Status	—	—	40	Self
21	Supersonic	Normal	Status	—	55	20	Normal
25	Stomp	Normal	Physical	65	100	20	Normal
31	Screech	Normal	Status	—	85	40	Normal
35	Roar	Normal	Status	—	—	20	Normal
41	Synchronoise	Psychic	Special	120	100	10	Adjacent
45	Rest	Psychic	Status	—	—	10	Self
45	Sleep Talk	Normal	Status	—	—	10	Self
50	Hyper Voice	Normal	Special	90	100	10	Many Others

● TM & HM MOVES

No.	Name	Type	Kind	Pow.	Acc.	PP	Range
TM05	Roar	Normal	Status	—	—	20	Normal
TM06	Toxic	Poison	Status	—	90	10	Normal
TM10	Hidden Power	Normal	Special	60	100	15	Normal
TM11	Sunny Day	Fire	Status	—	—	5	Both Sides
TM13	Ice Beam	Ice	Special	90	100	10	Normal
TM14	Blizzard	Ice	Special	110	70	5	Many Others
TM17	Protect	Normal	Status	—	—	10	Self
TM18	Rain Dance	Water	Status	—	—	5	Both Sides
TM21	Frustration	Normal	Physical	—	100	20	Normal
TM22	Solar Beam	Grass	Special	120	100	10	Normal
TM27	Return	Normal	Physical	—	100	20	Normal
TM30	Shadow Ball	Ghost	Special	80	100	15	Normal
TM32	Double Team	Normal	Status	—	—	15	Self
TM35	Flamethrower	Fire	Special	90	100	15	Normal
TM38	Fire Blast	Fire	Special	110	85	5	Normal
TM42	Facade	Normal	Physical	70	100	20	Normal
TM44	Rest	Psychic	Status	—	—	10	Self
TM45	Attract	Normal	Status	—	100	15	Normal
TM48	Round	Normal	Special	60	100	15	Normal
TM49	Echoed Voice	Normal	Special	40	100	15	Normal
TM56	Fling	Dark	Physical	—	100	10	Normal
TM59	Incinerate	Fire	Special	60	100	15	Many Others
TM67	Retaliate	Normal	Physical	70	100	5	Normal
TM87	Swagger	Normal	Status	—	90	15	Normal
TM88	Sleep Talk	Normal	Status	—	—	10	Self
TM90	Substitute	Normal	Status	—	—	10	Self
TM100	Confide	Normal	Status	—	—	20	Normal

● MOVES TAUGHT BY PEOPLE

Name	Type	Kind	Pow.	Acc.	PP	Range

● EGG MOVES

Name	Type	Kind	Pow.	Acc.	PP	Range
Take Down	Normal	Physical	90	85	20	Normal
Snore	Normal	Special	50	100	15	Normal
Extrasensory	Psychic	Special	80	100	20	Normal
Smelling Salts	Normal	Physical	70	100	10	Normal
Smokescreen	Normal	Status	—	100	20	Normal
Endeavor	Normal	Physical	—	100	5	Normal
Hammer Arm	Fighting	Physical	100	90	10	Normal
Fake Tears	Dark	Status	—	100	20	Normal
Circle Throw	Fighting	Physical	60	90	10	Normal
Disarming Voice	Fairy	Special	40	—	15	Many Others

AFTER THE HALL OF FAME

CENTRAL KALOS

140 | Whismur

COASTAL KALOS

MOUNTAIN KALOS

ADVENTURE DATA

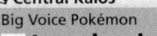

⌂ Central Kalos 141

Big Voice Pokémon

☑ **Loudred**

HEIGHT: 3'03"   WEIGHT: 89.3 lbs.
GENDER: ♂/♀

X It shouts loudly by inhaling air, and then uses its well-developed stomach muscles to exhale.

Y The shock waves from its cries can tip over trucks. It stamps its feet to power up.

TYPE Normal

ABILITY
Soundproof

HIDDEN ABILITY
Scrappy

STAT GROWTH RATES
HP	■■■
Attack	■■■■
Defense	■■
Sp. Atk	■■■
Sp. Def	■■
Speed	■■■

EGG GROUPS
Monster, Field

⌂ EVOLUTION

Lv. 20   Lv. 40

Whismur   Loudred   Exploud

ITEMS SOMETIMES HELD BY WILD POKÉMON
None

Damage taken in normal battles	
Normal	×1
Fire	×1
Water	×1
Grass	×1
Electric	×1
Ice	×1
Fighting	×2
Poison	×1
Ground	×1
Flying	×1
Psychic	×1
Bug	×1
Rock	×1
Ghost	×0
Dragon	×1
Dark	×1
Steel	×1
Fairy	×1

Damage taken in Inverse Battles	
Normal	×1
Fire	×1
Water	×1
Grass	×1
Electric	×1
Ice	×1
Fighting	×0.5
Poison	×1
Ground	×1
Flying	×1
Psychic	×1
Bug	×1
Rock	×1
Ghost	×2
Dragon	×1
Dark	×1
Steel	×1
Fairy	×1

Can be used in	
Inverse Battle	Battle Institute
—	Battle Maison
Battle Chateau	Random Matchup

Same form for ♂/♀

How to obtain for your Central Kalos Pokédex

Level up Whismur to Lv. 20.   Level up Whismur to Lv. 20.

X Y

● LEVEL-UP MOVES

Lv.	Name	Type	Kind	Pow.	Acc.	PP	Range
1	Pound	Normal	Physical	40	100	35	Normal
1	Uproar	Normal	Special	90	100	10	1 Random
1	Astonish	Ghost	Physical	30	100	15	Normal
1	Howl	Normal	Status	—	—	40	Self
5	Uproar	Normal	Special	90	100	10	1 Random
11	Astonish	Ghost	Physical	30	100	15	Normal
15	Howl	Normal	Status	—	—	40	Self
20	Bite	Dark	Physical	60	100	25	Normal
23	Supersonic	Normal	Status	—	55	20	Normal
29	Stomp	Normal	Physical	65	100	20	Normal
37	Screech	Normal	Status	—	85	40	Normal
43	Roar	Normal	Status	—	—	20	Normal
51	Synchronoise	Psychic	Special	120	100	10	Adjacent
57	Rest	Psychic	Status	—	—	10	Self
57	Sleep Talk	Normal	Status	—	—	10	Self
65	Hyper Voice	Normal	Special	90	100	10	Many Others

● TM & HM MOVES

No.	Name	Type	Kind	Pow.	Acc.	PP	Range
TM05	Roar	Normal	Status	—	—	20	Normal
TM06	Toxic	Poison	Status	—	90	10	Normal
TM10	Hidden Power	Normal	Special	60	100	15	Normal
TM11	Sunny Day	Fire	Status	—	—	5	Both Sides
TM12	Taunt	Dark	Status	—	100	20	Normal
TM13	Ice Beam	Ice	Special	90	100	10	Normal
TM14	Blizzard	Ice	Special	110	70	5	Many Others
TM17	Protect	Normal	Status	—	—	10	Self
TM18	Rain Dance	Water	Status	—	—	5	Both Sides
TM21	Frustration	Normal	Physical	—	100	20	Normal
TM22	Solar Beam	Grass	Special	120	100	10	Normal
TM23	Smack Down	Rock	Physical	50	100	15	Normal
TM26	Earthquake	Ground	Physical	100	100	10	Adjacent
TM27	Return	Normal	Physical	—	100	20	Normal
TM30	Shadow Ball	Ghost	Special	80	100	15	Normal
TM31	Brick Break	Fighting	Physical	75	100	15	Normal
TM32	Double Team	Normal	Status	—	—	15	Self
TM35	Flamethrower	Fire	Special	90	100	15	Normal
TM38	Fire Blast	Fire	Special	110	85	5	Normal
TM39	Rock Tomb	Rock	Physical	60	95	15	Normal
TM41	Torment	Dark	Status	—	100	15	Normal
TM42	Facade	Normal	Physical	70	100	20	Normal
TM44	Rest	Psychic	Status	—	—	10	Self
TM48	Round	Normal	Special	60	100	15	Normal
TM49	Echoed Voice	Normal	Special	40	100	15	Normal
TM50	Overheat	Fire	Special	130	90	5	Normal
TM56	Fling	Dark	Physical	—	100	10	Normal
TM59	Incinerate	Fire	Special	60	100	15	Many Others
TM67	Retaliate	Normal	Physical	70	100	5	Normal
TM78	Bulldoze	Ground	Physical	60	100	20	Adjacent
TM80	Rock Slide	Rock	Physical	75	90	10	Many Others
TM87	Swagger	Normal	Status	—	90	15	Normal

No.	Name	Type	Kind	Pow.	Acc.	PP	Range
TM88	Sleep Talk	Normal	Status	—	—	10	Self
TM90	Substitute	Normal	Status	—	—	10	Self
TM94	Rock Smash	Fighting	Physical	40	100	15	Normal
TM98	Power-Up Punch	Fighting	Physical	40	100	20	Normal
TM100	Confide	Normal	Status	—	—	20	Normal
HM04	Strength	Normal	Physical	80	100	15	Normal

● MOVES TAUGHT BY PEOPLE

Name	Type	Kind	Pow.	Acc.	PP	Range

Central Kalos
Loud Noise Pokémon   **142**

✅ Exploud

TYPE Normal

ABILITY
Soundproof

HIDDEN ABILITY
Scrappy

HEIGHT: 4'11"   WEIGHT: 185.2 lbs.
GENDER: ♂ / ♀

 Its howls can be heard over six miles away. It emits all sorts of noises from the ports on its body.

 Its roar in battle shakes the ground like a tremor—or like an earthquake has struck.

EVOLUTION

Lv. 20   Lv. 40

Whismur   Loudred   Exploud

STAT GROWTH RATES
HP   ▪▪▪▪
Attack ▪▪▪▪▪
Defense ▪▪▪
Sp. Atk ▪▪▪
Sp. Def ▪▪▪
Speed   ▪▪▪▪

EGG GROUPS
Monster, Field

ITEMS SOMETIMES HELD BY WILD POKÉMON
None

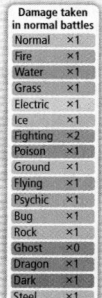

Damage taken in normal battles	
Normal	×1
Fire	×1
Water	×1
Grass	×1
Electric	×1
Ice	×1
Fighting	×2
Poison	×1
Ground	×1
Flying	×1
Psychic	×1
Bug	×1
Rock	×1
Ghost	×0
Dragon	×1
Dark	×1
Steel	×1
Fairy	×1

Damage taken in Inverse Battles	
Normal	×1
Fire	×1
Water	×1
Grass	×1
Electric	×1
Ice	×1
Fighting	×0.5
Poison	×1
Ground	×1
Flying	×1
Psychic	×1
Bug	×1
Rock	×1
Ghost	×2
Dragon	×1
Dark	×1
Steel	×1
Fairy	×1

Can be used in	
Inverse Battle	Battle Institute
—	Battle Maison
Battle Chateau	Random Matchup

Same form for ♂ / ♀

How to obtain for your Central Kalos Pokédex

Level up Loudred to Lv. 40.   Level up Loudred to Lv. 40.

X Y

● LEVEL-UP MOVES

Lv.	Name	Type	Kind	Pow.	Acc.	PP	Range
1	Boomburst	Normal	Special	140	100	10	Adjacent
1	Ice Fang	Ice	Physical	65	95	15	Normal
1	Fire Fang	Fire	Physical	65	95	15	Normal
1	Thunder Fang	Electric	Physical	65	95	15	Normal
1	Pound	Normal	Physical	40	100	35	Normal
1	Uproar	Normal	Special	90	100	10	1 Random
1	Astonish	Ghost	Physical	30	100	15	Normal
1	Howl	Normal	Status	—	—	40	Self
5	Uproar	Normal	Special	90	100	10	1 Random
11	Astonish	Ghost	Physical	30	100	15	Normal
15	Howl	Normal	Status	—	—	40	Self
20	Bite	Dark	Physical	60	100	25	Normal
23	Supersonic	Normal	Status	—	55	20	Normal
29	Stomp	Normal	Physical	65	100	20	Normal
37	Screech	Normal	Status	—	85	40	Normal
40	Crunch	Dark	Physical	80	100	15	Normal
45	Roar	Normal	Status	—	—	20	Normal
55	Synchronoise	Psychic	Special	120	100	10	Adjacent
55	Rest	Psychic	Status	—	—	10	Self
63	Sleep Talk	Normal	Status	—	—	10	Self
71	Hyper Voice	Normal	Special	90	100	10	Many Others
79	Hyper Beam	Normal	Special	150	90	5	Normal
85	Boomburst	Normal	Special	140	100	10	Adjacent

● TM & HM MOVES

No.	Name	Type	Kind	Pow.	Acc.	PP	Range
TM05	Roar	Normal	Status	—	—	20	Normal
TM06	Toxic	Poison	Status	—	90	10	Normal
TM10	Hidden Power	Normal	Special	60	100	15	Normal
TM11	Sunny Day	Fire	Status	—	—	5	Both Sides
TM12	Taunt	Dark	Status	—	100	20	Normal
TM13	Ice Beam	Ice	Special	90	100	10	Normal
TM14	Blizzard	Ice	Special	110	70	5	Many Others
TM15	Hyper Beam	Normal	Special	150	90	5	Normal
TM17	Protect	Normal	Status	—	—	10	Self
TM18	Rain Dance	Water	Status	—	—	5	Both Sides
TM21	Frustration	Normal	Physical	—	100	20	Normal
TM22	Solar Beam	Grass	Special	120	100	10	Normal
TM23	Smack Down	Rock	Physical	50	100	15	Normal
TM26	Earthquake	Ground	Physical	100	100	10	Adjacent
TM27	Return	Normal	Physical	—	100	20	Normal
TM30	Shadow Ball	Ghost	Special	80	100	15	Normal
TM31	Brick Break	Fighting	Physical	75	100	15	Normal
TM32	Double Team	Normal	Status	—	—	15	Self
TM35	Flamethrower	Fire	Special	90	100	15	Normal
TM38	Fire Blast	Fire	Special	110	85	5	Normal
TM39	Rock Tomb	Rock	Physical	60	95	15	Normal
TM41	Torment	Dark	Status	—	100	15	Normal
TM42	Facade	Normal	Physical	70	100	20	Normal
TM44	Rest	Psychic	Status	—	—	10	Self
TM45	Attract	Normal	Status	—	100	15	Normal
TM48	Round	Normal	Special	60	100	15	Normal
TM49	Echoed Voice	Normal	Special	40	100	15	Normal
TM50	Overheat	Fire	Special	130	90	5	Normal
TM52	Focus Blast	Fighting	Special	120	70	5	Normal
TM56	Fling	Dark	Physical	—	100	10	Normal
TM59	Incinerate	Fire	Special	60	100	15	Many Others
TM67	Retaliate	Normal	Physical	70	100	5	Normal
TM68	Giga Impact	Normal	Physical	150	90	5	Normal

No.	Name	Type	Kind	Pow.	Acc.	PP	Range
TM78	Bulldoze	Ground	Physical	60	100	20	Adjacent
TM80	Rock Slide	Rock	Physical	75	90	10	Many Others
TM87	Swagger	Normal	Status	—	90	15	Normal
TM88	Sleep Talk	Normal	Status	—	—	10	Self
TM90	Substitute	Normal	Status	—	—	10	Self
TM94	Rock Smash	Fighting	Physical	40	100	15	Normal
TM98	Power-Up Punch	Fighting	Physical	40	100	20	Normal
TM100	Confide	Normal	Status	—	—	20	Normal
HM03	Surf	Water	Special	90	100	15	Adjacent
HM04	Strength	Normal	Physical	80	100	15	Normal

● MOVES TAUGHT BY PEOPLE

Name	Type	Kind	Pow.	Acc.	PP	Range

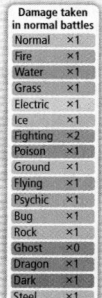

AFTER THE HALL OF FAME

CENTRAL KALOS

142

Exploud

COASTAL KALOS

MOUNTAIN KALOS

ADVENTURE DATA

AFTER THE HALL OF FAME

CENTRAL KALOS
143
Meditite

COASTAL KALOS

MOUNTAIN KALOS

ADVENTURE DATA

Central Kalos — 143

Meditate Pokémon
☑ **Meditite**

HEIGHT: 2'00" WEIGHT: 24.7 lbs.
GENDER: ♂/♀

TYPE Fighting | Psychic

ABILITY
Pure Power

HIDDEN ABILITY
Telepathy

STAT GROWTH RATES
HP	■■
Attack	■■
Defense	■■■
Sp. Atk	■■
Sp. Def	■■
Speed	■■■

EGG GROUP
Human-Like

X It always trains deep in mountains. It levitates when it heightens its spiritual power through meditation.

Y It eats just one berry a day. By enduring hunger, its spirit is tempered and made sharper.

EVOLUTION

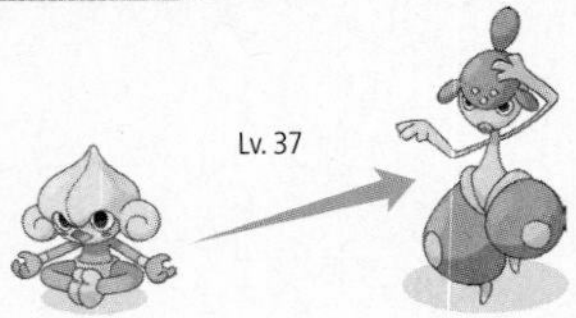

Meditite → Lv. 37 → Medicham

ITEMS SOMETIMES HELD BY WILD POKÉMON
None

Can be used in
Inverse Battle
—
Battle Chateau
Battle Institute
Battle Maison
Random Matchup

Damage taken in normal battles		Damage taken in Inverse Battles	
Normal	×1	Normal	×1
Fire	×1	Fire	×1
Water	×1	Water	×1
Grass	×1	Grass	×1
Electric	×1	Electric	×1
Ice	×1	Ice	×1
Fighting	×0.5	Fighting	×2
Poison	×1	Poison	×1
Ground	×1	Ground	×1
Flying	×2	Flying	×0.5
Psychic	×1	Psychic	×1
Bug	×1	Bug	×1
Rock	×0.5	Rock	×2
Ghost	×2	Ghost	×0.5
Dragon	×1	Dragon	×1
Dark	×1	Dark	×1
Steel	×1	Steel	×1
Fairy	×2	Fairy	×0.5

How to obtain for your Central Kalos Pokédex

X Catch in the Connecting Cave.

Y Catch in the Connecting Cave.

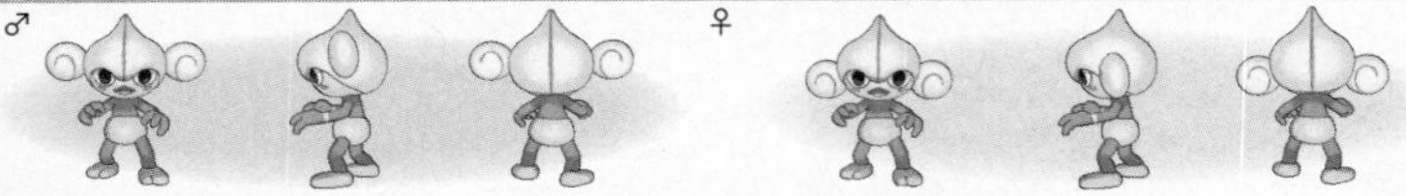

The protuberances on the male's head are located higher. The protuberances on the female's head are located lower.

● LEVEL-UP MOVES

Lv.	Name	Type	Kind	Pow.	Acc.	PP	Range
1	Bide	Normal	Physical	—	—	10	Self
4	Meditate	Psychic	Status	—	—	40	Self
8	Confusion	Psychic	Special	50	100	25	Normal
11	Detect	Fighting	Status	—	—	5	Self
15	Hidden Power	Normal	Special	60	100	15	Normal
18	Mind Reader	Normal	Status	—	—	5	Normal
22	Feint	Normal	Physical	30	100	10	Normal
25	Calm Mind	Psychic	Status	—	—	20	Self
29	Force Palm	Fighting	Physical	60	100	10	Normal
32	High Jump Kick	Fighting	Physical	130	90	10	Normal
36	Psych Up	Normal	Status	—	—	10	Normal
39	Acupressure	Normal	Status	—	—	30	Self/Ally
43	Power Trick	Psychic	Status	—	—	10	Self
46	Reversal	Fighting	Physical	—	100	15	Normal
50	Recover	Normal	Status	—	—	10	Self

● TM & HM MOVES

No.	Name	Type	Kind	Pow.	Acc.	PP	Range
TM03	Psyshock	Psychic	Special	80	100	10	Normal
TM04	Calm Mind	Psychic	Status	—	—	20	Self
TM06	Toxic	Poison	Status	—	90	10	Normal
TM08	Bulk Up	Fighting	Status	—	—	20	Self
TM10	Hidden Power	Normal	Special	60	100	15	Normal
TM11	Sunny Day	Fire	Status	—	—	5	Both Sides
TM16	Light Screen	Psychic	Status	—	—	30	Your Side
TM17	Protect	Normal	Status	—	—	10	Self
TM18	Rain Dance	Water	Status	—	—	5	Both Sides
TM21	Frustration	Normal	Physical	—	100	20	Normal
TM27	Return	Normal	Physical	—	100	20	Normal
TM29	Psychic	Psychic	Special	90	100	10	Normal
TM30	Shadow Ball	Ghost	Special	80	100	15	Normal
TM31	Brick Break	Fighting	Physical	75	100	15	Normal
TM32	Double Team	Normal	Status	—	—	15	Self
TM33	Reflect	Psychic	Status	—	—	20	Your Side
TM39	Rock Tomb	Rock	Physical	60	95	15	Normal
TM42	Facade	Normal	Physical	70	100	20	Normal
TM44	Rest	Psychic	Status	—	—	10	Self
TM45	Attract	Normal	Status	—	100	15	Normal
TM47	Low Sweep	Fighting	Physical	65	100	20	Normal
TM48	Round	Normal	Special	60	100	15	Normal
TM52	Focus Blast	Fighting	Special	120	70	5	Normal
TM56	Fling	Dark	Physical	—	100	10	Normal
TM67	Retaliate	Normal	Physical	70	100	5	Normal
TM70	Flash	Normal	Status	—	100	20	Normal
TM77	Psych Up	Normal	Status	—	—	10	Normal
TM80	Rock Slide	Rock	Physical	75	90	10	Many Others
TM84	Poison Jab	Poison	Physical	80	100	20	Normal
TM85	Dream Eater	Psychic	Special	100	100	15	Normal
TM86	Grass Knot	Grass	Special	—	100	20	Normal
TM87	Swagger	Normal	Status	—	90	15	Normal
TM88	Sleep Talk	Normal	Status	—	—	10	Self

No.	Name	Type	Kind	Pow.	Acc.	PP	Range
TM90	Substitute	Normal	Status	—	—	10	Self
TM94	Rock Smash	Fighting	Physical	40	100	15	Normal
TM98	Power-Up Punch	Fighting	Physical	40	100	20	Normal
TM100	Confide	Normal	Status	—	—	20	Normal
HM04	Strength	Normal	Physical	80	100	15	Normal

● MOVES TAUGHT BY PEOPLE

Name	Type	Kind	Pow.	Acc.	PP	Range

● EGG MOVES

Name	Type	Kind	Pow.	Acc.	PP	Range
Fire Punch	Fire	Physical	75	100	15	Normal
Thunder Punch	Electric	Physical	75	100	15	Normal
Ice Punch	Ice	Physical	75	100	15	Normal
Foresight	Normal	Status	—	—	40	Normal
Fake Out	Normal	Physical	40	100	10	Normal
Baton Pass	Normal	Status	—	—	40	Self
Dynamic Punch	Fighting	Physical	100	50	5	Normal
Power Swap	Psychic	Status	—	—	10	Normal
Guard Swap	Psychic	Status	—	—	10	Normal
Psycho Cut	Psychic	Physical	70	100	20	Normal
Bullet Punch	Steel	Physical	40	100	30	Normal
Drain Punch	Fighting	Physical	75	100	10	Normal
Secret Power	Normal	Physical	70	100	20	Normal
Quick Guard	Fighting	Status	—	—	15	Your Side

Central Kalos
Meditate Pokémon
✔ Medicham

144

HEIGHT: 4'03" WEIGHT: 69.4 lbs.
GENDER: ♂/♀

TYPE	Fighting	Psychic

ABILITY
Pure Power

HIDDEN ABILITY
Telepathy

STAT GROWTH RATES
HP	■■■
Attack	■■■
Defense	■■■
Sp. Atk	■■■
Sp. Def	■■■
Speed	■■■■

EGG GROUP
Human-Like

EVOLUTION

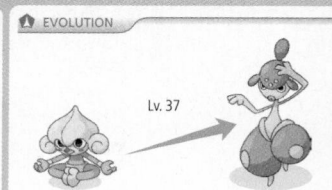

Meditite — Lv. 37 → Medicham

ITEMS SOMETIMES HELD BY WILD POKÉMON
None

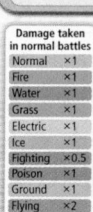
It elegantly avoids attacks with dance-like steps, then launches a devastating blow in the same motion.

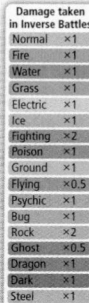
Through yoga training, it gained the psychic power to predict its foe's next move.

Damage taken in normal battles		Damage taken in Inverse Battles	
Normal	×1	Normal	×1
Fire	×1	Fire	×1
Water	×1	Water	×1
Grass	×1	Grass	×1
Electric	×1	Electric	×1
Ice	×1	Ice	×1
Fighting	×0.5	Fighting	×2
Poison	×1	Poison	×1
Ground	×1	Ground	×1
Flying	×2	Flying	×0.5
Psychic	×1	Psychic	×1
Bug	×1	Bug	×1
Rock	×0.5	Rock	×2
Ghost	×2	Ghost	×0.5
Dragon	×1	Dragon	×1
Dark	×1	Dark	×1
Steel	×1	Steel	×1
Fairy	×2	Fairy	×0.5

Can be used in
Inverse Battle

Battle Chateau
Battle Institute
Battle Maison
Random Matchup

How to obtain for your Central Kalos Pokédex

Level up Meditite to Lv. 37.	Level up Meditite to Lv. 37.
X	Y

♂ ♀

The male has a larger protuberance on top of its head than the female.

● LEVEL-UP MOVES

Lv.	Name	Type	Kind	Pow.	Acc.	PP	Range
1	Zen Headbutt	Psychic	Physical	80	90	15	Normal
1	Fire Punch	Fire	Physical	75	100	15	Normal
1	Thunder Punch	Electric	Physical	75	100	15	Normal
1	Ice Punch	Ice	Physical	75	100	15	Normal
1	Bide	Normal	Physical	—	—	10	Self
1	Meditate	Psychic	Status	—	—	40	Self
1	Confusion	Psychic	Special	50	100	25	Normal
1	Detect	Fighting	Status	—	—	5	Self
4	Meditate	Psychic	Status	—	—	40	Self
8	Confusion	Psychic	Special	50	100	25	Normal
11	Detect	Fighting	Status	—	—	5	Self
15	Hidden Power	Normal	Special	60	100	15	Normal
18	Mind Reader	Normal	Status	—	—	5	Normal
22	Feint	Normal	Physical	30	100	10	Normal
25	Calm Mind	Psychic	Status	—	—	20	Self
29	Force Palm	Fighting	Physical	60	100	10	Normal
32	High Jump Kick	Fighting	Physical	130	90	10	Normal
36	Psych Up	Normal	Status	—	—	10	Normal
42	Acupressure	Normal	Status	—	—	30	Self/Ally
49	Power Trick	Psychic	Status	—	—	10	Self
55	Reversal	Fighting	Physical	—	100	15	Normal
62	Recover	Normal	Status	—	—	10	Self

● TM & HM MOVES

No.	Name	Type	Kind	Pow.	Acc.	PP	Range
TM03	Psyshock	Psychic	Special	80	100	10	Normal
TM04	Calm Mind	Psychic	Status	—	—	20	Self
TM06	Toxic	Poison	Status	—	90	10	Normal
TM08	Bulk Up	Fighting	Status	—	—	20	Self
TM10	Hidden Power	Normal	Special	60	100	15	Normal
TM11	Sunny Day	Fire	Status	—	—	5	Both Sides
TM15	Hyper Beam	Normal	Special	150	90	5	Normal
TM16	Light Screen	Psychic	Status	—	—	30	Your Side
TM17	Protect	Normal	Status	—	—	10	Self
TM18	Rain Dance	Water	Status	—	—	5	Both Sides
TM21	Frustration	Normal	Physical	—	100	20	Normal
TM27	Return	Normal	Physical	—	100	20	Normal
TM29	Psychic	Psychic	Special	90	100	10	Normal
TM30	Shadow Ball	Ghost	Special	80	100	15	Normal
TM31	Brick Break	Fighting	Physical	75	100	15	Normal
TM32	Double Team	Normal	Status	—	—	15	Self
TM33	Reflect	Psychic	Status	—	—	20	Your Side
TM39	Rock Tomb	Rock	Physical	60	95	15	Normal
TM42	Facade	Normal	Physical	70	100	20	Normal
TM44	Rest	Psychic	Status	—	—	10	Self
TM45	Attract	Normal	Status	—	100	15	Normal
TM46	Thief	Dark	Physical	60	100	25	Normal
TM47	Low Sweep	Fighting	Physical	65	100	20	Normal
TM48	Round	Normal	Special	60	100	15	Normal
TM52	Focus Blast	Fighting	Special	120	70	5	Normal
TM53	Energy Ball	Grass	Special	90	100	10	Normal
TM56	Fling	Dark	Physical	—	100	10	Normal
TM67	Retaliate	Normal	Physical	70	100	5	Normal
TM68	Giga Impact	Normal	Physical	150	90	5	Normal
TM70	Flash	Normal	Status	—	100	20	Normal
TM77	Psych Up	Normal	Status	—	—	10	Normal
TM80	Rock Slide	Rock	Physical	75	90	10	Many Others
TM84	Poison Jab	Poison	Physical	80	100	20	Normal
TM85	Dream Eater	Psychic	Special	100	100	15	Normal
TM86	Grass Knot	Grass	Special	—	100	20	Normal
TM87	Swagger	Normal	Status	—	90	15	Normal
TM88	Sleep Talk	Normal	Status	—	—	10	Self
TM90	Substitute	Normal	Status	—	—	10	Self
TM94	Rock Smash	Fighting	Physical	40	100	15	Normal
TM98	Power-Up Punch	Fighting	Physical	40	100	20	Normal
TM100	Confide	Normal	Status	—	—	20	Normal
HM04	Strength	Normal	Physical	80	100	15	Normal

● MOVES TAUGHT BY PEOPLE

Name	Type	Kind	Pow.	Acc.	PP	Range

AFTER THE HALL OF FAME

CENTRAL KALOS

144 Medicham

COASTAL KALOS

MOUNTAIN KALOS

ADVENTURE DATA

Mega Evolution

Meditate Pokémon

☑ **Mega Medicham**

TYPE	**Fighting** **Psychic**

ABILITY
Pure Power

STAT GROWTH RATES

HP	▪▪▪
Attack	▪▪▪▪▪
Defense	▪▪▪▪
Sp. Atk	▪▪▪
Sp. Def	▪▪▪▪
Speed	▪▪▪▪▪

MEGA STONE REQUIRED

Medichamite
Obtain in Laverre City between 8 P.M. and 8:59 P.M., after entering the Hall of Fame and speaking with Professor Sycamore in Anistar City.

HEIGHT: 4'03"   WEIGHT: 69.4 lbs.   GENDER: ♂ / ♀

AFTER THE HALL OF FAME

CENTRAL KALOS

Mega Medicham

COASTAL KALOS

MOUNTAIN KALOS

ADVENTURE DATA

Damage taken in normal battles	
Normal	×1
Fire	×1
Water	×1
Grass	×1
Electric	×1
Ice	×1
Fighting	×0.5
Poison	×1
Ground	×1
Flying	×2
Psychic	×1
Bug	×1
Rock	×0.5
Ghost	×2
Dragon	×1
Dark	×1
Steel	×1
Fairy	×2

Damage taken in Inverse Battles	
Normal	×1
Fire	×1
Water	×1
Grass	×1
Electric	×1
Ice	×1
Fighting	×2
Poison	×1
Ground	×1
Flying	×0.5
Psychic	×1
Bug	×1
Rock	×2
Ghost	×0.5
Dragon	×1
Dark	×1
Steel	×1
Fairy	×0.5

Same form for ♂ / ♀

Can be used in	
Inverse Battle	Battle Institute
—	Battle Maison
Battle Chateau	Random Matchup

AFTER THE HALL OF FAME

CENTRAL KALOS

145 | Zubat

COASTAL KALOS

MOUNTAIN KALOS

ADVENTURE DATA

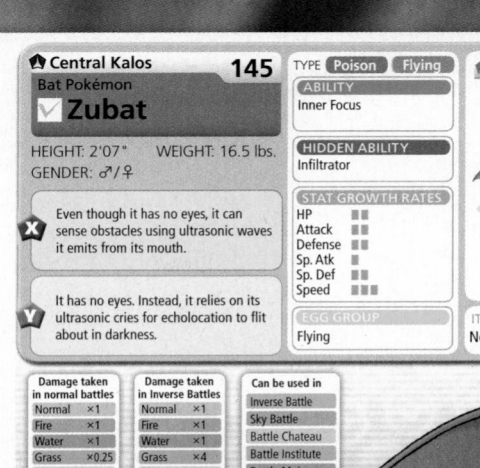

Central Kalos — 145

Bat Pokémon

☑ **Zubat**

HEIGHT: 2'07" WEIGHT: 16.5 lbs.
GENDER: ♂ / ♀

X Even though it has no eyes, it can sense obstacles using ultrasonic waves it emits from its mouth.

Y It has no eyes. Instead, it relies on its ultrasonic cries for echolocation to flit about in darkness.

TYPE Poison Flying

ABILITY
Inner Focus

HIDDEN ABILITY
Infiltrator

STAT GROWTH RATES
HP ■■
Attack ■■
Defense ■■
Sp. Atk ■
Sp. Def ■■
Speed ■■■

EGG GROUP
Flying

EVOLUTION

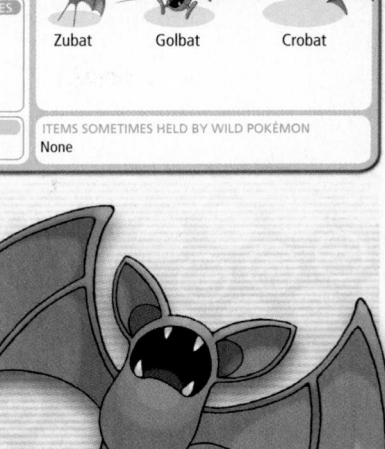

Lv. 22 — Level up with high friendship

Zubat → Golbat → Crobat

ITEMS SOMETIMES HELD BY WILD POKÉMON
None

Damage taken in normal battles		Damage taken in Inverse Battles	
Normal	×1	Normal	×1
Fire	×1	Fire	×1
Water	×1	Water	×1
Grass	×0.25	Grass	×4
Electric	×2	Electric	×0.5
Ice	×2	Ice	×0.5
Fighting	×0.25	Fighting	×4
Poison	×0.5	Poison	×2
Ground	×0	Ground	×1
Flying	×1	Flying	×1
Psychic	×2	Psychic	×0.5
Bug	×0.25	Bug	×4
Rock	×2	Rock	×0.5
Ghost	×1	Ghost	×1
Dragon	×1	Dragon	×1
Dark	×1	Dark	×1
Steel	×1	Steel	×1
Fairy	×0.5	Fairy	×2

Can be used in
- Inverse Battle
- Sky Battle
- Battle Chateau
- Battle Institute
- Battle Maison
- Random Matchup

How to obtain for your Central Kalos Pokédex

❶ Catch in the Connecting Cave.
❷ Catch in a Horde Encounter in the Connecting Cave.

❶ Catch in the Connecting Cave.
❷ Catch in a Horde Encounter in the Connecting Cave.

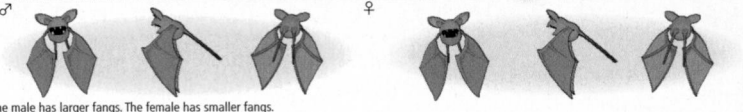

♂   ♀

The male has larger fangs. The female has smaller fangs.

● LEVEL-UP MOVES

Lv.	Name	Type	Kind	Pow.	Acc.	PP	Range
1	Leech Life	Bug	Physical	20	100	15	Normal
4	Supersonic	Normal	Status	—	55	20	Normal
8	Astonish	Ghost	Physical	30	100	15	Normal
12	Bite	Dark	Physical	60	100	25	Normal
15	Wing Attack	Flying	Physical	60	100	35	Normal
19	Confuse Ray	Ghost	Status	—	100	10	Normal
23	Swift	Normal	Special	60	—	20	Many Others
26	Air Cutter	Flying	Special	60	95	25	Many Others
30	Acrobatics	Flying	Physical	55	100	15	Normal
34	Mean Look	Normal	Status	—	—	5	Normal
37	Poison Fang	Poison	Physical	50	100	15	Normal
41	Haze	Ice	Status	—	—	30	Both Sides
45	Air Slash	Flying	Special	75	95	15	Normal

● TM & HM MOVES

No.	Name	Type	Kind	Pow.	Acc.	PP	Range
TM06	Toxic	Poison	Status	—	90	10	Normal
TM09	Venoshock	Poison	Special	65	100	10	Normal
TM10	Hidden Power	Normal	Special	60	100	15	Normal
TM11	Sunny Day	Fire	Status	—	—	5	Both Sides
TM12	Taunt	Dark	Status	—	100	20	Normal
TM17	Protect	Normal	Status	—	—	10	Self
TM18	Rain Dance	Water	Status	—	—	5	Both Sides
TM19	Roost	Flying	Status	—	—	10	Self
TM21	Frustration	Normal	Physical	—	100	20	Normal
TM27	Return	Normal	Physical	—	100	20	Normal
TM30	Shadow Ball	Ghost	Special	80	100	15	Normal
TM32	Double Team	Normal	Status	—	—	15	Self
TM36	Sludge Bomb	Poison	Special	90	100	10	Normal
TM40	Aerial Ace	Flying	Physical	60	—	20	Normal
TM41	Torment	Dark	Status	—	100	15	Normal
TM42	Facade	Normal	Physical	70	100	20	Normal
TM44	Rest	Psychic	Status	—	—	10	Self
TM45	Attract	Normal	Status	—	100	15	Normal
TM46	Thief	Dark	Physical	60	100	25	Normal
TM48	Round	Normal	Special	60	100	15	Normal
TM51	Steel Wing	Steel	Physical	70	90	25	Normal
TM62	Acrobatics	Flying	Physical	55	100	15	Normal
TM66	Payback	Dark	Physical	50	100	10	Normal
TM87	Swagger	Normal	Status	—	90	15	Normal
TM88	Sleep Talk	Normal	Status	—	—	10	Self
TM89	U-turn	Bug	Physical	70	100	20	Normal
TM90	Substitute	Normal	Status	—	—	10	Self
TM100	Confide	Normal	Status	—	—	20	Normal
HM02	Fly	Flying	Physical	90	95	15	Normal

● MOVES TAUGHT BY PEOPLE

Name	Type	Kind	Pow.	Acc.	PP	Range

● EGG MOVES

Name	Type	Kind	Pow.	Acc.	PP	Range
Quick Attack	Normal	Physical	40	100	30	Normal
Pursuit	Dark	Physical	40	100	20	Normal
Feint Attack	Dark	Physical	60	—	20	Normal
Gust	Flying	Special	40	100	35	Normal
Whirlwind	Normal	Status	—	—	20	Normal
Curse	Ghost	Status	—	—	10	Varies
Nasty Plot	Dark	Status	—	—	20	Self
Hypnosis	Psychic	Status	—	60	20	Normal
Zen Headbutt	Psychic	Physical	80	90	15	Normal
Brave Bird	Flying	Physical	120	100	15	Normal
Giga Drain	Grass	Special	75	100	10	Normal
Steel Wing	Steel	Physical	70	90	25	Normal
Defog	Flying	Status	—	—	15	Normal
Venom Drench	Poison	Status	—	100	20	Many Others

AFTER THE HALL OF FAME

CENTRAL KALOS

146

Golbat

COASTAL KALOS

MOUNTAIN KALOS

ADVENTURE DATA

🏠 Central Kalos   **146**
Bat Pokémon
☑ **Golbat**

HEIGHT: 5'03"   WEIGHT: 121.3 lbs.
GENDER: ♂/♀

TYPE Poison   Flying

ABILITY
Inner Focus

HIDDEN ABILITY
Infiltrator

STAT GROWTH RATES
HP	▪▪▪
Attack	▪▪▪▪
Defense	▪▪▪
Sp. Atk	▪▪▪
Sp. Def	▪▪▪
Speed	▪▪▪▪▪

EGG GROUP
Flying

X Once it bites, it will not stop draining energy from the victim even if it gets too heavy to fly.

Y Once it starts sucking blood, it does not stop until it is full. It flies at night in search of prey.

EVOLUTION

Zubat → Lv. 22 → Golbat → Level up with high friendship → Crobat

ITEMS SOMETIMES HELD BY WILD POKÉMON
None

Damage taken in normal battles		Damage taken in Inverse Battles	
Normal	×1	Normal	×1
Fire	×1	Fire	×1
Water	×1	Water	×1
Grass	×0.25	Grass	×4
Electric	×2	Electric	×0.5
Ice	×2	Ice	×0.5
Fighting	×0.25	Fighting	×4
Poison	×0.5	Poison	×2
Ground	×0	Ground	×1
Flying	×1	Flying	×1
Psychic	×2	Psychic	×0.5
Bug	×0.25	Bug	×4
Rock	×2	Rock	×0.5
Ghost	×1	Ghost	×1
Dragon	×1	Dragon	×1
Dark	×1	Dark	×1
Steel	×1	Steel	×1
Fairy	×0.5	Fairy	×2

Can be used in
Inverse Battle
Sky Battle
Battle Chateau
Battle Institute
Battle Maison
Random Matchup

How to obtain for your Central Kalos Pokédex

Level up Zubat to Lv. 22.   Level up Zubat to Lv. 22.

X   Y

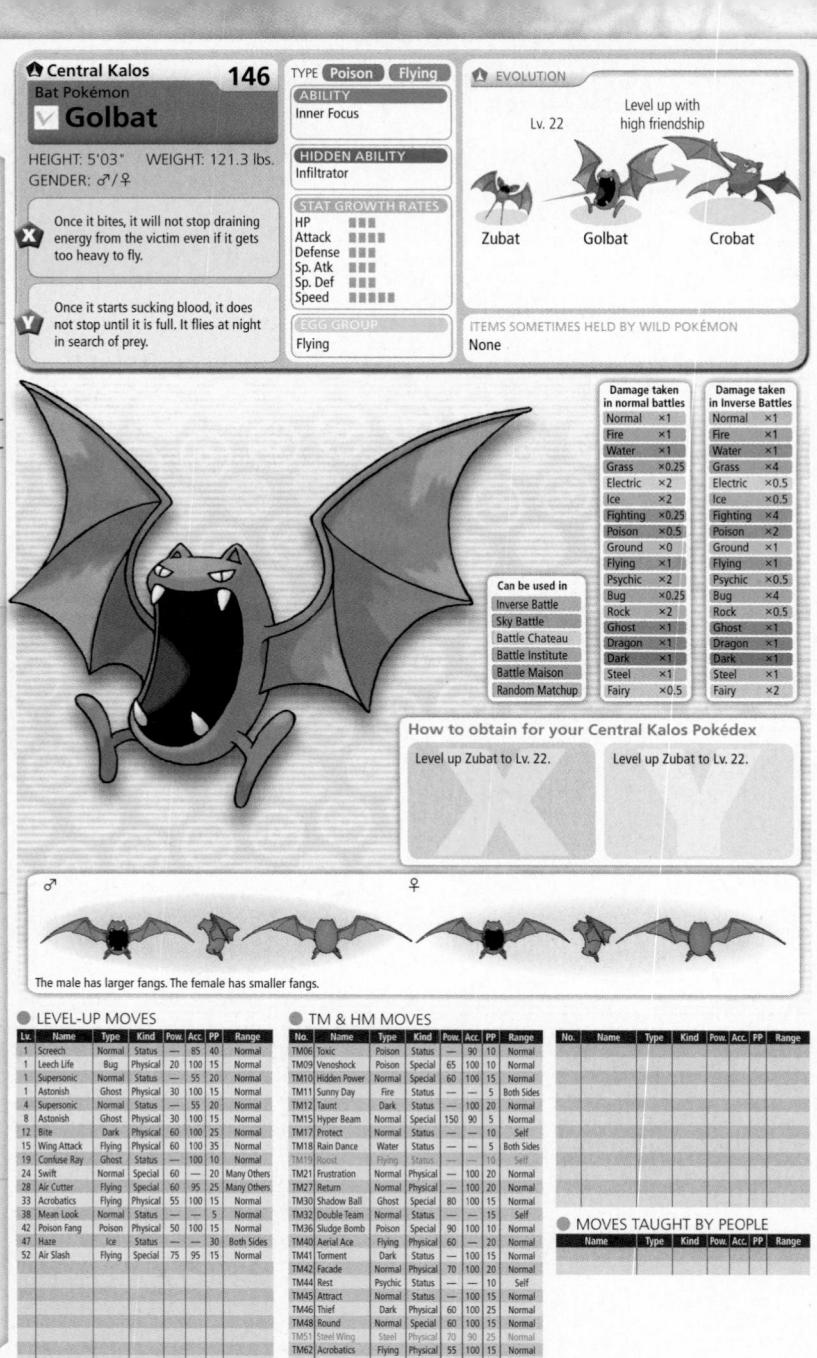

♂   ♀

The male has larger fangs. The female has smaller fangs.

● **LEVEL-UP MOVES**

Lv.	Name	Type	Kind	Pow.	Acc.	PP	Range
1	Screech	Normal	Status	—	85	40	Normal
1	Leech Life	Bug	Physical	20	100	15	Normal
1	Supersonic	Normal	Status	—	55	20	Normal
1	Astonish	Ghost	Physical	30	100	15	Normal
4	Supersonic	Normal	Status	—	55	20	Normal
8	Astonish	Ghost	Physical	30	100	15	Normal
12	Bite	Dark	Physical	60	100	25	Normal
15	Wing Attack	Flying	Physical	60	100	35	Normal
19	Confuse Ray	Ghost	Status	—	100	10	Normal
24	Swift	Normal	Special	60	—	20	Many Others
28	Air Cutter	Flying	Special	60	95	25	Many Others
33	Acrobatics	Flying	Physical	55	100	15	Normal
38	Mean Look	Normal	Status	—	—	5	Normal
42	Poison Fang	Poison	Physical	50	100	15	Normal
47	Haze	Ice	Status	—	—	30	Both Sides
52	Air Slash	Flying	Special	75	95	15	Normal

● **TM & HM MOVES**

No.	Name	Type	Kind	Pow.	Acc.	PP	Range
TM06	Toxic	Poison	Status	—	90	10	Normal
TM09	Venoshock	Poison	Special	65	100	10	Normal
TM10	Hidden Power	Normal	Special	60	100	15	Normal
TM11	Sunny Day	Fire	Status	—	—	5	Both Sides
TM12	Taunt	Dark	Status	—	100	20	Normal
TM15	Hyper Beam	Normal	Special	150	90	5	Normal
TM17	Protect	Normal	Status	—	—	10	Self
TM18	Rain Dance	Water	Status	—	—	5	Both Sides
TM19	Roost	Flying	Status	—	—	10	Self
TM21	Frustration	Normal	Physical	—	100	20	Normal
TM27	Return	Normal	Physical	—	100	20	Normal
TM30	Shadow Ball	Ghost	Special	80	100	15	Normal
TM32	Double Team	Normal	Status	—	—	15	Self
TM36	Sludge Bomb	Poison	Special	90	100	10	Normal
TM40	Aerial Ace	Flying	Physical	60	—	20	Normal
TM41	Torment	Dark	Status	—	100	15	Normal
TM42	Facade	Normal	Physical	70	100	20	Normal
TM44	Rest	Psychic	Status	—	—	10	Self
TM45	Attract	Normal	Status	—	100	15	Normal
TM46	Thief	Dark	Physical	60	100	25	Normal
TM48	Round	Normal	Special	60	100	15	Normal
TM51	Steel Wing	Steel	Physical	70	90	25	Normal
TM62	Acrobatics	Flying	Physical	55	100	15	Normal
TM66	Payback	Dark	Physical	50	100	10	Normal
TM68	Giga Impact	Normal	Physical	150	90	5	Normal
TM87	Swagger	Normal	Status	—	90	15	Normal
TM88	Sleep Talk	Normal	Status	—	—	10	Self
TM89	U-turn	Bug	Physical	70	100	20	Normal
TM90	Substitute	Normal	Status	—	—	10	Self
TM100	Confide	Normal	Status	—	—	20	Normal
HM02	Fly	Flying	Physical	90	95	15	Normal

● **MOVES TAUGHT BY PEOPLE**

Name	Type	Kind	Pow.	Acc.	PP	Range

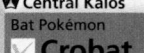 **Central Kalos** **147**

Bat Pokémon

☑ Crobat

HEIGHT: 5'11" WEIGHT: 165.3 lbs.
GENDER: ♂/♀

 It flies so silently through the dark on its four wings that it may not be noticed even when nearby.

 Having four wings allows it to fly more quickly and quietly so it can sneak up on prey without its noticing.

TYPE	Poison	Flying

ABILITY
Inner Focus

HIDDEN ABILITY
Infiltrator

STAT GROWTH RATES
HP	■■■
Attack	■■■
Defense	■■■■
Sp. Atk	■■■
Sp. Def	■■■
Speed	■■■■■■■

EGG GROUP
Flying

AFTER THE HALL OF FAME

CENTRAL KALOS

147 | Crobat

COASTAL K

MOUNTAIN KALOS

ADVENTURE DATA

EVOLUTION

	Lv. 22	Level up with high friendship
Zubat	Golbat	Crobat

ITEMS SOMETIMES HELD BY WILD POKÉMON
None

Damage taken in normal battles		Damage taken in Inverse Battles	
Normal	×1	Normal	×1
Fire	×1	Fire	×1
Water	×1	Water	×1
Grass	×0.25	Grass	×4
Electric	×2	Electric	×0.5
Ice	×2	Ice	×0.5
Fighting	×0.25	Fighting	×4
Poison	×0.5	Poison	×2
Ground	×0	Ground	×1
Flying	×1	Flying	×1
Psychic	×2	Psychic	×0.5
Bug	×0.25	Bug	×4
Rock	×2	Rock	×0.5
Ghost	×1	Ghost	×1
Dragon	×1	Dragon	×1
Dark	×1	Dark	×1
Steel	×1	Steel	×1
Fairy	×0.5	Fairy	×2

Can be used in	
Inverse Battle	Battle Institute
Sky Battle	Battle Maison
Battle Chateau	Random Matchup

Same form for ♂/♀

How to obtain for your Central Kalos Pokédex

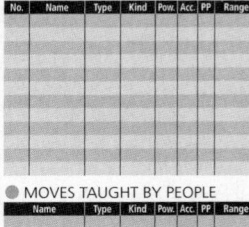

Level up Golbat with sufficiently high friendship.

Level up Golbat with sufficiently high friendship.

● LEVEL-UP MOVES

Lv.	Name	Type	Kind	Pow.	Acc.	PP	Range
1	Cross Poison	Poison	Physical	70	100	20	Normal
1	Screech	Normal	Status	—	85	40	Normal
1	Leech Life	Bug	Physical	20	100	15	Normal
1	Supersonic	Normal	Status	—	55	20	Normal
1	Astonish	Ghost	Physical	30	100	15	Normal
4	Supersonic	Normal	Status	—	55	20	Normal
8	Astonish	Ghost	Physical	30	100	15	Normal
12	Bite	Dark	Physical	60	100	25	Normal
15	Wing Attack	Flying	Physical	60	100	35	Normal
19	Confuse Ray	Ghost	Status	—	100	10	Normal
24	Swift	Normal	Special	60	—	20	Many Others
28	Air Cutter	Flying	Special	60	95	25	Many Others
33	Acrobatics	Flying	Physical	55	100	15	Normal
38	Mean Look	Normal	Status	—	—	5	Normal
42	Poison Fang	Poison	Physical	50	100	15	Normal
47	Haze	Ice	Status	—	—	30	Both Sides
52	Air Slash	Flying	Special	75	95	15	Normal

● TM & HM MOVES

No.	Name	Type	Kind	Pow.	Acc.	PP	Range
TM06	Toxic	Poison	Status	—	90	10	Normal
TM09	Venoshock	Poison	Special	65	100	10	Normal
TM10	Hidden Power	Normal	Special	60	100	15	Normal
TM11	Sunny Day	Fire	Status	—	—	5	Both Sides
TM12	Taunt	Dark	Status	—	100	20	Normal
TM15	Hyper Beam	Normal	Special	150	90	5	Normal
TM17	Protect	Normal	Status	—	—	10	Self
TM18	Rain Dance	Water	Status	—	—	5	Both Sides
TM19	Roost	Flying	Status	—	—	10	Self
TM21	Frustration	Normal	Physical	—	100	20	Normal
TM27	Return	Normal	Physical	—	100	20	Normal
TM30	Shadow Ball	Ghost	Special	80	100	15	Normal
TM32	Double Team	Normal	Status	—	—	15	Self
TM36	Sludge Bomb	Poison	Special	90	100	10	Normal
TM40	Aerial Ace	Flying	Physical	60	—	20	Normal
TM41	Torment	Dark	Status	—	100	15	Normal
TM42	Facade	Normal	Physical	70	100	20	Normal
TM44	Rest	Psychic	Status	—	—	10	Self
TM45	Attract	Normal	Status	—	100	15	Normal
TM46	Thief	Dark	Physical	60	100	25	Normal
TM48	Round	Normal	Special	60	100	15	Normal
TM51	Steel Wing	Steel	Physical	70	90	25	Normal
TM62	Acrobatics	Flying	Physical	55	100	15	Normal
TM66	Payback	Dark	Physical	50	100	10	Normal
TM68	Giga Impact	Normal	Physical	150	90	5	Normal
TM81	X-Scissor	Bug	Physical	80	100	15	Normal
TM87	Swagger	Normal	Status	—	90	15	Normal
TM88	Sleep Talk	Normal	Status	—	—	10	Self
TM89	U-turn	Bug	Physical	70	100	20	Normal
TM90	Substitute	Normal	Status	—	—	10	Self
TM97	Dark Pulse	Dark	Special	80	100	15	Normal
TM100	Confide	Normal	Status	—	—	20	Normal
HM02	Fly	Flying	Physical	90	95	15	Normal

● MOVES TAUGHT BY PEOPLE

Name	Type	Kind	Pow.	Acc.	PP	Range

AFTER THE HALL OF FAME

CENTRAL KALOS

148

Axew

COASTAL KALOS

MOUNTAIN KALOS

ADVENTURE DATA

⛰ Central Kalos 148

Tusk Pokémon

☑ **Axew**

HEIGHT: 2'00" WEIGHT: 39.7 lbs.
GENDER: ♂/♀

X They use their tusks to crush the berries they eat. Repeated regrowth makes their tusks strong and sharp.

Y They mark their territory by leaving gashes in trees with their tusks. If a tusk breaks, a new one grows in quickly.

TYPE Dragon

ABILITIES
Rivalry
Mold Breaker

HIDDEN ABILITY
Unnerve

STAT GROWTH RATES
HP	■■
Attack	■■■■
Defense	■■■
Sp. Atk	■
Sp. Def	■
Speed	■■■

EGG GROUPS
Monster, Dragon

↗ EVOLUTION

Lv. 38 → Lv. 48

Axew — Fraxure — Haxorus

ITEMS SOMETIMES HELD BY WILD POKÉMON
None

Can be used in	Damage taken in normal battles		Damage taken in Inverse Battles	
Inverse Battle	Normal	×1	Normal	×1
—	Fire	×0.5	Fire	×2
Battle Chateau	Water	×0.5	Water	×2
Battle Institute	Grass	×0.5	Grass	×2
Battle Maison	Electric	×0.5	Electric	×2
Random Matchup	Ice	×2	Ice	×0.5
	Fighting	×1	Fighting	×1
	Poison	×1	Poison	×1
	Ground	×1	Ground	×1
	Flying	×1	Flying	×1
	Psychic	×1	Psychic	×1
	Bug	×1	Bug	×1
	Rock	×1	Rock	×1
	Ghost	×1	Ghost	×1
	Dragon	×2	Dragon	×0.5
	Dark	×1	Dark	×1
	Steel	×1	Steel	×1
	Fairy	×2	Fairy	×0.5

How to obtain for your Central Kalos Pokédex

❶ Catch in the Connecting Cave.

❷ Catch in a Horde Encounter in the Connecting Cave.

❶ Catch in the Connecting Cave.

❷ Catch in a Horde Encounter in the Connecting Cave.

Same form for ♂ / ♀

● LEVEL-UP MOVES

Lv.	Name	Type	Kind	Pow.	Acc.	PP	Range
1	Scratch	Normal	Physical	40	100	35	Normal
4	Leer	Normal	Status	—	100	30	Many Others
7	Assurance	Dark	Physical	60	100	10	Normal
10	Dragon Rage	Dragon	Special	—	100	10	Normal
13	Dual Chop	Dragon	Physical	40	90	15	Normal
16	Scary Face	Normal	Status	—	100	10	Normal
20	Slash	Normal	Physical	70	100	20	Normal
24	False Swipe	Normal	Physical	40	100	40	Normal
28	Dragon Claw	Dragon	Physical	80	100	15	Normal
32	Dragon Dance	Dragon	Status	—	—	20	Self
36	Taunt	Dark	Status	—	100	20	Normal
41	Dragon Pulse	Dragon	Special	85	100	10	Normal
46	Swords Dance	Normal	Status	—	—	20	Self
50	Guillotine	Normal	Physical	—	30	5	Normal
56	Outrage	Dragon	Physical	120	100	10	1 Random
61	Giga Impact	Normal	Physical	150	90	5	Normal

● TM & HM MOVES

No.	Name	Type	Kind	Pow.	Acc.	PP	Range
TM01	Hone Claws	Dark	Status	—	—	15	Self
TM02	Dragon Claw	Dragon	Physical	80	100	15	Normal
TM05	Roar	Normal	Status	—	—	20	Normal
TM06	Toxic	Poison	Status	—	90	10	Normal
TM10	Hidden Power	Normal	Special	60	100	15	Normal
TM11	Sunny Day	Fire	Status	—	—	5	Both Sides
TM12	Taunt	Dark	Status	—	100	20	Normal
TM17	Protect	Normal	Status	—	—	10	Self
TM18	Rain Dance	Water	Status	—	—	5	Both Sides
TM21	Frustration	Normal	Physical	—	100	20	Normal
TM27	Return	Normal	Physical	—	100	20	Normal
TM28	Dig	Ground	Physical	80	100	10	Normal
TM32	Double Team	Normal	Status	—	—	15	Self
TM39	Rock Tomb	Rock	Physical	60	95	15	Normal
TM40	Aerial Ace	Flying	Physical	60	—	20	Normal
TM42	Facade	Normal	Physical	70	100	20	Normal
TM44	Rest	Psychic	Status	—	—	10	Self
TM45	Attract	Normal	Status	—	100	15	Normal
TM48	Round	Normal	Special	60	100	15	Normal
TM54	False Swipe	Normal	Physical	40	100	40	Normal
TM56	Fling	Dark	Physical	—	100	10	Normal
TM59	Incinerate	Fire	Special	60	100	15	Many Others
TM66	Payback	Dark	Physical	50	100	10	Normal
TM68	Giga Impact	Normal	Physical	150	90	5	Normal
TM75	Swords Dance	Normal	Status	—	—	20	Self
TM81	X-Scissor	Bug	Physical	80	100	15	Normal
TM84	Poison Jab	Poison	Physical	80	100	20	Normal
TM87	Swagger	Normal	Status	—	90	15	Normal
TM88	Sleep Talk	Normal	Status	—	—	10	Self
TM90	Substitute	Normal	Status	—	—	10	Self
TM94	Rock Smash	Fighting	Physical	40	100	15	Normal
TM100	Confide	Normal	Status	—	—	20	Normal
HM01	Cut	Normal	Physical	50	95	30	Normal

No.	Name	Type	Kind	Pow.	Acc.	PP	Range
HM04	Strength	Normal	Physical	80	100	15	Normal

● MOVES TAUGHT BY PEOPLE

Name	Type	Kind	Pow.	Acc.	PP	Range
Draco Meteor	Dragon	Special	130	90	5	Normal

● EGG MOVES

Name	Type	Kind	Pow.	Acc.	PP	Range
Counter	Fighting	Physical	—	100	20	Varies
Focus Energy	Normal	Status	—	—	30	Self
Reversal	Fighting	Physical	—	100	15	Normal
Endure	Normal	Status	—	—	10	Self
Razor Wind	Normal	Special	80	100	10	Many Others
Night Slash	Dark	Physical	70	100	15	Normal
Endeavor	Normal	Physical	—	100	5	Normal
Iron Tail	Steel	Physical	100	75	15	Normal
Dragon Pulse	Dragon	Special	85	100	10	Normal
Harden	Normal	Status	—	—	30	Self

AFTER THE HALL OF FAME

CENTRAL KALOS

149 Fraxure

COASTAL KALOS

MOUNTAIN KALOS

ADVENTURE DATA

Central Kalos 149

Axe Jaw Pokémon

Fraxure

HEIGHT: 3'03" WEIGHT: 79.4 lbs.
GENDER: ♂/♀

TYPE	Dragon

ABILITIES
Rivalry
Mold Breaker

HIDDEN ABILITY
Unnerve

STAT GROWTH RATES
HP ■■
Attack ■■■■■■
Defense ■■■
Sp. Atk ■■
Sp. Def ■■
Speed ■■■■

EGG GROUPS
Monster, Dragon

X Their tusks can shatter rocks. Territory battles between Fraxure can be intensely violent.

Y A broken tusk will not grow back, so it diligently sharpens its tusks on river rocks after the end of a battle.

EVOLUTION

Lv. 38   Lv. 48

Axew   Fraxure   Haxorus

ITEMS SOMETIMES HELD BY WILD POKÉMON
None

Damage taken in normal battles		Damage taken in Inverse Battles	
Normal	×1	Normal	×1
Fire	×0.5	Fire	×2
Water	×0.5	Water	×2
Grass	×0.5	Grass	×2
Electric	×0.5	Electric	×2
Ice	×2	Ice	×0.5
Fighting	×1	Fighting	×1
Poison	×1	Poison	×1
Ground	×1	Ground	×1
Flying	×1	Flying	×1
Psychic	×1	Psychic	×1
Bug	×1	Bug	×1
Rock	×1	Rock	×1
Ghost	×1	Ghost	×1
Dragon	×2	Dragon	×0.5
Dark	×1	Dark	×1
Steel	×1	Steel	×1
Fairy	×2	Fairy	×0.5

Can be used in
Inverse Battle

Battle Chateau
Battle Institute
Battle Maison
Random Matchup

How to obtain for your Central Kalos Pokédex

Level up Axew to Lv. 38.   Level up Axew to Lv. 38.

Same form for ♂/♀

● LEVEL-UP MOVES

Lv.	Name	Type	Kind	Pow.	Acc.	PP	Range
1	Scratch	Normal	Physical	40	100	35	Normal
1	Leer	Normal	Status	—	100	30	Many Others
1	Assurance	Dark	Physical	60	100	10	Normal
1	Dragon Rage	Dragon	Special	—	100	10	Normal
4	Leer	Normal	Status	—	100	30	Many Others
7	Assurance	Dark	Physical	60	100	10	Normal
10	Dragon Rage	Dragon	Special	—	100	10	Normal
13	Dual Chop	Dragon	Physical	40	90	15	Normal
16	Scary Face	Normal	Status	—	100	10	Normal
20	Slash	Normal	Physical	70	100	20	Normal
24	False Swipe	Normal	Physical	40	100	40	Normal
28	Dragon Claw	Dragon	Physical	80	100	15	Normal
32	Dragon Dance	Dragon	Status	—	—	20	Self
36	Taunt	Dark	Status	—	100	20	Normal
42	Dragon Pulse	Dragon	Special	85	100	10	Normal
48	Swords Dance	Normal	Status	—	—	20	Self
54	Guillotine	Normal	Physical	—	30	5	Normal
60	Outrage	Dragon	Physical	120	100	10	1 Random
66	Giga Impact	Normal	Physical	150	90	5	Normal

● TM & HM MOVES

No.	Name	Type	Kind	Pow.	Acc.	PP	Range
TM01	Hone Claws	Dark	Status	—	—	15	Self
TM02	Dragon Claw	Dragon	Physical	80	100	15	Normal
TM05	Roar	Normal	Status	—	—	20	Normal
TM06	Toxic	Poison	Status	—	90	10	Normal
TM10	Hidden Power	Normal	Special	60	100	15	Normal
TM11	Sunny Day	Fire	Status	—	—	5	Both Sides
TM12	Taunt	Dark	Status	—	100	20	Normal
TM17	Protect	Normal	Status	—	—	10	Self
TM18	Rain Dance	Water	Status	—	—	5	Both Sides
TM21	Frustration	Normal	Physical	—	100	20	Normal
TM27	Return	Normal	Physical	—	100	20	Normal
TM28	Dig	Ground	Physical	80	100	10	Normal
TM32	Double Team	Normal	Status	—	—	15	Self
TM39	Rock Tomb	Rock	Physical	60	95	15	Normal
TM40	Aerial Ace	Flying	Physical	60	—	20	Normal
TM42	Facade	Normal	Physical	70	100	20	Normal
TM44	Rest	Psychic	Status	—	—	10	Self
TM45	Attract	Normal	Status	—	100	15	Normal
TM48	Round	Normal	Special	60	100	15	Normal
TM54	False Swipe	Normal	Physical	40	100	40	Normal
TM56	Fling	Dark	Physical	—	100	10	Normal
TM59	Incinerate	Fire	Special	60	100	15	Many Others
TM65	Shadow Claw	Ghost	Physical	70	100	15	Normal
TM66	Payback	Dark	Physical	50	100	10	Normal
TM68	Giga Impact	Normal	Physical	150	90	5	Normal
TM75	Swords Dance	Normal	Status	—	—	20	Self
TM81	X-Scissor	Bug	Physical	80	100	15	Normal
TM82	Dragon Tail	Dragon	Physical	60	90	10	Normal
TM84	Poison Jab	Poison	Physical	80	100	20	Normal
TM87	Swagger	Normal	Status	—	90	15	Normal
TM88	Sleep Talk	Normal	Status	—	—	10	Self
TM90	Substitute	Normal	Status	—	—	10	Self
TM94	Rock Smash	Fighting	Physical	40	100	15	Normal
TM100	Confide	Normal	Status	—	—	20	Normal
HM01	Cut	Normal	Physical	50	95	30	Normal
HM04	Strength	Normal	Physical	80	100	15	Normal

● MOVES TAUGHT BY PEOPLE

Name	Type	Kind	Pow.	Acc.	PP	Range
Draco Meteor	Dragon	Special	130	90	5	Normal

AFTER THE HALL OF FAME

CENTRAL KALOS

150

Haxorus

COASTAL KALOS

MOUNTAIN KALOS

ADVENTURE DATA

🏠 Central Kalos — 150
Axe Jaw Pokémon
☑ **Haxorus**

HEIGHT: 5'11" WEIGHT: 232.6 lbs.
GENDER: ♂ / ♀

X They are kind but can be relentless when defending territory. They challenge foes with tusks that can cut steel.

Y Their sturdy tusks will stay sharp even if used to cut steel beams. These Pokémon are covered in hard armor.

TYPE Dragon

ABILITIES
Rivalry
Mold Breaker

HIDDEN ABILITY
Unnerve

STAT GROWTH RATES
HP	■■■
Attack	■■■■■■■
Defense	■■■■
Sp. Atk	■■■
Sp. Def	■■■
Speed	■■■■■

EGG GROUPS
Monster, Dragon

⬆ EVOLUTION

Axew — Lv. 38 → Fraxure — Lv. 48 → Haxorus

ITEMS SOMETIMES HELD BY WILD POKÉMON
None

Can be used in
- Inverse Battle
- —
- Battle Chateau
- Battle Institute
- Battle Maison
- Random Matchup

Damage taken in normal battles		Damage taken in Inverse Battles	
Normal	×1	Normal	×1
Fire	×0.5	Fire	×2
Water	×0.5	Water	×2
Grass	×0.5	Grass	×2
Electric	×0.5	Electric	×2
Ice	×2	Ice	×0.5
Fighting	×1	Fighting	×1
Poison	×1	Poison	×1
Ground	×1	Ground	×1
Flying	×1	Flying	×1
Psychic	×1	Psychic	×1
Bug	×1	Bug	×1
Rock	×1	Rock	×1
Ghost	×1	Ghost	×1
Dragon	×2	Dragon	×0.5
Dark	×1	Dark	×1
Steel	×1	Steel	×1
Fairy	×2	Fairy	×0.5

How to obtain for your Central Kalos Pokédex

X	Y
Level up Fraxure to Lv. 48.	Level up Fraxure to Lv. 48.

Same form for ♂ / ♀

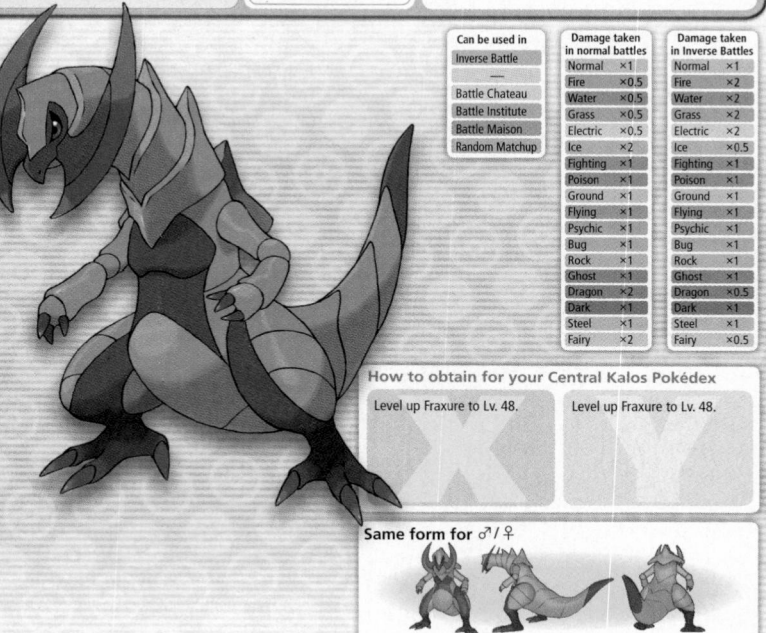

● LEVEL-UP MOVES

Lv.	Name	Type	Kind	Pow.	Acc.	PP	Range
1	Outrage	Dragon	Physical	120	100	10	1 Random
1	Scratch	Normal	Physical	40	100	35	Normal
1	Leer	Normal	Status	—	100	30	Many Others
1	Assurance	Dark	Physical	60	100	10	Normal
1	Dragon Rage	Dragon	Special	—	100	10	Normal
6	Leer	Normal	Status	—	100	30	Many Others
7	Assurance	Dark	Physical	60	100	10	Normal
10	Dragon Rage	Dragon	Special	—	100	10	Normal
13	Dual Chop	Dragon	Physical	40	90	15	Normal
16	Scary Face	Normal	Status	—	100	10	Normal
20	Slash	Normal	Physical	70	100	20	Normal
24	False Swipe	Normal	Physical	40	100	40	Normal
28	Dragon Claw	Dragon	Physical	80	100	15	Normal
32	Dragon Dance	Dragon	Status	—	—	20	Self
36	Taunt	Dark	Status	—	100	20	Normal
42	Dragon Pulse	Dragon	Special	85	100	10	Normal
50	Swords Dance	Normal	Status	—	—	20	Self
58	Guillotine	Normal	Physical	—	30	5	Normal
66	Outrage	Dragon	Physical	120	100	10	1 Random
74	Giga Impact	Normal	Physical	150	90	5	Normal

■ TM & HM MOVES

No.	Name	Type	Kind	Pow.	Acc.	PP	Range
TM01	Hone Claws	Dark	Status	—	—	15	Self
TM02	Dragon Claw	Dragon	Physical	80	100	15	Normal
TM05	Roar	Normal	Status	—	—	20	Normal
TM06	Toxic	Poison	Status	—	90	10	Normal
TM10	Hidden Power	Normal	Special	60	100	15	Normal
TM11	Sunny Day	Fire	Status	—	—	5	Both Sides
TM12	Taunt	Dark	Status	—	100	20	Normal
TM15	Hyper Beam	Normal	Special	150	90	5	Normal
TM17	Protect	Normal	Status	—	—	10	Self
TM18	Rain Dance	Water	Status	—	—	5	Both Sides
TM21	Frustration	Normal	Physical	—	100	20	Normal
TM26	Earthquake	Ground	Physical	100	100	10	Adjacent
TM27	Return	Normal	Physical	—	100	20	Normal
TM28	Dig	Ground	Physical	80	100	10	Normal
TM31	Brick Break	Fighting	Physical	75	100	15	Normal
TM32	Double Team	Normal	Status	—	—	15	Self
TM39	Rock Tomb	Rock	Physical	60	95	15	Normal
TM40	Aerial Ace	Flying	Physical	60	—	20	Normal
TM42	Facade	Normal	Physical	70	100	20	Normal
TM44	Rest	Psychic	Status	—	—	10	Self
TM45	Attract	Normal	Status	—	100	15	Normal
TM48	Round	Normal	Special	60	100	15	Normal
TM52	Focus Blast	Fighting	Special	120	70	5	Normal
TM54	False Swipe	Normal	Physical	40	100	40	Normal
TM56	Fling	Dark	Physical	—	100	10	Normal
TM59	Incinerate	Fire	Special	60	100	15	Many Others
TM65	Shadow Claw	Ghost	Physical	70	100	15	Normal
TM66	Payback	Dark	Physical	50	100	10	Normal
TM68	Giga Impact	Normal	Physical	150	90	5	Normal
TM75	Swords Dance	Normal	Status	—	—	20	Self
TM78	Bulldoze	Ground	Physical	60	100	20	Adjacent
TM80	Rock Slide	Rock	Physical	75	90	10	Many Others
TM81	X-Scissor	Bug	Physical	80	100	15	Normal

No.	Name	Type	Kind	Pow.	Acc.	PP	Range
TM82	Dragon Tail	Dragon	Physical	60	90	10	Normal
TM84	Poison Jab	Poison	Physical	80	100	20	Normal
TM86	Grass Knot	Grass	Special	—	100	20	Normal
TM87	Swagger	Normal	Status	—	90	15	Normal
TM88	Sleep Talk	Normal	Status	—	—	10	Self
TM90	Substitute	Normal	Status	—	—	10	Self
TM94	Rock Smash	Fighting	Physical	40	100	15	Normal
TM100	Confide	Normal	Status	—	—	20	Normal
HM01	Cut	Normal	Physical	50	95	30	Normal
HM03	Surf	Water	Special	90	100	15	Adjacent
HM04	Strength	Normal	Physical	80	100	15	Normal

● MOVES TAUGHT BY PEOPLE

Name	Type	Kind	Pow.	Acc.	PP	Range
Draco Meteor	Dragon	Special	130	90	5	Normal

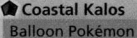 **Coastal Kalos** **001**

Balloon Pokémon

☑ **Drifloon**

HEIGHT: 1'04" WEIGHT: 2.6 lbs.
GENDER: ♂/♀

TYPE Ghost | Flying

ABILITIES
Aftermath
Unburden

HIDDEN ABILITY
Flare Boost

STAT GROWTH RATES
HP	▪▪▪▪
Attack	▪▪▪
Defense	▪▪
Sp. Atk	▪▪▪
Sp. Def	▪▪
Speed	▪▪▪▪

EGG GROUP
Amorphous

X A Pokémon formed by the spirits of people and Pokémon. It loves damp, humid seasons.

Y These Pokémon are called the "Signpost for Wandering Spirits." Children holding them sometimes vanish.

EVOLUTION

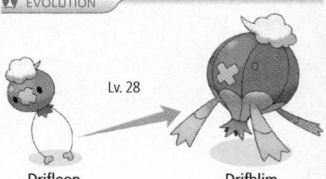

Drifloon — Lv. 28 → Drifblim

ITEMS SOMETIMES HELD BY WILD POKÉMON
None

Damage taken in normal battles		Damage taken in Inverse Battles		Can be used in
Normal	×0	Normal	×2	Inverse Battle
Fire	×1	Fire	×1	Sky Battle
Water	×1	Water	×1	Battle Chateau
Grass	×0.5	Grass	×2	Battle Institute
Electric	×2	Electric	×0.5	Battle Maison
Ice	×2	Ice	×0.5	Random Matchup
Fighting	×0	Fighting	×4	
Poison	×0.5	Poison	×2	
Ground	×0	Ground	×2	
Flying	×1	Flying	×1	
Psychic	×1	Psychic	×1	
Bug	×0.25	Bug	×4	
Rock	×2	Rock	×0.5	
Ghost	×2	Ghost	×0.5	
Dragon	×1	Dragon	×1	
Dark	×2	Dark	×0.5	
Steel	×1	Steel	×1	
Fairy	×1	Fairy	×1	

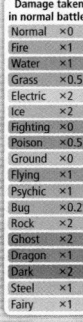

How to obtain for your Coastal Kalos Pokédex

❶ Catch in the tall grass on Route 8.
❷ Catch in the yellow flowers on Route 8.

❶ Catch in the tall grass on Route 8.
❷ Catch in the yellow flowers on Route 8.

Same form for ♂/♀

● **LEVEL-UP MOVES**

Lv.	Name	Type	Kind	Pow.	Acc.	PP	Range
1	Constrict	Normal	Physical	10	100	35	Normal
1	Minimize	Normal	Status	—	—	10	Self
4	Astonish	Ghost	Physical	30	100	15	Normal
8	Gust	Flying	Special	40	100	35	Normal
13	Focus Energy	Normal	Status	—	—	30	Self
16	Payback	Dark	Physical	50	100	10	Normal
20	Ominous Wind	Ghost	Special	60	100	5	Normal
23	Stockpile	Normal	Status	—	—	20	Self
27	Hex	Ghost	Special	65	100	10	Normal
32	Swallow	Normal	Status	—	—	10	Self
32	Spit Up	Normal	Special	—	100	10	Normal
36	Shadow Ball	Ghost	Special	80	100	15	Normal
40	Amnesia	Psychic	Status	—	—	20	Self
44	Baton Pass	Normal	Status	—	—	40	Self
50	Explosion	Normal	Physical	250	100	5	Adjacent

● **TM & HM MOVES**

No.	Name	Type	Kind	Pow.	Acc.	PP	Range
TM04	Calm Mind	Psychic	Status	—	—	20	Self
TM06	Toxic	Poison	Status	—	90	10	Normal
TM10	Hidden Power	Normal	Special	60	100	15	Normal
TM11	Sunny Day	Fire	Status	—	—	5	Both Sides
TM17	Protect	Normal	Status	—	—	10	Self
TM18	Rain Dance	Water	Status	—	—	5	Both Sides
TM21	Frustration	Normal	Physical	—	100	20	Normal
TM24	Thunderbolt	Electric	Special	90	100	15	Normal
TM25	Thunder	Electric	Special	110	70	10	Normal
TM27	Return	Normal	Physical	—	100	20	Normal
TM29	Psychic	Psychic	Special	90	100	10	Normal
TM30	Shadow Ball	Ghost	Special	80	100	15	Normal
TM32	Double Team	Normal	Status	—	—	15	Self
TM42	Facade	Normal	Physical	70	100	20	Normal
TM44	Rest	Psychic	Status	—	—	10	Self
TM45	Attract	Normal	Status	—	100	15	Normal
TM46	Thief	Dark	Physical	60	100	25	Normal
TM48	Round	Normal	Special	60	100	15	Normal
TM57	Charge Beam	Electric	Special	50	90	10	Normal
TM61	Will-O-Wisp	Fire	Status	—	85	15	Normal
TM62	Acrobatics	Flying	Physical	55	100	15	Normal
TM63	Embargo	Dark	Status	—	100	15	Normal
TM64	Explosion	Normal	Physical	250	100	5	Adjacent
TM66	Payback	Dark	Physical	50	100	10	Normal
TM70	Flash	Normal	Status	—	100	20	Normal
TM73	Thunder Wave	Electric	Status	—	100	20	Normal
TM74	Gyro Ball	Steel	Physical	—	100	5	Normal
TM77	Psych Up	Normal	Status	—	—	10	Normal
TM85	Dream Eater	Psychic	Special	100	100	15	Normal
TM87	Swagger	Normal	Status	—	90	15	Normal
TM88	Sleep Talk	Normal	Status	—	—	10	Self
TM90	Substitute	Normal	Status	—	—	10	Self
TM100	Confide	Normal	Status	—	—	20	Normal

No.	Name	Type	Kind	Pow.	Acc.	PP	Range
HM01	Cut	Normal	Physical	50	95	30	Normal

● **MOVES TAUGHT BY PEOPLE**

Name	Type	Kind	Pow.	Acc.	PP	Range

● **EGG MOVES**

Name	Type	Kind	Pow.	Acc.	PP	Range
Memento	Dark	Status	—	100	10	Normal
Body Slam	Normal	Physical	85	100	15	Normal
Destiny Bond	Ghost	Status	—	—	5	Self
Disable	Normal	Status	—	100	20	Normal
Haze	Ice	Status	—	—	30	Both Sides
Hypnosis	Psychic	Status	—	60	20	Normal
Weather Ball	Normal	Special	50	100	10	Normal
Clear Smog	Poison	Special	50	—	15	Normal
Defog	Flying	Status	—	—	15	Normal
Tailwind	Flying	Status	—	—	15	Your Side

AFTER THE HALL OF FAME

CENTRAL KALOS

COASTAL KALOS

001 Drifloon

MOUNTAIN KALOS

ADVENTURE DATA

AFTER THE HALL OF FAME

CENTRAL KALOS

COASTAL KALOS

002

Drifblim

MOUNTAIN KALOS

ADVENTURE DATA

Coastal Kalos 002

Blimp Pokémon

☑ Drifblim

HEIGHT: 3'11" WEIGHT: 33.1 lbs.
GENDER: ♂/♀

TYPE Ghost Flying

ABILITIES
Aftermath
Unburden

HIDDEN ABILITY
Flare Boost

It carries people and Pokémon when it flies. But since it only drifts, it can end up anywhere.

It's drowsy in daytime, but flies off in the evening in big groups. No one knows where they go.

STAT GROWTH RATES
HP
Attack
Defense
Sp. Atk
Sp. Def
Speed

EGG GROUP
Amorphous

EVOLUTION

Lv. 28

Drifloon → Drifblim

ITEMS SOMETIMES HELD BY WILD POKÉMON
None

Damage taken in normal battles	
Normal	×0
Fire	×1
Water	×1
Grass	×0.5
Electric	×2
Ice	×2
Fighting	×0
Poison	×0.5
Ground	×0
Flying	×1
Psychic	×1
Bug	×0.25
Rock	×2
Ghost	×2
Dragon	×1
Dark	×2
Steel	×1
Fairy	×1

Damage taken in Inverse Battles	
Normal	×2
Fire	×1
Water	×1
Grass	×2
Electric	×0.5
Ice	×0.5
Fighting	×4
Poison	×2
Ground	×2
Flying	×1
Psychic	×1
Bug	×4
Rock	×0.5
Ghost	×0.5
Dragon	×1
Dark	×0.5
Steel	×1
Fairy	×1

Can be used in	
Inverse Battle	Battle Institute
Sky Battle	Battle Maison
Battle Chateau	Random Matchup

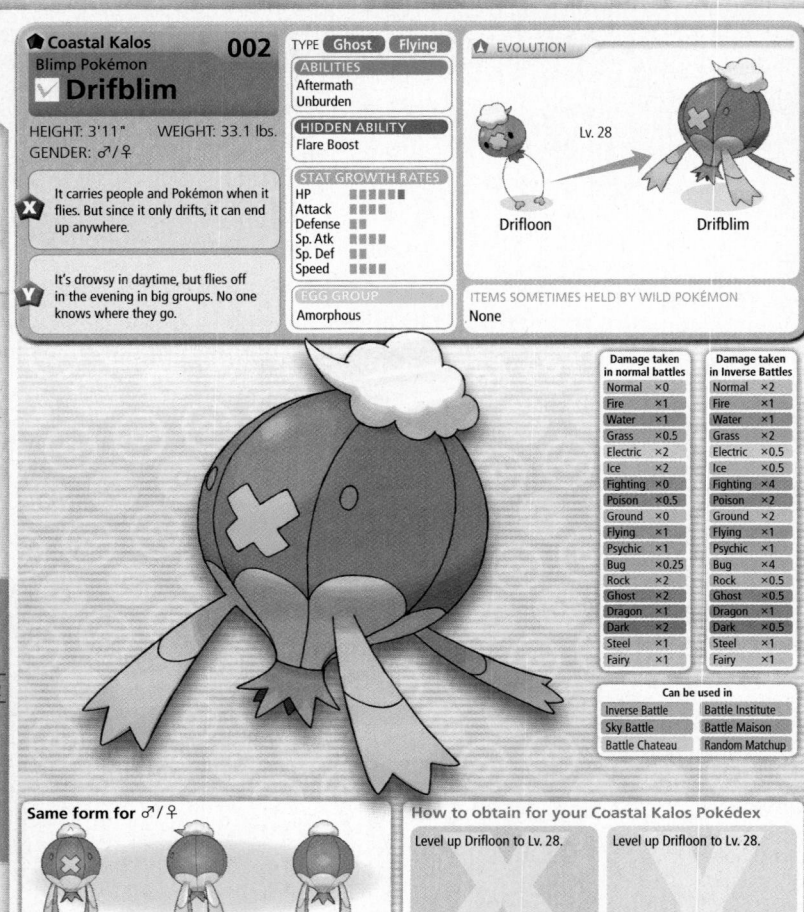

Same form for ♂/♀

How to obtain for your Coastal Kalos Pokédex
Level up Drifloon to Lv. 28. Level up Drifloon to Lv. 28.

● LEVEL-UP MOVES

Lv.	Name	Type	Kind	Pow.	Acc.	PP	Range
1	Phantom Force	Ghost	Physical	90	100	10	Normal
1	Constrict	Normal	Physical	10	100	35	Normal
1	Minimize	Normal	Status	—	—	10	Self
1	Astonish	Ghost	Physical	30	100	15	Normal
1	Gust	Flying	Special	40	100	35	Normal
4	Astonish	Ghost	Physical	30	100	15	Normal
8	Gust	Flying	Special	40	100	35	Normal
13	Focus Energy	Normal	Status	—	—	30	Self
16	Payback	Dark	Physical	50	100	10	Normal
20	Ominous Wind	Ghost	Special	60	100	5	Normal
25	Stockpile	Normal	Status	—	—	20	Self
27	Hex	Ghost	Special	65	100	10	Normal
34	Swallow	Normal	Status	—	—	10	Self
34	Spit Up	Normal	Special	—	100	10	Normal
40	Shadow Ball	Ghost	Special	80	100	15	Normal
46	Amnesia	Psychic	Status	—	—	20	Self
52	Baton Pass	Normal	Status	—	—	40	Self
60	Explosion	Normal	Physical	250	100	5	Adjacent
65	Phantom Force	Ghost	Physical	90	100	10	Normal

● TM & HM MOVES

No.	Name	Type	Kind	Pow.	Acc.	PP	Range
TM04	Calm Mind	Psychic	Status	—	—	20	Self
TM06	Toxic	Poison	Status	—	90	10	Normal
TM10	Hidden Power	Normal	Special	60	100	15	Normal
TM11	Sunny Day	Fire	Status	—	—	5	Both Sides
TM15	Hyper Beam	Normal	Special	150	90	5	Normal
TM17	Protect	Normal	Status	—	—	10	Self
TM18	Rain Dance	Water	Status	—	—	5	Both Sides
TM21	Frustration	Normal	Physical	—	100	20	Normal
TM24	Thunderbolt	Electric	Special	90	100	15	Normal
TM25	Thunder	Electric	Special	110	70	10	Normal
TM27	Return	Normal	Physical	—	100	20	Normal
TM29	Psychic	Psychic	Special	90	100	10	Normal
TM30	Shadow Ball	Ghost	Special	80	100	15	Normal
TM32	Double Team	Normal	Status	—	—	15	Self
TM42	Facade	Normal	Physical	70	100	20	Normal
TM44	Rest	Psychic	Status	—	—	10	Self
TM45	Attract	Normal	Status	—	100	15	Normal
TM46	Thief	Dark	Physical	60	100	25	Normal
TM48	Round	Normal	Special	60	100	15	Normal
TM57	Charge Beam	Electric	Special	50	90	10	Normal
TM61	Will-O-Wisp	Fire	Status	—	85	15	Normal
TM62	Acrobatics	Flying	Physical	55	100	15	Normal
TM63	Embargo	Dark	Status	—	100	15	Normal
TM64	Explosion	Normal	Physical	250	100	5	Adjacent
TM66	Payback	Dark	Physical	50	100	10	Normal
TM68	Giga Impact	Normal	Physical	150	90	5	Normal
TM70	Flash	Normal	Status	—	100	20	Normal
TM73	Thunder Wave	Electric	Status	—	100	20	Normal
TM74	Gyro Ball	Steel	Physical	—	100	5	Normal
TM77	Psych Up	Normal	Status	—	—	10	Normal
TM85	Dream Eater	Psychic	Special	100	100	15	Normal
TM87	Swagger	Normal	Status	—	90	15	Normal
TM88	Sleep Talk	Normal	Status	—	—	10	Self
TM90	Substitute	Normal	Status	—	—	10	Self
TM100	Confide	Normal	Status	—	—	20	Normal
HM01	Cut	Normal	Physical	50	95	30	Normal
HM02	Fly	Flying	Physical	90	95	15	Normal

● MOVES TAUGHT BY PEOPLE

Name	Type	Kind	Pow.	Acc.	PP	Range

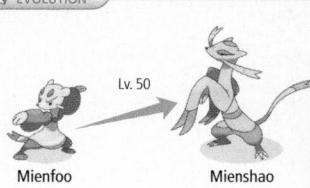

🍃 **Coastal Kalos** **003**
Martial Arts Pokémon
☑ **Mienfoo**

HEIGHT: 2'11" WEIGHT: 44.1 lbs.
GENDER: ♂/♀

TYPE Fighting

ABILITIES
Inner Focus
Regenerator

HIDDEN ABILITY
Reckless

STAT GROWTH RATES
HP	▮▮
Attack	▮▮▮▮
Defense	▮▮
Sp. Atk	▮▮▮
Sp. Def	▮▮
Speed	▮▮▮▮

EGG GROUPS
Field, Human-Like

EVOLUTION

Mienfoo → (Lv. 50) → Mienshao

ITEMS SOMETIMES HELD BY WILD POKÉMON
None

X It takes pride in the speed at which it can use moves. What it loses in power, it makes up for in quantity.

Y In fights, they dominate with onslaughts of flowing, continuous attacks. With their sharp claws, they cut enemies.

Damage taken in normal battles		Damage taken in Inverse Battles	
Normal	×1	Normal	×1
Fire	×1	Fire	×1
Water	×1	Water	×1
Grass	×1	Grass	×1
Electric	×1	Electric	×1
Ice	×1	Ice	×1
Fighting	×1	Fighting	×1
Poison	×1	Poison	×1
Ground	×1	Ground	×1
Flying	×2	Flying	×0.5
Psychic	×2	Psychic	×0.5
Bug	×0.5	Bug	×2
Rock	×0.5	Rock	×2
Ghost	×1	Ghost	×1
Dragon	×1	Dragon	×1
Dark	×0.5	Dark	×2
Steel	×1	Steel	×1
Fairy	×2	Fairy	×0.5

Can be used in	
Inverse Battle	Battle Institute
—	Battle Maison
Battle Chateau	Random Matchup

Same form for ♂/♀

How to obtain for your Coastal Kalos Pokédex

❶ Catch in the tall grass on Route 8.
❷ Catch in the yellow flowers on Route 8.

❶ Catch in the tall grass on Route 8.
❷ Catch in the yellow flowers on Route 8.

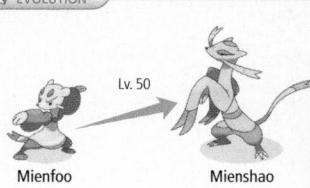

AFTER THE HALL OF FAME

CENTRAL KALOS

COASTAL KALOS

003 | Mienfoo

MOUNTAIN KALOS

ADVENTURE DATA

● **LEVEL-UP MOVES**

Lv.	Name	Type	Kind	Pow.	Acc.	PP	Range
1	Pound	Normal	Physical	40	100	35	Normal
5	Meditate	Psychic	Status	—	—	40	Self
9	Detect	Fighting	Status	—	—	5	Self
13	Fake Out	Normal	Physical	40	100	10	Normal
17	Double Slap	Normal	Physical	15	85	10	Normal
21	Swift	Normal	Special	60	—	20	Many Others
25	Calm Mind	Psychic	Status	—	—	20	Self
29	Force Palm	Fighting	Physical	60	100	10	Normal
33	Drain Punch	Fighting	Physical	75	100	10	Normal
37	Jump Kick	Fighting	Physical	100	95	10	Normal
41	U-turn	Bug	Physical	70	100	20	Normal
45	Quick Guard	Fighting	Status	—	—	15	Your Side
49	Bounce	Flying	Physical	85	85	5	Normal
50	High Jump Kick	Fighting	Physical	130	90	10	Normal
57	Reversal	Fighting	Physical	—	100	15	Normal
61	Aura Sphere	Fighting	Special	80	—	20	Normal

● **TM & HM MOVES**

No.	Name	Type	Kind	Pow.	Acc.	PP	Range
TM04	Calm Mind	Psychic	Status	—	—	20	Self
TM06	Toxic	Poison	Status	—	90	10	Normal
TM08	Bulk Up	Fighting	Status	—	—	20	Self
TM10	Hidden Power	Normal	Special	60	100	15	Normal
TM11	Sunny Day	Fire	Status	—	—	5	Both Sides
TM12	Taunt	Dark	Status	—	100	20	Normal
TM17	Protect	Normal	Status	—	—	10	Self
TM18	Rain Dance	Water	Status	—	—	5	Both Sides
TM21	Frustration	Normal	Physical	—	100	20	Normal
TM27	Return	Normal	Physical	—	100	20	Normal
TM28	Dig	Ground	Physical	80	100	10	Normal
TM31	Brick Break	Fighting	Physical	75	100	15	Normal
TM32	Double Team	Normal	Status	—	—	15	Self
TM33	Reflect	Psychic	Status	—	—	20	Your Side
TM39	Rock Tomb	Rock	Physical	60	95	15	Normal
TM40	Aerial Ace	Flying	Physical	60	—	20	Normal
TM42	Facade	Normal	Physical	70	100	20	Normal
TM44	Rest	Psychic	Status	—	—	10	Self
TM45	Attract	Normal	Status	—	100	15	Normal
TM47	Low Sweep	Fighting	Physical	65	100	20	Normal
TM48	Round	Normal	Special	60	100	15	Normal
TM52	Focus Blast	Fighting	Special	120	70	5	Normal
TM56	Fling	Dark	Physical	—	100	10	Normal
TM62	Acrobatics	Flying	Physical	55	100	15	Normal
TM66	Payback	Dark	Physical	50	100	10	Normal
TM67	Retaliate	Normal	Physical	70	100	5	Normal
TM71	Stone Edge	Rock	Physical	100	80	5	Normal
TM75	Swords Dance	Normal	Status	—	—	20	Self
TM77	Psych Up	Normal	Status	—	—	10	Normal
TM80	Rock Slide	Rock	Physical	75	90	10	Many Others
TM84	Poison Jab	Poison	Physical	80	100	20	Normal
TM86	Grass Knot	Grass	Special	—	100	20	Normal
TM87	Swagger	Normal	Status	—	90	15	Normal
TM88	Sleep Talk	Normal	Status	—	—	10	Self
TM89	U-turn	Bug	Physical	70	100	20	Normal
TM90	Substitute	Normal	Status	—	—	10	Self
TM94	Rock Smash	Fighting	Physical	40	100	15	Normal
TM98	Power-Up Punch	Fighting	Physical	40	100	20	Normal
TM100	Confide	Normal	Status	—	—	20	Normal
HM04	Strength	Normal	Physical	80	100	15	Normal

● **MOVES TAUGHT BY PEOPLE**

Name	Type	Kind	Pow.	Acc.	PP	Range

● **EGG MOVES**

Name	Type	Kind	Pow.	Acc.	PP	Range
Endure	Normal	Status	—	—	10	Self
Vital Throw	Fighting	Physical	70	—	10	Normal
Baton Pass	Normal	Status	—	—	40	Self
Smelling Salts	Normal	Physical	70	100	10	Normal
Low Kick	Fighting	Physical	—	100	20	Normal
Feint	Normal	Physical	30	100	10	Normal
Me First	Normal	Status	—	—	20	Varies
Knock Off	Dark	Physical	65	100	20	Normal
Ally Switch	Psychic	Status	—	—	15	Self

271

AFTER THE HALL OF FAME

CENTRAL KALOS

COASTAL KALOS

004

Mienshao

MOUNTAIN KALOS

ADVENTURE DATA

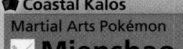

Coastal Kalos 004
Martial Arts Pokémon
☑ Mienshao

HEIGHT: 4'07" WEIGHT: 78.3 lbs.
GENDER: ♂/♀

X It wields the fur on its arms like a whip. Its arm attacks come with such rapidity that they cannot even be seen.

Y Using the long fur on its arms like whips, it launches into combo attacks that, once started, no one can stop.

TYPE Fighting

ABILITIES
Inner Focus
Regenerator

HIDDEN ABILITY
Reckless

STAT GROWTH RATES
HP ■■■
Attack ■■■■■■
Defense ■■■■
Sp. Atk ■■■■■
Sp. Def ■■■
Speed ■■■■■■

EGG GROUPS
Field, Human-Like

↑ EVOLUTION

Lv. 50

Mienfoo → Mienshao

ITEMS SOMETIMES HELD BY WILD POKÉMON
None

Can be used in
Inverse Battle
⎯⎯⎯
Battle Chateau
Battle Institute
Battle Maison
Random Matchup

Damage taken in normal battles	
Normal	×1
Fire	×1
Water	×1
Grass	×1
Electric	×1
Ice	×1
Fighting	×1
Poison	×1
Ground	×1
Flying	×2
Psychic	×2
Bug	×0.5
Rock	×0.5
Ghost	×1
Dragon	×1
Dark	×0.5
Steel	×1
Fairy	×2

Damage taken in Inverse Battles	
Normal	×1
Fire	×1
Water	×1
Grass	×1
Electric	×1
Ice	×1
Fighting	×1
Poison	×1
Ground	×1
Flying	×0.5
Psychic	×0.5
Bug	×2
Rock	×2
Ghost	×1
Dragon	×1
Dark	×2
Steel	×1
Fairy	×0.5

How to obtain for your Coastal Kalos Pokédex
Level up Mienfoo to Lv. 50.   Level up Mienfoo to Lv. 50.

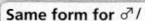

Same form for ♂/♀

● LEVEL-UP MOVES

Lv.	Name	Type	Kind	Pow.	Acc.	PP	Range
1	Aura Sphere	Fighting	Special	80	—	20	Normal
1	Reversal	Fighting	Physical	—	100	15	Normal
1	Pound	Normal	Physical	40	100	35	Normal
1	Meditate	Psychic	Status	—	—	40	Self
1	Detect	Fighting	Status	—	—	5	Self
1	Fake Out	Normal	Physical	40	100	10	Normal
5	Meditate	Psychic	Status	—	—	40	Self
9	Detect	Fighting	Status	—	—	5	Self
13	Fake Out	Normal	Physical	40	100	10	Normal
17	Double Slap	Normal	Physical	15	85	10	Normal
21	Swift	Normal	Special	60	—	20	Many Others
25	Calm Mind	Psychic	Status	—	—	20	Self
29	Force Palm	Fighting	Physical	60	100	10	Normal
33	Drain Punch	Fighting	Physical	75	100	10	Normal
37	Jump Kick	Fighting	Physical	100	95	10	Normal
41	U-turn	Bug	Physical	70	100	20	Normal
45	Wide Guard	Rock	Status	—	—	10	Your Side
49	Bounce	Flying	Physical	85	85	5	Normal
56	High Jump Kick	Fighting	Physical	130	90	10	Normal
63	Reversal	Fighting	Physical	—	100	15	Normal
70	Aura Sphere	Fighting	Special	80	—	20	Normal

● TM & HM MOVES

No.	Name	Type	Kind	Pow.	Acc.	PP	Range
TM04	Calm Mind	Psychic	Status	—	—	20	Self
TM06	Toxic	Poison	Status	—	90	10	Normal
TM08	Bulk Up	Fighting	Status	—	—	20	Self
TM10	Hidden Power	Normal	Special	60	100	15	Normal
TM11	Sunny Day	Fire	Status	—	—	5	Both Sides
TM12	Taunt	Dark	Status	—	100	20	Normal
TM15	Hyper Beam	Normal	Special	150	90	5	Normal
TM17	Protect	Normal	Status	—	—	10	Self
TM18	Rain Dance	Water	Status	—	—	5	Both Sides
TM21	Frustration	Normal	Physical	—	100	20	Normal
TM27	Return	Normal	Physical	—	100	20	Normal
TM28	Dig	Ground	Physical	80	100	10	Normal
TM31	Brick Break	Fighting	Physical	75	100	15	Normal
TM32	Double Team	Normal	Status	—	—	15	Self
TM33	Reflect	Psychic	Status	—	—	20	Your Side
TM39	Rock Tomb	Rock	Physical	60	95	15	Normal
TM40	Aerial Ace	Flying	Physical	60	—	20	Normal
TM42	Facade	Normal	Physical	70	100	20	Normal
TM44	Rest	Psychic	Status	—	—	10	Self
TM45	Attract	Normal	Status	—	100	15	Normal
TM47	Low Sweep	Fighting	Physical	65	100	20	Normal
TM48	Round	Normal	Special	60	100	15	Normal
TM52	Focus Blast	Fighting	Special	120	70	5	Normal
TM56	Fling	Dark	Physical	—	100	10	Normal
TM62	Acrobatics	Flying	Physical	55	100	15	Normal
TM66	Payback	Dark	Physical	50	100	10	Normal
TM67	Retaliate	Normal	Physical	70	100	5	Normal
TM68	Giga Impact	Normal	Physical	150	90	5	Normal
TM71	Stone Edge	Rock	Physical	100	80	5	Normal
TM75	Swords Dance	Normal	Status	—	—	20	Self
TM77	Psych Up	Normal	Status	—	—	10	Normal
TM80	Rock Slide	Rock	Physical	75	90	10	Many Others
TM84	Poison Jab	Poison	Physical	80	100	20	Normal

No.	Name	Type	Kind	Pow.	Acc.	PP	Range
TM86	Grass Knot	Grass	Special	—	100	20	Normal
TM87	Swagger	Normal	Status	—	90	15	Normal
TM88	Sleep Talk	Normal	Status	—	—	10	Self
TM89	U-turn	Bug	Physical	70	100	20	Normal
TM90	Substitute	Normal	Status	—	—	10	Self
TM94	Rock Smash	Fighting	Physical	40	100	15	Normal
TM98	Power-Up Punch	Fighting	Physical	40	100	20	Normal
TM100	Confide	Normal	Status	—	—	20	Normal
HM04	Strength	Normal	Physical	80	100	15	Normal

● MOVES TAUGHT BY PEOPLE

Name	Type	Kind	Pow.	Acc.	PP	Range

AFTER THE HALL OF FAME

CENTRAL KALOS

COASTAL KALOS

005 Zangoose

MOUNTAIN KALOS

ADVENTURE DATA

🐾 Coastal Kalos

005

Cat Ferret Pokémon

☑ Zangoose

HEIGHT: 4'03" WEIGHT: 88.8 lbs.
GENDER: ♂/♀

X It has feuded with Seviper for many generations. Its sharp claws are its biggest weapons.

Y Its fur would all stand on end if it smelled a Seviper nearby. Its sharp claws tear up its foes.

TYPE Normal

ABILITY
Immunity

HIDDEN ABILITY
Toxic Boost

STAT GROWTH RATES
HP	■■■
Attack	■■■■■■
Defense	■■■
Sp. Atk	■■■
Sp. Def	■■■
Speed	■■■■■

EGG GROUP
Field

EVOLUTION

Does not evolve

ITEMS SOMETIMES HELD BY WILD POKÉMON
Quick Claw

Damage taken in normal battles		Damage taken in Inverse Battles	
Normal	×1	Normal	×1
Fire	×1	Fire	×1
Water	×1	Water	×1
Grass	×1	Grass	×1
Electric	×1	Electric	×1
Ice	×1	Ice	×1
Fighting	×2	Fighting	×0.5
Poison	×1	Poison	×1
Ground	×1	Ground	×1
Flying	×1	Flying	×1
Psychic	×1	Psychic	×1
Bug	×1	Bug	×1
Rock	×1	Rock	×1
Ghost	×0	Ghost	×2
Dragon	×1	Dragon	×1
Dark	×1	Dark	×1
Steel	×1	Steel	×1
Fairy	×1	Fairy	×1

Can be used in	
Inverse Battle	Battle Institute
—	Battle Maison
Battle Chateau	Random Matchup

Same form for ♂/♀

How to obtain for your Coastal Kalos Pokédex

❶ Catch in the tall grass on Route 8.

❷ Catch in the yellow flowers on Route 8.

Catch in a Horde Encounter on Route 8.

● LEVEL-UP MOVES

Lv.	Name	Type	Kind	Pow.	Acc.	PP	Range
1	Scratch	Normal	Physical	40	100	35	Normal
1	Leer	Normal	Status	—	100	30	Many Others
5	Quick Attack	Normal	Physical	40	100	30	Normal
8	Fury Cutter	Bug	Physical	40	95	20	Normal
12	Pursuit	Dark	Physical	40	100	20	Normal
15	Slash	Normal	Physical	70	100	20	Normal
19	Embargo	Dark	Status	—	100	15	Normal
22	Crush Claw	Normal	Physical	75	95	10	Normal
26	Revenge	Fighting	Physical	60	100	10	Normal
29	False Swipe	Normal	Physical	40	100	40	Normal
33	Detect	Fighting	Status	—	—	5	Self
36	X-Scissor	Bug	Physical	80	100	15	Normal
40	Taunt	Dark	Status	—	100	20	Normal
43	Swords Dance	Normal	Status	—	—	20	Self
47	Close Combat	Fighting	Physical	120	100	5	Normal

● TM & HM MOVES

No.	Name	Type	Kind	Pow.	Acc.	PP	Range
TM01	Hone Claws	Dark	Status	—	—	15	Self
TM05	Roar	Normal	Status	—	—	20	Normal
TM06	Toxic	Poison	Status	—	90	10	Normal
TM10	Hidden Power	Normal	Special	60	100	15	Normal
TM11	Sunny Day	Fire	Status	—	—	5	Both Sides

No.	Name	Type	Kind	Pow.	Acc.	PP	Range
TM12	Taunt	Dark	Status	—	100	20	Normal
TM13	Ice Beam	Ice	Special	90	100	10	Normal
TM14	Blizzard	Ice	Special	110	70	5	Many Others
TM17	Protect	Normal	Status	—	—	10	Self
TM18	Rain Dance	Water	Status	—	—	5	Both Sides
TM21	Frustration	Normal	Physical	—	100	20	Normal
TM22	Solar Beam	Grass	Special	120	100	10	Normal
TM24	Thunderbolt	Electric	Special	90	100	15	Normal
TM25	Thunder	Electric	Special	110	70	10	Normal
TM27	Return	Normal	Physical	—	100	20	Normal
TM28	Dig	Ground	Physical	80	100	10	Normal
TM30	Shadow Ball	Ghost	Special	80	100	15	Normal
TM31	Brick Break	Fighting	Physical	75	100	15	Normal
TM32	Double Team	Normal	Status	—	—	15	Self
TM35	Flamethrower	Fire	Special	90	100	15	Normal
TM38	Fire Blast	Fire	Special	110	85	5	Normal
TM39	Rock Tomb	Rock	Physical	60	95	15	Normal
TM40	Aerial Ace	Flying	Physical	60	—	20	Normal
TM42	Facade	Normal	Physical	70	100	20	Normal
TM44	Rest	Psychic	Status	—	—	10	Self
TM45	Attract	Normal	Status	—	100	15	Normal
TM46	Thief	Dark	Physical	60	100	25	Normal
TM48	Round	Normal	Special	60	100	15	Normal
TM52	Focus Blast	Fighting	Special	120	70	5	Normal
TM54	False Swipe	Normal	Physical	40	100	40	Normal
TM56	Fling	Dark	Physical	—	100	10	Normal
TM59	Incinerate	Fire	Special	60	100	15	Many Others
TM63	Embargo	Dark	Status	—	100	15	Normal
TM65	Shadow Claw	Ghost	Physical	70	100	15	Normal
TM66	Payback	Dark	Physical	50	100	10	Normal
TM67	Retaliate	Normal	Physical	70	100	5	Normal
TM75	Swords Dance	Normal	Status	—	—	20	Self
TM80	Rock Slide	Rock	Physical	75	90	10	Many Others

No.	Name	Type	Kind	Pow.	Acc.	PP	Range
TM81	X-Scissor	Bug	Physical	80	100	15	Normal
TM84	Poison Jab	Poison	Physical	80	100	20	Normal
TM87	Swagger	Normal	Status	—	90	15	Normal
TM88	Sleep Talk	Normal	Status	—	—	10	Self
TM90	Substitute	Normal	Status	—	—	10	Self
TM94	Rock Smash	Fighting	Physical	40	100	15	Normal
TM98	Power-Up Punch	Fighting	Physical	40	100	20	Normal
TM100	Confide	Normal	Status	—	—	20	Normal
HM04	Strength	Normal	Physical	80	100	15	Normal

● MOVES TAUGHT BY PEOPLE

Name	Type	Kind	Pow.	Acc.	PP	Range

● EGG MOVES

Name	Type	Kind	Pow.	Acc.	PP	Range
Flail	Normal	Physical	—	100	15	Normal
Double Kick	Fighting	Physical	30	100	30	Normal
Razor Wind	Normal	Special	80	100	10	Many Others
Counter	Fighting	Physical	—	100	20	Varies
Curse	Ghost	Status	—	—	10	Varies
Fury Swipes	Normal	Physical	18	80	15	Normal
Night Slash	Dark	Physical	70	100	15	Normal
Metal Claw	Steel	Physical	50	95	35	Normal
Double Hit	Normal	Physical	35	90	10	Normal
Disable	Normal	Status	—	100	20	Normal
Iron Tail	Steel	Physical	100	75	15	Normal
Final Gambit	Fighting	Special	—	100	5	Normal
Feint	Normal	Physical	30	100	10	Normal
Quick Guard	Fighting	Status	—	—	15	Your Side

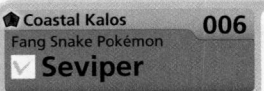

Coastal Kalos 006

Fang Snake Pokémon

Seviper

HEIGHT: 8'10" WEIGHT: 115.7 lbs.
GENDER: ♂/♀

X: In battle, it uses its bladed tail to counter any Zangoose. It secretes a deadly venom in its tail.

Y: Constant polishing makes the edge of the blade on its tail extremely sharp. It's Zangoose's archrival.

TYPE Poison

ABILITY
Shed Skin

HIDDEN ABILITY
Infiltrator

STAT GROWTH RATES
HP	■■■
Attack	■■■■■
Defense	■■■
Sp. Atk	■■■■■
Sp. Def	■■■
Speed	■■■■

EGG GROUPS
Field, Dragon

EVOLUTION
Does not evolve

ITEMS SOMETIMES HELD BY WILD POKÉMON
Persim Berry

Damage taken in normal battles		Damage taken in Inverse Battles	
Normal	×1	Normal	×1
Fire	×1	Fire	×1
Water	×1	Water	×1
Grass	×0.5	Grass	×2
Electric	×1	Electric	×1
Ice	×1	Ice	×1
Fighting	×0.5	Fighting	×2
Poison	×0.5	Poison	×2
Ground	×2	Ground	×0.5
Flying	×1	Flying	×1
Psychic	×2	Psychic	×0.5
Bug	×0.5	Bug	×2
Rock	×1	Rock	×1
Ghost	×1	Ghost	×1
Dragon	×1	Dragon	×1
Dark	×1	Dark	×1
Steel	×1	Steel	×1
Fairy	×0.5	Fairy	×2

Can be used in	
Inverse Battle	Battle Institute
—	Battle Maison
Battle Chateau	Random Matchup

Same form for ♂/♀

How to obtain for your Coastal Kalos Pokédex

Catch in a Horde Encounter on Route 8.

❶ Catch in the tall grass on Route 8.
❷ Catch in the yellow flowers on Route 8.

● LEVEL-UP MOVES

Lv.	Name	Type	Kind	Pow.	Acc.	PP	Range
1	Wrap	Normal	Physical	15	90	20	Normal
1	Swagger	Normal	Status	—	90	15	Normal
5	Bite	Dark	Physical	60	100	25	Normal
9	Lick	Ghost	Physical	30	100	30	Normal
12	Poison Tail	Poison	Physical	50	100	25	Normal
16	Screech	Normal	Status	—	85	40	Normal
20	Venoshock	Poison	Special	65	100	10	Normal
23	Glare	Normal	Status	—	100	30	Normal
27	Poison Fang	Poison	Physical	50	100	15	Normal
28	Venom Drench	Poison	Status	—	100	20	Many Others
31	Night Slash	Dark	Physical	70	100	15	Normal
34	Gastro Acid	Poison	Status	—	100	10	Normal
38	Haze	Ice	Status	—	—	30	Both Sides
42	Poison Jab	Poison	Physical	80	100	20	Normal
45	Crunch	Dark	Physical	80	100	15	Normal
46	Belch	Poison	Special	120	90	10	Normal
48	Coil	Poison	Status	—	—	20	Self
50	Wring Out	Normal	Special	—	100	5	Normal

● TM & HM MOVES

No.	Name	Type	Kind	Pow.	Acc.	PP	Range
TM06	Toxic	Poison	Status	—	90	10	Normal
TM09	Venoshock	Poison	Special	65	100	10	Normal
TM10	Hidden Power	Normal	Special	60	100	15	Normal
TM11	Sunny Day	Fire	Status	—	—	5	Both Sides
TM12	Taunt	Dark	Status	—	100	20	Normal
TM17	Protect	Normal	Status	—	—	10	Self
TM18	Rain Dance	Water	Status	—	—	5	Both Sides
TM21	Frustration	Normal	Physical	—	100	20	Normal
TM26	Earthquake	Ground	Physical	100	100	10	Adjacent
TM27	Return	Normal	Physical	—	100	20	Normal
TM28	Dig	Ground	Physical	80	100	10	Normal
TM32	Double Team	Normal	Status	—	—	15	Self
TM34	Sludge Wave	Poison	Special	95	100	10	Adjacent
TM35	Flamethrower	Fire	Special	90	100	15	Normal
TM36	Sludge Bomb	Poison	Special	90	100	10	Normal
TM42	Facade	Normal	Physical	70	100	20	Normal
TM44	Rest	Psychic	Status	—	—	10	Self
TM45	Attract	Normal	Status	—	100	15	Normal
TM46	Thief	Dark	Physical	60	100	25	Normal
TM48	Round	Normal	Special	60	100	15	Normal
TM66	Payback	Dark	Physical	50	100	10	Normal
TM67	Retaliate	Normal	Physical	70	100	5	Normal
TM78	Bulldoze	Ground	Physical	60	100	20	Adjacent
TM81	X-Scissor	Bug	Physical	80	100	15	Normal
TM82	Dragon Tail	Dragon	Physical	60	90	10	Normal
TM83	Infestation	Bug	Special	20	100	20	Normal
TM84	Poison Jab	Poison	Physical	80	100	20	Normal
TM87	Swagger	Normal	Status	—	90	15	Normal
TM88	Sleep Talk	Normal	Status	—	—	10	Self
TM90	Substitute	Normal	Status	—	—	10	Self
TM94	Rock Smash	Fighting	Physical	40	100	15	Normal
TM97	Dark Pulse	Dark	Special	80	100	15	Normal
TM100	Confide	Normal	Status	—	—	20	Normal

No.	Name	Type	Kind	Pow.	Acc.	PP	Range
HM04	Strength	Normal	Physical	80	100	15	Normal

● MOVES TAUGHT BY PEOPLE

Name	Type	Kind	Pow.	Acc.	PP	Range

● EGG MOVES

Name	Type	Kind	Pow.	Acc.	PP	Range
Stockpile	Normal	Status	—	—	20	Self
Swallow	Normal	Status	—	—	10	Self
Spit Up	Normal	Special	—	100	10	Normal
Body Slam	Normal	Physical	85	100	15	Normal
Scary Face	Normal	Status	—	100	10	Normal
Assurance	Dark	Physical	60	100	10	Normal
Night Slash	Dark	Physical	70	100	15	Normal
Switcheroo	Dark	Status	—	100	10	Normal
Iron Tail	Steel	Physical	100	75	15	Normal
Wring Out	Normal	Special	—	100	5	Normal
Punishment	Dark	Physical	—	100	5	Normal
Final Gambit	Fighting	Special	—	100	5	Normal

AFTER THE HALL OF FAME

CENTRAL KALOS

COASTAL KALOS

006

Seviper

MOUNTAIN KALOS

ADVENTURE DATA

274

AFTER THE HALL OF FAME

CENTRAL KALOS

COASTAL KALOS

007 | Spoink

MOUNTAIN KALOS

ADVENTURE DATA

🔺 **Coastal Kalos**

Bounce Pokémon

007

☑ **Spoink**

HEIGHT: 2'04" WEIGHT: 67.5 lbs.
GENDER: ♂/♀

TYPE **Psychic**

ABILITIES
Thick Fat
Own Tempo

HIDDEN ABILITY
Gluttony

STAT GROWTH RATES
HP	▪▪▪
Attack	▪▪
Defense	▪▪
Sp. Atk	▪▪▪
Sp. Def	▪▪▪
Speed	▪▪▪

EGG GROUP
Field

Ⓧ It bounces constantly, using its tail like a spring. The shock of bouncing keeps its heart beating.

Ⓨ It bounces around on its tail to keep its heart pumping. It carries a pearl from Clamperl on its head.

🔻 EVOLUTION

Spoink → Lv. 32 → Grumpig

ITEMS SOMETIMES HELD BY WILD POKÉMON
None

Damage taken in normal battles		Damage taken in Inverse Battles		Can be used in
Normal	×1	Normal	×1	Inverse Battle
Fire	×1	Fire	×1	—
Water	×1	Water	×1	Battle Chateau
Grass	×1	Grass	×1	Battle Institute
Electric	×1	Electric	×1	Battle Maison
Ice	×1	Ice	×1	Random Matchup
Fighting	×0.5	Fighting	×2	
Poison	×1	Poison	×1	
Ground	×1	Ground	×1	
Flying	×1	Flying	×1	
Psychic	×0.5	Psychic	×2	
Bug	×2	Bug	×0.5	
Rock	×1	Rock	×1	
Ghost	×2	Ghost	×0.5	
Dragon	×1	Dragon	×1	
Dark	×2	Dark	×0.5	
Steel	×1	Steel	×1	
Fairy	×1	Fairy	×1	

How to obtain for your Coastal Kalos Pokédex

❶ Catch in the tall grass on Route 8.
❷ Catch in the yellow flowers on Route 8.

❶ Catch in the tall grass on Route 8.
❷ Catch in the yellow flowers on Route 8.

Same form for ♂/♀

● **LEVEL-UP MOVES**

Lv.	Name	Type	Kind	Pow.	Acc.	PP	Range
1	Splash	Normal	Status	—	—	40	Self
7	Psywave	Psychic	Special	—	100	15	Normal
10	Odor Sleuth	Normal	Status	—	—	40	Normal
14	Psybeam	Psychic	Special	65	100	20	Normal
15	Psych Up	Normal	Status	—	—	10	Normal
18	Confuse Ray	Ghost	Status	—	100	10	Normal
21	Magic Coat	Psychic	Status	—	—	15	Self
26	Zen Headbutt	Psychic	Physical	80	90	15	Normal
29	Rest	Psychic	Status	—	—	10	Self
29	Snore	Normal	Special	50	100	15	Normal
33	Power Gem	Rock	Special	80	100	20	Normal
38	Psyshock	Psychic	Special	80	100	10	Normal
40	Payback	Dark	Physical	50	100	10	Normal
44	Psychic	Psychic	Special	90	100	10	Normal
50	Bounce	Flying	Physical	85	85	5	Normal

● **TM & HM MOVES**

No.	Name	Type	Kind	Pow.	Acc.	PP	Range
TM03	Psyshock	Psychic	Special	80	100	10	Normal
TM04	Calm Mind	Psychic	Status	—	—	20	Self
TM06	Toxic	Poison	Status	—	90	10	Normal
TM10	Hidden Power	Normal	Special	60	100	15	Normal
TM11	Sunny Day	Fire	Status	—	—	5	Both Sides
TM12	Taunt	Dark	Status	—	100	20	Normal
TM16	Light Screen	Psychic	Status	—	—	30	Your Side
TM17	Protect	Normal	Status	—	—	10	Self
TM18	Rain Dance	Water	Status	—	—	5	Both Sides
TM21	Frustration	Normal	Physical	—	100	20	Normal
TM27	Return	Normal	Physical	—	100	20	Normal
TM29	Psychic	Psychic	Special	90	100	10	Normal
TM30	Shadow Ball	Ghost	Special	80	100	15	Normal
TM32	Double Team	Normal	Status	—	—	15	Self
TM33	Reflect	Psychic	Status	—	—	20	Your Side
TM41	Torment	Dark	Status	—	100	15	Normal
TM42	Facade	Normal	Physical	70	100	20	Normal
TM44	Rest	Psychic	Status	—	—	10	Self
TM45	Attract	Normal	Status	—	100	15	Normal
TM46	Thief	Dark	Physical	60	100	25	Normal
TM48	Round	Normal	Special	60	100	15	Normal
TM57	Charge Beam	Electric	Special	50	90	10	Normal
TM66	Payback	Dark	Physical	50	100	10	Normal
TM70	Flash	Normal	Status	—	100	20	Normal
TM73	Thunder Wave	Electric	Status	—	100	20	Normal
TM77	Psych Up	Normal	Status	—	—	10	Normal
TM85	Dream Eater	Psychic	Special	100	100	15	Normal
TM86	Grass Knot	Grass	Special	—	100	20	Normal
TM87	Swagger	Normal	Status	—	90	15	Normal
TM88	Sleep Talk	Normal	Status	—	—	10	Self
TM90	Substitute	Normal	Status	—	—	10	Self
TM92	Trick Room	Psychic	Status	—	—	5	Both Sides
TM100	Confide	Normal	Status	—	—	20	Normal

No.	Name	Type	Kind	Pow.	Acc.	PP	Range

● **MOVES TAUGHT BY PEOPLE**

Name	Type	Kind	Pow.	Acc.	PP	Range

● **EGG MOVES**

Name	Type	Kind	Pow.	Acc.	PP	Range
Future Sight	Psychic	Special	120	100	10	Normal
Extrasensory	Psychic	Special	80	100	20	Normal
Trick	Psychic	Status	—	100	10	Normal
Zen Headbutt	Psychic	Physical	80	90	15	Normal
Amnesia	Psychic	Status	—	—	20	Self
Mirror Coat	Psychic	Special	—	100	20	Varies
Skill Swap	Psychic	Status	—	—	10	Normal
Whirlwind	Normal	Status	—	—	20	Normal
Lucky Chant	Normal	Status	—	—	30	Your Side
Endure	Normal	Status	—	—	10	Self
Simple Beam	Normal	Status	—	100	15	Normal

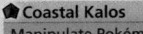

AFTER THE HALL OF FAME

CENTRAL KALOS

COASTAL KALOS

008

Grumpig

MOUNTAIN KALOS

ADVENTURE DATA

🏠 Coastal Kalos 008
Manipulate Pokémon
☑ **Grumpig**

HEIGHT: 2'11" WEIGHT: 157.6 lbs.
GENDER: ♂/♀

X It uses black pearls to amplify its psychic power. It does a strange dance to control foes' minds.

Y It uses black pearls to amplify its psychic power. It does an odd dance to gain control over foes.

TYPE [Psychic]

ABILITIES
Thick Fat
Own Tempo

HIDDEN ABILITY
Gluttony

STAT GROWTH RATES
HP ■■■
Attack ■■■
Defense ■■■
Sp. Atk ■■■■
Sp. Def ■■■■■
Speed ■■■■■

EGG GROUP
Field

🔼 EVOLUTION

Lv. 32

Spoink → Grumpig

ITEMS SOMETIMES HELD BY WILD POKÉMON
None

Damage taken in normal battles		Damage taken in Inverse Battles	
Normal	×1	Normal	×1
Fire	×1	Fire	×1
Water	×1	Water	×1
Grass	×1	Grass	×1
Electric	×1	Electric	×1
Ice	×1	Ice	×1
Fighting	×0.5	Fighting	×2
Poison	×1	Poison	×1
Ground	×1	Ground	×1
Flying	×1	Flying	×1
Psychic	×0.5	Psychic	×2
Bug	×2	Bug	×0.5
Rock	×1	Rock	×1
Ghost	×2	Ghost	×0.5
Dragon	×1	Dragon	×1
Dark	×2	Dark	×0.5
Steel	×1	Steel	×1
Fairy	×1	Fairy	×1

Can be used in	
Inverse Battle	Battle Institute
—	Battle Maison
Battle Chateau	Random Matchup

Same form for ♂ / ♀

How to obtain for your Coastal Kalos Pokédex

Level up Spoink to Lv. 32. Level up Spoink to Lv. 32.

X Y

● LEVEL-UP MOVES

Lv.	Name	Type	Kind	Pow.	Acc.	PP	Range
1	Splash	Normal	Status	—	—	40	Self
1	Pswave	Psychic	Special	—	100	15	Normal
1	Odor Sleuth	Normal	Status	—	—	40	Normal
1	Psybeam	Psychic	Special	65	100	20	Normal
7	Pswave	Psychic	Special	—	100	15	Normal
10	Odor Sleuth	Normal	Status	—	—	40	Normal
14	Psybeam	Psychic	Special	65	100	20	Normal
15	Psych Up	Normal	Status	—	—	10	Normal
18	Confuse Ray	Ghost	Status	—	100	10	Normal
21	Magic Coat	Psychic	Status	—	—	15	Self
26	Zen Headbutt	Psychic	Physical	80	90	15	Normal
29	Rest	Psychic	Status	—	—	10	Self
29	Snore	Normal	Special	50	100	15	Normal
35	Power Gem	Rock	Special	80	100	20	Normal
42	Psyshock	Psychic	Special	80	100	10	Normal
46	Payback	Dark	Physical	50	100	10	Normal
52	Psychic	Psychic	Special	90	100	10	Normal
60	Bounce	Flying	Physical	85	85	5	Normal

● TM & HM MOVES

No.	Name	Type	Kind	Pow.	Acc.	PP	Range
TM03	Psyshock	Psychic	Special	80	100	10	Normal
TM04	Calm Mind	Psychic	Status	—	—	20	Self
TM06	Toxic	Poison	Status	—	90	10	Normal
TM10	Hidden Power	Normal	Special	60	100	15	Normal
TM11	Sunny Day	Fire	Status	—	—	5	Both Sides
TM12	Taunt	Dark	Status	—	100	20	Normal
TM15	Hyper Beam	Normal	Special	150	90	5	Normal
TM16	Light Screen	Psychic	Status	—	—	30	Your Side
TM17	Protect	Normal	Status	—	—	10	Self
TM18	Rain Dance	Water	Status	—	—	5	Both Sides
TM21	Frustration	Normal	Physical	—	100	20	Normal
TM27	Return	Normal	Physical	—	100	20	Normal
TM29	Psychic	Psychic	Special	90	100	10	Normal
TM30	Shadow Ball	Ghost	Special	80	100	15	Normal
TM31	Brick Break	Fighting	Physical	75	100	15	Normal
TM32	Double Team	Normal	Status	—	—	15	Self
TM33	Reflect	Psychic	Status	—	—	20	Your Side
TM41	Torment	Dark	Status	—	100	15	Normal
TM42	Facade	Normal	Physical	70	100	20	Normal
TM44	Rest	Psychic	Status	—	—	10	Self
TM45	Attract	Normal	Status	—	100	15	Normal
TM46	Thief	Dark	Physical	60	100	25	Normal
TM48	Round	Normal	Special	60	100	15	Normal
TM52	Focus Blast	Fighting	Special	120	70	5	Normal
TM53	Energy Ball	Grass	Special	90	100	10	Normal
TM56	Fling	Dark	Physical	—	100	10	Normal
TM57	Charge Beam	Electric	Special	50	90	10	Normal
TM66	Payback	Dark	Physical	50	100	10	Normal
TM68	Giga Impact	Normal	Physical	150	90	5	Normal
TM70	Flash	Normal	Status	—	100	20	Normal
TM73	Thunder Wave	Electric	Status	—	100	20	Normal
TM77	Psych Up	Normal	Status	—	—	10	Normal
TM78	Bulldoze	Ground	Physical	60	100	20	Adjacent

No.	Name	Type	Kind	Pow.	Acc.	PP	Range
TM85	Dream Eater	Psychic	Special	100	100	15	Normal
TM86	Grass Knot	Grass	Special	—	100	20	Normal
TM87	Swagger	Normal	Status	—	90	15	Normal
TM88	Sleep Talk	Normal	Status	—	—	10	Self
TM90	Substitute	Normal	Status	—	—	10	Self
TM92	Trick Room	Psychic	Status	—	—	5	Both Sides
TM98	Power-Up Punch	Fighting	Physical	40	100	20	Normal
TM100	Confide	Normal	Status	—	—	20	Normal

● MOVES TAUGHT BY PEOPLE

Name	Type	Kind	Pow.	Acc.	PP	Range

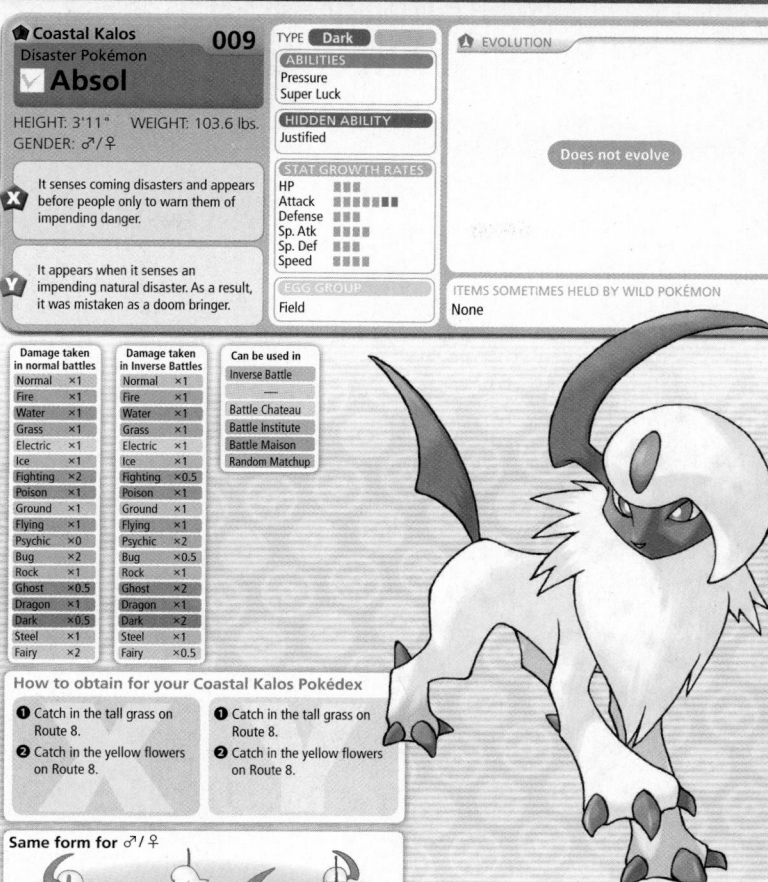

Coastal Kalos
009
Disaster Pokémon

Absol

HEIGHT: 3'11"   WEIGHT: 103.6 lbs.
GENDER: ♂/♀

X It senses coming disasters and appears before people only to warn them of impending danger.

Y It appears when it senses an impending natural disaster. As a result, it was mistaken as a doom bringer.

TYPE Dark

ABILITIES
Pressure
Super Luck

HIDDEN ABILITY
Justified

STAT GROWTH RATES
HP ■■■
Attack ■■■■■■■
Defense ■■■■
Sp. Atk ■■■
Sp. Def ■■■
Speed ■■■■

EGG GROUP
Field

EVOLUTION

Does not evolve

ITEMS SOMETIMES HELD BY WILD POKÉMON
None

Damage taken in normal battles	
Normal	×1
Fire	×1
Water	×1
Grass	×1
Electric	×1
Ice	×1
Fighting	×2
Poison	×1
Ground	×1
Flying	×1
Psychic	×0
Bug	×2
Rock	×1
Ghost	×0.5
Dragon	×1
Dark	×0.5
Steel	×1
Fairy	×2

Damage taken in Inverse Battles	
Normal	×1
Fire	×1
Water	×1
Grass	×1
Electric	×1
Ice	×1
Fighting	×0.5
Poison	×1
Ground	×1
Flying	×1
Psychic	×2
Bug	×0.5
Rock	×1
Ghost	×2
Dragon	×1
Dark	×2
Steel	×1
Fairy	×0.5

Can be used in
Inverse Battle
—
Battle Chateau
Battle Institute
Battle Maison
Random Matchup

How to obtain for your Coastal Kalos Pokédex

❶ Catch in the tall grass on Route 8.
❷ Catch in the yellow flowers on Route 8.

❶ Catch in the tall grass on Route 8.
❷ Catch in the yellow flowers on Route 8.

Same form for ♂/♀

● LEVEL-UP MOVES

Lv.	Name	Type	Kind	Pow.	Acc.	PP	Range
1	Perish Song	Normal	Status	—	—	5	Adjacent
1	Me First	Normal	Status	—	—	20	Varies
1	Razor Wind	Normal	Special	80	100	10	Many Others
1	Detect	Fighting	Status	—	—	5	Self
1	Taunt	Dark	Status	—	100	20	Normal
1	Scratch	Normal	Physical	40	100	35	Normal
1	Feint	Normal	Physical	30	100	10	Normal
4	Leer	Normal	Status	—	100	30	Many Others
9	Quick Attack	Normal	Physical	40	100	30	Normal
12	Pursuit	Dark	Physical	40	100	20	Normal
17	Taunt	Dark	Status	—	100	20	Normal
20	Bite	Dark	Physical	60	100	25	Normal
25	Double Team	Normal	Status	—	—	15	Self
28	Slash	Normal	Physical	70	100	20	Normal
33	Swords Dance	Normal	Status	—	—	20	Self
36	Future Sight	Psychic	Special	120	100	10	Normal
41	Sunny Day	Fire	Status	—	—	5	Both Sides
44	Detect	Fighting	Status	—	—	5	Self
47	Psycho Cut	Psychic	Physical	70	100	20	Normal
50	Sucker Punch	Dark	Physical	80	100	5	Normal
57	Razor Wind	Normal	Special	80	100	10	Many Others
60	Me First	Normal	Status	—	—	20	Varies
65	Perish Song	Normal	Status	—	—	5	Adjacent

● TM & HM MOVES

No.	Name	Type	Kind	Pow.	Acc.	PP	Range
TM01	Hone Claws	Dark	Status	—	—	15	Self
TM04	Calm Mind	Psychic	Status	—	—	20	Self
TM06	Toxic	Poison	Status	—	90	10	Normal
TM07	Hail	Ice	Status	—	—	10	Both Sides
TM10	Hidden Power	Normal	Special	60	100	15	Normal
TM11	Sunny Day	Fire	Status	—	—	5	Both Sides
TM12	Taunt	Dark	Status	—	100	20	Normal
TM13	Ice Beam	Ice	Special	90	100	10	Normal
TM14	Blizzard	Ice	Special	110	70	5	Many Others

No.	Name	Type	Kind	Pow.	Acc.	PP	Range
TM15	Hyper Beam	Normal	Special	150	90	5	Normal
TM17	Protect	Normal	Status	—	—	10	Self
TM18	Rain Dance	Water	Status	—	—	5	Both Sides
TM21	Frustration	Normal	Physical	—	100	20	Normal
TM24	Thunderbolt	Electric	Special	90	100	15	Normal
TM25	Thunder	Electric	Special	110	70	10	Normal
TM27	Return	Normal	Physical	—	100	20	Normal
TM30	Shadow Ball	Ghost	Special	80	100	15	Normal
TM32	Double Team	Normal	Status	—	—	15	Self
TM35	Flamethrower	Fire	Special	90	100	15	Normal
TM37	Sandstorm	Rock	Status	—	—	10	Both Sides
TM38	Fire Blast	Fire	Special	110	85	5	Normal
TM39	Rock Tomb	Rock	Physical	60	95	15	Normal
TM40	Aerial Ace	Flying	Physical	60	—	20	Normal
TM41	Torment	Dark	Status	—	100	15	Normal
TM42	Facade	Normal	Physical	70	100	20	Normal
TM44	Rest	Psychic	Status	—	—	10	Self
TM45	Attract	Normal	Status	—	100	15	Normal
TM46	Thief	Dark	Physical	60	100	25	Normal
TM48	Round	Normal	Special	60	100	15	Normal
TM49	Echoed Voice	Normal	Special	40	100	15	Normal
TM54	False Swipe	Normal	Physical	40	100	40	Normal
TM57	Charge Beam	Electric	Special	50	90	10	Normal
TM59	Incinerate	Fire	Special	60	100	15	Many Others
TM61	Will-O-Wisp	Fire	Status	—	85	15	Normal
TM65	Shadow Claw	Ghost	Physical	70	100	15	Normal
TM66	Payback	Dark	Physical	50	100	10	Normal
TM67	Retaliate	Normal	Physical	70	100	5	Normal
TM68	Giga Impact	Normal	Physical	150	90	5	Normal
TM70	Flash	Normal	Status	—	100	20	Normal
TM71	Stone Edge	Rock	Physical	100	80	5	Normal
TM73	Thunder Wave	Electric	Status	—	100	20	Normal
TM75	Swords Dance	Normal	Status	—	—	20	Self
TM77	Psych Up	Normal	Status	—	—	10	Normal
TM80	Rock Slide	Rock	Physical	75	90	10	Many Others

No.	Name	Type	Kind	Pow.	Acc.	PP	Range
TM81	X-Scissor	Bug	Physical	80	100	15	Normal
TM85	Dream Eater	Psychic	Special	100	100	15	Normal
TM87	Swagger	Normal	Status	—	90	15	Normal
TM88	Sleep Talk	Normal	Status	—	—	10	Self
TM90	Substitute	Normal	Status	—	—	10	Self
TM94	Rock Smash	Fighting	Physical	40	100	15	Normal
TM95	Snarl	Dark	Special	55	95	15	Many Others
TM97	Dark Pulse	Dark	Special	80	100	15	Normal
TM100	Confide	Normal	Status	—	—	20	Normal
HM01	Cut	Normal	Physical	50	95	30	Normal
HM04	Strength	Normal	Physical	80	100	15	Normal

● MOVES TAUGHT BY PEOPLE

Name	Type	Kind	Pow.	Acc.	PP	Range

● EGG MOVES

Name	Type	Kind	Pow.	Acc.	PP	Range
Baton Pass	Normal	Status	—	—	40	Self
Feint Attack	Dark	Physical	60	—	20	Normal
Double-Edge	Normal	Physical	120	100	15	Normal
Magic Coat	Psychic	Status	—	—	15	Self
Curse	Ghost	Status	—	—	10	Varies
Mean Look	Normal	Status	—	—	5	Normal
Zen Headbutt	Psychic	Physical	80	90	15	Normal
Punishment	Dark	Physical	—	100	5	Normal
Sucker Punch	Dark	Physical	80	100	5	Normal
Assurance	Dark	Physical	60	100	10	Normal
Me First	Normal	Status	—	—	20	Varies
Megahorn	Bug	Physical	120	85	10	Normal
Hex	Ghost	Special	65	100	10	Normal
Perish Song	Normal	Status	—	—	5	Adjacent
Play Rough	Fairy	Physical	90	90	10	Normal

AFTER THE HALL OF FAME

CENTRAL KALOS

COASTAL KALOS

Mega Absol

MOUNTAIN KALOS

ADVENTURE DATA

Mega Evolution

Disaster Pokémon

☑ **Mega Absol**

TYPE: Dark

ABILITY: Magic Bounce

HEIGHT: 3'11"   WEIGHT: 108.0 lbs.   GENDER: ♂/♀

STAT GROWTH RATES

HP	■■■
Attack	■■■■■■■
Defense	■■■■
Sp. Atk	■■■■■
Sp. Def	■■■■
Speed	■■■■■■

MEGA STONE REQUIRED

Absolite

Receive from Serena/Calem after defeating her/him in battle in Kiloude City, after entering the Hall of Fame (must take part in at least one battle in the Battle Maison first).

Damage taken in normal battles		Damage taken in Inverse Battles	
Normal	×1	Normal	×1
Fire	×1	Fire	×1
Water	×1	Water	×1
Grass	×1	Grass	×1
Electric	×1	Electric	×1
Ice	×1	Ice	×1
Fighting	×2	Fighting	×0.5
Poison	×1	Poison	×1
Ground	×1	Ground	×1
Flying	×1	Flying	×1
Psychic	×0	Psychic	×2
Bug	×2	Bug	×0.5
Rock	×1	Rock	×1
Ghost	×0.5	Ghost	×2
Dragon	×1	Dragon	×1
Dark	×0.5	Dark	×2
Steel	×1	Steel	×1
Fairy	×2	Fairy	×0.5

Can be used in	
Inverse Battle	Battle Institute
—	Battle Maison
Battle Chateau	Random Matchup

Same form for ♂/♀

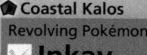 **Coastal Kalos**
Revolving Pokémon
010

☑Inkay

HEIGHT: 1'04" WEIGHT: 7.7 lbs.
GENDER: ♂ / ♀

X	Opponents who stare at the flashing of the light-emitting spots on its body become dazed and lose their will to fight.
Y	It flashes the light-emitting spots on its body, which drains its opponent's will to fight. It takes the opportunity to scuttle away and hide.

TYPE Dark Psychic

ABILITIES
Contrary
Suction Cups

HIDDEN ABILITY
Infiltrator

STAT GROWTH RATES
HP ▪▪
Attack ▪▪
Defense ▪▪
Sp. Atk ▪▪
Sp. Def ▪▪▪
Speed ▪▪▪

EGG GROUPS
Water 1, Water 2

ITEMS SOMETIMES HELD BY WILD POKÉMON
None

EVOLUTION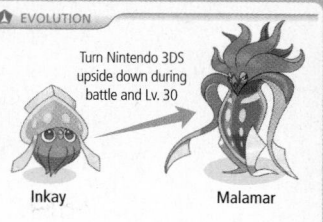

Turn Nintendo 3DS upside down during battle and Lv. 30

Inkay → Malamar

Damage taken in normal battles		Damage taken in Inverse Battles	
Normal	×1	Normal	×1
Fire	×1	Fire	×1
Water	×1	Water	×1
Grass	×1	Grass	×1
Electric	×1	Electric	×1
Ice	×1	Ice	×1
Fighting	×1	Fighting	×1
Poison	×1	Poison	×1
Ground	×1	Ground	×1
Flying	×1	Flying	×1
Psychic	×0	Psychic	×4
Bug	×4	Bug	×0.25
Rock	×1	Rock	×1
Ghost	×1	Ghost	×1
Dragon	×1	Dragon	×1
Dark	×1	Dark	×1
Steel	×1	Steel	×1
Fairy	×2	Fairy	×0.5

Can be used in	
Inverse Battle	Battle Institute
—	Battle Maison
Battle Chateau	Random Matchup

Same form for ♂ / ♀

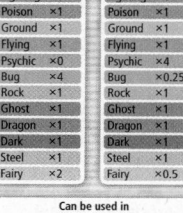

How to obtain for your Coastal Kalos Pokédex

❶ Catch in the tall grass on Route 8.
❷ Catch in the yellow flowers on Route 8.

❶ Catch in the tall grass on Route 8.
❷ Catch in the yellow flowers on Route 8.

● LEVEL-UP MOVES

Lv.	Name	Type	Kind	Pow.	Acc.	PP	Range
1	Tackle	Normal	Physical	50	100	35	Normal
1	Peck	Flying	Physical	35	100	35	Normal
1	Constrict	Normal	Physical	10	100	35	Normal
4	Reflect	Psychic	Status	—	—	20	Your Side
8	Foul Play	Dark	Physical	95	100	15	Normal
12	Swagger	Normal	Status	—	90	15	Normal
13	Psywave	Psychic	Special	—	100	15	Normal
15	Topsy-Turvy	Dark	Status	—	—	20	Normal
18	Hypnosis	Psychic	Status	—	60	20	Normal
21	Psybeam	Psychic	Special	65	100	20	Normal
23	Switcheroo	Dark	Status	—	100	10	Normal
27	Payback	Dark	Physical	50	100	10	Normal
31	Light Screen	Psychic	Status	—	—	30	Your Side
35	Pluck	Flying	Physical	60	100	20	Normal
39	Psycho Cut	Psychic	Physical	70	100	20	Normal
43	Slash	Normal	Physical	70	100	20	Normal
46	Night Slash	Dark	Physical	70	100	15	Normal
48	Superpower	Fighting	Physical	120	100	5	Normal

● TM & HM MOVES

No.	Name	Type	Kind	Pow.	Acc.	PP	Range
TM04	Calm Mind	Psychic	Status	—	—	20	Self
TM06	Toxic	Poison	Status	—	90	10	Normal
TM10	Hidden Power	Normal	Special	60	100	15	Normal
TM11	Sunny Day	Fire	Status	—	—	5	Both Sides
TM12	Taunt	Dark	Status	—	100	20	Normal
TM16	Light Screen	Psychic	Status	—	—	30	Your Side
TM17	Protect	Normal	Status	—	—	10	Self
TM18	Rain Dance	Water	Status	—	—	5	Both Sides
TM21	Frustration	Normal	Physical	—	100	20	Normal
TM24	Thunderbolt	Electric	Special	90	100	15	Normal
TM27	Return	Normal	Physical	—	100	20	Normal
TM29	Psychic	Psychic	Special	90	100	10	Normal
TM32	Double Team	Normal	Status	—	—	15	Self
TM33	Reflect	Psychic	Status	—	—	20	Your Side
TM35	Flamethrower	Fire	Special	90	100	15	Normal
TM40	Aerial Ace	Flying	Physical	60	—	20	Normal
TM41	Torment	Dark	Status	—	100	15	Normal
TM42	Facade	Normal	Physical	70	100	20	Normal
TM44	Rest	Psychic	Status	—	—	10	Self
TM45	Attract	Normal	Status	—	100	15	Normal
TM46	Thief	Dark	Physical	60	100	25	Normal
TM48	Round	Normal	Special	60	100	15	Normal
TM56	Fling	Dark	Physical	—	100	10	Normal
TM63	Embargo	Dark	Status	—	100	15	Normal
TM66	Payback	Dark	Physical	50	100	10	Normal
TM67	Retaliate	Normal	Physical	70	100	5	Normal
TM70	Flash	Normal	Status	—	100	20	Normal
TM77	Psych Up	Normal	Status	—	—	10	Self
TM80	Rock Slide	Rock	Physical	75	90	10	Many Others
TM87	Swagger	Normal	Status	—	90	15	Normal
TM88	Sleep Talk	Normal	Status	—	—	10	Self
TM90	Substitute	Normal	Status	—	—	10	Self
TM92	Trick Room	Psychic	Status	—	—	5	Both Sides

No.	Name	Type	Kind	Pow.	Acc.	PP	Range
TM97	Dark Pulse	Dark	Special	80	100	15	Normal
TM100	Confide	Normal	Status	—	—	20	Normal
HM01	Cut	Normal	Physical	50	95	30	Normal

● MOVES TAUGHT BY PEOPLE

Name	Type	Kind	Pow.	Acc.	PP	Range

● EGG MOVES

Name	Type	Kind	Pow.	Acc.	PP	Range
Simple Beam	Normal	Status	—	100	15	Normal
Power Split	Psychic	Status	—	—	10	Normal
Camouflage	Normal	Status	—	—	20	Self
Flatter	Dark	Status	—	100	15	Normal
Destiny Bond	Ghost	Status	—	—	5	Self

AFTER THE HALL OF FAME

CENTRAL KALOS

COASTAL KALOS

010 Inkay

MOUNTAIN KALOS

ADVENTURE DATA

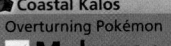

AFTER THE HALL OF FAME

CENTRAL KALOS

COASTAL KALOS

011

Malamar

MOUNTAIN KALOS

ADVENTURE DATA

Coastal Kalos 011
Overturning Pokémon
☑ Malamar

HEIGHT: 4'11" WEIGHT: 103.6 lbs.
GENDER: ♂/♀

X It wields the most compelling hypnotic powers of any Pokémon, and it forces others to do whatever it wants.

Y It lures its prey close with hypnotic motions, then wraps its tentacles around it before finishing it off with digestive fluids.

TYPE Dark | Psychic

ABILITIES
Contrary
Suction Cups

HIDDEN ABILITY
Infiltrator

STAT GROWTH RATES
HP	■■■■
Attack	■■■■■
Defense	■■■■
Sp. Atk	■■■
Sp. Def	■■■
Speed	■■■

EGG GROUPS
Water 1, Water 2

EVOLUTION

Turn Nintendo 3DS upside down during battle and Lv. 30

Inkay → Malamar

ITEMS SOMETIMES HELD BY WILD POKÉMON
None

Can be used in
Inverse Battle
━━━
Battle Chateau
Battle Institute
Battle Maison
Random Matchup

Damage taken in normal battles	
Normal	×1
Fire	×1
Water	×1
Grass	×1
Electric	×1
Ice	×1
Fighting	×1
Poison	×1
Ground	×1
Flying	×1
Psychic	×0
Bug	×4
Rock	×1
Ghost	×1
Dragon	×1
Dark	×1
Steel	×1
Fairy	×2

Damage taken in Inverse Battles	
Normal	×1
Fire	×1
Water	×1
Grass	×1
Electric	×1
Ice	×1
Fighting	×1
Poison	×1
Ground	×1
Flying	×1
Psychic	×4
Bug	×0.25
Rock	×1
Ghost	×1
Dragon	×1
Dark	×1
Steel	×1
Fairy	×0.5

How to obtain for your Coastal Kalos Pokédex

Turn your Nintendo 3DS system upside down for the entire battle in which you level up Inkay to Lv. 30.

Turn your Nintendo 3DS system upside down for the entire battle in which you level up Inkay to Lv. 30.

Same form for ♂/♀

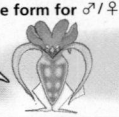

● LEVEL-UP MOVES

Lv.	Name	Type	Kind	Pow.	Acc.	PP	Range
1	Superpower	Fighting	Physical	120	100	5	Normal
1	Reversal	Fighting	Physical	—	100	15	Normal
1	Tackle	Normal	Physical	50	100	35	Normal
1	Peck	Flying	Physical	35	100	35	Normal
1	Constrict	Normal	Physical	10	100	35	Normal
4	Reflect	Psychic	Status	—	—	20	Your Side
8	Foul Play	Dark	Physical	95	100	15	Normal
12	Swagger	Normal	Status	—	90	15	Normal
13	Psywave	Psychic	Special	—	100	15	Normal
15	Topsy-Turvy	Dark	Status	—	—	20	Normal
18	Hypnosis	Psychic	Status	—	60	20	Normal
21	Psybeam	Psychic	Special	65	100	20	Normal
23	Switcheroo	Dark	Status	—	100	10	Normal
27	Payback	Dark	Physical	50	100	10	Normal
31	Light Screen	Psychic	Status	—	—	30	Your Side
35	Pluck	Flying	Physical	60	100	20	Normal
39	Psycho Cut	Psychic	Physical	70	100	20	Normal
43	Slash	Normal	Physical	70	100	20	Normal
46	Night Slash	Dark	Physical	70	100	15	Normal
48	Superpower	Fighting	Physical	120	100	5	Normal

● TM & HM MOVES

No.	Name	Type	Kind	Pow.	Acc.	PP	Range
TM03	Psyshock	Psychic	Special	80	100	10	Normal
TM04	Calm Mind	Psychic	Status	—	—	20	Self
TM06	Toxic	Poison	Status	—	90	10	Normal
TM10	Hidden Power	Normal	Special	60	100	15	Normal
TM11	Sunny Day	Fire	Status	—	—	5	Both Sides
TM12	Taunt	Dark	Status	—	100	20	Normal
TM15	Hyper Beam	Normal	Special	150	90	5	Normal
TM16	Light Screen	Psychic	Status	—	—	30	Your Side
TM17	Protect	Normal	Status	—	—	10	Self
TM18	Rain Dance	Water	Status	—	—	5	Both Sides
TM21	Frustration	Normal	Physical	—	100	20	Normal
TM24	Thunderbolt	Electric	Special	90	100	15	Normal
TM27	Return	Normal	Physical	—	100	20	Normal
TM29	Psychic	Psychic	Special	90	100	10	Normal
TM32	Double Team	Normal	Status	—	—	15	Self
TM33	Reflect	Psychic	Status	—	—	20	Your Side
TM35	Flamethrower	Fire	Special	90	100	15	Normal
TM40	Aerial Ace	Flying	Physical	60	—	20	Normal
TM41	Torment	Dark	Status	—	100	15	Normal
TM42	Facade	Normal	Physical	70	100	20	Normal
TM44	Rest	Psychic	Status	—	—	10	Self
TM45	Attract	Normal	Status	—	100	15	Normal
TM46	Thief	Dark	Physical	60	100	25	Normal
TM48	Round	Normal	Special	60	100	15	Normal
TM56	Fling	Dark	Physical	—	100	10	Normal
TM63	Embargo	Dark	Status	—	100	15	Normal
TM66	Payback	Dark	Physical	50	100	10	Normal
TM67	Retaliate	Normal	Physical	70	100	5	Normal
TM68	Giga Impact	Normal	Physical	150	90	5	Normal
TM70	Flash	Normal	Status	—	100	20	Normal
TM77	Psych Up	Normal	Status	—	—	10	Normal
TM80	Rock Slide	Rock	Physical	75	90	10	Many Others
TM87	Swagger	Normal	Status	—	90	15	Normal

No.	Name	Type	Kind	Pow.	Acc.	PP	Range
TM88	Sleep Talk	Normal	Status	—	—	10	Self
TM90	Substitute	Normal	Status	—	—	10	Self
TM92	Trick Room	Psychic	Status	—	—	5	Both Sides
TM97	Dark Pulse	Dark	Special	80	100	15	Normal
TM100	Confide	Normal	Status	—	—	20	Normal
HM01	Cut	Normal	Physical	50	95	30	Normal

● MOVES TAUGHT BY PEOPLE

Name	Type	Kind	Pow.	Acc.	PP	Range

Coastal Kalos

Meteorite Pokémon

Lunatone

012

HEIGHT: 3'03"   WEIGHT: 370.4 lbs.
GENDER: unknown

TYPE: Rock | Psychic

ABILITY
Levitate

HIDDEN ABILITY
None

STAT GROWTH RATES
HP ■■■
Attack ■■■
Defense ■■■
Sp. Atk ■■■■■
Sp. Def ■■■■
Speed ■■■■

EGG GROUP
Mineral

❌ Because it turns active on nights of the full moon, it is said to have some link to the lunar phases.

🅨 It was discovered at the site of a meteor strike 40 years ago. Its stare can lull its foes to sleep.

EVOLUTION

Does not evolve

ITEMS SOMETIMES HELD BY WILD POKÉMON
Moon Stone

Damage taken in normal battles	
Normal	×0.5
Fire	×0.5
Water	×2
Grass	×2
Electric	×1
Ice	×1
Fighting	×1
Poison	×0.5
Ground	×2
Flying	×0.5
Psychic	×0.5
Bug	×2
Rock	×1
Ghost	×2
Dragon	×1
Dark	×2
Steel	×2
Fairy	×1

Damage taken in Inverse Battles	
Normal	×2
Fire	×2
Water	×0.5
Grass	×0.5
Electric	×1
Ice	×1
Fighting	×1
Poison	×2
Ground	×0.5
Flying	×2
Psychic	×2
Bug	×0.5
Rock	×1
Ghost	×0.5
Dragon	×1
Dark	×0.5
Steel	×0.5
Fairy	×1

Can be used in	
Inverse Battle	Battle Institute
Sky Battle	Battle Maison
Battle Chateau	Random Matchup

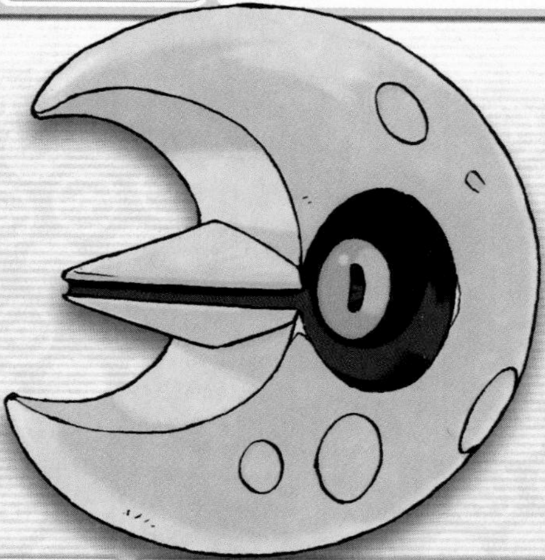

Gender unknown

 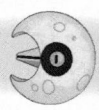 

How to obtain for your Coastal Kalos Pokédex

Catch in Glittering Cave.   Catch in Glittering Cave.

● LEVEL-UP MOVES

Lv.	Name	Type	Kind	Pow.	Acc.	PP	Range
1	Magic Room	Psychic	Status	—	—	10	Both Sides
1	Rock Throw	Rock	Physical	50	90	15	Normal
1	Tackle	Normal	Physical	50	100	35	Normal
1	Harden	Normal	Status	—	—	30	Self
1	Confusion	Psychic	Special	50	100	25	Normal
5	Rock Throw	Rock	Physical	50	90	15	Normal
9	Hypnosis	Psychic	Status	—	60	20	Normal
13	Rock Polish	Rock	Status	—	—	20	Self
17	Pyswave	Psychic	Special	—	100	15	Normal
21	Embargo	Dark	Status	—	100	15	Normal
25	Rock Slide	Rock	Physical	75	90	10	Many Others
29	Cosmic Power	Psychic	Status	—	—	20	Self
33	Psychic	Psychic	Special	90	100	10	Normal
37	Heal Block	Psychic	Status	—	100	15	Many Others
41	Stone Edge	Rock	Physical	100	80	5	Normal
45	Future Sight	Psychic	Special	120	100	10	Normal
49	Explosion	Normal	Physical	250	100	5	Adjacent
50	Moonblast	Fairy	Special	95	100	15	Normal
53	Magic Room	Psychic	Status	—	—	10	Both Sides

■ TM & HM MOVES

No.	Name	Type	Kind	Pow.	Acc.	PP	Range
TM03	Psyshock	Psychic	Special	80	100	10	Normal
TM04	Calm Mind	Psychic	Status	—	—	20	Self
TM06	Toxic	Poison	Status	—	90	10	Normal
TM10	Hidden Power	Normal	Special	60	100	15	Normal
TM13	Ice Beam	Ice	Special	90	100	10	Normal
TM14	Blizzard	Ice	Special	110	70	5	Many Others
TM15	Hyper Beam	Normal	Special	150	90	5	Normal
TM16	Light Screen	Psychic	Status	—	—	30	Your Side
TM17	Protect	Normal	Status	—	—	10	Self
TM18	Rain Dance	Water	Status	—	—	5	Both Sides
TM20	Safeguard	Normal	Status	—	—	25	Your Side
TM21	Frustration	Normal	Physical	—	100	20	Normal
TM23	Smack Down	Rock	Physical	50	100	15	Normal
TM26	Earthquake	Ground	Physical	100	100	10	Adjacent
TM27	Return	Normal	Physical	—	100	20	Normal
TM29	Psychic	Psychic	Special	90	100	10	Normal
TM30	Shadow Ball	Ghost	Special	80	100	15	Normal
TM32	Double Team	Normal	Status	—	—	15	Self
TM33	Reflect	Psychic	Status	—	—	20	Your Side
TM37	Sandstorm	Rock	Status	—	—	10	Both Sides
TM39	Rock Tomb	Rock	Physical	60	95	15	Normal
TM42	Facade	Normal	Physical	70	100	20	Normal
TM44	Rest	Psychic	Status	—	—	10	Self
TM48	Round	Normal	Special	60	100	15	Normal
TM57	Charge Beam	Electric	Special	50	90	10	Normal
TM62	Acrobatics	Flying	Physical	55	100	15	Normal
TM63	Embargo	Dark	Status	—	100	15	Normal
TM64	Explosion	Normal	Physical	250	100	5	Adjacent
TM68	Giga Impact	Normal	Physical	150	90	5	Normal
TM69	Rock Polish	Rock	Status	—	—	20	Self
TM70	Flash	Normal	Status	—	100	20	Normal
TM71	Stone Edge	Rock	Physical	100	80	5	Normal
TM74	Gyro Ball	Steel	Physical	—	100	5	Normal

No.	Name	Type	Kind	Pow.	Acc.	PP	Range
TM77	Psych Up	Normal	Status	—	—	10	Normal
TM78	Bulldoze	Ground	Physical	60	100	20	Adjacent
TM80	Rock Slide	Rock	Physical	75	90	10	Many Others
TM85	Dream Eater	Psychic	Special	100	100	15	Normal
TM86	Grass Knot	Grass	Special	—	100	20	Normal
TM87	Swagger	Normal	Status	—	90	15	Normal
TM88	Sleep Talk	Normal	Status	—	—	10	Self
TM90	Substitute	Normal	Status	—	—	10	Self
TM92	Trick Room	Psychic	Status	—	—	5	Both Sides
TM100	Confide	Normal	Status	—	—	20	Normal

● MOVES TAUGHT BY PEOPLE

Name	Type	Kind	Pow.	Acc.	PP	Range

● EGG MOVES

Name	Type	Kind	Pow.	Acc.	PP	Range

AFTER THE HALL OF FAME

CENTRAL KALOS

COASTAL KALOS

012 | Lunatone

MOUNTAIN KALOS

ADVENTURE DATA

AFTER THE HALL OF FAME

CENTRAL KALOS

COASTAL KALOS

013

Solrock

MOUNTAIN KALOS

ADVENTURE DATA

Coastal Kalos 013
Meteorite Pokémon
☑ Solrock

TYPE Rock Psychic

ABILITY
Levitate

HIDDEN ABILITY
None

HEIGHT: 3'11" WEIGHT: 339.5 lbs.
GENDER: unknown

X Solar energy is the source of its power, so it is strong during the daytime. When it spins, its body shines.

Y It absorbs solar energy during the day. Always expressionless, it can sense what its foe is thinking.

STAT GROWTH RATES
HP ▩▩▩
Attack ▩▩▩▩
Defense ▩▩▩▩
Sp. Atk ▩▩▩
Sp. Def ▩▩▩
Speed ▩▩▩▩

EGG GROUP
Mineral

EVOLUTION

Does not evolve

ITEMS SOMETIMES HELD BY WILD POKÉMON
Sun Stone

Can be used in
Inverse Battle
Sky Battle
Battle Chateau
Battle Institute
Battle Maison
Random Matchup

Damage taken in normal battles	
Normal	×0.5
Fire	×0.5
Water	×2
Grass	×2
Electric	×1
Ice	×1
Fighting	×1
Poison	×0.5
Ground	×2
Flying	×0.5
Psychic	×0.5
Bug	×2
Rock	×1
Ghost	×2
Dragon	×1
Dark	×2
Steel	×2
Fairy	×1

Damage taken in Inverse Battles	
Normal	×2
Fire	×2
Water	×0.5
Grass	×0.5
Electric	×1
Ice	×1
Fighting	×1
Poison	×2
Ground	×0.5
Flying	×2
Psychic	×2
Bug	×0.5
Rock	×1
Ghost	×0.5
Dragon	×1
Dark	×0.5
Steel	×0.5
Fairy	×1

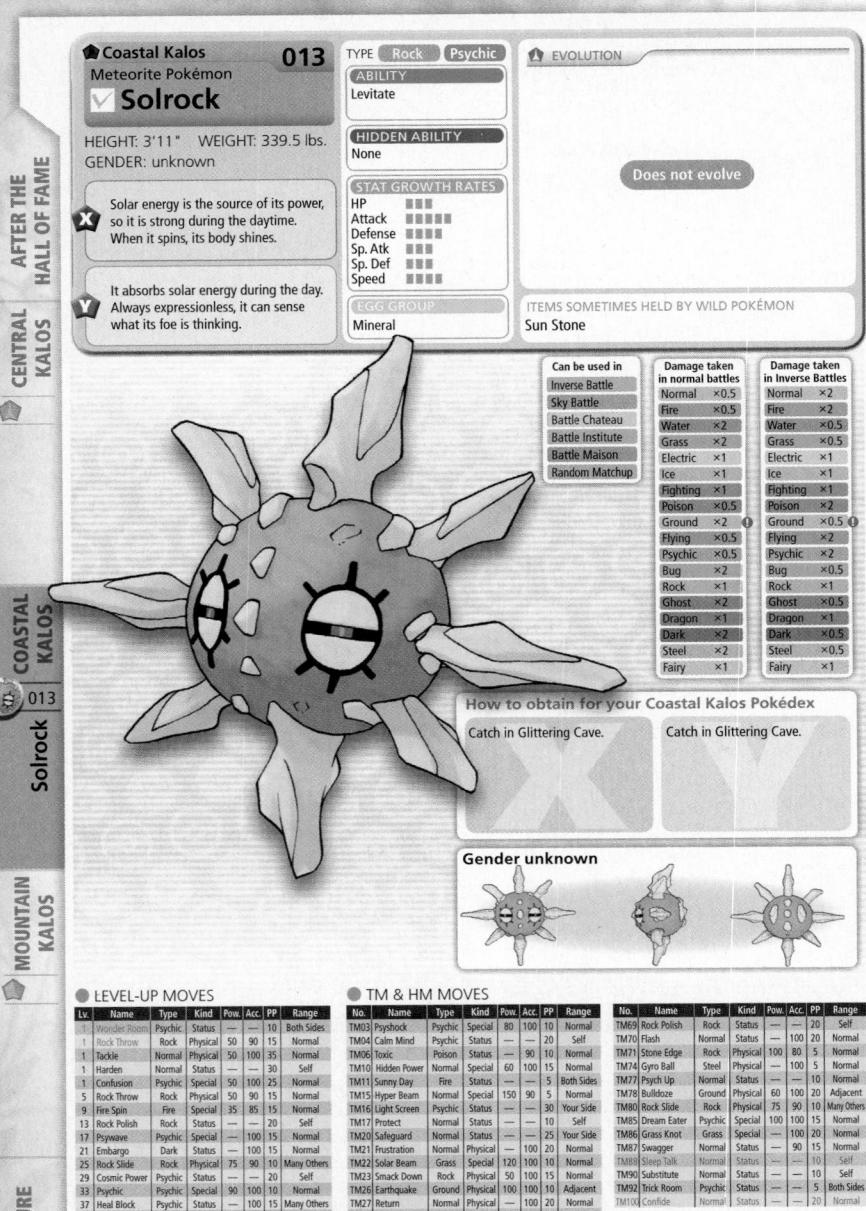

How to obtain for your Coastal Kalos Pokédex

Catch in Glittering Cave.

Catch in Glittering Cave.

Gender unknown

● LEVEL-UP MOVES

Lv.	Name	Type	Kind	Pow.	Acc.	PP	Range
1	Wonder Room	Psychic	Status	—	—	10	Both Sides
1	Rock Throw	Rock	Physical	50	90	15	Normal
1	Tackle	Normal	Physical	50	100	35	Normal
1	Harden	Normal	Status	—	—	30	Self
1	Confusion	Psychic	Special	50	100	25	Normal
5	Rock Throw	Rock	Physical	50	90	15	Normal
9	Fire Spin	Fire	Special	35	85	15	Normal
13	Rock Polish	Rock	Status	—	—	20	Self
17	Psywave	Psychic	Special	—	100	15	Normal
21	Embargo	Dark	Status	—	100	15	Normal
25	Rock Slide	Rock	Physical	75	90	10	Many Others
29	Cosmic Power	Psychic	Status	—	—	20	Self
33	Psychic	Psychic	Special	90	100	10	Normal
41	Stone Edge	Rock	Physical	100	80	5	Normal
45	Solar Beam	Grass	Special	120	100	10	Normal
49	Explosion	Normal	Physical	250	100	5	Adjacent
53	Wonder Room	Psychic	Status	—	—	10	Both Sides

● TM & HM MOVES

No.	Name	Type	Kind	Pow.	Acc.	PP	Range
TM03	Psyshock	Psychic	Special	80	100	10	Normal
TM04	Calm Mind	Psychic	Status	—	—	20	Self
TM06	Toxic	Poison	Status	—	90	10	Normal
TM10	Hidden Power	Normal	Special	60	100	15	Normal
TM11	Sunny Day	Fire	Status	—	—	5	Both Sides
TM15	Hyper Beam	Normal	Special	150	90	5	Normal
TM16	Light Screen	Psychic	Status	—	—	30	Your Side
TM17	Protect	Normal	Status	—	—	10	Self
TM20	Safeguard	Normal	Status	—	—	25	Your Side
TM21	Frustration	Normal	Physical	—	100	20	Normal
TM22	Solar Beam	Grass	Special	120	100	10	Normal
TM23	Smack Down	Rock	Physical	50	100	15	Normal
TM26	Earthquake	Ground	Physical	100	100	10	Adjacent
TM27	Return	Normal	Physical	—	100	20	Normal
TM29	Psychic	Psychic	Special	90	100	10	Normal
TM30	Shadow Ball	Ghost	Special	80	100	15	Normal
TM32	Double Team	Normal	Status	—	—	15	Self
TM33	Reflect	Psychic	Status	—	—	20	Your Side
TM35	Flamethrower	Fire	Special	90	100	15	Normal
TM37	Sandstorm	Rock	Status	—	—	10	Both Sides
TM38	Fire Blast	Fire	Special	110	85	5	Normal
TM39	Rock Tomb	Rock	Physical	60	95	15	Normal
TM42	Facade	Normal	Physical	70	100	20	Normal
TM44	Rest	Psychic	Status	—	—	10	Self
TM48	Round	Normal	Special	60	100	15	Normal
TM50	Overheat	Fire	Special	130	90	5	Normal
TM57	Charge Beam	Electric	Special	50	90	10	Normal
TM59	Incinerate	Fire	Special	60	100	15	Many Others
TM61	Will-O-Wisp	Fire	Status	—	85	15	Normal
TM62	Acrobatics	Flying	Physical	55	100	15	Normal
TM63	Embargo	Dark	Status	—	100	15	Normal
TM64	Explosion	Normal	Physical	250	100	5	Adjacent
TM68	Giga Impact	Normal	Physical	150	90	5	Normal

No.	Name	Type	Kind	Pow.	Acc.	PP	Range
TM69	Rock Polish	Rock	Status	—	—	20	Self
TM70	Flash	Normal	Status	—	100	20	Normal
TM71	Stone Edge	Rock	Physical	100	80	5	Normal
TM74	Gyro Ball	Steel	Physical	—	100	5	Normal
TM77	Psych Up	Normal	Status	—	—	10	Normal
TM78	Bulldoze	Ground	Physical	60	100	20	Many Others
TM80	Rock Slide	Rock	Physical	75	90	10	Many Others
TM85	Dream Eater	Psychic	Special	100	100	15	Normal
TM86	Grass Knot	Grass	Special	—	100	20	Normal
TM87	Swagger	Normal	Status	—	90	15	Normal
TM88	Sleep Talk	Normal	Status	—	—	10	Self
TM90	Substitute	Normal	Status	—	—	10	Self
TM92	Trick Room	Psychic	Status	—	—	5	Both Sides
TM100	Confide	Normal	Status	—	—	20	Normal

● MOVES TAUGHT BY PEOPLE

Name	Type	Kind	Pow.	Acc.	PP	Range

● EGG MOVES

Name	Type	Kind	Pow.	Acc.	PP	Range

AFTER THE HALL OF FAME

CENTRAL KALOS

COASTAL KALOS

014

Bagon

MOUNTAIN KALOS

ADVENTURE DATA

Coastal Kalos
Rock Head Pokémon
☑ Bagon

014

HEIGHT: 2'00" WEIGHT: 92.8 lbs.
GENDER: ♂/♀

X Its well-developed neck muscles and iron-like head can smash boulders into pieces.

Y Dreaming of one day flying, it practices by leaping off cliffs every day.

TYPE **Dragon**

ABILITY
Rock Head

HIDDEN ABILITY
Sheer Force

STAT GROWTH RATES
HP	■■
Attack	■■■■
Defense	■■■
Sp. Atk	■■
Sp. Def	■
Speed	■■■

EGG GROUP
Dragon

● EVOLUTION

Lv. 30   Lv. 50

Bagon   Shelgon   Salamence

ITEMS SOMETIMES HELD BY WILD POKÉMON
Dragon Fang

Damage taken in normal battles	
Normal	×1
Fire	×0.5
Water	×0.5
Grass	×0.5
Electric	×0.5
Ice	×2
Fighting	×1
Poison	×1
Ground	×1
Flying	×1
Psychic	×1
Bug	×1
Rock	×1
Ghost	×1
Dragon	×2
Dark	×1
Steel	×1
Fairy	×2

Damage taken in Inverse Battles	
Normal	×1
Fire	×2
Water	×2
Grass	×2
Electric	×2
Ice	×0.5
Fighting	×1
Poison	×1
Ground	×1
Flying	×1
Psychic	×1
Bug	×1
Rock	×1
Ghost	×1
Dragon	×0.5
Dark	×1
Steel	×1
Fairy	×0.5

Can be used in
Inverse Battle

Battle Chateau
Battle Institute
Battle Maison
Random Matchup

How to obtain for your Coastal Kalos Pokédex

❶ Catch in the tall grass on Route 8.
❷ Catch in the yellow flowers on Route 8.

❶ Catch in the tall grass on Route 8.
❷ Catch in the yellow flowers on Route 8.

Same form for ♂/♀

● LEVEL-UP MOVES

Lv.	Name	Type	Kind	Pow.	Acc.	PP	Range
1	Rage	Normal	Physical	20	100	20	Normal
5	Bite	Dark	Physical	60	100	25	Normal
10	Leer	Normal	Status	—	100	30	Many Others
16	Headbutt	Normal	Physical	70	100	15	Normal
20	Focus Energy	Normal	Status	—	—	30	Self
25	Ember	Fire	Special	40	100	25	Normal
31	Dragon Breath	Dragon	Special	60	100	20	Normal
35	Zen Headbutt	Psychic	Physical	80	90	15	Normal
40	Scary Face	Normal	Status	—	100	10	Normal
46	Crunch	Dark	Physical	80	100	15	Normal
50	Dragon Claw	Dragon	Physical	80	100	15	Normal
55	Double-Edge	Normal	Physical	120	100	15	Normal

● TM & HM MOVES

No.	Name	Type	Kind	Pow.	Acc.	PP	Range
TM01	Hone Claws	Dark	Status	—	—	15	Self
TM02	Dragon Claw	Dragon	Physical	80	100	15	Normal
TM05	Roar	Normal	Status	—	—	20	Normal
TM06	Toxic	Poison	Status	—	90	10	Normal
TM10	Hidden Power	Normal	Special	60	100	15	Normal
TM11	Sunny Day	Fire	Status	—	—	5	Both Sides
TM17	Protect	Normal	Status	—	—	10	Self
TM18	Rain Dance	Water	Status	—	—	5	Both Sides
TM21	Frustration	Normal	Physical	—	100	20	Normal
TM27	Return	Normal	Physical	—	100	20	Normal
TM31	Brick Break	Fighting	Physical	75	100	15	Normal
TM32	Double Team	Normal	Status	—	—	15	Self
TM35	Flamethrower	Fire	Special	90	100	15	Normal
TM38	Fire Blast	Fire	Special	110	85	5	Normal
TM39	Rock Tomb	Rock	Physical	60	95	15	Normal
TM40	Aerial Ace	Flying	Physical	60	—	20	Normal
TM42	Facade	Normal	Physical	70	100	20	Normal
TM44	Rest	Psychic	Status	—	—	10	Self
TM45	Attract	Normal	Status	—	100	15	Normal
TM48	Round	Normal	Special	60	100	15	Normal
TM59	Incinerate	Fire	Special	60	100	15	Many Others
TM65	Shadow Claw	Ghost	Physical	70	100	15	Normal
TM80	Rock Slide	Rock	Physical	75	90	10	Many Others
TM87	Swagger	Normal	Status	—	90	15	Normal
TM88	Sleep Talk	Normal	Status	—	—	10	Self
TM90	Substitute	Normal	Status	—	—	10	Self
TM94	Rock Smash	Fighting	Physical	40	100	15	Normal
TM100	Confide	Normal	Status	—	—	20	Normal
HM01	Cut	Normal	Physical	50	95	30	Normal
HM04	Strength	Normal	Physical	80	100	15	Normal

No.	Name	Type	Kind	Pow.	Acc.	PP	Range

● MOVES TAUGHT BY PEOPLE

Name	Type	Kind	Pow.	Acc.	PP	Range
Draco Meteor	Dragon	Special	130	90	5	Normal

● EGG MOVES

Name	Type	Kind	Pow.	Acc.	PP	Range
Hydro Pump	Water	Special	110	80	5	Normal
Thrash	Normal	Physical	120	100	10	1 Random
Dragon Rage	Dragon	Special	—	100	10	Normal
Twister	Dragon	Special	40	100	20	Many Others
Dragon Dance	Dragon	Status	—	—	20	Self
Fire Fang	Fire	Physical	65	95	15	Normal
Dragon Rush	Dragon	Physical	100	75	10	Normal
Dragon Pulse	Dragon	Special	85	100	10	Normal
Endure	Normal	Status	—	—	10	Self
Defense Curl	Normal	Status	—	—	40	Self

AFTER THE HALL OF FAME

CENTRAL KALOS

COASTAL KALOS

015

Shelgon

MOUNTAIN KALOS

ADVENTURE DATA

Coastal Kalos
Endurance Pokémon
☑ **Shelgon**

015

HEIGHT: 3'07" WEIGHT: 243.6 lbs.
GENDER: ♂/♀

TYPE Dragon

ABILITY
Rock Head

HIDDEN ABILITY
Overcoat

STAT GROWTH RATES
HP	■■■
Attack	■■■■■
Defense	■■■■
Sp. Atk	■■■
Sp. Def	■■
Speed	■■

EGG GROUP
Dragon

X Within its rugged shell, its cells have begun changing. The shell peels off the instant it evolves.

Y Its armored body makes all attacks bounce off. The armor is too tough, however, making it heavy and somewhat sluggish.

EVOLUTION

Lv. 30   Lv. 50

Bagon   Shelgon   Salamence

ITEMS SOMETIMES HELD BY WILD POKÉMON
None

Damage taken in normal battles		Damage taken in Inverse Battles	
Normal	×1	Normal	×1
Fire	×0.5	Fire	×2
Water	×0.5	Water	×2
Grass	×0.5	Grass	×2
Electric	×0.5	Electric	×2
Ice	×2	Ice	×0.5
Fighting	×1	Fighting	×1
Poison	×1	Poison	×1
Ground	×1	Ground	×1
Flying	×1	Flying	×1
Psychic	×1	Psychic	×1
Bug	×1	Bug	×1
Rock	×1	Rock	×1
Ghost	×1	Ghost	×1
Dragon	×2	Dragon	×0.5
Dark	×1	Dark	×1
Steel	×1	Steel	×1
Fairy	×2	Fairy	×0.5

Can be used in	
Inverse Battle	Battle Institute
—	Battle Maison
Battle Chateau	Random Matchup

Same form for ♂/♀

How to obtain for your Coastal Kalos Pokédex

Level up Bagon to Lv. 30.

Level up Bagon to Lv. 30.

● LEVEL-UP MOVES

Lv.	Name	Type	Kind	Pow.	Acc.	PP	Range
1	Rage	Normal	Physical	20	100	20	Normal
1	Bite	Dark	Physical	60	100	25	Normal
1	Leer	Normal	Status	—	100	30	Many Others
1	Headbutt	Normal	Physical	70	100	15	Normal
5	Bite	Dark	Physical	60	100	25	Normal
10	Leer	Normal	Status	—	100	30	Many Others
16	Headbutt	Normal	Physical	70	100	15	Normal
20	Focus Energy	Normal	Status	—	—	30	Self
25	Ember	Fire	Special	40	100	25	Normal
30	Protect	Normal	Status	—	—	10	Self
32	Dragon Breath	Dragon	Special	60	100	20	Normal
37	Zen Headbutt	Psychic	Physical	80	90	15	Normal
43	Scary Face	Normal	Status	—	100	10	Normal
50	Crunch	Dark	Physical	80	100	15	Normal
55	Dragon Claw	Dragon	Physical	80	100	15	Normal
61	Double-Edge	Normal	Physical	120	100	15	Normal

● TM & HM MOVES

No.	Name	Type	Kind	Pow.	Acc.	PP	Range
TM01	Hone Claws	Dark	Status	—	—	15	Self
TM02	Dragon Claw	Dragon	Physical	80	100	15	Normal
TM05	Roar	Normal	Status	—	—	20	Normal
TM06	Toxic	Poison	Status	—	90	10	Normal
TM10	Hidden Power	Normal	Special	60	100	15	Normal
TM11	Sunny Day	Fire	Status	—	—	5	Both Sides
TM17	Protect	Normal	Status	—	—	10	Self
TM18	Rain Dance	Water	Status	—	—	5	Both Sides
TM21	Frustration	Normal	Physical	—	100	20	Normal
TM27	Return	Normal	Physical	—	100	20	Normal
TM31	Brick Break	Fighting	Physical	75	100	15	Normal
TM32	Double Team	Normal	Status	—	—	15	Self
TM35	Flamethrower	Fire	Special	90	100	15	Normal
TM38	Fire Blast	Fire	Special	110	85	5	Normal
TM39	Rock Tomb	Rock	Physical	60	95	15	Normal
TM40	Aerial Ace	Flying	Physical	60	—	20	Normal
TM42	Facade	Normal	Physical	70	100	20	Normal
TM44	Rest	Psychic	Status	—	—	10	Self
TM45	Attract	Normal	Status	—	100	15	Normal
TM48	Round	Normal	Special	60	100	15	Normal
TM59	Incinerate	Fire	Special	60	100	15	Many Others
TM65	Shadow Claw	Ghost	Physical	70	100	15	Normal
TM80	Rock Slide	Rock	Physical	75	90	10	Many Others
TM87	Swagger	Normal	Status	—	90	15	Normal
TM90	Substitute	Normal	Status	—	—	10	Self
TM88	Sleep Talk	Normal	Status	—	—	10	Self
TM94	Rock Smash	Fighting	Physical	40	100	15	Normal
TM100	Confide	Normal	Status	—	—	20	Normal
HM01	Cut	Normal	Physical	50	95	30	Normal
HM04	Strength	Normal	Physical	80	100	15	Normal

No.	Name	Type	Kind	Pow.	Acc.	PP	Range

● MOVES TAUGHT BY PEOPLE

Name	Type	Kind	Pow.	Acc.	PP	Range
Draco Meteor	Dragon	Special	130	90	5	Normal

Coastal Kalos
Dragon Pokémon

016

 ## Salamence

HEIGHT: 4'11"   WEIGHT: 226.2 lbs.
GENDER: ♂ / ♀

TYPE	Dragon	Flying

ABILITY
Intimidate

HIDDEN ABILITY
Moxie

STAT GROWTH RATES
HP	■ ■ ■ ■
Attack	■ ■ ■ ■ ■ ■ ■
Defense	■ ■ ■ ■
Sp. Atk	■ ■ ■ ■ ■
Sp. Def	■ ■ ■
Speed	■ ■ ■ ■ ■

EGG GROUP
Dragon

EVOLUTION

Bagon   Lv. 30   Shelgon   Lv. 50   Salamence

ITEMS SOMETIMES HELD BY WILD POKÉMON
None

X It becomes uncontrollable if it is enraged. It destroys everything with shredding claws and fire.

Y It's uncontrollable if enraged. It flies around spouting flames and scorching fields and mountains.

Damage taken in normal battles		Damage taken in Inverse Battles	
Normal	×1	Normal	×1
Fire	×0.5	Fire	×2
Water	×0.5	Water	×2
Grass	×0.25	Grass	×4
Electric	×1	Electric	×1
Ice	×4	Ice	×0.25
Fighting	×0.5	Fighting	×2
Poison	×1	Poison	×1
Ground	×0	Ground	×2
Flying	×1	Flying	×1
Psychic	×1	Psychic	×1
Bug	×0.5	Bug	×2
Rock	×2	Rock	×0.5
Ghost	×1	Ghost	×1
Dragon	×2	Dragon	×0.5
Dark	×1	Dark	×1
Steel	×1	Steel	×1
Fairy	×2	Fairy	×0.5

Can be used in	
Inverse Battle	Battle Institute
Sky Battle	Battle Maison
Battle Chateau	Random Matchup

Same form for ♂ / ♀

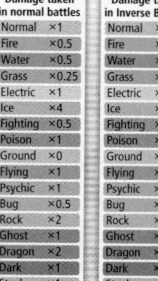

How to obtain for your Coastal Kalos Pokédex

X Level up Shelgon to Lv. 50.   **Y** Level up Shelgon to Lv. 50.

● LEVEL-UP MOVES

Lv.	Name	Type	Kind	Pow.	Acc.	PP	Range
1	Double-Edge	Normal	Physical	120	100	15	Normal
1	Fire Fang	Fire	Physical	65	95	15	Normal
1	Thunder Fang	Electric	Physical	65	95	15	Normal
1	Rage	Normal	Physical	20	100	20	Normal
1	Bite	Dark	Physical	60	100	25	Normal
1	Leer	Normal	Status	—	100	30	Many Others
1	Headbutt	Normal	Physical	70	100	15	Normal
5	Bite	Dark	Physical	60	100	25	Normal
10	Leer	Normal	Status	—	100	30	Many Others
16	Headbutt	Normal	Physical	70	100	15	Normal
20	Focus Energy	Normal	Status	—	—	30	Self
25	Ember	Fire	Special	40	100	25	Normal
30	Protect	Normal	Status	—	—	10	Self
32	Dragon Breath	Dragon	Special	60	100	20	Normal
37	Zen Headbutt	Psychic	Physical	80	90	15	Normal
43	Scary Face	Normal	Status	—	100	10	Normal
50	Fly	Flying	Physical	90	95	15	Normal
53	Crunch	Dark	Physical	80	100	15	Normal
61	Dragon Claw	Dragon	Physical	80	100	15	Normal
70	Double-Edge	Normal	Physical	120	100	15	Normal
80	Dragon Tail	Dragon	Physical	60	90	10	Normal

● TM & HM MOVES

No.	Name	Type	Kind	Pow.	Acc.	PP	Range
TM01	Hone Claws	Dark	Status	—	—	15	Self
TM02	Dragon Claw	Dragon	Physical	80	100	15	Normal
TM05	Roar	Normal	Status	—	—	20	Normal
TM06	Toxic	Poison	Status	—	90	10	Normal
TM10	Hidden Power	Normal	Special	60	100	15	Normal
TM11	Sunny Day	Fire	Status	—	—	5	Both Sides
TM15	Hyper Beam	Normal	Special	150	90	5	Normal
TM17	Protect	Normal	Status	—	—	10	Self
TM18	Rain Dance	Water	Status	—	—	5	Both Sides
TM19	Roost	Flying	Status	—	—	10	Self
TM21	Frustration	Normal	Physical	—	100	20	Normal
TM26	Earthquake	Ground	Physical	100	100	10	Adjacent
TM27	Return	Normal	Physical	—	100	20	Normal
TM31	Brick Break	Fighting	Physical	75	100	15	Normal
TM32	Double Team	Normal	Status	—	—	15	Self
TM35	Flamethrower	Fire	Special	90	100	15	Normal
TM38	Fire Blast	Fire	Special	110	85	5	Normal
TM39	Rock Tomb	Rock	Physical	60	95	15	Normal
TM40	Aerial Ace	Flying	Physical	60	—	20	Normal
TM42	Facade	Normal	Physical	70	100	20	Normal
TM44	Rest	Psychic	Status	—	—	10	Self
TM45	Attract	Normal	Status	—	100	15	Normal
TM48	Round	Normal	Special	60	100	15	Normal
TM51	Steel Wing	Steel	Physical	70	90	25	Normal
TM59	Incinerate	Fire	Special	60	100	15	Many Others
TM65	Shadow Claw	Ghost	Physical	70	100	15	Normal
TM68	Giga Impact	Normal	Physical	150	90	5	Normal
TM71	Stone Edge	Rock	Physical	100	80	5	Normal
TM78	Bulldoze	Ground	Physical	60	100	20	Adjacent
TM80	Rock Slide	Rock	Physical	75	90	10	Many Others
TM82	Dragon Tail	Dragon	Physical	60	90	10	Normal
TM87	Swagger	Normal	Status	—	90	15	Normal
TM88	Sleep Talk	Normal	Status	—	—	10	Self

No.	Name	Type	Kind	Pow.	Acc.	PP	Range
TM90	Substitute	Normal	Status	—	—	10	Self
TM94	Rock Smash	Fighting	Physical	40	100	15	Normal
TM100	Confide	Normal	Status	—	—	20	Normal
HM01	Cut	Normal	Physical	50	95	30	Normal
HM02	Fly	Flying	Physical	90	95	15	Normal
HM04	Strength	Normal	Physical	80	100	15	Normal

● MOVES TAUGHT BY PEOPLE

Name	Type	Kind	Pow.	Acc.	PP	Range
Draco Meteor	Dragon	Special	130	90	5	Normal

AFTER THE HALL OF FAME

CENTRAL KALOS

COASTAL KALOS

016 Salamence

MOUNTAIN KALOS

ADVENTURE DATA

AFTER THE HALL OF FAME

CENTRAL KALOS

COASTAL KALOS

017

Wingull

MOUNTAIN KALOS

ADVENTURE DATA

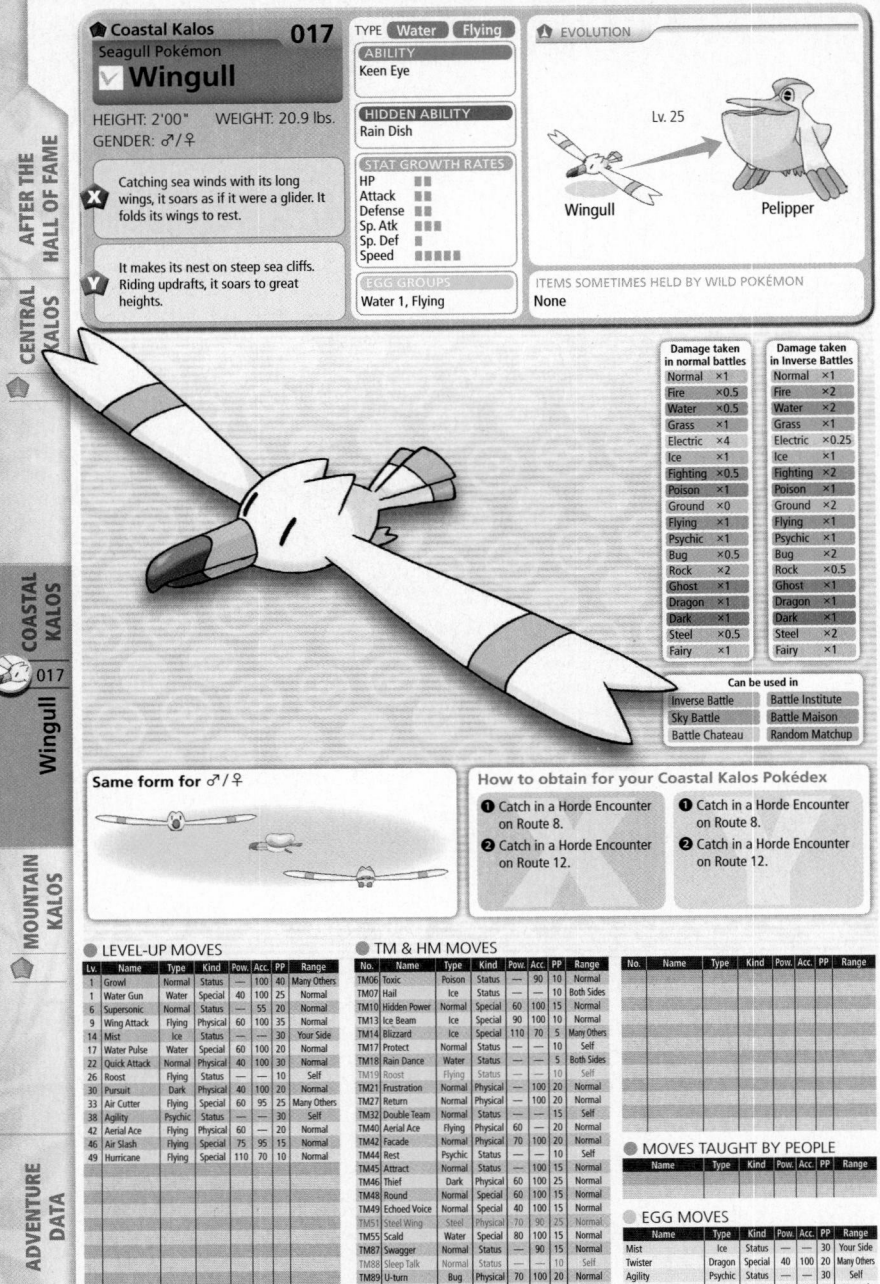

🏠 Coastal Kalos **017**
Seagull Pokémon
✓ Wingull

HEIGHT: 2'00" WEIGHT: 20.9 lbs.
GENDER: ♂/♀

X Catching sea winds with its long wings, it soars as if it were a glider. It folds its wings to rest.

Y It makes its nest on steep sea cliffs. Riding updrafts, it soars to great heights.

TYPE Water Flying

ABILITY
Keen Eye

HIDDEN ABILITY
Rain Dish

STAT GROWTH RATES
HP ▪▪
Attack ▪▪
Defense ▪▪
Sp. Atk ▪▪▪
Sp. Def ▪▪
Speed ▪▪▪▪▪

EGG GROUPS
Water 1, Flying

● EVOLUTION

Lv. 25

Wingull → Pelipper

ITEMS SOMETIMES HELD BY WILD POKÉMON
None

Damage taken in normal battles		Damage taken in Inverse Battles	
Normal	×1	Normal	×1
Fire	×0.5	Fire	×2
Water	×0.5	Water	×2
Grass	×1	Grass	×1
Electric	×4	Electric	×0.25
Ice	×1	Ice	×1
Fighting	×0.5	Fighting	×2
Poison	×1	Poison	×1
Ground	×0	Ground	×2
Flying	×1	Flying	×1
Psychic	×1	Psychic	×1
Bug	×0.5	Bug	×2
Rock	×2	Rock	×0.5
Ghost	×1	Ghost	×1
Dragon	×1	Dragon	×1
Dark	×1	Dark	×1
Steel	×0.5	Steel	×2
Fairy	×1	Fairy	×1

Can be used in	
Inverse Battle	Battle Institute
Sky Battle	Battle Maison
Battle Chateau	Random Matchup

Same form for ♂/♀

How to obtain for your Coastal Kalos Pokédex

❶ Catch in a Horde Encounter on Route 8.
❷ Catch in a Horde Encounter on Route 12.

❶ Catch in a Horde Encounter on Route 8.
❷ Catch in a Horde Encounter on Route 12.

● LEVEL-UP MOVES

Lv.	Name	Type	Kind	Pow.	Acc.	PP	Range
1	Growl	Normal	Status	—	100	40	Many Others
1	Water Gun	Water	Special	40	100	25	Normal
6	Supersonic	Normal	Status	—	55	20	Normal
9	Wing Attack	Flying	Physical	60	100	35	Normal
14	Mist	Ice	Status	—	—	30	Your Side
17	Water Pulse	Water	Special	60	100	20	Normal
22	Quick Attack	Normal	Physical	40	100	30	Normal
26	Roost	Flying	Status	—	—	10	Self
30	Pursuit	Dark	Physical	40	100	20	Normal
33	Air Cutter	Flying	Special	60	95	25	Many Others
38	Agility	Psychic	Status	—	—	30	Self
42	Aerial Ace	Flying	Physical	60	—	20	Normal
46	Air Slash	Flying	Special	75	95	15	Normal
49	Hurricane	Flying	Special	110	70	10	Normal

● TM & HM MOVES

No.	Name	Type	Kind	Pow.	Acc.	PP	Range
TM06	Toxic	Poison	Status	—	90	10	Normal
TM07	Hail	Ice	Status	—	—	10	Both Sides
TM10	Hidden Power	Normal	Special	60	100	15	Normal
TM13	Ice Beam	Ice	Special	90	100	10	Normal
TM14	Blizzard	Ice	Special	110	70	5	Many Others
TM17	Protect	Normal	Status	—	—	10	Self
TM18	Rain Dance	Water	Status	—	—	5	Both Sides
TM19	Roost	Flying	Status	—	—	10	Self
TM21	Frustration	Normal	Physical	—	100	20	Normal
TM27	Return	Normal	Physical	—	100	20	Normal
TM32	Double Team	Normal	Status	—	—	15	Self
TM40	Aerial Ace	Flying	Physical	60	—	20	Normal
TM42	Facade	Normal	Physical	70	100	20	Normal
TM44	Rest	Psychic	Status	—	—	10	Self
TM45	Attract	Normal	Status	—	100	15	Normal
TM48	Round	Normal	Special	60	100	15	Normal
TM49	Echoed Voice	Normal	Special	40	100	15	Normal
TM51	Steel Wing	Steel	Physical	70	90	25	Normal
TM55	Scald	Water	Special	80	100	15	Normal
TM87	Swagger	Normal	Status	—	90	15	Normal
TM88	Sleep Talk	Normal	Status	—	—	10	Self
TM89	U-turn	Bug	Physical	70	100	20	Normal
TM90	Substitute	Normal	Status	—	—	10	Self
TM100	Confide	Normal	Status	—	—	20	Normal
HM02	Fly	Flying	Physical	90	95	15	Normal

● MOVES TAUGHT BY PEOPLE

Name	Type	Kind	Pow.	Acc.	PP	Range

● EGG MOVES

Name	Type	Kind	Pow.	Acc.	PP	Range
Mist	Ice	Status	—	—	30	Your Side
Twister	Dragon	Special	40	100	20	Many Others
Agility	Psychic	Status	—	—	30	Self
Gust	Flying	Special	40	100	35	Normal
Water Sport	Water	Status	—	—	15	Both Sides
Aqua Ring	Water	Status	—	—	20	Self
Knock Off	Dark	Physical	65	100	20	Normal
Brine	Water	Special	65	100	10	Normal
Roost	Flying	Status	—	—	10	Self
Soak	Water	Status	—	100	20	Normal
Wide Guard	Rock	Status	—	—	10	Your Side

 **Coastal Kalos**

Water Bird Pokémon

018

 Pelipper

HEIGHT: 3'11"   WEIGHT: 61.7 lbs.
GENDER: ♂/♀

X It dips its large bill in the sea, then scoops up numerous prey along with water.

Y It is a messenger of the skies, carrying small Pokémon and eggs to safety in its bill.

TYPE: Water | Flying

ABILITY
Keen Eye

HIDDEN ABILITY
Rain Dish

STAT GROWTH RATES
HP
Attack
Defense
Sp. Atk
Sp. Def
Speed

EGG GROUPS
Water 1, Flying

EVOLUTION

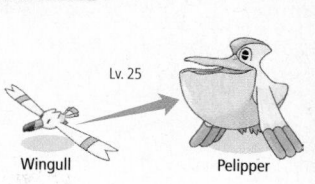

Lv. 25

Wingull → Pelipper

ITEMS SOMETIMES HELD BY WILD POKÉMON
None

Damage taken in normal battles		Damage taken in Inverse Battles	
Normal	×1	Normal	×1
Fire	×0.5	Fire	×2
Water	×0.5	Water	×2
Grass	×1	Grass	×1
Electric	×4	Electric	×0.25
Ice	×1	Ice	×1
Fighting	×0.5	Fighting	×2
Poison	×1	Poison	×1
Ground	×0	Ground	×2
Flying	×1	Flying	×1
Psychic	×1	Psychic	×1
Bug	×0.5	Bug	×2
Rock	×2	Rock	×0.5
Ghost	×1	Ghost	×1
Dragon	×1	Dragon	×1
Dark	×1	Dark	×1
Steel	×0.5	Steel	×2
Fairy	×1	Fairy	×1

Can be used in	
Inverse Battle	Battle Institute
Sky Battle	Battle Maison
Battle Chateau	Random Matchup

Same form for ♂/♀

How to obtain for your Coastal Kalos Pokédex

Level up Wingull to Lv. 25.   Level up Wingull to Lv. 25.

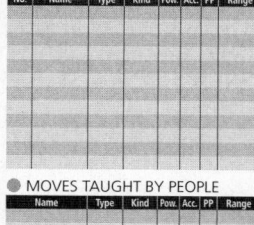

● **LEVEL-UP MOVES**

Lv.	Name	Type	Kind	Pow.	Acc.	PP	Range
1	Hydro Pump	Water	Special	110	80	5	Normal
1	Tailwind	Flying	Status	—	—	15	Your Side
1	Soak	Water	Status	—	100	20	Normal
1	Growl	Normal	Status	—	100	40	Many Others
1	Water Gun	Water	Special	40	100	25	Normal
1	Water Sport	Water	Status	—	—	15	Both Sides
1	Wing Attack	Flying	Physical	60	100	35	Normal
6	Supersonic	Normal	Status	—	55	20	Normal
9	Wing Attack	Flying	Physical	60	100	35	Normal
14	Mist	Ice	Status	—	—	30	Your Side
17	Water Pulse	Water	Special	60	100	20	Normal
22	Payback	Dark	Physical	50	100	10	Normal
25	Protect	Normal	Status	—	—	10	Self
28	Roost	Flying	Status	—	—	10	Self
34	Brine	Water	Special	65	100	10	Normal
39	Stockpile	Normal	Status	—	—	20	Self
39	Swallow	Normal	Status	—	—	10	Self
39	Spit Up	Normal	Special	—	100	10	Normal
46	Fling	Dark	Physical	—	100	10	Normal
52	Tailwind	Flying	Status	—	—	15	Your Side
58	Hydro Pump	Water	Special	110	80	5	Normal
63	Hurricane	Flying	Special	110	70	10	Normal

● **TM & HM MOVES**

No.	Name	Type	Kind	Pow.	Acc.	PP	Range
TM06	Toxic	Poison	Status	—	90	10	Normal
TM07	Hail	Ice	Status	—	—	10	Both Sides
TM10	Hidden Power	Normal	Special	60	100	15	Normal
TM13	Ice Beam	Ice	Special	90	100	10	Normal
TM14	Blizzard	Ice	Special	110	70	5	Many Others
TM15	Hyper Beam	Normal	Special	150	90	5	Normal
TM17	Protect	Normal	Status	—	—	10	Self
TM18	Rain Dance	Water	Status	—	—	5	Both Sides
TM19	Roost	Flying	Status	—	—	10	Self
TM21	Frustration	Normal	Physical	—	100	20	Normal
TM27	Return	Normal	Physical	—	100	20	Normal
TM32	Double Team	Normal	Status	—	—	15	Self
TM40	Aerial Ace	Flying	Physical	60	—	20	Normal
TM42	Facade	Normal	Physical	70	100	20	Normal
TM44	Rest	Psychic	Status	—	—	10	Self
TM45	Attract	Normal	Status	—	100	15	Normal
TM46	Thief	Dark	Physical	60	100	25	Normal
TM48	Round	Normal	Special	60	100	15	Normal
TM49	Echoed Voice	Normal	Special	40	100	15	Normal
TM51	Steel Wing	Steel	Physical	70	90	25	Normal
TM55	Scald	Water	Special	80	100	15	Normal
TM56	Fling	Dark	Physical	—	100	10	Normal
TM58	Sky Drop	Flying	Physical	60	100	10	Normal
TM66	Payback	Dark	Physical	50	100	10	Normal
TM68	Giga Impact	Normal	Physical	150	90	5	Normal
TM87	Swagger	Normal	Status	—	90	15	Normal
TM89	U-turn	Bug	Physical	70	100	20	Normal
TM90	Substitute	Normal	Status	—	—	10	Self
TM100	Confide	Normal	Status	—	—	20	Normal
HM02	Fly	Flying	Physical	90	95	15	Normal
HM03	Surf	Water	Special	90	100	15	Adjacent

● **MOVES TAUGHT BY PEOPLE**

Name	Type	Kind	Pow.	Acc.	PP	Range

AFTER THE HALL OF FAME

CENTRAL KALOS

COASTAL KALOS

018 | Pelipper

MOUNTAIN KALOS

ADVENTURE DATA

Coastal Kalos 019
Tiny Swallow Pokémon
☑ Taillow

HEIGHT: 1'00"　　WEIGHT: 5.1 lbs.
GENDER: ♂/♀

X It has a gutsy spirit that makes it bravely take on tough foes. It flies in search of warm climates.

Y It dislikes cold seasons. They migrate to other lands in search of warmth, flying over 180 miles a day.

TYPE **Normal** **Flying**

ABILITY
Guts

HIDDEN ABILITY
Scrappy

STAT GROWTH RATES
HP	■■
Attack	■■■
Defense	■■
Sp. Atk	■
Sp. Def	■
Speed	■■■■■

EGG GROUP
Flying

EVOLUTION

Taillow　　Lv. 22　　Swellow

ITEMS SOMETIMES HELD BY WILD POKÉMON
None

Damage taken in normal battles	
Normal	×1
Fire	×1
Water	×1
Grass	×0.5
Electric	×2
Ice	×2
Fighting	×1
Poison	×1
Ground	×0
Flying	×1
Psychic	×1
Bug	×0.5
Rock	×2
Ghost	×0
Dragon	×1
Dark	×1
Steel	×1
Fairy	×1

Damage taken in Inverse Battles	
Normal	×1
Fire	×1
Water	×1
Grass	×2
Electric	×0.5
Ice	×0.5
Fighting	×1
Poison	×1
Ground	×2
Flying	×1
Psychic	×1
Bug	×2
Rock	×0.5
Ghost	×2
Dragon	×1
Dark	×1
Steel	×1
Fairy	×1

Can be used in	
Inverse Battle	Battle Institute
—	Battle Maison
Battle Chateau	Random Matchup

Same form for ♂/♀

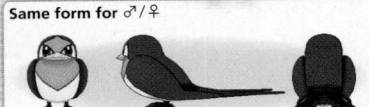

How to obtain for your Coastal Kalos Pokédex

X Catch in a Horde Encounter on Route 8.

Y Catch in a Horde Encounter on Route 8.

AFTER THE HALL OF FAME

CENTRAL KALOS

COASTAL KALOS
019
Taillow

MOUNTAIN KALOS

ADVENTURE DATA

● LEVEL-UP MOVES

Lv.	Name	Type	Kind	Pow.	Acc.	PP	Range
1	Peck	Flying	Physical	35	100	35	Normal
1	Growl	Normal	Status	—	100	40	Many Others
4	Focus Energy	Normal	Status	—	—	30	Self
7	Quick Attack	Normal	Physical	40	100	30	Normal
13	Wing Attack	Flying	Physical	60	100	35	Normal
19	Double Team	Normal	Status	—	—	15	Self
26	Endeavor	Normal	Physical	—	100	5	Normal
34	Aerial Ace	Flying	Physical	60	—	20	Normal
43	Agility	Psychic	Status	—	—	30	Self
53	Air Slash	Flying	Special	75	95	15	Normal

● TM & HM MOVES

No.	Name	Type	Kind	Pow.	Acc.	PP	Range
TM06	Toxic	Poison	Status	—	90	10	Normal
TM10	Hidden Power	Normal	Special	60	100	15	Normal
TM11	Sunny Day	Fire	Status	—	—	5	Both Sides
TM17	Protect	Normal	Status	—	—	10	Self
TM18	Rain Dance	Water	Status	—	—	5	Both Sides
TM19	Roost	Flying	Status	—	—	10	Self
TM21	Frustration	Normal	Physical	—	100	20	Normal
TM27	Return	Normal	Physical	—	100	20	Normal
TM32	Double Team	Normal	Status	—	—	15	Self
TM40	Aerial Ace	Flying	Physical	60	—	20	Normal
TM42	Facade	Normal	Physical	70	100	20	Normal
TM44	Rest	Psychic	Status	—	—	10	Self
TM45	Attract	Normal	Status	—	100	15	Normal
TM46	Thief	Dark	Physical	60	100	25	Normal
TM48	Round	Normal	Special	60	100	15	Normal
TM49	Echoed Voice	Normal	Special	40	100	15	Normal
TM51	Steel Wing	Steel	Physical	70	90	25	Normal
TM87	Swagger	Normal	Status	—	90	15	Normal
TM88	Sleep Talk	Normal	Status	—	—	10	Self
TM89	U-turn	Bug	Physical	70	100	20	Normal
TM90	Substitute	Normal	Status	—	—	10	Self
TM100	Confide	Normal	Status	—	—	20	Normal
HM02	Fly	Flying	Physical	90	95	15	Normal

● MOVES TAUGHT BY PEOPLE

Name	Type	Kind	Pow.	Acc.	PP	Range

● EGG MOVES

Name	Type	Kind	Pow.	Acc.	PP	Range
Pursuit	Dark	Physical	40	100	20	Normal
Supersonic	Normal	Status	—	55	20	Normal
Refresh	Normal	Status	—	—	20	Self
Mirror Move	Flying	Status	—	—	20	Normal
Rage	Normal	Physical	20	100	20	Normal
Sky Attack	Flying	Physical	140	90	5	Normal
Whirlwind	Normal	Status	—	—	20	Normal
Brave Bird	Flying	Physical	120	100	15	Normal
Roost	Flying	Status	—	—	10	Self
Steel Wing	Steel	Physical	70	90	25	Normal
Defog	Flying	Status	—	—	15	Normal
Boomburst	Normal	Special	140	100	10	Adjacent

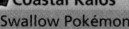

Coastal Kalos
Swallow Pokémon
☑ **Swellow**   **020**

HEIGHT: 2'04"   WEIGHT: 43.7 lbs.
GENDER: ♂/♀

X If its two tail feathers are standing at attention, it is proof of good health. It soars elegantly in the sky.

Y It dives at a steep angle as soon as it spots its prey. It catches its prey with sharp claws.

TYPE **Normal** **Flying**

ABILITY
Guts

HIDDEN ABILITY
Scrappy

STAT GROWTH RATES
HP
Attack
Defense
Sp. Atk
Sp. Def
Speed

EGG GROUP
Flying

ITEMS SOMETIMES HELD BY WILD POKÉMON
None

EVOLUTION

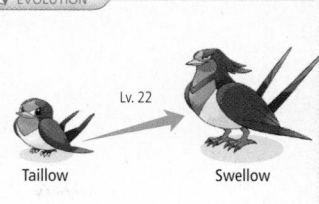

Taillow → Lv. 22 → Swellow

Damage taken in normal battles
Normal	×1
Fire	×1
Water	×1
Grass	×0.5
Electric	×2
Ice	×2
Fighting	×1
Poison	×1
Ground	×0
Flying	×1
Psychic	×1
Bug	×0.5
Rock	×2
Ghost	×0
Dragon	×1
Dark	×1
Steel	×1
Fairy	×1

Damage taken in Inverse Battles
Normal	×1
Fire	×1
Water	×1
Grass	×2
Electric	×0.5
Ice	×0.5
Fighting	×1
Poison	×1
Ground	×2
Flying	×1
Psychic	×1
Bug	×2
Rock	×0.5
Ghost	×2
Dragon	×1
Dark	×1
Steel	×1
Fairy	×1

Can be used in
Inverse Battle	Battle Institute
Sky Battle	Battle Maison
Battle Chateau	Random Matchup

Same form for ♂/♀

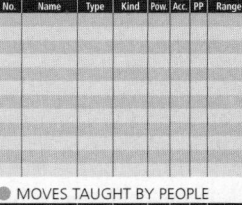

How to obtain for your Coastal Kalos Pokédex

Level up Taillow to Lv. 22.   Level up Taillow to Lv. 22.

● LEVEL-UP MOVES
Lv.	Name	Type	Kind	Pow.	Acc.	PP	Range
1	Air Slash	Flying	Special	75	95	15	Normal
1	Pluck	Flying	Physical	60	100	20	Normal
1	Peck	Flying	Physical	35	100	35	Normal
1	Growl	Normal	Status	—	100	40	Many Others
1	Focus Energy	Normal	Status	—	—	30	Self
1	Quick Attack	Normal	Physical	40	100	30	Normal
4	Focus Energy	Normal	Status	—	—	30	Self
7	Quick Attack	Normal	Physical	40	100	30	Normal
13	Wing Attack	Flying	Physical	60	100	35	Normal
19	Double Team	Normal	Status	—	—	15	Self
28	Endeavor	Normal	Physical	—	100	5	Normal
38	Aerial Ace	Flying	Physical	60	—	20	Normal
49	Agility	Psychic	Status	—	—	30	Self
61	Air Slash	Flying	Special	75	95	15	Normal

● TM & HM MOVES
No.	Name	Type	Kind	Pow.	Acc.	PP	Range
TM06	Toxic	Poison	Status	—	90	10	Normal
TM10	Hidden Power	Normal	Special	60	100	15	Normal
TM11	Sunny Day	Fire	Status	—	—	5	Both Sides
TM15	Hyper Beam	Normal	Special	150	90	5	Normal
TM17	Protect	Normal	Status	—	—	10	Self
TM18	Rain Dance	Water	Status	—	—	5	Both Sides
TM19	Roost	Flying	Status	—	—	10	Self
TM21	Frustration	Normal	Physical	—	100	20	Normal
TM27	Return	Normal	Physical	—	100	20	Normal
TM32	Double Team	Normal	Status	—	—	15	Self
TM40	Aerial Ace	Flying	Physical	60	—	20	Normal
TM42	Facade	Normal	Physical	70	100	20	Normal
TM44	Rest	Psychic	Status	—	—	10	Self
TM45	Attract	Normal	Status	—	100	15	Normal
TM46	Thief	Dark	Physical	60	100	25	Normal
TM48	Round	Normal	Special	60	100	15	Normal
TM49	Echoed Voice	Normal	Special	40	100	15	Normal
TM51	Steel Wing	Steel	Physical	70	90	25	Normal
TM68	Giga Impact	Normal	Physical	150	90	5	Normal
TM87	Swagger	Normal	Status	—	90	15	Normal
TM88	Sleep Talk	Normal	Status	—	—	10	Self
TM89	U-turn	Bug	Physical	70	100	20	Normal
TM90	Substitute	Normal	Status	—	—	10	Self
TM100	Confide	Normal	Status	—	—	20	Normal
HM02	Fly	Flying	Physical	90	95	15	Normal

No.	Name	Type	Kind	Pow.	Acc.	PP	Range

● MOVES TAUGHT BY PEOPLE
Name	Type	Kind	Pow.	Acc.	PP	Range

AFTER THE HALL OF FAME

CENTRAL KALOS

COASTAL KALOS

021

Binacle

MOUNTAIN KALOS

ADVENTURE DATA

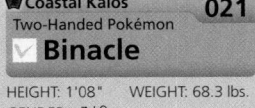

♠ Coastal Kalos

021

Two-Handed Pokémon

☑ Binacle

HEIGHT: 1'08" WEIGHT: 68.3 lbs.
GENDER: ♂/♀

X Two Binacle live together on one rock. When they fight, one of them will move to a different rock.

Y They stretch and then contract, yanking their rocks along with them in bold hops. They eat seaweed that washes up on the shoreline.

TYPE Rock | Water

ABILITIES
Tough Claws
Sniper

HIDDEN ABILITY
Pickpocket

STAT GROWTH RATES
HP	■■
Attack	■■■
Defense	■■■
Sp. Atk	■■
Sp. Def	■■
Speed	■■■

EGG GROUP
Water 3

♠ EVOLUTION

Binacle → Lv. 39 → Barbaracle

ITEMS SOMETIMES HELD BY WILD POKÉMON
None

	Damage taken in normal battles		Damage taken in Inverse Battles
Normal	×0.5	Normal	×2
Fire	×0.25	Fire	×4
Water	×1	Water	×1
Grass	×4	Grass	×0.25
Electric	×2	Electric	×0.5
Ice	×0.5	Ice	×2
Fighting	×2	Fighting	×0.5
Poison	×0.5	Poison	×2
Ground	×2	Ground	×0.5
Flying	×1	Flying	×1
Psychic	×1	Psychic	×1
Bug	×1	Bug	×1
Rock	×1	Rock	×1
Ghost	×1	Ghost	×1
Dragon	×1	Dragon	×1
Dark	×1	Dark	×1
Steel	×1	Steel	×1
Fairy	×1	Fairy	×1

Can be used in
Inverse Battle
—
Battle Chateau
Battle Institute
Battle Maison
Random Matchup

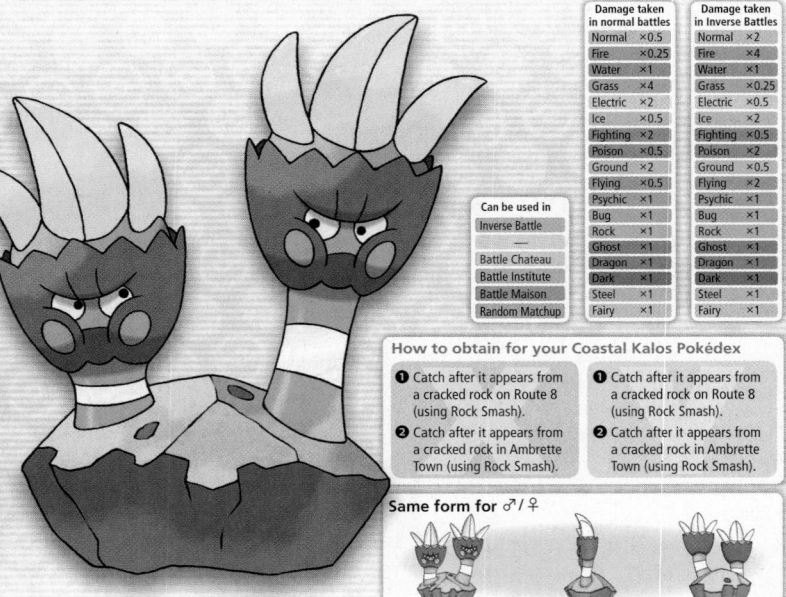

How to obtain for your Coastal Kalos Pokédex

❶ Catch after it appears from a cracked rock on Route 8 (using Rock Smash).

❷ Catch after it appears from a cracked rock in Ambrette Town (using Rock Smash).

❶ Catch after it appears from a cracked rock on Route 8 (using Rock Smash).

❷ Catch after it appears from a cracked rock in Ambrette Town (using Rock Smash).

Same form for ♂/♀

● LEVEL-UP MOVES

Lv.	Name	Type	Kind	Pow.	Acc.	PP	Range
1	Shell Smash	Normal	Status	—	—	15	Self
1	Scratch	Normal	Physical	40	100	35	Normal
1	Sand Attack	Ground	Status	—	100	15	Normal
4	Water Gun	Water	Special	40	100	25	Normal
7	Withdraw	Water	Status	—	—	40	Self
10	Fury Swipes	Normal	Physical	18	80	15	Normal
13	Slash	Normal	Physical	70	100	20	Normal
18	Mud-Slap	Ground	Special	20	100	10	Normal
20	Clamp	Water	Physical	35	85	15	Normal
24	Rock Polish	Rock	Status	—	—	20	Self
28	Ancient Power	Rock	Special	60	100	5	Normal
32	Hone Claws	Dark	Status	—	—	15	Self
37	Fury Cutter	Bug	Physical	40	95	20	Normal
41	Night Slash	Dark	Physical	70	100	15	Normal
45	Razor Shell	Water	Physical	75	95	10	Normal
49	Cross Chop	Fighting	Physical	100	80	5	Normal

● TM & HM MOVES

No.	Name	Type	Kind	Pow.	Acc.	PP	Range
TM01	Hone Claws	Dark	Status	—	—	15	Self
TM06	Toxic	Poison	Status	—	90	10	Normal
TM10	Hidden Power	Normal	Special	60	100	15	Normal
TM12	Taunt	Dark	Status	—	100	20	Normal
TM13	Ice Beam	Ice	Special	90	100	10	Normal
TM14	Blizzard	Ice	Special	110	70	5	Many Others
TM17	Protect	Normal	Status	—	—	10	Self
TM18	Rain Dance	Water	Status	—	—	5	Both Sides
TM20	Safeguard	Normal	Status	—	—	25	Your Side
TM21	Frustration	Normal	Physical	—	100	20	Normal
TM23	Smack Down	Rock	Physical	50	100	15	Normal
TM26	Earthquake	Ground	Physical	100	100	10	Adjacent
TM27	Return	Normal	Physical	—	100	20	Normal
TM28	Dig	Ground	Physical	80	100	10	Normal
TM31	Brick Break	Fighting	Physical	75	100	15	Normal
TM32	Double Team	Normal	Status	—	—	15	Self
TM34	Sludge Wave	Poison	Special	95	100	10	Adjacent
TM36	Sludge Bomb	Poison	Special	90	100	10	Normal
TM37	Sandstorm	Rock	Status	—	—	10	Both Sides
TM39	Rock Tomb	Rock	Physical	60	95	15	Normal
TM40	Aerial Ace	Flying	Physical	60	—	20	Normal
TM41	Torment	Dark	Status	—	100	15	Normal
TM42	Facade	Normal	Physical	70	100	20	Normal
TM44	Rest	Psychic	Status	—	—	10	Self
TM45	Attract	Normal	Status	—	100	15	Normal
TM46	Thief	Dark	Physical	60	100	25	Normal
TM48	Round	Normal	Special	60	100	15	Normal
TM54	False Swipe	Normal	Physical	40	100	40	Normal
TM55	Scald	Water	Special	80	100	15	Normal
TM56	Fling	Dark	Physical	—	100	10	Normal
TM63	Embargo	Dark	Status	—	100	15	Normal
TM65	Shadow Claw	Ghost	Physical	70	100	15	Normal
TM66	Payback	Dark	Physical	50	100	10	Normal
TM69	Rock Polish	Rock	Status	—	—	20	Self
TM71	Stone Edge	Rock	Physical	100	80	5	Normal
TM75	Swords Dance	Normal	Status	—	—	20	Self
TM78	Bulldoze	Ground	Physical	60	100	20	Adjacent
TM80	Rock Slide	Rock	Physical	75	90	10	Many Others
TM81	X-Scissor	Bug	Physical	80	100	15	Normal
TM83	Infestation	Bug	Special	20	100	20	Normal
TM84	Poison Jab	Poison	Physical	80	100	20	Normal
TM86	Grass Knot	Grass	Special	—	100	20	Normal
TM87	Swagger	Normal	Status	—	90	15	Normal
TM88	Sleep Talk	Normal	Status	—	—	10	Self
TM90	Substitute	Normal	Status	—	—	10	Self
TM94	Rock Smash	Fighting	Physical	40	100	15	Normal
TM96	Nature Power	Normal	Status	—	—	20	Normal

No.	Name	Type	Kind	Pow.	Acc.	PP	Range
TM98	Power-Up Punch	Fighting	Physical	40	100	20	Normal
TM100	Confide	Normal	Status	—	—	20	Normal
HM01	Cut	Normal	Physical	50	95	30	Normal
HM03	Surf	Water	Special	90	100	15	Adjacent
HM04	Strength	Normal	Physical	80	100	15	Normal

● MOVES TAUGHT BY PEOPLE

Name	Type	Kind	Pow.	Acc.	PP	Range

● EGG MOVES

Name	Type	Kind	Pow.	Acc.	PP	Range
Tickle	Normal	Status	—	100	20	Normal
Switcheroo	Dark	Status	—	100	10	Normal
Helping Hand	Normal	Status	—	—	20	1 Ally
Water Sport	Water	Status	—	—	15	Both Sides

🐚 Coastal Kalos
Collective Pokémon
022

☑ Barbaracle

HEIGHT: 4'03"　WEIGHT: 211.6 lbs.
GENDER: ♂ / ♀

TYPE | Rock | Water

ABILITIES
Tough Claws
Sniper

HIDDEN ABILITY
Pickpocket

STAT GROWTH RATES

HP	▪▪▪
Attack	▪▪▪▪
Defense	▪▪▪▪▪
Sp. Atk	▪▪▪
Sp. Def	▪▪▪▪
Speed	▪▪▪▪

EGG GROUP
Water 3

X When they evolve, two Binacle multiply into seven. They fight with the power of seven Binacle.

Y Barbaracle's legs and hands have minds of their own, and they will move independently. But they usually follow the head's orders.

⬆ EVOLUTION

Binacle　　Lv. 39 →　　Barbaracle

ITEMS SOMETIMES HELD BY WILD POKÉMON
None

Damage taken in normal battles		Damage taken in Inverse Battles	
Normal	×0.5	Normal	×2
Fire	×0.25	Fire	×4
Water	×1	Water	×1
Grass	×4	Grass	×0.25
Electric	×2	Electric	×0.5
Ice	×0.5	Ice	×2
Fighting	×2	Fighting	×0.5
Poison	×0.5	Poison	×2
Ground	×2	Ground	×0.5
Flying	×0.5	Flying	×2
Psychic	×1	Psychic	×1
Bug	×1	Bug	×1
Rock	×1	Rock	×1
Ghost	×1	Ghost	×1
Dragon	×1	Dragon	×1
Dark	×1	Dark	×1
Steel	×1	Steel	×1
Fairy	×1	Fairy	×1

Can be used in	
Inverse Battle	Battle Institute
—	Battle Maison
Battle Chateau	Random Matchup

Same form for ♂ / ♀

How to obtain for your Coastal Kalos Pokédex

Level up Binacle to Lv. 39.　|　Level up Binacle to Lv. 39.

X　**Y**

● LEVEL-UP MOVES

Lv.	Name	Type	Kind	Pow.	Acc.	PP	Range
1	Stone Edge	Rock	Physical	100	80	5	Normal
1	Skull Bash	Normal	Physical	130	100	10	Normal
1	Shell Smash	Normal	Status	—	—	15	Self
1	Scratch	Normal	Physical	40	100	35	Normal
1	Sand Attack	Ground	Status	—	100	15	Normal
4	Water Gun	Water	Special	40	100	25	Normal
7	Withdraw	Water	Status	—	—	40	Self
10	Fury Swipes	Normal	Physical	18	80	15	Normal
13	Slash	Normal	Physical	70	100	20	Normal
16	Mud-Slap	Ground	Special	20	100	10	Normal
20	Clamp	Water	Physical	35	85	15	Normal
24	Rock Polish	Rock	Status	—	—	20	Self
28	Ancient Power	Rock	Special	60	100	5	Normal
32	Hone Claws	Dark	Status	—	—	15	Self
37	Fury Cutter	Bug	Physical	40	95	20	Normal
42	Night Slash	Dark	Physical	70	100	15	Normal
48	Razor Shell	Water	Physical	75	95	10	Normal
55	Cross Chop	Fighting	Physical	100	80	5	Normal
60	Stone Edge	Rock	Physical	100	80	5	Normal
65	Skull Bash	Normal	Physical	130	100	10	Normal

● TM & HM MOVES

No.	Name	Type	Kind	Pow.	Acc.	PP	Range
TM01	Hone Claws	Dark	Status	—	—	15	Self
TM02	Dragon Claw	Dragon	Physical	80	100	15	Normal
TM06	Toxic	Poison	Status	—	90	10	Normal
TM08	Bulk Up	Fighting	Status	—	—	20	Self
TM10	Hidden Power	Normal	Special	60	100	15	Normal
TM12	Taunt	Dark	Status	—	100	20	Normal
TM13	Ice Beam	Ice	Special	90	100	10	Normal
TM14	Blizzard	Ice	Special	110	70	5	Many Others
TM15	Hyper Beam	Normal	Special	150	90	5	Normal
TM17	Protect	Normal	Status	—	—	10	Self

● TM & HM MOVES

No.	Name	Type	Kind	Pow.	Acc.	PP	Range
TM18	Rain Dance	Water	Status	—	—	5	Both Sides
TM20	Safeguard	Normal	Status	—	—	25	Your Side
TM21	Frustration	Normal	Physical	—	100	20	Normal
TM23	Smack Down	Rock	Physical	50	100	15	Normal
TM26	Earthquake	Ground	Physical	100	100	10	Adjacent
TM27	Return	Normal	Physical	—	100	20	Normal
TM28	Dig	Ground	Physical	80	100	10	Normal
TM31	Brick Break	Fighting	Physical	75	100	15	Normal
TM32	Double Team	Normal	Status	—	—	15	Self
TM34	Sludge Wave	Poison	Special	95	100	10	Adjacent
TM36	Sludge Bomb	Poison	Special	90	100	10	Normal
TM37	Sandstorm	Rock	Status	—	—	10	Both Sides
TM39	Rock Tomb	Rock	Physical	60	95	15	Normal
TM40	Aerial Ace	Flying	Physical	60	—	20	Normal
TM41	Torment	Dark	Status	—	100	15	Normal
TM42	Facade	Normal	Physical	70	100	20	Normal
TM44	Rest	Psychic	Status	—	—	10	Self
TM45	Attract	Normal	Status	—	100	15	Normal
TM46	Thief	Dark	Physical	60	100	25	Normal
TM48	Round	Normal	Special	60	100	15	Normal
TM52	Focus Blast	Fighting	Special	120	70	5	Normal
TM54	False Swipe	Normal	Physical	40	100	40	Normal
TM55	Scald	Water	Special	80	100	15	Normal
TM56	Fling	Dark	Physical	—	100	10	Normal
TM63	Embargo	Dark	Status	—	100	15	Normal
TM65	Shadow Claw	Ghost	Physical	70	100	15	Normal
TM66	Payback	Dark	Physical	50	100	10	Normal
TM68	Giga Impact	Normal	Physical	150	90	5	Normal
TM69	Rock Polish	Rock	Status	—	—	20	Self
TM71	Stone Edge	Rock	Physical	100	80	5	Normal
TM75	Swords Dance	Normal	Status	—	—	20	Self
TM78	Bulldoze	Ground	Physical	60	100	20	Adjacent
TM80	Rock Slide	Rock	Physical	75	90	10	Many Others

No.	Name	Type	Kind	Pow.	Acc.	PP	Range
TM81	X-Scissor	Bug	Physical	80	100	15	Normal
TM83	Infestation	Bug	Special	20	100	20	Normal
TM84	Poison Jab	Poison	Physical	80	100	20	Normal
TM86	Grass Knot	Grass	Special	—	100	20	Normal
TM87	Swagger	Normal	Status	—	90	15	Normal
TM88	Sleep Talk	Normal	Status	—	—	10	Self
TM90	Substitute	Normal	Status	—	—	10	Self
TM94	Rock Smash	Fighting	Physical	40	100	15	Normal
TM96	Nature Power	Normal	Status	—	—	20	Normal
TM98	Power-Up Punch	Fighting	Physical	40	100	20	Normal
TM100	Confide	Normal	Status	—	—	20	Normal
HM01	Cut	Normal	Physical	50	95	30	Normal
HM03	Surf	Water	Special	90	100	15	Adjacent
HM04	Strength	Normal	Physical	80	100	15	Normal

● MOVES TAUGHT BY PEOPLE

Name	Type	Kind	Pow.	Acc.	PP	Range

AFTER THE HALL OF FAME

CENTRAL KALOS

COASTAL KALOS

023

Dwebble

MOUNTAIN KALOS

ADVENTURE DATA

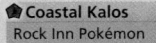

Dwebble

Coastal Kalos 023
Rock Inn Pokémon

HEIGHT: 1'00" WEIGHT: 32.0 lbs.
GENDER: ♂/♀

X It makes a hole in a suitable rock. If that rock breaks, the Pokémon remains agitated until it locates a replacement.

Y When it finds a stone of a suitable size, it secretes a liquid from its mouth to open up a hole to crawl into.

TYPE | Bug | Rock

ABILITIES
Sturdy
Shell Armor

HIDDEN ABILITY
Weak Armor

STAT GROWTH RATES
HP	■ ■
Attack	■ ■ ■
Defense	■ ■ ■ ■
Sp. Atk	■ ■
Sp. Def	■ ■
Speed	■ ■ ■

EGG GROUPS
Bug, Mineral

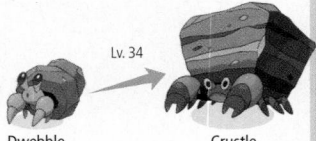

EVOLUTION

Dwebble → Lv. 34 → Crustle

ITEMS SOMETIMES HELD BY WILD POKÉMON
Hard Stone

Damage taken in normal battles		Damage taken in Inverse Battles	
Normal	×0.5	Normal	×2
Fire	×1	Fire	×1
Water	×2	Water	×0.5
Grass	×1	Grass	×1
Electric	×1	Electric	×1
Ice	×1	Ice	×1
Fighting	×1	Fighting	×1
Poison	×0.5	Poison	×2
Ground	×1	Ground	×1
Flying	×1	Flying	×1
Psychic	×1	Psychic	×1
Bug	×1	Bug	×1
Rock	×2	Rock	×0.5
Ghost	×1	Ghost	×1
Dragon	×1	Dragon	×1
Dark	×1	Dark	×1
Steel	×2	Steel	×0.5
Fairy	×1	Fairy	×1

Can be used in	
Inverse Battle	Battle Institute
—	Battle Maison
Battle Chateau	Random Matchup

Same form for ♂/♀

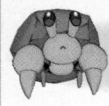

How to obtain for your Coastal Kalos Pokédex

❶ Catch after it appears from a cracked rock on Route 8 (using Rock Smash).

❷ Catch after it appears from a cracked rock in Ambrette Town (using Rock Smash).

❶ Catch after it appears from a cracked rock on Route 8 (using Rock Smash).

❷ Catch after it appears from a cracked rock in Ambrette Town (using Rock Smash).

LEVEL-UP MOVES

Lv.	Name	Type	Kind	Pow.	Acc.	PP	Range
1	Fury Cutter	Bug	Physical	40	95	20	Normal
5	Rock Blast	Rock	Physical	25	90	10	Normal
7	Withdraw	Water	Status	—	—	40	Self
11	Sand Attack	Ground	Status	—	100	15	Normal
13	Feint Attack	Dark	Physical	60	—	20	Normal
17	Smack Down	Rock	Physical	50	100	15	Normal
19	Rock Polish	Rock	Status	—	—	20	Self
23	Bug Bite	Bug	Physical	60	100	20	Normal
24	Stealth Rock	Rock	Status	—	—	20	Other Side
29	Rock Slide	Rock	Physical	75	90	10	Many Others
31	Slash	Normal	Physical	70	100	20	Normal
35	X-Scissor	Bug	Physical	80	100	15	Normal
37	Shell Smash	Normal	Status	—	—	15	Self
41	Flail	Normal	Physical	—	100	15	Normal
43	Rock Wrecker	Rock	Physical	150	90	5	Normal

TM & HM MOVES

No.	Name	Type	Kind	Pow.	Acc.	PP	Range
TM01	Hone Claws	Dark	Status	—	—	15	Self
TM06	Toxic	Poison	Status	—	90	10	Normal
TM10	Hidden Power	Normal	Special	60	100	15	Normal
TM17	Protect	Normal	Status	—	—	10	Self
TM21	Frustration	Normal	Physical	—	100	20	Normal
TM22	Solar Beam	Grass	Special	120	100	10	Normal
TM23	Smack Down	Rock	Physical	50	100	15	Normal
TM26	Earthquake	Ground	Physical	100	100	10	Adjacent
TM27	Return	Normal	Physical	—	100	20	Normal
TM28	Dig	Ground	Physical	80	100	10	Normal
TM32	Double Team	Normal	Status	—	—	15	Self
TM37	Sandstorm	Rock	Status	—	—	10	Both Sides
TM39	Rock Tomb	Rock	Physical	60	95	15	Normal
TM40	Aerial Ace	Flying	Physical	60	—	20	Normal
TM42	Facade	Normal	Physical	70	100	20	Normal
TM44	Rest	Psychic	Status	—	—	10	Self
TM45	Attract	Normal	Status	—	100	15	Normal
TM48	Round	Normal	Special	60	100	15	Normal
TM65	Shadow Claw	Ghost	Physical	70	100	15	Normal
TM69	Rock Polish	Rock	Status	—	—	20	Self
TM71	Stone Edge	Rock	Physical	100	80	5	Normal
TM75	Swords Dance	Normal	Status	—	—	20	Self
TM76	Struggle Bug	Bug	Special	50	100	20	Many Others
TM78	Bulldoze	Ground	Physical	60	100	20	Adjacent
TM80	Rock Slide	Rock	Physical	75	90	10	Many Others
TM81	X-Scissor	Bug	Physical	80	100	15	Normal
TM84	Poison Jab	Poison	Physical	80	100	20	Normal
TM87	Swagger	Normal	Status	—	90	15	Normal
TM88	Sleep Talk	Normal	Status	—	—	10	Self
TM90	Substitute	Normal	Status	—	—	10	Self
TM94	Rock Smash	Fighting	Physical	40	100	15	Normal
TM96	Nature Power	Normal	Status	—	—	20	Normal
TM100	Confide	Normal	Status	—	—	20	Normal

No.	Name	Type	Kind	Pow.	Acc.	PP	Range
HM01	Cut	Normal	Physical	50	95	30	Normal
HM04	Strength	Normal	Physical	80	100	15	Normal

MOVES TAUGHT BY PEOPLE

Name	Type	Kind	Pow.	Acc.	PP	Range

EGG MOVES

Name	Type	Kind	Pow.	Acc.	PP	Range
Endure	Normal	Status	—	—	10	Self
Iron Defense	Steel	Status	—	—	15	Self
Night Slash	Dark	Physical	70	100	15	Normal
Sand Tomb	Ground	Physical	35	85	15	Normal
Counter	Fighting	Physical	—	100	20	Varies
Curse	Ghost	Status	—	—	10	Varies
Spikes	Ground	Status	—	—	20	Other Side
Block	Normal	Status	—	—	5	Normal
Wide Guard	Rock	Status	—	—	10	Your Side
Rototiller	Ground	Status	—	—	10	Adjacent

COASTAL KALOS

024 Crustle

AFTER THE HALL OF FAME

CENTRAL KALOS

MOUNTAIN KALOS

ADVENTURE DATA

Coastal Kalos
Stone Home Pokémon

☑ Crustle

024

HEIGHT: 4'07" WEIGHT: 440.9 lbs.
GENDER: ♂/♀

X It possesses legs of enormous strength, enabling it to carry heavy slabs for many days, even when crossing arid land.

Y Competing for territory, Crustle fight viciously. The one whose boulder is broken is the loser of the battle.

TYPE	Bug	Rock

ABILITIES
Sturdy
Shell Armor

HIDDEN ABILITY
Weak Armor

STAT GROWTH RATES
HP	■■■
Attack	■■■■■
Defense	■■■■■
Sp. Atk	■■■
Sp. Def	■■■
Speed	■■■

EGG GROUPS
Bug, Mineral

EVOLUTION

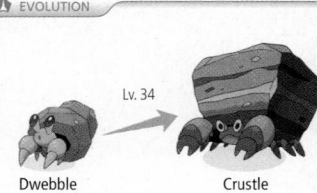

Dwebble → Crustle (Lv. 34)

ITEMS SOMETIMES HELD BY WILD POKÉMON
None

Damage taken in normal battles		Damage taken in Inverse Battles	
Normal	×0.5	Normal	×2
Fire	×1	Fire	×1
Water	×2	Water	×0.5
Grass	×1	Grass	×1
Electric	×1	Electric	×1
Ice	×1	Ice	×1
Fighting	×1	Fighting	×1
Poison	×0.5	Poison	×2
Ground	×1	Ground	×1
Flying	×1	Flying	×1
Psychic	×1	Psychic	×1
Bug	×1	Bug	×1
Rock	×2	Rock	×0.5
Ghost	×1	Ghost	×1
Dragon	×1	Dragon	×1
Dark	×1	Dark	×1
Steel	×2	Steel	×0.5
Fairy	×1	Fairy	×1

Can be used in	
Inverse Battle	Battle Institute
—	Battle Maison
Battle Chateau	Random Matchup

Same form for ♂/♀

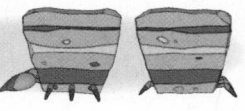

How to obtain for your Coastal Kalos Pokédex

Level up Dwebble to Lv. 34.

Level up Dwebble to Lv. 34.

● LEVEL-UP MOVES

Lv.	Name	Type	Kind	Pow.	Acc.	PP	Range
1	Shell Smash	Normal	Status	—	—	15	Self
1	Rock Blast	Rock	Physical	25	90	10	Normal
1	Withdraw	Water	Status	—	—	40	Self
1	Sand Attack	Ground	Status	—	100	15	Normal
5	Rock Blast	Rock	Physical	25	90	10	Normal
7	Withdraw	Water	Status	—	—	40	Self
11	Sand Attack	Ground	Status	—	100	15	Normal
13	Feint Attack	Dark	Physical	60	—	20	Normal
17	Smack Down	Rock	Physical	50	100	15	Normal
19	Rock Polish	Rock	Status	—	—	20	Self
23	Bug Bite	Bug	Physical	60	100	20	Normal
24	Stealth Rock	Rock	Status	—	—	20	Other Side
29	Rock Slide	Rock	Physical	75	90	10	Many Others
31	Slash	Normal	Physical	70	100	20	Normal
38	X-Scissor	Bug	Physical	80	100	15	Normal
43	Shell Smash	Normal	Status	—	—	15	Self
50	Flail	Normal	Physical	—	100	15	Normal
55	Rock Wrecker	Rock	Physical	150	90	5	Normal

● TM & HM MOVES

No.	Name	Type	Kind	Pow.	Acc.	PP	Range
TM01	Hone Claws	Dark	Status	—	—	15	Self
TM06	Toxic	Poison	Status	—	90	10	Normal
TM10	Hidden Power	Normal	Special	60	100	15	Normal
TM15	Hyper Beam	Normal	Special	150	90	5	Normal
TM17	Protect	Normal	Status	—	—	10	Self
TM21	Frustration	Normal	Physical	—	100	20	Normal
TM22	Solar Beam	Grass	Special	120	100	10	Normal
TM23	Smack Down	Rock	Physical	50	100	15	Normal
TM26	Earthquake	Ground	Physical	100	100	10	Adjacent
TM27	Return	Normal	Physical	—	100	20	Normal
TM28	Dig	Ground	Physical	80	100	10	Normal
TM32	Double Team	Normal	Status	—	—	15	Self
TM37	Sandstorm	Rock	Status	—	—	10	Both Sides
TM39	Rock Tomb	Rock	Physical	60	95	15	Normal
TM40	Aerial Ace	Flying	Physical	60	—	20	Normal
TM42	Facade	Normal	Physical	70	100	20	Normal
TM44	Rest	Psychic	Status	—	—	10	Self
TM45	Attract	Normal	Status	—	100	15	Normal
TM48	Round	Normal	Special	60	100	15	Normal
TM65	Shadow Claw	Ghost	Physical	70	100	15	Normal
TM68	Giga Impact	Normal	Physical	150	90	5	Normal
TM69	Rock Polish	Rock	Status	—	—	20	Self
TM71	Stone Edge	Rock	Physical	100	80	5	Normal
TM75	Swords Dance	Normal	Status	—	—	20	Self
TM76	Struggle Bug	Bug	Special	50	100	20	Many Others
TM78	Bulldoze	Ground	Physical	60	100	20	Adjacent
TM80	Rock Slide	Rock	Physical	75	90	10	Many Others
TM81	X-Scissor	Bug	Physical	80	100	15	Normal
TM84	Poison Jab	Poison	Physical	80	100	20	Normal
TM87	Swagger	Normal	Status	—	90	15	Normal
TM88	Sleep Talk	Normal	Status	—	—	10	Self
TM90	Substitute	Normal	Status	—	—	10	Self
TM94	Rock Smash	Fighting	Physical	40	100	15	Normal

No.	Name	Type	Kind	Pow.	Acc.	PP	Range
TM96	Nature Power	Normal	Status	—	—	20	Normal
TM100	Confide	Normal	Status	—	—	20	Normal
HM01	Cut	Normal	Physical	50	95	30	Normal
HM04	Strength	Normal	Physical	80	100	15	Normal

● MOVES TAUGHT BY PEOPLE

Name	Type	Kind	Pow.	Acc.	PP	Range

AFTER THE HALL OF FAME
CENTRAL KALOS
COASTAL KALOS
025
Tentacool
MOUNTAIN KALOS
ADVENTURE DATA

Coastal Kalos 025
Jellyfish Pokémon
Tentacool

HEIGHT: 2'11" WEIGHT: 100.3 lbs.
GENDER: ♂/♀

TYPE Water Poison

ABILITIES
Clear Body
Liquid Ooze

HIDDEN ABILITY
None

STAT GROWTH RATES
HP	■■
Attack	■■
Defense	■■
Sp. Atk	■■
Sp. Def	■■
Speed	■■■■

EGG GROUP
Water 3

Its body is virtually composed of water. It shoots strange beams from its crystal-like eyes.

Drifts in shallow seas. Anglers who hook them by accident are often punished by their stingers.

EVOLUTION
Tentacool → Lv. 30 → Tentacruel

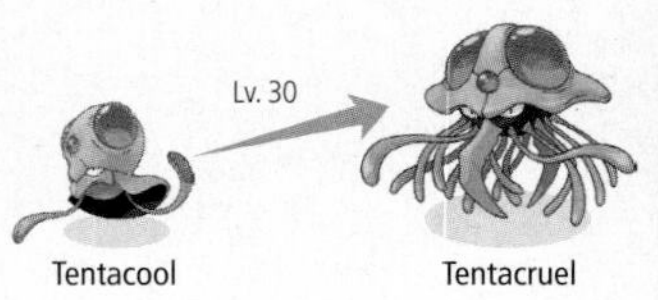

ITEMS SOMETIMES HELD BY WILD POKÉMON
Poison Barb

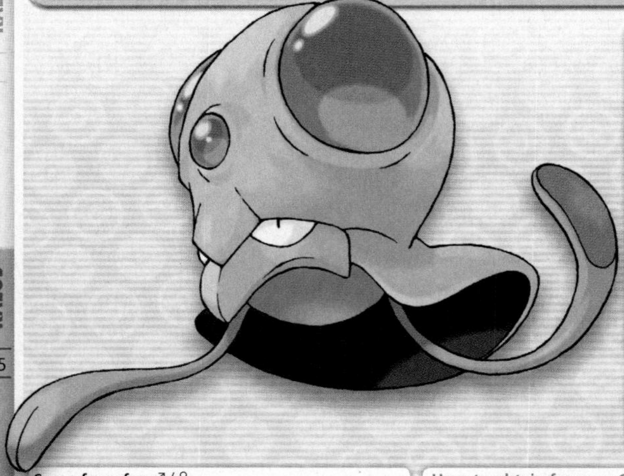

Damage taken in normal battles		Damage taken in Inverse Battles	
Normal	×1	Normal	×1
Fire	×0.5	Fire	×2
Water	×0.5	Water	×2
Grass	×1	Grass	×1
Electric	×2	Electric	×0.5
Ice	×0.5	Ice	×2
Fighting	×0.5	Fighting	×2
Poison	×0.5	Poison	×2
Ground	×2	Ground	×0.5
Flying	×1	Flying	×1
Psychic	×2	Psychic	×0.5
Bug	×0.5	Bug	×2
Rock	×1	Rock	×1
Ghost	×1	Ghost	×1
Dragon	×1	Dragon	×1
Dark	×1	Dark	×1
Steel	×0.5	Steel	×2
Fairy	×0.5	Fairy	×2

Can be used in	
Inverse Battle	Battle Institute
—	Battle Maison
Battle Chateau	Random Matchup

Same form for ♂/♀

How to obtain for your Coastal Kalos Pokédex
❶ Catch on the surface of the water on Route 8.
❷ Catch on the surface of the water in Ambrette Town.

❶ Catch on the surface of the water on Route 8.
❷ Catch on the surface of the water in Ambrette Town.

● LEVEL-UP MOVES
Lv.	Name	Type	Kind	Pow.	Acc.	PP	Range
1	Poison Sting	Poison	Physical	15	100	35	Normal
5	Supersonic	Normal	Status	—	55	20	Normal
8	Constrict	Normal	Physical	10	100	35	Normal
12	Acid	Poison	Special	40	100	30	Many Others
15	Toxic Spikes	Poison	Status	—	—	20	Other Side
19	Bubble Beam	Water	Special	65	100	20	Normal
22	Wrap	Normal	Physical	15	90	20	Normal
26	Acid Spray	Poison	Special	40	100	20	Normal
29	Barrier	Psychic	Status	—	—	20	Self
33	Water Pulse	Water	Special	60	100	20	Normal
36	Poison Jab	Poison	Physical	80	100	20	Normal
40	Screech	Normal	Status	—	85	40	Normal
43	Hex	Ghost	Special	65	100	10	Normal
47	Hydro Pump	Water	Special	110	80	5	Normal
50	Sludge Wave	Poison	Special	95	100	10	Adjacent
54	Wring Out	Normal	Special	—	100	5	Normal

● TM & HM MOVES
No.	Name	Type	Kind	Pow.	Acc.	PP	Range
TM06	Toxic	Poison	Status	—	90	10	Normal
TM07	Hail	Ice	Status	—	—	10	Both Sides
TM09	Venoshock	Poison	Special	65	100	10	Normal
TM10	Hidden Power	Normal	Special	60	100	15	Normal
TM13	Ice Beam	Ice	Special	90	100	10	Normal
TM14	Blizzard	Ice	Special	110	70	5	Many Others
TM17	Protect	Normal	Status	—	—	10	Self
TM18	Rain Dance	Water	Status	—	—	5	Both Sides
TM20	Safeguard	Normal	Status	—	—	25	Your Side
TM21	Frustration	Normal	Physical	—	100	20	Normal
TM27	Return	Normal	Physical	—	100	20	Normal
TM32	Double Team	Normal	Status	—	—	15	Self
TM34	Sludge Wave	Poison	Special	95	100	10	Adjacent
TM36	Sludge Bomb	Poison	Special	90	100	10	Normal
TM42	Facade	Normal	Physical	70	100	20	Normal
TM44	Rest	Psychic	Status	—	—	10	Self
TM45	Attract	Normal	Status	—	100	15	Normal
TM46	Thief	Dark	Physical	60	100	25	Normal
TM48	Round	Normal	Special	60	100	15	Normal
TM55	Scald	Water	Special	80	100	15	Normal
TM66	Payback	Dark	Physical	50	100	10	Normal
TM75	Swords Dance	Normal	Status	—	—	20	Self
TM83	Infestation	Bug	Special	20	100	20	Normal
TM84	Poison Jab	Poison	Physical	80	100	20	Normal
TM87	Swagger	Normal	Status	—	90	15	Normal
TM88	Sleep Talk	Normal	Status	—	—	10	Self
TM90	Substitute	Normal	Status	—	—	10	Self
TM99	Dazzling Gleam	Fairy	Special	80	100	10	Many Others
TM100	Confide	Normal	Status	—	—	20	Normal
HM01	Cut	Normal	Physical	50	95	30	Normal
HM03	Surf	Water	Special	90	100	15	Adjacent
HM05	Waterfall	Water	Physical	80	100	15	Normal

● MOVES TAUGHT BY PEOPLE
Name	Type	Kind	Pow.	Acc.	PP	Range

● EGG MOVES
Name	Type	Kind	Pow.	Acc.	PP	Range
Aurora Beam	Ice	Special	65	100	20	Normal
Mirror Coat	Psychic	Special	—	—	20	Varies
Rapid Spin	Normal	Physical	20	100	40	Normal
Haze	Ice	Status	—	—	30	Both Sides
Confuse Ray	Ghost	Status	—	100	10	Normal
Knock Off	Dark	Physical	65	100	20	Normal
Acupressure	Normal	Status	—	—	30	Self/Ally
Muddy Water	Water	Special	90	85	10	Many Others
Bubble	Water	Special	40	100	30	Many Others
Aqua Ring	Water	Status	—	—	20	Self
Tickle	Normal	Status	—	100	20	Normal

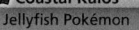

🔖 Coastal Kalos — 026

Jellyfish Pokémon

☑️ Tentacruel

HEIGHT: 5'03"　WEIGHT: 121.3 lbs.
GENDER: ♂ / ♀

 The tentacles are normally kept short. On hunts, they are extended to ensnare and immobilize prey.

 It has 80 tentacles that move about freely. They can sting, causing poisoning and sharp, stabbing pain.

TYPE | Water | Poison

ABILITIES
Clear Body
Liquid Ooze

HIDDEN ABILITY
None

STAT GROWTH RATES

HP	■■■
Attack	■■■■
Defense	■■■■
Sp. Atk	■■■■
Sp. Def	■■■■
Speed	■■■■■

EGG GROUP
Water 3

🔼 EVOLUTION

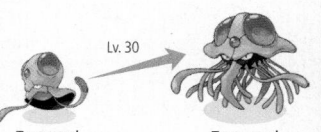

Tentacool　　　Lv. 30　　　Tentacruel

ITEMS SOMETIMES HELD BY WILD POKÉMON
None

Damage taken in normal battles

Normal	×1
Fire	×0.5
Water	×0.5
Grass	×1
Electric	×2
Ice	×0.5
Fighting	×0.5
Poison	×0.5
Ground	×2
Flying	×1
Psychic	×2
Bug	×0.5
Rock	×1
Ghost	×1
Dragon	×1
Dark	×1
Steel	×0.5
Fairy	×0.5

Damage taken in Inverse Battles

Normal	×1
Fire	×2
Water	×2
Grass	×1
Electric	×0.5
Ice	×2
Fighting	×2
Poison	×2
Ground	×0.5
Flying	×1
Psychic	×0.5
Bug	×2
Rock	×1
Ghost	×1
Dragon	×1
Dark	×1
Steel	×2
Fairy	×2

Can be used in

Inverse Battle	Battle Institute
----	Battle Maison
Battle Chateau	Random Matchup

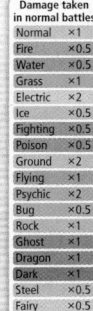

Same form for ♂ / ♀

How to obtain for your Coastal Kalos Pokédex

Level up Tentacool to Lv. 30.　　Level up Tentacool to Lv. 30.

● LEVEL-UP MOVES

Lv.	Name	Type	Kind	Pow.	Acc.	PP	Range
1	Reflect Type	Normal	Status	—	—	15	Normal
1	Wring Out	Normal	Special	—	100	5	Normal
1	Poison Sting	Poison	Physical	15	100	35	Normal
1	Supersonic	Normal	Status	—	55	20	Normal
1	Constrict	Normal	Physical	10	100	35	Normal
5	Supersonic	Normal	Status	—	55	20	Normal
8	Constrict	Normal	Physical	10	100	35	Normal
12	Acid	Poison	Special	40	100	30	Many Others
15	Toxic Spikes	Poison	Status	—	—	20	Other Side
19	Bubble Beam	Water	Special	65	100	20	Normal
22	Wrap	Normal	Physical	15	90	20	Normal
26	Acid Spray	Poison	Special	40	100	20	Normal
29	Barrier	Psychic	Status	—	—	20	Self
34	Water Pulse	Water	Special	60	100	20	Normal
38	Poison Jab	Poison	Physical	80	100	20	Normal
43	Screech	Normal	Status	—	85	40	Normal
47	Hex	Ghost	Special	65	100	10	Normal
52	Hydro Pump	Water	Special	110	80	5	Normal
56	Sludge Wave	Poison	Special	95	100	10	Adjacent
61	Wring Out	Normal	Special	—	100	5	Normal

● TM & HM MOVES

No.	Name	Type	Kind	Pow.	Acc.	PP	Range
TM06	Toxic	Poison	Status	—	90	10	Normal
TM07	Hail	Ice	Status	—	—	10	Both Sides
TM09	Venoshock	Poison	Special	65	100	10	Normal
TM10	Hidden Power	Normal	Special	60	100	15	Normal
TM13	Ice Beam	Ice	Special	90	100	10	Normal
TM14	Blizzard	Ice	Special	110	70	5	Many Others
TM15	Hyper Beam	Normal	Special	150	90	5	Normal
TM17	Protect	Normal	Status	—	—	10	Self
TM18	Rain Dance	Water	Status	—	—	5	Both Sides
TM20	Safeguard	Normal	Status	—	—	25	Your Side
TM21	Frustration	Normal	Physical	—	100	20	Normal
TM27	Return	Normal	Physical	—	100	20	Normal
TM32	Double Team	Normal	Status	—	—	15	Self
TM34	Sludge Wave	Poison	Special	95	100	10	Adjacent
TM36	Sludge Bomb	Poison	Special	90	100	10	Normal
TM42	Facade	Normal	Physical	70	100	20	Normal
TM44	Rest	Psychic	Status	—	—	10	Self
TM45	Attract	Normal	Status	—	100	15	Normal
TM46	Thief	Dark	Physical	60	100	25	Normal
TM48	Round	Normal	Special	60	100	15	Normal
TM55	Scald	Water	Special	80	100	15	Normal
TM66	Payback	Dark	Physical	50	100	10	Normal
TM68	Giga Impact	Normal	Physical	150	90	5	Normal
TM75	Swords Dance	Normal	Status	—	—	20	Self
TM83	Infestation	Bug	Special	20	100	20	Normal
TM84	Poison Jab	Poison	Physical	80	100	20	Normal
TM87	Swagger	Normal	Status	—	90	15	Normal
TM88	Sleep Talk	Normal	Status	—	—	10	Self
TM90	Substitute	Normal	Status	—	—	10	Self
TM99	Dazzling Gleam	Fairy	Special	80	100	10	Many Others
TM100	Confide	Normal	Status	—	—	20	Normal
HM01	Cut	Normal	Physical	50	95	30	Normal
HM03	Surf	Water	Special	90	100	15	Adjacent

No.	Name	Type	Kind	Pow.	Acc.	PP	Range
HM05	Waterfall	Water	Physical	80	100	15	Normal

● MOVES TAUGHT BY PEOPLE

Name	Type	Kind	Pow.	Acc.	PP	Range

AFTER THE HALL OF FAME

CENTRAL KALOS

COASTAL KALOS

026 | Tentacruel

MOUNTAIN KALOS

ADVENTURE DATA

AFTER THE HALL OF FAME

CENTRAL KALOS

COASTAL KALOS

027

Wailmer

MOUNTAIN KALOS

ADVENTURE DATA

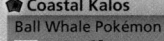

Coastal Kalos
Ball Whale Pokémon
☑ Wailmer

027

HEIGHT: 6'07" WEIGHT: 286.6 lbs.
GENDER: ♂/♀

TYPE	Water

ABILITIES
Water Veil
Oblivious

HIDDEN ABILITY
None

STAT GROWTH RATES

HP	■■■■■
Attack	■■■■
Defense	■■
Sp. Atk	■■■
Sp. Def	■■■
Speed	■■■

EGG GROUPS
Field, Water 2

X It bounces playfully like a ball. The more seawater it swallows, the higher it bounces.

Y It eats one ton of food every day. It plays by shooting stored seawater out its blowholes with great force.

⬆ EVOLUTION

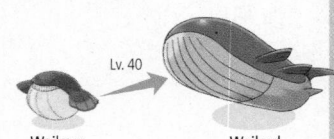

Wailmer → (Lv. 40) → Wailord

ITEMS SOMETIMES HELD BY WILD POKÉMON
None

Damage taken in normal battles		Damage taken in Inverse Battles	
Normal	×1	Normal	×1
Fire	×0.5	Fire	×2
Water	×0.5	Water	×2
Grass	×2	Grass	×0.5
Electric	×2	Electric	×0.5
Ice	×0.5	Ice	×2
Fighting	×1	Fighting	×1
Poison	×1	Poison	×1
Ground	×1	Ground	×1
Flying	×1	Flying	×1
Psychic	×1	Psychic	×1
Bug	×1	Bug	×1
Rock	×1	Rock	×1
Ghost	×1	Ghost	×1
Dragon	×1	Dragon	×1
Dark	×1	Dark	×1
Steel	×0.5	Steel	×2
Fairy	×1	Fairy	×1

Can be used in	
Inverse Battle	Battle Institute
—	Battle Maison
Battle Chateau	Random Matchup

Same form for ♂/♀

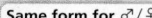

How to obtain for your Coastal Kalos Pokédex

❶ Catch on the surface of the water on Route 8.
❷ Catch on the surface of the water in Ambrette Town.

❶ Catch on the surface of the water on Route 8.
❷ Catch on the surface of the water in Ambrette Town.

● LEVEL-UP MOVES

Lv.	Name	Type	Kind	Pow.	Acc.	PP	Range
1	Splash	Normal	Status	—	—	40	Self
4	Growl	Normal	Status	—	100	40	Many Others
7	Water Gun	Water	Special	40	100	25	Normal
11	Rollout	Rock	Physical	30	90	20	Normal
14	Whirlpool	Water	Special	35	85	15	Normal
17	Astonish	Ghost	Physical	30	100	15	Normal
21	Water Pulse	Water	Special	60	100	20	Normal
24	Mist	Ice	Status	—	—	30	Your Side
27	Rest	Psychic	Status	—	—	10	Self
31	Brine	Water	Special	65	100	10	Normal
34	Water Spout	Water	Special	150	100	5	Many Others
37	Amnesia	Psychic	Status	—	—	20	Self
41	Dive	Water	Physical	80	100	10	Normal
44	Bounce	Flying	Physical	85	85	5	Normal
47	Hydro Pump	Water	Special	110	80	5	Normal
50	Heavy Slam	Steel	Physical	—	100	10	Normal

● TM & HM MOVES

No.	Name	Type	Kind	Pow.	Acc.	PP	Range
TM05	Roar	Normal	Status	—	—	20	Normal
TM06	Toxic	Poison	Status	—	90	10	Normal
TM07	Hail	Ice	Status	—	—	10	Both Sides
TM10	Hidden Power	Normal	Special	60	100	15	Normal
TM13	Ice Beam	Ice	Special	90	100	10	Normal
TM14	Blizzard	Ice	Special	110	70	5	Many Others
TM17	Protect	Normal	Status	—	—	10	Self
TM18	Rain Dance	Water	Status	—	—	5	Both Sides
TM21	Frustration	Normal	Physical	—	100	20	Normal
TM26	Earthquake	Ground	Physical	100	100	10	Adjacent
TM27	Return	Normal	Physical	—	100	20	Normal
TM32	Double Team	Normal	Status	—	—	15	Self
TM39	Rock Tomb	Rock	Physical	60	95	15	Normal
TM42	Facade	Normal	Physical	70	100	20	Normal
TM44	Rest	Psychic	Status	—	—	10	Self
TM45	Attract	Normal	Status	—	100	15	Normal
TM48	Round	Normal	Special	60	100	15	Normal
TM49	Echoed Voice	Normal	Special	40	100	15	Normal
TM55	Scald	Water	Special	80	100	15	Normal
TM78	Bulldoze	Ground	Physical	60	100	20	Adjacent
TM87	Swagger	Normal	Status	—	90	15	Normal
TM88	Sleep Talk	Normal	Status	—	—	10	Self
TM90	Substitute	Normal	Status	—	—	10	Self
TM94	Rock Smash	Fighting	Physical	40	100	15	Normal
TM100	Confide	Normal	Status	—	—	20	Normal
HM03	Surf	Water	Special	90	100	15	Adjacent
HM04	Strength	Normal	Physical	80	100	15	Normal
HM05	Waterfall	Water	Physical	80	100	15	Normal

● MOVES TAUGHT BY PEOPLE

Name	Type	Kind	Pow.	Acc.	PP	Range

● EGG MOVES

Name	Type	Kind	Pow.	Acc.	PP	Range
Double-Edge	Normal	Physical	120	100	15	Normal
Thrash	Normal	Physical	120	100	10	1 Random
Snore	Normal	Special	50	100	15	Normal
Sleep Talk	Normal	Status	—	—	10	Self
Curse	Ghost	Status	—	—	10	Varies
Fissure	Ground	Physical	—	30	5	Normal
Tickle	Normal	Status	—	100	20	Normal
Defense Curl	Normal	Status	—	—	40	Self
Body Slam	Normal	Physical	85	100	15	Normal
Aqua Ring	Water	Status	—	—	20	Self
Soak	Water	Status	—	100	20	Normal
Zen Headbutt	Psychic	Physical	80	90	15	Normal
Clear Smog	Poison	Special	50	—	15	Normal

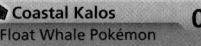

🏠 **Coastal Kalos** **028**
Float Whale Pokémon

✓ **Wailord**

HEIGHT: 47'07" WEIGHT: 877.4 lbs.
GENDER: ♂/♀

 It can sometimes knock out opponents with the shock created by breaching and crashing its big body onto the water.

 The biggest of all Pokémon. It can dive to a depth of almost 10,000 feet on only one breath.

TYPE Water

ABILITIES
Water Veil
Oblivious

HIDDEN ABILITY
None

STAT GROWTH RATES

HP	■■■■■
Attack	■■■■■
Defense	■■
Sp. Atk	■■■■
Sp. Def	■■
Speed	■■■

EGG GROUPS
Field, Water 2

EVOLUTION

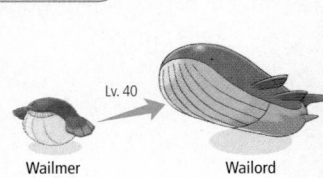

Lv. 40

Wailmer → Wailord

ITEMS SOMETIMES HELD BY WILD POKÉMON
None

Damage taken in normal battles		Damage taken in Inverse Battles	
Normal	×1	Normal	×1
Fire	×0.5	Fire	×2
Water	×0.5	Water	×2
Grass	×2	Grass	×0.5
Electric	×2	Electric	×0.5
Ice	×0.5	Ice	×2
Fighting	×1	Fighting	×1
Poison	×1	Poison	×1
Ground	×1	Ground	×1
Flying	×1	Flying	×1
Psychic	×1	Psychic	×1
Bug	×1	Bug	×1
Rock	×1	Rock	×1
Ghost	×1	Ghost	×1
Dragon	×1	Dragon	×1
Dark	×1	Dark	×1
Steel	×0.5	Steel	×2
Fairy	×1	Fairy	×1

Can be used in	
Inverse Battle	Battle Institute
—	Battle Maison
Battle Chateau	Random Matchup

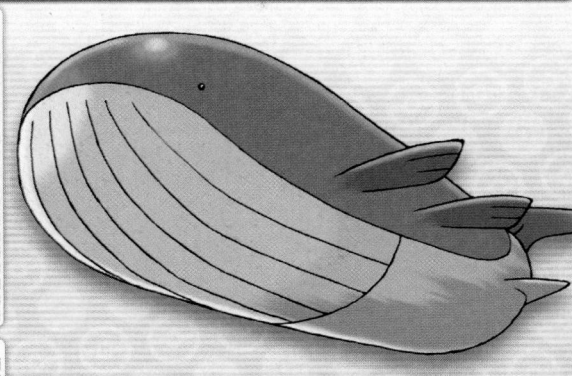

Same form for ♂/♀

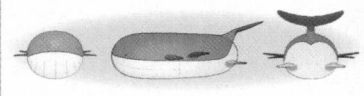

How to obtain for your Coastal Kalos Pokédex

Level up Wailmer to Lv. 40.	Level up Wailmer to Lv. 40.

● **LEVEL-UP MOVES**

Lv.	Name	Type	Kind	Pow.	Acc.	PP	Range
1	Splash	Normal	Status	—	—	40	Self
1	Growl	Normal	Status	—	100	40	Many Others
1	Water Gun	Water	Special	40	100	25	Normal
1	Rollout	Rock	Physical	30	90	20	Normal
4	Growl	Normal	Status	—	100	40	Many Others
7	Water Gun	Water	Special	40	100	25	Normal
11	Rollout	Rock	Physical	30	90	20	Normal
14	Whirlpool	Water	Special	35	85	15	Normal
17	Astonish	Ghost	Physical	30	100	15	Normal
21	Water Pulse	Water	Special	60	100	20	Normal
24	Mist	Ice	Status	—	—	30	Your Side
27	Rest	Psychic	Status	—	—	10	Self
31	Brine	Water	Special	65	100	10	Normal
34	Water Spout	Water	Special	150	100	5	Many Others
37	Amnesia	Psychic	Status	—	—	20	Self
46	Dive	Water	Physical	80	100	10	Normal
54	Bounce	Flying	Physical	85	85	5	Normal
62	Hydro Pump	Water	Special	110	80	5	Normal
70	Heavy Slam	Steel	Physical	—	100	10	Normal

● **TM & HM MOVES**

No.	Name	Type	Kind	Pow.	Acc.	PP	Range
TM05	Roar	Normal	Status	—	—	20	Normal
TM06	Toxic	Poison	Status	—	90	10	Normal
TM07	Hail	Ice	Status	—	—	10	Both Sides
TM10	Hidden Power	Normal	Special	60	100	15	Normal
TM13	Ice Beam	Ice	Special	90	100	10	Normal
TM14	Blizzard	Ice	Special	110	70	5	Many Others
TM15	Hyper Beam	Normal	Special	150	90	5	Normal
TM17	Protect	Normal	Status	—	—	10	Self
TM18	Rain Dance	Water	Status	—	—	5	Both Sides
TM21	Frustration	Normal	Physical	—	100	20	Normal
TM26	Earthquake	Ground	Physical	100	100	10	Adjacent
TM27	Return	Normal	Physical	—	100	20	Normal
TM32	Double Team	Normal	Status	—	—	15	Self
TM39	Rock Tomb	Rock	Physical	60	95	15	Normal
TM42	Facade	Normal	Physical	70	100	20	Normal
TM44	Rest	Psychic	Status	—	—	10	Self
TM45	Attract	Normal	Status	—	100	15	Normal
TM48	Round	Normal	Special	60	100	15	Normal
TM49	Echoed Voice	Normal	Special	40	100	15	Normal
TM55	Scald	Water	Special	80	100	15	Normal
TM68	Giga Impact	Normal	Physical	150	90	5	Normal
TM78	Bulldoze	Ground	Physical	60	100	20	Adjacent
TM87	Swagger	Normal	Status	—	90	15	Normal
TM88	Sleep Talk	Normal	Status	—	—	10	Self
TM90	Substitute	Normal	Status	—	—	10	Self
TM94	Rock Smash	Fighting	Physical	40	100	15	Normal
TM100	Confide	Normal	Status	—	—	20	Normal
HM03	Surf	Water	Special	90	100	15	Adjacent
HM04	Strength	Normal	Physical	80	100	15	Normal
HM05	Waterfall	Water	Physical	80	100	15	Normal

● **MOVES TAUGHT BY PEOPLE**

Name	Type	Kind	Pow.	Acc.	PP	Range

AFTER THE HALL OF FAME

CENTRAL KALOS

COASTAL KALOS

028

Wailord

MOUNTAIN KALOS

ADVENTURE DATA

AFTER THE HALL OF FAME

CENTRAL KALOS

COASTAL KALOS

029

Luvdisc

MOUNTAIN KALOS

ADVENTURE DATA

Coastal Kalos 029
Rendezvous Pokémon
☑ Luvdisc

HEIGHT: 2'00" WEIGHT: 19.2 lbs.
GENDER: ♂/♀

X It lives in warm seas. It is said that a couple finding this Pokémon will be blessed with eternal love.

Y During the spawning season, countless Luvdisc congregate at coral reefs, turning the waters pink.

TYPE Water

ABILITY
Swift Swim

HIDDEN ABILITY
None

STAT GROWTH RATES
HP	■■
Attack	■■
Defense	■■
Sp. Atk	■■
Sp. Def	■■
Speed	■■■■■

EGG GROUP
Water 2

EVOLUTION
Does not evolve

ITEMS SOMETIMES HELD BY WILD POKÉMON
Heart Scale

Damage taken in normal battles	
Normal	×1
Fire	×0.5
Water	×0.5
Grass	×2
Electric	×2
Ice	×0.5
Fighting	×1
Poison	×1
Ground	×1
Flying	×1
Psychic	×1
Bug	×1
Rock	×1
Ghost	×1
Dragon	×1
Dark	×1
Steel	×0.5
Fairy	×1

Damage taken in Inverse Battles	
Normal	×1
Fire	×2
Water	×2
Grass	×0.5
Electric	×0.5
Ice	×2
Fighting	×1
Poison	×1
Ground	×1
Flying	×1
Psychic	×1
Bug	×1
Rock	×1
Ghost	×1
Dragon	×1
Dark	×2
Steel	×2
Fairy	×1

Can be used in	
Inverse Battle	Battle Institute
—	Battle Maison
Battle Chateau	Random Matchup

Same form for ♂/♀

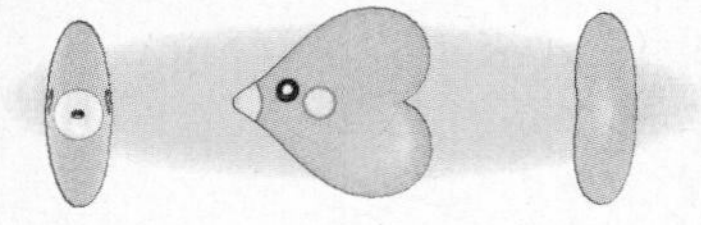

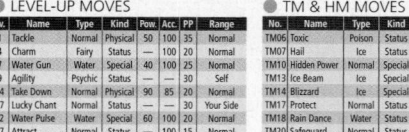

How to obtain for your Coastal Kalos Pokédex
❶ Catch using an Old Rod on Route 8.
❷ Catch using an Old Rod in Ambrette Town.

❶ Catch using an Old Rod on Route 8.
❷ Catch using an Old Rod in Ambrette Town.

● LEVEL-UP MOVES
Lv.	Name	Type	Kind	Pow.	Acc.	PP	Range
1	Tackle	Normal	Physical	50	100	35	Normal
4	Charm	Fairy	Status	—	100	20	Normal
7	Water Gun	Water	Special	40	100	25	Normal
9	Agility	Psychic	Status	—	—	30	Self
14	Take Down	Normal	Physical	90	85	20	Normal
17	Lucky Chant	Normal	Status	—	—	30	Your Side
22	Water Pulse	Water	Special	60	100	20	Normal
27	Attract	Normal	Status	—	100	15	Normal
31	Flail	Normal	Physical	—	100	15	Normal
37	Sweet Kiss	Fairy	Status	—	75	10	Normal
40	Hydro Pump	Water	Special	110	80	5	Normal
46	Aqua Ring	Water	Status	—	—	20	Self
50	Captivate	Normal	Status	—	100	20	Many Others
55	Safeguard	Normal	Status	—	—	25	Your Side

● TM & HM MOVES
No.	Name	Type	Kind	Pow.	Acc.	PP	Range
TM06	Toxic	Poison	Status	—	90	10	Normal
TM07	Hail	Ice	Status	—	—	10	Both Sides
TM10	Hidden Power	Normal	Special	60	100	15	Normal
TM13	Ice Beam	Ice	Special	90	100	10	Normal
TM14	Blizzard	Ice	Special	110	70	5	Many Others
TM17	Protect	Normal	Status	—	—	10	Self
TM18	Rain Dance	Water	Status	—	—	5	Both Sides
TM20	Safeguard	Normal	Status	—	—	25	Your Side
TM21	Frustration	Normal	Physical	—	100	20	Normal
TM27	Return	Normal	Physical	—	100	20	Normal
TM32	Double Team	Normal	Status	—	—	15	Self
TM42	Facade	Normal	Physical	70	100	20	Normal
TM44	Rest	Psychic	Status	—	—	10	Self
TM45	Attract	Normal	Status	—	100	15	Normal
TM48	Round	Normal	Special	60	100	15	Normal
TM55	Scald	Water	Special	80	100	15	Normal
TM77	Psych Up	Normal	Status	—	—	10	Normal
TM87	Swagger	Normal	Status	—	90	15	Normal
TM88	Sleep Talk	Normal	Status	—	—	10	Self
TM90	Substitute	Normal	Status	—	—	10	Self
TM100	Confide	Normal	Status	—	—	20	Normal
HM03	Surf	Water	Special	90	100	15	Adjacent
HM05	Waterfall	Water	Physical	80	100	15	Normal

● MOVES TAUGHT BY PEOPLE
Name	Type	Kind	Pow.	Acc.	PP	Range

● EGG MOVES
Name	Type	Kind	Pow.	Acc.	PP	Range
Splash	Normal	Status	—	—	40	Self
Supersonic	Normal	Status	—	55	20	Normal
Water Sport	Water	Status	—	—	15	Both Sides
Mud Sport	Ground	Status	—	—	15	Both Sides
Captivate	Normal	Status	—	100	20	Many Others
Aqua Ring	Water	Status	—	—	20	Self
Aqua Jet	Water	Physical	40	100	20	Normal
Heal Pulse	Psychic	Status	—	—	10	Normal
Brine	Water	Special	65	100	10	Normal
Entrainment	Normal	Status	—	100	15	Normal

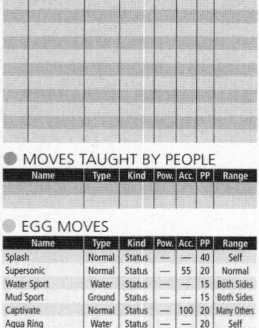

Coastal Kalos 030
Mock Kelp Pokémon

☑ **Skrelp**

TYPE [Poison] [Water]

HEIGHT: 1'08"   WEIGHT: 16.1 lbs.
GENDER: ♂/♀

ABILITIES
Poison Point
Poison Touch

HIDDEN ABILITY
None

STAT GROWTH RATES

HP	■■
Attack	■■■
Defense	■■
Sp. Atk	■■■
Sp. Def	■■■
Speed	■

EGG GROUPS
Water 1, Dragon

X — Camouflaged as rotten kelp, they spray liquid poison on prey that approaches unawares and then finish it off.

Y — It looks just like rotten kelp. It hides from foes while storing up power for its evolution.

⬆ EVOLUTION

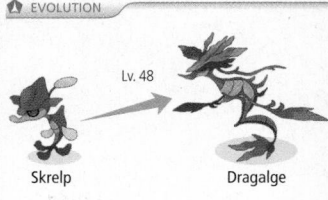

Skrelp   Lv. 48 →   Dragalge

ITEMS SOMETIMES HELD BY WILD POKÉMON
None

Damage taken in normal battles		Damage taken in Inverse Battles		Can be used in
Normal	×1	Normal	×1	Inverse Battle
Fire	×0.5	Fire	×2	—
Water	×0.5	Water	×2	Battle Chateau
Grass	×1	Grass	×1	Battle Institute
Electric	×2	Electric	×0.5	Battle Maison
Ice	×0.5	Ice	×2	Random Matchup
Fighting	×0.5	Fighting	×2	
Poison	×0.5	Poison	×2	
Ground	×2	Ground	×0.5	
Flying	×1	Flying	×1	
Psychic	×2	Psychic	×0.5	
Bug	×0.5	Bug	×2	
Rock	×1	Rock	×1	
Ghost	×1	Ghost	×1	
Dragon	×1	Dragon	×1	
Dark	×1	Dark	×1	
Steel	×0.5	Steel	×2	
Fairy	×0.5	Fairy	×2	

How to obtain for your Coastal Kalos Pokédex

Link Trade or transfer from another game.

❶ Catch using a Good Rod on Route 8.
❷ Catch using a Good Rod in Ambrette Town.

Same form for ♂/♀

● LEVEL-UP MOVES

Lv.	Name	Type	Kind	Pow.	Acc.	PP	Range
1	Tackle	Normal	Physical	50	100	35	Normal
1	Smokescreen	Normal	Status	—	100	20	Normal
1	Water Gun	Water	Special	40	100	25	Normal
5	Feint Attack	Dark	Physical	60	—	20	Normal
9	Tail Whip	Normal	Status	—	100	30	Many Others
12	Bubble	Water	Special	40	100	30	Many Others
15	Acid	Poison	Special	40	100	30	Many Others
19	Camouflage	Normal	Status	—	—	20	Self
23	Poison Tail	Poison	Physical	50	100	25	Normal
25	Water Pulse	Water	Special	60	100	20	Normal
28	Double Team	Normal	Status	—	—	15	Self
32	Toxic	Poison	Status	—	90	10	Normal
35	Aqua Tail	Water	Physical	90	90	10	Normal
38	Sludge Bomb	Poison	Special	90	100	10	Normal
42	Hydro Pump	Water	Special	110	80	5	Normal
49	Dragon Pulse	Dragon	Special	85	100	10	Normal

● TM & HM MOVES

No.	Name	Type	Kind	Pow.	Acc.	PP	Range
TM06	Toxic	Poison	Status	—	90	10	Normal
TM07	Hail	Ice	Status	—	—	10	Both Sides
TM09	Venoshock	Poison	Special	65	100	10	Normal
TM10	Hidden Power	Normal	Special	60	100	15	Normal
TM17	Protect	Normal	Status	—	—	10	Self
TM18	Rain Dance	Water	Status	—	—	5	Both Sides
TM21	Frustration	Normal	Physical	—	100	20	Normal
TM24	Thunderbolt	Electric	Special	90	100	15	Normal
TM27	Return	Normal	Physical	—	100	20	Normal
TM30	Shadow Ball	Ghost	Special	80	100	15	Normal
TM32	Double Team	Normal	Status	—	—	15	Self
TM34	Sludge Wave	Poison	Special	95	100	10	Adjacent
TM36	Sludge Bomb	Poison	Special	90	100	10	Normal
TM42	Facade	Normal	Physical	70	100	20	Normal
TM44	Rest	Psychic	Status	—	—	10	Self
TM45	Attract	Normal	Status	—	100	15	Normal
TM48	Round	Normal	Special	60	100	15	Normal
TM55	Scald	Water	Special	80	100	15	Normal
TM87	Swagger	Normal	Status	—	90	15	Normal
TM88	Sleep Talk	Normal	Status	—	—	10	Self
TM90	Substitute	Normal	Status	—	—	10	Self
TM100	Confide	Normal	Status	—	—	20	Normal
HM03	Surf	Water	Special	90	100	15	Adjacent
HM05	Waterfall	Water	Physical	80	100	15	Normal

No.	Name	Type	Kind	Pow.	Acc.	PP	Range

● MOVES TAUGHT BY PEOPLE

Name	Type	Kind	Pow.	Acc.	PP	Range

● EGG MOVES

Name	Type	Kind	Pow.	Acc.	PP	Range
Toxic Spikes	Poison	Status	—	—	20	Other Side
Play Rough	Fairy	Physical	90	90	10	Normal
Haze	Ice	Status	—	—	30	Both Sides
Acid Armor	Poison	Status	—	—	20	Self
Venom Drench	Poison	Status	—	100	20	Many Others

AFTER THE HALL OF FAME

CENTRAL KALOS

COASTAL KALOS

030 Skrelp

MOUNTAIN KALOS

ADVENTURE DATA

AFTER THE HALL OF FAME

CENTRAL KALOS

COASTAL KALOS
031
Dragalge

MOUNTAIN KALOS

ADVENTURE DATA

🏠 Coastal Kalos — 031

Mock Kelp Pokémon

☑ Dragalge

HEIGHT: 5'11" WEIGHT: 179.7 lbs.
GENDER: ♂/♀

TYPE Poison Dragon

ABILITIES
Poison Point
Poison Touch

HIDDEN ABILITY
None

STAT GROWTH RATES
HP	■■■
Attack	■■■■
Defense	■■■■
Sp. Atk	■■■■■
Sp. Def	■■■■■
Speed	■■■

EGG GROUPS
Water 1, Dragon

Ⅹ Their poison is strong enough to eat through the hull of a tanker, and they spit it indiscriminately at anything that enters their territory.

Ⅴ Tales are told of ships that wander into seas where Dragalge live, never to return.

⬆ EVOLUTION

Skrelp → (Lv. 48) → Dragalge

ITEMS SOMETIMES HELD BY WILD POKÉMON
None

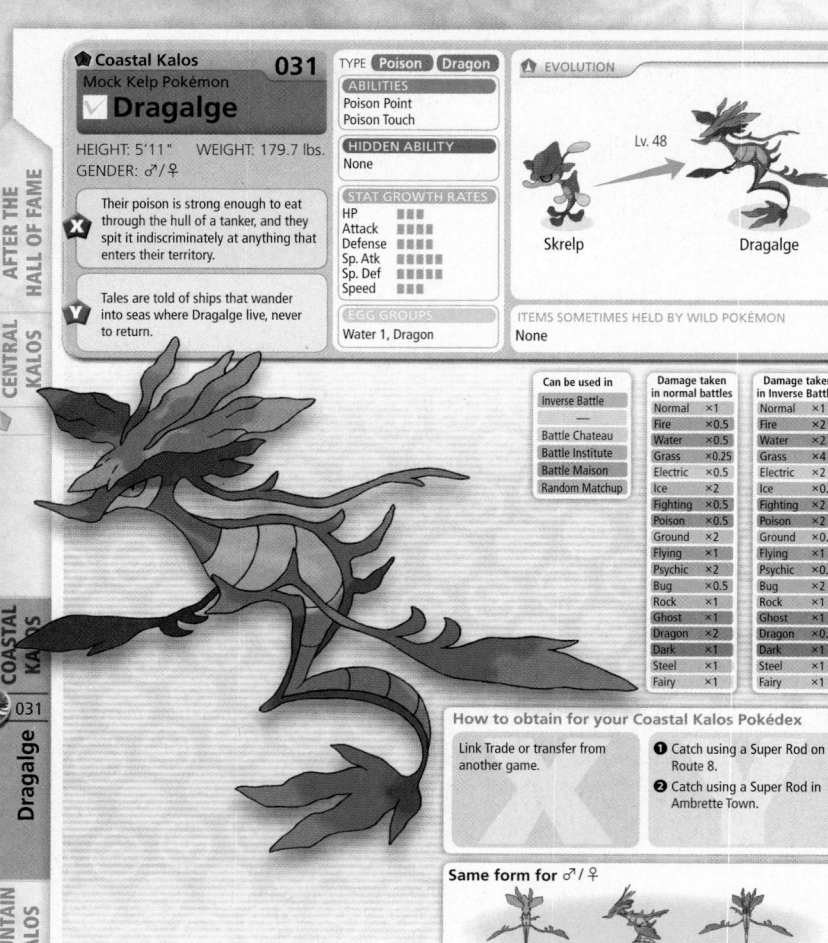

Can be used in
Inverse Battle
—
Battle Chateau
Battle Institute
Battle Maison
Random Matchup

Damage taken in normal battles	
Normal	×1
Fire	×0.5
Water	×0.5
Grass	×0.25
Electric	×0.5
Ice	×2
Fighting	×0.5
Poison	×0.5
Ground	×2
Flying	×1
Psychic	×2
Bug	×0.5
Rock	×1
Ghost	×1
Dragon	×2
Dark	×1
Steel	×1
Fairy	×1

Damage taken in Inverse Battles	
Normal	×1
Fire	×2
Water	×2
Grass	×4
Electric	×2
Ice	×0.5
Fighting	×2
Poison	×2
Ground	×0.5
Flying	×1
Psychic	×0.5
Bug	×2
Rock	×1
Ghost	×1
Dragon	×0.5
Dark	×1
Steel	×1
Fairy	×1

How to obtain for your Coastal Kalos Pokédex

Link Trade or transfer from another game.

❶ Catch using a Super Rod on Route 8.
❷ Catch using a Super Rod in Ambrette Town.

Same form for ♂/♀

● LEVEL-UP MOVES

Lv.	Name	Type	Kind	Pow.	Acc.	PP	Range
1	Dragon Tail	Dragon	Physical	60	90	10	Normal
1	Twister	Dragon	Special	40	100	20	Many Others
1	Tackle	Normal	Physical	50	100	35	Normal
1	Smokescreen	Normal	Status	—	100	20	Normal
1	Water Gun	Water	Special	40	100	25	Normal
5	Feint Attack	Dark	Physical	60	—	20	Normal
9	Tail Whip	Normal	Status	—	100	30	Many Others
12	Bubble	Water	Special	40	100	30	Many Others
15	Acid	Poison	Special	40	100	30	Many Others
19	Camouflage	Normal	Status	—	—	20	Self
23	Poison Tail	Poison	Physical	50	100	25	Normal
25	Water Pulse	Water	Special	60	100	20	Normal
28	Double Team	Normal	Status	—	—	15	Self
32	Toxic	Poison	Status	—	90	10	Normal
35	Aqua Tail	Water	Physical	90	90	10	Normal
42	Sludge Bomb	Poison	Special	90	100	10	Normal
42	Hydro Pump	Water	Special	110	80	5	Normal
53	Dragon Pulse	Dragon	Special	85	100	10	Normal
59	Dragon Tail	Dragon	Physical	60	90	10	Normal
67	Twister	Dragon	Special	40	100	20	Many Others

● TM & HM MOVES

No.	Name	Type	Kind	Pow.	Acc.	PP	Range
TM06	Toxic	Poison	Status	—	90	10	Normal
TM07	Hail	Ice	Status	—	—	10	Both Sides
TM09	Venoshock	Poison	Special	65	100	10	Normal
TM10	Hidden Power	Normal	Special	60	100	15	Normal
TM15	Hyper Beam	Normal	Special	150	90	5	Normal
TM17	Protect	Normal	Status	—	—	10	Self
TM18	Rain Dance	Water	Status	—	—	5	Both Sides
TM21	Frustration	Normal	Physical	—	100	20	Normal
TM24	Thunderbolt	Electric	Special	90	100	15	Normal
TM25	Thunder	Electric	Special	110	70	10	Normal
TM27	Return	Normal	Physical	—	100	20	Normal
TM30	Shadow Ball	Ghost	Special	80	100	15	Normal
TM32	Double Team	Normal	Status	—	—	15	Self
TM34	Sludge Wave	Poison	Special	95	100	10	Adjacent
TM36	Sludge Bomb	Poison	Special	90	100	10	Normal
TM42	Facade	Normal	Physical	70	100	20	Normal
TM44	Rest	Psychic	Status	—	—	10	Self
TM45	Attract	Normal	Status	—	100	15	Normal
TM48	Round	Normal	Special	60	100	15	Normal
TM52	Focus Blast	Fighting	Special	120	70	5	Normal
TM55	Scald	Water	Special	80	100	15	Normal
TM68	Giga Impact	Normal	Physical	150	90	5	Normal
TM82	Dragon Tail	Dragon	Physical	60	90	10	Normal
TM87	Swagger	Normal	Status	—	90	15	Normal
TM88	Sleep Talk	Normal	Status	—	—	10	Self
TM90	Substitute	Normal	Status	—	—	10	Self
TM100	Confide	Normal	Status	—	—	20	Normal
HM03	Surf	Water	Special	90	100	15	Adjacent
HM05	Waterfall	Water	Physical	80	100	15	Normal

● MOVES TAUGHT BY PEOPLE

Name	Type	Kind	Pow.	Acc.	PP	Range
Draco Meteor	Dragon	Special	130	90	5	Normal

AFTER THE HALL OF FAME

CENTRAL KALOS

COASTAL KALOS

032 Clauncher

MOUNTAIN KALOS

ADVENTURE DATA

 Coastal Kalos 032
Water Gun Pokémon

 Clauncher

HEIGHT: 1'08"   WEIGHT: 18.3 lbs.
GENDER: ♂ / ♀

X They knock down flying prey by firing compressed water from their massive claws like shooting a pistol.

Y Through controlled explosions of internal gas, it can expel water like a pistol shot. At close distances, it can shatter rock.

TYPE Water

ABILITY
Mega Launcher

HIDDEN ABILITY
None

STAT GROWTH RATES
HP	■ ■
Attack	■ ■ ■
Defense	■ ■ ■
Sp. Atk	■ ■ ■
Sp. Def	■ ■ ■
Speed	■ ■ ■

EGG GROUPS
Water 1, Water 3

EVOLUTION

Lv. 37

Clauncher   Clawitzer

ITEMS SOMETIMES HELD BY WILD POKÉMON
None

Damage taken in normal battles		Damage taken in Inverse Battles	
Normal	×1	Normal	×1
Fire	×0.5	Fire	×2
Water	×0.5	Water	×2
Grass	×2	Grass	×0.5
Electric	×2	Electric	×0.5
Ice	×0.5	Ice	×2
Fighting	×1	Fighting	×1
Poison	×1	Poison	×1
Ground	×1	Ground	×1
Flying	×1	Flying	×1
Psychic	×1	Psychic	×1
Bug	×1	Bug	×1
Rock	×1	Rock	×1
Ghost	×1	Ghost	×1
Dragon	×1	Dragon	×1
Dark	×1	Dark	×1
Steel	×0.5	Steel	×2
Fairy	×1	Fairy	×1

Can be used in	
Inverse Battle	Battle Institute
—	Battle Maison
Battle Chateau	Random Matchup

Same form for ♂ / ♀

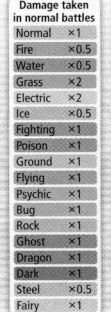

How to obtain for your Coastal Kalos Pokédex

❶ Catch using a Good Rod on Route 8.

❷ Catch using a Good Rod in Ambrette Town.

Link Trade or transfer from another game.

● **LEVEL-UP MOVES**
Lv.	Name	Type	Kind	Pow.	Acc.	PP	Range
1	Splash	Normal	Status	—	—	40	Self
1	Water Gun	Water	Special	40	100	25	Normal
7	Water Sport	Water	Status	—	—	15	Both Sides
9	Vice Grip	Normal	Physical	55	100	30	Normal
12	Bubble	Water	Special	40	100	30	Many Others
16	Flail	Normal	Physical	—	100	15	Normal
20	Bubble Beam	Water	Special	65	100	20	Normal
25	Swords Dance	Normal	Status	—	—	20	Self
30	Crabhammer	Water	Physical	100	90	10	Normal
34	Water Pulse	Water	Special	60	100	20	Normal
39	Smack Down	Rock	Physical	50	100	15	Normal
43	Aqua Jet	Water	Physical	40	100	20	Normal
48	Muddy Water	Water	Special	90	85	10	Many Others

● **TM & HM MOVES**
No.	Name	Type	Kind	Pow.	Acc.	PP	Range
TM06	Toxic	Poison	Status	—	90	10	Normal
TM09	Venoshock	Poison	Special	65	100	10	Normal
TM10	Hidden Power	Normal	Special	60	100	15	Normal
TM13	Ice Beam	Ice	Special	90	100	10	Normal
TM17	Protect	Normal	Status	—	—	10	Self
TM18	Rain Dance	Water	Status	—	—	5	Both Sides
TM21	Frustration	Normal	Physical	—	100	20	Normal
TM23	Smack Down	Rock	Physical	50	100	15	Normal
TM27	Return	Normal	Physical	—	100	20	Normal
TM32	Double Team	Normal	Status	—	—	15	Self
TM34	Sludge Wave	Poison	Special	95	100	10	Adjacent
TM36	Sludge Bomb	Poison	Special	90	100	10	Normal
TM42	Facade	Normal	Physical	70	100	20	Normal
TM44	Rest	Psychic	Status	—	—	10	Self
TM45	Attract	Normal	Status	—	100	15	Normal
TM48	Round	Normal	Special	60	100	15	Normal
TM55	Scald	Water	Special	80	100	15	Normal
TM75	Swords Dance	Normal	Status	—	—	20	Self
TM80	Rock Slide	Rock	Physical	75	90	10	Many Others
TM87	Swagger	Normal	Status	—	90	15	Normal
TM88	Sleep Talk	Normal	Status	—	—	10	Self
TM89	U-turn	Bug	Physical	70	100	20	Normal
TM90	Substitute	Normal	Status	—	—	10	Self
TM91	Flash Cannon	Steel	Special	80	100	10	Normal
TM100	Confide	Normal	Status	—	—	20	Normal
HM01	Cut	Normal	Physical	50	95	30	Normal
HM03	Surf	Water	Special	90	100	15	Adjacent
HM05	Waterfall	Water	Physical	80	100	15	Normal

No.	Name	Type	Kind	Pow.	Acc.	PP	Range

● **MOVES TAUGHT BY PEOPLE**
Name	Type	Kind	Pow.	Acc.	PP	Range

● **EGG MOVES**
Name	Type	Kind	Pow.	Acc.	PP	Range
Aqua Jet	Water	Physical	40	100	20	Normal
Entrainment	Normal	Status	—	100	15	Normal
Endure	Normal	Status	—	—	10	Self
Crabhammer	Water	Physical	100	90	10	Normal
Helping Hand	Normal	Status	—	—	20	1 Ally

AFTER THE HALL OF FAME

CENTRAL KALOS

COASTAL KALOS

033

Clawitzer

MOUNTAIN KALOS

ADVENTURE DATA

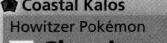

Coastal Kalos 033
Howitzer Pokémon

✓ Clawitzer

HEIGHT: 4'03" WEIGHT: 77.8 lbs.
GENDER: ♂/♀

X Their enormous claws launch cannonballs of water powerful enough to pierce tanker hulls.

Y By expelling water from the nozzle in the back of its claw, it can move at a speed of 60 knots.

TYPE	Water

ABILITY
Mega Launcher

HIDDEN ABILITY
None

STAT GROWTH RATES

HP	■■■
Attack	■■■
Defense	■■■
Sp. Atk	■■■■■
Sp. Def	■■■
Speed	■■■

EGG GROUPS
Water 1, Water 3

EVOLUTION

Lv. 37

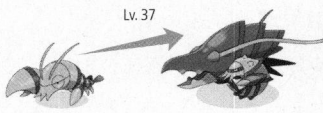

Clauncher → Clawitzer

ITEMS SOMETIMES HELD BY WILD POKÉMON
None

Damage taken in normal battles		Damage taken in Inverse Battles	
Normal	×1	Normal	×1
Fire	×0.5	Fire	×2
Water	×0.5	Water	×2
Grass	×2	Grass	×0.5
Electric	×2	Electric	×0.5
Ice	×0.5	Ice	×2
Fighting	×1	Fighting	×1
Poison	×1	Poison	×1
Ground	×1	Ground	×1
Flying	×1	Flying	×1
Psychic	×1	Psychic	×1
Bug	×1	Bug	×1
Rock	×1	Rock	×1
Ghost	×1	Ghost	×1
Dragon	×1	Dragon	×1
Dark	×1	Dark	×1
Steel	×0.5	Steel	×2
Fairy	×1	Fairy	×1

Can be used in	
Inverse Battle	Battle Institute
—	Battle Maison
Battle Chateau	Random Matchup

Same form for ♂/♀

How to obtain for your Coastal Kalos Pokédex

❶ Catch using a Super Rod on Route 8.
❷ Catch using a Super Rod in Ambrette Town.

Link Trade or transfer from another game.

● LEVEL-UP MOVES

Lv.	Name	Type	Kind	Pow.	Acc.	PP	Range
1	Heal Pulse	Psychic	Status	—	—	10	Normal
1	Dark Pulse	Dark	Special	80	100	15	Normal
1	Dragon Pulse	Dragon	Special	85	100	10	Normal
1	Aura Sphere	Fighting	Special	80	—	20	Normal
1	Splash	Normal	Status	—	—	40	Self
1	Water Gun	Water	Special	40	100	25	Normal
7	Water Sport	Water	Status	—	—	15	Both Sides
9	Vice Grip	Normal	Physical	55	100	30	Normal
12	Bubble	Water	Special	40	100	30	Many Others
16	Flail	Normal	Physical	—	100	15	Normal
20	Bubble Beam	Water	Special	65	100	20	Normal
25	Swords Dance	Normal	Status	—	—	20	Self
30	Crabhammer	Water	Physical	100	90	10	Normal
34	Water Pulse	Water	Special	60	100	20	Normal
42	Smack Down	Rock	Physical	50	100	15	Normal
47	Aqua Jet	Water	Physical	40	100	20	Normal
53	Muddy Water	Water	Special	90	85	10	Many Others
57	Dark Pulse	Dark	Special	80	100	15	Normal
63	Dragon Pulse	Dragon	Special	85	100	10	Normal
67	Aura Sphere	Fighting	Special	80	—	20	Normal

● TM & HM MOVES

No.	Name	Type	Kind	Pow.	Acc.	PP	Range
TM06	Toxic	Poison	Status	—	90	10	Normal
TM09	Venoshock	Poison	Special	65	100	10	Normal
TM10	Hidden Power	Normal	Special	60	100	15	Normal
TM13	Ice Beam	Ice	Special	90	100	10	Normal
TM15	Hyper Beam	Normal	Special	150	90	5	Normal
TM17	Protect	Normal	Status	—	—	10	Self
TM18	Rain Dance	Water	Status	—	—	5	Both Sides
TM21	Frustration	Normal	Physical	—	100	20	Normal
TM23	Smack Down	Rock	Physical	50	100	15	Normal
TM27	Return	Normal	Physical	—	100	20	Normal
TM30	Shadow Ball	Ghost	Special	80	100	15	Normal
TM32	Double Team	Normal	Status	—	—	15	Self
TM34	Sludge Wave	Poison	Special	95	100	10	Adjacent
TM36	Sludge Bomb	Poison	Special	90	100	10	Normal
TM42	Facade	Normal	Physical	70	100	20	Normal
TM44	Rest	Psychic	Status	—	—	10	Self
TM45	Attract	Normal	Status	—	100	15	Normal
TM48	Round	Normal	Special	60	100	15	Normal
TM52	Focus Blast	Fighting	Special	120	70	5	Normal
TM55	Scald	Water	Special	80	100	15	Normal
TM68	Giga Impact	Normal	Physical	150	90	5	Normal
TM75	Swords Dance	Normal	Status	—	—	20	Self
TM80	Rock Slide	Rock	Physical	75	90	10	Many Others
TM87	Swagger	Normal	Status	—	90	15	Normal
TM88	Sleep Talk	Normal	Status	—	—	10	Self
TM89	U-turn	Bug	Physical	70	100	20	Normal
TM90	Substitute	Normal	Status	—	—	10	Self
TM91	Flash Cannon	Steel	Special	80	100	10	Normal
TM97	Dark Pulse	Dark	Special	80	100	15	Normal
TM100	Confide	Normal	Status	—	—	20	Normal
HM01	Cut	Normal	Physical	50	95	30	Normal
HM03	Surf	Water	Special	90	100	15	Adjacent
HM05	Waterfall	Water	Physical	80	100	15	Normal

No.	Name	Type	Kind	Pow.	Acc.	PP	Range

● MOVES TAUGHT BY PEOPLE

Name	Type	Kind	Pow.	Acc.	PP	Range

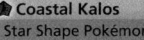 Coastal Kalos
Star Shape Pokémon

☑ **Staryu** **034**

HEIGHT: 2'07"   WEIGHT: 76.1 lbs.
GENDER: unknown

 Even if its body is torn, it can regenerate as long as the glowing central core remains intact.

It appears in large numbers by seashores. At night, its central core flashes with a red light.

TYPE Water

ABILITIES
Illuminate
Natural Cure

HIDDEN ABILITY
None

STAT GROWTH RATES
HP	■■
Attack	■■
Defense	■■■
Sp. Atk	■■■
Sp. Def	■■
Speed	■■■■■

EGG GROUP
Water 3

EVOLUTION

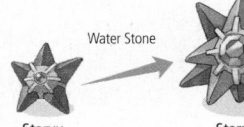

Water Stone

Staryu → Starmie

ITEMS SOMETIMES HELD BY WILD POKÉMON
Stardust

Damage taken in normal battles		Damage taken in Inverse Battles	
Normal	×1	Normal	×1
Fire	×0.5	Fire	×2
Water	×0.5	Water	×2
Grass	×2	Grass	×0.5
Electric	×2	Electric	×0.5
Ice	×0.5	Ice	×2
Fighting	×1	Fighting	×1
Poison	×1	Poison	×1
Ground	×1	Ground	×1
Flying	×1	Flying	×1
Psychic	×1	Psychic	×1
Bug	×1	Bug	×1
Rock	×1	Rock	×1
Ghost	×1	Ghost	×1
Dragon	×1	Dragon	×1
Dark	×1	Dark	×1
Steel	×0.5	Steel	×2
Fairy	×1	Fairy	×1

Can be used in	
Inverse Battle	Battle Institute
—	Battle Maison
Battle Chateau	Random Matchup

Gender unknown

How to obtain for your Coastal Kalos Pokédex

Catch using a Good Rod on Route 8. (X)

Link Trade or transfer from another game. (Y)

● LEVEL-UP MOVES

Lv.	Name	Type	Kind	Pow.	Acc.	PP	Range
1	Tackle	Normal	Physical	50	100	35	Normal
1	Harden	Normal	Status	—	—	30	Self
6	Water Gun	Water	Special	40	100	25	Normal
10	Rapid Spin	Normal	Physical	20	100	40	Normal
12	Recover	Normal	Status	—	—	10	Self
15	Camouflage	Normal	Status	—	—	20	Self
18	Swift	Normal	Special	60	—	20	Many Others
22	Bubble Beam	Water	Special	65	100	20	Normal
25	Minimize	Normal	Status	—	—	10	Self
30	Gyro Ball	Steel	Physical	—	100	5	Normal
33	Light Screen	Psychic	Status	—	—	30	Your Side
36	Brine	Water	Special	65	100	10	Normal
40	Reflect Type	Normal	Status	—	—	15	Normal
44	Power Gem	Rock	Special	80	100	20	Normal
48	Cosmic Power	Psychic	Status	—	—	20	Self
52	Hydro Pump	Water	Special	110	80	5	Normal

● TM & HM MOVES

No.	Name	Type	Kind	Pow.	Acc.	PP	Range
TM06	Toxic	Poison	Status	—	90	10	Normal
TM07	Hail	Ice	Status	—	—	10	Both Sides
TM10	Hidden Power	Normal	Special	60	100	15	Normal
TM13	Ice Beam	Ice	Special	90	100	10	Normal
TM14	Blizzard	Ice	Special	110	70	5	Many Others
TM16	Light Screen	Psychic	Status	—	—	30	Your Side
TM17	Protect	Normal	Status	—	—	10	Self
TM18	Rain Dance	Water	Status	—	—	5	Both Sides
TM21	Frustration	Normal	Physical	—	100	20	Normal
TM24	Thunderbolt	Electric	Special	90	100	15	Normal
TM25	Thunder	Electric	Special	110	70	10	Normal
TM27	Return	Normal	Physical	—	100	20	Normal
TM29	Psychic	Psychic	Special	90	100	10	Normal
TM32	Double Team	Normal	Status	—	—	15	Self
TM33	Reflect	Psychic	Status	—	—	20	Your Side
TM42	Facade	Normal	Physical	70	100	20	Normal
TM44	Rest	Psychic	Status	—	—	10	Self
TM48	Round	Normal	Special	60	100	15	Normal
TM55	Scald	Water	Special	80	100	15	Normal
TM70	Flash	Normal	Status	—	100	20	Normal
TM73	Thunder Wave	Electric	Status	—	100	20	Normal
TM74	Gyro Ball	Steel	Physical	—	100	5	Normal
TM77	Psych Up	Normal	Status	—	—	10	Normal
TM87	Swagger	Normal	Status	—	90	15	Normal
TM85	Sleep Talk	Normal	Status	—	—	10	Self
TM90	Substitute	Normal	Status	—	—	10	Self
TM91	Flash Cannon	Steel	Special	80	100	10	Normal
TM99	Dazzling Gleam	Fairy	Special	80	100	10	Many Others
TM100	Confide	Normal	Status	—	—	20	Normal
HM03	Surf	Water	Special	90	100	15	Adjacent
HM05	Waterfall	Water	Physical	80	100	15	Normal

No.	Name	Type	Kind	Pow.	Acc.	PP	Range

● MOVES TAUGHT BY PEOPLE

Name	Type	Kind	Pow.	Acc.	PP	Range

● EGG MOVES

Name	Type	Kind	Pow.	Acc.	PP	Range

AFTER THE HALL OF FAME
CENTRAL KALOS
COASTAL KALOS
034 Staryu
MOUNTAIN KALOS
ADVENTURE DATA

AFTER THE HALL OF FAME

CENTRAL KALOS

COASTAL KALOS

035

Starmie

MOUNTAIN KALOS

ADVENTURE DATA

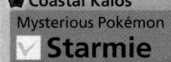

Coastal Kalos
Mysterious Pokémon
☑ Starmie

035

HEIGHT: 3'07" WEIGHT: 176.4 lbs.
GENDER: unknown

X Its central core glows with the seven colors of the rainbow. Some people value the core as a gem.

Y At the center of its body is a red core, which sends mysterious radio signals into the night sky.

TYPE Water Psychic

ABILITIES
Illuminate
Natural Cure

HIDDEN ABILITY
None

STAT GROWTH RATES
HP	■■■
Attack	■■■
Defense	■■■
Sp. Atk	■■■■
Sp. Def	■■■■
Speed	■■■■■

EGG GROUP
Water 3

EVOLUTION

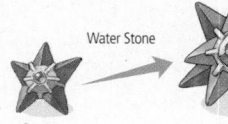

Water Stone

Staryu → Starmie

ITEMS SOMETIMES HELD BY WILD POKÉMON
Stardust, Star Piece

Damage taken in normal battles	
Normal	×1
Fire	×0.5
Water	×0.5
Grass	×2
Electric	×2
Ice	×0.5
Fighting	×0.5
Poison	×1
Ground	×1
Flying	×1
Psychic	×0.5
Bug	×2
Rock	×1
Ghost	×2
Dragon	×1
Dark	×2
Steel	×0.5
Fairy	×1

Damage taken in Inverse Battles	
Normal	×1
Fire	×2
Water	×2
Grass	×0.5
Electric	×0.5
Ice	×2
Fighting	×2
Poison	×1
Ground	×1
Flying	×1
Psychic	×1
Bug	×0.5
Rock	×1
Ghost	×0.5
Dragon	×1
Dark	×0.5
Steel	×2
Fairy	×1

Can be used in	
Inverse Battle	Battle Institute
—	Battle Maison
Battle Chateau	Random Matchup

Gender unknown

How to obtain for your Coastal Kalos Pokédex

❶ Catch using a Super Rod on Route 8.
❷ Use a Water Stone on Staryu.

❶ Link Trade or transfer from another game.
❷ Use a Water Stone on Staryu.

● LEVEL-UP MOVES

Lv.	Name	Type	Kind	Pow.	Acc.	PP	Range
1	Hydro Pump	Water	Special	110	80	5	Normal
1	Water Gun	Water	Special	40	100	25	Normal
1	Rapid Spin	Normal	Physical	20	100	40	Normal
1	Recover	Normal	Status	—	—	10	Self
1	Swift	Normal	Special	60	—	20	Many Others
22	Confuse Ray	Ghost	Status	—	100	10	Normal

● TM & HM MOVES

No.	Name	Type	Kind	Pow.	Acc.	PP	Range
TM03	Psyshock	Psychic	Special	80	100	10	Normal
TM06	Toxic	Poison	Status	—	90	10	Normal
TM07	Hail	Ice	Status	—	—	10	Both Sides
TM10	Hidden Power	Normal	Special	60	100	15	Normal
TM13	Ice Beam	Ice	Special	90	100	10	Normal
TM14	Blizzard	Ice	Special	110	70	5	Many Others
TM15	Hyper Beam	Normal	Special	150	90	5	Normal
TM16	Light Screen	Psychic	Status	—	—	30	Your Side
TM17	Protect	Normal	Status	—	—	10	Self
TM18	Rain Dance	Water	Status	—	—	5	Both Sides
TM21	Frustration	Normal	Physical	—	100	20	Normal
TM24	Thunderbolt	Electric	Special	90	100	15	Normal
TM25	Thunder	Electric	Special	110	70	10	Normal
TM27	Return	Normal	Physical	—	100	20	Normal
TM29	Psychic	Psychic	Special	90	100	10	Normal
TM32	Double Team	Normal	Status	—	—	15	Self
TM33	Reflect	Psychic	Status	—	—	20	Your Side
TM42	Facade	Normal	Physical	70	100	20	Normal
TM44	Rest	Psychic	Status	—	—	10	Self
TM48	Round	Normal	Special	60	100	15	Normal
TM55	Scald	Water	Special	80	100	15	Normal
TM68	Giga Impact	Normal	Physical	150	90	5	Normal
TM70	Flash	Normal	Status	—	100	20	Normal
TM73	Thunder Wave	Electric	Status	—	100	20	Normal
TM74	Gyro Ball	Steel	Physical	—	100	5	Normal
TM77	Psych Up	Normal	Status	—	—	10	Normal
TM85	Dream Eater	Psychic	Special	100	100	15	Normal
TM86	Grass Knot	Grass	Special	—	100	20	Normal
TM87	Swagger	Normal	Status	—	90	15	Normal
TM88	Sleep Talk	Normal	Status	—	—	10	Self
TM90	Substitute	Normal	Status	—	—	10	Self
TM91	Flash Cannon	Steel	Special	80	100	10	Normal
TM92	Trick Room	Psychic	Status	—	—	5	Both Sides

No.	Name	Type	Kind	Pow.	Acc.	PP	Range
TM99	Dazzling Gleam	Fairy	Special	80	100	10	Many Others
TM100	Confide	Normal	Status	—	—	20	Normal
HM03	Surf	Water	Special	90	100	15	Adjacent
HM05	Waterfall	Water	Physical	80	100	15	Normal

● MOVES TAUGHT BY PEOPLE

Name	Type	Kind	Pow.	Acc.	PP	Range

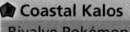 Coastal Kalos

Bivalve Pokémon

Shellder

036

HEIGHT: 1'00" WEIGHT: 8.8 lbs.
GENDER: ♂/♀

 Its hard shell repels any kind of attack. It is vulnerable only when its shell is open.

 Clamping onto an opponent reveals its vulnerable parts, so it uses this move only as a last resort.

TYPE Water

ABILITIES
Shell Armor
Skill Link

HIDDEN ABILITY
Overcoat

STAT GROWTH RATES
HP ▪▪
Attack ▪▪▪
Defense ▪▪▪▪
Sp. Atk ▪▪
Sp. Def ▪▪
Speed ▪▪

EGG GROUP
Water 3

 EVOLUTION

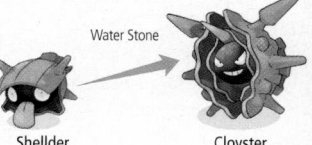

Water Stone

Shellder   Cloyster

ITEMS SOMETIMES HELD BY WILD POKÉMON
Pearl, Big Pearl

Damage taken in normal battles		Damage taken in Inverse Battles	
Normal	×1	Normal	×1
Fire	×0.5	Fire	×2
Water	×0.5	Water	×2
Grass	×2	Grass	×0.5
Electric	×2	Electric	×0.5
Ice	×0.5	Ice	×2
Fighting	×1	Fighting	×1
Poison	×1	Poison	×1
Ground	×1	Ground	×1
Flying	×1	Flying	×1
Psychic	×1	Psychic	×1
Bug	×1	Bug	×1
Rock	×1	Rock	×1
Ghost	×1	Ghost	×1
Dragon	×1	Dragon	×1
Dark	×1	Dark	×1
Steel	×0.5	Steel	×2
Fairy	×1	Fairy	×1

Can be used in	
Inverse Battle	Battle Institute
—	Battle Maison
Battle Chateau	Random Matchup

Same form for ♂/♀

How to obtain for your Coastal Kalos Pokédex

Link Trade or transfer from another game.

Catch using a Good Rod on Route 8.

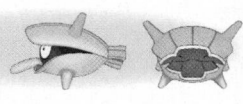

● LEVEL-UP MOVES

Lv.	Name	Type	Kind	Pow.	Acc.	PP	Range
1	Tackle	Normal	Physical	50	100	35	Normal
4	Withdraw	Water	Status	—	—	40	Self
8	Supersonic	Normal	Status	—	55	20	Normal
13	Icicle Spear	Ice	Physical	25	100	30	Normal
16	Protect	Normal	Status	—	—	10	Self
20	Leer	Normal	Status	—	100	30	Many Others
25	Clamp	Water	Physical	35	85	15	Normal
28	Ice Shard	Ice	Physical	40	100	30	Normal
32	Razor Shell	Water	Physical	75	95	10	Normal
37	Aurora Beam	Ice	Special	65	100	20	Normal
40	Whirlpool	Water	Special	35	85	15	Normal
44	Brine	Water	Special	65	100	10	Normal
49	Iron Defense	Steel	Status	—	—	15	Self
52	Ice Beam	Ice	Special	90	100	10	Normal
56	Shell Smash	Normal	Status	—	—	15	Self
61	Hydro Pump	Water	Special	110	80	5	Normal

● TM & HM MOVES

No.	Name	Type	Kind	Pow.	Acc.	PP	Range
TM06	Toxic	Poison	Status	—	90	10	Normal
TM07	Hail	Ice	Status	—	—	10	Both Sides
TM10	Hidden Power	Normal	Special	60	100	15	Normal
TM13	Ice Beam	Ice	Special	90	100	10	Normal
TM14	Blizzard	Ice	Special	110	70	5	Many Others
TM17	Protect	Normal	Status	—	—	10	Self
TM18	Rain Dance	Water	Status	—	—	5	Both Sides
TM21	Frustration	Normal	Physical	—	100	20	Normal
TM27	Return	Normal	Physical	—	100	20	Normal
TM32	Double Team	Normal	Status	—	—	15	Self
TM42	Facade	Normal	Physical	70	100	20	Normal
TM44	Rest	Psychic	Status	—	—	10	Self
TM45	Attract	Normal	Status	—	100	15	Normal
TM48	Round	Normal	Special	60	100	15	Normal
TM64	Explosion	Normal	Physical	250	100	5	Adjacent
TM66	Payback	Dark	Physical	50	100	10	Normal
TM87	Swagger	Normal	Status	—	90	15	Normal
TM88	Sleep Talk	Normal	Status	—	—	10	Self
TM90	Substitute	Normal	Status	—	—	10	Self
TM100	Confide	Normal	Status	—	—	20	Normal
HM03	Surf	Water	Special	90	100	15	Adjacent

● MOVES TAUGHT BY PEOPLE

Name	Type	Kind	Pow.	Acc.	PP	Range

● EGG MOVES

Name	Type	Kind	Pow.	Acc.	PP	Range
Bubble Beam	Water	Special	65	100	20	Normal
Take Down	Normal	Physical	90	85	20	Normal
Barrier	Psychic	Status	—	—	20	Self
Rapid Spin	Normal	Physical	20	100	40	Normal
Screech	Normal	Status	—	85	40	Normal
Icicle Spear	Ice	Physical	25	100	30	Normal
Mud Shot	Ground	Special	55	95	15	Normal
Rock Blast	Rock	Physical	25	90	10	Normal
Water Pulse	Water	Special	60	100	20	Normal
Aqua Ring	Water	Status	—	—	20	Self
Avalanche	Ice	Physical	60	100	10	Normal
Twineedle	Bug	Physical	25	100	20	Normal

AFTER THE HALL OF FAME

CENTRAL KALOS

COASTAL KALOS

036 Shellder

MOUNTAIN KALOS

ADVENTURE DATA

AFTER THE HALL OF FAME

CENTRAL KALOS

COASTAL KALOS

037

Cloyster

MOUNTAIN KALOS

ADVENTURE DATA

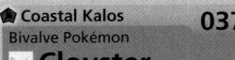

Coastal Kalos
Bivalve Pokémon

✓ Cloyster **037**

HEIGHT: 4'11" WEIGHT: 292.1 lbs.
GENDER: ♂/♀

TYPE Water | Ice

ABILITIES
Shell Armor
Skill Link

HIDDEN ABILITY
Overcoat

X Cloyster that live in seas with harsh tidal currents grow large, sharp spikes on their shells.

Y Its shell is extremely hard. It cannot be shattered, even with a bomb. The shell opens only when it is attacking.

STAT GROWTH RATES

HP	■■
Attack	■■■■■
Defense	■■■■■■■■■
Sp. Atk	■■■■
Sp. Def	■■
Speed	■■■■

EGG GROUP
Water 3

⬆ EVOLUTION

Water Stone

Shellder → Cloyster

ITEMS SOMETIMES HELD BY WILD POKÉMON
Pearl, Big Pearl

Damage taken in normal battles	
Normal	×1
Fire	×1
Water	×0.5
Grass	×2
Electric	×2
Ice	×0.25
Fighting	×2
Poison	×1
Ground	×1
Flying	×1
Psychic	×1
Bug	×1
Rock	×2
Ghost	×1
Dragon	×1
Dark	×1
Steel	×1
Fairy	×1

Damage taken in Inverse Battles	
Normal	×1
Fire	×1
Water	×2
Grass	×0.5
Electric	×0.5
Ice	×4
Fighting	×0.5
Poison	×1
Ground	×1
Flying	×1
Psychic	×1
Bug	×1
Rock	×0.5
Ghost	×1
Dragon	×1
Dark	×1
Steel	×1
Fairy	×1

Can be used in	
Inverse Battle	Battle Institute
—	Battle Maison
Battle Chateau	Random Matchup

Same form for ♂ / ♀

How to obtain for your Coastal Kalos Pokédex

❶ Link Trade or transfer from another game.
❷ Use a Water Stone on Shellder.

❶ Catch using a Super Rod on Route 8.
❷ Use a Water Stone on Shellder.

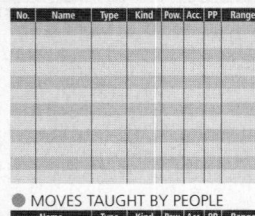

● LEVEL-UP MOVES

Lv.	Name	Type	Kind	Pow.	Acc.	PP	Range
1	Hydro Pump	Water	Special	110	80	5	Normal
1	Shell Smash	Normal	Status	—	—	15	Self
1	Toxic Spikes	Poison	Status	—	—	20	Other Side
1	Withdraw	Water	Status	—	—	40	Self
1	Supersonic	Normal	Status	—	55	20	Normal
1	Protect	Normal	Status	—	—	10	Self
1	Aurora Beam	Ice	Special	65	100	20	Normal
13	Spike Cannon	Normal	Physical	20	100	15	Normal
28	Spikes	Ground	Status	—	—	20	Other Side
50	Icicle Crash	Ice	Physical	85	90	10	Normal

● TM & HM MOVES

No.	Name	Type	Kind	Pow.	Acc.	PP	Range
TM06	Toxic	Poison	Status	—	90	10	Normal
TM07	Hail	Ice	Status	—	—	10	Both Sides
TM10	Hidden Power	Normal	Special	60	100	15	Normal
TM13	Ice Beam	Ice	Special	90	100	10	Normal
TM14	Blizzard	Ice	Special	110	70	5	Many Others
TM15	Hyper Beam	Normal	Special	150	90	5	Normal
TM17	Protect	Normal	Status	—	—	10	Self
TM18	Rain Dance	Water	Status	—	—	5	Both Sides
TM21	Frustration	Normal	Physical	—	100	20	Normal
TM27	Return	Normal	Physical	—	100	20	Normal
TM32	Double Team	Normal	Status	—	—	15	Self
TM41	Torment	Dark	Status	—	100	15	Normal
TM42	Facade	Normal	Physical	70	100	20	Normal
TM44	Rest	Psychic	Status	—	—	10	Self
TM45	Attract	Normal	Status	—	100	15	Normal
TM48	Round	Normal	Special	60	100	15	Normal
TM64	Explosion	Normal	Physical	250	100	5	Adjacent
TM66	Payback	Dark	Physical	50	100	10	Normal
TM68	Giga Impact	Normal	Physical	150	90	5	Normal
TM79	Frost Breath	Ice	Special	60	90	10	Normal
TM84	Poison Jab	Poison	Physical	80	100	20	Normal
TM87	Swagger	Normal	Status	—	90	15	Normal
TM88	Sleep Talk	Normal	Status	—	—	10	Self
TM90	Substitute	Normal	Status	—	—	10	Self
TM100	Confide	Normal	Status	—	—	20	Normal
HM03	Surf	Water	Special	90	100	15	Adjacent

No.	Name	Type	Kind	Pow.	Acc.	PP	Range

● MOVES TAUGHT BY PEOPLE

Name	Type	Kind	Pow.	Acc.	PP	Range

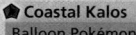

Coastal Kalos

038

Balloon Pokémon

Qwilfish

HEIGHT: 1'08" WEIGHT: 8.6 lbs.
GENDER: ♂/♀

X — To fire its poison spikes, it must inflate its body by drinking over 2.6 gallons of water all at once.

Y — The small spikes covering its body developed from scales. They inject a toxin that causes fainting.

TYPE	Water	Poison

ABILITIES
Poison Point
Swift Swim

HIDDEN ABILITY
None

STAT GROWTH RATES
HP	∎∎∎
Attack	∎∎∎∎∎
Defense	∎∎∎
Sp. Atk	∎∎∎
Sp. Def	∎∎
Speed	∎∎∎∎∎

EGG GROUP
Water 2

EVOLUTION

Does not evolve

ITEMS SOMETIMES HELD BY WILD POKÉMON
Poison Barb

Damage taken in normal battles		Damage taken in Inverse Battles	
Normal	×1	Normal	×1
Fire	×0.5	Fire	×2
Water	×0.5	Water	×2
Grass	×1	Grass	×1
Electric	×2	Electric	×0.5
Ice	×0.5	Ice	×2
Fighting	×0.5	Fighting	×2
Poison	×0.5	Poison	×2
Ground	×2	Ground	×0.5
Flying	×1	Flying	×1
Psychic	×2	Psychic	×0.5
Bug	×0.5	Bug	×2
Rock	×1	Rock	×1
Ghost	×1	Ghost	×1
Dragon	×1	Dragon	×1
Dark	×1	Dark	×1
Steel	×0.5	Steel	×2
Fairy	×0.5	Fairy	×2

Can be used in	
Inverse Battle	Battle Institute
—	Battle Maison
Battle Chateau	Random Matchup

Same form for ♂/♀

How to obtain for your Coastal Kalos Pokédex

Catch using a Super Rod on Route 8.

Catch using a Super Rod on Route 8.

● LEVEL-UP MOVES

Lv.	Name	Type	Kind	Pow.	Acc.	PP	Range
1	Fell Stinger	Bug	Physical	30	100	25	Normal
1	Hydro Pump	Water	Special	110	80	5	Normal
1	Destiny Bond	Ghost	Status	—	—	5	Self
1	Water Gun	Water	Special	40	100	25	Normal
1	Spikes	Ground	Status	—	—	20	Other Side
1	Tackle	Normal	Physical	50	100	35	Normal
1	Poison Sting	Poison	Physical	15	100	35	Normal
9	Harden	Normal	Status	—	—	30	Self
9	Minimize	Normal	Status	—	—	10	Self
13	Bubble	Water	Special	40	100	30	Many Others
17	Rollout	Rock	Physical	30	90	20	Normal
21	Toxic Spikes	Poison	Status	—	—	20	Other Side
25	Stockpile	Normal	Status	—	—	20	Self
25	Spit Up	Normal	Special	—	100	10	Normal
29	Revenge	Fighting	Physical	60	100	10	Normal
33	Brine	Water	Special	65	100	10	Normal
37	Pin Missile	Bug	Physical	25	95	20	Normal
41	Take Down	Normal	Physical	90	85	20	Normal
45	Aqua Tail	Water	Physical	90	90	10	Normal
49	Poison Jab	Poison	Physical	80	100	20	Normal
53	Destiny Bond	Ghost	Status	—	—	5	Self
57	Hydro Pump	Water	Special	110	80	5	Normal
60	Fell Stinger	Bug	Physical	30	100	25	Normal

● TM & HM MOVES

No.	Name	Type	Kind	Pow.	Acc.	PP	Range
TM06	Toxic	Poison	Status	—	90	10	Normal
TM07	Hail	Ice	Status	—	—	10	Both Sides
TM09	Venoshock	Poison	Special	65	100	10	Normal
TM10	Hidden Power	Normal	Special	60	100	15	Normal
TM12	Taunt	Dark	Status	—	100	20	Normal
TM13	Ice Beam	Ice	Special	90	100	10	Normal
TM14	Blizzard	Ice	Special	110	70	5	Many Others
TM17	Protect	Normal	Status	—	—	10	Self
TM18	Rain Dance	Water	Status	—	—	5	Both Sides
TM21	Frustration	Normal	Physical	—	100	20	Normal
TM27	Return	Normal	Physical	—	100	20	Normal
TM30	Shadow Ball	Ghost	Special	80	100	15	Normal
TM32	Double Team	Normal	Status	—	—	15	Self
TM34	Sludge Wave	Poison	Special	95	100	10	Adjacent
TM36	Sludge Bomb	Poison	Special	90	100	10	Normal
TM42	Facade	Normal	Physical	70	100	20	Normal
TM44	Rest	Psychic	Status	—	—	10	Self
TM45	Attract	Normal	Status	—	100	15	Normal
TM48	Round	Normal	Special	60	100	15	Normal
TM55	Scald	Water	Special	80	100	15	Normal
TM64	Explosion	Normal	Physical	250	100	5	Adjacent
TM66	Payback	Dark	Physical	50	100	10	Normal
TM73	Thunder Wave	Electric	Status	—	100	20	Normal
TM74	Gyro Ball	Steel	Physical	—	100	5	Normal
TM84	Poison Jab	Poison	Physical	80	100	20	Normal
TM87	Swagger	Normal	Status	—	90	15	Normal
TM88	Sleep Talk	Normal	Status	—	—	10	Self
TM90	Substitute	Normal	Status	—	—	10	Self
TM100	Confide	Normal	Status	—	—	20	Normal
HM03	Surf	Water	Special	90	100	15	Adjacent
HM05	Waterfall	Water	Physical	80	100	15	Normal

● MOVES TAUGHT BY PEOPLE

Name	Type	Kind	Pow.	Acc.	PP	Range

● EGG MOVES

Name	Type	Kind	Pow.	Acc.	PP	Range
Flail	Normal	Physical	—	100	15	Normal
Haze	Ice	Status	—	—	30	Both Sides
Bubble Beam	Water	Special	65	100	20	Normal
Supersonic	Normal	Status	—	55	20	Normal
Astonish	Ghost	Physical	30	100	15	Normal
Signal Beam	Bug	Special	75	100	15	Normal
Aqua Jet	Water	Physical	40	100	20	Normal
Water Pulse	Water	Special	60	100	20	Normal
Brine	Water	Special	65	100	10	Normal
Acid Spray	Poison	Special	40	100	20	Normal

AFTER THE HALL OF FAME

CENTRAL KALOS

COASTAL KALOS

038

Qwilfish

MOUNTAIN KALOS

ADVENTURE DATA

AFTER THE HALL OF FAME

CENTRAL KALOS

COASTAL KALOS

039

Horsea

MOUNTAIN KALOS

ADVENTURE DATA

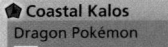

Coastal Kalos 039
Dragon Pokémon
✓ Horsea

HEIGHT: 1'04" WEIGHT: 17.6 lbs.
GENDER: ♂/♀

X Known to shoot down flying bugs with precision blasts of ink from the surface of the water.

Y It makes its nest in the shade of corals. If it senses danger, it spits murky ink and flees.

TYPE Water

ABILITIES
Swift Swim
Sniper

HIDDEN ABILITY
None

STAT GROWTH RATES
HP	■■
Attack	■■
Defense	■■
Sp. Atk	■■■
Sp. Def	■
Speed	■■■

EGG GROUPS
Water 1, Dragon

EVOLUTION
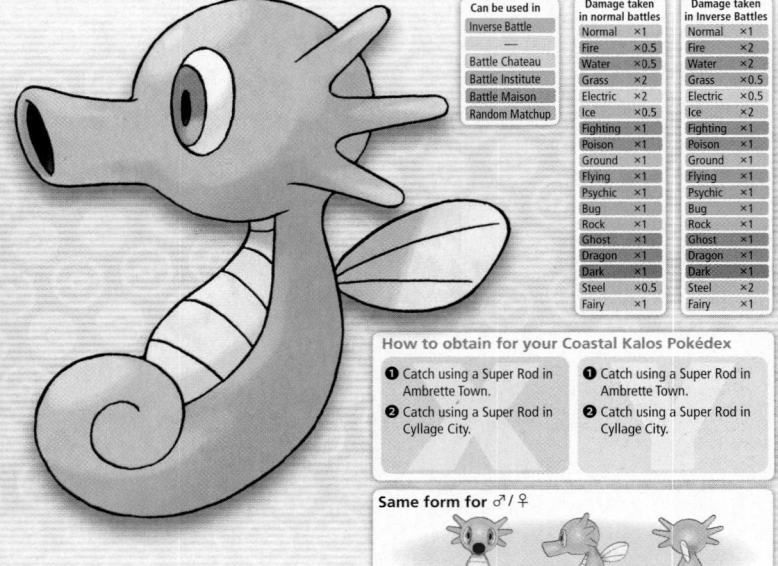

Horsea — Lv. 32 → Seadra — Link Trade with a Dragon Scale → Kingdra

ITEMS SOMETIMES HELD BY WILD POKÉMON
Dragon Scale

Can be used in
Inverse Battle
—
Battle Chateau
Battle Institute
Battle Maison
Random Matchup

Damage taken in normal battles
Normal	×1
Fire	×0.5
Water	×0.5
Grass	×2
Electric	×2
Ice	×0.5
Fighting	×1
Poison	×1
Ground	×1
Flying	×1
Psychic	×1
Bug	×1
Rock	×1
Ghost	×1
Dragon	×1
Dark	×1
Steel	×0.5
Fairy	×1

Damage taken in Inverse Battles
Normal	×1
Fire	×2
Water	×2
Grass	×0.5
Electric	×0.5
Ice	×2
Fighting	×1
Poison	×1
Ground	×1
Flying	×1
Psychic	×1
Bug	×1
Rock	×1
Ghost	×1
Dragon	×1
Dark	×2
Steel	×2
Fairy	×1

How to obtain for your Coastal Kalos Pokédex
❶ Catch using a Super Rod in Ambrette Town.
❷ Catch using a Super Rod in Cyllage City.

❶ Catch using a Super Rod in Ambrette Town.
❷ Catch using a Super Rod in Cyllage City.

Same form for ♂/♀

● LEVEL-UP MOVES
Lv.	Name	Type	Kind	Pow.	Acc.	PP	Range
1	Water Gun	Water	Special	40	100	25	Normal
4	Smokescreen	Normal	Status	—	100	20	Normal
8	Leer	Normal	Status	—	100	30	Many Others
11	Bubble	Water	Special	40	100	30	Many Others
14	Focus Energy	Normal	Status	—	—	30	Self
18	Bubble Beam	Water	Special	65	100	20	Normal
23	Agility	Psychic	Status	—	—	30	Self
26	Twister	Dragon	Special	40	100	20	Many Others
30	Brine	Water	Special	65	100	10	Normal
35	Hydro Pump	Water	Special	110	80	5	Normal
38	Dragon Dance	Dragon	Status	—	—	20	Self
42	Dragon Pulse	Dragon	Special	85	100	10	Normal

● TM & HM MOVES
No.	Name	Type	Kind	Pow.	Acc.	PP	Range
TM06	Toxic	Poison	Status	—	90	10	Normal
TM07	Hail	Ice	Status	—	—	10	Both Sides
TM10	Hidden Power	Normal	Special	60	100	15	Normal
TM13	Ice Beam	Ice	Special	90	100	10	Normal
TM14	Blizzard	Ice	Special	110	70	5	Many Others
TM17	Protect	Normal	Status	—	—	10	Self
TM18	Rain Dance	Water	Status	—	—	5	Both Sides
TM21	Frustration	Normal	Physical	—	100	20	Normal
TM27	Return	Normal	Physical	—	100	20	Normal
TM32	Double Team	Normal	Status	—	—	15	Self
TM42	Facade	Normal	Physical	70	100	20	Normal
TM44	Rest	Psychic	Status	—	—	10	Self
TM45	Attract	Normal	Status	—	100	15	Normal
TM48	Round	Normal	Special	60	100	15	Normal
TM55	Scald	Water	Special	80	100	15	Normal
TM87	Swagger	Normal	Status	—	90	15	Normal
TM88	Sleep Talk	Normal	Status	—	—	10	Self
TM90	Substitute	Normal	Status	—	—	10	Self
TM91	Flash Cannon	Steel	Special	80	100	10	Normal
TM100	Confide	Normal	Status	—	—	20	Normal
HM03	Surf	Water	Special	90	100	15	Adjacent
HM05	Waterfall	Water	Physical	80	100	15	Normal

● MOVES TAUGHT BY PEOPLE
Name	Type	Kind	Pow.	Acc.	PP	Range

● EGG MOVES
Name	Type	Kind	Pow.	Acc.	PP	Range
Flail	Normal	Physical	—	100	15	Normal
Aurora Beam	Ice	Special	65	100	20	Normal
Octazooka	Water	Special	65	85	10	Normal
Disable	Normal	Status	—	100	20	Normal
Splash	Normal	Status	—	—	40	Self
Dragon Rage	Dragon	Special	—	100	10	Normal
Dragon Breath	Dragon	Special	60	100	20	Normal
Signal Beam	Bug	Special	75	100	15	Normal
Razor Wind	Normal	Special	80	100	10	Many Others
Muddy Water	Water	Special	90	85	10	Many Others
Water Pulse	Water	Special	60	100	20	Normal
Clear Smog	Poison	Special	50	—	15	Normal
Outrage	Dragon	Physical	120	100	10	1 Random

Coastal Kalos **040**

Dragon Pokémon

☑ **Seadra**

HEIGHT: 3'11"   WEIGHT: 55.1 lbs.
GENDER: ♂/♀

X Its body bristles with sharp spikes. Carelessly trying to touch it could cause fainting from the spikes.

Y It is capable of swimming backwards by rapidly flapping its winglike pectoral fins and stout tail.

TYPE **Water**

ABILITIES
Poison Point
Sniper

HIDDEN ABILITY
None

STAT GROWTH RATES
HP   ■■
Attack ■■■
Defense ■■■■
Sp. Atk ■■■■■
Sp. Def ■■
Speed   ■■■■■

EGG GROUPS
Water 1, Dragon

EVOLUTION

Lv. 32   Link Trade with a Dragon Scale

Horsea   Seadra   Kingdra

ITEMS SOMETIMES HELD BY WILD POKÉMON
Dragon Scale

Damage taken in normal battles		Damage taken in Inverse Battles	
Normal	×1	Normal	×1
Fire	×0.5	Fire	×2
Water	×0.5	Water	×2
Grass	×2	Grass	×0.5
Electric	×2	Electric	×0.5
Ice	×0.5	Ice	×2
Fighting	×1	Fighting	×1
Poison	×1	Poison	×1
Ground	×1	Ground	×1
Flying	×1	Flying	×1
Psychic	×1	Psychic	×1
Bug	×1	Bug	×1
Rock	×1	Rock	×1
Ghost	×1	Ghost	×1
Dragon	×1	Dragon	×1
Dark	×1	Dark	×1
Steel	×0.5	Steel	×2
Fairy	×1	Fairy	×1

Can be used in
Inverse Battle
—
Battle Chateau
Battle Institute
Battle Maison
Random Matchup

How to obtain for your Coastal Kalos Pokédex

❶ Catch using a Super Rod in Ambrette Town or Cyllage City.
❷ Level up Horsea to Lv. 32.

❶ Catch using a Super Rod in Ambrette Town or Cyllage City.
❷ Level up Horsea to Lv. 32.

Same form for ♂/♀

● **LEVEL-UP MOVES**

Lv.	Name	Type	Kind	Pow.	Acc.	PP	Range
1	Water Gun	Water	Special	40	100	25	Normal
1	Smokescreen	Normal	Status	—	100	20	Normal
1	Leer	Normal	Status	—	100	30	Many Others
1	Bubble	Water	Special	40	100	30	Many Others
4	Smokescreen	Normal	Status	—	100	20	Normal
8	Leer	Normal	Status	—	100	30	Many Others
11	Bubble	Water	Special	40	100	30	Many Others
14	Focus Energy	Normal	Status	—	—	30	Self
18	Bubble Beam	Water	Special	65	100	20	Normal
23	Agility	Psychic	Status	—	—	30	Self
26	Twister	Dragon	Special	40	100	20	Many Others
30	Brine	Water	Special	65	100	10	Normal
40	Hydro Pump	Water	Special	110	80	5	Normal
48	Dragon Dance	Dragon	Status	—	—	20	Self
57	Dragon Pulse	Dragon	Special	85	100	10	Normal

● **TM & HM MOVES**

No.	Name	Type	Kind	Pow.	Acc.	PP	Range
TM06	Toxic	Poison	Status	—	90	10	Normal
TM07	Hail	Ice	Status	—	—	10	Both Sides
TM10	Hidden Power	Normal	Special	60	100	15	Normal
TM13	Ice Beam	Ice	Special	90	100	10	Normal
TM14	Blizzard	Ice	Special	110	70	5	Many Others
TM15	Hyper Beam	Normal	Special	150	90	5	Normal
TM17	Protect	Normal	Status	—	—	10	Self
TM18	Rain Dance	Water	Status	—	—	5	Both Sides
TM21	Frustration	Normal	Physical	—	100	20	Normal
TM27	Return	Normal	Physical	—	100	20	Normal
TM32	Double Team	Normal	Status	—	—	15	Self
TM42	Facade	Normal	Physical	70	100	20	Normal
TM44	Rest	Psychic	Status	—	—	10	Self
TM45	Attract	Normal	Status	—	100	15	Normal
TM48	Round	Normal	Special	60	100	15	Normal
TM55	Scald	Water	Special	80	100	15	Normal
TM68	Giga Impact	Normal	Physical	150	90	5	Normal
TM87	Swagger	Normal	Status	—	90	15	Normal
TM88	Sleep Talk	Normal	Status	—	—	10	Self
TM90	Substitute	Normal	Status	—	—	10	Self
TM91	Flash Cannon	Steel	Special	80	100	10	Normal
TM100	Confide	Normal	Status	—	—	20	Normal
HM03	Surf	Water	Special	90	100	15	Adjacent
HM05	Waterfall	Water	Physical	80	100	15	Normal

No.	Name	Type	Kind	Pow.	Acc.	PP	Range

● **MOVES TAUGHT BY PEOPLE**

Name	Type	Kind	Pow.	Acc.	PP	Range

AFTER THE HALL OF FAME

CENTRAL KALOS

COASTAL KALOS

040 Seadra

MOUNTAIN KALOS

ADVENTURE DATA

AFTER THE HALL OF FAME

CENTRAL KALOS

COASTAL KALOS

041

Kingdra

MOUNTAIN KALOS

ADVENTURE DATA

🏠 Coastal Kalos **041**
Dragon Pokémon
✅ **Kingdra**

HEIGHT: 5'11" WEIGHT: 335.1 lbs.
GENDER: ♂/♀

TYPE Water Dragon

ABILITIES
Swift Swim
Sniper

HIDDEN ABILITY
None

STAT GROWTH RATES
HP
Attack
Defense
Sp. Atk
Sp. Def
Speed

EGG GROUPS
Water 1, Dragon

❌ It is said that it usually hides in underwater caves. It can create whirlpools by yawning.

✅ It stores energy by sleeping at underwater depths at which no other life-forms can survive.

🔺 EVOLUTION

Lv. 32   Link Trade with a Dragon Scale

Horsea   Seadra   Kingdra

ITEMS SOMETIMES HELD BY WILD POKÉMON
None

	Damage taken in normal battles		Damage taken in Inverse Battles
Normal	×1	Normal	×1
Fire	×0.25	Fire	×4
Water	×0.25	Water	×4
Grass	×1	Grass	×1
Electric	×1	Electric	×1
Ice	×1	Ice	×1
Fighting	×1	Fighting	×1
Poison	×1	Poison	×1
Ground	×1	Ground	×1
Flying	×1	Flying	×1
Psychic	×1	Psychic	×1
Bug	×1	Bug	×1
Rock	×1	Rock	×1
Ghost	×1	Ghost	×1
Dragon	×2	Dragon	×0.5
Dark	×1	Dark	×1
Steel	×0.5	Steel	×2
Fairy	×2	Fairy	×0.5

Can be used in
Inverse Battle	Battle Institute
—	Battle Maison
Battle Chateau	Random Matchup

Same form for ♂/♀

How to obtain for your Coastal Kalos Pokédex
Receive Seadra with a Dragon Scale, and have it evolve.
Receive Seadra with a Dragon Scale, and have it evolve.

● **LEVEL-UP MOVES**

Lv.	Name	Type	Kind	Pow.	Acc.	PP	Range
1	Dragon Pulse	Dragon	Special	85	100	10	Normal
1	Yawn	Normal	Status	—	—	10	Normal
1	Water Gun	Water	Special	40	100	25	Normal
1	Smokescreen	Normal	Status	—	100	20	Normal
1	Leer	Normal	Status	—	100	30	Many Others
1	Bubble	Water	Special	40	100	30	Many Others
4	Smokescreen	Normal	Status	—	100	20	Normal
8	Leer	Normal	Status	—	100	30	Many Others
11	Bubble	Water	Special	40	100	30	Many Others
14	Focus Energy	Normal	Status	—	—	30	Self
18	Bubble Beam	Water	Special	65	100	20	Normal
23	Agility	Psychic	Status	—	—	30	Self
26	Twister	Dragon	Special	40	100	20	Many Others
30	Brine	Water	Special	65	100	10	Normal
40	Hydro Pump	Water	Special	110	80	5	Normal
48	Dragon Dance	Dragon	Status	—	—	20	Self
57	Dragon Pulse	Dragon	Special	85	100	10	Normal

● **TM & HM MOVES**

No.	Name	Type	Kind	Pow.	Acc.	PP	Range
TM06	Toxic	Poison	Status	—	90	10	Normal
TM07	Hail	Ice	Status	—	—	10	Both Sides
TM10	Hidden Power	Normal	Special	60	100	15	Normal
TM13	Ice Beam	Ice	Special	90	100	10	Normal
TM14	Blizzard	Ice	Special	110	70	5	Many Others
TM15	Hyper Beam	Normal	Special	150	90	5	Normal
TM17	Protect	Normal	Status	—	—	10	Self
TM18	Rain Dance	Water	Status	—	—	5	Both Sides
TM21	Frustration	Normal	Physical	—	100	20	Normal
TM27	Return	Normal	Physical	—	100	20	Normal
TM32	Double Team	Normal	Status	—	—	15	Self
TM42	Facade	Normal	Physical	70	100	20	Normal
TM44	Rest	Psychic	Status	—	—	10	Self
TM45	Attract	Normal	Status	—	100	15	Normal
TM48	Round	Normal	Special	60	100	15	Normal
TM55	Scald	Water	Special	80	100	15	Normal
TM60	Quash	Dark	Status	—	100	15	Normal
TM68	Giga Impact	Normal	Physical	150	90	5	Normal
TM87	Swagger	Normal	Status	—	90	15	Normal
TM88	Sleep Talk	Normal	Status	—	—	10	Self
TM90	Substitute	Normal	Status	—	—	10	Self
TM91	Flash Cannon	Steel	Special	80	100	10	Normal
TM100	Confide	Normal	Status	—	—	20	Normal
HM03	Surf	Water	Special	90	100	15	Adjacent
HM05	Waterfall	Water	Physical	80	100	15	Normal

No.	Name	Type	Kind	Pow.	Acc.	PP	Range

● **MOVES TAUGHT BY PEOPLE**

Name	Type	Kind	Pow.	Acc.	PP	Range
Draco Meteor	Dragon	Special	130	90	5	Normal

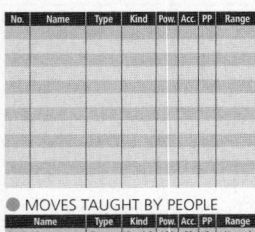

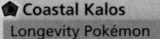

Coastal Kalos
Longevity Pokémon

042

☑ Relicanth

HEIGHT: 3'03" WEIGHT: 51.6 lbs.
GENDER: ♂/♀

X It has remained unchanged for 100 million years. It was discovered during a deep-sea exploration.

Y A rare Pokémon discovered during a deep-sea exploration. It has not changed in over 100 million years.

TYPE: Water | Rock

ABILITIES
Swift Swim
Rock Head

HIDDEN ABILITY
None

STAT GROWTH RATES
HP	■■■■
Attack	■■■■
Defense	■■■■■■■
Sp. Atk	■■
Sp. Def	■■■
Speed	■■■

EGG GROUPS
Water 1, Water 2

EVOLUTION

Does not evolve

ITEMS SOMETIMES HELD BY WILD POKÉMON
Deep Sea Scale

Damage taken in normal battles		Damage taken in Inverse Battles		Can be used in
Normal	×0.5	Normal	×2	Inverse Battle
Fire	×0.25	Fire	×4	—
Water	×1	Water	×1	Battle Chateau
Grass	×4	Grass	×0.25	Battle Institute
Electric	×2	Electric	×0.5	Battle Maison
Ice	×0.5	Ice	×2	Random Matchup
Fighting	×2	Fighting	×0.5	
Poison	×0.5	Poison	×2	
Ground	×2	Ground	×0.5	
Flying	×0.5	Flying	×2	
Psychic	×1	Psychic	×1	
Bug	×1	Bug	×1	
Rock	×1	Rock	×1	
Ghost	×1	Ghost	×1	
Dragon	×1	Dragon	×1	
Dark	×1	Dark	×1	
Steel	×1	Steel	×1	
Fairy	×1	Fairy	×1	

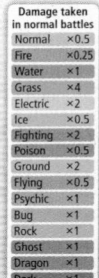

How to obtain for your Coastal Kalos Pokédex

❶ Catch using a Super Rod in Ambrette Town.
❷ Catch using a Super Rod in Cyllage City.

❶ Catch using a Super Rod in Ambrette Town.
❷ Catch using a Super Rod in Cyllage City.

♂
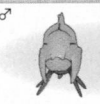  

♀

The male's cheeks hang lower than the female's cheeks.

● LEVEL-UP MOVES

Lv.	Name	Type	Kind	Pow.	Acc.	PP	Range
1	Head Smash	Rock	Physical	150	80	5	Normal
1	Hydro Pump	Water	Special	110	80	5	Normal
1	Ancient Power	Rock	Special	60	100	5	Normal
1	Mud Sport	Ground	Status	—	—	15	Both Sides
1	Tackle	Normal	Physical	50	100	35	Normal
1	Harden	Normal	Status	—	—	30	Self
8	Water Gun	Water	Special	40	100	25	Normal
15	Rock Tomb	Rock	Physical	60	95	15	Normal
22	Yawn	Normal	Status	—	—	10	Normal
29	Take Down	Normal	Physical	90	85	20	Normal
36	Mud Sport	Ground	Status	—	—	15	Both Sides
43	Ancient Power	Rock	Special	60	100	5	Normal
50	Double-Edge	Normal	Physical	120	100	15	Normal
57	Dive	Water	Physical	80	100	10	Normal
64	Rest	Psychic	Status	—	—	10	Self
71	Hydro Pump	Water	Special	110	80	5	Normal
78	Head Smash	Rock	Physical	150	80	5	Normal

● TM & HM MOVES

No.	Name	Type	Kind	Pow.	Acc.	PP	Range
TM04	Calm Mind	Psychic	Status	—	—	20	Self
TM06	Toxic	Poison	Status	—	90	10	Normal
TM07	Hail	Ice	Status	—	—	10	Both Sides
TM10	Hidden Power	Normal	Special	60	100	15	Normal
TM13	Ice Beam	Ice	Special	90	100	10	Normal
TM14	Blizzard	Ice	Special	110	70	5	Many Others
TM15	Hyper Beam	Normal	Special	150	90	5	Normal
TM17	Protect	Normal	Status	—	—	10	Self
TM18	Rain Dance	Water	Status	—	—	5	Both Sides
TM20	Safeguard	Normal	Status	—	—	25	Your Side
TM21	Frustration	Normal	Physical	—	100	20	Normal
TM23	Smack Down	Rock	Physical	50	100	15	Normal
TM26	Earthquake	Ground	Physical	100	100	10	Adjacent
TM27	Return	Normal	Physical	—	100	20	Normal
TM32	Double Team	Normal	Status	—	—	15	Self
TM37	Sandstorm	Rock	Status	—	—	10	Both Sides
TM39	Rock Tomb	Rock	Physical	60	95	15	Normal
TM42	Facade	Normal	Physical	70	100	20	Normal
TM44	Rest	Psychic	Status	—	—	10	Self
TM45	Attract	Normal	Status	—	100	15	Normal
TM48	Round	Normal	Special	60	100	15	Normal
TM55	Scald	Water	Special	80	100	15	Normal
TM68	Giga Impact	Normal	Physical	150	90	5	Normal
TM69	Rock Polish	Rock	Status	—	—	20	Self
TM71	Stone Edge	Rock	Physical	100	80	5	Normal
TM77	Psych Up	Normal	Status	—	—	10	Normal
TM78	Bulldoze	Ground	Physical	60	100	20	Adjacent
TM80	Rock Slide	Rock	Physical	75	90	10	Many Others
TM87	Swagger	Normal	Status	—	90	15	Normal
TM88	Sleep Talk	Normal	Status	—	—	10	Self
TM90	Substitute	Normal	Status	—	—	10	Self
TM94	Rock Smash	Fighting	Physical	40	100	15	Normal
TM100	Confide	Normal	Status	—	—	20	Normal

No.	Name	Type	Kind	Pow.	Acc.	PP	Range
HM03	Surf	Water	Special	90	100	15	Adjacent
HM05	Waterfall	Water	Physical	80	100	15	Normal

● MOVES TAUGHT BY PEOPLE

Name	Type	Kind	Pow.	Acc.	PP	Range

● EGG MOVES

Name	Type	Kind	Pow.	Acc.	PP	Range
Magnitude	Ground	Physical	—	100	30	Adjacent
Skull Bash	Normal	Physical	130	100	10	Normal
Water Sport	Water	Status	—	—	15	Both Sides
Amnesia	Psychic	Status	—	—	20	Self
Sleep Talk	Normal	Status	—	—	10	Self
Aqua Tail	Water	Physical	90	90	10	Normal
Snore	Normal	Special	50	100	15	Normal
Mud-Slap	Ground	Special	20	100	10	Normal
Muddy Water	Water	Special	90	85	10	Many Others
Mud Shot	Ground	Special	55	95	15	Normal
Brine	Water	Special	65	100	10	Normal
Zen Headbutt	Psychic	Physical	80	90	15	Normal

AFTER THE HALL OF FAME

CENTRAL KALOS

COASTAL KALOS

042 | Relicanth

MOUNTAIN KALOS

ADVENTURE DATA

AFTER THE HALL OF FAME

CENTRAL KALOS

COASTAL KALOS

043

Sandile

MOUNTAIN KALOS

ADVENTURE DATA

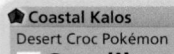

Coastal Kalos **043**

Desert Croc Pokémon

☑ **Sandile**

HEIGHT: 2'04"   WEIGHT: 33.5 lbs.
GENDER: ♂/♀

TYPE **Ground** **Dark**

ABILITIES
Intimidate
Moxie

HIDDEN ABILITY
Anger Point

STAT GROWTH RATES
HP	■■■
Attack	■■■■
Defense	■■
Sp. Atk	■■
Sp. Def	■■
Speed	■■■■

EGG GROUP
Field

X It moves along below the sand's surface, except for its nose and eyes. A dark membrane shields its eyes from the sun.

Y They live buried in the sands of the desert. The sun-warmed sands prevent their body temperature from dropping.

EVOLUTION

Lv. 29   Lv. 40

Sandile   Krokorok   Krookodile

ITEMS SOMETIMES HELD BY WILD POKÉMON
None

Damage taken in normal battles	
Normal	×1
Fire	×1
Water	×2
Grass	×2
Electric	×0
Ice	×2
Fighting	×2
Poison	×0.5
Ground	×1
Flying	×1
Psychic	×0
Bug	×2
Rock	×0.5
Ghost	×0.5
Dragon	×1
Dark	×0.5
Steel	×1
Fairy	×2

Damage taken in Inverse Battles	
Normal	×1
Fire	×1
Water	×0.5
Grass	×0.5
Electric	×2
Ice	×0.5
Fighting	×0.5
Poison	×2
Ground	×1
Flying	×1
Psychic	×2
Bug	×0.5
Rock	×2
Ghost	×2
Dragon	×1
Dark	×2
Steel	×1
Fairy	×0.5

Can be used in	
Inverse Battle	Battle Institute
—	Battle Maison
Battle Chateau	Random Matchup

Same form for ♂ / ♀

How to obtain for your Coastal Kalos Pokédex

Catch it when it pops out while you're riding Rhyhorn on Route 9.

Catch it when it pops out while you're riding Rhyhorn on Route 9.

● LEVEL-UP MOVES

Lv.	Name	Type	Kind	Pow.	Acc.	PP	Range
1	Leer	Normal	Status	—	100	30	Many Others
1	Rage	Normal	Physical	20	100	20	Normal
4	Bite	Dark	Physical	60	100	25	Normal
7	Sand Attack	Ground	Status	—	100	15	Normal
10	Torment	Dark	Status	—	100	15	Normal
13	Sand Tomb	Ground	Physical	35	85	15	Normal
16	Assurance	Dark	Physical	60	100	10	Normal
19	Mud-Slap	Ground	Special	20	100	10	Normal
22	Embargo	Dark	Status	—	100	15	Normal
25	Swagger	Normal	Status	—	90	15	Normal
28	Crunch	Dark	Physical	80	100	15	Normal
31	Dig	Ground	Physical	80	100	10	Normal
34	Scary Face	Normal	Status	—	100	10	Normal
37	Foul Play	Dark	Physical	95	100	15	Normal
40	Sandstorm	Rock	Status	—	—	10	Both Sides
43	Earthquake	Ground	Physical	100	100	10	Adjacent
46	Thrash	Normal	Physical	120	100	10	1 Random

● TM & HM MOVES

No.	Name	Type	Kind	Pow.	Acc.	PP	Range
TM01	Hone Claws	Dark	Status	—	—	15	Self
TM05	Roar	Normal	Status	—	—	20	Normal
TM06	Toxic	Poison	Status	—	90	10	Normal
TM10	Hidden Power	Normal	Special	60	100	15	Normal
TM12	Taunt	Dark	Status	—	100	20	Normal
TM17	Protect	Normal	Status	—	—	10	Self
TM21	Frustration	Normal	Physical	—	100	20	Normal
TM26	Earthquake	Ground	Physical	100	100	10	Adjacent
TM27	Return	Normal	Physical	—	100	20	Normal
TM28	Dig	Ground	Physical	80	100	10	Normal
TM32	Double Team	Normal	Status	—	—	15	Self
TM36	Sludge Bomb	Poison	Special	90	100	10	Normal
TM37	Sandstorm	Rock	Status	—	—	10	Both Sides
TM40	Rock Tomb	Rock	Physical	60	95	15	Normal
TM41	Torment	Dark	Status	—	100	15	Normal
TM42	Facade	Normal	Physical	70	100	20	Normal
TM44	Rest	Psychic	Status	—	—	10	Self
TM45	Attract	Normal	Status	—	100	15	Normal
TM46	Thief	Dark	Physical	60	100	25	Normal
TM48	Round	Normal	Special	60	100	15	Normal
TM59	Incinerate	Fire	Special	60	100	15	Many Others
TM63	Embargo	Dark	Status	—	100	15	Normal
TM66	Payback	Dark	Physical	50	100	10	Normal
TM67	Retaliate	Normal	Physical	70	100	5	Normal
TM71	Stone Edge	Rock	Physical	100	80	5	Normal
TM78	Bulldoze	Ground	Physical	60	100	20	Adjacent
TM80	Rock Slide	Rock	Physical	75	90	10	Many Others
TM87	Swagger	Normal	Status	—	90	15	Normal
TM88	Sleep Talk	Normal	Status	—	—	10	Self
TM90	Substitute	Normal	Status	—	—	10	Self
TM95	Snarl	Dark	Special	55	95	15	Many Others
TM97	Dark Pulse	Dark	Special	80	100	15	Normal
TM100	Confide	Normal	Status	—	—	20	Normal

No.	Name	Type	Kind	Pow.	Acc.	PP	Range
HM01	Cut	Normal	Physical	50	95	30	Normal

● MOVES TAUGHT BY PEOPLE

Name	Type	Kind	Pow.	Acc.	PP	Range

● EGG MOVES

Name	Type	Kind	Pow.	Acc.	PP	Range
Double-Edge	Normal	Physical	120	100	15	Normal
Rock Climb	Normal	Physical	90	85	20	Normal
Pursuit	Dark	Physical	40	100	20	Normal
Uproar	Normal	Special	90	100	10	1 Random
Fire Fang	Fire	Physical	65	95	15	Normal
Thunder Fang	Electric	Physical	65	95	15	Normal
Beat Up	Dark	Physical	—	100	10	Normal
Focus Energy	Normal	Status	—	—	30	Self
Counter	Fighting	Physical	—	100	20	Varies
Mean Look	Normal	Status	—	—	5	Normal
Me First	Normal	Status	—	—	20	Varies

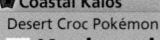
Desert Croc Pokémon

✓ **Krokorok**

044

HEIGHT: 3'03"   WEIGHT: 73.6 lbs.
GENDER: ♂/♀

| TYPE | Ground | Dark |

ABILITIES
Intimidate
Moxie

HIDDEN ABILITY
Anger Point

STAT GROWTH RATES
HP	■■■
Attack	■■■■
Defense	■■■
Sp. Atk	■■
Sp. Def	■■
Speed	■■■■

EGG GROUP
Field

🔺 EVOLUTION

Lv. 29   Lv. 40

Sandile   Krokorok   Krookodile

ITEMS SOMETIMES HELD BY WILD POKÉMON
None

X They live in groups of a few individuals. Protective membranes shield their eyes from sandstorms.

Y The special membrane covering its eyes can sense the heat of objects, so it can see its surroundings even in darkness.

Damage taken in normal battles		Damage taken in Inverse Battles	
Normal	×1	Normal	×1
Fire	×1	Fire	×1
Water	×2	Water	×0.5
Grass	×2	Grass	×0.5
Electric	×0	Electric	×2
Ice	×2	Ice	×0.5
Fighting	×2	Fighting	×0.5
Poison	×0.5	Poison	×2
Ground	×1	Ground	×1
Flying	×1	Flying	×1
Psychic	×0	Psychic	×2
Bug	×2	Bug	×0.5
Rock	×0.5	Rock	×2
Ghost	×0.5	Ghost	×2
Dragon	×1	Dragon	×1
Dark	×0.5	Dark	×2
Steel	×1	Steel	×1
Fairy	×2	Fairy	×0.5

Can be used in	
Inverse Battle	Battle Institute
—	Battle Maison
Battle Chateau	Random Matchup

Same form for ♂/♀

How to obtain for your Coastal Kalos Pokédex

Level up Sandile to Lv. 29.   Level up Sandile to Lv. 29.

● LEVEL-UP MOVES

Lv.	Name	Type	Kind	Pow.	Acc.	PP	Range
1	Leer	Normal	Status	—	100	30	Many Others
1	Rage	Normal	Physical	20	100	20	Normal
1	Bite	Dark	Physical	60	100	25	Normal
1	Sand Attack	Ground	Status	—	100	15	Normal
4	Bite	Dark	Physical	60	100	25	Normal
7	Sand Attack	Ground	Status	—	100	15	Normal
10	Torment	Dark	Status	—	100	15	Normal
13	Sand Tomb	Ground	Physical	35	85	15	Normal
16	Assurance	Dark	Physical	60	100	10	Normal
19	Mud-Slap	Ground	Special	20	100	10	Normal
22	Embargo	Dark	Status	—	100	15	Normal
25	Swagger	Normal	Status	—	90	15	Normal
28	Crunch	Dark	Physical	80	100	15	Normal
32	Dig	Ground	Physical	80	100	10	Normal
36	Scary Face	Normal	Status	—	100	10	Normal
40	Foul Play	Dark	Physical	95	100	15	Normal
44	Sandstorm	Rock	Status	—	—	10	Both Sides
48	Earthquake	Ground	Physical	100	100	10	Adjacent
52	Thrash	Normal	Physical	120	100	10	1 Random

● TM & HM MOVES

No.	Name	Type	Kind	Pow.	Acc.	PP	Range
TM01	Hone Claws	Dark	Status	—	—	15	Self
TM05	Roar	Normal	Status	—	—	20	Normal
TM06	Toxic	Poison	Status	—	90	10	Normal
TM10	Hidden Power	Normal	Special	60	100	15	Normal
TM12	Taunt	Dark	Status	—	100	20	Normal
TM17	Protect	Normal	Status	—	—	10	Self
TM21	Frustration	Normal	Physical	—	100	20	Normal
TM26	Earthquake	Ground	Physical	100	100	10	Adjacent
TM27	Return	Normal	Physical	—	100	20	Normal
TM28	Dig	Ground	Physical	80	100	10	Normal
TM31	Brick Break	Fighting	Physical	75	100	15	Normal
TM32	Double Team	Normal	Status	—	—	15	Self
TM36	Sludge Bomb	Poison	Special	90	100	10	Normal
TM37	Sandstorm	Rock	Status	—	—	10	Both Sides
TM39	Rock Tomb	Rock	Physical	60	95	15	Normal
TM41	Torment	Dark	Status	—	100	15	Normal
TM42	Facade	Normal	Physical	70	100	20	Normal
TM44	Rest	Psychic	Status	—	—	10	Self
TM45	Attract	Normal	Status	—	100	15	Normal
TM46	Thief	Dark	Physical	60	100	25	Normal
TM47	Low Sweep	Fighting	Physical	65	100	20	Normal
TM48	Round	Normal	Special	60	100	15	Normal
TM56	Fling	Dark	Physical	—	100	10	Normal
TM59	Incinerate	Fire	Special	60	100	15	Many Others
TM63	Embargo	Dark	Status	—	100	15	Normal
TM65	Shadow Claw	Ghost	Physical	70	100	15	Normal
TM66	Payback	Dark	Physical	50	100	10	Normal
TM67	Retaliate	Normal	Physical	70	100	5	Normal
TM71	Stone Edge	Rock	Physical	100	80	5	Normal
TM78	Bulldoze	Ground	Physical	60	100	20	Adjacent
TM80	Rock Slide	Rock	Physical	75	90	10	Many Others
TM86	Grass Knot	Grass	Special	—	100	20	Normal
TM87	Swagger	Normal	Status	—	90	15	Normal

No.	Name	Type	Kind	Pow.	Acc.	PP	Range
TM88	Sleep Talk	Normal	Status	—	—	10	Self
TM90	Substitute	Normal	Status	—	—	10	Self
TM94	Rock Smash	Fighting	Physical	40	100	15	Normal
TM95	Snarl	Dark	Special	55	95	15	Many Others
TM97	Dark Pulse	Dark	Special	80	100	15	Normal
TM98	Power-Up Punch	Fighting	Physical	40	100	20	Normal
TM100	Confide	Normal	Status	—	—	20	Normal
HM01	Cut	Normal	Physical	50	95	30	Normal
HM04	Strength	Normal	Physical	80	100	15	Normal

● MOVES TAUGHT BY PEOPLE

Name	Type	Kind	Pow.	Acc.	PP	Range

AFTER THE HALL OF FAME

CENTRAL KALOS

COASTAL KALOS

044 | Krokorok

MOUNTAIN KALOS

ADVENTURE DATA

AFTER THE HALL OF FAME

CENTRAL KALOS

COASTAL KALOS

045

Krookodile

MOUNTAIN KALOS

ADVENTURE DATA

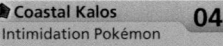

🌸 Coastal Kalos **045**

Intimidation Pokémon

☑ **Krookodile**

HEIGHT: 4'11" WEIGHT: 212.3 lbs.
GENDER: ♂/♀

TYPE Ground | Dark

ABILITIES
Intimidate
Moxie

HIDDEN ABILITY
Anger Point

STAT GROWTH RATES
HP	■■■■
Attack	■■■■■
Defense	■■■■
Sp. Atk	■■■
Sp. Def	■■■
Speed	■■■■■

EGG GROUP
Field

X Very violent Pokémon, they try to clamp down on anything that moves in front of their eyes.

Y They never allow prey to escape. Their jaws are so powerful, they can crush the body of an automobile.

🔼 EVOLUTION

Lv. 29   Lv. 40

Sandile   Krokorok   Krookodile

ITEMS SOMETIMES HELD BY WILD POKÉMON
None

Damage taken in normal battles	
Normal	×1
Fire	×1
Water	×2
Grass	×2
Electric	×0
Ice	×2
Fighting	×2
Poison	×0.5
Ground	×1
Flying	×1
Psychic	×0
Bug	×2
Rock	×0.5
Ghost	×0.5
Dragon	×1
Dark	×0.5
Steel	×1
Fairy	×2

Damage taken in Inverse Battles	
Normal	×1
Fire	×1
Water	×0.5
Grass	×0.5
Electric	×2
Ice	×0.5
Fighting	×0.5
Poison	×2
Ground	×1
Flying	×1
Psychic	×2
Bug	×0.5
Rock	×2
Ghost	×2
Dragon	×1
Dark	×2
Steel	×1
Fairy	×0.5

Can be used in	
Inverse Battle	Battle Institute
—	Battle Maison
Battle Chateau	Random Matchup

Same form for ♂/♀

How to obtain for your Coastal Kalos Pokédex

Level up Krokorok to Lv. 40. | Level up Krokorok to Lv. 40.

X   Y

● LEVEL-UP MOVES

Lv.	Name	Type	Kind	Pow.	Acc.	PP	Range
1	Outrage	Dragon	Physical	120	100	10	1 Random
1	Leer	Normal	Status	—	100	30	Many Others
1	Rage	Normal	Physical	20	100	20	Normal
1	Bite	Dark	Physical	60	100	25	Normal
1	Sand Attack	Ground	Status	—	100	15	Normal
4	Bite	Dark	Physical	60	100	25	Normal
7	Sand Attack	Ground	Status	—	100	15	Normal
10	Torment	Dark	Status	—	100	15	Normal
13	Sand Tomb	Ground	Physical	35	85	15	Normal
16	Assurance	Dark	Physical	60	100	10	Normal
19	Mud-Slap	Ground	Special	20	100	10	Normal
22	Embargo	Dark	Status	—	100	15	Normal
25	Swagger	Normal	Status	—	90	15	Normal
28	Crunch	Dark	Physical	80	100	15	Normal
32	Dig	Ground	Physical	80	100	10	Normal
36	Scary Face	Normal	Status	—	100	10	Normal
42	Foul Play	Dark	Physical	95	100	15	Normal
48	Sandstorm	Rock	Status	—	—	10	Both Sides
54	Earthquake	Ground	Physical	100	100	10	Adjacent
60	Outrage	Dragon	Physical	120	100	10	1 Random

● TM & HM MOVES

No.	Name	Type	Kind	Pow.	Acc.	PP	Range
TM01	Hone Claws	Dark	Status	—	—	15	Self
TM02	Dragon Claw	Dragon	Physical	80	100	15	Normal
TM05	Roar	Normal	Status	—	—	20	Normal
TM06	Toxic	Poison	Status	—	90	10	Normal
TM08	Bulk Up	Fighting	Status	—	—	20	Self
TM10	Hidden Power	Normal	Special	60	100	15	Normal
TM12	Taunt	Dark	Status	—	100	20	Normal
TM15	Hyper Beam	Normal	Special	150	90	5	Normal
TM17	Protect	Normal	Status	—	—	10	Self
TM21	Frustration	Normal	Physical	—	100	20	Normal
TM23	Smack Down	Rock	Physical	50	100	15	Normal
TM26	Earthquake	Ground	Physical	100	100	10	Adjacent
TM27	Return	Normal	Physical	—	100	20	Normal
TM28	Dig	Ground	Physical	80	100	10	Normal
TM31	Brick Break	Fighting	Physical	75	100	15	Normal
TM32	Double Team	Normal	Status	—	—	15	Self
TM36	Sludge Bomb	Poison	Special	90	100	10	Normal
TM37	Sandstorm	Rock	Status	—	—	10	Both Sides
TM39	Rock Tomb	Rock	Physical	60	95	15	Normal
TM40	Aerial Ace	Flying	Physical	60	—	20	Normal
TM41	Torment	Dark	Status	—	100	15	Normal
TM42	Facade	Normal	Physical	70	100	20	Normal
TM44	Rest	Psychic	Status	—	—	10	Self
TM45	Attract	Normal	Status	—	100	15	Normal
TM46	Thief	Dark	Physical	60	100	25	Normal
TM47	Low Sweep	Fighting	Physical	65	100	20	Normal
TM48	Round	Normal	Special	60	100	15	Normal
TM52	Focus Blast	Fighting	Special	120	70	5	Normal
TM56	Fling	Dark	Physical	—	100	10	Normal
TM59	Incinerate	Fire	Special	60	100	15	Many Others
TM63	Embargo	Dark	Status	—	100	15	Normal
TM65	Shadow Claw	Ghost	Physical	70	100	15	Normal
TM66	Payback	Dark	Physical	50	100	10	Normal

No.	Name	Type	Kind	Pow.	Acc.	PP	Range
TM67	Retaliate	Normal	Physical	70	100	5	Normal
TM68	Giga Impact	Normal	Physical	150	90	5	Normal
TM71	Stone Edge	Rock	Physical	100	80	5	Normal
TM78	Bulldoze	Ground	Physical	60	100	20	Adjacent
TM80	Rock Slide	Rock	Physical	75	90	10	Many Others
TM82	Dragon Tail	Dragon	Physical	60	90	10	Normal
TM86	Grass Knot	Grass	Special	—	100	20	Normal
TM87	Swagger	Normal	Status	—	90	15	Normal
TM88	Sleep Talk	Normal	Status	—	—	10	Self
TM90	Substitute	Normal	Status	—	—	10	Self
TM94	Rock Smash	Fighting	Physical	40	100	15	Normal
TM95	Snarl	Dark	Special	55	95	15	Many Others
TM97	Dark Pulse	Dark	Special	80	100	15	Normal
TM98	Power-Up Punch	Fighting	Physical	40	100	20	Normal
TM100	Confide	Normal	Status	—	—	20	Normal
HM01	Cut	Normal	Physical	50	95	30	Normal
HM04	Strength	Normal	Physical	80	100	15	Normal

● MOVES TAUGHT BY PEOPLE

Name	Type	Kind	Pow.	Acc.	PP	Range

Coastal Kalos **046**

Generator Pokémon

☑ Helioptile

HEIGHT: 1'08" WEIGHT: 13.2 lbs.
GENDER: ♂/♀

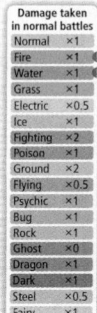

X They make their home in deserts. They can generate their energy from basking in the sun, so eating food is not a requirement.

Y The frills on either side of its head have cells that generate electricity when exposed to sunlight.

TYPE Electric Normal

ABILITIES
Dry Skin
Sand Veil

HIDDEN ABILITY
Solar Power

STAT GROWTH RATES
HP	■■
Attack	■■
Defense	■■
Sp. Atk	■■■
Sp. Def	■■
Speed	■■■■

EGG GROUPS
Monster, Dragon

● EVOLUTION

Helioptile — Sun Stone → Heliolisk

ITEMS SOMETIMES HELD BY WILD POKÉMON
None

Damage taken in normal battles		Damage taken in Inverse Battles	
Normal	×1	Normal	×1
Fire	×1	Fire	×1
Water	×1	Water	×1
Grass	×1	Grass	×1
Electric	×0.5	Electric	×2
Ice	×1	Ice	×1
Fighting	×2	Fighting	×0.5
Poison	×1	Poison	×1
Ground	×2	Ground	×0.5
Flying	×0.5	Flying	×2
Psychic	×1	Psychic	×1
Bug	×1	Bug	×1
Rock	×1	Rock	×1
Ghost	×0	Ghost	×2
Dragon	×1	Dragon	×1
Dark	×1	Dark	×1
Steel	×0.5	Steel	×2
Fairy	×1	Fairy	×1

Can be used in	
Inverse Battle	Battle Institute
—	Battle Maison
Battle Chateau	Random Matchup

Same form for ♂/♀

How to obtain for your Coastal Kalos Pokédex

Catch it when it pops out while you're riding Rhyhorn on Route 9.

Catch it when it pops out while you're riding Rhyhorn on Route 9.

● LEVEL-UP MOVES

Lv.	Name	Type	Kind	Pow.	Acc.	PP	Range
1	Pound	Normal	Physical	40	100	35	Normal
1	Tail Whip	Normal	Status	—	100	30	Many Others
6	Thunder Shock	Electric	Special	40	100	30	Normal
11	Charge	Electric	Status	—	—	20	Self
13	Mud-Slap	Ground	Special	20	100	10	Normal
17	Quick Attack	Normal	Physical	40	100	30	Normal
22	Razor Wind	Normal	Special	80	100	10	Many Others
25	Parabolic Charge	Electric	Special	50	100	20	Adjacent
31	Thunder Wave	Electric	Status	—	100	20	Normal
35	Bulldoze	Ground	Physical	60	100	20	Adjacent
40	Volt Switch	Electric	Special	70	100	20	Normal
45	Electrify	Electric	Status	—	—	20	Normal
49	Thunderbolt	Electric	Special	90	100	15	Normal

● TM & HM MOVES

No.	Name	Type	Kind	Pow.	Acc.	PP	Range
TM06	Toxic	Poison	Status	—	90	10	Normal
TM10	Hidden Power	Normal	Special	60	100	15	Normal
TM16	Light Screen	Psychic	Status	—	—	30	Your Side
TM17	Protect	Normal	Status	—	—	10	Self
TM18	Rain Dance	Water	Status	—	—	5	Both Sides
TM21	Frustration	Normal	Physical	—	100	20	Normal
TM24	Thunderbolt	Electric	Special	90	100	15	Normal
TM25	Thunder	Electric	Special	110	70	10	Normal
TM27	Return	Normal	Physical	—	100	20	Normal
TM28	Dig	Ground	Physical	80	100	10	Normal
TM32	Double Team	Normal	Status	—	—	15	Self
TM37	Sandstorm	Rock	Status	—	—	10	Both Sides
TM39	Rock Tomb	Rock	Physical	60	95	15	Normal
TM42	Facade	Normal	Physical	70	100	20	Normal
TM44	Rest	Psychic	Status	—	—	10	Self
TM45	Attract	Normal	Status	—	100	15	Normal
TM47	Low Sweep	Fighting	Physical	65	100	20	Normal
TM48	Round	Normal	Special	60	100	15	Normal
TM57	Charge Beam	Electric	Special	50	90	10	Normal
TM70	Flash	Normal	Status	—	100	20	Normal
TM72	Volt Switch	Electric	Special	70	100	20	Normal
TM73	Thunder Wave	Electric	Status	—	100	20	Normal
TM77	Psych Up	Normal	Status	—	—	10	Normal
TM78	Bulldoze	Ground	Physical	60	100	20	Adjacent
TM80	Rock Slide	Rock	Physical	75	90	10	Many Others
TM82	Dragon Tail	Dragon	Physical	60	90	10	Normal
TM86	Grass Knot	Grass	Special	—	100	20	Normal
TM87	Swagger	Normal	Status	—	90	15	Normal
TM88	Sleep Talk	Normal	Status	—	—	10	Self
TM89	U-turn	Bug	Physical	70	100	20	Normal
TM90	Substitute	Normal	Status	—	—	10	Self
TM93	Wild Charge	Electric	Physical	90	100	15	Normal
TM97	Dark Pulse	Dark	Special	80	100	15	Normal
TM100	Confide	Normal	Status	—	—	20	Normal
HM01	Cut	Normal	Physical	50	95	30	Normal
HM03	Surf	Water	Special	90	100	15	Adjacent

● MOVES TAUGHT BY PEOPLE

Name	Type	Kind	Pow.	Acc.	PP	Range

● EGG MOVES

Name	Type	Kind	Pow.	Acc.	PP	Range
Agility	Psychic	Status	—	—	30	Self
Glare	Normal	Status	—	100	30	Normal
Camouflage	Normal	Status	—	—	20	Self
Electric Terrain	Electric	Status	—	—	10	Both Sides

AFTER THE HALL OF FAME

CENTRAL KALOS

COASTAL KALOS

047

Heliolisk

MOUNTAIN KALOS

ADVENTURE DATA

🏠 **Coastal Kalos**   **047**
Generator Pokémon
☑ **Heliolisk**

HEIGHT: 3'03"   WEIGHT: 46.3 lbs.
GENDER: ♂/♀

TYPE (Electric) (Normal)

ABILITIES
Dry Skin
Sand Veil

HIDDEN ABILITY
Solar Power

⚡ EVOLUTION

Sun Stone

Helioptile   Heliolisk

❌ They flare their frills and generate energy. A single Heliolisk can generate sufficient electricity to power a skyscraper.

❓ It stimulates its muscles with electricity, boosting the strength in its legs and enabling it to run 100 yards in five seconds.

STAT GROWTH RATES

HP	▪▪▪
Attack	▪▪▪
Defense	▪▪▪
Sp. Atk	▪▪▪▪▪
Sp. Def	▪▪▪▪
Speed	▪▪▪▪▪

EGG GROUPS
Monster, Dragon

ITEMS SOMETIMES HELD BY WILD POKÉMON
None

Can be used in
Inverse Battle
—
Battle Chateau
Battle Institute
Battle Maison
Random Matchup

Damage taken in normal battles	
Normal	×1
Fire	×1
Water	×1
Grass	×1
Electric	×0.5
Ice	×1
Fighting	×2
Poison	×1
Ground	×2
Flying	×0.5
Psychic	×1
Bug	×1
Rock	×1
Ghost	×0
Dragon	×1
Dark	×1
Steel	×0.5
Fairy	×1

Damage taken in Inverse Battles	
Normal	×1
Fire	×1
Water	×1
Grass	×1
Electric	×2
Ice	×1
Fighting	×0.5
Poison	×1
Ground	×0.5
Flying	×2
Psychic	×1
Bug	×1
Rock	×1
Ghost	×2
Dragon	×1
Dark	×1
Steel	×2
Fairy	×1

How to obtain for your Coastal Kalos Pokédex

Use a Sun Stone on Helioptile.   Use a Sun Stone on Helioptile.

X   Y

Same form for ♂/♀

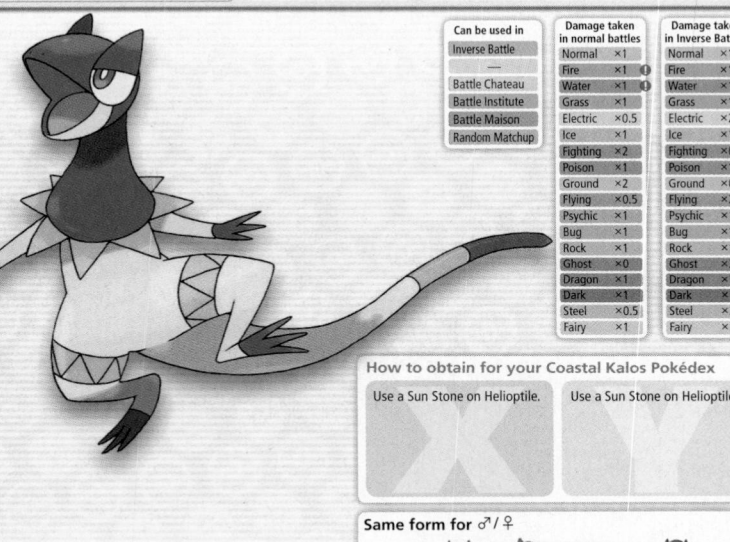

● LEVEL-UP MOVES

Lv.	Name	Type	Kind	Pow.	Acc.	PP	Range
1	Eerie Impulse	Electric	Status	—	100	15	Normal
1	Electrify	Electric	Status	—	—	20	Normal
1	Razor Wind	Normal	Special	80	100	10	Many Others
1	Quick Attack	Normal	Physical	40	100	30	Normal
1	Thunder	Electric	Special	110	70	10	Normal
1	Charge	Electric	Status	—	—	20	Self
1	Parabolic Charge	Electric	Special	50	100	20	Adjacent

● TM & HM MOVES

No.	Name	Type	Kind	Pow.	Acc.	PP	Range
TM06	Toxic	Poison	Status	—	90	10	Normal
TM10	Hidden Power	Normal	Special	60	100	15	Normal
TM15	Hyper Beam	Normal	Special	150	90	5	Normal
TM16	Light Screen	Psychic	Status	—	—	30	Your Side
TM17	Protect	Normal	Status	—	—	10	Self
TM18	Rain Dance	Water	Status	—	—	5	Both Sides
TM21	Frustration	Normal	Physical	—	100	20	Normal
TM24	Thunderbolt	Electric	Special	90	100	15	Normal
TM25	Thunder	Electric	Special	110	70	10	Normal
TM27	Return	Normal	Physical	—	100	20	Normal
TM28	Dig	Ground	Physical	80	100	10	Normal
TM32	Double Team	Normal	Status	—	—	15	Self
TM37	Sandstorm	Rock	Status	—	—	10	Both Sides
TM39	Rock Tomb	Rock	Physical	60	95	15	Normal
TM42	Facade	Normal	Physical	70	100	20	Normal
TM44	Rest	Psychic	Status	—	—	10	Self
TM45	Attract	Normal	Status	—	100	15	Normal
TM47	Low Sweep	Fighting	Physical	65	100	20	Normal
TM48	Round	Normal	Special	60	100	15	Normal
TM52	Focus Blast	Fighting	Special	120	70	5	Normal
TM57	Charge Beam	Electric	Special	50	90	10	Normal
TM68	Giga Impact	Normal	Physical	150	90	5	Normal
TM70	Flash	Normal	Status	—	100	20	Normal
TM72	Volt Switch	Electric	Special	70	100	20	Normal
TM73	Thunder Wave	Electric	Status	—	100	20	Normal
TM77	Psych Up	Normal	Status	—	—	10	Normal
TM78	Bulldoze	Ground	Physical	60	100	20	Adjacent
TM80	Rock Slide	Rock	Physical	75	90	10	Many Others
TM82	Dragon Tail	Dragon	Physical	60	90	10	Normal
TM86	Grass Knot	Grass	Special	—	100	20	Normal
TM87	Swagger	Normal	Status	—	90	15	Normal
TM88	Sleep Talk	Normal	Status	—	—	10	Self
TM89	U-turn	Bug	Physical	70	100	20	Normal

No.	Name	Type	Kind	Pow.	Acc.	PP	Range
TM90	Substitute	Normal	Status	—	—	10	Self
TM93	Wild Charge	Electric	Physical	90	100	15	Normal
TM97	Dark Pulse	Dark	Special	80	100	15	Normal
TM100	Confide	Normal	Status	—	—	20	Normal
HM01	Cut	Normal	Physical	50	95	30	Normal
HM03	Surf	Water	Special	90	100	15	Adjacent

● MOVES TAUGHT BY PEOPLE

Name	Type	Kind	Pow.	Acc.	PP	Range

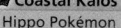 **Coastal Kalos**
Hippo Pokémon

☑ Hippopotas

048

HEIGHT: 2'07" WEIGHT: 109.1 lbs.
GENDER: ♂/♀

 It lives in arid places. Instead of perspiration, it expels grainy sand from its body.

 It enshrouds itself with sand to protect itself from germs. It does not enjoy getting wet.

TYPE Ground

ABILITY
Sand Stream

HIDDEN ABILITY
None

STAT GROWTH RATES
HP	■■■
Attack	■■■■
Defense	■■■
Sp. Atk	■■
Sp. Def	■■
Speed	■■

EGG GROUP
Field

EVOLUTION

Lv. 34

Hippopotas → Hippowdon

ITEMS SOMETIMES HELD BY WILD POKÉMON
None

Damage taken in normal battles	
Normal	×1
Fire	×1
Water	×2
Grass	×2
Electric	×0
Ice	×2
Fighting	×1
Poison	×0.5
Ground	×1
Flying	×1
Psychic	×1
Bug	×1
Rock	×0.5
Ghost	×1
Dragon	×1
Dark	×1
Steel	×1
Fairy	×1

Damage taken in Inverse Battles	
Normal	×1
Fire	×1
Water	×0.5
Grass	×0.5
Electric	×2
Ice	×0.5
Fighting	×1
Poison	×2
Ground	×1
Flying	×1
Psychic	×1
Bug	×1
Rock	×2
Ghost	×1
Dragon	×1
Dark	×1
Steel	×1
Fairy	×1

Can be used in
Inverse Battle

Battle Chateau
Battle Institute
Battle Maison
Random Matchup

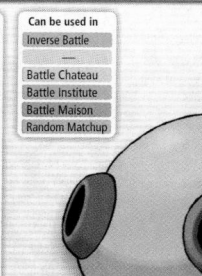

How to obtain for your Coastal Kalos Pokédex

Catch it when it pops out while you're riding Rhyhorn on Route 9.	Catch it when it pops out while you're riding Rhyhorn on Route 9.

♂     ♀

The male's body is mainly beige, and the female's body is mainly brown.

● LEVEL-UP MOVES

Lv.	Name	Type	Kind	Pow.	Acc.	PP	Range
1	Tackle	Normal	Physical	50	100	35	Normal
1	Sand Attack	Ground	Status	—	100	15	Normal
7	Bite	Dark	Physical	60	100	25	Normal
13	Yawn	Normal	Status	—	—	10	Normal
19	Take Down	Normal	Physical	90	85	20	Normal
19	Dig	Ground	Physical	80	100	10	Normal
25	Sand Tomb	Ground	Physical	35	85	15	Normal
31	Crunch	Dark	Physical	80	100	15	Normal
37	Earthquake	Ground	Physical	100	100	10	Adjacent
44	Double-Edge	Normal	Physical	120	100	15	Normal
50	Fissure	Ground	Physical	—	30	5	Normal

● TM & HM MOVES

No.	Name	Type	Kind	Pow.	Acc.	PP	Range
TM05	Roar	Normal	Status	—	—	20	Normal
TM06	Toxic	Poison	Status	—	90	10	Normal
TM10	Hidden Power	Normal	Special	60	100	15	Normal
TM11	Sunny Day	Fire	Status	—	—	5	Both Sides
TM17	Protect	Normal	Status	—	—	10	Self
TM21	Frustration	Normal	Physical	—	100	20	Normal
TM26	Earthquake	Ground	Physical	100	100	10	Adjacent
TM27	Return	Normal	Physical	—	100	20	Normal
TM28	Dig	Ground	Physical	80	100	10	Normal
TM32	Double Team	Normal	Status	—	—	15	Self
TM37	Sandstorm	Rock	Status	—	—	10	Both Sides
TM39	Rock Tomb	Rock	Physical	60	95	15	Normal
TM42	Facade	Normal	Physical	70	100	20	Normal
TM44	Rest	Psychic	Status	—	—	10	Self
TM45	Attract	Normal	Status	—	100	15	Normal
TM48	Round	Normal	Special	60	100	15	Normal
TM78	Bulldoze	Ground	Physical	60	100	20	Adjacent
TM80	Rock Slide	Rock	Physical	75	90	10	Many Others
TM87	Swagger	Normal	Status	—	90	15	Normal
TM88	Sleep Talk	Normal	Status	—	—	10	Self
TM90	Substitute	Normal	Status	—	—	10	Self
TM94	Rock Smash	Fighting	Physical	40	100	15	Normal
TM100	Confide	Normal	Status	—	—	20	Normal
HM04	Strength	Normal	Physical	80	100	15	Normal

● MOVES TAUGHT BY PEOPLE

Name	Type	Kind	Pow.	Acc.	PP	Range

● EGG MOVES

Name	Type	Kind	Pow.	Acc.	PP	Range
Stockpile	Normal	Status	—	—	20	Self
Swallow	Normal	Status	—	—	10	Self
Spit Up	Normal	Special	—	100	10	Normal
Curse	Ghost	Status	—	—	10	Varies
Slack Off	Normal	Status	—	—	10	Self
Body Slam	Normal	Physical	85	100	15	Normal
Sand Tomb	Ground	Physical	35	85	15	Normal
Revenge	Fighting	Physical	60	100	10	Normal
Sleep Talk	Normal	Status	—	—	10	Self
Whirlwind	Normal	Status	—	—	20	Normal

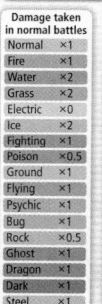 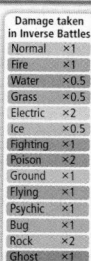

AFTER THE HALL OF FAME

CENTRAL KALOS

COASTAL KALOS

048 | Hippopotas

MOUNTAIN KALOS

ADVENTURE DATA

AFTER THE HALL OF FAME

CENTRAL KALOS

COASTAL KALOS

049 Hippowdon

MOUNTAIN KALOS

ADVENTURE DATA

Coastal Kalos

Heavyweight Pokémon

049

✔ Hippowdon

HEIGHT: 6'07" **WEIGHT:** 661.4 lbs.
GENDER: ♂/♀

TYPE Ground

ABILITY
Sand Stream

HIDDEN ABILITY
None

STAT GROWTH RATES
HP	■■■
Attack	■■■■■
Defense	■■■■■
Sp. Atk	■■■
Sp. Def	■■■
Speed	■■■

EGG GROUP
Field

X It brandishes its gaping mouth in a display of fearsome strength. It raises vast quantities of sand while attacking.

Y It blasts internally stored sand from ports on its body to create a towering twister for attack.

EVOLUTION

Hippopotas → Lv. 34 → Hippowdon

ITEMS SOMETIMES HELD BY WILD POKÉMON
None

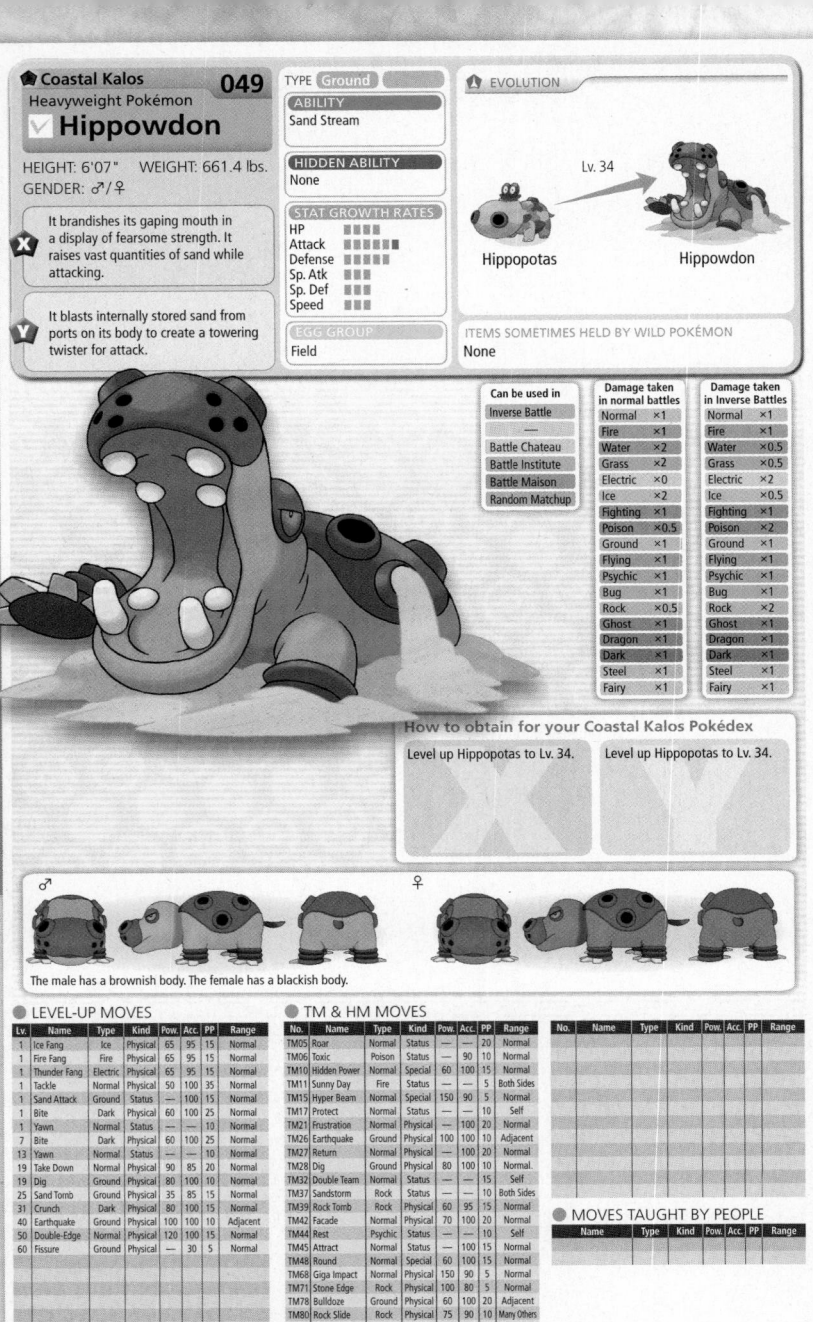

Can be used in
Inverse Battle
—
Battle Chateau
Battle Institute
Battle Maison
Random Matchup

Damage taken in normal battles		Damage taken in Inverse Battles	
Normal	×1	Normal	×1
Fire	×1	Fire	×1
Water	×2	Water	×0.5
Grass	×2	Grass	×0.5
Electric	×0	Electric	×1
Ice	×2	Ice	×0.5
Fighting	×1	Fighting	×1
Poison	×0.5	Poison	×2
Ground	×1	Ground	×1
Flying	×1	Flying	×1
Psychic	×1	Psychic	×1
Bug	×1	Bug	×1
Rock	×0.5	Rock	×2
Ghost	×1	Ghost	×1
Dragon	×1	Dragon	×1
Dark	×1	Dark	×1
Steel	×1	Steel	×1
Fairy	×1	Fairy	×1

How to obtain for your Coastal Kalos Pokédex

X	**Y**
Level up Hippopotas to Lv. 34.	Level up Hippopotas to Lv. 34.

♂ ♀

The male has a brownish body. The female has a blackish body.

● LEVEL-UP MOVES

Lv.	Name	Type	Kind	Pow.	Acc.	PP	Range
1	Ice Fang	Ice	Physical	65	95	15	Normal
1	Fire Fang	Fire	Physical	65	95	15	Normal
1	Thunder Fang	Electric	Physical	65	95	15	Normal
1	Tackle	Normal	Physical	50	100	35	Normal
1	Sand Attack	Ground	Status	—	100	15	Normal
1	Bite	Dark	Physical	60	100	25	Normal
1	Yawn	Normal	Status	—	—	10	Normal
7	Bite	Dark	Physical	60	100	25	Normal
13	Yawn	Normal	Status	—	—	10	Normal
19	Take Down	Normal	Physical	90	85	20	Normal
19	Dig	Ground	Physical	80	100	10	Normal
25	Sand Tomb	Ground	Physical	35	85	15	Normal
31	Crunch	Dark	Physical	80	100	15	Normal
41	Earthquake	Ground	Physical	100	100	10	Adjacent
50	Double-Edge	Normal	Physical	120	100	15	Normal
60	Fissure	Ground	Physical	—	30	5	Normal

● TM & HM MOVES

No.	Name	Type	Kind	Pow.	Acc.	PP	Range
TM05	Roar	Normal	Status	—	—	20	Normal
TM06	Toxic	Poison	Status	—	90	10	Normal
TM10	Hidden Power	Normal	Special	60	100	15	Normal
TM11	Sunny Day	Fire	Status	—	—	5	Both Sides
TM15	Hyper Beam	Normal	Special	150	90	5	Normal
TM17	Protect	Normal	Status	—	—	10	Self
TM21	Frustration	Normal	Physical	—	100	20	Normal
TM26	Earthquake	Ground	Physical	100	100	10	Adjacent
TM27	Return	Normal	Physical	—	100	20	Normal
TM28	Dig	Ground	Physical	80	100	10	Normal.
TM32	Double Team	Normal	Status	—	—	15	Self
TM37	Sandstorm	Rock	Status	—	—	10	Both Sides
TM39	Rock Tomb	Rock	Physical	60	95	15	Normal
TM42	Facade	Normal	Physical	70	100	20	Normal
TM44	Rest	Psychic	Status	—	—	10	Self
TM45	Attract	Normal	Status	—	100	15	Normal
TM48	Round	Normal	Special	60	100	15	Normal
TM68	Giga Impact	Normal	Physical	150	90	5	Normal
TM71	Stone Edge	Rock	Physical	100	80	5	Normal
TM78	Bulldoze	Ground	Physical	60	100	20	Adjacent
TM80	Rock Slide	Rock	Physical	75	90	10	Many Others
TM87	Swagger	Normal	Status	—	90	15	Normal
TM88	Sleep Talk	Normal	Status	—	—	10	Self
TM90	Substitute	Normal	Status	—	—	10	Self
TM94	Rock Smash	Fighting	Physical	40	100	15	Normal
TM100	Confide	Normal	Status	—	—	20	Normal
HM04	Strength	Normal	Physical	80	100	15	Normal

● MOVES TAUGHT BY PEOPLE

Name	Type	Kind	Pow.	Acc.	PP	Range

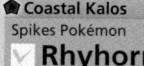

Coastal Kalos 050
Spikes Pokémon

☑ Rhyhorn

HEIGHT: 3'03"　WEIGHT: 253.5 lbs.
GENDER: ♂/♀

X Strong, but not too bright, this Pokémon can shatter even a skyscraper with its charging Tackles.

Y It is inept at turning because of its four short legs. It can only charge and run in one direction.

TYPE Ground | Rock

ABILITIES
Lightning Rod
Rock Head

HIDDEN ABILITY
Reckless

STAT GROWTH RATES
HP	■■■
Attack	■■■■
Defense	■■■■
Sp. Atk	■■■
Sp. Def	■
Speed	■■

EGG GROUPS
Monster, Field

EVOLUTION

Lv. 42 　Link Trade with Protector

Rhyhorn 　Rhydon 　Rhyperior

ITEMS SOMETIMES HELD BY WILD POKÉMON
None

Damage taken in normal battles		Damage taken in Inverse Battles	
Normal	×0.5	Normal	×2
Fire	×0.5	Fire	×2
Water	×4	Water	×0.25
Grass	×4	Grass	×0.25
Electric	×0	Electric	×2
Ice	×2	Ice	×0.5
Fighting	×2	Fighting	×0.5
Poison	×0.25	Poison	×4
Ground	×2	Ground	×0.5
Flying	×0.5	Flying	×2
Psychic	×1	Psychic	×1
Bug	×1	Bug	×1
Rock	×0.5	Rock	×2
Ghost	×1	Ghost	×1
Dragon	×1	Dragon	×1
Dark	×1	Dark	×1
Steel	×2	Steel	×0.5
Fairy	×1	Fairy	×1

Can be used in
Inverse Battle
—
Battle Chateau
Battle Institute
Battle Maison
Random Matchup

How to obtain for your Coastal Kalos Pokédex
Catch in Glittering Cave. | Catch in Glittering Cave.

♂　　　　　　　♀

The male has a longer horn. The female has a shorter horn.

● LEVEL-UP MOVES
Lv.	Name	Type	Kind	Pow.	Acc.	PP	Range
1	Horn Attack	Normal	Physical	65	100	25	Normal
1	Tail Whip	Normal	Status	—	100	30	Many Others
8	Stomp	Normal	Physical	65	100	20	Normal
12	Fury Attack	Normal	Physical	15	85	20	Normal
17	Scary Face	Normal	Status	—	100	10	Normal
23	Rock Blast	Rock	Physical	25	90	10	Normal
30	Bulldoze	Ground	Physical	60	100	20	Adjacent
34	Chip Away	Normal	Physical	70	100	20	Normal
41	Take Down	Normal	Physical	90	85	20	Normal
45	Drill Run	Ground	Physical	80	95	10	Normal
52	Stone Edge	Rock	Physical	100	80	5	Normal
56	Earthquake	Ground	Physical	100	100	10	Adjacent
63	Horn Drill	Normal	Physical	—	30	5	Normal
67	Megahorn	Bug	Physical	120	85	10	Normal

● TM & HM MOVES
No.	Name	Type	Kind	Pow.	Acc.	PP	Range
TM05	Roar	Normal	Status	—	—	20	Normal
TM06	Toxic	Poison	Status	—	90	10	Normal
TM10	Hidden Power	Normal	Special	60	100	15	Normal
TM11	Sunny Day	Fire	Status	—	—	5	Both Sides
TM13	Ice Beam	Ice	Special	90	100	10	Normal
TM14	Blizzard	Ice	Special	110	70	5	Many Others
TM17	Protect	Normal	Status	—	—	10	Self
TM18	Rain Dance	Water	Status	—	—	5	Both Sides
TM21	Frustration	Normal	Physical	—	100	20	Normal
TM24	Thunderbolt	Electric	Special	90	100	15	Normal
TM25	Thunder	Electric	Special	110	70	10	Normal
TM26	Earthquake	Ground	Physical	100	100	10	Adjacent
TM27	Return	Normal	Physical	—	100	20	Normal
TM28	Dig	Ground	Physical	80	100	10	Normal
TM32	Double Team	Normal	Status	—	—	15	Self
TM35	Flamethrower	Fire	Special	90	100	15	Normal
TM37	Sandstorm	Rock	Status	—	—	10	Both Sides
TM38	Fire Blast	Fire	Special	110	85	5	Normal
TM39	Rock Tomb	Rock	Physical	60	95	15	Normal
TM42	Facade	Normal	Physical	70	100	20	Normal
TM44	Rest	Psychic	Status	—	—	10	Self
TM45	Attract	Normal	Status	—	100	15	Normal
TM46	Thief	Dark	Physical	60	100	25	Normal
TM48	Round	Normal	Special	60	100	15	Normal
TM59	Incinerate	Fire	Special	60	100	15	Many Others
TM66	Payback	Dark	Physical	50	100	10	Normal
TM69	Rock Polish	Rock	Status	—	—	20	Self
TM71	Stone Edge	Rock	Physical	100	80	5	Normal
TM75	Swords Dance	Normal	Status	—	—	20	Self
TM78	Bulldoze	Ground	Physical	60	100	20	Adjacent
TM80	Rock Slide	Rock	Physical	75	90	10	Many Others
TM84	Poison Jab	Poison	Physical	80	100	20	Normal
TM87	Swagger	Normal	Status	—	90	15	Normal

No.	Name	Type	Kind	Pow.	Acc.	PP	Range
TM88	Sleep Talk	Normal	Status	—	—	10	Self
TM90	Substitute	Normal	Status	—	—	10	Self
TM94	Rock Smash	Fighting	Physical	40	100	15	Normal
TM100	Confide	Normal	Status	—	—	20	Normal
HM04	Strength	Normal	Physical	80	100	15	Normal

● MOVES TAUGHT BY PEOPLE
Name	Type	Kind	Pow.	Acc.	PP	Range

● EGG MOVES
Name	Type	Kind	Pow.	Acc.	PP	Range
Crunch	Dark	Physical	80	100	15	Normal
Reversal	Fighting	Physical	—	100	15	Normal
Counter	Fighting	Physical	—	100	20	Varies
Magnitude	Ground	Physical	—	100	30	Adjacent
Curse	Ghost	Status	—	—	10	Varies
Crush Claw	Normal	Physical	75	95	10	Normal
Dragon Rush	Dragon	Physical	100	75	10	Normal
Ice Fang	Ice	Physical	65	95	15	Normal
Fire Fang	Fire	Physical	65	95	15	Normal
Thunder Fang	Electric	Physical	65	95	15	Normal
Skull Bash	Normal	Physical	130	100	10	Normal
Iron Tail	Steel	Physical	100	75	15	Normal
Rock Climb	Normal	Physical	90	85	20	Normal
Rototiller	Ground	Status	—	—	10	Adjacent
Metal Burst	Steel	Physical	—	100	10	Varies
Guard Split	Psychic	Status	—	—	10	Normal

AFTER THE HALL OF FAME

CENTRAL KALOS

COASTAL KALOS

050 Rhyhorn

MOUNTAIN KALOS

ADVENTURE DATA

AFTER THE HALL OF FAME

CENTRAL KALOS

COASTAL KALOS

051

Rhydon

MOUNTAIN KALOS

ADVENTURE DATA

● Coastal Kalos 051
Drill Pokémon
☑ Rhydon

TYPE Ground Rock

ABILITIES
Lightning Rod
Rock Head

HIDDEN ABILITY
Reckless

HEIGHT: 6'03" WEIGHT: 264.6 lbs.
GENDER: ♂/♀

STAT GROWTH RATES
HP ▪▪▪▪
Attack ▪▪▪▪▪▪▪
Defense ▪▪▪▪▪
Sp. Atk ▪▪
Sp. Def ▪▪
Speed ▪▪

EGG GROUPS
Monster, Field

X: Protected by an armor-like hide, it is capable of living in molten lava of 3,600 degrees Fahrenheit.

Y: It begins walking on its hind legs after evolution. It can punch holes through boulders with its horn.

EVOLUTION
Rhyhorn → (Lv. 42) Rhydon → (Link Trade with Protector) Rhyperior

ITEMS SOMETIMES HELD BY WILD POKÉMON
None

Can be used in
Inverse Battle
—
Battle Chateau
Battle Institute
Battle Maison
Random Matchup

Damage taken in normal battles
Normal	×0.5
Fire	×0.5
Water	×4
Grass	×4
Electric	×0
Ice	×2
Fighting	×2
Poison	×0.25
Ground	×2
Flying	×0.5
Psychic	×1
Bug	×1
Rock	×0.5
Ghost	×1
Dragon	×1
Dark	×1
Steel	×2
Fairy	×1

Damage taken in Inverse Battles
Normal	×2
Fire	×2
Water	×0.25
Grass	×0.25
Electric	×2
Ice	×0.5
Fighting	×0.5
Poison	×4
Ground	×0.5
Flying	×2
Psychic	×1
Bug	×1
Rock	×2
Ghost	×1
Dragon	×1
Dark	×1
Steel	×0.5
Fairy	×1

How to obtain for your Coastal Kalos Pokédex
Level up Rhyhorn to Lv. 42. (X)
Level up Rhyhorn to Lv. 42. (Y)

The male has a longer horn on its face. The female has a shorter horn on its face.

● LEVEL-UP MOVES
Lv.	Name	Type	Kind	Pow.	Acc.	PP	Range
1	Megahorn	Bug	Physical	120	85	10	Normal
1	Horn Drill	Normal	Physical	—	30	5	Normal
1	Horn Attack	Normal	Physical	65	100	25	Normal
1	Tail Whip	Normal	Status	—	100	30	Many Others
1	Stomp	Normal	Physical	65	100	20	Normal
8	Fury Attack	Normal	Physical	15	85	20	Normal
8	Stomp	Normal	Physical	65	100	20	Normal
12	Fury Attack	Normal	Physical	15	85	20	Normal
19	Scary Face	Normal	Status	—	100	10	Normal
23	Rock Blast	Rock	Physical	25	90	10	Normal
30	Bulldoze	Ground	Physical	60	100	20	Adjacent
34	Chip Away	Normal	Physical	70	100	20	Normal
41	Take Down	Normal	Physical	90	85	20	Normal
42	Hammer Arm	Fighting	Physical	100	90	10	Normal
47	Fury Run	Ground	Physical	80	95	10	Normal
56	Stone Edge	Rock	Physical	100	80	5	Normal
62	Earthquake	Ground	Physical	100	100	10	Adjacent
71	Horn Drill	Normal	Physical	—	30	5	Normal
77	Megahorn	Bug	Physical	120	85	10	Normal

● TM & HM MOVES
No.	Name	Type	Kind	Pow.	Acc.	PP	Range
TM05	Roar	Normal	Status	—	—	20	Normal
TM06	Toxic	Poison	Status	—	90	10	Normal
TM10	Hidden Power	Normal	Special	60	100	15	Normal
TM11	Sunny Day	Fire	Status	—	—	5	Both Sides
TM13	Ice Beam	Ice	Special	90	100	10	Normal
TM14	Blizzard	Ice	Special	110	70	5	Many Others
TM15	Hyper Beam	Normal	Special	150	90	5	Normal
TM17	Protect	Normal	Status	—	—	10	Self
TM18	Rain Dance	Water	Status	—	—	5	Both Sides
TM21	Frustration	Normal	Physical	—	100	20	Normal
TM23	Smack Down	Rock	Physical	50	100	15	Normal
TM24	Thunderbolt	Electric	Special	90	100	15	Normal
TM25	Thunder	Electric	Special	110	70	10	Normal
TM26	Earthquake	Ground	Physical	100	100	10	Adjacent
TM27	Return	Normal	Physical	—	100	20	Normal
TM28	Dig	Ground	Physical	80	100	10	Normal
TM31	Brick Break	Fighting	Physical	75	100	15	Normal
TM32	Double Team	Normal	Status	—	—	15	Self
TM35	Flamethrower	Fire	Special	90	100	15	Normal
TM37	Sandstorm	Rock	Status	—	—	10	Both Sides
TM38	Fire Blast	Fire	Special	110	85	5	Normal
TM39	Rock Tomb	Rock	Physical	60	95	15	Normal
TM42	Facade	Normal	Physical	70	100	20	Normal
TM44	Rest	Psychic	Status	—	—	10	Self
TM45	Attract	Normal	Status	—	100	15	Normal
TM48	Round	Normal	Special	60	100	15	Normal
TM46	Thief	Dark	Physical	60	100	25	Normal
TM52	Focus Blast	Fighting	Special	120	70	5	Normal
TM56	Fling	Dark	Physical	—	100	10	Normal
TM59	Incinerate	Fire	Special	60	100	15	Many Others
TM65	Shadow Claw	Ghost	Physical	70	100	15	Normal
TM66	Payback	Dark	Physical	50	100	10	Normal
TM68	Giga Impact	Normal	Physical	150	90	5	Normal
TM69	Rock Polish	Rock	Status	—	—	20	Self
TM71	Stone Edge	Rock	Physical	100	80	5	Normal
TM75	Swords Dance	Normal	Status	—	—	20	Self
TM78	Bulldoze	Ground	Physical	60	100	20	Adjacent
TM80	Rock Slide	Rock	Physical	75	90	10	Many Others
TM82	Dragon Tail	Dragon	Physical	60	90	10	Normal
TM84	Poison Jab	Poison	Physical	80	100	20	Normal
TM87	Swagger	Normal	Status	—	90	15	Normal
TM88	Sleep Talk	Normal	Status	—	—	10	Self
TM90	Substitute	Normal	Status	—	—	10	Self
TM94	Rock Smash	Fighting	Physical	40	100	15	Normal
TM98	Power-Up Punch	Fighting	Physical	40	100	20	Normal
TM100	Confide	Normal	Status	—	—	20	Normal
HM01	Cut	Normal	Physical	50	95	30	Normal
HM03	Surf	Water	Special	90	100	15	Adjacent
HM04	Strength	Normal	Physical	80	100	15	Normal

● MOVES TAUGHT BY PEOPLE
Name	Type	Kind	Pow.	Acc.	PP	Range

🔶 Coastal Kalos 052

Drill Pokémon
Ⅴ **Rhyperior**

HEIGHT: 7'10" WEIGHT: 623.5 lbs.
GENDER: ♂/♀

 X From holes in its palms, it fires out Geodude. Its carapace can withstand volcanic eruptions.

 Y It puts rocks in holes in its palms and uses its muscles to shoot them. Geodude are shot at rare times.

TYPE	Ground	Rock

ABILITIES
Lightning Rod
Solid Rock

HIDDEN ABILITY
Reckless

STAT GROWTH RATES

Stat	
HP	■■■■
Attack	■■■■■
Defense	■■■■■■
Sp. Atk	■■■
Sp. Def	■■
Speed	■■

EGG GROUPS
Monster, Field

 EVOLUTION

Lv. 42 → Link Trade with Protector

Rhyhorn Rhydon Rhyperior

ITEMS SOMETIMES HELD BY WILD POKÉMON
None

Damage taken in normal battles		Damage taken in Inverse Battles	
Normal	×0.5	Normal	×2
Fire	×0.5	Fire	×2
Water	×4	Water	×0.25
Grass	×4	Grass	×0.25
Electric	×0	Electric	×2
Ice	×2	Ice	×0.5
Fighting	×2	Fighting	×0.5
Poison	×0.25	Poison	×4
Ground	×2	Ground	×0.5
Flying	×0.5	Flying	×2
Psychic	×1	Psychic	×1
Bug	×1	Bug	×1
Rock	×0.5	Rock	×2
Ghost	×1	Ghost	×1
Dragon	×1	Dragon	×1
Dark	×1	Dark	×1
Steel	×2	Steel	×0.5
Fairy	×1	Fairy	×1

Can be used in	
Inverse Battle	Battle Institute
—	Battle Maison
Battle Chateau	Random Matchup

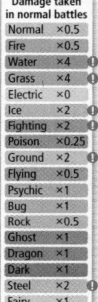

How to obtain for your Coastal Kalos Pokédex

Link Trade Rhydon while it is holding a Protector.

Link Trade Rhydon while it is holding a Protector.

♂ ♀

The male has a longer horn on top of its head. The female has a shorter horn on top of its head.

● LEVEL-UP MOVES

Lv.	Name	Type	Kind	Pow.	Acc.	PP	Range
1	Rock Wrecker	Rock	Physical	150	90	5	Normal
1	Megahorn	Bug	Physical	120	85	10	Normal
1	Horn Drill	Normal	Physical	—	30	5	Normal
1	Poison Jab	Poison	Physical	80	100	20	Normal
1	Horn Attack	Normal	Physical	65	100	25	Normal
1	Tail Whip	Normal	Status	—	100	30	Many Others
1	Stomp	Normal	Physical	65	100	20	Normal
1	Fury Attack	Normal	Physical	15	85	20	Normal
9	Stomp	Normal	Physical	65	100	20	Normal
19	Fury Attack	Normal	Physical	15	85	20	Normal
19	Scary Face	Normal	Status	—	100	10	Normal
23	Rock Blast	Rock	Physical	25	90	10	Normal
30	Chip Away	Normal	Physical	70	100	20	Normal
41	Take Down	Normal	Physical	90	85	20	Normal
42	Hammer Arm	Fighting	Physical	100	90	10	Normal
47	Drill Run	Ground	Physical	80	95	10	Normal
56	Stone Edge	Rock	Physical	100	80	5	Normal
62	Earthquake	Ground	Physical	100	100	10	Adjacent
71	Horn Drill	Normal	Physical	—	30	5	Normal
77	Megahorn	Bug	Physical	120	85	10	Normal
86	Rock Wrecker	Rock	Physical	150	90	5	Normal

● TM & HM MOVES

No.	Name	Type	Kind	Pow.	Acc.	PP	Range
TM05	Roar	Normal	Status	—	—	20	Normal
TM06	Toxic	Poison	Status	—	90	10	Normal
TM10	Hidden Power	Normal	Special	60	100	15	Normal
TM11	Sunny Day	Fire	Status	—	—	5	Both Sides
TM13	Ice Beam	Ice	Special	90	100	10	Normal
TM14	Blizzard	Ice	Special	110	70	5	Many Others
TM15	Hyper Beam	Normal	Special	150	90	5	Normal
TM17	Protect	Normal	Status	—	—	10	Self
TM18	Rain Dance	Water	Status	—	—	5	Both Sides
TM21	Frustration	Normal	Physical	—	100	20	Normal
TM23	Smack Down	Rock	Physical	50	100	15	Normal
TM24	Thunderbolt	Electric	Special	90	100	15	Normal
TM25	Thunder	Electric	Special	110	70	10	Normal
TM26	Earthquake	Ground	Physical	100	100	10	Adjacent
TM27	Return	Normal	Physical	—	100	20	Normal
TM28	Dig	Ground	Physical	80	100	10	Normal
TM31	Brick Break	Fighting	Physical	75	100	15	Normal
TM32	Double Team	Normal	Status	—	—	15	Self
TM35	Flamethrower	Fire	Special	90	100	15	Normal
TM37	Sandstorm	Rock	Status	—	—	10	Both Sides
TM38	Fire Blast	Fire	Special	110	85	5	Normal
TM39	Rock Tomb	Rock	Physical	60	95	15	Normal
TM42	Facade	Normal	Physical	70	100	20	Normal
TM44	Rest	Psychic	Status	—	—	10	Self
TM45	Attract	Normal	Status	—	100	15	Normal
TM46	Thief	Dark	Physical	60	100	25	Normal
TM48	Round	Normal	Special	60	100	15	Normal
TM52	Focus Blast	Fighting	Special	120	70	5	Normal
TM56	Fling	Dark	Physical	—	100	10	Normal
TM59	Incinerate	Fire	Special	60	100	15	Many Others
TM65	Shadow Claw	Ghost	Physical	70	100	15	Normal
TM66	Payback	Dark	Physical	50	100	10	Normal
TM68	Giga Impact	Normal	Physical	150	90	5	Normal

No.	Name	Type	Kind	Pow.	Acc.	PP	Range
TM69	Rock Polish	Rock	Status	—	—	20	Self
TM71	Stone Edge	Rock	Physical	100	80	5	Normal
TM75	Swords Dance	Normal	Status	—	—	20	Self
TM78	Bulldoze	Ground	Physical	60	100	20	Adjacent
TM80	Rock Slide	Rock	Physical	75	90	10	Many Others
TM82	Dragon Tail	Dragon	Physical	60	90	10	Normal
TM84	Poison Jab	Poison	Physical	80	100	20	Normal
TM87	Swagger	Normal	Status	—	90	15	Normal
TM88	Sleep Talk	Normal	Status	—	—	10	Self
TM90	Substitute	Normal	Status	—	—	10	Self
TM91	Flash Cannon	Steel	Special	80	100	10	Normal
TM94	Rock Smash	Fighting	Physical	40	100	15	Normal
TM96	Power-Up Punch	Fighting	Physical	40	100	20	Normal
TM100	Confide	Normal	Status	—	—	20	Normal
HM01	Cut	Normal	Physical	50	95	30	Normal
HM03	Surf	Water	Special	90	100	15	Adjacent
HM04	Strength	Normal	Physical	80	100	15	Normal

● MOVES TAUGHT BY PEOPLE

Name	Type	Kind	Pow.	Acc.	PP	Range

AFTER THE HALL OF FAME

CENTRAL KALOS

COASTAL KALOS

052 Rhyperior

MOUNTAIN KALOS

ADVENTURE DATA

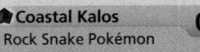

Coastal Kalos 053
Rock Snake Pokémon
☑ **Onix**

HEIGHT: 28'10" WEIGHT: 463.0 lbs.
GENDER: ♂/♀

X Burrows at high speed in search of food. The tunnels it leaves are used as homes by Diglett.

Y It usually lives underground. It searches for food while boring its way through the ground at 50 miles per hour.

TYPE Rock Ground

ABILITIES
Rock Head
Sturdy

HIDDEN ABILITY
Weak Armor

STAT GROWTH RATES
HP	▪▪
Attack	▪▪
Defense	▪▪▪▪▪▪▪
Sp. Atk	▪
Sp. Def	▪▪
Speed	▪▪▪

EGG GROUP
Mineral

EVOLUTION

Link Trade with Metal Coat

Onix → Steelix

ITEMS SOMETIMES HELD BY WILD POKÉMON
None

Can be used in
Inverse Battle
—
Battle Chateau
Battle Institute
Battle Maison
Random Matchup

Damage taken in normal battles	
Normal	×0.5
Fire	×0.5
Water	×4
Grass	×4
Electric	×0
Ice	×2
Fighting	×2
Poison	×0.25
Ground	×2
Flying	×0.5
Psychic	×1
Bug	×1
Rock	×0.5
Ghost	×1
Dragon	×1
Dark	×1
Steel	×2
Fairy	×1

Damage taken in Inverse Battles	
Normal	×2
Fire	×2
Water	×0.25
Grass	×0.25
Electric	×2
Ice	×0.5
Fighting	×0.5
Poison	×4
Ground	×0.5
Flying	×2
Psychic	×1
Bug	×2
Rock	×2
Ghost	×1
Dragon	×1
Dark	×1
Steel	×0.5
Fairy	×1

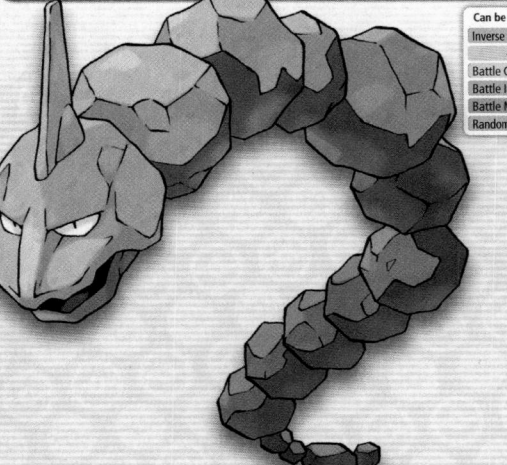

Same form for ♂/♀

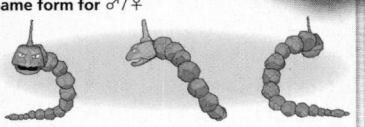

How to obtain for your Coastal Kalos Pokédex

❶ Catch in Glittering Cave.
❷ Catch after it appears from a cracked rock in the deepest part of Glittering Cave (using Rock Smash).

❶ Catch in Glittering Cave.
❷ Catch after it appears from a cracked rock in the deepest part of Glittering Cave (using Rock Smash).

● **LEVEL-UP MOVES**

Lv.	Name	Type	Kind	Pow.	Acc.	PP	Range
1	Mud Sport	Ground	Status	—	—	15	Both Sides
1	Tackle	Normal	Physical	50	100	35	Normal
1	Harden	Normal	Status	—	—	30	Self
1	Bind	Normal	Physical	15	85	20	Normal
4	Curse	Ghost	Status	—	—	10	Varies
7	Rock Throw	Rock	Physical	50	90	15	Normal
10	Rock Tomb	Rock	Physical	60	95	15	Normal
13	Rage	Normal	Physical	20	100	20	Normal
16	Stealth Rock	Rock	Status	—	—	20	Other Side
19	Rock Polish	Rock	Status	—	—	20	Self
20	Gyro Ball	Steel	Physical	—	100	5	Normal
22	Smack Down	Rock	Physical	50	100	15	Normal
25	Dragon Breath	Dragon	Special	60	100	20	Normal
28	Slam	Normal	Physical	80	75	20	Normal
31	Screech	Normal	Status	—	85	40	Normal
34	Rock Slide	Rock	Physical	75	90	10	Many Others
37	Sand Tomb	Ground	Physical	35	85	15	Normal
40	Iron Tail	Steel	Physical	100	75	15	Normal
43	Dig	Ground	Physical	80	100	10	Normal
46	Stone Edge	Rock	Physical	100	80	5	Normal
49	Double-Edge	Normal	Physical	120	100	15	Normal
52	Sandstorm	Rock	Status	—	—	10	Both Sides

● **TM & HM MOVES**

No.	Name	Type	Kind	Pow.	Acc.	PP	Range
TM05	Roar	Normal	Status	—	—	20	Normal
TM06	Toxic	Poison	Status	—	90	10	Normal
TM10	Hidden Power	Normal	Special	60	100	15	Normal
TM11	Sunny Day	Fire	Status	—	—	5	Both Sides
TM12	Taunt	Dark	Status	—	100	20	Normal
TM17	Protect	Normal	Status	—	—	10	Self
TM21	Frustration	Normal	Physical	—	100	20	Normal
TM23	Smack Down	Rock	Physical	50	100	15	Normal
TM26	Earthquake	Ground	Physical	100	100	10	Adjacent
TM27	Return	Normal	Physical	—	100	20	Normal
TM28	Dig	Ground	Physical	80	100	10	Normal
TM32	Double Team	Normal	Status	—	—	15	Self
TM37	Sandstorm	Rock	Status	—	—	10	Both Sides
TM39	Rock Tomb	Rock	Physical	60	95	15	Normal
TM41	Torment	Dark	Status	—	100	15	Normal
TM42	Facade	Normal	Physical	70	100	20	Normal
TM44	Rest	Psychic	Status	—	—	10	Self
TM45	Attract	Normal	Status	—	100	15	Normal
TM48	Round	Normal	Special	60	100	15	Normal
TM64	Explosion	Normal	Physical	250	100	5	Adjacent
TM66	Payback	Dark	Physical	50	100	10	Normal
TM69	Rock Polish	Rock	Status	—	—	20	Self
TM71	Stone Edge	Rock	Physical	100	80	5	Normal
TM74	Gyro Ball	Steel	Physical	—	100	5	Normal
TM77	Psych Up	Normal	Status	—	—	10	Normal
TM78	Bulldoze	Ground	Physical	60	100	20	Adjacent
TM80	Rock Slide	Rock	Physical	75	90	10	Many Others
TM82	Dragon Tail	Dragon	Physical	60	90	10	Normal
TM87	Swagger	Normal	Status	—	90	15	Normal
TM88	Sleep Talk	Normal	Status	—	—	10	Self
TM90	Substitute	Normal	Status	—	—	10	Self
TM91	Flash Cannon	Steel	Special	80	100	10	Normal
TM94	Rock Smash	Fighting	Physical	40	100	15	Normal

No.	Name	Type	Kind	Pow.	Acc.	PP	Range
TM96	Nature Power	Normal	Status	—	—	20	Normal
TM100	Confide	Normal	Status	—	—	20	Normal
HM04	Strength	Normal	Physical	80	100	15	Normal

● **MOVES TAUGHT BY PEOPLE**

Name	Type	Kind	Pow.	Acc.	PP	Range

● **EGG MOVES**

Name	Type	Kind	Pow.	Acc.	PP	Range
Flail	Normal	Physical	—	100	15	Normal
Block	Normal	Status	—	—	5	Normal
Defense Curl	Normal	Status	—	—	40	Self
Rollout	Rock	Physical	30	90	20	Normal
Rock Blast	Rock	Physical	25	90	10	Normal
Rock Climb	Normal	Physical	90	85	20	Normal
Heavy Slam	Steel	Physical	—	100	10	Normal
Stealth Rock	Rock	Status	—	—	20	Other Side
Rototiller	Ground	Status	—	—	10	Adjacent

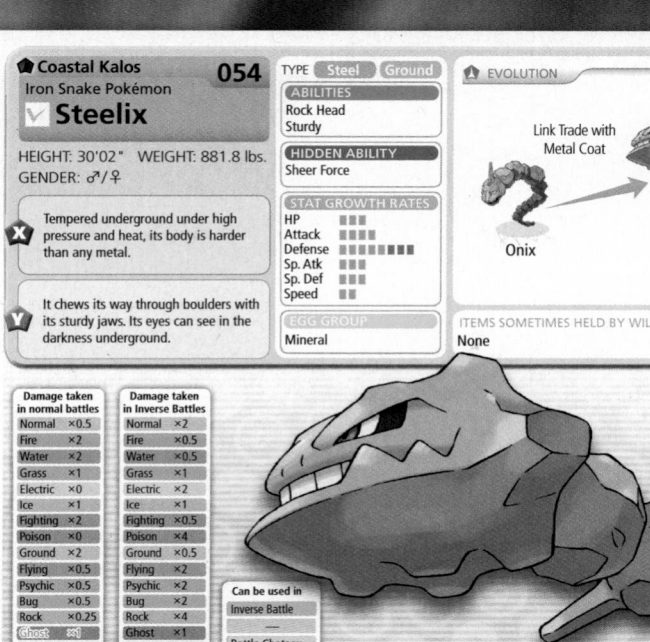

Coastal Kalos — 054
Iron Snake Pokémon
∨ Steelix

TYPE Steel / Ground

ABILITIES
Rock Head
Sturdy

HIDDEN ABILITY
Sheer Force

HEIGHT: 30'02" WEIGHT: 881.8 lbs.
GENDER: ♂/♀

X Tempered underground under high pressure and heat, its body is harder than any metal.

Y It chews its way through boulders with its sturdy jaws. Its eyes can see in the darkness underground.

STAT GROWTH RATES
HP	■■■
Attack	■■■■
Defense	■■■■■■■■
Sp. Atk	■■■
Sp. Def	■■■
Speed	■■

EGG GROUP
Mineral

EVOLUTION

Link Trade with Metal Coat

Onix → Steelix

ITEMS SOMETIMES HELD BY WILD POKÉMON
None

Damage taken in normal battles
Normal	×0.5
Fire	×2
Water	×2
Grass	×1
Electric	×0
Ice	×1
Fighting	×2
Poison	×0
Ground	×2
Flying	×0.5
Psychic	×0.5
Bug	×0.5
Rock	×0.25
Ghost	×1
Dragon	×0.5
Dark	×1
Steel	×0.5
Fairy	×0.5

Damage taken in Inverse Battles
Normal	×2
Fire	×0.5
Water	×0.5
Grass	×1
Electric	×2
Ice	×1
Fighting	×0.5
Poison	×4
Ground	×0.5
Flying	×2
Psychic	×2
Bug	×2
Rock	×4
Ghost	×1
Dragon	×2
Dark	×1
Steel	×2
Fairy	×2

Can be used in
Inverse Battle
—
Battle Chateau
Battle Institute
Battle Maison
Random Matchup

How to obtain for your Coastal Kalos Pokédex
♂
1. Trade the man in the Cyllage City Pokémon Center a Luvdisc.
2. Link Trade Onix while it is holding a Metal Coat.

♀
1. Trade the man in the Cyllage City Pokémon Center a Luvdisc.
2. Link Trade Onix while it is holding a Metal Coat.

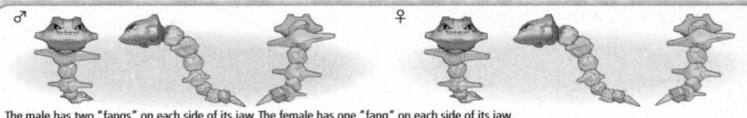

The male has two "fangs" on each side of its jaw. The female has one "fang" on each side of its jaw.

● LEVEL-UP MOVES
Lv.	Name	Type	Kind	Pow.	Acc.	PP	Range
1	Thunder Fang	Electric	Physical	65	95	15	Normal
1	Ice Fang	Ice	Physical	65	95	15	Normal
1	Fire Fang	Fire	Physical	65	95	15	Normal
1	Mud Sport	Ground	Status	—	—	15	Both Sides
1	Tackle	Normal	Physical	50	100	35	Normal
1	Harden	Normal	Status	—	—	30	Self
1	Bind	Normal	Physical	15	85	20	Normal
4	Curse	Ghost	Status	—	—	10	Varies
7	Rock Throw	Rock	Physical	50	90	15	Normal
10	Rock Tomb	Rock	Physical	60	95	15	Normal
13	Rage	Normal	Physical	20	100	20	Normal
16	Stealth Rock	Rock	Status	—	—	20	Other Side
19	Autotomize	Steel	Status	—	—	15	Self
20	Gyro Ball	Steel	Physical	—	100	5	Normal
22	Smack Down	Rock	Physical	50	100	15	Normal
25	Dragon Breath	Dragon	Special	60	100	20	Normal
28	Slam	Normal	Physical	80	75	20	Normal
31	Screech	Normal	Status	—	85	40	Normal
34	Rock Slide	Rock	Physical	75	90	10	Many Others
37	Crunch	Dark	Physical	80	100	15	Normal
40	Iron Tail	Steel	Physical	100	75	15	Normal
43	Dig	Ground	Physical	80	100	10	Normal
46	Stone Edge	Rock	Physical	100	80	5	Normal
49	Double-Edge	Normal	Physical	120	100	15	Normal
52	Sandstorm	Rock	Status	—	—	10	Both Sides

● TM & HM MOVES
No.	Name	Type	Kind	Pow.	Acc.	PP	Range
TM05	Roar	Normal	Status	—	—	20	Normal
TM06	Toxic	Poison	Status	—	90	10	Normal
TM10	Hidden Power	Normal	Special	60	100	15	Normal
TM11	Sunny Day	Fire	Status	—	—	5	Both Sides
TM12	Taunt	Dark	Status	—	100	20	Normal
TM15	Hyper Beam	Normal	Special	150	90	5	Normal
TM17	Protect	Normal	Status	—	—	10	Self
TM21	Frustration	Normal	Physical	—	100	20	Normal
TM23	Smack Down	Rock	Physical	50	100	15	Normal
TM26	Earthquake	Ground	Physical	100	100	10	Adjacent
TM27	Return	Normal	Physical	—	100	20	Normal
TM28	Dig	Ground	Physical	80	100	10	Normal
TM32	Double Team	Normal	Status	—	—	15	Self
TM37	Sandstorm	Rock	Status	—	—	10	Both Sides
TM39	Rock Tomb	Rock	Physical	60	95	15	Normal
TM41	Torment	Dark	Status	—	100	15	Normal
TM42	Facade	Normal	Physical	70	100	20	Normal
TM44	Rest	Psychic	Status	—	—	10	Self
TM45	Attract	Normal	Status	—	100	15	Normal
TM48	Round	Normal	Special	60	100	15	Normal
TM64	Explosion	Normal	Physical	250	100	5	Adjacent
TM66	Payback	Dark	Physical	50	100	10	Normal
TM68	Giga Impact	Normal	Physical	150	90	5	Normal
TM69	Rock Polish	Rock	Status	—	—	20	Self
TM71	Stone Edge	Rock	Physical	100	80	5	Normal
TM74	Gyro Ball	Steel	Physical	—	100	5	Normal
TM77	Psych Up	Normal	Status	—	—	10	Normal
TM78	Bulldoze	Ground	Physical	60	100	20	Adjacent
TM80	Rock Slide	Rock	Physical	75	90	10	Many Others
TM82	Dragon Tail	Dragon	Physical	60	90	10	Normal
TM87	Swagger	Normal	Status	—	90	15	Normal
TM88	Sleep Talk	Normal	Status	—	—	10	Self
TM90	Substitute	Normal	Status	—	—	10	Self
TM91	Flash Cannon	Steel	Special	80	100	10	Normal
TM94	Rock Smash	Fighting	Physical	40	100	15	Normal
TM96	Nature Power	Normal	Status	—	—	20	Normal
TM97	Dark Pulse	Dark	Special	80	100	15	Normal
TM100	Confide	Normal	Status	—	—	20	Normal
HM01	Cut	Normal	Physical	50	95	30	Normal
HM04	Strength	Normal	Physical	80	100	15	Normal

● MOVES TAUGHT BY PEOPLE
Name	Type	Kind	Pow.	Acc.	PP	Range

AFTER THE HALL OF FAME

CENTRAL KALOS

COASTAL KALOS

054 Steelix

MOUNTAIN KALOS

ADVENTURE DATA

AFTER THE HALL OF FAME

CENTRAL KALOS

COASTAL KALOS

055

Woobat

MOUNTAIN KALOS

ADVENTURE DATA

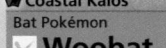

Coastal Kalos — 055

Bat Pokémon

✓ Woobat

HEIGHT: 1'04" WEIGHT: 4.6 lbs.
GENDER: ♂/♀

TYPE Psychic / Flying

ABILITIES
Unaware
Klutz

HIDDEN ABILITY
Simple

STAT GROWTH RATES
HP	▪▪
Attack	▪▪
Defense	▪▪
Sp. Atk	▪▪▪
Sp. Def	▪▪
Speed	▪▪▪▪

EGG GROUPS
Field, Flying

X Its habitat is dark forests and caves. It emits ultrasonic waves from its nose to learn about its surroundings.

Y The heart-shaped mark left on a body after a Woobat has been attached to it is said to bring good fortune.

EVOLUTION

Woobat → Level up with high friendship → Swoobat

ITEMS SOMETIMES HELD BY WILD POKÉMON
None

Damage taken in normal battles		Damage taken in Inverse Battles	
Normal	×1	Normal	×1
Fire	×1	Fire	×1
Water	×1	Water	×1
Grass	×0.5	Grass	×2
Electric	×2	Electric	×0.5
Ice	×2	Ice	×0.5
Fighting	×0.25	Fighting	×4
Poison	×1	Poison	×1
Ground	×0	Ground	×2
Flying	×1	Flying	×1
Psychic	×0.5	Psychic	×2
Bug	×1	Bug	×1
Rock	×2	Rock	×0.5
Ghost	×2	Ghost	×0.5
Dragon	×1	Dragon	×1
Dark	×2	Dark	×0.5
Steel	×1	Steel	×1
Fairy	×1	Fairy	×1

Can be used in	
Inverse Battle	Battle Institute
Sky Battle	Battle Maison
Battle Chateau	Random Matchup

Same form for ♂ / ♀

How to obtain for your Coastal Kalos Pokédex

❶ Catch when it ambushes you from the roof of Glittering Cave.

❷ Catch when it ambushes you from the roof of Reflection Cave.

❶ Catch when it ambushes you from the roof of Glittering Cave.

❷ Catch when it ambushes you from the roof of Reflection Cave.

● LEVEL-UP MOVES

Lv.	Name	Type	Kind	Pow.	Acc.	PP	Range
1	Confusion	Psychic	Special	50	100	25	Normal
4	Odor Sleuth	Normal	Status	—	—	40	Normal
8	Gust	Flying	Special	40	100	35	Normal
12	Assurance	Dark	Physical	60	100	10	Normal
15	Heart Stamp	Psychic	Physical	60	100	25	Normal
19	Imprison	Psychic	Status	—	—	10	Self
21	Air Cutter	Flying	Special	60	95	25	Many Others
25	Attract	Normal	Status	—	100	15	Normal
29	Amnesia	Psychic	Status	—	—	20	Self
29	Calm Mind	Psychic	Status	—	—	20	Self
32	Air Slash	Flying	Special	75	95	15	Normal
36	Future Sight	Psychic	Special	120	100	10	Normal
41	Psychic	Psychic	Special	90	100	10	Normal
47	Endeavor	Normal	Physical	—	100	5	Normal

● TM & HM MOVES

No.	Name	Type	Kind	Pow.	Acc.	PP	Range
TM03	Psyshock	Psychic	Special	80	100	10	Normal
TM04	Calm Mind	Psychic	Status	—	—	20	Self
TM06	Toxic	Poison	Status	—	90	10	Normal
TM10	Hidden Power	Normal	Special	60	100	15	Normal
TM12	Taunt	Dark	Status	—	100	20	Normal
TM16	Light Screen	Psychic	Status	—	—	30	Your Side
TM17	Protect	Normal	Status	—	—	10	Self
TM18	Rain Dance	Water	Status	—	—	5	Both Sides
TM19	Roost	Flying	Status	—	—	10	Self
TM20	Safeguard	Normal	Status	—	—	25	Your Side
TM21	Frustration	Normal	Physical	—	100	20	Normal
TM27	Return	Normal	Physical	—	100	20	Normal
TM29	Psychic	Psychic	Special	90	100	10	Normal
TM30	Shadow Ball	Ghost	Special	80	100	15	Normal
TM32	Double Team	Normal	Status	—	—	15	Self
TM33	Reflect	Psychic	Status	—	—	20	Your Side
TM40	Aerial Ace	Flying	Physical	60	—	20	Normal
TM41	Torment	Dark	Status	—	100	15	Normal
TM42	Facade	Normal	Physical	70	100	20	Normal
TM44	Rest	Psychic	Status	—	—	10	Self
TM45	Attract	Normal	Status	—	100	15	Normal
TM46	Thief	Dark	Physical	60	100	25	Normal
TM48	Round	Normal	Special	60	100	15	Normal
TM51	Steel Wing	Steel	Physical	70	90	25	Normal
TM53	Energy Ball	Grass	Special	90	100	10	Normal
TM57	Charge Beam	Electric	Special	50	90	10	Normal
TM62	Acrobatics	Flying	Physical	55	100	15	Normal
TM63	Embargo	Dark	Status	—	100	15	Normal
TM70	Flash	Normal	Status	—	100	20	Normal
TM73	Thunder Wave	Electric	Status	—	100	20	Normal
TM74	Gyro Ball	Steel	Physical	—	100	5	Normal
TM77	Psych Up	Normal	Status	—	—	10	Normal
TM85	Dream Eater	Psychic	Special	100	100	15	Normal

No.	Name	Type	Kind	Pow.	Acc.	PP	Range
TM87	Swagger	Normal	Status	—	90	15	Normal
TM88	Sleep Talk	Normal	Status	—	—	10	Self
TM89	U-turn	Bug	Physical	70	100	20	Normal
TM90	Substitute	Normal	Status	—	—	10	Self
TM92	Trick Room	Psychic	Status	—	—	5	Both Sides
TM100	Confide	Normal	Status	—	—	20	Normal
HM02	Fly	Flying	Physical	90	95	15	Normal

● MOVES TAUGHT BY PEOPLE

Name	Type	Kind	Pow.	Acc.	PP	Range

● EGG MOVES

Name	Type	Kind	Pow.	Acc.	PP	Range
Charm	Fairy	Status	—	100	20	Normal
Knock Off	Dark	Physical	65	100	20	Normal
Fake Tears	Dark	Status	—	100	20	Normal
Supersonic	Normal	Status	—	55	20	Normal
Synchronoise	Psychic	Special	120	100	10	Adjacent
Stored Power	Psychic	Special	20	100	10	Normal
Roost	Flying	Status	—	—	10	Self
Flatter	Dark	Status	—	100	15	Normal
Helping Hand	Normal	Status	—	—	20	1 Ally
Captivate	Normal	Status	—	100	20	Many Others
Venom Drench	Poison	Status	—	100	20	Many Others
Psycho Shift	Psychic	Status	—	100	10	Normal

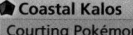

Coastal Kalos — 056

Courting Pokémon

☑ Swoobat

HEIGHT: 2'11" WEIGHT: 23.1 lbs.
GENDER: ♂/♀

X — It shakes its tail vigorously when it emits ultrasonic waves strong enough to reduce concrete to rubble.

Y — Anyone who comes into contact with the ultrasonic waves emitted by a courting male experiences a positive mood shift.

TYPE Psychic / Flying

ABILITIES
Unaware
Klutz

HIDDEN ABILITY
Simple

STAT GROWTH RATES
HP	■■■
Attack	■■■
Defense	■■■
Sp. Atk	■■■■
Sp. Def	■■
Speed	■■■■■

EGG GROUPS
Field, Flying

ITEMS SOMETIMES HELD BY WILD POKÉMON
None

⬆ EVOLUTION

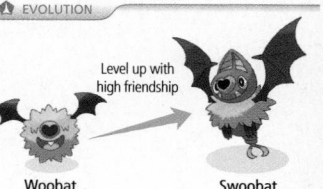

Woobat → (Level up with high friendship) → Swoobat

Damage taken in normal battles		Damage taken in Inverse Battles	
Normal	×1	Normal	×1
Fire	×1	Fire	×1
Water	×1	Water	×1
Grass	×0.5	Grass	×2
Electric	×2	Electric	×0.5
Ice	×2	Ice	×0.5
Fighting	×0.25	Fighting	×4
Poison	×1	Poison	×1
Ground	×0	Ground	×2
Flying	×1	Flying	×1
Psychic	×0.5	Psychic	×2
Bug	×1	Bug	×1
Rock	×2	Rock	×0.5
Ghost	×2	Ghost	×0.5
Dragon	×1	Dragon	×1
Dark	×2	Dark	×0.5
Steel	×1	Steel	×1
Fairy	×1	Fairy	×1

Can be used in
Inverse Battle
Sky Battle
Battle Chateau
Battle Institute
Battle Maison
Random Matchup

How to obtain for your Coastal Kalos Pokédex

Level up Woobat with sufficiently high friendship.

Level up Woobat with sufficiently high friendship.

Same form for ♂ / ♀

● LEVEL-UP MOVES

Lv.	Name	Type	Kind	Pow.	Acc.	PP	Range
1	Confusion	Psychic	Special	50	100	25	Normal
1	Odor Sleuth	Normal	Status	—	—	40	Normal
1	Gust	Flying	Special	40	100	35	Normal
4	Assurance	Dark	Physical	60	100	10	Normal
4	Odor Sleuth	Normal	Status	—	—	40	Normal
8	Gust	Flying	Special	40	100	35	Normal
12	Assurance	Dark	Physical	60	100	10	Normal
15	Heart Stamp	Psychic	Physical	60	100	25	Normal
19	Imprison	Psychic	Status	—	—	10	Self
21	Air Cutter	Flying	Special	60	95	25	Many Others
25	Attract	Normal	Status	—	100	15	Normal
29	Amnesia	Psychic	Status	—	—	20	Self
29	Calm Mind	Psychic	Status	—	—	20	Self
32	Air Slash	Flying	Special	75	95	15	Normal
36	Future Sight	Psychic	Special	120	100	10	Normal
41	Psychic	Psychic	Special	90	100	10	Normal
47	Endeavor	Normal	Physical	—	100	5	Normal

● TM & HM MOVES

No.	Name	Type	Kind	Pow.	Acc.	PP	Range
TM03	Psyshock	Psychic	Special	80	100	10	Normal
TM04	Calm Mind	Psychic	Status	—	—	20	Self
TM06	Toxic	Poison	Status	—	90	10	Normal
TM10	Hidden Power	Normal	Special	60	100	15	Normal
TM12	Taunt	Dark	Status	—	100	20	Normal
TM15	Hyper Beam	Normal	Special	150	90	5	Normal
TM16	Light Screen	Psychic	Status	—	—	30	Your Side
TM17	Protect	Normal	Status	—	—	10	Self
TM18	Rain Dance	Water	Status	—	—	5	Both Sides
TM19	Roost	Flying	Status	—	—	10	Self
TM20	Safeguard	Normal	Status	—	—	25	Your Side
TM21	Frustration	Normal	Physical	—	100	20	Normal
TM27	Return	Normal	Physical	—	100	20	Normal
TM29	Psychic	Psychic	Special	90	100	10	Normal
TM30	Shadow Ball	Ghost	Special	80	100	15	Normal
TM32	Double Team	Normal	Status	—	—	15	Self
TM33	Reflect	Psychic	Status	—	—	20	Your Side
TM40	Aerial Ace	Flying	Physical	60	—	20	Normal
TM41	Torment	Dark	Status	—	100	15	Normal
TM42	Facade	Normal	Physical	70	100	20	Normal
TM44	Rest	Psychic	Status	—	—	10	Self
TM45	Attract	Normal	Status	—	100	15	Normal
TM46	Thief	Dark	Physical	60	100	25	Normal
TM48	Round	Normal	Special	60	100	15	Normal
TM51	Steel Wing	Steel	Physical	70	90	25	Normal
TM53	Energy Ball	Grass	Special	90	100	10	Normal
TM57	Charge Beam	Electric	Special	50	90	10	Normal
TM62	Acrobatics	Flying	Physical	55	100	15	Normal
TM63	Embargo	Dark	Status	—	100	15	Normal
TM68	Giga Impact	Normal	Physical	150	90	5	Normal
TM70	Flash	Normal	Status	—	100	20	Normal
TM73	Thunder Wave	Electric	Status	—	100	20	Normal
TM74	Gyro Ball	Steel	Physical	—	100	5	Normal
TM77	Psych Up	Normal	Status	—	—	10	Normal
TM85	Dream Eater	Psychic	Special	100	100	15	Normal
TM87	Swagger	Normal	Status	—	90	15	Normal
TM88	Sleep Talk	Normal	Status	—	—	10	Self
TM89	U-turn	Bug	Physical	70	100	20	Normal
TM90	Substitute	Normal	Status	—	—	10	Self
TM92	Trick Room	Psychic	Status	—	—	5	Both Sides
TM100	Confide	Normal	Status	—	—	20	Normal
HM02	Fly	Flying	Physical	90	95	15	Normal

● MOVES TAUGHT BY PEOPLE

Name	Type	Kind	Pow.	Acc.	PP	Range

AFTER THE HALL OF FAME

CENTRAL KALOS

COASTAL KALOS

056 Swoobat

MOUNTAIN KALOS

ADVENTURE DATA

Coastal Kalos 057

Superpower Pokémon

☑ Machop

HEIGHT: 2'07" WEIGHT: 43.0 lbs.
GENDER: ♂/♀

X It hefts a Graveler repeatedly to strengthen its entire body. It uses every type of martial art.

Y Its whole body is composed of muscles. Even though it's the size of a human child, it can hurl 100 grown-ups.

TYPE Fighting

ABILITIES
Guts
No Guard

HIDDEN ABILITY
Steadfast

STAT GROWTH RATES
HP	■■■
Attack	■■■
Defense	■■
Sp. Atk	■■
Sp. Def	■■
Speed	■■

EGG GROUP
Human-Like

EVOLUTION

Machop — Lv. 28 → Machoke — Link Trade → Machamp

ITEMS SOMETIMES HELD BY WILD POKÉMON
None

Can be used in
Inverse Battle
—
Battle Chateau
Battle Institute
Battle Maison
Random Matchup

Damage taken in normal battles	
Normal	×1
Fire	×1
Water	×1
Grass	×1
Electric	×1
Ice	×1
Fighting	×1
Poison	×1
Ground	×1
Flying	×2
Psychic	×2
Bug	×0.5
Rock	×0.5
Ghost	×1
Dragon	×1
Dark	×0.5
Steel	×1
Fairy	×2

Damage taken in Inverse Battles	
Normal	×1
Fire	×1
Water	×1
Grass	×1
Electric	×1
Ice	×1
Fighting	×1
Poison	×1
Ground	×1
Flying	×0.5
Psychic	×0.5
Bug	×2
Rock	×2
Ghost	×1
Dragon	×1
Dark	×2
Steel	×1
Fairy	×0.5

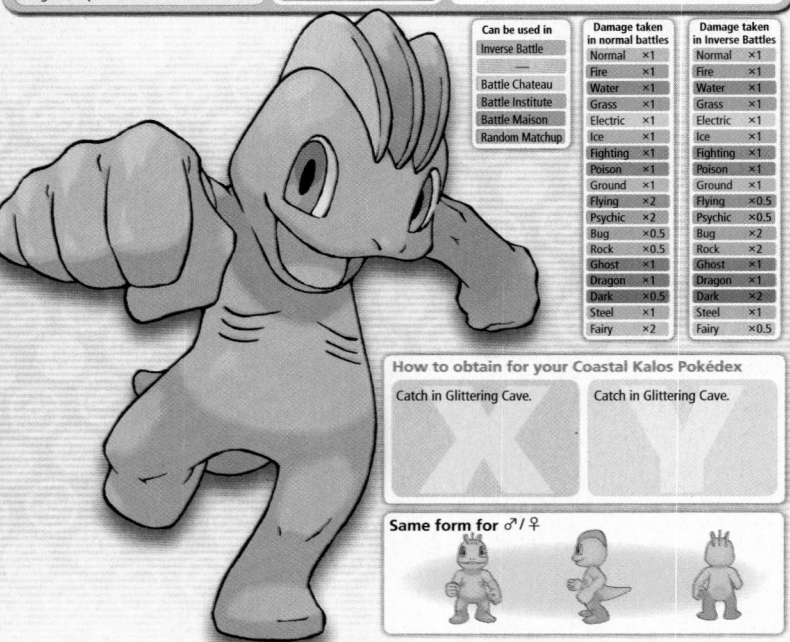

How to obtain for your Coastal Kalos Pokédex

X: Catch in Glittering Cave.

Y: Catch in Glittering Cave.

Same form for ♂/♀

LEVEL-UP MOVES

Lv.	Name	Type	Kind	Pow.	Acc.	PP	Range
1	Low Kick	Fighting	Physical	—	100	20	Normal
1	Leer	Normal	Status	—	100	30	Many Others
7	Focus Energy	Normal	Status	—	—	30	Self
10	Karate Chop	Fighting	Physical	50	100	25	Normal
13	Low Sweep	Fighting	Physical	65	100	20	Normal
19	Foresight	Normal	Status	—	—	40	Normal
22	Seismic Toss	Fighting	Physical	—	100	20	Normal
25	Revenge	Fighting	Physical	60	100	10	Normal
31	Vital Throw	Fighting	Physical	70	—	10	Normal
34	Submission	Fighting	Physical	80	80	20	Normal
37	Wake-Up Slap	Fighting	Physical	70	100	10	Normal
43	Cross Chop	Fighting	Physical	100	80	5	Normal
46	Scary Face	Normal	Status	—	100	10	Normal
49	Dynamic Punch	Fighting	Physical	100	50	5	Normal

TM & HM MOVES

No.	Name	Type	Kind	Pow.	Acc.	PP	Range
TM06	Toxic	Poison	Status	—	90	10	Normal
TM08	Bulk Up	Fighting	Status	—	—	20	Self
TM10	Hidden Power	Normal	Special	60	100	15	Normal
TM11	Sunny Day	Fire	Status	—	—	5	Both Sides
TM16	Light Screen	Psychic	Status	—	—	30	Your Side
TM17	Protect	Normal	Status	—	—	10	Self
TM18	Rain Dance	Water	Status	—	—	5	Both Sides
TM21	Frustration	Normal	Physical	—	100	20	Normal
TM23	Smack Down	Rock	Physical	50	100	15	Normal
TM26	Earthquake	Ground	Physical	100	100	10	Adjacent
TM27	Return	Normal	Physical	—	100	20	Normal
TM28	Dig	Ground	Physical	80	100	10	Normal
TM31	Brick Break	Fighting	Physical	75	100	15	Normal
TM32	Double Team	Normal	Status	—	—	15	Self
TM35	Flamethrower	Fire	Special	90	100	15	Normal
TM38	Fire Blast	Fire	Special	110	85	5	Normal
TM39	Rock Tomb	Rock	Physical	60	95	15	Normal
TM42	Facade	Normal	Physical	70	100	20	Normal
TM44	Rest	Psychic	Status	—	—	10	Self
TM45	Attract	Normal	Status	—	100	15	Normal
TM46	Thief	Dark	Physical	60	100	25	Normal
TM47	Low Sweep	Fighting	Physical	65	100	20	Normal
TM48	Round	Normal	Special	60	100	15	Normal
TM52	Focus Blast	Fighting	Special	120	70	5	Normal
TM56	Fling	Dark	Physical	—	100	10	Normal
TM59	Incinerate	Fire	Special	60	100	15	Many Others
TM66	Payback	Dark	Physical	50	100	10	Normal
TM67	Retaliate	Normal	Physical	70	100	5	Normal
TM78	Bulldoze	Ground	Physical	60	100	20	Adjacent
TM80	Rock Slide	Rock	Physical	75	90	10	Many Others
TM84	Poison Jab	Poison	Physical	80	100	20	Normal
TM87	Swagger	Normal	Status	—	90	15	Normal
TM88	Sleep Talk	Normal	Status	—	—	10	Self

No.	Name	Type	Kind	Pow.	Acc.	PP	Range
TM90	Substitute	Normal	Status	—	—	10	Self
TM94	Rock Smash	Fighting	Physical	40	100	15	Normal
TM98	Power-Up Punch	Fighting	Physical	40	100	20	Normal
TM100	Confide	Normal	Status	—	—	20	Normal
HM04	Strength	Normal	Physical	80	100	15	Normal

MOVES TAUGHT BY PEOPLE

Name	Type	Kind	Pow.	Acc.	PP	Range

EGG MOVES

Name	Type	Kind	Pow.	Acc.	PP	Range
Meditate	Psychic	Status	—	—	40	Self
Rolling Kick	Fighting	Physical	60	85	15	Normal
Encore	Normal	Status	—	100	5	Normal
Smelling Salts	Normal	Physical	70	100	10	Normal
Counter	Fighting	Physical	—	100	20	Varies
Close Combat	Fighting	Physical	120	100	5	Normal
Fire Punch	Fire	Physical	75	100	15	Normal
Thunder Punch	Electric	Physical	75	100	15	Normal
Ice Punch	Ice	Physical	75	100	15	Normal
Bullet Punch	Steel	Physical	40	100	30	Normal
Power Trick	Psychic	Status	—	—	10	Self
Heavy Slam	Steel	Physical	—	100	10	Normal
Knock Off	Dark	Physical	65	100	20	Normal
Tickle	Normal	Status	—	100	20	Normal
Quick Guard	Fighting	Status	—	—	15	Your Side

AFTER THE HALL OF FAME
CENTRAL KALOS
COASTAL KALOS
057
Machop
MOUNTAIN KALOS
ADVENTURE DATA

Coastal Kalos
Superpower Pokémon

Machoke **058**

 **TYPE** Fighting

ABILITIES
Guts
No Guard

HIDDEN ABILITY
Steadfast

HEIGHT: 4'11"   WEIGHT: 155.4 lbs.
GENDER: ♂/♀

X Its muscular body is so powerful, it must wear a power-save belt to be able to regulate its motions.

Y It can lift a dump truck with one hand. Using that power, it helps people with heavy jobs.

STAT GROWTH RATES

HP	■■■
Attack	■■■■■
Defense	■■■
Sp. Atk	■■
Sp. Def	■■■
Speed	■■■

EGG GROUP
Human-Like

EVOLUTION

Machop — Lv. 28 → Machoke — Link Trade → Machamp

ITEMS SOMETIMES HELD BY WILD POKÉMON
None

Damage taken in normal battles		Damage taken in Inverse Battles	
Normal	×1	Normal	×1
Fire	×1	Fire	×1
Water	×1	Water	×1
Grass	×1	Grass	×1
Electric	×1	Electric	×1
Ice	×1	Ice	×1
Fighting	×1	Fighting	×1
Poison	×1	Poison	×1
Ground	×1	Ground	×1
Flying	×2	Flying	×0.5
Psychic	×2	Psychic	×0.5
Bug	×0.5	Bug	×2
Rock	×0.5	Rock	×2
Ghost	×1	Ghost	×1
Dragon	×1	Dragon	×1
Dark	×0.5	Dark	×2
Steel	×1	Steel	×1
Fairy	×2	Fairy	×0.5

Can be used in
Inverse Battle
—
Battle Chateau
Battle Institute
Battle Maison
Random Matchup

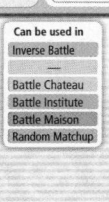

How to obtain for your Coastal Kalos Pokédex

Level up Machop to Lv. 28.	Level up Machop to Lv. 28.

Same form for ♂/♀

● LEVEL-UP MOVES

Lv.	Name	Type	Kind	Pow.	Acc.	PP	Range
1	Low Kick	Fighting	Physical	—	100	20	Normal
1	Leer	Normal	Status	—	100	30	Many Others
1	Focus Energy	Normal	Status	—	—	30	Self
1	Karate Chop	Fighting	Physical	50	100	25	Normal
7	Focus Energy	Normal	Status	—	—	30	Self
7	Karate Chop	Fighting	Physical	50	100	25	Normal
13	Low Sweep	Fighting	Physical	65	100	20	Normal
19	Foresight	Normal	Status	—	—	40	Normal
22	Seismic Toss	Fighting	Physical	—	100	20	Normal
25	Revenge	Fighting	Physical	60	100	10	Normal
32	Vital Throw	Fighting	Physical	70	—	10	Normal
36	Submission	Fighting	Physical	80	80	20	Normal
40	Wake-Up Slap	Fighting	Physical	70	100	10	Normal
44	Cross Chop	Fighting	Physical	100	80	5	Normal
51	Scary Face	Normal	Status	—	100	10	Normal
55	Dynamic Punch	Fighting	Physical	100	50	5	Normal

● TM & HM MOVES

No.	Name	Type	Kind	Pow.	Acc.	PP	Range
TM06	Toxic	Poison	Status	—	90	10	Normal
TM08	Bulk Up	Fighting	Status	—	—	20	Self
TM10	Hidden Power	Normal	Special	60	100	15	Normal
TM11	Sunny Day	Fire	Status	—	—	5	Both Sides
TM16	Light Screen	Psychic	Status	—	—	30	Your Side
TM17	Protect	Normal	Status	—	—	10	Self
TM18	Rain Dance	Water	Status	—	—	5	Both Sides
TM21	Frustration	Normal	Physical	—	100	20	Normal
TM23	Smack Down	Rock	Physical	50	100	15	Normal
TM26	Earthquake	Ground	Physical	100	100	10	Adjacent
TM27	Return	Normal	Physical	—	100	20	Normal
TM28	Dig	Ground	Physical	80	100	10	Normal
TM31	Brick Break	Fighting	Physical	75	100	15	Normal
TM32	Double Team	Normal	Status	—	—	15	Self
TM35	Flamethrower	Fire	Special	90	100	15	Normal
TM38	Fire Blast	Fire	Special	110	85	5	Normal
TM39	Rock Tomb	Rock	Physical	60	95	15	Normal
TM42	Facade	Normal	Physical	70	100	20	Normal
TM44	Rest	Psychic	Status	—	—	10	Self
TM45	Attract	Normal	Status	—	100	15	Normal
TM46	Thief	Dark	Physical	60	100	25	Normal
TM47	Low Sweep	Fighting	Physical	65	100	20	Normal
TM48	Round	Normal	Special	60	100	15	Normal
TM52	Focus Blast	Fighting	Special	120	70	5	Normal
TM56	Fling	Dark	Physical	—	100	10	Normal
TM59	Incinerate	Fire	Special	60	100	15	Many Others
TM66	Payback	Dark	Physical	50	100	10	Normal
TM67	Retaliate	Normal	Physical	70	100	5	Normal
TM78	Bulldoze	Ground	Physical	60	100	20	Adjacent
TM80	Rock Slide	Rock	Physical	75	90	10	Many Others
TM84	Poison Jab	Poison	Physical	80	100	20	Normal
TM87	Swagger	Normal	Status	—	90	15	Normal
TM88	Sleep Talk	Normal	Status	—	—	10	Self
TM90	Substitute	Normal	Status	—	—	10	Self
TM94	Rock Smash	Fighting	Physical	40	100	15	Normal
TM98	Power-Up Punch	Fighting	Physical	40	100	20	Normal
TM100	Confide	Normal	Status	—	—	20	Normal
HM04	Strength	Normal	Physical	80	100	15	Normal

● MOVES TAUGHT BY PEOPLE

Name	Type	Kind	Pow.	Acc.	PP	Range

AFTER THE HALL OF FAME

CENTRAL KALOS

COASTAL KALOS

058 Machoke

MOUNTAIN KALOS

ADVENTURE DATA

AFTER THE HALL OF FAME

CENTRAL KALOS

COASTAL KALOS

059

Machamp

MOUNTAIN KALOS

ADVENTURE DATA

♦ Coastal Kalos 059

Superpower Pokémon
☑ Machamp

HEIGHT: 5'03" WEIGHT: 286.6 lbs.
GENDER: ♂/♀

Ⓧ Its four ruggedly developed arms can launch a flurry of 1,000 punches in just two seconds.

Ⓨ It uses its four powerful arms to pin the limbs of its foe, then throws the victim over the horizon.

TYPE Fighting

ABILITIES
Guts
No Guard

HIDDEN ABILITY
Steadfast

STAT GROWTH RATES
HP	▪▪▪▪
Attack	▪▪▪▪▪▪▪
Defense	▪▪▪▪
Sp. Atk	▪▪▪
Sp. Def	▪▪▪▪
Speed	▪▪▪

EGG GROUP
Human-Like

⬆ EVOLUTION

Lv. 28   Link Trade

Machop   Machoke   Machamp

ITEMS SOMETIMES HELD BY WILD POKÉMON
None

Damage taken in normal battles		Damage taken in Inverse Battles	
Normal	×1	Normal	×1
Fire	×1	Fire	×1
Water	×1	Water	×1
Grass	×1	Grass	×1
Electric	×1	Electric	×1
Ice	×1	Ice	×1
Fighting	×1	Fighting	×1
Poison	×1	Poison	×1
Ground	×1	Ground	×1
Flying	×2	Flying	×0.5
Psychic	×2	Psychic	×0.5
Bug	×0.5	Bug	×2
Rock	×0.5	Rock	×2
Ghost	×1	Ghost	×1
Dragon	×1	Dragon	×1
Dark	×0.5	Dark	×2
Steel	×1	Steel	×1
Fairy	×2	Fairy	×0.5

Can be used in	
Inverse Battle	Battle Institute
—	Battle Maison
Battle Chateau	Random Matchup

Same form for ♂/♀

How to obtain for your Coastal Kalos Pokédex

Receive Machoke by Link Trade and have it evolve.

Receive Machoke by Link Trade and have it evolve.

● LEVEL-UP MOVES

Lv.	Name	Type	Kind	Pow.	Acc.	PP	Range
1	Wide Guard	Rock	Status	—	—	10	Your Side
1	Low Kick	Fighting	Physical	—	100	20	Normal
1	Leer	Normal	Status	—	100	30	Many Others
1	Focus Energy	Normal	Status	—	—	30	Self
1	Karate Chop	Fighting	Physical	50	100	25	Normal
7	Focus Energy	Normal	Status	—	—	30	Self
10	Karate Chop	Fighting	Physical	50	100	25	Normal
13	Low Sweep	Fighting	Physical	65	100	20	Normal
19	Foresight	Normal	Status	—	—	40	Normal
22	Seismic Toss	Fighting	Physical	—	100	20	Normal
25	Revenge	Fighting	Physical	60	100	10	Normal
32	Vital Throw	Fighting	Physical	70	—	10	Normal
36	Submission	Fighting	Physical	80	80	25	Normal
40	Wake-Up Slap	Fighting	Physical	70	100	10	Normal
44	Cross Chop	Fighting	Physical	100	80	5	Normal
51	Scary Face	Normal	Status	—	100	10	Normal
55	Dynamic Punch	Fighting	Physical	100	50	5	Normal

● TM & HM MOVES

No.	Name	Type	Kind	Pow.	Acc.	PP	Range
TM06	Toxic	Poison	Status	—	90	10	Normal
TM08	Bulk Up	Fighting	Status	—	—	20	Self
TM10	Hidden Power	Normal	Special	60	100	15	Normal
TM11	Sunny Day	Fire	Status	—	—	5	Both Sides
TM15	Hyper Beam	Normal	Special	150	90	5	Normal
TM16	Light Screen	Psychic	Status	—	—	30	Your Side
TM17	Protect	Normal	Status	—	—	10	Self
TM18	Rain Dance	Water	Status	—	—	5	Both Sides
TM21	Frustration	Normal	Physical	—	100	20	Normal
TM23	Smack Down	Rock	Physical	50	100	15	Normal
TM26	Earthquake	Ground	Physical	100	100	10	Adjacent
TM27	Return	Normal	Physical	—	100	20	Normal
TM28	Dig	Ground	Physical	80	100	10	Normal
TM31	Brick Break	Fighting	Physical	75	100	15	Normal
TM32	Double Team	Normal	Status	—	—	15	Self
TM35	Flamethrower	Fire	Special	90	100	15	Normal
TM38	Fire Blast	Fire	Special	110	85	5	Normal
TM39	Rock Tomb	Rock	Physical	60	95	15	Normal
TM42	Facade	Normal	Physical	70	100	20	Normal
TM44	Rest	Psychic	Status	—	—	10	Self
TM45	Attract	Normal	Status	—	100	15	Normal
TM46	Thief	Dark	Physical	60	100	25	Normal
TM47	Low Sweep	Fighting	Physical	65	100	20	Normal
TM48	Round	Normal	Special	60	100	15	Normal
TM52	Focus Blast	Fighting	Special	120	70	5	Normal
TM56	Fling	Dark	Physical	—	100	10	Normal
TM59	Incinerate	Fire	Special	60	100	15	Many Others
TM66	Payback	Dark	Physical	50	100	10	Normal
TM67	Retaliate	Normal	Physical	70	100	5	Normal
TM68	Giga Impact	Normal	Physical	150	90	5	Normal
TM71	Stone Edge	Rock	Physical	100	80	5	Normal
TM78	Bulldoze	Ground	Physical	60	100	20	Adjacent
TM80	Rock Slide	Rock	Physical	75	90	10	Many Others

No.	Name	Type	Kind	Pow.	Acc.	PP	Range
TM84	Poison Jab	Poison	Physical	80	100	20	Normal
TM87	Swagger	Normal	Status	—	90	15	Normal
TM88	Sleep Talk	Normal	Status	—	—	10	Self
TM90	Substitute	Normal	Status	—	—	10	Self
TM94	Rock Smash	Fighting	Physical	40	100	15	Normal
TM98	Power-Up Punch	Fighting	Physical	40	100	20	Normal
TM100	Confide	Normal	Status	—	—	20	Normal
HM04	Strength	Normal	Physical	80	100	15	Normal

● MOVES TAUGHT BY PEOPLE

Name	Type	Kind	Pow.	Acc.	PP	Range

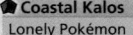 Coastal Kalos
Lonely Pokémon

060

 Cubone

HEIGHT: 1'04"　WEIGHT: 14.3 lbs.
GENDER: ♂/♀

 X It wears the skull of its dead mother on its head. When it becomes lonesome, it is said to cry loudly.

Y It always wears the skull of its dead mother, so no one has any idea what its hidden face looks like.

TYPE | Ground

ABILITIES
Rock Head
Lightning Rod

HIDDEN ABILITY
Battle Armor

STAT GROWTH RATES
HP	■■
Attack	■■■
Defense	■■■■
Sp. Atk	■■
Sp. Def	■■
Speed	■■

EGG GROUP
Monster

EVOLUTION

Cubone　　→ Lv. 28 →　　Marowak

ITEMS SOMETIMES HELD BY WILD POKÉMON
Thick Club

Damage taken in normal battles		Damage taken in Inverse Battles		Can be used in
Normal	×1	Normal	×1	Inverse Battle
Fire	×1	Fire	×1	—
Water	×2	Water	×0.5	Battle Chateau
Grass	×2	Grass	×0.5	Battle Institute
Electric	×0	Electric	×2	Battle Maison
Ice	×2	Ice	×0.5	Random Matchup
Fighting	×1	Fighting	×1	
Poison	×0.5	Poison	×2	
Ground	×1	Ground	×1	
Flying	×1	Flying	×1	
Psychic	×1	Psychic	×1	
Bug	×1	Bug	×1	
Rock	×0.5	Rock	×2	
Ghost	×1	Ghost	×1	
Dragon	×1	Dragon	×1	
Dark	×1	Dark	×1	
Steel	×1	Steel	×1	
Fairy	×1	Fairy	×1	

How to obtain for your Coastal Kalos Pokédex

Catch in Glittering Cave.	Catch in Glittering Cave.
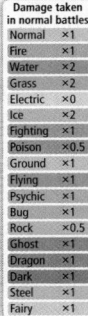	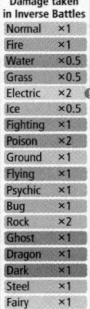

Same form for ♂/♀

● LEVEL-UP MOVES

Lv.	Name	Type	Kind	Pow.	Acc.	PP	Range
1	Growl	Normal	Status	—	100	40	Many Others
3	Tail Whip	Normal	Status	—	100	30	Many Others
7	Bone Club	Ground	Physical	65	85	20	Normal
11	Headbutt	Normal	Physical	70	100	15	Normal
13	Leer	Normal	Status	—	100	30	Many Others
17	Focus Energy	Normal	Status	—	—	30	Self
21	Bonemerang	Ground	Physical	50	90	10	Normal
23	Rage	Normal	Physical	20	100	20	Normal
27	False Swipe	Normal	Physical	40	100	40	Normal
31	Thrash	Normal	Physical	120	100	10	1 Random
33	Fling	Dark	Physical	—	100	10	Normal
37	Bone Rush	Ground	Physical	25	90	10	Normal
41	Endeavor	Normal	Physical	—	100	5	Normal
43	Double-Edge	Normal	Physical	120	100	15	Normal
47	Retaliate	Normal	Physical	70	100	5	Normal

● TM & HM MOVES

No.	Name	Type	Kind	Pow.	Acc.	PP	Range
TM06	Toxic	Poison	Status	—	90	10	Normal
TM10	Hidden Power	Normal	Special	60	100	15	Normal
TM11	Sunny Day	Fire	Status	—	—	5	Both Sides
TM13	Ice Beam	Ice	Special	90	100	10	Normal
TM14	Blizzard	Ice	Special	110	70	5	Many Others
TM17	Protect	Normal	Status	—	—	10	Self
TM21	Frustration	Normal	Physical	—	100	20	Normal
TM23	Smack Down	Rock	Physical	50	100	15	Normal
TM26	Earthquake	Ground	Physical	100	100	10	Adjacent
TM27	Return	Normal	Physical	—	100	20	Normal
TM28	Dig	Ground	Physical	80	100	10	Normal
TM31	Brick Break	Fighting	Physical	75	100	15	Normal
TM32	Double Team	Normal	Status	—	—	15	Self
TM35	Flamethrower	Fire	Special	90	100	15	Normal
TM37	Sandstorm	Rock	Status	—	—	10	Both Sides
TM38	Fire Blast	Fire	Special	110	85	5	Normal
TM39	Rock Tomb	Rock	Physical	60	95	15	Normal
TM40	Aerial Ace	Flying	Physical	60	—	20	Normal
TM42	Facade	Normal	Physical	70	100	20	Normal
TM44	Rest	Psychic	Status	—	—	10	Self
TM45	Attract	Normal	Status	—	100	15	Normal
TM46	Thief	Dark	Physical	60	100	25	Normal
TM48	Round	Normal	Special	60	100	15	Normal
TM49	Echoed Voice	Normal	Special	40	100	15	Normal
TM54	False Swipe	Normal	Physical	40	100	40	Normal
TM56	Fling	Dark	Physical	—	100	10	Normal
TM59	Incinerate	Fire	Special	60	100	15	Many Others
TM67	Retaliate	Normal	Physical	70	100	5	Normal
TM75	Swords Dance	Normal	Status	—	—	20	Self
TM78	Bulldoze	Ground	Physical	60	100	20	Adjacent
TM80	Rock Slide	Rock	Physical	75	90	10	Many Others
TM87	Swagger	Normal	Status	—	90	15	Normal
TM88	Sleep Talk	Normal	Status	—	—	10	Self

No.	Name	Type	Kind	Pow.	Acc.	PP	Range
TM90	Substitute	Normal	Status	—	—	10	Self
TM94	Rock Smash	Fighting	Physical	40	100	15	Normal
TM98	Power-Up Punch	Fighting	Physical	40	100	20	Normal
TM100	Confide	Normal	Status	—	—	20	Normal
HM04	Strength	Normal	Physical	80	100	15	Normal

● MOVES TAUGHT BY PEOPLE

Name	Type	Kind	Pow.	Acc.	PP	Range

● EGG MOVES

Name	Type	Kind	Pow.	Acc.	PP	Range
Ancient Power	Rock	Special	60	100	5	Normal
Belly Drum	Normal	Status	—	—	10	Self
Screech	Normal	Status	—	85	40	Normal
Skull Bash	Normal	Physical	130	100	10	Normal
Perish Song	Normal	Status	—	—	5	Adjacent
Double Kick	Fighting	Physical	30	100	30	Normal
Iron Head	Steel	Physical	80	100	15	Normal
Detect	Fighting	Status	—	—	5	Self
Endure	Normal	Status	—	—	10	Self
Chip Away	Normal	Physical	70	100	20	Normal

AFTER THE HALL OF FAME

CENTRAL KALOS

COASTAL KALOS

060 | Cubone

MOUNTAIN KALOS

ADVENTURE DATA

329

AFTER THE HALL OF FAME

CENTRAL KALOS

COASTAL KALOS

061

Marowak

MOUNTAIN KALOS

ADVENTURE DATA

Coastal Kalos
Bone Keeper Pokémon
⋁ Marowak
061

HEIGHT: 3'03"   WEIGHT: 99.2 lbs.
GENDER: ♂/♀

| TYPE | Ground |

ABILITIES
Rock Head
Lightning Rod

HIDDEN ABILITY
Battle Armor

STAT GROWTH RATES
HP	■■■
Attack	■■■
Defense	■■■■■
Sp. Atk	■■
Sp. Def	■■■
Speed	■■■

EGG GROUP
Monster

X It is small and was originally very weak. Its temperament turned ferocious when it began using bones.

Y The bone it holds is its key weapon. It throws the bone skillfully like a boomerang to KO targets.

↑ EVOLUTION
Cubone — Lv. 28 → Marowak

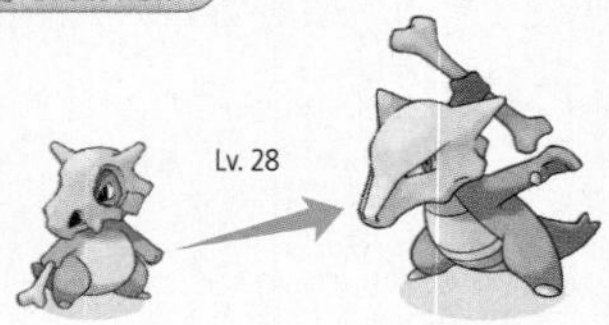

ITEMS SOMETIMES HELD BY WILD POKÉMON
None

Can be used in
Inverse Battle
—
Battle Chateau
Battle Institute
Battle Maison
Random Matchup

Damage taken in normal battles
Normal	×1
Fire	×1
Water	×2
Grass	×2
Electric	×0
Ice	×2
Fighting	×1
Poison	×0.5
Ground	×1
Flying	×1
Psychic	×1
Bug	×1
Rock	×0.5
Ghost	×1
Dragon	×1
Dark	×1
Steel	×1
Fairy	×1

Damage taken in Inverse Battles
Normal	×1
Fire	×1
Water	×0.5
Grass	×0.5
Electric	×2
Ice	×0.5
Fighting	×1
Poison	×2
Ground	×1
Flying	×1
Psychic	×1
Bug	×1
Rock	×2
Ghost	×1
Dragon	×1
Dark	×1
Steel	×1
Fairy	×1

Same form for ♂/♀

How to obtain for your Coastal Kalos Pokédex
Level up Cubone to Lv. 28.   Level up Cubone to Lv. 28.

● LEVEL-UP MOVES

Lv.	Name	Type	Kind	Pow.	Acc.	PP	Range
1	Growl	Normal	Status	—	100	40	Many Others
1	Tail Whip	Normal	Status	—	100	30	Many Others
1	Bone Club	Ground	Physical	65	85	20	Normal
1	Headbutt	Normal	Physical	70	100	15	Normal
3	Tail Whip	Normal	Status	—	100	30	Many Others
7	Bone Club	Ground	Physical	65	85	20	Normal
11	Headbutt	Normal	Physical	70	100	15	Normal
13	Leer	Normal	Status	—	100	30	Many Others
17	Focus Energy	Normal	Status	—	—	30	Self
21	Bonemerang	Ground	Physical	50	90	10	Normal
23	Rage	Normal	Physical	20	100	20	Normal
27	False Swipe	Normal	Physical	40	100	40	Normal
33	Thrash	Normal	Physical	120	100	10	1 Random
37	Fling	Dark	Physical	—	100	10	Normal
43	Bone Rush	Ground	Physical	25	90	10	Normal
49	Endeavor	Normal	Physical	—	100	5	Normal
53	Double-Edge	Normal	Physical	120	100	15	Normal
59	Retaliate	Normal	Physical	70	100	5	Normal

● TM & HM MOVES

No.	Name	Type	Kind	Pow.	Acc.	PP	Range
TM06	Toxic	Poison	Status	—	90	10	Normal
TM10	Hidden Power	Normal	Special	60	100	15	Normal
TM11	Sunny Day	Fire	Status	—	—	5	Both Sides
TM13	Ice Beam	Ice	Special	90	100	10	Normal
TM14	Blizzard	Ice	Special	110	70	5	Many Others
TM15	Hyper Beam	Normal	Special	150	90	5	Normal
TM17	Protect	Normal	Status	—	—	10	Self
TM21	Frustration	Normal	Physical	—	100	20	Normal
TM23	Smack Down	Rock	Physical	50	100	15	Normal
TM26	Earthquake	Ground	Physical	100	100	10	Adjacent
TM27	Return	Normal	Physical	—	100	20	Normal
TM28	Dig	Ground	Physical	80	100	10	Normal
TM31	Brick Break	Fighting	Physical	75	100	15	Normal
TM32	Double Team	Normal	Status	—	—	15	Self
TM35	Flamethrower	Fire	Special	90	100	15	Normal
TM37	Sandstorm	Rock	Status	—	—	10	Both Sides
TM38	Fire Blast	Fire	Special	110	85	5	Normal
TM39	Rock Tomb	Rock	Physical	60	95	15	Normal
TM40	Aerial Ace	Flying	Physical	60	—	20	Normal
TM42	Facade	Normal	Physical	70	100	20	Normal
TM44	Rest	Psychic	Status	—	—	10	Self
TM45	Attract	Normal	Status	—	100	15	Normal
TM46	Thief	Dark	Physical	60	100	25	Normal
TM48	Round	Normal	Special	60	100	15	Normal
TM49	Echoed Voice	Normal	Special	40	100	15	Normal
TM52	Focus Blast	Fighting	Special	120	70	5	Normal
TM54	False Swipe	Normal	Physical	40	100	40	Normal
TM56	Fling	Dark	Physical	—	100	10	Normal
TM59	Incinerate	Fire	Special	60	100	15	Many Others
TM67	Retaliate	Normal	Physical	70	100	5	Normal
TM68	Giga Impact	Normal	Physical	150	90	5	Normal
TM71	Stone Edge	Rock	Physical	100	80	5	Normal
TM75	Swords Dance	Normal	Status	—	—	20	Self

No.	Name	Type	Kind	Pow.	Acc.	PP	Range
TM78	Bulldoze	Ground	Physical	60	100	20	Adjacent
TM80	Rock Slide	Rock	Physical	75	90	10	Many Others
TM87	Swagger	Normal	Status	—	90	15	Normal
TM88	Sleep Talk	Normal	Status	—	—	10	Self
TM90	Substitute	Normal	Status	—	—	10	Self
TM94	Rock Smash	Fighting	Physical	40	100	15	Normal
TM98	Power-Up Punch	Fighting	Physical	40	100	20	Normal
TM100	Confide	Normal	Status	—	—	20	Normal
HM04	Strength	Normal	Physical	80	100	15	Normal

● MOVES TAUGHT BY PEOPLE

Name	Type	Kind	Pow.	Acc.	PP	Range

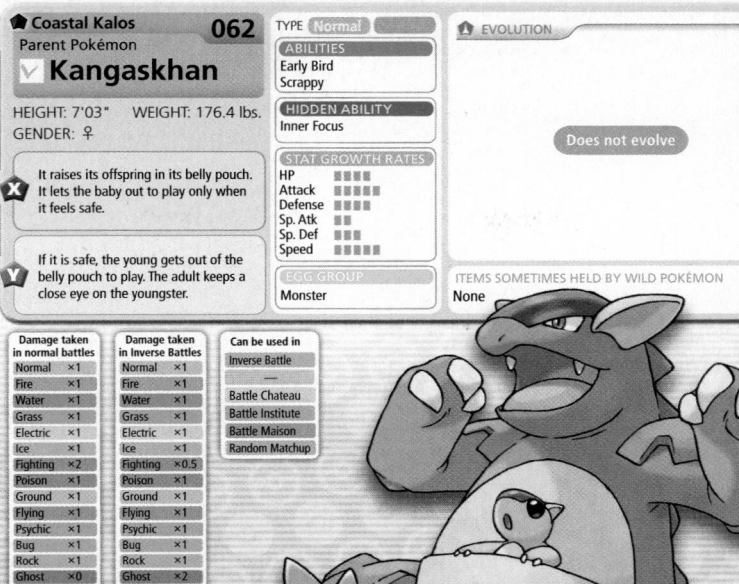

Coastal Kalos — 062
Parent Pokémon
🅥 Kangaskhan

HEIGHT: 7'03" WEIGHT: 176.4 lbs.
GENDER: ♀

X It raises its offspring in its belly pouch. It lets the baby out to play only when it feels safe.

Y If it is safe, the young gets out of the belly pouch to play. The adult keeps a close eye on the youngster.

TYPE Normal

ABILITIES
Early Bird
Scrappy

HIDDEN ABILITY
Inner Focus

STAT GROWTH RATES
HP	▪▪▪▪
Attack	▪▪▪▪▪
Defense	▪▪▪▪
Sp. Atk	▪▪
Sp. Def	▪▪
Speed	▪▪▪▪▪

EGG GROUP
Monster

EVOLUTION
Does not evolve

ITEMS SOMETIMES HELD BY WILD POKÉMON
None

Damage taken in normal battles		Damage taken in Inverse Battles	
Normal	×1	Normal	×1
Fire	×1	Fire	×1
Water	×1	Water	×1
Grass	×1	Grass	×1
Electric	×1	Electric	×1
Ice	×1	Ice	×1
Fighting	×2	Fighting	×0.5
Poison	×1	Poison	×1
Ground	×1	Ground	×1
Flying	×1	Flying	×1
Psychic	×1	Psychic	×1
Bug	×1	Bug	×1
Rock	×1	Rock	×1
Ghost	×0	Ghost	×2
Dragon	×1	Dragon	×1
Dark	×1	Dark	×1
Steel	×1	Steel	×1
Fairy	×1	Fairy	×1

Can be used in
Inverse Battle
——
Battle Chateau
Battle Institute
Battle Maison
Random Matchup

♀

How to obtain for your Coastal Kalos Pokédex

X	Y
Catch in Glittering Cave.	Catch in Glittering Cave.

● LEVEL-UP MOVES

Lv.	Name	Type	Kind	Pow.	Acc.	PP	Range
1	Comet Punch	Normal	Physical	18	85	15	Normal
1	Leer	Normal	Status	—	100	30	Many Others
7	Fake Out	Normal	Physical	40	100	10	Normal
10	Tail Whip	Normal	Status	—	100	30	Many Others
13	Bite	Dark	Physical	60	100	25	Normal
19	Double Hit	Normal	Physical	35	90	10	Normal
22	Rage	Normal	Physical	20	100	20	Normal
25	Mega Punch	Normal	Physical	80	85	20	Normal
31	Chip Away	Normal	Physical	70	100	20	Normal
34	Dizzy Punch	Normal	Physical	70	100	10	Normal
37	Crunch	Dark	Physical	80	100	15	Normal
43	Endure	Normal	Status	—	—	10	Self
46	Outrage	Dragon	Physical	120	100	10	1 Random
49	Sucker Punch	Dark	Physical	80	100	5	Normal
50	Reversal	Fighting	Physical	—	100	15	Normal

● TM & HM MOVES

No.	Name	Type	Kind	Pow.	Acc.	PP	Range
TM05	Roar	Normal	Status	—	—	20	Normal
TM06	Toxic	Poison	Status	—	90	10	Normal
TM07	Hail	Ice	Status	—	—	10	Both Sides
TM10	Hidden Power	Normal	Special	60	100	15	Normal
TM11	Sunny Day	Fire	Status	—	—	5	Both Sides
TM13	Ice Beam	Ice	Special	90	100	10	Normal
TM14	Blizzard	Ice	Special	110	70	5	Many Others
TM15	Hyper Beam	Normal	Special	150	90	5	Normal
TM17	Protect	Normal	Status	—	—	10	Self
TM18	Rain Dance	Water	Status	—	—	5	Both Sides
TM20	Safeguard	Normal	Status	—	—	25	Your Side
TM21	Frustration	Normal	Physical	—	100	20	Normal
TM22	Solar Beam	Grass	Special	120	100	10	Normal
TM24	Thunderbolt	Electric	Special	90	100	15	Normal
TM25	Thunder	Electric	Special	110	70	10	Normal
TM26	Earthquake	Ground	Physical	100	100	10	Adjacent
TM27	Return	Normal	Physical	—	100	20	Normal
TM28	Dig	Ground	Physical	80	100	10	Normal
TM30	Shadow Ball	Ghost	Special	80	100	15	Normal
TM31	Brick Break	Fighting	Physical	75	100	15	Normal
TM32	Double Team	Normal	Status	—	—	15	Self
TM35	Flamethrower	Fire	Special	90	100	15	Normal
TM37	Sandstorm	Rock	Status	—	—	10	Both Sides
TM38	Fire Blast	Fire	Special	110	85	5	Normal
TM39	Rock Tomb	Rock	Physical	60	95	15	Normal
TM40	Aerial Ace	Flying	Physical	60	—	20	Normal
TM42	Facade	Normal	Physical	70	100	20	Normal
TM44	Rest	Psychic	Status	—	—	10	Self
TM45	Attract	Normal	Status	—	100	15	Normal
TM48	Round	Normal	Special	60	100	15	Normal
TM49	Thief	Dark	Physical	60	100	25	Normal
TM52	Focus Blast	Fighting	Special	120	70	5	Normal
TM56	Fling	Dark	Physical	—	100	10	Normal
TM59	Incinerate	Fire	Special	60	100	15	Many Others
TM65	Shadow Claw	Ghost	Physical	70	100	15	Normal
TM67	Retaliate	Normal	Physical	70	100	5	Normal
TM68	Giga Impact	Normal	Physical	150	90	5	Normal
TM78	Bulldoze	Ground	Physical	60	100	20	Adjacent
TM80	Rock Slide	Rock	Physical	75	90	10	Many Others
TM87	Swagger	Normal	Status	—	90	15	Normal
TM88	Sleep Talk	Normal	Status	—	—	10	Self
TM90	Substitute	Normal	Status	—	—	10	Self
TM94	Rock Smash	Fighting	Physical	40	100	15	Normal
TM98	Power-Up Punch	Fighting	Physical	40	100	20	Normal
TM100	Confide	Normal	Status	—	—	20	Normal
HM01	Cut	Normal	Physical	50	95	30	Normal
HM03	Surf	Water	Special	90	100	15	Adjacent
HM04	Strength	Normal	Physical	80	100	15	Normal

● MOVES TAUGHT BY PEOPLE

Name	Type	Kind	Pow.	Acc.	PP	Range

● EGG MOVES

Name	Type	Kind	Pow.	Acc.	PP	Range
Stomp	Normal	Physical	65	100	20	Normal
Foresight	Normal	Status	—	—	40	Normal
Focus Energy	Normal	Status	—	—	30	Self
Disable	Normal	Status	—	100	20	Normal
Counter	Fighting	Physical	—	100	20	Varies
Crush Claw	Normal	Physical	75	95	10	Normal
Double-Edge	Normal	Physical	120	100	15	Normal
Endeavor	Normal	Physical	—	100	5	Normal
Hammer Arm	Fighting	Physical	100	90	10	Normal
Focus Punch	Fighting	Physical	150	100	20	Normal
Trump Card	Normal	Special	—	—	5	Normal
Uproar	Normal	Special	90	100	10	1 Random
Circle Throw	Fighting	Physical	60	90	10	Normal

AFTER THE HALL OF FAME

CENTRAL KALOS

COASTAL KALOS

062 | Kangaskhan

MOUNTAIN KALOS

ADVENTURE DATA

AFTER THE HALL OF FAME

CENTRAL KALOS

COASTAL KALOS

Mega Kangaskhan

MOUNTAIN

ADVENTURE DATA

Mega Evolution

Parent Pokémon

⋁ Mega Kangaskhan

TYPE	Normal

ABILITY
Parental Bond

STAT GROWTH RATES	
HP	▪▪▪▪▫
Attack	▪▪▪▪▪
Defense	▪▪▪▫
Sp. Atk	▪▪▪▫
Sp. Def	▪▪▪▫
Speed	▪▪▪▪▪

◉ MEGA STONE REQUIRED

Kangaskhanite
Obtain in Glittering Cave between 8 P.M. and 8:59 P.M., after entering the Hall of Fame and speaking with Professor Sycamore in Anistar City.

HEIGHT: 7'03"   WEIGHT: 220.5 lbs.   GENDER: ♀

Can be used in
Inverse Battle
—
Battle Chateau
Battle Institute
Battle Maison
Random Matchup

Damage taken in normal battles	
Normal	×1
Fire	×1
Water	×1
Grass	×1
Electric	×1
Ice	×1
Fighting	×2
Poison	×1
Ground	×1
Flying	×1
Psychic	×1
Bug	×1
Rock	×1
Ghost	×0
Dragon	×1
Dark	×1
Steel	×1
Fairy	×1

Damage taken in Inverse Battles	
Normal	×1
Fire	×1
Water	×1
Grass	×1
Electric	×1
Ice	×1
Fighting	×0.5
Poison	×1
Ground	×1
Flying	×1
Psychic	×1
Bug	×1
Rock	×1
Ghost	×2
Dragon	×1
Dark	×1
Steel	×1
Fairy	×1

♀

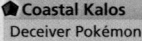 **Coastal Kalos**
Deceiver Pokémon

063

 Mawile

HEIGHT: 2'00" WEIGHT: 25.4 lbs.
GENDER: ♂/♀

 TYPE Steel Fairy

ABILITIES
Hyper Cutter
Intimidate

HIDDEN ABILITY
Sheer Force

STAT GROWTH RATES
HP	▪▪
Attack	▪▪▪▪
Defense	▪▪▪▪
Sp. Atk	▪▪▪
Sp. Def	▪▪
Speed	▪▪▪

EGG GROUPS
Field, Fairy

X It uses its docile-looking face to lull foes into complacency, then bites with its huge, relentless jaws.

Y Attached to its head is a huge set of jaws formed by horns. It can chew through iron beams.

▲ EVOLUTION

Does not evolve

ITEMS SOMETIMES HELD BY WILD POKÉMON
None

Damage taken in normal battles		Damage taken in Inverse Battles	
Normal	×0.5	Normal	×2
Fire	×2	Fire	×0.5
Water	×1	Water	×1
Grass	×0.5	Grass	×2
Electric	×1	Electric	×1
Ice	×0.5	Ice	×2
Fighting	×0	Fighting	×1
Poison	×0	Poison	×1
Ground	×2	Ground	×0.5
Flying	×0.5	Flying	×2
Psychic	×0.5	Psychic	×2
Bug	×0.25	Bug	×4
Rock	×0.5	Rock	×1
Ghost	×1	Ghost	×1
Dragon	×0	Dragon	×4
Dark	×0.5	Dark	×1
Steel	×1	Steel	×1
Fairy	×0.5	Fairy	×2

Can be used in	
Inverse Battle	Battle Institute
—	Battle Maison
Battle Chateau	Random Matchup

Same form for ♂/♀

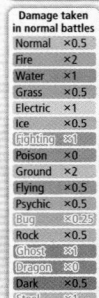

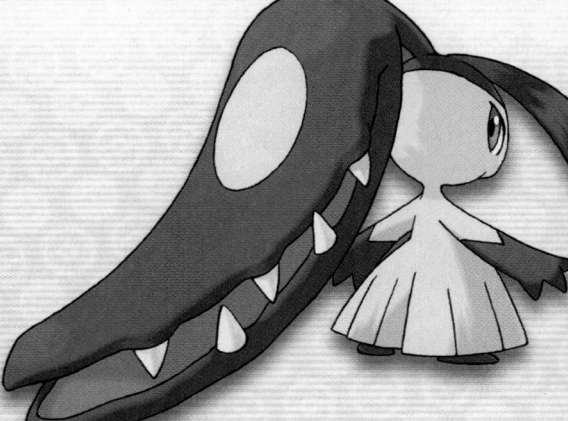

How to obtain for your Coastal Kalos Pokédex

Catch in Glittering Cave. Catch in Glittering Cave.

● **LEVEL-UP MOVES**
Lv.	Name	Type	Kind	Pow.	Acc.	PP	Range
1	Play Rough	Fairy	Physical	90	90	10	Normal
1	Iron Head	Steel	Physical	80	100	15	Normal
1	Taunt	Dark	Status	—	100	20	Normal
1	Growl	Normal	Status	—	100	40	Many Others
1	Fairy Wind	Fairy	Special	40	100	30	Normal
1	Astonish	Ghost	Physical	30	100	15	Normal
6	Fake Tears	Dark	Status	—	100	20	Normal
11	Bite	Dark	Physical	60	100	25	Normal
16	Sweet Scent	Normal	Status	—	100	20	Many Others
21	Vice Grip	Normal	Physical	55	100	30	Normal
26	Feint Attack	Dark	Physical	60	—	20	Normal
31	Baton Pass	Normal	Status	—	—	40	Self
36	Crunch	Dark	Physical	80	100	15	Normal
41	Iron Defense	Steel	Status	—	—	15	Self
46	Sucker Punch	Dark	Physical	80	100	5	Normal
50	Stockpile	Normal	Status	—	—	20	Self
50	Swallow	Normal	Status	—	—	10	Self
50	Spit Up	Normal	Special	—	100	10	Normal
56	Iron Head	Steel	Physical	80	100	15	Normal
60	Play Rough	Fairy	Physical	90	90	10	Normal

● **TM & HM MOVES**
No.	Name	Type	Kind	Pow.	Acc.	PP	Range
TM06	Toxic	Poison	Status	—	90	10	Normal
TM10	Hidden Power	Normal	Special	60	100	15	Normal

● **TM & HM MOVES**
No.	Name	Type	Kind	Pow.	Acc.	PP	Range
TM11	Sunny Day	Fire	Status	—	—	5	Both Sides
TM12	Taunt	Dark	Status	—	100	20	Normal
TM13	Ice Beam	Ice	Special	90	100	10	Normal
TM15	Hyper Beam	Normal	Special	150	90	5	Normal
TM17	Protect	Normal	Status	—	—	10	Self
TM18	Rain Dance	Water	Status	—	—	5	Both Sides
TM21	Frustration	Normal	Physical	—	100	20	Normal
TM22	Solar Beam	Grass	Special	120	100	10	Normal
TM27	Return	Normal	Physical	—	100	20	Normal
TM30	Shadow Ball	Ghost	Special	80	100	15	Normal
TM31	Brick Break	Fighting	Physical	75	100	15	Normal
TM32	Double Team	Normal	Status	—	—	15	Self
TM35	Flamethrower	Fire	Special	90	100	15	Normal
TM36	Sludge Bomb	Poison	Special	90	100	10	Normal
TM37	Sandstorm	Rock	Status	—	—	10	Both Sides
TM38	Fire Blast	Fire	Special	110	85	5	Normal
TM39	Rock Tomb	Rock	Physical	60	95	15	Normal
TM41	Torment	Dark	Status	—	100	15	Normal
TM42	Facade	Normal	Physical	70	100	20	Normal
TM44	Rest	Psychic	Status	—	—	10	Self
TM45	Attract	Normal	Status	—	100	15	Normal
TM48	Round	Normal	Special	60	100	15	Normal
TM52	Focus Blast	Fighting	Special	120	70	5	Normal
TM54	False Swipe	Normal	Physical	40	100	40	Normal
TM56	Fling	Dark	Physical	—	100	10	Normal
TM57	Charge Beam	Electric	Special	50	90	10	Normal
TM59	Incinerate	Fire	Special	60	100	15	Many Others
TM63	Embargo	Dark	Status	—	100	15	Normal
TM66	Payback	Dark	Physical	50	100	10	Normal
TM68	Giga Impact	Normal	Physical	150	90	5	Normal
TM71	Stone Edge	Rock	Physical	100	80	5	Normal
TM75	Swords Dance	Normal	Status	—	—	20	Self
TM77	Psych Up	Normal	Status	—	—	10	Normal
TM80	Rock Slide	Rock	Physical	75	90	10	Many Others
TM86	Grass Knot	Grass	Special	—	100	20	Normal
TM87	Swagger	Normal	Status	—	90	15	Normal
TM88	Sleep Talk	Normal	Status	—	—	10	Self
TM90	Substitute	Normal	Status	—	—	10	Self
TM91	Flash Cannon	Steel	Special	80	100	10	Normal
TM94	Rock Smash	Fighting	Physical	40	100	15	Normal
TM97	Dark Pulse	Dark	Special	80	100	15	Normal
TM98	Power-Up Punch	Fighting	Physical	40	100	20	Normal
TM100	Confide	Normal	Status	—	—	20	Normal
HM04	Strength	Normal	Physical	80	100	15	Normal

● **MOVES TAUGHT BY PEOPLE**
Name	Type	Kind	Pow.	Acc.	PP	Range

● **EGG MOVES**
Name	Type	Kind	Pow.	Acc.	PP	Range
Poison Fang	Poison	Physical	50	100	15	Normal
Ancient Power	Rock	Special	60	100	5	Normal
Tickle	Normal	Status	—	100	20	Normal
Sucker Punch	Dark	Physical	80	100	5	Normal
Ice Fang	Ice	Physical	65	95	15	Normal
Fire Fang	Fire	Physical	65	95	15	Normal
Thunder Fang	Electric	Physical	65	95	15	Normal
Punishment	Dark	Physical	—	100	5	Normal
Guard Swap	Psychic	Status	—	—	10	Normal
Captivate	Normal	Status	—	100	20	Many Others
Slam	Normal	Physical	80	75	20	Normal
Metal Burst	Steel	Physical	—	100	10	Varies
Misty Terrain	Fairy	Status	—	—	10	Both Sides
Seismic Toss	Fighting	Physical	—	100	20	Normal

AFTER THE HALL OF FAME

CENTRAL KALOS

COASTAL KALOS

063 | Mawile

MOUNTAIN KALOS

ADVENTURE DATA

Mega Mawile

Mega Evolution

Deceiver Pokémon

☑ Mega Mawile

TYPE	Steel	Fairy

ABILITY
Huge Power

STAT GROWTH RATES

HP	▪▪
Attack	▪▪▪▪▪
Defense	▪▪▪▪▪
Sp. Atk	▪▪▪
Sp. Def	▪▪▪▪
Speed	▪▪▪

MEGA STONE REQUIRED

Mawilite
Obtain in Camphrier Town's Shabboneau Castle between 8 P.M. and 8:59 P.M., after entering the Hall of Fame and speaking with Professor Sycamore in Anistar City.

HEIGHT: 3'03"   WEIGHT: 51.8 lbs.   GENDER: ♂/♀

Damage taken in normal battles	
Normal	×0.5
Fire	×2
Water	×1
Grass	×0.5
Electric	×1
Ice	×0.5
Fighting	×1
Poison	×0
Ground	×2
Flying	×0.5
Psychic	×0.5
Bug	×0.25
Rock	×0.5
Ghost	×1
Dragon	×0
Dark	×0.5
Steel	×1
Fairy	×0.5

Damage taken in Inverse Battles	
Normal	×2
Fire	×0.5
Water	×1
Grass	×2
Electric	×1
Ice	×2
Fighting	×1
Poison	×1
Ground	×0.5
Flying	×2
Psychic	×2
Bug	×4
Rock	×2
Ghost	×1
Dragon	×4
Dark	×2
Steel	×1
Fairy	×2

Can be used in
Inverse Battle
—
Battle Chateau
Battle Institute
Battle Maison
Random Matchup

Same form for ♂ / ♀

334

Coastal Kalos
Royal Heir Pokémon
☑ **Tyrunt** 064

HEIGHT: 2'07" WEIGHT: 57.3 lbs.
GENDER: ♂ / ♀

X	This Pokémon was restored from a fossil. If something that it doesn't like, it throws a tantrum and runs wild.
Y	Its immense jaws have enough destructive force that it can chew up an automobile. It lived 100 million years ago.

TYPE `Rock` `Dragon`

ABILITY
Strong Jaw

HIDDEN ABILITY
None

STAT GROWTH RATES
HP ■■■
Attack ■■■■■
Defense ■■■■
Sp. Atk ■■
Sp. Def ■■
Speed ■■■

EGG GROUPS
Monster, Dragon

EVOLUTION

Level up to Lv. 39 between 4 A.M. and 7:59 P.M.

Tyrunt → Tyrantrum

ITEMS SOMETIMES HELD BY WILD POKÉMON
None

Damage taken in normal battles		Damage taken in Inverse Battles	
Normal	×0.5	Normal	×2
Fire	×0.25	Fire	×4
Water	×1	Water	×1
Grass	×1	Grass	×1
Electric	×0.5	Electric	×2
Ice	×2	Ice	×0.5
Fighting	×2	Fighting	×0.5
Poison	×0.5	Poison	×2
Ground	×2	Ground	×0.5
Flying	×0.5	Flying	×2
Psychic	×1	Psychic	×1
Bug	×1	Bug	×1
Rock	×1	Rock	×1
Ghost	×1	Ghost	×1
Dragon	×2	Dragon	×0.5
Dark	×1	Dark	×1
Steel	×2	Steel	×0.5
Fairy	×2	Fairy	×0.5

Can be used in	
Inverse Battle	Battle Institute
—	Battle Maison
Battle Chateau	Random Matchup

Same form for ♂ / ♀

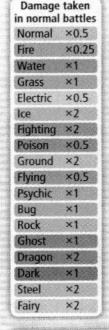

How to obtain for your Coastal Kalos Pokédex

❶ Receive Jaw Fossil from the assistant in Glittering Cave, then have it restored in Ambrette Town's Fossil Lab.
❷ Link Trade or transfer from another game.

❶ Receive Jaw Fossil from the assistant in Glittering Cave, then have it restored in Ambrette Town's Fossil Lab.
❷ Link Trade or transfer from another game.

● **LEVEL-UP MOVES**

Lv.	Name	Type	Kind	Pow.	Acc.	PP	Range
1	Tail Whip	Normal	Status	—	100	30	Many Others
1	Tackle	Normal	Physical	50	100	35	Normal
6	Roar	Normal	Status	—	—	20	Normal
10	Stomp	Normal	Physical	65	100	20	Normal
12	Bide	Normal	Physical	—	—	10	Self
15	Stealth Rock	Rock	Status	—	—	20	Other Side
17	Bite	Dark	Physical	60	100	25	Normal
20	Charm	Fairy	Status	—	100	20	Normal
26	Ancient Power	Rock	Special	60	100	5	Normal
30	Dragon Tail	Dragon	Physical	60	90	10	Normal
34	Crunch	Dark	Physical	80	100	15	Normal
37	Dragon Claw	Dragon	Physical	80	100	15	Normal
40	Thrash	Normal	Physical	120	100	10	1 Random
44	Earthquake	Ground	Physical	100	100	10	Adjacent
49	Horn Drill	Normal	Physical	—	30	5	Normal

● **TM & HM MOVES**

No.	Name	Type	Kind	Pow.	Acc.	PP	Range
TM01	Hone Claws	Dark	Status	—	—	15	Self
TM02	Dragon Claw	Dragon	Physical	80	100	15	Normal
TM05	Roar	Normal	Status	—	—	20	Normal
TM06	Toxic	Poison	Status	—	90	10	Normal
TM10	Hidden Power	Normal	Special	60	100	15	Both Sides
TM11	Sunny Day	Fire	Status	—	—	5	Both Sides
TM17	Protect	Normal	Status	—	—	10	Self
TM21	Frustration	Normal	Physical	—	100	20	Normal
TM26	Earthquake	Ground	Physical	100	100	10	Adjacent
TM27	Return	Normal	Physical	—	100	20	Normal
TM28	Dig	Ground	Physical	80	100	10	Normal
TM31	Brick Break	Fighting	Physical	75	100	15	Normal
TM32	Double Team	Normal	Status	—	—	15	Self
TM37	Sandstorm	Rock	Status	—	—	10	Both Sides
TM39	Rock Tomb	Rock	Physical	60	95	15	Normal
TM40	Aerial Ace	Flying	Physical	60	—	20	Normal
TM42	Facade	Normal	Physical	70	100	20	Normal
TM44	Rest	Psychic	Status	—	—	10	Self
TM45	Attract	Normal	Status	—	100	15	Normal
TM48	Round	Normal	Special	60	100	15	Normal
TM69	Rock Polish	Rock	Status	—	—	20	Self
TM71	Stone Edge	Rock	Physical	100	80	5	Normal
TM78	Bulldoze	Ground	Physical	60	100	20	Adjacent
TM80	Rock Slide	Rock	Physical	75	90	10	Many Others
TM82	Dragon Tail	Dragon	Physical	60	90	10	Normal
TM87	Swagger	Normal	Status	—	90	15	Normal
TM88	Sleep Talk	Normal	Status	—	—	10	Self
TM90	Substitute	Normal	Status	—	—	10	Self
TM94	Rock Smash	Fighting	Physical	40	100	15	Normal
TM97	Dark Pulse	Dark	Special	80	100	15	Normal
TM100	Confide	Normal	Status	—	—	20	Normal
HM04	Strength	Normal	Physical	80	100	15	Normal

● **MOVES TAUGHT BY PEOPLE**

Name	Type	Kind	Pow.	Acc.	PP	Range
Draco Meteor	Dragon	Special	130	90	5	Normal

● **EGG MOVES**

Name	Type	Kind	Pow.	Acc.	PP	Range
Dragon Dance	Dragon	Status	—	—	20	Self
Thunder Fang	Electric	Physical	65	95	15	Normal
Ice Fang	Ice	Physical	65	95	15	Normal
Poison Fang	Poison	Physical	50	100	15	Normal
Rock Polish	Rock	Status	—	—	20	Self
Fire Fang	Fire	Physical	65	95	15	Normal
Curse	Ghost	Status	—	—	10	Varies

AFTER THE HALL OF FAME

CENTRAL KALOS

COASTAL KALOS

065 Tyrantrum

MOUNTAIN KALOS

ADVENTURE DATA

🏠 Coastal Kalos — 065

Despot Pokémon

☑ Tyrantrum

HEIGHT: 8'02" WEIGHT: 595.2 lbs.
GENDER: ♂/♀

✗ Thanks to its gargantuan jaws, which could shred thick metal plates as if they were paper, it was invincible in the ancient world it once inhabited.

∨ Nothing could stop this Pokémon 100 million years ago, so it behaved like a king.

TYPE: Rock / Dragon

ABILITY
Strong Jaw

HIDDEN ABILITY
None

STAT GROWTH RATES
HP	■■■
Attack	■■■■■
Defense	■■■■■
Sp. Atk	■■■
Sp. Def	■■■
Speed	■■■■

EGG GROUPS
Monster, Dragon

☁ EVOLUTION
Level up to Lv. 39 between 4 A.M. and 7:59 P.M.

Tyrunt → Tyrantrum

ITEMS SOMETIMES HELD BY WILD POKÉMON
None

Damage taken in normal battles		Damage taken in Inverse Battles	
Normal	×0.5	Normal	×2
Fire	×0.25	Fire	×4
Water	×1	Water	×1
Grass	×1	Grass	×1
Electric	×0.5	Electric	×2
Ice	×2	Ice	×0.5
Fighting	×2	Fighting	×0.5
Poison	×0.5	Poison	×2
Ground	×2	Ground	×0.5
Flying	×2	Flying	×0.5
Psychic	×1	Psychic	×1
Bug	×1	Bug	×1
Rock	×1	Rock	×1
Ghost	×1	Ghost	×1
Dragon	×2	Dragon	×0.5
Dark	×1	Dark	×1
Steel	×2	Steel	×0.5
Fairy	×2	Fairy	×0.5

Can be used in	
Inverse Battle	Battle Institute
—	Battle Maison
Battle Chateau	Random Matchup

Same form for ♂/♀

How to obtain for your Coastal Kalos Pokédex
❶ Level up Tyrunt to Lv. 39 between 4 A.M. and 7:59 P.M.
❷ Link Trade or transfer from another game.

❶ Level up Tyrunt to Lv. 39 between 4 A.M. and 7:59 P.M.
❷ Link Trade or transfer from another game.

● LEVEL-UP MOVES
Lv.	Name	Type	Kind	Pow.	Acc.	PP	Range
1	Head Smash	Rock	Physical	150	80	5	Normal
1	Tail Whip	Normal	Status	—	100	30	Many Others
1	Tackle	Normal	Physical	50	100	35	Normal
6	Roar	Normal	Status	—	—	20	Normal
10	Stomp	Normal	Physical	65	100	20	Normal
12	Bide	Normal	Physical	—	—	10	Self
15	Stealth Rock	Rock	Status	—	—	20	Other Side
17	Bite	Dark	Physical	60	100	25	Normal
20	Charm	Fairy	Status	—	100	20	Normal
26	Ancient Power	Rock	Special	60	100	5	Normal
30	Dragon Tail	Dragon	Physical	60	90	10	Normal
34	Crunch	Dark	Physical	80	100	15	Normal
37	Dragon Claw	Dragon	Physical	80	100	15	Normal
42	Thrash	Normal	Physical	120	100	10	1 Random
47	Earthquake	Ground	Physical	100	100	10	Adjacent
53	Horn Drill	Normal	Physical	—	30	5	Normal
58	Head Smash	Rock	Physical	150	80	5	Normal
68	Rock Slide	Rock	Physical	75	90	10	Many Others
75	Giga Impact	Normal	Physical	150	90	5	Normal

● TM & HM MOVES
No.	Name	Type	Kind	Pow.	Acc.	PP	Range
TM01	Hone Claws	Dark	Status	—	—	15	Self
TM02	Dragon Claw	Dragon	Physical	80	100	15	Normal
TM05	Roar	Normal	Status	—	—	20	Normal
TM06	Toxic	Poison	Status	—	90	10	Normal
TM10	Hidden Power	Normal	Special	60	100	15	Normal
TM11	Sunny Day	Fire	Status	—	—	5	Both Sides
TM15	Hyper Beam	Normal	Special	150	90	5	Normal
TM17	Protect	Normal	Status	—	—	10	Self
TM21	Frustration	Normal	Physical	—	100	20	Normal
TM26	Earthquake	Ground	Physical	100	100	10	Adjacent
TM27	Return	Normal	Physical	—	100	20	Normal
TM28	Dig	Ground	Physical	80	100	10	Normal
TM31	Brick Break	Fighting	Physical	75	100	15	Normal
TM32	Double Team	Normal	Status	—	—	15	Self
TM37	Sandstorm	Rock	Status	—	—	10	Both Sides
TM39	Rock Tomb	Rock	Physical	60	95	15	Normal
TM40	Aerial Ace	Flying	Physical	60	—	20	Normal
TM42	Facade	Normal	Physical	70	100	20	Normal
TM44	Rest	Psychic	Status	—	—	10	Self
TM45	Attract	Normal	Status	—	100	15	Normal
TM48	Round	Normal	Special	60	100	15	Normal
TM68	Giga Impact	Normal	Physical	150	90	5	Normal
TM69	Rock Polish	Rock	Status	—	—	20	Self
TM71	Stone Edge	Rock	Physical	100	80	5	Normal
TM78	Bulldoze	Ground	Physical	60	100	20	Adjacent
TM80	Rock Slide	Rock	Physical	75	90	10	Many Others
TM82	Dragon Tail	Dragon	Physical	60	90	10	Normal
TM87	Swagger	Normal	Status	—	90	15	Normal
TM88	Sleep Talk	Normal	Status	—	—	10	Self
TM90	Substitute	Normal	Status	—	—	10	Self
TM94	Rock Smash	Fighting	Physical	40	100	15	Normal
TM97	Dark Pulse	Dark	Special	80	100	15	Normal
TM100	Confide	Normal	Status	—	—	20	Normal

No.	Name	Type	Kind	Pow.	Acc.	PP	Range
HM04	Strength	Normal	Physical	80	100	15	Normal

● MOVES TAUGHT BY PEOPLE
Name	Type	Kind	Pow.	Acc.	PP	Range

Coastal Kalos
Tundra Pokémon

✓ Amaura

066

HEIGHT: 4'03" WEIGHT: 55.6 lbs.
GENDER: ♂/♀

TYPE	Rock	Ice

ABILITY
Refrigerate

HIDDEN ABILITY
None

AFTER THE HALL OF FAME

CENTRAL KALOS

COASTAL KALOS

066 Amaura

MOUNTAIN KALOS

ADVENTURE DATA

▲ EVOLUTION

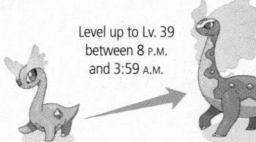

Level up to Lv. 39 between 8 P.M. and 3:59 A.M.

Amaura → Aurorus

X This ancient Pokémon was restored from part of its body that had been frozen in ice for over 100 million years.

Y This calm Pokémon lived in a cold land where there were no violent predators like Tyrantrum.

STAT GROWTH RATES

HP	■ ■ ■
Attack	■ ■ ■
Defense	■ ■
Sp. Atk	■ ■ ■
Sp. Def	■ ■ ■
Speed	■ ■ ■

EGG GROUP
Monster

ITEMS SOMETIMES HELD BY WILD POKÉMON
None

Damage taken in normal battles		Damage taken in Inverse Battles	
Normal	×0.5	Normal	×2
Fire	×1	Fire	×1
Water	×2	Water	×0.5
Grass	×2	Grass	×0.5
Electric	×1	Electric	×1
Ice	×0.5	Ice	×2
Fighting	×4	Fighting	×0.25
Poison	×0.5	Poison	×2
Ground	×2	Ground	×0.5
Flying	×0.5	Flying	×2
Psychic	×1	Psychic	×1
Bug	×1	Bug	×1
Rock	×2	Rock	×0.5
Ghost	×1	Ghost	×1
Dragon	×1	Dragon	×1
Dark	×1	Dark	×1
Steel	×4	Steel	×0.25
Fairy	×1	Fairy	×1

Can be used in
Inverse Battle
—
Battle Chateau
Battle Institute
Battle Maison
Random Matchup

How to obtain for your Coastal Kalos Pokédex

❶ Receive Sail Fossil from the assistant in Glittering Cave, then have it restored in Ambrette Town's Fossil Lab.
❷ Link Trade or transfer from another game.

❶ Receive Sail Fossil from the assistant in Glittering Cave, then have it restored in Ambrette Town's Fossil Lab.
❷ Link Trade or transfer from another game.

Same form for ♂/♀

● LEVEL-UP MOVES

Lv.	Name	Type	Kind	Pow.	Acc.	PP	Range
1	Growl	Normal	Status	—	100	40	Many Others
1	Powder Snow	Ice	Special	40	100	25	Many Others
5	Thunder Wave	Electric	Status	—	100	20	Normal
10	Rock Throw	Rock	Physical	50	90	15	Normal
13	Icy Wind	Ice	Special	55	95	15	Many Others
15	Take Down	Normal	Physical	90	85	20	Normal
18	Mist	Ice	Status	—	—	30	Your Side
22	Aurora Beam	Ice	Special	65	100	20	Normal
26	Ancient Power	Rock	Special	60	100	5	Normal
30	Round	Normal	Special	60	100	15	Normal
34	Avalanche	Ice	Physical	60	100	10	Normal
38	Hail	Ice	Status	—	—	10	Both Sides
41	Nature Power	Normal	Status	—	—	20	Normal
44	Encore	Normal	Status	—	100	5	Normal
47	Light Screen	Psychic	Status	—	—	30	Your Side
50	Ice Beam	Ice	Special	90	100	10	Normal
57	Hyper Beam	Normal	Special	150	90	5	Normal
65	Blizzard	Ice	Special	110	70	5	Many Others

● TM & HM MOVES

No.	Name	Type	Kind	Pow.	Acc.	PP	Range
TM04	Calm Mind	Psychic	Status	—	—	20	Self
TM05	Roar	Normal	Status	—	—	20	Normal
TM06	Toxic	Poison	Status	—	90	10	Normal
TM07	Hail	Ice	Status	—	—	10	Both Sides
TM10	Hidden Power	Normal	Special	60	100	15	Normal
TM13	Ice Beam	Ice	Special	90	100	10	Normal
TM14	Blizzard	Ice	Special	110	70	5	Many Others
TM15	Hyper Beam	Normal	Special	150	90	5	Normal
TM16	Light Screen	Psychic	Status	—	—	30	Your Side
TM17	Protect	Normal	Status	—	—	10	Self
TM18	Rain Dance	Water	Status	—	—	5	Both Sides
TM20	Safeguard	Normal	Status	—	—	25	Your Side
TM21	Frustration	Normal	Physical	—	100	20	Normal
TM24	Thunderbolt	Electric	Special	90	100	15	Normal
TM27	Return	Normal	Physical	—	100	20	Normal
TM32	Double Team	Normal	Status	—	—	15	Self
TM33	Reflect	Psychic	Status	—	—	20	Your Side
TM37	Sandstorm	Rock	Status	—	—	10	Both Sides
TM39	Rock Tomb	Rock	Physical	60	95	15	Normal
TM42	Facade	Normal	Physical	70	100	20	Normal
TM44	Rest	Psychic	Status	—	—	10	Self
TM45	Attract	Normal	Status	—	100	15	Normal
TM48	Round	Normal	Special	60	100	15	Normal
TM49	Echoed Voice	Normal	Special	40	100	15	Normal
TM57	Charge Beam	Electric	Special	50	90	10	Normal
TM69	Rock Polish	Rock	Status	—	—	20	Self
TM70	Flash	Normal	Status	—	100	20	Normal
TM71	Stone Edge	Rock	Physical	100	80	5	Normal
TM73	Thunder Wave	Electric	Status	—	100	20	Normal
TM77	Psych Up	Normal	Status	—	—	10	Normal
TM78	Bulldoze	Ground	Physical	60	100	20	Adjacent
TM79	Frost Breath	Ice	Special	60	90	10	Normal
TM80	Rock Slide	Rock	Physical	75	90	10	Many Others
TM82	Dragon Tail	Dragon	Physical	60	90	10	Normal
TM85	Dream Eater	Psychic	Special	100	100	15	Normal
TM87	Swagger	Normal	Status	—	90	15	Normal
TM88	Sleep Talk	Normal	Status	—	—	10	Self
TM90	Substitute	Normal	Status	—	—	10	Self
TM91	Flash Cannon	Steel	Special	80	100	10	Normal
TM94	Rock Smash	Fighting	Physical	40	100	15	Normal
TM96	Nature Power	Normal	Status	—	—	20	Normal
TM95	Dark Pulse	Dark	Special	80	100	15	Normal
TM100	Confide	Normal	Status	—	—	20	Normal

● MOVES TAUGHT BY PEOPLE

Name	Type	Kind	Pow.	Acc.	PP	Range

● EGG MOVES

Name	Type	Kind	Pow.	Acc.	PP	Range
Haze	Ice	Status	—	—	30	Both Sides
Barrier	Psychic	Status	—	—	20	Self
Mirror Coat	Psychic	Special	—	100	20	Varies
Magnet Rise	Electric	Status	—	—	10	Self
Discharge	Electric	Special	80	100	15	Adjacent

AFTER THE HALL OF FAME

CENTRAL KALOS

COASTAL KALOS

067

Aururos

MOUNTAIN KALOS

ADVENTURE DATA

🌿 Coastal Kalos   **067**

Tundra Pokémon

☑ **Aururos**

HEIGHT: 8'10"   WEIGHT: 496.0 lbs.
GENDER: ♂ / ♀

❌ The diamond-shaped crystals on its body expel air as cold as -240 degrees Fahrenheit, surrounding its enemies and encasing them in ice.

V Using its diamond-shaped crystals, it can instantly create a wall of ice to block an opponent's attack.

TYPE Rock Ice

ABILITY
Refrigerate

HIDDEN ABILITY
None

STAT GROWTH RATES

HP	■■■■■
Attack	■■■■
Defense	■■
Sp. Atk	■■■■■
Sp. Def	■■■■
Speed	■■■

EGG GROUP
Monster

EVOLUTION

Level up to Lv. 39 between 8 P.M. and 3:59 A.M.

Amaura → Aururos

ITEMS SOMETIMES HELD BY WILD POKÉMON
None

Can be used in

Inverse Battle

—

Battle Chateau
Battle Institute
Battle Maison
Random Matchup

Damage taken in normal battles	
Normal	×0.5
Fire	×1
Water	×2
Grass	×2
Electric	×1
Ice	×0.5
Fighting	×4
Poison	×0.5
Ground	×2
Flying	×0.5
Psychic	×1
Bug	×1
Rock	×1
Ghost	×1
Dragon	×1
Dark	×1
Steel	×4
Fairy	×1

Damage taken in Inverse Battles	
Normal	×2
Fire	×1
Water	×0.5
Grass	×0.5
Electric	×1
Ice	×2
Fighting	×0.25
Poison	×2
Ground	×0.5
Flying	×2
Psychic	×1
Bug	×1
Rock	×0.5
Ghost	×1
Dragon	×1
Dark	×1
Steel	×0.25
Fairy	×1

How to obtain for your Coastal Kalos Pokédex

❶ Level up Amaura to Lv. 39 between 8 P.M. and 3:59 A.M.
❷ Link Trade or transfer from another game.

❶ Level up Amaura to Lv. 39 between 8 P.M. and 3:59 A.M.
❷ Link Trade or transfer from another game.

Same form for ♂ / ♀

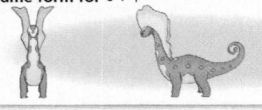

● LEVEL-UP MOVES

Lv.	Name	Type	Kind	Pow.	Acc.	PP	Range
1	Freeze-Dry	Ice	Special	70	100	20	Normal
1	Growl	Normal	Status	—	100	40	Many Others
1	Powder Snow	Ice	Special	40	100	25	Many Others
5	Thunder Wave	Electric	Status	—	100	20	Normal
10	Rock Throw	Rock	Physical	50	90	15	Normal
13	Icy Wind	Ice	Special	55	95	15	Many Others
15	Take Down	Normal	Physical	90	85	20	Normal
18	Mist	Ice	Status	—	—	30	Your Side
20	Aurora Beam	Ice	Special	65	100	20	Normal
26	Ancient Power	Rock	Special	60	100	5	Normal
30	Round	Normal	Special	60	100	15	Normal
34	Avalanche	Ice	Physical	60	100	10	Normal
38	Hail	Ice	Status	—	—	10	Both Sides
43	Nature Power	Normal	Status	—	—	20	Normal
46	Encore	Normal	Status	—	100	5	Normal
50	Light Screen	Psychic	Status	—	—	30	Your Side
56	Ice Beam	Ice	Special	90	100	10	Normal
63	Hyper Beam	Normal	Special	150	90	5	Normal
74	Blizzard	Ice	Special	110	70	5	Many Others
77	Freeze-Dry	Ice	Special	70	100	20	Normal

● TM & HM MOVES

No.	Name	Type	Kind	Pow.	Acc.	PP	Range
TM04	Calm Mind	Psychic	Status	—	—	20	Self
TM05	Roar	Normal	Status	—	—	20	Normal
TM06	Toxic	Poison	Status	—	90	10	Normal
TM07	Hail	Ice	Status	—	—	10	Both Sides
TM10	Hidden Power	Normal	Special	60	100	15	Normal
TM13	Ice Beam	Ice	Special	90	100	10	Normal
TM14	Blizzard	Ice	Special	110	70	5	Many Others
TM15	Hyper Beam	Normal	Special	150	90	5	Normal
TM16	Light Screen	Psychic	Status	—	—	30	Your Side
TM17	Protect	Normal	Status	—	—	10	Self
TM18	Rain Dance	Water	Status	—	—	5	Both Sides
TM20	Safeguard	Normal	Status	—	—	25	Your Side
TM21	Frustration	Normal	Physical	—	100	20	Normal
TM24	Thunderbolt	Electric	Special	90	100	15	Normal
TM25	Thunder	Electric	Special	110	70	10	Normal
TM26	Earthquake	Ground	Physical	100	100	10	Adjacent
TM27	Return	Normal	Physical	—	100	20	Normal
TM29	Psychic	Psychic	Special	90	100	10	Normal
TM32	Double Team	Normal	Status	—	—	15	Self
TM33	Reflect	Psychic	Status	—	—	20	Your Side
TM37	Sandstorm	Rock	Status	—	—	10	Both Sides
TM39	Rock Tomb	Rock	Physical	60	95	15	Normal
TM42	Facade	Normal	Physical	70	100	20	Normal
TM44	Rest	Psychic	Status	—	—	10	Self
TM45	Attract	Normal	Status	—	100	15	Normal
TM48	Round	Normal	Special	60	100	15	Normal
TM49	Echoed Voice	Normal	Special	40	100	15	Normal
TM57	Charge Beam	Electric	Special	50	90	10	Normal
TM68	Giga Impact	Normal	Physical	150	90	5	Normal
TM69	Rock Polish	Rock	Status	—	—	20	Self
TM70	Flash	Normal	Status	—	100	20	Normal
TM71	Stone Edge	Rock	Physical	100	80	5	Normal
TM73	Thunder Wave	Electric	Status	—	100	20	Normal
TM77	Psych Up	Normal	Status	—	—	10	Normal
TM78	Bulldoze	Ground	Physical	60	100	20	Adjacent
TM79	Frost Breath	Ice	Special	60	90	10	Normal
TM80	Rock Slide	Rock	Physical	75	90	10	Many Others
TM82	Dragon Tail	Dragon	Physical	60	90	10	Normal
TM85	Dream Eater	Psychic	Special	100	100	15	Normal
TM87	Swagger	Normal	Status	—	90	15	Normal
TM88	Sleep Talk	Normal	Status	—	—	10	Self
TM90	Substitute	Normal	Status	—	—	10	Self
TM91	Flash Cannon	Steel	Special	80	100	10	Normal
TM94	Rock Smash	Fighting	Physical	40	100	15	Normal
TM96	Nature Power	Normal	Status	—	—	20	Normal
TM97	Dark Pulse	Dark	Special	80	100	15	Normal
TM100	Confide	Normal	Status	—	—	20	Normal

● MOVES TAUGHT BY PEOPLE

Name	Type	Kind	Pow.	Acc.	PP	Range

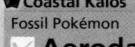 **Coastal Kalos**
Fossil Pokémon

068

☑ **Aerodactyl**

HEIGHT: 5'11" WEIGHT: 130.1 lbs.
GENDER: ♂/♀

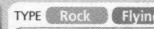 **TYPE** Rock Flying

ABILITIES
Rock Head
Pressure

HIDDEN ABILITY
Unnerve

STAT GROWTH RATES
HP	■■■
Attack	■■■■■
Defense	■■■■
Sp. Atk	■■■
Sp. Def	■■■
Speed	■■■■■■■

EGG GROUP
Flying

 X It was regenerated from a dinosaur's genetic matter that was found in amber. It flies with high-pitched cries.

Y This vicious Pokémon is said to have flown in ancient skies while shrieking high-pitched cries.

⬆ EVOLUTION

Does not evolve

ITEMS SOMETIMES HELD BY WILD POKÉMON
None

Damage taken in normal battles		Damage taken in Inverse Battles	
Normal	×0.5	Normal	×2
Fire	×1	Fire	×2
Water	×2	Water	×0.5
Grass	×1	Grass	×1
Electric	×2	Electric	×0.5
Ice	×2	Ice	×0.5
Fighting	×1	Fighting	×1
Poison	×0.5	Poison	×2
Ground	×0	Ground	×1
Flying	×0.5	Flying	×2
Psychic	×1	Psychic	×1
Bug	×0.5	Bug	×2
Rock	×1	Rock	×0.5
Ghost	×1	Ghost	×1
Dragon	×1	Dragon	×1
Dark	×1	Dark	×1
Steel	×2	Steel	×0.5
Fairy	×1	Fairy	×1

Can be used in
Inverse Battle	Battle Institute
Sky Battle	Battle Maison
Battle Chateau	Random Matchup

Same form for ♂/♀

How to obtain for your Coastal Kalos Pokédex

Smash a rock and obtain an Old Amber in Glittering Cave, and then have it restored in Ambrette Town's Fossil Lab.

Smash a rock and obtain an Old Amber in Glittering Cave, and then have it restored in Ambrette Town's Fossil Lab.

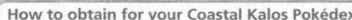

● LEVEL-UP MOVES

Lv.	Name	Type	Kind	Pow.	Acc.	PP	Range
1	Iron Head	Steel	Physical	80	100	15	Normal
1	Ice Fang	Ice	Physical	65	95	15	Normal
1	Fire Fang	Fire	Physical	65	95	15	Normal
1	Thunder Fang	Electric	Physical	65	95	15	Normal
1	Wing Attack	Flying	Physical	60	100	35	Normal
1	Supersonic	Normal	Status	—	55	20	Normal
1	Bite	Dark	Physical	60	100	25	Normal
1	Scary Face	Normal	Status	—	100	10	Normal
9	Roar	Normal	Status	—	—	20	Normal
17	Agility	Psychic	Status	—	—	30	Self
25	Ancient Power	Rock	Special	60	100	5	Normal
33	Crunch	Dark	Physical	80	100	15	Normal
41	Take Down	Normal	Physical	90	85	20	Normal
49	Sky Drop	Flying	Physical	60	100	10	Normal
57	Iron Head	Steel	Physical	80	100	15	Normal
65	Hyper Beam	Normal	Special	150	90	5	Normal
73	Rock Slide	Rock	Physical	75	90	10	Many Others
81	Giga Impact	Normal	Physical	150	90	5	Normal

● TM & HM MOVES

No.	Name	Type	Kind	Pow.	Acc.	PP	Range
TM01	Hone Claws	Dark	Status	—	—	15	Self
TM02	Dragon Claw	Dragon	Physical	80	100	15	Normal
TM05	Roar	Normal	Status	—	—	20	Normal
TM06	Toxic	Poison	Status	—	90	10	Normal
TM10	Hidden Power	Normal	Special	60	100	15	Normal
TM11	Sunny Day	Fire	Status	—	—	5	Both Sides
TM12	Taunt	Dark	Status	—	100	20	Normal
TM15	Hyper Beam	Normal	Special	150	90	5	Normal
TM17	Protect	Normal	Status	—	—	10	Self
TM18	Rain Dance	Water	Status	—	—	5	Both Sides
TM19	Roost	Flying	Status	—	—	10	Self
TM21	Frustration	Normal	Physical	—	100	20	Normal
TM23	Smack Down	Rock	Physical	50	100	15	Normal
TM26	Earthquake	Ground	Physical	100	100	10	Adjacent
TM27	Return	Normal	Physical	—	100	20	Normal
TM32	Double Team	Normal	Status	—	—	15	Self
TM35	Flamethrower	Fire	Special	90	100	15	Normal
TM37	Sandstorm	Rock	Status	—	—	10	Both Sides
TM38	Fire Blast	Fire	Special	110	85	5	Normal
TM39	Rock Tomb	Rock	Physical	60	95	15	Normal
TM40	Aerial Ace	Flying	Physical	60	—	20	Normal
TM41	Torment	Dark	Status	—	100	15	Normal
TM42	Facade	Normal	Physical	70	100	20	Normal
TM44	Rest	Psychic	Status	—	—	10	Self
TM45	Attract	Normal	Status	—	100	15	Normal
TM46	Thief	Dark	Physical	60	100	25	Normal
TM48	Round	Normal	Special	60	100	15	Normal
TM51	Steel Wing	Steel	Physical	70	90	25	Normal
TM58	Sky Drop	Flying	Physical	60	100	10	Normal
TM59	Incinerate	Fire	Special	60	100	15	Many Others
TM66	Payback	Dark	Physical	50	100	10	Normal
TM68	Giga Impact	Normal	Physical	150	90	5	Normal
TM69	Rock Polish	Rock	Status	—	—	20	Self

No.	Name	Type	Kind	Pow.	Acc.	PP	Range
TM71	Stone Edge	Rock	Physical	100	80	5	Normal
TM78	Bulldoze	Ground	Physical	60	100	20	Adjacent
TM80	Rock Slide	Rock	Physical	75	90	10	Many Others
TM87	Swagger	Normal	Status	—	90	15	Normal
TM88	Sleep Talk	Normal	Status	—	—	10	Self
TM90	Substitute	Normal	Status	—	—	10	Self
TM94	Rock Smash	Fighting	Physical	40	100	15	Normal
TM100	Confide	Normal	Status	—	—	20	Normal
HM02	Fly	Flying	Physical	90	95	15	Normal
HM04	Strength	Normal	Physical	80	100	15	Normal

● MOVES TAUGHT BY PEOPLE

Name	Type	Kind	Pow.	Acc.	PP	Range

● EGG MOVES

Name	Type	Kind	Pow.	Acc.	PP	Range
Whirlwind	Normal	Status	—	—	20	Normal
Pursuit	Dark	Physical	40	100	20	Normal
Foresight	Normal	Status	—	—	40	Normal
Steel Wing	Steel	Physical	70	90	25	Normal
Dragon Breath	Dragon	Special	60	100	20	Normal
Curse	Ghost	Status	—	—	10	Varies
Assurance	Dark	Physical	60	100	10	Normal
Roost	Flying	Status	—	—	10	Self
Tailwind	Flying	Status	—	—	15	Your Side
Wide Guard	Rock	Status	—	—	10	Your Side

AFTER THE HALL OF FAME

CENTRAL KALOS

COASTAL KALOS

068 | Aerodactyl

MOUNTAIN KALOS

ADVENTURE DATA

Mega Evolution

Fossil Pokémon

☑ Mega Aerodactyl

TYPE	Rock	Flying

ABILITY
Tough Claws

STAT GROWTH RATES

HP	■■■
Attack	■■■■■■■
Defense	■■■■
Sp. Atk	■■■
Sp. Def	■■■■
Speed	■■■■■■■■

MEGA STONE REQUIRED

Aerodactylite
Talk to a male Scientist in Ambrette Town's Fossil Lab to receive it (after meeting the assistant in Glittering Cave).

HEIGHT: 6'11" WEIGHT: 174.2 lbs. GENDER: ♂ / ♀

Damage taken in normal battles	
Normal	×0.5
Fire	×0.5
Water	×2
Grass	×1
Electric	×2
Ice	×2
Fighting	×1
Poison	×0.5
Ground	×0
Flying	×0.5
Psychic	×1
Bug	×0.5
Rock	×2
Ghost	×1
Dragon	×1
Dark	×1
Steel	×2
Fairy	×1

Damage taken in Inverse Battles	
Normal	×2
Fire	×2
Water	×0.5
Grass	×1
Electric	×0.5
Ice	×0.5
Fighting	×1
Poison	×2
Ground	×1
Flying	×2
Psychic	×1
Bug	×2
Rock	×0.5
Ghost	×1
Dragon	×1
Dark	×1
Steel	×0.5
Fairy	×1

Can be used in
Inverse Battle
Sky Battle
Battle Chateau
Battle Institute
Battle Maison
Random Matchup

Same form for ♂ / ♀

AFTER THE HALL OF FAME

CENTRAL KALOS

COASTAL KALOS

Mega Aerodactyl

MOUNTAIN KALOS

ADVENTURE DATA

Coastal Kalos — 069
Thorn Seed Pokémon
Ferroseed

HEIGHT: 2'00" WEIGHT: 41.4 lbs.
GENDER: ♂/♀

TYPE Grass | Steel

ABILITY
Iron Barbs

HIDDEN ABILITY
None

STAT GROWTH RATES
HP ■■
Attack ■■■
Defense ■■■■
Sp. Atk ■
Sp. Def ■
Speed ■■■■

EGG GROUPS
Grass, Mineral

X When threatened, it attacks by shooting a barrage of spikes, which gives it a chance to escape by rolling away.

Y It absorbs the iron it finds in the rock while clinging to the ceiling. It shoots spikes when in danger.

EVOLUTION

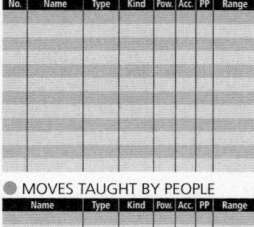

Ferroseed → Lv. 40 → Ferrothorn

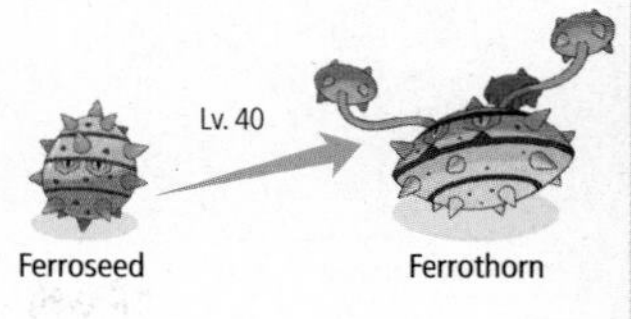

ITEMS SOMETIMES HELD BY WILD POKÉMON
Sticky Barb

Damage taken in normal battles	
Normal	×0.5
Fire	×4
Water	×0.5
Grass	×0.25
Electric	×0.5
Ice	×1
Fighting	×2
Poison	×0
Ground	×1
Flying	×1
Psychic	×0.5
Bug	×1
Rock	×0.5
Ghost	×1
Dragon	×0.5
Dark	×1
Steel	×0.5
Fairy	×0.5

Damage taken in Inverse Battles	
Normal	×2
Fire	×0.25
Water	×2
Grass	×4
Electric	×2
Ice	×1
Fighting	×0.5
Poison	×1
Ground	×1
Flying	×1
Psychic	×2
Bug	×1
Rock	×2
Ghost	×1
Dragon	×2
Dark	×1
Steel	×2
Fairy	×2

Can be used in
Inverse Battle
—
Battle Chateau
Battle Institute
Battle Maison
Random Matchup

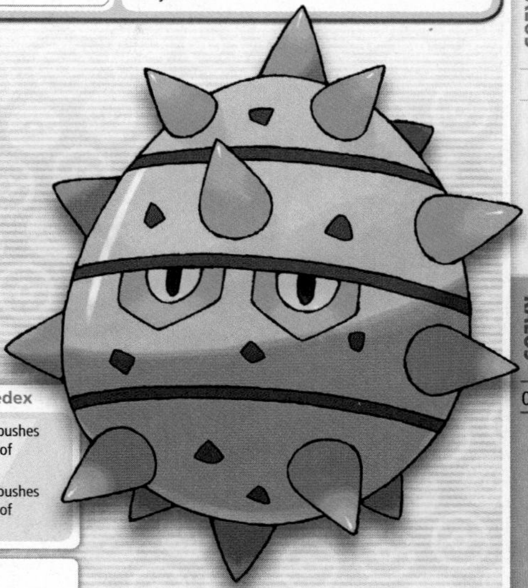

How to obtain for your Coastal Kalos Pokédex

❶ Catch when it ambushes you from the roof of Glittering Cave.
❷ Catch when it ambushes you from the roof of Reflection Cave.

❶ Catch when it ambushes you from the roof of Glittering Cave.
❷ Catch when it ambushes you from the roof of Reflection Cave.

Same form for ♂/♀

● LEVEL-UP MOVES

Lv.	Name	Type	Kind	Pow.	Acc.	PP	Range
1	Tackle	Normal	Physical	50	100	35	Normal
1	Harden	Normal	Status	—	—	30	Self
6	Rollout	Rock	Physical	30	90	20	Normal
9	Curse	Ghost	Status	—	—	10	Varies
14	Metal Claw	Steel	Physical	50	95	35	Normal
18	Pin Missile	Bug	Physical	25	95	20	Normal
21	Gyro Ball	Steel	Physical	—	100	5	Normal
26	Iron Defense	Steel	Status	—	—	15	Self
30	Mirror Shot	Steel	Special	65	85	10	Normal
35	Ingrain	Grass	Status	—	—	20	Self
38	Self-Destruct	Normal	Physical	200	100	5	Adjacent
43	Iron Head	Steel	Physical	80	100	15	Normal
47	Payback	Dark	Physical	50	100	10	Normal
52	Flash Cannon	Steel	Special	80	100	10	Normal
55	Explosion	Normal	Physical	250	100	5	Adjacent

● TM & HM MOVES

No.	Name	Type	Kind	Pow.	Acc.	PP	Range
TM01	Hone Claws	Dark	Status	—	—	15	Self
TM06	Toxic	Poison	Status	—	90	10	Normal
TM10	Hidden Power	Normal	Special	60	100	15	Normal
TM11	Sunny Day	Fire	Status	—	—	5	Both Sides
TM17	Protect	Normal	Status	—	—	10	Self
TM21	Frustration	Normal	Physical	—	100	20	Normal
TM22	Solar Beam	Grass	Special	120	100	10	Normal
TM24	Thunderbolt	Electric	Special	90	100	15	Normal
TM27	Return	Normal	Physical	—	100	20	Normal
TM32	Double Team	Normal	Status	—	—	15	Self
TM42	Facade	Normal	Physical	70	100	20	Normal
TM44	Rest	Psychic	Status	—	—	10	Self
TM48	Round	Normal	Special	60	100	15	Normal
TM53	Energy Ball	Grass	Special	90	100	10	Normal
TM64	Explosion	Normal	Physical	250	100	5	Adjacent
TM66	Payback	Dark	Physical	50	100	10	Normal
TM69	Rock Polish	Rock	Status	—	—	20	Self
TM70	Flash	Normal	Status	—	100	20	Normal
TM73	Thunder Wave	Electric	Status	—	100	20	Normal
TM74	Gyro Ball	Steel	Physical	—	100	5	Normal
TM84	Poison Jab	Poison	Physical	80	100	20	Normal
TM87	Swagger	Normal	Status	—	90	15	Normal
TM88	Sleep Talk	Normal	Status	—	—	10	Self
TM90	Substitute	Normal	Status	—	—	10	Self
TM91	Flash Cannon	Steel	Special	80	100	10	Normal
TM94	Rock Smash	Fighting	Physical	40	100	15	Normal
TM96	Nature Power	Normal	Status	—	—	20	Normal
TM100	Confide	Normal	Status	—	—	20	Normal

No.	Name	Type	Kind	Pow.	Acc.	PP	Range

● MOVES TAUGHT BY PEOPLE

Name	Type	Kind	Pow.	Acc.	PP	Range

● EGG MOVES

Name	Type	Kind	Pow.	Acc.	PP	Range
Bullet Seed	Grass	Physical	25	100	30	Normal
Leech Seed	Grass	Status	—	90	10	Normal
Spikes	Ground	Status	—	—	20	Other Side
Worry Seed	Grass	Status	—	100	10	Normal
Seed Bomb	Grass	Physical	80	100	15	Normal
Gravity	Psychic	Status	—	—	5	Both Sides
Rock Climb	Normal	Physical	90	85	20	Normal
Stealth Rock	Rock	Status	—	—	20	Other Side
Acid Spray	Poison	Special	40	100	20	Normal

AFTER THE HALL OF FAME

CENTRAL KALOS

COASTAL KALOS

069 | Ferroseed

MOUNTAIN KALOS

ADVENTURE DATA

AFTER THE HALL OF FAME

CENTRAL KALOS

COASTAL KALOS
070

Ferrothorn

MOUNTAIN KALOS

ADVENTURE DATA

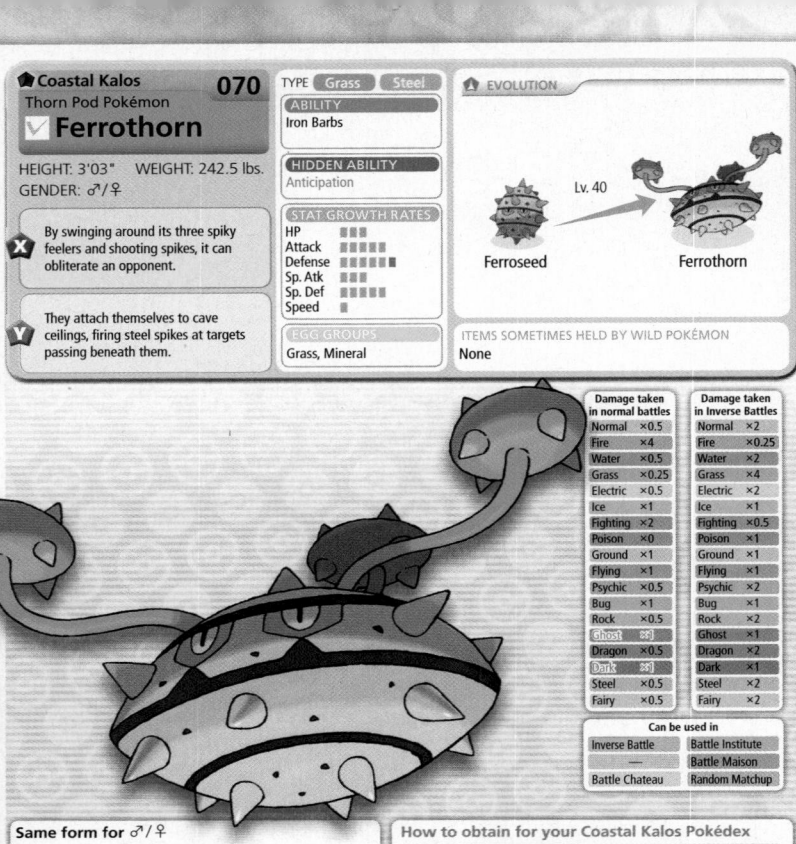

Coastal Kalos 070
Thorn Pod Pokémon
Ferrothorn

HEIGHT: 3'03" WEIGHT: 242.5 lbs.
GENDER: ♂/♀

X By swinging around its three spiky feelers and shooting spikes, it can obliterate an opponent.

Y They attach themselves to cave ceilings, firing steel spikes at targets passing beneath them.

TYPE Grass | Steel

ABILITY
Iron Barbs

HIDDEN ABILITY
Anticipation

STAT GROWTH RATES
HP	■■■
Attack	■■■■■
Defense	■■■■■■
Sp. Atk	■■■
Sp. Def	■■■■■
Speed	■

EGG GROUPS
Grass, Mineral

EVOLUTION

Ferroseed — Lv. 40 → Ferrothorn

ITEMS SOMETIMES HELD BY WILD POKÉMON
None

	Damage taken in normal battles		Damage taken in Inverse Battles
Normal	×0.5	Normal	×2
Fire	×4	Fire	×0.25
Water	×0.5	Water	×2
Grass	×0.25	Grass	×4
Electric	×0.5	Electric	×2
Ice	×1	Ice	×1
Fighting	×2	Fighting	×0.5
Poison	×0	Poison	×1
Ground	×1	Ground	×1
Flying	×1	Flying	×1
Psychic	×0.5	Psychic	×2
Bug	×1	Bug	×1
Rock	×0.5	Rock	×2
Ghost	×1	Ghost	×1
Dragon	×0.5	Dragon	×2
Dark	×1	Dark	×1
Steel	×0.5	Steel	×2
Fairy	×0.5	Fairy	×2

Can be used in
Inverse Battle	Battle Institute
—	Battle Maison
Battle Chateau	Random Matchup

Same form for ♂/♀

How to obtain for your Coastal Kalos Pokédex
| Level up Ferroseed to Lv. 40. | Level up Ferroseed to Lv. 40. |

● LEVEL-UP MOVES

Lv.	Name	Type	Kind	Pow.	Acc.	PP	Range
1	Rock Climb	Normal	Physical	90	85	20	Normal
1	Tackle	Normal	Physical	50	100	35	Normal
1	Harden	Normal	Status	—	—	30	Self
1	Rollout	Rock	Physical	30	90	20	Normal
6	Rollout	Rock	Physical	30	90	20	Normal
9	Curse	Ghost	Status	—	—	10	Varies
14	Metal Claw	Steel	Physical	50	95	35	Normal
18	Pin Missile	Bug	Physical	25	95	20	Normal
21	Gyro Ball	Steel	Physical	—	100	5	Normal
26	Iron Defense	Steel	Status	—	—	15	Self
30	Mirror Shot	Steel	Special	65	85	10	Normal
35	Ingrain	Grass	Status	—	—	20	Self
38	Self-Destruct	Normal	Physical	200	100	5	Adjacent
40	Power Whip	Grass	Physical	120	85	10	Normal
46	Iron Head	Steel	Physical	80	100	15	Normal
53	Payback	Dark	Physical	50	100	10	Normal
61	Flash Cannon	Steel	Special	80	100	10	Normal
67	Explosion	Normal	Physical	250	100	5	Adjacent

● TM & HM MOVES

No.	Name	Type	Kind	Pow.	Acc.	PP	Range
TM01	Hone Claws	Dark	Status	—	—	15	Self
TM06	Toxic	Poison	Status	—	90	10	Normal
TM10	Hidden Power	Normal	Special	60	100	15	Normal
TM11	Sunny Day	Fire	Status	—	—	5	Both Sides
TM15	Hyper Beam	Normal	Special	150	90	5	Normal
TM17	Protect	Normal	Status	—	—	10	Self
TM21	Frustration	Normal	Physical	—	100	20	Normal
TM22	Solar Beam	Grass	Special	120	100	10	Normal
TM24	Thunderbolt	Electric	Special	90	100	15	Normal
TM25	Thunder	Electric	Special	110	70	10	Normal
TM27	Return	Normal	Physical	—	100	20	Normal
TM32	Double Team	Normal	Status	—	—	15	Self
TM37	Sandstorm	Rock	Status	—	—	10	Both Sides
TM40	Aerial Ace	Flying	Physical	60	—	20	Normal
TM42	Facade	Normal	Physical	70	100	20	Normal
TM44	Rest	Psychic	Status	—	—	10	Self
TM48	Round	Normal	Special	60	100	15	Normal
TM53	Energy Ball	Grass	Special	90	100	10	Normal
TM64	Explosion	Normal	Physical	250	100	5	Adjacent
TM65	Shadow Claw	Ghost	Physical	70	100	15	Normal
TM66	Payback	Dark	Physical	50	100	10	Normal
TM68	Giga Impact	Normal	Physical	150	90	5	Normal
TM69	Rock Polish	Rock	Status	—	—	20	Self
TM70	Flash	Normal	Status	—	100	20	Normal
TM73	Thunder Wave	Electric	Status	—	100	20	Normal
TM74	Gyro Ball	Steel	Physical	—	100	5	Normal
TM75	Swords Dance	Normal	Status	—	—	20	Self
TM78	Bulldoze	Ground	Physical	60	100	20	Adjacent
TM84	Poison Jab	Poison	Physical	80	100	20	Normal
TM86	Grass Knot	Grass	Special	—	100	20	Normal
TM87	Swagger	Normal	Status	—	90	15	Normal
TM88	Sleep Talk	Normal	Status	—	—	10	Self
TM90	Substitute	Normal	Status	—	—	10	Self

No.	Name	Type	Kind	Pow.	Acc.	PP	Range
TM91	Flash Cannon	Steel	Special	80	100	10	Normal
TM94	Rock Smash	Fighting	Physical	40	100	15	Normal
TM96	Nature Power	Normal	Status	—	—	20	Normal
TM100	Confide	Normal	Status	—	—	20	Normal
HM01	Cut	Normal	Physical	50	95	30	Normal
HM04	Strength	Normal	Physical	80	100	15	Normal

● MOVES TAUGHT BY PEOPLE

Name	Type	Kind	Pow.	Acc.	PP	Range

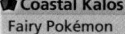

Coastal Kalos 071

Fairy Pokémon

Snubbull

HEIGHT: 2'00" WEIGHT: 17.2 lbs.
GENDER: ♂/♀

X It has an active, playful nature. Many women like to frolic with it because of its affectionate ways.

Y Small Pokémon flee from its scary face. It is, however, considered by women to be cute.

TYPE Fairy

ABILITIES
Intimidate
Run Away

HIDDEN ABILITY
Rattled

STAT GROWTH RATES
HP	■■■
Attack	■■■■
Defense	■■
Sp. Atk	■■
Sp. Def	■■
Speed	■■

EGG GROUPS
Field, Fairy

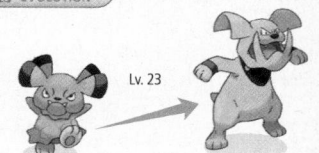

EVOLUTION

Snubbull → Lv. 23 → Granbull

ITEMS SOMETIMES HELD BY WILD POKÉMON
None

Damage taken in normal battles		Damage taken in Inverse Battles		Can be used in
Normal	×1	Normal	×1	Inverse Battle
Fire	×1	Fire	×1	——
Water	×1	Water	×1	Battle Chateau
Grass	×1	Grass	×1	Battle Institute
Electric	×1	Electric	×1	Battle Maison
Ice	×1	Ice	×1	Random Matchup
Fighting	×0.5	Fighting	×2	
Poison	×2	Poison	×0.5	
Ground	×1	Ground	×1	
Flying	×1	Flying	×1	
Psychic	×1	Psychic	×1	
Bug	×0.5	Bug	×2	
Rock	×1	Rock	×1	
Ghost	×1	Ghost	×1	
Dragon	×0	Dragon	×1	
Dark	×0.5	Dark	×2	
Steel	×2	Steel	×0.5	
Fairy	×1	Fairy	×1	

How to obtain for your Coastal Kalos Pokédex

❶ Catch in the tall grass on Route 10.
❷ Catch in the yellow flowers on Route 10.

❶ Catch in the tall grass on Route 10.
❷ Catch in the yellow flowers on Route 10.

Same form for ♂/♀

● LEVEL-UP MOVES

Lv.	Name	Type	Kind	Pow.	Acc.	PP	Range
1	Ice Fang	Ice	Physical	65	95	15	Normal
1	Fire Fang	Fire	Physical	65	95	15	Normal
1	Thunder Fang	Electric	Physical	65	95	15	Normal
1	Tackle	Normal	Physical	50	100	35	Normal
1	Scary Face	Normal	Status	—	100	10	Normal
1	Charm	Fairy	Status	—	100	20	Normal
7	Bite	Dark	Physical	60	100	25	Normal
13	Lick	Ghost	Physical	30	100	30	Normal
19	Headbutt	Normal	Physical	70	100	15	Normal
25	Roar	Normal	Status	—	—	20	Normal
31	Rage	Normal	Physical	20	100	20	Normal
37	Play Rough	Fairy	Physical	90	90	10	Normal
43	Payback	Dark	Physical	50	100	10	Normal
49	Crunch	Dark	Physical	80	100	15	Normal

● TM & HM MOVES

No.	Name	Type	Kind	Pow.	Acc.	PP	Range
TM05	Roar	Normal	Status	—	—	20	Normal
TM06	Toxic	Poison	Status	—	90	10	Normal

● TM & HM MOVES

No.	Name	Type	Kind	Pow.	Acc.	PP	Range
TM08	Bulk Up	Fighting	Status	—	—	20	Self
TM10	Hidden Power	Normal	Special	60	100	15	Normal
TM11	Sunny Day	Fire	Status	—	—	5	Both Sides
TM12	Taunt	Dark	Status	—	100	20	Normal
TM17	Protect	Normal	Status	—	—	10	Self
TM18	Rain Dance	Water	Status	—	—	5	Both Sides
TM21	Frustration	Normal	Physical	—	100	20	Normal
TM22	Solar Beam	Grass	Special	120	100	10	Normal
TM24	Thunderbolt	Electric	Special	90	100	15	Normal
TM25	Thunder	Electric	Special	110	70	10	Normal
TM26	Earthquake	Ground	Physical	100	100	10	Adjacent
TM27	Return	Normal	Physical	—	100	20	Normal
TM28	Dig	Ground	Physical	80	100	10	Normal
TM30	Shadow Ball	Ghost	Special	80	100	15	Normal
TM31	Brick Break	Fighting	Physical	75	100	15	Normal
TM32	Double Team	Normal	Status	—	—	15	Self
TM33	Reflect	Psychic	Status	—	—	20	Your Side
TM35	Flamethrower	Fire	Special	90	100	15	Normal
TM36	Sludge Bomb	Poison	Special	90	100	10	Normal
TM38	Fire Blast	Fire	Special	110	85	5	Normal
TM41	Torment	Dark	Status	—	100	15	Normal
TM42	Facade	Normal	Physical	70	100	20	Normal
TM44	Rest	Psychic	Status	—	—	10	Self
TM45	Attract	Normal	Status	—	100	15	Normal
TM46	Thief	Dark	Physical	60	100	25	Normal
TM48	Round	Normal	Special	60	100	15	Normal
TM50	Overheat	Fire	Special	130	90	5	Normal
TM56	Fling	Dark	Physical	—	100	10	Normal
TM61	Incinerate	Fire	Special	60	100	15	Many Others
TM66	Payback	Dark	Physical	50	100	10	Normal
TM67	Retaliate	Normal	Physical	70	100	5	Normal
TM73	Thunder Wave	Electric	Status	—	100	20	Normal
TM78	Bulldoze	Ground	Physical	60	100	20	Adjacent

No.	Name	Type	Kind	Pow.	Acc.	PP	Range
TM87	Swagger	Normal	Status	—	90	15	Normal
TM88	Sleep Talk	Normal	Status	—	—	10	Self
TM90	Substitute	Normal	Status	—	—	10	Self
TM93	Wild Charge	Electric	Physical	90	100	15	Normal
TM94	Rock Smash	Fighting	Physical	40	100	15	Normal
TM95	Snarl	Dark	Special	55	95	15	Many Others
TM98	Power-Up Punch	Fighting	Physical	40	100	20	Normal
TM99	Dazzling Gleam	Fairy	Special	80	100	10	Many Others
TM100	Confide	Normal	Status	—	—	20	Normal
HM04	Strength	Normal	Physical	80	100	15	Normal

● MOVES TAUGHT BY PEOPLE

Name	Type	Kind	Pow.	Acc.	PP	Range

● EGG MOVES

Name	Type	Kind	Pow.	Acc.	PP	Range
Metronome	Normal	Status	—	—	10	Self
Feint Attack	Dark	Physical	60	—	20	Normal
Present	Normal	Physical	—	90	15	Normal
Crunch	Dark	Physical	80	100	15	Normal
Heal Bell	Normal	Status	—	—	5	Your Party
Snore	Normal	Special	50	100	15	Normal
Smelling Salts	Normal	Physical	70	100	10	Normal
Close Combat	Fighting	Physical	120	100	5	Normal
Ice Fang	Ice	Physical	65	95	15	Normal
Fire Fang	Fire	Physical	65	95	15	Normal
Thunder Fang	Electric	Physical	65	95	15	Normal
Focus Punch	Fighting	Physical	150	100	20	Normal
Double-Edge	Normal	Physical	120	100	15	Normal
Mimic	Normal	Status	—	100	10	Normal
Fake Tears	Dark	Status	—	100	20	Normal

AFTER THE HALL OF FAME

CENTRAL KALOS

COASTAL KALOS

071 Snubbull

MOUNTAIN KALOS

ADVENTURE DATA

AFTER THE HALL OF FAME

CENTRAL KALOS

COASTAL KALOS

072

Granbull

MOUNTAIN KALOS

ADVENTURE DATA

🌊 Coastal Kalos

Fairy Pokémon

072

✅ **Granbull**

HEIGHT: 4'07" WEIGHT: 107.4 lbs.
GENDER: ♂ / ♀

TYPE Fairy

ABILITIES
Intimidate
Quick Feet

HIDDEN ABILITY
Rattled

STAT GROWTH RATES
HP ▪▪▪
Attack ▪▪▪▪▪
Defense ▪▪▪
Sp. Atk ▪▪▪
Sp. Def ▪▪▪
Speed ▪▪▪

EGG GROUPS
Field, Fairy

Ⓧ It is timid in spite of its looks. If it becomes enraged, however, it will strike with its huge fangs.

Ⓨ It can make most any Pokémon run away simply by opening its mouth wide to reveal its big fangs.

🔺 EVOLUTION

Snubbull — Lv. 23 → Granbull

ITEMS SOMETIMES HELD BY WILD POKÉMON
None

Can be used in
Inverse Battle
—
Battle Chateau
Battle Institute
Battle Maison
Random Matchup

Damage taken in normal battles
Normal	×1
Fire	×1
Water	×1
Grass	×1
Electric	×1
Ice	×1
Fighting	×0.5
Poison	×2
Ground	×1
Flying	×1
Psychic	×1
Bug	×0.5
Rock	×1
Ghost	×0
Dragon	×0
Dark	×0.5
Steel	×2
Fairy	×1

Damage taken in Inverse Battles
Normal	×1
Fire	×1
Water	×1
Grass	×1
Electric	×1
Ice	×1
Fighting	×2
Poison	×0.5
Ground	×1
Flying	×1
Psychic	×1
Bug	×2
Rock	×1
Ghost	×1
Dragon	×2
Dark	×2
Steel	×0.5
Fairy	×1

How to obtain for your Coastal Kalos Pokédex

Level up Snubbull to Lv. 23. | Level up Snubbull to Lv. 23.

Same form for ♂ / ♀

● LEVEL-UP MOVES

Lv.	Name	Type	Kind	Pow.	Acc.	PP	Range
1	Outrage	Dragon	Physical	120	100	10	1 Random
1	Ice Fang	Ice	Physical	65	95	15	Normal
1	Fire Fang	Fire	Physical	65	95	15	Normal
1	Thunder Fang	Electric	Physical	65	95	15	Normal
1	Tackle	Normal	Physical	50	100	35	Normal
1	Scary Face	Normal	Status	—	100	10	Normal
1	Tail Whip	Normal	Status	—	100	30	Many Others
1	Charm	Fairy	Status	—	100	20	Normal
7	Bite	Dark	Physical	60	100	25	Normal
13	Lick	Ghost	Physical	30	100	30	Normal
19	Headbutt	Normal	Physical	70	100	15	Normal
27	Roar	Normal	Status	—	—	20	Normal
35	Rage	Normal	Physical	20	100	20	Normal
43	Play Rough	Fairy	Physical	90	90	10	Normal
51	Payback	Dark	Physical	50	100	10	Normal
59	Crunch	Dark	Physical	80	100	15	Normal
67	Outrage	Dragon	Physical	120	100	10	1 Random

● TM & HM MOVES

No.	Name	Type	Kind	Pow.	Acc.	PP	Range
TM05	Roar	Normal	Status	—	—	20	Normal
TM06	Toxic	Poison	Status	—	90	10	Normal
TM08	Bulk Up	Fighting	Status	—	—	20	Self
TM10	Hidden Power	Normal	Special	60	100	15	Normal
TM11	Sunny Day	Fire	Status	—	—	5	Both Sides
TM12	Taunt	Dark	Status	—	100	20	Normal
TM15	Hyper Beam	Normal	Special	150	90	5	Normal
TM17	Protect	Normal	Status	—	—	10	Self
TM18	Rain Dance	Water	Status	—	—	5	Both Sides
TM21	Frustration	Normal	Physical	—	100	20	Normal
TM22	Solar Beam	Grass	Special	120	100	10	Normal
TM24	Thunderbolt	Electric	Special	90	100	15	Normal
TM25	Thunder	Electric	Special	110	70	10	Normal
TM26	Earthquake	Ground	Physical	100	100	10	Adjacent
TM27	Return	Normal	Physical	—	100	20	Normal
TM28	Dig	Ground	Physical	80	100	10	Normal
TM30	Shadow Ball	Ghost	Special	80	100	15	Normal
TM31	Brick Break	Fighting	Physical	75	100	15	Normal
TM32	Double Team	Normal	Status	—	—	15	Self
TM33	Reflect	Psychic	Status	—	—	20	Your Side
TM35	Flamethrower	Fire	Special	90	100	15	Normal
TM36	Sludge Bomb	Poison	Special	90	100	10	Normal
TM38	Fire Blast	Fire	Special	110	85	5	Normal
TM39	Rock Tomb	Rock	Physical	60	95	15	Normal
TM41	Torment	Dark	Status	—	100	15	Normal
TM42	Facade	Normal	Physical	70	100	20	Normal
TM44	Rest	Psychic	Status	—	—	10	Self
TM45	Attract	Normal	Status	—	100	15	Normal
TM46	Thief	Dark	Physical	60	100	25	Normal
TM48	Round	Normal	Special	60	100	15	Normal
TM50	Overheat	Fire	Special	130	90	5	Normal
TM52	Focus Blast	Fighting	Special	120	70	5	Normal
TM56	Fling	Dark	Physical	—	100	10	Normal

No.	Name	Type	Kind	Pow.	Acc.	PP	Range
TM59	Incinerate	Fire	Special	60	100	15	Many Others
TM66	Payback	Dark	Physical	50	100	10	Normal
TM67	Retaliate	Normal	Physical	70	100	5	Normal
TM68	Giga Impact	Normal	Physical	150	90	5	Normal
TM71	Stone Edge	Rock	Physical	100	80	5	Normal
TM73	Thunder Wave	Electric	Status	—	100	20	Normal
TM78	Bulldoze	Ground	Physical	60	100	20	Adjacent
TM80	Rock Slide	Rock	Physical	75	90	10	Many Others
TM87	Swagger	Normal	Status	—	90	15	Normal
TM88	Sleep Talk	Normal	Status	—	—	10	Self
TM90	Substitute	Normal	Status	—	—	10	Self
TM93	Wild Charge	Electric	Physical	90	100	15	Normal
TM94	Rock Smash	Fighting	Physical	40	100	15	Normal
TM95	Snarl	Dark	Special	55	95	15	Many Others
TM98	Power-Up Punch	Fighting	Physical	40	100	20	Normal
TM99	Dazzling Gleam	Fairy	Special	80	100	10	Many Others
TM100	Confide	Normal	Status	—	—	20	Normal
HM04	Strength	Normal	Physical	80	100	15	Normal

● MOVES TAUGHT BY PEOPLE

Name	Type	Kind	Pow.	Acc.	PP	Range

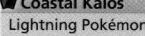

Coastal Kalos

073

Lightning Pokémon

▽ Electrike

HEIGHT: 2'00" WEIGHT: 33.5 lbs.
GENDER: ♂/♀

X Using electricity stored in its fur, it stimulates its muscles to heighten its reaction speed.

Y It stores static electricity in its fur for discharging. It gives off sparks if a storm approaches.

TYPE Electric

ABILITIES
Static
Lightning Rod

HIDDEN ABILITY
Minus

STAT GROWTH RATES
HP	■■
Attack	■■
Defense	■■
Sp. Atk	■■■
Sp. Def	■■
Speed	■■■■

EGG GROUP
Field

EVOLUTION

Lv. 26

Electrike → Manectric

ITEMS SOMETIMES HELD BY WILD POKÉMON
None

Damage taken in normal battles		Damage taken in Inverse Battles	
Normal	×1	Normal	×1
Fire	×1	Fire	×1
Water	×1	Water	×1
Grass	×1	Grass	×1
Electric	×0.5	Electric	×2
Ice	×1	Ice	×1
Fighting	×1	Fighting	×1
Poison	×1	Poison	×1
Ground	×2	Ground	×0.5
Flying	×0.5	Flying	×2
Psychic	×1	Psychic	×1
Bug	×1	Bug	×1
Rock	×1	Rock	×1
Ghost	×1	Ghost	×1
Dragon	×1	Dragon	×1
Dark	×1	Dark	×1
Steel	×0.5	Steel	×2
Fairy	×1	Fairy	×1

Can be used in
Inverse Battle	Battle Institute
—	Battle Maison
Battle Chateau	Random Matchup

Same form for ♂/♀

How to obtain for your Coastal Kalos Pokédex

Link Trade or transfer from another game.

❶ Catch in the tall grass on Route 10.
❷ Catch in the yellow flowers on Route 10.

● LEVEL-UP MOVES

Lv.	Name	Type	Kind	Pow.	Acc.	PP	Range
1	Tackle	Normal	Physical	50	100	35	Normal
4	Thunder Wave	Electric	Status	—	100	20	Normal
9	Leer	Normal	Status	—	100	30	Many Others
12	Howl	Normal	Status	—	—	40	Self
17	Quick Attack	Normal	Physical	40	100	30	Normal
20	Spark	Electric	Physical	65	100	20	Normal
25	Odor Sleuth	Normal	Status	—	—	40	Normal
28	Bite	Dark	Physical	60	100	25	Normal
33	Thunder Fang	Electric	Physical	65	95	15	Normal
36	Roar	Normal	Status	—	—	20	Normal
41	Discharge	Electric	Special	80	100	15	Adjacent
44	Charge	Electric	Status	—	—	20	Self
49	Wild Charge	Electric	Physical	90	100	15	Normal
52	Thunder	Electric	Special	110	70	10	Normal

● TM & HM MOVES

No.	Name	Type	Kind	Pow.	Acc.	PP	Range
TM05	Roar	Normal	Status	—	—	20	Normal
TM06	Toxic	Poison	Status	—	90	10	Normal
TM10	Hidden Power	Normal	Special	60	100	15	Normal
TM16	Light Screen	Psychic	Status	—	—	30	Your Side
TM17	Protect	Normal	Status	—	—	10	Self
TM18	Rain Dance	Water	Status	—	—	5	Both Sides
TM21	Frustration	Normal	Physical	—	100	20	Normal
TM24	Thunderbolt	Electric	Special	90	100	15	Normal
TM25	Thunder	Electric	Special	110	70	10	Normal
TM27	Return	Normal	Physical	—	100	20	Normal
TM32	Double Team	Normal	Status	—	—	15	Self
TM35	Flamethrower	Fire	Special	90	100	15	Normal
TM42	Facade	Normal	Physical	70	100	20	Normal
TM44	Rest	Psychic	Status	—	—	10	Self
TM45	Attract	Normal	Status	—	100	15	Normal
TM46	Thief	Dark	Physical	60	100	25	Normal
TM48	Round	Normal	Special	60	100	15	Normal
TM57	Charge Beam	Electric	Special	50	90	10	Normal
TM70	Flash	Normal	Status	—	100	20	Normal
TM72	Volt Switch	Electric	Special	70	100	20	Normal
TM73	Thunder Wave	Electric	Status	—	100	20	Normal
TM87	Swagger	Normal	Status	—	90	15	Normal
TM86	Sleep Talk	Normal	Status	—	—	10	Self
TM90	Substitute	Normal	Status	—	—	10	Self
TM93	Wild Charge	Electric	Physical	90	100	15	Normal
TM95	Snarl	Dark	Special	55	95	15	Many Others
TM100	Confide	Normal	Status	—	—	20	Normal
HM04	Strength	Normal	Physical	80	100	15	Normal

● MOVES TAUGHT BY PEOPLE

Name	Type	Kind	Pow.	Acc.	PP	Range

● EGG MOVES

Name	Type	Kind	Pow.	Acc.	PP	Range
Crunch	Dark	Physical	80	100	15	Normal
Headbutt	Normal	Physical	70	100	15	Normal
Uproar	Normal	Special	90	100	10	1 Random
Curse	Ghost	Status	—	—	10	Varies
Swift	Normal	Special	60	—	20	Many Others
Discharge	Electric	Special	80	100	15	Adjacent
Ice Fang	Ice	Physical	65	95	15	Normal
Fire Fang	Fire	Physical	65	95	15	Normal
Thunder Fang	Electric	Physical	65	95	15	Normal
Switcheroo	Dark	Status	—	100	10	Normal
Electro Ball	Electric	Special	—	100	10	Normal
Shock Wave	Electric	Special	60	—	20	Normal
Flame Burst	Fire	Special	70	100	15	Normal
Eerie Impulse	Electric	Status	—	100	15	Normal

AFTER THE HALL OF FAME

CENTRAL KALOS

COASTAL KALOS

073 Electrike

MOUNTAIN KALOS

ADVENTURE DATA

AFTER THE HALL OF FAME

CENTRAL KALOS

COASTAL KALOS

074 Manectric

MOUNTAIN KALOS

ADVENTURE DATA

🐾 Coastal Kalos 074

Discharge Pokémon

☑ Manectric

HEIGHT: 4'11"　　WEIGHT: 88.6 lbs.
GENDER: ♂/♀

TYPE Electric

ABILITIES
Static
Lightning Rod

HIDDEN ABILITY
Minus

STAT GROWTH RATES
HP	■■■
Attack	■■■
Defense	■■■
Sp. Atk	■■■■■
Sp. Def	■■■
Speed	■■■■■

EGG GROUP
Field

❌ It rarely appears before people. It is said to nest where lightning has fallen.

🅨 It discharges electricity from its mane. It creates a thundercloud overhead to drop lightning bolts.

⬆ EVOLUTION

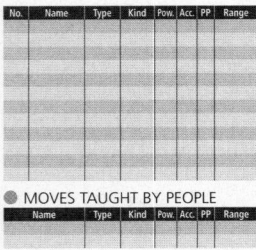

Electrike　　Lv. 26　　Manectric

ITEMS SOMETIMES HELD BY WILD POKÉMON
None

Can be used in
Inverse Battle
—
Battle Chateau
Battle Institute
Battle Maison
Random Matchup

Damage taken in normal battles	
Normal	×1
Fire	×1
Water	×1
Grass	×1
Electric	×0.5
Ice	×1
Fighting	×1
Poison	×1
Ground	×2
Flying	×0.5
Psychic	×1
Bug	×1
Rock	×1
Ghost	×1
Dragon	×1
Dark	×1
Steel	×0.5
Fairy	×1

Damage taken in Inverse Battles	
Normal	×1
Fire	×1
Water	×1
Grass	×1
Electric	×2
Ice	×1
Fighting	×1
Poison	×1
Ground	×0.5
Flying	×2
Psychic	×1
Bug	×1
Rock	×1
Ghost	×1
Dragon	×1
Dark	×2
Steel	×2
Fairy	×1

How to obtain for your Coastal Kalos Pokédex

X Link Trade or transfer from another game.

Y Level up Electrike to Lv. 26.

Same form for ♂/♀

● LEVEL-UP MOVES

Lv.	Name	Type	Kind	Pow.	Acc.	PP	Range
1	Electric Terrain	Electric	Status	—	—	10	Both Sides
1	Fire Fang	Fire	Physical	65	95	15	Normal
1	Tackle	Normal	Physical	50	100	35	Normal
1	Thunder Wave	Electric	Status	—	100	20	Normal
1	Leer	Normal	Status	—	100	30	Many Others
4	Howl	Normal	Status	—	—	40	Self
4	Thunder Wave	Electric	Status	—	100	20	Normal
9	Leer	Normal	Status	—	100	30	Many Others
12	Howl	Normal	Status	—	—	40	Self
17	Quick Attack	Normal	Physical	40	100	30	Normal
20	Spark	Electric	Physical	65	100	20	Normal
25	Odor Sleuth	Normal	Status	—	—	40	Normal
30	Bite	Dark	Physical	60	100	25	Normal
37	Thunder Fang	Electric	Physical	65	95	15	Normal
42	Roar	Normal	Status	—	—	20	Normal
49	Discharge	Electric	Special	80	100	15	Adjacent
54	Charge	Electric	Status	—	—	20	Self
61	Wild Charge	Electric	Physical	90	100	15	Normal
66	Thunder	Electric	Special	110	70	10	Normal
70	Electric Terrain	Electric	Status	—	—	10	Both Sides

● TM & HM MOVES

No.	Name	Type	Kind	Pow.	Acc.	PP	Range
TM05	Roar	Normal	Status	—	—	20	Normal
TM06	Toxic	Poison	Status	—	90	10	Normal
TM10	Hidden Power	Normal	Special	60	100	15	Normal
TM15	Hyper Beam	Normal	Special	150	90	5	Normal
TM16	Light Screen	Psychic	Status	—	—	30	Your Side
TM17	Protect	Normal	Status	—	—	10	Self
TM18	Rain Dance	Water	Status	—	—	5	Both Sides
TM21	Frustration	Normal	Physical	—	100	20	Normal
TM24	Thunderbolt	Electric	Special	90	100	15	Normal
TM25	Thunder	Electric	Special	110	70	10	Normal
TM27	Return	Normal	Physical	—	100	20	Normal
TM32	Double Team	Normal	Status	—	—	15	Self
TM35	Flamethrower	Fire	Special	90	100	15	Normal
TM42	Facade	Normal	Physical	70	100	20	Normal
TM44	Rest	Psychic	Status	—	—	10	Self
TM45	Attract	Normal	Status	—	100	15	Normal
TM46	Thief	Dark	Physical	60	100	25	Normal
TM48	Round	Normal	Special	60	100	15	Normal
TM50	Overheat	Fire	Special	130	90	5	Normal
TM57	Charge Beam	Electric	Special	50	90	10	Normal
TM68	Giga Impact	Normal	Physical	150	90	5	Normal
TM70	Flash	Normal	Status	—	100	20	Normal
TM72	Volt Switch	Electric	Special	70	100	20	Normal
TM73	Thunder Wave	Electric	Status	—	100	20	Normal
TM87	Swagger	Normal	Status	—	90	15	Normal
TM88	Sleep Talk	Normal	Status	—	—	10	Self
TM90	Substitute	Normal	Status	—	—	10	Self
TM93	Wild Charge	Electric	Physical	90	100	15	Normal
TM95	Snarl	Dark	Special	55	95	15	Many Others
TM100	Confide	Normal	Status	—	—	20	Normal
HM04	Strength	Normal	Physical	80	100	15	Normal

● MOVES TAUGHT BY PEOPLE

Name	Type	Kind	Pow.	Acc.	PP	Range

Mega Evolution

Discharge Pokémon
☑ Mega Manectric

TYPE	Electric	

ABILITY
Intimidate

STAT GROWTH RATES

HP	▪▪▪
Attack	▪▪▪▪
Defense	▪▪▪▪
Sp. Atk	▪▪▪▪▪▪▪
Sp. Def	▪▪▪
Speed	▪▪▪▪▪▪▪▪

MEGA STONE REQUIRED

Manectite
Obtain on Route 16 between 8 P.M. and 8:59 P.M., after entering the Hall of Fame and speaking with Professor Sycamore in Anistar City (in *Pokémon X*).

HEIGHT: 5'11"   WEIGHT: 97.0 lbs.   GENDER: ♂/♀

Damage taken in normal battles	
Normal	×1
Fire	×1
Water	×1
Grass	×1
Electric	×0.5
Ice	×1
Fighting	×1
Poison	×1
Ground	×2
Flying	×0.5
Psychic	×1
Bug	×1
Rock	×1
Ghost	×1
Dragon	×1
Dark	×1
Steel	×0.5
Fairy	×1

Damage taken in Inverse Battles	
Normal	×1
Fire	×1
Water	×1
Grass	×1
Electric	×2
Ice	×1
Fighting	×1
Poison	×1
Ground	×0.5
Flying	×2
Psychic	×1
Bug	×1
Rock	×1
Ghost	×1
Dragon	×1
Dark	×1
Steel	×2
Fairy	×1

Can be used in
Inverse Battle
—
Battle Chateau
Battle Institute
Battle Maison
Random Matchup

Same form for ♂/♀

AFTER THE HALL OF FAME

CENTRAL KALOS

COASTAL KALOS

075

Houndour

MOUNTAIN KALOS

ADVENTURE DATA

Coastal Kalos 075

Dark Pokémon

☑ Houndour

HEIGHT: 2'00" WEIGHT: 23.8 lbs.
GENDER: ♂/♀

X Around dawn, its ominous howl echoes through the area to announce that this is its territory.

Y To corner prey, they check each other's location using barks that only they can understand.

TYPE: Dark / Fire

ABILITIES
Early Bird
Flash Fire

HIDDEN ABILITY
Unnerve

STAT GROWTH RATES
HP
Attack
Defense
Sp. Atk
Sp. Def
Speed

EGG GROUP
Field

EVOLUTION

Houndour — Lv. 24 → Houndoom

ITEMS SOMETIMES HELD BY WILD POKÉMON
None

Damage taken in normal battles		Damage taken in Inverse Battles	
Normal	×1	Normal	×1
Fire	×0.5	Fire	×2
Water	×2	Water	×0.5
Grass	×0.5	Grass	×2
Electric	×1	Electric	×1
Ice	×0.5	Ice	×2
Fighting	×2	Fighting	×0.5
Poison	×1	Poison	×1
Ground	×2	Ground	×0.5
Flying	×1	Flying	×1
Psychic	×0	Psychic	×2
Bug	×1	Bug	×1
Rock	×2	Rock	×0.5
Ghost	×0.5	Ghost	×2
Dragon	×1	Dragon	×1
Dark	×0.5	Dark	×2
Steel	×0.5	Steel	×2
Fairy	×1	Fairy	×1

Can be used in	
Inverse Battle	Battle Institute
—	Battle Maison
Battle Chateau	Random Matchup

Same form for ♂/♀

How to obtain for your Coastal Kalos Pokédex

❶ Catch in the tall grass on Route 10.

❷ Catch in the yellow flowers on Route 10.

Link Trade or transfer from another game.

● LEVEL-UP MOVES

Lv.	Name	Type	Kind	Pow.	Acc.	PP	Range
1	Leer	Normal	Status	—	100	30	Many Others
1	Ember	Fire	Special	40	100	25	Normal
4	Howl	Normal	Status	—	—	40	Self
8	Smog	Poison	Special	30	70	20	Normal
13	Roar	Normal	Status	—	—	20	Normal
16	Bite	Dark	Physical	60	100	25	Normal
20	Odor Sleuth	Normal	Status	—	—	40	Normal
25	Beat Up	Dark	Physical	—	100	10	Normal
28	Fire Fang	Fire	Physical	65	95	15	Normal
32	Feint Attack	Dark	Physical	60	—	20	Normal
37	Embargo	Dark	Status	—	100	15	Normal
40	Foul Play	Dark	Physical	95	100	15	Normal
44	Flamethrower	Fire	Special	90	100	15	Normal
49	Crunch	Dark	Physical	80	100	15	Normal
52	Nasty Plot	Dark	Status	—	—	20	Self
56	Inferno	Fire	Special	100	50	5	Normal

● TM & HM MOVES

No.	Name	Type	Kind	Pow.	Acc.	PP	Range
TM05	Roar	Normal	Status	—	—	20	Normal
TM06	Toxic	Poison	Status	—	90	10	Normal
TM10	Hidden Power	Normal	Special	60	100	15	Normal
TM11	Sunny Day	Fire	Status	—	—	5	Both Sides
TM12	Taunt	Dark	Status	—	100	20	Normal
TM17	Protect	Normal	Status	—	—	10	Self
TM21	Frustration	Normal	Physical	—	100	20	Normal
TM22	Solar Beam	Grass	Special	120	100	10	Normal
TM27	Return	Normal	Physical	—	100	20	Normal
TM30	Shadow Ball	Ghost	Special	80	100	15	Normal
TM32	Double Team	Normal	Status	—	—	15	Self
TM35	Flamethrower	Fire	Special	90	100	15	Normal
TM36	Sludge Bomb	Poison	Special	90	100	10	Normal
TM38	Fire Blast	Fire	Special	110	85	5	Normal
TM41	Torment	Dark	Status	—	100	15	Normal
TM42	Facade	Normal	Physical	70	100	20	Normal
TM43	Flame Charge	Fire	Physical	50	100	20	Normal
TM44	Rest	Psychic	Status	—	—	10	Self
TM45	Attract	Normal	Status	—	100	15	Normal
TM46	Thief	Dark	Physical	60	100	25	Normal
TM48	Round	Normal	Special	60	100	15	Normal
TM50	Overheat	Fire	Special	130	90	5	Normal
TM59	Incinerate	Fire	Special	60	100	15	Many Others
TM61	Will-O-Wisp	Fire	Status	—	85	15	Normal
TM63	Embargo	Dark	Status	—	100	15	Normal
TM66	Payback	Dark	Physical	50	100	10	Normal
TM67	Retaliate	Normal	Physical	70	100	5	Normal
TM85	Dream Eater	Psychic	Special	100	100	15	Normal
TM87	Swagger	Normal	Status	—	90	15	Normal
TM88	Sleep Talk	Normal	Status	—	—	10	Self
TM90	Substitute	Normal	Status	—	—	10	Self
TM94	Rock Smash	Fighting	Physical	40	100	15	Normal
TM95	Snarl	Dark	Special	55	95	15	Many Others

No.	Name	Type	Kind	Pow.	Acc.	PP	Range
TM97	Dark Pulse	Dark	Special	80	100	15	Normal
TM100	Confide	Normal	Status	—	—	20	Normal

● MOVES TAUGHT BY PEOPLE

Name	Type	Kind	Pow.	Acc.	PP	Range

● EGG MOVES

Name	Type	Kind	Pow.	Acc.	PP	Range
Fire Spin	Fire	Special	35	85	15	Normal
Rage	Normal	Physical	20	100	20	Normal
Pursuit	Dark	Physical	40	100	20	Normal
Counter	Fighting	Physical	—	100	20	Varies
Spite	Ghost	Status	—	100	10	Normal
Reversal	Fighting	Physical	—	100	15	Normal
Beat Up	Dark	Physical	—	100	10	Normal
Fire Fang	Fire	Physical	65	95	15	Normal
Thunder Fang	Electric	Physical	65	95	15	Normal
Nasty Plot	Dark	Status	—	—	20	Self
Punishment	Dark	Physical	—	100	5	Normal
Feint	Normal	Physical	30	100	10	Normal
Sucker Punch	Dark	Physical	80	100	5	Normal
Destiny Bond	Ghost	Status	—	—	5	Self

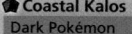

Coastal Kalos
076
Dark Pokémon
Houndoom

HEIGHT: 4'07"   WEIGHT: 77.2 lbs.
GENDER: ♂/♀

X Long ago, people imagined its eerie howls to be the call of the grim reaper.

Y The flames it breathes when angry contain toxins. If they cause a burn, it will hurt forever.

TYPE [Dark] [Fire]

ABILITIES
Early Bird
Flash Fire

HIDDEN ABILITY
Unnerve

STAT GROWTH RATES
HP	■■■
Attack	■■■■■
Defense	■■■
Sp. Atk	■■■■■
Sp. Def	■■■
Speed	■■■■■

EGG GROUP
Field

 EVOLUTION

Lv. 24

Houndour → Houndoom

ITEMS SOMETIMES HELD BY WILD POKÉMON
None

Damage taken in normal battles		Damage taken in Inverse Battles	
Normal	×1	Normal	×1
Fire	×0.5	Fire	×2
Water	×2	Water	×0.5
Grass	×0.5	Grass	×2
Electric	×1	Electric	×1
Ice	×0.5	Ice	×2
Fighting	×2	Fighting	×0.5
Poison	×1	Poison	×1
Ground	×2	Ground	×0.5
Flying	×1	Flying	×1
Psychic	×0	Psychic	×2
Bug	×1	Bug	×1
Rock	×2	Rock	×0.5
Ghost	×0.5	Ghost	×2
Dragon	×1	Dragon	×1
Dark	×0.5	Dark	×2
Steel	×0.5	Steel	×2
Fairy	×1	Fairy	×1

Can be used in
Inverse Battle
Battle Chateau
Battle Institute
Battle Maison
Random Matchup

How to obtain for your Coastal Kalos Pokédex
Level up Houndour to Lv. 24.

Link Trade or transfer from another game.

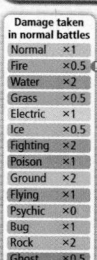
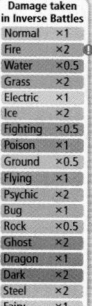
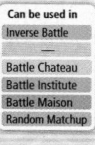

♂   ♀

The male has larger horns. The female has smaller horns.

● LEVEL-UP MOVES
Lv.	Name	Type	Kind	Pow.	Acc.	PP	Range
1	Inferno	Fire	Special	100	50	5	Normal
1	Nasty Plot	Dark	Status	—	—	20	Self
1	Thunder Fang	Electric	Physical	65	95	15	Normal
1	Leer	Normal	Status	—	100	30	Many Others
1	Ember	Fire	Special	40	100	25	Normal
1	Howl	Normal	Status	—	—	40	Self
1	Smog	Poison	Special	30	70	20	Normal
4	Howl	Normal	Status	—	—	40	Self
8	Smog	Poison	Special	30	70	20	Normal
13	Roar	Normal	Status	—	—	20	Normal
16	Bite	Dark	Physical	60	100	25	Normal
21	Odor Sleuth	Normal	Status	—	—	40	Normal
26	Beat Up	Dark	Physical	—	100	10	Normal
30	Fire Fang	Fire	Physical	65	95	15	Normal
35	Feint Attack	Dark	Physical	60	—	20	Normal
41	Embargo	Dark	Status	—	100	15	Normal
45	Foul Play	Dark	Physical	95	100	15	Normal
52	Flamethrower	Fire	Special	90	100	15	Normal
56	Crunch	Dark	Physical	80	100	15	Normal
60	Nasty Plot	Dark	Status	—	—	20	Self
65	Inferno	Fire	Special	100	50	5	Normal

● TM & HM MOVES
No.	Name	Type	Kind	Pow.	Acc.	PP	Range
TM05	Roar	Normal	Status	—	—	20	Normal
TM06	Toxic	Poison	Status	—	90	10	Normal
TM10	Hidden Power	Normal	Special	60	100	15	Normal
TM11	Sunny Day	Fire	Status	—	—	5	Both Sides
TM12	Taunt	Dark	Status	—	100	20	Normal
TM15	Hyper Beam	Normal	Special	150	90	5	Normal
TM17	Protect	Normal	Status	—	—	10	Self
TM21	Frustration	Normal	Physical	—	100	20	Normal
TM22	Solar Beam	Grass	Special	120	100	10	Normal
TM27	Return	Normal	Physical	—	100	20	Normal
TM30	Shadow Ball	Ghost	Special	80	100	15	Normal
TM32	Double Team	Normal	Status	—	—	15	Self
TM35	Flamethrower	Fire	Special	90	100	15	Normal
TM36	Sludge Bomb	Poison	Special	90	100	10	Normal
TM38	Fire Blast	Fire	Special	110	85	5	Normal
TM41	Torment	Dark	Status	—	100	15	Normal
TM42	Facade	Normal	Physical	70	100	20	Normal
TM43	Flame Charge	Fire	Physical	50	100	20	Normal
TM44	Rest	Psychic	Status	—	—	10	Self
TM45	Attract	Normal	Status	—	100	15	Normal
TM46	Thief	Dark	Physical	60	100	25	Normal
TM48	Round	Normal	Special	60	100	15	Normal
TM50	Overheat	Fire	Special	130	90	5	Normal
TM59	Incinerate	Fire	Special	60	100	15	Many Others
TM61	Will-O-Wisp	Fire	Status	—	85	15	Normal
TM63	Embargo	Dark	Status	—	100	15	Normal
TM66	Payback	Dark	Physical	50	100	10	Normal
TM67	Retaliate	Normal	Physical	70	100	5	Normal
TM68	Giga Impact	Normal	Physical	150	90	5	Normal
TM85	Dream Eater	Psychic	Special	100	100	15	Normal
TM87	Swagger	Normal	Status	—	90	15	Normal
TM88	Sleep Talk	Normal	Status	—	—	10	Self
TM90	Substitute	Normal	Status	—	—	10	Self

No.	Name	Type	Kind	Pow.	Acc.	PP	Range
TM94	Rock Smash	Fighting	Physical	40	100	15	Normal
TM95	Snarl	Dark	Special	55	95	15	Many Others
TM97	Dark Pulse	Dark	Special	80	100	15	Normal
TM100	Confide	Normal	Status	—	—	20	Normal
HM04	Strength	Normal	Physical	80	100	15	Normal

● MOVES TAUGHT BY PEOPLE
Name	Type	Kind	Pow.	Acc.	PP	Range

AFTER THE HALL OF FAME

CENTRAL KALOS

COASTAL KALOS

076

Houndoom

MOUNTAIN KALOS

ADVENTURE DATA

AFTER THE HALL OF FAME

CENTRAL KALOS

COASTAL KALOS

Mega Houndoom

MOUNTAIN KALOS

ADVENTURE DATA

Mega Evolution

Dark Pokémon

✓ **Mega Houndoom**

HEIGHT: 6'03"   WEIGHT: 109.1 lbs.   GENDER: ♂ / ♀

TYPE	Dark	Fire

ABILITY
Solar Power

STAT GROWTH RATES

HP	▪▪▪
Attack	▪▪▪▪▪
Defense	▪▪▪▪
Sp. Atk	▪▪▪▪▪▪▪
Sp. Def	▪▪▪▪
Speed	▪▪▪▪▪▪

⬤ MEGA STONE REQUIRED

Houndoominite

Obtain on Route 16 between 8 P.M. and 8:59 P.M., after entering the Hall of Fame and speaking with Professor Sycamore in Anistar City (in *Pokémon Y*).

Damage taken in normal battles	
Normal	×1
Fire	×0.5
Water	×2
Grass	×0.5
Electric	×1
Ice	×0.5
Fighting	×2
Poison	×1
Ground	×2
Flying	×1
Psychic	×0
Bug	×1
Rock	×2
Ghost	×0.5
Dragon	×1
Dark	×0.5
Steel	×0.5
Fairy	×1

Damage taken in Inverse Battles	
Normal	×1
Fire	×2
Water	×0.5
Grass	×2
Electric	×1
Ice	×2
Fighting	×0.5
Poison	×1
Ground	×0.5
Flying	×1
Psychic	×2
Bug	×1
Rock	×0.5
Ghost	×2
Dragon	×1
Dark	×2
Steel	×2
Fairy	×1

Can be used in

Inverse Battle

Battle Chateau
Battle Institute
Battle Maison
Random Matchup

Same form for ♂ / ♀

350

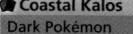

Coastal Kalos
Dark Pokémon

Houndoom

076

HEIGHT: 4'07" WEIGHT: 77.2 lbs.
GENDER: ♂/♀

 Long ago, people imagined its eerie howls to be the call of the grim reaper.

Y The flames it breathes when angry contain toxins. If they cause a burn, it will hurt forever.

TYPE Dark / Fire

ABILITIES
Early Bird
Flash Fire

HIDDEN ABILITY
Unnerve

STAT GROWTH RATES
HP	■■■
Attack	■■■■■
Defense	■■
Sp. Atk	■■■■■
Sp. Def	■■■
Speed	■■■■■

EGG GROUP
Field

EVOLUTION

Houndour — Lv. 24 → Houndoom

ITEMS SOMETIMES HELD BY WILD POKÉMON
None

AFTER THE HALL OF FAME

CENTRAL KALOS

COASTAL KALOS

076 Houndoom

MOUNTAIN KALOS

ADVENTURE DATA

Damage taken in normal battles		Damage taken in Inverse Battles		Can be used in
Normal	×1	Normal	×1	Inverse Battle
Fire	×0.5	Fire	×2	—
Water	×2	Water	×0.5	Battle Chateau
Grass	×0.5	Grass	×2	Battle Institute
Electric	×1	Electric	×1	Battle Maison
Ice	×0.5	Ice	×2	Random Matchup
Fighting	×2	Fighting	×0.5	
Poison	×1	Poison	×1	
Ground	×2	Ground	×0.5	
Flying	×1	Flying	×1	
Psychic	×0	Psychic	×2	
Bug	×1	Bug	×1	
Rock	×2	Rock	×0.5	
Ghost	×0.5	Ghost	×2	
Dragon	×1	Dragon	×1	
Dark	×0.5	Dark	×2	
Steel	×0.5	Steel	×2	
Fairy	×1	Fairy	×1	

How to obtain for your Coastal Kalos Pokédex

Level up Houndour to Lv. 24.

Link Trade or transfer from another game.

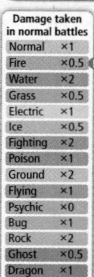
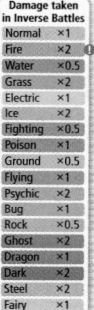
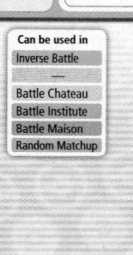

♂

♀

The male has larger horns. The female has smaller horns.

● LEVEL-UP MOVES

Lv.	Name	Type	Kind	Pow.	Acc.	PP	Range
1	Inferno	Fire	Special	100	50	5	Normal
1	Nasty Plot	Dark	Status	—	—	20	Self
1	Thunder Fang	Electric	Physical	65	95	15	Normal
1	Leer	Normal	Status	—	100	30	Many Others
1	Ember	Fire	Special	40	100	25	Normal
1	Howl	Normal	Status	—	—	40	Self
1	Smog	Poison	Special	30	70	20	Normal
4	Howl	Normal	Status	—	—	40	Self
8	Smog	Poison	Special	30	70	20	Normal
13	Roar	Normal	Status	—	—	20	Normal
16	Bite	Dark	Physical	60	100	25	Normal
20	Odor Sleuth	Normal	Status	—	—	40	Normal
26	Beat Up	Dark	Physical	—	100	10	Normal
30	Fire Fang	Fire	Physical	65	95	15	Normal
35	Feint Attack	Dark	Physical	60	—	20	Normal
41	Embargo	Dark	Status	—	100	15	Normal
45	Foul Play	Dark	Physical	95	100	15	Normal
50	Flamethrower	Fire	Special	90	100	15	Normal
56	Crunch	Dark	Physical	80	100	15	Normal
60	Nasty Plot	Dark	Status	—	—	20	Self
65	Inferno	Fire	Special	100	50	5	Normal

● TM & HM MOVES

No.	Name	Type	Kind	Pow.	Acc.	PP	Range
TM05	Roar	Normal	Status	—	—	20	Normal
TM06	Toxic	Poison	Status	—	90	10	Normal
TM10	Hidden Power	Normal	Special	60	100	15	Normal
TM11	Sunny Day	Fire	Status	—	—	5	Both Sides
TM12	Taunt	Dark	Status	—	100	20	Normal
TM15	Hyper Beam	Normal	Special	150	90	5	Normal
TM17	Protect	Normal	Status	—	—	10	Self
TM21	Frustration	Normal	Physical	—	100	20	Normal
TM22	Solar Beam	Grass	Special	120	100	10	Normal
TM27	Return	Normal	Physical	—	100	20	Normal
TM30	Shadow Ball	Ghost	Special	80	100	15	Normal
TM32	Double Team	Normal	Status	—	—	15	Self
TM35	Flamethrower	Fire	Special	90	100	15	Normal
TM36	Sludge Bomb	Poison	Special	90	100	10	Normal
TM38	Fire Blast	Fire	Special	110	85	5	Normal
TM41	Torment	Dark	Status	—	100	15	Normal
TM42	Facade	Normal	Physical	70	100	20	Normal
TM43	Flame Charge	Fire	Physical	50	100	20	Normal
TM44	Rest	Psychic	Status	—	—	10	Self
TM45	Attract	Normal	Status	—	100	15	Normal
TM46	Thief	Dark	Physical	60	100	25	Normal
TM48	Round	Normal	Special	60	100	15	Normal
TM50	Overheat	Fire	Special	130	90	5	Normal
TM59	Incinerate	Fire	Special	60	100	15	Many Others
TM61	Will-O-Wisp	Fire	Status	—	85	15	Normal
TM63	Embargo	Dark	Status	—	100	15	Normal
TM66	Payback	Dark	Physical	50	100	10	Normal
TM67	Retaliate	Normal	Physical	70	100	5	Normal
TM68	Giga Impact	Normal	Physical	150	90	5	Normal
TM85	Dream Eater	Psychic	Special	100	100	15	Normal
TM87	Swagger	Normal	Status	—	90	15	Normal
TM88	Sleep Talk	Normal	Status	—	—	10	Self
TM90	Substitute	Normal	Status	—	—	10	Self

No.	Name	Type	Kind	Pow.	Acc.	PP	Range
TM94	Rock Smash	Fighting	Physical	40	100	15	Normal
TM95	Snarl	Dark	Special	55	95	15	Many Others
TM97	Dark Pulse	Dark	Special	80	100	15	Normal
TM100	Confide	Normal	Status	—	—	20	Normal
HM04	Strength	Normal	Physical	80	100	15	Normal

● MOVES TAUGHT BY PEOPLE

Name	Type	Kind	Pow.	Acc.	PP	Range

AFTER THE HALL OF FAME

CENTRAL KALOS

COASTAL KALOS

Mega Houndoom

MOUNTAIN KALOS

ADVENTURE DATA

Mega Evolution

Dark Pokémon

☑ **Mega Houndoom**

HEIGHT: 6'03"　　WEIGHT: 109.1 lbs.　　GENDER: ♂ / ♀

TYPE	Dark	Fire

ABILITY
Solar Power

STAT GROWTH RATES

HP	▪▪▪
Attack	▪▪▪▪▪
Defense	▪▪▪▪
Sp. Atk	▪▪▪▪▪▪▪
Sp. Def	▪▪▪▪
Speed	▪▪▪▪▪▪

⬤ MEGA STONE REQUIRED

Houndoominite

Obtain on Route 16 between 8 P.M. and 8:59 P.M., after entering the Hall of Fame and speaking with Professor Sycamore in Anistar City (in *Pokémon Y*).

Damage taken in normal battles

Normal	×1
Fire	×0.5
Water	×2
Grass	×0.5
Electric	×1
Ice	×0.5
Fighting	×2
Poison	×1
Ground	×2
Flying	×1
Psychic	×0
Bug	×1
Rock	×2
Ghost	×0.5
Dragon	×1
Dark	×0.5
Steel	×0.5
Fairy	×1

Damage taken in Inverse Battles

Normal	×1
Fire	×2
Water	×0.5
Grass	×2
Electric	×1
Ice	×2
Fighting	×0.5
Poison	×1
Ground	×0.5
Flying	×1
Psychic	×2
Bug	×1
Rock	×0.5
Ghost	×2
Dragon	×1
Dark	×2
Steel	×2
Fairy	×1

Can be used in

Inverse Battle
—
Battle Chateau
Battle Institute
Battle Maison
Random Matchup

Same form for ♂ / ♀

⬟ Coastal Kalos

Evolution Pokémon

☑ Eevee

077

HEIGHT: 1'00" WEIGHT: 14.3 lbs.
GENDER: ♂/♀

X A rare Pokémon that adapts to harsh environments by taking on different evolutionary forms.

Y Thanks to its unstable genetic makeup, this special Pokémon conceals many different possible evolutions.

TYPE Normal

ABILITIES
Run Away
Adaptability

HIDDEN ABILITY
Anticipation

STAT GROWTH RATES
HP	■■
Attack	■■■
Defense	■■
Sp. Atk	■■
Sp. Def	■■
Speed	■■■

EGG GROUP
Field

⬘ EVOLUTION

Eevee	Espeon — Level up Eevee between 4 A.M. and 7:59 P.M. with high friendship.	Glaceon — Level up Eevee near the ice-covered rock in the Frost Cavern.
Vaporeon — Use a Water Stone on Eevee.	Umbreon — Level up Eevee between 8 P.M. and 3:59 A.M. with high friendship.	Sylveon — Level up an affectionate Eevee and have it learn a Fairy-type move. Or teach an affectionate Eevee a Fairy-type move, and then level it up.
Jolteon — Use a Thunder Stone on Eevee.	Leafeon — Level up Eevee near the moss-covered rock on Route 20.	
Flareon — Use a Fire Stone on Eevee.		

ITEMS SOMETIMES HELD BY WILD POKÉMON
None

Damage taken in normal battles		Damage taken in Inverse Battles	
Normal	×1	Normal	×1
Fire	×1	Fire	×1
Water	×1	Water	×1
Grass	×1	Grass	×1
Electric	×1	Electric	×1
Ice	×1	Ice	×1
Fighting	×2	Fighting	×0.5
Poison	×1	Poison	×1
Ground	×1	Ground	×1
Flying	×1	Flying	×1
Psychic	×1	Psychic	×1
Bug	×1	Bug	×1
Rock	×1	Rock	×1
Ghost	×0	Ghost	×2
Dragon	×1	Dragon	×1
Dark	×1	Dark	×1
Steel	×1	Steel	×1
Fairy	×1	Fairy	×1

Can be used in	
Inverse Battle	Battle Institute
—	Battle Maison
Battle Chateau	Random Matchup

Same form for ♂/♀

How to obtain for your Coastal Kalos Pokédex

❶ Catch in the yellow flowers on Route 10.
❷ Catch in the tall grass on Route 10.

❶ Catch in the yellow flowers on Route 10.
❷ Catch in the tall grass on Route 10.

● LEVEL-UP MOVES

Lv.	Name	Type	Kind	Pow.	Acc.	PP	Range
1	Helping Hand	Normal	Status	—	—	20	1 Ally
1	Growl	Normal	Status	—	100	40	Many Others
1	Tackle	Normal	Physical	50	100	35	Normal
1	Tail Whip	Normal	Status	—	100	30	Many Others
5	Sand Attack	Ground	Status	—	100	15	Normal
9	Baby-Doll Eyes	Fairy	Status	—	100	30	Normal
10	Swift	Normal	Special	60	—	20	Many Others
13	Quick Attack	Normal	Physical	40	100	30	Normal
17	Bite	Dark	Physical	60	100	25	Normal
20	Refresh	Normal	Status	—	—	20	Self
23	Covet	Normal	Physical	60	100	25	Normal
25	Take Down	Normal	Physical	90	85	20	Normal
29	Charm	Fairy	Status	—	100	20	Normal
33	Baton Pass	Normal	Status	—	—	40	Self
37	Double-Edge	Normal	Physical	120	100	15	Normal
41	Last Resort	Normal	Physical	140	100	5	Normal
45	Trump Card	Normal	Special	—	—	5	Normal

● TM & HM MOVES

No.	Name	Type	Kind	Pow.	Acc.	PP	Range
TM06	Toxic	Poison	Status	—	90	10	Normal
TM10	Hidden Power	Normal	Special	60	100	15	Normal
TM11	Sunny Day	Fire	Status	—	—	5	Both Sides
TM17	Protect	Normal	Status	—	—	10	Self
TM18	Rain Dance	Water	Status	—	—	5	Both Sides
TM21	Frustration	Normal	Physical	—	100	20	Normal
TM27	Return	Normal	Physical	—	100	20	Normal
TM28	Dig	Ground	Physical	80	100	10	Normal
TM30	Shadow Ball	Ghost	Special	80	100	15	Normal
TM32	Double Team	Normal	Status	—	—	15	Self
TM42	Facade	Normal	Physical	70	100	20	Normal
TM44	Rest	Psychic	Status	—	—	10	Self
TM45	Attract	Normal	Status	—	100	15	Normal
TM48	Round	Normal	Special	60	100	15	Normal
TM49	Echoed Voice	Normal	Special	40	100	15	Normal
TM67	Retaliate	Normal	Physical	70	100	5	Normal
TM87	Swagger	Normal	Status	—	90	15	Normal
TM88	Sleep Talk	Normal	Status	—	—	10	Self
TM90	Substitute	Normal	Status	—	—	10	Self
TM100	Confide	Normal	Status	—	—	20	Normal

● MOVES TAUGHT BY PEOPLE

Name	Type	Kind	Pow.	Acc.	PP	Range

● EGG MOVES

Name	Type	Kind	Pow.	Acc.	PP	Range
Charm	Fairy	Status	—	100	20	Normal
Flail	Normal	Physical	—	100	15	Normal
Endure	Normal	Status	—	—	10	Self
Curse	Ghost	Status	—	—	10	Varies
Tickle	Normal	Status	—	100	20	Normal
Wish	Normal	Status	—	—	10	Self
Yawn	Normal	Status	—	—	10	Normal
Fake Tears	Dark	Status	—	100	20	Normal
Covet	Normal	Physical	60	100	25	Normal
Detect	Fighting	Status	—	—	5	Self
Natural Gift	Normal	Physical	—	100	15	Normal
Stored Power	Psychic	Special	20	100	10	Normal
Synchronoise	Psychic	Special	120	100	10	Adjacent
Captivate	Normal	Status	—	100	20	Many Others

AFTER THE HALL OF FAME

CENTRAL KALOS

COASTAL KALOS

078

Vaporeon

MOUNTAIN KALOS

ADVENTURE DATA

🏠 **Coastal Kalos**
Bubble Jet Pokémon
078

☑ **Vaporeon**

HEIGHT: 3'03" WEIGHT: 63.9 lbs.
GENDER: ♂/♀

X It prefers beautiful shores. With cells similar to water molecules, it could melt in water.

Y It has evolved to be suitable for an aquatic life. It can invisibly melt away into water.

TYPE Water

ABILITY
Water Absorb

HIDDEN ABILITY
Hydration

STAT GROWTH RATES
HP	▪▪▪▪▪
Attack	▪▪▪
Defense	▪▪▪
Sp. Atk	▪▪▪▪▪
Sp. Def	▪▪▪▪
Speed	▪▪▪

EGG GROUP
Field

🔄 **EVOLUTION**

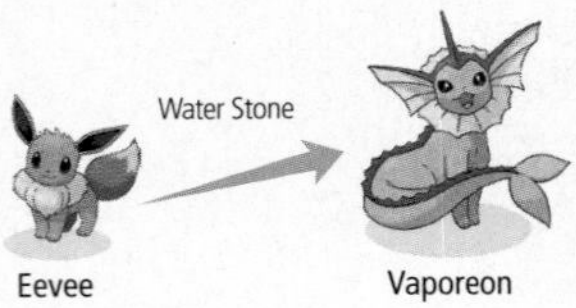

Eevee → Water Stone → Vaporeon

ITEMS SOMETIMES HELD BY WILD POKÉMON
None

Damage taken in normal battles		Damage taken in Inverse Battles	
Normal	×1	Normal	×1
Fire	×0.5	Fire	×2
Water	×0.5 ◀	Water	×2 ◀
Grass	×2	Grass	×0.5
Electric	×2	Electric	×0.5
Ice	×0.5	Ice	×2
Fighting	×1	Fighting	×1
Poison	×1	Poison	×1
Ground	×1	Ground	×1
Flying	×1	Flying	×1
Psychic	×1	Psychic	×1
Bug	×1	Bug	×1
Rock	×1	Rock	×1
Ghost	×1	Ghost	×1
Dragon	×1	Dragon	×1
Dark	×1	Dark	×1
Steel	×0.5	Steel	×2
Fairy	×1	Fairy	×1

Can be used in	
Inverse Battle	Battle Institute
—	Battle Maison
Battle Chateau	Random Matchup

Same form for ♂/♀

How to obtain for your Coastal Kalos Pokédex

Use a Water Stone on Eevee. Use a Water Stone on Eevee.

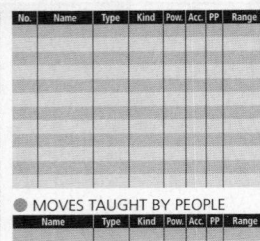

● **LEVEL-UP MOVES**

Lv.	Name	Type	Kind	Pow.	Acc.	PP	Range
1	Helping Hand	Normal	Status	—	—	20	1 Ally
1	Tackle	Normal	Physical	50	100	35	Normal
1	Tail Whip	Normal	Status	—	100	30	Many Others
5	Sand Attack	Ground	Status	—	100	15	Normal
9	Water Gun	Water	Special	40	100	25	Normal
13	Quick Attack	Normal	Physical	40	100	30	Normal
17	Water Pulse	Water	Special	60	100	20	Normal
20	Aurora Beam	Ice	Special	65	100	20	Normal
25	Aqua Ring	Water	Status	—	—	20	Self
29	Acid Armor	Poison	Status	—	—	20	Self
33	Haze	Ice	Status	—	—	30	Both Sides
37	Muddy Water	Water	Special	90	85	10	Many Others
41	Last Resort	Normal	Physical	140	100	5	Normal
45	Hydro Pump	Water	Special	110	80	5	Normal

● **TM & HM MOVES**

No.	Name	Type	Kind	Pow.	Acc.	PP	Range
TM05	Roar	Normal	Status	—	—	20	Normal
TM06	Toxic	Poison	Status	—	90	10	Normal
TM07	Hail	Ice	Status	—	—	10	Both Sides
TM10	Hidden Power	Normal	Special	60	100	15	Normal
TM11	Sunny Day	Fire	Status	—	—	5	Both Sides
TM13	Ice Beam	Ice	Special	90	100	10	Normal
TM14	Blizzard	Ice	Special	110	70	5	Many Others
TM15	Hyper Beam	Normal	Special	150	90	5	Normal
TM17	Protect	Normal	Status	—	—	10	Self
TM18	Rain Dance	Water	Status	—	—	5	Both Sides
TM21	Frustration	Normal	Physical	—	100	20	Normal
TM27	Return	Normal	Physical	—	100	20	Normal
TM28	Dig	Ground	Physical	80	100	10	Normal
TM30	Shadow Ball	Ghost	Special	80	100	15	Normal
TM32	Double Team	Normal	Status	—	—	15	Self
TM42	Facade	Normal	Physical	70	100	20	Normal
TM44	Rest	Psychic	Status	—	—	10	Self
TM45	Attract	Normal	Status	—	100	15	Normal
TM48	Round	Normal	Special	60	100	15	Normal
TM49	Echoed Voice	Normal	Special	40	100	15	Normal
TM55	Scald	Water	Special	80	100	15	Normal
TM67	Retaliate	Normal	Physical	70	100	5	Normal
TM68	Giga Impact	Normal	Physical	150	90	5	Normal
TM87	Swagger	Normal	Status	—	90	15	Normal
TM88	Sleep Talk	Normal	Status	—	—	10	Self
TM90	Substitute	Normal	Status	—	—	10	Self
TM94	Rock Smash	Fighting	Physical	40	100	15	Normal
TM100	Confide	Normal	Status	—	—	20	Normal
HM03	Surf	Water	Special	90	100	15	Adjacent
HM04	Strength	Normal	Physical	80	100	15	Normal
HM05	Waterfall	Water	Physical	80	100	15	Normal

No.	Name	Type	Kind	Pow.	Acc.	PP	Range

● **MOVES TAUGHT BY PEOPLE**

Name	Type	Kind	Pow.	Acc.	PP	Range

🔺 Coastal Kalos 079

Lightning Pokémon

☑ **Jolteon**

HEIGHT: 2'07"   WEIGHT: 54.0 lbs.
GENDER: ♂/♀

TYPE Electric

ABILITY
Volt Absorb

HIDDEN ABILITY
Quick Feet

STAT GROWTH RATES
HP	▪▪▪
Attack	▪▪▪
Defense	▪▪▪
Sp. Atk	▪▪▪▪▪
Sp. Def	▪▪▪▪
Speed	▪▪▪▪▪▪▪

EGG GROUP
Field

Ⓧ Every hair on its body starts to stand sharply on end if it becomes charged with electricity.

Ⓨ It accumulates negative ions in the atmosphere to blast out 10,000-volt lightning bolts.

🔺 EVOLUTION

Eevee → Thunder Stone → Jolteon

ITEMS SOMETIMES HELD BY WILD POKÉMON
None

Damage taken in normal battles		Damage taken in Inverse Battles	
Normal	×1	Normal	×1
Fire	×1	Fire	×1
Water	×1	Water	×1
Grass	×1	Grass	×1
Electric	×0.5 ❶	Electric	×2 ❶
Ice	×1	Ice	×1
Fighting	×1	Fighting	×1
Poison	×1	Poison	×1
Ground	×2	Ground	×0.5
Flying	×0.5	Flying	×2
Psychic	×1	Psychic	×1
Bug	×1	Bug	×1
Rock	×1	Rock	×1
Ghost	×1	Ghost	×1
Dragon	×1	Dragon	×1
Dark	×1	Dark	×1
Steel	×0.5	Steel	×2
Fairy	×1	Fairy	×1

Can be used in	
Inverse Battle	Battle Institute
—	Battle Maison
Battle Chateau	Random Matchup

Same form for ♂/♀

How to obtain for your Coastal Kalos Pokédex

Use a Thunder Stone on Eevee.   (X)   Use a Thunder Stone on Eevee.   (Y)

AFTER THE HALL OF FAME

CENTRAL KALOS

COASTAL KALOS

079 Jolteon

MOUNTAIN KALOS

ADVENTURE DATA

● LEVEL-UP MOVES

Lv.	Name	Type	Kind	Pow.	Acc.	PP	Range
1	Helping Hand	Normal	Status	—	—	20	1 Ally
1	Tackle	Normal	Physical	50	100	35	Normal
1	Tail Whip	Normal	Status	—	100	30	Many Others
5	Sand Attack	Ground	Status	—	100	15	Normal
9	Thunder Shock	Electric	Special	40	100	30	Normal
13	Quick Attack	Normal	Physical	40	100	30	Normal
17	Double Kick	Fighting	Physical	30	100	30	Normal
20	Thunder Fang	Electric	Physical	65	95	15	Normal
25	Pin Missile	Bug	Physical	25	95	20	Normal
29	Agility	Psychic	Status	—	—	30	Self
33	Thunder Wave	Electric	Status	—	100	20	Normal
37	Discharge	Electric	Special	80	100	15	Adjacent
41	Last Resort	Normal	Physical	140	100	5	Normal
45	Thunder	Electric	Special	110	70	10	Normal

● TM & HM MOVES

No.	Name	Type	Kind	Pow.	Acc.	PP	Range
TM05	Roar	Normal	Status	—	—	20	Normal
TM06	Toxic	Poison	Status	—	90	10	Normal
TM10	Hidden Power	Normal	Special	60	100	15	Normal
TM11	Sunny Day	Fire	Status	—	—	5	Both Sides
TM15	Hyper Beam	Normal	Special	150	90	5	Normal
TM16	Light Screen	Psychic	Status	—	—	30	Your Side
TM17	Protect	Normal	Status	—	—	10	Self
TM18	Rain Dance	Water	Status	—	—	5	Both Sides
TM21	Frustration	Normal	Physical	—	100	20	Normal
TM24	Thunderbolt	Electric	Special	90	100	15	Normal
TM25	Thunder	Electric	Special	110	70	10	Normal
TM27	Return	Normal	Physical	—	100	20	Normal
TM28	Dig	Ground	Physical	80	100	10	Normal
TM30	Shadow Ball	Ghost	Special	80	100	15	Normal
TM32	Double Team	Normal	Status	—	—	15	Self
TM42	Facade	Normal	Physical	70	100	20	Normal
TM44	Rest	Psychic	Status	—	—	10	Self
TM45	Attract	Normal	Status	—	100	15	Normal
TM48	Round	Normal	Special	60	100	15	Normal
TM49	Echoed Voice	Normal	Special	40	100	15	Normal
TM57	Charge Beam	Electric	Special	50	90	10	Normal
TM67	Retaliate	Normal	Physical	70	100	5	Normal
TM68	Giga Impact	Normal	Physical	150	90	5	Normal
TM70	Flash	Normal	Status	—	100	20	Normal
TM72	Volt Switch	Electric	Special	70	100	20	Normal
TM73	Thunder Wave	Electric	Status	—	100	20	Normal
TM87	Swagger	Normal	Status	—	90	15	Normal
TM88	Sleep Talk	Normal	Status	—	—	10	Self
TM90	Substitute	Normal	Status	—	—	10	Self
TM93	Wild Charge	Electric	Physical	90	100	15	Normal
TM94	Rock Smash	Fighting	Physical	40	100	15	Normal
TM100	Confide	Normal	Status	—	—	20	Normal
HM04	Strength	Normal	Physical	80	100	15	Normal

No.	Name	Type	Kind	Pow.	Acc.	PP	Range

● MOVES TAUGHT BY PEOPLE

Name	Type	Kind	Pow.	Acc.	PP	Range

AFTER THE HALL OF FAME

CENTRAL KALOS

COASTAL KALOS

080

Flareon

MOUNTAIN KALOS

ADVENTURE DATA

Coastal Kalos 080
Flame Pokémon
☑ Flareon

HEIGHT: 2'11"   WEIGHT: 55.1 lbs.
GENDER: ♂/♀

X It has a flame sac in its body. Its body temperature tops 1,650 degrees Fahrenheit before battle.

Y It has a flame bag inside its body. After inhaling deeply, it blows out flames of nearly 3,000 degrees Fahrenheit.

TYPE Fire

ABILITY
Flash Fire

HIDDEN ABILITY
Guts

STAT GROWTH RATES
HP ■■■
Attack ■■■■■■■
Defense ■■■
Sp. Atk ■■■■
Sp. Def ■■■■■■
Speed ■■■■

EGG GROUP
Field

EVOLUTION
Eevee — Fire Stone → Flareon

ITEMS SOMETIMES HELD BY WILD POKÉMON
None

Damage taken in normal battles		Damage taken in Inverse Battles	
Normal	×1	Normal	×1
Fire	×0.5	Fire	×2
Water	×2	Water	×0.5
Grass	×0.5	Grass	×2
Electric	×1	Electric	×1
Ice	×0.5	Ice	×2
Fighting	×1	Fighting	×1
Poison	×1	Poison	×1
Ground	×2	Ground	×0.5
Flying	×1	Flying	×1
Psychic	×1	Psychic	×1
Bug	×0.5	Bug	×2
Rock	×2	Rock	×0.5
Ghost	×1	Ghost	×1
Dragon	×1	Dragon	×1
Dark	×1	Dark	×1
Steel	×0.5	Steel	×2
Fairy	×0.5	Fairy	×2

Can be used in	
Inverse Battle	Battle Institute
—	Battle Maison
Battle Chateau	Random Matchup

Same form for ♂/♀

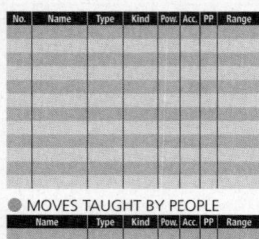

How to obtain for your Coastal Kalos Pokédex
X: Use a Fire Stone on Eevee.
Y: Use a Fire Stone on Eevee.

● LEVEL-UP MOVES

Lv.	Name	Type	Kind	Pow.	Acc.	PP	Range
1	Helping Hand	Normal	Status	—	—	20	1 Ally
1	Tackle	Normal	Physical	50	100	35	Normal
1	Tail Whip	Normal	Status	—	100	30	Many Others
5	Sand Attack	Ground	Status	—	100	15	Normal
9	Ember	Fire	Special	40	100	25	Normal
13	Quick Attack	Normal	Physical	40	100	30	Normal
17	Bite	Dark	Physical	60	100	25	Normal
20	Fire Fang	Fire	Physical	65	95	15	Normal
25	Fire Spin	Fire	Special	35	85	15	Normal
29	Scary Face	Normal	Status	—	100	10	Normal
33	Smog	Poison	Special	30	70	20	Normal
37	Lava Plume	Fire	Special	80	100	15	Adjacent
41	Last Resort	Normal	Physical	140	100	5	Normal
45	Flare Blitz	Fire	Physical	120	100	15	Normal

● TM & HM MOVES

No.	Name	Type	Kind	Pow.	Acc.	PP	Range
TM05	Roar	Normal	Status	—	—	20	Normal
TM06	Toxic	Poison	Status	—	90	10	Normal
TM10	Hidden Power	Normal	Special	60	100	15	Normal
TM11	Sunny Day	Fire	Status	—	—	5	Both Sides
TM15	Hyper Beam	Normal	Special	150	90	5	Normal
TM17	Protect	Normal	Status	—	—	10	Self
TM18	Rain Dance	Water	Status	—	—	5	Both Sides
TM21	Frustration	Normal	Physical	—	100	20	Normal
TM27	Return	Normal	Physical	—	100	20	Normal
TM28	Dig	Ground	Physical	80	100	10	Normal
TM30	Shadow Ball	Ghost	Special	80	100	15	Normal
TM32	Double Team	Normal	Status	—	—	15	Self
TM35	Flamethrower	Fire	Special	90	100	15	Normal
TM38	Fire Blast	Fire	Special	110	85	5	Normal
TM42	Facade	Normal	Physical	70	100	20	Normal
TM43	Flame Charge	Fire	Physical	50	100	20	Normal
TM44	Rest	Psychic	Status	—	—	10	Self
TM45	Attract	Normal	Status	—	100	15	Normal
TM48	Round	Normal	Special	60	100	15	Normal
TM49	Echoed Voice	Normal	Special	40	100	15	Normal
TM50	Overheat	Fire	Special	130	90	5	Normal
TM59	Incinerate	Fire	Special	60	100	15	Many Others
TM61	Will-O-Wisp	Fire	Status	—	85	15	Normal
TM67	Retaliate	Normal	Physical	70	100	5	Normal
TM68	Giga Impact	Normal	Physical	150	90	5	Normal
TM87	Swagger	Normal	Status	—	90	15	Normal
TM88	Sleep Talk	Normal	Status	—	—	10	Self
TM90	Substitute	Normal	Status	—	—	10	Self
TM94	Rock Smash	Fighting	Physical	40	100	15	Normal
TM100	Confide	Normal	Status	—	—	20	Normal
HM04	Strength	Normal	Physical	80	100	15	Normal

● MOVES TAUGHT BY PEOPLE

Name	Type	Kind	Pow.	Acc.	PP	Range

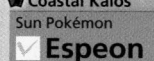

Coastal Kalos

Sun Pokémon

081

☑ Espeon

HEIGHT: 2'11" WEIGHT: 58.4 lbs.
GENDER: ♂/♀

X The tip of its forked tail quivers when it is predicting its opponent's next move.

Y Its fur is so sensitive, it can feel minute shifts in the air and predict the weather...and its foes' thoughts.

TYPE **Psychic**

ABILITY
Synchronize

HIDDEN ABILITY
Magic Bounce

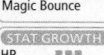

STAT GROWTH RATES
HP	■■■
Attack	■■■
Defense	■■■
Sp. Atk	■■■■■■
Sp. Def	■■■■
Speed	■■■■■

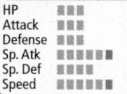

EGG GROUP
Field

EVOLUTION

Level up between
4 A.M. and 7:59 P.M.
with high friendship

Eevee → Espeon

ITEMS SOMETIMES HELD BY WILD POKÉMON
None

Damage taken in normal battles	
Normal	×1
Fire	×1
Water	×1
Grass	×1
Electric	×1
Ice	×1
Fighting	×0.5
Poison	×1
Ground	×1
Flying	×1
Psychic	×0.5
Bug	×2
Rock	×1
Ghost	×2
Dragon	×1
Dark	×2
Steel	×1
Fairy	×1

Damage taken in Inverse Battles	
Normal	×1
Fire	×1
Water	×1
Grass	×1
Electric	×1
Ice	×1
Fighting	×2
Poison	×1
Ground	×1
Flying	×1
Psychic	×2
Bug	×0.5
Rock	×1
Ghost	×0.5
Dragon	×1
Dark	×0.5
Steel	×1
Fairy	×1

Can be used in	
Inverse Battle	Battle Institute
—	Battle Maison
Battle Chateau	Random Matchup

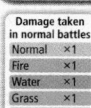

Same form for ♂/♀

How to obtain for your Coastal Kalos Pokédex

Level up Eevee between 4 A.M. and 7:59 P.M. with high friendship.

Level up Eevee between 4 A.M. and 7:59 P.M. with high friendship.

AFTER THE HALL OF FAME

CENTRAL KALOS

COASTAL KALOS

081 Espeon

MOUNTAIN KALOS

ADVENTURE DATA

● LEVEL-UP MOVES

Lv.	Name	Type	Kind	Pow.	Acc.	PP	Range
1	Helping Hand	Normal	Status	—	—	20	1 Ally
1	Tackle	Normal	Physical	50	100	35	Normal
1	Tail Whip	Normal	Status	—	100	30	Many Others
5	Sand Attack	Ground	Status	—	100	15	Normal
9	Confusion	Psychic	Special	50	100	25	Normal
13	Quick Attack	Normal	Physical	40	100	30	Normal
17	Swift	Normal	Special	60	—	20	Many Others
20	Psybeam	Psychic	Special	65	100	20	Normal
25	Future Sight	Psychic	Special	120	100	10	Normal
29	Psych Up	Normal	Status	—	—	10	Normal
33	Morning Sun	Normal	Status	—	—	5	Self
37	Psychic	Psychic	Special	90	100	10	Normal
41	Last Resort	Normal	Physical	140	100	5	Normal
45	Power Swap	Psychic	Status	—	—	10	Normal

● TM & HM MOVES

No.	Name	Type	Kind	Pow.	Acc.	PP	Range
TM03	Psyshock	Psychic	Special	80	100	10	Normal
TM04	Calm Mind	Psychic	Status	—	—	20	Self
TM06	Toxic	Poison	Status	—	90	10	Normal
TM10	Hidden Power	Normal	Special	60	100	15	Normal
TM11	Sunny Day	Fire	Status	—	—	5	Both Sides
TM15	Hyper Beam	Normal	Special	150	90	5	Normal
TM16	Light Screen	Psychic	Status	—	—	30	Your Side
TM17	Protect	Normal	Status	—	—	10	Self
TM18	Rain Dance	Water	Status	—	—	5	Both Sides
TM21	Frustration	Normal	Physical	—	100	20	Normal
TM27	Return	Normal	Physical	—	100	20	Normal
TM28	Dig	Ground	Physical	80	100	10	Normal
TM29	Psychic	Psychic	Special	90	100	10	Normal
TM30	Shadow Ball	Ghost	Special	80	100	15	Normal
TM32	Double Team	Normal	Status	—	—	15	Self
TM33	Reflect	Psychic	Status	—	—	20	Your Side
TM42	Facade	Normal	Physical	70	100	20	Normal
TM44	Rest	Psychic	Status	—	—	10	Self
TM45	Attract	Normal	Status	—	100	15	Normal
TM48	Round	Normal	Special	60	100	15	Normal
TM49	Echoed Voice	Normal	Special	40	100	15	Normal
TM67	Retaliate	Normal	Physical	70	100	5	Normal
TM68	Giga Impact	Normal	Physical	150	90	5	Normal
TM70	Flash	Normal	Status	—	100	20	Normal
TM77	Psych Up	Normal	Status	—	—	10	Normal
TM85	Dream Eater	Psychic	Special	100	100	15	Normal
TM86	Grass Knot	Grass	Special	—	100	20	Normal
TM87	Swagger	Normal	Status	—	90	15	Normal
TM88	Sleep Talk	Normal	Status	—	—	10	Self
TM90	Substitute	Normal	Status	—	—	10	Self
TM92	Trick Room	Psychic	Status	—	—	5	Both Sides
TM99	Dazzling Gleam	Fairy	Special	80	100	10	Many Others
TM100	Confide	Normal	Status	—	—	20	Normal

No.	Name	Type	Kind	Pow.	Acc.	PP	Range
HM01	Cut	Normal	Physical	50	95	30	Normal

● MOVES TAUGHT BY PEOPLE

Name	Type	Kind	Pow.	Acc.	PP	Range

AFTER THE HALL OF FAME

CENTRAL KALOS

COASTAL KALOS

082 Umbreon

MOUNTAIN KALOS

ADVENTURE DATA

⬠ Coastal Kalos 082
Moonlight Pokémon
☑ Umbreon

HEIGHT: 3'03" WEIGHT: 59.5 lbs.
GENDER: ♂/♀

X The light of the moon changed Eevee's genetic structure. It lurks in darkness for prey.

Y When exposed to the moon's aura, the rings on its body glow faintly and it's filled with a mysterious power.

TYPE Dark

ABILITY
Synchronize

HIDDEN ABILITY
Inner Focus

STAT GROWTH RATES
HP	▪▪▪▪
Attack	▪▪▪
Defense	▪▪▪▪▪
Sp. Atk	▪▪▪
Sp. Def	▪▪▪▪▪
Speed	▪▪▪▪

EGG GROUP
Field

🔼 EVOLUTION

Level up between 8 P.M. and 3:59 A.M. with high friendship

Eevee → Umbreon

ITEMS SOMETIMES HELD BY WILD POKÉMON
None

Damage taken in normal battles		Damage taken in Inverse Battles	
Normal	×1	Normal	×1
Fire	×1	Fire	×1
Water	×1	Water	×1
Grass	×1	Grass	×1
Electric	×1	Electric	×1
Ice	×1	Ice	×1
Fighting	×2	Fighting	×0.5
Poison	×1	Poison	×1
Ground	×1	Ground	×1
Flying	×1	Flying	×1
Psychic	×0	Psychic	×2
Bug	×2	Bug	×0.5
Rock	×1	Rock	×1
Ghost	×0.5	Ghost	×2
Dragon	×1	Dragon	×1
Dark	×0.5	Dark	×2
Steel	×1	Steel	×1
Fairy	×2	Fairy	×0.5

Can be used in	
Inverse Battle	Battle Institute
—	Battle Maison
Battle Chateau	Random Matchup

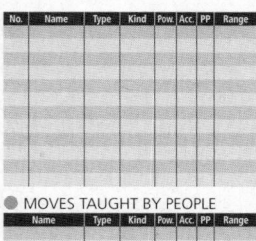

Same form for ♂/♀

How to obtain for your Coastal Kalos Pokédex

X Level up Eevee between 8 P.M. and 3:59 A.M. with high friendship.

Y Level up Eevee between 8 P.M. and 3:59 A.M. with high friendship.

● LEVEL-UP MOVES

Lv.	Name	Type	Kind	Pow.	Acc.	PP	Range
1	Helping Hand	Normal	Status	—	—	20	1 Ally
1	Tackle	Normal	Physical	50	100	35	Normal
1	Tail Whip	Normal	Status	—	100	30	Many Others
5	Sand Attack	Ground	Status	—	100	15	Normal
9	Pursuit	Dark	Physical	40	100	20	Normal
13	Quick Attack	Normal	Physical	40	100	30	Normal
17	Confuse Ray	Ghost	Status	—	100	10	Normal
20	Feint Attack	Dark	Physical	60	—	20	Normal
25	Assurance	Dark	Physical	60	100	10	Normal
29	Screech	Normal	Status	—	85	40	Normal
33	Moonlight	Fairy	Status	—	—	5	Self
37	Mean Look	Normal	Status	—	—	5	Normal
41	Last Resort	Normal	Physical	140	100	5	Normal
45	Guard Swap	Psychic	Status	—	—	10	Normal

● TM & HM MOVES

No.	Name	Type	Kind	Pow.	Acc.	PP	Range
TM06	Toxic	Poison	Status	—	90	10	Normal
TM10	Hidden Power	Normal	Special	60	100	15	Normal
TM11	Sunny Day	Fire	Status	—	—	5	Both Sides
TM12	Taunt	Dark	Status	—	100	20	Normal
TM15	Hyper Beam	Normal	Special	150	90	5	Normal
TM17	Protect	Normal	Status	—	—	10	Self
TM18	Rain Dance	Water	Status	—	—	5	Both Sides
TM21	Frustration	Normal	Physical	—	100	20	Normal
TM27	Return	Normal	Physical	—	100	20	Normal
TM28	Dig	Ground	Physical	80	100	10	Normal
TM29	Psychic	Psychic	Special	90	100	10	Normal
TM30	Shadow Ball	Ghost	Special	80	100	15	Normal
TM32	Double Team	Normal	Status	—	—	15	Self
TM41	Torment	Dark	Status	—	100	15	Normal
TM44	Facade	Normal	Physical	70	100	20	Normal
TM44	Rest	Psychic	Status	—	—	10	Self
TM45	Attract	Normal	Status	—	100	15	Normal
TM48	Round	Normal	Special	60	100	15	Normal
TM49	Echoed Voice	Normal	Special	40	100	15	Normal
TM66	Payback	Dark	Physical	50	100	10	Normal
TM67	Retaliate	Normal	Physical	70	100	5	Normal
TM68	Giga Impact	Normal	Physical	150	90	5	Normal
TM70	Flash	Normal	Status	—	100	20	Normal
TM77	Psych Up	Normal	Status	—	—	10	Normal
TM85	Dream Eater	Psychic	Special	100	100	15	Normal
TM87	Swagger	Normal	Status	—	90	15	Normal
TM88	Sleep Talk	Normal	Status	—	—	10	Self
TM90	Substitute	Normal	Status	—	—	10	Self
TM95	Snarl	Dark	Special	55	95	15	Many Others
TM97	Dark Pulse	Dark	Special	80	100	15	Normal
TM100	Confide	Normal	Status	—	—	20	Normal
HM01	Cut	Normal	Physical	50	95	30	Normal

No.	Name	Type	Kind	Pow.	Acc.	PP	Range

● MOVES TAUGHT BY PEOPLE

Name	Type	Kind	Pow.	Acc.	PP	Range

Coastal Kalos
Verdant Pokémon
☑ Leafeon

083

HEIGHT: 3'03" WEIGHT: 56.2 lbs.
GENDER: ♂/♀

X When you see Leafeon asleep in a patch of sunshine, you'll know it is using photosynthesis to produce clean air.

Y Just like a plant, it uses photosynthesis. As a result, it is always enveloped in clear air.

TYPE Grass

ABILITY
Leaf Guard

HIDDEN ABILITY
Chlorophyll

STAT GROWTH RATES
HP	▪▪▪
Attack	▪▪▪▪▪▪
Defense	▪▪▪▪▪▪
Sp. Atk	▪▪▪
Sp. Def	▪▪▪
Speed	▪▪▪▪▪

EGG GROUP
Field

EVOLUTION

Level up near the moss-covered rock on Route 20

Eevee → Leafeon

ITEMS SOMETIMES HELD BY WILD POKÉMON
None

Damage taken in normal battles	
Normal	×1
Fire	×2
Water	×0.5
Grass	×0.5
Electric	×0.5
Ice	×2
Fighting	×1
Poison	×2
Ground	×0.5
Flying	×2
Psychic	×1
Bug	×2
Rock	×1
Ghost	×1
Dragon	×1
Dark	×1
Steel	×1
Fairy	×1

Damage taken in Inverse Battles	
Normal	×1
Fire	×0.5
Water	×2
Grass	×2
Electric	×2
Ice	×0.5
Fighting	×1
Poison	×0.5
Ground	×2
Flying	×0.5
Psychic	×1
Bug	×0.5
Rock	×1
Ghost	×1
Dragon	×1
Dark	×1
Steel	×1
Fairy	×1

Can be used in	
Inverse Battle	Battle Institute
—	Battle Maison
Battle Chateau	Random Matchup

Same form for ♂ / ♀

How to obtain for your Coastal Kalos Pokédex

Level up Eevee near the moss-covered rock on Route 20.

Level up Eevee near the moss-covered rock on Route 20.

● LEVEL-UP MOVES

Lv.	Name	Type	Kind	Pow.	Acc.	PP	Range
1	Tail Whip	Normal	Status	—	100	30	Many Others
1	Tackle	Normal	Physical	50	100	35	Normal
1	Helping Hand	Normal	Status	—	—	20	1 Ally
5	Sand Attack	Ground	Status	—	100	15	Normal
9	Razor Leaf	Grass	Physical	55	95	25	Many Others
13	Quick Attack	Normal	Physical	40	100	30	Normal
17	Grass Whistle	Grass	Status	—	55	15	Normal
20	Magical Leaf	Grass	Special	60	—	20	Normal
25	Giga Drain	Grass	Special	75	100	10	Normal
29	Swords Dance	Normal	Status	—	—	20	Self
33	Synthesis	Grass	Status	—	—	5	Self
37	Sunny Day	Fire	Status	—	—	5	Both Sides
41	Last Resort	Normal	Physical	140	100	5	Normal
45	Leaf Blade	Grass	Physical	90	100	15	Normal

● TM & HM MOVES

No.	Name	Type	Kind	Pow.	Acc.	PP	Range
TM05	Roar	Normal	Status	—	—	20	Normal
TM06	Toxic	Poison	Status	—	90	10	Normal
TM10	Hidden Power	Normal	Special	60	100	15	Normal
TM11	Sunny Day	Fire	Status	—	—	5	Both Sides
TM15	Hyper Beam	Normal	Special	150	90	5	Normal
TM17	Protect	Normal	Status	—	—	10	Self
TM18	Rain Dance	Water	Status	—	—	5	Both Sides
TM21	Frustration	Normal	Physical	—	100	20	Normal
TM22	Solar Beam	Grass	Special	120	100	10	Normal
TM27	Return	Normal	Physical	—	100	20	Normal
TM28	Dig	Ground	Physical	80	100	10	Normal
TM30	Shadow Ball	Ghost	Special	80	100	15	Normal
TM32	Double Team	Normal	Status	—	—	15	Self
TM42	Aerial Ace	Flying	Physical	60	—	20	Normal
TM44	Rest	Psychic	Status	—	—	10	Self
TM45	Attract	Normal	Status	—	100	15	Normal
TM48	Round	Normal	Special	60	100	15	Normal
TM49	Echoed Voice	Normal	Special	40	100	15	Normal
TM53	Energy Ball	Grass	Special	90	100	10	Normal
TM67	Retaliate	Normal	Physical	70	100	5	Normal
TM68	Giga Impact	Normal	Physical	150	90	5	Normal
TM70	Flash	Normal	Status	—	100	20	Normal
TM75	Swords Dance	Normal	Status	—	—	20	Self
TM81	X-Scissor	Bug	Physical	80	100	15	Normal
TM86	Grass Knot	Grass	Special	—	100	20	Normal
TM87	Swagger	Normal	Status	—	90	15	Normal
TM88	Sleep Talk	Normal	Status	—	—	10	Self
TM90	Substitute	Normal	Status	—	—	10	Self
TM94	Rock Smash	Fighting	Physical	40	100	15	Normal
TM96	Nature Power	Normal	Status	—	—	20	Normal
TM100	Confide	Normal	Status	—	—	20	Normal
HM04	Strength	Normal	Physical	80	100	15	Normal

No.	Name	Type	Kind	Pow.	Acc.	PP	Range

● MOVES TAUGHT BY PEOPLE

Name	Type	Kind	Pow.	Acc.	PP	Range

AFTER THE HALL OF FAME

CENTRAL KALOS

COASTAL KALOS

084

Glaceon

MOUNTAIN KALOS

ADVENTURE DATA

Coastal Kalos
Fresh Snow Pokémon
084

✓ **Glaceon**

HEIGHT: 2'07" WEIGHT: 57.1 lbs.
GENDER: ♂/♀

TYPE Ice

ABILITY
Snow Cloak

HIDDEN ABILITY
Ice Body

STAT GROWTH RATES
HP	■■■
Attack	■■■
Defense	■■■■
Sp. Atk	■■■■■
Sp. Def	■■■■
Speed	■■■■

EGG GROUP
Field

X By controlling its body heat, it can freeze the atmosphere around it to make a diamond-dust flurry.

Y It lowers its body heat to freeze its fur. The hairs then become like needles it can fire.

EVOLUTION

Level up near the ice-covered rock in Frost Cavern

Eevee → Glaceon

ITEMS SOMETIMES HELD BY WILD POKÉMON
None

Damage taken in normal battles		Damage taken in Inverse Battles	
Normal	×1	Normal	×1
Fire	×2	Fire	×0.5
Water	×1	Water	×1
Grass	×1	Grass	×1
Electric	×1	Electric	×1
Ice	×0.5	Ice	×2
Fighting	×2	Fighting	×0.5
Poison	×1	Poison	×1
Ground	×1	Ground	×1
Flying	×1	Flying	×1
Psychic	×1	Psychic	×1
Bug	×1	Bug	×1
Rock	×2	Rock	×0.5
Ghost	×1	Ghost	×1
Dragon	×1	Dragon	×1
Dark	×1	Dark	×1
Steel	×2	Steel	×0.5
Fairy	×1	Fairy	×1

Can be used in	
Inverse Battle	Battle Institute
—	Battle Maison
Battle Chateau	Random Matchup

Same form for ♂/♀

How to obtain for your Coastal Kalos Pokédex

Level up Eevee near the ice-covered rock in Frost Cavern.

Level up Eevee near the ice-covered rock in Frost Cavern.

● LEVEL-UP MOVES

Lv.	Name	Type	Kind	Pow.	Acc.	PP	Range
1	Helping Hand	Normal	Status	—	—	20	1 Ally
1	Tackle	Normal	Physical	50	100	35	Normal
1	Tail Whip	Normal	Status	—	100	30	Many Others
5	Sand Attack	Ground	Status	—	100	15	Normal
9	Icy Wind	Ice	Special	55	95	15	Many Others
13	Quick Attack	Normal	Physical	40	100	30	Normal
17	Bite	Dark	Physical	60	100	25	Normal
20	Ice Fang	Ice	Physical	65	95	15	Normal
25	Ice Shard	Ice	Physical	40	100	30	Normal
29	Barrier	Psychic	Status	—	—	20	Self
33	Mirror Coat	Psychic	Special	—	100	20	Varies
37	Hail	Ice	Status	—	—	10	Both Sides
41	Last Resort	Normal	Physical	140	100	5	Normal
45	Blizzard	Ice	Special	110	70	5	Many Others

● TM & HM MOVES

No.	Name	Type	Kind	Pow.	Acc.	PP	Range
TM05	Roar	Normal	Status	—	—	20	Normal
TM06	Toxic	Poison	Status	—	90	10	Normal
TM07	Hail	Ice	Status	—	—	10	Both Sides
TM10	Hidden Power	Normal	Special	60	100	15	Normal
TM11	Sunny Day	Fire	Status	—	—	5	Both Sides
TM13	Ice Beam	Ice	Special	90	100	10	Normal
TM14	Blizzard	Ice	Special	110	70	5	Many Others
TM15	Hyper Beam	Normal	Special	150	90	5	Normal
TM17	Protect	Normal	Status	—	—	10	Self
TM18	Rain Dance	Water	Status	—	—	5	Both Sides
TM21	Frustration	Normal	Physical	—	100	20	Normal
TM27	Return	Normal	Physical	—	100	20	Normal
TM28	Dig	Ground	Physical	80	100	10	Normal
TM30	Shadow Ball	Ghost	Special	80	100	15	Normal
TM32	Double Team	Normal	Status	—	—	15	Self
TM42	Facade	Normal	Physical	70	100	20	Normal
TM44	Rest	Psychic	Status	—	—	10	Self
TM45	Attract	Normal	Status	—	100	15	Normal
TM48	Round	Normal	Special	60	100	15	Normal
TM49	Echoed Voice	Normal	Special	40	100	15	Normal
TM67	Retaliate	Normal	Physical	70	100	5	Normal
TM68	Giga Impact	Normal	Physical	150	90	5	Normal
TM79	Frost Breath	Ice	Special	60	90	10	Normal
TM87	Swagger	Normal	Status	—	90	15	Normal
TM88	Sleep Talk	Normal	Status	—	—	10	Self
TM90	Substitute	Normal	Status	—	—	10	Self
TM94	Rock Smash	Fighting	Physical	40	100	15	Normal
TM100	Confide	Normal	Status	—	—	20	Normal
HM04	Strength	Normal	Physical	80	100	15	Normal

No.	Name	Type	Kind	Pow.	Acc.	PP	Range

● MOVES TAUGHT BY PEOPLE

Name	Type	Kind	Pow.	Acc.	PP	Range

Coastal Kalos **085**
Intertwining Pokémon
 Sylveon

TYPE Fairy

ABILITY
Cute Charm

HIDDEN ABILITY
Pixilate

STAT GROWTH RATES
HP	▪▪▪
Attack	▪▪▪
Defense	▪▪▪
Sp. Atk	▪▪▪▪
Sp. Def	▪▪▪▪▪
Speed	▪▪▪

EGG GROUP
Field

HEIGHT: 3'03"   WEIGHT: 51.8 lbs.
GENDER: ♂/♀

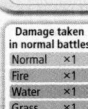 It sends a soothing aura from its ribbonlike feelers to calm fights.

It wraps its ribbonlike feelers around the arm of its beloved Trainer and walks with him or her.

EVOLUTION

High affection with a Fairy-type move

Eevee → Sylveon

ITEMS SOMETIMES HELD BY WILD POKÉMON
None

Damage taken in normal battles		Damage taken in Inverse Battles	
Normal	×1	Normal	×1
Fire	×1	Fire	×1
Water	×1	Water	×1
Grass	×1	Grass	×1
Electric	×1	Electric	×1
Ice	×1	Ice	×1
Fighting	×0.5	Fighting	×2
Poison	×2	Poison	×0.5
Ground	×1	Ground	×1
Flying	×1	Flying	×1
Psychic	×1	Psychic	×1
Bug	×0.5	Bug	×2
Rock	×1	Rock	×1
Ghost	×1	Ghost	×1
Dragon	×0	Dragon	×2
Dark	×0.5	Dark	×2
Steel	×2	Steel	×0.5
Fairy	×1	Fairy	×1

Can be used in	
Inverse Battle	Battle Institute
—	Battle Maison
Battle Chateau	Random Matchup

Same form for ♂/♀

How to obtain for your Coastal Kalos Pokédex

Level up an Eevee that is affectionate from playing Pokémon-Amie, and have it learn a Fairy-type move. Alternatively, teach it a Fairy-type move first, then level it up after ensuring that it is very affectionate.

Level up an Eevee that is affectionate from playing Pokémon-Amie, and have it learn a Fairy-type move. Alternatively, teach it a Fairy-type move first, then level it up after ensuring that it is very affectionate.

● **LEVEL-UP MOVES**
Lv.	Name	Type	Kind	Pow.	Acc.	PP	Range
1	Disarming Voice	Fairy	Special	40	—	15	Many Others
1	Tail Whip	Normal	Status	—	100	30	Many Others
1	Tackle	Normal	Physical	50	100	35	Normal
1	Helping Hand	Normal	Status	—	—	20	1 Ally
5	Sand Attack	Ground	Status	—	100	15	Normal
9	Fairy Wind	Fairy	Special	40	100	30	Normal
13	Quick Attack	Normal	Physical	40	100	30	Normal
17	Swift	Normal	Special	60	—	20	Many Others
20	Draining Kiss	Fairy	Special	50	100	10	Normal
25	Skill Swap	Psychic	Status	—	—	10	Normal
29	Misty Terrain	Fairy	Status	—	—	10	Both Sides
33	Light Screen	Psychic	Status	—	—	30	Your Side
37	Moonblast	Fairy	Special	95	100	15	Normal
41	Last Resort	Normal	Physical	140	100	5	Normal
45	Psych Up	Normal	Status	—	—	10	Normal

● **TM & HM MOVES**
No.	Name	Type	Kind	Pow.	Acc.	PP	Range
TM03	Psyshock	Psychic	Special	80	100	10	Normal
TM04	Calm Mind	Psychic	Status	—	—	20	Self
TM06	Toxic	Poison	Status	—	90	10	Normal
TM10	Hidden Power	Normal	Special	60	100	15	Normal
TM11	Sunny Day	Fire	Status	—	—	5	Both Sides
TM15	Hyper Beam	Normal	Special	150	90	5	Normal
TM16	Light Screen	Psychic	Status	—	—	30	Your Side
TM17	Protect	Normal	Status	—	—	10	Self
TM18	Rain Dance	Water	Status	—	—	5	Both Sides
TM20	Safeguard	Normal	Status	—	—	25	Your Side
TM21	Frustration	Normal	Physical	—	100	20	Normal
TM27	Return	Normal	Physical	—	100	20	Normal
TM28	Dig	Ground	Physical	80	100	10	Normal
TM30	Shadow Ball	Ghost	Special	80	100	15	Normal
TM32	Double Team	Normal	Status	—	—	15	Self
TM33	Reflect	Psychic	Status	—	—	20	Your Side
TM42	Facade	Normal	Physical	70	100	20	Normal
TM44	Rest	Psychic	Status	—	—	10	Self
TM45	Attract	Normal	Status	—	100	15	Normal
TM48	Round	Normal	Special	60	100	15	Normal
TM49	Echoed Voice	Normal	Special	40	100	15	Normal
TM67	Retaliate	Normal	Physical	70	100	5	Normal
TM68	Giga Impact	Normal	Physical	150	90	5	Normal
TM70	Flash	Normal	Status	—	100	20	Normal
TM77	Psych Up	Normal	Status	—	—	10	Normal
TM87	Swagger	Normal	Status	—	90	15	Normal
TM88	Sleep Talk	Normal	Status	—	—	10	Self
TM90	Substitute	Normal	Status	—	—	10	Self
TM99	Dazzling Gleam	Fairy	Special	80	100	10	Many Others
TM100	Confide	Normal	Status	—	—	20	Normal
HM01	Cut	Normal	Physical	50	95	30	Normal

No.	Name	Type	Kind	Pow.	Acc.	PP	Range

● **MOVES TAUGHT BY PEOPLE**
Name	Type	Kind	Pow.	Acc.	PP	Range

AFTER THE HALL OF FAME

CENTRAL KALOS

COASTAL KALOS

085 Sylveon

MOUNTAIN KALOS

ADVENTURE DATA

AFTER THE HALL OF FAME
CENTRAL KALOS
COASTAL KALOS
086
Emolga
MOUNTAIN KALOS
ADVENTURE DATA

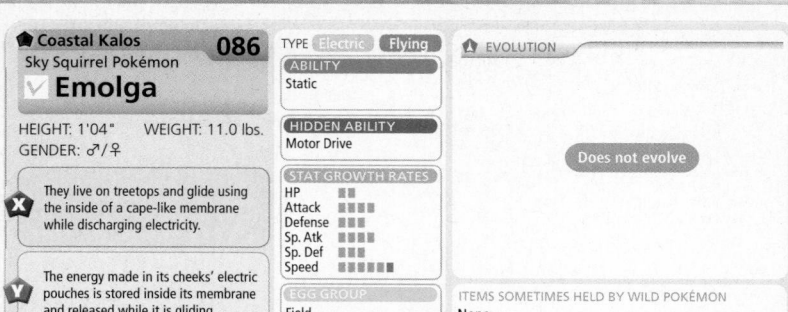

🍂 **Coastal Kalos** **086**
Sky Squirrel Pokémon
Emolga

HEIGHT: 1'04"   WEIGHT: 11.0 lbs.
GENDER: ♂/♀

TYPE Electric Flying

ABILITY
Static

HIDDEN ABILITY
Motor Drive

STAT GROWTH RATES
HP
Attack
Defense
Sp. Atk
Sp. Def
Speed

EGG GROUP
Field

EVOLUTION
Does not evolve

X They live on treetops and glide using the inside of a cape-like membrane while discharging electricity.

Y The energy made in its cheeks' electric pouches is stored inside its membrane and released while it is gliding.

ITEMS SOMETIMES HELD BY WILD POKÉMON
None

Damage taken in normal battles		Damage taken in Inverse Battles	
Normal	×1	Normal	×1
Fire	×1	Fire	×1
Water	×1	Water	×1
Grass	×0.5	Grass	×2
Electric	×1	Electric	×1
Ice	×2	Ice	×0.5
Fighting	×0.5	Fighting	×2
Poison	×1	Poison	×1
Ground	×0	Ground	×1
Flying	×0.5	Flying	×2
Psychic	×1	Psychic	×1
Bug	×0.5	Bug	×2
Rock	×2	Rock	×0.5
Ghost	×1	Ghost	×1
Dragon	×1	Dragon	×1
Dark	×1	Dark	×1
Steel	×0.5	Steel	×2
Fairy	×1	Fairy	×1

Can be used in	
Inverse Battle	Battle Institute
Sky Battle	Battle Maison
Battle Chateau	Random Matchup

Same form for ♂/♀

How to obtain for your Coastal Kalos Pokédex
❶ Catch in the tall grass on Route 10.
❷ Catch in the yellow flowers on Route 10.

❶ Catch in the tall grass on Route 10.
❷ Catch in the yellow flowers on Route 10.

● **LEVEL-UP MOVES**

Lv.	Name	Type	Kind	Pow.	Acc.	PP	Range
1	Thunder Shock	Electric	Special	40	100	30	Normal
4	Quick Attack	Normal	Physical	40	100	30	Normal
7	Tail Whip	Normal	Status	—	100	30	Many Others
10	Charge	Electric	Status	—	—	20	Self
13	Spark	Electric	Physical	65	100	20	Normal
15	Nuzzle	Electric	Physical	20	100	20	Normal
16	Pursuit	Dark	Physical	40	100	20	Normal
19	Double Team	Normal	Status	—	—	15	Self
22	Shock Wave	Electric	Special	60	—	20	Normal
26	Electro Ball	Electric	Special	—	100	10	Normal
30	Acrobatics	Flying	Physical	55	100	15	Normal
34	Light Screen	Psychic	Status	—	—	30	Your Side
38	Encore	Normal	Status	—	100	5	Normal
42	Volt Switch	Electric	Special	70	100	20	Normal
46	Agility	Psychic	Status	—	—	30	Self
50	Discharge	Electric	Special	80	100	15	Adjacent

● **TM & HM MOVES**

No.	Name	Type	Kind	Pow.	Acc.	PP	Range
TM06	Toxic	Poison	Status	—	90	10	Normal
TM10	Hidden Power	Normal	Special	60	100	15	Normal
TM12	Taunt	Dark	Status	—	100	20	Normal
TM16	Light Screen	Psychic	Status	—	—	30	Your Side
TM17	Protect	Normal	Status	—	—	10	Self
TM18	Rain Dance	Water	Status	—	—	5	Both Sides
TM19	Roost	Flying	Status	—	—	10	Self
TM21	Frustration	Normal	Physical	—	100	20	Normal
TM24	Thunderbolt	Electric	Special	90	100	15	Normal
TM25	Thunder	Electric	Special	110	70	10	Normal
TM27	Return	Normal	Physical	—	100	20	Normal
TM32	Double Team	Normal	Status	—	—	15	Self
TM40	Aerial Ace	Flying	Physical	60	—	20	Normal
TM42	Facade	Normal	Physical	70	100	20	Normal
TM44	Rest	Psychic	Status	—	—	10	Self
TM45	Attract	Normal	Status	—	100	15	Normal
TM48	Round	Normal	Special	60	100	15	Normal
TM56	Fling	Dark	Physical	—	100	10	Normal
TM57	Charge Beam	Electric	Special	50	90	10	Normal
TM62	Acrobatics	Flying	Physical	55	100	15	Normal
TM70	Flash	Normal	Status	—	100	20	Normal
TM72	Volt Switch	Electric	Special	70	100	20	Normal
TM73	Thunder Wave	Electric	Status	—	100	20	Normal
TM87	Swagger	Normal	Status	—	90	15	Normal
TM88	Sleep Talk	Normal	Status	—	—	10	Self
TM89	U-turn	Bug	Physical	70	100	20	Normal
TM90	Substitute	Normal	Status	—	—	10	Self
TM93	Wild Charge	Electric	Physical	90	100	15	Normal
TM100	Confide	Normal	Status	—	—	20	Normal
HM01	Cut	Normal	Physical	50	95	30	Normal

No.	Name	Type	Kind	Pow.	Acc.	PP	Range

● **MOVES TAUGHT BY PEOPLE**

Name	Type	Kind	Pow.	Acc.	PP	Range

● **EGG MOVES**

Name	Type	Kind	Pow.	Acc.	PP	Range
Roost	Flying	Status	—	—	10	Self
Iron Tail	Steel	Physical	100	75	15	Normal
Astonish	Ghost	Physical	30	100	15	Normal
Air Slash	Flying	Special	75	95	15	Normal
Shock Wave	Electric	Special	60	—	20	Normal
Charm	Fairy	Status	—	100	20	Normal
Covet	Normal	Physical	60	100	25	Normal
Tickle	Normal	Status	—	100	20	Normal
Baton Pass	Normal	Status	—	—	40	Self
Ion Deluge	Electric	Status	—	—	25	Both Sides

AFTER THE HALL OF FAME

CENTRAL KALOS

COASTAL KALOS

087 | Yanma

MOUNTAIN KALOS

ADVENTURE DATA

🔺 Coastal Kalos — 087
Clear Wing Pokémon
☑ Yanma

HEIGHT: 3'11"　　WEIGHT: 83.8 lbs.
GENDER: ♂/♀

X Its eyes can see 360 degrees without moving its head. It won't miss prey—even those behind it.

Y If it flaps its wings really fast, it can generate shock waves that will shatter windows in the area.

TYPE Bug | Flying

ABILITIES
Speed Boost
Compound Eyes

HIDDEN ABILITY
Frisk

STAT GROWTH RATES
HP	■■■
Attack	■■■
Defense	■■
Sp. Atk	■■■■
Sp. Def	■■
Speed	■■■■■

EGG GROUP
Bug

🔺 EVOLUTION

Lv. 33 with Ancient Power

Yanma　→　Yanmega

ITEMS SOMETIMES HELD BY WILD POKÉMON
Wide Lens

Damage taken in normal battles		Damage taken in Inverse Battles	
Normal	×1	Normal	×1
Fire	×2	Fire	×0.5
Water	×1	Water	×1
Grass	×0.25	Grass	×4
Electric	×2	Electric	×0.5
Ice	×2	Ice	×0.5
Fighting	×0.25	Fighting	×4
Poison	×1	Poison	×1
Ground	×0	Ground	×4
Flying	×2	Flying	×0.5
Psychic	×1	Psychic	×1
Bug	×0.5	Bug	×2
Rock	×4	Rock	×0.25
Ghost	×1	Ghost	×1
Dragon	×1	Dragon	×1
Dark	×1	Dark	×1
Steel	×1	Steel	×1
Fairy	×1	Fairy	×1

Can be used in	
Inverse Battle	Battle Institute
Sky Battle	Battle Maison
Battle Chateau	Random Matchup

Same form for ♂/♀

How to obtain for your Coastal Kalos Pokédex

Catch in a Horde Encounter on Route 10. **X**

Catch in a Horde Encounter on Route 10. **Y**

● LEVEL-UP MOVES

Lv.	Name	Type	Kind	Pow.	Acc.	PP	Range
1	Tackle	Normal	Physical	50	100	35	Normal
1	Foresight	Normal	Status	—	—	40	Normal
6	Quick Attack	Normal	Physical	40	100	30	Normal
11	Double Team	Normal	Status	—	—	15	Self
14	Sonic Boom	Normal	Special	—	90	20	Normal
17	Detect	Fighting	Status	—	—	5	Self
22	Supersonic	Normal	Status	—	55	20	Normal
27	Uproar	Normal	Special	90	100	10	1 Random
30	Pursuit	Dark	Physical	40	100	20	Normal
33	Ancient Power	Rock	Special	60	100	5	Normal
38	Hypnosis	Psychic	Status	—	60	20	Normal
43	Wing Attack	Flying	Physical	60	100	35	Normal
46	Screech	Normal	Status	—	85	40	Normal
49	U-turn	Bug	Physical	70	100	20	Normal
54	Air Slash	Flying	Special	75	95	15	Normal
57	Bug Buzz	Bug	Special	90	100	10	Normal

● TM & HM MOVES

No.	Name	Type	Kind	Pow.	Acc.	PP	Range
TM06	Toxic	Poison	Status	—	90	10	Normal
TM10	Hidden Power	Normal	Special	60	100	15	Normal
TM11	Sunny Day	Fire	Status	—	—	5	Both Sides
TM17	Protect	Normal	Status	—	—	10	Self
TM19	Roost	Flying	Status	—	—	10	Self
TM21	Frustration	Normal	Physical	—	100	20	Normal
TM22	Solar Beam	Grass	Special	120	100	10	Normal
TM27	Return	Normal	Physical	—	100	20	Normal
TM29	Psychic	Psychic	Special	90	100	10	Normal
TM30	Shadow Ball	Ghost	Special	80	100	15	Normal
TM32	Double Team	Normal	Status	—	—	15	Self
TM40	Aerial Ace	Flying	Physical	60	—	20	Normal
TM42	Facade	Normal	Physical	70	100	20	Normal
TM44	Rest	Psychic	Status	—	—	10	Self
TM45	Attract	Normal	Status	—	100	15	Normal
TM46	Thief	Dark	Physical	60	100	25	Normal
TM48	Round	Normal	Special	60	100	15	Normal
TM51	Steel Wing	Steel	Physical	70	90	25	Normal
TM70	Flash	Normal	Status	—	100	20	Normal
TM85	Dream Eater	Psychic	Special	100	100	15	Normal
TM87	Swagger	Normal	Status	—	90	15	Normal
TM88	Sleep Talk	Normal	Status	—	—	10	Self
TM89	U-turn	Bug	Physical	70	100	20	Normal
TM90	Substitute	Normal	Status	—	—	10	Self
TM100	Confide	Normal	Status	—	—	20	Normal

● MOVES TAUGHT BY PEOPLE

Name	Type	Kind	Pow.	Acc.	PP	Range

● EGG MOVES

Name	Type	Kind	Pow.	Acc.	PP	Range
Whirlwind	Normal	Status	—	—	20	Normal
Reversal	Fighting	Physical	—	100	15	Normal
Leech Life	Bug	Physical	20	100	15	Normal
Signal Beam	Bug	Special	75	100	15	Normal
Silver Wind	Bug	Special	60	100	5	Normal
Feint	Normal	Physical	30	100	10	Normal
Feint Attack	Dark	Physical	60	—	20	Normal
Pursuit	Dark	Physical	40	100	20	Normal
Double-Edge	Normal	Physical	120	100	15	Normal
Secret Power	Normal	Physical	70	100	20	Normal

AFTER THE HALL OF FAME

CENTRAL KALOS

COASTAL KALOS

088

Yanmega

MOUNTAIN KALOS

ADVENTURE DATA

🏔 Coastal Kalos 088
Ogre Darner Pokémon
✓ Yanmega

HEIGHT: 6'03" WEIGHT: 113.5 lbs.
GENDER: ♂/♀

| TYPE | Bug | Flying |

ABILITIES
Speed Boost
Tinted Lens

HIDDEN ABILITY
Frisk

STAT GROWTH RATES
HP	▪▪▪▪
Attack	▪▪▪▪
Defense	▪▪▪▪
Sp. Atk	▪▪▪▪▪▪▪
Sp. Def	▪▪
Speed	▪▪▪▪▪

EGG GROUP
Bug

❌ It prefers to battle by biting apart foes' heads instantly while flying by at high speed.

🔺 This six-legged Pokémon is easily capable of transporting an adult in flight. The wings on its tail help it stay balanced.

EVOLUTION

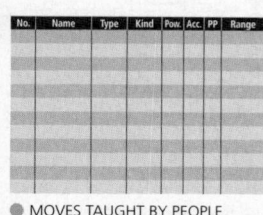

Lv. 33 with Ancient Power

Yanma → Yanmega

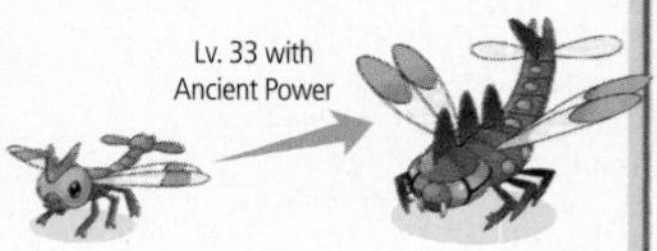

ITEMS SOMETIMES HELD BY WILD POKÉMON
None

	Damage taken in normal battles		Damage taken in Inverse Battles
Normal	×1	Normal	×1
Fire	×2	Fire	×0.5
Water	×1	Water	×1
Grass	×0.25	Grass	×4
Electric	×2	Electric	×0.5
Ice	×2	Ice	×0.5
Fighting	×0.25	Fighting	×4
Poison	×1	Poison	×1
Ground	×0	Ground	×4
Flying	×2	Flying	×0.5
Psychic	×1	Psychic	×1
Bug	×0.5	Bug	×2
Rock	×4	Rock	×0.25
Ghost	×1	Ghost	×1
Dragon	×1	Dragon	×1
Dark	×1	Dark	×1
Steel	×1	Steel	×1
Fairy	×1	Fairy	×1

Can be used in
Inverse Battle	Battle Institute
Sky Battle	Battle Maison
Battle Chateau	Random Matchup

Same form for ♂/♀

How to obtain for your Coastal Kalos Pokédex
Level up Yanma to Lv. 33, and have it learn Ancient Power. Alternatively, teach it Ancient Power first and then level it up.

Level up Yanma to Lv. 33, and have it learn Ancient Power. Alternatively, teach it Ancient Power first and then level it up.

● LEVEL-UP MOVES

Lv.	Name	Type	Kind	Pow.	Acc.	PP	Range
1	Bug Buzz	Bug	Special	90	100	10	Normal
1	Air Slash	Flying	Special	75	95	15	Normal
1	Night Slash	Dark	Physical	70	100	15	Normal
1	Bug Bite	Bug	Physical	60	100	20	Normal
1	Tackle	Normal	Physical	50	100	35	Normal
1	Foresight	Normal	Status	—	—	40	Normal
1	Quick Attack	Normal	Physical	40	100	30	Normal
1	Double Team	Normal	Status	—	—	15	Self
6	Quick Attack	Normal	Physical	40	100	30	Normal
11	Double Team	Normal	Status	—	—	15	Self
14	Sonic Boom	Normal	Special	—	90	20	Normal
17	Detect	Fighting	Status	—	—	5	Self
22	Supersonic	Normal	Status	—	55	20	Normal
27	Uproar	Normal	Special	90	100	10	1 Random
30	Pursuit	Dark	Physical	40	100	20	Normal
33	Ancient Power	Rock	Special	60	100	5	Normal
38	Feint	Normal	Physical	30	100	10	Normal
43	Slash	Normal	Physical	70	100	20	Normal
46	Screech	Normal	Status	—	85	40	Normal
49	U-turn	Bug	Physical	70	100	20	Normal
54	Air Slash	Flying	Special	75	95	15	Normal
57	Bug Buzz	Bug	Special	90	100	10	Normal

● TM & HM MOVES

No.	Name	Type	Kind	Pow.	Acc.	PP	Range
TM06	Toxic	Poison	Status	—	90	10	Normal
TM10	Hidden Power	Normal	Special	60	100	15	Normal
TM11	Sunny Day	Fire	Status	—	—	5	Both Sides
TM15	Hyper Beam	Normal	Special	150	90	5	Normal
TM17	Protect	Normal	Status	—	—	10	Self
TM19	Roost	Flying	Status	—	—	10	Self
TM21	Frustration	Normal	Physical	—	100	20	Normal
TM22	Solar Beam	Grass	Special	120	100	10	Normal
TM27	Return	Normal	Physical	—	100	20	Normal
TM29	Psychic	Psychic	Special	90	100	10	Normal
TM30	Shadow Ball	Ghost	Special	80	100	15	Normal
TM32	Double Team	Normal	Status	—	—	15	Self
TM40	Aerial Ace	Flying	Physical	60	—	20	Normal
TM44	Rest	Psychic	Status	—	—	10	Self
TM45	Attract	Normal	Status	—	100	15	Normal
TM46	Thief	Dark	Physical	60	100	25	Normal
TM48	Round	Normal	Special	60	100	15	Normal
TM51	Steel Wing	Steel	Physical	70	90	25	Normal
TM68	Giga Impact	Normal	Physical	150	90	5	Normal
TM70	Flash	Normal	Status	—	100	20	Normal
TM76	Struggle Bug	Bug	Special	50	100	20	Many Others
TM77	Psych Up	Normal	Status	—	—	10	Normal
TM85	Dream Eater	Psychic	Special	100	100	15	Normal
TM87	Swagger	Normal	Status	—	90	15	Normal
TM88	Sleep Talk	Normal	Status	—	—	10	Self
TM89	U-turn	Bug	Physical	70	100	20	Normal
TM90	Substitute	Normal	Status	—	—	10	Self
TM100	Confide	Normal	Status	—	—	20	Normal

No.	Name	Type	Kind	Pow.	Acc.	PP	Range

● MOVES TAUGHT BY PEOPLE

Name	Type	Kind	Pow.	Acc.	PP	Range

AFTER THE HALL OF FAME

CENTRAL KALOS

COASTAL KALOS

089

Hawlucha

MOUNTAIN KALOS

ADVENTURE DATA

 Coastal Kalos

Wrestling Pokémon

Hawlucha 089

HEIGHT: 2'07" WEIGHT: 47.4 lbs.
GENDER: ♂/♀

X Although its body is small, its proficient fighting skills enable it to keep up with big bruisers like Machamp and Hariyama.

Y With its wings, it controls its position in the air. It likes to attack from above, a maneuver that is difficult to defend against.

TYPE Fighting Flying

ABILITIES
Limber
Unburden

HIDDEN ABILITY
Mold Breaker

STAT GROWTH RATES
HP ■■■
Attack ■■■■■
Defense ■■■
Sp. Atk ■■■
Sp. Def ■■■
Speed ■■■■■■

EGG GROUP
Human-Like

EVOLUTION

Does not evolve

ITEMS SOMETIMES HELD BY WILD POKÉMON
King's Rock

Damage taken in normal battles		Damage taken in Inverse Battles	
Normal	×1	Normal	×1
Fire	×1	Fire	×1
Water	×1	Water	×1
Grass	×0.5	Grass	×2
Electric	×2	Electric	×0.5
Ice	×2	Ice	×0.5
Fighting	×0.5	Fighting	×2
Poison	×1	Poison	×1
Ground	×0	Ground	×2
Flying	×2	Flying	×0.5
Psychic	×2	Psychic	×0.5
Bug	×0.25	Bug	×4
Rock	×1	Rock	×1
Ghost	×1	Ghost	×1
Dragon	×1	Dragon	×1
Dark	×0.5	Dark	×2
Steel	×1	Steel	×1
Fairy	×2	Fairy	×0.5

Can be used in	
Inverse Battle	Battle Institute
—	Battle Maison
Battle Chateau	Random Matchup

Same form for ♂/♀

How to obtain for your Coastal Kalos Pokédex

❶ Catch in the tall grass on Route 10.
❷ Catch in the yellow flowers on Route 10.

❶ Catch in the tall grass on Route 10.
❷ Catch in the yellow flowers on Route 10.

● LEVEL-UP MOVES

Lv.	Name	Type	Kind	Pow.	Acc.	PP	Range
1	Detect	Fighting	Status	—	—	5	Self
1	Tackle	Normal	Physical	50	100	35	Normal
1	Hone Claws	Dark	Status	—	—	15	Self
4	Karate Chop	Fighting	Physical	50	100	25	Normal
8	Wing Attack	Flying	Physical	60	100	35	Normal
12	Roost	Flying	Status	—	—	10	Self
16	Aerial Ace	Flying	Physical	60	—	20	Normal
20	Encore	Normal	Status	—	100	5	Normal
24	Fling	Dark	Physical	—	100	10	Normal
28	Flying Press	Fighting	Physical	80	95	10	Normal
32	Bounce	Flying	Physical	85	85	5	Normal
36	Endeavor	Normal	Physical	—	100	5	Normal
40	Feather Dance	Flying	Status	—	100	15	Normal
44	High Jump Kick	Fighting	Physical	130	90	10	Normal
48	Sky Attack	Flying	Physical	140	90	5	Normal
52	Sky Drop	Flying	Physical	60	100	10	Normal
60	Swords Dance	Normal	Status	—	—	20	Self

● TM & HM MOVES

No.	Name	Type	Kind	Pow.	Acc.	PP	Range
TM01	Hone Claws	Dark	Status	—	—	15	Self
TM06	Toxic	Poison	Status	—	90	10	Normal
TM08	Bulk Up	Fighting	Status	—	—	20	Self
TM10	Hidden Power	Normal	Special	60	100	15	Normal
TM11	Sunny Day	Fire	Status	—	—	5	Both Sides
TM12	Taunt	Dark	Status	—	100	20	Normal
TM17	Protect	Normal	Status	—	—	10	Self
TM18	Rain Dance	Water	Status	—	—	5	Both Sides
TM19	Roost	Flying	Status	—	—	10	Self
TM21	Frustration	Normal	Physical	—	100	20	Normal
TM27	Return	Normal	Physical	—	100	20	Normal
TM28	Dig	Ground	Physical	80	100	10	Normal
TM31	Brick Break	Fighting	Physical	75	100	15	Normal
TM32	Double Team	Normal	Status	—	—	15	Self
TM39	Rock Tomb	Rock	Physical	60	95	15	Normal
TM40	Aerial Ace	Flying	Physical	60	—	20	Normal
TM41	Torment	Dark	Status	—	100	15	Normal
TM42	Facade	Normal	Physical	70	100	20	Normal
TM44	Rest	Psychic	Status	—	—	10	Self
TM45	Attract	Normal	Status	—	100	15	Normal
TM47	Low Sweep	Fighting	Physical	65	100	20	Normal
TM48	Round	Normal	Special	60	100	15	Normal
TM51	Steel Wing	Steel	Physical	70	90	25	Normal
TM52	Focus Blast	Fighting	Special	120	70	5	Normal
TM54	False Swipe	Normal	Physical	40	100	40	Normal
TM56	Fling	Dark	Physical	—	100	10	Normal
TM58	Sky Drop	Flying	Physical	60	100	10	Normal
TM62	Acrobatics	Flying	Physical	55	100	15	Normal
TM66	Payback	Dark	Physical	50	100	10	Normal
TM67	Retaliate	Normal	Physical	70	100	5	Normal
TM68	Giga Impact	Normal	Physical	150	90	5	Normal
TM71	Stone Edge	Rock	Physical	100	80	5	Normal
TM75	Swords Dance	Normal	Status	—	—	20	Self

No.	Name	Type	Kind	Pow.	Acc.	PP	Range
TM80	Rock Slide	Rock	Physical	75	90	10	Many Others
TM81	X-Scissor	Bug	Physical	80	100	15	Normal
TM84	Poison Jab	Poison	Physical	80	100	20	Normal
TM86	Grass Knot	Grass	Special	—	100	20	Normal
TM87	Swagger	Normal	Status	—	90	15	Normal
TM88	Sleep Talk	Normal	Status	—	—	10	Self
TM89	U-turn	Bug	Physical	70	100	20	Normal
TM90	Substitute	Normal	Status	—	—	10	Self
TM94	Rock Smash	Fighting	Physical	40	100	15	Normal
TM98	Power-Up Punch	Fighting	Physical	40	100	20	Normal
TM100	Confide	Normal	Status	—	—	20	Normal
HM01	Cut	Normal	Physical	50	95	30	Normal
HM02	Fly	Flying	Physical	90	95	15	Normal
HM04	Strength	Normal	Physical	80	100	15	Normal

● MOVES TAUGHT BY PEOPLE

Name	Type	Kind	Pow.	Acc.	PP	Range

● EGG MOVES

Name	Type	Kind	Pow.	Acc.	PP	Range
Agility	Psychic	Status	—	—	30	Self
Me First	Normal	Status	—	—	20	Varies
Ally Switch	Psychic	Status	—	—	15	Self
Entrainment	Normal	Status	—	100	15	Normal
Mud Sport	Ground	Status	—	—	15	Both Sides
Baton Pass	Normal	Status	—	—	40	Self
Quick Guard	Fighting	Status	—	—	15	Your Side

AFTER THE HALL OF FAME

CENTRAL KALOS

COASTAL KALOS

090
Sigilyph

MOUNTAIN KALOS

ADVENTURE DATA

Coastal Kalos 090

Avianoid Pokémon

Sigilyph

TYPE **Psychic** **Flying**

HEIGHT: 4'07" WEIGHT: 30.9 lbs.
GENDER: ♂/♀

ABILITIES
Wonder Skin
Magic Guard

HIDDEN ABILITY
Tinted Lens

STAT GROWTH RATES
HP ■■■
Attack ■■■
Defense ■■■■
Sp. Atk ■■■■■
Sp. Def ■■■
Speed ■■■■■

EGG GROUP
Flying

X The guardians of an ancient city, they use their psychic power to attack enemies that invade their territory.

Y The guardians of an ancient city, they always fly the same route while keeping watch for invaders.

EVOLUTION

Does not evolve

ITEMS SOMETIMES HELD BY WILD POKÉMON
None

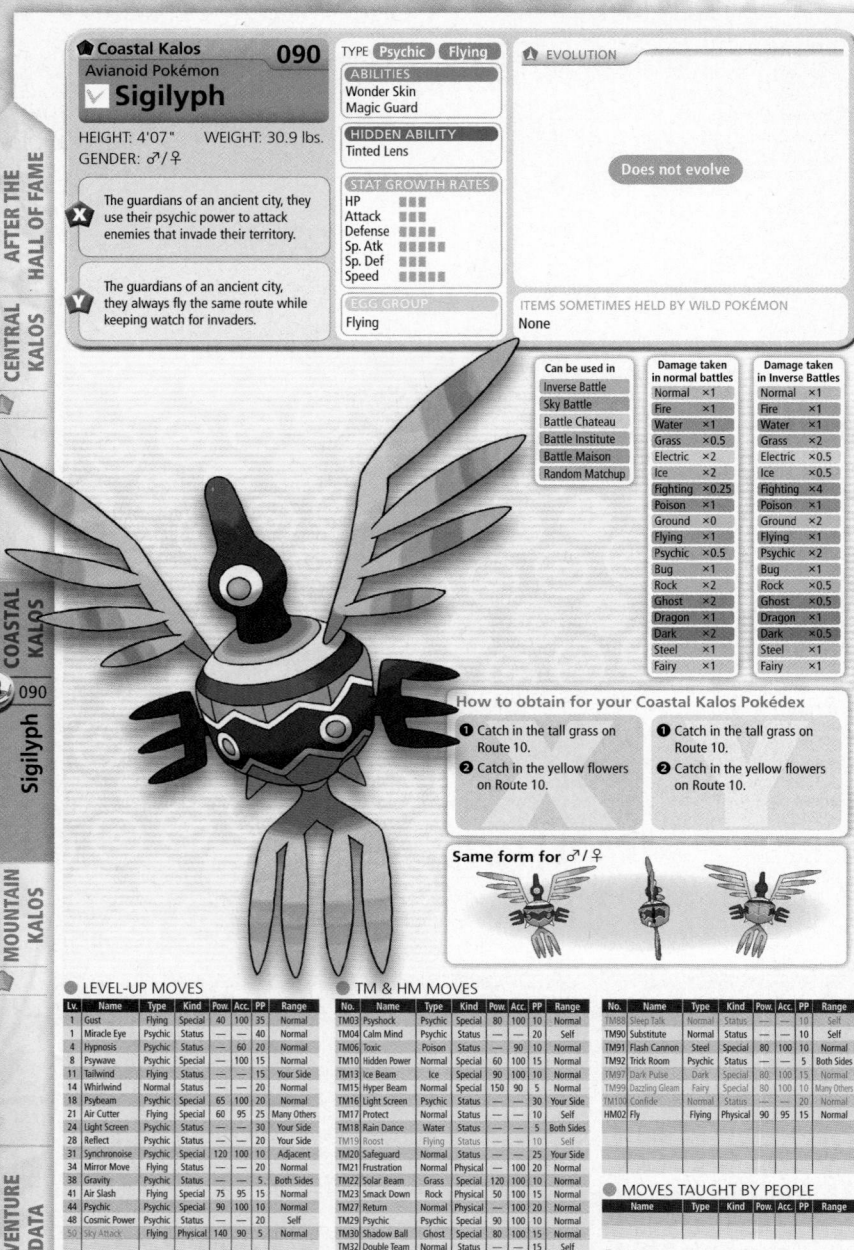

Can be used in
- Inverse Battle
- Sky Battle
- Battle Chateau
- Battle Institute
- Battle Maison
- Random Matchup

Damage taken in normal battles	
Normal	×1
Fire	×1
Water	×1
Grass	×0.5
Electric	×2
Ice	×2
Fighting	×0.25
Poison	×1
Ground	×0
Flying	×1
Psychic	×0.5
Bug	×2
Rock	×2
Ghost	×2
Dragon	×1
Dark	×2
Steel	×1
Fairy	×1

Damage taken in Inverse Battles	
Normal	×1
Fire	×1
Water	×1
Grass	×2
Electric	×0.5
Ice	×0.5
Fighting	×4
Poison	×1
Ground	×2
Flying	×1
Psychic	×2
Bug	×1
Rock	×0.5
Ghost	×0.5
Dragon	×1
Dark	×0.5
Steel	×1
Fairy	×1

How to obtain for your Coastal Kalos Pokédex

❶ Catch in the tall grass on Route 10.
❷ Catch in the yellow flowers on Route 10.

❶ Catch in the tall grass on Route 10.
❷ Catch in the yellow flowers on Route 10.

Same form for ♂/♀

● LEVEL-UP MOVES

Lv.	Name	Type	Kind	Pow.	Acc.	PP	Range
1	Gust	Flying	Special	40	100	35	Normal
1	Miracle Eye	Psychic	Status	—	—	40	Normal
4	Hypnosis	Psychic	Status	—	60	20	Normal
8	Psywave	Psychic	Special	—	100	15	Normal
11	Tailwind	Flying	Status	—	—	15	Your Side
14	Whirlwind	Normal	Status	—	—	20	Normal
18	Psybeam	Psychic	Special	65	100	20	Normal
21	Air Cutter	Flying	Special	60	95	25	Many Others
24	Light Screen	Psychic	Status	—	—	30	Your Side
28	Reflect	Psychic	Status	—	—	20	Your Side
31	Synchronoise	Psychic	Special	120	100	10	Adjacent
34	Mirror Move	Flying	Status	—	—	20	Normal
38	Gravity	Psychic	Status	—	—	5	Both Sides
41	Air Slash	Flying	Special	75	95	15	Normal
44	Psychic	Psychic	Special	90	100	10	Normal
48	Cosmic Power	Psychic	Status	—	—	20	Self
50	Sky Attack	Flying	Physical	140	90	5	Normal

● TM & HM MOVES

No.	Name	Type	Kind	Pow.	Acc.	PP	Range
TM03	Psyshock	Psychic	Special	80	100	10	Normal
TM04	Calm Mind	Psychic	Status	—	—	20	Self
TM06	Toxic	Poison	Status	—	90	10	Normal
TM10	Hidden Power	Normal	Special	60	100	15	Normal
TM13	Ice Beam	Ice	Special	90	100	10	Normal
TM15	Hyper Beam	Normal	Special	150	90	5	Normal
TM16	Light Screen	Psychic	Status	—	—	30	Your Side
TM17	Protect	Normal	Status	—	—	10	Self
TM18	Rain Dance	Water	Status	—	—	5	Both Sides
TM19	Roost	Flying	Status	—	—	10	Self
TM20	Safeguard	Normal	Status	—	—	25	Your Side
TM21	Frustration	Normal	Physical	—	100	20	Normal
TM22	Solar Beam	Grass	Special	120	100	10	Normal
TM23	Smack Down	Rock	Physical	50	100	15	Normal
TM27	Return	Normal	Physical	—	100	20	Normal
TM29	Psychic	Psychic	Special	90	100	10	Normal
TM30	Shadow Ball	Ghost	Special	80	100	15	Normal
TM32	Double Team	Normal	Status	—	—	15	Self
TM33	Reflect	Psychic	Status	—	—	20	Your Side
TM40	Aerial Ace	Flying	Physical	60	—	20	Normal
TM42	Facade	Normal	Physical	70	100	20	Normal
TM44	Rest	Psychic	Status	—	—	10	Self
TM45	Attract	Normal	Status	—	100	15	Normal
TM46	Thief	Dark	Physical	60	100	25	Normal
TM48	Round	Normal	Special	60	100	15	Normal
TM51	Steel Wing	Steel	Physical	70	90	25	Normal
TM53	Energy Ball	Grass	Special	90	100	10	Normal
TM57	Charge Beam	Electric	Special	50	90	10	Normal
TM70	Flash	Normal	Status	—	100	20	Normal
TM73	Thunder Wave	Electric	Status	—	100	20	Normal
TM77	Psych Up	Normal	Status	—	—	10	Self
TM85	Dream Eater	Psychic	Special	100	100	15	Normal
TM87	Swagger	Normal	Status	—	90	15	Normal

No.	Name	Type	Kind	Pow.	Acc.	PP	Range
TM88	Sleep Talk	Normal	Status	—	—	10	Self
TM90	Substitute	Normal	Status	—	—	10	Self
TM91	Flash Cannon	Steel	Special	80	100	10	Normal
TM92	Trick Room	Psychic	Status	—	—	5	Both Sides
TM97	Dark Pulse	Dark	Special	80	100	15	Normal
TM99	Dazzling Gleam	Fairy	Special	80	100	10	Many Others
TM100	Confide	Normal	Status	—	—	20	Normal
HM02	Fly	Flying	Physical	90	95	15	Normal

● MOVES TAUGHT BY PEOPLE

Name	Type	Kind	Pow.	Acc.	PP	Range

● EGG MOVES

Name	Type	Kind	Pow.	Acc.	PP	Range
Stored Power	Psychic	Special	20	100	10	Normal
Psycho Shift	Psychic	Status	—	100	10	Normal
Ancient Power	Rock	Special	60	100	5	Normal
Steel Wing	Steel	Physical	70	90	25	Normal
Roost	Flying	Status	—	—	10	Self
Skill Swap	Psychic	Status	—	—	10	Normal
Future Sight	Psychic	Special	120	100	10	Normal

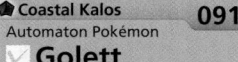

Coastal Kalos 091
Automaton Pokémon
☑ Golett

HEIGHT: 3'03" WEIGHT: 202.8 lbs.
GENDER: unknown

X The energy that burns inside it enables it to move, but no one has yet been able to identify this energy.

Y Ancient science fashioned this Pokémon from clay. It's been active for thousands of years.

TYPE Ground / Ghost

ABILITIES
Iron Fist
Klutz

HIDDEN ABILITY
No Good

STAT GROWTH RATES
HP	■■■
Attack	■■■■
Defense	■■■
Sp. Atk	■■
Sp. Def	■■
Speed	■■

EGG GROUP
Mineral

EVOLUTION

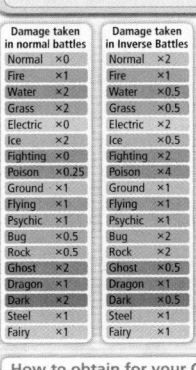

Golett → Lv. 43 → Golurk

ITEMS SOMETIMES HELD BY WILD POKÉMON
Light Clay

AFTER THE HALL OF FAME

CENTRAL KALOS

COASTAL KALOS

091 Golett

MOUNTAIN KALOS

ADVENTURE DATA

Damage taken in normal battles		Damage taken in Inverse Battles	
Normal	×0	Normal	×2
Fire	×1	Fire	×1
Water	×2	Water	×0.5
Grass	×2	Grass	×0.5
Electric	×0	Electric	×2
Ice	×1	Ice	×0.5
Fighting	×0	Fighting	×2
Poison	×0.25	Poison	×4
Ground	×1	Ground	×1
Flying	×1	Flying	×1
Psychic	×1	Psychic	×1
Bug	×0.5	Bug	×2
Rock	×1	Rock	×2
Ghost	×2	Ghost	×0.5
Dragon	×1	Dragon	×1
Dark	×2	Dark	×0.5
Steel	×1	Steel	×1
Fairy	×1	Fairy	×1

Can be used in
Inverse Battle
—
Battle Chateau
Battle Institute
Battle Maison
Random Matchup

How to obtain for your Coastal Kalos Pokédex

❶ Catch in the tall grass on Route 10.
❷ Catch in the yellow flowers on Route 10.

❶ Catch in the tall grass on Route 10.
❷ Catch in the yellow flowers on Route 10.

Gender unknown

● LEVEL-UP MOVES

Lv.	Name	Type	Kind	Pow.	Acc.	PP	Range
1	Pound	Normal	Physical	40	100	35	Normal
1	Astonish	Ghost	Physical	30	100	15	Normal
1	Defense Curl	Normal	Status	—	—	40	Self
5	Mud-Slap	Ground	Special	20	100	10	Normal
9	Rollout	Rock	Physical	30	90	20	Normal
13	Shadow Punch	Ghost	Physical	60	—	20	Normal
17	Iron Defense	Steel	Status	—	—	15	Self
21	Mega Punch	Normal	Physical	80	85	20	Normal
25	Magnitude	Ground	Physical	—	100	30	Adjacent
30	Dynamic Punch	Fighting	Physical	100	50	5	Normal
35	Night Shade	Ghost	Special	—	100	15	Normal
40	Curse	Ghost	Status	—	—	10	Varies
45	Earthquake	Ground	Physical	100	100	10	Adjacent
50	Hammer Arm	Fighting	Physical	100	90	10	Normal
55	Focus Punch	Fighting	Physical	150	100	20	Normal

● TM & HM MOVES

No.	Name	Type	Kind	Pow.	Acc.	PP	Range
TM06	Toxic	Poison	Status	—	90	10	Normal
TM10	Hidden Power	Normal	Special	60	100	15	Normal
TM13	Ice Beam	Ice	Special	90	100	10	Normal
TM17	Protect	Normal	Status	—	—	10	Self
TM18	Rain Dance	Water	Status	—	—	5	Both Sides
TM20	Safeguard	Normal	Status	—	—	25	Your Side
TM21	Frustration	Normal	Physical	—	100	20	Normal
TM26	Earthquake	Ground	Physical	100	100	10	Adjacent
TM27	Return	Normal	Physical	—	100	20	Normal
TM29	Psychic	Psychic	Special	90	100	10	Normal
TM30	Shadow Ball	Ghost	Special	80	100	15	Normal
TM31	Brick Break	Fighting	Physical	75	100	15	Normal
TM32	Double Team	Normal	Status	—	—	15	Self
TM39	Rock Tomb	Rock	Physical	60	95	15	Normal
TM42	Facade	Normal	Physical	70	100	20	Normal
TM44	Rest	Psychic	Status	—	—	10	Self
TM46	Thief	Dark	Physical	60	100	25	Normal
TM47	Low Sweep	Fighting	Physical	65	100	20	Normal
TM48	Round	Normal	Special	60	100	15	Normal
TM52	Focus Blast	Fighting	Special	120	70	5	Normal
TM56	Fling	Dark	Physical	—	100	10	Normal
TM69	Rock Polish	Rock	Status	—	—	20	Self
TM70	Flash	Normal	Status	—	100	20	Normal
TM74	Gyro Ball	Steel	Physical	—	100	5	Normal
TM78	Bulldoze	Ground	Physical	60	100	20	Adjacent
TM80	Rock Slide	Rock	Physical	75	90	10	Many Others
TM86	Grass Knot	Grass	Special	—	100	20	Normal
TM87	Swagger	Normal	Status	—	90	15	Normal
TM88	Sleep Talk	Normal	Status	—	—	10	Self
TM90	Substitute	Normal	Status	—	—	10	Self
TM94	Rock Smash	Fighting	Physical	40	100	15	Normal
TM98	Power-Up Punch	Fighting	Physical	40	100	20	Normal
TM100	Confide	Normal	Status	—	—	20	Normal

No.	Name	Type	Kind	Pow.	Acc.	PP	Range
HM04	Strength	Normal	Physical	80	100	15	Normal

● MOVES TAUGHT BY PEOPLE

Name	Type	Kind	Pow.	Acc.	PP	Range

● EGG MOVES

Name	Type	Kind	Pow.	Acc.	PP	Range

AFTER THE HALL OF FAME

CENTRAL KALOS

COASTAL KALOS

092

Golurk

MOUNTAIN KALOS

ADVENTURE DATA

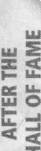

Coastal Kalos 092
Automaton Pokémon
☑ Golurk

HEIGHT: 9'02" WEIGHT: 727.5 lbs.
GENDER: unknown

X It is said that Golurk were ordered to protect people and Pokémon by the ancient people who made them.

Y It flies across the sky at Mach speeds. Removing the seal on its chest makes its internal energy go out of control.

TYPE Ground / Ghost

ABILITIES
Iron Fist
Klutz

HIDDEN ABILITY
No Grd

STAT GROWTH RATES
HP	■■■
Attack	■■■■■
Defense	■■■■
Sp. Atk	■■
Sp. Def	■■■
Speed	■■

EGG GROUP
Mineral

EVOLUTION

Golett → Lv. 43 → Golurk

ITEMS SOMETIMES HELD BY WILD POKÉMON
None

Can be used in
Inverse Battle
—
Battle Chateau
Battle Institute
Battle Maison
Random Matchup

Damage taken in normal battles	
Normal	×0
Fire	×1
Water	×2
Grass	×2
Electric	×0
Ice	×2
Fighting	×0
Poison	×0.25
Ground	×1
Flying	×1
Psychic	×1
Bug	×0.5
Rock	×0.5
Ghost	×2
Dragon	×1
Dark	×2
Steel	×1
Fairy	×1

Damage taken in Inverse Battles	
Normal	×2
Fire	×1
Water	×0.5
Grass	×0.5
Electric	×2
Ice	×0.5
Fighting	×2
Poison	×4
Ground	×1
Flying	×1
Psychic	×1
Bug	×2
Rock	×2
Ghost	×0.5
Dragon	×0.5
Dark	×0.5
Steel	×1
Fairy	×1

How to obtain for your Coastal Kalos Pokédex
Level up Golett to Lv. 43. | Level up Golett to Lv. 43.

Gender unknown

● LEVEL-UP MOVES

Lv.	Name	Type	Kind	Pow.	Acc.	PP	Range
1	Phantom Force	Ghost	Physical	90	100	10	Normal
1	Focus Punch	Fighting	Physical	150	100	20	Normal
1	Pound	Normal	Physical	40	100	35	Normal
1	Astonish	Ghost	Physical	30	100	15	Normal
1	Defense Curl	Normal	Status	—	—	40	Self
1	Mud-Slap	Ground	Special	20	100	10	Normal
5	Mud-Slap	Ground	Special	20	100	10	Normal
9	Rollout	Rock	Physical	30	90	20	Normal
13	Shadow Punch	Ghost	Physical	60	—	20	Normal
17	Iron Defense	Steel	Status	—	—	15	Self
21	Mega Punch	Normal	Physical	80	85	20	Normal
25	Magnitude	Ground	Physical	—	100	30	Adjacent
30	Dynamic Punch	Fighting	Physical	100	50	5	Normal
35	Night Shade	Ghost	Special	—	100	15	Normal
40	Curse	Ghost	Status	—	—	10	Varies
43	Heavy Slam	Steel	Physical	—	100	10	Normal
50	Earthquake	Ground	Physical	100	100	10	Adjacent
60	Hammer Arm	Fighting	Physical	100	90	10	Normal
70	Focus Punch	Fighting	Physical	150	100	20	Normal
75	Phantom Force	Ghost	Physical	90	100	10	Normal

● TM & HM MOVES

No.	Name	Type	Kind	Pow.	Acc.	PP	Range
TM06	Toxic	Poison	Status	—	90	10	Normal
TM10	Hidden Power	Normal	Special	60	100	15	Normal
TM13	Ice Beam	Ice	Special	90	100	10	Normal
TM15	Hyper Beam	Normal	Special	150	90	5	Normal
TM17	Protect	Normal	Status	—	—	10	Self
TM18	Rain Dance	Water	Status	—	—	5	Both Sides
TM21	Frustration	Normal	Physical	—	100	20	Normal
TM22	Solar Beam	Grass	Special	120	100	10	Normal
TM24	Thunderbolt	Electric	Special	90	100	15	Normal
TM26	Earthquake	Ground	Physical	100	100	10	Adjacent
TM27	Return	Normal	Physical	—	100	20	Normal
TM29	Psychic	Psychic	Special	90	100	10	Normal
TM30	Shadow Ball	Ghost	Special	80	100	15	Normal
TM31	Brick Break	Fighting	Physical	75	100	15	Normal
TM32	Double Team	Normal	Status	—	—	15	Self
TM39	Rock Tomb	Rock	Physical	60	95	15	Normal
TM42	Facade	Normal	Physical	70	100	20	Normal
TM44	Rest	Psychic	Status	—	—	10	Self
TM46	Thief	Dark	Physical	60	100	25	Normal
TM47	Low Sweep	Fighting	Physical	65	100	20	Normal
TM48	Round	Normal	Special	60	100	15	Normal
TM52	Focus Blast	Fighting	Special	120	70	5	Normal
TM56	Fling	Dark	Physical	—	100	10	Normal
TM57	Charge Beam	Electric	Special	50	90	10	Normal
TM68	Giga Impact	Normal	Physical	150	90	5	Normal
TM69	Rock Polish	Rock	Status	—	—	20	Self
TM70	Flash	Normal	Status	—	100	20	Normal
TM74	Gyro Ball	Steel	Physical	—	100	5	Normal
TM78	Bulldoze	Ground	Physical	60	100	20	Adjacent
TM80	Rock Slide	Rock	Physical	75	90	10	Many Others
TM86	Grass Knot	Grass	Special	—	100	20	Normal

No.	Name	Type	Kind	Pow.	Acc.	PP	Range
TM87	Swagger	Normal	Status	—	90	15	Normal
TM88	Sleep Talk	Normal	Status	—	—	10	Self
TM90	Substitute	Normal	Status	—	—	10	Self
TM91	Flash Cannon	Steel	Special	80	100	10	Normal
TM94	Rock Smash	Fighting	Physical	40	100	15	Normal
TM98	Power-Up Punch	Fighting	Physical	40	100	20	Normal
TM100	Confide	Normal	Status	—	—	20	Normal
HM02	Fly	Flying	Physical	90	95	15	Normal
HM04	Strength	Normal	Physical	80	100	15	Normal

● MOVES TAUGHT BY PEOPLE

Name	Type	Kind	Pow.	Acc.	PP	Range

Coastal Kalos
Compass Pokémon

Nosepass **093**

HEIGHT: 3'03" WEIGHT: 213.8 lbs.
GENDER: ♂/♀

X Its magnetic nose always faces north and draws iron objects to its body to protect itself better.

Y Its magnetic nose consistently faces north. Travelers check Nosepass to get their bearings.

 TYPE Rock

ABILITIES
Sturdy
Magnet Pull

HIDDEN ABILITY
Sand Force

STAT GROWTH RATES
HP	▪▪
Attack	▪▪
Defense	▪▪▪▪▪▪
Sp. Atk	▪▪
Sp. Def	▪▪▪▪
Speed	▪▪

EGG GROUP
Mineral

EVOLUTION

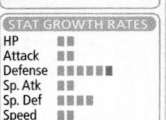

Level up on Route 13

Nosepass → Probopass

ITEMS SOMETIMES HELD BY WILD POKÉMON
Hard Stone

Damage taken in normal battles		Damage taken in Inverse Battles	
Normal	×0.5	Normal	×2
Fire	×0.5	Fire	×2
Water	×2	Water	×0.5
Grass	×2	Grass	×0.5
Electric	×1	Electric	×1
Ice	×1	Ice	×1
Fighting	×2	Fighting	×0.5
Poison	×0.5	Poison	×2
Ground	×2	Ground	×0.5
Flying	×0.5	Flying	×2
Psychic	×1	Psychic	×1
Bug	×1	Bug	×1
Rock	×1	Rock	×1
Ghost	×1	Ghost	×1
Dragon	×1	Dragon	×1
Dark	×1	Dark	×1
Steel	×2	Steel	×0.5
Fairy	×1	Fairy	×1

Can be used in	
Inverse Battle	Battle Institute
—	Battle Maison
Battle Chateau	Random Matchup

Same form for ♂/♀

How to obtain for your Coastal Kalos Pokédex

Catch in a Horde Encounter on Route 10.

Catch in a Horde Encounter on Route 10.

● LEVEL-UP MOVES

Lv.	Name	Type	Kind	Pow.	Acc.	PP	Range
1	Tackle	Normal	Physical	50	100	35	Normal
4	Harden	Normal	Status	—	—	30	Self
8	Block	Normal	Status	—	—	5	Normal
11	Rock Throw	Rock	Physical	50	90	15	Normal
15	Thunder Wave	Electric	Status	—	100	20	Normal
18	Rock Blast	Rock	Physical	25	90	10	Normal
22	Rest	Psychic	Status	—	—	10	Self
25	Spark	Electric	Physical	65	100	20	Normal
29	Rock Slide	Rock	Physical	75	90	10	Many Others
32	Power Gem	Rock	Special	80	100	20	Normal
36	Sandstorm	Rock	Status	—	—	10	Both Sides
39	Discharge	Electric	Special	80	100	15	Adjacent
43	Earth Power	Ground	Special	90	100	10	Normal
46	Stone Edge	Rock	Physical	100	80	5	Normal
50	Lock-On	Normal	Status	—	—	5	Normal
50	Zap Cannon	Electric	Special	120	50	5	Normal

● TM & HM MOVES

No.	Name	Type	Kind	Pow.	Acc.	PP	Range
TM06	Toxic	Poison	Status	—	90	10	Normal
TM10	Hidden Power	Normal	Special	60	100	15	Normal
TM11	Sunny Day	Fire	Status	—	—	5	Both Sides
TM12	Taunt	Dark	Status	—	100	20	Normal
TM17	Protect	Normal	Status	—	—	10	Self
TM21	Frustration	Normal	Physical	—	100	20	Normal
TM23	Smack Down	Rock	Physical	50	100	15	Normal
TM24	Thunderbolt	Electric	Special	90	100	15	Normal
TM25	Thunder	Electric	Special	110	70	10	Normal
TM26	Earthquake	Ground	Physical	100	100	10	Adjacent
TM27	Return	Normal	Physical	—	100	20	Normal
TM32	Double Team	Normal	Status	—	—	15	Self
TM37	Sandstorm	Rock	Status	—	—	10	Both Sides
TM39	Rock Tomb	Rock	Physical	60	95	15	Normal
TM41	Torment	Dark	Status	—	100	15	Normal
TM42	Facade	Normal	Physical	70	100	20	Normal
TM44	Rest	Psychic	Status	—	—	10	Self
TM45	Attract	Normal	Status	—	100	15	Normal
TM48	Round	Normal	Special	60	100	15	Normal
TM64	Explosion	Normal	Physical	250	100	5	Adjacent
TM69	Rock Polish	Rock	Status	—	—	20	Self
TM71	Stone Edge	Rock	Physical	100	80	5	Normal
TM72	Volt Switch	Electric	Special	70	100	20	Normal
TM73	Thunder Wave	Electric	Status	—	100	20	Normal
TM78	Bulldoze	Ground	Physical	60	100	20	Adjacent
TM80	Rock Slide	Rock	Physical	75	90	10	Many Others
TM87	Swagger	Normal	Status	—	90	15	Normal
TM88	Sleep Talk	Normal	Status	—	—	10	Self
TM90	Substitute	Normal	Status	—	—	10	Self
TM94	Rock Smash	Fighting	Physical	40	100	15	Normal
TM99	Dazzling Gleam	Fairy	Special	80	100	10	Many Others
TM100	Confide	Normal	Status	—	—	20	Normal
HM04	Strength	Normal	Physical	80	100	15	Normal

No.	Name	Type	Kind	Pow.	Acc.	PP	Range

● MOVES TAUGHT BY PEOPLE

Name	Type	Kind	Pow.	Acc.	PP	Range

● EGG MOVES

Name	Type	Kind	Pow.	Acc.	PP	Range
Magnitude	Ground	Physical	—	100	30	Adjacent
Rollout	Rock	Physical	30	90	20	Normal
Double-Edge	Normal	Physical	120	100	15	Normal
Block	Normal	Status	—	—	5	Normal
Stealth Rock	Rock	Status	—	—	20	Other Side
Endure	Normal	Status	—	—	10	Self
Wide Guard	Rock	Status	—	—	10	Your Side

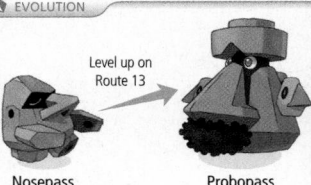

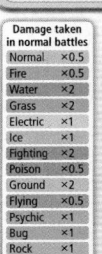

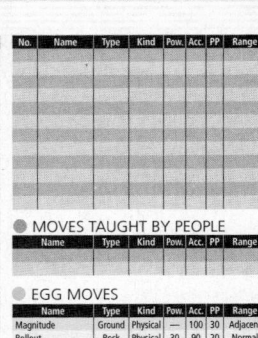

AFTER THE HALL OF FAME

CENTRAL KALOS

COASTAL KALOS

093 | Nosepass

MOUNTAIN KALOS

ADVENTURE DATA

367

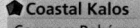

Coastal Kalos 094
Compass Pokémon
V Probopass

HEIGHT: 4'07"   WEIGHT: 749.6 lbs.
GENDER: ♂/♀

TYPE	Rock	Steel

ABILITIES
Sturdy
Magnet Pull

HIDDEN ABILITY
Sand Force

STAT GROWTH RATES
HP ▪▪▪
Attack ▪▪▪
Defense ▪▪▪▪▪▪
Sp. Atk ▪▪▪▪
Sp. Def ▪▪▪▪▪
Speed ▪▪

EGG GROUP
Mineral

X It exudes strong magnetism from all over. It controls three small units called Mini-Noses.

Y It freely controls three small units called Mini-Noses using magnetic force.

EVOLUTION

Level up on Route 13

Nosepass → Probopass

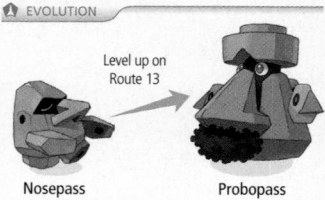

ITEMS SOMETIMES HELD BY WILD POKÉMON
None

Damage taken in normal battles	
Normal	×0.25
Fire	×1
Water	×2
Grass	×1
Electric	×1
Ice	×0.5
Fighting	×4
Poison	×0
Ground	×4
Flying	×0.25
Psychic	×0.5
Bug	×0.5
Rock	×0.5
Ghost	×1
Dragon	×0.5
Dark	×1
Steel	×1
Fairy	×0.5

Damage taken in Inverse Battles	
Normal	×4
Fire	×1
Water	×0.5
Grass	×1
Electric	×1
Ice	×2
Fighting	×0.25
Poison	×1
Ground	×0.25
Flying	×4
Psychic	×2
Bug	×2
Rock	×2
Ghost	×1
Dragon	×2
Dark	×1
Steel	×1
Fairy	×2

Can be used in	
Inverse Battle	Battle Institute
—	Battle Maison
Battle Chateau	Random Matchup

Same form for ♂/♀

How to obtain for your Coastal Kalos Pokédex

Level up Nosepass on Route 13.   Level up Nosepass on Route 13.

● LEVEL-UP MOVES

Lv.	Name	Type	Kind	Pow.	Acc.	PP	Range
1	Magnet Rise	Electric	Status	—	—	10	Self
1	Gravity	Psychic	Status	—	—	5	Both Sides
1	Tackle	Normal	Physical	50	100	35	Normal
1	Iron Defense	Steel	Status	—	—	15	Self
1	Block	Normal	Status	—	—	5	Normal
1	Magnet Bomb	Steel	Physical	60	—	20	Normal
4	Iron Defense	Steel	Status	—	—	15	Self
8	Block	Normal	Status	—	—	5	Normal
11	Magnet Bomb	Steel	Physical	60	—	20	Normal
15	Thunder Wave	Electric	Status	—	100	20	Normal
18	Rock Blast	Rock	Physical	25	90	10	Normal
22	Rest	Psychic	Status	—	—	10	Self
25	Spark	Electric	Physical	65	100	20	Normal
29	Rock Slide	Rock	Physical	75	90	10	Many Others
32	Power Gem	Rock	Special	80	100	20	Normal
36	Sandstorm	Rock	Status	—	—	10	Both Sides
39	Discharge	Electric	Special	80	100	15	Adjacent
43	Earth Power	Ground	Special	90	100	10	Normal
46	Stone Edge	Rock	Physical	100	80	5	Normal
50	Lock-On	Normal	Status	—	—	5	Normal
50	Zap Cannon	Electric	Special	120	50	5	Normal

● TM & HM MOVES

No.	Name	Type	Kind	Pow.	Acc.	PP	Range
TM06	Toxic	Poison	Status	—	90	10	Normal
TM10	Hidden Power	Normal	Special	60	100	15	Normal
TM11	Sunny Day	Fire	Status	—	—	5	Both Sides
TM12	Taunt	Dark	Status	—	100	20	Normal
TM15	Hyper Beam	Normal	Special	150	90	5	Normal
TM17	Protect	Normal	Status	—	—	10	Self
TM21	Frustration	Normal	Physical	—	100	20	Normal
TM23	Smack Down	Rock	Physical	50	100	15	Normal
TM24	Thunderbolt	Electric	Special	90	100	15	Normal
TM25	Thunder	Electric	Special	110	70	10	Normal
TM26	Earthquake	Ground	Physical	100	100	10	Adjacent
TM27	Return	Normal	Physical	—	100	20	Normal
TM32	Double Team	Normal	Status	—	—	15	Self
TM37	Sandstorm	Rock	Status	—	—	10	Both Sides
TM39	Rock Tomb	Rock	Physical	60	95	15	Normal
TM41	Torment	Dark	Status	—	100	15	Normal
TM42	Facade	Normal	Physical	70	100	20	Normal
TM44	Rest	Psychic	Status	—	—	10	Self
TM45	Attract	Normal	Status	—	100	15	Normal
TM48	Round	Normal	Special	60	100	15	Normal
TM64	Explosion	Normal	Physical	250	100	5	Adjacent
TM68	Giga Impact	Normal	Physical	150	90	5	Normal
TM69	Rock Polish	Rock	Status	—	—	20	Self
TM71	Stone Edge	Rock	Physical	100	80	5	Normal
TM72	Volt Switch	Electric	Special	70	100	20	Normal
TM73	Thunder Wave	Electric	Status	—	100	20	Normal
TM78	Bulldoze	Ground	Physical	60	100	20	Adjacent
TM80	Rock Slide	Rock	Physical	75	90	10	Many Others
TM87	Swagger	Normal	Status	—	90	15	Normal
TM88	Sleep Talk	Normal	Status	—	—	10	Self
TM90	Substitute	Normal	Status	—	—	10	Self
TM91	Flash Cannon	Steel	Special	80	100	10	Normal
TM94	Rock Smash	Fighting	Physical	40	100	15	Normal

No.	Name	Type	Kind	Pow.	Acc.	PP	Range
TM99	Dazzling Gleam	Fairy	Special	80	100	10	Many Others
TM100	Confide	Normal	Status	—	—	20	Normal
HM04	Strength	Normal	Physical	80	100	15	Normal

● MOVES TAUGHT BY PEOPLE

Name	Type	Kind	Pow.	Acc.	PP	Range

AFTER THE HALL OF FAME

CENTRAL KALOS

COASTAL KALOS

094

Probopass

MOUNTAIN KALOS

ADVENTURE DATA

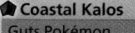

Coastal Kalos 095

Guts Pokémon

 Makuhita

HEIGHT: 3'03" WEIGHT: 190.5 lbs.
GENDER: ♂/♀

X It toughens up by slamming into thick trees over and over. It gains a sturdy body and dauntless spirit.

Y It grows stronger by enduring harsh training. It is a gutsy Pokémon that can withstand any attack.

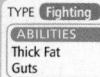

TYPE Fighting

ABILITIES
Thick Fat
Guts

HIDDEN ABILITY
Sheer Force

STAT GROWTH RATES
HP	■■■
Attack	■■■
Defense	■■
Sp. Atk	■
Sp. Def	■
Speed	■■

EGG GROUP
Human-Like

EVOLUTION

Makuhita — Lv. 24 → Hariyama

ITEMS SOMETIMES HELD BY WILD POKÉMON
None

Damage taken in normal battles		Damage taken in Inverse Battles	
Normal	×1	Normal	×1
Fire	×1	Fire	×1
Water	×1	Water	×1
Grass	×1	Grass	×1
Electric	×1	Electric	×1
Ice	×1	Ice	×1
Fighting	×1	Fighting	×1
Poison	×1	Poison	×1
Ground	×1	Ground	×1
Flying	×2	Flying	×0.5
Psychic	×2	Psychic	×0.5
Bug	×0.5	Bug	×2
Rock	×0.5	Rock	×2
Ghost	×1	Ghost	×1
Dragon	×1	Dragon	×1
Dark	×0.5	Dark	×2
Steel	×1	Steel	×1
Fairy	×2	Fairy	×0.5

Can be used in	
Inverse Battle	Battle Institute
—	Battle Maison
Battle Chateau	Random Matchup

Same form for ♂/♀

How to obtain for your Coastal Kalos Pokédex

Leave a Hariyama at the Pokémon Day Care, and hatch the Egg that is found.

Leave a Hariyama at the Pokémon Day Care, and hatch the Egg that is found.

● LEVEL-UP MOVES

Lv.	Name	Type	Kind	Pow.	Acc.	PP	Range
1	Tackle	Normal	Physical	50	100	35	Normal
1	Focus Energy	Normal	Status	—	—	30	Self
4	Sand Attack	Ground	Status	—	100	15	Normal
7	Arm Thrust	Fighting	Physical	15	100	20	Normal
10	Vital Throw	Fighting	Physical	70	—	10	Normal
13	Fake Out	Normal	Physical	40	100	10	Normal
16	Whirlwind	Normal	Status	—	—	20	Normal
19	Knock Off	Dark	Physical	65	100	20	Normal
22	Smelling Salts	Normal	Physical	70	100	10	Normal
25	Belly Drum	Normal	Status	—	—	10	Self
28	Force Palm	Fighting	Physical	60	100	10	Normal
31	Seismic Toss	Fighting	Physical	—	100	20	Normal
34	Wake-Up Slap	Fighting	Physical	70	100	10	Normal
37	Endure	Normal	Status	—	—	10	Self
40	Close Combat	Fighting	Physical	120	100	5	Normal
43	Reversal	Fighting	Physical	—	100	15	Normal
46	Heavy Slam	Steel	Physical	—	100	10	Normal

● TM & HM MOVES

No.	Name	Type	Kind	Pow.	Acc.	PP	Range
TM06	Toxic	Poison	Status	—	90	10	Normal
TM08	Bulk Up	Fighting	Status	—	—	20	Self
TM10	Hidden Power	Normal	Special	60	100	15	Normal
TM11	Sunny Day	Fire	Status	—	—	5	Both Sides
TM17	Protect	Normal	Status	—	—	10	Self
TM18	Rain Dance	Water	Status	—	—	5	Both Sides
TM21	Frustration	Normal	Physical	—	100	20	Normal
TM23	Smack Down	Rock	Physical	50	100	15	Normal
TM26	Earthquake	Ground	Physical	100	100	10	Adjacent
TM27	Return	Normal	Physical	—	100	20	Normal
TM28	Dig	Ground	Physical	80	100	10	Normal
TM31	Brick Break	Fighting	Physical	75	100	15	Normal
TM32	Double Team	Normal	Status	—	—	15	Self
TM39	Rock Tomb	Rock	Physical	60	95	15	Normal
TM42	Facade	Normal	Physical	70	100	20	Normal
TM44	Rest	Psychic	Status	—	—	10	Self
TM45	Attract	Normal	Status	—	100	15	Normal
TM47	Low Sweep	Fighting	Physical	65	100	20	Normal
TM48	Round	Normal	Special	60	100	15	Normal
TM52	Focus Blast	Fighting	Special	120	70	5	Normal
TM56	Fling	Dark	Physical	—	100	10	Normal
TM67	Retaliate	Normal	Physical	70	100	5	Normal
TM78	Bulldoze	Ground	Physical	60	100	20	Adjacent
TM80	Rock Slide	Rock	Physical	75	90	10	Many Others
TM84	Poison Jab	Poison	Physical	80	100	20	Normal
TM87	Swagger	Normal	Status	—	90	15	Normal
TM89	Sleep Talk	Normal	Status	—	—	10	Self
TM90	Substitute	Normal	Status	—	—	10	Self
TM94	Rock Smash	Fighting	Physical	40	100	15	Normal
TM98	Power-Up Punch	Fighting	Physical	40	100	20	Normal
TM100	Confide	Normal	Status	—	—	20	Normal
HM03	Surf	Water	Special	90	100	15	Adjacent
HM04	Strength	Normal	Physical	80	100	15	Normal

● MOVES TAUGHT BY PEOPLE

Name	Type	Kind	Pow.	Acc.	PP	Range

● EGG MOVES

Name	Type	Kind	Pow.	Acc.	PP	Range
Feint Attack	Dark	Physical	60	—	20	Normal
Detect	Fighting	Status	—	—	5	Self
Foresight	Normal	Status	—	—	40	Normal
Helping Hand	Normal	Status	—	—	20	1 Ally
Cross Chop	Fighting	Physical	100	80	5	Normal
Revenge	Fighting	Physical	60	100	10	Normal
Dynamic Punch	Fighting	Physical	100	50	5	Normal
Counter	Fighting	Physical	—	100	20	Varies
Wake-Up Slap	Fighting	Physical	70	100	10	Normal
Bullet Punch	Steel	Physical	40	100	30	Normal
Feint	Normal	Physical	30	100	10	Normal
Wide Guard	Rock	Status	—	—	10	Your Side
Focus Punch	Fighting	Physical	150	100	20	Normal
Chip Away	Normal	Physical	70	100	20	Normal

AFTER THE HALL OF FAME

CENTRAL KALOS

COASTAL KALOS

095 Makuhita

MOUNTAIN KALOS

ADVENTURE DATA

AFTER THE HALL OF FAME

CENTRAL KALOS

COASTAL KALOS
096
Hariyama

MOUNTAIN KALOS

ADVENTURE DATA

🍂 **Coastal Kalos** **096**

Arm Thrust Pokémon

☑ **Hariyama**

HEIGHT: 7'07" WEIGHT: 559.5 lbs.
GENDER: ♂ / ♀

TYPE Fighting

ABILITIES
Thick Fat
Guts

HIDDEN ABILITY
Sheer Force

STAT GROWTH RATES

HP	■■■■■
Attack	■■■■■
Defense	■■■
Sp. Atk	■■
Sp. Def	■■■
Speed	■■■

EGG GROUP
Human-Like

🔺 **EVOLUTION**

Lv. 24

Makuhita → Hariyama

ITEMS SOMETIMES HELD BY WILD POKÉMON
King's Rock

X It stomps on the ground to build power. It can send a 10-ton truck flying with a straight-arm punch.

Y It loves to match power with big-bodied Pokémon. It can knock a truck flying with its arm thrusts.

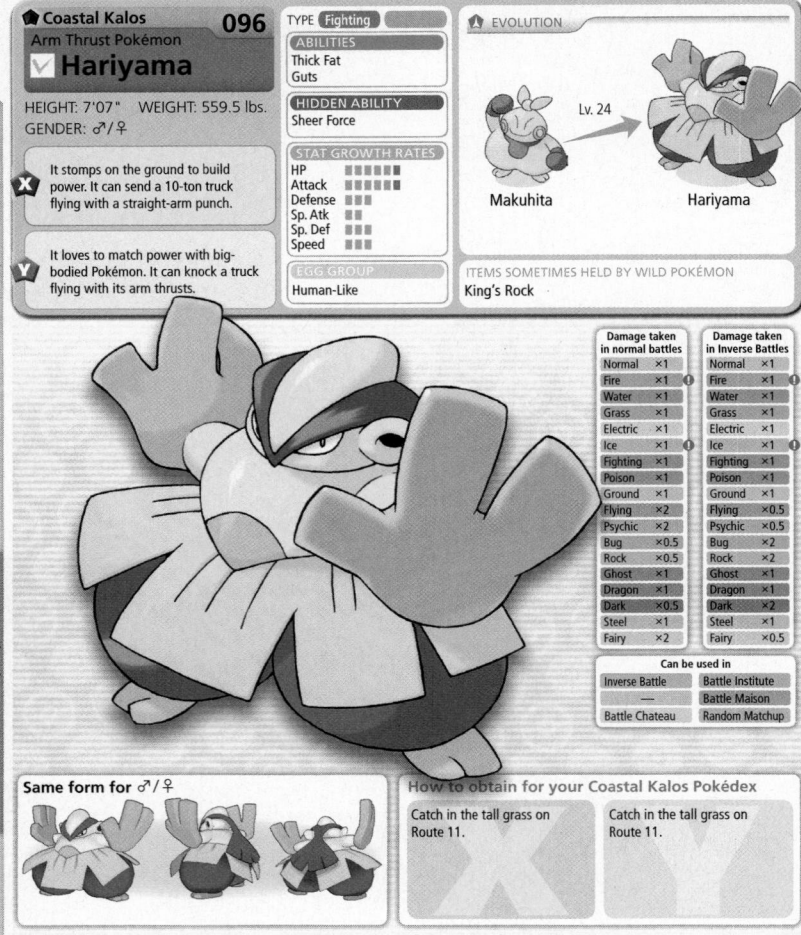

Damage taken in normal battles	
Normal	×1
Fire	×1
Water	×1
Grass	×1
Electric	×1
Ice	×1
Fighting	×1
Poison	×1
Ground	×1
Flying	×2
Psychic	×2
Bug	×0.5
Rock	×0.5
Ghost	×1
Dragon	×1
Dark	×0.5
Steel	×1
Fairy	×2

Damage taken in Inverse Battles	
Normal	×1
Fire	×1
Water	×1
Grass	×1
Electric	×1
Ice	×1
Fighting	×1
Poison	×1
Ground	×1
Flying	×0.5
Psychic	×0.5
Bug	×2
Rock	×2
Ghost	×1
Dragon	×1
Dark	×2
Steel	×1
Fairy	×0.5

Can be used in	
Inverse Battle	Battle Institute
—	Battle Maison
Battle Chateau	Random Matchup

Same form for ♂ / ♀

How to obtain for your Coastal Kalos Pokédex

Catch in the tall grass on Route 11.

Catch in the tall grass on Route 11.

● **LEVEL-UP MOVES**

Lv.	Name	Type	Kind	Pow.	Acc.	PP	Range
1	Brine	Water	Special	65	100	10	Normal
1	Tackle	Normal	Physical	50	100	35	Normal
1	Focus Energy	Normal	Status	—	—	30	Self
1	Sand Attack	Ground	Status	—	100	15	Normal
1	Arm Thrust	Fighting	Physical	15	100	20	Normal
4	Sand Attack	Ground	Status	—	100	15	Normal
7	Arm Thrust	Fighting	Physical	15	100	20	Normal
10	Vital Throw	Fighting	Physical	70	—	10	Normal
13	Fake Out	Normal	Physical	40	100	10	Normal
16	Whirlwind	Normal	Status	—	—	20	Normal
19	Knock Off	Dark	Physical	65	100	20	Normal
22	Smelling Salts	Normal	Physical	70	100	10	Normal
27	Belly Drum	Normal	Status	—	—	10	Self
32	Force Palm	Fighting	Physical	60	100	10	Normal
37	Seismic Toss	Fighting	Physical	—	100	20	Normal
42	Wake-Up Slap	Fighting	Physical	70	100	10	Normal
47	Endure	Normal	Status	—	—	10	Self
52	Close Combat	Fighting	Physical	120	100	5	Normal
57	Reversal	Fighting	Physical	—	100	15	Normal
62	Heavy Slam	Steel	Physical	—	100	10	Normal

● **TM & HM MOVES**

No.	Name	Type	Kind	Pow.	Acc.	PP	Range
TM06	Toxic	Poison	Status	—	90	10	Normal
TM08	Bulk Up	Fighting	Status	—	—	20	Self
TM10	Hidden Power	Normal	Special	60	100	15	Normal
TM11	Sunny Day	Fire	Status	—	—	5	Both Sides
TM15	Hyper Beam	Normal	Special	150	90	5	Normal
TM17	Protect	Normal	Status	—	—	10	Self
TM18	Rain Dance	Water	Status	—	—	5	Both Sides
TM21	Frustration	Normal	Physical	—	100	20	Normal
TM23	Smack Down	Rock	Physical	50	100	15	Normal
TM26	Earthquake	Ground	Physical	100	100	10	Adjacent
TM27	Return	Normal	Physical	—	100	20	Normal
TM28	Dig	Ground	Physical	80	100	10	Normal
TM31	Brick Break	Fighting	Physical	75	100	15	Normal
TM32	Double Team	Normal	Status	—	—	15	Self
TM39	Rock Tomb	Rock	Physical	60	95	15	Normal
TM42	Facade	Normal	Physical	70	100	20	Normal
TM44	Rest	Psychic	Status	—	—	10	Self
TM45	Attract	Normal	Status	—	100	15	Normal
TM47	Low Sweep	Fighting	Physical	65	100	20	Normal
TM48	Round	Normal	Special	60	100	15	Normal
TM52	Focus Blast	Fighting	Special	120	70	5	Normal
TM56	Fling	Dark	Physical	—	100	10	Normal
TM66	Payback	Dark	Physical	50	100	10	Normal
TM67	Retaliate	Normal	Physical	70	100	5	Normal
TM68	Giga Impact	Normal	Physical	150	90	5	Normal
TM71	Stone Edge	Rock	Physical	100	80	5	Normal
TM78	Bulldoze	Ground	Physical	60	100	20	Adjacent
TM80	Rock Slide	Rock	Physical	75	90	10	Many Others
TM84	Poison Jab	Poison	Physical	80	100	20	Normal
TM87	Swagger	Normal	Status	—	90	15	Normal
TM88	Sleep Talk	Normal	Status	—	—	10	Self
TM90	Substitute	Normal	Status	—	—	10	Self
TM94	Rock Smash	Fighting	Physical	40	100	15	Normal

No.	Name	Type	Kind	Pow.	Acc.	PP	Range
TM98	Power-Up Punch	Fighting	Physical	40	100	20	Normal
TM100	Confide	Normal	Status	—	—	20	Normal
HM03	Surf	Water	Special	90	100	15	Adjacent
HM04	Strength	Normal	Physical	80	100	15	Normal

● **MOVES TAUGHT BY PEOPLE**

Name	Type	Kind	Pow.	Acc.	PP	Range

Coastal Kalos

AFTER THE HALL OF FAME

CENTRAL KALOS

COASTAL KALOS

097 Throh

MOUNTAIN KALOS

ADVENTURE DATA

Coastal Kalos 097

Judo Pokémon

 Throh

HEIGHT: 4'03"   WEIGHT: 122.4 lbs.
GENDER: ♂

X When it tightens its belt, it becomes stronger. Wild Throh use vines to weave their own belts.

Y When it encounters a foe bigger than itself, it wants to throw it. It changes belts as it gets stronger.

TYPE Fighting

ABILITIES
Guts
Inner Focus

HIDDEN ABILITY
Mold Breaker

STAT GROWTH RATES

HP	■■■■■
Attack	■■■■■
Defense	■■■■
Sp. Atk	■
Sp. Def	■■■■
Speed	■■■

EGG GROUP
Human-Like

EVOLUTION

Does not evolve

ITEMS SOMETIMES HELD BY WILD POKÉMON
Black Belt

Damage taken in normal battles	
Normal	×1
Fire	×1
Water	×1
Grass	×1
Electric	×1
Ice	×1
Fighting	×1
Poison	×1
Ground	×1
Flying	×2
Psychic	×2
Bug	×0.5
Rock	×0.5
Ghost	×1
Dragon	×1
Dark	×0.5
Steel	×1
Fairy	×2

Damage taken in Inverse Battles	
Normal	×1
Fire	×1
Water	×1
Grass	×1
Electric	×1
Ice	×1
Fighting	×1
Poison	×1
Ground	×1
Flying	×0.5
Psychic	×0.5
Bug	×2
Rock	×2
Ghost	×1
Dragon	×2
Dark	×2
Steel	×1
Fairy	×0.5

Can be used in	
Inverse Battle	Battle Institute
—	Battle Maison
Battle Chateau	Random Matchup

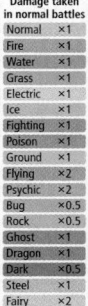
♂

How to obtain for your Coastal Kalos Pokédex

Link Trade or transfer from another game.

Catch in the tall grass on Route 11.

● LEVEL-UP MOVES

Lv.	Name	Type	Kind	Pow.	Acc.	PP	Range
1	Bind	Normal	Physical	15	85	20	Normal
1	Leer	Normal	Status	—	100	30	Many Others
5	Bide	Normal	Physical	—	—	10	Self
9	Focus Energy	Normal	Status	—	—	30	Self
13	Seismic Toss	Fighting	Physical	—	100	20	Normal
17	Vital Throw	Fighting	Physical	70	—	10	Normal
21	Revenge	Fighting	Physical	60	100	10	Normal
25	Storm Throw	Fighting	Physical	60	100	10	Normal
29	Body Slam	Normal	Physical	85	100	15	Normal
33	Bulk Up	Fighting	Status	—	—	20	Self
37	Circle Throw	Fighting	Physical	60	90	10	Normal
41	Endure	Normal	Status	—	—	10	Self
45	Wide Guard	Rock	Status	—	—	10	Your Side
48	Superpower	Fighting	Physical	120	100	5	Normal
50	Reversal	Fighting	Physical	—	100	15	Normal

● TM & HM MOVES

No.	Name	Type	Kind	Pow.	Acc.	PP	Range
TM06	Toxic	Poison	Status	—	90	10	Normal
TM08	Bulk Up	Fighting	Status	—	—	20	Self
TM10	Hidden Power	Normal	Special	60	100	15	Normal
TM11	Sunny Day	Fire	Status	—	—	5	Both Sides
TM12	Taunt	Dark	Status	—	100	20	Normal
TM17	Protect	Normal	Status	—	—	10	Self
TM18	Rain Dance	Water	Status	—	—	5	Both Sides
TM21	Frustration	Normal	Physical	—	100	20	Normal
TM26	Earthquake	Ground	Physical	100	100	10	Adjacent
TM27	Return	Normal	Physical	—	100	20	Normal
TM28	Dig	Ground	Physical	80	100	10	Normal
TM31	Brick Break	Fighting	Physical	75	100	15	Normal
TM32	Double Team	Normal	Status	—	—	15	Self
TM39	Rock Tomb	Rock	Physical	60	95	15	Normal
TM42	Facade	Normal	Physical	70	100	20	Normal
TM44	Rest	Psychic	Status	—	—	10	Self
TM45	Attract	Normal	Status	—	100	15	Normal
TM47	Low Sweep	Fighting	Physical	65	100	20	Normal
TM48	Round	Normal	Special	60	100	15	Normal
TM52	Focus Blast	Fighting	Special	120	70	5	Normal
TM56	Fling	Dark	Physical	—	100	10	Normal
TM66	Payback	Dark	Physical	50	100	10	Normal
TM67	Retaliate	Normal	Physical	70	100	5	Normal
TM68	Giga Impact	Normal	Physical	150	90	5	Normal
TM71	Stone Edge	Rock	Physical	100	80	5	Normal
TM78	Bulldoze	Ground	Physical	60	100	20	Adjacent
TM80	Rock Slide	Rock	Physical	75	90	10	Many Others
TM84	Poison Jab	Poison	Physical	80	100	20	Normal
TM86	Grass Knot	Grass	Special	—	100	20	Normal
TM87	Swagger	Normal	Status	—	90	15	Normal
TM88	Sleep Talk	Normal	Status	—	—	10	Self
TM90	Substitute	Normal	Status	—	—	10	Self
TM94	Rock Smash	Fighting	Physical	40	100	15	Normal

No.	Name	Type	Kind	Pow.	Acc.	PP	Range
TM98	Power-Up Punch	Fighting	Physical	40	100	20	Normal
TM100	Confide	Normal	Status	—	—	20	Normal
HM04	Strength	Normal	Physical	80	100	15	Normal

● MOVES TAUGHT BY PEOPLE

Name	Type	Kind	Pow.	Acc.	PP	Range

● EGG MOVES

Name	Type	Kind	Pow.	Acc.	PP	Range

AFTER THE HALL OF FAME

CENTRAL KALOS

COASTAL KALOS

098

Sawk

MOUNTAIN KALOS

ADVENTURE DATA

Coastal Kalos — 098

Sawk
Karate Pokémon

HEIGHT: 4'07" WEIGHT: 112.4 lbs.
GENDER: ♂

TYPE: **Fighting**

ABILITIES
Sturdy
Inner Focus

HIDDEN ABILITY
Mold Breaker

X Desiring the strongest karate chop, they seclude themselves in mountains and train without sleeping.

Y Tying their belts gets them pumped and makes their punches more destructive. Disturbing their training angers them.

STAT GROWTH RATES
HP	■■■
Attack	■■■■■■
Defense	■■■
Sp. Atk	■
Sp. Def	■■■
Speed	■■■■■

EGG GROUP
Human-Like

EVOLUTION

Does not evolve

ITEMS SOMETIMES HELD BY WILD POKÉMON
Black Belt

Can be used in
Inverse Battle
—
Battle Chateau
Battle Institute
Battle Maison
Random Matchup

Damage taken in normal battles		Damage taken in Inverse Battles	
Normal	×1	Normal	×1
Fire	×1	Fire	×1
Water	×1	Water	×1
Grass	×1	Grass	×1
Electric	×1	Electric	×1
Ice	×1	Ice	×1
Fighting	×1	Fighting	×1
Poison	×1	Poison	×1
Ground	×1	Ground	×1
Flying	×2	Flying	×0.5
Psychic	×2	Psychic	×0.5
Bug	×0.5	Bug	×2
Rock	×0.5	Rock	×2
Ghost	×1	Ghost	×1
Dragon	×1	Dragon	×1
Dark	×0.5	Dark	×2
Steel	×1	Steel	×1
Fairy	×2	Fairy	×0.5

How to obtain for your Coastal Kalos Pokédex
Catch in the tall grass on Route 11.

Link Trade or transfer from another game.

♂

● LEVEL-UP MOVES

Lv.	Name	Type	Kind	Pow.	Acc.	PP	Range
1	Rock Smash	Fighting	Physical	40	100	15	Normal
1	Leer	Normal	Status	—	100	30	Many Others
5	Bide	Normal	Physical	—	—	10	Self
9	Focus Energy	Normal	Status	—	—	30	Self
13	Double Kick	Fighting	Physical	30	100	30	Normal
17	Low Sweep	Fighting	Physical	65	100	20	Normal
21	Counter	Fighting	Physical	—	100	20	Varies
25	Karate Chop	Fighting	Physical	50	100	25	Normal
29	Brick Break	Fighting	Physical	75	100	15	Normal
33	Bulk Up	Fighting	Status	—	—	20	Self
37	Retaliate	Normal	Physical	70	100	5	Normal
41	Endure	Normal	Status	—	—	10	Self
45	Quick Guard	Fighting	Status	—	—	15	Your Side
48	Close Combat	Fighting	Physical	120	100	5	Normal
50	Reversal	Fighting	Physical	—	100	15	Normal

● TM & HM MOVES

No.	Name	Type	Kind	Pow.	Acc.	PP	Range
TM06	Toxic	Poison	Status	—	90	10	Normal
TM08	Bulk Up	Fighting	Status	—	—	20	Self
TM10	Hidden Power	Normal	Special	60	100	15	Normal
TM11	Sunny Day	Fire	Status	—	—	5	Both Sides
TM12	Taunt	Dark	Status	—	100	20	Normal
TM17	Protect	Normal	Status	—	—	10	Self
TM18	Rain Dance	Water	Status	—	—	5	Both Sides
TM21	Frustration	Normal	Physical	—	100	20	Normal
TM26	Earthquake	Ground	Physical	100	100	10	Adjacent
TM27	Return	Normal	Physical	—	100	20	Normal
TM28	Dig	Ground	Physical	80	100	10	Normal
TM31	Brick Break	Fighting	Physical	75	100	15	Normal
TM32	Double Team	Normal	Status	—	—	15	Self
TM39	Rock Tomb	Rock	Physical	60	95	15	Normal
TM42	Facade	Normal	Physical	70	100	20	Normal
TM44	Rest	Psychic	Status	—	—	10	Self
TM45	Attract	Normal	Status	—	100	15	Normal
TM47	Low Sweep	Fighting	Physical	65	100	20	Normal
TM48	Round	Normal	Special	60	100	15	Normal
TM52	Focus Blast	Fighting	Special	120	70	5	Normal
TM56	Fling	Dark	Physical	—	100	10	Normal
TM66	Payback	Dark	Physical	50	100	10	Normal
TM67	Retaliate	Normal	Physical	70	100	5	Normal
TM68	Giga Impact	Normal	Physical	150	90	5	Normal
TM71	Stone Edge	Rock	Physical	100	80	5	Normal
TM78	Bulldoze	Ground	Physical	60	100	20	Adjacent
TM80	Rock Slide	Rock	Physical	75	90	10	Many Others
TM84	Poison Jab	Poison	Physical	80	100	20	Normal
TM86	Grass Knot	Grass	Special	—	100	20	Normal
TM87	Swagger	Normal	Status	—	90	15	Normal
TM88	Sleep Talk	Normal	Status	—	—	10	Self
TM90	Substitute	Normal	Status	—	—	10	Self
TM94	Rock Smash	Fighting	Physical	40	100	15	Normal

No.	Name	Type	Kind	Pow.	Acc.	PP	Range
TM98	Power-Up Punch	Fighting	Physical	40	100	20	Normal
TM100	Confide	Normal	Status	—	—	20	Normal
HM04	Strength	Normal	Physical	80	100	15	Normal

● MOVES TAUGHT BY PEOPLE

Name	Type	Kind	Pow.	Acc.	PP	Range

● EGG MOVES

Name	Type	Kind	Pow.	Acc.	PP	Range

Starly

Coastal Kalos — **099**
Starling Pokémon

HEIGHT: 1'00" WEIGHT: 4.4 lbs.
GENDER: ♂/♀

TYPE	Normal	Flying

ABILITY
Keen Eye

HIDDEN ABILITY
Reckless

STAT GROWTH RATES
HP	■ ■
Attack	■ ■ ■
Defense	■ ■
Sp. Atk	■
Sp. Def	■
Speed	■ ■ ■

EGG GROUP
Flying

X: They flock in great numbers. Though small, they flap their wings with great power.

Y: They flock around mountains and fields, chasing after bug Pokémon. Their singing is noisy and annoying.

EVOLUTION

Starly — Lv. 14 → Staravia — Lv. 34 → Staraptor

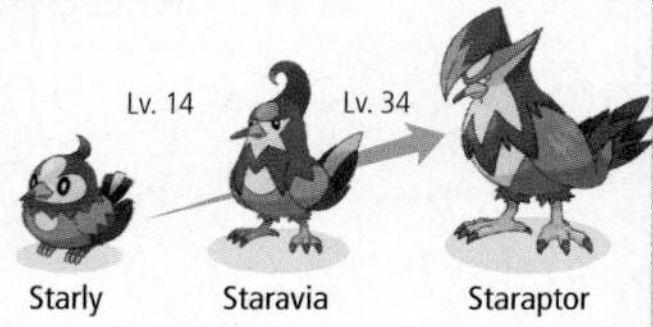

ITEMS SOMETIMES HELD BY WILD POKÉMON
None

AFTER THE HALL OF FAME

CENTRAL KALOS

COASTAL KALOS

099 Starly

MOUNTAIN KALOS

ADVENTURE DATA

Damage taken in normal battles		Damage taken in Inverse Battles		Can be used in
Normal	×1	Normal	×1	Inverse Battle
Fire	×1	Fire	×1	—
Water	×1	Water	×1	Battle Chateau
Grass	×0.5	Grass	×2	Battle Institute
Electric	×2	Electric	×0.5	Battle Maison
Ice	×2	Ice	×0.5	Random Matchup
Fighting	×1	Fighting	×1	
Poison	×1	Poison	×1	
Ground	×0	Ground	×2	
Flying	×1	Flying	×1	
Psychic	×1	Psychic	×1	
Bug	×0.5	Bug	×2	
Rock	×2	Rock	×0.5	
Ghost	×0	Ghost	×2	
Dragon	×1	Dragon	×1	
Dark	×1	Dark	×1	
Steel	×1	Steel	×1	
Fairy	×1	Fairy	×1	

How to obtain for your Coastal Kalos Pokédex

Catch in a Horde Encounter on Route 11.

Catch in a Horde Encounter on Route 11.

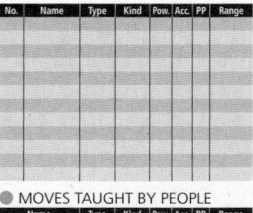

♂ ♀

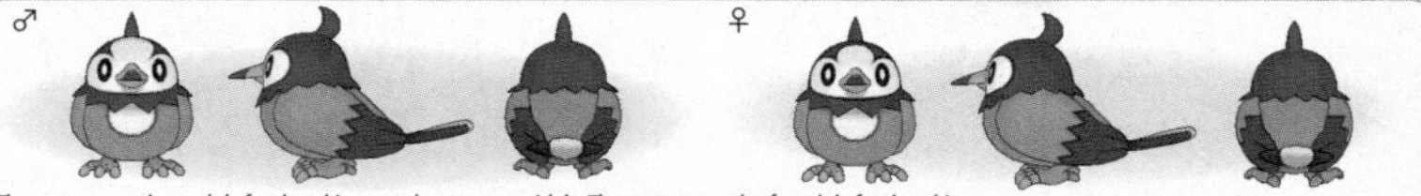

The pattern on the male's forehead is spread out more widely. The pattern on the female's forehead is narrower.

● LEVEL-UP MOVES

Lv.	Name	Type	Kind	Pow.	Acc.	PP	Range
1	Tackle	Normal	Physical	50	100	35	Normal
1	Growl	Normal	Status	—	100	40	Many Others
5	Quick Attack	Normal	Physical	40	100	30	Normal
9	Wing Attack	Flying	Physical	60	100	35	Normal
13	Double Team	Normal	Status	—	—	15	Self
17	Endeavor	Normal	Physical	—	100	5	Normal
21	Whirlwind	Normal	Status	—	—	20	Normal
25	Aerial Ace	Flying	Physical	60	—	20	Normal
29	Take Down	Normal	Physical	90	85	20	Normal
33	Agility	Psychic	Status	—	—	30	Self
37	Brave Bird	Flying	Physical	120	100	15	Normal
41	Final Gambit	Fighting	Special	—	100	5	Normal

● TM & HM MOVES

No.	Name	Type	Kind	Pow.	Acc.	PP	Range
TM06	Toxic	Poison	Status	—	90	10	Normal
TM10	Hidden Power	Normal	Special	60	100	15	Normal
TM11	Sunny Day	Fire	Status	—	—	5	Both Sides
TM17	Protect	Normal	Status	—	—	10	Self
TM18	Rain Dance	Water	Status	—	—	5	Both Sides
TM19	Roost	Flying	Status	—	—	10	Self
TM21	Frustration	Normal	Physical	—	100	20	Normal
TM27	Return	Normal	Physical	—	100	20	Normal
TM32	Double Team	Normal	Status	—	—	15	Self
TM40	Aerial Ace	Flying	Physical	60	—	20	Normal
TM42	Facade	Normal	Physical	70	100	20	Normal
TM44	Rest	Psychic	Status	—	—	10	Self
TM45	Attract	Normal	Status	—	100	15	Normal
TM46	Thief	Dark	Physical	60	100	25	Normal
TM48	Round	Normal	Special	60	100	15	Normal
TM49	Echoed Voice	Normal	Special	40	100	15	Normal
TM51	Steel Wing	Steel	Physical	70	90	25	Normal
TM87	Swagger	Normal	Status	—	90	15	Normal
TM88	Sleep Talk	Normal	Status	—	—	10	Self
TM89	U-turn	Bug	Physical	70	100	20	Normal
TM90	Substitute	Normal	Status	—	—	10	Self
TM100	Confide	Normal	Status	—	—	20	Normal
HM02	Fly	Flying	Physical	90	95	15	Normal

● MOVES TAUGHT BY PEOPLE

Name	Type	Kind	Pow.	Acc.	PP	Range

● EGG MOVES

Name	Type	Kind	Pow.	Acc.	PP	Range
Feather Dance	Flying	Status	—	100	15	Normal
Fury Attack	Normal	Physical	15	85	20	Normal
Pursuit	Dark	Physical	40	100	20	Normal
Astonish	Ghost	Physical	30	100	15	Normal
Sand Attack	Ground	Status	—	100	15	Normal
Foresight	Normal	Status	—	—	40	Normal
Double-Edge	Normal	Physical	120	100	15	Normal
Steel Wing	Steel	Physical	70	90	25	Normal
Uproar	Normal	Special	90	100	10	1 Random
Roost	Flying	Status	—	—	10	Self
Detect	Fighting	Status	—	—	5	Self
Revenge	Fighting	Physical	60	100	10	Normal
Mirror Move	Flying	Status	—	—	20	Normal

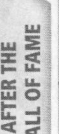

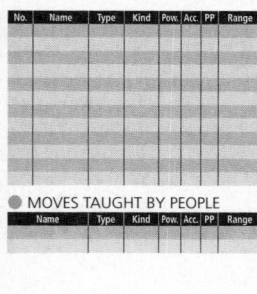

AFTER THE HALL OF FAME

CENTRAL KALOS

COASTAL KALOS

100

Staravia

MOUNTAIN KALOS

ADVENTURE DATA

🔺 **Coastal Kalos** **100**

Starling Pokémon

☑ **Staravia**

HEIGHT: 2'00" WEIGHT: 34.2 lbs.
GENDER: ♂ / ♀

TYPE Normal Flying

ABILITY
Intimidate

HIDDEN ABILITY
Reckless

STAT GROWTH RATES

HP	■■
Attack	■■■■
Defense	■■
Sp. Atk	■■
Sp. Def	■■
Speed	■■■■

EGG GROUP
Flying

⚡ EVOLUTION

Starly → Lv. 14 → Staravia → Lv. 34 → Staraptor

Ⓧ	They maintain huge flocks, although fierce scuffles break out between various flocks.
Ⓨ	It lives in forests and fields. Squabbles over territory occur when flocks collide.

ITEMS SOMETIMES HELD BY WILD POKÉMON
None

Can be used in
Inverse Battle
Sky Battle
Battle Chateau
Battle Institute
Battle Maison
Random Matchup

Damage taken in normal battles

Normal	×1
Fire	×1
Water	×1
Grass	×0.5
Electric	×2
Ice	×2
Fighting	×1
Poison	×1
Ground	×0
Flying	×1
Psychic	×1
Bug	×0.5
Rock	×2
Ghost	×0
Dragon	×1
Dark	×1
Steel	×1
Fairy	×1

Damage taken in Inverse Battles

Normal	×1
Fire	×1
Water	×1
Grass	×2
Electric	×0.5
Ice	×0.5
Fighting	×1
Poison	×1
Ground	×2
Flying	×1
Psychic	×1
Bug	×2
Rock	×0.5
Ghost	×2
Dragon	×1
Dark	×1
Steel	×1
Fairy	×1

How to obtain for your Coastal Kalos Pokédex

❶ Catch in the tall grass on Route 11.
❷ Level up Starly to Lv. 14.

❶ Catch in the tall grass on Route 11.
❷ Level up Starly to Lv. 14.

♂   ♀

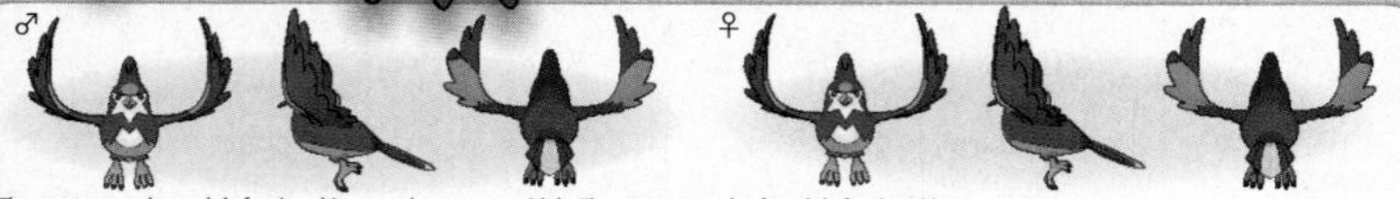

The pattern on the male's forehead is spread out more widely. The pattern on the female's forehead is narrower.

● **LEVEL-UP MOVES**

Lv.	Name	Type	Kind	Pow.	Acc.	PP	Range
1	Tackle	Normal	Physical	50	100	35	Normal
1	Growl	Normal	Status	—	100	40	Many Others
1	Quick Attack	Normal	Physical	40	100	30	Normal
5	Quick Attack	Normal	Physical	40	100	30	Normal
9	Wing Attack	Flying	Physical	60	100	35	Normal
13	Double Team	Normal	Status	—	—	15	Self
18	Endeavor	Normal	Physical	—	100	5	Normal
23	Whirlwind	Normal	Status	—	—	20	Normal
28	Aerial Ace	Flying	Physical	60	—	20	Normal
33	Take Down	Normal	Physical	90	85	20	Normal
38	Agility	Psychic	Status	—	—	30	Self
43	Brave Bird	Flying	Physical	120	100	15	Normal
48	Final Gambit	Fighting	Special	—	100	5	Normal

● **TM & HM MOVES**

No.	Name	Type	Kind	Pow.	Acc.	PP	Range
TM06	Toxic	Poison	Status	—	90	10	Normal
TM10	Hidden Power	Normal	Special	60	100	15	Normal
TM11	Sunny Day	Fire	Status	—	—	5	Both Sides
TM17	Protect	Normal	Status	—	—	10	Self
TM18	Rain Dance	Water	Status	—	—	5	Both Sides
TM19	Roost	Flying	Status	—	—	10	Self
TM21	Frustration	Normal	Physical	—	100	20	Normal
TM27	Return	Normal	Physical	—	100	20	Normal
TM32	Double Team	Normal	Status	—	—	15	Self
TM40	Aerial Ace	Flying	Physical	60	—	20	Normal
TM42	Facade	Normal	Physical	70	100	20	Normal
TM44	Rest	Psychic	Status	—	—	10	Self
TM45	Attract	Normal	Status	—	100	15	Normal
TM46	Thief	Dark	Physical	60	100	25	Normal
TM48	Round	Normal	Special	60	100	15	Normal
TM49	Echoed Voice	Normal	Special	40	100	15	Normal
TM51	Steel Wing	Steel	Physical	70	90	25	Normal
TM67	Retaliate	Normal	Physical	70	100	5	Normal
TM87	Swagger	Normal	Status	—	90	15	Normal
TM88	Sleep Talk	Normal	Status	—	—	10	Self
TM89	U-turn	Bug	Physical	70	100	20	Normal
TM90	Substitute	Normal	Status	—	—	10	Self
TM100	Confide	Normal	Status	—	—	20	Normal
HM02	Fly	Flying	Physical	90	95	15	Normal

No.	Name	Type	Kind	Pow.	Acc.	PP	Range

● **MOVES TAUGHT BY PEOPLE**

Name	Type	Kind	Pow.	Acc.	PP	Range

🍂 Coastal Kalos
Predator Pokémon
☑ Staraptor
101

HEIGHT: 3'11"   WEIGHT: 54.9 lbs.
GENDER: ♂/♀

| TYPE | Normal | Flying |

ABILITY
Intimidate

HIDDEN ABILITY
Reckless

STAT GROWTH RATES
HP	■■■
Attack	■■■■■■
Defense	■■■
Sp. Atk	■■
Sp. Def	■■■
Speed	■■■■■

EGG GROUP
Flying

❌ The muscles in its wings and legs are strong. It can easily fly while gripping a small Pokémon.

🅨 When Staravia evolve into Staraptor, they leave the flock to live alone. They have sturdy wings.

⬆ EVOLUTION

Starly — Lv. 14 → Staravia — Lv. 34 → Staraptor

ITEMS SOMETIMES HELD BY WILD POKÉMON
None

Damage taken in normal battles		Damage taken in Inverse Battles		Can be used in
Normal	×1	Normal	×1	Inverse Battle
Fire	×1	Fire	×1	Sky Battle
Water	×1	Water	×1	Battle Chateau
Grass	×0.5	Grass	×2	Battle Institute
Electric	×2	Electric	×0.5	Battle Maison
Ice	×2	Ice	×0.5	Random Matchup
Fighting	×1	Fighting	×1	
Poison	×1	Poison	×1	
Ground	×0	Ground	×2	
Flying	×1	Flying	×1	
Psychic	×1	Psychic	×1	
Bug	×0.5	Bug	×2	
Rock	×2	Rock	×0.5	
Ghost	×0	Ghost	×2	
Dragon	×1	Dragon	×1	
Dark	×1	Dark	×1	
Steel	×1	Steel	×1	
Fairy	×1	Fairy	×1	

How to obtain for your Coastal Kalos Pokédex

❌ Level up Staravia to Lv. 34.   🅨 Level up Staravia to Lv. 34.

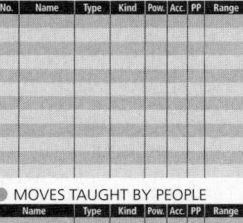

♂   ♀

The pattern on the male's forehead is spread out more widely. The pattern on the female's forehead is narrower.

● LEVEL-UP MOVES

Lv.	Name	Type	Kind	Pow.	Acc.	PP	Range
1	Tackle	Normal	Physical	50	100	35	Normal
1	Growl	Normal	Status	—	100	40	Many Others
1	Quick Attack	Normal	Physical	40	100	30	Normal
1	Wing Attack	Flying	Physical	60	100	35	Normal
5	Quick Attack	Normal	Physical	40	100	30	Normal
9	Wing Attack	Flying	Physical	60	100	35	Normal
13	Double Team	Normal	Status	—	—	15	Self
18	Endeavor	Normal	Physical	—	100	5	Normal
23	Whirlwind	Normal	Status	—	—	20	Normal
28	Aerial Ace	Flying	Physical	60	—	20	Normal
33	Take Down	Normal	Physical	90	85	20	Normal
34	Close Combat	Fighting	Physical	120	100	5	Normal
41	Agility	Psychic	Status	—	—	30	Self
49	Brave Bird	Flying	Physical	120	100	15	Normal
57	Final Gambit	Fighting	Special	—	100	5	Normal

■ TM & HM MOVES

No.	Name	Type	Kind	Pow.	Acc.	PP	Range
TM06	Toxic	Poison	Status	—	90	10	Normal
TM10	Hidden Power	Normal	Special	60	100	15	Normal
TM11	Sunny Day	Fire	Status	—	—	5	Both Sides
TM15	Hyper Beam	Normal	Special	150	90	5	Normal
TM17	Protect	Normal	Status	—	—	10	Self
TM18	Rain Dance	Water	Status	—	—	5	Both Sides
TM19	Roost	Flying	Status	—	—	10	Self
TM21	Frustration	Normal	Physical	—	100	20	Normal
TM27	Return	Normal	Physical	—	100	20	Normal
TM32	Double Team	Normal	Status	—	—	15	Self
TM40	Aerial Ace	Flying	Physical	60	—	20	Normal
TM42	Facade	Normal	Physical	70	100	20	Normal
TM44	Rest	Psychic	Status	—	—	10	Self
TM45	Attract	Normal	Status	—	100	15	Normal
TM46	Thief	Dark	Physical	60	100	25	Normal
TM48	Round	Normal	Special	60	100	15	Normal
TM49	Echoed Voice	Normal	Special	40	100	15	Normal
TM51	Steel Wing	Steel	Physical	70	90	25	Normal
TM67	Retaliate	Normal	Physical	70	100	5	Normal
TM68	Giga Impact	Normal	Physical	150	90	5	Normal
TM87	Swagger	Normal	Status	—	90	15	Normal
TM88	Sleep Talk	Normal	Status	—	—	10	Self
TM89	U-turn	Bug	Physical	70	100	20	Normal
TM90	Substitute	Normal	Status	—	—	10	Self
TM100	Confide	Normal	Status	—	—	20	Normal
HM02	Fly	Flying	Physical	90	95	15	Normal

No.	Name	Type	Kind	Pow.	Acc.	PP	Range

● MOVES TAUGHT BY PEOPLE

Name	Type	Kind	Pow.	Acc.	PP	Range

AFTER THE HALL OF FAME

CENTRAL KALOS

COASTAL KALOS

101 | Staraptor

MOUNTAIN KALOS

ADVENTURE DATA

AFTER THE HALL OF FAME

CENTRAL KALOS

COASTAL KALOS

102

Stunky

MOUNTAIN KALOS

ADVENTURE DATA

Coastal Kalos 102

Skunk Pokémon

✓ Stunky

HEIGHT: 1'04" WEIGHT: 42.3 lbs.
GENDER: ♂/♀

X It sprays a foul fluid from its rear. Its stench spreads over a mile radius, driving Pokémon away.

Y It protects itself by spraying a noxious fluid from its rear. The stench lingers for 24 hours.

TYPE Poison Dark

ABILITIES
Stench
Aftermath

HIDDEN ABILITY
Keen Eye

STAT GROWTH RATES

HP	■■■
Attack	■■■
Defense	■■
Sp. Atk	■■
Sp. Def	■■
Speed	■■■■

EGG GROUP
Field

EVOLUTION

Lv. 34

Stunky → Skuntank

ITEMS SOMETIMES HELD BY WILD POKÉMON
None

Damage taken in normal battles	
Normal	×1
Fire	×1
Water	×1
Grass	×0.5
Electric	×1
Ice	×1
Fighting	×1
Poison	×0.5
Ground	×2
Flying	×1
Psychic	×0
Bug	×1
Rock	×1
Ghost	×0.5
Dragon	×1
Dark	×0.5
Steel	×1
Fairy	×1

Damage taken in Inverse Battles	
Normal	×1
Fire	×1
Water	×1
Grass	×2
Electric	×1
Ice	×1
Fighting	×1
Poison	×2
Ground	×0.5
Flying	×1
Psychic	×1
Bug	×1
Rock	×1
Ghost	×2
Dragon	×1
Dark	×2
Steel	×1
Fairy	×1

Can be used in	
Inverse Battle	Battle Institute
—	Battle Maison
Battle Chateau	Random Matchup

Same form for ♂/♀

How to obtain for your Coastal Kalos Pokédex

❶ Catch in the tall grass on Route 11.
❷ Catch in a Horde Encounter on Route 11.

❶ Catch in the tall grass on Route 11.
❷ Catch in a Horde Encounter on Route 11.

● LEVEL-UP MOVES

Lv.	Name	Type	Kind	Pow.	Acc.	PP	Range
1	Scratch	Normal	Physical	40	100	35	Normal
1	Focus Energy	Normal	Status	—	—	30	Self
4	Poison Gas	Poison	Status	—	90	40	Many Others
7	Screech	Normal	Status	—	85	40	Normal
10	Fury Swipes	Normal	Physical	18	80	15	Normal
14	Smokescreen	Normal	Status	—	100	20	Normal
18	Feint	Normal	Physical	30	100	10	Normal
22	Slash	Normal	Physical	70	100	20	Normal
27	Toxic	Poison	Status	—	90	10	Normal
32	Acid Spray	Poison	Special	40	100	20	Normal
37	Night Slash	Dark	Physical	70	100	15	Normal
43	Memento	Dark	Status	—	100	10	Normal
46	Belch	Poison	Special	120	90	10	Normal
49	Explosion	Normal	Physical	250	100	5	Adjacent

● TM & HM MOVES

No.	Name	Type	Kind	Pow.	Acc.	PP	Range
TM01	Hone Claws	Dark	Status	—	—	15	Self
TM05	Roar	Normal	Status	—	—	20	Normal
TM06	Toxic	Poison	Status	—	90	10	Normal
TM09	Venoshock	Poison	Special	65	100	10	Normal
TM10	Hidden Power	Normal	Special	60	100	15	Normal
TM11	Sunny Day	Fire	Status	—	—	5	Both Sides
TM12	Taunt	Dark	Status	—	100	20	Normal
TM17	Protect	Normal	Status	—	—	10	Self
TM18	Rain Dance	Water	Status	—	—	5	Both Sides
TM21	Frustration	Normal	Physical	—	100	20	Normal
TM27	Return	Normal	Physical	—	100	20	Normal
TM28	Dig	Ground	Physical	80	100	10	Normal
TM30	Shadow Ball	Ghost	Special	80	100	15	Normal
TM32	Double Team	Normal	Status	—	—	15	Self
TM35	Flamethrower	Fire	Special	90	100	15	Normal
TM36	Sludge Bomb	Poison	Special	90	100	10	Normal
TM38	Fire Blast	Fire	Special	110	85	5	Normal
TM41	Torment	Dark	Status	—	100	15	Normal
TM42	Facade	Normal	Physical	70	100	20	Normal
TM44	Rest	Psychic	Status	—	—	10	Self
TM45	Attract	Normal	Status	—	100	15	Normal
TM46	Thief	Dark	Physical	60	100	25	Normal
TM48	Round	Normal	Special	60	100	15	Normal
TM59	Incinerate	Fire	Special	60	100	15	Many Others
TM64	Explosion	Normal	Physical	250	100	5	Adjacent
TM65	Shadow Claw	Ghost	Physical	70	100	15	Normal
TM66	Payback	Dark	Physical	50	100	10	Normal
TM87	Swagger	Normal	Status	—	90	15	Normal
TM88	Sleep Talk	Normal	Status	—	—	10	Self
TM90	Substitute	Normal	Status	—	—	10	Self
TM94	Rock Smash	Fighting	Physical	40	100	15	Normal
TM95	Snarl	Dark	Special	55	95	15	Many Others
TM97	Dark Pulse	Dark	Special	80	100	15	Normal

No.	Name	Type	Kind	Pow.	Acc.	PP	Range
TM100	Confide	Normal	Status	—	—	20	Normal
HM01	Cut	Normal	Physical	50	95	30	Normal

● MOVES TAUGHT BY PEOPLE

Name	Type	Kind	Pow.	Acc.	PP	Range

● EGG MOVES

Name	Type	Kind	Pow.	Acc.	PP	Range
Pursuit	Dark	Physical	40	100	20	Normal
Leer	Normal	Status	—	100	30	Many Others
Smog	Poison	Special	30	70	20	Normal
Double-Edge	Normal	Physical	120	100	15	Normal
Crunch	Dark	Physical	80	100	15	Normal
Scary Face	Normal	Status	—	100	10	Normal
Astonish	Ghost	Physical	30	100	15	Normal
Punishment	Dark	Physical	—	100	5	Normal
Haze	Ice	Status	—	—	30	Both Sides
Iron Tail	Steel	Physical	100	75	15	Normal
Foul Play	Dark	Physical	95	100	15	Normal
Flame Burst	Fire	Special	70	100	15	Normal
Play Rough	Fairy	Physical	90	90	10	Normal

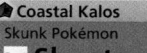

Coastal Kalos — 103

Skunk Pokémon

☑ **Skuntank**

HEIGHT: 3'03" WEIGHT: 83.8 lbs.
GENDER: ♂/♀

X — It sprays a vile-smelling fluid from the tip of its tail to attack. Its range is over 160 feet.

Y — It sprays a stinky fluid from its tail. The fluid smells worse the longer it is allowed to fester.

TYPE **Poison** **Dark**

ABILITIES
Stench
Aftermath

HIDDEN ABILITY
Keen Eye

STAT GROWTH RATES
HP	▪▪▪
Attack	▪▪▪▪▪
Defense	▪▪▪
Sp. Atk	▪▪▪
Sp. Def	▪▪▪
Speed	▪▪▪▪▪

EGG GROUP
Field

EVOLUTION

Stunky → Lv. 34 → Skuntank

ITEMS SOMETIMES HELD BY WILD POKÉMON
None

Damage taken in normal battles		Damage taken in Inverse Battles	
Normal	×1	Normal	×1
Fire	×1	Fire	×1
Water	×1	Water	×1
Grass	×0.5	Grass	×2
Electric	×1	Electric	×1
Ice	×1	Ice	×1
Fighting	×1	Fighting	×1
Poison	×0.5	Poison	×2
Ground	×2	Ground	×0.5
Flying	×1	Flying	×1
Psychic	×0	Psychic	×1
Bug	×1	Bug	×1
Rock	×1	Rock	×1
Ghost	×0.5	Ghost	×2
Dragon	×1	Dragon	×1
Dark	×0.5	Dark	×2
Steel	×1	Steel	×1
Fairy	×1	Fairy	×1

Can be used in	
Inverse Battle	Battle Institute
—	Battle Maison
Battle Chateau	Random Matchup

Same form for ♂/♀

How to obtain for your Coastal Kalos Pokédex

Level up Stunky to Lv. 34. Level up Stunky to Lv. 34.

● LEVEL-UP MOVES

Lv.	Name	Type	Kind	Pow.	Acc.	PP	Range
1	Scratch	Normal	Physical	40	100	35	Normal
1	Focus Energy	Normal	Status	—	—	30	Self
1	Poison Gas	Poison	Status	—	90	40	Many Others
4	Poison Gas	Poison	Status	—	90	40	Many Others
7	Screech	Normal	Status	—	85	40	Normal
9	Fury Swipes	Normal	Physical	18	80	15	Normal
14	Smokescreen	Normal	Status	—	100	20	Normal
18	Feint	Normal	Physical	30	100	10	Normal
22	Slash	Normal	Physical	70	100	20	Normal
27	Toxic	Poison	Status	—	90	10	Normal
32	Acid Spray	Poison	Special	40	100	20	Normal
34	Flamethrower	Fire	Special	90	100	15	Normal
41	Night Slash	Dark	Physical	70	100	15	Normal
51	Memento	Dark	Status	—	100	10	Normal
56	Belch	Poison	Special	120	90	10	Normal
61	Explosion	Normal	Physical	250	100	5	Adjacent

● TM & HM MOVES

No.	Name	Type	Kind	Pow.	Acc.	PP	Range
TM01	Hone Claws	Dark	Status	—	—	15	Self
TM05	Roar	Normal	Status	—	—	20	Normal
TM06	Toxic	Poison	Status	—	90	10	Normal
TM09	Venoshock	Poison	Special	65	100	10	Normal
TM10	Hidden Power	Normal	Special	60	100	15	Normal
TM11	Sunny Day	Fire	Status	—	—	5	Both Sides
TM12	Taunt	Dark	Status	—	100	20	Normal
TM15	Hyper Beam	Normal	Special	150	90	5	Normal
TM17	Protect	Normal	Status	—	—	10	Self
TM18	Rain Dance	Water	Status	—	—	5	Both Sides
TM21	Frustration	Normal	Physical	—	100	20	Normal
TM27	Return	Normal	Physical	—	100	20	Normal
TM28	Dig	Ground	Physical	80	100	10	Normal
TM30	Shadow Ball	Ghost	Special	80	100	15	Normal
TM32	Double Team	Normal	Status	—	—	15	Self
TM35	Flamethrower	Fire	Special	90	100	15	Normal
TM36	Sludge Bomb	Poison	Special	90	100	10	Normal
TM38	Fire Blast	Fire	Special	110	85	5	Normal
TM41	Torment	Dark	Status	—	100	15	Normal
TM42	Facade	Normal	Physical	70	100	20	Normal
TM44	Rest	Psychic	Status	—	—	10	Self
TM45	Attract	Normal	Status	—	100	15	Normal
TM46	Thief	Dark	Physical	60	100	25	Normal
TM48	Round	Normal	Special	60	100	15	Normal
TM59	Incinerate	Fire	Special	60	100	15	Many Others
TM64	Explosion	Normal	Physical	250	100	5	Adjacent
TM65	Shadow Claw	Ghost	Physical	70	100	15	Normal
TM66	Payback	Dark	Physical	50	100	10	Normal
TM68	Giga Impact	Normal	Physical	150	90	5	Normal
TM84	Poison Jab	Poison	Physical	80	100	20	Normal
TM87	Swagger	Normal	Status	—	90	15	Normal
TM88	Sleep Talk	Normal	Status	—	—	10	Self
TM90	Substitute	Normal	Status	—	—	10	Self

No.	Name	Type	Kind	Pow.	Acc.	PP	Range
TM94	Rock Smash	Fighting	Physical	40	100	15	Normal
TM95	Snarl	Dark	Special	55	95	15	Many Others
TM97	Dark Pulse	Dark	Special	80	100	15	Normal
TM100	Confide	Normal	Status	—	—	20	Normal
HM01	Cut	Normal	Physical	50	95	30	Normal
HM04	Strength	Normal	Physical	80	100	15	Normal

● MOVES TAUGHT BY PEOPLE

Name	Type	Kind	Pow.	Acc.	PP	Range

AFTER THE HALL OF FAME

CENTRAL KALOS

COASTAL KALOS

103 | Skuntank

MOUNTAIN KALOS

ADVENTURE DATA

AFTER THE HALL OF FAME

CENTRAL KALOS

COASTAL KALOS

104

Nidoran ♀

MOUNTAIN KALOS

ADVENTURE DATA

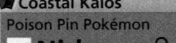

Coastal Kalos 104
Poison Pin Pokémon
☑ Nidoran ♀

HEIGHT: 1'04" WEIGHT: 15.4 lbs.
GENDER: ♀

X Although small, its venomous barbs render this Pokémon dangerous. The female has smaller horns.

Y Small and very docile, it protects itself with its small, poisonous horn when attacked.

TYPE **Poison**

ABILITIES
Poison Point
Rivalry

HIDDEN ABILITY
Hustle

STAT GROWTH RATES
HP ▪▪
Attack ▪▪
Defense ▪▪
Sp. Atk ▪▪
Sp. Def ▪▪
Speed ▪▪

EGG GROUPS
Monster, Field

EVOLUTION

Nidoran ♀ — Lv. 16 → Nidorina — Moon Stone → Nidoqueen

ITEMS SOMETIMES HELD BY WILD POKÉMON
None

Damage taken in normal battles		Damage taken in Inverse Battles	
Normal	×1	Normal	×1
Fire	×1	Fire	×1
Water	×1	Water	×1
Grass	×0.5	Grass	×2
Electric	×1	Electric	×1
Ice	×1	Ice	×1
Fighting	×0.5	Fighting	×2
Poison	×0.5	Poison	×2
Ground	×2	Ground	×0.5
Flying	×1	Flying	×1
Psychic	×2	Psychic	×0.5
Bug	×0.5	Bug	×2
Rock	×1	Rock	×1
Ghost	×1	Ghost	×1
Dragon	×1	Dragon	×1
Dark	×1	Dark	×1
Steel	×1	Steel	×1
Fairy	×0.5	Fairy	×2

Can be used in	
Inverse Battle	Battle Institute
—	Battle Maison
Battle Chateau	Random Matchup

♀

How to obtain for your Coastal Kalos Pokédex

Catch in a Horde Encounter on Route 11.	Catch in a Horde Encounter on Route 11.

● LEVEL-UP MOVES

Lv.	Name	Type	Kind	Pow.	Acc.	PP	Range
1	Growl	Normal	Status	—	100	40	Many Others
1	Scratch	Normal	Physical	40	100	35	Normal
7	Tail Whip	Normal	Status	—	100	30	Many Others
9	Double Kick	Fighting	Physical	30	100	30	Normal
13	Poison Sting	Poison	Physical	15	100	35	Normal
19	Fury Swipes	Normal	Physical	18	80	15	Normal
21	Bite	Dark	Physical	60	100	25	Normal
25	Helping Hand	Normal	Status	—	—	20	1 Ally
31	Toxic Spikes	Poison	Status	—	—	20	Other Side
33	Flatter	Dark	Status	—	100	15	Normal
37	Crunch	Dark	Physical	80	100	15	Normal
43	Captivate	Normal	Status	—	100	20	Many Others
45	Poison Fang	Poison	Physical	50	100	15	Normal

● TM & HM MOVES

No.	Name	Type	Kind	Pow.	Acc.	PP	Range
TM01	Hone Claws	Dark	Status	—	—	15	Self
TM06	Toxic	Poison	Status	—	90	10	Normal
TM09	Venoshock	Poison	Special	65	100	10	Normal
TM10	Hidden Power	Normal	Special	60	100	15	Normal
TM11	Sunny Day	Fire	Status	—	—	5	Both Sides
TM13	Ice Beam	Ice	Special	90	100	10	Normal
TM14	Blizzard	Ice	Special	110	70	5	Many Others
TM17	Protect	Normal	Status	—	—	10	Self
TM18	Rain Dance	Water	Status	—	—	5	Both Sides
TM21	Frustration	Normal	Physical	—	100	20	Normal
TM24	Thunderbolt	Electric	Special	90	100	15	Normal
TM25	Thunder	Electric	Special	110	70	10	Normal
TM27	Return	Normal	Physical	—	100	20	Normal
TM28	Dig	Ground	Physical	80	100	10	Normal
TM32	Double Team	Normal	Status	—	—	15	Self
TM36	Sludge Bomb	Poison	Special	90	100	10	Normal
TM40	Aerial Ace	Flying	Physical	60	—	20	Normal
TM42	Facade	Normal	Physical	70	100	20	Normal
TM44	Rest	Psychic	Status	—	—	10	Self
TM45	Attract	Normal	Status	—	100	15	Normal
TM46	Thief	Dark	Physical	60	100	25	Normal
TM48	Round	Normal	Special	60	100	15	Normal
TM49	Echoed Voice	Normal	Special	40	100	15	Normal
TM65	Shadow Claw	Ghost	Physical	70	100	15	Normal
TM84	Poison Jab	Poison	Physical	80	100	20	Normal
TM87	Swagger	Normal	Status	—	90	15	Normal
TM88	Sleep Talk	Normal	Status	—	—	10	Self
TM90	Substitute	Normal	Status	—	—	10	Self
TM94	Rock Smash	Fighting	Physical	40	100	15	Normal
TM100	Confide	Normal	Status	—	—	20	Normal
HM01	Cut	Normal	Physical	50	95	30	Normal
HM04	Strength	Normal	Physical	80	100	15	Normal

No.	Name	Type	Kind	Pow.	Acc.	PP	Range

● MOVES TAUGHT BY PEOPLE

Name	Type	Kind	Pow.	Acc.	PP	Range

● EGG MOVES

Name	Type	Kind	Pow.	Acc.	PP	Range
Supersonic	Normal	Status	—	55	20	Normal
Disable	Normal	Status	—	100	20	Normal
Take Down	Normal	Physical	90	85	20	Normal
Focus Energy	Normal	Status	—	—	30	Self
Charm	Fairy	Status	—	100	20	Normal
Counter	Fighting	Physical	—	100	20	Varies
Beat Up	Dark	Physical	—	100	10	Normal
Pursuit	Dark	Physical	40	100	20	Normal
Skull Bash	Normal	Physical	130	100	10	Normal
Iron Tail	Steel	Physical	100	75	15	Normal
Poison Tail	Poison	Physical	50	100	25	Normal
Endure	Normal	Status	—	—	10	Self
Chip Away	Normal	Physical	70	100	20	Normal
Venom Drench	Poison	Status	—	100	20	Many Others

AFTER THE HALL OF FAME

CENTRAL KALOS

COASTAL KALOS

105 | Nidorina

MOUNTAIN KALOS

ADVENTURE DATA

Coastal Kalos
Poison Pin Pokémon **105**

 Nidorina

HEIGHT: 2'07" WEIGHT: 44.1 lbs.
GENDER: ♀

 The female has a gentle temperament. It emits ultrasonic cries that have the power to befuddle foes.

The female has a gentle temperament. It emits ultrasonic cries that have the power to befuddle foes.

When feeding its young, it first chews the food into a paste, then spits it out for the offspring.

 TYPE **Poison**

ABILITIES
Poison Point
Rivalry

HIDDEN ABILITY
Hustle

STAT GROWTH RATES
HP	■■■
Attack	■■■
Defense	■■■
Sp. Atk	■■
Sp. Def	■■
Speed	■■■

EGG GROUP
No Eggs Discovered

 EVOLUTION

Lv. 16   Moon Stone

Nidoran ♀   Nidorina   Nidoqueen

ITEMS SOMETIMES HELD BY WILD POKÉMON
None

Damage taken in normal battles	
Normal	×1
Fire	×1
Water	×1
Grass	×0.5
Electric	×1
Ice	×1
Fighting	×0.5
Poison	×0.5
Ground	×2
Flying	×1
Psychic	×2
Bug	×0.5
Rock	×1
Ghost	×1
Dragon	×1
Dark	×1
Steel	×1
Fairy	×0.5

Damage taken in Inverse Battles	
Normal	×1
Fire	×1
Water	×1
Grass	×2
Electric	×1
Ice	×1
Fighting	×2
Poison	×2
Ground	×0.5
Flying	×1
Psychic	×0.5
Bug	×2
Rock	×1
Ghost	×1
Dragon	×1
Dark	×1
Steel	×1
Fairy	×2

Can be used in	
Inverse Battle	Battle Institute
—	Battle Maison
Battle Chateau	Random Matchup

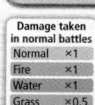 ♀

 ♀

How to obtain for your Coastal Kalos Pokédex

❶ Catch in the tall grass on Route 11.
❷ Level up Nidoran ♀ to Lv. 16.

❶ Catch in the tall grass on Route 11.
❷ Level up Nidoran ♀ to Lv. 16.

● LEVEL-UP MOVES

Lv.	Name	Type	Kind	Pow.	Acc.	PP	Range
1	Growl	Normal	Status	—	100	40	Many Others
1	Scratch	Normal	Physical	40	100	35	Normal
7	Tail Whip	Normal	Status	—	100	30	Many Others
9	Double Kick	Fighting	Physical	30	100	30	Normal
13	Poison Sting	Poison	Physical	15	100	35	Normal
20	Fury Swipes	Normal	Physical	18	80	15	Normal
23	Bite	Dark	Physical	60	100	25	Normal
28	Helping Hand	Normal	Status	—	—	20	1 Ally
35	Toxic Spikes	Poison	Status	—	—	20	Other Side
38	Flatter	Dark	Status	—	100	15	Normal
43	Crunch	Dark	Physical	80	100	15	Normal
50	Captivate	Normal	Status	—	100	20	Many Others
58	Poison Fang	Poison	Physical	50	100	15	Normal

● TM & HM MOVES

No.	Name	Type	Kind	Pow.	Acc.	PP	Range
TM01	Hone Claws	Dark	Status	—	—	15	Self
TM06	Toxic	Poison	Status	—	90	10	Normal
TM09	Venoshock	Poison	Special	65	100	10	Normal
TM10	Hidden Power	Normal	Special	60	100	15	Normal
TM11	Sunny Day	Fire	Status	—	—	5	Both Sides
TM13	Ice Beam	Ice	Special	90	100	10	Normal
TM14	Blizzard	Ice	Special	110	70	5	Many Others
TM17	Protect	Normal	Status	—	—	10	Self
TM18	Rain Dance	Water	Status	—	—	5	Both Sides
TM21	Frustration	Normal	Physical	—	100	20	Normal
TM24	Thunderbolt	Electric	Special	90	100	15	Normal
TM25	Thunder	Electric	Special	110	70	10	Normal
TM27	Return	Normal	Physical	—	100	20	Normal
TM28	Dig	Ground	Physical	80	100	10	Normal
TM32	Double Team	Normal	Status	—	—	15	Self
TM36	Sludge Bomb	Poison	Special	90	100	10	Normal
TM40	Aerial Ace	Flying	Physical	60	—	20	Normal
TM42	Facade	Normal	Physical	70	100	20	Normal
TM44	Rest	Psychic	Status	—	—	10	Self
TM45	Attract	Normal	Status	—	100	15	Normal
TM46	Thief	Dark	Physical	60	100	25	Normal
TM48	Round	Normal	Special	60	100	15	Normal
TM49	Echoed Voice	Normal	Special	40	100	15	Normal
TM65	Shadow Claw	Ghost	Physical	70	100	15	Normal
TM84	Poison Jab	Poison	Physical	80	100	20	Normal
TM87	Swagger	Normal	Status	—	90	15	Normal
TM88	Sleep Talk	Normal	Status	—	—	10	Self
TM90	Substitute	Normal	Status	—	—	10	Self
TM94	Rock Smash	Fighting	Physical	40	100	15	Normal
TM100	Confide	Normal	Status	—	—	20	Normal
HM01	Cut	Normal	Physical	50	95	30	Normal
HM04	Strength	Normal	Physical	80	100	15	Normal

No.	Name	Type	Kind	Pow.	Acc.	PP	Range

● MOVES TAUGHT BY PEOPLE

Name	Type	Kind	Pow.	Acc.	PP	Range

AFTER THE HALL OF FAME

CENTRAL KALOS

COASTAL KALOS

106

Nidoqueen

MOUNTAIN KALOS

ADVENTURE DATA

Coastal Kalos — 106

Drill Pokémon

Nidoqueen

HEIGHT: 4'03" WEIGHT: 132.3 lbs.
GENDER: ♀

TYPE Poison Ground

ABILITIES
Poison Point
Rivalry

HIDDEN ABILITY
Sheer Force

STAT GROWTH RATES
HP	▪▪▪▪
Attack	▪▪▪▪▪
Defense	▪▪▪▪
Sp. Atk	▪▪▪▪
Sp. Def	▪▪▪▪
Speed	▪▪▪▪

EGG GROUP
No Eggs Discovered

It uses its scaly, rugged body to seal the entrance of its nest and protect its young from predators.

The body is covered by stiff, needlelike scales. If it becomes excited, the needles bristle outwards.

EVOLUTION

Lv. 16 — Moon Stone

Nidoran ♀ → Nidorina → Nidoqueen

ITEMS SOMETIMES HELD BY WILD POKÉMON
None

♀

Damage taken in normal battles	
Normal	×1
Fire	×1
Water	×2
Grass	×1
Electric	×0
Ice	×2
Fighting	×0.5
Poison	×0.25
Ground	×2
Flying	×1
Psychic	×2
Bug	×0.5
Rock	×0.5
Ghost	×1
Dragon	×1
Dark	×1
Steel	×1
Fairy	×0.5

Damage taken in Inverse Battles	
Normal	×1
Fire	×1
Water	×0.5
Grass	×1
Electric	×2
Ice	×0.5
Fighting	×2
Poison	×4
Ground	×0.5
Flying	×1
Psychic	×0.5
Bug	×2
Rock	×2
Ghost	×1
Dragon	×1
Dark	×1
Steel	×1
Fairy	×2

Can be used in	
Inverse Battle	Battle Institute
—	Battle Maison
Battle Chateau	Random Matchup

How to obtain for your Coastal Kalos Pokédex

Use a Moon Stone on Nidorina. | Use a Moon Stone on Nidorina.

X Y

LEVEL-UP MOVES

Lv.	Name	Type	Kind	Pow.	Acc.	PP	Range
1	Superpower	Fighting	Physical	120	100	5	Normal
1	Scratch	Normal	Physical	40	100	35	Normal
1	Tail Whip	Normal	Status	—	100	30	Many Others
1	Double Kick	Fighting	Physical	30	100	30	Normal
1	Poison Sting	Poison	Physical	15	100	35	Normal
23	Chip Away	Normal	Physical	70	100	20	Normal
35	Body Slam	Normal	Physical	85	100	15	Normal
43	Earth Power	Ground	Special	90	100	10	Normal
58	Superpower	Fighting	Physical	120	100	5	Normal

TM & HM MOVES

No.	Name	Type	Kind	Pow.	Acc.	PP	Range
TM01	Hone Claws	Dark	Status	—	—	15	Self
TM05	Roar	Normal	Status	—	—	20	Normal
TM06	Toxic	Poison	Status	—	90	10	Normal
TM09	Venoshock	Poison	Special	65	100	10	Normal
TM10	Hidden Power	Normal	Special	60	100	15	Normal
TM11	Sunny Day	Fire	Status	—	—	5	Both Sides
TM12	Taunt	Dark	Status	—	100	20	Normal
TM13	Ice Beam	Ice	Special	90	100	10	Normal
TM14	Blizzard	Ice	Special	110	70	5	Many Others
TM15	Hyper Beam	Normal	Special	150	90	5	Normal
TM17	Protect	Normal	Status	—	—	10	Self
TM18	Rain Dance	Water	Status	—	—	5	Both Sides
TM21	Frustration	Normal	Physical	—	100	20	Normal
TM23	Smack Down	Rock	Physical	50	100	15	Normal
TM24	Thunderbolt	Electric	Special	90	100	15	Normal
TM25	Thunder	Electric	Special	110	70	10	Normal
TM26	Earthquake	Ground	Physical	100	100	10	Adjacent
TM27	Return	Normal	Physical	—	100	20	Normal
TM28	Dig	Ground	Physical	80	100	10	Normal
TM30	Shadow Ball	Ghost	Special	80	100	15	Normal
TM31	Brick Break	Fighting	Physical	75	100	15	Normal
TM32	Double Team	Normal	Status	—	—	15	Self
TM34	Sludge Wave	Poison	Special	95	100	10	Adjacent
TM35	Flamethrower	Fire	Special	90	100	15	Normal
TM36	Sludge Bomb	Poison	Special	90	100	10	Normal
TM37	Sandstorm	Rock	Status	—	—	10	Both Sides
TM38	Fire Blast	Fire	Special	110	85	5	Normal
TM39	Rock Tomb	Rock	Physical	60	95	15	Normal
TM40	Aerial Ace	Flying	Physical	60	—	20	Normal
TM41	Torment	Dark	Status	—	100	15	Normal
TM42	Facade	Normal	Physical	70	100	20	Normal
TM44	Rest	Psychic	Status	—	—	10	Self
TM45	Attract	Normal	Status	—	100	15	Normal

No.	Name	Type	Kind	Pow.	Acc.	PP	Range
TM46	Thief	Dark	Physical	60	100	25	Normal
TM48	Round	Normal	Special	60	100	15	Normal
TM49	Echoed Voice	Normal	Special	40	100	15	Normal
TM52	Focus Blast	Fighting	Special	120	70	5	Normal
TM56	Fling	Dark	Physical	—	100	10	Normal
TM59	Incinerate	Fire	Special	60	100	15	Many Others
TM60	Quash	Dark	Status	—	100	15	Normal
TM65	Shadow Claw	Ghost	Physical	70	100	15	Normal
TM68	Giga Impact	Normal	Physical	150	90	5	Normal
TM71	Stone Edge	Rock	Physical	100	80	5	Normal
TM78	Bulldoze	Ground	Physical	60	100	20	Adjacent
TM80	Rock Slide	Rock	Physical	75	90	10	Many Others
TM82	Dragon Tail	Dragon	Physical	60	90	10	Normal
TM84	Poison Jab	Poison	Physical	80	100	20	Normal
TM87	Swagger	Normal	Status	—	90	15	Normal
TM88	Sleep Talk	Normal	Status	—	—	10	Self
TM90	Substitute	Normal	Status	—	—	10	Self
TM94	Rock Smash	Fighting	Physical	40	100	15	Normal
TM98	Power-Up Punch	Fighting	Physical	40	100	20	Normal
TM100	Confide	Normal	Status	—	—	20	Normal
HM01	Cut	Normal	Physical	50	95	30	Normal
HM03	Surf	Water	Special	90	100	15	Adjacent
HM04	Strength	Normal	Physical	80	100	15	Normal

MOVES TAUGHT BY PEOPLE

Name	Type	Kind	Pow.	Acc.	PP	Range

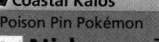

Coastal Kalos

Poison Pin Pokémon

107

☑ Nidoran♂

HEIGHT: 1'08" WEIGHT: 19.8 lbs.
GENDER: ♂

 It scans its surroundings by raising its ears out of the grass. Its toxic horn is for protection.

 Its large ears are flapped like wings when it is listening to distant sounds. It extends toxic barbs when angered.

TYPE Poison

ABILITIES
Poison Point
Rivalry

HIDDEN ABILITY
Hustle

STAT GROWTH RATES
HP	■■
Attack	■■■
Defense	■■
Sp. Atk	■■
Sp. Def	■■
Speed	■■■

EGG GROUPS
Monster, Field

⬆ EVOLUTION

Lv. 16   Moon Stone

Nidoran ♂   Nidorino   Nidoking

ITEMS SOMETIMES HELD BY WILD POKÉMON
None

Damage taken in normal battles	
Normal	×1
Fire	×1
Water	×1
Grass	×0.5
Electric	×1
Ice	×1
Fighting	×0.5
Poison	×0.5
Ground	×2
Flying	×1
Psychic	×2
Bug	×0.5
Rock	×1
Ghost	×1
Dragon	×1
Dark	×1
Steel	×1
Fairy	×0.5

Damage taken in Inverse Battles	
Normal	×1
Fire	×1
Water	×1
Grass	×2
Electric	×1
Ice	×1
Fighting	×2
Poison	×2
Ground	×0.5
Flying	×1
Psychic	×0.5
Bug	×2
Rock	×1
Ghost	×1
Dragon	×1
Dark	×1
Steel	×1
Fairy	×2

Can be used in	
Inverse Battle	Battle Institute
—	Battle Maison
Battle Chateau	Random Matchup

♂

How to obtain for your Coastal Kalos Pokédex

Catch in a Horde Encounter on Route 11.

Catch in a Horde Encounter on Route 11.

● LEVEL-UP MOVES

Lv.	Name	Type	Kind	Pow.	Acc.	PP	Range
1	Leer	Normal	Status	—	100	30	Many Others
1	Peck	Flying	Physical	35	100	35	Normal
7	Focus Energy	Normal	Status	—	—	30	Self
9	Double Kick	Fighting	Physical	30	100	30	Normal
13	Poison Sting	Poison	Physical	15	100	35	Normal
19	Fury Attack	Normal	Physical	15	85	20	Normal
21	Horn Attack	Normal	Physical	65	100	25	Normal
25	Helping Hand	Normal	Status	—	—	20	1 Ally
31	Toxic Spikes	Poison	Status	—	—	20	Other Side
33	Flatter	Dark	Status	—	100	15	Normal
37	Poison Jab	Poison	Physical	80	100	20	Normal
43	Captivate	Normal	Status	—	100	20	Many Others
45	Horn Drill	Normal	Physical	—	30	5	Normal

● TM & HM MOVES

No.	Name	Type	Kind	Pow.	Acc.	PP	Range
TM01	Hone Claws	Dark	Status	—	—	15	Self
TM06	Toxic	Poison	Status	—	90	10	Normal
TM09	Venoshock	Poison	Special	65	100	10	Normal
TM10	Hidden Power	Normal	Special	60	100	15	Normal
TM11	Sunny Day	Fire	Status	—	—	5	Both Sides
TM13	Ice Beam	Ice	Special	90	100	10	Normal
TM14	Blizzard	Ice	Special	110	70	5	Many Others
TM17	Protect	Normal	Status	—	—	10	Self
TM18	Rain Dance	Water	Status	—	—	5	Both Sides
TM21	Frustration	Normal	Physical	—	100	20	Normal
TM24	Thunderbolt	Electric	Special	90	100	15	Normal
TM25	Thunder	Electric	Special	110	70	10	Normal
TM27	Return	Normal	Physical	—	100	20	Normal
TM28	Dig	Ground	Physical	80	100	10	Normal
TM32	Double Team	Normal	Status	—	—	15	Self
TM36	Sludge Bomb	Poison	Special	90	100	10	Normal
TM42	Facade	Normal	Physical	70	100	20	Normal
TM44	Rest	Psychic	Status	—	—	10	Self
TM45	Attract	Normal	Status	—	100	15	Normal
TM46	Thief	Dark	Physical	60	100	25	Normal
TM48	Round	Normal	Special	60	100	15	Normal
TM49	Echoed Voice	Normal	Special	40	100	15	Normal
TM65	Shadow Claw	Ghost	Physical	70	100	15	Normal
TM84	Poison Jab	Poison	Physical	80	100	20	Normal
TM87	Swagger	Normal	Status	—	90	15	Normal
TM88	Sleep Talk	Normal	Status	—	—	10	Self
TM90	Substitute	Normal	Status	—	—	10	Self
TM94	Rock Smash	Fighting	Physical	40	100	15	Normal
TM100	Confide	Normal	Status	—	—	20	Normal
HM01	Cut	Normal	Physical	50	95	30	Normal
HM04	Strength	Normal	Physical	80	100	15	Normal

● MOVES TAUGHT BY PEOPLE

Name	Type	Kind	Pow.	Acc.	PP	Range

● EGG MOVES

Name	Type	Kind	Pow.	Acc.	PP	Range
Counter	Fighting	Physical	—	100	20	Varies
Disable	Normal	Status	—	100	20	Normal
Supersonic	Normal	Status	—	55	20	Normal
Take Down	Normal	Physical	90	85	20	Normal
Amnesia	Psychic	Status	—	—	20	Self
Confusion	Psychic	Special	50	100	25	Normal
Beat Up	Dark	Physical	—	100	10	Normal
Sucker Punch	Dark	Physical	80	100	5	Normal
Head Smash	Rock	Physical	150	80	5	Normal
Iron Tail	Steel	Physical	100	75	15	Normal
Poison Tail	Poison	Physical	50	100	25	Normal
Endure	Normal	Status	—	—	10	Self
Chip Away	Normal	Physical	70	100	20	Normal
Venom Drench	Poison	Status	—	100	20	Many Others

AFTER THE HALL OF FAME

CENTRAL KALOS

COASTAL KALOS

107 | Nidoran ♂

MOUNTAIN KALOS

ADVENTURE DATA

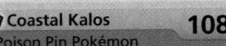

Coastal Kalos 108
Poison Pin Pokémon
✓ Nidorino

HEIGHT: 2'11" WEIGHT: 43.0 lbs.
GENDER: ♂

TYPE	Poison

ABILITIES
Poison Point
Rivalry

HIDDEN ABILITY
Hustle

STAT GROWTH RATES
HP	■■■
Attack	■■■
Defense	■■■
Sp. Atk	■■■
Sp. Def	■■
Speed	■■■■

EGG GROUPS
Monster, Field

X It raises its big ears to check its surroundings. If it senses anything, it attacks immediately.

Y An aggressive Pokémon that is quick to attack. The horn on its head secretes a powerful venom.

⬆ EVOLUTION

Lv. 16   Moon Stone

Nidoran ♂   Nidorino   Nidoking

ITEMS SOMETIMES HELD BY WILD POKÉMON
None

Damage taken in normal battles		Damage taken in Inverse Battles	
Normal	×1	Normal	×1
Fire	×1	Fire	×1
Water	×1	Water	×1
Grass	×0.5	Grass	×2
Electric	×1	Electric	×1
Ice	×1	Ice	×1
Fighting	×0.5	Fighting	×2
Poison	×0.5	Poison	×2
Ground	×2	Ground	×0.5
Flying	×1	Flying	×1
Psychic	×2	Psychic	×0.5
Bug	×0.5	Bug	×2
Rock	×1	Rock	×1
Ghost	×1	Ghost	×1
Dragon	×1	Dragon	×1
Dark	×1	Dark	×1
Steel	×1	Steel	×1
Fairy	×0.5	Fairy	×2

Can be used in	
Inverse Battle	Battle Institute
—	Battle Maison
Battle Chateau	Random Matchup

♂

How to obtain for your Coastal Kalos Pokédex

❶ Catch in the tall grass on Route 11.
❷ Level up Nidoran ♂ to Lv. 16.

❶ Catch in the tall grass on Route 11.
❷ Level up Nidoran ♂ to Lv. 16.

● LEVEL-UP MOVES

Lv.	Name	Type	Kind	Pow.	Acc.	PP	Range
1	Leer	Normal	Status	—	100	30	Many Others
1	Peck	Flying	Physical	35	100	35	Normal
7	Focus Energy	Normal	Status	—	—	30	Self
9	Double Kick	Fighting	Physical	30	100	30	Normal
13	Poison Sting	Poison	Physical	15	100	35	Normal
20	Fury Attack	Normal	Physical	15	85	20	Normal
23	Horn Attack	Normal	Physical	65	100	25	Normal
28	Helping Hand	Normal	Status	—	—	20	1 Ally
35	Toxic Spikes	Poison	Status	—	—	20	Other Side
38	Flatter	Dark	Status	—	100	15	Normal
43	Poison Jab	Poison	Physical	80	100	20	Normal
50	Captivate	Normal	Status	—	100	20	Many Others
58	Horn Drill	Normal	Physical	—	30	5	Normal

● TM & HM MOVES

No.	Name	Type	Kind	Pow.	Acc.	PP	Range
TM01	Hone Claws	Dark	Status	—	—	15	Self
TM06	Toxic	Poison	Status	—	90	10	Normal
TM09	Venoshock	Poison	Special	65	100	10	Normal
TM10	Hidden Power	Normal	Special	60	100	15	Normal
TM11	Sunny Day	Fire	Status	—	—	5	Both Sides
TM13	Ice Beam	Ice	Special	90	100	10	Normal
TM14	Blizzard	Ice	Special	110	70	5	Many Others
TM17	Protect	Normal	Status	—	—	10	Self
TM18	Rain Dance	Water	Status	—	—	5	Both Sides
TM21	Frustration	Normal	Physical	—	100	20	Normal
TM24	Thunderbolt	Electric	Special	90	100	15	Normal
TM25	Thunder	Electric	Special	110	70	10	Normal
TM27	Return	Normal	Physical	—	100	20	Normal
TM28	Dig	Ground	Physical	80	100	10	Normal
TM32	Double Team	Normal	Status	—	—	15	Self
TM36	Sludge Bomb	Poison	Special	90	100	10	Normal
TM42	Facade	Normal	Physical	70	100	20	Normal
TM44	Rest	Psychic	Status	—	—	10	Self
TM45	Attract	Normal	Status	—	100	15	Normal
TM46	Thief	Dark	Physical	60	100	25	Normal
TM48	Round	Normal	Special	60	100	15	Normal
TM49	Echoed Voice	Normal	Special	40	100	15	Normal
TM65	Shadow Claw	Ghost	Physical	70	100	15	Normal
TM84	Poison Jab	Poison	Physical	80	100	20	Normal
TM87	Swagger	Normal	Status	—	90	15	Normal
TM88	Sleep Talk	Normal	Status	—	—	10	Self
TM90	Substitute	Normal	Status	—	—	10	Self
TM94	Rock Smash	Fighting	Physical	40	100	15	Normal
TM100	Confide	Normal	Status	—	—	20	Normal
HM01	Cut	Normal	Physical	50	95	30	Normal
HM04	Strength	Normal	Physical	80	100	15	Normal

No.	Name	Type	Kind	Pow.	Acc.	PP	Range

● MOVES TAUGHT BY PEOPLE

Name	Type	Kind	Pow.	Acc.	PP	Range

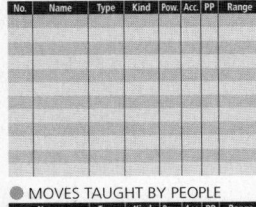

AFTER THE HALL OF FAME

CENTRAL KALOS

COASTAL KALOS

108

Nidorino

MOUNTAIN KALOS

ADVENTURE DATA

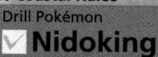

Coastal Kalos 109

Drill Pokémon

☑ Nidoking

HEIGHT: 4'07" WEIGHT: 136.7 lbs.
GENDER: ♂

TYPE Poison | Ground

ABILITIES
Poison Point
Rivalry

HIDDEN ABILITY
Sheer Force

 It is recognized by its rock-hard hide and its extended horn. Be careful with the horn, as it contains venom.

 One swing of its mighty tail can snap a telephone pole as if it were a matchstick.

STAT GROWTH RATES
HP	■■■
Attack	■■■■■
Defense	■■■
Sp. Atk	■■■■
Sp. Def	■■■
Speed	■■■■■

EGG GROUPS
Monster, Field

EVOLUTION

Lv. 16   Moon Stone

Nidoran ♂   Nidorino   Nidoking

ITEMS SOMETIMES HELD BY WILD POKÉMON
None

Damage taken in normal battles	
Normal	×1
Fire	×1
Water	×2
Grass	×1
Electric	×0
Ice	×2
Fighting	×0.5
Poison	×0.25
Ground	×2
Flying	×1
Psychic	×2
Bug	×0.5
Rock	×0.5
Ghost	×1
Dragon	×1
Dark	×1
Steel	×1
Fairy	×0.5

Damage taken in Inverse Battles	
Normal	×1
Fire	×1
Water	×0.5
Grass	×1
Electric	×2
Ice	×0.5
Fighting	×2
Poison	×4
Ground	×0.5
Flying	×1
Psychic	×0.5
Bug	×2
Rock	×2
Ghost	×1
Dragon	×1
Dark	×1
Steel	×1
Fairy	×2

Can be used in	
Inverse Battle	Battle Institute
—	Battle Maison
Battle Chateau	Random Matchup

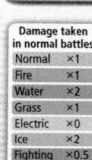

♂

How to obtain for your Coastal Kalos Pokédex

X: Use a Moon Stone on Nidorino.

Y: Use a Moon Stone on Nidorino.

● LEVEL-UP MOVES

Lv.	Name	Type	Kind	Pow.	Acc.	PP	Range
1	Megahorn	Bug	Physical	120	85	10	Normal
1	Peck	Flying	Physical	35	100	35	Normal
1	Focus Energy	Normal	Status	—	—	30	Self
1	Double Kick	Fighting	Physical	30	100	30	Normal
1	Poison Sting	Poison	Physical	15	100	35	Normal
23	Chip Away	Normal	Physical	70	100	20	Normal
35	Thrash	Normal	Physical	120	100	10	1 Random
43	Earth Power	Ground	Special	90	100	10	Normal
58	Megahorn	Bug	Physical	120	85	10	Normal

● TM & HM MOVES

No.	Name	Type	Kind	Pow.	Acc.	PP	Range
TM01	Hone Claws	Dark	Status	—	—	15	Self
TM05	Roar	Normal	Status	—	—	20	Normal
TM06	Toxic	Poison	Status	—	90	10	Normal
TM09	Venoshock	Poison	Special	65	100	10	Normal
TM10	Hidden Power	Normal	Special	60	100	15	Normal
TM11	Sunny Day	Fire	Status	—	—	5	Both Sides
TM12	Taunt	Dark	Status	—	100	20	Normal
TM13	Ice Beam	Ice	Special	90	100	10	Normal
TM14	Blizzard	Ice	Special	110	70	5	Many Others
TM15	Hyper Beam	Normal	Special	150	90	5	Normal
TM17	Protect	Normal	Status	—	—	10	Self
TM18	Rain Dance	Water	Status	—	—	5	Both Sides
TM21	Frustration	Normal	Physical	—	100	20	Normal
TM23	Smack Down	Rock	Physical	50	100	15	Normal
TM24	Thunderbolt	Electric	Special	90	100	15	Normal
TM25	Thunder	Electric	Special	110	70	10	Normal
TM26	Earthquake	Ground	Physical	100	100	10	Adjacent
TM27	Return	Normal	Physical	—	100	20	Normal
TM28	Dig	Ground	Physical	80	100	10	Normal
TM30	Shadow Ball	Ghost	Special	80	100	15	Normal
TM31	Brick Break	Fighting	Physical	75	100	15	Normal
TM32	Double Team	Normal	Status	—	—	15	Self
TM34	Sludge Wave	Poison	Special	95	100	10	Adjacent
TM35	Flamethrower	Fire	Special	90	100	15	Normal
TM36	Sludge Bomb	Poison	Special	90	100	10	Normal
TM37	Sandstorm	Rock	Status	—	—	10	Both Sides
TM38	Fire Blast	Fire	Special	110	85	5	Normal
TM39	Rock Tomb	Rock	Physical	60	95	15	Normal
TM41	Torment	Dark	Status	—	100	15	Normal
TM42	Facade	Normal	Physical	70	100	20	Normal
TM44	Rest	Psychic	Status	—	—	10	Self
TM45	Attract	Normal	Status	—	100	15	Normal
TM46	Thief	Dark	Physical	60	100	25	Normal

No.	Name	Type	Kind	Pow.	Acc.	PP	Range
TM48	Round	Normal	Special	60	100	15	Normal
TM49	Echoed Voice	Normal	Special	40	100	15	Normal
TM52	Focus Blast	Fighting	Special	120	70	5	Normal
TM56	Fling	Dark	Physical	—	100	10	Normal
TM59	Incinerate	Fire	Special	60	100	15	Many Others
TM60	Quash	Dark	Status	—	100	15	Normal
TM65	Shadow Claw	Ghost	Physical	70	100	15	Normal
TM68	Giga Impact	Normal	Physical	150	90	5	Normal
TM71	Stone Edge	Rock	Physical	100	80	5	Normal
TM78	Bulldoze	Ground	Physical	60	100	20	Adjacent
TM80	Rock Slide	Rock	Physical	75	90	10	Many Others
TM82	Dragon Tail	Dragon	Physical	60	90	10	Normal
TM84	Poison Jab	Poison	Physical	80	100	20	Normal
TM87	Swagger	Normal	Status	—	90	15	Normal
TM88	Sleep Talk	Normal	Status	—	—	10	Self
TM90	Substitute	Normal	Status	—	—	10	Self
TM94	Rock Smash	Fighting	Physical	40	100	15	Normal
TM98	Power-Up Punch	Fighting	Physical	40	100	20	Normal
TM100	Confide	Normal	Status	—	—	20	Normal
HM01	Cut	Normal	Physical	50	95	30	Normal
HM03	Surf	Water	Special	90	100	15	Adjacent
HM04	Strength	Normal	Physical	80	100	15	Normal

● MOVES TAUGHT BY PEOPLE

Name	Type	Kind	Pow.	Acc.	PP	Range

AFTER THE HALL OF FAME

CENTRAL KALOS

COASTAL KALOS

109 Nidoking

MOUNTAIN KALOS

ADVENTURE DATA

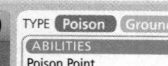

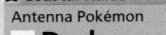

Coastal Kalos 110
Antenna Pokémon
∨ Dedenne

HEIGHT: 0'08" **WEIGHT:** 4.9 lbs.
GENDER: ♂/♀

TYPE Electric | Fairy

ABILITIES
Cheek Pouch
Pickup

HIDDEN ABILITY
Plus

EVOLUTION

Does not evolve

Ⓧ Its whiskers serve as antennas. By sending and receiving electrical waves, it can communicate with others over vast distances.

Ⓨ It uses its tail to absorb electricity from power plants or from outlets in houses, and then it fires the electricity from its whiskers.

STAT GROWTH RATES
HP ■ ■ ■
Attack ■ ■ ■
Defense ■ ■ ■
Sp. Atk ■ ■ ■ ■
Sp. Def ■ ■ ■
Speed ■ ■ ■ ■ ■

EGG GROUPS
Field, Fairy

ITEMS SOMETIMES HELD BY WILD POKÉMON
None

Damage taken in normal battles		Damage taken in Inverse Battles	
Normal	×1	Normal	×1
Fire	×1	Fire	×1
Water	×1	Water	×1
Grass	×1	Grass	×1
Electric	×0.5	Electric	×2
Ice	×1	Ice	×1
Fighting	×0.5	Fighting	×2
Poison	×2	Poison	×0.5
Ground	×2	Ground	×0.5
Flying	×0.5	Flying	×2
Psychic	×1	Psychic	×1
Bug	×0.5	Bug	×2
Rock	×1	Rock	×1
Ghost	×1	Ghost	×1
Dragon	×0	Dragon	×2
Dark	×0.5	Dark	×2
Steel	×1	Steel	×1
Fairy	×1	Fairy	×1

Can be used in	
Inverse Battle	Battle Institute
—	Battle Maison
Battle Chateau	Random Matchup

Same form for ♂/♀

How to obtain for your Coastal Kalos Pokédex

Ⓧ Catch in the tall grass on Route 11.

Ⓨ Catch in the tall grass on Route 11.

● LEVEL-UP MOVES

Lv.	Name	Type	Kind	Pow.	Acc.	PP	Range
1	Tackle	Normal	Physical	50	100	35	Normal
1	Tail Whip	Normal	Status	—	100	30	Many Others
7	Thunder Shock	Electric	Special	40	100	30	Normal
11	Charge	Electric	Status	—	—	20	Self
14	Charm	Fairy	Status	—	100	20	Normal
17	Parabolic Charge	Electric	Special	50	100	20	Adjacent
20	Nuzzle	Electric	Physical	20	100	20	Normal
23	Thunder Wave	Electric	Status	—	100	20	Normal
26	Volt Switch	Electric	Special	70	100	20	Normal
30	Rest	Psychic	Status	—	—	10	Self
31	Snore	Normal	Special	50	100	15	Normal
34	Charge Beam	Electric	Special	50	90	10	Normal
39	Entrainment	Normal	Status	—	100	15	Normal
42	Play Rough	Fairy	Physical	90	90	10	Normal
45	Thunder	Electric	Special	110	70	10	Normal
50	Discharge	Electric	Special	80	100	15	Adjacent

● TM & HM MOVES

No.	Name	Type	Kind	Pow.	Acc.	PP	Range
TM06	Toxic	Poison	Status	—	90	10	Normal
TM10	Hidden Power	Normal	Special	60	100	15	Normal
TM11	Sunny Day	Fire	Status	—	—	5	Both Sides
TM17	Protect	Normal	Status	—	—	10	Self
TM18	Rain Dance	Water	Status	—	—	5	Both Sides
TM21	Frustration	Normal	Physical	—	100	20	Normal
TM24	Thunderbolt	Electric	Special	90	100	15	Normal
TM25	Thunder	Electric	Special	110	70	10	Normal
TM27	Return	Normal	Physical	—	100	20	Normal
TM28	Dig	Ground	Physical	80	100	10	Normal
TM32	Double Team	Normal	Status	—	—	15	Self
TM40	Aerial Ace	Flying	Physical	60	—	20	Normal
TM42	Facade	Normal	Physical	70	100	20	Normal
TM44	Rest	Psychic	Status	—	—	10	Self
TM45	Attract	Normal	Status	—	100	15	Normal
TM46	Thief	Dark	Physical	60	100	25	Normal
TM48	Round	Normal	Special	60	100	15	Normal
TM56	Fling	Dark	Physical	—	100	10	Normal
TM57	Charge Beam	Electric	Special	50	90	10	Normal
TM67	Retaliate	Normal	Physical	70	100	5	Normal
TM68	Giga Impact	Normal	Physical	150	90	5	Normal
TM70	Flash	Normal	Status	—	100	20	Normal
TM72	Volt Switch	Electric	Special	70	100	20	Normal
TM73	Thunder Wave	Electric	Status	—	100	20	Normal
TM86	Grass Knot	Grass	Special	—	100	20	Normal
TM87	Swagger	Normal	Status	—	90	15	Normal
TM88	Sleep Talk	Normal	Status	—	—	10	Self
TM89	U-turn	Bug	Physical	70	100	20	Normal
TM90	Substitute	Normal	Status	—	—	10	Self
TM93	Wild Charge	Electric	Physical	90	100	15	Normal
TM100	Confide	Normal	Status	—	—	20	Normal
HM01	Cut	Normal	Physical	50	95	30	Normal

No.	Name	Type	Kind	Pow.	Acc.	PP	Range

● MOVES TAUGHT BY PEOPLE

Name	Type	Kind	Pow.	Acc.	PP	Range

● EGG MOVES

Name	Type	Kind	Pow.	Acc.	PP	Range
Eerie Impulse	Electric	Status	—	100	15	Normal
Covet	Normal	Physical	60	100	25	Normal
Helping Hand	Normal	Status	—	—	20	1 Ally
Natural Gift	Normal	Physical	—	100	15	Normal

AFTER THE HALL OF FAME

CENTRAL KALOS

COASTAL KALOS
110
Dedenne

MOUNTAIN KALOS

ADVENTURE DATA

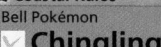

⬟ **Coastal Kalos** **111**
Bell Pokémon
☑ **Chingling**

HEIGHT: 0'08"   WEIGHT: 1.3 lbs.
GENDER: ♂/♀

TYPE Psychic

ABILITY
Levitate

HIDDEN ABILITY
None

STAT GROWTH RATES
HP ▪▪
Attack ▪▪
Defense ▪▪
Sp. Atk ▪▪▪
Sp. Def ▪▪
Speed ▪▪▪

EGG GROUP
No Eggs Discovered

⬆ EVOLUTION

Level up between
8 P.M. and 3:59 A.M.
with high friendship

Chingling → Chimecho

Ⓧ Each time it hops, it makes a ringing sound. It deafens foes by emitting high-frequency cries.

Ⓨ There is an orb inside its mouth. When it hops, the orb bounces all over and makes a ringing sound.

ITEMS SOMETIMES HELD BY WILD POKÉMON
None

Damage taken in normal battles	
Normal	×1
Fire	×1
Water	×1
Grass	×1
Electric	×1
Ice	×1
Fighting	×0.5
Poison	×1
Ground	×1 ⓘ
Flying	×1
Psychic	×0.5
Bug	×2
Rock	×1
Ghost	×2
Dragon	×1
Dark	×2
Steel	×1
Fairy	×1

Damage taken in Inverse Battles	
Normal	×1
Fire	×1
Water	×1
Grass	×1
Electric	×1
Ice	×1
Fighting	×2
Poison	×1
Ground	×1 ⓘ
Flying	×1
Psychic	×2
Bug	×0.5
Rock	×1
Ghost	×0.5
Dragon	×1
Dark	×0.5
Steel	×1
Fairy	×1

Can be used in	
Inverse Battle	Battle Institute
Sky Battle	Battle Maison
Battle Chateau	Random Matchup

Same form for ♂/♀

How to obtain for your Coastal Kalos Pokédex

❶ Catch in the tall grass on Route 11.
❷ Catch in Reflection Cave.

❶ Catch in the tall grass on Route 11.
❷ Catch in Reflection Cave.

● **LEVEL-UP MOVES**

Lv.	Name	Type	Kind	Pow.	Acc.	PP	Range
1	Wrap	Normal	Physical	15	90	20	Normal
6	Growl	Normal	Status	—	100	40	Many Others
9	Astonish	Ghost	Physical	30	100	15	Normal
14	Confusion	Psychic	Special	50	100	25	Normal
17	Uproar	Normal	Special	90	100	10	1 Random
22	Last Resort	Normal	Physical	140	100	5	Normal
25	Entrainment	Normal	Status	—	100	15	Normal

● **TM & HM MOVES**

No.	Name	Type	Kind	Pow.	Acc.	PP	Range
TM03	Psyshock	Psychic	Special	80	100	10	Normal
TM04	Calm Mind	Psychic	Status	—	—	20	Self
TM06	Toxic	Poison	Status	—	90	10	Normal
TM10	Hidden Power	Normal	Special	60	100	15	Normal
TM11	Sunny Day	Fire	Status	—	—	5	Both Sides
TM12	Taunt	Dark	Status	—	100	20	Normal
TM16	Light Screen	Psychic	Status	—	—	30	Your Side
TM17	Protect	Normal	Status	—	—	10	Self
TM18	Rain Dance	Water	Status	—	—	5	Both Sides
TM20	Safeguard	Normal	Status	—	—	25	Your Side
TM21	Frustration	Normal	Physical	—	100	20	Normal
TM27	Return	Normal	Physical	—	100	20	Normal
TM29	Psychic	Psychic	Special	90	100	10	Normal
TM30	Shadow Ball	Ghost	Special	80	100	15	Normal
TM32	Double Team	Normal	Status	—	—	15	Self
TM33	Reflect	Psychic	Status	—	—	20	Your Side
TM41	Torment	Dark	Status	—	100	15	Normal
TM42	Facade	Normal	Physical	70	100	20	Normal
TM44	Rest	Psychic	Status	—	—	10	Self
TM45	Attract	Normal	Status	—	100	15	Normal
TM48	Round	Normal	Special	60	100	15	Normal
TM49	Echoed Voice	Normal	Special	40	100	15	Normal
TM57	Charge Beam	Electric	Special	50	90	10	Normal
TM70	Flash	Normal	Status	—	100	20	Normal
TM73	Thunder Wave	Electric	Status	—	100	20	Normal
TM77	Psych Up	Normal	Status	—	—	10	Normal
TM85	Dream Eater	Psychic	Special	100	100	15	Normal
TM86	Grass Knot	Grass	Special	—	100	20	Normal
TM87	Swagger	Normal	Status	—	90	15	Normal
TM88	Sleep Talk	Normal	Status	—	—	10	Self
TM90	Substitute	Normal	Status	—	—	10	Self
TM92	Trick Room	Psychic	Status	—	—	5	Both Sides
TM99	Dazzling Gleam	Fairy	Special	80	100	10	Many Others

No.	Name	Type	Kind	Pow.	Acc.	PP	Range
TM100	Confide	Normal	Status	—	—	20	Normal

● **MOVES TAUGHT BY PEOPLE**

Name	Type	Kind	Pow.	Acc.	PP	Range

● **EGG MOVES**

Name	Type	Kind	Pow.	Acc.	PP	Range
Disable	Normal	Status	—	100	20	Normal
Curse	Ghost	Status	—	—	10	Varies
Hypnosis	Psychic	Status	—	60	20	Normal
Wish	Normal	Status	—	—	10	Self
Future Sight	Psychic	Special	120	100	10	Normal
Recover	Normal	Status	—	—	10	Self
Stored Power	Psychic	Special	20	100	10	Normal
Skill Swap	Psychic	Status	—	—	10	Normal
Cosmic Power	Psychic	Status	—	—	20	Self

AFTER THE HALL OF FAME

CENTRAL KALOS

COASTAL KALOS

111 Chingling

MOUNTAIN KALOS

ADVENTURE DATA

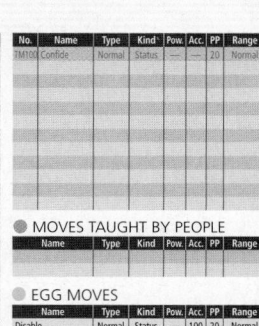

AFTER THE HALL OF FAME

CENTRAL KALOS

COASTAL KALOS

112

Chimecho

MOUNTAIN KALOS

ADVENTURE DATA

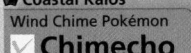

Coastal Kalos **112**
Wind Chime Pokémon
☑ **Chimecho**

HEIGHT: 2'00"   WEIGHT: 2.2 lbs.
GENDER: ♂/♀

X It uses the sucker on its head to hang from a tree or from eaves. It can produce seven different tones.

Y Emitting ultrasonic cries, it floats on winds to travel great distances.

TYPE Psychic

ABILITY
Levitate

HIDDEN ABILITY
None

STAT GROWTH RATES
HP	▪▪▪
Attack	▪▪▪
Defense	▪▪▪
Sp. Atk	▪▪▪▪▪
Sp. Def	▪▪▪
Speed	▪▪▪▪

EGG GROUP
Amorphous

EVOLUTION

Level up between 8 P.M. and 3:59 A.M. with high friendship

Chingling → Chimecho

ITEMS SOMETIMES HELD BY WILD POKÉMON
None

Can be used in
- Inverse Battle
- Sky Battle
- Battle Chateau
- Battle Institute
- Battle Maison
- Random Matchup

Damage taken in normal battles	
Normal	×1
Fire	×1
Water	×1
Grass	×1
Electric	×1
Ice	×1
Fighting	×0.5
Poison	×1
Ground	×1 ❗
Flying	×1
Psychic	×0.5
Bug	×2
Rock	×2
Ghost	×2
Dragon	×1
Dark	×2
Steel	×1
Fairy	×1

Damage taken in Inverse Battles	
Normal	×1
Fire	×1
Water	×1
Grass	×1
Electric	×1
Ice	×1
Fighting	×2
Poison	×1
Ground	×1 ❗
Flying	×1
Psychic	×2
Bug	×0.5
Rock	×1
Ghost	×0.5
Dragon	×1
Dark	×0.5
Steel	×1
Fairy	×1

How to obtain for your Coastal Kalos Pokédex

Level up Chingling between 8 P.M. and 3:59 A.M. with high friendship.

Level up Chingling between 8 P.M. and 3:59 A.M. with high friendship.

Same form for ♂/♀

● LEVEL-UP MOVES

Lv.	Name	Type	Kind	Pow.	Acc.	PP	Range
1	Healing Wish	Psychic	Status	—	—	10	Self
1	Synchronoise	Psychic	Special	120	100	10	Adjacent
1	Wrap	Normal	Physical	15	90	20	Normal
6	Growl	Normal	Status	—	100	40	Many Others
9	Astonish	Ghost	Physical	30	100	15	Normal
14	Confusion	Psychic	Special	50	100	25	Normal
17	Uproar	Normal	Special	90	100	10	1 Random
22	Take Down	Normal	Physical	90	85	20	Normal
25	Yawn	Normal	Status	—	—	10	Normal
30	Psywave	Psychic	Special	—	100	15	Normal
33	Double-Edge	Normal	Physical	120	100	15	Normal
38	Heal Bell	Normal	Status	—	—	5	Your Party
41	Safeguard	Normal	Status	—	—	25	Your Side
46	Extrasensory	Psychic	Special	80	100	20	Normal
49	Heal Pulse	Psychic	Status	—	—	10	Normal
54	Synchronoise	Psychic	Special	120	100	10	Adjacent
57	Healing Wish	Psychic	Status	—	—	10	Self

● TM & HM MOVES

No.	Name	Type	Kind	Pow.	Acc.	PP	Range
TM03	Psyshock	Psychic	Special	80	100	10	Normal
TM04	Calm Mind	Psychic	Status	—	—	20	Self
TM06	Toxic	Poison	Status	—	90	10	Normal
TM10	Hidden Power	Normal	Special	60	100	15	Normal
TM11	Sunny Day	Fire	Status	—	—	5	Both Sides
TM12	Taunt	Dark	Status	—	100	20	Normal
TM16	Light Screen	Psychic	Status	—	—	30	Your Side
TM17	Protect	Normal	Status	—	—	10	Self
TM18	Rain Dance	Water	Status	—	—	5	Both Sides
TM20	Safeguard	Normal	Status	—	—	25	Your Side
TM21	Frustration	Normal	Physical	—	100	20	Normal
TM27	Return	Normal	Physical	—	100	20	Normal
TM29	Psychic	Psychic	Special	90	100	10	Normal
TM30	Shadow Ball	Ghost	Special	80	100	15	Normal
TM32	Double Team	Normal	Status	—	—	15	Self
TM33	Reflect	Psychic	Status	—	—	20	Your Side
TM41	Torment	Dark	Status	—	100	15	Normal
TM42	Facade	Normal	Physical	70	100	20	Normal
TM44	Rest	Psychic	Status	—	—	10	Self
TM45	Attract	Normal	Status	—	100	15	Normal
TM48	Round	Normal	Special	60	100	15	Normal
TM49	Echoed Voice	Normal	Special	40	100	15	Normal
TM53	Energy Ball	Grass	Special	90	100	10	Normal
TM57	Charge Beam	Electric	Special	50	90	10	Normal
TM70	Flash	Normal	Status	—	100	20	Normal
TM73	Thunder Wave	Electric	Status	—	100	20	Normal
TM77	Psych Up	Normal	Status	—	—	10	Normal
TM85	Dream Eater	Psychic	Special	100	100	15	Normal
TM86	Grass Knot	Grass	Special	—	100	20	Normal
TM87	Swagger	Normal	Status	—	90	15	Normal
TM88	Sleep Talk	Normal	Status	—	—	10	Self
TM90	Substitute	Normal	Status	—	—	10	Self
TM92	Trick Room	Psychic	Status	—	—	5	Both Sides

No.	Name	Type	Kind	Pow.	Acc.	PP	Range
TM99	Dazzling Gleam	Fairy	Special	80	100	10	Many Others
TM100	Confide	Normal	Status	—	—	20	Normal

● MOVES TAUGHT BY PEOPLE

Name	Type	Kind	Pow.	Acc.	PP	Range

● EGG MOVES

Name	Type	Kind	Pow.	Acc.	PP	Range
Disable	Normal	Status	—	100	20	Normal
Curse	Ghost	Status	—	—	10	Varies
Hypnosis	Psychic	Status	—	60	20	Normal
Wish	Normal	Status	—	—	10	Self
Future Sight	Psychic	Special	120	100	10	Normal
Recover	Normal	Status	—	—	10	Self
Stored Power	Psychic	Special	20	100	10	Normal
Skill Swap	Psychic	Status	—	—	10	Normal
Cosmic Power	Psychic	Status	—	—	20	Self

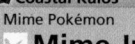

Coastal Kalos 113
Mime Pokémon
Mime Jr.

HEIGHT: 2'00" WEIGHT: 28.7 lbs.
GENDER: ♂ / ♀

| TYPE | Psychic | Fairy |

ABILITIES
Soundproof
Filter

HIDDEN ABILITY
Technician

STAT GROWTH RATES
HP	▮
Attack	▮
Defense	▮▮
Sp. Atk	▮▮▮
Sp. Def	▮▮▮▮
Speed	▮▮▮

EGG GROUP
No Eggs Discovered

EVOLUTION

Mime Jr. → Lv. 15 with Mimic → Mr. Mime

X In an attempt to confuse its enemy, it mimics the enemy's movements. Then it wastes no time in making itself scarce!

Y It habitually mimics foes. Once mimicked, the foe cannot take its eyes off this Pokémon.

ITEMS SOMETIMES HELD BY WILD POKÉMON
None

Damage taken in normal battles
Normal	×1
Fire	×1
Water	×1
Grass	×1
Electric	×1
Ice	×1
Fighting	×0.25
Poison	×2
Ground	×1
Flying	×1
Psychic	×0.5
Bug	×1
Rock	×1
Ghost	×2
Dragon	×0
Dark	×1
Steel	×2
Fairy	×1

Damage taken in Inverse Battles
Normal	×1
Fire	×1
Water	×1
Grass	×1
Electric	×1
Ice	×1
Fighting	×4
Poison	×0.5
Ground	×1
Flying	×1
Psychic	×2
Bug	×1
Rock	×1
Ghost	×0.5
Dragon	×2
Dark	×1
Steel	×0.5
Fairy	×1

Can be used in
Inverse Battle	Battle Institute
—	Battle Maison
Battle Chateau	Random Matchup

Same form for ♂ / ♀

How to obtain for your Coastal Kalos Pokédex
Catch in a Horde Encounter in Reflection Cave.

Catch in a Horde Encounter in Reflection Cave.

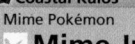
AFTER THE HALL OF FAME

CENTRAL KALOS

COASTAL KALOS

113 Mime Jr.

MOUNTAIN KALOS

ADVENTURE DATA

● LEVEL-UP MOVES
Lv.	Name	Type	Kind	Pow.	Acc.	PP	Range
1	Tickle	Normal	Status	—	100	20	Normal
1	Barrier	Psychic	Status	—	—	20	Self
1	Confusion	Psychic	Special	50	100	25	Normal
4	Copycat	Normal	Status	—	—	20	Self
8	Meditate	Psychic	Status	—	—	40	Self
11	Double Slap	Normal	Physical	15	85	10	Normal
15	Mimic	Normal	Status	—	—	10	Normal
18	Encore	Normal	Status	—	100	5	Normal
22	Light Screen	Psychic	Status	—	—	30	Your Side
22	Reflect	Psychic	Status	—	—	20	Your Side
25	Psybeam	Psychic	Special	65	100	20	Normal
29	Substitute	Normal	Status	—	—	10	Self
32	Recycle	Normal	Status	—	—	10	Self
36	Trick	Psychic	Status	—	100	10	Normal
39	Psychic	Psychic	Special	90	100	10	Normal
43	Role Play	Psychic	Status	—	—	10	Normal
46	Baton Pass	Normal	Status	—	—	40	Self
50	Safeguard	Normal	Status	—	—	25	Your Side

● TM & HM MOVES
No.	Name	Type	Kind	Pow.	Acc.	PP	Range
TM03	Psyshock	Psychic	Special	80	100	10	Normal
TM04	Calm Mind	Psychic	Status	—	—	20	Self
TM06	Toxic	Poison	Status	—	90	10	Normal
TM10	Hidden Power	Normal	Special	60	100	15	Normal
TM11	Sunny Day	Fire	Status	—	—	5	Both Sides
TM12	Taunt	Dark	Status	—	100	20	Normal
TM16	Light Screen	Psychic	Status	—	—	30	Your Side
TM17	Protect	Normal	Status	—	—	10	Self
TM18	Rain Dance	Water	Status	—	—	5	Both Sides
TM20	Safeguard	Normal	Status	—	—	25	Your Side
TM21	Frustration	Normal	Physical	—	100	20	Normal
TM22	Solar Beam	Grass	Special	120	100	10	Normal
TM24	Thunderbolt	Electric	Special	90	100	15	Normal
TM25	Thunder	Electric	Special	110	70	10	Normal
TM27	Return	Normal	Physical	—	100	20	Normal
TM29	Psychic	Psychic	Special	90	100	10	Normal
TM30	Shadow Ball	Ghost	Special	80	100	15	Normal
TM31	Brick Break	Fighting	Physical	75	100	15	Normal
TM32	Double Team	Normal	Status	—	—	15	Self
TM33	Reflect	Psychic	Status	—	—	20	Your Side
TM41	Torment	Dark	Status	—	100	15	Normal
TM42	Facade	Normal	Physical	70	100	20	Normal
TM44	Rest	Psychic	Status	—	—	10	Self
TM45	Attract	Normal	Status	—	100	15	Normal
TM46	Thief	Dark	Physical	60	100	25	Normal
TM48	Round	Normal	Special	60	100	15	Normal
TM56	Fling	Dark	Physical	—	100	10	Normal
TM57	Charge Beam	Electric	Special	50	90	10	Normal
TM70	Flash	Normal	Status	—	100	20	Normal
TM73	Thunder Wave	Electric	Status	—	100	20	Normal
TM77	Psych Up	Normal	Status	—	—	10	Normal
TM83	Infestation	Bug	Special	20	100	20	Normal
TM85	Dream Eater	Psychic	Special	100	100	15	Normal

No.	Name	Type	Kind	Pow.	Acc.	PP	Range
TM86	Grass Knot	Grass	Special	—	100	20	Normal
TM87	Swagger	Normal	Status	—	90	15	Normal
TM88	Sleep Talk	Normal	Status	—	—	10	Self
TM90	Substitute	Normal	Status	—	—	10	Self
TM92	Trick Room	Psychic	Status	—	—	5	Both Sides
TM100	Confide	Normal	Status	—	—	20	Normal

● MOVES TAUGHT BY PEOPLE
Name	Type	Kind	Pow.	Acc.	PP	Range

● EGG MOVES
Name	Type	Kind	Pow.	Acc.	PP	Range
Future Sight	Psychic	Special	120	100	10	Normal
Hypnosis	Psychic	Status	—	60	10	Normal
Mimic	Normal	Status	—	—	10	Normal
Fake Out	Normal	Physical	40	100	10	Normal
Trick	Psychic	Status	—	100	10	Normal
Confuse Ray	Ghost	Status	—	100	10	Normal
Wake-Up Slap	Fighting	Physical	70	100	10	Normal
Teeter Dance	Normal	Status	—	100	20	Adjacent
Healing Wish	Psychic	Status	—	—	10	Self
Charm	Fairy	Status	—	100	20	Normal
Nasty Plot	Dark	Status	—	—	20	Self
Power Split	Psychic	Status	—	—	10	Normal
Magic Room	Psychic	Status	—	—	10	Both Sides
Icy Wind	Ice	Special	55	95	15	Many Others

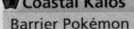

Coastal Kalos 114

Barrier Pokémon

☑ Mr. Mime

TYPE Psychic / Fairy

HEIGHT: 4'03" WEIGHT: 120.1 lbs.
GENDER: ♂/♀

ABILITIES
Soundproof
Filter

HIDDEN ABILITY
Technician

STAT GROWTH RATES
HP	▪▪
Attack	▪▪
Defense	▪▪▪
Sp. Atk	▪▪▪▪▪
Sp. Def	▪▪▪▪▪
Speed	▪▪▪▪▪

EGG GROUP
Human-Like

X Emanations from its fingertips solidify the air into invisible walls that repel even harsh attacks.

Y It is adept at conning people. It is said to be able to create walls out of thin air by miming.

▲ EVOLUTION

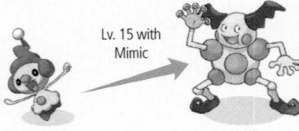

Mime Jr. — Lv. 15 with Mimic → Mr. Mime

ITEMS SOMETIMES HELD BY WILD POKÉMON
None

Damage taken in normal battles		Damage taken in Inverse Battles	
Normal	×1	Normal	×1
Fire	×1	Fire	×1
Water	×1	Water	×1
Grass	×1	Grass	×1
Electric	×1	Electric	×1
Ice	×1	Ice	×1
Fighting	×0.25	Fighting	×4
Poison	×2	Poison	×0.5
Ground	×1	Ground	×1
Flying	×1	Flying	×1
Psychic	×0.5	Psychic	×2
Bug	×1	Bug	×1
Rock	×1	Rock	×1
Ghost	×2	Ghost	×0.5
Dragon	×1	Dragon	×2
Dark	×1	Dark	×2
Steel	×2	Steel	×0.5
Fairy	×1	Fairy	×1

Can be used in	
Inverse Battle	Battle Institute
—	Battle Maison
Battle Chateau	Random Matchup

Same form for ♂/♀

How to obtain for your Coastal Kalos Pokédex

❶ Catch in Reflection Cave.
❷ Level up Mime Jr. to Lv. 15, and have it learn Mimic. Alternatively, teach it Mimic first and then level it up.

❶ Catch in Reflection Cave.
❷ Level up Mime Jr. to Lv. 15, and have it learn Mimic. Alternatively, teach it Mimic first and then level it up.

● LEVEL-UP MOVES

Lv.	Name	Type	Kind	Pow.	Acc.	PP	Range
1	Misty Terrain	Fairy	Status	—	—	10	Both Sides
1	Magical Leaf	Grass	Special	60	—	20	Normal
1	Quick Guard	Fighting	Status	—	—	15	Your Side
1	Wide Guard	Rock	Status	—	—	10	Your Side
1	Power Swap	Psychic	Status	—	—	10	Normal
1	Guard Swap	Psychic	Status	—	—	10	Normal
1	Barrier	Psychic	Status	—	—	20	Self
1	Confusion	Psychic	Special	50	100	25	Normal
4	Copycat	Normal	Status	—	—	20	Self
8	Meditate	Psychic	Status	—	—	40	Self
11	Double Slap	Normal	Physical	15	85	10	Normal
15	Mimic	Normal	Status	—	—	10	Normal
15	Psywave	Psychic	Special	—	100	15	Normal
18	Encore	Normal	Status	—	100	5	Normal
22	Light Screen	Psychic	Status	—	—	30	Your Side
22	Reflect	Psychic	Status	—	—	20	Your Side
25	Psybeam	Psychic	Special	65	100	20	Normal
29	Substitute	Normal	Status	—	—	10	Self
32	Recycle	Normal	Status	—	—	10	Self
36	Trick	Psychic	Status	—	100	10	Normal
39	Psychic	Psychic	Special	90	100	10	Normal
43	Role Play	Psychic	Status	—	—	10	Normal
46	Baton Pass	Normal	Status	—	—	40	Self
50	Safeguard	Normal	Status	—	—	25	Your Side

● TM & HM MOVES

No.	Name	Type	Kind	Pow.	Acc.	PP	Range
TM03	Psyshock	Psychic	Special	80	100	10	Normal
TM04	Calm Mind	Psychic	Status	—	—	20	Self
TM06	Toxic	Poison	Status	—	90	10	Normal
TM10	Hidden Power	Normal	Special	60	100	15	Normal
TM11	Sunny Day	Fire	Status	—	—	5	Both Sides
TM12	Taunt	Dark	Status	—	100	20	Normal
TM15	Hyper Beam	Normal	Special	150	90	5	Normal
TM16	Light Screen	Psychic	Status	—	—	30	Your Side
TM17	Protect	Normal	Status	—	—	10	Self
TM18	Rain Dance	Water	Status	—	—	5	Both Sides
TM20	Safeguard	Normal	Status	—	—	25	Your Side
TM21	Frustration	Normal	Physical	—	100	20	Normal
TM22	Solar Beam	Grass	Special	120	100	10	Normal
TM24	Thunderbolt	Electric	Special	90	100	15	Normal
TM25	Thunder	Electric	Special	110	70	10	Normal
TM27	Return	Normal	Physical	—	100	20	Normal
TM29	Psychic	Psychic	Special	90	100	10	Normal
TM30	Shadow Ball	Ghost	Special	80	100	15	Normal
TM31	Brick Break	Fighting	Physical	75	100	15	Normal
TM32	Double Team	Normal	Status	—	—	15	Self
TM33	Reflect	Psychic	Status	—	—	20	Your Side
TM40	Aerial Ace	Flying	Physical	60	—	20	Normal
TM41	Torment	Dark	Status	—	100	15	Normal
TM42	Facade	Normal	Physical	70	100	20	Normal
TM44	Rest	Psychic	Status	—	—	10	Self
TM45	Attract	Normal	Status	—	100	15	Normal
TM46	Thief	Dark	Physical	60	100	25	Normal
TM48	Round	Normal	Special	60	100	15	Normal
TM52	Focus Blast	Fighting	Special	120	70	5	Normal
TM53	Energy Ball	Grass	Special	90	100	10	Normal
TM56	Fling	Dark	Physical	—	100	10	Normal
TM57	Charge Beam	Electric	Special	50	90	10	Normal
TM66	Payback	Dark	Physical	50	100	10	Normal
TM68	Giga Impact	Normal	Physical	150	90	5	Normal

No.	Name	Type	Kind	Pow.	Acc.	PP	Range
TM70	Flash	Normal	Status	—	100	20	Normal
TM73	Thunder Wave	Electric	Status	—	100	20	Normal
TM77	Psych Up	Normal	Status	—	—	10	Normal
TM83	Infestation	Bug	Special	20	100	20	Normal
TM85	Dream Eater	Psychic	Special	100	100	15	Normal
TM86	Grass Knot	Grass	Special	—	100	20	Normal
TM87	Swagger	Normal	Status	—	90	15	Normal
TM88	Sleep Talk	Normal	Status	—	—	10	Self
TM90	Substitute	Normal	Status	—	—	10	Self
TM92	Trick Room	Psychic	Status	—	—	5	Both Sides
TM98	Power-Up Punch	Fighting	Physical	40	100	20	Normal
TM99	Dazzling Gleam	Fairy	Special	80	100	10	Many Others
TM100	Confide	Normal	Status	—	—	20	Normal

● MOVES TAUGHT BY PEOPLE

Name	Type	Kind	Pow.	Acc.	PP	Range

● EGG MOVES

Name	Type	Kind	Pow.	Acc.	PP	Range
Future Sight	Psychic	Special	120	100	10	Normal
Hypnosis	Psychic	Status	—	60	20	Normal
Mimic	Normal	Status	—	—	10	Normal
Fake Out	Normal	Physical	40	100	10	Normal
Trick	Psychic	Status	—	100	10	Normal
Confuse Ray	Ghost	Status	—	100	10	Normal
Wake-Up Slap	Fighting	Physical	70	100	10	Normal
Teeter Dance	Normal	Status	—	100	20	Adjacent
Nasty Plot	Dark	Status	—	—	20	Self
Power Split	Psychic	Status	—	—	10	Normal
Magic Room	Psychic	Status	—	—	10	Both Sides
Icy Wind	Ice	Special	55	95	15	Many Others

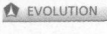

AFTER THE HALL OF FAME

CENTRAL KALOS

COASTAL KALOS

114

Mr. Mime

MOUNTAIN KALOS

ADVENTURE DATA

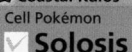

Coastal Kalos

115

Cell Pokémon

☑ Solosis

HEIGHT: 1'00" WEIGHT: 2.2 lbs.
GENDER: ♂/♀

X Because their bodies are enveloped in a special liquid, they are fine in any environment, no matter how severe.

Y They drive away attackers by unleashing psychic powers. They can use telepathy to talk with others.

TYPE Psychic

ABILITIES
Overcoat
Magic Guard

HIDDEN ABILITY
Regenerator

STAT GROWTH RATES
HP	■■
Attack	■■
Defense	■■
Sp. Atk	■■■■■
Sp. Def	■■
Speed	■

EGG GROUP
Amorphous

⬆ EVOLUTION

Lv. 32 → Lv. 41

Solosis — Duosion — Reuniclus

ITEMS SOMETIMES HELD BY WILD POKÉMON
None

Damage taken in normal battles		Damage taken in Inverse Battles	
Normal	×1	Normal	×1
Fire	×1	Fire	×1
Water	×1	Water	×1
Grass	×1	Grass	×1
Electric	×1	Electric	×1
Ice	×1	Ice	×1
Fighting	×0.5	Fighting	×2
Poison	×1	Poison	×1
Ground	×1	Ground	×1
Flying	×1	Flying	×1
Psychic	×0.5	Psychic	×2
Bug	×2	Bug	×0.5
Rock	×1	Rock	×1
Ghost	×2	Ghost	×0.5
Dragon	×1	Dragon	×1
Dark	×2	Dark	×0.5
Steel	×1	Steel	×1
Fairy	×1	Fairy	×1

Can be used in	
Inverse Battle	Battle Institute
—	Battle Maison
Battle Chateau	Random Matchup

Same form for ♂/♀

How to obtain for your Coastal Kalos Pokédex

Catch in Reflection Cave.

Catch in Reflection Cave.

 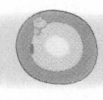

● LEVEL-UP MOVES

Lv.	Name	Type	Kind	Pow.	Acc.	PP	Range
1	Psywave	Psychic	Special	—	100	15	Normal
3	Reflect	Psychic	Status	—	—	20	Your Side
7	Rollout	Rock	Physical	30	90	20	Normal
10	Snatch	Dark	Status	—	—	10	Self
14	Hidden Power	Normal	Special	60	100	15	Normal
16	Light Screen	Psychic	Status	—	—	30	Your Side
19	Charm	Fairy	Status	—	100	20	Normal
24	Recover	Normal	Status	—	—	10	Self
25	Psyshock	Psychic	Special	80	100	10	Normal
28	Endeavor	Normal	Physical	—	100	5	Normal
31	Future Sight	Psychic	Special	120	100	10	Normal
33	Pain Split	Normal	Status	—	—	20	Normal
37	Psychic	Psychic	Special	90	100	10	Normal
40	Skill Swap	Psychic	Status	—	—	10	Normal
46	Heal Block	Psychic	Status	—	100	15	Many Others
48	Wonder Room	Psychic	Status	—	—	10	Both Sides

● TM & HM MOVES

No.	Name	Type	Kind	Pow.	Acc.	PP	Range
TM03	Psyshock	Psychic	Special	80	100	10	Normal
TM04	Calm Mind	Psychic	Status	—	—	20	Self
TM06	Toxic	Poison	Status	—	90	10	Normal
TM10	Hidden Power	Normal	Special	60	100	15	Normal
TM16	Light Screen	Psychic	Status	—	—	30	Your Side
TM17	Protect	Normal	Status	—	—	10	Self
TM18	Rain Dance	Water	Status	—	—	5	Both Sides
TM20	Safeguard	Normal	Status	—	—	25	Your Side
TM21	Frustration	Normal	Physical	—	100	20	Normal
TM25	Thunder	Electric	Special	110	70	10	Normal
TM27	Return	Normal	Physical	—	100	20	Normal
TM29	Psychic	Psychic	Special	90	100	10	Normal
TM30	Shadow Ball	Ghost	Special	80	100	15	Normal
TM32	Double Team	Normal	Status	—	—	15	Self
TM33	Reflect	Psychic	Status	—	—	20	Your Side
TM39	Rock Tomb	Rock	Physical	60	95	15	Normal
TM42	Facade	Normal	Physical	70	100	20	Normal
TM44	Rest	Psychic	Status	—	—	10	Self
TM45	Attract	Normal	Status	—	100	15	Normal
TM48	Round	Normal	Special	60	100	15	Normal
TM53	Energy Ball	Grass	Special	90	100	10	Normal
TM63	Embargo	Dark	Status	—	100	15	Normal
TM64	Explosion	Normal	Physical	250	100	5	Adjacent
TM70	Flash	Normal	Status	—	100	20	Normal
TM73	Thunder Wave	Electric	Status	—	100	20	Normal
TM74	Gyro Ball	Steel	Physical	—	100	5	Normal
TM77	Psych Up	Normal	Status	—	—	10	Normal
TM80	Rock Slide	Rock	Physical	75	90	10	Many Others
TM83	Infestation	Bug	Special	20	100	20	Normal
TM85	Dream Eater	Psychic	Special	100	100	15	Normal
TM87	Swagger	Normal	Status	—	90	15	Normal
TM88	Sleep Talk	Normal	Status	—	—	10	Self
TM90	Substitute	Normal	Status	—	—	10	Self

No.	Name	Type	Kind	Pow.	Acc.	PP	Range
TM91	Flash Cannon	Steel	Special	80	100	10	Normal
TM92	Trick Room	Psychic	Status	—	—	5	Both Sides
TM100	Confide	Normal	Status	—	—	20	Normal

● MOVES TAUGHT BY PEOPLE

Name	Type	Kind	Pow.	Acc.	PP	Range

● EGG MOVES

Name	Type	Kind	Pow.	Acc.	PP	Range
Night Shade	Ghost	Special	—	100	15	Normal
Astonish	Ghost	Physical	30	100	15	Normal
Confuse Ray	Ghost	Status	—	100	10	Normal
Acid Armor	Poison	Status	—	—	20	Self
Trick	Psychic	Status	—	100	10	Normal
Imprison	Psychic	Status	—	—	10	Self
Secret Power	Normal	Physical	70	100	20	Normal
Helping Hand	Normal	Status	—	—	20	1 Ally

AFTER THE HALL OF FAME

CENTRAL KALOS

COASTAL KALOS

115 | Solosis

MOUNTAIN KALOS

ADVENTURE DATA

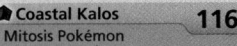

AFTER THE HALL OF FAME

CENTRAL KALOS

COASTAL KALOS

116

Duosion

MOUNTAIN KALOS

ADVENTURE DATA

Coastal Kalos 116
Mitosis Pokémon
☑ Duosion

TYPE Psychic

ABILITIES
Overcoat
Magic Guard

HIDDEN ABILITY
Regenerator

HEIGHT: 2'00" WEIGHT: 17.6 lbs.
GENDER: ♂/♀

X Since they have two divided brains, at times they suddenly try to take two different actions at once.

Y When their two divided brains think the same thoughts, their psychic power is maximized.

STAT GROWTH RATES
HP	▦▦▦
Attack	▦▦
Defense	▦▦
Sp. Atk	▦▦▦▦▦
Sp. Def	▦▦▦
Speed	▦▦

EGG GROUP
Amorphous

EVOLUTION

Solosis → Lv. 32 → Duosion → Lv. 41 → Reuniclus

ITEMS SOMETIMES HELD BY WILD POKÉMON
None

Damage taken in normal battles		Damage taken in Inverse Battles	
Normal	×1	Normal	×1
Fire	×1	Fire	×1
Water	×1	Water	×1
Grass	×1	Grass	×1
Electric	×1	Electric	×1
Ice	×1	Ice	×1
Fighting	×0.5	Fighting	×2
Poison	×1	Poison	×1
Ground	×1	Ground	×1
Flying	×1	Flying	×1
Psychic	×0.5	Psychic	×2
Bug	×2	Bug	×0.5
Rock	×1	Rock	×1
Ghost	×2	Ghost	×0.5
Dragon	×1	Dragon	×1
Dark	×2	Dark	×0.5
Steel	×1	Steel	×1
Fairy	×1	Fairy	×1

Can be used in	
Inverse Battle	Battle Institute
—	Battle Maison
Battle Chateau	Random Matchup

Same form for ♂/♀

How to obtain for your Coastal Kalos Pokédex

Level up Solosis to Lv. 32. (X)

Level up Solosis to Lv. 32. (Y)

● LEVEL-UP MOVES

Lv.	Name	Type	Kind	Pow.	Acc.	PP	Range
1	Psywave	Psychic	Special	—	100	15	Normal
1	Reflect	Psychic	Status	—	—	20	Your Side
1	Rollout	Rock	Physical	30	90	20	Normal
1	Snatch	Dark	Status	—	—	10	Self
3	Reflect	Psychic	Status	—	—	20	Your Side
7	Rollout	Rock	Physical	30	90	20	Normal
10	Snatch	Dark	Status	—	—	10	Self
14	Hidden Power	Normal	Special	60	100	15	Normal
16	Light Screen	Psychic	Status	—	—	30	Your Side
19	Charm	Fairy	Status	—	100	20	Normal
24	Recover	Normal	Status	—	—	10	Self
25	Psyshock	Psychic	Special	80	100	10	Normal
28	Endeavor	Normal	Physical	—	100	5	Normal
31	Future Sight	Psychic	Special	120	100	10	Normal
34	Pain Split	Normal	Status	—	—	20	Normal
39	Psychic	Psychic	Special	90	100	10	Normal
43	Skill Swap	Psychic	Status	—	—	10	Normal
50	Heal Block	Psychic	Status	—	100	15	Many Others
53	Wonder Room	Psychic	Status	—	—	10	Both Sides

● TM & HM MOVES

No.	Name	Type	Kind	Pow.	Acc.	PP	Range
TM03	Psyshock	Psychic	Special	80	100	10	Normal
TM04	Calm Mind	Psychic	Status	—	—	20	Self
TM06	Toxic	Poison	Status	—	90	10	Normal
TM10	Hidden Power	Normal	Special	60	100	15	Normal
TM16	Light Screen	Psychic	Status	—	—	30	Your Side
TM17	Protect	Normal	Status	—	—	10	Self
TM18	Rain Dance	Water	Status	—	—	5	Both Sides
TM20	Safeguard	Normal	Status	—	—	25	Your Side
TM21	Frustration	Normal	Physical	—	100	20	Normal
TM25	Thunder	Electric	Special	110	70	10	Normal
TM27	Return	Normal	Physical	—	100	20	Normal
TM29	Psychic	Psychic	Special	90	100	10	Normal
TM30	Shadow Ball	Ghost	Special	80	100	15	Normal
TM32	Double Team	Normal	Status	—	—	15	Self
TM33	Reflect	Psychic	Status	—	—	20	Your Side
TM39	Rock Tomb	Rock	Physical	60	95	15	Normal
TM42	Facade	Normal	Physical	70	100	20	Normal
TM44	Rest	Psychic	Status	—	—	10	Self
TM45	Attract	Normal	Status	—	100	15	Normal
TM48	Round	Normal	Special	60	100	15	Normal
TM53	Energy Ball	Grass	Special	90	100	10	Normal
TM63	Embargo	Dark	Status	—	100	15	Normal
TM64	Explosion	Normal	Physical	250	100	5	Adjacent
TM70	Flash	Normal	Status	—	100	20	Normal
TM73	Thunder Wave	Electric	Status	—	100	20	Normal
TM74	Gyro Ball	Steel	Physical	—	100	5	Normal
TM77	Psych Up	Normal	Status	—	—	10	Normal
TM80	Rock Slide	Rock	Physical	75	90	10	Many Others
TM83	Infestation	Bug	Special	20	100	20	Normal
TM85	Dream Eater	Psychic	Special	100	100	15	Normal
TM87	Swagger	Normal	Status	—	90	15	Normal
TM88	Sleep Talk	Normal	Status	—	—	10	Self
TM90	Substitute	Normal	Status	—	—	10	Self

No.	Name	Type	Kind	Pow.	Acc.	PP	Range
TM91	Flash Cannon	Steel	Special	80	100	10	Normal
TM92	Trick Room	Psychic	Status	—	—	5	Both Sides
TM100	Confide	Normal	Status	—	—	20	Normal

● MOVES TAUGHT BY PEOPLE

Name	Type	Kind	Pow.	Acc.	PP	Range

117

Multiplying Pokémon

Reuniclus

TYPE Psychic

ABILITIES
Overcoat
Magic Guard

HIDDEN ABILITY
Regenerator

HEIGHT: 3'03" WEIGHT: 44.3 lbs.
GENDER: ♂/♀

X They use psychic power to control their arms, which are made of a special liquid. They can crush boulders psychically.

Y When Reuniclus shake hands, a network forms between their brains, increasing their psychic power.

STAT GROWTH RATES
HP	■■■■
Attack	■■■
Defense	■■■
Sp. Atk	■■■■■
Sp. Def	■■■■
Speed	■■

EGG GROUP
Amorphous

EVOLUTION

Lv. 32 → Lv. 41

Solosis — Duosion — Reuniclus

ITEMS SOMETIMES HELD BY WILD POKÉMON
None

Damage taken in normal battles		Damage taken in Inverse Battles	
Normal	×1	Normal	×1
Fire	×1	Fire	×1
Water	×1	Water	×1
Grass	×1	Grass	×1
Electric	×1	Electric	×1
Ice	×1	Ice	×1
Fighting	×0.5	Fighting	×2
Poison	×1	Poison	×1
Ground	×1	Ground	×1
Flying	×1	Flying	×1
Psychic	×0.5	Psychic	×2
Bug	×2	Bug	×0.5
Rock	×1	Rock	×1
Ghost	×2	Ghost	×0.5
Dragon	×1	Dragon	×1
Dark	×2	Dark	×0.5
Steel	×1	Steel	×1
Fairy	×1	Fairy	×1

Can be used in	
Inverse Battle	Battle Institute
—	Battle Maison
Battle Chateau	Random Matchup

Same form for ♂/♀

How to obtain for your Coastal Kalos Pokédex

Level up Duosion to Lv. 41.   Level up Duosion to Lv. 41.

LEVEL-UP MOVES
Lv.	Name	Type	Kind	Pow.	Acc.	PP	Range
1	Psywave	Psychic	Special	—	100	15	Normal
1	Reflect	Psychic	Status	—	—	20	Your Side
1	Rollout	Rock	Physical	30	90	20	Normal
1	Snatch	Dark	Status	—	—	10	Self
3	Reflect	Psychic	Status	—	—	20	Your Side
7	Rollout	Rock	Physical	30	90	20	Normal
10	Snatch	Dark	Status	—	—	10	Self
14	Hidden Power	Normal	Special	60	100	15	Normal
16	Light Screen	Psychic	Status	—	—	30	Your Side
19	Charm	Fairy	Status	—	100	20	Normal
24	Recover	Normal	Status	—	—	10	Self
25	Psyshock	Psychic	Special	80	100	10	Normal
28	Endeavor	Normal	Physical	—	100	5	Normal
31	Future Sight	Psychic	Special	120	100	10	Normal
34	Pain Split	Normal	Status	—	—	20	Normal
39	Psychic	Psychic	Special	90	100	10	Normal
41	Dizzy Punch	Normal	Physical	70	100	10	Normal
45	Skill Swap	Psychic	Status	—	—	10	Normal
54	Heal Block	Psychic	Status	—	100	15	Many Others
59	Wonder Room	Psychic	Status	—	—	10	Both Sides

TM & HM MOVES
No.	Name	Type	Kind	Pow.	Acc.	PP	Range
TM03	Psyshock	Psychic	Special	80	100	10	Normal
TM04	Calm Mind	Psychic	Status	—	—	20	Self
TM06	Toxic	Poison	Status	—	90	10	Normal
TM10	Hidden Power	Normal	Special	60	100	15	Normal
TM15	Hyper Beam	Normal	Special	150	90	5	Normal
TM16	Light Screen	Psychic	Status	—	—	30	Your Side
TM17	Protect	Normal	Status	—	—	10	Self
TM18	Rain Dance	Water	Status	—	—	5	Both Sides
TM20	Safeguard	Normal	Status	—	—	25	Your Side
TM21	Frustration	Normal	Physical	—	100	20	Normal
TM25	Thunder	Electric	Special	110	70	10	Normal
TM27	Return	Normal	Physical	—	100	20	Normal
TM29	Psychic	Psychic	Special	90	100	10	Normal
TM30	Shadow Ball	Ghost	Special	80	100	15	Normal
TM32	Double Team	Normal	Status	—	—	15	Self
TM33	Reflect	Psychic	Status	—	—	20	Your Side
TM39	Rock Tomb	Rock	Physical	60	95	15	Normal
TM42	Facade	Normal	Physical	70	100	20	Normal
TM44	Rest	Psychic	Status	—	—	10	Self
TM45	Attract	Normal	Status	—	100	15	Normal
TM48	Round	Normal	Special	60	100	15	Normal
TM52	Focus Blast	Fighting	Special	120	70	5	Normal
TM53	Energy Ball	Grass	Special	90	100	10	Normal
TM56	Fling	Dark	Physical	—	100	10	Normal
TM63	Embargo	Dark	Status	—	100	15	Normal
TM64	Explosion	Normal	Physical	250	100	5	Adjacent
TM68	Giga Impact	Normal	Physical	150	90	5	Normal
TM70	Flash	Normal	Status	—	100	20	Normal
TM73	Thunder Wave	Electric	Status	—	100	20	Normal
TM74	Gyro Ball	Steel	Physical	—	100	5	Normal
TM77	Psych Up	Normal	Status	—	—	10	Normal
TM80	Rock Slide	Rock	Physical	75	90	10	Many Others
TM83	Infestation	Bug	Special	20	100	20	Normal
TM85	Dream Eater	Psychic	Special	100	100	15	Normal
TM86	Grass Knot	Grass	Special	—	100	20	Normal
TM87	Swagger	Normal	Status	—	90	15	Normal
TM88	Sleep Talk	Normal	Status	—	—	10	Self
TM90	Substitute	Normal	Status	—	—	10	Self
TM91	Flash Cannon	Steel	Special	80	100	10	Normal
TM92	Trick Room	Psychic	Status	—	—	5	Both Sides
TM94	Rock Smash	Fighting	Physical	40	100	15	Normal
TM98	Power-Up Punch	Fighting	Physical	40	100	20	Normal
TM100	Confide	Normal	Status	—	—	20	Normal
HM04	Strength	Normal	Physical	80	100	15	Normal

MOVES TAUGHT BY PEOPLE
Name	Type	Kind	Pow.	Acc.	PP	Range

AFTER THE HALL OF FAME

CENTRAL KALOS

COASTAL KALOS

118

Wynaut

MOUNTAIN KALOS

ADVENTURE DATA

Coastal Kalos 118

Bright Pokémon

☑ Wynaut

HEIGHT: 2'00"   WEIGHT: 30.9 lbs.
GENDER: ♂/♀

X It tends to move in a pack with others. They cluster in a tight group to sleep in a cave.

Y It grows strong by pushing up against others en masse. It loves eating sweet fruit.

TYPE Psychic

ABILITY
Shadow Tag

HIDDEN ABILITY
Telepathy

STAT GROWTH RATES
HP	▪▪▪▪
Attack	▪
Defense	▪
Sp. Atk	▪▪
Sp. Def	▪▪
Speed	▪

EGG GROUP
No Eggs Discovered

EVOLUTION

Wynaut — Lv. 15 → Wobbuffet

ITEMS SOMETIMES HELD BY WILD POKÉMON
None

Damage taken in normal battles		Damage taken in Inverse Battles	
Normal	×1	Normal	×1
Fire	×1	Fire	×1
Water	×1	Water	×1
Grass	×1	Grass	×1
Electric	×1	Electric	×1
Ice	×1	Ice	×1
Fighting	×0.5	Fighting	×2
Poison	×1	Poison	×1
Ground	×1	Ground	×1
Flying	×1	Flying	×1
Psychic	×0.5	Psychic	×2
Bug	×2	Bug	×0.5
Rock	×1	Rock	×1
Ghost	×2	Ghost	×0.5
Dragon	×1	Dragon	×1
Dark	×2	Dark	×0.5
Steel	×1	Steel	×1
Fairy	×1	Fairy	×1

Can be used in	
Inverse Battle	Battle Institute
—	Battle Maison
Battle Chateau	Random Matchup

Same form for ♂/♀

How to obtain for your Coastal Kalos Pokédex

Have Wobbuffet hold Lax Incense and leave it at the Pokémon Day Care, and hatch the Egg that is found.

Have Wobbuffet hold Lax Incense and leave it at the Pokémon Day Care, and hatch the Egg that is found.

● LEVEL-UP MOVES

Lv.	Name	Type	Kind	Pow.	Acc.	PP	Range
1	Splash	Normal	Status	—	—	40	Self
1	Charm	Fairy	Status	—	100	20	Normal
1	Encore	Normal	Status	—	100	5	Normal
15	Counter	Fighting	Physical	—	100	20	Varies
15	Mirror Coat	Psychic	Special	—	100	20	Varies
15	Safeguard	Normal	Status	—	—	25	Your Side
15	Destiny Bond	Ghost	Status	—	—	5	Self

● TM & HM MOVES

No.	Name	Type	Kind	Pow.	Acc.	PP	Range
TM20	Safeguard	Normal	Status	—	—	25	Your Side

No.	Name	Type	Kind	Pow.	Acc.	PP	Range

● MOVES TAUGHT BY PEOPLE

Name	Type	Kind	Pow.	Acc.	PP	Range

● EGG MOVES

Name	Type	Kind	Pow.	Acc.	PP	Range

AFTER THE HALL OF FAME

CENTRAL KALOS

COASTAL KALOS

119 Wobbuffet

MOUNTAIN KALOS

ADVENTURE DATA

🏔 Coastal Kalos — 119

Patient Pokémon

☑ Wobbuffet

HEIGHT: 4'03" WEIGHT: 62.8 lbs.
GENDER: ♂/♀

X It hates light and shock. If attacked, it inflates its body to build up its counterstrike.

Y To keep its pitch-black tail hidden, it lives quietly in the darkness. It is never first to attack.

TYPE Psychic

ABILITY
Shadow Tag

HIDDEN ABILITY
Telepathy

STAT GROWTH RATES
HP	▪▪▪▪▪▪▪
Attack	▪▪
Defense	▪▪▪
Sp. Atk	▪▪
Sp. Def	▪▪
Speed	▪▪

EGG GROUP
Amorphous

EVOLUTION

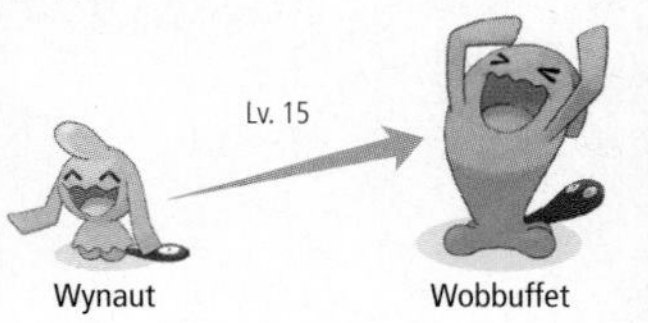

Wynaut → Lv. 15 → Wobbuffet

ITEMS SOMETIMES HELD BY WILD POKÉMON
None

Damage taken in normal battles		Damage taken in Inverse Battles	
Normal	×1	Normal	×1
Fire	×1	Fire	×1
Water	×1	Water	×1
Grass	×1	Grass	×1
Electric	×1	Electric	×1
Ice	×1	Ice	×1
Fighting	×0.5	Fighting	×2
Poison	×1	Poison	×1
Ground	×1	Ground	×1
Flying	×1	Flying	×1
Psychic	×0.5	Psychic	×2
Bug	×2	Bug	×0.5
Rock	×1	Rock	×1
Ghost	×2	Ghost	×0.5
Dragon	×1	Dragon	×1
Dark	×2	Dark	×0.5
Steel	×1	Steel	×1
Fairy	×1	Fairy	×1

Can be used in
Inverse Battle
—
Battle Chateau
Battle Institute
Battle Maison
Random Matchup

How to obtain for your Coastal Kalos Pokédex

Catch in Reflection Cave.	Catch in Reflection Cave.
X	Y

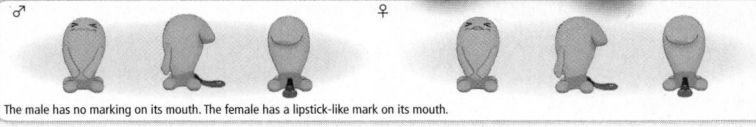

The male has no marking on its mouth. The female has a lipstick-like mark on its mouth.

● LEVEL-UP MOVES

Lv.	Name	Type	Kind	Pow.	Acc.	PP	Range
1	Counter	Fighting	Physical	—	100	20	Varies
1	Mirror Coat	Psychic	Special	—	100	20	Varies
1	Safeguard	Normal	Status	—	—	25	Your Side
1	Destiny Bond	Ghost	Status	—	—	5	Self

● TM & HM MOVES

No.	Name	Type	Kind	Pow.	Acc.	PP	Range
TM20	Safeguard	Normal	Status	—	—	25	Your Side

● MOVES TAUGHT BY PEOPLE

Name	Type	Kind	Pow.	Acc.	PP	Range

● EGG MOVES

Name	Type	Kind	Pow.	Acc.	PP	Range

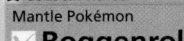

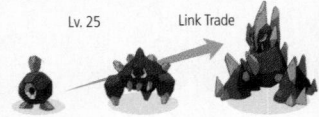

Coastal Kalos
Mantle Pokémon
☑ Roggenrola
120

HEIGHT: 1'04" **WEIGHT:** 39.7 lbs.
GENDER: ♂/♀

TYPE Rock

ABILITY
Sturdy

HIDDEN ABILITY
Sand Force

X Its ear is hexagonal in shape. Compressed underground, its body is as hard as steel.

Y They were discovered a hundred years ago in an earthquake fissure. Inside each one is an energy core.

STAT GROWTH RATES
HP	■■
Attack	■■■■
Defense	■■■■
Sp. Atk	■
Sp. Def	■
Speed	■

EGG GROUP
Mineral

EVOLUTION

Roggenrola → (Lv. 25) Boldore → (Link Trade) Gigalith

ITEMS SOMETIMES HELD BY WILD POKÉMON
Everstone, Hard Stone

Damage taken in normal battles	
Normal	×0.5
Fire	×0.5
Water	×2
Grass	×2
Electric	×1
Ice	×1
Fighting	×2
Poison	×0.5
Ground	×2
Flying	×0.5
Psychic	×1
Bug	×1
Rock	×1
Ghost	×1
Dragon	×1
Dark	×1
Steel	×2
Fairy	×1

Damage taken in Inverse Battles	
Normal	×2
Fire	×2
Water	×0.5
Grass	×0.5
Electric	×1
Ice	×1
Fighting	×0.5
Poison	×2
Ground	×0.5
Flying	×2
Psychic	×1
Bug	×1
Rock	×1
Ghost	×1
Dragon	×1
Dark	×1
Steel	×0.5
Fairy	×1

Can be used in	
Inverse Battle	Battle Institute
—	Battle Maison
Battle Chateau	Random Matchup

Same form for ♂/♀

How to obtain for your Coastal Kalos Pokédex
❶ Catch in Reflection Cave.
❷ Catch in a Horde Encounter in Reflection Cave.

❶ Catch in Reflection Cave.
❷ Catch in a Horde Encounter in Reflection Cave.

● LEVEL-UP MOVES
Lv.	Name	Type	Kind	Pow.	Acc.	PP	Range
1	Tackle	Normal	Physical	50	100	35	Normal
4	Harden	Normal	Status	—	—	30	Self
7	Sand Attack	Ground	Status	—	100	15	Normal
10	Headbutt	Normal	Physical	70	100	15	Normal
14	Rock Blast	Rock	Physical	25	90	10	Normal
17	Mud-Slap	Ground	Special	20	100	10	Normal
20	Iron Defense	Steel	Status	—	—	15	Self
23	Smack Down	Rock	Physical	50	100	15	Normal
27	Rock Slide	Rock	Physical	75	90	10	Many Others
30	Stealth Rock	Rock	Status	—	—	20	Other Side
33	Sandstorm	Rock	Status	—	—	10	Both Sides
36	Stone Edge	Rock	Physical	100	80	5	Normal
40	Explosion	Normal	Physical	250	100	5	Adjacent

● TM & HM MOVES
No.	Name	Type	Kind	Pow.	Acc.	PP	Range
TM06	Toxic	Poison	Status	—	90	10	Normal
TM10	Hidden Power	Normal	Special	60	100	15	Normal
TM17	Protect	Normal	Status	—	—	10	Self
TM21	Frustration	Normal	Physical	—	100	20	Normal
TM23	Smack Down	Rock	Physical	50	100	15	Normal
TM26	Earthquake	Ground	Physical	100	100	10	Adjacent
TM27	Return	Normal	Physical	—	100	20	Normal
TM32	Double Team	Normal	Status	—	—	15	Self
TM37	Sandstorm	Rock	Status	—	—	10	Both Sides
TM39	Rock Tomb	Rock	Physical	60	95	15	Normal
TM42	Facade	Normal	Physical	70	100	20	Normal
TM44	Rest	Psychic	Status	—	—	10	Self
TM48	Round	Normal	Special	60	100	15	Normal
TM64	Explosion	Normal	Physical	250	100	5	Adjacent
TM69	Rock Polish	Rock	Status	—	—	20	Self
TM71	Stone Edge	Rock	Physical	100	80	5	Normal
TM78	Bulldoze	Ground	Physical	60	100	20	Adjacent
TM80	Rock Slide	Rock	Physical	75	90	10	Many Others
TM87	Swagger	Normal	Status	—	90	15	Normal
TM88	Sleep Talk	Normal	Status	—	—	10	Self
TM90	Substitute	Normal	Status	—	—	10	Self
TM91	Flash Cannon	Steel	Special	80	100	10	Normal
TM94	Rock Smash	Fighting	Physical	40	100	15	Normal
TM96	Nature Power	Normal	Status	—	—	20	Normal
TM100	Confide	Normal	Status	—	—	20	Normal
HM04	Strength	Normal	Physical	80	100	15	Normal

● MOVES TAUGHT BY PEOPLE
Name	Type	Kind	Pow.	Acc.	PP	Range

● EGG MOVES
Name	Type	Kind	Pow.	Acc.	PP	Range
Magnitude	Ground	Physical	—	100	30	Adjacent
Curse	Ghost	Status	—	—	10	Varies
Autotomize	Steel	Status	—	—	15	Self
Rock Tomb	Rock	Physical	60	95	15	Normal
Lock-On	Normal	Status	—	—	5	Normal
Heavy Slam	Steel	Physical	—	100	10	Normal
Take Down	Normal	Physical	90	85	20	Normal
Gravity	Psychic	Status	—	—	5	Both Sides
Wide Guard	Rock	Status	—	—	10	Your Side

AFTER THE HALL OF FAME

CENTRAL KALOS

COASTAL KALOS

120
Roggenrola

MOUNTAIN KALOS

ADVENTURE DATA

AFTER THE HALL OF FAME

CENTRAL KALOS

COASTAL KALOS

121

Boldore

MOUNTAIN KALOS

ADVENTURE DATA

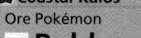

Coastal Kalos — 121
Ore Pokémon
Boldore

HEIGHT: 2'11" WEIGHT: 224.9 lbs.
GENDER: ♂/♀

TYPE: Rock

ABILITY
Sturdy

HIDDEN ABILITY
Sand Force

STAT GROWTH RATES
HP	■■■
Attack	■■■■■
Defense	■■■■■
Sp. Atk	■■
Sp. Def	■■
Speed	■

EGG GROUP
Mineral

EVOLUTION

Roggenrola → Lv. 25 Boldore → Link Trade Gigalith

X: Because its energy was too great to be contained, the energy leaked and formed orange crystals.

Y: When it is healthy, its core sticks out. Always facing the same way, it swiftly moves front to back and left to right.

ITEMS SOMETIMES HELD BY WILD POKÉMON
None

Damage taken in normal battles		Damage taken in Inverse Battles	
Normal	×0.5	Normal	×2
Fire	×0.5	Fire	×2
Water	×2	Water	×0.5
Grass	×2	Grass	×0.5
Electric	×1	Electric	×1
Ice	×1	Ice	×1
Fighting	×2	Fighting	×0.5
Poison	×0.5	Poison	×2
Ground	×2	Ground	×0.5
Flying	×0.5	Flying	×2
Psychic	×1	Psychic	×1
Bug	×1	Bug	×1
Rock	×1	Rock	×1
Ghost	×1	Ghost	×1
Dragon	×1	Dragon	×1
Dark	×1	Dark	×1
Steel	×2	Steel	×0.5
Fairy	×1	Fairy	×1

Can be used in	
Inverse Battle	Battle Institute
—	Battle Maison
Battle Chateau	Random Matchup

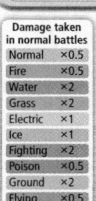

Same form for ♂/♀

How to obtain for your Coastal Kalos Pokédex

Level up Roggenrola to Lv. 25.	Level up Roggenrola to Lv. 25.

● LEVEL-UP MOVES

Lv.	Name	Type	Kind	Pow.	Acc.	PP	Range
1	Tackle	Normal	Physical	50	100	35	Normal
1	Harden	Normal	Status	—	—	30	Self
1	Sand Attack	Ground	Status	—	100	15	Normal
1	Headbutt	Normal	Physical	70	100	15	Normal
4	Harden	Normal	Status	—	—	30	Self
7	Sand Attack	Ground	Status	—	100	15	Normal
10	Headbutt	Normal	Physical	70	100	15	Normal
14	Rock Blast	Rock	Physical	25	90	10	Normal
17	Mud-Slap	Ground	Special	20	100	10	Normal
20	Iron Defense	Steel	Status	—	—	15	Self
23	Smack Down	Rock	Physical	50	100	15	Many Others
25	Power Gem	Rock	Special	80	100	20	Normal
30	Rock Slide	Rock	Physical	75	90	10	Many Others
36	Stealth Rock	Rock	Status	—	—	20	Other Side
42	Sandstorm	Rock	Status	—	—	10	Both Sides
48	Stone Edge	Rock	Physical	100	80	5	Normal
55	Explosion	Normal	Physical	250	100	5	Adjacent

● TM & HM MOVES

No.	Name	Type	Kind	Pow.	Acc.	PP	Range
TM06	Toxic	Poison	Status	—	90	10	Normal
TM10	Hidden Power	Normal	Special	60	100	15	Normal
TM17	Protect	Normal	Status	—	—	10	Self
TM21	Frustration	Normal	Physical	—	100	20	Normal
TM23	Smack Down	Rock	Physical	50	100	15	Normal
TM26	Earthquake	Ground	Physical	100	100	10	Adjacent
TM27	Return	Normal	Physical	—	100	20	Normal
TM32	Double Team	Normal	Status	—	—	15	Self
TM37	Sandstorm	Rock	Status	—	—	10	Both Sides
TM39	Rock Tomb	Rock	Physical	60	95	15	Normal
TM42	Facade	Normal	Physical	70	100	20	Normal
TM44	Rest	Psychic	Status	—	—	10	Self
TM45	Attract	Normal	Status	—	100	15	Normal
TM48	Round	Normal	Special	60	100	15	Normal
TM64	Explosion	Normal	Physical	250	100	5	Adjacent
TM69	Rock Polish	Rock	Status	—	—	20	Self
TM71	Stone Edge	Rock	Physical	100	80	5	Normal
TM78	Bulldoze	Ground	Physical	60	100	20	Adjacent
TM80	Rock Slide	Rock	Physical	75	90	10	Many Others
TM87	Swagger	Normal	Status	—	90	15	Normal
TM88	Sleep Talk	Normal	Status	—	—	10	Self
TM90	Substitute	Normal	Status	—	—	10	Self
TM91	Flash Cannon	Steel	Special	80	100	10	Normal
TM94	Rock Smash	Fighting	Physical	40	100	15	Normal
TM96	Nature Power	Normal	Status	—	—	20	Normal
TM100	Confide	Normal	Status	—	—	20	Normal
HM04	Strength	Normal	Physical	80	100	15	Normal

No.	Name	Type	Kind	Pow.	Acc.	PP	Range

● MOVES TAUGHT BY PEOPLE

Name	Type	Kind	Pow.	Acc.	PP	Range

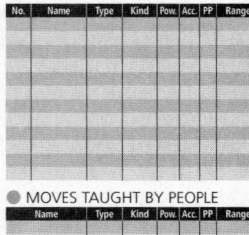

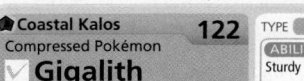

Coastal Kalos 122
Compressed Pokémon
☑ **Gigalith**

HEIGHT: 5'07" WEIGHT: 573.2 lbs.
GENDER: ♂/♀

TYPE	Rock	

ABILITY
Sturdy

HIDDEN ABILITY
Sand Force

STAT GROWTH RATES

HP	■■■
Attack	■■■■■■■
Defense	■■■■■■■■
Sp. Atk	■■■
Sp. Def	■■■
Speed	■■

EGG GROUP
Mineral

❌ The solar rays it absorbs are processed in its energy core and fired as a ball of light.

❌ Compressing the energy from its internal core lets it fire off an attack capable of blowing away a mountain.

EVOLUTION

Lv. 25 → Link Trade

Roggenrola → Boldore → Gigalith

ITEMS SOMETIMES HELD BY WILD POKÉMON
None

Damage taken in normal battles	
Normal	×0.5
Fire	×0.5
Water	×2
Grass	×2
Electric	×1
Ice	×1
Fighting	×2
Poison	×0.5
Ground	×2
Flying	×0.5
Psychic	×1
Bug	×1
Rock	×1
Ghost	×1
Dragon	×1
Dark	×1
Steel	×2
Fairy	×1

Damage taken in Inverse Battles	
Normal	×2
Fire	×2
Water	×0.5
Grass	×0.5
Electric	×1
Ice	×1
Fighting	×0.5
Poison	×2
Ground	×0.5
Flying	×2
Psychic	×1
Bug	×1
Rock	×1
Ghost	×1
Dragon	×1
Dark	×1
Steel	×0.5
Fairy	×1

Can be used in	
Inverse Battle	Battle Institute
—	Battle Maison
Battle Chateau	Random Matchup

Same form for ♂/♀

How to obtain for your Coastal Kalos Pokédex

Receive Boldore by Link Trade, and have it evolve.

Receive Boldore by Link Trade, and have it evolve.

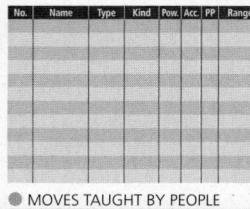

● LEVEL-UP MOVES

Lv.	Name	Type	Kind	Pow.	Acc.	PP	Range
1	Tackle	Normal	Physical	50	100	35	Normal
1	Harden	Normal	Status	—	—	30	Self
1	Sand Attack	Ground	Status	—	100	15	Normal
1	Headbutt	Normal	Physical	70	100	15	Normal
4	Harden	Normal	Status	—	—	30	Self
7	Sand Attack	Ground	Status	—	100	15	Normal
10	Headbutt	Normal	Physical	70	100	15	Normal
14	Rock Blast	Rock	Physical	25	90	10	Normal
17	Mud-Slap	Ground	Special	20	100	10	Normal
20	Iron Defense	Steel	Status	—	—	15	Self
23	Smack Down	Rock	Physical	50	100	15	Normal
25	Power Gem	Rock	Special	80	100	20	Normal
30	Rock Slide	Rock	Physical	75	90	10	Many Others
36	Stealth Rock	Rock	Status	—	—	20	Other Side
42	Sandstorm	Rock	Status	—	—	10	Both Sides
48	Stone Edge	Rock	Physical	100	80	5	Normal
55	Explosion	Normal	Physical	250	100	5	Adjacent

● TM & HM MOVES

No.	Name	Type	Kind	Pow.	Acc.	PP	Range
TM06	Toxic	Poison	Status	—	90	10	Normal
TM10	Hidden Power	Normal	Special	60	100	15	Normal
TM15	Hyper Beam	Normal	Special	150	90	5	Normal
TM17	Protect	Normal	Status	—	—	10	Self
TM21	Frustration	Normal	Physical	—	100	20	Normal
TM22	Solar Beam	Grass	Special	120	100	10	Normal
TM23	Smack Down	Rock	Physical	50	100	15	Normal
TM26	Earthquake	Ground	Physical	100	100	10	Adjacent
TM27	Return	Normal	Physical	—	100	20	Normal
TM32	Double Team	Normal	Status	—	—	15	Self
TM37	Sandstorm	Rock	Status	—	—	10	Both Sides
TM39	Rock Tomb	Rock	Physical	60	95	15	Normal
TM42	Facade	Normal	Physical	70	100	20	Normal
TM44	Rest	Psychic	Status	—	—	10	Self
TM45	Attract	Normal	Status	—	100	15	Normal
TM48	Round	Normal	Special	60	100	15	Normal
TM64	Explosion	Normal	Physical	250	100	5	Adjacent
TM68	Giga Impact	Normal	Physical	150	90	5	Normal
TM69	Rock Polish	Rock	Status	—	—	20	Self
TM71	Stone Edge	Rock	Physical	100	80	5	Normal
TM78	Bulldoze	Ground	Physical	60	100	20	Adjacent
TM80	Rock Slide	Rock	Physical	75	90	10	Many Others
TM87	Swagger	Normal	Status	—	90	15	Normal
TM88	Sleep Talk	Normal	Status	—	—	10	Self
TM90	Substitute	Normal	Status	—	—	10	Self
TM91	Flash Cannon	Steel	Special	80	100	10	Normal
TM94	Rock Smash	Fighting	Physical	40	100	15	Normal
TM96	Nature Power	Normal	Status	—	—	20	Normal
TM100	Confide	Normal	Status	—	—	20	Normal
HM04	Strength	Normal	Physical	80	100	15	Normal

No.	Name	Type	Kind	Pow.	Acc.	PP	Range

● MOVES TAUGHT BY PEOPLE

Name	Type	Kind	Pow.	Acc.	PP	Range

AFTER THE HALL OF FAME

CENTRAL KALOS

COASTAL KALOS

122

Gigalith

MOUNTAIN KALOS

ADVENTURE DATA

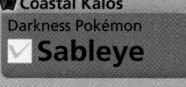

Coastal Kalos

123

Darkness Pokémon

☑ **Sableye**

HEIGHT: 1'08" WEIGHT: 24.3 lbs.
GENDER: ♂/♀

AFTER THE
HALL OF FAME

CENTRAL
KALOS

COASTAL
KALOS

123
Sableye

MOUNTAIN
KALOS

ADVENTURE
DATA

TYPE	Dark	Ghost

ABILITIES
Keen Eye
Stall

HIDDEN ABILITY
Prankster

STAT GROWTH RATES
HP ▪▪
Attack ▪▪▪▪
Defense ▪▪▪
Sp. Atk ▪▪▪
Sp. Def ▪▪▪
Speed ▪▪▪

EGG GROUP
Human-Like

EVOLUTION

Does not evolve

ITEMS SOMETIMES HELD BY WILD POKÉMON
None

 It hides in the darkness of caves. Its diet of gems has transformed its eyes into gemstones.

 It dwells in the darkness of caves. It uses its sharp claws to dig up gems to nourish itself.

Damage taken in normal battles

Normal	×0
Fire	×1
Water	×1
Grass	×1
Electric	×1
Ice	×1
Fighting	×0
Poison	×0.5
Ground	×1
Flying	×1
Psychic	×0
Bug	×1
Rock	×1
Ghost	×1
Dragon	×1
Dark	×1
Steel	×1
Fairy	×2

Damage taken in Inverse Battles

Normal	×2
Fire	×1
Water	×1
Grass	×1
Electric	×1
Ice	×1
Fighting	×1
Poison	×2
Ground	×1
Flying	×1
Psychic	×2
Bug	×1
Rock	×1
Ghost	×1
Dragon	×1
Dark	×1
Steel	×1
Fairy	×0.5

Can be used in

Inverse Battle	Battle Institute
—	Battle Maison
Battle Chateau	Random Matchup

Same form for ♂/♀

How to obtain for your Coastal Kalos Pokédex

Catch in Reflection Cave.

Catch in Reflection Cave.

● LEVEL-UP MOVES

Lv.	Name	Type	Kind	Pow.	Acc.	PP	Range
1	Mean Look	Normal	Status	—	—	5	Normal
1	Zen Headbutt	Psychic	Physical	80	90	15	Normal
1	Leer	Normal	Status	—	100	30	Many Others
1	Scratch	Normal	Physical	40	100	35	Normal
4	Foresight	Normal	Status	—	—	40	Normal
8	Night Shade	Ghost	Special	—	100	15	Normal
11	Astonish	Ghost	Physical	30	100	15	Normal
15	Fury Swipes	Normal	Physical	18	80	15	Normal
18	Fake Out	Normal	Physical	40	100	10	Normal
22	Detect	Fighting	Status	—	—	5	Self
25	Shadow Sneak	Ghost	Physical	40	100	30	Normal
29	Knock Off	Dark	Physical	65	100	20	Normal
32	Feint Attack	Dark	Physical	60	—	20	Normal
36	Punishment	Dark	Physical	—	100	5	Normal
39	Shadow Claw	Ghost	Physical	70	100	15	Normal
43	Power Gem	Rock	Special	80	100	20	Normal
46	Confuse Ray	Ghost	Status	—	100	10	Normal
50	Foul Play	Dark	Physical	95	100	15	Normal
53	Zen Headbutt	Psychic	Physical	80	90	15	Normal
57	Shadow Ball	Ghost	Special	80	100	15	Normal
60	Mean Look	Normal	Status	—	—	5	Normal

● TM & HM MOVES

No.	Name	Type	Kind	Pow.	Acc.	PP	Range
TM01	Hone Claws	Dark	Status	—	—	15	Self
TM04	Calm Mind	Psychic	Status	—	—	20	Self
TM06	Toxic	Poison	Status	—	90	10	Normal
TM10	Hidden Power	Normal	Special	60	100	15	Normal
TM11	Sunny Day	Fire	Status	—	—	5	Both Sides
TM12	Taunt	Dark	Status	—	100	20	Normal
TM17	Protect	Normal	Status	—	—	10	Self
TM18	Rain Dance	Water	Status	—	—	5	Both Sides
TM21	Frustration	Normal	Physical	—	100	20	Normal
TM27	Return	Normal	Physical	—	100	20	Normal
TM28	Dig	Ground	Physical	80	100	10	Normal
TM29	Psychic	Psychic	Special	90	100	10	Normal
TM30	Shadow Ball	Ghost	Special	80	100	15	Normal
TM31	Brick Break	Fighting	Physical	75	100	15	Normal
TM32	Double Team	Normal	Status	—	—	15	Self
TM39	Rock Tomb	Rock	Physical	60	95	15	Normal
TM40	Aerial Ace	Flying	Physical	60	—	20	Normal
TM41	Torment	Dark	Status	—	100	15	Normal
TM42	Facade	Normal	Physical	70	100	20	Normal
TM44	Rest	Psychic	Status	—	—	10	Self
TM46	Thief	Dark	Physical	60	100	25	Normal
TM47	Low Sweep	Fighting	Physical	65	100	20	Normal
TM48	Round	Normal	Special	60	100	15	Normal
TM56	Fling	Dark	Physical	—	100	10	Normal
TM59	Incinerate	Fire	Special	60	100	15	Many Others
TM61	Will-O-Wisp	Fire	Status	—	85	15	Normal
TM63	Embargo	Dark	Status	—	100	15	Normal
TM65	Shadow Claw	Ghost	Physical	70	100	15	Normal
TM66	Payback	Dark	Physical	50	100	10	Normal
TM67	Retaliate	Normal	Physical	70	100	5	Normal
TM70	Flash	Normal	Status	—	100	20	Normal
TM77	Psych Up	Normal	Status	—	—	10	Normal

No.	Name	Type	Kind	Pow.	Acc.	PP	Range
TM84	Poison Jab	Poison	Physical	80	100	20	Normal
TM85	Dream Eater	Psychic	Special	100	100	15	Normal
TM87	Swagger	Normal	Status	—	90	15	Normal
TM88	Sleep Talk	Normal	Status	—	—	10	Self
TM90	Substitute	Normal	Status	—	—	10	Self
TM94	Rock Smash	Fighting	Physical	40	100	15	Normal
TM95	Snarl	Dark	Special	55	95	15	Many Others
TM97	Dark Pulse	Dark	Special	80	100	15	Normal
TM98	Power-Up Punch	Fighting	Physical	40	100	20	Normal
TM99	Dazzling Gleam	Fairy	Special	80	100	10	Many Others
TM100	Confide	Normal	Status	—	—	20	Normal
HM01	Cut	Normal	Physical	50	95	30	Normal

● MOVES TAUGHT BY PEOPLE

Name	Type	Kind	Pow.	Acc.	PP	Range

● EGG MOVES

Name	Type	Kind	Pow.	Acc.	PP	Range
Recover	Normal	Status	—	—	10	Self
Moonlight	Fairy	Status	—	—	5	Self
Nasty Plot	Dark	Status	—	—	20	Self
Flatter	Dark	Status	—	100	15	Normal
Feint	Normal	Physical	30	100	10	Normal
Sucker Punch	Dark	Physical	80	100	5	Normal
Trick	Psychic	Status	—	100	10	Normal
Captivate	Normal	Status	—	100	20	Many Others
Mean Look	Normal	Status	—	—	5	Normal
Metal Burst	Steel	Physical	—	100	10	Varies
Imprison	Psychic	Status	—	—	10	Self

AFTER THE HALL OF FAME

CENTRAL KALOS

COASTAL KALOS

124

Carbink

MOUNTAIN KALOS

ADVENTURE DATA

🔺 Coastal Kalos

Jewel Pokémon

✔ Carbink

124

HEIGHT: 1'00"   WEIGHT: 12.6 lbs.
GENDER: unknown

X Born from the temperatures and pressures deep underground, it fires beams from the stone in its head.

Y It has slept underground for hundreds of millions of years since its birth. It's occasionally found during the excavation of caves.

TYPE Rock Fairy

ABILITY
Clear Body

HIDDEN ABILITY
Sturdy

STAT GROWTH RATES
HP	▮▮
Attack	▮▮▮
Defense	▮▮▮▮▮
Sp. Atk	▮▮
Sp. Def	▮▮▮▮▮
Speed	▮▮▮

EGG GROUPS
Fairy, Mineral

EVOLUTION

Does not evolve

ITEMS SOMETIMES HELD BY WILD POKÉMON
None

Damage taken in normal battles		Damage taken in Inverse Battles	
Normal	×0.5	Normal	×2
Fire	×0.5	Fire	×2
Water	×2	Water	×0.5
Grass	×2	Grass	×0.5
Electric	×1	Electric	×1
Ice	×1	Ice	×1
Fighting	×1	Fighting	×1
Poison	×1	Poison	×1
Ground	×2	Ground	×0.5
Flying	×0.5	Flying	×2
Psychic	×1	Psychic	×1
Bug	×0.5	Bug	×2
Rock	×1	Rock	×1
Ghost	×1	Ghost	×1
Dragon	×0	Dragon	×2
Dark	×0.5	Dark	×2
Steel	×4	Steel	×0.25
Fairy	×1	Fairy	×1

Can be used in	
Inverse Battle	Battle Institute
—	Battle Maison
Battle Chateau	Random Matchup

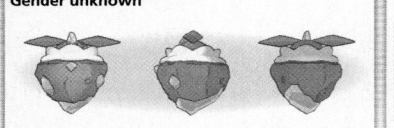

Gender unknown

How to obtain for your Coastal Kalos Pokédex

❶ Catch in Reflection Cave.
❷ Catch in a Horde Encounter in Reflection Cave.

❶ Catch in Reflection Cave.
❷ Catch in a Horde Encounter in Reflection Cave.

● LEVEL-UP MOVES

Lv.	Name	Type	Kind	Pow.	Acc.	PP	Range
1	Tackle	Normal	Physical	50	100	35	Normal
1	Harden	Normal	Status	—	—	30	Self
5	Rock Throw	Rock	Physical	50	90	15	Normal
8	Sharpen	Normal	Status	—	—	30	Self
12	Smack Down	Rock	Physical	50	100	15	Normal
18	Reflect	Psychic	Status	—	—	20	Your Side
21	Stealth Rock	Rock	Status	—	—	20	Other Side
27	Guard Split	Psychic	Status	—	—	10	Normal
31	Ancient Power	Rock	Special	60	100	5	Normal
35	Flail	Normal	Physical	—	100	15	Normal
40	Skill Swap	Psychic	Status	—	—	10	Normal
46	Power Gem	Rock	Special	80	100	20	Normal
49	Stone Edge	Rock	Physical	100	80	5	Normal
50	Moonblast	Fairy	Special	95	100	15	Normal
60	Light Screen	Psychic	Status	—	—	30	Your Side
70	Safeguard	Normal	Status	—	—	25	Your Side

■ TM & HM MOVES

No.	Name	Type	Kind	Pow.	Acc.	PP	Range
TM04	Calm Mind	Psychic	Status	—	—	20	Self
TM06	Toxic	Poison	Status	—	90	10	Normal
TM07	Hail	Ice	Status	—	—	10	Both Sides
TM10	Hidden Power	Normal	Special	60	100	15	Normal
TM11	Sunny Day	Fire	Status	—	—	5	Both Sides
TM16	Light Screen	Psychic	Status	—	—	30	Your Side
TM17	Protect	Normal	Status	—	—	10	Self
TM20	Safeguard	Normal	Status	—	—	25	Your Side
TM21	Frustration	Normal	Physical	—	100	20	Normal
TM23	Smack Down	Rock	Physical	50	100	15	Normal
TM27	Return	Normal	Physical	—	100	20	Normal
TM29	Psychic	Psychic	Special	90	100	10	Normal
TM32	Double Team	Normal	Status	—	—	15	Self
TM33	Reflect	Psychic	Status	—	—	20	Your Side
TM37	Sandstorm	Rock	Status	—	—	10	Both Sides
TM39	Rock Tomb	Rock	Physical	60	95	15	Normal
TM42	Facade	Normal	Physical	70	100	20	Normal
TM44	Rest	Psychic	Status	—	—	10	Self
TM48	Round	Normal	Special	60	100	15	Normal
TM64	Explosion	Normal	Physical	250	100	5	Adjacent
TM69	Rock Polish	Rock	Status	—	—	20	Self
TM70	Flash	Normal	Status	—	100	20	Normal
TM71	Stone Edge	Rock	Physical	100	80	5	Normal
TM74	Gyro Ball	Steel	Physical	—	100	5	Normal
TM77	Psych Up	Normal	Status	—	—	10	Self
TM80	Rock Slide	Rock	Physical	75	90	10	Many Others
TM87	Swagger	Normal	Status	—	90	15	Normal
TM88	Sleep Talk	Normal	Status	—	—	10	Self
TM90	Substitute	Normal	Status	—	—	10	Self
TM92	Trick Room	Psychic	Status	—	—	5	Both Sides
TM96	Nature Power	Normal	Status	—	—	20	Normal
TM99	Dazzling Gleam	Fairy	Special	80	100	10	Many Others
TM100	Confide	Normal	Status	—	—	20	Normal

● MOVES TAUGHT BY PEOPLE

Name	Type	Kind	Pow.	Acc.	PP	Range

● EGG MOVES

Name	Type	Kind	Pow.	Acc.	PP	Range

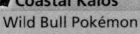
♠ Coastal Kalos
Wild Bull Pokémon
125

☑ **Tauros**

HEIGHT: 4'07" WEIGHT: 194.9 lbs.
GENDER: ♂

 After heightening its will to fight by whipping itself with its three tails, it charges at full speed.

 When it is about to tackle, it whips its body repeatedly with its three long tails.

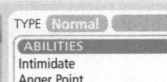

TYPE Normal

ABILITIES
Intimidate
Anger Point

HIDDEN ABILITY
Sheer Force

STAT GROWTH RATES
HP	■■■
Attack	■■■■■
Defense	■■■■
Sp. Atk	■■
Sp. Def	■■■
Speed	■■■■■■

EGG GROUP
Field

EVOLUTION

Does not evolve

ITEMS SOMETIMES HELD BY WILD POKÉMON
None

Damage taken in normal battles		Damage taken in Inverse Battles	
Normal	×1	Normal	×1
Fire	×1	Fire	×1
Water	×1	Water	×1
Grass	×1	Grass	×1
Electric	×1	Electric	×1
Ice	×1	Ice	×1
Fighting	×2	Fighting	×0.5
Poison	×1	Poison	×1
Ground	×1	Ground	×1
Flying	×1	Flying	×1
Psychic	×1	Psychic	×1
Bug	×1	Bug	×1
Rock	×1	Rock	×1
Ghost	×0	Ghost	×2
Dragon	×1	Dragon	×1
Dark	×1	Dark	×1
Steel	×1	Steel	×1
Fairy	×1	Fairy	×1

Can be used in	
Inverse Battle	Battle Institute
—	Battle Maison
Battle Chateau	Random Matchup

♂

How to obtain for your Coastal Kalos Pokédex
❶ Catch in the tall grass on Route 12.
❷ Catch in the yellow flowers on Route 12.

❶ Catch in the tall grass on Route 12.
❷ Catch in the yellow flowers on Route 12.

● **LEVEL-UP MOVES**

Lv.	Name	Type	Kind	Pow.	Acc.	PP	Range
1	Tackle	Normal	Physical	50	100	35	Normal
1	Tail Whip	Normal	Status	—	100	30	Many Others
5	Rage	Normal	Physical	20	100	20	Normal
8	Horn Attack	Normal	Physical	65	100	25	Normal
11	Scary Face	Normal	Status	—	100	10	Normal
15	Pursuit	Dark	Physical	40	100	20	Normal
19	Rest	Psychic	Status	—	—	10	Self
24	Payback	Dark	Physical	50	100	10	Normal
29	Work Up	Normal	Status	—	—	30	Self
35	Zen Headbutt	Psychic	Physical	80	90	15	Normal
41	Take Down	Normal	Physical	90	85	20	Normal
48	Swagger	Normal	Status	—	90	15	Normal
50	Thrash	Normal	Physical	120	100	10	1 Random
63	Giga Impact	Normal	Physical	150	90	5	Normal

● **TM & HM MOVES**

No.	Name	Type	Kind	Pow.	Acc.	PP	Range
TM06	Toxic	Poison	Status	—	90	10	Normal
TM10	Hidden Power	Normal	Special	60	100	15	Normal
TM11	Sunny Day	Fire	Status	—	—	5	Both Sides
TM13	Ice Beam	Ice	Special	90	100	10	Normal
TM14	Blizzard	Ice	Special	110	70	5	Many Others
TM15	Hyper Beam	Normal	Special	150	90	5	Normal
TM17	Protect	Normal	Status	—	—	10	Self
TM18	Rain Dance	Water	Status	—	—	5	Both Sides
TM21	Frustration	Normal	Physical	—	100	20	Normal
TM22	Solar Beam	Grass	Special	120	100	10	Normal
TM24	Thunderbolt	Electric	Special	90	100	15	Normal
TM25	Thunder	Electric	Special	110	70	10	Normal
TM26	Earthquake	Ground	Physical	100	100	10	Adjacent
TM27	Return	Normal	Physical	—	100	20	Normal
TM32	Double Team	Normal	Status	—	—	15	Self
TM35	Flamethrower	Fire	Special	90	100	15	Normal
TM37	Sandstorm	Rock	Status	—	—	10	Both Sides
TM38	Fire Blast	Fire	Special	110	85	5	Normal
TM39	Rock Tomb	Rock	Physical	60	95	15	Normal
TM42	Facade	Normal	Physical	70	100	20	Normal
TM44	Rest	Psychic	Status	—	—	10	Self
TM45	Attract	Normal	Status	—	100	15	Normal
TM48	Round	Normal	Special	60	100	15	Normal
TM59	Incinerate	Fire	Special	60	100	15	Many Others
TM66	Payback	Dark	Physical	50	100	10	Normal
TM67	Retaliate	Normal	Physical	70	100	5	Normal
TM68	Giga Impact	Normal	Physical	150	90	5	Normal
TM71	Stone Edge	Rock	Physical	100	80	5	Normal
TM78	Bulldoze	Ground	Physical	60	100	20	Adjacent
TM80	Rock Slide	Rock	Physical	75	90	10	Many Others
TM87	Swagger	Normal	Status	—	90	15	Normal
TM88	Sleep Talk	Normal	Status	—	—	10	Self
TM90	Substitute	Normal	Status	—	—	10	Self

No.	Name	Type	Kind	Pow.	Acc.	PP	Range
TM93	Wild Charge	Electric	Physical	90	100	15	Normal
TM94	Rock Smash	Fighting	Physical	40	100	15	Normal
TM100	Confide	Normal	Status	—	—	20	Normal
HM03	Surf	Water	Special	90	100	15	Adjacent
HM04	Strength	Normal	Physical	80	100	15	Normal

● **MOVES TAUGHT BY PEOPLE**

Name	Type	Kind	Pow.	Acc.	PP	Range

● **EGG MOVES**

Name	Type	Kind	Pow.	Acc.	PP	Range

AFTER THE HALL OF FAME

CENTRAL KALOS

COASTAL KALOS

125 Tauros

MOUNTAIN KALOS

ADVENTURE DATA

Coastal Kalos
Milk Cow Pokémon
☑ Miltank

126

HEIGHT: 3'11" WEIGHT: 166.4 lbs.
GENDER: ♀

X If it is around babies, the milk it produces contains much more nutrition than usual.

Y Its milk is packed with nutrition, making it the ultimate beverage for the sick or weary.

TYPE Normal

ABILITIES
Thick Fat
Scrappy

HIDDEN ABILITY
Sap Sipper

STAT GROWTH RATES
HP	■■■
Attack	■■■
Defense	■■■■
Sp. Atk	■■
Sp. Def	■■
Speed	■■■■

EGG GROUP
Field

EVOLUTION

Does not evolve

ITEMS SOMETIMES HELD BY WILD POKÉMON
Moomoo Milk

Damage taken in normal battles	
Normal	×1
Fire	×1
Water	×1
Grass	×1
Electric	×1
Ice	×1
Fighting	×2
Poison	×1
Ground	×1
Flying	×1
Psychic	×1
Bug	×1
Rock	×1
Ghost	×0
Dragon	×1
Dark	×1
Steel	×1
Fairy	×1

Damage taken in Inverse Battles	
Normal	×1
Fire	×1
Water	×1
Grass	×1
Electric	×1
Ice	×1
Fighting	×0.5
Poison	×1
Ground	×1
Flying	×1
Psychic	×1
Bug	×1
Rock	×1
Ghost	×2
Dragon	×1
Dark	×1
Steel	×1
Fairy	×1

Can be used in	
Inverse Battle	Battle Institute
—	Battle Maison
Battle Chateau	Random Matchup

♀

How to obtain for your Coastal Kalos Pokédex

❶ Catch in the tall grass on Route 12.
❷ Catch in the yellow flowers on Route 12.

❶ Catch in the tall grass on Route 12.
❷ Catch in the yellow flowers on Route 12.

● LEVEL-UP MOVES

Lv.	Name	Type	Kind	Pow.	Acc.	PP	Range
1	Tackle	Normal	Physical	50	100	35	Normal
3	Growl	Normal	Status	—	100	40	Many Others
5	Defense Curl	Normal	Status	—	—	40	Self
8	Stomp	Normal	Physical	65	100	20	Normal
11	Milk Drink	Normal	Status	—	—	10	Self
15	Bide	Normal	Physical	—	—	10	Self
19	Rollout	Rock	Physical	30	90	20	Normal
24	Body Slam	Normal	Physical	85	100	15	Normal
29	Zen Headbutt	Psychic	Physical	80	90	15	Normal
35	Captivate	Normal	Status	—	100	20	Many Others
41	Gyro Ball	Steel	Physical	—	100	5	Normal
48	Heal Bell	Normal	Status	—	—	5	Your Party
50	Wake-Up Slap	Fighting	Physical	70	100	10	Normal

● TM & HM MOVES

No.	Name	Type	Kind	Pow.	Acc.	PP	Range
TM06	Toxic	Poison	Status	—	90	10	Normal
TM10	Hidden Power	Normal	Special	60	100	15	Normal
TM11	Sunny Day	Fire	Status	—	—	5	Both Sides
TM13	Ice Beam	Ice	Special	90	100	10	Normal
TM14	Blizzard	Ice	Special	110	70	5	Many Others
TM15	Hyper Beam	Normal	Special	150	90	5	Normal
TM17	Protect	Normal	Status	—	—	10	Self
TM18	Rain Dance	Water	Status	—	—	5	Both Sides
TM21	Frustration	Normal	Physical	—	100	20	Normal
TM22	Solar Beam	Grass	Special	120	100	10	Normal
TM24	Thunderbolt	Electric	Special	90	100	15	Normal
TM25	Thunder	Electric	Special	110	70	10	Normal
TM26	Earthquake	Ground	Physical	100	100	10	Adjacent
TM27	Return	Normal	Physical	—	100	20	Normal
TM30	Shadow Ball	Ghost	Special	80	100	15	Normal
TM31	Brick Break	Fighting	Physical	75	100	15	Normal
TM32	Double Team	Normal	Status	—	—	15	Self
TM37	Sandstorm	Rock	Status	—	—	10	Both Sides
TM39	Rock Tomb	Rock	Physical	60	95	15	Normal
TM42	Facade	Normal	Physical	70	100	20	Normal
TM44	Rest	Psychic	Status	—	—	10	Self
TM45	Attract	Normal	Status	—	100	15	Normal
TM48	Round	Normal	Special	60	100	15	Normal
TM49	Echoed Voice	Normal	Special	40	100	15	Normal
TM52	Focus Blast	Fighting	Special	120	70	5	Normal
TM56	Fling	Dark	Physical	—	100	10	Normal
TM67	Retaliate	Normal	Physical	70	100	5	Normal
TM68	Giga Impact	Normal	Physical	150	90	5	Normal
TM73	Thunder Wave	Electric	Status	—	100	20	Normal
TM74	Gyro Ball	Steel	Physical	—	100	5	Normal
TM77	Psych Up	Normal	Status	—	—	10	Normal
TM78	Bulldoze	Ground	Physical	60	100	20	Adjacent
TM80	Rock Slide	Rock	Physical	75	90	10	Many Others

No.	Name	Type	Kind	Pow.	Acc.	PP	Range
TM87	Swagger	Normal	Status	—	90	15	Normal
TM88	Sleep Talk	Normal	Status	—	—	10	Self
TM90	Substitute	Normal	Status	—	—	10	Self
TM94	Rock Smash	Fighting	Physical	40	100	15	Normal
TM98	Power-Up Punch	Fighting	Physical	40	100	20	Normal
TM100	Confide	Normal	Status	—	—	20	Normal
HM03	Surf	Water	Special	90	100	15	Adjacent
HM04	Strength	Normal	Physical	80	100	15	Normal

● MOVES TAUGHT BY PEOPLE

Name	Type	Kind	Pow.	Acc.	PP	Range

● EGG MOVES

Name	Type	Kind	Pow.	Acc.	PP	Range
Present	Normal	Physical	—	90	15	Normal
Reversal	Fighting	Physical	—	100	15	Normal
Seismic Toss	Fighting	Physical	—	100	20	Normal
Endure	Normal	Status	—	—	10	Self
Curse	Ghost	Status	—	—	10	Varies
Helping Hand	Normal	Status	—	—	20	1 Ally
Sleep Talk	Normal	Status	—	—	10	Self
Dizzy Punch	Normal	Physical	70	100	10	Normal
Hammer Arm	Fighting	Physical	100	90	10	Normal
Double-Edge	Normal	Physical	120	100	15	Normal
Punishment	Dark	Physical	—	100	5	Normal
Natural Gift	Normal	Physical	—	100	15	Normal
Heart Stamp	Psychic	Physical	60	100	25	Normal
Belch	Poison	Special	120	90	10	Normal

AFTER THE HALL OF FAME

CENTRAL KALOS

COASTAL KALOS

126

Miltank

MOUNTAIN KALOS

ADVENTURE DATA

Coastal Kalos 127
Wool Pokémon

✔ Mareep

HEIGHT: 2'00"　　WEIGHT: 17.2 lbs.
GENDER: ♂/♀

X Its fluffy coat swells to double when static electricity builds up. Touching it can be shocking.

Y It stores lots of air in its soft fur, allowing it to stay cool in summer and warm in winter.

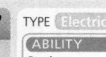

TYPE [Electric]

ABILITY
Static

HIDDEN ABILITY
Plus

STAT GROWTH RATES
HP	▪▪
Attack	▪▪
Defense	▪▪
Sp. Atk	▪▪▪
Sp. Def	▪▪
Speed	▪▪

EGG GROUPS
Monster, Field

⬆ EVOLUTION

Lv. 15　　Lv. 30

Mareep　　Flaaffy　　Ampharos

ITEMS SOMETIMES HELD BY WILD POKÉMON
None

Damage taken in normal battles	
Normal	×1
Fire	×1
Water	×1
Grass	×1
Electric	×0.5
Ice	×1
Fighting	×1
Poison	×1
Ground	×2
Flying	×0.5
Psychic	×1
Bug	×1
Rock	×1
Ghost	×1
Dragon	×1
Dark	×1
Steel	×0.5
Fairy	×1

Damage taken in Inverse Battles	
Normal	×1
Fire	×1
Water	×1
Grass	×1
Electric	×2
Ice	×1
Fighting	×1
Poison	×1
Ground	×0.5
Flying	×2
Psychic	×1
Bug	×1
Rock	×1
Ghost	×1
Dragon	×1
Dark	×1
Steel	×2
Fairy	×1

Can be used in	
Inverse Battle	Battle Institute
—	Battle Maison
Battle Chateau	Random Matchup

Same form for ♂/♀

How to obtain for your Coastal Kalos Pokédex

X Catch in a Horde Encounter on Route 12.

Y Catch in a Horde Encounter on Route 12.

● LEVEL-UP MOVES

Lv.	Name	Type	Kind	Pow.	Acc.	PP	Range
1	Tackle	Normal	Physical	50	100	35	Normal
1	Growl	Normal	Status	—	100	40	Many Others
4	Thunder Wave	Electric	Status	—	100	20	Normal
8	Thunder Shock	Electric	Special	40	100	30	Normal
11	Cotton Spore	Grass	Status	—	100	40	Many Others
15	Charge	Electric	Status	—	—	20	Self
18	Take Down	Normal	Physical	90	85	20	Normal
22	Electro Ball	Electric	Special	—	100	10	Normal
25	Confuse Ray	Ghost	Status	—	100	10	Normal
29	Power Gem	Rock	Special	80	100	20	Normal
32	Discharge	Electric	Special	80	100	15	Adjacent
36	Cotton Guard	Grass	Status	—	—	10	Self
39	Signal Beam	Bug	Special	75	100	15	Normal
43	Light Screen	Psychic	Status	—	—	30	Your Side
46	Thunder	Electric	Special	110	70	10	Normal

● TM & HM MOVES

No.	Name	Type	Kind	Pow.	Acc.	PP	Range
TM06	Toxic	Poison	Status	—	90	10	Normal
TM10	Hidden Power	Normal	Special	60	100	15	Normal
TM16	Light Screen	Psychic	Status	—	—	30	Your Side
TM17	Protect	Normal	Status	—	—	10	Self
TM18	Rain Dance	Water	Status	—	—	5	Both Sides
TM20	Safeguard	Normal	Status	—	—	25	Your Side
TM21	Frustration	Normal	Physical	—	100	20	Normal
TM24	Thunderbolt	Electric	Special	90	100	15	Normal
TM25	Thunder	Electric	Special	110	70	10	Normal
TM27	Return	Normal	Physical	—	100	20	Normal
TM32	Double Team	Normal	Status	—	—	15	Self
TM42	Facade	Normal	Physical	70	100	20	Normal
TM44	Rest	Psychic	Status	—	—	10	Self
TM45	Attract	Normal	Status	—	100	15	Normal
TM48	Round	Normal	Special	60	100	15	Normal
TM49	Echoed Voice	Normal	Special	40	100	15	Normal
TM57	Charge Beam	Electric	Special	50	90	10	Normal
TM70	Flash	Normal	Status	—	100	20	Normal
TM73	Thunder Wave	Electric	Status	—	100	20	Normal
TM87	Swagger	Normal	Status	—	90	15	Normal
TM88	Sleep Talk	Normal	Status	—	—	10	Self
TM90	Substitute	Normal	Status	—	—	10	Self
TM93	Wild Charge	Electric	Physical	90	100	15	Normal
TM100	Confide	Normal	Status	—	—	20	Normal

● MOVES TAUGHT BY PEOPLE

Name	Type	Kind	Pow.	Acc.	PP	Range

● EGG MOVES

Name	Type	Kind	Pow.	Acc.	PP	Range
Take Down	Normal	Physical	90	85	20	Normal
Body Slam	Normal	Physical	85	100	15	Normal
Screech	Normal	Status	—	85	40	Normal
Odor Sleuth	Normal	Status	—	—	40	Normal
Charge	Electric	Status	—	—	20	Self
Flatter	Dark	Status	—	100	15	Normal
Sand Attack	Ground	Status	—	100	15	Normal
Iron Tail	Steel	Physical	100	75	15	Normal
After You	Normal	Status	—	—	15	Normal
Agility	Psychic	Status	—	—	30	Self
Eerie Impulse	Electric	Status	—	100	15	Normal
Electric Terrain	Electric	Status	—	—	10	Both Sides

AFTER THE HALL OF FAME

CENTRAL KALOS

COASTAL KALOS

128

Flaaffy

MOUNTAIN KALOS

ADVENTURE DATA

Coastal Kalos 128
Wool Pokémon

☑ Flaaffy

HEIGHT: 2'07" WEIGHT: 29.3 lbs.
GENDER: ♂/♀

TYPE Electric

ABILITY
Static

HIDDEN ABILITY
Plus

X Its fluffy fleece easily stores electricity. Its rubbery hide keeps it from being electrocuted.

Y If its coat becomes fully charged with electricity, its tail lights up. It fires hair that zaps on impact.

STAT GROWTH RATES

HP	▪▪▪
Attack	▪▪▪
Defense	▪▪▪
Sp. Atk	▪▪▪
Sp. Def	▪▪▪
Speed	▪▪▪

EGG GROUPS
Monster, Field

EVOLUTION

Lv. 15   Lv. 30

Mareep → Flaaffy → Ampharos

ITEMS SOMETIMES HELD BY WILD POKÉMON
None

Can be used in
Inverse Battle
—
Battle Chateau
Battle Institute
Battle Maison
Random Matchup

Damage taken in normal battles		Damage taken in Inverse Battles	
Normal	×1	Normal	×1
Fire	×1	Fire	×1
Water	×1	Water	×1
Grass	×1	Grass	×1
Electric	×0.5	Electric	×2
Ice	×1	Ice	×1
Fighting	×1	Fighting	×1
Poison	×1	Poison	×1
Ground	×2	Ground	×0.5
Flying	×0.5	Flying	×2
Psychic	×1	Psychic	×1
Bug	×1	Bug	×1
Rock	×1	Rock	×1
Ghost	×1	Ghost	×1
Dragon	×1	Dragon	×1
Dark	×1	Dark	×1
Steel	×0.5	Steel	×2
Fairy	×1	Fairy	×1

How to obtain for your Coastal Kalos Pokédex

Level up Mareep to Lv. 15.	Level up Mareep to Lv. 15.

Same form for ♂/♀

● LEVEL-UP MOVES

Lv.	Name	Type	Kind	Pow.	Acc.	PP	Range
1	Tackle	Normal	Physical	50	100	35	Normal
1	Growl	Normal	Status	—	100	40	Many Others
1	Thunder Wave	Electric	Status	—	100	20	Normal
4	Thunder Wave	Electric	Status	—	100	20	Normal
8	Thunder Shock	Electric	Special	40	100	30	Normal
11	Cotton Spore	Grass	Status	—	100	40	Many Others
16	Charge	Electric	Status	—	—	20	Self
20	Take Down	Normal	Physical	90	85	20	Normal
25	Electro Ball	Electric	Special	—	100	10	Normal
29	Confuse Ray	Ghost	Status	—	100	10	Normal
34	Power Gem	Rock	Special	80	100	20	Normal
43	Discharge	Electric	Special	80	100	15	Adjacent
43	Cotton Guard	Grass	Status	—	—	10	Self
47	Signal Beam	Bug	Special	75	100	15	Normal
52	Light Screen	Psychic	Status	—	—	30	Your Side
56	Thunder	Electric	Special	110	70	10	Normal

● TM & HM MOVES

No.	Name	Type	Kind	Pow.	Acc.	PP	Range
TM06	Toxic	Poison	Status	—	90	10	Normal
TM10	Hidden Power	Normal	Special	60	100	15	Normal
TM16	Light Screen	Psychic	Status	—	—	30	Your Side
TM17	Protect	Normal	Status	—	—	10	Self
TM18	Rain Dance	Water	Status	—	—	5	Both Sides
TM20	Safeguard	Normal	Status	—	—	25	Your Side
TM21	Frustration	Normal	Physical	—	100	20	Normal
TM24	Thunderbolt	Electric	Special	90	100	15	Normal
TM25	Thunder	Electric	Special	110	70	10	Normal
TM27	Return	Normal	Physical	—	100	20	Normal
TM31	Brick Break	Fighting	Physical	75	100	15	Normal
TM32	Double Team	Normal	Status	—	—	15	Self
TM42	Facade	Normal	Physical	70	100	20	Normal
TM44	Rest	Psychic	Status	—	—	10	Self
TM45	Attract	Normal	Status	—	100	15	Normal
TM48	Round	Normal	Special	60	100	15	Normal
TM49	Echoed Voice	Normal	Special	40	100	15	Normal
TM56	Fling	Dark	Physical	—	100	10	Normal
TM57	Charge Beam	Electric	Special	50	90	10	Normal
TM70	Flash	Normal	Status	—	100	20	Normal
TM72	Volt Switch	Electric	Special	70	100	20	Normal
TM73	Thunder Wave	Electric	Status	—	100	20	Normal
TM87	Swagger	Normal	Status	—	90	15	Normal
TM88	Sleep Talk	Normal	Status	—	—	10	Self
TM90	Substitute	Normal	Status	—	—	10	Self
TM93	Wild Charge	Electric	Physical	90	100	15	Normal
TM94	Rock Smash	Fighting	Physical	40	100	15	Normal
TM98	Power-Up Punch	Fighting	Physical	40	100	20	Normal
TM100	Confide	Normal	Status	—	—	20	Normal
HM04	Strength	Normal	Physical	80	100	15	Normal

● MOVES TAUGHT BY PEOPLE

Name	Type	Kind	Pow.	Acc.	PP	Range

AFTER THE HALL OF FAME

CENTRAL KALOS

COASTAL KALOS

129 Ampharos

MOUNTAIN KALOS

ADVENTURE DATA

🏔 Coastal Kalos 129

Light Pokémon

☑ **Ampharos**

HEIGHT: 4'07" WEIGHT: 135.6 lbs.
GENDER: ♂/♀

X The tail's tip shines brightly and can be seen from far away. It acts as a beacon for lost people.

Y The tail's tip shines brightly and can be seen from far away. It acts as a beacon for lost people.

TYPE Electric

ABILITY
Static

HIDDEN ABILITY
Plus

STAT GROWTH RATES
HP	▪▪▪▪
Attack	▪▪▪▪
Defense	▪▪▪
Sp. Atk	▪▪▪▪▪▪
Sp. Def	▪▪▪▪
Speed	▪▪▪

EGG GROUPS
Monster, Field

EVOLUTION

Lv. 15   Lv. 30

Mareep → Flaaffy → Ampharos

ITEMS SOMETIMES HELD BY WILD POKÉMON
None

Damage taken in normal battles	
Normal	×1
Fire	×1
Water	×1
Grass	×1
Electric	×0.5
Ice	×1
Fighting	×1
Poison	×1
Ground	×2
Flying	×0.5
Psychic	×1
Bug	×1
Rock	×1
Ghost	×1
Dragon	×1
Dark	×1
Steel	×0.5
Fairy	×1

Damage taken in Inverse Battles	
Normal	×1
Fire	×1
Water	×1
Grass	×1
Electric	×2
Ice	×1
Fighting	×1
Poison	×1
Ground	×0.5
Flying	×2
Psychic	×1
Bug	×1
Rock	×1
Ghost	×1
Dragon	×1
Dark	×1
Steel	×2
Fairy	×1

Can be used in
Inverse Battle
—
Battle Chateau
Battle Institute
Battle Maison
Random Matchup

How to obtain for your Coastal Kalos Pokédex

Level up Flaaffy to Lv. 30.

Level up Flaaffy to Lv. 30.

Same form for ♂/♀

● LEVEL-UP MOVES

Lv.	Name	Type	Kind	Pow.	Acc.	PP	Range
1	Zap Cannon	Electric	Special	120	50	5	Normal
1	Magnetic Flux	Electric	Status	—	—	20	Your Party
1	Ion Deluge	Electric	Status	—	—	25	Both Sides
1	Dragon Pulse	Dragon	Special	85	100	10	Normal
1	Fire Punch	Fire	Physical	75	100	15	Normal
1	Tackle	Normal	Physical	50	100	35	Normal
1	Growl	Normal	Status	—	100	40	Many Others
1	Thunder Wave	Electric	Status	—	100	20	Normal
1	Thunder Shock	Electric	Special	40	100	30	Normal
4	Thunder Wave	Electric	Status	—	100	20	Normal
8	Thunder Shock	Electric	Special	40	100	30	Normal
11	Cotton Spore	Grass	Status	—	100	40	Many Others
16	Charge	Electric	Status	—	—	20	Self
20	Take Down	Normal	Physical	90	85	20	Normal
25	Electro Ball	Electric	Special	—	100	10	Normal
29	Confuse Ray	Ghost	Status	—	100	10	Normal
30	Thunder Punch	Electric	Physical	75	100	15	Normal
35	Power Gem	Rock	Special	80	100	20	Normal
40	Discharge	Electric	Special	80	100	15	Adjacent
46	Cotton Guard	Grass	Status	—	—	10	Self
51	Signal Beam	Bug	Special	75	100	15	Normal
57	Light Screen	Psychic	Status	—	—	30	Your Side
62	Thunder	Electric	Special	110	70	10	Normal
65	Dragon Pulse	Dragon	Special	85	100	10	Normal

● TM & HM MOVES

No.	Name	Type	Kind	Pow.	Acc.	PP	Range
TM06	Toxic	Poison	Status	—	90	10	Normal
TM10	Hidden Power	Normal	Special	60	100	15	Normal
TM15	Hyper Beam	Normal	Special	150	90	5	Normal
TM16	Light Screen	Psychic	Status	—	—	30	Your Side
TM17	Protect	Normal	Status	—	—	10	Self
TM18	Rain Dance	Water	Status	—	—	5	Both Sides
TM20	Safeguard	Normal	Status	—	—	25	Your Side
TM21	Frustration	Normal	Physical	—	100	20	Normal
TM24	Thunderbolt	Electric	Special	90	100	15	Normal
TM25	Thunder	Electric	Special	110	70	10	Normal
TM27	Return	Normal	Physical	—	100	20	Normal
TM31	Brick Break	Fighting	Physical	75	100	15	Normal
TM32	Double Team	Normal	Status	—	—	15	Self
TM42	Facade	Normal	Physical	70	100	20	Normal
TM44	Rest	Psychic	Status	—	—	10	Self
TM45	Attract	Normal	Status	—	100	15	Normal
TM48	Round	Normal	Special	60	100	15	Normal
TM49	Echoed Voice	Normal	Special	40	100	15	Normal
TM52	Focus Blast	Fighting	Special	120	70	5	Normal
TM56	Fling	Dark	Physical	—	100	10	Normal
TM57	Charge Beam	Electric	Special	50	90	10	Normal
TM68	Giga Impact	Normal	Physical	150	90	5	Normal
TM70	Flash	Normal	Status	—	100	20	Normal
TM72	Volt Switch	Electric	Special	70	100	20	Normal
TM73	Thunder Wave	Electric	Status	—	100	20	Normal
TM78	Bulldoze	Ground	Physical	60	100	20	Adjacent
TM87	Swagger	Normal	Status	—	90	15	Normal
TM88	Sleep Talk	Normal	Status	—	—	10	Self
TM90	Substitute	Normal	Status	—	—	10	Self
TM93	Wild Charge	Electric	Physical	90	100	15	Normal
TM94	Rock Smash	Fighting	Physical	40	100	15	Normal
TM98	Power-Up Punch	Fighting	Physical	40	100	20	Normal
TM100	Confide	Normal	Status	—	—	20	Normal

No.	Name	Type	Kind	Pow.	Acc.	PP	Range
HM04	Strength	Normal	Physical	80	100	15	Normal

● MOVES TAUGHT BY PEOPLE

Name	Type	Kind	Pow.	Acc.	PP	Range

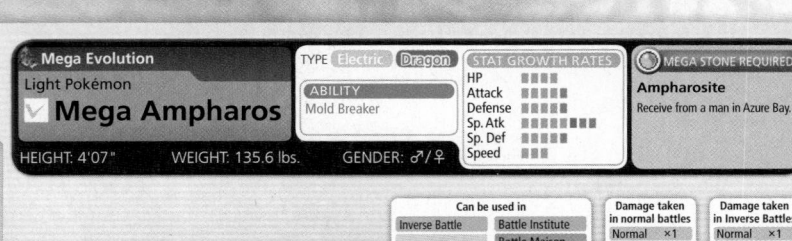

AFTER THE HALL OF FAME

CENTRAL KALOS

COASTAL KALOS

Mega Ampharos

MOUNTAIN KALOS

ADVENTURE DATA

Mega Evolution

Light Pokémon

☑ **Mega Ampharos**

HEIGHT: 4'07" WEIGHT: 135.6 lbs. GENDER: ♂/♀

TYPE: Electric Dragon

ABILITY
Mold Breaker

STAT GROWTH RATES
HP
Attack
Defense
Sp. Atk
Sp. Def
Speed

MEGA STONE REQUIRED
Ampharosite
Receive from a man in Azure Bay.

Can be used in

Inverse Battle	Battle Institute
—	Battle Maison
Battle Chateau	Random Matchup

Damage taken in normal battles

Normal	×1
Fire	×0.5
Water	×0.5
Grass	×0.5
Electric	×0.25
Ice	×2
Fighting	×1
Poison	×1
Ground	×2
Flying	×0.5
Psychic	×1
Bug	×1
Rock	×1
Ghost	×1
Dragon	×2
Dark	×1
Steel	×0.5
Fairy	×2

Damage taken in Inverse Battles

Normal	×1
Fire	×2
Water	×2
Grass	×2
Electric	×4
Ice	×0.5
Fighting	×1
Poison	×1
Ground	×0.5
Flying	×2
Psychic	×1
Bug	×1
Rock	×1
Ghost	×1
Dragon	×0.5
Dark	×1
Steel	×2
Fairy	×0.5

Same form for ♂/♀

AFTER THE HALL OF FAME

CENTRAL KALOS

COASTAL KALOS

130 Pinsir

MOUNTAIN KALOS

ADVENTURE DATA

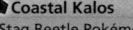

Coastal Kalos 130
Stag Beetle Pokémon
☑ **Pinsir**

HEIGHT: 4'11" WEIGHT: 121.3 lbs.
GENDER: ♂/♀

TYPE Bug

ABILITIES
Hyper Cutter
Mold Breaker

HIDDEN ABILITY
Moxie

STAT GROWTH RATES
HP	■■■
Attack	■■■■■■
Defense	■■■■
Sp. Atk	■■■
Sp. Def	■■■
Speed	■■■■■

EGG GROUP
Bug

EVOLUTION

Does not evolve

X It grips prey with its pincers until the prey is torn in half. What it can't tear, it tosses far.

Y It swings its long pincer horns wildly to attack. During cold periods, it hides deep in forests.

ITEMS SOMETIMES HELD BY WILD POKÉMON
None

Damage taken in normal battles		Damage taken in Inverse Battles	
Normal	×1	Normal	×1
Fire	×2	Fire	×0.5
Water	×1	Water	×1
Grass	×0.5	Grass	×2
Electric	×1	Electric	×1
Ice	×1	Ice	×1
Fighting	×0.5	Fighting	×2
Poison	×1	Poison	×1
Ground	×0.5	Ground	×2
Flying	×2	Flying	×0.5
Psychic	×1	Psychic	×1
Bug	×1	Bug	×1
Rock	×2	Rock	×0.5
Ghost	×1	Ghost	×1
Dragon	×1	Dragon	×1
Dark	×1	Dark	×1
Steel	×1	Steel	×1
Fairy	×1	Fairy	×1

Can be used in	
Inverse Battle	Battle Institute
—	Battle Maison
Battle Chateau	Random Matchup

Same form for ♂/♀

How to obtain for your Coastal Kalos Pokédex
1. Catch in the tall grass on Route 12.
2. Catch in the yellow flowers on Route 12.

Link Trade or transfer from another game.

● LEVEL-UP MOVES
Lv.	Name	Type	Kind	Pow.	Acc.	PP	Range
1	Vice Grip	Normal	Physical	55	100	30	Normal
1	Focus Energy	Normal	Status	—	—	30	Self
4	Bind	Normal	Physical	15	85	20	Normal
8	Seismic Toss	Fighting	Physical	—	100	20	Normal
11	Harden	Normal	Status	—	—	30	Self
15	Revenge	Fighting	Physical	60	100	10	Normal
18	Brick Break	Fighting	Physical	75	100	15	Normal
22	Vital Throw	Fighting	Physical	70	—	10	Normal
26	Submission	Fighting	Physical	80	80	20	Normal
29	X-Scissor	Bug	Physical	80	100	15	Normal
32	Storm Throw	Fighting	Physical	60	100	10	Normal
36	Thrash	Normal	Physical	120	100	10	1 Random
40	Swords Dance	Normal	Status	—	—	20	Self
43	Superpower	Fighting	Physical	120	100	5	Normal
47	Guillotine	Normal	Physical	—	30	5	Normal

● TM & HM MOVES
No.	Name	Type	Kind	Pow.	Acc.	PP	Range
TM06	Toxic	Poison	Status	—	90	10	Normal
TM08	Bulk Up	Fighting	Status	—	—	20	Self
TM10	Hidden Power	Normal	Special	60	100	15	Normal
TM11	Sunny Day	Fire	Status	—	—	5	Both Sides
TM15	Hyper Beam	Normal	Special	150	90	5	Normal
TM17	Protect	Normal	Status	—	—	10	Self
TM18	Rain Dance	Water	Status	—	—	5	Both Sides
TM21	Frustration	Normal	Physical	—	100	20	Normal
TM23	Smack Down	Rock	Physical	50	100	15	Normal
TM26	Earthquake	Ground	Physical	100	100	10	Adjacent
TM27	Return	Normal	Physical	—	100	20	Normal
TM28	Dig	Ground	Physical	80	100	10	Normal
TM31	Brick Break	Fighting	Physical	75	100	15	Normal
TM32	Double Team	Normal	Status	—	—	15	Self
TM39	Rock Tomb	Rock	Physical	60	95	15	Normal
TM42	Facade	Normal	Physical	70	100	20	Normal
TM44	Rest	Psychic	Status	—	—	10	Self
TM45	Attract	Normal	Status	—	100	15	Normal
TM46	Thief	Dark	Physical	60	100	25	Normal
TM48	Round	Normal	Special	60	100	15	Normal
TM52	Focus Blast	Fighting	Special	120	70	5	Normal
TM54	False Swipe	Normal	Physical	40	100	40	Normal
TM56	Fling	Dark	Physical	—	100	10	Normal
TM68	Giga Impact	Normal	Physical	150	90	5	Normal
TM71	Stone Edge	Rock	Physical	100	80	5	Normal
TM75	Swords Dance	Normal	Status	—	—	20	Self
TM76	Struggle Bug	Bug	Special	50	100	20	Many Others
TM78	Bulldoze	Ground	Physical	60	100	20	Adjacent
TM80	Rock Slide	Rock	Physical	75	90	10	Many Others
TM81	X-Scissor	Bug	Physical	80	100	15	Normal
TM87	Swagger	Normal	Status	—	90	15	Normal
TM88	Sleep Talk	Normal	Status	—	—	10	Self
TM90	Substitute	Normal	Status	—	—	10	Self

No.	Name	Type	Kind	Pow.	Acc.	PP	Range
TM94	Rock Smash	Fighting	Physical	40	100	15	Normal
TM100	Confide	Normal	Status	—	—	20	Normal
HM01	Cut	Normal	Physical	50	95	30	Normal
HM04	Strength	Normal	Physical	80	100	15	Normal

● MOVES TAUGHT BY PEOPLE
Name	Type	Kind	Pow.	Acc.	PP	Range

● EGG MOVES
Name	Type	Kind	Pow.	Acc.	PP	Range
Fury Attack	Normal	Physical	15	85	20	Normal
Flail	Normal	Physical	—	100	15	Normal
Feint Attack	Dark	Physical	60	—	20	Normal
Quick Attack	Normal	Physical	40	100	30	Normal
Close Combat	Fighting	Physical	120	100	5	Normal
Feint	Normal	Physical	30	100	10	Normal
Me First	Normal	Status	—	—	20	Varies
Bug Bite	Bug	Physical	60	100	20	Normal
Superpower	Fighting	Physical	120	100	5	Normal

AFTER THE HALL OF FAME

CENTRAL KALOS

COASTAL KALOS

Mega Pinsir

MOUNTAIN KALOS

ADVENTURE DATA

Mega Evolution

Stag Beetle Pokémon

☑ Mega Pinsir

TYPE	Bug	Flying

ABILITY
Aerilate

STAT GROWTH RATES

HP	▪▪▪
Attack	▪▪▪▪▪▪
Defense	▪▪▪▪▪
Sp. Atk	▪▪▪▪
Sp. Def	▪▪▪▪
Speed	▪▪▪▪▪▪

MEGA STONE REQUIRED

Pinsirite
Obtain in Santalune Forest between 8 P.M. and 8:59 P.M., after entering the Hall of Fame and speaking with Professor Sycamore in Anistar City (in *Pokémon X*).

HEIGHT: 5'07"   WEIGHT: 130.1 lbs.   GENDER: ♂/♀

Damage taken in normal battles	
Normal	×1
Fire	×2
Water	×1
Grass	×0.25
Electric	×2
Ice	×2
Fighting	×0.25
Poison	×1
Ground	×0
Flying	×2
Psychic	×1
Bug	×0.5
Rock	×4
Ghost	×1
Dragon	×1
Dark	×1
Steel	×1
Fairy	×1

Damage taken in Inverse Battles	
Normal	×1
Fire	×0.5
Water	×1
Grass	×4
Electric	×0.5
Ice	×0.5
Fighting	×4
Poison	×1
Ground	×4
Flying	×0.5
Psychic	×1
Bug	×2
Rock	×0.25
Ghost	×1
Dragon	×1
Dark	×1
Steel	×1
Fairy	×1

Same form for ♂/♀

Can be used in	
Inverse Battle	Battle Institute
—	Battle Maison
Battle Chateau	Random Matchup

AFTER THE HALL OF FAME

CENTRAL KALOS

COASTAL KALOS

131 Heracross

MOUNTAIN KALOS

ADVENTURE DATA

Coastal Kalos 131
Single Horn Pokémon
∨ Heracross

HEIGHT: 4'11"   WEIGHT: 119.0 lbs.
GENDER: ♂/♀

TYPE	Bug	Fighting

ABILITIES
Swarm
Guts

HIDDEN ABILITY
Moxie

STAT GROWTH RATES
HP ■■■
Attack ■■■■■■
Defense ■■■
Sp. Atk ■■
Sp. Def ■■■
Speed ■■■■■

EGG GROUP
Bug

EVOLUTION

Does not evolve

ITEMS SOMETIMES HELD BY WILD POKÉMON
None

X This powerful Pokémon thrusts its prized horn under its enemies' bellies, then lifts and throws them.

Y With its Herculean powers, it can easily throw around an object that is 100 times its own weight.

Damage taken in normal battles		Damage taken in Inverse Battles	
Normal	×1	Normal	×1
Fire	×2	Fire	×0.5
Water	×1	Water	×1
Grass	×0.5	Grass	×2
Electric	×1	Electric	×1
Ice	×1	Ice	×1
Fighting	×0.5	Fighting	×2
Poison	×1	Poison	×1
Ground	×0.5	Ground	×2
Flying	×4	Flying	×0.25
Psychic	×2	Psychic	×0.5
Bug	×0.5	Bug	×2
Rock	×1	Rock	×1
Ghost	×1	Ghost	×1
Dragon	×1	Dragon	×1
Dark	×0.5	Dark	×2
Steel	×1	Steel	×1
Fairy	×2	Fairy	×0.5

Can be used in
Inverse Battle
—
Battle Chateau
Battle Institute
Battle Maison
Random Matchup

How to obtain for your Coastal Kalos Pokédex

Link Trade or transfer from another game.

❶ Catch in the tall grass on Route 12.
❷ Catch in the yellow flowers on Route 12.

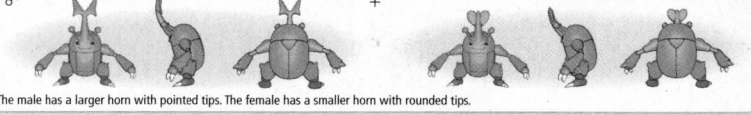

The male has a larger horn with pointed tips. The female has a smaller horn with rounded tips.

● LEVEL-UP MOVES

Lv.	Name	Type	Kind	Pow.	Acc.	PP	Range
1	Arm Thrust	Fighting	Physical	15	100	20	Normal
1	Bullet Seed	Grass	Physical	25	100	30	Normal
1	Night Slash	Dark	Physical	70	100	15	Normal
1	Tackle	Normal	Physical	50	100	35	Normal
1	Leer	Normal	Status	—	100	30	Many Others
1	Horn Attack	Normal	Physical	65	100	25	Normal
1	Endure	Normal	Status	—	—	10	Self
7	Fury Attack	Normal	Physical	15	85	20	Normal
10	Aerial Ace	Flying	Physical	60	—	20	Normal
16	Chip Away	Normal	Physical	70	100	20	Normal
19	Counter	Fighting	Physical	—	100	20	Varies
25	Brick Break	Fighting	Physical	75	100	15	Normal
28	Take Down	Normal	Physical	90	85	20	Normal
31	Pin Missile	Bug	Physical	25	95	20	Normal
34	Close Combat	Fighting	Physical	120	100	5	Normal
37	Feint	Normal	Physical	30	100	10	Normal
43	Reversal	Fighting	Physical	—	100	15	Normal
46	Megahorn	Bug	Physical	120	85	10	Normal

● TM & HM MOVES

No.	Name	Type	Kind	Pow.	Acc.	PP	Range
TM06	Toxic	Poison	Status	—	90	10	Normal
TM08	Bulk Up	Fighting	Status	—	—	20	Self
TM09	Venoshock	Poison	Special	65	100	10	Normal
TM10	Hidden Power	Normal	Special	60	100	15	Normal
TM11	Sunny Day	Fire	Status	—	—	5	Both Sides
TM15	Hyper Beam	Normal	Special	150	90	5	Normal
TM17	Protect	Normal	Status	—	—	10	Self
TM18	Rain Dance	Water	Status	—	—	5	Both Sides
TM21	Frustration	Normal	Physical	—	100	20	Normal
TM23	Smack Down	Rock	Physical	50	100	15	Normal
TM26	Earthquake	Ground	Physical	100	100	10	Adjacent
TM27	Return	Normal	Physical	—	100	20	Normal
TM28	Dig	Ground	Physical	80	100	10	Normal
TM31	Brick Break	Fighting	Physical	75	100	15	Normal
TM32	Double Team	Normal	Status	—	—	15	Self
TM39	Rock Tomb	Rock	Physical	60	95	15	Normal
TM40	Aerial Ace	Flying	Physical	60	—	20	Normal
TM42	Facade	Normal	Physical	70	100	20	Normal
TM44	Rest	Psychic	Status	—	—	10	Self
TM45	Attract	Normal	Status	—	100	15	Normal
TM46	Thief	Dark	Physical	60	100	25	Normal
TM48	Round	Normal	Special	60	100	15	Normal
TM52	Focus Blast	Fighting	Special	120	70	5	Normal
TM54	False Swipe	Normal	Physical	40	100	40	Normal
TM56	Fling	Dark	Physical	—	100	10	Normal
TM65	Shadow Claw	Ghost	Physical	70	100	15	Normal
TM67	Retaliate	Normal	Physical	70	100	5	Normal
TM68	Giga Impact	Normal	Physical	150	90	5	Normal
TM71	Stone Edge	Rock	Physical	100	80	5	Normal
TM75	Swords Dance	Normal	Status	—	—	20	Self
TM76	Struggle Bug	Bug	Special	30	100	20	Many Others
TM78	Bulldoze	Ground	Physical	60	100	20	Adjacent
TM80	Rock Slide	Rock	Physical	75	90	10	Many Others

No.	Name	Type	Kind	Pow.	Acc.	PP	Range
TM87	Swagger	Normal	Status	—	90	15	Normal
TM88	Sleep Talk	Normal	Status	—	—	10	Self
TM90	Substitute	Normal	Status	—	—	10	Self
TM94	Rock Smash	Fighting	Physical	40	100	15	Normal
TM100	Confide	Normal	Status	—	—	20	Normal
HM01	Cut	Normal	Physical	50	95	30	Normal
HM04	Strength	Normal	Physical	80	100	15	Normal

● MOVES TAUGHT BY PEOPLE

Name	Type	Kind	Pow.	Acc.	PP	Range

● EGG MOVES

Name	Type	Kind	Pow.	Acc.	PP	Range
Harden	Normal	Status	—	—	30	Self
Bide	Normal	Physical	—	—	10	Self
Flail	Normal	Physical	—	100	15	Normal
Revenge	Fighting	Physical	60	100	10	Normal
Pursuit	Dark	Physical	40	100	20	Normal
Double-Edge	Normal	Physical	120	100	15	Normal
Seismic Toss	Fighting	Physical	—	100	20	Normal
Focus Punch	Fighting	Physical	150	100	20	Normal
Megahorn	Bug	Physical	120	85	10	Normal
Rock Blast	Rock	Physical	25	90	10	Normal

AFTER THE HALL OF FAME

CENTRAL KALOS

COASTAL KALOS

Mega Heracross

MOUNTAIN KALOS

ADVENTURE DATA

Mega Evolution

Single Horn Pokémon

☑ Mega Heracross

HEIGHT: 5'07"   WEIGHT: 137.8 lbs.   GENDER: ♂/♀

TYPE: **Bug** **Fighting**

ABILITY
Skill Link

STAT GROWTH RATES	
HP	■■■
Attack	■■■■■■■■
Defense	■■■■■
Sp. Atk	■■
Sp. Def	■■■■
Speed	■■■■

🟤 MEGA STONE REQUIRED

Heracronite

Obtain in Santalune Forest between 8 P.M. and 8:59 P.M., after entering the Hall of Fame and speaking with Professor Sycamore in Anistar City (in *Pokémon Y*).

Damage taken in normal battles	
Normal	×1
Fire	×2
Water	×1
Grass	×0.5
Electric	×1
Ice	×1
Fighting	×0.5
Poison	×1
Ground	×0.5
Flying	×4
Psychic	×2
Bug	×0.5
Rock	×1
Ghost	×1
Dragon	×1
Dark	×0.5
Steel	×1
Fairy	×2

Damage taken in Inverse Battles	
Normal	×1
Fire	×0.5
Water	×1
Grass	×2
Electric	×1
Ice	×1
Fighting	×2
Poison	×1
Ground	×2
Flying	×0.25
Psychic	×0.5
Bug	×2
Rock	×1
Ghost	×1
Dragon	×1
Dark	×1
Steel	×1
Fairy	×0.5

Can be used in	
Inverse Battle	Battle Institute
—	Battle Maison
Battle Chateau	Random Matchup

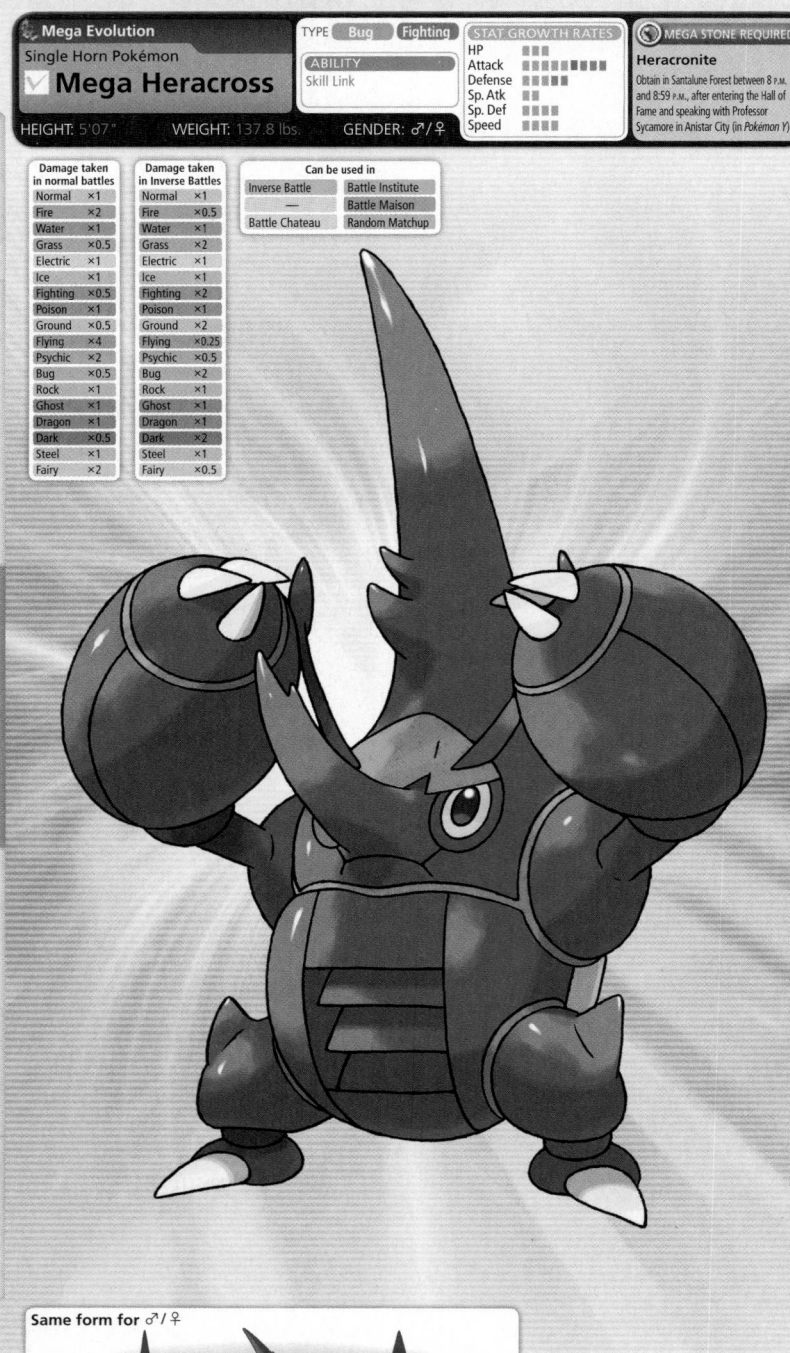

Same form for ♂/♀

EleSquirrel Pokémon

✓ Pachirisu

HEIGHT: 1'04" WEIGHT: 8.6 lbs.
GENDER: ♂/♀

X It makes fur balls that crackle with static electricity. It stores them with berries in tree holes.

Y A pair may be seen rubbing their cheek pouches together in an effort to share stored electricity.

TYPE **Electric**

ABILITIES
Run Away
Pickup

HIDDEN ABILITY
Volt Absorb

STAT GROWTH RATES
HP	■ ■ ■
Attack	■ ■
Defense	■ ■ ■
Sp. Atk	■ ■
Sp. Def	■ ■ ■ ■
Speed	■ ■ ■ ■ ■

EGG GROUPS
Field, Fairy

EVOLUTION

Does not evolve

ITEMS SOMETIMES HELD BY WILD POKÉMON
None

Damage taken in normal battles		Damage taken in Inverse Battles	
Normal	×1	Normal	×1
Fire	×1	Fire	×1
Water	×1	Water	×1
Grass	×1	Grass	×1
Electric	×0.5	Electric	×2
Ice	×1	Ice	×1
Fighting	×1	Fighting	×1
Poison	×1	Poison	×1
Ground	×2	Ground	×0.5
Flying	×0.5	Flying	×2
Psychic	×1	Psychic	×1
Bug	×1	Bug	×1
Rock	×1	Rock	×1
Ghost	×1	Ghost	×1
Dragon	×1	Dragon	×1
Dark	×1	Dark	×1
Steel	×0.5	Steel	×2
Fairy	×1	Fairy	×1

Can be used in
Inverse Battle
—
Battle Chateau
Battle Institute
Battle Maison
Random Matchup

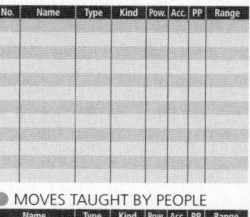

How to obtain for your Coastal Kalos Pokédex

① Catch in the tall grass on Route 12.
② Catch in the yellow flowers on Route 12.

① Catch in the tall grass on Route 12.
② Catch in the yellow flowers on Route 12.

♂   ♀

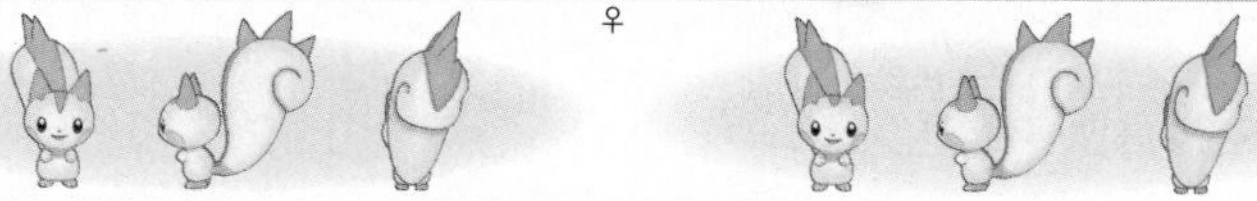

The pattern on the male's forehead is spread out more widely. The pattern on the female's forehead is narrower.

● LEVEL-UP MOVES

Lv.	Name	Type	Kind	Pow.	Acc.	PP	Range
1	Growl	Normal	Status	—	100	40	Many Others
1	Bide	Normal	Physical	—	—	10	Self
5	Quick Attack	Normal	Physical	40	100	30	Normal
9	Charm	Fairy	Status	—	100	20	Normal
13	Spark	Electric	Physical	65	100	20	Normal
17	Endure	Normal	Status	—	—	10	Self
19	Nuzzle	Electric	Physical	20	100	20	Normal
21	Swift	Normal	Special	60	—	20	Many Others
25	Electro Ball	Electric	Special	—	100	10	Normal
29	Sweet Kiss	Fairy	Status	—	75	10	Normal
33	Thunder Wave	Electric	Status	—	100	20	Normal
37	Super Fang	Normal	Physical	90	90	10	Normal
41	Discharge	Electric	Special	80	100	15	Adjacent
45	Last Resort	Normal	Physical	140	100	5	Normal
49	Hyper Fang	Normal	Physical	80	90	15	Normal

● TM & HM MOVES

No.	Name	Type	Kind	Pow.	Acc.	PP	Range
TM06	Toxic	Poison	Status	—	90	10	Normal
TM10	Hidden Power	Normal	Special	60	100	15	Normal
TM16	Light Screen	Psychic	Status	—	—	30	Your Side
TM17	Protect	Normal	Status	—	—	10	Self
TM18	Rain Dance	Water	Status	—	—	5	Both Sides
TM21	Frustration	Normal	Physical	—	100	20	Normal
TM24	Thunderbolt	Electric	Special	90	100	15	Normal
TM25	Thunder	Electric	Special	110	70	10	Normal
TM27	Return	Normal	Physical	—	100	20	Normal
TM28	Dig	Ground	Physical	80	100	10	Normal
TM32	Double Team	Normal	Status	—	—	15	Self
TM42	Facade	Normal	Physical	70	100	20	Normal
TM44	Rest	Psychic	Status	—	—	10	Self
TM45	Attract	Normal	Status	—	100	15	Normal
TM48	Round	Normal	Special	60	100	15	Normal
TM49	Echoed Voice	Normal	Special	40	100	15	Normal
TM56	Fling	Dark	Physical	—	100	10	Normal
TM70	Flash	Normal	Status	—	100	20	Normal
TM72	Volt Switch	Electric	Special	70	100	20	Normal
TM73	Thunder Wave	Electric	Status	—	100	20	Normal
TM86	Grass Knot	Grass	Special	—	100	20	Normal
TM87	Swagger	Normal	Status	—	90	15	Normal
TM88	Sleep Talk	Normal	Status	—	—	10	Self
TM89	U-turn	Bug	Physical	70	100	20	Normal
TM90	Substitute	Normal	Status	—	—	10	Self
TM100	Confide	Normal	Status	—	—	20	Normal
HM01	Cut	Normal	Physical	50	95	30	Normal

● MOVES TAUGHT BY PEOPLE

Name	Type	Kind	Pow.	Acc.	PP	Range

● EGG MOVES

Name	Type	Kind	Pow.	Acc.	PP	Range
Covet	Normal	Physical	60	100	25	Normal
Bite	Dark	Physical	60	100	25	Normal
Fake Tears	Dark	Status	—	100	20	Normal
Defense Curl	Normal	Status	—	—	40	Self
Rollout	Rock	Physical	30	90	20	Normal
Flatter	Dark	Status	—	100	15	Normal
Flail	Normal	Physical	—	100	15	Normal
Iron Tail	Steel	Physical	100	75	15	Normal
Tail Whip	Normal	Status	—	100	30	Many Others
Follow Me	Normal	Status	—	—	20	Self
Charge	Electric	Status	—	—	20	Self
Bestow	Normal	Status	—	—	15	Normal
Ion Deluge	Electric	Status	—	—	25	Both Sides

AFTER THE HALL OF FAME

CENTRAL KALOS

COASTAL KALOS

133

Slowpoke

MOUNTAIN KALOS

ADVENTURE DATA

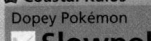

Coastal Kalos   133
Dopey Pokémon
✓ Slowpoke

HEIGHT: 3'11" WEIGHT: 79.4 lbs.
GENDER: ♂/♀

TYPE Water Psychic

ABILITIES
Oblivious
Own Tempo

HIDDEN ABILITY
Regenerator

STAT GROWTH RATES
HP	▪▪▪▪
Attack	▪▪▪
Defense	▪▪▪
Sp. Atk	▪▪
Sp. Def	▪▪
Speed	▪

EGG GROUPS
Monster, Water 1

X It is always vacantly lost in thought, but no one knows what it is thinking about. It is good at fishing with its tail.

Y It lazes vacantly near water. If something bites its tail, it won't even notice for a whole day.

EVOLUTION

Slowpoke → Lv. 37 → Slowbro
Slowpoke → Link Trade with a King's Rock → Slowking

ITEMS SOMETIMES HELD BY WILD POKÉMON
Lagging Tail

Damage taken in normal battles		Damage taken in Inverse Battles	
Normal	×1	Normal	×1
Fire	×0.5	Fire	×2
Water	×0.5	Water	×2
Grass	×2	Grass	×0.5
Electric	×2	Electric	×0.5
Ice	×0.5	Ice	×2
Fighting	×0.5	Fighting	×2
Poison	×1	Poison	×1
Ground	×1	Ground	×1
Flying	×1	Flying	×1
Psychic	×0.5	Psychic	×2
Bug	×2	Bug	×0.5
Rock	×1	Rock	×1
Ghost	×1	Ghost	×1
Dragon	×1	Dragon	×1
Dark	×2	Dark	×0.5
Steel	×0.5	Steel	×2
Fairy	×1	Fairy	×1

Can be used in	
Inverse Battle	Battle Institute
----	Battle Maison
Battle Chateau	Random Matchup

Same form for ♂/♀

How to obtain for your Coastal Kalos Pokédex

❶ Catch in the tall grass on Route 12.
❷ Catch in the yellow flowers on Route 12.

❶ Catch in the tall grass on Route 12.
❷ Catch in the yellow flowers on Route 12.

● LEVEL-UP MOVES

Lv.	Name	Type	Kind	Pow.	Acc.	PP	Range
1	Curse	Ghost	Status	—	—	10	Varies
1	Yawn	Normal	Status	—	—	10	Normal
1	Tackle	Normal	Physical	50	100	35	Normal
5	Growl	Normal	Status	—	100	40	Many Others
9	Water Gun	Water	Special	40	100	25	Normal
14	Confusion	Psychic	Special	50	100	25	Normal
19	Disable	Normal	Status	—	100	20	Normal
23	Headbutt	Normal	Physical	70	100	15	Normal
28	Water Pulse	Water	Special	60	100	20	Normal
32	Zen Headbutt	Psychic	Physical	80	90	15	Normal
36	Slack Off	Normal	Status	—	—	10	Self
41	Amnesia	Psychic	Status	—	—	20	Self
45	Psychic	Psychic	Special	90	100	10	Normal
49	Rain Dance	Water	Status	—	—	5	Both Sides
54	Psych Up	Normal	Status	—	—	10	Normal
58	Heal Pulse	Psychic	Status	—	—	10	Normal

● TM & HM MOVES

No.	Name	Type	Kind	Pow.	Acc.	PP	Range
TM03	Psyshock	Psychic	Special	80	100	10	Normal
TM04	Calm Mind	Psychic	Status	—	—	20	Self
TM06	Toxic	Poison	Status	—	90	10	Normal
TM07	Hail	Ice	Status	—	—	10	Both Sides
TM10	Hidden Power	Normal	Special	60	100	15	Normal
TM11	Sunny Day	Fire	Status	—	—	5	Both Sides
TM13	Ice Beam	Ice	Special	90	100	10	Normal
TM14	Blizzard	Ice	Special	110	70	5	Many Others
TM16	Light Screen	Psychic	Status	—	—	30	Your Side
TM17	Protect	Normal	Status	—	—	10	Self
TM18	Rain Dance	Water	Status	—	—	5	Both Sides
TM20	Safeguard	Normal	Status	—	—	25	Your Side
TM21	Frustration	Normal	Physical	—	100	20	Normal
TM26	Earthquake	Ground	Physical	100	100	10	Adjacent
TM27	Return	Normal	Physical	—	100	20	Normal
TM28	Dig	Ground	Physical	80	100	10	Normal
TM29	Psychic	Psychic	Special	90	100	10	Normal
TM30	Shadow Ball	Ghost	Special	80	100	15	Normal
TM32	Double Team	Normal	Status	—	—	15	Self
TM35	Flamethrower	Fire	Special	90	100	15	Normal
TM38	Fire Blast	Fire	Special	110	85	5	Normal
TM42	Facade	Normal	Physical	70	100	20	Normal
TM44	Rest	Psychic	Status	—	—	10	Self
TM45	Attract	Normal	Status	—	100	15	Normal
TM48	Round	Normal	Special	60	100	15	Normal
TM49	Echoed Voice	Normal	Special	40	100	15	Normal
TM55	Scald	Water	Special	80	100	15	Normal
TM59	Incinerate	Fire	Special	60	100	15	Many Others
TM70	Flash	Normal	Status	—	100	20	Normal
TM73	Thunder Wave	Electric	Status	—	100	20	Normal
TM77	Psych Up	Normal	Status	—	—	10	Normal
TM78	Bulldoze	Ground	Physical	60	100	20	Adjacent
TM85	Dream Eater	Psychic	Special	100	100	15	Normal
TM86	Grass Knot	Grass	Special	—	100	20	Normal
TM87	Swagger	Normal	Status	—	90	15	Normal
TM88	Sleep Talk	Normal	Status	—	—	10	Self
TM90	Substitute	Normal	Status	—	—	10	Self
TM92	Trick Room	Psychic	Status	—	—	5	Both Sides
TM100	Confide	Normal	Status	—	—	20	Normal
HM03	Surf	Water	Special	90	100	15	Adjacent
HM04	Strength	Normal	Physical	80	100	15	Normal

● MOVES TAUGHT BY PEOPLE

Name	Type	Kind	Pow.	Acc.	PP	Range

● EGG MOVES

Name	Type	Kind	Pow.	Acc.	PP	Range
Belly Drum	Normal	Status	—	—	10	Self
Future Sight	Psychic	Special	120	100	10	Normal
Stomp	Normal	Physical	65	100	20	Normal
Mud Sport	Ground	Status	—	—	15	Both Sides
Sleep Talk	Normal	Status	—	—	10	Self
Snore	Normal	Special	50	100	15	Normal
Me First	Normal	Status	—	—	20	Varies
Block	Normal	Status	—	—	5	Normal
Zen Headbutt	Psychic	Physical	80	90	15	Normal
Wonder Room	Psychic	Status	—	—	10	Both Sides
Belch	Poison	Special	120	90	10	Normal

AFTER THE HALL OF FAME

CENTRAL KALOS

COASTAL KALOS

134 | Slowbro

MOUNTAIN KALOS

ADVENTURE DATA

◆ Coastal Kalos 134
Hermit Crab Pokémon
☑ Slowbro

TYPE Water Psychic

ABILITIES
Oblivious
Own Tempo

HIDDEN ABILITY
Regenerator

HEIGHT: 5'03"   WEIGHT: 173.1 lbs.
GENDER: ♂/♀

STAT GROWTH RATES
HP	▪▪▪▪
Attack	▪▪▪▪
Defense	▪▪▪▪▪
Sp. Atk	▪▪▪▪▪
Sp. Def	▪▪▪▪
Speed	▪▪

EGG GROUPS
Monster, Water 1

⊗ An attached Shellder won't let go because of the tasty flavor that oozes out of its tail.

Ⓨ When a Slowpoke went hunting in the sea, its tail was bitten by a Shellder. That made it evolve into Slowbro.

▲ EVOLUTION

Slowpoke — Lv. 37 → Slowbro

Slowpoke — Link Trade with a King's Rock → Slowking

ITEMS SOMETIMES HELD BY WILD POKÉMON
None

Damage taken in normal battles	
Normal	×1
Fire	×0.5
Water	×0.5
Grass	×2
Electric	×2
Ice	×0.5
Fighting	×0.5
Poison	×1
Ground	×1
Flying	×1
Psychic	×0.5
Bug	×2
Rock	×1
Ghost	×2
Dragon	×1
Dark	×2
Steel	×0.5
Fairy	×1

Damage taken in Inverse Battles	
Normal	×1
Fire	×2
Water	×2
Grass	×0.5
Electric	×0.5
Ice	×2
Fighting	×2
Poison	×1
Ground	×1
Flying	×1
Psychic	×2
Bug	×0.5
Rock	×1
Ghost	×0.5
Dragon	×1
Dark	×0.5
Steel	×2
Fairy	×1

Can be used in	
Inverse Battle	Battle Institute
—	Battle Maison
Battle Chateau	Random Matchup

Same form for ♂/♀

How to obtain for your Coastal Kalos Pokédex
Level up Slowpoke to Lv. 37.   Level up Slowpoke to Lv. 37.

● LEVEL-UP MOVES

Lv.	Name	Type	Kind	Pow.	Acc.	PP	Range
1	Heal Pulse	Psychic	Status	—	—	10	Normal
1	Curse	Ghost	Status	—	—	10	Varies
1	Yawn	Normal	Status	—	—	10	Normal
1	Tackle	Normal	Physical	50	100	35	Normal
1	Growl	Normal	Status	—	100	40	Many Others
5	Growl	Normal	Status	—	100	40	Many Others
9	Water Gun	Water	Special	40	100	25	Normal
14	Confusion	Psychic	Special	50	100	25	Normal
19	Disable	Normal	Status	—	100	20	Normal
23	Headbutt	Normal	Physical	70	100	15	Normal
28	Water Pulse	Water	Special	60	100	20	Normal
32	Zen Headbutt	Psychic	Physical	80	90	15	Normal
36	Slack Off	Normal	Status	—	—	10	Self
37	Withdraw	Water	Status	—	—	40	Self
43	Amnesia	Psychic	Status	—	—	20	Self
49	Psychic	Psychic	Special	90	100	10	Normal
55	Rain Dance	Water	Status	—	—	5	Both Sides
61	Psych Up	Normal	Status	—	—	10	Self
68	Heal Pulse	Psychic	Status	—	—	10	Normal

● TM & HM MOVES

No.	Name	Type	Kind	Pow.	Acc.	PP	Range
TM03	Psyshock	Psychic	Special	80	100	10	Normal
TM04	Calm Mind	Psychic	Status	—	—	20	Self
TM06	Toxic	Poison	Status	—	90	10	Normal
TM07	Hail	Ice	Status	—	—	10	Both Sides
TM10	Hidden Power	Normal	Special	60	100	15	Normal
TM11	Sunny Day	Fire	Status	—	—	5	Both Sides
TM13	Ice Beam	Ice	Special	90	100	10	Normal
TM14	Blizzard	Ice	Special	110	70	5	Many Others
TM15	Hyper Beam	Normal	Special	150	90	5	Normal
TM17	Protect	Normal	Status	—	—	10	Self
TM16	Light Screen	Psychic	Status	—	—	30	Your Side
TM18	Rain Dance	Water	Status	—	—	5	Both Sides
TM20	Safeguard	Normal	Status	—	—	25	Your Side
TM21	Frustration	Normal	Physical	—	100	20	Normal
TM26	Earthquake	Ground	Physical	100	100	10	Adjacent
TM27	Return	Normal	Physical	—	100	20	Normal
TM28	Dig	Ground	Physical	80	100	10	Normal
TM29	Psychic	Psychic	Special	90	100	10	Normal
TM30	Shadow Ball	Ghost	Special	80	100	15	Normal
TM31	Brick Break	Fighting	Physical	75	100	15	Normal
TM32	Double Team	Normal	Status	—	—	15	Self
TM35	Flamethrower	Fire	Special	90	100	15	Normal
TM38	Fire Blast	Fire	Special	110	85	5	Normal
TM40	Aerial Ace	Flying	Physical	60	—	20	Normal
TM42	Facade	Normal	Physical	70	100	20	Normal
TM44	Rest	Psychic	Status	—	—	10	Self
TM45	Attract	Normal	Status	—	100	15	Normal
TM48	Round	Normal	Special	60	100	15	Normal
TM49	Echoed Voice	Normal	Special	40	100	15	Normal
TM52	Focus Blast	Fighting	Special	120	70	5	Normal
TM55	Scald	Water	Special	80	100	15	Normal
TM56	Fling	Dark	Physical	—	100	10	Normal
TM59	Incinerate	Fire	Special	60	100	15	Many Others

No.	Name	Type	Kind	Pow.	Acc.	PP	Range
TM68	Giga Impact	Normal	Physical	150	90	5	Normal
TM70	Flash	Normal	Status	—	100	20	Normal
TM73	Thunder Wave	Electric	Status	—	100	20	Normal
TM77	Psych Up	Normal	Status	—	—	10	Normal
TM78	Bulldoze	Ground	Physical	60	100	20	Adjacent
TM85	Dream Eater	Psychic	Special	100	100	15	Normal
TM86	Grass Knot	Grass	Special	—	100	20	Normal
TM87	Swagger	Normal	Status	—	90	15	Normal
TM88	Sleep Talk	Normal	Status	—	—	10	Self
TM90	Substitute	Normal	Status	—	—	10	Self
TM92	Trick Room	Psychic	Status	—	—	5	Both Sides
TM94	Rock Smash	Fighting	Physical	40	100	15	Normal
TM100	Confide	Normal	Status	—	—	20	Normal
HM03	Surf	Water	Special	90	100	15	Adjacent
HM04	Strength	Normal	Physical	80	100	15	Normal

● MOVES TAUGHT BY PEOPLE

Name	Type	Kind	Pow.	Acc.	PP	Range

AFTER THE HALL OF FAME

CENTRAL KALOS

COASTAL KALOS

135

Slowking

MOUNTAIN KALOS

ADVENTURE DATA

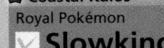

Coastal Kalos
Royal Pokémon

135

Slowking

TYPE: Water / Psychic

ABILITIES
Oblivious
Own Tempo

HIDDEN ABILITY
Regenerator

HEIGHT: 6'07" WEIGHT: 175.3 lbs.
GENDER: ♂/♀

X It has incredible intellect and intuition. Whatever the situation, it remains calm and collected.

Y When its head was bitten, toxins entered Slowpoke's head and unlocked an extraordinary power.

STAT GROWTH RATES
HP	▪▪▪▪
Attack	▪▪▪▪
Defense	▪▪▪▪
Sp. Atk	▪▪▪▪▪
Sp. Def	▪▪▪▪▪
Speed	▪▪

EGG GROUPS
Monster, Water 1

EVOLUTION

Slowpoke → (Lv. 37) Slowbro
Slowpoke → (Link Trade with a King's Rock) Slowking

ITEMS SOMETIMES HELD BY WILD POKÉMON
None

Can be used in
Inverse Battle
—
Battle Chateau
Battle Institute
Battle Maison
Random Matchup

Damage taken in normal battles	
Normal	×1
Fire	×0.5
Water	×0.5
Grass	×2
Electric	×2
Ice	×0.5
Fighting	×0.5
Poison	×1
Ground	×1
Flying	×1
Psychic	×0.5
Bug	×2
Rock	×1
Ghost	×2
Dragon	×1
Dark	×2
Steel	×1
Fairy	×1

Damage taken in Inverse Battles	
Normal	×1
Fire	×2
Water	×2
Grass	×0.5
Electric	×0.5
Ice	×2
Fighting	×2
Poison	×1
Ground	×1
Flying	×1
Psychic	×2
Bug	×0.5
Rock	×1
Ghost	×0.5
Dragon	×1
Dark	×0.5
Steel	×2
Fairy	×1

How to obtain for your Coastal Kalos Pokédex

Receive Slowpoke with a King's Rock by Link Trade, and have it evolve.

Receive Slowpoke with a King's Rock by Link Trade, and have it evolve.

Same form for ♂/♀

● LEVEL-UP MOVES

Lv.	Name	Type	Kind	Pow.	Acc.	PP	Range
1	Heal Pulse	Psychic	Status	—	—	10	Normal
1	Power Gem	Rock	Special	80	100	20	Normal
1	Hidden Power	Normal	Special	60	100	15	Varies
1	Curse	Ghost	Status	—	—	10	Varies
1	Yawn	Normal	Status	—	—	10	Normal
1	Tackle	Normal	Physical	50	100	35	Normal
5	Growl	Normal	Status	—	100	40	Many Others
9	Water Gun	Water	Special	40	100	25	Normal
14	Confusion	Psychic	Special	50	100	25	Normal
19	Disable	Normal	Status	—	100	20	Normal
23	Headbutt	Normal	Physical	70	100	15	Normal
28	Water Pulse	Water	Special	60	100	20	Normal
32	Zen Headbutt	Psychic	Physical	80	90	15	Normal
36	Nasty Plot	Dark	Status	—	—	20	Self
41	Swagger	Normal	Status	—	90	15	Normal
45	Psychic	Psychic	Special	90	100	10	Normal
49	Trump Card	Normal	Special	—	—	5	Normal
54	Psych Up	Normal	Status	—	—	10	Normal
58	Heal Pulse	Psychic	Status	—	—	10	Normal

● TM & HM MOVES

No.	Name	Type	Kind	Pow.	Acc.	PP	Range
TM03	Psyshock	Psychic	Special	80	100	10	Normal
TM04	Calm Mind	Psychic	Status	—	—	20	Self
TM06	Toxic	Poison	Status	—	90	10	Normal
TM07	Hail	Ice	Status	—	—	10	Both Sides
TM10	Hidden Power	Normal	Special	60	100	15	Normal
TM11	Sunny Day	Fire	Status	—	—	5	Both Sides
TM13	Ice Beam	Ice	Special	90	100	10	Normal
TM14	Blizzard	Ice	Special	110	70	5	Many Others
TM15	Hyper Beam	Normal	Special	150	90	5	Normal
TM16	Light Screen	Psychic	Status	—	—	30	Your Side
TM17	Protect	Normal	Status	—	—	10	Self
TM18	Rain Dance	Water	Status	—	—	5	Both Sides
TM20	Safeguard	Normal	Status	—	—	25	Your Side
TM21	Frustration	Normal	Physical	—	100	20	Normal
TM26	Earthquake	Ground	Physical	100	100	10	Adjacent
TM27	Return	Normal	Physical	—	100	20	Normal
TM28	Dig	Ground	Physical	80	100	10	Normal
TM29	Psychic	Psychic	Special	90	100	10	Normal
TM30	Shadow Ball	Ghost	Special	80	100	15	Normal
TM31	Brick Break	Fighting	Physical	75	100	15	Normal
TM32	Double Team	Normal	Status	—	—	15	Self
TM35	Flamethrower	Fire	Special	90	100	15	Normal
TM38	Fire Blast	Fire	Special	110	85	5	Normal
TM42	Facade	Normal	Physical	70	100	20	Normal
TM44	Rest	Psychic	Status	—	—	10	Self
TM45	Attract	Normal	Status	—	100	15	Normal
TM48	Round	Normal	Special	60	100	15	Normal
TM49	Echoed Voice	Normal	Special	40	100	15	Normal
TM52	Focus Blast	Fighting	Special	120	70	5	Normal
TM55	Scald	Water	Special	80	100	15	Normal
TM56	Fling	Dark	Physical	—	100	10	Normal
TM59	Incinerate	Fire	Special	60	100	15	Many Others
TM60	Quash	Dark	Status	—	100	15	Normal

No.	Name	Type	Kind	Pow.	Acc.	PP	Range
TM68	Giga Impact	Normal	Physical	150	90	5	Normal
TM70	Flash	Normal	Status	—	100	20	Normal
TM73	Thunder Wave	Electric	Status	—	100	20	Normal
TM77	Psych Up	Normal	Status	—	—	10	Normal
TM78	Bulldoze	Ground	Physical	60	100	20	Adjacent
TM82	Dragon Tail	Dragon	Physical	60	90	10	Normal
TM85	Dream Eater	Psychic	Special	100	100	15	Normal
TM86	Grass Knot	Grass	Special	—	100	20	Normal
TM87	Swagger	Normal	Status	—	90	15	Normal
TM88	Sleep Talk	Normal	Status	—	—	10	Self
TM90	Substitute	Normal	Status	—	—	10	Self
TM92	Trick Room	Psychic	Status	—	—	5	Both Sides
TM94	Rock Smash	Fighting	Physical	40	100	15	Normal
TM98	Power-Up Punch	Fighting	Physical	40	100	20	Normal
TM100	Confide	Normal	Status	—	—	20	Normal
HM03	Surf	Water	Special	90	100	15	Adjacent
HM04	Strength	Normal	Physical	80	100	15	Normal

● MOVES TAUGHT BY PEOPLE

Name	Type	Kind	Pow.	Acc.	PP	Range

Coastal Kalos

136

Egg Pokémon

☑ Exeggcute

HEIGHT: 1'04"   WEIGHT: 5.5 lbs.
GENDER: ♂/♀

TYPE	Grass	Psychic

ABILITY
Chlorophyll

HIDDEN ABILITY
Harvest

STAT GROWTH RATES
HP	▮▮▮
Attack	▮▮
Defense	▮▮▮▮
Sp. Atk	▮▮▮
Sp. Def	▮▮▮
Speed	▮▮

EGG GROUP
Grass

X Its six eggs converse using telepathy. They can quickly gather if they become separated.

Y Even though it appears to be eggs of some sort, it was discovered to be a life-form more like plant seeds.

EVOLUTION

Leaf Stone

Exeggcute → Exeggutor

ITEMS SOMETIMES HELD BY WILD POKÉMON
None

Damage taken in normal battles
Normal	×1
Fire	×2
Water	×0.5
Grass	×0.5
Electric	×0.5
Ice	×2
Fighting	×0.5
Poison	×2
Ground	×0.5
Flying	×2
Psychic	×0.5
Bug	×4
Rock	×1
Ghost	×2
Dragon	×1
Dark	×2
Steel	×1
Fairy	×1

Damage taken in Inverse Battles
Normal	×1
Fire	×0.5
Water	×2
Grass	×2
Electric	×2
Ice	×0.5
Fighting	×2
Poison	×0.5
Ground	×2
Flying	×0.5
Psychic	×2
Bug	×0.25
Rock	×1
Ghost	×0.5
Dragon	×1
Dark	×0.5
Steel	×1
Fairy	×1

Can be used in
Inverse Battle	Battle Institute
—	Battle Maison
Battle Chateau	Random Matchup

Same form for ♂/♀

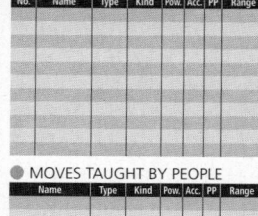

How to obtain for your Coastal Kalos Pokédex

❶ Catch in the tall grass on Route 12.
❷ Catch in the yellow flowers on Route 12.

❶ Catch in the tall grass on Route 12.
❷ Catch in the yellow flowers on Route 12.

AFTER THE HALL OF FAME

CENTRAL KALOS

COASTAL KALOS

136

Exeggcute

MOUNTAIN KALOS

ADVENTURE DATA

● LEVEL-UP MOVES

Lv.	Name	Type	Kind	Pow.	Acc.	PP	Range
1	Barrage	Normal	Physical	15	85	20	Normal
1	Uproar	Normal	Special	90	100	10	1 Random
1	Hypnosis	Psychic	Status	—	60	20	Normal
7	Reflect	Psychic	Status	—	—	20	Your Side
11	Leech Seed	Grass	Status	—	90	10	Normal
17	Bullet Seed	Grass	Physical	25	100	30	Normal
19	Stun Spore	Grass	Status	—	75	30	Normal
21	Poison Powder	Poison	Status	—	75	35	Normal
23	Sleep Powder	Grass	Status	—	75	15	Normal
27	Confusion	Psychic	Special	50	100	25	Normal
33	Worry Seed	Grass	Status	—	100	10	Normal
37	Natural Gift	Normal	Physical	—	100	15	Normal
43	Solar Beam	Grass	Special	120	100	10	Normal
47	Extrasensory	Psychic	Special	80	100	20	Normal
50	Bestow	Normal	Status	—	—	15	Normal

● TM & HM MOVES

No.	Name	Type	Kind	Pow.	Acc.	PP	Range
TM06	Toxic	Poison	Status	—	90	10	Normal
TM10	Hidden Power	Normal	Special	60	100	15	Normal
TM11	Sunny Day	Fire	Status	—	—	5	Both Sides
TM16	Light Screen	Psychic	Status	—	—	30	Your Side
TM17	Protect	Normal	Status	—	—	10	Self
TM21	Frustration	Normal	Physical	—	100	20	Normal
TM22	Solar Beam	Grass	Special	120	100	10	Normal
TM27	Return	Normal	Physical	—	100	20	Normal
TM29	Psychic	Psychic	Special	90	100	10	Normal
TM32	Double Team	Normal	Status	—	—	15	Self
TM33	Reflect	Psychic	Status	—	—	20	Your Side
TM36	Sludge Bomb	Poison	Special	90	100	10	Normal
TM42	Facade	Normal	Physical	70	100	20	Normal
TM44	Rest	Psychic	Status	—	—	10	Self
TM45	Attract	Normal	Status	—	100	15	Normal
TM46	Thief	Dark	Physical	60	100	25	Normal
TM48	Round	Normal	Special	60	100	15	Normal
TM53	Energy Ball	Grass	Special	90	100	10	Normal
TM64	Explosion	Normal	Physical	250	100	5	Adjacent
TM70	Flash	Normal	Status	—	100	20	Normal
TM75	Swords Dance	Normal	Status	—	—	20	Self
TM77	Psych Up	Normal	Status	—	—	10	Normal
TM83	Infestation	Bug	Special	20	100	20	Normal
TM85	Dream Eater	Psychic	Special	100	100	15	Normal
TM86	Grass Knot	Grass	Special	—	100	20	Normal
TM87	Swagger	Normal	Status	—	90	15	Normal
TM88	Sleep Talk	Normal	Status	—	—	10	Self
TM90	Substitute	Normal	Status	—	—	10	Self
TM92	Trick Room	Psychic	Status	—	—	5	Both Sides
TM96	Nature Power	Normal	Status	—	—	20	Normal
TM100	Confide	Normal	Status	—	—	20	Normal
HM04	Strength	Normal	Physical	80	100	15	Normal

● MOVES TAUGHT BY PEOPLE

Name	Type	Kind	Pow.	Acc.	PP	Range

● EGG MOVES

Name	Type	Kind	Pow.	Acc.	PP	Range
Synthesis	Grass	Status	—	—	5	Self
Moonlight	Fairy	Status	—	—	5	Self
Ancient Power	Rock	Special	60	100	5	Normal
Ingrain	Grass	Status	—	—	20	Self
Curse	Ghost	Status	—	—	10	Varies
Nature Power	Normal	Status	—	—	20	Normal
Lucky Chant	Normal	Status	—	—	30	Your Side
Leaf Storm	Grass	Special	130	90	5	Normal
Power Swap	Psychic	Status	—	—	10	Normal
Giga Drain	Grass	Special	75	100	10	Normal
Skill Swap	Psychic	Status	—	—	10	Normal
Natural Gift	Normal	Physical	—	100	15	Normal
Block	Normal	Status	—	—	5	Normal
Grassy Terrain	Grass	Status	—	—	10	Both Sides

🌴 Coastal Kalos **137**
Coconut Pokémon
✓ **Exeggutor**

HEIGHT: 6'07" WEIGHT: 264.6 lbs.
GENDER: ♂/♀

TYPE Grass Psychic

ABILITY
Chlorophyll

HIDDEN ABILITY
Harvest

STAT GROWTH RATES
HP	■■■■
Attack	■■■■
Defense	■■■■
Sp. Atk	■■■■■■
Sp. Def	■■■
Speed	■■■

EGG GROUP
Grass

X Its three heads think independently. However, they are friendly and never appear to squabble.

Y It is called "The Walking Jungle." If a head grows too big, it falls off and becomes an Exeggcute.

⚡ EVOLUTION

Exeggcute → Leaf Stone → Exeggutor

ITEMS SOMETIMES HELD BY WILD POKÉMON
None

Damage taken in normal battles
Normal	×1
Fire	×2
Water	×0.5
Grass	×0.5
Electric	×0.5
Ice	×2
Fighting	×0.5
Poison	×2
Ground	×0.5
Flying	×2
Psychic	×0.5
Bug	×4
Rock	×1
Ghost	×1
Dragon	×1
Dark	×2
Steel	×1
Fairy	×1

Damage taken in inverse Battles
Normal	×1
Fire	×0.5
Water	×2
Grass	×2
Electric	×2
Ice	×0.5
Fighting	×2
Poison	×0.5
Ground	×2
Flying	×0.5
Psychic	×2
Bug	×0.25
Rock	×1
Ghost	×0.5
Dragon	×1
Dark	×0.5
Steel	×1
Fairy	×1

Can be used in
Inverse Battle	Battle Institute
—	Battle Maison
Battle Chateau	Random Matchup

Same form for ♂/♀

How to obtain for your Coastal Kalos Pokédex

Use a Leaf Stone on Exeggcute.	Use a Leaf Stone on Exeggcute.
X	Y

● LEVEL-UP MOVES

Lv.	Name	Type	Kind	Pow.	Acc.	PP	Range
1	Seed Bomb	Grass	Physical	80	100	15	Normal
1	Barrage	Normal	Physical	15	85	20	Normal
1	Hypnosis	Psychic	Status	—	60	20	Normal
1	Confusion	Psychic	Special	50	100	25	Normal
1	Stomp	Normal	Physical	65	100	20	Normal
17	Psyshock	Psychic	Special	80	100	10	Normal
27	Egg Bomb	Normal	Physical	100	75	10	Normal
37	Wood Hammer	Grass	Physical	120	100	15	Normal
47	Leaf Storm	Grass	Special	130	90	5	Normal

● TM & HM MOVES

No.	Name	Type	Kind	Pow.	Acc.	PP	Range
TM03	Psyshock	Psychic	Special	80	100	10	Normal
TM06	Toxic	Poison	Status	—	90	10	Normal
TM10	Hidden Power	Normal	Special	60	100	15	Normal
TM11	Sunny Day	Fire	Status	—	—	5	Both Sides
TM15	Hyper Beam	Normal	Special	150	90	5	Normal
TM16	Light Screen	Psychic	Status	—	—	30	Your Side
TM17	Protect	Normal	Status	—	—	10	Self
TM21	Frustration	Normal	Physical	—	100	20	Normal
TM22	Solar Beam	Grass	Special	120	100	10	Normal
TM27	Return	Normal	Physical	—	100	20	Normal
TM29	Psychic	Psychic	Special	90	100	10	Normal
TM32	Double Team	Normal	Status	—	—	15	Self
TM33	Reflect	Psychic	Status	—	—	20	Your Side
TM36	Sludge Bomb	Poison	Special	90	100	10	Normal
TM42	Facade	Normal	Physical	70	100	20	Normal
TM44	Rest	Psychic	Status	—	—	10	Self
TM45	Attract	Normal	Status	—	100	15	Normal
TM46	Thief	Dark	Physical	60	100	25	Normal
TM48	Round	Normal	Special	60	100	15	Normal
TM53	Energy Ball	Grass	Special	90	100	10	Normal
TM64	Explosion	Normal	Physical	250	100	5	Adjacent
TM68	Giga Impact	Normal	Physical	150	90	5	Normal
TM70	Flash	Normal	Status	—	100	20	Normal
TM75	Swords Dance	Normal	Status	—	—	20	Self
TM77	Psych Up	Normal	Status	—	—	10	Normal
TM83	Infestation	Bug	Special	20	100	20	Normal
TM85	Dream Eater	Psychic	Special	100	100	15	Normal
TM86	Grass Knot	Grass	Special	—	100	20	Normal
TM87	Swagger	Normal	Status	—	90	15	Normal
TM88	Sleep Talk	Normal	Status	—	—	10	Self
TM90	Substitute	Normal	Status	—	—	10	Self
TM92	Trick Room	Psychic	Status	—	—	5	Both Sides
TM96	Nature Power	Normal	Status	—	—	20	Normal

No.	Name	Type	Kind	Pow.	Acc.	PP	Range
TM100	Confide	Normal	Status	—	—	20	Normal
HM04	Strength	Normal	Physical	80	100	15	Normal

● MOVES TAUGHT BY PEOPLE

Name	Type	Kind	Pow.	Acc.	PP	Range

AFTER THE HALL OF FAME

CENTRAL KALOS

COASTAL KALOS

137

Exeggutor

MOUNTAIN KALOS

ADVENTURE DATA

♠ Coastal Kalos
Music Note Pokémon
☑ Chatot
138

HEIGHT: 1'08" WEIGHT: 4.2 lbs.
GENDER: ♂/♀

TYPE	Normal	Flying

ABILITIES
Keen Eye
Tangled Feet

HIDDEN ABILITY
None

STAT GROWTH RATES
HP	■■■
Attack	■■■
Defense	■■
Sp. Atk	■■■■■
Sp. Def	■■
Speed	■■■■■

EGG GROUP
Flying

ⓧ It mimics the cries of other Pokémon to trick them into thinking it's one of them. This way they won't attack it.

ⓨ It can learn and speak human words. If they gather, they all learn the same saying.

EVOLUTION

Does not evolve

ITEMS SOMETIMES HELD BY WILD POKÉMON
Metronome

Damage taken in normal battles	
Normal	×1
Fire	×1
Water	×1
Grass	×0.5
Electric	×2
Ice	×2
Fighting	×1
Poison	×1
Ground	×0
Flying	×1
Psychic	×1
Bug	×0.5
Rock	×2
Ghost	×0
Dragon	×1
Dark	×1
Steel	×1
Fairy	×1

Damage taken in Inverse Battles	
Normal	×1
Fire	×1
Water	×1
Grass	×2
Electric	×0.5
Ice	×0.5
Fighting	×1
Poison	×1
Ground	×2
Flying	×1
Psychic	×1
Bug	×2
Rock	×0.5
Ghost	×2
Dragon	×1
Dark	×1
Steel	×1
Fairy	×1

Can be used in	
Inverse Battle	Battle Institute
—	Battle Maison
Battle Chateau	Random Matchup

Same form for ♂/♀

How to obtain for your Coastal Kalos Pokédex

❶ Catch in the tall grass on Route 12.
❷ Catch in the yellow flowers on Route 12.

❶ Catch in the tall grass on Route 12.
❷ Catch in the yellow flowers on Route 12.

● LEVEL-UP MOVES

Lv.	Name	Type	Kind	Pow.	Acc.	PP	Range
1	Hyper Voice	Normal	Special	90	100	10	Many Others
1	Chatter	Flying	Special	65	100	20	Normal
1	Confide	Normal	Status	—	—	20	Normal
1	Taunt	Dark	Status	—	100	20	Normal
5	Peck	Flying	Physical	35	100	35	Normal
5	Growl	Normal	Status	—	100	40	Many Others
9	Mirror Move	Flying	Status	—	—	20	Normal
13	Sing	Normal	Status	—	55	15	Normal
17	Fury Attack	Normal	Physical	15	85	20	Normal
21	Chatter	Flying	Special	65	100	20	Normal
25	Taunt	Dark	Status	—	100	20	Normal
29	Round	Normal	Special	60	100	15	Normal
33	Mimic	Normal	Status	—	—	10	Normal
37	Echoed Voice	Normal	Special	40	100	15	Normal
41	Roost	Flying	Status	—	—	10	Self
45	Uproar	Normal	Special	90	100	10	1 Random
49	Synchronoise	Psychic	Special	120	100	10	Adjacent
50	Feather Dance	Flying	Status	—	100	15	Normal
57	Hyper Voice	Normal	Special	90	100	10	Many Others

● TM & HM MOVES

No.	Name	Type	Kind	Pow.	Acc.	PP	Range
TM06	Toxic	Poison	Status	—	90	10	Normal
TM10	Hidden Power	Normal	Special	60	100	15	Normal
TM11	Sunny Day	Fire	Status	—	—	5	Both Sides
TM12	Taunt	Dark	Status	—	100	20	Normal
TM17	Protect	Normal	Status	—	—	10	Self
TM18	Rain Dance	Water	Status	—	—	5	Both Sides
TM19	Roost	Flying	Status	—	—	10	Self
TM21	Frustration	Normal	Physical	—	100	20	Normal
TM27	Return	Normal	Physical	—	100	20	Normal
TM32	Double Team	Normal	Status	—	—	15	Self
TM40	Aerial Ace	Flying	Physical	60	—	20	Normal
TM41	Torment	Dark	Status	—	100	15	Normal
TM42	Facade	Normal	Physical	70	100	20	Normal
TM44	Rest	Psychic	Status	—	—	10	Self
TM45	Attract	Normal	Status	—	100	15	Normal
TM46	Thief	Dark	Physical	60	100	25	Normal
TM48	Round	Normal	Special	60	100	15	Normal
TM49	Echoed Voice	Normal	Special	40	100	15	Normal
TM51	Steel Wing	Steel	Physical	70	90	25	Normal
TM87	Swagger	Normal	Status	—	90	15	Normal
TM88	Sleep Talk	Normal	Status	—	—	10	Self
TM89	U-turn	Bug	Physical	70	100	20	Normal
TM90	Substitute	Normal	Status	—	—	10	Self
TM100	Confide	Normal	Status	—	—	20	Normal
HM02	Fly	Flying	Physical	90	95	15	Normal

No.	Name	Type	Kind	Pow.	Acc.	PP	Range

● MOVES TAUGHT BY PEOPLE

Name	Type	Kind	Pow.	Acc.	PP	Range

● EGG MOVES

Name	Type	Kind	Pow.	Acc.	PP	Range
Encore	Normal	Status	—	100	5	Normal
Night Shade	Ghost	Special	—	100	15	Normal
Agility	Psychic	Status	—	—	30	Self
Nasty Plot	Dark	Status	—	—	20	Self
Supersonic	Normal	Status	—	55	20	Normal
Steel Wing	Steel	Physical	70	90	25	Normal
Sleep Talk	Normal	Status	—	—	10	Self
Defog	Flying	Status	—	—	15	Normal
Air Cutter	Flying	Special	60	95	25	Many Others
Boomburst	Normal	Special	140	100	10	Adjacent

AFTER THE HALL OF FAME

CENTRAL KALOS

COASTAL KALOS

138 Chatot

MOUNTAIN KALOS

ADVENTURE DATA

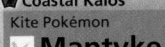

Coastal Kalos **139**

Kite Pokémon

✓ Mantyke

HEIGHT: 3'03" WEIGHT: 143.3 lbs.
GENDER: ♂/♀

TYPE Water | Flying

ABILITIES
Swift Swim
Water Absorb

HIDDEN ABILITY
None

STAT GROWTH RATES
HP	■■
Attack	■
Defense	■■
Sp. Atk	■■■
Sp. Def	■■■■■
Speed	■■■

EGG GROUP
No Eggs Discovered

The pattern on its back varies by region. It often swims in a school of Remoraid.

When it swims close to the surface of the ocean, people aboard ships are able to observe the pattern on its back.

EVOLUTION

Level up with Remoraid in your party

Mantyke → Mantine

ITEMS SOMETIMES HELD BY WILD POKÉMON
None

Damage taken in normal battles		Damage taken in Inverse Battles	
Normal	×1	Normal	×1
Fire	×0.5	Fire	×2
Water	×0.5	Water	×2
Grass	×1	Grass	×1
Electric	×4	Electric	×0.25
Ice	×1	Ice	×1
Fighting	×0.5	Fighting	×2
Poison	×1	Poison	×1
Ground	×0	Ground	×2
Flying	×1	Flying	×1
Psychic	×1	Psychic	×1
Bug	×0.5	Bug	×2
Rock	×2	Rock	×0.5
Ghost	×1	Ghost	×1
Dragon	×1	Dragon	×1
Dark	×1	Dark	×1
Steel	×0.5	Steel	×1
Fairy	×1	Fairy	×1

Can be used in
Inverse Battle	Battle Institute
Sky Battle	Battle Maison
Battle Chateau	Random Matchup

Same form for ♂/♀

How to obtain for your Coastal Kalos Pokédex

❶ Catch on the surface of the water in Shalour City.
❷ Catch on the surface of the water on Route 12.

❶ Catch on the surface of the water in Shalour City.
❷ Catch on the surface of the water on Route 12.

● LEVEL-UP MOVES

Lv.	Name	Type	Kind	Pow.	Acc.	PP	Range
1	Tackle	Normal	Physical	50	100	35	Normal
1	Bubble	Water	Special	40	100	30	Many Others
3	Supersonic	Normal	Status	—	55	20	Normal
7	Bubble Beam	Water	Special	65	100	20	Normal
11	Confuse Ray	Ghost	Status	—	100	10	Normal
14	Wing Attack	Flying	Physical	60	100	35	Normal
16	Headbutt	Normal	Physical	70	100	15	Normal
19	Water Pulse	Water	Special	60	100	20	Normal
23	Wide Guard	Rock	Status	—	—	10	Your Side
27	Take Down	Normal	Physical	90	85	20	Normal
32	Agility	Psychic	Status	—	—	30	Self
36	Air Slash	Flying	Special	75	95	15	Normal
39	Aqua Ring	Water	Status	—	—	20	Self
46	Bounce	Flying	Physical	85	85	5	Normal
49	Hydro Pump	Water	Special	110	80	5	Normal

● TM & HM MOVES

No.	Name	Type	Kind	Pow.	Acc.	PP	Range
TM06	Toxic	Poison	Status	—	90	10	Normal
TM07	Hail	Ice	Status	—	—	10	Both Sides
TM10	Hidden Power	Normal	Special	60	100	15	Normal
TM13	Ice Beam	Ice	Special	90	100	10	Normal
TM14	Blizzard	Ice	Special	110	70	5	Many Others
TM17	Protect	Normal	Status	—	—	10	Self
TM18	Rain Dance	Water	Status	—	—	5	Both Sides
TM21	Frustration	Normal	Physical	—	100	20	Normal
TM26	Earthquake	Ground	Physical	100	100	10	Adjacent
TM27	Return	Normal	Physical	—	100	20	Normal
TM32	Double Team	Normal	Status	—	—	15	Self
TM40	Aerial Ace	Flying	Physical	60	—	20	Normal
TM42	Facade	Normal	Physical	70	100	20	Normal
TM44	Rest	Psychic	Status	—	—	10	Self
TM45	Attract	Normal	Status	—	100	15	Normal
TM48	Round	Normal	Special	60	100	15	Normal
TM55	Scald	Water	Special	80	100	15	Normal
TM62	Acrobatics	Flying	Physical	55	100	15	Normal
TM78	Bulldoze	Ground	Physical	60	100	20	Adjacent
TM80	Rock Slide	Rock	Physical	75	90	10	Many Others
TM87	Swagger	Normal	Status	—	90	15	Normal
TM88	Sleep Talk	Normal	Status	—	—	10	Self
TM90	Substitute	Normal	Status	—	—	10	Self
TM100	Confide	Normal	Status	—	—	20	Normal
HM03	Surf	Water	Special	90	100	15	Adjacent
HM05	Waterfall	Water	Physical	80	100	15	Normal

No.	Name	Type	Kind	Pow.	Acc.	PP	Range

● MOVES TAUGHT BY PEOPLE

Name	Type	Kind	Pow.	Acc.	PP	Range

● EGG MOVES

Name	Type	Kind	Pow.	Acc.	PP	Range
Twister	Dragon	Special	40	100	20	Many Others
Hydro Pump	Water	Special	110	80	5	Normal
Haze	Ice	Status	—	—	30	Both Sides
Slam	Normal	Physical	80	75	20	Normal
Mud Sport	Ground	Status	—	—	15	Both Sides
Mirror Coat	Psychic	Special	—	100	20	Varies
Water Sport	Water	Status	—	—	15	Both Sides
Splash	Normal	Status	—	—	40	Self
Signal Beam	Bug	Special	75	100	15	Normal
Wide Guard	Rock	Status	—	—	10	Your Side
Amnesia	Psychic	Status	—	—	20	Self
Tailwind	Flying	Status	—	—	15	Your Side

AFTER THE HALL OF FAME

CENTRAL KALOS

COASTAL KALOS
139
Mantyke

MOUNTAIN KALOS

ADVENTURE DATA

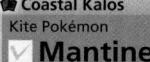

🏆 Coastal Kalos   140

Kite Pokémon

☑ **Mantine**

HEIGHT: 6'11"   WEIGHT: 485.0 lbs.
GENDER: ♂/♀

X If it builds up enough speed swimming, it can fly over 300 feet out of the water from the surface of the ocean.

Y While elegantly swimming in the sea, it ignores Remoraid that cling to its fins seeking food scraps.

TYPE `Water` `Flying`

ABILITIES
Swift Swim
Water Absorb

HIDDEN ABILITY
None

STAT GROWTH RATES
HP ■■■
Attack ■■
Defense ■■■
Sp. Atk ■■■■
Sp. Def ■■■■■
Speed ■■■■

EGG GROUP
Water 1

⬆ EVOLUTION

Level up with Remoraid in your party

Mantyke   Mantine

ITEMS SOMETIMES HELD BY WILD POKÉMON
None

Damage taken in normal battles		Damage taken in Inverse Battles	
Normal	×1	Normal	×1
Fire	×0.5	Fire	×2
Water	×0.5	Water	×2
Grass	×1	Grass	×1
Electric	×4	Electric	×0.25
Ice	×1	Ice	×1
Fighting	×0.5	Fighting	×2
Poison	×1	Poison	×1
Ground	×0	Ground	×2
Flying	×1	Flying	×1
Psychic	×1	Psychic	×1
Bug	×0.5	Bug	×2
Rock	×2	Rock	×0.5
Ghost	×1	Ghost	×1
Dragon	×1	Dragon	×1
Dark	×1	Dark	×1
Steel	×0.5	Steel	×2
Fairy	×1	Fairy	×1

Can be used in	
Inverse Battle	Battle Institute
Sky Battle	Battle Maison
Battle Chateau	Random Matchup

Same form for ♂/♀

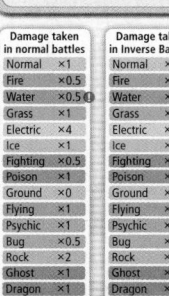

How to obtain for your Coastal Kalos Pokédex

| Level up Mantyke with Remoraid in your party. | Level up Mantyke with Remoraid in your party. |

X   **Y**

● LEVEL-UP MOVES

Lv.	Name	Type	Kind	Pow.	Acc.	PP	Range
1	Psybeam	Psychic	Special	65	100	20	Normal
1	Bullet Seed	Grass	Physical	25	100	30	Normal
1	Signal Beam	Bug	Special	75	100	15	Normal
1	Tackle	Normal	Physical	50	100	35	Normal
1	Bubble	Water	Special	40	100	30	Many Others
1	Supersonic	Normal	Status	—	55	20	Normal
1	Bubble Beam	Water	Special	65	100	20	Normal
3	Supersonic	Normal	Status	—	55	20	Normal
7	Bubble Beam	Water	Special	65	100	20	Normal
11	Confuse Ray	Ghost	Status	—	100	10	Normal
14	Wing Attack	Flying	Physical	60	100	35	Normal
16	Headbutt	Normal	Physical	70	100	15	Normal
19	Water Pulse	Water	Special	60	100	20	Normal
23	Wide Guard	Rock	Status	—	—	10	Your Side
27	Take Down	Normal	Physical	90	85	20	Normal
32	Agility	Psychic	Status	—	—	30	Self
36	Air Slash	Flying	Special	75	95	15	Normal
39	Aqua Ring	Water	Status	—	—	20	Self
46	Bounce	Flying	Physical	85	85	5	Normal
49	Hydro Pump	Water	Special	110	80	5	Normal

■ TM & HM MOVES

No.	Name	Type	Kind	Pow.	Acc.	PP	Range
TM06	Toxic	Poison	Status	—	90	10	Normal
TM07	Hail	Ice	Status	—	—	10	Both Sides
TM10	Hidden Power	Normal	Special	60	100	15	Normal
TM13	Ice Beam	Ice	Special	90	100	10	Normal
TM14	Blizzard	Ice	Special	110	70	5	Many Others
TM15	Hyper Beam	Normal	Special	150	90	5	Normal
TM17	Protect	Normal	Status	—	—	10	Self
TM18	Rain Dance	Water	Status	—	—	5	Both Sides
TM21	Frustration	Normal	Physical	—	100	20	Normal
TM26	Earthquake	Ground	Physical	100	100	10	Adjacent
TM27	Return	Normal	Physical	—	100	20	Normal
TM32	Double Team	Normal	Status	—	—	15	Self
TM39	Rock Tomb	Rock	Physical	60	95	15	Normal
TM40	Aerial Ace	Flying	Physical	60	—	20	Normal
TM42	Facade	Normal	Physical	70	100	20	Normal
TM44	Rest	Psychic	Status	—	—	10	Self
TM45	Attract	Normal	Status	—	100	15	Normal
TM48	Round	Normal	Special	60	100	15	Normal
TM55	Scald	Water	Special	80	100	15	Normal
TM62	Acrobatics	Flying	Physical	55	100	15	Normal
TM68	Giga Impact	Normal	Physical	150	90	5	Normal
TM78	Bulldoze	Ground	Physical	60	100	20	Adjacent
TM80	Rock Slide	Rock	Physical	75	90	10	Many Others
TM87	Swagger	Normal	Status	—	90	15	Normal
TM88	Sleep Talk	Normal	Status	—	—	10	Self
TM90	Substitute	Normal	Status	—	—	10	Self
TM100	Confide	Normal	Status	—	—	20	Normal
HM03	Surf	Water	Special	90	100	15	Adjacent
HM05	Waterfall	Water	Physical	80	100	15	Normal

● MOVES TAUGHT BY PEOPLE

Name	Type	Kind	Pow.	Acc.	PP	Range

● EGG MOVES

Name	Type	Kind	Pow.	Acc.	PP	Range
Twister	Dragon	Special	40	100	20	Many Others
Hydro Pump	Water	Special	110	80	5	Normal
Haze	Ice	Status	—	—	30	Both Sides
Slam	Normal	Physical	80	75	20	Normal
Mud Sport	Ground	Status	—	—	15	Both Sides
Mirror Coat	Psychic	Special	—	100	20	Varies
Water Sport	Water	Status	—	—	15	Both Sides
Splash	Normal	Status	—	—	40	Self
Wide Guard	Rock	Status	—	—	10	Your Side
Amnesia	Psychic	Status	—	—	20	Self

AFTER THE HALL OF FAME

CENTRAL KALOS

COASTAL KALOS

140 | Mantine

MOUNTAIN KALOS

ADVENTURE DATA

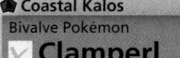

Coastal Kalos
Bivalve Pokémon

Clamperl

141

HEIGHT: 1'04" WEIGHT: 115.7 lbs.
GENDER: ♂/♀

X — When it evolves, it makes a mysterious pearl that amplifies psychic powers when it's held.

Y — It is protected by a sturdy shell. Once in a lifetime, it makes a magnificent pearl.

TYPE Water

ABILITY
Shell Armor

HIDDEN ABILITY
None

STAT GROWTH RATES
HP	■■
Attack	■■■
Defense	■■■■
Sp. Atk	■■■■
Sp. Def	■■
Speed	■■

EGG GROUP
Water 1

EVOLUTION

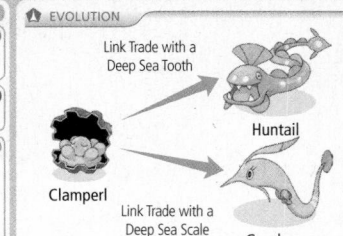

Clamperl → Link Trade with a Deep Sea Tooth → Huntail

Clamperl → Link Trade with a Deep Sea Scale → Gorebyss

ITEMS SOMETIMES HELD BY WILD POKÉMON
Big Pearl

Damage taken in normal battles		Damage taken in Inverse Battles	
Normal	×1	Normal	×1
Fire	×0.5	Fire	×2
Water	×0.5	Water	×2
Grass	×2	Grass	×0.5
Electric	×2	Electric	×0.5
Ice	×0.5	Ice	×2
Fighting	×1	Fighting	×1
Poison	×1	Poison	×1
Ground	×1	Ground	×1
Flying	×1	Flying	×1
Psychic	×1	Psychic	×1
Bug	×1	Bug	×1
Rock	×1	Rock	×1
Ghost	×1	Ghost	×1
Dragon	×1	Dragon	×1
Dark	×1	Dark	×1
Steel	×0.5	Steel	×2
Fairy	×1	Fairy	×1

Can be used in	
Inverse Battle	Battle Institute
—	Battle Maison
Battle Chateau	Random Matchup

Same form for ♂/♀

How to obtain for your Coastal Kalos Pokédex

X — Catch using a Good Rod on Route 12.

Y — Catch using a Good Rod on Route 12.

● LEVEL-UP MOVES

Lv.	Name	Type	Kind	Pow.	Acc.	PP	Range
1	Clamp	Water	Physical	35	85	15	Normal
1	Water Gun	Water	Special	40	100	25	Normal
1	Whirlpool	Water	Special	35	85	15	Normal
1	Iron Defense	Steel	Status	—	—	15	Self
50	Shell Smash	Normal	Status	—	—	15	Self

● TM & HM MOVES

No.	Name	Type	Kind	Pow.	Acc.	PP	Range
TM06	Toxic	Poison	Status	—	90	10	Normal
TM07	Hail	Ice	Status	—	—	10	Both Sides
TM10	Hidden Power	Normal	Special	60	100	15	Normal
TM13	Ice Beam	Ice	Special	90	100	10	Normal
TM14	Blizzard	Ice	Special	110	70	5	Many Others
TM17	Protect	Normal	Status	—	—	10	Self
TM18	Rain Dance	Water	Status	—	—	5	Both Sides
TM21	Frustration	Normal	Physical	—	100	20	Normal
TM27	Return	Normal	Physical	—	100	20	Normal
TM32	Double Team	Normal	Status	—	—	15	Self
TM42	Facade	Normal	Physical	70	100	20	Normal
TM44	Rest	Psychic	Status	—	—	10	Self
TM45	Attract	Normal	Status	—	100	15	Normal
TM48	Round	Normal	Special	60	100	15	Normal
TM55	Scald	Water	Special	80	100	15	Normal
TM87	Swagger	Normal	Status	—	90	15	Normal
TM88	Sleep Talk	Normal	Status	—	—	10	Self
TM90	Substitute	Normal	Status	—	—	10	Self
TM100	Confide	Normal	Status	—	—	20	Normal
HM03	Surf	Water	Special	90	100	15	Adjacent
HM05	Waterfall	Water	Physical	80	100	15	Normal

No.	Name	Type	Kind	Pow.	Acc.	PP	Range

● MOVES TAUGHT BY PEOPLE

Name	Type	Kind	Pow.	Acc.	PP	Range

● EGG MOVES

Name	Type	Kind	Pow.	Acc.	PP	Range
Refresh	Normal	Status	—	—	20	Self
Mud Sport	Ground	Status	—	—	15	Both Sides
Body Slam	Normal	Physical	85	100	15	Normal
Supersonic	Normal	Status	—	55	20	Normal
Barrier	Psychic	Status	—	—	20	Self
Confuse Ray	Ghost	Status	—	100	10	Normal
Aqua Ring	Water	Status	—	—	20	Self
Muddy Water	Water	Special	90	85	10	Many Others
Water Pulse	Water	Special	60	100	20	Normal
Brine	Water	Special	65	100	10	Normal
Endure	Normal	Status	—	—	10	Self

Sidebar:

AFTER THE HALL OF FAME

CENTRAL KALOS

COASTAL KALOS

141

Clamperl

MOUNTAIN KALOS

ADVENTURE DATA

Deep Sea Pokémon
☑ Huntail

HEIGHT: 5'07" **WEIGHT:** 59.5 lbs.
GENDER: ♂/♀

X It lives deep in the sea where no light ever filters down. It lights up its small fishlike tail to attract prey.

Y It lives deep in the sea. With a tail shaped like a small fish, it attracts unsuspecting prey.

TYPE Water

ABILITY
Swift Swim

HIDDEN ABILITY
None

STAT GROWTH RATES
HP	▓▓
Attack	▓▓▓▓
Defense	▓▓▓▓▓
Sp. Atk	▓▓▓▓▓
Sp. Def	▓▓▓
Speed	▓▓▓

EGG GROUP
Water 1

EVOLUTION

Link Trade with a Deep Sea Tooth → Huntail

Clamperl

Link Trade with a Deep Sea Scale → Gorebyss

ITEMS SOMETIMES HELD BY WILD POKÉMON
Deep Sea Tooth

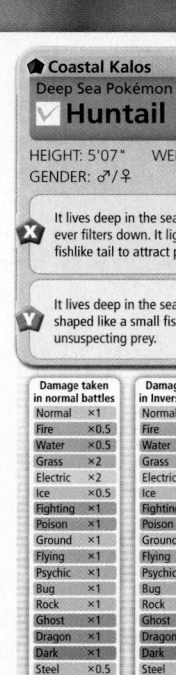

Damage taken in normal battles		Damage taken in Inverse Battles	
Normal	×1	Normal	×1
Fire	×0.5	Fire	×2
Water	×0.5	Water	×2
Grass	×2	Grass	×0.5
Electric	×2	Electric	×0.5
Ice	×0.5	Ice	×2
Fighting	×1	Fighting	×1
Poison	×1	Poison	×1
Ground	×1	Ground	×1
Flying	×1	Flying	×1
Psychic	×1	Psychic	×1
Bug	×1	Bug	×1
Rock	×1	Rock	×1
Ghost	×1	Ghost	×1
Dragon	×1	Dragon	×1
Dark	×1	Dark	×1
Steel	×0.5	Steel	×2
Fairy	×1	Fairy	×1

Can be used in	
Inverse Battle	Battle Institute
—	Battle Maison
Battle Chateau	Random Matchup

Same form for ♂/♀

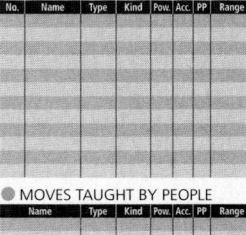

How to obtain for your Coastal Kalos Pokédex
❶ Catch using a Super Rod on Route 12.
❷ Receive Clamperl with a Deep Sea Tooth by Link Trade, and have it evolve.

Receive Clamperl with a Deep Sea Tooth by Link Trade, and have it evolve.

● LEVEL-UP MOVES
Lv.	Name	Type	Kind	Pow.	Acc.	PP	Range
1	Whirlpool	Water	Special	35	85	15	Normal
6	Bite	Dark	Physical	60	100	25	Normal
10	Screech	Normal	Status	—	85	40	Normal
15	Water Pulse	Water	Special	60	100	20	Normal
19	Scary Face	Normal	Status	—	100	10	Normal
24	Ice Fang	Ice	Physical	65	95	15	Normal
28	Brine	Water	Special	65	100	10	Normal
33	Baton Pass	Normal	Status	—	—	40	Self
37	Dive	Water	Physical	80	100	10	Normal
42	Crunch	Dark	Physical	80	100	15	Normal
46	Aqua Tail	Water	Physical	90	90	10	Normal
50	Hydro Pump	Water	Special	110	80	5	Normal

● TM & HM MOVES
No.	Name	Type	Kind	Pow.	Acc.	PP	Range
TM06	Toxic	Poison	Status	—	90	10	Normal
TM07	Hail	Ice	Status	—	—	10	Both Sides
TM10	Hidden Power	Normal	Special	60	100	15	Normal
TM13	Ice Beam	Ice	Special	90	100	10	Normal
TM14	Blizzard	Ice	Special	110	70	5	Many Others
TM15	Hyper Beam	Normal	Special	150	90	5	Normal
TM17	Protect	Normal	Status	—	—	10	Self
TM18	Rain Dance	Water	Status	—	—	5	Both Sides
TM21	Frustration	Normal	Physical	—	100	20	Normal
TM27	Return	Normal	Physical	—	100	20	Normal
TM32	Double Team	Normal	Status	—	—	15	Self
TM39	Rock Tomb	Rock	Physical	60	95	15	Normal
TM42	Facade	Normal	Physical	70	100	20	Normal
TM44	Rest	Psychic	Status	—	—	10	Self
TM45	Attract	Normal	Status	—	100	15	Normal
TM48	Round	Normal	Special	60	100	15	Normal
TM55	Scald	Water	Special	80	100	15	Normal
TM68	Giga Impact	Normal	Physical	150	90	5	Normal
TM83	Infestation	Bug	Special	20	100	20	Normal
TM87	Swagger	Normal	Status	—	90	15	Normal
TM88	Sleep Talk	Normal	Status	—	—	10	Self
TM90	Substitute	Normal	Status	—	—	10	Self
TM100	Confide	Normal	Status	—	—	20	Normal
HM03	Surf	Water	Special	90	100	15	Adjacent
HM05	Waterfall	Water	Physical	80	100	15	Normal

No.	Name	Type	Kind	Pow.	Acc.	PP	Range

● MOVES TAUGHT BY PEOPLE
Name	Type	Kind	Pow.	Acc.	PP	Range

AFTER THE HALL OF FAME

CENTRAL KALOS

COASTAL KALOS

143

Gorebyss

MOUNTAIN KALOS

ADVENTURE DATA

Coastal Kalos 143
South Sea Pokémon
☑ Gorebyss

HEIGHT: 5'11" WEIGHT: 49.8 lbs.
GENDER: ♂/♀

X It lives at the bottom of the sea. In the springtime, its pink body turns more vivid for some reason.

Y Its swimming form is exquisitely elegant. With its thin mouth, it feeds on seaweed that grows between rocks.

TYPE Water

ABILITY
Swift Swim

HIDDEN ABILITY
Hydration

STAT GROWTH RATES
HP	■■
Attack	■■
Defense	■■■■
Sp. Atk	■■■■■■
Sp. Def	■■■■
Speed	■■■

EGG GROUP
Water 1

EVOLUTION

Clamperl → Link Trade with a Deep Sea Tooth → Huntail

Clamperl → Link Trade with a Deep Sea Scale → Gorebyss

ITEMS SOMETIMES HELD BY WILD POKÉMON
Deep Sea Scale

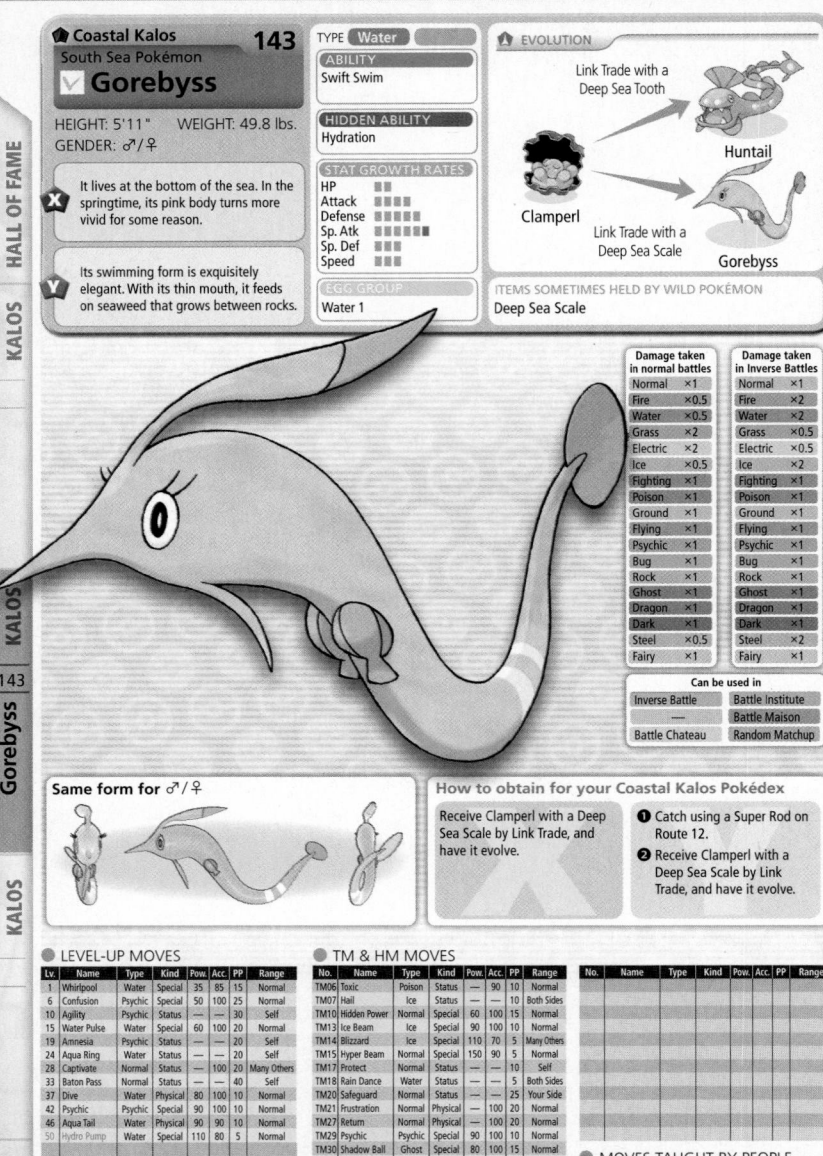

Damage taken in normal battles	
Normal	×1
Fire	×0.5
Water	×0.5
Grass	×2
Electric	×2
Ice	×0.5
Fighting	×1
Poison	×1
Ground	×1
Flying	×1
Psychic	×1
Bug	×1
Rock	×1
Ghost	×1
Dragon	×1
Dark	×1
Steel	×0.5
Fairy	×1

Damage taken in Inverse Battles	
Normal	×1
Fire	×2
Water	×2
Grass	×0.5
Electric	×0.5
Ice	×2
Fighting	×1
Poison	×1
Ground	×1
Flying	×1
Psychic	×1
Bug	×1
Rock	×1
Ghost	×1
Dragon	×1
Dark	×1
Steel	×2
Fairy	×1

Can be used in	
Inverse Battle	Battle Institute
—	Battle Maison
Battle Chateau	Random Matchup

Same form for ♂/♀

How to obtain for your Coastal Kalos Pokédex

Receive Clamperl with a Deep Sea Scale by Link Trade, and have it evolve.

❶ Catch using a Super Rod on Route 12.
❷ Receive Clamperl with a Deep Sea Scale by Link Trade, and have it evolve.

● LEVEL-UP MOVES

Lv.	Name	Type	Kind	Pow.	Acc.	PP	Range
1	Whirlpool	Water	Special	35	85	15	Normal
6	Confusion	Psychic	Special	50	100	25	Normal
10	Agility	Psychic	Status	—	—	30	Self
15	Water Pulse	Water	Special	60	100	20	Normal
19	Amnesia	Psychic	Status	—	—	20	Self
24	Aqua Ring	Water	Status	—	—	20	Self
28	Captivate	Normal	Status	—	100	20	Many Others
33	Baton Pass	Normal	Status	—	—	40	Self
37	Dive	Water	Physical	80	100	10	Normal
42	Psychic	Psychic	Special	90	100	10	Normal
46	Aqua Tail	Water	Physical	90	90	10	Normal
50	Hydro Pump	Water	Special	110	80	5	Normal

● TM & HM MOVES

No.	Name	Type	Kind	Pow.	Acc.	PP	Range
TM06	Toxic	Poison	Status	—	90	10	Normal
TM07	Hail	Ice	Status	—	—	10	Both Sides
TM10	Hidden Power	Normal	Special	60	100	15	Normal
TM13	Ice Beam	Ice	Special	90	100	10	Normal
TM14	Blizzard	Ice	Special	110	70	5	Many Others
TM15	Hyper Beam	Normal	Special	150	90	5	Normal
TM17	Protect	Normal	Status	—	—	10	Self
TM18	Rain Dance	Water	Status	—	—	5	Both Sides
TM20	Safeguard	Normal	Status	—	—	25	Your Side
TM21	Frustration	Normal	Physical	—	100	20	Normal
TM27	Return	Normal	Physical	—	100	20	Normal
TM29	Psychic	Psychic	Special	90	100	10	Normal
TM30	Shadow Ball	Ghost	Special	80	100	15	Normal
TM32	Double Team	Normal	Status	—	—	15	Self
TM42	Facade	Normal	Physical	70	100	20	Normal
TM44	Rest	Psychic	Status	—	—	10	Self
TM45	Attract	Normal	Status	—	100	15	Normal
TM48	Round	Normal	Special	60	100	15	Normal
TM55	Scald	Water	Special	80	100	15	Normal
TM68	Giga Impact	Normal	Physical	150	90	5	Normal
TM77	Psych Up	Normal	Status	—	—	10	Normal
TM83	Infestation	Bug	Special	20	100	20	Normal
TM87	Swagger	Normal	Status	—	90	15	Normal
TM88	Sleep Talk	Normal	Status	—	—	10	Self
TM90	Substitute	Normal	Status	—	—	10	Self
TM100	Confide	Normal	Status	—	—	20	Normal
HM03	Surf	Water	Special	90	100	15	Adjacent
HM05	Waterfall	Water	Physical	80	100	15	Normal

No.	Name	Type	Kind	Pow.	Acc.	PP	Range

● MOVES TAUGHT BY PEOPLE

Name	Type	Kind	Pow.	Acc.	PP	Range

Coastal Kalos 144
Jet Pokémon
Remoraid

HEIGHT: 2'00" WEIGHT: 26.5 lbs.
GENDER: ♂/♀

X It has superb accuracy. The water it shoots out can strike moving prey from more than 300 feet away.

Y Using its dorsal fin as a suction pad, it clings to a Mantine's underside to scavenge for leftovers.

TYPE Water

ABILITIES
Hustle
Sniper

HIDDEN ABILITY
Moody

STAT GROWTH RATES
HP	■ ■
Attack	■ ■ ■
Defense	■ ■ ■
Sp. Atk	■ ■ ■
Sp. Def	■ ■
Speed	■ ■ ■ ■

EGG GROUPS
Water 1, Water 2

EVOLUTION

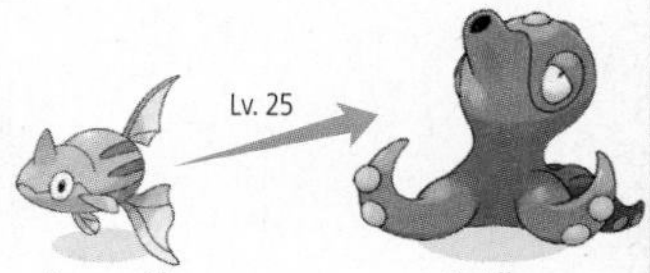

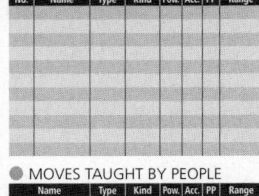

Remoraid → Lv. 25 → Octillery

ITEMS SOMETIMES HELD BY WILD POKÉMON
None

Damage taken in normal battles		Damage taken in Inverse Battles		Can be used in
Normal	×1	Normal	×1	Inverse Battle
Fire	×0.5	Fire	×2	—
Water	×0.5	Water	×2	Battle Chateau
Grass	×2	Grass	×0.5	Battle Institute
Electric	×2	Electric	×0.5	Battle Maison
Ice	×0.5	Ice	×2	Random Matchup
Fighting	×1	Fighting	×1	
Poison	×1	Poison	×1	
Ground	×1	Ground	×1	
Flying	×1	Flying	×1	
Psychic	×1	Psychic	×1	
Bug	×1	Bug	×1	
Rock	×1	Rock	×1	
Ghost	×1	Ghost	×1	
Dragon	×1	Dragon	×1	
Dark	×1	Dark	×1	
Steel	×0.5	Steel	×2	
Fairy	×1	Fairy	×1	

How to obtain for your Coastal Kalos Pokédex
❶ Catch using a Good Rod in Shalour City.
❷ Catch using a Good Rod on Route 12.

❶ Catch using a Good Rod in Shalour City.
❷ Catch using a Good Rod on Route 12.

Same form for ♂/♀

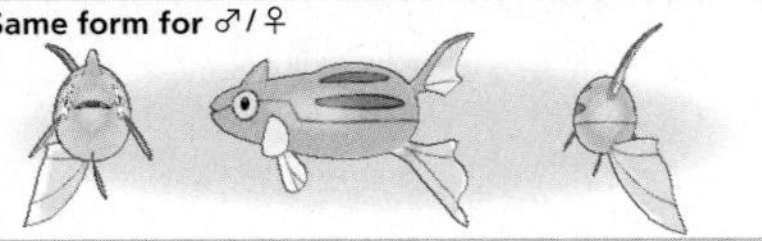

● LEVEL-UP MOVES
Lv.	Name	Type	Kind	Pow.	Acc.	PP	Range
1	Water Gun	Water	Special	40	100	25	Normal
6	Lock-On	Normal	Status	—	—	5	Normal
10	Psybeam	Psychic	Special	65	100	20	Normal
14	Aurora Beam	Ice	Special	65	100	20	Normal
18	Bubble Beam	Water	Special	65	100	20	Normal
22	Focus Energy	Normal	Status	—	—	30	Self
26	Water Pulse	Water	Special	60	100	20	Normal
30	Signal Beam	Bug	Special	75	100	15	Normal
34	Ice Beam	Ice	Special	90	100	10	Normal
38	Bullet Seed	Grass	Physical	25	100	30	Normal
42	Hydro Pump	Water	Special	110	80	5	Normal
46	Hyper Beam	Normal	Special	150	90	5	Normal
50	Soak	Water	Status	—	100	20	Normal

● TM & HM MOVES
No.	Name	Type	Kind	Pow.	Acc.	PP	Range
TM06	Toxic	Poison	Status	—	90	10	Normal
TM10	Hidden Power	Normal	Special	60	100	15	Normal
TM11	Sunny Day	Fire	Status	—	—	5	Both Sides
TM13	Ice Beam	Ice	Special	90	100	10	Normal
TM14	Blizzard	Ice	Special	110	70	5	Many Others
TM15	Hyper Beam	Normal	Special	150	90	5	Normal
TM17	Protect	Normal	Status	—	—	10	Self
TM18	Rain Dance	Water	Status	—	—	5	Both Sides
TM21	Frustration	Normal	Physical	—	100	20	Normal
TM23	Smack Down	Rock	Physical	50	100	15	Normal
TM27	Return	Normal	Physical	—	100	20	Normal
TM29	Psychic	Psychic	Special	90	100	10	Normal
TM32	Double Team	Normal	Status	—	—	15	Self
TM35	Flamethrower	Fire	Special	90	100	15	Normal
TM38	Fire Blast	Fire	Special	110	85	5	Normal
TM42	Facade	Normal	Physical	70	100	20	Normal
TM44	Rest	Psychic	Status	—	—	10	Self
TM45	Attract	Normal	Status	—	100	15	Normal
TM46	Thief	Dark	Physical	60	100	25	Normal
TM48	Round	Normal	Special	60	100	15	Normal
TM55	Scald	Water	Special	80	100	15	Normal
TM57	Charge Beam	Electric	Special	50	90	10	Normal
TM59	Incinerate	Fire	Special	60	100	15	Many Others
TM73	Thunder Wave	Electric	Status	—	100	20	Normal
TM87	Swagger	Normal	Status	—	90	15	Normal
TM88	Sleep Talk	Normal	Status	—	—	10	Self
TM90	Substitute	Normal	Status	—	—	10	Self
TM100	Confide	Normal	Status	—	—	20	Normal
HM03	Surf	Water	Special	90	100	15	Adjacent
HM05	Waterfall	Water	Physical	80	100	15	Normal

● MOVES TAUGHT BY PEOPLE
Name	Type	Kind	Pow.	Acc.	PP	Range

● EGG MOVES
Name	Type	Kind	Pow.	Acc.	PP	Range
Aurora Beam	Ice	Special	65	100	20	Normal
Octazooka	Water	Special	65	85	10	Normal
Supersonic	Normal	Status	—	55	20	Normal
Haze	Ice	Status	—	—	30	Both Sides
Screech	Normal	Status	—	85	40	Normal
Rock Blast	Rock	Physical	25	90	10	Normal
Snore	Normal	Special	50	100	15	Normal
Flail	Normal	Physical	—	100	15	Normal
Water Spout	Water	Special	150	100	5	Many Others
Mud Shot	Ground	Special	55	95	15	Normal
Swift	Normal	Special	60	—	20	Many Others
Acid Spray	Poison	Special	40	100	20	Normal
Water Pulse	Water	Special	60	100	20	Normal
Entrainment	Normal	Status	—	100	15	Normal

AFTER THE HALL OF FAME

CENTRAL KALOS

COASTAL KALOS

145

Octillery

MOUNTAIN KALOS

ADVENTURE DATA

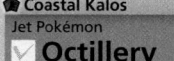

Coastal Kalos 145
Jet Pokémon
Octillery

HEIGHT: 2'11"   WEIGHT: 62.8 lbs.
GENDER: ♂/♀

TYPE Water

ABILITIES
Suction Cups
Sniper

HIDDEN ABILITY
Moody

STAT GROWTH RATES

HP	■■■
Attack	■■■■■
Defense	■■■
Sp. Atk	■■■■■
Sp. Def	■■■
Speed	■■■

EGG GROUPS
Water 1, Water 2

X It has a tendency to want to be in holes. It prefers rock crags or pots and sprays ink from them before attacking.

Y It traps foes with the suction cups on its tentacles, then smashes them with its rock-hard head.

EVOLUTION

Remoraid → (Lv. 25) → Octillery

ITEMS SOMETIMES HELD BY WILD POKÉMON
None

Can be used in
Inverse Battle
—
Battle Chateau
Battle Institute
Battle Maison
Random Matchup

Damage taken in normal battles	
Normal	×1
Fire	×0.5
Water	×0.5
Grass	×2
Electric	×2
Ice	×0.5
Fighting	×1
Poison	×1
Ground	×1
Flying	×1
Psychic	×1
Bug	×1
Rock	×1
Ghost	×1
Dragon	×1
Dark	×1
Steel	×0.5
Fairy	×1

Damage taken in Inverse Battles	
Normal	×1
Fire	×2
Water	×2
Grass	×0.5
Electric	×0.5
Ice	×2
Fighting	×1
Poison	×1
Ground	×1
Flying	×1
Psychic	×1
Bug	×1
Rock	×1
Ghost	×1
Dragon	×1
Dark	×1
Steel	×2
Fairy	×1

How to obtain for your Coastal Kalos Pokédex

❶ Catch using a Super Rod in Shalour City or on Route 12.
❷ Level up Remoraid to Lv. 25.

❶ Catch using a Super Rod in Shalour City or on Route 12.
❷ Level up Remoraid to Lv. 25.

♂   ♀

The male has larger suckers. The female has smaller suckers.

● LEVEL-UP MOVES

Lv.	Name	Type	Kind	Pow.	Acc.	PP	Range
1	Gunk Shot	Poison	Physical	120	80	5	Normal
1	Rock Blast	Rock	Physical	25	90	10	Normal
1	Water Gun	Water	Special	40	100	25	Normal
1	Constrict	Normal	Physical	10	100	35	Normal
1	Psybeam	Psychic	Special	65	100	20	Normal
1	Aurora Beam	Ice	Special	65	100	20	Normal
6	Constrict	Normal	Physical	10	100	35	Normal
10	Psybeam	Psychic	Special	65	100	20	Normal
14	Aurora Beam	Ice	Special	65	100	20	Normal
18	Bubble Beam	Water	Special	65	100	20	Normal
22	Focus Energy	Normal	Status	—	—	30	Self
25	Octazooka	Water	Special	65	85	10	Normal
28	Wring Out	Normal	Special	—	100	5	Normal
34	Signal Beam	Bug	Special	75	100	15	Normal
40	Ice Beam	Ice	Special	90	100	10	Normal
46	Bullet Seed	Grass	Physical	25	100	30	Normal
52	Hydro Pump	Water	Special	110	80	5	Normal
58	Hyper Beam	Normal	Special	150	90	5	Normal
64	Soak	Water	Status	—	100	20	Normal

● TM & HM MOVES

No.	Name	Type	Kind	Pow.	Acc.	PP	Range
TM06	Toxic	Poison	Status	—	90	10	Normal
TM10	Hidden Power	Normal	Special	60	100	15	Normal
TM11	Sunny Day	Fire	Status	—	—	5	Both Sides
TM13	Ice Beam	Ice	Special	90	100	10	Normal
TM14	Blizzard	Ice	Special	110	70	5	Many Others
TM15	Hyper Beam	Normal	Special	150	90	5	Normal
TM17	Protect	Normal	Status	—	—	10	Self
TM18	Rain Dance	Water	Status	—	—	5	Both Sides
TM21	Frustration	Normal	Physical	—	100	20	Normal
TM23	Smack Down	Rock	Physical	50	100	15	Normal
TM27	Return	Normal	Physical	—	100	20	Normal
TM29	Psychic	Psychic	Special	90	100	10	Normal
TM32	Double Team	Normal	Status	—	—	15	Self
TM34	Sludge Wave	Poison	Special	95	100	10	Adjacent
TM35	Flamethrower	Fire	Special	90	100	15	Normal
TM36	Sludge Bomb	Poison	Special	90	100	10	Normal
TM38	Fire Blast	Fire	Special	110	85	5	Normal
TM42	Facade	Normal	Physical	70	100	20	Normal
TM44	Rest	Psychic	Status	—	—	10	Self
TM45	Attract	Normal	Status	—	100	15	Normal
TM46	Thief	Dark	Physical	60	100	25	Normal
TM48	Round	Normal	Special	60	100	15	Normal
TM53	Energy Ball	Grass	Special	90	100	10	Normal
TM55	Scald	Water	Special	80	100	15	Normal
TM57	Charge Beam	Electric	Special	50	90	10	Normal
TM59	Incinerate	Fire	Special	60	100	15	Many Others
TM66	Payback	Dark	Physical	50	100	10	Normal
TM68	Giga Impact	Normal	Physical	150	90	5	Normal
TM73	Thunder Wave	Electric	Status	—	100	20	Normal
TM87	Swagger	Normal	Status	—	90	15	Normal
TM88	Sleep Talk	Normal	Status	—	—	10	Self
TM90	Substitute	Normal	Status	—	—	10	Self
TM91	Flash Cannon	Steel	Special	80	100	10	Normal

No.	Name	Type	Kind	Pow.	Acc.	PP	Range
TM100	Confide	Normal	Status	—	—	20	Normal
HM03	Surf	Water	Special	90	100	15	Adjacent
HM05	Waterfall	Water	Physical	80	100	15	Normal

● MOVES TAUGHT BY PEOPLE

Name	Type	Kind	Pow.	Acc.	PP	Range

AFTER THE HALL OF FAME

CENTRAL KALOS

COASTAL KALOS

146 | Corsola

MOUNTAIN KALOS

ADVENTURE DATA

🐚 Coastal Kalos
Coral Pokémon

✔ Corsola
146

HEIGHT: 2'00"   WEIGHT: 11.0 lbs.
GENDER: ♂/♀

TYPE | Water | Rock

ABILITIES
Hustle
Natural Cure

HIDDEN ABILITY
Regenerator

STAT GROWTH RATES
HP ■■
Attack ■■■
Defense ■■■■
Sp. Atk ■■■
Sp. Def ■■■■
Speed ■■

EGG GROUPS
Water 1, Water 3

EVOLUTION

Does not evolve

> X It continuously sheds and grows. The tip of its head is prized as a treasure because of its beauty.

> Y They prefer unpolluted southern seas. Their coral branches lose their color and deteriorate in dirty water.

ITEMS SOMETIMES HELD BY WILD POKÉMON
Hard Stone

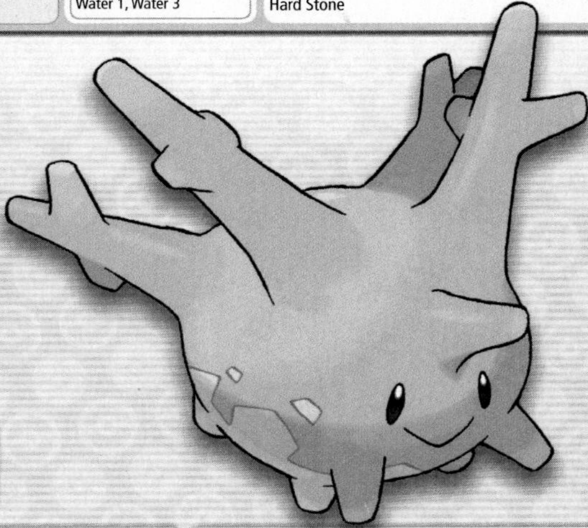

Damage taken in normal battles		Damage taken in Inverse Battles	
Normal	×0.5	Normal	×2
Fire	×0.25	Fire	×4
Water	×1	Water	×1
Grass	×4	Grass	×0.25
Electric	×2	Electric	×0.5
Ice	×0.5	Ice	×2
Fighting	×2	Fighting	×0.5
Poison	×0.5	Poison	×2
Ground	×2	Ground	×0.5
Flying	×0.5	Flying	×2
Psychic	×1	Psychic	×1
Bug	×1	Bug	×1
Rock	×1	Rock	×1
Ghost	×1	Ghost	×1
Dragon	×1	Dragon	×1
Dark	×1	Dark	×1
Steel	×1	Steel	×1
Fairy	×1	Fairy	×1

Can be used in	
Inverse Battle	Battle Institute
—	Battle Maison
Battle Chateau	Random Matchup

Same form for ♂ / ♀

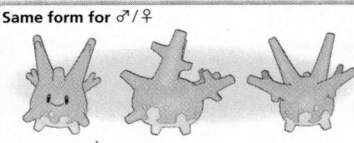

How to obtain for your Coastal Kalos Pokédex

Catch using a Super Rod on Route 12.

Catch using a Super Rod on Route 12.

● LEVEL-UP MOVES

Lv.	Name	Type	Kind	Pow.	Acc.	PP	Range
1	Tackle	Normal	Physical	50	100	35	Normal
4	Harden	Normal	Status	—	—	30	Self
8	Bubble	Water	Special	40	100	30	Many Others
10	Recover	Normal	Status	—	—	10	Self
13	Refresh	Normal	Status	—	—	20	Self
17	Bubble Beam	Water	Special	65	100	20	Normal
20	Ancient Power	Rock	Special	60	100	5	Normal
23	Lucky Chant	Normal	Status	—	—	30	Your Side
27	Spike Cannon	Normal	Physical	20	100	15	Normal
29	Iron Defense	Steel	Status	—	—	15	Self
31	Rock Blast	Rock	Physical	25	90	10	Normal
35	Endure	Normal	Status	—	—	10	Self
38	Aqua Ring	Water	Status	—	—	20	Self
41	Power Gem	Rock	Special	80	100	20	Normal
45	Mirror Coat	Psychic	Special	—	100	20	Varies
47	Earth Power	Ground	Special	90	100	10	Normal
50	Flail	Normal	Physical	—	100	15	Normal

● TM & HM MOVES

No.	Name	Type	Kind	Pow.	Acc.	PP	Range
TM04	Calm Mind	Psychic	Status	—	—	20	Self
TM06	Toxic	Poison	Status	—	90	10	Normal
TM07	Hail	Ice	Status	—	—	10	Both Sides
TM10	Hidden Power	Normal	Special	60	100	15	Normal
TM11	Sunny Day	Fire	Status	—	—	5	Both Sides
TM13	Ice Beam	Ice	Special	90	100	10	Normal
TM14	Blizzard	Ice	Special	110	70	5	Many Others
TM16	Light Screen	Psychic	Status	—	—	30	Your Side
TM17	Protect	Normal	Status	—	—	10	Self
TM18	Rain Dance	Water	Status	—	—	5	Both Sides
TM20	Safeguard	Normal	Status	—	—	25	Your Side
TM21	Frustration	Normal	Physical	—	100	20	Normal
TM26	Earthquake	Ground	Physical	100	100	10	Adjacent
TM27	Return	Normal	Physical	—	100	20	Normal
TM28	Dig	Ground	Physical	80	100	10	Normal
TM29	Psychic	Psychic	Special	90	100	10	Normal
TM30	Shadow Ball	Ghost	Special	80	100	15	Normal
TM32	Double Team	Normal	Status	—	—	15	Self
TM33	Reflect	Psychic	Status	—	—	20	Your Side
TM37	Sandstorm	Rock	Status	—	—	10	Both Sides
TM39	Rock Tomb	Rock	Physical	60	95	15	Normal
TM42	Facade	Normal	Physical	70	100	20	Normal
TM44	Rest	Psychic	Status	—	—	10	Self
TM45	Attract	Normal	Status	—	100	15	Normal
TM48	Round	Normal	Special	60	100	15	Normal
TM55	Scald	Water	Special	80	100	15	Normal
TM64	Explosion	Normal	Physical	250	100	5	Adjacent
TM69	Rock Polish	Rock	Status	—	—	20	Self
TM71	Stone Edge	Rock	Physical	100	80	5	Normal
TM78	Bulldoze	Ground	Physical	60	100	20	Adjacent
TM80	Rock Slide	Rock	Physical	75	90	10	Many Others
TM87	Swagger	Normal	Status	—	90	15	Normal
TM88	Sleep Talk	Normal	Status	—	—	10	Self

No.	Name	Type	Kind	Pow.	Acc.	PP	Range
TM90	Substitute	Normal	Status	—	—	10	Self
TM94	Rock Smash	Fighting	Physical	40	100	15	Normal
TM96	Nature Power	Normal	Status	—	—	20	Normal
TM100	Confide	Normal	Status	—	—	20	Normal
HM03	Surf	Water	Special	90	100	15	Adjacent
HM04	Strength	Normal	Physical	80	100	15	Normal

● MOVES TAUGHT BY PEOPLE

Name	Type	Kind	Pow.	Acc.	PP	Range

● EGG MOVES

Name	Type	Kind	Pow.	Acc.	PP	Range
Screech	Normal	Status	—	85	40	Normal
Mist	Ice	Status	—	—	30	Your Side
Amnesia	Psychic	Status	—	—	20	Self
Barrier	Psychic	Status	—	—	20	Self
Ingrain	Grass	Status	—	—	20	Self
Confuse Ray	Ghost	Status	—	100	10	Normal
Icicle Spear	Ice	Physical	25	100	30	Normal
Nature Power	Normal	Status	—	—	20	Normal
Aqua Ring	Water	Status	—	—	20	Self
Curse	Ghost	Status	—	—	10	Varies
Bide	Normal	Physical	—	—	10	Self
Water Pulse	Water	Special	60	100	20	Normal
Head Smash	Rock	Physical	150	80	5	Normal
Camouflage	Normal	Status	—	—	20	Self

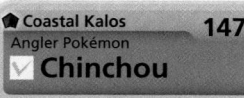

Coastal Kalos 147

Angler Pokémon

☑ Chinchou

HEIGHT: 1'08" WEIGHT: 26.5 lbs.
GENDER: ♂/♀

X On the dark ocean floor, its only means of communication is its constantly flashing lights.

Y It shoots positive and negative electricity between the tips of its two antennae and zaps its enemies.

TYPE Water | Electric

ABILITIES
Volt Absorb
Illuminate

HIDDEN ABILITY
None

STAT GROWTH RATES
HP	■■■
Attack	■■■
Defense	■■
Sp. Atk	■■
Sp. Def	■■■
Speed	■■■■

EGG GROUP
Water 2

EVOLUTION

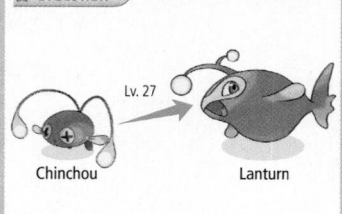

Chinchou — Lv. 27 → Lanturn

ITEMS SOMETIMES HELD BY WILD POKÉMON
Deep Sea Scale

Damage taken in normal battles		Damage taken in Inverse Battles	
Normal	×1	Normal	×1
Fire	×0.5	Fire	×2
Water	×0.5	Water	×2
Grass	×2	Grass	×0.5
Electric	×1 ❶	Electric	×1 ❶
Ice	×0.5	Ice	×2
Fighting	×1	Fighting	×1
Poison	×1	Poison	×1
Ground	×2	Ground	×0.5
Flying	×0.5	Flying	×2
Psychic	×1	Psychic	×1
Bug	×1	Bug	×1
Rock	×1	Rock	×1
Ghost	×1	Ghost	×1
Dragon	×1	Dragon	×1
Dark	×1	Dark	×1
Steel	×0.25	Steel	×4
Fairy	×1	Fairy	×1

Can be used in	
Inverse Battle	Battle Institute
—	Battle Maison
Battle Chateau	Random Matchup

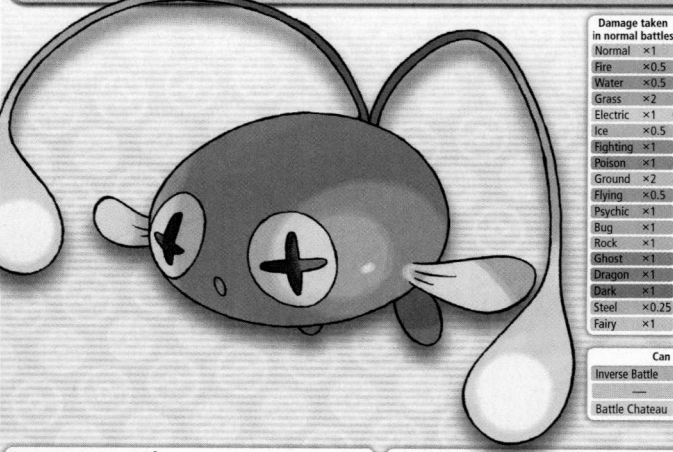

Same form for ♂/♀

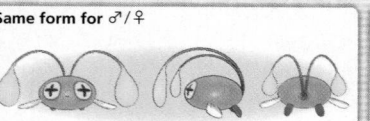

How to obtain for your Coastal Kalos Pokédex

❶ Catch using a Good Rod in Shalour City.
❷ Catch using a Good Rod in Azure Bay.

❶ Catch using a Good Rod in Shalour City.
❷ Catch using a Good Rod in Azure Bay.

● LEVEL-UP MOVES

Lv.	Name	Type	Kind	Pow.	Acc.	PP	Range
1	Water Gun	Water	Special	40	100	25	Normal
1	Supersonic	Normal	Status	—	55	20	Normal
6	Thunder Wave	Electric	Status	—	100	20	Normal
9	Flail	Normal	Physical	—	100	15	Normal
12	Bubble	Water	Special	40	100	30	Many Others
17	Confuse Ray	Ghost	Status	—	100	10	Normal
20	Spark	Electric	Physical	65	100	20	Normal
23	Take Down	Normal	Physical	90	85	20	Normal
28	Electro Ball	Electric	Special	—	100	10	Normal
31	Bubble Beam	Water	Special	65	100	20	Normal
34	Signal Beam	Bug	Special	75	100	15	Normal
39	Discharge	Electric	Special	80	100	15	Adjacent
42	Aqua Ring	Water	Status	—	—	20	Self
45	Hydro Pump	Water	Special	110	80	5	Normal
47	Ion Deluge	Electric	Status	—	—	25	Both Sides
50	Charge	Electric	Status	—	—	20	Self

● TM & HM MOVES

No.	Name	Type	Kind	Pow.	Acc.	PP	Range
TM06	Toxic	Poison	Status	—	90	10	Normal
TM07	Hail	Ice	Status	—	—	10	Both Sides
TM10	Hidden Power	Normal	Special	60	100	15	Normal
TM13	Ice Beam	Ice	Special	90	100	10	Normal
TM14	Blizzard	Ice	Special	110	70	5	Many Others
TM17	Protect	Normal	Status	—	—	10	Self
TM18	Rain Dance	Water	Status	—	—	5	Both Sides
TM21	Frustration	Normal	Physical	—	100	20	Normal
TM24	Thunderbolt	Electric	Special	90	100	15	Normal
TM25	Thunder	Electric	Special	110	70	10	Normal
TM27	Return	Normal	Physical	—	100	20	Normal
TM32	Double Team	Normal	Status	—	—	15	Self
TM42	Facade	Normal	Physical	70	100	20	Normal
TM44	Rest	Psychic	Status	—	—	10	Self
TM45	Attract	Normal	Status	—	100	15	Normal
TM48	Round	Normal	Special	60	100	15	Normal
TM55	Scald	Water	Special	80	100	15	Normal
TM57	Charge Beam	Electric	Special	50	90	10	Normal
TM70	Flash	Normal	Status	—	100	20	Normal
TM72	Volt Switch	Electric	Special	70	100	20	Normal
TM73	Thunder Wave	Electric	Status	—	100	20	Normal
TM87	Swagger	Normal	Status	—	90	15	Normal
TM88	Sleep Talk	Normal	Status	—	—	10	Self
TM90	Substitute	Normal	Status	—	—	10	Self
TM93	Wild Charge	Electric	Physical	90	100	15	Normal
TM99	Dazzling Gleam	Fairy	Special	80	100	10	Many Others
TM100	Confide	Normal	Status	—	—	20	Normal
HM03	Surf	Water	Special	90	100	15	Adjacent
HM05	Waterfall	Water	Physical	80	100	15	Normal

● MOVES TAUGHT BY PEOPLE

Name	Type	Kind	Pow.	Acc.	PP	Range

● EGG MOVES

Name	Type	Kind	Pow.	Acc.	PP	Range
Flail	Normal	Physical	—	100	15	Normal
Screech	Normal	Status	—	85	40	Normal
Amnesia	Psychic	Status	—	—	20	Self
Psybeam	Psychic	Special	65	100	20	Normal
Whirlpool	Water	Special	35	85	15	Normal
Agility	Psychic	Status	—	—	30	Self
Mist	Ice	Status	—	—	30	Your Side
Shock Wave	Electric	Special	60	—	20	Normal
Brine	Water	Special	65	100	10	Normal
Water Pulse	Water	Special	60	100	20	Normal
Soak	Water	Status	—	100	20	Normal

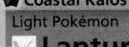

Coastal Kalos

148

Light Pokémon

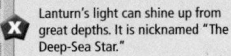
Lanturn

HEIGHT: 3'11" WEIGHT: 49.6 lbs.
GENDER: ♂/♀

TYPE Water Electric

ABILITIES
Volt Absorb
Illuminate

HIDDEN ABILITY
None

STAT GROWTH RATES
HP	▪▪▪▪▪
Attack	▪▪▪
Defense	▪▪▪
Sp. Atk	▪▪▪▪
Sp. Def	▪▪▪
Speed	▪▪▪▪

EGG GROUP
Water 2

X Lanturn's light can shine from great depths. It is nicknamed "The Deep-Sea Star."

Y It blinds prey with an intense burst of light. With the prey incapacitated, the Pokémon swallows it in a single gulp.

EVOLUTION

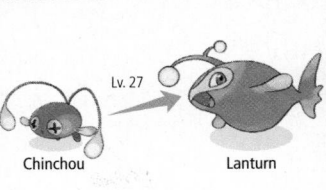

Chinchou → (Lv. 27) → Lanturn

ITEMS SOMETIMES HELD BY WILD POKÉMON
Deep Sea Scale

Damage taken in normal battles		Damage taken in Inverse Battles	
Normal	×1	Normal	×1
Fire	×0.5	Fire	×2
Water	×0.5	Water	×2
Grass	×2	Grass	×0.5
Electric	×1 ❶	Electric	×1 ❶
Ice	×0.5	Ice	×2
Fighting	×1	Fighting	×1
Poison	×1	Poison	×1
Ground	×2	Ground	×0.5
Flying	×0.5	Flying	×2
Psychic	×1	Psychic	×1
Bug	×1	Bug	×1
Rock	×1	Rock	×1
Ghost	×1	Ghost	×1
Dragon	×1	Dragon	×1
Dark	×1	Dark	×1
Steel	×0.25	Steel	×4
Fairy	×1	Fairy	×1

Can be used in	
Inverse Battle	Battle Institute
—	Battle Maison
Battle Chateau	Random Matchup

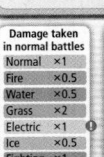

Same form for ♂/♀

How to obtain for your Coastal Kalos Pokédex

❶ Catch using a Super Rod in Shalour City or Azure Bay.
❷ Level up Chinchou to Lv. 27.

❶ Catch using a Super Rod in Shalour City or Azure Bay.
❷ Level up Chinchou to Lv. 27.

AFTER THE HALL OF FAME

CENTRAL KALOS

COASTAL KALOS

148 Lanturn

MOUNTAIN KALOS

ADVENTURE DATA

● LEVEL-UP MOVES

Lv.	Name	Type	Kind	Pow.	Acc.	PP	Range
1	Eerie Impulse	Electric	Status	—	100	15	Normal
1	Water Gun	Water	Special	40	100	25	Normal
1	Supersonic	Normal	Status	—	55	20	Normal
1	Thunder Wave	Electric	Status	—	100	20	Normal
6	Thunder Wave	Electric	Status	—	100	20	Normal
9	Flail	Normal	Physical	—	100	15	Normal
12	Bubble	Water	Special	40	100	30	Many Others
17	Confuse Ray	Ghost	Status	—	100	10	Normal
20	Spark	Electric	Physical	65	100	20	Normal
23	Take Down	Normal	Physical	90	85	20	Normal
27	Stockpile	Normal	Status	—	—	20	Self
27	Swallow	Normal	Status	—	—	10	Self
27	Spit Up	Normal	Special	—	100	10	Normal
30	Electro Ball	Electric	Special	—	100	10	Normal
35	Bubble Beam	Water	Special	65	100	20	Normal
40	Signal Beam	Bug	Special	75	100	15	Normal
47	Discharge	Electric	Special	80	100	15	Adjacent
52	Aqua Ring	Water	Status	—	—	20	Self
57	Hydro Pump	Water	Special	110	80	5	Normal
60	Ion Deluge	Electric	Status	—	—	25	Both Sides
64	Charge	Electric	Status	—	—	20	Self

● TM & HM MOVES

No.	Name	Type	Kind	Pow.	Acc.	PP	Range
TM06	Toxic	Poison	Status	—	90	10	Normal
TM07	Hail	Ice	Status	—	—	10	Both Sides
TM10	Hidden Power	Normal	Special	60	100	15	Normal
TM13	Ice Beam	Ice	Special	90	100	10	Normal
TM14	Blizzard	Ice	Special	110	70	5	Many Others
TM15	Hyper Beam	Normal	Special	150	90	5	Normal
TM17	Protect	Normal	Status	—	—	10	Self
TM18	Rain Dance	Water	Status	—	—	5	Both Sides
TM21	Frustration	Normal	Physical	—	100	20	Normal
TM24	Thunderbolt	Electric	Special	90	100	15	Normal
TM25	Thunder	Electric	Special	110	70	10	Normal
TM27	Return	Normal	Physical	—	100	20	Normal
TM32	Double Team	Normal	Status	—	—	15	Self
TM42	Facade	Normal	Physical	70	100	20	Normal
TM44	Rest	Psychic	Status	—	—	10	Self
TM45	Attract	Normal	Status	—	100	15	Normal
TM48	Round	Normal	Special	60	100	15	Normal
TM55	Scald	Water	Special	80	100	15	Normal
TM57	Charge Beam	Electric	Special	50	90	10	Normal
TM68	Giga Impact	Normal	Physical	150	90	5	Normal
TM70	Flash	Normal	Status	—	100	20	Normal
TM72	Volt Switch	Electric	Special	70	100	20	Normal
TM73	Thunder Wave	Electric	Status	—	100	20	Normal
TM87	Swagger	Normal	Status	—	90	15	Normal
TM88	Sleep Talk	Normal	Status	—	—	10	Self
TM90	Substitute	Normal	Status	—	—	10	Self
TM93	Wild Charge	Electric	Physical	90	100	15	Normal
TM99	Dazzling Gleam	Fairy	Special	80	100	10	Many Others
TM100	Confide	Normal	Status	—	—	20	Normal
HM03	Surf	Water	Special	90	100	15	Adjacent
HM05	Waterfall	Water	Physical	80	100	15	Normal

No.	Name	Type	Kind	Pow.	Acc.	PP	Range

● MOVES TAUGHT BY PEOPLE

Name	Type	Kind	Pow.	Acc.	PP	Range

AFTER THE HALL OF FAME

CENTRAL KALOS

COASTAL KALOS

149

Alomomola

MOUNTAIN KALOS

ADVENTURE DATA

Coastal Kalos 149
Caring Pokémon
☑ Alomomola

HEIGHT: 3'11" WEIGHT: 69.7 lbs.
GENDER: ♂/♀

X Floating in the open sea is how they live. When they find a wounded Pokémon, they embrace it and bring it to shore.

Y It gently holds injured and weak Pokémon in its fins. Its special membrane heals their wounds.

TYPE **Water**

ABILITIES
Healer
Hydration

HIDDEN ABILITY
None

STAT GROWTH RATES

HP	▪▪▪▪▪▪
Attack	▪▪▪▪
Defense	▪▪▪▪
Sp. Atk	▪▪
Sp. Def	▪▪
Speed	▪▪▪▪

EGG GROUPS
Water 1, Water 2

EVOLUTION

Does not evolve

ITEMS SOMETIMES HELD BY WILD POKÉMON
None

Can be used in
Inverse Battle
—
Battle Chateau
Battle Institute
Battle Maison
Random Matchup

Damage taken in normal battles	
Normal	×1
Fire	×0.5
Water	×0.5
Grass	×2
Electric	×2
Ice	×0.5
Fighting	×1
Poison	×1
Ground	×1
Flying	×1
Psychic	×1
Bug	×1
Rock	×1
Ghost	×1
Dragon	×1
Dark	×1
Steel	×0.5
Fairy	×1

Damage taken in Inverse Battles	
Normal	×1
Fire	×2
Water	×2
Grass	×0.5
Electric	×0.5
Ice	×2
Fighting	×1
Poison	×1
Ground	×1
Flying	×1
Psychic	×1
Bug	×1
Rock	×1
Ghost	×1
Dragon	×1
Dark	×1
Steel	×2
Fairy	×1

How to obtain for your Coastal Kalos Pokédex

❶ Catch using a Super Rod in Shalour City.

❷ Catch using a Super Rod in Azure Bay.

❶ Catch using a Super Rod in Shalour City.

❷ Catch using a Super Rod in Azure Bay.

Same form for ♂/♀

LEVEL-UP MOVES

Lv.	Name	Type	Kind	Pow.	Acc.	PP	Range
1	Hydro Pump	Water	Special	110	80	5	Normal
1	Wide Guard	Rock	Status	—	—	10	Your Side
1	Healing Wish	Psychic	Status	—	—	10	Self
1	Pound	Normal	Physical	40	100	35	Normal
1	Water Sport	Water	Status	—	—	15	Both Sides
5	Aqua Ring	Water	Status	—	—	20	Self
9	Aqua Jet	Water	Physical	40	100	20	Normal
13	Double Slap	Normal	Physical	15	85	10	Normal
17	Heal Pulse	Psychic	Status	—	—	10	Normal
21	Protect	Normal	Status	—	—	10	Self
25	Water Pulse	Water	Special	60	100	20	Normal
29	Wake-Up Slap	Fighting	Physical	70	100	10	Normal
33	Soak	Water	Status	—	100	20	Normal
37	Wish	Normal	Status	—	—	10	Self
41	Brine	Water	Special	65	100	10	Normal
45	Safeguard	Normal	Status	—	—	25	Your Side
49	Helping Hand	Normal	Status	—	—	20	1 Ally
53	Wide Guard	Rock	Status	—	—	10	Your Side
57	Healing Wish	Psychic	Status	—	—	10	Self
61	Hydro Pump	Water	Special	110	80	5	Normal

TM & HM MOVES

No.	Name	Type	Kind	Pow.	Acc.	PP	Range
TM04	Calm Mind	Psychic	Status	—	—	20	Self
TM06	Toxic	Poison	Status	—	90	10	Normal
TM07	Hail	Ice	Status	—	—	10	Both Sides
TM10	Hidden Power	Normal	Special	60	100	15	Normal
TM13	Ice Beam	Ice	Special	90	100	10	Normal
TM14	Blizzard	Ice	Special	110	70	5	Many Others
TM16	Light Screen	Psychic	Status	—	—	30	Your Side
TM17	Protect	Normal	Status	—	—	10	Self
TM18	Rain Dance	Water	Status	—	—	5	Both Sides
TM20	Safeguard	Normal	Status	—	—	25	Your Side
TM21	Frustration	Normal	Physical	—	100	20	Normal
TM27	Return	Normal	Physical	—	100	20	Normal
TM29	Psychic	Psychic	Special	90	100	10	Normal
TM30	Shadow Ball	Ghost	Special	80	100	15	Normal
TM32	Double Team	Normal	Status	—	—	15	Self
TM42	Facade	Normal	Physical	70	100	20	Normal
TM44	Rest	Psychic	Status	—	—	10	Self
TM45	Attract	Normal	Status	—	100	15	Normal
TM48	Round	Normal	Special	60	100	15	Normal
TM55	Scald	Water	Special	80	100	15	Normal
TM77	Psych Up	Normal	Status	—	—	10	Self
TM87	Swagger	Normal	Status	—	90	15	Normal
TM88	Sleep Talk	Normal	Status	—	—	10	Self
TM90	Substitute	Normal	Status	—	—	10	Self
TM100	Confide	Normal	Status	—	—	20	Normal
HM03	Surf	Water	Special	90	100	15	Adjacent
HM05	Waterfall	Water	Physical	80	100	15	Normal

MOVES TAUGHT BY PEOPLE

Name	Type	Kind	Pow.	Acc.	PP	Range

EGG MOVES

Name	Type	Kind	Pow.	Acc.	PP	Range
Pain Split	Normal	Status	—	—	20	Normal
Refresh	Normal	Status	—	—	20	Self
Tickle	Normal	Status	—	100	20	Normal
Mirror Coat	Psychic	Special	—	100	20	Varies
Mist	Ice	Status	—	—	30	Your Side
Endure	Normal	Status	—	—	10	Self

AFTER THE HALL OF FAME

CENTRAL KALOS

COASTAL KALOS | 150

Lapras

MOUNTAIN KALOS

ADVENTURE DATA

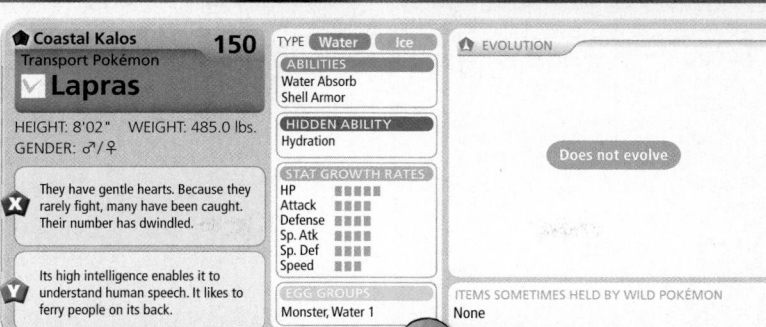

Coastal Kalos 150
Transport Pokémon
Lapras

HEIGHT: 8'02" WEIGHT: 485.0 lbs.
GENDER: ♂/♀

X They have gentle hearts. Because they rarely fight, many have been caught. Their number has dwindled.

Y Its high intelligence enables it to understand human speech. It likes to ferry people on its back.

TYPE Water | Ice

ABILITIES
Water Absorb
Shell Armor

HIDDEN ABILITY
Hydration

STAT GROWTH RATES
HP
Attack
Defense
Sp. Atk
Sp. Def
Speed

EGG GROUPS
Monster, Water 1

EVOLUTION

Does not evolve

ITEMS SOMETIMES HELD BY WILD POKÉMON
None

Damage taken in normal battles		Damage taken in Inverse Battles	
Normal	×1	Normal	×1
Fire	×1	Fire	×1
Water	×0.5	Water	×2
Grass	×2	Grass	×0.5
Electric	×2	Electric	×0.5
Ice	×0.25	Ice	×4
Fighting	×2	Fighting	×0.5
Poison	×1	Poison	×1
Ground	×1	Ground	×1
Flying	×1	Flying	×1
Psychic	×1	Psychic	×1
Bug	×1	Bug	×1
Rock	×2	Rock	×0.5
Ghost	×1	Ghost	×1
Dragon	×1	Dragon	×1
Dark	×1	Dark	×1
Steel	×1	Steel	×1
Fairy	×1	Fairy	×1

Can be used in	
Inverse Battle	Battle Institute
—	Battle Maison
Battle Chateau	Random Matchup

Same form for ♂/♀

How to obtain for your Coastal Kalos Pokédex

❶ Receive it from a man on Route 12.
❷ Catch on the surface of the water on Route 12.

❶ Receive it from a man on Route 12.
❷ Catch on the surface of the water on Route 12.

● LEVEL-UP MOVES

Lv.	Name	Type	Kind	Pow.	Acc.	PP	Range
1	Sing	Normal	Status	—	55	15	Normal
1	Growl	Normal	Status	—	100	40	Many Others
1	Water Gun	Water	Special	40	100	25	Normal
4	Mist	Ice	Status	—	—	30	Your Side
7	Confuse Ray	Ghost	Status	—	100	10	Normal
10	Ice Shard	Ice	Physical	40	100	30	Normal
14	Water Pulse	Water	Special	60	100	20	Normal
18	Body Slam	Normal	Physical	85	100	15	Normal
22	Rain Dance	Water	Status	—	—	5	Both Sides
27	Perish Song	Normal	Status	—	—	5	Adjacent
32	Ice Beam	Ice	Special	90	100	10	Normal
37	Brine	Water	Special	65	100	10	Normal
43	Safeguard	Normal	Status	—	—	25	Your Side
47	Hydro Pump	Water	Special	110	80	5	Normal
50	Sheer Cold	Ice	Special	—	30	5	Normal

● TM & HM MOVES

No.	Name	Type	Kind	Pow.	Acc.	PP	Range
TM05	Roar	Normal	Status	—	—	20	Normal
TM06	Toxic	Poison	Status	—	90	10	Normal
TM07	Hail	Ice	Status	—	—	10	Both Sides
TM10	Hidden Power	Normal	Special	60	100	15	Normal
TM13	Ice Beam	Ice	Special	90	100	10	Normal
TM14	Blizzard	Ice	Special	110	70	5	Many Others
TM15	Hyper Beam	Normal	Special	150	90	5	Normal
TM17	Protect	Normal	Status	—	—	10	Self
TM18	Rain Dance	Water	Status	—	—	5	Both Sides
TM20	Safeguard	Normal	Status	—	—	25	Your Side
TM21	Frustration	Normal	Physical	—	100	20	Normal
TM24	Thunderbolt	Electric	Special	90	100	15	Normal
TM25	Thunder	Electric	Special	110	70	10	Normal
TM27	Return	Normal	Physical	—	100	20	Normal
TM29	Psychic	Psychic	Special	90	100	10	Normal
TM32	Double Team	Normal	Status	—	—	15	Self
TM42	Facade	Normal	Physical	70	100	20	Normal
TM44	Rest	Psychic	Status	—	—	10	Self
TM45	Attract	Normal	Status	—	100	15	Normal
TM48	Round	Normal	Special	60	100	15	Normal
TM49	Echoed Voice	Normal	Special	40	100	15	Normal
TM68	Giga Impact	Normal	Physical	150	90	5	Normal
TM78	Bulldoze	Ground	Physical	60	100	20	Adjacent
TM79	Frost Breath	Ice	Special	60	90	10	Normal
TM85	Dream Eater	Psychic	Special	100	100	15	Normal
TM87	Swagger	Normal	Status	—	90	15	Normal
TM88	Sleep Talk	Normal	Status	—	—	10	Self
TM90	Substitute	Normal	Status	—	—	10	Self
TM94	Rock Smash	Fighting	Physical	40	100	15	Normal
TM100	Confide	Normal	Status	—	—	20	Normal
HM03	Surf	Water	Special	90	100	15	Adjacent
HM04	Strength	Normal	Physical	80	100	15	Normal
HM05	Waterfall	Water	Physical	80	100	15	Normal

● MOVES TAUGHT BY PEOPLE

Name	Type	Kind	Pow.	Acc.	PP	Range

● EGG MOVES

Name	Type	Kind	Pow.	Acc.	PP	Range
Foresight	Normal	Status	—	—	40	Normal
Tickle	Normal	Status	—	100	20	Normal
Refresh	Normal	Status	—	—	20	Self
Dragon Dance	Dragon	Status	—	—	20	Self
Curse	Ghost	Status	—	—	10	Varies
Sleep Talk	Normal	Status	—	—	10	Self
Horn Drill	Normal	Physical	—	30	5	Normal
Ancient Power	Rock	Special	60	100	5	Normal
Whirlpool	Water	Special	35	85	15	Normal
Fissure	Ground	Physical	—	30	5	Normal
Dragon Pulse	Dragon	Special	85	100	10	Normal
Avalanche	Ice	Physical	60	100	10	Normal
Future Sight	Psychic	Special	120	100	10	Normal
Freeze-Dry	Ice	Special	70	100	20	Normal

AFTER THE HALL OF FAME

CENTRAL KALOS

COASTAL KALOS

151

Articuno

MOUNTAIN KALOS

ADVENTURE DATA

Coastal Kalos — 151
Freeze Pokémon

☑ Articuno

HEIGHT: 5'07" WEIGHT: 122.1 lbs.
GENDER: unknown

TYPE Ice Flying

ABILITY
Pressure

HIDDEN ABILITY
None

STAT GROWTH RATES
HP
Attack
Defense
Sp. Atk
Sp. Def
Speed

EGG GROUP
No Eggs Discovered

X A legendary bird Pokémon. It can create blizzards by freezing moisture in the air.

Y A legendary bird Pokémon that is said to appear to doomed people who are lost in icy mountains.

EVOLUTION
Does not evolve

ITEMS SOMETIMES HELD BY WILD POKÉMON
None

Damage taken in normal battles	
Normal	×1
Fire	×2
Water	×1
Grass	×0.5
Electric	×2
Ice	×1
Fighting	×1
Poison	×1
Ground	×0
Flying	×1
Psychic	×1
Bug	×0.5
Rock	×4
Ghost	×1
Dragon	×1
Dark	×1
Steel	×2
Fairy	×1

Damage taken in Inverse Battles	
Normal	×1
Fire	×0.5
Water	×1
Grass	×2
Electric	×0.5
Ice	×1
Fighting	×1
Poison	×1
Ground	×2
Flying	×1
Psychic	×1
Bug	×2
Rock	×0.25
Ghost	×1
Dragon	×1
Dark	×1
Steel	×0.5
Fairy	×1

Can be used in	
Inverse Battle	Battle Institute
Sky Battle	Battle Maison
Battle Chateau	Random Matchup

Gender unknown

How to obtain for your Coastal Kalos Pokédex

❶ After entering the Hall of Fame, encounter it on the the roads and water surfaces of the Kalos region 11 times, then catch it in Azure Bay (if you chose Chespin at the beginning of the game).

❷ Link Trade or transfer from another game.

❶ After entering the Hall of Fame, encounter it on the the roads and water surfaces of the Kalos region 11 times, then catch it in Azure Bay (if you chose Chespin at the beginning of the game).

❷ Link Trade or transfer from another game.

● LEVEL-UP MOVES

Lv.	Name	Type	Kind	Pow.	Acc.	PP	Range
1	Roost	Flying	Status	—	—	10	Self
1	Hurricane	Flying	Special	110	70	10	Normal
1	Freeze-Dry	Ice	Special	70	100	20	Normal
1	Tailwind	Flying	Status	—	—	15	Your Side
1	Sheer Cold	Ice	Special	—	30	5	Normal
1	Gust	Flying	Special	40	100	35	Normal
1	Powder Snow	Ice	Special	40	100	25	Many Others
8	Mist	Ice	Status	—	—	30	Your Side
15	Ice Shard	Ice	Physical	40	100	30	Normal
22	Mind Reader	Normal	Status	—	5	Normal
29	Ancient Power	Rock	Special	60	100	5	Normal
36	Agility	Psychic	Status	—	—	30	Self
43	Ice Beam	Ice	Special	90	100	10	Normal
50	Reflect	Psychic	Status	—	—	20	Your Side
57	Hail	Ice	Status	—	—	10	Both Sides
64	Tailwind	Flying	Status	—	—	15	Your Side
71	Blizzard	Ice	Special	110	70	5	Many Others
78	Sheer Cold	Ice	Special	—	30	5	Normal
85	Roost	Flying	Status	—	—	10	Self
92	Hurricane	Flying	Special	110	70	10	Normal

● TM & HM MOVES

No.	Name	Type	Kind	Pow.	Acc.	PP	Range
TM05	Roar	Normal	Status	—	—	20	Normal
TM06	Toxic	Poison	Status	—	90	10	Normal
TM07	Hail	Ice	Status	—	—	10	Both Sides
TM10	Hidden Power	Normal	Special	60	100	15	Normal
TM11	Sunny Day	Fire	Status	—	—	5	Both Sides
TM13	Ice Beam	Ice	Special	90	100	10	Normal
TM14	Blizzard	Ice	Special	110	70	5	Many Others
TM15	Hyper Beam	Normal	Special	150	90	5	Normal
TM17	Protect	Normal	Status	—	—	10	Self
TM18	Rain Dance	Water	Status	—	—	5	Both Sides
TM19	Roost	Flying	Status	—	—	10	Self
TM21	Frustration	Normal	Physical	—	100	20	Normal
TM27	Return	Normal	Physical	—	100	20	Normal
TM32	Double Team	Normal	Status	—	—	15	Self
TM33	Reflect	Psychic	Status	—	—	20	Your Side
TM37	Sandstorm	Rock	Status	—	—	10	Both Sides
TM40	Aerial Ace	Flying	Physical	60	—	20	Normal
TM42	Facade	Normal	Physical	70	100	20	Normal
TM44	Rest	Psychic	Status	—	—	10	Self
TM48	Round	Normal	Special	60	100	15	Normal
TM51	Steel Wing	Steel	Physical	70	90	25	Normal
TM58	Sky Drop	Flying	Physical	60	100	10	Normal
TM68	Giga Impact	Normal	Physical	150	90	5	Normal
TM79	Frost Breath	Ice	Special	60	90	10	Normal
TM87	Swagger	Normal	Status	—	90	15	Normal
TM88	Sleep Talk	Normal	Status	—	—	10	Self
TM89	U-turn	Bug	Physical	70	100	20	Normal
TM90	Substitute	Normal	Status	—	—	10	Self
TM94	Rock Smash	Fighting	Physical	40	100	15	Normal
TM100	Confide	Normal	Status	—	—	20	Normal
HM02	Fly	Flying	Physical	90	95	15	Normal

No.	Name	Type	Kind	Pow.	Acc.	PP	Range

● MOVES TAUGHT BY PEOPLE

Name	Type	Kind	Pow.	Acc.	PP	Range

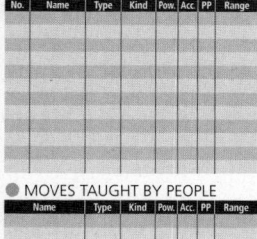

Electric Pokémon

☑ Zapdos

HEIGHT: 5'03" WEIGHT: 116.0 lbs.
GENDER: unknown

X A legendary bird Pokémon that is said to appear from clouds while dropping enormous lightning bolts.

Y A legendary bird Pokémon that is said to live in thunderclouds. It freely controls lightning bolts.

TYPE	Electric	Flying

ABILITY
Pressure

HIDDEN ABILITY
None

STAT GROWTH RATES

HP	■■■■
Attack	■■■■■
Defense	■■■■
Sp. Atk	■■■■■■
Sp. Def	■■■■
Speed	■■■■■

EGG GROUP
No Eggs Discovered

EVOLUTION

Does not evolve

ITEMS SOMETIMES HELD BY WILD POKÉMON
None

Damage taken in normal battles		Damage taken in Inverse Battles	
Normal	×1	Normal	×1
Fire	×1	Fire	×1
Water	×1	Water	×1
Grass	×0.5	Grass	×2
Electric	×1	Electric	×1
Ice	×2	Ice	×0.5
Fighting	×0.5	Fighting	×2
Poison	×1	Poison	×1
Ground	×0	Ground	×1
Flying	×1	Flying	×2
Psychic	×1	Psychic	×1
Bug	×0.5	Bug	×2
Rock	×2	Rock	×0.5
Ghost	×1	Ghost	×1
Dragon	×1	Dragon	×1
Dark	×1	Dark	×1
Steel	×0.5	Steel	×2
Fairy	×1	Fairy	×1

Can be used in	
Inverse Battle	Battle Institute
Sky Battle	Battle Maison
Battle Chateau	Random Matchup

Gender unknown

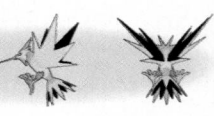

How to obtain for your Coastal Kalos Pokédex

❶ After entering the Hall of Fame, encounter it on the the roads and water surfaces of the Kalos region 11 times, then catch it in Azure Bay (if you chose Fennekin at the beginning of the game).

❷ Link Trade or transfer from another game.

❶ After entering the Hall of Fame, encounter it on the the roads and water surfaces of the Kalos region 11 times, then catch it in Azure Bay (if you chose Fennekin at the beginning of the game).

❷ Link Trade or transfer from another game.

● LEVEL-UP MOVES

Lv.	Name	Type	Kind	Pow.	Acc.	PP	Range
1	Roost	Flying	Status	—	—	10	Self
1	Zap Cannon	Electric	Special	120	50	5	Normal
1	Drill Peck	Flying	Physical	80	100	20	Normal
1	Peck	Flying	Physical	35	100	35	Normal
1	Thunder Shock	Electric	Special	40	100	30	Normal
8	Thunder Wave	Electric	Status	—	100	20	Normal
15	Detect	Fighting	Status	—	—	5	Self
22	Pluck	Flying	Physical	60	100	20	Normal
29	Ancient Power	Rock	Special	60	100	5	Normal
36	Charge	Electric	Status	—	—	20	Self
43	Agility	Psychic	Status	—	—	30	Self
50	Discharge	Electric	Special	80	100	15	Adjacent
57	Rain Dance	Water	Status	—	—	5	Both Sides
64	Light Screen	Psychic	Status	—	—	30	Your Side
71	Drill Peck	Flying	Physical	80	100	20	Normal
78	Thunder	Electric	Special	110	70	10	Normal
85	Roost	Flying	Status	—	—	10	Self
92	Zap Cannon	Electric	Special	120	50	5	Normal

● TM & HM MOVES

No.	Name	Type	Kind	Pow.	Acc.	PP	Range
TM05	Roar	Normal	Status	—	—	20	Normal
TM06	Toxic	Poison	Status	—	90	10	Normal
TM10	Hidden Power	Normal	Special	60	100	15	Normal
TM11	Sunny Day	Fire	Status	—	—	5	Both Sides
TM15	Hyper Beam	Normal	Special	150	90	5	Normal
TM16	Light Screen	Psychic	Status	—	—	30	Your Side
TM17	Protect	Normal	Status	—	—	10	Self
TM18	Rain Dance	Water	Status	—	—	5	Both Sides
TM19	Roost	Flying	Status	—	—	10	Self
TM21	Frustration	Normal	Physical	—	100	20	Normal
TM24	Thunderbolt	Electric	Special	90	100	15	Normal
TM25	Thunder	Electric	Special	110	70	10	Normal
TM27	Return	Normal	Physical	—	100	20	Normal
TM32	Double Team	Normal	Status	—	—	15	Self
TM40	Aerial Ace	Flying	Physical	60	—	20	Normal
TM42	Facade	Normal	Physical	70	100	20	Normal
TM44	Rest	Psychic	Status	—	—	10	Self
TM48	Round	Normal	Special	60	100	15	Normal
TM51	Steel Wing	Steel	Physical	70	90	25	Normal
TM57	Charge Beam	Electric	Special	50	90	10	Normal
TM58	Sky Drop	Flying	Physical	60	100	10	Normal
TM68	Giga Impact	Normal	Physical	150	90	5	Normal
TM70	Flash	Normal	Status	—	100	20	Normal
TM72	Volt Switch	Electric	Special	70	100	20	Normal
TM73	Thunder Wave	Electric	Status	—	100	20	Normal
TM87	Swagger	Normal	Status	—	90	15	Normal
TM88	Sleep Talk	Normal	Status	—	—	10	Self
TM89	U-turn	Bug	Physical	70	100	20	Normal
TM90	Substitute	Normal	Status	—	—	10	Self
TM93	Wild Charge	Electric	Physical	90	100	15	Normal
TM94	Rock Smash	Fighting	Physical	40	100	15	Normal
TM100	Confide	Normal	Status	—	—	20	Normal

No.	Name	Type	Kind	Pow.	Acc.	PP	Range
HM02	Fly	Flying	Physical	90	95	15	Normal

● MOVES TAUGHT BY PEOPLE

Name	Type	Kind	Pow.	Acc.	PP	Range

AFTER THE HALL OF FAME

CENTRAL KALOS

COASTAL KALOS

153

Moltres

MOUNTAIN KALOS

ADVENTURE DATA

Coastal Kalos 153
Flame Pokémon

☑ Moltres

HEIGHT: 6'07" WEIGHT: 132.3 lbs.
GENDER: unknown

X It is said to be the legendary bird Pokémon of fire. Every flap of its wings creates a dazzling flare of flames.

Y One of the legendary bird Pokémon. It is said that its appearance indicates the coming of spring.

TYPE Fire Flying

ABILITY
Pressure

HIDDEN ABILITY
None

STAT GROWTH RATES

HP	■■■
Attack	■■■■
Defense	■■■
Sp. Atk	■■■■■
Sp. Def	■■■■
Speed	■■■■

EGG GROUP
No Eggs Discovered

EVOLUTION

Does not evolve

ITEMS SOMETIMES HELD BY WILD POKÉMON
None

Damage taken in normal battles		Damage taken in Inverse Battles	
Normal	×1	Normal	×1
Fire	×0.5	Fire	×2
Water	×2	Water	×0.5
Grass	×0.25	Grass	×4
Electric	×2	Electric	×0.5
Ice	×1	Ice	×1
Fighting	×0.5	Fighting	×2
Poison	×1	Poison	×1
Ground	×0	Ground	×1
Flying	×1	Flying	×1
Psychic	×1	Psychic	×1
Bug	×0.25	Bug	×4
Rock	×4	Rock	×0.25
Ghost	×1	Ghost	×1
Dragon	×1	Dragon	×1
Dark	×1	Dark	×1
Steel	×0.5	Steel	×2
Fairy	×0.5	Fairy	×2

Can be used in	
Inverse Battle	Battle Institute
Sky Battle	Battle Maison
Battle Chateau	Random Matchup

Gender unknown

How to obtain for your Coastal Kalos Pokédex

❶ After entering the Hall of Fame, encounter it on the the roads and water surfaces of the Kalos region 11 times, then catch it in Azure Bay (if you chose Froakie at the beginning of the game).

❷ Link Trade or transfer from another game.

❶ After entering the Hall of Fame, encounter it on the the roads and water surfaces of the Kalos region 11 times, then catch it in Azure Bay (if you chose Froakie at the beginning of the game).

❷ Link Trade or transfer from another game.

● LEVEL-UP MOVES

Lv.	Name	Type	Kind	Pow.	Acc.	PP	Range
1	Roost	Flying	Status	—	—	10	Self
1	Hurricane	Flying	Special	110	70	10	Normal
1	Sky Attack	Flying	Physical	140	90	5	Normal
1	Heat Wave	Fire	Special	95	90	10	Many Others
1	Wing Attack	Flying	Physical	60	100	35	Normal
1	Ember	Fire	Special	40	100	25	Normal
8	Fire Spin	Fire	Special	35	85	15	Normal
15	Agility	Psychic	Status	—	—	30	Self
22	Endure	Normal	Status	—	—	10	Self
29	Ancient Power	Rock	Special	60	100	5	Normal
36	Flamethrower	Fire	Special	90	100	15	Normal
43	Safeguard	Normal	Status	—	—	25	Your Side
50	Air Slash	Flying	Special	75	95	15	Normal
57	Sunny Day	Fire	Status	—	—	5	Both Sides
64	Heat Wave	Fire	Special	95	90	10	Many Others
71	Solar Beam	Grass	Special	120	100	10	Normal
78	Sky Attack	Flying	Physical	140	90	5	Normal
85	Roost	Flying	Status	—	—	10	Self
92	Hurricane	Flying	Special	110	70	10	Normal

● TM & HM MOVES

No.	Name	Type	Kind	Pow.	Acc.	PP	Range
TM05	Roar	Normal	Status	—	—	20	Normal
TM06	Toxic	Poison	Status	—	90	10	Normal
TM10	Hidden Power	Normal	Special	60	100	15	Normal
TM11	Sunny Day	Fire	Status	—	—	5	Both Sides
TM15	Hyper Beam	Normal	Special	150	90	5	Normal
TM17	Protect	Normal	Status	—	—	10	Self
TM18	Rain Dance	Water	Status	—	—	5	Both Sides
TM19	Roost	Flying	Status	—	—	10	Self
TM20	Safeguard	Normal	Status	—	—	25	Your Side
TM21	Frustration	Normal	Physical	—	100	20	Normal
TM22	Solar Beam	Grass	Special	120	100	10	Normal
TM27	Return	Normal	Physical	—	100	20	Normal
TM32	Double Team	Normal	Status	—	—	15	Self
TM35	Flamethrower	Fire	Special	90	100	15	Normal
TM37	Sandstorm	Rock	Status	—	—	10	Both Sides
TM38	Fire Blast	Fire	Special	110	85	5	Normal
TM40	Aerial Ace	Flying	Physical	60	—	20	Normal
TM42	Facade	Normal	Physical	70	100	20	Normal
TM43	Flame Charge	Fire	Physical	50	100	20	Normal
TM44	Rest	Psychic	Status	—	—	10	Self
TM48	Round	Normal	Special	60	100	15	Normal
TM50	Overheat	Fire	Special	130	90	5	Normal
TM51	Steel Wing	Steel	Physical	70	90	25	Normal
TM58	Sky Drop	Flying	Physical	60	100	10	Normal
TM59	Incinerate	Fire	Special	60	100	15	Many Others
TM61	Will-O-Wisp	Fire	Status	—	85	15	Normal
TM68	Giga Impact	Normal	Physical	150	90	5	Normal
TM87	Swagger	Normal	Status	—	90	15	Normal
TM88	Sleep Talk	Normal	Status	—	—	10	Self
TM89	U-turn	Bug	Physical	70	100	20	Normal
TM90	Substitute	Normal	Status	—	—	10	Self
TM94	Rock Smash	Fighting	Physical	40	100	15	Normal
TM100	Confide	Normal	Status	—	—	20	Normal

No.	Name	Type	Kind	Pow.	Acc.	PP	Range
HM02	Fly	Flying	Physical	90	95	15	Normal

● MOVES TAUGHT BY PEOPLE

Name	Type	Kind	Pow.	Acc.	PP	Range

♠ Mountain Kalos 001

Mole Pokémon

☑ **Diglett**

HEIGHT: 0'08"   WEIGHT: 1.8 lbs.
GENDER: ♂/♀

| TYPE | Ground |

ABILITIES
Sand Veil
Arena Trap

HIDDEN ABILITY
Sand Force

STAT GROWTH RATES
HP ▪
Attack ▪▪▪
Defense ▪
Sp. Atk ▪▪
Sp. Def ▪▪
Speed ▪▪▪▪▪

EGG GROUP
Field

⊗ Lives about one yard underground where it feeds on plant roots. It sometimes appears aboveground.

▽ Its skin is very thin. If it is exposed to light, its blood heats up, causing it to grow weak.

▲ EVOLUTION

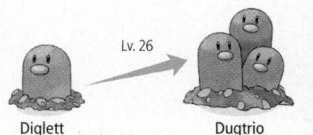

Lv. 26

Diglett → Dugtrio

ITEMS SOMETIMES HELD BY WILD POKÉMON
None

Damage taken in normal battles		Damage taken in Inverse Battles	
Normal	×1	Normal	×1
Fire	×1	Fire	×1
Water	×2	Water	×0.5
Grass	×2	Grass	×0.5
Electric	×0	Electric	×2
Ice	×2	Ice	×0.5
Fighting	×1	Fighting	×1
Poison	×0.5	Poison	×2
Ground	×1	Ground	×1
Flying	×1	Flying	×1
Psychic	×1	Psychic	×1
Bug	×1	Bug	×1
Rock	×0.5	Rock	×2
Ghost	×1	Ghost	×1
Dragon	×1	Dragon	×1
Dark	×1	Dark	×1
Steel	×1	Steel	×1
Fairy	×1	Fairy	×1

Can be used in	
Inverse Battle	Battle Institute
—	Battle Maison
Battle Chateau	Random Matchup

Same form for ♂/♀

How to obtain for your Mountain Kalos Pokédex

Leave Dugtrio at the Pokémon Day Care, and hatch the Egg that is found.

Leave Dugtrio at the Pokémon Day Care, and hatch the Egg that is found.

● LEVEL-UP MOVES

Lv.	Name	Type	Kind	Pow.	Acc.	PP	Range
1	Scratch	Normal	Physical	40	100	35	Normal
1	Sand Attack	Ground	Status	—	100	15	Normal
4	Growl	Normal	Status	—	100	40	Many Others
7	Astonish	Ghost	Physical	30	100	15	Normal
12	Mud-Slap	Ground	Special	20	100	10	Normal
15	Magnitude	Ground	Physical	—	100	30	Adjacent
18	Bulldoze	Ground	Physical	60	100	20	Adjacent
23	Sucker Punch	Dark	Physical	80	100	5	Normal
26	Mud Bomb	Ground	Special	65	85	10	Normal
29	Earth Power	Ground	Special	90	100	10	Normal
34	Dig	Ground	Physical	80	100	10	Normal
37	Slash	Normal	Physical	70	100	20	Normal
40	Earthquake	Ground	Physical	100	100	10	Adjacent
45	Fissure	Ground	Physical	—	30	5	Normal

● TM & HM MOVES

No.	Name	Type	Kind	Pow.	Acc.	PP	Range
TM01	Hone Claws	Dark	Status	—	—	15	Self
TM06	Toxic	Poison	Status	—	90	10	Normal
TM10	Hidden Power	Normal	Special	60	100	15	Normal
TM11	Sunny Day	Fire	Status	—	—	5	Both Sides
TM17	Protect	Normal	Status	—	—	10	Self
TM21	Frustration	Normal	Physical	—	100	20	Normal
TM26	Earthquake	Ground	Physical	100	100	10	Adjacent
TM27	Return	Normal	Physical	—	100	20	Normal
TM28	Dig	Ground	Physical	80	100	10	Normal
TM32	Double Team	Normal	Status	—	—	15	Self
TM36	Sludge Bomb	Poison	Special	90	100	10	Normal
TM37	Sandstorm	Rock	Status	—	—	10	Both Sides
TM39	Rock Tomb	Rock	Physical	60	95	15	Normal
TM40	Aerial Ace	Flying	Physical	60	—	20	Normal
TM42	Facade	Normal	Physical	70	100	20	Normal
TM44	Rest	Psychic	Status	—	—	10	Self
TM45	Attract	Normal	Status	—	100	15	Normal
TM46	Thief	Dark	Physical	60	100	25	Normal
TM48	Round	Normal	Special	60	100	15	Normal
TM49	Echoed Voice	Normal	Special	40	100	15	Normal
TM65	Shadow Claw	Ghost	Physical	70	100	15	Normal
TM78	Bulldoze	Ground	Physical	60	100	20	Adjacent
TM80	Rock Slide	Rock	Physical	75	90	10	Many Others
TM87	Swagger	Normal	Status	—	90	15	Normal
TM88	Sleep Talk	Normal	Status	—	—	10	Self
TM90	Substitute	Normal	Status	—	—	10	Self
TM94	Rock Smash	Fighting	Physical	40	100	15	Normal
TM100	Confide	Normal	Status	—	—	20	Normal
HM01	Cut	Normal	Physical	50	95	30	Normal

No.	Name	Type	Kind	Pow.	Acc.	PP	Range

● MOVES TAUGHT BY PEOPLE

Name	Type	Kind	Pow.	Acc.	PP	Range

● EGG MOVES

Name	Type	Kind	Pow.	Acc.	PP	Range
Feint Attack	Dark	Physical	60	—	20	Normal
Screech	Normal	Status	—	85	40	Normal
Ancient Power	Rock	Special	60	100	5	Normal
Pursuit	Dark	Physical	40	100	20	Normal
Beat Up	Dark	Physical	—	100	10	Normal
Uproar	Normal	Special	90	100	10	1 Random
Mud Bomb	Ground	Special	65	85	10	Normal
Astonish	Ghost	Physical	30	100	15	Normal
Reversal	Fighting	Physical	—	100	15	Normal
Headbutt	Normal	Physical	70	100	15	Normal
Endure	Normal	Status	—	—	10	Self
Final Gambit	Fighting	Special	—	100	5	Normal
Memento	Dark	Status	—	100	10	Normal

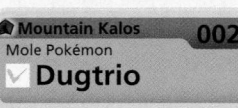

Mountain Kalos 002

Mole Pokémon

✓ **Dugtrio**

TYPE: Ground

ABILITIES
Sand Veil
Arena Trap

HIDDEN ABILITY
Sand Force

HEIGHT: 2'04" WEIGHT: 73.4 lbs.
GENDER: ♂ / ♀

X In battle, it digs through the ground and strikes the unsuspecting foe from an unexpected direction.

Y Extremely powerful, they can dig through even the hardest ground to a depth of over 60 miles.

STAT GROWTH RATES
HP	■■
Attack	■■■■
Defense	■■■
Sp. Atk	■■
Sp. Def	■■■
Speed	■■■■■■

EGG GROUP
Field

⬆ EVOLUTION

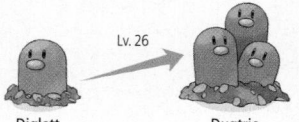

Diglett → Lv. 26 → Dugtrio

ITEMS SOMETIMES HELD BY WILD POKÉMON
Soft Sand

Damage taken in normal battles		Damage taken in Inverse Battles	
Normal	×1	Normal	×1
Fire	×1	Fire	×1
Water	×2	Water	×0.5
Grass	×2	Grass	×0.5
Electric	×0	Electric	×2
Ice	×2	Ice	×0.5
Fighting	×1	Fighting	×1
Poison	×0.5	Poison	×2
Ground	×1	Ground	×1
Flying	×1	Flying	×1
Psychic	×1	Psychic	×1
Bug	×1	Bug	×1
Rock	×0.5	Rock	×2
Ghost	×1	Ghost	×1
Dragon	×1	Dragon	×1
Dark	×1	Dark	×1
Steel	×1	Steel	×1
Fairy	×1	Fairy	×1

Can be used in	
Inverse Battle	Battle Institute
—	Battle Maison
Battle Chateau	Random Matchup

Same form for ♂ / ♀

How to obtain for your Mountain Kalos Pokédex

Catch when it pops out of a cloud of dust on Route 13.	Catch when it pops out of a cloud of dust on Route 13.

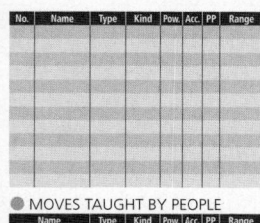

● LEVEL-UP MOVES

Lv.	Name	Type	Kind	Pow.	Acc.	PP	Range
1	Rototiller	Ground	Status	—	—	10	Adjacent
1	Night Slash	Dark	Physical	70	100	15	Normal
1	Tri Attack	Normal	Special	80	100	10	Normal
1	Scratch	Normal	Physical	40	100	35	Normal
1	Sand Attack	Ground	Status	—	100	15	Normal
1	Growl	Normal	Status	—	100	40	Many Others
4	Growl	Normal	Status	—	100	40	Many Others
7	Astonish	Ghost	Physical	30	100	15	Normal
12	Mud-Slap	Ground	Special	20	100	10	Normal
15	Magnitude	Ground	Physical	—	100	30	Adjacent
18	Bulldoze	Ground	Physical	60	100	20	Adjacent
23	Sucker Punch	Dark	Physical	80	100	5	Normal
26	Sand Tomb	Ground	Physical	35	85	15	Normal
28	Mud Bomb	Ground	Special	65	85	10	Normal
33	Earth Power	Ground	Special	90	100	10	Normal
42	Dig	Ground	Physical	80	100	10	Normal
45	Slash	Normal	Physical	70	100	20	Normal
50	Earthquake	Ground	Physical	100	100	10	Adjacent
57	Fissure	Ground	Physical	—	30	5	Normal

● TM & HM MOVES

No.	Name	Type	Kind	Pow.	Acc.	PP	Range
TM01	Hone Claws	Dark	Status	—	—	15	Self
TM06	Toxic	Poison	Status	—	90	10	Normal
TM10	Hidden Power	Normal	Special	60	100	15	Normal
TM11	Sunny Day	Fire	Status	—	—	5	Both Sides
TM15	Hyper Beam	Normal	Special	150	90	5	Normal
TM17	Protect	Normal	Status	—	—	10	Self
TM21	Frustration	Normal	Physical	—	100	20	Normal
TM26	Earthquake	Ground	Physical	100	100	10	Adjacent
TM27	Return	Normal	Physical	—	100	20	Normal
TM28	Dig	Ground	Physical	80	100	10	Normal
TM32	Double Team	Normal	Status	—	—	15	Self
TM34	Sludge Wave	Poison	Special	95	100	10	Adjacent
TM36	Sludge Bomb	Poison	Special	90	100	10	Normal
TM37	Sandstorm	Rock	Status	—	—	10	Both Sides
TM39	Rock Tomb	Rock	Physical	60	95	15	Normal
TM40	Aerial Ace	Flying	Physical	60	—	20	Normal
TM42	Facade	Normal	Physical	70	100	20	Normal
TM44	Rest	Psychic	Status	—	—	10	Self
TM45	Attract	Normal	Status	—	100	15	Normal
TM46	Thief	Dark	Physical	60	100	25	Normal
TM48	Round	Normal	Special	60	100	15	Normal
TM49	Echoed Voice	Normal	Special	40	100	15	Normal
TM65	Shadow Claw	Ghost	Physical	70	100	15	Normal
TM68	Giga Impact	Normal	Physical	150	90	5	Normal
TM71	Stone Edge	Rock	Physical	100	80	5	Normal
TM78	Bulldoze	Ground	Physical	60	100	20	Adjacent
TM80	Rock Slide	Rock	Physical	75	90	10	Many Others
TM87	Swagger	Normal	Status	—	90	15	Normal
TM88	Sleep Talk	Normal	Status	—	—	10	Self
TM90	Substitute	Normal	Status	—	—	10	Self
TM94	Rock Smash	Fighting	Physical	40	100	15	Normal
TM100	Confide	Normal	Status	—	—	20	Normal
HM01	Cut	Normal	Physical	50	95	30	Normal

No.	Name	Type	Kind	Pow.	Acc.	PP	Range

● MOVES TAUGHT BY PEOPLE

Name	Type	Kind	Pow.	Acc.	PP	Range

AFTER THE HALL OF FAME

CENTRAL KALOS

COASTAL KALOS

MOUNTAIN KALOS

002 Dugtrio

ADVENTURE DATA

Mountain Kalos **003**

Ant Pit Pokémon

☑ Trapinch

HEIGHT: 2'04"   WEIGHT: 33.1 lbs.
GENDER: ♂/♀

 It lives in arid deserts. It makes a sloping pit trap in sand where it patiently awaits prey.

It makes an inescapable conical pit and lies in wait at the bottom for prey to come tumbling down.

TYPE **Ground**

ABILITIES
Hyper Cutter
Arena Trap

HIDDEN ABILITY
Sheer Force

STAT GROWTH RATES
HP	■■
Attack	■■■■■
Defense	■■
Sp. Atk	■■
Sp. Def	■■
Speed	■

EGG GROUP
Bug

⚑ EVOLUTION

Trapinch → Lv. 35 → Vibrava → Lv. 45 → Flygon

ITEMS SOMETIMES HELD BY WILD POKÉMON
Soft Sand

Damage taken in normal battles		Damage taken in Inverse Battles	
Normal	×1	Normal	×1
Fire	×1	Fire	×1
Water	×2	Water	×0.5
Grass	×2	Grass	×0.5
Electric	×0	Electric	×2
Ice	×2	Ice	×0.5
Fighting	×1	Fighting	×1
Poison	×0.5	Poison	×2
Ground	×1	Ground	×1
Flying	×1	Flying	×1
Psychic	×1	Psychic	×1
Bug	×1	Bug	×1
Rock	×0.5	Rock	×2
Ghost	×1	Ghost	×1
Dragon	×1	Dragon	×1
Dark	×1	Dark	×1
Steel	×1	Steel	×1
Fairy	×1	Fairy	×1

Can be used in	
Inverse Battle	Battle Institute
—	Battle Maison
Battle Chateau	Random Matchup

Same form for ♂/♀

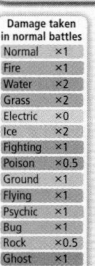

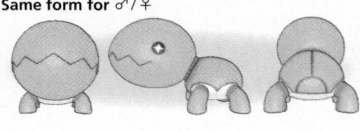

How to obtain for your Mountain Kalos Pokédex

Catch when it pops out of a cloud of dust on Route 13.

Catch when it pops out of a cloud of dust on Route 13.

● LEVEL-UP MOVES

Lv.	Name	Type	Kind	Pow.	Acc.	PP	Range
1	Fissure	Ground	Physical	—	30	5	Normal
1	Superpower	Fighting	Physical	120	100	5	Normal
1	Feint	Normal	Physical	30	100	10	Normal
1	Bite	Dark	Physical	60	100	25	Normal
4	Sand Attack	Ground	Status	—	100	15	Normal
7	Feint Attack	Dark	Physical	60	—	20	Normal
10	Sand Tomb	Ground	Physical	35	85	15	Normal
13	Mud-Slap	Ground	Special	20	100	10	Normal
17	Bide	Normal	Physical	—	—	10	Self
21	Bulldoze	Ground	Physical	60	100	20	Adjacent
25	Rock Slide	Rock	Physical	75	90	10	Many Others
29	Dig	Ground	Physical	80	100	10	Normal
34	Crunch	Dark	Physical	80	100	15	Normal
39	Earth Power	Ground	Special	90	100	10	Normal
44	Sandstorm	Rock	Status	—	—	10	Both Sides
49	Hyper Beam	Normal	Special	150	90	5	Normal
55	Earthquake	Ground	Physical	100	100	10	Adjacent
61	Feint	Normal	Physical	30	100	10	Normal
67	Superpower	Fighting	Physical	120	100	5	Normal
73	Fissure	Ground	Physical	—	30	5	Normal

● TM & HM MOVES

No.	Name	Type	Kind	Pow.	Acc.	PP	Range
TM06	Toxic	Poison	Status	—	90	10	Normal
TM10	Hidden Power	Normal	Special	60	100	15	Normal
TM11	Sunny Day	Fire	Status	—	—	5	Both Sides
TM15	Hyper Beam	Normal	Special	150	90	5	Normal
TM17	Protect	Normal	Status	—	—	10	Self
TM21	Frustration	Normal	Physical	—	100	20	Normal
TM22	Solar Beam	Grass	Special	120	100	10	Normal
TM26	Earthquake	Ground	Physical	100	100	10	Adjacent
TM27	Return	Normal	Physical	—	100	20	Normal
TM28	Dig	Ground	Physical	80	100	10	Normal
TM32	Double Team	Normal	Status	—	—	15	Self
TM37	Sandstorm	Rock	Status	—	—	10	Both Sides
TM39	Rock Tomb	Rock	Physical	60	95	15	Normal
TM42	Facade	Normal	Physical	70	100	20	Normal
TM44	Rest	Psychic	Status	—	—	10	Self
TM45	Attract	Normal	Status	—	100	15	Normal
TM48	Round	Normal	Special	60	100	15	Normal
TM76	Struggle Bug	Bug	Special	50	100	20	Many Others
TM78	Bulldoze	Ground	Physical	60	100	20	Adjacent
TM80	Rock Slide	Rock	Physical	75	90	10	Many Others
TM87	Swagger	Normal	Status	—	90	15	Normal
TM88	Sleep Talk	Normal	Status	—	—	10	Self
TM90	Substitute	Normal	Status	—	—	10	Self
TM94	Rock Smash	Fighting	Physical	40	100	15	Normal
TM100	Confide	Normal	Status	—	—	20	Normal
HM04	Strength	Normal	Physical	80	100	15	Normal

No.	Name	Type	Kind	Pow.	Acc.	PP	Range

● MOVES TAUGHT BY PEOPLE

Name	Type	Kind	Pow.	Acc.	PP	Range

● EGG MOVES

Name	Type	Kind	Pow.	Acc.	PP	Range
Focus Energy	Normal	Status	—	—	30	Self
Quick Attack	Normal	Physical	40	100	30	Normal
Gust	Flying	Special	40	100	35	Normal
Flail	Normal	Physical	—	100	15	Normal
Fury Cutter	Bug	Physical	40	95	20	Normal
Mud Shot	Ground	Special	55	95	15	Normal
Endure	Normal	Status	—	—	10	Self
Earth Power	Ground	Special	90	100	10	Normal
Bug Bite	Bug	Physical	60	100	20	Normal
Signal Beam	Bug	Special	75	100	15	Normal

AFTER THE HALL OF FAME

CENTRAL KALOS

COASTAL KALOS

MOUNTAIN KALOS

004

Vibrava

ADVENTURE DATA

Mountain Kalos — 004

Vibration Pokémon

Vibrava

HEIGHT: 3'07"　WEIGHT: 33.7 lbs.
GENDER: ♂/♀

X The ultrasonic waves it generates by rubbing its two wings together cause severe headaches.

Y It generates ultrasonic waves by violently flapping its wings. After making its prey faint, it melts the prey with acid.

TYPE Ground　Dragon

ABILITY
Levitate

HIDDEN ABILITY
None

STAT GROWTH RATES

HP	■■
Attack	■■■■
Defense	■■
Sp. Atk	■■
Sp. Def	■■
Speed	■■■■

EGG GROUP
Bug

EVOLUTION

Trapinch — Lv. 35 → Vibrava — Lv. 45 → Flygon

ITEMS SOMETIMES HELD BY WILD POKÉMON
None

Damage taken in normal battles		Damage taken in Inverse Battles	
Normal	×1	Normal	×1
Fire	×0.5	Fire	×2
Water	×1	Water	×1
Grass	×1	Grass	×1
Electric	×0	Electric	×4
Ice	×4	Ice	×0.25
Fighting	×1	Fighting	×1
Poison	×0.5	Poison	×1
Ground	×1 ❶	Ground	×1 ❶
Flying	×1	Flying	×1
Psychic	×1	Psychic	×1
Bug	×1	Bug	×1
Rock	×0.5	Rock	×2
Ghost	×1	Ghost	×1
Dragon	×2	Dragon	×0.5
Dark	×1	Dark	×1
Steel	×1	Steel	×1
Fairy	×2	Fairy	×0.5

Can be used in	
Inverse Battle	Battle Institute
Sky Battle	Battle Maison
Battle Chateau	Random Matchup

Same form for ♂/♀

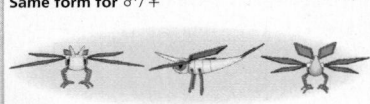

How to obtain for your Mountain Kalos Pokédex

Level up Trapinch to Lv. 35.	Level up Trapinch to Lv. 35.

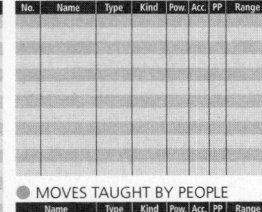

● LEVEL-UP MOVES

Lv.	Name	Type	Kind	Pow.	Acc.	PP	Range
1	Sonic Boom	Normal	Special	—	90	20	Normal
1	Sand Attack	Ground	Status	—	100	15	Normal
1	Feint Attack	Dark	Physical	60	—	20	Normal
1	Sand Tomb	Ground	Physical	35	85	15	Normal
4	Sand Attack	Ground	Status	—	100	15	Normal
7	Feint Attack	Dark	Physical	60	—	20	Normal
10	Sand Tomb	Ground	Physical	35	85	15	Normal
10	Mud-Slap	Ground	Special	20	100	10	Normal
17	Bide	Normal	Physical	—	—	10	Self
21	Bulldoze	Ground	Physical	60	100	20	Adjacent
25	Rock Slide	Rock	Physical	75	90	10	Many Others
29	Supersonic	Normal	Status	—	55	20	Normal
34	Screech	Normal	Status	—	85	40	Normal
35	Dragon Breath	Dragon	Special	60	100	20	Normal
39	Earth Power	Ground	Special	90	100	10	Normal
44	Sandstorm	Rock	Status	—	—	10	Both Sides
49	Hyper Beam	Normal	Special	150	90	5	Normal

● TM & HM MOVES

No.	Name	Type	Kind	Pow.	Acc.	PP	Range
TM06	Toxic	Poison	Status	—	90	10	Normal
TM10	Hidden Power	Normal	Special	60	100	15	Normal
TM11	Sunny Day	Fire	Status	—	—	5	Both Sides
TM15	Hyper Beam	Normal	Special	150	90	5	Normal
TM17	Protect	Normal	Status	—	—	10	Self
TM19	Roost	Flying	Status	—	—	10	Self
TM21	Frustration	Normal	Physical	—	100	20	Normal
TM22	Solar Beam	Grass	Special	120	100	10	Normal
TM26	Earthquake	Ground	Physical	100	100	10	Adjacent
TM27	Return	Normal	Physical	—	100	20	Normal
TM28	Dig	Ground	Physical	80	100	10	Normal
TM32	Double Team	Normal	Status	—	—	15	Self
TM37	Sandstorm	Rock	Status	—	—	10	Both Sides
TM39	Rock Tomb	Rock	Physical	60	95	15	Normal
TM42	Facade	Normal	Physical	70	100	20	Normal
TM44	Rest	Psychic	Status	—	—	10	Self
TM45	Attract	Normal	Status	—	100	15	Normal
TM48	Round	Normal	Special	60	100	15	Normal
TM51	Steel Wing	Steel	Physical	70	90	25	Normal
TM76	Struggle Bug	Bug	Special	50	100	20	Many Others
TM78	Bulldoze	Ground	Physical	60	100	20	Adjacent
TM80	Rock Slide	Rock	Physical	75	90	10	Many Others
TM87	Swagger	Normal	Status	—	90	15	Normal
TM88	Sleep Talk	Normal	Status	—	—	10	Self
TM89	U-turn	Bug	Physical	70	100	20	Normal
TM90	Substitute	Normal	Status	—	—	10	Self
TM94	Rock Smash	Fighting	Physical	40	100	15	Normal
TM100	Confide	Normal	Status	—	—	20	Normal
HM02	Fly	Flying	Physical	90	95	15	Normal
HM04	Strength	Normal	Physical	80	100	15	Normal

● MOVES TAUGHT BY PEOPLE

Name	Type	Kind	Pow.	Acc.	PP	Range
Draco Meteor	Dragon	Special	130	90	5	Normal

Mountain Kalos 005

Mystic Pokémon

V Flygon

HEIGHT: 6'07" WEIGHT: 180.8 lbs.
GENDER: ♂/♀

X It hides itself by kicking up desert sand with its wings. Red covers shield its eyes from sand.

Y Known as "The Desert Spirit," this Pokémon hides in the sandstorms it causes by beating its wings.

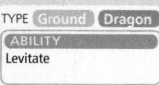

TYPE Ground Dragon

ABILITY
Levitate

HIDDEN ABILITY
None

STAT GROWTH RATES
HP	▪▪▪
Attack	▪▪▪▪
Defense	▪▪▪▪
Sp. Atk	▪▪▪▪
Sp. Def	▪▪▪
Speed	▪▪▪▪▪

EGG GROUP
Bug

EVOLUTION

	Lv. 35	Lv. 45
Trapinch	Vibrava	Flygon

ITEMS SOMETIMES HELD BY WILD POKÉMON
None

Damage taken in normal battles		Damage taken in Inverse Battles	
Normal	×1	Normal	×1
Fire	×0.5	Fire	×2
Water	×1	Water	×1
Grass	×1	Grass	×1
Electric	×0	Electric	×4
Ice	×4	Ice	×0.25
Fighting	×1	Fighting	×1
Poison	×0.5	Poison	×2
Ground	×1	Ground	×1
Flying	×1	Flying	×1
Psychic	×1	Psychic	×1
Bug	×1	Bug	×1
Rock	×0.5	Rock	×2
Ghost	×1	Ghost	×1
Dragon	×2	Dragon	×0.5
Dark	×1	Dark	×1
Steel	×1	Steel	×1
Fairy	×2	Fairy	×0.5

Can be used in	
Inverse Battle	Battle Institute
Sky Battle	Battle Maison
Battle Chateau	Random Matchup

Same form for ♂/♀

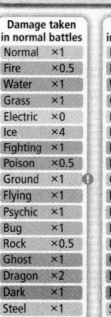

How to obtain for your Mountain Kalos Pokédex

Level up Vibrava to Lv. 45.	Level up Vibrava to Lv. 45.

● LEVEL-UP MOVES

Lv.	Name	Type	Kind	Pow.	Acc.	PP	Range
1	Sonic Boom	Normal	Special	—	90	20	Normal
1	Sand Attack	Ground	Status	—	100	15	Normal
1	Feint Attack	Dark	Physical	60	—	20	Normal
1	Sand Tomb	Ground	Physical	35	85	15	Normal
4	Sand Attack	Ground	Status	—	100	15	Normal
7	Feint Attack	Dark	Physical	60	—	20	Normal
10	Sand Tomb	Ground	Physical	35	85	15	Normal
13	Mud-Slap	Ground	Special	20	100	10	Normal
17	Bide	Normal	Physical	—	—	10	Self
21	Bulldoze	Ground	Physical	60	100	20	Adjacent
25	Rock Slide	Rock	Physical	75	90	10	Many Others
29	Supersonic	Normal	Status	—	55	20	Normal
34	Screech	Normal	Status	—	85	40	Normal
35	Dragon Breath	Dragon	Special	60	100	20	Normal
39	Earth Power	Ground	Special	90	100	10	Normal
44	Sandstorm	Rock	Status	—	—	10	Both Sides
45	Dragon Tail	Dragon	Physical	60	90	10	Normal
49	Hyper Beam	Normal	Special	150	90	5	Normal
55	Dragon Claw	Dragon	Physical	80	100	15	Normal

● TM & HM MOVES

No.	Name	Type	Kind	Pow.	Acc.	PP	Range
TM01	Hone Claws	Dark	Status	—	—	15	Self
TM02	Dragon Claw	Dragon	Physical	80	100	15	Normal
TM06	Toxic	Poison	Status	—	90	10	Normal
TM10	Hidden Power	Normal	Special	60	100	15	Normal
TM11	Sunny Day	Fire	Status	—	—	5	Both Sides
TM15	Hyper Beam	Normal	Special	150	90	5	Normal
TM17	Protect	Normal	Status	—	—	10	Self
TM19	Roost	Flying	Status	—	—	10	Self
TM21	Frustration	Normal	Physical	—	100	20	Normal
TM22	Solar Beam	Grass	Special	120	100	10	Normal
TM26	Earthquake	Ground	Physical	100	100	10	Adjacent
TM27	Return	Normal	Physical	—	100	20	Normal
TM28	Dig	Ground	Physical	80	100	10	Normal
TM32	Double Team	Normal	Status	—	—	15	Self
TM35	Flamethrower	Fire	Special	90	100	15	Normal
TM37	Sandstorm	Rock	Status	—	—	10	Both Sides
TM38	Fire Blast	Fire	Special	110	85	5	Normal
TM39	Rock Tomb	Rock	Physical	60	95	15	Normal
TM40	Aerial Ace	Flying	Physical	60	—	20	Normal
TM42	Facade	Normal	Physical	70	100	20	Normal
TM44	Rest	Psychic	Status	—	—	10	Self
TM45	Attract	Normal	Status	—	100	15	Normal
TM48	Round	Normal	Special	60	100	15	Normal
TM51	Steel Wing	Steel	Physical	70	90	25	Normal
TM59	Incinerate	Fire	Special	60	100	15	Many Others
TM68	Giga Impact	Normal	Physical	150	90	5	Normal
TM71	Stone Edge	Rock	Physical	100	80	5	Normal
TM76	Struggle Bug	Bug	Special	50	100	20	Many Others
TM78	Bulldoze	Ground	Physical	60	100	20	Adjacent
TM80	Rock Slide	Rock	Physical	75	90	10	Many Others
TM82	Dragon Tail	Dragon	Physical	60	90	10	Normal
TM87	Swagger	Normal	Status	—	90	15	Normal
TM88	Sleep Talk	Normal	Status	—	—	10	Self

No.	Name	Type	Kind	Pow.	Acc.	PP	Range
TM89	U-turn	Bug	Physical	70	100	20	Normal
TM90	Substitute	Normal	Status	—	—	10	Self
TM94	Rock Smash	Fighting	Physical	40	100	15	Normal
TM98	Power-Up Patch	Fighting	Physical	40	100	20	Normal
TM100	Confide	Normal	Status	—	—	20	Normal
HM02	Fly	Flying	Physical	90	95	15	Normal
HM04	Strength	Normal	Physical	80	100	15	Normal

● MOVES TAUGHT BY PEOPLE

Name	Type	Kind	Pow.	Acc.	PP	Range
Draco Meteor	Dragon	Special	130	90	5	Normal

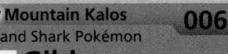

Mountain Kalos 006
Land Shark Pokémon
☑ Gible

HEIGHT: 2'04" WEIGHT: 45.2 lbs.
GENDER: ♂/♀

TYPE **Dragon** **Ground**

ABILITY
Sand Veil

HIDDEN ABILITY
Rough Skin

STAT GROWTH RATES
HP	■■■
Attack	■■■■
Defense	■■
Sp. Atk	■■
Sp. Def	■■
Speed	■■

EGG GROUPS
Monster, Dragon

X: It nests in horizontal holes warmed by geothermal heat. Foes who get too close can expect to be pounced on and bitten.

Y: It nests in small, horizontal holes in cave walls. It pounces to catch prey that stray too close.

EVOLUTION

Gible — Lv. 24 → Gabite — Lv. 48 → Garchomp

ITEMS SOMETIMES HELD BY WILD POKÉMON
None

Can be used in
Inverse Battle
—
Battle Chateau
Battle Institute
Battle Maison
Random Matchup

Damage taken in normal battles	
Normal	×1
Fire	×0.5
Water	×1
Grass	×1
Electric	×0
Ice	×4
Fighting	×1
Poison	×0.5
Ground	×1
Flying	×1
Psychic	×1
Bug	×1
Rock	×0.5
Ghost	×1
Dragon	×2
Dark	×1
Steel	×1
Fairy	×2

Damage taken in Inverse Battles	
Normal	×1
Fire	×2
Water	×1
Grass	×1
Electric	×1
Ice	×0.25
Fighting	×1
Poison	×2
Ground	×1
Flying	×1
Psychic	×1
Bug	×1
Rock	×2
Ghost	×1
Dragon	×0.5
Dark	×1
Steel	×1
Fairy	×0.5

How to obtain for your Mountain Kalos Pokédex

X: Catch when it pops out of a cloud of dust on Route 13.

Y: Catch when it pops out of a cloud of dust on Route 13.

♂    ♀

The male has a notch in its back fin. The female has no notch in its back fin.

006 Gible

● LEVEL-UP MOVES

Lv.	Name	Type	Kind	Pow.	Acc.	PP	Range
1	Tackle	Normal	Physical	50	100	35	Normal
3	Sand Attack	Ground	Status	—	100	15	Normal
7	Dragon Rage	Dragon	Special	—	100	10	Normal
13	Sandstorm	Rock	Status	—	—	10	Both Sides
15	Take Down	Normal	Physical	90	85	20	Normal
19	Sand Tomb	Ground	Physical	35	85	15	Normal
25	Slash	Normal	Physical	70	100	20	Normal
27	Dragon Claw	Dragon	Physical	80	100	15	Normal
31	Dig	Ground	Physical	80	100	10	Normal
37	Dragon Rush	Dragon	Physical	100	75	10	Normal

● TM & HM MOVES

No.	Name	Type	Kind	Pow.	Acc.	PP	Range
TM01	Hone Claws	Dark	Status	—	—	15	Self
TM02	Dragon Claw	Dragon	Physical	80	100	15	Normal
TM05	Roar	Normal	Status	—	—	20	Normal
TM06	Toxic	Poison	Status	—	90	10	Normal
TM10	Hidden Power	Normal	Special	60	100	15	Normal
TM11	Sunny Day	Fire	Status	—	—	5	Both Sides
TM17	Protect	Normal	Status	—	—	10	Self
TM18	Rain Dance	Water	Status	—	—	5	Both Sides
TM21	Frustration	Normal	Physical	—	100	20	Normal
TM26	Earthquake	Ground	Physical	100	100	10	Adjacent
TM27	Return	Normal	Physical	—	100	20	Normal
TM28	Dig	Ground	Physical	80	100	10	Normal
TM32	Double Team	Normal	Status	—	—	15	Self
TM35	Flamethrower	Fire	Special	90	100	15	Normal
TM37	Sandstorm	Rock	Status	—	—	10	Both Sides
TM38	Fire Blast	Fire	Special	110	85	5	Normal
TM39	Rock Tomb	Rock	Physical	60	95	15	Normal
TM40	Aerial Ace	Flying	Physical	60	—	20	Normal
TM42	Facade	Normal	Physical	70	100	20	Normal
TM44	Rest	Psychic	Status	—	—	10	Self
TM45	Attract	Normal	Status	—	100	15	Normal
TM48	Round	Normal	Special	60	100	15	Normal
TM59	Incinerate	Fire	Special	60	100	15	Many Others
TM65	Shadow Claw	Ghost	Physical	70	100	15	Normal
TM71	Stone Edge	Rock	Physical	100	80	5	Normal
TM78	Bulldoze	Ground	Physical	60	100	20	Adjacent
TM80	Rock Slide	Rock	Physical	75	90	10	Many Others
TM87	Swagger	Normal	Status	—	90	15	Normal
TM88	Sleep Talk	Normal	Status	—	—	10	Self
TM90	Substitute	Normal	Status	—	—	10	Self
TM94	Rock Smash	Fighting	Physical	40	100	15	Normal
TM100	Confide	Normal	Status	—	—	20	Normal
HM01	Cut	Normal	Physical	50	95	30	Normal

No.	Name	Type	Kind	Pow.	Acc.	PP	Range
HM04	Strength	Normal	Physical	80	100	15	Normal

● MOVES TAUGHT BY PEOPLE

Name	Type	Kind	Pow.	Acc.	PP	Range
Draco Meteor	Dragon	Special	130	90	5	Normal

● EGG MOVES

Name	Type	Kind	Pow.	Acc.	PP	Range
Dragon Breath	Dragon	Special	60	100	20	Normal
Outrage	Dragon	Physical	120	100	10	1 Random
Twister	Dragon	Special	40	100	20	Many Others
Scary Face	Normal	Status	—	100	10	Normal
Double-Edge	Normal	Physical	120	100	15	Normal
Thrash	Normal	Physical	120	100	10	1 Random
Metal Claw	Steel	Physical	50	95	35	Normal
Sand Tomb	Ground	Physical	35	85	15	Normal
Body Slam	Normal	Physical	85	100	15	Normal
Iron Head	Steel	Physical	80	100	15	Normal
Mud Shot	Ground	Special	55	95	15	Normal
Rock Climb	Normal	Physical	90	85	20	Normal
Iron Tail	Steel	Physical	100	75	15	Normal

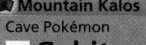

Mountain Kalos 007
Cave Pokémon

Gabite ✓

HEIGHT: 4'07" WEIGHT: 123.5 lbs.
GENDER: ♂/♀

TYPE Dragon Ground

ABILITY
Sand Veil

HIDDEN ABILITY
Rough Skin

STAT GROWTH RATES
HP	■■
Attack	■■■■
Defense	■■■
Sp. Atk	■■
Sp. Def	■■
Speed	■■■■

EGG GROUPS
Monster, Dragon

 It loves sparkly things. It seeks treasures in caves and hoards the loot in its nest.

 As it digs to expand its nest, it habitually digs up gems that it then hoards in its nest.

EVOLUTION

Lv. 24 Lv. 48

Gible — Gabite — Garchomp

ITEMS SOMETIMES HELD BY WILD POKÉMON
None

Damage taken in normal battles		Damage taken in Inverse Battles		Can be used in
Normal	×1	Normal	×1	Inverse Battle
Fire	×0.5	Fire	×2	—
Water	×1	Water	×1	Battle Chateau
Grass	×1	Grass	×1	Battle Institute
Electric	×0	Electric	×4	Battle Maison
Ice	×4	Ice	×0.25	Random Matchup
Fighting	×1	Fighting	×1	
Poison	×0.5	Poison	×2	
Ground	×1	Ground	×1	
Flying	×1	Flying	×1	
Psychic	×1	Psychic	×1	
Bug	×1	Bug	×1	
Rock	×0.5	Rock	×2	
Ghost	×1	Ghost	×1	
Dragon	×2	Dragon	×0.5	
Dark	×1	Dark	×1	
Steel	×1	Steel	×1	
Fairy	×2	Fairy	×0.5	

How to obtain for your Mountain Kalos Pokédex

Level up Gible to Lv. 24.	Level up Gible to Lv. 24.

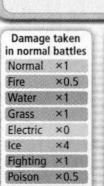

♂    ♀

The male has a notch in its back fin. The female has no notch in its back fin.

● LEVEL-UP MOVES

Lv.	Name	Type	Kind	Pow.	Acc.	PP	Range
1	Tackle	Normal	Physical	50	100	35	Normal
1	Sand Attack	Ground	Status	—	100	15	Normal
3	Sand Attack	Ground	Status	—	100	15	Normal
7	Dragon Rage	Dragon	Special	—	100	10	Normal
13	Sandstorm	Rock	Status	—	—	10	Both Sides
15	Take Down	Normal	Physical	90	85	20	Normal
19	Sand Tomb	Ground	Physical	35	85	15	Normal
24	Dual Chop	Dragon	Physical	40	90	15	Normal
28	Slash	Normal	Physical	70	100	20	Normal
33	Dragon Claw	Dragon	Physical	80	100	15	Normal
40	Dig	Ground	Physical	80	100	10	Normal
49	Dragon Rush	Dragon	Physical	100	75	10	Normal

■ TM & HM MOVES

No.	Name	Type	Kind	Pow.	Acc.	PP	Range
TM01	Hone Claws	Dark	Status	—	—	15	Self
TM02	Dragon Claw	Dragon	Physical	80	100	15	Normal
TM05	Roar	Normal	Status	—	—	20	Normal
TM06	Toxic	Poison	Status	—	90	10	Normal
TM10	Hidden Power	Normal	Special	60	100	15	Normal
TM11	Sunny Day	Fire	Status	—	—	5	Both Sides
TM17	Protect	Normal	Status	—	—	10	Self
TM18	Rain Dance	Water	Status	—	—	5	Both Sides
TM21	Frustration	Normal	Physical	—	100	20	Normal
TM26	Earthquake	Ground	Physical	100	100	10	Adjacent
TM27	Return	Normal	Physical	—	100	20	Normal
TM28	Dig	Ground	Physical	80	100	10	Normal
TM32	Double Team	Normal	Status	—	—	15	Self
TM35	Flamethrower	Fire	Special	90	100	15	Normal
TM37	Sandstorm	Rock	Status	—	—	10	Both Sides
TM38	Fire Blast	Fire	Special	110	85	5	Normal
TM39	Rock Tomb	Rock	Physical	60	95	15	Normal
TM40	Aerial Ace	Flying	Physical	60	—	20	Normal
TM42	Facade	Normal	Physical	70	100	20	Normal
TM44	Rest	Psychic	Status	—	—	10	Self
TM45	Attract	Normal	Status	—	100	15	Normal
TM48	Round	Normal	Special	60	100	15	Normal
TM59	Incinerate	Fire	Special	60	100	15	Many Others
TM65	Shadow Claw	Ghost	Physical	70	100	15	Normal
TM71	Stone Edge	Rock	Physical	100	80	5	Normal
TM78	Bulldoze	Ground	Physical	60	100	20	Adjacent
TM80	Rock Slide	Rock	Physical	75	90	10	Many Others
TM87	Swagger	Normal	Status	—	90	15	Normal
TM88	Sleep Talk	Normal	Status	—	—	10	Self
TM90	Substitute	Normal	Status	—	—	10	Self
TM94	Rock Smash	Fighting	Physical	40	100	15	Normal
TM100	Confide	Normal	Status	—	—	20	Normal
HM01	Cut	Normal	Physical	50	95	30	Normal

No.	Name	Type	Kind	Pow.	Acc.	PP	Range
HM04	Strength	Normal	Physical	80	100	15	Normal

● MOVES TAUGHT BY PEOPLE

Name	Type	Kind	Pow.	Acc.	PP	Range
Draco Meteor	Dragon	Special	130	90	5	Normal

AFTER THE HALL OF FAME

CENTRAL KALOS

COASTAL KALOS

MOUNTAIN KALOS

008

Garchomp

ADVENTURE DATA

Mountain Kalos 008
Mach Pokémon
☑ Garchomp

HEIGHT: 6'03" WEIGHT: 209.4 lbs.
GENDER: ♂/♀

TYPE Dragon Ground

ABILITY
Sand Veil

HIDDEN ABILITY
Rough Skin

STAT GROWTH RATES
HP	■■■■
Attack	■■■■■
Defense	■■■■
Sp. Atk	■■■■
Sp. Def	■■■■
Speed	■■■■■

EGG GROUPS
Monster, Dragon

X When it folds up its body and extends its wings, it looks like a jet plane. It flies at sonic speed.

Y It flies at speeds equal to a jet fighter plane. It never allows its prey to escape.

EVOLUTION
Gible → Lv. 24 → Gabite → Lv. 48 → Garchomp

ITEMS SOMETIMES HELD BY WILD POKÉMON
None

Can be used in
Inverse Battle
—
Battle Chateau
Battle Institute
Battle Maison
Random Matchup

Damage taken in normal battles
Normal	×1	Fire	×0.5	Water	×1	Grass	×1	Electric	×0	Ice	×4	Fighting	×1	Poison	×0.5	Ground	×1	Flying	×1	Psychic	×1	Bug	×1	Rock	×0.5	Ghost	×1	Dragon	×2	Dark	×1	Steel	×1	Fairy	×2

Damage taken in Inverse Battles
Normal	×1	Fire	×2	Water	×1	Grass	×1	Electric	×4	Ice	×0.25	Fighting	×1	Poison	×2	Ground	×1	Flying	×1	Psychic	×1	Bug	×1	Rock	×2	Ghost	×1	Dragon	×0.5	Dark	×1	Steel	×1	Fairy	×0.5

How to obtain for your Mountain Kalos Pokédex
X: Level up Gabite to Lv. 48. Y: Level up Gabite to Lv. 48.

The male has a notch in its back fin. The female has no notch in its back fin.

LEVEL-UP MOVES
Lv.	Name	Type	Kind	Pow.	Acc.	PP	Range
1	Fire Fang	Fire	Physical	65	95	15	Normal
1	Tackle	Normal	Physical	50	100	35	Normal
1	Sand Attack	Ground	Status	—	100	15	Normal
1	Dragon Rage	Dragon	Special	—	100	10	Normal
1	Sandstorm	Rock	Status	—	—	10	Both Sides
3	Sand Attack	Ground	Status	—	100	15	Normal
7	Dragon Rage	Dragon	Special	—	100	10	Normal
13	Sandstorm	Rock	Status	—	—	10	Both Sides
15	Take Down	Normal	Physical	90	85	20	Normal
19	Sand Tomb	Ground	Physical	35	85	15	Normal
24	Dual Chop	Dragon	Physical	40	90	15	Normal
28	Slash	Normal	Physical	70	100	20	Normal
33	Dragon Claw	Dragon	Physical	80	100	15	Normal
40	Dig	Ground	Physical	80	100	10	Normal
48	Crunch	Dark	Physical	80	100	15	Normal
55	Dragon Rush	Dragon	Physical	100	75	10	Normal

TM & HM MOVES
No.	Name	Type	Kind	Pow.	Acc.	PP	Range
TM01	Hone Claws	Dark	Status	—	—	15	Self
TM02	Dragon Claw	Dragon	Physical	80	100	15	Normal
TM05	Roar	Normal	Status	—	—	20	Normal
TM06	Toxic	Poison	Status	—	90	10	Normal
TM10	Hidden Power	Normal	Special	60	100	15	Normal
TM11	Sunny Day	Fire	Status	—	—	5	Both Sides
TM15	Hyper Beam	Normal	Special	150	90	5	Normal
TM17	Protect	Normal	Status	—	—	10	Self
TM18	Rain Dance	Water	Status	—	—	5	Both Sides
TM21	Frustration	Normal	Physical	—	100	20	Normal
TM26	Earthquake	Ground	Physical	100	100	10	Adjacent
TM27	Return	Normal	Physical	—	100	20	Normal
TM28	Dig	Ground	Physical	80	100	10	Normal
TM31	Brick Break	Fighting	Physical	75	100	15	Normal
TM32	Double Team	Normal	Status	—	—	15	Self
TM35	Flamethrower	Fire	Special	90	100	15	Normal
TM37	Sandstorm	Rock	Status	—	—	10	Both Sides
TM38	Fire Blast	Fire	Special	110	85	5	Normal
TM39	Rock Tomb	Rock	Physical	60	95	15	Normal
TM40	Aerial Ace	Flying	Physical	60	—	20	Normal
TM42	Facade	Normal	Physical	70	100	20	Normal
TM44	Rest	Psychic	Status	—	—	10	Self
TM45	Attract	Normal	Status	—	100	15	Normal
TM48	Round	Normal	Special	60	100	15	Normal
TM54	False Swipe	Normal	Physical	40	100	40	Normal
TM56	Fling	Dark	Physical	—	100	10	Normal
TM59	Incinerate	Fire	Special	60	100	15	Many Others
TM65	Shadow Claw	Ghost	Physical	70	100	15	Normal
TM68	Giga Impact	Normal	Physical	150	90	5	Normal
TM71	Stone Edge	Rock	Physical	100	80	5	Normal
TM75	Swords Dance	Normal	Status	—	—	20	Self
TM78	Bulldoze	Ground	Physical	60	100	20	Adjacent
TM80	Rock Slide	Rock	Physical	75	90	10	Many Others
TM82	Dragon Tail	Dragon	Physical	60	90	10	Normal
TM84	Poison Jab	Poison	Physical	80	100	20	Normal
TM87	Swagger	Normal	Status	—	90	15	Normal
TM88	Sleep Talk	Normal	Status	—	—	10	Self
TM90	Substitute	Normal	Status	—	—	10	Self
TM94	Rock Smash	Fighting	Physical	40	100	15	Normal
TM100	Confide	Normal	Status	—	—	20	Normal
HM01	Cut	Normal	Physical	50	95	30	Normal
HM03	Surf	Water	Special	90	100	15	Normal
HM04	Strength	Normal	Physical	80	100	15	Normal

MOVES TAUGHT BY PEOPLE
Name	Type	Kind	Pow.	Acc.	PP	Range
Draco Meteor	Dragon	Special	130	90	5	Normal

438

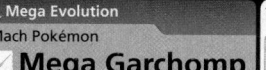

Mega Evolution

Mach Pokémon

☑ **Mega Garchomp**

TYPE **Dragon** **Ground**

ABILITY
Sand Force

STAT GROWTH RATES

HP	▪▪▪▪
Attack	▪▪▪▪▪▪▪▪▪
Defense	▪▪▪▪▪
Sp. Atk	▪▪▪▪▪▪
Sp. Def	▪▪▪▪
Speed	▪▪▪▪▪

MEGA STONE REQUIRED

Garchompite

Obtain on Victory Road between 8 P.M. and 8:59 P.M., after entering the Hall of Fame and speaking with Professor Sycamore in Anistar City.

HEIGHT: 6'03" WEIGHT: 209.4 lbs. GENDER: ♂/♀

Damage taken in normal battles	
Normal	×1
Fire	×0.5
Water	×1
Grass	×1
Electric	×0
Ice	×4
Fighting	×1
Poison	×0.5
Ground	×1
Flying	×1
Psychic	×1
Bug	×1
Rock	×0.5
Ghost	×1
Dragon	×2
Dark	×1
Steel	×1
Fairy	×2

Damage taken in Inverse Battles	
Normal	×1
Fire	×2
Water	×1
Grass	×1
Electric	×4
Ice	×0.25
Fighting	×1
Poison	×2
Ground	×1
Flying	×1
Psychic	×1
Bug	×1
Rock	×2
Ghost	×1
Dragon	×0.5
Dark	×1
Steel	×1
Fairy	×0.5

Can be used in
Inverse Battle
—
Battle Chateau
Battle Institute
Battle Maison
Random Matchup

Same form for ♂/♀

Mountain Kalos 009
Rock Pokémon
☑ Geodude

HEIGHT: 1'04" WEIGHT: 44.1 lbs.
GENDER: ♂/♀

X Found in fields and mountains. Mistaking them for boulders, people often step or trip on them.

Y It is impossible to distinguish from rocks. It slams against others in contests of hardness.

TYPE: Rock · Ground

ABILITIES
Rock Head
Sturdy

HIDDEN ABILITY
Sand Veil

STAT GROWTH RATES
HP	▪▪
Attack	▪▪▪▪
Defense	▪▪▪▪
Sp. Atk	▪
Sp. Def	▪
Speed	▪

EGG GROUP
Mineral

EVOLUTION

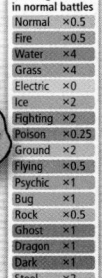

Lv. 25 — Link Trade

Geodude → Graveler → Golem

ITEMS SOMETIMES HELD BY WILD POKÉMON
Everstone

Damage taken in normal battles		Damage taken in Inverse Battles	
Normal	×0.5	Normal	×2
Fire	×0.5	Fire	×2
Water	×4	Water	×0.25
Grass	×4	Grass	×0.25
Electric	×0	Electric	×2
Ice	×2	Ice	×0.5
Fighting	×2	Fighting	×0.5
Poison	×0.25	Poison	×4
Ground	×2	Ground	×0.5
Flying	×0.5	Flying	×2
Psychic	×1	Psychic	×1
Bug	×1	Bug	×1
Rock	×0.5	Rock	×2
Ghost	×1	Ghost	×1
Dragon	×1	Dragon	×1
Dark	×1	Dark	×1
Steel	×2	Steel	×0.5
Fairy	×1	Fairy	×1

Can be used in	
Inverse Battle	Battle Institute
—	Battle Maison
Battle Chateau	Random Matchup

Same form for ♂/♀

How to obtain for your Mountain Kalos Pokédex

❶ Catch in a Horde Encounter on Route 18.
❷ Catch in a Horde Encounter in Terminus Cave.

❶ Catch in a Horde Encounter on Route 18.
❷ Catch in a Horde Encounter in Terminus Cave.

009 Geodude

● LEVEL-UP MOVES

Lv.	Name	Type	Kind	Pow.	Acc.	PP	Range
1	Tackle	Normal	Physical	50	100	35	Normal
1	Defense Curl	Normal	Status	—	—	40	Self
4	Mud Sport	Ground	Status	—	—	15	Both Sides
8	Rock Polish	Rock	Status	—	—	20	Self
11	Rollout	Rock	Physical	30	90	20	Normal
15	Magnitude	Ground	Physical	—	100	30	Adjacent
18	Rock Throw	Rock	Physical	50	90	15	Normal
22	Rock Blast	Rock	Physical	25	90	10	Normal
25	Smack Down	Rock	Physical	50	100	15	Normal
29	Self-Destruct	Normal	Physical	200	100	5	Adjacent
32	Bulldoze	Ground	Physical	60	100	20	Adjacent
36	Stealth Rock	Rock	Status	—	—	20	Other Side
39	Earthquake	Ground	Physical	100	100	10	Adjacent
43	Explosion	Normal	Physical	250	100	5	Adjacent
46	Double-Edge	Normal	Physical	120	100	15	Normal
50	Stone Edge	Rock	Physical	100	80	5	Normal

● TM & HM MOVES

No.	Name	Type	Kind	Pow.	Acc.	PP	Range
TM06	Toxic	Poison	Status	—	90	10	Normal
TM10	Hidden Power	Normal	Special	60	100	15	Normal
TM11	Sunny Day	Fire	Status	—	—	5	Both Sides
TM17	Protect	Normal	Status	—	—	10	Self
TM21	Frustration	Normal	Physical	—	100	20	Normal
TM23	Smack Down	Rock	Physical	50	100	15	Normal
TM26	Earthquake	Ground	Physical	100	100	10	Adjacent
TM27	Return	Normal	Physical	—	100	20	Normal
TM28	Dig	Ground	Physical	80	100	10	Normal
TM31	Brick Break	Fighting	Physical	75	100	15	Normal
TM32	Double Team	Normal	Status	—	—	15	Self
TM35	Flamethrower	Fire	Special	90	100	15	Normal
TM37	Sandstorm	Rock	Status	—	—	10	Both Sides
TM38	Fire Blast	Fire	Special	110	85	5	Normal
TM39	Rock Tomb	Rock	Physical	60	95	15	Normal
TM42	Facade	Normal	Physical	70	100	20	Normal
TM44	Rest	Psychic	Status	—	—	10	Self
TM45	Attract	Normal	Status	—	100	15	Normal
TM48	Round	Normal	Special	60	100	15	Normal
TM56	Fling	Dark	Physical	—	100	10	Normal
TM59	Incinerate	Fire	Special	60	100	15	Normal
TM64	Explosion	Normal	Physical	250	100	5	Adjacent
TM69	Rock Polish	Rock	Status	—	—	20	Self
TM71	Stone Edge	Rock	Physical	100	80	5	Normal
TM74	Gyro Ball	Steel	Physical	—	100	5	Normal
TM78	Bulldoze	Ground	Physical	60	100	20	Adjacent
TM80	Rock Slide	Rock	Physical	75	90	10	Many Others
TM87	Swagger	Normal	Status	—	90	15	Normal
TM88	Sleep Talk	Normal	Status	—	—	10	Self
TM90	Substitute	Normal	Status	—	—	10	Self
TM94	Rock Smash	Fighting	Physical	40	100	15	Normal
TM96	Nature Power	Normal	Status	—	—	20	Normal
TM98	Power-Up Punch	Fighting	Physical	40	100	20	Normal

No.	Name	Type	Kind	Pow.	Acc.	PP	Range
TM100	Confide	Normal	Status	—	—	20	Normal
HM04	Strength	Normal	Physical	80	100	15	Normal

● MOVES TAUGHT BY PEOPLE

Name	Type	Kind	Pow.	Acc.	PP	Range

● EGG MOVES

Name	Type	Kind	Pow.	Acc.	PP	Range
Mega Punch	Normal	Physical	80	85	20	Normal
Block	Normal	Status	—	—	5	Normal
Hammer Arm	Fighting	Physical	100	90	10	Normal
Flail	Normal	Physical	—	100	15	Normal
Curse	Ghost	Status	—	—	10	Varies
Focus Punch	Fighting	Physical	150	100	20	Normal
Rock Climb	Normal	Physical	90	85	20	Normal
Endure	Normal	Status	—	—	10	Self
Autotomize	Steel	Status	—	—	15	Self
Wide Guard	Rock	Status	—	—	10	Your Side

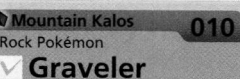

Mountain Kalos 010

Rock Pokémon

☑ Graveler

HEIGHT: 3'03"   WEIGHT: 231.5 lbs.
GENDER: ♂/♀

X With a free and uncaring nature, it doesn't mind if pieces break off while it rolls down mountains.

Y Rolls down slopes to move. It rolls over any obstacle without slowing or changing its direction.

TYPE Rock | Ground

ABILITIES
Rock Head
Sturdy

HIDDEN ABILITY
Sand Veil

STAT GROWTH RATES

HP	■■
Attack	■■■■■
Defense	■■■■■
Sp. Atk	■■
Sp. Def	■■
Speed	■■

EGG GROUP
Mineral

⬆ EVOLUTION

Geodude   Graveler   Golem

Lv. 25   Link Trade

ITEMS SOMETIMES HELD BY WILD POKÉMON
Everstone

Damage taken in normal battles		Damage taken in Inverse Battles	
Normal	×0.5	Normal	×2
Fire	×0.5	Fire	×2
Water	×4	Water	×0.25
Grass	×4	Grass	×0.25
Electric	×0	Electric	×2
Ice	×2	Ice	×0.5
Fighting	×2	Fighting	×0.5
Poison	×0.25	Poison	×4
Ground	×2	Ground	×0.5
Flying	×0.5	Flying	×2
Psychic	×1	Psychic	×1
Bug	×1	Bug	×1
Rock	×0.5	Rock	×2
Ghost	×1	Ghost	×1
Dragon	×1	Dragon	×1
Dark	×1	Dark	×1
Steel	×2	Steel	×0.5
Fairy	×1	Fairy	×1

Can be used in

Inverse Battle	Battle Institute
—	Battle Maison
Battle Chateau	Random Matchup

Same form for ♂/♀

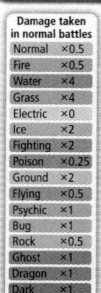

How to obtain for your Mountain Kalos Pokédex

❶ Catch after it appears from a cracked rock on Route 13 or Route 18 (using Rock Smash).

❷ Level up Geodude to Lv. 25.

❶ Catch after it appears from a cracked rock on Route 13 or Route 18 (using Rock Smash).

❷ Level up Geodude to Lv. 25.

● LEVEL-UP MOVES

Lv.	Name	Type	Kind	Pow.	Acc.	PP	Range
1	Tackle	Normal	Physical	50	100	35	Normal
1	Defense Curl	Normal	Status	—	—	40	Self
1	Mud Sport	Ground	Status	—	—	15	Both Sides
1	Rock Polish	Rock	Status	—	—	20	Self
4	Mud Sport	Ground	Status	—	—	15	Both Sides
8	Rock Polish	Rock	Status	—	—	20	Self
11	Rollout	Rock	Physical	30	90	20	Normal
15	Magnitude	Ground	Physical	—	100	30	Adjacent
18	Rock Throw	Rock	Physical	50	90	15	Normal
22	Rock Blast	Rock	Physical	25	90	10	Normal
27	Smack Down	Rock	Physical	50	100	15	Normal
31	Self-Destruct	Normal	Physical	200	100	5	Adjacent
36	Bulldoze	Ground	Physical	60	100	20	Adjacent
42	Stealth Rock	Rock	Status	—	—	20	Other Side
47	Earthquake	Ground	Physical	100	100	10	Adjacent
53	Explosion	Normal	Physical	250	100	5	Adjacent
58	Double-Edge	Normal	Physical	120	100	15	Normal
64	Stone Edge	Rock	Physical	100	80	5	Normal

● TM & HM MOVES

No.	Name	Type	Kind	Pow.	Acc.	PP	Range
TM06	Toxic	Poison	Status	—	90	10	Normal
TM10	Hidden Power	Normal	Special	60	100	15	Normal
TM11	Sunny Day	Fire	Status	—	—	5	Both Sides
TM17	Protect	Normal	Status	—	—	10	Self
TM21	Frustration	Normal	Physical	—	100	20	Normal
TM23	Smack Down	Rock	Physical	50	100	15	Normal
TM26	Earthquake	Ground	Physical	100	100	10	Adjacent
TM27	Return	Normal	Physical	—	100	20	Normal
TM28	Dig	Ground	Physical	80	100	10	Normal
TM31	Brick Break	Fighting	Physical	75	100	15	Normal
TM32	Double Team	Normal	Status	—	—	15	Self
TM35	Flamethrower	Fire	Special	90	100	15	Normal
TM37	Sandstorm	Rock	Status	—	—	10	Both Sides
TM38	Fire Blast	Fire	Special	110	85	5	Normal
TM39	Rock Tomb	Rock	Physical	60	95	15	Normal
TM42	Facade	Normal	Physical	70	100	20	Normal
TM44	Rest	Psychic	Status	—	—	10	Self
TM45	Attract	Normal	Status	—	100	15	Normal
TM48	Round	Normal	Special	60	100	15	Normal
TM56	Fling	Dark	Physical	—	100	10	Normal
TM59	Incinerate	Fire	Special	60	100	15	Many Others
TM64	Explosion	Normal	Physical	250	100	5	Adjacent
TM69	Rock Polish	Rock	Status	—	—	20	Self
TM71	Stone Edge	Rock	Physical	100	80	5	Normal
TM74	Gyro Ball	Steel	Physical	—	100	5	Normal
TM78	Bulldoze	Ground	Physical	60	100	20	Adjacent
TM80	Rock Slide	Rock	Physical	75	90	10	Many Others
TM87	Swagger	Normal	Status	—	90	15	Normal
TM88	Sleep Talk	Normal	Status	—	—	10	Self
TM90	Substitute	Normal	Status	—	—	10	Self
TM94	Rock Smash	Fighting	Physical	40	100	15	Normal
TM96	Nature Power	Normal	Status	—	—	20	Normal
TM98	Power-Up Punch	Fighting	Physical	40	100	20	Normal

No.	Name	Type	Kind	Pow.	Acc.	PP	Range
TM100	Confide	Normal	Status	—	—	20	Normal
HM04	Strength	Normal	Physical	80	100	15	Normal

● MOVES TAUGHT BY PEOPLE

Name	Type	Kind	Pow.	Acc.	PP	Range

Mountain Kalos 011

Megaton Pokémon

✓ Golem

HEIGHT: 4'07"　WEIGHT: 661.4 lbs.
GENDER: ♂/♀

X It tumbles down mountains, leaving grooves from peak to base. Stay clear of these grooves.

Y Even dynamite can't harm its hard, boulder-like body. It sheds its hide just once a year.

TYPE: Rock　Ground

ABILITIES
Rock Head
Sturdy

HIDDEN ABILITY
Sand Veil

STAT GROWTH RATES
HP	■■■
Attack	■■■■■
Defense	■■■■■■
Sp. Atk	■■■
Sp. Def	■■■
Speed	■■■

EGG GROUP
Mineral

EVOLUTION

Lv. 25 — Geodude → Graveler — Link Trade → Golem

ITEMS SOMETIMES HELD BY WILD POKÉMON
None

Damage taken in normal battles
Normal	×0.5
Fire	×0.5
Water	×4
Grass	×4
Electric	×0
Ice	×2
Fighting	×2
Poison	×0.25
Ground	×2
Flying	×0.5
Psychic	×1
Bug	×1
Rock	×0.5
Ghost	×1
Dragon	×1
Dark	×1
Steel	×2
Fairy	×1

Damage taken in Inverse Battles
Normal	×2
Fire	×2
Water	×0.25
Grass	×0.25
Electric	×2
Ice	×0.5
Fighting	×0.5
Poison	×4
Ground	×0.5
Flying	×2
Psychic	×1
Bug	×1
Rock	×2
Ghost	×1
Dragon	×1
Dark	×1
Steel	×0.5
Fairy	×1

Can be used in
Inverse Battle	Battle Institute
—	Battle Maison
Battle Chateau	Random Matchup

Same form for ♂/♀

How to obtain for your Mountain Kalos Pokédex

Receive Graveler by Link Trade, and have it evolve. (X)

Receive Graveler by Link Trade, and have it evolve. (Y)

011

Golem

● LEVEL-UP MOVES

Lv.	Name	Type	Kind	Pow.	Acc.	PP	Range
1	Heavy Slam	Steel	Physical	—	100	10	Normal
1	Tackle	Normal	Physical	50	100	35	Normal
1	Defense Curl	Normal	Status	—	—	40	Self
1	Mud Sport	Ground	Status	—	—	15	Both Sides
1	Rock Polish	Rock	Status	—	—	20	Self
4	Mud Sport	Ground	Status	—	—	15	Both Sides
8	Rock Polish	Rock	Status	—	—	20	Self
11	Steamroller	Bug	Physical	65	100	20	Normal
15	Magnitude	Ground	Physical	—	100	30	Adjacent
18	Rock Throw	Rock	Physical	50	90	15	Normal
22	Rock Blast	Rock	Physical	25	90	10	Normal
27	Smack Down	Rock	Physical	50	100	15	Normal
31	Self-Destruct	Normal	Physical	200	100	5	Adjacent
36	Bulldoze	Ground	Physical	60	100	20	Adjacent
42	Stealth Rock	Rock	Status	—	—	20	Other Side
47	Earthquake	Ground	Physical	100	100	10	Adjacent
53	Explosion	Normal	Physical	250	100	5	Adjacent
58	Double-Edge	Normal	Physical	120	100	15	Normal
64	Stone Edge	Rock	Physical	100	80	5	Normal
69	Heavy Slam	Steel	Physical	—	100	10	Normal

● TM & HM MOVES

No.	Name	Type	Kind	Pow.	Acc.	PP	Range
TM05	Roar	Normal	Status	—	—	20	Normal
TM06	Toxic	Poison	Status	—	90	10	Normal
TM10	Hidden Power	Normal	Special	60	100	15	Normal
TM11	Sunny Day	Fire	Status	—	—	5	Both Sides
TM15	Hyper Beam	Normal	Special	150	90	5	Normal
TM17	Protect	Normal	Status	—	—	10	Self
TM21	Frustration	Normal	Physical	—	100	20	Normal
TM23	Smack Down	Rock	Physical	50	100	15	Normal
TM26	Earthquake	Ground	Physical	100	100	10	Adjacent
TM27	Return	Normal	Physical	—	100	20	Normal
TM28	Dig	Ground	Physical	80	100	10	Normal
TM31	Brick Break	Fighting	Physical	75	100	15	Normal
TM32	Double Team	Normal	Status	—	—	15	Self
TM35	Flamethrower	Fire	Special	90	100	15	Normal
TM37	Sandstorm	Rock	Status	—	—	10	Both Sides
TM38	Fire Blast	Fire	Special	110	85	5	Normal
TM39	Rock Tomb	Rock	Physical	60	95	15	Normal
TM42	Facade	Normal	Physical	70	100	20	Normal
TM44	Rest	Psychic	Status	—	—	10	Self
TM45	Attract	Normal	Status	—	100	15	Normal
TM48	Round	Normal	Special	60	100	15	Normal
TM52	Focus Blast	Fighting	Special	120	70	5	Normal
TM56	Fling	Dark	Physical	—	100	10	Normal
TM59	Incinerate	Fire	Special	60	100	15	Many Others
TM64	Explosion	Normal	Physical	250	100	5	Adjacent
TM68	Giga Impact	Normal	Physical	150	90	5	Normal
TM69	Rock Polish	Rock	Status	—	—	20	Self
TM71	Stone Edge	Rock	Physical	100	80	5	Normal
TM74	Gyro Ball	Steel	Physical	—	100	5	Normal
TM78	Bulldoze	Ground	Physical	60	100	20	Adjacent
TM80	Rock Slide	Rock	Physical	75	90	10	Many Others
TM87	Swagger	Normal	Status	—	90	15	Normal
TM88	Sleep Talk	Normal	Status	—	—	10	Self

No.	Name	Type	Kind	Pow.	Acc.	PP	Range
TM90	Substitute	Normal	Status	—	—	10	Self
TM94	Rock Smash	Fighting	Physical	40	100	15	Normal
TM96	Nature Power	Normal	Status	—	—	20	Normal
TM98	Power-Up Punch	Fighting	Physical	40	100	20	Normal
TM100	Confide	Normal	Status	—	—	20	Normal
HM04	Strength	Normal	Physical	80	100	15	Normal

● MOVES TAUGHT BY PEOPLE

Name	Type	Kind	Pow.	Acc.	PP	Range

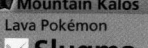
Lava Pokémon

☑ Slugma

012

HEIGHT: 2'04"   WEIGHT: 77.2 lbs.
GENDER: ♂/♀

X A common sight in volcanic areas, it slowly slithers around in a constant search for warm places.

Y Its body is made of magma. If it doesn't keep moving, its body will cool and harden.

TYPE	Fire

ABILITIES
Magma Armor
Flame Body

HIDDEN ABILITY
Weak Armor

STAT GROWTH RATES
HP	■ ■
Attack	■ ■
Defense	■ ■
Sp. Atk	■ ■ ■
Sp. Def	■ ■
Speed	■

EGG GROUP
Amorphous

⬆ EVOLUTION

Slugma — Lv. 38 → Magcargo

ITEMS SOMETIMES HELD BY WILD POKÉMON
None

Damage taken in normal battles		Damage taken in Inverse Battles	
Normal	×1	Normal	×1
Fire	×0.5	Fire	×2
Water	×2	Water	×0.5
Grass	×0.5	Grass	×2
Electric	×1	Electric	×1
Ice	×0.5	Ice	×2
Fighting	×1	Fighting	×1
Poison	×1	Poison	×1
Ground	×2	Ground	×0.5
Flying	×1	Flying	×1
Psychic	×1	Psychic	×1
Bug	×0.5	Bug	×2
Rock	×2	Rock	×0.5
Ghost	×1	Ghost	×1
Dragon	×1	Dragon	×1
Dark	×1	Dark	×1
Steel	×0.5	Steel	×2
Fairy	×0.5	Fairy	×2

Can be used in	
Inverse Battle	Battle Institute
—	Battle Maison
Battle Chateau	Random Matchup

Same form for ♂/♀

How to obtain for your Mountain Kalos Pokédex

Catch after it appears from a cracked rock on Route 13 (using Rock Smash).

Catch after it appears from a cracked rock on Route 13 (using Rock Smash).

● LEVEL-UP MOVES

Lv.	Name	Type	Kind	Pow.	Acc.	PP	Range
1	Yawn	Normal	Status	—	—	10	Normal
1	Smog	Poison	Special	30	70	20	Normal
5	Ember	Fire	Special	40	100	25	Normal
10	Rock Throw	Rock	Physical	50	90	15	Normal
14	Harden	Normal	Status	—	—	30	Self
19	Recover	Normal	Status	—	—	10	Self
23	Flame Burst	Fire	Special	70	100	15	Normal
28	Ancient Power	Rock	Special	60	100	5	Normal
32	Amnesia	Psychic	Status	—	—	20	Self
37	Lava Plume	Fire	Special	80	100	15	Adjacent
41	Rock Slide	Rock	Physical	75	90	10	Many Others
46	Body Slam	Normal	Physical	85	100	15	Normal
50	Flamethrower	Fire	Special	90	100	15	Normal
55	Earth Power	Ground	Special	90	100	10	Normal

● TM & HM MOVES

No.	Name	Type	Kind	Pow.	Acc.	PP	Range
TM06	Toxic	Poison	Status	—	90	10	Normal
TM10	Hidden Power	Normal	Special	60	100	15	Normal
TM11	Sunny Day	Fire	Status	—	—	5	Both Sides
TM16	Light Screen	Psychic	Status	—	—	30	Your Side
TM17	Protect	Normal	Status	—	—	10	Self
TM21	Frustration	Normal	Physical	—	100	20	Normal
TM27	Return	Normal	Physical	—	100	20	Normal
TM32	Double Team	Normal	Status	—	—	15	Self
TM33	Reflect	Psychic	Status	—	—	20	Your Side
TM35	Flamethrower	Fire	Special	90	100	15	Normal
TM38	Fire Blast	Fire	Special	110	85	5	Normal
TM39	Rock Tomb	Rock	Physical	60	95	15	Normal
TM42	Facade	Normal	Physical	70	100	20	Normal
TM43	Flame Charge	Fire	Physical	50	100	20	Normal
TM44	Rest	Psychic	Status	—	—	10	Self
TM45	Attract	Normal	Status	—	100	15	Normal
TM48	Round	Normal	Special	60	100	15	Normal
TM50	Overheat	Fire	Special	130	90	5	Normal
TM59	Incinerate	Fire	Special	60	100	15	Many Others
TM61	Will-O-Wisp	Fire	Status	—	85	15	Normal
TM80	Rock Slide	Rock	Physical	75	90	10	Many Others
TM83	Infestation	Bug	Special	20	100	20	Normal
TM87	Swagger	Normal	Status	—	90	15	Normal
TM88	Sleep Talk	Normal	Status	—	—	10	Self
TM90	Substitute	Normal	Status	—	—	10	Self
TM94	Rock Smash	Fighting	Physical	40	100	15	Normal
TM96	Nature Power	Normal	Status	—	—	20	Normal
TM100	Confide	Normal	Status	—	—	20	Normal

● MOVES TAUGHT BY PEOPLE

Name	Type	Kind	Pow.	Acc.	PP	Range

● EGG MOVES

Name	Type	Kind	Pow.	Acc.	PP	Range
Acid Armor	Poison	Status	—	—	20	Self
Heat Wave	Fire	Special	95	90	10	Many Others
Curse	Ghost	Status	—	—	10	Varies
Smokescreen	Normal	Status	—	100	20	Normal
Memento	Dark	Status	—	100	10	Normal
Stockpile	Normal	Status	—	—	20	Self
Spit Up	Normal	Special	—	100	10	Normal
Swallow	Normal	Status	—	—	10	Self
Rollout	Rock	Physical	30	90	20	Normal
Inferno	Fire	Special	100	50	5	Normal
Earth Power	Ground	Special	90	100	10	Normal
Guard Swap	Psychic	Status	—	—	10	Normal

AFTER THE HALL OF FAME

CENTRAL KALOS

COASTAL KALOS

MOUNTAIN KALOS

012 | Slugma

ADVENTURE DATA

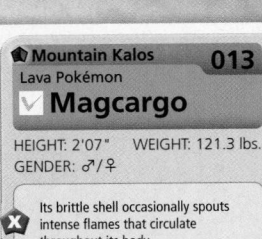

🏔 Mountain Kalos — 013

Lava Pokémon

☑ Magcargo

HEIGHT: 2'07" WEIGHT: 121.3 lbs.
GENDER: ♂/♀

TYPE	Fire	Rock

ABILITIES
Magma Armor
Flame Body

HIDDEN ABILITY
Weak Armor

STAT GROWTH RATES

HP	▪▪
Attack	▪▪▪
Defense	▪▪▪▪▪
Sp. Atk	▪▪▪▪
Sp. Def	▪▪▪
Speed	▪▪

EGG GROUP
Amorphous

X Its brittle shell occasionally spouts intense flames that circulate throughout its body.

Y Its body is as hot as lava and is always billowing. Flames will occasionally burst from its shell.

⚡ EVOLUTION

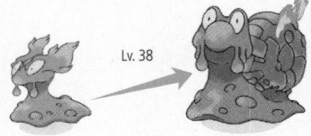

Slugma → Lv. 38 → Magcargo

ITEMS SOMETIMES HELD BY WILD POKÉMON
None

Damage taken in normal battles	
Normal	×0.5
Fire	×0.25
Water	×4
Grass	×1
Electric	×1
Ice	×0.5
Fighting	×2
Poison	×0.5
Ground	×4
Flying	×0.5
Psychic	×1
Bug	×1
Rock	×2
Ghost	×1
Dragon	×1
Dark	×1
Steel	×1
Fairy	×0.5

Damage taken in Inverse Battles	
Normal	×2
Fire	×4
Water	×0.25
Grass	×1
Electric	×1
Ice	×2
Fighting	×0.5
Poison	×2
Ground	×0.25
Flying	×2
Psychic	×1
Bug	×2
Rock	×0.5
Ghost	×1
Dragon	×1
Dark	×1
Steel	×1
Fairy	×2

Can be used in	
Inverse Battle	Battle Institute
—	Battle Maison
Battle Chateau	Random Matchup

Same form for ♂/♀

How to obtain for your Mountain Kalos Pokédex

X Level up Slugma to Lv. 38.

Y Level up Slugma to Lv. 38.

● LEVEL-UP MOVES

Lv.	Name	Type	Kind	Pow.	Acc.	PP	Range
1	Earth Power	Ground	Special	90	100	10	Normal
1	Yawn	Normal	Status	—	—	10	Normal
1	Smog	Poison	Special	30	70	20	Normal
1	Ember	Fire	Special	40	100	25	Normal
1	Rock Throw	Rock	Physical	50	90	15	Normal
5	Ember	Fire	Special	40	100	25	Normal
10	Rock Throw	Rock	Physical	50	90	15	Normal
14	Harden	Normal	Status	—	—	30	Self
19	Recover	Normal	Status	—	—	10	Self
23	Flame Burst	Fire	Special	70	100	15	Normal
28	Ancient Power	Rock	Special	60	100	5	Normal
32	Amnesia	Psychic	Status	—	—	20	Self
37	Lava Plume	Fire	Special	80	100	15	Adjacent
38	Shell Smash	Normal	Status	—	—	15	Self
44	Rock Slide	Rock	Physical	75	90	10	Many Others
52	Body Slam	Normal	Physical	85	100	15	Normal
59	Flamethrower	Fire	Special	90	100	15	Normal
67	Earth Power	Ground	Special	90	100	10	Normal

● TM & HM MOVES

No.	Name	Type	Kind	Pow.	Acc.	PP	Range
TM06	Toxic	Poison	Status	—	90	10	Normal
TM10	Hidden Power	Normal	Special	60	100	15	Normal
TM11	Sunny Day	Fire	Status	—	—	5	Both Sides
TM15	Hyper Beam	Normal	Special	150	90	5	Normal
TM16	Light Screen	Psychic	Status	—	—	30	Your Side
TM17	Protect	Normal	Status	—	—	10	Self
TM21	Frustration	Normal	Physical	—	100	20	Normal
TM22	Solar Beam	Grass	Special	120	100	10	Normal
TM23	Smack Down	Rock	Physical	50	100	15	Normal
TM26	Earthquake	Ground	Physical	100	100	10	Adjacent
TM27	Return	Normal	Physical	—	100	20	Normal
TM32	Double Team	Normal	Status	—	—	15	Self
TM33	Reflect	Psychic	Status	—	—	20	Your Side
TM35	Flamethrower	Fire	Special	90	100	15	Normal
TM37	Sandstorm	Rock	Status	—	—	10	Both Sides
TM38	Fire Blast	Fire	Special	110	85	5	Normal
TM39	Rock Tomb	Rock	Physical	60	95	15	Normal
TM42	Facade	Normal	Physical	70	100	20	Normal
TM43	Flame Charge	Fire	Physical	50	100	20	Normal
TM44	Rest	Psychic	Status	—	—	10	Self
TM45	Attract	Normal	Status	—	100	15	Normal
TM48	Round	Normal	Special	60	100	15	Normal
TM50	Overheat	Fire	Special	130	90	5	Normal
TM59	Incinerate	Fire	Special	60	100	15	Many Others
TM61	Will-O-Wisp	Fire	Status	—	85	15	Normal
TM64	Explosion	Normal	Physical	250	100	5	Adjacent
TM68	Giga Impact	Normal	Physical	150	90	5	Normal
TM69	Rock Polish	Rock	Status	—	—	20	Self
TM71	Stone Edge	Rock	Physical	100	80	5	Normal
TM74	Gyro Ball	Steel	Physical	—	100	5	Normal
TM78	Bulldoze	Ground	Physical	60	100	20	Adjacent
TM80	Rock Slide	Rock	Physical	75	90	10	Many Others
TM85	Infestation	Bug	Special	20	100	20	Normal

No.	Name	Type	Kind	Pow.	Acc.	PP	Range
TM87	Swagger	Normal	Status	—	90	15	Normal
TM88	Sleep Talk	Normal	Status	—	—	10	Self
TM90	Substitute	Normal	Status	—	—	10	Self
TM94	Rock Smash	Fighting	Physical	40	100	15	Normal
TM96	Nature Power	Normal	Status	—	—	20	Normal
TM100	Confide	Normal	Status	—	—	20	Normal
HM04	Strength	Normal	Physical	80	100	15	Normal

● MOVES TAUGHT BY PEOPLE

Name	Type	Kind	Pow.	Acc.	PP	Range

AFTER THE HALL OF FAME
CENTRAL KALOS
COASTAL KALOS
MOUNTAIN KALOS
013 Magcargo
ADVENTURE DATA

Mold Pokémon
014

☑ **Shuckle**

HEIGHT: 2'00"   WEIGHT: 45.2 lbs.
GENDER: ♂/♀

TYPE	Bug	Rock

ABILITIES
Sturdy
Gluttony

HIDDEN ABILITY
Contrary

STAT GROWTH RATES
HP	▮
Attack	▮
Defense	▮▮▮▮▮▮▮▮▮
Sp. Atk	▮
Sp. Def	▮▮▮▮▮▮▮▮▮
Speed	▮

EGG GROUP
Bug

EVOLUTION
Does not evolve

ITEMS SOMETIMES HELD BY WILD POKÉMON
Berry Juice

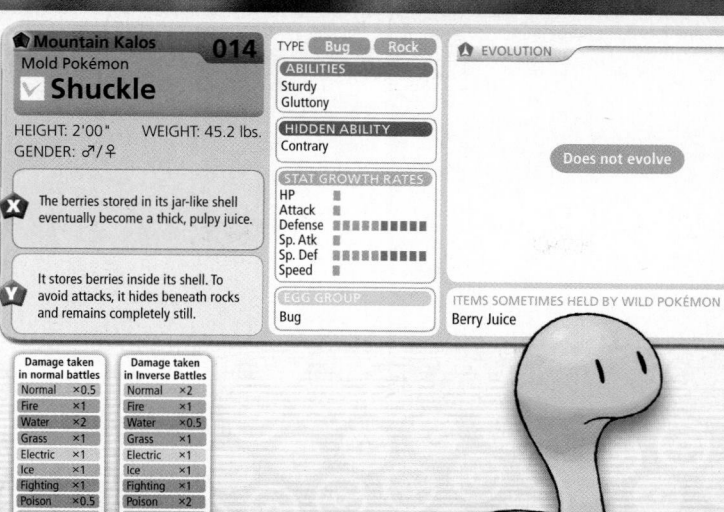

Ⓧ The berries stored in its jar-like shell eventually become a thick, pulpy juice.

Ⓨ It stores berries inside its shell. To avoid attacks, it hides beneath rocks and remains completely still.

Damage taken in normal battles	
Normal	×0.5
Fire	×1
Water	×2
Grass	×1
Electric	×1
Ice	×1
Fighting	×1
Poison	×0.5
Ground	×1
Flying	×1
Psychic	×1
Bug	×1
Rock	×2
Ghost	×1
Dragon	×1
Dark	×1
Steel	×2
Fairy	×1

Damage taken in Inverse Battles	
Normal	×2
Fire	×1
Water	×0.5
Grass	×1
Electric	×1
Ice	×1
Fighting	×1
Poison	×2
Ground	×1
Flying	×1
Psychic	×1
Bug	×1
Rock	×0.5
Ghost	×1
Dragon	×1
Dark	×1
Steel	×0.5
Fairy	×1

Can be used in	
Inverse Battle	Battle Institute
—	Battle Maison
Battle Chateau	Random Matchup

Same form for ♂/♀

How to obtain for your Mountain Kalos Pokédex

❶ Catch after it appears from a cracked rock on Route 18 (using Rock Smash).
❷ Catch after it appears from a cracked rock in Terminus Cave (using Rock Smash).

❶ Catch after it appears from a cracked rock on Route 18 (using Rock Smash).
❷ Catch after it appears from a cracked rock in Terminus Cave (using Rock Smash).

AFTER THE HALL OF FAME
CENTRAL KALOS
COASTAL KALOS
MOUNTAIN KALOS
014 ☑ Shuckle
ADVENTURE DATA

● **LEVEL-UP MOVES**

Lv.	Name	Type	Kind	Pow.	Acc.	PP	Range
1	Sticky Web	Bug	Status	—	—	20	Other Side
1	Withdraw	Water	Status	—	—	40	Self
1	Constrict	Normal	Physical	10	100	35	Normal
1	Bide	Normal	Physical	—	—	10	Self
1	Rollout	Rock	Physical	30	90	20	Normal
5	Encore	Normal	Status	—	100	5	Normal
9	Wrap	Normal	Physical	15	90	20	Normal
12	Struggle Bug	Bug	Special	50	100	20	Many Others
16	Safeguard	Normal	Status	—	—	25	Your Side
20	Rest	Psychic	Status	—	—	10	Self
23	Rock Throw	Rock	Physical	50	90	15	Normal
27	Gastro Acid	Poison	Status	—	100	10	Normal
31	Power Trick	Psychic	Status	—	—	10	Self
34	Shell Smash	Normal	Status	—	—	15	Self
38	Rock Slide	Rock	Physical	75	90	10	Many Others
42	Bug Bite	Bug	Physical	60	100	20	Normal
45	Power Split	Psychic	Status	—	—	10	Normal
45	Guard Split	Psychic	Status	—	—	10	Normal
49	Stone Edge	Rock	Physical	100	80	5	Normal
53	Sticky Web	Bug	Status	—	—	20	Other Side

● **TM & HM MOVES**

No.	Name	Type	Kind	Pow.	Acc.	PP	Range
TM06	Toxic	Poison	Status	—	90	10	Normal
TM09	Venoshock	Poison	Special	65	100	10	Normal
TM10	Hidden Power	Normal	Special	60	100	15	Normal
TM11	Sunny Day	Fire	Status	—	—	5	Both Sides
TM17	Protect	Normal	Status	—	—	10	Self
TM20	Safeguard	Normal	Status	—	—	25	Your Side
TM21	Frustration	Normal	Physical	—	100	20	Normal
TM23	Smack Down	Rock	Physical	50	100	15	Normal
TM26	Earthquake	Ground	Physical	100	100	10	Adjacent
TM27	Return	Normal	Physical	—	100	20	Normal
TM28	Dig	Ground	Physical	80	100	10	Normal
TM32	Double Team	Normal	Status	—	—	15	Self
TM34	Sludge Wave	Poison	Special	95	100	10	Adjacent
TM36	Sludge Bomb	Poison	Special	90	100	10	Normal
TM37	Sandstorm	Rock	Status	—	—	10	Both Sides
TM39	Rock Tomb	Rock	Physical	60	95	15	Normal
TM42	Facade	Normal	Physical	70	100	20	Normal
TM44	Rest	Psychic	Status	—	—	10	Self
TM45	Attract	Normal	Status	—	100	15	Normal
TM48	Round	Normal	Special	60	100	15	Normal
TM69	Rock Polish	Rock	Status	—	—	20	Self
TM70	Flash	Normal	Status	—	100	20	Normal
TM71	Stone Edge	Rock	Physical	100	80	5	Normal
TM74	Gyro Ball	Steel	Physical	—	100	5	Normal
TM76	Struggle Bug	Bug	Special	50	100	20	Many Others
TM78	Bulldoze	Ground	Physical	60	100	20	Adjacent
TM80	Rock Slide	Rock	Physical	75	90	10	Many Others
TM83	Infestation	Bug	Special	20	100	20	Normal
TM87	Swagger	Normal	Status	—	90	15	Normal
TM88	Sleep Talk	Normal	Status	—	—	10	Self
TM90	Substitute	Normal	Status	—	—	10	Self
TM94	Rock Smash	Fighting	Physical	40	100	15	Normal
TM100	Confide	Normal	Status	—	—	20	Normal

No.	Name	Type	Kind	Pow.	Acc.	PP	Range
HM04	Strength	Normal	Physical	80	100	15	Normal

● **MOVES TAUGHT BY PEOPLE**

Name	Type	Kind	Pow.	Acc.	PP	Range

● **EGG MOVES**

Name	Type	Kind	Pow.	Acc.	PP	Range
Sweet Scent	Normal	Status	—	100	20	Many Others
Knock Off	Dark	Physical	65	100	20	Normal
Helping Hand	Normal	Status	—	—	20	1 Ally
Acupressure	Normal	Status	—	—	30	Self/Ally
Sand Tomb	Ground	Physical	35	85	15	Normal
Mud-Slap	Ground	Special	20	100	10	Normal
Acid	Poison	Special	40	100	30	Many Others
Rock Blast	Rock	Physical	25	90	10	Normal
Final Gambit	Fighting	Special	—	100	5	Normal

Mountain Kalos 015
Scorpion Pokémon
Skorupi

HEIGHT: 2'07" WEIGHT: 26.5 lbs.
GENDER: ♂ / ♀

TYPE Poison | Bug

ABILITIES
Battle Armor
Sniper

HIDDEN ABILITY
Keen Eye

STAT GROWTH RATES
HP ■■
Attack ■■■
Defense ■■■■
Sp. Atk ■
Sp. Def ■■
Speed ■■■■

EGG GROUPS
Bug, Water 3

X It grips prey with its tail claws and injects poison. It tenaciously hangs on until the poison takes.

Y It burrows under the sand to lie in wait for prey. Its tail claws can inject its prey with a savage poison.

EVOLUTION

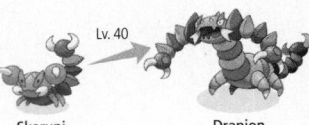

Skorupi — Lv. 40 → Drapion

ITEMS SOMETIMES HELD BY WILD POKÉMON
Poison Barb

Damage taken in normal battles	
Normal	×1
Fire	×2
Water	×1
Grass	×0.25
Electric	×1
Ice	×1
Fighting	×0.25
Poison	×0.5
Ground	×1
Flying	×2
Psychic	×2
Bug	×0.5
Rock	×2
Ghost	×1
Dragon	×1
Dark	×1
Steel	×1
Fairy	×0.5

Damage taken in Inverse Battles	
Normal	×1
Fire	×0.5
Water	×1
Grass	×4
Electric	×1
Ice	×1
Fighting	×4
Poison	×2
Ground	×1
Flying	×0.5
Psychic	×0.5
Bug	×2
Rock	×0.5
Ghost	×1
Dragon	×1
Dark	×1
Steel	×1
Fairy	×2

Can be used in	
Inverse Battle	Battle Institute
—	Battle Maison
Battle Chateau	Random Matchup

Same form for ♂ / ♀

How to obtain for your Mountain Kalos Pokédex

❶ Catch in the tall grass on Route 14.

❷ Catch in the tall grass on Route 15.

❶ Catch in the tall grass on Route 14.

❷ Catch in the tall grass on Route 15.

Skorupi 015

● LEVEL-UP MOVES

Lv.	Name	Type	Kind	Pow.	Acc.	PP	Range
1	Bite	Dark	Physical	60	100	25	Normal
1	Poison Sting	Poison	Physical	15	100	35	Normal
1	Leer	Normal	Status	—	100	30	Many Others
5	Knock Off	Dark	Physical	65	100	20	Normal
9	Pin Missile	Bug	Physical	25	95	20	Normal
13	Acupressure	Normal	Status	—	—	30	Self/Ally
16	Pursuit	Dark	Physical	40	100	20	Normal
20	Bug Bite	Bug	Physical	60	100	20	Normal
23	Poison Fang	Poison	Physical	50	100	15	Normal
27	Venoshock	Poison	Special	65	100	10	Normal
30	Hone Claws	Dark	Status	—	—	15	Self
34	Toxic Spikes	Poison	Status	—	—	20	Other Side
38	Night Slash	Dark	Physical	70	100	15	Normal
41	Scary Face	Normal	Status	—	100	10	Normal
45	Crunch	Dark	Physical	80	100	15	Normal
47	Fell Stinger	Bug	Physical	30	100	25	Normal
49	Cross Poison	Poison	Physical	70	100	20	Normal

● TM & HM MOVES

No.	Name	Type	Kind	Pow.	Acc.	PP	Range
TM01	Hone Claws	Dark	Status	—	—	15	Self
TM06	Toxic	Poison	Status	—	90	10	Normal
TM09	Venoshock	Poison	Special	65	100	10	Normal
TM10	Hidden Power	Normal	Special	60	100	15	Normal
TM11	Sunny Day	Fire	Status	—	—	5	Both Sides
TM12	Taunt	Dark	Status	—	100	20	Normal
TM17	Protect	Normal	Status	—	—	10	Self
TM18	Rain Dance	Water	Status	—	—	5	Both Sides
TM21	Frustration	Normal	Physical	—	100	20	Normal
TM27	Return	Normal	Physical	—	100	20	Normal
TM28	Dig	Ground	Physical	80	100	10	Normal
TM30	Shadow Ball	Ghost	Special	80	100	15	Normal
TM31	Brick Break	Fighting	Physical	75	100	15	Normal
TM32	Double Team	Normal	Status	—	—	15	Self
TM36	Sludge Bomb	Poison	Special	90	100	10	Normal
TM39	Rock Tomb	Rock	Physical	60	95	15	Normal
TM40	Aerial Ace	Flying	Physical	60	—	20	Normal
TM41	Torment	Dark	Status	—	100	15	Normal
TM42	Facade	Normal	Physical	70	100	20	Normal
TM44	Rest	Psychic	Status	—	—	10	Self
TM45	Attract	Normal	Status	—	100	15	Normal
TM46	Thief	Dark	Physical	60	100	25	Normal
TM48	Round	Normal	Special	60	100	15	Normal
TM54	False Swipe	Normal	Physical	40	100	40	Normal
TM56	Fling	Dark	Physical	—	100	10	Normal
TM66	Payback	Dark	Physical	50	100	10	Normal
TM70	Flash	Normal	Status	—	100	20	Normal
TM75	Swords Dance	Normal	Status	—	—	20	Self
TM76	Struggle Bug	Bug	Special	50	100	20	Many Others
TM81	X-Scissor	Bug	Physical	80	100	15	Normal
TM83	Infestation	Bug	Special	20	100	20	Normal
TM84	Poison Jab	Poison	Physical	80	100	20	Normal
TM87	Swagger	Normal	Status	—	90	15	Normal

No.	Name	Type	Kind	Pow.	Acc.	PP	Range
TM88	Sleep Talk	Normal	Status	—	—	10	Self
TM90	Substitute	Normal	Status	—	—	10	Self
TM94	Rock Smash	Fighting	Physical	40	100	15	Normal
TM97	Dark Pulse	Dark	Special	80	100	15	Normal
TM100	Confide	Normal	Status	—	—	20	Normal
HM01	Cut	Normal	Physical	50	95	30	Normal
HM04	Strength	Normal	Physical	80	100	15	Normal

● MOVES TAUGHT BY PEOPLE

Name	Type	Kind	Pow.	Acc.	PP	Range

● EGG MOVES

Name	Type	Kind	Pow.	Acc.	PP	Range
Feint Attack	Dark	Physical	60	—	20	Normal
Screech	Normal	Status	—	85	40	Normal
Sand Attack	Ground	Status	—	100	15	Normal
Slash	Normal	Physical	70	100	20	Normal
Confuse Ray	Ghost	Status	—	100	10	Normal
Whirlwind	Normal	Status	—	—	20	Normal
Agility	Psychic	Status	—	—	30	Self
Pursuit	Dark	Physical	40	100	20	Normal
Night Slash	Dark	Physical	70	100	15	Normal
Iron Tail	Steel	Physical	100	75	15	Normal
Twineedle	Bug	Physical	25	100	20	Normal
Poison Tail	Poison	Physical	50	100	25	Normal

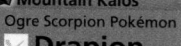

Mountain Kalos
Ogre Scorpion Pokémon **016**

Drapion

TYPE Poison Dark

ABILITIES
Battle Armor
Sniper

HIDDEN ABILITY
Keen Eye

HEIGHT: 4'03" WEIGHT: 135.6 lbs.
GENDER: ♂ / ♀

 It takes pride in its strength. Even though it can tear foes apart, it finishes them off with powerful poison.

 It has the power in its clawed arms to make scrap of a car. The tips of its claws release poison.

STAT GROWTH RATES
HP	■■■
Attack	■■■■
Defense	■■■■■
Sp. Atk	■■■
Sp. Def	■■■
Speed	■■■■

EGG GROUPS
Bug, Water 3

EVOLUTION

Skorupi → Lv. 40 Drapion

ITEMS SOMETIMES HELD BY WILD POKÉMON
Poison Barb

Damage taken in normal battles	
Normal	×1
Fire	×1
Water	×1
Grass	×0.5
Electric	×1
Ice	×1
Fighting	×1
Poison	×0.5
Ground	×2
Flying	×1
Psychic	×0
Bug	×1
Rock	×1
Ghost	×0.5
Dragon	×1
Dark	×0.5
Steel	×1
Fairy	×1

Damage taken in Inverse Battles	
Normal	×1
Fire	×1
Water	×1
Grass	×2
Electric	×1
Ice	×1
Fighting	×1
Poison	×2
Ground	×0.5
Flying	×1
Psychic	×1
Bug	×1
Rock	×1
Ghost	×2
Dragon	×1
Dark	×2
Steel	×1
Fairy	×1

Can be used in	
Inverse Battle	Battle Institute
—	Battle Maison
Battle Chateau	Random Matchup

Same form for ♂ / ♀

How to obtain for your Mountain Kalos Pokédex
❶ Catch in the yellow or purple flowers on Route 19.
❷ Level up Skorupi to Lv. 40.

❶ Catch in the yellow or purple flowers on Route 19.
❷ Level up Skorupi to Lv. 40.

AFTER THE HALL OF FAME

CENTRAL KALOS

COASTAL KALOS

MOUNTAIN KALOS

016 Drapion

ADVENTURE DATA

● **LEVEL-UP MOVES**

Lv.	Name	Type	Kind	Pow.	Acc.	PP	Range
1	Thunder Fang	Electric	Physical	65	95	15	Normal
1	Ice Fang	Ice	Physical	65	95	15	Normal
1	Fire Fang	Fire	Physical	65	95	15	Normal
1	Bite	Dark	Physical	60	100	25	Normal
1	Poison Sting	Poison	Physical	15	100	35	Normal
1	Leer	Normal	Status	—	100	30	Many Others
1	Knock Off	Dark	Physical	65	100	20	Normal
5	Knock Off	Dark	Physical	65	100	20	Normal
9	Pin Missile	Bug	Physical	25	95	20	Normal
13	Acupressure	Normal	Status	—	—	30	Self/Ally
16	Pursuit	Dark	Physical	40	100	20	Normal
20	Bug Bite	Bug	Physical	60	100	20	Normal
23	Poison Fang	Poison	Physical	50	100	15	Normal
27	Venoshock	Poison	Special	65	100	10	Normal
30	Hone Claws	Dark	Status	—	—	15	Self
34	Toxic Spikes	Poison	Status	—	—	20	Other Side
39	Night Slash	Dark	Physical	70	100	15	Normal
43	Scary Face	Normal	Status	—	100	10	Normal
49	Crunch	Dark	Physical	80	100	15	Normal
53	Fell Stinger	Bug	Physical	30	100	25	Normal
57	Cross Poison	Poison	Physical	70	100	20	Normal

● **TM & HM MOVES**

No.	Name	Type	Kind	Pow.	Acc.	PP	Range
TM01	Hone Claws	Dark	Status	—	—	15	Self
TM05	Roar	Normal	Status	—	—	20	Normal
TM06	Toxic	Poison	Status	—	90	10	Normal
TM09	Venoshock	Poison	Special	65	100	10	Normal
TM10	Hidden Power	Normal	Special	60	100	15	Normal
TM11	Sunny Day	Fire	Status	—	—	5	Both Sides
TM12	Taunt	Dark	Status	—	100	20	Normal
TM15	Hyper Beam	Normal	Special	150	90	5	Normal
TM17	Protect	Normal	Status	—	—	10	Self
TM18	Rain Dance	Water	Status	—	—	5	Both Sides
TM21	Frustration	Normal	Physical	—	100	20	Normal
TM26	Earthquake	Ground	Physical	100	100	10	Adjacent
TM27	Return	Normal	Physical	—	100	20	Normal
TM28	Dig	Ground	Physical	80	100	10	Normal
TM30	Shadow Ball	Ghost	Special	80	100	15	Normal
TM31	Brick Break	Fighting	Physical	75	100	15	Normal
TM32	Double Team	Normal	Status	—	—	15	Self
TM36	Sludge Bomb	Poison	Special	90	100	10	Normal
TM39	Rock Tomb	Rock	Physical	60	95	15	Normal
TM40	Aerial Ace	Flying	Physical	60	—	20	Normal
TM41	Torment	Dark	Status	—	100	15	Normal
TM42	Facade	Normal	Physical	70	100	20	Normal
TM44	Rest	Psychic	Status	—	—	10	Self
TM45	Attract	Normal	Status	—	100	15	Normal
TM46	Thief	Dark	Physical	60	100	25	Normal
TM48	Round	Normal	Special	60	100	15	Normal
TM54	False Swipe	Normal	Physical	40	100	40	Normal
TM56	Fling	Dark	Physical	—	100	10	Normal
TM66	Payback	Dark	Physical	50	100	10	Normal
TM67	Retaliate	Normal	Physical	70	100	5	Normal
TM68	Giga Impact	Normal	Physical	150	90	5	Normal
TM70	Flash	Normal	Status	—	100	20	Normal
TM75	Swords Dance	Normal	Status	—	—	20	Self

No.	Name	Type	Kind	Pow.	Acc.	PP	Range
TM76	Struggle Bug	Bug	Special	50	100	20	Many Others
TM78	Bulldoze	Ground	Physical	60	100	20	Adjacent
TM80	Rock Slide	Rock	Physical	75	90	10	Many Others
TM81	X-Scissor	Bug	Physical	80	100	15	Normal
TM83	Infestation	Bug	Special	20	100	20	Normal
TM84	Poison Jab	Poison	Physical	80	100	20	Normal
TM87	Swagger	Normal	Status	—	90	15	Normal
TM88	Sleep Talk	Normal	Status	—	—	10	Self
TM90	Substitute	Normal	Status	—	—	10	Self
TM94	Rock Smash	Fighting	Physical	40	100	15	Normal
TM95	Snarl	Dark	Special	55	95	15	Many Others
TM97	Dark Pulse	Dark	Special	80	100	15	Normal
TM100	Confide	Normal	Status	—	—	20	Normal
HM01	Cut	Normal	Physical	50	95	30	Normal
HM04	Strength	Normal	Physical	80	100	15	Normal

● **MOVES TAUGHT BY PEOPLE**

Name	Type	Kind	Pow.	Acc.	PP	Range

AFTER THE HALL OF FAME

CENTRAL KALOS

COASTAL KALOS

MOUNTAIN KALOS

ADVENTURE DATA

Mountain Kalos 017
Water Fish Pokémon
☑ Wooper

HEIGHT: 1'04"   WEIGHT: 18.7 lbs.
GENDER: ♂/♀

✗ This Pokémon lives in cold water. It will leave the water to search for food when it gets cold outside.

Y When the temperature cools in the evening, they emerge from water to seek food along the shore.

TYPE Water Ground

ABILITIES
Damp
Water Absorb

HIDDEN ABILITY
Unaware

STAT GROWTH RATES
HP	▪▪
Attack	▪▪
Defense	▪▪
Sp. Atk	▪
Sp. Def	▪
Speed	▪

EGG GROUPS
Water 1, Field

EVOLUTION

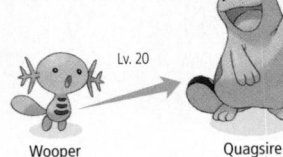

Wooper   Lv. 20   Quagsire

ITEMS SOMETIMES HELD BY WILD POKÉMON
None

Can be used in
Inverse Battle
—
Battle Chateau
Battle Institute
Battle Maison
Random Matchup

Damage taken in normal battles	
Normal	×1
Fire	×0.5
Water	×1
Grass	×4
Electric	×0
Ice	×1
Fighting	×1
Poison	×0.5
Ground	×1
Flying	×1
Psychic	×1
Bug	×1
Rock	×0.5
Ghost	×1
Dragon	×1
Dark	×1
Steel	×0.5
Fairy	×1

Damage taken in Inverse Battles	
Normal	×1
Fire	×1
Water	×1
Grass	×0.25
Electric	×1
Ice	×1
Fighting	×1
Poison	×2
Ground	×1
Flying	×1
Psychic	×1
Bug	×1
Rock	×2
Ghost	×1
Dragon	×1
Dark	×1
Steel	×2
Fairy	×1

How to obtain for your Mountain Kalos Pokédex

Leave Quagsire at the Pokémon Day Care, and hatch the Egg that is found.

Leave Quagsire at the Pokémon Day Care, and hatch the Egg that is found.

♂     ♀

The male has more abundant frills on its head. The female has less abundant frills on its head.

● LEVEL-UP MOVES

Lv.	Name	Type	Kind	Pow.	Acc.	PP	Range
1	Water Gun	Water	Special	40	100	25	Normal
5	Tail Whip	Normal	Status	—	100	30	Many Others
5	Mud Sport	Ground	Status	—	—	15	Both Sides
9	Mud Shot	Ground	Special	55	95	15	Normal
15	Slam	Normal	Physical	80	75	20	Normal
19	Mud Bomb	Ground	Special	65	85	10	Normal
23	Amnesia	Psychic	Status	—	—	20	Self
29	Yawn	Normal	Status	—	—	10	Normal
33	Earthquake	Ground	Physical	100	100	10	Adjacent
37	Rain Dance	Water	Status	—	—	5	Both Sides
43	Mist	Ice	Status	—	—	30	Your Side
43	Haze	Ice	Status	—	—	30	Both Sides
47	Muddy Water	Water	Special	90	85	10	Many Others

● TM & HM MOVES

No.	Name	Type	Kind	Pow.	Acc.	PP	Range
TM06	Toxic	Poison	Status	—	90	10	Normal
TM07	Hail	Ice	Status	—	—	10	Both Sides
TM10	Hidden Power	Normal	Special	60	100	15	Normal
TM13	Ice Beam	Ice	Special	90	100	10	Normal
TM14	Blizzard	Ice	Special	110	70	5	Many Others
TM17	Protect	Normal	Status	—	—	10	Self
TM18	Rain Dance	Water	Status	—	—	5	Both Sides
TM20	Safeguard	Normal	Status	—	—	25	Your Side
TM21	Frustration	Normal	Physical	—	100	20	Normal
TM26	Earthquake	Ground	Physical	100	100	10	Adjacent
TM27	Return	Normal	Physical	—	100	20	Normal
TM28	Dig	Ground	Physical	80	100	10	Normal
TM32	Double Team	Normal	Status	—	—	15	Self
TM34	Sludge Wave	Poison	Special	95	100	10	Adjacent
TM36	Sludge Bomb	Poison	Special	90	100	10	Normal
TM37	Sandstorm	Rock	Status	—	—	10	Both Sides
TM42	Facade	Normal	Physical	70	100	20	Normal
TM44	Rest	Psychic	Status	—	—	10	Self
TM45	Attract	Normal	Status	—	100	15	Normal
TM48	Round	Normal	Special	60	100	15	Normal
TM55	Scald	Water	Special	80	100	15	Normal
TM70	Flash	Normal	Status	—	100	20	Normal
TM78	Bulldoze	Ground	Physical	60	100	20	Adjacent
TM83	Infestation	Bug	Special	20	100	20	Normal
TM87	Swagger	Normal	Status	—	90	15	Normal
TM88	Sleep Talk	Normal	Status	—	—	10	Self
TM90	Substitute	Normal	Status	—	—	10	Self
TM94	Rock Smash	Fighting	Physical	40	100	15	Normal
TM100	Confide	Normal	Status	—	—	20	Normal
HM03	Surf	Water	Special	90	100	15	Adjacent
HM05	Waterfall	Water	Special	80	100	15	Normal

● MOVES TAUGHT BY PEOPLE

Name	Type	Kind	Pow.	Acc.	PP	Range

● EGG MOVES

Name	Type	Kind	Pow.	Acc.	PP	Range
Body Slam	Normal	Physical	85	100	15	Normal
Ancient Power	Rock	Special	60	100	5	Normal
Curse	Ghost	Status	—	—	10	Varies
Mud Sport	Ground	Status	—	—	15	Both Sides
Stockpile	Normal	Status	—	—	20	Self
Swallow	Normal	Status	—	—	10	Self
Spit Up	Normal	Special	—	100	10	Normal
Counter	Fighting	Physical	—	100	20	Varies
Encore	Normal	Status	—	100	5	Normal
Double Kick	Fighting	Physical	30	100	30	Normal
Recover	Normal	Status	—	—	10	Self
After You	Normal	Status	—	—	15	Normal
Sleep Talk	Normal	Status	—	—	10	Self
Acid Spray	Poison	Special	40	100	20	Normal
Guard Swap	Psychic	Status	—	—	10	Normal
Eerie Impulse	Electric	Status	—	100	15	Normal

Wooper 017

Mountain Kalos
018
Water Fish Pokémon
☑ **Quagsire**

HEIGHT: 4'07" WEIGHT: 165.3 lbs.
GENDER: ♂ / ♀

X It has a sluggish nature. It lies at the river's bottom, waiting for prey to stray into its mouth.

Y This carefree Pokémon has an easygoing nature. While swimming, it always bumps into boat hulls.

TYPE Water Ground

ABILITIES
Damp
Water Absorb

HIDDEN ABILITY
Unaware

STAT GROWTH RATES
HP	■■■■
Attack	■■■■
Defense	■■■■
Sp. Atk	■■■
Sp. Def	■■■
Speed	■■

EGG GROUPS
Water 1, Field

EVOLUTION

Wooper → Lv. 20 → Quagsire

ITEMS SOMETIMES HELD BY WILD POKÉMON
None

Damage taken in normal battles		Damage taken in Inverse Battles	
Normal	×1	Normal	×1
Fire	×0.5	Fire	×2
Water	×1	Water	×1
Grass	×4	Grass	×0.25
Electric	×0	Electric	×1
Ice	×1	Ice	×1
Fighting	×1	Fighting	×1
Poison	×0.5	Poison	×2
Ground	×1	Ground	×1
Flying	×1	Flying	×1
Psychic	×1	Psychic	×1
Bug	×1	Bug	×1
Rock	×0.5	Rock	×2
Ghost	×1	Ghost	×1
Dragon	×1	Dragon	×1
Dark	×1	Dark	×1
Steel	×0.5	Steel	×2
Fairy	×1	Fairy	×1

Can be used in
Inverse Battle
————
Battle Chateau
Battle Institute
Battle Maison
Random Matchup

How to obtain for your Mountain Kalos Pokédex

❶ Catch on the surface of the water or in the swamps along Route 14.
❷ Level up Wooper to Lv. 20.

❶ Catch on the surface of the water or in the swamps along Route 14.
❷ Level up Wooper to Lv. 20.

♂   ♀

The male has larger fins on its back. The female has smaller fins on its back.

● LEVEL-UP MOVES

Lv.	Name	Type	Kind	Pow.	Acc.	PP	Range
1	Water Gun	Water	Special	40	100	25	Normal
1	Tail Whip	Normal	Status	—	100	30	Many Others
1	Mud Sport	Ground	Status	—	—	15	Both Sides
5	Mud Sport	Ground	Status	—	—	15	Both Sides
9	Mud Shot	Ground	Special	55	95	15	Normal
15	Slam	Normal	Physical	80	75	20	Normal
19	Mud Bomb	Ground	Special	65	85	10	Normal
24	Amnesia	Psychic	Status	—	—	20	Self
31	Yawn	Normal	Status	—	—	10	Normal
36	Earthquake	Ground	Physical	100	100	10	Adjacent
41	Rain Dance	Water	Status	—	—	5	Both Sides
48	Mist	Ice	Status	—	—	30	Your Side
48	Haze	Ice	Status	—	—	30	Both Sides
53	Muddy Water	Water	Special	90	85	10	Many Others

● TM & HM MOVES

No.	Name	Type	Kind	Pow.	Acc.	PP	Range
TM06	Toxic	Poison	Status	—	90	10	Normal
TM07	Hail	Ice	Status	—	—	10	Both Sides
TM10	Hidden Power	Normal	Special	60	100	15	Normal
TM13	Ice Beam	Ice	Special	90	100	10	Normal
TM14	Blizzard	Ice	Special	110	70	5	Many Others
TM15	Hyper Beam	Normal	Special	150	90	5	Normal
TM17	Protect	Normal	Status	—	—	10	Self
TM18	Rain Dance	Water	Status	—	—	5	Both Sides
TM20	Safeguard	Normal	Status	—	—	25	Your Side
TM21	Frustration	Normal	Physical	—	100	20	Normal
TM26	Earthquake	Ground	Physical	100	100	10	Adjacent
TM27	Return	Normal	Physical	—	100	20	Normal
TM28	Dig	Ground	Physical	80	100	10	Normal
TM31	Brick Break	Fighting	Physical	75	100	15	Normal
TM32	Double Team	Normal	Status	—	—	15	Self
TM34	Sludge Wave	Poison	Special	95	100	10	Adjacent
TM36	Sludge Bomb	Poison	Special	90	100	10	Normal
TM37	Sandstorm	Rock	Status	—	—	10	Both Sides
TM39	Rock Tomb	Rock	Physical	60	95	15	Normal
TM42	Facade	Normal	Physical	70	100	20	Normal
TM44	Rest	Psychic	Status	—	—	10	Self
TM45	Attract	Normal	Status	—	100	15	Normal
TM46	Thief	Dark	Physical	60	100	25	Normal
TM48	Round	Normal	Special	60	100	15	Normal
TM52	Focus Blast	Fighting	Special	120	70	5	Normal
TM55	Scald	Water	Special	80	100	15	Normal
TM56	Fling	Dark	Physical	—	100	10	Normal
TM68	Giga Impact	Normal	Physical	150	90	5	Normal
TM70	Flash	Normal	Status	—	100	20	Normal
TM71	Stone Edge	Rock	Physical	100	80	5	Normal
TM78	Bulldoze	Ground	Physical	60	100	20	Adjacent
TM80	Rock Slide	Rock	Physical	75	90	10	Many Others
TM83	Infestation	Bug	Special	20	100	20	Normal

No.	Name	Type	Kind	Pow.	Acc.	PP	Range
TM87	Swagger	Normal	Status	—	90	15	Normal
TM88	Sleep Talk	Normal	Status	—	—	10	Self
TM90	Substitute	Normal	Status	—	—	10	Self
TM94	Rock Smash	Fighting	Physical	40	100	15	Normal
TM98	Power-Up Punch	Fighting	Physical	40	100	20	Normal
TM100	Confide	Normal	Status	—	—	20	Normal
HM03	Surf	Water	Special	90	100	15	Adjacent
HM04	Strength	Normal	Physical	80	100	15	Normal
HM05	Waterfall	Water	Physical	80	100	15	Normal

● MOVES TAUGHT BY PEOPLE

Name	Type	Kind	Pow.	Acc.	PP	Range

AFTER THE HALL OF FAME

CENTRAL KALOS

COASTAL KALOS

MOUNTAIN KALOS

018 | Quagsire

ADVENTURE DATA

Mountain Kalos — 019

Soft Tissue Pokémon

Goomy

HEIGHT: 1'00" WEIGHT: 6.2 lbs.
GENDER: ♂ / ♀

TYPE Dragon

ABILITIES
Sap Sipper
Hydration

HIDDEN ABILITY
Gooey

STAT GROWTH RATES
HP
Attack
Defense
Sp. Atk
Sp. Def
Speed

EGG GROUP
Dragon

X The weakest Dragon-type Pokémon, it lives in damp, shady places, so its body doesn't dry out.

Y It's covered in a slimy membrane that makes any punches or kicks slide off it harmlessly.

EVOLUTION

Lv. 40 → Lv. 50 in a place where it is raining

Goomy — Sliggoo — Goodra

ITEMS SOMETIMES HELD BY WILD POKÉMON
None

Damage taken in normal battles		Damage taken in Inverse Battles	
Normal	×1	Normal	×1
Fire	×0.5	Fire	×2
Water	×0.5	Water	×2
Grass	×0.5	Grass	×2
Electric	×0.5	Electric	×2
Ice	×2	Ice	×0.5
Fighting	×1	Fighting	×1
Poison	×1	Poison	×1
Ground	×1	Ground	×1
Flying	×1	Flying	×1
Psychic	×1	Psychic	×1
Bug	×1	Bug	×1
Rock	×1	Rock	×1
Ghost	×1	Ghost	×1
Dragon	×2	Dragon	×0.5
Dark	×1	Dark	×1
Steel	×1	Steel	×1
Fairy	×2	Fairy	×0.5

Can be used in	
Inverse Battle	Battle Institute
—	Battle Maison
Battle Chateau	Random Matchup

Same form for ♂ / ♀

How to obtain for your Mountain Kalos Pokédex

X
1. Catch in the tall grass on Route 14.
2. Catch in the swamps along Route 14.

Y
1. Catch in the tall grass on Route 14.
2. Catch in the swamps along Route 14.

LEVEL-UP MOVES

Lv.	Name	Type	Kind	Pow.	Acc.	PP	Range
1	Tackle	Normal	Physical	50	100	35	Normal
1	Bubble	Water	Special	40	100	30	Many Others
5	Absorb	Grass	Special	20	100	25	Normal
9	Protect	Normal	Status	—	—	10	Self
13	Bide	Normal	Physical	—	—	10	Self
18	Dragon Breath	Dragon	Special	60	100	20	Normal
25	Rain Dance	Water	Status	—	—	5	Both Sides
28	Flail	Normal	Physical	—	100	15	Normal
32	Body Slam	Normal	Physical	85	100	15	Normal
38	Muddy Water	Water	Special	90	85	10	Many Others
42	Dragon Pulse	Dragon	Special	85	100	10	Normal

TM & HM MOVES

No.	Name	Type	Kind	Pow.	Acc.	PP	Range
TM06	Toxic	Poison	Status	—	90	10	Normal
TM10	Hidden Power	Normal	Special	60	100	15	Normal
TM11	Sunny Day	Fire	Status	—	—	5	Both Sides
TM17	Protect	Normal	Status	—	—	10	Self
TM18	Rain Dance	Water	Status	—	—	5	Both Sides
TM21	Frustration	Normal	Physical	—	100	20	Normal
TM24	Thunderbolt	Electric	Special	90	100	15	Normal
TM27	Return	Normal	Physical	—	100	20	Normal
TM32	Double Team	Normal	Status	—	—	15	Self
TM34	Sludge Wave	Poison	Special	95	100	10	Adjacent
TM36	Sludge Bomb	Poison	Special	90	100	10	Normal
TM42	Facade	Normal	Physical	70	100	20	Normal
TM44	Rest	Psychic	Status	—	—	10	Self
TM45	Attract	Normal	Status	—	100	15	Normal
TM48	Round	Normal	Special	60	100	15	Normal
TM80	Rock Slide	Rock	Physical	75	90	10	Many Others
TM83	Infestation	Bug	Special	20	100	20	Normal
TM87	Swagger	Normal	Status	—	90	15	Normal
TM88	Sleep Talk	Normal	Status	—	—	10	Self
TM90	Substitute	Normal	Status	—	—	10	Self
TM100	Confide	Normal	Status	—	—	20	Normal

MOVES TAUGHT BY PEOPLE

Name	Type	Kind	Pow.	Acc.	PP	Range
Draco Meteor	Dragon	Special	130	90	5	Normal

EGG MOVES

Name	Type	Kind	Pow.	Acc.	PP	Range
Acid Armor	Poison	Status	—	—	20	Self
Curse	Ghost	Status	—	—	10	Varies
Iron Tail	Steel	Physical	100	75	15	Normal
Poison Tail	Poison	Physical	50	100	25	Normal
Counter	Fighting	Physical	—	100	20	Varies
Endure	Normal	Status	—	—	10	Self

Goomy
019

AFTER THE HALL OF FAME

CENTRAL KALOS

COASTAL KALOS

MOUNTAIN KALOS

ADVENTURE DATA

450

Mountain Kalos 020

Soft Tissue Pokémon

☑ **Sliggoo**

HEIGHT: 2'07" WEIGHT: 38.6 lbs.
GENDER: ♂/♀

TYPE Dragon

ABILITIES
Sap Sipper
Hydration

HIDDEN ABILITY
Gooey

STAT GROWTH RATES
HP	■■■
Attack	■■■■
Defense	■■
Sp. Atk	■■■■
Sp. Def	■■■■■
Speed	■■■

EGG GROUP
Dragon

X It drives away opponents by excreting a sticky liquid that can dissolve anything. Its eyes devolved, so it can't see anything.

Y Its four horns are a high-performance radar system. It uses them to sense sounds and smells, rather than using ears or a nose.

EVOLUTION

Goomy — Lv. 40 → Sliggoo — Lv. 50 in a place where it is raining → Goodra

ITEMS SOMETIMES HELD BY WILD POKÉMON
None

Damage taken in normal battles		Damage taken in Inverse Battles	
Normal	×1	Normal	×1
Fire	×0.5	Fire	×2
Water	×0.5	Water	×2
Grass	×0.5	Grass	×2
Electric	×0.5	Electric	×2
Ice	×2	Ice	×0.5
Fighting	×1	Fighting	×1
Poison	×1	Poison	×1
Ground	×1	Ground	×1
Flying	×1	Flying	×1
Psychic	×1	Psychic	×1
Bug	×1	Bug	×1
Rock	×1	Rock	×1
Ghost	×1	Ghost	×1
Dragon	×2	Dragon	×0.5
Dark	×1	Dark	×1
Steel	×1	Steel	×1
Fairy	×2	Fairy	×0.5

Can be used in
Inverse Battle
—
Battle Chateau
Battle Institute
Battle Maison
Random Matchup

How to obtain for your Mountain Kalos Pokédex

❶ Catch in the yellow flowers or in the swamps along Route 19.
❷ Level up Goomy to Lv. 40.

❶ Catch in the yellow flowers or the swamps along Route 19.
❷ Level up Goomy to Lv. 40.

Same form for ♂/♀

● LEVEL-UP MOVES

Lv.	Name	Type	Kind	Pow.	Acc.	PP	Range
1	Tackle	Normal	Physical	50	100	35	Normal
1	Bubble	Water	Special	40	100	30	Many Others
5	Absorb	Grass	Special	20	100	25	Normal
9	Protect	Normal	Status	—	—	10	Self
13	Bide	Normal	Physical	—	—	10	Self
18	Dragon Breath	Dragon	Special	60	100	20	Normal
25	Rain Dance	Water	Status	—	—	5	Both Sides
28	Flail	Normal	Physical	—	100	15	Normal
32	Body Slam	Normal	Physical	85	100	15	Normal
38	Muddy Water	Water	Special	90	85	10	Many Others
47	Dragon Pulse	Dragon	Special	85	100	10	Normal

● TM & HM MOVES

No.	Name	Type	Kind	Pow.	Acc.	PP	Range
TM06	Toxic	Poison	Status	—	90	10	Normal
TM10	Hidden Power	Normal	Special	60	100	15	Normal
TM11	Sunny Day	Fire	Status	—	—	5	Both Sides
TM13	Ice Beam	Ice	Special	90	100	10	Normal
TM14	Blizzard	Ice	Special	110	70	5	Many Others
TM17	Protect	Normal	Status	—	—	10	Self
TM18	Rain Dance	Water	Status	—	—	5	Both Sides
TM21	Frustration	Normal	Physical	—	100	20	Normal
TM24	Thunderbolt	Electric	Special	90	100	15	Normal
TM27	Return	Normal	Physical	—	100	20	Normal
TM32	Double Team	Normal	Status	—	—	15	Self
TM34	Sludge Wave	Poison	Special	95	100	10	Adjacent
TM36	Sludge Bomb	Poison	Special	90	100	10	Normal
TM42	Facade	Normal	Physical	70	100	20	Normal
TM44	Rest	Psychic	Status	—	—	10	Self
TM45	Attract	Normal	Status	—	100	15	Normal
TM48	Round	Normal	Special	60	100	15	Normal
TM80	Rock Slide	Rock	Physical	75	90	10	Many Others
TM83	Infestation	Bug	Special	20	100	20	Normal
TM87	Swagger	Normal	Status	—	90	15	Normal
TM88	Sleep Talk	Normal	Status	—	—	10	Self
TM90	Substitute	Normal	Status	—	—	10	Self
TM100	Confide	Normal	Status	—	—	20	Normal

No.	Name	Type	Kind	Pow.	Acc.	PP	Range

● MOVES TAUGHT BY PEOPLE

Name	Type	Kind	Pow.	Acc.	PP	Range
Draco Meteor	Dragon	Special	130	90	5	Normal

AFTER THE HALL OF FAME

CENTRAL KALOS

COASTAL KALOS

MOUNTAIN KALOS

020 Sliggoo

ADVENTURE DATA

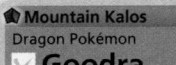

Mountain Kalos

021

Dragon Pokémon

☑ Goodra

HEIGHT: 6'07" WEIGHT: 331.8 lbs.
GENDER: ♂/♀

X This very friendly Dragon-type Pokémon will hug its beloved Trainer, leaving that Trainer covered in sticky slime.

Y It attacks with retractable horns. It throws a punch that's the equivalent of the force of a hundred pro boxers.

TYPE **Dragon**

ABILITIES
Sap Sipper
Hydration

HIDDEN ABILITY
Gooey

STAT GROWTH RATES
HP	▪▪▪▪
Attack	▪▪▪▪▪
Defense	▪▪▪
Sp. Atk	▪▪▪▪
Sp. Def	▪▪▪▪▪▪
Speed	▪▪▪

EGG GROUP
Dragon

EVOLUTION

Goomy → (Lv. 40) → Sliggoo → (Lv. 50 in a place where it is raining) → Goodra

ITEMS SOMETIMES HELD BY WILD POKÉMON
None

Damage taken in normal battles	
Normal	×1
Fire	×0.5
Water	×0.5
Grass	×0.5
Electric	×0.5
Ice	×2
Fighting	×1
Poison	×1
Ground	×1
Flying	×1
Psychic	×1
Bug	×1
Rock	×1
Ghost	×1
Dragon	×2
Dark	×1
Steel	×1
Fairy	×2

Damage taken in Inverse Battles	
Normal	×1
Fire	×2
Water	×2
Grass	×2
Electric	×2
Ice	×0.5
Fighting	×1
Poison	×1
Ground	×1
Flying	×1
Psychic	×1
Bug	×1
Rock	×1
Ghost	×1
Dragon	×0.5
Dark	×1
Steel	×1
Fairy	×0.5

Can be used in	
Inverse Battle	Battle Institute
—	Battle Maison
Battle Chateau	Random Matchup

Same form for ♂/♀

How to obtain for your Mountain Kalos Pokédex

Level up Sliggoo to Lv. 50 in a place where it is raining.

Level up Sliggoo to Lv. 50 in a place where it is raining.

021

Goodra

● LEVEL-UP MOVES

Lv.	Name	Type	Kind	Pow.	Acc.	PP	Range
1	Outrage	Dragon	Physical	120	100	10	1 Random
1	Feint	Normal	Physical	30	100	10	Normal
1	Tackle	Normal	Physical	50	100	35	Normal
1	Bubble	Water	Special	40	100	30	Many Others
5	Absorb	Grass	Special	20	100	25	Normal
9	Protect	Normal	Status	—	—	10	Self
13	Bide	Normal	Physical	—	—	10	Self
18	Dragon Breath	Dragon	Special	60	100	20	Normal
25	Rain Dance	Water	Status	—	—	5	Both Sides
28	Flail	Normal	Physical	—	100	15	Normal
32	Body Slam	Normal	Physical	85	100	15	Normal
38	Muddy Water	Water	Special	90	85	10	Many Others
47	Dragon Pulse	Dragon	Special	85	100	10	Normal
50	Aqua Tail	Water	Physical	90	90	10	Normal
55	Power Whip	Grass	Physical	120	85	10	Normal
63	Outrage	Dragon	Physical	120	100	10	1 Random

● TM & HM MOVES

No.	Name	Type	Kind	Pow.	Acc.	PP	Range
TM06	Toxic	Poison	Status	—	90	10	Normal
TM07	Hail	Ice	Status	—	—	10	Both Sides
TM10	Hidden Power	Normal	Special	60	100	15	Normal
TM11	Sunny Day	Fire	Status	—	—	5	Both Sides
TM13	Ice Beam	Ice	Special	90	100	10	Normal
TM14	Blizzard	Ice	Special	110	70	5	Many Others
TM15	Hyper Beam	Normal	Special	150	90	5	Normal
TM17	Protect	Normal	Status	—	—	10	Self
TM18	Rain Dance	Water	Status	—	—	5	Both Sides
TM21	Frustration	Normal	Physical	—	100	20	Normal
TM24	Thunderbolt	Electric	Special	90	100	15	Normal
TM25	Thunder	Electric	Special	110	70	10	Normal
TM26	Earthquake	Ground	Physical	100	100	10	Adjacent
TM27	Return	Normal	Physical	—	100	20	Normal
TM32	Double Team	Normal	Status	—	—	15	Self
TM34	Sludge Wave	Poison	Special	95	100	10	Adjacent
TM35	Flamethrower	Fire	Special	90	100	15	Normal
TM36	Sludge Bomb	Poison	Special	90	100	10	Normal
TM38	Fire Blast	Fire	Special	110	85	5	Normal
TM42	Facade	Normal	Physical	70	100	20	Normal
TM44	Rest	Psychic	Status	—	—	10	Self
TM45	Attract	Normal	Status	—	100	15	Normal
TM48	Round	Normal	Special	60	100	15	Normal
TM52	Focus Blast	Fighting	Special	120	70	5	Normal
TM59	Incinerate	Fire	Special	60	100	15	Many Others
TM68	Giga Impact	Normal	Physical	150	90	5	Normal
TM78	Bulldoze	Ground	Physical	60	100	20	Adjacent
TM80	Rock Slide	Rock	Physical	75	90	10	Many Others
TM82	Dragon Tail	Dragon	Physical	60	90	10	Normal
TM83	Infestation	Bug	Special	20	100	20	Normal
TM87	Swagger	Normal	Status	—	90	15	Normal
TM88	Sleep Talk	Normal	Status	—	—	10	Self
TM90	Substitute	Normal	Status	—	—	10	Self

No.	Name	Type	Kind	Pow.	Acc.	PP	Range
TM94	Rock Smash	Fighting	Physical	40	100	15	Normal
TM100	Confide	Normal	Status	—	—	20	Normal
HM04	Strength	Normal	Physical	80	100	15	Normal

● MOVES TAUGHT BY PEOPLE

Name	Type	Kind	Pow.	Acc.	PP	Range
Draco Meteor	Dragon	Special	130	90	5	Normal

Mountain Kalos
Clamping Pokémon
022

Karrablast

HEIGHT: 1'08"   WEIGHT: 13.0 lbs.
GENDER: ♂/♀

TYPE Bug

ABILITIES
Swarm
Shed Skin

HIDDEN ABILITY
No Guard

STAT GROWTH RATES
HP	■■
Attack	■■■■
Defense	■■
Sp. Atk	■■
Sp. Def	■■
Speed	■■■

EGG GROUP
Bug

X These mysterious Pokémon evolve when they receive electrical stimulation while they are in the same place as Shelmet.

Y For some reason they evolve when they receive electrical energy while they are attacking Shelmet.

EVOLUTION

Karrablast → Link Trade for Shelmet → Escavalier

ITEMS SOMETIMES HELD BY WILD POKÉMON
None

Damage taken in normal battles
Normal	×1
Fire	×2
Water	×1
Grass	×0.5
Electric	×1
Ice	×1
Fighting	×0.5
Poison	×1
Ground	×0.5
Flying	×2
Psychic	×1
Bug	×1
Rock	×2
Ghost	×1
Dragon	×1
Dark	×1
Steel	×1
Fairy	×1

Damage taken in Inverse Battles
Normal	×1
Fire	×0.5
Water	×1
Grass	×2
Electric	×1
Ice	×1
Fighting	×2
Poison	×1
Ground	×2
Flying	×0.5
Psychic	×1
Bug	×1
Rock	×0.5
Ghost	×1
Dragon	×1
Dark	×1
Steel	×1
Fairy	×1

Can be used in
Inverse Battle
————
Battle Chateau
Battle Institute
Battle Maison
Random Matchup

How to obtain for your Mountain Kalos Pokédex
❶ Catch in the tall grass on Route 14.
❷ Catch in the swamps along Route 14.

❶ Catch in the tall grass on Route 14.
❷ Catch in the swamps along Route 14.

Same form for ♂/♀

● LEVEL-UP MOVES
Lv.	Name	Type	Kind	Pow.	Acc.	PP	Range
1	Peck	Flying	Physical	35	100	35	Normal
4	Leer	Normal	Status	—	100	30	Many Others
8	Endure	Normal	Status	—	—	10	Self
13	Fury Cutter	Bug	Physical	40	95	20	Normal
16	Fury Attack	Normal	Physical	15	85	20	Normal
20	Headbutt	Normal	Physical	70	100	15	Normal
25	False Swipe	Normal	Physical	40	100	40	Normal
28	Bug Buzz	Bug	Special	90	100	10	Normal
32	Slash	Normal	Physical	70	100	20	Normal
37	Take Down	Normal	Physical	90	85	20	Normal
40	Scary Face	Normal	Status	—	100	10	Normal
44	X-Scissor	Bug	Physical	80	100	15	Normal
49	Flail	Normal	Physical	—	100	15	Normal
52	Swords Dance	Normal	Status	—	—	20	Self
56	Double-Edge	Normal	Physical	120	100	15	Normal

● TM & HM MOVES
No.	Name	Type	Kind	Pow.	Acc.	PP	Range
TM06	Toxic	Poison	Status	—	90	10	Normal
TM10	Hidden Power	Normal	Special	60	100	15	Normal
TM17	Protect	Normal	Status	—	—	10	Self
TM18	Rain Dance	Water	Status	—	—	5	Both Sides
TM21	Frustration	Normal	Physical	—	100	20	Normal
TM27	Return	Normal	Physical	—	100	20	Normal
TM32	Double Team	Normal	Status	—	—	15	Self
TM40	Aerial Ace	Flying	Physical	60	—	20	Normal
TM42	Facade	Normal	Physical	70	100	20	Normal
TM44	Rest	Psychic	Status	—	—	10	Self
TM45	Attract	Normal	Status	—	100	15	Normal
TM48	Round	Normal	Special	60	100	15	Normal
TM53	Energy Ball	Grass	Special	90	100	10	Normal
TM54	False Swipe	Normal	Physical	40	100	40	Normal
TM75	Swords Dance	Normal	Status	—	—	20	Self
TM76	Struggle Bug	Bug	Special	50	100	20	Many Others
TM81	X-Scissor	Bug	Physical	80	100	15	Normal
TM83	Infestation	Bug	Special	20	100	20	Normal
TM84	Poison Jab	Poison	Physical	80	100	20	Normal
TM87	Swagger	Normal	Status	—	90	15	Normal
TM88	Sleep Talk	Normal	Status	—	—	10	Self
TM90	Substitute	Normal	Status	—	—	10	Self
TM100	Confide	Normal	Status	—	—	20	Normal
HM01	Cut	Normal	Physical	50	95	30	Normal

● MOVES TAUGHT BY PEOPLE
Name	Type	Kind	Pow.	Acc.	PP	Range

● EGG MOVES
Name	Type	Kind	Pow.	Acc.	PP	Range
Megahorn	Bug	Physical	120	85	10	Normal
Pursuit	Dark	Physical	40	100	20	Normal
Counter	Fighting	Physical	—	100	20	Varies
Horn Attack	Normal	Physical	65	100	25	Normal
Feint Attack	Dark	Physical	60	—	20	Normal
Bug Bite	Bug	Physical	60	100	20	Normal
Screech	Normal	Status	—	85	40	Normal
Knock Off	Dark	Physical	65	100	20	Normal
Drill Run	Ground	Physical	80	95	10	Normal

🔺 Mountain Kalos 023

Cavalry Pokémon

⋁ Escavalier

HEIGHT: 3'03" WEIGHT: 72.8 lbs.
GENDER: ♂/♀

TYPE	Bug	Steel

ABILITIES
Swarm
Shell Armor

HIDDEN ABILITY
Overcoat

X Wearing the shell covering they stole from Shelmet, they defend themselves and attack with two lances.

Y These Pokémon evolve by wearing the shell covering of a Shelmet. The steel armor protects their whole body.

STAT GROWTH RATES

HP	▪▪▪
Attack	▪▪▪▪▪▪▪
Defense	▪▪▪▪▪
Sp. Atk	▪▪▪
Sp. Def	▪▪▪▪
Speed	▪

EGG GROUP
Bug

🔺 EVOLUTION

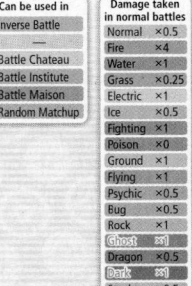

Karrablast → Link Trade for Shelmet → Escavalier

ITEMS SOMETIMES HELD BY WILD POKÉMON
None

Can be used in
Inverse Battle
—
Battle Chateau
Battle Institute
Battle Maison
Random Matchup

Damage taken in normal battles	
Normal	×0.5
Fire	×4
Water	×1
Grass	×0.25
Electric	×1
Ice	×0.5
Fighting	×1
Poison	×0
Ground	×1
Flying	×1
Psychic	×0.5
Bug	×1
Rock	×1
Ghost	×1
Dragon	×0.5
Dark	×1
Steel	×0.5
Fairy	×0.5

Damage taken in Inverse Battles	
Normal	×2
Fire	×0.25
Water	×1
Grass	×4
Electric	×1
Ice	×2
Fighting	×1
Poison	×2
Ground	×1
Flying	×1
Psychic	×2
Bug	×2
Rock	×1
Ghost	×1
Dragon	×2
Dark	×1
Steel	×2
Fairy	×2

How to obtain for your Mountain Kalos Pokédex

Trade your Shelmet in return for a Karrablast in a Link Trade, and have the Karrablast evolve.

Trade your Shelmet in return for a Karrablast in a Link Trade, and have the Karrablast evolve.

Same form for ♂/♀

 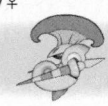 

023
Escavalier

● LEVEL-UP MOVES

Lv.	Name	Type	Kind	Pow.	Acc.	PP	Range
1	Double-Edge	Normal	Physical	120	100	15	Normal
1	Fell Stinger	Bug	Physical	30	100	25	Normal
1	Peck	Flying	Physical	35	100	35	Normal
1	Leer	Normal	Status	—	100	30	Many Others
1	Quick Guard	Fighting	Status	—	—	15	Your Side
1	Twineedle	Bug	Physical	25	100	20	Normal
4	Leer	Normal	Status	—	100	30	Many Others
8	Quick Guard	Fighting	Status	—	—	15	Your Side
13	Twineedle	Bug	Physical	25	100	20	Normal
16	Fury Attack	Normal	Physical	15	85	20	Normal
20	Headbutt	Normal	Physical	70	100	15	Normal
25	False Swipe	Normal	Physical	40	100	40	Normal
28	Bug Buzz	Bug	Special	90	100	10	Normal
32	Slash	Normal	Physical	70	100	20	Normal
37	Iron Head	Steel	Physical	80	100	15	Normal
40	Iron Defense	Steel	Status	—	—	15	Self
44	X-Scissor	Bug	Physical	80	100	15	Normal
49	Reversal	Fighting	Physical	—	100	15	Normal
52	Swords Dance	Normal	Status	—	—	20	Self
56	Giga Impact	Normal	Physical	150	90	5	Normal
60	Fell Stinger	Bug	Physical	30	100	25	Normal

● TM & HM MOVES

No.	Name	Type	Kind	Pow.	Acc.	PP	Range
TM06	Toxic	Poison	Status	—	90	10	Normal
TM10	Hidden Power	Normal	Special	60	100	15	Normal
TM15	Hyper Beam	Normal	Special	150	90	5	Normal
TM17	Protect	Normal	Status	—	—	10	Self
TM18	Rain Dance	Water	Status	—	—	5	Both Sides
TM21	Frustration	Normal	Physical	—	100	20	Normal
TM27	Return	Normal	Physical	—	100	20	Normal
TM32	Double Team	Normal	Status	—	—	15	Self
TM40	Aerial Ace	Flying	Physical	60	—	20	Normal
TM42	Facade	Normal	Physical	70	100	20	Normal
TM44	Rest	Psychic	Status	—	—	10	Self
TM45	Attract	Normal	Status	—	100	15	Normal
TM48	Round	Normal	Special	60	100	15	Normal
TM52	Focus Blast	Fighting	Special	120	70	5	Normal
TM53	Energy Ball	Grass	Special	90	100	10	Normal
TM54	False Swipe	Normal	Physical	40	100	40	Normal
TM68	Giga Impact	Normal	Physical	150	90	5	Normal
TM75	Swords Dance	Normal	Status	—	—	20	Self
TM76	Struggle Bug	Bug	Special	50	100	20	Many Others
TM81	X-Scissor	Bug	Physical	80	100	15	Normal
TM83	Infestation	Bug	Special	20	100	20	Normal
TM84	Poison Jab	Poison	Physical	80	100	20	Normal
TM87	Swagger	Normal	Status	—	90	15	Normal
TM88	Sleep Talk	Normal	Status	—	—	10	Self
TM90	Substitute	Normal	Status	—	—	10	Self
TM94	Rock Smash	Fighting	Physical	40	100	15	Normal
TM100	Confide	Normal	Status	—	—	20	Normal
HM01	Cut	Normal	Physical	50	95	30	Normal

● MOVES TAUGHT BY PEOPLE

Name	Type	Kind	Pow.	Acc.	PP	Range

Mountain Kalos 024

Snail Pokémon

☑ Shelmet

HEIGHT: 1'04" **WEIGHT:** 17.0 lbs.
GENDER: ♂/♀

TYPE Bug

ABILITIES
Hydration
Shell Armor

HIDDEN ABILITY
Overcoat

STAT GROWTH RATES
HP	■■
Attack	■■
Defense	■■■■
Sp. Atk	■■
Sp. Def	■■■
Speed	■■

EGG GROUP
Bug

Ⓧ When it and Karrablast are together, and both receive electrical stimulation, they both evolve.

Ⓨ It evolves when bathed in an electric-like energy along with Karrablast. The reason is still unknown.

⬆ EVOLUTION

Link Trade for Karrablast

Shelmet → Accelgor

ITEMS SOMETIMES HELD BY WILD POKÉMON
None

Damage taken in normal battles		Damage taken in Inverse Battles	
Normal	×1	Normal	×1
Fire	×2	Fire	×0.5
Water	×1	Water	×1
Grass	×0.5	Grass	×2
Electric	×1	Electric	×1
Ice	×1	Ice	×1
Fighting	×0.5	Fighting	×2
Poison	×1	Poison	×1
Ground	×0.5	Ground	×2
Flying	×2	Flying	×0.5
Psychic	×1	Psychic	×1
Bug	×1	Bug	×1
Rock	×2	Rock	×0.5
Ghost	×1	Ghost	×1
Dragon	×1	Dragon	×1
Dark	×1	Dark	×1
Steel	×1	Steel	×1
Fairy	×1	Fairy	×1

Can be used in	
Inverse Battle	Battle Institute
—	Battle Maison
Battle Chateau	Random Matchup

Same form for ♂/♀

How to obtain for your Mountain Kalos Pokédex

❶ Catch in the tall grass on Route 14.
❷ Catch in the swamps along Route 14.

❶ Catch in the tall grass on Route 14.
❷ Catch in the swamps along Route 14.

● LEVEL-UP MOVES

Lv.	Name	Type	Kind	Pow.	Acc.	PP	Range
1	Leech Life	Bug	Physical	20	100	15	Normal
4	Acid	Poison	Special	40	100	30	Many Others
8	Bide	Normal	Physical	—	—	10	Self
13	Curse	Ghost	Status	—	—	10	Varies
16	Struggle Bug	Bug	Special	50	100	20	Many Others
20	Mega Drain	Grass	Special	40	100	15	Normal
25	Yawn	Normal	Status	—	—	10	Normal
28	Protect	Normal	Status	—	—	10	Self
32	Acid Armor	Poison	Status	—	—	20	Self
37	Giga Drain	Grass	Special	75	100	10	Normal
40	Body Slam	Normal	Physical	85	100	15	Normal
44	Bug Buzz	Bug	Special	90	100	10	Normal
49	Recover	Normal	Status	—	—	10	Self
50	Guard Swap	Psychic	Status	—	—	10	Normal
56	Final Gambit	Fighting	Special	—	100	5	Normal

● TM & HM MOVES

No.	Name	Type	Kind	Pow.	Acc.	PP	Range
TM06	Toxic	Poison	Status	—	90	10	Normal
TM09	Venoshock	Poison	Special	65	100	10	Normal
TM10	Hidden Power	Normal	Special	60	100	15	Normal
TM17	Protect	Normal	Status	—	—	10	Self
TM18	Rain Dance	Water	Status	—	—	5	Both Sides
TM21	Frustration	Normal	Physical	—	100	20	Normal
TM27	Return	Normal	Physical	—	100	20	Normal
TM32	Double Team	Normal	Status	—	—	15	Self
TM36	Sludge Bomb	Poison	Special	90	100	10	Normal
TM42	Facade	Normal	Physical	70	100	20	Normal
TM44	Rest	Psychic	Status	—	—	10	Self
TM45	Attract	Normal	Status	—	100	15	Normal
TM48	Round	Normal	Special	60	100	15	Normal
TM53	Energy Ball	Grass	Special	90	100	10	Normal
TM76	Struggle Bug	Bug	Special	50	100	20	Many Others
TM83	Infestation	Bug	Special	20	100	20	Normal
TM87	Swagger	Normal	Status	—	90	15	Normal
TM88	Sleep Talk	Normal	Status	—	—	10	Self
TM90	Substitute	Normal	Status	—	—	10	Self
TM100	Confide	Normal	Status	—	—	20	Normal

● MOVES TAUGHT BY PEOPLE

Name	Type	Kind	Pow.	Acc.	PP	Range

● EGG MOVES

Name	Type	Kind	Pow.	Acc.	PP	Range
Endure	Normal	Status	—	—	10	Self
Baton Pass	Normal	Status	—	—	40	Self
Double-Edge	Normal	Physical	120	100	15	Normal
Encore	Normal	Status	—	100	5	Normal
Guard Split	Psychic	Status	—	—	10	Normal
Mind Reader	Normal	Status	—	—	5	Normal
Mud-Slap	Ground	Special	20	100	10	Normal
Spikes	Ground	Status	—	—	20	Other Side
Feint	Normal	Physical	30	100	10	Normal
Pursuit	Dark	Physical	40	100	20	Normal

AFTER THE HALL OF FAME
CENTRAL KALOS
COASTAL KALOS
MOUNTAIN KALOS
024 Shelmet
ADVENTURE DATA

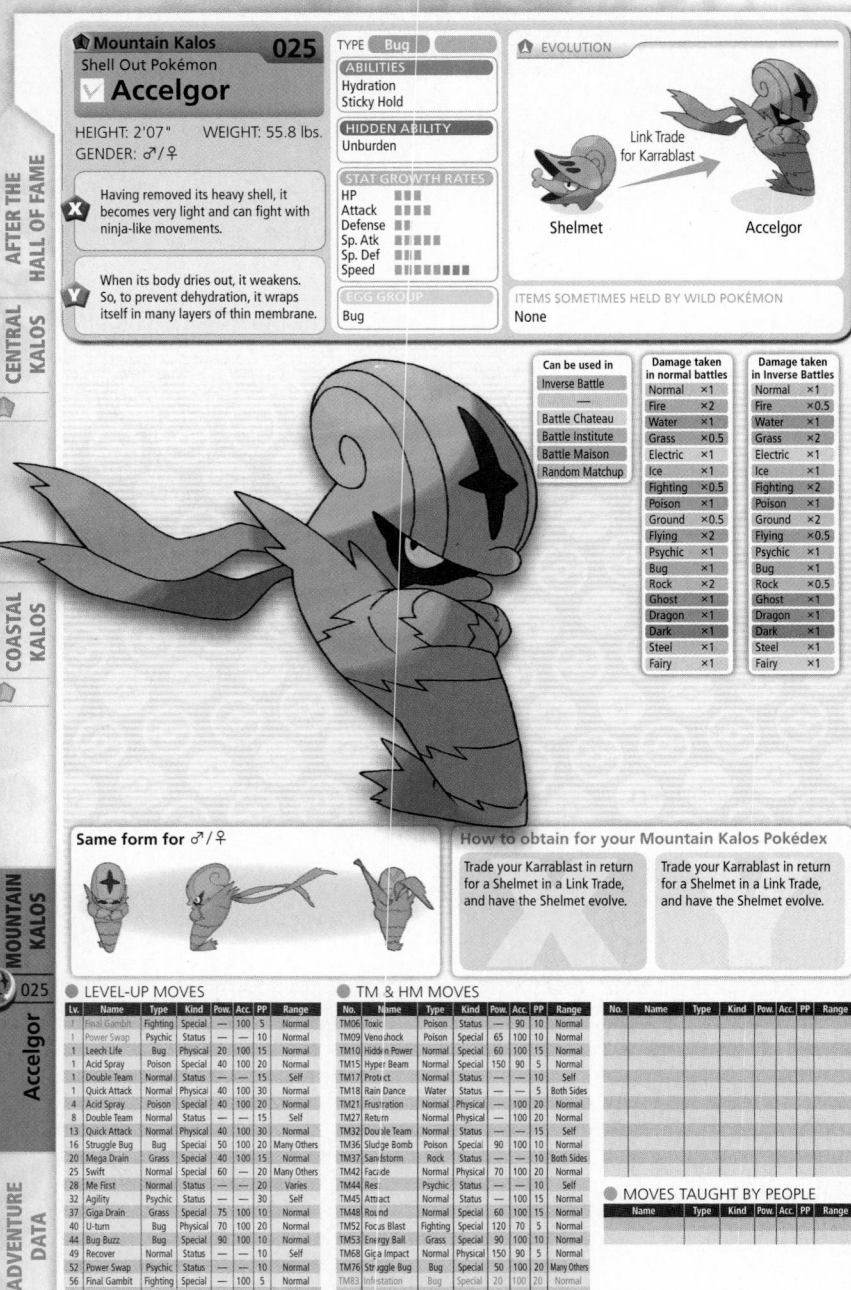

♠ Mountain Kalos — 025

Shell Out Pokémon

☑ **Accelgor**

HEIGHT: 2'07"   WEIGHT: 55.8 lbs.
GENDER: ♂/♀

X Having removed its heavy shell, it becomes very light and can fight with ninja-like movements.

Y When its body dries out, it weakens. So, to prevent dehydration, it wraps itself in many layers of thin membrane.

TYPE Bug

ABILITIES
Hydration
Sticky Hold

HIDDEN ABILITY
Unburden

STAT GROWTH RATES
HP	■■■
Attack	■■■■
Defense	■■
Sp. Atk	■■■■■
Sp. Def	■■■
Speed	■■■■■■■■

EGG GROUP
Bug

EVOLUTION

Shelmet → (Link Trade for Karrablast) → Accelgor

ITEMS SOMETIMES HELD BY WILD POKÉMON
None

Can be used in
Inverse Battle
—
Battle Chateau
Battle Institute
Battle Maison
Random Matchup

Damage taken in normal battles	
Normal	×1
Fire	×2
Water	×1
Grass	×0.5
Electric	×1
Ice	×1
Fighting	×0.5
Poison	×1
Ground	×0.5
Flying	×2
Psychic	×1
Bug	×1
Rock	×2
Ghost	×1
Dragon	×1
Dark	×1
Steel	×1
Fairy	×1

Damage taken in Inverse Battles	
Normal	×1
Fire	×0.5
Water	×1
Grass	×2
Electric	×1
Ice	×1
Fighting	×2
Poison	×1
Ground	×2
Flying	×0.5
Psychic	×1
Bug	×1
Rock	×0.5
Ghost	×1
Dragon	×1
Dark	×1
Steel	×1
Fairy	×1

Same form for ♂/♀

How to obtain for your Mountain Kalos Pokédex

Trade your Karrablast in return for a Shelmet in a Link Trade, and have the Shelmet evolve.

Trade your Karrablast in return for a Shelmet in a Link Trade, and have the Shelmet evolve.

025

Accelgor

● LEVEL-UP MOVES

Lv.	Name	Type	Kind	Pow.	Acc.	PP	Range
1	Final Gambit	Fighting	Special	—	100	5	Normal
1	Power Swap	Psychic	Status	—	—	10	Normal
1	Leech Life	Bug	Physical	20	100	15	Normal
1	Acid Spray	Poison	Special	40	100	20	Normal
1	Double Team	Normal	Status	—	—	15	Self
1	Quick Attack	Normal	Physical	40	100	30	Normal
4	Acid Spray	Poison	Special	40	100	20	Normal
8	Double Team	Normal	Status	—	—	15	Self
13	Quick Attack	Normal	Physical	40	100	30	Normal
16	Struggle Bug	Bug	Special	50	100	20	Many Others
20	Mega Drain	Grass	Special	40	100	15	Normal
25	Swift	Normal	Special	60	—	20	Many Others
28	Me First	Normal	Status	—	—	20	Varies
32	Agility	Psychic	Status	—	—	30	Self
37	Giga Drain	Grass	Special	75	100	10	Normal
40	U-turn	Bug	Physical	70	100	20	Normal
44	Bug Buzz	Bug	Special	90	100	10	Normal
49	Recover	Normal	Status	—	—	10	Self
52	Power Swap	Psychic	Status	—	—	10	Normal
56	Final Gambit	Fighting	Special	—	100	5	Normal

● TM & HM MOVES

No.	Name	Type	Kind	Pow.	Acc.	PP	Range
TM06	Toxic	Poison	Status	—	90	10	Normal
TM09	Venoshock	Poison	Special	65	100	10	Normal
TM10	Hidden Power	Normal	Special	60	100	15	Normal
TM15	Hyper Beam	Normal	Special	150	90	5	Normal
TM17	Protect	Normal	Status	—	—	10	Self
TM18	Rain Dance	Water	Status	—	—	5	Both Sides
TM21	Frustration	Normal	Physical	—	100	20	Normal
TM27	Return	Normal	Physical	—	100	20	Normal
TM32	Double Team	Normal	Status	—	—	15	Self
TM36	Sludge Bomb	Poison	Special	90	100	10	Normal
TM37	Sandstorm	Rock	Status	—	—	10	Both Sides
TM42	Facade	Normal	Physical	70	100	20	Normal
TM44	Rest	Psychic	Status	—	—	10	Self
TM45	Attract	Normal	Status	—	100	15	Normal
TM48	Round	Normal	Special	60	100	15	Normal
TM52	Focus Blast	Fighting	Special	120	70	5	Normal
TM53	Energy Ball	Grass	Special	90	100	10	Normal
TM68	Giga Impact	Normal	Physical	150	90	5	Normal
TM76	Struggle Bug	Bug	Special	50	100	20	Many Others
TM83	Infestation	Bug	Special	20	100	20	Normal
TM87	Swagger	Normal	Status	—	90	15	Normal
TM88	Sleep Talk	Normal	Status	—	—	10	Self
TM89	U-turn	Bug	Physical	70	100	20	Normal
TM90	Substitute	Normal	Status	—	—	10	Self
TM100	Confide	Normal	Status	—	—	20	Normal

No.	Name	Type	Kind	Pow.	Acc.	PP	Range

● MOVES TAUGHT BY PEOPLE

Name	Type	Kind	Pow.	Acc.	PP	Range

Mountain Kalos — 026

Flower Pokémon

☑ Bellsprout

HEIGHT: 2'04"　WEIGHT: 8.8 lbs.
GENDER: ♂/♀

X Even though its body is extremely skinny, it is blindingly fast when catching its prey.

Y Its bud looks like a human face. Because of the bud, it is rumored to be a type of legendary mandrake plant.

TYPE: Grass / Poison

ABILITY
Chlorophyll

HIDDEN ABILITY
Gluttony

STAT GROWTH RATES
HP ▪▪
Attack ▪▪▪▪
Defense ▪▪
Sp. Atk ▪▪▪
Sp. Def ▪▪▪
Speed ▪▪

EGG GROUP
Grass

EVOLUTION

Lv. 21 / Leaf Stone

Bellsprout — Weepinbell — Victreebel

ITEMS SOMETIMES HELD BY WILD POKÉMON
None

Damage taken in normal battles		Damage taken in Inverse Battles	
Normal	×1	Normal	×1
Fire	×2	Fire	×0.5
Water	×0.5	Water	×2
Grass	×0.25	Grass	×4
Electric	×0.5	Electric	×2
Ice	×2	Ice	×0.5
Fighting	×0.5	Fighting	×2
Poison	×1	Poison	×1
Ground	×1	Ground	×1
Flying	×2	Flying	×0.5
Psychic	×2	Psychic	×0.5
Bug	×1	Bug	×1
Rock	×1	Rock	×1
Ghost	×1	Ghost	×1
Dragon	×1	Dragon	×1
Dark	×1	Dark	×1
Steel	×1	Steel	×1
Fairy	×0.5	Fairy	×2

Can be used in	
Inverse Battle	Battle Institute
—	Battle Maison
Battle Chateau	Random Matchup

Same form for ♂/♀

How to obtain for your Mountain Kalos Pokédex

Catch in a Horde Encounter on Route 14. | Catch in a Horde Encounter on Route 14.

LEVEL-UP MOVES

Lv.	Name	Type	Kind	Pow.	Acc.	PP	Range
1	Vine Whip	Grass	Physical	45	100	25	Normal
7	Growth	Normal	Status	—	—	20	Self
11	Wrap	Normal	Physical	15	90	20	Normal
13	Sleep Powder	Grass	Status	—	75	15	Normal
15	Poison Powder	Poison	Status	—	75	35	Normal
17	Stun Spore	Grass	Status	—	75	30	Normal
23	Acid	Poison	Special	40	100	30	Many Others
27	Knock Off	Dark	Physical	65	100	20	Normal
29	Sweet Scent	Normal	Status	—	100	20	Many Others
35	Gastro Acid	Poison	Status	—	100	10	Normal
39	Razor Leaf	Grass	Physical	55	95	25	Many Others
41	Slam	Normal	Physical	80	75	20	Normal
47	Wring Out	Normal	Special	—	100	5	Normal

TM & HM MOVES

No.	Name	Type	Kind	Pow.	Acc.	PP	Range
TM06	Toxic	Poison	Status	—	90	10	Normal
TM09	Venoshock	Poison	Special	65	100	10	Normal
TM10	Hidden Power	Normal	Special	60	100	15	Normal
TM11	Sunny Day	Fire	Status	—	—	5	Both Sides
TM17	Protect	Normal	Status	—	—	10	Self
TM21	Frustration	Normal	Physical	—	100	20	Normal
TM22	Solar Beam	Grass	Special	120	100	10	Normal
TM27	Return	Normal	Physical	—	100	20	Normal
TM32	Double Team	Normal	Status	—	—	15	Self
TM33	Reflect	Psychic	Status	—	—	20	Your Side
TM36	Sludge Bomb	Poison	Special	90	100	10	Normal
TM42	Facade	Normal	Physical	70	100	20	Normal
TM44	Rest	Psychic	Status	—	—	10	Self
TM45	Attract	Normal	Status	—	100	15	Normal
TM46	Thief	Dark	Physical	60	100	25	Normal
TM48	Round	Normal	Special	60	100	15	Normal
TM53	Energy Ball	Grass	Special	90	100	10	Normal
TM70	Flash	Normal	Status	—	100	20	Normal
TM75	Swords Dance	Normal	Status	—	—	20	Self
TM83	Infestation	Bug	Special	20	100	20	Normal
TM86	Grass Knot	Grass	Special	—	100	20	Normal
TM87	Swagger	Normal	Status	—	90	15	Normal
TM88	Sleep Talk	Normal	Status	—	—	10	Self
TM90	Substitute	Normal	Status	—	—	10	Self
TM96	Nature Power	Normal	Status	—	—	20	Normal
TM100	Confide	Normal	Status	—	—	20	Normal
HM01	Cut	Normal	Physical	50	95	30	Normal

MOVES TAUGHT BY PEOPLE

Name	Type	Kind	Pow.	Acc.	PP	Range

EGG MOVES

Name	Type	Kind	Pow.	Acc.	PP	Range
Encore	Normal	Status	—	100	5	Normal
Synthesis	Grass	Status	—	—	5	Self
Leech Life	Bug	Physical	20	100	15	Normal
Ingrain	Grass	Status	—	—	20	Self
Magical Leaf	Grass	Special	60	—	20	Normal
Worry Seed	Grass	Status	—	100	10	Normal
Tickle	Normal	Status	—	100	20	Normal
Weather Ball	Normal	Special	50	100	10	Normal
Bullet Seed	Grass	Physical	25	100	30	Normal
Natural Gift	Normal	Physical	—	100	15	Normal
Giga Drain	Grass	Special	75	100	10	Normal
Clear Smog	Poison	Special	50	—	15	Normal
Power Whip	Grass	Physical	120	85	10	Normal
Acid Spray	Poison	Special	40	100	20	Normal
Belch	Poison	Special	120	90	10	Normal

AFTER THE HALL OF FAME

CENTRAL KALOS

COASTAL KALOS

MOUNTAIN KALOS

027

Weepinbell

ADVENTURE DATA

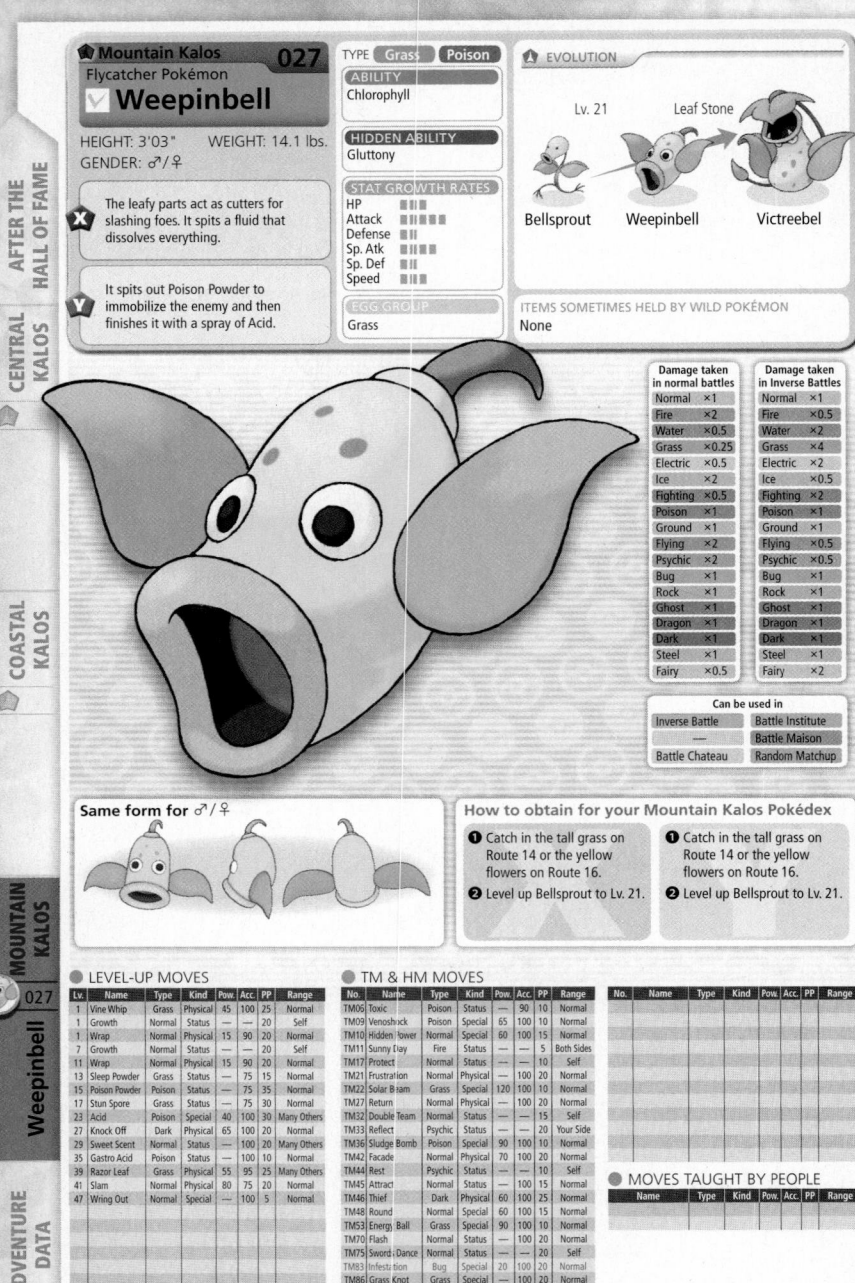

Mountain Kalos 027

Flycatcher Pokémon

Weepinbell

HEIGHT: 3'03" WEIGHT: 14.1 lbs.
GENDER: ♂/♀

X The leafy parts act as cutters for slashing foes. It spits a fluid that dissolves everything.

Y It spits out Poison Powder to immobilize the enemy and then finishes it with a spray of Acid.

TYPE: Grass / Poison

ABILITY
Chlorophyll

HIDDEN ABILITY
Gluttony

STAT GROWTH RATES
HP
Attack
Defense
Sp. Atk
Sp. Def
Speed

EGG GROUP
Grass

EVOLUTION

Lv. 21 Leaf Stone

Bellsprout Weepinbell Victreebel

ITEMS SOMETIMES HELD BY WILD POKÉMON
None

Damage taken in normal battles	
Normal	×1
Fire	×2
Water	×0.5
Grass	×0.25
Electric	×0.5
Ice	×2
Fighting	×0.5
Poison	×1
Ground	×1
Flying	×2
Psychic	×2
Bug	×1
Rock	×1
Ghost	×1
Dragon	×1
Dark	×1
Steel	×1
Fairy	×0.5

Damage taken in Inverse Battles	
Normal	×1
Fire	×0.5
Water	×2
Grass	×4
Electric	×2
Ice	×0.5
Fighting	×2
Poison	×1
Ground	×1
Flying	×0.5
Psychic	×0.5
Bug	×1
Rock	×1
Ghost	×1
Dragon	×1
Dark	×1
Steel	×1
Fairy	×2

Can be used in	
Inverse Battle	Battle Institute
—	Battle Maison
Battle Chateau	Random Matchup

Same form for ♂/♀

How to obtain for your Mountain Kalos Pokédex

❶ Catch in the tall grass on Route 14 or the yellow flowers on Route 16.
❷ Level up Bellsprout to Lv. 21.

❶ Catch in the tall grass on Route 14 or the yellow flowers on Route 16.
❷ Level up Bellsprout to Lv. 21.

● LEVEL-UP MOVES

Lv.	Name	Type	Kind	Pow.	Acc.	PP	Range
1	Vine Whip	Grass	Physical	45	100	25	Normal
1	Growth	Normal	Status	—	—	20	Self
1	Wrap	Normal	Physical	15	90	20	Normal
7	Growth	Normal	Status	—	—	20	Self
11	Wrap	Normal	Physical	15	90	20	Normal
13	Sleep Powder	Grass	Status	—	75	15	Normal
15	Poison Powder	Poison	Status	—	75	35	Normal
17	Stun Spore	Grass	Status	—	75	30	Normal
23	Acid	Poison	Special	40	100	30	Many Others
27	Knock Off	Dark	Physical	65	100	20	Normal
29	Sweet Scent	Normal	Status	—	100	20	Many Others
35	Gastro Acid	Poison	Status	—	100	10	Normal
39	Razor Leaf	Grass	Physical	55	95	25	Many Others
41	Slam	Normal	Physical	80	75	20	Normal
47	Wring Out	Normal	Special	—	100	5	Normal

● TM & HM MOVES

No.	Name	Type	Kind	Pow.	Acc.	PP	Range
TM06	Toxic	Poison	Status	—	90	10	Normal
TM09	Venoshock	Poison	Special	65	100	10	Normal
TM10	Hidden Power	Normal	Special	60	100	15	Normal
TM11	Sunny Day	Fire	Status	—	—	5	Both Sides
TM17	Protect	Normal	Status	—	—	10	Self
TM21	Frustration	Normal	Physical	—	100	20	Normal
TM22	Solar Beam	Grass	Special	120	100	10	Normal
TM27	Return	Normal	Physical	—	100	20	Normal
TM32	Double Team	Normal	Status	—	—	15	Self
TM33	Reflect	Psychic	Status	—	—	20	Your Side
TM36	Sludge Bomb	Poison	Special	90	100	10	Normal
TM42	Facade	Normal	Physical	70	100	20	Normal
TM44	Rest	Psychic	Status	—	—	10	Self
TM45	Attract	Normal	Status	—	100	15	Normal
TM46	Thief	Dark	Physical	60	100	25	Normal
TM48	Round	Normal	Special	60	100	15	Normal
TM53	Energy Ball	Grass	Special	90	100	10	Normal
TM70	Flash	Normal	Status	—	100	20	Normal
TM75	Swords Dance	Normal	Status	—	—	20	Self
TM83	Infestation	Bug	Special	20	100	20	Normal
TM86	Grass Knot	Grass	Special	—	100	20	Normal
TM87	Swagger	Normal	Status	—	90	15	Normal
TM88	Sleep Talk	Normal	Status	—	—	10	Self
TM90	Substitute	Normal	Status	—	—	10	Self
TM96	Nature Power	Normal	Status	—	—	20	Normal
TM100	Confide	Normal	Status	—	—	20	Normal
HM01	Cut	Normal	Physical	50	95	30	Normal

No.	Name	Type	Kind	Pow.	Acc.	PP	Range

● MOVES TAUGHT BY PEOPLE

Name	Type	Kind	Pow.	Acc.	PP	Range

Mountain Kalos — 028

Victreebel
Flycatcher Pokémon

HEIGHT: 5'07" WEIGHT: 34.2 lbs.
GENDER: ♂/♀

X: Said to live in huge colonies deep in jungles, although no one has ever returned from there.

Y: Once ingested into this Pokémon's body, even the hardest object will melt into nothing.

TYPE Grass | Poison

ABILITY
Chlorophyll

HIDDEN ABILITY
Gluttony

STAT GROWTH RATES
HP	■■■
Attack	■■■■■
Defense	■■■
Sp. Atk	■■■■■
Sp. Def	■■■
Speed	■■■■

EGG GROUP
Grass

EVOLUTION

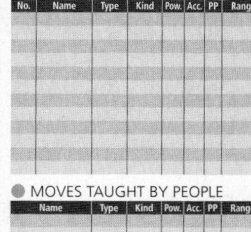

Lv. 21 — Leaf Stone

Bellsprout — Weepinbell — Victreebel

ITEMS SOMETIMES HELD BY WILD POKÉMON
None

Damage taken in normal battles		Damage taken in Inverse Battles	
Normal	×1	Normal	×1
Fire	×2	Fire	×0.5
Water	×0.5	Water	×2
Grass	×0.25	Grass	×4
Electric	×0.5	Electric	×2
Ice	×2	Ice	×0.5
Fighting	×0.5	Fighting	×2
Poison	×1	Poison	×1
Ground	×1	Ground	×1
Flying	×2	Flying	×0.5
Psychic	×2	Psychic	×0.5
Bug	×1	Bug	×1
Rock	×1	Rock	×1
Ghost	×1	Ghost	×1
Dragon	×1	Dragon	×1
Dark	×1	Dark	×1
Steel	×1	Steel	×1
Fairy	×0.5	Fairy	×2

Can be used in	
Inverse Battle	Battle Institute
—	Battle Maison
Battle Chateau	Random Matchup

Same form for ♂/♀

How to obtain for your Mountain Kalos Pokédex
Use a Leaf Stone on Weepinbell. Use a Leaf Stone on Weepinbell.

● LEVEL-UP MOVES
Lv.	Name	Type	Kind	Pow.	Acc.	PP	Range
1	Stockpile	Normal	Status	—	—	20	Self
1	Swallow	Normal	Status	—	—	10	Self
1	Spit Up	Normal	Special	—	100	10	Normal
1	Vine Whip	Grass	Physical	45	100	25	Normal
1	Sleep Powder	Grass	Status	—	75	15	Normal
1	Sweet Scent	Normal	Status	—	100	20	Many Others
1	Razor Leaf	Grass	Physical	55	95	25	Many Others
27	Leaf Tornado	Grass	Special	65	90	10	Normal
47	Leaf Storm	Grass	Special	130	90	5	Normal
47	Leaf Blade	Grass	Physical	90	100	15	Normal

● TM & HM MOVES
No.	Name	Type	Kind	Pow.	Acc.	PP	Range
TM06	Toxic	Poison	Status	—	90	10	Normal
TM09	Venoshock	Poison	Special	65	100	10	Normal
TM10	Hidden Power	Normal	Special	60	100	15	Normal
TM11	Sunny Day	Fire	Status	—	—	5	Both Sides
TM15	Hyper Beam	Normal	Special	150	90	5	Normal
TM17	Protect	Normal	Status	—	—	10	Self
TM21	Frustration	Normal	Physical	—	100	20	Normal
TM22	Solar Beam	Grass	Special	120	100	10	Normal
TM27	Return	Normal	Physical	—	100	20	Normal
TM32	Double Team	Normal	Status	—	—	15	Self
TM33	Reflect	Psychic	Status	—	—	20	Your Side
TM36	Sludge Bomb	Poison	Special	90	100	10	Normal
TM42	Facade	Normal	Physical	70	100	20	Normal
TM44	Rest	Psychic	Status	—	—	10	Self
TM45	Attract	Normal	Status	—	100	15	Normal
TM46	Thief	Dark	Physical	60	100	25	Normal
TM48	Round	Normal	Special	60	100	15	Normal
TM53	Energy Ball	Grass	Special	90	100	10	Normal
TM68	Giga Impact	Normal	Physical	150	90	5	Normal
TM70	Flash	Normal	Status	—	100	20	Normal
TM75	Swords Dance	Normal	Status	—	—	20	Self
TM83	Infestation	Bug	Special	20	100	20	Normal
TM86	Grass Knot	Grass	Special	—	100	20	Normal
TM87	Swagger	Normal	Status	—	90	15	Normal
TM88	Sleep Talk	Normal	Status	—	—	10	Self
TM90	Substitute	Normal	Status	—	—	10	Self
TM96	Nature Power	Normal	Status	—	—	20	Normal
TM100	Confide	Normal	Status	—	—	20	Normal
HM01	Cut	Normal	Physical	50	95	30	Normal

● MOVES TAUGHT BY PEOPLE
Name	Type	Kind	Pow.	Acc.	PP	Range

AFTER THE HALL OF FAME

CENTRAL KALOS

COASTAL KALOS

MOUNTAIN KALOS

028 | Victreebel

ADVENTURE DATA

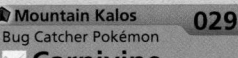

🏔 Mountain Kalos 029
Bug Catcher Pokémon
☑ **Carnivine**

HEIGHT: 4'07" WEIGHT: 59.5 lbs.
GENDER: ♂/♀

TYPE	Grass

ABILITY
Levitate

HIDDEN ABILITY
None

STAT GROWTH RATES
HP	▮▮▮
Attack	▮▮▮▮▮
Defense	▮▮▮
Sp. Atk	▮▮▮▮
Sp. Def	▮▮▮
Speed	▮▮▮

EGG GROUP
Grass

X It attracts prey with its sweet-smelling saliva, then chomps down. It takes a whole day to eat prey.

Y It binds itself to trees in marshes. It attracts prey with its sweet-smelling drool and gulps them down.

🔼 EVOLUTION

Does not evolve

ITEMS SOMETIMES HELD BY WILD POKÉMON
None

Damage taken in normal battles		Damage taken in Inverse Battles	
Normal	×1	Normal	×1
Fire	×2	Fire	×0.5
Water	×0.5	Water	×2
Grass	×0.5	Grass	×2
Electric	×0.5	Electric	×2
Ice	×2	Ice	×0.5
Fighting	×1	Fighting	×1
Poison	×2	Poison	×0.5
Ground	×0.5 🔾	Ground	×2 🔾
Flying	×2	Flying	×0.5
Psychic	×1	Psychic	×1
Bug	×2	Bug	×0.5
Rock	×1	Rock	×1
Ghost	×1	Ghost	×1
Dragon	×1	Dragon	×1
Dark	×1	Dark	×1
Steel	×1	Steel	×1
Fairy	×1	Fairy	×1

Can be used in	
Inverse Battle	Battle Institute
Sky Battle	Battle Maison
Battle Chateau	Random Matchup

Same form for ♂/♀

How to obtain for your Mountain Kalos Pokédex

❶ Catch in the tall grass on Route 14.
❷ Catch in the swamps along Route 14.

❶ Catch in the tall grass on Route 14.
❷ Catch in the swamps along Route 14.

029

Carnivine

● LEVEL-UP MOVES

Lv.	Name	Type	Kind	Pow.	Acc.	PP	Range
1	Bind	Normal	Physical	15	85	20	Normal
1	Growth	Normal	Status	—	—	20	Self
7	Bite	Dark	Physical	60	100	25	Normal
11	Vine Whip	Grass	Physical	45	100	25	Normal
17	Sweet Scent	Normal	Status	—	100	20	Many Others
21	Ingrain	Grass	Status	—	—	20	Self
27	Feint Attack	Dark	Physical	60	—	20	Normal
31	Leaf Tornado	Grass	Special	65	90	10	Normal
37	Stockpile	Normal	Status	—	—	20	Self
37	Spit Up	Normal	Special	—	100	10	Normal
37	Swallow	Normal	Status	—	—	10	Self
41	Crunch	Dark	Physical	80	100	15	Normal
47	Wring Out	Normal	Special	—	100	5	Normal
50	Power Whip	Grass	Physical	120	85	10	Normal

● TM & HM MOVES

No.	Name	Type	Kind	Pow.	Acc.	PP	Range
TM06	Toxic	Poison	Status	—	90	10	Normal
TM10	Hidden Power	Normal	Special	60	100	15	Normal
TM11	Sunny Day	Fire	Status	—	—	5	Both Sides
TM15	Hyper Beam	Normal	Special	150	90	5	Normal
TM17	Protect	Normal	Status	—	—	10	Self
TM21	Frustration	Normal	Physical	—	100	20	Normal
TM22	Solar Beam	Grass	Special	120	100	10	Normal
TM27	Return	Normal	Physical	—	100	20	Normal
TM32	Double Team	Normal	Status	—	—	15	Self
TM36	Sludge Bomb	Poison	Special	90	100	10	Normal
TM42	Facade	Normal	Physical	70	100	20	Normal
TM44	Rest	Psychic	Status	—	—	10	Self
TM45	Attract	Normal	Status	—	100	15	Normal
TM46	Thief	Dark	Physical	60	100	25	Normal
TM48	Round	Normal	Special	60	100	15	Normal
TM53	Energy Ball	Grass	Special	90	100	10	Normal
TM56	Fling	Dark	Physical	—	100	10	Normal
TM66	Payback	Dark	Physical	50	100	10	Normal
TM68	Giga Impact	Normal	Physical	150	90	5	Normal
TM70	Flash	Normal	Status	—	100	20	Normal
TM75	Swords Dance	Normal	Status	—	—	20	Self
TM83	Infestation	Bug	Special	20	100	20	Normal
TM86	Grass Knot	Grass	Special	—	100	20	Normal
TM87	Swagger	Normal	Status	—	90	15	Normal
TM88	Sleep Talk	Normal	Status	—	—	10	Self
TM90	Substitute	Normal	Status	—	—	10	Self
TM96	Nature Power	Normal	Status	—	—	20	Normal
TM100	Confide	Normal	Status	—	—	20	Normal
HM01	Cut	Normal	Physical	50	95	30	Normal

● MOVES TAUGHT BY PEOPLE

Name	Type	Kind	Pow.	Acc.	PP	Range

● EGG MOVES

Name	Type	Kind	Pow.	Acc.	PP	Range
Sleep Powder	Grass	Status	—	75	15	Normal
Stun Spore	Grass	Status	—	75	30	Normal
Razor Leaf	Grass	Physical	55	95	25	Many Others
Slam	Normal	Physical	80	75	20	Normal
Synthesis	Grass	Status	—	—	5	Self
Magical Leaf	Grass	Special	60	—	20	Normal
Leech Seed	Grass	Status	—	90	10	Normal
Worry Seed	Grass	Status	—	100	10	Normal
Giga Drain	Grass	Special	75	100	10	Normal
Rage Powder	Bug	Status	—	—	20	Self
Grass Whistle	Grass	Status	—	55	15	Normal

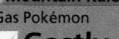

Mountain Kalos 030

Gas Pokémon

☑ **Gastly**

HEIGHT: 4'03"   WEIGHT: 0.2 lbs.
GENDER: ♂/♀

TYPE	Ghost	Poison

ABILITY
Levitate

HIDDEN ABILITY
None

STAT GROWTH RATES
HP	■■
Attack	■■
Defense	■■
Sp. Atk	■■■■■
Sp. Def	■■
Speed	■■■■

EGG GROUP
Amorphous

⚅ Its body is made of gas. Despite lacking substance, it can envelop an opponent of any size and cause suffocation.

⚅ Born from gases, anyone would faint if engulfed by its gaseous body, which contains poison.

EVOLUTION

Lv. 25   Link Trade

Gastly   Haunter   Gengar

ITEMS SOMETIMES HELD BY WILD POKÉMON
None

Damage taken in normal battles		Damage taken in Inverse Battles	
Normal	×0	Normal	×2
Fire	×1	Fire	×1
Water	×1	Water	×1
Grass	×0.5	Grass	×2
Electric	×1	Electric	×1
Ice	×1	Ice	×1
Fighting	×0	Fighting	×4
Poison	×0.25	Poison	×4
Ground	×2	Ground	×0.5
Flying	×1	Flying	×1
Psychic	×2	Psychic	×0.5
Bug	×0.25	Bug	×4
Rock	×1	Rock	×1
Ghost	×2	Ghost	×0.5
Dragon	×1	Dragon	×1
Dark	×2	Dark	×0.5
Steel	×1	Steel	×1
Fairy	×0.5	Fairy	×2

Can be used in	
Inverse Battle	Battle Institute
Sky Battle	Battle Maison
Battle Chateau	Random Matchup

Same form for ♂/♀

How to obtain for your Mountain Kalos Pokédex

Leave Haunter or Gengar at the Pokémon Day Care, and hatch the Egg that is found.

Leave Haunter or Gengar at the Pokémon Day Care, and hatch the Egg that is found.

AFTER THE HALL OF FAME

CENTRAL KALOS

COASTAL KALOS

MOUNTAIN KALOS

030 Gastly

ADVENTURE DATA

● LEVEL-UP MOVES

Lv.	Name	Type	Kind	Pow.	Acc.	PP	Range
1	Hypnosis	Psychic	Status	—	60	20	Normal
1	Lick	Ghost	Physical	30	100	30	Normal
5	Spite	Ghost	Status	—	100	10	Normal
8	Mean Look	Normal	Status	—	—	5	Normal
12	Curse	Ghost	Status	—	—	10	Varies
15	Night Shade	Ghost	Special	—	100	15	Normal
19	Confuse Ray	Ghost	Status	—	100	10	Normal
22	Sucker Punch	Dark	Physical	80	100	5	Normal
26	Payback	Dark	Physical	50	100	10	Normal
29	Shadow Ball	Ghost	Special	80	100	15	Normal
33	Dream Eater	Psychic	Special	100	100	15	Normal
36	Dark Pulse	Dark	Special	80	100	15	Normal
40	Destiny Bond	Ghost	Status	—	—	5	Self
43	Hex	Ghost	Special	65	100	10	Normal
47	Nightmare	Ghost	Status	—	100	15	Normal

■ TM & HM MOVES

No.	Name	Type	Kind	Pow.	Acc.	PP	Range
TM06	Toxic	Poison	Status	—	90	10	Normal
TM09	Venoshock	Poison	Special	65	100	10	Normal
TM10	Hidden Power	Normal	Special	60	100	15	Normal
TM11	Sunny Day	Fire	Status	—	—	5	Both Sides
TM12	Taunt	Dark	Status	—	100	20	Normal
TM17	Protect	Normal	Status	—	—	10	Self
TM18	Rain Dance	Water	Status	—	—	5	Both Sides
TM21	Frustration	Normal	Physical	—	100	20	Normal
TM24	Thunderbolt	Electric	Special	90	100	15	Normal
TM27	Return	Normal	Physical	—	100	20	Normal
TM29	Psychic	Psychic	Special	90	100	10	Normal
TM30	Shadow Ball	Ghost	Special	80	100	15	Normal
TM32	Double Team	Normal	Status	—	—	15	Self
TM36	Sludge Bomb	Poison	Special	90	100	10	Normal
TM41	Torment	Dark	Status	—	100	15	Normal
TM42	Facade	Normal	Physical	70	100	20	Normal
TM44	Rest	Psychic	Status	—	—	10	Self
TM45	Attract	Normal	Status	—	100	15	Normal
TM46	Thief	Dark	Physical	60	100	25	Normal
TM48	Round	Normal	Special	60	100	15	Normal
TM53	Energy Ball	Grass	Special	90	100	10	Normal
TM61	Will-O-Wisp	Fire	Status	—	85	15	Normal
TM63	Embargo	Dark	Status	—	100	15	Normal
TM64	Explosion	Normal	Physical	250	100	5	Adjacent
TM66	Payback	Dark	Physical	50	100	10	Normal
TM77	Psych Up	Normal	Status	—	—	10	Normal
TM85	Dream Eater	Psychic	Special	100	100	15	Normal
TM87	Swagger	Normal	Status	—	90	15	Normal
TM88	Sleep Talk	Normal	Status	—	—	10	Self
TM90	Substitute	Normal	Status	—	—	10	Self
TM92	Trick Room	Psychic	Status	—	—	5	Both Sides
TM97	Dark Pulse	Dark	Special	80	100	15	Normal

No.	Name	Type	Kind	Pow.	Acc.	PP	Range
TM99	Dazzling Gleam	Fairy	Special	80	100	10	Many Others
TM100	Confide	Normal	Status	—	—	20	Normal

● MOVES TAUGHT BY PEOPLE

Name	Type	Kind	Pow.	Acc.	PP	Range

● EGG MOVES

Name	Type	Kind	Pow.	Acc.	PP	Range
Psywave	Psychic	Special	—	100	15	Normal
Perish Song	Normal	Status	—	—	5	Adjacent
Haze	Ice	Status	—	—	30	Both Sides
Astonish	Ghost	Physical	30	100	15	Normal
Grudge	Ghost	Status	—	—	5	Self
Fire Punch	Fire	Physical	75	100	15	Normal
Ice Punch	Ice	Physical	75	100	15	Normal
Thunder Punch	Electric	Physical	75	100	15	Normal
Disable	Normal	Status	—	100	20	Normal
Scary Face	Normal	Status	—	100	10	Normal
Clear Smog	Poison	Special	50	—	15	Normal
Smog	Poison	Special	30	70	20	Normal
Reflect Type	Normal	Status	—	—	15	Normal

🏔 **Mountain Kalos** 031

Gas Pokémon

Ⓥ **Haunter**

HEIGHT: 5'03"　　WEIGHT: 0.2 lbs.
GENDER: ♂/♀

X If you get the feeling of being watched in darkness when nobody is around, Haunter is there.

Y It licks with its gaseous tongue to steal the victim's life force. It lurks in darkness for prey.

TYPE　Ghost　Poison

ABILITY
Levitate

HIDDEN ABILITY
None

STAT GROWTH RATES
HP	■■
Attack	■■
Defense	■■
Sp. Atk	■■■■
Sp. Def	■■
Speed	■■■■■

EGG GROUP
Amorphous

🧬 EVOLUTION

Lv. 25　　Link Trade

Gastly　　　Haunter　　　Gengar

ITEMS SOMETIMES HELD BY WILD POKÉMON
None

Damage taken in normal battles	
Normal	×0
Fire	×1
Water	×1
Grass	×0.5
Electric	×1
Ice	×1
Fighting	×0
Poison	×0.25
Ground	×2 ❶
Flying	×1
Psychic	×2
Bug	×0.25
Rock	×1
Ghost	×2
Dragon	×1
Dark	×2
Steel	×1
Fairy	×0.5

Damage taken in Inverse Battles	
Normal	×2
Fire	×1
Water	×1
Grass	×2
Electric	×1
Ice	×1
Fighting	×4
Poison	×4
Ground	×0.5 ❶
Flying	×1
Psychic	×0.5
Bug	×4
Rock	×1
Ghost	×0.5
Dragon	×1
Dark	×0.5
Steel	×1
Fairy	×2

Can be used in
Inverse Battle	Battle Institute
Sky Battle	Battle Maison
Battle Chateau	Random Matchup

Same form for ♂/♀

How to obtain for your Mountain Kalos Pokédex

❶ Catch in the tall grass on Route 14.
❷ Catch on Frost Cavern 1F.

❶ Catch in the tall grass on Route 14.
❷ Catch on Frost Cavern 1F.

● **LEVEL-UP MOVES**

Lv.	Name	Type	Kind	Pow.	Acc.	PP	Range
1	Hypnosis	Psychic	Status	—	60	20	Normal
1	Lick	Ghost	Physical	30	100	30	Normal
5	Spite	Ghost	Status	—	100	10	Normal
5	Spite	Ghost	Status	—	100	10	Normal
8	Mean Look	Normal	Status	—	—	5	Normal
12	Curse	Ghost	Status	—	—	10	Varies
15	Night Shade	Ghost	Special	—	100	15	Normal
19	Confuse Ray	Ghost	Status	—	100	10	Normal
22	Sucker Punch	Dark	Physical	80	100	5	Normal
25	Shadow Punch	Ghost	Physical	60	—	20	Normal
28	Payback	Dark	Physical	50	100	10	Normal
33	Shadow Ball	Ghost	Special	80	100	15	Normal
38	Dream Eater	Psychic	Special	100	100	15	Normal
44	Dark Pulse	Dark	Special	80	100	15	Normal
50	Destiny Bond	Ghost	Status	—	—	5	Self
55	Hex	Ghost	Special	65	100	10	Normal
61	Nightmare	Ghost	Status	—	100	15	Normal

● **TM & HM MOVES**

No.	Name	Type	Kind	Pow.	Acc.	PP	Range
TM06	Toxic	Poison	Status	—	90	10	Normal
TM09	Venoshock	Poison	Special	65	100	10	Normal
TM10	Hidden Power	Normal	Special	60	100	15	Normal
TM11	Sunny Day	Fire	Status	—	—	5	Both Sides
TM12	Taunt	Dark	Status	—	100	20	Normal
TM17	Protect	Normal	Status	—	—	10	Self
TM18	Rain Dance	Water	Status	—	—	5	Both Sides
TM21	Frustration	Normal	Physical	—	100	20	Normal
TM24	Thunderbolt	Electric	Special	90	100	15	Normal
TM27	Return	Normal	Physical	—	100	20	Normal
TM29	Psychic	Psychic	Special	90	100	10	Normal
TM30	Shadow Ball	Ghost	Special	80	100	15	Normal
TM32	Double Team	Normal	Status	—	—	15	Self
TM36	Sludge Bomb	Poison	Special	90	100	10	Normal
TM41	Torment	Dark	Status	—	100	15	Normal
TM42	Facade	Normal	Physical	70	100	20	Normal
TM44	Rest	Psychic	Status	—	—	10	Self
TM45	Attract	Normal	Status	—	100	15	Normal
TM46	Thief	Dark	Physical	60	100	25	Normal
TM48	Round	Normal	Special	60	100	15	Normal
TM53	Energy Ball	Grass	Special	90	100	10	Normal
TM56	Fling	Dark	Physical	—	100	10	Normal
TM61	Will-O-Wisp	Fire	Status	—	85	15	Normal
TM63	Embargo	Dark	Status	—	100	15	Normal
TM64	Explosion	Normal	Physical	250	100	5	Adjacent
TM65	Shadow Claw	Ghost	Physical	70	100	15	Normal
TM66	Payback	Dark	Physical	50	100	10	Normal
TM77	Psych Up	Normal	Status	—	—	10	Normal
TM83	Infestation	Bug	Special	20	100	20	Normal
TM84	Poison Jab	Poison	Physical	80	100	20	Normal
TM85	Dream Eater	Psychic	Special	100	100	15	Normal
TM87	Swagger	Normal	Status	—	90	15	Normal
TM88	Sleep Talk	Normal	Status	—	—	10	Self

No.	Name	Type	Kind	Pow.	Acc.	PP	Range
TM90	Substitute	Normal	Status	—	—	10	Self
TM92	Trick Room	Psychic	Status	—	—	5	Both Sides
TM97	Dark Pulse	Dark	Special	80	100	15	Normal
TM99	Dazzling Gleam	Fairy	Special	80	100	10	Many Others
TM100	Confide	Normal	Status	—	—	20	Normal

● **MOVES TAUGHT BY PEOPLE**

Name	Type	Kind	Pow.	Acc.	PP	Range

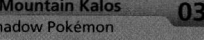

Mountain Kalos 032
Shadow Pokémon
☑ **Gengar**

HEIGHT: 4'11" WEIGHT: 89.3 lbs.
GENDER: ♂/♀

TYPE **Ghost** **Poison**

ABILITY
Levitate

HIDDEN ABILITY
None

X It hides in shadows. It is said that if Gengar is hiding, it cools the area by nearly 10 degrees Fahrenheit.

Y Hiding in people's shadows at night, it absorbs their heat. The chill it causes makes the victims shake.

STAT GROWTH RATES
HP	■■■
Attack	■■■
Defense	■■■
Sp. Atk	■■■■■
Sp. Def	■■■
Speed	■■■■■

EGG GROUP
Amorphous

▲ EVOLUTION

Lv. 25 Link Trade

Gastly   Haunter   Gengar

ITEMS SOMETIMES HELD BY WILD POKÉMON
None

Damage taken in normal battles
Normal	×0
Fire	×1
Water	×1
Grass	×0.5
Electric	×1
Ice	×1
Fighting	×0
Poison	×0.25
Ground	×2
Flying	×1
Psychic	×2
Bug	×0.25
Rock	×1
Ghost	×2
Dragon	×1
Dark	×2
Steel	×1
Fairy	×0.5

Damage taken in Inverse Battles
Normal	×2
Fire	×1
Water	×1
Grass	×2
Electric	×1
Ice	×1
Fighting	×4
Poison	×4
Ground	×0.5
Flying	×1
Psychic	×0.5
Bug	×4
Rock	×1
Ghost	×0.5
Dragon	×1
Dark	×0.5
Steel	×1
Fairy	×2

Can be used in
Inverse Battle
——
Battle Chateau
Battle Institute
Battle Maison
Random Matchup

How to obtain for your Mountain Kalos Pokédex

Receive Haunter by Link Trade, and have it evolve.

Receive Haunter by Link Trade, and have it evolve.

Same form for ♂/♀

● LEVEL-UP MOVES

Lv.	Name	Type	Kind	Pow.	Acc.	PP	Range
1	Hypnosis	Psychic	Status	—	60	20	Normal
1	Lick	Ghost	Physical	30	100	30	Normal
1	Spite	Ghost	Status	—	100	10	Normal
5	Spite	Ghost	Status	—	100	10	Normal
8	Mean Look	Normal	Status	—	—	5	Normal
12	Curse	Ghost	Status	—	—	10	Varies
15	Night Shade	Ghost	Special	—	100	15	Normal
19	Confuse Ray	Ghost	Status	—	100	10	Normal
22	Sucker Punch	Dark	Physical	80	100	5	Normal
25	Shadow Punch	Ghost	Physical	60	—	20	Normal
28	Payback	Dark	Physical	50	100	10	Normal
33	Shadow Ball	Ghost	Special	80	100	15	Normal
39	Dream Eater	Psychic	Special	100	100	15	Normal
44	Dark Pulse	Dark	Special	80	100	15	Normal
50	Destiny Bond	Ghost	Status	—	—	5	Self
55	Hex	Ghost	Special	65	100	10	Normal
61	Nightmare	Ghost	Status	—	100	15	Normal

● TM & HM MOVES

No.	Name	Type	Kind	Pow.	Acc.	PP	Range
TM06	Toxic	Poison	Status	—	90	10	Normal
TM09	Venoshock	Poison	Special	65	100	10	Normal
TM10	Hidden Power	Normal	Special	60	100	15	Normal
TM11	Sunny Day	Fire	Status	—	—	5	Both Sides
TM12	Taunt	Dark	Status	—	100	20	Normal
TM15	Hyper Beam	Normal	Special	150	90	5	Normal
TM17	Protect	Normal	Status	—	—	10	Self
TM18	Rain Dance	Water	Status	—	—	5	Both Sides
TM21	Frustration	Normal	Physical	—	100	20	Normal
TM24	Thunderbolt	Electric	Special	90	100	15	Normal
TM25	Thunder	Electric	Special	110	70	10	Normal
TM27	Return	Normal	Physical	—	100	20	Normal
TM29	Psychic	Psychic	Special	90	100	10	Normal
TM30	Shadow Ball	Ghost	Special	80	100	15	Normal
TM31	Brick Break	Fighting	Physical	75	100	15	Normal
TM32	Double Team	Normal	Status	—	—	15	Self
TM36	Sludge Bomb	Poison	Special	90	100	10	Normal
TM41	Torment	Dark	Status	—	100	15	Normal
TM42	Facade	Normal	Physical	70	100	20	Normal
TM44	Rest	Psychic	Status	—	—	10	Self
TM45	Attract	Normal	Status	—	100	15	Normal
TM46	Thief	Dark	Physical	60	100	25	Normal
TM48	Round	Normal	Special	60	100	15	Normal
TM52	Focus Blast	Fighting	Special	120	70	5	Normal
TM53	Energy Ball	Grass	Special	90	100	10	Normal
TM56	Fling	Dark	Physical	—	100	10	Normal
TM61	Will-O-Wisp	Fire	Status	—	85	15	Normal
TM63	Embargo	Dark	Status	—	100	15	Normal
TM64	Explosion	Normal	Physical	250	100	5	Adjacent
TM65	Shadow Claw	Ghost	Physical	70	100	15	Normal
TM66	Payback	Dark	Physical	50	100	10	Normal
TM68	Giga Impact	Normal	Physical	150	90	5	Normal
TM77	Psych Up	Normal	Status	—	—	10	Normal

No.	Name	Type	Kind	Pow.	Acc.	PP	Range
TM83	Infestation	Bug	Special	20	100	20	Normal
TM84	Poison Jab	Poison	Physical	80	100	20	Normal
TM85	Dream Eater	Psychic	Special	100	100	15	Normal
TM87	Swagger	Normal	Status	—	90	15	Normal
TM88	Sleep Talk	Normal	Status	—	—	10	Self
TM90	Substitute	Normal	Status	—	—	10	Self
TM92	Trick Room	Psychic	Status	—	—	5	Both Sides
TM94	Rock Smash	Fighting	Physical	40	100	15	Normal
TM97	Dark Pulse	Dark	Special	80	100	15	Normal
TM98	Power-Up Punch	Fighting	Physical	40	100	20	Normal
TM99	Dazzling Gleam	Fairy	Special	80	100	10	Many Others
TM100	Confide	Normal	Status	—	—	20	Normal
HM04	Strength	Normal	Physical	80	100	15	Normal

● MOVES TAUGHT BY PEOPLE

Name	Type	Kind	Pow.	Acc.	PP	Range

AFTER THE HALL OF FAME

CENTRAL KALOS

CRYSTAL KALOS

MOUNTAIN KALOS

032 Gengar

ADVENTURE DATA

AFTER THE HALL OF FAME

CENTRAL KALOS

COASTAL KALOS

MOUNTAIN KALOS

Mega Gengar

ADVENTURE DATA

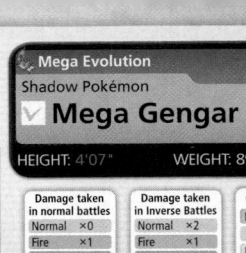

Mega Evolution

Shadow Pokémon

☑ **Mega Gengar**

HEIGHT: 4'07"   WEIGHT: 89.3 lbs.   GENDER: ♂/♀

TYPE: Ghost / Poison

ABILITY
Shadow Tag

STAT GROWTH RATES

Stat	Growth
HP	■■■
Attack	■■■
Defense	■■■■
Sp. Atk	■■■■■■■■
Sp. Def	■■■■
Speed	■■■■■■■

MEGA STONE REQUIRED

Gengarite

Receive from a woman in Laverre City if you talk to her after having Gastly, Haunter, or Gengar registered in your Pokédex.

Damage taken in normal battles	
Normal	×0
Fire	×1
Water	×1
Grass	×0.5
Electric	×1
Ice	×1
Fighting	×0
Poison	×0.25
Ground	×2
Flying	×1
Psychic	×2
Bug	×0.25
Rock	×1
Ghost	×2
Dragon	×1
Dark	×2
Steel	×1
Fairy	×0.5

Damage taken in Inverse Battles	
Normal	×2
Fire	×1
Water	×1
Grass	×2
Electric	×1
Ice	×1
Fighting	×4
Poison	×4
Ground	×0.5
Flying	×1
Psychic	×0.5
Bug	×4
Rock	×1
Ghost	×0.5
Dragon	×1
Dark	×0.5
Steel	×1
Fairy	×2

Can be used in
Inverse Battle
—
Battle Chateau
Battle Institute
Battle Maison
Random Matchup

Same form for ♂/♀

AFTER THE HALL OF FAME

CENTRAL KALOS

COASTAL KALOS

MOUNTAIN KALOS

033

Poliwag

ADVENTURE DATA

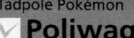

Mountain Kalos — 033
Poliwag
Tadpole Pokémon

TYPE Water

HEIGHT: 2'00" WEIGHT: 27.3 lbs.
GENDER: ♂/♀

ABILITIES
Water Absorb
Damp

HIDDEN ABILITY
Swift Swim

Its slick black skin is thin and damp. A part of its internal organs can be seen through the skin as a spiral pattern.

The direction of the spiral on the belly differs by area. It is more adept at swimming than walking.

STAT GROWTH RATES
HP	■■
Attack	■■■
Defense	■■
Sp. Atk	■■
Sp. Def	■■
Speed	■■■■■

EGG GROUP
Water 1

EVOLUTION

Poliwag — Lv. 25 → Poliwhirl — Water Stone → Poliwrath

Poliwhirl — Link Trade with a King's Rock → Politoed

ITEMS SOMETIMES HELD BY WILD POKÉMON
None

Damage taken in normal battles		Damage taken in Inverse Battles	
Normal	×1	Normal	×1
Fire	×0.5	Fire	×2
Water	×0.5	Water	×2
Grass	×2	Grass	×0.5
Electric	×2	Electric	×0.5
Ice	×0.5	Ice	×2
Fighting	×1	Fighting	×1
Poison	×1	Poison	×1
Ground	×1	Ground	×1
Flying	×1	Flying	×1
Psychic	×1	Psychic	×1
Bug	×1	Bug	×1
Rock	×1	Rock	×1
Ghost	×1	Ghost	×1
Dragon	×1	Dragon	×1
Dark	×1	Dark	×1
Steel	×0.5	Steel	×2
Fairy	×1	Fairy	×1

Can be used in	
Inverse Battle	Battle Institute
—	Battle Maison
Battle Chateau	Random Matchup

Same form for ♂/♀

How to obtain for your Mountain Kalos Pokédex

❶ Catch using an Old Rod on Route 14.
❷ Catch using an Old Rod in Laverre City.

❶ Catch using an Old Rod on Route 14.
❷ Catch using an Old Rod in Laverre City.

LEVEL-UP MOVES

Lv.	Name	Type	Kind	Pow.	Acc.	PP	Range
1	Water Sport	Water	Status	—	—	15	Both Sides
5	Water Gun	Water	Special	40	100	25	Normal
8	Hypnosis	Psychic	Status	—	60	20	Normal
11	Bubble	Water	Special	40	100	30	Many Others
15	Double Slap	Normal	Physical	15	85	10	Normal
18	Rain Dance	Water	Status	—	—	5	Both Sides
21	Body Slam	Normal	Physical	85	100	15	Normal
25	Bubble Beam	Water	Special	65	100	20	Normal
28	Mud Shot	Ground	Special	55	95	15	Normal
31	Belly Drum	Normal	Status	—	—	10	Self
35	Wake-Up Slap	Fighting	Physical	70	100	10	Normal
38	Hydro Pump	Water	Special	110	80	5	Normal
41	Mud Bomb	Ground	Special	65	85	10	Normal

TM & HM MOVES

No.	Name	Type	Kind	Pow.	Acc.	PP	Range
TM06	Toxic	Poison	Status	—	90	10	Normal
TM07	Hail	Ice	Status	—	—	10	Both Sides
TM10	Hidden Power	Normal	Special	60	100	15	Normal
TM13	Ice Beam	Ice	Special	90	100	10	Normal
TM14	Blizzard	Ice	Special	110	70	5	Many Others
TM17	Protect	Normal	Status	—	—	10	Self
TM18	Rain Dance	Water	Status	—	—	5	Both Sides
TM21	Frustration	Normal	Physical	—	100	20	Normal
TM27	Return	Normal	Physical	—	100	20	Normal
TM28	Dig	Ground	Physical	80	100	10	Normal
TM29	Psychic	Psychic	Special	90	100	10	Normal
TM32	Double Team	Normal	Status	—	—	15	Self
TM42	Facade	Normal	Physical	70	100	20	Normal
TM44	Rest	Psychic	Status	—	—	10	Self
TM45	Attract	Normal	Status	—	100	15	Normal
TM46	Thief	Dark	Physical	60	100	25	Normal
TM48	Round	Normal	Special	60	100	15	Normal
TM55	Scald	Water	Special	80	100	15	Normal
TM87	Swagger	Normal	Status	—	90	15	Normal
TM88	Sleep Talk	Normal	Status	—	—	10	Self
TM90	Substitute	Normal	Status	—	—	10	Self
TM100	Confide	Normal	Status	—	—	20	Normal
HM03	Surf	Water	Special	90	100	15	Adjacent
HM05	Waterfall	Water	Physical	80	100	15	Normal

MOVES TAUGHT BY PEOPLE

Name	Type	Kind	Pow.	Acc.	PP	Range

EGG MOVES

Name	Type	Kind	Pow.	Acc.	PP	Range
Mist	Ice	Status	—	—	30	Your Side
Splash	Normal	Status	—	—	40	Self
Bubble Beam	Water	Special	65	100	20	Normal
Haze	Ice	Status	—	—	30	Both Sides
Mind Reader	Normal	Status	—	—	5	Normal
Water Sport	Water	Status	—	—	15	Both Sides
Ice Ball	Ice	Physical	30	90	20	Normal
Mud Shot	Ground	Special	55	95	15	Normal
Refresh	Normal	Status	—	—	20	Self
Endeavor	Normal	Physical	—	100	5	Normal
Encore	Normal	Status	—	100	5	Normal
Endure	Normal	Status	—	—	10	Self
Water Pulse	Water	Special	60	100	20	Normal

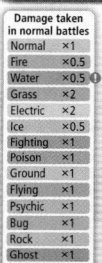

Mountain Kalos 034
Tadpole Pokémon
✓ Poliwhirl

HEIGHT: 3'03" WEIGHT: 44.1 lbs.
GENDER: ♂/♀

X It can live in or out of water. When out of water, it constantly sweats to keep its body slimy.

Y Its two legs are well developed. Even though it can live on the ground, it prefers living in water.

TYPE Water

ABILITIES
Water Absorb
Damp

HIDDEN ABILITY
Swift Swim

STAT GROWTH RATES
HP ▪▪▪
Attack ▪▪▪
Defense ▪▪▪
Sp. Atk ▪▪
Sp. Def ▪▪
Speed ▪▪▪▪▪

EGG GROUP
Water 1

EVOLUTION

Poliwag — Lv. 25 → Poliwhirl — Water Stone → Poliwrath
Link Trade with a King's Rock → Politoed

ITEMS SOMETIMES HELD BY WILD POKÉMON
King's Rock

Damage taken in normal battles		Damage taken in Inverse Battles	
Normal	×1	Normal	×1
Fire	×0.5	Fire	×2
Water	×0.5	Water	×2
Grass	×2	Grass	×0.5
Electric	×2	Electric	×0.5
Ice	×0.5	Ice	×2
Fighting	×1	Fighting	×1
Poison	×1	Poison	×1
Ground	×1	Ground	×1
Flying	×1	Flying	×1
Psychic	×1	Psychic	×1
Bug	×1	Bug	×1
Rock	×1	Rock	×1
Ghost	×1	Ghost	×1
Dragon	×1	Dragon	×1
Dark	×1	Dark	×1
Steel	×0.5	Steel	×2
Fairy	×1	Fairy	×1

Can be used in	
Inverse Battle	Battle Institute
—	Battle Maison
Battle Chateau	Random Matchup

Same form for ♂/♀

How to obtain for your Mountain Kalos Pokédex
1. Catch using a Good Rod on Route 14 or in Laverre City.
2. Level up Poliwag to Lv. 25.

1. Catch using a Good Rod on Route 14 or in Laverre City.
2. Level up Poliwag to Lv. 25.

● LEVEL-UP MOVES

Lv.	Name	Type	Kind	Pow.	Acc.	PP	Range
1	Water Sport	Water	Status	—	—	15	Both Sides
1	Water Gun	Water	Special	40	100	25	Normal
1	Hypnosis	Psychic	Status	—	60	20	Normal
5	Water Gun	Water	Special	40	100	25	Normal
8	Hypnosis	Psychic	Status	—	60	20	Normal
11	Bubble	Water	Special	40	100	30	Many Others
15	Double Slap	Normal	Physical	15	85	10	Normal
18	Rain Dance	Water	Status	—	—	5	Both Sides
21	Body Slam	Normal	Physical	85	100	15	Normal
27	Bubble Beam	Water	Special	65	100	20	Normal
32	Mud Shot	Ground	Special	55	95	15	Normal
37	Belly Drum	Normal	Status	—	—	10	Self
43	Wake-Up Slap	Fighting	Physical	70	100	10	Normal
48	Hydro Pump	Water	Special	110	80	5	Normal
53	Mud Bomb	Ground	Special	65	85	10	Normal

● TM & HM MOVES

No.	Name	Type	Kind	Pow.	Acc.	PP	Range
TM06	Toxic	Poison	Status	—	90	10	Normal
TM07	Hail	Ice	Status	—	—	10	Both Sides
TM10	Hidden Power	Normal	Special	60	100	15	Normal
TM13	Ice Beam	Ice	Special	90	100	10	Normal
TM14	Blizzard	Ice	Special	110	70	5	Many Others
TM17	Protect	Normal	Status	—	—	10	Self
TM18	Rain Dance	Water	Status	—	—	5	Both Sides
TM21	Frustration	Normal	Physical	—	100	20	Normal
TM26	Earthquake	Ground	Physical	100	100	10	Adjacent
TM27	Return	Normal	Physical	—	100	20	Normal
TM28	Dig	Ground	Physical	80	100	10	Normal
TM29	Psychic	Psychic	Special	90	100	10	Normal
TM31	Brick Break	Fighting	Physical	75	100	15	Normal
TM32	Double Team	Normal	Status	—	—	15	Self
TM42	Facade	Normal	Physical	70	100	20	Normal
TM44	Rest	Psychic	Status	—	—	10	Self
TM45	Attract	Normal	Status	—	100	15	Normal
TM46	Thief	Dark	Physical	60	100	25	Normal
TM48	Round	Normal	Special	60	100	15	Normal
TM55	Scald	Water	Special	80	100	15	Normal
TM56	Fling	Dark	Physical	—	100	10	Normal
TM78	Bulldoze	Ground	Physical	60	100	20	Adjacent
TM87	Swagger	Normal	Status	—	90	15	Normal
TM88	Sleep Talk	Normal	Status	—	—	10	Self
TM90	Substitute	Normal	Status	—	—	10	Self
TM94	Rock Smash	Fighting	Physical	40	100	15	Normal
TM98	Power-Up Punch	Fighting	Physical	40	100	20	Normal
TM100	Confide	Normal	Status	—	—	20	Normal
HM03	Surf	Water	Special	90	100	15	Adjacent
HM04	Strength	Normal	Physical	80	100	15	Normal
HM05	Waterfall	Water	Physical	80	100	15	Normal

No.	Name	Type	Kind	Pow.	Acc.	PP	Range

● MOVES TAUGHT BY PEOPLE

Name	Type	Kind	Pow.	Acc.	PP	Range

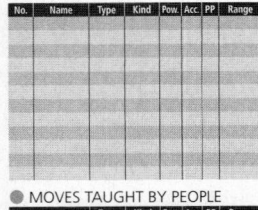

AFTER THE HALL OF FAME

CENTRAL KALOS

COASTAL KALOS

MOUNTAIN KALOS

034 Poliwhirl

ADVENTURE DATA

466

MOUNTAIN KALOS

035

Poliwrath

AFTER THE HALL OF FAME

CENTRAL KALOS

COASTAL KALOS

ADVENTURE DATA

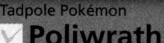

Mountain Kalos 035
Tadpole Pokémon

☑ **Poliwrath**

HEIGHT: 4'03" WEIGHT: 119.0 lbs.
GENDER: ♂/♀

 With its extremely tough muscles, it can keep swimming in the Pacific Ocean without resting.

 A swimmer adept at both the front crawl and breaststroke. Easily overtakes the best human swimmers.

TYPE **Water** **Fighting**

ABILITIES
Water Absorb
Damp

HIDDEN ABILITY
Swift Swim

STAT GROWTH RATES
HP	■■■■
Attack	■■■■■
Defense	■■■■
Sp. Atk	■■■
Sp. Def	■■■■
Speed	■■■■

EGG GROUP
Water 1

EVOLUTION

Water Stone

Lv. 25

Poliwag — Poliwhirl

Poliwrath

Link Trade with a King's Rock

Politoed

ITEMS SOMETIMES HELD BY WILD POKÉMON
King's Rock

Damage taken in normal battles			Damage taken in Inverse Battles	
Normal	×1		Normal	×1
Fire	×0.5		Fire	×2
Water	×0.5 ❶		Water	×2 ❶
Grass	×2		Grass	×0.5
Electric	×2		Electric	×0.5
Ice	×0.5		Ice	×2
Fighting	×1		Fighting	×1
Poison	×1		Poison	×1
Ground	×1		Ground	×1
Flying	×2		Flying	×0.5
Psychic	×2		Psychic	×0.5
Bug	×0.5		Bug	×2
Rock	×0.5		Rock	×2
Ghost	×1		Ghost	×1
Dragon	×1		Dragon	×1
Dark	×0.5		Dark	×2
Steel	×0.5		Steel	×2
Fairy	×2		Fairy	×0.5

Can be used in	
Inverse Battle	Battle Institute
—	Battle Maison
Battle Chateau	Random Matchup

Same form for ♂/♀

How to obtain for your Mountain Kalos Pokédex

❶ Catch using a Super Rod on Victory Road (Inside 4).

❷ Use a Water Stone on Poliwhirl.

❶ Catch using a Super Rod on Victory Road (Inside 4).

❷ Use a Water Stone on Poliwhirl.

LEVEL-UP MOVES

Lv.	Name	Type	Kind	Pow.	Acc.	PP	Range
1	Circle Throw	Fighting	Physical	60	90	10	Normal
1	Bubble Beam	Water	Special	65	100	20	Normal
1	Hypnosis	Psychic	Status	—	60	20	Normal
1	Double Slap	Normal	Physical	15	85	10	Normal
1	Submission	Fighting	Physical	80	80	20	Normal
32	Dynamic Punch	Fighting	Physical	100	50	5	Normal
43	Mind Reader	Normal	Status	—	—	5	Normal
53	Circle Throw	Fighting	Physical	60	90	10	Normal

TM & HM MOVES

No.	Name	Type	Kind	Pow.	Acc.	PP	Range
TM06	Toxic	Poison	Status	—	90	10	Normal
TM07	Hail	Ice	Status	—	—	10	Both Sides
TM08	Bulk Up	Fighting	Status	—	—	20	Self
TM10	Hidden Power	Normal	Special	60	100	15	Normal
TM13	Ice Beam	Ice	Special	90	100	10	Normal
TM14	Blizzard	Ice	Special	110	70	5	Many Others
TM15	Hyper Beam	Normal	Special	150	90	5	Normal
TM17	Protect	Normal	Status	—	—	10	Self
TM18	Rain Dance	Water	Status	—	—	5	Both Sides
TM21	Frustration	Normal	Physical	—	100	20	Normal
TM26	Earthquake	Ground	Physical	100	100	10	Adjacent
TM27	Return	Normal	Physical	—	100	20	Normal
TM28	Dig	Ground	Physical	80	100	10	Normal
TM29	Psychic	Psychic	Special	90	100	10	Normal
TM31	Brick Break	Fighting	Physical	75	100	15	Normal
TM32	Double Team	Normal	Status	—	—	15	Self
TM39	Rock Tomb	Rock	Physical	60	95	15	Normal
TM42	Facade	Normal	Physical	70	100	20	Normal
TM44	Rest	Psychic	Status	—	—	10	Self
TM45	Attract	Normal	Status	—	100	15	Normal
TM46	Thief	Dark	Physical	60	100	25	Normal
TM47	Low Sweep	Fighting	Physical	65	100	20	Normal
TM48	Round	Normal	Special	60	100	15	Normal
TM52	Focus Blast	Fighting	Special	120	70	5	Normal
TM55	Scald	Water	Special	80	100	15	Normal
TM56	Fling	Dark	Physical	—	100	10	Normal
TM66	Payback	Dark	Physical	50	100	10	Normal
TM68	Giga Impact	Normal	Physical	150	90	5	Normal
TM78	Bulldoze	Ground	Physical	60	100	20	Adjacent
TM80	Rock Slide	Rock	Physical	75	90	10	Many Others
TM84	Poison Jab	Poison	Physical	80	100	20	Normal
TM87	Swagger	Normal	Status	—	90	15	Normal
TM88	Sleep Talk	Normal	Status	—	—	10	Self

No.	Name	Type	Kind	Pow.	Acc.	PP	Range
TM90	Substitute	Normal	Status	—	—	10	Self
TM94	Rock Smash	Fighting	Physical	40	100	15	Normal
TM98	Power-Up Punch	Fighting	Physical	40	100	20	Normal
TM100	Confide	Normal	Status	—	—	20	Normal
HM03	Surf	Water	Special	90	100	15	Adjacent
HM04	Strength	Normal	Physical	80	100	15	Normal
HM05	Waterfall	Water	Physical	80	100	15	Normal

MOVES TAUGHT BY PEOPLE

Name	Type	Kind	Pow.	Acc.	PP	Range

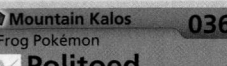

Mountain Kalos **036**

Frog Pokémon

☑ **Politoed**

HEIGHT: 3'07" WEIGHT: 74.7 lbs.
GENDER: ♂/♀

X Whenever three or more of these get together, they sing in a loud voice that sounds like bellowing.

Y If Poliwag and Poliwhirl hear its echoing cry, they respond by gathering from far and wide.

TYPE Water

ABILITIES
Water Absorb
Damp

HIDDEN ABILITY
Drizzle

STAT GROWTH RATES
HP	■■■■
Attack	■■■
Defense	■■■
Sp. Atk	■■■
Sp. Def	■■■■
Speed	■■■

EGG GROUP
Water 1

EVOLUTION

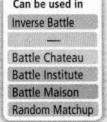

Poliwag → (Lv. 25) Poliwhirl → (Water Stone) Poliwrath
Poliwhirl → (Link Trade with a King's Rock) Politoed

ITEMS SOMETIMES HELD BY WILD POKÉMON
King's Rock

Can be used in
Inverse Battle
—
Battle Chateau
Battle Institute
Battle Maison
Random Matchup

Damage taken in normal battles	
Normal	×1
Fire	×0.5
Water	×0.5
Grass	×2
Electric	×2
Ice	×0.5
Fighting	×1
Poison	×1
Ground	×1
Flying	×1
Psychic	×1
Bug	×1
Rock	×1
Ghost	×1
Dragon	×1
Dark	×1
Steel	×0.5
Fairy	×1

Damage taken in Inverse Battles	
Normal	×1
Fire	×2
Water	×2
Grass	×0.5
Electric	×0.5
Ice	×2
Fighting	×1
Poison	×1
Ground	×1
Flying	×1
Psychic	×1
Bug	×1
Rock	×1
Ghost	×1
Dragon	×1
Dark	×1
Steel	×2
Fairy	×1

How to obtain for your Mountain Kalos Pokédex

❶ Catch using a Super Rod on Route 19.
❷ Receive Poliwhirl with a King's Rock by Link Trade, and have it evolve.

❶ Catch using a Super Rod on Route 19.
❷ Receive Poliwhirl with a King's Rock by Link Trade, and have it evolve.

♂    ♀

The male has larger vocal sacs on its cheeks. The female has smaller vocal sacs on its cheeks.

● **LEVEL-UP MOVES**

Lv.	Name	Type	Kind	Pow.	Acc.	PP	Range
1	Bubble Beam	Water	Special	65	100	20	Normal
1	Hypnosis	Psychic	Status	—	60	20	Normal
1	Double Slap	Normal	Physical	15	85	10	Normal
1	Perish Song	Normal	Status	—	—	5	Adjacent
27	Swagger	Normal	Status	—	90	15	Normal
37	Bounce	Flying	Physical	85	85	5	Normal
48	Hyper Voice	Normal	Special	90	100	10	Many Others

● **TM & HM MOVES**

No.	Name	Type	Kind	Pow.	Acc.	PP	Range
TM06	Toxic	Poison	Status	—	90	10	Normal
TM07	Hail	Ice	Status	—	—	10	Both Sides
TM10	Hidden Power	Normal	Special	60	100	15	Normal
TM13	Ice Beam	Ice	Special	90	100	10	Normal
TM14	Blizzard	Ice	Special	110	70	5	Many Others
TM15	Hyper Beam	Normal	Special	150	90	5	Normal
TM17	Protect	Normal	Status	—	—	10	Self
TM18	Rain Dance	Water	Status	—	—	5	Both Sides
TM21	Frustration	Normal	Physical	—	100	20	Normal
TM26	Earthquake	Ground	Physical	100	100	10	Adjacent
TM27	Return	Normal	Physical	—	100	20	Normal
TM28	Dig	Ground	Physical	80	100	10	Normal
TM29	Psychic	Psychic	Special	90	100	10	Normal
TM31	Brick Break	Fighting	Physical	75	100	15	Normal
TM32	Double Team	Normal	Status	—	—	15	Self
TM42	Facade	Normal	Physical	70	100	20	Normal
TM44	Rest	Psychic	Status	—	—	10	Self
TM45	Attract	Normal	Status	—	100	15	Normal
TM46	Thief	Dark	Physical	60	100	25	Normal
TM48	Round	Normal	Special	60	100	15	Normal
TM49	Echoed Voice	Normal	Special	40	100	15	Normal
TM52	Focus Blast	Fighting	Special	120	70	5	Normal
TM55	Scald	Water	Special	80	100	15	Normal
TM56	Fling	Dark	Physical	—	100	10	Normal
TM66	Payback	Dark	Physical	50	100	10	Normal
TM68	Giga Impact	Normal	Physical	150	90	5	Normal
TM78	Bulldoze	Ground	Physical	60	100	20	Adjacent
TM87	Swagger	Normal	Status	—	90	15	Normal
TM88	Sleep Talk	Normal	Status	—	—	10	Self
TM90	Substitute	Normal	Status	—	—	10	Self
TM94	Rock Smash	Fighting	Physical	40	100	15	Normal
TM98	Power-Up Punch	Fighting	Physical	40	100	20	Normal
TM100	Confide	Normal	Status	—	—	20	Normal

No.	Name	Type	Kind	Pow.	Acc.	PP	Range
HM03	Surf	Water	Special	90	100	15	Adjacent
HM04	Strength	Normal	Physical	80	100	15	Normal
HM05	Waterfall	Water	Physical	80	100	15	Normal

● **MOVES TAUGHT BY PEOPLE**

Name	Type	Kind	Pow.	Acc.	PP	Range

AFTER THE HALL OF FAME

CENTRAL KALOS

COASTAL KALOS

MOUNTAIN KALOS
036
Politoed

ADVENTURE DATA

Mountain Kalos

Snake Pokémon

⌄ Ekans

037

HEIGHT: 6'07" WEIGHT: 15.2 lbs.
GENDER: ♂/♀

X The older it gets, the longer it grows. At night, it wraps its long body around tree branches to rest.

Y Moving silently and stealthily, it eats the eggs of birds, such as Pidgey and Spearow, whole.

TYPE Poison

ABILITIES
Intimidate
Shed Skin

HIDDEN ABILITY
Unnerve

STAT GROWTH RATES
HP	■■
Attack	■■■
Defense	■■
Sp. Atk	■■
Sp. Def	■■
Speed	■■■

EGG GROUPS
Field, Dragon

EVOLUTION

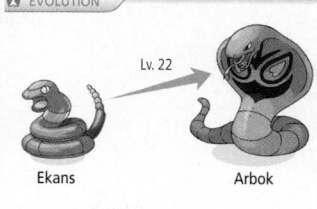

Lv. 22

Ekans → Arbok

ITEMS SOMETIMES HELD BY WILD POKÉMON
None

Damage taken in normal battles		Damage taken in Inverse Battles	
Normal	×1	Normal	×1
Fire	×1	Fire	×1
Water	×1	Water	×1
Grass	×0.5	Grass	×2
Electric	×1	Electric	×1
Ice	×1	Ice	×1
Fighting	×0.5	Fighting	×2
Poison	×0.5	Poison	×2
Ground	×2	Ground	×0.5
Flying	×1	Flying	×1
Psychic	×2	Psychic	×0.5
Bug	×0.5	Bug	×2
Rock	×1	Rock	×1
Ghost	×1	Ghost	×1
Dragon	×1	Dragon	×1
Dark	×1	Dark	×1
Steel	×1	Steel	×1
Fairy	×0.5	Fairy	×2

Can be used in
Inverse Battle	Battle Institute
—	Battle Maison
Battle Chateau	Random Matchup

Same form for ♂/♀

How to obtain for your Mountain Kalos Pokédex

Catch in a Horde Encounter on Route 14.

Catch in a Horde Encounter on Route 14.

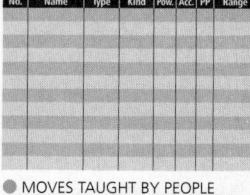

● LEVEL-UP MOVES

Lv.	Name	Type	Kind	Pow.	Acc.	PP	Range
1	Wrap	Normal	Physical	15	90	20	Normal
1	Leer	Normal	Status	—	100	30	Many Others
4	Poison Sting	Poison	Physical	15	100	35	Normal
9	Bite	Dark	Physical	60	100	25	Normal
12	Glare	Normal	Status	—	100	30	Normal
17	Screech	Normal	Status	—	85	40	Normal
20	Acid	Poison	Special	40	100	30	Many Others
25	Stockpile	Normal	Status	—	—	20	Self
25	Swallow	Normal	Status	—	—	10	Self
25	Spit Up	Normal	Special	—	100	10	Normal
28	Acid Spray	Poison	Special	40	100	20	Normal
33	Mud Bomb	Ground	Special	65	85	10	Normal
36	Gastro Acid	Poison	Status	—	100	10	Normal
38	Belch	Poison	Special	120	90	10	Normal
41	Haze	Ice	Status	—	—	30	Both Sides
44	Coil	Poison	Status	—	—	20	Self
49	Gunk Shot	Poison	Physical	120	80	5	Normal

● TM & HM MOVES

No.	Name	Type	Kind	Pow.	Acc.	PP	Range
TM06	Toxic	Poison	Status	—	90	10	Normal
TM09	Venoshock	Poison	Special	65	100	10	Normal
TM10	Hidden Power	Normal	Special	60	100	15	Normal
TM11	Sunny Day	Fire	Status	—	—	5	Both Sides
TM17	Protect	Normal	Status	—	—	10	Self
TM18	Rain Dance	Water	Status	—	—	5	Both Sides
TM21	Frustration	Normal	Physical	—	100	20	Normal
TM26	Earthquake	Ground	Physical	100	100	10	Adjacent
TM27	Return	Normal	Physical	—	100	20	Normal
TM28	Dig	Ground	Physical	80	100	10	Normal
TM32	Double Team	Normal	Status	—	—	15	Self
TM34	Sludge Wave	Poison	Special	95	100	10	Adjacent
TM36	Sludge Bomb	Poison	Special	90	100	10	Normal
TM39	Rock Tomb	Rock	Physical	60	95	15	Normal
TM41	Torment	Dark	Status	—	100	15	Normal
TM42	Facade	Normal	Physical	70	100	20	Normal
TM44	Rest	Psychic	Status	—	—	10	Self
TM45	Attract	Normal	Status	—	100	15	Normal
TM46	Thief	Dark	Physical	60	100	25	Normal
TM48	Round	Normal	Special	60	100	15	Normal
TM66	Payback	Dark	Physical	50	100	10	Normal
TM78	Bulldoze	Ground	Physical	60	100	20	Adjacent
TM80	Rock Slide	Rock	Physical	75	90	10	Many Others
TM83	Infestation	Bug	Special	20	100	20	Normal
TM84	Poison Jab	Poison	Physical	80	100	20	Normal
TM87	Swagger	Normal	Status	—	90	15	Normal
TM88	Sleep Talk	Normal	Status	—	—	10	Self
TM90	Substitute	Normal	Status	—	—	10	Self
TM97	Dark Pulse	Dark	Special	80	100	15	Normal
TM100	Confide	Normal	Status	—	—	20	Normal
HM04	Strength	Normal	Physical	80	100	15	Normal

● MOVES TAUGHT BY PEOPLE

Name	Type	Kind	Pow.	Acc.	PP	Range

● EGG MOVES

Name	Type	Kind	Pow.	Acc.	PP	Range
Pursuit	Dark	Physical	40	100	20	Normal
Slam	Normal	Physical	80	75	20	Normal
Spite	Ghost	Status	—	100	10	Normal
Beat Up	Dark	Physical	—	100	10	Normal
Poison Fang	Poison	Physical	50	100	15	Normal
Scary Face	Normal	Status	—	100	10	Normal
Poison Tail	Poison	Physical	50	100	25	Normal
Disable	Normal	Status	—	100	20	Normal
Switcheroo	Dark	Status	—	100	10	Normal
Iron Tail	Steel	Physical	100	75	15	Normal
Sucker Punch	Dark	Physical	80	100	5	Normal
Snatch	Dark	Status	—	—	10	Self

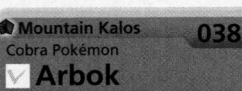

🔴 Mountain Kalos 038

Cobra Pokémon

☑ Arbok

HEIGHT: 11'06" WEIGHT: 143.3 lbs.
GENDER: ♂/♀

X The pattern on its belly appears to be a frightening face. Weak foes will flee just at the sight of the pattern.

Y To intimidate foes, it spreads its chest wide and makes eerie sounds by expelling air from its mouth.

TYPE Poison

ABILITIES
Intimidate
Shed Skin

HIDDEN ABILITY
Unnerve

STAT GROWTH RATES
HP	▪▪▪
Attack	▪▪▪▪
Defense	▪▪▪
Sp. Atk	▪▪▪
Sp. Def	▪▪▪
Speed	▪▪▪▪

EGG GROUPS
Field, Dragon

⬆ EVOLUTION

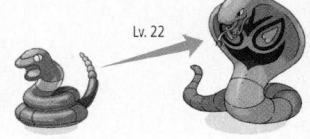

Ekans — Lv. 22 → Arbok

ITEMS SOMETIMES HELD BY WILD POKÉMON
None

Damage taken in normal battles		Damage taken in Inverse Battles	
Normal	×1	Normal	×1
Fire	×1	Fire	×1
Water	×1	Water	×1
Grass	×0.5	Grass	×2
Electric	×1	Electric	×1
Ice	×1	Ice	×1
Fighting	×0.5	Fighting	×2
Poison	×0.5	Poison	×2
Ground	×2	Ground	×0.5
Flying	×1	Flying	×1
Psychic	×2	Psychic	×0.5
Bug	×0.5	Bug	×2
Rock	×1	Rock	×1
Ghost	×1	Ghost	×1
Dragon	×1	Dragon	×1
Dark	×1	Dark	×1
Steel	×1	Steel	×1
Fairy	×0.5	Fairy	×2

Can be used in	
Inverse Battle	Battle Institute
—	Battle Maison
Battle Chateau	Random Matchup

Same form for ♂/♀

How to obtain for your Mountain Kalos Pokédex

❶ Catch in a Horde Encounter on Route 19.
❷ Level up Ekans to Lv. 22.

❶ Catch in a Horde Encounter on Route 19.
❷ Level up Ekans to Lv. 22.

● LEVEL-UP MOVES

Lv.	Name	Type	Kind	Pow.	Acc.	PP	Range
1	Ice Fang	Ice	Physical	65	95	15	Normal
1	Thunder Fang	Electric	Physical	65	95	15	Normal
1	Fire Fang	Fire	Physical	65	95	15	Normal
1	Wrap	Normal	Physical	15	90	20	Normal
1	Leer	Normal	Status	—	100	30	Many Others
1	Poison Sting	Poison	Physical	15	100	35	Normal
1	Bite	Dark	Physical	60	100	25	Normal
4	Poison Sting	Poison	Physical	15	100	35	Normal
9	Bite	Dark	Physical	60	100	25	Normal
12	Glare	Normal	Status	—	100	30	Normal
17	Screech	Normal	Status	—	85	40	Normal
20	Acid	Poison	Special	40	100	30	Many Others
22	Crunch	Dark	Physical	80	100	15	Normal
27	Stockpile	Normal	Status	—	—	20	Self
27	Swallow	Normal	Status	—	—	10	Self
27	Spit Up	Normal	Special	—	100	10	Normal
32	Acid Spray	Poison	Special	40	100	20	Normal
39	Mud Bomb	Ground	Special	65	85	10	Normal
44	Gastro Acid	Poison	Status	—	100	10	Normal
48	Belch	Poison	Special	120	90	10	Normal
51	Haze	Ice	Status	—	—	30	Both Sides
56	Coil	Poison	Status	—	—	20	Self
63	Gunk Shot	Poison	Physical	120	80	5	Normal

● TM & HM MOVES

No.	Name	Type	Kind	Pow.	Acc.	PP	Range
TM06	Toxic	Poison	Status	—	90	10	Normal
TM09	Venoshock	Poison	Special	65	100	10	Normal
TM10	Hidden Power	Normal	Special	60	100	15	Normal
TM11	Sunny Day	Fire	Status	—	—	5	Both Sides
TM15	Hyper Beam	Normal	Special	150	90	5	Normal
TM17	Protect	Normal	Status	—	—	10	Self
TM18	Rain Dance	Water	Status	—	—	5	Both Sides
TM21	Frustration	Normal	Physical	—	100	20	Normal
TM26	Earthquake	Ground	Physical	100	100	10	Adjacent
TM27	Return	Normal	Physical	—	100	20	Normal
TM28	Dig	Ground	Physical	80	100	10	Normal
TM32	Double Team	Normal	Status	—	—	15	Self
TM34	Sludge Wave	Poison	Special	95	100	10	Adjacent
TM36	Sludge Bomb	Poison	Special	90	100	10	Normal
TM39	Rock Tomb	Rock	Physical	60	95	15	Normal
TM41	Torment	Dark	Status	—	100	15	Normal
TM42	Facade	Normal	Physical	70	100	20	Normal
TM44	Rest	Psychic	Status	—	—	10	Self
TM45	Attract	Normal	Status	—	100	15	Normal
TM46	Thief	Dark	Physical	60	100	25	Normal
TM48	Round	Normal	Special	60	100	15	Normal
TM66	Payback	Dark	Physical	50	100	10	Normal
TM68	Giga Impact	Normal	Physical	150	90	5	Normal
TM78	Bulldoze	Ground	Physical	60	100	20	Adjacent
TM80	Rock Slide	Rock	Physical	75	90	10	Many Others
TM82	Dragon Tail	Dragon	Physical	60	90	10	Normal
TM83	Infestation	Bug	Special	20	100	20	Normal
TM84	Poison Jab	Poison	Physical	80	100	20	Normal
TM87	Swagger	Normal	Status	—	90	15	Normal
TM88	Sleep Talk	Normal	Status	—	—	10	Self
TM90	Substitute	Normal	Status	—	—	10	Self
TM97	Dark Pulse	Dark	Special	80	100	15	Normal
TM100	Confide	Normal	Status	—	—	20	Normal

No.	Name	Type	Kind	Pow.	Acc.	PP	Range
HM04	Strength	Normal	Physical	80	100	15	Normal

● MOVES TAUGHT BY PEOPLE

Name	Type	Kind	Pow.	Acc.	PP	Range

Left sidebar:

AFTER THE HALL OF FAME

CENTRAL KALOS

COASTAL KALOS

MOUNTAIN KALOS

038

Arbok

ADVENTURE DATA

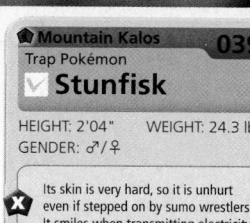

Mountain Kalos — 039

Trap Pokémon

☑ Stunfisk

HEIGHT: 2'04" WEIGHT: 24.3 lbs.
GENDER: ♂/♀

X Its skin is very hard, so it is unhurt even if stepped on by sumo wrestlers. It smiles when transmitting electricity.

Y It conceals itself in the mud of the seashore. Then it waits. When prey touch it, it delivers a jolt of electricity.

TYPE: Ground / Electric

ABILITIES
Static
Limber

HIDDEN ABILITY
Sand Veil

STAT GROWTH RATES
HP ▪▪▪▪
Attack ▪▪▪
Defense ▪▪▪▪
Sp. Atk ▪▪▪▪
Sp. Def ▪▪▪▪
Speed ▪▪

EGG GROUPS
Water 1, Amorphous

EVOLUTION

Does not evolve

ITEMS SOMETIMES HELD BY WILD POKÉMON
Soft Sand

Damage taken in normal battles		Damage taken in Inverse Battles	
Normal	×1	Normal	×1
Fire	×1	Fire	×1
Water	×2	Water	×0.5
Grass	×2	Grass	×0.5
Electric	×0	Electric	×4
Ice	×2	Ice	×0.5
Fighting	×1	Fighting	×1
Poison	×0.5	Poison	×2
Ground	×2	Ground	×0.5
Flying	×0.5	Flying	×2
Psychic	×1	Psychic	×1
Bug	×1	Bug	×1
Rock	×0.5	Rock	×2
Ghost	×1	Ghost	×1
Dragon	×1	Dragon	×1
Dark	×1	Dark	×1
Steel	×0.5	Steel	×2
Fairy	×1	Fairy	×1

Can be used in	
Inverse Battle	Battle Institute
—	Battle Maison
Battle Chateau	Random Matchup

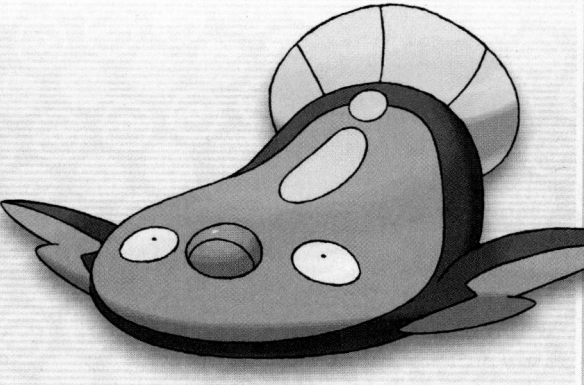

Same form for ♂/♀

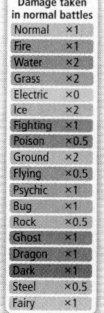

How to obtain for your Mountain Kalos Pokédex

❶ Catch in the swamps along Route 14.
❷ Catch on the surface of the water on Route 14.

❶ Catch in the swamps along Route 14.
❷ Catch on the surface of the water on Route 14.

● LEVEL-UP MOVES

Lv.	Name	Type	Kind	Pow.	Acc.	PP	Range
1	Fissure	Ground	Physical	—	30	5	Normal
1	Flail	Normal	Physical	—	100	15	Normal
1	Tackle	Normal	Physical	50	100	35	Normal
1	Water Gun	Water	Special	40	100	25	Normal
1	Mud-Slap	Ground	Special	20	100	10	Normal
5	Mud Sport	Ground	Status	—	—	15	Both Sides
5	Bide	Normal	Physical	—	—	10	Self
9	Thunder Shock	Electric	Special	40	100	30	Normal
13	Mud Shot	Ground	Special	55	95	15	Normal
17	Camouflage	Normal	Status	—	—	20	Self
21	Mud Bomb	Ground	Special	65	85	10	Normal
25	Discharge	Electric	Special	80	100	15	Adjacent
30	Endure	Normal	Status	—	—	10	Self
35	Bounce	Flying	Physical	85	85	5	Normal
40	Muddy Water	Water	Special	90	85	10	Many Others
45	Thunderbolt	Electric	Special	90	100	15	Normal
50	Revenge	Fighting	Physical	60	100	10	Normal
55	Flail	Normal	Physical	—	100	15	Normal
61	Fissure	Ground	Physical	—	30	5	Normal

● TM & HM MOVES

No.	Name	Type	Kind	Pow.	Acc.	PP	Range
TM06	Toxic	Poison	Status	—	90	10	Normal
TM10	Hidden Power	Normal	Special	60	100	15	Normal
TM17	Protect	Normal	Status	—	—	10	Self
TM18	Rain Dance	Water	Status	—	—	5	Both Sides
TM21	Frustration	Normal	Physical	—	100	20	Normal
TM24	Thunderbolt	Electric	Special	90	100	15	Normal
TM25	Thunder	Electric	Special	110	70	10	Normal
TM26	Earthquake	Ground	Physical	100	100	10	Adjacent
TM27	Return	Normal	Physical	—	100	20	Normal
TM28	Dig	Ground	Physical	80	100	10	Normal
TM32	Double Team	Normal	Status	—	—	15	Self
TM34	Sludge Wave	Poison	Special	95	100	10	Adjacent
TM36	Sludge Bomb	Poison	Special	90	100	10	Normal
TM37	Sandstorm	Rock	Status	—	—	10	Both Sides
TM39	Rock Tomb	Rock	Physical	60	95	15	Normal
TM42	Facade	Normal	Physical	70	100	20	Normal
TM44	Rest	Psychic	Status	—	—	10	Self
TM45	Attract	Normal	Status	—	100	15	Normal
TM48	Round	Normal	Special	60	100	15	Normal
TM55	Scald	Water	Special	80	100	15	Normal
TM66	Payback	Dark	Physical	50	100	10	Normal
TM70	Flash	Normal	Status	—	100	20	Normal
TM71	Stone Edge	Rock	Physical	100	80	5	Normal
TM73	Thunder Wave	Electric	Status	—	100	20	Normal
TM78	Bulldoze	Ground	Physical	60	100	20	Adjacent
TM80	Rock Slide	Rock	Physical	75	90	10	Many Others
TM83	Infestation	Bug	Special	20	100	20	Normal
TM87	Swagger	Normal	Status	—	90	15	Normal
TM88	Sleep Talk	Normal	Status	—	—	10	Self
TM90	Substitute	Normal	Status	—	—	10	Self
TM100	Confide	Normal	Status	—	—	20	Normal
HM03	Surf	Water	Special	90	100	15	Adjacent

No.	Name	Type	Kind	Pow.	Acc.	PP	Range

● MOVES TAUGHT BY PEOPLE

Name	Type	Kind	Pow.	Acc.	PP	Range

● EGG MOVES

Name	Type	Kind	Pow.	Acc.	PP	Range
Shock Wave	Electric	Special	60	—	20	Normal
Earth Power	Ground	Special	90	100	10	Normal
Yawn	Normal	Status	—	—	10	Normal
Sleep Talk	Normal	Status	—	—	10	Self
Astonish	Ghost	Physical	30	100	15	Normal
Curse	Ghost	Status	—	—	10	Varies
Spite	Ghost	Status	—	—	10	Normal
Spark	Electric	Physical	65	100	20	Normal
Pain Split	Normal	Status	—	—	20	Normal
Eerie Impulse	Electric	Status	—	100	15	Normal
Reflect Type	Normal	Status	—	—	15	Normal
Me First	Normal	Status	—	—	20	Varies

AFTER THE HALL OF FAME

CENTRAL KALOS

COASTAL KALOS

MOUNTAIN KALOS

039 Stunfisk

ADVENTURE DATA

Mountain Kalos 040
Whiskers Pokémon

✓ **Barboach**

HEIGHT: 1'04" WEIGHT: 4.2 lbs.
GENDER: ♂/♀

X It coats its entire body with a slimy fluid so it can squirm and slip away if grabbed.

Y Its whiskers make a superb radar. They are used to locate prey, even in the murkiest of water.

TYPE **Water** **Ground**

ABILITIES
Oblivious
Anticipation

HIDDEN ABILITY
None

STAT GROWTH RATES
HP	■■
Attack	■■■
Defense	■■
Sp. Atk	■■
Sp. Def	■■
Speed	■■■

EGG GROUP
Water 2

EVOLUTION

Lv. 30

Barboach → Whiscash

ITEMS SOMETIMES HELD BY WILD POKÉMON
None

Damage taken in normal battles	
Normal	×1
Fire	×0.5
Water	×1
Grass	×4
Electric	×0
Ice	×1
Fighting	×1
Poison	×0.5
Ground	×1
Flying	×1
Psychic	×1
Bug	×1
Rock	×0.5
Ghost	×1
Dragon	×1
Dark	×1
Steel	×0.5
Fairy	×1

Damage taken in Inverse Battles	
Normal	×1
Fire	×2
Water	×1
Grass	×0.25
Electric	×1
Ice	×1
Fighting	×1
Poison	×2
Ground	×1
Flying	×1
Psychic	×1
Bug	×1
Rock	×2
Ghost	×1
Dragon	×1
Dark	×1
Steel	×2
Fairy	×1

Can be used in	
Inverse Battle	Battle Institute
—	Battle Maison
Battle Chateau	Random Matchup

Same form for ♂/♀

How to obtain for your Mountain Kalos Pokédex

❶ Catch using a Good Rod on Route 14.
❷ Catch using a Good Rod on Route 19.

❶ Catch using a Good Rod on Route 14.
❷ Catch using a Good Rod on Route 19.

● LEVEL-UP MOVES

Lv.	Name	Type	Kind	Pow.	Acc.	PP	Range
1	Mud-Slap	Ground	Special	20	100	10	Normal
6	Mud Sport	Ground	Status	—	—	15	Both Sides
6	Water Sport	Water	Status	—	—	15	Both Sides
10	Water Gun	Water	Special	40	100	25	Normal
14	Mud Bomb	Ground	Special	65	85	10	Normal
18	Amnesia	Psychic	Status	—	—	20	Self
22	Water Pulse	Water	Special	60	100	20	Normal
26	Magnitude	Ground	Physical	—	100	30	Adjacent
31	Rest	Psychic	Status	—	—	10	Self
31	Snore	Normal	Special	50	100	15	Normal
35	Aqua Tail	Water	Physical	90	90	10	Normal
39	Earthquake	Ground	Physical	100	100	10	Adjacent
43	Future Sight	Psychic	Special	120	100	10	Normal
47	Fissure	Ground	Physical	—	30	5	Normal

● TM & HM MOVES

No.	Name	Type	Kind	Pow.	Acc.	PP	Range
TM06	Toxic	Poison	Status	—	90	10	Normal
TM07	Hail	Ice	Status	—	—	10	Both Sides
TM10	Hidden Power	Normal	Special	60	100	15	Normal
TM13	Ice Beam	Ice	Special	90	100	10	Normal
TM14	Blizzard	Ice	Special	110	70	5	Many Others
TM17	Protect	Normal	Status	—	—	10	Self
TM18	Rain Dance	Water	Status	—	—	5	Both Sides
TM21	Frustration	Normal	Physical	—	100	20	Normal
TM26	Earthquake	Ground	Physical	100	100	10	Adjacent
TM27	Return	Normal	Physical	—	100	20	Normal
TM32	Double Team	Normal	Status	—	—	15	Self
TM37	Sandstorm	Rock	Status	—	—	10	Both Sides
TM39	Rock Tomb	Rock	Physical	60	95	15	Normal
TM42	Facade	Normal	Physical	70	100	20	Normal
TM44	Rest	Psychic	Status	—	—	10	Self
TM45	Attract	Normal	Status	—	100	15	Normal
TM48	Round	Normal	Special	60	100	15	Normal
TM55	Scald	Water	Special	80	100	15	Normal
TM78	Bulldoze	Ground	Physical	60	100	20	Adjacent
TM87	Swagger	Normal	Status	—	90	15	Normal
TM88	Sleep Talk	Normal	Status	—	—	10	Self
TM90	Substitute	Normal	Status	—	—	10	Self
TM100	Confide	Normal	Status	—	—	20	Normal
HM03	Surf	Water	Special	90	100	15	Adjacent
HM05	Waterfall	Water	Physical	80	100	15	Normal

No.	Name	Type	Kind	Pow.	Acc.	PP	Range

● MOVES TAUGHT BY PEOPLE

Name	Type	Kind	Pow.	Acc.	PP	Range

● EGG MOVES

Name	Type	Kind	Pow.	Acc.	PP	Range
Thrash	Normal	Physical	120	100	10	1 Random
Whirlpool	Water	Special	35	85	15	Normal
Spark	Electric	Physical	65	100	20	Normal
Hydro Pump	Water	Special	110	80	5	Normal
Flail	Normal	Physical	—	100	15	Normal
Take Down	Normal	Physical	90	85	20	Normal
Dragon Dance	Dragon	Status	—	—	20	Self
Earth Power	Ground	Special	90	100	10	Normal
Mud Shot	Ground	Special	55	95	15	Normal
Muddy Water	Water	Special	90	85	10	Many Others

AFTER THE HALL OF FAME

CENTRAL KALOS

COASTAL KALOS

MOUNTAIN KALOS

040

Barboach

ADVENTURE DATA

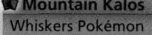

Mountain Kalos 041
Whiskers Pokémon

✓ Whiscash

HEIGHT: 2'11"   WEIGHT: 52.0 lbs.
GENDER: ♂ / ♀

X It claims a large swamp to itself. If a foe comes near it, it sets off tremors by thrashing around.

Y It makes its nest at the bottom of swamps. It will eat anything—if it is alive, Whiscash will eat it.

TYPE **Water** **Ground**

ABILITIES
Oblivious
Anticipation

HIDDEN ABILITY
None

STAT GROWTH RATES
HP	■■■
Attack	■■■
Defense	■■■
Sp. Atk	■■■■
Sp. Def	■■■
Speed	■■■

EGG GROUP
Water 2

⚑ EVOLUTION

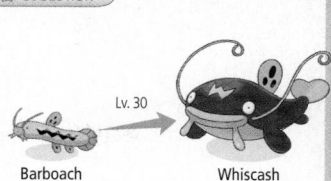

Barboach   Lv. 30   Whiscash

ITEMS SOMETIMES HELD BY WILD POKÉMON
None

Damage taken in normal battles		Damage taken in Inverse Battles	
Normal	×1	Normal	×1
Fire	×0.5	Fire	×2
Water	×1	Water	×1
Grass	×4	Grass	×0.25
Electric	×0	Electric	×1
Ice	×1	Ice	×1
Fighting	×1	Fighting	×1
Poison	×0.5	Poison	×2
Ground	×1	Ground	×1
Flying	×1	Flying	×1
Psychic	×1	Psychic	×1
Bug	×1	Bug	×1
Rock	×0.5	Rock	×2
Ghost	×1	Ghost	×1
Dragon	×1	Dragon	×1
Dark	×1	Dark	×1
Steel	×0.5	Steel	×2
Fairy	×1	Fairy	×1

Can be used in	
Inverse Battle	Battle Institute
—	Battle Maison
Battle Chateau	Random Matchup

Same form for ♂ / ♀

How to obtain for your Mountain Kalos Pokédex
❶ Catch using a Super Rod on Route 14 or Route 19.
❷ Level up Barboach to Lv. 30.

❶ Catch using a Super Rod on Route 14 or Route 19.
❷ Level up Barboach to Lv. 30.

● LEVEL-UP MOVES
Lv.	Name	Type	Kind	Pow.	Acc.	PP	Range
1	Zen Headbutt	Psychic	Physical	80	90	15	Normal
1	Tickle	Normal	Status	—	100	20	Normal
1	Mud-Slap	Ground	Special	20	100	10	Normal
1	Water Sport	Water	Status	—	—	15	Both Sides
6	Mud Sport	Ground	Status	—	—	15	Both Sides
6	Water Sport	Water	Status	—	—	15	Both Sides
10	Water Gun	Water	Special	40	100	25	Normal
14	Mud Bomb	Ground	Special	65	85	10	Normal
18	Amnesia	Psychic	Status	—	—	20	Self
22	Water Pulse	Water	Special	60	100	20	Normal
26	Magnitude	Ground	Physical	—	100	30	Adjacent
33	Rest	Psychic	Status	—	—	10	Self
33	Snore	Normal	Special	50	100	15	Normal
39	Aqua Tail	Water	Physical	90	90	10	Normal
45	Earthquake	Ground	Physical	100	100	10	Adjacent
51	Future Sight	Psychic	Special	120	100	10	Normal
57	Fissure	Ground	Physical	—	30	5	Normal

● TM & HM MOVES
No.	Name	Type	Kind	Pow.	Acc.	PP	Range
TM06	Toxic	Poison	Status	—	90	10	Normal
TM07	Hail	Ice	Status	—	—	10	Both Sides
TM10	Hidden Power	Normal	Special	60	100	15	Normal
TM13	Ice Beam	Ice	Special	90	100	10	Normal
TM14	Blizzard	Ice	Special	110	70	5	Many Others
TM15	Hyper Beam	Normal	Special	150	90	5	Normal
TM17	Protect	Normal	Status	—	—	10	Self
TM18	Rain Dance	Water	Status	—	—	5	Both Sides
TM21	Frustration	Normal	Physical	—	100	20	Normal
TM26	Earthquake	Ground	Physical	100	100	10	Adjacent
TM27	Return	Normal	Physical	—	100	20	Normal
TM32	Double Team	Normal	Status	—	—	15	Self
TM37	Sandstorm	Rock	Status	—	—	10	Both Sides
TM39	Rock Tomb	Rock	Physical	60	95	15	Normal
TM42	Facade	Normal	Physical	70	100	20	Normal
TM44	Rest	Psychic	Status	—	—	10	Self
TM45	Attract	Normal	Status	—	100	15	Normal
TM48	Round	Normal	Special	60	100	15	Normal
TM55	Scald	Water	Special	80	100	15	Normal
TM68	Giga Impact	Normal	Physical	150	90	5	Normal
TM71	Stone Edge	Rock	Physical	100	80	5	Normal
TM78	Bulldoze	Ground	Physical	60	100	20	Adjacent
TM80	Rock Slide	Rock	Physical	75	90	10	Many Others
TM87	Swagger	Normal	Status	—	90	15	Normal
TM88	Sleep Talk	Normal	Status	—	—	10	Self
TM90	Substitute	Normal	Status	—	—	10	Self
TM94	Rock Smash	Fighting	Physical	40	100	15	Normal
TM100	Confide	Normal	Status	—	—	20	Normal
HM03	Surf	Water	Special	90	100	15	Adjacent
HM04	Strength	Normal	Physical	80	100	15	Normal
HM05	Waterfall	Water	Physical	80	100	15	Normal

No.	Name	Type	Kind	Pow.	Acc.	PP	Range

● MOVES TAUGHT BY PEOPLE
Name	Type	Kind	Pow.	Acc.	PP	Range

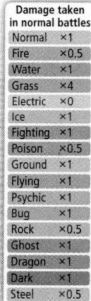

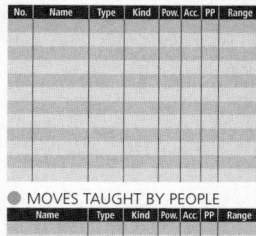

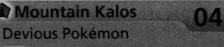

Mountain Kalos 042
Devious Pokémon

✓ Purrloin

HEIGHT: 1'04"   WEIGHT: 22.3 lbs.
GENDER: ♂/♀

X Its cute act is a ruse. When victims let down their guard, they find their items taken. It attacks with sharp claws.

Y They steal from people for fun, but their victims can't help but forgive them. Their deceptively cute act is perfect.

TYPE **Dark**

ABILITIES
Limber
Unburden

HIDDEN ABILITY
Prankster

STAT GROWTH RATES
HP	■■
Attack	■■■
Defense	■■
Sp. Atk	■■
Sp. Def	■■
Speed	■■■■

EGG GROUP
Field

⚐ EVOLUTION

Purrloin   Lv. 20 →   Liepard

ITEMS SOMETIMES HELD BY WILD POKÉMON
None

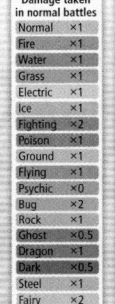

Damage taken in normal battles		Damage taken in Inverse Battles	
Normal	×1	Normal	×1
Fire	×1	Fire	×1
Water	×1	Water	×1
Grass	×1	Grass	×1
Electric	×1	Electric	×1
Ice	×1	Ice	×1
Fighting	×2	Fighting	×0.5
Poison	×1	Poison	×1
Ground	×1	Ground	×1
Flying	×1	Flying	×1
Psychic	×0	Psychic	×2
Bug	×2	Bug	×0.5
Rock	×1	Rock	×1
Ghost	×0.5	Ghost	×2
Dragon	×1	Dragon	×1
Dark	×0.5	Dark	×2
Steel	×1	Steel	×1
Fairy	×2	Fairy	×0.5

Can be used in	
Inverse Battle	Battle Institute
—	Battle Maison
Battle Chateau	Random Matchup

Same form for ♂/♀

How to obtain for your Mountain Kalos Pokédex

Link Trade or transfer from another game.

Leave Liepard at the Pokémon Day Care, and hatch the Egg that is found.

● LEVEL-UP MOVES

Lv.	Name	Type	Kind	Pow.	Acc.	PP	Range
1	Scratch	Normal	Physical	40	100	35	Normal
3	Growl	Normal	Status	—	100	40	Many Others
6	Assist	Normal	Status	—	—	20	Self
10	Sand Attack	Ground	Status	—	100	15	Normal
12	Fury Swipes	Normal	Physical	18	80	15	Normal
15	Pursuit	Dark	Physical	40	100	20	Normal
19	Torment	Dark	Status	—	100	15	Normal
21	Fake Out	Normal	Physical	40	100	10	Normal
24	Hone Claws	Dark	Status	—	—	15	Self
28	Assurance	Dark	Physical	60	100	10	Normal
30	Slash	Normal	Physical	70	100	20	Normal
33	Captivate	Normal	Status	—	100	20	Many Others
37	Night Slash	Dark	Physical	70	100	15	Normal
39	Snatch	Dark	Status	—	—	10	Self
42	Nasty Plot	Dark	Status	—	—	20	Self
46	Sucker Punch	Dark	Physical	80	100	5	Normal
49	Play Rough	Fairy	Physical	90	90	10	Normal

● TM & HM MOVES

No.	Name	Type	Kind	Pow.	Acc.	PP	Range
TM01	Hone Claws	Dark	Status	—	—	15	Self
TM06	Toxic	Poison	Status	—	90	10	Normal
TM10	Hidden Power	Normal	Special	60	100	15	Normal
TM11	Sunny Day	Fire	Status	—	—	5	Both Sides
TM12	Taunt	Dark	Status	—	100	20	Normal
TM17	Protect	Normal	Status	—	—	10	Self
TM18	Rain Dance	Water	Status	—	—	5	Both Sides
TM21	Frustration	Normal	Physical	—	100	20	Normal
TM27	Return	Normal	Physical	—	100	20	Normal
TM30	Shadow Ball	Ghost	Special	80	100	15	Normal
TM32	Double Team	Normal	Status	—	—	15	Self
TM40	Aerial Ace	Flying	Physical	60	—	20	Normal
TM41	Torment	Dark	Status	—	100	15	Normal
TM42	Facade	Normal	Physical	70	100	20	Normal
TM44	Rest	Psychic	Status	—	—	10	Self
TM45	Attract	Normal	Status	—	100	15	Normal
TM46	Thief	Dark	Physical	60	100	25	Normal
TM48	Round	Normal	Special	60	100	15	Normal
TM49	Echoed Voice	Normal	Special	40	100	15	Normal
TM63	Embargo	Dark	Status	—	100	15	Normal
TM65	Shadow Claw	Ghost	Physical	70	100	15	Normal
TM66	Payback	Dark	Physical	50	100	10	Normal
TM73	Thunder Wave	Electric	Status	—	100	20	Normal
TM77	Psych Up	Normal	Status	—	—	10	Normal
TM85	Dream Eater	Psychic	Special	100	100	15	Normal
TM86	Grass Knot	Grass	Special	—	100	20	Normal
TM87	Swagger	Normal	Status	—	90	15	Normal
TM88	Sleep Talk	Normal	Status	—	—	10	Self
TM89	U-turn	Bug	Physical	70	100	20	Normal
TM90	Substitute	Normal	Status	—	—	10	Self
TM95	Snarl	Dark	Special	55	95	15	Many Others
TM97	Dark Pulse	Dark	Special	80	100	15	Normal
TM100	Confide	Normal	Status	—	—	20	Normal

● MOVES TAUGHT BY PEOPLE

Name	Type	Kind	Pow.	Acc.	PP	Range

● EGG MOVES

Name	Type	Kind	Pow.	Acc.	PP	Range
Pay Day	Normal	Physical	40	100	20	Normal
Foul Play	Dark	Physical	95	100	15	Normal
Feint Attack	Dark	Physical	60	—	20	Normal
Fake Tears	Dark	Status	—	100	20	Normal
Charm	Fairy	Status	—	100	20	Normal
Encore	Normal	Status	—	100	5	Normal
Yawn	Normal	Status	—	—	10	Normal
Covet	Normal	Physical	60	100	25	Normal
Copycat	Normal	Status	—	—	20	Self

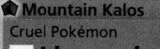

Mountain Kalos 043
Cruel Pokémon
☑ **Liepard**

HEIGHT: 3'07" WEIGHT: 82.7 lbs.
GENDER: ♂/♀

TYPE Dark

ABILITIES
Limber
Unburden

HIDDEN ABILITY
Prankster

X — Their beautiful form comes from the muscles they have developed. They run silently in the night.

Y — Stealthily, it sneaks up on its target, striking from behind before its victim has a chance to react.

STAT GROWTH RATES
HP	■■■
Attack	■■■■■
Defense	■■
Sp. Atk	■■■■
Sp. Def	■■
Speed	■■■■■■

EGG GROUP
Field

EVOLUTION

Purrloin — Lv. 20 → Liepard

ITEMS SOMETIMES HELD BY WILD POKÉMON
None

Damage taken in normal battles		Damage taken in Inverse Battles	
Normal	×1	Normal	×1
Fire	×1	Fire	×1
Water	×1	Water	×1
Grass	×1	Grass	×1
Electric	×1	Electric	×1
Ice	×1	Ice	×1
Fighting	×2	Fighting	×0.5
Poison	×1	Poison	×1
Ground	×1	Ground	×1
Flying	×1	Flying	×1
Psychic	×0	Psychic	×2
Bug	×1	Bug	×0.5
Rock	×1	Rock	×1
Ghost	×0.5	Ghost	×2
Dragon	×1	Dragon	×1
Dark	×0.5	Dark	×2
Steel	×1	Steel	×1
Fairy	×2	Fairy	×0.5

Can be used in	
Inverse Battle	Battle Institute
—	Battle Maison
Battle Chateau	Random Matchup

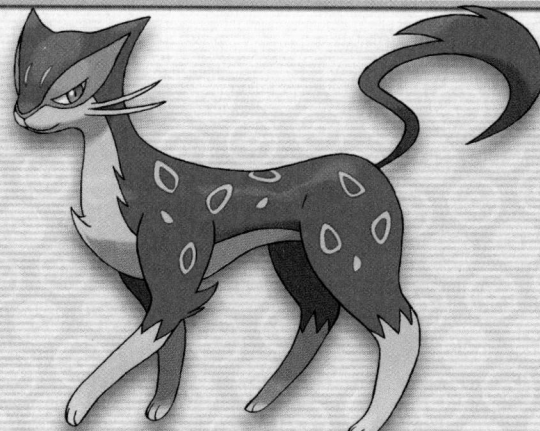

Same form for ♂/♀

How to obtain for your Mountain Kalos Pokédex

Link Trade or transfer from another game.

❶ Catch in the tall grass on Route 15.
❷ Catch in the red flowers on Route 15.

● LEVEL-UP MOVES
Lv.	Name	Type	Kind	Pow.	Acc.	PP	Range
1	Scratch	Normal	Physical	40	100	35	Normal
1	Growl	Normal	Status	—	100	40	Many Others
1	Assist	Normal	Status	—	—	20	Self
1	Sand Attack	Ground	Status	—	100	15	Normal
3	Growl	Normal	Status	—	100	40	Many Others
6	Assist	Normal	Status	—	—	20	Self
8	Sand Attack	Ground	Status	—	100	15	Normal
10	Fury Swipes	Normal	Physical	18	80	15	Normal
12	Pursuit	Dark	Physical	40	100	20	Normal
15	Torment	Dark	Status	—	100	15	Normal
19	Fake Out	Normal	Physical	40	100	10	Normal
22	Hone Claws	Dark	Status	—	—	15	Self
26	Assurance	Dark	Physical	60	100	10	Normal
31	Slash	Normal	Physical	70	100	20	Normal
34	Taunt	Dark	Status	—	100	20	Normal
38	Night Slash	Dark	Physical	70	100	15	Normal
43	Snatch	Dark	Status	—	—	10	Self
47	Nasty Plot	Dark	Status	—	—	20	Self
50	Sucker Punch	Dark	Physical	80	100	5	Normal
55	Play Rough	Fairy	Physical	90	90	10	Normal
58							

● TM & HM MOVES
No.	Name	Type	Kind	Pow.	Acc.	PP	Range
TM01	Hone Claws	Dark	Status	—	—	15	Self
TM06	Toxic	Poison	Status	—	90	10	Normal
TM10	Hidden Power	Normal	Special	60	100	15	Normal
TM11	Sunny Day	Fire	Status	—	—	5	Both Sides
TM12	Taunt	Dark	Status	—	100	20	Normal
TM15	Hyper Beam	Normal	Special	150	90	5	Normal
TM17	Protect	Normal	Status	—	—	10	Self
TM18	Rain Dance	Water	Status	—	—	5	Both Sides
TM21	Frustration	Normal	Physical	—	100	20	Normal
TM27	Return	Normal	Physical	—	100	20	Normal
TM30	Shadow Ball	Ghost	Special	80	100	15	Normal
TM32	Double Team	Normal	Status	—	—	15	Self
TM40	Aerial Ace	Flying	Physical	60	—	20	Normal
TM41	Torment	Dark	Status	—	100	15	Normal
TM42	Facade	Normal	Physical	70	100	20	Normal
TM44	Rest	Psychic	Status	—	—	10	Self
TM45	Attract	Normal	Status	—	100	15	Normal
TM46	Thief	Dark	Physical	60	100	25	Normal
TM48	Round	Normal	Special	60	100	15	Normal
TM49	Echoed Voice	Normal	Special	40	100	15	Normal
TM63	Embargo	Dark	Status	—	100	15	Normal
TM65	Shadow Claw	Ghost	Physical	70	100	15	Normal
TM66	Payback	Dark	Physical	50	100	10	Normal
TM68	Giga Impact	Normal	Physical	150	90	5	Normal
TM73	Thunder Wave	Electric	Status	—	100	20	Normal
TM77	Psych Up	Normal	Status	—	—	10	Self
TM85	Dream Eater	Psychic	Special	100	100	15	Normal
TM86	Grass Knot	Grass	Special	—	100	20	Normal
TM87	Swagger	Normal	Status	—	90	15	Normal
TM88	Sleep Talk	Normal	Status	—	—	10	Self
TM89	U-turn	Bug	Physical	70	100	20	Normal
TM90	Substitute	Normal	Status	—	—	10	Self
TM94	Rock Smash	Fighting	Physical	40	100	15	Normal

No.	Name	Type	Kind	Pow.	Acc.	PP	Range
TM95	Snarl	Dark	Special	55	95	15	Many Others
TM97	Dark Pulse	Dark	Special	80	100	15	Normal
TM100	Confide	Normal	Status	—	—	20	Normal
HM01	Cut	Normal	Physical	50	95	30	Normal

● MOVES TAUGHT BY PEOPLE
Name	Type	Kind	Pow.	Acc.	PP	Range

AFTER THE HALL OF FAME

CENTRAL KALOS

COASTAL KALOS

MOUNTAIN KALOS

043 Liepard

ADVENTURE DATA

Mountain Kalos — 044
Bite Pokémon
☑ Poochyena

HEIGHT: 1'08"   WEIGHT: 30.0 lbs.
GENDER: ♂/♀

TYPE Dark

ABILITIES
Run Away
Quick Feet

HIDDEN ABILITY
Rattled

X	A Pokémon with a persistent nature, it chases its chosen prey until the prey becomes exhausted.
Y	It has a very tenacious nature. Its acute sense of smell lets it chase a chosen prey without ever losing track.

STAT GROWTH RATES
HP	■■
Attack	■■■
Defense	■■
Sp. Atk	■
Sp. Def	■
Speed	■■

EGG GROUP
Field

EVOLUTION

Poochyena → Lv. 18 → Mightyena

ITEMS SOMETIMES HELD BY WILD POKÉMON
None

Damage taken in normal battles		Damage taken in Inverse Battles	
Normal	×1	Normal	×1
Fire	×1	Fire	×1
Water	×1	Water	×1
Grass	×1	Grass	×1
Electric	×1	Electric	×1
Ice	×1	Ice	×1
Fighting	×2	Fighting	×0.5
Poison	×1	Poison	×1
Ground	×1	Ground	×1
Flying	×1	Flying	×1
Psychic	×0	Psychic	×2
Bug	×2	Bug	×0.5
Rock	×1	Rock	×1
Ghost	×0.5	Ghost	×2
Dragon	×1	Dragon	×1
Dark	×0.5	Dark	×2
Steel	×1	Steel	×1
Fairy	×2	Fairy	×0.5

Can be used in	
Inverse Battle	Battle Institute
—	Battle Maison
Battle Chateau	Random Matchup

Same form for ♂/♀

How to obtain for your Mountain Kalos Pokédex

Leave Mightyena at the Pokémon Day Care, and hatch the Egg that is found.

Link Trade or transfer from another game.

● LEVEL-UP MOVES

Lv.	Name	Type	Kind	Pow.	Acc.	PP	Range
1	Tackle	Normal	Physical	50	100	35	Normal
5	Howl	Normal	Status	—	—	40	Self
9	Sand Attack	Ground	Status	—	100	15	Normal
13	Bite	Dark	Physical	60	100	25	Normal
17	Odor Sleuth	Normal	Status	—	—	40	Normal
21	Roar	Normal	Status	—	—	20	Normal
25	Swagger	Normal	Status	—	90	15	Normal
29	Assurance	Dark	Physical	60	100	10	Normal
33	Scary Face	Normal	Status	—	100	10	Normal
37	Taunt	Dark	Status	—	100	20	Normal
41	Embargo	Dark	Status	—	100	15	Normal
45	Take Down	Normal	Physical	90	85	20	Normal
49	Sucker Punch	Dark	Physical	80	100	5	Normal
53	Crunch	Dark	Physical	80	100	15	Normal

● TM & HM MOVES

No.	Name	Type	Kind	Pow.	Acc.	PP	Range
TM05	Roar	Normal	Status	—	—	20	Normal
TM06	Toxic	Poison	Status	—	90	10	Normal
TM10	Hidden Power	Normal	Special	60	100	15	Normal
TM11	Sunny Day	Fire	Status	—	—	5	Both Sides
TM12	Taunt	Dark	Status	—	100	20	Normal
TM17	Protect	Normal	Status	—	—	10	Self
TM18	Rain Dance	Water	Status	—	—	5	Both Sides
TM21	Frustration	Normal	Physical	—	100	20	Normal
TM27	Return	Normal	Physical	—	100	20	Normal
TM28	Dig	Ground	Physical	80	100	10	Normal
TM30	Shadow Ball	Ghost	Special	80	100	15	Normal
TM32	Double Team	Normal	Status	—	—	15	Self
TM41	Torment	Dark	Status	—	100	15	Normal
TM42	Facade	Normal	Physical	70	100	20	Normal
TM44	Rest	Psychic	Status	—	—	10	Self
TM45	Attract	Normal	Status	—	100	15	Normal
TM46	Thief	Dark	Physical	60	100	25	Normal
TM48	Round	Normal	Special	60	100	15	Normal
TM59	Incinerate	Fire	Special	60	100	15	Many Others
TM63	Embargo	Dark	Status	—	100	15	Normal
TM66	Payback	Dark	Physical	50	100	10	Normal
TM67	Retaliate	Normal	Physical	70	100	5	Normal
TM87	Swagger	Normal	Status	—	90	15	Normal
TM88	Sleep Talk	Normal	Status	—	—	10	Self
TM90	Substitute	Normal	Status	—	—	10	Self
TM94	Rock Smash	Fighting	Physical	40	100	15	Normal
TM95	Snarl	Dark	Special	55	95	15	Many Others
TM97	Dark Pulse	Dark	Special	80	100	15	Normal
TM100	Confide	Normal	Status	—	—	20	Normal

● MOVES TAUGHT BY PEOPLE

Name	Type	Kind	Pow.	Acc.	PP	Range

● EGG MOVES

Name	Type	Kind	Pow.	Acc.	PP	Range
Astonish	Ghost	Physical	30	100	15	Normal
Poison Fang	Poison	Physical	50	100	15	Normal
Covet	Normal	Physical	60	100	25	Normal
Leer	Normal	Status	—	100	30	Many Others
Yawn	Normal	Status	—	—	10	Normal
Sucker Punch	Dark	Physical	80	100	5	Normal
Ice Fang	Ice	Physical	65	95	15	Normal
Fire Fang	Fire	Physical	65	95	15	Normal
Thunder Fang	Electric	Physical	65	95	15	Normal
Me First	Normal	Status	—	—	20	Varies
Snatch	Dark	Status	—	—	10	Self
Sleep Talk	Normal	Status	—	—	10	Self
Play Rough	Fairy	Physical	90	90	10	Normal

AFTER THE HALL OF FAME

CENTRAL KALOS

COASTAL KALOS

MOUNTAIN KALOS

044

Poochyena

ADVENTURE DATA

Mountain Kalos
Bite Pokémon
045
☑ **Mightyena**

HEIGHT: 3'03" WEIGHT: 81.6 lbs.
GENDER: ♂/♀

 X It will always obey the commands of a skilled Trainer. Its behavior arises from its living in packs in ancient times.

Y It chases down prey in a pack of around ten. They defeat foes with perfectly coordinated teamwork.

TYPE **Dark**

ABILITIES
Intimidate
Quick Feet

HIDDEN ABILITY
Moxie

STAT GROWTH RATES
HP	▪▪▪
Attack	▪▪▪▪▪
Defense	▪▪▪
Sp. Atk	▪▪▪
Sp. Def	▪▪▪
Speed	▪▪▪▪

EGG GROUP
Field

🔼 EVOLUTION

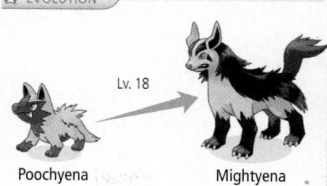

Lv. 18

Poochyena → Mightyena

ITEMS SOMETIMES HELD BY WILD POKÉMON
None

Damage taken in normal battles		Damage taken in Inverse Battles	
Normal	×1	Normal	×1
Fire	×1	Fire	×1
Water	×1	Water	×1
Grass	×1	Grass	×1
Electric	×1	Electric	×1
Ice	×1	Ice	×1
Fighting	×2	Fighting	×0.5
Poison	×1	Poison	×1
Ground	×1	Ground	×1
Flying	×1	Flying	×1
Psychic	×0	Psychic	×2
Bug	×1	Bug	×0.5
Rock	×1	Rock	×1
Ghost	×0.5	Ghost	×2
Dragon	×1	Dragon	×1
Dark	×0.5	Dark	×2
Steel	×1	Steel	×1
Fairy	×2	Fairy	×0.5

Can be used in	
Inverse Battle	Battle Institute
—	Battle Maison
Battle Chateau	Random Matchup

Same form for ♂/♀

How to obtain for your Mountain Kalos Pokédex

❶ Catch in the tall grass on Route 15.

❷ Catch in the red flowers on Route 15.

Link Trade or transfer from another game.

● LEVEL-UP MOVES

Lv.	Name	Type	Kind	Pow.	Acc.	PP	Range
1	Crunch	Dark	Physical	80	100	15	Normal
1	Tackle	Normal	Physical	50	100	35	Normal
1	Howl	Normal	Status	—	—	40	Self
1	Sand Attack	Ground	Status	—	100	15	Normal
1	Bite	Dark	Physical	60	100	25	Normal
5	Howl	Normal	Status	—	—	40	Self
9	Sand Attack	Ground	Status	—	100	15	Normal
13	Bite	Dark	Physical	60	100	25	Normal
17	Odor Sleuth	Normal	Status	—	—	40	Normal
22	Roar	Normal	Status	—	—	20	Normal
27	Swagger	Normal	Status	—	90	15	Normal
32	Assurance	Dark	Physical	60	100	10	Normal
37	Scary Face	Normal	Status	—	100	10	Normal
42	Taunt	Dark	Status	—	100	20	Normal
47	Embargo	Dark	Status	—	100	15	Normal
52	Take Down	Normal	Physical	90	85	20	Normal
57	Thief	Dark	Physical	60	100	25	Normal
62	Sucker Punch	Dark	Physical	80	100	5	Normal
65	Crunch	Dark	Physical	80	100	15	Normal

● TM & HM MOVES

No.	Name	Type	Kind	Pow.	Acc.	PP	Range
TM05	Roar	Normal	Status	—	—	20	Normal
TM06	Toxic	Poison	Status	—	90	10	Normal
TM10	Hidden Power	Normal	Special	60	100	15	Normal
TM11	Sunny Day	Fire	Status	—	—	5	Both Sides
TM12	Taunt	Dark	Status	—	100	20	Normal
TM15	Hyper Beam	Normal	Special	150	90	5	Normal
TM17	Protect	Normal	Status	—	—	10	Self
TM18	Rain Dance	Water	Status	—	—	5	Both Sides
TM21	Frustration	Normal	Physical	—	100	20	Normal
TM27	Return	Normal	Physical	—	100	20	Normal
TM28	Dig	Ground	Physical	80	100	10	Normal
TM30	Shadow Ball	Ghost	Special	80	100	15	Normal
TM32	Double Team	Normal	Status	—	—	15	Self
TM41	Torment	Dark	Status	—	100	15	Normal
TM42	Facade	Normal	Physical	70	100	20	Normal
TM44	Rest	Psychic	Status	—	—	10	Self
TM46	Thief	Dark	Physical	60	100	25	Normal
TM48	Round	Normal	Special	60	100	15	Normal
TM59	Incinerate	Fire	Special	60	100	15	Many Others
TM63	Embargo	Dark	Status	—	100	15	Normal
TM66	Payback	Dark	Physical	50	100	10	Normal
TM67	Retaliate	Normal	Physical	70	100	5	Normal
TM68	Giga Impact	Normal	Physical	150	90	5	Normal
TM87	Swagger	Normal	Status	—	90	15	Normal
TM88	Sleep Talk	Normal	Status	—	—	10	Self
TM90	Substitute	Normal	Status	—	—	10	Self
TM94	Rock Smash	Fighting	Physical	40	100	15	Normal
TM95	Snarl	Dark	Special	55	95	15	Many Others
TM97	Dark Pulse	Dark	Special	80	100	15	Normal
TM100	Confide	Normal	Status	—	—	20	Normal
HM04	Strength	Normal	Physical	80	100	15	Normal

● MOVES TAUGHT BY PEOPLE

Name	Type	Kind	Pow.	Acc.	PP	Range

045 Mightyena

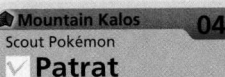

Mountain Kalos 046

Scout Pokémon

✓ Patrat

HEIGHT: 1'08"   WEIGHT: 25.6 lbs.
GENDER: ♂/♀

X Using food stored in cheek pouches, they can keep watch for days. They use their tails to communicate with others.

Y Extremely cautious, one of them will always be on the lookout, but it won't notice a foe coming from behind.

TYPE Normal

ABILITIES
Run Away
Keen Eye

HIDDEN ABILITY
Analytic

STAT GROWTH RATES
HP ▪▪
Attack ▪▪
Defense ▪▪
Sp. Atk ▪▪
Sp. Def ▪▪
Speed ▪▪

EGG GROUP
Field

ITEMS SOMETIMES HELD BY WILD POKÉMON
None

EVOLUTION

Patrat → Lv. 20 → Watchog

Damage taken in normal battles		Damage taken in Inverse Battles	
Normal	×1	Normal	×1
Fire	×1	Fire	×1
Water	×1	Water	×1
Grass	×1	Grass	×1
Electric	×1	Electric	×1
Ice	×1	Ice	×1
Fighting	×2	Fighting	×0.5
Poison	×1	Poison	×1
Ground	×1	Ground	×1
Flying	×1	Flying	×1
Psychic	×1	Psychic	×1
Bug	×1	Bug	×1
Rock	×1	Rock	×1
Ghost	×0	Ghost	×2
Dragon	×1	Dragon	×1
Dark	×1	Dark	×1
Steel	×1	Steel	×1
Fairy	×1	Fairy	×1

Can be used in	
Inverse Battle	Battle Institute
—	Battle Maison
Battle Chateau	Random Matchup

Same form for ♂ / ♀

How to obtain for your Mountain Kalos Pokédex

Leave Watchog at the Pokémon Day Care, and hatch the Egg that is found.

Leave Watchog at the Pokémon Day Care, and hatch the Egg that is found.

● LEVEL-UP MOVES

Lv.	Name	Type	Kind	Pow.	Acc.	PP	Range
1	Tackle	Normal	Physical	50	100	35	Normal
3	Leer	Normal	Status	—	100	30	Many Others
6	Bite	Dark	Physical	60	100	25	Normal
8	Bide	Normal	Physical	—	—	10	Self
11	Detect	Fighting	Status	—	—	5	Self
13	Sand Attack	Ground	Status	—	100	15	Normal
16	Crunch	Dark	Physical	80	100	15	Normal
18	Hypnosis	Psychic	Status	—	60	20	Normal
21	Super Fang	Normal	Physical	—	90	10	Normal
23	After You	Normal	Status	—	—	15	Normal
26	Work Up	Normal	Status	—	—	30	Self
28	Hyper Fang	Normal	Physical	80	90	15	Normal
31	Mean Look	Normal	Status	—	—	5	Normal
33	Baton Pass	Normal	Status	—	—	40	Self
36	Slam	Normal	Physical	80	75	20	Normal

● TM & HM MOVES

No.	Name	Type	Kind	Pow.	Acc.	PP	Range
TM06	Toxic	Poison	Status	—	90	10	Normal
TM10	Hidden Power	Normal	Special	60	100	15	Normal
TM11	Sunny Day	Fire	Status	—	—	5	Both Sides
TM17	Protect	Normal	Status	—	—	10	Self
TM18	Rain Dance	Water	Status	—	—	5	Both Sides
TM21	Frustration	Normal	Physical	—	100	20	Normal
TM24	Thunderbolt	Electric	Special	90	100	15	Normal
TM27	Return	Normal	Physical	—	100	20	Normal
TM28	Dig	Ground	Physical	80	100	10	Normal
TM30	Shadow Ball	Ghost	Special	80	100	15	Normal
TM32	Double Team	Normal	Status	—	—	15	Self
TM42	Facade	Normal	Physical	70	100	20	Normal
TM44	Rest	Psychic	Status	—	—	10	Self
TM45	Attract	Normal	Status	—	100	15	Normal
TM48	Round	Normal	Special	60	100	15	Normal
TM56	Fling	Dark	Physical	—	100	10	Normal
TM67	Retaliate	Normal	Physical	70	100	5	Normal
TM75	Swords Dance	Normal	Status	—	—	20	Self
TM86	Grass Knot	Grass	Special	—	100	20	Normal
TM87	Swagger	Normal	Status	—	90	15	Normal
TM88	Sleep Talk	Normal	Status	—	—	10	Self
TM90	Substitute	Normal	Status	—	—	10	Self
TM100	Confide	Normal	Status	—	—	20	Normal
HM01	Cut	Normal	Physical	50	95	30	Normal

● MOVES TAUGHT BY PEOPLE

Name	Type	Kind	Pow.	Acc.	PP	Range

● EGG MOVES

Name	Type	Kind	Pow.	Acc.	PP	Range
Foresight	Normal	Status	—	—	40	Normal
Iron Tail	Steel	Physical	100	75	15	Normal
Screech	Normal	Status	—	85	40	Normal
Assurance	Dark	Physical	60	100	10	Normal
Pursuit	Dark	Physical	40	100	20	Normal
Revenge	Fighting	Physical	60	100	10	Normal
Flail	Normal	Physical	—	100	15	Normal

AFTER THE HALL OF FAME

CENTRAL KALOS

COASTAL KALOS

MOUNTAIN KALOS

046

Patrat

ADVENTURE DATA

✔ Watchog

HEIGHT: 3'07" **WEIGHT:** 59.5 lbs.
GENDER: ♂/♀

TYPE Normal

ABILITIES
Illuminate
Keen Eye

HIDDEN ABILITY
Analytic

STAT GROWTH RATES
HP	▪▪▪
Attack	▪▪▪▪
Defense	▪▪▪
Sp. Atk	▪▪▪
Sp. Def	▪▪▪
Speed	▪▪▪▪

EGG GROUP
Field

X Using luminescent matter, it makes its eyes and body glow and stuns attacking opponents.

Y When they see an enemy, their tails stand high, and they spit the seeds of berries stored in their cheek pouches.

EVOLUTION

Patrat → Lv. 20 → Watchog

ITEMS SOMETIMES HELD BY WILD POKÉMON
None

Damage taken in normal battles		Damage taken in Inverse Battles	
Normal	×1	Normal	×1
Fire	×1	Fire	×1
Water	×1	Water	×1
Grass	×1	Grass	×1
Electric	×1	Electric	×1
Ice	×1	Ice	×1
Fighting	×2	Fighting	×0.5
Poison	×1	Poison	×1
Ground	×1	Ground	×1
Flying	×1	Flying	×1
Psychic	×1	Psychic	×1
Bug	×1	Bug	×1
Rock	×1	Rock	×1
Ghost	×0	Ghost	×2
Dragon	×1	Dragon	×1
Dark	×1	Dark	×1
Steel	×1	Steel	×1
Fairy	×1	Fairy	×1

Can be used in
Inverse Battle

Battle Chateau
Battle Institute
Battle Maison
Random Matchup

How to obtain for your Mountain Kalos Pokédex

❶ Catch in the tall grass on Route 15.
❷ Catch in the red flowers on Route 15.

❶ Catch in the tall grass on Route 15.
❷ Catch in the red flowers on Route 15.

Same form for ♂/♀

● LEVEL-UP MOVES

Lv.	Name	Type	Kind	Pow.	Acc.	PP	Range
1	Rototiller	Ground	Status	—	—	10	Adjacent
1	Tackle	Normal	Physical	50	100	35	Normal
1	Leer	Normal	Status	—	100	30	Many Others
1	Bite	Dark	Physical	60	100	25	Normal
1	Low Kick	Fighting	Physical	—	100	20	Normal
3	Leer	Normal	Status	—	100	30	Many Others
6	Bite	Dark	Physical	60	100	25	Normal
8	Bide	Normal	Physical	—	—	10	Self
11	Detect	Fighting	Status	—	—	5	Self
13	Sand Attack	Ground	Status	—	100	15	Normal
16	Crunch	Dark	Physical	80	100	15	Normal
18	Hypnosis	Psychic	Status	—	60	20	Normal
20	Confuse Ray	Ghost	Status	—	100	10	Normal
22	Super Fang	Normal	Physical	—	90	10	Normal
25	After You	Normal	Status	—	—	15	Normal
29	Psych Up	Normal	Status	—	—	10	Normal
32	Hyper Fang	Normal	Physical	80	90	15	Normal
36	Mean Look	Normal	Status	—	—	5	Normal
39	Baton Pass	Normal	Status	—	—	40	Self
43	Slam	Normal	Physical	80	75	20	Normal

● TM & HM MOVES

No.	Name	Type	Kind	Pow.	Acc.	PP	Range
TM06	Toxic	Poison	Status	—	90	10	Normal
TM10	Hidden Power	Normal	Special	60	100	15	Normal
TM11	Sunny Day	Fire	Status	—	—	5	Both Sides
TM15	Hyper Beam	Normal	Special	150	90	5	Normal
TM16	Light Screen	Psychic	Status	—	—	30	Your Side
TM17	Protect	Normal	Status	—	—	10	Self
TM18	Rain Dance	Water	Status	—	—	5	Both Sides
TM21	Frustration	Normal	Physical	—	100	20	Normal
TM24	Thunderbolt	Electric	Special	90	100	15	Normal
TM25	Thunder	Electric	Special	110	70	10	Normal
TM27	Return	Normal	Physical	—	100	20	Normal
TM28	Dig	Ground	Physical	80	100	10	Normal
TM30	Shadow Ball	Ghost	Special	80	100	15	Normal
TM32	Double Team	Normal	Status	—	—	15	Self
TM35	Flamethrower	Fire	Special	90	100	15	Normal
TM42	Facade	Normal	Physical	70	100	20	Normal
TM44	Rest	Psychic	Status	—	—	10	Self
TM45	Attract	Normal	Status	—	100	15	Normal
TM48	Round	Normal	Special	60	100	15	Normal
TM52	Focus Blast	Fighting	Special	120	70	5	Normal
TM56	Fling	Dark	Physical	—	100	10	Normal
TM67	Retaliate	Normal	Physical	70	100	5	Normal
TM68	Giga Impact	Normal	Physical	150	90	5	Normal
TM70	Flash	Normal	Status	—	100	20	Normal
TM73	Thunder Wave	Electric	Status	—	100	20	Normal
TM75	Swords Dance	Normal	Status	—	—	20	Self
TM77	Psych Up	Normal	Status	—	—	10	Normal
TM85	Dream Eater	Psychic	Special	100	100	15	Normal
TM86	Grass Knot	Grass	Special	—	100	20	Normal
TM87	Swagger	Normal	Status	—	90	15	Normal
TM88	Sleep Talk	Normal	Status	—	—	10	Self
TM90	Substitute	Normal	Status	—	—	10	Self
TM94	Rock Smash	Fighting	Physical	40	100	15	Normal
TM98	Power-Up Punch	Fighting	Physical	40	100	20	Normal
TM100	Confide	Normal	Status	—	—	20	Normal
HM01	Cut	Normal	Physical	50	95	30	Normal
HM04	Strength	Normal	Physical	80	100	15	Normal

● MOVES TAUGHT BY PEOPLE

Name	Type	Kind	Pow.	Acc.	PP	Range

AFTER THE HALL OF FAME

CENTRAL KALOS

COASTAL KALOS

MOUNTAIN KALOS

047 Watchog

ADVENTURE DATA

Mountain Kalos 048

Sharp Blade Pokémon

☑ **Pawniard**

HEIGHT: 1'08"   WEIGHT: 22.5 lbs.
GENDER: ♂/♀

| TYPE | Dark | Steel |

ABILITIES
Defiant
Inner Focus

HIDDEN ABILITY
Pressure

STAT GROWTH RATES
HP ■■
Attack ■■■■
Defense ■■■
Sp. Atk ■■
Sp. Def ■■
Speed ■■■

EGG GROUP
Human-Like

X Blades comprise this Pokémon's entire body. If battling dulls the blades, it sharpens them on stones by the river.

Y Ignoring their injuries, groups attack by sinking the blades that cover their bodies into their prey.

EVOLUTION

Pawniard — Lv. 52 → Bisharp

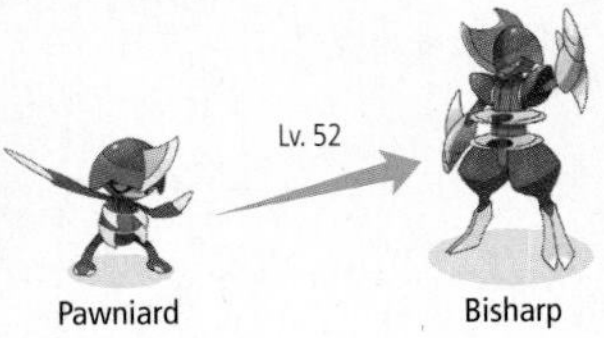

ITEMS SOMETIMES HELD BY WILD POKÉMON
None

Damage taken in normal battles		Damage taken in Inverse Battles	
Normal	×0.5	Normal	×2
Fire	×2	Fire	×0.5
Water	×1	Water	×1
Grass	×0.5	Grass	×2
Electric	×1	Electric	×1
Ice	×0.5	Ice	×2
Fighting	×4	Fighting	×0.25
Poison	×0	Poison	×2
Ground	×2	Ground	×0.5
Flying	×0.5	Flying	×2
Psychic	×0	Psychic	×4
Bug	×1	Bug	×1
Rock	×0.5	Rock	×2
Ghost	×0.5	Ghost	×2
Dragon	×0.5	Dragon	×2
Dark	×0.5	Dark	×2
Steel	×0.5	Steel	×2
Fairy	×1	Fairy	×1

Can be used in	
Inverse Battle	Battle Institute
—	Battle Maison
Battle Chateau	Random Matchup

Same form for ♂/♀

How to obtain for your Mountain Kalos Pokédex

❶ Catch in the tall grass on Route 15.
❷ Catch in the red flowers on Route 15.

❶ Catch in the tall grass on Route 15.
❷ Catch in the red flowers on Route 15.

048
Pawniard

● LEVEL-UP MOVES

Lv.	Name	Type	Kind	Pow.	Acc.	PP	Range
1	Scratch	Normal	Physical	40	100	35	Normal
6	Leer	Normal	Status	—	100	30	Many Others
9	Fury Cutter	Bug	Physical	40	95	20	Normal
14	Torment	Dark	Status	—	100	15	Normal
17	Feint Attack	Dark	Physical	60	—	20	Normal
22	Scary Face	Normal	Status	—	100	10	Normal
25	Metal Claw	Steel	Physical	50	95	35	Normal
30	Slash	Normal	Physical	70	100	20	Normal
33	Assurance	Dark	Physical	60	100	10	Normal
38	Metal Sound	Steel	Status	—	85	40	Normal
41	Embargo	Dark	Status	—	100	15	Normal
46	Iron Defense	Steel	Status	—	—	15	Self
49	Night Slash	Dark	Physical	70	100	15	Normal
54	Iron Head	Steel	Physical	80	100	15	Normal
57	Swords Dance	Normal	Status	—	—	20	Self
62	Guillotine	Normal	Physical	—	30	5	Normal

● TM & HM MOVES

No.	Name	Type	Kind	Pow.	Acc.	PP	Range
TM01	Hone Claws	Dark	Status	—	—	15	Self
TM06	Toxic	Poison	Status	—	90	10	Normal
TM10	Hidden Power	Normal	Special	60	100	15	Normal
TM12	Taunt	Dark	Status	—	100	20	Normal
TM17	Protect	Normal	Status	—	—	10	Self
TM18	Rain Dance	Water	Status	—	—	5	Both Sides
TM21	Frustration	Normal	Physical	—	100	20	Normal
TM27	Return	Normal	Physical	—	100	20	Normal
TM28	Dig	Ground	Physical	80	100	10	Normal
TM31	Brick Break	Fighting	Physical	75	100	15	Normal
TM32	Double Team	Normal	Status	—	—	15	Self
TM37	Sandstorm	Rock	Status	—	—	10	Both Sides
TM39	Rock Tomb	Rock	Physical	60	95	15	Normal
TM40	Aerial Ace	Flying	Physical	60	—	20	Normal
TM41	Torment	Dark	Status	—	100	15	Normal
TM42	Facade	Normal	Physical	70	100	20	Normal
TM44	Rest	Psychic	Status	—	—	10	Self
TM46	Thief	Dark	Physical	60	100	25	Normal
TM47	Low Sweep	Fighting	Physical	65	100	20	Normal
TM48	Round	Normal	Special	60	100	15	Normal
TM54	False Swipe	Normal	Physical	40	100	40	Normal
TM56	Fling	Dark	Physical	—	100	10	Normal
TM63	Embargo	Dark	Status	—	100	15	Normal
TM65	Shadow Claw	Ghost	Physical	70	100	15	Normal
TM66	Payback	Dark	Physical	50	100	10	Normal
TM67	Retaliate	Normal	Physical	70	100	5	Normal
TM69	Rock Polish	Rock	Status	—	—	20	Self
TM73	Thunder Wave	Electric	Status	—	100	20	Normal
TM75	Swords Dance	Normal	Status	—	—	20	Self
TM81	X-Scissor	Bug	Physical	80	100	15	Normal
TM84	Poison Jab	Poison	Physical	80	100	20	Normal
TM86	Grass Knot	Grass	Special	—	100	20	Normal

No.	Name	Type	Kind	Pow.	Acc.	PP	Range
TM87	Swagger	Normal	Status	—	90	15	Normal
TM88	Sleep Talk	Normal	Status	—	—	10	Self
TM90	Substitute	Normal	Status	—	—	10	Self
TM94	Rock Smash	Fighting	Physical	40	100	15	Normal
TM95	Snarl	Dark	Special	55	95	15	Many Others
TM97	Dark Pulse	Dark	Special	80	100	15	Normal
TM98	Power-Up Punch	Fighting	Physical	40	100	20	Normal
TM100	Confide	Normal	Status	—	—	20	Normal
HM01	Cut	Normal	Physical	50	95	30	Normal

● MOVES TAUGHT BY PEOPLE

Name	Type	Kind	Pow.	Acc.	PP	Range

● EGG MOVES

Name	Type	Kind	Pow.	Acc.	PP	Range
Revenge	Fighting	Physical	60	100	10	Normal
Sucker Punch	Dark	Physical	80	100	5	Normal
Pursuit	Dark	Physical	40	100	20	Normal
Headbutt	Normal	Physical	70	100	15	Normal
Stealth Rock	Rock	Status	—	—	20	Other Side
Psycho Cut	Psychic	Physical	70	100	20	Normal
Mean Look	Normal	Status	—	—	5	Normal
Quick Guard	Fighting	Status	—	—	15	Your Side

Mountain Kalos 049
Sword Blade Pokémon
☑ **Bisharp**

HEIGHT: 5'03" WEIGHT: 154.3 lbs.
GENDER: ♂/♀

TYPE Dark Steel

ABILITIES
Defiant
Inner Focus

HIDDEN ABILITY
Pressure

STAT GROWTH RATES
HP ■■■
Attack ■■■■■
Defense ■■■■
Sp. Atk ■■■
Sp. Def ■■■
Speed ■■■■

EGG GROUP
Human-Like

EVOLUTION

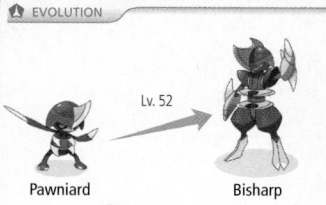

Lv. 52

Pawniard → Bisharp

 X This pitiless Pokémon commands a group of Pawniard to hound prey into immobility. It then moves in to finish the prey off.

Y Bisharp pursues prey in the company of a large group of Pawniard. Then Bisharp finishes off the prey.

ITEMS SOMETIMES HELD BY WILD POKÉMON
None

Damage taken in normal battles	
Normal	×0.5
Fire	×2
Water	×1
Grass	×0.5
Electric	×1
Ice	×0.5
Fighting	×4
Poison	×0
Ground	×2
Flying	×0.5
Psychic	×0
Bug	×1
Rock	×0.5
Ghost	×0.5
Dragon	×0.5
Dark	×0.5
Steel	×0.5
Fairy	×1

Damage taken in Inverse Battles	
Normal	×2
Fire	×0.5
Water	×1
Grass	×2
Electric	×1
Ice	×2
Fighting	×0.25
Poison	×2
Ground	×0.5
Flying	×2
Psychic	×4
Bug	×1
Rock	×2
Ghost	×2
Dragon	×2
Dark	×2
Steel	×2
Fairy	×1

Can be used in
Inverse Battle
—
—
Battle Chateau
Battle Institute
Battle Maison
Random Matchup

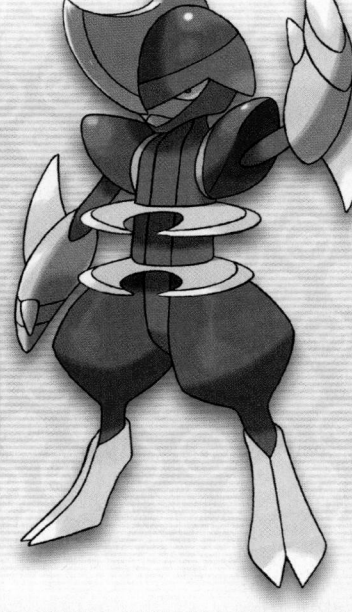

How to obtain for your Mountain Kalos Pokédex

❶ Trade a Jigglypuff with a woman in a house in Snowbelle City.
❷ Level up Pawniard to Lv. 52.

❶ Trade a Jigglypuff with a woman in a house in Snowbelle City.
❷ Level up Pawniard to Lv. 52.

Same form for ♂/♀

● LEVEL-UP MOVES

Lv.	Name	Type	Kind	Pow.	Acc.	PP	Range
1	Guillotine	Normal	Physical	—	30	5	Normal
1	Iron Head	Steel	Physical	80	100	15	Normal
1	Metal Burst	Steel	Physical	—	100	10	Varies
1	Scratch	Normal	Physical	40	100	35	Normal
1	Leer	Normal	Status	—	100	30	Many Others
1	Fury Cutter	Bug	Physical	40	95	20	Normal
1	Torment	Dark	Status	—	100	15	Normal
6	Leer	Normal	Status	—	100	30	Many Others
9	Fury Cutter	Bug	Physical	40	95	20	Normal
14	Torment	Dark	Status	—	100	15	Normal
17	Feint Attack	Dark	Physical	60	—	20	Normal
22	Scary Face	Normal	Status	—	100	10	Normal
25	Metal Claw	Steel	Physical	50	95	35	Normal
30	Slash	Normal	Physical	70	100	20	Normal
33	Assurance	Dark	Physical	60	100	10	Normal
38	Metal Sound	Steel	Status	—	85	40	Normal
41	Embargo	Dark	Status	—	100	15	Normal
46	Iron Defense	Steel	Status	—	—	15	Self
49	Night Slash	Dark	Physical	70	100	15	Normal
57	Iron Head	Steel	Physical	80	100	15	Normal
63	Swords Dance	Normal	Status	—	—	20	Self
71	Guillotine	Normal	Physical	—	30	5	Normal

● TM & HM MOVES

No.	Name	Type	Kind	Pow.	Acc.	PP	Range
TM01	Hone Claws	Dark	Status	—	—	15	Self
TM06	Toxic	Poison	Status	—	90	10	Normal
TM10	Hidden Power	Normal	Special	60	100	15	Normal
TM12	Taunt	Dark	Status	—	100	20	Normal
TM15	Hyper Beam	Normal	Special	150	90	5	Normal
TM17	Protect	Normal	Status	—	—	10	Self
TM18	Rain Dance	Water	Status	—	—	5	Both Sides
TM21	Frustration	Normal	Physical	—	100	20	Normal
TM27	Return	Normal	Physical	—	100	20	Normal
TM28	Dig	Ground	Physical	80	100	10	Normal
TM31	Brick Break	Fighting	Physical	75	100	15	Normal
TM32	Double Team	Normal	Status	—	—	15	Self
TM37	Sandstorm	Rock	Status	—	—	10	Both Sides
TM39	Rock Tomb	Rock	Physical	60	95	15	Normal
TM40	Aerial Ace	Flying	Physical	60	—	20	Normal
TM41	Torment	Dark	Status	—	100	15	Normal
TM42	Facade	Normal	Physical	70	100	20	Normal
TM44	Rest	Psychic	Status	—	—	10	Self
TM45	Attract	Normal	Status	—	100	15	Normal
TM46	Thief	Dark	Physical	60	100	25	Normal
TM47	Low Sweep	Fighting	Physical	65	100	20	Normal
TM48	Round	Normal	Special	60	100	15	Normal
TM52	Focus Blast	Fighting	Special	120	70	5	Normal
TM54	False Swipe	Normal	Physical	40	100	40	Normal
TM56	Fling	Dark	Physical	—	100	10	Normal
TM63	Embargo	Dark	Status	—	100	15	Normal
TM65	Shadow Claw	Ghost	Physical	70	100	15	Normal
TM66	Payback	Dark	Physical	50	100	10	Normal
TM67	Retaliate	Normal	Physical	70	100	5	Normal
TM68	Giga Impact	Normal	Physical	150	90	5	Normal
TM69	Rock Polish	Rock	Status	—	—	20	Self
TM71	Stone Edge	Rock	Physical	100	80	5	Normal
TM73	Thunder Wave	Electric	Status	—	100	20	Normal

No.	Name	Type	Kind	Pow.	Acc.	PP	Range
TM75	Swords Dance	Normal	Status	—	—	20	Self
TM81	X-Scissor	Bug	Physical	80	100	15	Normal
TM84	Poison Jab	Poison	Physical	80	100	20	Normal
TM86	Grass Knot	Grass	Special	—	100	20	Normal
TM87	Swagger	Normal	Status	—	90	15	Normal
TM88	Sleep Talk	Normal	Status	—	—	10	Self
TM90	Substitute	Normal	Status	—	—	10	Self
TM94	Rock Smash	Fighting	Physical	40	100	15	Normal
TM95	Snarl	Dark	Special	55	95	15	Many Others
TM97	Dark Pulse	Dark	Special	80	100	15	Normal
TM98	Power-Up Punch	Fighting	Physical	40	100	20	Normal
TM100	Confide	Normal	Status	—	—	20	Normal
HM01	Cut	Normal	Physical	50	95	30	Normal

● MOVES TAUGHT BY PEOPLE

Name	Type	Kind	Pow.	Acc.	PP	Range

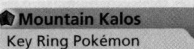

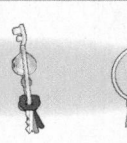

AFTER THE HALL OF FAME

CENTRAL KALOS

COASTAL KALOS

MOUNTAIN KALOS

050

Klefki

ADVENTURE DATA

Mountain Kalos 050
Klefki
Key Ring Pokémon

HEIGHT: 0'08" WEIGHT: 6.6 lbs.
GENDER: ♂/♀

X These key collectors threaten any attackers by fiercely jingling their keys at them.

Y It never lets go of a key that it likes, so people give it the keys to vaults and safes as a way to prevent crime.

TYPE: Steel / Fairy

ABILITY
Prankster

HIDDEN ABILITY
Magician

STAT GROWTH RATES
HP	■■
Attack	■■■
Defense	■■■■
Sp. Atk	■■■■
Sp. Def	■■■■
Speed	■■■■

EGG GROUP
Mineral

EVOLUTION
Does not evolve

ITEMS SOMETIMES HELD BY WILD POKÉMON
None

Damage taken in normal battles		Damage taken in Inverse Battles	
Normal	×0.5	Normal	×2
Fire	×2	Fire	×0.5
Water	×1	Water	×1
Grass	×0.5	Grass	×2
Electric	×1	Electric	×1
Ice	×0.5	Ice	×2
Fighting	×1	Fighting	×1
Poison	×0	Poison	×1
Ground	×2	Ground	×0.5
Flying	×0.5	Flying	×2
Psychic	×0.5	Psychic	×2
Bug	×0.25	Bug	×4
Rock	×0.5	Rock	×2
Ghost	×1	Ghost	×1
Dragon	×0	Dragon	×4
Dark	×0.5	Dark	×2
Steel	×1	Steel	×1
Fairy	×0.5	Fairy	×2

Can be used in	
Inverse Battle	Battle Institute
—	Battle Maison
Battle Chateau	Random Matchup

Same form for ♂/♀

How to obtain for your Mountain Kalos Pokédex
❶ Catch in the tall grass on Route 15.
❷ Catch in the red flowers on Route 15.

❶ Catch in the tall grass on Route 15.
❷ Catch in the red flowers on Route 15.

LEVEL-UP MOVES
Lv.	Name	Type	Kind	Pow.	Acc.	PP	Range
1	Fairy Lock	Fairy	Status	—	—	10	Both Sides
1	Tackle	Normal	Physical	50	100	35	Normal
5	Fairy Wind	Fairy	Special	40	100	30	Normal
8	Astonish	Ghost	Physical	30	100	15	Normal
12	Metal Sound	Steel	Status	—	85	40	Normal
15	Spikes	Ground	Status	—	—	20	Other Side
18	Draining Kiss	Fairy	Special	50	100	10	Normal
23	Crafty Shield	Fairy	Status	—	—	10	Your Side
27	Foul Play	Dark	Physical	95	100	15	Normal
32	Torment	Dark	Status	—	100	15	Normal
34	Mirror Shot	Steel	Special	65	85	10	Normal
36	Imprison	Psychic	Status	—	—	10	Self
40	Recycle	Normal	Status	—	—	10	Self
43	Play Rough	Fairy	Physical	90	90	10	Normal
44	Magic Room	Psychic	Status	—	—	10	Both Sides
50	Heal Block	Psychic	Status	—	100	15	Many Others

TM & HM MOVES
No.	Name	Type	Kind	Pow.	Acc.	PP	Range
TM03	Psyshock	Psychic	Special	80	100	10	Normal
TM04	Calm Mind	Psychic	Status	—	—	20	Self
TM06	Toxic	Poison	Status	—	90	10	Normal
TM10	Hidden Power	Normal	Special	60	100	15	Normal
TM11	Sunny Day	Fire	Status	—	—	5	Both Sides
TM15	Hyper Beam	Normal	Special	150	90	5	Normal
TM16	Light Screen	Psychic	Status	—	—	30	Your Side
TM17	Protect	Normal	Status	—	—	10	Self
TM18	Rain Dance	Water	Status	—	—	5	Both Sides
TM21	Frustration	Normal	Physical	—	100	20	Normal
TM27	Return	Normal	Physical	—	100	20	Normal
TM29	Psychic	Psychic	Special	90	100	10	Normal
TM32	Double Team	Normal	Status	—	—	15	Self
TM33	Reflect	Psychic	Status	—	—	20	Your Side
TM41	Torment	Dark	Status	—	100	15	Normal
TM42	Facade	Normal	Physical	70	100	20	Normal
TM44	Rest	Psychic	Status	—	—	10	Self
TM45	Attract	Normal	Status	—	100	15	Normal
TM46	Thief	Dark	Physical	60	100	25	Normal
TM48	Round	Normal	Special	60	100	15	Normal
TM68	Giga Impact	Normal	Physical	150	90	5	Normal
TM73	Thunder Wave	Electric	Status	—	100	20	Normal
TM77	Psych Up	Normal	Status	—	—	10	Normal
TM87	Swagger	Normal	Status	—	90	15	Normal
TM88	Sleep Talk	Normal	Status	—	—	10	Self
TM90	Substitute	Normal	Status	—	—	10	Self
TM91	Flash Cannon	Steel	Special	80	100	10	Normal
TM99	Dazzling Gleam	Fairy	Special	80	100	10	Many Others
TM100	Confide	Normal	Status	—	—	20	Normal
HM01	Cut	Normal	Physical	50	95	30	Normal

No.	Name	Type	Kind	Pow.	Acc.	PP	Range

MOVES TAUGHT BY PEOPLE
Name	Type	Kind	Pow.	Acc.	PP	Range

EGG MOVES
Name	Type	Kind	Pow.	Acc.	PP	Range
Switcheroo	Dark	Status	—	100	10	Normal
Thief	Dark	Physical	60	100	25	Normal
Lock-On	Normal	Status	—	—	5	Normal
Iron Defense	Steel	Status	—	—	15	Self

Mountain Kalos
Darkness Pokémon
✓ Murkrow 051

HEIGHT: 1'08" WEIGHT: 4.6 lbs.
GENDER: ♂/♀

TYPE Dark Flying

ABILITIES
Insomnia
Super Luck

HIDDEN ABILITY
Prankster

STAT GROWTH RATES
HP ■■■
Attack ■■■■
Defense ■■
Sp. Atk ■■■■
Sp. Def ■■
Speed ■■■■■

EGG GROUP
Flying

EVOLUTION

Murkrow — Dusk Stone → Honchkrow

ITEMS SOMETIMES HELD BY WILD POKÉMON
None

X — It hides any shiny object it finds in a secret location. Murkrow and Meowth loot one another's stashes.

Y — Feared and loathed by many, it is believed to bring misfortune to all those who see it at night.

Damage taken in normal battles	
Normal	×1
Fire	×1
Water	×1
Grass	×0.5
Electric	×2
Ice	×2
Fighting	×1
Poison	×1
Ground	×0
Flying	×1
Psychic	×0
Bug	×1
Rock	×2
Ghost	×0.5
Dragon	×1
Dark	×0.5
Steel	×1
Fairy	×2

Damage taken in Inverse Battles	
Normal	×1
Fire	×1
Water	×1
Grass	×2
Electric	×0.5
Ice	×0.5
Fighting	×1
Poison	×1
Ground	×2
Flying	×1
Psychic	×2
Bug	×1
Rock	×0.5
Ghost	×2
Dragon	×1
Dark	×2
Steel	×1
Fairy	×0.5

Can be used in
Inverse Battle
—
Battle Chateau
Battle Institute
Battle Maison
Random Matchup

How to obtain for your Mountain Kalos Pokédex

① Catch in a Horde Encounter on Route 15.
② Catch in a Horde Encounter on Route 16.

① Catch in a Horde Encounter on Route 15.
② Catch in a Horde Encounter on Route 16.

 ♂   ♀

The male has a larger cockscomb. The female has a smaller cockscomb.

● LEVEL-UP MOVES

Lv.	Name	Type	Kind	Pow.	Acc.	PP	Range
1	Peck	Flying	Physical	35	100	35	Normal
1	Astonish	Ghost	Physical	30	100	15	Normal
5	Pursuit	Dark	Physical	40	100	20	Normal
11	Haze	Ice	Status	—	—	30	Both Sides
15	Wing Attack	Flying	Physical	60	100	35	Normal
21	Night Shade	Ghost	Special	—	100	15	Normal
25	Assurance	Dark	Physical	60	100	10	Normal
31	Taunt	Dark	Status	—	100	20	Normal
35	Feint Attack	Dark	Physical	60	—	20	Normal
41	Mean Look	Normal	Status	—	—	5	Normal
45	Foul Play	Dark	Physical	95	100	15	Normal
51	Tailwind	Flying	Status	—	—	15	Your Side
55	Sucker Punch	Dark	Physical	80	100	5	Normal
61	Torment	Dark	Status	—	100	15	Normal
65	Quash	Dark	Status	—	100	15	Normal

● TM & HM MOVES

No.	Name	Type	Kind	Pow.	Acc.	PP	Range
TM04	Calm Mind	Psychic	Status	—	—	20	Self
TM06	Toxic	Poison	Status	—	90	10	Normal
TM10	Hidden Power	Normal	Special	60	100	15	Normal
TM11	Sunny Day	Fire	Status	—	—	5	Both Sides
TM12	Taunt	Dark	Status	—	100	20	Normal
TM17	Protect	Normal	Status	—	—	10	Self
TM18	Rain Dance	Water	Status	—	—	5	Both Sides
TM19	Roost	Flying	Status	—	—	10	Self
TM21	Frustration	Normal	Physical	—	100	20	Normal
TM27	Return	Normal	Physical	—	100	20	Normal
TM29	Psychic	Psychic	Special	90	100	10	Normal
TM30	Shadow Ball	Ghost	Special	80	100	15	Normal
TM32	Double Team	Normal	Status	—	—	15	Self
TM40	Aerial Ace	Flying	Physical	60	—	20	Normal
TM41	Torment	Dark	Status	—	100	15	Normal
TM42	Facade	Normal	Physical	70	100	20	Normal
TM44	Rest	Psychic	Status	—	—	10	Self
TM45	Attract	Normal	Status	—	100	15	Normal
TM46	Thief	Dark	Physical	60	100	25	Normal
TM48	Round	Normal	Special	60	100	15	Normal
TM51	Steel Wing	Steel	Physical	70	90	25	Normal
TM60	Quash	Dark	Status	—	100	15	Normal
TM63	Embargo	Dark	Status	—	100	15	Normal
TM66	Payback	Dark	Physical	50	100	10	Normal
TM67	Retaliate	Normal	Physical	70	100	5	Normal
TM73	Thunder Wave	Electric	Status	—	100	20	Normal
TM77	Psych Up	Normal	Status	—	—	10	Normal
TM85	Dream Eater	Psychic	Special	100	100	15	Normal
TM87	Swagger	Normal	Status	—	90	15	Normal
TM88	Sleep Talk	Normal	Status	—	—	10	Self
TM90	Substitute	Normal	Status	—	—	10	Self
TM95	Snarl	Dark	Special	55	95	15	Many Others
TM97	Dark Pulse	Dark	Special	80	100	15	Normal

No.	Name	Type	Kind	Pow.	Acc.	PP	Range
TM100	Confide	Normal	Status	—	—	20	Normal
HM02	Fly	Flying	Physical	90	95	15	Normal

● MOVES TAUGHT BY PEOPLE

Name	Type	Kind	Pow.	Acc.	PP	Range

● EGG MOVES

Name	Type	Kind	Pow.	Acc.	PP	Range
Whirlwind	Normal	Status	—	—	20	Normal
Drill Peck	Flying	Physical	80	100	20	Normal
Mirror Move	Flying	Status	—	—	20	Normal
Wing Attack	Flying	Physical	60	100	35	Normal
Sky Attack	Flying	Physical	140	90	5	Normal
Confuse Ray	Ghost	Status	—	100	10	Normal
Feather Dance	Flying	Status	—	100	15	Normal
Perish Song	Normal	Status	—	—	5	Adjacent
Psycho Shift	Psychic	Status	—	100	10	Normal
Screech	Normal	Status	—	85	40	Normal
Feint Attack	Dark	Physical	60	—	20	Normal
Brave Bird	Flying	Physical	120	100	15	Normal
Roost	Flying	Status	—	—	10	Self
Assurance	Dark	Physical	60	100	10	Normal
Flatter	Dark	Status	—	100	15	Normal

AFTER THE HALL OF FAME

CENTRAL KALOS

COASTAL KALOS

MOUNTAIN KALOS

051 Murkrow

ADVENTURE DATA

Mountain Kalos 052
Big Boss Pokémon
☑ **Honchkrow**

HEIGHT: 2'11" WEIGHT: 60.2 lbs.
GENDER: ♂/♀

TYPE Dark Flying

ABILITIES
Insomnia
Super Luck

HIDDEN ABILITY
Moxie

STAT GROWTH RATES
HP	■■■■
Attack	■■■■■■
Defense	■■
Sp. Atk	■■■■■
Sp. Def	■■
Speed	■■■■

EGG GROUP
Flying

X If one utters a deep cry, many Murkrow gather quickly. For this, it is called "Summoner of Night."

Y Becoming active at night, it is known to swarm with numerous Murkrow in tow.

EVOLUTION

Murkrow — Dusk Stone → Honchkrow

ITEMS SOMETIMES HELD BY WILD POKÉMON
None

Damage taken in normal battles	
Normal	×1
Fire	×1
Water	×1
Grass	×0.5
Electric	×2
Ice	×2
Fighting	×1
Poison	×1
Ground	×0
Flying	×1
Psychic	×0
Bug	×1
Rock	×2
Ghost	×0.5
Dragon	×1
Dark	×0.5
Steel	×1
Fairy	×2

Damage taken in Inverse Battles	
Normal	×1
Fire	×1
Water	×1
Grass	×2
Electric	×0.5
Ice	×0.5
Fighting	×1
Poison	×1
Ground	×2
Flying	×1
Psychic	×2
Bug	×1
Rock	×0.5
Ghost	×2
Dragon	×1
Dark	×2
Steel	×1
Fairy	×0.5

Can be used in	
Inverse Battle	Battle Institute
Sky Battle	Battle Maison
Battle Chateau	Random Matchup

Same form for ♂/♀

How to obtain for your Mountain Kalos Pokédex

X	Y
Use a Dusk Stone on Murkrow.	Use a Dusk Stone on Murkrow.

● LEVEL-UP MOVES

Lv.	Name	Type	Kind	Pow.	Acc.	PP	Range
1	Night Slash	Dark	Physical	70	100	15	Normal
1	Sucker Punch	Dark	Physical	80	100	5	Normal
1	Astonish	Ghost	Physical	30	100	15	Normal
1	Pursuit	Dark	Physical	40	100	20	Normal
1	Haze	Ice	Status	—	—	30	Both Sides
1	Wing Attack	Flying	Physical	60	100	35	Normal
25	Swagger	Normal	Status	—	90	15	Normal
35	Nasty Plot	Dark	Status	—	—	20	Self
45	Foul Play	Dark	Physical	95	100	15	Normal
55	Night Slash	Dark	Physical	70	100	15	Normal
65	Quash	Dark	Status	—	100	15	Normal
75	Dark Pulse	Dark	Special	80	100	15	Normal

● TM & HM MOVES

No.	Name	Type	Kind	Pow.	Acc.	PP	Range
TM04	Calm Mind	Psychic	Status	—	—	20	Self
TM06	Toxic	Poison	Status	—	90	10	Normal
TM10	Hidden Power	Normal	Special	60	100	15	Normal
TM11	Sunny Day	Fire	Status	—	—	5	Both Sides
TM12	Taunt	Dark	Status	—	100	20	Normal
TM15	Hyper Beam	Normal	Special	150	90	5	Normal
TM17	Protect	Normal	Status	—	—	10	Self
TM18	Rain Dance	Water	Status	—	—	5	Both Sides
TM19	Roost	Flying	Status	—	—	10	Self
TM21	Frustration	Normal	Physical	—	100	20	Normal
TM27	Return	Normal	Physical	—	100	20	Normal
TM29	Psychic	Psychic	Special	90	100	10	Normal
TM30	Shadow Ball	Ghost	Special	80	100	15	Normal
TM32	Double Team	Normal	Status	—	—	15	Self
TM40	Aerial Ace	Flying	Physical	60	—	20	Normal
TM41	Torment	Dark	Status	—	100	15	Normal
TM42	Facade	Normal	Physical	70	100	20	Normal
TM44	Rest	Psychic	Status	—	—	10	Self
TM45	Attract	Normal	Status	—	100	15	Normal
TM46	Thief	Dark	Physical	60	100	25	Normal
TM48	Round	Normal	Special	60	100	15	Normal
TM51	Steel Wing	Steel	Physical	70	90	25	Normal
TM59	Incinerate	Fire	Special	60	100	15	Many Others
TM60	Quash	Dark	Status	—	100	15	Normal
TM63	Embargo	Dark	Status	—	100	15	Normal
TM66	Payback	Dark	Physical	50	100	10	Normal
TM67	Retaliate	Normal	Physical	70	100	5	Normal
TM68	Giga Impact	Normal	Physical	150	90	5	Normal
TM73	Thunder Wave	Electric	Status	—	100	20	Normal
TM77	Psych Up	Normal	Status	—	—	10	Normal
TM85	Dream Eater	Psychic	Special	100	100	15	Normal
TM87	Swagger	Normal	Status	—	90	15	Normal
TM88	Sleep Talk	Normal	Status	—	—	10	Self

No.	Name	Type	Kind	Pow.	Acc.	PP	Range
TM90	Substitute	Normal	Status	—	—	10	Self
TM95	Snarl	Dark	Special	55	95	15	Many Others
TM97	Dark Pulse	Dark	Special	80	100	15	Normal
TM100	Confide	Normal	Status	—	—	20	Normal
HM02	Fly	Flying	Physical	90	95	15	Normal

● MOVES TAUGHT BY PEOPLE

Name	Type	Kind	Pow.	Acc.	PP	Range

Honchkrow

052

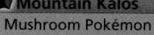
Mushroom Pokémon

Foongus

053

HEIGHT: 0'08" WEIGHT: 2.2 lbs.
GENDER: ♂/♀

TYPE Grass | Poison

ABILITY
Effect Spore

HIDDEN ABILITY
Regenerator

STAT GROWTH RATES
HP	■■■
Attack	■■■
Defense	■■
Sp. Atk	■■■
Sp. Def	■■
Speed	■

EGG GROUP
Grass

X It lures people in with its Poké Ball pattern, then releases poison spores. Why it resembles a Poké Ball is unknown.

Y It lures Pokémon with its pattern that looks just like a Poké Ball, then releases poison spores.

EVOLUTION

Foongus — Lv. 39 → Amoonguss

ITEMS SOMETIMES HELD BY WILD POKÉMON
Tiny Mushroom, Big Mushroom

Damage taken in normal battles		Damage taken in Inverse Battles	
Normal	×1	Normal	×1
Fire	×2	Fire	×0.5
Water	×0.5	Water	×2
Grass	×0.25	Grass	×4
Electric	×0.5	Electric	×2
Ice	×2	Ice	×0.5
Fighting	×0.5	Fighting	×2
Poison	×1	Poison	×1
Ground	×1	Ground	×1
Flying	×2	Flying	×0.5
Psychic	×2	Psychic	×0.5
Bug	×1	Bug	×1
Rock	×1	Rock	×1
Ghost	×1	Ghost	×1
Dragon	×1	Dragon	×1
Dark	×1	Dark	×1
Steel	×1	Steel	×1
Fairy	×0.5	Fairy	×2

Can be used in	
Inverse Battle	Battle Institute
—	Battle Maison
Battle Chateau	Random Matchup

Same form for ♂/♀

 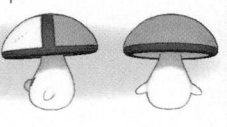

How to obtain for your Mountain Kalos Pokédex

❶ Catch in the tall grass on Route 15.
❷ Catch in the red flowers on Route 15.

❶ Catch in the tall grass on Route 15.
❷ Catch in the red flowers on Route 15.

● LEVEL-UP MOVES

Lv.	Name	Type	Kind	Pow.	Acc.	PP	Range
1	Absorb	Grass	Special	20	100	25	Normal
6	Growth	Normal	Status	—	—	20	Self
8	Astonish	Ghost	Physical	30	100	15	Normal
12	Bide	Normal	Physical	—	—	10	Self
15	Mega Drain	Grass	Special	40	100	15	Normal
18	Ingrain	Grass	Status	—	—	20	Self
20	Feint Attack	Dark	Physical	60	—	20	Normal
24	Sweet Scent	Normal	Status	—	100	20	Many Others
28	Giga Drain	Grass	Special	75	100	10	Normal
32	Toxic	Poison	Status	—	90	10	Normal
35	Synthesis	Grass	Status	—	—	5	Self
39	Clear Smog	Poison	Special	50	—	15	Normal
43	Solar Beam	Grass	Special	120	100	10	Normal
45	Rage Powder	Bug	Status	—	—	20	Self
50	Spore	Grass	Status	—	100	15	Normal

● TM & HM MOVES

No.	Name	Type	Kind	Pow.	Acc.	PP	Range
TM06	Toxic	Poison	Status	—	90	10	Normal
TM09	Venoshock	Poison	Special	65	100	10	Normal
TM10	Hidden Power	Normal	Special	60	100	15	Normal
TM11	Sunny Day	Fire	Status	—	—	5	Both Sides
TM17	Protect	Normal	Status	—	—	10	Self
TM18	Rain Dance	Water	Status	—	—	5	Both Sides
TM21	Frustration	Normal	Physical	—	100	20	Normal
TM22	Solar Beam	Grass	Special	120	100	10	Normal
TM27	Return	Normal	Physical	—	100	20	Normal
TM32	Double Team	Normal	Status	—	—	15	Self
TM36	Sludge Bomb	Poison	Special	90	100	10	Normal
TM42	Facade	Normal	Physical	70	100	20	Normal
TM44	Rest	Psychic	Status	—	—	10	Self
TM45	Attract	Normal	Status	—	100	15	Normal
TM48	Round	Normal	Special	60	100	15	Normal
TM53	Energy Ball	Grass	Special	90	100	10	Normal
TM66	Payback	Dark	Physical	50	100	10	Normal
TM70	Flash	Normal	Status	—	100	20	Normal
TM86	Grass Knot	Grass	Special	—	100	20	Normal
TM87	Swagger	Normal	Status	—	90	15	Normal
TM88	Sleep Talk	Normal	Status	—	—	10	Self
TM90	Substitute	Normal	Status	—	—	10	Self
TM96	Nature Power	Normal	Status	—	—	20	Normal
TM100	Confide	Normal	Status	—	—	20	Normal

● MOVES TAUGHT BY PEOPLE

Name	Type	Kind	Pow.	Acc.	PP	Range

● EGG MOVES

Name	Type	Kind	Pow.	Acc.	PP	Range
Gastro Acid	Poison	Status	—	100	10	Normal
Growth	Normal	Status	—	—	20	Self
Poison Powder	Poison	Status	—	75	35	Normal
Stun Spore	Grass	Status	—	75	30	Normal
Rollout	Rock	Physical	30	90	20	Normal
Defense Curl	Normal	Status	—	—	40	Self
Endure	Normal	Status	—	—	10	Self
Body Slam	Normal	Physical	85	100	15	Normal

AFTER THE HALL OF FAME

CENTRAL KALOS

COASTAL KALOS

MOUNTAIN KALOS

053 Foongus

ADVENTURE DATA

AFTER THE HALL OF FAME

CENTRAL KALOS

COASTAL KALOS

MOUNTAIN KALOS
054
Amoonguss

ADVENTURE DATA

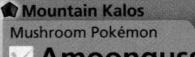

🍄 Mountain Kalos **054**
Mushroom Pokémon

☑ **Amoonguss**

HEIGHT: 2'00"   WEIGHT: 23.1 lbs.
GENDER: ♂/♀

TYPE Grass Poison

ABILITY
Effect Spore

HIDDEN ABILITY
Regenerator

STAT GROWTH RATES
HP	▪▪▪▪▪
Attack	▪▪▪▪
Defense	▪▪▪▪
Sp. Atk	▪▪▪▪
Sp. Def	▪▪▪
Speed	▪▪

EGG GROUP
Grass

X	They show off their Poké Ball caps to lure prey, but very few Pokémon are fooled by this.

Y	It lures prey close by dancing and waving its arm caps, which resemble Poké Balls, in a swaying motion.

EVOLUTION

Foongus →(Lv. 39)→ Amoonguss

ITEMS SOMETIMES HELD BY WILD POKÉMON
Tiny Mushroom, Big Mushroom

Damage taken in normal battles	
Normal	×1
Fire	×2
Water	×0.5
Grass	×0.25
Electric	×0.5
Ice	×2
Fighting	×0.5
Poison	×1
Ground	×1
Flying	×2
Psychic	×2
Bug	×1
Rock	×1
Ghost	×1
Dragon	×1
Dark	×1
Steel	×1
Fairy	×0.5

Damage taken in Inverse Battles	
Normal	×1
Fire	×0.5
Water	×2
Grass	×4
Electric	×2
Ice	×0.5
Fighting	×2
Poison	×1
Ground	×1
Flying	×0.5
Psychic	×0.5
Bug	×1
Rock	×1
Ghost	×1
Dragon	×1
Dark	×1
Steel	×1
Fairy	×2

Can be used in	
Inverse Battle	Battle Institute
—	Battle Maison
Battle Chateau	Random Matchup

Same form for ♂/♀

How to obtain for your Mountain Kalos Pokédex

❶ Catch in the tall grass or the red flowers on Route 20.
❷ Level up Foongus to Lv. 39.

❶ Catch in the tall grass or red flowers on Route 20.
❷ Level up Foongus to Lv. 39.

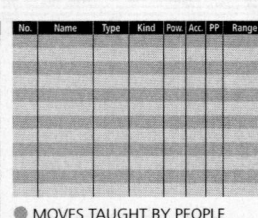

● **LEVEL-UP MOVES**

Lv.	Name	Type	Kind	Pow.	Acc.	PP	Range
1	Absorb	Grass	Special	20	100	25	Normal
1	Growth	Normal	Status	—	—	20	Self
1	Astonish	Ghost	Physical	30	100	15	Normal
1	Bide	Normal	Physical	—	—	10	Self
6	Growth	Normal	Status	—	—	20	Self
8	Astonish	Ghost	Physical	30	100	15	Normal
12	Bide	Normal	Physical	—	—	10	Self
15	Mega Drain	Grass	Special	40	100	15	Normal
18	Ingrain	Grass	Status	—	—	20	Self
20	Feint Attack	Dark	Physical	60	—	20	Normal
24	Sweet Scent	Normal	Status	—	100	20	Many Others
28	Giga Drain	Grass	Special	75	100	10	Normal
32	Toxic	Poison	Status	—	90	10	Normal
35	Synthesis	Grass	Status	—	—	5	Self
43	Clear Smog	Poison	Special	50	—	15	Normal
49	Solar Beam	Grass	Special	120	100	10	Normal
54	Rage Powder	Bug	Status	—	—	20	Self
62	Spore	Grass	Status	—	100	15	Normal

● **TM & HM MOVES**

No.	Name	Type	Kind	Pow.	Acc.	PP	Range
TM06	Toxic	Poison	Status	—	90	10	Normal
TM09	Venoshock	Poison	Special	65	100	10	Normal
TM10	Hidden Power	Normal	Special	60	100	15	Normal
TM11	Sunny Day	Fire	Status	—	—	5	Both Sides
TM15	Hyper Beam	Normal	Special	150	90	5	Normal
TM17	Protect	Normal	Status	—	—	10	Self
TM18	Rain Dance	Water	Status	—	—	5	Both Sides
TM21	Frustration	Normal	Physical	—	100	20	Normal
TM22	Solar Beam	Grass	Special	120	100	10	Normal
TM27	Return	Normal	Physical	—	100	20	Normal
TM32	Double Team	Normal	Status	—	—	15	Self
TM36	Sludge Bomb	Poison	Special	90	100	10	Normal
TM42	Facade	Normal	Physical	70	100	20	Normal
TM44	Rest	Psychic	Status	—	—	10	Self
TM45	Attract	Normal	Status	—	100	15	Normal
TM48	Round	Normal	Special	60	100	15	Normal
TM53	Energy Ball	Grass	Special	90	100	10	Normal
TM66	Payback	Dark	Physical	50	100	10	Normal
TM68	Giga Impact	Normal	Physical	150	90	5	Normal
TM70	Flash	Normal	Status	—	100	20	Normal
TM86	Grass Knot	Grass	Special	—	100	20	Normal
TM87	Swagger	Normal	Status	—	90	15	Normal
TM88	Sleep Talk	Normal	Status	—	—	10	Self
TM90	Substitute	Normal	Status	—	—	10	Self
TM96	Nature Power	Normal	Status	—	—	20	Normal
TM100	Confide	Normal	Status	—	—	20	Normal

No.	Name	Type	Kind	Pow.	Acc.	PP	Range

● **MOVES TAUGHT BY PEOPLE**

Name	Type	Kind	Pow.	Acc.	PP	Range

Mountain Kalos **055**
Water Weed Pokémon

☑ **Lotad**

HEIGHT: 1'08" WEIGHT: 5.7 lbs.
GENDER: ♂/♀

X It looks like an aquatic plant and serves as a ferry to Pokémon that can't swim.

Y It searches about for clean water. If it does not drink water for too long, the leaf on its head wilts.

TYPE Water Grass

ABILITIES
Swift Swim
Rain Dish

HIDDEN ABILITY
Own Tempo

STAT GROWTH RATES
HP	■■
Attack	■■
Defense	■■
Sp. Atk	■■
Sp. Def	■■
Speed	■■

EGG GROUPS
Water 1, Grass

ITEMS SOMETIMES HELD BY WILD POKÉMON
None

EVOLUTION

Lv. 14 Water Stone

Lotad → Lombre → Ludicolo

Damage taken in normal battles		Damage taken in Inverse Battles	
Normal	×1	Normal	×1
Fire	×1	Fire	×1
Water	×0.25	Water	×4
Grass	×1	Grass	×1
Electric	×1	Electric	×1
Ice	×1	Ice	×1
Fighting	×1	Fighting	×1
Poison	×2	Poison	×0.5
Ground	×0.5	Ground	×2
Flying	×2	Flying	×0.5
Psychic	×1	Psychic	×1
Bug	×2	Bug	×0.5
Rock	×1	Rock	×1
Ghost	×1	Ghost	×1
Dragon	×1	Dragon	×1
Dark	×1	Dark	×1
Steel	×0.5	Steel	×2
Fairy	×1	Fairy	×1

Can be used in	
Inverse Battle	Battle Institute
—	Battle Maison
Battle Chateau	Random Matchup

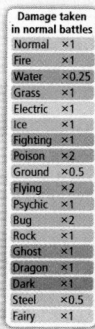

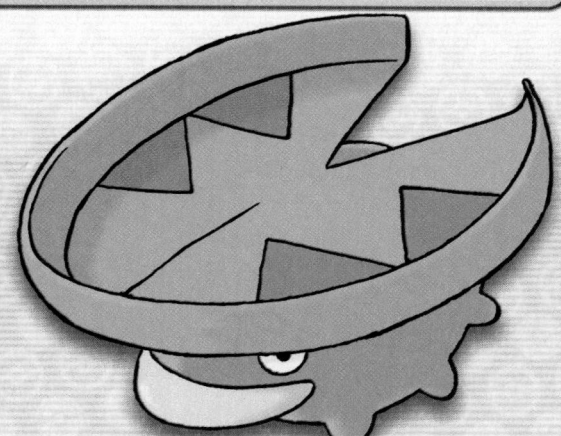

Same form for ♂/♀

How to obtain for your Mountain Kalos Pokédex

Leave Lombre or Ludicolo at the Pokémon Day Care, and hatch the Egg that is found.

Leave Lombre or Ludicolo at the Pokémon Day Care, and hatch the Egg that is found.

● LEVEL-UP MOVES

Lv.	Name	Type	Kind	Pow.	Acc.	PP	Range
1	Astonish	Ghost	Physical	30	100	15	Normal
3	Growl	Normal	Status	—	100	40	Many Others
5	Absorb	Grass	Special	20	100	25	Normal
7	Nature Power	Normal	Status	—	—	20	Normal
11	Mist	Ice	Status	—	—	30	Your Side
15	Natural Gift	Normal	Physical	—	100	15	Normal
19	Mega Drain	Grass	Special	40	100	15	Normal
25	Bubble Beam	Water	Special	65	100	20	Normal
31	Zen Headbutt	Psychic	Physical	80	90	15	Normal
37	Rain Dance	Water	Status	—	—	5	Both Sides
45	Energy Ball	Grass	Special	90	100	10	Normal

● TM & HM MOVES

No.	Name	Type	Kind	Pow.	Acc.	PP	Range
TM06	Toxic	Poison	Status	—	90	10	Normal
TM07	Hail	Ice	Status	—	—	10	Both Sides
TM10	Hidden Power	Normal	Special	60	100	15	Normal
TM11	Sunny Day	Fire	Status	—	—	5	Both Sides
TM13	Ice Beam	Ice	Special	90	100	10	Normal
TM14	Blizzard	Ice	Special	110	70	5	Many Others
TM17	Protect	Normal	Status	—	—	10	Self
TM18	Rain Dance	Water	Status	—	—	5	Both Sides
TM21	Frustration	Normal	Physical	—	100	20	Normal
TM22	Solar Beam	Grass	Special	120	100	10	Normal
TM27	Return	Normal	Physical	—	100	20	Normal
TM32	Double Team	Normal	Status	—	—	15	Self
TM42	Facade	Normal	Physical	70	100	20	Normal
TM44	Rest	Psychic	Status	—	—	10	Self
TM45	Attract	Normal	Status	—	100	15	Normal
TM46	Thief	Dark	Physical	60	100	25	Normal
TM48	Round	Normal	Special	60	100	15	Normal
TM49	Echoed Voice	Normal	Special	40	100	15	Normal
TM53	Energy Ball	Grass	Special	90	100	10	Normal
TM55	Scald	Water	Special	80	100	15	Normal
TM70	Flash	Normal	Status	—	100	20	Normal
TM75	Swords Dance	Normal	Status	—	—	20	Self
TM86	Grass Knot	Grass	Special	—	100	20	Normal
TM87	Swagger	Normal	Status	—	90	15	Normal
TM88	Sleep Talk	Normal	Status	—	—	10	Self
TM90	Substitute	Normal	Status	—	—	10	Self
TM96	Nature Power	Normal	Status	—	—	20	Normal
TM100	Confide	Normal	Status	—	—	20	Normal
HM03	Surf	Water	Special	90	100	15	Adjacent

● MOVES TAUGHT BY PEOPLE

Name	Type	Kind	Pow.	Acc.	PP	Range

● EGG MOVES

Name	Type	Kind	Pow.	Acc.	PP	Range
Synthesis	Grass	Status	—	—	5	Self
Razor Leaf	Grass	Physical	55	95	25	Many Others
Sweet Scent	Normal	Status	—	100	20	Many Others
Leech Seed	Grass	Status	—	90	10	Normal
Flail	Normal	Physical	—	100	15	Normal
Water Gun	Water	Special	40	100	25	Normal
Tickle	Normal	Status	—	100	20	Normal
Counter	Fighting	Physical	—	100	20	Varies
Giga Drain	Grass	Special	75	100	10	Normal
Teeter Dance	Normal	Status	—	100	20	Adjacent

AFTER THE HALL OF FAME

CENTRAL KALOS

COASTAL KALOS

MOUNTAIN KALOS

055 Lotad

ADVENTURE DATA

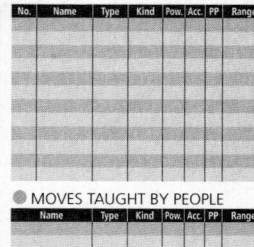

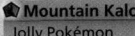 Mountain Kalos 056

Jolly Pokémon

Lombre

HEIGHT: 3'11"   WEIGHT: 71.6 lbs.
GENDER: ♂ / ♀

X It lives at the water's edge where it is sunny. It sleeps on a bed of water-grass by day and becomes active at night.

Y It has a mischievous spirit. If it spots an angler, it will tug on the fishing line to interfere.

TYPE: Water | Grass

ABILITIES
Swift Swim
Rain Dish

HIDDEN ABILITY
Own Tempo

STAT GROWTH RATES
HP	■■■
Attack	■■■
Defense	■■■
Sp. Atk	■■■
Sp. Def	■■■
Speed	■■■

EGG GROUPS
Water 1, Grass

EVOLUTION

Lotad — Lv. 14 → Lombre — Water Stone → Ludicolo

ITEMS SOMETIMES HELD BY WILD POKÉMON
None

Damage taken in normal battles	
Normal	×1
Fire	×1
Water	×0.25
Grass	×1
Electric	×1
Ice	×1
Fighting	×1
Poison	×2
Ground	×0.5
Flying	×2
Psychic	×1
Bug	×2
Rock	×1
Ghost	×1
Dragon	×1
Dark	×1
Steel	×0.5
Fairy	×1

Damage taken in Inverse Battles	
Normal	×1
Fire	×1
Water	×4
Grass	×1
Electric	×1
Ice	×1
Fighting	×1
Poison	×0.5
Ground	×2
Flying	×0.5
Psychic	×1
Bug	×0.5
Rock	×1
Ghost	×1
Dragon	×1
Dark	×1
Steel	×2
Fairy	×1

Can be used in	
Inverse Battle	Battle Institute
—	Battle Maison
Battle Chateau	Random Matchup

Same form for ♂ / ♀

How to obtain for your Mountain Kalos Pokédex

❶ Catch on the surface of the water on Route 15.

❷ Catch on the surface of the water on Route 16.

❶ Catch on the surface of the water on Route 15.

❷ Catch on the surface of the water on Route 16.

056

Lombre

● LEVEL-UP MOVES

Lv.	Name	Type	Kind	Pow.	Acc.	PP	Range
1	Astonish	Ghost	Physical	30	100	15	Normal
3	Growl	Normal	Status	—	100	40	Many Others
5	Absorb	Grass	Special	20	100	25	Normal
9	Nature Power	Normal	Status	—	—	20	Normal
11	Fake Out	Normal	Physical	40	100	10	Normal
15	Fury Swipes	Normal	Physical	18	80	15	Normal
19	Water Sport	Water	Status	—	—	15	Both Sides
25	Bubble Beam	Water	Special	65	100	20	Normal
31	Zen Headbutt	Psychic	Physical	80	90	15	Normal
37	Uproar	Normal	Special	90	100	10	1 Random
45	Hydro Pump	Water	Special	110	80	5	Normal

● TM & HM MOVES

No.	Name	Type	Kind	Pow.	Acc.	PP	Range
TM01	Hone Claws	Dark	Status	—	—	15	Self
TM06	Toxic	Poison	Status	—	90	10	Normal
TM07	Hail	Ice	Status	—	—	10	Both Sides
TM10	Hidden Power	Normal	Special	60	100	15	Normal
TM11	Sunny Day	Fire	Status	—	—	5	Both Sides
TM13	Ice Beam	Ice	Special	90	100	10	Normal
TM14	Blizzard	Ice	Special	110	70	5	Many Others
TM17	Protect	Normal	Status	—	—	10	Self
TM18	Rain Dance	Water	Status	—	—	5	Both Sides
TM21	Frustration	Normal	Physical	—	100	20	Normal
TM22	Solar Beam	Grass	Special	120	100	10	Normal
TM27	Return	Normal	Physical	—	100	20	Normal
TM31	Brick Break	Fighting	Physical	75	100	15	Normal
TM32	Double Team	Normal	Status	—	—	15	Self
TM42	Facade	Normal	Physical	70	100	20	Normal
TM44	Rest	Psychic	Status	—	—	10	Self
TM45	Attract	Normal	Status	—	100	15	Normal
TM46	Thief	Dark	Physical	60	100	25	Normal
TM48	Round	Normal	Special	60	100	15	Normal
TM49	Echoed Voice	Normal	Special	40	100	15	Normal
TM53	Energy Ball	Grass	Special	90	100	10	Normal
TM55	Scald	Water	Special	80	100	15	Normal
TM56	Fling	Dark	Physical	—	100	10	Normal
TM70	Flash	Normal	Status	—	100	20	Normal
TM75	Swords Dance	Normal	Status	—	—	20	Self
TM86	Grass Knot	Grass	Special	—	100	20	Normal
TM87	Swagger	Normal	Status	—	90	15	Normal
TM88	Sleep Talk	Normal	Status	—	—	10	Self
TM90	Substitute	Normal	Status	—	—	10	Self
TM94	Rock Smash	Fighting	Physical	40	100	15	Normal
TM96	Nature Power	Normal	Status	—	—	20	Normal
TM98	Power-Up Punch	Fighting	Physical	40	100	20	Normal
TM100	Confide	Normal	Status	—	—	20	Normal

No.	Name	Type	Kind	Pow.	Acc.	PP	Range
HM03	Surf	Water	Special	90	100	15	Adjacent
HM04	Strength	Normal	Physical	80	100	15	Normal
HM05	Waterfall	Water	Physical	80	100	15	Normal

● MOVES TAUGHT BY PEOPLE

Name	Type	Kind	Pow.	Acc.	PP	Range

AFTER THE
HALL OF FAME

CENTRAL
KALOS

COASTAL
KALOS

MOUNTAIN
KALOS

057

Ludicolo

ADVENTURE
DATA

★ Mountain Kalos 057
Carefree Pokémon
☑ Ludicolo

HEIGHT: 4'11" WEIGHT: 121.3 lbs.
GENDER: ♂/♀

X If it hears festive music, all its muscles fill with energy. It can't help breaking out into a dance.

Y The rhythm of bright, festive music activates Ludicolo's cells, making it more powerful.

TYPE Water Grass

ABILITIES
Swift Swim
Rain Dish

HIDDEN ABILITY
Own Tempo

STAT GROWTH RATES
HP ■■■
Attack ■■■■
Defense ■■■
Sp. Atk ■■■
Sp. Def ■■■■
Speed ■■■■

EGG GROUPS
Water 1, Grass

⚡ EVOLUTION

Lv. 14 Water Stone

Lotad Lombre Ludicolo

ITEMS SOMETIMES HELD BY WILD POKÉMON
None

Damage taken in normal battles		Damage taken in Inverse Battles		Can be used in
Normal	×1	Normal	×1	Inverse Battle
Fire	×1	Fire	×1	—
Water	×0.25	Water	×4	Battle Chateau
Grass	×1	Grass	×1	Battle Institute
Electric	×1	Electric	×1	Battle Maison
Ice	×1	Ice	×1	Random Matchup
Fighting	×1	Fighting	×1	
Poison	×2	Poison	×0.5	
Ground	×0.5	Ground	×2	
Flying	×2	Flying	×0.5	
Psychic	×1	Psychic	×1	
Bug	×2	Bug	×0.5	
Rock	×1	Rock	×1	
Ghost	×1	Ghost	×1	
Dragon	×1	Dragon	×1	
Dark	×1	Dark	×1	
Steel	×0.5	Steel	×2	
Fairy	×1	Fairy	×1	

How to obtain for your Mountain Kalos Pokédex

Use a Water Stone on Lombre. Use a Water Stone on Lombre.

  ♂ ♀

The zigzag patterns are larger on the male's body. The zigzag patterns are smaller on the female's body.

● LEVEL-UP MOVES

Lv.	Name	Type	Kind	Pow.	Acc.	PP	Range
1	Astonish	Ghost	Physical	30	100	15	Normal
1	Growl	Normal	Status	—	100	40	Many Others
1	Mega Drain	Grass	Special	40	100	15	Normal
1	Nature Power	Normal	Status	—	—	20	Normal

● TM & HM MOVES

No.	Name	Type	Kind	Pow.	Acc.	PP	Range
TM01	Hone Claws	Dark	Status	—	—	15	Self
TM06	Toxic	Poison	Status	—	90	10	Normal
TM07	Hail	Ice	Status	—	—	10	Both Sides
TM10	Hidden Power	Normal	Special	60	100	15	Normal
TM11	Sunny Day	Fire	Status	—	—	5	Both Sides
TM13	Ice Beam	Ice	Special	90	100	10	Normal
TM14	Blizzard	Ice	Special	110	70	5	Many Others
TM15	Hyper Beam	Normal	Special	150	90	5	Normal
TM17	Protect	Normal	Status	—	—	10	Self
TM18	Rain Dance	Water	Status	—	—	5	Both Sides
TM21	Frustration	Normal	Physical	—	100	20	Normal
TM22	Solar Beam	Grass	Special	120	100	10	Normal
TM27	Return	Normal	Physical	—	100	20	Normal
TM31	Brick Break	Fighting	Physical	75	100	15	Normal
TM32	Double Team	Normal	Status	—	—	15	Self
TM42	Facade	Normal	Physical	70	100	20	Normal
TM44	Rest	Psychic	Status	—	—	10	Self
TM45	Attract	Normal	Status	—	100	15	Normal
TM46	Thief	Dark	Physical	60	100	25	Normal
TM48	Round	Normal	Special	60	100	15	Normal
TM49	Echoed Voice	Normal	Special	40	100	15	Normal
TM52	Focus Blast	Fighting	Special	120	70	5	Normal
TM53	Energy Ball	Grass	Special	90	100	10	Normal
TM55	Scald	Water	Special	80	100	15	Normal
TM56	Fling	Dark	Physical	—	100	10	Normal
TM68	Giga Impact	Normal	Physical	150	90	5	Normal
TM70	Flash	Normal	Status	—	100	20	Normal
TM75	Swords Dance	Normal	Status	—	—	20	Self
TM86	Grass Knot	Grass	Special	—	100	20	Normal
TM87	Swagger	Normal	Status	—	90	15	Normal
TM88	Sleep Talk	Normal	Status	—	—	10	Self
TM90	Substitute	Normal	Status	—	—	10	Self
TM94	Rock Smash	Fighting	Physical	40	100	15	Normal

No.	Name	Type	Kind	Pow.	Acc.	PP	Range
TM96	Nature Power	Normal	Status	—	—	20	Normal
TM98	Power-Up Punch	Fighting	Physical	40	100	20	Normal
TM100	Confide	Normal	Status	—	—	20	Normal
HM03	Surf	Water	Special	90	100	15	Adjacent
HM04	Strength	Normal	Physical	80	100	15	Normal
HM05	Waterfall	Water	Physical	80	100	15	Normal

● MOVES TAUGHT BY PEOPLE

Name	Type	Kind	Pow.	Acc.	PP	Range

🏔 Mountain Kalos 058
Sea Weasel Pokémon
☑ Buizel

HEIGHT: 2'04"   WEIGHT: 65.0 lbs.
GENDER: ♂/♀

X It swims by rotating its two tails like a screw. When it dives, its flotation sac collapses.

Y It inflates the flotation sac around its neck and pokes its head out of the water to see what is going on.

TYPE | Water

ABILITY
Swift Swim

HIDDEN ABILITY
Water Veil

STAT GROWTH RATES
HP ▪▪▪
Attack ▪▪▪
Defense ▪▪
Sp. Atk ▪▪▪
Sp. Def ▪▪
Speed ▪▪▪▪▪

EGG GROUPS
Water 1, Field

🔄 EVOLUTION

Buizel → Lv. 26 → Floatzel

ITEMS SOMETIMES HELD BY WILD POKÉMON
None

	Damage taken in normal battles		Damage taken in Inverse Battles
Normal	×1	Normal	×1
Fire	×0.5	Fire	×2
Water	×0.5	Water	×2
Grass	×2	Grass	×0.5
Electric	×2	Electric	×0.5
Ice	×0.5	Ice	×2
Fighting	×1	Fighting	×1
Poison	×1	Poison	×1
Ground	×1	Ground	×1
Flying	×1	Flying	×1
Psychic	×1	Psychic	×1
Bug	×1	Bug	×1
Rock	×1	Rock	×1
Ghost	×1	Ghost	×1
Dragon	×1	Dragon	×1
Dark	×1	Dark	×1
Steel	×0.5	Steel	×2
Fairy	×1	Fairy	×1

Can be used in
Inverse Battle
—
Battle Chateau
Battle Institute
Battle Maison
Random Matchup

How to obtain for your Mountain Kalos Pokédex

Leave Floatzel at the Pokémon Day Care, and hatch the Egg that is found.

Leave Floatzel at the Pokémon Day Care, and hatch the Egg that is found.

The male has two marks on its back. The female has one mark on its back.

🔵 058 Buizel

● LEVEL-UP MOVES

Lv.	Name	Type	Kind	Pow.	Acc.	PP	Range
1	Sonic Boom	Normal	Special	—	90	20	Normal
4	Growl	Normal	Status	—	100	40	Many Others
7	Water Sport	Water	Status	—	—	15	Both Sides
11	Quick Attack	Normal	Physical	40	100	30	Normal
15	Water Gun	Water	Special	40	100	25	Normal
18	Pursuit	Dark	Physical	40	100	20	Normal
21	Swift	Normal	Special	60	—	20	Many Others
24	Aqua Jet	Water	Physical	40	100	20	Normal
27	Double Hit	Normal	Physical	35	90	10	Normal
31	Whirlpool	Water	Special	35	85	15	Normal
35	Razor Wind	Normal	Special	80	100	10	Many Others
38	Aqua Tail	Water	Physical	90	90	10	Normal
41	Agility	Psychic	Status	—	—	30	Self
45	Hydro Pump	Water	Special	110	80	5	Normal

● TM & HM MOVES

No.	Name	Type	Kind	Pow.	Acc.	PP	Range
TM06	Toxic	Poison	Status	—	90	10	Normal
TM07	Hail	Ice	Status	—	—	10	Both Sides
TM08	Bulk Up	Fighting	Status	—	—	20	Self
TM10	Hidden Power	Normal	Special	60	100	15	Normal
TM13	Ice Beam	Ice	Special	90	100	10	Normal
TM14	Blizzard	Ice	Special	110	70	5	Many Others
TM17	Protect	Normal	Status	—	—	10	Self
TM18	Rain Dance	Water	Status	—	—	5	Both Sides
TM21	Frustration	Normal	Physical	—	100	20	Normal
TM27	Return	Normal	Physical	—	100	20	Normal
TM28	Dig	Ground	Physical	80	100	10	Normal
TM31	Brick Break	Fighting	Physical	75	100	15	Normal
TM32	Double Team	Normal	Status	—	—	15	Self
TM39	Rock Tomb	Rock	Physical	60	95	15	Normal
TM42	Facade	Normal	Physical	70	100	20	Normal
TM44	Rest	Psychic	Status	—	—	10	Self
TM45	Attract	Normal	Status	—	100	15	Normal
TM48	Round	Normal	Special	60	100	15	Normal
TM49	Echoed Voice	Normal	Special	40	100	15	Normal
TM55	Scald	Water	Special	80	100	15	Normal
TM87	Swagger	Normal	Status	—	90	15	Normal
TM88	Sleep Talk	Normal	Status	—	—	10	Self
TM90	Substitute	Normal	Status	—	—	10	Self
TM94	Rock Smash	Fighting	Physical	40	100	15	Normal
TM98	Power-Up Punch	Fighting	Physical	40	100	20	Normal
TM100	Confide	Normal	Status	—	—	20	Normal
HM03	Surf	Water	Special	90	100	15	Adjacent
HM04	Strength	Normal	Physical	80	100	15	Normal
HM05	Waterfall	Water	Physical	80	100	15	Normal

No.	Name	Type	Kind	Pow.	Acc.	PP	Range

● MOVES TAUGHT BY PEOPLE

Name	Type	Kind	Pow.	Acc.	PP	Range

● EGG MOVES

Name	Type	Kind	Pow.	Acc.	PP	Range
Mud-Slap	Ground	Special	20	100	10	Normal
Headbutt	Normal	Physical	70	100	15	Normal
Fury Swipes	Normal	Physical	18	80	15	Normal
Slash	Normal	Physical	70	100	20	Normal
Odor Sleuth	Normal	Status	—	—	40	Normal
Double Slap	Normal	Physical	15	85	10	Normal
Fury Cutter	Bug	Physical	40	95	20	Normal
Baton Pass	Normal	Status	—	—	40	Self
Aqua Tail	Water	Physical	90	90	10	Normal
Aqua Ring	Water	Status	—	—	20	Self
Me First	Normal	Status	—	—	20	Varies
Switcheroo	Dark	Status	—	100	10	Normal
Tail Slap	Normal	Physical	25	85	10	Normal
Soak	Water	Status	—	100	20	Normal

Mountain Kalos
Sea Weasel Pokémon

059

☑ Floatzel

HEIGHT: 3'07" WEIGHT: 73.9 lbs.
GENDER: ♂/♀

X It floats using its well-developed flotation sac. It assists in the rescues of drowning people.

Y Its flotation sac developed as a result of pursuing aquatic prey. It can double as a rubber raft.

TYPE | Water

ABILITY
Swift Swim

HIDDEN ABILITY
Water Veil

STAT GROWTH RATES
HP	■■■
Attack	■■■■■
Defense	■■■
Sp. Atk	■■■
Sp. Def	■■
Speed	■■■■■■

EGG GROUPS
Water 1, Field

EVOLUTION

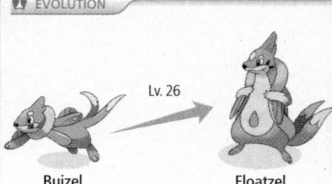

Buizel → Lv. 26 → Floatzel

ITEMS SOMETIMES HELD BY WILD POKÉMON
None

Damage taken in normal battles		Damage taken in Inverse Battles		Can be used in
Normal	×1	Normal	×1	Inverse Battle
Fire	×0.5	Fire	×2	—
Water	×0.5	Water	×2	Battle Chateau
Grass	×2	Grass	×0.5	Battle Institute
Electric	×2	Electric	×0.5	Battle Maison
Ice	×0.5	Ice	×2	Random Matchup
Fighting	×1	Fighting	×1	
Poison	×1	Poison	×1	
Ground	×1	Ground	×1	
Flying	×1	Flying	×1	
Psychic	×1	Psychic	×1	
Bug	×1	Bug	×1	
Rock	×1	Rock	×1	
Ghost	×1	Ghost	×1	
Dragon	×1	Dragon	×1	
Dark	×1	Dark	×1	
Steel	×0.5	Steel	×2	
Fairy	×1	Fairy	×1	

How to obtain for your Mountain Kalos Pokédex

❶ Catch on the surface of the water on Route 15.
❷ Catch in the yellow flowers on Route 16.

❶ Catch on the surface of the water on Route 15.
❷ Catch in the yellow flowers on Route 16.

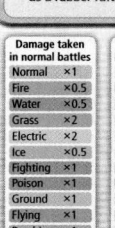

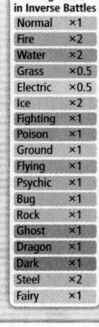

♂   ♀

The male has two marks on its back. The female has one mark on its back.

● LEVEL-UP MOVES

Lv.	Name	Type	Kind	Pow.	Acc.	PP	Range
1	Ice Fang	Ice	Physical	65	95	15	Normal
1	Crunch	Dark	Physical	80	100	15	Normal
1	Sonic Boom	Normal	Special	—	90	20	Normal
1	Growl	Normal	Status	—	100	40	Many Others
1	Water Sport	Water	Status	—	—	15	Both Sides
1	Quick Attack	Normal	Physical	40	100	30	Normal
4	Growl	Normal	Status	—	100	40	Many Others
7	Water Sport	Water	Status	—	—	15	Both Sides
11	Quick Attack	Normal	Physical	40	100	30	Normal
15	Water Gun	Water	Special	40	100	25	Normal
18	Pursuit	Dark	Physical	40	100	20	Normal
21	Swift	Normal	Special	60	—	20	Many Others
24	Aqua Jet	Water	Physical	40	100	20	Normal
29	Double Hit	Normal	Physical	35	90	10	Normal
35	Whirlpool	Water	Special	35	85	15	Normal
41	Razor Wind	Normal	Special	80	100	10	Many Others
46	Aqua Tail	Water	Physical	90	90	10	Normal
51	Agility	Psychic	Status	—	—	30	Self
57	Hydro Pump	Water	Special	110	80	5	Normal

● TM & HM MOVES

No.	Name	Type	Kind	Pow.	Acc.	PP	Range
TM05	Roar	Normal	Status	—	—	20	Normal
TM06	Toxic	Poison	Status	—	90	10	Normal
TM07	Hail	Ice	Status	—	—	10	Both Sides
TM08	Bulk Up	Fighting	Status	—	—	20	Self
TM10	Hidden Power	Normal	Special	60	100	15	Normal
TM12	Taunt	Dark	Status	—	100	20	Normal
TM13	Ice Beam	Ice	Special	90	100	10	Normal
TM14	Blizzard	Ice	Special	110	70	5	Many Others
TM15	Hyper Beam	Normal	Special	150	90	5	Normal
TM17	Protect	Normal	Status	—	—	10	Self
TM18	Rain Dance	Water	Status	—	—	5	Both Sides
TM21	Frustration	Normal	Physical	—	100	20	Normal
TM27	Return	Normal	Physical	—	100	20	Normal
TM28	Dig	Ground	Physical	80	100	10	Normal
TM31	Brick Break	Fighting	Physical	75	100	15	Normal
TM32	Double Team	Normal	Status	—	—	15	Self
TM39	Rock Tomb	Rock	Physical	60	95	15	Normal
TM41	Torment	Dark	Status	—	100	15	Normal
TM42	Facade	Normal	Physical	70	100	20	Normal
TM44	Rest	Psychic	Status	—	—	10	Self
TM45	Attract	Normal	Status	—	100	15	Normal
TM48	Round	Normal	Special	60	100	15	Normal
TM49	Echoed Voice	Normal	Special	40	100	15	Normal
TM52	Focus Blast	Fighting	Special	120	70	5	Normal
TM55	Scald	Water	Special	80	100	15	Normal
TM66	Payback	Dark	Physical	50	100	10	Normal
TM68	Giga Impact	Normal	Physical	150	90	5	Normal
TM87	Swagger	Normal	Status	—	90	15	Normal
TM88	Sleep Talk	Normal	Status	—	—	10	Self
TM90	Substitute	Normal	Status	—	—	10	Self
TM94	Rock Smash	Fighting	Physical	40	100	15	Normal
TM98	Power-Up Punch	Fighting	Physical	40	100	20	Normal
TM100	Confide	Normal	Status	—	—	20	Normal

No.	Name	Type	Kind	Pow.	Acc.	PP	Range
HM03	Surf	Water	Special	90	100	15	Adjacent
HM04	Strength	Normal	Physical	80	100	15	Normal
HM05	Waterfall	Water	Physical	80	100	15	Normal

● MOVES TAUGHT BY PEOPLE

Name	Type	Kind	Pow.	Acc.	PP	Range

Mountain Kalos — 060
Hostile Pokémon
☑ Basculin

HEIGHT: 3'03" WEIGHT: 39.7 lbs.
GENDER: ♂/♀

X Red- and blue-striped Basculin are very violent and always fighting. They are also remarkably tasty.

Y Red and blue Basculin usually do not get along, but sometimes members of one school mingle with the other's school.

Red-Striped Form
TYPE: Water

ABILITIES
Reckless
Adaptability

HIDDEN ABILITY
None

STAT GROWTH RATES
HP ■■■
Attack ■■■■■
Defense ■■■
Sp. Atk ■■■■
Sp. Def ■■
Speed ■■■■■

EGG GROUP
Water 2

Blue-Striped Form
TYPE: Water

ABILITIES
Rock Head
Adaptability

HIDDEN ABILITY
None

STAT GROWTH RATES
HP ■■■
Attack ■■■■■
Defense ■■■
Sp. Atk ■■■■
Sp. Def ■■
Speed ■■■■■

EGG GROUP
Water 2

EVOLUTION
Does not evolve

ITEMS SOMETIMES HELD BY WILD POKÉMON
Deep Sea Tooth

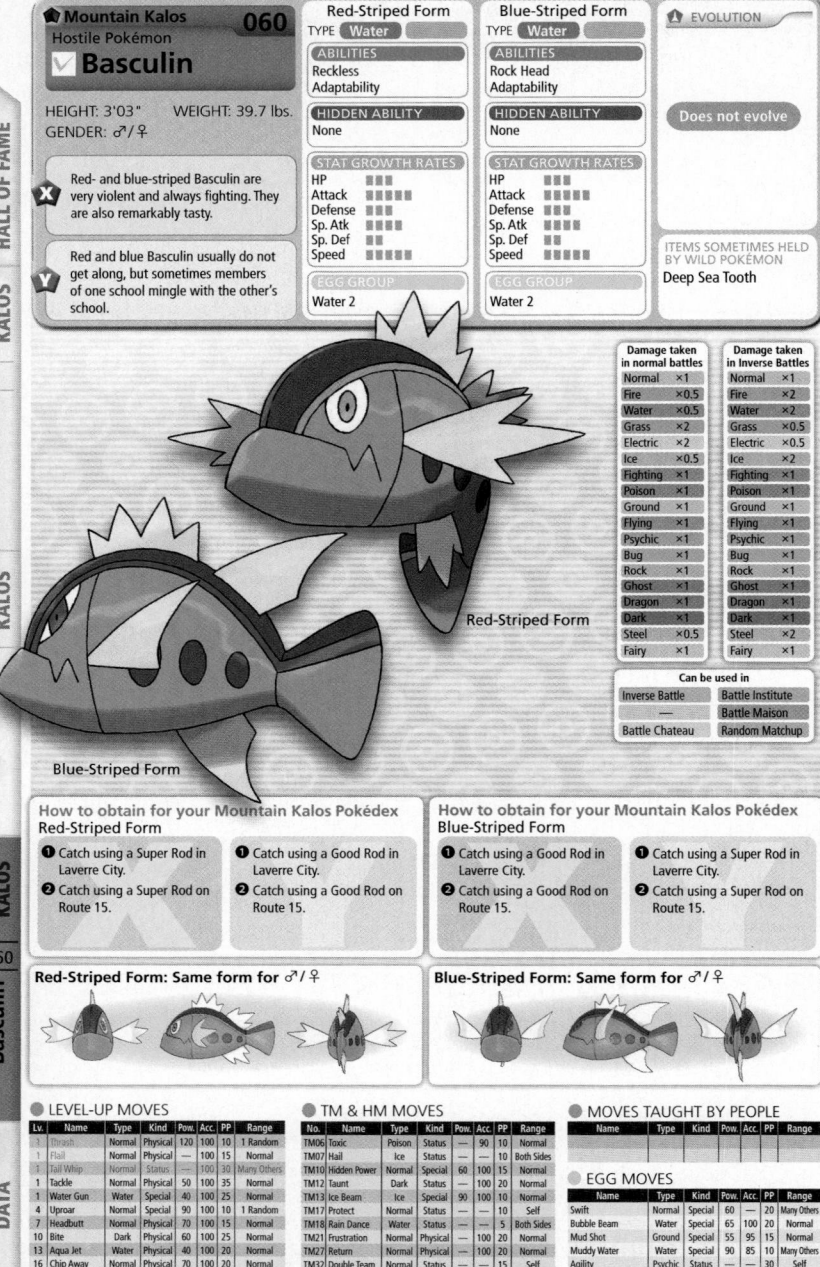

Red-Striped Form

Blue-Striped Form

	Damage taken in normal battles	Damage taken in Inverse Battles
Normal	×1	×1
Fire	×0.5	×2
Water	×0.5	×2
Grass	×2	×0.5
Electric	×2	×0.5
Ice	×0.5	×2
Fighting	×1	×1
Poison	×1	×1
Ground	×1	×1
Flying	×1	×1
Psychic	×1	×1
Bug	×1	×1
Rock	×1	×1
Ghost	×1	×1
Dragon	×1	×1
Dark	×1	×1
Steel	×0.5	×2
Fairy	×1	×1

Can be used in	
Inverse Battle	Battle Institute
—	Battle Maison
Battle Chateau	Random Matchup

How to obtain for your Mountain Kalos Pokédex Red-Striped Form
❶ Catch using a Super Rod in Laverre City.
❷ Catch using a Super Rod on Route 15.
❶ Catch using a Good Rod in Laverre City.
❷ Catch using a Good Rod on Route 15.

How to obtain for your Mountain Kalos Pokédex Blue-Striped Form
❶ Catch using a Good Rod in Laverre City.
❷ Catch using a Good Rod on Route 15.
❶ Catch using a Super Rod in Laverre City.
❷ Catch using a Super Rod on Route 15.

Red-Striped Form: Same form for ♂/♀

Blue-Striped Form: Same form for ♂/♀

060
Basculin

● LEVEL-UP MOVES

Lv.	Name	Type	Kind	Pow.	Acc.	PP	Range
1	Thrash	Normal	Physical	120	100	10	1 Random
1	Flail	Normal	Physical	—	100	15	Normal
1	Tail Whip	Normal	Status	—	100	30	Many Others
1	Tackle	Normal	Physical	50	100	35	Normal
1	Water Gun	Water	Special	40	100	25	Normal
4	Uproar	Normal	Special	90	100	10	1 Random
7	Headbutt	Normal	Physical	70	100	15	Normal
10	Bite	Dark	Physical	60	100	25	Normal
13	Aqua Jet	Water	Physical	40	100	20	Normal
16	Chip Away	Normal	Physical	70	100	20	Normal
20	Take Down	Normal	Physical	90	85	20	Normal
24	Crunch	Dark	Physical	80	100	15	Normal
28	Aqua Tail	Water	Physical	90	90	10	Normal
32	Soak	Water	Status	—	100	20	Normal
36	Double-Edge	Normal	Physical	120	100	15	Normal
41	Scary Face	Normal	Status	—	100	10	Normal
46	Flail	Normal	Physical	—	100	15	Normal
50	Final Gambit	Fighting	Special	—	100	5	Normal
56	Thrash	Normal	Physical	120	100	10	1 Random

● TM & HM MOVES

No.	Name	Type	Kind	Pow.	Acc.	PP	Range
TM06	Toxic	Poison	Status	—	90	10	Normal
TM07	Hail	Ice	Status	—	—	10	Both Sides
TM10	Hidden Power	Normal	Special	60	100	15	Normal
TM12	Taunt	Dark	Status	—	100	20	Normal
TM13	Ice Beam	Ice	Special	90	100	10	Normal
TM17	Protect	Normal	Status	—	—	10	Self
TM18	Rain Dance	Water	Status	—	—	5	Both Sides
TM21	Frustration	Normal	Physical	—	100	20	Normal
TM27	Return	Normal	Physical	—	100	20	Normal
TM32	Double Team	Normal	Status	—	—	15	Self
TM42	Facade	Normal	Physical	70	100	20	Normal
TM44	Rest	Psychic	Status	—	—	10	Self
TM45	Attract	Normal	Status	—	100	15	Normal
TM48	Round	Normal	Special	60	100	15	Normal
TM55	Scald	Water	Special	80	100	15	Normal
TM87	Swagger	Normal	Status	—	90	15	Normal
TM88	Sleep Talk	Normal	Status	—	—	10	Self
TM90	Substitute	Normal	Status	—	—	10	Self
TM100	Confide	Normal	Status	—	—	20	Normal
HM01	Cut	Normal	Physical	50	95	30	Normal
HM03	Surf	Water	Special	90	100	15	Normal
HM05	Waterfall	Water	Physical	80	100	15	Normal

● MOVES TAUGHT BY PEOPLE

Name	Type	Kind	Pow.	Acc.	PP	Range

● EGG MOVES

Name	Type	Kind	Pow.	Acc.	PP	Range
Swift	Normal	Special	60	—	20	Many Others
Bubble Beam	Water	Special	65	100	20	Normal
Mud Shot	Ground	Special	55	95	15	Normal
Muddy Water	Water	Special	90	85	10	Many Others
Agility	Psychic	Status	—	—	30	Self
Whirlpool	Water	Special	35	85	15	Normal
Rage	Normal	Physical	20	100	20	Normal
Brine	Water	Special	65	100	10	Normal
Revenge	Fighting	Physical	60	100	10	Normal

🏔 Mountain Kalos — 061
Stump Pokémon
☑ **Phantump**

HEIGHT: 1'04" WEIGHT: 15.4 lbs.
GENDER: ♂/♀

| TYPE | Ghost | Grass |

ABILITIES
Natural Cure
Frisk

HIDDEN ABILITY
Harvest

STAT GROWTH RATES
HP ■■
Attack ■■■■
Defense ■■
Sp. Atk ■■
Sp. Def ■■
Speed ■■

EGG GROUPS
Grass, Amorphous

ITEMS SOMETIMES HELD BY WILD POKÉMON
None

ⓧ These Pokémon are created when spirits possess rotten tree stumps. They prefer to live in abandoned forests.

ⓨ According to old tales, these Pokémon are stumps possessed by the spirits of children who died while lost in the forest.

EVOLUTION

Phantump → Link Trade → Trevenant

Damage taken in normal battles		Damage taken in Inverse Battles	
Normal	×0	Normal	×2
Fire	×2	Fire	×0.5
Water	×0.5	Water	×2
Grass	×0.5	Grass	×2
Electric	×0.5	Electric	×2
Ice	×2	Ice	×0.5
Fighting	×0	Fighting	×2
Poison	×1	Poison	×1
Ground	×0.5	Ground	×2
Flying	×2	Flying	×0.5
Psychic	×1	Psychic	×1
Bug	×1	Bug	×1
Rock	×1	Rock	×1
Ghost	×2	Ghost	×0.5
Dragon	×1	Dragon	×1
Dark	×2	Dark	×0.5
Steel	×1	Steel	×1
Fairy	×1	Fairy	×1

Can be used in
Inverse Battle
——
Battle Chateau
Battle Institute
Battle Maison
Random Matchup

How to obtain for your Mountain Kalos Pokédex

❶ Catch in the very tall grass on Route 16.
❷ Catch in the yellow flowers on Route 16.

❶ Catch in the very tall grass on Route 16.
❷ Catch in the yellow flowers on Route 16.

Same form for ♂/♀

● LEVEL-UP MOVES

Lv.	Name	Type	Kind	Pow.	Acc.	PP	Range
1	Tackle	Normal	Physical	50	100	35	Normal
1	Confuse Ray	Ghost	Status	—	100	10	Normal
5	Astonish	Ghost	Physical	30	100	15	Normal
8	Growth	Normal	Status	—	—	20	Self
13	Ingrain	Grass	Status	—	—	20	Self
19	Feint Attack	Dark	Physical	60	—	20	Normal
23	Leech Seed	Grass	Status	—	90	10	Normal
28	Curse	Ghost	Status	—	—	10	Varies
31	Will-O-Wisp	Fire	Status	—	85	15	Normal
35	Forest's Curse	Grass	Status	—	100	20	Normal
39	Destiny Bond	Ghost	Status	—	—	5	Self
45	Phantom Force	Ghost	Physical	90	100	10	Normal
49	Wood Hammer	Grass	Physical	120	100	15	Normal
54	Horn Leech	Grass	Physical	75	100	10	Normal

● TM & HM MOVES

No.	Name	Type	Kind	Pow.	Acc.	PP	Range
TM06	Toxic	Poison	Status	—	90	10	Normal
TM10	Hidden Power	Normal	Special	60	100	15	Normal
TM11	Sunny Day	Fire	Status	—	—	5	Both Sides
TM17	Protect	Normal	Status	—	—	10	Self
TM20	Safeguard	Normal	Status	—	—	25	Your Side
TM21	Frustration	Normal	Physical	—	100	20	Normal
TM22	Solar Beam	Grass	Special	120	100	10	Normal
TM27	Return	Normal	Physical	—	100	20	Normal
TM28	Dig	Ground	Physical	80	100	10	Normal
TM29	Psychic	Psychic	Special	90	100	10	Normal
TM30	Shadow Ball	Ghost	Special	80	100	15	Normal
TM32	Double Team	Normal	Status	—	—	15	Self
TM33	Reflect	Psychic	Status	—	—	20	Your Side
TM42	Facade	Normal	Physical	70	100	20	Normal
TM44	Rest	Psychic	Status	—	—	10	Self
TM45	Attract	Normal	Status	—	100	15	Normal
TM46	Thief	Dark	Physical	60	100	25	Normal
TM48	Round	Normal	Special	60	100	15	Normal
TM53	Energy Ball	Grass	Special	90	100	10	Normal
TM61	Will-O-Wisp	Fire	Status	—	85	15	Normal
TM65	Shadow Claw	Ghost	Physical	70	100	15	Normal
TM78	Bulldoze	Ground	Physical	60	100	20	Adjacent
TM80	Rock Slide	Rock	Physical	75	90	10	Many Others
TM84	Poison Jab	Poison	Physical	80	100	20	Normal
TM85	Dream Eater	Psychic	Special	100	100	15	Normal
TM86	Grass Knot	Grass	Special	—	100	20	Normal
TM87	Swagger	Normal	Status	—	90	15	Normal
TM88	Sleep Talk	Normal	Status	—	—	10	Self
TM90	Substitute	Normal	Status	—	—	10	Self
TM92	Trick Room	Psychic	Status	—	—	5	Both Sides
TM94	Rock Smash	Fighting	Physical	40	100	15	Normal
TM96	Nature Power	Normal	Status	—	—	20	Normal
TM97	Dark Pulse	Dark	Special	80	100	15	Normal

No.	Name	Type	Kind	Pow.	Acc.	PP	Range
TM100	Confide	Normal	Status	—	—	20	Normal
HM01	Cut	Normal	Physical	50	95	30	Normal
HM04	Strength	Normal	Physical	80	100	15	Normal

● MOVES TAUGHT BY PEOPLE

Name	Type	Kind	Pow.	Acc.	PP	Range

● EGG MOVES

Name	Type	Kind	Pow.	Acc.	PP	Range
Grudge	Ghost	Status	—	—	5	Self
Bestow	Normal	Status	—	—	15	Normal
Imprison	Psychic	Status	—	—	10	Self
Venom Drench	Poison	Status	—	100	20	Many Others

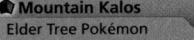

Mountain Kalos — 062
Trevenant
Elder Tree Pokémon

HEIGHT: 4'11" WEIGHT: 156.5 lbs.
GENDER: ♂/♀

TYPE	Ghost	Grass

ABILITIES
Natural Cure
Frisk

HIDDEN ABILITY
Harvest

X It can control trees at will. It will trap people who harm the forest, so they can never leave.

Y Using its roots as a nervous system, it controls the trees in the forest. It's kind to the Pokémon that reside in its body.

STAT GROWTH RATES
HP ■■■
Attack ■■■■■■
Defense ■■■
Sp. Atk ■■■
Sp. Def ■■■
Speed ■■■

EGG GROUPS
Grass, Amorphous

▲ EVOLUTION

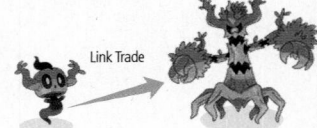

Phantump → (Link Trade) → Trevenant

ITEMS SOMETIMES HELD BY WILD POKÉMON
None

	Damage taken in normal battles		Damage taken in Inverse Battles
Normal	×0	Normal	×2
Fire	×2	Fire	×0.5
Water	×0.5	Water	×2
Grass	×0.5	Grass	×2
Electric	×0.5	Electric	×2
Ice	×2	Ice	×0.5
Fighting	×0	Fighting	×2
Poison	×1	Poison	×1
Ground	×0.5	Ground	×2
Flying	×2	Flying	×0.5
Psychic	×1	Psychic	×1
Bug	×1	Bug	×1
Rock	×1	Rock	×1
Ghost	×2	Ghost	×0.5
Dragon	×1	Dragon	×1
Dark	×2	Dark	×0.5
Steel	×1	Steel	×1
Fairy	×1	Fairy	×1

Can be used in	
Inverse Battle	Battle Institute
—	Battle Maison
Battle Chateau	Random Matchup

Same form for ♂ / ♀

How to obtain for your Mountain Kalos Pokédex

❶ Catch in the tall grass or red flowers on Route 20.
❷ Receive Phantump by Link Trade, and have it evolve.

❶ Catch in the tall grass or red flowers on Route 20.
❷ Receive Phantump by Link Trade, and have it evolve.

● LEVEL-UP MOVES

Lv.	Name	Type	Kind	Pow.	Acc.	PP	Range
1	Horn Leech	Grass	Physical	75	100	10	Normal
1	Tackle	Normal	Physical	50	100	35	Normal
1	Confuse Ray	Ghost	Status	—	100	10	Normal
5	Astonish	Ghost	Physical	30	100	15	Normal
8	Growth	Normal	Status	—	—	20	Self
13	Ingrain	Grass	Status	—	—	20	Self
19	Feint Attack	Dark	Physical	60	—	20	Normal
23	Leech Seed	Grass	Status	—	90	10	Normal
28	Curse	Ghost	Status	—	—	10	Varies
31	Will-O-Wisp	Fire	Status	—	85	15	Normal
35	Forest's Curse	Grass	Status	—	100	20	Normal
39	Destiny Bond	Ghost	Status	—	—	5	Self
44	Phantom Force	Ghost	Physical	90	100	10	Normal
49	Wood Hammer	Grass	Physical	120	100	15	Normal
55	Shadow Claw	Ghost	Physical	70	100	15	Normal
62	Horn Leech	Grass	Physical	75	100	10	Normal

● TM & HM MOVES

No.	Name	Type	Kind	Pow.	Acc.	PP	Range
TM01	Hone Claws	Dark	Status	—	—	15	Self
TM04	Calm Mind	Psychic	Status	—	—	20	Self
TM06	Toxic	Poison	Status	—	90	10	Normal
TM10	Hidden Power	Normal	Special	60	100	15	Normal
TM11	Sunny Day	Fire	Status	—	—	5	Both Sides
TM15	Hyper Beam	Normal	Special	150	90	5	Normal
TM17	Protect	Normal	Status	—	—	10	Self
TM20	Safeguard	Normal	Status	—	—	25	Your Side
TM21	Frustration	Normal	Physical	—	100	20	Normal
TM22	Solar Beam	Grass	Special	120	100	10	Normal
TM26	Earthquake	Ground	Physical	100	100	10	Adjacent
TM27	Return	Normal	Physical	—	100	20	Normal
TM28	Dig	Ground	Physical	80	100	10	Normal
TM29	Psychic	Psychic	Special	90	100	10	Normal
TM30	Shadow Ball	Ghost	Special	80	100	15	Normal
TM32	Double Team	Normal	Status	—	—	15	Self
TM33	Reflect	Psychic	Status	—	—	20	Your Side
TM42	Facade	Normal	Physical	70	100	20	Normal
TM44	Rest	Psychic	Status	—	—	10	Self
TM45	Attract	Normal	Status	—	100	15	Normal
TM46	Thief	Dark	Physical	60	100	25	Normal
TM48	Round	Normal	Special	60	100	15	Normal
TM52	Focus Blast	Fighting	Special	120	70	5	Normal
TM53	Energy Ball	Grass	Special	90	100	10	Normal
TM61	Will-O-Wisp	Fire	Status	—	85	15	Normal
TM65	Shadow Claw	Ghost	Physical	70	100	15	Normal
TM68	Giga Impact	Normal	Physical	150	90	5	Normal
TM78	Bulldoze	Ground	Physical	60	100	20	Adjacent
TM80	Rock Slide	Rock	Physical	75	90	10	Many Others
TM81	X-Scissor	Bug	Physical	80	100	15	Normal
TM84	Poison Jab	Poison	Physical	80	100	20	Normal
TM85	Dream Eater	Psychic	Special	100	100	15	Normal
TM86	Grass Knot	Grass	Special	—	100	20	Normal

No.	Name	Type	Kind	Pow.	Acc.	PP	Range
TM87	Swagger	Normal	Status	—	90	15	Normal
TM88	Sleep Talk	Normal	Status	—	—	10	Self
TM90	Substitute	Normal	Status	—	—	10	Self
TM92	Trick Room	Psychic	Status	—	—	5	Both Sides
TM94	Rock Smash	Fighting	Physical	40	100	15	Normal
TM96	Nature Power	Normal	Status	—	—	20	Normal
TM97	Dark Pulse	Dark	Special	80	100	15	Normal
TM98	Power-Up Punch	Fighting	Physical	40	100	20	Normal
TM100	Confide	Normal	Status	—	—	20	Normal
HM01	Cut	Normal	Physical	50	95	30	Normal
HM04	Strength	Normal	Physical	80	100	15	Normal

● MOVES TAUGHT BY PEOPLE

Name	Type	Kind	Pow.	Acc.	PP	Range

AFTER THE HALL OF FAME

CENTRAL KALOS

COASTAL KALOS

MOUNTAIN KALOS

062

Trevenant

ADVENTURE DATA

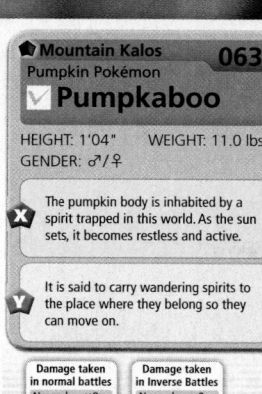

Mountain Kalos **063**
Pumpkin Pokémon
Pumpkaboo

HEIGHT: 1'04" WEIGHT: 11.0 lbs.
GENDER: ♂/♀

TYPE Ghost | Grass

ABILITIES
Pickup
Frisk

HIDDEN ABILITY
Insomnia

EGG GROUP
Amorphous

X The pumpkin body is inhabited by a spirit trapped in this world. As the sun sets, it becomes restless and active.

Y It is said to carry wandering spirits to the place where they belong so they can move on.

EVOLUTION

Link Trade

Pumpkaboo → Gourgeist

ITEMS SOMETIMES HELD BY WILD POKÉMON
None

Damage taken in normal battles		Damage taken in Inverse Battles	
Normal	×0	Normal	×2
Fire	×2	Fire	×0.5
Water	×0.5	Water	×2
Grass	×0.5	Grass	×2
Electric	×0.5	Electric	×2
Ice	×2	Ice	×0.5
Fighting	×0	Fighting	×2
Poison	×1	Poison	×1
Ground	×0.5	Ground	×2
Flying	×2	Flying	×0.5
Psychic	×1	Psychic	×1
Bug	×1	Bug	×1
Rock	×1	Rock	×1
Ghost	×2	Ghost	×0.5
Dragon	×1	Dragon	×1
Dark	×2	Dark	×0.5
Steel	×1	Steel	×1
Fairy	×1	Fairy	×1

Can be used in	
Inverse Battle	Battle Institute
—	Battle Maison
Battle Chateau	Random Matchup

How to obtain for your Mountain Kalos Pokédex

Catch in the very tall grass on Route 16.	Catch in the very tall grass on Route 16.

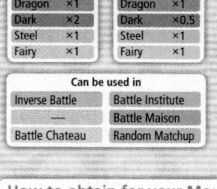

● **LEVEL-UP MOVES**

Lv.	Name	Type	Kind	Pow.	Acc.	PP	Range
1	Trick	Psychic	Status	—	100	10	Normal
1	Astonish	Ghost	Physical	30	100	15	Normal
1	Confuse Ray	Ghost	Status	—	100	10	Normal
4	Scary Face	Normal	Status	—	100	10	Normal
6	Trick-or-Treat	Ghost	Status	—	100	20	Normal
11	Worry Seed	Grass	Status	—	100	10	Normal
16	Razor Leaf	Grass	Physical	55	95	25	Many Others
20	Leech Seed	Grass	Status	—	90	10	Normal
23	Trick-or-Treat	Ghost	Status	—	100	20	Normal
26	Bullet Seed	Grass	Physical	25	100	30	Normal
30	Shadow Sneak	Ghost	Physical	40	100	30	Normal
36	Shadow Ball	Ghost	Special	80	100	15	Normal
40	Trick-or-Treat	Ghost	Status	—	100	20	Normal
42	Pain Split	Normal	Status	—	—	20	Normal
48	Seed Bomb	Grass	Physical	80	100	15	Normal

● **TM & HM MOVES**

No.	Name	Type	Kind	Pow.	Acc.	PP	Range
TM06	Toxic	Poison	Status	—	90	10	Normal
TM10	Hidden Power	Normal	Special	60	100	15	Normal
TM11	Sunny Day	Fire	Status	—	—	5	Both Sides
TM16	Light Screen	Psychic	Status	—	—	30	Your Side
TM17	Protect	Normal	Status	—	—	10	Self
TM20	Safeguard	Normal	Status	—	—	25	Your Side
TM21	Frustration	Normal	Physical	—	100	20	Normal
TM22	Solar Beam	Grass	Special	120	100	10	Normal
TM27	Return	Normal	Physical	—	100	20	Normal
TM29	Psychic	Psychic	Special	90	100	10	Normal
TM30	Shadow Ball	Ghost	Special	80	100	15	Normal
TM32	Double Team	Normal	Status	—	—	15	Self
TM35	Flamethrower	Fire	Special	90	100	15	Normal
TM36	Sludge Bomb	Poison	Special	90	100	10	Normal
TM38	Fire Blast	Fire	Special	110	85	5	Normal
TM42	Facade	Normal	Physical	70	100	20	Normal
TM43	Flame Charge	Fire	Physical	50	100	20	Normal
TM44	Rest	Psychic	Status	—	—	10	Self
TM45	Attract	Normal	Status	—	100	15	Normal
TM46	Thief	Dark	Physical	60	100	25	Normal
TM48	Round	Normal	Special	60	100	15	Normal
TM53	Energy Ball	Grass	Special	90	100	10	Normal
TM57	Charge Beam	Electric	Special	50	90	10	Normal
TM59	Incinerate	Fire	Special	60	100	15	Many Others
TM61	Will-O-Wisp	Fire	Status	—	85	15	Normal
TM64	Explosion	Normal	Physical	250	100	5	Adjacent
TM70	Flash	Normal	Status	—	100	20	Normal
TM74	Gyro Ball	Steel	Physical	—	100	5	Normal
TM80	Rock Slide	Rock	Physical	75	90	10	Many Others
TM85	Dream Eater	Psychic	Special	100	100	15	Normal
TM86	Grass Knot	Grass	Special	—	100	20	Normal
TM87	Swagger	Normal	Status	—	90	15	Normal
TM88	Sleep Talk	Normal	Status	—	—	10	Self

No.	Name	Type	Kind	Pow.	Acc.	PP	Range
TM90	Substitute	Normal	Status	—	—	10	Self
TM92	Trick Room	Psychic	Status	—	—	5	Both Sides
TM94	Rock Smash	Fighting	Physical	40	100	15	Normal
TM96	Nature Power	Normal	Status	—	—	20	Normal
TM97	Dark Pulse	Dark	Special	80	100	15	Normal
TM100	Confide	Normal	Status	—	—	20	Normal

● **MOVES TAUGHT BY PEOPLE**

Name	Type	Kind	Pow.	Acc.	PP	Range

● **EGG MOVES**

Name	Type	Kind	Pow.	Acc.	PP	Range
Disable	Normal	Status	—	100	20	Normal
Bestow	Normal	Status	—	—	15	Normal
Destiny Bond	Ghost	Status	—	—	5	Self

AFTER THE HALL OF FAME

CENTRAL KALOS

COASTAL KALOS

MOUNTAIN KALOS

063

Pumpkaboo

ADVENTURE DATA

◯ Pumpkaboo Come in Different Sizes

Pumpkaboo specimens can come in many varying sizes.

There are four different sizes you may encounter.

Small Size: same form for ♂/♀
HEIGHT: 1'00"   WEIGHT: 7.7 lbs.

STAT GROWTH RATES
HP
Attack
Defense
Sp. Atk
Sp. Def
Speed

Same form for ♂/♀
HEIGHT: 1'04"   WEIGHT: 11.0 lbs.

STAT GROWTH RATES
HP
Attack
Defense
Sp. Atk
Sp. Def
Speed

Large Size: same form for ♂/♀
HEIGHT: 1'08"   WEIGHT: 16.5 lbs.

STAT GROWTH RATES
HP
Attack
Defense
Sp. Atk
Sp. Def
Speed

Super Size: same form for ♂/♀
HEIGHT: 2'07"   WEIGHT: 33.1 lbs.

STAT GROWTH RATES
HP
Attack
Defense
Sp. Atk
Sp. Def
Speed

✓ Gourgeist

TYPE	Ghost	Grass

ABILITIES
Pickup
Frisk

HIDDEN ABILITY
Insomnia

EGG GROUP
Amorphous

HEIGHT: 2'11"   WEIGHT: 27.6 lbs.
GENDER: ♂ / ♀

X Singing in eerie voices, they wander town streets on the night of the new moon. Anyone who hears their song is cursed.

Y It enwraps its prey in its hairlike arms. It sings joyfully as it observes the suffering of its prey.

EVOLUTION

Link Trade

Pumpkaboo → Gourgeist

ITEMS SOMETIMES HELD BY WILD POKÉMON
None

Damage taken in normal battles

Normal	×0
Fire	×2
Water	×0.5
Grass	×0.5
Electric	×0.5
Ice	×2
Fighting	×0
Poison	×1
Ground	×0.5
Flying	×2
Psychic	×1
Bug	×1
Rock	×1
Ghost	×1
Dragon	×1
Dark	×2
Steel	×1
Fairy	×1

Damage taken in Inverse Battles

Normal	×2
Fire	×0.5
Water	×2
Grass	×2
Electric	×2
Ice	×0.5
Fighting	×2
Poison	×1
Ground	×2
Flying	×0.5
Psychic	×1
Bug	×1
Rock	×1
Ghost	×0.5
Dragon	×1
Dark	×0.5
Steel	×1
Fairy	×1

Can be used in

Inverse Battle

Battle Chateau
Battle Institute
Battle Maison
Random Matchup

How to obtain for your Mountain Kalos Pokédex

Receive Pumpkaboo by Link Trade, and have it evolve.

Receive Pumpkaboo by Link Trade, and have it evolve.

● LEVEL-UP MOVES

Lv.	Name	Type	Kind	Pow.	Acc.	PP	Range
1	Explosion	Normal	Physical	250	100	5	Adjacent
1	Phantom Force	Ghost	Physical	90	100	10	Normal
1	Trick	Psychic	Status	—	100	10	Normal
1	Astonish	Ghost	Physical	30	100	15	Normal
1	Confuse Ray	Ghost	Status	—	100	10	Normal
4	Scary Face	Normal	Status	—	100	10	Normal
6	Trick-or-Treat	Ghost	Status	—	100	20	Normal
11	Worry Seed	Grass	Status	—	100	10	Normal
16	Razor Leaf	Grass	Physical	55	95	25	Many Others
20	Leech Seed	Grass	Status	—	90	10	Normal
23	Trick-or-Treat	Ghost	Status	—	100	20	Normal
26	Bullet Seed	Grass	Physical	25	100	30	Normal
30	Shadow Sneak	Ghost	Physical	40	100	30	Normal
36	Shadow Ball	Ghost	Special	80	100	15	Normal
40	Trick-or-Treat	Ghost	Status	—	100	20	Normal
42	Pain Split	Normal	Status	—	—	20	Normal
48	Seed Bomb	Grass	Physical	80	100	15	Normal
57	Phantom Force	Ghost	Physical	90	100	10	Normal
63	Trick-or-Treat	Ghost	Status	—	100	20	Normal
70	Shadow Ball	Ghost	Special	80	100	15	Normal
75	Explosion	Normal	Physical	250	100	5	Adjacent

● TM & HM MOVES

No.	Name	Type	Kind	Pow.	Acc.	PP	Range
TM06	Toxic	Poison	Status	—	90	10	Normal
TM10	Hidden Power	Normal	Special	60	100	15	Normal
TM11	Sunny Day	Fire	Status	—	—	5	Both Sides
TM15	Hyper Beam	Normal	Special	150	90	5	Normal
TM16	Light Screen	Psychic	Status	—	—	30	Your Side
TM17	Protect	Normal	Status	—	—	10	Self
TM20	Safeguard	Normal	Status	—	—	25	Your Side
TM21	Frustration	Normal	Physical	—	100	20	Normal
TM22	Solar Beam	Grass	Special	120	100	10	Normal
TM27	Return	Normal	Physical	—	100	20	Normal
TM29	Psychic	Psychic	Special	90	100	10	Normal
TM30	Shadow Ball	Ghost	Special	80	100	15	Normal
TM32	Double Team	Normal	Status	—	—	15	Self
TM35	Flamethrower	Fire	Special	90	100	15	Normal
TM36	Sludge Bomb	Poison	Special	90	100	10	Normal
TM38	Fire Blast	Fire	Special	110	85	5	Normal
TM42	Facade	Normal	Physical	70	100	20	Normal
TM43	Flame Charge	Fire	Physical	50	100	20	Normal
TM44	Rest	Psychic	Status	—	—	10	Self
TM45	Attract	Normal	Status	—	100	15	Normal
TM46	Thief	Dark	Physical	60	100	25	Normal
TM48	Round	Normal	Special	60	100	15	Normal
TM52	Focus Blast	Fighting	Special	120	70	5	Normal
TM53	Energy Ball	Grass	Special	90	100	10	Normal
TM57	Charge Beam	Electric	Special	50	90	10	Normal
TM59	Incinerate	Fire	Special	60	100	15	Many Others
TM61	Will-O-Wisp	Fire	Status	—	85	15	Normal
TM64	Explosion	Normal	Physical	250	100	5	Adjacent
TM68	Giga Impact	Normal	Physical	150	90	5	Normal
TM70	Flash	Normal	Status	—	100	20	Normal
TM74	Gyro Ball	Steel	Physical	—	100	5	Normal
TM80	Rock Slide	Rock	Physical	75	90	10	Many Others
TM85	Dream Eater	Psychic	Special	100	100	15	Normal

No.	Name	Type	Kind	Pow.	Acc.	PP	Range
TM86	Grass Knot	Grass	Special	—	100	20	Normal
TM87	Swagger	Normal	Status	—	90	15	Normal
TM88	Sleep Talk	Normal	Status	—	—	10	Self
TM90	Substitute	Normal	Status	—	—	10	Self
TM92	Trick Room	Psychic	Status	—	—	5	Both Sides
TM94	Rock Smash	Fighting	Physical	40	100	15	Normal
TM96	Nature Power	Normal	Status	—	—	20	Normal
TM97	Dark Pulse	Dark	Special	80	100	15	Normal
TM100	Confide	Normal	Status	—	—	20	Normal

● MOVES TAUGHT BY PEOPLE

Name	Type	Kind	Pow.	Acc.	PP	Range

AFTER THE HALL OF FAME

CENTRAL KALOS

COASTAL KALOS

MOUNTAIN KALOS

064

Gourgeist

ADVENTURE DATA

Gourgeist Come in Different Sizes

Gourgeist specimens can come in many varying sizes.

They do not all appear in nature, but instead can be evolved from Pumpkaboo that are obtained by Link Trade and evolved.

Small Size: same form for ♂/♀
HEIGHT: 2'04"   WEIGHT: 20.9 lbs.

STAT GROWTH RATES
HP
Attack
Defense
Sp. Atk
Sp. Def
Speed

Same form for ♂/♀
HEIGHT: 2'11"   WEIGHT: 27.6 lbs.

STAT GROWTH RATES
HP
Attack
Defense
Sp. Atk
Sp. Def
Speed

Large Size: same form for ♂/♀
HEIGHT: 3'07"   WEIGHT: 30.9 lbs.

STAT GROWTH RATES
HP
Attack
Defense
Sp. Atk
Sp. Def
Speed

Super Size: same form for ♂/♀
HEIGHT: 5'07"   WEIGHT: 86.0 lbs.

STAT GROWTH RATES
HP
Attack
Defense
Sp. Atk
Sp. Def
Speed

Mountain Kalos 065

Candle Pokémon

☑ Litwick

HEIGHT: 1'00" WEIGHT: 6.8 lbs.
GENDER: ♂/♀

TYPE	Ghost	Fire

ABILITIES
Flash Fire
Flame Body

HIDDEN ABILITY
Infiltrator

STAT GROWTH RATES
HP	■ ■
Attack	■ ■
Defense	■ ■
Sp. Atk	■ ■ ■
Sp. Def	■ ■
Speed	■

EGG GROUP
Amorphous

X While shining a light and pretending to be a guide, it leeches off the life force of any who follow it.

Y Litwick shines a light that absorbs the life energy of people and Pokémon, which becomes the fuel that it burns.

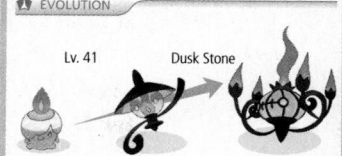

EVOLUTION

Lv. 41   Dusk Stone

Litwick   Lampent   Chandelure

ITEMS SOMETIMES HELD BY WILD POKÉMON
None

Damage taken in normal battles		Damage taken in Inverse Battles		Can be used in
Normal	×0	Normal	×2	Inverse Battle
Fire	×0.5	Fire	×2	—
Water	×2	Water	×0.5	Battle Chateau
Grass	×0.5	Grass	×2	Battle Institute
Electric	×1	Electric	×1	Battle Maison
Ice	×0.5	Ice	×2	Random Matchup
Fighting	×0	Fighting	×2	
Poison	×0.5	Poison	×2	
Ground	×2	Ground	×0.5	
Flying	×1	Flying	×1	
Psychic	×1	Psychic	×1	
Bug	×0.25	Bug	×4	
Rock	×2	Rock	×0.5	
Ghost	×2	Ghost	×0.5	
Dragon	×1	Dragon	×1	
Dark	×2	Dark	×0.5	
Steel	×0.5	Steel	×2	
Fairy	×0.5	Fairy	×2	

How to obtain for your Mountain Kalos Pokédex

Catch in the Lost Hotel.   Catch in the Lost Hotel.

Same form for ♂/♀

● LEVEL-UP MOVES

Lv.	Name	Type	Kind	Pow.	Acc.	PP	Range
1	Ember	Fire	Special	40	100	25	Normal
1	Astonish	Ghost	Physical	30	100	15	Normal
3	Minimize	Normal	Status	—	—	10	Self
5	Smog	Poison	Special	30	70	20	Normal
7	Fire Spin	Fire	Special	35	85	15	Normal
10	Confuse Ray	Ghost	Status	—	100	10	Normal
13	Night Shade	Ghost	Special	—	100	15	Normal
16	Will-O-Wisp	Fire	Status	—	85	15	Normal
20	Flame Burst	Fire	Special	70	100	15	Normal
24	Imprison	Psychic	Status	—	—	10	Self
28	Hex	Ghost	Special	65	100	10	Normal
33	Memento	Dark	Status	—	100	10	Normal
38	Inferno	Fire	Special	100	50	5	Normal
43	Curse	Ghost	Status	—	—	10	Varies
49	Shadow Ball	Ghost	Special	80	100	15	Normal
55	Pain Split	Normal	Status	—	—	20	Normal
61	Overheat	Fire	Special	130	90	5	Normal

● TM & HM MOVES

No.	Name	Type	Kind	Pow.	Acc.	PP	Range
TM04	Calm Mind	Psychic	Status	—	—	20	Self
TM06	Toxic	Poison	Status	—	90	10	Normal
TM10	Hidden Power	Normal	Special	60	100	15	Normal
TM11	Sunny Day	Fire	Status	—	—	5	Both Sides
TM12	Taunt	Dark	Status	—	100	20	Normal
TM17	Protect	Normal	Status	—	—	10	Self
TM20	Safeguard	Normal	Status	—	—	25	Your Side
TM21	Frustration	Normal	Physical	—	100	20	Normal
TM22	Solar Beam	Grass	Special	120	100	10	Normal
TM27	Return	Normal	Physical	—	100	20	Normal
TM29	Psychic	Psychic	Special	90	100	10	Normal
TM30	Shadow Ball	Ghost	Special	80	100	15	Normal
TM32	Double Team	Normal	Status	—	—	15	Self
TM35	Flamethrower	Fire	Special	90	100	15	Normal
TM38	Fire Blast	Fire	Special	110	85	5	Normal
TM42	Facade	Normal	Physical	70	100	20	Normal
TM43	Flame Charge	Fire	Physical	50	100	20	Normal
TM44	Rest	Psychic	Status	—	—	10	Self
TM45	Attract	Normal	Status	—	100	15	Normal
TM46	Thief	Dark	Physical	60	100	25	Normal
TM48	Round	Normal	Special	60	100	15	Normal
TM50	Overheat	Fire	Special	130	90	5	Normal
TM53	Energy Ball	Grass	Special	90	100	10	Normal
TM59	Incinerate	Fire	Special	60	100	15	Many Others
TM61	Will-O-Wisp	Fire	Status	—	85	15	Normal
TM63	Embargo	Dark	Status	—	100	15	Normal
TM66	Payback	Dark	Physical	50	100	10	Normal
TM70	Flash	Normal	Status	—	100	20	Normal
TM77	Psych Up	Normal	Status	—	—	10	Normal
TM85	Dream Eater	Psychic	Special	100	100	15	Normal
TM87	Swagger	Normal	Status	—	90	15	Normal
TM88	Sleep Talk	Normal	Status	—	—	10	Self
TM90	Substitute	Normal	Status	—	—	10	Self

No.	Name	Type	Kind	Pow.	Acc.	PP	Range
TM92	Trick Room	Psychic	Status	—	—	5	Both Sides
TM97	Dark Pulse	Dark	Special	80	100	15	Normal
TM100	Confide	Normal	Status	—	—	20	Normal

● MOVES TAUGHT BY PEOPLE

Name	Type	Kind	Pow.	Acc.	PP	Range

● EGG MOVES

Name	Type	Kind	Pow.	Acc.	PP	Range
Acid Armor	Poison	Status	—	—	20	Self
Heat Wave	Fire	Special	95	90	10	Many Others
Haze	Ice	Status	—	—	30	Both Sides
Endure	Normal	Status	—	—	10	Self
Captivate	Normal	Status	—	100	20	Many Others
Acid	Poison	Special	40	100	30	Many Others
Clear Smog	Poison	Special	50	—	15	Normal
Power Split	Psychic	Status	—	—	10	Normal

AFTER THE HALL OF FAME

CENTRAL KALOS

COASTAL KALOS

MOUNTAIN KALOS

065 Litwick

ADVENTURE DATA

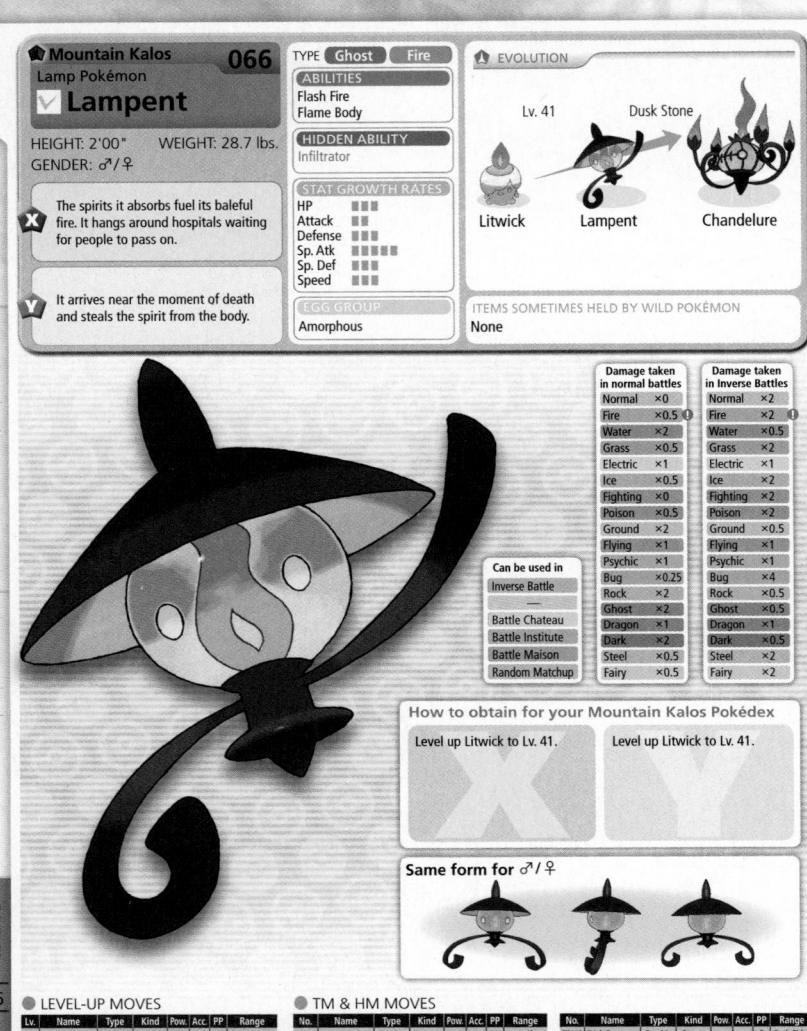

Mountain Kalos 066

Lamp Pokémon

Lampent

TYPE: Ghost / Fire

HEIGHT: 2'00" **WEIGHT:** 28.7 lbs.
GENDER: ♂/♀

ABILITIES
Flash Fire
Flame Body

HIDDEN ABILITY
Infiltrator

X: The spirits it absorbs fuel its baleful fire. It hangs around hospitals waiting for people to pass on.

Y: It arrives near the moment of death and steals the spirit from the body.

STAT GROWTH RATES
HP ■■■
Attack ■■
Defense ■■
Sp. Atk ■■■■■
Sp. Def ■■■
Speed ■■■

EGG GROUP
Amorphous

EVOLUTION
Litwick → (Lv. 41) Lampent → (Dusk Stone) Chandelure

ITEMS SOMETIMES HELD BY WILD POKÉMON: None

Damage taken in normal battles		Damage taken in Inverse Battles	
Normal	×0	Normal	×2
Fire	×0.5	Fire	×2
Water	×2	Water	×0.5
Grass	×0.5	Grass	×2
Electric	×1	Electric	×1
Ice	×0.5	Ice	×2
Fighting	×0	Fighting	×2
Poison	×0.5	Poison	×2
Ground	×2	Ground	×0.5
Flying	×1	Flying	×1
Psychic	×1	Psychic	×1
Bug	×0.25	Bug	×4
Rock	×2	Rock	×0.5
Ghost	×2	Ghost	×0.5
Dragon	×1	Dragon	×1
Dark	×2	Dark	×0.5
Steel	×0.5	Steel	×2
Fairy	×0.5	Fairy	×2

Can be used in
Inverse Battle
—
Battle Chateau
Battle Institute
Battle Maison
Random Matchup

How to obtain for your Mountain Kalos Pokédex
X: Level up Litwick to Lv. 41.
Y: Level up Litwick to Lv. 41.

Same form for ♂/♀

LEVEL-UP MOVES

Lv.	Name	Type	Kind	Pow.	Acc.	PP	Range
1	Ember	Fire	Special	40	100	25	Normal
1	Astonish	Ghost	Physical	30	100	15	Normal
1	Minimize	Normal	Status	—	—	10	Self
1	Smog	Poison	Special	30	70	20	Normal
3	Minimize	Normal	Status	—	—	10	Self
5	Smog	Poison	Special	30	70	20	Normal
7	Fire Spin	Fire	Special	35	85	15	Normal
10	Confuse Ray	Ghost	Status	—	100	10	Normal
13	Night Shade	Ghost	Special	—	100	15	Normal
16	Will-O-Wisp	Fire	Status	—	85	15	Normal
20	Flame Burst	Fire	Special	70	100	15	Normal
24	Imprison	Psychic	Status	—	—	10	Self
28	Hex	Ghost	Special	65	100	10	Normal
33	Memento	Dark	Status	—	100	10	Normal
38	Inferno	Fire	Special	100	50	5	Normal
45	Curse	Ghost	Status	—	—	10	Varies
53	Shadow Ball	Ghost	Special	80	100	15	Normal
61	Pain Split	Normal	Status	—	—	20	Normal
69	Overheat	Fire	Special	130	90	5	Normal

TM & HM MOVES

No.	Name	Type	Kind	Pow.	Acc.	PP	Range
TM04	Calm Mind	Psychic	Status	—	—	20	Self
TM06	Toxic	Poison	Status	—	90	10	Normal
TM10	Hidden Power	Normal	Special	60	100	15	Normal
TM11	Sunny Day	Fire	Status	—	—	5	Both Sides
TM12	Taunt	Dark	Status	—	100	20	Normal
TM17	Protect	Normal	Status	—	—	10	Self
TM20	Safeguard	Normal	Status	—	—	25	Your Side
TM21	Frustration	Normal	Physical	—	100	20	Normal
TM22	Solar Beam	Grass	Special	120	100	10	Normal
TM27	Return	Normal	Physical	—	100	20	Normal
TM29	Psychic	Psychic	Special	90	100	10	Normal
TM30	Shadow Ball	Ghost	Special	80	100	15	Normal
TM32	Double Team	Normal	Status	—	—	15	Self
TM35	Flamethrower	Fire	Special	90	100	15	Normal
TM38	Fire Blast	Fire	Special	110	85	5	Normal
TM42	Facade	Normal	Physical	70	100	20	Normal
TM43	Flame Charge	Fire	Physical	50	100	20	Normal
TM44	Rest	Psychic	Status	—	—	10	Self
TM45	Attract	Normal	Status	—	100	15	Normal
TM46	Thief	Dark	Physical	60	100	25	Normal
TM48	Round	Normal	Special	60	100	15	Normal
TM50	Overheat	Fire	Special	130	90	5	Normal
TM53	Energy Ball	Grass	Special	90	100	10	Normal
TM59	Incinerate	Fire	Special	60	100	15	Many Others
TM61	Will-O-Wisp	Fire	Status	—	85	15	Normal
TM63	Embargo	Dark	Status	—	100	15	Normal
TM66	Payback	Dark	Physical	50	100	10	Normal
TM70	Flash	Normal	Status	—	100	20	Normal
TM77	Psych Up	Normal	Status	—	—	10	Normal
TM85	Dream Eater	Psychic	Special	100	100	15	Normal
TM87	Swagger	Normal	Status	—	90	15	Normal
TM88	Sleep Talk	Normal	Status	—	—	10	Self
TM90	Substitute	Normal	Status	—	—	10	Self
TM92	Trick Room	Psychic	Status	—	—	5	Both Sides
TM97	Dark Pulse	Dark	Special	80	100	15	Normal
TM100	Confide	Normal	Status	—	—	20	Normal

MOVES TAUGHT BY PEOPLE

Name	Type	Kind	Pow.	Acc.	PP	Range

500

Luring Pokémon

Chandelure

HEIGHT: 3'03"   WEIGHT: 75.6 lbs.
GENDER: ♂/♀

X Being consumed in Chandelure's flame burns up the spirit, leaving the body behind.

Y The spirits burned up in its ominous flame lose their way and wander this world forever.

TYPE: Ghost | Fire

ABILITIES
Flash Fire
Flame Body

HIDDEN ABILITY
Infiltrator

STAT GROWTH RATES
HP	■■■
Attack	■■■
Defense	■■■■
Sp. Atk	■■■■■■■
Sp. Def	■■■■
Speed	■■■■

EGG GROUP
Amorphous

EVOLUTION

Lv. 41 — Dusk Stone

Litwick → Lampent → Chandelure

ITEMS SOMETIMES HELD BY WILD POKÉMON
None

Damage taken in normal battles	
Normal	×0
Fire	×0.5
Water	×2
Grass	×0.5
Electric	×1
Ice	×0.5
Fighting	×0
Poison	×0.5
Ground	×2
Flying	×1
Psychic	×1
Bug	×0.25
Rock	×2
Ghost	×2
Dragon	×1
Dark	×2
Steel	×0.5
Fairy	×0.5

Damage taken in Inverse Battles	
Normal	×2
Fire	×2
Water	×0.5
Grass	×2
Electric	×1
Ice	×2
Fighting	×2
Poison	×2
Ground	×0.5
Flying	×1
Psychic	×1
Bug	×4
Rock	×0.5
Ghost	×0.5
Dragon	×1
Dark	×0.5
Steel	×2
Fairy	×2

Can be used in
Inverse Battle
—
Battle Chateau
Battle Institute
Battle Maison
Random Matchup

How to obtain for your Mountain Kalos Pokédex

Use a Dusk Stone on Lampent. | Use a Dusk Stone on Lampent.

X   Y

Same form for ♂/♀

LEVEL-UP MOVES

Lv.	Name	Type	Kind	Pow.	Acc.	PP	Range
1	Pain Split	Normal	Status	—	—	20	Normal
1	Smog	Poison	Special	30	70	20	Normal
1	Confuse Ray	Ghost	Status	—	100	10	Normal
1	Flame Burst	Fire	Special	70	100	15	Normal
1	Hex	Ghost	Special	65	100	10	Normal

TM & HM MOVES

No.	Name	Type	Kind	Pow.	Acc.	PP	Range
TM04	Calm Mind	Psychic	Status	—	—	20	Self
TM06	Toxic	Poison	Status	—	90	10	Normal
TM10	Hidden Power	Normal	Special	60	100	15	Normal
TM11	Sunny Day	Fire	Status	—	—	5	Normal
TM12	Taunt	Dark	Status	—	100	20	Normal
TM15	Hyper Beam	Normal	Special	150	90	5	Normal
TM17	Protect	Normal	Status	—	—	10	Self
TM20	Safeguard	Normal	Status	—	—	25	Your Side
TM21	Frustration	Normal	Physical	—	100	20	Normal
TM22	Solar Beam	Grass	Special	120	100	10	Normal
TM27	Return	Normal	Physical	—	100	20	Normal
TM29	Psychic	Psychic	Special	90	100	10	Normal
TM30	Shadow Ball	Ghost	Special	80	100	15	Normal
TM32	Double Team	Normal	Status	—	—	15	Self
TM35	Flamethrower	Fire	Special	90	100	15	Normal
TM38	Fire Blast	Fire	Special	110	85	5	Normal
TM42	Facade	Normal	Physical	70	100	20	Normal
TM43	Flame Charge	Fire	Physical	50	100	20	Normal
TM44	Rest	Psychic	Status	—	—	10	Self
TM45	Attract	Normal	Status	—	100	15	Normal
TM46	Thief	Dark	Physical	60	100	25	Normal
TM48	Round	Normal	Special	60	100	15	Normal
TM50	Overheat	Fire	Special	130	90	5	Normal
TM53	Energy Ball	Grass	Special	90	100	10	Normal
TM59	Incinerate	Fire	Special	60	100	15	Many Others
TM61	Will-O-Wisp	Fire	Status	—	85	15	Normal
TM63	Embargo	Dark	Status	—	100	15	Normal
TM66	Payback	Dark	Physical	50	100	10	Normal
TM68	Giga Impact	Normal	Physical	150	90	5	Normal
TM70	Flash	Normal	Status	—	100	20	Normal
TM77	Psych Up	Normal	Status	—	—	10	Normal
TM85	Dream Eater	Psychic	Special	100	100	15	Normal
TM87	Swagger	Normal	Status	—	90	15	Normal

No.	Name	Type	Kind	Pow.	Acc.	PP	Range
TM88	Sleep Talk	Normal	Status	—	—	10	Self
TM90	Substitute	Normal	Status	—	—	10	Self
TM92	Trick Room	Psychic	Status	—	—	5	Both Sides
TM97	Dark Pulse	Dark	Special	80	100	15	Normal
TM100	Confide	Normal	Status	—	—	20	Normal

MOVES TAUGHT BY PEOPLE

Name	Type	Kind	Pow.	Acc.	PP	Range

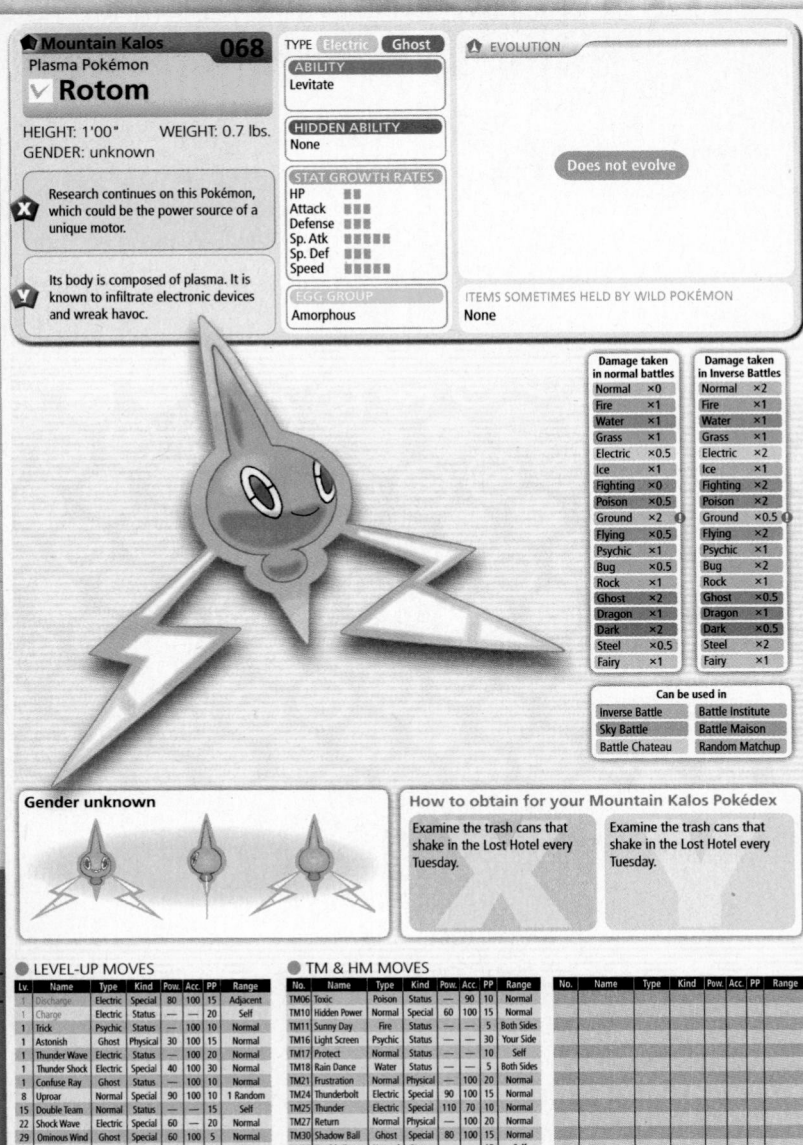

Mountain Kalos — 068

Plasma Pokémon

Rotom

TYPE Electric Ghost

ABILITY
Levitate

HIDDEN ABILITY
None

HEIGHT: 1'00" WEIGHT: 0.7 lbs.
GENDER: unknown

Research continues on this Pokémon, which could be the power source of a unique motor.

Its body is composed of plasma. It is known to infiltrate electronic devices and wreak havoc.

STAT GROWTH RATES
HP	▪▪
Attack	▪▪▪
Defense	▪▪▪
Sp. Atk	▪▪▪▪▪
Sp. Def	▪▪▪▪▪
Speed	▪▪▪▪▪

EGG GROUP
Amorphous

EVOLUTION
Does not evolve

ITEMS SOMETIMES HELD BY WILD POKÉMON
None

Damage taken in normal battles		Damage taken in Inverse Battles	
Normal	×0	Normal	×2
Fire	×1	Fire	×1
Water	×1	Water	×1
Grass	×1	Grass	×1
Electric	×0.5	Electric	×2
Ice	×1	Ice	×1
Fighting	×0	Fighting	×2
Poison	×0.5	Poison	×2
Ground	×2	Ground	×0.5
Flying	×0.5	Flying	×2
Psychic	×1	Psychic	×1
Bug	×1	Bug	×2
Rock	×1	Rock	×1
Ghost	×2	Ghost	×0.5
Dragon	×1	Dragon	×1
Dark	×2	Dark	×0.5
Steel	×0.5	Steel	×2
Fairy	×1	Fairy	×1

Can be used in
Inverse Battle	Battle Institute
Sky Battle	Battle Maison
Battle Chateau	Random Matchup

Gender unknown

How to obtain for your Mountain Kalos Pokédex

X Examine the trash cans that shake in the Lost Hotel every Tuesday.

Y Examine the trash cans that shake in the Lost Hotel every Tuesday.

LEVEL-UP MOVES

Lv.	Name	Type	Kind	Pow.	Acc.	PP	Range
1	Discharge	Electric	Special	80	100	15	Adjacent
1	Charge	Electric	Status	—	—	20	Self
1	Trick	Psychic	Status	—	100	10	Normal
1	Astonish	Ghost	Physical	30	100	15	Normal
1	Thunder Wave	Electric	Status	—	100	20	Normal
1	Thunder Shock	Electric	Special	40	100	30	Normal
1	Confuse Ray	Ghost	Status	—	100	10	Normal
8	Uproar	Normal	Special	90	100	10	1 Random
15	Double Team	Normal	Status	—	—	15	Self
22	Shock Wave	Electric	Special	60	—	20	Normal
29	Ominous Wind	Ghost	Special	60	100	5	Normal
36	Substitute	Normal	Status	—	—	10	Self
43	Electro Ball	Electric	Special	—	100	10	Normal
50	Hex	Ghost	Special	65	100	10	Normal
57	Charge	Electric	Status	—	—	20	Self
64	Discharge	Electric	Special	80	100	15	Adjacent

TM & HM MOVES

No.	Name	Type	Kind	Pow.	Acc.	PP	Range
TM06	Toxic	Poison	Status	—	90	10	Normal
TM10	Hidden Power	Normal	Special	60	100	15	Normal
TM11	Sunny Day	Fire	Status	—	—	5	Both Sides
TM16	Light Screen	Psychic	Status	—	—	30	Your Side
TM17	Protect	Normal	Status	—	—	10	Self
TM18	Rain Dance	Water	Status	—	—	5	Both Sides
TM21	Frustration	Normal	Physical	—	100	20	Normal
TM24	Thunderbolt	Electric	Special	90	100	15	Normal
TM25	Thunder	Electric	Special	110	70	10	Normal
TM27	Return	Normal	Physical	—	100	20	Normal
TM30	Shadow Ball	Ghost	Special	80	100	15	Normal
TM32	Double Team	Normal	Status	—	—	15	Self
TM33	Reflect	Psychic	Status	—	—	20	Your Side
TM42	Facade	Normal	Physical	70	100	20	Normal
TM44	Rest	Psychic	Status	—	—	10	Self
TM46	Thief	Dark	Physical	60	100	25	Normal
TM48	Round	Normal	Special	60	100	15	Normal
TM57	Charge Beam	Electric	Special	50	90	10	Normal
TM61	Will-O-Wisp	Fire	Status	—	85	15	Normal
TM70	Flash	Normal	Status	—	100	20	Normal
TM72	Volt Switch	Electric	Special	70	100	20	Normal
TM73	Thunder Wave	Electric	Status	—	100	20	Normal
TM77	Psych Up	Normal	Status	—	—	10	Normal
TM85	Dream Eater	Psychic	Special	100	100	15	Normal
TM87	Swagger	Normal	Status	—	90	15	Normal
TM88	Sleep Talk	Normal	Status	—	—	10	Self
TM90	Substitute	Normal	Status	—	—	10	Self
TM97	Dark Pulse	Dark	Special	80	100	15	Normal
TM100	Confide	Normal	Status	—	—	20	Normal

MOVES TAUGHT BY PEOPLE

Name	Type	Kind	Pow.	Acc.	PP	Range

Note: Rotom's form can be changed by letting it investigate different appliances, which can be found in cardboard boxes on the second floor of Professor Sycamore's Pokémon Lab in Lumiose City. Examining a microwave will make it Heat Rotom; a washing machine, Wash Rotom; a refrigerator, Frost Rotom; a fan, Fan Rotom; a lawnmower, Mow Rotom.

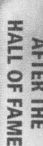

Mountain Kalos — 068

Plasma Pokémon

∨ Rotom
Heat Rotom

HEIGHT: 1'00"　　**WEIGHT:** 0.7 lbs.
GENDER: unknown

TYPE Electric | Fire

ABILITY
Levitate

HIDDEN ABILITY
None

X Research continues on this Pokémon, which could be the power source of a unique motor.

Y Its body is composed of plasma. It is known to infiltrate electronic devices and wreak havoc.

STAT GROWTH RATES
HP	■ ■
Attack	■ ■ ■
Defense	■ ■ ■ ■
Sp. Atk	■ ■ ■ ■ ■
Sp. Def	■ ■ ■ ■
Speed	■ ■ ■ ■ ■

EGG GROUP
Amorphous

EVOLUTION

Does not evolve

ITEMS SOMETIMES HELD BY WILD POKÉMON
None

Damage taken in normal battles		Damage taken in Inverse Battles	
Normal	×1	Normal	×1
Fire	×0.5	Fire	×2
Water	×2	Water	×0.5
Grass	×0.5	Grass	×2
Electric	×0.5	Electric	×2
Ice	×0.5	Ice	×2
Fighting	×1	Fighting	×1
Poison	×1	Poison	×1
Ground	×4	Ground	×0.25
Flying	×0.5	Flying	×2
Psychic	×1	Psychic	×1
Bug	×0.5	Bug	×2
Rock	×2	Rock	×0.5
Ghost	×1	Ghost	×1
Dragon	×1	Dragon	×1
Dark	×1	Dark	×1
Steel	×0.25	Steel	×4
Fairy	×0.5	Fairy	×2

Can be used in	
Inverse Battle	Battle Institute
Sky Battle	Battle Maison
Battle Chateau	Random Matchup

Gender unknown

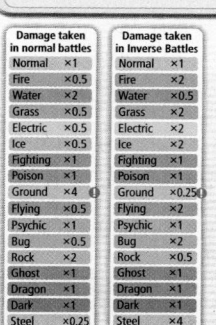

How to obtain for your Mountain Kalos Pokédex

X Examine the trash cans that shake in the Lost Hotel every Tuesday.

Y Examine the trash cans that shake in the Lost Hotel every Tuesday.

● LEVEL-UP MOVES

Lv.	Name	Type	Kind	Pow.	Acc.	PP	Range
1	Discharge	Electric	Special	80	100	15	Adjacent
1	Charge	Electric	Status	—	—	20	Self
1	Trick	Psychic	Status	—	100	10	Normal
1	Astonish	Ghost	Physical	30	100	15	Normal
1	Thunder Wave	Electric	Status	—	100	20	Normal
1	Thunder Shock	Electric	Special	40	100	30	Normal
1	Confuse Ray	Ghost	Status	—	100	10	Normal
8	Uproar	Normal	Special	90	100	10	1 Random
15	Double Team	Normal	Status	—	—	15	Self
22	Shock Wave	Electric	Special	60	—	20	Normal
29	Ominous Wind	Ghost	Special	60	100	5	Normal
36	Substitute	Normal	Status	—	—	10	Self
43	Electro Ball	Electric	Special	—	100	10	Normal
50	Hex	Ghost	Special	65	100	10	Normal
57	Charge	Electric	Status	—	—	20	Self
64	Discharge	Electric	Special	80	100	15	Adjacent
◆	Overheat	Fire	Special	130	90	5	Normal

● TM & HM MOVES

No.	Name	Type	Kind	Pow.	Acc.	PP	Range
TM06	Toxic	Poison	Status	—	90	10	Normal
TM10	Hidden Power	Normal	Special	60	100	15	Normal
TM11	Sunny Day	Fire	Status	—	—	5	Both Sides
TM16	Light Screen	Psychic	Status	—	—	30	Your Side
TM17	Protect	Normal	Status	—	—	10	Self
TM18	Rain Dance	Water	Status	—	—	5	Both Sides
TM21	Frustration	Normal	Physical	—	100	20	Normal
TM24	Thunderbolt	Electric	Special	90	100	15	Normal
TM25	Thunder	Electric	Special	110	70	10	Normal
TM30	Shadow Ball	Ghost	Special	80	100	15	Normal
TM32	Double Team	Normal	Status	—	—	15	Self
TM33	Reflect	Psychic	Status	—	—	20	Your Side
TM42	Facade	Normal	Physical	70	100	20	Normal
TM44	Rest	Psychic	Status	—	—	10	Self
TM46	Thief	Dark	Physical	60	100	25	Normal
TM48	Round	Normal	Special	60	100	15	Normal
TM57	Charge Beam	Electric	Special	50	90	10	Normal
TM61	Will-O-Wisp	Fire	Status	—	85	15	Normal
TM70	Flash	Normal	Status	—	100	20	Normal
TM72	Volt Switch	Electric	Special	70	100	20	Normal
TM73	Thunder Wave	Electric	Status	—	100	20	Normal
TM77	Psych Up	Normal	Status	—	—	10	Normal
TM85	Dream Eater	Psychic	Special	100	100	15	Normal
TM87	Swagger	Normal	Status	—	90	15	Normal
TM88	Sleep Talk	Normal	Status	—	—	10	Self
TM90	Substitute	Normal	Status	—	—	10	Self
TM97	Dark Pulse	Dark	Special	80	100	15	Normal
TM100	Confide	Normal	Status	—	—	20	Normal

● MOVES TAUGHT BY PEOPLE

Name	Type	Kind	Pow.	Acc.	PP	Range

◆ This move can only be learned when Rotom has changed forms. If it returns to being normal Rotom, it will forget this move.
Note: Rotom's form can be changed by letting it investigate different appliances, which can be found in cardboard boxes on the second floor of Professor Sycamore's Pokémon Lab in Lumiose City. Examining a microwave will make it Heat Rotom; a washing machine, Wash Rotom; a refrigerator, Frost Rotom; a fan, Fan Rotom; a lawnmower, Mow Rotom.

AFTER THE HALL OF FAME

CENTRAL KALOS

COASTAL KALOS

MOUNTAIN KALOS

068 Rotom Heat Rotom

ADVENTURE DATA

Mountain Kalos 068
Plasma Pokémon
Rotom
Wash Rotom

HEIGHT: 1'00" WEIGHT: 0.7 lbs.
GENDER: unknown

X Research continues on this Pokémon, which could be the power source of a unique motor.

Y Its body is composed of plasma. It is known to infiltrate electronic devices and wreak havoc.

TYPE Electric Water

ABILITY
Levitate

HIDDEN ABILITY
None

STAT GROWTH RATES
HP	■■
Attack	■■■
Defense	■■■■■
Sp. Atk	■■■■■
Sp. Def	■■■■
Speed	■■■■■

EGG GROUP
Amorphous

EVOLUTION
Does not evolve

ITEMS SOMETIMES HELD BY WILD POKÉMON
None

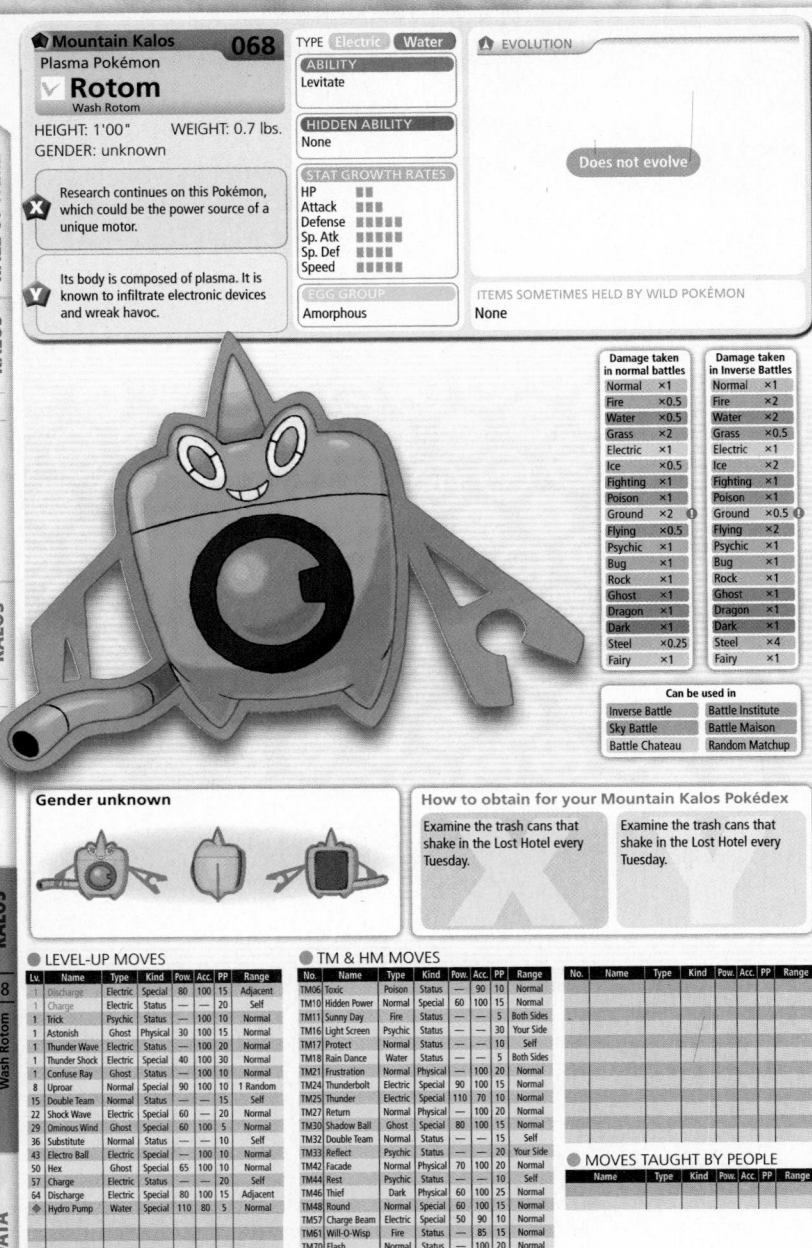

Damage taken in normal battles		Damage taken in Inverse Battles	
Normal	×1	Normal	×1
Fire	×0.5	Fire	×2
Water	×0.5	Water	×0.5
Grass	×2	Grass	×0.5
Electric	×1	Electric	×1
Ice	×0.5	Ice	×2
Fighting	×1	Fighting	×1
Poison	×1	Poison	×1
Ground	×2 ❶	Ground	×0.5 ❶
Flying	×0.5	Flying	×2
Psychic	×1	Psychic	×1
Bug	×1	Bug	×1
Rock	×1	Rock	×1
Ghost	×1	Ghost	×1
Dragon	×1	Dragon	×1
Dark	×1	Dark	×1
Steel	×0.25	Steel	×4
Fairy	×1	Fairy	×1

Can be used in	
Inverse Battle	Battle Institute
Sky Battle	Battle Maison
Battle Chateau	Random Matchup

Gender unknown

How to obtain for your Mountain Kalos Pokédex

Examine the trash cans that shake in the Lost Hotel every Tuesday.

Examine the trash cans that shake in the Lost Hotel every Tuesday.

● LEVEL-UP MOVES
Lv.	Name	Type	Kind	Pow.	Acc.	PP	Range
1	Discharge	Electric	Special	80	100	15	Adjacent
1	Charge	Electric	Status	—	—	20	Self
1	Trick	Psychic	Status	—	100	10	Normal
1	Astonish	Ghost	Physical	30	100	15	Normal
1	Thunder Wave	Electric	Status	—	100	20	Normal
1	Thunder Shock	Electric	Special	40	100	30	Normal
1	Confuse Ray	Ghost	Status	—	100	10	Normal
8	Uproar	Normal	Special	90	100	10	1 Random
15	Double Team	Normal	Status	—	—	15	Self
22	Shock Wave	Electric	Special	60	—	20	Normal
29	Ominous Wind	Ghost	Special	60	100	5	Normal
36	Substitute	Normal	Status	—	—	10	Self
43	Electro Ball	Electric	Special	—	100	10	Normal
50	Hex	Ghost	Special	65	100	10	Normal
57	Charge	Electric	Status	—	—	20	Self
64	Discharge	Electric	Special	80	100	15	Adjacent
◆	Hydro Pump	Water	Special	110	80	5	Normal

■ TM & HM MOVES
No.	Name	Type	Kind	Pow.	Acc.	PP	Range
TM06	Toxic	Poison	Status	—	90	10	Normal
TM10	Hidden Power	Normal	Special	60	100	15	Normal
TM11	Sunny Day	Fire	Status	—	—	5	Both Sides
TM16	Light Screen	Psychic	Status	—	—	30	Your Side
TM17	Protect	Normal	Status	—	—	10	Self
TM18	Rain Dance	Water	Status	—	—	5	Both Sides
TM21	Frustration	Normal	Physical	—	100	20	Normal
TM24	Thunderbolt	Electric	Special	90	100	15	Normal
TM25	Thunder	Electric	Special	110	70	10	Normal
TM27	Return	Normal	Physical	—	100	20	Normal
TM30	Shadow Ball	Ghost	Special	80	100	15	Normal
TM32	Double Team	Normal	Status	—	—	15	Self
TM33	Reflect	Psychic	Status	—	—	20	Your Side
TM42	Facade	Normal	Physical	70	100	20	Normal
TM44	Rest	Psychic	Status	—	—	10	Self
TM46	Thief	Dark	Physical	60	100	25	Normal
TM48	Round	Normal	Special	60	100	15	Normal
TM57	Charge Beam	Electric	Special	50	90	10	Normal
TM61	Will-O-Wisp	Fire	Status	—	85	15	Normal
TM70	Flash	Normal	Status	—	100	20	Normal
TM72	Volt Switch	Electric	Special	70	100	20	Normal
TM73	Thunder Wave	Electric	Status	—	100	20	Normal
TM77	Psych Up	Normal	Status	—	—	10	Normal
TM85	Dream Eater	Psychic	Special	100	100	15	Normal
TM87	Swagger	Normal	Status	—	90	15	Normal
TM88	Sleep Talk	Normal	Status	—	—	10	Self
TM90	Substitute	Normal	Status	—	—	10	Self
TM97	Dark Pulse	Dark	Special	80	100	15	Normal
TM100	Confide	Normal	Status	—	—	20	Normal

No.	Name	Type	Kind	Pow.	Acc.	PP	Range

● MOVES TAUGHT BY PEOPLE
Name	Type	Kind	Pow.	Acc.	PP	Range

◆ This move can only be learned when Rotom has changed forms. If it returns to being normal Rotom, it will forget this move.

Note: Rotom's form can be changed by letting it investigate different appliances, which can be found in cardboard boxes on the second floor of Professor Sycamore's Pokémon Lab in Lumiose City. Examining a microwave will make it Heat Rotom; a washing machine, Wash Rotom; a refrigerator, Frost Rotom; a fan, Fan Rotom; a lawnmower, Mow Rotom.

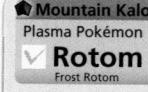
Plasma Pokémon

☑ Rotom
Frost Rotom

HEIGHT: 1'00"　　WEIGHT: 0.7 lbs.
GENDER: unknown

068

X Research continues on this Pokémon, which could be the power source of a unique motor.

Y Its body is composed of plasma. It is known to infiltrate electronic devices and wreak havoc.

TYPE: Electric / Ice

ABILITY
Levitate

HIDDEN ABILITY
None

STAT GROWTH RATES
HP	■ ■
Attack	■ ■ ■
Defense	■ ■ ■ ■ ■
Sp. Atk	■ ■ ■ ■ ■
Sp. Def	■ ■ ■ ■
Speed	■ ■ ■ ■ ■

EGG GROUP
Amorphous

EVOLUTION

Does not evolve

ITEMS SOMETIMES HELD BY WILD POKÉMON
None

AFTER THE HALL OF FAME

CENTRAL KALOS

COASTAL KALOS

MOUNTAIN KALOS

068
Rotom
Frost Rotom

ADVENTURE DATA

Damage taken in normal battles		Damage taken in Inverse Battles	
Normal	×1	Normal	×1
Fire	×2	Fire	×0.5
Water	×1	Water	×1
Grass	×1	Grass	×1
Electric	×0.5	Electric	×2
Ice	×0.5	Ice	×2
Fighting	×2	Fighting	×0.5
Poison	×1	Poison	×1
Ground	×2	Ground	×0.5
Flying	×0.5	Flying	×2
Psychic	×1	Psychic	×1
Bug	×1	Bug	×1
Rock	×2	Rock	×0.5
Ghost	×1	Ghost	×1
Dragon	×1	Dragon	×1
Dark	×1	Dark	×1
Steel	×1	Steel	×1
Fairy	×1	Fairy	×1

Can be used in	
Inverse Battle	Battle Institute
Sky Battle	Battle Maison
Battle Chateau	Random Matchup

Gender unknown

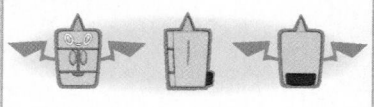

How to obtain for your Mountain Kalos Pokédex

X Examine the trash cans that shake in the Lost Hotel every Tuesday.

Y Examine the trash cans that shake in the Lost Hotel every Tuesday.

● LEVEL-UP MOVES

Lv.	Name	Type	Kind	Pow.	Acc.	PP	Range
1	Discharge	Electric	Special	80	100	15	Adjacent
1	Charge	Electric	Status	—	—	20	Self
1	Trick	Psychic	Status	—	100	10	Normal
1	Astonish	Ghost	Physical	30	100	15	Normal
1	Thunder Wave	Electric	Status	—	100	20	Normal
1	Thunder Shock	Electric	Special	40	100	30	Normal
1	Confuse Ray	Ghost	Status	—	100	10	Normal
8	Uproar	Normal	Special	90	100	10	1 Random
15	Double Team	Normal	Status	—	—	15	Self
22	Shock Wave	Electric	Special	60	—	20	Normal
29	Ominous Wind	Ghost	Special	60	100	5	Normal
36	Substitute	Normal	Status	—	—	10	Self
43	Electro Ball	Electric	Special	—	100	10	Normal
50	Hex	Ghost	Special	65	100	10	Normal
57	Charge	Electric	Status	—	—	20	Self
64	Discharge	Electric	Special	80	100	15	Adjacent
◆	Blizzard	Ice	Special	110	70	5	Many Others

● TM & HM MOVES

No.	Name	Type	Kind	Pow.	Acc.	PP	Range
TM06	Toxic	Poison	Status	—	90	10	Normal
TM10	Hidden Power	Normal	Special	60	100	15	Normal
TM11	Sunny Day	Fire	Status	—	—	5	Both Sides
TM16	Light Screen	Psychic	Status	—	—	30	Your Side
TM17	Protect	Normal	Status	—	—	10	Self
TM18	Rain Dance	Water	Status	—	—	5	Both Sides
TM21	Frustration	Normal	Physical	—	100	20	Normal
TM24	Thunderbolt	Electric	Special	90	100	15	Normal
TM25	Thunder	Electric	Special	110	70	10	Normal
TM27	Return	Normal	Physical	—	100	20	Normal
TM30	Shadow Ball	Ghost	Special	80	100	15	Normal
TM32	Double Team	Normal	Status	—	—	15	Self
TM33	Reflect	Psychic	Status	—	—	20	Your Side
TM42	Facade	Normal	Physical	70	100	20	Normal
TM44	Rest	Psychic	Status	—	—	10	Self
TM46	Thief	Dark	Physical	60	100	25	Normal
TM48	Round	Normal	Special	60	100	15	Normal
TM57	Charge Beam	Electric	Special	50	90	10	Normal
TM61	Will-O-Wisp	Fire	Status	—	85	15	Normal
TM70	Flash	Normal	Status	—	100	20	Normal
TM72	Volt Switch	Electric	Special	70	100	20	Normal
TM73	Thunder Wave	Electric	Status	—	100	20	Normal
TM77	Psych Up	Normal	Status	—	—	10	Normal
TM85	Dream Eater	Psychic	Special	100	100	15	Normal
TM87	Swagger	Normal	Status	—	90	15	Normal
TM88	Sleep Talk	Normal	Status	—	—	10	Self
TM90	Substitute	Normal	Status	—	—	10	Self
TM97	Dark Pulse	Dark	Special	80	100	15	Normal
TM100	Confide	Normal	Status	—	—	20	Normal

No.	Name	Type	Kind	Pow.	Acc.	PP	Range

● MOVES TAUGHT BY PEOPLE

Name	Type	Kind	Pow.	Acc.	PP	Range

◆ This move can only be learned when Rotom has changed forms. If it returns to being normal Rotom, it will forget this move.
Note: Rotom's form can be changed by letting it investigate different appliances, which can be found in cardboard boxes on the second floor of Professor Sycamore's Pokémon Lab in Lumiose City. Examining a microwave will make it Heat Rotom; a washing machine, Wash Rotom; a refrigerator, Frost Rotom; a fan, Fan Rotom; a lawnmower, Mow Rotom.

AFTER THE HALL OF FAME

CENTRAL KALOS

COASTAL KALOS

MOUNTAIN KALOS

068

Rotom
Fan Rotom

ADVENTURE DATA

⬟ Mountain Kalos 068

Plasma Pokémon

∨ **Rotom**
Fan Rotom

HEIGHT: 1'00" WEIGHT: 0.7 lbs.
GENDER: unknown

X Research continues on this Pokémon, which could be the power source of a unique motor.

Y Its body is composed of plasma. It is known to infiltrate electronic devices and wreak havoc.

TYPE Electric Flying

ABILITY
Levitate

HIDDEN ABILITY
None

STAT GROWTH RATES
HP	▦▦
Attack	▦▦▦
Defense	▦▦▦
Sp. Atk	▦▦▦▦▦
Sp. Def	▦▦▦▦▦
Speed	▦▦▦▦▦

EGG GROUP
Amorphous

⬛ EVOLUTION

Does not evolve

ITEMS SOMETIMES HELD BY WILD POKÉMON
None

Damage taken in normal battles		Damage taken in Inverse Battles	
Normal	×1	Normal	×1
Fire	×1	Fire	×1
Water	×1	Water	×1
Grass	×0.5	Grass	×2
Electric	×1	Electric	×1
Ice	×2	Ice	×0.5
Fighting	×0.5	Fighting	×2
Poison	×1	Poison	×1
Ground	×0	Ground	×1
Flying	×0.5	Flying	×2
Psychic	×1	Psychic	×1
Bug	×0.5	Bug	×2
Rock	×2	Rock	×0.5
Ghost	×1	Ghost	×1
Dragon	×1	Dragon	×1
Dark	×1	Dark	×1
Steel	×0.5	Steel	×2
Fairy	×1	Fairy	×1

Can be used in	
Inverse Battle	Battle Institute
Sky Battle	Battle Maison
Battle Chateau	Random Matchup

Gender unknown

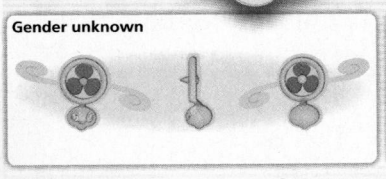

How to obtain for your Mountain Kalos Pokédex

Examine the trash cans that shake in the Lost Hotel every Tuesday.

Examine the trash cans that shake in the Lost Hotel every Tuesday.

● LEVEL-UP MOVES

Lv.	Name	Type	Kind	Pow.	Acc.	PP	Range
1	Discharge	Electric	Special	80	100	15	Adjacent
1	Charge	Electric	Status	—	—	20	Self
1	Trick	Psychic	Status	—	100	10	Normal
1	Astonish	Ghost	Physical	30	100	15	Normal
1	Thunder Wave	Electric	Status	—	100	20	Normal
1	Thunder Shock	Electric	Special	40	100	30	Normal
1	Confuse Ray	Ghost	Status	—	100	10	Normal
8	Uproar	Normal	Special	90	100	10	1 Random
15	Double Team	Normal	Status	—	—	15	Self
22	Shock Wave	Electric	Special	60	—	20	Normal
29	Ominous Wind	Ghost	Special	60	100	5	Normal
36	Substitute	Normal	Status	—	—	10	Self
43	Electro Ball	Electric	Special	—	100	10	Normal
50	Hex	Ghost	Special	65	100	10	Normal
57	Charge	Electric	Status	—	—	20	Self
64	Discharge	Electric	Special	80	100	15	Adjacent
◆	Air Slash	Flying	Special	75	95	15	Normal

● TM & HM MOVES

No.	Name	Type	Kind	Pow.	Acc.	PP	Range
TM06	Toxic	Poison	Status	—	90	10	Normal
TM10	Hidden Power	Normal	Special	60	100	15	Normal
TM11	Sunny Day	Fire	Status	—	—	5	Both Sides
TM16	Light Screen	Psychic	Status	—	—	30	Your Side
TM17	Protect	Normal	Status	—	—	10	Self
TM18	Rain Dance	Water	Status	—	—	5	Both Sides
TM21	Frustration	Normal	Physical	—	100	20	Normal
TM24	Thunderbolt	Electric	Special	90	100	15	Normal
TM25	Thunder	Electric	Special	110	70	10	Normal
TM27	Return	Normal	Physical	—	100	20	Normal
TM30	Shadow Ball	Ghost	Special	80	100	15	Normal
TM32	Double Team	Normal	Status	—	—	15	Self
TM33	Reflect	Psychic	Status	—	—	20	Your Side
TM42	Facade	Normal	Physical	70	100	20	Normal
TM44	Rest	Psychic	Status	—	—	10	Self
TM46	Thief	Dark	Physical	60	100	25	Normal
TM48	Round	Normal	Special	60	100	15	Normal
TM57	Charge Beam	Electric	Special	50	90	10	Normal
TM61	Will-O-Wisp	Fire	Status	—	85	15	Normal
TM70	Flash	Normal	Status	—	100	20	Normal
TM72	Volt Switch	Electric	Special	70	100	20	Normal
TM73	Thunder Wave	Electric	Status	—	100	20	Normal
TM77	Psych Up	Normal	Status	—	—	10	Normal
TM85	Dream Eater	Psychic	Special	100	100	15	Normal
TM87	Swagger	Normal	Status	—	90	15	Normal
TM88	Sleep Talk	Normal	Status	—	—	10	Self
TM90	Substitute	Normal	Status	—	—	10	Self
TM97	Dark Pulse	Dark	Special	80	100	15	Normal
TM100	Confide	Normal	Status	—	—	20	Normal

No.	Name	Type	Kind	Pow.	Acc.	PP	Range

● MOVES TAUGHT BY PEOPLE

Name	Type	Kind	Pow.	Acc.	PP	Range

◆ This move can only be learned when Rotom has changed forms. If it returns to being normal Rotom, it will forget this move.
Note: Rotom's form can be changed by letting it investigate different appliances, which can be found in cardboard boxes on the second floor of Professor Sycamore's Pokémon Lab in Lumiose City. Examining a microwave will make it Heat Rotom; a washing machine, Wash Rotom; a refrigerator, Frost Rotom; a fan, Fan Rotom; a lawnmower, Mow Rotom.

Mountain Kalos 068
Plasma Pokémon
☑ Rotom
Mow Rotom

HEIGHT: 1'00" WEIGHT: 0.7 lbs.
GENDER: unknown

X Research continues on this Pokémon, which could be the power source of a unique motor.

Y Its body is composed of plasma. It is known to infiltrate electronic devices and wreak havoc.

TYPE Electric | Grass

ABILITY
Levitate

HIDDEN ABILITY
None

STAT GROWTH RATES
HP	■■
Attack	■■
Defense	■■■■■
Sp. Atk	■■■■■
Sp. Def	■■■■
Speed	■■■■■

EGG GROUP
Amorphous

EVOLUTION

Does not evolve

ITEMS SOMETIMES HELD BY WILD POKÉMON
None

Damage taken in normal battles		Damage taken in Inverse Battles	
Normal	×1	Normal	×1
Fire	×2	Fire	×0.5
Water	×0.5	Water	×2
Grass	×0.5	Grass	×2
Electric	×0.25	Electric	×4
Ice	×2	Ice	×0.5
Fighting	×1	Fighting	×1
Poison	×2	Poison	×0.5
Ground	×1 ⓘ	Ground	×1 ⓘ
Flying	×1	Flying	×1
Psychic	×1	Psychic	×1
Bug	×2	Bug	×0.5
Rock	×1	Rock	×1
Ghost	×1	Ghost	×1
Dragon	×1	Dragon	×1
Dark	×1	Dark	×1
Steel	×0.5	Steel	×2
Fairy	×1	Fairy	×1

Can be used in	
Inverse Battle	Battle Institute
Sky Battle	Battle Maison
Battle Chateau	Random Matchup

Gender unknown

How to obtain for your Mountain Kalos Pokédex
Examine the trash cans that shake in the Lost Hotel every Tuesday.

Examine the trash cans that shake in the Lost Hotel every Tuesday.

● LEVEL-UP MOVES

Lv.	Name	Type	Kind	Pow.	Acc.	PP	Range
1	Discharge	Electric	Special	80	100	15	Adjacent
1	Charge	Electric	Status	—	—	20	Self
1	Trick	Psychic	Status	—	100	10	Normal
1	Astonish	Ghost	Physical	30	100	15	Normal
1	Thunder Wave	Electric	Status	—	100	20	Normal
1	Thunder Shock	Electric	Special	40	100	30	Normal
1	Confuse Ray	Ghost	Status	—	100	10	Normal
8	Uproar	Normal	Special	90	100	10	1 Random
15	Double Team	Normal	Status	—	—	15	Self
22	Shock Wave	Electric	Special	60	—	20	Normal
29	Ominous Wind	Ghost	Special	60	100	5	Normal
36	Substitute	Normal	Status	—	—	10	Self
43	Electro Ball	Electric	Special	—	100	10	Normal
50	Hex	Ghost	Special	65	100	10	Normal
57	Charge	Electric	Status	—	—	20	Self
64	Discharge	Electric	Special	80	100	15	Adjacent
◆	Leaf Storm	Grass	Special	130	90	5	Normal

● TM & HM MOVES

No.	Name	Type	Kind	Pow.	Acc.	PP	Range
TM06	Toxic	Poison	Status	—	90	10	Normal
TM10	Hidden Power	Normal	Special	60	100	15	Normal
TM11	Sunny Day	Fire	Status	—	—	5	Both Sides
TM16	Light Screen	Psychic	Status	—	—	30	Your Side
TM17	Protect	Normal	Status	—	—	10	Self
TM18	Rain Dance	Water	Status	—	—	5	Both Sides
TM21	Frustration	Normal	Physical	—	100	20	Normal
TM24	Thunderbolt	Electric	Special	90	100	15	Normal
TM25	Thunder	Electric	Special	110	70	10	Normal
TM27	Return	Normal	Physical	—	100	20	Normal
TM30	Shadow Ball	Ghost	Special	80	100	15	Normal
TM32	Double Team	Normal	Status	—	—	15	Self
TM33	Reflect	Psychic	Status	—	—	20	Your Side
TM42	Facade	Normal	Physical	70	100	20	Normal
TM44	Rest	Psychic	Status	—	—	10	Self
TM46	Thief	Dark	Physical	60	100	25	Normal
TM48	Round	Normal	Special	60	100	15	Normal
TM57	Charge Beam	Electric	Special	50	90	10	Normal
TM61	Will-O-Wisp	Fire	Status	—	85	15	Normal
TM70	Flash	Normal	Status	—	100	20	Normal
TM72	Volt Switch	Electric	Special	70	100	20	Normal
TM73	Thunder Wave	Electric	Status	—	100	20	Normal
TM77	Psych Up	Normal	Status	—	—	10	Normal
TM85	Dream Eater	Psychic	Special	100	100	15	Normal
TM87	Swagger	Normal	Status	—	90	15	Normal
TM88	Sleep Talk	Normal	Status	—	—	10	Self
TM90	Substitute	Normal	Status	—	—	10	Self
TM97	Dark Pulse	Dark	Special	80	100	15	Normal
TM100	Confide	Normal	Status	—	—	20	Normal

● MOVES TAUGHT BY PEOPLE

Name	Type	Kind	Pow.	Acc.	PP	Range

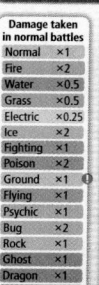

◆ This move can only be learned when Rotom has changed forms. If it returns to being normal Rotom, it will forget this move.
Note: Rotom's form can be changed by letting it investigate different appliances, which can be found in cardboard boxes on the second floor of Professor Sycamore's Pokémon Lab in Lumiose City. Examining a microwave will make it Heat Rotom; a washing machine, Wash Rotom; a refrigerator, Frost Rotom; a fan, Fan Rotom; a lawnmower, Mow Rotom.

AFTER THE HALL OF FAME

CENTRAL KALOS

COASTAL KALOS

MOUNTAIN KALOS

068 Rotom Mow Rotom

ADVENTURE DATA

Mountain Kalos 069
Magnet Pokémon
✓ Magnemite

HEIGHT: 1'00"　　WEIGHT: 13.2 lbs.
GENDER: unknown

X The units at the sides of its body generate antigravity energy to keep it aloft in the air.

Y It moves while constantly hovering. It discharges Thunder Wave and so on from the units at its sides.

TYPE Electric | Steel

ABILITIES
Magnet Pull
Sturdy

HIDDEN ABILITY
Analytic

STAT GROWTH RATES
HP	■
Attack	■■
Defense	■■
Sp. Atk	■■■■■
Sp. Def	■■
Speed	■■■

EGG GROUP
Mineral

EVOLUTION

Magnemite　　Lv. 30　　Magneton　　Level up on Route 13　　Magnezone

ITEMS SOMETIMES HELD BY WILD POKÉMON
None

Damage taken in normal battles	
Normal	×0.5
Fire	×2
Water	×1
Grass	×0.5
Electric	×0.5
Ice	×0.5
Fighting	×2
Poison	×0
Ground	×4
Flying	×0.25
Psychic	×0.5
Bug	×0.5
Rock	×0.5
Ghost	×1
Dragon	×0.5
Dark	×1
Steel	×0.25
Fairy	×0.5

Damage taken in Inverse Battles	
Normal	×2
Fire	×0.5
Water	×1
Grass	×2
Electric	×2
Ice	×2
Fighting	×0.5
Poison	×2
Ground	×0.25
Flying	×4
Psychic	×2
Bug	×2
Rock	×2
Ghost	×1
Dragon	×2
Dark	×1
Steel	×4
Fairy	×2

Can be used in
Inverse Battle	Battle Institute
—	Battle Maison
Battle Chateau	Random Matchup

Gender unknown

How to obtain for your Mountain Kalos Pokédex

Leave Magneton or Magnezone at the Pokémon Day Care with Ditto, and hatch the Egg that is found.

Leave Magneton or Magnezone at the Pokémon Day Care with Ditto, and hatch the Egg that is found.

● LEVEL-UP MOVES

Lv.	Name	Type	Kind	Pow.	Acc.	PP	Range
1	Tackle	Normal	Physical	50	100	35	Normal
4	Supersonic	Normal	Status	—	55	20	Normal
7	Thunder Shock	Electric	Special	40	100	30	Normal
11	Sonic Boom	Normal	Special	—	90	20	Normal
15	Thunder Wave	Electric	Status	—	100	20	Normal
18	Magnet Bomb	Steel	Physical	60	—	20	Normal
21	Spark	Electric	Physical	65	100	20	Normal
25	Mirror Shot	Steel	Special	65	85	10	Normal
29	Metal Sound	Steel	Status	—	85	40	Normal
32	Electro Ball	Electric	Special	—	100	10	Normal
35	Flash Cannon	Steel	Special	80	100	10	Normal
39	Screech	Normal	Status	—	85	40	Normal
43	Discharge	Electric	Special	80	100	15	Adjacent
46	Lock-On	Normal	Status	—	—	5	Normal
49	Magnet Rise	Electric	Status	—	—	10	Self
53	Gyro Ball	Steel	Physical	—	100	5	Normal
57	Zap Cannon	Electric	Special	120	50	5	Normal

● TM & HM MOVES

No.	Name	Type	Kind	Pow.	Acc.	PP	Range
TM06	Toxic	Poison	Status	—	90	10	Normal
TM10	Hidden Power	Normal	Special	60	100	15	Normal
TM11	Sunny Day	Fire	Status	—	—	5	Both Sides
TM16	Light Screen	Psychic	Status	—	—	30	Your Side
TM17	Protect	Normal	Status	—	—	10	Self
TM18	Rain Dance	Water	Status	—	—	5	Both Sides
TM21	Frustration	Normal	Physical	—	100	20	Normal
TM24	Thunderbolt	Electric	Special	90	100	15	Normal
TM25	Thunder	Electric	Special	110	70	10	Normal
TM27	Return	Normal	Physical	—	100	20	Normal
TM32	Double Team	Normal	Status	—	—	15	Self
TM33	Reflect	Psychic	Status	—	—	20	Your Side
TM42	Facade	Normal	Physical	70	100	20	Normal
TM44	Rest	Psychic	Status	—	—	10	Self
TM48	Round	Normal	Special	60	100	15	Normal
TM57	Charge Beam	Electric	Special	50	90	10	Normal
TM64	Explosion	Normal	Physical	250	100	5	Adjacent
TM70	Flash	Normal	Status	—	100	20	Normal
TM72	Volt Switch	Electric	Special	70	100	20	Normal
TM73	Thunder Wave	Electric	Status	—	100	20	Normal
TM74	Gyro Ball	Steel	Physical	—	100	5	Normal
TM77	Psych Up	Normal	Status	—	—	10	Normal
TM87	Swagger	Normal	Status	—	90	15	Normal
TM88	Sleep Talk	Normal	Status	—	—	10	Self
TM90	Substitute	Normal	Status	—	—	10	Self
TM91	Flash Cannon	Steel	Special	80	100	10	Normal
TM93	Wild Charge	Electric	Physical	90	100	15	Normal
TM100	Confide	Normal	Status	—	—	20	Normal

No.	Name	Type	Kind	Pow.	Acc.	PP	Range

● MOVES TAUGHT BY PEOPLE

Name	Type	Kind	Pow.	Acc.	PP	Range

● EGG MOVES

Name	Type	Kind	Pow.	Acc.	PP	Range

Mountain Kalos

Magnet Pokémon

070

 Magneton

HEIGHT: 3'03" WEIGHT: 132.3 lbs.
GENDER: unknown

X A linked cluster formed of several Magnemite. It discharges powerful magnetic waves at high voltage.

Y Generates strange radio signals. It raises the temperature by 3.6 degrees Fahrenheit within 3,300 feet.

TYPE Electric | Steel

ABILITIES
Magnet Pull
Sturdy

HIDDEN ABILITY
Analytic

STAT GROWTH RATES
HP	■■
Attack	■■■
Defense	■■■
Sp. Atk	■■■■■
Sp. Def	■■■
Speed	■■■■

EGG GROUP
Mineral

EVOLUTION

Lv. 30 → Level up on Route 13

Magnemite → Magneton → Magnezone

ITEMS SOMETIMES HELD BY WILD POKÉMON
Metal Coat

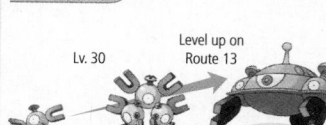

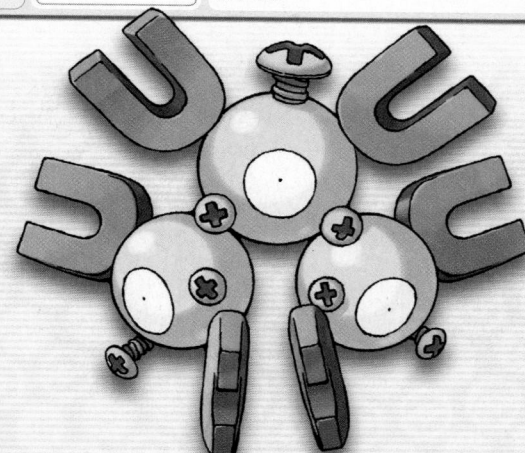

Damage taken in normal battles		Damage taken in Inverse Battles	
Normal	×0.5	Normal	×2
Fire	×2	Fire	×0.5
Water	×1	Water	×1
Grass	×0.5	Grass	×2
Electric	×0.5	Electric	×2
Ice	×0.5	Ice	×2
Fighting	×2	Fighting	×0.5
Poison	×0	Poison	×2
Ground	×4	Ground	×0.25
Flying	×0.25	Flying	×4
Psychic	×0.5	Psychic	×2
Bug	×0.5	Bug	×2
Rock	×0.5	Rock	×2
Ghost		Ghost	×1
Dragon	×0.5	Dragon	×2
Dark		Dark	×1
Steel	×0.25	Steel	×4
Fairy	×0.5	Fairy	×2

Can be used in	
Inverse Battle	Battle Institute
—	Battle Maison
Battle Chateau	Random Matchup

Gender unknown

 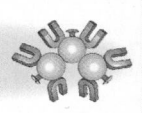

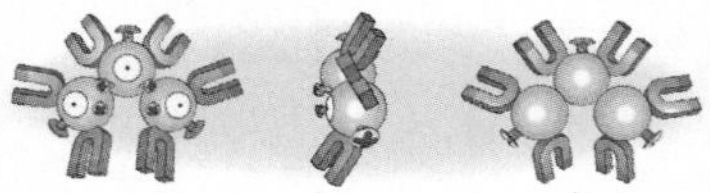

How to obtain for your Mountain Kalos Pokédex

Catch in the Lost Hotel. | Catch in the Lost Hotel.

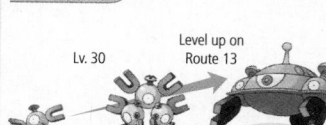

● LEVEL-UP MOVES

Lv.	Name	Type	Kind	Pow.	Acc.	PP	Range
1	Zap Cannon	Electric	Special	120	50	5	Normal
1	Tri Attack	Normal	Special	80	100	10	Normal
1	Tackle	Normal	Physical	50	100	35	Normal
1	Supersonic	Normal	Status	—	55	20	Normal
1	Thunder Shock	Electric	Special	40	100	30	Normal
1	Sonic Boom	Normal	Special	—	90	20	Normal
4	Supersonic	Normal	Status	—	55	20	Normal
7	Thunder Shock	Electric	Special	40	100	30	Normal
11	Electric Terrain	Electric	Status	—	—	10	Both Sides
15	Thunder Wave	Electric	Status	—	100	20	Normal
18	Magnet Bomb	Steel	Physical	60	—	20	Normal
21	Spark	Electric	Physical	65	100	20	Normal
25	Mirror Shot	Steel	Special	65	85	10	Normal
29	Metal Sound	Steel	Status	—	85	40	Normal
34	Electro Ball	Electric	Special	—	100	10	Normal
39	Flash Cannon	Steel	Special	80	100	10	Normal
45	Screech	Normal	Status	—	85	40	Normal
51	Discharge	Electric	Special	80	100	15	Adjacent
56	Lock-On	Normal	Status	—	—	5	Normal
62	Magnet Rise	Electric	Status	—	—	10	Self
67	Gyro Ball	Steel	Physical	—	100	5	Normal
73	Zap Cannon	Electric	Special	120	50	5	Normal

● TM & HM MOVES

No.	Name	Type	Kind	Pow.	Acc.	PP	Range
TM06	Toxic	Poison	Status	—	90	10	Normal
TM10	Hidden Power	Normal	Special	60	100	15	Normal
TM11	Sunny Day	Fire	Status	—	—	5	Both Sides
TM15	Hyper Beam	Normal	Special	150	90	5	Normal
TM16	Light Screen	Psychic	Status	—	—	30	Your Side
TM17	Protect	Normal	Status	—	—	10	Self
TM18	Rain Dance	Water	Status	—	—	5	Both Sides
TM21	Frustration	Normal	Physical	—	100	20	Normal
TM24	Thunderbolt	Electric	Special	90	100	15	Normal
TM25	Thunder	Electric	Special	110	70	10	Normal
TM27	Return	Normal	Physical	—	100	20	Normal
TM32	Double Team	Normal	Status	—	—	15	Self
TM33	Reflect	Psychic	Status	—	—	20	Your Side
TM42	Facade	Normal	Physical	70	100	20	Normal
TM44	Rest	Psychic	Status	—	—	10	Self
TM48	Round	Normal	Special	60	100	15	Normal
TM57	Charge Beam	Electric	Special	50	90	10	Normal
TM64	Explosion	Normal	Physical	250	100	5	Adjacent
TM68	Giga Impact	Normal	Physical	150	90	5	Normal
TM70	Flash	Normal	Status	—	100	20	Normal
TM72	Volt Switch	Electric	Special	70	100	20	Normal
TM73	Thunder Wave	Electric	Status	—	100	20	Normal
TM74	Gyro Ball	Steel	Physical	—	100	5	Normal
TM77	Psych Up	Normal	Status	—	—	10	Normal
TM87	Swagger	Normal	Status	—	90	15	Normal
TM88	Sleep Talk	Normal	Status	—	—	10	Self
TM90	Substitute	Normal	Status	—	—	10	Self
TM91	Flash Cannon	Steel	Special	80	100	10	Normal
TM93	Wild Charge	Electric	Physical	90	100	15	Normal
TM100	Confide	Normal	Status	—	—	20	Normal

No.	Name	Type	Kind	Pow.	Acc.	PP	Range

● MOVES TAUGHT BY PEOPLE

Name	Type	Kind	Pow.	Acc.	PP	Range

 070 Magneton

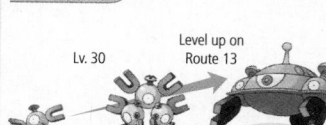

AFTER THE HALL OF FAME

CENTRAL KALOS

COASTAL KALOS

MOUNTAIN KALOS

070 | Magneton

ADVENTURE DATA

🔺 Mountain Kalos 071

Magnet Area Pokémon

✓ Magnezone

HEIGHT: 3'11" WEIGHT: 396.8 lbs.
GENDER: unknown

❌ Sometimes the magnetism emitted by Magnezone is too strong, making them attract each other so they cannot move.

✓ It evolved from exposure to a special magnetic field. Three units generate magnetism.

TYPE Electric Steel

ABILITIES
Magnet Pull
Sturdy

HIDDEN ABILITY
Analytic

STAT GROWTH RATES
HP	■■■
Attack	■■■
Defense	■■■■
Sp. Atk	■■■■■■
Sp. Def	■■■■
Speed	■■■

EGG GROUP
Mineral

🔺 EVOLUTION

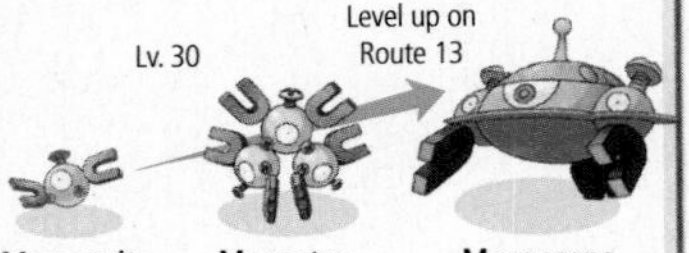

Lv. 30

Level up on Route 13

Magnemite   Magneton   Magnezone

ITEMS SOMETIMES HELD BY WILD POKÉMON
None

Damage taken in normal battles	
Normal	×0.5
Fire	×2
Water	×1
Grass	×0.5
Electric	×0.5
Ice	×0.5
Fighting	×2
Poison	×0
Ground	×4
Flying	×0.25
Psychic	×0.5
Bug	×0.5
Rock	×0.5
Ghost	×1
Dragon	×0.5
Dark	×1
Steel	×0.25
Fairy	×0.5

Damage taken in Inverse Battles	
Normal	×2
Fire	×0.5
Water	×1
Grass	×2
Electric	×2
Ice	×2
Fighting	×0.5
Poison	×2
Ground	×0.25
Flying	×4
Psychic	×2
Bug	×2
Rock	×2
Ghost	×1
Dragon	×2
Dark	×1
Steel	×4
Fairy	×2

Can be used in	
Inverse Battle	Battle Institute
—	Battle Maison
Battle Chateau	Random Matchup

Gender unknown

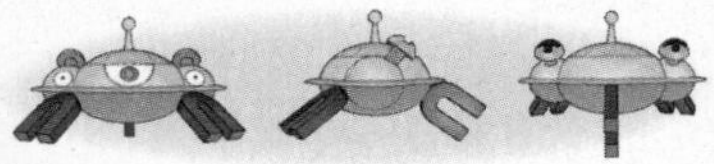

How to obtain for your Mountain Kalos Pokédex

Level up Magneton on Route 13.

Level up Magneton on Route 13.

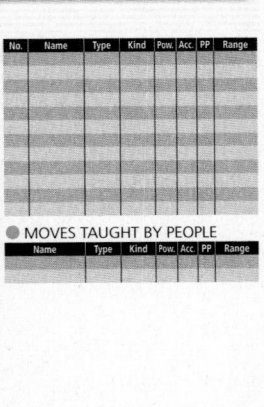

● LEVEL-UP MOVES

Lv.	Name	Type	Kind	Pow.	Acc.	PP	Range
1	Zap Cannon	Electric	Special	120	50	5	Normal
1	Magnetic Flux	Electric	Status	—	—	20	Your Party
1	Mirror Coat	Psychic	Special	—	100	20	Varies
1	Barrier	Psychic	Status	—	—	20	Self
1	Tackle	Normal	Physical	50	100	35	Normal
1	Supersonic	Normal	Status	—	55	20	Normal
1	Sonic Boom	Normal	Special	—	90	20	Normal
4	Supersonic	Normal	Status	—	55	20	Normal
7	Thunder Shock	Electric	Special	40	100	30	Normal
11	Electric Terrain	Electric	Status	—	—	10	Both Sides
15	Thunder Wave	Electric	Status	—	100	20	Normal
18	Magnet Bomb	Steel	Physical	60	—	20	Normal
21	Spark	Electric	Physical	65	100	20	Normal
25	Mirror Shot	Steel	Special	65	85	10	Normal
29	Metal Sound	Steel	Status	—	85	40	Normal
34	Electro Ball	Electric	Special	—	100	10	Normal
39	Flash Cannon	Steel	Special	80	100	10	Normal
45	Screech	Normal	Status	—	85	40	Normal
51	Discharge	Electric	Special	80	100	15	Adjacent
56	Lock-On	Normal	Status	—	—	5	Normal
62	Magnet Rise	Electric	Status	—	—	10	Self
67	Gyro Ball	Steel	Physical	—	100	5	Normal
73	Zap Cannon	Electric	Special	120	50	5	Normal

● TM & HM MOVES

No.	Name	Type	Kind	Pow.	Acc.	PP	Range
TM06	Toxic	Poison	Status	—	90	10	Normal
TM10	Hidden Power	Normal	Special	60	100	15	Normal
TM11	Sunny Day	Fire	Status	—	—	5	Both Sides
TM15	Hyper Beam	Normal	Special	150	90	5	Normal
TM16	Light Screen	Psychic	Status	—	—	30	Your Side
TM17	Protect	Normal	Status	—	—	10	Self
TM18	Rain Dance	Water	Status	—	—	5	Both Sides
TM21	Frustration	Normal	Physical	—	100	20	Normal
TM24	Thunderbolt	Electric	Special	90	100	15	Normal
TM25	Thunder	Electric	Special	110	70	10	Normal
TM27	Return	Normal	Physical	—	100	20	Normal
TM32	Double Team	Normal	Status	—	—	15	Self
TM33	Reflect	Psychic	Status	—	—	20	Your Side
TM42	Facade	Normal	Physical	70	100	20	Normal
TM44	Rest	Psychic	Status	—	—	10	Self
TM48	Round	Normal	Special	60	100	15	Normal
TM57	Charge Beam	Electric	Special	50	90	10	Normal
TM64	Explosion	Normal	Physical	250	100	5	Adjacent
TM68	Giga Impact	Normal	Physical	150	90	5	Normal
TM70	Flash	Normal	Status	—	100	20	Normal
TM72	Volt Switch	Electric	Special	70	100	20	Normal
TM73	Thunder Wave	Electric	Status	—	100	20	Normal
TM74	Gyro Ball	Steel	Physical	—	100	5	Normal
TM77	Psych Up	Normal	Status	—	—	10	Normal
TM87	Swagger	Normal	Status	—	90	15	Normal
TM88	Sleep Talk	Normal	Status	—	—	10	Self
TM90	Substitute	Normal	Status	—	—	10	Self
TM91	Flash Cannon	Steel	Special	80	100	10	Normal
TM93	Wild Charge	Electric	Physical	90	100	15	Normal
TM100	Confide	Normal	Status	—	—	20	Normal

No.	Name	Type	Kind	Pow.	Acc.	PP	Range

● MOVES TAUGHT BY PEOPLE

Name	Type	Kind	Pow.	Acc.	PP	Range

Magnezone 071

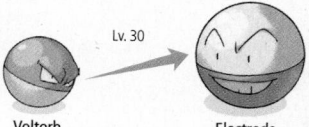

♠ Mountain Kalos 072
Ball Pokémon
☑ Voltorb

HEIGHT: 1'08" WEIGHT: 22.9 lbs.
GENDER: unknown

X It was discovered when Poké Balls were introduced. It is said that there is some connection.

Y Usually found in power plants. Easily mistaken for a Poké Ball, it has zapped many people.

TYPE Electric

ABILITIES
Soundproof
Static

HIDDEN ABILITY
Aftermath

STAT GROWTH RATES
HP ▪▪
Attack ▪▪
Defense ▪▪
Sp. Atk ▪▪▪
Sp. Def ▪▪
Speed ▪▪▪▪▪

EGG GROUP
Mineral

🔺 EVOLUTION

Lv. 30

Voltorb → Electrode

ITEMS SOMETIMES HELD BY WILD POKÉMON
None

Damage taken in normal battles		Damage taken in Inverse Battles	
Normal	×1	Normal	×1
Fire	×1	Fire	×1
Water	×1	Water	×1
Grass	×1	Grass	×1
Electric	×0.5	Electric	×2
Ice	×1	Ice	×1
Fighting	×1	Fighting	×1
Poison	×1	Poison	×1
Ground	×2	Ground	×0.5
Flying	×0.5	Flying	×2
Psychic	×1	Psychic	×1
Bug	×1	Bug	×1
Rock	×1	Rock	×1
Ghost	×1	Ghost	×1
Dragon	×1	Dragon	×1
Dark	×1	Dark	×1
Steel	×0.5	Steel	×2
Fairy	×1	Fairy	×1

Can be used in	
Inverse Battle	Battle Institute
—	Battle Maison
Battle Chateau	Random Matchup

Gender unknown

 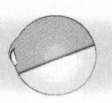 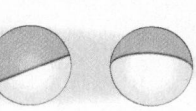

How to obtain for your Mountain Kalos Pokédex

Leave Electrode at the Pokémon Day Care with Ditto, and hatch the Egg that is found.

Leave Electrode at the Pokémon Day Care with Ditto, and hatch the Egg that is found.

● LEVEL-UP MOVES

Lv.	Name	Type	Kind	Pow.	Acc.	PP	Range
1	Charge	Electric	Status	—	—	20	Self
5	Tackle	Normal	Physical	50	100	35	Normal
8	Sonic Boom	Normal	Special	—	90	20	Normal
10	Eerie Impulse	Electric	Status	—	100	15	Normal
12	Spark	Electric	Physical	65	100	20	Normal
15	Rollout	Rock	Physical	30	90	20	Normal
19	Screech	Normal	Status	—	85	40	Normal
22	Charge Beam	Electric	Special	50	90	10	Normal
26	Light Screen	Psychic	Status	—	—	30	Your Side
29	Electro Ball	Electric	Special	—	100	10	Normal
33	Self-Destruct	Normal	Physical	200	100	5	Adjacent
36	Swift	Normal	Special	60	—	20	Many Others
40	Magnet Rise	Electric	Status	—	—	10	Self
43	Gyro Ball	Steel	Physical	—	100	5	Normal
47	Explosion	Normal	Physical	250	100	5	Adjacent
50	Mirror Coat	Psychic	Special	—	100	20	Varies

● TM & HM MOVES

No.	Name	Type	Kind	Pow.	Acc.	PP	Range
TM06	Toxic	Poison	Status	—	90	10	Normal
TM10	Hidden Power	Normal	Special	60	100	15	Normal
TM12	Taunt	Dark	Status	—	100	20	Normal
TM16	Light Screen	Psychic	Status	—	—	30	Your Side
TM17	Protect	Normal	Status	—	—	10	Self
TM18	Rain Dance	Water	Status	—	—	5	Both Sides
TM21	Frustration	Normal	Physical	—	100	20	Normal
TM24	Thunderbolt	Electric	Special	90	100	15	Normal
TM25	Thunder	Electric	Special	110	70	10	Normal
TM27	Return	Normal	Physical	—	100	20	Normal
TM32	Double Team	Normal	Status	—	—	15	Self
TM41	Torment	Dark	Status	—	100	15	Normal
TM42	Facade	Normal	Physical	70	100	20	Normal
TM44	Rest	Psychic	Status	—	—	10	Self
TM46	Thief	Dark	Physical	60	100	25	Normal
TM48	Round	Normal	Special	60	100	15	Normal
TM57	Charge Beam	Electric	Special	50	90	10	Normal
TM64	Explosion	Normal	Physical	250	100	5	Adjacent
TM70	Flash	Normal	Status	—	100	20	Normal
TM72	Volt Switch	Electric	Special	70	100	20	Normal
TM73	Thunder Wave	Electric	Status	—	100	20	Normal
TM74	Gyro Ball	Steel	Physical	—	100	5	Normal
TM87	Swagger	Normal	Status	—	90	15	Normal
TM88	Sleep Talk	Normal	Status	—	—	10	Self
TM90	Substitute	Normal	Status	—	—	10	Self
TM93	Wild Charge	Electric	Physical	90	100	15	Normal
TM100	Confide	Normal	Status	—	—	20	Normal

● MOVES TAUGHT BY PEOPLE

Name	Type	Kind	Pow.	Acc.	PP	Range

● EGG MOVES

Name	Type	Kind	Pow.	Acc.	PP	Range

AFTER THE HALL OF FAME

CENTRAL KALOS

COASTAL KALOS

MOUNTAIN KALOS

072 Voltorb

ADVENTURE DATA

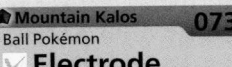

Ball Pokémon

✓ Electrode

HEIGHT: 3'11" WEIGHT: 146.8 lbs.
GENDER: unknown

TYPE Electric

ABILITIES
Soundproof
Static

HIDDEN ABILITY
Aftermath

STAT GROWTH RATES
HP	■■■
Attack	■■■
Defense	■■■
Sp. Atk	■■■■
Sp. Def	■■■
Speed	■■■■■■■

EGG GROUP
Mineral

X It explodes in response to even minor stimuli. It is feared, with the nickname of "The Bomb Ball."

Y It stores an overflowing amount of electric energy inside its body. Even a small shock makes it explode.

EVOLUTION

Lv. 30

Voltorb → Electrode

ITEMS SOMETIMES HELD BY WILD POKÉMON
None

Damage taken in normal battles	
Normal	×1
Fire	×1
Water	×1
Grass	×1
Electric	×0.5
Ice	×1
Fighting	×1
Poison	×1
Ground	×2
Flying	×0.5
Psychic	×1
Bug	×1
Rock	×1
Ghost	×1
Dragon	×1
Dark	×1
Steel	×0.5
Fairy	×1

Damage taken in Inverse Battles	
Normal	×1
Fire	×1
Water	×1
Grass	×1
Electric	×2
Ice	×1
Fighting	×1
Poison	×1
Ground	×0.5
Flying	×2
Psychic	×1
Bug	×1
Rock	×1
Ghost	×1
Dragon	×1
Dark	×1
Steel	×2
Fairy	×1

Can be used in	
Inverse Battle	Battle Institute
—	Battle Maison
Battle Chateau	Random Matchup

Gender unknown

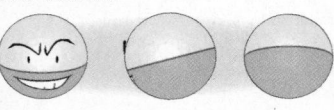

How to obtain for your Mountain Kalos Pokédex

Catch in the Lost Hotel.

Catch in the Lost Hotel.

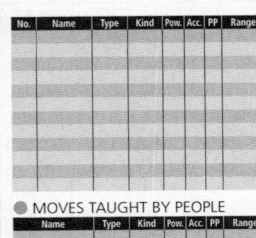

AFTER THE HALL OF FAME

CENTRAL KALOS

COASTAL KALOS

MOUNTAIN KALOS

073

Electrode

ADVENTURE DATA

● LEVEL-UP MOVES

Lv.	Name	Type	Kind	Pow.	Acc.	PP	Range
1	Magnetic Flux	Electric	Status	—	—	20	Your Party
1	Charge	Electric	Status	—	—	20	Self
1	Tackle	Normal	Physical	50	100	35	Normal
1	Sonic Boom	Normal	Special	—	90	20	Normal
1	Spark	Electric	Physical	65	100	20	Normal
1	Tackle	Normal	Physical	50	100	35	Normal
8	Eerie Impulse	Electric	Status	—	100	15	Normal
12	Spark	Electric	Physical	65	100	20	Normal
15	Rollout	Rock	Physical	30	90	20	Normal
19	Screech	Normal	Status	—	85	40	Normal
22	Charge Beam	Electric	Special	50	90	10	Normal
26	Light Screen	Psychic	Status	—	—	30	Your Side
29	Electro Ball	Electric	Special	—	100	10	Normal
35	Self-Destruct	Normal	Physical	200	100	5	Adjacent
40	Swift	Normal	Special	60	—	20	Many Others
46	Magnet Rise	Electric	Status	—	—	10	Self
51	Gyro Ball	Steel	Physical	—	100	5	Normal
57	Explosion	Normal	Physical	250	100	5	Adjacent
62	Mirror Coat	Psychic	Special	—	100	20	Varies

● TM & HM MOVES

No.	Name	Type	Kind	Pow.	Acc.	PP	Range
TM06	Toxic	Poison	Status	—	90	10	Normal
TM10	Hidden Power	Normal	Special	60	100	15	Normal
TM12	Taunt	Dark	Status	—	100	20	Normal
TM15	Hyper Beam	Normal	Special	150	90	5	Normal
TM16	Light Screen	Psychic	Status	—	—	30	Your Side
TM17	Protect	Normal	Status	—	—	10	Self
TM18	Rain Dance	Water	Status	—	—	5	Both Sides
TM21	Frustration	Normal	Physical	—	100	20	Normal
TM24	Thunderbolt	Electric	Special	90	100	15	Normal
TM25	Thunder	Electric	Special	110	70	10	Normal
TM27	Return	Normal	Physical	—	100	20	Normal
TM32	Double Team	Normal	Status	—	—	15	Self
TM41	Torment	Dark	Status	—	100	15	Normal
TM42	Facade	Normal	Physical	70	100	20	Normal
TM44	Rest	Psychic	Status	—	—	10	Self
TM46	Thief	Dark	Physical	60	100	25	Normal
TM48	Round	Normal	Special	60	100	15	Normal
TM57	Charge Beam	Electric	Special	50	90	10	Normal
TM64	Explosion	Normal	Physical	250	100	5	Adjacent
TM68	Giga Impact	Normal	Physical	150	90	5	Normal
TM70	Flash	Normal	Status	—	100	20	Normal
TM72	Volt Switch	Electric	Special	70	100	20	Normal
TM73	Thunder Wave	Electric	Status	—	100	20	Normal
TM74	Gyro Ball	Steel	Physical	—	100	5	Normal
TM87	Swagger	Normal	Status	—	90	15	Normal
TM88	Sleep Talk	Normal	Status	—	—	10	Self
TM90	Substitute	Normal	Status	—	—	10	Self
TM93	Wild Charge	Electric	Physical	90	100	15	Normal
TM100	Confide	Normal	Status	—	—	20	Normal

No.	Name	Type	Kind	Pow.	Acc.	PP	Range

● MOVES TAUGHT BY PEOPLE

Name	Type	Kind	Pow.	Acc.	PP	Range

Trash Bag Pokémon

☑ Trubbish

TYPE Poison

ABILITIES
Stench
Sticky Hold

HIDDEN ABILITY
Aftermath

HEIGHT: 2'00" WEIGHT: 68.3 lbs.
GENDER: ♂/♀

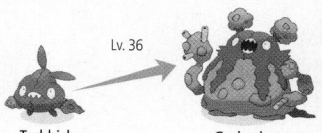

EVOLUTION

Lv. 36

Trubbish → Garbodor

X The combination of garbage bags and industrial waste caused the chemical reaction that created this Pokémon.

Y Inhaling the gas they belch will make you sleep for a week. They prefer unsanitary places.

STAT GROWTH RATES
HP	■■
Attack	■■■
Defense	■■■
Sp. Atk	■■
Sp. Def	■■■
Speed	■■■■

EGG GROUP
Mineral

ITEMS SOMETIMES HELD BY WILD POKÉMON
Black Sludge

Damage taken in normal battles		Damage taken in Inverse Battles	
Normal	×1	Normal	×1
Fire	×1	Fire	×1
Water	×1	Water	×1
Grass	×0.5	Grass	×2
Electric	×1	Electric	×1
Ice	×1	Ice	×1
Fighting	×0.5	Fighting	×2
Poison	×0.5	Poison	×2
Ground	×2	Ground	×0.5
Flying	×1	Flying	×1
Psychic	×2	Psychic	×0.5
Bug	×0.5	Bug	×2
Rock	×1	Rock	×1
Ghost	×1	Ghost	×1
Dragon	×1	Dragon	×1
Dark	×1	Dark	×1
Steel	×1	Steel	×1
Fairy	×0.5	Fairy	×2

Can be used in	
Inverse Battle	Battle Institute
—	Battle Maison
Battle Chateau	Random Matchup

Same form for ♂/♀

How to obtain for your Mountain Kalos Pokédex

Examine the trash cans that shake in the Lost Hotel.

Examine the trash cans that shake in the Lost Hotel.

● LEVEL-UP MOVES

Lv.	Name	Type	Kind	Pow.	Acc.	PP	Range
1	Pound	Normal	Physical	40	100	35	Normal
1	Poison Gas	Poison	Status	—	90	40	Many Others
3	Recycle	Normal	Status	—	—	10	Self
7	Toxic Spikes	Poison	Status	—	—	20	Other Side
12	Acid Spray	Poison	Special	40	100	20	Normal
14	Double Slap	Normal	Physical	15	85	10	Normal
18	Sludge	Poison	Special	65	100	20	Normal
23	Stockpile	Normal	Status	—	—	20	Self
23	Swallow	Normal	Status	—	—	10	Self
25	Take Down	Normal	Physical	90	85	20	Normal
29	Sludge Bomb	Poison	Special	90	100	10	Normal
34	Clear Smog	Poison	Special	50	—	15	Normal
36	Toxic	Poison	Status	—	90	10	Normal
40	Amnesia	Psychic	Status	—	—	20	Self
42	Belch	Poison	Special	120	90	10	Normal
45	Gunk Shot	Poison	Physical	120	80	5	Normal
47	Explosion	Normal	Physical	250	100	5	Adjacent

● TM & HM MOVES

No.	Name	Type	Kind	Pow.	Acc.	PP	Range
TM06	Toxic	Poison	Status	—	90	10	Normal
TM09	Venoshock	Poison	Special	65	100	10	Normal
TM10	Hidden Power	Normal	Special	60	100	15	Normal
TM11	Sunny Day	Fire	Status	—	—	5	Both Sides
TM17	Protect	Normal	Status	—	—	10	Self
TM18	Rain Dance	Water	Status	—	—	5	Both Sides
TM21	Frustration	Normal	Physical	—	100	20	Normal
TM27	Return	Normal	Physical	—	100	20	Normal
TM32	Double Team	Normal	Status	—	—	15	Self
TM34	Sludge Wave	Poison	Special	95	100	10	Adjacent
TM36	Sludge Bomb	Poison	Special	90	100	10	Normal
TM42	Facade	Normal	Physical	70	100	20	Normal
TM44	Rest	Psychic	Status	—	—	10	Self
TM45	Attract	Normal	Status	—	100	15	Normal
TM46	Thief	Dark	Physical	60	100	25	Normal
TM48	Round	Normal	Special	60	100	15	Normal
TM64	Explosion	Normal	Physical	250	100	5	Adjacent
TM66	Payback	Dark	Physical	50	100	10	Normal
TM83	Infestation	Bug	Special	20	100	20	Normal
TM87	Swagger	Normal	Status	—	90	15	Normal
TM88	Sleep Talk	Normal	Status	—	—	10	Self
TM90	Substitute	Normal	Status	—	—	10	Self
TM97	Dark Pulse	Dark	Special	80	100	15	Normal
TM100	Confide	Normal	Status	—	—	20	Normal

● MOVES TAUGHT BY PEOPLE

Name	Type	Kind	Pow.	Acc.	PP	Range

● EGG MOVES

Name	Type	Kind	Pow.	Acc.	PP	Range
Spikes	Ground	Status	—	—	20	Other Side
Rollout	Rock	Physical	30	90	20	Normal
Haze	Ice	Status	—	—	30	Both Sides
Curse	Ghost	Status	—	—	10	Varies
Rock Blast	Rock	Physical	25	90	10	Normal
Sand Attack	Ground	Status	—	100	15	Normal
Mud Sport	Ground	Status	—	—	15	Both Sides
Self-Destruct	Normal	Physical	200	100	5	Adjacent

AFTER THE HALL OF FAME

CENTRAL KALOS

COASTAL KALOS

MOUNTAIN KALOS

074 | Trubbish

ADVENTURE DATA

🏔 Mountain Kalos 075
Trash Heap Pokémon
✓ Garbodor

HEIGHT: 6'03" WEIGHT: 236.6 lbs.
GENDER: ♂/♀

X It clenches opponents with its left arm and finishes them off with foul-smelling poison gas belched from its mouth.

Y Consuming garbage makes new kinds of poison gases and liquids inside their bodies.

TYPE **Poison**

ABILITIES
Stench
Weak Armor

HIDDEN ABILITY
Aftermath

STAT GROWTH RATES
HP ⬛⬛⬛
Attack ⬛⬛⬛⬛
Defense ⬛⬛⬛⬛
Sp. Atk ⬛⬛⬛
Sp. Def ⬛⬛⬛
Speed ⬛⬛⬛⬛

EGG GROUP
Mineral

⬆ EVOLUTION

Trubbish → Lv. 36 → Garbodor

ITEMS SOMETIMES HELD BY WILD POKÉMON
Black Sludge, Nugget

Damage taken in normal battles		Damage taken in Inverse Battles	
Normal	×1	Normal	×1
Fire	×1	Fire	×1
Water	×1	Water	×1
Grass	×0.5	Grass	×2
Electric	×1	Electric	×1
Ice	×1	Ice	×1
Fighting	×0.5	Fighting	×1
Poison	×0.5	Poison	×2
Ground	×2	Ground	×0.5
Flying	×1	Flying	×1
Psychic	×2	Psychic	×0.5
Bug	×0.5	Bug	×2
Rock	×1	Rock	×1
Ghost	×1	Ghost	×1
Dragon	×1	Dragon	×1
Dark	×1	Dark	×1
Steel	×1	Steel	×1
Fairy	×0.5	Fairy	×2

Can be used in	
Inverse Battle	Battle Institute
—	Battle Maison
Battle Chateau	Random Matchup

Same form for ♂/♀

How to obtain for your Mountain Kalos Pokédex

❶ Examine the trash cans that shake in the Lost Hotel or the Pokémon Village.

❷ Level up Trubbish to Lv. 36.

❶ Examine the trash cans that shake in the Lost Hotel or the Pokémon Village.

❷ Level up Trubbish to Lv. 36.

● LEVEL-UP MOVES

Lv.	Name	Type	Kind	Pow.	Acc.	PP	Range
1	Pound	Normal	Physical	40	100	35	Normal
1	Poison Gas	Poison	Status	—	90	40	Many Others
1	Recycle	Normal	Status	—	—	10	Self
1	Toxic Spikes	Poison	Status	—	—	20	Other Side
3	Recycle	Normal	Status	—	—	10	Self
7	Toxic Spikes	Poison	Status	—	—	20	Other Side
12	Acid Spray	Poison	Special	40	100	20	Normal
14	Double Slap	Normal	Physical	15	85	10	Normal
18	Sludge	Poison	Special	65	100	20	Normal
23	Stockpile	Normal	Status	—	—	20	Self
23	Swallow	Normal	Status	—	—	10	Self
25	Body Slam	Normal	Physical	85	100	15	Normal
29	Sludge Bomb	Poison	Special	90	100	10	Normal
34	Clear Smog	Poison	Special	50	—	15	Normal
39	Toxic	Poison	Status	—	90	10	Normal
46	Amnesia	Psychic	Status	—	—	20	Self
49	Belch	Poison	Special	120	90	10	Normal
54	Gunk Shot	Poison	Physical	120	80	5	Normal
59	Explosion	Normal	Physical	250	100	5	Adjacent

● TM & HM MOVES

No.	Name	Type	Kind	Pow.	Acc.	PP	Range
TM06	Toxic	Poison	Status	—	90	10	Normal
TM09	Venoshock	Poison	Special	65	100	10	Normal
TM10	Hidden Power	Normal	Special	60	100	15	Normal
TM11	Sunny Day	Fire	Status	—	—	5	Both Sides
TM15	Hyper Beam	Normal	Special	150	90	5	Normal
TM17	Protect	Normal	Status	—	—	10	Self
TM18	Rain Dance	Water	Status	—	—	5	Both Sides
TM21	Frustration	Normal	Physical	—	100	20	Normal
TM22	Solar Beam	Grass	Special	120	100	10	Normal
TM23	Smack Down	Rock	Physical	50	100	15	Normal
TM24	Thunderbolt	Electric	Special	90	100	15	Normal
TM27	Return	Normal	Physical	—	100	20	Normal
TM29	Psychic	Psychic	Special	90	100	10	Normal
TM32	Double Team	Normal	Status	—	—	15	Self
TM34	Sludge Wave	Poison	Special	95	100	10	Adjacent
TM36	Sludge Bomb	Poison	Special	90	100	10	Normal
TM42	Facade	Normal	Physical	70	100	20	Normal
TM44	Rest	Psychic	Status	—	—	10	Self
TM45	Attract	Normal	Status	—	100	15	Normal
TM46	Thief	Dark	Physical	60	100	25	Normal
TM48	Round	Normal	Special	60	100	15	Normal
TM52	Focus Blast	Fighting	Special	120	70	5	Normal
TM56	Fling	Dark	Physical	—	100	10	Normal
TM64	Explosion	Normal	Physical	250	100	5	Adjacent
TM66	Payback	Dark	Physical	50	100	10	Normal
TM68	Giga Impact	Normal	Physical	150	90	5	Normal
TM69	Rock Polish	Rock	Status	—	—	20	Self
TM83	Infestation	Bug	Special	20	100	20	Normal
TM87	Swagger	Normal	Status	—	90	15	Normal
TM88	Sleep Talk	Normal	Status	—	—	10	Self
TM90	Substitute	Normal	Status	—	—	10	Self
TM97	Dark Pulse	Dark	Special	80	100	15	Normal
TM100	Confide	Normal	Status	—	—	20	Normal

No.	Name	Type	Kind	Pow.	Acc.	PP	Range

● MOVES TAUGHT BY PEOPLE

Name	Type	Kind	Pow.	Acc.	PP	Range

Mountain Kalos 076
Pig Pokémon
☑ Swinub

HEIGHT: 1'04" WEIGHT: 14.3 lbs.
GENDER: ♂/♀

TYPE [Ice] [Ground]

ABILITIES
Oblivious
Snow Cloak

HIDDEN ABILITY
Thick Fat

STAT GROWTH RATES
HP	■■
Attack	■■■
Defense	■■
Sp. Atk	■
Sp. Def	■
Speed	■■■

EGG GROUP
Field

X It rubs its snout on the ground to find and dig up food. It sometimes discovers hot springs.

Y If it smells something enticing, it dashes off headlong to find the source of the aroma.

EVOLUTION

Swinub — Lv. 33 → Piloswine — Level up with Ancient Power* → Mamoswine

ITEMS SOMETIMES HELD BY WILD POKÉMON
None

Damage taken in normal battles		Damage taken in Inverse Battles	
Normal	×1	Normal	×1
Fire	×2	Fire	×0.5
Water	×2	Water	×0.5
Grass	×2	Grass	×0.5
Electric	×0	Electric	×2
Ice	×1	Ice	×1
Fighting	×2	Fighting	×0.5
Poison	×0.5	Poison	×2
Ground	×1	Ground	×1
Flying	×1	Flying	×1
Psychic	×1	Psychic	×1
Bug	×1	Bug	×1
Rock	×1	Rock	×1
Ghost	×1	Ghost	×1
Dragon	×1	Dragon	×1
Dark	×1	Dark	×1
Steel	×2	Steel	×0.5
Fairy	×1	Fairy	×1

Can be used in	
Inverse Battle	Battle Institute
—	Battle Maison
Battle Chateau	Random Matchup

Same form for ♂/♀

How to obtain for your Mountain Kalos Pokédex

Leave Piloswine or Mamoswine at the Pokémon Day Care, and hatch the Egg that is found.

Leave Piloswine or Mamoswine at the Pokémon Day Care, and hatch the Egg that is found.

● LEVEL-UP MOVES

Lv.	Name	Type	Kind	Pow.	Acc.	PP	Range
1	Tackle	Normal	Physical	50	100	35	Normal
1	Odor Sleuth	Normal	Status	—	—	40	Normal
5	Mud Sport	Ground	Status	—	—	15	Both Sides
8	Powder Snow	Ice	Special	40	100	25	Many Others
11	Mud-Slap	Ground	Special	20	100	10	Normal
14	Endure	Normal	Status	—	—	10	Self
18	Mud Bomb	Ground	Special	65	85	10	Normal
21	Icy Wind	Ice	Special	55	95	15	Many Others
24	Ice Shard	Ice	Physical	40	100	30	Normal
28	Take Down	Normal	Physical	90	85	20	Normal
35	Mist	Ice	Status	—	—	30	Your Side
37	Earthquake	Ground	Physical	100	100	10	Adjacent
40	Flail	Normal	Physical	—	100	15	Normal
44	Blizzard	Ice	Special	110	70	5	Many Others
48	Amnesia	Psychic	Status	—	—	20	Self

● TM & HM MOVES

No.	Name	Type	Kind	Pow.	Acc.	PP	Range
TM05	Roar	Normal	Status	—	—	20	Normal
TM06	Toxic	Poison	Status	—	90	10	Normal
TM07	Hail	Ice	Status	—	—	10	Both Sides
TM10	Hidden Power	Normal	Special	60	100	15	Normal
TM13	Ice Beam	Ice	Special	90	100	10	Normal
TM14	Blizzard	Ice	Special	110	70	5	Many Others
TM15	Light Screen	Psychic	Status	—	—	30	Your Side
TM17	Protect	Normal	Status	—	—	10	Self
TM18	Rain Dance	Water	Status	—	—	5	Both Sides
TM21	Frustration	Normal	Physical	—	100	20	Normal
TM26	Earthquake	Ground	Physical	100	100	10	Adjacent
TM27	Return	Normal	Physical	—	100	20	Normal
TM28	Dig	Ground	Physical	80	100	10	Normal
TM32	Double Team	Normal	Status	—	—	15	Self
TM33	Reflect	Psychic	Status	—	—	20	Your Side
TM37	Sandstorm	Rock	Status	—	—	10	Both Sides
TM39	Rock Tomb	Rock	Physical	60	95	15	Normal
TM42	Facade	Normal	Physical	70	100	20	Normal
TM44	Rest	Psychic	Status	—	—	10	Self
TM45	Attract	Normal	Status	—	100	15	Normal
TM48	Round	Normal	Special	60	100	15	Normal
TM78	Bulldoze	Ground	Physical	60	100	20	Adjacent
TM80	Rock Slide	Rock	Physical	75	90	10	Many Others
TM87	Swagger	Normal	Status	—	90	15	Normal
TM88	Sleep Talk	Normal	Status	—	—	10	Self
TM90	Substitute	Normal	Status	—	—	10	Self
TM94	Rock Smash	Fighting	Physical	40	100	15	Normal
TM100	Confide	Normal	Status	—	—	20	Normal
HM04	Strength	Normal	Physical	80	100	15	Normal

● MOVES TAUGHT BY PEOPLE

Name	Type	Kind	Pow.	Acc.	PP	Range

● EGG MOVES

Name	Type	Kind	Pow.	Acc.	PP	Range
Take Down	Normal	Physical	90	85	20	Normal
Bite	Dark	Physical	60	100	25	Normal
Body Slam	Normal	Physical	85	100	15	Normal
Ancient Power	Rock	Special	60	100	5	Normal
Mud Shot	Ground	Special	55	95	15	Normal
Icicle Spear	Ice	Physical	25	100	30	Normal
Double-Edge	Normal	Physical	120	100	15	Normal
Fissure	Ground	Physical	—	30	5	Normal
Curse	Ghost	Status	—	—	10	Varies
Avalanche	Ice	Physical	60	100	10	Normal
Stealth Rock	Rock	Status	—	—	20	Other Side
Icicle Crash	Ice	Physical	85	90	10	Normal
Freeze-Dry	Ice	Special	70	100	20	Normal

*Give Madam Reminder in Dendemille Town a Heart Scale to have her teach Piloswine the move Ancient Power.

AFTER THE HALL OF FAME

CENTRAL KALOS

COASTAL KALOS

MOUNTAIN KALOS

076 Swinub

ADVENTURE DATA

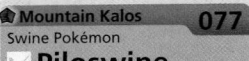

Mountain Kalos 077
Swine Pokémon

☑ Piloswine

HEIGHT: 3'07"   WEIGHT: 123.0 lbs.
GENDER: ♂/♀

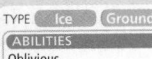

TYPE Ice Ground

ABILITIES
Oblivious
Snow Cloak

HIDDEN ABILITY
Thick Fat

STAT GROWTH RATES
HP	■■■■
Attack	■■■■■
Defense	■■■■
Sp. Atk	■■■
Sp. Def	■■■
Speed	■■■

EGG GROUP
Field

X Although its legs are short, its rugged hooves prevent it from slipping, even on icy ground.

Y Because the long hair all over its body obscures its sight, it just keeps charging repeatedly.

EVOLUTION

| Swinub | Lv. 33 → | Piloswine | Level up with Ancient Power* → | Mamoswine |

ITEMS SOMETIMES HELD BY WILD POKÉMON
None

Can be used in
Inverse Battle
—
Battle Chateau
Battle Institute
Battle Maison
Random Matchup

Damage taken in normal battles
Normal	×1
Fire	×2
Water	×2
Grass	×2
Electric	×0
Ice	×1
Fighting	×2
Poison	×0.5
Ground	×1
Flying	×1
Psychic	×1
Bug	×1
Rock	×1
Ghost	×1
Dragon	×1
Dark	×1
Steel	×2
Fairy	×1

Damage taken in Inverse Battles
Normal	×1
Fire	×0.5
Water	×0.5
Grass	×0.5
Electric	×2
Ice	×1
Fighting	×0.5
Poison	×2
Ground	×1
Flying	×1
Psychic	×1
Bug	×1
Rock	×1
Ghost	×1
Dragon	×1
Dark	×1
Steel	×0.5
Fairy	×1

How to obtain for your Mountain Kalos Pokédex

❶ Catch on Frost Cavern 1F.	❶ Catch on Frost Cavern 1F.
❷ Catch on Frost Cavern 2F.	❷ Catch on Frost Cavern 2F.

♂   ♀

The male has longer tusks. The female has shorter tusks.

● LEVEL-UP MOVES
Lv.	Name	Type	Kind	Pow.	Acc.	PP	Range
1	Ancient Power	Rock	Special	60	100	5	Normal
1	Peck	Flying	Physical	35	100	35	Normal
1	Odor Sleuth	Normal	Status	—	—	40	Normal
1	Mud Sport	Ground	Status	—	—	15	Both Sides
1	Powder Snow	Ice	Special	40	100	25	Many Others
5	Mud Sport	Ground	Status	—	—	15	Both Sides
8	Powder Snow	Ice	Special	40	100	25	Many Others
11	Mud-Slap	Ground	Special	20	100	10	Normal
14	Endure	Normal	Status	—	—	10	Self
18	Mud Bomb	Ground	Special	65	85	10	Normal
21	Icy Wind	Ice	Special	55	95	15	Many Others
24	Ice Fang	Ice	Physical	65	95	15	Normal
28	Take Down	Normal	Physical	90	85	20	Normal
33	Fury Attack	Normal	Physical	15	85	20	Normal
37	Mist	Ice	Status	—	—	30	Your Side
41	Thrash	Normal	Physical	120	100	10	1 Random
46	Earthquake	Ground	Physical	100	100	10	Adjacent
52	Blizzard	Ice	Special	110	70	5	Many Others
58	Amnesia	Psychic	Status	—	—	20	Self

● TM & HM MOVES
No.	Name	Type	Kind	Pow.	Acc.	PP	Range
TM05	Roar	Normal	Status	—	—	20	Normal
TM06	Toxic	Poison	Status	—	90	10	Normal
TM07	Hail	Ice	Status	—	—	10	Both Sides
TM10	Hidden Power	Normal	Special	60	100	15	Normal
TM13	Ice Beam	Ice	Special	90	100	10	Normal
TM14	Blizzard	Ice	Special	110	70	5	Many Others
TM15	Hyper Beam	Normal	Special	150	90	5	Normal
TM16	Light Screen	Psychic	Status	—	—	30	Your Side
TM17	Protect	Normal	Status	—	—	10	Self
TM18	Rain Dance	Water	Status	—	—	5	Both Sides
TM21	Frustration	Normal	Physical	—	100	20	Normal
TM26	Earthquake	Ground	Physical	100	100	10	Adjacent
TM27	Return	Normal	Physical	—	100	20	Normal
TM28	Dig	Ground	Physical	80	100	10	Normal
TM32	Double Team	Normal	Status	—	—	15	Self
TM33	Reflect	Psychic	Status	—	—	20	Your Side
TM37	Sandstorm	Rock	Status	—	—	10	Both Sides
TM39	Rock Tomb	Rock	Physical	60	95	15	Normal
TM42	Facade	Normal	Physical	70	100	20	Normal
TM44	Rest	Psychic	Status	—	—	10	Self
TM45	Attract	Normal	Status	—	100	15	Normal
TM48	Round	Normal	Special	60	100	15	Normal
TM68	Giga Impact	Normal	Physical	150	90	5	Normal
TM71	Stone Edge	Rock	Physical	100	80	5	Normal
TM78	Bulldoze	Ground	Physical	60	100	20	Adjacent
TM80	Rock Slide	Rock	Physical	75	90	10	Many Others
TM87	Swagger	Normal	Status	—	90	15	Normal
TM88	Sleep Talk	Normal	Status	—	—	10	Self
TM90	Substitute	Normal	Status	—	—	10	Self
TM94	Rock Smash	Fighting	Physical	40	100	15	Normal
TM100	Confide	Normal	Status	—	—	20	Normal
HM04	Strength	Normal	Physical	80	100	15	Normal

No.	Name	Type	Kind	Pow.	Acc.	PP	Range

● MOVES TAUGHT BY PEOPLE
Name	Type	Kind	Pow.	Acc.	PP	Range

AFTER THE HALL OF FAME
CENTRAL KALOS
COASTAL KALOS
MOUNTAIN KALOS
077
Piloswine
ADVENTURE DATA

*Give Madam Reminder in Dendemille Town a Heart Scale to have her teach Piloswine the move Ancient Power.

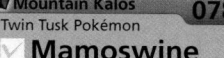

Twin Tusk Pokémon

☑ **Mamoswine**

HEIGHT: 8'02" WEIGHT: 641.5 lbs.
GENDER: ♂/♀

❌ A frozen Mamoswine was dug from ice dating back 10,000 years. This Pokémon has been around a long, long, long time.

🔽 Its impressive tusks are made of ice. The population thinned when it turned warm after the ice age.

TYPE	Ice	Ground

ABILITIES
Oblivious
Snow Cloak

HIDDEN ABILITY
Thick Fat

STAT GROWTH RATES
HP	▪▪▪▪
Attack	▪▪▪▪▪▪▪
Defense	▪▪▪▪
Sp. Atk	▪▪▪
Sp. Def	▪▪▪
Speed	▪▪▪▪

EGG GROUP
Field

⬥ EVOLUTION

Lv. 33 ➤ Level up with Ancient Power*

Swinub — Piloswine — Mamoswine

ITEMS SOMETIMES HELD BY WILD POKÉMON
None

Damage taken in normal battles			Damage taken in Inverse Battles			Can be used in
Normal	×1		Normal	×1		Inverse Battle
Fire	×2		Fire	×0.5		—
Water	×2		Water	×0.5		Battle Chateau
Grass	×2		Grass	×0.5		Battle Institute
Electric	×0		Electric	×2		Battle Maison
Ice	×1		Ice	×1		Random Matchup
Fighting	×2		Fighting	×0.5		
Poison	×0.5		Poison	×2		
Ground	×1		Ground	×1		
Flying	×1		Flying	×1		
Psychic	×1		Psychic	×1		
Bug	×1		Bug	×1		
Rock	×1		Rock	×1		
Ghost	×1		Ghost	×1		
Dragon	×1		Dragon	×1		
Dark	×1		Dark	×1		
Steel	×2		Steel	×0.5		
Fairy	×1		Fairy	×1		

How to obtain for your Mountain Kalos Pokédex

Have Piloswine learn Ancient Power, then level it up.	Have Piloswine learn Ancient Power, then level it up.

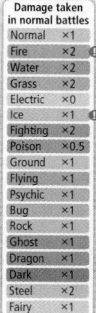
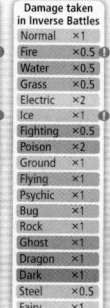

♂   ♀

The male has longer tusks. The female has shorter tusks.

● LEVEL-UP MOVES

Lv.	Name	Type	Kind	Pow.	Acc.	PP	Range
1	Scary Face	Normal	Status	—	100	10	Normal
1	Ancient Power	Rock	Special	60	100	5	Normal
1	Peck	Flying	Physical	35	100	35	Normal
1	Odor Sleuth	Normal	Status	—	—	40	Normal
1	Mud Sport	Ground	Status	—	—	15	Both Sides
1	Powder Snow	Ice	Special	40	100	25	Many Others
5	Mud Sport	Ground	Status	—	—	15	Both Sides
8	Powder Snow	Ice	Special	40	100	25	Many Others
11	Mud-Slap	Ground	Special	20	100	10	Normal
14	Endure	Normal	Status	—	—	10	Self
18	Mud Bomb	Ground	Special	65	85	10	Normal
21	Hail	Ice	Status	—	—	10	Both Sides
24	Ice Fang	Ice	Physical	65	95	15	Normal
28	Take Down	Normal	Physical	90	85	20	Normal
33	Double Hit	Normal	Physical	35	90	10	Normal
37	Mist	Ice	Status	—	—	30	Your Side
41	Thrash	Normal	Physical	120	100	10	1 Random
46	Earthquake	Ground	Physical	100	100	10	Adjacent
52	Blizzard	Ice	Special	110	70	5	Many Others
58	Scary Face	Normal	Status	—	100	10	Normal

● TM & HM MOVES

No.	Name	Type	Kind	Pow.	Acc.	PP	Range
TM05	Roar	Normal	Status	—	—	20	Normal
TM06	Toxic	Poison	Status	—	90	10	Normal
TM07	Hail	Ice	Status	—	—	10	Both Sides
TM10	Hidden Power	Normal	Special	60	100	15	Normal
TM13	Ice Beam	Ice	Special	90	100	10	Normal
TM14	Blizzard	Ice	Special	110	70	5	Many Others
TM15	Hyper Beam	Normal	Special	150	90	5	Normal
TM16	Light Screen	Psychic	Status	—	—	30	Your Side
TM17	Protect	Normal	Status	—	—	10	Self
TM18	Rain Dance	Water	Status	—	—	5	Both Sides
TM21	Frustration	Normal	Physical	—	100	20	Normal
TM26	Earthquake	Ground	Physical	100	100	10	Adjacent
TM27	Return	Normal	Physical	—	100	20	Normal
TM28	Dig	Ground	Physical	80	100	10	Normal
TM32	Double Team	Normal	Status	—	—	15	Self
TM33	Reflect	Psychic	Status	—	—	20	Your Side
TM37	Sandstorm	Rock	Status	—	—	10	Both Sides
TM39	Rock Tomb	Rock	Physical	60	95	15	Normal
TM42	Facade	Normal	Physical	70	100	20	Normal
TM44	Rest	Psychic	Status	—	—	10	Self
TM45	Attract	Normal	Status	—	100	15	Normal
TM48	Round	Normal	Special	60	100	15	Normal
TM68	Giga Impact	Normal	Physical	150	90	5	Normal
TM71	Stone Edge	Rock	Physical	100	80	5	Normal
TM78	Bulldoze	Ground	Physical	60	100	20	Adjacent
TM80	Rock Slide	Rock	Physical	75	90	10	Many Others
TM87	Swagger	Normal	Status	—	90	15	Normal
TM88	Sleep Talk	Normal	Status	—	—	10	Self
TM90	Substitute	Normal	Status	—	—	10	Self
TM94	Rock Smash	Fighting	Physical	40	100	15	Normal
TM100	Confide	Normal	Status	—	—	20	Normal
HM04	Strength	Normal	Physical	80	100	15	Normal

No.	Name	Type	Kind	Pow.	Acc.	PP	Range

● MOVES TAUGHT BY PEOPLE

Name	Type	Kind	Pow.	Acc.	PP	Range

*Give Madam Reminder in Dendemille Town a Heart Scale to have her teach Piloswine the move Ancient Power.

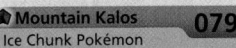

Mountain Kalos — 079

Ice Chunk Pokémon

Bergmite

HEIGHT: 3'03" WEIGHT: 219.4 lbs.
GENDER: ♂/♀

X It blocks opponents' attacks with the ice that shields its body. It uses cold air to repair any cracks with new ice.

Y Using air of -150 degrees Fahrenheit, they freeze opponents solid. They live in herds above the snow line on mountains.

TYPE: Ice

ABILITIES
Own Tempo
Ice Body

HIDDEN ABILITY
Sturdy

STAT GROWTH RATES
HP ■■
Attack ■■■■
Defense ■■■■
Sp. Atk ■■
Sp. Def ■■
Speed ■■

EGG GROUP
Monster

EVOLUTION

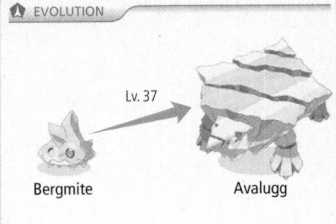

Bergmite → (Lv. 37) → Avalugg

ITEMS SOMETIMES HELD BY WILD POKÉMON
None

	Damage taken in normal battles		Damage taken in Inverse Battles
Normal	×1	Normal	×1
Fire	×2	Fire	×0.5
Water	×1	Water	×1
Grass	×1	Grass	×1
Electric	×1	Electric	×2
Ice	×0.5	Ice	×2
Fighting	×2	Fighting	×0.5
Poison	×1	Poison	×1
Ground	×1	Ground	×1
Flying	×1	Flying	×1
Psychic	×1	Psychic	×1
Bug	×1	Bug	×1
Rock	×2	Rock	×0.5
Ghost	×1	Ghost	×1
Dragon	×1	Dragon	×1
Dark	×1	Dark	×1
Steel	×2	Steel	×0.5
Fairy	×1	Fairy	×1

Can be used in

Inverse Battle	Battle Institute
—	Battle Maison
Battle Chateau	Random Matchup

Same form for ♂/♀

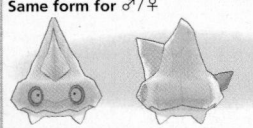

How to obtain for your Mountain Kalos Pokédex

❶ Catch on Frost Cavern 1F.
❷ Catch on Frost Cavern 2F.

❶ Catch on Frost Cavern 1F.
❷ Catch on Frost Cavern 2F.

LEVEL-UP MOVES

Lv.	Name	Type	Kind	Pow.	Acc.	PP	Range
1	Tackle	Normal	Physical	50	100	35	Normal
1	Bite	Dark	Physical	60	100	25	Normal
1	Harden	Normal	Status	—	—	30	Self
5	Powder Snow	Ice	Special	40	100	25	Many Others
10	Icy Wind	Ice	Special	55	95	15	Many Others
15	Take Down	Normal	Physical	90	85	20	Normal
20	Sharpen	Normal	Status	—	—	30	Self
22	Curse	Ghost	Status	—	—	10	Varies
26	Ice Fang	Ice	Physical	65	95	15	Normal
30	Ice Ball	Ice	Physical	30	90	20	Normal
35	Rapid Spin	Normal	Physical	20	100	40	Normal
39	Avalanche	Ice	Physical	60	100	10	Normal
43	Blizzard	Ice	Special	110	70	5	Many Others
47	Recover	Normal	Status	—	—	10	Self
49	Double-Edge	Normal	Physical	120	100	15	Normal

TM & HM MOVES

No.	Name	Type	Kind	Pow.	Acc.	PP	Range
TM06	Toxic	Poison	Status	—	90	10	Normal
TM07	Hail	Ice	Status	—	—	10	Both Sides
TM10	Hidden Power	Normal	Special	60	100	15	Normal
TM13	Ice Beam	Ice	Special	90	100	10	Normal
TM14	Blizzard	Ice	Special	110	70	5	Many Others
TM17	Protect	Normal	Status	—	—	10	Self
TM18	Rain Dance	Water	Status	—	—	5	Both Sides
TM20	Safeguard	Normal	Status	—	—	25	Your Side
TM21	Frustration	Normal	Physical	—	100	20	Normal
TM27	Return	Normal	Physical	—	100	20	Normal
TM32	Double Team	Normal	Status	—	—	15	Self
TM39	Rock Tomb	Rock	Physical	60	95	15	Normal
TM42	Facade	Normal	Physical	70	100	20	Normal
TM44	Rest	Psychic	Status	—	—	10	Self
TM45	Attract	Normal	Status	—	100	15	Normal
TM48	Round	Normal	Special	60	100	15	Normal
TM69	Rock Polish	Rock	Status	—	—	20	Self
TM70	Flash	Normal	Status	—	100	20	Normal
TM71	Stone Edge	Rock	Physical	100	80	5	Normal
TM74	Gyro Ball	Steel	Special	—	100	5	Normal
TM79	Frost Breath	Ice	Special	60	90	10	Normal
TM80	Rock Slide	Rock	Physical	75	90	10	Many Others
TM87	Swagger	Normal	Status	—	90	15	Normal
TM88	Sleep Talk	Normal	Status	—	—	10	Self
TM90	Substitute	Normal	Status	—	—	10	Self
TM91	Flash Cannon	Steel	Special	80	100	10	Normal
TM94	Rock Smash	Fighting	Physical	40	100	15	Normal
TM100	Confide	Normal	Status	—	—	20	Normal
HM03	Surf	Water	Special	90	100	15	Adjacent
HM04	Strength	Normal	Physical	80	100	15	Normal

MOVES TAUGHT BY PEOPLE

Name	Type	Kind	Pow.	Acc.	PP	Range

EGG MOVES

Name	Type	Kind	Pow.	Acc.	PP	Range
Recover	Normal	Status	—	—	10	Self
Mist	Ice	Status	—	—	30	Your Side
Barrier	Psychic	Status	—	—	20	Self
Mirror Coat	Psychic	Special	—	100	20	Varies

AFTER THE HALL OF FAME

CENTRAL KALOS

COASTAL KALOS

MOUNTAIN KALOS

079

Bergmite

ADVENTURE DATA

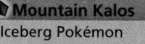

Mountain Kalos
Iceberg Pokémon
080

 Avalugg

HEIGHT: 6'07"   WEIGHT: 1113.3 lbs.
GENDER: ♂/♀

 Its ice-covered body is as hard as steel. Its cumbersome frame crushes anything that stands in its way.

The way several Bergmite huddle on its back makes it look like an aircraft carrier made of ice.

TYPE Ice

ABILITIES
Own Tempo
Ice Body

HIDDEN ABILITY
Sturdy

STAT GROWTH RATES
HP	▪▪▪▪
Attack	▪▪▪▪▪▪
Defense	▪▪▪▪▪▪▪▪
Sp. Atk	▪▪
Sp. Def	▪▪
Speed	▪▪

EGG GROUP
Monster

EVOLUTION

Bergmite — Lv. 37 → Avalugg

ITEMS SOMETIMES HELD BY WILD POKÉMON
None

Damage taken in normal battles		Damage taken in Inverse Battles	
Normal	×1	Normal	×1
Fire	×2	Fire	×0.5
Water	×1	Water	×1
Grass	×1	Grass	×1
Electric	×1	Electric	×1
Ice	×0.5	Ice	×2
Fighting	×2	Fighting	×0.5
Poison	×1	Poison	×1
Ground	×1	Ground	×1
Flying	×1	Flying	×1
Psychic	×1	Psychic	×1
Bug	×1	Bug	×1
Rock	×2	Rock	×0.5
Ghost	×1	Ghost	×1
Dragon	×1	Dragon	×1
Dark	×1	Dark	×1
Steel	×2	Steel	×0.5
Fairy	×1	Fairy	×1

Can be used in	
Inverse Battle	Battle Institute
—	Battle Maison
Battle Chateau	Random Matchup

Same form for ♂/♀

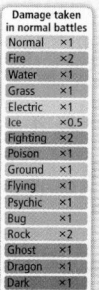

How to obtain for your Mountain Kalos Pokédex

Level up Bergmite to Lv. 37.   Level up Bergmite to Lv. 37.

● LEVEL-UP MOVES

Lv.	Name	Type	Kind	Pow.	Acc.	PP	Range
1	Iron Defense	Steel	Status	—	—	15	Self
1	Crunch	Dark	Physical	80	100	15	Normal
1	Skull Bash	Normal	Physical	130	100	10	Normal
1	Tackle	Normal	Physical	50	100	35	Normal
1	Bite	Dark	Physical	60	100	25	Normal
1	Harden	Normal	Status	—	—	30	Self
5	Powder Snow	Ice	Special	40	100	25	Many Others
10	Icy Wind	Ice	Special	55	95	15	Many Others
15	Take Down	Normal	Physical	90	85	20	Normal
20	Sharpen	Normal	Status	—	—	30	Self
22	Curse	Ghost	Status	—	—	10	Varies
26	Ice Fang	Ice	Physical	65	95	15	Normal
30	Ice Ball	Ice	Physical	30	90	20	Normal
35	Rapid Spin	Normal	Physical	20	100	40	Normal
42	Avalanche	Ice	Physical	60	100	10	Normal
46	Blizzard	Ice	Special	110	70	5	Many Others
51	Recover	Normal	Status	—	—	10	Self
56	Double-Edge	Normal	Physical	120	100	15	Normal
60	Skull Bash	Normal	Physical	130	100	10	Normal
65	Crunch	Dark	Physical	80	100	15	Normal

● TM & HM MOVES

No.	Name	Type	Kind	Pow.	Acc.	PP	Range
TM05	Roar	Normal	Status	—	—	20	Normal
TM06	Toxic	Poison	Status	—	90	10	Normal
TM07	Hail	Ice	Status	—	—	10	Both Sides
TM10	Hidden Power	Normal	Special	60	100	15	Normal
TM13	Ice Beam	Ice	Special	90	100	10	Normal
TM14	Blizzard	Ice	Special	110	70	5	Many Others
TM15	Hyper Beam	Normal	Special	150	90	5	Normal
TM17	Protect	Normal	Status	—	—	10	Self
TM18	Rain Dance	Water	Status	—	—	5	Both Sides
TM20	Safeguard	Normal	Status	—	—	25	Your Side
TM21	Frustration	Normal	Physical	—	100	20	Normal
TM26	Earthquake	Ground	Physical	100	100	10	Adjacent
TM27	Return	Normal	Physical	—	100	20	Normal
TM32	Double Team	Normal	Status	—	—	15	Self
TM39	Rock Tomb	Rock	Physical	60	95	15	Normal
TM42	Facade	Normal	Physical	70	100	20	Normal
TM44	Rest	Psychic	Status	—	—	10	Self
TM45	Attract	Normal	Status	—	100	15	Normal
TM48	Round	Normal	Special	60	100	15	Normal
TM68	Giga Impact	Normal	Physical	150	90	5	Normal
TM69	Rock Polish	Rock	Status	—	—	20	Self
TM70	Flash	Normal	Status	—	100	20	Normal
TM71	Stone Edge	Rock	Physical	100	80	5	Normal
TM74	Gyro Ball	Steel	Physical	—	100	5	Normal
TM78	Bulldoze	Ground	Physical	60	100	20	Adjacent
TM79	Frost Breath	Ice	Special	60	90	10	Normal
TM80	Rock Slide	Rock	Physical	75	90	10	Many Others
TM87	Swagger	Normal	Status	—	90	15	Normal
TM88	Sleep Talk	Normal	Status	—	—	10	Self
TM90	Substitute	Normal	Status	—	—	10	Self
TM91	Flash Cannon	Steel	Special	80	100	10	Normal
TM94	Rock Smash	Fighting	Physical	40	100	15	Normal
TM100	Confide	Normal	Status	—	—	20	Normal

No.	Name	Type	Kind	Pow.	Acc.	PP	Range
HM03	Surf	Water	Special	90	100	15	Adjacent
HM04	Strength	Normal	Physical	80	100	15	Normal

● MOVES TAUGHT BY PEOPLE

Name	Type	Kind	Pow.	Acc.	PP	Range

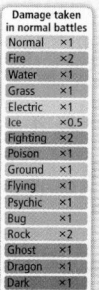

AFTER THE HALL OF FAME

CENTRAL KALOS

COASTAL KALOS

MOUNTAIN KALOS

080 | Avalugg

ADVENTURE DATA

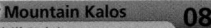

Mountain Kalos 081

Chill Pokémon

Cubchoo

HEIGHT: 1'08" WEIGHT: 18.7 lbs.
GENDER: ♂/♀

X Its nose is always running. It sniffs the snot back up because the mucus provides the raw material for its moves.

Y Their snot is a barometer of health. When healthy, their snot is sticky and the power of their ice moves increases.

TYPE: Ice

ABILITY
Snow Cloak

HIDDEN ABILITY
Rattled

STAT GROWTH RATES
HP ▪▪
Attack ▪▪▪▪
Defense ▪▪▪
Sp. Atk ▪▪▪
Sp. Def ▪▪
Speed ▪▪

EGG GROUP
Field

EVOLUTION

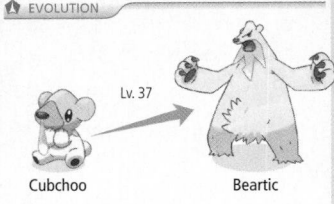

Cubchoo — Lv. 37 → Beartic

ITEMS SOMETIMES HELD BY WILD POKÉMON
None

Damage taken in normal battles	
Normal	×1
Fire	×2
Water	×1
Grass	×1
Electric	×1
Ice	×0.5
Fighting	×2
Poison	×1
Ground	×1
Flying	×1
Psychic	×1
Bug	×1
Rock	×2
Ghost	×1
Dragon	×1
Dark	×1
Steel	×2
Fairy	×1

Damage taken in Inverse Battles	
Normal	×1
Fire	×0.5
Water	×1
Grass	×1
Electric	×1
Ice	×2
Fighting	×0.5
Poison	×1
Ground	×1
Flying	×1
Psychic	×1
Bug	×1
Rock	×0.5
Ghost	×1
Dragon	×1
Dark	×1
Steel	×0.5
Fairy	×1

Can be used in	
Inverse Battle	Battle Institute
——	Battle Maison
Battle Chateau	Random Matchup

Same form for ♂/♀

How to obtain for your Mountain Kalos Pokédex

❶ Catch in a Horde Encounter on Frost Cavern 1F.
❷ Catch in a Horde Encounter on Frost Cavern 2F.

❶ Catch in a Horde Encounter on Frost Cavern 1F.
❷ Catch in a Horde Encounter on Frost Cavern 2F.

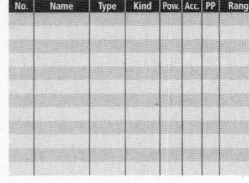

081 Cubchoo

● LEVEL-UP MOVES

Lv.	Name	Type	Kind	Pow.	Acc.	PP	Range
1	Growl	Normal	Status	—	100	40	Many Others
5	Powder Snow	Ice	Special	40	100	25	Many Others
9	Bide	Normal	Physical	—	—	10	Self
13	Icy Wind	Ice	Special	55	95	15	Many Others
15	Play Nice	Normal	Status	—	—	20	Normal
17	Fury Swipes	Normal	Physical	18	80	15	Normal
21	Brine	Water	Special	65	100	10	Normal
25	Endure	Normal	Status	—	—	10	Self
29	Charm	Fairy	Status	—	100	20	Normal
33	Slash	Normal	Physical	70	100	20	Normal
36	Flail	Normal	Physical	—	100	15	Normal
41	Rest	Psychic	Status	—	—	10	Self
45	Blizzard	Ice	Special	110	70	5	Many Others
49	Hail	Ice	Status	—	—	10	Both Sides
53	Thrash	Normal	Physical	120	100	10	1 Random
57	Sheer Cold	Ice	Special	—	30	5	Normal

● TM & HM MOVES

No.	Name	Type	Kind	Pow.	Acc.	PP	Range
TM01	Hone Claws	Dark	Status	—	—	15	Self
TM06	Toxic	Poison	Status	—	90	10	Normal
TM07	Hail	Ice	Status	—	—	10	Both Sides
TM10	Hidden Power	Normal	Special	60	100	15	Normal
TM13	Ice Beam	Ice	Special	90	100	10	Normal
TM14	Blizzard	Ice	Special	110	70	5	Many Others
TM17	Protect	Normal	Status	—	—	10	Self
TM18	Rain Dance	Water	Status	—	—	5	Both Sides
TM21	Frustration	Normal	Physical	—	100	20	Normal
TM27	Return	Normal	Physical	—	100	20	Normal
TM28	Dig	Ground	Physical	80	100	10	Normal
TM32	Double Team	Normal	Status	—	—	15	Self
TM39	Rock Tomb	Rock	Physical	60	95	15	Normal
TM40	Aerial Ace	Flying	Physical	60	—	20	Normal
TM42	Facade	Normal	Physical	70	100	20	Normal
TM44	Rest	Psychic	Status	—	—	10	Self
TM45	Attract	Normal	Status	—	100	15	Normal
TM48	Round	Normal	Special	60	100	15	Normal
TM49	Echoed Voice	Normal	Special	40	100	15	Normal
TM56	Fling	Dark	Physical	—	100	10	Normal
TM65	Shadow Claw	Ghost	Physical	70	100	15	Normal
TM79	Frost Breath	Ice	Special	60	90	10	Normal
TM86	Grass Knot	Grass	Special	—	100	20	Normal
TM87	Swagger	Normal	Status	—	90	15	Normal
TM88	Sleep Talk	Normal	Status	—	—	10	Self
TM90	Substitute	Normal	Status	—	—	10	Self
TM94	Rock Smash	Fighting	Physical	40	100	15	Normal
TM98	Power-Up Punch	Fighting	Physical	40	100	20	Normal
TM100	Confide	Normal	Status	—	—	20	Normal
HM01	Cut	Normal	Physical	50	95	30	Normal
HM03	Surf	Water	Special	90	100	15	Adjacent
HM04	Strength	Normal	Physical	80	100	15	Normal

No.	Name	Type	Kind	Pow.	Acc.	PP	Range

● MOVES TAUGHT BY PEOPLE

Name	Type	Kind	Pow.	Acc.	PP	Range

● EGG MOVES

Name	Type	Kind	Pow.	Acc.	PP	Range
Yawn	Normal	Status	—	—	10	Normal
Avalanche	Ice	Physical	60	100	10	Normal
Encore	Normal	Status	—	100	5	Normal
Ice Punch	Ice	Physical	75	100	15	Normal
Night Slash	Dark	Physical	70	100	15	Normal
Assurance	Dark	Physical	60	100	10	Normal
Sleep Talk	Normal	Status	—	—	10	Self
Focus Punch	Fighting	Physical	150	100	20	Normal
Play Rough	Fairy	Physical	90	90	10	Normal

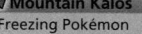 **Mountain Kalos**

Freezing Pokémon

Beartic

082

HEIGHT: 8'06"   WEIGHT: 573.2 lbs.
GENDER: ♂/♀

TYPE	Ice

ABILITY
Snow Cloak

HIDDEN ABILITY
Swift Swim

STAT GROWTH RATES

HP	■■■■
Attack	■■■■■■
Defense	■■■■
Sp. Atk	■■■
Sp. Def	■■■
Speed	■■■

EGG GROUP
Field

(X) They love the cold seas of the north. They create pathways across the ocean waters by freezing their own breath.

(Y) It freezes its breath to create fangs and claws of ice to fight with. Cold northern areas are its habitat.

EVOLUTION

Cubchoo — Lv. 37 → Beartic

ITEMS SOMETIMES HELD BY WILD POKÉMON
None

Damage taken in normal battles	
Normal	×1
Fire	×2
Water	×1
Grass	×1
Electric	×1
Ice	×0.5
Fighting	×2
Poison	×1
Ground	×1
Flying	×1
Psychic	×1
Bug	×1
Rock	×2
Ghost	×1
Dragon	×1
Dark	×1
Steel	×2
Fairy	×1

Damage taken in Inverse Battles	
Normal	×1
Fire	×0.5
Water	×1
Grass	×1
Electric	×1
Ice	×2
Fighting	×0.5
Poison	×1
Ground	×1
Flying	×1
Psychic	×1
Bug	×1
Rock	×0.5
Ghost	×1
Dragon	×1
Dark	×1
Steel	×0.5
Fairy	×1

Can be used in	
Inverse Battle	Battle Institute
—	Battle Maison
Battle Chateau	Random Matchup

Same form for ♂/♀

How to obtain for your Mountain Kalos Pokédex

❶ Catch on Frost Cavern 1F or 2F.
❷ Level up Cubchoo to Lv. 37.

❶ Catch on Frost Cavern 1F or 2F.
❷ Level up Cubchoo to Lv. 37.

● LEVEL-UP MOVES

Lv.	Name	Type	Kind	Pow.	Acc.	PP	Range
1	Sheer Cold	Ice	Special	—	30	5	Normal
1	Thrash	Normal	Physical	120	100	10	1 Random
1	Superpower	Fighting	Physical	120	100	5	Normal
1	Aqua Jet	Water	Physical	40	100	20	Normal
1	Growl	Normal	Status	—	100	40	Many Others
1	Powder Snow	Ice	Special	40	100	25	Many Others
1	Bide	Normal	Physical	—	—	10	Self
1	Icy Wind	Ice	Special	55	95	15	Many Others
9	Play Nice	Normal	Status	—	—	20	Normal
13	Icy Wind	Ice	Special	55	95	15	Many Others
17	Fury Swipes	Normal	Physical	18	80	15	Normal
21	Brine	Water	Special	65	100	10	Normal
25	Endure	Normal	Status	—	—	10	Self
29	Swagger	Normal	Status	—	90	15	Normal
33	Slash	Normal	Physical	70	100	20	Normal
36	Flail	Normal	Physical	—	100	15	Normal
37	Icicle Crash	Ice	Physical	85	90	10	Normal
41	Rest	Psychic	Status	—	—	10	Self
45	Blizzard	Ice	Special	110	70	5	Many Others
53	Hail	Ice	Status	—	—	10	Both Sides
59	Thrash	Normal	Physical	120	100	10	1 Random
66	Sheer Cold	Ice	Special	—	30	5	Normal

● TM & HM MOVES

No.	Name	Type	Kind	Pow.	Acc.	PP	Range
TM01	Hone Claws	Dark	Status	—	—	15	Self
TM05	Roar	Normal	Status	—	—	20	Normal
TM06	Toxic	Poison	Status	—	90	10	Normal
TM07	Hail	Ice	Status	—	—	10	Both Sides
TM08	Bulk Up	Fighting	Status	—	—	20	Self
TM10	Hidden Power	Normal	Special	60	100	15	Normal
TM12	Taunt	Dark	Status	—	100	20	Normal
TM13	Ice Beam	Ice	Special	90	100	10	Normal
TM14	Blizzard	Ice	Special	110	70	5	Many Others
TM15	Hyper Beam	Normal	Special	150	90	5	Normal
TM17	Protect	Normal	Status	—	—	10	Self
TM18	Rain Dance	Water	Status	—	—	5	Both Sides
TM21	Frustration	Normal	Physical	—	100	20	Normal
TM27	Return	Normal	Physical	—	100	20	Normal
TM28	Dig	Ground	Physical	80	100	10	Normal
TM31	Brick Break	Fighting	Physical	75	100	15	Normal
TM32	Double Team	Normal	Status	—	—	15	Self
TM39	Rock Tomb	Rock	Physical	60	95	15	Normal
TM40	Aerial Ace	Flying	Physical	60	—	20	Normal
TM41	Torment	Dark	Status	—	100	15	Normal
TM42	Facade	Normal	Physical	70	100	20	Normal
TM44	Rest	Psychic	Status	—	—	10	Self
TM45	Attract	Normal	Status	—	100	15	Normal
TM48	Round	Normal	Special	60	100	15	Normal
TM49	Echoed Voice	Normal	Special	40	100	15	Normal
TM52	Focus Blast	Fighting	Special	120	70	5	Normal
TM56	Fling	Dark	Physical	—	100	10	Normal
TM65	Shadow Claw	Ghost	Physical	70	100	15	Normal
TM68	Giga Impact	Normal	Physical	150	90	5	Normal
TM71	Stone Edge	Rock	Physical	100	80	5	Normal
TM75	Swords Dance	Normal	Status	—	—	20	Self
TM78	Bulldoze	Ground	Physical	60	100	20	Adjacent
TM79	Frost Breath	Ice	Special	60	90	10	Normal
TM80	Rock Slide	Rock	Physical	75	90	10	Many Others

No.	Name	Type	Kind	Pow.	Acc.	PP	Range
TM86	Grass Knot	Grass	Special	—	100	20	Normal
TM87	Swagger	Normal	Status	—	90	15	Normal
TM88	Sleep Talk	Normal	Status	—	—	10	Self
TM90	Substitute	Normal	Status	—	—	10	Self
TM94	Rock Smash	Fighting	Physical	40	100	15	Normal
TM98	Power-Up Punch	Fighting	Physical	40	100	20	Normal
TM100	Confide	Normal	Status	—	—	20	Normal
HM01	Cut	Normal	Physical	50	95	30	Normal
HM03	Surf	Water	Special	90	100	15	Adjacent
HM04	Strength	Normal	Physical	80	100	15	Normal

● MOVES TAUGHT BY PEOPLE

Name	Type	Kind	Pow.	Acc.	PP	Range

AFTER THE HALL OF FAME

CENTRAL KALOS

COASTAL KALOS

MOUNTAIN KALOS

ADVENTURE DATA

083

Smoochum

Mountain Kalos 083
Kiss Pokémon
☑ **Smoochum**

HEIGHT: 1'04" WEIGHT: 13.2 lbs.
GENDER: ♀

TYPE Ice Psychic

ABILITIES
Oblivious
Forewarn

HIDDEN ABILITY
Hydration

STAT GROWTH RATES
HP	■■
Attack	■■
Defense	■
Sp. Atk	■■■■
Sp. Def	■■■
Speed	■■■■

EGG GROUP
No Eggs Discovered

X · Its lips are the most sensitive part of its body. It always uses its lips first to examine things.

Y · It tests everything by touching with its lips, which remember what it likes and dislikes.

EVOLUTION

Smoochum → Lv. 30 → Jynx

ITEMS SOMETIMES HELD BY WILD POKÉMON
None

Damage taken in normal battles		Damage taken in Inverse Battles	
Normal	×1	Normal	×1
Fire	×2	Fire	×0.5
Water	×1	Water	×1
Grass	×1	Grass	×1
Electric	×1	Electric	×1
Ice	×0.5	Ice	×2
Fighting	×1	Fighting	×1
Poison	×1	Poison	×1
Ground	×1	Ground	×1
Flying	×1	Flying	×1
Psychic	×0.5	Psychic	×2
Bug	×2	Bug	×0.5
Rock	×2	Rock	×0.5
Ghost	×2	Ghost	×0.5
Dragon	×1	Dragon	×1
Dark	×2	Dark	×0.5
Steel	×2	Steel	×0.5
Fairy	×1	Fairy	×1

Can be used in	
Inverse Battle	Battle Institute
—	Battle Maison
Battle Chateau	Random Matchup

♀

How to obtain for your Mountain Kalos Pokédex

❶ Catch in a Horde Encounter on Frost Cavern 1F.
❷ Catch in a Horde Encounter on Frost Cavern 2F.

❶ Catch in a Horde Encounter on Frost Cavern 1F.
❷ Catch in a Horde Encounter on Frost Cavern 2F.

● **LEVEL-UP MOVES**

Lv.	Name	Type	Kind	Pow.	Acc.	PP	Range
1	Pound	Normal	Physical	40	100	35	Normal
5	Lick	Ghost	Physical	30	100	30	Normal
8	Sweet Kiss	Fairy	Status	—	75	10	Normal
11	Powder Snow	Ice	Special	40	100	25	Many Others
15	Confusion	Psychic	Special	50	100	25	Normal
18	Sing	Normal	Status	—	55	15	Normal
21	Heart Stamp	Psychic	Physical	60	100	25	Normal
25	Mean Look	Normal	Status	—	—	5	Normal
28	Fake Tears	Dark	Status	—	100	20	Normal
31	Lucky Chant	Normal	Status	—	—	30	Your Side
35	Avalanche	Ice	Physical	60	100	10	Normal
38	Psychic	Psychic	Special	90	100	10	Normal
41	Copycat	Normal	Status	—	—	20	Self
45	Perish Song	Normal	Status	—	—	5	Adjacent
48	Blizzard	Ice	Special	110	70	5	Many Others

● **TM & HM MOVES**

No.	Name	Type	Kind	Pow.	Acc.	PP	Range
TM03	Psyshock	Psychic	Special	80	100	10	Normal
TM04	Calm Mind	Psychic	Status	—	—	20	Self
TM06	Toxic	Poison	Status	—	90	10	Normal
TM07	Hail	Ice	Status	—	—	10	Both Sides
TM10	Hidden Power	Normal	Special	60	100	15	Normal
TM13	Ice Beam	Ice	Special	90	100	10	Normal
TM14	Blizzard	Ice	Special	110	70	5	Many Others
TM16	Light Screen	Psychic	Status	—	—	30	Your Side
TM17	Protect	Normal	Status	—	—	10	Self
TM18	Rain Dance	Water	Status	—	—	5	Both Sides
TM21	Frustration	Normal	Physical	—	100	20	Normal
TM27	Return	Normal	Physical	—	100	20	Normal
TM29	Psychic	Psychic	Special	90	100	10	Normal
TM30	Shadow Ball	Ghost	Special	80	100	15	Normal
TM32	Double Team	Normal	Status	—	—	15	Self
TM33	Reflect	Psychic	Status	—	—	20	Your Side
TM42	Facade	Normal	Physical	70	100	20	Normal
TM44	Rest	Psychic	Status	—	—	10	Self
TM45	Attract	Normal	Status	—	100	15	Normal
TM46	Thief	Dark	Physical	60	100	25	Normal
TM48	Round	Normal	Special	60	100	15	Normal
TM49	Echoed Voice	Normal	Special	40	100	15	Normal
TM56	Fling	Dark	Physical	—	100	10	Normal
TM66	Payback	Dark	Physical	50	100	10	Normal
TM70	Flash	Normal	Status	—	100	20	Normal
TM77	Psych Up	Normal	Status	—	—	10	Self
TM79	Frost Breath	Ice	Special	60	90	10	Normal
TM85	Dream Eater	Psychic	Special	100	100	15	Normal
TM86	Grass Knot	Grass	Special	—	100	20	Normal
TM87	Swagger	Normal	Status	—	90	15	Normal
TM88	Sleep Talk	Normal	Status	—	—	10	Self
TM90	Substitute	Normal	Status	—	—	10	Self
TM92	Trick Room	Psychic	Status	—	—	5	Both Sides

No.	Name	Type	Kind	Pow.	Acc.	PP	Range
TM100	Confide	Normal	Status	—	—	20	Normal

● **MOVES TAUGHT BY PEOPLE**

Name	Type	Kind	Pow.	Acc.	PP	Range

● **EGG MOVES**

Name	Type	Kind	Pow.	Acc.	PP	Range
Meditate	Psychic	Status	—	—	40	Self
Fake Out	Normal	Physical	40	100	10	Normal
Wish	Normal	Status	—	—	10	Self
Ice Punch	Ice	Physical	75	100	10	Normal
Miracle Eye	Psychic	Status	—	—	40	Normal
Nasty Plot	Dark	Status	—	—	20	Self
Wake-Up Slap	Fighting	Physical	70	100	10	Normal
Captivate	Normal	Status	—	100	20	Many Others

Mountain Kalos 084
Human Shape Pokémon
✓ Jynx

HEIGHT: 4'07" WEIGHT: 89.5 lbs.
GENDER: ♀

TYPE Ice | Psychic

ABILITIES
Oblivious
Forewarn

HIDDEN ABILITY
Dry Skin

STAT GROWTH RATES
HP	■■■
Attack	■■■
Defense	■■
Sp. Atk	■■■■■
Sp. Def	■■■■
Speed	■■■■

EGG GROUP
Human-Like

X It wiggles its hips as it walks. It can cause people to dance in unison with it.

Y It speaks using a language that sounds human. Research is underway to determine what is being said.

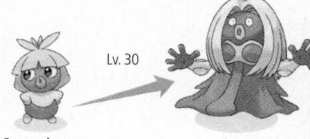

EVOLUTION

Smoochum → (Lv. 30) → Jynx

ITEMS SOMETIMES HELD BY WILD POKÉMON
None

Damage taken in normal battles		Damage taken in Inverse Battles	
Normal	×1	Normal	×1
Fire	×2	Fire	×0.5
Water	×1	Water	×1
Grass	×1	Grass	×1
Electric	×1	Electric	×1
Ice	×0.5	Ice	×2
Fighting	×1	Fighting	×1
Poison	×1	Poison	×1
Ground	×1	Ground	×1
Flying	×1	Flying	×1
Psychic	×0.5	Psychic	×2
Bug	×2	Bug	×0.5
Rock	×2	Rock	×0.5
Ghost	×2	Ghost	×0.5
Dragon	×1	Dragon	×1
Dark	×2	Dark	×0.5
Steel	×2	Steel	×0.5
Fairy	×1	Fairy	×1

Can be used in	
Inverse Battle	Battle Institute
—	Battle Maison
Battle Chateau	Random Matchup

♀

How to obtain for your Mountain Kalos Pokédex

❶ Catch on Frost Cavern 1F or 2F.
❷ Level up Smoochum to Lv. 30.

❶ Catch on Frost Cavern 1F or 2F.
❷ Level up Smoochum to Lv. 30.

● LEVEL-UP MOVES

Lv.	Name	Type	Kind	Pow.	Acc.	PP	Range
1	Draining Kiss	Fairy	Special	50	100	10	Normal
1	Perish Song	Normal	Status	—	—	5	Adjacent
1	Pound	Normal	Physical	40	100	35	Normal
1	Lick	Ghost	Physical	30	100	30	Normal
1	Lovely Kiss	Normal	Status	—	75	10	Normal
1	Powder Snow	Ice	Special	40	100	25	Many Others
5	Lick	Ghost	Physical	30	100	30	Normal
8	Lovely Kiss	Normal	Status	—	75	10	Normal
11	Powder Snow	Ice	Special	40	100	25	Many Others
15	Double Slap	Normal	Physical	15	85	10	Normal
18	Ice Punch	Ice	Physical	75	100	15	Normal
21	Heart Stamp	Psychic	Physical	60	100	25	Normal
25	Mean Look	Normal	Status	—	—	5	Normal
28	Fake Tears	Dark	Status	—	100	20	Normal
33	Wake-Up Slap	Fighting	Physical	70	100	10	Normal
39	Avalanche	Ice	Physical	60	100	10	Normal
44	Body Slam	Normal	Physical	85	100	15	Normal
49	Wring Out	Normal	Special	—	100	5	Normal
55	Perish Song	Normal	Status	—	—	5	Adjacent
60	Blizzard	Ice	Special	110	70	5	Many Others

● TM & HM MOVES

No.	Name	Type	Kind	Pow.	Acc.	PP	Range
TM03	Psyshock	Psychic	Special	80	100	10	Normal
TM04	Calm Mind	Psychic	Status	—	—	20	Self
TM06	Toxic	Poison	Status	—	90	10	Normal
TM07	Hail	Ice	Status	—	—	10	Both Sides
TM10	Hidden Power	Normal	Special	60	100	15	Normal
TM12	Taunt	Dark	Status	—	100	20	Normal
TM13	Ice Beam	Ice	Special	90	100	10	Normal
TM14	Blizzard	Ice	Special	110	70	5	Many Others
TM15	Hyper Beam	Normal	Special	150	90	5	Normal
TM16	Light Screen	Psychic	Status	—	—	30	Your Side
TM17	Protect	Normal	Status	—	—	10	Self
TM18	Rain Dance	Water	Status	—	—	5	Both Sides
TM21	Frustration	Normal	Physical	—	100	20	Normal
TM27	Return	Normal	Physical	—	100	20	Normal
TM29	Psychic	Psychic	Special	90	100	10	Normal
TM30	Shadow Ball	Ghost	Special	80	100	15	Normal
TM31	Brick Break	Fighting	Physical	75	100	15	Normal
TM32	Double Team	Normal	Status	—	—	15	Self
TM33	Reflect	Psychic	Status	—	—	20	Your Side
TM41	Torment	Dark	Status	—	100	15	Normal
TM42	Facade	Normal	Physical	70	100	20	Normal
TM44	Rest	Psychic	Status	—	—	10	Self
TM45	Attract	Normal	Status	—	100	15	Normal
TM46	Thief	Dark	Physical	60	100	25	Normal
TM48	Round	Normal	Special	60	100	15	Normal
TM49	Echoed Voice	Normal	Special	40	100	15	Normal
TM52	Focus Blast	Fighting	Special	120	70	5	Normal
TM53	Energy Ball	Grass	Special	90	100	10	Normal
TM56	Fling	Dark	Physical	—	100	10	Normal
TM66	Payback	Dark	Physical	50	100	10	Normal
TM68	Giga Impact	Normal	Physical	150	90	5	Normal
TM70	Flash	Normal	Status	—	100	20	Normal
TM77	Psych Up	Normal	Status	—	—	10	Normal

No.	Name	Type	Kind	Pow.	Acc.	PP	Range
TM79	Frost Breath	Ice	Special	60	90	10	Normal
TM85	Dream Eater	Psychic	Special	100	100	15	Normal
TM86	Grass Knot	Grass	Special	—	100	20	Normal
TM87	Swagger	Normal	Status	—	90	15	Normal
TM88	Sleep Talk	Normal	Status	—	—	10	Self
TM90	Substitute	Normal	Status	—	—	10	Self
TM92	Trick Room	Psychic	Status	—	—	5	Both Sides
TM98	Power-Up Punch	Fighting	Physical	40	100	20	Normal
TM100	Confide	Normal	Status	—	—	20	Normal

Name	Type	Kind	Pow.	Acc.	PP	Range

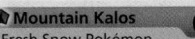

Mountain Kalos
Fresh Snow Pokémon
☑ Vanillite 085

HEIGHT: 1'04" WEIGHT: 12.6 lbs.
GENDER: ♂ / ♀

X The temperature of their breath is -58 degrees Fahrenheit. They create snow crystals and make snow fall in the areas around them.

Y This Pokémon formed from icicles bathed in energy from the morning sun. It sleeps buried in snow.

TYPE Ice

ABILITY
Ice Body

HIDDEN ABILITY
Weak Armor

STAT GROWTH RATES
HP	▪▪
Attack	▪▪
Defense	▪▪
Sp. Atk	▪▪▪
Sp. Def	▪▪▪
Speed	▪▪▪

EGG GROUP
Mineral

EVOLUTION

Lv. 35 → Lv. 47

Vanillite Vanillish Vanilluxe

ITEMS SOMETIMES HELD BY WILD POKÉMON
None

Damage taken in normal battles		Damage taken in Inverse Battles	
Normal	×1	Normal	×1
Fire	×2	Fire	×0.5
Water	×1	Water	×1
Grass	×1	Grass	×1
Electric	×1	Electric	×1
Ice	×0.5	Ice	×2
Fighting	×2	Fighting	×0.5
Poison	×1	Poison	×1
Ground	×1	Ground	×1
Flying	×1	Flying	×1
Psychic	×1	Psychic	×1
Bug	×1	Bug	×1
Rock	×2	Rock	×0.5
Ghost	×1	Ghost	×1
Dragon	×1	Dragon	×1
Dark	×1	Dark	×1
Steel	×2	Steel	×0.5
Fairy	×1	Fairy	×1

Can be used in	
Inverse Battle	Battle Institute
—	Battle Maison
Battle Chateau	Random Matchup

Same form for ♂ / ♀

How to obtain for your Mountain Kalos Pokédex

❶ Catch in a Horde Encounter on Frost Cavern 1F.
❷ Catch in a Horde Encounter on Frost Cavern 2F.

❶ Catch in a Horde Encounter on Frost Cavern 1F.
❷ Catch in a Horde Encounter on Frost Cavern 2F.

● LEVEL-UP MOVES

Lv.	Name	Type	Kind	Pow.	Acc.	PP	Range
1	Icicle Spear	Ice	Physical	25	100	30	Normal
4	Harden	Normal	Status	—	—	30	Self
7	Astonish	Ghost	Physical	30	100	15	Normal
10	Uproar	Normal	Special	90	100	10	1 Random
13	Icy Wind	Ice	Special	55	95	15	Many Others
16	Mist	Ice	Status	—	—	30	Your Side
19	Avalanche	Ice	Physical	60	100	10	Normal
22	Taunt	Dark	Status	—	100	20	Normal
26	Mirror Shot	Steel	Special	65	85	10	Normal
31	Acid Armor	Poison	Status	—	—	20	Self
35	Ice Beam	Ice	Special	90	100	10	Normal
40	Hail	Ice	Status	—	—	10	Both Sides
44	Mirror Coat	Psychic	Special	—	100	20	Varies
49	Blizzard	Ice	Special	110	70	5	Many Others
53	Sheer Cold	Ice	Special	—	30	5	Normal

● TM & HM MOVES

No.	Name	Type	Kind	Pow.	Acc.	PP	Range
TM06	Toxic	Poison	Status	—	90	10	Normal
TM07	Hail	Ice	Status	—	—	10	Both Sides
TM10	Hidden Power	Normal	Special	60	100	15	Normal
TM12	Taunt	Dark	Status	—	100	20	Normal
TM13	Ice Beam	Ice	Special	90	100	10	Normal
TM14	Blizzard	Ice	Special	110	70	5	Many Others
TM16	Light Screen	Psychic	Status	—	—	30	Your Side
TM17	Protect	Normal	Status	—	—	10	Self
TM18	Rain Dance	Water	Status	—	—	5	Both Sides
TM21	Frustration	Normal	Physical	—	100	20	Normal
TM27	Return	Normal	Physical	—	100	20	Normal
TM32	Double Team	Normal	Status	—	—	15	Self
TM42	Facade	Normal	Physical	70	100	20	Normal
TM44	Rest	Psychic	Status	—	—	10	Self
TM45	Attract	Normal	Status	—	100	15	Normal
TM48	Round	Normal	Special	60	100	15	Normal
TM64	Explosion	Normal	Physical	250	100	5	Adjacent
TM79	Frost Breath	Ice	Special	60	90	10	Normal
TM87	Swagger	Normal	Status	—	90	15	Normal
TM88	Sleep Talk	Normal	Status	—	—	10	Self
TM90	Substitute	Normal	Status	—	—	10	Self
TM91	Flash Cannon	Steel	Special	80	100	10	Normal
TM100	Confide	Normal	Status	—	—	20	Normal

● MOVES TAUGHT BY PEOPLE

Name	Type	Kind	Pow.	Acc.	PP	Range

● EGG MOVES

Name	Type	Kind	Pow.	Acc.	PP	Range
Water Pulse	Water	Special	60	100	20	Normal
Natural Gift	Normal	Physical	—	100	15	Normal
Imprison	Psychic	Status	—	—	10	Self
Autotomize	Steel	Status	—	—	15	Self
Iron Defense	Steel	Status	—	—	15	Self
Magnet Rise	Electric	Status	—	—	10	Self
Ice Shard	Ice	Physical	40	100	30	Normal
Powder Snow	Ice	Special	40	100	25	Many Others

AFTER THE HALL OF FAME

CENTRAL KALOS

COASTAL KALOS

MOUNTAIN KALOS

085 Vanillite

ADVENTURE DATA

Mountain Kalos **086**

Icy Snow Pokémon

☑ **Vanillish**

HEIGHT: 3'07" WEIGHT: 90.4 lbs.
GENDER: ♂/♀

 🅧 They cool down the surrounding air and create ice particles, which they use to freeze their foes.

🅨 Snowy mountains are this Pokémon's habitat. During an ancient ice age, they moved to southern areas.

TYPE Ice

ABILITY
Ice Body

HIDDEN ABILITY
Weak Armor

STAT GROWTH RATES

HP	■■
Attack	■■■
Defense	■■■
Sp. Atk	■■■■
Sp. Def	■■■
Speed	■■■

EGG GROUP
Mineral

EVOLUTION

Lv. 35	Lv. 47
Vanillite	Vanillish	Vanilluxe

ITEMS SOMETIMES HELD BY WILD POKÉMON
None

Damage taken in normal battles	
Normal	×1
Fire	×2
Water	×1
Grass	×1
Electric	×1
Ice	×0.5
Fighting	×2
Poison	×1
Ground	×1
Flying	×1
Psychic	×1
Bug	×1
Rock	×2
Ghost	×1
Dragon	×1
Dark	×1
Steel	×2
Fairy	×1

Damage taken in Inverse Battles	
Normal	×1
Fire	×0.5
Water	×1
Grass	×1
Electric	×1
Ice	×2
Fighting	×0.5
Poison	×1
Ground	×1
Flying	×1
Psychic	×1
Bug	×1
Rock	×0.5
Ghost	×1
Dragon	×1
Dark	×1
Steel	×0.5
Fairy	×1

Can be used in
Inverse Battle
—
Battle Chateau
Battle Institute
Battle Maison
Random Matchup

How to obtain for your Mountain Kalos Pokédex

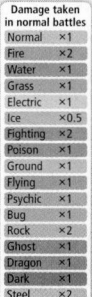 Level up Vanillite to Lv. 35.

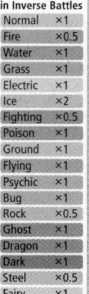 Level up Vanillite to Lv. 35.

Same form for ♂/♀

● **LEVEL-UP MOVES**

Lv.	Name	Type	Kind	Pow.	Acc.	PP	Range
1	Icicle Spear	Ice	Physical	25	100	30	Normal
1	Harden	Normal	Status	—	—	30	Self
1	Astonish	Ghost	Physical	30	100	15	Normal
1	Uproar	Normal	Special	90	100	10	1 Random
4	Harden	Normal	Status	—	—	30	Self
7	Astonish	Ghost	Physical	30	100	15	Normal
10	Uproar	Normal	Special	90	100	10	1 Random
13	Icy Wind	Ice	Special	55	95	15	Many Others
16	Mist	Ice	Status	—	—	30	Your Side
19	Avalanche	Ice	Physical	60	100	10	Normal
22	Taunt	Dark	Status	—	100	20	Normal
26	Mirror Shot	Steel	Special	65	85	10	Normal
31	Acid Armor	Poison	Status	—	—	20	Self
36	Ice Beam	Ice	Special	90	100	10	Normal
42	Hail	Ice	Status	—	—	10	Both Sides
47	Mirror Coat	Psychic	Special	—	100	20	Varies
53	Blizzard	Ice	Special	110	70	5	Many Others
58	Sheer Cold	Ice	Special	—	30	5	Normal

● **TM & HM MOVES**

No.	Name	Type	Kind	Pow.	Acc.	PP	Range
TM06	Toxic	Poison	Status	—	90	10	Normal
TM07	Hail	Ice	Status	—	—	10	Both Sides
TM10	Hidden Power	Normal	Special	60	100	15	Normal
TM12	Taunt	Dark	Status	—	100	20	Normal
TM13	Ice Beam	Ice	Special	90	100	10	Normal
TM14	Blizzard	Ice	Special	110	70	5	Many Others
TM16	Light Screen	Psychic	Status	—	—	30	Your Side
TM17	Protect	Normal	Status	—	—	10	Self
TM18	Rain Dance	Water	Status	—	—	5	Both Sides
TM21	Frustration	Normal	Physical	—	100	20	Normal
TM27	Return	Normal	Physical	—	100	20	Normal
TM32	Double Team	Normal	Status	—	—	15	Self
TM42	Facade	Normal	Physical	70	100	20	Normal
TM44	Rest	Psychic	Status	—	—	10	Self
TM45	Attract	Normal	Status	—	100	15	Normal
TM48	Round	Normal	Special	60	100	15	Normal
TM64	Explosion	Normal	Physical	250	100	5	Adjacent
TM79	Frost Breath	Ice	Special	60	90	10	Normal
TM87	Swagger	Normal	Status	—	90	15	Normal
TM88	Sleep Talk	Normal	Status	—	—	10	Self
TM90	Substitute	Normal	Status	—	—	10	Self
TM91	Flash Cannon	Steel	Special	80	100	10	Normal
TM100	Confide	Normal	Status	—	—	20	Normal

No.	Name	Type	Kind	Pow.	Acc.	PP	Range

● **MOVES TAUGHT BY PEOPLE**

Name	Type	Kind	Pow.	Acc.	PP	Range

AFTER THE HALL OF FAME

CENTRAL KALOS

COASTAL KALOS

MOUNTAIN KALOS

086 Vanillish

ADVENTURE DATA

Mountain Kalos 087
Snowstorm Pokémon
☑ Vanilluxe

HEIGHT: 4'03" WEIGHT: 126.8 lbs.
GENDER: ♂/♀

| TYPE | Ice |

ABILITY
Ice Body

HIDDEN ABILITY
Weak Armor

X If both heads get angry simultaneously, this Pokémon expels a blizzard, burying everything in snow.

Y Swallowing large amounts of water, they make snow clouds inside their bodies and, when angry, cause violent blizzards.

STAT GROWTH RATES
HP ▪▪▪
Attack ▪▪▪▪▪
Defense ▪▪▪▪
Sp. Atk ▪▪▪▪▪
Sp. Def ▪▪▪▪▪
Speed ▪▪▪▪

EGG GROUP
Mineral

⬆ EVOLUTION

Lv. 35   Lv. 47

Vanillite   Vanillish   Vanilluxe

ITEMS SOMETIMES HELD BY WILD POKÉMON
None

Damage taken in normal battles	
Normal	×1
Fire	×2
Water	×1
Grass	×1
Electric	×1
Ice	×0.5
Fighting	×2
Poison	×1
Ground	×1
Flying	×1
Psychic	×1
Bug	×1
Rock	×2
Ghost	×1
Dragon	×1
Dark	×1
Steel	×2
Fairy	×1

Damage taken in Inverse Battles	
Normal	×1
Fire	×0.5
Water	×1
Grass	×1
Electric	×1
Ice	×2
Fighting	×0.5
Poison	×1
Ground	×1
Flying	×1
Psychic	×1
Bug	×1
Rock	×0.5
Ghost	×1
Dragon	×1
Dark	×1
Steel	×0.5
Fairy	×1

Can be used in
Inverse Battle
—
Battle Chateau
Battle Institute
Battle Maison
Random Matchup

How to obtain for your Mountain Kalos Pokédex
Level up Vanillish to Lv. 47.   Level up Vanillish to Lv. 47.

Same form for ♂/♀

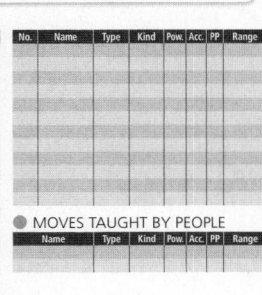

● LEVEL-UP MOVES

Lv.	Name	Type	Kind	Pow.	Acc.	PP	Range
1	Sheer Cold	Ice	Special	—	30	5	Normal
1	Freeze-Dry	Ice	Special	70	100	20	Normal
1	Weather Ball	Normal	Special	50	100	10	Normal
1	Icicle Spear	Ice	Physical	25	100	30	Normal
1	Harden	Normal	Status	—	—	30	Self
1	Astonish	Ghost	Physical	30	100	15	Normal
1	Uproar	Normal	Special	90	100	10	1 Random
4	Harden	Normal	Status	—	—	30	Self
7	Astonish	Ghost	Physical	30	100	15	Normal
10	Uproar	Normal	Special	90	100	10	1 Random
13	Icy Wind	Ice	Special	55	95	15	Many Others
16	Mist	Ice	Status	—	—	30	Your Side
19	Avalanche	Ice	Physical	60	100	10	Normal
22	Taunt	Dark	Status	—	100	20	Normal
26	Mirror Shot	Steel	Special	65	85	10	Normal
31	Acid Armor	Poison	Status	—	—	20	Self
36	Ice Beam	Ice	Special	90	100	10	Normal
42	Hail	Ice	Status	—	—	10	Both Sides
50	Mirror Coat	Psychic	Special	—	—	20	Varies
59	Blizzard	Ice	Special	110	70	5	Many Others
67	Sheer Cold	Ice	Special	—	30	5	Normal

● TM & HM MOVES

No.	Name	Type	Kind	Pow.	Acc.	PP	Range
TM06	Toxic	Poison	Status	—	90	10	Normal
TM07	Hail	Ice	Status	—	—	10	Both Sides
TM10	Hidden Power	Normal	Special	60	100	15	Normal
TM12	Taunt	Dark	Status	—	100	20	Normal
TM13	Ice Beam	Ice	Special	90	100	10	Normal
TM14	Blizzard	Ice	Special	110	70	5	Many Others
TM15	Hyper Beam	Normal	Special	150	90	5	Normal
TM16	Light Screen	Psychic	Status	—	—	30	Your Side
TM17	Protect	Normal	Status	—	—	10	Self
TM18	Rain Dance	Water	Status	—	—	5	Both Sides
TM21	Frustration	Normal	Physical	—	100	20	Normal
TM27	Return	Normal	Physical	—	100	20	Normal
TM32	Double Team	Normal	Status	—	—	15	Self
TM42	Facade	Normal	Physical	70	100	20	Normal
TM44	Rest	Psychic	Status	—	—	10	Self
TM45	Attract	Normal	Status	—	100	15	Normal
TM48	Round	Normal	Special	60	100	15	Normal
TM64	Explosion	Normal	Physical	250	100	5	Adjacent
TM68	Giga Impact	Normal	Physical	150	90	5	Normal
TM79	Frost Breath	Ice	Special	60	90	10	Normal
TM87	Swagger	Normal	Status	—	90	15	Normal
TM88	Sleep Talk	Normal	Status	—	—	10	Self
TM90	Substitute	Normal	Status	—	—	10	Self
TM91	Flash Cannon	Steel	Special	80	100	10	Normal
TM100	Confide	Normal	Status	—	—	20	Normal

● MOVES TAUGHT BY PEOPLE

Name	Type	Kind	Pow.	Acc.	PP	Range

AFTER THE HALL OF FAME

CENTRAL KALOS

COASTAL KALOS

MOUNTAIN KALOS

088

Snover

ADVENTURE DATA

Mountain Kalos
088
Frost Tree Pokémon
Snover

HEIGHT: 3'03"   WEIGHT: 111.3 lbs.
GENDER: ♂/♀

X During cold seasons, it migrates to the mountain's lower reaches. It returns to the snow-covered summit in the spring.

Y In the spring, it grows berries with the texture of frozen treats around its belly.

TYPE Grass   Ice

ABILITY
Snow Warning

HIDDEN ABILITY
Soundproof

STAT GROWTH RATES
HP	■■■
Attack	■■
Defense	■■
Sp. Atk	■■■
Sp. Def	■■■
Speed	■■

EGG GROUPS
Monster, Grass

EVOLUTION

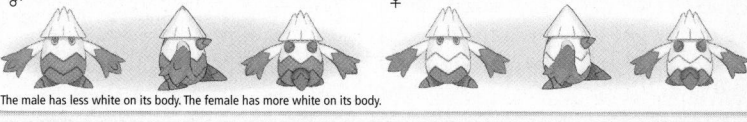

Snover → Abomasnow (Lv. 40)

ITEMS SOMETIMES HELD BY WILD POKÉMON
Never-Melt Ice

Damage taken in normal battles
Normal	×1
Fire	×4
Water	×0.5
Grass	×0.5
Electric	×0.5
Ice	×1
Fighting	×2
Poison	×2
Ground	×0.5
Flying	×2
Psychic	×1
Bug	×2
Rock	×2
Ghost	×1
Dragon	×1
Dark	×1
Steel	×2
Fairy	×1

Damage taken in Inverse Battles
Normal	×1
Fire	×0.25
Water	×2
Grass	×2
Electric	×2
Ice	×1
Fighting	×0.5
Poison	×0.5
Ground	×2
Flying	×0.5
Psychic	×1
Bug	×0.5
Rock	×0.5
Ghost	×1
Dragon	×1
Dark	×1
Steel	×0.5
Fairy	×1

Can be used in
Inverse Battle

Battle Chateau
Battle Institute
Battle Maison
Random Matchup

How to obtain for your Mountain Kalos Pokédex

Catch when it pops out while you're riding Mamoswine on Route 17.

Catch when it pops out while you're riding Mamoswine on Route 17.

♂   ♀

The male has less white on its body. The female has more white on its body.

● LEVEL-UP MOVES

Lv.	Name	Type	Kind	Pow.	Acc.	PP	Range
1	Powder Snow	Ice	Special	40	100	25	Many Others
1	Leer	Normal	Status	—	100	30	Many Others
5	Razor Leaf	Grass	Physical	55	95	25	Many Others
9	Icy Wind	Ice	Special	55	95	15	Many Others
13	Grass Whistle	Grass	Status	—	55	15	Normal
17	Swagger	Normal	Status	—	90	15	Normal
21	Mist	Ice	Status	—	—	30	Your Side
26	Ice Shard	Ice	Physical	40	100	30	Normal
31	Ingrain	Grass	Status	—	—	20	Self
36	Wood Hammer	Grass	Physical	120	100	15	Normal
41	Blizzard	Ice	Special	110	70	5	Many Others
46	Sheer Cold	Ice	Special	—	30	5	Normal

● TM & HM MOVES

No.	Name	Type	Kind	Pow.	Acc.	PP	Range
TM06	Toxic	Poison	Status	—	90	10	Normal
TM07	Hail	Ice	Status	—	—	10	Both Sides
TM10	Hidden Power	Normal	Special	60	100	15	Normal
TM13	Ice Beam	Ice	Special	90	100	10	Normal
TM14	Blizzard	Ice	Special	110	70	5	Many Others
TM16	Light Screen	Psychic	Status	—	—	30	Your Side
TM17	Protect	Normal	Status	—	—	10	Self
TM18	Rain Dance	Water	Status	—	—	5	Both Sides
TM20	Safeguard	Normal	Status	—	—	25	Your Side
TM21	Frustration	Normal	Physical	—	100	20	Normal
TM22	Solar Beam	Grass	Special	120	100	10	Normal
TM27	Return	Normal	Physical	—	100	20	Normal
TM30	Shadow Ball	Ghost	Special	80	100	15	Normal
TM32	Double Team	Normal	Status	—	—	15	Self
TM42	Facade	Normal	Physical	70	100	20	Normal
TM44	Rest	Psychic	Status	—	—	10	Self
TM45	Attract	Normal	Status	—	100	15	Normal
TM48	Round	Normal	Special	60	100	15	Normal
TM53	Energy Ball	Grass	Special	90	100	10	Normal
TM70	Flash	Normal	Status	—	100	20	Normal
TM75	Swords Dance	Normal	Status	—	—	20	Self
TM79	Frost Breath	Ice	Special	60	90	10	Normal
TM86	Grass Knot	Grass	Special	—	100	20	Normal
TM87	Swagger	Normal	Status	—	90	15	Normal
TM88	Sleep Talk	Normal	Status	—	—	10	Self
TM90	Substitute	Normal	Status	—	—	10	Self
TM100	Confide	Normal	Status	—	—	20	Normal

● MOVES TAUGHT BY PEOPLE

Name	Type	Kind	Pow.	Acc.	PP	Range

● EGG MOVES

Name	Type	Kind	Pow.	Acc.	PP	Range
Leech Seed	Grass	Status	—	90	10	Normal
Magical Leaf	Grass	Special	60	—	20	Normal
Seed Bomb	Grass	Physical	80	100	15	Normal
Growth	Normal	Status	—	—	20	Self
Double-Edge	Normal	Physical	120	100	15	Normal
Mist	Ice	Status	—	—	30	Your Side
Stomp	Normal	Physical	65	100	20	Normal
Skull Bash	Normal	Physical	130	100	10	Normal
Avalanche	Ice	Physical	60	100	10	Normal
Natural Gift	Normal	Physical	—	100	15	Normal
Bullet Seed	Grass	Physical	25	100	30	Normal

Mountain Kalos 089
Frost Tree Pokémon
☑ Abomasnow

HEIGHT: 7'03"   WEIGHT: 298.7 lbs.
GENDER: ♂ / ♀

X It blankets wide areas in snow by whipping up blizzards. It is also known as "The Ice Monster."

Y It lives a quiet life on mountains that are perpetually covered in snow. It hides itself by whipping up blizzards.

TYPE (Grass) (Ice)

ABILITY
Snow Warning

HIDDEN ABILITY
Soundproof

STAT GROWTH RATES
HP	■■■■
Attack	■■■■
Defense	■■■■
Sp. Atk	■■■■■
Sp. Def	■■■■
Speed	■■■

EGG GROUPS
Monster, Grass

EVOLUTION

Snover — Lv. 40 → Abomasnow

ITEMS SOMETIMES HELD BY WILD POKÉMON
Never-Melt Ice

Damage taken in normal battles		Damage taken in Inverse Battles	
Normal	×1	Normal	×1
Fire	×4	Fire	×0.25
Water	×0.5	Water	×2
Grass	×0.5	Grass	×2
Electric	×0.5	Electric	×2
Ice	×1	Ice	×1
Fighting	×2	Fighting	×0.5
Poison	×2	Poison	×0.5
Ground	×0.5	Ground	×2
Flying	×2	Flying	×0.5
Psychic	×1	Psychic	×1
Bug	×2	Bug	×0.5
Rock	×2	Rock	×0.5
Ghost	×1	Ghost	×1
Dragon	×1	Dragon	×1
Dark	×1	Dark	×1
Steel	×2	Steel	×0.5
Fairy	×1	Fairy	×1

Can be used in
Inverse Battle
—
Battle Chateau
Battle Institute
Battle Maison
Random Matchup

How to obtain for your Mountain Kalos Pokédex

❶ Catch when it pops out while you're riding Mamoswine on Route 17.
❷ Level up Snover to Lv. 40.

❶ Catch when it pops out while you're riding Mamoswine on Route 17.
❷ Level up Snover to Lv. 40.

♂   ♀

The male has a shorter fringe on its chest. The female has a longer fringe on its chest.

089

Abomasnow

● LEVEL-UP MOVES

Lv.	Name	Type	Kind	Pow.	Acc.	PP	Range
1	Ice Punch	Ice	Physical	75	100	15	Normal
1	Powder Snow	Ice	Special	40	100	25	Many Others
1	Leer	Normal	Status	—	100	30	Many Others
1	Razor Leaf	Grass	Physical	55	95	25	Many Others
5	Razor Leaf	Grass	Physical	55	95	25	Many Others
9	Icy Wind	Ice	Special	55	95	15	Many Others
9	Icy Wind	Ice	Special	55	95	15	Many Others
13	Grass Whistle	Grass	Status	—	55	15	Normal
17	Swagger	Normal	Status	—	90	15	Normal
21	Mist	Ice	Status	—	—	30	Your Side
26	Ice Shard	Ice	Physical	40	100	30	Normal
31	Ingrain	Grass	Status	—	—	20	Self
36	Wood Hammer	Grass	Physical	120	100	15	Normal
47	Blizzard	Ice	Special	110	70	5	Many Others
58	Sheer Cold	Ice	Special	—	30	5	Normal

● TM & HM MOVES

No.	Name	Type	Kind	Pow.	Acc.	PP	Range
TM06	Toxic	Poison	Status	—	90	10	Normal
TM07	Hail	Ice	Status	—	—	10	Both Sides
TM10	Hidden Power	Normal	Special	60	100	15	Normal
TM13	Ice Beam	Ice	Special	90	100	10	Normal
TM14	Blizzard	Ice	Special	110	70	5	Many Others
TM15	Hyper Beam	Normal	Special	150	90	5	Normal
TM16	Light Screen	Psychic	Status	—	—	30	Your Side
TM17	Protect	Normal	Status	—	—	10	Self
TM18	Rain Dance	Water	Status	—	—	5	Both Sides
TM20	Safeguard	Normal	Status	—	—	25	Your Side
TM21	Frustration	Normal	Physical	—	100	20	Normal
TM22	Solar Beam	Grass	Special	120	100	10	Normal
TM26	Earthquake	Ground	Physical	100	100	10	Adjacent
TM27	Return	Normal	Physical	—	100	20	Normal
TM30	Shadow Ball	Ghost	Special	80	100	15	Normal
TM31	Brick Break	Fighting	Physical	75	100	15	Normal
TM32	Double Team	Normal	Status	—	—	15	Self
TM39	Rock Tomb	Rock	Physical	60	95	15	Normal
TM42	Facade	Normal	Physical	70	100	20	Normal
TM44	Rest	Psychic	Status	—	—	10	Self
TM45	Attract	Normal	Status	—	100	15	Normal
TM48	Round	Normal	Special	60	100	15	Normal
TM52	Focus Blast	Fighting	Special	120	70	5	Normal
TM53	Energy Ball	Grass	Special	90	100	10	Normal
TM56	Fling	Dark	Physical	—	100	10	Normal
TM68	Giga Impact	Normal	Physical	150	90	5	Normal
TM70	Flash	Normal	Status	—	100	20	Normal
TM75	Swords Dance	Normal	Status	—	—	20	Self
TM78	Bulldoze	Ground	Physical	60	100	20	Adjacent
TM79	Frost Breath	Ice	Special	60	90	10	Normal
TM80	Rock Slide	Rock	Physical	75	90	10	Many Others
TM86	Grass Knot	Grass	Special	—	100	20	Normal
TM87	Swagger	Normal	Status	—	90	15	Normal

No.	Name	Type	Kind	Pow.	Acc.	PP	Range
TM88	Sleep Talk	Normal	Status	—	—	10	Self
TM90	Substitute	Normal	Status	—	—	10	Self
TM94	Rock Smash	Fighting	Physical	40	100	15	Normal
TM100	Confide	Normal	Status	—	—	20	Normal
HM04	Strength	Normal	Physical	80	100	15	Normal

● MOVES TAUGHT BY PEOPLE

Name	Type	Kind	Pow.	Acc.	PP	Range

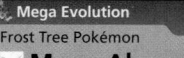

Mega Evolution

Frost Tree Pokémon

☑ **Mega Abomasnow**

TYPE	Grass	Ice

ABILITY
Snow Warning

STAT GROWTH RATES

HP	■■■■
Attack	■■■■■■
Defense	■■■■■
Sp. Atk	■■■■■■
Sp. Def	■■■■
Speed	■■

MEGA STONE REQUIRED

Abomasite
Receive from Abomasnow in Frost Cavern, after saving it from Team Flare.

HEIGHT: 8'10"　　WEIGHT: 407.9 lbs.　　GENDER: ♂/♀

Damage taken in normal battles	
Normal	×1
Fire	×4
Water	×0.5
Grass	×0.5
Electric	×0.5
Ice	×1
Fighting	×2
Poison	×2
Ground	×0.5
Flying	×2
Psychic	×1
Bug	×2
Rock	×2
Ghost	×1
Dragon	×1
Dark	×1
Steel	×2
Fairy	×1

Damage taken in Inverse Battles	
Normal	×1
Fire	×0.25
Water	×2
Grass	×2
Electric	×2
Ice	×1
Fighting	×0.5
Poison	×0.5
Ground	×2
Flying	×0.5
Psychic	×1
Bug	×0.5
Rock	×0.5
Ghost	×1
Dragon	×1
Dark	×1
Steel	×0.5
Fairy	×1

Can be used in
Inverse Battle
—
Battle Chateau
Battle Institute
Battle Maison
Random Matchup

AFTER THE HALL OF FAME

CENTRAL KALOS

COASTAL KALOS

MOUNTAIN KALOS　Mega Abomasnow

ADVENTURE DATA

Same form for ♂/♀

🔺 **Mountain Kalos** 090
Delivery Pokémon
☑ **Delibird**

HEIGHT: 2'11" WEIGHT: 35.3 lbs.
GENDER: ♂/♀

TYPE Ice Flying

ABILITIES
Vital Spirit
Hustle

HIDDEN ABILITY
Insomnia

EVOLUTION

Does not evolve

❌	It carries food rolled up in its tail. It has the habit of sharing food with people lost in mountains.
❌	It carries food all day long. When someone is lost in the mountains, it shares that food.

STAT GROWTH RATES

HP	▪▪
Attack	▪▪▪
Defense	▪▪
Sp. Atk	▪▪▪
Sp. Def	▪▪
Speed	▪▪▪▪

EGG GROUPS
Water 1, Field

ITEMS SOMETIMES HELD BY WILD POKÉMON
None

Can be used in

Inverse Battle

—

Battle Chateau
Battle Institute
Battle Maison
Random Matchup

Damage taken in normal battles		Damage taken in Inverse Battles	
Normal	×1	Normal	×1
Fire	×2	Fire	×0.5
Water	×1	Water	×1
Grass	×0.5	Grass	×2
Electric	×2	Electric	×0.5
Ice	×1	Ice	×1
Fighting	×1	Fighting	×1
Poison	×1	Poison	×1
Ground	×0	Ground	×2
Flying	×1	Flying	×1
Psychic	×1	Psychic	×1
Bug	×0.5	Bug	×2
Rock	×4	Rock	×0.25
Ghost	×1	Ghost	×1
Dragon	×1	Dragon	×1
Dark	×1	Dark	×1
Steel	×2	Steel	×0.5
Fairy	×1	Fairy	×1

How to obtain for your Mountain Kalos Pokédex

Catch when it pops out while you're riding Mamoswine on Route 17.

Catch when it pops out while you're riding Mamoswine on Route 17.

Same form for ♂/♀

● **LEVEL-UP MOVES**

Lv.	Name	Type	Kind	Pow.	Acc.	PP	Range
1	Present	Normal	Physical	—	90	15	Normal

● **TM & HM MOVES**

No.	Name	Type	Kind	Pow.	Acc.	PP	Range
TM06	Toxic	Poison	Status	—	90	10	Normal
TM07	Hail	Ice	Status	—	—	10	Both Sides
TM10	Hidden Power	Normal	Special	60	100	15	Normal
TM13	Ice Beam	Ice	Special	90	100	10	Normal
TM14	Blizzard	Ice	Special	110	70	5	Many Others
TM17	Protect	Normal	Status	—	—	10	Self
TM18	Rain Dance	Water	Status	—	—	5	Both Sides
TM21	Frustration	Normal	Physical	—	100	20	Normal
TM27	Return	Normal	Physical	—	100	20	Normal
TM31	Brick Break	Fighting	Physical	75	100	15	Normal
TM32	Double Team	Normal	Status	—	—	15	Self
TM40	Aerial Ace	Flying	Physical	60	—	20	Normal
TM42	Facade	Normal	Physical	70	100	20	Normal
TM44	Rest	Psychic	Status	—	—	10	Self
TM45	Attract	Normal	Status	—	100	15	Normal
TM46	Thief	Dark	Physical	60	100	25	Normal
TM48	Round	Normal	Special	60	100	15	Normal
TM56	Fling	Dark	Physical	—	100	10	Normal
TM79	Frost Breath	Ice	Special	60	90	10	Normal
TM87	Swagger	Normal	Status	—	90	15	Normal
TM88	Sleep Talk	Normal	Status	—	—	10	Self
TM90	Substitute	Normal	Status	—	—	10	Self
TM98	Power-Up Punch	Fighting	Physical	40	100	20	Normal
TM100	Confide	Normal	Status	—	—	20	Normal
HM02	Fly	Flying	Physical	90	95	15	Normal

No.	Name	Type	Kind	Pow.	Acc.	PP	Range

● **MOVES TAUGHT BY PEOPLE**

Name	Type	Kind	Pow.	Acc.	PP	Range

● **EGG MOVES**

Name	Type	Kind	Pow.	Acc.	PP	Range
Aurora Beam	Ice	Special	65	100	20	Normal
Quick Attack	Normal	Physical	40	100	30	Normal
Future Sight	Psychic	Special	120	100	10	Normal
Splash	Normal	Status	—	—	40	Self
Rapid Spin	Normal	Physical	20	100	40	Normal
Ice Ball	Ice	Physical	30	90	20	Normal
Ice Shard	Ice	Physical	40	100	30	Normal
Ice Punch	Ice	Physical	75	100	15	Normal
Fake Out	Normal	Physical	40	100	10	Normal
Bestow	Normal	Status	—	—	15	Normal
Icy Wind	Ice	Special	55	95	15	Many Others
Freeze-Dry	Ice	Special	70	100	20	Normal
Destiny Bond	Ghost	Status	—	—	5	Self
Spikes	Ground	Status	—	—	20	Other Side

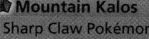

Mountain Kalos
Sharp Claw Pokémon
✅ Sneasel

091

HEIGHT: 2'11" WEIGHT: 61.7 lbs.
GENDER: ♂/♀

TYPE	Dark	Ice

ABILITIES
Inner Focus
Keen Eye

HIDDEN ABILITY
Pickpocket

STAT GROWTH RATES

HP	▪▪
Attack	▪▪▪▪▪
Defense	▪▪▪
Sp. Atk	▪▪
Sp. Def	▪▪▪
Speed	▪▪▪▪▪▪

EGG GROUP
Field

X It feeds on eggs stolen from nests. Its sharply hooked claws rip vulnerable spots on prey.

Y Its paws conceal sharp claws. If attacked, it suddenly extends the claws and startles its enemy.

EVOLUTION
Level up with a Razor Claw between 8 P.M. and 3:59 A.M.

Sneasel → Weavile

ITEMS SOMETIMES HELD BY WILD POKÉMON
Grip Claw, Quick Claw

Damage taken in normal battles		Damage taken in Inverse Battles	
Normal	×1	Normal	×1
Fire	×2	Fire	×0.5
Water	×1	Water	×1
Grass	×1	Grass	×1
Electric	×1	Electric	×1
Ice	×0.5	Ice	×2
Fighting	×4	Fighting	×0.25
Poison	×1	Poison	×1
Ground	×1	Ground	×1
Flying	×1	Flying	×1
Psychic	×0	Psychic	×2
Bug	×2	Bug	×0.5
Rock	×2	Rock	×0.5
Ghost	×0.5	Ghost	×2
Dragon	×1	Dragon	×1
Dark	×0.5	Dark	×2
Steel	×1	Steel	×0.5
Fairy	×2	Fairy	×0.5

Can be used in
Inverse Battle
—
Battle Chateau
Battle Institute
Battle Maison
Random Matchup

How to obtain for your Mountain Kalos Pokédex

Catch when it pops out while you're riding Mamoswine on Route 17.

Catch when it pops out while you're riding Mamoswine on Route 17.

♂

♀

The male has larger ears. The female has smaller ears.

● LEVEL-UP MOVES

Lv.	Name	Type	Kind	Pow.	Acc.	PP	Range
1	Scratch	Normal	Physical	40	100	35	Normal
1	Leer	Normal	Status	—	100	30	Many Others
1	Taunt	Dark	Status	—	100	20	Normal
8	Quick Attack	Normal	Physical	40	100	30	Normal
10	Feint Attack	Dark	Physical	60	—	20	Normal
14	Icy Wind	Ice	Special	55	95	15	Many Others
16	Fury Swipes	Normal	Physical	18	80	15	Normal
20	Agility	Psychic	Status	—	—	30	Self
22	Metal Claw	Steel	Physical	50	95	35	Normal
26	Hone Claws	Dark	Status	—	—	15	Self
28	Beat Up	Dark	Physical	—	100	10	Normal
32	Screech	Normal	Status	—	85	40	Normal
35	Slash	Normal	Physical	70	100	20	Normal
40	Snatch	Dark	Status	—	—	10	Self
44	Punishment	Dark	Physical	—	100	5	Normal
47	Ice Shard	Ice	Physical	40	100	30	Normal

● TM & HM MOVES

No.	Name	Type	Kind	Pow.	Acc.	PP	Range
TM01	Hone Claws	Dark	Status	—	—	15	Self
TM04	Calm Mind	Psychic	Status	—	—	20	Self
TM06	Toxic	Poison	Status	—	90	10	Normal
TM07	Hail	Ice	Status	—	—	10	Both Sides
TM10	Hidden Power	Normal	Special	60	100	15	Normal
TM11	Sunny Day	Fire	Status	—	—	5	Both Sides
TM12	Taunt	Dark	Status	—	100	20	Normal
TM13	Ice Beam	Ice	Special	90	100	10	Normal
TM14	Blizzard	Ice	Special	110	70	5	Many Others
TM17	Protect	Normal	Status	—	—	10	Self
TM18	Rain Dance	Water	Status	—	—	5	Both Sides
TM21	Frustration	Normal	Physical	—	100	20	Normal
TM27	Return	Normal	Physical	—	100	20	Normal
TM28	Dig	Ground	Physical	80	100	10	Normal
TM30	Shadow Ball	Ghost	Special	80	100	15	Normal
TM31	Brick Break	Fighting	Physical	75	100	15	Normal
TM32	Double Team	Normal	Status	—	—	15	Self
TM33	Reflect	Psychic	Status	—	—	20	Your Side
TM40	Aerial Ace	Flying	Physical	60	—	20	Normal
TM41	Torment	Dark	Status	—	100	15	Normal
TM42	Facade	Normal	Physical	70	100	20	Normal
TM44	Rest	Psychic	Status	—	—	10	Self
TM45	Attract	Normal	Status	—	100	15	Normal
TM46	Thief	Dark	Physical	60	100	25	Normal
TM47	Low Sweep	Fighting	Physical	65	100	20	Normal
TM48	Round	Normal	Special	60	100	15	Normal
TM54	False Swipe	Normal	Physical	40	100	40	Normal
TM56	Fling	Dark	Physical	—	100	10	Normal
TM63	Embargo	Dark	Status	—	100	15	Normal
TM65	Shadow Claw	Ghost	Physical	70	100	15	Normal
TM66	Payback	Dark	Physical	50	100	10	Normal
TM67	Retaliate	Normal	Physical	70	100	5	Normal
TM75	Swords Dance	Normal	Status	—	—	20	Self
TM77	Psych Up	Normal	Status	—	—	10	Normal
TM81	X-Scissor	Bug	Physical	80	100	15	Normal
TM84	Poison Jab	Poison	Physical	80	100	20	Normal
TM85	Dream Eater	Psychic	Special	100	100	15	Normal
TM87	Swagger	Normal	Status	—	90	15	Normal
TM88	Sleep Talk	Normal	Status	—	—	10	Self
TM90	Substitute	Normal	Status	—	—	10	Self
TM94	Rock Smash	Fighting	Physical	40	100	15	Normal
TM95	Snarl	Dark	Special	55	95	15	Many Others
TM97	Dark Pulse	Dark	Special	80	100	15	Normal
TM98	Power-Up Punch	Fighting	Physical	40	100	20	Normal
TM100	Confide	Normal	Status	—	—	20	Normal
HM01	Cut	Normal	Physical	50	95	30	Normal
HM03	Surf	Water	Special	90	100	15	Adjacent
HM04	Strength	Normal	Physical	80	100	15	Normal

● MOVES TAUGHT BY PEOPLE

Name	Type	Kind	Pow.	Acc.	PP	Range

● EGG MOVES

Name	Type	Kind	Pow.	Acc.	PP	Range
Counter	Fighting	Physical	—	100	20	Varies
Spite	Ghost	Status	—	100	10	Normal
Foresight	Normal	Status	—	—	40	Normal
Bite	Dark	Physical	60	100	25	Normal
Crush Claw	Normal	Physical	75	95	10	Normal
Fake Out	Normal	Physical	40	100	10	Normal
Double Hit	Normal	Physical	35	90	10	Normal
Punishment	Dark	Physical	—	100	5	Normal
Pursuit	Dark	Physical	40	100	20	Normal
Ice Shard	Ice	Physical	40	100	30	Normal
Ice Punch	Ice	Physical	75	100	15	Normal
Assist	Normal	Status	—	—	20	Self
Avalanche	Ice	Physical	60	100	10	Normal
Feint	Normal	Physical	30	100	10	Normal
Icicle Crash	Ice	Physical	85	90	10	Normal

AFTER THE HALL OF FAME
CENTRAL KALOS
COASTAL KALOS
MOUNTAIN KALOS
091 Sneasel
ADVENTURE DATA

AFTER THE HALL OF FAME

CENTRAL KALOS

COASTAL KALOS

MOUNTAIN KALOS
092

Weavile

ADVENTURE DATA

Mountain Kalos
092

Sharp Claw Pokémon

Weavile

HEIGHT: 3'07"   WEIGHT: 75.0 lbs.
GENDER: ♂/♀

TYPE	Dark	Ice

ABILITY
Pressure

HIDDEN ABILITY
Pickpocket

STAT GROWTH RATES
HP	■■■
Attack	■■■■■
Defense	■■■
Sp. Atk	■■
Sp. Def	■■
Speed	■■■■■■

EGG GROUP
Field

X It lives in snowy regions. It carves patterns in trees with its claws as a signal to others.

Y They live in cold regions, forming groups of four or five that hunt prey with impressive coordination.

EVOLUTION

Level up with a Razor Claw between 8 P.M. and 3:59 A.M.

Sneasel → Weavile

ITEMS SOMETIMES HELD BY WILD POKÉMON
None

Can be used in
- Inverse Battle
- —
- Battle Chateau
- Battle Institute
- Battle Maison
- Random Matchup

Damage taken in normal battles	
Normal	×1
Fire	×2
Water	×1
Grass	×1
Electric	×1
Ice	×0.5
Fighting	×4
Poison	×1
Ground	×1
Flying	×1
Psychic	×0
Bug	×2
Rock	×2
Ghost	×0.5
Dragon	×1
Dark	×0.5
Steel	×2
Fairy	×2

Damage taken in Inverse Battles	
Normal	×1
Fire	×0.5
Water	×1
Grass	×1
Electric	×1
Ice	×2
Fighting	×0.25
Poison	×1
Ground	×1
Flying	×1
Psychic	×2
Bug	×0.5
Rock	×0.5
Ghost	×2
Dragon	×1
Dark	×2
Steel	×0.5
Fairy	×0.5

How to obtain for your Mountain Kalos Pokédex

Level up Sneasel between 8 P.M. and 3:59 A.M. while it is holding a Razor Claw.

Level up Sneasel between 8 P.M. and 3:59 A.M. while it is holding a Razor Claw.

The male has larger ears. The female has smaller ears.

● LEVEL-UP MOVES

Lv.	Name	Type	Kind	Pow.	Acc.	PP	Range
1	Embargo	Dark	Status	—	100	15	Normal
1	Revenge	Fighting	Physical	60	100	10	Normal
1	Assurance	Dark	Physical	60	100	10	Normal
1	Scratch	Normal	Physical	40	100	35	Normal
1	Leer	Normal	Status	—	100	30	Many Others
1	Taunt	Dark	Status	—	100	20	Normal
4	Quick Attack	Normal	Physical	40	100	30	Normal
8	Quick Attack	Normal	Physical	40	100	30	Normal
10	Feint Attack	Dark	Physical	60	—	20	Normal
14	Icy Wind	Ice	Special	55	95	15	Many Others
16	Fury Swipes	Normal	Physical	18	80	15	Normal
20	Nasty Plot	Dark	Status	—	—	20	Self
22	Metal Claw	Steel	Physical	50	95	35	Normal
25	Hone Claws	Dark	Status	—	—	15	Self
28	Fling	Dark	Physical	—	100	10	Normal
32	Screech	Normal	Status	—	85	40	Normal
35	Night Slash	Dark	Physical	70	100	15	Normal
40	Snatch	Dark	Status	—	—	10	Self
44	Punishment	Dark	Physical	—	100	5	Normal
47	Dark Pulse	Dark	Special	80	100	15	Normal

● TM & HM MOVES

No.	Name	Type	Kind	Pow.	Acc.	PP	Range
TM01	Hone Claws	Dark	Status	—	—	15	Self
TM04	Calm Mind	Psychic	Status	—	—	20	Self
TM06	Toxic	Poison	Status	—	90	10	Normal
TM07	Hail	Ice	Status	—	—	10	Both Sides
TM10	Hidden Power	Normal	Special	60	100	15	Normal
TM11	Sunny Day	Fire	Status	—	—	5	Both Sides
TM12	Taunt	Dark	Status	—	100	20	Normal
TM13	Ice Beam	Ice	Special	90	100	10	Normal
TM14	Blizzard	Ice	Special	110	70	5	Many Others
TM15	Hyper Beam	Normal	Special	150	90	5	Normal
TM17	Protect	Normal	Status	—	—	10	Self
TM18	Rain Dance	Water	Status	—	—	5	Both Sides
TM21	Frustration	Normal	Physical	—	100	20	Normal
TM27	Return	Normal	Physical	—	100	20	Normal
TM28	Dig	Ground	Physical	80	100	10	Normal
TM30	Shadow Ball	Ghost	Special	80	100	15	Normal
TM31	Brick Break	Fighting	Physical	75	100	15	Normal
TM32	Double Team	Normal	Status	—	—	15	Self
TM33	Reflect	Psychic	Status	—	—	20	Your Side
TM40	Aerial Ace	Flying	Physical	60	—	20	Normal
TM41	Torment	Dark	Status	—	100	15	Normal
TM42	Facade	Normal	Physical	70	100	20	Normal
TM44	Rest	Psychic	Status	—	—	10	Self
TM45	Attract	Normal	Status	—	100	15	Normal
TM46	Thief	Dark	Physical	60	100	25	Normal
TM47	Low Sweep	Fighting	Physical	65	100	20	Normal
TM48	Round	Normal	Special	60	100	15	Normal
TM52	Focus Blast	Fighting	Special	120	70	5	Normal
TM54	False Swipe	Normal	Physical	40	100	40	Normal
TM56	Fling	Dark	Physical	—	100	10	Normal
TM63	Embargo	Dark	Status	—	100	15	Normal
TM65	Shadow Claw	Ghost	Physical	70	100	15	Normal
TM66	Payback	Dark	Physical	50	100	10	Normal

No.	Name	Type	Kind	Pow.	Acc.	PP	Range
TM67	Retaliate	Normal	Physical	70	100	5	Normal
TM68	Giga Impact	Normal	Physical	150	90	5	Normal
TM75	Swords Dance	Normal	Status	—	—	20	Self
TM77	Psych Up	Normal	Status	—	—	10	Normal
TM81	X-Scissor	Bug	Physical	80	100	15	Normal
TM84	Poison Jab	Poison	Physical	80	100	20	Normal
TM85	Dream Eater	Psychic	Special	100	100	15	Normal
TM87	Swagger	Normal	Status	—	90	15	Normal
TM88	Sleep Talk	Normal	Status	—	—	10	Self
TM90	Substitute	Normal	Status	—	—	10	Self
TM94	Rock Smash	Fighting	Physical	40	100	15	Normal
TM95	Snarl	Dark	Special	55	95	15	Many Others
TM97	Dark Pulse	Dark	Special	80	100	15	Normal
TM98	Power-Up Punch	Fighting	Physical	40	100	20	Normal
TM100	Confide	Normal	Status	—	—	20	Normal
HM01	Cut	Normal	Physical	50	95	30	Normal
HM03	Surf	Water	Special	90	100	15	Adjacent
HM04	Strength	Normal	Physical	80	100	15	Normal

● MOVES TAUGHT BY PEOPLE

Name	Type	Kind	Pow.	Acc.	PP	Range

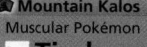

⛰ Mountain Kalos

Muscular Pokémon

093

✓ Timburr

HEIGHT: 2'00" WEIGHT: 27.6 lbs.
GENDER: ♂/♀

X These Pokémon appear at building sites and help out with construction. They always carry squared logs.

Y Always carrying squared logs, they help out with construction. As they grow, they carry bigger logs.

TYPE **Fighting**

ABILITIES
Guts
Sheer Force

HIDDEN ABILITY
Iron Fist

STAT GROWTH RATES
HP	■■■
Attack	■■■■
Defense	■■■
Sp. Atk	■
Sp. Def	■■
Speed	■■

EGG GROUP
Human-Like

⚑ EVOLUTION

Lv. 25   Link Trade

Timburr   Gurdurr   Conkeldurr

ITEMS SOMETIMES HELD BY WILD POKÉMON
None

Damage taken in normal battles		Damage taken in Inverse Battles	
Normal	×1	Normal	×1
Fire	×1	Fire	×1
Water	×1	Water	×1
Grass	×1	Grass	×1
Electric	×1	Electric	×1
Ice	×1	Ice	×1
Fighting	×1	Fighting	×1
Poison	×1	Poison	×1
Ground	×1	Ground	×1
Flying	×2	Flying	×0.5
Psychic	×2	Psychic	×0.5
Bug	×0.5	Bug	×2
Rock	×0.5	Rock	×2
Ghost	×1	Ghost	×1
Dragon	×1	Dragon	×1
Dark	×0.5	Dark	×2
Steel	×1	Steel	×1
Fairy	×2	Fairy	×0.5

Can be used in	
Inverse Battle	Battle Institute
—	Battle Maison
Battle Chateau	Random Matchup

Same form for ♂/♀

How to obtain for your Mountain Kalos Pokédex

Leave Gurdurr or Conkeldurr at the Pokémon Day Care, and hatch the Egg that is found.

Leave Gurdurr or Conkeldurr at the Pokémon Day Care, and hatch the Egg that is found.

● **LEVEL-UP MOVES**

Lv.	Name	Type	Kind	Pow.	Acc.	PP	Range
1	Pound	Normal	Physical	40	100	35	Normal
1	Leer	Normal	Status	—	100	30	Many Others
4	Focus Energy	Normal	Status	—	—	30	Self
8	Bide	Normal	Physical	—	—	10	Self
12	Low Kick	Fighting	Physical	—	100	20	Normal
16	Rock Throw	Rock	Physical	50	90	15	Normal
20	Wake-Up Slap	Fighting	Physical	70	100	10	Normal
24	Chip Away	Normal	Physical	70	100	20	Normal
28	Bulk Up	Fighting	Status	—	—	20	Self
31	Rock Slide	Rock	Physical	75	90	10	Many Others
34	Dynamic Punch	Fighting	Physical	100	50	5	Normal
37	Scary Face	Normal	Status	—	100	10	Normal
40	Hammer Arm	Fighting	Physical	100	90	10	Normal
43	Stone Edge	Rock	Physical	100	80	5	Normal
46	Focus Punch	Fighting	Physical	150	100	20	Normal
49	Superpower	Fighting	Physical	120	100	5	Normal

● **TM & HM MOVES**

No.	Name	Type	Kind	Pow.	Acc.	PP	Range
TM06	Toxic	Poison	Status	—	90	10	Normal
TM08	Bulk Up	Fighting	Status	—	—	20	Self
TM10	Hidden Power	Normal	Special	60	100	15	Normal
TM11	Sunny Day	Fire	Status	—	—	5	Both Sides
TM12	Taunt	Dark	Status	—	100	20	Normal
TM17	Protect	Normal	Status	—	—	10	Self
TM18	Rain Dance	Water	Status	—	—	5	Both Sides
TM21	Frustration	Normal	Physical	—	100	20	Normal
TM23	Smack Down	Rock	Physical	50	100	15	Normal
TM27	Return	Normal	Physical	—	100	20	Normal
TM28	Dig	Ground	Physical	80	100	10	Normal
TM31	Brick Break	Fighting	Physical	75	100	15	Normal
TM32	Double Team	Normal	Status	—	—	15	Self
TM39	Rock Tomb	Rock	Physical	60	95	15	Normal
TM42	Facade	Normal	Physical	70	100	20	Normal
TM44	Rest	Psychic	Status	—	—	10	Self
TM45	Attract	Normal	Status	—	100	15	Normal
TM47	Low Sweep	Fighting	Physical	65	100	20	Normal
TM48	Round	Normal	Special	60	100	15	Normal
TM52	Focus Blast	Fighting	Special	120	70	5	Normal
TM56	Fling	Dark	Physical	—	100	10	Normal
TM66	Payback	Dark	Physical	50	100	10	Normal
TM67	Retaliate	Normal	Physical	70	100	5	Normal
TM71	Stone Edge	Rock	Physical	100	80	5	Normal
TM80	Rock Slide	Rock	Physical	75	90	10	Many Others
TM84	Poison Jab	Poison	Physical	80	100	20	Normal
TM86	Grass Knot	Grass	Special	—	100	20	Normal
TM87	Swagger	Normal	Status	—	90	15	Normal
TM88	Sleep Talk	Normal	Status	—	—	10	Self
TM90	Substitute	Normal	Status	—	—	10	Self
TM94	Rock Smash	Fighting	Physical	40	100	15	Normal
TM98	Power-Up Punch	Fighting	Physical	40	100	20	Normal
TM100	Confide	Normal	Status	—	—	20	Normal

No.	Name	Type	Kind	Pow.	Acc.	PP	Range
HM04	Strength	Normal	Physical	80	100	15	Normal

● **MOVES TAUGHT BY PEOPLE**

Name	Type	Kind	Pow.	Acc.	PP	Range

● **EGG MOVES**

Name	Type	Kind	Pow.	Acc.	PP	Range
Drain Punch	Fighting	Physical	75	100	10	Normal
Endure	Normal	Status	—	—	10	Self
Counter	Fighting	Physical	—	100	20	Varies
Comet Punch	Normal	Physical	18	85	15	Normal
Foresight	Normal	Status	—	—	40	Normal
Smelling Salts	Normal	Physical	70	100	10	Normal
Detect	Fighting	Status	—	—	5	Self
Wide Guard	Rock	Status	—	—	10	Your Side
Force Palm	Fighting	Physical	60	100	10	Normal
Reversal	Fighting	Physical	—	100	15	Normal
Mach Punch	Fighting	Physical	40	100	30	Normal

Mountain Kalos
Muscular Pokémon
✓ Gurdurr

094

HEIGHT: 3'11" WEIGHT: 88.2 lbs.
GENDER: ♂/♀

X With strengthened bodies, they skillfully wield steel beams to take down buildings.

Y This Pokémon is so muscular and strongly built that even a group of wrestlers could not make it budge an inch.

TYPE: **Fighting**

ABILITIES
Guts
Sheer Force

HIDDEN ABILITY
Iron Fist

STAT GROWTH RATES
HP	■■■
Attack	■■■■■
Defense	■■■■
Sp. Atk	■■
Sp. Def	■■
Speed	■■

EGG GROUP
Human-Like

EVOLUTION

Lv. 25   Link Trade

Timburr   Gurdurr   Conkeldurr

ITEMS SOMETIMES HELD BY WILD POKÉMON
None

Damage taken in normal battles		Damage taken in Inverse Battles	
Normal	×1	Normal	×1
Fire	×1	Fire	×1
Water	×1	Water	×1
Grass	×1	Grass	×1
Electric	×1	Electric	×1
Ice	×1	Ice	×1
Fighting	×1	Fighting	×1
Poison	×1	Poison	×1
Ground	×1	Ground	×1
Flying	×2	Flying	×0.5
Psychic	×2	Psychic	×0.5
Bug	×0.5	Bug	×2
Rock	×0.5	Rock	×2
Ghost	×1	Ghost	×1
Dragon	×1	Dragon	×1
Dark	×0.5	Dark	×2
Steel	×1	Steel	×1
Fairy	×2	Fairy	×0.5

Can be used in
Inverse Battle

Battle Chateau
Battle Institute
Battle Maison
Random Matchup

How to obtain for your Mountain Kalos Pokédex

❶ Catch in the tall grass on Route 18.
❷ Catch in the red flowers on Route 18.

❶ Catch in the tall grass on Route 18.
❷ Catch in the red flowers on Route 18.

Same form for ♂/♀

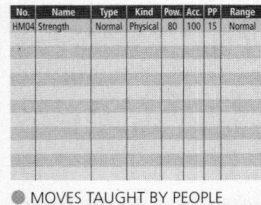

● LEVEL-UP MOVES

Lv.	Name	Type	Kind	Pow.	Acc.	PP	Range
1	Pound	Normal	Physical	40	100	35	Normal
1	Leer	Normal	Status	—	100	30	Many Others
1	Focus Energy	Normal	Status	—	—	30	Self
1	Bide	Normal	Physical	—	—	10	Self
4	Focus Energy	Normal	Status	—	—	30	Self
8	Bide	Normal	Physical	—	—	10	Self
12	Low Kick	Fighting	Physical	—	100	20	Normal
16	Rock Throw	Rock	Physical	50	90	15	Normal
20	Wake-Up Slap	Fighting	Physical	70	100	10	Normal
24	Chip Away	Normal	Physical	70	100	20	Normal
29	Bulk Up	Fighting	Status	—	—	20	Self
33	Rock Slide	Rock	Physical	75	90	10	Many Others
37	Dynamic Punch	Fighting	Physical	100	50	5	Normal
41	Scary Face	Normal	Status	—	100	10	Normal
45	Hammer Arm	Fighting	Physical	100	90	10	Normal
49	Stone Edge	Rock	Physical	100	80	5	Normal
53	Focus Punch	Fighting	Physical	150	100	20	Normal
57	Superpower	Fighting	Physical	120	100	5	Normal

● TM & HM MOVES

No.	Name	Type	Kind	Pow.	Acc.	PP	Range
TM06	Toxic	Poison	Status	—	90	10	Normal
TM08	Bulk Up	Fighting	Status	—	—	20	Self
TM10	Hidden Power	Normal	Special	60	100	15	Normal
TM11	Sunny Day	Fire	Status	—	—	5	Both Sides
TM12	Taunt	Dark	Status	—	100	20	Normal
TM17	Protect	Normal	Status	—	—	10	Self
TM18	Rain Dance	Water	Status	—	—	5	Both Sides
TM21	Frustration	Normal	Physical	—	100	20	Normal
TM23	Smack Down	Rock	Physical	50	100	15	Normal
TM27	Return	Normal	Physical	—	100	20	Normal
TM28	Dig	Ground	Physical	80	100	10	Normal
TM31	Brick Break	Fighting	Physical	75	100	15	Normal
TM32	Double Team	Normal	Status	—	—	15	Self
TM39	Rock Tomb	Rock	Physical	60	95	15	Normal
TM42	Facade	Normal	Physical	70	100	20	Normal
TM44	Rest	Psychic	Status	—	—	10	Self
TM45	Attract	Normal	Status	—	100	15	Normal
TM47	Low Sweep	Fighting	Physical	65	100	20	Normal
TM48	Round	Normal	Special	60	100	15	Normal
TM52	Focus Blast	Fighting	Special	120	70	5	Normal
TM56	Fling	Dark	Physical	—	100	10	Normal
TM66	Payback	Dark	Physical	50	100	10	Normal
TM67	Retaliate	Normal	Physical	70	100	5	Normal
TM71	Stone Edge	Rock	Physical	100	80	5	Normal
TM80	Rock Slide	Rock	Physical	75	90	10	Many Others
TM84	Poison Jab	Poison	Physical	80	100	20	Normal
TM86	Grass Knot	Grass	Special	—	100	20	Normal
TM87	Swagger	Normal	Status	—	90	15	Normal
TM88	Sleep Talk	Normal	Status	—	—	10	Self
TM90	Substitute	Normal	Status	—	—	10	Self
TM94	Rock Smash	Fighting	Physical	40	100	15	Normal
TM98	Power-Up Punch	Fighting	Physical	40	100	20	Normal
TM100	Confide	Normal	Status	—	—	20	Normal

No.	Name	Type	Kind	Pow.	Acc.	PP	Range
HM04	Strength	Normal	Physical	80	100	15	Normal

● MOVES TAUGHT BY PEOPLE

Name	Type	Kind	Pow.	Acc.	PP	Range

Mountain Kalos 095
Muscular Pokémon
Conkeldurr

HEIGHT: 4'07" WEIGHT: 191.8 lbs.
GENDER: ♂/♀

X It is thought that Conkeldurr taught humans how to make concrete more than 2,000 years ago.

Y Rather than rely on force, they master moves that utilize the centrifugal force of spinning concrete.

TYPE Fighting

ABILITIES
Guts
Sheer Force

HIDDEN ABILITY
Iron Fist

STAT GROWTH RATES
HP ▪▪▪▪
Attack ▪▪▪▪▪▪▪▪
Defense ▪▪▪▪
Sp. Atk ▪▪▪
Sp. Def ▪▪▪
Speed ▪▪▪

EGG GROUP
Human-Like

EVOLUTION

Lv. 25 — Link Trade

Timburr — Gurdurr — Conkeldurr

ITEMS SOMETIMES HELD BY WILD POKÉMON
None

Damage taken in normal battles		Damage taken in Inverse Battles	
Normal	×1	Normal	×1
Fire	×1	Fire	×1
Water	×1	Water	×1
Grass	×1	Grass	×1
Electric	×1	Electric	×1
Ice	×1	Ice	×1
Fighting	×1	Fighting	×1
Poison	×1	Poison	×1
Ground	×1	Ground	×1
Flying	×2	Flying	×0.5
Psychic	×2	Psychic	×0.5
Bug	×0.5	Bug	×2
Rock	×0.5	Rock	×2
Ghost	×1	Ghost	×1
Dragon	×1	Dragon	×1
Dark	×0.5	Dark	×2
Steel	×1	Steel	×1
Fairy	×2	Fairy	×0.5

Can be used in	
Inverse Battle	Battle Institute
—	Battle Maison
Battle Chateau	Random Matchup

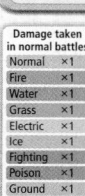

Same form for ♂ / ♀

 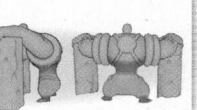

How to obtain for your Mountain Kalos Pokédex

Receive Gurdurr by Link Trade, and have it evolve.

Receive Gurdurr by Link Trade, and have it evolve.

AFTER THE HALL OF FAME

CENTRAL KALOS

COASTAL KALOS

MOUNTAIN KALOS

095

Conkeldurr

ADVENTURE DATA

● LEVEL-UP MOVES

Lv.	Name	Type	Kind	Pow.	Acc.	PP	Range
1	Pound	Normal	Physical	40	100	35	Normal
1	Leer	Normal	Status	—	100	30	Many Others
1	Focus Energy	Normal	Status	—	—	30	Self
1	Bide	Normal	Physical	—	—	10	Self
4	Focus Energy	Normal	Status	—	—	30	Self
8	Bide	Normal	Physical	—	—	10	Self
12	Low Kick	Fighting	Physical	—	100	20	Normal
16	Rock Throw	Rock	Physical	50	90	15	Normal
20	Wake-Up Slap	Fighting	Physical	70	100	10	Normal
24	Chip Away	Normal	Physical	70	100	20	Normal
29	Bulk Up	Fighting	Status	—	—	20	Self
33	Rock Slide	Rock	Physical	75	90	10	Many Others
37	Dynamic Punch	Fighting	Physical	100	50	5	Normal
41	Scary Face	Normal	Status	—	100	10	Normal
45	Hammer Arm	Fighting	Physical	100	90	10	Normal
49	Stone Edge	Rock	Physical	100	80	5	Normal
53	Focus Punch	Fighting	Physical	150	100	20	Normal
57	Superpower	Fighting	Physical	120	100	5	Normal

● TM & HM MOVES

No.	Name	Type	Kind	Pow.	Acc.	PP	Range
TM06	Toxic	Poison	Status	—	90	10	Normal
TM08	Bulk Up	Fighting	Status	—	—	20	Self
TM10	Hidden Power	Normal	Special	60	100	15	Normal
TM11	Sunny Day	Fire	Status	—	—	5	Both Sides
TM12	Taunt	Dark	Status	—	100	20	Normal
TM15	Hyper Beam	Normal	Special	150	90	5	Normal
TM17	Protect	Normal	Status	—	—	10	Self
TM18	Rain Dance	Water	Status	—	—	5	Both Sides
TM21	Frustration	Normal	Physical	—	100	20	Normal
TM23	Smack Down	Rock	Physical	50	100	15	Normal
TM26	Earthquake	Ground	Physical	100	100	10	Adjacent
TM27	Return	Normal	Physical	—	100	20	Normal
TM28	Dig	Ground	Physical	80	100	10	Normal
TM31	Brick Break	Fighting	Physical	75	100	15	Normal
TM32	Double Team	Normal	Status	—	—	15	Self
TM39	Rock Tomb	Rock	Physical	60	95	15	Normal
TM42	Facade	Normal	Physical	70	100	20	Normal
TM44	Rest	Psychic	Status	—	—	10	Self
TM45	Attract	Normal	Status	—	100	15	Normal
TM47	Low Sweep	Fighting	Physical	65	100	20	Normal
TM48	Round	Normal	Special	60	100	15	Normal
TM52	Focus Blast	Fighting	Special	120	70	5	Normal
TM56	Fling	Dark	Physical	—	100	10	Normal
TM66	Payback	Dark	Physical	50	100	10	Normal
TM67	Retaliate	Normal	Physical	70	100	5	Normal
TM68	Giga Impact	Normal	Physical	150	90	5	Normal
TM71	Stone Edge	Rock	Physical	100	80	5	Normal
TM78	Bulldoze	Ground	Physical	60	100	20	Adjacent
TM80	Rock Slide	Rock	Physical	75	90	10	Many Others
TM84	Poison Jab	Poison	Physical	80	100	20	Normal
TM86	Grass Knot	Grass	Special	—	100	20	Normal
TM87	Swagger	Normal	Status	—	90	15	Normal
TM88	Sleep Talk	Normal	Status	—	—	10	Self
TM90	Substitute	Normal	Status	—	—	10	Self
TM94	Rock Smash	Fighting	Physical	40	100	15	Normal
TM98	Power-Up Punch	Fighting	Physical	40	100	20	Normal
TM100	Confide	Normal	Status	—	—	20	Normal
HM04	Strength	Normal	Physical	80	100	15	Normal

● MOVES TAUGHT BY PEOPLE

Name	Type	Kind	Pow.	Acc.	PP	Range

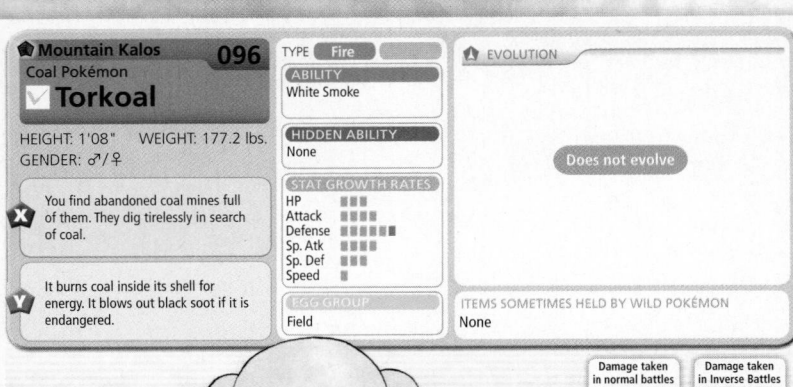

Mountain Kalos 096
Coal Pokémon
☑ Torkoal

HEIGHT: 1'08" WEIGHT: 177.2 lbs.
GENDER: ♂/♀

| TYPE | Fire |

ABILITY
White Smoke

HIDDEN ABILITY
None

X — You find abandoned coal mines full of them. They dig tirelessly in search of coal.

Y — It burns coal inside its shell for energy. It blows out black soot if it is endangered.

STAT GROWTH RATES

HP	▪▪▪
Attack	▪▪▪
Defense	▪▪▪▪▪▪▪
Sp. Atk	▪▪▪
Sp. Def	▪▪▪
Speed	▪

EGG GROUP
Field

EVOLUTION

Does not evolve

ITEMS SOMETIMES HELD BY WILD POKÉMON
None

Damage taken in normal battles		Damage taken in Inverse Battles	
Normal	×1	Normal	×1
Fire	×0.5	Fire	×2
Water	×2	Water	×0.5
Grass	×0.5	Grass	×2
Electric	×1	Electric	×1
Ice	×0.5	Ice	×2
Fighting	×1	Fighting	×1
Poison	×1	Poison	×1
Ground	×2	Ground	×0.5
Flying	×1	Flying	×1
Psychic	×1	Psychic	×1
Bug	×0.5	Bug	×2
Rock	×2	Rock	×0.5
Ghost	×1	Ghost	×1
Dragon	×1	Dragon	×1
Dark	×1	Dark	×1
Steel	×0.5	Steel	×2
Fairy	×0.5	Fairy	×2

Can be used in	
Inverse Battle	Battle Institute
—	Battle Maison
Battle Chateau	Random Matchup

Same form for ♂/♀

How to obtain for your Mountain Kalos Pokédex

❶ Catch in the tall grass on Route 18.
❷ Catch in the red flowers on Route 18.

❶ Catch in the tall grass on Route 18.
❷ Catch in the red flowers on Route 18.

● LEVEL-UP MOVES

Lv.	Name	Type	Kind	Pow.	Acc.	PP	Range
1	Inferno	Fire	Special	100	50	5	Normal
1	Heat Wave	Fire	Special	95	90	10	Many Others
1	Protect	Normal	Status	—	—	10	Self
1	Flail	Normal	Physical	—	100	15	Normal
1	Shell Smash	Normal	Status	—	—	15	Self
1	Ember	Fire	Special	40	100	25	Normal
4	Smog	Poison	Special	30	70	20	Normal
7	Withdraw	Water	Status	—	—	40	Self
12	Curse	Ghost	Status	—	—	10	Varies
17	Fire Spin	Fire	Special	35	85	15	Normal
20	Smokescreen	Normal	Status	—	100	20	Normal
23	Flame Wheel	Fire	Physical	60	100	25	Normal
25	Rapid Spin	Normal	Physical	20	100	40	Normal
28	Flamethrower	Fire	Special	90	100	15	Normal
33	Body Slam	Normal	Physical	85	100	15	Normal
36	Protect	Normal	Status	—	—	10	Self
39	Lava Plume	Fire	Special	80	100	15	Adjacent
44	Iron Defense	Steel	Status	—	—	15	Self
49	Amnesia	Psychic	Status	—	—	20	Self
52	Flail	Normal	Physical	—	100	15	Normal
55	Heat Wave	Fire	Special	95	90	10	Many Others
60	Inferno	Fire	Special	100	50	5	Normal
65	Shell Smash	Normal	Status	—	—	15	Self

● TM & HM MOVES

No.	Name	Type	Kind	Pow.	Acc.	PP	Range
TM06	Toxic	Poison	Status	—	90	10	Normal
TM10	Hidden Power	Normal	Special	60	100	15	Normal
TM11	Sunny Day	Fire	Status	—	—	5	Both Sides
TM15	Hyper Beam	Normal	Special	150	90	5	Normal
TM17	Protect	Normal	Status	—	—	10	Self
TM21	Frustration	Normal	Physical	—	100	20	Normal
TM22	Solar Beam	Grass	Special	120	100	10	Normal
TM26	Earthquake	Ground	Physical	100	100	10	Adjacent
TM27	Return	Normal	Physical	—	100	20	Normal
TM32	Double Team	Normal	Status	—	—	15	Self
TM35	Flamethrower	Fire	Special	90	100	15	Normal
TM36	Sludge Bomb	Poison	Special	90	100	10	Normal
TM38	Fire Blast	Fire	Special	110	85	5	Normal
TM39	Rock Tomb	Rock	Physical	60	95	15	Normal
TM42	Facade	Normal	Physical	70	100	20	Normal
TM43	Flame Charge	Fire	Physical	50	100	20	Normal
TM44	Rest	Psychic	Status	—	—	10	Self
TM45	Attract	Normal	Status	—	100	15	Normal
TM48	Round	Normal	Special	60	100	15	Normal
TM50	Overheat	Fire	Special	130	90	5	Normal
TM59	Incinerate	Fire	Special	60	100	15	Many Others
TM61	Will-O-Wisp	Fire	Status	—	85	15	Normal
TM64	Explosion	Normal	Physical	250	100	5	Adjacent
TM68	Giga Impact	Normal	Physical	150	90	5	Normal
TM71	Stone Edge	Rock	Physical	100	80	5	Normal
TM74	Gyro Ball	Steel	Physical	—	100	5	Normal
TM78	Bulldoze	Ground	Physical	60	100	20	Adjacent
TM80	Rock Slide	Rock	Physical	75	90	10	Many Others
TM87	Swagger	Normal	Status	—	90	15	Normal
TM88	Sleep Talk	Normal	Status	—	—	10	Self
TM90	Substitute	Normal	Status	—	—	10	Self
TM94	Rock Smash	Fighting	Physical	40	100	15	Normal
TM96	Nature Power	Normal	Status	—	—	20	Normal

No.	Name	Type	Kind	Pow.	Acc.	PP	Range
TM100	Confide	Normal	Status	—	—	20	Normal
HM04	Strength	Normal	Physical	80	100	15	Normal

● MOVES TAUGHT BY PEOPLE

Name	Type	Kind	Pow.	Acc.	PP	Range

● EGG MOVES

Name	Type	Kind	Pow.	Acc.	PP	Range
Eruption	Fire	Special	150	100	5	Many Others
Endure	Normal	Status	—	—	10	Self
Sleep Talk	Normal	Status	—	—	10	Self
Yawn	Normal	Status	—	—	10	Normal
Fissure	Ground	Physical	—	30	5	Normal
Skull Bash	Normal	Physical	130	100	10	Normal
Flame Burst	Fire	Special	70	100	15	Normal
Clear Smog	Poison	Special	50	—	15	Normal
Superpower	Fighting	Physical	120	100	5	Normal

Mountain Kalos 097
Mouse Pokémon

☑ Sandshrew

HEIGHT: 2'00" WEIGHT: 26.5 lbs.
GENDER: ♂/♀

X It burrows and lives underground. If threatened, it curls itself up into a ball for protection.

Y Disliking water, it lives in deep burrows in arid areas. It can roll itself instantly into a ball.

TYPE Ground

ABILITY
Sand Veil

HIDDEN ABILITY
Sand Rush

STAT GROWTH RATES
HP	▪▪
Attack	▪▪▪
Defense	▪▪▪▪
Sp. Atk	▪
Sp. Def	▪
Speed	▪▪

EGG GROUP
Field

EVOLUTION

Lv. 22

Sandshrew → Sandslash

ITEMS SOMETIMES HELD BY WILD POKÉMON
None

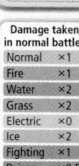

Damage taken in normal battles		Damage taken in Inverse Battles	
Normal	×1	Normal	×1
Fire	×1	Fire	×1
Water	×2	Water	×0.5
Grass	×2	Grass	×0.5
Electric	×0	Electric	×2
Ice	×2	Ice	×0.5
Fighting	×1	Fighting	×1
Poison	×0.5	Poison	×2
Ground	×1	Ground	×1
Flying	×1	Flying	×1
Psychic	×1	Psychic	×1
Bug	×1	Bug	×1
Rock	×0.5	Rock	×2
Ghost	×1	Ghost	×1
Dragon	×1	Dragon	×1
Dark	×1	Dark	×1
Steel	×1	Steel	×1
Fairy	×1	Fairy	×1

Can be used in	
Inverse Battle	Battle Institute
-----	Battle Maison
Battle Chateau	Random Matchup

Same form for ♂ / ♀

How to obtain for your Mountain Kalos Pokédex

Leave Sandslash at the Pokémon Day Care, and hatch the Egg that is found.	Leave Sandslash at the Pokémon Day Care, and hatch the Egg that is found.

● LEVEL-UP MOVES

Lv.	Name	Type	Kind	Pow.	Acc.	PP	Range
1	Scratch	Normal	Physical	40	100	35	Normal
1	Defense Curl	Normal	Status	—	—	40	Self
3	Sand Attack	Ground	Status	—	100	15	Normal
5	Poison Sting	Poison	Physical	15	100	35	Normal
7	Rollout	Rock	Physical	30	90	20	Normal
9	Rapid Spin	Normal	Physical	20	100	40	Normal
11	Swift	Normal	Special	60	—	20	Many Others
14	Fury Cutter	Bug	Physical	40	95	20	Normal
17	Magnitude	Ground	Physical	—	100	30	Adjacent
20	Fury Swipes	Normal	Physical	18	80	15	Normal
23	Sand Tomb	Ground	Physical	35	85	15	Normal
26	Slash	Normal	Physical	70	100	20	Normal
30	Dig	Ground	Physical	80	100	10	Normal
34	Gyro Ball	Steel	Physical	—	100	5	Normal
38	Swords Dance	Normal	Status	—	—	20	Self
42	Sandstorm	Rock	Status	—	—	10	Both Sides
46	Earthquake	Ground	Physical	100	100	10	Adjacent

● TM & HM MOVES

No.	Name	Type	Kind	Pow.	Acc.	PP	Range
TM01	Hone Claws	Dark	Status	—	—	15	Self
TM06	Toxic	Poison	Status	—	90	10	Normal
TM10	Hidden Power	Normal	Special	60	100	15	Normal
TM11	Sunny Day	Fire	Status	—	—	5	Both Sides
TM17	Protect	Normal	Status	—	—	10	Self
TM20	Safeguard	Normal	Status	—	—	25	Your Side
TM21	Frustration	Normal	Physical	—	100	20	Normal
TM26	Earthquake	Ground	Physical	100	100	10	Adjacent
TM27	Return	Normal	Physical	—	100	20	Normal
TM28	Dig	Ground	Physical	80	100	10	Normal
TM31	Brick Break	Fighting	Physical	75	100	15	Normal
TM32	Double Team	Normal	Status	—	—	15	Self
TM37	Sandstorm	Rock	Status	—	—	10	Both Sides
TM39	Rock Tomb	Rock	Physical	60	95	15	Normal
TM40	Aerial Ace	Flying	Physical	60	—	20	Normal
TM42	Facade	Normal	Physical	70	100	20	Normal
TM44	Rest	Psychic	Status	—	—	10	Self
TM45	Attract	Normal	Status	—	100	15	Normal
TM46	Thief	Dark	Physical	60	100	25	Normal
TM48	Round	Normal	Special	60	100	15	Normal
TM56	Fling	Dark	Physical	—	100	10	Normal
TM65	Shadow Claw	Ghost	Physical	70	100	15	Normal
TM74	Gyro Ball	Steel	Physical	—	100	5	Normal
TM75	Swords Dance	Normal	Status	—	—	20	Self
TM78	Bulldoze	Ground	Physical	60	100	20	Adjacent
TM80	Rock Slide	Rock	Physical	75	90	10	Many Others
TM81	X-Scissor	Bug	Physical	80	100	15	Normal
TM84	Poison Jab	Poison	Physical	80	100	20	Normal
TM87	Swagger	Normal	Status	—	90	15	Normal
TM88	Sleep Talk	Normal	Status	—	—	10	Self
TM90	Substitute	Normal	Status	—	—	10	Self
TM94	Rock Smash	Fighting	Physical	40	100	15	Normal
TM100	Confide	Normal	Status	—	—	20	Normal

No.	Name	Type	Kind	Pow.	Acc.	PP	Range
HM01	Cut	Normal	Physical	50	95	30	Normal
HM04	Strength	Normal	Physical	80	100	15	Normal

● MOVES TAUGHT BY PEOPLE

Name	Type	Kind	Pow.	Acc.	PP	Range

● EGG MOVES

Name	Type	Kind	Pow.	Acc.	PP	Range
Flail	Normal	Physical	—	100	15	Normal
Counter	Fighting	Physical	—	100	20	Varies
Rapid Spin	Normal	Physical	20	100	40	Normal
Metal Claw	Steel	Physical	50	95	35	Normal
Crush Claw	Normal	Physical	75	95	10	Normal
Night Slash	Dark	Physical	70	100	15	Normal
Mud Shot	Ground	Special	55	95	15	Normal
Endure	Normal	Status	—	—	10	Self
Chip Away	Normal	Physical	70	100	20	Normal
Rock Climb	Normal	Physical	90	85	20	Normal
Rototiller	Ground	Status	—	—	10	Adjacent

AFTER THE HALL OF FAME

CENTRAL KALOS

COASTAL KALOS

MOUNTAIN KALOS

098

Sandslash

ADVENTURE DATA

🏔 Mountain Kalos **098**

Mouse Pokémon

✓ Sandslash

HEIGHT: 3'03" WEIGHT: 65.0 lbs.
GENDER: ♂/♀

X	If it digs at an incredible pace, it may snap off its spikes and claws. They grow back in a day.
Y	Curls up into a spiny ball when threatened. It can roll while curled up to attack or escape.

TYPE Ground

ABILITY
Sand Veil

HIDDEN ABILITY
Sand Rush

STAT GROWTH RATES
HP ■■■
Attack ■■■■
Defense ■■■■■
Sp. Atk ■■
Sp. Def ■■
Speed ■■■■

EGG GROUP
Field

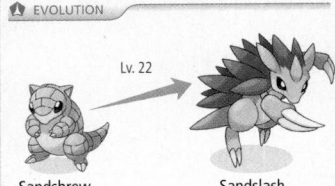

⬆ EVOLUTION

Lv. 22

Sandshrew → Sandslash

ITEMS SOMETIMES HELD BY WILD POKÉMON
Quick Claw

Damage taken in normal battles		Damage taken in Inverse Battles	
Normal	×1	Normal	×1
Fire	×1	Fire	×1
Water	×2	Water	×0.5
Grass	×2	Grass	×0.5
Electric	×0	Electric	×2
Ice	×2	Ice	×0.5
Fighting	×1	Fighting	×1
Poison	×0.5	Poison	×2
Ground	×1	Ground	×1
Flying	×1	Flying	×1
Psychic	×1	Psychic	×1
Bug	×1	Bug	×1
Rock	×0.5	Rock	×2
Ghost	×1	Ghost	×1
Dragon	×1	Dragon	×1
Dark	×1	Dark	×1
Steel	×1	Steel	×1
Fairy	×1	Fairy	×1

Can be used in	
Inverse Battle	Battle Institute
—	Battle Maison
Battle Chateau	Random Matchup

Same form for ♂/♀

How to obtain for your Mountain Kalos Pokédex

❶ Catch in the tall grass on Route 18.
❷ Catch in the red flowers on Route 18.

❶ Catch in the tall grass on Route 18.
❷ Catch in the red flowers on Route 18.

● LEVEL-UP MOVES

Lv.	Name	Type	Kind	Pow.	Acc.	PP	Range
1	Scratch	Normal	Physical	40	100	35	Normal
1	Defense Curl	Normal	Status	—	—	40	Self
3	Sand Attack	Ground	Status	—	100	15	Normal
5	Poison Sting	Poison	Physical	15	100	35	Normal
5	Sand Attack	Ground	Status	—	100	15	Normal
5	Poison Sting	Poison	Physical	15	100	35	Normal
7	Rollout	Rock	Physical	30	90	20	Normal
9	Rapid Spin	Normal	Physical	20	100	40	Normal
11	Swift	Normal	Special	60	—	20	Many Others
14	Fury Cutter	Bug	Physical	40	95	20	Normal
17	Magnitude	Ground	Physical	—	100	30	Adjacent
20	Fury Swipes	Normal	Physical	18	80	15	Normal
22	Crush Claw	Normal	Physical	75	95	10	Normal
23	Sand Tomb	Ground	Physical	35	85	15	Normal
26	Slash	Normal	Physical	70	100	20	Normal
30	Dig	Ground	Physical	80	100	10	Normal
34	Gyro Ball	Steel	Physical	—	100	5	Normal
38	Swords Dance	Normal	Status	—	—	20	Self
42	Sandstorm	Rock	Status	—	—	10	Both Sides
46	Earthquake	Ground	Physical	100	100	10	Adjacent

● TM & HM MOVES

No.	Name	Type	Kind	Pow.	Acc.	PP	Range
TM01	Hone Claws	Dark	Status	—	—	15	Self
TM06	Toxic	Poison	Status	—	90	10	Normal
TM10	Hidden Power	Normal	Special	60	100	15	Normal
TM11	Sunny Day	Fire	Status	—	—	5	Both Sides
TM15	Hyper Beam	Normal	Special	150	90	5	Normal
TM17	Protect	Normal	Status	—	—	10	Self
TM20	Safeguard	Normal	Status	—	—	25	Your Side
TM21	Frustration	Normal	Physical	—	100	20	Normal
TM26	Earthquake	Ground	Physical	100	100	10	Adjacent
TM27	Return	Normal	Physical	—	100	20	Normal
TM28	Dig	Ground	Physical	80	100	10	Normal
TM31	Brick Break	Fighting	Physical	75	100	15	Normal
TM32	Double Team	Normal	Status	—	—	15	Self
TM37	Sandstorm	Rock	Status	—	—	10	Both Sides
TM39	Rock Tomb	Rock	Physical	60	95	15	Normal
TM40	Aerial Ace	Flying	Physical	60	—	20	Normal
TM42	Facade	Normal	Physical	70	100	20	Normal
TM44	Rest	Psychic	Status	—	—	10	Self
TM45	Attract	Normal	Status	—	100	15	Normal
TM46	Thief	Dark	Physical	60	100	25	Normal
TM48	Round	Normal	Special	60	100	15	Normal
TM52	Focus Blast	Fighting	Special	120	70	5	Normal
TM56	Fling	Dark	Physical	—	100	10	Normal
TM65	Shadow Claw	Ghost	Physical	70	100	15	Normal
TM68	Giga Impact	Normal	Physical	150	90	5	Normal
TM71	Stone Edge	Rock	Physical	100	80	5	Normal
TM74	Gyro Ball	Steel	Physical	—	100	5	Normal
TM75	Swords Dance	Normal	Status	—	—	20	Self
TM78	Bulldoze	Ground	Physical	60	100	20	Adjacent
TM80	Rock Slide	Rock	Physical	75	90	10	Many Others
TM81	X-Scissor	Bug	Physical	80	100	15	Normal
TM84	Poison Jab	Poison	Physical	80	100	20	Normal
TM87	Swagger	Normal	Status	—	90	15	Normal

No.	Name	Type	Kind	Pow.	Acc.	PP	Range
TM88	Sleep Talk	Normal	Status	—	—	10	Self
TM90	Substitute	Normal	Status	—	—	10	Self
TM94	Rock Smash	Fighting	Physical	40	100	15	Normal
TM100	Confide	Normal	Status	—	—	20	Normal
HM01	Cut	Normal	Physical	50	95	30	Normal
HM04	Strength	Normal	Physical	80	100	15	Normal

● MOVES TAUGHT BY PEOPLE

Name	Type	Kind	Pow.	Acc.	PP	Range

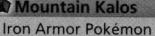 **Mountain Kalos** **099**

Iron Armor Pokémon

☑ **Aron**

HEIGHT: 1'04" WEIGHT: 132.3 lbs.
GENDER: ♂/♀

 It usually lives deep in mountains. However, hunger may drive it to eat railroad tracks and cars.

 When it evolves, it sheds the steel carapace that covers its whole body and develops a new one.

TYPE Steel Rock

ABILITIES
Sturdy
Rock Head

HIDDEN ABILITY
Heavy Metal

STAT GROWTH RATES
HP	▪▪
Attack	▪▪▪▪
Defense	▪▪▪▪
Sp. Atk	▪▪
Sp. Def	▪▪
Speed	▪▪

EGG GROUP
Monster

EVOLUTION

	Lv. 32	Lv. 42
Aron	Lairon	Aggron

ITEMS SOMETIMES HELD BY WILD POKÉMON
None

Damage taken in normal battles		Damage taken in Inverse Battles	
Normal	×0.25	Normal	×4
Fire	×1	Fire	×1
Water	×2	Water	×0.5
Grass	×1	Grass	×1
Electric	×1	Electric	×1
Ice	×0.5	Ice	×2
Fighting	×4	Fighting	×0.25
Poison	×0	Poison	×4
Ground	×4	Ground	×0.25
Flying	×0.25	Flying	×4
Psychic	×0.5	Psychic	×2
Bug	×0.5	Bug	×2
Rock	×0.5	Rock	×2
Ghost	×1	Ghost	×1
Dragon	×0.5	Dragon	×2
Dark	×1	Dark	×1
Steel	×1	Steel	×1
Fairy	×0.5	Fairy	×2

Can be used in	
Inverse Battle	Battle Institute
—	Battle Maison
Battle Chateau	Random Matchup

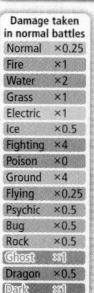

Same form for ♂/♀

  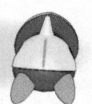

How to obtain for your Mountain Kalos Pokédex

Catch in a Horde Encounter in Terminus Cave.

Link Trade or transfer from another game.

● **LEVEL-UP MOVES**

Lv.	Name	Type	Kind	Pow.	Acc.	PP	Range
1	Tackle	Normal	Physical	50	100	35	Normal
1	Harden	Normal	Status	—	—	30	Self
4	Mud-Slap	Ground	Special	20	100	10	Normal
8	Headbutt	Normal	Physical	70	100	15	Normal
11	Metal Claw	Steel	Physical	50	95	35	Normal
15	Iron Defense	Steel	Status	—	—	15	Self
18	Roar	Normal	Status	—	—	20	Normal
22	Take Down	Normal	Physical	90	85	20	Normal
25	Iron Head	Steel	Physical	80	100	15	Normal
29	Protect	Normal	Status	—	—	10	Self
32	Metal Sound	Steel	Status	—	85	40	Normal
36	Iron Tail	Steel	Physical	100	75	15	Normal
39	Autotomize	Steel	Status	—	—	15	Self
43	Heavy Slam	Steel	Physical	—	100	10	Normal
46	Double-Edge	Normal	Physical	120	100	15	Normal
50	Metal Burst	Steel	Physical	—	100	10	Varies

● **TM & HM MOVES**

No.	Name	Type	Kind	Pow.	Acc.	PP	Range
TM01	Hone Claws	Dark	Status	—	—	15	Self
TM05	Roar	Normal	Status	—	—	20	Normal
TM06	Toxic	Poison	Status	—	90	10	Normal
TM10	Hidden Power	Normal	Special	60	100	15	Normal
TM11	Sunny Day	Fire	Status	—	—	5	Both Sides
TM17	Protect	Normal	Status	—	—	10	Self
TM18	Rain Dance	Water	Status	—	—	5	Both Sides
TM21	Frustration	Normal	Physical	—	100	20	Normal
TM26	Earthquake	Ground	Physical	100	100	10	Adjacent
TM27	Return	Normal	Physical	—	100	20	Normal
TM28	Dig	Ground	Physical	80	100	10	Normal
TM32	Double Team	Normal	Status	—	—	15	Self
TM37	Sandstorm	Rock	Status	—	—	10	Both Sides
TM39	Rock Tomb	Rock	Physical	60	95	15	Normal
TM40	Aerial Ace	Flying	Physical	60	—	20	Normal
TM42	Facade	Normal	Physical	70	100	20	Normal
TM44	Rest	Psychic	Status	—	—	10	Self
TM45	Attract	Normal	Status	—	100	15	Normal
TM48	Round	Normal	Special	60	100	15	Normal
TM65	Shadow Claw	Ghost	Physical	70	100	15	Normal
TM69	Rock Polish	Rock	Status	—	—	20	Self
TM78	Bulldoze	Ground	Physical	60	100	20	Adjacent
TM80	Rock Slide	Rock	Physical	75	90	10	Many Others
TM87	Swagger	Normal	Status	—	90	15	Normal
TM88	Sleep Talk	Normal	Status	—	—	10	Self
TM90	Substitute	Normal	Status	—	—	10	Self
TM94	Rock Smash	Fighting	Physical	40	100	15	Normal
TM100	Confide	Normal	Status	—	—	20	Normal
HM01	Cut	Normal	Physical	50	95	30	Normal
HM04	Strength	Normal	Physical	80	100	15	Normal

No.	Name	Type	Kind	Pow.	Acc.	PP	Range

● **MOVES TAUGHT BY PEOPLE**

Name	Type	Kind	Pow.	Acc.	PP	Range

● **EGG MOVES**

Name	Type	Kind	Pow.	Acc.	PP	Range
Endeavor	Normal	Physical	—	100	5	Normal
Body Slam	Normal	Physical	85	100	15	Normal
Stomp	Normal	Physical	65	100	20	Normal
Smelling Salts	Normal	Physical	70	100	10	Normal
Curse	Ghost	Status	—	—	10	Varies
Screech	Normal	Status	—	85	40	Normal
Iron Head	Steel	Physical	80	100	15	Normal
Dragon Rush	Dragon	Physical	100	75	10	Normal
Head Smash	Rock	Physical	150	80	5	Normal
Superpower	Fighting	Physical	120	100	5	Normal
Stealth Rock	Rock	Status	—	—	20	Other Side
Reversal	Fighting	Physical	—	100	15	Normal

AFTER THE HALL OF FAME

CENTRAL KALOS

COASTAL KALOS

MOUNTAIN KALOS

099 Aron

ADVENTURE DATA

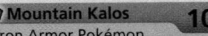

Mountain Kalos 100

Iron Armor Pokémon

Lairon

HEIGHT: 2'11" WEIGHT: 264.6 lbs.
GENDER: ♂/♀

X It loves iron ore. Groups of them fight for territory by bashing one another with their steel bodies.

Y It habitually shows off its strength with the size of sparks it creates by ramming its steel body into boulders.

TYPE Steel / Rock

ABILITIES
Sturdy
Rock Head

HIDDEN ABILITY
Heavy Metal

STAT GROWTH RATES
HP	■■■
Attack	■■■■
Defense	■■■■■■
Sp. Atk	■■
Sp. Def	■■
Speed	■■

EGG GROUP
Monster

EVOLUTION

Aron — Lv. 32 → Lairon — Lv. 42 → Aggron

ITEMS SOMETIMES HELD BY WILD POKÉMON
Hard Stone

Damage taken in normal battles		Damage taken in Inverse Battles	
Normal	×0.25	Normal	×4
Fire	×1	Fire	×1
Water	×2	Water	×0.5
Grass	×1	Grass	×1
Electric	×1	Electric	×1
Ice	×0.5	Ice	×2
Fighting	×4	Fighting	×0.25
Poison	×0	Poison	×4
Ground	×4	Ground	×0.25
Flying	×0.25	Flying	×4
Psychic	×0.5	Psychic	×2
Bug	×0.5	Bug	×2
Rock	×0.5	Rock	×2
Ghost	×1	Ghost	×1
Dragon	×0.5	Dragon	×2
Dark	×1	Dark	×1
Steel	×1	Steel	×1
Fairy	×0.5	Fairy	×2

Can be used in	
Inverse Battle	Battle Institute
—	Battle Maison
Battle Chateau	Random Matchup

Same form for ♂/♀

How to obtain for your Mountain Kalos Pokédex

❶ Catch in the tall grass or red flowers on Route 18.
❷ Level up Aron to Lv. 32.

❶ Link Trade or transfer from another game.
❷ Level up Aron to Lv. 32.

LEVEL-UP MOVES

Lv.	Name	Type	Kind	Pow.	Acc.	PP	Range
1	Tackle	Normal	Physical	50	100	35	Normal
1	Harden	Normal	Status	—	—	30	Self
1	Mud-Slap	Ground	Special	20	100	10	Normal
1	Headbutt	Normal	Physical	70	100	15	Normal
4	Mud-Slap	Ground	Special	20	100	10	Normal
8	Headbutt	Normal	Physical	70	100	15	Normal
11	Metal Claw	Steel	Physical	50	95	35	Normal
15	Iron Defense	Steel	Status	—	—	15	Self
18	Roar	Normal	Status	—	—	20	Normal
22	Take Down	Normal	Physical	90	85	20	Normal
25	Iron Head	Steel	Physical	80	100	15	Normal
29	Protect	Normal	Status	—	—	10	Self
34	Metal Sound	Steel	Status	—	85	40	Normal
40	Iron Tail	Steel	Physical	100	75	15	Normal
45	Autotomize	Steel	Status	—	—	15	Self
51	Heavy Slam	Steel	Physical	—	100	10	Normal
56	Double-Edge	Normal	Physical	120	100	15	Normal
62	Metal Burst	Steel	Physical	—	100	10	Varies

TM & HM MOVES

No.	Name	Type	Kind	Pow.	Acc.	PP	Range
TM01	Hone Claws	Dark	Status	—	—	15	Self
TM05	Roar	Normal	Status	—	—	20	Normal
TM06	Toxic	Poison	Status	—	90	10	Normal
TM10	Hidden Power	Normal	Special	60	100	15	Normal
TM11	Sunny Day	Fire	Status	—	—	5	Both Sides
TM17	Protect	Normal	Status	—	—	10	Self
TM18	Rain Dance	Water	Status	—	—	5	Both Sides
TM21	Frustration	Normal	Physical	—	100	20	Normal
TM26	Earthquake	Ground	Physical	100	100	10	Adjacent
TM27	Return	Normal	Physical	—	100	20	Normal
TM28	Dig	Ground	Physical	80	100	10	Normal
TM32	Double Team	Normal	Status	—	—	15	Self
TM37	Sandstorm	Rock	Status	—	—	10	Both Sides
TM39	Rock Tomb	Rock	Physical	60	95	15	Normal
TM40	Aerial Ace	Flying	Physical	60	—	20	Normal
TM42	Facade	Normal	Physical	70	100	20	Normal
TM44	Rest	Psychic	Status	—	—	10	Self
TM45	Attract	Normal	Status	—	100	15	Normal
TM48	Round	Normal	Special	60	100	15	Normal
TM65	Shadow Claw	Ghost	Physical	70	100	15	Normal
TM69	Rock Polish	Rock	Status	—	—	20	Self
TM71	Stone Edge	Rock	Physical	100	80	5	Normal
TM78	Bulldoze	Ground	Physical	60	100	20	Adjacent
TM80	Rock Slide	Rock	Physical	75	90	10	Many Others
TM87	Swagger	Normal	Status	—	90	15	Normal
TM88	Sleep Talk	Normal	Status	—	—	10	Self
TM90	Substitute	Normal	Status	—	—	10	Self
TM94	Rock Smash	Fighting	Physical	40	100	15	Normal
TM100	Confide	Normal	Status	—	—	20	Normal
HM01	Cut	Normal	Physical	50	95	30	Normal
HM04	Strength	Normal	Physical	80	100	15	Normal

MOVES TAUGHT BY PEOPLE

Name	Type	Kind	Pow.	Acc.	PP	Range

🏔 Mountain Kalos 101

Iron Armor Pokémon

☑ Aggron

HEIGHT: 6'11" WEIGHT: 793.7 lbs.
GENDER: ♂ / ♀

TYPE Steel Rock

ABILITIES
Sturdy
Rock Head

HIDDEN ABILITY
Heavy Metal

STAT GROWTH RATES

HP	■■■
Attack	■■■■■
Defense	■■■■■■■■
Sp. Atk	■■■
Sp. Def	■■■
Speed	■■■

EGG GROUP
Monster

Ⓧ It claims an entire mountain as its own. The more wounds it has, the more it has battled, so don't take it lightly.

Ⓨ While seeking iron for food, it digs tunnels by breaking through bedrock with its steel horns.

⚡ EVOLUTION

Aron — Lv. 32 — Lairon — Lv. 42 — Aggron

ITEMS SOMETIMES HELD BY WILD POKÉMON
None

Damage taken in normal battles

Normal	×0.25
Fire	×1
Water	×2
Grass	×1
Electric	×1
Ice	×0.5
Fighting	×4
Poison	×0
Ground	×4
Flying	×0.25
Psychic	×0.5
Bug	×0.5
Rock	×0.5
Ghost	×1
Dragon	×0.5
Dark	×1
Steel	×1
Fairy	×0.5

Damage taken in Inverse Battles

Normal	×4
Fire	×1
Water	×0.5
Grass	×1
Electric	×1
Ice	×2
Fighting	×0.25
Poison	×4
Ground	×0.25
Flying	×4
Psychic	×2
Bug	×2
Rock	×2
Ghost	×1
Dragon	×2
Dark	×1
Steel	×1
Fairy	×2

Can be used in

Inverse Battle	Battle Institute
—	Battle Maison
Battle Chateau	Random Matchup

Same form for ♂ / ♀

How to obtain for your Mountain Kalos Pokédex

Level up Lairon to Lv. 42.

❶ Link Trade or transfer from another game.
❷ Level up Lairon to Lv. 42.

● LEVEL-UP MOVES

Lv.	Name	Type	Kind	Pow.	Acc.	PP	Range
1	Tackle	Normal	Physical	50	100	35	Normal
1	Harden	Normal	Status	—	—	30	Self
1	Mud-Slap	Ground	Special	20	100	10	Normal
1	Headbutt	Normal	Physical	70	100	15	Normal
4	Mud-Slap	Ground	Special	20	100	10	Normal
8	Headbutt	Normal	Physical	70	100	15	Normal
11	Metal Claw	Steel	Physical	50	95	35	Normal
15	Iron Defense	Steel	Status	—	—	15	Self
18	Roar	Normal	Status	—	—	20	Normal
22	Take Down	Normal	Physical	90	85	20	Normal
25	Iron Head	Steel	Physical	80	100	15	Normal
29	Protect	Normal	Status	—	—	10	Self
34	Metal Sound	Steel	Status	—	85	40	Normal
40	Iron Tail	Steel	Physical	100	75	15	Normal
48	Autotomize	Steel	Status	—	—	15	Self
57	Heavy Slam	Steel	Physical	—	100	10	Normal
65	Double-Edge	Normal	Physical	120	100	15	Normal
74	Metal Burst	Steel	Physical	—	100	10	Varies

● TM & HM MOVES

No.	Name	Type	Kind	Pow.	Acc.	PP	Range
TM01	Hone Claws	Dark	Status	—	—	15	Self
TM02	Dragon Claw	Dragon	Physical	80	100	15	Normal
TM05	Roar	Normal	Status	—	—	20	Normal

No.	Name	Type	Kind	Pow.	Acc.	PP	Range
TM06	Toxic	Poison	Status	—	90	10	Normal
TM10	Hidden Power	Normal	Special	60	100	15	Normal
TM11	Sunny Day	Fire	Status	—	—	5	Both Sides
TM12	Taunt	Dark	Status	—	100	20	Normal
TM13	Ice Beam	Ice	Special	90	100	10	Normal
TM14	Blizzard	Ice	Special	110	70	5	Many Others
TM15	Hyper Beam	Normal	Special	150	90	5	Normal
TM17	Protect	Normal	Status	—	—	10	Self
TM18	Rain Dance	Water	Status	—	—	5	Both Sides
TM21	Frustration	Normal	Physical	—	100	20	Normal
TM22	Solar Beam	Grass	Special	120	100	10	Normal
TM23	Smack Down	Rock	Physical	50	100	15	Normal
TM24	Thunderbolt	Electric	Special	90	100	15	Normal
TM25	Thunder	Electric	Special	110	70	10	Normal
TM26	Earthquake	Ground	Physical	100	100	10	Adjacent
TM27	Return	Normal	Physical	—	100	20	Normal
TM28	Dig	Ground	Physical	80	100	10	Normal
TM31	Brick Break	Fighting	Physical	75	100	15	Normal
TM32	Double Team	Normal	Status	—	—	15	Self
TM35	Flamethrower	Fire	Special	90	100	15	Normal
TM37	Sandstorm	Rock	Status	—	—	10	Both Sides
TM38	Fire Blast	Fire	Special	110	85	5	Normal
TM39	Rock Tomb	Rock	Physical	60	95	15	Normal
TM40	Aerial Ace	Flying	Physical	60	—	20	Normal
TM42	Facade	Normal	Physical	70	100	20	Normal
TM44	Rest	Psychic	Status	—	—	10	Self
TM45	Attract	Normal	Status	—	100	15	Normal
TM48	Round	Normal	Special	60	100	15	Normal
TM52	Focus Blast	Fighting	Special	120	70	5	Normal
TM56	Fling	Dark	Physical	—	100	10	Normal
TM59	Incinerate	Fire	Special	60	100	15	Many Others
TM65	Shadow Claw	Ghost	Physical	70	100	15	Normal
TM66	Payback	Dark	Physical	50	100	10	Normal

No.	Name	Type	Kind	Pow.	Acc.	PP	Range
TM68	Giga Impact	Normal	Physical	150	90	5	Normal
TM69	Rock Polish	Rock	Status	—	—	20	Self
TM71	Stone Edge	Rock	Physical	100	80	5	Normal
TM73	Thunder Wave	Electric	Status	—	100	20	Normal
TM78	Bulldoze	Ground	Physical	60	100	20	Adjacent
TM80	Rock Slide	Rock	Physical	75	90	10	Many Others
TM82	Dragon Tail	Dragon	Physical	60	90	10	Normal
TM87	Swagger	Normal	Status	—	90	15	Normal
TM88	Sleep Talk	Normal	Status	—	—	10	Self
TM90	Substitute	Normal	Status	—	—	10	Self
TM91	Flash Cannon	Steel	Special	80	100	10	Normal
TM94	Rock Smash	Fighting	Physical	40	100	15	Normal
TM97	Dark Pulse	Dark	Special	80	100	15	Normal
TM98	Power-Up Punch	Fighting	Physical	40	100	20	Normal
TM100	Confide	Normal	Status	—	—	20	Normal
HM01	Cut	Normal	Physical	50	95	30	Normal
HM03	Surf	Water	Special	90	100	15	Adjacent
HM04	Strength	Normal	Physical	80	100	15	Normal

● MOVES TAUGHT BY PEOPLE

Name	Type	Kind	Pow.	Acc.	PP	Range

AFTER THE HALL OF FAME

CENTRAL KALOS

COASTAL KALOS

MOUNTAIN KALOS

101 Aggron

ADVENTURE DATA

AFTER THE
HALL OF FAME

CENTRAL
KALOS

COASTAL
KALOS

MOUNTAIN
KALOS

Mega Aggron

ADVENTURE
DATA

Mega Evolution

Iron Armor Pokémon

☑ Mega Aggron

TYPE Steel

ABILITY
Filter

HEIGHT: 7'03"   WEIGHT: 870.8 lbs.   GENDER: ♂/♀

STAT GROWTH RATES

HP	▪▪▪
Attack	▪▪▪▪▪▪
Defense	▪▪▪▪▪▪▪▪
Sp. Atk	▪▪▪
Sp. Def	▪▪▪
Speed	▪▪▪

MEGA STONE REQUIRED

Aggronite
Obtain in Cyllage City between 8 P.M. and 8:59 P.M., after entering the Hall of Fame and speaking with Professor Sycamore in Anistar City (in *Pokémon Y*).

Can be used in

Inverse Battle
—
Battle Chateau
Battle Institute
Battle Maison
Random Matchup

Damage taken in normal battles		Damage taken in Inverse Battles	
Normal	×0.5	Normal	×2
Fire	×2	Fire	×0.5
Water	×1	Water	×1
Grass	×0.5	Grass	×2
Electric	×1	Electric	×1
Ice	×0.5	Ice	×2
Fighting	×2	Fighting	×0.5
Poison	×0	Poison	×2
Ground	×2	Ground	×0.5
Flying	×0.5	Flying	×2
Psychic	×0.5	Psychic	×2
Bug	×0.5	Bug	×2
Rock	×0.5	Rock	×2
Ghost	×1	Ghost	×1
Dragon	×0.5	Dragon	×2
Dark	×1	Dark	×1
Steel	×0.5	Steel	×2
Fairy	×0.5	Fairy	×2

Same form for ♂/♀

102

Rock Skin Pokémon

☑ Larvitar

HEIGHT: 2'00"   WEIGHT: 158.7 lbs.
GENDER: ♂/♀

TYPE `Rock` `Ground`

ABILITY
Guts

HIDDEN ABILITY
Sand Veil

STAT GROWTH RATES
HP	▪▪
Attack	▪▪
Defense	▪▪
Sp. Atk	▪▪
Sp. Def	▪▪
Speed	▪▪

EGG GROUP
Monster

X It feeds on soil. After it has eaten a large mountain, it falls asleep so it can grow.

Y Born deep underground, it comes aboveground and becomes a pupa once it has finished eating the surrounding soil.

◆ EVOLUTION

Lv. 30   Lv. 55

Larvitar   Pupitar   Tyranitar

ITEMS SOMETIMES HELD BY WILD POKÉMON
None

Damage taken in normal battles	
Normal	×0.5
Fire	×0.5
Water	×4
Grass	×4
Electric	×0
Ice	×2
Fighting	×2
Poison	×0.25
Ground	×2
Flying	×0.5
Psychic	×1
Bug	×1
Rock	×0.5
Ghost	×1
Dragon	×1
Dark	×1
Steel	×2
Fairy	×1

Damage taken in Inverse Battles	
Normal	×2
Fire	×2
Water	×0.25
Grass	×0.25
Electric	×2
Ice	×0.5
Fighting	×2
Poison	×4
Ground	×0.5
Flying	×2
Psychic	×1
Bug	×1
Rock	×2
Ghost	×1
Dragon	×1
Dark	×1
Steel	×0.5
Fairy	×1

Can be used in
Inverse Battle
—
—
Battle Chateau
Battle Institute
Battle Maison
Random Matchup

How to obtain for your Mountain Kalos Pokédex

Link Trade or transfer from another game.

Catch in a Horde Encounter in Terminus Cave.

Same form for ♂ / ♀

● LEVEL-UP MOVES

Lv.	Name	Type	Kind	Pow.	Acc.	PP	Range
1	Bite	Dark	Physical	60	100	25	Normal
1	Leer	Normal	Status	—	100	30	Many Others
5	Sandstorm	Rock	Status	—	—	10	Both Sides
10	Screech	Normal	Status	—	85	40	Normal
14	Chip Away	Normal	Physical	70	100	20	Normal
19	Rock Slide	Rock	Physical	75	90	10	Many Others
23	Scary Face	Normal	Status	—	100	10	Normal
28	Thrash	Normal	Physical	120	100	10	1 Random
32	Dark Pulse	Dark	Special	80	100	15	Normal
37	Payback	Dark	Physical	50	100	10	Normal
41	Crunch	Dark	Physical	80	100	15	Normal
46	Earthquake	Ground	Physical	100	100	10	Adjacent
50	Stone Edge	Rock	Physical	100	80	5	Normal
55	Hyper Beam	Normal	Special	150	90	5	Normal

● TM & HM MOVES

No.	Name	Type	Kind	Pow.	Acc.	PP	Range
TM06	Toxic	Poison	Status	—	90	10	Normal
TM10	Hidden Power	Normal	Special	60	100	15	Normal
TM11	Sunny Day	Fire	Status	—	—	5	Both Sides
TM12	Taunt	Dark	Status	—	100	20	Normal
TM15	Hyper Beam	Normal	Special	150	90	5	Normal
TM17	Protect	Normal	Status	—	—	10	Self
TM18	Rain Dance	Water	Status	—	—	5	Both Sides
TM21	Frustration	Normal	Physical	—	100	20	Normal
TM23	Smack Down	Rock	Physical	50	100	15	Normal
TM26	Earthquake	Ground	Physical	100	100	10	Adjacent
TM27	Return	Normal	Physical	—	100	20	Normal
TM28	Dig	Ground	Physical	80	100	10	Normal
TM31	Brick Break	Fighting	Physical	75	100	15	Normal
TM32	Double Team	Normal	Status	—	—	15	Self
TM37	Sandstorm	Rock	Status	—	—	10	Both Sides
TM39	Rock Tomb	Rock	Physical	60	95	15	Normal
TM41	Torment	Dark	Status	—	100	15	Normal
TM42	Facade	Normal	Physical	70	100	20	Normal
TM44	Rest	Psychic	Status	—	—	10	Self
TM45	Attract	Normal	Status	—	100	15	Normal
TM48	Round	Normal	Special	60	100	15	Normal
TM66	Payback	Dark	Physical	50	100	10	Normal
TM67	Retaliate	Normal	Physical	70	100	5	Normal
TM69	Rock Polish	Rock	Status	—	—	20	Self
TM71	Stone Edge	Rock	Physical	100	80	5	Normal
TM78	Bulldoze	Ground	Physical	60	100	20	Adjacent
TM80	Rock Slide	Rock	Physical	75	90	10	Many Others
TM87	Swagger	Normal	Status	—	90	15	Normal
TM88	Sleep Talk	Normal	Status	—	—	10	Self
TM90	Substitute	Normal	Status	—	—	10	Self
TM94	Rock Smash	Fighting	Physical	40	100	15	Normal
TM95	Snarl	Dark	Special	55	95	15	Many Others
TM97	Dark Pulse	Dark	Special	80	100	15	Normal
TM98	Power-Up Punch	Fighting	Physical	40	100	20	Normal
TM100	Confide	Normal	Status	—	—	20	Normal

● MOVES TAUGHT BY PEOPLE

Name	Type	Kind	Pow.	Acc.	PP	Range

● EGG MOVES

Name	Type	Kind	Pow.	Acc.	PP	Range
Pursuit	Dark	Physical	40	100	20	Normal
Stomp	Normal	Physical	65	100	20	Normal
Outrage	Dragon	Physical	120	100	10	1 Random
Focus Energy	Normal	Status	—	—	30	Self
Ancient Power	Rock	Special	60	100	5	Normal
Dragon Dance	Dragon	Status	—	—	20	Self
Curse	Ghost	Status	—	—	10	Varies
Iron Defense	Steel	Status	—	—	15	Self
Assurance	Dark	Physical	60	100	10	Normal
Iron Head	Steel	Physical	80	100	15	Normal
Stealth Rock	Rock	Status	—	—	20	Other Side
Iron Tail	Steel	Physical	100	75	15	Normal

AFTER THE HALL OF FAME

CENTRAL KALOS

COASTAL KALOS

MOUNTAIN KALOS

102 Larvitar

ADVENTURE DATA

543

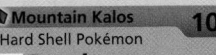

Mountain Kalos

Hard Shell Pokémon

103

☑ **Pupitar**

HEIGHT: 3'11" WEIGHT: 335.1 lbs.
GENDER: ♂/♀

TYPE Rock Ground

ABILITY
Shed Skin

HIDDEN ABILITY
None

STAT GROWTH RATES
HP	■■■
Attack	■■■
Defense	■■■
Sp. Atk	■■■
Sp. Def	■■■
Speed	■■■

EGG GROUP
Monster

X Its body is as hard as bedrock. By venting pressurized gas, it can launch itself like a rocket.

Y Its shell is as hard as sheet rock, and it is also very strong. Its thrashing can topple a mountain.

EVOLUTION

Larvitar — Lv. 30 → Pupitar — Lv. 55 → Tyranitar

ITEMS SOMETIMES HELD BY WILD POKÉMON
None

Can be used in
Inverse Battle
—
Battle Chateau
Battle Institute
Battle Maison
Random Matchup

Damage taken in normal battles
Normal	×0.5
Fire	×0.5
Water	×4
Grass	×4
Electric	×0
Ice	×2
Fighting	×2
Poison	×0.25
Ground	×2
Flying	×0.5
Psychic	×1
Bug	×1
Rock	×0.5
Ghost	×1
Dragon	×1
Dark	×1
Steel	×2
Fairy	×1

Damage taken in Inverse Battles
Normal	×2
Fire	×2
Water	×0.25
Grass	×0.25
Electric	×2
Ice	×0.5
Fighting	×0.5
Poison	×4
Ground	×0.5
Flying	×2
Psychic	×1
Bug	×1
Rock	×2
Ghost	×1
Dragon	×1
Dark	×1
Steel	×0.5
Fairy	×1

How to obtain for your Mountain Kalos Pokédex

Link Trade or transfer from another game.

❶ Catch in the tall grass or red flowers on Route 18.
❷ Level up Larvitar to Lv. 30.

Same form for ♂/♀

● **LEVEL-UP MOVES**

Lv.	Name	Type	Kind	Pow.	Acc.	PP	Range
1	Bite	Dark	Physical	60	100	25	Normal
1	Leer	Normal	Status	—	100	30	Many Others
1	Sandstorm	Rock	Status	—	—	10	Both Sides
1	Screech	Normal	Status	—	85	40	Normal
5	Sandstorm	Rock	Status	—	—	10	Both Sides
10	Screech	Normal	Status	—	85	40	Normal
14	Chip Away	Normal	Physical	70	100	20	Normal
19	Rock Slide	Rock	Physical	75	90	10	Many Others
23	Scary Face	Normal	Status	—	100	10	Normal
28	Thrash	Normal	Physical	120	100	10	1 Random
34	Dark Pulse	Dark	Special	80	100	15	Normal
41	Payback	Dark	Physical	50	100	10	Normal
47	Crunch	Dark	Physical	80	100	15	Normal
54	Earthquake	Ground	Physical	100	100	10	Adjacent
60	Stone Edge	Rock	Physical	100	80	5	Normal
67	Hyper Beam	Normal	Special	150	90	5	Normal

● **TM & HM MOVES**

No.	Name	Type	Kind	Pow.	Acc.	PP	Range
TM06	Toxic	Poison	Status	—	90	10	Normal
TM10	Hidden Power	Normal	Special	60	100	15	Normal
TM11	Sunny Day	Fire	Status	—	—	5	Both Sides
TM12	Taunt	Dark	Status	—	100	20	Normal
TM15	Hyper Beam	Normal	Special	150	90	5	Normal
TM17	Protect	Normal	Status	—	—	10	Self
TM18	Rain Dance	Water	Status	—	—	5	Both Sides
TM21	Frustration	Normal	Physical	—	100	20	Normal
TM23	Smack Down	Rock	Physical	50	100	15	Normal
TM26	Earthquake	Ground	Physical	100	100	10	Adjacent
TM27	Return	Normal	Physical	—	100	20	Normal
TM28	Dig	Ground	Physical	80	100	10	Normal
TM31	Brick Break	Fighting	Physical	75	100	15	Normal
TM32	Double Team	Normal	Status	—	—	15	Self
TM37	Sandstorm	Rock	Status	—	—	10	Both Sides
TM39	Rock Tomb	Rock	Physical	60	95	15	Normal
TM41	Torment	Dark	Status	—	100	15	Normal
TM42	Facade	Normal	Physical	70	100	20	Normal
TM44	Rest	Psychic	Status	—	—	10	Self
TM45	Attract	Normal	Status	—	100	15	Normal
TM48	Round	Normal	Special	60	100	15	Normal
TM66	Payback	Dark	Physical	50	100	10	Normal
TM67	Retaliate	Normal	Physical	70	100	5	Normal
TM69	Rock Polish	Rock	Status	—	—	20	Self
TM71	Stone Edge	Rock	Physical	100	80	5	Normal
TM78	Bulldoze	Ground	Physical	60	100	20	Adjacent
TM80	Rock Slide	Rock	Physical	75	90	10	Many Others
TM87	Swagger	Normal	Status	—	90	15	Normal
TM88	Sleep Talk	Normal	Status	—	—	10	Self
TM90	Substitute	Normal	Status	—	—	10	Self
TM94	Rock Smash	Fighting	Physical	40	100	15	Normal
TM95	Snarl	Dark	Special	55	95	15	Many Others
TM97	Dark Pulse	Dark	Special	80	100	15	Normal

No.	Name	Type	Kind	Pow.	Acc.	PP	Range
TM98	Power-Up Punch	Fighting	Physical	40	100	20	Normal
TM100	Confide	Normal	Status	—	—	20	Normal

● **MOVES TAUGHT BY PEOPLE**

Name	Type	Kind	Pow.	Acc.	PP	Range

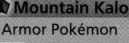

Mountain Kalos — 104
Armor Pokémon
∨ Tyranitar

HEIGHT: 6'07" WEIGHT: 445.3 lbs.
GENDER: ♂/♀

 In just one of its mighty hands, it has the power to make the ground shake and mountains crumble.

 If it rampages, it knocks down mountains and buries rivers. Maps must be redrawn afterward.

TYPE	Rock	Dark

ABILITY
Sand Stream

HIDDEN ABILITY
Unnerve

STAT GROWTH RATES
HP	■■■■
Attack	■■■■■■■
Defense	■■■■■
Sp. Atk	■■■■■
Sp. Def	■■■■
Speed	■■■

EGG GROUP
Monster

EVOLUTION

Lv. 30 → Lv. 55
Larvitar — Pupitar — Tyranitar

ITEMS SOMETIMES HELD BY WILD POKÉMON
None

Damage taken in normal battles	
Normal	×0.5
Fire	×0.5
Water	×2
Grass	×2
Electric	×1
Ice	×1
Fighting	×4
Poison	×0.5
Ground	×2
Flying	×0.5
Psychic	×0
Bug	×2
Rock	×1
Ghost	×2
Dragon	×1
Dark	×0.5
Steel	×2
Fairy	×2

Damage taken in Inverse Battles	
Normal	×2
Fire	×2
Water	×0.5
Grass	×0.5
Electric	×1
Ice	×1
Fighting	×0.25
Poison	×2
Ground	×0.5
Flying	×2
Psychic	×2
Bug	×0.5
Rock	×1
Ghost	×2
Dragon	×1
Dark	×2
Steel	×0.5
Fairy	×0.5

Can be used in
Inverse Battle
—
Battle Chateau
Battle Institute
Battle Maison
Random Matchup

How to obtain for your Mountain Kalos Pokédex

Link Trade or transfer from another game.	Level up Pupitar to Lv. 55.
X	Y

Same form for ♂/♀

● LEVEL-UP MOVES

Lv.	Name	Type	Kind	Pow.	Acc.	PP	Range
1	Thunder Fang	Electric	Physical	65	95	15	Normal
1	Ice Fang	Ice	Physical	65	95	15	Normal
1	Fire Fang	Fire	Physical	65	95	15	Normal
1	Bite	Dark	Physical	60	100	25	Normal
1	Leer	Normal	Status	—	100	30	Many Others
1	Sandstorm	Rock	Status	—	—	10	Both Sides
5	Screech	Normal	Status	—	85	40	Normal
5	Sandstorm	Rock	Status	—	—	10	Both Sides
5	Screech	Normal	Status	—	85	40	Normal
10	Screech	Normal	Status	—	85	40	Normal
14	Chip Away	Normal	Physical	70	100	20	Normal
19	Rock Slide	Rock	Physical	75	90	10	Many Others
23	Scary Face	Normal	Status	—	100	10	Normal
28	Thrash	Normal	Physical	120	100	10	1 Random
34	Dark Pulse	Dark	Special	80	100	15	Normal
41	Payback	Dark	Physical	50	100	10	Normal
47	Crunch	Dark	Physical	80	100	15	Normal
54	Earthquake	Ground	Physical	100	100	10	Adjacent
63	Stone Edge	Rock	Physical	100	80	5	Normal
73	Hyper Beam	Normal	Special	150	90	5	Normal
82	Giga Impact	Normal	Physical	150	90	5	Normal

● TM & HM MOVES

No.	Name	Type	Kind	Pow.	Acc.	PP	Range
TM01	Hone Claws	Dark	Status	—	—	15	Self
TM02	Dragon Claw	Dragon	Physical	80	100	15	Normal
TM05	Roar	Normal	Status	—	—	20	Normal
TM06	Toxic	Poison	Status	—	90	10	Normal
TM10	Hidden Power	Normal	Special	60	100	15	Normal
TM11	Sunny Day	Fire	Status	—	—	5	Both Sides
TM12	Taunt	Dark	Status	—	100	20	Normal
TM13	Ice Beam	Ice	Special	90	100	10	Normal
TM14	Blizzard	Ice	Special	110	70	5	Many Others
TM15	Hyper Beam	Normal	Special	150	90	5	Normal
TM17	Protect	Normal	Status	—	—	10	Self
TM18	Rain Dance	Water	Status	—	—	5	Both Sides
TM21	Frustration	Normal	Physical	—	100	20	Normal
TM23	Smack Down	Rock	Physical	50	100	15	Normal
TM24	Thunderbolt	Electric	Special	90	100	15	Normal
TM25	Thunder	Electric	Special	110	70	10	Normal
TM26	Earthquake	Ground	Physical	100	100	10	Adjacent
TM27	Return	Normal	Physical	—	100	20	Normal
TM28	Dig	Ground	Physical	80	100	10	Normal
TM31	Brick Break	Fighting	Physical	75	100	15	Normal
TM32	Double Team	Normal	Status	—	—	15	Self
TM35	Flamethrower	Fire	Special	90	100	15	Normal
TM37	Sandstorm	Rock	Status	—	—	10	Both Sides
TM38	Fire Blast	Fire	Special	110	85	5	Normal
TM39	Rock Tomb	Rock	Physical	60	95	15	Normal
TM40	Aerial Ace	Flying	Physical	60	—	20	Normal
TM41	Torment	Dark	Status	—	100	15	Normal
TM42	Facade	Normal	Physical	70	100	20	Normal
TM44	Rest	Psychic	Status	—	—	10	Self
TM45	Attract	Normal	Status	—	100	15	Normal
TM48	Round	Normal	Special	60	100	15	Normal
TM52	Focus Blast	Fighting	Special	120	70	5	Normal
TM56	Fling	Dark	Physical	—	100	10	Normal
TM59	Incinerate	Fire	Special	60	100	15	Many Others
TM65	Shadow Claw	Ghost	Physical	70	100	15	Normal
TM66	Payback	Dark	Physical	50	100	10	Normal
TM67	Retaliate	Normal	Physical	70	100	5	Normal
TM68	Giga Impact	Normal	Physical	150	90	5	Normal
TM69	Rock Polish	Rock	Status	—	—	20	Self
TM71	Stone Edge	Rock	Physical	100	80	5	Normal
TM73	Thunder Wave	Electric	Status	—	100	20	Normal
TM78	Bulldoze	Ground	Physical	60	100	20	Adjacent
TM80	Rock Slide	Rock	Physical	75	90	10	Many Others
TM82	Dragon Tail	Dragon	Physical	60	90	10	Normal
TM87	Swagger	Normal	Status	—	90	15	Normal
TM88	Sleep Talk	Normal	Status	—	—	10	Self
TM90	Substitute	Normal	Status	—	—	10	Self
TM94	Rock Smash	Fighting	Physical	40	100	15	Normal
TM95	Snarl	Dark	Special	55	95	15	Many Others
TM97	Dark Pulse	Dark	Special	80	100	15	Normal
TM98	Power-Up Punch	Fighting	Physical	40	100	20	Normal
TM100	Confide	Normal	Status	—	—	20	Normal
HM01	Cut	Normal	Physical	50	95	30	Normal
HM03	Surf	Water	Special	90	100	15	Adjacent
HM04	Strength	Normal	Physical	80	100	15	Normal

● MOVES TAUGHT BY PEOPLE

Name	Type	Kind	Pow.	Acc.	PP	Range

AFTER THE HALL OF FAME

CENTRAL KALOS

COASTAL KALOS

MOUNTAIN KALOS

Mega Tyranitar

ADVENTURE DATA

Mega Evolution

Armor Pokémon

☑ **Mega Tyranitar**

TYPE	Rock / Dark

ABILITY
Sand Stream

HEIGHT: 8'02"   WEIGHT: 562.2 lbs.   GENDER: ♂/♀

STAT GROWTH RATES
HP
Attack
Defense
Sp. Atk
Sp. Def
Speed

MEGA STONE REQUIRED

Tyranitarite
Obtain in Cyllage City between 8 P.M. and 8:59 P.M., after entering the Hall of Fame and speaking with Professor Sycamore in Anistar City (in *Pokémon X*).

Damage taken in normal battles	
Normal	×0.5
Fire	×0.5
Water	×2
Grass	×2
Electric	×1
Ice	×1
Fighting	×4
Poison	×0.5
Ground	×2
Flying	×0.5
Psychic	×0
Bug	×2
Rock	×1
Ghost	×0.5
Dragon	×1
Dark	×0.5
Steel	×2
Fairy	×2

Damage taken in Inverse Battles	
Normal	×2
Fire	×2
Water	×0.5
Grass	×0.5
Electric	×1
Ice	×1
Fighting	×0.25
Poison	×2
Ground	×0.5
Flying	×2
Psychic	×2
Bug	×0.5
Rock	×1
Ghost	×2
Dragon	×1
Dark	×2
Steel	×0.5
Fairy	×0.5

Can be used in
Inverse Battle
—
Battle Chateau
Battle Institute
Battle Maison
Random Matchup

Same form for ♂/♀

Mountain Kalos **105**
Anteater Pokémon

 Heatmor

HEIGHT: 4'07" WEIGHT: 127.9 lbs.
GENDER: ♂/♀

X Using their very hot, flame-covered tongues, they burn through Durant's steel bodies and consume their insides.

Y It draws in air through its tail, transforms it into fire, and uses it like a tongue. It melts Durant and eats them.

TYPE Fire

ABILITIES
Gluttony
Flash Fire

HIDDEN ABILITY
White Smoke

STAT GROWTH RATES
HP	■■■
Attack	■■■■
Defense	■■■
Sp. Atk	■■■■
Sp. Def	■■■
Speed	■■■■

EGG GROUP
Field

EVOLUTION

Does not evolve

ITEMS SOMETIMES HELD BY WILD POKÉMON
None

Damage taken in normal battles		Damage taken in Inverse Battles	
Normal	×1	Normal	×1
Fire	×0.5	Fire	×2
Water	×2	Water	×0.5
Grass	×0.5	Grass	×2
Electric	×1	Electric	×1
Ice	×0.5	Ice	×2
Fighting	×1	Fighting	×1
Poison	×1	Poison	×1
Ground	×2	Ground	×0.5
Flying	×1	Flying	×1
Psychic	×1	Psychic	×1
Bug	×0.5	Bug	×2
Rock	×2	Rock	×0.5
Ghost	×1	Ghost	×1
Dragon	×1	Dragon	×1
Dark	×1	Dark	×1
Steel	×0.5	Steel	×2
Fairy	×0.5	Fairy	×2

Can be used in	
Inverse Battle	Battle Institute
—	Battle Maison
Battle Chateau	Random Matchup

Same form for ♂/♀

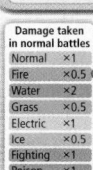

How to obtain for your Mountain Kalos Pokédex

❶ Catch in the tall grass on Route 18.
❷ Catch in the red flowers on Route 18.

❶ Catch in the tall grass on Route 18.
❷ Catch in the red flowers on Route 18.

● **LEVEL-UP MOVES**

Lv.	Name	Type	Kind	Pow.	Acc.	PP	Range
1	Inferno	Fire	Special	100	50	5	Normal
1	Hone Claws	Dark	Status	—	—	15	Self
1	Tackle	Normal	Physical	50	100	35	Normal
1	Incinerate	Fire	Special	60	100	15	Many Others
1	Lick	Ghost	Physical	30	100	30	Normal
6	Odor Sleuth	Normal	Status	—	—	40	Normal
11	Bind	Normal	Physical	15	85	20	Normal
16	Fire Spin	Fire	Special	35	85	15	Normal
21	Fury Swipes	Normal	Physical	18	80	15	Normal
26	Snatch	Dark	Status	—	—	10	Self
31	Flame Burst	Fire	Special	70	100	15	Normal
36	Bug Bite	Bug	Physical	60	100	20	Normal
41	Slash	Normal	Physical	70	100	20	Normal
44	Amnesia	Psychic	Status	—	—	20	Self
47	Flamethrower	Fire	Special	90	100	15	Normal
50	Stockpile	Normal	Status	—	—	20	Self
50	Spit Up	Normal	Special	—	100	10	Normal
50	Swallow	Normal	Status	—	—	10	Self
61	Inferno	Fire	Special	100	50	5	Normal

● **TM & HM MOVES**

No.	Name	Type	Kind	Pow.	Acc.	PP	Range
TM01	Hone Claws	Dark	Status	—	—	15	Self
TM06	Toxic	Poison	Status	—	90	10	Normal
TM10	Hidden Power	Normal	Special	60	100	15	Normal
TM11	Sunny Day	Fire	Status	—	—	5	Both Sides
TM12	Taunt	Dark	Status	—	100	20	Normal
TM17	Protect	Normal	Status	—	—	10	Self
TM18	Rain Dance	Water	Status	—	—	5	Both Sides
TM21	Frustration	Normal	Physical	—	100	20	Normal
TM22	Solar Beam	Grass	Special	120	100	10	Normal
TM27	Return	Normal	Physical	—	100	20	Normal
TM28	Dig	Ground	Physical	80	100	10	Normal
TM32	Double Team	Normal	Status	—	—	15	Self
TM35	Flamethrower	Fire	Special	90	100	15	Normal
TM38	Fire Blast	Fire	Special	110	85	5	Normal
TM39	Rock Tomb	Rock	Physical	60	95	15	Normal
TM40	Aerial Ace	Flying	Physical	60	—	20	Normal
TM42	Facade	Normal	Physical	70	100	20	Normal
TM44	Rest	Psychic	Status	—	—	10	Self
TM45	Attract	Normal	Status	—	100	15	Normal
TM46	Thief	Dark	Physical	60	100	25	Normal
TM48	Round	Normal	Special	60	100	15	Normal
TM52	Focus Blast	Fighting	Special	120	70	5	Normal
TM56	Fling	Dark	Physical	—	100	10	Normal
TM59	Incinerate	Fire	Special	60	100	15	Many Others
TM61	Will-O-Wisp	Fire	Status	—	85	15	Normal
TM65	Shadow Claw	Ghost	Physical	70	100	15	Normal
TM68	Giga Impact	Normal	Physical	150	90	5	Normal
TM87	Swagger	Normal	Status	—	90	15	Normal
TM88	Sleep Talk	Normal	Status	—	—	10	Self
TM90	Substitute	Normal	Status	—	—	10	Self
TM94	Rock Smash	Fighting	Physical	40	100	15	Normal
TM98	Power-Up Punch	Fighting	Physical	40	100	20	Normal
TM100	Confide	Normal	Status	—	—	20	Normal

No.	Name	Type	Kind	Pow.	Acc.	PP	Range
HM01	Cut	Normal	Physical	50	95	30	Normal

● **MOVES TAUGHT BY PEOPLE**

Name	Type	Kind	Pow.	Acc.	PP	Range

● **EGG MOVES**

Name	Type	Kind	Pow.	Acc.	PP	Range
Pursuit	Dark	Physical	40	100	20	Normal
Wrap	Normal	Physical	15	90	20	Normal
Night Slash	Dark	Physical	70	100	15	Normal
Curse	Ghost	Status	—	—	10	Varies
Body Slam	Normal	Physical	85	100	15	Normal
Heat Wave	Fire	Special	95	90	10	Many Others
Feint Attack	Dark	Physical	60	—	20	Normal
Sucker Punch	Dark	Physical	80	100	5	Normal
Tickle	Normal	Status	—	100	20	Normal
Sleep Talk	Normal	Status	—	—	10	Self
Belch	Poison	Special	120	90	10	Normal

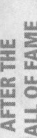

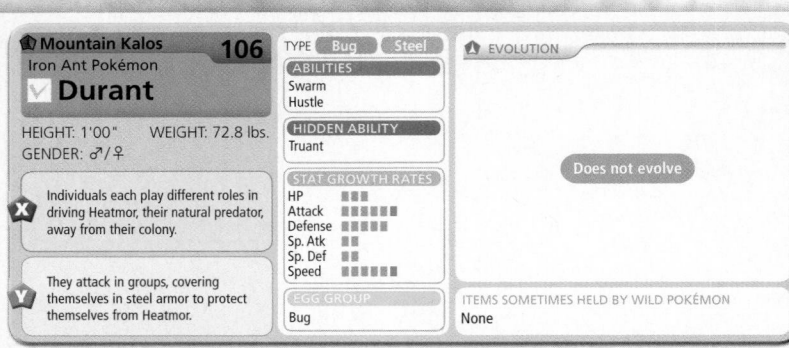

Mountain Kalos 106
Iron Ant Pokémon
☑ Durant

HEIGHT: 1'00" WEIGHT: 72.8 lbs.
GENDER: ♂/♀

TYPE Bug Steel

ABILITIES
Swarm
Hustle

HIDDEN ABILITY
Truant

STAT GROWTH RATES
HP ▪▪▪
Attack ▪▪▪▪▪
Defense ▪▪▪▪▪
Sp. Atk ▪▪
Sp. Def ▪▪
Speed ▪▪▪▪▪

EGG GROUP
Bug

EVOLUTION

Does not evolve

X Individuals each play different roles in driving Heatmor, their natural predator, away from their colony.

Y They attack in groups, covering themselves in steel armor to protect themselves from Heatmor.

ITEMS SOMETIMES HELD BY WILD POKÉMON
None

Can be used in
Inverse Battle

Battle Chateau
Battle Institute
Battle Maison
Random Matchup

Damage taken in normal battles	
Normal	×0.5
Fire	×4
Water	×1
Grass	×0.25
Electric	×1
Ice	×0.5
Fighting	×1
Poison	×0
Ground	×1
Flying	×1
Psychic	×0.5
Bug	×0.5
Rock	×1
Ghost	×1
Dragon	×0.5
Dark	×1
Steel	×0.5
Fairy	×0.5

Damage taken in Inverse Battles	
Normal	×2
Fire	×0.25
Water	×1
Grass	×4
Electric	×1
Ice	×2
Fighting	×1
Poison	×2
Ground	×1
Flying	×1
Psychic	×2
Bug	×2
Rock	×1
Ghost	×1
Dragon	×1
Dark	×1
Steel	×2
Fairy	×2

Same form for ♂/♀

How to obtain for your Mountain Kalos Pokédex

X:
❶ Catch in the tall grass on Route 18.
❷ Catch in the red flowers on Route 18.

Y:
❶ Catch in the tall grass on Route 18.
❷ Catch in the red flowers on Route 18.

● LEVEL-UP MOVES

Lv.	Name	Type	Kind	Pow.	Acc.	PP	Range
1	Guillotine	Normal	Physical	—	30	5	Normal
1	Iron Defense	Steel	Status	—	—	15	Self
1	Metal Sound	Steel	Status	—	85	40	Normal
1	Vice Grip	Normal	Physical	55	100	30	Normal
1	Sand Attack	Ground	Status	—	100	15	Normal
6	Fury Cutter	Bug	Physical	40	95	20	Normal
11	Bite	Dark	Physical	60	100	25	Normal
16	Agility	Psychic	Status	—	—	30	Self
21	Metal Claw	Steel	Physical	50	95	35	Normal
26	Bug Bite	Bug	Physical	60	100	20	Normal
31	Crunch	Dark	Physical	80	100	15	Normal
36	Iron Head	Steel	Physical	80	100	15	Normal
41	Dig	Ground	Physical	80	100	10	Normal
46	Entrainment	Normal	Status	—	100	15	Normal
51	X-Scissor	Bug	Physical	80	100	15	Normal
56	Iron Defense	Steel	Status	—	—	15	Self
61	Guillotine	Normal	Physical	—	30	5	Normal
66	Metal Sound	Steel	Status	—	85	40	Normal

● TM & HM MOVES

No.	Name	Type	Kind	Pow.	Acc.	PP	Range
TM01	Hone Claws	Dark	Status	—	—	15	Self
TM06	Toxic	Poison	Status	—	90	10	Normal
TM10	Hidden Power	Normal	Special	60	100	15	Normal
TM17	Protect	Normal	Status	—	—	10	Self
TM21	Frustration	Normal	Physical	—	100	20	Normal
TM27	Return	Normal	Physical	—	100	20	Normal
TM28	Dig	Ground	Physical	80	100	10	Normal
TM32	Double Team	Normal	Status	—	—	15	Self
TM37	Sandstorm	Rock	Status	—	—	10	Both Sides
TM39	Rock Tomb	Rock	Physical	60	95	15	Normal
TM40	Aerial Ace	Flying	Physical	60	—	20	Normal
TM42	Facade	Normal	Physical	70	100	20	Normal
TM44	Rest	Psychic	Status	—	—	10	Self
TM45	Attract	Normal	Status	—	100	15	Normal
TM48	Round	Normal	Special	60	100	15	Normal
TM53	Energy Ball	Grass	Special	90	100	10	Normal
TM65	Shadow Claw	Ghost	Physical	70	100	15	Normal
TM67	Retaliate	Normal	Physical	70	100	5	Normal
TM68	Giga Impact	Normal	Physical	150	90	5	Normal
TM69	Rock Polish	Rock	Status	—	—	20	Self
TM71	Stone Edge	Rock	Physical	100	80	5	Normal
TM73	Thunder Wave	Electric	Status	—	100	20	Normal
TM76	Struggle Bug	Bug	Special	50	100	20	Many Others
TM80	Rock Slide	Rock	Physical	75	90	10	Many Others
TM81	X-Scissor	Bug	Physical	80	100	15	Normal
TM87	Swagger	Normal	Status	—	90	15	Normal
TM88	Sleep Talk	Normal	Status	—	—	10	Self
TM90	Substitute	Normal	Status	—	—	10	Self
TM91	Flash Cannon	Steel	Special	80	100	10	Normal
TM94	Rock Smash	Fighting	Physical	40	100	15	Normal
TM100	Confide	Normal	Status	—	—	20	Normal
HM01	Cut	Normal	Physical	50	95	30	Normal
HM04	Strength	Normal	Physical	80	100	15	Normal

No.	Name	Type	Kind	Pow.	Acc.	PP	Range

● MOVES TAUGHT BY PEOPLE

Name	Type	Kind	Pow.	Acc.	PP	Range

● EGG MOVES

Name	Type	Kind	Pow.	Acc.	PP	Range
Screech	Normal	Status	—	85	40	Normal
Endure	Normal	Status	—	—	10	Self
Rock Climb	Normal	Physical	90	85	20	Normal
Baton Pass	Normal	Status	—	—	40	Self
Thunder Fang	Electric	Physical	65	95	15	Normal
Feint Attack	Dark	Physical	60	—	20	Normal

AFTER THE HALL OF FAME

CENTRAL KALOS

COASTAL KALOS

MOUNTAIN KALOS

106 Durant

ADVENTURE DATA

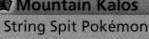

Mountain Kalos 107
String Spit Pokémon
☑ Spinarak

HEIGHT: 1'08" WEIGHT: 18.7 lbs.
GENDER: ♂/♀

It spins a web using fine—but durable—thread. It then waits patiently for prey to be trapped.

It lies still in the same pose for days in its web, waiting for its unsuspecting prey to wander close.

TYPE Bug Poison

ABILITIES
Swarm
Insomnia

HIDDEN ABILITY
Sniper

STAT GROWTH RATES
HP	■■
Attack	■■■
Defense	■■
Sp. Atk	■■
Sp. Def	■■
Speed	■■

EGG GROUP
Bug

EVOLUTION

Lv. 22

Spinarak → Ariados

ITEMS SOMETIMES HELD BY WILD POKÉMON
None

Damage taken in normal battles		Damage taken in Inverse Battles	
Normal	×1	Normal	×1
Fire	×2	Fire	×0.5
Water	×1	Water	×1
Grass	×0.25	Grass	×4
Electric	×1	Electric	×1
Ice	×1	Ice	×1
Fighting	×0.25	Fighting	×4
Poison	×0.5	Poison	×2
Ground	×1	Ground	×1
Flying	×2	Flying	×0.5
Psychic	×2	Psychic	×0.5
Bug	×0.5	Bug	×2
Rock	×2	Rock	×0.5
Ghost	×1	Ghost	×1
Dragon	×1	Dragon	×1
Dark	×1	Dark	×1
Steel	×1	Steel	×1
Fairy	×0.5	Fairy	×2

Can be used in	
Inverse Battle	Battle Institute
—	Battle Maison
Battle Chateau	Random Matchup

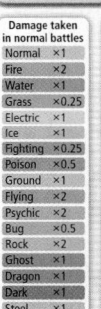

Same form for ♂/♀

How to obtain for your Mountain Kalos Pokédex

Leave Ariados at the Pokémon Day Care, and hatch the Egg that is found.

Leave Ariados at the Pokémon Day Care, and hatch the Egg that is found.

● LEVEL-UP MOVES

Lv.	Name	Type	Kind	Pow.	Acc.	PP	Range
1	Poison Sting	Poison	Physical	15	100	35	Normal
1	String Shot	Bug	Status	—	95	40	Many Others
5	Scary Face	Normal	Status	—	100	10	Normal
8	Constrict	Normal	Physical	10	100	35	Normal
12	Leech Life	Bug	Physical	20	100	15	Normal
15	Night Shade	Ghost	Special	—	100	15	Normal
19	Shadow Sneak	Ghost	Physical	40	100	30	Normal
22	Fury Swipes	Normal	Physical	18	80	15	Normal
26	Sucker Punch	Dark	Physical	80	100	5	Normal
29	Spider Web	Bug	Status	—	—	10	Normal
33	Agility	Psychic	Status	—	—	30	Self
36	Pin Missile	Bug	Physical	25	95	20	Normal
40	Psychic	Psychic	Special	90	100	10	Normal
43	Poison Jab	Poison	Physical	80	100	20	Normal
47	Cross Poison	Poison	Physical	70	100	20	Normal
50	Sticky Web	Bug	Status	—	—	20	Other Side

● TM & HM MOVES

No.	Name	Type	Kind	Pow.	Acc.	PP	Range
TM01	Hone Claws	Dark	Status	—	—	15	Self
TM06	Toxic	Poison	Status	—	90	10	Normal
TM09	Venoshock	Poison	Special	65	100	10	Normal
TM10	Hidden Power	Normal	Special	60	100	15	Normal
TM11	Sunny Day	Fire	Status	—	—	5	Both Sides
TM17	Protect	Normal	Status	—	—	10	Self
TM21	Frustration	Normal	Physical	—	100	20	Normal
TM22	Solar Beam	Grass	Special	120	100	10	Normal
TM27	Return	Normal	Physical	—	100	20	Normal
TM28	Dig	Ground	Physical	80	100	10	Normal
TM29	Psychic	Psychic	Special	90	100	10	Normal
TM32	Double Team	Normal	Status	—	—	15	Self
TM36	Sludge Bomb	Poison	Special	90	100	10	Normal
TM42	Facade	Normal	Physical	70	100	20	Normal
TM44	Rest	Psychic	Status	—	—	10	Self
TM45	Attract	Normal	Status	—	100	15	Normal
TM46	Thief	Dark	Physical	60	100	25	Normal
TM48	Round	Normal	Special	60	100	15	Normal
TM70	Flash	Normal	Status	—	100	20	Normal
TM76	Struggle Bug	Bug	Special	50	100	20	Many Others
TM81	X-Scissor	Bug	Physical	80	100	15	Normal
TM83	Infestation	Bug	Special	20	100	20	Normal
TM84	Poison Jab	Poison	Physical	80	100	20	Normal
TM87	Swagger	Normal	Status	—	90	15	Normal
TM88	Sleep Talk	Normal	Status	—	—	10	Self
TM90	Substitute	Normal	Status	—	—	10	Self
TM100	Confide	Normal	Status	—	—	20	Normal

● MOVES TAUGHT BY PEOPLE

Name	Type	Kind	Pow.	Acc.	PP	Range

● EGG MOVES

Name	Type	Kind	Pow.	Acc.	PP	Range
Psybeam	Psychic	Special	65	100	20	Normal
Disable	Normal	Status	—	100	20	Normal
Sonic Boom	Normal	Special	—	90	20	Normal
Baton Pass	Normal	Status	—	—	40	Self
Pursuit	Dark	Physical	40	100	20	Normal
Signal Beam	Bug	Special	75	100	15	Normal
Toxic Spikes	Poison	Status	—	—	20	Other Side
Twineedle	Bug	Physical	25	100	20	Normal
Electroweb	Electric	Special	55	95	15	Many Others
Rage Powder	Bug	Status	—	—	20	Self
Night Slash	Dark	Physical	70	100	15	Normal
Megahorn	Bug	Physical	120	85	10	Normal

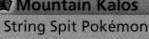

AFTER THE HALL OF FAME

CENTRAL KALOS

COASTAL KALOS

MOUNTAIN KALOS

108

Ariados

ADVENTURE DATA

Mountain Kalos 108
Long Leg Pokémon

☑ Ariados

HEIGHT: 3'07"　WEIGHT: 73.9 lbs.
GENDER: ♂/♀

TYPE Bug | Poison

ABILITIES
Swarm
Insomnia

HIDDEN ABILITY
Sniper

STAT GROWTH RATES
HP	■■■
Attack	■■■■
Defense	■■■
Sp. Atk	■■■
Sp. Def	■■■
Speed	■■

EGG GROUP
Bug

⚠ EVOLUTION

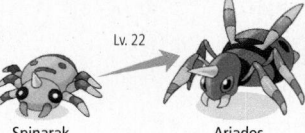

Spinarak — Lv. 22 → Ariados

X It spins string not only from its rear but also from its mouth. It's hard to tell which end is which.

Y It attaches silk to its prey and sets it free. Later, it tracks the silk to the prey and its friends.

ITEMS SOMETIMES HELD BY WILD POKÉMON
None

Damage taken in normal battles	
Normal	×1
Fire	×2
Water	×1
Grass	×0.25
Electric	×1
Ice	×1
Fighting	×0.25
Poison	×0.5
Ground	×1
Flying	×2
Psychic	×2
Bug	×0.5
Rock	×2
Ghost	×1
Dragon	×1
Dark	×1
Steel	×1
Fairy	×0.5

Damage taken in Inverse Battles	
Normal	×1
Fire	×0.5
Water	×1
Grass	×4
Electric	×1
Ice	×1
Fighting	×4
Poison	×2
Ground	×1
Flying	×0.5
Psychic	×0.5
Bug	×2
Rock	×0.5
Ghost	×1
Dragon	×1
Dark	×1
Steel	×1
Fairy	×2

Can be used in
Inverse Battle	Battle Institute
—	Battle Maison
Battle Chateau	Random Matchup

Same form for ♂/♀

How to obtain for your Mountain Kalos Pokédex

❶ Catch when it ambushes you from the roof of Terminus Cave.
❷ Catch when it ambushes you from the roof of the caves along Victory Road.

❶ Catch when it ambushes you from the roof of Terminus Cave.
❷ Catch when it ambushes you from the roof of the caves along Victory Road.

● LEVEL-UP MOVES

Lv.	Name	Type	Kind	Pow.	Acc.	PP	Range
1	Venom Drench	Poison	Status	—	100	20	Many Others
1	Fell Stinger	Bug	Physical	30	100	25	Normal
1	Bug Bite	Bug	Physical	60	100	20	Normal
1	Poison Sting	Poison	Physical	15	100	35	Normal
1	String Shot	Bug	Status	—	95	40	Many Others
1	Scary Face	Normal	Status	—	100	10	Normal
1	Constrict	Normal	Physical	10	100	35	Normal
5	Scary Face	Normal	Status	—	100	10	Normal
8	Constrict	Normal	Physical	10	100	35	Normal
12	Leech Life	Bug	Physical	20	100	15	Normal
15	Night Shade	Ghost	Special	—	100	15	Normal
19	Shadow Sneak	Ghost	Physical	40	100	30	Normal
23	Fury Swipes	Normal	Physical	18	80	15	Normal
28	Spider Web	Bug	Status	—	—	10	Normal
32	Sucker Punch	Dark	Physical	80	100	5	Normal
37	Agility	Psychic	Status	—	—	30	Self
41	Pin Missile	Bug	Physical	25	95	20	Normal
46	Psychic	Psychic	Special	90	100	10	Normal
50	Poison Jab	Poison	Physical	80	100	20	Normal
55	Cross Poison	Poison	Physical	70	100	20	Normal
58	Sticky Web	Bug	Status	—	—	20	Other Side

● TM & HM MOVES

No.	Name	Type	Kind	Pow.	Acc.	PP	Range
TM01	Hone Claws	Dark	Status	—	—	15	Self
TM06	Toxic	Poison	Status	—	90	10	Normal
TM09	Venoshock	Poison	Special	65	100	10	Normal
TM10	Hidden Power	Normal	Special	60	100	15	Normal
TM11	Sunny Day	Fire	Status	—	—	5	Both Sides
TM15	Hyper Beam	Normal	Special	150	90	5	Normal
TM17	Protect	Normal	Status	—	—	10	Self
TM21	Frustration	Normal	Physical	—	100	20	Normal
TM22	Solar Beam	Grass	Special	120	100	10	Normal
TM27	Return	Normal	Physical	—	100	20	Normal
TM28	Dig	Ground	Physical	80	100	10	Normal
TM29	Psychic	Psychic	Special	90	100	10	Normal
TM32	Double Team	Normal	Status	—	—	15	Self
TM36	Sludge Bomb	Poison	Special	90	100	10	Normal
TM42	Facade	Normal	Physical	70	100	20	Normal
TM44	Rest	Psychic	Status	—	—	10	Self
TM45	Attract	Normal	Status	—	100	15	Normal
TM46	Thief	Dark	Physical	60	100	25	Normal
TM48	Round	Normal	Special	60	100	15	Normal
TM68	Giga Impact	Normal	Physical	150	90	5	Normal
TM70	Flash	Normal	Status	—	100	20	Normal
TM76	Struggle Bug	Bug	Special	50	100	20	Many Others
TM81	X-Scissor	Bug	Physical	80	100	15	Normal
TM83	Infestation	Bug	Special	20	100	20	Normal
TM84	Poison Jab	Poison	Physical	80	100	20	Normal
TM87	Swagger	Normal	Status	—	90	15	Normal
TM88	Sleep Talk	Normal	Status	—	—	10	Self
TM90	Substitute	Normal	Status	—	—	10	Self
TM100	Confide	Normal	Status	—	—	20	Normal

No.	Name	Type	Kind	Pow.	Acc.	PP	Range

● MOVES TAUGHT BY PEOPLE

Name	Type	Kind	Pow.	Acc.	PP	Range

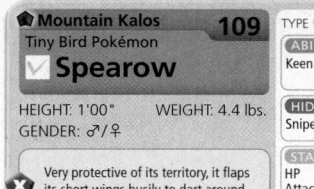

♦ Mountain Kalos **109**

Tiny Bird Pokémon

☑ **Spearow**

HEIGHT: 1'00"　　WEIGHT: 4.4 lbs.
GENDER: ♂/♀

X Very protective of its territory, it flaps its short wings busily to dart around at high speed.

Y Eats bugs in grassy areas. It has to flap its short wings at high speed to stay airborne.

TYPE Normal Flying

ABILITY
Keen Eye

HIDDEN ABILITY
Sniper

STAT GROWTH RATES
HP	■■
Attack	■■■
Defense	■■
Sp. Atk	■■
Sp. Def	■
Speed	■■■■

EGG GROUP
Flying

EVOLUTION

Spearow　　　Lv. 20　　　Fearow

ITEMS SOMETIMES HELD BY WILD POKÉMON
None

Damage taken in normal battles		Damage taken in Inverse Battles	
Normal	×1	Normal	×1
Fire	×1	Fire	×1
Water	×1	Water	×1
Grass	×0.5	Grass	×2
Electric	×2	Electric	×0.5
Ice	×2	Ice	×0.5
Fighting	×1	Fighting	×1
Poison	×1	Poison	×1
Ground	×0	Ground	×2
Flying	×1	Flying	×1
Psychic	×1	Psychic	×1
Bug	×0.5	Bug	×2
Rock	×2	Rock	×0.5
Ghost	×0	Ghost	×2
Dragon	×1	Dragon	×1
Dark	×1	Dark	×1
Steel	×1	Steel	×1
Fairy	×1	Fairy	×1

Can be used in	
Inverse Battle	Battle Institute
—	Battle Maison
Battle Chateau	Random Matchup

Same form for ♂/♀

How to obtain for your Mountain Kalos Pokédex

Leave Fearow at the Pokémon Day Care, and hatch the Egg that is found.

Leave Fearow at the Pokémon Day Care, and hatch the Egg that is found.

● LEVEL-UP MOVES

Lv.	Name	Type	Kind	Pow.	Acc.	PP	Range
1	Peck	Flying	Physical	35	100	35	Normal
1	Growl	Normal	Status	—	100	40	Many Others
5	Leer	Normal	Status	—	100	30	Many Others
9	Fury Attack	Normal	Physical	15	85	20	Normal
13	Pursuit	Dark	Physical	40	100	20	Normal
17	Aerial Ace	Flying	Physical	60	—	20	Normal
21	Mirror Move	Flying	Status	—	—	20	Normal
25	Agility	Psychic	Status	—	—	30	Self
29	Assurance	Dark	Physical	60	100	10	Normal
33	Roost	Flying	Status	—	—	10	Self
37	Drill Peck	Flying	Physical	80	100	20	Normal

● TM & HM MOVES

No.	Name	Type	Kind	Pow.	Acc.	PP	Range
TM06	Toxic	Poison	Status	—	90	10	Normal
TM10	Hidden Power	Normal	Special	60	100	15	Normal
TM11	Sunny Day	Fire	Status	—	—	5	Both Sides
TM17	Protect	Normal	Status	—	—	10	Self
TM18	Rain Dance	Water	Status	—	—	5	Both Sides
TM19	Roost	Flying	Status	—	—	10	Self
TM21	Frustration	Normal	Physical	—	100	20	Normal
TM27	Return	Normal	Physical	—	100	20	Normal
TM32	Double Team	Normal	Status	—	—	15	Self
TM40	Aerial Ace	Flying	Physical	60	—	20	Normal
TM42	Facade	Normal	Physical	70	100	20	Normal
TM44	Rest	Psychic	Status	—	—	10	Self
TM45	Attract	Normal	Status	—	100	15	Normal
TM46	Thief	Dark	Physical	60	100	25	Normal
TM48	Round	Normal	Special	60	100	15	Normal
TM49	Echoed Voice	Normal	Special	40	100	15	Normal
TM51	Steel Wing	Steel	Physical	70	90	25	Normal
TM54	False Swipe	Normal	Physical	40	100	40	Normal
TM87	Swagger	Normal	Status	—	90	15	Normal
TM88	Sleep Talk	Normal	Status	—	—	10	Self
TM89	U-turn	Bug	Physical	70	100	20	Normal
TM90	Substitute	Normal	Status	—	—	10	Self
TM100	Confide	Normal	Status	—	—	20	Normal
HM02	Fly	Flying	Physical	90	95	15	Normal

● MOVES TAUGHT BY PEOPLE

Name	Type	Kind	Pow.	Acc.	PP	Range

● EGG MOVES

Name	Type	Kind	Pow.	Acc.	PP	Range
Feint Attack	Dark	Physical	60	—	20	Normal
Scary Face	Normal	Status	—	100	10	Normal
Quick Attack	Normal	Physical	40	100	30	Normal
Tri Attack	Normal	Special	80	100	10	Normal
Astonish	Ghost	Physical	30	100	15	Normal
Sky Attack	Flying	Physical	140	90	5	Normal
Whirlwind	Normal	Status	—	—	20	Normal
Uproar	Normal	Special	90	100	10	1 Random
Feather Dance	Flying	Status	—	100	15	Normal
Steel Wing	Steel	Physical	70	90	25	Normal
Razor Wind	Normal	Special	80	100	10	Many Others

AFTER THE HALL OF FAME

CENTRAL KALOS

COASTAL KALOS

MOUNTAIN KALOS

109 | Spearow

ADVENTURE DATA

110 Fearow
Beak Pokémon

☑ **Fearow**

HEIGHT: 3'11" WEIGHT: 83.8 lbs.
GENDER: ♂/♀

TYPE Normal / Flying

ABILITY
Keen Eye

HIDDEN ABILITY
Sniper

STAT GROWTH RATES
HP	■■■
Attack	■■■■■
Defense	■■■
Sp. Atk	■■■
Sp. Def	■■■
Speed	■■■■■

EGG GROUP
Flying

X: With its huge and magnificent wings, it can keep aloft without ever having to land for rest.

Y: It has the stamina to fly all day on its broad wings. It fights by using its sharp beak.

EVOLUTION

Spearow → Lv. 20 → Fearow

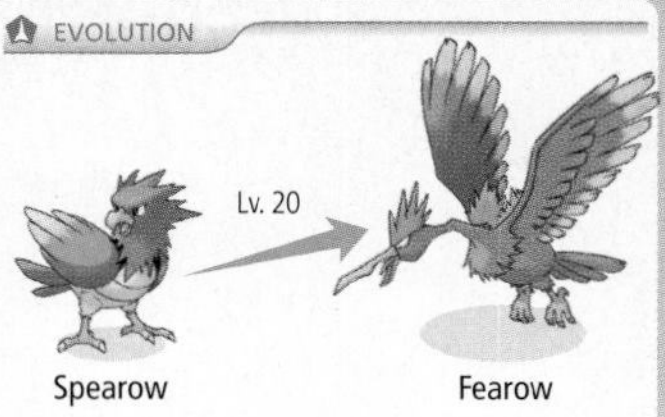

ITEMS SOMETIMES HELD BY WILD POKÉMON
Sharp Beak

Damage taken in normal battles
Normal	×1
Fire	×1
Water	×1
Grass	×0.5
Electric	×2
Ice	×2
Fighting	×1
Poison	×1
Ground	×0
Flying	×1
Psychic	×1
Bug	×0.5
Rock	×2
Ghost	×0
Dragon	×1
Dark	×1
Steel	×1
Fairy	×1

Damage taken in Inverse Battles
Normal	×1
Fire	×1
Water	×1
Grass	×2
Electric	×0.5
Ice	×0.5
Fighting	×1
Poison	×1
Ground	×2
Flying	×1
Psychic	×1
Bug	×2
Rock	×0.5
Ghost	×2
Dragon	×1
Dark	×1
Steel	×1
Fairy	×1

Can be used in
Inverse Battle	Battle Institute
Sky Battle	Battle Maison
Battle Chateau	Random Matchup

Same form for ♂/♀

How to obtain for your Mountain Kalos Pokédex
X: Catch when it ambushes you outside on Victory Road.
Y: Catch when it ambushes you outside on Victory Road.

LEVEL-UP MOVES
Lv.	Name	Type	Kind	Pow.	Acc.	PP	Range
1	Drill Run	Ground	Physical	80	95	10	Normal
1	Pluck	Flying	Physical	60	100	20	Normal
1	Peck	Flying	Physical	35	100	35	Normal
1	Growl	Normal	Status	—	100	40	Many Others
1	Leer	Normal	Status	—	100	30	Many Others
1	Fury Attack	Normal	Physical	15	85	20	Normal
5	Leer	Normal	Status	—	100	30	Many Others
9	Fury Attack	Normal	Physical	15	85	20	Normal
13	Pursuit	Dark	Physical	40	100	20	Normal
17	Aerial Ace	Flying	Physical	60	—	20	Normal
23	Mirror Move	Flying	Status	—	—	20	Normal
29	Agility	Psychic	Status	—	—	30	Self
35	Assurance	Dark	Physical	60	100	10	Normal
41	Roost	Flying	Status	—	—	10	Self
47	Drill Peck	Flying	Physical	80	100	20	Normal
53	Drill Run	Ground	Physical	80	95	10	Normal

TM & HM MOVES
No.	Name	Type	Kind	Pow.	Acc.	PP	Range
TM06	Toxic	Poison	Status	—	90	10	Normal
TM10	Hidden Power	Normal	Special	60	100	15	Normal
TM11	Sunny Day	Fire	Status	—	—	5	Both Sides
TM15	Hyper Beam	Normal	Special	150	90	5	Normal
TM17	Protect	Normal	Status	—	—	10	Self
TM18	Rain Dance	Water	Status	—	—	5	Both Sides
TM19	Roost	Flying	Status	—	—	10	Self
TM21	Frustration	Normal	Physical	—	100	20	Normal
TM27	Return	Normal	Physical	—	100	20	Normal
TM32	Double Team	Normal	Status	—	—	15	Self
TM40	Aerial Ace	Flying	Physical	60	—	20	Normal
TM42	Facade	Normal	Physical	70	100	20	Normal
TM44	Rest	Psychic	Status	—	—	10	Self
TM45	Attract	Normal	Status	—	100	15	Normal
TM46	Thief	Dark	Physical	60	100	25	Normal
TM48	Round	Normal	Special	60	100	15	Normal
TM49	Echoed Voice	Normal	Special	40	100	15	Normal
TM51	Steel Wing	Steel	Physical	70	90	25	Normal
TM54	False Swipe	Normal	Physical	40	100	40	Normal
TM68	Giga Impact	Normal	Physical	150	90	5	Normal
TM87	Swagger	Normal	Status	—	90	15	Normal
TM88	Sleep Talk	Normal	Status	—	—	10	Self
TM89	U-turn	Bug	Physical	70	100	20	Normal
TM90	Substitute	Normal	Status	—	—	10	Self
TM100	Confide	Normal	Status	—	—	20	Normal
HM02	Fly	Flying	Physical	90	95	15	Normal

MOVES TAUGHT BY PEOPLE
Name	Type	Kind	Pow.	Acc.	PP	Range

Crystallizing Pokémon

☑ Cryogonal

HEIGHT: 3'07"   WEIGHT: 326.3 lbs.
GENDER: unknown

X They are born in snow clouds. They use chains made of ice crystals to capture prey.

Y They are composed of ice crystals. They capture prey with chains of ice, freezing the prey at -148 degrees Fahrenheit.

TYPE	Ice

ABILITY
Levitate

HIDDEN ABILITY
None

STAT GROWTH RATES
HP	■■■
Attack	■■■
Defense	■■
Sp. Atk	■■■■■
Sp. Def	■■■■■
Speed	■■■■■

EGG GROUP
Mineral

EVOLUTION

Does not evolve

ITEMS SOMETIMES HELD BY WILD POKÉMON
Never-Melt Ice

Damage taken in normal battles		Damage taken in Inverse Battles	
Normal	×1	Normal	×1
Fire	×2	Fire	×0.5
Water	×1	Water	×1
Grass	×1	Grass	×1
Electric	×1	Electric	×1
Ice	×0.5	Ice	×2
Fighting	×2	Fighting	×0.5
Poison	×1	Poison	×1
Ground	×1 ❶	Ground	×1 ❶
Flying	×1	Flying	×1
Psychic	×1	Psychic	×1
Bug	×1	Bug	×1
Rock	×2	Rock	×0.5
Ghost	×1	Ghost	×1
Dragon	×1	Dragon	×1
Dark	×1	Dark	×1
Steel	×2	Steel	×0.5
Fairy	×1	Fairy	×1

Can be used in	
Inverse Battle	Battle Institute
Sky Battle	Battle Maison
Battle Chateau	Random Matchup

Gender unknown

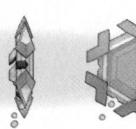

How to obtain for your Mountain Kalos Pokédex

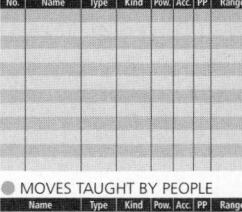

❶ Catch on Frost Cavern 1F.
❷ Catch on Frost Cavern 2F.

❶ Catch on Frost Cavern 1F.
❷ Catch on Frost Cavern 3F.

● LEVEL-UP MOVES

Lv.	Name	Type	Kind	Pow.	Acc.	PP	Range
1	Sheer Cold	Ice	Special	—	30	5	Normal
1	Night Slash	Dark	Physical	70	100	15	Normal
1	Ice Shard	Ice	Physical	40	100	30	Normal
1	Mist	Ice	Status	—	—	30	Your Side
1	Haze	Ice	Status	—	—	30	Both Sides
1	Bind	Normal	Physical	15	85	20	Normal
5	Ice Shard	Ice	Physical	40	100	30	Normal
9	Sharpen	Normal	Status	—	—	30	Self
13	Rapid Spin	Normal	Physical	20	100	40	Normal
17	Icy Wind	Ice	Special	55	95	15	Many Others
21	Mist	Ice	Status	—	—	30	Your Side
21	Haze	Ice	Status	—	—	30	Both Sides
25	Aurora Beam	Ice	Special	65	100	20	Normal
29	Acid Armor	Poison	Status	—	—	20	Self
33	Ice Beam	Ice	Special	90	100	10	Normal
37	Light Screen	Psychic	Status	—	—	30	Your Side
37	Reflect	Psychic	Status	—	—	20	Your Side
41	Slash	Normal	Physical	70	100	20	Normal
45	Confuse Ray	Ghost	Status	—	100	10	Normal
49	Recover	Normal	Status	—	—	10	Self
50	Freeze-Dry	Ice	Special	70	100	20	Normal
53	Solar Beam	Grass	Special	120	100	10	Normal
57	Night Slash	Dark	Physical	70	100	15	Normal
61	Sheer Cold	Ice	Special	—	30	5	Normal

● TM & HM MOVES

No.	Name	Type	Kind	Pow.	Acc.	PP	Range
TM06	Toxic	Poison	Status	—	90	10	Normal
TM07	Hail	Ice	Status	—	—	10	Both Sides
TM10	Hidden Power	Normal	Special	60	100	15	Normal
TM13	Ice Beam	Ice	Special	90	100	10	Normal
TM14	Blizzard	Ice	Special	110	70	5	Many Others
TM15	Hyper Beam	Normal	Special	150	90	5	Normal
TM16	Light Screen	Psychic	Status	—	—	30	Your Side
TM17	Protect	Normal	Status	—	—	10	Self
TM18	Rain Dance	Water	Status	—	—	5	Both Sides
TM21	Frustration	Normal	Physical	—	100	20	Normal
TM22	Solar Beam	Grass	Special	120	100	10	Normal
TM27	Return	Normal	Physical	—	100	20	Normal
TM32	Double Team	Normal	Status	—	—	15	Self
TM33	Reflect	Psychic	Status	—	—	20	Your Side
TM42	Facade	Normal	Physical	70	100	20	Normal
TM44	Rest	Psychic	Status	—	—	10	Self
TM45	Attract	Normal	Status	—	100	15	Normal
TM48	Round	Normal	Special	60	100	15	Normal
TM62	Acrobatics	Flying	Physical	55	100	15	Normal
TM64	Explosion	Normal	Physical	250	100	5	Adjacent
TM79	Frost Breath	Ice	Special	60	90	10	Normal
TM84	Poison Jab	Poison	Physical	80	100	20	Normal
TM87	Swagger	Normal	Status	—	90	15	Normal
TM88	Sleep Talk	Normal	Status	—	—	10	Self
TM90	Substitute	Normal	Status	—	—	10	Self
TM91	Flash Cannon	Steel	Special	80	100	10	Normal
TM100	Confide	Normal	Status	—	—	20	Normal

● MOVES TAUGHT BY PEOPLE

Name	Type	Kind	Pow.	Acc.	PP	Range

AFTER THE HALL OF FAME

CENTRAL KALOS

COASTAL KALOS

MOUNTAIN KALOS

ADVENTURE DATA

Skarmory

112

⬛ Mountain Kalos — 112

Armor Bird Pokémon

☑ Skarmory

HEIGHT: 5'07" WEIGHT: 111.3 lbs.
GENDER: ♂/♀

X After nesting in bramble bushes, the wings of its chicks grow hard from scratches by thorns.

Y Despite being clad entirely in iron-hard armor, it flies at speeds over 180 mph.

TYPE Steel Flying

ABILITIES
Keen Eye
Sturdy

HIDDEN ABILITY
Weak Armor

STAT GROWTH RATES
HP	■■■
Attack	■■■■
Defense	■■■■■■■
Sp. Atk	■■
Sp. Def	■■■
Speed	■■■■

EGG GROUP
Flying

EVOLUTION

Does not evolve

ITEMS SOMETIMES HELD BY WILD POKÉMON
None

Damage taken in normal battles		Damage taken in Inverse Battles	
Normal	×0.5	Normal	×2
Fire	×2	Fire	×0.5
Water	×1	Water	×1
Grass	×0.25	Grass	×4
Electric	×2	Electric	×0.5
Ice	×1	Ice	×1
Fighting	×1	Fighting	×1
Poison	×0	Poison	×2
Ground	×0	Ground	×1
Flying	×0.5	Flying	×2
Psychic	×0.5	Psychic	×2
Bug	×0.25	Bug	×4
Rock	×1	Rock	×1
Ghost	×1	Ghost	×1
Dragon	×0.5	Dragon	×2
Dark	×1	Dark	×1
Steel	×0.5	Steel	×2
Fairy	×0.5	Fairy	×2

Can be used in	
Inverse Battle	Battle Institute
Sky Battle	Battle Maison
Battle Chateau	Random Matchup

Same form for ♂ / ♀

How to obtain for your Mountain Kalos Pokédex

Catch when it ambushes you outside on Victory Road.	Catch when it ambushes you outside on Victory Road.

● LEVEL-UP MOVES

Lv.	Name	Type	Kind	Pow.	Acc.	PP	Range
1	Leer	Normal	Status	—	100	30	Many Others
1	Peck	Flying	Physical	35	100	35	Normal
6	Sand Attack	Ground	Status	—	100	15	Normal
9	Swift	Normal	Special	60	—	20	Many Others
12	Agility	Psychic	Status	—	—	30	Self
17	Fury Attack	Normal	Physical	15	85	20	Normal
20	Feint	Normal	Physical	30	100	10	Normal
23	Air Cutter	Flying	Special	60	95	25	Many Others
28	Spikes	Ground	Status	—	—	20	Other Side
31	Metal Sound	Steel	Status	—	85	40	Normal
34	Steel Wing	Steel	Physical	70	90	25	Normal
39	Autotomize	Steel	Status	—	—	15	Self
42	Air Slash	Flying	Special	75	95	15	Normal
45	Slash	Normal	Physical	70	100	20	Normal
50	Night Slash	Dark	Physical	70	100	15	Normal

● TM & HM MOVES

No.	Name	Type	Kind	Pow.	Acc.	PP	Range
TM05	Roar	Normal	Status	—	—	20	Normal
TM06	Toxic	Poison	Status	—	90	10	Normal
TM10	Hidden Power	Normal	Special	60	100	15	Normal
TM11	Sunny Day	Fire	Status	—	—	5	Both Sides
TM12	Taunt	Dark	Status	—	100	20	Normal
TM17	Protect	Normal	Status	—	—	10	Self
TM19	Roost	Flying	Status	—	—	10	Self
TM21	Frustration	Normal	Physical	—	100	20	Normal
TM27	Return	Normal	Physical	—	100	20	Normal
TM32	Double Team	Normal	Status	—	—	15	Self
TM37	Sandstorm	Rock	Status	—	—	10	Both Sides
TM39	Rock Tomb	Rock	Physical	60	95	15	Normal
TM40	Aerial Ace	Flying	Physical	60	—	20	Normal
TM41	Torment	Dark	Status	—	100	15	Normal
TM42	Facade	Normal	Physical	70	100	20	Normal
TM44	Rest	Psychic	Status	—	—	10	Self
TM45	Attract	Normal	Status	—	100	15	Normal
TM46	Thief	Dark	Physical	60	100	25	Normal
TM48	Round	Normal	Special	60	100	15	Normal
TM51	Steel Wing	Steel	Physical	70	90	25	Normal
TM58	Sky Drop	Flying	Physical	60	100	10	Normal
TM66	Payback	Dark	Physical	50	100	10	Normal
TM70	Flash	Normal	Status	—	100	20	Normal
TM75	Swords Dance	Normal	Status	—	—	20	Self
TM80	Rock Slide	Rock	Physical	75	90	10	Many Others
TM81	X-Scissor	Bug	Physical	80	100	15	Normal
TM87	Swagger	Normal	Status	—	90	15	Normal
TM88	Sleep Talk	Normal	Status	—	—	10	Self
TM90	Substitute	Normal	Status	—	—	10	Self
TM91	Flash Cannon	Steel	Special	80	100	10	Normal
TM94	Rock Smash	Fighting	Physical	40	100	15	Normal
TM97	Dark Pulse	Dark	Special	80	100	15	Normal
TM100	Confide	Normal	Status	—	—	20	Normal

No.	Name	Type	Kind	Pow.	Acc.	PP	Range
HM01	Cut	Normal	Physical	50	95	30	Normal
HM02	Fly	Flying	Physical	90	95	15	Normal

● MOVES TAUGHT BY PEOPLE

Name	Type	Kind	Pow.	Acc.	PP	Range

● EGG MOVES

Name	Type	Kind	Pow.	Acc.	PP	Range
Drill Peck	Flying	Physical	80	100	20	Normal
Pursuit	Dark	Physical	40	100	20	Normal
Whirlwind	Normal	Status	—	—	20	Normal
Sky Attack	Flying	Physical	140	90	5	Normal
Curse	Ghost	Status	—	—	10	Varies
Brave Bird	Flying	Physical	120	100	15	Normal
Assurance	Dark	Physical	60	100	10	Normal
Guard Swap	Psychic	Status	—	—	10	Normal
Stealth Rock	Rock	Status	—	—	20	Other Side
Endure	Normal	Status	—	—	10	Self

AFTER THE HALL OF FAME

CENTRAL KALOS

COASTAL KALOS

MOUNTAIN KALOS

113

Noibat

ADVENTURE DATA

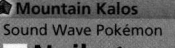

Mountain Kalos 113
Sound Wave Pokémon
☑ Noibat

HEIGHT: 1'08" WEIGHT: 17.6 lbs.
GENDER: ♂/♀

X They live in pitch-black caves. Their enormous ears can emit ultrasonic waves of 200,000 hertz.

Y Even a robust wrestler will become dizzy and unable to stand when exposed to its 200,000-hertz ultrasonic waves.

TYPE Flying Dragon

ABILITIES
Frisk
Infiltrator

HIDDEN ABILITY
Telepathy

STAT GROWTH RATES
HP	■ ■
Attack	■ ■
Defense	■ ■
Sp. Atk	■ ■
Sp. Def	■ ■
Speed	■ ■ ■

EGG GROUP
Flying

⭐ EVOLUTION

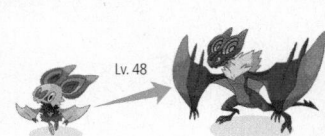

Lv. 48

Noibat → Noivern

ITEMS SOMETIMES HELD BY WILD POKÉMON
None

Damage taken in normal battles		Damage taken in Inverse Battles	
Normal	×1	Normal	×1
Fire	×0.5	Fire	×2
Water	×0.5	Water	×2
Grass	×0.25	Grass	×4
Electric	×1	Electric	×1
Ice	×4	Ice	×0.25
Fighting	×0.5	Fighting	×2
Poison	×1	Poison	×1
Ground	×0	Ground	×2
Flying	×1	Flying	×1
Psychic	×1	Psychic	×1
Bug	×1	Bug	×2
Rock	×2	Rock	×0.5
Ghost	×1	Ghost	×1
Dragon	×2	Dragon	×0.5
Dark	×1	Dark	×1
Steel	×1	Steel	×1
Fairy	×2	Fairy	×0.5

Can be used in	
Inverse Battle	Battle Institute
Sky Battle	Battle Maison
Battle Chateau	Random Matchup

Same form for ♂/♀

How to obtain for your Mountain Kalos Pokédex

❶ Catch when it ambushes you from the roof of Terminus Cave.

❷ Catch when it ambushes you from the roof of the caves along Victory Road.

❶ Catch when it ambushes you from the roof of Terminus Cave.

❷ Catch when it ambushes you from the roof of the caves along Victory Road.

● LEVEL-UP MOVES
Lv.	Name	Type	Kind	Pow.	Acc.	PP	Range
1	Screech	Normal	Status	—	85	40	Normal
1	Supersonic	Normal	Status	—	55	20	Normal
1	Tackle	Normal	Physical	50	100	35	Normal
5	Leech Life	Bug	Physical	20	100	15	Normal
11	Gust	Flying	Special	40	100	35	Normal
13	Bite	Dark	Physical	60	100	25	Normal
16	Wing Attack	Flying	Physical	60	100	35	Normal
23	Agility	Psychic	Status	—	—	30	Self
23	Air Cutter	Flying	Special	60	95	25	Many Others
27	Roost	Flying	Status	—	—	10	Self
31	Razor Wind	Normal	Special	80	100	10	Many Others
35	Tailwind	Flying	Status	—	—	15	Your Side
40	Whirlwind	Normal	Status	—	—	20	Normal
43	Super Fang	Normal	Physical	—	90	10	Normal
48	Air Slash	Flying	Special	75	95	15	Normal
58	Hurricane	Flying	Special	110	70	10	Normal

● TM & HM MOVES
No.	Name	Type	Kind	Pow.	Acc.	PP	Range
TM06	Toxic	Poison	Status	—	90	10	Normal
TM10	Hidden Power	Normal	Special	60	100	15	Normal
TM11	Sunny Day	Fire	Status	—	—	5	Both Sides
TM12	Taunt	Dark	Status	—	100	20	Normal
TM17	Protect	Normal	Status	—	—	10	Self
TM19	Roost	Flying	Status	—	—	10	Self
TM21	Frustration	Normal	Physical	—	100	20	Normal
TM22	Solar Beam	Grass	Special	120	100	10	Normal
TM27	Return	Normal	Physical	—	100	20	Normal
TM29	Psychic	Psychic	Special	90	100	10	Normal
TM30	Shadow Ball	Ghost	Special	80	100	15	Normal
TM31	Brick Break	Fighting	Physical	75	100	15	Normal
TM32	Double Team	Normal	Status	—	—	15	Self
TM40	Aerial Ace	Flying	Physical	60	—	20	Normal
TM41	Torment	Dark	Status	—	100	15	Normal
TM44	Rest	Psychic	Status	—	—	10	Self
TM45	Attract	Normal	Status	—	100	15	Normal
TM46	Thief	Dark	Physical	60	100	25	Normal
TM48	Round	Normal	Special	60	100	15	Normal
TM49	Echoed Voice	Normal	Special	40	100	15	Normal
TM51	Steel Wing	Steel	Physical	70	90	25	Normal
TM62	Acrobatics	Flying	Physical	55	100	15	Normal
TM65	Shadow Claw	Ghost	Physical	70	100	15	Normal
TM81	X-Scissor	Bug	Physical	80	100	15	Normal
TM85	Dream Eater	Psychic	Special	100	100	15	Normal
TM87	Swagger	Normal	Status	—	90	15	Normal
TM88	Sleep Talk	Normal	Status	—	—	10	Self
TM89	U-turn	Bug	Physical	70	100	20	Normal
TM90	Substitute	Normal	Status	—	—	10	Self
TM93	Wild Charge	Electric	Physical	90	100	15	Normal
TM97	Dark Pulse	Dark	Special	80	100	15	Normal
TM100	Confide	Normal	Status	—	—	20	Normal

No.	Name	Type	Kind	Pow.	Acc.	PP	Range
HM01	Cut	Normal	Physical	50	95	30	Normal
HM02	Fly	Flying	Physical	90	95	15	Normal

● MOVES TAUGHT BY PEOPLE
Name	Type	Kind	Pow.	Acc.	PP	Range
Draco Meteor	Dragon	Special	130	90	5	Normal

● EGG MOVES
Name	Type	Kind	Pow.	Acc.	PP	Range
Switcheroo	Dark	Status	—	100	10	Normal
Snatch	Dark	Status	—	—	10	Self
Outrage	Dragon	Physical	120	100	10	1 Random
Tailwind	Flying	Status	—	—	15	Your Side

Mountain Kalos 114
Sound Wave Pokémon
☑ **Noivern**

HEIGHT: 4'11" WEIGHT: 187.4 lbs.
GENDER: ♂/♀

TYPE Flying Dragon

ABILITIES
Frisk
Infiltrator

HIDDEN ABILITY
Telepathy

STAT GROWTH RATES
HP ▮▮▮
Attack ▮▮▮
Defense ▮▮▮
Sp. Atk ▮▮▮▮▮
Sp. Def ▮▮▮
Speed ▮▮▮▮▮▮▮

EGG GROUP
Flying

X They fly around on moonless nights and attack careless prey. Nothing can beat them in a battle in the dark.

Y The ultrasonic waves it emits from its ears can reduce a large boulder to pebbles. It swoops out of the dark to attack.

EVOLUTION

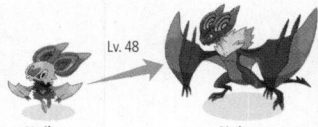

Noibat → Lv. 48 → Noivern

ITEMS SOMETIMES HELD BY WILD POKÉMON
None

Damage taken in normal battles		Damage taken in Inverse Battles	
Normal	×1	Normal	×1
Fire	×0.5	Fire	×2
Water	×0.5	Water	×2
Grass	×0.25	Grass	×4
Electric	×1	Electric	×1
Ice	×4	Ice	×0.25
Fighting	×0.5	Fighting	×2
Poison	×1	Poison	×1
Ground	×0	Ground	×2
Flying	×1	Flying	×1
Psychic	×1	Psychic	×1
Bug	×0.5	Bug	×2
Rock	×2	Rock	×0.5
Ghost	×1	Ghost	×1
Dragon	×2	Dragon	×0.5
Dark	×1	Dark	×1
Steel	×1	Steel	×1
Fairy	×2	Fairy	×0.5

Can be used in	
Inverse Battle	Battle Institute
Sky Battle	Battle Maison
Battle Chateau	Random Matchup

Same form for ♂/♀

How to obtain for your Mountain Kalos Pokédex

Level up Noibat to Lv. 48.	Level up Noibat to Lv. 48.
X	Y

114 Noivern

● LEVEL-UP MOVES

Lv.	Name	Type	Kind	Pow.	Acc.	PP	Range
1	Moonlight	Fairy	Status	—	—	5	Self
1	Boomburst	Normal	Special	140	100	10	Adjacent
1	Dragon Pulse	Dragon	Special	85	100	10	Normal
1	Hurricane	Flying	Special	110	70	10	Normal
1	Screech	Normal	Status	—	85	40	Normal
1	Supersonic	Normal	Status	—	55	20	Normal
1	Tackle	Normal	Physical	50	100	35	Normal
5	Leech Life	Bug	Physical	20	100	15	Normal
11	Gust	Flying	Special	40	100	35	Normal
13	Bite	Dark	Physical	60	100	25	Normal
16	Wing Attack	Flying	Physical	60	100	35	Normal
18	Agility	Psychic	Status	—	—	30	Self
23	Air Cutter	Flying	Special	60	95	25	Many Others
27	Roost	Flying	Status	—	—	10	Self
31	Razor Wind	Normal	Special	80	100	10	Many Others
35	Tailwind	Flying	Status	—	—	15	Your Side
40	Whirlwind	Normal	Status	—	—	20	Normal
43	Super Fang	Normal	Physical	—	90	10	Normal
53	Air Slash	Flying	Special	75	95	15	Normal
62	Hurricane	Flying	Special	110	70	10	Normal
70	Dragon Pulse	Dragon	Special	85	100	10	Normal
75	Boomburst	Normal	Special	140	100	10	Adjacent

● TM & HM MOVES

No.	Name	Type	Kind	Pow.	Acc.	PP	Range
TM01	Hone Claws	Dark	Status	—	—	15	Self
TM02	Dragon Claw	Dragon	Physical	80	100	15	Normal
TM06	Toxic	Poison	Status	—	90	10	Normal
TM10	Hidden Power	Normal	Special	60	100	15	Normal
TM11	Sunny Day	Fire	Status	—	—	5	Both Sides
TM12	Taunt	Dark	Status	—	100	20	Normal
TM15	Hyper Beam	Normal	Special	150	90	5	Normal
TM17	Protect	Normal	Status	—	—	10	Self
TM19	Roost	Flying	Status	—	—	10	Self
TM21	Frustration	Normal	Physical	—	100	20	Normal
TM22	Solar Beam	Grass	Special	120	100	10	Normal
TM27	Return	Normal	Physical	—	100	20	Normal
TM29	Psychic	Psychic	Special	90	100	10	Normal
TM30	Shadow Ball	Ghost	Special	80	100	15	Normal
TM31	Brick Break	Fighting	Physical	75	100	15	Normal
TM32	Double Team	Normal	Status	—	—	15	Self
TM35	Flamethrower	Fire	Special	90	100	15	Normal
TM40	Aerial Ace	Flying	Physical	60	—	20	Normal
TM41	Torment	Dark	Status	—	100	15	Normal
TM42	Facade	Normal	Physical	70	100	20	Normal
TM44	Rest	Psychic	Status	—	—	10	Self
TM45	Attract	Normal	Status	—	100	15	Normal
TM46	Thief	Dark	Physical	60	100	25	Normal
TM48	Round	Normal	Special	60	100	15	Normal
TM49	Echoed Voice	Normal	Special	40	100	15	Normal
TM51	Steel Wing	Steel	Physical	70	90	25	Normal
TM52	Focus Blast	Fighting	Special	120	70	5	Normal
TM62	Acrobatics	Flying	Physical	55	100	15	Normal
TM65	Shadow Claw	Ghost	Physical	70	100	15	Normal
TM68	Giga Impact	Normal	Physical	150	90	5	Normal
TM81	X-Scissor	Bug	Physical	80	100	15	Normal
TM85	Dream Eater	Psychic	Special	100	100	15	Normal
TM87	Swagger	Normal	Status	—	90	15	Normal
TM88	Sleep Talk	Normal	Status	—	—	10	Self
TM89	U-turn	Bug	Physical	70	100	20	Normal
TM90	Substitute	Normal	Status	—	—	10	Self
TM93	Wild Charge	Electric	Physical	90	100	15	Normal
TM97	Dark Pulse	Dark	Special	80	100	15	Normal
TM100	Confide	Normal	Status	—	—	20	Normal
HM01	Cut	Normal	Physical	50	95	30	Normal
HM02	Fly	Flying	Physical	90	95	15	Normal

● MOVES TAUGHT BY PEOPLE

Name	Type	Kind	Pow.	Acc.	PP	Range
Draco Meteor	Dragon	Special	130	90	5	Normal

AFTER THE HALL OF FAME

CENTRAL KALOS

COASTAL KALOS

MOUNTAIN KALOS

115 | Gligar

ADVENTURE DATA

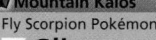

Mountain Kalos 115
Fly Scorpion Pokémon
✓ Gligar

HEIGHT: 3'07" WEIGHT: 142.9 lbs.
GENDER: ♂/♀

TYPE Ground / Flying

ABILITIES
Hyper Cutter
Sand Veil

HIDDEN ABILITY
Immunity

STAT GROWTH RATES
HP ▪▪▪
Attack ▪▪▪
Defense ▪▪▪▪▪
Sp. Atk ▪▪
Sp. Def ▪▪▪
Speed ▪▪▪▪▪

EGG GROUP
Bug

 X
It usually clings to cliffs. When it spots its prey, it spreads its wings and glides down to attack.

 Y
It flies straight at its target's face, then clamps down on the startled victim to inject poison.

EVOLUTION

Level up with a Razor Fang between 8 P.M. and 3:59 A.M.

Gligar → Gliscor

ITEMS SOMETIMES HELD BY WILD POKÉMON
None

Damage taken in normal battles		Damage taken in Inverse Battles	
Normal	×1	Normal	×1
Fire	×1	Fire	×1
Water	×2	Water	×0.5
Grass	×1	Grass	×1
Electric	×0	Electric	×1
Ice	×4	Ice	×0.25
Fighting	×0.5	Fighting	×2
Poison	×0.5	Poison	×2
Ground	×0	Ground	×2
Flying	×1	Flying	×1
Psychic	×1	Psychic	×1
Bug	×0.5	Bug	×2
Rock	×1	Rock	×1
Ghost	×1	Ghost	×1
Dragon	×1	Dragon	×1
Dark	×1	Dark	×1
Steel	×1	Steel	×1
Fairy	×1	Fairy	×1

Can be used in
Inverse Battle
Sky Battle
Battle Chateau
Battle Institute
Battle Maison
Random Matchup

How to obtain for your Mountain Kalos Pokédex

Catch in a Horde Encounter on Route 19.

Catch in a Horde Encounter on Route 19.

X Y

 ♂    ♀

The male has a larger stinger on its tail. The female has a smaller stinger on its tail.

● LEVEL-UP MOVES

Lv.	Name	Type	Kind	Pow.	Acc.	PP	Range
1	Poison Sting	Poison	Physical	15	100	35	Normal
4	Sand Attack	Ground	Status	—	100	15	Normal
7	Harden	Normal	Status	—	—	30	Self
10	Knock Off	Dark	Physical	65	100	20	Normal
13	Quick Attack	Normal	Physical	40	100	30	Normal
16	Fury Cutter	Bug	Physical	40	95	20	Normal
19	Feint Attack	Dark	Physical	60	—	20	Normal
22	Acrobatics	Flying	Physical	55	100	15	Normal
27	Slash	Normal	Physical	70	100	20	Normal
30	U-turn	Bug	Physical	70	100	20	Normal
35	Screech	Normal	Status	—	85	40	Normal
40	X-Scissor	Bug	Physical	80	100	15	Normal
45	Sky Uppercut	Fighting	Physical	85	90	15	Normal
50	Swords Dance	Normal	Status	—	—	20	Self
55	Guillotine	Normal	Physical	—	30	5	Normal

● TM & HM MOVES

No.	Name	Type	Kind	Pow.	Acc.	PP	Range
TM01	Hone Claws	Dark	Status	—	—	15	Self
TM06	Toxic	Poison	Status	—	90	10	Normal
TM09	Venoshock	Poison	Special	65	100	10	Normal
TM10	Hidden Power	Normal	Special	60	100	15	Normal
TM11	Sunny Day	Fire	Status	—	—	5	Both Sides
TM12	Taunt	Dark	Status	—	100	20	Normal
TM17	Protect	Normal	Status	—	—	10	Self
TM18	Rain Dance	Water	Status	—	—	5	Both Sides
TM19	Roost	Flying	Status	—	—	10	Self
TM21	Frustration	Normal	Physical	—	100	20	Normal
TM27	Return	Normal	Physical	—	100	20	Normal
TM28	Dig	Ground	Physical	80	100	10	Normal
TM31	Brick Break	Fighting	Physical	75	100	15	Normal
TM32	Double Team	Normal	Status	—	—	15	Self
TM36	Sludge Bomb	Poison	Special	90	100	10	Normal
TM37	Sandstorm	Rock	Status	—	—	10	Both Sides
TM39	Rock Tomb	Rock	Physical	60	95	15	Normal
TM40	Aerial Ace	Flying	Physical	60	—	20	Normal
TM41	Torment	Dark	Status	—	100	15	Normal
TM42	Facade	Normal	Physical	70	100	20	Normal
TM44	Rest	Psychic	Status	—	—	10	Self
TM45	Attract	Normal	Status	—	100	15	Normal
TM46	Thief	Dark	Physical	60	100	25	Normal
TM48	Round	Normal	Special	60	100	15	Normal
TM51	Steel Wing	Steel	Physical	70	90	25	Normal
TM54	False Swipe	Normal	Physical	40	100	40	Normal
TM56	Fling	Dark	Physical	—	100	10	Normal
TM62	Acrobatics	Flying	Physical	55	100	15	Normal
TM66	Payback	Dark	Physical	50	100	10	Normal
TM69	Rock Polish	Rock	Status	—	—	20	Self
TM71	Stone Edge	Rock	Physical	100	80	5	Normal
TM75	Swords Dance	Normal	Status	—	—	20	Self
TM76	Struggle Bug	Bug	Special	30	100	20	Many Others
TM78	Bulldoze	Ground	Physical	60	100	20	Adjacent
TM80	Rock Slide	Rock	Physical	75	90	10	Many Others
TM81	X-Scissor	Bug	Physical	80	100	15	Normal
TM84	Poison Jab	Poison	Physical	80	100	20	Normal
TM87	Swagger	Normal	Status	—	90	15	Normal
TM88	Sleep Talk	Normal	Status	—	—	10	Self
TM89	U-turn	Bug	Physical	70	100	20	Normal
TM90	Substitute	Normal	Status	—	—	10	Self
TM94	Rock Smash	Fighting	Physical	40	100	15	Normal
TM97	Dark Pulse	Dark	Special	80	100	15	Normal
TM100	Confide	Normal	Status	—	—	20	Normal
HM01	Cut	Normal	Physical	50	95	30	Normal
HM04	Strength	Normal	Physical	80	100	15	Normal

● MOVES TAUGHT BY PEOPLE

Name	Type	Kind	Pow.	Acc.	PP	Range

● EGG MOVES

Name	Type	Kind	Pow.	Acc.	PP	Range
Metal Claw	Steel	Physical	50	95	35	Normal
Wing Attack	Flying	Physical	60	100	35	Normal
Razor Wind	Normal	Special	80	100	10	Many Others
Counter	Fighting	Physical	—	100	20	Varies
Sand Tomb	Ground	Physical	35	85	15	Normal
Agility	Psychic	Status	—	—	30	Self
Baton Pass	Normal	Status	—	—	40	Self
Double-Edge	Normal	Physical	120	100	15	Normal
Feint	Normal	Physical	30	100	10	Normal
Night Slash	Dark	Physical	70	100	15	Normal
Cross Poison	Poison	Physical	70	100	20	Normal
Power Trick	Psychic	Status	—	—	10	Self
Rock Climb	Normal	Physical	90	85	20	Normal
Poison Tail	Poison	Physical	50	100	25	Normal

Mountain Kalos 116

Fang Scorpion Pokémon

✔ Gliscor

HEIGHT: 6'07" WEIGHT: 93.7 lbs.
GENDER: ♂/♀

X It observes prey while hanging inverted from branches. When the chance presents itself, it swoops!

Y Its flight is soundless. It uses its lengthy tail to carry off its prey... Then its elongated fangs do the rest.

TYPE Ground Flying

ABILITIES
Hyper Cutter
Sand Veil

HIDDEN ABILITY
Poison Heal

STAT GROWTH RATES
HP	■■■
Attack	■■■■
Defense	■■■■■
Sp. Atk	■■
Sp. Def	■■
Speed	■■■■■

EGG GROUP
Bug

⬆ EVOLUTION

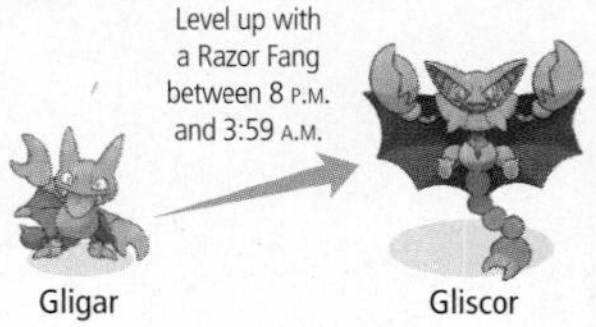

Level up with a Razor Fang between 8 P.M. and 3:59 A.M.

Gligar → Gliscor

ITEMS SOMETIMES HELD BY WILD POKÉMON
None

Can be used in
Inverse Battle
Sky Battle
Battle Chateau
Battle Institute
Battle Maison
Random Matchup

Damage taken in normal battles	
Normal	×1
Fire	×1
Water	×2
Grass	×1
Electric	×0
Ice	×4
Fighting	×0.5
Poison	×0.5
Ground	×0
Flying	×1
Psychic	×1
Bug	×0.5
Rock	×1
Ghost	×1
Dragon	×1
Dark	×1
Steel	×1
Fairy	×1

Damage taken in Inverse Battles	
Normal	×1
Fire	×1
Water	×0.5
Grass	×1
Electric	×1
Ice	×0.25
Fighting	×2
Poison	×2
Ground	×2
Flying	×1
Psychic	×1
Bug	×2
Rock	×1
Ghost	×1
Dragon	×1
Dark	×1
Steel	×1
Fairy	×1

How to obtain for your Mountain Kalos Pokédex

Level up Gligar between 8 P.M. and 3:59 A.M. while it is holding a Razor Fang.

Level up Gligar between 8 P.M. and 3:59 A.M. while it is holding a Razor Fang.

Same form for ♂/♀

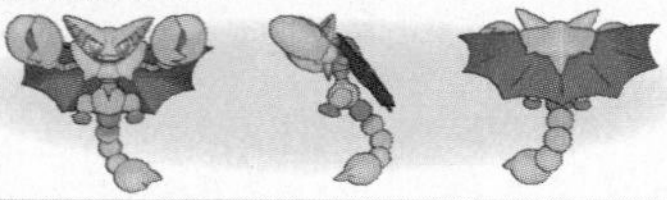

116

Gliscor

ADVENTURE DATA

● LEVEL-UP MOVES

Lv.	Name	Type	Kind	Pow.	Acc.	PP	Range
1	Guillotine	Normal	Physical	—	30	5	Normal
1	Thunder Fang	Electric	Physical	65	95	15	Normal
1	Ice Fang	Ice	Physical	65	95	15	Normal
1	Fire Fang	Fire	Physical	65	95	15	Normal
1	Poison Jab	Poison	Physical	80	100	20	Normal
1	Sand Attack	Ground	Status	—	100	15	Normal
1	Harden	Normal	Status	—	—	30	Self
1	Knock Off	Dark	Physical	65	100	20	Normal
4	Sand Attack	Ground	Status	—	100	15	Normal
7	Harden	Normal	Status	—	—	30	Self
10	Knock Off	Dark	Physical	65	100	20	Normal
13	Quick Attack	Normal	Physical	40	100	30	Normal
16	Fury Cutter	Bug	Physical	40	95	20	Normal
19	Feint Attack	Dark	Physical	60	—	20	Normal
22	Acrobatics	Flying	Physical	55	100	15	Normal
27	Night Slash	Dark	Physical	70	100	15	Normal
30	U-turn	Bug	Physical	70	100	20	Normal
35	Screech	Normal	Status	—	85	40	Normal
40	K-Scissor	Bug	Physical	80	100	15	Normal
45	Sky Uppercut	Fighting	Physical	85	90	15	Normal
50	Swords Dance	Normal	Status	—	—	20	Self
55	Guillotine	Normal	Physical	—	30	5	Normal

● TM & HM MOVES

No.	Name	Type	Kind	Pow.	Acc.	PP	Range
TM01	Hone Claws	Dark	Status	—	—	15	Self
TM06	Toxic	Poison	Status	—	90	10	Normal
TM09	Venoshock	Poison	Special	65	100	10	Normal
TM10	Hidden Power	Normal	Special	60	100	15	Normal
TM11	Sunny Day	Fire	Status	—	—	5	Both Sides
TM12	Taunt	Dark	Status	—	100	20	Normal
TM15	Hyper Beam	Normal	Special	150	90	5	Normal
TM17	Protect	Normal	Status	—	—	10	Self
TM18	Rain Dance	Water	Status	—	—	5	Both Sides
TM19	Roost	Flying	Status	—	—	10	Self
TM21	Frustration	Normal	Physical	—	100	20	Normal
TM26	Earthquake	Ground	Physical	100	100	10	Adjacent
TM27	Return	Normal	Physical	—	100	20	Normal
TM28	Dig	Ground	Physical	80	100	10	Normal
TM31	Brick Break	Fighting	Physical	75	100	15	Normal
TM32	Double Team	Normal	Status	—	—	15	Self
TM36	Sludge Bomb	Poison	Special	90	100	10	Normal
TM37	Sandstorm	Rock	Status	—	—	10	Both Sides
TM39	Rock Tomb	Rock	Physical	60	95	15	Normal
TM40	Aerial Ace	Flying	Physical	60	—	20	Normal
TM41	Torment	Dark	Status	—	100	15	Normal
TM42	Facade	Normal	Physical	70	100	20	Normal
TM44	Rest	Psychic	Status	—	—	10	Self
TM45	Attract	Normal	Status	—	100	15	Normal
TM46	Thief	Dark	Physical	60	100	25	Normal
TM48	Round	Normal	Special	60	100	15	Normal
TM51	Steel Wing	Steel	Physical	70	90	25	Normal
TM54	False Swipe	Normal	Physical	40	100	40	Normal
TM56	Fling	Dark	Physical	—	100	10	Normal
TM62	Acrobatics	Flying	Physical	55	100	15	Normal
TM66	Payback	Dark	Physical	50	100	10	Normal
TM68	Giga Impact	Normal	Physical	150	90	5	Normal
TM69	Rock Polish	Rock	Status	—	—	20	Self

No.	Name	Type	Kind	Pow.	Acc.	PP	Range
TM71	Stone Edge	Rock	Physical	100	80	5	Normal
TM75	Swords Dance	Normal	Status	—	—	20	Self
TM76	Struggle Bug	Bug	Special	50	100	20	Many Others
TM78	Bulldoze	Ground	Physical	60	100	20	Adjacent
TM80	Rock Slide	Rock	Physical	75	90	10	Many Others
TM81	X-Scissor	Bug	Physical	80	100	15	Normal
TM84	Poison Jab	Poison	Physical	80	100	20	Normal
TM87	Swagger	Normal	Status	—	90	15	Normal
TM88	Sleep Talk	Normal	Status	—	—	10	Self
TM89	U-turn	Bug	Physical	70	100	20	Normal
TM90	Substitute	Normal	Status	—	—	10	Self
TM94	Rock Smash	Fighting	Physical	40	100	15	Normal
TM97	Dark Pulse	Dark	Special	80	100	15	Normal
TM100	Confide	Normal	Status	—	—	20	Normal
HM01	Cut	Normal	Physical	50	95	30	Normal
HM04	Strength	Normal	Physical	80	100	15	Normal

● MOVES TAUGHT BY PEOPLE

Name	Type	Kind	Pow.	Acc.	PP	Range

Owl Pokémon

☑ Hoothoot

HEIGHT: 2'04" WEIGHT: 46.7 lbs.
GENDER: ♂/♀

X It has a perfect sense of time. Whatever happens, it keeps rhythm by precisely tilting its head in time.

Y It always stands on one foot. It changes feet so fast, the movement can rarely be seen.

TYPE Normal / Flying

ABILITIES
Insomnia
Keen Eye

HIDDEN ABILITY
Tinted Lens

STAT GROWTH RATES
HP	■■
Attack	■■
Defense	■■
Sp. Atk	■■
Sp. Def	■■
Speed	■■■

EGG GROUP
Flying

EVOLUTION

Hoothoot → Lv. 20 → Noctowl

ITEMS SOMETIMES HELD BY WILD POKÉMON
None

Damage taken in normal battles		Damage taken in Inverse Battles	
Normal	×1	Normal	×1
Fire	×1	Fire	×1
Water	×1	Water	×1
Grass	×0.5	Grass	×2
Electric	×2	Electric	×0.5
Ice	×2	Ice	×0.5
Fighting	×1	Fighting	×1
Poison	×1	Poison	×1
Ground	×0	Ground	×2
Flying	×1	Flying	×1
Psychic	×1	Psychic	×1
Bug	×0.5	Bug	×2
Rock	×2	Rock	×0.5
Ghost	×0	Ghost	×2
Dragon	×1	Dragon	×1
Dark	×1	Dark	×1
Steel	×1	Steel	×1
Fairy	×1	Fairy	×1

Can be used in
Inverse Battle
—
Battle Chateau
Battle Institute
Battle Maison
Random Matchup

How to obtain for your Mountain Kalos Pokédex

Leave Noctowl at the Pokémon Day Care, and hatch the Egg that is found.

Leave Noctowl at the Pokémon Day Care, and hatch the Egg that is found.

Same form for ♂/♀

● LEVEL-UP MOVES

Lv.	Name	Type	Kind	Pow.	Acc.	PP	Range
1	Tackle	Normal	Physical	50	100	35	Normal
1	Growl	Normal	Status	—	100	40	Many Others
1	Foresight	Normal	Status	—	—	40	Normal
5	Hypnosis	Psychic	Status	—	60	20	Normal
9	Peck	Flying	Physical	35	100	35	Normal
13	Uproar	Normal	Special	90	100	10	1 Random
17	Reflect	Psychic	Status	—	—	20	Your Side
21	Confusion	Psychic	Special	50	100	25	Normal
25	Echoed Voice	Normal	Special	40	100	15	Normal
29	Take Down	Normal	Physical	90	85	20	Normal
33	Air Slash	Flying	Special	75	95	15	Normal
37	Zen Headbutt	Psychic	Physical	80	90	15	Normal
41	Synchronoise	Psychic	Special	120	100	10	Adjacent
45	Extrasensory	Psychic	Special	80	100	20	Normal
49	Psycho Shift	Psychic	Status	—	100	10	Normal
53	Roost	Flying	Status	—	—	10	Self
57	Dream Eater	Psychic	Special	100	100	15	Normal

● TM & HM MOVES

No.	Name	Type	Kind	Pow.	Acc.	PP	Range
TM06	Toxic	Poison	Status	—	90	10	Normal
TM10	Hidden Power	Normal	Special	60	100	15	Normal
TM11	Sunny Day	Fire	Status	—	—	5	Both Sides
TM17	Protect	Normal	Status	—	—	10	Self
TM18	Rain Dance	Water	Status	—	—	5	Both Sides
TM19	Roost	Flying	Status	—	—	10	Self
TM21	Frustration	Normal	Physical	—	100	20	Normal
TM27	Return	Normal	Physical	—	100	20	Normal
TM29	Psychic	Psychic	Special	90	100	10	Normal
TM30	Shadow Ball	Ghost	Special	80	100	15	Normal
TM32	Double Team	Normal	Status	—	—	15	Self
TM33	Reflect	Psychic	Status	—	—	20	Your Side
TM40	Aerial Ace	Flying	Physical	60	—	20	Normal
TM42	Facade	Normal	Physical	70	100	20	Normal
TM44	Rest	Psychic	Status	—	—	10	Self
TM45	Attract	Normal	Status	—	100	15	Normal
TM46	Thief	Dark	Physical	60	100	25	Normal
TM48	Round	Normal	Special	60	100	15	Normal
TM49	Echoed Voice	Normal	Special	40	100	15	Normal
TM51	Steel Wing	Steel	Physical	70	90	25	Normal
TM77	Psych Up	Normal	Status	—	—	10	Normal
TM85	Dream Eater	Psychic	Special	100	100	15	Normal
TM87	Swagger	Normal	Status	—	90	15	Normal
TM88	Sleep Talk	Normal	Status	—	—	10	Self
TM90	Substitute	Normal	Status	—	—	10	Self
TM100	Confide	Normal	Status	—	—	20	Normal
HM02	Fly	Flying	Physical	90	95	15	Normal

● MOVES TAUGHT BY PEOPLE

Name	Type	Kind	Pow.	Acc.	PP	Range

● EGG MOVES

Name	Type	Kind	Pow.	Acc.	PP	Range
Mirror Move	Flying	Status	—	—	20	Normal
Supersonic	Normal	Status	—	55	20	Normal
Feint Attack	Dark	Physical	60	—	20	Normal
Wing Attack	Flying	Physical	60	100	35	Normal
Whirlwind	Normal	Status	—	—	20	Normal
Sky Attack	Flying	Physical	140	90	5	Normal
Feather Dance	Flying	Status	—	100	15	Normal
Agility	Psychic	Status	—	—	30	Self
Night Shade	Ghost	Special	—	100	15	Normal
Defog	Flying	Status	—	—	15	Normal

AFTER THE HALL OF FAME
CENTRAL KALOS
COASTAL KALOS
MOUNTAIN KALOS
117 Hoothoot
ADVENTURE DATA

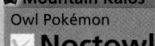

Mountain Kalos 118
Owl Pokémon
☑ Noctowl

HEIGHT: 5'03" WEIGHT: 89.9 lbs.
GENDER: ♂/♀

TYPE: Normal / Flying

ABILITIES
Insomnia
Keen Eye

HIDDEN ABILITY
Tinted Lens

STAT GROWTH RATES
HP	■■■■
Attack	■■■
Defense	■■
Sp. Atk	■■■■
Sp. Def	■■■
Speed	■■■■

EGG GROUP
Flying

X Its eyes are specially adapted. They concentrate even faint light and enable it to see in the dark.

Y When it needs to think, it rotates its head 180 degrees to sharpen its intellectual power.

EVOLUTION

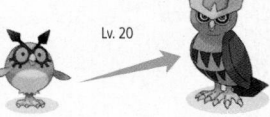

Hoothoot — Lv. 20 → Noctowl

ITEMS SOMETIMES HELD BY WILD POKÉMON
None

Can be used in
Inverse Battle
Sky Battle
Battle Chateau
Battle Institute
Battle Maison
Random Matchup

Damage taken in normal battles		Damage taken in Inverse Battles	
Normal	×1	Normal	×1
Fire	×1	Fire	×1
Water	×1	Water	×1
Grass	×0.5	Grass	×2
Electric	×2	Electric	×0.5
Ice	×2	Ice	×0.5
Fighting	×1	Fighting	×1
Poison	×1	Poison	×1
Ground	×0	Ground	×2
Flying	×1	Flying	×1
Psychic	×1	Psychic	×1
Bug	×0.5	Bug	×2
Rock	×2	Rock	×0.5
Ghost	×0	Ghost	×2
Dragon	×1	Dragon	×1
Dark	×1	Dark	×1
Steel	×1	Steel	×1
Fairy	×1	Fairy	×1

How to obtain for your Mountain Kalos Pokédex

① Catch in the tall grass on Route 20.
② Catch in the red flowers on Route 20.

① Catch in the tall grass on Route 20.
② Catch in the red flowers on Route 20.

Same form for ♂/♀

● LEVEL-UP MOVES

Lv.	Name	Type	Kind	Pow.	Acc.	PP	Range
1	Dream Eater	Psychic	Special	100	100	15	Normal
1	Sky Attack	Flying	Physical	140	90	5	Normal
1	Tackle	Normal	Physical	50	100	35	Normal
1	Growl	Normal	Status	—	100	40	Many Others
1	Foresight	Normal	Status	—	—	40	Normal
1	Hypnosis	Psychic	Status	—	60	20	Normal
5	Hypnosis	Psychic	Status	—	60	20	Normal
9	Peck	Flying	Physical	35	100	35	Normal
13	Uproar	Normal	Special	90	100	10	1 Random
17	Reflect	Psychic	Status	—	—	20	Your Side
22	Confusion	Psychic	Special	50	100	25	Normal
27	Echoed Voice	Normal	Special	40	100	15	Normal
32	Take Down	Normal	Physical	90	85	20	Normal
37	Air Slash	Flying	Special	75	95	15	Normal
42	Zen Headbutt	Psychic	Physical	80	90	15	Normal
47	Synchronoise	Psychic	Special	120	100	10	Adjacent
52	Extrasensory	Psychic	Special	80	100	20	Normal
57	Psycho Shift	Psychic	Status	—	100	10	Normal
62	Roost	Flying	Status	—	—	10	Self
67	Dream Eater	Psychic	Special	100	100	15	Normal

● TM & HM MOVES

No.	Name	Type	Kind	Pow.	Acc.	PP	Range
TM06	Toxic	Poison	Status	—	90	10	Normal
TM10	Hidden Power	Normal	Special	60	100	15	Normal
TM11	Sunny Day	Fire	Status	—	—	5	Both Sides
TM15	Hyper Beam	Normal	Special	150	90	5	Normal
TM17	Protect	Normal	Status	—	—	10	Self
TM18	Rain Dance	Water	Status	—	—	5	Both Sides
TM19	Roost	Flying	Status	—	—	10	Self
TM21	Frustration	Normal	Physical	—	100	20	Normal
TM27	Return	Normal	Physical	—	100	20	Normal
TM29	Psychic	Psychic	Special	90	100	10	Normal
TM30	Shadow Ball	Ghost	Special	80	100	15	Normal
TM32	Double Team	Normal	Status	—	—	15	Self
TM33	Reflect	Psychic	Status	—	—	20	Your Side
TM40	Aerial Ace	Flying	Physical	60	—	20	Normal
TM42	Facade	Normal	Physical	70	100	20	Normal
TM44	Rest	Psychic	Status	—	—	10	Self
TM45	Attract	Normal	Status	—	100	15	Normal
TM46	Thief	Dark	Physical	60	100	25	Normal
TM48	Round	Normal	Special	60	100	15	Normal
TM49	Echoed Voice	Normal	Special	40	100	15	Normal
TM51	Steel Wing	Steel	Physical	70	90	25	Normal
TM68	Giga Impact	Normal	Physical	150	90	5	Normal
TM77	Psych Up	Normal	Status	—	—	10	Normal
TM85	Dream Eater	Psychic	Special	100	100	15	Normal
TM87	Swagger	Normal	Status	—	90	15	Normal
TM88	Sleep Talk	Normal	Status	—	—	10	Self
TM90	Substitute	Normal	Status	—	—	10	Self
TM100	Confide	Normal	Status	—	—	20	Normal
HM02	Fly	Flying	Physical	90	95	15	Normal

● MOVES TAUGHT BY PEOPLE

Name	Type	Kind	Pow.	Acc.	PP	Range

🏔 Mountain Kalos **119**
Balloon Pokémon
☑ **Igglybuff**

HEIGHT: 1'00" WEIGHT: 2.2 lbs.
GENDER: ♂/♀

ⓧ Instead of walking with its short legs, it moves around by bouncing on its soft, tender body.

ⓨ It has a very soft body. If it starts to roll, it will bounce all over and be impossible to stop.

TYPE Normal Fairy

TYPE Normal Fairy

ABILITIES
Cute Charm
Competitive

HIDDEN ABILITY
Friend Guard

STAT GROWTH RATES
HP	▪▪▪▪
Attack	▪▪
Defense	▪
Sp. Atk	▪▪
Sp. Def	▪
Speed	▪

EGG GROUP
No Eggs Discovered

▲ EVOLUTION

Level up with high friendship → Moon Stone →

Igglybuff Jigglypuff Wigglytuff

ITEMS SOMETIMES HELD BY WILD POKÉMON
None

Damage taken in normal battles		Damage taken in Inverse Battles	
Normal	×1	Normal	×1
Fire	×1	Fire	×1
Water	×1	Water	×1
Grass	×1	Grass	×1
Electric	×1	Electric	×1
Ice	×1	Ice	×1
Fighting	×1	Fighting	×1
Poison	×2	Poison	×0.5
Ground	×1	Ground	×1
Flying	×1	Flying	×1
Psychic	×1	Psychic	×1
Bug	×0.5	Bug	×2
Rock	×1	Rock	×1
Ghost	×0	Ghost	×2
Dragon	×0	Dragon	×2
Dark	×0.5	Dark	×2
Steel	×2	Steel	×0.5
Fairy	×1	Fairy	×1

Can be used in	
Inverse Battle	Battle Institute
—	Battle Maison
Battle Chateau	Random Matchup

Same form for ♂/♀

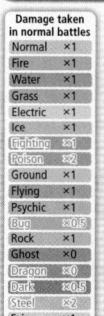

How to obtain for your Mountain Kalos Pokédex

Leave Jigglypuff or Wigglytuff at the Pokémon Day Care, and hatch the Egg that is found.

Leave Jigglypuff or Wigglytuff at the Pokémon Day Care, and hatch the Egg that is found.

● LEVEL-UP MOVES

Lv.	Name	Type	Kind	Pow.	Acc.	PP	Range
1	Sing	Normal	Status	—	55	15	Normal
1	Charm	Fairy	Status	—	100	20	Normal
5	Defense Curl	Normal	Status	—	—	40	Self
9	Pound	Normal	Physical	40	100	35	Normal
13	Sweet Kiss	Fairy	Status	—	75	10	Normal
17	Copycat	Normal	Status	—	—	20	Self

● TM & HM MOVES

No.	Name	Type	Kind	Pow.	Acc.	PP	Range
TM06	Toxic	Poison	Status	—	90	10	Normal
TM10	Hidden Power	Normal	Special	60	100	15	Normal
TM11	Sunny Day	Fire	Status	—	—	5	Both Sides
TM16	Light Screen	Psychic	Status	—	—	30	Your Side
TM17	Protect	Normal	Status	—	—	10	Self
TM18	Rain Dance	Water	Status	—	—	5	Both Sides
TM20	Safeguard	Normal	Status	—	—	25	Your Side
TM21	Frustration	Normal	Physical	—	100	20	Normal
TM22	Solar Beam	Grass	Special	120	100	10	Normal
TM27	Return	Normal	Physical	—	100	20	Normal
TM28	Dig	Ground	Physical	80	100	10	Normal
TM29	Psychic	Psychic	Special	90	100	10	Normal
TM30	Shadow Ball	Ghost	Special	80	100	15	Normal
TM32	Double Team	Normal	Status	—	—	15	Self
TM33	Reflect	Psychic	Status	—	—	20	Your Side
TM35	Flamethrower	Fire	Special	90	100	15	Normal
TM38	Fire Blast	Fire	Special	110	85	5	Normal
TM42	Facade	Normal	Physical	70	100	20	Normal
TM44	Rest	Psychic	Status	—	—	10	Self
TM45	Attract	Normal	Status	—	100	15	Normal
TM48	Round	Normal	Special	60	100	15	Normal
TM49	Echoed Voice	Normal	Special	40	100	15	Normal
TM56	Fling	Dark	Physical	—	100	10	Normal
TM59	Incinerate	Fire	Special	60	100	15	Many Others
TM70	Flash	Normal	Status	—	100	20	Normal
TM73	Thunder Wave	Electric	Status	—	100	20	Normal
TM77	Psych Up	Normal	Status	—	—	10	Normal
TM85	Dream Eater	Psychic	Special	100	100	15	Normal
TM86	Grass Knot	Grass	Special	—	100	20	Normal
TM87	Swagger	Normal	Status	—	90	15	Normal
TM88	Sleep Talk	Normal	Status	—	—	10	Self
TM90	Substitute	Normal	Status	—	—	10	Self
TM93	Wild Charge	Electric	Physical	90	100	15	Normal

No.	Name	Type	Kind	Pow.	Acc.	PP	Range
TM100	Confide	Normal	Status	—	—	20	Normal

● MOVES TAUGHT BY PEOPLE

Name	Type	Kind	Pow.	Acc.	PP	Range

● EGG MOVES

Name	Type	Kind	Pow.	Acc.	PP	Range
Perish Song	Normal	Status	—	—	5	Adjacent
Present	Normal	Physical	—	90	15	Normal
Feint Attack	Dark	Physical	60	—	20	Normal
Wish	Normal	Status	—	—	10	Self
Fake Tears	Dark	Status	—	100	20	Normal
Last Resort	Normal	Physical	140	100	5	Normal
Covet	Normal	Physical	60	100	25	Normal
Gravity	Psychic	Status	—	—	5	Both Sides
Sleep Talk	Normal	Status	—	—	10	Self
Captivate	Normal	Status	—	100	20	Many Others
Punishment	Dark	Physical	—	100	5	Normal
Misty Terrain	Fairy	Status	—	—	10	Both Sides
Heal Pulse	Psychic	Status	—	—	10	Normal

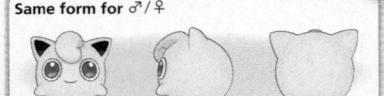

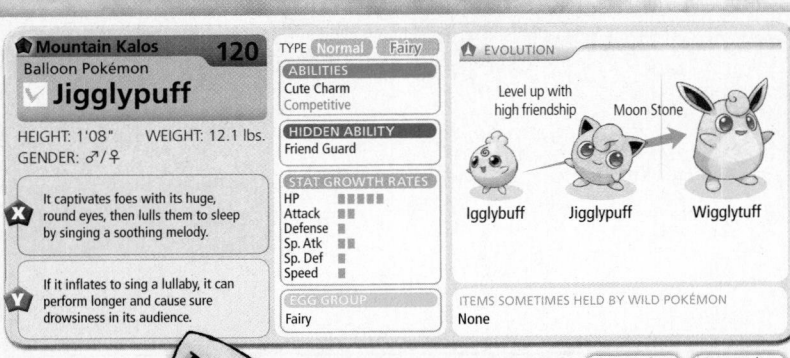

Jigglypuff

Mountain Kalos 120
Balloon Pokémon
☑ **Jigglypuff**

HEIGHT: 1'08" WEIGHT: 12.1 lbs.
GENDER: ♂/♀

X It captivates foes with its huge, round eyes, then lulls them to sleep by singing a soothing melody.

Y If it inflates to sing a lullaby, it can perform longer and cause sure drowsiness in its audience.

TYPE: Normal / Fairy

ABILITIES
Cute Charm
Competitive

HIDDEN ABILITY
Friend Guard

STAT GROWTH RATES
HP	▪▪▪▪▪
Attack	▪▪
Defense	▪▪
Sp. Atk	▪▪
Sp. Def	▪▪
Speed	▪

EGG GROUP
Fairy

EVOLUTION

Level up with high friendship → Moon Stone →

Igglybuff Jigglypuff Wigglytuff

ITEMS SOMETIMES HELD BY WILD POKÉMON
None

Damage taken in normal battles		Damage taken in Inverse Battles	
Normal	×1	Normal	×1
Fire	×1	Fire	×1
Water	×1	Water	×1
Grass	×1	Grass	×1
Electric	×1	Electric	×1
Ice	×1	Ice	×1
Fighting	×1	Fighting	×1
Poison	×2	Poison	×0.5
Ground	×1	Ground	×1
Flying	×1	Flying	×1
Psychic	×1	Psychic	×1
Bug	×0.5	Bug	×2
Rock	×1	Rock	×1
Ghost	×0	Ghost	×2
Dragon	×0	Dragon	×2
Dark	×0.5	Dark	×2
Steel	×2	Steel	×0.5
Fairy	×1	Fairy	×1

Can be used in	
Inverse Battle	Battle Institute
—	Battle Maison
Battle Chateau	Random Matchup

Same form for ♂/♀

How to obtain for your Mountain Kalos Pokédex

❶ Catch in the tall grass on Route 20.
❷ Catch in the red flowers on Route 20.

❶ Catch in the tall grass on Route 20.
❷ Catch in the red flowers on Route 20.

● LEVEL-UP MOVES

Lv.	Name	Type	Kind	Pow.	Acc.	PP	Range
1	Sing	Normal	Status	—	55	15	Normal
5	Defense Curl	Normal	Status	—	—	40	Self
7	Pound	Normal	Physical	40	100	35	Normal
10	Play Nice	Normal	Status	—	—	20	Normal
13	Disable	Normal	Status	—	100	20	Normal
17	Round	Normal	Special	60	100	15	Normal
21	Rollout	Rock	Physical	30	90	20	Normal
25	Double Slap	Normal	Physical	15	85	10	Normal
29	Rest	Psychic	Status	—	—	10	Self
33	Body Slam	Normal	Physical	85	100	15	Normal
37	Gyro Ball	Steel	Physical	—	100	5	Normal
41	Wake-Up Slap	Fighting	Physical	70	100	10	Normal
45	Mimic	Normal	Status	—	—	10	Normal
48	Hyper Voice	Normal	Special	90	100	10	Many Others
50	Disarming Voice	Fairy	Special	40	—	15	Many Others
53	Double-Edge	Normal	Physical	120	100	15	Normal

● TM & HM MOVES

No.	Name	Type	Kind	Pow.	Acc.	PP	Range
TM06	Toxic	Poison	Status	—	90	10	Normal
TM10	Hidden Power	Normal	Special	60	100	15	Normal
TM11	Sunny Day	Fire	Status	—	—	5	Both Sides
TM13	Ice Beam	Ice	Special	90	100	10	Normal
TM14	Blizzard	Ice	Special	110	70	5	Many Others
TM16	Light Screen	Psychic	Status	—	—	30	Your Side
TM17	Protect	Normal	Status	—	—	10	Self
TM18	Rain Dance	Water	Status	—	—	5	Both Sides
TM20	Safeguard	Normal	Status	—	—	25	Your Side
TM21	Frustration	Normal	Physical	—	100	20	Normal
TM22	Solar Beam	Grass	Special	120	100	10	Normal
TM24	Thunderbolt	Electric	Special	90	100	15	Normal
TM25	Thunder	Electric	Special	110	70	10	Normal
TM27	Return	Normal	Physical	—	100	20	Normal
TM28	Dig	Ground	Physical	80	100	10	Normal
TM29	Psychic	Psychic	Special	90	100	10	Normal
TM30	Shadow Ball	Ghost	Special	80	100	15	Normal
TM31	Brick Break	Fighting	Physical	75	100	15	Normal
TM32	Double Team	Normal	Status	—	—	15	Self
TM33	Reflect	Psychic	Status	—	—	20	Your Side
TM35	Flamethrower	Fire	Special	90	100	15	Normal
TM38	Fire Blast	Fire	Special	110	85	5	Normal
TM42	Facade	Normal	Physical	70	100	20	Normal
TM44	Rest	Psychic	Status	—	—	10	Self
TM45	Attract	Normal	Status	—	100	15	Normal
TM48	Round	Normal	Special	60	100	15	Normal
TM49	Echoed Voice	Normal	Special	40	100	15	Normal
TM56	Fling	Dark	Physical	—	100	10	Normal
TM57	Charge Beam	Electric	Special	50	90	10	Normal
TM59	Incinerate	Fire	Special	60	100	15	Many Others
TM67	Retaliate	Normal	Physical	70	100	5	Normal
TM70	Flash	Normal	Status	—	100	20	Normal
TM73	Thunder Wave	Electric	Status	—	100	20	Normal

No.	Name	Type	Kind	Pow.	Acc.	PP	Range
TM74	Gyro Ball	Steel	Physical	—	100	5	Normal
TM77	Psych Up	Normal	Status	—	—	10	Normal
TM85	Dream Eater	Psychic	Special	100	100	15	Normal
TM86	Grass Knot	Grass	Special	—	100	20	Normal
TM87	Swagger	Normal	Status	—	90	15	Normal
TM88	Sleep Talk	Normal	Status	—	—	10	Self
TM90	Substitute	Normal	Status	—	—	10	Self
TM93	Wild Charge	Electric	Physical	90	100	15	Normal
TM96	Power-Up Punch	Fighting	Physical	40	100	20	Normal
TM99	Dazzling Gleam	Fairy	Special	80	100	10	Many Others
TM100	Confide	Normal	Status	—	—	20	Normal
HM04	Strength	Normal	Physical	80	100	15	Normal

● MOVES TAUGHT BY PEOPLE

Name	Type	Kind	Pow.	Acc.	PP	Range

AFTER THE HALL OF FAME

CENTRAL KALOS

COASTAL KALOS

MOUNTAIN KALOS

ADVENTURE DATA

120

Jigglypuff

🏔 Mountain Kalos
Balloon Pokémon

121

∨ Wigglytuff

HEIGHT: 3'03" WEIGHT: 26.5 lbs.
GENDER: ♂/♀

TYPE Normal Fairy

ABILITIES
Cute Charm
Competitive

HIDDEN ABILITY
Frisk

⬆ EVOLUTION

Level up with
high friendship   Moon Stone

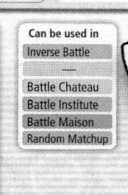

Igglybuff   Jigglypuff   Wigglytuff

X Their fur feels so good that if two of them snuggle together, they won't want to be separated.

Y The body is soft and rubbery. When angered, it will suck in air and inflate itself to an enormous size.

STAT GROWTH RATES
HP	▪▪▪▪
Attack	▪▪▪▪
Defense	▪▪
Sp. Atk	▪▪▪▪
Sp. Def	▪▪
Speed	▪▪▪

EGG GROUP
Fairy

ITEMS SOMETIMES HELD BY WILD POKÉMON
None

Damage taken in normal battles	
Normal	×1
Fire	×1
Water	×1
Grass	×1
Electric	×1
Ice	×1
Fighting	×1
Poison	×2
Ground	×1
Flying	×1
Psychic	×1
Bug	×0.5
Rock	×1
Ghost	×0
Dragon	×0
Dark	×0.5
Steel	×2
Fairy	×1

Damage taken in Inverse Battles	
Normal	×1
Fire	×1
Water	×1
Grass	×1
Electric	×1
Ice	×1
Fighting	×1
Poison	×0.5
Ground	×1
Flying	×1
Psychic	×1
Bug	×2
Rock	×1
Ghost	×2
Dragon	×2
Dark	×2
Steel	×0.5
Fairy	×1

Can be used in
Inverse Battle
—
Battle Chateau
Battle Institute
Battle Maison
Random Matchup

How to obtain for your Mountain Kalos Pokédex

Use a Moon Stone on Jigglypuff. Use a Moon Stone on Jigglypuff.

X   Y

Same form for ♂/♀

● LEVEL-UP MOVES
Lv.	Name	Type	Kind	Pow.	Acc.	PP	Range
1	Double-Edge	Normal	Physical	120	100	15	Normal
1	Play Rough	Fairy	Physical	90	90	10	Normal
1	Sing	Normal	Status	—	55	15	Normal
1	Disable	Normal	Status	—	100	20	Normal
1	Defense Curl	Normal	Status	—	—	40	Self
1	Double Slap	Normal	Physical	15	85	10	Normal

● TM & HM MOVES
No.	Name	Type	Kind	Pow.	Acc.	PP	Range
TM06	Toxic	Poison	Status	—	90	10	Normal
TM10	Hidden Power	Normal	Special	60	100	15	Normal
TM11	Sunny Day	Fire	Status	—	—	5	Both Sides
TM13	Ice Beam	Ice	Special	90	100	10	Normal
TM14	Blizzard	Ice	Special	110	70	5	Many Others
TM15	Hyper Beam	Normal	Special	150	90	5	Normal
TM16	Light Screen	Psychic	Status	—	—	30	Your Side
TM17	Protect	Normal	Status	—	—	10	Self
TM18	Rain Dance	Water	Status	—	—	5	Both Sides
TM20	Safeguard	Normal	Status	—	—	25	Your Side
TM21	Frustration	Normal	Physical	—	100	20	Normal
TM22	Solar Beam	Grass	Special	120	100	10	Normal
TM24	Thunderbolt	Electric	Special	90	100	15	Normal
TM25	Thunder	Electric	Special	110	70	10	Normal
TM27	Return	Normal	Physical	—	100	20	Normal
TM28	Dig	Ground	Physical	80	100	10	Normal
TM29	Psychic	Psychic	Special	90	100	10	Normal
TM30	Shadow Ball	Ghost	Special	80	100	15	Normal
TM31	Brick Break	Fighting	Physical	75	100	15	Normal
TM32	Double Team	Normal	Status	—	—	15	Self
TM33	Reflect	Psychic	Status	—	—	20	Your Side
TM35	Flamethrower	Fire	Special	90	100	15	Normal
TM38	Fire Blast	Fire	Special	110	85	5	Normal
TM42	Facade	Normal	Physical	70	100	20	Normal
TM44	Rest	Psychic	Status	—	—	10	Self
TM45	Attract	Normal	Status	—	100	15	Normal
TM48	Round	Normal	Special	60	100	15	Normal
TM49	Echoed Voice	Normal	Special	40	100	15	Normal
TM52	Focus Blast	Fighting	Special	120	70	5	Normal
TM56	Fling	Dark	Physical	—	100	10	Normal
TM57	Charge Beam	Electric	Special	50	90	10	Normal
TM59	Incinerate	Fire	Special	60	100	15	Many Others
TM67	Retaliate	Normal	Physical	70	100	5	Normal
TM68	Giga Impact	Normal	Physical	150	90	5	Normal
TM70	Flash	Normal	Status	—	100	20	Normal
TM73	Thunder Wave	Electric	Status	—	100	20	Normal
TM74	Gyro Ball	Steel	Physical	—	100	5	Normal
TM77	Psych Up	Normal	Status	—	—	10	Normal
TM85	Dream Eater	Psychic	Special	100	100	15	Normal
TM86	Grass Knot	Grass	Special	—	100	20	Normal
TM87	Swagger	Normal	Status	—	90	15	Normal
TM88	Sleep Talk	Normal	Status	—	—	10	Self
TM90	Substitute	Normal	Status	—	—	10	Self
TM93	Wild Charge	Electric	Physical	90	100	15	Normal
TM98	Power-Up Punch	Fighting	Physical	40	100	20	Normal
TM99	Dazzling Gleam	Fairy	Special	80	100	10	Many Others
TM100	Confide	Normal	Status	—	—	20	Normal
HM04	Strength	Normal	Physical	80	100	15	Normal

● MOVES TAUGHT BY PEOPLE
Name	Type	Kind	Pow.	Acc.	PP	Range

AFTER THE HALL OF FAME

CENTRAL KALOS

COASTAL KALOS

MOUNTAIN KALOS

121 Wigglytuff

ADVENTURE DATA

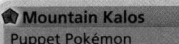

Mountain Kalos 122
Puppet Pokémon
☑ Shuppet

HEIGHT: 2'00" WEIGHT: 5.1 lbs.
GENDER: ♂/♀

TYPE Ghost

ABILITIES
Insomnia
Frisk

HIDDEN ABILITY
Cursed Body

STAT GROWTH RATES
HP	■■
Attack	■■■■
Defense	■■
Sp. Atk	■■■
Sp. Def	■
Speed	■■■

EGG GROUP
Amorphous

⬆ EVOLUTION

Lv. 37

Shuppet → Banette

ITEMS SOMETIMES HELD BY WILD POKÉMON
None

X It uses its horn to feed on envy and malice—or so it's said. It's very active at night.

Y It loves vengeful emotions and hangs in rows under the eaves of houses where vengeful people live.

Damage taken in normal battles		Damage taken in Inverse Battles	
Normal	×0	Normal	×2
Fire	×1	Fire	×1
Water	×1	Water	×1
Grass	×1	Grass	×1
Electric	×1	Electric	×1
Ice	×1	Ice	×1
Fighting	×0	Fighting	×2
Poison	×0.5	Poison	×2
Ground	×1	Ground	×1
Flying	×1	Flying	×1
Psychic	×1	Psychic	×1
Bug	×0.5	Bug	×2
Rock	×1	Rock	×1
Ghost	×2	Ghost	×0.5
Dragon	×1	Dragon	×1
Dark	×2	Dark	×0.5
Steel	×1	Steel	×1
Fairy	×1	Fairy	×1

Can be used in	
Inverse Battle	Battle Institute
—	Battle Maison
Battle Chateau	Random Matchup

Same form for ♂/♀

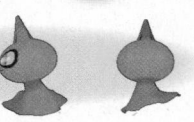

How to obtain for your Mountain Kalos Pokédex

Leave Banette at the Pokémon Day Care, and hatch the Egg that is found.

Leave Banette at the Pokémon Day Care, and hatch the Egg that is found.

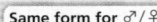

● LEVEL-UP MOVES

Lv.	Name	Type	Kind	Pow.	Acc.	PP	Range
1	Knock Off	Dark	Physical	65	100	20	Normal
4	Screech	Normal	Status	—	85	40	Normal
7	Night Shade	Ghost	Special	—	100	15	Normal
10	Spite	Ghost	Status	—	100	10	Normal
13	Will-O-Wisp	Fire	Status	—	85	15	Normal
16	Shadow Sneak	Ghost	Physical	40	100	30	Normal
19	Curse	Ghost	Status	—	—	10	Varies
22	Feint Attack	Dark	Physical	60	—	20	Normal
26	Hex	Ghost	Special	65	100	10	Normal
30	Shadow Ball	Ghost	Special	80	100	15	Normal
34	Sucker Punch	Dark	Physical	80	100	5	Normal
38	Embargo	Dark	Status	—	100	15	Normal
42	Snatch	Dark	Status	—	—	10	Self
46	Grudge	Ghost	Status	—	—	5	Self
50	Trick	Psychic	Status	—	100	10	Normal

● TM & HM MOVES

No.	Name	Type	Kind	Pow.	Acc.	PP	Range
TM04	Calm Mind	Psychic	Status	—	—	20	Self
TM06	Toxic	Poison	Status	—	90	10	Normal
TM10	Hidden Power	Normal	Special	60	100	15	Normal
TM11	Sunny Day	Fire	Status	—	—	5	Both Sides
TM12	Taunt	Dark	Status	—	100	20	Normal
TM17	Protect	Normal	Status	—	—	10	Self
TM18	Rain Dance	Water	Status	—	—	5	Both Sides
TM21	Frustration	Normal	Physical	—	100	20	Normal
TM24	Thunderbolt	Electric	Special	90	100	15	Normal
TM25	Thunder	Electric	Special	110	70	10	Normal
TM27	Return	Normal	Physical	—	100	20	Normal
TM29	Psychic	Psychic	Special	90	100	10	Normal
TM30	Shadow Ball	Ghost	Special	80	100	15	Normal
TM32	Double Team	Normal	Status	—	—	15	Self
TM41	Torment	Dark	Status	—	100	15	Normal
TM42	Facade	Normal	Physical	70	100	20	Normal
TM44	Rest	Psychic	Status	—	—	10	Self
TM45	Attract	Normal	Status	—	100	15	Normal
TM46	Thief	Dark	Physical	60	100	25	Normal
TM48	Round	Normal	Special	60	100	15	Normal
TM57	Charge Beam	Electric	Special	50	90	10	Normal
TM61	Will-O-Wisp	Fire	Status	—	85	15	Normal
TM63	Embargo	Dark	Status	—	100	15	Normal
TM66	Payback	Dark	Physical	50	100	10	Normal
TM70	Flash	Normal	Status	—	100	20	Normal
TM73	Thunder Wave	Electric	Status	—	100	20	Normal
TM77	Psych Up	Normal	Status	—	—	10	Normal
TM85	Dream Eater	Psychic	Special	100	100	15	Normal
TM87	Swagger	Normal	Status	—	90	15	Normal
TM88	Sleep Talk	Normal	Status	—	—	10	Self
TM90	Substitute	Normal	Status	—	—	10	Self
TM92	Trick Room	Psychic	Status	—	—	5	Both Sides
TM97	Dark Pulse	Dark	Special	80	100	15	Normal

No.	Name	Type	Kind	Pow.	Acc.	PP	Range
TM99	Dazzling Gleam	Fairy	Special	80	100	10	Many Others
TM100	Confide	Normal	Status	—	—	20	Normal

● MOVES TAUGHT BY PEOPLE

Name	Type	Kind	Pow.	Acc.	PP	Range

● EGG MOVES

Name	Type	Kind	Pow.	Acc.	PP	Range
Disable	Normal	Status	—	100	20	Normal
Destiny Bond	Ghost	Status	—	—	5	Self
Foresight	Normal	Status	—	—	40	Normal
Astonish	Ghost	Physical	30	100	15	Normal
Imprison	Psychic	Status	—	—	10	Self
Pursuit	Dark	Physical	40	100	20	Normal
Shadow Sneak	Ghost	Physical	40	100	30	Normal
Confuse Ray	Ghost	Status	—	100	10	Normal
Ominous Wind	Ghost	Special	60	100	5	Normal
Gunk Shot	Poison	Physical	120	80	5	Normal
Phantom Force	Ghost	Physical	90	100	10	Normal

AFTER THE HALL OF FAME

CENTRAL KALOS

COASTAL KALOS

MOUNTAIN KALOS

122

Shuppet

ADVENTURE DATA

Mountain Kalos

AFTER THE HALL OF FAME

CENTRAL KALOS

COASTAL KALOS

MOUNTAIN KALOS | 123 | Banette

ADVENTURE DATA

Mountain Kalos

Marionette Pokémon

☑ **Banette**

123

HEIGHT: 3'07"   WEIGHT: 27.6 lbs.
GENDER: ♂/♀

X — A doll that became a Pokémon over its grudge from being junked. It seeks the child that disowned it.

Y — Strong feelings of hatred turned a puppet into a Pokémon. If it opens its mouth, its cursed energy escapes.

TYPE Ghost

ABILITIES
Insomnia
Frisk

HIDDEN ABILITY
Cursed Body

STAT GROWTH RATES
HP	■■■
Attack	■■■■■
Defense	■■■
Sp. Atk	■■■■
Sp. Def	■■■
Speed	■■■

EGG GROUP
Amorphous

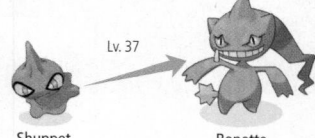

EVOLUTION

Shuppet → Lv. 37 → Banette

ITEMS SOMETIMES HELD BY WILD POKÉMON
Spell Tag

Damage taken in normal battles
Normal	×0
Fire	×1
Water	×1
Grass	×1
Electric	×1
Ice	×1
Fighting	×0
Poison	×0.5
Ground	×1
Flying	×1
Psychic	×1
Bug	×0.5
Rock	×1
Ghost	×2
Dragon	×1
Dark	×2
Steel	×1
Fairy	×1

Damage taken in Inverse Battles
Normal	×2
Fire	×1
Water	×1
Grass	×1
Electric	×1
Ice	×1
Fighting	×2
Poison	×2
Ground	×1
Flying	×1
Psychic	×1
Bug	×2
Rock	×2
Ghost	×0.5
Dragon	×1
Dark	×0.5
Steel	×1
Fairy	×1

Can be used in
Inverse Battle	Battle Institute
—	Battle Maison
Battle Chateau	Random Matchup

Same form for ♂/♀

How to obtain for your Mountain Kalos Pokédex

Examine the trash cans that shake in the Pokémon Village every Thursday.

Examine the trash cans that shake in the Pokémon Village every Thursday.

● LEVEL-UP MOVES

Lv.	Name	Type	Kind	Pow.	Acc.	PP	Range
1	Knock Off	Dark	Physical	65	100	20	Normal
1	Screech	Normal	Status	—	85	40	Normal
1	Night Shade	Ghost	Special	—	100	15	Normal
1	Curse	Ghost	Status	—	—	10	Varies
4	Screech	Normal	Status	—	85	40	Normal
7	Night Shade	Ghost	Special	—	100	15	Normal
10	Spite	Ghost	Status	—	100	10	Normal
13	Will-O-Wisp	Fire	Status	—	85	15	Normal
16	Shadow Sneak	Ghost	Physical	40	100	30	Normal
19	Curse	Ghost	Status	—	—	10	Varies
22	Feint Attack	Dark	Physical	60	—	20	Normal
26	Hex	Ghost	Special	65	100	10	Normal
30	Shadow Ball	Ghost	Special	80	100	15	Normal
34	Sucker Punch	Dark	Physical	80	100	5	Normal
40	Embargo	Dark	Status	—	100	15	Normal
46	Snatch	Dark	Status	—	—	10	Self
52	Grudge	Ghost	Status	—	—	5	Self
58	Trick	Psychic	Status	—	100	10	Normal

● TM & HM MOVES

No.	Name	Type	Kind	Pow.	Acc.	PP	Range
TM04	Calm Mind	Psychic	Status	—	—	20	Self
TM06	Toxic	Poison	Status	—	90	10	Normal
TM10	Hidden Power	Normal	Special	60	100	15	Normal
TM11	Sunny Day	Fire	Status	—	—	5	Both Sides
TM12	Taunt	Dark	Status	—	100	20	Normal
TM15	Hyper Beam	Normal	Special	150	90	5	Normal
TM17	Protect	Normal	Status	—	—	10	Self
TM18	Rain Dance	Water	Status	—	—	5	Both Sides
TM21	Frustration	Normal	Physical	—	100	20	Normal
TM24	Thunderbolt	Electric	Special	90	100	15	Normal
TM25	Thunder	Electric	Special	110	70	10	Normal
TM27	Return	Normal	Physical	—	100	20	Normal
TM29	Psychic	Psychic	Special	90	100	10	Normal
TM30	Shadow Ball	Ghost	Special	80	100	15	Normal
TM32	Double Team	Normal	Status	—	—	15	Self
TM41	Torment	Dark	Status	—	100	15	Normal
TM42	Facade	Normal	Physical	70	100	20	Normal
TM44	Rest	Psychic	Status	—	—	10	Self
TM45	Attract	Normal	Status	—	100	15	Normal
TM46	Thief	Dark	Physical	60	100	25	Normal
TM48	Round	Normal	Special	60	100	15	Normal
TM56	Fling	Dark	Physical	—	100	10	Normal
TM57	Charge Beam	Electric	Special	50	90	10	Normal
TM61	Will-O-Wisp	Fire	Status	—	85	15	Normal
TM63	Embargo	Dark	Status	—	100	15	Normal
TM65	Shadow Claw	Ghost	Physical	70	100	15	Normal
TM66	Payback	Dark	Physical	50	100	10	Normal
TM68	Giga Impact	Normal	Physical	150	90	5	Normal
TM70	Flash	Normal	Status	—	100	20	Normal
TM73	Thunder Wave	Electric	Status	—	100	20	Normal
TM77	Psych Up	Normal	Status	—	—	10	Normal
TM83	Infestation	Bug	Special	20	100	20	Normal
TM85	Dream Eater	Psychic	Special	100	100	15	Normal
TM87	Swagger	Normal	Status	—	90	15	Normal
TM88	Sleep Talk	Normal	Status	—	—	10	Self
TM90	Substitute	Normal	Status	—	—	10	Self
TM92	Trick Room	Psychic	Status	—	—	5	Both Sides
TM97	Dark Pulse	Dark	Special	80	100	15	Normal
TM99	Dazzling Gleam	Fairy	Special	80	100	10	Many Others
TM100	Confide	Normal	Status	—	—	20	Normal

● MOVES TAUGHT BY PEOPLE

Name	Type	Kind	Pow.	Acc.	PP	Range

AFTER THE HALL OF FAME

CENTRAL KALOS

COASTAL KALOS

MOUNTAIN KALOS

Mega Banette

ADVENTURE DATA

Mega Evolution

Marionette Pokémon

☑ Mega Banette

TYPE	Ghost

ABILITY
Prankster

HEIGHT: 3'11"   WEIGHT: 28.7 lbs.   GENDER: ♂/♀

STAT GROWTH RATES

HP	▩▩▩
Attack	▩▩▩▩▩▩▩▩
Defense	▩▩▩
Sp. Atk	▩▩▩▩▩
Sp. Def	▩▩▩
Speed	▩▩▩▩

⬡ MEGA STONE REQUIRED

Banettite
Obtain in Route 22's Chamber of Emptiness between 8 P.M. and 8:59 P.M., after entering the Hall of Fame and speaking with Professor Sycamore in Anistar City.

Damage taken in normal battles		Damage taken in Inverse Battles	
Normal	×0	Normal	×2
Fire	×1	Fire	×1
Water	×1	Water	×1
Grass	×1	Grass	×1
Electric	×1	Electric	×1
Ice	×1	Ice	×1
Fighting	×0	Fighting	×2
Poison	×0.5	Poison	×2
Ground	×1	Ground	×1
Flying	×1	Flying	×1
Psychic	×1	Psychic	×1
Bug	×0.5	Bug	×2
Rock	×1	Rock	×1
Ghost	×2	Ghost	×0.5
Dragon	×1	Dragon	×1
Dark	×2	Dark	×0.5
Steel	×1	Steel	×1
Fairy	×1	Fairy	×1

Can be used in	
Inverse Battle	Battle Institute
—	Battle Maison
Battle Chateau	Random Matchup

Same form for ♂/♀

Mountain Kalos
Tricky Fox Pokémon
☑ Zorua

124

HEIGHT: 2'04" WEIGHT: 27.6 lbs.
GENDER: ♂ / ♀

❌ It changes so it looks just like its foe, tricks it, and then uses that opportunity to flee.

Ⓨ To protect themselves from danger, they hide their true identities by transforming into people and Pokémon.

TYPE Dark

ABILITY
Illusion

HIDDEN ABILITY
None

STAT GROWTH RATES
HP	▮▮
Attack	▮▮▮
Defense	▮▮
Sp. Atk	▮▮▮▮
Sp. Def	▮▮
Speed	▮▮▮▮

EGG GROUP
Field

EVOLUTION

Zorua → Lv. 30 → Zoroark

ITEMS SOMETIMES HELD BY WILD POKÉMON
None

Damage taken in normal battles		Damage taken in Inverse Battles	
Normal	×1	Normal	×1
Fire	×1	Fire	×1
Water	×1	Water	×1
Grass	×1	Grass	×1
Electric	×1	Electric	×1
Ice	×1	Ice	×1
Fighting	×2	Fighting	×0.5
Poison	×1	Poison	×1
Ground	×1	Ground	×1
Flying	×1	Flying	×1
Psychic	×0	Psychic	×2
Bug	×2	Bug	×0.5
Rock	×1	Rock	×1
Ghost	×0.5	Ghost	×2
Dragon	×1	Dragon	×1
Dark	×0.5	Dark	×2
Steel	×1	Steel	×1
Fairy	×2	Fairy	×0.5

Can be used in	
Inverse Battle	Battle Institute
—	Battle Maison
Battle Chateau	Random Matchup

Same form for ♂ / ♀

How to obtain for your Mountain Kalos Pokédex

Leave Zoroark at the Pokémon Day Care, and hatch the Egg that is found.

Leave Zoroark at the Pokémon Day Care, and hatch the Egg that is found.

● LEVEL-UP MOVES
Lv.	Name	Type	Kind	Pow.	Acc.	PP	Range
1	Scratch	Normal	Physical	40	100	35	Normal
1	Leer	Normal	Status	—	100	30	Many Others
5	Pursuit	Dark	Physical	40	100	20	Normal
9	Fake Tears	Dark	Status	—	100	20	Normal
13	Fury Swipes	Normal	Physical	18	80	15	Normal
17	Feint Attack	Dark	Physical	60	—	20	Normal
21	Scary Face	Normal	Status	—	100	10	Normal
25	Taunt	Dark	Status	—	100	20	Normal
29	Foul Play	Dark	Physical	95	100	15	Normal
33	Torment	Dark	Status	—	100	15	Normal
37	Agility	Psychic	Status	—	—	30	Self
41	Embargo	Dark	Status	—	100	15	Normal
45	Punishment	Dark	Physical	—	100	5	Normal
49	Nasty Plot	Dark	Status	—	—	20	Self
53	Imprison	Psychic	Status	—	—	10	Self
57	Night Daze	Dark	Special	85	95	10	Normal

● TM & HM MOVES
No.	Name	Type	Kind	Pow.	Acc.	PP	Range
TM01	Hone Claws	Dark	Status	—	—	15	Self
TM04	Calm Mind	Psychic	Status	—	—	20	Self
TM05	Roar	Normal	Status	—	—	20	Normal
TM06	Toxic	Poison	Status	—	90	10	Normal
TM10	Hidden Power	Normal	Special	60	100	15	Normal
TM11	Sunny Day	Fire	Status	—	—	5	Both Sides
TM12	Taunt	Dark	Status	—	100	20	Normal
TM17	Protect	Normal	Status	—	—	10	Self
TM18	Rain Dance	Water	Status	—	—	5	Both Sides
TM21	Frustration	Normal	Physical	—	100	20	Normal
TM27	Return	Normal	Physical	—	100	20	Normal
TM28	Dig	Ground	Physical	80	100	10	Normal
TM30	Shadow Ball	Ghost	Special	80	100	15	Normal
TM32	Double Team	Normal	Status	—	—	15	Self
TM40	Aerial Ace	Flying	Physical	60	—	20	Normal
TM41	Torment	Dark	Status	—	100	15	Normal
TM42	Facade	Normal	Physical	70	100	20	Normal
TM44	Rest	Psychic	Status	—	—	10	Self
TM45	Attract	Normal	Status	—	100	15	Normal
TM46	Thief	Dark	Physical	60	100	25	Normal
TM48	Round	Normal	Special	60	100	15	Normal
TM56	Fling	Dark	Physical	—	100	10	Normal
TM59	Incinerate	Fire	Special	60	100	15	Many Others
TM63	Embargo	Dark	Status	—	100	15	Normal
TM66	Payback	Dark	Physical	50	100	10	Normal
TM67	Retaliate	Normal	Physical	70	100	5	Normal
TM75	Swords Dance	Normal	Status	—	—	20	Self
TM77	Psych Up	Normal	Status	—	—	10	Normal
TM86	Grass Knot	Grass	Special	—	100	20	Normal
TM87	Swagger	Normal	Status	—	90	15	Normal
TM88	Sleep Talk	Normal	Status	—	—	10	Self
TM89	U-turn	Bug	Physical	70	100	20	Normal
TM90	Substitute	Normal	Status	—	—	10	Self

No.	Name	Type	Kind	Pow.	Acc.	PP	Range
TM95	Snarl	Dark	Special	55	95	15	Many Others
TM97	Dark Pulse	Dark	Special	80	100	15	Normal
TM100	Confide	Normal	Status	—	—	20	Normal
HM01	Cut	Normal	Physical	50	95	30	Normal

● MOVES TAUGHT BY PEOPLE
Name	Type	Kind	Pow.	Acc.	PP	Range

● EGG MOVES
Name	Type	Kind	Pow.	Acc.	PP	Range
Detect	Fighting	Status	—	—	5	Self
Captivate	Normal	Status	—	100	20	Many Others
Dark Pulse	Dark	Special	80	100	15	Normal
Snatch	Dark	Status	—	—	10	Self
Memento	Dark	Status	—	100	10	Normal
Sucker Punch	Dark	Physical	80	100	5	Normal
Extrasensory	Psychic	Special	80	100	20	Normal
Counter	Fighting	Physical	—	100	20	Varies
Copycat	Normal	Status	—	—	20	Self

AFTER THE HALL OF FAME

CENTRAL KALOS

COASTAL KALOS

MOUNTAIN KALOS

124 Zorua

ADVENTURE DATA

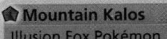

AFTER THE HALL OF FAME

CENTRAL KALOS

COASTAL KALOS

MOUNTAIN KALOS

125

Zoroark

ADVENTURE DATA

Mountain Kalos 125
Illusion Fox Pokémon
☑ Zoroark

HEIGHT: 5'03" WEIGHT: 178.8 lbs.
GENDER: ♂/♀

TYPE Dark

ABILITY
Illusion

HIDDEN ABILITY
None

X Each has the ability to fool a large group of people simultaneously. They protect their lair with illusory scenery.

Y Bonds between these Pokémon are very strong. It protects the safety of its pack by tricking its opponents.

STAT GROWTH RATES
HP	■■■
Attack	■■■■■
Defense	■■■
Sp. Atk	■■■■■■
Sp. Def	■■■
Speed	■■■■■■

EGG GROUP
Field

EVOLUTION

Zorua → Lv. 30 → Zoroark

ITEMS SOMETIMES HELD BY WILD POKÉMON
None

Damage taken in normal battles		Damage taken in Inverse Battles	
Normal	×1	Normal	×1
Fire	×1	Fire	×1
Water	×1	Water	×1
Grass	×1	Grass	×1
Electric	×1	Electric	×1
Ice	×1	Ice	×1
Fighting	×2	Fighting	×0.5
Poison	×1	Poison	×1
Ground	×1	Ground	×1
Flying	×1	Flying	×1
Psychic	×0	Psychic	×2
Bug	×2	Bug	×0.5
Rock	×1	Rock	×1
Ghost	×0.5	Ghost	×2
Dragon	×1	Dragon	×1
Dark	×0.5	Dark	×2
Steel	×1	Steel	×1
Fairy	×2	Fairy	×0.5

Can be used in	
Inverse Battle	Battle Institute
—	Battle Maison
Battle Chateau	Random Matchup

Same form for ♂/♀

How to obtain for your Mountain Kalos Pokédex

❶ Catch in the tall grass on Route 20.
❷ Catch in the yellow flowers in the Pokémon Village.

❶ Catch in the tall grass on Route 20.
❷ Catch in the yellow flowers in the Pokémon Village.

● LEVEL-UP MOVES

Lv.	Name	Type	Kind	Pow.	Acc.	PP	Range
1	Night Daze	Dark	Special	85	95	10	Normal
1	Imprison	Psychic	Status	—	—	10	Self
1	U-turn	Bug	Physical	70	100	20	Normal
1	Scratch	Normal	Physical	40	100	35	Normal
1	Leer	Normal	Status	—	100	30	Many Others
1	Pursuit	Dark	Physical	40	100	20	Normal
1	Hone Claws	Dark	Status	—	—	15	Self
5	Pursuit	Dark	Physical	40	100	20	Normal
9	Hone Claws	Dark	Status	—	—	15	Self
13	Fury Swipes	Normal	Physical	18	80	15	Normal
17	Feint Attack	Dark	Physical	60	—	20	Normal
21	Scary Face	Normal	Status	—	100	10	Normal
25	Taunt	Dark	Status	—	100	20	Normal
29	Foul Play	Dark	Physical	95	100	15	Normal
30	Night Slash	Dark	Physical	70	100	15	Normal
34	Torment	Dark	Status	—	100	15	Normal
39	Agility	Psychic	Status	—	—	30	Self
44	Embargo	Dark	Status	—	100	15	Normal
49	Punishment	Dark	Physical	—	100	5	Normal
54	Nasty Plot	Dark	Status	—	—	20	Self
59	Imprison	Psychic	Status	—	—	10	Self
64	Night Daze	Dark	Special	85	95	10	Normal

● TM & HM MOVES

No.	Name	Type	Kind	Pow.	Acc.	PP	Range
TM01	Hone Claws	Dark	Status	—	—	15	Self
TM04	Calm Mind	Psychic	Status	—	—	20	Self
TM05	Roar	Normal	Status	—	—	20	Normal
TM06	Toxic	Poison	Status	—	90	10	Normal
TM10	Hidden Power	Normal	Special	60	100	15	Normal
TM11	Sunny Day	Fire	Status	—	—	5	Both Sides
TM12	Taunt	Dark	Status	—	100	20	Normal
TM15	Hyper Beam	Normal	Special	150	90	5	Normal
TM17	Protect	Normal	Status	—	—	10	Self
TM18	Rain Dance	Water	Status	—	—	5	Both Sides
TM21	Frustration	Normal	Physical	—	100	20	Normal
TM27	Return	Normal	Physical	—	100	20	Normal
TM28	Dig	Ground	Physical	80	100	10	Normal
TM30	Shadow Ball	Ghost	Special	80	100	15	Normal
TM32	Double Team	Normal	Status	—	—	15	Self
TM35	Flamethrower	Fire	Special	90	100	15	Normal
TM40	Aerial Ace	Flying	Physical	60	—	20	Normal
TM41	Torment	Dark	Status	—	100	15	Normal
TM42	Facade	Normal	Physical	70	100	20	Normal
TM44	Rest	Psychic	Status	—	—	10	Self
TM45	Attract	Normal	Status	—	100	15	Normal
TM46	Thief	Dark	Physical	60	100	25	Normal
TM47	Low Sweep	Fighting	Physical	65	100	20	Normal
TM48	Round	Normal	Special	60	100	15	Normal
TM52	Focus Blast	Fighting	Special	120	70	5	Normal
TM56	Fling	Dark	Physical	—	100	10	Normal
TM59	Incinerate	Fire	Special	60	100	15	Many Others
TM63	Embargo	Dark	Status	—	100	15	Normal
TM65	Shadow Claw	Ghost	Physical	70	100	15	Normal
TM66	Payback	Dark	Physical	50	100	10	Normal
TM67	Retaliate	Normal	Physical	70	100	5	Normal
TM68	Giga Impact	Normal	Physical	150	90	5	Normal
TM75	Swords Dance	Normal	Status	—	—	20	Self
TM77	Psych Up	Normal	Status	—	—	10	Normal
TM86	Grass Knot	Grass	Special	—	100	20	Normal
TM87	Swagger	Normal	Status	—	90	15	Normal
TM88	Sleep Talk	Normal	Status	—	—	10	Self
TM89	U-turn	Bug	Physical	70	100	20	Normal
TM90	Substitute	Normal	Status	—	—	10	Self
TM94	Rock Smash	Fighting	Physical	40	100	15	Normal
TM95	Snarl	Dark	Special	55	95	15	Many Others
TM97	Dark Pulse	Dark	Special	80	100	15	Normal
TM100	Confide	Normal	Status	—	—	20	Normal
HM01	Cut	Normal	Physical	50	95	30	Normal

● MOVES TAUGHT BY PEOPLE

Name	Type	Kind	Pow.	Acc.	PP	Range

Mountain Kalos **126**
Fixation Pokémon
 Gothita

HEIGHT: 1'04" WEIGHT: 12.8 lbs.
GENDER: ♂/♀

X Their ribbonlike feelers increase their psychic power. They are always staring at something.

Y They intently observe both Trainers and Pokémon. Apparently, they are looking at something that only Gothita can see.

TYPE **Psychic**

ABILITIES
Frisk
Competitive

HIDDEN ABILITY
Shadow Tag

STAT GROWTH RATES
HP	■■
Attack	■■
Defense	■■
Sp. Atk	■■■
Sp. Def	■■■
Speed	■■■

EGG GROUP
Human-Like

EVOLUTION

Gothita	Gothorita	Gothitelle
	Lv. 32	Lv. 41

ITEMS SOMETIMES HELD BY WILD POKÉMON
None

Damage taken in normal battles		Damage taken in Inverse Battles		Can be used in
Normal	×1	Normal	×1	Inverse Battle
Fire	×1	Fire	×1	—
Water	×1	Water	×1	Battle Chateau
Grass	×1	Grass	×1	Battle Institute
Electric	×1	Electric	×1	Battle Maison
Ice	×1	Ice	×1	Random Matchup
Fighting	×0.5	Fighting	×2	
Poison	×1	Poison	×1	
Ground	×1	Ground	×1	
Flying	×1	Flying	×1	
Psychic	×0.5	Psychic	×2	
Bug	×2	Bug	×0.5	
Rock	×1	Rock	×1	
Ghost	×2	Ghost	×0.5	
Dragon	×1	Dragon	×1	
Dark	×2	Dark	×0.5	
Steel	×1	Steel	×1	
Fairy	×1	Fairy	×1	

How to obtain for your Mountain Kalos Pokédex

Leave Gothorita or Gothitelle at the Pokémon Day Care, and hatch the Egg that is found.

Leave Gothorita or Gothitelle at the Pokémon Day Care, and hatch the Egg that is found.

Same form for ♂/♀

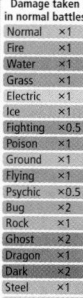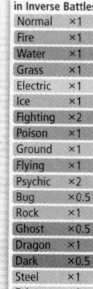

● **LEVEL-UP MOVES**

Lv.	Name	Type	Kind	Pow.	Acc.	PP	Range
1	Pound	Normal	Physical	40	100	35	Normal
2	Confusion	Psychic	Special	50	100	25	Normal
7	Tickle	Normal	Status	—	100	20	Normal
8	Play Nice	Normal	Status	—	—	20	Normal
10	Fake Tears	Dark	Status	—	100	20	Normal
14	Double Slap	Normal	Physical	15	85	10	Normal
16	Psybeam	Psychic	Special	65	100	10	Normal
19	Embargo	Dark	Status	—	100	15	Normal
24	Feint Attack	Dark	Physical	60	—	20	Normal
25	Psyshock	Psychic	Special	80	100	10	Normal
28	Flatter	Dark	Status	—	100	15	Normal
31	Future Sight	Psychic	Special	120	100	10	Normal
33	Heal Block	Psychic	Status	—	100	15	Many Others
37	Psychic	Psychic	Special	90	100	10	Normal
40	Telekinesis	Psychic	Status	—	—	15	Normal
46	Charm	Fairy	Status	—	100	20	Normal
48	Magic Room	Psychic	Status	—	—	10	Both Sides

● **TM & HM MOVES**

No.	Name	Type	Kind	Pow.	Acc.	PP	Range
TM03	Psyshock	Psychic	Special	80	100	10	Normal
TM04	Calm Mind	Psychic	Status	—	—	20	Self
TM06	Toxic	Poison	Status	—	90	10	Normal
TM10	Hidden Power	Normal	Special	60	100	15	Normal
TM12	Taunt	Dark	Status	—	100	20	Normal
TM16	Light Screen	Psychic	Status	—	—	30	Your Side
TM17	Protect	Normal	Status	—	—	10	Self
TM18	Rain Dance	Water	Status	—	—	5	Both Sides
TM20	Safeguard	Normal	Status	—	—	25	Your Side
TM21	Frustration	Normal	Physical	—	100	20	Normal
TM24	Thunderbolt	Electric	Special	90	100	15	Normal
TM27	Return	Normal	Physical	—	100	20	Normal
TM29	Psychic	Psychic	Special	90	100	10	Normal
TM30	Shadow Ball	Ghost	Special	80	100	15	Normal
TM32	Double Team	Normal	Status	—	—	15	Self
TM33	Reflect	Psychic	Status	—	—	20	Your Side
TM39	Rock Tomb	Rock	Physical	60	95	15	Normal
TM41	Torment	Dark	Status	—	100	15	Normal
TM42	Facade	Normal	Physical	70	100	20	Normal
TM44	Rest	Psychic	Status	—	—	10	Self
TM45	Attract	Normal	Status	—	100	15	Normal
TM46	Thief	Dark	Physical	60	100	25	Normal
TM48	Round	Normal	Special	60	100	15	Normal
TM53	Energy Ball	Grass	Special	90	100	10	Normal
TM56	Fling	Dark	Physical	—	100	10	Normal
TM57	Charge Beam	Electric	Special	50	90	10	Normal
TM63	Embargo	Dark	Status	—	100	15	Normal
TM66	Payback	Dark	Physical	50	100	10	Normal
TM70	Flash	Normal	Status	—	100	20	Normal
TM73	Thunder Wave	Electric	Status	—	100	20	Normal
TM77	Psych Up	Normal	Status	—	—	10	Normal
TM80	Rock Slide	Rock	Physical	75	90	10	Many Others
TM85	Dream Eater	Psychic	Special	100	100	15	Normal
TM86	Grass Knot	Grass	Special	—	100	20	Normal
TM87	Swagger	Normal	Status	—	90	15	Normal
TM88	Sleep Talk	Normal	Status	—	—	10	Self
TM90	Substitute	Normal	Status	—	—	10	Self
TM92	Trick Room	Psychic	Status	—	—	5	Both Sides
TM100	Confide	Normal	Status	—	—	20	Normal

● **MOVES TAUGHT BY PEOPLE**

Name	Type	Kind	Pow.	Acc.	PP	Range

● **EGG MOVES**

Name	Type	Kind	Pow.	Acc.	PP	Range
Mirror Coat	Psychic	Special	—	100	20	Varies
Uproar	Normal	Special	90	100	10	1 Random
Miracle Eye	Psychic	Status	—	—	40	Normal
Captivate	Normal	Status	—	100	20	Many Others
Mean Look	Normal	Status	—	—	5	Normal
Dark Pulse	Dark	Special	80	100	15	Normal
Heal Pulse	Psychic	Status	—	—	10	Normal

AFTER THE HALL OF FAME

CENTRAL KALOS

COASTAL KALOS

MOUNTAIN KALOS

126

Gothita

ADVENTURE DATA

AFTER THE HALL OF FAME

CENTRAL KALOS

COASTAL KALOS

MOUNTAIN KALOS
127

Gothorita

ADVENTURE DATA

⛰ Mountain Kalos 127

Manipulate Pokémon

☑ **Gothorita**

HEIGHT: 2'04" WEIGHT: 39.7 lbs.
GENDER: ♂ / ♀

X Starlight is the source of their power. At night, they mark star positions by using psychic power to float stones.

Y According to many old tales, it creates friends for itself by controlling sleeping children on starry nights.

TYPE **Psychic**

ABILITIES
Frisk
Competitive

HIDDEN ABILITY
Shadow Tag

STAT GROWTH RATES
HP	▮▮▮
Attack	▮▮
Defense	▮▮▮
Sp. Atk	▮▮▮
Sp. Def	▮▮▮▮
Speed	▮▮▮

EGG GROUP
Human-Like

🔺 EVOLUTION

Lv. 32   Lv. 41

Gothita   Gothorita   Gothitelle

ITEMS SOMETIMES HELD BY WILD POKÉMON
None

Can be used in
Inverse Battle
—
Battle Chateau
Battle Institute
Battle Maison
Random Matchup

Damage taken in normal battles	
Normal	×1
Fire	×1
Water	×1
Grass	×1
Electric	×1
Ice	×1
Fighting	×0.5
Poison	×1
Ground	×1
Flying	×1
Psychic	×0.5
Bug	×2
Rock	×1
Ghost	×2
Dragon	×1
Dark	×2
Steel	×1
Fairy	×1

Damage taken in Inverse Battles	
Normal	×1
Fire	×1
Water	×1
Grass	×1
Electric	×1
Ice	×1
Fighting	×2
Poison	×1
Ground	×1
Flying	×1
Psychic	×2
Bug	×0.5
Rock	×1
Ghost	×0.5
Dragon	×1
Dark	×0.5
Steel	×1
Fairy	×1

How to obtain for your Mountain Kalos Pokédex

❶ Catch in the tall grass on Route 20.
❷ Catch in the red flowers on Route 20.

❶ Catch in the tall grass on Route 20.
❷ Catch in the red flowers on Route 20.

Same form for ♂ / ♀

● LEVEL-UP MOVES

Lv.	Name	Type	Kind	Pow.	Acc.	PP	Range
1	Pound	Normal	Physical	40	100	35	Normal
1	Confusion	Psychic	Special	50	100	25	Normal
1	Tickle	Normal	Status	—	100	20	Normal
1	Play Nice	Normal	Status	—	—	20	Normal
3	Confusion	Psychic	Special	50	100	25	Normal
7	Tickle	Normal	Status	—	100	20	Normal
10	Fake Tears	Dark	Status	—	100	20	Normal
14	Double Slap	Normal	Physical	15	85	10	Normal
16	Psybeam	Psychic	Special	65	100	10	Normal
19	Embargo	Dark	Status	—	100	15	Normal
24	Feint Attack	Dark	Physical	60	—	20	Normal
25	Psyshock	Psychic	Special	80	100	10	Normal
28	Flatter	Dark	Status	—	100	15	Normal
31	Future Sight	Psychic	Special	120	100	10	Normal
34	Heal Block	Psychic	Status	—	100	15	Many Others
39	Psychic	Psychic	Special	90	100	10	Normal
43	Telekinesis	Psychic	Status	—	—	15	Normal
50	Charm	Fairy	Status	—	100	20	Normal
53	Magic Room	Psychic	Status	—	—	10	Both Sides

● TM & HM MOVES

No.	Name	Type	Kind	Pow.	Acc.	PP	Range
TM03	Psyshock	Psychic	Special	80	100	10	Normal
TM04	Calm Mind	Psychic	Status	—	—	20	Self
TM06	Toxic	Poison	Status	—	90	10	Normal
TM10	Hidden Power	Normal	Special	60	100	15	Normal
TM12	Taunt	Dark	Status	—	100	20	Normal
TM16	Light Screen	Psychic	Status	—	—	30	Your Side
TM17	Protect	Normal	Status	—	—	10	Self
TM18	Rain Dance	Water	Status	—	—	5	Both Sides
TM20	Safeguard	Normal	Status	—	—	25	Your Side
TM21	Frustration	Normal	Physical	—	100	20	Normal
TM24	Thunderbolt	Electric	Special	90	100	15	Normal
TM27	Return	Normal	Physical	—	100	20	Normal
TM29	Psychic	Psychic	Special	90	100	10	Normal
TM30	Shadow Ball	Ghost	Special	80	100	15	Normal
TM32	Double Team	Normal	Status	—	—	15	Self
TM33	Reflect	Psychic	Status	—	—	20	Your Side
TM39	Rock Tomb	Rock	Physical	60	95	15	Normal
TM41	Torment	Dark	Status	—	100	15	Normal
TM42	Facade	Normal	Physical	70	100	20	Normal
TM44	Rest	Psychic	Status	—	—	10	Self
TM45	Attract	Normal	Status	—	100	15	Normal
TM46	Thief	Dark	Physical	60	100	25	Normal
TM48	Round	Normal	Special	60	100	15	Normal
TM53	Energy Ball	Grass	Special	90	100	10	Normal
TM56	Fling	Dark	Physical	—	100	10	Normal
TM57	Charge Beam	Electric	Special	50	90	10	Normal
TM63	Embargo	Dark	Status	—	100	15	Normal
TM66	Payback	Dark	Physical	50	100	10	Normal
TM70	Flash	Normal	Status	—	100	20	Normal
TM73	Thunder Wave	Electric	Status	—	100	20	Normal
TM77	Psych Up	Normal	Status	—	—	10	Normal
TM80	Rock Slide	Rock	Physical	75	90	10	Many Others
TM85	Dream Eater	Psychic	Special	100	100	15	Normal
TM86	Grass Knot	Grass	Special	—	100	20	Normal
TM87	Swagger	Normal	Status	—	90	15	Normal
TM88	Sleep Talk	Normal	Status	—	—	10	Self
TM90	Substitute	Normal	Status	—	—	10	Self
TM92	Trick Room	Psychic	Status	—	—	5	Both Sides
TM100	Confide	Normal	Status	—	—	20	Normal

● MOVES TAUGHT BY PEOPLE

Name	Type	Kind	Pow.	Acc.	PP	Range

Mountain Kalos **128**

Astral Body Pokémon

 # Gothitelle

HEIGHT: 4'11"   WEIGHT: 97.0 lbs.
GENDER: ♂/♀

X Starry skies thousands of light-years away are visible in the space distorted by their intense psychic power.

Y They can predict the future from the placement and movement of the stars. They can see Trainers' life spans.

TYPE Psychic

ABILITIES
Frisk
Competitive

HIDDEN ABILITY
Shadow Tag

STAT GROWTH RATES
HP	■■■
Attack	■■■
Defense	■■■
Sp. Atk	■■■■■
Sp. Def	■■■■■
Speed	■■■■

EGG GROUP
Human-Like

EVOLUTION

Gothita → Lv. 32 → Gothorita → Lv. 41 → Gothitelle

ITEMS SOMETIMES HELD BY WILD POKÉMON
None

Damage taken in normal battles		Damage taken in Inverse Battles	
Normal	×1	Normal	×1
Fire	×1	Fire	×1
Water	×1	Water	×1
Grass	×1	Grass	×1
Electric	×1	Electric	×1
Ice	×1	Ice	×1
Fighting	×0.5	Fighting	×2
Poison	×1	Poison	×1
Ground	×1	Ground	×1
Flying	×1	Flying	×1
Psychic	×0.5	Psychic	×2
Bug	×2	Bug	×0.5
Rock	×1	Rock	×1
Ghost	×2	Ghost	×0.5
Dragon	×1	Dragon	×1
Dark	×2	Dark	×0.5
Steel	×1	Steel	×1
Fairy	×1	Fairy	×1

Can be used in
Inverse Battle
——
Battle Chateau
Battle Institute
Battle Maison
Random Matchup

How to obtain for your Mountain Kalos Pokédex

Level up Gothorita to Lv. 41.	Level up Gothorita to Lv. 41.
X	Y

Same form for ♂/♀

● LEVEL-UP MOVES

Lv.	Name	Type	Kind	Pow.	Acc.	PP	Range
1	Pound	Normal	Physical	40	100	35	Normal
1	Confusion	Psychic	Special	50	100	25	Normal
1	Tickle	Normal	Status	—	100	20	Normal
3	Play Nice	Normal	Status	—	—	20	Normal
3	Confusion	Psychic	Special	50	100	25	Normal
7	Tickle	Normal	Status	—	100	20	Normal
10	Fake Tears	Dark	Status	—	100	20	Normal
14	Double Slap	Normal	Physical	15	85	10	Normal
16	Psybeam	Psychic	Special	65	100	20	Normal
19	Embargo	Dark	Status	—	100	15	Normal
24	Feint Attack	Dark	Physical	60	—	20	Normal
25	Psyshock	Psychic	Special	80	100	10	Normal
28	Flatter	Dark	Status	—	100	15	Normal
31	Future Sight	Psychic	Special	120	100	10	Normal
34	Heal Block	Psychic	Status	—	100	15	Many Others
39	Psychic	Psychic	Special	90	100	10	Normal
45	Telekinesis	Psychic	Status	—	—	15	Normal
54	Charm	Fairy	Status	—	100	20	Normal
59	Magic Room	Psychic	Status	—	—	10	Both Sides

● TM & HM MOVES

No.	Name	Type	Kind	Pow.	Acc.	PP	Range
TM03	Psyshock	Psychic	Special	80	100	10	Normal
TM04	Calm Mind	Psychic	Status	—	—	20	Self
TM06	Toxic	Poison	Status	—	90	10	Normal
TM10	Hidden Power	Normal	Special	60	100	15	Normal
TM12	Taunt	Dark	Status	—	100	20	Normal
TM15	Hyper Beam	Normal	Special	150	90	5	Normal
TM16	Light Screen	Psychic	Status	—	—	30	Your Side
TM17	Protect	Normal	Status	—	—	10	Self
TM18	Rain Dance	Water	Status	—	—	5	Both Sides
TM20	Safeguard	Normal	Status	—	—	25	Your Side
TM21	Frustration	Normal	Physical	—	100	20	Normal
TM24	Thunderbolt	Electric	Special	90	100	15	Normal
TM27	Return	Normal	Physical	—	100	20	Normal
TM29	Psychic	Psychic	Special	90	100	10	Normal
TM30	Shadow Ball	Ghost	Special	80	100	15	Normal
TM31	Brick Break	Fighting	Physical	75	100	15	Normal
TM32	Double Team	Normal	Status	—	—	15	Self
TM33	Reflect	Psychic	Status	—	—	20	Your Side
TM41	Torment	Dark	Status	—	100	15	Normal
TM42	Facade	Normal	Physical	70	100	20	Normal
TM44	Rest	Psychic	Status	—	—	10	Self
TM45	Attract	Normal	Status	—	100	15	Normal
TM46	Thief	Dark	Physical	60	100	25	Normal
TM47	Low Sweep	Fighting	Physical	65	100	20	Normal
TM48	Round	Normal	Special	60	100	15	Normal
TM53	Energy Ball	Grass	Special	90	100	10	Normal
TM56	Fling	Dark	Physical	—	100	10	Normal
TM57	Charge Beam	Electric	Special	50	90	10	Normal
TM63	Embargo	Dark	Status	—	100	15	Normal
TM66	Payback	Dark	Physical	50	100	10	Normal
TM68	Giga Impact	Normal	Physical	150	90	5	Normal
TM70	Flash	Normal	Status	—	100	20	Normal

No.	Name	Type	Kind	Pow.	Acc.	PP	Range
TM73	Thunder Wave	Electric	Status	—	100	20	Normal
TM77	Psych Up	Normal	Status	—	—	10	Normal
TM80	Rock Slide	Rock	Physical	75	90	10	Many Others
TM85	Dream Eater	Psychic	Special	100	100	15	Normal
TM86	Grass Knot	Grass	Special	—	100	20	Normal
TM87	Swagger	Normal	Status	—	90	15	Normal
TM88	Sleep Talk	Normal	Status	—	—	10	Self
TM90	Substitute	Normal	Status	—	—	10	Self
TM92	Trick Room	Psychic	Status	—	—	5	Both Sides
TM98	Power-Up Punch	Fighting	Physical	40	100	20	Normal
TM100	Confide	Normal	Status	—	—	20	Normal

● MOVES TAUGHT BY PEOPLE

Name	Type	Kind	Pow.	Acc.	PP	Range

AFTER THE HALL OF FAME
CENTRAL KALOS
COASTAL KALOS
MOUNTAIN KALOS
128
Gothitelle
ADVENTURE DATA

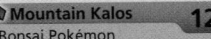
Bonsai Pokémon

∨ **Bonsly**

HEIGHT: 1'08" WEIGHT: 33.1 lbs.
GENDER: ♂/♀

TYPE **Rock**

ABILITIES
Sturdy
Rock Head

HIDDEN ABILITY
Rattled

STAT GROWTH RATES
HP	▪▪
Attack	▪▪▪▪
Defense	▪▪▪▪
Sp. Atk	▪
Sp. Def	▪
Speed	▪▪

EGG GROUP
No Eggs Discovered

X It prefers arid environments. It leaks water from its eyes to adjust its body's fluid levels.

Y It prefers an arid atmosphere. It leaks water that looks like tears when adjusting its moisture level.

⬆ EVOLUTION

Lv. 15 with Mimic

Bonsly → Sudowoodo

ITEMS SOMETIMES HELD BY WILD POKÉMON
None

Can be used in
Inverse Battle

Battle Chateau
Battle Institute
Battle Maison
Random Matchup

Damage taken in normal battles	
Normal	×0.5
Fire	×0.5
Water	×2
Grass	×2
Electric	×1
Ice	×1
Fighting	×2
Poison	×0.5
Ground	×2
Flying	×0.5
Psychic	×1
Bug	×1
Rock	×1
Ghost	×1
Dragon	×1
Dark	×1
Steel	×2
Fairy	×1

Damage taken in Inverse Battles	
Normal	×2
Fire	×2
Water	×0.5
Grass	×0.5
Electric	×1
Ice	×1
Fighting	×0.5
Poison	×2
Ground	×0.5
Flying	×2
Psychic	×1
Bug	×1
Rock	×1
Ghost	×1
Dragon	×1
Dark	×1
Steel	×0.5
Fairy	×1

How to obtain for your Mountain Kalos Pokédex

Have Sudowoodo hold Rock Incense and leave it at the Pokémon Day Care, and hatch the Egg that is found.

Have Sudowoodo hold Rock Incense and leave it at the Pokémon Day Care, and hatch the Egg that is found.

Same form for ♂/♀

● LEVEL-UP MOVES
Lv.	Name	Type	Kind	Pow.	Acc.	PP	Range
1	Fake Tears	Dark	Status	—	100	20	Normal
1	Copycat	Normal	Status	—	—	20	Self
5	Flail	Normal	Physical	—	100	15	Normal
8	Low Kick	Fighting	Physical	—	100	20	Normal
12	Rock Throw	Rock	Physical	50	90	15	Normal
15	Mimic	Normal	Status	—	—	10	Normal
19	Feint Attack	Dark	Physical	60	—	20	Normal
22	Rock Tomb	Rock	Physical	60	95	15	Normal
26	Block	Normal	Status	—	—	5	Normal
29	Rock Slide	Rock	Physical	75	90	10	Many Others
33	Counter	Fighting	Physical	—	100	20	Varies
36	Sucker Punch	Dark	Physical	80	100	5	Normal
40	Double-Edge	Normal	Physical	120	100	15	Normal

● TM & HM MOVES
No.	Name	Type	Kind	Pow.	Acc.	PP	Range
TM04	Calm Mind	Psychic	Status	—	—	20	Self
TM06	Toxic	Poison	Status	—	90	10	Normal
TM10	Hidden Power	Normal	Special	60	100	15	Normal
TM11	Sunny Day	Fire	Status	—	—	5	Both Sides
TM17	Protect	Normal	Status	—	—	10	Self
TM21	Frustration	Normal	Physical	—	100	20	Normal
TM23	Smack Down	Rock	Physical	50	100	15	Normal
TM27	Return	Normal	Physical	—	100	20	Normal
TM28	Dig	Ground	Physical	80	100	10	Normal
TM31	Brick Break	Fighting	Physical	75	100	15	Normal
TM32	Double Team	Normal	Status	—	—	15	Self
TM37	Sandstorm	Rock	Status	—	—	10	Both Sides
TM39	Rock Tomb	Rock	Physical	60	95	15	Normal
TM42	Facade	Normal	Physical	70	100	20	Normal
TM44	Rest	Psychic	Status	—	—	10	Self
TM45	Attract	Normal	Status	—	100	15	Normal
TM46	Thief	Dark	Physical	60	100	25	Normal
TM48	Round	Normal	Special	60	100	15	Normal
TM64	Explosion	Normal	Physical	250	100	5	Adjacent
TM69	Rock Polish	Rock	Status	—	—	20	Self
TM77	Psych Up	Normal	Status	—	—	10	Normal
TM80	Rock Slide	Rock	Physical	75	90	10	Many Others
TM87	Swagger	Normal	Status	—	90	15	Normal
TM88	Sleep Talk	Normal	Status	—	—	10	Self
TM90	Substitute	Normal	Status	—	—	10	Self
TM96	Nature Power	Normal	Status	—	—	20	Normal
TM100	Confide	Normal	Status	—	—	20	Normal

● MOVES TAUGHT BY PEOPLE
Name	Type	Kind	Pow.	Acc.	PP	Range

● EGG MOVES
Name	Type	Kind	Pow.	Acc.	PP	Range
Self-Destruct	Normal	Physical	200	100	5	Adjacent
Headbutt	Normal	Physical	70	100	15	Normal
Harden	Normal	Status	—	—	30	Self
Defense Curl	Normal	Status	—	—	40	Self
Rollout	Rock	Physical	30	90	20	Normal
Sand Tomb	Ground	Physical	35	85	15	Normal
Stealth Rock	Rock	Status	—	—	20	Other Side
Curse	Ghost	Status	—	—	10	Varies
Endure	Normal	Status	—	—	10	Self

130

Imitation Pokémon

☑ Sudowoodo

HEIGHT: 3'11" WEIGHT: 83.8 lbs.
GENDER: ♂/♀

TYPE Rock

ABILITIES
Sturdy
Rock Head

HIDDEN ABILITY
Rattled

STAT GROWTH RATES
HP	■■■
Attack	■■■■■
Defense	■■■■■
Sp. Atk	■
Sp. Def	■
Speed	■■

EGG GROUP
Mineral

X Although it always pretends to be a tree, its composition appears more similar to rock than to vegetation.

Y It disguises itself as a tree to avoid attack. It hates water, so it will disappear if it starts raining.

EVOLUTION

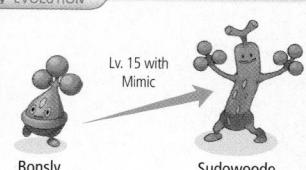

Bonsly → Lv. 15 with Mimic → Sudowoodo

ITEMS SOMETIMES HELD BY WILD POKÉMON
None

Damage taken in normal battles		Damage taken in Inverse Battles	
Normal	×0.5	Normal	×2
Fire	×0.5	Fire	×2
Water	×2	Water	×0.5
Grass	×2	Grass	×0.5
Electric	×1	Electric	×1
Ice	×1	Ice	×1
Fighting	×2	Fighting	×0.5
Poison	×0.5	Poison	×2
Ground	×2	Ground	×0.5
Flying	×1	Flying	×2
Psychic	×1	Psychic	×1
Bug	×1	Bug	×1
Rock	×1	Rock	×1
Ghost	×1	Ghost	×1
Dragon	×1	Dragon	×1
Dark	×1	Dark	×1
Steel	×2	Steel	×0.5
Fairy	×1	Fairy	×1

Can be used in
Inverse Battle
—
Battle Chateau
Battle Institute
Battle Maison
Random Matchup

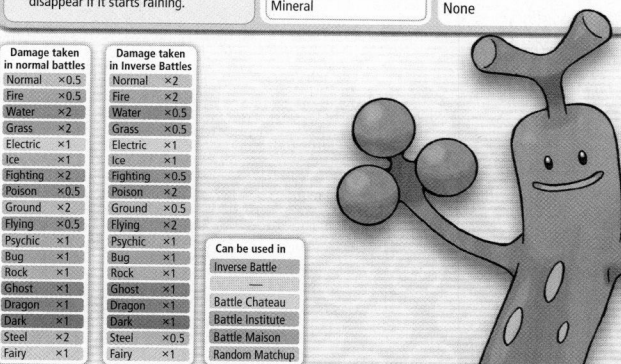

How to obtain for your Mountain Kalos Pokédex
❶ Catch in a Horde Encounter on Route 20.
❷ Level up Bonsly to Lv. 15, and have it learn Mimic. Alternatively, teach it Mimic first and then level it up.

❶ Catch in a Horde Encounter on Route 20.
❷ Level up Bonsly to Lv. 15, and have it learn Mimic. Alternatively, teach it Mimic first and then level it up.

♂   ♀

The male has larger horns. The female has smaller horns.

● LEVEL-UP MOVES
Lv.	Name	Type	Kind	Pow.	Acc.	PP	Range
1	Wood Hammer	Grass	Physical	120	100	15	Normal
1	Copycat	Normal	Status	—	—	20	Self
1	Flail	Normal	Physical	—	100	15	Normal
1	Low Kick	Fighting	Physical	—	100	20	Normal
1	Rock Throw	Rock	Physical	50	90	15	Normal
5	Flail	Normal	Physical	—	100	15	Normal
8	Low Kick	Fighting	Physical	—	100	20	Normal
12	Rock Throw	Rock	Physical	50	90	15	Normal
15	Mimic	Normal	Status	—	—	10	Normal
15	Slam	Normal	Physical	80	75	20	Normal
19	Feint Attack	Dark	Physical	60	—	20	Normal
22	Rock Tomb	Rock	Physical	60	95	15	Normal
26	Block	Normal	Status	—	—	5	Normal
29	Rock Slide	Rock	Physical	75	90	10	Many Others
33	Counter	Fighting	Physical	—	100	20	Varies
36	Sucker Punch	Dark	Physical	80	100	5	Normal
40	Double-Edge	Normal	Physical	120	100	15	Normal
43	Stone Edge	Rock	Physical	100	80	5	Normal
47	Hammer Arm	Fighting	Physical	100	90	10	Normal

● TM & HM MOVES
No.	Name	Type	Kind	Pow.	Acc.	PP	Range
TM04	Calm Mind	Psychic	Status	—	—	20	Self
TM06	Toxic	Poison	Status	—	90	10	Normal
TM10	Hidden Power	Normal	Special	60	100	15	Normal
TM11	Sunny Day	Fire	Status	—	—	5	Both Sides
TM12	Taunt	Dark	Status	—	100	20	Normal
TM17	Protect	Normal	Status	—	—	10	Self
TM21	Frustration	Normal	Physical	—	100	20	Normal
TM23	Smack Down	Rock	Physical	50	100	15	Normal
TM26	Earthquake	Ground	Physical	100	100	10	Adjacent
TM27	Return	Normal	Physical	—	100	20	Normal
TM28	Dig	Ground	Physical	80	100	10	Normal
TM31	Brick Break	Fighting	Physical	75	100	15	Normal
TM32	Double Team	Normal	Status	—	—	15	Self
TM37	Sandstorm	Rock	Status	—	—	10	Both Sides
TM39	Rock Tomb	Rock	Physical	60	95	15	Normal
TM41	Torment	Dark	Status	—	100	15	Normal
TM42	Facade	Normal	Physical	70	100	20	Normal
TM44	Rest	Psychic	Status	—	—	10	Self
TM45	Attract	Normal	Status	—	100	15	Normal
TM46	Thief	Dark	Physical	60	100	25	Normal
TM48	Round	Normal	Special	60	100	15	Normal
TM56	Fling	Dark	Physical	—	100	10	Normal
TM64	Explosion	Normal	Physical	250	100	5	Adjacent
TM69	Rock Polish	Rock	Status	—	—	20	Self
TM71	Stone Edge	Rock	Physical	100	80	5	Normal
TM77	Psych Up	Normal	Status	—	—	10	Normal
TM78	Bulldoze	Ground	Physical	60	100	20	Adjacent
TM80	Rock Slide	Rock	Physical	75	90	10	Many Others
TM87	Swagger	Normal	Status	—	90	15	Normal
TM88	Sleep Talk	Normal	Status	—	—	10	Self
TM90	Substitute	Normal	Status	—	—	10	Self
TM94	Rock Smash	Fighting	Physical	40	100	15	Normal
TM96	Nature Power	Normal	Status	—	—	20	Normal

No.	Name	Type	Kind	Pow.	Acc.	PP	Range
TM98	Power-Up Punch	Fighting	Physical	40	100	20	Normal
TM100	Confide	Normal	Status	—	—	20	Normal
HM04	Strength	Normal	Physical	80	100	15	Normal

● MOVES TAUGHT BY PEOPLE
Name	Type	Kind	Pow.	Acc.	PP	Range

● EGG MOVES
Name	Type	Kind	Pow.	Acc.	PP	Range
Self-Destruct	Normal	Physical	200	100	5	Adjacent
Headbutt	Normal	Physical	70	100	15	Normal
Harden	Normal	Status	—	—	30	Self
Defense Curl	Normal	Status	—	—	40	Self
Rollout	Rock	Physical	30	90	20	Normal
Sand Tomb	Ground	Physical	35	85	15	Normal
Stealth Rock	Rock	Status	—	—	20	Other Side
Curse	Ghost	Status	—	—	10	Varies
Endure	Normal	Status	—	—	10	Self

AFTER THE HALL OF FAME

CENTRAL KALOS

COASTAL KALOS

MOUNTAIN KALOS

130 Sudowoodo

ADVENTURE DATA

Mountain Kalos 131
Spot Panda Pokémon
☑ **Spinda**

HEIGHT: 3'07" WEIGHT: 11.0 lbs.
GENDER: ♂/♀

TYPE Normal

ABILITIES
Own Tempo
Tangled Feet

HIDDEN ABILITY
Contrary

EVOLUTION

Does not evolve

X No two Spinda have the same pattern of spots. Its tottering step foils the aim of foes.

Y The chances of two Spinda having identical spot patterns is less than one in four billion.

STAT GROWTH RATES
HP	■■■
Attack	■■■
Defense	■■■
Sp. Atk	■■■
Sp. Def	■■■
Speed	■■■

EGG GROUPS
Field, Human-Like

ITEMS SOMETIMES HELD BY WILD POKÉMON
None

Damage taken in normal battles		Damage taken in Inverse Battles	
Normal	×1	Normal	×1
Fire	×1	Fire	×1
Water	×1	Water	×1
Grass	×1	Grass	×1
Electric	×1	Electric	×1
Ice	×1	Ice	×1
Fighting	×2	Fighting	×0.5
Poison	×1	Poison	×1
Ground	×1	Ground	×1
Flying	×1	Flying	×1
Psychic	×1	Psychic	×1
Bug	×1	Bug	×1
Rock	×1	Rock	×1
Ghost	×0	Ghost	×2
Dragon	×1	Dragon	×1
Dark	×1	Dark	×1
Steel	×1	Steel	×1
Fairy	×1	Fairy	×1

Can be used in	
Inverse Battle	Battle Institute
—	Battle Maison
Battle Chateau	Random Matchup

Same form for ♂/♀

How to obtain for your Mountain Kalos Pokédex

❶ Catch in the red flowers on Route 21.
❷ Catch in the purple flowers on Route 21.

❶ Catch in the red flowers on Route 21.
❷ Catch in the purple flowers on Route 21.

131
Spinda

● LEVEL-UP MOVES

Lv.	Name	Type	Kind	Pow.	Acc.	PP	Range
1	Tackle	Normal	Physical	50	100	35	Normal
5	Uproar	Normal	Special	90	100	10	1 Random
10	Copycat	Normal	Status	—	—	20	Self
14	Feint Attack	Dark	Physical	60	—	20	Normal
19	Psybeam	Psychic	Special	65	100	20	Normal
23	Hypnosis	Psychic	Status	—	60	20	Normal
28	Dizzy Punch	Normal	Physical	70	100	10	Normal
32	Sucker Punch	Dark	Physical	80	100	5	Normal
37	Teeter Dance	Normal	Status	—	100	20	Adjacent
41	Psych Up	Normal	Status	—	—	10	Normal
46	Double-Edge	Normal	Physical	120	100	15	Normal
50	Flail	Normal	Physical	—	100	15	Normal
50	Thrash	Normal	Physical	120	100	10	1 Random

● TM & HM MOVES

No.	Name	Type	Kind	Pow.	Acc.	PP	Range
TM04	Calm Mind	Psychic	Status	—	—	20	Self
TM06	Toxic	Poison	Status	—	90	10	Normal
TM10	Hidden Power	Normal	Special	60	100	15	Normal
TM11	Sunny Day	Fire	Status	—	—	5	Both Sides
TM17	Protect	Normal	Status	—	—	10	Self
TM18	Rain Dance	Water	Status	—	—	5	Both Sides
TM20	Safeguard	Normal	Status	—	—	25	Your Side
TM21	Frustration	Normal	Physical	—	100	20	Normal
TM27	Return	Normal	Physical	—	100	20	Normal
TM28	Dig	Ground	Physical	80	100	10	Normal
TM29	Psychic	Psychic	Special	90	100	10	Normal
TM30	Shadow Ball	Ghost	Special	80	100	15	Normal
TM31	Brick Break	Fighting	Physical	75	100	15	Normal
TM32	Double Team	Normal	Status	—	—	15	Self
TM39	Rock Tomb	Rock	Physical	60	95	15	Normal
TM42	Facade	Normal	Physical	70	100	20	Normal
TM44	Rest	Psychic	Status	—	—	10	Self
TM45	Attract	Normal	Status	—	100	15	Normal
TM46	Thief	Dark	Physical	60	100	25	Normal
TM48	Round	Normal	Special	60	100	15	Normal
TM56	Fling	Dark	Physical	—	100	10	Normal
TM67	Retaliate	Normal	Physical	70	100	5	Normal
TM70	Flash	Normal	Status	—	100	20	Normal
TM77	Psych Up	Normal	Status	—	—	10	Normal
TM80	Rock Slide	Rock	Physical	75	90	10	Many Others
TM85	Dream Eater	Psychic	Special	100	100	15	Normal
TM87	Swagger	Normal	Status	—	90	15	Normal
TM90	Substitute	Normal	Status	—	—	10	Self
TM92	Trick Room	Psychic	Status	—	—	5	Both Sides
TM93	Wild Charge	Electric	Physical	90	100	15	Normal
TM94	Rock Smash	Fighting	Physical	40	100	15	Normal
TM98	Power-Up Punch	Fighting	Physical	40	100	20	Normal
TM100	Confide	Normal	Status	—	—	20	Normal

No.	Name	Type	Kind	Pow.	Acc.	PP	Range
HM04	Strength	Normal	Physical	80	100	15	Normal

● MOVES TAUGHT BY PEOPLE

Name	Type	Kind	Pow.	Acc.	PP	Range

● EGG MOVES

Name	Type	Kind	Pow.	Acc.	PP	Range
Encore	Normal	Status	—	100	5	Normal
Assist	Normal	Status	—	—	20	Self
Disable	Normal	Status	—	100	20	Normal
Baton Pass	Normal	Status	—	—	40	Self
Wish	Normal	Status	—	—	10	Self
Trick	Psychic	Status	—	100	10	Normal
Smelling Salts	Normal	Physical	70	100	10	Normal
Fake Out	Normal	Physical	40	100	10	Normal
Role Play	Psychic	Status	—	—	10	Normal
Psycho Cut	Psychic	Physical	70	100	20	Normal
Fake Tears	Dark	Status	—	100	20	Normal
Rapid Spin	Normal	Physical	20	100	40	Normal
Icy Wind	Ice	Special	55	95	15	Many Others
Water Pulse	Water	Special	60	100	20	Normal
Psycho Shift	Psychic	Status	—	100	10	Normal
Guard Split	Psychic	Status	—	—	10	Normal

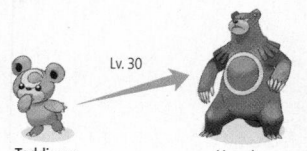

Mountain Kalos

132

Little Bear Pokémon

☑ Teddiursa

HEIGHT: 2'00" WEIGHT: 19.4 lbs.
GENDER: ♂/♀

TYPE Normal

ABILITIES
Pickup
Quick Feet

HIDDEN ABILITY
Honey Gather

STAT GROWTH RATES
HP	■■■
Attack	■■■■
Defense	■■
Sp. Atk	■■
Sp. Def	■■
Speed	■■

EGG GROUP
Field

EVOLUTION

Teddiursa → Lv. 30 → Ursaring

ITEMS SOMETIMES HELD BY WILD POKÉMON
None

X If it finds honey, its crescent mark glows. It always licks its paws because they're soaked with honey.

Y Before food becomes scarce in wintertime, its habit is to hoard food in many hidden locations.

Damage taken in normal battles	
Normal	×1
Fire	×1
Water	×1
Grass	×1
Electric	×1
Ice	×1
Fighting	×2
Poison	×1
Ground	×1
Flying	×1
Psychic	×1
Bug	×1
Rock	×1
Ghost	×0
Dragon	×1
Dark	×1
Steel	×1
Fairy	×1

Damage taken in Inverse Battles	
Normal	×1
Fire	×1
Water	×1
Grass	×1
Electric	×1
Ice	×1
Fighting	×0.5
Poison	×1
Ground	×1
Flying	×1
Psychic	×1
Bug	×1
Rock	×1
Ghost	×2
Dragon	×1
Dark	×1
Steel	×1
Fairy	×1

Can be used in	
Inverse Battle	Battle Institute
—	Battle Maison
Battle Chateau	Random Matchup

Same form for ♂/♀

How to obtain for your Mountain Kalos Pokédex

Leave Ursaring at the Pokémon Day Care, and hatch the Egg that is found.

Leave Ursaring at the Pokémon Day Care, and hatch the Egg that is found.

● LEVEL-UP MOVES

Lv.	Name	Type	Kind	Pow.	Acc.	PP	Range
1	Fling	Dark	Physical	—	100	10	Normal
1	Covet	Normal	Physical	60	100	25	Normal
1	Scratch	Normal	Physical	40	100	35	Normal
1	Baby-Doll Eyes	Fairy	Status	—	100	30	Normal
1	Lick	Ghost	Physical	30	100	30	Normal
1	Fake Tears	Dark	Status	—	100	20	Normal
8	Fury Swipes	Normal	Physical	18	80	15	Normal
15	Feint Attack	Dark	Physical	60	—	20	Normal
22	Sweet Scent	Normal	Status	—	100	20	Many Others
25	Play Nice	Normal	Status	—	—	20	Normal
29	Slash	Normal	Physical	70	100	20	Normal
36	Charm	Fairy	Status	—	100	20	Normal
43	Rest	Psychic	Status	—	—	10	Self
43	Snore	Normal	Special	50	100	15	Normal
50	Thrash	Normal	Physical	120	100	10	1 Random
57	Fling	Dark	Physical	—	100	10	Normal

● TM & HM MOVES

No.	Name	Type	Kind	Pow.	Acc.	PP	Range
TM01	Hone Claws	Dark	Status	—	—	15	Self
TM05	Roar	Normal	Status	—	—	20	Normal
TM06	Toxic	Poison	Status	—	90	10	Normal
TM08	Bulk Up	Fighting	Status	—	—	20	Self
TM10	Hidden Power	Normal	Special	60	100	15	Normal
TM11	Sunny Day	Fire	Status	—	—	5	Both Sides
TM12	Taunt	Dark	Status	—	100	20	Normal
TM17	Protect	Normal	Status	—	—	10	Self
TM18	Rain Dance	Water	Status	—	—	5	Both Sides
TM21	Frustration	Normal	Physical	—	100	20	Normal
TM27	Return	Normal	Physical	—	100	20	Normal
TM26	Earthquake	Ground	Physical	100	100	10	Adjacent
TM28	Dig	Ground	Physical	80	100	10	Normal
TM31	Brick Break	Fighting	Physical	75	100	15	Normal
TM32	Double Team	Normal	Status	—	—	15	Self
TM39	Rock Tomb	Rock	Physical	60	95	15	Normal
TM40	Aerial Ace	Flying	Physical	60	—	20	Normal
TM41	Torment	Dark	Status	—	100	15	Normal
TM42	Facade	Normal	Physical	70	100	20	Normal
TM44	Rest	Psychic	Status	—	—	10	Self
TM45	Attract	Normal	Status	—	100	15	Normal
TM46	Thief	Dark	Physical	60	100	25	Normal
TM48	Round	Normal	Special	60	100	15	Normal
TM56	Fling	Dark	Physical	—	100	10	Normal
TM65	Shadow Claw	Ghost	Physical	70	100	15	Normal
TM66	Payback	Dark	Physical	50	100	10	Normal
TM67	Retaliate	Normal	Physical	70	100	5	Normal
TM75	Swords Dance	Normal	Status	—	—	20	Self
TM78	Bulldoze	Ground	Physical	60	100	20	Adjacent
TM80	Rock Slide	Rock	Physical	75	90	10	Many Others
TM87	Swagger	Normal	Status	—	90	15	Normal
TM88	Sleep Talk	Normal	Status	—	—	10	Self
TM90	Substitute	Normal	Status	—	—	10	Self

No.	Name	Type	Kind	Pow.	Acc.	PP	Range
TM94	Rock Smash	Fighting	Physical	40	100	15	Normal
TM98	Power-Up Punch	Fighting	Physical	40	100	20	Normal
TM100	Confide	Normal	Status	—	—	20	Normal
HM01	Cut	Normal	Physical	50	95	30	Normal
HM04	Strength	Normal	Physical	80	100	15	Normal

● MOVES TAUGHT BY PEOPLE

Name	Type	Kind	Pow.	Acc.	PP	Range

● EGG MOVES

Name	Type	Kind	Pow.	Acc.	PP	Range
Crunch	Dark	Physical	80	100	15	Normal
Take Down	Normal	Physical	90	85	20	Normal
Seismic Toss	Fighting	Physical	—	100	20	Normal
Counter	Fighting	Physical	—	100	20	Varies
Metal Claw	Steel	Physical	50	95	35	Normal
Fake Tears	Dark	Status	—	100	20	Normal
Yawn	Normal	Status	—	—	10	Normal
Sleep Talk	Normal	Status	—	—	10	Self
Cross Chop	Fighting	Physical	100	80	5	Normal
Double-Edge	Normal	Physical	120	100	15	Normal
Close Combat	Fighting	Physical	120	100	5	Normal
Night Slash	Dark	Physical	70	100	15	Normal
Belly Drum	Normal	Status	—	—	10	Self
Chip Away	Normal	Physical	70	100	20	Normal
Play Rough	Fairy	Physical	90	90	10	Normal

AFTER THE HALL OF FAME

CENTRAL KALOS

COASTAL KALOS

MOUNTAIN KALOS

132 Teddiursa

ADVENTURE DATA

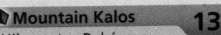

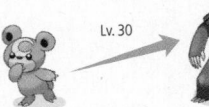

⛰ Mountain Kalos 133
Hibernator Pokémon
☑ Ursaring

HEIGHT: 5'11" WEIGHT: 277.3 lbs.
GENDER: ♂/♀

X With its ability to distinguish any aroma, it unfailingly finds all food buried deep underground.

Y Although it has a large body, it is quite skilled at climbing trees. It eats and sleeps in the treetops.

TYPE Normal

ABILITIES
Guts
Quick Feet

HIDDEN ABILITY
Unnerve

STAT GROWTH RATES
HP
Attack
Defense
Sp. Atk
Sp. Def
Speed

EGG GROUP
Field

● EVOLUTION

Teddiursa → Lv. 30 → Ursaring

ITEMS SOMETIMES HELD BY WILD POKÉMON
None

Can be used in
Inverse Battle
—
Battle Chateau
Battle Institute
Battle Maison
Random Matchup

Damage taken in normal battles		Damage taken in Inverse Battles	
Normal	×1	Normal	×1
Fire	×1	Fire	×1
Water	×1	Water	×1
Grass	×1	Grass	×1
Electric	×1	Electric	×1
Ice	×1	Ice	×1
Fighting	×2	Fighting	×0.5
Poison	×1	Poison	×1
Ground	×1	Ground	×1
Flying	×1	Flying	×1
Psychic	×1	Psychic	×1
Bug	×1	Bug	×1
Rock	×1	Rock	×1
Ghost	×0	Ghost	×2
Dragon	×1	Dragon	×1
Dark	×1	Dark	×1
Steel	×1	Steel	×1
Fairy	×1	Fairy	×1

How to obtain for your Mountain Kalos Pokédex

❶ Catch in the red flowers on Route 21.

❷ Catch in the purple flowers on Route 21.

❶ Catch in the red flowers on Route 21.

❷ Catch in the purple flowers on Route 21.

♂

♀

The male has a shorter fringe on its shoulders. The female has a longer fringe on its shoulders.

● LEVEL-UP MOVES

Lv.	Name	Type	Kind	Pow.	Acc.	PP	Range
1	Hammer Arm	Fighting	Physical	100	90	10	Normal
1	Covet	Normal	Physical	60	100	25	Normal
1	Scratch	Normal	Physical	40	100	35	Normal
1	Leer	Normal	Status	—	100	30	Many Others
1	Lick	Ghost	Physical	30	100	30	Normal
1	Fake Tears	Dark	Status	—	100	20	Normal
8	Fury Swipes	Normal	Physical	18	80	15	Normal
15	Feint Attack	Dark	Physical	60	—	20	Normal
22	Sweet Scent	Normal	Status	—	100	20	Many Others
25	Play Nice	Normal	Status	—	—	20	Normal
29	Slash	Normal	Physical	70	100	20	Normal
38	Scary Face	Normal	Status	—	100	10	Normal
47	Rest	Psychic	Status	—	—	10	Self
49	Snore	Normal	Special	50	100	15	Normal
58	Thrash	Normal	Physical	120	100	10	1 Random
67	Hammer Arm	Fighting	Physical	100	90	10	Normal

● TM & HM MOVES

No.	Name	Type	Kind	Pow.	Acc.	PP	Range
TM01	Hone Claws	Dark	Status	—	—	15	Self
TM05	Roar	Normal	Status	—	—	20	Normal
TM06	Toxic	Poison	Status	—	90	10	Normal
TM08	Bulk Up	Fighting	Status	—	—	20	Self
TM10	Hidden Power	Normal	Special	60	100	15	Normal
TM11	Sunny Day	Fire	Status	—	—	5	Both Sides
TM12	Taunt	Dark	Status	—	100	20	Normal
TM15	Hyper Beam	Normal	Special	150	90	5	Normal
TM17	Protect	Normal	Status	—	—	10	Self
TM18	Rain Dance	Water	Status	—	—	5	Both Sides
TM21	Frustration	Normal	Physical	—	100	20	Normal
TM23	Smack Down	Rock	Physical	50	100	15	Normal
TM26	Earthquake	Ground	Physical	100	100	10	Adjacent
TM27	Return	Normal	Physical	—	100	20	Normal
TM28	Dig	Ground	Physical	80	100	10	Normal
TM31	Brick Break	Fighting	Physical	75	100	15	Normal
TM32	Double Team	Normal	Status	—	—	15	Self
TM39	Rock Tomb	Rock	Physical	60	95	15	Normal
TM40	Aerial Ace	Flying	Physical	60	—	20	Normal
TM41	Torment	Dark	Status	—	100	15	Normal
TM42	Facade	Normal	Physical	70	100	20	Normal
TM44	Rest	Psychic	Status	—	—	10	Self
TM45	Attract	Normal	Status	—	100	15	Normal
TM46	Thief	Dark	Physical	60	100	25	Normal
TM48	Round	Normal	Special	60	100	15	Normal
TM52	Focus Blast	Fighting	Special	120	70	5	Normal
TM56	Fling	Dark	Physical	—	100	10	Normal
TM65	Shadow Claw	Ghost	Physical	70	100	15	Normal
TM66	Payback	Dark	Physical	50	100	10	Normal
TM67	Retaliate	Normal	Physical	70	100	5	Normal
TM68	Giga Impact	Normal	Physical	150	90	5	Normal
TM71	Stone Edge	Rock	Physical	100	80	5	Normal
TM75	Swords Dance	Normal	Status	—	—	20	Self
TM78	Bulldoze	Ground	Physical	60	100	20	Adjacent
TM80	Rock Slide	Rock	Physical	75	90	10	Many Others
TM87	Swagger	Normal	Status	—	90	15	Normal
TM88	Sleep Talk	Normal	Status	—	—	10	Self
TM90	Substitute	Normal	Status	—	—	10	Self
TM94	Rock Smash	Fighting	Physical	40	100	15	Normal
TM98	Power-Up Punch	Fighting	Physical	40	100	20	Normal
TM100	Confide	Normal	Status	—	—	20	Normal
HM01	Cut	Normal	Physical	50	95	30	Normal
HM04	Strength	Normal	Physical	80	100	15	Normal

● MOVES TAUGHT BY PEOPLE

Name	Type	Kind	Pow.	Acc.	PP	Range

AFTER THE HALL OF FAME

CENTRAL KALOS

COASTAL KALOS

MOUNTAIN KALOS

133 Ursaring

ADVENTURE DATA

Mountain Kalos — 134
Licking Pokémon

Lickitung

HEIGHT: 3'11" WEIGHT: 144.4 lbs.
GENDER: ♂/♀

X Its long tongue, slathered with a gooey saliva, sticks to anything, so it is very useful.

Y Its tongue is twice the length of its body. It can be moved like an arm for grabbing food and attacking.

TYPE Normal

ABILITIES
Own Tempo
Oblivious

HIDDEN ABILITY
Cloud Nine

STAT GROWTH RATES
HP	▪▪▪▪
Attack	▪▪▪
Defense	▪▪▪
Sp. Atk	▪▪▪
Sp. Def	▪▪▪
Speed	▪▪

EGG GROUP
Monster

EVOLUTION

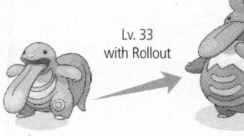

Lickitung → Lv. 33 with Rollout → Lickilicky

ITEMS SOMETIMES HELD BY WILD POKÉMON
Lagging Tail

Damage taken in normal battles		Damage taken in Inverse Battles	
Normal	×1	Normal	×1
Fire	×1	Fire	×1
Water	×1	Water	×1
Grass	×1	Grass	×1
Electric	×1	Electric	×1
Ice	×1	Ice	×1
Fighting	×2	Fighting	×0.5
Poison	×1	Poison	×1
Ground	×1	Ground	×1
Flying	×1	Flying	×1
Psychic	×1	Psychic	×1
Bug	×1	Bug	×1
Rock	×1	Rock	×1
Ghost	×0	Ghost	×2
Dragon	×1	Dragon	×1
Dark	×1	Dark	×1
Steel	×1	Steel	×1
Fairy	×1	Fairy	×1

Can be used in	
Inverse Battle	Battle Institute
—	Battle Maison
Battle Chateau	Random Matchup

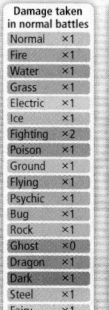

Same form for ♂/♀

How to obtain for your Mountain Kalos Pokédex

❶ Catch in the caves along Victory Road.
❷ Catch in a Horde Encounter in the caves along Victory Road.

❶ Catch in the caves along Victory Road.
❷ Catch in a Horde Encounter in the caves along Victory Road.

● LEVEL-UP MOVES
Lv.	Name	Type	Kind	Pow.	Acc.	PP	Range
1	Lick	Ghost	Physical	30	100	30	Normal
5	Supersonic	Normal	Status	—	55	20	Normal
9	Defense Curl	Normal	Status	—	—	40	Self
13	Knock Off	Dark	Physical	65	100	20	Normal
17	Wrap	Normal	Physical	15	90	20	Normal
21	Stomp	Normal	Physical	65	100	20	Normal
25	Disable	Normal	Status	—	100	20	Normal
29	Slam	Normal	Physical	80	75	20	Normal
33	Rollout	Rock	Physical	30	90	20	Normal
37	Chip Away	Normal	Physical	70	100	20	Normal
41	Me First	Normal	Status	—	—	20	Varies
45	Refresh	Normal	Status	—	—	20	Self
49	Screech	Normal	Status	—	85	40	Normal
53	Power Whip	Grass	Physical	120	85	10	Normal
57	Wring Out	Normal	Special	—	100	5	Normal

● TM & HM MOVES
No.	Name	Type	Kind	Pow.	Acc.	PP	Range
TM06	Toxic	Poison	Status	—	90	10	Normal
TM10	Hidden Power	Normal	Special	60	100	15	Normal
TM11	Sunny Day	Fire	Status	—	—	5	Both Sides
TM13	Ice Beam	Ice	Special	90	100	10	Normal
TM14	Blizzard	Ice	Special	110	70	5	Many Others
TM15	Hyper Beam	Normal	Special	150	90	5	Normal
TM17	Protect	Normal	Status	—	—	10	Self
TM18	Rain Dance	Water	Status	—	—	5	Both Sides
TM21	Frustration	Normal	Physical	—	100	20	Normal
TM22	Solar Beam	Grass	Special	120	100	10	Normal
TM24	Thunderbolt	Electric	Special	90	100	15	Normal
TM25	Thunder	Electric	Special	110	70	10	Normal
TM26	Earthquake	Ground	Physical	100	100	10	Adjacent
TM27	Return	Normal	Physical	—	100	20	Normal
TM28	Dig	Ground	Physical	80	100	10	Normal
TM30	Shadow Ball	Ghost	Special	80	100	15	Normal
TM31	Brick Break	Fighting	Physical	75	100	15	Normal
TM32	Double Team	Normal	Status	—	—	15	Self
TM35	Flamethrower	Fire	Special	90	100	15	Normal
TM37	Sandstorm	Rock	Status	—	—	10	Both Sides
TM38	Fire Blast	Fire	Special	110	85	5	Normal
TM39	Rock Tomb	Rock	Physical	60	95	15	Normal
TM42	Facade	Normal	Physical	70	100	20	Normal
TM44	Rest	Psychic	Status	—	—	10	Self
TM45	Attract	Normal	Status	—	100	15	Normal
TM46	Thief	Dark	Physical	60	100	25	Normal
TM48	Round	Normal	Special	60	100	15	Normal
TM56	Fling	Dark	Physical	—	100	10	Normal
TM59	Incinerate	Fire	Special	60	100	15	Many Others
TM67	Retaliate	Normal	Physical	70	100	5	Normal
TM68	Giga Impact	Normal	Physical	150	90	5	Normal
TM75	Swords Dance	Normal	Status	—	—	20	Self
TM77	Psych Up	Normal	Status	—	—	10	Normal

No.	Name	Type	Kind	Pow.	Acc.	PP	Range
TM78	Bulldoze	Ground	Physical	60	100	20	Adjacent
TM80	Rock Slide	Rock	Physical	75	90	10	Many Others
TM82	Dragon Tail	Dragon	Physical	60	90	10	Normal
TM85	Dream Eater	Psychic	Special	100	100	15	Normal
TM87	Swagger	Normal	Status	—	90	15	Normal
TM88	Sleep Talk	Normal	Status	—	—	10	Self
TM90	Substitute	Normal	Status	—	—	10	Self
TM94	Rock Smash	Fighting	Physical	40	100	15	Normal
TM98	Power-Up Punch	Fighting	Physical	40	100	20	Normal
TM100	Confide	Normal	Status	—	—	20	Normal
HM01	Cut	Normal	Physical	50	95	30	Normal
HM03	Surf	Water	Special	90	100	15	Adjacent
HM04	Strength	Normal	Physical	80	100	15	Normal

● MOVES TAUGHT BY PEOPLE
Name	Type	Kind	Pow.	Acc.	PP	Range

● EGG MOVES
Name	Type	Kind	Pow.	Acc.	PP	Range
Belly Drum	Normal	Status	—	—	10	Self
Magnitude	Ground	Physical	—	100	30	Adjacent
Body Slam	Normal	Physical	85	100	15	Normal
Curse	Ghost	Status	—	—	10	Varies
Smelling Salts	Normal	Physical	70	100	10	Normal
Sleep Talk	Normal	Status	—	—	10	Self
Snore	Normal	Special	50	100	15	Normal
Amnesia	Psychic	Status	—	—	20	Self
Hammer Arm	Fighting	Physical	100	90	10	Normal
Muddy Water	Water	Special	90	85	10	Many Others
Zen Headbutt	Psychic	Physical	80	90	15	Normal
Belch	Poison	Special	120	90	10	Normal

AFTER THE HALL OF FAME
CENTRAL KALOS
COASTAL KALOS
MOUNTAIN KALOS
134 Lickitung
ADVENTURE DATA

🔼 Mountain Kalos **135**

Licking Pokémon

☑ **Lickilicky**

HEIGHT: 5'07" WEIGHT: 308.6 lbs.
GENDER: ♂/♀

X It wraps things with its extensible tongue. Getting too close to it will leave you soaked with drool.

Y Their saliva contains lots of components that can dissolve anything. The numbness caused by their lick does not dissipate.

TYPE Normal

ABILITIES
Own Tempo
Oblivious

HIDDEN ABILITY
Cloud Nine

STAT GROWTH RATES
HP	■■■■
Attack	■■■■
Defense	■■■■
Sp. Atk	■■■■
Sp. Def	■■■■
Speed	■■■

EGG GROUP
Monster

🔼 EVOLUTION

Lickitung → Lv. 33 with Rollout → Lickilicky

ITEMS SOMETIMES HELD BY WILD POKÉMON
None

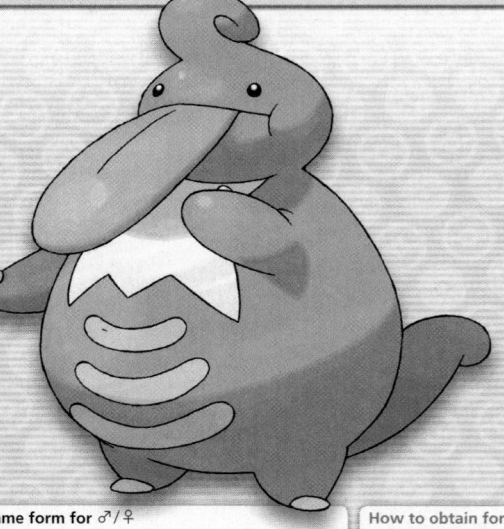

Damage taken in normal battles	
Normal	×1
Fire	×1
Water	×1
Grass	×1
Electric	×1
Ice	×1
Fighting	×2
Poison	×1
Ground	×1
Flying	×1
Psychic	×1
Bug	×1
Rock	×1
Ghost	×0
Dragon	×1
Dark	×1
Steel	×1
Fairy	×1

Damage taken in Inverse Battles	
Normal	×1
Fire	×1
Water	×1
Grass	×1
Electric	×1
Ice	×1
Fighting	×0.5
Poison	×1
Ground	×1
Flying	×1
Psychic	×1
Bug	×1
Rock	×1
Ghost	×2
Dragon	×1
Dark	×1
Steel	×1
Fairy	×1

Can be used in	
Inverse Battle	Battle Institute
—	Battle Maison
Battle Chateau	Random Matchup

Same form for ♂/♀

How to obtain for your Mountain Kalos Pokédex

Level up Lickitung to Lv. 33, and have it learn Rollout. Alternatively, teach it Rollout and then have it level up.

Level up Lickitung to Lv. 33, and have it learn Rollout. Alternatively, teach it Rollout and then have it level up.

135

Lickilicky

● LEVEL-UP MOVES

Lv.	Name	Type	Kind	Pow.	Acc.	PP	Range
1	Wring Out	Normal	Special	—	100	5	Normal
1	Power Whip	Grass	Physical	120	85	10	Normal
1	Lick	Ghost	Physical	30	100	30	Normal
5	Supersonic	Normal	Status	—	55	20	Normal
9	Defense Curl	Normal	Status	—	—	40	Self
13	Knock Off	Dark	Physical	65	100	20	Normal
17	Wrap	Normal	Physical	15	90	20	Normal
21	Stomp	Normal	Physical	65	100	20	Normal
25	Disable	Normal	Status	—	100	20	Normal
29	Slam	Normal	Physical	80	75	20	Normal
33	Rollout	Rock	Physical	30	90	20	Normal
37	Chip Away	Normal	Physical	70	100	20	Normal
41	Me First	Normal	Status	—	—	20	Varies
45	Refresh	Normal	Status	—	—	20	Self
49	Screech	Normal	Status	—	85	40	Normal
53	Power Whip	Grass	Physical	120	85	10	Normal
57	Wring Out	Normal	Special	—	100	5	Normal
61	Gyro Ball	Steel	Physical	—	100	5	Normal

● TM & HM MOVES

No.	Name	Type	Kind	Pow.	Acc.	PP	Range
TM06	Toxic	Poison	Status	—	90	10	Normal
TM10	Hidden Power	Normal	Special	60	100	15	Normal
TM11	Sunny Day	Fire	Status	—	—	5	Both Sides
TM13	Ice Beam	Ice	Special	90	100	10	Normal
TM14	Blizzard	Ice	Special	110	70	5	Many Others
TM15	Hyper Beam	Normal	Special	150	90	5	Normal
TM17	Protect	Normal	Status	—	—	10	Self
TM18	Rain Dance	Water	Status	—	—	5	Both Sides
TM21	Frustration	Normal	Physical	—	100	20	Normal
TM22	Solar Beam	Grass	Special	120	100	10	Normal
TM24	Thunderbolt	Electric	Special	90	100	15	Normal
TM25	Thunder	Electric	Special	110	70	10	Normal
TM26	Earthquake	Ground	Physical	100	100	10	Adjacent
TM27	Return	Normal	Physical	—	100	20	Normal
TM28	Dig	Ground	Physical	80	100	10	Normal
TM30	Shadow Ball	Ghost	Special	80	100	15	Normal
TM31	Brick Break	Fighting	Physical	75	100	15	Normal
TM32	Double Team	Normal	Status	—	—	15	Self
TM35	Flamethrower	Fire	Special	90	100	15	Normal
TM37	Sandstorm	Rock	Status	—	—	10	Both Sides
TM38	Fire Blast	Fire	Special	110	85	5	Normal
TM39	Rock Tomb	Rock	Physical	60	95	15	Normal
TM42	Facade	Normal	Physical	70	100	20	Normal
TM44	Rest	Psychic	Status	—	—	10	Self
TM45	Attract	Normal	Status	—	100	15	Normal
TM46	Thief	Dark	Physical	60	100	25	Normal
TM48	Round	Normal	Special	60	100	15	Normal
TM52	Focus Blast	Fighting	Special	120	70	5	Normal
TM56	Fling	Dark	Physical	—	100	10	Normal
TM59	Incinerate	Fire	Special	60	100	15	Many Others
TM64	Explosion	Normal	Physical	250	100	5	Adjacent
TM67	Retaliate	Normal	Physical	70	100	5	Normal
TM68	Giga Impact	Normal	Physical	150	90	5	Normal

No.	Name	Type	Kind	Pow.	Acc.	PP	Range
TM74	Gyro Ball	Steel	Physical	—	100	5	Normal
TM75	Swords Dance	Normal	Status	—	—	20	Self
TM77	Psych Up	Normal	Status	—	—	10	Normal
TM78	Bulldoze	Ground	Physical	60	100	20	Adjacent
TM80	Rock Slide	Rock	Physical	75	90	10	Many Others
TM82	Dragon Tail	Dragon	Physical	60	90	10	Normal
TM85	Dream Eater	Psychic	Special	100	100	15	Normal
TM87	Swagger	Normal	Status	—	90	15	Normal
TM88	Sleep Talk	Normal	Status	—	—	10	Self
TM90	Substitute	Normal	Status	—	—	10	Self
TM94	Rock Smash	Fighting	Physical	40	100	15	Normal
TM98	Power-Up Punch	Fighting	Physical	40	100	20	Normal
TM100	Confide	Normal	Status	—	—	20	Normal
HM01	Cut	Normal	Physical	50	95	30	Normal
HM03	Surf	Water	Special	90	100	15	Adjacent
HM04	Strength	Normal	Physical	80	100	15	Normal

● MOVES TAUGHT BY PEOPLE

Name	Type	Kind	Pow.	Acc.	PP	Range

AFTER THE HALL OF FAME

CENTRAL KALOS

COASTAL KALOS

MOUNTAIN KALOS

ADVENTURE DATA

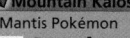

Mountain Kalos 136

Mantis Pokémon

Scyther

HEIGHT: 4'11" WEIGHT: 123.5 lbs.
GENDER: ♂/♀

X	It tears and shreds prey with its wickedly sharp scythes. It very rarely spreads its wings to fly.
Y	It slashes through grass with its sharp scythes, moving too fast for the human eye to track.

TYPE Bug Flying

ABILITIES
Swarm
Technician

HIDDEN ABILITY
Steadfast

STAT GROWTH RATES
HP ▪▪▪
Attack ▪▪▪▪▪▪
Defense ▪▪▪▪
Sp. Atk ▪▪▪
Sp. Def ▪▪▪
Speed ▪▪▪▪▪▪

EGG GROUP
Bug

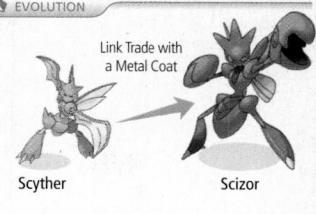

EVOLUTION

Link Trade with a Metal Coat

Scyther → Scizor

ITEMS SOMETIMES HELD BY WILD POKÉMON
None

Damage taken in normal battles		Damage taken in Inverse Battles	
Normal	×1	Normal	×1
Fire	×2	Fire	×0.5
Water	×1	Water	×1
Grass	×0.25	Grass	×4
Electric	×2	Electric	×0.5
Ice	×2	Ice	×0.5
Fighting	×0.25	Fighting	×4
Poison	×1	Poison	×1
Ground	×0	Ground	×4
Flying	×2	Flying	×0.5
Psychic	×1	Psychic	×1
Bug	×0.5	Bug	×2
Rock	×4	Rock	×0.25
Ghost	×1	Ghost	×1
Dragon	×1	Dragon	×1
Dark	×1	Dark	×1
Steel	×1	Steel	×1
Fairy	×1	Fairy	×1

Can be used in
Inverse Battle
Sky Battle
Battle Chateau
Battle Institute
Battle Maison
Random Matchup

How to obtain for your Mountain Kalos Pokédex

X	**Y**
❶ Catch in the red flowers on Route 21.	❶ Catch in the red flowers on Route 21.
❷ Catch in the purple flowers on Route 21.	❷ Catch in the purple flowers on Route 21.

♂   ♀

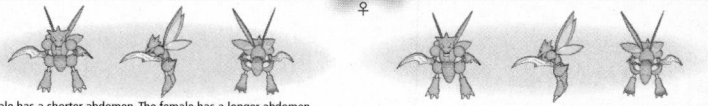

The male has a shorter abdomen. The female has a longer abdomen.

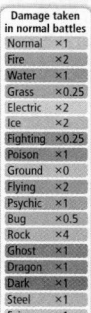

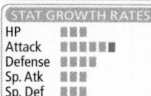

AFTER THE HALL OF FAME

CENTRAL KALOS

COASTAL KALOS

MOUNTAIN KALOS

136

Scyther

ADVENTURE DATA

● LEVEL-UP MOVES

Lv.	Name	Type	Kind	Pow.	Acc.	PP	Range
1	Vacuum Wave	Fighting	Special	40	100	30	Normal
1	Quick Attack	Normal	Physical	40	100	30	Normal
1	Leer	Normal	Status	—	100	30	Many Others
5	Focus Energy	Normal	Status	—	—	30	Self
9	Pursuit	Dark	Physical	40	100	20	Normal
13	False Swipe	Normal	Physical	40	100	40	Normal
17	Agility	Psychic	Status	—	—	30	Self
21	Wing Attack	Flying	Physical	60	100	35	Normal
25	Fury Cutter	Bug	Physical	40	95	20	Normal
29	Slash	Normal	Physical	70	100	20	Normal
33	Razor Wind	Normal	Special	80	100	10	Many Others
37	Double Team	Normal	Status	—	—	15	Self
41	X-Scissor	Bug	Physical	80	100	15	Normal
45	Night Slash	Dark	Physical	70	100	15	Normal
49	Double Hit	Normal	Physical	35	90	10	Normal
53	Air Slash	Flying	Special	75	95	15	Normal
57	Swords Dance	Normal	Status	—	—	20	Self
61	Feint	Normal	Physical	30	100	10	Normal

● TM & HM MOVES

No.	Name	Type	Kind	Pow.	Acc.	PP	Range
TM06	Toxic	Poison	Status	—	90	10	Normal
TM10	Hidden Power	Normal	Special	60	100	15	Normal
TM11	Sunny Day	Fire	Status	—	—	5	Both Sides
TM15	Hyper Beam	Normal	Special	150	90	5	Normal
TM16	Light Screen	Psychic	Status	—	—	30	Your Side
TM17	Protect	Normal	Status	—	—	10	Self
TM18	Rain Dance	Water	Status	—	—	5	Both Sides
TM19	Roost	Flying	Status	—	—	10	Self
TM20	Safeguard	Normal	Status	—	—	25	Your Side
TM21	Frustration	Normal	Physical	—	100	20	Normal
TM27	Return	Normal	Physical	—	100	20	Normal
TM31	Brick Break	Fighting	Physical	75	100	15	Normal
TM32	Double Team	Normal	Status	—	—	15	Self
TM40	Aerial Ace	Flying	Physical	60	—	20	Normal
TM42	Facade	Normal	Physical	70	100	20	Normal
TM44	Rest	Psychic	Status	—	—	10	Self
TM45	Attract	Normal	Status	—	100	15	Normal
TM46	Thief	Dark	Physical	60	100	25	Normal
TM48	Round	Normal	Special	60	100	15	Normal
TM51	Steel Wing	Steel	Physical	70	90	25	Normal
TM54	False Swipe	Normal	Physical	40	100	40	Normal
TM68	Giga Impact	Normal	Physical	150	90	5	Normal
TM75	Swords Dance	Normal	Status	—	—	20	Self
TM76	Struggle Bug	Bug	Special	50	100	20	Many Others
TM81	X-Scissor	Bug	Physical	80	100	15	Normal
TM87	Swagger	Normal	Status	—	90	15	Normal
TM88	Sleep Talk	Normal	Status	—	—	10	Self
TM89	U-turn	Bug	Physical	70	100	20	Normal
TM90	Substitute	Normal	Status	—	—	10	Self
TM94	Rock Smash	Fighting	Physical	40	100	15	Normal
TM100	Confide	Normal	Status	—	—	20	Normal
HM01	Cut	Normal	Physical	50	95	30	Normal

● MOVES TAUGHT BY PEOPLE

Name	Type	Kind	Pow.	Acc.	PP	Range

● EGG MOVES

Name	Type	Kind	Pow.	Acc.	PP	Range
Counter	Fighting	Physical	—	100	20	Varies
Baton Pass	Normal	Status	—	—	40	Self
Razor Wind	Normal	Special	80	100	10	Many Others
Reversal	Fighting	Physical	—	100	15	Normal
Endure	Normal	Status	—	—	10	Self
Silver Wind	Bug	Special	60	100	5	Normal
Bug Buzz	Bug	Special	90	100	10	Normal
Night Slash	Dark	Physical	70	100	15	Normal
Defog	Flying	Status	—	—	15	Normal
Steel Wing	Steel	Physical	70	90	25	Normal
Quick Guard	Fighting	Status	—	—	15	Your Side

Mountain Kalos 137
Pincer Pokémon
Scizor

HEIGHT: 5'11" WEIGHT: 260.1 lbs.
GENDER: ♂/♀

TYPE: Bug / Steel

ABILITIES
Swarm
Technician

HIDDEN ABILITY
Light Metal

STAT GROWTH RATES
HP
Attack
Defense
Sp. Atk
Sp. Def
Speed

EGG GROUP
Bug

X: This Pokémon's pincers, which contain steel, can crush any hard object it gets ahold of into bits.

Y: It has a steel-hard body. It intimidates foes by upraising its eye-patterned pincers.

EVOLUTION
Link Trade with a Metal Coat
Scyther → Scizor

ITEMS SOMETIMES HELD BY WILD POKÉMON
None

Can be used in
Inverse Battle
—
Battle Chateau
Battle Institute
Battle Maison
Random Matchup

Damage taken in normal battles		Damage taken in Inverse Battles	
Normal	×0.5	Normal	×2
Fire	×4	Fire	×0.25
Water	×1	Water	×1
Grass	×0.25	Grass	×4
Electric	×1	Electric	×1
Ice	×0.5	Ice	×2
Fighting	×1	Fighting	×1
Poison	×0	Poison	×1
Ground	×1	Ground	×1
Flying	×1	Flying	×1
Psychic	×0.5	Psychic	×2
Bug	×0.5	Bug	×2
Rock	×1	Rock	×1
Ghost	×1	Ghost	×1
Dragon	×0.5	Dragon	×2
Dark	×1	Dark	×1
Steel	×0.5	Steel	×1
Fairy	×0.5	Fairy	×2

How to obtain for your Mountain Kalos Pokédex

Receive Scyther by Link Trade while it is holding a Metal Coat, and have it evolve.

Receive Scyther by Link Trade while it is holding a Metal Coat, and have it evolve.

♂ ♀

The male has a shorter abdomen. The female has a longer abdomen.

137
Scizor

● LEVEL-UP MOVES

Lv.	Name	Type	Kind	Pow.	Acc.	PP	Range
1	Feint	Normal	Physical	30	100	10	Normal
1	Bullet Punch	Steel	Physical	40	100	30	Normal
1	Quick Attack	Normal	Physical	40	100	30	Normal
1	Leer	Normal	Status	—	100	30	Many Others
5	Focus Energy	Normal	Status	—	—	30	Self
9	Pursuit	Dark	Physical	40	100	20	Normal
13	False Swipe	Normal	Physical	40	100	40	Normal
17	Agility	Psychic	Status	—	—	30	Self
21	Metal Claw	Steel	Physical	50	95	35	Normal
25	Fury Cutter	Bug	Physical	40	95	20	Normal
29	Slash	Normal	Physical	70	100	20	Normal
33	Razor Wind	Normal	Special	80	100	10	Many Others
37	Iron Defense	Steel	Status	—	—	15	Self
41	X-Scissor	Bug	Physical	80	100	15	Normal
45	Double Hit	Normal	Physical	35	90	10	Normal
50	Iron Head	Steel	Physical	80	100	15	Normal
57	Swords Dance	Normal	Status	—	—	20	Self
61	Feint	Normal	Physical	30	100	10	Normal

● TM & HM MOVES

No.	Name	Type	Kind	Pow.	Acc.	PP	Range
TM06	Toxic	Poison	Status	—	90	10	Normal
TM09	Venoshock	Poison	Special	65	100	10	Normal
TM10	Hidden Power	Normal	Special	60	100	15	Normal
TM11	Sunny Day	Fire	Status	—	—	5	Both Sides
TM15	Hyper Beam	Normal	Special	150	90	5	Normal
TM16	Light Screen	Psychic	Status	—	—	30	Your Side
TM17	Protect	Normal	Status	—	—	10	Self
TM18	Rain Dance	Water	Status	—	—	5	Both Sides
TM19	Roost	Flying	Status	—	—	10	Self
TM20	Safeguard	Normal	Status	—	—	25	Your Side
TM21	Frustration	Normal	Physical	—	100	20	Normal
TM27	Return	Normal	Physical	—	100	20	Normal
TM31	Brick Break	Fighting	Physical	75	100	15	Normal
TM32	Double Team	Normal	Status	—	—	15	Self
TM37	Sandstorm	Rock	Status	—	—	10	Both Sides
TM40	Aerial Ace	Flying	Physical	60	—	20	Normal
TM42	Facade	Normal	Physical	70	100	20	Normal
TM44	Rest	Psychic	Status	—	—	10	Self
TM45	Attract	Normal	Status	—	100	15	Normal
TM46	Thief	Dark	Physical	60	100	25	Normal
TM48	Round	Normal	Special	60	100	15	Normal
TM51	Steel Wing	Steel	Physical	70	90	25	Normal
TM54	False Swipe	Normal	Physical	40	100	40	Normal
TM56	Fling	Dark	Physical	—	100	10	Normal
TM62	Acrobatics	Flying	Physical	55	100	15	Normal
TM68	Giga Impact	Normal	Physical	150	90	5	Normal
TM75	Swords Dance	Normal	Status	—	—	20	Self
TM76	Struggle Bug	Bug	Special	50	100	20	Many Others
TM81	X-Scissor	Bug	Physical	80	100	15	Normal
TM87	Swagger	Normal	Status	—	90	15	Normal
TM88	Sleep Talk	Normal	Status	—	—	10	Self
TM89	U-turn	Bug	Physical	70	100	20	Normal
TM90	Substitute	Normal	Status	—	—	10	Self
TM91	Flash Cannon	Steel	Special	80	100	10	Normal
TM94	Rock Smash	Fighting	Physical	40	100	15	Normal
TM100	Confide	Normal	Status	—	—	20	Normal
HM01	Cut	Normal	Physical	50	95	30	Normal
HM04	Strength	Normal	Physical	80	100	15	Normal

● MOVES TAUGHT BY PEOPLE

Name	Type	Kind	Pow.	Acc.	PP	Range

580

Mega Evolution

Pincer Pokémon

☑ Mega Scizor

TYPE	Bug	Steel

ABILITY
Technician

HEIGHT: 6'07" WEIGHT: 275.6 lbs. GENDER: ♂/♀

STAT GROWTH RATES

HP	▪▪▪
Attack	▪▪▪▪▪▪▪
Defense	▪▪▪▪▪▪
Sp. Atk	▪▪▪
Sp. Def	▪▪▪▪
Speed	▪▪▪▪

⊙ MEGA STONE REQUIRED

Scizorite
Obtain in Frost Cavern between 8 P.M. and 8:59 P.M., after entering the Hall of Fame and speaking with Professor Sycamore in Anistar City.

Damage taken in normal battles	
Normal	×0.5
Fire	×4
Water	×1
Grass	×0.25
Electric	×1
Ice	×0.5
Fighting	×1
Poison	×0
Ground	×1
Flying	×1
Psychic	×0.5
Bug	×0.5
Rock	×1
Ghost	×1
Dragon	×0.5
Dark	×1
Steel	×0.5
Fairy	×0.5

Damage taken in Inverse Battles	
Normal	×2
Fire	×0.25
Water	×1
Grass	×4
Electric	×1
Ice	×2
Fighting	×1
Poison	×2
Ground	×1
Flying	×1
Psychic	×2
Bug	×2
Rock	×1
Ghost	×1
Dragon	×2
Dark	×1
Steel	×2
Fairy	×2

Can be used in
Inverse Battle
—
Battle Chateau
Battle Institute
Battle Maison
Random Matchup

Same form for ♂/♀

AFTER THE HALL OF FAME

CENTRAL KALOS

COASTAL ⋯S

MOUNTAIN KALOS Mega Scizor

ADVENTURE DATA

581

Mountain Kalos — 138
Transform Pokémon
✓ Ditto

HEIGHT: 1'00" WEIGHT: 8.8 lbs.
GENDER: unknown

X It has the ability to reconstitute its entire cellular structure to transform into whatever it sees.

Y It can freely recombine its own cellular structure to transform into other life-forms.

TYPE Normal

ABILITY
Limber

HIDDEN ABILITY
Imposter

STAT GROWTH RATES
HP ■■
Attack ■■■
Defense ■■
Sp. Atk ■■
Sp. Def ■■
Speed ■■■

EGG GROUP
Ditto

EVOLUTION
Does not evolve

ITEMS SOMETIMES HELD BY WILD POKÉMON
Quick Powder, Metal Powder

Damage taken in normal battles		Damage taken in Inverse Battles	
Normal	×1	Normal	×1
Fire	×1	Fire	×1
Water	×1	Water	×1
Grass	×1	Grass	×1
Electric	×1	Electric	×1
Ice	×1	Ice	×1
Fighting	×2	Fighting	×0.5
Poison	×1	Poison	×1
Ground	×1	Ground	×1
Flying	×1	Flying	×1
Psychic	×1	Psychic	×1
Bug	×1	Bug	×1
Rock	×1	Rock	×1
Ghost	×0	Ghost	×2
Dragon	×1	Dragon	×1
Dark	×1	Dark	×1
Steel	×1	Steel	×1
Fairy	×1	Fairy	×1

Can be used in	
Inverse Battle	Battle Institute
—	Battle Maison
Battle Chateau	Random Matchup

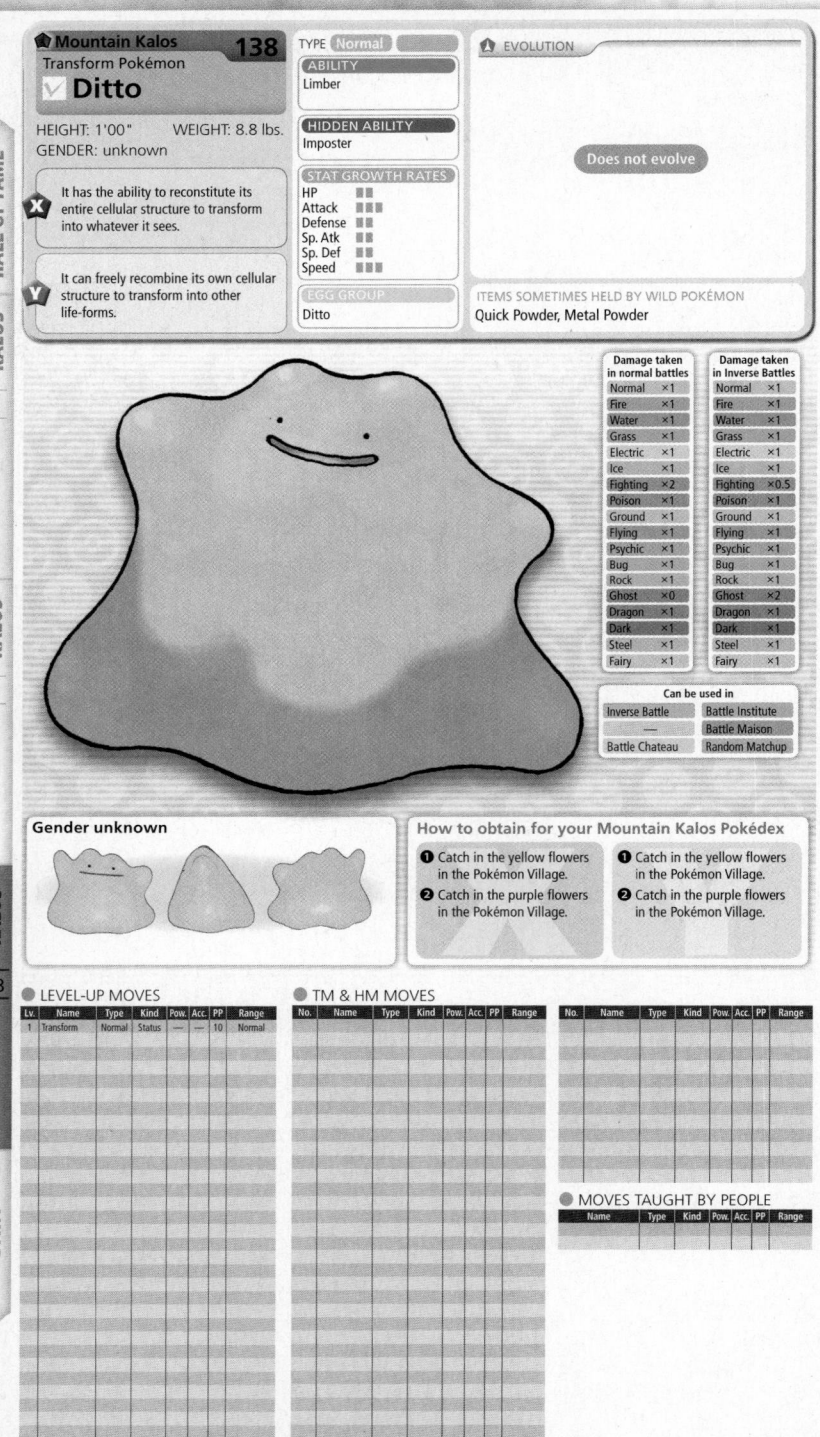

Gender unknown

How to obtain for your Mountain Kalos Pokédex
1 Catch in the yellow flowers in the Pokémon Village.
2 Catch in the purple flowers in the Pokémon Village.

1 Catch in the yellow flowers in the Pokémon Village.
2 Catch in the purple flowers in the Pokémon Village.

138 Ditto

● LEVEL-UP MOVES
Lv.	Name	Type	Kind	Pow.	Acc.	PP	Range
1	Transform	Normal	Status	—	—	10	Normal

● TM & HM MOVES
No.	Name	Type	Kind	Pow.	Acc.	PP	Range

● MOVES TAUGHT BY PEOPLE
Name	Type	Kind	Pow.	Acc.	PP	Range

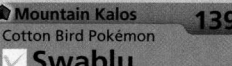

Mountain Kalos 139
Cotton Bird Pokémon
✓ **Swablu**

HEIGHT: 1'04" WEIGHT: 2.6 lbs.
GENDER: ♂/♀

X For some reason, it likes to land on people's heads softly and act like it's a hat.

Y It constantly grooms its cotton-like wings. It takes a shower to clean itself if it becomes dirty.

TYPE Normal Flying

ABILITY
Natural Cure

HIDDEN ABILITY
Cloud Nine

STAT GROWTH RATES
HP	■■
Attack	■■
Defense	■■■
Sp. Atk	■■
Sp. Def	■■■
Speed	■■■

EGG GROUPS
Flying, Dragon

EVOLUTION

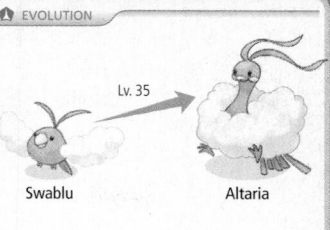

Lv. 35

Swablu → Altaria

ITEMS SOMETIMES HELD BY WILD POKÉMON
None

Damage taken in normal battles		Damage taken in Inverse Battles	
Normal	×1	Normal	×1
Fire	×1	Fire	×1
Water	×1	Water	×1
Grass	×0.5	Grass	×2
Electric	×2	Electric	×0.5
Ice	×2	Ice	×0.5
Fighting	×1	Fighting	×1
Poison	×1	Poison	×1
Ground	×0	Ground	×2
Flying	×1	Flying	×1
Psychic	×1	Psychic	×1
Bug	×0.5	Bug	×2
Rock	×2	Rock	×0.5
Ghost	×0	Ghost	×2
Dragon	×1	Dragon	×1
Dark	×1	Dark	×1
Steel	×1	Steel	×1
Fairy	×1	Fairy	×1

Can be used in
Inverse Battle	Battle Institute
Sky Battle	Battle Maison
Battle Chateau	Random Matchup

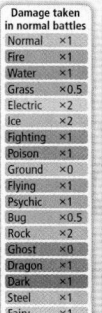 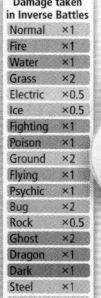

Same form for ♂/♀

How to obtain for your Mountain Kalos Pokédex

Catch in a Horde Encounter on Route 21.

Catch in a Horde Encounter on Route 21.

AFTER THE HALL OF FAME

CENTRAL KALOS

COASTAL KALOS

MOUNTAIN KALOS

139

Swablu

ADVENTURE DATA

● LEVEL-UP MOVES

Lv.	Name	Type	Kind	Pow.	Acc.	PP	Range
1	Peck	Flying	Physical	35	100	35	Normal
1	Growl	Normal	Status	—	100	40	Many Others
4	Astonish	Ghost	Physical	30	100	15	Normal
8	Sing	Normal	Status	—	55	15	Normal
10	Fury Attack	Normal	Physical	15	85	20	Normal
13	Safeguard	Normal	Status	—	—	25	Your Side
15	Mist	Ice	Status	—	—	30	Your Side
18	Round	Normal	Special	60	100	15	Normal
21	Natural Gift	Normal	Physical	—	100	15	Normal
25	Take Down	Normal	Physical	90	85	20	Normal
29	Refresh	Normal	Status	—	—	20	Self
34	Mirror Move	Flying	Status	—	—	20	Normal
39	Cotton Guard	Grass	Status	—	—	10	Self
42	Dragon Pulse	Dragon	Special	85	100	10	Normal
48	Perish Song	Normal	Status	—	—	5	Adjacent
50	Moonblast	Fairy	Special	95	100	15	Normal

● TM & HM MOVES

No.	Name	Type	Kind	Pow.	Acc.	PP	Range
TM06	Toxic	Poison	Status	—	90	10	Normal
TM10	Hidden Power	Normal	Special	60	100	15	Normal
TM11	Sunny Day	Fire	Status	—	—	5	Both Sides
TM13	Ice Beam	Ice	Special	90	100	10	Normal
TM17	Protect	Normal	Status	—	—	10	Self
TM18	Rain Dance	Water	Status	—	—	5	Both Sides
TM19	Roost	Flying	Status	—	—	10	Self
TM20	Safeguard	Normal	Status	—	—	25	Your Side
TM21	Frustration	Normal	Physical	—	100	20	Normal
TM22	Solar Beam	Grass	Special	120	100	10	Normal
TM27	Return	Normal	Physical	—	100	20	Normal
TM32	Double Team	Normal	Status	—	—	15	Self
TM40	Aerial Ace	Flying	Physical	60	—	20	Normal
TM42	Facade	Normal	Physical	70	100	20	Normal
TM44	Rest	Psychic	Status	—	—	10	Self
TM45	Attract	Normal	Status	—	100	15	Normal
TM46	Thief	Dark	Physical	60	100	25	Normal
TM48	Round	Normal	Special	60	100	15	Normal
TM49	Echoed Voice	Normal	Special	40	100	15	Normal
TM51	Steel Wing	Steel	Physical	70	90	25	Normal
TM77	Psych Up	Normal	Status	—	—	10	Normal
TM85	Dream Eater	Psychic	Special	100	100	15	Normal
TM87	Swagger	Normal	Status	—	90	15	Normal
TM88	Sleep Talk	Normal	Status	—	—	10	Self
TM90	Substitute	Normal	Status	—	—	10	Self
TM99	Dazzling Gleam	Fairy	Special	80	100	10	Many Others
TM100	Confide	Normal	Status	—	—	20	Normal
HM02	Fly	Flying	Physical	90	95	15	Normal

● MOVES TAUGHT BY PEOPLE

Name	Type	Kind	Pow.	Acc.	PP	Range

● EGG MOVES

Name	Type	Kind	Pow.	Acc.	PP	Range
Agility	Psychic	Status	—	—	30	Self
Haze	Ice	Status	—	—	30	Both Sides
Pursuit	Dark	Physical	40	100	20	Normal
Rage	Normal	Physical	20	100	20	Normal
Feather Dance	Flying	Status	—	100	15	Normal
Dragon Rush	Dragon	Physical	100	75	10	Normal
Power Swap	Psychic	Status	—	—	10	Normal
Roost	Flying	Status	—	—	10	Self
Hyper Voice	Normal	Special	90	100	10	Many Others
Steel Wing	Steel	Physical	70	90	25	Normal

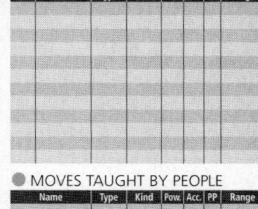

Mountain Kalos 140
Altaria
Humming Pokémon

HEIGHT: 3'07" WEIGHT: 45.4 lbs.
GENDER: ♂/♀

X It flies gracefully through the sky. Its melodic humming makes you feel like you're in a dream.

Y On sunny days, it flies freely through the sky and blends into the clouds. It sings in a beautiful soprano.

TYPE Dragon Flying

ABILITY
Natural Cure

HIDDEN ABILITY
Cloud Nine

STAT GROWTH RATES
HP	■■■
Attack	■■■
Defense	■■■■
Sp. Atk	■■■
Sp. Def	■■■
Speed	■■■

EGG GROUPS
Flying, Dragon

EVOLUTION

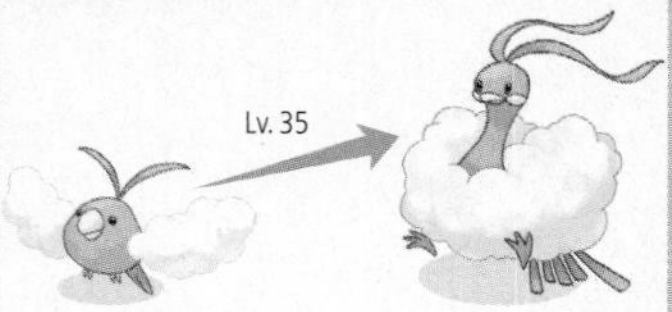

Lv. 35

Swablu → Altaria

ITEMS SOMETIMES HELD BY WILD POKÉMON
None

Damage taken in normal battles		Damage taken in Inverse Battles	
Normal	×1	Normal	×1
Fire	×0.5	Fire	×2
Water	×0.5	Water	×2
Grass	×0.25	Grass	×4
Electric	×1	Electric	×1
Ice	×4	Ice	×0.25
Fighting	×0.5	Fighting	×2
Poison	×1	Poison	×1
Ground	×0	Ground	×2
Flying	×1	Flying	×1
Psychic	×1	Psychic	×1
Bug	×0.5	Bug	×2
Rock	×2	Rock	×0.5
Ghost	×1	Ghost	×1
Dragon	×2	Dragon	×0.5
Dark	×1	Dark	×1
Steel	×1	Steel	×1
Fairy	×2	Fairy	×0.5

Can be used in	
Inverse Battle	Battle Institute
Sky Battle	Battle Maison
Battle Chateau	Random Matchup

Same form for ♂/♀

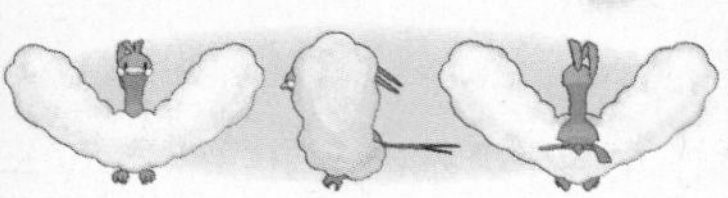

How to obtain for your Mountain Kalos Pokédex

❶ Catch in the red or purple flowers on Route 21.
❷ Level up Swablu to Lv. 35.

❶ Catch in the red or purple flowers on Route 21.
❷ Level up Swablu to Lv. 35.

140

Altaria

LEVEL-UP MOVES

Lv.	Name	Type	Kind	Pow.	Acc.	PP	Range
1	Sky Attack	Flying	Physical	140	90	5	Normal
1	Pluck	Flying	Physical	60	100	20	Normal
1	Peck	Flying	Physical	35	100	35	Normal
1	Growl	Normal	Status	—	100	40	Many Others
1	Astonish	Ghost	Physical	30	100	15	Normal
1	Sing	Normal	Status	—	55	15	Normal
4	Astonish	Ghost	Physical	30	100	15	Normal
8	Sing	Normal	Status	—	55	15	Normal
10	Fury Attack	Normal	Physical	15	85	20	Normal
13	Safeguard	Normal	Status	—	—	25	Your Side
15	Mist	Ice	Status	—	—	30	Your Side
18	Round	Normal	Special	60	100	15	Normal
21	Natural Gift	Normal	Physical	—	100	15	Normal
25	Take Down	Normal	Physical	90	85	20	Normal
29	Refresh	Normal	Status	—	—	20	Self
34	Dragon Dance	Dragon	Status	—	—	20	Self
38	Dragon Breath	Dragon	Special	60	100	20	Normal
42	Cotton Guard	Grass	Status	—	—	10	Self
48	Dragon Pulse	Dragon	Special	85	100	10	Normal
57	Perish Song	Normal	Status	—	—	5	Adjacent
60	Moonblast	Fairy	Special	95	100	15	Normal
64	Sky Attack	Flying	Physical	140	90	5	Normal

TM & HM MOVES

No.	Name	Type	Kind	Pow.	Acc.	PP	Range
TM01	Hone Claws	Dark	Status	—	—	15	Self
TM02	Dragon Claw	Dragon	Physical	80	100	15	Normal
TM05	Roar	Normal	Status	—	—	20	Normal
TM06	Toxic	Poison	Status	—	90	10	Normal
TM10	Hidden Power	Normal	Special	60	100	15	Normal
TM11	Sunny Day	Fire	Status	—	—	5	Both Sides
TM13	Ice Beam	Ice	Special	90	100	10	Normal
TM15	Hyper Beam	Normal	Special	150	90	5	Normal
TM17	Protect	Normal	Status	—	—	10	Self
TM18	Rain Dance	Water	Status	—	—	5	Both Sides
TM19	Roost	Flying	Status	—	—	10	Self
TM20	Safeguard	Normal	Status	—	—	25	Your Side
TM21	Frustration	Normal	Physical	—	100	20	Normal
TM22	Solar Beam	Grass	Special	120	100	10	Normal
TM26	Earthquake	Ground	Physical	100	100	10	Adjacent
TM27	Return	Normal	Physical	—	100	20	Normal
TM32	Double Team	Normal	Status	—	—	15	Self
TM35	Flamethrower	Fire	Special	90	100	15	Normal
TM38	Fire Blast	Fire	Special	110	85	5	Normal
TM40	Aerial Ace	Flying	Physical	60	—	20	Normal
TM42	Facade	Normal	Physical	70	100	20	Normal
TM44	Rest	Psychic	Status	—	—	10	Self
TM45	Attract	Normal	Status	—	100	15	Normal
TM46	Thief	Dark	Physical	60	100	25	Normal
TM48	Round	Normal	Special	60	100	15	Normal
TM49	Echoed Voice	Normal	Special	40	100	15	Normal
TM51	Steel Wing	Steel	Physical	70	90	25	Normal
TM59	Incinerate	Fire	Special	60	100	15	Many Others
TM68	Giga Impact	Normal	Physical	150	90	5	Normal
TM77	Psych Up	Normal	Status	—	—	10	Normal
TM78	Bulldoze	Ground	Physical	60	100	20	Adjacent
TM85	Dream Eater	Psychic	Special	100	100	15	Normal
TM87	Swagger	Normal	Status	—	90	15	Normal

No.	Name	Type	Kind	Pow.	Acc.	PP	Range
TM88	Sleep Talk	Normal	Status	—	—	10	Self
TM90	Substitute	Normal	Status	—	—	10	Self
TM94	Rock Smash	Fighting	Physical	40	100	15	Normal
TM99	Dazzling Gleam	Fairy	Special	80	100	10	Many Others
TM100	Confide	Normal	Status	—	—	20	Normal
HM02	Fly	Flying	Physical	90	95	15	Normal

MOVES TAUGHT BY PEOPLE

Name	Type	Kind	Pow.	Acc.	PP	Range
Draco Meteor	Dragon	Special	130	90	5	Normal

Cave Pokémon
☑ Druddigon

141

HEIGHT: 5'03" WEIGHT: 306.4 lbs.
GENDER: ♂/♀

TYPE Dragon

ABILITIES
Rough Skin
Sheer Force

HIDDEN ABILITY
Mold Breaker

STAT GROWTH RATES
HP	■■■
Attack	■■■■■■
Defense	■■■■
Sp. Atk	■■■
Sp. Def	■■■■
Speed	■■■

EGG GROUPS
Dragon, Monster

⬆ EVOLUTION

Does not evolve

 X It races through narrow caves, using its sharp claws to catch prey. The skin on its face is harder than a rock.

Y It warms its body by absorbing sunlight with its wings. When its body temperature falls, it can no longer move.

ITEMS SOMETIMES HELD BY WILD POKÉMON
Dragon Fang

Damage taken in normal battles		Damage taken in Inverse Battles	
Normal	×1	Normal	×1
Fire	×0.5	Fire	×2
Water	×0.5	Water	×2
Grass	×0.5	Grass	×2
Electric	×0.5	Electric	×2
Ice	×2	Ice	×0.5
Fighting	×1	Fighting	×1
Poison	×1	Poison	×1
Ground	×1	Ground	×1
Flying	×1	Flying	×1
Psychic	×1	Psychic	×1
Bug	×1	Bug	×1
Rock	×1	Rock	×1
Ghost	×1	Ghost	×1
Dragon	×2	Dragon	×0.5
Dark	×1	Dark	×1
Steel	×1	Steel	×1
Fairy	×2	Fairy	×0.5

Can be used in	
Inverse Battle	Battle Institute
—	Battle Maison
Battle Chateau	Random Matchup

Same form for ♂ / ♀

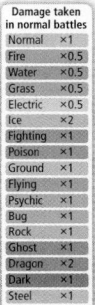

How to obtain for your Mountain Kalos Pokédex

X Catch in the caves along Victory Road.

Y Catch in the caves along Victory Road.

● LEVEL-UP MOVES

Lv.	Name	Type	Kind	Pow.	Acc.	PP	Range
1	Leer	Normal	Status	—	100	30	Many Others
1	Scratch	Normal	Physical	40	100	35	Normal
5	Hone Claws	Dark	Status	—	—	15	Self
9	Bite	Dark	Physical	60	100	25	Normal
13	Scary Face	Normal	Status	—	100	10	Normal
18	Dragon Rage	Dragon	Special	—	100	10	Normal
21	Slash	Normal	Physical	70	100	20	Normal
25	Crunch	Dark	Physical	80	100	15	Normal
27	Dragon Claw	Dragon	Physical	80	100	15	Normal
31	Chip Away	Normal	Physical	70	100	20	Normal
35	Revenge	Fighting	Physical	60	100	10	Normal
40	Night Slash	Dark	Physical	70	100	15	Normal
45	Dragon Tail	Dragon	Physical	60	90	10	Normal
49	Rock Climb	Normal	Physical	90	85	20	Normal
55	Superpower	Fighting	Physical	120	100	5	Normal
62	Outrage	Dragon	Physical	120	100	10	1 Random

● TM & HM MOVES

No.	Name	Type	Kind	Pow.	Acc.	PP	Range
TM01	Hone Claws	Dark	Status	—	—	15	Self
TM02	Dragon Claw	Dragon	Physical	80	100	15	Normal
TM05	Roar	Normal	Status	—	—	20	Normal
TM06	Toxic	Poison	Status	—	90	10	Normal
TM10	Hidden Power	Normal	Special	60	100	15	Normal
TM11	Sunny Day	Fire	Status	—	—	5	Both Sides

No.	Name	Type	Kind	Pow.	Acc.	PP	Range
TM15	Hyper Beam	Normal	Special	150	90	5	Normal
TM17	Protect	Normal	Status	—	—	10	Self
TM18	Rain Dance	Water	Status	—	—	5	Both Sides
TM21	Frustration	Normal	Physical	—	100	20	Normal
TM23	Smack Down	Rock	Physical	50	100	15	Normal
TM26	Earthquake	Ground	Physical	100	100	10	Adjacent
TM27	Return	Normal	Physical	—	100	20	Normal
TM28	Dig	Ground	Physical	80	100	10	Normal
TM32	Double Team	Normal	Status	—	—	15	Self
TM35	Flamethrower	Fire	Special	90	100	15	Normal
TM36	Sludge Bomb	Poison	Special	90	100	10	Normal
TM39	Rock Tomb	Rock	Physical	60	95	15	Normal
TM40	Aerial Ace	Flying	Physical	60	—	20	Normal
TM41	Torment	Dark	Status	—	100	15	Normal
TM42	Facade	Normal	Physical	70	100	20	Normal
TM44	Rest	Psychic	Status	—	—	10	Self
TM45	Attract	Normal	Status	—	100	15	Normal
TM48	Round	Normal	Special	60	100	15	Normal
TM52	Focus Blast	Fighting	Special	120	70	5	Normal
TM56	Fling	Dark	Physical	—	100	10	Normal
TM57	Charge Beam	Electric	Special	50	90	10	Normal
TM59	Incinerate	Fire	Special	60	100	15	Many Others
TM65	Shadow Claw	Ghost	Physical	70	100	15	Normal
TM66	Payback	Dark	Physical	50	100	10	Normal
TM67	Retaliate	Normal	Physical	70	100	5	Normal
TM68	Giga Impact	Normal	Physical	150	90	5	Normal
TM78	Bulldoze	Ground	Physical	60	100	20	Adjacent
TM80	Rock Slide	Rock	Physical	75	90	10	Many Others
TM82	Dragon Tail	Dragon	Physical	60	90	10	Normal
TM87	Swagger	Normal	Status	—	90	15	Normal
TM88	Sleep Talk	Normal	Status	—	—	10	Self
TM90	Substitute	Normal	Status	—	—	10	Self

No.	Name	Type	Kind	Pow.	Acc.	PP	Range
TM91	Flash Cannon	Steel	Special	80	100	10	Normal
TM94	Rock Smash	Fighting	Physical	40	100	15	Normal
TM95	Snarl	Dark	Special	55	95	15	Many Others
TM97	Dark Pulse	Dark	Special	80	100	15	Normal
TM98	Power-Up Punch	Fighting	Physical	40	100	20	Normal
TM100	Confide	Normal	Status	—	—	20	Normal
HM01	Cut	Normal	Physical	50	95	30	Normal
HM03	Surf	Water	Special	90	100	15	Adjacent
HM04	Strength	Normal	Physical	80	100	15	Normal

● MOVES TAUGHT BY PEOPLE

Name	Type	Kind	Pow.	Acc.	PP	Range

● EGG MOVES

Name	Type	Kind	Pow.	Acc.	PP	Range
Fire Fang	Fire	Physical	65	95	15	Normal
Thunder Fang	Electric	Physical	65	95	15	Normal
Crush Claw	Normal	Physical	75	95	10	Normal
Feint Attack	Dark	Physical	60	—	20	Normal
Pursuit	Dark	Physical	40	100	20	Normal
Iron Tail	Steel	Physical	100	75	15	Normal
Poison Tail	Poison	Physical	50	100	25	Normal
Snatch	Dark	Status	—	—	10	Self
Metal Claw	Steel	Physical	50	95	35	Normal
Glare	Normal	Status	—	100	30	Normal
Sucker Punch	Dark	Physical	80	100	5	Normal

Mountain Kalos 142
Irate Pokémon
☑ Deino

HEIGHT: 2'07" WEIGHT: 38.1 lbs.
GENDER: ♂/♀

X They cannot see, so they tackle and bite to learn about their surroundings. Their bodies are covered in wounds.

Y Lacking sight, it's unaware of its surroundings, so it bumps into things and eats anything that moves.

TYPE	Dark	Dragon

ABILITY
Hustle

HIDDEN ABILITY
None

STAT GROWTH RATES
HP	■■
Attack	■■■
Defense	■■
Sp. Atk	■■
Sp. Def	■■
Speed	■■

EGG GROUP
Dragon

EVOLUTION

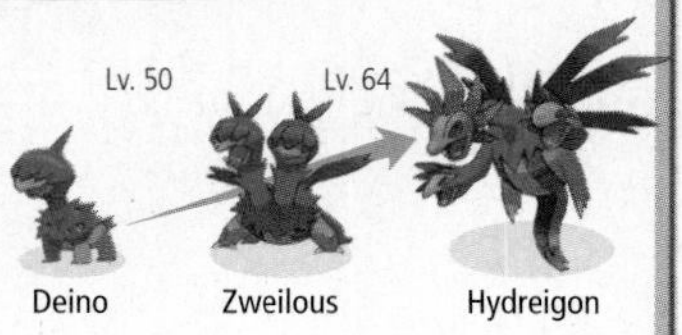

Lv. 50   Lv. 64

Deino   Zweilous   Hydreigon

ITEMS SOMETIMES HELD BY WILD POKÉMON
None

Damage taken in normal battles		Damage taken in Inverse Battles	
Normal	×1	Normal	×1
Fire	×0.5	Fire	×2
Water	×0.5	Water	×2
Grass	×0.5	Grass	×2
Electric	×0.5	Electric	×2
Ice	×2	Ice	×0.5
Fighting	×2	Fighting	×0.5
Poison	×1	Poison	×1
Ground	×1	Ground	×1
Flying	×1	Flying	×1
Psychic	×0	Psychic	×2
Bug	×2	Bug	×0.5
Rock	×1	Rock	×1
Ghost	×1	Ghost	×2
Dragon	×2	Dragon	×0.5
Dark	×0.5	Dark	×2
Steel	×1	Steel	×1
Fairy	×4	Fairy	×0.25

Can be used in	
Inverse Battle	Battle Institute
—	Battle Maison
Battle Chateau	Random Matchup

Same form for ♂/♀

How to obtain for your Mountain Kalos Pokédex

Leave Zweilous or Hydreigon at the Pokémon Day Care, and hatch the Egg that is found.

Leave Zweilous or Hydreigon at the Pokémon Day Care, and hatch the Egg that is found.

LEVEL-UP MOVES

Lv.	Name	Type	Kind	Pow.	Acc.	PP	Range
1	Tackle	Normal	Physical	50	100	35	Normal
1	Dragon Rage	Dragon	Special	—	100	10	Normal
4	Focus Energy	Normal	Status	—	—	30	Self
9	Bite	Dark	Physical	60	100	25	Normal
12	Headbutt	Normal	Physical	70	100	15	Normal
17	Dragon Breath	Dragon	Special	60	100	20	Normal
20	Roar	Normal	Status	—	—	20	Normal
25	Crunch	Dark	Physical	80	100	15	Normal
28	Slam	Normal	Physical	80	75	20	Normal
32	Dragon Pulse	Dragon	Special	85	100	10	Normal
38	Work Up	Normal	Status	—	—	30	Self
42	Dragon Rush	Dragon	Physical	100	75	10	Normal
48	Body Slam	Normal	Physical	85	100	15	Normal
50	Scary Face	Normal	Status	—	100	10	Normal
58	Hyper Voice	Normal	Special	90	100	10	Many Others
62	Outrage	Dragon	Physical	120	100	10	1 Random

TM & HM MOVES

No.	Name	Type	Kind	Pow.	Acc.	PP	Range
TM05	Roar	Normal	Status	—	—	20	Normal
TM06	Toxic	Poison	Status	—	90	10	Normal
TM10	Hidden Power	Normal	Special	60	100	15	Normal
TM11	Sunny Day	Fire	Status	—	—	5	Both Sides
TM12	Taunt	Dark	Status	—	100	20	Normal
TM17	Protect	Normal	Status	—	—	10	Self
TM18	Rain Dance	Water	Status	—	—	5	Both Sides
TM21	Frustration	Normal	Physical	—	100	20	Normal
TM27	Return	Normal	Physical	—	100	20	Normal
TM32	Double Team	Normal	Status	—	—	15	Self
TM41	Torment	Dark	Status	—	100	15	Normal
TM42	Facade	Normal	Physical	70	100	20	Normal
TM44	Rest	Psychic	Status	—	—	10	Self
TM45	Attract	Normal	Status	—	100	15	Normal
TM46	Thief	Dark	Physical	60	100	25	Normal
TM48	Round	Normal	Special	60	100	15	Normal
TM59	Incinerate	Fire	Special	60	100	15	Many Others
TM73	Thunder Wave	Electric	Status	—	100	20	Normal
TM77	Psych Up	Normal	Status	—	—	10	Normal
TM82	Dragon Tail	Dragon	Physical	60	90	10	Normal
TM87	Swagger	Normal	Status	—	90	15	Normal
TM88	Sleep Talk	Normal	Status	—	—	10	Self
TM90	Substitute	Normal	Status	—	—	10	Self
TM94	Rock Smash	Fighting	Physical	40	100	15	Normal
TM97	Dark Pulse	Dark	Special	80	100	15	Normal
TM100	Confide	Normal	Status	—	—	20	Normal
HM04	Strength	Normal	Physical	80	100	15	Normal

MOVES TAUGHT BY PEOPLE

Name	Type	Kind	Pow.	Acc.	PP	Range
Draco Meteor	Dragon	Special	130	90	5	Normal

EGG MOVES

Name	Type	Kind	Pow.	Acc.	PP	Range
Fire Fang	Fire	Physical	65	95	15	Normal
Thunder Fang	Electric	Physical	65	95	15	Normal
Ice Fang	Ice	Physical	65	95	15	Normal
Double Hit	Normal	Physical	35	90	10	Normal
Astonish	Ghost	Physical	30	100	15	Normal
Earth Power	Ground	Special	90	100	10	Normal
Screech	Normal	Status	—	85	40	Normal
Head Smash	Rock	Physical	150	80	5	Normal
Assurance	Dark	Physical	60	100	10	Normal
Dark Pulse	Dark	Special	80	100	15	Normal

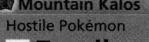

⬆ Mountain Kalos

Hostile Pokémon **143**
☑ Zweilous

HEIGHT: 4'07" WEIGHT: 110.2 lbs.
GENDER: ♂/♀

X The two heads do not get along. Whichever head eats more than the other gets to be the leader.

Y After it has eaten up all the food in its territory, it moves to another area. Its two heads do not get along.

TYPE	Dark	Dragon

ABILITY
Hustle

HIDDEN ABILITY
None

STAT GROWTH RATES
HP	▪▪▪
Attack	▪▪▪▪
Defense	▪▪▪
Sp. Atk	▪▪▪
Sp. Def	▪▪▪
Speed	▪▪▪

EGG GROUP
Dragon

⬆ EVOLUTION

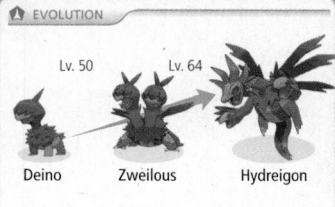

	Lv. 50		Lv. 64	
Deino		Zweilous		Hydreigon

ITEMS SOMETIMES HELD BY WILD POKÉMON
None

Damage taken in normal battles		Damage taken in Inverse Battles	
Normal	×1	Normal	×1
Fire	×0.5	Fire	×2
Water	×0.5	Water	×2
Grass	×0.5	Grass	×2
Electric	×0.5	Electric	×2
Ice	×2	Ice	×0.5
Fighting	×2	Fighting	×0.5
Poison	×1	Poison	×1
Ground	×1	Ground	×1
Flying	×1	Flying	×1
Psychic	×0	Psychic	×2
Bug	×2	Bug	×0.5
Rock	×1	Rock	×1
Ghost	×0.5	Ghost	×2
Dragon	×2	Dragon	×0.5
Dark	×0.5	Dark	×2
Steel	×1	Steel	×1
Fairy	×4	Fairy	×0.25

Can be used in	
Inverse Battle	Battle Institute
—	Battle Maison
Battle Chateau	Random Matchup

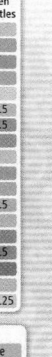

Same form for ♂/♀

How to obtain for your Mountain Kalos Pokédex

Catch in the caves along Victory Road.	Catch in the caves along Victory Road.
X	**Y**

● LEVEL-UP MOVES

Lv.	Name	Type	Kind	Pow.	Acc.	PP	Range
1	Double Hit	Normal	Physical	35	90	10	Normal
1	Dragon Rage	Dragon	Special	—	100	10	Normal
1	Focus Energy	Normal	Status	—	—	30	Self
1	Bite	Dark	Physical	60	100	25	Normal
4	Focus Energy	Normal	Status	—	—	30	Self
9	Bite	Dark	Physical	60	100	25	Normal
12	Headbutt	Normal	Physical	70	100	15	Normal
17	Dragon Breath	Dragon	Special	60	100	20	Normal
20	Roar	Normal	Status	—	—	20	Normal
25	Crunch	Dark	Physical	80	100	15	Normal
28	Slam	Normal	Physical	80	75	20	Normal
32	Dragon Pulse	Dragon	Special	85	100	10	Normal
38	Work Up	Normal	Status	—	—	30	Self
42	Dragon Rush	Dragon	Physical	100	75	10	Normal
48	Body Slam	Normal	Physical	85	100	15	Normal
55	Scary Face	Normal	Status	—	100	10	Normal
64	Hyper Voice	Normal	Special	90	100	10	Many Others
71	Outrage	Dragon	Physical	120	100	10	1 Random

● TM & HM MOVES

No.	Name	Type	Kind	Pow.	Acc.	PP	Range
TM05	Roar	Normal	Status	—	—	20	Normal
TM06	Toxic	Poison	Status	—	90	10	Normal
TM10	Hidden Power	Normal	Special	60	100	15	Normal
TM11	Sunny Day	Fire	Status	—	—	5	Both Sides
TM12	Taunt	Dark	Status	—	100	20	Normal
TM17	Protect	Normal	Status	—	—	10	Self
TM18	Rain Dance	Water	Status	—	—	5	Both Sides
TM21	Frustration	Normal	Physical	—	100	20	Normal
TM27	Return	Normal	Physical	—	100	20	Normal
TM32	Double Team	Normal	Status	—	—	15	Self
TM41	Torment	Dark	Status	—	100	15	Normal
TM42	Facade	Normal	Physical	70	100	20	Normal
TM44	Rest	Psychic	Status	—	—	10	Self
TM45	Attract	Normal	Status	—	100	15	Normal
TM46	Thief	Dark	Physical	60	100	25	Normal
TM48	Round	Normal	Special	60	100	15	Normal
TM59	Incinerate	Fire	Special	60	100	15	Many Others
TM73	Thunder Wave	Electric	Status	—	100	20	Normal
TM77	Psych Up	Normal	Status	—	—	10	Normal
TM82	Dragon Tail	Dragon	Physical	60	90	10	Normal
TM87	Swagger	Normal	Status	—	90	15	Normal
TM88	Sleep Talk	Normal	Status	—	—	10	Self
TM90	Substitute	Normal	Status	—	—	10	Self
TM94	Rock Smash	Fighting	Physical	40	100	15	Normal
TM97	Dark Pulse	Dark	Special	80	100	15	Normal
TM100	Confide	Normal	Status	—	—	20	Normal
HM04	Strength	Normal	Physical	80	100	15	Normal

● MOVES TAUGHT BY PEOPLE

Name	Type	Kind	Pow.	Acc.	PP	Range
Draco Meteor	Dragon	Special	130	90	5	Normal

Mountain Kalos 144
Brutal Pokémon
☑ Hydreigon

TYPE **Dark** **Dragon**

ABILITY
Levitate

HIDDEN ABILITY
None

HEIGHT: 5'11"   WEIGHT: 352.7 lbs.
GENDER: ♂ / ♀

X The heads on their arms do not have brains. They use all three heads to consume and destroy everything.

Y It responds to movement by attacking. This scary, three-headed Pokémon devours everything in its path!

STAT GROWTH RATES
HP	▪▪▪▪
Attack	▪▪▪▪
Defense	▪▪▪▪
Sp. Atk	▪▪▪▪▪
Sp. Def	▪▪▪▪
Speed	▪▪▪▪

EGG GROUP
Dragon

EVOLUTION

Lv. 50   Lv. 64

Deino   Zweilous   Hydreigon

ITEMS SOMETIMES HELD BY WILD POKÉMON
None

Damage taken in normal battles
Normal	×1
Fire	×0.5
Water	×0.5
Grass	×0.5
Electric	×0.5
Ice	×2
Fighting	×2
Poison	×1
Ground	×1
Flying	×1
Psychic	×0
Bug	×2
Rock	×1
Ghost	×1
Dragon	×2
Dark	×0.5
Steel	×1
Fairy	×4

Damage taken in Inverse Battles
Normal	×1
Fire	×2
Water	×2
Grass	×2
Electric	×2
Ice	×0.5
Fighting	×0.5
Poison	×1
Ground	×1
Flying	×1
Psychic	×2
Bug	×0.5
Rock	×2
Ghost	×2
Dragon	×0.5
Dark	×2
Steel	×1
Fairy	×0.25

Can be used in
Inverse Battle
Sky Battle
Battle Chateau
Battle Institute
Battle Maison
Random Matchup

How to obtain for your Mountain Kalos Pokédex

Catch it when it ambushes you outside on Victory Road.

Catch it when it ambushes you outside on Victory Road.

Same form for ♂ / ♀

● LEVEL-UP MOVES

Lv.	Name	Type	Kind	Pow.	Acc.	PP	Range
1	Outrage	Dragon	Physical	120	100	10	1 Random
1	Hyper Voice	Normal	Special	90	100	10	Many Others
1	Tri Attack	Normal	Special	80	100	10	Normal
1	Focus Energy	Normal	Status	—	—	30	Self
1	Dragon Rage	Dragon	Special	—	100	10	Normal
1	Bite	Dark	Physical	60	100	25	Normal
4	Focus Energy	Normal	Status	—	—	30	Self
9	Bite	Dark	Physical	60	100	25	Normal
12	Headbutt	Normal	Physical	70	100	15	Normal
17	Dragon Breath	Dragon	Special	60	100	20	Normal
20	Roar	Normal	Status	—	—	20	Normal
25	Crunch	Dark	Physical	80	100	15	Normal
32	Slam	Normal	Physical	80	75	20	Normal
32	Dragon Pulse	Dragon	Special	85	100	10	Normal
38	Work Up	Normal	Status	—	—	30	Self
42	Dragon Rush	Dragon	Physical	100	75	10	Normal
48	Body Slam	Normal	Physical	85	100	15	Normal
55	Scary Face	Normal	Status	—	100	10	Normal
68	Hyper Voice	Normal	Special	90	100	10	Many Others
79	Outrage	Dragon	Physical	120	100	10	1 Random

● TM & HM MOVES

No.	Name	Type	Kind	Pow.	Acc.	PP	Range
TM05	Roar	Normal	Status	—	—	20	Normal
TM06	Toxic	Poison	Status	—	90	10	Normal
TM10	Hidden Power	Normal	Special	60	100	15	Normal
TM11	Sunny Day	Fire	Status	—	—	5	Both Sides
TM12	Taunt	Dark	Status	—	100	20	Normal
TM15	Hyper Beam	Normal	Special	150	90	5	Normal
TM17	Protect	Normal	Status	—	—	10	Self
TM18	Rain Dance	Water	Status	—	—	5	Both Sides
TM19	Roost	Flying	Status	—	—	10	Self
TM21	Frustration	Normal	Physical	—	100	20	Normal
TM26	Earthquake	Ground	Physical	100	100	10	Adjacent
TM27	Return	Normal	Physical	—	100	20	Normal
TM32	Double Team	Normal	Status	—	—	15	Self
TM33	Reflect	Psychic	Status	—	—	20	Your Side
TM35	Flamethrower	Fire	Special	90	100	15	Normal
TM38	Fire Blast	Fire	Special	110	85	5	Normal
TM39	Rock Tomb	Rock	Physical	60	95	15	Normal
TM41	Torment	Dark	Status	—	100	15	Normal
TM42	Facade	Normal	Physical	70	100	20	Normal
TM44	Rest	Psychic	Status	—	—	10	Self
TM45	Attract	Normal	Status	—	100	15	Normal
TM46	Thief	Dark	Physical	60	100	25	Normal
TM48	Round	Normal	Special	60	100	15	Normal
TM49	Echoed Voice	Normal	Special	40	100	15	Normal
TM51	Steel Wing	Steel	Physical	70	90	25	Normal
TM52	Focus Blast	Fighting	Special	120	70	5	Normal
TM57	Charge Beam	Electric	Special	50	90	10	Normal
TM59	Incinerate	Fire	Special	60	100	15	Many Others
TM62	Acrobatics	Flying	Physical	55	100	15	Normal
TM66	Payback	Dark	Physical	50	100	10	Normal
TM68	Giga Impact	Normal	Physical	150	90	5	Normal
TM71	Stone Edge	Rock	Physical	100	80	5	Normal
TM73	Thunder Wave	Electric	Status	—	100	20	Normal
TM77	Psych Up	Normal	Status	—	—	10	Normal
TM78	Bulldoze	Ground	Physical	60	100	20	Adjacent
TM80	Rock Slide	Rock	Physical	75	90	10	Many Others
TM82	Dragon Tail	Dragon	Physical	60	90	10	Normal
TM87	Swagger	Normal	Status	—	90	15	Normal
TM88	Sleep Talk	Normal	Status	—	—	10	Self
TM89	U-turn	Bug	Physical	70	100	20	Normal
TM90	Substitute	Normal	Status	—	—	10	Self
TM91	Flash Cannon	Steel	Special	80	100	10	Normal
TM94	Rock Smash	Fighting	Physical	40	100	15	Normal
TM97	Dark Pulse	Dark	Special	80	100	15	Normal
TM100	Confide	Normal	Status	—	—	20	Normal
HM02	Fly	Flying	Physical	90	95	15	Normal
HM03	Surf	Water	Special	90	100	15	Adjacent
HM04	Strength	Normal	Physical	80	100	15	Normal

● MOVES TAUGHT BY PEOPLE

Name	Type	Kind	Pow.	Acc.	PP	Range
Draco Meteor	Dragon	Special	130	90	5	Normal

Dragon Pokémon

 Dratini

HEIGHT: 5'11"   WEIGHT: 7.3 lbs.
GENDER: ♂/♀

TYPE Dragon

ABILITY
Shed Skin

HIDDEN ABILITY
Marvel Scale

STAT GROWTH RATES
HP	▪▪
Attack	▪▪▪
Defense	▪▪
Sp. Atk	▪▪
Sp. Def	▪▪
Speed	▪▪▪

EGG GROUPS
Water 1, Dragon

 It is called the "Mirage Pokémon" because so few have seen it. Its shed skin has been found.

Ⓨ This Pokémon is full of life energy. It continually sheds its skin and grows steadily larger.

EVOLUTION

Lv. 30   Lv. 55

Dratini   Dragonair   Dragonite

ITEMS SOMETIMES HELD BY WILD POKÉMON
Dragon Scale

Damage taken in normal battles	
Normal	×1
Fire	×0.5
Water	×0.5
Grass	×0.5
Electric	×0.5
Ice	×2
Fighting	×1
Poison	×1
Ground	×1
Flying	×1
Psychic	×1
Bug	×1
Rock	×1
Ghost	×1
Dragon	×2
Dark	×1
Steel	×1
Fairy	×2

Damage taken in Inverse Battles	
Normal	×1
Fire	×2
Water	×2
Grass	×2
Electric	×2
Ice	×0.5
Fighting	×1
Poison	×1
Ground	×1
Flying	×1
Psychic	×1
Bug	×1
Rock	×1
Ghost	×1
Dragon	×0.5
Dark	×1
Steel	×1
Fairy	×0.5

Can be used in	
Inverse Battle	Battle Institute
—	Battle Maison
Battle Chateau	Random Matchup

Same form for ♂/♀

How to obtain for your Mountain Kalos Pokédex

Catch using a Good Rod on Route 21.

Catch using a Good Rod on Route 21.

● LEVEL-UP MOVES

Lv.	Name	Type	Kind	Pow.	Acc.	PP	Range
1	Wrap	Normal	Physical	15	90	20	Normal
1	Leer	Normal	Status	—	100	30	Many Others
5	Thunder Wave	Electric	Status	—	100	20	Normal
11	Twister	Dragon	Special	40	100	20	Many Others
15	Dragon Rage	Dragon	Special	—	100	10	Normal
21	Slam	Normal	Physical	80	75	20	Normal
25	Agility	Psychic	Status	—	—	30	Self
31	Dragon Tail	Dragon	Physical	60	90	10	Normal
35	Aqua Tail	Water	Physical	90	90	10	Normal
41	Dragon Rush	Dragon	Physical	100	75	10	Normal
45	Safeguard	Normal	Status	—	—	25	Your Side
51	Dragon Dance	Dragon	Status	—	—	20	Self
55	Outrage	Dragon	Physical	120	100	10	1 Random
61	Hyper Beam	Normal	Special	150	90	5	Normal

● TM & HM MOVES

No.	Name	Type	Kind	Pow.	Acc.	PP	Range
TM06	Toxic	Poison	Status	—	90	10	Normal
TM07	Hail	Ice	Status	—	—	10	Both Sides
TM10	Hidden Power	Normal	Special	60	100	15	Normal
TM11	Sunny Day	Fire	Status	—	—	5	Both Sides
TM13	Ice Beam	Ice	Special	90	100	10	Normal
TM14	Blizzard	Ice	Special	110	70	5	Many Others
TM15	Hyper Beam	Normal	Special	150	90	5	Normal
TM16	Light Screen	Psychic	Status	—	—	30	Your Side
TM17	Protect	Normal	Status	—	—	10	Self
TM18	Rain Dance	Water	Status	—	—	5	Both Sides
TM20	Safeguard	Normal	Status	—	—	25	Your Side
TM21	Frustration	Normal	Physical	—	100	20	Normal
TM24	Thunderbolt	Electric	Special	90	100	15	Normal
TM25	Thunder	Electric	Special	110	70	10	Normal
TM27	Return	Normal	Physical	—	100	20	Normal
TM32	Double Team	Normal	Status	—	—	15	Self
TM35	Flamethrower	Fire	Special	90	100	15	Normal
TM38	Fire Blast	Fire	Special	110	85	5	Normal
TM42	Facade	Normal	Physical	70	100	20	Normal
TM44	Rest	Psychic	Status	—	—	10	Self
TM45	Attract	Normal	Status	—	100	15	Normal
TM48	Round	Normal	Special	60	100	15	Normal
TM59	Incinerate	Fire	Special	60	100	15	Many Others
TM73	Thunder Wave	Electric	Status	—	100	20	Normal
TM82	Dragon Tail	Dragon	Physical	60	90	10	Normal
TM87	Swagger	Normal	Status	—	90	15	Normal
TM88	Sleep Talk	Normal	Status	—	—	10	Self
TM90	Substitute	Normal	Status	—	—	10	Self
TM100	Confide	Normal	Status	—	—	20	Normal
HM03	Surf	Water	Special	90	100	15	Adjacent
HM05	Waterfall	Water	Physical	80	100	15	Normal

● MOVES TAUGHT BY PEOPLE

Name	Type	Kind	Pow.	Acc.	PP	Range
Draco Meteor	Dragon	Special	130	90	5	Normal

● EGG MOVES

Name	Type	Kind	Pow.	Acc.	PP	Range
Mist	Ice	Status	—	—	30	Your Side
Haze	Ice	Status	—	—	30	Both Sides
Supersonic	Normal	Status	—	55	20	Normal
Dragon Breath	Dragon	Special	60	100	20	Normal
Dragon Dance	Dragon	Status	—	—	20	Self
Dragon Rush	Dragon	Physical	100	75	10	Normal
Extreme Speed	Normal	Physical	80	100	5	Normal
Water Pulse	Water	Special	60	100	20	Normal
Aqua Jet	Water	Physical	40	100	20	Normal
Dragon Pulse	Dragon	Special	85	100	10	Normal
Iron Tail	Steel	Physical	100	75	15	Normal

AFTER THE HALL OF FAME

CENTRAL KALOS

COASTAL KALOS

MOUNTAIN KALOS

145 | Dratini

ADVENTURE DATA

Mountain Kalos 146
Dragon Pokémon
▽ Dragonair

HEIGHT: 13'01"　WEIGHT: 36.4 lbs.
GENDER: ♂/♀

Its crystalline orbs appear to give this Pokémon the power to freely control the weather.

A mystical Pokémon that exudes a gentle aura. It is said to have the ability to change the weather.

TYPE **Dragon**

ABILITY
Shed Skin

HIDDEN ABILITY
Marvel Scale

STAT GROWTH RATES
HP	■■■
Attack	■■■■
Defense	■■■
Sp. Atk	■■■
Sp. Def	■■■
Speed	■■■■

EGG GROUPS
Water 1, Dragon

EVOLUTION

Dratini　Lv. 30　Dragonair　Lv. 55　Dragonite

ITEMS SOMETIMES HELD BY WILD POKÉMON
Dragon Scale

Damage taken in normal battles	
Normal	×1
Fire	×0.5
Water	×0.5
Grass	×0.5
Electric	×0.5
Ice	×2
Fighting	×1
Poison	×1
Ground	×1
Flying	×1
Psychic	×1
Bug	×1
Rock	×1
Ghost	×1
Dragon	×2
Dark	×1
Steel	×1
Fairy	×2

Damage taken in Inverse Battles	
Normal	×1
Fire	×2
Water	×2
Grass	×2
Electric	×2
Ice	×0.5
Fighting	×1
Poison	×1
Ground	×1
Flying	×1
Psychic	×1
Bug	×1
Rock	×1
Ghost	×1
Dragon	×0.5
Dark	×1
Steel	×1
Fairy	×0.5

Can be used in	
Inverse Battle	Battle Institute
—	Battle Maison
Battle Chateau	Random Matchup

Same form for ♂/♀

How to obtain for your Mountain Kalos Pokédex

❶ Catch using a Super Rod on Route 21.
❷ Level up Dratini to Lv. 30.

❶ Catch using a Super Rod on Route 21.
❷ Level up Dratini to Lv. 30.

● LEVEL-UP MOVES

Lv.	Name	Type	Kind	Pow.	Acc.	PP	Range
1	Wrap	Normal	Physical	15	90	20	Normal
1	Leer	Normal	Status	—	100	30	Many Others
1	Thunder Wave	Electric	Status	—	100	20	Normal
1	Twister	Dragon	Special	40	100	20	Many Others
5	Thunder Wave	Electric	Status	—	100	20	Normal
11	Twister	Dragon	Special	40	100	20	Many Others
15	Dragon Rage	Dragon	Special	—	100	10	Normal
21	Slam	Normal	Physical	80	75	20	Normal
25	Agility	Psychic	Status	—	—	30	Self
33	Dragon Tail	Dragon	Physical	60	90	10	Normal
39	Aqua Tail	Water	Physical	90	90	10	Normal
47	Dragon Rush	Dragon	Physical	100	75	10	Normal
53	Safeguard	Normal	Status	—	—	25	Your Side
61	Dragon Dance	Dragon	Status	—	—	20	Self
67	Outrage	Dragon	Physical	120	100	10	1 Random
75	Hyper Beam	Normal	Special	150	90	5	Normal

● TM & HM MOVES

No.	Name	Type	Kind	Pow.	Acc.	PP	Range
TM06	Toxic	Poison	Status	—	90	10	Normal
TM07	Hail	Ice	Status	—	—	10	Both Sides
TM10	Hidden Power	Normal	Special	60	100	15	Normal
TM11	Sunny Day	Fire	Status	—	—	5	Both Sides
TM13	Ice Beam	Ice	Special	90	100	10	Normal
TM14	Blizzard	Ice	Special	110	70	5	Many Others
TM15	Hyper Beam	Normal	Special	150	90	5	Normal
TM16	Light Screen	Psychic	Status	—	—	30	Your Side
TM17	Protect	Normal	Status	—	—	10	Self
TM18	Rain Dance	Water	Status	—	—	5	Both Sides
TM20	Safeguard	Normal	Status	—	—	25	Your Side
TM21	Frustration	Normal	Physical	—	100	20	Normal
TM24	Thunderbolt	Electric	Special	90	100	15	Normal
TM25	Thunder	Electric	Special	110	70	10	Normal
TM27	Return	Normal	Physical	—	100	20	Normal
TM32	Double Team	Normal	Status	—	—	15	Self
TM35	Flamethrower	Fire	Special	90	100	15	Normal
TM38	Fire Blast	Fire	Special	110	85	5	Normal
TM42	Facade	Normal	Physical	70	100	20	Normal
TM44	Rest	Psychic	Status	—	—	10	Self
TM45	Attract	Normal	Status	—	100	15	Normal
TM48	Round	Normal	Special	60	100	15	Normal
TM59	Incinerate	Fire	Special	60	100	15	Many Others
TM73	Thunder Wave	Electric	Status	—	100	20	Normal
TM82	Dragon Tail	Dragon	Physical	60	90	10	Normal
TM87	Swagger	Normal	Status	—	90	15	Normal
TM88	Sleep Talk	Normal	Status	—	—	10	Self
TM90	Substitute	Normal	Status	—	—	10	Self
TM100	Confide	Normal	Status	—	—	20	Normal
HM03	Surf	Water	Special	90	100	15	Adjacent
HM05	Waterfall	Water	Physical	80	100	15	Normal

● MOVES TAUGHT BY PEOPLE

Name	Type	Kind	Pow.	Acc.	PP	Range
Draco Meteor	Dragon	Special	130	90	5	Normal

Mountain Kalos
147
Dragon Pokémon
 Dragonite

HEIGHT: 7'03"   WEIGHT: 463.0 lbs.
GENDER: ♂/♀

TYPE	Dragon	Flying

ABILITY
Inner Focus

HIDDEN ABILITY
Multiscale

STAT GROWTH RATES

HP	■■■
Attack	■■■■■■■
Defense	■■■■
Sp. Atk	■■■■
Sp. Def	■■■■
Speed	■■■■

EGG GROUPS
Water 1, Dragon

X It can fly in spite of its big and bulky physique. It circles the globe in just 16 hours.

Y It is said to make its home somewhere in the sea. It guides crews of shipwrecks to shore.

▲ EVOLUTION

	Lv. 30	Lv. 55
Dratini	Dragonair	Dragonite

ITEMS SOMETIMES HELD BY WILD POKÉMON
None

Damage taken in normal battles		Damage taken in Inverse Battles	
Normal	×1	Normal	×1
Fire	×0.5	Fire	×2
Water	×0.5	Water	×2
Grass	×0.25	Grass	×4
Electric	×1	Electric	×1
Ice	×4	Ice	×0.25
Fighting	×0.5	Fighting	×2
Poison	×1	Poison	×1
Ground	×0	Ground	×2
Flying	×1	Flying	×1
Psychic	×1	Psychic	×1
Bug	×0.5	Bug	×2
Rock	×2	Rock	×0.5
Ghost	×1	Ghost	×1
Dragon	×2	Dragon	×0.5
Dark	×1	Dark	×1
Steel	×1	Steel	×1
Fairy	×2	Fairy	×0.5

Can be used in	
Inverse Battle	Battle Institute
Sky Battle	Battle Maison
Battle Chateau	Random Matchup

Same form for ♂/♀

How to obtain for your Mountain Kalos Pokédex

Level up Dragonair to Lv. 55.   Level up Dragonair to Lv. 55.

X   Y

● LEVEL-UP MOVES

Lv.	Name	Type	Kind	Pow.	Acc.	PP	Range
1	Hurricane	Flying	Special	110	70	10	Many Others
1	Fire Punch	Fire	Physical	75	100	15	Normal
1	Thunder Punch	Electric	Physical	75	100	15	Normal
1	Roost	Flying	Status	—	—	10	Self
1	Wrap	Normal	Physical	15	90	20	Normal
1	Leer	Normal	Status	—	100	30	Many Others
1	Thunder Wave	Electric	Status	—	100	20	Normal
1	Twister	Dragon	Special	40	100	20	Many Others
5	Thunder Wave	Electric	Status	—	100	20	Normal
11	Twister	Dragon	Special	40	100	20	Many Others
15	Dragon Rage	Dragon	Special	—	100	10	Normal
21	Slam	Normal	Physical	80	75	20	Normal
25	Agility	Psychic	Status	—	—	30	Self
33	Dragon Tail	Dragon	Physical	60	90	10	Normal
39	Aqua Tail	Water	Physical	90	90	10	Normal
47	Dragon Rush	Dragon	Physical	100	75	10	Normal
53	Safeguard	Normal	Status	—	—	25	Your Side
55	Wing Attack	Flying	Physical	60	100	35	Normal
61	Dragon Dance	Dragon	Status	—	—	20	Self
67	Outrage	Dragon	Physical	120	100	10	1 Random
75	Hyper Beam	Normal	Special	150	90	5	Normal
81	Hurricane	Flying	Special	110	70	10	Many Others

● TM & HM MOVES

No.	Name	Type	Kind	Pow.	Acc.	PP	Range
TM01	Hone Claws	Dark	Status	—	—	15	Self
TM02	Dragon Claw	Dragon	Physical	80	100	15	Normal
TM05	Roar	Normal	Status	—	—	20	Normal
TM06	Toxic	Poison	Status	—	90	10	Normal
TM07	Hail	Ice	Status	—	—	10	Both Sides
TM10	Hidden Power	Normal	Special	60	100	15	Normal
TM11	Sunny Day	Fire	Status	—	—	5	Both Sides
TM13	Ice Beam	Ice	Special	90	100	10	Normal

No.	Name	Type	Kind	Pow.	Acc.	PP	Range
TM14	Blizzard	Ice	Special	110	70	5	Many Others
TM15	Hyper Beam	Normal	Special	150	90	5	Normal
TM16	Light Screen	Psychic	Status	—	—	30	Your Side
TM17	Protect	Normal	Status	—	—	10	Self
TM18	Rain Dance	Water	Status	—	—	5	Both Sides
TM19	Roost	Flying	Status	—	—	10	Self
TM20	Safeguard	Normal	Status	—	—	25	Your Side
TM21	Frustration	Normal	Physical	—	100	20	Normal
TM24	Thunderbolt	Electric	Special	90	100	15	Normal
TM25	Thunder	Electric	Special	110	70	10	Normal
TM26	Earthquake	Ground	Physical	100	100	10	Adjacent
TM27	Return	Normal	Physical	—	100	20	Normal
TM31	Brick Break	Fighting	Physical	75	100	15	Normal
TM32	Double Team	Normal	Status	—	—	15	Self
TM35	Flamethrower	Fire	Special	90	100	15	Normal
TM37	Sandstorm	Rock	Status	—	—	10	Both Sides
TM38	Fire Blast	Fire	Special	110	85	5	Normal
TM39	Rock Tomb	Rock	Physical	60	95	15	Normal
TM40	Aerial Ace	Flying	Physical	60	—	20	Normal
TM42	Facade	Normal	Physical	70	100	20	Normal
TM44	Rest	Psychic	Status	—	—	10	Self
TM45	Attract	Normal	Status	—	100	15	Normal
TM48	Round	Normal	Special	60	100	15	Normal
TM51	Steel Wing	Steel	Physical	70	90	25	Normal
TM52	Focus Blast	Fighting	Special	120	70	5	Normal
TM56	Fling	Dark	Physical	—	100	10	Normal
TM58	Sky Drop	Flying	Physical	60	100	10	Normal
TM59	Incinerate	Fire	Special	60	100	15	Many Others
TM68	Giga Impact	Normal	Physical	150	90	5	Normal
TM71	Stone Edge	Rock	Physical	100	80	5	Normal
TM73	Thunder Wave	Electric	Status	—	100	20	Normal
TM78	Bulldoze	Ground	Physical	60	100	20	Adjacent
TM80	Rock Slide	Rock	Physical	75	90	10	Many Others

No.	Name	Type	Kind	Pow.	Acc.	PP	Range
TM82	Dragon Tail	Dragon	Physical	60	90	10	Normal
TM87	Swagger	Normal	Status	—	90	15	Normal
TM88	Sleep Talk	Normal	Status	—	—	10	Self
TM90	Substitute	Normal	Status	—	—	10	Self
TM94	Rock Smash	Fighting	Physical	40	100	15	Normal
TM98	Power-Up Punch	Fighting	Physical	40	100	20	Normal
TM100	Confide	Normal	Status	—	—	20	Normal
HM01	Cut	Normal	Physical	50	95	30	Normal
HM02	Fly	Flying	Physical	90	95	15	Normal
HM03	Surf	Water	Special	90	100	15	Adjacent
HM04	Strength	Normal	Physical	80	100	15	Normal
HM05	Waterfall	Water	Physical	80	100	15	Normal

● MOVES TAUGHT BY PEOPLE

Name	Type	Kind	Pow.	Acc.	PP	Range
Draco Meteor	Dragon	Special	130	90	5	Normal

AFTER THE HALL OF FAME

CENTRAL KALOS

COASTAL KALOS

MOUNTAIN KALOS

147 Dragonite

ADVENTURE DATA

AFTER THE HALL OF FAME

CENTRAL KALOS

COASTAL KALOS

MOUNTAIN KALOS

148

Xerneas

ADVENTURE DATA

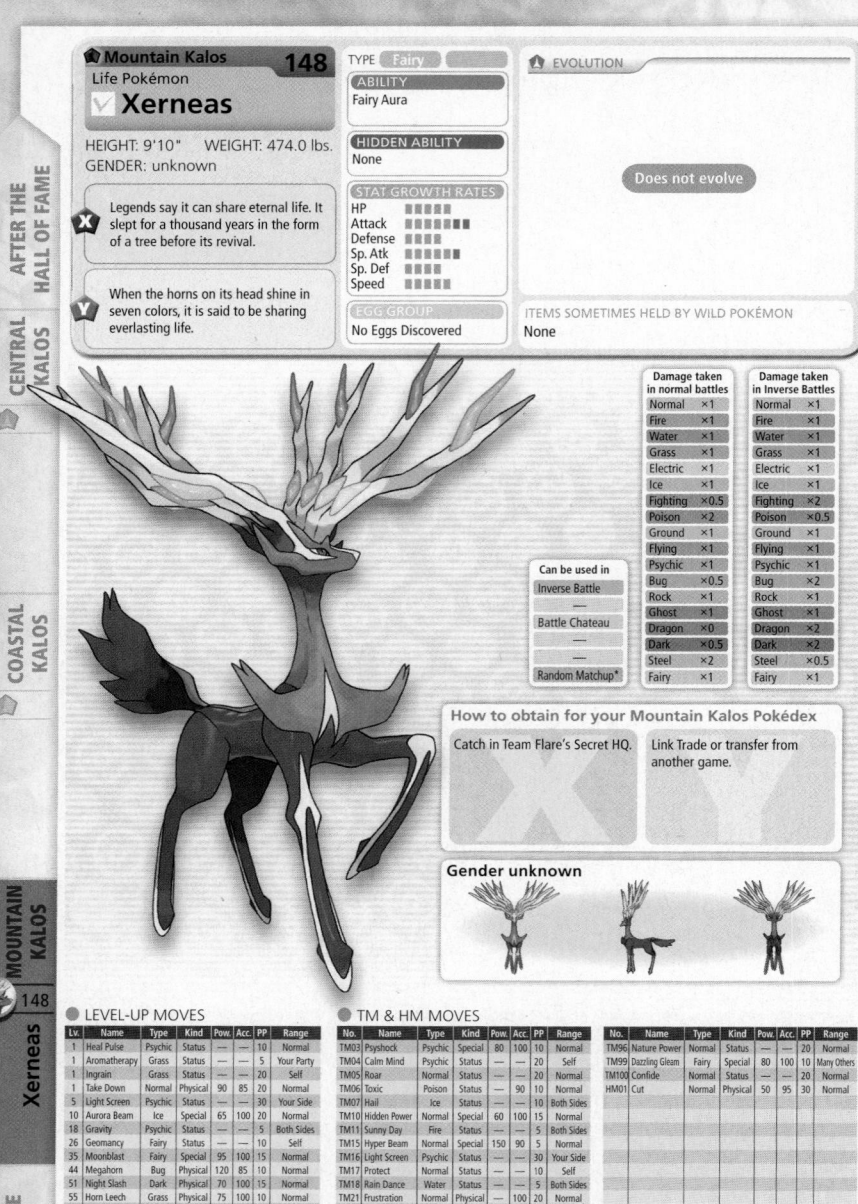

Mountain Kalos 148
Life Pokémon

☑ Xerneas

HEIGHT: 9'10"   WEIGHT: 474.0 lbs.
GENDER: unknown

X Legends say it can share eternal life. It slept for a thousand years in the form of a tree before its revival.

Y When the horns on its head shine in seven colors, it is said to be sharing everlasting life.

TYPE Fairy

ABILITY
Fairy Aura

HIDDEN ABILITY
None

STAT GROWTH RATES
HP ▪▪▪▪▪
Attack ▪▪▪▪▪▪▪
Defense ▪▪▪▪
Sp. Atk ▪▪▪▪▪▪
Sp. Def ▪▪▪▪▪▪
Speed ▪▪▪▪▪

EGG GROUP
No Eggs Discovered

EVOLUTION

Does not evolve

ITEMS SOMETIMES HELD BY WILD POKÉMON
None

Damage taken in normal battles		Damage taken in Inverse Battles	
Normal	×1	Normal	×1
Fire	×1	Fire	×1
Water	×1	Water	×1
Grass	×1	Grass	×1
Electric	×1	Electric	×1
Ice	×1	Ice	×1
Fighting	×0.5	Fighting	×2
Poison	×2	Poison	×0.5
Ground	×1	Ground	×1
Flying	×1	Flying	×1
Psychic	×1	Psychic	×1
Bug	×0.5	Bug	×2
Rock	×1	Rock	×1
Ghost	×1	Ghost	×1
Dragon	×0	Dragon	×2
Dark	×0.5	Dark	×2
Steel	×2	Steel	×0.5
Fairy	×1	Fairy	×1

Can be used in
| Inverse Battle |
| — |
| Battle Chateau |
| — |
| — |
| Random Matchup* |

How to obtain for your Mountain Kalos Pokédex

Catch in Team Flare's Secret HQ.

Link Trade or transfer from another game.

Gender unknown

● LEVEL-UP MOVES

Lv.	Name	Type	Kind	Pow.	Acc.	PP	Range
1	Heal Pulse	Psychic	Status	—	—	10	Normal
1	Aromatherapy	Grass	Status	—	—	5	Your Party
1	Ingrain	Grass	Status	—	—	20	Self
1	Take Down	Normal	Physical	90	85	20	Normal
5	Light Screen	Psychic	Status	—	—	30	Your Side
10	Aurora Beam	Ice	Special	65	100	20	Normal
18	Gravity	Psychic	Status	—	—	5	Both Sides
26	Geomancy	Fairy	Status	—	—	10	Self
35	Moonblast	Fairy	Special	95	100	15	Normal
44	Megahorn	Bug	Physical	120	85	10	Normal
51	Night Slash	Dark	Physical	70	100	15	Normal
55	Horn Leech	Grass	Physical	75	100	10	Normal
59	Psych Up	Normal	Status	—	—	10	Normal
63	Misty Terrain	Fairy	Status	—	—	10	Both Sides
72	Nature Power	Normal	Status	—	—	20	Normal
80	Close Combat	Fighting	Physical	120	100	5	Normal
88	Giga Impact	Normal	Physical	150	90	5	Normal
93	Outrage	Dragon	Physical	120	100	10	1 Random

● TM & HM MOVES

No.	Name	Type	Kind	Pow.	Acc.	PP	Range
TM03	Psyshock	Psychic	Special	80	100	10	Normal
TM04	Calm Mind	Psychic	Status	—	—	20	Self
TM05	Roar	Normal	Status	—	—	20	Normal
TM06	Toxic	Poison	Status	—	90	10	Normal
TM07	Hail	Ice	Status	—	—	10	Both Sides
TM10	Hidden Power	Normal	Special	60	100	15	Normal
TM11	Sunny Day	Fire	Status	—	—	5	Both Sides
TM15	Hyper Beam	Normal	Special	150	90	5	Normal
TM16	Light Screen	Psychic	Status	—	—	30	Your Side
TM17	Protect	Normal	Status	—	—	10	Self
TM18	Rain Dance	Water	Status	—	—	5	Both Sides
TM21	Frustration	Normal	Physical	—	100	20	Normal
TM24	Thunderbolt	Electric	Special	90	100	15	Normal
TM25	Thunder	Electric	Special	110	70	10	Normal
TM27	Return	Normal	Physical	—	100	20	Normal
TM29	Psychic	Psychic	Special	90	100	10	Normal
TM32	Double Team	Normal	Status	—	—	15	Self
TM33	Reflect	Psychic	Status	—	—	20	Your Side
TM42	Facade	Normal	Physical	70	100	20	Normal
TM44	Rest	Psychic	Status	—	—	10	Self
TM48	Round	Normal	Special	60	100	15	Normal
TM49	Echoed Voice	Normal	Special	40	100	15	Normal
TM52	Focus Blast	Fighting	Special	120	70	5	Normal
TM68	Giga Impact	Normal	Physical	150	90	5	Normal
TM70	Flash	Normal	Status	—	100	20	Normal
TM73	Thunder Wave	Electric	Status	—	100	20	Normal
TM77	Psych Up	Normal	Status	—	—	10	Normal
TM80	Rock Slide	Rock	Physical	75	90	10	Many Others
TM86	Grass Knot	Grass	Special	—	100	20	Normal
TM87	Swagger	Normal	Status	—	90	15	Normal
TM88	Sleep Talk	Normal	Status	—	—	10	Self
TM90	Substitute	Normal	Status	—	—	10	Self
TM91	Flash Cannon	Steel	Special	80	100	10	Normal
TM96	Nature Power	Normal	Status	—	—	20	Normal
TM99	Dazzling Gleam	Fairy	Special	80	100	10	Many Others
TM100	Confide	Normal	Status	—	—	20	Normal
HM01	Cut	Normal	Physical	50	95	30	Normal

● MOVES TAUGHT BY PEOPLE

Name	Type	Kind	Pow.	Acc.	PP	Range

*This Pokémon can only be used in Free Battles.

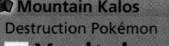

Mountain Kalos **149**

Destruction Pokémon

☑ Yveltal

HEIGHT: 19'00" WEIGHT: 447.5 lbs.
GENDER: unknown

X When this legendary Pokémon's wings and tail feathers spread wide and glow red, it absorbs the life force of living creatures.

Y When its life comes to an end, it absorbs the life energy of every living thing and turns into a cocoon once more.

TYPE **Dark** **Flying**

ABILITY
Dark Aura

HIDDEN ABILITY
None

STAT GROWTH RATES
HP	▪▪▪▪▪
Attack	▪▪▪▪▪▪
Defense	▪▪▪▪
Sp. Atk	▪▪▪▪▪▪
Sp. Def	▪▪▪▪
Speed	▪▪▪▪▪

EGG GROUP
No Eggs Discovered

EVOLUTION

Does not evolve

ITEMS SOMETIMES HELD BY WILD POKÉMON
None

Damage taken in normal battles		Damage taken in Inverse Battles	
Normal	×1	Normal	×1
Fire	×1	Fire	×1
Water	×1	Water	×1
Grass	×0.5	Grass	×2
Electric	×2	Electric	×0.5
Ice	×2	Ice	×0.5
Fighting	×1	Fighting	×1
Poison	×1	Poison	×1
Ground	×0	Ground	×2
Flying	×1	Flying	×1
Psychic	×0	Psychic	×2
Bug	×1	Bug	×1
Rock	×2	Rock	×0.5
Ghost	×1	Ghost	×1
Dragon	×1	Dragon	×1
Dark	×0.5	Dark	×2
Steel	×1	Steel	×1
Fairy	×2	Fairy	×0.5

Can be used in
Inverse Battle
Sky Battle
Battle Chateau
—
—
Random Matchup*

How to obtain for your Mountain Kalos Pokédex

Link Trade or transfer from another game.

Catch in Team Flare's Secret HQ.

Gender unknown

● LEVEL-UP MOVES

Lv.	Name	Type	Kind	Pow.	Acc.	PP	Range
1	Hurricane	Flying	Special	110	70	10	Normal
1	Razor Wind	Normal	Special	80	100	10	Many Others
1	Taunt	Dark	Status	—	100	20	Normal
1	Roost	Flying	Status	—	—	10	Self
5	Double Team	Normal	Status	—	—	15	Self
10	Air Slash	Flying	Special	75	95	15	Normal
18	Snarl	Dark	Special	55	95	15	Many Others
26	Oblivion Wing	Flying	Special	80	100	10	Normal
35	Disable	Normal	Status	—	100	20	Normal
44	Dark Pulse	Dark	Special	80	100	15	Normal
51	Foul Play	Dark	Physical	95	100	15	Normal
55	Phantom Force	Ghost	Physical	90	100	10	Normal
59	Psychic	Psychic	Special	90	100	10	Normal
63	Dragon Rush	Dragon	Physical	100	75	10	Normal
72	Focus Blast	Fighting	Special	120	70	5	Normal
80	Sucker Punch	Dark	Physical	80	100	5	Normal
88	Hyper Beam	Normal	Special	150	90	5	Normal
93	Sky Attack	Flying	Physical	140	90	5	Normal

● TM & HM MOVES

No.	Name	Type	Kind	Pow.	Acc.	PP	Range
TM01	Hone Claws	Dark	Status	—	—	15	Self
TM02	Dragon Claw	Dragon	Physical	80	100	15	Normal
TM06	Toxic	Poison	Status	—	90	10	Normal
TM10	Hidden Power	Normal	Special	60	100	15	Normal
TM11	Sunny Day	Fire	Status	—	—	5	Both Sides
TM12	Taunt	Dark	Status	—	100	20	Normal
TM15	Hyper Beam	Normal	Special	150	90	5	Normal
TM17	Protect	Normal	Status	—	—	10	Self
TM18	Rain Dance	Water	Status	—	—	5	Both Sides
TM19	Roost	Flying	Status	—	—	10	Self
TM21	Frustration	Normal	Physical	—	100	20	Normal
TM27	Return	Normal	Physical	—	100	20	Normal
TM29	Psychic	Psychic	Special	90	100	10	Normal
TM30	Shadow Ball	Ghost	Special	80	100	15	Normal
TM32	Double Team	Normal	Status	—	—	15	Self
TM40	Aerial Ace	Flying	Physical	60	—	20	Normal
TM41	Torment	Dark	Status	—	100	15	Normal
TM42	Facade	Normal	Physical	70	100	20	Normal
TM44	Rest	Psychic	Status	—	—	10	Self
TM46	Thief	Dark	Physical	60	100	25	Normal
TM48	Round	Normal	Special	60	100	15	Normal
TM51	Steel Wing	Steel	Physical	70	90	25	Normal
TM52	Focus Blast	Fighting	Special	120	70	5	Normal
TM58	Sky Drop	Flying	Physical	60	100	10	Normal
TM62	Acrobatics	Flying	Physical	55	100	15	Normal
TM63	Embargo	Dark	Status	—	100	15	Normal
TM65	Shadow Claw	Ghost	Physical	70	100	15	Normal
TM68	Giga Impact	Normal	Physical	150	90	5	Normal
TM80	Rock Slide	Rock	Physical	75	90	10	Many Others
TM85	Dream Eater	Psychic	Special	100	100	15	Normal
TM87	Swagger	Normal	Status	—	90	15	Normal
TM88	Sleep Talk	Normal	Status	—	—	10	Self
TM89	U-turn	Bug	Physical	70	100	20	Normal

No.	Name	Type	Kind	Pow.	Acc.	PP	Range
TM90	Substitute	Normal	Status	—	—	10	Self
TM95	Snarl	Dark	Special	55	95	15	Many Others
TM97	Dark Pulse	Dark	Special	80	100	15	Normal
TM100	Confide	Normal	Status	—	—	20	Normal
HM01	Cut	Normal	Physical	50	95	30	Normal
HM02	Fly	Flying	Physical	90	95	15	Normal

● MOVES TAUGHT BY PEOPLE

Name	Type	Kind	Pow.	Acc.	PP	Range

*This Pokémon can only be used in Free Battles.

🔺 Mountain Kalos 150
Order Pokémon
☑ **Zygarde**

HEIGHT: 16'05" WEIGHT: 672.4 lbs.
GENDER: unknown

TYPE Dragon Ground

ABILITY
Aura Break

HIDDEN ABILITY
None

❌ When the Kalos region's ecosystem falls into disarray, it appears and reveals its secret power.

🔽 It's hypothesized that it's monitoring those who destroy the ecosystem from deep in the cave where it lives.

STAT GROWTH RATES
HP
Attack
Defense
Sp. Atk
Sp. Def
Speed

EGG GROUP
No Eggs Discovered

EVOLUTION
Does not evolve

ITEMS SOMETIMES HELD BY WILD POKÉMON
None

Damage taken in normal battles		Damage taken in Inverse Battles	
Normal	×1	Normal	×1
Fire	×0.5	Fire	×2
Water	×1	Water	×1
Grass	×1	Grass	×1
Electric	×0	Electric	×4
Ice	×4	Ice	×0.25
Fighting	×1	Fighting	×1
Poison	×0.5	Poison	×2
Ground	×1	Ground	×1
Flying	×1	Flying	×1
Psychic	×1	Psychic	×1
Bug	×1	Bug	×1
Rock	×0.5	Rock	×2
Ghost	×1	Ghost	×1
Dragon	×2	Dragon	×0.5
Dark	×1	Dark	×1
Steel	×1	Steel	×1
Fairy	×2	Fairy	×0.5

Can be used in	
Inverse Battle	—
Battle Chateau	Random Matchup*

Gender unknown

How to obtain for your Mountain Kalos Pokédex
Catch in the deepest part of Terminus Cave, after entering the Hall of Fame.

Catch in the deepest part of Terminus Cave, after entering the Hall of Fame.

● LEVEL-UP MOVES

Lv.	Name	Type	Kind	Pow.	Acc.	PP	Range
1	Glare	Normal	Status	—	100	30	Normal
1	Bulldoze	Ground	Physical	60	100	20	Adjacent
1	Dragon Breath	Dragon	Special	60	100	20	Normal
1	Bite	Dark	Physical	60	100	25	Normal
5	Safeguard	Normal	Status	—	—	25	Your Side
10	Dig	Ground	Physical	80	100	10	Normal
18	Bind	Normal	Physical	15	85	20	Normal
26	Land's Wrath	Ground	Physical	90	100	10	Many Others
35	Sandstorm	Rock	Status	—	—	10	Both Sides
44	Haze	Ice	Status	—	—	30	Both Sides
51	Crunch	Dark	Physical	80	100	15	Normal
57	Earthquake	Ground	Physical	100	100	10	Adjacent
59	Camouflage	Normal	Status	—	—	20	Self
63	Dragon Pulse	Dragon	Special	85	100	10	Normal
72	Dragon Dance	Dragon	Status	—	—	20	Self
80	Coil	Poison	Status	—	—	20	Self
88	Extreme Speed	Normal	Physical	80	100	5	Normal
93	Outrage	Dragon	Physical	120	100	10	1 Random

● TM & HM MOVES

No.	Name	Type	Kind	Pow.	Acc.	PP	Range
TM06	Toxic	Poison	Status	—	90	10	Normal
TM10	Hidden Power	Normal	Special	60	100	15	Normal
TM11	Sunny Day	Fire	Status	—	—	5	Both Sides
TM15	Hyper Beam	Normal	Special	150	90	5	Normal
TM17	Protect	Normal	Status	—	—	10	Self
TM20	Safeguard	Normal	Status	—	—	25	Your Side
TM21	Frustration	Normal	Physical	—	100	20	Normal
TM26	Earthquake	Ground	Physical	100	100	10	Adjacent
TM27	Return	Normal	Physical	—	100	20	Normal
TM28	Dig	Ground	Physical	80	100	10	Normal
TM31	Brick Break	Fighting	Physical	75	100	15	Normal
TM32	Double Team	Normal	Status	—	—	15	Self
TM34	Sludge Wave	Poison	Special	95	100	10	Adjacent
TM37	Sandstorm	Rock	Status	—	—	10	Both Sides
TM42	Facade	Normal	Physical	70	100	20	Normal
TM44	Rest	Psychic	Status	—	—	10	Self
TM48	Round	Normal	Special	60	100	15	Normal
TM52	Focus Blast	Fighting	Special	120	70	5	Normal
TM68	Giga Impact	Normal	Physical	150	90	5	Normal
TM71	Stone Edge	Rock	Physical	100	80	5	Normal
TM78	Bulldoze	Ground	Physical	60	100	20	Adjacent
TM80	Rock Slide	Rock	Physical	75	90	10	Many Others
TM82	Dragon Tail	Dragon	Physical	60	90	10	Normal
TM86	Grass Knot	Grass	Special	—	100	20	Normal
TM87	Swagger	Normal	Status	—	90	15	Normal
TM88	Sleep Talk	Normal	Status	—	—	10	Self
TM90	Substitute	Normal	Status	—	—	10	Self
TM94	Rock Smash	Fighting	Physical	40	100	15	Normal
TM100	Confide	Normal	Status	—	—	20	Normal
HM04	Strength	Normal	Physical	80	100	15	Normal

● MOVES TAUGHT BY PEOPLE

Name	Type	Kind	Pow.	Acc.	PP	Range
Draco Meteor	Dragon	Special	130	90	5	Normal

Zygarde 150

*This Pokémon can only be used in Free Battles.

AFTER THE HALL OF FAME

CENTRAL KALOS

COASTAL KALOS

MOUNTAIN KALOS

151 | Mewtwo

ADVENTURE DATA

⛰ Mountain Kalos
Genetic Pokémon
☑ Mewtwo
151

HEIGHT: 6'07"　WEIGHT: 269.0 lbs.
GENDER: unknown

TYPE Psychic

ABILITY
Pressure

HIDDEN ABILITY
None

STAT GROWTH RATES
HP ▪▪▪▪
Attack ▪▪▪▪
Defense ▪▪▪▪
Sp. Atk ▪▪▪▪▪▪▪▪
Sp. Def ▪▪▪▪
Speed ▪▪▪▪▪▪▪

EGG GROUP
No Eggs Discovered

EVOLUTION

Does not evolve

ITEMS SOMETIMES HELD BY WILD POKÉMON
None

X It was created by a scientist after years of horrific gene-splicing and DNA-engineering experiments.

Y A Pokémon created by recombining Mew's genes. It's said to have the most savage heart among Pokémon.

Damage taken in normal battles		Damage taken in Inverse Battles		Can be used in
Normal	×1	Normal	×1	Inverse Battle
Fire	×1	Fire	×1	—
Water	×1	Water	×1	Battle Chateau
Grass	×1	Grass	×1	—
Electric	×1	Electric	×1	
Ice	×1	Ice	×1	Random Matchup*
Fighting	×0.5	Fighting	×2	
Poison	×1	Poison	×1	
Ground	×1	Ground	×1	
Flying	×1	Flying	×1	
Psychic	×0.5	Psychic	×2	
Bug	×2	Bug	×0.5	
Rock	×1	Rock	×1	
Ghost	×2	Ghost	×0.5	
Dragon	×1	Dragon	×1	
Dark	×2	Dark	×0.5	
Steel	×1	Steel	×1	
Fairy	×1	Fairy	×1	

How to obtain for your Mountain Kalos Pokédex

Catch in the Unknown Dungeon in the Pokémon Village, after entering the Hall of Fame.

Catch in the Unknown Dungeon in the Pokémon Village, after entering the Hall of Fame.

Gender unknown

● LEVEL-UP MOVES

Lv.	Name	Type	Kind	Pow.	Acc.	PP	Range
1	Confusion	Psychic	Special	50	100	25	Normal
1	Disable	Normal	Status	—	100	20	Normal
1	Safeguard	Normal	Status	—	—	25	Your Side
8	Swift	Normal	Special	60	—	20	Many Others
15	Future Sight	Psychic	Special	120	100	10	Normal
22	Psych Up	Normal	Status	—	—	10	Normal
29	Miracle Eye	Psychic	Status	—	—	40	Normal
36	Psycho Cut	Psychic	Physical	70	100	20	Normal
43	Power Swap	Psychic	Status	—	—	10	Normal
43	Guard Swap	Psychic	Status	—	—	10	Normal
50	Recover	Normal	Status	—	—	10	Self
57	Psychic	Psychic	Special	90	100	10	Normal
64	Barrier	Psychic	Status	—	—	20	Self
70	Aura Sphere	Fighting	Special	80	—	20	Normal
79	Amnesia	Psychic	Status	—	—	20	Self
86	Mist	Ice	Status	—	—	30	Your Side
93	Me First	Normal	Status	—	—	20	Varies
100	Psystrike	Psychic	Special	100	100	10	Normal

● TM & HM MOVES

No.	Name	Type	Kind	Pow.	Acc.	PP	Range
TM03	Psyshock	Psychic	Special	80	100	10	Normal
TM04	Calm Mind	Psychic	Status	—	—	20	Self
TM06	Toxic	Poison	Status	—	90	10	Normal
TM07	Hail	Ice	Status	—	—	10	Both Sides
TM08	Bulk Up	Fighting	Status	—	—	20	Self
TM10	Hidden Power	Normal	Special	60	100	15	Normal
TM11	Sunny Day	Fire	Status	—	—	5	Both Sides
TM12	Taunt	Dark	Status	—	100	20	Normal
TM13	Ice Beam	Ice	Special	90	100	10	Normal
TM14	Blizzard	Ice	Special	110	70	5	Many Others
TM15	Hyper Beam	Normal	Special	150	90	5	Normal
TM16	Light Screen	Psychic	Status	—	—	30	Your Side

No.	Name	Type	Kind	Pow.	Acc.	PP	Range
TM17	Protect	Normal	Status	—	—	10	Self
TM18	Rain Dance	Water	Status	—	—	5	Both Sides
TM20	Safeguard	Normal	Status	—	—	25	Your Side
TM21	Frustration	Normal	Physical	—	100	20	Normal
TM22	Solar Beam	Grass	Special	120	100	10	Normal
TM24	Thunderbolt	Electric	Special	90	100	15	Normal
TM25	Thunder	Electric	Special	110	70	10	Normal
TM26	Earthquake	Ground	Physical	100	100	10	Adjacent
TM27	Return	Normal	Physical	—	100	20	Normal
TM29	Psychic	Psychic	Special	90	100	10	Normal
TM30	Shadow Ball	Ghost	Special	80	100	15	Normal
TM31	Brick Break	Fighting	Physical	75	100	15	Normal
TM32	Double Team	Normal	Status	—	—	15	Self
TM33	Reflect	Psychic	Status	—	—	20	Your Side
TM35	Flamethrower	Fire	Special	90	100	15	Normal
TM37	Sandstorm	Rock	Status	—	—	10	Both Sides
TM38	Fire Blast	Fire	Special	110	85	5	Normal
TM39	Rock Tomb	Rock	Physical	60	95	15	Normal
TM40	Aerial Ace	Flying	Physical	60	—	20	Normal
TM41	Torment	Dark	Status	—	100	15	Normal
TM42	Facade	Normal	Physical	70	100	20	Normal
TM44	Rest	Psychic	Status	—	—	10	Self
TM47	Low Sweep	Fighting	Physical	65	100	20	Normal
TM48	Round	Normal	Special	60	100	15	Normal
TM52	Focus Blast	Fighting	Special	120	70	5	Normal
TM53	Energy Ball	Grass	Special	90	100	10	Normal
TM56	Fling	Dark	Physical	—	100	10	Normal
TM57	Charge Beam	Electric	Special	50	90	10	Normal
TM58	Incinerate	Fire	Special	60	100	15	Many Others
TM61	Will-O-Wisp	Fire	Status	—	85	15	Normal
TM63	Embargo	Dark	Status	—	100	15	Normal
TM68	Giga Impact	Normal	Physical	150	90	5	Normal
TM70	Flash	Normal	Status	—	100	20	Normal

No.	Name	Type	Kind	Pow.	Acc.	PP	Range
TM71	Stone Edge	Rock	Physical	100	80	5	Normal
TM73	Thunder Wave	Electric	Status	—	100	20	Normal
TM77	Psych Up	Normal	Status	—	—	10	Normal
TM78	Bulldoze	Ground	Physical	60	100	20	Adjacent
TM80	Rock Slide	Rock	Physical	75	90	10	Many Others
TM84	Poison Jab	Poison	Physical	80	100	20	Normal
TM85	Dream Eater	Psychic	Special	100	100	15	Normal
TM86	Grass Knot	Grass	Special	—	100	20	Normal
TM87	Swagger	Normal	Status	—	90	15	Normal
TM88	Sleep Talk	Normal	Status	—	—	10	Self
TM90	Substitute	Normal	Status	—	—	10	Self
TM92	Trick Room	Psychic	Status	—	—	5	Both Sides
TM94	Rock Smash	Fighting	Physical	40	100	15	Normal
TM98	Power-Up Punch	Fighting	Physical	40	100	20	Normal
TM100	Confide	Normal	Status	—	—	20	Normal
HM04	Strength	Normal	Physical	80	100	15	Normal

● MOVES TAUGHT BY PEOPLE

Name	Type	Kind	Pow.	Acc.	PP	Range

*This Pokémon can only be used in Free Battles.

AFTER THE HALL OF FAME

CENTRAL KALOS

COASTAL KALOS

MOUNTAIN KALOS

Mega Mewtwo X

ADVENTURE DATA

Mega Evolution

Genetic Pokémon

∨ **Mega Mewtwo X**

HEIGHT: 7'07"　　WEIGHT: 280.0 lbs.　　GENDER: unknown

TYPE Psychic Fighting

ABILITY
Steadfast

STAT GROWTH RATES

HP	■■■■
Attack	■■■■■■■■
Defense	■■■■
Sp. Atk	■■■■■■■
Sp. Def	■■■■
Speed	■■■■■■■

MEGA STONE REQUIRED

Mewtwonite X
Catch Mewtwo in the Unknown Dungeon in the Pokémon Village, after entering the Hall of Fame (in *Pokémon X*).

Damage taken in normal battles

Normal	×1
Fire	×1
Water	×1
Grass	×1
Electric	×1
Ice	×1
Fighting	×0.5
Poison	×1
Ground	×1
Flying	×2
Psychic	×1
Bug	×1
Rock	×0.5
Ghost	×2
Dragon	×1
Dark	×1
Steel	×1
Fairy	×2

Damage taken in Inverse Battles

Normal	×1
Fire	×1
Water	×1
Grass	×1
Electric	×1
Ice	×1
Fighting	×2
Poison	×1
Ground	×1
Flying	×0.5
Psychic	×1
Bug	×1
Rock	×2
Ghost	×0.5
Dragon	×1
Dark	×1
Steel	×1
Fairy	×0.5

Can be used in

Inverse Battle	—
—	—
Battle Chateau	Random Matchup*

Gender unknown

*This Pokémon can only be used in Free Battles.

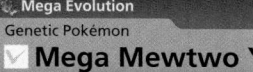

Mega Evolution

Genetic Pokémon

✓ **Mega Mewtwo Y**

TYPE	**Psychic**
ABILITY	Insomnia

STAT GROWTH RATES

HP	▪▪▪▪
Attack	▪▪▪▪▪▪▪
Defense	▪▪▪
Sp. Atk	▪▪▪▪▪▪▪▪▪
Sp. Def	▪▪▪▪
Speed	▪▪▪▪▪▪▪

MEGA STONE REQUIRED

Mewtwonite Y
Catch Mewtwo in the Unknown Dungeon in the Pokémon Village, after entering the Hall of Fame (in *Pokémon Y*).

HEIGHT: 4'11"   WEIGHT: 72.8 lbs.   GENDER: unknown

Damage taken in normal battles		Damage taken in Inverse Battles	
Normal	×1	Normal	×1
Fire	×1	Fire	×1
Water	×1	Water	×1
Grass	×1	Grass	×1
Electric	×1	Electric	×1
Ice	×1	Ice	×1
Fighting	×0.5	Fighting	×2
Poison	×1	Poison	×1
Ground	×1	Ground	×1
Flying	×1	Flying	×1
Psychic	×0.5	Psychic	×2
Bug	×2	Bug	×0.5
Rock	×1	Rock	×1
Ghost	×2	Ghost	×0.5
Dragon	×1	Dragon	×1
Dark	×2	Dark	×0.5
Steel	×1	Steel	×1
Fairy	×1	Fairy	×1

Can be used in	
Inverse Battle	—
—	—
Battle Chateau	Random Matchup*

Gender unknown

*This Pokémon can only be used in Free Battles.

AFTER THE
HALL OF FAME

CENTRAL
KALOS

COASTAL
KALOS

MOUNTAIN
KALOS

ADVENTURE
DATA

How and Where to Meet Special Pokémon

Among the Pokémon in the Kalos region, there are some precious Pokémon that you can meet only once during your adventure. But if you defeat them in battle or run from battle, you'll be able to catch them after you enter the Hall of Fame. Learn how to make these special Pokémon reappear!

Pokémon		Level	Location	Held item	How to meet it again if you defeat it in battle or run from battle
Snorlax		Lv. 15	Route 7	Sitrus Berry	Defeat the Elite Four and the Champion at the Pokémon League. It comes back until you catch it.
Xerneas		Lv. 50	Team Flare Secret HQ (X)	—	Battle it until you catch it on the spot.
Yveltal		Lv. 50	Team Flare Secret HQ (Y)	—	Battle it until you catch it on the spot.
Articuno		Lv. 70	Sea Spirit's Den in Azure Bay (if you chose Chespin at the beginning of the journey)	—	Defeat the Elite Four and the Champion at the Pokémon League. See note below.
Zapdos		Lv. 70	Sea Spirit's Den in Azure Bay (if you chose Fennekin at the beginning of the journey)	—	Defeat the Elite Four and the Champion at the Pokémon League. See note below.
Moltres		Lv. 70	Sea Spirit's Den in Azure Bay (if you chose Froakie at the beginning of the journey)	—	Defeat the Elite Four and the Champion at the Pokémon League. See note below.
Zygarde		Lv. 70	Terminus Cave	—	Defeat the Elite Four and the Champion at the Pokémon League. It comes back until you catch it.
Mewtwo		Lv. 70	Unknown Dungeon in Pokémon Village	—	Defeat the Elite Four and the Champion at the Pokémon League. It comes back until you catch it.

Note: Articuno, Zapdos, or Moltres will start wandering around the Kalos region after you enter the Hall of Fame. You must encounter the Pokémon 11 times in the field. Then it will move to the Sea Spirit's Den in Azure Bay, and you can catch it there. If you lose against it in battle, the Pokémon will stay there and you can try again. If you defeat it or run away, you'll have to enter the Hall of Fame again and wander around Kalos to encounter it 11 more times. So it might be wise to save the game before your battle!

Pokémon Moves

Explanations of the Move List

Move .... The move's name

Type .... The move's type

Kind .... Physical moves deal more damage when a Pokémon's Attack is high. Special moves deal more damage when a Pokémon's Sp. Atk is high. Status moves cause effects, such as status conditions.

Pow. .... The move's attack power

Acc. .... The move's accuracy

PP .... How many times the move can be used

Range .... The number and types of targets the move affects

DA .... Moves that make direct contact with the target

Long .... Moves that can target the Pokémon on the other side during Triple Battles

Range Guide

Normal: The move affects the selected target.

Self: The move affects only the user.

1 Ally: The move affects an adjacent ally in Double, Triple, and Multi Battles.

Self/Ally: The move affects the user or one of its allies at random.

Your Party: The move affects your entire party, including party Pokémon who are still in their Poké Balls.

1 Random: The move affects one of the opposing Pokémon at random.

Many Others: The move affects multiple Pokémon at the same time.

Adjacent: The move affects the surrounding Pokémon at the same time.

Your Side: The move affects the side of the field where your Pokémon are.

Other Side: The move affects the opponent's side of the field.

Both Sides: The move affects the entire playing field without regard to opposing and ally Pokémon.

Varies: The move is influenced by things like the opposing Pokémon's move or the user's type, so the effect and range are not fixed.

A

Move	Type	Kind	Pow.	Acc.	PP	Range	DA	Long	Effect
Absorb	Grass	Special	20	100	25	Normal	—	—	Restores HP by up to half of the damage dealt to the target.
Acid	Poison	Special	40	100	30	Many Others	—	—	A 10% chance of lowering the targets' Sp. Def by 1. Its power is reduced by 25% when it hits multiple Pokémon.
Acid Armor	Poison	Status	—	—	20	Self	—	—	Raises the user's Defense by 2.
Acid Spray	Poison	Special	40	100	20	Normal	—	—	Lowers the target's Sp. Def by 2.
Acrobatics	Flying	Physical	55	100	15	Normal	○	○	This move's power is doubled if the user isn't holding an item.
Acupressure	Normal	Status	—	—	30	Self/Ally	—	—	Raises a random stat by 2.
Aerial Ace	Flying	Physical	60	—	20	Normal	○	—	A sure hit.
After You	Normal	Status	—	—	15	Normal	—	—	The user helps the target and makes it use its move right after the user, regardless of its Speed. It fails if the target was going to use its move right after anyway, or if the target has already used its move this turn.
Agility	Psychic	Status	—	—	30	Self	—	—	Raises the user's Speed by 2.
Air Cutter	Flying	Special	60	95	25	Many Others	—	—	Critical hits land more easily. Its power is reduced by 25% when it hits multiple Pokémon.
Air Slash	Flying	Special	75	95	15	Normal	—	○	A 30% chance of making the target flinch (unable to use moves on that turn).
Ally Switch	Psychic	Status	—	—	15	Self	—	—	The user switches places with an ally. It fails if the user or target is in the middle (works only when the target is on the other end).
Amnesia	Psychic	Status	—	—	20	Self	—	—	Raises the user's Sp. Def by 2.
Ancient Power	Rock	Special	60	100	5	Normal	—	—	A 10% chance of raising the user's Attack, Defense, Speed, Sp. Atk, and Sp. Def stats by 1.
Aqua Jet	Water	Physical	40	100	20	Normal	○	—	Always strikes first. The user with the higher Speed goes first if similar moves are used.
Aqua Ring	Water	Status	—	—	20	Self	—	—	Restores 1/16 of max HP every turn.
Aqua Tail	Water	Physical	90	90	10	Normal	○	—	A regular attack.
Arm Thrust	Fighting	Physical	15	100	20	Normal	○	—	Attacks 2–5 times in a row in a single turn.
Aromatherapy	Grass	Status	—	—	5	Your Party	—	○	Heals status conditions of all your Pokémon, including those in your party.
Aromatic Mist	Fairy	Status	—	—	20	1 Ally	—	—	Raises one ally's Sp. Def by 1.
Assist	Normal	Status	—	—	20	Self	—	—	Uses a random move from one of the Pokémon in your party that is not in battle.
Assurance	Dark	Physical	60	100	10	Normal	○	—	Move's power is doubled if the target has already taken some damage in the same turn.
Astonish	Ghost	Physical	30	100	15	Normal	○	—	A 30% chance of making the target flinch (unable to use moves on that turn).
Attack Order	Bug	Physical	90	100	15	Normal	—	—	Critical hits land more easily.
Attract	Normal	Status	—	100	15	Normal	—	—	Leaves the target unable to attack 50% of the time. Only works if the user and the target are of different genders.
Aura Sphere	Fighting	Special	80	—	20	Normal	—	○	A sure hit.
Aurora Beam	Ice	Special	65	100	20	Normal	—	—	A 10% chance of lowering the target's Attack by 1.
Autotomize	Steel	Status	—	—	15	Self	—	—	Raises the user's Speed by 2 and lowers its weight by 220 lbs.
Avalanche	Ice	Physical	60	100	10	Normal	○	—	Always strikes last. This move's power is doubled if the user has taken damage from the target that turn.

B

Move	Type	Kind	Pow.	Acc.	PP	Range	DA	Long	Effect
Baby-Doll Eyes	Fairy	Status	—	100	30	Normal	—	—	Always strikes first. Lowers the target's Attack by 1.
Barrage	Normal	Physical	15	85	20	Normal	—	—	Attacks 2–5 times in a row in a single turn.
Barrier	Psychic	Status	—	—	20	Self	—	—	Raises the user's Defense by 2.
Baton Pass	Normal	Status	—	—	40	Self	—	—	User swaps out with an ally Pokémon and passes along any stat changes.
Beat Up	Dark	Physical	—	100	10	Normal	—	—	Attacks once for each Pokémon in your party, including the user. Does not count Pokémon that have fainted or have status conditions.
Belch	Poison	Special	120	90	10	Normal	—	—	Cannot be used without first eating a Berry.
Belly Drum	Normal	Status	—	—	10	Self	—	—	The user loses half of its maximum HP but raises its Attack to the maximum.
Bestow	Normal	Status	—	—	15	Normal	—	—	If the target is not holding an item and the user is, the user can give that item to the target. Fails if the user is not holding an item or the target is holding an item.
Bide	Normal	Physical	—	—	10	Self	○	—	Inflicts twice the damage received during the next 2 turns. Cannot choose moves during those 2 turns.
Bind	Normal	Physical	15	85	20	Normal	○	—	Inflicts damage equal to 1/8 the target's max HP for 4–5 turns. The target cannot flee during that time.
Bite	Dark	Physical	60	100	25	Normal	○	—	A 30% chance of making the target flinch (unable to use moves on that turn).
Blast Burn	Fire	Special	150	90	5	Normal	—	—	The user can't move during the next turn. If the target is Frozen, it will be thawed.
Blaze Kick	Fire	Physical	85	90	10	Normal	○	—	A 10% chance of inflicting the Burned status condition on the target. Critical hits land more easily. If the target is Frozen, it will be thawed.
Blizzard	Ice	Special	110	70	5	Many Others	—	—	A 10% chance of inflicting the Frozen status condition on the targets. Is 100% accurate in the hail weather condition. Its power is reduced by 25% when it hits multiple Pokémon.
Block	Normal	Status	—	—	5	Normal	—	—	The target cannot escape. If used during a Trainer battle, the opposing Trainer cannot switch Pokémon.
Body Slam	Normal	Physical	85	100	15	Normal	○	—	A 30% chance of inflicting the Paralysis status condition on the target. If the target has used Minimize, this move will be a sure hit and its power will be doubled.
Bone Club	Ground	Physical	65	85	20	Normal	—	—	A 10% chance of making the target flinch (unable to use moves on that turn).
Bone Rush	Ground	Physical	25	90	10	Normal	—	—	Attacks 2–5 times in a row in a single turn.
Bonemerang	Ground	Physical	50	90	10	Normal	—	—	Attacks twice in a row in a single turn.
Boomburst	Normal	Special	140	100	10	Adjacent	—	—	Its power is weaker when it hits multiple Pokémon. Strikes the target even if it is using Substitute.
Bounce	Flying	Physical	85	85	5	Normal	○	—	The user flies into the air on the first turn and attacks on the second. A 30% chance of inflicting the Paralysis status condition on the target.
Brave Bird	Flying	Physical	120	100	15	Normal	○	○	The user takes 1/3 of the damage inflicted.
Brick Break	Fighting	Physical	75	100	15	Normal	○	—	This move is not affected by Reflect. It removes the effect of Reflect and Light Screen.
Brine	Water	Special	65	100	10	Normal	—	—	This move's power is doubled if the target's HP is at half or below.
Bubble	Water	Special	40	100	30	Many Others	—	—	A 10% chance of lowering the targets' Speed by 1. Its power is reduced by 25% when it hits multiple Pokémon.
Bubble Beam	Water	Special	65	100	20	Normal	—	—	A 10% chance of lowering the target's Speed by 1.
Bug Bite	Bug	Physical	60	100	20	Normal	—	—	If the target is holding a Berry with a battle effect, the user eats that Berry and uses its effect.
Bug Buzz	Bug	Special	90	100	10	Normal	—	—	A 10% chance of lowering the target's Sp. Def by 1. Strikes the target even if it is using Substitute.
Bulk Up	Fighting	Status	—	—	20	Self	—	—	Raises the user's Attack and Defense by 1.
Bulldoze	Ground	Physical	60	100	20	Adjacent	—	—	Lowers the targets' Speed by 1. Its power is reduced by 25% when it hits multiple Pokémon.
Bullet Punch	Steel	Physical	40	100	30	Normal	○	—	Always strikes first. The user with the higher Speed goes first if similar moves are used.
Bullet Seed	Grass	Physical	25	100	30	Normal	—	—	Attacks 2–5 times in a row in a single turn.

C

Move	Type	Kind	Pow.	Acc.	PP	Range	DA	Long	Effect
Calm Mind	Psychic	Status	—	—	20	Self	—	—	Raises the user's Sp. Atk and Sp. Def by 1.
Camouflage	Normal	Status	—	—	20	Self	—	—	Changes the user's type to match the environment: Cave: Rock type Dirt/Sand/Swamp: Ground type Electric Terrain: Electric type Grass / Grassy Terrain: Grass type Indoors / Sky Battle / Link: Normal type Misty Terrain: Fairy type Snow/Ice: Ice type Water Surface / Puddle / Shoal: Water type
Captivate	Normal	Status	—	100	20	Many Others	—	—	Lowers the target's Sp. Atk by 2. Only works if the user and the target are of different genders.
Charge	Electric	Status	—	—	20	Self	—	—	Doubles the attack power of an Electric-type move used the next turn. Raises the user's Sp. Def by 1.

Move	Type	Kind	Pow.	Acc.	PP	Range	DA	Long	Effect
Charge Beam	Electric	Special	50	90	10	Normal	—	—	A 70% chance of raising the user's Sp. Atk by 1.
Charm	Fairy	Status	—	100	20	Normal	—	—	Lowers the target's Attack by 2.
Chatter	Flying	Special	65	100	20	Normal	—	○	When the user is Chatot, this move also inflicts the Confused status condition on the target. Strikes the target even if it is using Substitute.
Chip Away	Normal	Physical	70	100	20	Normal	○	—	Damage dealt is not affected by the opposing Pokémon's stat changes.
Circle Throw	Fighting	Physical	60	90	10	Normal	○	—	Always strikes last. Ends wild Pokémon battles after attacking. When battling multiple wild Pokémon or if the wild Pokémon's level is higher than the user's, no additional effect takes place. In a battle with a Trainer, this move forces another Pokémon to switch in. If there is no Pokémon to switch in, no additional effect takes place.
Clamp	Water	Physical	35	85	15	Normal	○	—	Inflicts damage equal to 1/8 the target's max HP for 4–5 turns. The target cannot flee during that time.
Clear Smog	Poison	Special	50	—	15	Normal	—	—	Eliminates every stat change of the target.
Close Combat	Fighting	Physical	120	100	5	Normal	○	—	Lowers the user's Defense and Sp. Def by 1.
Coil	Poison	Status	—	—	20	Self	—	—	Raises the user's Attack, Defense, and accuracy by 1.
Comet Punch	Normal	Physical	18	85	15	Normal	○	—	Attacks 2–5 times in a row in a single turn.
Confide	Normal	Status	—	—	20	Normal	—	—	A sure hit. Lowers the target's Sp. Atk by 1. Strikes the target even if it is using Detect, King's Shield, Mat Block, Protect, Spiky Shield, or Substitute.
Confuse Ray	Ghost	Status	—	100	10	Normal	—	—	Inflicts the Confused status condition on the target.
Confusion	Psychic	Special	50	100	25	Normal	—	—	A 10% chance of inflicting the Confused status condition on the target.
Constrict	Normal	Physical	10	100	35	Normal	○	—	A 10% chance of lowering the target's Speed by 1.
Copycat	Normal	Status	—	—	20	Self	—	—	Uses the last move used.
Cosmic Power	Psychic	Status	—	—	20	Self	—	—	Raises the user's Defense and Sp. Def by 1.
Cotton Guard	Grass	Status	—	—	10	Self	—	—	Raises the user's Defense by 3.
Cotton Spore	Grass	Status	—	100	40	Many Others	—	—	Lowers the targets' Speed by 2.
Counter	Fighting	Physical	—	100	20	Varies	—	—	If the user is attacked physically, this move inflicts twice the damage done to the user. Always strikes last.
Covet	Normal	Physical	60	100	25	Normal	○	—	When the target is holding an item and the user is not, the user can steal that item. A regular attack if the target is not holding an item.
Crabhammer	Water	Physical	100	90	10	Normal	○	—	Critical hits land more easily.
Crafty Shield	Fairy	Status	—	—	10	Your Side	—	—	Protects the user and allies from status moves used in the same turn. Does not protect against damage-dealing moves.
Cross Chop	Fighting	Physical	100	80	5	Normal	○	—	Critical hits land more easily.
Cross Poison	Poison	Physical	70	100	20	Normal	○	—	Critical hits land more easily. A 10% chance of inflicting the Poison status condition on the target.
Crunch	Dark	Physical	80	100	15	Normal	○	—	A 20% chance of lowering the target's Defense by 1.
Crush Claw	Normal	Physical	75	95	10	Normal	○	—	A 50% chance of lowering the target's Defense by 1.
Curse	Ghost	Status	—	—	10	Varies	—	—	Lowers the user's Speed by 1 and raises its Attack and Defense by 1. If used by a Ghost-type Pokémon, the user loses half of its maximum HP, but the move lowers the target's HP by 1/4 of its maximum every turn.
Cut	Normal	Physical	50	95	30	Normal	○	—	A regular attack.

D

Move	Type	Kind	Pow.	Acc.	PP	Range	DA	Long	Effect
Dark Pulse	Dark	Special	80	100	15	Normal	—	○	Has a 20% chance of making the target flinch (unable to use moves on that turn).
Dazzling Gleam	Fairy	Special	80	100	10	Many Others	—	—	Its power is weaker when it hits multiple Pokémon.
Defend Order	Bug	Status	—	—	10	Self	—	—	Raises the user's Defense and Sp. Def by 1.
Defense Curl	Normal	Status	—	—	40	Self	—	—	Raises the user's Defense by 1.
Defog	Flying	Status	—	—	15	Normal	—	—	Lowers the target's evasion by 1. Nullifies the effects of Light Screen, Reflect, Safeguard, Mist, Spikes, Toxic Spikes, and Stealth Rock on the target's side.
Destiny Bond	Ghost	Status	—	—	5	Self	—	—	If the user faints due to damage from a Pokémon, that Pokémon faints as well.
Detect	Fighting	Status	—	—	5	Self	—	—	The user evades all moves that turn. If used in succession, its chance of failing rises.
Dig	Ground	Physical	80	100	10	Normal	○	—	The user burrows underground on the first turn and attacks on the second.
Disable	Normal	Status	—	100	20	Normal	—	—	The target can't use the move it just used for 4 turns.
Disarming Voice	Fairy	Special	40	—	15	Many Others	—	—	A sure hit. Strikes the target even if it is using Substitute. Its power is weaker when it hits multiple Pokémon.
Discharge	Electric	Special	80	100	15	Adjacent	—	—	A 30% chance of inflicting the Paralysis status condition on the targets. Its power is reduced by 25% when it hits multiple Pokémon.
Dive	Water	Physical	80	100	10	Normal	○	—	The user dives deep on the first turn and attacks on the second.
Dizzy Punch	Normal	Physical	70	100	10	Normal	○	—	A 20% chance of inflicting the Confused status condition on the target.
Double Hit	Normal	Physical	35	90	10	Normal	○	—	Attacks twice in a row in a single turn.
Double Kick	Fighting	Physical	30	100	30	Normal	○	—	Attacks twice in a row in a single turn.

Pokémon Moves

AFTER THE HALL OF FAME

CENTRAL KALOS

COASTAL KALOS

MOUNTAIN KALOS

ADVENTURE DATA

Move	Type	Kind	Pow.	Acc.	PP	Range	DA	Long	Effect
Double Slap	Normal	Physical	15	85	10	Normal	—	—	Attacks 2–5 times in a row in a single turn.
Double Team	Normal	Status	—	—	15	Self	—	—	Raises the user's evasion by 1.
Double-Edge	Normal	Physical	120	100	15	Normal	○	—	The user takes 1/3 of the damage inflicted.
Draco Meteor	Dragon	Special	130	90	5	Normal	—	—	Lowers the user's Sp. Atk by 2.
Dragon Breath	Dragon	Special	60	100	20	Normal	—	—	A 30% chance of inflicting the Paralysis status condition on the target.
Dragon Claw	Dragon	Physical	80	100	15	Normal	○	—	A regular attack.
Dragon Dance	Dragon	Status	—	—	20	Self	—	—	Raises the user's Attack and Speed by 1.
Dragon Pulse	Dragon	Special	85	100	10	Normal	—	○	A regular attack.
Dragon Rage	Dragon	Special	—	100	10	Normal	—	—	Deals a fixed 40 points of damage.
Dragon Rush	Dragon	Physical	100	75	10	Normal	○	—	A 20% chance of making the target flinch (unable to use moves on that turn). If the target has used Minimize, this move will be a sure hit and its power will be doubled.
Dragon Tail	Dragon	Physical	60	90	10	Normal	○	—	Ends wild Pokémon battles after attacking. When battling multiple wild Pokémon or if the wild Pokémon's level is higher than the user's, no additional effect takes place. In a battle with a Trainer, this move forces another Pokémon to switch in. If there is no Pokémon to switch in, no additional effect takes place.
Drain Punch	Fighting	Physical	75	100	10	Normal	○	—	Restores HP by up to half of the damage dealt to the target.
Draining Kiss	Fairy	Special	50	100	10	Normal	○	—	Restores HP by up to 3/4 of the damage dealt to the target.
Dream Eater	Psychic	Special	100	100	15	Normal	—	—	Only works when the target is asleep. Restores HP by up to half of the damage dealt to the target.
Drill Peck	Flying	Physical	80	100	20	Normal	○	○	A regular attack.
Drill Run	Ground	Physical	80	95	10	Normal	○	—	Critical hits land more easily.
Dual Chop	Dragon	Physical	40	90	15	Normal	○	—	Attacks twice in a row in a single turn.
Dynamic Punch	Fighting	Physical	100	50	5	Normal	○	—	Inflicts the Confused status condition on the target.

E

Move	Type	Kind	Pow.	Acc.	PP	Range	DA	Long	Effect
Earth Power	Ground	Special	90	100	10	Normal	—	—	A 10% chance of lowering the target's Sp. Def by 1.
Earthquake	Ground	Physical	100	100	10	Adjacent	—	—	Does twice the damage if targets are underground due to using Dig. Its power is reduced by 25% when it hits multiple Pokémon.
Echoed Voice	Normal	Special	40	100	15	Normal	—	—	If this move is used every turn, no matter which Pokémon uses it, its power increases (max 200). If no Pokémon uses it in a turn, the power returns to normal. Strikes the target even if it is using Substitute.
Eerie Impulse	Electric	Status	—	100	15	Normal	—	—	Lowers the target's Sp. Atk by 2.
Egg Bomb	Normal	Physical	100	75	10	Normal	—	—	A regular attack.
Electric Terrain	Electric	Status	—	—	10	Both Sides	—	—	Electrifies the field for 5 turns. During that time, Pokémon on the ground will be able to do 50% more damage with Electric-type moves and cannot fall asleep.
Electrify	Electric	Status	—	—	20	Normal	—	—	Changes any attack used by the target in the same turn into an Electric-type move.
Electro Ball	Electric	Special	—	100	10	Normal	—	—	The faster the user is than the target, the greater the move's power (max 150).
Electroweb	Electric	Special	55	95	15	Many Others	—	—	Lowers the targets' Speed by 1. Its power is reduced by 25% when it hits multiple Pokémon.
Embargo	Dark	Status	—	100	15	Normal	—	—	The target can't use items for 5 turns. The Trainer also can't use items on that Pokémon.
Ember	Fire	Special	40	100	25	Normal	—	—	A 10% chance of inflicting the Burned status condition on the target. If the target is Frozen, it will be thawed.
Encore	Normal	Status	—	100	5	Normal	—	—	The target is forced to keep using the last move it used. This effect lasts 3 turns.
Endeavor	Normal	Physical	—	100	5	Normal	○	—	Inflicts damage equal to the target's HP minus the user's HP.
Endure	Normal	Status	—	—	10	Self	—	—	Leaves the user with 1 HP when hit by a move that would KO it. If used in succession, its chance of failing rises.
Energy Ball	Grass	Special	90	100	10	Normal	—	—	A 10% chance of lowering the target's Sp. Def by 1.
Entrainment	Normal	Status	—	100	15	Normal	—	—	Makes the target's Ability the same as the user's. Fails with certain Abilities, however.
Eruption	Fire	Special	150	100	5	Many Others	—	—	If the user's HP is low, this move has lower attack power. If the targets are Frozen, they will be thawed. Its power is reduced by 25% when it hits multiple Pokémon.
Explosion	Normal	Physical	250	100	5	Adjacent	—	—	The user faints after using it. Its power is reduced by 25% when it hits multiple Pokémon.
Extrasensory	Psychic	Special	80	100	20	Normal	—	—	A 10% chance of making the target flinch (unable to use moves on that turn).
Extreme Speed	Normal	Physical	80	100	5	Normal	○	—	Always strikes first. Faster than other moves that strike first, except for Fake Out. (If two Pokémon use this move, the one with the higher Speed goes first.)

F

Move	Type	Kind	Pow.	Acc.	PP	Range	DA	Long	Effect
Facade	Normal	Physical	70	100	20	Normal	○	—	This move's power is doubled if the user has a Paralysis, Poison, or Burned status condition.
Fairy Lock	Fairy	Status	—	—	10	Both Sides	—	—	The target cannot escape during the next turn. If used during a Trainer battle, the opposing Trainer cannot switch Pokémon.

Move	Type	Kind	Pow.	Acc.	PP	Range	DA	Long	Effect
Fairy Wind	Fairy	Special	40	100	30	Normal	—	—	A regular attack.
Fake Out	Normal	Physical	40	100	10	Normal	○	—	Always strikes first and makes the target flinch (unable to use moves on that turn). Only works on the first turn after the user is sent out. Faster than other moves that strike first.
Fake Tears	Dark	Status	—	100	20	Normal	—	—	Lowers the target's Sp. Def by 2.
False Swipe	Normal	Physical	40	100	40	Normal	○	—	Always leaves 1 HP, even if the damage would have made the target faint.
Feather Dance	Flying	Status	—	100	15	Normal	—	—	Lowers the target's Attack by 2.
Feint	Normal	Physical	30	100	10	Normal	—	—	Always strikes first. Faster than other moves that strike first, except Fake Out. If two Pokémon use this move, or if the other Pokémon uses the move Extreme Speed, the one with the higher Speed goes first. Strikes the target even if it is using Detect, King's Shield, Mat Block, Protect, Quick Guard, Spiky Shield, or Wide Guard, and eliminates the effects of those moves.
Feint Attack	Dark	Physical	60	—	20	Normal	—	—	A sure hit.
Fell Stinger	Bug	Physical	30	100	25	Normal	—	—	When the Pokémon knocks out an opponent with this move, its Attack goes up 2.
Final Gambit	Fighting	Special	—	100	5	Normal	○	—	Does damage to the target equal to the user's remaining HP. If the move lands, the user faints. If the move does not land, the user will not faint.
Fire Blast	Fire	Special	110	85	5	Normal	—	—	A 10% chance of inflicting the Burned status condition on the target. If the target is Frozen, it will be thawed.
Fire Fang	Fire	Physical	65	95	15	Normal	○	—	A 10% chance of inflicting the Burned status condition or making the target flinch (unable to use moves on that turn). If the target is Frozen, it will be thawed.
Fire Pledge	Fire	Special	80	100	10	Normal	—	—	When combined with Water Pledge or Grass Pledge, the power and effect change. If combined with Water Pledge, the power is 150 and it becomes a Water-type move. This makes it more likely that your team's moves will have additional effects for 4 turns. If combined with Grass Pledge, the power is 150 and it remains a Fire-type move. This damages opposing Pokémon, except Fire types, for 4 turns. If the target is Frozen, it will be thawed.
Fire Punch	Fire	Physical	75	100	15	Normal	○	—	A 10% chance of inflicting the Burned status condition on the target. If the target is Frozen, it will be thawed.
Fire Spin	Fire	Special	35	85	15	Normal	—	—	Inflicts damage equal to 1/8 the target's max HP for 4–5 turns. The target cannot flee during that time. If the target is Frozen, it will be thawed.
Fissure	Ground	Physical	—	30	5	Normal	—	—	The target faints with one hit if the user's level is equal to or greater than the target's level. The higher the user's level is compared to the target's, the more accurate the move is.
Flail	Normal	Physical	—	100	15	Normal	○	—	The lower the user's HP is, the greater the move's power becomes (max 200).
Flame Burst	Fire	Special	70	100	15	Normal	—	—	It deals damage equal to 1/16 of the max HP of any Pokémon next to the target during Double or Triple Battles. If the target is Frozen, it will be thawed.
Flame Charge	Fire	Physical	50	100	20	Normal	○	—	Raises the user's Speed by 1. If the target is Frozen, it will be thawed.
Flame Wheel	Fire	Physical	60	100	25	Normal	○	—	A 10% chance of inflicting the Burned status condition on the target. If the target is Frozen, it will be thawed. This move can be used even if the user is Frozen. If the user is Frozen, this also thaws the user.
Flamethrower	Fire	Special	90	100	15	Normal	—	—	A 10% chance of inflicting the Burned status condition on the target. If the target is Frozen, it will be thawed.
Flare Blitz	Fire	Physical	120	100	15	Normal	○	—	User takes 1/3 of the damage done to the target. A 10% chance of inflicting the Burned status condition on the target. If the target is Frozen, it will be thawed. This move can be used even if the user is Frozen. If the user is Frozen, this also thaws the user.
Flash	Normal	Status	—	100	20	Normal	—	—	Lowers the target's accuracy by 1.
Flash Cannon	Steel	Special	80	100	10	Normal	—	—	A 10% chance of lowering the target's Sp. Def by 1.
Flatter	Dark	Status	—	100	15	Normal	—	—	Inflicts the Confused status condition on the target, but also raises its Sp. Atk by 1.
Fling	Dark	Physical	—	100	10	Normal	—	—	The user attacks by throwing its held item at the target. Power and effect vary depending on the item.
Flower Shield	Fairy	Status	—	—	10	Adjacent	—	○	Raises the Defense of any Grass-type Pokémon by 1.
Fly	Flying	Physical	90	95	15	Normal	○	○	The user flies into the air on the first turn and attacks on the second.
Flying Press	Fighting	Physical	80	95	10	Normal	○	○	This move is both Fighting type and Flying type. If the target has used Minimize, it will be a sure hit and its power will be doubled.
Focus Blast	Fighting	Special	120	70	5	Normal	—	—	A 10% chance of lowering the target's Sp. Def by 1.
Focus Energy	Normal	Status	—	—	30	Self	—	—	Heightens the critical-hit ratio of the user's subsequent moves.
Focus Punch	Fighting	Physical	150	100	20	Normal	○	—	Always strikes last. The move misses if the user is hit before this move lands.
Follow Me	Normal	Status	—	—	20	Self	—	—	This move goes first. Opposing Pokémon aim only at the user.
Force Palm	Fighting	Physical	60	100	10	Normal	○	—	A 30% chance of inflicting the Paralysis status condition on the target.
Foresight	Normal	Status	—	—	40	Normal	—	—	Attacks land easily regardless of the target's evasion. Makes Ghost-type Pokémon vulnerable to Normal- and Fighting-type moves.

Move	Type	Kind	Pow.	Acc.	PP	Range	DA	Long	Effect
Forest's Curse	Grass	Status	—	100	20	Normal	—	—	Gives the target the Grass type.
Foul Play	Dark	Physical	95	100	15	Normal	○	—	The user turns the target's power against it. Damage varies depending on the target's Attack and Defense.
Freeze-Dry	Ice	Special	70	100	20	Normal	—	—	Super effective even against Water-type Pokémon. A 10% chance of inflicting the Frozen status condition.
Frenzy Plant	Grass	Special	150	90	5	Normal	—	—	The user can't move during the next turn.
Frost Breath	Ice	Special	60	90	10	Normal	—	—	Always delivers a critical hit.
Frustration	Normal	Physical	—	100	20	Normal	○	—	The lower the user's friendship, the greater this move's power (max 102).
Fury Attack	Normal	Physical	15	85	20	Normal	○	—	Attacks 2–5 times in a row in a single turn.
Fury Cutter	Bug	Physical	40	95	20	Normal	○	—	This move doubles in power with every successful hit (max 120). Power returns to normal once it misses.
Fury Swipes	Normal	Physical	18	80	15	Normal	○	—	Attacks 2–5 times in a row in a single turn.
Future Sight	Psychic	Special	120	100	10	Normal	—	—	Attacks the target after 2 turns. This move is affected by the target's type.

G

Move	Type	Kind	Pow.	Acc.	PP	Range	DA	Long	Effect
Gastro Acid	Poison	Status	—	100	10	Normal	—	—	Disables the target's Ability.
Geomancy	Fairy	Status	—	—	10	Self	—	—	Builds power on the first turn and increases the user's Sp. Atk, Sp. Def, and Speed by 2 on the second.
Giga Drain	Grass	Special	75	100	10	Normal	—	—	Restores HP by up to half of the damage dealt to the target.
Giga Impact	Normal	Physical	150	90	5	Normal	○	—	The user can't move during the next turn.
Glare	Normal	Status	—	100	30	Normal	—	—	Inflicts the Paralysis status condition on the target.
Grass Knot	Grass	Special	—	100	20	Normal	○	—	The heavier the target is compared to the user, the greater the move's power becomes (max 120).
Grass Pledge	Grass	Special	80	100	10	Normal	—	—	When combined with Water Pledge or Fire Pledge, the power and effect change. If combined with Water Pledge, the power is 150 and it remains a Grass-type move. This lowers the Speed of opposing Pokémon for 4 turns. If combined with Fire Pledge, the power is 150 and it becomes a Fire-type move. This damages all non-Fire types for 4 turns. If the target is Frozen, it will be thawed.
Grass Whistle	Grass	Status	—	55	15	Normal	—	—	Inflicts the Sleep status condition on the target. Strikes the target even if it is using Substitute.
Grassy Terrain	Grass	Status	—	—	10	Both Sides	—	—	Covers the field with grass for 5 turns. During that time, Pokémon on the ground will be able to do 50% more damage with Grass-type moves and will recover 1/16 of the Pokémon's maximum HP each turn.
Gravity	Psychic	Status	—	—	5	Both Sides	—	—	Raises the accuracy of all Pokémon in battle for 5 turns. Ground-type moves will now hit a Pokémon with the Levitate Ability or a Flying-type Pokémon. Prevents the use of Bounce, Fly, High Jump Kick, Jump Kick, Magnet Rise, Sky Drop, Splash, and Telekinesis. Pulls any airborne Pokémon to the ground.
Growl	Normal	Status	—	100	40	Many Others	—	—	Lowers the target's Attack by 1. Strikes the target even if it is using Substitute.
Growth	Normal	Status	—	—	20	Self	—	—	Raises the user's Attack and Sp. Atk by 1. Raises them by 2 when the weather condition is sunny.
Grudge	Ghost	Status	—	—	5	Self	—	—	Any move that causes the user to faint will have its PP dropped to 0.
Guard Split	Psychic	Status	—	—	10	Normal	—	—	The user and the target's Defense and Sp. Def are added, then divided equally between them.
Guard Swap	Psychic	Status	—	—	10	Normal	—	—	Swaps Defense and Sp. Def changes between the user and the target.
Guillotine	Normal	Physical	—	30	5	Normal	○	—	The target faints with one hit if the user's level is equal to or greater than the target's level. The higher the user's level is compared to the target's, the more accurate the move is.
Gunk Shot	Poison	Physical	120	80	5	Normal	○	—	A 30% chance of inflicting the Poison status condition on the target.
Gust	Flying	Special	40	100	35	Normal	—	○	It even hits Pokémon that are in the sky due to using moves such as Fly and Bounce, dealing them twice the usual damage.
Gyro Ball	Steel	Physical	—	100	5	Normal	○	—	The slower the user is than the target, the greater this move's power becomes (max 150).

H

Move	Type	Kind	Pow.	Acc.	PP	Range	DA	Long	Effect
Hail	Ice	Status	—	—	10	Both Sides	—	—	Changes the weather condition to hail for 5 turns, dealing damage every turn equal to 1/16 of its max HP to each Pokémon in the field that is not an Ice type.
Hammer Arm	Fighting	Physical	100	90	10	Normal	○	—	Lowers the user's Speed by 1.
Harden	Normal	Status	—	—	30	Self	—	—	Raises the user's Defense by 1.
Haze	Ice	Status	—	—	30	Both Sides	—	—	Eliminates every stat change of the targets.
Head Smash	Rock	Physical	150	80	5	Normal	○	—	The user takes 1/2 of the damage inflicted.
Headbutt	Normal	Physical	70	100	15	Normal	○	—	A 30% chance of making the target flinch (unable to use moves on that turn).

Move	Type	Kind	Pow.	Acc.	PP	Range	DA	Long	Effect
Heal Bell	Normal	Status	—	—	5	Your Party	—	○	Heals status conditions of all your Pokémon, including those in your party. Affects the target even if it is using Substitute.
Heal Block	Psychic	Status	—	100	15	Many Others	—	—	Targets cannot have HP restored by moves, Abilities, or held items for 5 turns.
Heal Order	Bug	Status	—	—	10	Self	—	—	Restores HP by up to half of the user's maximum HP.
Heal Pulse	Psychic	Status	—	—	10	Normal	—	○	Restores the target's HP by up to half of its maximum HP.
Healing Wish	Psychic	Status	—	—	10	Self	—	—	The user faints, but fully heals the next Pokémon's HP and status conditions.
Heart Stamp	Psychic	Physical	60	100	25	Normal	○	—	A 30% chance of making the target flinch (unable to use moves on that turn).
Heat Wave	Fire	Special	95	90	10	Many Others	—	—	A 10% chance of inflicting the Burned status condition on the targets. If the targets are Frozen, they will be thawed. Its power is reduced by 25% when it hits multiple Pokémon.
Heavy Slam	Steel	Physical	—	100	10	Normal	○	—	The heavier the user is compared to the target, the greater the move's power becomes (max 120).
Helping Hand	Normal	Status	—	—	20	1 Ally	—	—	Always strikes first. Strengthens the attack power of one ally's moves by 50%.
Hex	Ghost	Special	65	100	10	Normal	—	—	Deals twice the usual damage to a target affected by status conditions.
Hidden Power	Normal	Special	60	100	15	Normal	—	—	Type changes depending on the user.
High Jump Kick	Fighting	Physical	130	90	10	Normal	○	—	If this move misses, the user loses half of its maximum HP.
Hone Claws	Dark	Status	—	—	15	Self	—	—	Raises Attack and accuracy by 1.
Horn Attack	Normal	Physical	65	100	25	Normal	○	—	A regular attack.
Horn Drill	Normal	Physical	—	30	5	Normal	○	—	The target faints with one hit if the user's level is equal to or greater than the target's level. The higher the user's level is compared to the target's, the more accurate the move is.
Horn Leech	Grass	Physical	75	100	10	Normal	○	—	Restores HP by up to half of the damage dealt to the target.
Howl	Normal	Status	—	—	40	Self	—	—	Raises the user's Attack by 1.
Hurricane	Flying	Special	110	70	10	Normal	—	○	A 30% chance of inflicting the Confused status condition on the target. Is 100% accurate in the rain weather condition and 50% accurate in the sunny weather condition. It can hit Pokémon that are in the sky due to using moves such as Fly and Bounce.
Hydro Cannon	Water	Special	150	90	5	Normal	—	—	The user can't move during the next turn.
Hydro Pump	Water	Special	110	80	5	Normal	—	—	A regular attack.
Hyper Beam	Normal	Special	150	90	5	Normal	—	—	The user can't move during the next turn.
Hyper Fang	Normal	Physical	80	90	15	Normal	○	—	A 10% chance of making the target flinch (unable to use moves on that turn).
Hyper Voice	Normal	Special	90	100	10	Many Others	—	—	Strikes the target even if it is using Substitute. Its power is reduced by 25% when it hits multiple Pokémon.
Hypnosis	Psychic	Status	—	60	20	Normal	—	—	Inflicts the Sleep status condition on the target.

I

Move	Type	Kind	Pow.	Acc.	PP	Range	DA	Long	Effect
Ice Ball	Ice	Physical	30	90	20	Normal	○	—	Attacks consecutively over 5 turns or until it misses. Cannot choose other moves during this time. Damage dealt doubles with each successful hit (max 480). Does twice the damage if used after Defense Curl.
Ice Beam	Ice	Special	90	100	10	Normal	—	—	A 10% chance of inflicting the Frozen status condition on the target.
Ice Fang	Ice	Physical	65	95	15	Normal	○	—	A 10% chance of inflicting the Frozen status condition or making the target flinch (unable to use moves on that turn).
Ice Punch	Ice	Physical	75	100	15	Normal	○	—	A 10% chance of inflicting the Frozen status condition on the target.
Ice Shard	Ice	Physical	40	100	30	Normal	—	—	Always strikes first. The user with the higher Speed goes first if similar moves are used.
Icicle Crash	Ice	Physical	85	90	10	Normal	—	—	A 30% chance of making the target flinch (unable to use moves on that turn).
Icicle Spear	Ice	Physical	25	100	30	Normal	—	—	Attacks 2–5 times in a row in a single turn.
Icy Wind	Ice	Special	55	95	15	Many Others	—	—	Lowers the targets' Speed by 1. Its power is reduced by 25% when it hits multiple Pokémon.
Imprison	Psychic	Status	—	—	10	Self	—	—	Opposing Pokémon cannot use a move if the user knows that move as well.
Incinerate	Fire	Special	60	100	15	Many Others	—	—	Burns up the Berry or Normal Gem being held by each of the targets, which makes them unusable. If the targets are Frozen, they will be thawed. Its power is reduced by 25% when it hits multiple Pokémon.
Inferno	Fire	Special	100	50	5	Normal	—	—	Inflicts the Burned status condition on the target. If the target is Frozen, it will be thawed.
Infestation	Bug	Special	20	100	20	Normal	○	—	Inflicts damage equal to 1/8 the target's max HP for 4–5 turns. The target cannot flee during that time.
Ingrain	Grass	Status	—	—	20	Self	—	—	Restores 1/16 of max HP every turn. The user cannot be switched out after using this move. Ground-type moves will now hit the user even if it is a Flying-type Pokémon or has the Levitate Ability.
Ion Deluge	Electric	Status	—	—	25	Both Sides	—	—	Changes any Normal-type moves used in the same turn into Electric-type moves.
Iron Defense	Steel	Status	—	—	15	Self	—	—	Raises the user's Defense by 2.

Move	Type	Kind	Pow.	Acc.	PP	Range	DA	Long	Effect
Iron Head	Steel	Physical	80	100	15	Normal	○	—	A 30% chance of making the target flinch (unable to use moves on that turn).
Iron Tail	Steel	Physical	100	75	15	Normal	○	—	A 30% chance of lowering the target's Defense by 1.

J

Move	Type	Kind	Pow.	Acc.	PP	Range	DA	Long	Effect
Jump Kick	Fighting	Physical	100	95	10	Normal	○	—	If this move misses, the user loses half of its maximum HP.

K

Move	Type	Kind	Pow.	Acc.	PP	Range	DA	Long	Effect
Karate Chop	Fighting	Physical	50	100	25	Normal	○	—	Critical hits land more easily.
Kinesis	Psychic	Status	—	80	15	Normal	—	—	Lowers the target's accuracy by 1.
King's Shield	Steel	Status	—	—	10	Self	—	—	The user evades all attacks that turn. If an opposing Pokémon uses a move that makes direct contact, its Attack will be lowered by 2.
Knock Off	Dark	Physical	65	100	20	Normal	○	—	The target drops its held item. It gets the item back after the battle. This move does 50% more damage to opponents holding items.

L

Move	Type	Kind	Pow.	Acc.	PP	Range	DA	Long	Effect
Land's Wrath	Ground	Physical	90	100	10	Many Others	—	—	Its power is weaker when it hits multiple Pokémon.
Last Resort	Normal	Physical	140	100	5	Normal	○	—	Fails unless the user has used each of its other moves at least once.
Lava Plume	Fire	Special	80	100	15	Adjacent	—	—	A 30% chance of inflicting the Burned status condition on the targets. If the targets are Frozen, they will be thawed. Its power is reduced by 25% when it hits multiple Pokémon.
Leaf Blade	Grass	Physical	90	100	15	Normal	○	—	Critical hits land more easily.
Leaf Storm	Grass	Special	130	90	5	Normal	—	—	Lowers the user's Sp. Atk by 2.
Leaf Tornado	Grass	Special	65	90	10	Normal	—	—	A 50% chance of lowering the target's accuracy by 1.
Leech Life	Bug	Physical	20	100	15	Normal	○	—	Restores HP by up to half of the damage dealt to the target.
Leech Seed	Grass	Status	—	90	10	Normal	—	—	Steals 1/8 of the target's max HP every turn and absorbs it to restore the user. Keeps working even after the user switches out. Does not work on Grass types.
Leer	Normal	Status	—	100	30	Many Others	—	—	Lowers the targets' Defense by 1.
Lick	Ghost	Physical	30	100	30	Normal	○	—	A 30% chance of inflicting the Paralysis status condition on the target.
Light Screen	Psychic	Status	—	—	30	Your Side	—	—	Halves the damage to the Pokémon on your side from special moves. Effect lasts 5 turns even if the user is switched out. Effect is weaker in Double and Triple Battles.
Lock-On	Normal	Status	—	—	5	Normal	—	—	The user's next move will be a sure hit.
Lovely Kiss	Normal	Status	—	75	10	Normal	—	—	Inflicts the Sleep status condition on the target.
Low Kick	Fighting	Physical	—	100	20	Normal	○	—	The heavier the target is compared to the user, the greater the move's power becomes (max 120).
Low Sweep	Fighting	Physical	65	100	20	Normal	○	—	Lowers the target's Speed by 1.
Lucky Chant	Normal	Status	—	—	30	Your Side	—	—	The Pokémon on your side take no critical hits for 5 turns.

M

Move	Type	Kind	Pow.	Acc.	PP	Range	DA	Long	Effect
Mach Punch	Fighting	Physical	40	100	30	Normal	○	—	Always strikes first. The user with the higher Speed goes first if similar moves are used.
Magic Coat	Psychic	Status	—	—	15	Self	—	—	Always strikes first. Reflects moves with effects like Leech Seed or those that inflict status conditions such as Sleep, Poison, Paralysis, or Confused.
Magic Room	Psychic	Status	—	—	10	Both Sides	—	—	Always strikes last. No held items will have any effect for 5 turns. Fling cannot be used to throw items while Magic Room is in effect. The effect ends if the move is used again.
Magical Leaf	Grass	Special	60	—	20	Normal	—	—	A sure hit.
Magnet Bomb	Steel	Physical	60	—	20	Normal	—	—	A sure hit.
Magnet Rise	Electric	Status	—	—	10	Self	—	—	Nullifies Ground-type moves for 5 turns.
Magnetic Flux	Electric	Status	—	—	20	Your Party	—	○	Raises the Defense and Sp. Def of allies with either the Plus or Minus Abilities.
Magnitude	Ground	Physical	—	100	30	Adjacent	—	—	This move's power varies among 10, 30, 50, 70, 90, 110, and 150. Does twice the damage if targets are underground due to using Dig. Its power is reduced by 25% when it hits multiple Pokémon.
Mat Block	Fighting	Status	—	—	10	Your Side	—	—	Protects the user and allies from damage-dealing moves used in the same turn. Does not protect against status moves.
Me First	Normal	Status	—	—	20	Varies	—	—	Copies the target's chosen move and uses it with 50% greater power. Fails if it does not strike first.
Mean Look	Normal	Status	—	—	5	Normal	—	—	The target cannot escape. If used during a Trainer battle, the opposing Trainer cannot switch Pokémon.
Meditate	Psychic	Status	—	—	40	Self	—	—	Raises the user's Attack by 1.
Mega Drain	Grass	Special	40	100	15	Normal	—	—	Restores HP by up to half of the damage dealt to the target.

Move	Type	Kind	Pow.	Acc.	PP	Range	DA	Long	Effect
Mega Punch	Normal	Physical	80	85	20	Normal	○	—	A regular attack.
Megahorn	Bug	Physical	120	85	10	Normal	○	—	A regular attack.
Memento	Dark	Status	—	100	10	Normal	—	—	The user faints, but the target's Attack and Sp. Atk are lowered by 2.
Metal Burst	Steel	Physical	—	100	10	Varies	—	—	Targets the Pokémon that most recently damaged the user with a move. Inflicts 1.5 times the damage taken.
Metal Claw	Steel	Physical	50	95	35	Normal	○	—	A 10% chance of raising the user's Attack by 1.
Metal Sound	Steel	Status	—	85	40	Normal	—	—	Lowers the target's Sp. Def by 2. Strikes the target even if it is using Substitute.
Metronome	Normal	Status	—	—	10	Self	—	—	Uses one move randomly chosen from all possible moves.
Milk Drink	Normal	Status	—	—	10	Self	—	—	Restores HP by up to half of the user's maximum HP.
Mimic	Normal	Status	—	—	10	Normal	—	—	Copies the target's last-used move (copied move has a PP of 5). Fails if used before the opposing Pokémon uses a move.
Mind Reader	Normal	Status	—	—	5	Normal	—	—	The user's next move will be a sure hit.
Minimize	Normal	Status	—	—	10	Self	—	—	Raises the user's evasion by 2.
Miracle Eye	Psychic	Status	—	—	40	Normal	—	—	Attacks land easily regardless of the target's evasion. Makes Dark-type Pokémon vulnerable to Psychic-type moves.
Mirror Coat	Psychic	Special	—	100	20	Varies	—	—	If the user is attacked with a special move, this move inflicts twice the damage done to the user. Always strikes last.
Mirror Move	Flying	Status	—	—	20	Normal	—	—	Uses the last move that the target used.
Mirror Shot	Steel	Special	65	85	10	Normal	—	—	A 30% chance of lowering the target's accuracy by 1.
Mist	Ice	Status	—	—	30	Your Side	—	—	Protects against stat-lowering moves and additional effects for 5 turns.
Misty Terrain	Fairy	Status	—	—	10	Both Sides	—	—	Covers the field with mist for 5 turns. During that time, Pokémon on the ground take half damage from Dragon-type moves and cannot be afflicted with new status conditions.
Moonblast	Fairy	Special	95	100	15	Normal	—	—	A 30% chance of lowering the target's Sp. Atk by 1.
Moonlight	Fairy	Status	—	—	5	Self	—	—	Recovers 1/2 of the user's maximum HP in normal weather conditions. Recovers 2/3 of the user's maximum HP in sunny weather conditions. Recovers 1/4 of the user's maximum HP in rain/sandstorm/hail weather conditions.
Morning Sun	Normal	Status	—	—	5	Self	—	—	Recovers 1/2 of the user's maximum HP in normal weather conditions. Recovers 2/3 of the user's maximum HP in sunny weather conditions. Recovers 1/4 of the user's maximum HP in rain/sandstorm/hail weather conditions.
Mud Bomb	Ground	Special	65	85	10	Normal	—	—	A 30% chance of lowering the target's accuracy by 1.
Mud Shot	Ground	Special	55	95	15	Normal	—	—	Lowers the target's Speed by 1.
Mud Sport	Ground	Status	—	—	15	Both Sides	—	—	Lowers the power of Electric-type moves to 1/3 of normal for 5 turns.
Muddy Water	Water	Special	90	85	10	Many Others	—	—	A 30% chance of lowering the targets' accuracy by 1. Its power is reduced by 25% when it hits multiple Pokémon.
Mud-Slap	Ground	Special	20	100	10	Normal	—	—	Lowers the target's accuracy by 1.
Mystical Fire	Fire	Special	65	100	10	Normal	—	—	Lowers the target's Sp. Atk by 1.

N

Move	Type	Kind	Pow.	Acc.	PP	Range	DA	Long	Effect
Nasty Plot	Dark	Status	—	—	20	Self	—	—	Raises the user's Sp. Atk by 2.
Natural Gift	Normal	Physical	—	100	15	Normal	—	—	This move's type and power change according to the Berry held by the user. The Berry is consumed when this move is used. This move fails if the user is not holding a Berry.
Nature Power	Normal	Status	—	—	20	Normal	—	—	This move varies depending on the environment: Cave: Power Gem / Dirt/Sand: Earth Power / Grass / Grassy Terrain: Energy Ball / Electric Terrain: Thunderbolt / Ice: Ice Beam / Indoors / Sky Battle / Link Battle: Tri Attack / Misty Terrain: Moonblast / Snow: Frost Breath / Swamp: Mud Bomb / Water Surface / Puddles / Shoals: Hydro Pump
Needle Arm	Grass	Physical	60	100	15	Normal	○	—	A 30% chance of making the target flinch (unable to use moves on that turn).
Night Daze	Dark	Special	85	95	10	Normal	—	—	A 40% chance of lowering the target's accuracy by 1.
Night Shade	Ghost	Special	—	100	15	Normal	—	—	Deals a fixed amount of damage equal to the user's level.
Night Slash	Dark	Physical	70	100	15	Normal	○	—	Critical hits land more easily.
Nightmare	Ghost	Status	—	100	15	Normal	—	—	Lowers the target's HP by 1/4 of maximum after each turn. Fails if the target is not asleep.
Noble Roar	Normal	Status	—	100	30	Normal	—	—	Lowers the target's Attack and Sp. Atk by 1. Strikes the target even if it is using Substitute.
Nuzzle	Electric	Physical	20	100	20	Normal	○	—	Inflicts the Paralysis status condition on the target.

O

Move	Type	Kind	Pow.	Acc.	PP	Range	DA	Long	Effect
Oblivion Wing	Flying	Special	80	100	10	Normal	—	○	Restores HP by up to 3/4 of the damage dealt to the target.
Octazooka	Water	Special	65	85	10	Normal	—	—	A 50% chance of lowering the target's accuracy by 1.

Move	Type	Kind	Pow.	Acc.	PP	Range	DA	Long	Effect
Odor Sleuth	Normal	Status	—	—	40	Normal	—	—	Attacks land easily regardless of the target's evasion. Makes Ghost-type Pokémon vulnerable to Normal- and Fighting-type moves.
Ominous Wind	Ghost	Special	60	100	5	Normal	—	—	A 10% chance of raising the user's Attack, Defense, Speed, Sp. Atk, and Sp. Def stats by 1.
Outrage	Dragon	Physical	120	100	10	1 Random	○	—	Attacks consecutively over 2–3 turns. Cannot choose other moves during this time. The user becomes Confused after using this move.
Overheat	Fire	Special	130	90	5	Normal	—	—	Lowers the user's Sp. Atk by 2. If the target is Frozen, it will be thawed.

P

Move	Type	Kind	Pow.	Acc.	PP	Range	DA	Long	Effect
Pain Split	Normal	Status	—	—	20	Normal	—	—	The user and target's HP are added, then divided equally between them.
Parabolic Charge	Electric	Special	50	100	20	Adjacent	—	—	Restores HP by up to half of the damage dealt to the target. Its power is weaker when it hits multiple Pokémon.
Parting Shot	Dark	Status	—	100	20	Normal	—	—	Lowers the target's Attack and Sp. Atk. After attacking, user switches out with another Pokémon in the party. Strikes the target even if it is using Substitute.
Pay Day	Normal	Physical	40	100	20	Normal	—	—	Increases the amount of prize money received after battle (the user's level, multiplied by the number of attacks, multiplied by 5).
Payback	Dark	Physical	50	100	10	Normal	○	—	This move's power is doubled if the user strikes after the target.
Peck	Flying	Physical	35	100	35	Normal	○	○	A regular attack.
Perish Song	Normal	Status	—	—	5	Adjacent	—	○	All adjacent Pokémon in battle will faint after 3 turns, unless switched out. Strikes the target even if it is using Substitute.
Petal Blizzard	Grass	Physical	90	100	15	Adjacent	—	—	Its power is weaker when it hits multiple Pokémon.
Petal Dance	Grass	Special	120	100	10	1 Random	○	—	Attacks consecutively over 2–3 turns. Cannot choose other moves during this time. The user becomes Confused after using this move.
Phantom Force	Ghost	Physical	90	100	10	Normal	○	—	User disappears on the first turn and attacks on the second. Strikes the target even if it is using Detect, King's Shield, Mat Block, Protect, or Spiky Shield. If the target has used Minimize, it will be a sure hit and its power will be doubled.
Pin Missile	Bug	Physical	25	95	20	Normal	—	—	Attacks 2–5 times in a row in a single turn.
Play Nice	Normal	Status	—	—	20	Normal	—	—	A sure hit. Lowers the target's Attack by 1. Strikes the target even if it is using Detect, King's Shield, Mat Block, Protect, Spiky Shield, or Substitute.
Play Rough	Fairy	Physical	90	90	10	Normal	○	—	A 10% chance of lowering the target's Attack by 1.
Pluck	Flying	Physical	60	100	20	Normal	○	○	If the target is holding a Berry with a battle effect, the user eats that Berry and uses its effect.
Poison Fang	Poison	Physical	50	100	15	Normal	○	—	A 50% chance of inflicting the Badly Poisoned status condition on the target. Damage from being Badly Poisoned increases with every turn.
Poison Gas	Poison	Status	—	90	40	Many Others	—	—	Inflicts the Poison status condition on the targets.
Poison Jab	Poison	Physical	80	100	20	Normal	○	—	A 30% chance of inflicting the Poison status condition on the target.
Poison Powder	Poison	Status	—	75	35	Normal	—	—	Inflicts the Poison status condition on the targets.
Poison Sting	Poison	Physical	15	100	35	Normal	○	—	A 30% chance of inflicting the Poison status condition on the target.
Poison Tail	Poison	Physical	50	100	25	Normal	○	—	A 10% chance of inflicting the Poison status condition on the target. Critical hits land more easily.
Pound	Normal	Physical	40	100	35	Normal	○	—	A regular attack.
Powder	Bug	Status	—	100	20	Normal	—	—	Deals damage equal to 1/4 of max HP if the target uses a Fire-type move in the same turn.
Powder Snow	Ice	Special	40	100	25	Many Others	—	—	A 10% chance of inflicting the Frozen status condition on the targets. Its power is reduced by 25% when it hits multiple Pokémon.
Power Gem	Rock	Special	80	100	20	Normal	—	—	A regular attack.
Power Split	Psychic	Status	—	—	10	Normal	—	—	The user and the target's Attack and Sp. Atk are added, then divided equally between them.
Power Swap	Psychic	Status	—	—	10	Normal	—	—	Swaps Attack and Sp. Atk changes between the user and the target.
Power Trick	Psychic	Status	—	—	10	Self	—	—	Swaps original Attack and Defense stats (does not swap stat changes).
Power Whip	Grass	Physical	120	85	10	Normal	○	—	A regular attack.
Power-Up Punch	Fighting	Physical	40	100	20	Normal	○	—	Raises the user's Attack by 1.
Present	Normal	Physical	—	90	15	Normal	—	—	This move's power varies among 40 (40% chance), 80 (30% chance), and 120 (10% chance). It also has a 20% chance of healing the target by 1/4 of its maximum HP.
Protect	Normal	Status	—	—	10	Self	—	—	The user evades all moves that turn. If used in succession, its chance of failing rises.
Psybeam	Psychic	Special	65	100	20	Normal	—	—	A 10% chance of inflicting the Confused status condition on the target.
Psych Up	Normal	Status	—	—	10	Normal	—	—	Copies the target's stat changes to the user.
Psychic	Psychic	Special	90	100	10	Normal	—	—	A 10% chance of lowering the target's Sp. Def by 1.

Move	Type	Kind	Pow.	Acc.	PP	Range	DA	Long	Effect
Psycho Cut	Psychic	Physical	70	100	20	Normal	—	—	Critical hits land more easily.
Psycho Shift	Psychic	Status	—	100	10	Normal	—	—	Shifts the user's Paralysis, Poison, Badly Poisoned, Burned, or Sleep status conditions to the target and heals the user.
Psyshock	Psychic	Special	80	100	10	Normal	—	—	Damage depends on the user's Sp. Atk and the target's Defense.
Psystrike	Psychic	Special	100	100	10	Normal	—	—	Damage depends on the user's Sp. Atk and the target's Defense.
Psywave	Psychic	Special	—	100	15	Normal	—	—	Inflicts damage equal to the user's level multiplied by a random value between 0.5 and 1.5.
Punishment	Dark	Physical	—	100	5	Normal	○	—	With each level that the target's stats increase, the move's power becomes greater (max 200).
Pursuit	Dark	Physical	40	100	20	Normal	○	—	Does twice the usual damage if the target is switching out.

Q

Move	Type	Kind	Pow.	Acc.	PP	Range	DA	Long	Effect
Quash	Dark	Status	—	100	15	Normal	—	—	The user suppresses the target and makes it move last that turn. Fails if the target has already used its move that turn.
Quick Attack	Normal	Physical	40	100	30	Normal	○	—	Always strikes first. The user with the higher Speed goes first if similar moves are used.
Quick Guard	Fighting	Status	—	—	15	Your Side	—	—	Protects the user and its allies from first-strike moves.
Quiver Dance	Bug	Status	—	—	20	Self	—	—	Raises the user's Sp. Atk, Sp. Def, and Speed by 1.

R

Move	Type	Kind	Pow.	Acc.	PP	Range	DA	Long	Effect
Rage	Normal	Physical	20	100	20	Normal	○	—	Attack rises by 1 with each hit the user takes.
Rage Powder	Bug	Status	—	—	20	Self	—	—	This move goes first. Opposing Pokémon aim only at the user.
Rain Dance	Water	Status	—	—	5	Both Sides	—	—	Changes the weather condition to rain for 5 turns, strengthening Water-type moves by 50% and reducing the power of Fire-type moves by 50%.
Rapid Spin	Normal	Physical	20	100	40	Normal	○	—	Releases the user from moves such as Bind, Leech Seed, Spikes, and Wrap.
Razor Leaf	Grass	Physical	55	95	25	Many Others	—	—	Critical hits land more easily. Its power is reduced by 25% when it hits multiple Pokémon.
Razor Shell	Water	Physical	75	95	10	Normal	○	—	A 50% chance of lowering the target's Defense by 1.
Razor Wind	Normal	Special	80	100	10	Many Others	—	—	The user stores power on the first turn and attacks on the second. Critical hits land more easily. Its power is reduced by 25% when it hits multiple Pokémon.
Recover	Normal	Status	—	—	10	Self	—	—	Restores HP by up to half of the user's maximum HP.
Recycle	Normal	Status	—	—	10	Self	—	—	A held item that has been used can be used again.
Reflect	Psychic	Status	—	—	20	Your Side	—	—	Halves the damage to the Pokémon on your side from physical moves. Effect lasts 5 turns even if the user is switched out. Effect is weaker in Double and Triple Battles.
Reflect Type	Normal	Status	—	—	15	Normal	—	—	The user becomes the same type as the target.
Refresh	Normal	Status	—	—	20	Self	—	—	Heals Poison, Badly Poisoned, Paralysis, and Burned conditions.
Rest	Psychic	Status	—	—	10	Self	—	—	Fully restores HP, but makes the user sleep for 2 turns.
Retaliate	Normal	Physical	70	100	5	Normal	○	—	This move's power is doubled if an ally fainted in the previous turn.
Return	Normal	Physical	—	100	20	Normal	○	—	This move's power is affected by friendship. The higher the user's friendship, the greater the move's power (max 102).
Revenge	Fighting	Physical	60	100	10	Normal	○	—	This move's power is doubled if the user has taken damage from the target that turn.
Reversal	Fighting	Physical	—	100	15	Normal	○	—	The lower the user's HP is, the greater the move's power becomes (max 200).
Roar	Normal	Status	—	—	20	Normal	—	—	Ends wild Pokémon battles. If the opposing Pokémon's level is higher than the user's, this move fails. In a Double Battle with Pokémon, this move fails. In a battle with a Trainer, this move forces the opposing Trainer to switch Pokémon. When there is no Pokémon to switch in, this move fails. Strikes the target even if it is using Detect, King's Shield, Mat Block, Protect, Spiky Shield, or Substitute.
Rock Blast	Rock	Physical	25	90	10	Normal	—	—	Attacks 2–5 times in a row in a single turn.
Rock Climb	Normal	Physical	90	85	20	Normal	○	—	A 20% chance of inflicting the Confused status condition on the target.
Rock Polish	Rock	Status	—	—	20	Self	—	—	Raises the user's Speed by 2.
Rock Slide	Rock	Physical	75	90	10	Many Others	—	—	A 30% chance of making the targets flinch (unable to use moves on that turn). Its power is reduced by 25% when it hits multiple Pokémon.
Rock Smash	Fighting	Physical	40	100	15	Normal	○	—	A 50% chance of lowering the target's Defense by 1.
Rock Throw	Rock	Physical	50	90	15	Normal	—	—	A regular attack.
Rock Tomb	Rock	Physical	60	95	15	Normal	—	—	Lowers the target's Speed by 1.
Rock Wrecker	Rock	Physical	150	90	5	Normal	—	—	The user can't move during the next turn.
Role Play	Psychic	Status	—	—	10	Normal	—	—	Copies the target's Ability. Fails with certain Abilities, however.
Rolling Kick	Fighting	Physical	60	85	15	Normal	○	—	A 30% chance of making the target flinch (unable to use moves on that turn).

Move	Type	Kind	Pow.	Acc.	PP	Range	DA	Long	Effect
Rollout	Rock	Physical	30	90	20	Normal	○	—	Attacks consecutively over 5 turns or until it misses. Cannot choose other moves during this time. Damage dealt doubles with every successful hit (max 480). Does twice the damage if used after Defense Curl.
Roost	Flying	Status	—	—	10	Self	—	—	Restores HP by up to half of the user's maximum HP, but takes away the Flying type from the user for that turn.
Rototiller	Ground	Status	—	—	10	Adjacent	—	○	Raises the Attack and Sp. Atk of Grass-type Pokémon by 1.
Round	Normal	Special	60	100	15	Normal	—	—	When multiple Pokémon use this move in a turn, the first one to use it is followed immediately by the others. Attack's power is doubled when following another Pokémon using the same move. Strikes the target even if it is using Substitute.

S

Move	Type	Kind	Pow.	Acc.	PP	Range	DA	Long	Effect
Sacred Sword	Fighting	Physical	90	100	15	Normal	○	—	Ignores the stat changes of the opposing Pokémon, except for Speed.
Safeguard	Normal	Status	—	—	25	Your Side	—	—	Protects the Pokémon on your side from status conditions for 5 turns. Effects last even if the user switches out.
Sand Attack	Ground	Status	—	100	15	Normal	—	—	Lowers the target's accuracy by 1.
Sand Tomb	Ground	Physical	35	85	15	Normal	—	—	Inflicts damage equal to 1/8 the target's max HP for 4–5 turns. The target cannot flee during that time.
Sandstorm	Rock	Status	—	—	10	Both Sides	—	—	Changes the weather condition to sandstorm for 5 turns. Raises the Sp. Def of Rock-type Pokémon by 50% for the length of the sandstorm. All Pokémon other than Rock, Steel, and Ground types take damage each turn equal to 1/16 of their max HP.
Scald	Water	Special	80	100	15	Normal	—	—	A 30% chance of inflicting the Burned status condition on the target. This move can be used even when the user is Frozen. Using this move will thaw the user, relieving the Frozen status condition.
Scary Face	Normal	Status	—	100	10	Normal	—	—	Lowers the targets' Speed by 2.
Scratch	Normal	Physical	40	100	35	Normal	○	—	A regular attack.
Screech	Normal	Status	—	85	40	Normal	—	—	Lowers the target's Defense by 2. Strikes the target even if it is using Substitute.
Secret Power	Normal	Physical	70	100	20	Normal	—	—	A 30% chance of one of the following additional effects, depending on the environment: Cave: Target flinches Dirt/Sand: Lowers accuracy by 1 Grass/Grassy Terrain: Sleep status condition Indoors / Sky Battle / Electric Terrain / Link Battle: Inflicts Paralysis status condition Misty Terrain: Lowers Sp. Atk by 1 Snow/Ice: Inflicts Frozen status condition Swamp: Lowers Speed by 1 Water Surface / Puddles / Shoals: Lowers Attack by 1
Seed Bomb	Grass	Physical	80	100	15	Normal	—	—	A regular attack.
Seismic Toss	Fighting	Physical	—	100	20	Normal	○	—	Deals a fixed amount of damage equal to the user's level.
Self-Destruct	Normal	Physical	200	100	5	Adjacent	—	—	The user faints after using it. Its power is reduced by 25% when it hits multiple Pokémon.
Shadow Ball	Ghost	Special	80	100	15	Normal	—	—	A 20% chance of lowering the target's Sp. Def by 1.
Shadow Claw	Ghost	Physical	70	100	15	Normal	○	—	Critical hits land more easily.
Shadow Punch	Ghost	Physical	60	—	20	Normal	○	—	A sure hit.
Shadow Sneak	Ghost	Physical	40	100	30	Normal	○	—	Always strikes first. The user with the higher Speed goes first if similar moves are used.
Sharpen	Normal	Status	—	—	30	Self	—	—	Raises the user's Attack by 1.
Sheer Cold	Ice	Special	—	30	5	Normal	—	—	The target faints with one hit if the user's level is equal to or greater than the target's level. The higher the user's level is compared to the target's, the more accurate the move is.
Shell Smash	Normal	Status	—	—	15	Self	—	—	Lowers the user's Defense and Sp. Def by 1 and raises the user's Attack, Sp. Atk, and Speed by 2.
Shock Wave	Electric	Special	60	—	20	Normal	—	—	A sure hit.
Signal Beam	Bug	Special	75	100	15	Normal	—	—	A 10% chance of inflicting the Confused status condition on the target.
Silver Wind	Bug	Special	60	100	5	Normal	—	—	A 10% chance of raising the user's Attack, Defense, Speed, Sp. Atk, and Sp. Def stats by 1.
Simple Beam	Normal	Status	—	100	15	Normal	—	—	Changes the target's Ability to Simple. Fails with certain Abilities, however.
Sing	Normal	Status	—	55	15	Normal	—	—	Inflicts the Sleep status condition on the target. Strikes the target even if it is using Substitute.
Sketch	Normal	Status	—	—	1	Normal	—	—	Copies the last move used by the target. The user then forgets Sketch and learns the new move.
Skill Swap	Psychic	Status	—	—	10	Normal	—	—	Swaps Abilities between the user and target. Fails with certain Abilities, however.
Skull Bash	Normal	Physical	130	100	10	Normal	○	—	Builds power on the first turn and attacks on the second. It raises the user's Defense stat by 1 on the first turn.
Sky Attack	Flying	Physical	140	90	5	Normal	—	○	Builds power on the first turn and attacks on the second. Critical hits land more easily. A 30% chance of making the target flinch (unable to use moves on that turn).

Move	Type	Kind	Pow.	Acc.	PP	Range	DA	Long	Effect
Sky Drop	Flying	Physical	60	100	10	Normal	○	○	The user takes the target into the sky, and then damages it by dropping it during the next turn. Does not damage Flying-type Pokémon. Pokémon weighing over 440.9 lbs. cannot be lifted.
Sky Uppercut	Fighting	Physical	85	90	15	Normal	○	—	It even hits Pokémon that are in the sky due to having used moves such as Fly and Bounce.
Slack Off	Normal	Status	—	—	10	Self	—	—	Restores HP by up to half of the user's maximum HP.
Slam	Normal	Physical	80	75	20	Normal	○	—	A regular attack.
Slash	Normal	Physical	70	100	20	Normal	○	—	Critical hits land more easily.
Sleep Powder	Grass	Status	—	75	15	Normal	—	—	Inflicts the Sleep status condition on the target.
Sleep Talk	Normal	Status	—	—	10	Self	—	—	Only works when the user is asleep. Randomly uses one of the user's moves.
Sludge	Poison	Special	65	100	20	Normal	—	—	A 30% chance of inflicting the Poison status condition on the target.
Sludge Bomb	Poison	Special	90	100	10	Normal	—	—	A 30% chance of inflicting the Poison status condition on the target.
Sludge Wave	Poison	Special	95	100	10	Adjacent	—	—	A 10% chance of inflicting the Poison status condition on the targets. Its power is reduced by 25% when it hits multiple Pokémon.
Smack Down	Rock	Physical	50	100	15	Normal	—	—	Ground-type moves will now hit a Pokémon with the Levitate Ability or a Flying-type Pokémon. They will also hit a Pokémon that is in the sky due to using a move such as Fly or Bounce.
Smelling Salts	Normal	Physical	70	100	10	Normal	○	—	Deals twice the usual damage to targets with Paralysis, but heals that status condition.
Smog	Poison	Special	30	70	20	Normal	—	—	A 40% chance of inflicting the Poison status condition on the target.
Smokescreen	Normal	Status	—	100	20	Normal	—	—	Lowers the target's accuracy by 1.
Snarl	Dark	Special	55	95	15	Many Others	—	—	Lowers the targets' Sp. Atk by 1. Its power is weaker when it hits multiple Pokémon. Strikes the target even if it is using Substitute.
Snatch	Dark	Status	—	—	10	Self	—	—	Steals the effects of recovery or stat-changing moves used by the target on that turn and applies them to the user.
Snore	Normal	Special	50	100	15	Normal	—	—	Only works when the user is asleep. A 30% chance of making the target flinch (unable to use moves on that turn). Strikes the target even if it is using Substitute.
Soak	Water	Status	—	100	20	Normal	—	—	Changes the target's type to Water.
Solar Beam	Grass	Special	120	100	10	Normal	—	—	Builds power on the first turn and attacks on the second. In sunny weather conditions, attacks on first turn. In rain/sandstorm/hail weather conditions, the power is halved.
Sonic Boom	Normal	Special	—	90	20	Normal	—	—	Deals a fixed 20 points of damage.
Spark	Electric	Physical	65	100	20	Normal	○	—	A 30% chance of inflicting the Paralysis status condition on the target.
Spider Web	Bug	Status	—	—	10	Normal	—	—	The target cannot escape. If used during a Trainer battle, the opposing Trainer cannot switch Pokémon.
Spike Cannon	Normal	Physical	20	100	15	Normal	—	—	Attacks 2–5 times in a row in a single turn.
Spikes	Ground	Status	—	—	20	Other Side	—	—	Damages Pokémon as they are sent out to the opposing side. Power rises with each use, up to 3 times (1st time: 1/8 of maximum HP; 2nd time: 1/6 of maximum HP; 3rd time: 1/4 of maximum HP). Ineffective against Flying-type Pokémon and Pokémon with the Levitate Ability.
Spiky Shield	Grass	Status	—	—	10	Self	—	—	The user takes no damage in the same turn this move is used. If an opposing Pokémon uses a move that makes direct contact, the attacker will be damaged for 1/8 of its maximum HP.
Spit Up	Normal	Special	—	100	10	Normal	—	—	The more times the user has used Stockpile, the greater the move's power becomes (max 300). Fails if the user has not used Stockpile first. Nullifies Defense and Sp. Def stat increases caused by Stockpile.
Spite	Ghost	Status	—	100	10	Normal	—	—	Takes 4 points from the PP of the target's last used move.
Splash	Normal	Status	—	—	40	Self	—	—	No effect.
Spore	Grass	Status	—	100	15	Normal	—	—	Inflicts the Sleep status condition on the target.
Stealth Rock	Rock	Status	—	—	20	Other Side	—	—	Damages Pokémon as they are sent out to the opposing side. Damage is subject to type matchups.
Steamroller	Bug	Physical	65	100	20	Normal	○	—	A 30% chance of making the targets flinch (unable to use moves on that turn). If the target has used Minimize, this move will be a sure hit and its power will be doubled.
Steel Wing	Steel	Physical	70	90	25	Normal	○	—	A 10% chance of raising the user's Defense by 1.
Sticky Web	Bug	Status	—	—	20	Other Side	—	—	Lowers the Speed of any Pokémon sent out to the opposing side by 1.
Stockpile	Normal	Status	—	—	20	Self	—	—	Raises the user's Defense and Sp. Def by 1. Can be used up to 3 times.
Stomp	Normal	Physical	65	100	20	Normal	○	—	A 30% chance of making the targets flinch (unable to use moves on that turn). If the target has used Minimize, this move will be a sure hit and its power will be doubled.
Stone Edge	Rock	Physical	100	80	5	Normal	—	—	Critical hits land more easily.
Stored Power	Psychic	Special	20	100	10	Normal	—	—	With each level that the user's stats increase, the move's power increases by 20 (max 860).
Storm Throw	Fighting	Physical	60	100	10	Normal	○	—	Always delivers a critical hit.
Strength	Normal	Physical	80	100	15	Normal	○	—	A regular attack.
String Shot	Bug	Status	—	95	40	Many Others	—	—	Lowers the targets' Speed by 2.

Move	Type	Kind	Pow.	Acc.	PP	Range	DA	Long	Effect
Struggle	Normal	Physical	50	—	1	Normal	○	—	This move becomes available when all other moves are out of PP. The user takes damage equal to 1/4 of its maximum HP. Inflicts damage regardless of type matchup.
Struggle Bug	Bug	Special	50	100	20	Many Others	—	—	Lowers the targets' Sp. Atk by 1. Its power is weaker when it hits multiple Pokémon.
Stun Spore	Grass	Status	—	75	30	Normal	—	—	Inflicts the Paralysis status condition on the target.
Submission	Fighting	Physical	80	80	20	Normal	○	—	The user takes 1/4 of the damage inflicted.
Substitute	Normal	Status	—	—	10	Self	—	—	Uses 1/4 of maximum HP to create a copy of the user.
Sucker Punch	Dark	Physical	80	100	5	Normal	○	—	This move attacks first and deals damage only if the target's chosen move is an attack move.
Sunny Day	Fire	Status	—	—	5	Both Sides	—	—	Changes the weather condition to sunny for 5 turns, strengthening Fire-type moves by 50% and reducing the power of Water-type moves by 50%.
Super Fang	Normal	Physical	—	90	10	Normal	○	—	Halves the target's HP.
Superpower	Fighting	Physical	120	100	5	Normal	○	—	Lowers the user's Attack and Defense by 1.
Supersonic	Normal	Status	—	55	20	Normal	—	—	Inflicts the Confused status condition on the target. Strikes the target even if it is using Substitute.
Surf	Water	Special	90	100	15	Adjacent	—	—	Does twice the damage if the target is using Dive when attacked. Its power is weaker when it hits multiple Pokémon.
Swagger	Normal	Status	—	90	15	Normal	—	—	Inflicts the Confused status condition on the target, but also raises its Attack by 2.
Swallow	Normal	Status	—	—	10	Self	—	—	Restores HP, the amount of which is determined by how many times the user has used Stockpile. Fails if the user has not used Stockpile first. Nullifies Defense and Sp. Def stat increases caused by Stockpile.
Sweet Kiss	Fairy	Status	—	75	10	Normal	—	—	Inflicts the Confused status condition on the target.
Sweet Scent	Normal	Status	—	100	20	Many Others	—	—	Lowers the targets' evasion by 2.
Swift	Normal	Special	60	—	20	Many Others	—	—	A sure hit. Its power is weaker when it hits multiple Pokémon.
Switcheroo	Dark	Status	—	100	10	Normal	—	—	Swaps items between the user and the target.
Swords Dance	Normal	Status	—	—	20	Self	—	—	Raises the user's Attack by 2.
Synchronoise	Psychic	Special	120	100	10	Adjacent	—	—	Inflicts damage on any Pokémon of the same type as the user. Its power is weaker when it hits multiple Pokémon.
Synthesis	Grass	Status	—	—	5	Self	—	—	Recovers 1/2 of the user's maximum HP in normal weather conditions. Recovers 2/3 of the user's maximum HP in sunny weather conditions. Recovers 1/4 of the user's maximum HP in rain/sandstorm/hail weather conditions.

T

Move	Type	Kind	Pow.	Acc.	PP	Range	DA	Long	Effect
Tackle	Normal	Physical	50	100	35	Normal	○	—	A regular attack.
Tail Glow	Bug	Status	—	—	20	Self	—	—	Raises the user's Sp. Atk by 3.
Tail Slap	Normal	Physical	25	85	10	Normal	○	—	Attacks 2–5 times in a row in a single turn.
Tail Whip	Normal	Status	—	100	30	Many Others	—	—	Lowers the targets' Defense by 1.
Tailwind	Flying	Status	—	—	15	Your Side	—	—	Doubles the Speed of the Pokémon on your side for 4 turns.
Take Down	Normal	Physical	90	85	20	Normal	○	—	The user takes 1/4 of the damage inflicted.
Taunt	Dark	Status	—	100	20	Normal	—	—	Prevents the target from using anything other than attack moves for 3 turns.
Teeter Dance	Normal	Status	—	100	20	Adjacent	—	—	Inflicts the Confused status condition on the target.
Telekinesis	Psychic	Status	—	—	15	Normal	—	—	Makes the target float for 3 turns. All moves land regardless of their accuracy except for Ground-type moves and one-hit KO moves such as Fissure, Guillotine, Horn Drill, and Sheer Cold.
Teleport	Psychic	Status	—	—	20	Self	—	—	Ends wild Pokémon battles.
Thief	Dark	Physical	60	100	25	Normal	○	—	When the target is holding an item and the user is not, the user can steal that item. When the target is not holding an item, this move will function as a normal attack.
Thrash	Normal	Physical	120	100	10	1 Random	○	—	Attacks consecutively over 2–3 turns. Cannot choose other moves during this time. The user becomes Confused after using this move.
Thunder	Electric	Special	110	70	10	Normal	—	—	A 30% chance of inflicting the Paralysis status condition on the target. Is 100% accurate in the rain weather condition and 50% accurate in the sunny weather condition. It hits even Pokémon that are in the sky due to using moves such as Fly and Bounce.
Thunder Fang	Electric	Physical	65	95	15	Normal	○	—	A 10% chance of making the target flinch (unable to use moves on that turn).
Thunder Punch	Electric	Physical	75	100	15	Normal	○	—	A 10% chance of inflicting the Paralysis status condition on the target.
Thunder Shock	Electric	Special	40	100	30	Normal	—	—	A 10% chance of inflicting the Paralysis status condition on the target.
Thunder Wave	Electric	Status	—	100	20	Normal	—	—	Inflicts the Paralysis status condition on the target. Does not work on Ground types.
Thunderbolt	Electric	Special	90	100	15	Normal	—	—	A 10% chance of inflicting the Paralysis status condition on the target.
Tickle	Normal	Status	—	100	20	Normal	—	—	Lowers the target's Attack and Defense by 1.
Topsy-Turvy	Dark	Status	—	—	20	Normal	—	—	Reverses the effects of any stat changes affecting the target.
Torment	Dark	Status	—	100	15	Normal	—	—	Makes the target unable to use the same move twice in a row.

Pokémon Moves

Move	Type	Kind	Pow.	Acc.	PP	Range	DA	Long	Effect
Toxic	Poison	Status	—	90	10	Normal	—	—	Inflicts the Badly Poisoned status condition on the target. Damage from being Badly Poisoned increases with every turn. It never misses if used by a Poison-type Pokémon.
Toxic Spikes	Poison	Status	—	—	20	Other Side	—	—	Lays a trap of poison spikes on the opposing side that inflict the Poison status condition on Pokémon that switch into battle. Using Toxic Spikes twice inflicts the Badly Poisoned condition. The damage from the Badly Poisoned condition increases every turn. Toxic Spikes' effects end when a Poison-type Pokémon switches into battle. Ineffective against Flying-type Pokémon and Pokémon with the Levitate Ability.
Transform	Normal	Status	—	—	10	Normal	—	—	The user transforms into the target. The user has the same moves and Ability as the target (all moves have 5 PP).
Tri Attack	Normal	Special	80	100	10	Normal	—	—	A 20% chance of inflicting the Paralysis, Burned, or Frozen status condition on the target.
Trick	Psychic	Status	—	100	10	Normal	—	—	Swaps items between the user and the target.
Trick Room	Psychic	Status	—	—	5	Both Sides	—	—	Always strikes last. For 5 turns, Pokémon with lower Speed go first. First-strike moves still go first. Self-canceling if used again while Trick Room is still in effect.
Trick-or-Treat	Ghost	Status	—	100	20	Normal	—	—	Gives the target the Ghost type in addition to its original type(s).
Trump Card	Normal	Special	—	—	5	Normal	○	—	A sure hit. The lower the user's PP is, the greater the move's power becomes (max 200).
Twineedle	Bug	Physical	25	100	20	Normal	—	—	Attacks twice in a row in a single turn. A 20% chance of inflicting the Poison status condition on the target.
Twister	Dragon	Special	40	100	20	Many Others	—	—	A 20% chance of making the targets flinch (unable to use moves on that turn). Does twice the damage if the targets are in the sky due to moves such as Fly or Bounce. Its power is weaker when it hits multiple Pokémon.

U

Move	Type	Kind	Pow.	Acc.	PP	Range	DA	Long	Effect
Uproar	Normal	Special	90	100	10	1 Random	—	—	The user makes an uproar for 3 turns. During that time, no Pokémon can fall asleep. Strikes the target even if it is using Substitute.
U-turn	Bug	Physical	70	100	20	Normal	○	—	After attacking, the user switches out with another Pokémon in the party.

V

Move	Type	Kind	Pow.	Acc.	PP	Range	DA	Long	Effect
Vacuum Wave	Fighting	Special	40	100	30	Normal	—	—	Always strikes first. The user with the higher Speed goes first if similar moves are used.
Venom Drench	Poison	Status	—	100	20	Many Others	—	—	Lowers the Attack, Sp. Atk, and Speed of opposing Pokémon afflicted with Poison or Badly Poisoned status conditions by 1.
Venoshock	Poison	Special	65	100	10	Normal	—	—	Does twice the damage to a target that has the Poison or Badly Poisoned status condition.
Vice Grip	Normal	Physical	55	100	30	Normal	○	—	A regular attack.
Vine Whip	Grass	Physical	45	100	25	Normal	○	—	A regular attack.
Vital Throw	Fighting	Physical	70	—	10	Normal	○	—	Always strikes later than normal, but has perfect accuracy.
Volt Switch	Electric	Special	70	100	20	Normal	—	—	After attacking, the user switches out with another Pokémon in the party.
Volt Tackle	Electric	Physical	120	100	15	Normal	○	—	The user takes 1/3 of the damage inflicted. A 10% chance of inflicting the Paralysis status condition on the target.

W

Move	Type	Kind	Pow.	Acc.	PP	Range	DA	Long	Effect
Wake-Up Slap	Fighting	Physical	70	100	10	Normal	○	—	Does twice the usual damage to a sleeping target, but heals that status condition.
Water Gun	Water	Special	40	100	25	Normal	—	—	A regular attack.
Water Pledge	Water	Special	80	100	10	Normal	—	—	When combined with Fire Pledge or Grass Pledge, the power and effect change. If combined with Fire Pledge, the power is 150 and it remains a Water-type move. This makes it more likely that your team's moves will have additional effects for 4 turns. If combined with Grass Pledge, the power is 150 and it becomes a Grass-type move. This lowers the Speed of opposing Pokémon for 4 turns.
Water Pulse	Water	Special	60	100	20	Normal	—	○	A 20% chance of inflicting the Confused status condition on the target.
Water Shuriken	Water	Physical	15	100	20	Normal	—	—	Always strikes first. The user with the higher Speed goes first if similar moves are used. Attacks 2–5 times in a row in a single turn.
Water Sport	Water	Status	—	—	15	Both Sides	—	—	Lowers the power of Fire-type moves to 1/3 of normal for 5 turns.
Water Spout	Water	Special	150	100	5	Many Others	—	—	If the user's HP is low, this move has lower power. Its power is weaker when it hits multiple Pokémon.
Waterfall	Water	Physical	80	100	15	Normal	○	—	A 20% chance of making the target flinch (unable to use moves on that turn).

AFTER THE HALL OF FAME

CENTRAL KALOS

COASTAL KALOS

MOUNTAIN KALOS

ADVENTURE DATA

Move	Type	Kind	Pow.	Acc.	PP	Range	DA	Long	Effect
Weather Ball	Normal	Special	50	100	10	Normal	—	—	In special weather conditions, this move's type changes and its attack power doubles. Sunny weather condition: Fire type. Rain weather condition: Water type. Hail weather condition: Ice type. Sandstorm weather condition: Rock type.
Whirlpool	Water	Special	35	85	15	Normal	—	—	Inflicts damage equal to 1/8 the target's max HP for 4–5 turns. The target cannot flee during that time. Does twice the damage if the target is using Dive when attacked.
Whirlwind	Normal	Status	—	—	20	Normal	—	—	Ends wild Pokémon battles. If the opposing Pokémon's level is higher than the user's, this move fails. In a Double Battle with wild Pokémon, this move fails. In a battle with a Trainer, this move forces the opposing Trainer to switch Pokémon. When there are no Pokémon to switch in, this move fails. Strikes the target even if it is using Detect, King's Shield, Mat Block, Protect, or Spiky Shield.
Wide Guard	Rock	Status	—	—	10	Your Side	—	—	Protects your side from any moves used that turn that target multiple Pokémon.
Wild Charge	Electric	Physical	90	100	15	Normal	○	—	The user takes 1/4 of the damage inflicted.
Will-O-Wisp	Fire	Status	—	85	15	Normal	—	—	Inflicts the Burned status condition on the target.
Wing Attack	Flying	Physical	60	100	35	Normal	○	○	A regular attack.
Wish	Normal	Status	—	—	10	Self	—	—	Restores 1/2 of maximum HP at the end of the next turn. Works even if the user has switched out.
Withdraw	Water	Status	—	—	40	Self	—	—	Raises the user's Defense by 1.
Wonder Room	Psychic	Status	—	—	10	Both Sides	—	—	Always strikes last. Each Pokémon's Defense and Sp. Def stats are swapped for 5 turns. The effect ends if the move is used again.
Wood Hammer	Grass	Physical	120	100	15	Normal	○	—	The user takes 1/3 of the damage inflicted.
Work Up	Normal	Status	—	—	30	Self	—	—	Raises the user's Attack and Sp. Atk by 1.
Worry Seed	Grass	Status	—	100	10	Normal	—	—	Changes the target's Ability to Insomnia. Fails with certain Abilities, however.
Wrap	Normal	Physical	15	90	20	Normal	○	—	Inflicts damage equal to 1/8 the target's max HP for 4–5 turns. The target cannot flee during that time.
Wring Out	Normal	Special	—	100	5	Normal	○	—	The more HP the target has left, the greater the move's power becomes (max 120).

XYZ

Move	Type	Kind	Pow.	Acc.	PP	Range	DA	Long	Effect
X-Scissor	Bug	Physical	80	100	15	Normal	○	—	A regular attack.
Yawn	Normal	Status	—	—	10	Normal	—	—	Inflicts the Sleep status condition on the target at the end of the next turn unless the target switches out.
Zap Cannon	Electric	Special	120	50	5	Normal	—	—	Inflicts the Paralysis status condition on the target.
Zen Headbutt	Psychic	Physical	80	90	15	Normal	○	—	A 20% chance of making the target flinch (unable to use moves on that turn).

Field Moves

Move	Effects in the field
Cut	Cuts down thorny trees so your party may pass.
Dig	Pulls you out of spaces like caves, returning you to the last entrance you went through.
Flash	Enables you to see farther and makes you less likely to encounter wild Pokémon in caves. The effect lasts until you exit the cave.
Fly	Whisks you instantly to a town or city you've visited before.
Milk Drink	Distributes part of the user's own HP among teammates.
Rock Smash	Smashes cracked rocks and walls so your party may pass. Smashed rocks may contain items or wild Pokémon.
Strength	Allows you to move large rocks and push them into holes to create new paths.
Surf	Allows you to move across the surface of a body of water.
Sweet Scent	Attracts wild Pokémon and makes them attack. If you are in an area prone to Horde Encounters, a horde of Pokémon will definitely appear.
Teleport	Transports you to the last Pokémon Center you used (cannot be used in caves or similar locations.)
Waterfall	Allows you to climb up and down waterfalls.

How to Obtain TMs

No.	Move	How to obtain	Price
1	Hone Claws	Route 5	—
2	Dragon Claw	Victory Road (Outside)	—
3	Psyshock	Victory Road (Inside)	—
4	Calm Mind	Defeat Olympia at the Anistar City Pokémon Gym	—
5	Roar	Get for 24 BP at the Battle Maison in Kiloude City	—
6	Toxic	From a woman on Route 14	—
7	Hail	Shalour City Poké Mart	50,000
8	Bulk Up	From a Battle Girl in a house in Snowbelle City	—
9	Venoshock	Route 6	—
10	Hidden Power	From a man in a house in Anistar City	—
11	Sunny Day	Lumiose City South Boulevard Poké Mart	50,000
12	Taunt	From a Team Flare Grunt in Lysandre Labs	—
13	Ice Beam	Defeat Wulfric at the Snowbelle City Pokémon Gym	—
14	Blizzard	Anistar City Poké Mart	70,000
15	Hyper Beam	Anistar City Poké Mart	90,000
16	Light Screen	Kiloude City Poké Mart	30,000
17	Protect	From the Butler in Parfum Palace	—
18	Rain Dance	Lumiose City South Boulevard Poké Mart	50,000
19	Roost	Route 8	—
20	Safeguard	Shalour City Poké Mart	30,000
21	Frustration	From a Backpacker in the Connecting Cave	—
22	Solar Beam	Route 21	—
23	Smack Down	Get for 32 BP at the Battle Maison in Kiloude City	—
24	Thunderbolt	Defeat Clemont at the Lumiose City Pokémon Gym	—
25	Thunder	Anistar City Poké Mart	70,000
26	Earthquake	Route 22	—
27	Return	From Dexio on Route 4	—
28	Dig	Shalour City Poké Mart	10,000
29	Psychic	Pokémon Village	—
30	Shadow Ball	Terminus Cave B2F	—
31	Brick Break	Terminus Cave B1F	—
32	Double Team	From a woman in Anistar City Pokémon Center (talk to her between 4 A.M. and 10:59 A.M.)	—
33	Reflect	Kiloude City Poké Mart	30,000
34	Sludge Wave	Get for 32 BP at the Battle Maison in Kiloude City	—
35	Flamethrower	From a woman in Anistar City Pokémon Center (talk to her between 11 A.M. and 5:59 P.M.)	—
36	Sludge Bomb	Route 19	—
37	Sandstorm	Shalour City Poké Mart	50,000
38	Fire Blast	Anistar City Poké Mart	70,000
39	Rock Tomb	Defeat Grant at the Cyllage City Pokémon Gym	—
40	Aerial Ace	Connecting Cave	—
41	Torment	From a boy in Laverre City	—
42	Facade	From a boy in a house in Dendemille Town	—
43	Flame Charge	From a Worker in Kalos Power Plant (after defeating Team Flare)	—
44	Rest	From a man in Hotel Cyllage in Cyllage City	—
45	Attract	From a girl at Baa de Mer Ranch on Route 12	—
46	Thief	From a woman in Cassius's house in Camphrier Town	—
47	Low Sweep	From a man in the Tower of Mastery in Shalour City	—
48	Round	Get for 16 BP at the Battle Maison in Kiloude City	—
49	Echoed Voice	From a woman on Hotel Richissime 5F in Lumiose City	—
50	Overheat	Kiloude City Poké Mart	80,000
51	Steel Wing	Get for 32 BP at the Battle Maison in Kiloude City	—
52	Focus Blast	Anistar City Poké Mart	10,000
53	Energy Ball	Route 20	—
54	False Swipe	From a Scientist at the Pokémon Lab in Lumiose City (when you've seen 20+ Central Kalos Pokémon)	—
55	Scald	Correctly answer the quiz given by a girl in Couriway Hotel in Couriway Town	—
56	Fling	From a woman in the Lost Hotel	—
57	Charge Beam	Route 13	—
58	Sky Drop	From a woman in a house in Kiloude City	—
59	Incinerate	Get for 16 BP at the Battle Maison in Kiloude City	—
60	Quash	Get for 24 BP at the Battle Maison in Kiloude City	—
61	Will-O-Wisp	Route 14	—
62	Acrobatics	Correctly answer the quiz given by a woman in Coumarine City	—
63	Embargo	Correctly answer the quiz given by a woman in Coumarine City	—
64	Explosion	Get for 48 BP at the Battle Maison in Kiloude City	—
65	Shadow Claw	Glittering Cave	—
66	Payback	From an old man in Geosenge Town Pokémon Center	—
67	Retaliate	Get for 48 BP at the Battle Maison in Kiloude City	—
68	Giga Impact	Kiloude City Poké Mart	90,000
69	Rock Polish	Route 11	—
70	Flash	From Tierno in Reflection Cave	—
71	Stone Edge	Frost Cavern (Outside)	—

Left margin tabs: AFTER THE HALL OF FAME · CENTRAL KALOS · COASTAL KALOS · MOUNTAIN KALOS · ADVENTURE DATA

No.	Move	How to obtain	Price
72	Volt Switch	Get for 48 BP at the Battle Maison in Kiloude City	—
73	Thunder Wave	Route 10	—
74	Gyro Ball	Reflection Cave B2F	—
75	Swords Dance	Lumiose City South Boulevard Poké Mart	10,000
76	Struggle Bug	Lumiose City South Boulevard Poké Mart	10,000
77	Psych Up	From a woman in Anistar City Pokémon Center (talk to her between 6 P.M. and 7:59 P.M.)	—
78	Bulldoze	Lumiose City South Boulevard Poké Mart	10,000
79	Frost Breath	Frost Cavern 2F	—
80	Rock Slide	Couriway Town	—
81	X-Scissor	Azure Bay	—
82	Dragon Tail	From a man in Lumiose Museum in Lumiose City	—
83	Infestation	Defeat Viola at the Santalune City Pokémon Gym	—
84	Poison Jab	Shalour City Poké Mart	10,000
85	Dream Eater	Get for 48 BP at the Battle Maison in Kiloude City	—
86	Grass Knot	Defeat Ramos at the Coumarine City Pokémon Gym	—
87	Swagger	Get for 24 BP at the Battle Maison in Kiloude City	—
88	Sleep Talk	From a woman in Hotel Cyllage in Cyllage City	—
89	U-turn	From an old woman in Couriway Town	—
90	Substitute	From a woman in Anistar City Pokémon Center (talk to her between 8 P.M. and 3:59 A.M.)	—
91	Flash Cannon	From a girl in a house in Kiloude City	—
92	Trick Room	Correctly answer the quiz given by a woman in Coumarine City	—
93	Wild Charge	Kiloude City Poké Mart	50,000
94	Rock Smash	From a woman in Ambrette Town	—
95	Snarl	Lost Hotel	—
96	Nature Power	From a woman in Hotel Ambrette in Ambrette Town	—
97	Dark Pulse	Route 15	—
98	Power-Up Punch	Defeat Korrina at the Shalour City Pokémon Gym	—
99	Dazzling Gleam	Defeat Valerie at the Laverre City Pokémon Gym	—
100	Confide	Correctly answer the quiz given by a woman in Coumarine City	—

How to Obtain HMs

No.	Move	How to obtain	Price
1	Cut	Parfum Palace courtyard	—
2	Fly	From Professor Sycamore in Coumarine City	—
3	Surf	From Serena/Calem in Shalour City	—
4	Strength	From Grant in Cyllage City	—
5	Waterfall	From Shauna on Route 19	—

Moves Taught by Others and Where to Learn Them

Move	Location
Blast Burn	Move Tutor's house in Snowbelle City (talk to the old man inside)
Draco Meteor	Move Tutor's house on Route 21 (talk to the Black Belt inside)
Fire Pledge	Move Tutor's house in Laverre City (talk to the man inside)
Frenzy Plant	Move Tutor's house in Snowbelle City (talk to the old man inside)
Grass Pledge	Move Tutor's house in Laverre City (talk to the man inside)
Hydro Cannon	Move Tutor's house in Snowbelle City (talk to the old man inside)
Water Pledge	Move Tutor's house in Laverre City (talk to the man inside)

AFTER THE HALL OF FAME

CENTRAL KALOS

COASTAL KALOS

MOUNTAIN KALOS

ADVENTURE DATA

A

Ability	Effect in battle	Effect when the Pokémon is the lead in your party
Adaptability	The power boost received by using a move of the same type as the Pokémon will be 100% instead of 50%.	—
Aerilate	Changes Normal-type moves to Flying type and increases their power by 30%.	—
Aftermath	Knocks off 1/4 of the attacking Pokémon's maximum HP when a direct attack causes the Pokémon to faint.	—
Analytic	The power of its move is increased by 30% when the Pokémon moves last.	—
Anger Point	Raises the Pokémon's Attack to the maximum when hit by a critical hit.	—
Anticipation	Warns if your opponent's Pokémon has supereffective moves or one-hit KO moves when the Pokémon enters battle.	—
Arena Trap	Prevents the opponent's Pokémon from fleeing or switching out. Ineffective against Flying-type Pokémon and Pokémon with the Levitate Ability.	Makes it easier to encounter wild Pokémon.
Aroma Veil	Protects the team from Attract, Disable, Encore, Heal Block, Taunt, and Torment.	—
Aura Break	Reverses the effects of the Fairy Aura Ability and lowers the power of Fairy-type moves by 25%. Reverses the Dark Aura Ability and lowers the power of Dark-type moves by 25%.	—

B

Ability	Effect in battle	Effect when the Pokémon is the lead in your party
Battle Armor	Opposing Pokémon's moves will not hit critically.	—
Big Pecks	Prevents Defense from being lowered.	—
Blaze	Raises the power of Fire-type moves by 50% when the Pokémon's HP drops to 1/3 or less.	—
Bulletproof	Protects against Acid Spray, Aura Sphere, Barrage, Bullet Seed, Egg Bomb, Electro Ball, Energy Ball, Focus Blast, Gyro Ball, Ice Ball, Magnet Bomb, Mist Ball, Mud Bomb, Octazooka, Rock Wrecker, Searing Shot, Seed Bomb, Shadow Ball, Sludge Bomb, Weather Ball, and Zap Cannon.	—

C

Ability	Effect in battle	Effect when the Pokémon is the lead in your party
Cheek Pouch	Eating a Berry not only grants its usual benefits, but also restores 1/3 of the Pokémon's maximum HP.	—
Chlorophyll	Doubles Speed in the sunny weather condition.	—
Clear Body	Protects against stat-lowering moves and Abilities.	—
Cloud Nine	Eliminates effects of weather on Pokémon.	—
Color Change	Changes the Pokémon's type into the type of the move that just hit it.	—
Competitive	When an opponent's move or Ability lowers the Pokémon's stats, the Pokémon's Sp. Atk rises by 2.	—
Compound Eyes	Raises accuracy by 30%.	Raises encounter rate with wild Pokémon holding items.
Contrary	Makes stat changes have an opposite effect (increase instead of decrease and vice versa).	—
Cursed Body	Provides a 30% chance of inflicting Disable on the move the opponent used to hit the Pokémon.	—
Cute Charm	Provides a 30% chance of inflicting the Infatuated status condition when hit with a direct attack.	Raises encounter rate of wild Pokémon of the opposite gender.

D

Ability	Effect in battle	Effect when the Pokémon is the lead in your party
Damp	Prevents Pokémon on either side from using Explosion or Self-Destruct. Nullifies the Aftermath Ability.	—
Dark Aura	Raises the power of Dark-type moves by 1/3. Affects all Pokémon in the field.	—
Defiant	When an opponent's move or Ability lowers the Pokémon's stats, the Pokémon's Attack rises by 2.	—
Drizzle	Makes the weather rain for five turns when the Pokémon enters battle.	—
Drought	Makes the weather sunny for five turns when the Pokémon enters battle.	—
Dry Skin	Restores HP by 1/4 of the Pokémon's maximum HP when the Pokémon is hit by a Water-type move. Restores HP by 1/8 of its maximum HP at the end of every turn in the rain weather condition. However, the damage the Pokémon receives from Fire-type moves increases by 25%. Takes damage of 1/8 of its maximum HP at the end of every turn in the sunny weather condition.	—

E

Ability	Effect in battle	Effect when the Pokémon is the lead in your party
Early Bird	Causes the Pokémon to wake quickly from the Sleep status condition.	—
Effect Spore	Provides a 30% chance of inflicting the Poison, Paralysis, or Sleep status conditions when hit with a direct attack.	—

F

Ability	Effect in battle	Effect when the Pokémon is the lead in your party
Fairy Aura	Raises the power of Fairy-type moves by 1/3. Affects all Pokémon in the field.	—
Filter	Decreases the damage received from supereffective moves by 25%.	—
Flame Body	Provides a 30% chance of inflicting the Burned status condition when hit with a direct attack.	Facilitates hatching Eggs in your party.
Flare Boost	Increases the power of special moves by 50% when Burned.	—
Flash Fire	When the Pokémon is hit by a Fire-type move, rather than taking damage, its Fire-type moves increase power by 50%.	—
Flower Veil	Grass-type allies cannot have their stats lowered, and they are protected from being inflicted with status conditions.	—
Forewarn	Reveals a move an opponent knows when the Pokémon enters battle. Damaging attack moves with high power are prioritized.	—
Friend Guard	Reduces damage done to allies by 25%.	—
Frisk	Checks an opponent's held item when the Pokémon enters battle.	—
Fur Coat	Halves the damage taken from physical moves.	—

G

Ability	Effect in battle	Effect when the Pokémon is the lead in your party
Gale Wings	Gives priority to Flying-type moves.	—
Gluttony	Allows the Pokémon to use its held Berry sooner when it has low HP.	—
Gooey	Lowers the Speed of an attacker who makes direct contact by 1.	—
Grass Pelt	Raises Defense by 50% when the field is affected by Grassy Terrain.	—
Guts	Attack stat rises by 50% when the Pokémon is affected by a status condition.	—

H

Ability	Effect in battle	Effect when the Pokémon is the lead in your party
Harvest	Provides at every turn end a 50% chance of restoring the Berry the Pokémon used, and a 100% chance when the weather condition is sunny.	—
Healer	At the end of every turn, it provides a 33% chance that an ally Pokémon's status condition will be healed.	—
Heavy Metal	Doubles the Pokémon's weight.	—
Honey Gather	If the Pokémon isn't holding an item, it will sometimes be left holding Honey after a battle (even if it didn't participate). Its chance of finding Honey increases with its level.	—
Huge Power	Doubles Attack.	—
Hustle	Raises Attack by 50%, but lowers the accuracy of the Pokémon's physical moves by 20%.	Makes it easier to encounter high-level wild Pokémon.
Hydration	Cures status conditions at the end of each turn during the rain weather condition.	—
Hyper Cutter	Prevents Attack from being lowered.	—

I

Ability	Effect in battle	Effect when the Pokémon is the lead in your party
Ice Body	Restores HP by 1/16 of the Pokémon's maximum HP at the end of every turn in the hail weather condition.	—
Illuminate	No effect.	Makes it easier to encounter wild Pokémon.
Illusion	Appears in battle disguised as the last Pokémon in the party.	—
Immunity	Protects against the Poison status condition.	—
Imposter	Transforms itself into the Pokémon it is facing as it enters battle.	—
Infiltrator	Moves can hit even if the target used Light Screen, Mist, Reflect, Safeguard, or Substitute.	—
Inner Focus	The Pokémon doesn't flinch as an additional effect of a move.	—
Insomnia	Protects against the Sleep status condition.	—
Intimidate	When this Pokémon enters battle, it lowers the opposing Pokémon's Attack by 1.	Lowers encounter rate with low-level wild Pokémon.
Iron Barbs	Knocks off 1/8 of the attacking Pokémon's HP when the Pokémon makes a direct attack.	—
Iron Fist	Increases the power of Bullet Punch, Comet Punch, Dizzy Punch, Drain Punch, Dynamic Punch, Fire Punch, Focus Punch, Hammer Arm, Ice Punch, Mach Punch, Mega Punch, Power-Up Punch, Shadow Punch, Sky Uppercut, and Thunder Punch by 20%.	—

J

Ability	Effect in battle	Effect when the Pokémon is the lead in your party
Justified	When the Pokémon is hit by a Dark-type move, Attack goes up by 1.	—

K

Ability	Effect in battle	Effect when the Pokémon is the lead in your party
Keen Eye	Prevents accuracy from being lowered. Ignores evasiveness-raising moves.	Lowers encounter rate with low-level wild Pokémon.
Klutz	Causes the Pokémon's held items to have no effect.	—

L

Ability	Effect in battle	Effect when the Pokémon is the lead in your party
Leaf Guard	Protects the Pokémon from status conditions when in the sunny weather condition.	—
Levitate	Gives full immunity from all Ground-type moves.	—
Light Metal	Halves the Pokémon's weight.	—
Lightning Rod	Draws all Electric-type moves to the Pokémon. When the Pokémon is hit by an Electric-type move, rather than taking damage, its Sp. Atk goes up by 1 .	—
Limber	Protects against the Paralysis status condition.	—
Liquid Ooze	When an opposing Pokémon uses an HP-draining move, it damages the user instead.	—

M

Ability	Effect in battle	Effect when the Pokémon is the lead in your party
Magic Bounce	Reflects status moves.	—
Magic Guard	The Pokémon will not take damage from anything other than a direct attack. Nullifies the Aftermath, Iron Barbs, Liquid Ooze, and Rough Skin Abilities, the hail and sandstorm weather conditions, and the Burned, Poison, and Badly Poisoned status conditions. The effects of Bind, Clamp, Curse, Fire Pledge, Fire Spin, Flame Burst, Infestation, Leech Seed, Nightmare, Sand Tomb, Spikes, Stealth Rock, Whirlpool, and Wrap are negated, as are the item effects from Black Sludge, Life Orb, Rocky Helmet, and Sticky Barb. The Pokémon also receives no recoil or move-failure damage from attacks.	—
Magician	The Pokémon seizes the item of an opponent it hits with a move. Fails if the Pokémon is already holding an item.	—
Magma Armor	Prevents the Frozen status condition.	Facilitates hatching Eggs in your party.
Magnet Pull	Prevents Steel-type opponents from fleeing or switching out.	Raises encounter rate with wild Steel-type Pokémon.
Marvel Scale	Defense stat increases by 50% when the Pokémon is affected by a status condition.	—
Mega Launcher	Raises the power of Aura Sphere, Dark Pulse, Dragon Pulse, and Water Pulse by 50%. Heal Pulse will restore 75% of the target's maximum HP.	—
Minus	Raises Sp. Atk by 50% when another ally has the Ability Plus or Minus.	—
Mold Breaker	Allows the Pokémon to use moves on targets regardless of their Abilities. Does not nullify Abilities that have effects after an attack. For example, the Pokémon can score a critical hit against a target with Battle Armor, but it will still take damage from Rough Skin.	—
Moody	Raises one stat by 2 and lowers another by 1 at the end of every turn.	—
Motor Drive	When the Pokémon is hit by an Electric-type move, rather than taking damage, its Speed goes up by 1.	—
Moxie	When the Pokémon knocks out an opponent with a move, Attack goes up 1.	—
Multiscale	Halves damage when HP is full.	—

N

Ability	Effect in battle	Effect when the Pokémon is the lead in your party
Natural Cure	Cures the Pokémon's status conditions when it switches out.	—
No Guard	Moves used by or against the Pokémon always strike their targets.	Makes it easier to encounter wild Pokémon.
Normalize	Changes all of the Pokémon's moves to Normal-type.	—

O

Ability	Effect in battle	Effect when the Pokémon is the lead in your party
Oblivious	Protects against the Infatuated status condition. Immune to Captivate and Taunt.	—
Overcoat	Protects the Pokémon from weather damage, such as hail and sandstorm. Protects it from Cotton Spore, Poison Powder, Powder, Rage Powder, Sleep Powder, Spore, and Stun Spore. Immune to the Effect Spore Ability.	—
Overgrow	Raises the power of Grass-type moves by 50% when the Pokémon's HP drops to 1/3 or less.	—
Own Tempo	Protects against the Confused status condition.	—

P

Ability	Effect in battle	Effect when the Pokémon is the lead in your party
Parental Bond	Causes attacks to strike twice, with the second hit dealing only half the normal damage. Does not affect moves that naturally strike multiple times or moves that strike multiple targets.	—
Pickpocket	Steals an item when hit with a direct attack. It fails if the Pokémon is already holding an item.	—
Pickup	At the end of every turn, the Pokémon picks up the item that the opposing Pokémon used that turn. Fails if the Pokémon is already holding an item.	If the Pokémon has no held item, it sometimes picks one up after battle (even if it didn't participate). It picks up different items depending on its level.
Pixilate	Changes Normal-type moves to Fairy-type and increases their power by 30%.	—
Plus	Raises Sp. Atk by 50% when another ally has the Ability Plus or Minus.	—

Ability	Effect in battle	Effect when the Pokémon is the lead in your party
Poison Heal	Restores 1/8 of the Pokémon's maximum HP at the end of every turn if the Pokémon has the Poison or Badly Poisoned status condition rather than taking damage.	—
Poison Point	Provides a 30% chance of inflicting the Poison status condition when the Pokémon is hit by a direct attack.	—
Poison Touch	Provides a 30% chance of inflicting the Poison status condition when the Pokémon uses a direct attack.	—
Prankster	Gives priority to status moves.	—
Pressure	When the Pokémon is hit by an opponent's move, it depletes 1 additional PP from that move.	Makes it easier to encounter high-level wild Pokémon.
Protean	Changes the Pokémon's type to the same type as the move it has just used.	—
Pure Power	Doubles its Attack stat.	—

Q

Ability	Effect in battle	Effect when the Pokémon is the lead in your party
Quick Feet	Increases Speed by 50% when the Pokémon is affected by status conditions.	Lowers wild Pokémon encounter rate.

R

Ability	Effect in battle	Effect when the Pokémon is the lead in your party
Rain Dish	Restores HP by 1/16 of the Pokémon's maximum HP at the end of every turn in the rain weather condition.	—
Rattled	When the Pokémon is hit by a Ghost-, Dark-, or Bug-type move, Speed goes up by 1.	—
Reckless	Raises the power of moves by 20% with recoil damage.	—
Refrigerate	Changes Normal-type moves to Ice type and increases their power by 30%.	—
Regenerator	Restores 1/3 its maximum HP when withdrawn from battle.	—
Rivalry	If the target is the same gender, the Pokémon's Attack goes up by 25%. If the target is of the opposite gender, its Attack goes down by 25%. No effect when the gender is unknown.	—
Rock Head	No recoil damage from moves like Take Down and Double-Edge.	—
Rough Skin	Knocks off 1/8 of the attacking Pokémon's maximum HP when the Pokémon makes a direct attack.	—
Run Away	Allows the Pokémon to always escape from a battle with a wild Pokémon.	—

S

Ability	Effect in battle	Effect when the Pokémon is the lead in your party
Sand Force	Raises the power of Ground-, Rock-, and Steel-type moves by 30% in the sandstorm weather condition. Sandstorm does not damage the Pokémon.	—
Sand Rush	Doubles Speed in the sandstorm weather condition. Sandstorm does not damage the Pokémon.	—
Sand Stream	Makes the weather sandstorm for five turns when the Pokémon enters battle.	—
Sand Veil	The accuracy of the opposing Pokémon's move decreases by 20% in the sandstorm weather condition. Sandstorm does not damage the Pokémon with this Ability.	Lowers encounter rate with wild Pokémon in the sandstorm weather condition.
Sap Sipper	When the Pokémon is hit by a Grass-type move, rather than taking damage, its Attack goes up by 1.	—
Scrappy	Allows the Pokémon to hit Ghost-type Pokémon with Normal- and Fighting-type moves. (The type matchup changes from "It's not very effective..." to normal.)	—
Serene Grace	Doubles chances of moves inflicting additional effects.	—
Shadow Tag	Prevents the opposing Pokémon from fleeing or switching out. If both your and the opposing Pokémon have this Ability, the effect is canceled.	—
Shed Skin	At the end of every turn, provides a 33% chance of curing the Pokémon's status conditions.	—
Sheer Force	When moves with an additional effect are used, power increases by 30%, but the additional effect is lost.	—
Shell Armor	Opposing Pokémon's moves will not hit critically.	—
Shield Dust	Protects the Pokémon from additional effects of moves.	—
Simple	Doubles the effects of stat changes.	—
Skill Link	Moves that strike successively strike the maximum number of times (2–5 times means it always strikes 5 times).	—
Sniper	Moves that deliver a critical hit deal 125% more damage.	—
Snow Cloak	The accuracy of the opposing Pokémon's move decreases by 20% in the hail weather condition. Hail does not damage Pokémon with this Ability.	Lowers encounter rate with wild Pokémon in the hail weather condition.
Snow Warning	Makes the weather hail for five turns when the Pokémon enters battle.	—
Solar Power	Raises Sp. Atk by 50%, but takes damage of 1/8 of the Pokémon's maximum HP at the end of every turn in the sunny weather condition.	—
Solid Rock	Decreases the damage received from supereffective moves by 25%.	—
Soundproof	Protects the Pokémon from sound-based moves: Boomburst, Bug Buzz, Chatter, Confide, Disarming Voice, Echoed Voice, Grass Whistle, Growl, Heal Bell, Hyper Voice, Metal Sound, Noble Roar, Parting Shot, Perish Song, Roar, Round, Screech, Sing, Snarl, Snore, Supersonic, Uproar.	—
Speed Boost	Raises Speed by 1 at the end of every turn.	—
Stall	The Pokémon's moves are used last in the turn.	—

Pokémon Abilities

Ability	Effect in battle	Effect when the Pokémon is the lead in your party
Stance Change	Changes from Shield Forme to Blade Forme when an attack move is used. Changes from Blade Forme to Shield Forme when King's Shield is used.	—
Static	A 30% chance of inflicting the Paralysis status condition when hit with a direct attack.	Raises encounter rate with wild Electric-type Pokémon.
Steadfast	Raises Speed by 1 every time the Pokémon flinches.	—
Stench	Has a 10% chance of making the target flinch when the Pokémon uses a move to deal damage.	Lowers wild Pokémon encounter rate.
Sticky Hold	Prevents the Pokémon's held item from being stolen.	Makes Pokémon bite more often when fishing.
Strong Jaw	Raises the power of Bite, Crunch, Fire Fang, Hyper Fang, Ice Fang, Poison Fang, and Thunder Fang by 50%.	—
Sturdy	Protects the Pokémon against one-hit KO moves like Horn Drill and Sheer Cold. Leaves the Pokémon with 1 HP if hit by a move that would knock it out when its HP is full.	—
Suction Cups	Nullifies moves like Dragon Tail, Roar, and Whirlwind, which would force Pokémon to switch out.	Makes Pokémon bite more often when fishing.
Super Luck	Heightens the critical-hit ratio of the Pokémon's moves.	—
Swarm	Raises the power of Bug-type moves by 50% when the Pokémon's HP drops to 1/3 or less.	—
Sweet Veil	Protects the team against the Sleep status condition.	—
Swift Swim	Doubles Speed in the rain weather condition.	—
Symbiosis	When an ally uses its item, the Pokémon gives its own item to that ally.	—
Synchronize	When the Pokémon receives the Poison, Paralysis, or Burned status condition, this inflicts the same condition.	Raises encounter rate with wild Pokémon with the same Nature.

T

Ability	Effect in battle	Effect when the Pokémon is the lead in your party
Tangled Feet	Raises evasion when the Pokémon has the Confused status condition.	—
Technician	If the move's power is 60 or less, its power will increase by 50%. Also takes effect if a move's power is altered by itself or by another move.	—
Telepathy	Prevents damage from allies.	—
Thick Fat	Halves damage from Fire- and Ice-type moves.	—
Tinted Lens	Nullifies the type disadvantage of the Pokémon's not-very-effective moves: 1/2 damage turns into regular damage, 1/4 damage turns into 1/2 damage.	—
Torrent	Raises the power of Water-type moves by 50% when the Pokémon's HP drops to 1/3 or less.	—
Tough Claws	Raises the power of direct attacks by 30%.	—
Toxic Boost	Increases the power of physical moves by 50% when it has the Poison or Badly Poisoned status condition.	—
Trace	Makes the Pokémon's Ability the same as the opponent's, except for certain Abilities like Trace.	—
Truant	Allows the Pokémon to use a move only once every other turn.	—

U

Ability	Effect in battle	Effect when the Pokémon is the lead in your party
Unaware	Ignores the stat changes of the opposing Pokémon, except Speed.	—
Unburden	Doubles Speed if the Pokémon loses or consumes a held item. Its Speed returns to normal if the Pokémon holds another item. No effect if the Pokémon starts out with no held item.	—
Unnerve	Prevent the opposing Pokémon from eating Berries.	—

V

Ability	Effect in battle	Effect when the Pokémon is the lead in your party
Vital Spirit	Protects against the Sleep status condition.	Makes it easier to encounter high-level wild Pokémon.
Volt Absorb	When the Pokémon is hit by an Electric-type move, HP is restored by 25% of its maximum HP rather than taking damage.	—

W

Ability	Effect in battle	Effect when the Pokémon is the lead in your party
Water Absorb	When the Pokémon is hit by a Water-type move, HP is restored by 25% of its maximum HP rather than taking damage.	—
Water Veil	Prevents the Burned status condition.	—
Weak Armor	When the Pokémon is hit by a physical attack, Defense goes down by 1, but Speed goes up by 1.	—
White Smoke	Protects against stat-lowering moves and Abilities.	Lowers wild Pokémon encounter rate.
Wonder Guard	Protects the Pokémon against all moves except supereffective ones.	—
Wonder Skin	Makes status moves more likely to miss.	—

Items Picked Up with the Pickup Ability

Item	Level of Pokémon with Pickup Ability									
	Lv. 1									Lv. 100
Potion	◎									
Antidote	○	◎								
Super Potion	○	○	◎							
Great Ball	○	○	○	◎						
Repel	○	○	○	○	◎					
Escape Rope	○	○	○	○	○	◎				
Full Heal	○	○	○	○	○	○	◎			
Hyper Potion	○	○	○	○	○	○	○	◎		
Ultra Ball	△	△	○	○	○	○	○	○	◎	
Revive		△	△	○	○	○	○	○	○	◎
Rare Candy			△	△	○	○	○	○	○	○
Sun Stone				△	△	○	○	○	○	○
Moon Stone					△	△	○	○	○	○
Heart Scale						△	△	○	○	○
Full Restore			▲	▲			△	△	○	○
Max Revive								△	△	○
PP Up									△	△
Max Elixir										△
Nugget	▲	▲								
King's Rock		▲	▲							
Ether				▲	▲					
Iron Ball					▲	▲				
Prism Scale						▲	▲	▲	▲	▲
Elixir							▲	▲		
Leftovers									▲	▲

◎ Often found ○ Sometimes found △ Rarely found ▲ Almost never found

Pokémon's Natures

Each individual Pokémon has a Nature, which affects how its stats grow when it levels up.

Pokémon's stats	ATTACK	DEFENSE	SPEED	SP. ATK	SP. DEF
Adamant	○			▲	
Bashful					
Bold	▲	○			
Brave	○		▲		
Calm	▲				○
Careful				▲	○
Docile					
Gentle		▲			○
Hardy					
Hasty		▲	○		
Impish		○		▲	
Jolly			○	▲	
Lax		○			▲
Lonely	○	▲			
Mild		▲		○	
Modest	▲			○	
Naive			○		▲
Naughty	○				▲
Quiet			▲	○	
Quirky					
Rash				○	▲
Relaxed		○	▲		
Sassy			▲		○
Serious					
Timid	▲		○		

○ Gains more upon leveling up
▲ Gains less upon leveling up

Pokémon's Characteristics

On top of having a Nature, each individual Pokémon has a Characteristic. This also affects how the Pokémon's stats grow when it levels up.

Stat that grows easily	Characteristic
HP	Loves to eat.
	Takes plenty of siestas.
	Nods off a lot.
	Scatters things often.
	Likes to relax.

Stat that grows easily	Characteristic
ATTACK	Proud of its power.
	Likes to thrash about.
	A little quick tempered.
	Likes to fight.
	Quick tempered.

Stat that grows easily	Characteristic
DEFENSE	Sturdy body.
	Capable of taking hits.
	Highly persistent.
	Good endurance.
	Good perseverance.

Stat that grows easily	Characteristic
SPEED	Likes to run.
	Alert to sounds.
	Impetuous and silly.
	Somewhat of a clown.
	Quick to flee.

Stat that grows easily	Characteristic
SP. ATK	Highly curious.
	Mischievous.
	Thoroughly cunning.
	Often lost in thought.
	Very finicky.

Stat that grows easily	Characteristic
SP. DEF	Strong willed.
	Somewhat vain.
	Strongly defiant.
	Hates to lose.
	Somewhat stubborn.

Base Stats Raised through Defeating Wild Pokémon in Kalos

Kalos No.	Pokémon	HP	ATTACK	DEFENSE	SP. ATK	SP. DEF	SPEED
Central Kalos Pokédex 010	Bunnelby	—	—	—	—	—	O
Central Kalos Pokédex 011	Diggersby	O	—	—	—	—	—
Central Kalos Pokédex 012	Zigzagoon	—	—	—	—	—	O
Central Kalos Pokédex 014	Fletchling	—	—	—	—	—	O
Central Kalos Pokédex 017	Pidgey	—	—	—	—	—	O
Central Kalos Pokédex 020	Scatterbug	—	—	O	—	—	—
Central Kalos Pokédex 023	Caterpie	O	—	—	—	—	—
Central Kalos Pokédex 024	Metapod	—	—	O	—	—	—
Central Kalos Pokédex 026	Weedle	—	—	—	—	—	O
Central Kalos Pokédex 027	Kakuna	—	—	O	—	—	—
Central Kalos Pokédex 029	Pansage	—	—	—	—	—	O
Central Kalos Pokédex 031	Pansear	—	—	—	—	—	O
Central Kalos Pokédex 033	Panpour	—	—	—	—	—	O
Central Kalos Pokédex 036	Pikachu	—	—	—	—	—	O
Central Kalos Pokédex 038	Bidoof	O	—	—	—	—	—
Central Kalos Pokédex 039	Bibarel	—	O	—	—	—	—
Central Kalos Pokédex 040	Dunsparce	O	—	—	—	—	—
Central Kalos Pokédex 041	Azurill	O	—	—	—	—	—
Central Kalos Pokédex 042	Marill	O	—	—	—	—	—
Central Kalos Pokédex 043	Azumarill	O	—	—	—	—	—
Central Kalos Pokédex 044	Burmy	—	—	—	—	O	—
Central Kalos Pokédex 048	Masquerain	—	—	—	O	O	—
Central Kalos Pokédex 049	Magikarp	—	—	—	—	—	O
Central Kalos Pokédex 050	Gyarados	—	O	—	—	—	—
Central Kalos Pokédex 051	Corphish	—	O	—	—	—	—
Central Kalos Pokédex 052	Crawdaunt	—	O	—	—	—	—
Central Kalos Pokédex 053	Goldeen	—	O	—	—	—	—
Central Kalos Pokédex 054	Seaking	—	O	—	—	—	—
Central Kalos Pokédex 055	Carvanha	—	O	—	—	—	—
Central Kalos Pokédex 056	Sharpedo	—	O	—	—	—	—
Central Kalos Pokédex 057	Litleo	—	—	—	O	—	—
Central Kalos Pokédex 059	Psyduck	—	—	—	O	—	—
Central Kalos Pokédex 061	Farfetch'd	—	O	—	—	—	—
Central Kalos Pokédex 062	Riolu	—	O	—	—	—	—
Central Kalos Pokédex 064	Ralts	—	—	—	O	—	—
Central Kalos Pokédex 068	Flabébé	—	—	—	—	O	—
Central Kalos Pokédex 071	Budew	—	—	—	O	—	—
Central Kalos Pokédex 072	Roselia	—	—	—	O	—	—
Central Kalos Pokédex 074	Ledyba	—	—	—	—	O	—
Central Kalos Pokédex 076	Combee	—	—	—	—	—	O
Central Kalos Pokédex 078	Skitty	—	—	—	—	—	O
Central Kalos Pokédex 089	Skiddo	O	—	—	—	—	—
Central Kalos Pokédex 091	Pancham	—	O	—	—	—	—
Central Kalos Pokédex 093	Furfrou	—	—	—	—	—	O
Central Kalos Pokédex 094	Doduo	—	O	—	—	—	—
Central Kalos Pokédex 096	Plusle	—	—	—	—	—	O
Central Kalos Pokédex 097	Minun	—	—	—	—	—	O
Central Kalos Pokédex 098	Gulpin	O	—	—	—	—	—
Central Kalos Pokédex 100	Scraggy	—	O	—	—	—	—
Central Kalos Pokédex 102	Abra	—	—	—	O	—	—
Central Kalos Pokédex 105	Oddish	—	—	—	O	—	—
Central Kalos Pokédex 109	Sentret	—	O	—	—	—	—
Central Kalos Pokédex 111	Nincada	—	—	O	—	—	—
Central Kalos Pokédex 114	Espurr	—	—	—	—	—	O
Central Kalos Pokédex 116	Kecleon	—	—	—	—	O	—
Central Kalos Pokédex 117	Honedge	—	—	O	—	—	—
Central Kalos Pokédex 120	Venipede	—	—	O	—	—	—
Central Kalos Pokédex 123	Audino	O	—	—	—	—	—
Central Kalos Pokédex 124	Smeargle	—	—	—	—	—	O
Central Kalos Pokédex 125	Croagunk	—	O	—	—	—	—
Central Kalos Pokédex 127	Ducklett	O	—	—	—	—	—
Central Kalos Pokédex 129	Spritzee	O	—	—	—	—	—
Central Kalos Pokédex 131	Swirlix	—	—	—	O	—	—
Central Kalos Pokédex 133	Volbeat	—	—	—	—	—	O
Central Kalos Pokédex 134	Illumise	—	—	—	—	—	O
Central Kalos Pokédex 135	Hoppip	—	—	—	—	O	—
Central Kalos Pokédex 140	Whismur	O	—	—	—	—	—
Central Kalos Pokédex 143	Meditite	—	—	—	—	—	O
Central Kalos Pokédex 145	Zubat	—	—	—	—	—	O
Central Kalos Pokédex 148	Axew	—	O	—	—	—	—

Base Stats Raised through Defeating Wild Pokémon in the Kalos Region

Kalos No.	Pokémon	HP	ATTACK	DEFENSE	SP. ATK	SP. DEF	SPEED
Coastal Kalos Pokédex 001	Drifloon	○	—	—	—	—	—
Coastal Kalos Pokédex 003	Mienfoo	—	○	—	—	—	—
Coastal Kalos Pokédex 005	Zangoose	—	○	—	—	—	—
Coastal Kalos Pokédex 006	Seviper	—	○	—	○	—	—
Coastal Kalos Pokédex 007	Spoink	—	—	—	—	○	—
Coastal Kalos Pokédex 009	Absol	—	○	—	—	—	—
Coastal Kalos Pokédex 010	Inkay	—	○	—	—	—	—
Coastal Kalos Pokédex 012	Lunatone	—	—	—	○	—	—
Coastal Kalos Pokédex 013	Solrock	—	○	—	—	—	—
Coastal Kalos Pokédex 014	Bagon	—	○	—	—	—	—
Coastal Kalos Pokédex 017	Wingull	—	—	—	—	—	○
Coastal Kalos Pokédex 019	Taillow	—	—	—	—	—	○
Coastal Kalos Pokédex 021	Binacle	—	○	—	—	—	—
Coastal Kalos Pokédex 023	Dwebble	—	—	○	—	—	—
Coastal Kalos Pokédex 025	Tentacool	—	—	—	—	○	—
Coastal Kalos Pokédex 027	Wailmer	○	—	—	—	—	—
Coastal Kalos Pokédex 029	Luvdisc	—	—	—	—	—	○
Coastal Kalos Pokédex 030	Skrelp	—	—	—	—	○	—
Coastal Kalos Pokédex 031	Dragalge	—	—	—	—	○	—
Coastal Kalos Pokédex 032	Clauncher	—	—	—	○	—	—
Coastal Kalos Pokédex 033	Clawitzer	—	—	—	○	—	—
Coastal Kalos Pokédex 034	Staryu	—	—	—	—	—	○
Coastal Kalos Pokédex 035	Starmie	—	—	—	—	—	○
Coastal Kalos Pokédex 036	Shellder	—	—	○	—	—	—
Coastal Kalos Pokédex 037	Cloyster	—	—	○	—	—	—
Coastal Kalos Pokédex 038	Qwilfish	—	○	—	—	—	—
Coastal Kalos Pokédex 039	Horsea	—	—	—	○	—	—
Coastal Kalos Pokédex 040	Seadra	—	—	○	○	—	—
Coastal Kalos Pokédex 042	Relicanth	○	—	○	—	—	—
Coastal Kalos Pokédex 043	Sandile	—	○	—	—	—	—
Coastal Kalos Pokédex 046	Helioptile	—	—	—	—	—	○
Coastal Kalos Pokédex 048	Hippopotas	—	—	○	—	—	—
Coastal Kalos Pokédex 050	Rhyhorn	—	—	○	—	—	—
Coastal Kalos Pokédex 053	Onix	—	—	○	—	—	—
Coastal Kalos Pokédex 055	Woobat	—	—	—	—	—	○
Coastal Kalos Pokédex 057	Machop	—	○	—	—	—	—
Coastal Kalos Pokédex 060	Cubone	—	—	○	—	—	—
Coastal Kalos Pokédex 062	Kangaskhan	○	—	—	—	—	—
Coastal Kalos Pokédex 063	Mawile	—	○	○	—	—	—
Coastal Kalos Pokédex 069	Ferroseed	—	—	○	—	—	—
Coastal Kalos Pokédex 071	Snubbull	—	○	—	—	—	—
Coastal Kalos Pokédex 073	Electrike	—	—	—	—	—	○
Coastal Kalos Pokédex 075	Houndour	—	—	—	○	—	—
Coastal Kalos Pokédex 077	Eevee	—	—	—	—	○	—
Coastal Kalos Pokédex 086	Emolga	—	—	—	—	—	○
Coastal Kalos Pokédex 087	Yanma	—	—	—	—	—	○
Coastal Kalos Pokédex 089	Hawlucha	—	○	—	—	—	—
Coastal Kalos Pokédex 090	Sigilyph	—	—	—	○	—	—
Coastal Kalos Pokédex 091	Golett	—	○	—	—	—	—
Coastal Kalos Pokédex 093	Nosepass	—	—	○	—	—	—
Coastal Kalos Pokédex 096	Hariyama	○	—	—	—	—	—
Coastal Kalos Pokédex 097	Throh	○	—	—	—	—	—
Coastal Kalos Pokédex 098	Sawk	—	○	—	—	—	—
Coastal Kalos Pokédex 099	Starly	—	—	—	—	—	○
Coastal Kalos Pokédex 100	Staravia	—	—	—	—	—	○
Coastal Kalos Pokédex 102	Stunky	—	—	—	—	—	○
Coastal Kalos Pokédex 104	Nidoran ♀	○	—	—	—	—	—
Coastal Kalos Pokédex 105	Nidorina	○	—	—	—	—	—
Coastal Kalos Pokédex 107	Nidoran ♂	—	○	—	—	—	—
Coastal Kalos Pokédex 108	Nidorino	—	○	—	—	—	—
Coastal Kalos Pokédex 110	Dedenne	—	—	—	—	—	○
Coastal Kalos Pokédex 111	Chingling	—	—	—	—	○	—
Coastal Kalos Pokédex 113	Mime Jr.	—	—	—	—	○	—
Coastal Kalos Pokédex 114	Mr. Mime	—	—	—	—	○	—
Coastal Kalos Pokédex 115	Solosis	—	—	—	○	—	—
Coastal Kalos Pokédex 119	Wobbuffet	○	—	—	—	—	—
Coastal Kalos Pokédex 120	Roggenrola	—	—	○	—	—	—
Coastal Kalos Pokédex 123	Sableye	—	○	○	—	—	—
Coastal Kalos Pokédex 124	Carbink	—	—	—	—	○	—
Coastal Kalos Pokédex 125	Tauros	—	○	—	—	—	○
Coastal Kalos Pokédex 126	Miltank	—	—	○	—	—	—

AFTER THE HALL OF FAME
CENTRAL KALOS
COASTAL KALOS
MOUNTAIN KALOS
ADVENTURE DATA

Kalos No.	Pokémon	HP	ATTACK	DEFENSE	SP. ATK	SP. DEF	SPEED
Coastal Kalos Pokédex 127	Mareep	—	—	—	○	—	—
Coastal Kalos Pokédex 130	Pinsir	—	○	—	—	—	—
Coastal Kalos Pokédex 131	Heracross	—	○	—	—	—	—
Coastal Kalos Pokédex 132	Pachirisu	—	—	—	—	—	○
Coastal Kalos Pokédex 133	Slowpoke	○	—	—	—	—	—
Coastal Kalos Pokédex 136	Exeggcute	—	—	○	—	—	—
Coastal Kalos Pokédex 138	Chatot	—	○	—	—	—	—
Coastal Kalos Pokédex 139	Mantyke	—	—	—	—	○	—
Coastal Kalos Pokédex 141	Clamperl	—	—	○	—	—	—
Coastal Kalos Pokédex 142	Huntail	—	○	○	—	—	—
Coastal Kalos Pokédex 143	Gorebyss	—	—	—	○	—	—
Coastal Kalos Pokédex 144	Remoraid	—	—	—	—	○	—
Coastal Kalos Pokédex 145	Octillery	—	◎	—	○	—	—
Coastal Kalos Pokédex 146	Corsola	—	—	○	—	—	—
Coastal Kalos Pokédex 147	Chinchou	○	—	—	—	—	—
Coastal Kalos Pokédex 148	Lanturn	○	—	—	—	—	—
Coastal Kalos Pokédex 149	Alomomola	○	—	—	—	—	—
Coastal Kalos Pokédex 150	Lapras	○	—	—	—	—	—
Mountain Kalos Pokédex 002	Dugtrio	—	—	—	—	—	○
Mountain Kalos Pokédex 003	Trapinch	—	○	—	—	—	—
Mountain Kalos Pokédex 006	Gible	—	○	—	—	—	—
Mountain Kalos Pokédex 009	Geodude	—	—	○	—	—	—
Mountain Kalos Pokédex 010	Graveler	—	—	○	—	—	—
Mountain Kalos Pokédex 012	Slugma	—	—	—	○	—	—
Mountain Kalos Pokédex 014	Shuckle	—	—	○	—	○	—
Mountain Kalos Pokédex 015	Skorupi	—	—	○	—	—	—
Mountain Kalos Pokédex 016	Drapion	—	—	○	—	—	—
Mountain Kalos Pokédex 018	Quagsire	○	—	—	—	—	—
Mountain Kalos Pokédex 019	Goomy	—	—	—	—	○	—
Mountain Kalos Pokédex 020	Sliggoo	—	—	—	—	○	—
Mountain Kalos Pokédex 022	Karrablast	—	○	—	—	—	—
Mountain Kalos Pokédex 024	Shelmet	—	—	○	—	—	—
Mountain Kalos Pokédex 026	Bellsprout	—	○	—	—	—	—
Mountain Kalos Pokédex 027	Weepinbell	—	○	—	—	—	—
Mountain Kalos Pokédex 029	Carnivine	—	○	—	—	—	—
Mountain Kalos Pokédex 031	Haunter	—	—	—	○	—	—
Mountain Kalos Pokédex 033	Poliwag	—	—	—	—	—	○
Mountain Kalos Pokédex 034	Poliwhirl	—	—	—	—	—	○
Mountain Kalos Pokédex 035	Poliwrath	—	—	○	—	—	—
Mountain Kalos Pokédex 036	Politoed	—	—	—	—	○	—
Mountain Kalos Pokédex 037	Ekans	—	○	—	—	—	—
Mountain Kalos Pokédex 038	Arbok	—	○	—	—	—	—
Mountain Kalos Pokédex 039	Stunfisk	○	—	—	—	—	—
Mountain Kalos Pokédex 040	Barboach	○	—	—	—	—	—
Mountain Kalos Pokédex 041	Whiscash	○	—	—	—	—	—
Mountain Kalos Pokédex 043	Liepard	—	—	—	—	—	○
Mountain Kalos Pokédex 045	Mightyena	—	○	—	—	—	—
Mountain Kalos Pokédex 047	Watchog	—	○	—	—	—	—
Mountain Kalos Pokédex 048	Pawniard	—	○	—	—	—	—
Mountain Kalos Pokédex 050	Klefki	—	—	○	—	—	—
Mountain Kalos Pokédex 051	Murkrow	—	—	—	—	—	○
Mountain Kalos Pokédex 053	Foongus	○	—	—	—	—	—
Mountain Kalos Pokédex 054	Amoonguss	○	—	—	—	—	—
Mountain Kalos Pokédex 056	Lombre	—	—	—	—	○	—
Mountain Kalos Pokédex 059	Floatzel	—	—	—	—	—	○
Mountain Kalos Pokédex 060	Basculin	—	—	—	—	—	○
Mountain Kalos Pokédex 061	Phantump	—	○	—	—	—	—
Mountain Kalos Pokédex 062	Trevenant	—	○	—	—	—	—
Mountain Kalos Pokédex 063	Pumpkaboo	—	—	○	—	—	—
Mountain Kalos Pokédex 065	Litwick	—	—	—	○	—	—
Mountain Kalos Pokédex 068	Rotom	—	—	—	○	—	○
Mountain Kalos Pokédex 070	Magneton	—	—	—	○	—	—
Mountain Kalos Pokédex 073	Electrode	—	—	—	—	—	○
Mountain Kalos Pokédex 074	Trubbish	—	—	—	—	—	○
Mountain Kalos Pokédex 075	Garbodor	—	○	—	—	—	—
Mountain Kalos Pokédex 077	Piloswine	○	○	—	—	—	—
Mountain Kalos Pokédex 079	Bergmite	—	—	○	—	—	—
Mountain Kalos Pokédex 081	Cubchoo	—	○	—	—	—	—
Mountain Kalos Pokédex 082	Beartic	—	○	—	—	—	—
Mountain Kalos Pokédex 083	Smoochum	—	—	—	—	○	—
Mountain Kalos Pokédex 084	Jynx	—	—	—	—	○	—

Kalos No.	Pokémon	HP	ATTACK	DEFENSE	SP. ATK	SP. DEF	SPEED
Mountain Kalos Pokédex 085	Vanillite	—	—	—	O	—	—
Mountain Kalos Pokédex 088	Snover	—	O	—	—	—	—
Mountain Kalos Pokédex 089	Abomasnow	—	—	O	O	—	—
Mountain Kalos Pokédex 090	Delibird	—	—	—	—	—	O
Mountain Kalos Pokédex 091	Sneasel	—	—	—	—	—	O
Mountain Kalos Pokédex 094	Gurdurr	—	O	—	—	—	—
Mountain Kalos Pokédex 096	Torkoal	—	—	O	—	—	—
Mountain Kalos Pokédex 098	Sandslash	—	—	O	—	—	—
Mountain Kalos Pokédex 099	Aron	—	—	O	—	—	—
Mountain Kalos Pokédex 100	Lairon	—	—	O	—	—	—
Mountain Kalos Pokédex 102	Larvitar	—	O	—	—	—	—
Mountain Kalos Pokédex 103	Pupitar	—	O	—	—	—	—
Mountain Kalos Pokédex 105	Heatmor	—	—	—	O	—	—
Mountain Kalos Pokédex 106	Durant	—	—	O	—	—	—
Mountain Kalos Pokédex 108	Ariados	—	O	—	—	—	—
Mountain Kalos Pokédex 110	Fearow	—	—	—	—	—	O
Mountain Kalos Pokédex 111	Cryogonal	—	—	—	—	O	—
Mountain Kalos Pokédex 112	Skarmory	—	—	O	—	—	—
Mountain Kalos Pokédex 113	Noibat	—	—	—	—	—	O
Mountain Kalos Pokédex 115	Gligar	—	—	O	—	—	—
Mountain Kalos Pokédex 118	Noctowl	O	—	—	—	—	—
Mountain Kalos Pokédex 120	Jigglypuff	O	—	—	—	—	—
Mountain Kalos Pokédex 123	Banette	—	O	—	—	—	—
Mountain Kalos Pokédex 125	Zoroark	—	—	—	O	—	—
Mountain Kalos Pokédex 127	Gothorita	—	—	—	—	O	—
Mountain Kalos Pokédex 130	Sudowoodo	—	—	O	—	—	—
Mountain Kalos Pokédex 131	Spinda	—	—	—	O	—	—
Mountain Kalos Pokédex 133	Ursaring	—	O	—	—	—	—
Mountain Kalos Pokédex 134	Lickitung	O	—	—	—	—	—
Mountain Kalos Pokédex 136	Scyther	—	O	—	—	—	—
Mountain Kalos Pokédex 138	Ditto	O	—	—	—	—	—
Mountain Kalos Pokédex 139	Swablu	—	—	—	—	O	—
Mountain Kalos Pokédex 140	Altaria	—	—	—	—	O	—
Mountain Kalos Pokédex 141	Druddigon	—	O	—	—	—	—
Mountain Kalos Pokédex 143	Zweilous	—	O	—	—	—	—
Mountain Kalos Pokédex 144	Hydreigon	—	—	—	—	O	—
Mountain Kalos Pokédex 145	Dratini	—	O	—	—	—	—
Mountain Kalos Pokédex 146	Dragonair	—	O	—	—	—	—

Defeating One of These Wild Pokémon Will Raise the HP Base Stat

Pokémon	Where they appear	Pokémon	Where they appear	Pokémon	Where they appear
Alomomola	Shalour City (Super Rod)	Hariyama	Route 11 (Tall Grass)	Nidoran ♀	Route 11 (Horde Encounter)
Amoonguss	Route 20 (Tall Grass)	Jigglypuff	Route 20 (Tall Grass)	Nidorina	Route 11 (Tall Grass)
Audino	Route 6 (Ambush)	Kangaskhan	Glittering Cave	Noctowl	Route 20 (Tall Grass)
Azumarill	Route 22 (Yellow Flowers)	Lanturn	Shalour City (Super Rod)	Piloswine	Frost Cavern (Inside)
Azurill	Route 22 (Tall Grass)	Lapras	Route 12 (Water Surface)	Quagsire	Route 14 (Water Surface)
Barboach	Route 14 (Good Rod)	Lickitung	Victory Road (Inside)	Relicanth	Cyllage City (Super Rod)
Bidoof	Route 3 (Tall Grass)	Marill	Route 3 (Water Surface)	Skiddo	Route 5 (Purple Flowers)
Caterpie	Santalune Forest (Tall Grass)			Slowpoke	Route 12 (Tall Grass)
Chinchou	Shalour City (Good Rod)			Spritzee	Route 7 (Tall Grass: X)
Diggersby	Route 22 (Yellow Flowers)			Stunfisk	Route 14 (Swamp)
Ditto	Pokémon Village (Yellow Flowers)			Throh	Route 11 (Tall Grass: Y)
Drifloon	Route 8 (Tall Grass)			Wailmer	Route 8 (Water Surface)
Ducklett	Route 7 (Tall Grass)			Whiscash	Route 14 (Super Rod)
Dunsparce	Route 3 (Tall Grass)			Whismur	Connecting Cave
Foongus	Route 15 (Tall Grass)			Wobbuffet	Reflection Cave
Gulpin	Route 5 (Tall Grass)				

Defeating One of These Wild Pokémon Will Raise the Attack Base Stat

Pokémon	Where they appear	Pokémon	Where they appear	Pokémon	Where they appear
Abomasnow	Route 17 (Ride Mamoswine)	Garbodor	Lost Hotel (Trash Can)	Pupitar	Route 18 (Red Flowers: Y)
Absol	Route 8 (Yellow Flowers)	Gible	Route 13	Qwilfish	Route 8 (Super Rod)
Arbok	Route 19 (Horde Encounter)	Goldeen	Route 3 (Good Rod)	Riolu	Route 22 (Tall Grass)
Ariados	Terminus Cave (Ambush)	Golett	Route 10 (Tall Grass)	Sableye	Reflection Cave
Axew	Connecting Cave	Gurdurr	Route 18 (Tall Grass)	Sandile	Route 9 (Ride Rhyhorn)
Bagon	Route 8 (Tall Grass)	Gyarados	Route 3 (Super Rod)	Sawk	Route 11 (Tall Grass: X)
Banette	Pokémon Village (Trash Can: Thursdays)	Hawlucha	Route 10 (Tall Grass)	Scraggy	Route 5 (Horde Encounter)
Beartic	Frost Cavern (Inside)	Heracross	Route 12 (Tall Grass: Y)	Scyther	Route 21 (Red Flowers)
Bellsprout	Route 14 (Horde Encounter)	Huntail	Route 12 (Super Rod: X)	Seaking	Route 3 (Super Rod)
Bibarel	Route 22 (Yellow Flowers)	Inkay	Route 8 (Tall Grass)	Sentret	Route 6 (Very Tall Grass)
Binacle	Route 8 (Rock Smash)	Karrablast	Route 14 (Tall Grass)	Seviper	Route 8 (Tall Grass: Y)
Carnivine	Route 14 (Tall Grass)	Larvitar	Terminus Cave (Horde Encounter: Y)	Sharpedo	Route 22 (Super Rod)
Carvanha	Route 22 (Good Rod)	Machop	Glittering Cave	Snover	Route 17 (Ride Mamoswine)
Chatot	Route 12 (Tall Grass)	Mawile	Glittering Cave	Snubbull	Route 10 (Yellow Flowers)
Corphish	Route 3 (Good Rod)	Mienfoo	Route 8 (Yellow Flowers)	Solrock	Glittering Cave
Crawdaunt	Route 3 (Super Rod)	Mightyena	Route 15 (Tall Grass: X)	Tauros	Route 12 (Yellow Flowers)
Croagunk	Route 7 (Tall Grass)	Nidoran♂	Route 11 (Horde Encounter)	Trapinch	Route 13
Cubchoo	Frost Cavern (Cave: Horde Encounter)	Nidorino	Route 11 (Tall Grass)	Trevenant	Route 20 (Red Flowers)
Doduo	Route 5 (Tall Grass)	Octillery	Shalour City (Super Rod)	Ursaring	Route 21 (Red Flowers)
Dragonair	Route 21 (Super Rod)	Pancham	Route 5 (Purple Flowers)	Watchog	Route 15 (Red Flowers)
Dratini	Route 21 (Good Rod)	Pawniard	Lost Hotel	Weepinbell	Route 14 (Tall Grass)
Druddigon	Victory Road (Inside)	Phantump	Route 16 (Yellow Flowers)	Zangoose	Route 8 (Tall Grass: X)
Ekans	Route 14 (Horde Encounter)	Piloswine	Frost Cavern (Inside)	Zweilous	Victory Road (Inside)
Farfetch'd	Route 22 (Tall Grass)	Pinsir	Route 12 (Tall Grass: X)		

Defeating One of These Wild Pokémon Will Raise the Defense Base Stat

Pokémon	Where they appear	Pokémon	Where they appear	Pokémon	Where they appear
Aron	Terminus Cave (Horde Encounter: X)	Hippopotas	Route 9 (Ride Rhyhorn)	Rhyhorn	Glittering Cave
Bergmite	Frost Cavern (Inside)	Honedge	Route 6 (Very Tall Grass)	Roggenrola	Reflection Cave
Carbink	Reflection Cave	Huntail	Route 12 (Super Rod: X)	Sableye	Reflection Cave
Clamperl	Route 12 (Good Rod)	Kakuna	Santalune Forest (Tall Grass: X)	Sandslash	Route 18 (Red Flowers)
Cloyster	Route 8 (Super Rod: Y)	Klefki	Lost Hotel	Scatterbug	Route 2 (Tall Grass)
Corsola	Route 12 (Super Rod)	Lairon	Route 18 (Red Flowers: X)	Seadra	Cyllage City (Super Rod)
Cubone	Glittering Cave	Mawile	Glittering Cave	Shellder	Route 8 (Good Rod: Y)
Drapion	Route 19 (Purple Flowers)	Metapod	Santalune Forest (Tall Grass: Y)	Shelmet	Route 14 (Tall Grass)
Durant	Terminus Cave	Miltank	Route 12 (Yellow Flowers)	Shuckle	Route 18 (Rock Smash)
Dwebble	Cyllage City (Rock Smash)	Nincada	Route 6 (Very Tall Grass)	Skarmory	Victory Road (Ambush)
Exeggcute	Route 12 (Tall Grass)	Nosepass	Route 10 (Horde Encounter)	Skorupi	Route 14 (Tall Grass)
Ferroseed	Glittering Cave (Ambush)	Onix	Glittering Cave	Sudowoodo	Route 20 (Horde Encounter)
Geodude	Route 18 (Horde Encounter)	Poliwrath	Victory Road (Cave: Super Rod)	Swirlix	Route 7 (Tall Grass: X)
Gligar	Route 19 (Horde Encounter)	Pumpkaboo	Route 16 (Very Tall Grass)	Torkoal	Route 18 (Tall Grass)
Graveler	Route 13 (Rock Smash)	Relicanth	Cyllage City (Super Rod)	Venipede	Route 6 (Ambush)

Defeating One of These Wild Pokémon Will Raise the Sp. Attack Base Stat

Pokémon	Where they appear	Pokémon	Where they appear	Pokémon	Where they appear
Abomasnow	Route 17 (Ride Mamoswine)	Litleo	Route 22 (Tall Grass)	Seadra	Cyllage City (Super Rod)
Abra	Route 5 (Tall Grass)	Litwick	Lost Hotel	Seviper	Route 8 (Tall Grass: Y)
Budew	Route 4 (Yellow Flowers)	Lunatone	Glittering Cave	Sigilyph	Route 10 (Tall Grass)
Chingling	Route 11 (Tall Grass)	Magneton	Lost Hotel	Slugma	Route 13 (Rock Smash)
Clauncher	Cyllage City (Good Rod: X)	Mareep	Route 12 (Horde Encounter)	Smoochum	Frost Cavern (Cave: Horde Encounter)
Clawitzer	Cyllage City (Super Rod: X)	Masquerain	Route 3 (Water Surface)	Solosis	Reflection Cave
Gorebyss	Route 12 (Super Rod: Y)	Octillery	Shalour City (Super Rod)	Spinda	Route 21 (Red Flowers)
Haunter	Frost Cavern (Inside)	Oddish	Route 6 (Very Tall Grass)	Vanillite	Frost Cavern (Cave: Horde Encounter)
Heatmor	Route 18 (Tall Grass)	Psyduck	Route 22 (Water Surface)	Zoroark	Pokémon Village (Yellow Flowers)
Horsea	Cyllage City (Good Rod)	Ralts	Route 4 (Yellow Flowers)		
Houndour	Route 10 (Yellow Flowers: X)	Remoraid	Shalour City (Good Rod)		
Hydreigon	Victory Road (Ambush)	Roselia	Route 7 (Tall Grass)		
Jynx	Frost Cavern (Inside)	Rotom	Lost Hotel (Trash Can: Tuesdays)		

AFTER THE
HALL OF FAME

CENTRAL
KALOS

COASTAL
KALOS

MOUNTAIN
KALOS

ADVENTURE
DATA

Defeating One of These Wild Pokémon Will Raise the Sp. Defense Base Stat

Pokémon	Where they appear
Altaria	Route 21 (Red Flowers)
Burmy	Route 3 (Tall Grass)
Carbink	Reflection Cave
Corsola	Route 12 (Super Rod)
Cryogonal	Frost Cavern 2F
Dragalge	Cyllage City (Super Rod: V)
Eevee	Route 10 (Yellow Flowers)
Flabébé	Route 4 (Yellow Flowers)
Goomy	Route 14 (Swamp)
Gothorita	Route 20 (Red Flowers)
Hoppip	Route 7 (Horde Encounter)
Kecleon	Route 6 (Very Tall Grass)
Ledyba	Route 4 (Red Flowers)

Pokémon	Where they appear
Lombre	Route 15 (Water Surface)
Mantyke	Shalour City (Water Surface)
Masquerain	Route 3 (Water Surface)
Mime Jr.	Reflection Cave (Horde Encounter)
Mr. Mime	Reflection Cave
Politoed	Route 19 (Super Rod)
Shuckle	Route 18 (Rock Smash)
Skrelp	Cyllage City (Good Rod: V)
Sliggoo	Route 19 (Yellow Flowers)
Spoink	Route 8 (Tall Grass)
Swablu	Route 21 (Horde Encounter)
Tentacool	Cyllage City (Water Surface)

Defeating One of These Wild Pokémon Will Raise the Speed Base Stat

Pokémon	Where they appear
Basculin	Laverre City (Good Rod)
Bunnelby	Route 2 (Tall Grass)
Combee	Route 4 (Yellow Flowers)
Dedenne	Route 11 (Tall Grass)
Delibird	Route 17 (Ride Mamoswine)
Dugtrio	Route 13 (Ambush)
Electrike	Route 10 (Yellow Flowers: V)
Electrode	Lost Hotel
Emolga	Route 10 (Tall Grass)
Espurr	Route 6 (Very Tall Grass)
Fearow	Victory Road (Ambush)
Fletchling	Route 2 (Tall Grass)
Floatzel	Route 21 (Purple Flowers)
Furfrou	Route 5 (Tall Grass)
Helioptile	Route 9 (Ride Rhyhorn)
Illumise	Route 7 (Tall Grass)
Liepard	Route 15 (Tall Grass: V)
Luvdisc	Cyllage City (Old Rod)
Magikarp	Route 3 (Old Rod)
Meditite	Connecting Cave
Minun	Route 5 (Horde Encounter)
Murkrow	Route 15 (Horde Encounter)
Noibat	Terminus Cave (Ambush)
Pachirisu	Route 12 (Tall Grass)
Panpour	Santalune Forest (Tall Grass)
Pansage	Santalune Forest (Tall Grass)

Pokémon	Where they appear
Pansear	Santalune Forest (Tall Grass)
Pidgey	Route 2 (Tall Grass)
Pikachu	Santalune Forest (Tall Grass)
Plusle	Route 5 (Horde Encounter)
Poliwag	Laverre City (Old Rod)
Poliwhirl	Laverre City (Super Rod)
Rotom	Lost Hotel (Trash Can: Tuesdays)
Skitty	Route 4 (Yellow Flowers)
Smeargle	Route 7 (Tall Grass)
Sneasel	Route 17 (Ride Mamoswine)
Staravia	Route 11 (Tall Grass)
Starly	Route 11 (Horde Encounter)
Starmie	Route 8 (Super Rod: X)
Staryu	Route 8 (Good Rod: X)
Stunky	Route 11 (Tall Grass)
Taillow	Route 8 (Horde Encounter)
Tauros	Route 12 (Yellow Flowers)
Trubbish	Lost Hotel (Trash Can)
Volbeat	Route 7 (Tall Grass)
Weedle	Santalune Forest (Tall Grass)
Wingull	Route 8 (Horde Encounter)
Woobat	Glittering Cave (Ambush)
Yanma	Route 10 (Horde Encounter)
Zigzagoon	Route 2 (Tall Grass)
Zubat	Connecting Cave

A

Item	Description	How to obtain	Price
Ability Capsule	Allows a Pokémon with two Abilities to switch between these Abilities.	Get for 200 BP in Kiloude City's Battle Maison	—
Abomasite	When held, it allows Abomasnow to Mega Evolve into Mega Abomasnow during battle.	Talk to Abomasnow in the Frost Cavern (after you chase away Team Flare)	—
Absolite	When held, it allows Absol to Mega Evolve into Mega Absol during battle.	Receive from Serena/Calem in Kiloude City (after entering the Hall of Fame)	—
Absorb Bulb	Raises the holder's Sp. Atk by 1 when it is hit by a Water-type move. It goes away after use.	Get for 32 BP in Kiloude City's Battle Maison	—
Adamant Orb	When held by Dialga, it boosts the power of Dragon- and Steel-type moves.	Terminus Cave: Zygarde's Chamber	—
Aerodactylite	When held, it allows Aerodactyl to Mega Evolve into Mega Aerodactyl during battle.	Receive from the assistant in Ambrette Town's Fossil Lab (after exploring Glittering Cave)	—
Aggronite	When held, it allows Aggron to Mega Evolve into Mega Aggron during battle.	Find in Cyllage City Pokémon Gym between 8 P.M. and 8:59 P.M. (after entering the Hall of Fame) *Pokémon Y only	—
Air Balloon	The holder floats and Ground-type moves will no longer hit the holder. The balloon pops when the holder is hit by an attack.	Get for 48 BP in Kiloude City's Battle Maison	—
Alakazite	When held, it allows Alakazam to Mega Evolve into Mega Alakazam during battle.	Find in Reflection Cave between 8 P.M. and 8:59 P.M. (after entering the Hall of Fame)	—
Amaze Mulch	Mulch to be used in a Berry Field. Combines the effects of Rich, Surprise, and Boost Mulch.	Add either a Kee Berry or Maranga Berry to the mix in the composter when making compost in the Berry fields	—
Ampharosite	When held, it allows Ampharos to Mega Evolve into Mega Ampharos during battle.	Receive from an old man in Azure Bay	—
Amulet Coin	Doubles the prize money from a battle if the Pokémon holding it joins in.	Find in one of the small rooms in Parfum Palace	—
Antidote	Cures the Poison status condition.	Buy at Poké Marts (after obtaining first Gym Badge)	100
Armor Fossil	A Pokémon Fossil. When restored, it becomes Shieldon.	Use Rock Smash to break cracked rocks deep within Glittering Cave (after entering the Hall of Fame)	—
Assault Vest	Raises Sp. Def when held, but prevents the use of status moves.	Get for 48 BP in Kiloude City's Battle Maison	—
Awakening	Cures the Sleep status condition.	Buy at Poké Marts (after obtaining first Gym Badge)	250

B

Item	Description	How to obtain	Price
Balm Mushroom	A fragrant mushroom. It can be sold at shops for 6,250.	Win at Lumiose City's Restaurant Le Wow (after entering the Hall of Fame)	—
Banettite	When held, it allows Banette to Mega Evolve into Mega Banette during battle.	Find in Route 22's Chamber of Emptiness between 8 P.M. and 8:59 P.M. (after entering the Hall of Fame)	—
Berry Juice	Restores the HP of one Pokémon by 20 points.	Receive from a woman in Camphrier Town / Get for 10 Poké Miles in Lumiose City's Pokémon Center	—
Big Mushroom	A big mushroom. It can be sold at shops for 2,500.	Win at Lumiose City's Restaurant Le Yeah / Route 14 / Sometimes held by wild Amoonguss and Foongus	—
Big Nugget	A big nugget of pure gold. It can be sold at shops for 10,000.	Receive from the president of the Poké Ball Factory / Win at Lumiose City's Sushi High Roller (after entering the Hall of Fame)	—
Big Pearl	A big pearl. It can be sold at shops for 3,750.	Find in Azure Bay / Sometimes held by wild Clamperl, Cloyster, or Shellder	—
Big Root	When the holder uses an HP-draining move, it increases the amount of HP recovered by 30%.	Find in Dendemille Town	—
Binding Band	When held, the damage done to targets every turn becomes 1/6 of their max HP by moves like Bind or Wrap.	Get for 48 BP in Kiloude City's Battle Maison	—
Black Belt	When held by a Pokémon, it boosts the power of Fighting-type moves by 20%.	Reflection Cave B2F / Sometimes held by wild Sawk or Throh	—
Black Glasses	When held by a Pokémon, it boosts the power of Dark-type moves by 20%.	Lysandre Labs	—
Black Sludge	If the holder is a Poison-type Pokémon, it restores 1/16 of its maximum HP every turn. If the holder is any other type, it loses 1/8 of its maximum HP every turn.	Sometimes held by wild Croagunk and Trubbish / Often held by wild Garbodor	—
Blastoisinite	When held, it allows Blastoise to Mega Evolve into Mega Blastoise during battle.	Receive from Professor Sycamore in Lumiose City (if you chose Squirtle) / Buy at Lumiose City's Stone Emporium	Varies ◆
Boost Mulch	Mulch to be used in a Berry field. It increases the Berry harvest that can be grown by diligent watering.	Add two Berries of the same color to the composter when making compost in the Berry fields	—
Bright Powder	Boosts the holder's evasion.	Get for 48 BP in Kiloude City's Battle Maison	—
Burn Heal	Cures the Burned status condition.	Buy at Poké Marts (after obtaining first Gym Badge)	250

AFTER THE HALL OF FAME

CENTRAL KALOS

COASTAL KALOS

MOUNTAIN KALOS

ADVENTURE DATA

AFTER THE
HALL OF FAME

CENTRAL
KALOS

COASTAL
KALOS

MOUNTAIN
KALOS

ADVENTURE
DATA

C

	Item	Description	How to obtain	Price
	Calcium	Raises the base Sp. Atk stat of a Pokémon.	Buy at the Poké Mart in Laverre City / Get for 2 BP in Kiloude City's Battle Maison	9,800
	Carbos	Raises the base Speed stat of a Pokémon.	Buy at the Poké Mart in Laverre City / Get for 2 BP in Kiloude City's Battle Maison	9,800
	Cell Battery	Increases Attack by 1 when the holder is hit with Electric-type moves. It goes away after use.	Get for 32 BP in Kiloude City's Battle Maison	—
	Charcoal	When held by a Pokémon, it boosts the power of Fire-type moves by 20%.	Win from a woman in Couriway Town for answering a quiz (if you chose Fennekin as your initial Pokémon partner)	—
	Charizardite X	When held, it allows Charizard to Mega Evolve into Mega Charizard X during battle.	Receive from Professor Sycamore in Lumiose City (if you chose Charmander) / Buy at Lumiose City's Stone Emporium *Pokémon X only	Varies
	Charizardite Y	When held, it allows Charizard to Mega Evolve into Mega Charizard Y during battle.	Receive from Professor Sycamore in Lumiose City (if you chose Charmander) / Buy at Lumiose City's Stone Emporium *Pokémon Y only	Varies
	Choice Band	The holder can use only one of its moves, but the power of physical moves increases by 50%.	Get for 48 BP in Kiloude City's Battle Maison	—
	Choice Scarf	The holder can use only one of its moves, but Speed increases by 50%.	Get for 48 BP in Kiloude City's Battle Maison	—
	Choice Specs	The holder can use only one of its moves, but the power of special moves increases by 50%.	Get for 48 BP in Kiloude City's Battle Maison	—
	Claw Fossil	A Pokémon Fossil. When restored, it becomes Anorith.	Use Rock Smash to break cracked rocks deep within Glittering Cave (after entering the Hall of Fame) *Pokémon X only	—
	Cleanse Tag	Helps keep wild Pokémon away if the holder is the first one in the party.	Route 14	—
	Clever Wing	Slightly raises the base Sp. Def stat of a Pokémon. It can be used until the stat reaches its maximum value.	Win for achieving Beginner Rank, Novice Rank, or Normal Rank in Lumiose City's Battle Institute	—
	Comet Shard	A shard that fell to the ground when a comet approached. It can be sold at shops for 15,000.	Entrust the old man in Anistar City with a Pokémon of Lv. 5 or below before entering the Hall of Fame, and then return to his house later	—
	Cover Fossil	A Pokémon Fossil. When restored, it becomes Tirtouga.	Use Rock Smash to break cracked rocks deep within Glittering Cave (after entering the Hall of Fame)	—

D

	Item	Description	How to obtain	Price
	Damp Rock	Extends the duration of the move Rain Dance by three turns when held.	Route 14	—
	Dawn Stone	It can evolve male Kirlia.	Route 3 / Win from an Inverse Battle on Route 18	—
	Deep Sea Scale	When held by Clamperl, it doubles Sp. Def. Link Trade Clamperl while it holds the Deep Sea Scale to evolve it into Gorebyss.	Azure Bay / Sometimes held by wild Chinchou, Relicanth, or others	—
	Deep Sea Tooth	When held by Clamperl, it doubles Sp. Atk. Link Trade Clamperl while it holds the Deep Sea Tooth to evolve it into Huntail.	Azure Bay / Sometimes held by wild Carvanha, Sharpedo, or others	—
	Destiny Knot	When a Pokémon holding it is inflicted with Infatuation, the Pokémon shares the condition with its attacker. (A Pokémon holding a Destiny Knot in the Pokémon Day Care will pass five of the stats from it and the other Pokémon in the Pokémon Day Care, which they had when they hatched, to the Pokémon Egg that is found.)	Receive from Maid in Cyllage City's Hotel Cyllage	—
	Dire Hit	Significantly raises the critical-hit ratio of the Pokémon on which it is used. It can be used only once.	Buy at the Poké Mart in Santalune City	650
	Dome Fossil	A Pokémon Fossil. When restored, it becomes Kabuto.	Use Rock Smash to break cracked rocks deep within Glittering Cave (after entering the Hall of Fame) *Pokémon Y only	—
	Draco Plate	When held by a Pokémon, it boosts the power of Dragon-type moves by 20%. (When held by Arceus, it shifts Arceus's type to Dragon type.)	Find on Route 22	—
	Dragon Fang	When held by a Pokémon, it boosts the power of Dragon-type moves by 20%.	In the fourth cave on Victory Road / Sometimes held by wild Bagon or Druddigon	—
	Dragon Scale	Link Trade Seadra while it holds the Dragon Scale to evolve it into Kingdra.	Terminus Cave Small Chamber 1 / Sometimes held by wild Dratini, Horsea, or Seadra	—
	Dread Plate	When held by a Pokémon, it boosts the power of Dark-type moves by 20%. (When held by Arceus, it shifts Arceus's type to Dark type.)	Lost Hotel	—
	Dubious Disc	Link Trade Porygon2 while it holds the Dubious Disc to evolve it into Porygon-Z.	Get for 32 BP in Kiloude City's Battle Maison	—
	Dusk Stone	It can evolve Doublade, Lampent, and Murkrow.	Terminus Cave B2F / Receive from a Team Flare Grunt in Laverre City (after entering the Hall of Fame)	—

E

Item	Description	How to obtain	Price
Earth Plate	When held by a Pokémon, it boosts the power of Ground-type moves by 20%. (When held by Arceus, it shifts Arceus's type to Ground type.)	Reflection Cave B2F	—
Eject Button	If the holder is hit by an attack, it switches places with a party Pokémon. It goes away after use.	Get for 32 BP in Kiloude City's Battle Maison	—
Electirizer	Link Trade Electabuzz while it holds the Electirizer to evolve it into Electivire.	Get for 32 BP in Kiloude City's Battle Maison	—
Elixir	Restores the PP of all of a Pokémon's moves by 10 points.	Route 22 / Terminus Cave B2F / Route 21	—
Energy Powder	Restores the HP of one Pokémon by 50 points. Very bitter (lowers a Pokémon's friendship).	Buy from Lumiose City's Herboriste	500
Energy Root	Restores the HP of one Pokémon by 200 points. Very bitter (lowers a Pokémon's friendship).	Buy from Lumiose City's Herboriste	800
Escape Rope	Use it to escape instantly from a cave or a dungeon.	Buy at Poké Marts (after obtaining first Gym Badge) / Glittering Cave	550
Ether	Restores the PP of a Pokémon's move by 10 points.	Route 4 / Parfum Palace / Laverre City / Frost Cavern 3F	—
Everstone	Prevents the Pokémon that holds it from evolving.	Receive from woman in Geosenge Town / Often held by wild Roggenrola / Sometimes held by wild Geodude or Graveler	—
Eviolite	Raises Defense and Sp. Def by 50% when held by a Pokémon that can still evolve.	Receive from a man in Shalour City (if you have seen 40 or more Pokémon in the Coastal Kalos Pokédex)	—
Expert Belt	Raises the power of supereffective moves by 20%.	Receive from a woman on 3F in an office building in Lumiose City	—

F

Item	Description	How to obtain	Price
Fire Stone	It can evolve Eevee and Pansear.	Route 12 / Buy at Lumiose City's Stone Emporium / Win from an Inverse Battle on Route 18	2,100
Fist Plate	When held by a Pokémon, it boosts the power of Fighting-type moves by 20%. (When held by Arceus, it shifts Arceus's type to Fighting type.)	Route 16	—
Flame Orb	Inflicts the Burned status condition on the holder during battle.	Get for 16 BP in Kiloude City's Battle Maison	—
Flame Plate	When held by a Pokémon, it boosts the power of Fire-type moves by 20%. (When held by Arceus, it shifts Arceus's type to Fire type.)	Route 13	—
Float Stone	Halves the holder's weight.	Use Rock Slide or Hyper Voice in battles where rocks appear in the background (in the Connecting Cave, Terminus Cave, or other locations)	—
Focus Band	Has a 10% chance of leaving the holder with 1 HP when it receives damage that would cause it to faint.	Get for 48 BP in Kiloude City's Battle Maison	—
Focus Sash	A holder with full HP is left with 1 HP when it is hit by a move that would cause it to faint.	Get for 48 BP in Kiloude City's Battle Maison	—
Fresh Water	Restores the HP of one Pokémon by 50 points.	Buy from a man in the Kalos Power Plant (discounted to 100 after you chase away Team Flare) / Buy from a man in Couriway Town	300
Full Heal	Cures all status conditions.	Buy at Poké Marts (after obtaining third Gym Badge)	600
Full Incense	When held by a Pokémon, it makes the holder move later.	Buy from the incense seller in Coumarine City	9,600
Full Restore	Fully restores the HP and heals any status conditions of a single Pokémon.	Buy at Poké Marts (after obtaining fifth Gym Badge)	3,000

G

Item	Description	How to obtain	Price
Garchompite	When held, it allows Garchomp to Mega Evolve into Mega Garchomp during battle.	Find on Victory Road between 8 P.M. and 8:59 P.M. (after entering the Hall of Fame)	—
Gardevoirite	When held, it allows Gardevoir to Mega Evolve into Mega Gardevoir during battle.	Receive with the Ralts that you get in a trade with Diantha in Lumiose City's Café Soleil (after entering the Hall of Fame)	—
Gengarite	When held, it allows Gengar to Mega Evolve into Mega Gengar during battle.	Receive from a woman in Laverre City (after having seen Gastly, Haunter, or Gengar)	—
Genius Wing	Slightly raises the base Sp. Atk stat of a Pokémon. It can be used until the stat reaches its maximum value.	Win for achieving Beginner Rank, Novice Rank, or Normal Rank in Lumiose City's Battle Institute	—
Grip Claw	Extends the duration of moves like Bind and Wrap.	Often held by wild Sneasel	—
Griseous Orb	When held by Giratina, it changes it into its Origin Forme, and boosts the power of Dragon- and Ghost-type moves by 20%.	Terminus Cave: Zygarde's Chamber	—
Guard Spec.	Prevents stat reduction among the Trainer's party Pokémon for five turns.	Buy at the Poké Mart in Santalune City	700
Gyaradosite	When held, it allows Gyarados to Mega Evolve into Mega Gyarados during battle.	Find in Couriway Town between 8 P.M. and 8:59 P.M. (after entering the Hall of Fame)	—

AFTER THE HALL OF FAME

CENTRAL KALOS

COASTAL KALOS

MOUNTAIN KALOS

ADVENTURE DATA

H

Item	Description	How to obtain	Price
Hard Stone	When held by a Pokémon, it boosts the power of Rock-type moves by 20%.	Glittering Cave / Sometimes held by wild Pokémon such as Dwebble, Nosepass, or others	—
Heal Powder	Cures all status conditions. Very bitter (lowers a Pokémon's friendship).	Buy from Lumiose City's Herboriste	450
Health Wing	Slightly raises the base HP stat of a Pokémon. It can be used until the stat reaches its maximum value.	Win for achieving Beginner Rank, Novice Rank, or Normal Rank in Lumiose City's Battle Institute	—
Heart Scale	Give one to Madam Reminder in Dendemille Town, and she will have your Pokémon remember a move it has forgotten.	Route 8 / Outside the Frost Cavern / Often held by wild Luvdisc / Receive from Tierno every day in Coumarine City (after entering the Hall of Fame)	—
Heat Rock	When held by a Pokémon, it extends the duration of the move Sunny Day by three turns.	Terminus Cave B1F	—
Helix Fossil	A Pokémon Fossil. When restored, it becomes Omanyte.	Use Rock Smash to break cracked rocks deep within Glittering Cave (after entering the Hall of Fame) *Pokémon Y only*	—
Heracronite	When held, it allows Heracross to Mega Evolve into Mega Heracross during battle.	Find in Santalune Forest between 8 P.M. and 8:59 P.M. (after entering the Hall of Fame) *Pokémon Y only*	—
Honey	Attracts wild Pokémon where wild Pokémon can appear, and causes a Horde Encounter.	Receive from Trevor on Route 5 / Sometimes held by wild Combee	—
Houndoominite	When held, it allows Houndoom to Mega Evolve into Mega Houndoom during battle.	Find on Route 16 between 8 P.M. and 8:59 P.M. (after entering the Hall of Fame) *Pokémon Y only*	—
HP Up	Raises the base HP stat of a Pokémon.	Buy at the Poké Mart in Laverre City / Get for 2 BP in Kiloude City's Battle Maison	9,800
Hyper Potion	Restores the HP of one Pokémon by 200 points.	Buy at Poké Marts (after obtaining second Gym Badge)	1,200

I

Item	Description	How to obtain	Price
Ice Heal	Cures the Frozen status condition.	Buy at Poké Marts (after obtaining first Gym Badge)	250
Icicle Plate	When held by a Pokémon, it boosts the power of Ice-type moves by 20%. (When held by Arceus, it shifts Arceus's type to Ice type.)	Route 17	—
Icy Rock	Extends the duration of the move Hail by 3 turns when held.	Frost Cavern 1F	—
Insect Plate	When held by a Pokémon, it boosts the power of Bug-type moves by 20%. (When held by Arceus, it shifts Arceus's type to Bug type.)	Route 21	—
Iron	Raises the base Defense stat of a Pokémon.	Buy at the Poké Mart in Laverre City / Get for 2 BP in Kiloude City's Battle Maison	9,800
Iron Ball	Halves the holder's Speed. If the holder has the Levitate Ability or is a Flying-type Pokémon, Ground-type moves can hit it.	Get for 48 BP in Kiloude City's Battle Maison	—
Iron Plate	When held by a Pokémon, it boosts the power of Steel-type moves by 20%. (When held by Arceus, it shifts Arceus's type to Steel type.)	Terminus Cave B2F	—

J

Item	Description	How to obtain	Price
Jaw Fossil	A Pokémon Fossil. When restored, it becomes Tyrunt.	Receive from the assistant in Glittering Cave	—

K

Item	Description	How to obtain	Price
Kangaskhanite	When held, it allows Kangaskhan to Mega Evolve into Mega Kangaskhan during battle.	Find in Glittering Cave between 8 P.M. and 8:59 P.M. (after entering the Hall of Fame)	—
King's Rock	When the holder damages a target with an attack, there is a 10% chance the target will flinch.	Receive from Lysandre in Lumiose City's Lysandre Café / Sometimes held by wild Pokémon such as Hariyama, Hawlucha, or others	—

L

Item	Description	How to obtain	Price
Lagging Tail	When held by a Pokémon, it makes it move later.	Sometimes held by wild Lickitung or Slowpoke	—
Lava Cookie	Lavaridge Town's famous specialty. Cures all status conditions.	Receive from a visitor from the Hoenn region met at various hotels	—
Lax Incense	Boosts the holder's evasion.	Buy from the incense seller in Coumarine City	9,600
Leaf Stone	It can evolve Exeggcute, Gloom, Pansage, and Weepinbell.	Route 8 / Buy at Lumiose City's Stone Emporium / Win from an Inverse Battle on Route 18	2,100
Leftovers	It restores 1/16 of the holder's maximum HP every turn.	Route 12	—

Item	Description	How to obtain	Price
Lemonade	Restores the HP of one Pokémon by 80 points.	It can be won by clearing Secret Super-Training Regimens in S.T.	—
Life Orb	Lowers the holder's HP each time it attacks, but raises the power of moves by 30%.	Get for 48 BP in Kiloude City's Battle Maison	—
Light Ball	Doubles Attack and Sp. Atk stats when held by Pikachu.	Sometimes held by wild Pikachu	—
Light Clay	Extends the duration of moves like Reflect and Light Screen.	Sometimes held by wild Golett	—
Lucarionite	When held, it allows Lucario to Mega Evolve into Mega Lucario during battle.	Held by the Lucario you receive from Lady Korrina in Shalour City	—
Luck Incense	Doubles prize money from a battle if the holding Pokémon joins in.	Buy from the incense seller in Coumarine City	9,600
Lucky Egg	Increases the number of Experience Points received from battle by 50%.	Receive from a woman in Coumarine City's Coumarine Hotel	—
Luminous Moss	Increases Sp. Def by 1 when the holder is hit with Water-type moves. It goes away after use.	Use Hyper Voice or Rock Slide in battles in Glittering Cave where you see mossy rocks in the background	—
Lumiose Galette	A popular pastry sold in Lumiose City. Cures all status conditions for one Pokémon.	Lumiose City's Galette Stand	100
Lustrous Orb	When held by Palkia, it boosts the power of Dragon- and Water-type moves.	Terminus Cave: Zygarde's Chamber	—

M

Item	Description	How to obtain	Price
Macho Brace	Halves Speed, but makes it easier to raise base stats.	Route 15	—
Magmarizer	Link Trade Magmar while it holds the Magmarizer to evolve it into Magmortar.	Get for 32 BP in Kiloude City's Battle Maison	—
Magnet	When held by a Pokémon, it boosts the power of Electric-type moves by 20%.	Receive from a woman in the Kalos Power Plant (after you chase away Team Flare)	—
Manectite	When held, it allows Manectric to Mega Evolve into Mega Manectric during battle.	Find on Route 16 between 8 P.M. and 8:59 P.M. (after entering the Hall of Fame) *Pokémon X only	—
Mawilite	When held, it allows Mawile to Mega Evolve into Mega Mawile during battle.	Find in Camphrier Town's Shabboneau Castle between 8 P.M. and 8:59 P.M. (after entering the Hall of Fame)	—
Max Elixir	Completely restores the PP of all of a Pokémon's moves.	Victory Road (Outside)	—
Max Ether	Completely restores the PP of a Pokémon's move.	Shalour City / Poké Ball Factory / Route 18 / Pokémon Village	—
Max Potion	Completely restores the HP of a single Pokémon.	Buy at Poké Marts (after obtaining fourth Gym Badge)	2,500
Max Repel	Prevents weak wild Pokémon from appearing for 250 steps after its use.	Buy at Poké Marts (after obtaining third Gym Badge).	700
Max Revive	Revives a fainted Pokémon and fully restores its HP.	Poké Ball Factory / Find on Route 19 / Receive from Serena/Calem on Victory Road	—
Meadow Plate	When held by a Pokémon, it boosts the power of Grass-type moves by 20%. (When held by Arceus, it shifts Arceus's type to Grass type.)	Route 20	—
Medichamite	When held, it allows Medicham to Mega Evolve into Mega Medicham during battle.	Find in Laverre City between 8 P.M. and 8:59 P.M. (after entering the Hall of Fame)	—
Mental Herb	The holder can cure itself of the Infatuated status condition. The Pokémon can also heal from Disable, Encore, Taunt, Torment, and Heal Block. It goes away after use.	Sometimes held by wild Pancham	—
Metal Coat	When held by a Pokémon, it boosts the power of Steel-type moves by 20%. Link Trade Onix or Scyther while they hold a Metal Coat to evolve them.	In the Poké Ball Factory / Sometimes held by wild Magneton	—
Metal Powder	When held by Ditto, Defense doubles.	Sometimes held by wild Ditto	—
Metronome	When held by a Pokémon, it raises the power of a move used consecutively by that Pokémon (max 200).	Receive from a man in Coumarine City's Hillcrest Station / Sometimes held by wild Chatot	—
Mewtwonite X	When held, it allows Mewtwo to Mega Evolve into Mega Mewtwo X during battle.	Catch Mewtwo in the Unknown Dungeon in the Pokémon Village (after entering the Hall of Fame) *Pokémon X only	—
Mewtwonite Y	When held, it allows Mewtwo to Mega Evolve into Mega Mewtwo Y during battle.	Catch Mewtwo in the Unknown Dungeon within the Pokémon Village (after entering the Hall of Fame) *Pokémon Y only	—
Mind Plate	When held by a Pokémon, it boosts the power of Psychic-type moves by 20%. (When held by Arceus, it shifts Arceus's type to Psychic type.)	Route 10	—
Miracle Seed	When held by a Pokémon, it boosts the power of Grass-type moves by 20%.	Berry fields on Route 7 / Win from a woman in Couriway Town for answering a quiz (if you chose Chespin)	—
Moomoo Milk	Restores the HP of one Pokémon by 100 points.	Buy from a woman in Dendemille Town / May receive as a bonus when buying freshly baked Lumiose Galettes at Lumiose City's Galette Stand	500

Item	Description	How to obtain	Price
Moon Stone	It can evolve Jigglypuff, Nidorina, Nidorino, and Skitty.	Win as a prize for a victorious Inverse Battle in the Inverse House on Route 18 / Sometimes held by wild Lunatone	—
Muscle Band	When held by a Pokémon, it boosts the power of physical moves by 10%.	Get for 48 BP in Kiloude City's Battle Maison	—
Muscle Wing	Raises the base Attack stat of a Pokémon by a little. It can be used until the stat reaches its maximum value.	Win for achieving Beginner Rank, Novice Rank, or Normal Rank in Lumiose City's Battle Institute	—
Mystic Water	When held by a Pokémon, it boosts the power of Water-type moves by 20%.	Win from a woman in Couriway Town for answering a quiz (if you chose Froakie)	—

N

Item	Description	How to obtain	Price
Never-Melt Ice	When held by a Pokémon, it boosts the power of Ice-type moves by 20%.	Frost Cavern 2F / Sometimes held by wild Abomasnow, Cryogonal, or Snover	—
Normal Gem	When held by a Pokémon, it boosts the power of a Normal-type move by 30% one time. It goes away after use.	Terminus Cave (using Dowsing Machine)	—
Nugget	A nugget of pure gold. It can be sold at shops for 5,000.	Sometimes held by wild Garbodor / Find in Kiloude City (after entering the Hall of Fame)	—

O

Item	Description	How to obtain	Price
Odd Incense	When held by a Pokémon, it boosts the power of Psychic-type moves by 20%.	Buy from the incense seller in Coumarine City	9,600
Old Amber	A piece of amber that contains genetic material. When restored, it becomes Aerodactyl.	Use Rock Smash to break cracked rocks deep within Glittering Cave	—
Oval Stone	Level up Happiny between 4 A.M. and 7:59 P.M. while it holds the Oval Stone to evolve it into Chansey.	Find in the Unknown Dungeon in the Pokémon Village (using the Dowsing Machine after entering the Hall of Fame)	—

P

Item	Description	How to obtain	Price
Paralyze Heal	Cures the Paralysis status condition.	Buy at Poké Marts (after obtaining first Gym Badge)	200
Pearl	A pretty pearl. It can be sold at shops for 700.	Ambrette Town / Often held by wild Cloyster and Shellder	—
Pearl String	Very large pearls that sparkle in a pretty silver collar. It can be sold at shops for 7,500.	If you have a Furfrou in your party that has kept the same trim for 15 days or more, talk to a woman in Lumiose City's Café Woof	—
Pinsirite	When held, it allows Pinsir to Mega Evolve into Mega Pinsir during battle.	Find in Santalune Forest between 8 P.M. and 8:59 P.M. (after entering the Hall of Fame) *Pokémon X only	—
Pixie Plate	When held by a Pokémon, it boosts the power of Fairy-type moves by 20%. (When held by Arceus, it shifts Arceus's type to Fairy type.)	Pokémon Village	—
Plume Fossil	A Pokémon Fossil. When restored, it becomes Archen.	Use Rock Smash to break cracked rocks deep within Glittering Cave (after entering the Hall of Fame)	—
Poison Barb	When held by a Pokémon, it boosts the power of Poison-type moves by 20%.	Route 4 / Sometimes held by wild Budew, Roselia, Venipede, or others	—
Poké Doll	Ensures that the holder can successfully run from a wild Pokémon encounter.	Show the man in Laverre City a Pokémon with a height of 1'00" or less. Show the woman in Laverre City a Pokémon with a height of 9'10" or greater.	—
Poké Toy	Ensures that the holder can successfully run from a wild Pokémon encounter.	Correctly identify the Pokémon cry imitated by the woman in Coumarine City	—
Potion	Restores the HP of one Pokémon by 20 points.	Buy at the Potion shop in Aquacorde Town / Buy at Poké Marts (from the start)	300
Power Anklet	Halves the holder's Speed, but makes the Speed base stat easier to raise.	Get for 16 BP in Kiloude City's Battle Maison	—
Power Band	Halves the holder's Speed, but makes the Sp. Def base stat easier to raise.	Get for 16 BP in Kiloude City's Battle Maison	—
Power Belt	Halves the holder's Speed, but makes the Defense base stat easier to raise.	Get for 16 BP in Kiloude City's Battle Maison	—
Power Bracer	Halves the holder's Speed, but makes the Attack base stat easier to raise.	Get for 16 BP in Kiloude City's Battle Maison	—
Power Herb	The holder can immediately use a move that requires a one-turn charge. It goes away after use.	Get for 32 BP in Kiloude City's Battle Maison	—
Power Lens	Halves the holder's Speed, but makes the Sp. Atk base stat easier to raise.	Get for 16 BP in Kiloude City's Battle Maison	—
Power Weight	Halves the holder's Speed, but makes the HP base stat easier to raise.	Get for 16 BP in Kiloude City's Battle Maison	—
PP Max	Increases the max number of PP as high as it will go.	Win second prize in Lumiose City's Loto-ID Center / Get as a reward for meeting 21 or more of the same Pokémon using the Poké Radar	—

Item	Description	How to obtain	Price
PP Up	Increases the max number of PP by one level.	Route 7 / Route 15 / Route 18 / Route 19 / Victory Road (Outside) / Win third prize in Lumiose City's Loto-ID Center	—
Pretty Wing	A pretty wing. It can be sold at shops for 100.	Talk to Fletchling in Pokémon Village	—
Prism Scale	Link Trade Feebas while it holds the Prism Scale to evolve it into Milotic.	Receive from a girl on 4F in an office building in Lumiose City if you have 10 or more items of clothing	—
Protector	Link Trade Rhydon while it holds the Protector to evolve it into Rhyperior.	Lost Hotel / Get for 32 BP in Kiloude City's Battle Maison	—
Protein	Raises the base Attack stat of a Pokémon.	Buy at the Poké Mart in Laverre City / Get for 2 BP in Kiloude City's Battle Maison	9,800
Pure Incense	Helps keep wild Pokémon away if the holder is the first one in the party.	Buy from the incense seller in Coumarine City	9,600

Q

Item	Description	How to obtain	Price
Quick Claw	Allows the holder to strike first sometimes.	Receive from a woman in an office building in Lumiose City 1F / Sometimes held by wild Sandslash, Sneasel, or Zangoose	—
Quick Powder	When held by Ditto, Speed doubles.	Often held by wild Ditto	—

R

Item	Description	How to obtain	Price
Rage Candy Bar	Mahogany Town's famous snack. Restores the HP of one Pokémon by 20.	Receive from a visitor from the Johto region met at various hotels	—
Rare Bone	A rare bone. It can be sold at shops for 5,000.	Route 19	—
Rare Candy	Raises a Pokémon's level by 1.	Route 13 / Route 14 / Route 16 / Route 17 / Lysandre Labs / Couriway Town / Route 21	—
Razor Claw	Boosts the holder's critical-hit ratio. ●	Get for 48 BP in Kiloude City's Battle Maison	—
Razor Fang	When the holder hits a target with an attack, there is a 10% chance the target will flinch. ★	Get for 48 BP in Kiloude City's Battle Maison	—
Reaper Cloth	Link Trade Dusclops while it holds the Reaper Cloth to evolve it into Dusknoir.	Terminus Cave B1F / Get for 32 BP in Kiloude City's Battle Maison	—
Red Card	If the holder is hit by an attack, the opposing Trainer is forced to switch out the attacking Pokémon. It goes away after use.	Get for 32 BP in Kiloude City's Battle Maison	—
Repel	Prevents weak wild Pokémon from appearing for 100 steps after its use.	Buy at Poké Marts (after obtaining first Gym Badge)	350
Resist Wing	Slightly raises the base Defense stat of a Pokémon. It can be used until the stat reaches its maximum value.	Win for achieving Beginner Rank, Novice Rank, or Normal Rank in Lumiose City's Battle Institute	—
Revival Herb	Revives a fainted Pokémon. Very bitter (lowers a Pokémon's friendship).	Buy from Lumiose City's Herboriste	2,800
Revive	Revives a fainted Pokémon and restores half of its HP.	Buy at Poké Marts (after obtaining second Gym Badge) / Break cracked rocks using Rock Smash	1,500
Rich Mulch	Mulch to be used in a Berry field. It increases the Berry harvest without the need for particularly diligent care.	Add three Berries of different colors to the composter when making compost in the Berry fields	—
Ring Target	Moves that would otherwise have no effect will hit the holder.	Get for 32 BP in Kiloude City's Battle Maison	—
Rock Incense	When held by a Pokémon, it boosts the power of Rock-type moves by 20%.	Buy from the incense seller in Coumarine City	9,600
Rocky Helmet	When the bearer is hit with an attack that makes direct contact, it damages the attacker for 1/6 of its maximum HP.	Receive from a woman in the Ambrette Town gate	—
Root Fossil	A Pokémon Fossil. When restored, it becomes Lileep.	Use Rock Smash to break cracked rocks deep within Glittering Cave (after entering the Hall of Fame) *Pokémon X only	—
Rose Incense	When held by a Pokémon, it boosts the power of Grass-type moves by 20%.	Buy from the incense seller in Coumarine City	9,600

S

Item	Description	How to obtain	Price
Sachet	Link Trade Spritzee while it holds the Sachet to evolve it into Aromatisse.	Receive from a man in Cyllage City (*Pokémon Y only*) / Find on Route 12 / Get for 32 BP in Kiloude City's Battle Maison	—
Safety Goggles	Protects the Pokémon from weather damage, such as hail and sandstorm. Protects it from Cotton Spore, Poison Powder, Powder, Rage Powder, Sleep Powder, Spore, and Stun Spore. Immune to the Effect Spore Ability.	Get for 48 BP in Kiloude City's Battle Maison	—
Sail Fossil	A Pokémon Fossil. When restored, it becomes Amaura.	Receive from the assistant in Glittering Cave	—
Scizorite	When held, it allows Scizor to Mega Evolve into Mega Scizor during battle.	Find in the Frost Cavern between 8 P.M. and 8:59 P.M. (after entering the Hall of Fame)	—

Items

	Item	Description	How to obtain	Price
	Scope Lens	Boosts the holder's critical-hit ratio.	Get for 48 BP in Kiloude City's Battle Maison	—
	Sea Incense	When held by a Pokémon, it boosts the power of Water-type moves by 20%.	Buy from the incense seller in Coumarine City	9,600
	Sharp Beak	When held by a Pokémon, it boosts the power of Flying-type moves by 20%.	Route 5 / Sometimes held by wild Doduo or Fearow	—
	Shed Shell	Always allows the holder to be switched out.	Sometimes held by wild Scraggy	—
	Shell Bell	Restores the holder's HP by up to 1/8th of the damage dealt to the target.	Receive from an old man in Dendemille Town (if you have registered 70 or more Pokémon in the Mountain Kalos Pokédex)	—
	Shiny Stone	It can evolve Floette and Roselia.	Route 12 / Win from an Inverse Battle on Route 18	—
	Silk Scarf	When held by a Pokémon, it boosts the power of Normal-type moves by 20%.	Receive from an old man in Coumarine City	—
	Silver Powder	When held by a Pokémon, it boosts the power of Bug-type moves by 20%.	Route 7 / Sometimes held by wild Masquerain	—
	Skull Fossil	A Pokémon Fossil. When restored, it becomes Cranidos.	Use Rock Smash to break cracked rocks deep within Glittering Cave (after entering the Hall of Fame)	—
	Sky Plate	When held by a Pokémon, it boosts the power of Flying-type moves by 20%. (When held by Arceus, it shifts Arceus's type to Flying type.)	Coumarine City	—
	Smoke Ball	Allows the holder to successfully run away from wild Pokémon.	Lost Hotel	—
	Smooth Rock	Extends the duration of the move Sandstorm by three turns when held.	Route 13	—
	Snowball	Increases Attack by 1 when the holder is hit with Ice-type moves. It goes away after use.	Use Hyper Voice or Rock Slide in battles outside the Frost Cavern and along Route 17 where you see piles of snow in the background	—
	Soda Pop	Restores the HP of one Pokémon by 60 points.	Receive from a woman in Cyllage City	300
	Soft Sand	When held by a Pokémon, it boosts the power of Ground-type moves by 20%.	Geosenge Town / Sometimes held by wild Dugtrio, Stunfisk, or Trapinch	—
	Soothe Bell	The holder's friendship improves more quickly.	Receive from a woman in Shalour City (when the lead Pokémon in your party has high friendship)	—
	Spell Tag	When held by a Pokémon, it boosts the power of Ghost-type moves by 20%.	On Route 14 / Sometimes held by wild Banette	—
	Splash Plate	When held by a Pokémon, it boosts the power of Water-type moves by 20%. (When held by Arceus, it shifts Arceus's type to Water type.)	Azure Bay	—
	Spooky Plate	When held by a Pokémon, it boosts the power of Ghost-type moves by 20%. (When held by Arceus, it shifts Arceus's type to Ghost type.)	Chamber of Emptiness on Route 22	—
	Star Piece	A red gem. It can be sold at shops for 4,900.	Camphrier Town / Terminus Cave B1F / Sometimes held by wild Starmie	—
	Stardust	Lovely, red-colored sand. It can be sold at shops for 1,000.	Always held by wild Staryu / Often held by wild Starmie	—
	Stick	When held by Farfetch'd, it raises the critical-hit ratio of its moves.	Sometimes held by wild Farfetch'd	—
	Sticky Barb	Damages the holder by 1/8 of its max HP every turn. It can stick to an opponent that it makes direct contact with.	Sometimes held by wild Ferroseed	—
	Stone Plate	When held by a Pokémon, it boosts the power of Rock-type moves by 20%. (When held by Arceus, it shifts Arceus's type to Rock type.)	Find on Route 15	—
	Sun Stone	It can evolve Gloom and Helioptile.	Get from the Hiker in Shalour City in exchange for the Intriguing Stone / Route 13 / Sometimes held by wild Solrock	—
	Super Potion	Restores the HP of one Pokémon by 50 points.	Buy at Poké Marts (after obtaining first Gym Badge)	700
	Super Repel	Prevents weak wild Pokémon from appearing for 200 steps after its use.	Buy at Poké Marts (after obtaining second Gym Badge)	500
	Surprise Mulch	Mulch to be used in a Berry Field. Ensures that a mutation will occur if you have planted two Berry trees next to each other that can give rise to a mutation.	Add three Berries of the same color to the composter when making compost in the Berry fields	—
	Sweet Heart	Restores the HP of one Pokémon by 20 points.	Receive from a woman in Camphrier Town	—
	Swift Wing	Slightly raises the base Speed stat of a Pokémon. It can be used until the stat reaches its maximum value.	Win for achieving Beginner Rank, Novice Rank, or Normal Rank in Lumiose City's Battle Institute	—

T

	Item	Description	How to obtain	Price
	Thick Club	When held by Cubone or Marowak, the power of physical moves is doubled.	Sometimes held by wild Cubone	—
	Thunder Stone	It can evolve Pikachu and Eevee.	Route 10 / Win in an Inverse Battle on Route 18	—

Item	Description	How to obtain	Price
Tiny Mushroom	A tiny mushroom. It can be sold at shops for 250.	Win at Lumiose City's Restaurant Le Nah / Route 7 / Sometimes held by wild Amoonguss or Foongus	—
Toxic Orb	Inflicts the Badly Poisoned status condition on the holder during battle.	Get for 16 BP in Kiloude City's Battle Maison	—
Toxic Plate	When held by a Pokémon, it boosts the power of Poison-type moves by 20%. (When held by Arceus, it shifts Arceus's type to Poison type.)	Route 19	—
Twisted Spoon	When held by a Pokémon, it boosts the power of Psychic-type moves by 20%.	Lost Hotel / Sometimes held by wild Abra	—
Tyranitarite	When held, it allows Tyranitar to Mega Evolve into Mega Tyranitar during battle.	Find in Cyllage City Pokémon Gym between 8 P.M. and 8:59 P.M. (after entering the Hall of Fame) *Pokémon X only	—

U

Item	Description	How to obtain	Price
Up-Grade	Link Trade Porygon while it holds the Up-Grade to evolve it into Porygon2.	Get for 32 BP in Kiloude City's Battle Maison	—

V

Item	Description	How to obtain	Price
Venusaurite	When held, it allows Venusaur to Mega Evolve into Mega Venusaur during battle.	Receive from Professor Sycamore in Lumiose City (if you chose Bulbasaur) / Buy at Lumiose City's Stone Emporium	Varies ◆

W

Item	Description	How to obtain	Price
Water Stone	It can evolve Eevee, Lombre, Panpour, Poliwhirl, Sheldler, and Staryu.	Route 8 / Buy at Lumiose City's Stone Emporium / Win from an Inverse Battle on Route 18	2,100
Wave Incense	When held by a Pokémon, it boosts the power of Water-type moves by 20%.	Buy from the incense seller in Coumarine City	9,600
Weakness Policy	Increases Attack and Sp. Atk by 2 if the holder is hit with a move that it's weak to.	Get for 32 BP in Kiloude City's Battle Maison	—
Whipped Dream	Link Trade Swirlix while it holds a Whipped Dream to evolve it into Slurpuff.	Receive from a man in Cyllage City (*Pokémon X only*) / Find on Route 12 / Get for 32 BP in Kiloude City's Battle Maison	—
White Herb	Restores lowered stats. It goes away after use.	Get for 32 BP in Kiloude City's Battle Maison	—
Wide Lens	Raises the holder's accuracy by 10%.	Get for 48 BP in Kiloude City's Battle Maison / Sometimes held by wild Yanma	—
Wise Glasses	When held by a Pokémon, it boosts the power of special moves by 10%.	Get for 48 BP in Kiloude City's Battle Maison	—

X

Item	Description	How to obtain	Price
X Accuracy	Raises the accuracy of a Pokémon on which it is used.	Buy at the Poké Mart in Santalune City	950
X Attack	Raises the Attack stat of a Pokémon by 1.	Buy at the Poké Mart in Santalune City	500
X Defense	Raises the Defense stat of a Pokémon by 1.	Buy at the Poké Mart in Santalune City	550
X Sp. Atk	Raises the Sp. Atk stat of a Pokémon by 1.	Buy at the Poké Mart in Santalune City	350
X Sp. Def	Raises the Sp. Def stat of a Pokémon by 1.	Buy at the Poké Mart in Santalune City	350
X Speed	Raises the Speed of a Pokémon by 1.	Buy at the Poké Mart in Santalune City	350

Z

Item	Description	How to obtain	Price
Zap Plate	When held by a Pokémon, it boosts the power of Electric-type moves by 20%. (When held by Arceus, it shifts Arceus's type to Electric type.)	Kalos Power Plant	—
Zinc	Raises the base Sp. Def stat of a Pokémon.	Buy at the Poké Mart in Laverre City / Get for 2 BP in Kiloude City's Battle Maison	9,800
Zoom Lens	Raises the holder's accuracy by 20% when it moves after the opposing Pokémon.	Get for 48 BP in Kiloude City's Battle Maison	—

◆ The price will be affected by how stylish you are considered to be. The lowest possible price is 10,000.
● If you give Sneasel the Razor Claw to hold and level it up between 8 P.M. and 3:59 A.M., it will evolve into Weavile.
★ If you give Gligar the Razor Fang to hold and level it up between 8 P.M. and 3:59 A.M., it will evolve into Gliscor.

Key Items

Item	Description	How to obtain	Price
Adventure Rules	This book contains all the points a new Trainer needs to know on a journey. It was handmade by a kind friend.	Receive from Serena/Calem on Route 3	—
Bicycle	A folding Bicycle that enables a rider to get around much faster than dashing.	Receive from the Cycle Shop in Cyllage City	—
Dowsing Machine	It searches for hidden items in the area and emits different lights and sounds when it detects something.	Receive from the Swimmer ♀ on Route 8 (after exploring Glittering Cave)	—
Elevator Key	A card key that activates the elevator in Lysandre Labs. It is emblazoned with Team Flare's logo.	Receive from Mable in Lysandre Labs after defeating her in battle	—
Exp. Share	When it is switched to ON, all of the Pokémon in your party will receive Exp. Points, even if they themselves do not battle.	Receive from Alexa in Santalune City (after defeating the Santalune City Gym Leader)	—
Good Rod	A nice, new fishing rod. You can use it to fish for Pokémon from the waterside.	Receive from the fishing enthusiast in Coumarine City	—
Holo Caster	A device that allows users to receive and view hologram clips at any time.	Receive from your mom in Vaniville Town (after visiting Aquacorde Town)	—
Honor of Kalos	A precious symbol that is awarded only to an individual who has done great things for the Kalos region.	Enter the Hall of Fame	—
Intriguing Stone	A rather curious stone that might appear to be valuable to some. It's all in the eye of the beholder.	Receive from Tierno in Shalour City	—
Lens Case	A rather chic-looking case for carrying contact lenses.	Receive from a woman in Lumiose City's PR Video Studio	—
Looker Ticket	A ticket that was handmade by Looker. It's decorated with a liberal amount of glittery paint.	Obtain in the first chapter of Looker's tale (after entering the Hall of Fame)	—
Mega Ring	A bracelet containing an untold power that somehow enables Pokémon carrying Mega Stones to Mega Evolve in battle.	Receive from Successor Korrina in Shalour City (after defeating the Shalour City Gym Leader)	—
Old Rod	An old and beat-up fishing rod. You can use it to fish for Pokémon from the waterside.	Receive from fishing enthusiast in Ambrette Town's Ambrette Aquarium	—
Oval Charm	An oval charm said to increase the chance of Pokémon Eggs being found at the Day Care.	Have Professor Sycamore evaluate your Pokédex in his Pokémon Lab in Lumiose City (after you have found all of the Pokémon in the Kalos region)	—
Poké Flute	A flute that can be played with a beautiful tone. It wakes sleeping Pokémon.	Borrow from the owner of Parfum Palace (after catching the owner's Furfrou)	—
Poké Radar	A tool that can search out Pokémon that are hiding in the tall grass. Its battery is recharged as you walk. (Using the Roller Skates will not recharge the battery and cancels the Poké Radar.)	Receive from a man in the Sycamore Pokémon Lab in Lumiose City (after entering the Hall of Fame)	—
Power Plant Pass	This pass serves as an ID card for gaining access to the power plant that lies along Route 13.	Find on Route 13	—
Prof's Letter	A letter that Professor Sycamore wrote to your mother. A faint but pleasant scent seems to cling to the paper.	Receive from Tierno in Aquacorde Town	—
Roller Skates	Attaches roller skates to the bottom of your shoes, allowing you to glide quickly around and perform tricks.	Receive from Roller Skater Rinka in Santalune City	—
Sprinklotad	A watering can shaped like Lotad. It helps promote the healthy growth of any Berries planted in good, soft soil.	Receive from the man at the Berry fields on Route 7	—
Super Rod	An awesome, high-tech fishing rod. You can use it to fish for Pokémon from the waterside.	Receive from the Fisherman located in the fishing shack on Route 16	—
TMV Pass	A commuter pass that allows the holder to ride the TMV between Lumiose City and Kiloude City at any time.	Receive from Professor Sycamore in Lumiose Station (after entering the Hall of Fame)	—
Town Map	A very convenient map that can be viewed anytime. It even shows you your present location in the region.	Receive from your mom in Vaniville Town (after visiting Aquacorde Town)	—
Vs. Recorder	An amazing device that can record a battle between friends or the battles at certain special battle facilities.	Receive from an old man in Kiloude City	—

Poké Balls

Item	Description	How to obtain	Price
Poké Ball	A device for catching wild Pokémon.	Buy in Poké Ball shop in Aquacorde Town and at Poké Marts (from the start)	200
Great Ball	A Poké Ball that provides a higher Pokémon catch rate than a standard Poké Ball can.	Buy at Poké Marts (after obtaining first Gym Badge)	600
Ultra Ball	A Poké Ball that provides a higher Pokémon catch rate than a Great Ball can.	Buy at Poké Marts (after obtaining third Gym Badge)	1,200
Master Ball	A Poké Ball that will catch any wild Pokémon without fail.	Receive from the president of the Poké Ball Factory / Win jackpot in Lumiose City's Loto-ID Center	—
Premier Ball	A rare Poké Ball made to celebrate an event of some sort.	Buy 10 or more Poké Balls at a time / Buy at Lumiose City's Poké Ball Boutique	200
Heal Ball	A remedial Poké Ball that restores the HP of a Pokémon caught with it and eliminates any status conditions.	Buy at Poké Marts in Lumiose City (South Boulevard) and Snowbelle City / Receive from a girl in Lumiose City's Poké Ball Boutique	300
Net Ball	A Poké Ball that is more effective when attempting to catch Water- or Bug-type Pokémon.	Buy at Poké Marts in Cyllage City, Lumiose City (South Boulevard), and Snowbelle City / Buy at Lumiose City's Poké Ball Boutique	1,000
Nest Ball	A Poké Ball that becomes more effective the lower the level of the wild Pokémon.	Buy at Poké Marts in Cyllage City, Lumiose City (South Boulevard), and Snowbelle City / Buy at Lumiose City's Poké Ball Boutique	1,000
Quick Ball	A Poké Ball that has a more successful catch rate if used at the start of a wild encounter.	Buy at Poké Marts in Coumarine City and Snowbelle City / Buy at Lumiose City's Poké Ball Boutique	1,000
Dusk Ball	A Poké Ball that makes it easier to catch wild Pokémon in caves or at night (between 8 P.M. and 3:59 A.M.).	Buy at Poké Marts in Cyllage City and Snowbelle City / Buy at Lumiose City's Poké Ball Boutique	1,000
Timer Ball	A Poké Ball that becomes progressively more effective the more turns that are taken in battle.	Buy at Poké Marts in Coumarine City and Snowbelle City / Buy at Lumiose City's Poké Ball Boutique	1,000
Repeat Ball	A Poké Ball that works especially well on a Pokémon species that has been caught before.	Buy at Poké Marts in Coumarine City and Snowbelle City / Buy at Lumiose City's Poké Ball Boutique/ Receive from Sina in Coumarine City / Find on Route 21	1,000
Dive Ball	A Poké Ball that works especially well when catching Pokémon that live underwater.	Buy at Lumiose City's Poké Ball Boutique / Receive from man in Ambrette Town (in exchange for a Poké Ball) / Azure Bay	1,000
Luxury Ball	A Poké Ball that makes a wild Pokémon quickly grow friendlier after being caught.	Buy at Lumiose City's Poké Ball Boutique / Receive from a woman in Lumiose City's Pokémon Lab / Receive from a girl in Lumiose City's Poké Ball Boutique	1,000

Items Held by Wild Pokémon in Kalos

Sometimes Pokémon that appear in the wild hold items. When you catch a Pokémon that's holding an item, you get that item. Some items, such as Grip Claw, Light Clay, and Sticky Barb, can't be obtained in any other way.

Kalos No.	Pokémon	Always holding	Often holding	Sometimes holding
Central Kalos Pokédex 036	Pikachu	—	—	Light Ball
Central Kalos Pokédex 048	Masquerain	—	—	Silver Powder
Central Kalos Pokédex 055	Carvanha	—	—	Deep Sea Tooth
Central Kalos Pokédex 056	Sharpedo	—	—	Deep Sea Tooth
Central Kalos Pokédex 061	Farfetch'd	—	—	Stick
Central Kalos Pokédex 071	Budew	—	—	Poison Barb
Central Kalos Pokédex 072	Roselia	—	—	Poison Barb
Central Kalos Pokédex 076	Combee	—	—	Honey
Central Kalos Pokédex 091	Pancham	—	—	Mental Herb
Central Kalos Pokédex 094	Doduo	—	—	Sharp Beak
Central Kalos Pokédex 098	Gulpin	—	—	Oran Berry
Central Kalos Pokédex 100	Scraggy	—	—	Shed Shell
Central Kalos Pokédex 102	Abra	—	—	Twisted Spoon
Central Kalos Pokédex 104	Alakazam	—	—	Twisted Spoon
Central Kalos Pokédex 120	Venipede	—	—	Poison Barb
Central Kalos Pokédex 123	Audino	—	Oran Berry	Sitrus Berry
Central Kalos Pokédex 125	Croagunk	—	—	Black Sludge
Coastal Kalos Pokédex 005	Zangoose	—	—	Quick Claw
Coastal Kalos Pokédex 006	Seviper	Persim Berry	—	—
Coastal Kalos Pokédex 012	Lunatone	—	—	Moon Stone
Coastal Kalos Pokédex 013	Solrock	—	—	Sun Stone
Coastal Kalos Pokédex 014	Bagon	—	—	Dragon Fang
Coastal Kalos Pokédex 023	Dwebble	—	—	Hard Stone
Coastal Kalos Pokédex 025	Tentacool	—	—	Poison Barb
Coastal Kalos Pokédex 029	Luvdisc	—	Heart Scale	—
Coastal Kalos Pokédex 034	Staryu	Stardust	—	—
Coastal Kalos Pokédex 035	Starmie	—	Stardust	Star Piece
Coastal Kalos Pokédex 036	Shellder	—	Pearl	Big Pearl
Coastal Kalos Pokédex 037	Cloyster	—	Pearl	Big Pearl
Coastal Kalos Pokédex 038	Qwilfish	—	—	Poison Barb
Coastal Kalos Pokédex 039	Horsea	—	—	Dragon Scale
Coastal Kalos Pokédex 040	Seadra	—	—	Dragon Scale
Coastal Kalos Pokédex 042	Relicanth	—	—	Deep Sea Scale
Coastal Kalos Pokédex 060	Cubone	—	—	Thick Club
Coastal Kalos Pokédex 069	Ferroseed	—	—	Sticky Barb
Coastal Kalos Pokédex 087	Yanma	—	—	Wide Lens
Coastal Kalos Pokédex 089	Hawlucha	—	—	King's Rock
Coastal Kalos Pokédex 091	Golett	—	—	Light Clay
Coastal Kalos Pokédex 093	Nosepass	—	—	Hard Stone
Coastal Kalos Pokédex 096	Hariyama	—	—	King's Rock
Coastal Kalos Pokédex 097	Throh	—	—	Black Belt
Coastal Kalos Pokédex 098	Sawk	—	—	Black Belt
Coastal Kalos Pokédex 120	Roggenrola	—	Everstone	Hard Stone
Coastal Kalos Pokédex 126	Miltank	Moomoo Milk	—	—
Coastal Kalos Pokédex 133	Slowpoke	—	—	Lagging Tail
Coastal Kalos Pokédex 138	Chatot	—	—	Metronome
Coastal Kalos Pokédex 141	Clamperl	—	—	Big Pearl
Coastal Kalos Pokédex 142	Huntail	—	—	Deep Sea Tooth
Coastal Kalos Pokédex 143	Gorebyss	—	—	Deep Sea Scale
Coastal Kalos Pokédex 146	Corsola	—	—	Hard Stone
Coastal Kalos Pokédex 147	Chinchou	—	—	Deep Sea Scale
Coastal Kalos Pokédex 148	Lanturn	—	—	Deep Sea Scale

Kalos No.	Pokémon	Always holding	Often holding	Sometimes holding
Mountain Kalos Pokédex 002	Dugtrio	—	—	Soft Sand
Mountain Kalos Pokédex 003	Trapinch	—	—	Soft Sand
Mountain Kalos Pokédex 009	Geodude	—	—	Everstone
Mountain Kalos Pokédex 010	Graveler	—	—	Everstone
Mountain Kalos Pokédex 014	Shuckle	Berry Juice	—	—
Mountain Kalos Pokédex 015	Skorupi	—	—	Poison Barb
Mountain Kalos Pokédex 016	Drapion	—	—	Poison Barb
Mountain Kalos Pokédex 034	Poliwhirl	—	—	King's Rock
Mountain Kalos Pokédex 035	Poliwrath	—	—	King's Rock
Mountain Kalos Pokédex 036	Politoed	—	—	King's Rock
Mountain Kalos Pokédex 039	Stunfisk	—	—	Soft Sand
Mountain Kalos Pokédex 053	Foongus	—	Tiny Mushroom	Big Mushroom
Mountain Kalos Pokédex 054	Amoonguss	—	Tiny Mushroom	Big Mushroom
Mountain Kalos Pokédex 060	Basculin	—	—	Deep Sea Tooth
Mountain Kalos Pokédex 070	Magneton	—	—	Metal Coat
Mountain Kalos Pokédex 074	Trubbish	—	—	Black Sludge
Mountain Kalos Pokédex 075	Garbodor	—	Black Sludge	Nugget
Mountain Kalos Pokédex 088	Snover	—	—	Never-Melt Ice
Mountain Kalos Pokédex 089	Abomasnow	—	—	Never-Melt Ice
Mountain Kalos Pokédex 091	Sneasel	—	Grip Claw	Quick Claw
Mountain Kalos Pokédex 098	Sandslash	—	—	Quick Claw
Mountain Kalos Pokédex 099	Aron	—	—	Hard Stone
Mountain Kalos Pokédex 100	Lairon	—	—	Hard Stone
Mountain Kalos Pokédex 110	Fearow	—	—	Sharp Beak
Mountain Kalos Pokédex 111	Cryogonal	—	—	Never-Melt Ice
Mountain Kalos Pokédex 123	Banette	—	—	Spell Tag
Mountain Kalos Pokédex 134	Lickitung	—	—	Lagging Tail
Mountain Kalos Pokédex 138	Ditto	—	Quick Powder	Metal Powder
Mountain Kalos Pokédex 141	Druddigon	—	—	Dragon Fang
Mountain Kalos Pokédex 145	Dratini	—	—	Dragon Scale
Mountain Kalos Pokédex 146	Dragonair	—	—	Dragon Scale

Berries That Restore HP, PP, and Status Conditions

	Berry	Color	Time to mature	Min. yield	Max. yield	Possible mutation	Mutating neighbor	Pests	
	Aguav Berry	Green	24 hrs	3	15	Grepa Berry	Figy Berry	Burmy	
	Aspear Berry	Yellow	24 hrs	4	15	Hondew Berry	Leppa Berry	Combee	
	Cheri Berry	Red	24 hrs	4	15	—	—	Ledyba	
	Chesto Berry	Purple	24 hrs	4	15	Kelpsy Berry	Persim Berry	Illumise	
	Figy Berry	Red	24 hrs	3	15	Grepa Berry	Aguav Berry	Ledyba	
	Iapapa Berry	Yellow	24 hrs	3	15	Pomeg Berry	Mago Berry	Combee	
	Leppa Berry	Red	24 hrs	2	15	Hondew Berry	Aspear Berry	Ledyba	
	Lum Berry	Green	48 hrs	3	20	Tamato Berry	Sitrus Berry	Burmy	
	Mago Berry	Pink	24 hrs	3	15	Pomeg Berry	Iapapa Berry	Spewpa	
	Oran Berry	Blue	24 hrs	4	15	Qualot Berry	Pecha Berry	Volbeat	
	Pecha Berry	Pink	24 hrs	4	15	Qualot Berry	Oran Berry	Spewpa	
	Persim Berry	Pink	24 hrs	4	15	Kelpsy Berry	Chesto Berry	Spewpa	
	Rawst Berry	Green	24 hrs	4	15	—	—	Burmy	
	Sitrus Berry	Yellow	48 hrs	3	20	Tamato Berry	Lum Berry	Combee	
	Wiki Berry	Purple	24 hrs	3	15	—	—	Illumise	

Berries That Lower Base Stats

	Berry	Color	Time to mature	Min. yield	Max. yield	Possible mutation	Mutating neighbor	Pests	
	Grepa Berry	Yellow	48 hrs	1	20	Salac Berry	Roseli Berry	Combee	
	Hondew Berry	Green	48 hrs	1	20	Liechi Berry	Yache Berry	Burmy	
	Kelpsy Berry	Blue	48 hrs	1	20	Apicot Berry	Wacan Berry	Volbeat	
	Pomeg Berry	Red	48 hrs	1	20	Petaya Berry	Kasib Berry	Ledyba	
	Qualot Berry	Yellow	48 hrs	1	20	Ganlon Berry	Tanga Berry	Combee	
	Tamato Berry	Red	48 hrs	1	20	—	—	Ledyba	

Berries That Change the Damage Taken by the Holder

	Berry	Color	Time to mature	Min. yield	Max. yield	Possible mutation	Mutating neighbor	Pests	
	Babiri Berry	Green	48 hrs	3	20	—	—	Burmy	
	Charti Berry	Yellow	48 hrs	3	20	—	—	Combee	
	Chilan Berry	Yellow	48 hrs	3	20	—	—	Combee	
	Chople Berry	Red	48 hrs	3	20	—	—	Ledyba	
	Coba Berry	Blue	48 hrs	3	20	—	—	Volbeat	

Effects	How to obtain	Berry
Holder restores some of its HP when its HP falls to half or less, but Pokémon of certain Natures gain the Confused status condition.	The Berry tree on Route 6	Aguav Berry
Holder can heal itself of the Frozen status condition.	The Berry tree on Route 12 / Show a man in Camphrier Town the type of Pokémon he wishes to see / The unattended stand in Coumarine City	Aspear Berry
Holder can heal itself of the Paralysis status condition.	Show a man in Camphrier Town the type of Pokémon he wishes to see / The unattended stand in Coumarine City	Cheri Berry
Holder can heal itself of the Sleep status condition.	Show a man in Camphrier Town the type of Pokémon he wishes to see / The unattended stand in Coumarine City	Chesto Berry
Holder restores its HP when its HP falls to half or less, but Pokémon of certain Natures gain the Confused status condition.	The Berry tree on Route 21	Figy Berry
Holder restores some of its HP when its HP falls to half or less, but Pokémon of certain Natures gain the Confused status condition.	The Berry tree on Route 10	Iapapa Berry
Holder restores 10 PP to a move when that move's PP reaches 0.	The Berry tree on Route 15	Leppa Berry
Holder can heal itself of any status condition.	The Berry tree on Route 16	Lum Berry
Holder restores some of its HP when its HP falls to half or less, but Pokémon of certain Natures gain the Confused status condition.	The Berry tree on Route 8	Mago Berry
Holder restores its HP by 10 when its HP falls to half or less.	The Berry tree on Route 5 / Defeat Inver in the house on Route 18 / Visit the Berry farmer for the first time	Oran Berry
Holder can heal itself of the Poison status condition.	Show a man in Camphrier Town the type of Pokémon he wishes to see / The unattended stand in Coumarine City / Visit the Berry farmer for the first time	Pecha Berry
Holder can heal itself of the Confused status condition.	The Berry tree on Route 7	Persim Berry
Holder can heal itself of the Burned status condition.	Show a man in Camphrier Town the type of Pokémon he wishes to see / The unattended stand in Coumarine City	Rawst Berry
Holder restores its HP by 1/4 of its max HP when its HP falls to half or less.	The Berry tree on Route 11 / Defeat Inver in the house on Route 18	Sitrus Berry
Holder restores some of its HP when its HP falls to half or less, but Pokémon of certain Natures gain the Confused status condition.	Use Blizzard, Air Cutter, or Twister during battle when you see a tree with purple Berries on certain routes including 5, 6, 7, 10, 11, and 22	Wiki Berry

Effects	How to obtain	Berry
Slightly raises the Pokémon's friendship, but lowers its base Sp. Def stat.	Sudden mutation	Grepa Berry
Slightly raises the Pokémon's friendship, but lowers its base Sp. Atk stat.	Sudden mutation	Hondew Berry
Slightly raises the Pokémon's friendship, but lowers its base Attack stat.	Sudden mutation	Kelpsy Berry
Slightly raises the Pokémon's friendship, but lowers its base HP stat.	Sudden mutation	Pomeg Berry
Slightly raises the Pokémon's friendship, but lowers its base Defense stat.	Sudden mutation	Qualot Berry
Slightly raises the Pokémon's friendship, but lowers its base Speed stat.	Sudden mutation	Tamato Berry

Effects	How to obtain	Berry
Halves damage the holder takes from supereffective Steel-type moves.	Defeat Inver in the house on Route 18	Babiri Berry
Halves damage the holder takes from supereffective Rock-type moves.	Talk to a boy in a house in Cyllage City / Defeat Inver in the house on Route 18	Charti Berry
Halves damage the holder takes from Normal-type moves.	Defeat Inver in the house on Route 18	Chilan Berry
Halves damage the holder takes from supereffective Fighting-type moves.	Talk to Furfrou in Pokémon Village / Defeat Inver in the house on Route 18	Chople Berry
Halves damage the holder takes from supereffective Flying-type moves.	Defeat Inver in the house on Route 18	Coba Berry

Berries

Berries That Change the Damage Taken by the Holder

	Berry	Color	Time to mature	Min. yield	Max. yield	Possible mutation	Mutating neighbor	Pests	
	Colbur Berry	Purple	48 hrs	3	20	—	—	Illumise	
	Haban Berry	Red	48 hrs	3	20	—	—	Ledyba	
	Kasib Berry	Purple	48 hrs	3	20	Petaya Berry	Pomeg Berry	Illumise	
	Kebia Berry	Green	48 hrs	3	20	—	—	Burmy	
	Occa Berry	Red	48 hrs	3	20	—	—	Ledyba	
	Passho Berry	Blue	48 hrs	3	20	—	—	Volbeat	
	Payapa Berry	Purple	48 hrs	3	20	—	—	Illumise	
	Rindo Berry	Green	48 hrs	3	20	—	—	Burmy	
	Roseli Berry	Pink	48 hrs	3	20	Salac Berry	Grepa Berry	Spewpa	
	Shuca Berry	Yellow	48 hrs	3	20	—	—	Combee	
	Tanga Berry	Green	48 hrs	3	20	Ganlon Berry	Qualot Berry	Burmy	
	Wacan Berry	Yellow	48 hrs	3	20	Apicot Berry	Kelpsy Berry	Combee	
	Yache Berry	Blue	48 hrs	3	20	Liechi Berry	Hondew Berry	Volbeat	

Berries That Change Stats

	Berry	Color	Time to mature	Min. yield	Max. yield	Possible mutation	Mutating neighbor	Pests	
	Apicot Berry	Blue	96 hrs	1	10	—	—	Volbeat	
	Ganlon Berry	Purple	96 hrs	1	10	Kee Berry	Liechi Berry	Illumise	
	Kee Berry	Yellow	96 hrs	1	10	—	—	Combee	
	Lansat Berry	Red	120 hrs	1	5	—	—	Ledyba	
	Liechi Berry	Red	96 hrs	1	10	Kee Berry	Ganlon Berry	Ledyba	
	Maranga Berry	Blue	96 hrs	1	10	—	—	Volbeat	
	Petaya Berry	Pink	96 hrs	1	10	Maranga Berry	Salac Berry	Spewpa	
	Salac Berry	Green	96 hrs	1	10	Maranga Berry	Petaya Berry	Burmy	
	Starf Berry	Green	120 hrs	1	5	—	—	Burmy	

Effects	How to obtain	Berry
Halves damage the holder takes from supereffective Dark-type moves.	Defeat Inver in the house on Route 18	Colbur Berry
Halves damage the holder takes from supereffective Dragon-type moves.	Defeat Inver in the house on Route 18	Haban Berry
Halves damage the holder takes from supereffective Ghost-type moves.	The Berry tree on Route 20 / Defeat Inver in the house on Route 18	Kasib Berry
Halves damage the holder takes from supereffective Poison-type moves.	Defeat Inver in the house on Route 18	Kebia Berry
Halves damage the holder takes from supereffective Fire-type moves.	Defeat Inver in the house on Route 18	Occa Berry
Halves damage the holder takes from supereffective Water-type moves.	Defeat Inver in the house on Route 18	Passho Berry
Halves damage the holder takes from supereffective Psychic-type moves.	Defeat Inver in the house on Route 18	Payapa Berry
Halves damage the holder takes from supereffective Grass-type moves.	Defeat Inver in the house on Route 18	Rindo Berry
Halves damage the holder takes from supereffective Fairy-type moves.	The Berry tree on Route 14 / Defeat Inver in the house on Route 18	Roseli Berry
Halves damage the holder takes from supereffective Ground-type moves.	Defeat Inver in the house on Route 18	Shuca Berry
Halves damage the holder takes from supereffective Bug-type moves.	The Berry tree on Route 22 / Defeat Inver in the house on Route 18	Tanga Berry
Halves damage the holder takes from supereffective Electric-type moves.	The Berry tree on Route 18 / Defeat Inver in the house on Route 18	Wacan Berry
Halves damage the holder takes from supereffective Ice-type moves.	The Berry tree on Route 19 / Defeat Inver in the house on Route 18	Yache Berry

Effects	How to obtain	Berry
Holder's Sp. Def goes up 1 when its HP falls to half or less.	Sudden mutation	Apicot Berry
Holder raises its Defense stat by 1 when its HP becomes low.	Sudden mutation	Ganlon Berry
When the holder takes damage from a physical attack, the holder's Defense goes up by 1.	Sudden mutation	Kee Berry
Raises the critical-hit ratio of the holder's attacks when its HP falls to half or less.	At the Battle Maison, win 100 battles in a row in a given format (for example, Super Single Battle), and then talk to the girl at the entrance	Lansat Berry
Holder raises its Attack stat by 1 when its HP becomes low.	Sudden mutation	Liechi Berry
When the holder takes damage from a special attack, the holder's Sp. Def goes up by 1.	Sudden mutation	Maranga Berry
Raises the holder's Sp. Atk stat by 1 when its HP becomes low.	Sudden mutation	Petaya Berry
Holder raises its Speed stat by 1 when its HP becomes low.	Sudden mutation	Salac Berry
Raises one of the holder's stats by 2 when its HP falls to half or less.	At the Battle Maison, win 200 battles in a row in a given format (for example, Super Single Battle), and then talk to the girl at the entrance	Starf Berry

Items Obtained by Destroying Trees and Rocks

Items can sometimes be found in special circumstances during battle. When you see certain trees, rocks, or other objects in the background of a battle, use the recommended moves to destroy these objects, and you may be able to find an item in the rubble.

Item	Trees and rocks your Pokémon can destroy	Places where trees and rocks are found	Moves needed to destroy trees and rocks
Aguav Berry	Tree bearing green Berries	Route 5, 6, 7, 10, 11, 22 / Pokémon Village / Victory Road (Outside)	Blizzard / Air Cutter / Twister
Aspear Berry	Tree bearing yellow Berries	Route 8, 9, 13, 18, 19	Blizzard / Air Cutter / Twister
Babiri Berry	Tree bearing green Berries	Route 5, 6, 7, 10, 11, 22 / Pokémon Village / Victory Road (Outside)	Blizzard / Air Cutter / Twister
Charti Berry	Tree bearing yellow Berries	Route 8, 9, 13, 18, 19	Blizzard / Air Cutter / Twister
Cheri Berry	Tree bearing red Berries	Ambrette Town (fishing) / Route 8 (Rock Smash) / Azure Bay (tall grass) / fishing (sandy beaches)	Blizzard / Air Cutter / Twister
Chesto Berry	Tree bearing purple Berries	Route 5, 6, 7, 10, 11, 22 / Pokémon Village / Victory Road (Outside)	Blizzard / Air Cutter / Twister
Chilan Berry	Tree bearing yellow Berries	Route 8, 9, 13, 18, 19	Blizzard / Air Cutter / Twister
Chople Berry	Tree bearing red Berries	Ambrette Town (fishing) / Route 8 (Rock Smash) / Azure Bay (tall grass) / fishing (sandy beaches)	Blizzard / Air Cutter / Twister
Coba Berry	Tree bearing blue Berries	Frost Cavern (Outside) / Route 17	Blizzard / Air Cutter / Twister
Colbur Berry	Tree bearing purple Berries	Route 5, 6, 7, 10, 11, 22 / Pokémon Village / Victory Road (Outside)	Blizzard / Air Cutter / Twister
Damp Rock	Slim rock	Connecting Cave / Chamber of Emptiness / Sea Spirit's Den / Terminus Cave / Unknown Dungeon / Victory Road (Inside)	Surf / Muddy Water / Water Spout
Figy Berry	Tree bearing red Berries	Ambrette Town (fishing) / Route 8 (Rock Smash) / Azure Bay (tall grass) / fishing (sandy beaches)	Blizzard / Air Cutter / Twister
Fire Stone	Jagged rock	Route 8, 9, 13, 18, 19	Rock Slide / Hyper Voice
Float Stone	Jagged rock	Connecting Cave / Chamber of Emptiness / Sea Spirit's Den / Terminus Cave / Unknown Dungeon / Victory Road (Inside)	Rock Slide / Hyper Voice
Haban Berry	Tree bearing red Berries	Ambrette Town (fishing) / Route 8 (Rock Smash) / Azure Bay (tall grass) / fishing (sandy beaches)	Blizzard / Air Cutter / Twister
Hard Stone	Jagged rock	Connecting Cave / Chamber of Emptiness / Sea Spirit's Den / Terminus Cave / Unknown Dungeon / Victory Road (Inside)	Rock Slide / Hyper Voice
Heat Rock	Round rock	Route 8, 9, 13, 18, 19	Heat Wave / Eruption / Lava Plume
Iapapa Berry	Tree bearing yellow Berries	Route 8, 9, 13, 18, 19	Blizzard / Air Cutter / Twister
Kasib Berry	Tree bearing purple Berries	Route 5, 6, 7, 10, 11, 22 / Pokémon Village / Victory Road (Outside)	Blizzard / Air Cutter / Twister
Kebia Berry	Tree bearing green Berries	Route 5, 6, 7, 10, 11, 22 / Pokémon Village / Victory Road (Outside)	Blizzard / Air Cutter / Twister
Leaf Stone	Jagged rock	Route 8, 9, 13, 18, 19	Rock Slide / Hyper Voice
Leppa Berry	Tree bearing red Berries	Ambrette Town (fishing) / Route 8 (Rock Smash) / Azure Bay (tall grass) / fishing (sandy beaches)	Blizzard / Air Cutter / Twister
Lum Berry	Tree bearing green Berries	Route 5, 6, 7, 10, 11, 22 / Pokémon Village / Victory Road (Outside)	Blizzard / Air Cutter / Twister
Luminous Moss	Mossy Rock	Glittering Cave	Rock Slide / Hyper Voice
Mago Berry	Tree bearing pink Berries	Ambrette Town (fishing) / Route 8 (Rock Smash) / Azure Bay (tall grass) / fishing (sandy beaches)	Blizzard / Air Cutter / Twister
Mental Herb	Grass	Route 5, 6, 7, 10, 11, 22 / Pokémon Village / Victory Road (Outside)	Petal Blizzard / Razor Leaf
Never-Melt Ice	Iceberg	Frost Cavern (Outside) / Route 17	Rock Slide / Hyper Voice
Occa Berry	Tree bearing red Berries	Ambrette Town (fishing) / Route 8 (Rock Smash) / Azure Bay (tall grass) / fishing (sandy beaches)	Blizzard / Air Cutter / Twister
Oran Berry	Tree bearing blue Berries	Frost Cavern (Outside) / Route 17	Blizzard / Air Cutter / Twister
Passho Berry	Tree bearing blue Berries	Frost Cavern (Outside) / Route 17	Blizzard / Air Cutter / Twister
Payapa Berry	Tree bearing purple Berries	Route 5, 6, 7, 10, 11, 22 / Pokémon Village / Victory Road (Outside)	Blizzard / Air Cutter / Twister
Pecha Berry	Tree bearing pink Berries	Ambrette Town (fishing) / Route 8 (Rock Smash) / Azure Bay (tall grass) / fishing (sandy beaches)	Blizzard / Air Cutter / Twister
Persim Berry	Tree bearing pink Berries	Ambrette Town (fishing) / Route 8 (Rock Smash) / Azure Bay (tall grass) / fishing (sandy beaches)	Blizzard / Air Cutter / Twister
Power Herb	Grass	Route 5, 6, 7, 10, 11, 22 / Pokémon Village / Victory Road (Outside)	Petal Blizzard / Razor Leaf
Rawst Berry	Tree bearing green Berries	Route 5, 6, 7, 10, 11, 22 / Pokémon Village / Victory Road (Outside)	Blizzard / Air Cutter / Twister
Rindo Berry	Tree bearing green Berries	Route 5, 6, 7, 10, 11, 22 / Pokémon Village / Victory Road (Outside)	Blizzard / Air Cutter / Twister
Shuca Berry	Tree bearing yellow Berries	Route 8, 9, 13, 18, 19	Blizzard / Air Cutter / Twister
Sitrus Berry	Tree bearing yellow Berries	Route 8, 9, 13, 18, 19	Blizzard / Air Cutter / Twister

Item	Trees and rocks your Pokémon can destroy	Places where trees and rocks are found	Moves needed to destroy trees and rocks
Snowball	Snow Mound	Frost Cavern (Outside) / Route 17	Rock Slide / Hyper Voice
Soft Sand	Sand Mound	Ambrette Town (fishing) / Route 8 (Rock Smash) / Azure Bay (tall grass) / fishing (sandy beaches)	Rock Slide / Hyper Voice
Stardust	Sand Mound	Ambrette Town (fishing) / Route 8 (Rock Smash) / Azure Bay (tall grass) / fishing (sandy beaches)	Rock Slide / Hyper Voice
Tanga Berry	Tree bearing green Berries	Route 5, 6, 7, 10, 11, 22 / Pokémon Village / Victory Road (Outside)	Blizzard / Air Cutter / Twister
Thunder Stone	Jagged rock	Route 8, 9, 13, 18, 19	Rock Slide / Hyper Voice
Wacan Berry	Tree bearing yellow Berries	Route 8, 9, 13, 18, 19	Blizzard / Air Cutter / Twister
Water Stone	Jagged rock	Route 8, 9, 13, 18, 19	Rock Slide / Hyper Voice
White Herb	Grass	Route 5, 6, 7, 10, 11, 22 / Pokémon Village / Victory Road (Outside)	Petal Blizzard / Razor Leaf
Wiki Berry	Tree bearing purple Berries	Route 5, 6, 7, 10, 11, 22 / Pokémon Village / Victory Road (Outside)	Blizzard / Air Cutter / Twister
Yache Berry	Tree bearing blue Berries	Frost Cavern (Outside) / Route 17	Blizzard / Air Cutter / Twister

◆ On sandy beaches, sometimes trees and rocks that can be destroyed appear during battle. These trees and rocks won't appear when sandy beaches are not available, such as on Route 19.

Items Obtained by Using the Rock Smash Field Move

Item	Places where rocks are found
Armor Fossil	Glittering Cave (lowest level; after entering the Hall of Fame)
Big Pearl	Any rock
Claw Fossil	Glittering Cave (lowest level; after entering the Hall of Fame: X)
Cover Fossil	Glittering Cave (lowest level; after entering the Hall of Fame)
Dome Fossil	Glittering Cave (lowest level; after entering the Hall of Fame: Y)
Ether	Any rock
Hard Stone	Any rock
Heart Scale	Any rock
Helix Fossil	Glittering Cave (lowest level; after entering the Hall of Fame: Y)

Item	Places where rocks are found
Max Ether	Any rock
Max Revive	Any rock
Old Amber	Glittering Cave (lowest level)
Pearl	Any rock
Plume Fossil	Glittering Cave (lowest level; after entering the Hall of Fame)
Revive	Any rock
Root Fossil	Glittering Cave (lowest level; after entering the Hall of Fame: X)
Skull Fossil	Glittering Cave (lowest level; after entering the Hall of Fame)
Soft Sand	Any rock
Star Piece	Any rock

Items Obtained by Checking a Shaking Trash Can

● **Lost Hotel (Trash Can 1)**

Item	Frequency
Dusk Ball	○
Escape Rope	○
HP Up	△
Iron	△
Max Elixir	▲
Protein	△
Super Repel	○

● **Lost Hotel (Trash Can 2)**

Item	Frequency
Big Nugget	▲
Calcium	△
Carbos	△
Escape Rope	○
Max Repel	○
Nugget	○
Zinc	△

● **Pokémon Village (Trash Can 1)**

Item	Frequency
Big Mushroom	△
Honey	○
Max Revive	△
Mental Herb	△
Poké Toy	△
Pretty Wing	○
Tiny Mushroom	○

● **Pokémon Village (Trash Can 2)**

Item	Frequency
Balm Mushroom	△
Big Mushroom	○
Eviolite	▲
Heal Powder	△
Honey	○
Prism Scale	○
Revival Herb	△

○ Often found
△ Sometimes found
▲ Rarely found

◆Trash Can 2 in the Lost Hotel shakes only on Tuesdays. Trash Can 2 in the Pokémon Village shakes only on Thursdays.

The number in the brackets is the level at which the Pokémon learns the move. [E] is an Egg Move, [TM] is a Technical Machine Move, [HM] is a Hidden Machine Move, and [T] is a move that someone teaches the Pokémon. Form(e) names of Pokémon such as Wormadam and Rotom are in parentheses.

A

	Move	Pokémon that can learn it					
Grass	Absorb	Amoonguss [1]	Budew [1]	Foongus [1]	Gloom [1]	Goodra [5]	Goomy [5]
		Lombre [5]	Lotad [5]	Oddish [1]	Roselia [1]	Sliggoo [5]	
Poison	Acid	Arbok [20]	Bellsprout [23]	Dragalge [15]	Ekans [20]	Gloom [1, 9]	Litwick [E]
		Oddish [9]	Shelmet [4]	Shuckle [15]	Skrelp [15]	Tentacool [12]	Tentacruel [12]
		Weepinbell [23]					
	Acid Armor	Cryogonal [29]	Goomy [E]	Gulpin [E]	Litwick [E]	Shelmet [32]	Skrelp [E]
		Slugma [E]	Solosis [E]	Vanillish [31]	Vanillite [31]	Vanilluxe [31]	Vaporeon [29]
	Acid Spray	Accelgor [1, 4]	Arbok [32]	Bellsprout [E]	Ekans [28]	Ferroseed [E]	Garbodor [12]
		Gulpin [34]	Qwilfish [E]	Remoraid [E]	Skuntank [32]	Stunky [32]	Swalot [38]
		Tentacool [26]	Tentacruel [26]	Trubbish [12]	Wooper [E]		
Flying	Acrobatics (TM62)	Beedrill [TM]	Butterfree [TM]	Crobat [33, TM]	Cryogonal [TM]	Drifblim [TM]	Drifloon [TM]
		Emolga [30, TM]	Farfetch'd [37, TM]	Fletchinder [42, TM]	Fletchling [39, TM]	Froakie [TM]	Frogadier [TM]
		Gligar [22, TM]	Gliscor [22, TM]	Golbat [33, TM]	Greninja [TM]	Hawlucha [TM]	Hoppip [28, TM]
		Hydreigon [TM]	Illumise [TM]	Jumpluff [34, TM]	Ledian [TM]	Ledyba [TM]	Lunatone [TM]
		Mantine [TM]	Mantyke [TM]	Mienfoo [TM]	Mienshao [TM]	Mothim [TM]	Noibat [TM]
		Noivern [TM]	Panpour [31, TM]	Pansage [31, TM]	Pansear [31, TM]	Scizor [TM]	Simipour [TM]
		Simisage [TM]	Simisear [TM]	Skiploom [32, TM]	Solrock [TM]	Swoobat [TM]	Talonflame [44, TM]
		Vespiquen [TM]	Vivillon [TM]	Volbeat [TM]	Woobat [TM]	Yveltal [TM]	Zubat [30, TM]
Normal	Acupressure	Croagunk [E]	Dodrio [28]	Doduo [28]	Drapion [13]	Medicham [42]	Meditite [39]
		Shuckle [E]	Skorupi [13]	Tentacool [E]			
Flying	Aerial Ace (TM40)	Absol [TM]	Aegislash [1, TM]	Aerodactyl [TM]	Aggron [TM]	Altaria [TM]	Aron [TM]
		Articuno [TM]	Axew [TM]	Bagon [TM]	Barbaracle [TM]	Beartic [TM]	Beedrill [TM]
		Binacle [TM]	Bisharp [TM]	Butterfree [TM]	Charizard [TM]	Charmander [TM]	Charmeleon [TM]
		Chatot [TM]	Chesnaught [TM]	Chespin [TM]	Corphish [TM]	Crawdaunt [TM]	Crobat [TM]
		Crustle [TM]	Cubchoo [TM]	Cubone [TM]	Dedenne [TM]	Delibird [TM]	Diglett [TM]
		Dodrio [TM]	Doduo [TM]	Doublade [22, TM]	Durant [TM]	Dwebble [TM]	Druddigon [TM]
		Ducklett [15, TM]	Dugtrio [TM]	Dunsparce [TM]	Dragonite [TM]	Drapion [TM]	Escavalier [TM]
		Farfetch'd [9, TM]	Fearow [17, TM]	Ferrothorn [TM]	Fletchinder [TM]	Fletchling [TM]	Flygon [TM]
		Fraxure [TM]	Froakie [TM]	Frogadier [TM]	Gabite [TM]	Gallade [TM]	Garchomp [TM]
		Gible [TM]	Gligar [TM]	Gliscor [TM]	Gogoat [1, 65, TM]	Golbat [TM]	Golduck [TM]
		Greninja [TM]	Hawlucha [16, TM]	Haxorus [TM]	Heatmor [TM]	Heracross [10, TM]	Honchkrow [TM]
		Honedge [22, TM]	Hoothoot [TM]	Hoppip [TM]	Illumise [TM]	Inkay [TM]	Jumpluff [TM]
		Kangaskhan [TM]	Karrablast [TM]	Kecleon [TM]	Krookodile [TM]	Lairon [TM]	Leafeon [TM]
		Ledian [TM]	Ledyba [TM]	Liepard [TM]	Malamar [TM]	Mantine [TM]	Mantyke [TM]
		Marowak [TM]	Masquerain [TM]	Mewtwo [TM]	Mienfoo [TM]	Mienshao [TM]	Moltres [TM]
		Mothim [TM]	Mr. Mime [TM]	Murkrow [TM]	Nidoqueen [TM]	Nidoran♀ [TM]	Nidorina [TM]
		Nincada [TM]	Ninjask [TM]	Noctowl [TM]	Noibat [TM]	Noivern [TM]	Pancham [TM]
		Pangoro [TM]	Pawniard [TM]	Pelipper [TM]	Pidgeot [TM]	Pidgeotto [TM]	Pidgey [TM]
		Psyduck [TM]	Purrloin [TM]	Quilladin [TM]	Sableye [TM]	Salamence [TM]	Sandshrew [TM]
		Sandslash [TM]	Scizor [TM]	Scyther [TM]	Shedinja [TM]	Shelgon [TM]	Sigilyph [TM]
		Skarmory [TM]	Skiploom [TM]	Skorupi [TM]	Slowbro [TM]	Sneasel [TM]	Spearow [17, TM]
		Staraptor [28, TM]	Staravia [28, TM]	Starly [25, TM]	Swablu [TM]	Swanna [15, TM]	Swellow [38, TM]
		Swoobat [TM]	Taillow [34, TM]	Talonflame [TM]	Teddiursa [TM]	Tyranitar [TM]	Tyrantrum [TM]
		Tyrunt [TM]	Ursaring [TM]	Vespiquen [TM]	Vivillon [TM]	Volbeat [TM]	Weavile [TM]
		Wingull [42, TM]	Woobat [TM]	Yanma [TM]	Yanmega [TM]	Yveltal [TM]	Zangoose [TM]
		Zapdos [TM]	Zoroark [TM]	Zorua [TM]	Zubat [TM]		
Normal	After You	Audino [40]	Mareep [E]	Munchlax [E]	Oddish [E]	Patrat [23]	Snorlax [E]
		Swirlix [E]	Watchog [25]	Wooper [E]			
Psychic	Agility	Accelgor [32]	Aerodactyl [17]	Ariados [37]	Articuno [36]	Basculin [E]	Beedrill [31]
		Buizel [41]	Bunnelby [41]	Carvanha [36]	Chatot [E]	Chinchou [31]	Diggersby [1]
		Dodrio [41]	Doduo [37]	Dragonair [25]	Dragonite [25]	Dratini [25]	Dunsparce [E]
		Durant [16]	Emolga [46]	Farfetch'd [31]	Fearow [29]	Fletchinder [13]	Fletchling [13]
		Floatzel [51]	Gligar [E]	Goldeen [47]	Gorebyss [10]	Hawlucha [E]	Helioptile [E]
		Hoothoot [E]	Horsea [23]	Jolteon [29]	Kingdra [23]	Ledian [36]	Ledyba [30]
		Luvdisc [9]	Mantine [32]	Mantyke [32]	Mareep [E]	Minun [48]	Moltres [15]
		Ninjask [38]	Noibat [18]	Noivern [29]	Pidgeot [32]	Pidgeotto [32]	Pidgey [29]
		Pikachu [37]	Plusle [48]	Riolu [E]	Scizor [17]	Scolipede [33]	Scyther [17]
		Seadra [33]	Seaking [56]	Sharpedo [45]	Skarmory [12]	Skorupi [E]	Sneasel [20]
		Spearow [25]	Spinarak [33]	Staraptor [41]	Staravia [38]	Starly [33]	Surskit [31]
		Swablu [E]	Swellow [49]	Taillow [43]	Talonflame [13]	Venipede [29]	Whirlipede [32]
		Wingull [38, E]	Zapdos [43]	Zoroark [39]	Zorua [37]		

	Move	Pokémon that can learn it					
Flying	Air Cutter	Charmander [E]	Chatot [E]	Crobat [28]	Ducklett [E]	Farfetch'd [21]	Golbat [28]
		Noibat [23]	Noivern [23]	Pidgey [E]	Sigilyph [21]	Skarmory [23]	Swoobat [21]
		Wingull [33]	Woobat [21]	Zubat [26]			
	Air Slash	Charizard [1]	Crobat [52]	Ducklett [27]	Emolga [E]	Farfetch'd [49]	Golbat [52]
		Hoothoot [33]	Mantine [36]	Mantyke [36]	Masquerain [47]	Moltres [50]	Mothim [41]
		Noctowl [37]	Noibat [48]	Noivern [53]	Pidgeot [62]	Pidgeotto [57]	Pidgey [49, E]
		Rotom (Fan) ◆	Scyther [50]	Sigilyph [41]	Skarmory [42]	Swanna [27]	Swellow [1, 61]
		Swoobat [32]	Taillow [53]	Vespiquen [37]	Wingull [46]	Woobat [32]	Yanma [54]
		Yanmega [1, 54]	Yveltal [10]	Zubat [45]			
Psychic	Ally Switch	Abra [E]	Alakazam [24]	Hawlucha [E]	Kadabra [24]	Mienfoo [E]	Ralts [E]
	Amnesia	Audino [E]	Barboach [18]	Bibarel [33]	Bidoof [29]	Bulbasaur [E]	Chinchou [E]
		Corsola [E]	Drifblim [46]	Drifloon [40]	Furret [42]	Garbodor [46]	Golduck [49]
		Gorebyss [19]	Gulpin [17]	Heatmor [44]	Hoppip [E]	Lickitung [E]	Magcargo [32]
		Mantine [E]	Mantyke [E]	Marill [E]	Mewtwo [79]	Munchlax [9]	Nidoran♂ [E]
		Pansear [25]	Piloswine [58]	Psyduck [43]	Quagsire [24]	Relicanth [E]	Scraggy [E]
		Sentret [36]	Slowbro [43]	Slowpoke [41]	Slugma [32]	Snorlax [9]	Spoink [E]
		Swalot [17]	Swinub [48]	Swoobat [29]	Torkoal [49]	Trubbish [40]	Wailmer [37]
		Wailord [37]	Whiscash [18]	Woobat [29]	Wooper [23]		
Rock	Ancient Power	Aerodactyl [25]	Amaura [26]	Articuno [29]	Aurorus [26]	Barbaracle [28]	Binacle [28]
		Carbink [31]	Carvanha [E]	Charmander [E]	Corphish [E]	Corsola [20]	Cubone [E]
		Diglett [E]	Dunsparce [19, E]	Exeggcute [E]	Kecleon [1, 55]	Lapras [E]	Larvitar [E]
		Magcargo [28]	Mamoswine [1]	Mawile [E]	Moltres [29]	Piloswine [1]	Relicanth [1, 43]
		Sigilyph [E]	Slugma [28]	Swinub [E]	Tyrantrum [26]	Tyrunt [26]	Wooper [E]
		Yanma [33]	Yanmega [33]	Zapdos [29]			
Water	Aqua Jet	Alomomola [9]	Basculin [13]	Beartic [E]	Buizel [24]	Carvanha [31]	Clauncher [43, E]
		Clawitzer [47]	Corphish [E]	Dratini [E]	Floatzel [24]	Golduck [1]	Luvdisc [E]
		Marill [E]	Qwilfish [E]	Sharpedo [34]	Squirtle [E]	Surskit [E]	
	Aqua Ring	Alomomola [31]	Azumarill [31]	Buizel [E]	Chinchou [42]	Clamperl [E]	Corsola [38, E]
		Ducklett [24]	Goldeen [27]	Gorebyss [24]	Lanturn [52]	Luvdisc [46, E]	Mantine [39]
		Mantyke [39]	Marill [28]	Panpour [E]	Seaking [27]	Shellder [E]	Squirtle [E]
		Swanna [24]	Tentacool [E]	Vaporeon [25]	Wailmer [E]	Wingull [E]	
	Aqua Tail	Azumarill [21]	Barboach [35]	Basculin [28]	Bidoof [E]	Blastoise [32]	Buizel [38, E]
		Dragalge [35]	Dragonair [39]	Dragonite [39]	Dratini [35]	Floatzel [46]	Goldeen [E]
		Golduck [32]	Goodra [50]	Gorebyss [46]	Gyarados [35]	Huntail [46]	Marill [20]
		Panpour [E]	Psyduck [32]	Qwilfish [45]	Relicanth [E]	Skrelp [35]	Squirtle [28]
		Wartortle [32]	Whiscash [39]				
Fighting	Arm Thrust	Hariyama [1, 7]	Heracross [1]	Makuhita [7]	Pancham [7]	Pangoro [7]	
Grass	Aromatherapy	Aromatisse [25]	Flabébé [33]	Floette [38]	Florges [1]	Hoppip [E]	Roselia [43]
		Slurpuff [26]	Spritzee [25]	Swirlix [26]	Vileplume [1]	Vivillon [31]	Xerneas [1]
Fairy	Aromatic Mist	Aromatisse [1]					
Normal	Assist	Espurr [E]	Liepard [1, 6]	Purrloin [6]	Sentret [E]	Skitty [22]	Sneasel [E]
		Spinda [E]					
Dark	Assurance	Absol [E]	Aerodactyl [E]	Axew [7]	Beedrill [34]	Bisharp [33]	Carvanha [26]
		Cubchoo [E]	Deino [E]	Doduo [E]	Fearow [35]	Fraxure [1, 7]	Haxorus [1, 7]
		Krokorok [16]	Krookodile [16]	Larvitar [E]	Liepard [31]	Mightyena [32]	Murkrow [25, E]
		Patrat [E]	Pawniard [33]	Poochyena [29]	Purrloin [28]	Sandile [16]	Seviper [E]
		Sharpedo [26]	Skarmory [E]	Spearow [29]	Swoobat [1, 12]	Umbreon [25]	Weavile [1]
		Woobat [12]					
Ghost	Astonish	Altaria [1, 4]	Amoonguss [1, 8]	Chimecho [9]	Chingling [9]	Croagunk [1]	Crobat [1, 8]
		Deino [E]	Diglett [7, E]	Drifblim [1, 4]	Drifloon [4]	Dugtrio [7]	Dunsparce [E]
		Emolga [E]	Exploud [1, 11]	Foongus [8]	Gastly [E]	Golbat [1, 8]	Golett [1]
		Golurk [1]	Gourgeist [1]	Honchkrow [1]	Kecleon [1]	Klefki [8]	Lampent [1]
		Litwick [1]	Lombre [1]	Lotad [1]	Loudred [1, 11]	Ludicolo [1]	Mawile [1]
		Murkrow [1]	Panpour [E]	Pansage [1]	Pansear [E]	Phantump [1]	Poochyena [1]
		Pumpkaboo [1]	Qwilfish [E]	Rotom (Fan) [1]	Rotom (Frost) [1]	Rotom (Heat) [1]	Rotom (Mow) [1]
		Rotom (Wash) [1]	Rotom [1]	Sableye [11]	Shuppet [E]	Solosis [1]	Spearow [E]
		Starly [E]	Stunfisk [E]	Stunky [E]	Swablu [4]	Toxicroak [1]	Trevenant [5]
		Vanillish [1, 7]	Vanillite [7]	Vanilluxe [1, 7]	Wailmer [17]	Wailord [17]	Whismur [11]
		Zubat [8]					
Bug	Attack Order	Vespiquen [45]					

◆ When Rotom becomes Fan Rotom, it learns the move Air Slash. When it changes back to Rotom, it forgets the move.

Move	Pokémon that can learn it				
Normal / Attract (TM45)	Abomasnow [TM]	Abra [TM]	Absol [TM]	Accelgor [TM]	Aegislash [TM]	Aerodactyl [TM]
	Aggron [TM]	Alakazam [TM]	Alomomola [TM]	Altaria [TM]	Amaura [TM]	Amoonguss [TM]
	Ampharos [TM]	Arbok [TM]	Ariados [TM]	Aromatisse [29, TM]	Aron [TM]	Audino [15, TM]
	Aurorus [TM]	Avalugg [TM]	Axew [TM]	Azumarill [TM]	Azurill [TM]	Bagon [TM]
	Banette [TM]	Barbaracle [TM]	Barboach [TM]	Basculin [TM]	Beartic [TM]	Beedrill [TM]
	Bellossom [TM]	Bellsprout [TM]	Bergmite [TM]	Bibarel [TM]	Bidoof [TM]	Binacle [TM]
	Bisharp [TM]	Blastoise [TM]	Boldore [TM]	Bonsly [TM]	Braixen [TM]	Budew [TM]
	Buizel [TM]	Bulbasaur [TM]	Bunnelby [TM]	Butterfree [TM]	Carnivine [TM]	Carvanha [TM]
	Chandelure [TM]	Charizard [TM]	Charmander [TM]	Charmeleon [TM]	Chatot [TM]	Chesnaught [TM]
	Chespin [TM]	Chimecho [TM]	Chinchou [TM]	Chingling [TM]	Clamperl [TM]	Clauncher [TM]
	Clawitzer [TM]	Cloyster [TM]	Conkeldurr [TM]	Corphish [TM]	Corsola [TM]	Crawdaunt [TM]
	Croagunk [TM]	Crobat [TM]	Crustle [TM]	Cryogonal [TM]	Cubchoo [TM]	Cubone [TM]
	Dedenne [TM]	Deino [TM]	Delcatty [1, TM]	Delibird [TM]	Delphox [TM]	Diggersby [TM]
	Diglett [TM]	Dodrio [TM]	Doduo [TM]	Doublade [TM]	Dragalge [TM]	Dragonair [TM]
	Dragonite [TM]	Drapion [TM]	Dratini [TM]	Drifblim [TM]	Drifloon [TM]	Druddigon [TM]
	Ducklett [TM]	Dugtrio [TM]	Dunsparce [TM]	Duosion [TM]	Durant [TM]	Dwebble [TM]
	Eevee [TM]	Ekans [TM]	Electrike [TM]	Emolga [TM]	Escavalier [TM]	Espeon [TM]
	Espurr [TM]	Exeggcute [TM]	Exeggutor [TM]	Exploud [TM]	Farfetch'd [TM]	Fearow [TM]
	Fennekin [TM]	Flaaffy [TM]	Flabébé [TM]	Flareon [TM]	Fletchinder [TM]	Fletchling [TM]
	Floatzel [TM]	Floette [TM]	Florges [TM]	Flygon [TM]	Foongus [TM]	Fraxure [TM]
	Froakie [TM]	Frogadier [TM]	Furfrou [TM]	Furret [TM]	Gabite [TM]	Gallade [TM]
	Garbodor [TM]	Garchomp [TM]	Gardevoir [TM]	Gastly [TM]	Gengar [TM]	Geodude [TM]
	Gible [TM]	Gigalith [TM]	Glaceon [TM]	Gligar [TM]	Gliscor [TM]	Gloom [TM]
	Gogoat [TM]	Golbat [TM]	Goldeen [TM]	Golduck [TM]	Golem [TM]	Goodra [TM]
	Goomy [TM]	Gorebyss [TM]	Gothita [TM]	Gothitelle [TM]	Gothorita [TM]	Gourgeist [TM]
	Granbull [TM]	Graveler [TM]	Greninja [TM]	Grumpig [TM]	Gulpin [TM]	Gurdurr [TM]
	Gyarados [TM]	Hariyama [TM]	Haunter [TM]	Hawlucha [TM]	Haxorus [TM]	Heatmor [TM]
	Heliolisk [TM]	Helioptile [TM]	Heracross [TM]	Hippopotas [TM]	Hippowdon [TM]	Honchkrow [TM]
	Honedge [TM]	Hoothoot [TM]	Hoppip [TM]	Horsea [TM]	Houndoom [TM]	Houndour [TM]
	Huntail [TM]	Hydreigon [TM]	Igglybuff [TM]	Illumise [TM]	Inkay [TM]	Ivysaur [TM]
	Jigglypuff [TM]	Jolteon [TM]	Jumpluff [TM]	Jynx [TM]	Kadabra [TM]	Kangaskhan [TM]
	Karrablast [TM]	Kecleon [TM]	Kingdra [TM]	Kirlia [TM]	Klefki [TM]	Krokorok [TM]
	Krookodile [TM]	Lairon [TM]	Lampent [TM]	Lanturn [TM]	Lapras [TM]	Larvitar [TM]
	Leafeon [TM]	Ledian [TM]	Ledyba [TM]	Lickilicky [TM]	Lickitung [TM]	Liepard [TM]
	Linoone [TM]	Litleo [TM]	Litwick [TM]	Lombre [TM]	Lotad [TM]	Loudred [TM]
	Lucario [TM]	Ludicolo [TM]	Luvdisc [27, TM]	Machamp [TM]	Machoke [TM]	Machop [TM]
	Magcargo [TM]	Makuhita [TM]	Malamar [TM]	Mamoswine [TM]	Manectric [TM]	Mantine [TM]
	Mantyke [TM]	Mareep [TM]	Marill [TM]	Marowak [TM]	Masquerain [TM]	Mawile [TM]
	Medicham [TM]	Meditite [TM]	Meowstic (Female) [TM]	Meowstic (Male) [TM]	Mienfoo [TM]	Mienshao [TM]
	Mightyena [TM]	Miltank [TM]	Mime Jr. [TM]	Minun [TM]	Mothim [TM]	Mr. Mime [TM]
	Munchlax [TM]	Murkrow [TM]	Nidoking [TM]	Nidoqueen [TM]	Nidoran ♀ [TM]	Nidoran ♂ [TM]
	Nidorina [TM]	Nidorino [TM]	Ninjask [TM]	Noctowl [TM]	Noibat [TM]	Noivern [TM]
	Nosepass [TM]	Octillery [TM]	Oddish [TM]	Onix [TM]	Pachirisu [TM]	Pancham [TM]
	Pangoro [TM]	Panpour [TM]	Pansage [TM]	Pansear [TM]	Patrat [TM]	Pawniard [TM]
	Pelipper [TM]	Phantump [TM]	Pichu [TM]	Pidgeot [TM]	Pidgeotto [TM]	Pidgey [TM]
	Pikachu [TM]	Piloswine [TM]	Pinsir [TM]	Plusle [TM]	Politoed [TM]	Poliwag [TM]
	Poliwhirl [TM]	Poliwrath [TM]	Poochyena [TM]	Probopass [TM]	Psyduck [TM]	Pumpkaboo [TM]
	Pupitar [TM]	Purrloin [TM]	Pyroar [TM]	Quagsire [TM]	Quilladin [TM]	Qwilfish [TM]
	Raichu [TM]	Ralts [TM]	Relicanth [TM]	Remoraid [TM]	Reuniclus [TM]	Rhydon [TM]
	Rhyhorn [TM]	Rhyperior [TM]	Riolu [TM]	Roggenrola [TM]	Roselia [TM]	Roserade [TM]
	Sableye [TM]	Salamence [TM]	Sandile [TM]	Sandshrew [TM]	Sandslash [TM]	Sawk [TM]
	Scizor [TM]	Scolipede [TM]	Scrafty [TM]	Scraggy [TM]	Scyther [TM]	Seadra [TM]
	Seaking [TM]	Sentret [TM]	Seviper [TM]	Sharpedo [TM]	Shelgon [TM]	Shellder [TM]
	Shelmet [TM]	Shuckle [TM]	Shuppet [TM]	Sigilyph [TM]	Simipour [TM]	Simisage [TM]
	Simisear [TM]	Skarmory [TM]	Skiddo [TM]	Skiploom [TM]	Skitty [8, TM]	Skorupi [TM]
	Skrelp [TM]	Skuntank [TM]	Sliggoo [TM]	Slowbro [TM]	Slowking [TM]	Slowpoke [TM]
	Slugma [TM]	Slurpuff [TM]	Smoochum [TM]	Sneasel [TM]	Snorlax [TM]	Snover [TM]
	Snubbull [TM]	Solosis [TM]	Spearow [TM]	Spinarak [TM]	Spinda [TM]	Spoink [TM]
	Spritzee [29, TM]	Squirtle [TM]	Staraptor [TM]	Staravia [TM]	Starly [TM]	Steelix [TM]
	Stunfisk [TM]	Stunky [TM]	Sudowoodo [TM]	Surskit [TM]	Swablu [TM]	Swalot [TM]
	Swanna [TM]	Swellow [TM]	Swinub [TM]	Swirlix [TM]	Swoobat [25, TM]	Sylveon [TM]
	Taillow [TM]	Talonflame [TM]	Tauros [TM]	Teddiursa [TM]	Tentacool [TM]	Tentacruel [TM]
	Throh [TM]	Timburr [TM]	Torkoal [TM]	Toxicroak [TM]	Trapinch [TM]	Trevenant [TM]
	Trubbish [TM]	Tyranitar [TM]	Tyrantrum [TM]	Tyrunt [TM]	Umbreon [TM]	Ursaring [TM]
	Vanillish [TM]	Vanillite [TM]	Vanilluxe [TM]	Vaporeon [TM]	Venipede [TM]	Venusaur [TM]
	Vespiquen [TM]	Vibrava [TM]	Victreebel [TM]	Vileplume [TM]	Vivillon [TM]	Volbeat [TM]
	Wailmer [TM]	Wailord [TM]	Wartortle [TM]	Watchog [TM]	Weavile [TM]	Weepinbell [TM]
	Whirlipede [TM]	Whiscash [TM]	Whismur [TM]	Wigglytuff [TM]	Wingull [TM]	Woobat [25, TM]
	Wooper [TM]	Wormadam (Plant) [41, TM]	Wormadam (Sand) [41, TM]	Wormadam (Trash) [41, TM]	Yanma [TM]	Yanmega [TM]
	Zangoose [TM]	Zigzagoon [TM]	Zoroark [TM]	Zorua [TM]	Zubat [TM]	Zweilous [TM]

Type	Move	Pokémon that can learn it					
Fighting	Aura Sphere	Clawitzer [1, 67]	Lucario [1, 42]	Mewtwo [70]	Mienfoo [61]	Mienshao [1, 70]	Squirtle [E]
Ice	Aurora Beam	Amaura [20]	Aurorus [20]	Cloyster [1]	Cryogonal [25]	Delibird [E]	Horsea [E]
		Octillery [1, 14]	Remoraid [14, E]	Shellder [37]	Tentacool [E]	Vaporeon [20]	Xerneas [10]
Steel	Autotomize	Aegislash [1]	Aggron [48]	Aron [39]	Doublade [18]	Geodude [E]	Honedge [18]
		Lairon [45]	Roggenrola [E]	Skarmory [39]	Steelix [19]	Vanillite [E]	
Ice	Avalanche	Amaura [34]	Aurorus [34]	Avalugg [42]	Bergmite [39]	Cubchoo [E]	Jynx [39]
		Lapras [E]	Shellder [E]	Smoochum [35]	Sneasel [E]	Snover [E]	Swinub [E]
		Vanillish [19]	Vanillite [19]	Vanilluxe [19]			

B

Type	Move	Pokémon that can learn it					
Fairy	Baby-Doll Eyes	Eevee [9]	Furfrou [9]	Teddiursa [1]	Zigzagoon [11]		
Normal	Barrage	Exeggcute [1]	Exeggutor [1]				
Psychic	Barrier	Abra [E]	Amaura [E]	Bergmite [E]	Clamperl [E]	Corsola [E]	Espurr [E]
		Glaceon [29]	Magnezone [1]	Mewtwo [64]	Mime Jr. [1]	Mr. Mime [1]	Shellder [E]
		Tentacool [29]	Tentacruel [29]				
Normal	Baton Pass	Absol [E]	Buizel [E]	Drifblim [52]	Drifloon [44]	Durant [E]	Eevee [33]
		Emolga [E]	Furret [46]	Gligar [E]	Gorebyss [33]	Hawlucha [E]	Huntail [33]
		Illumise [E]	Ledian [24]	Ledyba [22]	Mawile [31]	Meditite [E]	Mienfoo [E]
		Mime Jr. [46]	Minun [44]	Mr. Mime [46]	Ninjask [45]	Patrat [33]	Plusle [44]
		Scolipede [30]	Scyther [E]	Sentret [39]	Shelmet [E]	Skitty [E]	Spinarak [E]
		Spinda [E]	Surskit [43]	Volbeat [E]	Watchog [39]		
Dark	Beat Up	Charmander [E]	Diglett [E]	Ekans [E]	Houndoom [26]	Houndour [25, E]	Nidoran♀ [E]
		Nidoran♂ [E]	Sandile [E]	Sneasel [28]			
Poison	Belch	Arbok [48]	Bellsprout [E]	Croagunk [47]	Ekans [38]	Garbodor [49]	Gulpin [40]
		Heatmor [E]	Lickitung [E]	Miltank [E]	Munchlax [E]	Seviper [46]	Skuntank [56]
		Slowpoke [E]	Snorlax [E]	Stunky [46]	Swalot [46]	Toxicroak [58]	Trubbish [42]
Normal	Belly Drum	Charmander [E]	Chesnaught [1]	Chespin [E]	Cubone [E]	Hariyama [27]	Lickitung [E]
		Linoone [59]	Makuhita [25]	Marill [E]	Munchlax [44]	Poliwag [31]	Poliwhirl [37]
		Slowpoke [E]	Snorlax [44]	Swirlix [E]	Teddiursa [E]	Zigzagoon [45]	
Normal	Bestow	Audino [E]	Delibird [E]	Exeggcute [50]	Froakie [E]	Linoone [41]	Pachirisu [E]
		Phantump [E]	Pichu [E]	Pumpkaboo [E]	Zigzagoon [33]		
Normal	Bide	Amoonguss [1, 12]	Beartic [1]	Conkeldurr [1, 8]	Corsola [E]	Cubchoo [9]	Dunsparce [E]
		Flygon [17]	Foongus [12]	Goodra [13]	Goomy [13]	Gurdurr [1, 8]	Heracross [E]
		Ledyba [E]	Medicham [1]	Meditite [1]	Miltank [15]	Pachirisu [1]	Patrat [8]
		Pichu [E]	Sawk [5]	Shelmet [E]	Shuckle [1]	Sliggoo [13]	Stunfisk [5]
		Throh [5]	Timburr [8]	Trapinch [1]	Tyrantrum [12]	Tyrunt [12]	Vibrava [17]
		Watchog [8]					
	Bind	Carnivine [1]	Cryogonal [1]	Heatmor [11]	Kecleon [4]	Onix [1]	Pinsir [4]
		Steelix [1]	Throh [1]	Zygarde [18]			
Dark	Bite	Absol [20]	Aerodactyl [1]	Arbok [1, 9]	Avalugg [E]	Bagon [5]	Basculin [10]
		Bergmite [1]	Blastoise [16]	Carnivine [7]	Carvanha [1]	Charmander [E]	Chesnaught [11]
		Chespin [11]	Crobat [12]	Deino [9]	Drapion [1]	Druddigon [9]	Dunsparce [E]
		Durant [11]	Eevee [17]	Ekans [9]	Electrike [28]	Exploud [20]	Flareon [17]
		Furfrou [22]	Glaceon [17]	Golbat [12]	Granbull [7]	Gyarados [20]	Hippopotas [7]
		Hippowdon [1, 7]	Houndoom [16]	Houndour [16]	Huntail [6]	Hydreigon [1, 9]	Kangaskhan [13]
		Krokorok [1, 4]	Krookodile [1, 4]	Larvitar [1]	Loudred [20]	Manectric [30]	Mawile [11]
		Mightyena [1, 13]	Nidoran♀ [21]	Nidorina [23]	Noibat [13]	Noivern [13]	Pachirisu [E]
		Panpour [19]	Pansage [19]	Pansear [19]	Patrat [6]	Poochyena [13]	Pupitar [1]
		Quilladin [11]	Riolu [E]	Salamence [1, 5]	Sandile [4]	Seviper [E]	Sharpedo [1]
		Shelgon [1, 5]	Skorupi [1]	Sneasel [E]	Snubbull [7]	Squirtle [16]	Swinub [E]
		Trapinch [1]	Tyranitar [1]	Tyrantrum [17]	Tyrunt [17]	Wartortle [16]	Watchog [1, 6]
		Zubat [12]	Zweilous [1, 9]	Zygarde [1]			
Fire	Blast Burn	Charizard [T]	Delphox [T]				
	Blaze Kick	Riolu [E]					
Ice	Blizzard (TM14)	Abomasnow [47, TM]	Absol [TM]	Aggron [TM]	Alomomola [TM]	Amaura [65, TM]	Articuno [71, TM]
		Audino [TM]	Aurorus [74, TM]	Avalugg [46, TM]	Azumarill [TM]	Azurill [TM]	Barbaracle [TM]
		Barboach [TM]	Beartic [45, TM]	Bergmite [43, TM]	Bibarel [TM]	Bidoof [TM]	Binacle [TM]
		Blastoise [TM]	Buizel [TM]	Carvanha [TM]	Chinchou [TM]	Clamperl [TM]	Cloyster [TM]
		Corphish [TM]	Corsola [TM]	Crawdaunt [TM]	Cryogonal [TM]	Cubchoo [45, TM]	Cubone [TM]
		Delcatty [TM]	Delibird [TM]	Dragonair [TM]	Dragonite [TM]	Dratini [TM]	Dunsparce [TM]
		Exploud [TM]	Floatzel [TM]	Froakie [TM]	Frogadier [TM]	Furret [TM]	Glaceon [45, TM]
		Goldeen [TM]	Golduck [TM]	Goodra [TM]	Gorebyss [TM]	Greninja [TM]	Gyarados [TM]
		Horsea [TM]	Huntail [TM]	Jigglypuff [TM]	Jynx [60, TM]	Kangaskhan [TM]	Kecleon [TM]
		Kingdra [TM]	Lanturn [TM]	Lapras [TM]	Lickilicky [TM]	Lickitung [TM]	Linoone [TM]
		Lombre [TM]	Lotad [TM]	Loudred [TM]	Ludicolo [TM]	Lunatone [TM]	Luvdisc [TM]
		Mamoswine [52, TM]	Mantine [TM]	Mantyke [TM]	Marill [TM]	Marowak [TM]	Masquerain [TM]

AFTER THE HALL OF FAME · CENTRAL KALOS · COASTAL KALOS · MOUNTAIN KALOS · ADVENTURE DATA

Move	Pokémon that can learn it					
Ice						
Blizzard (TM14)	Mewtwo [TM]	Miltank [TM]	Munchlax [TM]	Nidoking [TM]	Nidoqueen [TM]	Nidoran♀ [TM]
	Nidoran♂ [TM]	Nidorina [TM]	Nidorino [TM]	Octillery [TM]	Panpour [TM]	Pelipper [TM]
	Piloswine [52, TM]	Politoed [TM]	Poliwag [TM]	Poliwhirl [TM]	Poliwrath [TM]	Psyduck [TM]
	Quagsire [52, TM]	Qwilfish [TM]	Relicanth [TM]	Remoraid [TM]	Rhydon [TM]	Rhyhorn [TM]
	Rhyperior [TM]	Rotom (Frost) ◆	Seadra [TM]	Seaking [TM]	Sharpedo [TM]	Shellder [TM]
	Simipour [TM]	Skitty [TM]	Sliggoo [TM]	Slowbro [TM]	Slowking [TM]	Slowpoke [TM]
	Smoochum [48, TM]	Sneasel [TM]	Snorlax [TM]	Snover [41, TM]	Squirtle [TM]	Starmie [TM]
	Staryu [TM]	Surskit [TM]	Swinub [44, TM]	Tauros [TM]	Tentacool [TM]	Tentacruel [TM]
	Tyranitar [TM]	Vanillish [53, TM]	Vanillite [49, TM]	Vanilluxe [59, TM]	Vaporeon [TM]	Wailmer [TM]
	Wailord [TM]	Wartortle [TM]	Weavile [TM]	Whiscash [TM]	Whismur [TM]	Wigglytuff [TM]
	Wingull [TM]	Wooper [TM]	Zangoose [TM]	Zigzagoon [TM]		
Normal						
Block	Bonsly [26]	Dwebble [E]	Exeggcute [E]	Geodude [E]	Nosepass [8, E]	Onix [E]
	Probopass [1, 8]	Slowpoke [E]	Snorlax [E]	Sudowoodo [26]		
Body Slam	Aron [E]	Azurill [E]	Chesnaught [48]	Chespin [42]	Clamperl [E]	Corphish [E]
	Deino [48]	Drifloon [E]	Foongus [E]	Garbodor [25]	Gible [E]	Goldeen [E]
	Goodra [32]	Goomy [32]	Heatmor [E]	Hippopotas [E]	Hydreigon [48]	Jigglypuff [33]
	Jynx [44]	Lapras [18]	Lickitung [E]	Magcargo [52]	Mareep [E]	Marill [E]
	Miltank [24]	Munchlax [25]	Nidoqueen [35]	Pancham [33]	Pangoro [35]	Poliwag [21]
	Poliwhirl [21]	Quilladin [48]	Seviper [E]	Shelmet [40]	Sliggoo [32]	Slugma [46]
	Snorlax [25]	Swalot [26]	Swinub [E]	Throh [29]	Torkoal [33]	Wailmer [46]
	Wooper [E]	Zweilous [48]				
Ground						
Bone Club	Cubone [7]	Marowak [1, 7]				
Bone Rush	Cubone [37]	Lucario [29]	Marowak [43]			
Bonemerang	Cubone [21]	Marowak [21]				
Normal						
Boomburst	Chatot [E]	Exploud [1, 85]	Noivern [1, 75]	Taillow [E]		
Flying						
Bounce	Azurill [23]	Bunnelby [38]	Diggersby [42]	Froakie [39]	Frogadier [44]	Grumpig [60]
	Hawlucha [49]	Hoppip [46]	Jumpluff [64]	Mantine [46]	Mantyke [46]	Mienfoo [49]
	Mienshao [49]	Politoed [37]	Skiploom [56]	Spoink [50]	Stunfisk [35]	Wailmer [44]
	Wailord [54]					
Brave Bird	Doduo [E]	Ducklett [41]	Farfetch'd [1, 55]	Murkrow [E]	Pidgey [E]	Skarmory [E]
	Staraptor [49]	Staravia [43]	Starly [37]	Swanna [47]	Taillow [E]	Talonflame [1, 64]
	Zubat [E]					
Fighting						
Brick Break (TM31)	Abomasnow [TM]	Aegislash [TM]	Aggron [TM]	Ampharos [TM]	Azumarill [TM]	Bagon [TM]
	Barbaracle [TM]	Beartic [TM]	Beedrill [TM]	Binacle [TM]	Bisharp [TM]	Blastoise [TM]
	Bonsly [TM]	Buizel [TM]	Bunnelby [TM]	Charizard [TM]	Charmander [TM]	Charmeleon [TM]
	Chesnaught [TM]	Chespin [TM]	Conkeldurr [TM]	Corphish [TM]	Crawdaunt [TM]	Croagunk [TM]
	Cubone [TM]	Delibird [TM]	Diggersby [TM]	Doublade [TM]	Dragonite [TM]	Drapion [TM]
	Exploud [TM]	Flaaffy [TM]	Floatzel [TM]	Furret [TM]	Gallade [TM]	Garchomp [TM]
	Gengar [TM]	Geodude [TM]	Gligar [TM]	Gliscor [TM]	Gogoat [TM]	Golduck [TM]
	Golem [TM]	Golett [TM]	Golurk [TM]	Gothitelle [TM]	Granbull [TM]	Graveler [TM]
	Grumpig [TM]	Gurdurr [TM]	Hariyama [TM]	Haxorus [TM]	Heracross [25, TM]	Honedge [TM]
	Illumise [TM]	Jigglypuff [TM]	Jynx [TM]	Kangaskhan [TM]	Kecleon [TM]	Krokorok [TM]
	Krookodile [TM]	Larvitar [TM]	Ledian [TM]	Ledyba [TM]	Lickilicky [TM]	Lickitung [TM]
	Lombre [TM]	Loudred [TM]	Lucario [TM]	Ludicolo [TM]	Machamp [TM]	Machoke [TM]
	Machop [TM]	Makuhita [TM]	Marill [TM]	Marowak [TM]	Mawile [TM]	Medicham [TM]
	Meditite [TM]	Mewtwo [TM]	Mienfoo [TM]	Mienshao [TM]	Miltank [TM]	Mime Jr. [TM]
	Mr. Mime [TM]	Munchlax [TM]	Nidoking [TM]	Nidoqueen [TM]	Noibat [TM]	Noivern [TM]
	Pancham [TM]	Pangoro [TM]	Pawniard [TM]	Pikachu [TM]	Pinsir [18, TM]	Politoed [TM]
	Poliwhirl [TM]	Poliwrath [TM]	Psyduck [TM]	Pupitar [TM]	Quagsire [TM]	Quilladin [TM]
	Raichu [TM]	Rhydon [TM]	Rhyperior [TM]	Riolu [TM]	Sableye [TM]	Salamence [TM]
	Sandshrew [TM]	Sandslash [TM]	Sawk [29, TM]	Scizor [TM]	Scrafty [20, TM]	Scraggy [20, TM]
	Scyther [TM]	Sentret [TM]	Shelgon [TM]	Simipour [TM]	Simisage [TM]	Simisear [TM]
	Skiddo [TM]	Skorupi [TM]	Slowbro [TM]	Slowking [TM]	Sneasel [TM]	Snorlax [TM]
	Snubbull [TM]	Spinda [TM]	Squirtle [TM]	Sudowoodo [TM]	Teddiursa [TM]	Throh [TM]
	Timburr [TM]	Toxicroak [TM]	Tyranitar [TM]	Tyrantrum [TM]	Tyrunt [TM]	Ursaring [TM]
	Volbeat [TM]	Wartortle [TM]	Weavile [TM]	Wigglytuff [TM]	Zangoose [TM]	Zygarde [TM]
Water						
Brine	Alomomola [41]	Basculin [E]	Beartic [21]	Carvanha [E]	Chinchou [E]	Clamperl [E]
	Cubchoo [21]	Ducklett [E]	Hariyama [1]	Horsea [30]	Huntail [28]	Kingdra [30]
	Lapras [37]	Luvdisc [E]	Panpour [34]	Pelipper [34]	Qwilfish [33, E]	Relicanth [E]
	Seadra [30]	Shellder [44]	Squirtle [E]	Staryu [36]	Wailmer [31]	Wailord [31]
	Wingull [E]					
Bubble	Azumarill [7]	Azurill [7]	Blastoise [13]	Chinchou [12]	Clauncher [12]	Clawitzer [12]
	Corphish [1]	Corsola [8]	Crawdaunt [1]	Dragalge [12]	Froakie [5]	Frogadier [5]
	Goodra [1]	Goomy [1]	Greninja [5]	Horsea [11]	Kingdra [1, 11]	Lanturn [12]
	Mantine [1]	Mantyke [1]	Marill [7]	Masquerain [1]	Poliwag [11]	Poliwhirl [11]
	Qwilfish [13]	Seadra [1, 11]	Skrelp [12]	Sliggoo [1]	Squirtle [13]	Surskit [1]
	Tentacool [E]	Wartortle [13]				

◆ When Rotom becomes Frost Rotom, it learns the move Blizzard. When it changes back to Rotom, it forgets the move.

	Move	Pokémon that can learn it					
Water	Bubble Beam	Azumarill [13]	Azurill [13]	Basculin [E]	Chinchou [31]	Clauncher [20]	Clawitzer [20]
		Corphish [20]	Corsola [17]	Crawdaunt [20]	Ducklett [19]	Horsea [18]	Kingdra [18]
		Lanturn [35]	Lombre [25]	Lotad [25]	Mantine [1, 7]	Mantyke [7]	Marill [13]
		Octillery [18]	Politoed [1]	Poliwag [25, E]	Poliwhirl [27]	Poliwrath [1]	Qwilfish [E]
		Remoraid [18]	Seadra [18]	Shellder [E]	Staryu [22]	Surskit [25]	Swanna [19]
		Tentacool [19]	Tentacruel [19]				
Bug	Bug Bite	Ariados [1]	Burmy [15]	Caterpie [15]	Combee [13]	Crustle [23]	Drapion [20]
		Durant [26]	Dwebble [23]	Heatmor [36]	Karrablast [E]	Ledyba [E]	Mothim [15]
		Nincada [E]	Ninjask [1]	Pinsir [E]	Scatterbug [15]	Scolipede [23]	Shuckle [42]
		Skorupi [20]	Surskit [E]	Trapinch [E]	Venipede [22]	Weedle [15]	Whirlipede [23]
		Wormadam (Plant) [15]	Wormadam (Sand) [15]	Wormadam (Trash) [15]	Yanmega [1]		
Bug	Bug Buzz	Accelgor [44]	Butterfree [42]	Combee [29]	Escavalier [28]	Illumise [41, E]	Karrablast [28]
		Ledian [53]	Ledyba [41, E]	Masquerain [1, 61]	Mothim [47]	Nincada [E]	Scyther [E]
		Shelmet [44]	Vivillon [35]	Volbeat [41, E]	Yanma [57]	Yanmega [1, 57]	
Fighting	Bulk Up (TM08)	Barbaracle [TM]	Beartic [TM]	Buizel [TM]	Bunnelby [TM]	Chesnaught [44, TM]	Chespin [39, TM]
		Conkeldurr [29, TM]	Croagunk [TM]	Diggersby [TM]	Floatzel [TM]	Gallade [TM]	Gogoat [34, TM]
		Granbull [TM]	Gurdurr [29, TM]	Hariyama [TM]	Hawlucha [TM]	Heracross [TM]	Krookodile [TM]
		Lucario [TM]	Machamp [TM]	Machoke [TM]	Machop [TM]	Makuhita [TM]	Medicham [TM]
		Meditite [TM]	Mewtwo [TM]	Mienfoo [TM]	Mienshao [TM]	Pancham [TM]	Pangoro [TM]
		Pinsir [TM]	Poliwrath [TM]	Quilladin [44, TM]	Riolu [TM]	Sawk [33, TM]	Scrafty [TM]
		Scraggy [TM]	Skiddo [34, TM]	Snubbull [TM]	Talonflame [TM]	Teddiursa [TM]	Throh [33, TM]
		Timburr [28, TM]	Toxicroak [TM]	Ursaring [TM]			
Ground	Bulldoze (TM78)	Abomasnow [TM]	Aerodactyl [TM]	Aggron [TM]	Altaria [TM]	Amaura [TM]	Ampharos [TM]
		Arbok [TM]	Aron [TM]	Aurorus [TM]	Avalugg [TM]	Azumarill [TM]	Barbaracle [TM]
		Barboach [TM]	Beartic [TM]	Bibarel [TM]	Binacle [TM]	Blastoise [TM]	Boldore [TM]
		Bunnelby [TM]	Charizard [TM]	Chesnaught [TM]	Chespin [TM]	Conkeldurr [TM]	Corsola [TM]
		Croagunk [TM]	Crustle [TM]	Cubone [TM]	Diggersby [1, TM]	Diglett [18, TM]	Dragonite [TM]
		Drapion [TM]	Druddigon [TM]	Dugtrio [18, TM]	Dunsparce [TM]	Dwebble [TM]	Ekans [TM]
		Exploud [TM]	Ferrothorn [TM]	Flygon [21, TM]	Gabite [TM]	Gallade [TM]	Garchomp [TM]
		Geodude [32, TM]	Gible [TM]	Gigalith [TM]	Gligar [TM]	Gliscor [TM]	Gogoat [26, TM]
		Golem [36, TM]	Golett [TM]	Golurk [TM]	Goodra [TM]	Granbull [TM]	Graveler [36, TM]
		Grumpig [TM]	Gyarados [TM]	Hariyama [TM]	Haxorus [TM]	Heliolisk [TM]	Helioptile [35, TM]
		Heracross [TM]	Hippopotas [TM]	Hippowdon [TM]	Hydreigon [TM]	Kangaskhan [TM]	Krokorok [TM]
		Krookodile [TM]	Lairon [TM]	Lapras [TM]	Larvitar [TM]	Lickilicky [TM]	Lickitung [TM]
		Litleo [TM]	Loudred [TM]	Lucario [TM]	Lunatone [TM]	Machamp [TM]	Machoke [TM]
		Machop [TM]	Magcargo [TM]	Makuhita [TM]	Mamoswine [TM]	Mantine [TM]	Mantyke [TM]
		Marowak [TM]	Mewtwo [TM]	Miltank [TM]	Munchlax [TM]	Nidoking [TM]	Nidoqueen [TM]
		Nosepass [TM]	Onix [TM]	Pancham [TM]	Pangoro [TM]	Phantump [TM]	Piloswine [TM]
		Pinsir [TM]	Politoed [TM]	Poliwhirl [TM]	Poliwrath [TM]	Probopass [TM]	Pupitar [TM]
		Pyroar [TM]	Quagsire [TM]	Quilladin [TM]	Relicanth [TM]	Rhydon [30, TM]	Rhyhorn [30, TM]
		Rhyperior [TM]	Riolu [TM]	Roggenrola [TM]	Salamence [TM]	Sandile [TM]	Sandshrew [TM]
		Sandslash [TM]	Sawk [TM]	Scolipede [TM]	Seviper [TM]	Sharpedo [TM]	Shuckle [TM]
		Skiddo [26, TM]	Slowbro [TM]	Slowking [TM]	Slowpoke [TM]	Snorlax [TM]	Snubbull [TM]
		Solrock [TM]	Steelix [TM]	Stunfisk [TM]	Sudowoodo [TM]	Swalot [TM]	Swinub [TM]
		Tauros [TM]	Teddiursa [TM]	Throh [TM]	Torkoal [TM]	Toxicroak [TM]	Trapinch [21, TM]
		Trevenant [TM]	Tyranitar [TM]	Tyrantrum [TM]	Tyrunt [TM]	Ursaring [TM]	Venusaur [TM]
		Vibrava [21, TM]	Wailmer [TM]	Wailord [TM]	Whiscash [TM]	Wooper [TM]	Wormadam (Sand) [TM]
		Zygarde [1, TM]					
Steel	Bullet Punch	Croagunk [E]	Machop [E]	Makuhita [E]	Meditite [E]	Riolu [E]	Scizor [1]
Grass	Bullet Seed	Bellsprout [E]	Exeggcute [17]	Ferroseed [E]	Gourgeist [26]	Heracross [1]	Hoppip [19]
		Jumpluff [20]	Mantine [1]	Octillery [46]	Pansage [E]	Pumpkaboo [26]	Remoraid [38]
		Roselia [E]	Skiploom [20]	Snover [E]			

C

	Move	Pokémon that can learn it					
Psychic	Calm Mind (TM04)	Abra [TM]	Absol [TM]	Alakazam [42, TM]	Alomomola [TM]	Amaura [TM]	Aromatisse [17, TM]
		Audino [TM]	Aurorus [TM]	Banette [TM]	Bonsly [TM]	Carbink [TM]	Chandelure [TM]
		Chimecho [TM]	Chingling [TM]	Corsola [TM]	Delcatty [TM]	Delphox [TM]	Drifblim [TM]
		Drifloon [TM]	Dunsparce [TM]	Duosion [TM]	Espeon [TM]	Espurr [TM]	Flabébé [TM]
		Floette [TM]	Florges [TM]	Gallade [TM]	Gardevoir [33, TM]	Golduck [TM]	Gothita [TM]
		Gothitelle [TM]	Gothorita [TM]	Grumpig [TM]	Honchkrow [TM]	Inkay [TM]	Jynx [TM]
		Kadabra [TM]	Kirlia [31, TM]	Klefki [TM]	Lampent [TM]	Litwick [TM]	Lucario [47, TM]
		Lunatone [TM]	Malamar [TM]	Medicham [25, TM]	Meditite [25, TM]	Meowstic (Female) [TM]	Meowstic (Male) [TM]
		Mewtwo [TM]	Mienfoo [25, TM]	Mienshao [25, TM]	Mime Jr. [TM]	Mr. Mime [TM]	Murkrow [TM]
		Psyduck [TM]	Ralts [28, TM]	Relicanth [TM]	Reuniclus [TM]	Sableye [TM]	Shuppet [TM]
		Sigilyph [TM]	Skitty [TM]	Slowbro [TM]	Slowking [TM]	Slowpoke [TM]	Slurpuff [TM]
		Smoochum [TM]	Sneasel [TM]	Solosis [TM]	Solrock [TM]	Spinda [TM]	Spoink [TM]
		Spritzee [17, TM]	Sudowoodo [TM]	Swirlix [TM]	Swoobat [29, TM]	Sylveon [TM]	Trevenant [TM]
		Vivillon [TM]	Weavile [TM]	Woobat [29, TM]	Xerneas [TM]	Zoroark [TM]	Zorua [TM]

AFTER THE HALL OF FAME

CENTRAL KALOS

COASTAL KALOS

MOUNTAIN KALOS

ADVENTURE DATA

	Move	Pokémon that can learn it					
Normal	Camouflage	Azurill [E]	Corsola [E]	Dragalge [19]	Flabébé [E]	Froakie [E]	Helioptile [E]
		Inkay [E]	Kecleon [E]	Marill [E]	Mothim [35]	Skrelp [19]	Staryu [15]
		Stunfisk [17]	Zygarde [59]				
	Captivate	Butterfree [40]	Eevee [E]	Flabébé [E]	Furfrou [E]	Gardevoir [60]	Gorebyss [28]
		Gothita [E]	Igglybuff [E]	Illumise [E]	Litwick [E]	Luvdisc [50, E]	Mawile [E]
		Miltank [35]	Nidoran♀ [43]	Nidoran♂ [43]	Nidorina [50]	Nidorino [50]	Purrloin [33]
		Sableye [E]	Sentret [E]	Skitty [46, E]	Smoochum [E]	Spritzee [E]	Vespiquen [41]
		Woobat [E]	Wormadam (Plant) [35]	Wormadam (Sand) [35]	Wormadam (Trash) [35]	Zorua [E]	
Electric	Charge	Ampharos [16]	Chinchou [50]	Dedenne [11]	Electrike [44]	Electrode [1]	Emolga [10]
		Flaaffy [16]	Heliolisk [7]	Helioptile [11]	Lanturn [64]	Manectric [54]	Mareep [15, E]
		Minun [38]	Pachirisu [E]	Pichu [E]	Plusle [38]	Rotom (Fan) [1, 57]	Rotom (Frost) [1, 57]
		Rotom (Heat) [1, 57]	Rotom (Mow) [1, 57]	Rotom (Wash) [1, 57]	Rotom [1, 57]	Voltorb [1]	Zapdos [36]
Electric	Charge Beam (TM57)	Abra [TM]	Absol [TM]	Alakazam [TM]	Amaura [TM]	Ampharos [TM]	Aromatisse [TM]
		Audino [TM]	Aurorus [TM]	Banette [TM]	Bibarel [TM]	Bidoof [TM]	Chimecho [TM]
		Chinchou [TM]	Chingling [TM]	Dedenne [34, TM]	Delcatty [37]	Drifblim [TM]	Drifloon [TM]
		Druddigon [TM]	Dunsparce [TM]	Electrike [TM]	Electrode [22, TM]	Emolga [TM]	Espurr [TM]
		Flaaffy [TM]	Furfrou [TM]	Furret [TM]	Gallade [TM]	Gardevoir [TM]	Golurk [TM]
		Gothita [TM]	Gothitelle [TM]	Gothorita [TM]	Gourgeist [TM]	Grumpig [TM]	Heliolisk [TM]
		Helioptile [TM]	Hydreigon [TM]	Illumise [TM]	Jigglypuff [TM]	Jolteon [TM]	Kadabra [TM]
		Kecleon [TM]	Kirlia [TM]	Lanturn [TM]	Linoone [TM]	Lunatone [TM]	Magnemite [TM]
		Magneton [TM]	Magnezone [TM]	Manectric [TM]	Mareep [TM]	Mawile [TM]	Meowstic (Female) [28, TM]
		Meowstic (Male) [TM]	Mewtwo [TM]	Mime Jr. [TM]	Minun [TM]	Mr. Mime [TM]	Octillery [TM]
		Pachirisu [TM]	Pichu [TM]	Pikachu [TM]	Plusle [TM]	Pumpkaboo [TM]	Raichu [TM]
		Ralts [TM]	Remoraid [TM]	Rotom (Fan) [TM]	Rotom (Frost) [TM]	Rotom (Heat) [TM]	Rotom (Mow) [TM]
		Rotom (Wash) [TM]	Rotom [TM]	Sentret [TM]	Shuppet [TM]	Sigilyph [TM]	Skitty [TM]
		Solrock [TM]	Spoink [TM]	Spritzee [TM]	Swoobat [TM]	Volbeat [TM]	Voltorb [22, TM]
		Wigglytuff [TM]	Woobat [TM]	Zapdos [TM]	Zigzagoon [TM]		
Fairy	Charm	Aromatisse [35]	Azurill [10]	Bulbasaur [E]	Cubchoo [29]	Dedenne [14]	Duosion [19]
		Eevee [29, E]	Emolga [E]	Furfrou [38]	Gothita [46]	Gothitelle [54]	Gothorita [50]
		Granbull [1]	Igglybuff [1]	Illumise [E]	Kirlia [50]	Luvdisc [4]	Meowstic (Male) [28]
		Mime Jr. [E]	Minun [21]	Munchlax [E]	Nidoran♀ [E]	Oddish [E]	Pachirisu [9]
		Pichu [1]	Purrloin [E]	Ralts [43]	Reuniclus [E]	Sentret [E]	Skitty [25]
		Snorlax [E]	Snubbull [1]	Solosis [19]	Spritzee [35]	Teddiursa [36]	Tyrantrum [20]
		Tyrunt [20]	Woobat [E]	Wynaut [1]	Zigzagoon [E]		
Flying	Chatter	Chatot [1, 21]					
Normal	Chip Away	Basculin [16]	Conkeldurr [24]	Corphish [E]	Cubone [E]	Druddigon [31]	Gurdurr [24]
		Heracross [16]	Kangaskhan [31]	Larvitar [14]	Lickilicky [37]	Lickitung [37]	Makuhita [E]
		Munchlax [17]	Nidoking [23]	Nidoqueen [23]	Nidoran♀ [E]	Nidoran♂ [E]	Pupitar [14]
		Rhydon [34]	Rhyhorn [34]	Rhyperior [30]	Sandshrew [E]	Scrafty [27]	Scraggy [27]
		Snorlax [17]	Teddiursa [E]	Timburr [24]	Tyranitar [14]		
Fighting	Circle Throw	Kangaskhan [E]	Pancham [25]	Pangoro [25]	Poliwrath [1, 53]	Riolu [E]	Throh [37]
		Whismur [E]					
Water	Clamp	Barbaracle [20]	Binacle [20]	Clamperl [1]	Shellder [25]		
Poison	Clear Smog	Amoonguss [43]	Bellsprout [E]	Drifloon [E]	Foongus [39]	Garbodor [34]	Gastly [E]
		Horsea [E]	Litwick [E]	Psyduck [E]	Torkoal [E]	Trubbish [34]	Wailmer [E]
Fighting	Close Combat	Gallade [1, 59]	Hariyama [52]	Heracross [34]	Lucario [1, 55]	Machop [E]	Makuhita [40]
		Pinsir [E]	Sawk [48]	Snubbull [E]	Staraptor [34]	Teddiursa [E]	Xerneas [80]
		Zangoose [47]					
Poison	Coil	Arbok [56]	Dunsparce [37]	Ekans [44]	Seviper [48]	Zygarde [80]	
Normal	Comet Punch	Kangaskhan [1]	Ledian [1, 9]	Ledyba [9]	Pancham [15]	Pangoro [15]	Timburr [E]
Normal	Confide (TM100)	Abomasnow [TM]	Abra [TM]	Absol [TM]	Accelgor [TM]	Aegislash [TM]	Aerodactyl [TM]
		Aggron [TM]	Alakazam [TM]	Alomomola [TM]	Altaria [TM]	Amaura [TM]	Amoonguss [TM]
		Ampharos [TM]	Arbok [TM]	Ariados [TM]	Aromatisse [TM]	Aron [TM]	Articuno [TM]
		Audino [TM]	Aurorus [TM]	Avalugg [TM]	Axew [TM]	Azumarill [TM]	Azurill [TM]
		Bagon [TM]	Banette [TM]	Barbaracle [TM]	Barboach [TM]	Basculin [TM]	Beartic [TM]
		Beedrill [TM]	Bellossom [TM]	Bellsprout [TM]	Bergmite [TM]	Bibarel [TM]	Bidoof [TM]
		Binacle [TM]	Bisharp [TM]	Blastoise [TM]	Boldore [TM]	Bonsly [TM]	Braixen [TM]
		Budew [TM]	Buizel [TM]	Bulbasaur [TM]	Bunnelby [TM]	Butterfree [TM]	Carbink [TM]
		Carnivine [TM]	Carvanha [TM]	Chandelure [TM]	Charizard [TM]	Charmander [TM]	Charmeleon [TM]
		Chatot [1, TM]	Chesnaught [TM]	Chespin [TM]	Chimecho [TM]	Chinchou [TM]	Chingling [TM]
		Clamperl [TM]	Clauncher [TM]	Clawitzer [TM]	Cloyster [TM]	Conkeldurr [TM]	Corphish [TM]
		Corsola [TM]	Crawdaunt [TM]	Croagunk [TM]	Crobat [TM]	Crustle [TM]	Cryogonal [TM]
		Cubchoo [TM]	Cubone [TM]	Dedenne [TM]	Deino [TM]	Delcatty [TM]	Delibird [TM]

Move	Pokémon that can learn it

Normal — Confide (TM100)

Delphox [TM], Diggersby [TM], Diglett [TM], Dodrio [TM], Doduo [TM], Doublade [TM], Dragalge [TM], Dragonair [TM], Dragonite [TM], Drapion [TM], Dratini [TM], Drifblim [TM], Drifloon [TM], Druddigon [TM], Ducklett [TM], Dugtrio [TM], Dunsparce [TM], Duosion [TM], Durant [TM], Dwebble [TM], Eevee [TM], Ekans [TM], Electrike [TM], Electrode [TM], Emolga [TM], Escavalier [TM], Espeon [TM], Espurr [TM], Exeggcute [TM], Exeggutor [TM], Exploud [TM], Farfetch'd [TM], Fearow [TM], Fennekin [TM], Ferroseed [TM], Ferrothorn [TM], Flaaffy [TM], Flabébé [TM], Flareon [TM], Fletchinder [TM], Fletchling [TM], Floatzel [TM], Floette [TM], Florges [TM], Flygon [TM], Foongus [TM], Fraxure [TM], Froakie [TM], Frogadier [TM], Furfrou [TM], Furret [TM], Gabite [TM], Gallade [TM], Garbodor [TM], Garchomp [TM], Gardevoir [TM], Gastly [TM], Gengar [TM], Geodude [TM], Gible [TM], Gigalith [TM], Glaceon [TM], Gligar [TM], Gliscor [TM], Gloom [TM], Gogoat [TM], Golbat [TM], Goldeen [TM], Golduck [TM], Golem [TM], Golett [TM], Golurk [TM], Goodra [TM], Goomy [TM], Gorebyss [TM], Gothita [TM], Gothitelle [TM], Gothorita [TM], Gourgeist [TM], Granbull [TM], Graveler [TM], Greninja [TM], Grumpig [TM], Gulpin [TM], Gurdurr [TM], Gyarados [TM], Hariyama [TM], Haunter [TM], Hawlucha [TM], Haxorus [TM], Heatmor [TM], Heliolisk [TM], Helioptile [TM], Heracross [TM], Hippopotas [TM], Hippowdon [TM], Honchkrow [TM], Honedge [TM], Hoothoot [TM], Hoppip [TM], Horsea [TM], Houndoom [TM], Houndour [TM], Huntail [TM], Hydreigon [TM], Igglybuff [TM], Illumise [TM], Inkay [TM], Ivysaur [TM], Jigglypuff [TM], Jolteon [TM], Jumpluff [TM], Jynx [TM], Kadabra [TM], Kangaskhan [TM], Karrablast [TM], Kecleon [TM], Kingdra [TM], Kirlia [TM], Klefki [TM], Krokorok [TM], Krookodile [TM], Lairon [TM], Lampent [TM], Lanturn [TM], Lapras [TM], Larvitar [TM], Leafeon [TM], Ledian [TM], Ledyba [TM], Lickilicky [TM], Lickitung [TM], Liepard [TM], Linoone [TM], Litleo [TM], Litwick [TM], Lombre [TM], Lotad [TM], Loudred [TM], Lucario [TM], Ludicolo [TM], Lunatone [TM], Luvdisc [TM], Machamp [TM], Machoke [TM], Machop [TM], Magcargo [TM], Magnemite [TM], Magneton [TM], Magnezone [TM], Makuhita [TM], Malamar [TM], Mamoswine [TM], Manectric [TM], Mantine [TM], Mantyke [TM], Mareep [TM], Marill [TM], Marowak [TM], Masquerain [TM], Mawile [TM], Medicham [TM], Meditite [TM], Meowstic (Female) [TM], Meowstic (Male) [TM], Mewtwo [TM], Mienfoo [TM], Mienshao [TM], Mightyena [TM], Miltank [TM], Mime Jr. [TM], Minun [TM], Moltres [TM], Mothim [TM], Mr. Mime [TM], Munchlax [TM], Murkrow [TM], Nidoking [TM], Nidoqueen [TM], Nidoran ♀ [TM], Nidoran♂ [TM], Nidorina [TM], Nidorino [TM], Nincada [TM], Ninjask [TM], Noctowl [TM], Noibat [TM], Noivern [TM], Nosepass [TM], Octillery [TM], Oddish [TM], Onix [TM], Pachirisu [TM], Pancham [TM], Pangoro [TM], Panpour [TM], Pansage [TM], Pansear [TM], Patrat [TM], Pawniard [TM], Pelipper [TM], Phantump [TM], Phanpy [TM]... Pichu [TM], Pidgeot [TM], Pidgeotto [TM], Pidgey [TM], Pikachu [TM], Piloswine [TM], Pinsir [TM], Pluslе [TM], Politoed [TM], Poliwag [TM], Poliwhirl [TM], Poliwrath [TM], Poochyena [TM], Probopass [TM], Psyduck [TM], Pumpkaboo [TM], Pupitar [TM], Purrloin [TM], Pyroar [TM], Quagsire [TM], Quilladin [TM], Qwilfish [TM], Raichu [TM], Ralts [TM], Relicanth [TM], Remoraid [TM], Reuniclus [TM], Rhydon [TM], Rhyhorn [TM], Rhyperior [TM], Riolu [TM], Roggenrola [TM], Roselia [TM], Roserade [TM], Rotom (Fan) [TM], Rotom (Frost) [TM], Rotom (Heat) [TM], Rotom (Mow) [TM], Rotom (Wash) [TM], Rotom [TM], Sableye [TM], Salamence [TM], Sandile [TM], Sandshrew [TM], Sandslash [TM], Sawk [TM], Scizor [TM], Scolipede [TM], Scrafty [TM], Scraggy [TM], Scyther [TM], Seadra [TM], Seaking [TM], Sentret [TM], Seviper [TM], Sharpedo [TM], Shedinja [TM], Shelgon [TM], Shellder [TM], Shelmet [TM], Shuckle [TM], Shuppet [TM], Sigilyph [TM], Simipour [TM], Simisage [TM], Simisear [TM], Skarmory [TM], Skiddo [TM], Skiploom [TM], Skitty [TM], Skorupi [TM], Skrelp [TM], Skuntank [TM], Sliggoo [TM], Slowbro [TM], Slowking [TM], Slowpoke [TM], Slugma [TM], Slurpuff [TM], Smoochum [TM], Sneasel [TM], Snorlax [TM], Snover [TM], Snubbull [TM], Solosis [TM], Solrock [TM], Spearow [TM], Spinarak [TM], Spinda [TM], Spoink [TM], Spritzee [TM], Squirtle [TM], Staraptor [TM], Staravia [TM], Starly [TM], Starmie [TM], Staryu [TM], Steelix [TM], Stunfisk [TM], Stunky [TM], Sudowoodo [TM], Surskit [TM], Swablu [TM], Swalot [TM], Swanna [TM], Swellow [TM], Swinub [TM], Swirlix [TM], Swoobat [TM], Sylveon [TM], Taillow [TM], Talonflame [TM], Tauros [TM], Teddiursa [TM], Tentacool [TM], Tentacruel [TM], Throh [TM], Timburr [TM], Torkoal [TM], Toxicroak [TM], Trapinch [TM], Trevenant [TM], Trubbish [TM], Tyranitar [TM], Tyrantrum [TM], Tyrunt [TM], Umbreon [TM], Ursaring [TM], Vanillish [TM], Vanillite [TM], Vanilluxe [TM], Vaporeon [TM], Venipede [TM], Venusaur [TM], Vespiquen [TM], Vibrava [TM], Victreebel [TM], Vileplume [TM], Vivillon [TM], Volbeat [TM], Voltorb [TM], Wailmer [TM], Wailord [TM], Wartortle [TM], Watchog [TM], Weavile [TM], Weepinbell [TM], Whirlipede [TM], Whiscash [TM], Whismur [TM], Wigglytuff [TM], Wingull [TM], Woobat [TM], Wooper [TM], Wormadam (Plant) [TM], Wormadam (Sand) [TM], Wormadam (Trash) [TM], Xerneas [TM], Yanma [TM], Yanmega [TM], Yveltal [TM], Zangoose [TM], Zapdos [TM], Zigzagoon [TM], Zoroark [TM], Zorua [TM], Zubat [TM], Zweilous [TM], Zygarde [TM]

Ghost — Confuse Ray

Ampharos [29], Chandelure [1], Chinchou [17], Clamperl [E], Corsola [E], Crobat [19], Cryogonal [45], Flaaffy [29], Gastly [19], Gengar [19], Golbat [19], Gourgeist [1], Grumpig [18], Haunter [19], Illumise [9], Lampent [1], Lanturn [17], Lapras [7], Litwick [10], Mantine [11], Mantyke [11], Mareep [25], Mime Jr. [E], Mr. Mime [E], Murkrow [E], Phantump [1], Psyduck [E], Pumpkaboo [1], Ralts [E], Rotom (Fan) [1], Rotom (Frost) [1], Rotom (Heat) [1], Rotom (Mow) [1], Rotom (Wash) [1], Rotom [1], Sableye [1], Shedinja [31], Shuppet [E], Skorupi [E], Solosis [E], Spoink [18], Starmie [22], Tentacool [E], Trevenant [1], Umbreon [17], Vespiquen [1], Volbeat [9], Watchog [20], Zubat [19]

	Move	Pokémon that can learn it					
Psychic	Confusion	Alakazam [1, 16]	Butterfree [1, 10]	Chimecho [14]	Chingling [14]	Espeon [9]	Espurr [9]
		Exeggcute [27]	Exeggutor [1]	Gallade [1, 6]	Gardevoir [1, 6]	Golduck [15]	Gorebyss [6]
		Gothita [3]	Gothitelle [1, 3]	Gothorita [1, 3]	Hoothoot [21]	Hoppip [E]	Kadabra [1, 16]
		Kirlia [1, 6]	Lunatone [1]	Medicham [1, 8]	Meditite [8]	Meowstic (Female) [9]	Meowstic (Male) [9]
		Mewtwo [1]	Mime Jr. [1]	Mothim [23]	Mr. Mime [1]	Nidorino♂ [E]	Noctowl [22]
		Psyduck [15]	Ralts [6]	Slowbro [14]	Slowking [14]	Slowpoke [14]	Smoochum [15]
		Solrock [1]	Swoobat [1]	Woobat [1]	Wormadam (Plant) [23]	Wormadam (Sand) [23]	Wormadam (Trash) [23]
Normal	Constrict	Ariados [1, 8]	Drifblim [1]	Drifloon [1]	Inkay [1]	Malamar [1]	Octillery [1, 6]
		Shuckle [1]	Spinarak [8]	Tentacool [8]	Tentacruel [1, 8]		
	Copycat	Azurill [E]	Bonsly [1]	Flabébé [E]	Igglybuff [17]	Mime Jr. [4]	Minun [24]
		Mr. Mime [4]	Plusle [24]	Purrloin [E]	Riolu [19]	Skitty [18]	Smoochum [41]
		Spinda [10]	Sudowoodo [1]	Swirlix [E]	Zorua [E]		
Psychic	Cosmic Power	Chimecho [E]	Chingling [E]	Lunatone [29]	Sigilyph [48]	Skitty [E]	Solrock [29]
		Staryu [48]					
Grass	Cotton Guard	Altaria [42]	Ampharos [46]	Flaaffy [43]	Furfrou [48]	Hoppip [E]	Mareep [36]
		Slurpuff [41]	Swablu [39]	Swirlix [41]			
	Cotton Spore	Ampharos [11]	Budew [E]	Flaaffy [11]	Hoppip [34]	Jumpluff [44]	Mareep [11]
		Roselia [40]	Skiploom [40]	Slurpuff [17]	Swirlix [17]		
Fighting	Counter	Axew [E]	Bonsly [33]	Charmander [E]	Croagunk [E]	Dwebble [E]	Gligar [E]
		Goomy [E]	Heracross [19]	Houndour [E]	Kangaskhan [E]	Karrablast [E]	Lotad [E]
		Lucario [6]	Machop [E]	Makuhita [E]	Munchlax [E]	Nidoran♀ [E]	Nidoran♂ [E]
		Rhyhorn [E]	Riolu [6]	Sandile [E]	Sandshrew [E]	Sawk [21]	Scraggy [E]
		Scyther [E]	Sneasel [E]	Snorlax [E]	Sudowoodo [33]	Teddiursa [E]	Timburr [E]
		Wobbuffet [1]	Wooper [E]	Wynaut [15]	Zangoose [E]	Zorua [E]	
Normal	Covet	Dedenne [E]	Eevee [23, E]	Emolga [E]	Espurr [5]	Farfetch'd [E]	Igglybuff [E]
		Illumise [45]	Linoone [35]	Meowstic (Female) [5]	Meowstic (Male) [5]	Pachirisu [E]	Panpour [E]
		Pansage [E]	Pansear [E]	Poochyena [E]	Purrloin [E]	Sentret [E]	Skitty [36]
		Teddiursa [1]	Ursaring [1]	Zigzagoon [29]			
Water	Crabhammer	Clauncher [30, E]	Clawitzer [30]	Corphish [38]	Crawdaunt [44]		
Fairy	Crafty Shield	Klefki [23]					
Fighting	Cross Chop	Barbaracle [55]	Binacle [49]	Croagunk [E]	Machamp [44]	Machoke [44]	Machop [43]
		Makuhita [E]	Psyduck [E]	Riolu [E]	Teddiursa [E]		
Poison	Cross Poison	Ariados [55]	Crobat [1]	Drapion [57]	Gligar [E]	Skorupi [49]	Spinarak [47]
Dark	Crunch	Aerodactyl [33]	Arbok [22]	Avalugg [1, 65]	Bagon [46]	Basculin [24]	Carnivine [41]
		Carvanha [28]	Charmander [E]	Corphish [47]	Crawdaunt [57]	Deino [25]	Drapion [49]
		Druddigon [25]	Durant [31]	Electrike [E]	Exploud [40]	Floatzel [1]	Garchomp [48]
		Granbull [59]	Hippopotas [31]	Hippowdon [31]	Houndoom [56]	Houndour [49]	Huntail [42]
		Hydreigon [25]	Kangaskhan [37]	Krokorok [28]	Krookodile [28]	Larvitar [41]	Litleo [39]
		Mawile [36]	Mightyena [1, 65]	Nidoran♀ [37]	Nidorina [43]	Pancham [39]	Pangoro [42]
		Panpour [43]	Pansage [43]	Pansear [43]	Patrat [16]	Poochyena [53]	Pupitar [47]
		Pyroar [42]	Rhyhorn [E]	Riolu [E]	Salamence [53]	Sandile [28]	Scrafty [38]
		Scraggy [38]	Seviper [45]	Sharpedo [28]	Shelgon [50]	Skorupi [45]	Snorlax [49]
		Snubbull [49, E]	Steelix [E]	Stunky [E]	Teddiursa [E]	Trapinch [34]	Tyranitar [47]
		Tyrantrum [34]	Tyrunt [34]	Watchog [16]	Zweilous [25]	Zygarde [51]	
Normal	Crush Claw	Druddigon [E]	Kangaskhan [E]	Rhyhorn [E]	Sandshrew [E]	Sandslash [22]	Sneasel [E]
		Zangoose [22]					
Ghost	Curse	Absol [E]	Aerodactyl [E]	Aron [E]	Avalugg [22]	Banette [1, 19]	Bergmite [22]
		Bibarel [53]	Bidoof [45]	Bonsly [E]	Bulbasaur [E]	Chespin [E]	Chimecho [E]
		Chingling [E]	Corsola [E]	Dunsparce [E]	Dwebble [E]	Eevee [E]	Electrike [E]
		Exeggcute [E]	Farfetch'd [E]	Ferroseed [9]	Ferrothorn [1, 9]	Gastly [12]	Gengar [12]
		Geodude [E]	Golett [40]	Golurk [40]	Goomy [E]	Gulpin [E]	Haunter [12]
		Heatmor [E]	Hippopotas [E]	Lampent [45]	Lapras [E]	Larvitar [E]	Lickitung [E]
		Litwick [43]	Miltank [E]	Munchlax [E]	Onix [4]	Phantump [28]	Rhyhorn [E]
		Roggenrola [E]	Shelmet [13]	Shuppet [19]	Skarmory [E]	Slowbro [1]	Slowking [1]
		Slowpoke [1]	Slugma [E]	Snorlax [E]	Steelix [4]	Stunfisk [E]	Sudowoodo [E]
		Swinub [E]	Torkoal [12]	Trevenant [28]	Trubbish [E]	Tyrunt [E]	Wailmer [E]
		Wooper [E]	Zangoose [E]	Zubat [E]			
Normal	Cut (HM01)	Absol [HM]	Aegislash [HM]	Aggron [HM]	Axew [HM]	Bagon [HM]	
		Barbaracle [HM]	Basculin [HM]	Beartic [HM]	Beedrill [HM]	Bellossom [HM]	Bellsprout [HM]
		Bibarel [HM]	Bidoof [HM]	Binacle [HM]	Bisharp [HM]	Braixen [HM]	Budew [HM]
		Bulbasaur [HM]	Bunnelby [HM]	Carnivine [HM]	Charizard [HM]	Charmander [HM]	Charmeleon [HM]
		Chesnaught [HM]	Chespin [HM]	Clauncher [HM]	Clawitzer [HM]	Corphish [HM]	Crawdaunt [HM]
		Crustle [HM]	Cubchoo [HM]	Dedenne [HM]	Delphox [HM]	Diggersby [HM]	Diglett [HM]
		Doublade [HM]	Dragonite [HM]	Drapion [HM]	Drifblim [HM]	Drifloon [HM]	Druddigon [HM]
		Dugtrio [HM]	Durant [HM]	Dwebble [HM]	Emolga [HM]	Escavalier [HM]	Espeon [HM]
		Espurr [HM]	Farfetch'd [HM]	Fennekin [HM]	Ferrothorn [HM]	Fraxure [HM]	Froakie [HM]
		Frogadier [HM]	Furret [HM]	Gabite [HM]	Gallade [HM]	Garchomp [HM]	Gible [HM]

AFTER THE HALL OF FAME

CENTRAL KALOS

COASTAL KALOS

MOUNTAIN KALOS

ADVENTURE DATA

	Move	Pokémon that can learn it					
Normal	Cut (HM01)	Gligar [HM]	Gliscor [HM]	Gloom [HM]	Greninja [HM]	Hawlucha [HM]	Haxorus [HM]
		Heatmor [HM]	Heliolisk [HM]	Helioptile [HM]	Heracross [HM]	Honedge [HM]	Inkay [HM]
		Ivysaur [HM]	Kangaskhan [HM]	Karrablast [HM]	Kecleon [HM]	Klefki [HM]	Krokorok [HM]
		Krookodile [HM]	Lairon [HM]	Lickilicky [HM]	Lickitung [HM]	Liepard [HM]	Linoone [HM]
		Malamar [HM]	Meowstic (Female) [HM]	Meowstic (Male) [HM]	Nidoking [HM]	Nidoqueen [HM]	Nidoran ♀ [HM]
		Nidoran♂ [HM]	Nidorina [HM]	Nidorino [HM]	Nincada [HM]	Ninjask [HM]	Noibat [HM]
		Noivern [HM]	Oddish [HM]	Pachirisu [HM]	Pancham [HM]	Pangoro [HM]	Panpour [HM]
		Pansage [HM]	Pansear [HM]	Patrat [HM]	Pawniard [HM]	Phantump [HM]	Pinsir [HM]
		Purrloin [HM]	Quilladin [HM]	Rhydon [HM]	Rhyperior [HM]	Roselia [HM]	Roserade [HM]
		Sableye [HM]	Salamence [HM]	Sandile [HM]	Sandshrew [HM]	Sandslash [HM]	Scizor [HM]
		Scolipede [HM]	Scyther [HM]	Sentret [HM]	Shedinja [HM]	Shelgon [HM]	Simipour [HM]
		Simisage [HM]	Simisear [HM]	Skarmory [HM]	Skorupi [HM]	Skuntank [HM]	Sneasel [HM]
		Steelix [HM]	Stunky [HM]	Sylveon [HM]	Teddiursa [HM]	Tentacool [HM]	Tentacruel [HM]
		Toxicroak [HM]	Trevenant [HM]	Tyranitar [HM]	Umbreon [HM]	Ursaring [HM]	Venusaur [HM]
		Vespiquen [HM]	Victreebel [HM]	Vileplume [HM]	Watchog [HM]	Weavile [HM]	Weepinbell [HM]
		Xerneas [HM]	Yveltal [HM]	Zigzagoon [HM]	Zoroark [HM]	Zorua [HM]	

D

	Move	Pokémon that can learn it					
Dark	Dark Pulse (TM97)	Absol [TM]	Aggron [TM]	Amaura [TM]	Arbok [TM]	Aurorus [TM]	Banette [TM]
		Bisharp [TM]	Blastoise [TM]	Carvanha [TM]	Chandelure [TM]	Clawitzer [1, 57, TM]	Crawdaunt [TM]
		Croagunk [TM]	Crobat [TM]	Deino [TM, E]	Drapion [TM]	Druddigon [TM]	Ekans [TM]
		Espurr [TM]	Frogadier [TM]	Furfrou [TM]	Garbodor [TM]	Gastly [36, TM]	Gengar [44, TM]
		Gligar [TM]	Gliscor [TM]	Gothita [E]	Gourgeist [TM]	Greninja [TM]	Gyarados [TM]
		Haunter [44, TM]	Heliolisk [TM]	Helioptile [TM]	Honchkrow [75, TM]	Houndoom [TM]	Houndour [TM]
		Hydreigon [TM]	Inkay [TM]	Krokorok [TM]	Krookodile [TM]	Lampent [TM]	Larvitar [32, TM]
		Liepard [TM]	Litleo [TM]	Litwick [TM]	Lucario [TM]	Malamar [TM]	Mawile [TM]
		Meowstic (Female) [TM]	Meowstic (Male) [TM]	Mightyena [TM]	Murkrow [TM]	Noibat [TM]	Noivern [TM]
		Pancham [TM]	Pangoro [TM]	Pawniard [TM]	Phantump [TM]	Poochyena [TM]	Pumpkaboo [TM]
		Pupitar [34, TM]	Purrloin [TM]	Pyroar [TM]	Rotom (Fan) [TM]	Rotom (Frost) [TM]	Rotom (Heat) [TM]
		Rotom (Mow) [TM]	Rotom (Wash) [TM]	Rotom [TM]	Sableye [TM]	Sandile [TM]	Scrafty [TM]
		Scraggy [TM]	Seviper [TM]	Sharpedo [TM]	Shuppet [TM]	Sigilyph [TM]	Skarmory [TM]
		Skorupi [TM]	Skuntank [TM]	Sneasel [TM]	Steelix [TM]	Stunky [TM]	Toxicroak [TM]
		Trevenant [TM]	Trubbish [TM]	Tyranitar [34, TM]	Tyrantrum [TM]	Tyrunt [TM]	Umbreon [TM]
		Weavile [47, TM]	Yveltal [44, TM]	Zoroark [TM]	Zorua [TM, E]	Zweilous [TM]	
Fairy	Dazzling Gleam (TM99)	Abra [TM]	Alakazam [TM]	Altaria [TM]	Aromatisse [TM]	Audino [TM]	Banette [TM]
		Bellossom [TM]	Budew [TM]	Carbink [TM]	Chimecho [TM]	Chinchou [TM]	Chingling [TM]
		Espeon [TM]	Flabébé [TM]	Floette [TM]	Florges [TM]	Gallade [TM]	Gardevoir [TM]
		Gastly [TM]	Gengar [TM]	Gloom [TM]	Granbull [TM]	Haunter [TM]	Hoppip [TM]
		Illumise [TM]	Jigglypuff [TM]	Jumpluff [TM]	Kadabra [TM]	Kirlia [TM]	Klefki [TM]
		Lanturn [TM]	Mr. Mime [TM]	Nosepass [TM]	Oddish [TM]	Probopass [TM]	Ralts [TM]
		Roselia [TM]	Roserade [TM]	Sableye [TM]	Shuppet [TM]	Sigilyph [TM]	Skiploom [TM]
		Slurpuff [TM]	Snubbull [TM]	Spritzee [TM]	Starmie [TM]	Staryu [TM]	Swablu [TM]
		Swirlix [TM]	Sylveon [TM]	Tentacool [TM]	Tentacruel [TM]	Vileplume [TM]	Volbeat [TM]
		Wigglytuff [TM]	Xerneas [TM]				
Bug	Defend Order	Vespiquen [17]					
Normal	Defense Curl	Azumarill [10]	Bagon [E]	Bibarel [9]	Bidoof [9, E]	Bonsly [E]	Bunnelby [E]
		Chespin [E]	Dunsparce [1]	Foongus [E]	Furret [1, 4]	Geodude [1]	Golem [1]
		Golett [1]	Golurk [1]	Graveler [1]	Igglybuff [5]	Jigglypuff [5]	Lickilicky [9]
		Lickitung [9]	Marill [10]	Miltank [5]	Munchlax [4]	Onix [E]	Pachirisu [E]
		Sandshrew [1]	Sandslash [1]	Scolipede [1]	Sentret [4]	Skiddo [E]	Snorlax [4]
		Sudowoodo [E]	Venipede [1]	Wailmer [E]	Whirlipede [1]	Wigglytuff [1]	
Flying	Defog	Chatot [E]	Drifloon [E]	Ducklett [6]	Hoothoot [E]	Pidgey [E]	Scyther [E]
		Swanna [1, 6]	Taillow [E]	Zubat [E]			
Ghost	Destiny Bond	Carvanha [E]	Delibird [E]	Drifloon [E]	Gastly [40]	Gengar [50]	Gulpin [E]
		Haunter [50]	Honedge [E]	Houndour [E]	Inkay [E]	Phantump [39]	Pumpkaboo [E]
		Qwilfish [1, 53]	Ralts [E]	Shuppet [E]	Trevenant [39]	Vespiquen [1, 53]	Wobbuffet [1]
		Wynaut [15]					
Fighting	Detect	Absol [1, 44]	Cubone [E]	Eevee [E]	Hawlucha [1]	Lucario [1]	Makuhita [E]
		Medicham [1, 11]	Meditite [11]	Mienfoo [9]	Mienshao [1, 9]	Patrat [11]	Riolu [E]
		Sableye [22]	Scraggy [E]	Starly [E]	Timburr [E]	Watchog [11]	Yanma [17]
		Yanmega [17]	Zangoose [33]	Zapdos [15]	Zorua [E]		

Pokémon Moves Reverse Lookup

Move	Pokémon that can learn it					
Dig (TM28) — Ground	Aggron [TM]	Arbok [TM]	Ariados [TM]	Aron [TM]	Audino [TM]	Axew [TM]
	Azumarill [TM]	Barbaracle [TM]	Beartic [TM]	Bibarel [TM]	Bidoof [TM]	Binacle [TM]
	Bisharp [TM]	Blastoise [TM]	Bonsly [TM]	Buizel [TM]	Bunnelby [33, TM]	Charizard [TM]
	Charmander [TM]	Charmeleon [TM]	Chesnaught [TM]	Chespin [TM]	Conkeldurr [TM]	Corphish [TM]
	Corsola [TM]	Crawdaunt [TM]	Croagunk [TM]	Crustle [TM]	Cubchoo [TM]	Cubone [TM]
	Dedenne [TM]	Delcatty [TM]	Diggersby [37, TM]	Diglett [34, TM]	Drapion [TM]	Druddigon [TM]
	Dugtrio [40, TM]	Dunsparce [31, TM]	Durant [41, TM]	Dwebble [TM]	Eevee [TM]	Ekans [TM]
	Espeon [TM]	Flareon [TM]	Floatzel [TM]	Flygon [TM]	Fraxure [TM]	Froakie [TM]
	Frogadier [TM]	Furfrou [TM]	Furret [TM]	Gabite [40, TM]	Garchomp [40, TM]	Geodude [TM]
	Gible [31, TM]	Glaceon [TM]	Gligar [TM]	Gliscor [TM]	Gogoat [TM]	Golduck [TM]
	Golem [TM]	Granbull [TM]	Graveler [TM]	Greninja [TM]	Gurdurr [TM]	Hariyama [TM]
	Hawlucha [TM]	Haxorus [TM]	Heatmor [TM]	Helioptile [TM]	Heracross [TM]	
	Hippopotas [19, TM]	Hippowdon [19, TM]	Igglybuff [TM]	Jigglypuff [TM]	Jolteon [TM]	Kangaskhan [TM]
	Kecleon [TM]	Krokorok [32, TM]	Krookodile [32, TM]	Lairon [TM]	Larvitar [TM]	Leafeon [TM]
	Ledian [TM]	Ledyba [TM]	Lickilicky [TM]	Lickitung [TM]	Linoone [TM]	Litleo [TM]
	Lucario [TM]	Machamp [TM]	Machoke [TM]	Machop [TM]	Makuhita [TM]	Mamoswine [TM]
	Marill [TM]	Marowak [TM]	Meowstic (Female) [TM]	Meowstic (Male) [TM]	Mienfoo [TM]	Mienshao [TM]
	Mightyena [TM]	Nidoking [TM]	Nidoqueen [TM]	Nidoran♀ [TM]	Nidoran♂ [TM]	Nidorina [TM]
	Nidorino [TM]	Nincada [45, TM]	Ninjask [TM]	Onix [43, TM]	Pachirisu [TM]	Pancham [TM]
	Pangoro [TM]	Panpour [TM]	Pansage [TM]	Pansear [TM]	Patrat [TM]	Pawniard [TM]
	Phantump [TM]	Pikachu [TM]	Piloswine [TM]	Pinsir [TM]	Politoed [TM]	Poliwag [TM]
	Poliwhirl [TM]	Poliwrath [TM]	Poochyena [TM]	Psyduck [TM]	Pupitar [TM]	Pyroar [TM]
	Quagsire [TM]	Quilladin [TM]	Raichu [TM]	Rhydon [TM]	Rhyhorn [TM]	Rhyperior [TM]
	Riolu [TM]	Sableye [TM]	Sandile [31, TM]	Sandshrew [30, TM]	Sandslash [30, TM]	Sawk [TM]
	Scolipede [TM]	Scrafty [TM]	Scraggy [TM]	Sentret [TM]	Seviper [TM]	Shedinja [TM]
	Shuckle [TM]	Simipour [TM]	Simisage [TM]	Simisear [TM]	Skiddo [TM]	Skitty [TM]
	Skorupi [TM]	Skuntank [TM]	Slowbro [TM]	Slowking [TM]	Slowpoke [TM]	Sneasel [TM]
	Snubbull [TM]	Spinarak [TM]	Spinda [TM]	Squirtle [TM]	Steelix [43, TM]	Stunfisk [TM]
	Stunky [TM]	Sudowoodo [TM]	Swinub [TM]	Sylveon [TM]	Teddiursa [TM]	Throh [TM]
	Timburr [TM]	Toxicroak [TM]	Trapinch [29, TM]	Trevenant [TM]	Tyranitar [TM]	Tyrantrum [TM]
	Tyrunt [TM]	Umbreon [TM]	Ursaring [TM]	Vaporeon [TM]	Vibrava [TM]	Wartortle [TM]
	Watchog [TM]	Weavile [TM]	Wigglytuff [TM]	Wooper [TM]	Wormadam (Sand) [TM]	Zangoose [TM]
	Zigzagoon [TM]	Zoroark [TM]	Zorua [TM]	Zygarde [10, TM]		
Disable — Normal	Alakazam [18]	Chimecho [E]	Chingling [E]	Drifloon [E]	Ekans [E]	Gastly [E]
	Golduck [11]	Horsea [E]	Jigglypuff [13]	Kadabra [18]	Kangaskhan [E]	Kecleon [E]
	Lickilicky [25]	Lickitung [25]	Mewtwo [1]	Nidoran♀ [E]	Nidoran♂ [E]	Psyduck [11]
	Pumpkaboo [E]	Ralts [E]	Shuppet [E]	Slowbro [19]	Slowking [19]	Slowpoke [19]
	Spinarak [E]	Spinda [E]	Spritzee [E]	Wigglytuff [1]	Yveltal [35]	Zangoose [E]
Disarming Voice — Fairy	Aromatisse [53]	Espurr [22]	Florges [1]	Jigglypuff [50]	Meowstic (Female) [22]	Meowstic (Male) [22]
	Panpour [E]	Pansage [E]	Pansear [E]	Pichu [E]	Spritzee [50]	Sylveon [1]
	Whismur [E]					
Discharge — Electric	Amaura [E]	Ampharos [40]	Chinchou [39]	Dedenne [50]	Electrike [41, E]	Emolga [50]
	Flaaffy [38]	Jolteon [37]	Lanturn [47]	Magnemite [43]	Magneton [51]	Magnezone [51]
	Manectric [49]	Mareep [32]	Minun [39]	Nosepass [39]	Pachirisu [41]	Pikachu [42]
	Plusle [E]	Probopass [39]	Rotom (Fan) [1, 64]	Rotom (Frost) [1, 64]	Rotom (Heat) [1, 64]	Rotom (Mow) [1, 64]
	Rotom (Wash) [1, 64]	Rotom [1, 64]	Stunfisk [25]	Zapdos [50]		
Dive — Water	Gorebyss [37]	Huntail [37]	Relicanth [57]	Wailmer [41]	Wailord [46]	
Dizzy Punch	Kangaskhan [34]	Kecleon [E]	Ledyba [E]	Miltank [E]	Reuniclus [41]	Spinda [28]
	Volbeat [E]					
Double Hit	Buizel [27]	Deino [E]	Doduo [32]	Floatzel [29]	Kangaskhan [19]	Mamoswine [33]
	Scizor [49]	Scyther [49]	Sneasel [E]	Zangoose [E]	Zweilous [1]	
	Bunnelby [20]	Cubone [E]	Diggersby [20]	Jolteon [17]	Nidoking [1]	Nidoqueen [1]
	Nidoran♀ [9]	Nidoran♂ [9]	Nidorina [9]	Nidorino [9]	Sawk [13]	Wooper [E]
	Zangoose [E]					
Double Slap — Normal	Alomomola [13]	Audino [10]	Buizel [E]	Bunnelby [10]	Delcatty [1]	Garbodor [14]
	Gothita [14]	Gothitelle [14]	Gothorita [14]	Jigglypuff [25]	Jynx [15]	Mienfoo [17]
	Mienshao [17]	Mime Jr. [11]	Mr. Mime [11]	Pichu [E]	Politoed [1]	Poliwag [15]
	Poliwhirl [15]	Poliwrath [1]	Skitty [15]	Trubbish [14]	Wigglytuff [1]	
Double Team (TM32)	Abomasnow [TM]	Abra [TM]	Absol [25, TM]	Accelgor [1, 8, TM]	Aegislash [TM]	Aerodactyl [TM]
	Aggron [TM]	Alakazam [TM]	Alomomola [TM]	Altaria [TM]	Amaura [TM]	Amoonguss [TM]
	Ampharos [TM]	Arbok [TM]	Ariados [TM]	Aromatisse [TM]	Aron [TM]	Articuno [TM]
	Audino [TM]	Aurorus [TM]	Avalugg [TM]	Axew [TM]	Azumarill [TM]	Azurill [TM]
	Bagon [TM]	Banette [TM]	Barbaracle [TM]	Barboach [TM]	Basculin [TM]	Beartic [TM]
	Beedrill [TM]	Bellossom [TM]	Bellsprout [TM]	Bergmite [TM]	Bibarel [TM]	Bidoof [TM]
	Binacle [TM]	Bisharp [TM]	Blastoise [TM]	Boldore [TM]	Bonsly [TM]	Braixen [TM]
	Budew [TM]	Buizel [TM]	Bulbasaur [TM]	Bunnelby [TM]	Butterfree [TM]	Carbink [TM]
	Carnivine [TM]	Carvanha [TM]	Chandelure [TM]	Charizard [TM]	Charmander [TM]	Charmeleon [TM]

Move	Pokémon that can learn it				
Double Team (TM32) *(Normal)*	Chatot [TM]	Chesnaught [TM]	Chespin [TM]	Chimecho [TM]	Chinchou [TM]	Chingling [TM]
	Clamperl [TM]	Clauncher [TM]	Clawitzer [TM]	Cloyster [TM]	Conkeldurr [TM]	Corphish [TM]
	Corsola [TM]	Crawdaunt [TM]	Croagunk [TM]	Crobat [TM]	Crustle [TM]	Cryogonal [TM]
	Cubchoo [TM]	Cubone [TM]	Dedenne [TM]	Deino [TM]	Delcatty [TM]	Delibird [TM]
	Delphox [TM]	Diggersby [TM]	Diglett [TM]	Dodrio [TM]	Doduo [TM]	Doublade [TM]
	Dragalge [28, TM]	Dragonair [TM]	Dragonite [TM]	Drapion [TM]	Dratini [TM]	Drifblim [TM]
	Drifloon [TM]	Druddigon [TM]	Ducklett [TM]	Dugtrio [TM]	Dunsparce [TM]	Duosion [TM]
	Durant [TM]	Dwebble [TM]	Eevee [TM]	Ekans [TM]	Electrike [TM]	Electrode [TM]
	Emolga [19, TM]	Escavalier [TM]	Espeon [TM]	Espurr [TM]	Exeggcute [TM]	Exeggutor [TM]
	Exploud [TM]	Farfetch'd [TM]	Fearow [TM]	Fennekin [TM]	Ferroseed [TM]	Ferrothorn [TM]
	Flaaffy [TM]	Flabébé [TM]	Flareon [TM]	Fletchinder [TM]	Fletchling [TM]	Floatzel [TM]
	Floette [TM]	Florges [TM]	Flygon [TM]	Foongus [TM]	Fraxure [TM]	Froakie [43, TM]
	Frogadier [48, TM]	Furfrou [TM]	Furret [TM]	Gabite [TM]	Gallade [1, 10, TM]	Garbodor [TM]
	Garchomp [TM]	Gardevoir [1, 10, TM]	Gastly [TM]	Gengar [TM]	Geodude [TM]	Gible [TM]
	Gigalith [TM]	Glaceon [TM]	Gligar [TM]	Gliscor [TM]	Gloom [TM]	Gogoat [TM]
	Golbat [TM]	Goldeen [TM]	Golduck [TM]	Golem [TM]	Golett [TM]	Golurk [TM]
	Goodra [TM]	Goomy [TM]	Gorebyss [TM]	Gothita [TM]	Gothitelle [TM]	Gothorita [TM]
	Gourgeist [TM]	Granbull [TM]	Graveler [TM]	Greninja [52, TM]	Grumpig [TM]	Gulpin [TM]
	Gurdurr [TM]	Gyarados [TM]	Hariyama [TM]	Haunter [TM]	Hawlucha [TM]	Haxorus [TM]
	Heatmor [TM]	Heliolisk [TM]	Helioptile [TM]	Heracross [TM]	Hippopotas [TM]	Hippowdon [TM]
	Honchkrow [TM]	Honedge [TM]	Hoothoot [TM]	Hoppip [TM]	Horsea [TM]	Houndoom [TM]
	Houndour [TM]	Huntail [TM]	Hydreigon [TM]	Igglybuff [TM]	Illumise [TM]	Inkay [TM]
	Ivysaur [TM]	Jigglypuff [TM]	Jolteon [TM]	Jumpluff [TM]	Jynx [TM]	Kadabra [TM]
	Kangaskhan [TM]	Karrablast [TM]	Kecleon [TM]	Kingdra [TM]	Kirlia [1, 10, TM]	Klefki [TM]
	Krokorok [TM]	Krookodile [TM]	Lairon [TM]	Lampent [TM]	Lanturn [TM]	Lapras [TM]
	Larvitar [TM]	Leafeon [TM]	Ledian [TM]	Ledyba [TM]	Lickilicky [TM]	Lickitung [TM]
	Liepard [TM]	Linoone [TM]	Litleo [TM]	Litwick [TM]	Lombre [TM]	Lotad [TM]
	Loudred [TM]	Lucario [TM]	Ludicolo [TM]	Lunatone [TM]	Luvdisc [TM]	Machamp [TM]
	Machoke [TM]	Machop [TM]	Magcargo [TM]	Magnemite [TM]	Magneton [TM]	Magnezone [TM]
	Makuhita [TM]	Malamar [TM]	Mamoswine [TM]	Manectric [TM]	Mantine [TM]	Mantyke [TM]
	Mareep [TM]	Marill [TM]	Marowak [TM]	Masquerain [TM]	Mawile [TM]	Medicham [TM]
	Meditite [TM]	Meowstic (Female) [TM]	Meowstic (Male) [TM]	Mewtwo [TM]	Mienfoo [TM]	Mienshao [TM]
	Mightyena [TM]	Miltank [TM]	Mime Jr. [TM]	Minun [TM]	Moltres [TM]	Mothim [TM]
	Mr. Mime [TM]	Munchlax [TM]	Murkrow [TM]	Nidoking [TM]	Nidoqueen [TM]	Nidoran♀ [TM]
	Nidoran♂ [TM]	Nidorina [TM]	Nidorino [TM]	Nincada [TM]	Ninjask [20, TM]	Noctowl [TM]
	Noibat [TM]	Noivern [TM]	Nosepass [TM]	Octillery [TM]	Oddish [TM]	Onix [TM]
	Pachirisu [TM]	Pancham [TM]	Pangoro [TM]	Panpour [TM]	Pansage [TM]	Pansear [TM]
	Patrat [TM]	Pawniard [TM]	Pelipper [TM]	Phantump [TM]	Pichu [TM]	Pidgeot [TM]
	Pidgeotto [TM]	Pidgey [TM]	Pikachu [21, TM]	Piloswine [TM]	Pinsir [TM]	Plusle [TM]
	Politoed [TM]	Poliwag [TM]	Poliwhirl [TM]	Poliwrath [TM]	Poochyena [TM]	Probopass [TM]
	Psyduck [TM]	Pumpkaboo [TM]	Pupitar [TM]	Purrloin [TM]	Pyroar [TM]	Quagsire [TM]
	Quilladin [TM]	Qwilfish [TM]	Raichu [TM]	Ralts [10, TM]	Relicanth [TM]	Remoraid [TM]
	Reuniclus [TM]	Rhydon [TM]	Rhyhorn [TM]	Rhyperior [TM]	Riolu [TM]	Roggenrola [TM]
	Roselia [TM]	Roserade [TM]	Rotom (Fan) [15, TM]	Rotom (Frost) [15, TM]	Rotom (Heat) [15, TM]	Rotom (Mow) [15, TM]
	Rotom (Wash) [15, TM]	Rotom [15, TM]	Sableye [TM]	Salamence [TM]	Sandile [TM]	Sandshrew [TM]
	Sandslash [TM]	Sawk [TM]	Scizor [TM]	Scolipede [TM]	Scrafty [TM]	Scraggy [TM]
	Scyther [37, TM]	Seadra [TM]	Seaking [TM]	Sentret [TM]	Seviper [TM]	Sharpedo [TM]
	Shedinja [TM]	Shelgon [TM]	Shellder [TM]	Shelmet [TM]	Shuckle [TM]	Shuppet [TM]
	Sigilyph [TM]	Simipour [TM]	Simisage [TM]	Simisear [TM]	Skarmory [TM]	Skiddo [TM]
	Skiploom [TM]	Skitty [TM]	Skorupi [TM]	Skrelp [28, TM]	Skuntank [TM]	Sliggoo [TM]
	Slowbro [TM]	Slowking [TM]	Slowpoke [TM]	Slugma [TM]	Slurpuff [TM]	Smoochum [TM]
	Sneasel [TM]	Snorlax [TM]	Snover [TM]	Snubbull [TM]	Solosis [TM]	Solrock [TM]
	Spearow [TM]	Spinarak [TM]	Spinda [TM]	Spoink [TM]	Spritzee [TM]	Squirtle [TM]
	Staraptor [13, TM]	Staravia [13, TM]	Starly [13, TM]	Starmie [TM]	Staryu [TM]	Steelix [TM]
	Stunfisk [TM]	Stunky [TM]	Sudowoodo [TM]	Surskit [TM]	Swablu [TM]	Swalot [TM]
	Swanna [TM]	Swellow [19, TM]	Swinub [TM]	Swirlix [TM]	Swoobat [TM]	Sylveon [TM]
	Taillow [19, TM]	Talonflame [TM]	Tauros [TM]	Teddiursa [TM]	Tentacool [TM]	Tentacruel [TM]
	Throh [TM]	Timburr [TM]	Torkoal [TM]	Toxicroak [TM]	Trapinch [TM]	Trevenant [TM]
	Trubbish [TM]	Tyranitar [TM]	Tyrantrum [TM]	Tyrunt [TM]	Umbreon [TM]	Ursaring [TM]
	Vanillish [TM]	Vanillite [TM]	Vanilluxe [TM]	Vaporeon [TM]	Venipede [TM]	Venusaur [TM]
	Vespiquen [TM]	Vibrava [TM]	Victreebel [TM]	Vileplume [TM]	Vivillon [TM]	Volbeat [5, TM]
	Voltorb [TM]	Wailmer [TM]	Wailord [TM]	Wartortle [TM]	Watchog [TM]	Weavile [TM]
	Weepinbell [TM]	Whirlipede [TM]	Whiscash [TM]	Whismur [TM]	Wigglytuff [TM]	Wingull [TM]
	Woobat [TM]	Wooper [TM]	Wormadam (Plant) [TM]	Wormadam (Sand) [TM]	Wormadam (Trash) [TM]	Xerneas [TM]
	Yanma [11, TM]	Yanmega [1, 11, TM]	Yveltal [5, TM]	Zangoose [TM]	Zapdos [TM]	Zigzagoon [TM]
	Zoroark [TM]	Zorua [TM]	Zubat [TM]	Zweilous [TM]	Zygarde [TM]	

Move	Pokémon that can learn it					
Normal						
Double-Edge	Absol [E]	Aggron [65]	Aron [46]	Audino [50]	Avalugg [56]	Azumarill [25]
	Bagon [55]	Basculin [36]	Bergmite [49]	Bidoof [E]	Bonsly [40]	Bulbasaur [27]
	Carvanha [E]	Chimecho [33]	Corphish [E]	Cubone [43]	Dunsparce [34]	Eevee [37]
	Escavalier [1]	Geodude [46]	Gible [E]	Gligar [E]	Gogoat [40]	Golem [58]
	Graveler [58]	Heracross [E]	Hippopotas [44]	Hippowdon [50]	Hoppip [E]	Ivysaur [31]
	Jigglypuff [53]	Kangaskhan [E]	Karrablast [56]	Lairon [56]	Ledian [48]	Ledyba [38]
	Marill [23]	Marowak [53]	Miltank [E]	Munchlax [E]	Nosepass [E]	Onix [49]
	Relicanth [50]	Salamence [1, 70]	Sandile [E]	Scolipede [55]	Sentret [E]	Shelgon [61]
	Shelmet [E]	Skiddo [38]	Skitty [42]	Snorlax [E]	Snover [E]	Snubbull [E]
	Spinda [46]	Starly [E]	Steelix [49]	Stunky [E]	Sudowoodo [40]	Swinub [E]
	Teddiursa [E]	Venipede [43]	Venusaur [31]	Volbeat [45]	Wailmer [E]	Whirlipede [50]
	Wigglytuff [1]	Yanma [E]				
Dragon						
Draco Meteor	Altaria [T]	Axew [T]	Bagon [T]	Deino [T]	Dragalge [T]	Dragonair [T]
	Dragonite [T]	Dratini [T]	Druddigon [T]	Flygon [T]	Fraxure [T]	Gabite [T]
	Garchomp [T]	Gible [T]	Goodra [T]	Goomy [T]	Haxorus [T]	Hydreigon [T]
	Kingdra [T]	Noibat [T]	Noivern [T]	Salamence [T]	Shelgon [T]	Sliggoo [T]
	Tyrantrum [T]	Tyrunt [T]	Vibrava [T]	Zweilous [T]	Zygarde [T]	
Dragon Breath	Aerodactyl [E]	Altaria [35]	Bagon [31]	Deino [17]	Dratini [E]	Flygon [35]
	Gible [E]	Goodra [18]	Goomy [18]	Horsea [E]	Hydreigon [17]	Onix [25]
	Salamence [32]	Shelgon [32]	Sliggoo [18]	Steelix [25]	Vibrava [35]	Zweilous [17]
	Zygarde [1]					
Dragon Claw (TM02)	Aerodactyl [TM]	Aggron [TM]	Altaria [TM]	Axew [28, TM]	Bagon [50, TM]	Barbaracle [TM]
	Charizard [1, TM]	Charmander [TM]	Charmeleon [TM]	Chesnaught [TM]	Dragonite [TM]	Druddigon [27, TM]
	Flygon [55, TM]	Fraxure [28, TM]	Gabite [33, TM]	Garchomp [33, TM]	Gible [27, TM]	Haxorus [28, TM]
	Krookodile [TM]	Noivern [TM]	Pangoro [TM]	Salamence [61, TM]	Scrafty [TM]	Scraggy [TM]
	Shelgon [55, TM]	Tyranitar [TM]	Tyrantrum [37, TM]	Tyrunt [37, TM]	Yveltal [TM]	
Dragon Dance	Altaria [34]	Axew [32]	Bagon [E]	Barboach [E]	Charmander [E]	Corphish [E]
	Dragonair [61]	Dragonite [61]	Dratini [51, E]	Fraxure [32]	Gyarados [44]	Haxorus [32]
	Horsea [38]	Kingdra [48]	Lapras [E]	Larvitar [E]	Scraggy [E]	Seadra [48]
	Tyrunt [E]	Zygarde [72]				
Dragon Pulse	Altaria [48]	Ampharos [1, 65]	Axew [41, E]	Bagon [E]	Charmander [E]	Clawitzer [1, 63]
	Deino [32]	Dragalge [53]	Dratini [E]	Fraxure [42]	Goodra [47]	Goomy [42]
	Haxorus [42]	Horsea [42]	Hydreigon [32]	Kingdra [1, 57]	Lapras [E]	Lucario [1, 60]
	Noivern [1, 70]	Seadra [57]	Skrelp [49]	Sliggoo [47]	Squirtle [E]	Swablu [42]
	Zweilous [32]	Zygarde [63]				
Dragon Rage	Axew [10]	Bagon [E]	Charizard [17]	Charmander [16]	Charmeleon [17]	Deino [1]
	Dragonair [15]	Dragonite [15]	Dratini [15]	Druddigon [18]	Fraxure [1, 10]	Gabite [7]
	Garchomp [1, 7]	Gible [7]	Gyarados [23]	Haxorus [1, 10]	Horsea [E]	Hydreigon [1]
	Zweilous [1]					
Dragon Rush	Aron [E]	Bagon [E]	Charmander [E]	Deino [42]	Dragonair [47]	Dragonite [47]
	Dratini [41, E]	Gabite [49]	Garchomp [55]	Gible [37]	Hydreigon [42]	Rhyhorn [E]
	Swablu [E]	Yveltal [63]	Zweilous [42]			
Dragon Tail (TM82)	Aggron [TM]	Amaura [TM]	Arbok [TM]	Aurorus [TM]	Blastoise [TM]	Charizard [TM]
	Deino [TM]	Dragalge [1, 59, TM]	Dragonair [33, TM]	Dragonite [33, TM]	Dratini [31, TM]	Druddigon [45, TM]
	Flygon [45, TM]	Fraxure [TM]	Garchomp [TM]	Goodra [TM]	Gyarados [TM]	Haxorus [TM]
	Heliolisk [TM]	Helioptile [TM]	Hydreigon [TM]	Krookodile [TM]	Lickilicky [TM]	Lickitung [TM]
	Nidoking [TM]	Nidoqueen [TM]	Onix [TM]	Rhydon [TM]	Rhyperior [TM]	Salamence [80, TM]
	Scrafty [TM]	Scraggy [TM]	Seviper [TM]	Slowking [TM]	Steelix [TM]	Tyranitar [TM]
	Tyrantrum [30, TM]	Tyrunt [30, TM]	Zweilous [TM]	Zygarde [TM]		
Fighting						
Drain Punch	Croagunk [E]	Ledyba [E]	Meditite [E]	Mienfoo [33]	Mienshao [33]	Scraggy [E]
	Timburr [E]					
Fairy						
Draining Kiss	Aromatisse [21]	Audino [E]	Jynx [1]	Klefki [18]	Slurpuff [31]	Spritzee [21]
	Swirlix [31]	Sylveon [20]	Vivillon [25]			
Psychic						
Dream Eater (TM85)	Abra [TM]	Absol [TM]	Alakazam [TM]	Altaria [TM]	Amaura [TM]	Aromatisse [TM]
	Audino [TM]	Aurorus [TM]	Banette [TM]	Braixen [TM]	Butterfree [TM]	Chandelure [TM]
	Chimecho [TM]	Chingling [TM]	Delcatty [TM]	Delphox [TM]	Drifblim [TM]	Drifloon [TM]
	Dunsparce [TM]	Duosion [TM]	Espeon [TM]	Espurr [TM]	Exeggcute [TM]	Exeggutor [TM]
	Fennekin [TM]	Gallade [TM]	Gardevoir [73, TM]	Gastly [33, TM]	Gengar [39, TM]	Gothita [TM]
	Gothitelle [TM]	Gothorita [TM]	Gourgeist [TM]	Grumpig [TM]	Gulpin [TM]	Haunter [39, TM]
	Honchkrow [TM]	Hoothoot [57, TM]	Houndoom [TM]	Houndour [TM]	Igglybuff [TM]	Jigglypuff [TM]
	Jynx [TM]	Kadabra [TM]	Kirlia [59, TM]	Lampent [TM]	Lapras [TM]	Lickilicky [TM]
	Lickitung [TM]	Liepard [TM]	Litwick [TM]	Lunatone [TM]	Medicham [TM]	Meditite [TM]
	Meowstic (Female) [TM]	Meowstic (Male) [TM]	Mewtwo [TM]	Mime Jr. [TM]	Mothim [TM]	Mr. Mime [TM]
	Murkrow [TM]	Noctowl [1, 67, TM]	Noibat [TM]	Noivern [TM]	Phantump [TM]	Pumpkaboo [TM]
	Purrloin [TM]	Ralts [49, TM]	Reuniclus [TM]	Rotom (Fan) [TM]	Rotom (Frost) [TM]	Rotom (Heat) [TM]
	Rotom (Mow) [TM]	Rotom (Wash) [TM]	Rotom [TM]	Sableye [TM]	Shedinja [TM]	Shuppet [TM]
	Sigilyph [TM]	Skitty [TM]	Slowbro [TM]	Slowking [TM]	Slowpoke [TM]	Slurpuff [TM]
	Smoochum [TM]	Sneasel [TM]	Solosis [TM]	Solrock [TM]	Spinda [TM]	Spoink [TM]

	Move	Pokémon that can learn it					
Psychic	Dream Eater (TM85)	Spritzee [TM]	Starmie [TM]	Swablu [TM]	Swalot [TM]	Swirlix [TM]	Swoobat [TM]
		Trevenant [TM]	Umbreon [TM]	Vivillon [TM]	Watchog [TM]	Weavile [TM]	Wigglytuff [TM]
		Woobat [TM]	Wormadam (Plant) [TM]	Wormadam (Sand) [TM]	Wormadam (Trash) [TM]	Yanma [TM]	Yanmega [TM]
		Yveltal [TM]					
Flying	Drill Peck	Dodrio [47]	Doduo [41]	Fearow [47]	Murkrow [E]	Skarmory [E]	Spearow [37]
		Zapdos [1, 71]					
Ground	Drill Run	Dunsparce [43]	Fearow [1, 53]	Karrablast [E]	Rhydon [47]	Rhyhorn [45]	Rhyperior [47]
Dragon	Dual Chop	Axew [13]	Fraxure [13]	Gabite [24]	Garchomp [24]	Haxorus [13]	
Fighting	Dynamic Punch	Conkeldurr [37]	Croagunk [E]	Golett [30]	Golurk [30]	Gurdurr [37]	Machamp [55]
		Machoke [55]	Machop [49]	Makuhita [E]	Meditite [E]	Poliwrath [32]	Timburr [34]

E

	Move	Pokémon that can learn it					
Ground	Earth Power	Barboach [E]	Corsola [47]	Deino [E]	Diglett [29]	Dugtrio [33]	Flygon [39]
		Magcargo [1, 67]	Nidoking [43]	Nidoqueen [43]	Nosepass [43]	Probopass [43]	Slugma [55, E]
		Stunfisk [E]	Trapinch [39, E]	Vibrava [39]			
Ground	Earthquake (TM26)	Abomasnow [TM]	Aerodactyl [TM]	Aggron [TM]	Altaria [TM]	Arbok [TM]	Aron [TM]
		Aurorus [TM]	Avalugg [TM]	Barbaracle [TM]	Barboach [39, TM]	Binacle [TM]	Blastoise [TM]
		Boldore [TM]	Bunnelby [49, TM]	Charizard [TM]	Chesnaught [TM]	Conkeldurr [TM]	Corsola [TM]
		Croagunk [TM]	Crustle [TM]	Cubone [TM]	Diggersby [57, TM]	Diglett [40, TM]	Dragonite [TM]
		Drapion [TM]	Druddigon [TM]	Dugtrio [50, TM]	Dunsparce [TM]	Dwebble [TM]	Ekans [TM]
		Exploud [TM]	Flygon [TM]	Gabite [TM]	Gallade [TM]	Garchomp [TM]	Geodude [39, TM]
		Gible [TM]	Gigalith [TM]	Gligar [TM]	Gliscor [TM]	Gogoat [60, TM]	Golem [47, TM]
		Golett [45, TM]	Golurk [50, TM]	Goodra [TM]	Granbull [TM]	Graveler [47, TM]	Gyarados [TM]
		Hariyama [TM]	Haxorus [TM]	Heracross [TM]	Hippopotas [37, TM]	Hippowdon [40, TM]	Hydreigon [TM]
		Kangaskhan [TM]	Krokorok [48, TM]	Krookodile [54, TM]	Lairon [TM]	Larvitar [46, TM]	Lickilicky [TM]
		Lickitung [TM]	Loudred [TM]	Lucario [TM]	Lunatone [TM]	Machamp [TM]	Machoke [TM]
		Machop [TM]	Magcargo [TM]	Makuhita [TM]	Mamoswine [46, TM]	Mantine [TM]	Mantyke [TM]
		Marowak [TM]	Mewtwo [TM]	Miltank [TM]	Munchlax [TM]	Nidoking [TM]	Nidoqueen [TM]
		Nosepass [TM]	Onix [TM]	Pangoro [TM]	Piloswine [46, TM]	Pinsir [TM]	Politoed [TM]
		Poliwhirl [TM]	Poliwrath [TM]	Probopass [TM]	Pupitar [54, TM]	Quagsire [36, TM]	Relicanth [TM]
		Rhydon [62, TM]	Rhyhorn [56, TM]	Rhyperior [62, TM]	Riolu [TM]	Roggenrola [TM]	Salamence [TM]
		Sandile [43, TM]	Sandshrew [46, TM]	Sandslash [46, TM]	Sawk [TM]	Scolipede [TM]	Seviper [TM]
		Sharpedo [TM]	Shuckle [TM]	Slowbro [TM]	Slowking [TM]	Slowpoke [TM]	Snorlax [TM]
		Snubbull [TM]	Solrock [TM]	Steelix [TM]	Stunfisk [TM]	Sudowoodo [TM]	Swalot [TM]
		Swinub [37, TM]	Tauros [TM]	Teddiursa [TM]	Throh [TM]	Torkoal [TM]	Toxicroak [TM]
		Trapinch [55, TM]	Trevenant [TM]	Tyranitar [54, TM]	Tyrantrum [47, TM]	Tyrunt [44, TM]	Ursaring [TM]
		Venusaur [TM]	Vibrava [TM]	Wailmer [TM]	Wailord [TM]	Whiscash [45, TM]	Wooper [33, TM]
		Wormadam (Sand) [TM]	Zygarde [55, TM]				
Normal	Echoed Voice (TM49)	Absol [TM]	Altaria [TM]	Amaura [TM]	Ampharos [TM]	Aromatisse [13, TM]	Audino [TM]
		Aurorus [TM]	Beartic [TM]	Bibarel [TM]	Bidoof [TM]	Braixen [TM]	Buizel [TM]
		Bulbasaur [TM]	Charizard [TM]	Charmander [TM]	Charmeleon [TM]	Chatot [37, TM]	Chimecho [TM]
		Chingling [TM]	Cubchoo [TM]	Cubone [TM]	Delcatty [TM]	Delphox [TM]	Diglett [TM]
		Dodrio [TM]	Doduo [TM]	Dugtrio [TM]	Eevee [TM]	Espeon [TM]	Espurr [TM]
		Exploud [TM]	Fearow [TM]	Fennekin [TM]	Flaaffy [TM]	Flabébé [TM]	Flareon [TM]
		Floatzel [TM]	Floette [TM]	Florges [TM]	Froakie [TM]	Frogadier [TM]	Furfrou [TM]
		Furret [TM]	Gallade [TM]	Gardevoir [TM]	Glaceon [TM]	Greninja [TM]	Hoothoot [25, TM]
		Hydreigon [TM]	Igglybuff [TM]	Ivysaur [TM]	Jigglypuff [TM]	Jolteon [TM]	Jynx [TM]
		Kirlia [TM]	Lapras [TM]	Leafeon [TM]	Liepard [TM]	Linoone [TM]	Litleo [33, TM]
		Lombre [TM]	Lotad [TM]	Loudred [TM]	Ludicolo [TM]	Mareep [TM]	Marowak [TM]
		Meowstic (Female) [TM]	Meowstic (Male) [TM]	Miltank [TM]	Minun [TM]	Nidoking [TM]	Nidoqueen [TM]
		Nidoran♀ [TM]	Nidoran♂ [TM]	Nidorina [TM]	Nidorino [TM]	Noctowl [27, TM]	Noibat [TM]
		Noivern [TM]	Pachirisu [TM]	Pancham [TM]	Pangoro [TM]	Pelipper [TM]	Pichu [TM]
		Pikachu [TM]	Plusle [TM]	Politoed [TM]	Purrloin [TM]	Pyroar [33, TM]	Raichu [TM]
		Ralts [TM]	Sentret [TM]	Skitty [TM]	Slowbro [TM]	Slowking [TM]	Slowpoke [TM]
		Smoochum [TM]	Spearow [TM]	Spritzee [13, TM]	Staraptor [TM]	Staravia [TM]	Starly [TM]
		Swablu [TM]	Swellow [TM]	Sylveon [TM]	Taillow [TM]	Umbreon [TM]	Vaporeon [TM]
		Venusaur [TM]	Wailmer [TM]	Wailord [TM]	Whismur [TM]	Wigglytuff [TM]	Wingull [TM]
		Xerneas [TM]	Zigzagoon [TM]				
Electric	Eerie Impulse	Dedenne [E]	Electrike [E]	Electrode [8]	Heliolisk [1]	Lanturn [1]	Mareep [E]
		Stunfisk [E]	Voltorb [10]	Wooper [E]			

AFTER THE HALL OF FAME

CENTRAL KALOS

COASTAL KALOS

MOUNTAIN KALOS

ADVENTURE DATA

	Move	Pokémon that can learn it					
Normal	Egg Bomb	Exeggutor [27]					
Electric	Electric Terrain Electrify	Helioptile [E] Heliolisk [1]	Magneton [11] Helioptile [45]	Magnezone [11]	Manectric [1, 70]	Mareep [E]	
Electric	Electro Ball	Ampharos [25] Lanturn [30] Pachirisu [25] Rotom (Mow) [43]	Chinchou [28] Magnemite [32] Pikachu [18] Rotom (Wash) [43]	Electrike [E] Magneton [34] Plusle [29] Rotom [43]	Electrode [29] Magnezone [34] Rotom (Fan) [43] Voltorb [29]	Emolga [26] Mareep [22] Rotom (Frost) [43]	Flaaffy [25] Minun [29] Rotom (Heat) [43]
Electric	Electroweb	Spinarak [E]					
Dark	Embargo (TM63)	Abra [TM] Braixen [TM] Duosion [TM] Gothorita [19, TM] Kadabra [TM] Lunatone [21, TM] Pangoro [TM] Sandile [22, TM] Toxicroak [TM] Zorua [41, TM]	Alakazam [TM] Chandelure [TM] Fennekin [TM] Haunter [TM] Krokorok [22, TM] Malamar [TM] Pawniard [41, TM] Shuppet [38, TM] Weavile [1, TM]	Banette [40, TM] Croagunk [TM] Gastly [TM] Honchkrow [TM] Krookodile [22, TM] Mawile [TM] Poochyena [41, TM] Sneasel [TM] Woobat [TM]	Barbaracle [TM] Delphox [TM] Gengar [TM] Houndoom [41, TM] Lampent [TM] Mewtwo [TM] Purrloin [TM] Solosis [TM] Yveltal [TM]	Binacle [TM] Drifblim [TM] Gothita [19, TM] Houndour [37, TM] Liepard [TM] Mightyena [47, TM] Reuniclus [TM] Solrock [21, TM] Zangoose [19, TM]	Bisharp [41, TM] Drifloon [TM] Gothitelle [19, TM] Inkay [TM] Litwick [TM] Murkrow [TM] Sableye [TM] Swoobat [TM] Zoroark [44, TM]
Fire	Ember	Bagon [25] Fennekin [5] Litleo [5] Shelgon [25]	Braixen [5] Flareon [9] Litwick [1] Slugma [5]	Charizard [1, 7] Fletchinder [17] Magcargo [1, 5] Talonflame [17]	Charmander [7] Houndoom [1] Moltres [1] Torkoal [1]	Charmeleon [1, 7] Houndour [1] Pyroar [5]	Delphox [5] Lampent [1] Salamence [25]
Normal	Encore	Abra [E] Chatot [E] Illumise [25, E] Pichu [E] Shelmet [E] Wynaut [1]	Amaura [44] Cubchoo [E] Ledyba [E] Plusle [17] Shuckle [5]	Audino [E] Emolga [38] Machop [E] Poliwag [E] Spinda [E]	Aurorus [46] Gulpin [23] Mime Jr. [18] Psyduck [E] Swalot [23]	Azurill [E] Hawlucha [20] Minun [17] Purrloin [E] Volbeat [E]	Bellsprout [E] Hoppip [E] Mr. Mime [18] Ralts [E] Wooper [E]
Normal	Endeavor	Aron [E] Doduo [46, E] Marowak [49] Staraptor [18] Taillow [26]	Axew [E] Dunsparce [46] Poliwag [E] Staravia [18] Whismur [5]	Beedrill [40] Duosion [28] Pyroar [28] Starly [17] Woobat [47]	Corphish [E] Hawlucha [36] Reuniclus [28] Swellow [28]	Cubone [41] Kangaskhan [E] Slurpuff [21] Swirlix [21]	Dodrio [54] Litleo [28] Solosis [28] Swoobat [47]
Normal	Endure	Alomomola [E] Bulbasaur [E] Diglett [E] Geodude [E] Karrablast [8] Moltres [22] Pichu [E] Scyther [E] Surskit [E]	Axew [E] Clamperl [E] Dunsparce [40] Goomy [E] Litwick [E] Nidoran♀ [E] Piloswine [14] Shelmet [E] Swinub [14]	Bagon [E] Clauncher [E] Durant [E] Hariyama [47] Makuhita [37] Nidoran♂ [E] Poliwag [E] Skarmory [E] Throh [E]	Beartic [25] Corsola [35] Dwebble [E] Heracross [1] Mamoswine [14] Nincada [E] Riolu [1] Spoink [E] Timburr [E]	Bidoof [E] Cubchoo [25] Eevee [E] Hoppip [E] Mienfoo [E] Nosepass [E] Sandshrew [E] Stunfisk [30] Torkoal [E]	Bonsly [E] Cubone [E] Foongus [E] Kangaskhan [43] Miltank [E] Pachirisu [17] Sawk [41] Sudowoodo [E] Trapinch [E]
Grass	Energy Ball (TM53)	Abomasnow [TM] Bellossom [TM] Chandelure [TM] Escavalier [TM] Flabébé [TM] Gengar [TM] Gourgeist [TM] Jynx [TM] Lombre [TM] Meowstic (Male) [TM] Pansage [TM] Roserade [TM] Slurpuff [36, TM] Trevenant [TM] Woobat [TM]	Abra [TM] Bellsprout [TM] Chesnaught [TM] Espurr [TM] Floette [TM] Gloom [TM] Grumpig [TM] Kadabra [TM] Lotad [45, TM] Mewtwo [TM] Phantump [TM] Shelmet [TM] Snover [TM] Venusaur [TM] Wormadam (Plant) [TM]	Accelgor [TM] Budew [TM] Chespin [TM] Exeggcute [TM] Florges [TM] Gogoat [TM] Haunter [TM] Karrablast [TM] Ludicolo [TM] Mothim [TM] Pumpkaboo [TM] Sigilyph [TM] Solosis [TM] Victreebel [TM]	Alakazam [TM] Bulbasaur [TM] Chimecho [TM] Exeggutor [TM] Foongus [TM] Gothita [TM] Hoppip [TM] Lampent [TM] Masquerain [TM] Mr. Mime [TM] Quilladin [TM] Simisage [TM] Spritzee [TM] Vileplume [TM]	Amoonguss [TM] Butterfree [TM] Duosion [TM] Ferroseed [TM] Gardevoir [TM] Gothitelle [TM] Ivysaur [TM] Leafeon [TM] Medicham [TM] Octillery [TM] Reuniclus [TM] Skiddo [TM] Swirlix [36, TM] Vivillon [TM]	Aromatisse [TM] Carnivine [TM] Durant [TM] Ferrothorn [TM] Gastly [TM] Gothorita [TM] Jumpluff [TM] Litwick [TM] Meowstic (Female) [TM] Oddish [TM] Roselia [TM] Skiploom [TM] Swoobat [TM] Weepinbell [TM]
Normal	Entrainment	Audino [25] Litleo [E] Remoraid [E]	Chingling [25] Luvdisc [E]	Clauncher [E] Minun [1, 63]	Dedenne [39] Pancham [42]	Durant [46] Pangoro [1, 45]	Hawlucha [E] Plusle [1, 63]
Fire	Eruption	Torkoal [E]					

	Move	Pokémon that can learn it					
Normal	Explosion (TM64)	Boldore [55, TM]	Bonsly [TM]	Carbink [TM]	Cloyster [TM]	Corsola [TM]	Cryogonal [TM]
		Drifblim [60, TM]	Drifloon [50, TM]	Duosion [TM]	Electrode [57, TM]	Exeggcute [TM]	Exeggutor [TM]
		Ferroseed [55, TM]	Ferrothorn [67, TM]	Garbodor [59, TM]	Gastly [TM]	Gengar [TM]	Geodude [43, TM]
		Gigalith [TM]	Golem [53, TM]	Gourgeist [1, 75, TM]	Graveler [53, TM]	Gulpin [TM]	Haunter [TM]
		Lickilicky [TM]	Lunatone [49, TM]	Magcargo [TM]	Magnemite [TM]	Magneton [TM]	Magnezone [TM]
		Nosepass [TM]	Onix [TM]	Probopass [TM]	Pumpkaboo [TM]	Qwilfish [TM]	Reuniclus [TM]
		Roggenrola [40, TM]	Shellder [TM]	Skuntank [61, TM]	Solosis [TM]	Solrock [49, TM]	Steelix [TM]
		Stunky [49, TM]	Sudowoodo [TM]	Swalot [TM]	Torkoal [TM]	Trubbish [47, TM]	Vanillish [TM]
		Vanillite [TM]	Vanilluxe [TM]	Voltorb [47, TM]			
Psychic	Extrasensory	Budew [E]	Chimecho [46]	Exeggcute [47]	Greninja [49]	Hoothoot [45]	Meowstic (Female) [35]
		Noctowl [52]	Spoink [E]	Whismur [E]	Zorua [E]		
Normal	Extreme Speed	Dratini [E]	Lucario [1, 65]	Zygarde [88]			

F

	Move	Pokémon that can learn it					
Normal	Facade (TM42)	Abomasnow [TM]	Abra [TM]	Absol [TM]	Accelgor [TM]	Aegislash [TM]	Aerodactyl [TM]
		Aggron [TM]	Alakazam [TM]	Alomomola [TM]	Altaria [TM]	Amaura [TM]	Amoonguss [TM]
		Ampharos [TM]	Arbok [TM]	Ariados [TM]	Aromatisse [TM]	Aron [TM]	Articuno [TM]
		Audino [TM]	Aurorus [TM]	Avalugg [TM]	Axew [TM]	Azumarill [TM]	Azurill [TM]
		Bagon [TM]	Banette [TM]	Barbaracle [TM]	Barboach [TM]	Basculin [TM]	Beartic [TM]
		Beedrill [TM]	Bellossom [TM]	Bellsprout [TM]	Bergmite [TM]	Bibarel [TM]	Bidoof [TM]
		Binacle [TM]	Bisharp [TM]	Blastoise [TM]	Boldore [TM]	Bonsly [TM]	Braixen [TM]
		Budew [TM]	Buizel [TM]	Bulbasaur [TM]	Bunnelby [47, TM]	Butterfree [TM]	Carbink [TM]
		Carnivine [TM]	Carvanha [TM]	Chandelure [TM]	Charizard [TM]	Charmander [TM]	Charmeleon [TM]
		Chatot [TM]	Chesnaught [TM]	Chespin [TM]	Chimecho [TM]	Chinchou [TM]	Chingling [TM]
		Clamperl [TM]	Clauncher [TM]	Clawitzer [TM]	Cloyster [TM]	Conkeldurr [TM]	Corphish [TM]
		Corsola [TM]	Crawdaunt [TM]	Croagunk [TM]	Crobat [TM]	Crustle [TM]	Cryogonal [TM]
		Cubchoo [TM]	Cubone [TM]	Dedenne [TM]	Deino [TM]	Delcatty [TM]	Delibird [TM]
		Delphox [TM]	Diggersby [53, TM]	Diglett [TM]	Dodrio [TM]	Doduo [TM]	Doublade [TM]
		Dragalge [TM]	Dragonair [TM]	Dragonite [TM]	Drapion [TM]	Dratini [TM]	Drifblim [TM]
		Drifloon [TM]	Druddigon [TM]	Ducklett [TM]	Dugtrio [TM]	Dunsparce [TM]	Duosion [TM]
		Durant [TM]	Dwebble [TM]	Eevee [TM]	Ekans [TM]	Electrike [TM]	Electrode [TM]
		Emolga [TM]	Escavalier [TM]	Espeon [TM]	Espurr [TM]	Exeggcute [TM]	Exeggutor [TM]
		Exploud [TM]	Farfetch'd [TM]	Fearow [TM]	Fennekin [TM]	Ferroseed [TM]	Ferrothorn [TM]
		Flaaffy [TM]	Flabébé [TM]	Flareon [TM]	Fletchinder [TM]	Fletchling [TM]	Floatzel [TM]
		Floette [TM]	Florges [TM]	Flygon [TM]	Foongus [TM]	Fraxure [TM]	Froakie [TM]
		Frogadier [TM]	Furfrou [TM]	Furret [TM]	Gabite [TM]	Gallade [TM]	Garbodor [TM]
		Garchomp [TM]	Gardevoir [TM]	Gastly [TM]	Gengar [TM]	Geodude [TM]	Gible [TM]
		Gigalith [TM]	Glaceon [TM]	Gligar [TM]	Gliscor [TM]	Gloom [TM]	Gogoat [TM]
		Golbat [TM]	Goldeen [TM]	Golduck [TM]	Golem [TM]	Golett [TM]	Golurk [TM]
		Goodra [TM]	Goomy [TM]	Gorebyss [TM]	Gothita [TM]	Gothitelle [TM]	Gothorita [TM]
		Gourgeist [TM]	Granbull [TM]	Graveler [TM]	Greninja [TM]	Grumpig [TM]	Gulpin [TM]
		Gurdurr [TM]	Gyarados [TM]	Hariyama [TM]	Haunter [TM]	Hawlucha [TM]	Haxorus [TM]
		Heatmor [TM]	Heliolisk [TM]	Helioptile [TM]	Heracross [TM]	Hippopotas [TM]	Hippowdon [TM]
		Honchkrow [TM]	Honedge [TM]	Hoothoot [TM]	Hoppip [TM]	Horsea [TM]	Houndoom [TM]
		Houndour [TM]	Huntail [TM]	Hydreigon [TM]	Igglybuff [TM]	Illumise [TM]	Inkay [TM]
		Ivysaur [TM]	Jigglypuff [TM]	Jolteon [TM]	Jumpluff [TM]	Jynx [TM]	Kadabra [TM]
		Kangaskhan [TM]	Karrablast [TM]	Kecleon [TM]	Kingdra [TM]	Kirlia [TM]	Klefki [TM]
		Krokorok [TM]	Krookodile [TM]	Lairon [TM]	Lampent [TM]	Lanturn [TM]	Lapras [TM]
		Larvitar [TM]	Leafeon [TM]	Ledian [TM]	Ledyba [TM]	Lickilicky [TM]	Lickitung [TM]
		Liepard [TM]	Linoone [TM]	Litleo [TM]	Litwick [TM]	Lombre [TM]	Lotad [TM]
		Loudred [TM]	Lucario [TM]	Ludicolo [TM]	Lunatone [TM]	Luvdisc [TM]	Machamp [TM]
		Machoke [TM]	Machop [TM]	Magcargo [TM]	Magnemite [TM]	Magneton [TM]	Magnezone [TM]
		Makuhita [TM]	Malamar [TM]	Mamoswine [TM]	Manectric [TM]	Mantine [TM]	Mantyke [TM]
		Mareep [TM]	Marill [TM]	Marowak [TM]	Masquerain [TM]	Mawile [TM]	Medicham [TM]
		Meditite [TM]	Meowstic (Female) [TM]	Meowstic (Male) [TM]	Mewtwo [TM]	Mienfoo [TM]	Mienshao [TM]
		Mightyena [TM]	Miltank [TM]	Mime Jr. [TM]	Minun [TM]	Moltres [TM]	Mothim [TM]
		Mr. Mime [TM]	Munchlax [TM]	Murkrow [TM]	Nidoking [TM]	Nidoqueen [TM]	Nidoran ♀ [TM]
		Nidoran ♂ [TM]	Nidorina [TM]	Nidorino [TM]	Nincada [TM]	Ninjask [TM]	Noctowl [TM]
		Noibat [TM]	Noivern [TM]	Nosepass [TM]	Octillery [TM]	Oddish [TM]	Onix [TM]
		Pachirisu [TM]	Pancham [TM]	Pangoro [TM]	Panpour [TM]	Pansage [TM]	Pansear [TM]
		Patrat [TM]	Pawniard [TM]	Pelipper [TM]	Phantump [TM]	Pichu [TM]	Pidgeot [TM]
		Pidgeotto [TM]	Pidgey [TM]	Pikachu [TM]	Piloswine [TM]	Pinsir [TM]	Plusle [TM]
		Politoed [TM]	Poliwag [TM]	Poliwhirl [TM]	Poliwrath [TM]	Poochyena [TM]	Probopass [TM]
		Psyduck [TM]	Pumpkaboo [TM]	Pupitar [TM]	Purrloin [TM]	Pyroar [TM]	Quagsire [TM]
		Quilladin [TM]	Qwilfish [TM]	Raichu [TM]	Ralts [TM]	Relicanth [TM]	Remoraid [TM]
		Reuniclus [TM]	Rhydon [TM]	Rhyhorn [TM]	Rhyperior [TM]	Riolu [TM]	Roggenrola [TM]
		Roselia [TM]	Roserade [TM]	Rotom (Fan) [TM]	Rotom (Frost) [TM]	Rotom (Heat) [TM]	Rotom (Mow) [TM]

	Move	Pokémon that can learn it					
Normal	Facade (TM42)	Rotom (Wash) [TM]	Rotom [TM]	Sableye [TM]	Salamence [TM]	Sandile [TM]	Sandshrew [TM]
		Sandslash [TM]	Sawk [TM]	Scizor [TM]	Scolipede [TM]	Scrafty [45, TM]	Scraggy [42, TM]
		Scyther [TM]	Seadra [TM]	Seaking [TM]	Sentret [TM]	Seviper [TM]	Sharpedo [TM]
		Shedinja [TM]	Shelgon [TM]	Shellder [TM]	Shelmet [TM]	Shuckle [TM]	Shuppet [TM]
		Sigilyph [TM]	Simipour [TM]	Simisage [TM]	Simisear [TM]	Skarmory [TM]	Skiddo [TM]
		Skiploom [TM]	Skitty [TM]	Skorupi [TM]	Skrelp [TM]	Skuntank [TM]	Sliggoo [TM]
		Slowbro [TM]	Slowking [TM]	Slowpoke [TM]	Slugma [TM]	Slurpuff [TM]	Smoochum [TM]
		Sneasel [TM]	Snorlax [TM]	Snover [TM]	Snubbull [TM]	Solosis [TM]	Solrock [TM]
		Spearow [TM]	Spinarak [TM]	Spinda [TM]	Spoink [TM]	Spritzee [TM]	Squirtle [TM]
		Staraptor [TM]	Staravia [TM]	Starly [TM]	Starmie [TM]	Staryu [TM]	Steelix [TM]
		Stunfisk [TM]	Stunky [TM]	Sudowoodo [TM]	Surskit [TM]	Swablu [TM]	Swalot [TM]
		Swanna [TM]	Swellow [TM]	Swinub [TM]	Swirlix [TM]	Swoobat [TM]	Sylveon [TM]
		Taillow [TM]	Talonflame [TM]	Tauros [TM]	Teddiursa [TM]	Tentacool [TM]	Tentacruel [TM]
		Throh [TM]	Timburr [TM]	Torkoal [TM]	Toxicroak [TM]	Trapinch [TM]	Trevenant [TM]
		Trubbish [TM]	Tyranitar [TM]	Tyrantrum [TM]	Tyrunt [TM]	Umbreon [TM]	Ursaring [TM]
		Vanillish [TM]	Vanillite [TM]	Vanilluxe [TM]	Vaporeon [TM]	Venipede [TM]	Venusaur [TM]
		Vespiquen [TM]	Vibrava [TM]	Victreebel [TM]	Vileplume [TM]	Vivillon [TM]	Volbeat [TM]
		Voltorb [TM]	Wailmer [TM]	Wailord [TM]	Wartortle [TM]	Watchog [TM]	Weavile [TM]
		Weepinbell [TM]	Whirlipede [TM]	Whiscash [TM]	Whismur [TM]	Wigglytuff [TM]	Wingull [TM]
		Woobat [TM]	Wooper [TM]	Wormadam (Plant) [TM]	Wormadam (Sand) [TM]	Wormadam (Trash) [TM]	Xerneas [TM]
		Yanma [TM]	Yanmega [TM]	Yveltal [TM]	Zangoose [TM]	Zapdos [TM]	Zigzagoon [TM]
		Zoroark [TM]	Zorua [TM]	Zubat [TM]	Zweilous [TM]	Zygarde [TM]	
Fairy	Fairy Lock	Klefki [1]					
Fairy	Fairy Wind	Aromatisse [1]	Flabébé [6]	Floette [6]	Hoppip [10]	Jumpluff [10]	Klefki [5]
		Mawile [1]	Skiploom [10]	Slurpuff [5]	Spritzee [1]	Swirlix [5]	Sylveon [9]
Normal	Fake Out	Croagunk [E]	Delcatty [1]	Delibird [E]	Espurr [19]	Hariyama [13]	Kangaskhan [7]
		Kecleon [E]	Liepard [22]	Lombre [11]	Makuhita [13]	Meditite [E]	Meowstic (Female) [19]
		Meowstic (Male) [E]	Mienfoo [13]	Mienshao [1, 13]	Mime Jr. [E]	Mr. Mime [E]	Pichu [E]
		Purrloin [21]	Sableye [18]	Scraggy [E]	Skitty [1, E]	Smoochum [E]	Sneasel [E]
		Spinda [E]	Squirtle [E]				
Dark	Fake Tears	Azurill [E]	Bonsly [1]	Eevee [E]	Gothita [10]	Gothitelle [10]	Gothorita [10]
		Igglybuff [E]	Illumise [E]	Jynx [28]	Mawile [6]	Minun [35]	Pachirisu [E]
		Plusle [35]	Purrloin [E]	Skitty [E]	Slurpuff [10]	Smoochum [28]	Snubbull [E]
		Spinda [E]	Swirlix [10]	Teddiursa [1, E]	Ursaring [1]	Whismur [E]	Woobat [E]
		Zorua [9]					
Normal	False Swipe (TM54)	Absol [TM]	Aegislash [TM]	Axew [24, TM]	Barbaracle [TM]	Beedrill [TM]	Binacle [TM]
		Bisharp [TM]	Corphish [TM]	Crawdaunt [TM]	Cubone [27, TM]	Doublade [TM]	Drapion [TM]
		Escavalier [25, TM]	Farfetch'd [45, TM]	Fearow [TM]	Fraxure [24, TM]	Gallade [50, TM]	Garchomp [TM]
		Gligar [TM]	Gliscor [TM]	Hawlucha [TM]	Haxorus [24, TM]	Heracross [TM]	Honedge [TM]
		Karrablast [25, TM]	Marowak [27, TM]	Mawile [TM]	Nincada [25, TM]	Ninjask [TM]	Pancham [TM]
		Pangoro [TM]	Pawniard [TM]	Pinsir [TM]	Scizor [13, TM]	Scyther [13, TM]	Shedinja [TM]
		Skorupi [TM]	Sneasel [TM]	Spearow [TM]	Weavile [TM]	Zangoose [29, TM]	
Flying	Feather Dance	Chatot [50]	Ducklett [21]	Farfetch'd [E]	Hawlucha [40]	Hoothoot [E]	Murkrow [E]
		Pidgeot [27]	Pidgeotto [27]	Pidgey [25]	Spearow [E]	Starly [E]	Swablu [E]
		Swanna [21]					
Normal	Feint	Absol [1]	Chesnaught [1]	Croagunk [E]	Farfetch'd [43]	Gallade [45]	Gligar [E]
		Goodra [1]	Heracross [37]	Houndour [1]	Kecleon [14]	Lucario [11]	Makuhita [1]
		Medicham [22]	Meditite [22]	Mienfoo [E]	Pikachu [34]	Pinsir [E]	Riolu [11]
		Sableye [E]	Scizor [1, 61]	Scyther [61]	Sharpedo [1]	Shelmet [E]	Skarmory [20]
		Skuntank [18]	Sneasel [E]	Stunky [18]	Trapinch [1, 61]	Yanma [E]	Yanmega [38]
		Zangoose [E]					
Dark	Feint Attack	Absol [E]	Amoonguss [20]	Banette [22]	Bisharp [19]	Bonsly [19]	Carnivine [27]
		Croagunk [17]	Crustle [13]	Diglett [E]	Doduo [E]	Dragalge [5]	Druddigon [E]
		Durant [E]	Dwebble [13]	Flygon [1, 7]	Foongus [20]	Gligar [19]	Gliscor [19]
		Gothita [24]	Gothitelle [24]	Gothorita [24]	Greninja [33]	Heatmor [E]	Hoothoot [E]
		Houndoom [35]	Houndour [32]	Igglybuff [E]	Karrablast [E]	Kecleon [7]	Makuhita [E]
		Mawile [26]	Murkrow [35, E]	Nincada [E]	Pawniard [17]	Phantump [19]	Pidgey [E]
		Pinsir [E]	Purrloin [E]	Sableye [E]	Scrafty [1, 9]	Scraggy [9, E]	Shuppet [22]
		Skitty [29]	Skorupi [E]	Skrelp [5]	Sneasel [10]	Snubbull [E]	Spearow [E]
		Spinda [14]	Sudowoodo [19]	Teddiursa [15]	Toxicroak [17]	Trapinch [7]	Trevenant [19]
		Umbreon [20]	Ursaring [15]	Vibrava [1, 7]	Weavile [10]	Yanma [E]	Zoroark [17]
		Zorua [17]	Zubat [E]				
Bug	Fell Stinger	Ariados [1]	Beedrill [45]	Drapion [53]	Escavalier [1, 60]	Qwilfish [1, 60]	Skorupi [47]
		Surskit [E]	Vespiquen [1, 57]				
Fighting	Final Gambit	Accelgor [1, 56]	Basculin [50]	Diglett [E]	Nincada [E]	Riolu [50]	Seviper [E]
		Shelmet [56]	Shuckle [E]	Staraptor [57]	Staravia [48]	Starly [41]	Zangoose [E]

AFTER THE
HALL OF FAME

CENTRAL
KALOS

COASTAL
KALOS

MOUNTAIN
KALOS

ADVENTURE
DATA

Move	Pokémon that can learn it					
Fire Blast (TM38)	Absol [TM]	Aerodactyl [TM]	Aggron [TM]	Altaria [TM]	Audino [TM]	Bagon [TM]
	Braixen [55, TM]	Chandelure [TM]	Charizard [TM]	Charmander [TM]	Charmeleon [TM]	Cubone [TM]
	Delphox [61, TM]	Dragonair [TM]	Dragonite [TM]	Dratini [TM]	Dunsparce [TM]	Exploud [TM]
	Fennekin [48, TM]	Flareon [TM]	Fletchinder [TM]	Flygon [TM]	Gabite [TM]	Garchomp [TM]
	Geodude [TM]	Gible [TM]	Golem [TM]	Goodra [TM]	Gourgeist [TM]	Granbull [TM]
	Graveler [TM]	Gyarados [TM]	Heatmor [TM]	Houndoom [TM]	Houndour [TM]	Hydreigon [TM]
	Igglybuff [TM]	Jigglypuff [TM]	Kangaskhan [TM]	Kecleon [TM]	Lampent [TM]	Lickilicky [TM]
	Lickitung [TM]	Litleo [TM]	Litwick [TM]	Loudred [TM]	Machamp [TM]	Machoke [TM]
	Machop [TM]	Magcargo [TM]	Marowak [TM]	Mawile [TM]	Mewtwo [TM]	Moltres [TM]
	Munchlax [TM]	Nidoking [TM]	Nidoqueen [TM]	Octillery [TM]	Pansear [34, TM]	Pumpkaboo [TM]
	Pyroar [TM]	Remoraid [TM]	Rhydon [TM]	Rhyhorn [TM]	Rhyperior [TM]	Salamence [TM]
	Shelgon [TM]	Simisear [TM]	Skuntank [TM]	Slowbro [TM]	Slowking [TM]	Slowpoke [TM]
	Slugma [TM]	Snorlax [TM]	Snubbull [TM]	Solrock [TM]	Stunky [TM]	Talonflame [TM]
	Tauros [TM]	Torkoal [TM]	Tyranitar [TM]	Whismur [TM]	Wigglytuff [TM]	Zangoose [TM]
Fire Fang	Aerodactyl [1]	Arbok [1]	Bagon [E]	Charizard [28]	Charmander [25]	Charmeleon [28]
	Deino [E]	Drapion [1]	Druddigon [E]	Electrike [E]	Exploud [1]	Flareon [20]
	Garchomp [1]	Gliscor [1]	Granbull [1]	Hippowdon [1]	Houndoom [30]	Houndour [28, E]
	Litleo [23]	Manectric [1]	Mawile [E]	Poochyena [E]	Pyroar [23]	Rhyhorn [E]
	Salamence [1]	Sandile [E]	Snubbull [1, E]	Steelix [1]	Tyranitar [1]	Tyrunt [E]
Fire Pledge	Braixen [T]	Charizard [T]	Charmander [T]	Charmeleon [T]	Delphox [T]	Fennekin [T]
Fire Punch	Abra [E]	Ampharos [1]	Dragonite [1]	Gastly [E]	Machop [E]	Medicham [1]
	Meditite [E]	Pansear [E]	Scraggy [E]			
Fire Spin	Braixen [22]	Charizard [56]	Charmander [43]	Charmeleon [50]	Delphox [22]	Fennekin [20]
	Flareon [25]	Heatmor [16]	Houndour [E]	Lampent [7]	Litleo [E]	Litwick [7]
	Moltres [8]	Pansear [E]	Solrock [9]	Torkoal [17]		
Fissure	Barboach [47]	Diglett [45]	Dugtrio [57]	Hippopotas [50]	Hippowdon [60]	Lapras [E]
	Snorlax [E]	Stunfisk [1, 61]	Swinub [E]	Torkoal [E]	Trapinch [1, 73]	Wailmer [E]
	Whiscash [57]	Wormadam (Sand) [47]				
Flail	Aromatisse [38]	Barboach [E]	Basculin [1, 46]	Beartic [36]	Bonsly [5]	Bunnelby [29]
	Carbink [35]	Chinchou [9, E]	Clauncher [16]	Clawitzer [16]	Corsola [50]	Crustle [50]
	Cubchoo [36]	Diggersby [31]	Doduo [E]	Dunsparce [49]	Dwebble [41]	Eevee [E]
	Farfetch'd [E]	Fletchinder [16]	Fletchling [16]	Geodude [E]	Goldeen [21]	Goodra [28]
	Goomy [28]	Heracross [E]	Horsea [E]	Karrablast [49]	Lanturn [9]	Lotad [E]
	Luvdisc [31]	Magikarp [30]	Oddish [E]	Onix [E]	Pachirisu [E]	Patrat [E]
	Pichu [E]	Pinsir [E]	Qwilfish [E]	Remoraid [E]	Sandshrew [E]	Seaking [21]
	Sliggoo [28]	Spinda [50]	Spritzee [38]	Squirtle [E]	Stunfisk [1, 55]	Sudowoodo [1, 5]
	Swinub [40]	Talonflame [16]	Torkoal [1, 52]	Trapinch [E]	Wormadam (Plant) [38]	Wormadam (Sand) [38]
	Wormadam (Trash) [38]	Zangoose [E]	Zigzagoon [37]			
Flame Burst	Chandelure [1]	Charizard [32]	Charmander [28]	Charmeleon [32]	Electrike [E]	Heatmor [31]
	Lampent [20]	Litwick [20]	Magcargo [23]	Pansear [22]	Simisear [1]	Slugma [23]
	Stunky [E]	Torkoal [E]				
Flame Charge (TM43)	Braixen [14, TM]	Chandelure [TM]	Charizard [TM]	Charmander [TM]	Charmeleon [TM]	Delphox [14, TM]
	Fennekin [14, TM]	Flareon [TM]	Fletchinder [38, TM]	Fletchling [34, TM]	Gourgeist [TM]	Houndoom [TM]
	Houndour [TM]	Lampent [TM]	Litleo [TM]	Litwick [TM]	Magcargo [TM]	Moltres [TM]
	Pansear [TM]	Pumpkaboo [TM]	Pyroar [TM]	Simisear [TM]	Slugma [TM]	Talonflame [39, TM]
	Torkoal [TM]					
Flame Wheel	Torkoal [23]					
Flamethrower (TM35)	Absol [TM]	Aerodactyl [TM]	Aggron [TM]	Altaria [TM]	Audino [TM]	Bagon [TM]
	Braixen [41, TM]	Chandelure [TM]	Charizard [47, TM]	Charmander [37, TM]	Charmeleon [43, TM]	Cubone [TM]
	Delphox [42, TM]	Dragonair [TM]	Dragonite [TM]	Dratini [TM]	Druddigon [TM]	Dunsparce [TM]
	Electrike [TM]	Exploud [TM]	Fennekin [35, TM]	Flareon [TM]	Fletchinder [TM]	Flygon [TM]
	Furret [TM]	Gabite [TM]	Garchomp [TM]	Geodude [TM]	Gible [TM]	Golem [TM]
	Goodra [TM]	Gourgeist [TM]	Granbull [TM]	Graveler [TM]	Gyarados [TM]	Heatmor [47, TM]
	Houndoom [50, TM]	Houndour [44, TM]	Hydreigon [TM]	Igglybuff [TM]	Inkay [TM]	Jigglypuff [TM]
	Kangaskhan [TM]	Kecleon [TM]	Lampent [TM]	Lickilicky [TM]	Lickitung [TM]	Litleo [36, TM]
	Litwick [TM]	Loudred [TM]	Machamp [TM]	Machoke [TM]	Machop [TM]	Magcargo [59, TM]
	Malamar [TM]	Manectric [TM]	Marowak [TM]	Mawile [TM]	Mewtwo [TM]	Moltres [36, TM]
	Munchlax [TM]	Nidoking [TM]	Nidoqueen [TM]	Noivern [TM]	Octillery [TM]	Pansear [TM]
	Pumpkaboo [TM]	Pyroar [38, TM]	Remoraid [TM]	Rhydon [TM]	Rhyhorn [TM]	Rhyperior [TM]
	Salamence [TM]	Sentret [TM]	Seviper [TM]	Shelgon [TM]	Simisear [TM]	Skuntank [34, TM]
	Slowbro [TM]	Slowking [TM]	Slowpoke [TM]	Slugma [50, TM]	Slurpuff [TM]	Snorlax [TM]
	Snubbull [TM]	Solrock [TM]	Stunky [TM]	Swirlix [TM]	Talonflame [TM]	Tauros [TM]
	Torkoal [28, TM]	Tyranitar [TM]	Watchog [TM]	Whismur [TM]	Wigglytuff [TM]	Zangoose [TM]
	Zoroark [TM]					
Flare Blitz	Charizard [1, 77]	Charmander [E]	Flareon [45]	Talonflame [1]		

AFTER THE HALL OF FAME

CENTRAL KALOS

COASTAL KALOS

MOUNTAIN KALOS

ADVENTURE DATA

Move	Pokémon that can learn it					
Flash Cannon (TM91) *(Steel)*	Aegislash [TM]	Aggron [TM]	Amaura [TM]	Aromatisse [TM]	Aurorus [TM]	Avalugg [TM]
	Bergmite [TM]	Blastoise [1, TM]	Boldore [TM]	Clauncher [TM]	Clawitzer [TM]	Cryogonal [TM]
	Doublade [TM]	Druddigon [TM]	Duosion [TM]	Durant [TM]	Ferroseed [52, TM]	Ferrothorn [61, TM]
	Gigalith [TM]	Golurk [TM]	Honedge [TM]	Horsea [TM]	Hydreigon [TM]	Kingdra [TM]
	Klefki [TM]	Lucario [TM]	Magnemite [35, TM]	Magneton [39, TM]	Magnezone [39, TM]	Mawile [TM]
	Octillery [TM]	Onix [TM]	Probopass [TM]	Reuniclus [TM]	Rhyperior [TM]	Roggenrola [TM]
	Scizor [TM]	Seadra [TM]	Sigilyph [TM]	Skarmory [TM]	Solosis [TM]	Spritzee [TM]
	Starmie [TM]	Staryu [TM]	Steelix [TM]	Vanillish [TM]	Vanillite [TM]	Vanilluxe [TM]
	Wormadam (Trash) [TM]	Xerneas [TM]				
Flash (TM70) *(Normal)*	Abomasnow [TM]	Abra [TM]	Absol [TM]	Alakazam [TM]	Amaura [TM]	Amoonguss [TM]
	Ampharos [TM]	Ariados [TM]	Aromatisse [TM]	Audino [TM]	Aurorus [TM]	Avalugg [TM]
	Banette [TM]	Beedrill [TM]	Bellossom [TM]	Bellsprout [TM]	Bergmite [TM]	Budew [TM]
	Bulbasaur [TM]	Butterfree [TM]	Carbink [TM]	Carnivine [TM]	Chandelure [TM]	Chesnaught [TM]
	Chespin [TM]	Chimecho [TM]	Chinchou [TM]	Chingling [TM]	Dedenne [TM]	Delcatty [TM]
	Drapion [TM]	Drifblim [TM]	Drifloon [TM]	Duosion [TM]	Electrike [TM]	Electrode [TM]
	Emolga [TM]	Espeon [TM]	Espurr [TM]	Exeggcute [TM]	Exeggutor [TM]	Ferroseed [TM]
	Ferrothorn [TM]	Flaaffy [TM]	Flabébé [TM]	Floette [TM]	Florges [TM]	Foongus [TM]
	Furfrou [TM]	Gallade [TM]	Gardevoir [TM]	Gloom [TM]	Golduck [TM]	Golett [TM]
	Golurk [TM]	Gothita [TM]	Gothitelle [TM]	Gothorita [TM]	Gourgeist [TM]	Grumpig [TM]
	Heliolisk [TM]	Helioptile [TM]	Hoppip [TM]	Igglybuff [TM]	Illumise [TM]	Inkay [TM]
	Ivysaur [TM]	Jigglypuff [TM]	Jolteon [TM]	Jumpluff [TM]	Jynx [TM]	Kadabra [TM]
	Kecleon [TM]	Kirlia [TM]	Lampent [TM]	Lanturn [TM]	Leafeon [TM]	Ledian [TM]
	Ledyba [TM]	Litwick [TM]	Lombre [TM]	Lotad [TM]	Ludicolo [TM]	Lunatone [TM]
	Magnemite [TM]	Magneton [TM]	Magnezone [TM]	Malamar [TM]	Manectric [TM]	Mareep [TM]
	Masquerain [TM]	Medicham [TM]	Meditite [TM]	Meowstic (Female) [TM]	Meowstic (Male) [TM]	Mewtwo [TM]
	Mime Jr. [TM]	Minun [TM]	Mothim [TM]	Mr. Mime [TM]	Nincada [TM]	Ninjask [TM]
	Oddish [TM]	Pachirisu [TM]	Pansage [TM]	Pichu [TM]	Pikachu [TM]	Plusle [TM]
	Psyduck [TM]	Pumpkaboo [TM]	Quagsire [TM]	Quilladin [TM]	Raichu [TM]	Ralts [TM]
	Reuniclus [TM]	Roselia [TM]	Roserade [TM]	Rotom (Fan) [TM]	Rotom (Frost) [TM]	Rotom (Heat) [TM]
	Rotom (Mow) [TM]	Rotom (Wash) [TM]	Rotom [TM]	Sableye [TM]	Shedinja [TM]	Shuckle [TM]
	Shuppet [TM]	Sigilyph [TM]	Simisage [TM]	Skarmory [TM]	Skiploom [TM]	Skitty [TM]
	Skorupi [TM]	Slowbro [TM]	Slowking [TM]	Slowpoke [TM]	Slurpuff [TM]	Smoochum [TM]
	Snover [TM]	Solosis [TM]	Solrock [TM]	Spinarak [TM]	Spinda [TM]	Spoink [TM]
	Spritzee [TM]	Starmie [TM]	Staryu [TM]	Stunfisk [TM]	Surskit [TM]	Swirlix [TM]
	Swoobat [TM]	Sylveon [TM]	Umbreon [TM]	Venusaur [TM]	Vespiquen [TM]	Victreebel [TM]
	Vileplume [TM]	Vivillon [TM]	Volbeat [1, TM]	Voltorb [TM]	Watchog [TM]	Weepinbell [TM]
	Wigglytuff [TM]	Woobat [TM]	Wooper [TM]	Wormadam (Plant) [TM]	Wormadam (Sand) [TM]	Wormadam (Trash) [TM]
	Xerneas [TM]	Yanma [TM]	Yanmega [TM]	Zapdos [TM]		
Flatter	Croagunk [50]	Gothita [28]	Gothitelle [28]	Gothorita [28]	Illumise [29]	Inkay [E]
	Mareep [E]	Murkrow [E]	Nidoran♀ [33]	Nidoran♂ [33]	Nidorina [38]	Nidorino [38]
	Pachirisu [E]	Sableye [E]	Toxicroak [62]	Woobat [E]		
Fling (TM56) *(Dark)*	Abomasnow [TM]	Abra [TM]	Aggron [TM]	Alakazam [TM]	Ampharos [TM]	Audino [TM]
	Axew [TM]	Azumarill [TM]	Banette [TM]	Barbaracle [TM]	Beartic [TM]	Bellossom [TM]
	Bibarel [TM]	Binacle [TM]	Bisharp [TM]	Blastoise [TM]	Bunnelby [TM]	Carnivine [TM]
	Charizard [TM]	Charmander [TM]	Charmeleon [TM]	Chesnaught [TM]	Chespin [TM]	Conkeldurr [TM]
	Corphish [TM]	Crawdaunt [TM]	Croagunk [TM]	Cubchoo [TM]	Cubone [33, TM]	Dedenne [TM]
	Delibird [TM]	Diggersby [TM]	Dragonite [TM]	Drapion [TM]	Druddigon [TM]	Emolga [TM]
	Exploud [TM]	Flaaffy [TM]	Fraxure [TM]	Froakie [25, TM]	Frogadier [28, TM]	Furret [TM]
	Gallade [TM]	Garbodor [TM]	Garchomp [TM]	Gardevoir [TM]	Gengar [TM]	Geodude [TM]
	Gligar [TM]	Gliscor [TM]	Gloom [TM]	Golduck [TM]	Golem [TM]	Golett [TM]
	Golurk [TM]	Gothita [TM]	Gothitelle [TM]	Gothorita [TM]	Granbull [TM]	Graveler [TM]
	Greninja [TM]	Grumpig [TM]	Gurdurr [TM]	Hariyama [TM]	Haunter [TM]	Hawlucha [24, TM]
	Haxorus [TM]	Heatmor [TM]	Heracross [TM]	Igglybuff [TM]	Illumise [TM]	Inkay [TM]
	Jigglypuff [TM]	Jynx [TM]	Kadabra [TM]	Kangaskhan [TM]	Kecleon [TM]	Kirlia [TM]
	Krokorok [TM]	Krookodile [TM]	Ledian [TM]	Ledyba [TM]	Lickilicky [TM]	Lickitung [TM]
	Linoone [65, TM]	Lombre [TM]	Loudred [TM]	Lucario [TM]	Ludicolo [TM]	Machamp [TM]
	Machoke [TM]	Machop [TM]	Makuhita [TM]	Malamar [TM]	Marill [TM]	Marowak [37, TM]
	Mawile [TM]	Medicham [TM]	Meditite [TM]	Mewtwo [TM]	Mienfoo [TM]	Mienshao [TM]
	Miltank [TM]	Mime Jr. [TM]	Minun [TM]	Mr. Mime [TM]	Munchlax [41, TM]	Nidoking [TM]
	Nidoqueen [TM]	Pachirisu [TM]	Pancham [TM]	Pangoro [TM]	Panpour [28, TM]	Pansage [28, TM]
	Pansear [28, TM]	Patrat [TM]	Pawniard [TM]	Pelipper [46, TM]	Pichu [TM]	Pikachu [TM]
	Pinsir [TM]	Plusle [TM]	Politoed [TM]	Poliwhirl [TM]	Poliwrath [TM]	Psyduck [TM]
	Quagsire [TM]	Quilladin [TM]	Raichu [TM]	Ralts [TM]	Reuniclus [TM]	Rhydon [TM]
	Rhyperior [TM]	Riolu [TM]	Sableye [TM]	Sandshrew [TM]	Sandslash [TM]	Sawk [TM]
	Scizor [TM]	Scrafty [TM]	Scraggy [TM]	Sentret [TM]	Simipour [TM]	Simisage [TM]
	Simisear [TM]	Skorupi [TM]	Slowbro [TM]	Slowking [TM]	Smoochum [TM]	Sneasel [TM]
	Snorlax [TM]	Snubbull [TM]	Spinda [TM]	Squirtle [TM]	Sudowoodo [TM]	Teddiursa [1, 57, TM]
	Throh [TM]	Timburr [TM]	Toxicroak [TM]	Tyranitar [TM]	Ursaring [TM]	Vespiquen [TM]
	Vileplume [TM]	Volbeat [TM]	Wartortle [TM]	Watchog [TM]	Weavile [28, TM]	Whismur [TM]
	Wigglytuff [TM]	Zangoose [TM]	Zigzagoon [49, TM]	Zoroark [TM]	Zorua [TM]	

Type	Move	Pokémon that can learn it					
Fairy	Flower Shield	Florges [1]					
Flying	Fly (HM02)	Aerodactyl [HM]	Altaria [HM]	Articuno [HM]	Charizard [HM]	Chatot [HM]	Crobat [HM]
		Delibird [HM]	Dodrio [HM]	Doduo [HM]	Dragonite [HM]	Drifblim [HM]	Ducklett [HM]
		Farfetch'd [HM]	Fearow [HM]	Fletchinder [HM]	Fletchling [HM]	Flygon [HM]	Golbat [HM]
		Golurk [HM]	Hawlucha [HM]	Honchkrow [HM]	Hoothoot [HM]	Hydreigon [HM]	Moltres [HM]
		Murkrow [HM]	Noctowl [HM]	Noibat [HM]	Noivern [HM]	Pelipper [HM]	Pidgeot [HM]
		Pidgeotto [HM]	Pidgey [HM]	Salamence [50, HM]	Sigilyph [HM]	Skarmory [HM]	Spearow [HM]
		Staraptor [HM]	Staravia [HM]	Starly [HM]	Swablu [HM]	Swanna [HM]	Swellow [HM]
		Swoobat [HM]	Taillow [HM]	Talonflame [HM]	Vibrava [HM]	Wingull [HM]	Woobat [HM]
		Yveltal [HM]	Zapdos [HM]	Zubat [HM]			
Fighting	Flying Press	Hawlucha [28]					
Fighting	Focus Blast (TM52)	Abomasnow [TM]	Accelgor [TM]	Aggron [TM]	Alakazam [TM]	Ampharos [TM]	Azumarill [TM]
		Barbaracle [TM]	Beartic [TM]	Bisharp [TM]	Blastoise [TM]	Charizard [TM]	Chesnaught [TM]
		Clawitzer [TM]	Conkeldurr [TM]	Croagunk [TM]	Dragalge [TM]	Dragonite [TM]	Druddigon [TM]
		Escavalier [TM]	Exploud [TM]	Floatzel [TM]	Furret [TM]	Gallade [TM]	Garbodor [TM]
		Gardevoir [TM]	Gengar [TM]	Golduck [TM]	Golem [TM]	Golett [TM]	Golurk [TM]
		Goodra [TM]	Gourgeist [TM]	Granbull [TM]	Grumpig [TM]	Gurdurr [TM]	Hariyama [TM]
		Hawlucha [TM]	Haxorus [TM]	Heatmor [TM]	Heliolisk [TM]	Heracross [TM]	Hydreigon [TM]
		Jynx [TM]	Kangaskhan [TM]	Krookodile [TM]	Ledian [TM]	Lickilicky [TM]	Lucario [TM]
		Ludicolo [TM]	Machamp [TM]	Machoke [TM]	Machop [TM]	Makuhita [TM]	Marowak [TM]
		Mawile [TM]	Medicham [TM]	Meditite [TM]	Mewtwo [TM]	Mienfoo [TM]	Mienshao [TM]
		Miltank [TM]	Mr. Mime [TM]	Nidoking [TM]	Nidoqueen [TM]	Noivern [TM]	Pangoro [TM]
		Pinsir [TM]	Politoed [TM]	Poliwrath [TM]	Quagsire [TM]	Raichu [TM]	Reuniclus [TM]
		Rhydon [TM]	Rhyperior [TM]	Riolu [TM]	Sandslash [TM]	Sawk [TM]	Scrafty [TM]
		Scraggy [TM]	Simipour [TM]	Simisage [TM]	Simisear [TM]	Slowbro [TM]	Slowking [TM]
		Snorlax [TM]	Throh [TM]	Timburr [TM]	Toxicroak [TM]	Trevenant [TM]	Tyranitar [TM]
		Ursaring [TM]	Watchog [TM]	Weavile [TM]	Wigglytuff [TM]	Xerneas [TM]	Yveltal [72, TM]
		Zangoose [TM]	Zoroark [TM]	Zygarde [TM]			
Normal	Focus Energy	Axew [E]	Bagon [20]	Beedrill [20]	Carvanha [8]	Conkeldurr [1, 4]	Cubone [17]
		Deino [4]	Drifblim [13]	Drifloon [13]	Gurdurr [1, 4]	Hariyama [1]	Horsea [14]
		Hydreigon [1, 4]	Kangaskhan [E]	Kingdra [14]	Larvitar [E]	Machamp [1, 7]	Machoke [1, 7]
		Machop [7]	Makuhita [1]	Marowak [17]	Nidoking [1]	Nidoran♀ [7]	Nidoran♂ [7]
		Nidorino [7]	Octillery [22]	Pinsir [1]	Remoraid [22]	Salamence [20]	Sandile [E]
		Sawk [9]	Scizor [5]	Scyther [5]	Seadra [14]	Sentret [E]	Sharpedo [1, 8]
		Shelgon [20]	Skuntank [1]	Stunky [1]	Swellow [1, 3]	Taillow [4]	Throh [9]
		Timburr [4]	Trapinch [E]	Zweilous [1, 4]			
Fighting	Focus Punch	Charmander [E]	Conkeldurr [53]	Cubchoo [E]	Geodude [E]	Golett [55]	Golurk [1, 70]
		Gurdurr [53]	Heracross [E]	Kangaskhan [E]	Ledyba [E]	Makuhita [E]	Scrafty [58]
		Scraggy [48]	Snubbull [E]	Timburr [46]			
Normal	Follow Me	Furret [21]	Pachirisu [E]	Riolu [E]	Sentret [19]		
Fighting	Force Palm	Hariyama [32]	Makuhita [28]	Medicham [29]	Meditite [29]	Mienfoo [29]	Mienshao [29]
		Riolu [15]	Timburr [E]				
Normal	Foresight	Aerodactyl [E]	Farfetch'd [E]	Furret [1]	Hoothoot [1]	Kangaskhan [E]	Lapras [E]
		Lucario [1]	Machamp [19]	Machoke [19]	Machop [19]	Makuhita [E]	Meditite [E]
		Noctowl [1]	Patrat [E]	Pidgey [E]	Psyduck [E]	Riolu [1]	Sableye [4]
		Sentret [1]	Shuppet [E]	Skitty [4]	Sneasel [E]	Squirtle [E]	Starly [E]
		Surskit [E]	Timburr [E]	Yanma [1]	Yanmega [1]		
Grass	Forest's Curse	Phantump [35]	Trevenant [35]				
Dark	Foul Play	Honchkrow [45]	Houndoom [45]	Houndour [40]	Inkay [8]	Kecleon [E]	Klefki [27]
		Krokorok [40]	Krookodile [42]	Malamar [8]	Murkrow [45]	Pancham [E]	Purrloin [E]
		Sableye [50]	Sandile [37]	Stunky [E]	Yveltal [51]	Zoroark [29]	Zorua [29]
Ice	Freeze-Dry	Articuno [1]	Aurorus [1, 77]	Cryogonal [50]	Delibird [E]	Lapras [E]	Swinub [E]
		Vanilluxe [1]					
Grass	Frenzy Plant	Chesnaught [T]	Venusaur [T]				
Ice	Frost Breath (TM79)	Abomasnow [TM]	Amaura [TM]	Articuno [TM]	Aurorus [TM]	Avalugg [TM]	Beartic [TM]
		Bergmite [TM]	Cloyster [TM]	Cryogonal [TM]	Cubchoo [TM]	Delibird [TM]	Glaceon [TM]
		Jynx [TM]	Lapras [TM]	Smoochum [TM]	Snover [TM]	Vanillish [TM]	Vanillite [TM]
		Vanilluxe [TM]					
Normal	Frustration (TM21)	Abomasnow [TM]	Abra [TM]	Absol [TM]	Accelgor [TM]	Aegislash [TM]	Aerodactyl [TM]
		Aggron [TM]	Alakazam [TM]	Alomomola [TM]	Altaria [TM]	Amaura [TM]	Amoonguss [TM]
		Ampharos [TM]	Arbok [TM]	Ariados [TM]	Aromatisse [TM]	Aron [TM]	Articuno [TM]
		Audino [TM]	Aurorus [TM]	Avalugg [TM]	Axew [TM]	Azumarill [TM]	Azurill [TM]
		Bagon [TM]	Banette [TM]	Barbaracle [TM]	Barboach [TM]	Basculin [TM]	Beartic [TM]
		Beedrill [TM]	Bellossom [TM]	Bellsprout [TM]	Bergmite [TM]	Bibarel [TM]	Bidoof [TM]
		Binacle [TM]	Bisharp [TM]	Blastoise [TM]	Boldore [TM]	Bonsly [TM]	Braixen [TM]
		Budew [TM]	Buizel [TM]	Bulbasaur [TM]	Bunnelby [TM]	Butterfree [TM]	Carbink [TM]
		Carnivine [TM]	Carvanha [TM]	Chandelure [TM]	Charizard [TM]	Charmander [TM]	Charmeleon [TM]
		Chatot [TM]	Chesnaught [TM]	Chespin [TM]	Chimecho [TM]	Chinchou [TM]	Chingling [TM]

AFTER THE HALL OF FAME

CENTRAL KALOS

COASTAL KALOS

MOUNTAIN KALOS

ADVENTURE DATA

Move	Pokémon that can learn it					
Frustration (TM21) *(Normal)*	Clamperl [TM]	Clauncher [TM]	Clawitzer [TM]	Cloyster [TM]	Conkeldurr [TM]	Corphish [TM]
	Corsola [TM]	Crawdaunt [TM]	Croagunk [TM]	Crobat [TM]	Crustle [TM]	Cryogonal [TM]
	Cubchoo [TM]	Cubone [TM]	Dedenne [TM]	Deino [TM]	Delcatty [TM]	Delibird [TM]
	Delphox [TM]	Diggersby [TM]	Diglett [TM]	Dodrio [TM]	Doduo [TM]	Doublade [TM]
	Dragalge [TM]	Dragonair [TM]	Dragonite [TM]	Drapion [TM]	Dratini [TM]	Drifblim [TM]
	Drifloon [TM]	Druddigon [TM]	Ducklett [TM]	Dugtrio [TM]	Dunsparce [TM]	Duosion [TM]
	Durant [TM]	Dwebble [TM]	Eevee [TM]	Ekans [TM]	Electrike [TM]	Electrode [TM]
	Emolga [TM]	Escavalier [TM]	Espeon [TM]	Espurr [TM]	Exeggcute [TM]	Exeggutor [TM]
	Exploud [TM]	Farfetch'd [TM]	Fearow [TM]	Fennekin [TM]	Ferroseed [TM]	Ferrothorn [TM]
	Flaaffy [TM]	Flabébé [TM]	Flareon [TM]	Fletchinder [TM]	Fletchling [TM]	Floatzel [TM]
	Floette [TM]	Florges [TM]	Flygon [TM]	Foongus [TM]	Fraxure [TM]	Froakie [TM]
	Frogadier [TM]	Furfrou [TM]	Furret [TM]	Gabite [TM]	Gallade [TM]	Garbodor [TM]
	Garchomp [TM]	Gardevoir [TM]	Gastly [TM]	Gengar [TM]	Geodude [TM]	Gible [TM]
	Gigalith [TM]	Glaceon [TM]	Gligar [TM]	Gliscor [TM]	Gloom [TM]	Gogoat [TM]
	Golbat [TM]	Goldeen [TM]	Golduck [TM]	Golem [TM]	Golett [TM]	Golurk [TM]
	Goodra [TM]	Goomy [TM]	Gorebyss [TM]	Gothita [TM]	Gothitelle [TM]	Gothorita [TM]
	Gourgeist [TM]	Granbull [TM]	Graveler [TM]	Greninja [TM]	Grumpig [TM]	Gulpin [TM]
	Gurdurr [TM]	Gyarados [TM]	Hariyama [TM]	Haunter [TM]	Hawlucha [TM]	Haxorus [TM]
	Heatmor [TM]	Heliolisk [TM]	Helioptile [TM]	Heracross [TM]	Hippopotas [TM]	Hippowdon [TM]
	Honchkrow [TM]	Honedge [TM]	Hoothoot [TM]	Hoppip [TM]	Horsea [TM]	Houndoom [TM]
	Houndour [TM]	Huntail [TM]	Hydreigon [TM]	Igglybuff [TM]	Illumise [TM]	Inkay [TM]
	Ivysaur [TM]	Jigglypuff [TM]	Jolteon [TM]	Jumpluff [TM]	Jynx [TM]	Kadabra [TM]
	Kangaskhan [TM]	Karrablast [TM]	Kecleon [TM]	Kingdra [TM]	Kirlia [TM]	Klefki [TM]
	Krokorok [TM]	Krookodile [TM]	Lairon [TM]	Lampent [TM]	Lanturn [TM]	Lapras [TM]
	Larvitar [TM]	Leafeon [TM]	Ledian [TM]	Ledyba [TM]	Lickilicky [TM]	Lickitung [TM]
	Liepard [TM]	Linoone [TM]	Litleo [TM]	Litwick [TM]	Lombre [TM]	Lotad [TM]
	Loudred [TM]	Lucario [TM]	Ludicolo [TM]	Lunatone [TM]	Luvdisc [TM]	Machamp [TM]
	Machoke [TM]	Machop [TM]	Magcargo [TM]	Magnemite [TM]	Magneton [TM]	Magnezone [TM]
	Makuhita [TM]	Malamar [TM]	Mamoswine [TM]	Manectric [TM]	Mantine [TM]	Mantyke [TM]
	Mareep [TM]	Marill [TM]	Marowak [TM]	Masquerain [TM]	Mawile [TM]	Medicham [TM]
	Meditite [TM]	Meowstic (Female) [TM]	Meowstic (Male) [TM]	Mewtwo [TM]	Mienfoo [TM]	Mienshao [TM]
	Mightyena [TM]	Miltank [TM]	Mime Jr. [TM]	Minun [TM]	Moltres [TM]	Mothim [TM]
	Mr. Mime [TM]	Munchlax [TM]	Murkrow [TM]	Nidoking [TM]	Nidoqueen [TM]	Nidoran ♀ [TM]
	Nidoran♂ [TM]	Nidorina [TM]	Nidorino [TM]	Nincada [TM]	Ninjask [TM]	Noctowl [TM]
	Noibat [TM]	Noivern [TM]	Nosepass [TM]	Octillery [TM]	Oddish [TM]	Onix [TM]
	Pachirisu [TM]	Pancham [TM]	Pangoro [TM]	Panpour [TM]	Pansage [TM]	Pansear [TM]
	Patrat [TM]	Pawniard [TM]	Pelipper [TM]	Phantump [TM]	Pichu [TM]	Pidgeot [TM]
	Pidgeotto [TM]	Pidgey [TM]	Pikachu [TM]	Piloswine [TM]	Pinsir [TM]	Plusle [TM]
	Politoed [TM]	Poliwag [TM]	Poliwhirl [TM]	Poliwrath [TM]	Poochyena [TM]	Probopass [TM]
	Psyduck [TM]	Pumpkaboo [TM]	Pupitar [TM]	Purrloin [TM]	Pyroar [TM]	Quagsire [TM]
	Quilladin [TM]	Qwilfish [TM]	Raichu [TM]	Ralts [TM]	Relicanth [TM]	Remoraid [TM]
	Reuniclus [TM]	Rhydon [TM]	Rhyhorn [TM]	Rhyperior [TM]	Riolu [TM]	Roggenrola [TM]
	Roselia [TM]	Roserade [TM]	Rotom (Fan) [TM]	Rotom (Frost) [TM]	Rotom (Heat) [TM]	Rotom (Mow) [TM]
	Rotom (Wash) [TM]	Rotom [TM]	Sableye [TM]	Salamence [TM]	Sandile [TM]	Sandshrew [TM]
	Sandslash [TM]	Sawk [TM]	Scizor [TM]	Scolipede [TM]	Scrafty [TM]	Scraggy [TM]
	Scyther [TM]	Seadra [TM]	Seaking [TM]	Sentret [TM]	Seviper [TM]	Sharpedo [TM]
	Shedinja [TM]	Shelgon [TM]	Shellder [TM]	Shelmet [TM]	Shuckle [TM]	Shuppet [TM]
	Sigilyph [TM]	Simipour [TM]	Simisage [TM]	Simisear [TM]	Skarmory [TM]	Skiddo [TM]
	Skiploom [TM]	Skitty [TM]	Skorupi [TM]	Skrelp [TM]	Skuntank [TM]	Sliggoo [TM]
	Slowbro [TM]	Slowking [TM]	Slowpoke [TM]	Slugma [TM]	Slurpuff [TM]	Smoochum [TM]
	Sneasel [TM]	Snorlax [TM]	Snover [TM]	Snubbull [TM]	Solosis [TM]	Solrock [TM]
	Spearow [TM]	Spinarak [TM]	Spinda [TM]	Spoink [TM]	Spritzee [TM]	Squirtle [TM]
	Staraptor [TM]	Staravia [TM]	Starly [TM]	Starmie [TM]	Staryu [TM]	Steelix [TM]
	Stunfisk [TM]	Stunky [TM]	Sudowoodo [TM]	Surskit [TM]	Swablu [TM]	Swalot [TM]
	Swanna [TM]	Swellow [TM]	Swinub [TM]	Swirlix [TM]	Swoobat [TM]	Sylveon [TM]
	Taillow [TM]	Talonflame [TM]	Tauros [TM]	Teddiursa [TM]	Tentacool [TM]	Tentacruel [TM]
	Throh [TM]	Timburr [TM]	Torkoal [TM]	Toxicroak [TM]	Trapinch [TM]	Trevenant [TM]
	Trubbish [TM]	Tyranitar [TM]	Tyrantrum [TM]	Tyrunt [TM]	Umbreon [TM]	Ursaring [TM]
	Vanillish [TM]	Vanillite [TM]	Vanilluxe [TM]	Vaporeon [TM]	Venipede [TM]	Venusaur [TM]
	Vespiquen [TM]	Vibrava [TM]	Victreebel [TM]	Vileplume [TM]	Vivillon [TM]	Volbeat [TM]
	Voltorb [TM]	Wailmer [TM]	Wailord [TM]	Wartortle [TM]	Watchog [TM]	Weavile [TM]
	Weepinbell [TM]	Whirlipede [TM]	Whiscash [TM]	Whismur [TM]	Wigglytuff [TM]	Wingull [TM]
	Woobat [TM]	Wooper [TM]	Wormadam (Plant) [TM]	Wormadam (Sand) [TM]	Wormadam (Trash) [TM]	Xerneas [TM]
	Yanma [TM]	Yanmega [TM]	Yveltal [TM]	Zangoose [TM]	Zapdos [TM]	Zigzagoon [TM]
	Zoroark [TM]	Zorua [TM]	Zubat [TM]	Zweilous [TM]	Zygarde [TM]	
Fury Attack	Altaria [10]	Beedrill [1, 10]	Chatot [17]	Dodrio [14]	Doduo [14]	Escavalier [16]
	Farfetch'd [7]	Fearow [1, 9]	Goldeen [31]	Heracross [7]	Karrablast [16]	Nidoran♂ [19]
	Nidorino [20]	Piloswine [33]	Pinsir [E]	Rhydon [1, 12]	Rhyhorn [12]	Rhyperior [1, 19]
	Seaking [31]	Skarmory [17]	Spearow [9]	Starly [E]	Swablu [10]	

	Move	Pokémon that can learn it					
Bug	Fury Cutter	Aegislash [1]	Barbaracle [37]	Binacle [37]	Bisharp [1, 9]	Buizel [E]	Doublade [5]
		Durant [6]	Dwebble [1]	Farfetch'd [1]	Gallade [37]	Gligar [16]	Gliscor [16]
		Honedge [5]	Karrablast [13]	Ninjask [20]	Pawniard [9]	Sandshrew [14]	Sandslash [14]
		Scizor [25]	Scyther [25]	Trapinch [E]	Vespiquen [5]	Zangoose [8]	
Normal	Fury Swipes	Ariados [23]	Barbaracle [10]	Beartic [17]	Bidoof [E]	Binacle [10]	Buizel [E]
		Cubchoo [17]	Furret [13]	Golduck [22]	Heatmor [21]	Kecleon [10]	Liepard [12]
		Linoone [29]	Lombre [15]	Nidoran ♀ [19]	Nidorina [20]	Nincada [14]	Ninjask [14]
		Panpour [13]	Pansage [13]	Pansear [13]	Psyduck [22]	Purrloin [10]	Sableye [15]
		Sandshrew [20]	Sandslash [20]	Sentret [13]	Shedinja [14]	Simipour [1]	Simisage [1]
		Simisear [1]	Skuntank [10]	Sneasel [16]	Spinarak [22]	Stunky [10]	Teddiursa [8]
		Ursaring [8]	Vespiquen [13]	Weavile [16]	Zangoose [E]	Zoroark [13]	Zorua [13]
Psychic	Future Sight	Absol [36]	Alakazam [48]	Barboach [43]	Chimecho [E]	Chingling [E]	Delibird [E]
		Delphox [1, 69]	Duosion [31]	Espeon [25]	Gardevoir [53]	Gothita [31]	Gothitelle [31]
		Gothorita [31]	Kadabra [48]	Kirlia [45]	Lapras [E]	Lunatone [45]	Marill [E]
		Meowstic (Female) [50]	Mewtwo [15]	Mime Jr. [E]	Mr. Mime [E]	Psyduck [E]	Ralts [39]
		Reuniclus [31]	Sigilyph [E]	Slowpoke [E]	Solosis [31]	Spoink [E]	Swoobat [36]
		Whiscash [51]	Woobat [36]				

G

	Move	Pokémon that can learn it					
Poison	Gastro Acid	Arbok [44]	Bellsprout [35]	Ekans [36]	Foongus [E]	Gulpin [49]	Seviper [34]
		Shuckle [27]	Swalot [59]	Weepinbell [35]			
Fairy	Geomancy	Xerneas [26]					
Grass	Giga Drain	Accelgor [37]	Amoonguss [28]	Bellsprout [E]	Budew [E]	Bulbasaur [E]	Carnivine [E]
		Exeggcute [E]	Foongus [28]	Gloom [47]	Hoppip [43]	Jumpluff [59]	Leafeon [25]
		Lotad [E]	Oddish [37]	Roselia [25, 8]	Shelmet [37]	Skiploom [52]	Zubat [E]
Normal	Giga Impact (TM68)	Abomasnow [TM]	Absol [TM]	Accelgor [TM]	Aegislash [TM]	Aerodactyl [81, TM]	Aggron [TM]
		Alakazam [TM]	Altaria [TM]	Amoonguss [TM]	Ampharos [TM]	Arbok [TM]	Ariados [TM]
		Aromatisse [TM]	Articuno [TM]	Aurorus [TM]	Avalugg [TM]	Axew [61, TM]	Azumarill [TM]
		Banette [TM]	Barbaracle [TM]	Beartic [TM]	Beedrill [TM]	Bellossom [TM]	Bibarel [TM]
		Bisharp [TM]	Blastoise [TM]	Butterfree [TM]	Carnivine [TM]	Chandelure [TM]	Charizard [TM]
		Chesnaught [70, TM]	Clawitzer [TM]	Cloyster [TM]	Conkeldurr [TM]	Crawdaunt [TM]	Crobat [TM]
		Crustle [TM]	Dedenne [TM]	Delcatty [TM]	Delphox [TM]	Diggersby [TM]	Dodrio [TM]
		Dragalge [TM]	Dragonite [TM]	Drapion [TM]	Drifblim [TM]	Druddigon [TM]	Dugtrio [TM]
		Durant [TM]	Electrode [TM]	Escavalier [56, TM]	Espeon [TM]	Exeggutor [TM]	Exploud [TM]
		Fearow [TM]	Ferrothorn [TM]	Flareon [TM]	Floatzel [TM]	Florges [TM]	Flygon [TM]
		Fraxure [66, TM]	Furfrou [TM]	Furret [TM]	Gallade [TM]	Garbodor [TM]	Garchomp [TM]
		Gardevoir [TM]	Gengar [TM]	Gigalith [TM]	Glaceon [TM]	Gliscor [TM]	Gogoat [TM]
		Golbat [TM]	Golduck [TM]	Golem [TM]	Golurk [TM]	Goodra [TM]	Gorebyss [TM]
		Gothitelle [TM]	Gourgeist [TM]	Granbull [TM]	Greninja [TM]	Grumpig [TM]	Gyarados [TM]
		Hariyama [TM]	Hawlucha [TM]	Haxorus [74, TM]	Heatmor [TM]	Heliolisk [TM]	Heracross [TM]
		Hippowdon [TM]	Honchkrow [TM]	Houndoom [TM]	Huntail [TM]	Hydreigon [TM]	Jolteon [TM]
		Jumpluff [TM]	Jynx [TM]	Kangaskhan [TM]	Kingdra [TM]	Klefki [TM]	Krookodile [TM]
		Lanturn [TM]	Lapras [TM]	Leafeon [TM]	Ledian [TM]	Lickilicky [TM]	Lickitung [TM]
		Liepard [TM]	Linoone [TM]	Lucario [TM]	Ludicolo [TM]	Lunatone [TM]	Machamp [TM]
		Magcargo [TM]	Magneton [TM]	Magnezone [TM]	Malamar [TM]	Mamoswine [TM]	Manectric [TM]
		Mantine [TM]	Marowak [TM]	Masquerain [TM]	Mawile [TM]	Medicham [TM]	Meowstic (Female) [TM]
		Meowstic (Male) [TM]	Mewtwo [TM]	Mienshao [TM]	Mightyena [TM]	Miltank [TM]	Moltres [TM]
		Mothim [TM]	Mr. Mime [TM]	Nidoking [TM]	Nidoqueen [TM]	Ninjask [TM]	Noctowl [TM]
		Noivern [TM]	Octillery [TM]	Pangoro [TM]	Pelipper [TM]	Pidgeot [TM]	Piloswine [TM]
		Pinsir [TM]	Politoed [TM]	Poliwrath [TM]	Probopass [TM]	Pyroar [TM]	Quagsire [TM]
		Raichu [TM]	Relicanth [TM]	Reuniclus [TM]	Rhydon [TM]	Rhyperior [TM]	Roserade [TM]
		Salamence [TM]	Sandslash [TM]	Sawk [TM]	Scizor [TM]	Scolipede [TM]	Scrafty [TM]
		Scyther [TM]	Seadra [TM]	Seaking [TM]	Sharpedo [TM]	Shedinja [TM]	Simipour [TM]
		Simisage [TM]	Simisear [TM]	Skuntank [TM]	Slowbro [TM]	Slowking [TM]	Slurpuff [TM]
		Snorlax [57, TM]	Solrock [TM]	Staraptor [TM]	Starmie [TM]	Steelix [TM]	Swalot [TM]
		Swanna [TM]	Swellow [TM]	Swoobat [TM]	Sylveon [TM]	Talonflame [TM]	Tauros [63, TM]
		Tentacruel [TM]	Throh [TM]	Torkoal [TM]	Toxicroak [TM]	Trevenant [TM]	Tyranitar [82, TM]
		Tyrantrum [75, TM]	Umbreon [TM]	Ursaring [TM]	Vanilluxe [TM]	Vaporeon [TM]	Venusaur [TM]
		Vespiquen [TM]	Victreebel [TM]	Vileplume [TM]	Vivillon [TM]	Wailord [TM]	Watchog [TM]
		Weavile [TM]	Whiscash [TM]	Wigglytuff [TM]	Wormadam (Plant) [TM]	Wormadam (Sand) [TM]	Wormadam (Trash) [TM]
		Xerneas [88, TM]	Yanmega [TM]	Yveltal [TM]	Zapdos [TM]	Zoroark [TM]	Zygarde [TM]
Normal	Glare	Arbok [12]	Druddigon [E]	Dunsparce [28]	Ekans [12]	Heliotile [E]	Seviper [23]
		Zygarde [1]					

Pokémon Moves Reverse Lookup

Type	Move	Pokémon that can learn it					
Grass	Grass Knot (TM86)	Abomasnow [TM]	Abra [TM]	Alakazam [TM]	Amoonguss [TM]	Audino [TM]	Azumarill [TM]
		Barbaracle [TM]	Beartic [TM]	Bellossom [TM]	Bellsprout [TM]	Bibarel [TM]	Bidoof [TM]
		Binacle [TM]	Bisharp [TM]	Braixen [TM]	Budew [TM]	Bulbasaur [TM]	Bunnelby [TM]
		Carnivine [TM]	Chesnaught [TM]	Chespin [TM]	Chimecho [TM]	Chingling [TM]	Conkeldurr [TM]
		Cubchoo [TM]	Dedenne [TM]	Delcatty [TM]	Delphox [TM]	Diggersby [TM]	Espeon [TM]
		Exeggcute [TM]	Exeggutor [TM]	Fennekin [TM]	Ferrothorn [TM]	Flabébé [TM]	Floette [TM]
		Florges [1, TM]	Foongus [TM]	Froakie [TM]	Frogadier [TM]	Furfrou [TM]	Furret [TM]
		Gallade [TM]	Gardevoir [TM]	Gloom [TM]	Gogoat [TM]	Golett [TM]	Golurk [TM]
		Gothita [TM]	Gothitelle [TM]	Gothorita [TM]	Gourgeist [TM]	Greninja [TM]	Grumpig [TM]
		Gurdurr [TM]	Hawlucha [TM]	Haxorus [TM]	Heliolisk [TM]	Helioptile [TM]	Hoppip [TM]
		Igglybuff [TM]	Ivysaur [TM]	Jigglypuff [TM]	Jumpluff [TM]	Jynx [TM]	Kadabra [TM]
		Kecleon [TM]	Kirlia [TM]	Krokorok [TM]	Krookodile [TM]	Leafeon [TM]	Liepard [TM]
		Linoone [TM]	Lombre [TM]	Lotad [TM]	Ludicolo [TM]	Lunatone [TM]	Marill [TM]
		Mawile [TM]	Medicham [TM]	Meditite [TM]	Mewtwo [TM]	Mienfoo [TM]	Mienshao [TM]
		Mime Jr. [TM]	Minun [TM]	Mr. Mime [TM]	Oddish [TM]	Pachirisu [TM]	Pancham [TM]
		Pangoro [TM]	Panpour [TM]	Pansage [34, TM]	Pansear [TM]	Patrat [TM]	Pawniard [TM]
		Phantump [TM]	Pichu [TM]	Pikachu [TM]	Plusle [TM]	Pumpkaboo [TM]	Purrloin [TM]
		Quilladin [TM]	Raichu [TM]	Ralts [TM]	Reuniclus [TM]	Roselia [TM]	Roserade [TM]
		Sawk [TM]	Scrafty [TM]	Scraggy [TM]	Sentret [TM]	Simipour [TM]	Simisage [TM]
		Simisear [TM]	Skiddo [TM]	Skiploom [TM]	Skitty [TM]	Slowbro [TM]	Slowking [TM]
		Slowpoke [TM]	Smoochum [TM]	Snover [TM]	Solrock [TM]	Spoink [TM]	Starmie [TM]
		Throh [TM]	Timburr [TM]	Trevenant [TM]	Venusaur [TM]	Victreebel [TM]	Vileplume [TM]
		Watchog [TM]	Weepinbell [TM]	Wigglytuff [TM]	Wormadam (Plant) [TM]	Xerneas [TM]	Zigzagoon [TM]
		Zoroark [TM]	Zorua [TM]	Zygarde [TM]			
	Grass Pledge	Bulbasaur [T]	Chesnaught [T]	Chespin [T]	Ivysaur [T]	Quilladin [T]	Venusaur [T]
	Grass Whistle	Abomasnow [13]	Budew [E]	Bulbasaur [E]	Carnivine [E]	Leafeon [17]	Pansage [E]
		Roselia [22, E]	Snover [13]				
	Grassy Terrain	Bulbasaur [E]	Exeggcute [E]	Flabébé [24]	Floette [27]	Florges [1]	Gloom [56]
		Hoppip [E]	Oddish [45]	Roserade [1]			
Psychic	Gravity	Ferroseed [E]	Igglybuff [E]	Probopass [1]	Roggenrola [E]	Sigilyph [38]	Xerneas [18]
Normal	Growl	Altaria [1]	Amaura [1]	Ampharos [1]	Audino [1]	Aurorus [1]	Beartic [1]
		Bibarel [1, 5]	Bidoof [5]	Buizel [4]	Bulbasaur [3]	Charizard [1]	Charmander [1]
		Charmeleon [1]	Chatot [5]	Chesnaught [1]	Chespin [1]	Chimecho [6]	Chingling [6]
		Cubchoo [1]	Cubone [1]	Diglett [4]	Dodrio [1]	Doduo [1]	Dugtrio [1, 4]
		Eevee [1]	Fearow [1]	Flaaffy [1]	Fletchinder [1]	Fletchling [1]	Floatzel [1, 4]
		Froakie [1]	Frogadier [1]	Furfrou [1]	Gardevoir [1]	Greninja [1]	Hoothoot [1]
		Ivysaur [1, 3]	Kirlia [1]	Lapras [1]	Liepard [1, 3]	Linoone [1]	Lombre [3]
		Lotad [3]	Ludicolo [1]	Mareep [1]	Marowak [1]	Mawile [1]	Miltank [3]
		Minun [1]	Nidoran ♀ [1]	Nidorina [1]	Noctowl [1]	Pachirisu [1]	Pelipper [1]
		Pikachu [1]	Plusle [1]	Purrloin [1]	Quilladin [1]	Ralts [1]	Skitty [1]
		Slowbro [1, 5]	Slowking [5]	Slowpoke [1]	Spearow [1]	Staraptor [1]	Staravia [1]
		Starly [1]	Swablu [1]	Swellow [1]	Taillow [1]	Talonflame [1]	Venusaur [1, 3]
		Wailmer [4]	Wailord [1, 4]	Wingull [1]	Zigzagoon [1]		
	Growth	Amoonguss [1, 6]	Bellsprout [7]	Budew [4]	Bulbasaur [25]	Carnivine [1]	Foongus [6, E]
		Gogoat [1]	Illumise [E]	Ivysaur [28]	Phantump [8]	Roselia [4]	Skiddo [1]
		Snover [E]	Trevenant [8]	Venusaur [28]	Weepinbell [1, 7]	Wormadam (Plant) [29]	
Ghost	Grudge	Banette [52]	Gastly [E]	Phantump [E]	Ralts [E]	Shedinja [43]	Shuppet [46]
Psychic	Guard Split	Abra [E]	Carbink [27]	Rhyhorn [E]	Shelmet [E]	Shuckle [45]	Spinda [E]
	Guard Swap	Abra [E]	Mawile [E]	Meditite [E]	Mewtwo [43]	Mr. Mime [1]	Shelmet [50]
		Skarmory [E]	Slugma [E]	Umbreon [45]	Wooper [E]		
Normal	Guillotine	Axew [50]	Bisharp [1, 71]	Corphish [53]	Crawdaunt [1, 65]	Durant [1, 61]	Fraxure [54]
		Gligar [55]	Gliscor [1, 55]	Haxorus [58]	Pawniard [62]	Pinsir [47]	
Poison	Gunk Shot	Arbok [63]	Ekans [49]	Garbodor [54]	Gulpin [59, E]	Octillery [1]	Shuppet [E]
		Swalot [1, 73]	Trubbish [45]				
Flying	Gust	Articuno [1]	Butterfree [16]	Combee [1]	Drifblim [1, 8]	Drifloon [8]	Ducklett [1]
		Farfetch'd [E]	Masquerain [22]	Mothim [26]	Nincada [E]	Noibat [11]	Noivern [11]
		Pidgeot [1, 9]	Pidgeotto [1, 9]	Pidgey [9]	Sigilyph [1]	Swoobat [1, 8]	Trapinch [E]
		Vespiquen [1]	Vivillon [1]	Wingull [E]	Woobat [8]	Zubat [E]	

Move	Pokémon that can learn it					
Gyro Ball (TM74)	Aegislash [TM]	Aromatisse [TM]	Avalugg [TM]	Bergmite [TM]	Blastoise [TM]	Carbink [TM]
	Chesnaught [TM]	Chespin [TM]	Doublade [TM]	Drifblim [TM]	Drifloon [TM]	Dunsparce [TM]
	Duosion [TM]	Electrode [51, TM]	Ferroseed [21, TM]	Ferrothorn [21, TM]	Geodude [TM]	Golem [TM]
	Golett [TM]	Golurk [TM]	Gourgeist [TM]	Graveler [TM]	Honedge [TM]	Jigglypuff [37, TM]
	Lickilicky [61, TM]	Lunatone [TM]	Magcargo [TM]	Magnemite [53, TM]	Magneton [67, TM]	Magnezone [67, TM]
	Miltank [41, TM]	Onix [20, TM]	Pumpkaboo [TM]	Quilladin [TM]	Qwilfish [TM]	Reuniclus [TM]
	Sandshrew [34, TM]	Sandslash [34, TM]	Scolipede [TM]	Shuckle [TM]	Solosis [TM]	Solrock [TM]
	Spritzee [TM]	Squirtle [TM]	Starmie [TM]	Staryu [30, TM]	Steelix [20, TM]	Swoobat [TM]
	Torkoal [TM]	Venipede [TM]	Voltorb [43, TM]	Wartortle [TM]	Whirlipede [TM]	Wigglytuff [TM]
	Woobat [TM]	Wormadam (Trash) [TM]				

H

Move	Pokémon that can learn it					
Hail (TM07)	Abomasnow [TM]	Absol [TM]	Alomomola [TM]	Amaura [38, TM]	Articuno [57, TM]	Aurorus [38, TM]
	Avalugg [TM]	Azumarill [TM]	Azurill [TM]	Barboach [TM]	Basculin [TM]	Beartic [53, TM]
	Bergmite [TM]	Blastoise [TM]	Buizel [TM]	Carbink [TM]	Carvanha [TM]	Chinchou [TM]
	Clamperl [TM]	Cloyster [TM]	Corphish [TM]	Corsola [TM]	Crawdaunt [TM]	Cryogonal [TM]
	Cubchoo [49, TM]	Delibird [TM]	Dragalge [TM]	Dragonair [TM]	Dragonite [TM]	Dratini [TM]
	Ducklett [TM]	Floatzel [TM]	Glaceon [37, TM]	Goldeen [TM]	Golduck [TM]	Goodra [TM]
	Gorebyss [TM]	Gyarados [TM]	Horsea [TM]	Huntail [TM]	Jynx [TM]	Kangaskhan [TM]
	Kingdra [TM]	Lanturn [TM]	Lapras [TM]	Lombre [TM]	Lotad [TM]	Ludicolo [TM]
	Luvdisc [TM]	Mamoswine [21, TM]	Mantine [TM]	Mantyke [TM]	Marill [TM]	Mewtwo [TM]
	Panpour [TM]	Pelipper [TM]	Piloswine [TM]	Politoed [TM]	Poliwag [TM]	Poliwhirl [TM]
	Poliwrath [TM]	Psyduck [TM]	Quagsire [TM]	Qwilfish [TM]	Relicanth [TM]	Seadra [TM]
	Seaking [TM]	Sharpedo [TM]	Shellder [TM]	Simipour [TM]	Skrelp [TM]	Slowbro [TM]
	Slowking [TM]	Slowpoke [TM]	Smoochum [TM]	Sneasel [TM]	Snover [TM]	Squirtle [TM]
	Starmie [TM]	Staryu [TM]	Swanna [TM]	Swinub [TM]	Tentacool [TM]	Tentacruel [TM]
	Vanillish [42, TM]	Vanillite [40, TM]	Vanilluxe [42, TM]	Vaporeon [TM]	Wailmer [TM]	Wailord [TM]
	Wartortle [TM]	Weavile [TM]	Whiscash [TM]	Wingull [TM]	Wooper [TM]	Xerneas [TM]
Hammer Arm	Chesnaught [1, 60]	Conkeldurr [45]	Diggersby [1, 60]	Geodude [E]	Golett [50]	Golurk [60]
	Gurdurr [45]	Kangaskhan [E]	Lickitung [45]	Miltank [E]	Pangoro [1, 57]	Rhydon [42]
	Rhyperior [42]	Sudowoodo [47]	Timburr [40]	Ursaring [1, 67]	Whismur [E]	
Harden	Aggron [1]	Aron [1]	Avalugg [1]	Axew [E]	Bergmite [1]	Boldore [1, 4]
	Bonsly [E]	Carbink [1]	Corphish [7]	Corsola [4]	Crawdaunt [1, 7]	
	Ferrothorn [1]	Gigalith [1, 4]	Gligar [7]	Gliscor [1, 7]	Heracross [E]	Kakuna [1, 7]
	Lairon [1]	Lunatone [1]	Magcargo [14]	Metapod [1, 7]	Nincada [1]	Ninjask [1]
	Nosepass [4]	Onix [11]	Pinsir [11]	Qwilfish [9]	Relicanth [1]	Roggenrola [4]
	Shedinja [1]	Slugma [14]	Solrock [1]	Spewpa [1]	Staryu [1]	Steelix [1]
	Sudowoodo [E]	Vanillish [1, 4]	Vanillite [4]	Vanilluxe [1, 4]	Wormadam (Sand) [29]	
Haze	Amaura [E]	Arbok [51]	Crobat [47]	Cryogonal [1, 21]	Doduo [E]	Dratini [E]
	Drifloon [E]	Ekans [41]	Gastly [E]	Golbat [47]	Goldeen [E]	Greninja [56]
	Honchkrow [1]	Litwick [E]	Mantine [E]	Mantyke [E]	Murkrow [11]	Poliwag [E]
	Quagsire [48]	Qwilfish [E]	Remoraid [E]	Seviper [38]	Skrelp [E]	Squirtle [E]
	Stunky [E]	Surskit [37]	Swablu [E]	Tentacool [E]	Trubbish [E]	Vaporeon [33]
	Wooper [43]	Zubat [41]	Zygarde [44]			
Head Smash	Aegislash [1]	Aron [E]	Corsola [E]	Deino [E]	Nidoran♂ [E]	Relicanth [1, 78]
	Scrafty [65]	Scraggy [50]	Tyrantrum [1, 58]			
Headbutt	Aggron [1, 8]	Aron [8]	Bagon [16]	Basculin [7]	Bibarel [18]	Bidoof [17]
	Boldore [1, 10]	Bonsly [E]	Buizel [E]	Croagunk [E]	Cubone [11]	Deino [12]
	Diglett [E]	Dunsparce [E]	Electrike [E]	Escavalier [20]	Furfrou [12]	Gigalith [1, 10]
	Granbull [19]	Hydreigon [12]	Karrablast [20]	Lairon [1, 8]	Linoone [1, 9]	Litleo [11]
	Mantine [16]	Mantyke [16]	Marowak [1, 11]	Pawniard [16]	Pyroar [11]	Roggenrola [10]
	Salamence [1, 16]	Scrafty [12]	Scraggy [12]	Shelgon [1, 16]	Slowbro [23]	Slowking [23]
	Slowpoke [23]	Snubbull [19]	Sudowoodo [E]	Zigzagoon [9]	Zweilous [12]	
Heal Bell	Audino [E]	Chimecho [38]	Miltank [48]	Skitty [39]	Snubbull [E]	
Heal Block	Duosion [50]	Gothita [33]	Gothitelle [34]	Gothorita [34]	Klefki [50]	Lunatone [37]
	Reuniclus [54]	Shedinja [50]	Solosis [46]	Solrock [37]		
Heal Order	Vespiquen [29]					
Heal Pulse	Alomomola [17]	Aromatisse [1]	Audino [35]	Chimecho [49]	Clawitzer [1]	Gallade [25]
	Gardevoir [25]	Gothita [E]	Igglybuff [1]	Kirlia [25]	Lucario [51]	Luvdisc [E]
	Ralts [23]	Slowbro [1, 68]	Slowking [1, 58]	Slowpoke [58]	Xerneas [1]	
Healing Wish	Alomomola [1, 57]	Audino [E]	Chimecho [1, 57]	Gardevoir [E]	Mime Jr. [E]	
Heart Stamp	Jynx [21]	Miltank [E]	Smoochum [21]	Swoobat [15]	Woobat [15]	
Heat Wave	Charizard [1, 71]	Fennekin [E]	Heatmor [E]	Litwick [E]	Moltres [1, 64]	Pansear [E]
	Slugma [E]	Torkoal [1, 55]				

AFTER THE HALL OF FAME

CENTRAL KALOS

COASTAL KALOS

MOUNTAIN KALOS

ADVENTURE DATA

Move	Pokémon that can learn it					
Steel — **Heavy Slam**	Aggron [57]	Aron [43]	Golem [1, 69]	Golurk [43]	Hariyama [62]	Lairon [51]
	Machop [E]	Makuhita [46]	Onix [E]	Roggenrola [E]	Snorlax [50]	Wailmer [50]
	Wailord [70]					
Normal — **Helping Hand**	Alomomola [49]	Audino [1]	Azumarill [16]	Azurill [16]	Binacle [E]	Clauncher [E]
	Dedenne [E]	Eevee [1]	Espeon [1]	Flareon [1]	Furret [17]	Gallade [39]
	Glaceon [1]	Hoppip [E]	Illumise [33]	Jolteon [1]	Leafeon [1]	Makuhita [E]
	Marill [16]	Meowstic (Male) [1]	Miltank [E]	Minun [10]	Nidoran♀ [25]	Nidoran♂ [25]
	Nidorina [28]	Nidorino [28]	Plusle [10]	Sentret [16]	Shuckle [E]	Skitty [E]
	Solosis [E]	Sylveon [1]	Umbreon [1]	Vaporeon [1]	Volbeat [33]	Woobat [E]
	Zigzagoon [E]					
Ghost — **Hex**	Absol [E]	Banette [26]	Chandelure [1]	Drifblim [27]	Drifloon [27]	Dunsparce [1]
	Gastly [43]	Gengar [55]	Haunter [55]	Lampent [28]	Litwick [28]	Rotom (Fan) [50]
	Rotom (Frost) [50]	Rotom (Heat) [50]	Rotom (Mow) [50]	Rotom (Wash) [50]	Rotom [50]	Shuppet [26]
	Tentacool [43]	Tentacruel [47]				
Normal — **Hidden Power (TM10)**	Abomasnow [TM]	Abra [TM]	Absol [TM]	Accelgor [TM]	Aegislash [TM]	Aerodactyl [TM]
	Aggron [TM]	Alakazam [TM]	Alomomola [TM]	Altaria [TM]	Amaura [TM]	Amoonguss [TM]
	Ampharos [TM]	Arbok [TM]	Ariados [TM]	Aromatisse [TM]	Aron [TM]	Articuno [TM]
	Audino [TM]	Aurorus [TM]	Avalugg [TM]	Axew [TM]	Azumarill [TM]	Azurill [TM]
	Bagon [TM]	Banette [TM]	Barbaracle [TM]	Barboach [TM]	Basculin [TM]	Beartic [TM]
	Beedrill [TM]	Bellossom [TM]	Bellsprout [TM]	Bergmite [TM]	Bibarel [TM]	Bidoof [TM]
	Binacle [TM]	Bisharp [TM]	Blastoise [TM]	Boldore [TM]	Bonsly [TM]	Braixen [TM]
	Budew [TM]	Buizel [TM]	Bulbasaur [TM]	Bunnelby [TM]	Burmy [20, TM]	Butterfree [TM]
	Carbink [TM]	Carnivine [TM]	Carvanha [TM]	Chandelure [TM]	Charizard [TM]	Charmander [TM]
	Charmeleon [TM]	Chatot [TM]	Chesnaught [TM]	Chespin [TM]	Chimecho [TM]	Chinchou [TM]
	Chingling [TM]	Clamperl [TM]	Clauncher [TM]	Clawitzer [TM]	Cloyster [TM]	Conkeldurr [TM]
	Corphish [TM]	Corsola [TM]	Crawdaunt [TM]	Croagunk [TM]	Crobat [TM]	Crustle [TM]
	Cryogonal [TM]	Cubchoo [TM]	Cubone [TM]	Dedenne [TM]	Deino [TM]	Delcatty [TM]
	Delibird [TM]	Delphox [TM]	Diggersby [TM]	Diglett [TM]	Dodrio [TM]	Doduo [TM]
	Doublade [TM]	Dragalge [TM]	Dragonair [TM]	Dragonite [TM]	Drapion [TM]	Dratini [TM]
	Drifblim [TM]	Drifloon [TM]	Druddigon [TM]	Ducklett [TM]	Dugtrio [TM]	Dunsparce [TM]
	Duosion [14, TM]	Durant [TM]	Dwebble [TM]	Eevee [TM]	Ekans [TM]	Electrike [TM]
	Electrode [TM]	Emolga [TM]	Escavalier [TM]	Espeon [TM]	Espurr [TM]	Exeggcute [TM]
	Exeggutor [TM]	Exploud [TM]	Farfetch'd [TM]	Fearow [TM]	Fennekin [TM]	Ferroseed [TM]
	Ferrothorn [TM]	Flaaffy [TM]	Flabébé [TM]	Flareon [TM]	Fletchinder [TM]	Fletchling [TM]
	Floatzel [TM]	Floette [TM]	Florges [TM]	Flygon [TM]	Foongus [TM]	Fraxure [TM]
	Froakie [TM]	Frogadier [TM]	Furfrou [TM]	Furret [TM]	Gabite [TM]	Gallade [TM]
	Garbodor [TM]	Garchomp [TM]	Gardevoir [TM]	Gastly [TM]	Gengar [TM]	Geodude [TM]
	Gible [TM]	Gigalith [TM]	Glaceon [TM]	Gligar [TM]	Gliscor [TM]	Gloom [TM]
	Gogoat [TM]	Golbat [TM]	Goldeen [TM]	Golduck [TM]	Golem [TM]	Golett [TM]
	Golurk [TM]	Goodra [TM]	Goomy [TM]	Gorebyss [TM]	Gothita [TM]	Gothitelle [TM]
	Gothorita [TM]	Gourgeist [TM]	Granbull [TM]	Graveler [TM]	Greninja [TM]	Grumpig [TM]
	Gulpin [TM]	Gurdurr [TM]	Gyarados [TM]	Hariyama [TM]	Haunter [TM]	Hawlucha [TM]
	Haxorus [TM]	Heatmor [TM]	Heliolisk [TM]	Helioptile [TM]	Heracross [TM]	Hippopotas [TM]
	Hippowdon [TM]	Honchkrow [TM]	Honedge [TM]	Hoothoot [TM]	Hoppip [TM]	Horsea [TM]
	Houndoom [TM]	Houndour [TM]	Huntail [TM]	Hydreigon [TM]	Igglybuff [TM]	Illumise [TM]
	Inkay [TM]	Ivysaur [TM]	Jigglypuff [TM]	Jolteon [TM]	Jumpluff [TM]	Jynx [TM]
	Kadabra [TM]	Kangaskhan [TM]	Karrablast [TM]	Kecleon [TM]	Kingdra [TM]	Kirlia [TM]
	Klefki [TM]	Krokorok [TM]	Krookodile [TM]	Lairon [TM]	Lampent [TM]	Lanturn [TM]
	Lapras [TM]	Larvitar [TM]	Leafeon [TM]	Ledian [TM]	Ledyba [TM]	Lickilicky [TM]
	Lickitung [TM]	Liepard [TM]	Linoone [TM]	Litleo [TM]	Litwick [TM]	Lombre [TM]
	Lotad [TM]	Loudred [TM]	Lucario [TM]	Ludicolo [TM]	Lunatone [TM]	Luvdisc [TM]
	Machamp [TM]	Machoke [TM]	Machop [TM]	Magcargo [TM]	Magnemite [TM]	Magneton [TM]
	Magnezone [TM]	Makuhita [TM]	Malamar [TM]	Mamoswine [TM]	Manectric [TM]	Mantine [TM]
	Mantyke [TM]	Mareep [TM]	Marill [TM]	Marowak [TM]	Masquerain [TM]	Mawile [TM]
	Medicham [15, TM]	Meditite [15, TM]	Meowstic (Female) [TM]	Meowstic (Male) [TM]	Mewtwo [TM]	Mienfoo [TM]
	Mienshao [TM]	Mightyena [TM]	Miltank [TM]	Mime Jr. [TM]	Minun [TM]	Moltres [TM]
	Mothim [20, TM]	Mr. Mime [TM]	Munchlax [TM]	Murkrow [TM]	Nidoking [TM]	Nidoqueen [TM]
	Nidoran♀ [TM]	Nidoran♂ [TM]	Nidorina [TM]	Nidorino [TM]	Nincada [TM]	Ninjask [TM]
	Noctowl [TM]	Noibat [TM]	Noivern [TM]	Nosepass [TM]	Octillery [TM]	Oddish [TM]
	Onix [TM]	Pachirisu [TM]	Pancham [TM]	Pangoro [TM]	Panpour [TM]	Pansage [TM]
	Pansear [TM]	Patrat [TM]	Pawniard [TM]	Pelipper [TM]	Phantump [TM]	Pichu [TM]
	Pidgeot [TM]	Pidgeotto [TM]	Pidgey [TM]	Pikachu [TM]	Piloswine [TM]	Pinsir [TM]
	Plusle [TM]	Politoed [TM]	Poliwag [TM]	Poliwhirl [TM]	Poliwrath [TM]	Poochyena [TM]
	Probopass [TM]	Psyduck [TM]	Pumpkaboo [TM]	Pupitar [TM]	Purrloin [TM]	Pyroar [TM]
	Quagsire [TM]	Quilladin [TM]	Qwilfish [TM]	Raichu [TM]	Ralts [TM]	Relicanth [TM]
	Remoraid [TM]	Reuniclus [14, TM]	Rhydon [TM]	Rhyhorn [TM]	Rhyperior [TM]	Riolu [TM]
	Roggenrola [TM]	Roselia [TM]	Roserade [TM]	Rotom (Fan) [TM]	Rotom (Frost) [TM]	Rotom (Heat) [TM]
	Rotom (Mow) [TM]	Rotom (Wash) [TM]	Rotom [TM]	Sableye [TM]	Salamence [TM]	Sandile [TM]
	Sandshrew [TM]	Sandslash [TM]	Sawk [TM]	Scizor [TM]	Scolipede [TM]	Scrafty [TM]
	Scraggy [TM]	Scyther [TM]	Seadra [TM]	Seaking [TM]	Sentret [TM]	Seviper [TM]
	Sharpedo [TM]	Shedinja [TM]	Shelgon [TM]	Shellder [TM]	Shelmet [TM]	Shuckle [TM]
	Shuppet [TM]	Sigilyph [TM]	Simipour [TM]	Simisage [TM]	Simisear [TM]	Skarmory [TM]

Type	Move	Pokémon that can learn it					
Normal	Hidden Power (TM10)	Skiddo [TM]	Skiploom [TM]	Skitty [TM]	Skorupi [TM]	Skrelp [TM]	Skuntank [TM]
		Sliggoo [TM]	Slowbro [TM]	Slowking [1, TM]	Slowpoke [TM]	Slugma [TM]	Slurpuff [TM]
		Smoochum [TM]	Sneasel [TM]	Snorlax [TM]	Snover [TM]	Snubbull [TM]	Solosis [14, TM]
		Solrock [TM]	Spearow [TM]	Spinarak [TM]	Spinda [TM]	Spoink [TM]	Spritzee [TM]
		Squirtle [TM]	Staraptor [TM]	Staravia [TM]	Starly [TM]	Starmie [TM]	Staryu [TM]
		Steelix [TM]	Stunfisk [TM]	Stunky [TM]	Sudowoodo [TM]	Surskit [TM]	Swablu [TM]
		Swalot [TM]	Swanna [TM]	Swellow [TM]	Swinub [TM]	Swirlix [TM]	Swoobat [TM]
		Sylveon [TM]	Taillow [TM]	Talonflame [TM]	Tauros [TM]	Teddiursa [TM]	Tentacool [TM]
		Tentacruel [TM]	Throh [TM]	Timburr [TM]	Torkoal [TM]	Toxicroak [TM]	Trapinch [TM]
		Trevenant [TM]	Trubbish [TM]	Tyranitar [TM]	Tyrantrum [TM]	Tyrunt [TM]	Umbreon [TM]
		Ursaring [TM]	Vanillish [TM]	Vanillite [TM]	Vanilluxe [TM]	Vaporeon [TM]	Venipede [TM]
		Venusaur [TM]	Vespiquen [TM]	Vibrava [TM]	Victreebel [TM]	Vileplume [TM]	Vivillon [TM]
		Volbeat [TM]	Voltorb [TM]	Wailmer [TM]	Wailord [TM]	Wartortle [TM]	Watchog [TM]
		Weavile [TM]	Weepinbell [TM]	Whirlipede [TM]	Whiscash [TM]	Whismur [TM]	Wigglytuff [TM]
		Wingull [TM]	Woobat [TM]	Wooper [TM]	Wormadam (Plant) [20, TM]	Wormadam (Sand) [20, TM]	Wormadam (Trash) [20, TM]
		Xerneas [TM]	Yanma [TM]	Yanmega [TM]	Yveltal [TM]	Zangoose [TM]	Zapdos [TM]
		Zigzagoon [TM]	Zoroark [TM]	Zorua [TM]	Zubat [TM]	Zweilous [TM]	Zygarde [TM]
Fighting	High Jump Kick	Hawlucha [44]	Medicham [32]	Meditite [32]	Mienfoo [50]	Mienshao [56]	Riolu [E]
		Scrafty [31]	Scraggy [31]				
Dark	Hone Claws (TM01)	Absol [TM]	Aerodactyl [TM]	Aggron [TM]	Altaria [TM]	Ariados [TM]	Aron [TM]
		Axew [TM]	Bagon [TM]	Barbaracle [32, TM]	Beartic [TM]	Binacle [32, TM]	Bisharp [TM]
		Charizard [TM]	Charmander [TM]	Charmeleon [TM]	Chesnaught [TM]	Corphish [TM]	Crawdaunt [TM]
		Crustle [TM]	Cubchoo [TM]	Diglett [TM]	Dragonite [TM]	Drapion [30, TM]	Druddigon [5, TM]
		Dugtrio [TM]	Durant [TM]	Dwebble [TM]	Ferroseed [TM]	Ferrothorn [TM]	Flygon [TM]
		Fraxure [TM]	Furret [TM]	Gabite [TM]	Garchomp [TM]	Gible [TM]	Gligar [TM]
		Gliscor [TM]	Golduck [TM]	Hawlucha [1, TM]	Haxorus [TM]	Heatmor [1, TM]	Kecleon [TM]
		Krokorok [TM]	Krookodile [TM]	Lairon [TM]	Liepard [26, TM]	Linoone [TM]	Lombre [TM]
		Lucario [TM]	Ludicolo [TM]	Nidoking [TM]	Nidoqueen [TM]	Nidoran♀ [TM]	Nidoran♂ [TM]
		Nidorina [TM]	Nidorino [TM]	Nincada [TM]	Ninjask [TM]	Noivern [TM]	Pangoro [TM]
		Panpour [TM]	Pansage [TM]	Pansear [TM]	Pawniard [TM]	Psyduck [TM]	Purrloin [24, TM]
		Quilladin [TM]	Sableye [TM]	Salamence [TM]	Sandile [TM]	Sandshrew [TM]	Sandslash [TM]
		Sentret [TM]	Shedinja [TM]	Shelgon [TM]	Simipour [TM]	Simisage [TM]	Simisear [TM]
		Skorupi [30, TM]	Skuntank [TM]	Sneasel [25, TM]	Spinarak [TM]	Stunky [TM]	Talonflame [TM]
		Teddiursa [TM]	Trevenant [TM]	Tyranitar [TM]	Tyrantrum [TM]	Tyrunt [TM]	Ursaring [TM]
		Vespiquen [TM]	Weavile [25, TM]	Yveltal [TM]	Zangoose [TM]	Zigzagoon [TM]	Zoroark [1, 9, TM]
		Zorua [TM]					
Normal	Horn Attack	Goldeen [11]	Heracross [1]	Karrablast [E]	Nidoran♂ [21]	Nidorino [23]	Rhydon [1]
		Rhyhorn [1]	Rhyperior [1]	Seaking [11]	Tauros [8]		
Normal	Horn Drill	Goldeen [41]	Lapras [E]	Nidoran♂ [45]	Nidorino [58]	Rhydon [1, 71]	Rhyhorn [63]
		Rhyperior [1, 71]	Seaking [47]	Tyrantrum [53]	Tyrunt [49]		
Grass	Horn Leech	Gogoat [47]	Phantump [54]	Skiddo [42]	Trevenant [1, 62]	Xerneas [55]	
Normal	Howl	Braixen [11]	Delphox [11]	Electrike [12]	Exploud [1, 15]	Fennekin [11]	Houndoom [1, 4]
		Houndour [4]	Loudred [1, 15]	Manectric [1, 12]	Mightyena [1, 5]	Poochyena [5]	Whismur [15]
Flying	Hurricane	Articuno [1, 92]	Dragonite [1, 81]	Ducklett [46]	Moltres [1, 92]	Noibat [58]	Noivern [1, 62]
		Pelipper [63]	Pidgeot [1, 68]	Pidgeotto [62]	Pidgey [53]	Swanna [55]	Vivillon [50]
		Wingull [49]	Yveltal [1]				
Water	Hydro Cannon	Blastoise [T]	Greninja [T]				
Water	Hydro Pump	Alomomola [1, 61]	Azumarill [46]	Bagon [E]	Barboach [E]	Blastoise [60]	Buizel [45]
		Carvanha [E]	Chinchou [45]	Cloyster [1]	Dragalge [42]	Floatzel [57]	Froakie [48]
		Frogadier [55]	Goldeen [E]	Golduck [50]	Gorebyss [50]	Greninja [60]	Gyarados [41]
		Horsea [35]	Huntail [50]	Kingdra [40]	Lanturn [57]	Lapras [47]	Lombre [45]
		Luvdisc [40]	Mantine [49, E]	Mantyke [49, E]	Marill [40]	Octillery [52]	Panpour [E]
		Pelipper [1, 58]	Poliwag [38]	Poliwhirl [48]	Psyduck [46]	Qwilfish [1, 57]	Relicanth [1, 71]
		Remoraid [42]	Rotom (Wash) ♦	Seadra [40]	Shellder [61]	Skrelp [42]	Squirtle [40]
		Starmie [1]	Staryu [52]	Surskit [E]	Tentacool [47]	Tentacruel [52]	Vaporeon [45]
		Wailmer [47]	Wailord [62]	Wartortle [48]			
Normal	Hyper Beam (TM15)	Abomasnow [TM]	Absol [TM]	Accelgor [TM]	Aegislash [TM]	Aerodactyl [65, TM]	Aggron [TM]
		Alakazam [TM]	Altaria [TM]	Amaura [57, TM]	Amoonguss [TM]	Ampharos [TM]	Arbok [TM]
		Ariados [TM]	Aromatisse [TM]	Articuno [TM]	Audino [TM]	Aurorus [63, TM]	Avalugg [TM]
		Azumarill [TM]	Banette [TM]	Barbaracle [TM]	Beartic [TM]	Beedrill [TM]	Bellossom [TM]
		Bibarel [TM]	Bisharp [TM]	Blastoise [TM]	Butterfree [TM]	Carnivine [TM]	Chandelure [TM]
		Charizard [TM]	Chesnaught [TM]	Clawitzer [TM]	Cloyster [TM]	Conkeldurr [TM]	Crawdaunt [TM]
		Crobat [TM]	Crustle [TM]	Cryogonal [TM]	Delcatty [TM]	Delphox [TM]	Diggersby [TM]
		Dodrio [TM]	Dragalge [TM]	Dragonair [75, TM]	Dragonite [75, TM]	Drapion [TM]	Dratini [61, TM]
		Drifblim [TM]	Druddigon [TM]	Dugtrio [TM]	Electrode [TM]	Escavalier [TM]	Espeon [TM]
		Exeggutor [TM]	Exploud [79, TM]	Fearow [TM]	Ferrothorn [TM]	Flareon [TM]	Floatzel [TM]
		Florges [TM]	Flygon [49, TM]	Furret [TM]	Gallade [TM]	Garbodor [TM]	Garchomp [TM]
		Gardevoir [TM]	Gengar [TM]	Gigalith [TM]	Glaceon [TM]	Gliscor [TM]	Gogoat [TM]

◆ When Rotom becomes Wash Rotom, it learns the move Hydro Pump. When it changes back to Rotom, it forgets the move.

AFTER THE HALL OF FAME

CENTRAL KALOS

COASTAL KALOS

MOUNTAIN KALOS

ADVENTURE DATA

AFTER THE HALL OF FAME · CENTRAL KALOS · COASTAL KALOS · MOUNTAIN KALOS · ADVENTURE DATA

Normal

Move	Pokémon that can learn it					
Hyper Beam (TM15)	Golbat [TM]	Golduck [TM]	Golem [TM]	Golurk [TM]	Goodra [TM]	Gorebyss [TM]
	Gothitelle [TM]	Gourgeist [TM]	Granbull [TM]	Greninja [TM]	Grumpig [TM]	Gyarados [47, TM]
	Hariyama [TM]	Haxorus [TM]	Heliolisk [TM]	Heracross [TM]	Hippowdon [TM]	Honchkrow [TM]
	Houndoom [TM]	Huntail [TM]	Hydreigon [TM]	Jolteon [TM]	Jumpluff [TM]	Jynx [TM]
	Kangaskhan [TM]	Kingdra [TM]	Klefki [TM]	Krookodile [TM]	Lanturn [TM]	Lapras [TM]
	Larvitar [55, TM]	Leafeon [TM]	Ledian [TM]	Lickilicky [TM]	Lickitung [TM]	Liepard [TM]
	Linoone [TM]	Lucario [TM]	Ludicolo [TM]	Lunatone [TM]	Machamp [TM]	Magcargo [TM]
	Magneton [TM]	Magnezone [TM]	Malamar [TM]	Mamoswine [TM]	Manectric [TM]	Mantine [TM]
	Marowak [TM]	Masquerain [TM]	Mawile [TM]	Medicham [TM]	Meowstic (Female) [TM]	Meowstic (Male) [TM]
	Mewtwo [TM]	Mienshao [TM]	Mightyena [TM]	Miltank [TM]	Moltres [TM]	Mothim [TM]
	Mr. Mime [TM]	Nidoking [TM]	Nidoqueen [TM]	Ninjask [TM]	Noctowl [TM]	Noivern [TM]
	Octillery [58, TM]	Pangoro [TM]	Pelipper [TM]	Pidgeot [TM]	Piloswine [TM]	Pinsir [TM]
	Politoed [TM]	Poliwrath [TM]	Probopass [TM]	Pupitar [67, TM]	Pyroar [1, TM]	Quagsire [TM]
	Raichu [TM]	Relicanth [TM]	Remoraid [46, TM]	Reuniclus [TM]	Rhydon [TM]	Rhyperior [TM]
	Roserade [TM]	Salamence [TM]	Sandslash [TM]	Scizor [TM]	Scolipede [TM]	Scrafty [TM]
	Scyther [TM]	Seadra [TM]	Seaking [TM]	Sharpedo [TM]	Shedinja [TM]	Sigilyph [TM]
	Simipour [TM]	Simisage [TM]	Simisear [TM]	Skuntank [TM]	Slowbro [TM]	Slowking [TM]
	Slurpuff [TM]	Snorlax [TM]	Solrock [TM]	Staraptor [TM]	Starmie [TM]	Steelix [TM]
	Swalot [TM]	Swanna [TM]	Swellow [TM]	Swoobat [TM]	Sylveon [TM]	Talonflame [TM]
	Tauros [TM]	Tentacruel [TM]	Torkoal [TM]	Toxicroak [TM]	Trapinch [49, TM]	Trevenant [TM]
	Tyranitar [73, TM]	Tyrantrum [TM]	Umbreon [TM]	Ursaring [TM]	Vanilluxe [TM]	Vaporeon [TM]
	Venusaur [TM]	Vespiquen [TM]	Vibrava [49, TM]	Victreebel [TM]	Vileplume [TM]	Vivillon [TM]
	Wailord [TM]	Watchog [TM]	Weavile [TM]	Whiscash [TM]	Wigglytuff [TM]	Wormadam (Plant) [TM]
	Wormadam (Sand) [TM]	Wormadam (Trash) [TM]	Xerneas [TM]	Yanmega [TM]	Yveltal [88, TM]	Zapdos [TM]
	Zoroark [TM]	Zygarde [TM]				
Hyper Fang	Bibarel [23]	Bidoof [21]	Pachirisu [49]	Patrat [28]	Watchog [32]	
Hyper Voice	Chatot [1, 57]	Deino [58]	Exploud [71]	Furret [56]	Hydreigon [1, 68]	Jigglypuff [48]
	Litleo [43]	Loudred [65]	Politoed [48]	Pyroar [48]	Sentret [47]	Swablu [E]
	Whismur [50]	Zweilous [64]				

Psychic

Move	Pokémon that can learn it					
Hypnosis	Chimecho [E]	Chingling [E]	Drifloon [E]	Exeggcute [1]	Exeggutor [1]	Fennekin [E]
	Gardevoir [65]	Gastly [1]	Gengar [1]	Haunter [1]	Hoothoot [5]	Inkay [18]
	Kirlia [53]	Lunatone [9]	Malamar [18]	Mime Jr. [E]	Mr. Mime [1, 5]	Noctowl [1, 5]
	Patrat [18]	Politoed [1]	Poliwag [8]	Poliwhirl [1, 8]	Poliwrath [1]	Psyduck [E]
	Ralts [45]	Sigilyph [4]	Spinda [23]	Watchog [18]	Yanma [38]	Zubat [E]

I

Ice

Move	Pokémon that can learn it					
Ice Ball	Avalugg [30]	Bergmite [30]	Delibird [E]	Poliwag [E]		
Ice Beam (TM13)	Abomasnow [TM]	Absol [TM]	Aggron [TM]	Alomomola [TM]	Altaria [TM]	Amaura [50, TM]
	Articuno [43, TM]	Audino [TM]	Aurorus [56, TM]	Avalugg [TM]	Barbaracle [TM]	Barboach [TM]
	Basculin [TM]	Beartic [TM]	Bergmite [TM]	Bibarel [TM]	Bidoof [TM]	Binacle [TM]
	Blastoise [TM]	Buizel [TM]	Carvanha [TM]	Chinchou [TM]	Clamperl [TM]	Clauncher [TM]
	Clawitzer [TM]	Cloyster [TM]	Corphish [TM]	Corsola [TM]	Crawdaunt [TM]	Cryogonal [33, TM]
	Cubchoo [TM]	Cubone [TM]	Delcatty [TM]	Delibird [TM]	Dragonair [TM]	Dragonite [TM]
	Dratini [TM]	Ducklett [TM]	Dunsparce [TM]	Exploud [TM]	Floatzel [TM]	Froakie [TM]
	Frogadier [TM]	Furret [TM]	Glaceon [TM]	Goldeen [TM]	Golduck [TM]	Golett [TM]
	Golurk [TM]	Goodra [TM]	Gorebyss [TM]	Greninja [TM]	Gulpin [TM]	Gyarados [TM]
	Horsea [TM]	Huntail [TM]	Jigglypuff [TM]	Jynx [TM]	Kangaskhan [TM]	Kecleon [TM]
	Kingdra [TM]	Lanturn [TM]	Lapras [32, TM]	Lickilicky [TM]	Lickitung [TM]	Linoone [TM]
	Lombre [TM]	Lotad [TM]	Loudred [TM]	Ludicolo [TM]	Lunatone [TM]	Luvdisc [TM]
	Mamoswine [TM]	Mantine [TM]	Mantyke [TM]	Marill [TM]	Marowak [TM]	Masquerain [TM]
	Mawile [TM]	Mewtwo [TM]	Miltank [TM]	Munchlax [TM]	Nidoking [TM]	Nidoqueen [TM]
	Nidoran ♀ [TM]	Nidoran ♂ [TM]	Nidorina [TM]	Nidorino [TM]	Octillery [40, TM]	Panpour [TM]
	Pelipper [TM]	Piloswine [TM]	Politoed [TM]	Poliwag [TM]	Poliwhirl [TM]	Poliwrath [TM]
	Psyduck [TM]	Quagsire [TM]	Qwilfish [TM]	Relicanth [TM]	Remoraid [34, TM]	Rhydon [TM]
	Rhyhorn [TM]	Rhyperior [TM]	Seadra [TM]	Seaking [TM]	Sentret [TM]	Sharpedo [TM]
	Shellder [52, TM]	Sigilyph [TM]	Simipour [TM]	Skitty [TM]	Sliggoo [TM]	Slowbro [TM]
	Slowking [TM]	Slowpoke [TM]	Smoochum [TM]	Sneasel [TM]	Snorlax [TM]	Snover [TM]
	Squirtle [TM]	Starmie [TM]	Staryu [TM]	Surskit [TM]	Swablu [TM]	Swalot [TM]
	Swanna [TM]	Swinub [TM]	Tauros [TM]	Tentacool [TM]	Tentacruel [TM]	Tyranitar [TM]
	Vanillish [36, TM]	Vanillite [35, TM]	Vanilluxe [36, TM]	Vaporeon [TM]	Wailmer [TM]	Wailord [TM]
	Wartortle [TM]	Weavile [TM]	Whiscash [TM]	Whismur [TM]	Wigglytuff [TM]	Wingull [TM]
	Wooper [TM]	Zangoose [TM]	Zigzagoon [TM]			
Ice Fang	Aerodactyl [1]	Arbok [1]	Avalugg [26]	Bergmite [26]	Carvanha [16]	Deino [E]
	Drapion [1]	Electrike [E]	Exploud [1]	Floatzel [1]	Glaceon [20]	Gliscor [1]
	Granbull [1]	Gyarados [32]	Hippowdon [1]	Huntail [24]	Mamoswine [24]	Mawile [1]
	Piloswine [24]	Poochyena [E]	Rhyhorn [1]	Sharpedo [16]	Snubbull [1, E]	Steelix [1]
	Tyranitar [1]	Tyrunt [E]				
Ice Punch	Abomasnow [1]	Abra [E]	Cubchoo [E]	Delibird [E]	Gastly [E]	Jynx [18]
	Machop [E]	Medicham [1]	Meditite [E]	Scraggy [E]	Smoochum [E]	Sneasel [E]

Type	Move		Pokémon that can learn it				
Ice	Ice Shard	Abomasnow [26]	Articuno [15]	Cryogonal [1, 5]	Delibird [E]	Glaceon [25]	Lapras [10]
		Shellder [28]	Sneasel [47, E]	Snover [26]	Swinub [24]	Vanillite [E]	
	Icicle Crash	Beartic [37]	Cloyster [50]	Sneasel [E]	Swinub [E]		
		Corsola [E]	Shellder [13, E]	Swinub [E]	Vanillish [1]	Vanillite [1]	Vanilluxe [1]
	Icy Wind	Abomasnow [1, 9]	Amaura [13]	Aurorus [13]	Avalugg [10]	Beartic [1, 13]	Bergmite [10]
		Cryogonal [17]	Cubchoo [13]	Delibird [E]	Glaceon [9]	Mime Jr. [E]	Mr. Mime [13]
		Piloswine [21]	Sneasel [14]	Snover [9]	Spinda [E]	Swinub [21]	Vanillish [13]
		Vanillite [13]	Vanilluxe [13]	Weavile [14]			
Psychic	Imprison	Gardevoir [45]	Kirlia [39]	Klefki [36]	Lampent [24]	Litwick [24]	Meowstic (Male) [45]
		Phantump [E]	Ralts [34]	Sableye [E]	Shuppet [E]	Solosis [E]	Swoobat [19]
		Vanillite [E]	Woobat [19]	Zoroark [1, 59]	Zorua [53]		
Fire	Incinerate (TM59)	Absol [TM]	Aerodactyl [TM]	Aggron [TM]	Altaria [TM]	Audino [TM]	Axew [TM]
		Bagon [TM]	Braixen [TM]	Chandelure [TM]	Charizard [TM]	Charmander [TM]	Charmeleon [TM]
		Cubone [TM]	Deino [TM]	Delphox [TM]	Dragonair [TM]	Dragonite [TM]	Dratini [TM]
		Druddigon [TM]	Dunsparce [TM]	Exploud [TM]	Fennekin [TM]	Flareon [TM]	Fletchinder [TM]
		Flygon [TM]	Fraxure [TM]	Gabite [TM]	Garchomp [TM]	Geodude [TM]	Gible [TM]
		Golem [TM]	Goodra [TM]	Gourgeist [TM]	Granbull [TM]	Graveler [TM]	Gyarados [TM]
		Haxorus [TM]	Heatmor [1, TM]	Honchkrow [TM]	Houndoom [TM]	Houndour [TM]	Hydreigon [TM]
		Igglybuff [TM]	Jigglypuff [TM]	Kangaskhan [TM]	Kecleon [TM]	Krokorok [TM]	Krookodile [TM]
		Lampent [TM]	Lickilicky [TM]	Lickitung [TM]	Litleo [46, TM]	Litwick [TM]	Loudred [TM]
		Machamp [TM]	Machoke [TM]	Machop [TM]	Magcargo [TM]	Marowak [TM]	Mawile [TM]
		Mewtwo [TM]	Mightyena [TM]	Moltres [TM]	Munchlax [TM]	Nidoking [TM]	Nidoqueen [TM]
		Octillery [TM]	Pansear [10, TM]	Poochyena [TM]	Pumpkaboo [TM]	Pyroar [51, TM]	Remoraid [TM]
		Rhydon [TM]	Rhyhorn [TM]	Rhyperior [TM]	Sableye [TM]	Salamence [TM]	Sandile [TM]
		Scrafty [TM]	Scraggy [TM]	Sheigon [TM]	Simisear [TM]	Skuntank [TM]	Slowbro [TM]
		Slowking [TM]	Slowpoke [TM]	Slugma [TM]	Snorlax [TM]	Snubbull [TM]	Solrock [TM]
		Stunky [TM]	Talonflame [TM]	Tauros [TM]	Torkoal [TM]	Tyranitar [TM]	Whismur [TM]
		Wigglytuff [TM]	Zangoose [TM]	Zoroark [TM]	Zorua [TM]	Zweilous [TM]	
	Inferno	Charizard [62]	Charmander [46]	Charmeleon [54]	Heatmor [1, 61]	Houndoom [1, 65]	Houndour [56]
		Lampent [38]	Litwick [38]	Slugma [E]	Torkoal [1, 60]		
Bug	Infestation (TM83)	Accelgor [TM]	Arbok [TM]	Ariados [TM]	Banette [TM]	Barbaracle [TM]	Beedrill [TM]
		Bellossom [TM]	Bellsprout [TM]	Binacle [TM]	Butterfree [TM]	Carnivine [TM]	Drapion [TM]
		Duosion [TM]	Ekans [TM]	Escavalier [TM]	Exeggcute [TM]	Exeggutor [TM]	Garbodor [TM]
		Gastly [TM]	Gengar [TM]	Gloom [TM]	Goodra [TM]	Goomy [TM]	Gorebyss [TM]
		Gulpin [TM]	Haunter [TM]	Hoppip [TM]	Huntail [TM]	Jumpluff [TM]	Karrablast [TM]
		Ledian [TM]	Ledyba [TM]	Magcargo [TM]	Masquerain [TM]	Mime Jr. [TM]	Mothim [TM]
		Mr. Mime [TM]	Oddish [TM]	Pangoro [TM]	Quagsire [TM]	Reuniclus [TM]	Scolipede [TM]
		Seviper [TM]	Shelmet [TM]	Shuckle [TM]	Skiploom [TM]	Skorupi [TM]	Sliggoo [TM]
		Slugma [TM]	Solosis [TM]	Spinarak [TM]	Stunfisk [TM]	Surskit [TM]	Swalot [TM]
		Tentacool [TM]	Tentacruel [TM]	Trubbish [TM]	Venipede [TM]	Vespiquen [TM]	Victreebel [TM]
		Vileplume [TM]	Vivillon [TM]	Weepinbell [TM]	Whirlipede [TM]	Wooper [TM]	Wormadam (Plant) [TM]
		Wormadam (Sand) [TM]	Wormadam (Trash) [TM]				
Grass	Ingrain	Abomasnow [31]	Amoonguss [18]	Bellsprout [E]	Bulbasaur [E]	Carnivine [21]	Corsola [E]
		Exeggcute [E]	Ferroseed [35]	Ferrothorn [35]	Foongus [18]	Oddish [E]	Phantump [13]
		Roselia [34]	Snover [31]	Trevenant [13]	Xerneas [1]		
Electric	Ion Deluge	Ampharos [1]	Chinchou [47]	Emolga [E]	Lanturn [60]	Pachirisu [E]	
Steel	Iron Defense	Aegislash [1]	Aggron [15]	Aron [15]	Avalugg [1]	Bisharp [46]	Blastoise [46]
		Boldore [20]	Clamperl [1]	Corsola [29]	Doublade [32]	Durant [1, 56]	Dwebble [E]
		Escavalier [40]	Ferroseed [26]	Ferrothorn [26]	Gigalith [20]	Golett [17]	Golurk [17]
		Honedge [32]	Klefki [E]	Lairon [15]	Larvitar [4]	Mawile [41]	Pawniard [46]
		Probopass [1, 4]	Riolu [E]	Roggenrola [20]	Scizor [37]	Shellder [49]	Squirtle [34]
		Torkoal [44]	Vanillite [E]	Wartortle [40]	Whirlipede [22]		
	Iron Head	Aegislash [1]	Aerodactyl [1, 57]	Aggron [25]	Aron [25, E]	Bisharp [1, 57]	Cubone [E]
		Doublade [45]	Durant [36]	Escavalier [37]	Ferroseed [43]	Ferrothorn [46]	Gible [E]
		Honedge [42]	Lairon [25]	Larvitar [E]	Mawile [1, 56]	Pawniard [54]	Scizor [50]
		Wormadam (Trash) [47]					
	Iron Tail	Aggron [40]	Aron [36]	Axew [E]	Dratini [E]	Druddigon [E]	Ekans [E]
		Emolga [E]	Gible [E]	Goomy [E]	Lairon [40]	Larvitar [E]	Mareep [E]
		Nidoran ♀ [E]	Nidoran ♂ [E]	Onix [40]	Pachirisu [E]	Patrat [E]	Rhyhorn [E]
		Sentret [E]	Seviper [E]	Skorupi [E]	Steelix [40]	Stunky [E]	Zangoose [E]

J

Type	Move		Pokémon that can learn it				
Fighting	Jump Kick	Mienfoo [37]	Mienshao [37]				

AFTER THE HALL OF FAME

CENTRAL KALOS

COASTAL KALOS

MOUNTAIN KALOS

ADVENTURE DATA

K

	Move	Pokémon that can learn it				
Fighting	Karate Chop	Hawlucha [4]	Machamp [1, 10]	Machoke [1, 10]	Machop [10]	Pancham [12]	Pangoro [12]
		Sawk [25]					
Psychic	Kinesis	Alakazam [1]	Kadabra [1]				
Steel	King's Shield	Aegislash [1]					
Dark	Knock Off	Abra [E]	Banette [1]	Bellsprout [27]	Corphish [26, E]	Crawdaunt [26]	Drapion [1, 5]
		Farfetch'd [13]	Gligar [10]	Gliscor [1, 10]	Hariyama [19]	Karrablast [E]	Ledyba [E]
		Lickilicky [13]	Lickitung [13]	Machop [E]	Makuhita [19]	Mienfoo [E]	Sableye [29]
		Shuckle [E]	Shuppet [1]	Skorupi [5]	Tentacool [E]	Weepinbell [27]	Wingull [E]
		Woobat [E]					

L

	Move	Pokémon that can learn it				
Ground	Land's Wrath	Zygarde [26]					
Normal	Last Resort	Audino [1, 55]	Chingling [22]	Eevee [41]	Espeon [41]	Flareon [41]	Glaceon [41]
		Igglybuff [E]	Jolteon [41]	Leafeon [41]	Munchlax [1, 57]	Pachirisu [45]	Plusle [50]
		Sentret [E]	Skitty [E]	Sylveon [41]	Umbreon [41]	Vaporeon [41]	
Fire	Lava Plume	Flareon [37]	Magcargo [37]	Slugma [37]	Torkoal [39]		
Grass	Leaf Blade	Bellossom [1]	Farfetch'd [E]	Gallade [1]	Gogoat [55]	Leafeon [45]	Skiddo [45]
		Victreebel [47]					
	Leaf Storm	Bellossom [1, 53]	Budew [E]	Bulbasaur [E]	Exeggcute [E]	Exeggutor [47]	Pansage [E]
	Leaf Storm	Roselia [E]	Rotom (Mow) ◆	Victreebel [47]	Wormadam (Plant) [47]		
	Leaf Tornado	Carnivine [31]	Victreebel [27]				
Bug	Leech Life	Accelgor [1]	Ariados [12]	Bellsprout [E]	Crobat [1]	Golbat [1]	Nincada [5]
		Ninjask [1, 5]	Noibat [5]	Noivern [5]	Shedinja [5]	Shelmet [1]	Spinarak [12]
		Yanma [1]	Zubat [1]				
Grass	Leech Seed	Bulbasaur [7]	Carnivine [E]	Chesnaught [15]	Chespin [15]	Exeggcute [11]	Ferroseed [E]
		Gogoat [12]	Gourgeist [20]	Hoppip [22]	Ivysaur [1, 7]	Jumpluff [24]	Lotad [E]
		Pansage [16]	Phantump [23]	Pumpkaboo [20]	Quilladin [15]	Roselia [16]	Skiddo [12]
		Skiploom [24]	Snover [E]	Trevenant [23]	Venusaur [1, 7]		
Normal	Leer	Abomasnow [1]	Absol [4]	Arbok [1]	Axew [4]	Bagon [10]	Bisharp [1, 6]
		Bunnelby [1]	Carvanha [1]	Conkeldurr [1]	Corphish [13]	Crawdaunt [1, 13]	Cubone [13]
		Diggersby [1]	Dragonair [1]	Dragonite [1]	Drapion [1]	Dratini [1]	Druddigon [1]
		Ekans [1]	Electrike [9]	Escavalier [1, 4]	Espurr [1]	Farfetch'd [1]	Fearow [1, 5]
		Fraxure [1, 4]	Gallade [1]	Gurdurr [1]	Gyarados [26]	Haxorus [1, 4]	Heracross [1]
		Horsea [8]	Houndoom [1]	Houndour [1]	Kangaskhan [1]	Karrablast [4]	Kingdra [1, 8]
		Krokorok [1]	Krookodile [1, 9]	Larvitar [1]	Litleo [1]	Machamp [1]	Machoke [1]
		Machop [1]	Manectric [1, 9]	Marowak [13]	Meowstic (Female) [1]	Meowstic (Male) [1]	Nidoran♂ [1]
		Nidorino [1]	Pancham [1]	Pangoro [1]	Panpour [4]	Pansage [4]	Pansear [4]
		Patrat [3]	Pawniard [6]	Poochyena [E]	Pupitar [1]	Pyroar [1]	Sableye [1]
		Salamence [1, 10]	Sandile [1]	Sawk [1]	Scizor [1]	Scrafty [1]	Scraggy [1]
		Scyther [1]	Seadra [1, 8]	Sharpedo [1]	Shelgon [1, 10]	Shellder [20]	Simipour [1]
		Simisage [1]	Simisear [1]	Skarmory [1]	Skorupi [1]	Sneasel [1]	Snover [1]
		Spearow [5]	Stunky [E]	Throh [1]	Timburr [1]	Tyranitar [1]	Ursaring [1]
		Watchog [1, 3]	Weavile [1]	Zangoose [1]	Zoroark [1]	Zorua [1]	
Ghost	Lick	Froakie [10]	Frogadier [10]	Gastly [1]	Gengar [1]	Granbull [13]	Greninja [10]
		Haunter [1]	Heatmor [1]	Jynx [1, 5]	Kecleon [1]	Lickilicky [1]	Lickitung [1]
		Munchlax [1, 12, E]	Panpour [7]	Pansage [7]	Pansear [7]	Seviper [9]	Simipour [1]
		Simisage [1]	Simisear [1]	Smoochum [5]	Snorlax [12, E]	Snubbull [13]	Teddiursa [1]
		Ursaring [1]					
Psychic	Light Screen (TM16)	Abomasnow [TM]	Abra [TM]	Alakazam [TM]	Alomomola [TM]	Amaura [47, TM]	Ampharos [57, TM]
		Aromatisse [TM]	Audino [TM]	Aurorus [50, TM]	Azumarill [TM]	Azurill [TM]	Braixen [30, TM]
		Bulbasaur [TM]	Carbink [60, TM]	Chimecho [TM]	Chingling [TM]	Corsola [TM]	Cryogonal [37, TM]
		Delphox [30, TM]	Dragonair [TM]	Dragonite [TM]	Dratini [TM]	Duosion [16, TM]	Electrike [TM]
		Electrode [26, TM]	Emolga [34, TM]	Espeon [TM]	Espurr [13, TM]	Exeggcute [TM]	Exeggutor [TM]
		Fennekin [27, TM]	Flaaffy [52, TM]	Florges [TM]	Gallade [TM]	Gardevoir [TM]	Golduck [TM]
		Gothita [TM]	Gothitelle [TM]	Gothorita [TM]	Grumpig [TM]	Helioptile [TM]	Heliolisk [TM]
		Helioptile [TM]	Igglybuff [TM]	Illumise [TM]	Inkay [31, TM]	Ivysaur [TM]	Jigglypuff [TM]
		Jolteon [TM]	Jynx [TM]	Kadabra [TM]	Kirlia [TM]	Klefki [TM]	Ledian [14, TM]
		Ledyba [14, TM]	Lunatone [TM]	Machamp [TM]	Machoke [TM]	Machop [TM]	Magcargo [TM]
		Magnemite [TM]	Magneton [TM]	Magnezone [TM]	Malamar [31, TM]	Mamoswine [TM]	Manectric [TM]
		Mareep [43, TM]	Marill [TM]	Medicham [TM]	Meditite [TM]	Meowstic (Female) [13, TM]	Meowstic (Male) [13, TM]
		Mewtwo [TM]	Mime Jr. [22, TM]	Minun [TM]	Mr. Mime [22, TM]	Pachirisu [TM]	Pichu [TM]
		Pikachu [45, TM]	Piloswine [TM]	Plusle [TM]	Psyduck [TM]	Pumpkaboo [TM]	Raichu [TM]

◆ When Rotom becomes Mow Rotom, it learns the move Leaf Storm. When it changes back to Rotom, it forgets the move.

Move	Pokémon that can learn it					
Light Screen (TM16) *(Psychic)*	Ralts [TM]	Reuniclus [16, TM]	Rotom (Fan) [TM]	Rotom (Frost) [TM]	Rotom (Heat) [TM]	Rotom (Mow) [TM]
	Rotom (Wash) [TM]	Rotom [TM]	Scizor [TM]	Scyther [TM]	Sigilyph [24, TM]	Slowbro [TM]
	Slowking [TM]	Slowpoke [TM]	Slugma [TM]	Slurpuff [58, TM]	Smoochum [TM]	Snover [TM]
	Solosis [16, TM]	Solrock [TM]	Spoink [TM]	Spritzee [TM]	Starmie [TM]	Staryu [33, TM]
	Swinub [TM]	Swirlix [58, TM]	Swoobat [TM]	Sylveon [33, TM]	Vanillish [TM]	Vanillite [TM]
	Vanilluxe [TM]	Venusaur [TM]	Vivillon [1, TM]	Volbeat [TM]	Voltorb [26, TM]	Watchog [TM]
	Wigglytuff [TM]	Woobat [TM]	Xerneas [5, TM]	Zapdos [64, TM]		
Lock-On *(Normal)*	Klefki [E]	Magnemite [46]	Magneton [56]	Magnezone [56]	Nosepass [50]	Probopass [50]
	Remoraid [6]	Roggenrola [E]				
Lovely Kiss	Jynx [1, 8]					
Low Kick	Bonsly [8]	Conkeldurr [12]	Gurdurr [12]	Machamp [1]	Machoke [1]	Machop [1]
	Mienfoo [E]	Panpour [E]	Pansage [E]	Pansear [E]	Riolu [E]	Scrafty [1]
	Scraggy [1]	Sudowoodo [1, 8]	Timburr [12]	Watchog [1]		
Low Sweep (TM47) *(Fighting)*	Bisharp [TM]	Chesnaught [TM]	Chespin [TM]	Conkeldurr [TM]	Croagunk [TM]	Gallade [TM]
	Golduck [TM]	Golett [TM]	Golurk [TM]	Gothitelle [TM]	Gurdurr [TM]	Hariyama [TM]
	Hawlucha [TM]	Heliolisk [TM]	Helioptile [TM]	Krokorok [TM]	Krookodile [TM]	Lucario [TM]
	Machamp [13, TM]	Machoke [13, TM]	Machop [13, TM]	Makuhita [TM]	Medicham [TM]	Meditite [TM]
	Mewtwo [TM]	Mienfoo [TM]	Mienshao [TM]	Pancham [TM]	Pangoro [70, TM]	Panpour [TM]
	Pansage [TM]	Pansear [TM]	Pawniard [TM]	Poliwrath [TM]	Quilladin [TM]	Riolu [TM]
	Sableye [TM]	Sawk [17, TM]	Scrafty [TM]	Scraggy [TM]	Simipour [TM]	Simisage [TM]
	Simisear [TM]	Sneasel [TM]	Throh [TM]	Timburr [TM]	Toxicroak [TM]	Weavile [TM]
	Zoroark [TM]					
Lucky Chant *(Normal)*	Audino [E]	Braixen [27]	Corsola [23]	Delphox [27]	Ducklett [E]	Exeggcute [E]
	Fennekin [25]	Flabébé [10]	Floette [10]	Florges [1]	Gloom [29]	Kirlia [17]
	Luvdisc [17]	Minun [E]	Oddish [25]	Pichu [E]	Plusle [E]	Ralts [17]
	Smoochum [31]	Spoink [E]				

M

Move	Pokémon that can learn it					
Mach Punch *(Fighting)*	Ledian [17]	Ledyba [17]	Timburr [E]			
Magic Coat *(Psychic)*	Absol [E]	Dunsparce [E]	Fennekin [E]	Grumpig [21]	Kecleon [E]	Spoink [21]
Magic Room *(Psychic)*	Braixen [53]	Delphox [58]	Fennekin [46]	Gothita [48]	Gothitelle [59]	Gothorita [53]
	Klefki [44]	Lunatone [1, 53]	Mime Jr. [E]	Mr. Mime [E]		
Magical Leaf *(Grass)*	Bellossom [23]	Bellsprout [E]	Bulbasaur [E]	Carnivine [E]	Flabébé [22]	Floette [25]
	Florges [1]	Gardevoir [22]	Kirlia [22]	Leafeon [20]	Meowstic (Female) [1]	Mr. Mime [1]
	Pansage [E]	Ralts [21]	Roselia [19]	Roserade [E]	Snover [E]	
Magnet Bomb *(Steel)*	Magnemite [18]	Magneton [18]	Magnezone [18]	Probopass [1, 11]		
Magnet Rise *(Electric)*	Amaura [E]	Electrode [46]	Magnemite [49]	Magneton [62]	Magnezone [62]	Probopass [1]
	Vanillite [E]	Voltorb [40]				
Magnetic Flux *(Electric)*	Ampharos [1]	Electrode [1]	Magnezone [1]			
Magnitude *(Ground)*	Barboach [26]	Diglett [15]	Dugtrio [15]	Geodude [15]	Golem [15]	Golett [25]
	Golurk [25]	Graveler [15]	Lickitung [15]	Nosepass [E]	Relicanth [E]	Rhyhorn [E]
	Roggenrola [E]	Sandshrew [17]	Sandslash [17]	Whiscash [26]		
Mat Block *(Fighting)*	Greninja [1]					
Me First *(Normal)*	Absol [1, 60, E]	Accelgor [28]	Buizel [E]	Croagunk [E]	Ducklett [E]	Fletchinder [46]
	Fletchling [41]	Furret [50]	Hawlucha [E]	Lickilicky [41]	Lickitung [41]	Lucario [37]
	Meowstic (Female) [1]	Mewtwo [93]	Mienfoo [E]	Pancham [E]	Pinsir [E]	Poochyena [E]
	Sandile [E]	Sentret [42]	Slowpoke [E]	Stunfisk [E]	Talonflame [49]	
Mean Look	Absol [E]	Crobat [38]	Gastly [8]	Gengar [8]	Golbat [38]	Gothita [E]
	Haunter [8]	Jynx [25]	Meowstic (Male) [1]	Murkrow [41]	Patrat [31]	Pawniard [E]
	Ralts [E]	Sableye [1, 60, E]	Sandile [E]	Smoochum [25]	Umbreon [37]	Watchog [36]
	Zubat [34]					
Meditate *(Psychic)*	Croagunk [E]	Machop [E]	Medicham [1, 4]	Meditite [4]	Mienfoo [5]	Mienshao [1, 5]
	Mime Jr. [8]	Mr. Mime [8]	Smoochum [E]			
Mega Drain *(Grass)*	Accelgor [20]	Amoonguss [15]	Bellossom [1]	Budew [13]	Foongus [15]	Gloom [23]
	Hoppip [25]	Jumpluff [29]	Lotad [19]	Ludicolo [1]	Oddish [21]	Roselia [13]
	Roserade [1]	Shelmet [20]	Skiploom [28]	Vileplume [1]		
Mega Punch *(Normal)*	Geodude [E]	Golett [21]	Golurk [21]	Kangaskhan [25]		
Megahorn *(Bug)*	Absol [E]	Goldeen [57]	Heracross [46, E]	Nidoking [1, 58]	Rhydon [1, 77]	Rhyhorn [67]
	Rhyperior [1, 77]	Scolipede [1, 65]	Seaking [1, 72]	Spinarak [E]	Xerneas [44]	
Memento *(Dark)*	Diglett [E]	Drifloon [24]	Hoppip [49]	Jumpluff [69]	Lampent [33]	Litwick [33]
	Ralts [E]	Skiploom [60]	Skuntank [51]	Slugma [E]	Stunky [43]	Zorua [E]
Metal Burst *(Steel)*	Aggron [74]	Aron [50]	Bisharp [1]	Lairon [62]	Mawile [E]	Rhyhorn [E]
	Sableye [E]					

Pokémon Moves Reverse Lookup

Type	Move	Pokémon that can learn it					
Steel	Metal Claw	Aggron [11]	Aron [11]	Bisharp [25]	Charmander [E]	Corphish [E]	Druddigon [E]
		Durant [21]	Ferroseed [14]	Ferrothorn [14]	Gible [E]	Gligar [E]	Lairon [11]
		Lucario [1]	Nincada [38]	Pawniard [25]	Sandshrew [E]	Scizor [21]	Sneasel [22]
		Teddiursa [E]	Weavile [22]	Zangoose [E]			
Steel	Metal Sound	Aggron [34]	Aron [32]	Bisharp [38]	Doublade [8]	Durant [1, 66]	Honedge [8, E]
		Klefki [12]	Lairon [34]	Lucario [24]	Magnemite [29]	Magneton [29]	Magnezone [29]
		Pawniard [38]	Skarmory [31]	Wormadam (Trash) [29]			
Normal	Metronome	Munchlax [1]	Snubbull [1]				
Normal	Milk Drink	Gogoat [58]	Miltank [11]	Skiddo [50, E]			
Normal	Mimic	Bonsly [15]	Chatot [33]	Furfrou [E]	Jigglypuff [45]	Mime Jr. [15, E]	Mr. Mime [15, E]
		Snubbull [E]	Sudowoodo [15]				
Normal	Mind Reader	Articuno [22]	Budew [E]	Froakie [E]	Medicham [18]	Meditite [18]	Nincada [19]
		Ninjask [19]	Poliwag [E]	Poliwrath [43]	Riolu [E]	Roselia [E]	Shedinja [19]
		Shelmet [E]	Surskit [E]				
Normal	Minimize	Drifblim [1]	Driffloon [1]	Lampent [1, 3]	Litwick [3]	Qwilfish [9]	Staryu [25]
Psychic	Miracle Eye	Alakazam [22]	Gothita [E]	Kadabra [22]	Meowstic (Male) [31]	Mewtwo [29]	Sigilyph [1]
		Smoochum [E]					
Psychic	Mirror Coat	Alomomola [E]	Amaura [E]	Bergmite [E]	Corsola [45]	Electrode [62]	Glaceon [33]
		Gothita [E]	Magnezone [1]	Mantine [E]	Mantyke [E]	Spoink [E]	Squirtle [E]
		Tentacool [E]	Vanillish [47]	Vanillite [44]	Vanilluxe [50]	Voltorb [50]	Wobbuffet [1]
		Wynaut [15]					
Flying	Mirror Move	Chatot [9]	Doduo [E]	Ducklett [E]	Farfetch'd [E]	Fearow [23]	Hoothoot [E]
		Murkrow [E]	Pidgeot [56]	Pidgeotto [52]	Pidgey [45]	Sigilyph [34]	Spearow [21]
		Starly [E]	Swablu [34]	Taillow [E]			
Steel	Mirror Shot	Ferroseed [30]	Ferrothorn [30]	Klefki [34]	Magnemite [25]	Magneton [25]	Magnezone [25]
		Vanillish [26]	Vanillite [26]	Vanilluxe [26]	Wormadam (Trash) [26]		
Ice	Mist	Abomasnow [21]	Alomomola [E]	Altaria [15]	Amaura [18]	Articuno [8]	Aurorus [18]
		Bergmite [E]	Chinchou [E]	Corsola [E]	Cryogonal [1, 21]	Dratini [E]	Lapras [4]
		Lotad [11]	Mamoswine [37]	Mewtwo [86]	Pelipper [14]	Piloswine [37]	Poliwag [E]
		Quagsire [48]	Snover [21, E]	Squirtle [37]	Surskit [37]	Swablu [15]	Swinub [35]
		Vanillish [16]	Vanillite [16]	Vanilluxe [16]	Wailmer [24]	Wailord [24]	Wingull [14, E]
		Wooper [43]					
Fairy	Misty Terrain	Aromatisse [42]	Flabébé [37]	Floette [43]	Florges [1]	Gardevoir [1]	Igglybuff [E]
		Mawile [E]	Meowstic (Male) [50]	Mr. Mime [1]	Ralts [E]	Spritzee [42]	Sylveon [29]
		Xerneas [63]					
Fairy	Moonblast	Altaria [60]	Aromatisse [31]	Carbink [50]	Flabébé [41]	Floette [46]	Florges [1]
		Gardevoir [1, 85]	Lunatone [50]	Spritzee [31]	Swablu [50]	Sylveon [37]	Xerneas [35]
Fairy	Moonlight	Exeggcute [E]	Gloom [41]	Illumise [13]	Noivern [1]	Oddish [33]	Sableye [E]
		Umbreon [33]	Volbeat [13]				
Normal	Morning Sun	Espeon [33]					
Ground	Mud Bomb	Arbok [39]	Barboach [14]	Croagunk [29]	Diglett [26, E]	Dugtrio [28]	Ekans [33]
		Mamoswine [18]	Piloswine [18]	Poliwag [41]	Poliwhirl [53]	Psyduck [E]	Quagsire [19]
		Skitty [E]	Stunfisk [21]	Swinub [18]	Toxicroak [29]	Whiscash [14]	Wooper [19]
Ground	Mud Shot	Barboach [E]	Basculin [E]	Bunnelby [18]	Chesnaught [41]	Chespin [35]	Diggersby [18]
		Gible [E]	Goldeen [E]	Poliwag [28, E]	Poliwhirl [32]	Quagsire [9]	Quilladin [39]
		Relicanth [E]	Remoraid [E]	Sandshrew [E]	Shellder [E]	Stunfisk [13]	Surskit [E]
		Swinub [E]	Trapinch [E]	Wooper [9]			
Ground	Mud Sport	Barboach [6]	Clamperl [E]	Corphish [E]	Ducklett [E]	Froakie [E]	Geodude [4]
		Goldeen [E]	Golem [1, 4]	Graveler [1, 4]	Hawlucha [E]	Linoone [23]	Luvdisc [E]
		Mamoswine [1, 5]	Mantine [E]	Mantyke [E]	Onix [1]	Panpour [E]	Piloswine [1, 5]
		Quagsire [1, 5]	Relicanth [1, 36]	Slowpoke [E]	Squirtle [E]	Steelix [1]	Stunfisk [1]
		Swinub [5]	Trubbish [E]	Whiscash [1, 6]	Wooper [5, E]	Zigzagoon [21]	
Water	Muddy Water	Azurill [E]	Barboach [E]	Basculin [E]	Clamperl [E]	Clauncher [48]	Clawitzer [53]
		Goodra [38]	Goomy [38]	Horsea [E]	Lickitung [E]	Marill [E]	Quagsire [53]
		Relicanth [E]	Sliggoo [38]	Squirtle [E]	Stunfisk [40]	Tentacool [E]	Vaporeon [37]
		Wooper [47]					
Ground	Mud-Slap	Aggron [1, 4]	Aron [4]	Barbaracle [18]	Barboach [1]	Binacle [18]	Boldore [17]
		Buizel [E]	Bunnelby [13]	Croagunk [3]	Diggersby [13]	Diglett [12]	Dugtrio [12]
		Farfetch'd [E]	Flygon [13]	Gigalith [17]	Goldeen [E]	Golett [5]	Golurk [1, 5]
		Gulpin [E]	Helioptile [13]	Krokorok [19]	Krookodile [19]	Lairon [1, 4]	Mamoswine [11]
		Nincada [31]	Piloswine [11]	Relicanth [E]	Roggenrola [17]	Sandile [19]	Shelmet [E]
		Shuckle [E]	Stunfisk [1]	Swinub [11]	Toxicroak [1, 3]	Trapinch [13]	Vibrava [13]
		Whiscash [1]	Zigzagoon [1]				
Fire	Mystical Fire	Delphox [36, 75]					

N

	Move	Pokémon that can learn it					
Dark	Nasty Plot	Chatot [E] Liepard [50] Pansear [E] Slowking [36] Zubat [E]	Croagunk [38] Mime Jr. [E] Pichu [18] Smoochum [E]	Honchkrow [35] Minun [1, 56] Pluslе [1, 56] Toxicroak [41]	Houndoom [1, 60] Mr. Mime [E] Purrloin [42] Weavile [20]	Houndour [52, E] Panpour [E] Riolu [47] Zoroark [54]	Kecleon [E] Pansage [E] Sableye [E] Zorua [49]
Normal	Natural Gift	Altaria [21] Exeggcute [37, E] Munchlax [49, E] Sentret [E]	Bellsprout [E] Fletchinder [31] Oddish [29] Snorlax [E]	Budew [E] Fletchling [29] Panpour [40] Snover [E]	Dedenne [E] Gloom [35] Pansage [40] Swablu [21]	Doduo [E] Lotad [15] Pansear [40] Talonflame [31]	Eevee [E] Miltank [E] Roselia [E] Vanillite [E]
Normal	Nature Power (TM96)	Amaura [41, 96] Binacle [TM] Carbink [TM] Crustle [TM] Ferrothorn [TM] Gigalith [TM] Ivysaur [TM] Oddish [TM, E] Roggenrola [TM] Steelix [TM] Vileplume [TM]	Amoonguss [TM] Boldore [TM] Carnivine [TM] Diggersby [TM] Flabébé [TM] Gloom [TM] Leafeon [TM] Onix [TM] Roselia [TM] Sudowoodo [TM] Weepinbell [TM]	Aurorus [43, TM] Bonsly [TM] Chesnaught [TM] Dwebble [TM] Floette [TM] Gogoat [TM] Lombre [7, TM] Pansage [TM] Roserade [TM] Torkoal [TM] Xerneas [72, TM]	Barbaracle [TM] Budew [TM] Chespin [TM] Exeggcute [TM, E] Florges [TM] Golem [TM] Lotad [7, TM] Phantump [TM] Simisage [TM] Trevenant [TM]	Bellossom [TM] Bulbasaur [TM, E] Corsola [TM, E] Exeggutor [TM] Foongus [TM] Gourgeist [TM] Ludicolo [1, TM] Pumpkaboo [TM] Skiddo [TM] Venusaur [TM]	Bellsprout [TM] Bunnelby [TM] Crawdaunt [TM] Ferroseed [TM] Geodude [TM] Graveler [TM] Magcargo [TM] Quilladin [TM] Slugma [TM] Victreebel [TM]
Grass	Needle Arm	Chesnaught [26]	Quilladin [26]				
Dark	Night Daze	Zoroark [1, 64]	Zorua [57]				
Ghost	Night Shade	Ariados [15] Golurk [35] Sableye [8]	Banette [1, 7] Haunter [15] Shuppet [7]	Chatot [E] Hoothoot [E] Solosis [E]	Gastly [15] Lampent [13] Spinarak [15]	Gengar [15] Litwick [13]	Golett [35] Murkrow [21]
Dark	Night Slash	Absol [41] Corphish [35] Druddigon [40] Gliscor [27] Inkay [46] Sandshrew [E] Skorupi [38, E] Xerneas [51]	Aegislash [1] Crawdaunt [39] Dugtrio [1] Greninja [1, 70] Liepard [43] Scizor [45] Skuntank [41] Yanmega [1]	Axew [E] Cryogonal [1, 57] Dwebble [E] Heatmor [E] Malamar [46] Scyther [45, E] Spinarak [E] Zangoose [E]	Barbaracle [44] Cubchoo [E] Farfetch'd [33, E] Heracross [1] Nincada [E] Seviper [31, E] Stunky [37] Zoroark [30]	Binacle [41] Doublade [36] Gallade [1] Honchkrow [1, 55] Pawniard [49] Sharpedo [1, 56] Teddiursa [E]	Bisharp [49] Drapion [38] Gligar [E] Honedge [35] Purrloin [37] Skarmory [50] Weavile [35]
Ghost	Nightmare	Gastly [47]	Gengar [61]	Haunter [61]			
Normal	Noble Roar	Litleo [15]	Pyroar [15]				
Electric	Nuzzle	Dedenne [20]	Emolga [15]	Minun [1]	Pachirisu [19]	Pikachu [23]	Plusle [1]

O

	Move	Pokémon that can learn it					
Flying	Oblivion Wing	Yveltal [26]					
Water	Octazooka	Horsea [E]	Octillery [25]	Remoraid [E]			
Normal	Odor Sleuth	Aromatisse [8] Furfrou [27] Mamoswine [1] Poochyena [17] Zigzagoon [17]	Bidoof [E] Grumpig [1, 10] Manectric [25] Spoink [10]	Buizel [E] Heatmor [6] Mareep [E] Spritzee [8]	Bunnelby [25] Houndoom [20] Mightyena [17] Swinub [1]	Diggersby [26] Houndour [20] Munchlax [1] Swoobat [1, 4]	Electrike [25] Linoone [17] Piloswine [1] Woobat [4]
Ghost	Ominous Wind	Drifblim [20] Rotom (Mow) [29]	Driffloon [20] Rotom (Wash) [29]	Masquerain [1] Rotom [29]	Rotom (Fan) [29] Shuppet [E]	Rotom (Frost) [29]	Rotom (Heat) [29]
Dragon	Outrage	Axew [56] Druddigon [62] Horsea [E] Xerneas [93]	Charmander [E] Fraxure [60] Hydreigon [1, 79] Zweilous [71]	Deino [62] Gible [E] Kangaskhan [46] Zygarde [93]	Dragonair [67] Goodra [1, 63] Krookodile [1, 60]	Dragonite [67] Granbull [1, 67] Larvitar [E]	Dratini [55] Haxorus [1, 66] Noibat [E]
Fire	Overheat (TM50)	Braixen [TM] Exploud [TM] Houndoom [TM] Magcargo [TM] Simisear [TM]	Chandelure [TM] Fennekin [TM] Houndour [TM] Manectric [TM] Slugma [TM]	Charizard [TM] Flareon [TM] Lampent [69, TM] Moltres [TM] Snubbull [TM]	Charmander [TM] Fletchinder [TM] Litleo [50, TM] Pansear [TM] Solrock [TM]	Charmeleon [TM] Fletchling [TM] Litwick [61, TM] Pyroar [57, TM] Talonflame [TM]	Delphox [TM] Granbull [TM] Loudred [TM] Rotom (Heat) [TM] ◆ Torkoal [TM]

◆ When Rotom becomes Heat Rotom, it learns the move Overheat. When it changes back to Rotom, it forgets the move.

P

Move	Pokémon that can learn it					
Pain Split (Normal)	Alomomola [E]	Chandelure [1]	Chesnaught [52]	Chespin [45]	Duosion [34]	Gourgeist [42]
	Gulpin [E]	Lampent [61]	Litwick [55]	Pumpkaboo [42]	Quilladin [52]	Reuniclus [34]
	Solosis [33]	Stunfisk [E]				
Parabolic Charge (Electric)	Dedenne [17]	Heliolisk [1]	Helioptile [25]			
Parting Shot (Dark)	Pancham [45]	Pangoro [48]				
Pay Day (Normal)	Purrloin [E]					
Payback (TM66) (Dark)	Absol [TM]	Aerodactyl [TM]	Aggron [TM]	Amoonguss [TM]	Arbok [TM]	Axew [TM]
	Banette [TM]	Barbaracle [TM]	Beedrill [TM]	Binacle [TM]	Bisharp [TM]	Bunnelby [TM]
	Carnivine [TM]	Carvanha [TM]	Chandelure [TM]	Chesnaught [TM]	Chespin [TM]	Cloyster [TM]
	Conkeldurr [TM]	Corphish [TM]	Crawdaunt [TM]	Croagunk [TM]	Crobat [TM]	Delcatty [TM]
	Diggersby [TM]	Dodrio [TM]	Drapion [TM]	Drifblim [16, TM]	Drifloon [16, TM]	Druddigon [TM]
	Ekans [TM]	Espurr [TM]	Ferroseed [47, TM]	Ferrothorn [53, TM]	Floatzel [TM]	Foongus [TM]
	Fraxure [TM]	Garbodor [TM]	Gastly [26, TM]	Gengar [28, TM]	Gligar [TM]	Gliscor [TM]
	Gogoat [TM]	Golbat [TM]	Gothita [TM]	Gothitelle [TM]	Gothorita [TM]	Granbull [51, TM]
	Grumpig [46, TM]	Gurdurr [TM]	Gyarados [TM]	Hariyama [TM]	Haunter [28, TM]	Hawlucha [TM]
	Haxorus [TM]	Honchkrow [TM]	Houndoom [TM]	Houndour [TM]	Hydreigon [TM]	Inkay [27, TM]
	Jynx [TM]	Krokorok [TM]	Krookodile [TM]	Lampent [TM]	Larvitar [37, TM]	Liepard [TM]
	Litleo [TM]	Litwick [TM]	Lucario [TM]	Machamp [TM]	Machoke [TM]	Machop [TM]
	Malamar [27, TM]	Mawile [TM]	Meowstic (Female) [TM]	Meowstic (Male) [TM]	Mienfoo [TM]	Mienshao [TM]
	Mightyena [TM]	Mr. Mime [TM]	Murkrow [TM]	Octillery [TM]	Onix [TM]	Pancham [TM]
	Pangoro [TM]	Panpour [TM]	Pansage [TM]	Pansear [TM]	Pawniard [TM]	Pelipper [22, TM]
	Politoed [TM]	Poliwrath [TM]	Poochyena [TM]	Pupitar [41, TM]	Purrloin [TM]	Pyroar [TM]
	Quilladin [TM]	Qwilfish [TM]	Rhydon [TM]	Rhyhorn [TM]	Rhyperior [TM]	Riolu [TM]
	Sableye [TM]	Sandile [TM]	Sawk [TM]	Scolipede [TM]	Scrafty [23, TM]	Scraggy [23, TM]
	Seviper [TM]	Sharpedo [TM]	Shellder [TM]	Shuppet [TM]	Simipour [TM]	Simisage [TM]
	Simisear [TM]	Skarmory [TM]	Skiddo [TM]	Skitty [TM]	Skorupi [TM]	Skuntank [TM]
	Smoochum [TM]	Sneasel [TM]	Snubbull [43, TM]	Spoink [40, TM]	Steelix [TM]	Stunfisk [TM]
	Stunky [TM]	Tauros [24, TM]	Teddiursa [TM]	Tentacool [TM]	Tentacruel [TM]	Throh [TM]
	Timburr [TM]	Toxicroak [TM]	Trubbish [TM]	Tyranitar [41, TM]	Umbreon [TM]	Ursaring [TM]
	Venipede [TM]	Weavile [TM]	Whirlipede [TM]	Zangoose [TM]	Zoroark [TM]	Zorua [TM]
	Zubat [TM]					
Peck (Flying)	Altaria [1]	Chatot [1]	Dodrio [1]	Doduo [1]	Escavalier [1]	Farfetch'd [1]
	Fearow [1]	Fletchinder [10]	Fletchling [10]	Goldeen [1]	Hoothoot [9]	Inkay [1]
	Karrablast [1]	Malamar [1]	Mamoswine [1]	Murkrow [1]	Nidoking [1]	Nidoran♂ [1]
	Nidorino [1]	Noctowl [9]	Piloswine [1]	Seaking [1]	Skarmory [1]	Spearow [1]
	Swablu [1]	Swellow [1]	Taillow [1]	Talonflame [10]	Zapdos [1]	
Perish Song (Normal)	Absol [1, 65, E]	Altaria [57]	Cubone [E]	Gastly [E]	Igglybuff [E]	Jynx [1, 55]
	Lapras [E]	Marill [E]	Murkrow [E]	Politoed [1]	Smoochum [45]	Swablu [48]
Petal Blizzard (Grass)	Bellossom [50]	Flabébé [28]	Floette [33]	Florges [1]	Gloom [50]	Roselia [50]
	Venusaur [50]	Vileplume [50]				
Petal Dance (Grass)	Bulbasaur [E]	Flabébé [45]	Floette [51]	Florges [1]	Gloom [53]	Oddish [41]
	Roselia [37]	Venusaur [32]	Vileplume [53]			
Phantom Force (Ghost)	Drifblim [1, 65]	Golurk [1, 75]	Gourgeist [1, 57]	Phantump [45]	Shedinja [47]	Shuppet [E]
	Trevenant [45]	Yveltal [55]				
Pin Missile (Bug)	Ariados [41]	Beedrill [28]	Budew [E]	Chesnaught [20]	Chespin [18]	Drapion [9]
	Ferroseed [18]	Ferrothorn [18]	Heracross [31]	Jolteon [25]	Quilladin [20]	Qwilfish [37]
	Roselia [E]	Skorupi [9]	Spinarak [36]	Venipede [E]	Zigzagoon [25]	
Play Nice (Normal)	Audino [1]	Beartic [9]	Cubchoo [15]	Gothita [8]	Gothitelle [1]	Gothorita [1]
	Illumise [1]	Jigglypuff [10]	Minun [1]	Panpour [1]	Pansage [1]	Pansear [1]
	Pikachu [7]	Plusle [1, 21]	Slurpuff [8]	Swirlix [8]	Teddiursa [25]	Ursaring [25]
Play Rough (Fairy)	Absol [42]	Azumarill [50]	Cubchoo [E]	Dedenne [42]	Granbull [43]	Klefki [43]
	Liepard [58]	Linoone [1]	Marill [45]	Mawile [1, 60]	Poochyena [E]	Purrloin [49]
	Skitty [49]	Skrelp [E]	Slurpuff [49]	Snubbull [37]	Stunky [E]	Swirlix [49]
	Teddiursa [E]	Wigglytuff [1]				
Pluck (Flying)	Altaria [1]	Dodrio [1]	Fearow [1]	Inkay [35]	Malamar [35]	Swellow [1]
	Zapdos [22]					
Poison Fang (Poison)	Crobat [42]	Drapion [23]	Ekans [E]	Golbat [42]	Mawile [E]	Nidoran♀ [45]
	Nidorina [58]	Poochyena [E]	Seviper [27]	Skorupi [23]	Tyrunt [E]	Zubat [37]
Poison Gas (Poison)	Garbodor [1]	Gulpin [9]	Skuntank [1, 4]	Stunky [4]	Swalot [1, 9]	Trubbish [1]

Move	Pokémon that can learn it				
Poison Jab (TM84)	Arbok [TM]	Ariados [50, TM]	Axew [TM]	Barbaracle [TM]	Beedrill [37, TM]	Binacle [TM]
	Bisharp [TM]	Chesnaught [TM]	Chespin [TM]	Cloyster [TM]	Conkeldurr [TM]	Croagunk [43, TM]
	Crustle [TM]	Cryogonal [TM]	Drapion [TM]	Dunsparce [TM]	Dwebble [TM]	Ekans [TM]
	Escavalier [TM]	Farfetch'd [1, TM]	Ferroseed [TM]	Ferrothorn [TM]	Fraxure [TM]	Gallade [TM]
	Garchomp [TM]	Gengar [TM]	Gligar [TM]	Gliscor [1, TM]	Goldeen [TM]	Gurdurr [TM]
	Hariyama [TM]	Haunter [TM]	Hawlucha [TM]	Haxorus [TM]	Karrablast [TM]	Lucario [TM]
	Machamp [TM]	Machoke [TM]	Machop [TM]	Makuhita [TM]	Medicham [TM]	Meditite [TM]
	Mewtwo [TM]	Mienfoo [TM]	Mienshao [TM]	Nidoking [TM]	Nidoqueen [TM]	Nidoran♀ [TM]
	Nidoran♂ [37, TM]	Nidorina [TM]	Nidorino [43, TM]	Pangoro [TM]	Pawniard [TM]	Phantump [TM]
	Poliwrath [TM]	Quilladin [TM]	Qwilfish [49, TM]	Rhydon [TM]	Rhyhorn [TM]	Rhyperior [1, TM]
	Riolu [TM]	Roselia [TM]	Roserade [TM]	Sableye [TM]	Sandshrew [TM]	Sandslash [TM]
	Sawk [TM]	Scolipede [TM]	Scrafty [TM]	Scraggy [TM]	Seaking [1, TM]	Seviper [42, TM]
	Sharpedo [TM]	Skorupi [TM]	Skuntank [TM]	Sneasel [TM]	Spinarak [43, TM]	Tentacool [36, TM]
	Tentacruel [38, TM]	Throh [TM]	Timburr [TM]	Toxicroak [49, TM]	Trevenant [TM]	Venipede [TM]
	Weavile [TM]	Whirlipede [TM]	Zangoose [TM]			
Poison Powder	Bellsprout [15]	Bulbasaur [13]	Butterfree [21]	Exeggcute [21]	Foongus [E]	Gloom [13]
	Hoppip [12]	Ivysaur [13]	Jumpluff [12]	Mothim [29]	Oddish [13]	Scatterbug [E]
	Skiploom [12]	Venusaur [13]	Vileplume [1]	Vivillon [1]	Weepinbell [15]	
Poison Sting	Arbok [1, 4]	Ariados [1]	Croagunk [8]	Drapion [1]	Ekans [1]	Gligar [1]
	Nidoking [1]	Nidoqueen [1]	Nidoran♀ [13]	Nidoran♂ [13]	Nidorina [13]	Nidorino [13]
	Qwilfish [1]	Roselia [7]	Roserade [1]	Sandshrew [5]	Sandslash [1]	Scolipede [1, 5]
	Skorupi [1]	Spinarak [1]	Tentacool [1]	Tentacruel [1]	Toxicroak [1, 8]	Venipede [5]
	Vespiquen [1]	Weedle [1]	Whirlipede [1, 5]			
Poison Tail	Dragalge [23]	Druddigon [23]	Ekans [31]	Gligar [E]	Goomy [E]	Nidoran♀ [E]
	Nidoran♂ [E]	Scolipede [19]	Seviper [12]	Skorupi [E]	Skrelp [23]	Venipede [19]
	Whirlipede [19]					
Pound	Alomomola [1]	Audino [1]	Conkeldurr [1]	Exploud [1]	Froakie [1]	Frogadier [1]
	Garbodor [1]	Golett [1]	Golurk [1]	Gothita [1]	Gothitelle [1]	Gothorita [1]
	Greninja [1]	Gulpin [1]	Gurdurr [1]	Helioptile [1]	Igglybuff [9]	Jigglypuff [7]
	Jynx [1]	Loudred [1]	Mienfoo [1]	Mienshao [1]	Smoochum [1]	Swalot [1]
	Timburr [1]	Trubbish [1]	Whismur [1]			
Powder	Vivillon [1, 55]					
Powder Snow	Abomasnow [1]	Amaura [1]	Articuno [1]	Aurorus [1]	Avalugg [5]	Beartic [1]
	Bergmite [5]	Cubchoo [5]	Jynx [1, 11]	Mamoswine [1, 8]	Piloswine [1, 8]	Smoochum [11]
	Snover [1]	Swinub [8]	Vanillite [E]			
Power Gem	Ampharos [35]	Boldore [25]	Carbink [46]	Corsola [41]	Flaaffy [34]	Gigalith [25]
	Grumpig [35]	Mareep [29]	Nosepass [32]	Probopass [32]	Sableye [43]	Slowking [1]
	Spoink [33]	Staryu [43]	Vespiquen [25]			
Power Split	Inkay [E]	Litwick [E]	Mime Jr. [E]	Mr. Mime [E]	Shuckle [45]	Surskit [E]
Power Swap	Accelgor [1, 52]	Espeon [45]	Exeggcute [E]	Meditite [E]	Mewtwo [43]	Mr. Mime [1]
	Swablu [E]					
Power Trick	Abra [E]	Aegislash [E]	Doublade [41]	Gligar [E]	Honedge [39]	Machop [E]
	Medicham [49]	Meditite [43]	Shuckle [31]			
Power Whip	Bellsprout [E]	Bulbasaur [E]	Carnivine [50]	Ferrothorn [40]	Goodra [55]	Lickilicky [1, 53]
	Lickitung [53]					
Power-Up Punch (TM98)	Aggron [TM]	Ampharos [TM]	Audino [TM]	Azumarill [TM]	Barbaracle [TM]	Beartic [TM]
	Binacle [TM]	Bisharp [TM]	Blastoise [TM]	Braixen [TM]	Buizel [TM]	Bunnelby [TM]
	Charizard [TM]	Charmander [TM]	Charmeleon [TM]	Chesnaught [TM]	Chespin [TM]	Conkeldurr [TM]
	Croagunk [TM]	Cubchoo [TM]	Cubone [TM]	Delibird [TM]	Delphox [TM]	Diggersby [TM]
	Dragonite [TM]	Druddigon [TM]	Exploud [TM]	Fennekin [TM]	Flaaffy [TM]	Floatzel [TM]
	Flygon [TM]	Froakie [TM]	Frogadier [TM]	Furret [TM]	Gallade [TM]	Gengar [TM]
	Geodude [TM]	Golduck [TM]	Golem [TM]	Golett [TM]	Golurk [TM]	Gothitelle [TM]
	Granbull [TM]	Graveler [TM]	Greninja [TM]	Grumpig [TM]	Gulpin [TM]	Gurdurr [TM]
	Hariyama [TM]	Hawlucha [TM]	Heatmor [TM]	Illumise [TM]	Jigglypuff [TM]	Jynx [TM]
	Kangaskhan [TM]	Kecleon [TM]	Krokorok [TM]	Krookodile [TM]	Larvitar [TM]	Ledian [TM]
	Ledyba [TM]	Lickilicky [TM]	Lickitung [TM]	Lombre [TM]	Loudred [TM]	Lucario [15, TM]
	Ludicolo [TM]	Machamp [TM]	Machoke [TM]	Machop [TM]	Makuhita [TM]	Marill [TM]
	Marowak [TM]	Mawile [TM]	Medicham [TM]	Meditite [TM]	Meowstic (Female) [TM]	Meowstic (Male) [TM]
	Mewtwo [TM]	Mienfoo [TM]	Mienshao [TM]	Miltank [TM]	Mr. Mime [TM]	Munchlax [TM]
	Nidoking [TM]	Nidoqueen [TM]	Pancham [TM]	Pangoro [TM]	Pawniard [TM]	Politoed [TM]
	Poliwhirl [TM]	Poliwrath [TM]	Psyduck [TM]	Pupitar [TM]	Quagsire [TM]	Quilladin [TM]
	Reuniclus [TM]	Rhydon [TM]	Rhyperior [TM]	Riolu [TM]	Sableye [TM]	Sawk [TM]
	Scrafty [TM]	Scraggy [TM]	Sentret [TM]	Simipour [TM]	Simisage [TM]	Simisear [TM]
	Slowking [TM]	Sneasel [TM]	Snorlax [TM]	Snubbull [TM]	Spinda [TM]	Squirtle [TM]
	Sudowoodo [TM]	Swalot [TM]	Teddiursa [TM]	Throh [TM]	Timburr [TM]	Toxicroak [TM]
	Trevenant [TM]	Tyranitar [TM]	Ursaring [TM]	Volbeat [TM]	Wartortle [TM]	Watchog [TM]
	Weavile [TM]	Wigglytuff [TM]	Zangoose [TM]			
Present	Delibird [1]	Igglybuff [E]	Marill [E]	Miltank [E]	Pichu [E]	Snubbull [E]

Pokémon Moves Reverse Lookup

Move	Pokémon that can learn it					
		Abomasnow [TM]	Abra [TM]	Absol [TM]	Accelgor [TM]	Aegislash [TM]	Aerodactyl [TM]
		Aggron [29, TM]	Alakazam [TM]	Alomomola [21, TM]	Altaria [TM]	Amaura [TM]	Amoonguss [TM]
		Ampharos [TM]	Arbok [TM]	Ariados [TM]	Aromatisse [TM]	Aron [29, TM]	Articuno [TM]
		Audino [TM]	Aurorus [TM]	Avalugg [TM]	Axew [TM]	Azumarill [TM]	Azurill [TM]
		Bagon [TM]	Banette [TM]	Barbaracle [TM]	Barboach [TM]	Basculin [TM]	Beartic [TM]
		Beedrill [TM]	Bellossom [TM]	Bellsprout [TM]	Bergmite [TM]	Bibarel [TM]	Bidoof [TM]
		Binacle [TM]	Bisharp [TM]	Blastoise [24, TM]	Boldore [TM]	Bonsly [TM]	Braixen [TM]
		Budew [TM]	Buizel [TM]	Bulbasaur [TM]	Bunnelby [TM]	Burmy [1, TM]	Butterfree [TM]
		Carbink [TM]	Carnivine [TM]	Carvanha [TM]	Chandelure [TM]	Charizard [TM]	Charmander [TM]
		Charmeleon [TM]	Chatot [TM]	Chesnaught [TM]	Chespin [TM]	Chimecho [TM]	Chinchou [TM]
		Chingling [TM]	Clamperl [TM]	Clauncher [TM]	Clawitzer [TM]	Cloyster [1, TM]	Conkeldurr [TM]
		Corphish [23, TM]	Corsola [TM]	Crawdaunt [23, TM]	Croagunk [TM]	Crobat [TM]	Crustle [TM]
		Cryogonal [TM]	Cubchoo [TM]	Cubone [TM]	Dedenne [TM]	Deino [TM]	Delcatty [TM]
		Delibird [TM]	Delphox [TM]	Diggersby [TM]	Diglett [TM]	Dodrio [TM]	Doduo [TM]
		Doublade [TM]	Dragalge [TM]	Dragonair [TM]	Dragonite [TM]	Drapion [TM]	Dratini [TM]
		Drifblim [TM]	Drifloon [TM]	Druddigon [TM]	Ducklett [TM]	Dugtrio [TM]	Dunsparce [TM]
		Duosion [TM]	Durant [TM]	Dwebble [TM]	Eevee [TM]	Ekans [TM]	Electrike [TM]
		Electrode [TM]	Emolga [TM]	Escavalier [TM]	Espeon [TM]	Espurr [TM]	Exeggcute [TM]
		Exeggutor [TM]	Exploud [TM]	Farfetch'd [TM]	Fearow [TM]	Fennekin [TM]	Ferroseed [TM]
		Ferrothorn [TM]	Flaaffy [TM]	Flabébé [TM]	Flareon [TM]	Fletchinder [TM]	Fletchling [TM]
		Floatzel [TM]	Floette [TM]	Florges [TM]	Flygon [TM]	Foongus [TM]	Fraxure [TM]
		Froakie [TM]	Frogadier [TM]	Furfrou [TM]	Furret [TM]	Gabite [TM]	Gallade [53, TM]
		Garbodor [TM]	Garchomp [TM]	Gardevoir [TM]	Gastly [TM]	Gengar [TM]	Geodude [TM]
		Gible [TM]	Gigalith [TM]	Glaceon [TM]	Gligar [TM]	Gliscor [TM]	Gloom [TM]
		Gogoat [TM]	Golbat [TM]	Goldeen [TM]	Golduck [TM]	Golem [TM]	Golett [TM]
		Golurk [TM]	Goodra [9, TM]	Goomy [9, TM]	Gorebyss [TM]	Gothita [TM]	Gothitelle [TM]
		Gothorita [TM]	Gourgeist [TM]	Granbull [TM]	Graveler [TM]	Greninja [TM]	Grumpig [TM]
		Gulpin [TM]	Gurdurr [TM]	Gyarados [TM]	Hariyama [TM]	Haunter [TM]	Hawlucha [TM]
		Haxorus [TM]	Heatmor [TM]	Helioptile [TM]	Heliolisk [TM]	Heracross [TM]	Hippopotas [TM]
	Protect (TM17)	Hippowdon [TM]	Honchkrow [TM]	Honedge [TM]	Hoothoot [TM]	Hoppip [TM]	Horsea [TM]
		Houndoom [TM]	Houndour [TM]	Huntail [TM]	Hydreigon [TM]	Igglybuff [TM]	Illumise [TM]
		Inkay [TM]	Ivysaur [TM]	Jigglypuff [TM]	Jolteon [TM]	Jumpluff [TM]	Jynx [TM]
		Kadabra [TM]	Kangaskhan [TM]	Karrablast [TM]	Kecleon [TM]	Kingdra [TM]	Kirlia [TM]
		Klefki [TM]	Krokorok [TM]	Krookodile [TM]	Lairon [29, TM]	Lampent [TM]	Lanturn [TM]
		Lapras [TM]	Larvitar [TM]	Leafeon [TM]	Ledian [TM]	Ledyba [TM]	Lickilicky [TM]
		Lickitung [TM]	Liepard [TM]	Linoone [TM]	Litleo [TM]	Litwick [TM]	Lombre [TM]
		Lotad [TM]	Loudred [TM]	Lucario [TM]	Ludicolo [TM]	Lunatone [TM]	Luvdisc [TM]
		Machamp [TM]	Machoke [TM]	Machop [TM]	Magcargo [TM]	Magnemite [TM]	Magneton [TM]
		Magnezone [TM]	Makuhita [TM]	Malamar [TM]	Mamoswine [TM]	Manectric [TM]	Mantine [TM]
		Mantyke [TM]	Mareep [TM]	Marill [TM]	Marowak [TM]	Masquerain [TM]	Mawile [TM]
		Medicham [TM]	Meditite [TM]	Meowstic (Female) [TM]	Meowstic (Male) [TM]	Mewtwo [TM]	Mienfoo [TM]
		Mienshao [TM]	Mightyena [TM]	Miltank [TM]	Mime Jr. [TM]	Minun [TM]	Moltres [TM]
		Mothim [10, TM]	Mr. Mime [TM]	Munchlax [TM]	Murkrow [TM]	Nidoking [TM]	Nidoqueen [TM]
		Nidoran♀ [TM]	Nidoran♂ [TM]	Nidorina [TM]	Nidorino [TM]	Nincada [TM]	Ninjask [TM]
		Noctowl [TM]	Noibat [TM]	Noivern [TM]	Nosepass [TM]	Octillery [TM]	Oddish [TM]
		Onix [TM]	Pachirisu [TM]	Pancham [TM]	Pangoro [TM]	Panpour [TM]	Pansage [TM]
		Pansear [TM]	Patrat [TM]	Pawniard [TM]	Pelipper [25, TM]	Phantump [TM]	Pichu [TM]
		Pidgeot [TM]	Pidgeotto [TM]	Pidgey [TM]	Pikachu [TM]	Piloswine [TM]	Pinsir [TM]
		Plusle [TM]	Politoed [TM]	Poliwag [TM]	Poliwhirl [TM]	Poliwrath [TM]	Poochyena [TM]
		Probopass [TM]	Psyduck [TM]	Pumpkaboo [TM]	Pupitar [TM]	Purrloin [TM]	Pyroar [TM]
		Quagsire [TM]	Quilladin [TM]	Qwilfish [TM]	Raichu [TM]	Ralts [TM]	Relicanth [TM]
		Remoraid [TM]	Reuniclus [TM]	Rhydon [TM]	Rhyhorn [TM]	Rhyperior [TM]	Riolu [TM]
		Roggenrola [TM]	Roselia [TM]	Roserade [TM]	Rotom (Fan) [TM]	Rotom (Frost) [TM]	Rotom (Heat) [TM]
		Rotom (Mow) [TM]	Rotom (Wash) [TM]	Rotom [TM]	Sableye [TM]	Salamence [30, TM]	Sandile [TM]
		Sandshrew [TM]	Sandslash [TM]	Sawk [TM]	Scizor [TM]	Scolipede [15, TM]	Scrafty [TM]
		Scraggy [TM]	Scyther [TM]	Seadra [TM]	Seaking [TM]	Sentret [TM]	Seviper [TM]
		Sharpedo [TM]	Shedinja [TM]	Shelgon [30, TM]	Shellder [16, TM]	Shelmet [28, TM]	Shuckle [TM]
		Shuppet [TM]	Sigilyph [TM]	Simipour [TM]	Simisage [TM]	Simisear [TM]	Skarmory [TM]
		Skiddo [TM]	Skiploom [TM]	Skitty [TM]	Skorupi [TM]	Skrelp [TM]	Skuntank [TM]
		Sliggoo [9, TM]	Slowbro [TM]	Slowking [TM]	Slowpoke [TM]	Slugma [TM]	Slurpuff [TM]
		Smoochum [TM]	Sneasel [TM]	Snorlax [TM]	Snover [TM]	Snubbull [TM]	Solosis [TM]
		Solrock [TM]	Spearow [TM]	Spewpa [9, TM]	Spinarak [TM]	Spinda [TM]	Spoink [TM]
		Spritzee [TM]	Squirtle [22, TM]	Staraptor [TM]	Staravia [TM]	Starly [TM]	Starmie [TM]
		Staryu [TM]	Steelix [TM]	Stunfisk [TM]	Stunky [TM]	Sudowoodo [TM]	Surskit [TM]
		Swablu [TM]	Swalot [TM]	Swanna [TM]	Swellow [TM]	Swinub [TM]	Swirlix [TM]
		Swoobat [TM]	Sylveon [TM]	Tailow [TM]	Talonflame [TM]	Tauros [TM]	Teddiursa [TM]
		Tentacool [TM]	Tentacruel [TM]	Throh [TM]	Timburr [TM]	Torkoal [1, 36, TM]	Toxicroak [TM]
		Trapinch [TM]	Trevenant [TM]	Trubbish [TM]	Tyranitar [TM]	Tyrantrum [TM]	Tyrunt [TM]
		Umbreon [TM]	Ursaring [TM]	Vanillish [TM]	Vanillite [TM]	Vanilluxe [TM]	Vaporeon [TM]
		Venipede [15, TM]	Venusaur [TM]	Vespiquen [TM]	Vibrava [TM]	Victreebel [TM]	Vileplume [TM]
		Vivillon [TM]	Volbeat [29, TM]	Voltorb [TM]	Wailmer [TM]	Wailord [TM]	Wartortle [24, TM]
		Watchog [TM]	Weavile [TM]	Weepinbell [TM]	Whirlipede [15, TM]	Whiscash [TM]	Whismur [TM]

Move	Pokémon that can learn it					
Normal						
Protect (TM17)	Wigglytuff [TM]	Wingull [TM]	Woobat [TM]	Wooper [TM]	Wormadam (Plant) [10, TM]	Wormadam (Sand) [10, TM]
	Wormadam (Trash) [10, TM]	Xerneas [TM]	Yanma [TM]	Yanmega [TM]	Yveltal [TM]	Zangoose [TM]
	Zapdos [TM]	Zigzagoon [TM]	Zoroark [TM]	Zorua [TM]	Zubat [TM]	Zweilous [TM]
	Zygarde [TM]					
Psychic						
Psybeam	Alakazam [28]	Braixen [18]	Butterfree [24]	Chinchou [E]	Delphox [18]	Espeon [20]
	Espurr [17]	Fennekin [17]	Goldeen [E]	Gothita [16]	Gothitelle [16]	Gothorita [16]
	Grumpig [1, 14]	Inkay [21]	Kadabra [28]	Kecleon [18]	Ledyba [E]	Malamar [21]
	Mantine [1]	Meowstic (Female) [17]	Meowstic (Male) [17]	Mime Jr. [25]	Mothim [32]	Mr. Mime [25]
	Octillery [1, 10]	Psyduck [E]	Remoraid [10]	Sigilyph [18]	Spinarak [E]	Spinda [19]
	Spoink [14]	Surskit [E]	Vivillon [17]	Wormadam (Plant) [32]	Wormadam (Sand) [32]	Wormadam (Trash) [32]
Normal						
Psych Up (TM77)	Abra [TM]	Absol [TM]	Alakazam [TM]	Alomomola [TM]	Altaria [TM]	Amaura [TM]
	Aromatisse [64, TM]	Audino [TM]	Aurorus [TM]	Banette [TM]	Bonsly [TM]	Braixen [TM]
	Budew [TM]	Butterfree [TM]	Carbink [TM]	Chandelure [TM]	Chimecho [TM]	Chingling [TM]
	Deino [TM]	Delcatty [TM]	Delphox [TM]	Drifblim [TM]	Drifloon [TM]	Dunsparce [TM]
	Duosion [TM]	Espeon [29, TM]	Espurr [TM]	Exeggcute [TM]	Exeggutor [TM]	Farfetch'd [TM]
	Fennekin [TM]	Gallade [TM]	Gardevoir [TM]	Gastly [TM]	Gengar [TM]	Golduck [43, TM]
	Gorebyss [TM]	Gothita [TM]	Gothitelle [TM]	Gothorita [TM]	Grumpig [15, TM]	Haunter [TM]
	Heliolisk [TM]	Helioptile [TM]	Honchkrow [TM]	Hoothoot [TM]	Hoppip [TM]	Hydreigon [TM]
	Igglybuff [TM]	Illumise [TM]	Inkay [TM]	Jigglypuff [TM]	Jumpluff [TM]	Jynx [TM]
	Kadabra [TM]	Kecleon [TM]	Kirlia [TM]	Klefki [TM]	Lampent [TM]	Lickilicky [TM]
	Lickitung [TM]	Liepard [TM]	Litwick [TM]	Lunatone [TM]	Luvdisc [TM]	Magnemite [TM]
	Magneton [TM]	Magnezone [TM]	Malamar [TM]	Masquerain [TM]	Mawile [TM]	Medicham [36, TM]
	Meditite [36, TM]	Meowstic (Female) [TM]	Meowstic (Male) [TM]	Mewtwo [22, TM]	Mienfoo [TM]	Mienshao [TM]
	Miltank [TM]	Mime Jr. [TM]	Mothim [TM]	Mr. Mime [TM]	Murkrow [TM]	Noctowl [TM]
	Onix [TM]	Psyduck [39, TM]	Purrloin [TM]	Ralts [TM]	Relicanth [TM]	Reuniclus [TM]
	Roselia [TM]	Roserade [TM]	Rotom (Fan) [TM]	Rotom (Frost) [TM]	Rotom (Heat) [TM]	Rotom (Mow) [TM]
	Rotom (Wash) [TM]	Rotom [TM]	Sableye [TM]	Shuppet [TM]	Sigilyph [TM]	Skiploom [TM]
	Skitty [TM]	Slowbro [62, TM]	Slowking [54, TM]	Slowpoke [54, TM]	Slurpuff [TM]	Smoochum [TM]
	Sneasel [TM]	Solosis [TM]	Solrock [TM]	Spinda [41, TM]	Spoink [15, TM]	Spritzee [TM]
	Starmie [TM]	Staryu [TM]	Steelix [TM]	Sudowoodo [TM]	Surskit [TM]	Swablu [TM]
	Swirlix [TM]	Swoobat [TM]	Sylveon [45, TM]	Umbreon [TM]	Vivillon [TM]	Volbeat [TM]
	Watchog [29, TM]	Weavile [TM]	Wigglytuff [TM]	Woobat [TM]	Wormadam (Plant) [TM]	Wormadam (Sand) [TM]
	Wormadam (Trash) [TM]	Xerneas [59, TM]	Yanmega [TM]	Zoroark [TM]	Zorua [TM]	Zweilous [TM]
Psychic						
Psychic (TM29)	Abra [TM]	Alakazam [46, TM]	Alomomola [TM]	Ariados [46, TM]	Aromatisse [48, TM]	Audino [TM]
	Aurorus [TM]	Banette [TM]	Braixen [48, TM]	Butterfree [TM]	Carbink [TM]	Chandelure [TM]
	Chimecho [TM]	Chingling [TM]	Corsola [TM]	Delphox [51, TM]	Drifblim [TM]	Drifloon [TM]
	Duosion [39, TM]	Espeon [37, TM]	Espurr [TM]	Exeggcute [TM]	Exeggutor [TM]	Fennekin [41, TM]
	Flabébé [TM]	Floette [TM]	Florges [TM]	Gallade [TM]	Garbodor [TM]	Gardevoir [40, TM]
	Gastly [TM]	Gengar [TM]	Golduck [TM]	Golett [TM]	Golurk [TM]	Gorebyss [42, TM]
	Gothita [37, TM]	Gothitelle [39, TM]	Gothorita [39, TM]	Gourgeist [TM]	Grumpig [52, TM]	Haunter [TM]
	Honchkrow [TM]	Hoothoot [TM]	Igglybuff [TM]	Inkay [TM]	Jigglypuff [TM]	Jynx [TM]
	Kadabra [46, TM]	Kirlia [36, TM]	Klefki [TM]	Lampent [TM]	Lapras [TM]	Litwick [TM]
	Lucario [TM]	Lunatone [33, TM]	Malamar [TM]	Medicham [TM]	Meditite [TM]	Meowstic (Female) [40, TM]
	Meowstic (Male) [40, TM]	Mewtwo [57, TM]	Mime Jr. [39, TM]	Mothim [44, TM]	Mr. Mime [39, TM]	Munchlax [TM]
	Murkrow [TM]	Noctowl [TM]	Noibat [TM]	Noivern [TM]	Octillery [TM]	Phantump [TM]
	Politoed [TM]	Poliwag [TM]	Poliwhirl [TM]	Poliwrath [TM]	Psyduck [TM]	Pumpkaboo [TM]
	Ralts [32, TM]	Remoraid [TM]	Reuniclus [39, TM]	Sableye [TM]	Shuppet [TM]	Sigilyph [44, TM]
	Slowbro [49, TM]	Slowking [45, TM]	Slowpoke [45, TM]	Slurpuff [TM]	Smoochum [38, TM]	Snorlax [TM]
	Solosis [37, TM]	Solrock [33, TM]	Spinarak [40, TM]	Spinda [TM]	Spoink [44, TM]	Spritzee [48, TM]
	Starmie [TM]	Staryu [TM]	Swirlix [TM]	Swoobat [41, TM]	Trevenant [TM]	Umbreon [TM]
	Vivillon [TM]	Wigglytuff [TM]	Woobat [41, TM]	Wormadam (Plant) [44, TM]	Wormadam (Sand) [44, TM]	Wormadam (Trash) [44, TM]
	Xerneas [TM]	Yanma [TM]	Yanmega [TM]	Yveltal [59, TM]		
Psycho Cut	Absol [47]	Alakazam [40]	Gallade [36]	Inkay [39]	Kadabra [40]	Malamar [39]
	Meditite [E]	Mewtwo [36]	Pawniard [E]	Spinda [E]		
Psycho Shift	Abra [E]	Hoothoot [49]	Murkrow [E]	Noctowl [57]	Sigilyph [E]	Spinda [E]
	Woobat [E]					
Psyshock (TM03)	Abra [TM]	Alakazam [TM]	Aromatisse [TM]	Audino [TM]	Braixen [34, TM]	Chimecho [TM]
	Chingling [TM]	Delphox [34, TM]	Duosion [25, TM]	Espeon [TM]	Espurr [25, TM]	Exeggutor [17, TM]
	Fennekin [31, TM]	Gallade [TM]	Gardevoir [TM]	Golduck [TM]	Gothita [25, TM]	Gothitelle [25, TM]
	Gothorita [25, TM]	Grumpig [42, TM]	Jynx [TM]	Kadabra [TM]	Kirlia [TM]	Klefki [TM]
	Lunatone [TM]	Malamar [TM]	Medicham [TM]	Meditite [TM]	Meowstic (Female) [25, TM]	Meowstic (Male) [25, TM]
	Mewtwo [TM]	Mime Jr. [TM]	Mr. Mime [TM]	Psyduck [TM]	Ralts [TM]	Reuniclus [25, TM]
	Sigilyph [TM]	Slowbro [TM]	Slowking [TM]	Slowpoke [TM]	Smoochum [TM]	Solosis [25, TM]
	Solrock [TM]	Spoink [38, TM]	Starmie [TM]	Swoobat [TM]	Sylveon [TM]	Woobat [TM]
	Xerneas [TM]					

685

Pokémon Moves Reverse Lookup

	Move	Pokémon that can learn it					
Psychic	Psystrike	Mewtwo [100]					
Psychic	Psywave	Chimecho [30]	Duosion [1]	Gastly [E]	Grumpig [1, 7]	Inkay [13]	Lunatone [17]
		Malamar [13]	Mr. Mime [15]	Reuniclus [1]	Sigilyph [8]	Solosis [1]	Solrock [17]
		Spoink [7]					
Dark	Punishment	Absol [E]	Houndour [E]	Igglybuff [E]	Mawile [E]	Miltank [E]	Sableye [36]
		Seviper [E]	Sneasel [44, E]	Stunky [E]	Weavile [44]	Zoroark [49]	Zorua [45]
Dark	Pursuit	Absol [E]	Aegislash [12]	Aerodactyl [E]	Beedrill [22]	Buizel [18]	Croagunk [15]
		Diglett [E]	Dodrio [19]	Doduo [19]	Doublade [13]	Drapion [16]	Druddigon [E]
		Dunsparce [10]	Ekans [E]	Emolga [16]	Fearow [13]	Floatzel [18]	Heatmor [E]
		Heracross [E]	Honchkrow [1]	Honedge [13]	Houndour [E]	Karrablast [E]	Larvitar [E]
		Liepard [15]	Munchlax [E]	Murkrow [5]	Nidoran♀ [E]	Patrat [E]	Pawniard [E]
		Pidgey [E]	Purrloin [15]	Sandile [E]	Scizor [9]	Scolipede [12]	Scyther [9]
		Sentret [E]	Shelmet [E]	Shuppet [E]	Skarmory [E]	Skorupi [16, E]	Sneasel [E]
		Snorlax [E]	Spearow [13]	Spinarak [E]	Starly [E]	Stunky [E]	Swablu [E]
		Taillow [E]	Tauros [15]	Toxicroak [15]	Umbreon [9]	Venipede [12]	Vespiquen [9]
		Whirlipede [12]	Wingull [30]	Yanma [30, E]	Yanmega [30]	Zangoose [12]	Zigzagoon [E]
		Zoroark [1, 5]	Zorua [5]	Zubat [E]			

Q

	Move	Pokémon that can learn it					
Dark	Quash (TM60)	Honchkrow [65, TM]	Kingdra [TM]	Murkrow [65, TM]	Nidoking [TM]	Nidoqueen [TM]	Pancham [E]
		Pangoro [TM]	Slowking [TM]	Vespiquen [TM]			
Normal	Quick Attack	Absol [9]	Accelgor [1, 13]	Bidoof [E]	Buizel [11]	Bunnelby [7]	Delibird [E]
		Diggersby [7]	Dodrio [1, 5]	Doduo [5, E]	Eevee [13]	Electrike [17]	Emolga [4]
		Espeon [13]	Farfetch'd [E]	Flareon [13]	Fletchinder [6]	Fletchling [6]	Floatzel [1, 11]
		Froakie [8]	Frogadier [8]	Furret [1, 7]	Glaceon [13]	Gligar [13]	Gliscor [13]
		Greninja [8]	Heliolisk [1]	Helioptile [17]	Illumise [17]	Jolteon [13]	Leafeon [13]
		Lucario [1]	Manectric [17]	Masquerain [1, 7]	Minun [7]	Pachirisu [5]	Pidgeot [1, 13]
		Pidgeotto [13]	Pidgey [13]	Pikachu [10]	Pinsir [E]	Plusle [7]	Raichu [E]
		Riolu [1]	Scizor [1]	Scyther [1]	Sentret [7]	Sneasel [8]	Spearow [E]
		Staraptor [1, 5]	Staravia [1, 5]	Starly [5]	Surskit [7]	Swellow [1, 7]	Sylveon [13]
		Taillow [7]	Talonflame [6]	Trapinch [E]	Umbreon [13]	Vaporeon [13]	Volbeat [17]
		Weavile [1, 8]	Wingull [22]	Yanma [6]	Yanmega [1, 6]	Zangoose [5]	Zubat [E]
Fighting	Quick Guard	Chespin [E]	Croagunk [E]	Escavalier [1, 8]	Fletchling [E]	Hawlucha [E]	Lucario [33]
		Machop [E]	Meditite [E]	Meowstic (Male) [1, 53]	Mienfoo [45]	Mr. Mime [1]	Pancham [E]
		Pawniard [E]	Sawk [45]	Scraggy [E]	Scyther [E]	Zangoose [E]	
Bug	Quiver Dance	Butterfree [46]	Masquerain [1, 68]	Mothim [50]	Vivillon [45]		

R

	Move	Pokémon that can learn it					
Normal	Rage	Bagon [1]	Basculin [E]	Beedrill [19]	Carvanha [6]	Cubone [23]	Dodrio [1, 10]
		Doduo [10]	Dunsparce [1]	Granbull [35]	Houndour [1]	Kangaskhan [22]	Krokorok [1]
		Krookodile [1]	Marowak [23]	Onix [13]	Salamence [1]	Sandile [1]	Sharpedo [1, 6]
		Shelgon [1]	Snubbull [31]	Steelix [13]	Swablu [1]	Taillow [1]	Tauros [5]
Bug	Rage Powder	Amoonguss [54]	Butterfree [34]	Carnivine [1]	Foongus [45]	Hoppip [31]	Jumpluff [39]
		Scatterbug [E]	Skiploom [36]	Spinarak [E]			
Water	Rain Dance (TM18)	Abomasnow [TM]	Abra [TM]	Absol [TM]	Accelgor [TM]	Aegislash [TM]	Aerodactyl [TM]
		Aggron [TM]	Alakazam [TM]	Alomomola [TM]	Altaria [TM]	Amaura [TM]	Amoonguss [TM]
		Ampharos [TM]	Arbok [TM]	Aromatisse [TM]	Aron [TM]	Articuno [TM]	Audino [TM]
		Aurorus [TM]	Avalugg [TM]	Axew [TM]	Azumarill [35, TM]	Azurill [TM]	Bagon [TM]
		Banette [TM]	Barbaracle [TM]	Barboach [TM]	Basculin [TM]	Beartic [TM]	Bergmite [TM]
		Bibarel [TM]	Bidoof [TM]	Binacle [TM]	Bisharp [TM]	Blastoise [53, TM]	Braixen [TM]
		Budew [TM]	Buizel [TM]	Butterfree [TM]	Carvanha [TM]	Chatot [TM]	Chimecho [TM]
		Chinchou [TM]	Chingling [TM]	Clamperl [TM]	Clauncher [TM]	Clawitzer [TM]	Cloyster [TM]
		Conkeldurr [TM]	Corphish [TM]	Corsola [TM]	Crawdaunt [TM]	Croagunk [TM]	Crobat [TM]
		Cryogonal [TM]	Cubchoo [TM]	Dedenne [TM]	Deino [TM]	Delcatty [TM]	Delibird [TM]
		Delphox [TM]	Doublade [TM]	Dragalge [TM]	Dragonair [TM]	Dragonite [TM]	Drapion [TM]
		Dratini [TM]	Drifblim [TM]	Drifloon [TM]	Druddigon [TM]	Ducklett [34, TM]	Dunsparce [TM]
		Duosion [TM]	Eevee [TM]	Ekans [TM]	Electrike [TM]	Electrode [TM]	Emolga [TM]
		Escavalier [TM]	Espeon [TM]	Espurr [TM]	Exploud [TM]	Fearow [TM]	Fennekin [TM]
		Flaaffy [TM]	Flabébé [TM]	Flareon [TM]	Floatzel [TM]	Floette [TM]	Florges [TM]
		Foongus [TM]	Fraxure [TM]	Froakie [TM]	Frogadier [TM]	Furfrou [TM]	Furret [TM]
		Gabite [TM]	Gallade [TM]	Garbodor [TM]	Garchomp [TM]	Gardevoir [TM]	Gastly [TM]
		Gengar [TM]	Gible [TM]	Glaceon [TM]	Gligar [TM]	Gliscor [TM]	Gogoat [TM]
		Golbat [TM]	Goldeen [TM]	Golduck [TM]	Golett [TM]	Golurk [TM]	Goodra [25, TM]
		Goomy [25, TM]	Gorebyss [TM]	Gothita [TM]	Gothitelle [TM]	Gothorita [TM]	Granbull [TM]
		Greninja [TM]	Grumpig [TM]	Gulpin [TM]	Gurdurr [TM]	Gyarados [38, TM]	Hariyama [TM]
		Haunter [TM]	Hawlucha [TM]	Haxorus [TM]	Heatmor [TM]	Heliolisk [TM]	Helioptile [TM]
		Heracross [TM]	Honchkrow [TM]	Honedge [TM]	Hoothoot [TM]	Horsea [TM]	Huntail [TM]
		Hydreigon [TM]	Igglybuff [TM]	Illumise [TM]	Inkay [TM]	Jigglypuff [TM]	Jolteon [TM]
		Jynx [TM]	Kadabra [TM]	Kangaskhan [TM]	Karrablast [TM]	Kecleon [TM]	Kingdra [TM]

Type	Move	Pokémon that can learn it					
Water	Rain Dance (TM18)	Kirlia [TM]	Klefki [TM]	Lairon [TM]	Lanturn [TM]	Lapras [22, TM]	Larvitar [TM]
		Leafeon [TM]	Lickilicky [TM]	Lickitung [TM]	Liepard [TM]	Linoone [TM]	Litleo [TM]
		Lombre [TM]	Lotad [37, TM]	Loudred [TM]	Lucario [TM]	Ludicolo [TM]	Lunatone [TM]
		Luvdisc [TM]	Machamp [TM]	Machoke [TM]	Machop [TM]	Magnemite [TM]	Magneton [TM]
		Magnezone [TM]	Makuhita [TM]	Malamar [TM]	Mamoswine [TM]	Manectric [TM]	Mantine [TM]
		Mantyke [TM]	Mareep [TM]	Marill [31, TM]	Masquerain [TM]	Mawile [TM]	Medicham [TM]
		Meditite [TM]	Meowstic (Female) [TM]	Meowstic (Male) [TM]	Mewtwo [TM]	Mienfoo [TM]	Mienshao [TM]
		Mightyena [TM]	Miltank [TM]	Mime Jr. [TM]	Minun [TM]	Moltres [TM]	Mothim [TM]
		Mr. Mime [TM]	Munchlax [TM]	Murkrow [TM]	Nidoking [TM]	Nidoqueen [TM]	Nidoran♀ [TM]
		Nidoran♂ [TM]	Nidorina [TM]	Nidorino [TM]	Noctowl [TM]	Octillery [TM]	Pachirisu [TM]
		Pancham [TM]	Pangoro [TM]	Panpour [TM]	Patrat [TM]	Pawniard [TM]	Pelipper [TM]
		Pichu [TM]	Pidgeot [TM]	Pidgeotto [TM]	Pidgey [TM]	Pikachu [TM]	Piloswine [TM]
		Pinsir [TM]	Plusle [TM]	Politoed [TM]	Poliwag [18, TM]	Poliwhirl [18, TM]	Poliwrath [TM]
		Poochyena [TM]	Psyduck [TM]	Pupitar [TM]	Purrloin [TM]	Pyroar [TM]	Quagsire [41, TM]
		Qwilfish [TM]	Raichu [TM]	Ralts [TM]	Relicanth [TM]	Remoraid [TM]	Reuniclus [TM]
		Rhydon [TM]	Rhyhorn [TM]	Rhyperior [TM]	Riolu [TM]	Roselia [TM]	Roserade [TM]
		Rotom (Fan) [TM]	Rotom (Frost) [TM]	Rotom (Heat) [TM]	Rotom (Mow) [TM]	Rotom (Wash) [TM]	Rotom [TM]
		Sableye [TM]	Salamence [TM]	Sawk [TM]	Scizor [TM]	Scrafty [TM]	Scraggy [TM]
		Scyther [TM]	Seadra [TM]	Seaking [TM]	Sentret [TM]	Seviper [TM]	Sharpedo [TM]
		Shelgon [TM]	Shellder [TM]	Shelmet [TM]	Shuppet [TM]	Sigilyph [TM]	Simipour [TM]
		Skiddo [TM]	Skitty [TM]	Skorupi [TM]	Skrelp [TM]	Skuntank [TM]	Sliggoo [25, TM]
		Slowbro [55, TM]	Slowking [TM]	Slowpoke [49, TM]	Slurpuff [TM]	Smoochum [TM]	Sneasel [TM]
		Snorlax [TM]	Snover [TM]	Snubbull [TM]	Solosis [TM]	Spearow [TM]	Spinda [TM]
		Spoink [TM]	Spritzee [TM]	Squirtle [37, TM]	Staraptor [TM]	Staravia [TM]	Starly [TM]
		Starmie [TM]	Staryu [TM]	Stunfisk [TM]	Stunky [TM]	Surskit [TM]	Swablu [TM]
		Swalot [TM]	Swanna [34, TM]	Swellow [TM]	Swinub [TM]	Swirlix [TM]	Swoobat [TM]
		Sylveon [TM]	Taillow [TM]	Tauros [TM]	Teddiursa [TM]	Tentacool [TM]	Tentacruel [TM]
		Throh [TM]	Timburr [TM]	Toxicroak [TM]	Trubbish [TM]	Tyranitar [TM]	Umbreon [TM]
		Ursaring [TM]	Vanillish [TM]	Vanillite [TM]	Vanilluxe [TM]	Vaporeon [TM]	Vespiquen [TM]
		Vivillon [TM]	Volbeat [TM]	Voltorb [TM]	Wailmer [TM]	Wailord [TM]	Wartortle [44, TM]
		Watchog [TM]	Weavile [TM]	Whiscash [TM]	Whismur [TM]	Wigglytuff [TM]	Wingull [TM]
		Woobat [TM]	Wooper [37, TM]	Wormadam (Plant) [TM]	Wormadam (Sand) [TM]	Wormadam (Trash) [TM]	Xerneas [TM]
		Yveltal [TM]	Zangoose [TM]	Zapdos [57, TM]	Zigzagoon [TM]	Zoroark [TM]	Zorua [TM]
		Zubat [TM]	Zweilous [TM]				
Normal	Rapid Spin	Avalugg [35]	Bergmite [35]	Blastoise [20]	Cryogonal [13]	Delibird [E]	Sandshrew [9, E]
		Sandslash [9]	Shellder [E]	Spinda [E]	Squirtle [19]	Starmie [1]	Staryu [10]
		Tentacool [E]	Torkoal [25]	Wartortle [20]			
Grass	Razor Leaf	Abomasnow [1, 5]	Bellossom [35]	Budew [E]	Bulbasaur [19]	Carnivine [E]	Flabébé [15]
		Floette [15]	Gogoat [13]	Gourgeist [16]	Ivysaur [20]	Leafeon [9]	Lotad [E]
		Oddish [E]	Pumpkaboo [16]	Roselia [E]	Skiddo [13]	Snover [5]	Venusaur [20]
		Victreebel [1]	Weepinbell [39]	Wormadam (Plant) [26]			
Water	Razor Shell	Barbaracle [48]	Binacle [45]	Shellder [32]			
Normal	Razor Wind	Absol [1, 57]	Axew [E]	Buizel [35]	Fletchinder [27]	Fletchling [25]	Floatzel [41]
		Gligar [E]	Heliolisk [1]	Helioptile [22]	Horsea [E]	Noibat [31]	Noivern [31]
		Scizor [33]	Scyther [33, E]	Spearow [E]	Talonflame [27]	Yveltal [E]	Zangoose [E]
	Recover	Accelgor [49]	Alakazam [36]	Avalugg [51]	Bergmite [47, E]	Chimecho [E]	Chingling [E]
		Corsola [10]	Cryogonal [49]	Duosion [24]	Kadabra [36]	Kecleon [E]	Magcargo [19]
		Medicham [62]	Meditite [50]	Mewtwo [50]	Reuniclus [24]	Sableye [E]	Shelmet [49]
		Slugma [19]	Solosis [24]	Starmie [1]	Staryu [12]	Wooper [E]	
	Recycle	Garbodor [1, 3]	Klefki [40]	Mime Jr. [32]	Mr. Mime [32]	Panpour [37]	Pansage [37]
		Pansear [37]	Trubbish [3]				
Psychic	Reflect (TM33)	Abra [TM]	Aegislash [TM]	Alakazam [30, TM]	Amaura [TM]	Aromatisse [57, TM]	Articuno [50, TM]
		Audino [TM]	Aurorus [TM]	Bellsprout [TM]	Carbink [18, TM]	Chesnaught [TM]	Chespin [TM]
		Chimecho [TM]	Chingling [TM]	Corsola [TM]	Cryogonal [37, TM]	Doublade [TM]	Duosion [1, 3, TM]
		Espeon [TM]	Espurr [TM]	Exeggcute [7, TM]	Exeggutor [TM]	Gallade [TM]	Gardevoir [TM]
		Gothita [TM]	Gothitelle [TM]	Gothorita [TM]	Granbull [TM]	Grumpig [TM]	Honedge [TM]
		Hoothoot [17, TM]	Hoppip [TM]	Hydreigon [TM]	Igglybuff [TM]	Inkay [4, TM]	Jigglypuff [TM]
		Jumpluff [TM]	Jynx [TM]	Kadabra [30, TM]	Kirlia [TM]	Klefki [TM]	Ledian [14, TM]
		Ledyba [14, TM]	Lunatone [TM]	Magcargo [TM]	Magnemite [TM]	Magneton [TM]	Magnezone [TM]
		Malamar [4, TM]	Mamoswine [TM]	Medicham [TM]	Meditite [TM]	Meowstic (Female) [TM]	Meowstic (Male) [35, TM]
		Mewtwo [TM]	Mienfoo [TM]	Mienshao [TM]	Mime Jr. [22, TM]	Mr. Mime [22, TM]	Noctowl [17, TM]
		Phantump [TM]	Piloswine [TM]	Quilladin [TM]	Ralts [TM]	Reuniclus [1, 3, TM]	Rotom (Fan) [TM]
		Rotom (Frost) [TM]	Rotom (Heat) [TM]	Rotom (Mow) [TM]	Rotom (Wash) [TM]	Rotom [TM]	Sigilyph [28, TM]
		Skiploom [TM]	Slugma [TM]	Smoochum [TM]	Sneasel [TM]	Snubbull [TM]	Solosis [3, TM]
		Solrock [TM]	Spoink [TM]	Spritzee [TM]	Trevenant [TM]	Victreebel [TM]	Weavile [TM]
		Wigglytuff [TM]	Woobat [TM]	Xerneas [TM]			

AFTER THE HALL OF FAME

CENTRAL KALOS

COASTAL KALOS

MOUNTAIN KALOS

ADVENTURE DATA

Pokémon Moves Reverse Lookup

	Move	Pokémon that can learn it				
Normal	Reflect Type	Gastly [E]	Staryu [40]	Stunfisk [E]	Tentacruel [1]	
	Refresh	Alomomola [E]	Altaria [29]	Audino [5]	Azurill [E]	Clamperl [E]	Corsola [13]
		Eevee [20]	Furfrou [E]	Lapras [E]	Lickilicky [45]	Lickitung [45]	Marill [E]
		Poliwag [E]	Psyduck [E]	Spritzee [E]	Squirtle [E]	Swablu [29]	Taillow [E]
Psychic	Rest (TM44)	Abomasnow [TM]	Abra [TM]	Absol [TM]	Accelgor [TM]	Aegislash [TM]	Aerodactyl [TM]
		Aggron [TM]	Alakazam [TM]	Alomomola [TM]	Altaria [TM]	Amaura [TM]	Amoonguss [TM]
		Ampharos [TM]	Arbok [TM]	Ariados [TM]	Aromatisse [TM]	Aron [TM]	Articuno [TM]
		Audino [TM]	Aurorus [TM]	Avalugg [TM]	Axew [TM]	Azumarill [TM]	Azurill [TM]
		Bagon [TM]	Banette [TM]	Barbaracle [TM]	Barboach [31, TM]	Basculin [TM]	Beartic [41, TM]
		Beedrill [TM]	Bellossom [TM]	Bellsprout [TM]	Bergmite [TM]	Bibarel [TM]	Bidoof [TM]
		Binacle [TM]	Bisharp [TM]	Blastoise [TM]	Boldore [TM]	Bonsly [TM]	Braixen [TM]
		Budew [TM]	Buizel [TM]	Bulbasaur [TM]	Bunnelby [TM]	Butterfree [TM]	Carbink [TM]
		Carnivine [TM]	Carvanha [TM]	Chandelure [TM]	Charizard [TM]	Charmander [TM]	Charmeleon [TM]
		Chatot [TM]	Chesnaught [TM]	Chespin [TM]	Chimecho [TM]	Chinchou [TM]	Chingling [TM]
		Clamperl [TM]	Clauncher [TM]	Clawitzer [TM]	Cloyster [TM]	Conkeldurr [TM]	Corphish [TM]
		Corsola [TM]	Crawdaunt [TM]	Croagunk [TM]	Crobat [TM]	Crustle [TM]	Cryogonal [TM]
		Cubchoo [41, TM]	Cubone [TM]	Dedenne [30, TM]	Deino [TM]	Delcatty [TM]	Delibird [TM]
		Delphox [TM]	Diggersby [TM]	Diglett [TM]	Dodrio [TM]	Doduo [TM]	Doublade [TM]
		Dragalge [TM]	Dragonair [TM]	Dragonite [TM]	Drapion [TM]	Dratini [TM]	Drifblim [TM]
		Driffloon [TM]	Druddigon [TM]	Ducklett [TM]	Dugtrio [TM]	Dunsparce [TM]	Duosion [TM]
		Durant [TM]	Dwebble [TM]	Eevee [TM]	Ekans [TM]	Electrike [TM]	Electrode [TM]
		Emolga [TM]	Escavalier [TM]	Espeon [TM]	Espurr [TM]	Exeggcute [TM]	Exeggutor [TM]
		Exploud [55, TM]	Farfetch'd [TM]	Fearow [TM]	Fennekin [TM]	Ferroseed [TM]	Ferrothorn [TM]
		Flaaffy [TM]	Flabébé [TM]	Flareon [TM]	Fletchinder [TM]	Fletchling [TM]	Floatzel [TM]
		Floette [TM]	Florges [TM]	Flygon [TM]	Foongus [TM]	Fraxure [TM]	Froakie [TM]
		Frogadier [TM]	Furfrou [TM]	Furret [32, TM]	Gabite [TM]	Gallade [TM]	Garbodor [TM]
		Garchomp [TM]	Gardevoir [TM]	Gastly [TM]	Gengar [TM]	Geodude [TM]	Gible [TM]
		Gigalith [TM]	Glaceon [TM]	Gligar [TM]	Gliscor [TM]	Gloom [TM]	Gogoat [TM]
		Golbat [TM]	Goldeen [TM]	Golduck [TM]	Golem [TM]	Golett [TM]	Golurk [TM]
		Goodra [TM]	Goomy [TM]	Gorebyss [TM]	Gothita [TM]	Gothitelle [TM]	Gothorita [TM]
		Gourgeist [TM]	Granbull [TM]	Graveler [TM]	Greninja [TM]	Grumpig [29, TM]	Gulpin [TM]
		Gurdurr [TM]	Gyarados [TM]	Hariyama [TM]	Haunter [TM]	Hawlucha [TM]	Haxorus [TM]
		Heatmor [TM]	Heliolisk [TM]	Helioptile [TM]	Heracross [TM]	Hippopotas [TM]	Hippowdon [TM]
		Honchkrow [TM]	Honedge [TM]	Hoothoot [TM]	Hoppip [TM]	Horsea [TM]	Houndoom [TM]
		Houndour [TM]	Huntail [TM]	Hydreigon [TM]	Igglybuff [TM]	Illumise [TM]	Inkay [TM]
		Ivysaur [TM]	Jigglypuff [29, TM]	Jolteon [TM]	Jumpluff [TM]	Jynx [TM]	Kadabra [TM]
		Kangaskhan [TM]	Karrablast [TM]	Kecleon [TM]	Kingdra [TM]	Kirlia [TM]	Klefki [TM]
		Krokorok [TM]	Krookodile [TM]	Lairon [TM]	Lampent [TM]	Lanturn [TM]	Lapras [TM]
		Larvitar [TM]	Leafeon [TM]	Ledian [TM]	Ledyba [TM]	Lickilicky [TM]	Lickitung [TM]
		Liepard [TM]	Linoone [53, TM]	Litleo [TM]	Litwick [TM]	Lombre [TM]	Lotad [TM]
		Loudred [57, TM]	Lucario [TM]	Ludicolo [TM]	Lunatone [TM]	Luvdisc [TM]	Machamp [TM]
		Machoke [TM]	Machop [TM]	Magcargo [TM]	Magnemite [TM]	Magneton [TM]	Magnezone [TM]
		Makuhita [TM]	Malamar [TM]	Mamoswine [TM]	Manectric [TM]	Mantine [TM]	Mantyke [TM]
		Mareep [TM]	Marill [TM]	Marowak [TM]	Masquerain [TM]	Mawile [TM]	Medicham [TM]
		Meditite [TM]	Meowstic (Female) [TM]	Meowstic (Male) [TM]	Mewtwo [TM]	Mienfoo [TM]	Mienshao [TM]
		Mightyena [TM]	Miltank [TM]	Mime Jr. [TM]	Minun [TM]	Moltres [TM]	Mothim [TM]
		Mr. Mime [TM]	Munchlax [TM]	Murkrow [TM]	Nidoking [TM]	Nidoqueen [TM]	Nidoran ♀ [TM]
		Nidoran♂ [TM]	Nidorina [TM]	Nidorino [TM]	Nincada [TM]	Ninjask [TM]	Noctowl [TM]
		Noibat [TM]	Noivern [TM]	Nosepass [22, TM]	Octillery [TM]	Oddish [TM]	Onix [TM]
		Pachirisu [TM]	Pancham [TM]	Pangoro [TM]	Panpour [TM]	Pansage [TM]	Pansear [TM]
		Patrat [TM]	Pawniard [TM]	Pelipper [TM]	Phantump [TM]	Pichu [TM]	Pidgeot [TM]
		Pidgeotto [TM]	Pidgey [TM]	Pikachu [TM]	Piloswine [TM]	Pinsir [TM]	Plusle [TM]
		Politoed [TM]	Poliwag [TM]	Poliwhirl [TM]	Poliwrath [TM]	Poochyena [TM]	Probopass [22, TM]
		Psyduck [TM]	Pumpkaboo [TM]	Pupitar [TM]	Purrloin [TM]	Pyroar [TM]	Quagsire [TM]
		Quilladin [TM]	Qwilfish [TM]	Raichu [TM]	Ralts [TM]	Relicanth [64, TM]	Remoraid [TM]
		Reuniclus [TM]	Rhydon [TM]	Rhyhorn [TM]	Rhyperior [TM]	Riolu [TM]	Roggenrola [TM]
		Roselia [TM]	Roserade [TM]	Rotom (Fan) [TM]	Rotom (Frost) [TM]	Rotom (Heat) [TM]	Rotom (Mow) [TM]
		Rotom (Wash) [TM]	Rotom [TM]	Sableye [TM]	Salamence [TM]	Sandile [TM]	Sandshrew [TM]
		Sandslash [TM]	Sawk [TM]	Scizor [TM]	Scolipede [TM]	Scrafty [TM]	Scraggy [TM]
		Scyther [TM]	Seadra [TM]	Seaking [TM]	Sentret [28, TM]	Seviper [TM]	Sharpedo [TM]
		Shedinja [TM]	Shelgon [TM]	Shellder [TM]	Shelmet [TM]	Shuckle [20, TM]	Shuppet [TM]
		Sigilyph [TM]	Simipour [TM]	Simisage [TM]	Simisear [TM]	Skarmory [TM]	Skiddo [TM]
		Skiploom [TM]	Skitty [TM]	Skorupi [TM]	Skrelp [TM]	Skuntank [TM]	Sliggoo [TM]
		Slowbro [TM]	Slowking [TM]	Slowpoke [TM]	Slugma [TM]	Slurpuff [TM]	Smoochum [TM]
		Sneasel [TM]	Snorlax [28, TM]	Snover [TM]	Snubbull [TM]	Solosis [TM]	Solrock [TM]
		Spearow [TM]	Spinarak [TM]	Spinda [TM]	Spoink [29, TM]	Spritzee [TM]	Squirtle [TM]
		Staraptor [TM]	Staravia [TM]	Starly [TM]	Starmie [TM]	Staryu [TM]	Steelix [TM]
		Stunfisk [TM]	Stunky [TM]	Sudowoodo [TM]	Surskit [TM]	Swablu [TM]	Swalot [TM]
		Swanna [TM]	Swellow [TM]	Swinub [TM]	Swirlix [TM]	Swoobat [TM]	Sylveon [TM]
		Taillow [TM]	Talonflame [TM]	Tauros [19, TM]	Teddiursa [43, TM]	Tentacool [TM]	Tentacruel [TM]
		Throh [TM]	Timburr [TM]	Torkoal [TM]	Toxicroak [TM]	Trapinch [TM]	Trevenant [TM]
		Trubbish [TM]	Tyranitar [TM]	Tyrantrum [TM]	Tyrunt [TM]	Umbreon [TM]	Ursaring [47, TM]
		Vanillish [TM]	Vanillite [TM]	Vanilluxe [TM]	Vaporeon [TM]	Venipede [TM]	Venusaur [TM]
		Vespiquen [TM]	Vibrava [TM]	Victreebel [TM]	Vileplume [TM]	Vivillon [TM]	Volbeat [TM]

Move	Pokémon that can learn it					
Rest (TM44) *(Psychic)*	Voltorb [TM]	Wailmer [27, TM]	Wailord [27, TM]	Wartortle [TM]	Watchog [TM]	Weavile [TM]
	Weepinbell [TM]	Whirlipede [TM]	Whiscash [33, TM]	Whismur [45, TM]	Wigglytuff [TM]	Wingull [TM]
	Woobat [TM]	Wooper [TM]	Wormadam (Plant) [TM]	Wormadam (Sand) [TM]	Wormadam (Trash) [TM]	Xerneas [TM]
	Yanma [TM]	Yanmega [TM]	Yveltal [TM]	Zangoose [TM]	Zapdos [TM]	Zigzagoon [41, TM]
	Zoroark [TM]	Zorua [TM]	Zubat [TM]	Zweilous [TM]	Zygarde [TM]	
Retaliate (TM67)	Absol [TM]	Aegislash [TM]	Audino [TM]	Bibarel [TM]	Bidoof [TM]	Bisharp [TM]
	Carvanha [TM]	Chesnaught [TM]	Chespin [TM]	Conkeldurr [TM]	Crawdaunt [TM]	Croagunk [TM]
	Cubone [47, TM]	Dedenne [TM]	Delcatty [TM]	Doublade [26, TM]	Drapion [TM]	Druddigon [TM]
	Dunsparce [TM]	Durant [TM]	Eevee [TM]	Espeon [TM]	Exploud [TM]	Farfetch'd [TM]
	Flareon [TM]	Furfrou [33, TM]	Furret [TM]	Gallade [TM]	Glaceon [TM]	Gogoat [TM]
	Granbull [TM]	Gurdurr [TM]	Hariyama [TM]	Hawlucha [TM]	Heracross [TM]	Honchkrow [TM]
	Honedge [26, TM]	Houndoom [TM]	Houndour [TM]	Inkay [TM]	Jigglypuff [TM]	Jolteon [TM]
	Kangaskhan [TM]	Kecleon [TM]	Krokorok [TM]	Krookodile [TM]	Larvitar [TM]	Leafeon [TM]
	Lickilicky [TM]	Lickitung [TM]	Linoone [TM]	Litleo [TM]	Loudred [TM]	Lucario [TM]
	Machamp [TM]	Machoke [TM]	Machop [TM]	Makuhita [TM]	Malamar [TM]	Marowak [59, TM]
	Medicham [TM]	Meditite [TM]	Mienfoo [TM]	Mienshao [TM]	Mightyena [TM]	Miltank [TM]
	Munchlax [TM]	Murkrow [TM]	Pancham [TM]	Pangoro [TM]	Patrat [TM]	Pawniard [TM]
	Poochyena [TM]	Pupitar [TM]	Pyroar [TM]	Quilladin [TM]	Riolu [TM]	Sableye [TM]
	Sandile [TM]	Sawk [37, TM]	Scrafty [TM]	Scraggy [TM]	Sneasel [TM]	Seviper [TM]
	Sharpedo [TM]	Skiddo [TM]	Skitty [TM]	Sneasel [TM]	Snorlax [TM]	Snubbull [TM]
	Spinda [TM]	Staraptor [TM]	Staravia [TM]	Sylveon [TM]	Tauros [TM]	Teddiursa [TM]
	Throh [TM]	Timburr [TM]	Toxicroak [TM]	Tyranitar [TM]	Umbreon [TM]	Ursaring [TM]
	Vaporeon [TM]	Watchog [TM]	Weavile [TM]	Whismur [TM]	Wigglytuff [TM]	Zangoose [TM]
	Zigzagoon [TM]	Zoroark [TM]	Zorua [TM]			
Return (TM27) *(Normal)*	Abomasnow [TM]	Abra [TM]	Absol [TM]	Accelgor [TM]	Aegislash [TM]	Aerodactyl [TM]
	Aggron [TM]	Alakazam [TM]	Alomomola [TM]	Altaria [TM]	Amaura [TM]	Amoonguss [TM]
	Ampharos [TM]	Arbok [TM]	Ariados [TM]	Aromatisse [TM]	Aron [TM]	Articuno [TM]
	Audino [TM]	Aurorus [TM]	Avalugg [TM]	Axew [TM]	Azumarill [TM]	Azurill [TM]
	Bagon [TM]	Banette [TM]	Barbaracle [TM]	Barboach [TM]	Basculin [TM]	Beartic [TM]
	Beedrill [TM]	Bellossom [TM]	Bellsprout [TM]	Bergmite [TM]	Bibarel [TM]	Bidoof [TM]
	Binacle [TM]	Bisharp [TM]	Blastoise [TM]	Boldore [TM]	Bonsly [TM]	Braixen [TM]
	Budew [TM]	Buizel [TM]	Bulbasaur [TM]	Bunnelby [TM]	Butterfree [TM]	Carbink [TM]
	Carnivine [TM]	Carvanha [TM]	Chandelure [TM]	Charizard [TM]	Charmander [TM]	Charmeleon [TM]
	Chatot [TM]	Chesnaught [TM]	Chespin [TM]	Chimecho [TM]	Chinchou [TM]	Chingling [TM]
	Clamperl [TM]	Clauncher [TM]	Clawitzer [TM]	Cloyster [TM]	Conkeldurr [TM]	Corphish [TM]
	Corsola [TM]	Crawdaunt [TM]	Croagunk [TM]	Crobat [TM]	Crustle [TM]	Cryogonal [TM]
	Cubchoo [TM]	Cubone [TM]	Dedenne [TM]	Deino [TM]	Delcatty [TM]	Delibird [TM]
	Delphox [TM]	Diggersby [TM]	Diglett [TM]	Dodrio [TM]	Doduo [TM]	Doublade [TM]
	Dragalge [TM]	Dragonair [TM]	Dragonite [TM]	Drapion [TM]	Dratini [TM]	Drifblim [TM]
	Drifloon [TM]	Druddigon [TM]	Ducklett [TM]	Dugtrio [TM]	Dunsparce [TM]	Duosion [TM]
	Durant [TM]	Dwebble [TM]	Eevee [TM]	Ekans [TM]	Electrike [TM]	Electrode [TM]
	Emolga [TM]	Escavalier [TM]	Espeon [TM]	Espurr [TM]	Exeggcute [TM]	Exeggutor [TM]
	Exploud [TM]	Farfetch'd [TM]	Fearow [TM]	Fennekin [TM]	Ferroseed [TM]	Ferrothorn [TM]
	Flaaffy [TM]	Flabébé [TM]	Flareon [TM]	Fletchinder [TM]	Fletchling [TM]	Floatzel [TM]
	Floette [TM]	Florges [TM]	Flygon [TM]	Foongus [TM]	Fraxure [TM]	Froakie [TM]
	Frogadier [TM]	Furfrou [TM]	Furret [TM]	Gabite [TM]	Gallade [TM]	Garbodor [TM]
	Garchomp [TM]	Gardevoir [TM]	Gastly [TM]	Gengar [TM]	Geodude [TM]	Gible [TM]
	Gigalith [TM]	Glaceon [TM]	Gligar [TM]	Gliscor [TM]	Gloom [TM]	Gogoat [TM]
	Golbat [TM]	Goldeen [TM]	Golduck [TM]	Golem [TM]	Golett [TM]	Golurk [TM]
	Goodra [TM]	Goomy [TM]	Gorebyss [TM]	Gothita [TM]	Gothitelle [TM]	Gothorita [TM]
	Gourgeist [TM]	Granbull [TM]	Graveler [TM]	Greninja [TM]	Grumpig [TM]	Gulpin [TM]
	Gurdurr [TM]	Gyarados [TM]	Hariyama [TM]	Haunter [TM]	Hawlucha [TM]	Haxorus [TM]
	Heatmor [TM]	Heliolisk [TM]	Helioptile [TM]	Heracross [TM]	Hippopotas [TM]	Hippowdon [TM]
	Honchkrow [TM]	Honedge [TM]	Hoothoot [TM]	Hoppip [TM]	Horsea [TM]	Houndoom [TM]
	Houndour [TM]	Huntail [TM]	Hydreigon [TM]	Igglybuff [TM]	Illumise [TM]	Inkay [TM]
	Ivysaur [TM]	Jigglypuff [TM]	Jolteon [TM]	Jumpluff [TM]	Jynx [TM]	Kadabra [TM]
	Kangaskhan [TM]	Karrablast [TM]	Kecleon [TM]	Kingdra [TM]	Kirlia [TM]	Klefki [TM]
	Krokorok [TM]	Krookodile [TM]	Lairon [TM]	Lampent [TM]	Lanturn [TM]	Lapras [TM]
	Larvitar [TM]	Leafeon [TM]	Ledian [TM]	Ledyba [TM]	Lickilicky [TM]	Lickitung [TM]
	Liepard [TM]	Linoone [TM]	Litleo [TM]	Litwick [TM]	Lombre [TM]	Lotad [TM]
	Loudred [TM]	Lucario [TM]	Ludicolo [TM]	Lunatone [TM]	Luvdisc [TM]	Machamp [TM]
	Machoke [TM]	Machop [TM]	Magcargo [TM]	Magnemite [TM]	Magneton [TM]	Magnezone [TM]
	Makuhita [TM]	Malamar [TM]	Mamoswine [TM]	Manectric [TM]	Mantine [TM]	Mantyke [TM]
	Mareep [TM]	Marill [TM]	Marowak [TM]	Masquerain [TM]	Mawile [TM]	Medicham [TM]
	Meditite [TM]	Meowstic (Female) [TM]	Meowstic (Male) [TM]	Mewtwo [TM]	Mienfoo [TM]	Mienshao [TM]
	Mightyena [TM]	Miltank [TM]	Mime Jr. [TM]	Minun [TM]	Moltres [TM]	Mothim [TM]
	Mr. Mime [TM]	Munchlax [TM]	Murkrow [TM]	Nidoking [TM]	Nidoqueen [TM]	Nidoran ♀ [TM]
	Nidoran♂ [TM]	Nidorina [TM]	Nidorino [TM]	Nincada [TM]	Ninjask [TM]	Noctowl [TM]
	Noibat [TM]	Noivern [TM]	Nosepass [TM]	Octillery [TM]	Oddish [TM]	Onix [TM]
	Pachirisu [TM]	Pancham [TM]	Pangoro [TM]	Panpour [TM]	Pansage [TM]	Pansear [TM]
	Patrat [TM]	Pawniard [TM]	Pelipper [TM]	Phantump [TM]	Pichu [TM]	Pidgeot [TM]
	Pidgeotto [TM]	Pidgey [TM]	Pikachu [TM]	Piloswine [TM]	Pinsir [TM]	Plusle [TM]

AFTER THE HALL OF FAME

CENTRAL KALOS

COASTAL KALOS

MOUNTAIN KALOS

ADVENTURE DATA

AFTER THE HALL OF FAME · CENTRAL KALOS · COASTAL KALOS · MOUNTAIN KALOS · ADVENTURE DATA

Type	Move	Pokémon that can learn it					
Normal	Return (TM27)	Politoed [TM]	Poliwag [TM]	Poliwhirl [TM]	Poliwrath [TM]	Poochyena [TM]	Probopass [TM]
		Psyduck [TM]	Pumpkaboo [TM]	Pupitar [TM]	Purrloin [TM]	Pyroar [TM]	Quagsire [TM]
		Quilladin [TM]	Qwilfish [TM]	Raichu [TM]	Ralts [TM]	Relicanth [TM]	Remoraid [TM]
		Reuniclus [TM]	Rhydon [TM]	Rhyhorn [TM]	Rhyperior [TM]	Riolu [TM]	Roggenrola [TM]
		Roselia [TM]	Roserade [TM]	Rotom (Fan) [TM]	Rotom (Frost) [TM]	Rotom (Heat) [TM]	Rotom (Mow) [TM]
		Rotom (Wash) [TM]	Rotom [TM]	Sableye [TM]	Salamence [TM]	Sandile [TM]	Sandshrew [TM]
		Sandslash [TM]	Sawk [TM]	Scizor [TM]	Scolipede [TM]	Scrafty [TM]	Scraggy [TM]
		Scyther [TM]	Seadra [TM]	Seaking [TM]	Sentret [TM]	Seviper [TM]	Sharpedo [TM]
		Shedinja [TM]	Shelgon [TM]	Shellder [TM]	Shelmet [TM]	Shuckle [TM]	Shuppet [TM]
		Sigilyph [TM]	Simipour [TM]	Simisage [TM]	Simisear [TM]	Skarmory [TM]	Skiddo [TM]
		Skiploom [TM]	Skitty [TM]	Skorupi [TM]	Skrelp [TM]	Skuntank [TM]	Sliggoo [TM]
		Slowbro [TM]	Slowking [TM]	Slowpoke [TM]	Slugma [TM]	Slurpuff [TM]	Smoochum [TM]
		Sneasel [TM]	Snorlax [TM]	Snover [TM]	Snubbull [TM]	Solosis [TM]	Solrock [TM]
		Spearow [TM]	Spinarak [TM]	Spinda [TM]	Spoink [TM]	Spritzee [TM]	Squirtle [TM]
		Staraptor [TM]	Staravia [TM]	Starly [TM]	Starmie [TM]	Staryu [TM]	Steelix [TM]
		Stunfisk [TM]	Stunky [TM]	Sudowoodo [TM]	Surskit [TM]	Swablu [TM]	Swalot [TM]
		Swanna [TM]	Swellow [TM]	Swinub [TM]	Swirlix [TM]	Swoobat [TM]	Sylveon [TM]
		Taillow [TM]	Talonflame [TM]	Tauros [TM]	Teddiursa [TM]	Tentacool [TM]	Tentacruel [TM]
		Throh [TM]	Timburr [TM]	Torkoal [TM]	Toxicroak [TM]	Trapinch [TM]	Trevenant [TM]
		Trubbish [TM]	Tyranitar [TM]	Tyrantrum [TM]	Tyrunt [TM]	Umbreon [TM]	Ursaring [TM]
		Vanillish [TM]	Vanillite [TM]	Vanilluxe [TM]	Vaporeon [TM]	Venipede [TM]	Venusaur [TM]
		Vespiquen [TM]	Vibrava [TM]	Victreebel [TM]	Vileplume [TM]	Vivillon [TM]	Volbeat [TM]
		Voltorb [TM]	Wailmer [TM]	Wailord [TM]	Wartortle [TM]	Watchog [TM]	Weavile [TM]
		Weepinbell [TM]	Whirlipede [TM]	Whiscash [TM]	Whismur [TM]	Wigglytuff [TM]	Wingull [TM]
		Woobat [TM]	Wooper [TM]	Wormadam (Plant) [TM]	Wormadam (Sand) [TM]	Wormadam (Trash) [TM]	Xerneas [TM]
		Yanma [TM]	Yanmega [TM]	Yveltal [TM]	Zangoose [TM]	Zapdos [TM]	Zigzagoon [TM]
		Zoroark [TM]	Zorua [TM]	Zubat [TM]	Zweilous [TM]	Zygarde [TM]	
Fighting	Revenge	Basculin [E]	Croagunk [22]	Druddigon [35]	Farfetch'd [E]	Heracross [E]	Hippopotas [E]
		Machamp [25]	Machoke [25]	Machop [25]	Makuhita [E]	Patrat [E]	Pawniard [E]
		Pinsir [15]	Qwilfish [22]	Starly [E]	Stunfisk [50]	Throh [21]	Toxicroak [22]
		Weavile [1]	Zangoose [26]				
		Aron [E]	Axew [E]	Diglett [E]	Escavalier [49]	Hariyama [57]	Heracross [43]
		Houndour [E]	Kangaskhan [50]	Makuhita [43]	Malamar [1]	Medicham [55]	Meditite [46]
		Mienfoo [57]	Mienshao [1, 63]	Miltank [E]	Pichu [E]	Rhyhorn [E]	Riolu [29]
		Sawk [50]	Scyther [E]	Sentret [E]	Throh [50]	Timburr [E]	Yanma [E]
Normal	Roar (TM05)	Aerodactyl [9, TM]	Aggron [18, TM]	Altaria [TM]	Amaura [TM]	Aron [18, TM]	Articuno [TM]
		Aurorus [TM]	Avalugg [TM]	Axew [TM]	Bagon [TM]	Beartic [TM]	Blastoise [TM]
		Charizard [TM]	Chesnaught [TM]	Chespin [TM]	Deino [20, TM]	Dragonite [TM]	Drapion [TM]
		Druddigon [TM]	Electrike [36, TM]	Exploud [45, TM]	Flareon [TM]	Floatzel [TM]	Fraxure [TM]
		Furfrou [TM]	Gabite [TM]	Garchomp [TM]	Gible [TM]	Glaceon [TM]	Gogoat [TM]
		Golem [TM]	Granbull [27, TM]	Gyarados [TM]	Haxorus [TM]	Hippopotas [TM]	Hippowdon [TM]
		Houndoom [13, TM]	Houndour [13, TM]	Hydreigon [20, TM]	Jolteon [TM]	Kangaskhan [TM]	Krokorok [TM]
		Krookodile [TM]	Lairon [18, TM]	Lapras [TM]	Leafeon [TM]	Linoone [TM]	Litleo [TM]
		Loudred [43, TM]	Lucario [TM]	Mamoswine [TM]	Manectric [42, TM]	Mightyena [22, TM]	Moltres [TM]
		Nidoking [TM]	Nidoqueen [TM]	Onix [TM]	Pancham [TM]	Pangoro [TM]	Piloswine [TM]
		Poochyena [21, TM]	Pyroar [TM]	Quilladin [TM]	Rhydon [TM]	Rhyhorn [TM]	Rhyperior [TM]
		Riolu [TM]	Salamence [TM]	Sandile [TM]	Scrafty [TM]	Scraggy [TM]	Sharpedo [TM]
		Shelgon [TM]	Skarmory [TM]	Skiddo [TM]	Skuntank [TM]	Snubbull [25, TM]	Steelix [TM]
		Stunky [TM]	Swinub [TM]	Teddiursa [TM]	Tyranitar [TM]	Tyrantrum [6, TM]	Tyrunt [6, TM]
		Ursaring [TM]	Vaporeon [TM]	Venusaur [TM]	Wailmer [TM]	Wailord [TM]	Whismur [35, TM]
		Xerneas [TM]	Zangoose [TM]	Zapdos [TM]	Zoroark [TM]	Zorua [TM]	Zweilous [20, TM]
Rock	Rock Blast	Boldore [14]	Corsola [31]	Crustle [1, 5]	Dwebble [5]	Geodude [22]	Gigalith [14]
		Golem [22]	Graveler [22]	Heracross [E]	Nosepass [18]	Octillery [1]	Onix [E]
		Probopass [18]	Remoraid [E]	Rhydon [23]	Rhyhorn [23]	Rhyperior [23]	Roggenrola [14]
		Shellder [E]	Shuckle [E]	Trubbish [E]	Wormadam (Sand) [26]		
Normal	Rock Climb	Bidoof [E]	Druddigon [49]	Durant [E]	Ferroseed [E]	Ferrothorn [1]	Geodude [E]
		Gible [E]	Gligar [E]	Onix [E]	Rhyhorn [E]	Sandile [E]	Sandshrew [E]
		Scolipede [50]	Scrafty [51]	Scraggy [45]	Venipede [40, E]	Whirlipede [46]	Zigzagoon [E]
Rock	Rock Polish (TM69)	Aerodactyl [TM]	Aggron [TM]	Amaura [TM]	Aron [TM]	Aurorus [TM]	Avalugg [TM]
		Barbaracle [24, TM]	Bergmite [TM]	Binacle [24, TM]	Bisharp [TM]	Boldore [TM]	Bonsly [TM]
		Carbink [TM]	Corsola [TM]	Crustle [19, TM]	Durant [TM]	Dwebble [19, TM]	Ferroseed [TM]
		Ferrothorn [TM]	Garbodor [TM]	Geodude [8, TM]	Gigalith [TM]	Gligar [TM]	Gliscor [TM]
		Golem [1, 8, TM]	Golett [TM]	Golurk [TM]	Graveler [1, 8, TM]	Lairon [TM]	Larvitar [TM]
		Lunatone [13, TM]	Magcargo [TM]	Nosepass [TM]	Onix [19, TM]	Pawniard [TM]	Probopass [TM]
		Pupitar [TM]	Relicanth [TM]	Rhydon [TM]	Rhyhorn [TM]	Rhyperior [TM]	Roggenrola [TM]
		Shuckle [TM]	Solrock [13, TM]	Steelix [TM]	Sudowoodo [TM]	Tyranitar [TM]	Tyrantrum [TM]
		Tyrunt [TM, E]					

Move	Pokémon that can learn it					
Rock Rock Slide (TM80)	Abomasnow [TM]	Absol [TM]	Aegislash [TM]	Aerodactyl [73, TM]	Aggron [TM]	Amaura [TM]
	Arbok [TM]	Aron [TM]	Aurorus [TM]	Avalugg [TM]	Bagon [TM]	Barbaracle [TM]
	Beartic [TM]	Bergmite [TM]	Binacle [TM]	Blastoise [TM]	Boldore [30, TM]	Bonsly [29, TM]
	Bunnelby [TM]	Carbink [TM]	Charizard [TM]	Charmander [TM]	Charmeleon [TM]	Chesnaught [TM]
	Chespin [TM]	Clauncher [TM]	Clawitzer [TM]	Conkeldurr [33, TM]	Corphish [TM]	Corsola [TM]
	Crawdaunt [TM]	Croagunk [TM]	Crustle [29, TM]	Cubone [TM]	Diggersby [TM]	Diglett [TM]
	Doublade [TM]	Dragonite [TM]	Drapion [TM]	Druddigon [TM]	Dugtrio [TM]	Dunsparce [TM]
	Duosion [TM]	Durant [TM]	Dwebble [29, TM]	Ekans [TM]	Exploud [TM]	Flygon [25, TM]
	Froakie [TM]	Frogadier [TM]	Gabite [TM]	Gallade [TM]	Garchomp [TM]	Geodude [TM]
	Gible [TM]	Gigalith [30, TM]	Gligar [TM]	Gliscor [TM]	Gogoat [TM]	Golem [TM]
	Golett [TM]	Golurk [TM]	Goodra [TM]	Goomy [TM]	Gothita [TM]	Gothitelle [TM]
	Gothorita [TM]	Gourgeist [TM]	Granbull [TM]	Graveler [TM]	Greninja [TM]	Gurdurr [33, TM]
	Hariyama [TM]	Hawlucha [TM]	Haxorus [TM]	Heliolisk [TM]	Helioptile [TM]	Heracross [TM]
	Hippopotas [TM]	Hippowdon [TM]	Honedge [TM]	Hydreigon [TM]	Inkay [TM]	Kangaskhan [TM]
	Kecleon [TM]	Krokorok [TM]	Krookodile [TM]	Lairon [TM]	Larvitar [19, TM]	Lickilicky [TM]
	Lickitung [TM]	Loudred [TM]	Lucario [TM]	Lunatone [25, TM]	Machamp [TM]	Machoke [TM]
	Machop [TM]	Magcargo [44, TM]	Makuhita [TM]	Malamar [TM]	Mamoswine [TM]	Mantine [TM]
	Mantyke [TM]	Marowak [TM]	Mawile [TM]	Medicham [TM]	Meditite [TM]	Mewtwo [TM]
	Mienfoo [TM]	Mienshao [TM]	Miltank [TM]	Munchlax [TM]	Nidoking [TM]	Nidoqueen [TM]
	Nosepass [29, TM]	Onix [34, TM]	Pancham [TM]	Pangoro [TM]	Phantump [TM]	Piloswine [TM]
	Pinsir [TM]	Poliwrath [TM]	Probopass [29, TM]	Pumpkaboo [TM]	Pupitar [19, TM]	Quagsire [TM]
	Quilladin [TM]	Relicanth [TM]	Reuniclus [TM]	Rhydon [TM]	Rhyhorn [TM]	Rhyperior [TM]
	Riolu [TM]	Roggenrola [27, TM]	Salamence [TM]	Sandile [TM]	Sandshrew [TM]	Sandslash [TM]
	Sawk [TM]	Scolipede [TM]	Scrafty [TM]	Scraggy [TM]	Shelgon [TM]	Shuckle [38, TM]
	Simipour [TM]	Simisage [TM]	Simisear [TM]	Skarmory [TM]	Skiddo [TM]	Sliggoo [TM]
	Slugma [41, TM]	Snorlax [TM]	Solosis [TM]	Solrock [25, TM]	Spinda [TM]	Steelix [34, TM]
	Stunfisk [TM]	Sudowoodo [29, TM]	Swinub [TM]	Tauros [TM]	Teddiursa [TM]	Throh [TM]
	Timburr [31, TM]	Torkoal [TM]	Toxicroak [TM]	Trapinch [25, TM]	Trevenant [TM]	Tyranitar [19, TM]
	Tyrantrum [68, TM]	Tyrunt [TM]	Ursaring [TM]	Vibrava [25, TM]	Whiscash [TM]	Xerneas [TM]
	Yveltal [TM]	Zangoose [TM]	Zygarde [TM]			
Fighting Rock Smash (TM94)	Abomasnow [TM]	Absol [TM]	Aegislash [TM]	Aerodactyl [TM]	Aggron [TM]	Altaria [TM]
	Amaura [TM]	Ampharos [TM]	Aron [TM]	Articuno [TM]	Aurorus [TM]	Avalugg [TM]
	Axew [TM]	Azumarill [TM]	Bagon [TM]	Barbaracle [TM]	Beartic [TM]	Beedrill [TM]
	Bergmite [TM]	Bibarel [TM]	Bidoof [TM]	Binacle [TM]	Bisharp [TM]	Blastoise [TM]
	Boldore [TM]	Buizel [TM]	Bulbasaur [TM]	Bunnelby [TM]	Charizard [TM]	Charmander [TM]
	Charmeleon [TM]	Chesnaught [TM]	Chespin [TM]	Conkeldurr [TM]	Corphish [TM]	Corsola [TM]
	Crawdaunt [TM]	Croagunk [TM]	Crustle [TM]	Cubchoo [TM]	Cubone [TM]	Deino [TM]
	Delcatty [TM]	Diggersby [TM]	Diglett [TM]	Doublade [TM]	Dragonite [TM]	Drapion [TM]
	Druddigon [TM]	Dugtrio [TM]	Dunsparce [TM]	Durant [TM]	Dwebble [TM]	Escavalier [TM]
	Exploud [TM]	Ferroseed [TM]	Ferrothorn [TM]	Flaaffy [TM]	Flareon [TM]	Floatzel [TM]
	Flygon [TM]	Fraxure [TM]	Froakie [TM]	Frogadier [TM]	Furfrou [TM]	Furret [TM]
	Gabite [TM]	Gallade [TM]	Garchomp [TM]	Gengar [TM]	Geodude [TM]	Gible [TM]
	Gigalith [TM]	Glaceon [TM]	Gligar [TM]	Gliscor [TM]	Gogoat [TM]	Golduck [TM]
	Golem [TM]	Golett [TM]	Golurk [TM]	Goodra [TM]	Gourgeist [TM]	Granbull [TM]
	Graveler [TM]	Greninja [TM]	Gulpin [TM]	Gurdurr [TM]	Gyarados [TM]	Hariyama [TM]
	Hawlucha [TM]	Haxorus [TM]	Heatmor [TM]	Heracross [TM]	Hippopotas [TM]	Hippowdon [TM]
	Honedge [TM]	Houndoom [TM]	Houndour [TM]	Hydreigon [TM]	Ivysaur [TM]	Jolteon [TM]
	Kangaskhan [TM]	Kecleon [TM]	Krokorok [TM]	Krookodile [TM]	Lairon [TM]	Lapras [TM]
	Larvitar [TM]	Leafeon [TM]	Ledian [TM]	Lickilicky [TM]	Lickitung [TM]	Liepard [TM]
	Linoone [TM]	Litleo [TM]	Lombre [TM]	Loudred [TM]	Lucario [TM]	Ludicolo [TM]
	Machamp [TM]	Machoke [TM]	Machop [TM]	Magcargo [TM]	Makuhita [TM]	Mamoswine [TM]
	Marill [TM]	Marowak [TM]	Mawile [TM]	Medicham [TM]	Meditite [TM]	Mewtwo [TM]
	Mienfoo [TM]	Mienshao [TM]	Mightyena [TM]	Miltank [TM]	Moltres [TM]	Munchlax [TM]
	Nidoking [TM]	Nidoqueen [TM]	Nidoran ♀ [TM]	Nidoran ♂ [TM]	Nidorina [TM]	Nidorino [TM]
	Nosepass [TM]	Onix [TM]	Pancham [TM]	Pangoro [TM]	Panpour [TM]	Pansage [TM]
	Pansear [TM]	Pawniard [TM]	Phantump [TM]	Pikachu [TM]	Piloswine [TM]	Pinsir [TM]
	Politoed [TM]	Poliwhirl [TM]	Poliwrath [TM]	Poochyena [TM]	Probopass [TM]	Psyduck [TM]
	Pumpkaboo [TM]	Pupitar [TM]	Pyroar [TM]	Quagsire [TM]	Quilladin [TM]	Raichu [TM]
	Relicanth [TM]	Reuniclus [TM]	Rhydon [TM]	Rhyhorn [TM]	Rhyperior [TM]	Riolu [TM]
	Roggenrola [TM]	Sableye [TM]	Salamence [TM]	Sandshrew [TM]	Sandslash [TM]	Sawk [1, TM]
	Scizor [TM]	Scolipede [TM]	Scrafty [TM]	Scraggy [TM]	Scyther [TM]	Seviper [TM]
	Sharpedo [TM]	Shelgon [TM]	Shuckle [TM]	Skorupi [TM]	Simisage [TM]	Simisear [TM]
	Skarmory [TM]	Skiddo [TM]	Simipour [TM]	Skuntank [TM]	Slowbro [TM]	Slowking [TM]
	Slugma [TM]	Sneasel [TM]	Snorlax [TM]	Snubbull [TM]	Spinda [TM]	Squirtle [TM]
	Steelix [TM]	Stunky [TM]	Sudowoodo [TM]	Swalot [TM]	Swinub [TM]	Tauros [TM]
	Teddiursa [TM]	Throh [TM]	Timburr [TM]	Torkoal [TM]	Toxicroak [TM]	Trapinch [TM]
	Trevenant [TM]	Tyranitar [TM]	Tyrantrum [TM]	Tyrunt [TM]	Ursaring [TM]	Vaporeon [TM]
	Venipede [TM]	Venusaur [TM]	Vibrava [TM]	Wailmer [TM]	Wailord [TM]	Wartortle [TM]
	Watchog [TM]	Weavile [TM]	Whirlipede [TM]	Whiscash [TM]	Wooper [TM]	Zangoose [TM]
	Zapdos [TM]	Zigzagoon [TM]	Zoroark [TM]	Zweilous [TM]	Zygarde [TM]	

AFTER THE HALL OF FAME

CENTRAL KALOS

COASTAL KALOS

MOUNTAIN KALOS

ADVENTURE DATA

Move	Pokémon that can learn it					
Rock Throw (Rock)	Amaura [10]	Aurorus [10]	Bonsly [12]	Carbink [5]	Conkeldurr [16]	Geodude [18]
	Golem [18]	Graveler [18]	Gurdurr [16]	Lunatone [1, 5]	Magcargo [1, 10]	Nosepass [11]
	Onix [7]	Shuckle [23]	Slugma [10]	Solrock [1, 5]	Steelix [7]	Sudowoodo [1, 12]
	Timburr [16]					
Rock Tomb (TM39) (Rock)	Abomasnow [TM]	Absol [TM]	Aerodactyl [TM]	Aggron [TM]	Amaura [TM]	Arbok [TM]
	Aron [TM]	Aurorus [TM]	Avalugg [TM]	Axew [TM]	Bagon [TM]	Barbaracle [TM]
	Barboach [TM]	Beartic [TM]	Bergmite [TM]	Binacle [TM]	Bisharp [TM]	Blastoise [TM]
	Boldore [TM]	Bonsly [22, TM]	Buizel [TM]	Bunnelby [TM]	Carbink [TM]	Charizard [TM]
	Charmander [TM]	Charmeleon [TM]	Chesnaught [TM]	Chespin [TM]	Conkeldurr [TM]	Corphish [TM]
	Corsola [TM]	Crawdaunt [TM]	Croagunk [TM]	Crustle [TM]	Cubchoo [TM]	Cubone [TM]
	Diggersby [TM]	Diglett [TM]	Dragonite [TM]	Drapion [TM]	Druddigon [TM]	Dugtrio [TM]
	Dunsparce [TM]	Duosion [TM]	Durant [TM]	Dwebble [TM]	Ekans [TM]	Exploud [TM]
	Floatzel [TM]	Flygon [TM]	Fraxure [TM]	Froakie [TM]	Frogadier [TM]	Gabite [TM]
	Gallade [TM]	Garchomp [TM]	Geodude [TM]	Gible [TM]	Gigalith [TM]	Gligar [TM]
	Gliscor [TM]	Golem [TM]	Golett [TM]	Golurk [TM]	Gothita [TM]	Gothitelle [TM]
	Gothorita [TM]	Granbull [TM]	Graveler [TM]	Greninja [TM]	Gurdurr [TM]	Hariyama [TM]
	Hawlucha [TM]	Haxorus [TM]	Heatmor [TM]	Heliolisk [TM]	Helioptile [TM]	Heracross [TM]
	Hippopotas [TM]	Hippowdon [TM]	Huntail [TM]	Hydreigon [TM]	Kangaskhan [TM]	Kecleon [TM]
	Krokorok [TM]	Krookodile [TM]	Lairon [TM]	Larvitar [TM]	Lickilicky [TM]	Lickitung [TM]
	Loudred [TM]	Lucario [TM]	Lunatone [TM]	Machamp [TM]	Machoke [TM]	Machop [TM]
	Magcargo [TM]	Makuhita [TM]	Mamoswine [TM]	Mantine [TM]	Marowak [TM]	Mawile [TM]
	Medicham [TM]	Meditite [TM]	Mewtwo [TM]	Mienfoo [TM]	Mienshao [TM]	Miltank [TM]
	Munchlax [TM]	Nidoking [TM]	Nidoqueen [TM]	Nosepass [TM]	Onix [10, TM]	Pancham [TM]
	Pangoro [TM]	Panpour [TM]	Pansage [TM]	Pansear [TM]	Pawniard [TM]	Piloswine [TM]
	Pinsir [TM]	Poliwrath [TM]	Probopass [TM]	Pupitar [TM]	Quagsire [TM]	Quilladin [TM]
	Relicanth [15, TM]	Reuniclus [TM]	Rhydon [TM]	Rhyhorn [TM]	Rhyperior [TM]	Riolu [TM]
	Roggenrola [TM, E]	Sableye [TM]	Salamence [TM]	Sandile [TM]	Sandshrew [TM]	Sandslash [TM]
	Sawk [TM]	Scolipede [TM]	Scrafty [TM]	Scraggy [TM]	Sharpedo [TM]	Shelgon [TM]
	Shuckle [TM]	Simipour [TM]	Simisage [TM]	Simisear [TM]	Skarmory [TM]	Skorupi [TM]
	Slugma [TM]	Snorlax [TM]	Solosis [TM]	Solrock [TM]	Spinda [TM]	Squirtle [TM]
	Steelix [10, TM]	Stunfisk [TM]	Sudowoodo [22, TM]	Swinub [TM]	Tauros [TM]	Teddiursa [TM]
	Throh [TM]	Timburr [TM]	Torkoal [TM]	Toxicroak [TM]	Trapinch [TM]	Tyranitar [TM]
	Tyrantrum [TM]	Tyrunt [TM]	Ursaring [TM]	Vibrava [TM]	Wailmer [TM]	Wailord [TM]
	Wartortle [TM]	Whiscash [TM]	Wormadam (Sand) [TM]	Zangoose [TM]		
Rock Wrecker	Crustle [55]	Dwebble [43]	Rhyperior [1, 86]			
Role Play (Psychic)	Delphox [1]	Furfrou [E]	Greninja [1]	Kadabra [42]	Meowstic (Female) [43]	Meowstic (Male) [43]
	Mime Jr. [43]	Mr. Mime [43]	Panpour [E]	Pansage [E]	Pansear [E]	Spinda [E]
Rolling Kick (Fighting)	Machop [E]					
Rollout (Rock)	Azumarill [10]	Bibarel [13]	Bidoof [13, E]	Bonsly [E]	Bunnelby [E]	Chesnaught [8]
	Chespin [8, E]	Dunsparce [4]	Duosion [1, 7]	Electrode [15]	Ferroseed [6]	Ferrothorn [1, 6]
	Foongus [E]	Geodude [11]	Golett [9]	Golurk [9]	Graveler [11]	Jigglypuff [21]
	Lickilicky [33]	Lickitung [33]	Marill [10]	Miltank [19]	Munchlax [36]	Nosepass [E]
	Onix [E]	Pachirisu [E]	Quilladin [8]	Qwilfish [17]	Reuniclus [1, 7]	Sandshrew [7]
	Sandslash [7]	Scolipede [1]	Shuckle [1]	Skiddo [E]	Slugma [E]	Snorlax [36]
	Solosis [7]	Sudowoodo [1]	Trubbish [E]	Venipede [1]	Voltorb [15]	Wailmer [11]
	Wailord [1, 11]	Whirlipede [1]				
Roost (TM19) (Flying)	Aerodactyl [TM, E]	Altaria [TM]	Articuno [1, 85, TM]	Beedrill [TM]	Butterfree [TM]	Charizard [TM]
	Chatot [41, TM]	Crobat [TM]	Dodrio [TM]	Doduo [TM]	Dragonite [1, TM]	Ducklett [30, TM]
	Dunsparce [25, TM]	Emolga [TM, E]	Farfetch'd [TM, E]	Fearow [41, TM]	Fletchinder [25, TM]	Fletchling [21, TM]
	Flygon [TM]	Gligar [TM]	Gliscor [TM]	Golbat [TM]	Hawlucha [12, TM]	Honchkrow [TM]
	Hoothoot [53, TM]	Hydreigon [TM]	Illumise [TM]	Ledian [TM]	Ledyba [TM]	Masquerain [TM]
	Moltres [1, 85, TM]	Mothim [TM]	Murkrow [TM, E]	Ninjask [TM]	Noctowl [62, TM]	Noibat [27, TM]
	Noivern [27, TM]	Pelipper [28, TM]	Pidgeot [44, TM]	Pidgeotto [42, TM]	Pidgey [37, TM]	Salamence [TM]
	Scizor [TM]	Scyther [TM]	Sigilyph [TM]	Skarmory [TM]	Spearow [33, TM]	Staraptor [TM]
	Staravia [TM]	Starly [TM, E]	Swablu [TM, E]	Swanna [30, TM]	Swellow [TM]	Swoobat [TM]
	Taillow [TM, E]	Talonflame [25, TM]	Vespiquen [TM]	Vibrava [TM]	Vivillon [TM]	Volbeat [TM]
	Wingull [26, TM, E]	Woobat [TM, E]	Yanma [TM]	Yanmega [TM]	Yveltal [1, TM]	Zapdos [1, 85, TM]
	Zubat [TM]					
Rototiller (Ground)	Bibarel [1]	Diggersby [1]	Dugtrio [1]	Dwebble [E]	Linoone [1]	Onix [E]
	Rhyhorn [E]	Sandshrew [E]	Watchog [1]			

Move	Pokémon that can learn it					
Normal Round (TM48)	Abomasnow [TM]	Abra [TM]	Absol [TM]	Accelgor [TM]	Aegislash [TM]	Aerodactyl [TM]
	Aggron [TM]	Alakazam [TM]	Alomomola [TM]	Altaria [18, TM]	Amaura [30, TM]	Amoonguss [TM]
	Ampharos [TM]	Arbok [TM]	Ariados [TM]	Aromatisse [TM]	Aron [TM]	Articuno [TM]
	Audino [TM]	Aurorus [30, TM]	Avalugg [TM]	Axew [TM]	Azumarill [TM]	Azurill [TM]
	Bagon [TM]	Banette [TM]	Barbaracle [TM]	Barboach [TM]	Basculin [TM]	Beartic [TM]
	Beedrill [TM]	Bellossom [TM]	Bellsprout [TM]	Bergmite [TM]	Bibarel [TM]	Bidoof [TM]
	Binacle [TM]	Bisharp [TM]	Blastoise [TM]	Boldore [TM]	Bonsly [TM]	Braixen [TM]
	Budew [TM]	Buizel [TM]	Bulbasaur [TM]	Bunnelby [TM]	Butterfree [TM]	Carbink [TM]
	Carnivine [TM]	Carvanha [TM]	Chandelure [TM]	Charizard [TM]	Charmander [TM]	Charmeleon [TM]
	Chatot [29, TM]	Chesnaught [TM]	Chespin [TM]	Chimecho [TM]	Chinchou [TM]	Chingling [TM]
	Clamperl [TM]	Clauncher [TM]	Clawitzer [TM]	Cloyster [TM]	Conkeldurr [TM]	Corphish [TM]
	Corsola [TM]	Crawdaunt [TM]	Croagunk [TM]	Crobat [TM]	Crustle [TM]	Cryogonal [TM]
	Cubchoo [TM]	Cubone [TM]	Dedenne [TM]	Deino [TM]	Delcatty [TM]	Delibird [TM]
	Delphox [TM]	Diggersby [TM]	Diglett [TM]	Dodrio [TM]	Doduo [TM]	Dragalge [TM]
	Dragonair [TM]	Dragonite [TM]	Drapion [TM]	Dratini [TM]	Drifblim [TM]	Drifloon [TM]
	Druddigon [TM]	Ducklett [TM]	Dugtrio [TM]	Dunsparce [TM]	Duosion [TM]	Durant [TM]
	Dwebble [TM]	Eevee [TM]	Ekans [TM]	Electrike [TM]	Electrode [TM]	Emolga [TM]
	Escavalier [TM]	Espeon [TM]	Espurr [TM]	Exeggcute [TM]	Exeggutor [TM]	Exploud [TM]
	Farfetch'd [TM]	Fearow [TM]	Fennekin [TM]	Ferroseed [TM]	Ferrothorn [TM]	Flaaffy [TM]
	Flabébé [TM]	Flareon [TM]	Fletchinder [TM]	Fletchling [TM]	Floatzel [TM]	Floette [TM]
	Florges [TM]	Flygon [TM]	Foongus [TM]	Fraxure [TM]	Froakie [21, TM]	Frogadier [23, TM]
	Furfrou [TM]	Furret [TM]	Gabite [TM]	Gallade [TM]	Garbodor [TM]	Garchomp [TM]
	Gardevoir [TM]	Gastly [TM]	Gengar [TM]	Geodude [TM]	Gible [TM]	Gigalith [TM]
	Glaceon [TM]	Gligar [TM]	Gliscor [TM]	Gloom [TM]	Gogoat [TM]	Golbat [TM]
	Goldeen [TM]	Golduck [TM]	Golem [TM]	Golett [TM]	Golurk [TM]	Goodra [TM]
	Goomy [TM]	Gorebyss [TM]	Gothita [TM]	Gothitelle [TM]	Gothorita [TM]	Gourgeist [TM]
	Granbull [TM]	Graveler [TM]	Greninja [TM]	Grumpig [TM]	Gulpin [TM]	Gurdurr [TM]
	Gyarados [TM]	Hariyama [TM]	Haunter [TM]	Hawlucha [TM]	Haxorus [TM]	Heatmor [TM]
	Heliolisk [TM]	Helioptile [TM]	Heracross [TM]	Hippopotas [TM]	Hippowdon [TM]	Honchkrow [TM]
	Hoothoot [TM]	Hoppip [TM]	Horsea [TM]	Houndoom [TM]	Houndour [TM]	Huntail [TM]
	Hydreigon [TM]	Igglybuff [TM]	Illumise [TM]	Inkay [TM]	Ivysaur [TM]	Jigglypuff [17, TM]
	Jolteon [TM]	Jumpluff [TM]	Jynx [TM]	Kadabra [TM]	Kangaskhan [TM]	Karrablast [TM]
	Kecleon [TM]	Kingdra [TM]	Kirlia [TM]	Klefki [TM]	Krokorok [TM]	Krookodile [TM]
	Lairon [TM]	Lampent [TM]	Lanturn [TM]	Lapras [TM]	Larvitar [TM]	Leafeon [TM]
	Ledian [TM]	Ledyba [TM]	Lickilicky [TM]	Lickitung [TM]	Liepard [TM]	Linoone [TM]
	Litleo [TM]	Litwick [TM]	Lombre [TM]	Lotad [TM]	Loudred [TM]	Lucario [TM]
	Ludicolo [TM]	Lunatone [TM]	Luvdisc [TM]	Machamp [TM]	Machoke [TM]	Machop [TM]
	Magcargo [TM]	Magnemite [TM]	Magneton [TM]	Magnezone [TM]	Makuhita [TM]	Malamar [TM]
	Mamoswine [TM]	Manectric [TM]	Mantine [TM]	Mantyke [TM]	Mareep [TM]	Marill [TM]
	Marowak [TM]	Masquerain [TM]	Mawile [TM]	Medicham [TM]	Meditite [TM]	Meowstic (Female) [TM]
	Meowstic (Male) [TM]	Mewtwo [TM]	Mienfoo [TM]	Mienshao [TM]	Mightyena [TM]	Miltank [TM]
	Mime Jr. [TM]	Minun [TM]	Moltres [TM]	Mothim [TM]	Mr. Mime [TM]	Munchlax [TM]
	Murkrow [TM]	Nidoking [TM]	Nidoqueen [TM]	Nidoran ♀ [TM]	Nidoran ♂ [TM]	Nidorina [TM]
	Nidorino [TM]	Nincada [TM]	Ninjask [TM]	Noctowl [TM]	Noibat [TM]	Noivern [TM]
	Nosepass [TM]	Octillery [TM]	Oddish [TM]	Onix [TM]	Pachirisu [TM]	Pancham [TM]
	Pangoro [TM]	Panpour [TM]	Pansage [TM]	Pansear [TM]	Patrat [TM]	Pawniard [TM]
	Pelipper [TM]	Phantump [TM]	Pichu [TM]	Pidgeot [TM]	Pidgeotto [TM]	Pidgey [TM]
	Pikachu [TM]	Piloswine [TM]	Pinsir [TM]	Plusle [TM]	Politoed [TM]	Poliwag [TM]
	Poliwhirl [TM]	Poliwrath [TM]	Poochyena [TM]	Probopass [TM]	Psyduck [TM]	Pumpkaboo [TM]
	Pupitar [TM]	Purrloin [TM]	Pyroar [TM]	Quagsire [TM]	Quilladin [TM]	Qwilfish [TM]
	Raichu [TM]	Ralts [TM]	Relicanth [TM]	Remoraid [TM]	Reuniclus [TM]	Rhydon [TM]
	Rhyhorn [TM]	Rhyperior [TM]	Riolu [TM]	Roggenrola [TM]	Roselia [TM]	Roserade [TM]
	Rotom (Fan) [TM]	Rotom (Frost) [TM]	Rotom (Heat) [TM]	Rotom (Mow) [TM]	Rotom (Wash) [TM]	Rotom [TM]
	Sableye [TM]	Salamence [TM]	Sandile [TM]	Sandshrew [TM]	Sandslash [TM]	Sawk [TM]
	Scizor [TM]	Scolipede [TM]	Scrafty [TM]	Scraggy [TM]	Scyther [TM]	Seadra [TM]
	Seaking [TM]	Sentret [TM]	Seviper [TM]	Sharpedo [TM]	Shedinja [TM]	Shelgon [TM]
	Shellder [TM]	Shelmet [TM]	Shuckle [TM]	Shuppet [TM]	Sigilyph [TM]	Simipour [TM]
	Simisage [TM]	Simisear [TM]	Skarmory [TM]	Skiddo [TM]	Skiploom [TM]	Skitty [TM]
	Skorupi [TM]	Skrelp [TM]	Skuntank [TM]	Sliggoo [TM]	Slowbro [TM]	Slowking [TM]
	Slowpoke [TM]	Slugma [TM]	Slurpuff [13, TM]	Smoochum [TM]	Sneasel [TM]	Snorlax [TM]
	Snover [TM]	Snubbull [TM]	Solosis [TM]	Solrock [TM]	Spearow [TM]	Spinarak [TM]
	Spinda [TM]	Spoink [TM]	Spritzee [TM]	Squirtle [TM]	Staraptor [TM]	Staravia [TM]
	Starly [TM]	Starmie [TM]	Staryu [TM]	Steelix [TM]	Stunfisk [TM]	Stunky [TM]
	Sudowoodo [TM]	Surskit [TM]	Swablu [18, TM]	Swalot [TM]	Swanna [TM]	Swellow [TM]
	Swinub [TM]	Swirlix [13, TM]	Swoobat [TM]	Sylveon [TM]	Taillow [TM]	Talonflame [TM]
	Tauros [TM]	Teddiursa [TM]	Tentacool [TM]	Tentacruel [TM]	Throh [TM]	Timburr [TM]
	Torkoal [TM]	Toxicroak [TM]	Trapinch [TM]	Trevenant [TM]	Trubbish [TM]	Tyranitar [TM]
	Tyrantrum [TM]	Tyrunt [TM]	Umbreon [TM]	Ursaring [TM]	Vanillish [TM]	Vanillite [TM]
	Vanilluxe [TM]	Vaporeon [TM]	Venipede [TM]	Venusaur [TM]	Vespiquen [TM]	Vibrava [TM]
	Victreebel [TM]	Vileplume [TM]	Vivillon [TM]	Volbeat [TM]	Voltorb [TM]	Wailmer [TM]
	Wailord [TM]	Wartortle [TM]	Watchog [TM]	Weavile [TM]	Weepinbell [TM]	Whirlipede [TM]
	Whiscash [TM]	Whismur [TM]	Wigglytuff [TM]	Wingull [TM]	Woobat [TM]	Wooper [TM]
	Wormadam (Plant) [TM]	Wormadam (Sand) [TM]	Wormadam (Trash) [TM]	Xerneas [TM]	Yanma [TM]	Yanmega [TM]
	Yveltal [TM]	Zangoose [TM]	Zapdos [TM]	Zigzagoon [TM]	Zoroark [TM]	Zorua [TM]
	Zubat [TM]	Zweilous [TM]	Zygarde [TM]			

S

Type	Move	Pokémon that can learn it					
Fighting	Sacred Sword	Aegislash [1]	Doublade [51]	Honedge [47]			
Normal	Safeguard (TM20)	Abomasnow [TM]	Abra [TM]	Alakazam [TM]	Alomomola [45, TM]	Altaria [13, TM]	Amaura [TM]
		Ampharos [TM]	Audino [TM]	Aurorus [TM]	Avalugg [TM]	Barbaracle [TM]	Bellossom [TM]
		Bergmite [TM]	Binacle [TM]	Braixen [TM]	Bulbasaur [TM]	Butterfree [36, TM]	Carbink [70, TM]
		Chandelure [53, TM]	Chimecho [41, TM]	Chingling [TM]	Corsola [TM]	Delcatty [TM]	Delphox [TM]
		Dragonair [53, TM]	Dragonite [53, TM]	Dratini [45, TM]	Duosion [TM]	Espurr [TM]	Fennekin [TM]
		Flaaffy [TM]	Flabébé [TM]	Floette [TM]	Florges [TM]	Gallade [TM]	Gardevoir [TM]
		Golett [TM]	Golurk [TM]	Gorebyss [TM]	Gothita [TM]	Gothitelle [TM]	Gothorita [TM]
		Gourgeist [TM]	Igglybuff [TM]	Ivysaur [TM]	Jigglypuff [TM]	Kadabra [TM]	Kangaskhan [TM]
		Kirlia [TM]	Klefki [TM]	Lampent [TM]	Lapras [43, TM]	Ledian [14, TM]	Ledyba [14, TM]
		Litwick [TM]	Lunatone [TM]	Luvdisc [55, TM]	Mareep [TM]	Meowstic (Female) [TM]	Meowstic (Male) [TM]
		Mewtwo [1, TM]	Mime Jr. [50, TM]	Moltres [43, TM]	Mothim [TM]	Mr. Mime [50, TM]	Phantump [TM]
		Pumpkaboo [TM]	Quagsire [TM]	Ralts [TM]	Relicanth [TM]	Reuniclus [TM]	Sandshrew [TM]
		Sandslash [TM]	Scizor [TM]	Scyther [TM]	Shuckle [16, TM]	Sigilyph [TM]	Skitty [TM]
		Slowbro [TM]	Slowking [TM]	Slowpoke [TM]	Slurpuff [67, TM]	Snover [TM]	Solosis [TM]
		Solrock [TM]	Spinda [TM]	Swablu [13, TM]	Swirlix [67, TM]	Swoobat [TM]	Sylveon [TM]
		Tentacool [TM]	Tentacruel [TM]	Trevenant [TM]	Venusaur [TM]	Vileplume [TM]	Vivillon [41, TM]
		Wigglytuff [TM]	Wobbuffet [1, TM]	Woobat [TM]	Wooper [TM]	Wormadam (Plant) [TM]	Wormadam (Sand) [TM]
		Wormadam (Trash) [TM]	Wynaut [15, TM]	Zygarde [5, TM]			
Ground	Sand Attack	Barbaracle [1]	Binacle [1]	Boldore [1, 7]	Crustle [1, 11]	Diglett [1]	Dugtrio [1]
		Durant [1]	Dwebble [11]	Eevee [5]	Espeon [5]	Farfetch'd [1]	Flareon [5]
		Flygon [1, 4]	Furfrou [5]	Gabite [1, 3]	Garchomp [1, 3]	Gible [3]	Gigalith [1, 7]
		Glaceon [5]	Gligar [4]	Gliscor [1, 4]	Hariyama [1, 4]	Hippopotas [1]	Hippowdon [1]
		Jolteon [5]	Krookodile [1, 7]	Krookodile [1, 7]	Leafeon [5]	Liepard [1, 10]	Linoone [13]
		Makuhita [4]	Mareep [E]	Mightyena [1, 9]	Nincada [9]	Ninjask [1, 9]	Patrat [13]
		Pidgeot [1, 5]	Pidgeotto [1, 5]	Pidgey [5]	Poochyena [1, 9]	Purrloin [10]	Roggenrola [7]
		Sandile [7]	Sandshrew [1, 3]	Sandslash [1, 3]	Scrafty [1, 5]	Scraggy [5]	Shedinja [9]
		Skarmory [6]	Skorupi [E]	Starly [E]	Sylveon [5]	Trapinch [4]	Trubbish [E]
		Umbreon [5]	Vaporeon [5]	Vibrava [1, 4]	Watchog [13]	Zigzagoon [13]	
	Sand Tomb	Bonsly [E]	Dugtrio [26]	Dwebble [E]	Flygon [1, 10]	Gabite [19]	Garchomp [19]
		Gible [19, E]	Gligar [E]	Hippopotas [25, E]	Hippowdon [25]	Krokorok [13]	Krookodile [13]
		Onix [37]	Sandile [13]	Sandshrew [23]	Sandslash [23]	Shuckle [E]	Sudowoodo [E]
		Trapinch [10]	Vibrava [1, 10]				
Rock	Sandstorm (TM37)	Absol [TM]	Accelgor [TM]	Aerodactyl [TM]	Aggron [TM]	Amaura [TM]	Aron [TM]
		Articuno [TM]	Aurorus [TM]	Barbaracle [TM]	Barboach [TM]	Binacle [TM]	Bisharp [TM]
		Boldore [42, TM]	Bonsly [TM]	Bunnelby [TM]	Carbink [TM]	Corsola [TM]	Crustle [TM]
		Cubone [TM]	Diggersby [TM]	Diglett [TM]	Dragonite [TM]	Dugtrio [TM]	Durant [TM]
		Dwebble [TM]	Ferrothorn [TM]	Flygon [44, TM]	Gabite [13, TM]	Garchomp [1, 13, TM]	Geodude [TM]
		Gible [13, TM]	Gigalith [42, TM]	Gligar [TM]	Gliscor [TM]	Golem [TM]	Graveler [TM]
		Gyarados [TM]	Heliolisk [TM]	Helioptile [TM]	Hippopotas [TM]	Hippowdon [TM]	Kangaskhan [TM]
		Krokorok [44, TM]	Krookodile [48, TM]	Lairon [TM]	Larvitar [5, TM]	Lickilicky [TM]	Lickitung [TM]
		Lunatone [TM]	Magcargo [TM]	Mamoswine [TM]	Marowak [TM]	Mawile [TM]	Mewtwo [TM]
		Miltank [TM]	Moltres [TM]	Munchlax [TM]	Nidoking [TM]	Nincada [TM]	Nincada [TM]
		Ninjask [TM]	Nosepass [36, TM]	Onix [52, TM]	Pawniard [TM]	Piloswine [TM]	Probopass [36, TM]
		Pupitar [1, 5, TM]	Quagsire [TM]	Relicanth [TM]	Rhydon [TM]	Rhyhorn [TM]	Rhyperior [TM]
		Roggenrola [33, TM]	Sandile [40, TM]	Sandshrew [42, TM]	Sandslash [42, TM]	Scizor [TM]	Shedinja [TM]
		Shuckle [TM]	Skarmory [TM]	Snorlax [TM]	Solrock [TM]	Steelix [52, TM]	Stunfisk [TM]
		Sudowoodo [TM]	Swinub [TM]	Tauros [TM]	Trapinch [44, TM]	Tyranitar [1, 5, TM]	Tyrantrum [TM]
		Tyrunt [TM]	Vibrava [44, TM]	Whiscash [TM]	Wooper [TM]	Wormadam (Sand) [TM]	Zapdos [TM]
		Zygarde [35, TM]					
Water	Scald (TM55)	Alomomola [TM]	Azumarill [TM]	Azurill [TM]	Barbaracle [TM]	Barboach [TM]	Basculin [TM]
		Bibarel [TM]	Binacle [TM]	Blastoise [TM]	Buizel [TM]	Carvanha [TM]	Chinchou [TM]
		Clamperl [TM]	Clauncher [TM]	Clawitzer [TM]	Corphish [TM]	Corsola [TM]	Crawdaunt [TM]
		Dragalge [TM]	Ducklett [TM]	Floatzel [TM]	Froakie [TM]	Frogadier [TM]	Goldeen [TM]
		Golduck [TM]	Gorebyss [TM]	Greninja [TM]	Gyarados [TM]	Horsea [TM]	Huntail [TM]
		Kingdra [TM]	Lanturn [TM]	Lombre [TM]	Lotad [TM]	Ludicolo [TM]	Luvdisc [TM]
		Mantine [TM]	Mantyke [TM]	Marill [TM]	Masquerain [TM]	Octillery [TM]	Panpour [22, TM]
		Pelipper [TM]	Politoed [TM]	Poliwag [TM]	Poliwhirl [TM]	Poliwrath [TM]	Psyduck [TM]
		Quagsire [TM]	Qwilfish [TM]	Relicanth [TM]	Remoraid [TM]	Seadra [TM]	Seaking [TM]
		Sharpedo [TM]	Simipour [1, TM]	Skrelp [TM]	Slowbro [TM]	Slowking [TM]	Slowpoke [TM]
		Squirtle [TM]	Starmie [TM]	Staryu [TM]	Stunfisk [TM]	Surskit [TM]	Swanna [TM]
		Tentacool [TM]	Tentacruel [TM]	Vaporeon [TM]	Wailmer [TM]	Wailord [TM]	Wartortle [TM]
		Whiscash [TM]	Wingull [TM]	Wooper [TM]			

Move	Pokémon that can learn it					
Scary Face	Aerodactyl [1]	Ariados [1, 5]	Axew [16]	Bagon [40]	Basculin [41]	Bisharp [22]
	Carvanha [11]	Charizard [21]	Charmander [19]	Charmeleon [21]	Conkeldurr [41]	Deino [50]
	Drapion [43]	Druddigon [13]	Ekans [E]	Flareon [29]	Fraxure [16]	Gastly [E]
	Gible [E]	Gourgeist [4]	Granbull [1]	Gurdurr [41]	Haxorus [16]	Huntail [19]
	Hydreigon [55]	Karrablast [40]	Krokorok [36]	Krookodile [41]	Larvitar [23]	Machamp [51]
	Machoke [51]	Machop [46]	Mamoswine [1, 58]	Masquerain [26]	Mightyena [37]	Pawniard [22]
	Poochyena [33]	Pumpkaboo [4]	Pupitar [23]	Rhydon [19]	Rhyhorn [19]	Rhyperior [19]
	Salamence [43]	Sandile [34]	Scrafty [34]	Scraggy [34]	Seviper [E]	Sharpedo [11]
	Shelgon [43]	Skorupi [41]	Snubbull [1]	Spearow [E]	Spinarak [5]	Stunky [E]
	Tauros [11]	Timburr [37]	Tyranitar [23]	Ursaring [38]	Zoroark [21]	Zorua [21]
	Zweilous [55]					
Scratch	Absol [1]	Axew [1]	Barbaracle [1]	Binacle [1]	Bisharp [1]	Braixen [1]
	Charizard [1]	Charmander [1]	Charmeleon [1]	Delphox [1]	Diglett [1]	Druddigon [1]
	Dugtrio [1]	Espurr [1]	Fraxure [1]	Furret [1]	Golduck [1]	Haxorus [1]
	Nidoran ♀ [1]	Kecleon [1]	Liepard [1]	Meowstic (Female) [1]	Meowstic (Male) [1]	Nidoqueen [1]
		Nidorina [1]	Nincada [1]	Ninjask [1]	Panpour [1]	Pansage [1]
	Pansear [1]	Pawniard [1]	Psyduck [1]	Purrloin [1]	Sableye [1]	Sandshrew [1]
	Sandslash [1]	Sentret [1]	Shedinja [1]	Skuntank [1]	Sneasel [1]	Stunky [1]
	Teddiursa [1]	Ursaring [1]	Weavile [1]	Zangoose [1]	Zoroark [1]	Zorua [1]
Screech	Arbok [17]	Aron [E]	Banette [1, 4]	Carvanha [18]	Chinchou [E]	Corsola [E]
	Crobat [1]	Cubone [E]	Deino [E]	Diglett [E]	Dunsparce [13]	Durant [E]
	Ekans [17]	Electrode [19]	Exploud [37]	Flygon [34]	Gligar [35]	Gliscor [35]
	Golbat [1]	Golduck [25]	Huntail [10]	Karrablast [E]	Kecleon [32]	Larvitar [10]
	Ledyba [E]	Lickilicky [49]	Lickitung [49]	Loudred [37]	Magnemite [39]	Magneton [45]
	Magnezone [45]	Mareep [E]	Munchlax [20]	Murkrow [E]	Ninjask [20]	Noibat [1]
	Noivern [24]	Onix [31]	Patrat [E]	Psyduck [25]	Pupitar [1, 10]	Remoraid [E]
	Riolu [24]	Scolipede [1, 8]	Seviper [16]	Sharpedo [18]	Shellder [E]	Shuppet [4]
	Skorupi [E]	Skuntank [7]	Sneasel [32]	Steelix [31]	Stunky [7]	Tentacool [40]
	Tentacruel [43]	Tyranitar [1, 10]	Umbreon [29]	Venipede [8]	Vibrava [34]	Voltorb [19]
	Weavile [32]	Whirlipede [1, 8]	Whismur [31]	Yanma [46]	Yanmega [46]	
Secret Power	Audino [20]	Dunsparce [E]	Meditite [E]	Oddish [E]	Psyduck [E]	Solosis [E]
	Yanma [E]					
Seed Bomb	Budew [E]	Bulbasaur [37]	Chesnaught [35]	Chespin [32]	Exeggutor [1]	Ferroseed [E]
	Gogoat [30]	Gourgeist [48]	Hoppip [E]	Pansage [22]	Pumpkaboo [48]	Quilladin [35]
	Roselia [E]	Simisage [1]	Skiddo [30]	Snover [E]		
Seismic Toss	Hariyama [37]	Heracross [E]	Machamp [22]	Machoke [22]	Machop [22]	Makuhita [31]
	Mawile [E]	Miltank [E]	Pinsir [8]	Teddiursa [E]	Throh [13]	Volbeat [E]
Self-Destruct	Bonsly [E]	Electrode [35]	Ferroseed [38]	Ferrothorn [38]	Geodude [29]	Golem [31]
	Graveler [31]	Munchlax [E]	Sudowoodo [E]	Trubbish [E]	Voltorb [33]	
Shadow Ball (TM30)	Abomasnow [TM]	Abra [TM]	Absol [TM]	Aegislash [TM]	Alakazam [TM]	Alomomola [TM]
	Audino [TM]	Banette [30, TM]	Bibarel [TM]	Bidoof [TM]	Budew [TM]	Butterfree [TM]
	Chandelure [TM]	Chimecho [TM]	Chingling [TM]	Clawitzer [TM]	Corsola [TM]	Croagunk [TM]
	Crobat [TM]	Delcatty [TM]	Delphox [1, TM]	Dragalge [TM]	Drapion [TM]	Drifblim [40, TM]
	Drifloon [36, TM]	Dunsparce [TM]	Duosion [TM]	Eevee [TM]	Espeon [TM]	Exploud [TM]
	Flareon [TM]	Furret [TM]	Gallade [TM]	Gardevoir [TM]	Gastly [29, TM]	Gengar [33, TM]
	Glaceon [TM]	Golbat [TM]	Golett [TM]	Golurk [TM]	Gorebyss [TM]	Gothita [TM]
	Gothitelle [TM]	Gothorita [TM]	Gourgeist [36, 70, TM]	Granbull [TM]	Grumpig [TM]	Gulpin [TM]
	Haunter [33, TM]	Honchkrow [TM]	Hoothoot [TM]	Houndoom [TM]	Houndour [TM]	Igglybuff [TM]
	Illumise [TM]	Jigglypuff [TM]	Jolteon [TM]	Jynx [TM]	Kadabra [TM]	Kangaskhan [TM]
	Kecleon [TM]	Kirlia [TM]	Lampent [53, TM]	Leafeon [TM]	Lickilicky [TM]	Lickitung [TM]
	Liepard [TM]	Linoone [TM]	Litwick [49, TM]	Loudred [TM]	Lucario [TM]	Lunatone [TM]
	Masquerain [TM]	Mawile [TM]	Medicham [TM]	Meditite [TM]	Meowstic (Female) [31, TM]	Meowstic (Male) [TM]
	Mewtwo [TM]	Mightyena [TM]	Miltank [TM]	Mime Jr. [TM]	Mothim [TM]	Mr. Mime [TM]
	Munchlax [TM]	Murkrow [TM]	Nidoking [TM]	Nidoqueen [TM]	Nincada [TM]	Ninjask [TM]
	Noctowl [TM]	Noibat [TM]	Noivern [TM]	Patrat [TM]	Phantump [TM]	Poochyena [TM]
	Pumpkaboo [36, TM]	Purrloin [TM]	Qwilfish [TM]	Ralts [TM]	Reuniclus [TM]	Roselia [TM]
	Roserade [TM]	Rotom (Fan) [TM]	Rotom (Frost) [TM]	Rotom (Heat) [TM]	Rotom (Mow) [TM]	Rotom (Wash) [TM]
	Rotom [TM]	Sableye [57, TM]	Sentret [TM]	Shedinja [59, TM]	Shuppet [30, TM]	Sigilyph [TM]
	Skitty [TM]	Skorupi [TM]	Skrelp [TM]	Skuntank [TM]	Slowbro [TM]	Slowking [TM]
	Slowpoke [TM]	Smoochum [TM]	Sneasel [TM]	Snorlax [TM]	Snover [TM]	Snubbull [TM]
	Solosis [TM]	Solrock [TM]	Spinda [TM]	Spoink [TM]	Stunky [TM]	Surskit [TM]
	Swalot [TM]	Swoobat [TM]	Sylveon [TM]	Toxicroak [TM]	Trevenant [TM]	Umbreon [TM]
	Vaporeon [TM]	Volbeat [TM]	Watchog [TM]	Weavile [TM]	Whismur [TM]	Wigglytuff [TM]
	Woobat [TM]	Wormadam (Plant) [TM]	Wormadam (Sand) [TM]	Wormadam (Trash) [TM]	Yanma [TM]	Yanmega [TM]
	Yveltal [TM]	Zangoose [TM]	Zigzagoon [TM]	Zoroark [TM]	Zorua [TM]	Zubat [TM]
	Absol [TM]	Aegislash [TM]	Aggron [TM]	Aron [TM]	Bagon [TM]	Banette [TM]
	Barbaracle [TM]	Beartic [TM]	Binacle [TM]	Bisharp [TM]	Charizard [1, TM]	Charmander [TM]
	Charmeleon [TM]	Chesnaught [TM]	Chespin [TM]	Crustle [TM]	Cubchoo [TM]	Diglett [TM]

AFTER THE HALL OF FAME

CENTRAL KALOS

COASTAL KALOS

MOUNTAIN KALOS

ADVENTURE DATA

Pokémon Moves Reverse Lookup

AFTER THE HALL OF FAME

CENTRAL KALOS

COASTAL KALOS

MOUNTAIN KALOS

ADVENTURE DATA

Type	Move	Pokémon that can learn it					
Ghost	Shadow Ball (TM30)	Doublade [TM]	Druddigon [TM]	Dugtrio [TM]	Durant [TM]	Dwebble [TM]	Ferrothorn [TM]
		Fraxure [TM]	Furret [TM]	Gabite [TM]	Garchomp [TM]	Gengar [TM]	Gible [TM]
		Golduck [TM]	Haunter [TM]	Haxorus [TM]	Heatmor [TM]	Heracross [TM]	Honedge [TM]
		Kangaskhan [TM]	Kecleon [49, TM]	Krokorok [TM]	Krookodile [TM]	Lairon [TM]	Liepard [TM]
		Linoone [TM]	Lucario [TM]	Nidoking [TM]	Nidoqueen [TM]	Nidoran♂ [TM]	Nidorina [TM]
		Nidorina [TM]	Nidorino [TM]	Noibat [TM]	Noivern [TM]	Pancham [TM]	Pangoro [TM]
		Panpour [TM]	Pansage [TM]	Pansear [TM]	Pawniard [TM]	Phantump [TM]	Psyduck [TM]
		Purrloin [TM]	Quilladin [TM]	Rhydon [TM]	Rhyperior [TM]	Riolu [TM]	Sableye [39, TM]
		Salamence [TM]	Sandshrew [TM]	Sandslash [TM]	Sentret [TM]	Shedinja [TM]	Shelgon [TM]
		Simipour [TM]	Simisage [TM]	Simisear [TM]	Skuntank [TM]	Sneasel [TM]	Stunky [TM]
		Teddiursa [TM]	Trevenant [55, TM]	Tyranitar [TM]	Ursaring [TM]	Weavile [TM]	Yveltal [TM]
		Zangoose [TM]	Zoroark [TM]				
	Shadow Punch	Gengar [25]	Golett [13]	Golurk [13]	Haunter [25]		
	Shadow Sneak	Aegislash [1]	Ariados [19]	Banette [16]	Doublade [20]	Gourgeist [30]	Greninja [23]
		Honedge [20, E]	Kecleon [22]	Pumpkaboo [30]	Ralts [E]	Sableye [25]	Shedinja [38]
		Shuppet [16, E]	Spinarak [19]				
Normal	Sharpen	Avalugg [20]	Bergmite [20]	Carbink [8]	Cryogonal [9]		
Ice	Sheer Cold	Abomasnow [58]	Articuno [1, 78]	Beartic [1, 66]	Cryogonal [1, 61]	Cubchoo [57]	Lapras [50]
		Snover [46]	Vanillish [58]	Vanillite [53]	Vanilluxe [1, 67]		
Normal	Shell Smash	Barbaracle [1]	Binacle [1]	Clamperl [50]	Cloyster [1]	Crustle [1, 43]	Dwebble [37]
		Magcargo [38]	Shellder [56]	Shuckle [34]	Torkoal [1, 65]		
Electric	Shock Wave	Chinchou [E]	Electrike [E]	Emolga [22, E]	Rotom (Fan) [22]	Rotom (Frost) [22]	Rotom (Heat) [22]
		Rotom (Mow) [22]	Rotom (Wash) [22]	Rotom [22]	Stunfisk [E]		
Bug	Signal Beam	Ampharos [51]	Chinchou [34]	Flaaffy [47]	Goldeen [E]	Horsea [E]	Lanturn [40]
		Mantine [1]	Mantyke [E]	Mareep [39]	Meowstic (Female) [45]	Octillery [34]	Qwilfish [E]
		Remoraid [30]	Spinarak [E]	Surskit [E]	Trapinch [E]	Volbeat [25]	Yanma [E]
	Silver Wind	Butterfree [28]	Illumise [E]	Ledian [29]	Ledyba [25, E]	Masquerain [40]	Mothim [38]
		Nincada [E]	Scyther [E]	Volbeat [E]	Yanma [E]		
	Simple Beam	Audino [45]	Farfetch'd [E]	Inkay [E]	Psyduck [E]	Skitty [E]	Spoink [E]
		Zigzagoon [E]					
Normal	Sing	Altaria [1, 8]	Azurill [E]	Chatot [13]	Delcatty [1]	Igglybuff [1]	Jigglypuff [1]
		Lapras [1]	Minun [E]	Plusle [E]	Skitty [11]	Smoochum [18]	Swablu [8]
		Wigglytuff [1]					
	Sketch	Smeargle [1]	Smeargle [11]	Smeargle [21]	Smeargle [31]	Smeargle [41]	Smeargle [51]
		Smeargle [61]	Smeargle [71]	Smeargle [81]	Smeargle [91]		
Psychic	Skill Swap	Abra [E]	Aromatisse [44]	Carbink [40]	Chimecho [E]	Chingling [E]	Duosion [43]
		Exeggcute [E]	Kecleon [E]	Ralts [E]	Reuniclus [45]	Sigilyph [E]	Solosis [40]
		Spoink [E]	Spritzee [44]	Sylveon [25]			
Normal	Skull Bash	Avalugg [1, 60]	Barbaracle [1, 65]	Bidoof [E]	Blastoise [39]	Bulbasaur [E]	Cubone [E]
		Goldeen [E]	Nidoran♀ [E]	Relicanth [E]	Rhyhorn [E]	Sharpedo [50]	Snover [E]
		Squirtle [31]	Torkoal [E]	Wartortle [36]			
Flying	Sky Attack	Altaria [1, 64]	Hawlucha [48]	Hoothoot [E]	Moltres [1, 78]	Murkrow [E]	Noctowl [1]
		Sigilyph [50]	Skarmory [E]	Spearow [E]	Taillow [E]	Yveltal [93]	
	Sky Drop (TM58)	Aerodactyl [49, TM]	Articuno [TM]	Charizard [TM]	Dragonite [TM]	Hawlucha [55, TM]	Moltres [TM]
		Pelipper [TM]	Skarmory [TM]	Yveltal [TM]	Zapdos [TM]		
Fighting	Sky Uppercut	Gligar [45]	Gliscor [45]	Pancham [48]	Pangoro [52]	Riolu [E]	
Normal	Slack Off	Hippopotas [E]	Slowbro [36]	Slowpoke [36]			
	Slam	Azurill [20, E]	Bellsprout [41]	Carnivine [E]	Deino [28]	Dragonair [21]	Dragonite [21]
		Dratini [21]	Ekans [E]	Furret [28]	Hydreigon [28]	Lickilicky [29]	Lickitung [29]
		Mantine [E]	Mantyke [E]	Mawile [28]	Onix [28]	Patrat [36]	Pikachu [26]
		Quagsire [15]	Sentret [25]	Steelix [28]	Sudowoodo [15]	Watchog [43]	Weepinbell [41]
		Wooper [15]	Zweilous [28]				
	Slash	Absol [28]	Aegislash [1]	Axew [20]	Barbaracle [13]	Beartic [33]	Binacle [13]
		Bisharp [30]	Buizel [E]	Charizard [41]	Charmander [34]	Charmeleon [39]	Crustle [31]
		Cryogonal [41]	Cubchoo [33]	Diglett [37]	Doublade [29]	Druddigon [21]	Dugtrio [45]
		Dwebble [31]	Escavalier [32]	Farfetch'd [19]	Fraxure [20]	Gabite [28]	Gallade [22]
		Garchomp [28]	Gible [25]	Gligar [27]	Haxorus [20]	Heatmor [41]	Honedge [29]
		Inkay [43]	Karrablast [32]	Kecleon [27]	Liepard [34]	Linoone [47]	Malamar [43]
		Ninjask [31]	Pancham [20]	Pangoro [20]	Pawniard [30]	Purrloin [30]	Sandshrew [26]
		Sandslash [26]	Scizor [29]	Scyther [29]	Sneasel [35]	Stunky [22]	Skarmory [45]
		Skorupi [E]	Skuntank [22]	Teddiursa [29]	Ursaring [29]		
		Vespiquen [21]	Yanmega [43]	Zangoose [15]			
Grass	Sleep Powder	Bellsprout [13]	Budew [E]	Bulbasaur [13]	Butterfree [12]	Carnivine [E]	Exeggcute [23]
		Gloom [17]	Hoppip [16]	Ivysaur [13]	Jumpluff [16]	Oddish [17]	Roselia [E]
		Skiploom [16]	Venusaur [13]	Victreebel [1]	Vivillon [1]	Weepinbell [13]	

Move	Pokémon that can learn it					
Normal — Sleep Talk (TM88)	Abomasnow [TM]	Abra [TM]	Absol [TM]	Accelgor [TM]	Aegislash [TM]	Aerodactyl [TM]
	Aggron [TM]	Alakazam [TM]	Alomomola [TM]	Altaria [TM]	Amaura [TM]	Amoonguss [TM]
	Ampharos [TM]	Arbok [TM]	Ariados [TM]	Aromatisse [TM]	Aron [TM]	Articuno [TM]
	Audino [TM, E]	Aurorus [TM]	Avalugg [TM]	Axew [TM]	Azumarill [TM]	Azurill [TM]
	Bagon [TM]	Banette [TM]	Barbaracle [TM]	Barboach [TM]	Basculin [TM]	Beartic [TM]
	Beedrill [TM]	Bellossom [TM]	Bellsprout [TM]	Bergmite [TM]	Bibarel [TM]	Bidoof [TM, E]
	Binacle [TM]	Bisharp [TM]	Blastoise [TM]	Boldore [TM]	Bonsly [TM]	Braixen [TM]
	Budew [TM]	Buizel [TM]	Bulbasaur [TM]	Bunnelby [TM]	Butterfree [TM]	Carbink [TM]
	Carnivine [TM]	Carvanha [TM]	Chandelure [TM]	Charizard [TM]	Charmander [TM]	Charmeleon [TM]
	Chatot [TM, E]	Chesnaught [TM]	Chespin [TM]	Chimecho [TM]	Chinchou [TM]	Chingling [TM]
	Clamperl [TM]	Clauncher [TM]	Clawitzer [TM]	Cloyster [TM]	Conkeldurr [TM]	Corphish [TM]
	Corsola [TM]	Crawdaunt [TM]	Croagunk [TM]	Crobat [TM]	Crustle [TM]	Cryogonal [TM]
	Cubchoo [TM, E]	Cubone [TM]	Dedenne [TM]	Deino [TM]	Delcatty [TM]	Delibird [TM]
	Delphox [TM]	Diggersby [TM]	Diglett [TM]	Dodrio [TM]	Doduo [TM]	Doublade [TM]
	Dragalge [TM]	Dragonair [TM]	Dragonite [TM]	Drapion [TM]	Dratini [TM]	Drifblim [TM]
	Drifloon [TM]	Druddigon [TM]	Ducklett [TM]	Dugtrio [TM]	Dunsparce [TM, E]	Duosion [TM]
	Durant [TM]	Dwebble [TM]	Eevee [TM]	Ekans [TM]	Electrike [TM]	Electrode [TM]
	Emolga [TM]	Escavalier [TM]	Espeon [TM]	Espurr [TM]	Exeggcute [TM]	Exeggutor [TM]
	Exploud [63, TM]	Farfetch'd [TM]	Fearow [TM]	Fennekin [TM]	Ferroseed [TM]	Ferrothorn [TM]
	Flaaffy [TM]	Flabébé [TM]	Flareon [TM]	Fletchinder [TM]	Fletchling [TM]	Floatzel [TM]
	Floette [TM]	Florges [TM]	Flygon [TM]	Foongus [TM]	Fraxure [TM]	Froakie [TM]
	Frogadier [TM]	Furfrou [TM]	Furret [TM]	Gabite [TM]	Gallade [TM]	Garbodor [TM]
	Garchomp [TM]	Gardevoir [TM]	Gastly [TM]	Gengar [TM]	Geodude [TM]	Gible [TM]
	Gigalith [TM]	Glaceon [TM]	Gligar [TM]	Gliscor [TM]	Gloom [TM]	Gogoat [TM]
	Golbat [TM]	Goldeen [TM, E]	Golduck [TM]	Golem [TM]	Golett [TM]	Golurk [TM]
	Goodra [TM]	Goomy [TM]	Gorebyss [TM]	Gothita [TM]	Gothitelle [TM]	Gothorita [TM]
	Gourgeist [TM]	Granbull [TM]	Graveler [TM]	Greninja [TM]	Grumpig [TM]	Gulpin [TM]
	Gurdurr [TM]	Gyarados [TM]	Hariyama [TM]	Haunter [TM]	Hawlucha [TM]	Haxorus [TM]
	Heatmor [TM, E]	Helioptile [TM]	Helioptile [TM]	Heracross [TM]	Hippopotas [TM, E]	Hippowdon [TM]
	Honchkrow [TM]	Honedge [TM]	Hoothoot [TM]	Hoppip [TM]	Horsea [TM]	Houndoom [TM]
	Houndour [TM]	Huntail [TM]	Hydreigon [TM]	Igglybuff [TM, E]	Illumise [TM]	Inkay [TM]
	Ivysaur [TM]	Jigglypuff [TM]	Jolteon [TM]	Jumpluff [TM]	Jynx [TM]	Kadabra [TM]
	Kangaskhan [TM]	Karrablast [TM]	Kecleon [TM]	Kingdra [TM]	Kirlia [TM]	Klefki [TM]
	Krokorok [TM]	Krookodile [TM]	Lairon [TM]	Lampent [TM]	Lanturn [TM]	Lapras [TM, E]
	Larvitar [TM]	Leafeon [TM]	Ledian [TM]	Ledyba [TM]	Lickilicky [TM]	Lickitung [TM, E]
	Liepard [TM]	Linoone [TM]	Litleo [TM]	Litwick [TM]	Lombre [TM]	Lotad [TM]
	Loudred [57, TM]	Lucario [TM]	Ludicolo [TM]	Lunatone [TM]	Luvdisc [TM]	Machamp [TM]
	Machoke [TM]	Machop [TM]	Magcargo [TM]	Magnemite [TM]	Magneton [TM]	Magnezone [TM]
	Makuhita [TM]	Malamar [TM]	Mamoswine [TM]	Manectric [TM]	Mantine [TM]	Mantyke [TM]
	Mareep [TM]	Marill [TM]	Marowak [TM]	Masquerain [TM]	Mawile [TM]	Medicham [TM]
	Meditite [TM]	Meowstic (Female) [TM]	Meowstic (Male) [TM]	Mewtwo [TM]	Mienfoo [TM]	Mienshao [TM]
	Mightyena [TM]	Miltank [TM, E]	Mime Jr. [TM]	Minun [TM]	Moltres [TM]	Mothim [TM]
	Mr. Mime [TM]	Munchlax [TM]	Murkrow [TM]	Nidoking [TM]	Nidoqueen [TM]	Nidoran♀ [TM]
	Nidoran♂ [TM]	Nidorina [TM]	Nidorino [TM]	Nincada [TM]	Ninjask [TM]	Noctowl [TM]
	Noibat [TM]	Noivern [TM]	Nosepass [TM]	Octillery [TM]	Oddish [TM]	Onix [TM]
	Pachirisu [TM]	Pancham [TM]	Pangoro [TM]	Panpour [TM]	Pansage [TM]	Pansear [TM, E]
	Patrat [TM]	Pawniard [TM]	Pelipper [TM]	Phantump [TM]	Pichu [TM]	Pidgeot [TM]
	Pidgeotto [TM]	Pidgey [TM]	Pikachu [TM]	Piloswine [TM]	Pinsir [TM]	Plusle [TM]
	Politoed [TM]	Poliwag [TM]	Poliwhirl [TM]	Poliwrath [TM]	Poochyena [TM, E]	Probopass [TM]
	Psyduck [TM, E]	Pumpkaboo [TM]	Pupitar [TM]	Purrloin [TM]	Pyroar [TM]	Quagsire [TM]
	Quilladin [TM]	Qwilfish [TM]	Raichu [TM]	Ralts [TM]	Relicanth [TM, E]	Remoraid [TM]
	Reuniclus [TM]	Rhydon [TM]	Rhyhorn [TM]	Rhyperior [TM]	Riolu [TM]	Roggenrola [TM]
	Roselia [TM]	Roserade [TM]	Rotom (Fan) [TM]	Rotom (Frost) [TM]	Rotom (Heat) [TM]	Rotom (Mow) [TM]
	Rotom (Wash) [TM]	Rotom [TM]	Sableye [TM]	Salamence [TM]	Sandile [TM]	Sandshrew [TM]
	Sandslash [TM]	Sawk [TM]	Scizor [TM]	Scolipede [TM]	Scrafty [TM]	Scraggy [TM]
	Scyther [TM]	Seadra [TM]	Seaking [TM]	Sentret [TM]	Seviper [TM]	Sharpedo [TM]
	Shedinja [TM]	Shelgon [TM]	Shellder [TM]	Shelmet [TM]	Shuckle [TM]	Shuppet [TM]
	Sigilyph [TM]	Simipour [TM]	Simisage [TM]	Simisear [TM]	Skarmory [TM]	Skiddo [TM]
	Skiploom [TM]	Skitty [TM]	Skorupi [TM]	Skrelp [TM]	Skuntank [TM]	Sliggoo [TM]
	Slowbro [TM]	Slowking [TM]	Slowpoke [TM, E]	Slugma [TM]	Slurpuff [TM]	Smoochum [TM]
	Sneasel [TM]	Snorlax [33, TM]	Snover [TM]	Snubbull [TM]	Solosis [TM]	Solrock [TM]
	Spearow [TM]	Spinarak [TM]	Spoink [TM]	Spritzee [TM]	Squirtle [TM]	Staraptor [TM]
	Staravia [TM]	Starly [TM]	Starmie [TM]	Staryu [TM]	Steelix [TM]	Stunfisk [TM, E]
	Stunky [TM]	Sudowoodo [TM]	Surskit [TM]	Swablu [TM]	Swalot [TM]	Swanna [TM]
	Swellow [TM]	Swinub [TM]	Swirlix [TM]	Swoobat [TM]	Sylveon [TM]	Taillow [TM]
	Talonflame [TM]	Tauros [TM]	Teddiursa [TM, E]	Tentacool [TM]	Tentacruel [TM]	Throh [TM]
	Timburr [TM]	Torkoal [TM, E]	Toxicroak [TM]	Trapinch [TM]	Trevenant [TM]	Trubbish [TM]
	Tyranitar [TM]	Tyrantrum [TM]	Tyrunt [TM]	Umbreon [TM]	Ursaring [TM]	Vanillish [TM]
	Vanillite [TM]	Vanilluxe [TM]	Vaporeon [TM]	Venipede [TM]	Venusaur [TM]	Vespiquen [TM]
	Vibrava [TM]	Victreebel [TM]	Vileplume [TM]	Vivillon [TM]	Volbeat [TM]	Voltorb [TM]
	Wailmer [TM, E]	Wailord [TM]	Wartortle [TM]	Watchog [TM]	Weavile [TM]	Weepinbell [TM]
	Whirlipede [TM]	Whiscash [TM]	Whismur [45, TM]	Wigglytuff [TM]	Wingull [TM]	Woobat [TM]

AFTER THE HALL OF FAME

CENTRAL KALOS

COASTAL KALOS

MOUNTAIN KALOS

ADVENTURE DATA

Move	Pokémon that can learn it					
Sleep Talk (TM88)	Wooper [TM, E]	Wormadam (Plant) [TM]	Wormadam (Sand) [TM]	Wormadam (Trash) [TM]	Xerneas [TM]	Yanma [TM]
	Yanmega [TM]	Yveltal [TM]	Zangoose [TM]	Zapdos [TM]	Zigzagoon [TM, E]	Zoroark [TM]
	Zorua [TM]	Zubat [TM]	Zweilous [TM]	Zygarde [TM]		
Sludge	Bulbasaur [E]	Garbodor [18]	Gulpin [14]	Swalot [1, 14]	Trubbish [18]	
Sludge Bomb (TM36)	Accelgor [TM]	Amoonguss [TM]	Arbok [TM]	Ariados [TM]	Barbaracle [TM]	Beedrill [TM]
	Bellossom [TM]	Bellsprout [TM]	Binacle [TM]	Budew [TM]	Bulbasaur [TM]	Bunnelby [TM]
	Carnivine [TM]	Chesnaught [TM]	Chespin [TM]	Clauncher [TM]	Clawitzer [TM]	Corphish [TM]
	Crawdaunt [TM]	Croagunk [45, TM]	Crobat [TM]	Diggersby [TM]	Diglett [TM]	Dragalge [38, TM]
	Drapion [TM]	Druddigon [TM]	Dugtrio [TM]	Ekans [TM]	Exeggcute [TM]	Exeggutor [TM]
	Foongus [TM]	Garbodor [29, TM]	Gastly [TM]	Gengar [TM]	Gligar [TM]	Gliscor [TM]
	Gloom [TM]	Golbat [TM]	Goodra [TM]	Goomy [TM]	Gourgeist [TM]	Granbull [TM]
	Gulpin [44, TM]	Haunter [TM]	Houndoom [TM]	Houndour [TM]	Ivysaur [TM]	Krokorok [TM]
	Krookodile [TM]	Mawile [TM]	Nidoking [TM]	Nidoqueen [TM]	Nidoran ♀ [TM]	Nidoran ♂ [TM]
	Nidorina [TM]	Nidorino [TM]	Octillery [TM]	Oddish [TM]	Pancham [TM]	Pangoro [TM]
	Pumpkaboo [TM]	Quagsire [TM]	Quilladin [TM]	Qwilfish [TM]	Roselia [TM]	Roserade [TM]
	Sandile [TM]	Scolipede [TM]	Scrafty [TM]	Scraggy [TM]	Seviper [TM]	Shelmet [TM]
	Shuckle [TM]	Skorupi [TM]	Skrelp [38, TM]	Skuntank [TM]	Sliggoo [TM]	Snubbull [TM]
	Spinarak [TM]	Stunfisk [TM]	Stunky [TM]	Swalot [52, TM]	Tentacool [TM]	Tentacruel [TM]
	Torkoal [TM]	Toxicroak [54, TM]	Trubbish [29, TM]	Venipede [TM]	Venusaur [TM]	Vespiquen [TM]
	Victreebel [TM]	Vileplume [TM]	Weepinbell [TM]	Whirlipede [TM]	Wooper [TM]	Zubat [TM]
Sludge Wave (TM34)	Arbok [TM]	Barbaracle [TM]	Binacle [TM]	Clauncher [TM]	Clawitzer [TM]	Crawdaunt [TM]
	Croagunk [TM]	Dragalge [TM]	Dugtrio [TM]	Ekans [TM]	Garbodor [TM]	Goodra [TM]
	Goomy [TM]	Gulpin [TM]	Nidoking [TM]	Nidoqueen [TM]	Octillery [TM]	Quagsire [TM]
	Qwilfish [TM]	Seviper [TM]	Shuckle [TM]	Skrelp [TM]	Sliggoo [TM]	Stunfisk [TM]
	Swalot [TM]	Tentacool [50, TM]	Tentacruel [56, TM]	Toxicroak [TM]	Trubbish [TM]	Wooper [TM]
	Zygarde [TM]					
Smack Down (TM23)	Aerodactyl [TM]	Aggron [TM]	Barbaracle [TM]	Binacle [TM]	Blastoise [TM]	Boldore [23, TM]
	Bonsly [TM]	Bunnelby [TM]	Carbink [12, TM]	Chesnaught [TM]	Chespin [TM]	Clauncher [39, TM]
	Clawitzer [42, TM]	Conkeldurr [TM]	Crustle [17, TM]	Cubone [TM]	Diggersby [TM]	Druddigon [TM]
	Dwebble [17, TM]	Exploud [TM]	Froakie [TM]	Frogadier [33, TM]	Garbodor [TM]	Geodude [25, TM]
	Gigalith [23, TM]	Golem [27, TM]	Graveler [27, TM]	Greninja [TM]	Gurdurr [TM]	Hariyama [TM]
	Heracross [TM]	Krookodile [TM]	Larvitar [TM]	Loudred [TM]	Lunatone [TM]	Machamp [TM]
	Machoke [TM]	Machop [TM]	Magcargo [TM]	Makuhita [TM]	Marowak [TM]	Nidoking [TM]
	Nidoqueen [TM]	Nosepass [TM]	Octillery [TM]	Onix [22, TM]	Pinsir [TM]	Probopass [TM]
	Pupitar [TM]	Quilladin [TM]	Relicanth [TM]	Remoraid [TM]	Rhydon [TM]	Rhyperior [TM]
	Roggenrola [23, TM]	Scrafty [TM]	Scraggy [TM]	Shuckle [TM]	Sigilyph [TM]	Snorlax [TM]
	Solrock [TM]	Steelix [22, TM]	Sudowoodo [TM]	Timburr [TM]	Tyranitar [TM]	Ursaring [TM]
Smelling Salts	Aron [E]	Croagunk [E]	Hariyama [22]	Lickitung [E]	Machop [E]	Makuhita [22]
	Mienfoo [E]	Snubbull [E]	Spinda [E]	Timburr [E]	Whismur [E]	
Smog	Chandelure [1]	Flareon [33]	Gastly [E]	Gulpin [E]	Houndoom [1, 8]	Houndour [8]
	Lampent [1, 5]	Litwick [5]	Magcargo [1]	Slugma [1]	Stunky [E]	Torkoal [4]
Smokescreen	Charizard [1, 10]	Charmander [10]	Charmeleon [10]	Dragalge [1]	Froakie [18]	Frogadier [20]
	Greninja [36]	Horsea [1]	Kingdra [1, 4]	Seadra [1, 4]	Skrelp [1]	Skuntank [14]
	Slugma [E]	Stunky [14]	Torkoal [20]	Whismur [E]		
Snarl (TM95)	Absol [TM]	Bisharp [TM]	Carvanha [TM]	Crawdaunt [TM]	Drapion [TM]	Druddigon [TM]
	Electrike [TM]	Furfrou [TM]	Granbull [TM]	Honchkrow [TM]	Houndoom [TM]	Houndour [TM]
	Krokorok [TM]	Krookodile [TM]	Larvitar [TM]	Liepard [TM]	Litleo [TM]	Manectric [TM]
	Mightyena [TM]	Murkrow [TM]	Pangoro [TM]	Pawniard [TM]	Poochyena [TM]	Pupitar [TM]
	Purrloin [TM]	Pyroar [TM]	Sableye [TM]	Sandile [TM]	Scrafty [TM]	Scraggy [TM]
	Sharpedo [TM]	Skuntank [TM]	Sneasel [TM]	Snubbull [TM]	Stunky [TM]	Tyranitar [TM]
	Umbreon [TM]	Weavile [TM]	Yveltal [18, TM]	Zoroark [TM]	Zorua [TM]	
Snatch	Banette [46]	Druddigon [E]	Duosion [1, 10]	Ekans [E]	Fletchling [E]	Heatmor [26]
	Kecleon [E]	Liepard [47]	Litleo [E]	Munchlax [1, 52]	Noibat [E]	Poochyena [E]
	Purrloin [39]	Reuniclus [1, 10]	Shuppet [42]	Sneasel [40]	Solosis [10]	Weavile [40]
	Zorua [E]					
Snore	Barboach [31]	Dedenne [31]	Dunsparce [E]	Grumpig [29]	Lickitung [E]	Relicanth [E]
	Remoraid [E]	Slowpoke [E]	Snorlax [28]	Snubbull [E]	Spoink [29]	Teddiursa [43]
	Ursaring [49]	Wailmer [E]	Whiscash [33]	Whismur [E]		
Soak	Alomomola [33]	Azurill [E]	Basculin [32]	Buizel [E]	Chinchou [E]	Goldeen [50]
	Golduck [38]	Octillery [64]	Pelipper [1]	Psyduck [36]	Remoraid [50]	Seaking [63]
	Wailmer [E]	Wingull [E]				

Move	Pokémon that can learn it					
Solar Beam (TM22) *(Grass)*	Abomasnow [TM]	Aggron [TM]	Altaria [TM]	Amoonguss [49, TM]	Ariados [TM]	Audino [TM]
	Beedrill [TM]	Bellossom [TM]	Bellsprout [TM]	Braixen [TM]	Budew [TM]	Bulbasaur [TM]
	Butterfree [TM]	Carnivine [TM]	Chandelure [TM]	Charizard [TM]	Chesnaught [TM]	Chespin [TM]
	Crustle [TM]	Cryogonal [53, TM]	Delcatty [TM]	Delphox [TM]	Dunsparce [TM]	Dwebble [TM]
	Exeggcute [43, TM]	Exeggutor [TM]	Exploud [TM]	Fennekin [TM]	Ferroseed [TM]	Ferrothorn [TM]
	Flabébé [48, TM]	Floette [58, TM]	Florges [TM]	Flygon [TM]	Foongus [43, TM]	Furret [TM]
	Garbodor [TM]	Gigalith [TM]	Gloom [TM]	Gogoat [TM]	Golurk [TM]	Gourgeist [TM]
	Granbull [TM]	Gulpin [TM]	Heatmor [TM]	Hoppip [TM]	Houndoom [TM]	Houndour [TM]
	Igglybuff [TM]	Illumise [TM]	Ivysaur [44, TM]	Jigglypuff [TM]	Jumpluff [TM]	Kangaskhan [TM]
	Kecleon [TM]	Lampent [TM]	Leafeon [TM]	Ledian [TM]	Ledyba [TM]	Lickilicky [TM]
	Lickitung [TM]	Litleo [TM]	Litwick [TM]	Lombre [TM]	Lotad [TM]	Loudred [TM]
	Ludicolo [TM]	Magcargo [TM]	Masquerain [TM]	Mawile [TM]	Mewtwo [TM]	Miltank [TM]
	Mime Jr. [TM]	Moltres [71, TM]	Mothim [TM]	Mr. Mime [TM]	Munchlax [TM]	Nincada [TM]
	Ninjask [TM]	Noibat [TM]	Noivern [TM]	Oddish [TM]	Pansage [TM]	Pansear [TM]
	Phantump [TM]	Pumpkaboo [TM]	Pyroar [TM]	Quilladin [TM]	Roselia [TM]	Roserade [TM]
	Scolipede [TM]	Sentret [TM]	Shedinja [TM]	Sigilyph [TM]	Simisage [TM]	Simisear [TM]
	Skiddo [TM]	Skiploom [TM]	Skitty [TM]	Snorlax [TM]	Snover [TM]	Snubbull [TM]
	Solrock [45, TM]	Spinarak [TM]	Surskit [TM]	Swablu [TM]	Swalot [TM]	Talonflame [TM]
	Tauros [TM]	Torkoal [TM]	Trapinch [TM]	Trevenant [TM]	Venipede [TM]	Venusaur [53, TM]
	Vibrava [TM]	Victreebel [TM]	Vileplume [65, TM]	Vivillon [TM]	Volbeat [TM]	Weepinbell [TM]
	Whirlipede [TM]	Whismur [TM]	Wigglytuff [TM]	Wormadam (Plant) [TM]	Yanma [TM]	Yanmega [TM]
	Zangoose [TM]					
Sonic Boom *(Normal)*	Buizel [1]	Electrode [1]	Floatzel [1]	Flygon [1]	Magnemite [11]	Magneton [1]
	Magnezone [1]	Spinarak [4]	Vibrava [1]	Voltorb [8]	Yanma [14]	Yanmega [14]
Spark *(Electric)*	Barboach [E]	Chinchou [20]	Electrike [20]	Electrode [1, 12]	Emolga [13]	Lanturn [20]
	Magnemite [21]	Magneton [21]	Magnezone [21]	Manectric [20]	Minun [15]	Nosepass [25]
	Pachirisu [13]	Plusle [15]	Probopass [25]	Stunfisk [E]	Voltorb [12]	
Spider Web *(Bug)*	Ariados [32]	Spinarak [29]				
Spike Cannon *(Normal)*	Cloyster [13]	Corsola [27]				
Spikes *(Ground)*	Budew [E]	Bunnelby [E]	Chespin [E]	Cloyster [28]	Delibird [E]	Dwebble [E]
	Ferroseed [E]	Greninja [28]	Klefki [15]	Qwilfish [1]	Roselia [E]	Shelmet [E]
	Skarmory [28]	Trubbish [E]	Venipede [E]			
Spiky Shield *(Grass)*	Chesnaught [36, 75]					
Spit Up *(Normal)*	Arbok [27]	Carnivine [37]	Drifblim [34]	Drifloon [32]	Ekans [25]	Gulpin [39]
	Heatmor [50]	Hippopotas [E]	Lanturn [27]	Mawile [50]	Pelipper [39]	Qwilfish [25]
	Seviper [E]	Slugma [E]	Swalot [45]	Victreebel [1]	Wooper [E]	
Spite *(Ghost)*	Banette [10]	Dunsparce [7]	Ekans [25]	Gastly [5]	Gengar [1, 5]	Haunter [1, 5]
	Houndour [E]	Shedinja [25]	Shuppet [10]	Sneasel [E]	Stunfisk [E]	
Splash *(Normal)*	Azurill [1]	Clauncher [1]	Clawitzer [1]	Delibird [E]	Grumpig [1]	Hoppip [1]
	Horsea [E]	Jumpluff [1]	Luvdisc [E]	Magikarp [1]	Mantine [E]	Mantyke [E]
	Poliwag [1]	Skiploom [1]	Spoink [1]	Wailmer [1]	Wailord [1]	Wynaut [1]
Spore *(Grass)*	Amoonguss [62]	Foongus [50]				
Stealth Rock *(Rock)*	Aron [E]	Boldore [36]	Bonsly [E]	Carbink [21]	Crustle [24]	Dwebble [24]
	Ferroseed [E]	Geodude [36]	Gigalith [36]	Golem [42]	Graveler [42]	Larvitar [E]
	Nosepass [E]	Onix [16, E]	Pawniard [E]	Roggenrola [30]	Skarmory [E]	Steelix [16]
	Sudowoodo [E]	Swinub [E]	Tyrantrum [15]	Tyrunt [15]		
Steamroller *(Bug)*	Golem [11]	Scolipede [39]	Venipede [33]	Whirlipede [37]		
Steel Wing (TM51) *(Steel)*	Aerodactyl [TM, E]	Altaria [TM]	Articuno [TM]	Charizard [TM]	Chatot [TM, E]	Crobat [TM]
	Dodrio [TM]	Doduo [TM]	Dragonite [TM]	Ducklett [TM, E]	Farfetch'd [TM, E]	Fearow [TM]
	Fletchinder [55, TM]	Fletchling [48, TM]	Flygon [TM]	Gligar [TM]	Gliscor [TM]	Golbat [TM]
	Hawlucha [TM]	Honchkrow [TM]	Hoothoot [TM]	Hydreigon [TM]	Moltres [TM]	Murkrow [TM]
	Noctowl [TM]	Noibat [TM]	Noivern [TM]	Pelipper [TM]	Pidgeot [TM]	Pidgeotto [TM]
	Pidgey [TM, E]	Salamence [TM]	Scizor [TM]	Scyther [TM, E]	Sigilyph [TM, E]	Skarmory [34, TM]
	Spearow [TM, E]	Staraptor [TM]	Staravia [TM]	Starly [TM, E]	Swablu [TM, E]	Swanna [TM]
	Swellow [TM]	Swoobat [TM]	Taillow [TM, E]	Talonflame [60, TM]	Vibrava [TM]	Wingull [TM]
	Woobat [TM]	Yanma [TM]	Yanmega [TM]	Yveltal [TM]	Zapdos [TM]	Zubat [TM, E]
Sticky Web *(Bug)*	Ariados [58]	Shuckle [1, 53]	Spinarak [50]	Surskit [46]		
Stockpile *(Normal)*	Arbok [27]	Carnivine [37]	Drifblim [25]	Drifloon [25]	Ekans [25]	Garbodor [23]
	Gulpin [39]	Heatmor [50]	Hippopotas [E]	Lanturn [27]	Mawile [50]	Munchlax [28]
	Pelipper [39]	Qwilfish [25]	Seviper [E]	Slugma [E]	Swalot [45]	Trubbish [23]
	Victreebel [1]	Wooper [E]				

	Move	Pokémon that can learn it					
Normal	Stomp	Aron [E]	Exeggutor [1]	Exploud [29]	Kangaskhan [E]	Larvitar [E]	Lickilicky [21]
		Lickitung [21]	Loudred [29]	Miltank [8]	Rhydon [1, 9]	Rhyhorn [8]	Rhyperior [1, 9]
		Slowpoke [E]	Snover [E]	Tyrantrum [10]	Tyrunt [10]	Whismur [25]	
Rock	Stone Edge (TM71)	Absol [TM]	Aerodactyl [TM]	Aggron [TM]	Amaura [TM]	Aurorus [TM]	Avalugg [TM]
		Barbaracle [1, 60, TM]	Beartic [TM]	Bergmite [TM]	Binacle [TM]	Bisharp [TM]	Boldore [48, TM]
		Bunnelby [TM]	Carbink [49, TM]	Chesnaught [TM]	Chespin [TM]	Conkeldurr [49, TM]	Corsola [TM]
		Crustle [TM]	Diggersby [TM]	Dragonite [TM]	Dugtrio [TM]	Durant [TM]	Dwebble [TM]
		Flygon [TM]	Gabite [TM]	Gallade [TM]	Garchomp [TM]	Geodude [50, TM]	Gible [TM]
		Gigalith [48, TM]	Gligar [TM]	Gliscor [TM]	Golem [64, TM]	Golurk [TM]	Granbull [TM]
		Graveler [64, TM]	Gurdurr [49, TM]	Gyarados [TM]	Hariyama [TM]	Hawlucha [TM]	Heracross [TM]
		Hippowdon [TM]	Hydreigon [TM]	Krokorok [TM]	Krookodile [TM]	Lairon [TM]	Larvitar [50, TM]
		Lucario [TM]	Lunatone [41, TM]	Machamp [TM]	Magcargo [TM]	Mamoswine [TM]	Marowak [TM]
		Mawile [TM]	Mewtwo [TM]	Mienfoo [TM]	Mienshao [TM]	Nidoking [TM]	Nidoqueen [TM]
		Nosepass [46, TM]	Onix [46, TM]	Pancham [TM]	Pangoro [TM]	Piloswine [TM]	Pinsir [TM]
		Proboposs [46, TM]	Pupitar [60, TM]	Quagsire [TM]	Quilladin [TM]	Relicanth [TM]	Rhydon [56, TM]
		Rhyhorn [52, TM]	Rhyperior [56, TM]	Roggenrola [36, TM]	Salamence [TM]	Sandile [TM]	Sandslash [TM]
		Sawk [TM]	Scrafty [TM]	Scraggy [TM]	Shuckle [49, TM]	Solrock [41, TM]	Steelix [46, TM]
		Stunfisk [TM]	Sudowoodo [43, TM]	Tauros [TM]	Throh [TM]	Timburr [43, TM]	Torkoal [TM]
		Toxicroak [TM]	Tyranitar [63, TM]	Tyrantrum [TM]	Tyrunt [TM]	Ursaring [TM]	Whiscash [TM]
		Zygarde [TM]					
Psychic	Stored Power	Chimecho [E]	Chingling [E]	Eevee [E]	Gallade [1, 64]	Gardevoir [1, 80]	Kirlia [64]
		Meowstic (Female) [1, 53]	Ralts [54]	Sigilyph [E]	Woobat [E]		
Fighting	Storm Throw	Pancham [E]	Pinsir [33]	Throh [25]			
Normal	Strength (HM04)	Abomasnow [HM]	Absol [HM]	Aerodactyl [HM]	Aggron [HM]	Ampharos [HM]	Arbok [HM]
		Aron [HM]	Avalugg [HM]	Axew [HM]	Azumarill [HM]	Bagon [HM]	Barbaracle [HM]
		Beartic [HM]	Bergmite [HM]	Bibarel [HM]	Binacle [HM]	Blastoise [HM]	Boldore [HM]
		Buizel [HM]	Bulbasaur [HM]	Bunnelby [HM]	Charizard [HM]	Charmander [HM]	Charmeleon [HM]
		Chesnaught [HM]	Chespin [HM]	Conkeldurr [HM]	Corphish [HM]	Corsola [HM]	Crawdaunt [HM]
		Croagunk [HM]	Crustle [HM]	Cubchoo [HM]	Cubone [HM]	Deino [HM]	Delcatty [HM]
		Diggersby [HM]	Dragonite [HM]	Drapion [HM]	Druddigon [HM]	Dunsparce [HM]	Durant [HM]
		Dwebble [HM]	Ekans [HM]	Electrike [HM]	Exeggcute [HM]	Exeggutor [HM]	Exploud [HM]
		Ferrothorn [HM]	Flaaffy [HM]	Flareon [HM]	Floatzel [HM]	Flygon [HM]	Fraxure [HM]
		Froakie [HM]	Frogadier [HM]	Furret [HM]	Gabite [HM]	Gallade [HM]	Garchomp [HM]
		Gengar [HM]	Geodude [HM]	Gible [HM]	Gigalith [HM]	Glaceon [HM]	Gligar [HM]
		Gliscor [HM]	Gogoat [HM]	Golduck [HM]	Golem [HM]	Golett [HM]	Golurk [HM]
		Goodra [HM]	Granbull [HM]	Graveler [HM]	Greninja [HM]	Gulpin [HM]	Gurdurr [HM]
		Gyarados [HM]	Hariyama [HM]	Hawlucha [HM]	Haxorus [HM]	Heracross [HM]	Hippopotas [HM]
		Hippowdon [HM]	Houndoom [HM]	Hydreigon [HM]	Ivysaur [HM]	Jigglypuff [HM]	Jolteon [HM]
		Kangaskhan [HM]	Kecleon [HM]	Krokorok [HM]	Krookodile [HM]	Lairon [HM]	Lapras [HM]
		Leafeon [HM]	Ledian [HM]	Lickilicky [HM]	Lickitung [HM]	Linoone [HM]	Litleo [HM]
		Lombre [HM]	Loudred [HM]	Lucario [HM]	Ludicolo [HM]	Machamp [HM]	Machoke [HM]
		Machop [HM]	Magcargo [HM]	Makuhita [HM]	Mamoswine [HM]	Manectric [HM]	Marill [HM]
		Marowak [HM]	Mawile [HM]	Medicham [HM]	Meditite [HM]	Mewtwo [HM]	Mienfoo [HM]
		Mienshao [HM]	Mightyena [HM]	Miltank [HM]	Munchlax [HM]	Nidoking [HM]	Nidoqueen [HM]
		Nidoran ♀ [HM]	Nidoran ♂ [HM]	Nidorina [HM]	Nidorino [HM]	Nosepass [HM]	Onix [HM]
		Pancham [HM]	Pangoro [HM]	Phantump [HM]	Pikachu [HM]	Piloswine [HM]	Pinsir [HM]
		Politoed [HM]	Poliwhirl [HM]	Poliwrath [HM]	Proboposs [HM]	Psyduck [HM]	Pyroar [HM]
		Quagsire [HM]	Quilladin [HM]	Raichu [HM]	Reuniclus [HM]	Rhydon [HM]	Rhyhorn [HM]
		Rhyperior [HM]	Riolu [HM]	Roggenrola [HM]	Salamence [HM]	Sandshrew [HM]	Sandslash [HM]
		Sawk [HM]	Scizor [HM]	Scolipede [HM]	Scrafty [HM]	Scraggy [HM]	Seviper [HM]
		Sharpedo [HM]	Shelgon [HM]	Shuckle [HM]	Skiddo [HM]	Skorupi [HM]	Skuntank [HM]
		Slowbro [HM]	Slowking [HM]	Slowpoke [HM]	Sneasel [HM]	Snorlax [HM]	Snubbull [HM]
		Spinda [HM]	Squirtle [HM]	Steelix [HM]	Sudowoodo [HM]	Swalot [HM]	Swinub [HM]
		Tauros [HM]	Teddiursa [HM]	Throh [HM]	Timburr [HM]	Torkoal [HM]	Toxicroak [HM]
		Trapinch [HM]	Trevenant [HM]	Tyranitar [HM]	Tyrantrum [HM]	Tyrunt [HM]	Ursaring [HM]
		Vaporeon [HM]	Venusaur [HM]	Vibrava [HM]	Wailmer [HM]	Wailord [HM]	Wartortle [HM]
		Watchog [HM]	Weavile [HM]	Whiscash [HM]	Wigglytuff [HM]	Zangoose [HM]	Zweilous [HM]
		Zygarde [HM]					
	String Shot	Ariados [1]	Caterpie [1]	Scatterbug [1]	Spinarak [1]	Weedle [1]	
Bug	Struggle Bug (TM76)	Accelgor [16, TM]	Ariados [TM]	Beedrill [TM]	Butterfree [TM]	Crustle [TM]	Drapion [TM]
		Durant [TM]	Dwebble [TM]	Escavalier [TM]	Flygon [TM]	Gligar [TM]	Gliscor [TM]
		Heracross [TM]	Illumise [TM]	Karrablast [TM]	Ledian [TM]	Ledyba [TM]	Masquerain [TM]
		Mothim [TM]	Nincada [TM]	Ninjask [TM]	Pinsir [TM]	Scizor [TM]	Scolipede [TM]
		Scyther [TM]	Shedinja [TM]	Shelmet [16, TM]	Shuckle [12, TM]	Skorupi [TM]	Spinarak [TM]
		Surskit [TM]	Trapinch [TM]	Venipede [TM]	Vespiquen [TM]	Vibrava [TM]	Vivillon [12, TM]
		Volbeat [TM]	Whirlipede [TM]	Wormadam (Plant) [TM]	Wormadam (Sand) [TM]	Wormadam (Trash) [TM]	Yanmega [TM]

	Move	Pokémon that can learn it					
Grass	Stun Spore	Bellossom [1]	Bellsprout [17]	Budew [10]	Butterfree [12]	Carnivine [E]	Exeggcute [19]
		Foongus [E]	Gloom [15]	Hoppip [14]	Jumpluff [14]	Masquerain [33]	Oddish [15]
		Roselia [10]	Scatterbug [6, E]	Skiploom [14]	Vileplume [1]	Vivillon [1]	Weepinbell [17]
Fighting	Submission	Machamp [36]	Machoke [36]	Machop [34]	Pinsir [26]	Poliwrath [1]	
Normal	Substitute (TM90)	Abomasnow [TM]	Abra [TM]	Absol [TM]	Accelgor [TM]	Aegislash [TM]	Aerodactyl [TM]
		Aggron [TM]	Alakazam [TM]	Alomomola [TM]	Altaria [TM]	Amaura [TM]	Amoonguss [TM]
		Ampharos [TM]	Arbok [TM]	Ariados [TM]	Aromatisse [TM]	Aron [TM]	Articuno [TM]
		Audino [TM]	Aurorus [TM]	Avalugg [TM]	Axew [TM]	Azumarill [TM]	Azurill [TM]
		Bagon [TM]	Banette [TM]	Barbaracle [TM]	Barboach [TM]	Basculin [TM]	Beartic [TM]
		Beedrill [TM]	Bellossom [TM]	Bellsprout [TM]	Bergmite [TM]	Bibarel [TM]	Bidoof [TM]
		Binacle [TM]	Bisharp [TM]	Blastoise [TM]	Boldore [TM]	Bonsly [TM]	Braixen [TM]
		Budew [TM]	Buizel [TM]	Bulbasaur [TM]	Bunnelby [TM]	Butterfree [TM]	Carbink [TM]
		Carnivine [TM]	Carvanha [TM]	Chandelure [TM]	Charizard [TM]	Charmander [TM]	Charmeleon [TM]
		Chatot [TM]	Chesnaught [TM]	Chespin [TM]	Chimecho [TM]	Chinchou [TM]	Chingling [TM]
		Clamperl [TM]	Clauncher [TM]	Clawitzer [TM]	Cloyster [TM]	Conkeldurr [TM]	Corphish [TM]
		Corsola [TM]	Crawdaunt [TM]	Croagunk [TM]	Crobat [TM]	Crustle [TM]	Cryogonal [TM]
		Cubchoo [TM]	Cubone [TM]	Dedenne [TM]	Deino [TM]	Delcatty [TM]	Delibird [TM]
		Delphox [TM]	Diggersby [TM]	Diglett [TM]	Dodrio [TM]	Doduo [TM]	Doublade [TM]
		Dragalge [TM]	Dragonair [TM]	Dragonite [TM]	Drapion [TM]	Dratini [TM]	Drifblim [TM]
		Drifloon [TM]	Druddigon [TM]	Ducklett [TM]	Dugtrio [TM]	Dunsparce [TM]	Duosion [TM]
		Durant [TM]	Dwebble [TM]	Eevee [TM]	Ekans [TM]	Electrike [TM]	Electrode [TM]
		Emolga [TM]	Escavalier [TM]	Espeon [TM]	Espurr [TM]	Exeggcute [TM]	Exeggutor [TM]
		Exploud [TM]	Farfetch'd [TM]	Fearow [TM]	Fennekin [TM]	Ferroseed [TM]	Ferrothorn [TM]
		Flaaffy [TM]	Flabébé [TM]	Flareon [TM]	Fletchinder [TM]	Fletchling [TM]	Floatzel [TM]
		Floette [TM]	Florges [TM]	Flygon [TM]	Foongus [TM]	Fraxure [TM]	Froakie [35, TM]
		Frogadier [38, TM]	Furfrou [TM]	Furret [TM]	Gabite [TM]	Gallade [TM]	Garbodor [TM]
		Garchomp [TM]	Gardevoir [TM]	Gastly [TM]	Gengar [TM]	Geodude [TM]	Gible [TM]
		Gigalith [TM]	Glaceon [TM]	Gligar [TM]	Gliscor [TM]	Gloom [TM]	Gogoat [TM]
		Golbat [TM]	Goldeen [TM]	Golduck [TM]	Golem [TM]	Golett [TM]	Golurk [TM]
		Goodra [TM]	Goomy [TM]	Gorebyss [TM]	Gothita [TM]	Gothitelle [TM]	Gothorita [TM]
		Gourgeist [TM]	Granbull [TM]	Graveler [TM]	Greninja [43, TM]	Grumpig [TM]	Gulpin [TM]
		Gurdurr [TM]	Gyarados [TM]	Hariyama [TM]	Haunter [TM]	Hawlucha [TM]	Haxorus [TM]
		Heatmor [TM]	Heliolisk [TM]	Helioptile [TM]	Heracross [TM]	Hippopotas [TM]	Hippowdon [TM]
		Honchkrow [TM]	Honedge [TM]	Hoothoot [TM]	Hoppip [TM]	Horsea [TM]	Houndoom [TM]
		Houndour [TM]	Huntail [TM]	Hydreigon [TM]	Igglybuff [TM]	Illumise [TM]	Inkay [TM]
		Ivysaur [TM]	Jigglypuff [TM]	Jolteon [TM]	Jumpluff [TM]	Jynx [TM]	Kadabra [TM]
		Kangaskhan [TM]	Karrablast [TM]	Kecleon [37, TM]	Kingdra [TM]	Kirlia [TM]	Klefki [TM]
		Krokorok [TM]	Krookodile [TM]	Lairon [TM]	Lampent [TM]	Lanturn [TM]	Lapras [TM]
		Larvitar [TM]	Leafeon [TM]	Ledian [TM]	Ledyba [TM]	Lickilicky [TM]	Lickitung [TM]
		Liepard [TM]	Linoone [TM]	Litleo [TM]	Litwick [TM]	Lombre [TM]	Lotad [TM]
		Loudred [TM]	Lucario [TM]	Ludicolo [TM]	Lunatone [TM]	Luvdisc [TM]	Machamp [TM]
		Machoke [TM]	Machop [TM]	Magcargo [TM]	Magnemite [TM]	Magneton [TM]	Magnezone [TM]
		Makuhita [TM]	Malamar [TM]	Mamoswine [TM]	Manectric [TM]	Mantine [TM]	Mantyke [TM]
		Mareep [TM]	Marill [TM]	Marowak [TM]	Masquerain [TM]	Mawile [TM]	Medicham [TM]
		Meditite [TM]	Meowstic (Female) [TM]	Meowstic (Male) [TM]	Mewtwo [TM]	Mienfoo [TM]	Mienshao [TM]
		Mightyena [TM]	Miltank [TM]	Mime Jr. [29, TM]	Minun [TM]	Moltres [TM]	Mothim [TM]
		Mr. Mime [29, TM]	Munchlax [TM]	Murkrow [TM]	Nidoking [TM]	Nidoqueen [TM]	Nidoran ♀ [TM]
		Nidoran ♂ [TM]	Nidorina [TM]	Nidorino [TM]	Nincada [TM]	Ninjask [TM]	Noctowl [TM]
		Noibat [TM]	Noivern [TM]	Nosepass [TM]	Octillery [TM]	Oddish [TM]	Onix [TM]
		Pachirisu [TM]	Pancham [TM]	Pangoro [TM]	Panpour [TM]	Pansage [TM]	Pansear [TM]
		Patrat [TM]	Pawniard [TM]	Pelipper [TM]	Phantump [TM]	Pichu [TM]	Pidgeot [TM]
		Pidgeotto [TM]	Pidgey [TM]	Pikachu [TM]	Piloswine [TM]	Pinsir [TM]	Pluse [TM]
		Politoed [TM]	Poliwag [TM]	Poliwhirl [TM]	Poliwrath [TM]	Poochyena [TM]	Probopass [TM]
		Psyduck [TM]	Pumpkaboo [TM]	Pupitar [TM]	Purrloin [TM]	Pyroar [TM]	Quagsire [TM]
		Quilladin [TM]	Qwilfish [TM]	Raichu [TM]	Ralts [TM]	Relicanth [TM]	Remoraid [TM]
		Reuniclus [TM]	Rhydon [TM]	Rhyhorn [TM]	Rhyperior [TM]	Riolu [TM]	Roggenrola [TM]
		Roselia [TM]	Roserade [TM]	Rotom (Fan) [36, TM]	Rotom (Frost) [36, TM]	Rotom (Heat) [36, TM]	Rotom (Mow) [36, TM]
		Rotom (Wash) [36, TM]	Rotom [36, TM]	Sableye [TM]	Salamence [TM]	Sandile [TM]	Sandshrew [TM]
		Sandslash [TM]	Sawk [TM]	Scizor [TM]	Scolipede [TM]	Scrafty [TM]	Scraggy [TM]
		Scyther [TM]	Seadra [TM]	Seaking [TM]	Sentret [TM]	Seviper [TM]	Sharpedo [TM]
		Shedinja [TM]	Shelgon [TM]	Shellder [TM]	Shelmet [TM]	Shuckle [TM]	Shuppet [TM]
		Sigilyph [TM]	Simipour [TM]	Simisage [TM]	Simisear [TM]	Skarmory [TM]	Skiddo [TM]
		Skiploom [TM]	Skitty [TM]	Skorupi [TM]	Skrelp [TM]	Skuntank [TM]	Sligoo [TM]
		Slowbro [TM]	Slowking [TM]	Slowpoke [TM]	Slugma [TM]	Slurpuff [TM]	Smoochum [TM]
		Sneasel [TM]	Snorlax [TM]	Snover [TM]	Snubbull [TM]	Solosis [TM]	Solrock [TM]
		Spearow [TM]	Spinarak [TM]	Spinda [TM]	Spoink [TM]	Spritzee [TM]	Squirtle [TM]
		Staraptor [TM]	Staravia [TM]	Starly [TM]	Starmie [TM]	Staryu [TM]	Steelix [TM]
		Stunfisk [TM]	Stunky [TM]	Sudowoodo [TM]	Surskit [TM]	Swablu [TM]	Swalot [TM]
		Swanna [TM]	Swellow [TM]	Swinub [TM]	Swirlix [TM]	Swoobat [TM]	Sylveon [TM]
		Taillow [TM]	Talonflame [TM]	Tauros [TM]	Teddiursa [TM]	Tentacool [TM]	Tentacruel [TM]

AFTER THE HALL OF FAME

CENTRAL KALOS

COASTAL KALOS

MOUNTAIN KALOS

ADVENTURE DATA

Move	Pokémon that can learn it					
Substitute (TM90) *Normal*	Throh [TM]	Timburr [TM]	Torkoal [TM]	Toxicroak [TM]	Trapinch [TM]	Trevenant [TM]
	Trubbish [TM]	Tyranitar [TM]	Tyrantrum [TM]	Tyrunt [TM]	Umbreon [TM]	Ursaring [TM]
	Vanillish [TM]	Vanillite [TM]	Vanilluxe [TM]	Vaporeon [TM]	Venipede [TM]	Venusaur [TM]
	Vespiquen [TM]	Vibrava [TM]	Victreebel [TM]	Vileplume [TM]	Vivillon [TM]	Volbeat [TM]
	Voltorb [TM]	Wailmer [TM]	Wailord [TM]	Wartortle [TM]	Watchog [TM]	Weavile [TM]
	Weepinbell [TM]	Whirlipede [TM]	Whiscash [TM]	Whismur [TM]	Wigglytuff [TM]	Wingull [TM]
	Woobat [TM]	Wooper [TM]	Wormadam (Plant) [TM]	Wormadam (Sand) [TM]	Wormadam (Trash) [TM]	Xerneas [TM]
	Yanma [TM]	Yanmega [TM]	Yveltal [TM]	Zangoose [TM]	Zapdos [TM]	Zigzagoon [TM]
	Zoroark [TM]	Zorua [TM]	Zubat [TM]	Zweilous [TM]	Zygarde [TM]	
Sucker Punch *Dark*	Absol [50, E]	Ariados [28]	Banette [34]	Bonsly [36]	Croagunk [31]	Diglett [23]
	Druddigon [E]	Dugtrio [23]	Ekans [E]	Furfrou [42]	Furret [36]	Gastly [22]
	Gengar [22]	Haunter [22]	Heatmor [E]	Honchkrow [1]	Houndour [E]	Kangaskhan [49]
	Kecleon [43]	Liepard [55]	Mawile [34]	Meowstic (Female) [48]	Meowstic (Male) [48]	Mightyena [62]
	Murkrow [55]	Nidoran♂ [E]	Pawniard [E]	Poochyena [49, E]	Purrloin [46]	Sableye [E]
	Sentret [31]	Shuppet [34]	Skitty [E]	Spinarak [26]	Spinda [32]	Sudowoodo [36]
	Toxicroak [31]	Yveltal [80]	Zorua [E]			
Sunny Day (TM11) *Fire*	Abra [TM]	Absol [TM]	Aegislash [TM]	Aerodactyl [TM]	Aggron [TM]	Alakazam [TM]
	Altaria [TM]	Amoonguss [TM]	Arbok [TM]	Ariados [TM]	Aromatisse [TM]	Aron [TM]
	Articuno [TM]	Audino [TM]	Axew [TM]	Bagon [TM]	Banette [TM]	Beedrill [TM]
	Bellossom [1, TM]	Bellsprout [TM]	Bibarel [TM]	Bidoof [TM]	Bonsly [TM]	Braixen [51, TM]
	Budew [TM]	Bulbasaur [TM]	Butterfree [TM]	Carbink [TM]	Carnivine [TM]	Chandelure [TM]
	Charizard [TM]	Charmander [TM]	Charmeleon [TM]	Chatot [TM]	Chesnaught [TM]	Chespin [TM]
	Chimecho [TM]	Chingling [TM]	Conkeldurr [TM]	Corsola [TM]	Croagunk [TM]	Crobat [TM]
	Cubone [TM]	Dedenne [TM]	Deino [TM]	Delcatty [TM]	Delphox [55, TM]	Diglett [TM]
	Dodrio [TM]	Doduo [TM]	Dragonair [TM]	Dragonite [TM]	Drapion [TM]	Dratini [TM]
	Drifblim [TM]	Drifloon [TM]	Druddigon [TM]	Dugtrio [TM]	Dunsparce [TM]	Eevee [TM]
	Ekans [TM]	Espeon [TM]	Espurr [TM]	Exeggcute [TM]	Exeggutor [TM]	Exploud [TM]
	Farfetch'd [TM]	Fearow [TM]	Fennekin [43, TM]	Ferroseed [TM]	Ferrothorn [TM]	Flabébé [TM]
	Flareon [TM]	Fletchinder [TM]	Fletchling [TM]	Floette [TM]	Florges [TM]	Flygon [TM]
	Foongus [TM]	Fraxure [TM]	Furfrou [TM]	Furret [TM]	Gabite [TM]	Gallade [TM]
	Garbodor [TM]	Garchomp [TM]	Gardevoir [TM]	Gastly [TM]	Gengar [TM]	Geodude [TM]
	Gible [TM]	Glaceon [TM]	Gligar [TM]	Gliscor [TM]	Gloom [TM]	Gogoat [TM]
	Golbat [TM]	Golem [TM]	Goodra [TM]	Goomy [TM]	Gourgeist [TM]	Granbull [TM]
	Graveler [TM]	Grumpig [TM]	Gulpin [TM]	Gurdurr [TM]	Hariyama [TM]	Haunter [TM]
	Hawlucha [TM]	Haxorus [TM]	Heatmor [TM]	Heracross [TM]	Hippopotas [TM]	Hippowdon [TM]
	Honchkrow [TM]	Hoothoot [TM]	Hoppip [TM]	Houndoom [TM]	Houndour [TM]	Hydreigon [TM]
	Igglybuff [TM]	Illumise [TM]	Inkay [TM]	Ivysaur [TM]	Jigglypuff [TM]	Jolteon [TM]
	Jumpluff [TM]	Kadabra [TM]	Kangaskhan [TM]	Kecleon [TM]	Kirlia [TM]	Klefki [TM]
	Lairon [TM]	Lampent [TM]	Larvitar [TM]	Leafeon [37, TM]	Ledian [TM]	Ledyba [TM]
	Lickilicky [TM]	Lickitung [TM]	Liepard [TM]	Linoone [TM]	Litleo [TM]	Litwick [TM]
	Lombre [TM]	Lotad [TM]	Loudred [TM]	Lucario [TM]	Ludicolo [TM]	Machamp [TM]
	Machoke [TM]	Machop [TM]	Magcargo [TM]	Magnemite [TM]	Magneton [TM]	Magnezone [TM]
	Makuhita [TM]	Malamar [TM]	Marowak [TM]	Masquerain [TM]	Mawile [TM]	Medicham [TM]
	Meditite [TM]	Meowstic (Female) [TM]	Meowstic (Male) [TM]	Mewtwo [TM]	Mienfoo [TM]	Mienshao [TM]
	Mightyena [TM]	Miltank [TM]	Mime Jr. [TM]	Moltres [57, TM]	Mothim [TM]	Mr. Mime [TM]
	Munchlax [TM]	Murkrow [TM]	Nidoking [TM]	Nidoqueen [TM]	Nidoran♀ [TM]	Nidoran♂ [TM]
	Nidorina [TM]	Nidorino [TM]	Nincada [TM]	Ninjask [TM]	Noctowl [TM]	Noibat [TM]
	Noivern [TM]	Nosepass [TM]	Octillery [TM]	Oddish [TM]	Onix [TM]	Pancham [TM]
	Pangoro [TM]	Pansage [TM]	Pansear [TM]	Patrat [TM]	Phantump [TM]	Pidgeot [TM]
	Pidgeotto [TM]	Pidgey [TM]	Pinsir [TM]	Poochyena [TM]	Probopass [TM]	Pumpkaboo [TM]
	Pupitar [TM]	Purrloin [TM]	Pyroar [TM]	Quilladin [TM]	Ralts [TM]	Remoraid [TM]
	Rhydon [TM]	Rhyhorn [TM]	Rhyperior [TM]	Riolu [TM]	Roselia [TM]	Roserade [TM]
	Rotom (Fan) [TM]	Rotom (Frost) [TM]	Rotom (Heat) [TM]	Rotom (Mow) [TM]	Rotom (Wash) [TM]	Rotom [TM]
	Sableye [TM]	Salamence [TM]	Sandshrew [TM]	Sandslash [TM]	Sawk [TM]	Scizor [TM]
	Scolipede [TM]	Scrafty [TM]	Scraggy [TM]	Scyther [TM]	Sentret [TM]	Seviper [TM]
	Shedinja [TM]	Shelgon [TM]	Shuckle [TM]	Shuppet [TM]	Simisage [TM]	Simisear [TM]
	Skarmory [TM]	Skiddo [TM]	Skiploom [TM]	Skitty [TM]	Skorupi [TM]	Skuntank [TM]
	Sliggoo [TM]	Slowbro [TM]	Slowking [TM]	Slowpoke [TM]	Slugma [TM]	Slurpuff [TM]
	Sneasel [TM]	Snorlax [TM]	Snubbull [TM]	Solrock [TM]	Spearow [TM]	Spinarak [TM]
	Spinda [TM]	Spoink [TM]	Spritzee [TM]	Staraptor [TM]	Staravia [TM]	Starly [TM]
	Steelix [TM]	Stunky [TM]	Sudowoodo [TM]	Surskit [TM]	Swablu [TM]	Swalot [TM]
	Swellow [TM]	Swirlix [TM]	Sylveon [TM]	Taillow [TM]	Talonflame [TM]	Tauros [TM]
	Teddiursa [TM]	Throh [TM]	Timburr [TM]	Torkoal [TM]	Toxicroak [TM]	Trapinch [TM]
	Trevenant [TM]	Trubbish [TM]	Tyranitar [TM]	Tyrantrum [TM]	Tyrunt [TM]	Umbreon [TM]
	Ursaring [TM]	Vaporeon [TM]	Venipede [TM]	Venusaur [TM]	Vespiquen [TM]	Vibrava [TM]
	Victreebel [TM]	Vileplume [TM]	Vivillon [TM]	Volbeat [TM]	Watchog [TM]	Weavile [TM]
	Weepinbell [TM]	Whirlipede [TM]	Whismur [TM]	Wigglytuff [TM]	Wormadam (Plant) [TM]	Wormadam (Sand) [TM]
	Wormadam (Trash) [TM]	Xerneas [TM]	Yanma [TM]	Yanmega [TM]	Yveltal [TM]	Zangoose [TM]
	Zapdos [TM]	Zigzagoon [TM]	Zoroark [TM]	Zorua [TM]	Zubat [TM]	Zweilous [TM]
	Zygarde [TM]					

Type	Move	Pokémon that can learn it					
Normal	Super Fang	Bibarel [43]	Bidoof [37]	Bunnelby [42]	Diggersby [48]	Noibat [43]	Noivern [43]
		Pachirisu [37]	Patrat [21]	Watchog [22]			
Fighting	Superpower	Aron [E]	Azumarill [42]	Beartic [1]	Bibarel [48]	Bidoof [41]	Conkeldurr [57]
		Corphish [E]	Druddigon [55]	Gurdurr [57]	Inkay [48]	Malamar [1, 48]	Marill [37, E]
		Nidoqueen [1, 58]	Pinsir [43, E]	Throh [48]	Timburr [49]	Torkoal [E]	Trapinch [1, 67]
Normal	Supersonic	Aerodactyl [1]	Butterfree [18]	Chatot [E]	Chinchou [1]	Clamperl [E]	Cloyster [1]
		Crobat [1, 4]	Doduo [E]	Dratini [E]	Exploud [23]	Flygon [29]	Golbat [1, 4]
		Goldeen [7]	Hoothoot [E]	Lanturn [1]	Ledian [1, 6]	Ledyba [6]	Lickilicky [5]
		Lickitung [5]	Loudred [23]	Luvdisc [E]	Magnemite [4]	Magneton [1, 4]	Magnezone [1, 4]
		Mantine [1, 3]	Mantyke [3]	Marill [E]	Nidoran♀ [E]	Nidoran♂ [E]	Noibat [1]
		Noivern [1]	Pelipper [6]	Qwilfish [E]	Remoraid [E]	Seaking [1, 7]	Shellder [8]
		Taillow [E]	Tentacool [5]	Tentacruel [1, 5]	Vibrava [29]	Vivillon [21]	Whismur [21]
		Wingull [6]	Woobat [E]	Yanma [22]	Yanmega [22]	Zubat [4]	
Water	Surf (HM03)	Aggron [HM]	Alomomola [HM]	Audino [HM]	Avalugg [HM]	Azumarill [HM]	Azurill [HM]
		Barbaracle [HM]	Barboach [HM]	Basculin [HM]	Beartic [HM]	Bergmite [HM]	Bibarel [HM]
		Binacle [HM]	Blastoise [HM]	Buizel [HM]	Bunnelby [HM]	Carvanha [HM]	Chinchou [HM]
		Clamperl [HM]	Clauncher [HM]	Clawitzer [HM]	Cloyster [HM]	Corphish [HM]	Corsola [HM]
		Crawdaunt [HM]	Cubchoo [HM]	Diggersby [HM]	Dragalge [HM]	Dragonair [HM]	Dragonite [HM]
		Dratini [HM]	Druddigon [HM]	Ducklett [HM]	Exploud [HM]	Floatzel [HM]	Froakie [HM]
		Frogadier [HM]	Furfrou [HM]	Furret [HM]	Garchomp [HM]	Gogoat [HM]	Goldeen [HM]
		Golduck [HM]	Gorebyss [HM]	Greninja [HM]	Gyarados [HM]	Hariyama [HM]	Haxorus [HM]
		Heliolisk [HM]	Helioptile [HM]	Horsea [HM]	Huntail [HM]	Kangaskhan [HM]	Kecleon [HM]
		Kingdra [HM]	Lanturn [HM]	Lapras [HM]	Lickilicky [HM]	Lickitung [HM]	Linoone [HM]
		Lombre [HM]	Lotad [HM]	Ludicolo [HM]	Luvdisc [HM]	Makuhita [HM]	Mantine [HM]
		Mantyke [HM]	Marill [HM]	Miltank [HM]	Munchlax [HM]	Nidoking [HM]	Nidoqueen [HM]
		Octillery [HM]	Pancham [HM]	Pangoro [HM]	Panpour [HM]	Pelipper [HM]	Politoed [HM]
		Poliwag [HM]	Poliwhirl [HM]	Poliwrath [HM]	Psyduck [HM]	Quagsire [HM]	Qwilfish [HM]
		Relicanth [HM]	Remoraid [HM]	Rhydon [HM]	Rhyperior [HM]	Seadra [HM]	Seaking [HM]
		Sentret [HM]	Sharpedo [HM]	Shellder [HM]	Simipour [HM]	Skiddo [HM]	Skrelp [HM]
		Slowbro [HM]	Slowking [HM]	Slowpoke [HM]	Slurpuff [HM]	Sneasel [HM]	Snorlax [HM]
		Squirtle [HM]	Starmie [HM]	Staryu [HM]	Stunfisk [HM]	Swanna [HM]	Swirlix [HM]
		Tauros [HM]	Tentacool [HM]	Tentacruel [HM]	Tyranitar [HM]	Vaporeon [HM]	Wailmer [HM]
		Wailord [HM]	Wartortle [HM]	Weavile [HM]	Whiscash [HM]	Wooper [HM]	Zigzagoon [HM]
Normal	Swagger (TM87)	Abomasnow [17, TM]	Abra [TM]	Absol [TM]	Accelgor [TM]	Aegislash [TM]	Aerodactyl [TM]
		Aggron [TM]	Alakazam [TM]	Alomomola [TM]	Altaria [TM]	Amaura [TM]	Amoonguss [TM]
		Ampharos [TM]	Arbok [TM]	Ariados [TM]	Aromatisse [TM]	Aron [TM]	Articuno [TM]
		Audino [TM]	Aurorus [TM]	Avalugg [TM]	Axew [TM]	Azumarill [TM]	Azurill [TM]
		Bagon [TM]	Banette [TM]	Barbaracle [TM]	Barboach [TM]	Basculin [TM]	Beartic [29, TM]
		Beedrill [TM]	Bellossom [TM]	Bellsprout [TM]	Bergmite [TM]	Bibarel [TM]	Bidoof [TM]
		Binacle [TM]	Bisharp [TM]	Blastoise [TM]	Boldore [TM]	Bonsly [TM]	Braixen [TM]
		Budew [TM]	Buizel [TM]	Bulbasaur [TM]	Bunnelby [TM]	Butterfree [TM]	Carbink [TM]
		Carnivine [TM]	Carvanha [21, TM]	Chandelure [TM]	Charizard [TM]	Charmander [TM]	Charmeleon [TM]
		Chatot [TM]	Chesnaught [TM]	Chespin [TM]	Chimecho [TM]	Chinchou [TM]	Chingling [TM]
		Clamperl [TM]	Clauncher [TM]	Clawitzer [TM]	Cloyster [TM]	Conkeldurr [TM]	Corphish [TM]
		Corsola [TM]	Crawdaunt [TM]	Croagunk [24, TM]	Crobat [TM]	Crustle [TM]	Cryogonal [TM]
		Cubchoo [TM]	Cubone [TM]	Dedenne [TM]	Deino [TM]	Delcatty [TM]	Delibird [TM]
		Delphox [TM]	Diggersby [TM]	Diglett [TM]	Dodrio [TM]	Doduo [TM]	Doublade [TM]
		Dragalge [TM]	Dragonair [TM]	Dragonite [TM]	Drapion [TM]	Dratini [TM]	Drifblim [TM]
		Drifloon [TM]	Druddigon [TM]	Ducklett [TM]	Dugtrio [TM]	Dunsparce [TM]	Duosion [TM]
		Durant [TM]	Dwebble [TM]	Eevee [TM]	Ekans [TM]	Electrike [TM]	Electrode [TM]
		Emolga [TM]	Escavalier [TM]	Espeon [TM]	Espurr [TM]	Exeggcute [TM]	Exeggutor [TM]
		Exploud [TM]	Farfetch'd [TM]	Fearow [TM]	Fennekin [TM]	Ferroseed [TM]	Ferrothorn [TM]
		Flaaffy [TM]	Flabébé [TM]	Flareon [TM]	Fletchinder [TM]	Fletchling [TM]	Floatzel [TM]
		Floette [TM]	Florges [TM]	Flygon [TM]	Foongus [TM]	Fraxure [TM]	Froakie [TM]
		Frogadier [TM]	Furfrou [TM]	Furret [TM]	Gabite [TM]	Gallade [TM]	Garbodor [TM]
		Garchomp [TM]	Gardevoir [TM]	Gastly [TM]	Gengar [TM]	Geodude [TM]	Gible [TM]
		Gigalith [TM]	Glaceon [TM]	Gligar [TM]	Gliscor [TM]	Gloom [TM]	Gogoat [TM]
		Golbat [TM]	Goldeen [TM]	Golduck [TM]	Golem [TM]	Golett [TM]	Golurk [TM]
		Goodra [TM]	Goomy [TM]	Gorebyss [TM]	Gothita [TM]	Gothitelle [TM]	Gothorita [TM]
		Gourgeist [TM]	Granbull [TM]	Graveler [TM]	Greninja [TM]	Grumpig [TM]	Gulpin [TM]
		Gurdurr [TM]	Gyarados [TM]	Hariyama [TM]	Haunter [TM]	Hawlucha [TM]	Haxorus [TM]
		Heatmor [TM]	Heliolisk [TM]	Helioptile [TM]	Heracross [TM]	Hippopotas [TM]	Hippowdon [TM]
		Honchkrow [25, TM]	Honedge [TM]	Hoothoot [TM]	Hoppip [TM]	Horsea [TM]	Houndoom [TM]
		Houndour [TM]	Huntail [TM]	Hydreigon [TM]	Igglybuff [TM]	Illumise [TM]	Inkay [12, TM]
		Ivysaur [TM]	Jigglypuff [TM]	Jolteon [TM]	Jumpluff [TM]	Jynx [TM]	Kadabra [TM]
		Kangaskhan [TM]	Karrablast [TM]	Kecleon [TM]	Kingdra [TM]	Kirlia [TM]	Klefki [TM]
		Krokorok [25, TM]	Krookodile [25, TM]	Lairon [TM]	Lampent [TM]	Lanturn [TM]	Lapras [TM]
		Larvitar [TM]	Leafeon [TM]	Ledian [TM]	Ledyba [TM]	Lickilicky [TM]	Lickitung [TM]
		Liepard [TM]	Linoone [TM]	Litleo [TM]	Litwick [TM]	Lombre [TM]	Lotad [TM]
		Loudred [TM]	Lucario [TM]	Ludicolo [TM]	Lunatone [TM]	Luvdisc [TM]	Machamp [TM]

AFTER THE HALL OF FAME

CENTRAL KALOS

COASTAL KALOS

MOUNTAIN KALOS

ADVENTURE DATA

Pokémon Moves Reverse Lookup

Move	Pokémon that can learn it					
Swagger (TM87) *(Normal)*	Machoke [TM]	Machop [TM]	Magcargo [TM]	Magnemite [TM]	Magneton [TM]	Magnezone [TM]
	Makuhita [TM]	Malamar [12, TM]	Mamoswine [TM]	Manectric [TM]	Mantine [TM]	Mantyke [TM]
	Mareep [TM]	Marill [TM]	Marowak [TM]	Masquerain [TM]	Mawile [TM]	Medicham [TM]
	Meditite [TM]	Meowstic (Female) [TM]	Meowstic (Male) [TM]	Mewtwo [TM]	Mienfoo [TM]	Mienshao [TM]
	Mightyena [27, TM]	Miltank [TM]	Mime Jr. [TM]	Minun [TM]	Moltres [TM]	Mothim [TM]
	Mr. Mime [TM]	Munchlax [TM]	Murkrow [TM]	Nidoking [TM]	Nidoqueen [TM]	Nidoran ♀ [TM]
	Nidoran♂ [TM]	Nidorina [TM]	Nidorino [TM]	Nincada [TM]	Ninjask [TM]	Noctowl [TM]
	Noibat [TM]	Noivern [TM]	Nosepass [TM]	Octillery [TM]	Oddish [TM]	Onix [TM]
	Pachirisu [TM]	Pancham [TM]	Pangoro [TM]	Panpour [TM]	Pansage [TM]	Pansear [TM]
	Patrat [TM]	Pawniard [TM]	Pelipper [TM]	Phantump [TM]	Pichu [TM]	Pidgeot [TM]
	Pidgeotto [TM]	Pidgey [TM]	Pikachu [TM]	Piloswine [TM]	Pinsir [TM]	Plusle [TM]
	Politoed [27, TM]	Poliwag [TM]	Poliwhirl [TM]	Poliwrath [TM]	Poochyena [25, TM]	Probopass [TM]
	Psyduck [TM]	Pumpkaboo [TM]	Pupitar [TM]	Purrloin [TM]	Pyroar [TM]	Quagsire [TM]
	Quilladin [TM]	Qwilfish [TM]	Raichu [TM]	Ralts [TM]	Relicanth [TM]	Remoraid [TM]
	Reuniclus [TM]	Rhydon [TM]	Rhyhorn [TM]	Rhyperior [TM]	Riolu [TM]	Roggenrola [TM]
	Roselia [TM]	Roserade [TM]	Rotom (Fan) [TM]	Rotom (Frost) [TM]	Rotom (Heat) [TM]	Rotom (Mow) [TM]
	Rotom (Wash) [TM]	Rotom [TM]	Sableye [TM]	Salamence [TM]	Sandile [25, TM]	Sandshrew [TM]
	Sandslash [TM]	Sawk [TM]	Scizor [TM]	Scolipede [TM]	Scrafty [16, TM]	Scraggy [16, TM]
	Scyther [TM]	Seadra [TM]	Seaking [TM]	Sentret [TM]	Seviper [1, TM]	Sharpedo [21, TM]
	Shedinja [TM]	Shelgon [TM]	Shellder [TM]	Shelmet [TM]	Shuckle [TM]	Shuppet [TM]
	Sigilyph [TM]	Simipour [TM]	Simisage [TM]	Simisear [TM]	Skarmory [TM]	Skiddo [TM]
	Skiploom [TM]	Skitty [TM]	Skorupi [TM]	Skrelp [TM]	Skuntank [TM]	Sliggoo [TM]
	Slowbro [TM]	Slowking [41, TM]	Slowpoke [TM]	Slugma [TM]	Slurpuff [TM]	Smoochum [TM]
	Sneasel [TM]	Snorlax [TM]	Snover [17, TM]	Snubbull [TM]	Solosis [TM]	Solrock [TM]
	Spearow [TM]	Spinarak [TM]	Spinda [TM]	Spoink [TM]	Spritzee [TM]	Squirtle [TM]
	Staraptor [TM]	Staravia [TM]	Starly [TM]	Starmie [TM]	Staryu [TM]	Steelix [TM]
	Stunfisk [TM]	Stunky [TM]	Sudowoodo [TM]	Surskit [TM]	Swablu [TM]	Swalot [TM]
	Swanna [TM]	Swellow [TM]	Swinub [TM]	Swirlix [TM]	Swoobat [TM]	Sylveon [TM]
	Taillow [TM]	Talonflame [TM]	Tauros [48, TM]	Teddiursa [TM]	Tentacool [TM]	Tentacruel [TM]
	Throh [TM]	Timburr [TM]	Torkoal [TM]	Toxicroak [24, TM]	Trapinch [TM]	Trevenant [TM]
	Trubbish [TM]	Tyranitar [TM]	Tyrantrum [TM]	Tyrunt [TM]	Umbreon [TM]	Ursaring [TM]
	Vanillish [TM]	Vanillite [TM]	Vanilluxe [TM]	Vaporeon [TM]	Venipede [TM]	Venusaur [TM]
	Vespiquen [49, TM]	Vibrava [TM]	Victreebel [TM]	Vileplume [TM]	Vivillon [TM]	Volbeat [TM]
	Voltorb [TM]	Wailmer [TM]	Wailord [TM]	Wartortle [TM]	Watchog [TM]	Weavile [TM]
	Weepinbell [TM]	Whirlipede [TM]	Whiscash [TM]	Whismur [TM]	Wigglytuff [TM]	Wingull [TM]
	Woobat [TM]	Wooper [TM]	Wormadam (Plant) [TM]	Wormadam (Sand) [TM]	Wormadam (Trash) [TM]	Xerneas [TM]
	Yanma [TM]	Yanmega [TM]	Yveltal [TM]	Zangoose [TM]	Zapdos [TM]	Zigzagoon [TM]
	Zoroark [TM]	Zorua [TM]	Zubat [TM]	Zweilous [TM]	Zygarde [TM]	
Swallow	Arbok [27]	Carnivine [37]	Drifblim [34]	Drifloon [32]	Ekans [25]	Garbodor [23]
	Gulpin [39]	Heatmor [50]	Hippopotas [E]	Lanturn [E]	Mawile [50]	Munchlax [33]
	Pelipper [39]	Seviper [E]	Slugma [E]	Swalot [45]	Trubbish [23]	Victreebel [1]
	Wooper [E]					
Sweet Kiss *(Fairy)*	Aromatisse [6]	Audino [E]	Igglybuff [13]	Luvdisc [37]	Minun [E]	Pachirisu [29]
	Pichu [10]	Plusle [E]	Smoochum [8]	Spritzee [6]		
Sweet Scent *(Normal)*	Amoonguss [24]	Aromatisse [1]	Bellossom [1]	Bellsprout [29]	Bulbasaur [21]	Carnivine [17]
	Combee [E]	Foongus [24]	Gloom [1, 5]	Illumise [5]	Ivysaur [23]	Lotad [E]
	Masquerain [1, 13]	Mawile [16]	Oddish [5]	Roselia [31]	Roserade [1]	Shuckle [E]
	Slurpuff [1]	Spritzee [1]	Surskit [13]	Swirlix [1]	Teddiursa [22]	Ursaring [22]
	Venusaur [1]	Vespiquen [1]	Victreebel [1]	Weepinbell [29]		
Swift	Accelgor [25]	Basculin [E]	Buizel [21]	Carvanha [E]	Crawdaunt [30]	Crobat [24]
	Eevee [10]	Electrike [E]	Electrode [40]	Espeon [17]	Floatzel [21]	Golbat [24]
	Ledian [41]	Ledyba [33]	Mewtwo [8]	Mienfoo [21]	Mienshao [22]	Minun [31]
	Pachirisu [21]	Plusle [31]	Remoraid [E]	Sandshrew [11]	Sandslash [11]	Skarmory [9]
	Starmie [1]	Staryu [18]	Sylveon [17]	Voltorb [36]	Zubat [23]	
Switcheroo *(Dark)*	Binacle [E]	Buizel [E]	Corphish [E]	Delphox [E]	Ekans [E]	Electrike [E]
	Inkay [23]	Klefki [E]	Linoone [1]	Malamar [23]	Noibat [E]	Seviper [E]
Swords Dance (TM75) *(Normal)*	Abomasnow [TM]	Absol [33, TM]	Aegislash [1, TM]	Axew [46, TM]	Barbaracle [TM]	
	Beedrill [TM]	Bellossom [TM]	Bellsprout [TM]	Binacle [TM]	Bisharp [63, TM]	Budew [TM]
	Bulbasaur [TM]	Carnivine [TM]	Charizard [TM]	Charmander [TM]	Charmeleon [TM]	Chesnaught [TM]
	Chespin [TM]	Clauncher [25, TM]	Clawitzer [25, TM]	Corphish [44, TM]	Crawdaunt [52, TM]	Crustle [TM]
	Cubone [TM]	Diggersby [1, TM]	Doublade [1, TM]	Drapion [TM]	Dwebble [TM]	Escavalier [52, TM]
	Exeggcute [TM]	Exeggutor [TM]	Farfetch'd [25, TM]	Ferrothorn [TM]	Fletchinder [TM]	Fletchling [TM]
	Fraxure [48, TM]	Gallade [31, TM]	Garchomp [TM]	Gligar [50, TM]	Gliscor [50, TM]	Gloom [TM]
	Hawlucha [60, TM]	Haxorus [50, TM]	Heracross [TM]	Honedge [1, TM]	Hoppip [TM]	Ivysaur [TM]
	Jumpluff [TM]	Karrablast [52, TM]	Leafeon [29, TM]	Ledian [TM]	Ledyba [TM]	Lickilicky [TM]
	Lickitung [TM]	Lombre [TM]	Lotad [TM]	Lucario [19, TM]	Ludicolo [TM]	Marowak [TM]
	Mawile [TM]	Mienfoo [TM]	Mienshao [TM]	Ninjask [25, TM]	Oddish [TM]	Pancham [TM]
	Pangoro [TM]	Patrat [TM]	Pawniard [57, TM]	Pinsir [40, TM]	Quilladin [TM]	Rhydon [TM]
	Rhyhorn [TM]	Rhyperior [TM]	Riolu [TM]	Roselia [TM]	Roserade [TM]	Sandshrew [38, TM]

	Move	Pokémon that can learn it					
Normal	Swords Dance (TM75)	Sandslash [38, TM]	Scizor [57, TM]	Scolipede [TM]	Scyther [57, TM]	Skarmory [TM]	Skiploom [TM]
		Skorupi [TM]	Sneasel [TM]	Snover [TM]	Talonflame [TM]	Teddiursa [TM]	Tentacool [TM]
		Tentacruel [TM]	Toxicroak [TM]	Ursaring [TM]	Venusaur [TM]	Victreebel [TM]	Vileplume [TM]
		Watchog [TM]	Weavile [TM]	Weepinbell [TM]	Zangoose [43, TM]	Zoroark [TM]	Zorua [TM]
Psychic	Synchronoise	Chatot [49]	Chimecho [1, 54]	Eevee [E]	Exploud [55]	Hoothoot [41]	Kecleon [1, 58]
		Loudred [51]	Noctowl [47]	Psyduck [E]	Ralts [E]	Sigilyph [31]	Whismur [41]
		Woobat [E]					
Grass	Synthesis	Amoonguss [35]	Bellsprout [E]	Budew [E]	Bulbasaur [33]	Carnivine [E]	Chespin [E]
		Exeggcute [E]	Foongus [35]	Gogoat [20]	Hoppip [4]	Ivysaur [39]	Jumpluff [1, 4]
		Leafeon [33]	Lotad [E]	Oddish [E]	Roselia [46, E]	Skiddo [20]	Skiploom [1, 4]
		Venusaur [45]					

T

	Move	Pokémon that can learn it					
Normal	Tackle	Aggron [1]	Ampharos [1]	Aron [1]	Avalugg [1]	Azumarill [1]	Basculin [1]
		Bergmite [1]	Bibarel [1]	Bidoof [1]	Blastoise [1]	Boldore [1]	Bulbasaur [1]
		Bunnelby [1]	Burmy [10]	Carbink [1]	Caterpie [1]	Chesnaught [1]	Chespin [1]
		Corsola [1]	Dedenne [1]	Deino [1]	Diggersby [1]	Doublade [1]	Dragalge [1]
		Eevee [1]	Electrike [1]	Electrode [1, 5]	Espeon [1]	Ferroseed [1]	Ferrothorn [1]
		Flaaffy [1]	Flabébé [1]	Flareon [1]	Fletchinder [1]	Fletchling [1]	Floette [1]
		Furfrou [1]	Gabite [1]	Garchomp [1]	Geodude [1]	Gible [1]	Gigalith [1]
		Glaceon [1]	Gogoat [1]	Golem [1]	Goodra [1]	Goomy [1]	Granbull [1]
		Graveler [1]	Hariyama [1]	Hawlucha [1]	Heatmor [1]	Heracross [1]	Hippopotas [1]
		Hippowdon [1]	Honedge [1]	Hoothoot [1]	Hoppip [8]	Illumise [1]	Inkay [1]
		Ivysaur [1]	Jolteon [1]	Jumpluff [1, 8]	Klefki [1]	Lairon [1]	Leafeon [1]
		Ledian [1]	Ledyba [1]	Linoone [1]	Litleo [1]	Lunatone [1]	Luvdisc [1]
		Magikarp [15]	Magnemite [1]	Magneton [1]	Magnezone [1]	Makuhita [1]	Malamar [1]
		Manectric [1]	Mantine [1]	Mantyke [1]	Mareep [1]	Marill [1]	Mightyena [1]
		Miltank [1]	Mothim [1]	Munchlax [1]	Noctowl [1]	Noibat [1]	Noivern [1]
		Nosepass [1]	Onix [1]	Pancham [1]	Pangoro [1]	Patrat [1]	Phantump [1]
		Pidgeot [1]	Pidgeotto [1]	Pidgey [1]	Poochyena [1]	Probopass [1]	Pyroar [1]
		Quilladin [1]	Qwilfish [1]	Relicanth [1]	Roggenrola [1]	Scatterbug [1]	Shellder [1]
		Skiddo [1]	Skiploom [1, 8]	Skitty [1]	Skrelp [1]	Sliggoo [1]	Slowbro [1]
		Slowking [1]	Slowpoke [1]	Slurpuff [1]	Snorlax [1]	Snubbull [1]	Solrock [1]
		Spinda [1]	Squirtle [1]	Staraptor [1]	Staravia [1]	Starly [1]	Staryu [1]
		Steelix [1]	Stunfisk [1]	Swinub [1]	Swirlix [1]	Sylveon [1]	Talonflame [1]
		Tauros [1]	Trevenant [1]	Tyrantrum [1]	Tyrunt [1]	Umbreon [1]	Vaporeon [1]
		Venusaur [1]	Volbeat [1]	Voltorb [5]	Wartortle [1]	Watchog [1]	Wormadam (Plant) [1]
		Wormadam (Sand) [1]	Wormadam (Trash) []	Yanma [1]	Yanmega [1]	Zigzagoon [1]	
Bug	Tail Glow	Volbeat [21]					
Normal	Tail Slap	Buizel [E]					
	Tail Whip	Azumarill [1, 2]	Azurill [2]	Basculin [1]	Blastoise [1, 4]	Braixen [1]	Cubone [3]
		Dedenne [1]	Delphox [1]	Dragalge [9]	Eevee [1]	Emolga [7]	Espeon [1]
		Fennekin [1]	Flareon [1]	Furfrou [15]	Glaceon [1]	Gogoat [9]	Goldeen [1]
		Golduck [1, 4]	Granbull [1]	Helioptile [1]	Hoppip [6]	Jolteon [1]	Jumpluff [1, 6]
		Kangaskhan [10]	Kecleon [1]	Leafeon [1]	Linoone [1, 5]	Marill [1]	Marowak [1, 3]
		Nidoqueen [1]	Nidoran♀ [7]	Nidorina [7]	Pachirisu [E]	Pichu [5]	Pikachu [1]
		Psyduck [4]	Quagsire [1]	Raichu [1]	Rhydon [1]	Rhyhorn [1]	Rhyperior [1]
		Seaking [1]	Skiddo [9]	Skiploom [1, 6]	Skitty [1]	Snubbull [1]	Umbreon [1]
		Squirtle [4]	Sylveon [1]	Tauros [3]	Tyrantrum [1]	Tyrunt [1]	Vaporeon [1]
		Vaporeon [1]	Wartortle [1, 4]	Wooper [1]	Zigzagoon [5]		
Flying	Tailwind	Aerodactyl [E]	Articuno [1, 64]	Butterfree [30]	Drifloon [E]	Ducklett [37]	Fletchinder [51]
		Fletchling [45, E]	Ledyba [E]	Mantyke [E]	Murkrow [50]	Noibat [35, E]	Noivern [35]
		Pelipper [1, 52]	Pidgeot [50]	Pidgeotto [47]	Pidgey [41]	Sigilyph [11]	Swanna [40]
		Talonflame [55]					
Normal	Take Down	Aerodactyl [41]	Aggron [22]	Altaria [25]	Amaura [15]	Ampharos [20]	Aron [22]
		Audino [30]	Aurorus [15]	Avalugg [15]	Barboach [E]	Basculin [20]	Bergmite [15]
		Bibarel [38]	Bidoof [33]	Bulbasaur [15]	Bunnelby [15]	Carvanha [38]	Chesnaught [30]
		Chespin [27]	Chimecho [22]	Chinchou [23]	Diggersby [15]	Dunsparce [22]	Eevee [25]
		Flaaffy [20]	Furfrou [35]	Gabite [15]	Garchomp [15]	Gible [15]	Gogoat [22]
		Heracross [28]	Hippopotas [19]	Hippowdon [19]	Hoothoot [29]	Ivysaur [15]	Karrablast [37]
		Lairon [22]	Lanturn [23]	Litleo [20]	Luvdisc [14]	Mamoswine [28]	Mantine [27]
		Mantyke [27]	Mareep [18, E]	Mightyena [52]	Nidoran♀ [E]	Nidoran♂ [E]	Noctowl [32]
		Piloswine [28]	Poochyena [45]	Pyroar [20]	Quilladin [30]	Qwilfish [E]	Relicanth [29]
		Rhydon [41]	Rhyhorn [41]	Rhyperior [41]	Roggenrola [E]	Shellder [E]	Skiddo [22]
		Staraptor [33]	Staravia [33]	Starly [29]	Swablu [25]	Swinub [28, E]	Tauros [41]
		Teddiursa [E]	Trubbish [25]	Venipede [E]	Venusaur [15]	Whismur [E]	Xerneas [1]

	Move	Pokémon that can learn it					
Dark	Taunt (TM12)	Abra [TM]	Absol [1, 17, TM]	Aerodactyl [TM]	Aggron [TM]	Alakazam [TM]	Axew [36, TM]
		Banette [TM]	Barbaracle [TM]	Basculin [TM]	Beartic [TM]	Bibarel [TM]	Bidoof [TM]
		Binacle [TM]	Bisharp [TM]	Carvanha [TM]	Chandelure [TM]	Chatot [1, 25, TM]	Chesnaught [TM]
		Chespin [TM]	Chimecho [TM]	Chingling [TM]	Conkeldurr [TM]	Corphish [32, TM]	Crawdaunt [34, TM]
		Croagunk [10, TM]	Crobat [TM]	Deino [TM]	Dodrio [TM]	Drapion [TM]	Druddigon [TM]
		Electrode [TM]	Emolga [TM]	Exploud [TM]	Fletchinder [TM]	Fletchling [TM]	Floatzel [TM]
		Fraxure [36, TM]	Froakie [TM]	Frogadier [TM]	Gallade [TM]	Gardevoir [TM]	Gastly [TM]
		Gengar [TM]	Gligar [TM]	Gliscor [TM]	Golbat [TM]	Gothita [TM]	Gothitelle [TM]
		Gothorita [TM]	Granbull [TM]	Greninja [TM]	Grumpig [TM]	Gurdurr [TM]	Gyarados [TM]
		Haunter [TM]	Hawlucha [TM]	Haxorus [36, TM]	Heatmor [TM]	Honchkrow [TM]	Houndoom [TM]
		Houndour [TM]	Hydreigon [TM]	Inkay [TM]	Jynx [TM]	Kadabra [TM]	Kirlia [TM]
		Krokorok [TM]	Krookodile [TM]	Lampent [TM]	Larvitar [TM]	Liepard [38, TM]	Litleo [TM]
		Litwick [TM]	Loudred [TM]	Malamar [TM]	Mawile [1, TM]	Mewtwo [TM]	Mienfoo [TM]
		Mienshao [TM]	Mightyena [42, TM]	Mime Jr. [TM]	Mr. Mime [TM]	Murkrow [31, TM]	Nidoking [TM]
		Nidoqueen [TM]	Noibat [TM]	Noivern [TM]	Nosepass [TM]	Onix [TM]	Pangoro [65, TM]
		Panpour [25, TM]	Pansage [TM]	Pansear [TM]	Pawniard [TM]	Poochyena [37, TM]	Probopass [TM]
		Pupitar [TM]	Purrloin [TM]	Pyroar [TM]	Quilladin [TM]	Qwilfish [TM]	Ralts [TM]
		Sableye [TM]	Sandile [TM]	Sawk [TM]	Scrafty [TM]	Scraggy [TM]	Seviper [TM]
		Sharpedo [40, TM]	Shuppet [TM]	Simipour [TM]	Simisage [TM]	Simisear [TM]	Skarmory [TM]
		Skorupi [TM]	Skuntank [TM]	Sneasel [1, TM]	Snubbull [TM]	Spoink [TM]	Steelix [TM]
		Stunky [TM]	Sudowoodo [TM]	Swoobat [TM]	Talonflame [TM]	Teddiursa [TM]	Throh [TM]
		Timburr [TM]	Toxicroak [10, TM]	Tyranitar [TM]	Umbreon [TM]	Ursaring [TM]	Vanillish [22, TM]
		Vanillite [22, TM]	Vanilluxe [22, TM]	Voltorb [TM]	Weavile [1, TM]	Woobat [TM]	Yveltal [1, TM]
		Zangoose [40, TM]	Zoroark [25, TM]	Zorua [25, TM]	Zubat [TM]	Zweilous [TM]	
Normal	Teeter Dance	Lotad [E]	Mime Jr. [E]	Mr. Mime [E]	Oddish [E]	Spinda [37]	
Psychic	Telekinesis	Alakazam [34]	Gothita [40]	Gothitelle [45]	Gothorita [43]	Kadabra [34]	
Psychic	Teleport	Abra [1]	Alakazam [1]	Gallade [1, 12]	Gardevoir [1, 12]	Kadabra [1]	Kirlia [1, 12]
		Ralts [12]					
Dark	Thief (TM46)	Abra [TM]	Absol [TM]	Aerodactyl [TM]	Alakazam [TM]	Altaria [TM]	Arbok [TM]
		Ariados [TM]	Banette [TM]	Barbaracle [TM]	Beedrill [TM]	Bellsprout [TM]	Bibarel [TM]
		Bidoof [TM]	Binacle [TM]	Bisharp [TM]	Bonsly [TM]	Braixen [TM]	Bunnelby [TM]
		Butterfree [TM]	Carnivine [TM]	Carvanha [TM]	Chandelure [TM]	Chatot [TM]	Croagunk [TM]
		Crobat [TM]	Cubone [TM]	Dedenne [TM]	Deino [TM]	Delibird [TM]	Delphox [TM]
		Diggersby [TM]	Diglett [TM]	Dodrio [TM]	Doduo [TM]	Drapion [TM]	Drifblim [TM]
		Drifloon [TM]	Dugtrio [TM]	Dunsparce [TM]	Ekans [TM]	Electrike [TM]	Electrode [TM]
		Exeggcute [TM]	Exeggutor [TM]	Farfetch'd [TM]	Fearow [TM]	Fennekin [TM]	Fletchinder [TM]
		Fletchling [TM]	Froakie [TM]	Frogadier [TM]	Furret [TM]	Gallade [TM]	Garbodor [TM]
		Gardevoir [TM]	Gastly [TM]	Gengar [TM]	Gligar [TM]	Gliscor [TM]	Golbat [TM]
		Golett [TM]	Golurk [TM]	Gothita [TM]	Gothitelle [TM]	Gothorita [TM]	Gourgeist [TM]
		Granbull [TM]	Greninja [TM]	Grumpig [TM]	Haunter [TM]	Heatmor [TM]	Heracross [TM]
		Honchkrow [TM]	Hoothoot [TM]	Houndoom [TM]	Houndour [TM]	Hydreigon [TM]	Illumise [TM]
		Inkay [TM]	Jynx [TM]	Kadabra [TM]	Kangaskhan [TM]	Kecleon [1, TM]	Kirlia [TM]
		Klefki [TM, E]	Krokorok [TM]	Krookodile [TM]	Lampent [TM]	Ledian [TM]	Ledyba [TM]
		Lickilicky [TM]	Lickitung [TM]	Liepard [TM]	Linoone [TM]	Litleo [TM]	Litwick [TM]
		Lombre [TM]	Lotad [TM]	Ludicolo [TM]	Machamp [TM]	Machoke [TM]	Machop [TM]
		Malamar [TM]	Manectric [TM]	Marowak [TM]	Masquerain [TM]	Mightyena [57, TM]	Mime Jr. [TM]
		Mothim [TM]	Mr. Mime [TM]	Murkrow [TM]	Nidoking [TM]	Nidoqueen [TM]	Nidoran♂ [TM]
		Nidoran♀ [TM]	Nidorina [TM]	Nidorino [TM]	Ninjask [TM]	Noctowl [TM]	Noibat [TM]
		Noivern [TM]	Octillery [TM]	Pangoro [TM]	Panpour [TM]	Pansage [TM]	Pansear [TM]
		Pawniard [TM]	Pelipper [TM]	Phantump [TM]	Pidgeot [TM]	Pidgeotto [TM]	Pidgey [TM]
		Pinsir [TM]	Politoed [TM]	Poliwag [TM]	Poliwhirl [TM]	Poliwrath [TM]	Poochyena [TM]
		Pumpkaboo [TM]	Purrloin [TM]	Pyroar [TM]	Quagsire [TM]	Raichu [TM]	Ralts [TM]
		Remoraid [TM]	Rhydon [TM]	Rhyhorn [TM]	Rhyperior [TM]	Rotom (Fan) [TM]	Rotom (Frost) [TM]
		Rotom (Heat) [TM]	Rotom (Mow) [TM]	Rotom (Wash) [TM]	Rotom [TM]	Sableye [TM]	Sandile [TM]
		Sandshrew [TM]	Sandslash [TM]	Scizor [TM]	Scrafty [TM]	Scyther [TM]	Sentret [TM]
		Seviper [TM]	Sharpedo [TM]	Shedinja [TM]	Shuppet [TM]	Sigilyph [TM]	Simipour [TM]
		Simisage [TM]	Simisear [TM]	Skarmory [TM]	Skorupi [TM]	Skuntank [TM]	Slurpuff [TM]
		Smoochum [TM]	Sneasel [TM]	Snubbull [TM]	Spearow [TM]	Spinarak [TM]	Spinda [TM]
		Spoink [TM]	Staraptor [TM]	Staravia [TM]	Starly [TM]	Stunky [TM]	Sudowoodo [TM]
		Surskit [TM]	Swablu [TM]	Swellow [TM]	Swirlix [TM]	Swoobat [TM]	Taillow [TM]
		Talonflame [TM]	Teddiursa [TM]	Tentacool [TM]	Tentacruel [TM]	Toxicroak [TM]	Trevenant [TM]
		Trubbish [TM]	Ursaring [TM]	Vespiquen [TM]	Victreebel [TM]	Vivillon [TM]	Volbeat [TM]
		Voltorb [TM]	Weavile [TM]	Weepinbell [TM]	Wingull [TM]	Woobat [TM]	Wormadam (Plant) [TM]
		Wormadam (Sand) [TM]	Wormadam (Trash) [TM]	Yanma [TM]	Yanmega [TM]	Yveltal [TM]	Zangoose [TM]
		Zigzagoon [TM]	Zoroark [TM]	Zorua [TM]	Zubat [TM]	Zweilous [TM]	

	Move	Pokémon that can learn it					
Normal	Thrash	Bagon [E]	Barboach [E]	Basculin [1, 56]	Beartic [1, 59]	Carvanha [E]	Cubchoo [53]
		Cubone [31]	Dodrio [60]	Doduo [50]	Gible [E]	Gyarados [1]	Krokorok [52]
		Larvitar [28]	Mamoswine [41]	Marowak [33]	Nidoking [35]	Piloswine [41]	Pinsir [36]
		Pupitar [28]	Sandile [46]	Spinda [50]	Tauros [50]	Teddiursa [50]	Tyranitar [28]
		Tyrantrum [42]	Tyrunt [40]	Ursaring [58]	Wailmer [E]		
Electric	Thunder Fang	Aerodactyl [1]	Arbok [1]	Deino [E]	Drapion [1]	Druddigon [E]	Durant [E]
		Electrike [33, E]	Exploud [1]	Gliscor [1]	Granbull [1]	Hippowdon [1]	Houndoom [1]
		Houndour [E]	Jolteon [20]	Manectric [37]	Mawile [E]	Poochyena [E]	Rhyhorn [E]
		Salamence [1]	Sandile [E]	Snubbull [1, 8]	Steelix [1]	Tyranitar [1]	Tyrunt [E]
	Thunder Punch	Abra [E]	Ampharos [30]	Dragonite [1]	Gastly [E]	Machop [E]	Medicham [1]
		Meditite [E]	Pichu [E]	Scraggy [E]			
	Thunder Shock	Ampharos [1, 8]	Dedenne [7]	Emolga [1]	Flaaffy [1, 8]	Helioptile [6]	Jolteon [9]
		Magnemite [7]	Magneton [1, 7]	Magnezone [7]	Mareep [8]	Pichu [1]	Pikachu [1]
		Raichu [1]	Rotom (Fan) [1]	Rotom (Frost) [1]	Rotom (Heat) [1]	Rotom (Mow) [1]	Rotom (Wash) [1]
		Rotom [1]	Stunfisk [9]	Zapdos [1]			
	Thunder (TM25)	Absol [TM]	Aggron [TM]	Ampharos [62, TM]	Aromatisse [TM]	Audino [TM]	Aurorus [TM]
		Banette [TM]	Bibarel [TM]	Bidoof [TM]	Chinchou [TM]	Dedenne [45, TM]	Delcatty [TM]
		Dragalge [TM]	Dragonair [TM]	Dragonite [TM]	Dratini [TM]	Drifblim [TM]	Drifloon [TM]
		Dunsparce [TM]	Duosion [TM]	Electrike [52, TM]	Electrode [TM]	Emolga [TM]	Ferrothorn [TM]
		Flaaffy [56, TM]	Furret [TM]	Gengar [TM]	Goodra [TM]	Granbull [TM]	Gyarados [TM]
		Heliolisk [1, TM]	Helioptile [TM]	Illumise [TM]	Jigglypuff [TM]	Jolteon [45, TM]	Kangaskhan [TM]
		Kecleon [TM]	Lanturn [TM]	Lapras [TM]	Lickilicky [TM]	Lickitung [TM]	Linoone [TM]
		Magnemite [TM]	Magneton [TM]	Magnezone [TM]	Manectric [66, TM]	Mareep [46, TM]	Mewtwo [TM]
		Miltank [TM]	Mime Jr. [TM]	Minun [42, TM]	Mr. Mime [TM]	Munchlax [TM]	Nidoking [TM]
		Nidoqueen [TM]	Nidoran♀ [TM]	Nidoran♂ [TM]	Nidorina [TM]	Nidorino [TM]	Nosepass [TM]
		Pachirisu [TM]	Pichu [TM]	Pikachu [50, TM]	Pluse [42, TM]	Probopass [TM]	Raichu [TM]
		Reuniclus [TM]	Rhydon [TM]	Rhyhorn [TM]	Rhyperior [TM]	Rotom (Fan) [TM]	Rotom (Frost) [TM]
		Rotom (Heat) [TM]	Rotom (Mow) [TM]	Rotom (Wash) [TM]	Rotom [TM]	Shuppet [TM]	Skitty [TM]
		Snorlax [TM]	Snubbull [TM]	Solosis [TM]	Starmie [TM]	Staryu [TM]	Stunfisk [TM]
		Tauros [TM]	Tyranitar [TM]	Volbeat [TM]	Voltorb [TM]	Watchog [TM]	Wigglytuff [TM]
		Xerneas [TM]	Zangoose [TM]	Zapdos [78, TM]	Zigzagoon [TM]		
	Thunder Wave (TM73)	Abra [TM]	Absol [TM]	Aggron [TM]	Alakazam [TM]	Amaura [5, TM]	Ampharos [1, 4, TM]
		Audino [TM]	Aurorus [TM]	Banette [TM]	Bibarel [TM]	Bidoof [TM]	Bisharp [TM]
		Chimecho [TM]	Chinchou [6, TM]	Chingling [TM]	Dedenne [23, TM]	Deino [TM]	Delcatty [TM]
		Dragonair [1, 5, TM]	Dragonite [1, 5, TM]	Dratini [5, TM]	Drifblim [TM]	Drifloon [TM]	Dunsparce [TM]
		Duosion [TM]	Durant [TM]	Electrike [4, TM]	Electrode [TM]	Emolga [TM]	Espurr [TM]
		Ferroseed [TM]	Ferrothorn [TM]	Flaaffy [1, 4, TM]	Furfrou [TM]	Gallade [TM]	Gardevoir [TM]
		Gothita [TM]	Gothitelle [TM]	Gothorita [TM]	Granbull [TM]	Grumpig [TM]	Gyarados [TM]
		Heliolisk [TM]	Helioptile [31, TM]	Honchkrow [TM]	Hydreigon [TM]	Igglybuff [TM]	Illumise [TM]
		Jigglypuff [TM]	Jolteon [33, TM]	Kadabra [TM]	Kecleon [TM]	Kirlia [TM]	Klefki [TM]
		Lanturn [1, 6, TM]	Liepard [TM]	Linoone [TM]	Magnemite [15, TM]	Magneton [15, TM]	Magnezone [15, TM]
		Manectric [1, 4, TM]	Mareep [4, TM]	Meowstic (Female) [TM]	Meowstic (Male) [TM]	Mewtwo [TM]	Miltank [TM]
		Mime Jr. [TM]	Minun [3, TM]	Mr. Mime [TM]	Murkrow [TM]	Nosepass [15, TM]	Octillery [TM]
		Pachirisu [33, TM]	Pawniard [TM]	Pichu [13, TM]	Pikachu [13, TM]	Pluse [3, TM]	Probopass [15, TM]
		Purrloin [TM]	Qwilfish [TM]	Raichu [TM]	Ralts [TM]	Remoraid [TM]	Reuniclus [TM]
		Rotom (Fan) [1, TM]	Rotom (Frost) [1, TM]	Rotom (Heat) [1, TM]	Rotom (Mow) [1, TM]	Rotom (Wash) [1, TM]	Rotom [1, TM]
		Shuppet [TM]	Sigilyph [TM]	Skitty [TM]	Slowbro [TM]	Slowking [TM]	Slowpoke [TM]
		Snubbull [TM]	Solosis [TM]	Spoink [TM]	Starmie [TM]	Staryu [TM]	Stunfisk [TM]
		Swoobat [TM]	Tyranitar [TM]	Volbeat [TM]	Voltorb [TM]	Watchog [TM]	Wigglytuff [TM]
		Woobat [TM]	Xerneas [TM]	Zapdos [8, TM]	Zigzagoon [TM]	Zweilous [TM]	
	Thunderbolt (TM24)	Absol [TM]	Aggron [TM]	Amaura [TM]	Ampharos [TM]	Aromatisse [TM]	Audino [TM]
		Aurorus [TM]	Banette [TM]	Bibarel [TM]	Bidoof [TM]	Chinchou [TM]	Dedenne [TM]
		Delcatty [TM]	Dragalge [TM]	Dragonair [TM]	Dragonite [TM]	Dratini [TM]	Drifblim [TM]
		Drifloon [TM]	Dunsparce [TM]	Electrike [TM]	Electrode [TM]	Emolga [TM]	Espurr [TM]
		Ferroseed [TM]	Ferrothorn [TM]	Flaaffy [TM]	Furret [TM]	Gallade [TM]	Garbodor [TM]
		Gardevoir [TM]	Gastly [TM]	Gengar [TM]	Golurk [TM]	Goodra [TM]	Goomy [TM]
		Gothita [TM]	Gothitelle [TM]	Gothorita [TM]	Granbull [TM]	Gyarados [TM]	Haunter [TM]
		Heliolisk [TM]	Helioptile [49, TM]	Illumise [TM]	Inkay [TM]	Jigglypuff [TM]	Jolteon [TM]
		Kangaskhan [TM]	Kecleon [TM]	Kirlia [TM]	Lanturn [TM]	Lapras [TM]	Lickilicky [TM]
		Lickitung [TM]	Linoone [TM]	Magnemite [TM]	Magneton [TM]	Magnezone [TM]	Malamar [TM]
		Manectric [TM]	Mareep [TM]	Meowstic (Female) [TM]	Meowstic (Male) [TM]	Mewtwo [TM]	Miltank [TM]
		Mime Jr. [TM]	Minun [TM]	Mr. Mime [TM]	Munchlax [TM]	Nidoking [TM]	Nidoqueen [TM]
		Nidoran♀ [TM]	Nidoran♂ [TM]	Nidorina [TM]	Nidorino [TM]	Nosepass [TM]	Pachirisu [TM]
		Patrat [TM]	Pichu [TM]	Pikachu [29, TM]	Pluse [TM]	Probopass [TM]	Raichu [1, TM]
		Ralts [TM]	Rhydon [TM]	Rhyhorn [TM]	Rhyperior [TM]	Rotom (Fan) [TM]	Rotom (Frost) [TM]
		Rotom (Heat) [TM]	Rotom (Mow) [TM]	Rotom (Wash) [TM]	Rotom [TM]	Sentret [TM]	Shuppet [TM]
		Skitty [TM]	Skrelp [TM]	Sliggoo [TM]	Slurpuff [TM]	Snorlax [TM]	Snubbull [TM]
		Spritzee [TM]	Starmie [TM]	Staryu [TM]	Stunfisk [45, TM]	Swirlix [TM]	Tauros [TM]
		Tyranitar [TM]	Volbeat [TM]	Voltorb [TM]	Watchog [TM]	Wigglytuff [TM]	Xerneas [TM]
		Zangoose [TM]	Zapdos [TM]	Zigzagoon [TM]			

Pokémon Moves Reverse Lookup

Move	Pokémon that can learn it					
Normal						
Tickle	Alomomola [E]	Azurill [E]	Bellsprout [E]	Binacle [E]	Eevee [E]	Emolga [E]
	Gothita [7]	Gothitelle [1, 7]	Gothorita [1, 7]	Heatmor [E]	Lapras [E]	Lotad [E]
	Machop [E]	Mawile [E]	Mime Jr. [1]	Oddish [E]	Panpour [E]	Pansage [E]
	Pansear [E]	Pichu [E]	Skitty [E]	Tentacool [E]	Wailmer [E]	Whiscash [1]
	Zigzagoon [E]					
Dark						
Topsy-Turvy	Inkay [15]	Malamar [15]				
Torment (TM41)	Abra [TM]	Absol [TM]	Aerodactyl [TM]	Alakazam [TM]	Arbok [TM]	Aromatisse [TM]
	Banette [TM]	Barbaracle [TM]	Binacle [TM]	Bisharp [1, 14, TM]	Bunnelby [TM]	Carvanha [TM]
	Chatot [TM]	Chimecho [TM]	Chingling [TM]	Cloyster [TM]	Croagunk [TM]	Crobat [TM]
	Deino [TM]	Diggersby [TM]	Dodrio [TM]	Drapion [TM]	Druddigon [TM]	Ekans [TM]
	Electrode [TM]	Espurr [TM]	Exploud [TM]	Floatzel [TM]	Gallade [TM]	Gardevoir [TM]
	Gastly [TM]	Gengar [TM]	Gligar [TM]	Gliscor [TM]	Golbat [TM]	Gothita [TM]
	Gothitelle [TM]	Gothorita [TM]	Granbull [TM]	Grumpig [TM]	Gyarados [TM]	Haunter [TM]
	Hawlucha [TM]	Honchkrow [TM]	Houndoom [TM]	Houndour [TM]	Hydreigon [TM]	Inkay [TM]
	Jynx [TM]	Kadabra [TM]	Kirlia [TM]	Klefki [32, TM]	Krokorok [10, TM]	Krookodile [10, TM]
	Larvitar [TM]	Liepard [19, TM]	Loudred [TM]	Malamar [TM]	Mawile [TM]	Meowstic (Female) [TM]
	Meowstic (Male) [TM]	Mewtwo [TM]	Mightyena [TM]	Mime Jr. [TM]	Mr. Mime [TM]	Murkrow [61, TM]
	Nidoking [TM]	Nidoqueen [TM]	Noibat [TM]	Noivern [TM]	Nosepass [TM]	Onix [TM]
	Pancham [TM]	Pangoro [TM]	Panpour [TM]	Pansage [25, TM]	Pansear [TM]	Pawniard [14, TM]
	Poochyena [TM]	Probopass [TM]	Pupitar [TM]	Purrloin [19, TM]	Ralts [TM]	Sableye [TM]
	Sandile [10, TM]	Scrafty [TM]	Scraggy [TM]	Sharpedo [TM]	Shuppet [TM]	Simipour [TM]
	Simisage [TM]	Simisear [TM]	Skarmory [TM]	Skorupi [TM]	Skuntank [TM]	Sneasel [TM]
	Snubbull [TM]	Spoink [TM]	Spritzee [TM]	Steelix [TM]	Stunky [TM]	Sudowoodo [TM]
	Swoobat [TM]	Teddiursa [TM]	Toxicroak [TM]	Tyranitar [TM]	Umbreon [TM]	Ursaring [TM]
	Voltorb [TM]	Weavile [TM]	Woobat [TM]	Yveltal [TM]	Zoroark [34, TM]	Zorua [33, TM]
	Zubat [TM]	Zweilous [TM]				
Poison						
Toxic Spikes	Beedrill [25]	Cloyster [1]	Drapion [34]	Froakie [E]	Garbodor [1, 7]	Nidoran♀ [31]
	Nidoran♂ [31]	Nidorina [35]	Nidorino [35]	Qwilfish [21]	Roselia [28]	Skorupi [34]
	Skrelp [E]	Spinarak [E]	Tentacool [15]	Tentacruel [15]	Trubbish [7]	Venipede [E]
Toxic (TM06)	Abomasnow [TM]	Abra [TM]	Absol [TM]	Accelgor [TM]	Aegislash [TM]	Aerodactyl [TM]
	Aggron [TM]	Alakazam [TM]	Alomomola [TM]	Altaria [TM]	Amaura [TM]	Amoonguss [32, TM]
	Ampharos [TM]	Arbok [TM]	Ariados [TM]	Aromatisse [TM]	Aron [TM]	Articuno [TM]
	Audino [TM]	Aurorus [TM]	Avalugg [TM]	Axew [TM]	Azumarill [TM]	Azurill [TM]
	Bagon [TM]	Banette [TM]	Barbaracle [TM]	Barboach [TM]	Basculin [TM]	Beartic [TM]
	Beedrill [TM]	Bellossom [TM]	Bellsprout [TM]	Bergmite [TM]	Bibarel [TM]	Bidoof [TM]
	Binacle [TM]	Bisharp [TM]	Blastoise [TM]	Boldore [TM]	Bonsly [TM]	Braixen [TM]
	Budew [TM]	Buizel [TM]	Bulbasaur [TM]	Bunnelby [TM]	Butterfree [TM]	Carbink [TM]
	Carnivine [TM]	Carvanha [TM]	Chandelure [TM]	Charizard [TM]	Charmander [TM]	Charmeleon [TM]
	Chatot [TM]	Chesnaught [TM]	Chespin [TM]	Chimecho [TM]	Chinchou [TM]	Chingling [TM]
	Clamperl [TM]	Clauncher [TM]	Clawitzer [TM]	Cloyster [TM]	Conkeldurr [TM]	Corphish [TM]
	Corsola [TM]	Crawdaunt [TM]	Croagunk [TM]	Crobat [TM]	Crustle [TM]	Cryogonal [TM]
	Cubchoo [TM]	Cubone [TM]	Dedenne [TM]	Deino [TM]	Delcatty [TM]	Delibird [TM]
	Delphox [TM]	Diggersby [TM]	Diglett [TM]	Dodrio [TM]	Doduo [TM]	Doublade [TM]
	Dragalge [32, TM]	Dragonair [TM]	Dragonite [TM]	Drapion [TM]	Dratini [TM]	Drifblim [TM]
	Drifloon [TM]	Druddigon [TM]	Ducklett [TM]	Dugtrio [TM]	Dunsparce [TM]	Duosion [TM]
	Durant [TM]	Dwebble [TM]	Eevee [TM]	Ekans [TM]	Electrike [TM]	Electrode [TM]
	Emolga [TM]	Escavalier [TM]	Espeon [TM]	Espurr [TM]	Exeggcute [TM]	Exeggutor [TM]
	Exploud [TM]	Farfetch'd [TM]	Fearow [TM]	Fennekin [TM]	Ferroseed [TM]	Ferrothorn [TM]
	Flaaffy [TM]	Flabébé [TM]	Flareon [TM]	Fletchinder [TM]	Fletchling [TM]	Floatzel [TM]
	Floette [TM]	Florges [TM]	Flygon [TM]	Foongus [32, TM]	Fraxure [TM]	Froakie [TM]
	Frogadier [TM]	Furfrou [TM]	Furret [TM]	Gabite [TM]	Gallade [TM]	Garbodor [39, TM]
	Garchomp [TM]	Gardevoir [TM]	Gastly [TM]	Gengar [TM]	Geodude [TM]	Gible [TM]
	Gigalith [TM]	Glaceon [TM]	Gligar [TM]	Gliscor [TM]	Gloom [TM]	Gogoat [TM]
	Golbat [TM]	Goldeen [TM]	Golduck [TM]	Golem [TM]	Golett [TM]	Golurk [TM]
	Goodra [TM]	Goomy [TM]	Gorebyss [TM]	Gothita [TM]	Gothitelle [TM]	Gothorita [TM]
	Gourgeist [TM]	Granbull [TM]	Graveler [TM]	Greninja [TM]	Grumpig [TM]	Gulpin [28, TM]
	Gurdurr [TM]	Gyarados [TM]	Hariyama [TM]	Haunter [TM]	Hawlucha [TM]	Haxorus [TM]
	Heatmor [TM]	Helioptile [TM]	Heracross [TM]	Hippopotas [TM]	Hippowdon [TM]	Horsea [TM]
	Honchkrow [TM]	Honedge [TM]	Hoothoot [TM]	Hoppip [TM]	Houndoom [TM]	Houndour [TM]
	Houndour [TM]	Huntail [TM]	Hydreigon [TM]	Igglybuff [TM]	Illumise [TM]	Inkay [TM]
	Ivysaur [TM]	Jigglypuff [TM]	Jolteon [TM]	Jumpluff [TM]	Jynx [TM]	Kadabra [TM]
	Kangaskhan [TM]	Karrablast [TM]	Kecleon [TM]	Kingdra [TM]	Kirlia [TM]	Klefki [TM]
	Krokorok [TM]	Krookodile [TM]	Lairon [TM]	Lampent [TM]	Lanturn [TM]	Lapras [TM]
	Larvitar [TM]	Leafeon [TM]	Ledian [TM]	Ledyba [TM]	Lickilicky [TM]	Lickitung [TM]
	Liepard [TM]	Linoone [TM]	Litleo [TM]	Litwick [TM]	Lombre [TM]	Lotad [TM]
	Loudred [TM]	Lucario [TM]	Ludicolo [TM]	Lunatone [TM]	Luvdisc [TM]	Machamp [TM]
	Machoke [TM]	Machop [TM]	Magcargo [TM]	Magnemite [TM]	Magneton [TM]	Magnezone [TM]
	Makuhita [TM]	Malamar [TM]	Mamoswine [TM]	Manectric [TM]	Mantine [TM]	Mantyke [TM]
	Mareep [TM]	Marill [TM]	Marowak [TM]	Masquerain [TM]	Mawile [TM]	Medicham [TM]
	Meditite [TM]	Meowstic (Female) [TM]	Meowstic (Male) [TM]	Mewtwo [TM]	Mienfoo [TM]	Mienshao [TM]
	Mightyena [TM]	Miltank [TM]	Mime Jr. [TM]	Minun [TM]	Moltres [TM]	Mothim [TM]
	Mr. Mime [TM]	Munchlax [TM]	Murkrow [TM]	Nidoking [TM]	Nidoqueen [TM]	Nidoran♀ [TM]

Type	Move	Pokémon that can learn it					
Poison	Toxic (TM06)	Nidoran♂ [TM]	Nidorina [TM]	Nidorino [TM]	Nincada [TM]	Ninjask [TM]	Noctowl [TM]
		Noibat [TM]	Noivern [TM]	Nosepass [TM]	Octillery [TM]	Oddish [TM]	Onix [TM]
		Pachirisu [TM]	Pancham [TM]	Pangoro [TM]	Panpour [TM]	Pansage [TM]	Pansear [TM]
		Patrat [TM]	Pawniard [TM]	Pelipper [TM]	Phantump [TM]	Pichu [TM]	Pidgeot [TM]
		Pidgeotto [TM]	Pidgey [TM]	Pikachu [TM]	Piloswine [TM]	Pinsir [TM]	Pluse [TM]
		Politoed [TM]	Poliwag [TM]	Poliwhirl [TM]	Poliwrath [TM]	Poochyena [TM]	Probopass [TM]
		Psyduck [TM]	Pumpkaboo [TM]	Pupitar [TM]	Purrloin [TM]	Pyroar [TM]	Quagsire [TM]
		Quilladin [TM]	Qwilfish [TM]	Raichu [TM]	Ralts [TM]	Relicanth [TM]	Remoraid [TM]
		Reuniclus [TM]	Rhydon [TM]	Rhyhorn [TM]	Rhyperior [TM]	Riolu [TM]	Roggenrola [TM]
		Roselia [40, TM]	Roserade [TM]	Rotom (Fan) [TM]	Rotom (Frost) [TM]	Rotom (Heat) [TM]	Rotom (Mow) [TM]
		Rotom (Wash) [TM]	Rotom [TM]	Sableye [TM]	Salamence [TM]	Sandile [TM]	Sandshrew [TM]
		Sandslash [TM]	Sawk [TM]	Scizor [TM]	Scolipede [44, TM]	Scrafty [TM]	Scraggy [TM]
		Scyther [TM]	Seadra [TM]	Seaking [TM]	Sentret [TM]	Seviper [TM]	Sharpedo [TM]
		Shedinja [TM]	Shelgon [TM]	Shellder [TM]	Shelmet [TM]	Shuckle [TM]	Shuppet [TM]
		Sigilyph [TM]	Simipour [TM]	Simisage [TM]	Simisear [TM]	Skarmory [TM]	Skiddo [TM]
		Skiploom [TM]	Skitty [TM]	Skorupi [TM]	Skrelp [32, TM]	Skuntank [27, TM]	Sliggoo [TM]
		Slowbro [TM]	Slowking [TM]	Slowpoke [TM]	Slugma [TM]	Slurpuff [TM]	Smoochum [TM]
		Sneasel [TM]	Snorlax [TM]	Snover [TM]	Snubbull [TM]	Solosis [TM]	Solrock [TM]
		Spearow [TM]	Spinarak [TM]	Spinda [TM]	Spoink [TM]	Spritzee [TM]	Squirtle [TM]
		Staraptor [TM]	Staravia [TM]	Starly [TM]	Starmie [TM]	Staryu [TM]	Steelix [TM]
		Stunfisk [TM]	Stunky [27, TM]	Sudowoodo [TM]	Surskit [TM]	Swablu [TM]	Swalot [30, TM]
		Swanna [TM]	Swellow [TM]	Swinub [TM]	Swirlix [TM]	Swoobat [TM]	Sylveon [TM]
		Taillow [TM]	Talonflame [TM]	Tauros [TM]	Teddiursa [TM]	Tentacool [TM]	Tentacruel [TM]
		Throh [TM]	Timburr [TM]	Torkoal [TM]	Toxicroak [TM]	Trapinch [TM]	Trevenant [TM]
		Trubbish [36, TM]	Tyranitar [TM]	Tyrantrum [TM]	Tyrunt [TM]	Umbreon [TM]	Ursaring [TM]
		Vanillish [TM]	Vanillite [TM]	Vanilluxe [TM]	Vaporeon [TM]	Venipede [36, TM]	Venusaur [TM]
		Vespiquen [33, TM]	Vibrava [TM]	Victreebel [TM]	Vileplume [TM]	Vivillon [TM]	Volbeat [TM]
		Voltorb [TM]	Wailmer [TM]	Wailord [TM]	Wartortle [TM]	Watchog [TM]	Weavile [TM]
		Weepinbell [TM]	Whirlipede [41, TM]	Whiscash [TM]	Whismur [TM]	Wigglytuff [TM]	Wingull [TM]
		Woobat [TM]	Wooper [TM]	Wormadam (Plant) [TM]	Wormadam (Sand) [TM]	Wormadam (Trash) [TM]	Xerneas [TM]
		Yanma [TM]	Yanmega [TM]	Yveltal [TM]	Zangoose [TM]	Zapdos [TM]	Zigzagoon [TM]
		Zoroark [TM]	Zorua [TM]	Zubat [TM]	Zweilous [TM]	Zygarde [TM]	
Normal	Transform	Ditto [1]					
Normal	Tri Attack	Dodrio [34]	Dugtrio [1]	Hydreigon [1]	Magneton [1]	Spearow [E]	
Psychic	Trick	Alakazam [50]	Banette [58]	Espurr [E]	Gourgeist [1]	Kadabra [50]	Kecleon [E]
		Mime Jr. [36, E]	Mr. Mime [36, E]	Pumpkaboo [1]	Rotom (Fan) [1]	Rotom (Frost) [1]	Rotom (Heat) [1]
		Rotom (Mow) [1]	Rotom (Wash) [1]	Rotom [1]	Sableye [E]	Sentret [E]	Shuppet [50]
		Solosis [E]	Spinda [E]	Spoink [E]	Volbeat [E]	Zigzagoon [E]	
Psychic	Trick Room (TM92)	Abra [TM]	Alakazam [TM]	Aromatisse [TM]	Audino [TM]	Banette [TM]	Carbink [TM]
		Chandelure [TM]	Chimecho [TM]	Chingling [TM]	Delphox [TM]	Duosion [TM]	Espeon [TM]
		Espurr [TM]	Exeggcute [TM]	Exeggutor [TM]	Gallade [TM]	Gardevoir [TM]	Gastly [TM]
		Gengar [TM]	Gothita [TM]	Gothitelle [TM]	Gothorita [TM]	Grumpig [TM]	Haunter [TM]
		Inkay [TM]	Jynx [TM]	Kadabra [TM]	Kecleon [TM]	Kirlia [TM]	
		Lampent [TM]	Litwick [TM]	Lunatone [TM]	Malamar [TM]	Meowstic (Female) [TM]	Meowstic (Male) [TM]
		Mewtwo [TM]	Mime Jr. [TM]	Mr. Mime [TM]	Phantump [TM]	Pumpkaboo [TM]	Ralts [TM]
		Reuniclus [TM]	Shuppet [TM]	Sigilyph [TM]	Slowbro [TM]	Slowking [TM]	Slowpoke [TM]
		Smoochum [TM]	Solosis [TM]	Solrock [TM]	Spinda [TM]	Spoink [TM]	Spritzee [TM]
		Starmie [TM]	Swoobat [TM]	Trevenant [TM]	Woobat [TM]		
Ghost	Trick-or-Treat	Gourgeist [6, 23, 40, 63]	Pumpkaboo [6, 23, 40]				
Normal	Trump Card	Corphish [E]	Dunsparce [E]	Eevee [45]	Farfetch'd [E]	Kangaskhan [E]	Minun [51]
		Slowking [49]					
Bug	Twineedle	Beedrill [16]	Escavalier [1, 13]	Shellder [E]	Skorupi [E]	Spinarak [E]	Venipede [E]
Dragon	Twister	Bagon [E]	Dragalge [1, 67]	Dragonair [1, 11]	Dragonite [1, 11]	Dratini [11]	Gible [E]
		Gyarados [29]	Horsea [26]	Kingdra [26]	Mantine [E]	Mantyke [E]	Pidgeot [22]
		Pidgeotto [22]	Pidgey [21]	Seadra [26]	Wingull [E]		

U

Type	Move	Pokémon that can learn it					
Normal	Uproar	Basculin [4]	Chatot [45]	Chimecho [17]	Chingling [17]	Diglett [E]	Dodrio [23]
		Doduo [23]	Electrike [E]	Exeggcute [1]	Exploud [1, 5]	Gothita [E]	Hoothoot [13]
		Kangaskhan [E]	Lombre [37]	Loudred [1, 5]	Noctowl [13]	Pidgey [E]	Rotom (Fan) [8]
		Rotom (Frost) [8]	Rotom (Heat) [8]	Rotom (Mow) [8]	Rotom (Wash) [8]	Rotom [8]	Sandile [E]
		Skitty [E]	Spearow [E]	Spinda [5]	Starly [E]	Vanillish [1, 10]	Vanillite [10]
		Vanilluxe [1, 10]	Whismur [5]	Yanma [27]	Yanmega [27]		

AFTER THE HALL OF FAME

CENTRAL KALOS

COASTAL KALOS

MOUNTAIN KALOS

ADVENTURE DATA

	Move	Pokémon that can learn it					
Bug	U-turn (TM89)	Accelgor [40, TM]	Articuno [TM]	Beedrill [TM]	Bunnelby [TM]	Butterfree [TM]	Chatot [TM]
		Clauncher [TM]	Clawitzer [TM]	Crobat [TM]	Dedenne [TM]	Diggersby [TM]	Emolga [TM]
		Farfetch'd [TM]	Fearow [TM]	Fletchinder [TM]	Fletchling [TM]	Flygon [TM]	Froakie [TM]
		Frogadier [TM]	Furfrou [TM]	Furret [TM]	Gligar [30, TM]	Gliscor [30, TM]	Golbat [TM]
		Greninja [TM]	Hawlucha [TM]	Heliolisk [TM]	Helioptile [TM]	Hoppip [37, TM]	Hydreigon [TM]
		Illumise [TM]	Jumpluff [49, TM]	Ledian [TM]	Ledyba [TM]	Liepard [TM]	Masquerain [TM]
		Mienfoo [41, TM]	Mienshao [41, TM]	Moltres [TM]	Mothim [TM]	Ninjask [TM]	Noibat [TM]
		Noivern [TM]	Pachirisu [TM]	Pelipper [TM]	Pidgeot [TM]	Pidgeotto [TM]	Pidgey [TM]
		Purrloin [TM]	Scizor [TM]	Scyther [TM]	Sentret [TM]	Skiploom [44, TM]	Spearow [TM]
		Staraptor [TM]	Staravia [TM]	Starly [TM]	Swellow [TM]	Swoobat [TM]	Taillow [TM]
		Talonflame [TM]	Vespiquen [TM]	Vibrava [TM]	Vivillon [TM]	Volbeat [TM]	Wingull [TM]
		Woobat [TM]	Yanma [49, TM]	Yanmega [49, TM]	Yveltal [TM]	Zapdos [TM]	Zoroark [1, TM]
		Zorua [TM]	Zubat [TM]				

V

	Move	Pokémon that can learn it					
Fighting	Vacuum Wave	Croagunk [E]	Riolu [E]	Scyther [1]			
Poison	Venom Drench	Ariados [1]	Gulpin [E]	Nidoran ♀ [E]	Nidoran ♂ [E]	Phantump [E]	Roserade [1]
		Scolipede [47]	Seviper [28]	Skrelp [E]	Whirlipede [43]	Woobat [E]	Zubat [E]
Poison	Venoshock (TM09)	Accelgor [TM]	Amoonguss [TM]	Arbok [TM]	Ariados [TM]	Beedrill [TM]	Bellossom [TM]
		Bellsprout [TM]	Budew [TM]	Bulbasaur [TM]	Butterfree [TM]	Clauncher [TM]	Clawitzer [TM]
		Croagunk [36, TM]	Crobat [TM]	Dragalge [TM]	Drapion [27, TM]	Ekans [TM]	Foongus [TM]
		Garbodor [TM]	Gastly [TM]	Gengar [TM]	Gligar [TM]	Gliscor [TM]	Gloom [TM]
		Golbat [TM]	Gulpin [TM]	Haunter [TM]	Heracross [TM]	Ivysaur [TM]	Mothim [TM]
		Nidoking [TM]	Nidoqueen [TM]	Nidoran ♀ [TM]	Nidoran ♂ [TM]	Nidorina [TM]	Nidorino [TM]
		Oddish [TM]	Qwilfish [TM]	Roselia [TM]	Roserade [TM]	Scizor [TM]	Scolipede [28, TM]
		Seviper [20, TM]	Shelmet [TM]	Shuckle [TM]	Skorupi [27, TM]	Skrelp [TM]	Skuntank [TM]
		Spinarak [TM]	Stunky [TM]	Swalot [TM]	Tentacool [TM]	Tentacruel [TM]	Toxicroak [36, TM]
		Trubbish [TM]	Venipede [26, 38, TM]	Venusaur [TM]	Vespiquen [TM]	Victreebel [TM]	Vileplume [TM]
		Weepinbell [TM]	Whirlipede [28, TM]	Wormadam (Plant) [TM]	Wormadam (Sand) [TM]	Wormadam (Trash) [TM]	Zubat [TM]
Normal	Vice Grip	Clauncher [9]	Clawitzer [9]	Corphish [10]	Crawdaunt [1, 10]	Durant [1]	Mawile [21]
		Pinsir [1]					
Grass	Vine Whip	Bellsprout [1]	Bulbasaur [9]	Carnivine [11]	Chesnaught [5]	Chespin [5]	Flabébé [1]
		Floette [1]	Gogoat [7]	Ivysaur [9]	Pansage [10]	Quilladin [5]	Skiddo [7]
		Venusaur [1, 9]	Victreebel [1]	Weepinbell [1]			
Fighting	Vital Throw	Hariyama [10]	Machamp [32]	Machoke [32]	Machop [31]	Makuhita [10]	Mienfoo [E]
		Pancham [27]	Pangoro [27]	Pinsir [22]	Throh [17]		
Electric	Volt Switch (TM72)	Ampharos [TM]	Chinchou [TM]	Dedenne [26, TM]	Electrike [TM]	Electrode [TM]	Emolga [42, TM]
		Flaaffy [TM]	Heliolisk [TM]	Helioptile [40, TM]	Jolteon [TM]	Lanturn [TM]	Magnemite [TM]
		Magneton [TM]	Magnezone [TM]	Manectric [TM]	Minun [TM]	Nosepass [TM]	Pachirisu [TM]
		Pichu [TM]	Pikachu [TM]	Plusle [TM]	Probopass [TM]	Raichu [TM]	Rotom (Fan) [TM]
		Rotom (Frost) [TM]	Rotom (Heat) [TM]	Rotom (Mow) [TM]	Rotom (Wash) [TM]	Rotom [TM]	Voltorb [TM]
		Zapdos [TM]					
	Volt Tackle	Pichu [E] ◆					

W

	Move	Pokémon that can learn it					
Fighting	Wake-Up Slap	Alomomola [29]	Conkeldurr [20]	Croagunk [E]	Gurdurr [20]	Hariyama [42]	Jigglypuff [41]
		Jynx [33]	Karrablast [E]	Machamp [40]	Machoke [40]	Machop [37]	Makuhita [34, E]
		Miltank [50]	Mime Jr. [E]	Mr. Mime [E]	Poliwag [35]	Poliwhirl [43]	Skitty [32]
		Smoochum [E]	Timburr [20]				
Water	Water Gun	Azumarill [29]	Azurill [1]	Barbaracle [4]	Barboach [10]	Basculin [1]	Bibarel [15]
		Binacle [4]	Blastoise [1, 7]	Buizel [15]	Chinchou [1]	Clamperl [1]	Clauncher [1]
		Clawitzer [1]	Dragalge [1]	Ducklett [1]	Floatzel [15]	Golduck [1, 8]	Horsea [1]
		Kingdra [1]	Lanturn [1]	Lapras [1]	Lotad [E]	Luvdisc [7]	Marill [1]
		Octillery [1]	Panpour [10]	Pelipper [1]	Poliwag [5]	Poliwhirl [1, 5]	Psyduck [8]
		Quagsire [1]	Qwilfish [1]	Relicanth [8]	Remoraid [1]	Seadra [1]	Skrelp [1]
		Slowbro [9]	Slowking [9]	Slowpoke [9]	Squirtle [1]	Starmie [1]	Staryu [6]
		Stunfisk [1]	Swanna [9]	Vaporeon [9]	Wailmer [7]	Wailord [1, 7]	Wartortle [1, 7]
		Whiscash [10]	Wingull [1]	Wooper [1]			
	Water Pledge	Blastoise [T]	Froakie [T]	Frogadier [T]	Greninja [T]	Squirtle [T]	Wartortle [T]

◆ To obtain an Egg from which the Pokémon that has learned Volt Tackle will hatch, one of the Pokémon at the Pokémon Day Care needs to be a Pikachu or Raichu holding the Light Ball. Sometimes wild Pikachu are holding this item.

Pokémon Moves Reverse Lookup

AFTER THE HALL OF FAME

CENTRAL KALOS

COASTAL KALOS

MOUNTAIN KALOS

ADVENTURE DATA

Move	Pokémon that can learn it					
Water Pulse	Alomomola [25]	Barboach [22]	Blastoise [28]	Chinchou [E]	Clamperl [E]	Clauncher [34]
	Clawitzer [34]	Corsola [E]	Dragalge [25]	Dratini [E]	Ducklett [13]	Froakie [14]
	Frogadier [14]	Goldeen [17]	Golduck [18]	Gorebyss [15]	Greninja [14]	Horsea [E]
	Huntail [15]	Lapras [14]	Luvdisc [22]	Mantine [19]	Mantyke [19]	Pelipper [17]
	Poliwag [E]	Psyduck [18]	Qwilfish [E]	Remoraid [26, E]	Seaking [17]	Shellder [E]
	Skrelp [25]	Slowbro [28]	Slowking [28]	Slowpoke [28]	Spinda [E]	Squirtle [25]
	Swanna [13]	Tentacool [33]	Tentacruel [34]	Vanillite [E]	Vaporeon [17]	Wailmer [21]
	Wailord [21]	Wartortle [28]	Whiscash [22]	Wingull [17]		
Water Shuriken	Greninja [36, 75]					
Water Sport	Alomomola [1]	Azumarill [1, 5]	Azurill [5, E]	Barboach [6]	Bidoof [E]	Binacle [E]
	Budew [7]	Buizel [E]	Clauncher [7]	Clawitzer [7]	Ducklett [3]	Floatzel [1, 7]
	Froakie [E]	Goldeen [1]	Golduck [E]	Lombre [19]	Luvdisc [E]	Mantine [E]
	Mantyke [E]	Marill [5, E]	Masquerain [1, 19]	Panpour [16]	Pelipper [1]	Poliwag [1, E]
	Poliwhirl [1]	Psyduck [1]	Relicanth [E]	Seaking [1]	Surskit [19]	Swanna [1, 3]
	Whiscash [1, 6]	Wingull [E]				
Water Spout	Remoraid [E]	Squirtle [E]	Wailmer [34]	Wailord [34]		
Waterfall (HM05)	Alomomola [HM]	Azumarill [HM]	Azurill [HM]	Barboach [HM]	Basculin [HM]	Bibarel [HM]
	Blastoise [HM]	Buizel [HM]	Carvanha [HM]	Chinchou [HM]	Clamperl [HM]	Clauncher [HM]
	Clawitzer [HM]	Corphish [HM]	Crawdaunt [HM]	Dragalge [HM]	Dragonair [HM]	Dragonite [HM]
	Dratini [HM]	Floatzel [HM]	Froakie [HM]	Frogadier [HM]	Goldeen [37, HM]	Golduck [HM]
	Gorebyss [HM]	Greninja [HM]	Gyarados [HM]	Horsea [HM]	Huntail [HM]	Kingdra [HM]
	Lanturn [HM]	Lapras [HM]	Lombre [HM]	Ludicolo [HM]	Luvdisc [HM]	Mantine [HM]
	Mantyke [HM]	Marill [HM]	Octillery [HM]	Panpour [HM]	Politoed [HM]	Poliwag [HM]
	Poliwhirl [HM]	Poliwrath [HM]	Psyduck [HM]	Quagsire [HM]	Qwilfish [HM]	Relicanth [HM]
	Remoraid [HM]	Seadra [HM]	Seaking [40, HM]	Sharpedo [HM]	Simipour [HM]	Skrelp [HM]
	Squirtle [HM]	Starmie [HM]	Staryu [HM]	Tentacool [HM]	Tentacruel [HM]	Vaporeon [HM]
	Wailmer [HM]	Wailord [HM]	Wartortle [HM]	Whiscash [HM]	Wooper [HM]	
Weather Ball	Bellsprout [E]	Drifloon [E]	Roserade [1]	Vanilluxe [1]		
Whirlpool	Barboach [E]	Basculin [E]	Buizel [31]	Chinchou [E]	Clamperl [1]	Floatzel [35]
	Gorebyss [1]	Huntail [1]	Lapras [E]	Shellder [40]	Wailmer [14]	Wailord [14]
Whirlwind	Aerodactyl [E]	Butterfree [22]	Hariyama [16]	Hippopotas [E]	Hoothoot [E]	Makuhita [16]
	Masquerain [1, 54]	Munchlax [E]	Murkrow [E]	Noibat [40]	Noivern [40]	Pidgeot [17]
	Pidgeotto [17]	Pidgey [17]	Sigilyph [14]	Skarmory [E]	Skorupi [E]	Snorlax [E]
	Spearow [E]	Spoink [E]	Staraptor [23]	Staravia [23]	Starly [21]	Taillow [E]
	Yanma [E]	Zubat [E]				
Wide Guard	Aerodactyl [E]	Alomomola [1, 53]	Dwebble [E]	Geodude [E]	Honedge [E]	Machamp [1]
	Makuhita [E]	Mantine [23, E]	Mantyke [23, E]	Mienshao [45]	Mr. Mime [1]	Nosepass [E]
	Roggenrola [E]	Throh [45]	Timburr [E]	Wingull [E]		
Wild Charge (TM93)	Ampharos [TM]	Audino [TM]	Bunnelby [TM]	Chinchou [TM]	Dedenne [TM]	Delcatty [TM]
	Diggersby [TM]	Dunsparce [TM]	Electrike [49, TM]	Electrode [TM]	Emolga [TM]	Flaaffy [TM]
	Furfrou [TM]	Gogoat [TM]	Granbull [TM]	Heliolisk [TM]	Helioptile [TM]	Igglybuff [TM]
	Jigglypuff [TM]	Jolteon [TM]	Lanturn [TM]	Litleo [TM]	Magnemite [TM]	Magneton [TM]
	Magnezone [TM]	Manectric [61, TM]	Mareep [TM]	Minun [TM]	Noibat [TM]	Noivern [TM]
	Pichu [TM]	Pikachu [TM]	Plusle [TM]	Pyroar [TM]	Raichu [TM]	Skiddo [TM]
	Skitty [TM]	Snorlax [TM]	Snubbull [TM]	Spinda [TM]	Tauros [TM]	Voltorb [TM]
	Wigglytuff [TM]	Zapdos [TM]				
Will-O-Wisp (TM61)	Absol [TM]	Banette [13, TM]	Braixen [45, TM]	Chandelure [TM]	Charizard [TM]	Charmander [TM]
	Charmeleon [TM]	Delphox [47, TM]	Drifblim [TM]	Drifloon [TM]	Fennekin [38, TM]	Flareon [TM]
	Fletchinder [TM]	Gallade [TM]	Gardevoir [TM]	Gastly [TM]	Gengar [TM]	Gourgeist [TM]
	Haunter [TM]	Heatmor [TM]	Houndoom [TM]	Houndour [TM]	Kirlia [TM]	Lampent [16, TM]
	Litleo [TM]	Litwick [16, TM]	Magcargo [TM]	Mewtwo [TM]	Moltres [TM]	Pansear [TM]
	Phantump [31, TM]	Pumpkaboo [TM]	Pyroar [TM]	Ralts [TM]	Rotom (Fan) [TM]	Rotom (Frost) [TM]
	Rotom (Heat) [TM]	Rotom (Mow) [TM]	Rotom (Wash) [TM]	Rotom [TM]	Sableye [TM]	Shedinja [TM]
	Shuppet [13, TM]	Simisear [TM]	Slugma [TM]	Solrock [TM]	Talonflame [TM]	Torkoal [TM]
	Trevenant [31, TM]					
Wing Attack	Aerodactyl [1]	Charizard [36]	Crobat [15]	Dragonite [55]	Ducklett [9]	Gligar [E]
	Golbat [15]	Hawlucha [8]	Honchkrow [1]	Hoothoot [E]	Mantine [14]	Mantyke [14]
	Moltres [1]	Murkrow [15, E]	Noibat [16]	Noivern [16]	Pelipper [1, 9]	Pidgeot [38]
	Pidgeotto [37]	Pidgey [33]	Scyther [21]	Staraptor [1, 9]	Staravia [9]	Starly [9]
	Swanna [1, 9]	Swellow [13]	Taillow [13]	Wingull [9]	Yanma [43]	Zubat [15]
Wish	Alomomola [37]	Audino [E]	Chimecho [E]	Chingling [E]	Eevee [E]	Fennekin [E]
	Flabébé [20]	Floette [20]	Florges [1]	Gardevoir [17]	Igglybuff [E]	Illumise [21]
	Minun [E]	Pichu [E]	Plusle [E]	Skitty [E]	Slurpuff [45]	Smoochum [E]
	Spinda [E]	Spritzee [E]	Swirlix [45]			
Withdraw	Barbaracle [7]	Binacle [7]	Blastoise [1, 10]	Cloyster [1]	Crustle [1, 7]	Dwebble [7]
	Shellder [4]	Shuckle [1]	Slowbro [37]	Squirtle [10]	Torkoal [7]	Wartortle [10]
Wonder Room	Duosion [53]	Golduck [60]	Psyduck [50]	Reuniclus [59]	Slowpoke [E]	Solosis [48]
	Solrock [1, 53]					

	Move	Pokémon that can learn it				
Grass	Wood Hammer	Abomasnow [36]	Chesnaught [55]	Chespin [48]	Exeggutor [37]	Phantump [49]	Quilladin [55]
		Snover [36]	Sudowoodo [1]	Trevenant [49]			
Normal	Work Up	Deino [38]	Furfrou [E]	Hydreigon [38]	Litleo [8]	Pancham [10]	Pangoro [10]
		Patrat [26]	Pyroar [8]	Tauros [29]	Zweilous [38]		
Grass	Worry Seed	Bellsprout [E]	Budew [16]	Bulbasaur [31]	Carnivine [E]	Exeggcute [33]	Ferroseed [E]
		Gogoat [16]	Gourgeist [11]	Hoppip [40, E]	Ivysaur [36]	Jumpluff [54]	Pumpkaboo [11]
		Skiddo [16]	Skiploom [48]	Venusaur [39]			
Normal	Wrap	Arbok [1]	Bellsprout [11]	Chimecho [1]	Chingling [1]	Dragonair [1]	Dragonite [1]
		Dratini [1]	Ekans [1]	Heatmor [E]	Lickilicky [1]	Lickitung [17]	Seviper [1]
		Shuckle [9]	Tentacool [22]	Tentacruel [22]	Weepinbell [1, 11]		
	Wring Out	Bellsprout [47]	Carnivine [47]	Gulpin [54]	Jynx [49]	Lickilicky [1, 57]	Lickitung [57]
		Octillery [28]	Seviper [50, E]	Swalot [1, 66]	Tentacool [54]	Tentacruel [1, 61]	Weepinbell [47]

X

	Move	Pokémon that can learn it				
Bug	X-Scissor (TM81)	Absol [TM]	Ariados [TM]	Axew [TM]	Barbaracle [TM]	Beedrill [TM]	Binacle [TM]
		Bisharp [TM]	Corphish [TM]	Crawdaunt [TM]	Croagunk [TM]	Crobat [TM]	Crustle [38, TM]
		Drapion [TM]	Durant [51, TM]	Dwebble [35, TM]	Escavalier [44, TM]	Fraxure [TM]	Gallade [TM]
		Gligar [40, TM]	Gliscor [40, TM]	Hawlucha [TM]	Haxorus [TM]	Karrablast [44, TM]	Leafeon [TM]
		Nincada [TM]	Ninjask [52, TM]	Noibat [TM]	Noivern [TM]	Pangoro [TM]	Pawniard [TM]
		Pinsir [29, TM]	Sandshrew [TM]	Sandslash [TM]	Scizor [41, TM]	Scolipede [TM]	Scyther [41, TM]
		Seviper [TM]	Shedinja [TM]	Skarmory [TM]	Skorupi [TM]	Sneasel [TM]	Spinarak [TM]
		Toxicroak [TM]	Trevenant [TM]	Vespiquen [TM]	Weavile [TM]	Zangoose [36, TM]	

Y

	Move	Pokémon that can learn it				
Normal	Yawn	Audino [E]	Bibarel [28]	Bidoof [25]	Chimecho [25]	Cubchoo [E]	Dunsparce [16]
		Eevee [E]	Espurr [E]	Gulpin [6]	Hippopotas [13]	Hippowdon [1, 13]	Kingdra [1]
		Litleo [E]	Magcargo [1]	Pansear [16]	Poochyena [E]	Psyduck [E]	Purrloin [E]
		Quagsire [31]	Relicanth [22]	Shelmet [25]	Slowbro [1]	Slowking [1]	Slowpoke [1]
		Slugma [1]	Snorlax [20]	Squirtle [E]	Stunfisk [E]	Swalot [1, 6]	Swirlix [E]
		Teddiursa [E]	Torkoal [E]	Wooper [29]			

Z

	Move	Pokémon that can learn it				
Electric	Zap Cannon	Ampharos [1]	Magnemite [57]	Magneton [1, 73]	Magnezone [1, 73]	Nosepass [50]	Probopass [50]
		Zapdos [1, 92]					
Psychic	Zen Headbutt	Absol [E]	Bagon [35]	Golduck [29]	Grumpig [26]	Hoothoot [37]	Illumise [37]
		Lickitung [E]	Lombre [31]	Lotad [31]	Medicham [1]	Miltank [29]	Munchlax [E]
		Noctowl [42]	Psyduck [29]	Relicanth [E]	Sableye [1, 53]	Salamence [37]	Scraggy [E]
		Shelgon [37]	Skitty [E]	Slowbro [32]	Slowking [32]	Slowpoke [32, E]	Spoink [26, E]
		Tauros [35]	Volbeat [37]	Wailmer [E]	Whiscash [1]	Zubat [E]	

Hidden Abilities are included. Note that Meowstic and Basculin have different Abilities depending on their forms, which are indicated in parentheses.

A

Ability	Pokémon that have this Ability				
Adaptability	Basculin (Blue)	Basculin (Red)	Corphish	Crawdaunt	Eevee	Mega Lucario
Aerilate	Mega Pinsir					
Aftermath	Drifblim	Drifloon	Electrode	Garbodor	Skuntank	Stunky
	Trubbish	Voltorb				
Analytic	Magnemite	Magneton	Magnezone	Patrat	Watchog	
Anger Point	Krokorok	Krookodile	Sandile	Tauros		
Anticipation	Barboach	Croagunk	Eevee	Ferrothorn	Toxicroak	Whiscash
	Wormadam					
Arena Trap	Diglett	Dugtrio	Trapinch			
Aroma Veil	Aromatisse	Spritzee				
Aura Break	Zygarde					

B

Ability	Pokémon that have this Ability				
Battle Armor	Cubone	Drapion	Marowak	Skorupi		
Big Pecks	Ducklett	Fletchling	Pidgeot	Pidgeotto	Pidgey	Swanna
Blaze	Braixen	Charizard	Charmander	Charmeleon	Delphox	Fennekin
	Pansear	Simisear				
Bulletproof	Chesnaught	Chespin	Quilladin			

C

Ability	Pokémon that have this Ability				
Cheek Pouch	Bunnelby	Dedenne	Diggersby			
Chlorophyll	Bellossom	Bellsprout	Bulbasaur	Exeggcute	Exeggutor	Gloom
	Hoppip	Ivysaur	Jumpluff	Leafeon	Oddish	Skiploom
	Venusaur	Victreebel	Vileplume	Weepinbell		
Clear Body	Carbink	Tentacool	Tentacruel			
Cloud Nine	Altaria	Golduck	Lickilicky	Lickitung	Psyduck	Swablu
Color Change	Kecleon					
Competitive	Gothita	Gothitelle	Gothorita	Igglybuff	Jigglypuff	Meowstic (F)
	Wigglytuff					
Compound Eyes	Butterfree	Nincada	Scatterbug	Vivillon	Yanma	
Contrary	Inkay	Malamar	Shuckle	Spinda		
Cursed Body	Banette	Shuppet				
Cute Charm	Delcatty	Igglybuff	Jigglypuff	Skitty	Sylveon	Wigglytuff

D

Ability	Pokémon that have this Ability				
Damp	Golduck	Politoed	Poliwag	Poliwhirl	Poliwrath	Psyduck
	Quagsire	Wooper				
Dark Aura	Yveltal					
Defiant	Bisharp	Farfetch'd	Pawniard			
Drizzle	Politoed					
Drought	Mega Charizard Y					
Dry Skin	Croagunk	Heliolisk	Helioptile	Jynx	Toxicroak	

E

Ability	Pokémon that have this Ability				
Early Bird	Dodrio	Doduo	Houndoom	Houndour	Kangaskhan	Ledian
	Ledyba					
Effect Spore	Amoonguss	Foongus	Vileplume			

F

Ability	Pokémon that have this Ability				
Fairy Aura	Xerneas					
Filter	Mega Aggron	Mime Jr.	Mr. Mime			
Flame Body	Chandelure	Fletchinder	Lampent	Litwick	Magcargo	Slugma
	Talonflame					
Flare Boost	Drifblim	Drifloon				
Flash Fire	Chandelure	Flareon	Heatmor	Houndoom	Houndour	Lampent
	Litwick					
Flower Veil	Flabébé	Floette	Florges			
Forewarn	Jynx	Smoochum				

AFTER THE HALL OF FAME

CENTRAL KALOS

COASTAL KALOS

MOUNTAIN KALOS

ADVENTURE DATA

Ability	Pokémon that have this Ability					
Friend Guard	Igglybuff	Jigglypuff	Scatterbug	Spewpa	Vivillon	
Frisk	Banette	Furret	Gothita	Gothitelle	Gothorita	
	Noibat	Noivern	Phantump	Pumpkaboo	Sentret	Gourgeist
	Trevenant	Wigglytuff	Yanma	Yanmega		Shuppet
Fur Coat	Furfrou					

G

Ability	Pokémon that have this Ability					
Gale Wings	Fletchinder	Fletchling	Talonflame			
Gluttony	Bellsprout	Gulpin	Heatmor	Linoone	Panpour	Pansage
	Pansear	Shuckle	Simipour	Simisage	Simisear	Swalot
	Victreebel	Weepinbell	Zigzagoon			
Gooey	Goodra	Goomy	Sliggoo			
Grass Pelt	Gogoat	Skiddo				
Guts	Conkeldurr	Flareon	Gurdurr	Hariyama	Heracross	Larvitar
	Machamp	Machoke	Machop	Makuhita	Swellow	Taillow
	Throh	Timburr	Ursaring			

H

Ability	Pokémon that have this Ability					
Harvest	Exeggcute	Exeggutor	Phantump	Trevenant		
Healer	Alomomola	Aromatisse	Audino	Bellossom	Spritzee	
Heavy Metal	Aggron	Aron	Lairon			
Honey Gather	Combee	Teddiursa				
Huge Power	Azumarill	Azurill	Bunnelby	Diggersby	Marill	Mega Mawile
Hustle	Combee	Corsola	Deino	Delibird	Durant	Nidoran ♂
	Nidoran ♂	Nidorina	Nidorino	Remoraid	Zweilous	
Hydration	Accelgor	Alomomola	Ducklett	Goodra	Goomy	Gorebyss
	Lapras	Shelmet	Sliggoo	Smoochum	Swanna	Vaporeon
Hyper Cutter	Corphish	Crawdaunt	Gligar	Gliscor	Mawile	Pinsir
	Trapinch					

I

Ability	Pokémon that have this Ability					
Ice Body	Avalugg	Bergmite	Glaceon	Vanillish	Vanillite	Vanilluxe
Illuminate	Chinchou	Lanturn	Starmie	Staryu	Volbeat	Watchog
Illusion	Zoroark	Zorua				
Immunity	Gligar	Snorlax	Zangoose			
Imposter	Ditto					
Infiltrator	Chandelure	Crobat	Espurr	Golbat	Hoppip	Jumpluff
	Lampent	Litwick	Meowstic (F)	Meowstic (M)	Ninjask	Noibat
	Noivern	Seviper	Skiploom	Zubat		
Inner Focus	Abra	Alakazam	Bisharp	Crobat	Dragonite	Farfetch'd
	Golbat	Kadabra	Kangaskhan	Lucario	Mienfoo	Mienshao
	Pawniard	Riolu	Sawk	Sneasel	Throh	Umbreon
	Zubat					
Insomnia	Ariados	Banette	Delibird	Gourgeist	Honchkrow	Hoothoot
	Mega Mewtwo Y	Murkrow	Noctowl	Pumpkaboo	Shuppet	Spinarak
Intimidate	Arbok	Ekans	Granbull	Gyarados	Krokorok	Krookodile
	Masquerain	Mawile	Mega Manectric	Mightyena	Salamence	Sandile
	Scrafty	Scraggy	Snubbull	Staraptor	Staravia	Tauros
Iron Barbs	Ferroseed	Ferrothorn				
Iron Fist	Conkeldurr	Golett	Golurk	Gurdurr	Ledian	Pancham
	Pangoro	Timburr				

J

Ability	Pokémon that have this Ability					
Justified	Absol	Gallade	Lucario			

K

Ability	Pokémon that have this Ability					
Keen Eye	Chatot	Drapion	Ducklett	Espurr	Farfetch'd	Fearow
	Furret	Hoothoot	Meowstic (F)	Meowstic (M)	Noctowl	Patrat
	Pelipper	Pidgeot	Pidgeotto	Pidgey	Sableye	Sentret
	Skarmory	Skorupi	Skuntank	Sneasel	Spearow	Starly
	Stunky	Swanna	Watchog	Wingull		
Klutz	Audino	Golett	Golurk	Swoobat	Woobat	

L

Ability	Pokémon that have this Ability					
Leaf Guard	Budew	Hoppip	Jumpluff	Leafeon	Roselia	Skiploom
Levitate	Carnivine	Chimecho	Chingling	Cryogonal	Flygon	Gastly
	Gengar	Haunter	Hydreigon	Lunatone	Rotom	Solrock
	Vibrava					
Light Metal	Scizor					
Lightning Rod	Cubone	Electrike	Manectric	Marowak	Pichu	Pikachu
	Plusle	Raichu	Rhydon	Rhyhorn	Rhyperior	
Limber	Ditto	Hawlucha	Liepard	Purrloin	Stunfisk	
Liquid Ooze	Gulpin	Swalot	Tentacool	Tentacruel		

M

Ability	Pokémon that have this Ability					
Magic Bounce	Espeon	Mega Absol				
Magic Guard	Abra	Alakazam	Duosion	Kadabra	Reuniclus	Sigilyph
	Solosis					
Magician	Braixen	Delphox	Fennekin	Klefki		
Magma Armor	Magcargo	Slugma				
Magnet Pull	Magnemite	Magneton	Magnezone	Nosepass	Probopass	
Marvel Scale	Dragonair	Dratini				
Mega Launcher	Clauncher	Clawitzer	Mega Blastoise			
Minus	Electrike	Manectric	Minun			
Mold Breaker	Axew	Druddigon	Fraxure	Hawlucha	Haxorus	Mega Ampharos
	Mega Gyarados	Pancham	Pangoro	Pinsir	Sawk	Throh
Moody	Bibarel	Bidoof	Octillery	Remoraid	Smeargle	
Motor Drive	Emolga					
Moxie	Gyarados	Heracross	Honchkrow	Krokorok	Krookodile	Mightyena
	Pinsir	Salamence	Sandile	Scrafty	Scraggy	
Multiscale	Dragonite					

N

Ability	Pokémon that have this Ability					
Natural Cure	Altaria	Budew	Corsola	Phantump	Roselia	Roserade
	Starmie	Staryu	Swablu	Trevenant		
No Guard	Doublade	Golett	Golurk	Honedge	Karrablast	Machamp
	Machoke	Machop				
Normalize	Delcatty	Skitty				

O

Ability	Pokémon that have this Ability					
Oblivious	Barboach	Illumise	Jynx	Lickilicky	Lickitung	Mamoswine
	Piloswine	Slowbro	Slowking	Slowpoke	Smoochum	Swinub
	Wailmer	Wailord	Whiscash			
Overcoat	Cloyster	Duosion	Escavalier	Reuniclus	Shelgon	Shellder
	Shelmet	Solosis				
Overgrow	Bulbasaur	Chesnaught	Chespin	Ivysaur	Pansage	Quilladin
	Simisage	Venusaur				
Own Tempo	Avalugg	Bergmite	Espurr	Grumpig	Lickilicky	Lickitung
	Lombre	Lotad	Ludicolo	Slowbro	Slowking	Slowpoke
	Smeargle	Spinda	Spoink			

P

Ability	Pokémon that have this Ability					
Parental Bond	Mega Kangaskhan					
Pickpocket	Barbaracle	Binacle	Sneasel	Weavile		
Pickup	Bunnelby	Dedenne	Diggersby	Gourgeist	Linoone	Munchlax
	Pachirisu	Pumpkaboo	Teddiursa	Zigzagoon		
Pixilate	Mega Gardevoir	Sylveon				
Plus	Ampharos	Dedenne	Flaaffy	Mareep	Plusle	
Poison Heal	Gliscor					
Poison Point	Budew	Dragalge	Nidoking	Nidoqueen	Nidoran ♀	Nidoran ♂
	Nidorina	Nidorino	Qwilfish	Roselia	Roserade	Scolipede
	Seadra	Skrelp	Venipede	Whirlipede		
Poison Touch	Croagunk	Dragalge	Skrelp	Toxicroak		
Prankster	Illumise	Klefki	Liepard	Mega Banette	Meowstic (M)	Murkrow
	Purrloin	Riolu	Sableye	Volbeat		
Pressure	Absol	Aerodactyl	Articuno	Bisharp	Mewtwo	Moltres
	Pawniard	Vespiquen	Weavile	Zapdos		
Protean	Froakie	Frogadier	Greninja	Kecleon		
Pure Power	Medicham	Meditite	Mega Medicham			

Pokémon Abilities Reverse Lookup

Q

Ability	Pokémon that have this Ability					
Quick Feet	Granbull	Jolteon	Linoone	Mightyena	Poochyena	Teddiursa
	Ursaring	Zigzagoon				

R

Ability	Pokémon that have this Ability					
Rain Dish	Blastoise	Lombre	Lotad	Ludicolo	Pelipper	Squirtle
	Surskit	Wartortle	Wingull			
Rattled	Bonsly	Cubchoo	Dunsparce	Granbull	Ledyba	Magikarp
	Poochyena	Snubbull	Sudowoodo	Whismur		
Reckless	Basculin (Red)	Mienfoo	Mienshao	Rhydon	Rhyhorn	Rhyperior
	Staraptor	Staravia	Starly			
Refrigerate	Amaura	Aurorus				
Regenerator	Amoonguss	Audino	Corsola	Duosion	Foongus	Mienfoo
	Mienshao	Reuniclus	Slowbro	Slowking	Slowpoke	Solosis
Rivalry	Axew	Fraxure	Haxorus	Litleo	Nidoking	Nidoqueen
	Nidoran♀	Nidoran♂	Nidorina	Nidorino	Pyroar	
Rock Head	Aerodactyl	Aggron	Aron	Bagon	Basculin (Blue)	Bonsly
	Cubone	Geodude	Golem	Graveler	Lairon	Marowak
	Onix	Relicanth	Rhydon	Rhyhorn	Shelgon	Steelix
	Sudowoodo					
Rough Skin	Carvanha	Druddigon	Gabite	Garchomp	Gible	Sharpedo
Run Away	Caterpie	Dodrio	Doduo	Dunsparce	Eevee	Furret
	Nincada	Oddish	Pachirisu	Patrat	Poochyena	Sentret
	Snubbull	Weedle				

S

Ability	Pokémon that have this Ability					
Sand Force	Boldore	Diglett	Dugtrio	Gigalith	Mega Garchomp	Nosepass
	Probopass	Roggenrola				
Sand Rush	Sandshrew	Sandslash				
Sand Stream	Hippopotas	Hippowdon	Mega Tyranitar	Tyranitar		
Sand Veil	Diglett	Dugtrio	Gabite	Garchomp	Geodude	Gible
	Gligar	Gliscor	Golem	Graveler	Heliolisk	Helioptile
	Larvitar	Sandshrew	Sandslash	Stunfisk		
Sap Sipper	Azumarill	Azurill	Gogoat	Goodra	Goomy	Marill
	Miltank	Skiddo	Sliggoo			
Scrappy	Exploud	Kangaskhan	Loudred	Miltank	Pancham	Pangoro
	Swellow	Taillow				
Serene Grace	Dunsparce					
Shadow Tag	Gothita	Gothitelle	Gothorita	Mega Gengar	Wobbuffet	Wynaut
Shed Skin	Arbok	Burmy	Dragonair	Dratini	Ekans	Kakuna
	Karrablast	Metapod	Pupitar	Scrafty	Scraggy	Seviper
	Spewpa					
Sheer Force	Bagon	Conkeldurr	Druddigon	Gurdurr	Hariyama	Makuhita
	Mawile	Nidoking	Nidoqueen	Steelix	Tauros	Timburr
	Trapinch					
Shell Armor	Clamperl	Cloyster	Corphish	Crawdaunt	Crustle	Dwebble
	Escavalier	Lapras	Shellder	Shelmet		
Shield Dust	Caterpie	Scatterbug	Vivillon	Weedle		
Simple	Bibarel	Bidoof	Swoobat	Woobat		
Skill Link	Cloyster	Mega Heracross	Shellder			
Sniper	Ariados	Barbaracle	Beedrill	Binacle	Drapion	Fearow
	Horsea	Kingdra	Octillery	Remoraid	Seadra	Skorupi
	Spearow	Spinarak				
Snow Cloak	Beartic	Cubchoo	Glaceon	Mamoswine	Piloswine	Swinub
Snow Warning	Abomasnow	Mega Abomasnow	Snover			
Solar Power	Charizard	Charmander	Charmeleon	Heliolisk	Helioptile	Mega Houndoom
Solid Rock	Rhyperior					
Soundproof	Abomasnow	Electrode	Exploud	Loudred	Mime Jr.	Mr. Mime
	Snover	Voltorb	Whismur			
Speed Boost	Ninjask	Scolipede	Venipede	Whirlipede	Yanma	Yanmega
Stall	Sableye					
Stance Change	Aegislash					
Static	Ampharos	Electrike	Electrode	Emolga	Flaaffy	Manectric
	Mareep	Pichu	Pikachu	Raichu	Stunfisk	Voltorb
Steadfast	Gallade	Lucario	Machamp	Machoke	Machop	Mega Mewtwo X
	Riolu	Scyther				
Stench	Garbodor	Gloom	Skuntank	Stunky	Trubbish	
Sticky Hold	Accelgor	Gulpin	Swalot	Trubbish		

AFTER THE HALL OF FAME

CENTRAL KALOS

COASTAL KALOS

MOUNTAIN KALOS

ADVENTURE DATA

Ability	Pokémon that have this Ability					
Strong Jaw	Tyrantrum	Tyrunt				
Sturdy	Aggron	Aron	Avalugg	Bergmite	Boldore	Bonsly
	Carbink	Crustle	Dwebble	Geodude	Gigalith	Golem
	Graveler	Lairon	Magnemite	Magneton	Magnezone	Nosepass
	Onix	Probopass	Roggenrola	Sawk	Shuckle	Skarmory
	Steelix	Sudowoodo				
Suction Cups	Inkay	Malamar	Octillery			
Super Luck	Absol	Honchkrow	Murkrow			
Swarm	Ariados	Beedrill	Durant	Escavalier	Heracross	Karrablast
	Ledian	Ledyba	Mothim	Scizor	Scolipede	Scyther
	Spinarak	Venipede	Volbeat	Whirlipede		
Sweet Veil	Slurpuff	Swirlix				
Swift Swim	Beartic	Buizel	Floatzel	Goldeen	Golduck	Gorebyss
	Horsea	Huntail	Kingdra	Lombre	Lotad	Ludicolo
	Luvdisc	Magikarp	Mantine	Mantyke	Poliwag	Poliwhirl
	Poliwrath	Psyduck	Qwilfish	Relicanth	Seaking	Surskit
Symbiosis	Flabébé	Floette	Florges			
Synchronize	Abra	Alakazam	Espeon	Gardevoir	Kadabra	Kirlia
	Ralts	Umbreon				

 T

Ability	Pokémon that have this Ability					
Tangled Feet	Chatot	Dodrio	Doduo	Pidgeot	Pidgeotto	Pidgey
	Spinda					
Technician	Mega Scizor	Mime Jr.	Mr. Mime	Roserade	Scizor	Scyther
	Smeargle					
Telepathy	Gardevoir	Kirlia	Medicham	Meditite	Noibat	Noivern
	Ralts	Wobbuffet	Wynaut			
Thick Fat	Azumarill	Azurill	Grumpig	Hariyama	Makuhita	Mamoswine
	Marill	Mega Venusaur	Miltank	Munchlax	Piloswine	Snorlax
	Spoink	Swinub				
Tinted Lens	Butterfree	Hoothoot	Illumise	Mothim	Noctowl	Sigilyph
	Yanmega					
Torrent	Blastoise	Froakie	Frogadier	Greninja	Panpour	Simipour
	Squirtle	Wartortle				
Tough Claws	Barbaracle	Binacle	Mega Aerodactyl	Mega Charizard X		
Toxic Boost	Zangoose					
Trace	Gardevoir	Kirlia	Mega Alakazam	Ralts		
Truant	Durant					

U

Ability	Pokémon that have this Ability					
Unaware	Bibarel	Bidoof	Quagsire	Swoobat	Woobat	Wooper
Unburden	Accelgor	Drifblim	Drifloon	Hawlucha	Liepard	Purrloin
	Slurpuff	Swirlix				
Unnerve	Aerodactyl	Arbok	Axew	Ekans	Fraxure	Haxorus
	Houndoom	Houndour	Litleo	Masquerain	Pyroar	Tyranitar
	Ursaring	Vespiquen				

V

Ability	Pokémon that have this Ability					
Vital Spirit	Delibird					
Volt Absorb	Chinchou	Jolteon	Lanturn	Minun	Pachirisu	

W

Ability	Pokémon that have this Ability					
Water Absorb	Lapras	Mantine	Mantyke	Politoed	Poliwag	Poliwhirl
	Poliwrath	Quagsire	Vaporeon	Wooper		
Water Veil	Buizel	Floatzel	Goldeen	Seaking	Wailmer	Wailord
Weak Armor	Crustle	Dwebble	Garbodor	Magcargo	Onix	Skarmory
	Slugma	Vanillish	Vanillite	Vanilluxe		
White Smoke	Heatmor	Torkoal				
Wonder Guard	Shedinja					
Wonder Skin	Delcatty	Sigilyph	Skitty			

A

Pokémon	Kalos Pokédex No.	National Pokédex No.	Type		Ability		Hidden Ability	
Abomasnow	Mountain 089	460	Grass	Ice	Snow Warning		Soundproof	
Abra	Central 102	63	Psychic		Synchronize	Inner Focus	Magic Guard	
Absol	Coastal 009	359	Dark		Pressure	Super Luck	Justified	
Accelgor	Mountain 025	617	Bug		Hydration	Sticky Hold	Unburden	
Aegislash (Blade)	Central 119	681	Steel	Ghost	Stance Change			
Aegislash (Shield)	Central 119	681	Steel	Ghost	Stance Change			
Aerodactyl	Coastal 068	142	Rock	Flying	Rock Head	Pressure	Unnerve	
Aggron	Mountain 101	306	Steel	Rock	Sturdy	Rock Head	Heavy Metal	
Alakazam	Central 104	65	Psychic		Synchronize	Inner Focus	Magic Guard	
Alomomola	Coastal 149	594	Water		Healer	Hydration		
Altaria	Mountain 140	334	Dragon	Flying	Natural Cure		Cloud Nine	
Amaura	Coastal 066	698	Rock	Ice	Refrigerate			
Amoonguss	Mountain 054	591	Grass	Poison	Effect Spore		Regenerator	
Ampharos	Coastal 129	181	Electric		Static		Plus	
Arbok	Mountain 038	24	Poison		Intimidate	Shed Skin	Unnerve	
Ariados	Mountain 108	168	Bug	Poison	Swarm	Insomnia	Sniper	
Aromatisse	Central 130	683	Fairy		Healer		Aroma Veil	
Aron	Mountain 099	304	Steel	Rock	Sturdy	Rock Head	Heavy Metal	
Articuno	Coastal 151	144	Ice	Flying	Pressure			
Audino	Central 123	531	Normal		Healer	Regenerator	Klutz	
Aurorus	Coastal 067	699	Rock	Ice	Refrigerate			
Avalugg	Mountain 080	713	Ice		Own Tempo	Ice Body	Sturdy	
Axew	Central 148	610	Dragon		Rivalry	Mold Breaker	Unnerve	
Azumarill	Central 043	184	Water	Fairy	Thick Fat	Huge Power	Sap Sipper	
Azurill	Central 041	298	Normal	Fairy	Thick Fat	Huge Power	Sap Sipper	

B

Pokémon	Kalos Pokédex No.	National Pokédex No.	Type		Ability		Hidden Ability	
Bagon	Coastal 014	371	Dragon		Rock Head		Sheer Force	
Banette	Mountain 123	354	Ghost		Insomnia	Frisk	Cursed Body	
Barbaracle	Coastal 022	689	Rock	Water	Tough Claws	Sniper	Pickpocket	
Barboach	Mountain 040	339	Water	Ground	Oblivious	Anticipation		
Basculin (Blue)	Mountain 060	550	Water		Rock Head	Adaptability		
Basculin (Red)	Mountain 060	550	Water		Reckless	Adaptability		
Beartic	Mountain 082	614	Ice		Snow Cloak		Swift Swim	
Beedrill	Central 028	15	Bug	Poison	Swarm		Sniper	
Bellossom	Central 108	182	Grass		Chlorophyll		Healer	
Bellsprout	Mountain 026	69	Grass	Poison	Chlorophyll		Gluttony	
Bergmite	Mountain 079	712	Ice		Own Tempo	Ice Body	Sturdy	
Bibarel	Central 039	400	Normal	Water	Simple	Unaware	Moody	
Bidoof	Central 038	399	Normal		Simple	Unaware	Moody	
Binacle	Coastal 021	688	Rock	Water	Tough Claws	Sniper	Pickpocket	
Bisharp	Mountain 049	625	Dark	Steel	Defiant	Inner Focus	Pressure	
Blastoise	Central 088	9	Water		Torrent		Rain Dish	
Boldore	Coastal 121	525	Rock		Sturdy		Sand Force	
Bonsly	Mountain 129	438	Rock		Sturdy	Rock Head	Rattled	
Braixen	Central 005	654	Fire		Blaze		Magician	
Budew	Central 071	406	Grass	Poison	Natural Cure	Poison Point	Leaf Guard	
Buizel	Mountain 058	418	Water		Swift Swim		Water Veil	
Bulbasaur	Central 080	1	Grass	Poison	Overgrow		Chlorophyll	
Bunnelby	Central 010	659	Normal		Pickup	Cheek Pouch	Huge Power	
Burmy	Central 044	412	Bug		Shed Skin			
Butterfree	Central 025	12	Bug	Flying	Compound Eyes		Tinted Lens	

C

Pokémon	Kalos Pokédex No.	National Pokédex No.	Type		Ability		Hidden Ability	
Carbink	Coastal 124	703	Rock	Fairy	Clear Body		Sturdy	
Carnivine	Mountain 029	455	Grass		Levitate			
Carvanha	Central 055	318	Water	Dark	Rough Skin			
Caterpie	Central 023	10	Bug		Shield Dust		Run Away	
Chandelure	Mountain 067	609	Ghost	Fire	Flash Fire	Flame Body	Infiltrator	
Charizard	Central 085	6	Fire	Flying	Blaze		Solar Power	
Charmander	Central 083	4	Fire		Blaze		Solar Power	
Charmeleon	Central 084	5	Fire		Blaze		Solar Power	
Chatot	Coastal 138	441	Normal	Flying	Keen Eye	Tangled Feet		
Chesnaught	Central 003	652	Grass	Fighting	Overgrow		Bulletproof	
Chespin	Central 001	650	Grass		Overgrow		Bulletproof	
Chimecho	Coastal 112	358	Psychic		Levitate			
Chinchou	Coastal 147	170	Water	Electric	Volt Absorb	Illuminate		
Chingling	Coastal 111	433	Psychic		Levitate			
Clamperl	Coastal 116	366	Water		Shell Armor			

Note: Types marked with ★ will do 4× the usual damage. Types appearing in ▬▬ may deal more or less damage depending on the Pokémon's Ability.

Weak against these move types						
★Fire	Fighting	Poison	Flying	Bug	Rock	Steel
Bug	Ghost	Dark				
Fighting	Bug	Fairy				
Fire	Flying	Rock				
Fire	Ground	Ghost	Dark			
Fire	Ground	Ghost	Dark			
Water	Electric	Ice	Rock	Steel		
★Fighting	★Ground	Water				
Bug	Ghost	Dark				
Grass	Electric					
★Ice	Rock	Dragon	Fairy			
★Fighting	★Steel	Water	Grass	Ground	Rock	
Fire	Ice	Flying	Psychic			
Ground						
Ground	Psychic					
Fire	Flying	Psychic	Rock			
Poison	Steel					
★Fighting	★Ground	Water				
★Rock	Fire	Electric	Steel			
Fighting						
★Fighting	★Steel	Water	Grass	Ground	Rock	
Fire	Fighting	Rock	Steel			
Ice	Dragon	Fairy				
Grass	Electric	Poison				
Poison	Steel					

Weak against these move types						
Ice	Dragon	Fairy				
Ghost	Dark					
★Grass	Electric	Fighting	Ground			
★Grass						
Grass	Electric					
Grass	Electric					
Fire	Fighting	Rock	Steel			
Fire	Flying	Psychic	Rock			
Fire	Ice	Poison	Flying	Bug		
Fire	Ice	Flying	Psychic			
Fire	Fighting	Rock	Steel			
Grass	Electric	Fighting				
Fighting						
★Grass	Electric	Fighting	Ground			
★Fighting	Fire	Ground				
Grass	Electric					
Water	Grass	Fighting	Ground	Steel		
Water	Grass	Fighting	Ground	Steel		
Water	Ground	Rock				
Fire	Ice	Flying	Psychic			
Grass	Electric					
Fire	Ice	Flying	Psychic			
Fighting						
Fire	Flying	Rock				
★Rock	Fire	Electric	Ice	Flying		

Weak against these move types						
★Steel	Water	Grass	Ground			
Fire	Ice	Poison	Flying	Bug		
Grass	Electric	Fighting	Bug	Fairy		
Fire	Flying	Rock				
Water	Ground	Rock	Ghost	Dark		
★Rock	Water	Electric				
Water	Ground	Rock				
Water	Ground	Rock				
Electric	Ice	Rock				
★Flying	Fire	Ice	Poison	Psychic	Fairy	
Fire	Ice	Poison	Flying	Bug		
Bug	Ghost	Dark				
Grass	Ground					
Bug	Ghost	Dark				
Grass	Electric					

AFTER THE HALL OF FAME

CENTRAL KALOS

COASTAL KALOS

MOUNTAIN KALOS

ADVENTURE DATA

AFTER THE HALL OF FAME

CENTRAL KALOS

COASTAL KALOS

MOUNTAIN KALOS

ADVENTURE DATA

Pokémon	Kalos Pokédex No.	National Pokédex No.	Type		Ability		Hidden Ability
Clauncher	Coastal 032	692	Water		Mega Launcher		
Clawitzer	Coastal 033	693	Water		Mega Launcher		
Cloyster	Coastal 037	91	Water	Ice	Shell Armor	Skill Link	Overcoat
Combee	Central 076	415	Bug	Flying	Honey Gather		Hustle
Conkeldurr	Mountain 095	534	Fighting		Guts	Sheer Force	Iron Fist
Corphish	Central 051	341	Water		Hyper Cutter	Shell Armor	Adaptability
Corsola	Coastal 146	222	Water	Rock	Hustle	Natural Cure	Regenerator
Crawdaunt	Central 052	342	Water	Dark	Hyper Cutter	Shell Armor	Adaptability
Croagunk	Central 125	453	Poison	Fighting	Anticipation	Dry Skin	Poison Touch
Crobat	Central 147	169	Poison	Flying	Inner Focus		Infiltrator
Crustle	Coastal 024	558	Bug	Rock	Sturdy	Shell Armor	Weak Armor
Cryogonal	Mountain 111	615	Ice		Levitate		
Cubchoo	Mountain 081	613	Ice		Snow Cloak		Rattled
Cubone	Coastal 060	104	Ground		Rock Head	Lightning Rod	Battle Armor

D

Pokémon	Kalos Pokédex No.	National Pokédex No.	Type		Ability		Hidden Ability
Dedenne	Coastal 110	702	Electric	Fairy	Cheek Pouch	Pickup	Plus
Deino	Mountain 142	633	Dark	Dragon	Hustle		
Delcatty	Central 079	301	Normal		Cute Charm	Normalize	Wonder Skin
Delibird	Mountain 090	225	Ice	Flying	Vital Spirit	Hustle	Insomnia
Delphox	Central 006	655	Fire	Psychic	Blaze		Magician
Diggersby	Central 011	660	Normal	Ground	Pickup	Cheek Pouch	Huge Power
Diglett	Mountain 001	50	Ground		Sand Veil	Arena Trap	Sand Force
Ditto	Mountain 138	132	Normal		Limber		Imposter
Dodrio	Central 095	85	Normal	Flying	Run Away	Early Bird	Tangled Feet
Doduo	Central 094	84	Normal	Flying	Run Away	Early Bird	Tangled Feet
Doublade	Central 118	680	Steel	Ghost	No Guard		
Dragalge	Coastal 031	691	Poison	Dragon	Poison Point	Poison Touch	
Dragonair	Mountain 146	148	Dragon		Shed Skin		Marvel Scale
Dragonite	Mountain 147	149	Dragon	Flying	Inner Focus		Multiscale
Drapion	Mountain 016	452	Poison	Dark	Battle Armor	Sniper	Keen Eye
Dratini	Mountain 145	147	Dragon		Shed Skin		Marvel Scale
Drifblim	Coastal 002	426	Ghost	Flying	Aftermath	Unburden	Flare Boost
Drifloon	Coastal 001	425	Ghost	Flying	Aftermath	Unburden	Flare Boost
Druddigon	Mountain 141	621	Dragon		Rough Skin	Sheer Force	Mold Breaker
Ducklett	Central 127	580	Water	Flying	Keen Eye	Big Pecks	Hydration
Dugtrio	Mountain 002	51	Ground		Sand Veil	Arena Trap	Sand Force
Dunsparce	Central 040	206	Normal		Serene Grace	Run Away	Rattled
Duosion	Coastal 116	578	Psychic		Overcoat	Magic Guard	Regenerator
Durant	Mountain 106	632	Bug	Steel	Swarm	Hustle	Truant
Dwebble	Coastal 023	557	Bug	Rock	Sturdy	Shell Armor	Weak Armor

E

Pokémon	Kalos Pokédex No.	National Pokédex No.	Type		Ability		Hidden Ability
Eevee	Coastal 077	133	Normal		Run Away	Adaptability	Anticipation
Ekans	Mountain 037	23	Poison		Intimidate	Shed Skin	Unnerve
Electrike	Coastal 073	309	Electric		Static	Lightning Rod	Minus
Electrode	Mountain 073	101	Electric		Soundproof	Static	Aftermath
Emolga	Coastal 086	587	Electric	Flying	Static		Motor Drive
Escavalier	Mountain 023	589	Bug	Steel	Swarm	Shell Armor	Overcoat
Espeon	Coastal 081	196	Psychic		Synchronize		Magic Bounce
Espurr	Central 114	677	Psychic		Keen Eye	Infiltrator	Own Tempo
Exeggcute	Coastal 136	102	Grass	Psychic	Chlorophyll		Harvest
Exeggutor	Coastal 137	103	Grass	Psychic	Chlorophyll		Harvest
Exploud	Central 142	295	Normal		Soundproof		Scrappy

F

Pokémon	Kalos Pokédex No.	National Pokédex No.	Type		Ability		Hidden Ability
Farfetch'd	Central 061	83	Normal	Flying	Keen Eye	Inner Focus	Defiant
Fearow	Mountain 110	22	Normal	Flying	Keen Eye		Sniper
Fennekin	Central 004	653	Fire		Blaze		Magician
Ferroseed	Coastal 069	597	Grass	Steel	Iron Barbs		
Ferrothorn	Coastal 070	598	Grass	Steel	Iron Barbs		Anticipation
Flaaffy	Coastal 128	180	Electric		Static		Plus
Flabébé	Central 068	669	Fairy		Flower Veil		Symbiosis
Flareon	Coastal 080	136	Fire		Flash Fire		Guts
Fletchinder	Central 015	662	Fire	Flying	Flame Body		Gale Wings
Fletchling	Central 014	661	Normal	Flying	Big Pecks		Gale Wings
Floatzel	Mountain 059	419	Water		Swift Swim		Water Veil
Floette	Central 069	670	Fairy		Flower Veil		Symbiosis

Note: Types marked with ★ will do 4× the usual damage. Types appearing in ▬ may deal more or less damage depending on the Pokémon's Ability.

Weak against these move types				
Grass	Electric			
Grass	Electric			
Grass	Electric	Fighting	Rock	
★Rock	Fire	Electric	Ice	Flying
Flying	Psychic	Fairy		
Grass	Electric			
★Grass	Electric	Fighting	Ground	
Grass	Electric	Fighting	Bug	Fairy
★Psychic	Ground	Flying		
Electric	Ice	Psychic	Rock	
Water	Rock	Steel		
Fire	Fighting	Rock	Steel	
Fire	Fighting	Rock	Steel	
Water	Grass	Ice		

Weak against these move types				
Poison	Ground			
★Fairy	Ice	Fighting	Bug	Dragon
Fighting				
★Rock	Fire	Electric	Steel	
Water	Ground	Rock	Ghost	Dark
Water	Grass	Ice	Fighting	
Water	Grass	Ice		
Fighting				
Electric	Ice	Rock		
Electric	Ice	Rock		
Fire	Ground	Ghost	Dark	
Ice	Ground	Psychic	Dragon	
Ice	Dragon	Fairy		
★Ice	Rock	Dragon	Fairy	
Ground				
Ice	Dragon	Fairy		
Electric	Ice	Rock	Ghost	Dark
Electric	Ice	Rock	Ghost	Dark
Ice	Dragon	Fairy		
★Electric	Rock			
Water	Grass	Ice		
Fighting				
Bug	Ghost	Dark		
★Fire				
Water	Rock	Steel		

Weak against these move types						
Fighting						
Ground	Psychic					
Ground						
Ground						
Ice	Rock					
★Fire						
Bug	Ghost	Dark				
Bug	Ghost	Dark				
★Bug	Fire	Ice	Poison	Flying	Ghost	Dark
★Bug	Fire	Ice	Poison	Flying	Ghost	Dark
Fighting						

Weak against these move types		
Electric	Ice	Rock
Electric	Ice	Rock
Water	Ground	Rock
★Fire	Fighting	
★Fire	Fighting	
Ground		
Poison	Steel	
Water	Ground	Rock
★Rock	Water	Electric
Electric	Ice	Rock
Grass	Electric	
Poison	Steel	

Pokémon Weakness Chart—Kalos Regional Pokédex

AFTER THE HALL OF FAME

Pokémon	Kalos Pokédex No.	National Pokédex No.	Type		Ability		Hidden Ability
Florges	Central 070	671	Fairy		Flower Veil		Symbiosis
Flygon	Mountain 005	330	Ground	Dragon	Levitate		
Foongus	Mountain 053	590	Grass	Poison	Effect Spore		Regenerator
Fraxure	Central 149	611	Dragon		Rivalry	Mold Breaker	Unnerve
Froakie	Central 007	656	Water		Torrent		Protean
Frogadier	Central 008	657	Water		Torrent		Protean
Furfrou	Central 093	676	Normal		Fur Coat		
Furret	Central 110	162	Normal		Run Away	Keen Eye	Frisk

G

CENTRAL KALOS

Pokémon	Kalos Pokédex No.	National Pokédex No.	Type		Ability		Hidden Ability
Gabite	Mountain 007	444	Dragon	Ground	Sand Veil		Rough Skin
Gallade	Central 067	475	Psychic	Fighting	Steadfast		Justified
Garbodor	Mountain 075	569	Poison		Stench	Weak Armor	Aftermath
Garchomp	Mountain 008	445	Dragon	Ground	Sand Veil		Rough Skin
Gardevoir	Central 066	282	Psychic	Fairy	Synchronize	Trace	Telepathy
Gastly	Mountain 030	92	Ghost	Poison	Levitate		
Gengar	Mountain 032	94	Ghost	Poison	Levitate		
Geodude	Mountain 009	74	Rock	Ground	Rock Head	Sturdy	Sand Veil
Gible	Mountain 006	443	Dragon	Ground	Sand Veil		Rough Skin
Gigalith	Coastal 122	526	Rock		Sturdy		Sand Force
Glaceon	Coastal 084	471	Ice		Snow Cloak		Ice Body
Gligar	Mountain 115	207	Ground	Flying	Hyper Cutter	Sand Veil	Immunity
Gliscor	Mountain 116	472	Ground	Flying	Hyper Cutter	Sand Veil	Poison Heal
Gloom	Central 106	44	Grass	Poison	Chlorophyll		Stench
Gogoat	Central 090	673	Grass		Sap Sipper		Grass Pelt
Golbat	Central 146	42	Poison	Flying	Inner Focus		Infiltrator
Goldeen	Central 053	118	Water		Swift Swim	Water Veil	
Golduck	Central 060	55	Water		Damp	Cloud Nine	Swift Swim
Golem	Mountain 011	76	Rock	Ground	Rock Head	Sturdy	Sand Veil
Golett	Coastal 091	622	Ground	Ghost	Iron Fist	Klutz	No Guard
Golurk	Coastal 092	623	Ground	Ghost	Iron Fist	Klutz	No Guard
Goodra	Mountain 021	706	Dragon		Sap Sipper	Hydration	Gooey
Goomy	Mountain 019	704	Dragon		Sap Sipper	Hydration	Gooey
Gorebyss	Coastal 143	368	Water		Swift Swim		Hydration
Gothita	Mountain 126	574	Psychic		Frisk	Competitive	Shadow Tag
Gothitelle	Mountain 128	576	Psychic		Frisk	Competitive	Shadow Tag
Gothorita	Mountain 127	575	Psychic		Frisk	Competitive	Shadow Tag
Gourgeist	Mountain 064	711	Ghost	Grass	Pickup	Frisk	Insomnia
Granbull	Coastal 072	210	Fairy		Intimidate	Quick Feet	Rattled
Graveler	Mountain 010	75	Rock	Ground	Rock Head	Sturdy	Sand Veil
Greninja	Central 009	658	Water	Dark	Torrent		Protean
Grumpig	Coastal 008	326	Psychic		Thick Fat	Own Tempo	
Gulpin	Central 098	316	Poison		Liquid Ooze	Sticky Hold	Gluttony
Gurdurr	Mountain 094	533	Fighting		Guts	Sheer Force	Iron Fist
Gyarados	Central 050	130	Water	Flying	Intimidate		Moxie

H

COASTAL KALOS

Pokémon	Kalos Pokédex No.	National Pokédex No.	Type		Ability		Hidden Ability
Hariyama	Coastal 096	297	Fighting		Thick Fat	Guts	Sheer Force
Haunter	Mountain 031	93	Ghost	Poison	Levitate		
Hawlucha	Coastal 089	701	Fighting	Flying	Limber	Unburden	Mold Breaker
Haxorus	Central 150	612	Dragon		Rivalry	Mold Breaker	Unnerve
Heatmor	Mountain 105	631	Fire		Gluttony	Flash Fire	White Smoke
Heliolisk	Coastal 047	695	Electric	Normal	Dry Skin	Sand Veil	Solar Power
Helioptile	Coastal 046	694	Electric	Normal	Dry Skin	Sand Veil	Solar Power
Heracross	Coastal 131	214	Bug	Fighting	Swarm	Guts	Moxie
Hippopotas	Coastal 048	449	Ground		Sand Stream		
Hippowdon	Coastal 049	450	Ground		Sand Stream		
Honchkrow	Mountain 052	430	Dark	Flying	Insomnia	Super Luck	Moxie
Honedge	Central 117	679	Steel	Ghost	No Guard		
Hoothoot	Mountain 117	163	Normal	Flying	Insomnia	Keen Eye	Tinted Lens
Hoppip	Central 135	187	Grass	Flying	Chlorophyll	Leaf Guard	Infiltrator
Horsea	Coastal 039	116	Water		Swift Swim	Sniper	
Houndoom	Coastal 076	229	Dark	Fire	Early Bird	Flash Fire	Unnerve
Houndour	Coastal 075	228	Dark	Fire	Early Bird	Flash Fire	Unnerve
Huntail	Coastal 142	367	Water		Swift Swim		
Hydreigon	Mountain 144	635	Dark	Dragon	Levitate		

MOUNTAIN KALOS / ADVENTURE DATA

Note: Types marked with ★ will do 4× the usual damage. Types appearing in ▬▬ may deal more or less damage depending on the Pokémon's Ability.

Weak against these move types					
Poison	Steel				
★Ice	Dragon	Fairy			
Fire	Ice	Flying	Psychic		
Ice	Dragon	Fairy			
Grass	Electric				
Grass	Electric				
Fighting					
Fighting					

Weak against these move types					
★Ice	Dragon	Fairy			
Flying	Ghost	Fairy			
Ground	Psychic				
★Ice	Dragon	Fairy			
Poison	Ghost	Steel			
Ground	Psychic	Ghost	Dark		
Ground	Psychic	Ghost	Dark		
★Water	★Grass	Ice	Fighting	Ground	Steel
★Ice	Dragon	Fairy			
Water	Grass	Fighting	Ground	Steel	
Fire	Fighting	Rock	Steel		
★Ice	Water				
★Ice	Water				
Fire	Ice	Flying	Psychic		
Fire	Ice	Poison	Flying	Bug	
Electric	Ice	Psychic	Rock		
Grass	Electric				
Grass	Electric				
★Water	★Grass	Ice	Fighting	Ground	Steel
Water	Grass	Ice	Ghost	Dark	
Water	Grass	Ice	Ghost	Dark	
Ice	Dragon	Fairy			
Ice	Dragon	Fairy			
Grass	Electric				
Bug	Ghost	Dark			
Bug	Ghost	Dark			
Bug	Ghost	Dark			
Fire	Ice	Flying	Ghost	Dark	
Poison	Steel				
★Water	★Grass	Ice	Fighting	Ground	Steel
Grass	Electric	Fighting	Bug	Fairy	
Bug	Ghost	Dark			
Ground	Psychic				
Flying	Psychic	Fairy			
★Electric	Rock				

Weak against these move types					
Flying	Psychic	Fairy			
Ground	Psychic	Ghost	Dark		
Electric	Ice	Flying	Psychic	Fairy	
Ice	Dragon	Fairy			
Water	Ground	Rock			
Fighting	Ground				
Fighting	Ground				
★Flying	Fire	Psychic	Fairy		
Water	Grass	Ice			
Water	Grass	Ice			
Electric	Ice	Rock	Fairy		
Fire	Ground	Ghost	Dark		
Electric	Ice	Rock			
★Ice	Fire	Poison	Flying	Rock	
Grass	Electric				
Water	Fighting	Ground	Rock		
Water	Fighting	Ground	Rock		
Grass	Electric				
★Fairy	Ice	Fighting	Bug	Dragon	

Pokémon Weakness Chart—Kalos Regional Pokédex

AFTER THE HALL OF FAME

CENTRAL KALOS

COASTAL KALOS

MOUNTAIN KALOS

ADVENTURE DATA

I

Pokémon	Kalos Pokédex No.	National Pokédex No.	Type		Ability		Hidden Ability
Igglybuff	Mountain 119	174	Normal	Fairy	Cute Charm	Competitive	Friend Guard
Illumise	Central 134	314	Bug		Oblivious	Tinted Lens	Prankster
Inkay	Coastal 010	686	Dark	Psychic	Contrary	Suction Cups	
Ivysaur	Central 081	2	Grass	Poison	Overgrow		Chlorophyll

J

Pokémon	Kalos Pokédex No.	National Pokédex No.	Type		Ability		Hidden Ability
Jigglypuff	Mountain 120	39	Normal	Fairy	Cute Charm	Competitive	Friend Guard
Jolteon	Coastal 079	135	Electric		Volt Absorb		Quick Feet
Jumpluff	Central 137	189	Grass	Flying	Chlorophyll	Leaf Guard	Infiltrator
Jynx	Mountain 084	124	Ice	Psychic	Oblivious	Forewarn	Dry Skin

K

Pokémon	Kalos Pokédex No.	National Pokédex No.	Type		Ability		Hidden Ability
Kadabra	Central 103	64	Psychic		Synchronize	Inner Focus	Magic Guard
Kakuna	Central 027	14	Bug	Poison	Shed Skin		
Kangaskhan	Coastal 062	115	Normal		Early Bird	Scrappy	Inner Focus
Karrablast	Mountain 022	588	Bug		Swarm	Shed Skin	No Guard
Kecleon	Central 116	352	Normal		Color Change		Protean
Kingdra	Coastal 041	230	Water	Dragon	Swift Swim	Sniper	
Kirlia	Central 065	281	Psychic	Fairy	Synchronize	Trace	Telepathy
Klefki	Mountain 050	707	Steel	Fairy	Prankster		Magician
Krokorok	Coastal 044	552	Ground	Dark	Intimidate	Moxie	Anger Point
Krookodile	Coastal 045	553	Ground	Dark	Intimidate	Moxie	Anger Point

L

Pokémon	Kalos Pokédex No.	National Pokédex No.	Type		Ability		Hidden Ability
Lairon	Mountain 100	305	Steel	Rock	Sturdy	Rock Head	Heavy Metal
Lampent	Mountain 066	608	Ghost	Fire	Flash Fire	Flame Body	Infiltrator
Lanturn	Coastal 148	171	Water	Electric	Volt Absorb	Illuminate	
Lapras	Coastal 150	131	Water	Ice	Water Absorb	Shell Armor	Hydration
Larvitar	Mountain 102	246	Rock	Ground	Guts		Sand Veil
Leafeon	Coastal 083	470	Grass		Leaf Guard		Chlorophyll
Ledian	Central 075	166	Bug	Flying	Swarm	Early Bird	Iron Fist
Ledyba	Central 074	165	Bug	Flying	Swarm	Early Bird	Rattled
Lickilicky	Mountain 135	463	Normal		Own Tempo	Oblivious	Cloud Nine
Lickitung	Mountain 134	108	Normal		Own Tempo	Oblivious	Cloud Nine
Liepard	Mountain 043	510	Dark		Limber	Unburden	Prankster
Linoone	Central 013	264	Normal		Pickup	Gluttony	Quick Feet
Litleo	Central 057	667	Fire	Normal	Rivalry	Unnerve	
Litwick	Mountain 065	607	Ghost	Fire	Flash Fire	Flame Body	Infiltrator
Lombre	Mountain 056	271	Water	Grass	Swift Swim	Rain Dish	Own Tempo
Lotad	Mountain 055	270	Water	Grass	Swift Swim	Rain Dish	Own Tempo
Loudred	Central 141	294	Normal		Soundproof		Scrappy
Lucario	Central 063	448	Fighting	Steel	Steadfast	Inner Focus	Justified
Ludicolo	Mountain 057	272	Water	Grass	Swift Swim	Rain Dish	Own Tempo
Lunatone	Coastal 012	337	Rock	Psychic	Levitate		
Luvdisc	Coastal 029	370	Water		Swift Swim		

M

Pokémon	Kalos Pokédex No.	National Pokédex No.	Type		Ability		Hidden Ability
Machamp	Coastal 059	68	Fighting		Guts	No Guard	Steadfast
Machoke	Coastal 058	67	Fighting		Guts	No Guard	Steadfast
Machop	Coastal 057	66	Fighting		Guts	No Guard	Steadfast
Magcargo	Mountain 013	219	Fire	Rock	Magma Armor	Flame Body	Weak Armor
Magikarp	Central 049	129	Water		Swift Swim		Rattled
Magnemite	Mountain 069	81	Electric	Steel	Magnet Pull	Sturdy	Analytic
Magneton	Mountain 070	82	Electric	Steel	Magnet Pull	Sturdy	Analytic
Magnezone	Mountain 071	462	Electric	Steel	Magnet Pull	Sturdy	Analytic
Makuhita	Coastal 095	296	Fighting		Thick Fat	Guts	Sheer Force
Malamar	Coastal 011	687	Dark	Psychic	Contrary	Suction Cups	
Mamoswine	Mountain 078	473	Ice	Ground	Oblivious	Snow Cloak	Thick Fat
Manectric	Coastal 074	310	Electric		Static	Lightning Rod	Minus
Mantine	Coastal 140	226	Water	Flying	Swift Swim	Water Absorb	
Mantyke	Coastal 139	458	Water	Flying	Swift Swim	Water Absorb	
Mareep	Coastal 127	179	Electric		Static		Plus
Marill	Central 042	183	Water	Fairy	Thick Fat	Huge Power	Sap Sipper
Marowak	Coastal 105	105	Ground		Rock Head	Lightning Rod	Battle Armor
Masquerain	Central 048	284	Bug	Flying	Intimidate		Unnerve

Note: Types marked with ★ will do 4× the usual damage. Types appearing in ▅▅ may deal more or less damage depending on the Pokémon's Ability.

Weak against these move types						
Poison	Steel					
Fire	Flying	Rock				
★Bug	Fairy					
Fire	Ice	Flying	Psychic			

Weak against these move types						
Poison	Steel					
Ground						
★Ice	Fire	Poison	Flying	Rock		
Fire	Bug	Rock	Ghost	Dark	Steel	

Weak against these move types						
Bug	Ghost	Dark				
Fire	Flying	Psychic	Rock			
Fighting						
Fire	Flying	Rock				
Fighting						
Dragon	Fairy					
Poison	Ghost	Steel				
Fire	Ground					
Water	Grass	Ice	Fighting	Bug	Fairy	
Water	Grass	Ice	Fighting	Bug	Fairy	

Weak against these move types						
★Fighting	★Ground	Water				
Water	Ground	Rock	Ghost	Dark		
Grass	Ground					
Grass	Electric	Fighting	Rock			
★Water	★Grass	Ice	Fighting	Ground	Steel	
Fire	Ice	Poison	Flying	Bug		
★Rock	Fire	Electric	Ice	Flying		
★Rock	Fire	Electric	Ice	Flying		
Fighting						
Fighting						
Fighting	Bug	Fairy				
Fighting						
Water	Fighting	Ground	Rock			
Water	Ground	Rock	Ghost	Dark		
Poison	Flying	Bug				
Poison	Flying	Bug				
Fighting						
Fire	Fighting	Ground				
Poison	Flying	Bug				
Water	Grass	Ground	Bug	Ghost	Dark	Steel
Grass	Electric					

Weak against these move types						
Flying	Psychic	Fairy				
Flying	Psychic	Fairy				
Flying	Psychic	Fairy				
★Water	★Ground	Fighting	Rock			
Grass	Electric					
★Ground	Fire	Fighting				
★Ground	Fire	Fighting				
★Ground	Fire	Fighting				
Flying	Psychic	Fairy				
★Bug	Fairy					
Fire	Water	Grass	Fighting	Steel		
Ground						
★Electric	Rock					
★Electric	Rock					
Ground						
Grass	Electric	Poison				
Water	Grass	Ice				
★Rock	Fire	Electric	Ice	Flying		

AFTER THE HALL OF FAME

CENTRAL KALOS

COASTAL KALOS

MOUNTAIN KALOS

ADVENTURE DATA

Pokémon	Kalos Pokédex No.	National Pokédex No.	Type		Ability		Hidden Ability
Mawile	Coastal 063	303	Steel	Fairy	Hyper Cutter	Intimidate	Sheer Force
Medicham	Central 144	308	Fighting	Psychic	Pure Power		Telepathy
Meditite	Central 143	307	Fighting	Psychic	Pure Power		Telepathy
Meowstic (F)	Central 115	678	Psychic		Keen Eye	Infiltrator	Competitive
Meowstic (M)	Central 115	678	Psychic		Keen Eye	Infiltrator	Prankster
Metapod	Central 024	11	Bug		Shed Skin		
Mewtwo	Mountain 151	150	Psychic		Pressure		
Mienfoo	Coastal 003	619	Fighting		Inner Focus	Regenerator	Reckless
Mienshao	Coastal 004	620	Fighting		Inner Focus	Regenerator	Reckless
Mightyena	Mountain 045	262	Dark		Intimidate	Quick Feet	Moxie
Miltank	Coastal 126	241	Normal		Thick Fat	Scrappy	Sap Sipper
Mime Jr.	Coastal 113	439	Psychic	Fairy	Soundproof	Filter	Technician
Minun	Central 097	312	Electric		Minus		Volt Absorb
Moltres	Coastal 153	146	Fire	Flying	Pressure		
Mothim	Central 046	414	Bug	Flying	Swarm		Tinted Lens
Mr. Mime	Coastal 114	122	Psychic	Fairy	Soundproof	Filter	Technician
Munchlax	Central 138	446	Normal		Pickup	Thick Fat	
Murkrow	Mountain 051	198	Dark	Flying	Insomnia	Super Luck	Prankster

N

Pokémon	Kalos Pokédex No.	National Pokédex No.	Type		Ability		Hidden Ability
Nidoking	Coastal 109	34	Poison	Ground	Poison Point	Rivalry	Sheer Force
Nidoqueen	Coastal 106	31	Poison	Ground	Poison Point	Rivalry	Sheer Force
Nidoran ♀	Coastal 104	29	Poison		Poison Point	Rivalry	Hustle
Nidoran ♂	Coastal 107	32	Poison		Poison Point	Rivalry	Hustle
Nidorina	Coastal 105	30	Poison		Poison Point	Rivalry	Hustle
Nidorino	Coastal 108	33	Poison		Poison Point	Rivalry	Hustle
Nincada	Central 111	290	Bug	Ground	Compound Eyes		Run Away
Ninjask	Central 112	291	Bug	Flying	Speed Boost		Infiltrator
Noctowl	Mountain 118	164	Normal	Flying	Insomnia	Keen Eye	Tinted Lens
Noibat	Mountain 113	714	Flying	Dragon	Frisk	Infiltrator	Telepathy
Noivern	Mountain 114	715	Flying	Dragon	Frisk	Infiltrator	Telepathy
Nosepass	Coastal 093	299	Rock		Sturdy	Magnet Pull	Sand Force

O

Pokémon	Kalos Pokédex No.	National Pokédex No.	Type		Ability		Hidden Ability
Octillery	Coastal 145	224	Water		Suction Cups	Sniper	Moody
Oddish	Central 105	43	Grass	Poison	Chlorophyll		Run Away
Onix	Coastal 053	95	Rock	Ground	Rock Head	Sturdy	Weak Armor

P

Pokémon	Kalos Pokédex No.	National Pokédex No.	Type		Ability		Hidden Ability
Pachirisu	Coastal 132	417	Electric		Run Away	Pickup	Volt Absorb
Pancham	Central 091	674	Fighting		Iron Fist	Mold Breaker	Scrappy
Pangoro	Central 092	675	Fighting	Dark	Iron Fist	Mold Breaker	Scrappy
Panpour	Central 033	515	Water		Gluttony		Torrent
Pansage	Central 029	511	Grass		Gluttony		Overgrow
Pansear	Central 031	513	Fire		Gluttony		Blaze
Patrat	Mountain 046	504	Normal		Run Away	Keen Eye	Analytic
Pawniard	Mountain 048	624	Dark	Steel	Defiant	Inner Focus	Pressure
Pelipper	Coastal 018	279	Water	Flying	Keen Eye		Rain Dish
Phantump	Mountain 061	708	Ghost	Grass	Natural Cure	Frisk	Harvest
Pichu	Central 035	172	Electric		Static		Lightning Rod
Pidgeot	Central 019	18	Normal	Flying	Keen Eye	Tangled Feet	Big Pecks
Pidgeotto	Central 018	17	Normal	Flying	Keen Eye	Tangled Feet	Big Pecks
Pidgey	Central 017	16	Normal	Flying	Keen Eye	Tangled Feet	Big Pecks
Pikachu	Central 036	25	Electric		Static		Lightning Rod
Piloswine	Mountain 077	221	Ice	Ground	Oblivious	Snow Cloak	Thick Fat
Pinsir	Coastal 130	127	Bug		Hyper Cutter	Mold Breaker	Moxie
Plusle	Central 096	311	Electric		Plus		Lightning Rod
Politoed	Mountain 036	186	Water		Water Absorb	Damp	Drizzle
Poliwag	Mountain 033	60	Water		Water Absorb	Damp	Swift Swim
Poliwhirl	Mountain 034	61	Water		Water Absorb	Damp	Swift Swim
Poliwrath	Mountain 035	62	Water	Fighting	Water Absorb	Damp	Swift Swim
Poochyena	Mountain 044	261	Dark		Run Away	Quick Feet	Rattled
Probopass	Coastal 094	476	Rock	Steel	Sturdy	Magnet Pull	Sand Force
Psyduck	Central 059	54	Water		Damp	Cloud Nine	Swift Swim
Pumpkaboo	Mountain 063	710	Ghost	Grass	Pickup	Frisk	Insomnia
Pupitar	Mountain 103	247	Rock	Ground	Shed Skin		
Purrloin	Mountain 042	509	Dark		Limber	Unburden	Prankster
Pyroar	Central 058	668	Fire	Normal	Rivalry	Unnerve	

Note: Types marked with ★ will do 4× the usual damage. Types appearing in ▬ may deal more or less damage depending on the Pokémon's Ability.

Weak against these move types						
Fire	Ground					
Flying	Ghost	Fairy				
Flying	Ghost	Fairy				
Bug	Ghost	Dark				
Bug	Ghost	Dark				
Fire	Flying	Rock				
Bug	Ghost	Dark				
Flying	Psychic	Fairy				
Flying	Psychic	Fairy				
Fighting	Bug	Fairy				
Fighting						
Poison	Ghost	Steel				
Ground						
★Rock	Water	Electric				
★Rock	Fire	Electric	Ice	Flying		
Poison	Ghost	Steel				
Fighting						
Electric	Ice	Rock	Fairy			

Weak against these move types						
Water	Ice	Ground	Psychic			
Water	Ice	Ground	Psychic			
Ground	Psychic					
Ground	Psychic					
Ground	Psychic					
Ground	Psychic					
Fire	Water	Ice	Flying			
★Rock	Fire	Electric	Ice	Flying		
Electric	Ice	Rock				
★Ice	Rock	Dragon	Fairy			
★Ice	Rock	Dragon	Fairy			
Water	Grass	Fighting	Ground	Steel		

Weak against these move types						
Grass	Electric					
Fire	Ice	Flying	Psychic			
★Water	★Grass	Ice	Fighting	Ground	Steel	

Weak against these move types						
Ground						
Flying	Psychic	Fairy				
★Fairy	Fighting	Flying				
Grass	Electric					
Fire	Ice	Poison	Flying	Bug		
Water	Ground	Rock				
Fighting						
★Fighting	Fire	Ground				
★Electric	Rock					
Fire	Ice	Flying	Ghost	Dark		
Ground						
Electric	Ice	Rock				
Electric	Ice	Rock				
Electric	Ice	Rock				
Ground						
Fire	Water	Grass	Fighting	Steel		
Fire	Flying	Rock				
Ground						
Grass	Electric					
Grass	Electric					
Grass	Electric					
Grass	Electric	Flying	Psychic	Fairy		
Fighting	Bug	Fairy				
★Fighting	★Ground	Water				
Grass	Electric					
Fire	Ice	Flying	Ghost	Dark		
★Water	★Grass	Ice	Fighting	Ground	Steel	
Fighting	Bug	Fairy				
Water	Fighting	Ground	Rock			

AFTER THE HALL OF FAME

CENTRAL KALOS

COASTAL KALOS

MOUNTAIN KALOS

ADVENTURE DATA

Q

Pokémon	Kalos Pokédex No.	National Pokédex No.	Type		Ability		Hidden Ability	
Quagsire	Mountain 018	195	Water	Ground	Damp	Water Absorb	Unaware	
Quilladin	Central 002	651	Grass		Overgrow		Bulletproof	
Qwilfish	Coastal 038	211	Water	Poison	Poison Point	Swift Swim		

R

Pokémon	Kalos Pokédex No.	National Pokédex No.	Type		Ability		Hidden Ability	
Raichu	Central 037	26	Electric		Static		Lightning Rod	
Ralts	Central 064	280	Psychic	Fairy	Synchronize	Trace	Telepathy	
Relicanth	Coastal 042	369	Water	Rock	Swift Swim	Rock Head		
Remoraid	Coastal 144	223	Water		Hustle	Sniper	Moody	
Reuniclus	Coastal 117	579	Psychic		Overcoat	Magic Guard	Regenerator	
Rhydon	Coastal 051	112	Ground	Rock	Lightning Rod	Rock Head	Reckless	
Rhyhorn	Coastal 050	111	Ground	Rock	Lightning Rod	Rock Head	Reckless	
Rhyperior	Coastal 052	464	Ground	Rock	Lightning Rod	Solid Rock	Reckless	
Riolu	Central 062	447	Fighting		Steadfast	Inner Focus	Prankster	
Roggenrola	Coastal 120	524	Rock		Sturdy		Sand Force	
Roselia	Central 072	315	Grass	Poison	Natural Cure	Poison Point	Leaf Guard	
Roserade	Central 073	407	Grass	Poison	Natural Cure	Poison Point	Technician	
Rotom	Mountain 068	479	Electric	Ghost	Levitate			
Rotom (Fan)	Mountain 068	479	Electric	Flying	Levitate			
Rotom (Frost)	Mountain 068	479	Electric	Ice	Levitate			
Rotom (Heat)	Mountain 068	479	Electric	Fire	Levitate			
Rotom (Mow)	Mountain 068	479	Electric	Grass	Levitate			
Rotom (Wash)	Mountain 068	479	Electric	Water	Levitate			

S

Pokémon	Kalos Pokédex No.	National Pokédex No.	Type		Ability		Hidden Ability	
Sableye	Coastal 123	302	Dark	Ghost	Keen Eye	Stall	Prankster	
Salamence	Coastal 016	373	Dragon	Flying	Intimidate		Moxie	
Sandile	Coastal 043	551	Ground	Dark	Intimidate	Moxie	Anger Point	
Sandshrew	Mountain 097	27	Ground		Sand Veil		Sand Rush	
Sandslash	Mountain 098	28	Ground		Sand Veil		Sand Rush	
Sawk	Coastal 098	539	Fighting		Sturdy	Inner Focus	Mold Breaker	
Scatterbug	Central 020	664	Bug		Shield Dust	Compound Eyes	Friend Guard	
Scizor	Mountain 137	212	Bug	Steel	Swarm	Technician	Light Metal	
Scolipede	Central 122	545	Bug	Poison	Poison Point	Swarm	Speed Boost	
Scrafty	Central 101	560	Dark	Fighting	Shed Skin	Moxie	Intimidate	
Scraggy	Central 100	559	Dark	Fighting	Shed Skin	Moxie	Intimidate	
Scyther	Mountain 136	123	Bug	Flying	Swarm	Technician	Steadfast	
Seadra	Coastal 040	117	Water		Poison Point	Sniper		
Seaking	Central 054	119	Water		Swift Swim	Water Veil		
Sentret	Central 109	161	Normal		Run Away	Keen Eye	Frisk	
Seviper	Coastal 006	336	Poison		Shed Skin		Infiltrator	
Sharpedo	Central 056	319	Water	Dark	Rough Skin			
Shedinja	Central 113	292	Bug	Ghost	Wonder Guard			
Shelgon	Coastal 015	372	Dragon		Rock Head		Overcoat	
Shellder	Coastal 036	90	Water		Shell Armor	Skill Link	Overcoat	
Shelmet	Mountain 024	616	Bug		Hydration	Shell Armor	Overcoat	
Shuckle	Mountain 014	213	Bug	Rock	Sturdy	Gluttony	Contrary	
Shuppet	Mountain 122	353	Ghost		Insomnia	Frisk	Cursed Body	
Sigilyph	Coastal 090	561	Psychic	Flying	Wonder Skin	Magic Guard	Tinted Lens	
Simipour	Central 034	516	Water		Gluttony		Torrent	
Simisage	Central 030	512	Grass		Gluttony		Overgrow	
Simisear	Central 032	514	Fire		Gluttony		Blaze	
Skarmory	Mountain 112	227	Steel	Flying	Keen Eye	Sturdy	Weak Armor	
Skiddo	Central 089	672	Grass		Sap Sipper		Grass Pelt	
Skiploom	Central 136	188	Grass	Flying	Chlorophyll	Leaf Guard	Infiltrator	
Skitty	Central 078	300	Normal		Cute Charm	Normalize	Wonder Skin	
Skorupi	Mountain 015	451	Poison	Bug	Battle Armor	Sniper	Keen Eye	
Skrelp	Coastal 030	690	Poison	Water	Poison Point	Poison Touch		
Skuntank	Coastal 103	435	Poison	Dark	Stench	Aftermath	Keen Eye	
Sliggoo	Mountain 020	705	Dragon		Sap Sipper	Hydration	Gooey	
Slowbro	Coastal 134	80	Water	Psychic	Oblivious	Own Tempo	Regenerator	
Slowking	Coastal 135	199	Water	Psychic	Oblivious	Own Tempo	Regenerator	
Slowpoke	Coastal 133	79	Water	Psychic	Oblivious	Own Tempo	Regenerator	
Slugma	Mountain 012	218	Fire		Magma Armor	Flame Body	Weak Armor	
Slurpuff	Central 132	685	Fairy		Sweet Veil		Unburden	
Smeargle	Central 124	235	Normal		Own Tempo	Technician	Moody	
Smoochum	Mountain 083	238	Ice	Psychic	Oblivious	Forewarn	Hydration	

Note: Types marked with ★ will do 4× the usual damage. Types appearing in ▬▬ may deal more or less damage depending on the Pokémon's Ability.

Weak against these move types					
★Grass					
Fire	Ice	Poison	Flying	Bug	
Electric	Ground	Psychic			

Weak against these move types					
Ground					
Poison	Ghost	Steel			
★Grass	Electric	Fighting	Ground		
Grass	Electric				
Bug	Ghost	Dark			
★Water	★Grass	Ice	Fighting	Ground	Steel
★Water	★Grass	Ice	Fighting	Ground	Steel
★Water	★Grass	Ice	Fighting	Ground	Steel
Flying	Psychic	Fairy			
Water	Grass	Fighting	Ground	Steel	
Fire	Ice	Flying	Psychic		
Fire	Ice	Flying	Psychic		
Ground	Ghost	Dark			
Ice	Rock				
Fire	Fighting	Ground	Rock		
★Ground	Water	Rock			
Fire	Ice	Poison	Bug		
Grass	Ground				

Weak against these move types					
Fairy					
★Ice	Rock	Dragon	Fairy		
Water	Grass	Ice	Fighting	Bug	Fairy
Water	Grass	Ice			
Water	Grass	Ice			
Flying	Psychic	Fairy			
Fire	Flying	Rock			
★Fire					
Fire	Flying	Psychic	Rock		
★Fairy	Fighting	Flying			
★Fairy	Fighting	Flying			
★Rock	Fire	Electric	Ice	Flying	
Grass	Electric				
Grass	Electric				
Fighting					
Ground	Psychic				
Grass	Electric	Fighting	Bug	Fairy	
Fire	Flying	Rock	Ghost	Dark	
Ice	Dragon	Fairy			
Grass	Electric				
Fire	Flying	Rock			
Water	Rock	Steel			
Ghost	Dark				
Electric	Ice	Rock	Ghost	Dark	
Grass	Electric				
Fire	Ice	Poison	Flying	Bug	
Water	Ground	Rock			
Fire	Electric				
Fire	Ice	Poison	Flying	Bug	
★Ice	Fire	Poison	Flying	Rock	
Fighting					
Fire	Flying	Psychic	Rock		
Electric	Ground	Psychic			
Ground					
Ice	Dragon	Fairy			
Grass	Electric	Bug	Ghost	Dark	
Grass	Electric	Bug	Ghost	Dark	
Grass	Electric	Bug	Ghost	Dark	
Water	Ground	Rock			
Poison	Steel				
Fighting					
Fire	Bug	Rock	Ghost	Dark	Steel

Pokémon	Kalos Pokédex No.	National Pokédex No.	Type		Ability		Hidden Ability
Sneasel	Mountain 091	215	Dark	Ice	Inner Focus	Keen Eye	Pickpocket
Snorlax	Central 139	143	Normal		Immunity	Thick Fat	
Snover	Mountain 088	459	Grass	Ice	Snow Warning		Soundproof
Snubbull	Coastal 071	209	Fairy		Intimidate	Run Away	Rattled
Solosis	Coastal 115	577	Psychic		Overcoat	Magic Guard	Regenerator
Solrock	Coastal 013	338	Rock	Psychic	Levitate		
Spearow	Mountain 109	21	Normal	Flying	Keen Eye		Sniper
Spewpa	Central 021	665	Bug		Shed Skin		Friend Guard
Spinarak	Mountain 107	167	Bug	Poison	Swarm	Insomnia	Sniper
Spinda	Mountain 131	327	Normal		Own Tempo	Tangled Feet	Contrary
Spoink	Coastal 007	325	Psychic		Thick Fat	Own Tempo	
Spritzee	Central 129	682	Fairy		Healer		Aroma Veil
Squirtle	Central 086	7	Water		Torrent		Rain Dish
Staraptor	Coastal 101	398	Normal	Flying	Intimidate		Reckless
Staravia	Coastal 100	397	Normal	Flying	Intimidate		Reckless
Starly	Coastal 099	396	Normal	Flying	Keen Eye		Reckless
Starmie	Coastal 035	121	Water	Psychic	Illuminate	Natural Cure	
Staryu	Coastal 034	120	Water		Illuminate	Natural Cure	
Steelix	Coastal 054	208	Steel	Ground	Rock Head	Sturdy	Sheer Force
Stunfisk	Mountain 039	618	Ground	Electric	Static	Limber	Sand Veil
Stunky	Coastal 102	434	Poison	Dark	Stench	Aftermath	Keen Eye
Sudowoodo	Mountain 130	185	Rock		Sturdy	Rock Head	Rattled
Surskit	Central 047	283	Bug	Water	Swift Swim		Rain Dish
Swablu	Mountain 139	333	Normal	Flying	Natural Cure		Cloud Nine
Swalot	Central 099	317	Poison		Liquid Ooze	Sticky Hold	Gluttony
Swanna	Central 128	581	Water	Flying	Keen Eye	Big Pecks	Hydration
Swellow	Coastal 020	277	Normal	Flying	Guts		Scrappy
Swinub	Mountain 076	220	Ice	Ground	Oblivious	Snow Cloak	Thick Fat
Swirlix	Central 131	684	Fairy		Sweet Veil		Unburden
Swoobat	Coastal 056	528	Psychic	Flying	Unaware	Klutz	Simple
Sylveon	Coastal 085	700	Fairy		Cute Charm		Pixilate

T

Pokémon	Kalos Pokédex No.	National Pokédex No.	Type		Ability		Hidden Ability
Taillow	Coastal 019	276	Normal	Flying	Guts		Scrappy
Talonflame	Central 016	663	Fire	Flying	Flame Body		Gale Wings
Tauros	Coastal 125	128	Normal		Intimidate	Anger Point	Sheer Force
Teddiursa	Mountain 132	216	Normal		Pickup	Quick Feet	Honey Gather
Tentacool	Coastal 025	72	Water	Poison	Clear Body	Liquid Ooze	
Tentacruel	Coastal 026	73	Water	Poison	Clear Body	Liquid Ooze	
Throh	Coastal 097	538	Fighting		Guts	Inner Focus	Mold Breaker
Timburr	Mountain 093	532	Fighting		Guts	Sheer Force	Iron Fist
Torkoal	Mountain 096	324	Fire		White Smoke		
Toxicroak	Central 126	454	Poison	Fighting	Anticipation	Dry Skin	Poison Touch
Trapinch	Mountain 003	328	Ground		Hyper Cutter	Arena Trap	Sheer Force
Trevenant	Mountain 062	709	Ghost	Grass	Natural Cure	Frisk	Harvest
Trubbish	Mountain 074	568	Poison		Stench	Sticky Hold	Aftermath
Tyranitar	Mountain 104	248	Rock	Dark	Sand Stream		Unnerve
Tyrantrum	Coastal 065	697	Rock	Dragon	Strong Jaw		
Tyrunt	Coastal 064	696	Rock	Dragon	Strong Jaw		

U

Pokémon	Kalos Pokédex No.	National Pokédex No.	Type		Ability		Hidden Ability
Umbreon	Coastal 082	197	Dark		Synchronize		Inner Focus
Ursaring	Mountain 133	217	Normal		Guts	Quick Feet	Unnerve

V

Pokémon	Kalos Pokédex No.	National Pokédex No.	Type		Ability		Hidden Ability
Vanillish	Mountain 086	583	Ice		Ice Body		Weak Armor
Vanillite	Mountain 085	582	Ice		Ice Body		Weak Armor
Vanilluxe	Mountain 087	584	Ice		Ice Body		Weak Armor
Vaporeon	Coastal 078	134	Water		Water Absorb		Hydration
Venipede	Central 120	543	Bug	Poison	Poison Point	Swarm	Speed Boost
Venusaur	Central 082	3	Grass	Poison	Overgrow		Chlorophyll
Vespiquen	Central 077	416	Bug	Flying	Pressure		Unnerve
Vibrava	Mountain 004	329	Ground	Dragon	Levitate		
Victreebel	Mountain 028	71	Grass	Poison	Chlorophyll		Gluttony
Vileplume	Central 107	45	Grass	Poison	Chlorophyll		Effect Spore
Vivillon	Central 022	666	Bug	Flying	Shield Dust	Compound Eyes	Friend Guard
Volbeat	Central 133	313	Bug		Illuminate	Swarm	Prankster
Voltorb	Mountain 072	100	Electric		Soundproof	Static	Aftermath

Note: Types marked with ★ will do 4× the usual damage. Types appearing in ▩ may deal more or less damage depending on the Pokémon's Ability.

	Weak against these move types					
★Fighting	Fire	Bug	Rock	Steel	Fairy	
Fighting						
★Fire	Fighting	Poison	Flying	Bug	Rock	Steel
Poison	Steel					
Bug	Ghost	Dark				
Water	Grass	Ground	Bug	Ghost	Dark	Steel
Electric	Ice	Rock				
Fire	Flying	Rock				
Fire	Flying	Psychic	Rock			
Fighting						
Bug	Ghost	Dark				
Poison	Steel					
Grass	Electric					
Electric	Ice	Rock				
Electric	Ice	Rock				
Electric	Ice	Rock				
Grass	Electric	Bug	Ghost	Dark		
Grass	Electric					
Fire	Water	Fighting	Ground			
Water	Grass	Ice	Ground			
Ground						
Water	Grass	Fighting	Ground	Steel		
Electric	Flying	Rock				
Electric	Ice	Rock				
Ground	Psychic					
★Electric	Rock					
Electric	Ice	Rock				
Fire	Water	Grass	Fighting	Steel		
Poison	Steel					
Electric	Ice	Rock	Ghost	Dark		
Poison	Steel					

	Weak against these move types					
Electric	Ice	Rock				
★Rock	Water	Electric				
Fighting						
Fighting						
Electric	Ground	Psychic				
Electric	Ground	Psychic				
Flying	Psychic	Fairy				
Flying	Psychic	Fairy				
Water	Ground	Rock				
★Psychic	Ground	Flying				
Water	Grass	Ice				
Fire	Ice	Flying	Ghost	Dark		
Ground	Psychic					
★Fighting	Water	Grass	Ground	Bug	Steel	Fairy
Ice	Fighting	Ground	Dragon	Steel	Fairy	
Ice	Fighting	Ground	Dragon	Steel	Fairy	

	Weak against these move types					
Fighting	Bug	Fairy				
Fighting						

	Weak against these move types					
Fire	Fighting	Rock	Steel			
Fire	Fighting	Rock	Steel			
Fire	Fighting	Rock	Steel			
Grass	Electric					
Fire	Flying	Psychic	Rock			
Fire	Ice	Flying	Psychic			
★Rock	Fire	Electric	Ice	Flying		
★Ice	Dragon	Fairy				
Fire	Ice	Flying	Psychic			
Fire	Ice	Flying	Psychic			
★Rock	Fire	Electric	Ice	Flying		
Fire	Flying	Rock				
Ground						

W

Pokémon	Kalos Pokédex No.	National Pokédex No.	Type		Ability		Hidden Ability	
Wailmer	Coastal 027	320	Water		Water Veil	Oblivious		
Wailord	Coastal 028	321	Water		Water Veil	Oblivious		
Wartortle	Central 087	8	Water		Torrent		Rain Dish	
Watchog	Mountain 047	505	Normal		Illuminate	Keen Eye	Analytic	
Weavile	Mountain 092	461	Dark	Ice	Pressure		Pickpocket	
Weedle	Central 026	13	Bug	Poison	Shield Dust		Run Away	
Weepinbell	Mountain 027	70	Grass	Poison	Chlorophyll		Gluttony	
Whirlipede	Central 121	544	Bug	Poison	Poison Point	Swarm	Speed Boost	
Whiscash	Mountain 041	340	Water	Ground	Oblivious	Anticipation		
Whismur	Central 140	293	Normal		Soundproof		Rattled	
Wigglytuff	Mountain 121	40	Normal	Fairy	Cute Charm	Competitive	Frisk	
Wingull	Coastal 017	278	Water	Flying	Keen Eye		Rain Dish	
Wobbuffet	Coastal 119	202	Psychic		Shadow Tag		Telepathy	
Woobat	Coastal 055	527	Psychic	Flying	Unaware	Klutz	Simple	
Wooper	Mountain 017	194	Water	Ground	Damp	Water Absorb	Unaware	
Wormadam (Plant)	Central 045	413	Bug	Grass	Anticipation			
Wormadam (Sand)	Central 045	413	Bug	Ground	Anticipation			
Wormadam (Trash)	Central 045	413	Bug	Steel	Anticipation			
Wynaut	Coastal 118	360	Psychic		Shadow Tag		Telepathy	

XYZ

Pokémon	Kalos Pokédex No.	National Pokédex No.	Type		Ability		Hidden Ability	
Xerneas	Mountain 148	716	Fairy		Fairy Aura			
Yanma	Coastal 087	193	Bug	Flying	Speed Boost	Compound Eyes	Frisk	
Yanmega	Coastal 088	469	Bug	Flying	Speed Boost	Tinted Lens	Frisk	
Yveltal	Mountain 149	717	Dark	Flying	Dark Aura			
Zangoose	Coastal 005	335	Normal		Immunity		Toxic Boost	
Zapdos	Coastal 152	145	Electric	Flying	Pressure			
Zigzagoon	Central 012	263	Normal		Pickup	Gluttony	Quick Feet	
Zoroark	Mountain 125	571	Dark		Illusion			
Zorua	Mountain 124	570	Dark		Illusion			
Zubat	Central 145	41	Poison	Flying	Inner Focus		Infiltrator	
Zweilous	Mountain 143	634	Dark	Dragon	Hustle			
Zygarde	Mountain 150	718	Dragon	Ground	Aura Break			

Mega-Evolved Pokémon

Pokémon	Kalos Pokédex No.	National Pokédex No.	Type		Ability		Hidden Ability	
Mega Abomasnow	Mountain 089	460	Grass	Ice	Snow Warning			
Mega Absol	Coastal 009	359	Dark		Magic Bounce			
Mega Aerodactyl	Coastal 068	142	Rock	Flying	Tough Claws			
Mega Aggron	Mountain 101	306	Steel		Filter			
Mega Alakazam	Central 104	65	Psychic		Trace			
Mega Ampharos	Coastal 129	181	Electric	Dragon	Mold Breaker			
Mega Banette	Mountain 123	354	Ghost		Prankster			
Mega Blastoise	Central 088	9	Water		Mega Launcher			
Mega Charizard X	Central 085	6	Fire	Dragon	Tough Claws			
Mega Charizard Y	Central 085	6	Fire	Flying	Drought			
Mega Garchomp	Mountain 008	445	Dragon	Ground	Sand Force			
Mega Gardevoir	Central 066	282	Psychic	Fairy	Pixilate			
Mega Gengar	Mountain 032	94	Ghost	Poison	Shadow Tag			
Mega Gyarados	Central 050	130	Water	Dark	Mold Breaker			
Mega Heracross	Coastal 131	214	Bug	Fighting	Skill Link			
Mega Houndoom	Coastal 076	229	Dark	Fire	Solar Power			
Mega Kangaskhan	Coastal 062	115	Normal		Parental Bond			
Mega Lucario	Central 063	448	Fighting	Steel	Adaptability			
Mega Manectric	Coastal 074	310	Electric		Intimidate			
Mega Mawile	Coastal 063	303	Steel	Fairy	Huge Power			
Mega Medicham	Central 144	308	Fighting	Psychic	Pure Power			
Mega Mewtwo X	Mountain 151	150	Psychic	Fighting	Steadfast			
Mega Mewtwo Y	Mountain 151	150	Psychic		Insomnia			
Mega Pinsir	Coastal 130	127	Bug	Flying	Aerilate			
Mega Scizor	Mountain 137	212	Bug	Steel	Technician			
Mega Tyranitar	Mountain 104	248	Rock	Dark	Sand Stream			
Mega Venusaur	Central 082	3	Grass	Poison	Thick Fat			

Note: Types marked with ★ will do 4× the usual damage. Types appearing in ▆▆▆ may deal more or less damage depending on the Pokémon's Ability.

Pokémon Weakness Chart—Kalos Regional Pokédex

	Weak against these move types				
Grass	Electric				
Grass	Electric				
Grass	Electric				
Fighting					
★Fighting	Fire	Bug	Rock	Steel	Fairy
Fire	Flying	Psychic	Rock		
Fire	Ice	Flying	Psychic		
Fire	Flying	Psychic	Rock		
★Grass					
Fighting					
Poison	Steel				
★Electric	Rock				
Bug	Ghost				
Electric	Ice	Rock	Ghost	Dark	
★Grass					
★Fire	★Flying	Ice	Poison	Bug	Rock
Fire	Water	Ice	Flying		
★Fire					
Bug	Ghost	Dark			

	Weak against these move types			
Poison	Steel			
★Rock	Fire	Electric	Ice	Flying
★Rock	Fire	Electric	Ice	Flying
Electric	Ice	Rock	Fairy	
Fighting				
Ice	Rock			
Fighting				
Fighting	Bug	Fairy		
Fighting	Bug	Fairy		
Electric	Ice	Psychic	Rock	
★Fairy	Ice	Fighting	Bug	Dragon
★Ice	Dragon	Fairy		

	Weak against these move types					
★Fire	Fighting	Poison	Flying	Bug	Rock	Steel
Fighting	Bug	Fairy				
Water	Electric	Ice	Rock	Steel		
Fire	Fighting	Ground				
Bug	Ghost	Dark				
Ice	Ground	Dragon	Fairy			
Ghost	Dark					
Grass	Electric					
Ground	Rock	Dragon				
★Rock	Water	Electric				
★Ice	Dragon	Fairy				
Poison	Ghost	Steel				
Ground	Psychic	Ghost	Dark			
Grass	Electric	Fighting	Bug	Fairy		
★Flying	Fire	Psychic	Fairy			
Water	Fighting	Ground	Rock			
Fighting						
Fire	Fighting	Ground				
Ground						
Fire	Ground					
Flying	Ghost	Fairy				
Flying	Ghost	Fairy				
Bug	Ghost	Dark				
★Rock	Fire	Electric	Ice	Flying		
★Fire						
★Fighting	Water	Grass	Ground	Bug	Steel	Fairy
Fire	Ice	Flying	Psychic			

733

Type Matchup Chart

Types are assigned both to moves and to the Pokémon themselves. These types can greatly affect the amount of damage dealt or received in battle, so if you learn how they line up against one another, you'll give yourself an edge in battle.

Attacking Pokémon's Move Type \ Defending Pokémon's Type	Normal	Fire	Water	Grass	Electric	Ice	Fighting	Poison	Ground	Flying	Psychic	Bug	Rock	Ghost	Dragon	Dark	Steel	Fairy
Normal													▲	×			▲	
Fire		▲	▲	●		●						●	▲		▲		●	
Water		●	▲	▲					●				●		▲			
Grass		▲	●	▲				▲	●	▲		▲	●		▲		▲	
Electric			●	▲	▲				×	●					▲			
Ice		▲	▲	●		▲			●	●					●		▲	
Fighting	●					●		▲		▲	▲	▲	●	×		●	●	▲
Poison				●				▲	▲				▲	▲			×	●
Ground		●		▲	●			●		×		▲	●				●	
Flying				●	▲		●					●	▲				▲	
Psychic							●	●			▲					×	▲	
Bug		▲		●			▲	▲		▲	●			▲		●	▲	▲
Rock		●				●	▲		▲	●		●					▲	
Ghost	×										●			●		▲		
Dragon															●		▲	×
Dark							▲				●			●		▲		▲
Steel		▲	▲		▲	●							●				▲	●
Fairy		▲					●	▲							●	●	▲	

Ineffective status conditions and moves depending on type

Type	Effect
Fire	• Cannot be afflicted with the Burned condition
Grass	• Immune to Leech Seed • Immune to powder and spore moves
Electric	• Cannot be afflicted with the Paralyzed condition
Ice	• Immune to the Frozen condition • Take no damage from hail
Poison	• Immune to the Poison and Badly Poisoned conditions • Immune to the Poison and Badly Poisoned conditions, when switching in with Toxic Spikes in play • Nullify Toxic Spikes (unless these Pokémon are also Flying type or have the Levitate Ability)
Ground	• Immune to Thunder Wave* • Take no damage from sandstorms
Flying	• Cannot be damaged by Spikes when switching in • Cannot be afflicted with a Poison or Badly Poisoned condition due to switching in with Toxic Spikes in play
Rock	• Take no damage from sandstorms • Speed goes up in a sandstorm
Ghost	• Cannot be affected by moves that prevent Pokémon from fleeing from battle
Steel	• Take no damage from sandstorms • Immune to the Poison and Badly Poisoned conditions • Immune to the Poison and Badly Poisoned conditions, when switching in with Toxic Spikes in play

Key

●	Very effective "It's super effective!"	× 2
No icon	Normal damage	× 1
▲	Not too effective "It's not very effective…"	× 1/2
×	No effect "It doesn't affect…"	× 0

* Types usually don't have effects on status moves, but Thunder Wave won't work against Ground-type Pokémon.

Inverse Type Matchup Chart

An Inverse Battle is a Pokémon battle in which type matchups will be reversed. For example, a Flying-type Pokémon is immune to Ground-type moves in a normal battle, but in an Inverse Battle, a Ground-type move can inflict twice the damage on a Flying-type Pokémon. You can try Inverse Battles in a house on Route 18.

Attacking Pokémon's Move Type ↓ / Defending Pokémon's Type →	Normal	Fire	Water	Grass	Electric	Ice	Fighting	Poison	Ground	Flying	Psychic	Bug	Rock	Ghost	Dragon	Dark	Steel	Fairy
Normal													◉	◉			◉	
Fire		◉	◉	△		△						△	◉		◉		△	
Water		△	◉	◉					△				△		◉			
Grass		◉	△	◉				◉	△	◉		◉	△		◉		◉	
Electric			△	◉	◉				◉	△					◉			
Ice		◉	◉	△		◉			△	△					△		◉	
Fighting	△					△		◉		◉	◉	◉	△	◉		△	△	◉
Poison				△				◉	◉				◉	◉			◉	△
Ground		△		◉	△			△		◉		◉	△				△	
Flying				△	◉		△					△	◉				◉	
Psychic							△	△			◉					◉	◉	
Bug		◉		△			◉	◉		◉	△			◉		△	◉	◉
Rock		△				△	◉		◉	△		△					◉	
Ghost	◉										△			△		◉		
Dragon															△		◉	◉
Dark							◉				△			△		◉		◉
Steel		◉	◉		◉	△							△				◉	△
Fairy		◉					△	◉							△	△	◉	

Location where you can enjoy an Inverse Battle

Challenge yourself once a day in a house on Route 18!

Would you care to try an Inverse Battle?

Speak to Psychic Inver in a house on Route 18 to try an Inverse Battle once a day. After a battle, you get a reward. Try it every day!

Key

◉	Very effective "It's super effective!"	× 2
No icon	Normal damage	× 1
△	Not too effective "It's not very effective…"	× 1/2

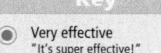

CREDITS

Original Japanese *Complete Kalos Pokédex*
Planning, Page Layout, Writing & Map Development: Shusuke Motomiya and ONEUP, Inc.
Art Direction, Design & Layout: RAGTIME CO., LTD.
DTPR: Plane Dot

PROJECT MANAGER
Emily Luty

EDITORS
Wolfgang Baur
Kellyn Ballard
Blaise Selby
Eric Haddock
Rachel Payne (Bridge Consulting)

RESEARCHERS & TRANSLATORS
Hisato Yamamori
Mikiko Ryu
Jillian Nonaka
Sayuri Munday

SCREENSHOTS
Antoin Johnson
Aaron Campion (Aerotek)
Jeff Hines (Bridge Consulting)

COVER DESIGNERS
Eric Medalle
Bridget O'Neill

ADDITIONAL CONTENT WRITER
Steve Stratton (Prima Games)

DESIGN & PRODUCTION
Prima Games
Donato Tica
Jamie Knight Bryson
Elise Winter
Mark Hughes
Kate Abbott

ACKNOWLEDGEMENTS
Chris Franc
Heather Dalgleish
Hiromi Kimura
J.C. Smith
Phaedra Long
Yasuhiro Usui

The Pokémon Company
INTERNATIONAL

The Official Kalos Region Pokédex & Postgame Adventure Guide

©2013 The Pokémon Company International.

ISBN: 978-0-804162-57-9

Published in the United States by
The Pokémon Company International
333 108th Ave NE Suite 1900
Bellevue, WA 98004 USA

1st Floor Building 4, Chiswick Park
566 Chiswick High Road
London, W4 5YE United Kingdom

Printed in the United States of America using materials
from the *Pokémon X & Pokémon Y*: Complete Kalos
Pokédex. Original Japanese Pokédex published in Japan
by OVERLAP, Inc.